DAVE & A...

Buying Un... ...es and
Autogr... ...ngles for 30 Years!
No Collection Is Too Big or Too Small
CONTACT US TODAY!

WILL TRAVEL ANYWHERE

FAST, FAIR OFFERS
(USUALLY WITHIN 24 HOURS)

PAID IN CASH
ON THE SPOT AVAILABLE

ALL TRANSACTIONS 100% CONFIDENTIAL

STOP PAYING CRAZY AUCTION FEES

CONTACT:

1-888-440-9787 x112

buying@dacardworld.com

55 Oriskany Dr.
Tonawanda, NY 14150

Mon.-Fri. | 9AM-5PM

WE'RE BUYING:

SPORTS CARDS

Paying Top Dollar for your Autograph Cards!

We are buying autograph cards valued at over $25
Rookies, Prospects, Current Stars, Hall Of Famers,
Autographed Patch Cards, Graded Autographed
Cards as well as Cut Autographed Cards!

- **Baseball:** Gleyber Torres, Mike Trout, Mickey Mantle,
Vladimir Guerrero Jr., Ronald Acuna, Juan Soto,
Aaron Judge, Barry Bonds, Wander Franco, & more!

- **Basketball:** Luka Doncic, Michael Jordan, Steph Curry,
Lebron James, Giannis Antetokounmpo, Ben Simmons,
Ja Morant, Larry Bird, Trae Young, Zion Williamson, & more!

- **Football:** Lamar Jackson, Tom Brady, Aaron Rodgers,
Christian McCaffrey, DeShaun Watson, Patrick Mahomes,
Randy Moss, Russell Wilson, Dak Prescott, & more!

- **Hockey:** Connor McDavid, Auston Matthews,
Wayne Gretzky, David Pastrnak, Jaromir,
Nathan Mackinnon, Sidney Crosby, & more!

We also buy Unopened Boxes and Cases of Sports
Cards and Entertainment Cards (All Years).

AUTOGRAPHED MEMORABILIA

- **Authenticated by:** PSA/DNA, JSA, Steiner,
Upper Deck Authenticated, TriStar, Leaf, GTSM,
and Mounted Memories/Fanatics

21ST EDITION 2022

BECKETT

THE #1 AUTHORITY ON COLLECTIBLES

GRADED
CARD PRICE GUIDE

THE HOBBY'S MOST RELIABLE AND RELIED UPON SOURCE ™

Founder: Dr. James Beckett III

Edited by the Price Guide Staff of BECKETT COLLECTIBLES

Beckett Collectibles LLC
4635 McEwen Dr.
Dallas, TX 75244
(972)991-6657
beckett.com

First Printing ISBN: 978-1-953801-12-8

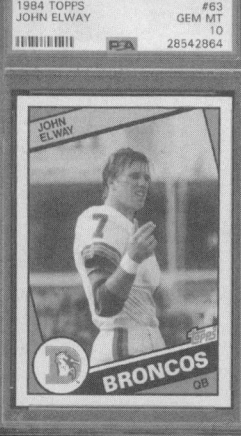

TABLE OF
CONTENTS

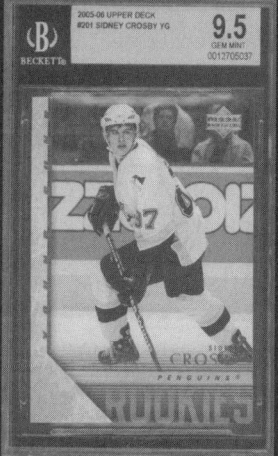

STAFF

EDITORIAL

MIKE PAYNE
Editorial Director

RYAN CRACKNELL
Hobby Editor

ERIC KNAGG
Graphic Design

COLLECTIBLES DATA PUBLISHING

BRIAN FLEISCHER
Manager | Sr. Market Analyst

PRICE GUIDE STAFF
Lloyd Almonguera, Ryan Altubar, Matt Bible, Jeff Camay, Steve Dalton, Justin Grunert, Junel Magale, Eric Norton, Kristian Redulla, Arsenio Tan, Sam Zimmer

ADVERTISING

TED BARKER
Senior Sales Executive
tbarker@beckett.com
972.448.9147

ALEX SORIANO
Advertising Sales Executive
alex@beckett.com
619.392.5299

BECKETT GRADING SERVICES

JEROMY MURRAY
VP, Grading & Authentication
4635 McEwen Road,
Dallas, TX 75244
jmurray@beckett.com

GRADING SALES/ SHOW STAFF

DEREK FICKEN
Midwest/Southeast
Regional Sales Manager
dficken@beckett.com
Office: 972.448.9144

NEW YORK OFFICE
484 White Plains Rd, 2nd Floor,
Eastchester, N.Y. 10709

CHARLES STABILE
Northeast Regional
Sales Manager
cstabile@beckett.com
Office: 914.268.0533

CALIFORNIA OFFICE
17900 Sky Park Circle, Suite
200, Irvine, CA 92614

MICHAEL GARDNER
Western Regional
Sales Manager
mgardner@beckett.com
Office: 714.200.1934
Fax: 714.388.3741

DONGWOON LEE
Asia/Pacific Sales Manager
dongwoonl@beckett.com
Cell +82.10.6826.6868

Grading Customer Service:
972.448.9188 or
grading@beckett.com

BECKETT DIGITAL STUDIO

DANIEL MOSCOSO

OPERATIONS

ALBERTO CHAVEZ
Sr. Logistics & Facilities
Manager

EDITORIAL, PRODUCTION & SALES OFFICE

4635 McEwen Road,
Dallas TX 75244
972.991.6657
beckett.com

© 2022 by Beckett Media,
LLC. All rights reserved.

Reproduction of any material
from this issue in whole or in
part is strictly prohibited.

Subscriptions, address chang-
es, renewals, missing or dam-
aged copies - 866.287.9383

239.653.0225 Foreign inquires
subscriptions@beckett.com

BECKETT COLLECTIBLES, LLC

SANDEEP DUA - President
JEROMY MURRAY - President -
Beckett Collectibles

How to Use

What's listed?

Beckett Graded Card Price Guide features a multi-sport format comprised of baseball, basketball, football, golf, hockey and Magic the Gathering. Our goal is to include all significant professionally graded cards from 1887-present.

What's not listed?

Unlike the raw card price guides featured within our magazine titles, Beckett Graded Card Price Guide focuses solely on material that is most frequently submitted to the top professional grading companies.

How do I find what I'm looking for?

The Price Guide is structured alphabetically by sport (baseball first, followed by basketball then football, etc.) and chronologically within each sport.

Why aren't prices listed for every condition?

After analyzing market conditions, it was determined that eight columns for vintage and four columns for modern era material best captured the range of graded cards trading hands in collectible condition. There's little need to list values for graded NM or ExMt modern era cards because material in less than NmMt condition is rarely submitted for grading. Conversely, Mint and Gem Mint graded cards are so rare in many vintage sets that providing accurate values is nearly impossible.

Why are some fields blank within the pricing grids?

Because the Price Guide is based on real-world transactions, we've deliberately left fields blank where populations are too low to derive consistent valuations. Rather than list highly dubious values for "low population" cards, we've chosen to augment the pricing grids for each set by reporting historical sales on significant rarities at the end of each set listing.

Additionally, prices are not listed for some low-end cards valued under $4 (about half the cost to grade a card). If you see a blank field for a low-end condition, you can assume the card is worth less than five dollars in that grade.

Why are vintage common cards individually listed but not modern era singles in the pricing grids?

We've gone to great lengths to extensively research market conditions for commons and minor stars. In vintage releases with a healthy community of set builders, the impact of Population Reports can be significant on the values of scarce commons and minor stars in high grade so we've included prices for every card. Frankly, it's pretty easy to figure out how much a 1957 Topps Mickey Mantle is worth in NM or NmMt since there are plenty of copies in circulation. But the task is tougher when determining the value for the Max Surkont card in similar condition - there are only a handful of high-end copies available and they sell at a premium.

There are relatively few graded card set builders for modern era releases thus the truncated listings.

How do I differentiate values between the various grading companies?

The market for professionally graded sports cards is today predominantly comprised of three companies BGS/BVG, PSA and SGC. Rather than try to break down listings for every card in every condition by every company (a bewildering option on the printed page and a virtual impossibility given the inherent inconsistencies in trading volume), we've chosen to simplify matters by providing the value that the card is most commonly traded for in that grade.

The catch is that not all company's cards always trade for equal value (in equal grade) from the various eras. We approached this dilemma by looking at market share as the primary arbiter of value. For example, the majority of 1950s graded baseball cards circulating within the secondary market are encapsulated by PSA, thus the values we list for these cards largely reflect PSA trading levels. Conversely, SGC has a significant presence and status in tobacco-era material, thus the values we list for this material is demonstrably based upon SGC transactions. In the modern era material, BGS is a market leader and the listed values are thus noticeably based on transactions of BGS cards.

None of this, however, clarifies values for the consumer dealing in vintage Beckett graded cards or modern-era SGC material. To that effect, we've added some specific sales listings to the beginning of the pricing grid for each applicable set. It's here that you'll find specific information for companies with lower trading volume in that era for some key cards, illuminating potential differences in the sales levels listed in the pricing grid.

How do I reference PSA cards with qualifiers?

In general, PSA cards with qualifiers sell for about two levels lower than the grade on the label for post-WWII material (i.e. a PSA 7 OC will sell for about the same as a standard PSA 5) and one level below the grade on the label for pre-WWII material. We don't list specific values for these cards due to low trading volume on the secondary market. Significant PSA cards with qualifiers will, however, be referenced within our sales notes at the end of each set listing.

Where do you get your sales information from?

Every card sale from every major auction house over the past few years (Goodwin, Heritage, Lelands, Legendary, Memory Lane, Mile High, Robert Edward, etc.) has been gathered and analyzed. The unending stream of sales from eBay and other online community-based auctions also have been reviewed. Dealers at the leading shows across America have and will continue to be interviewed by our staff of analysts throughout the year.

Furthermore, a community message board on beckett.com devoted specifically to pricing is available to all. If you've got some feedback, wish to voice your opinion or simply want to provide some sales data, you'll have a venue to do so on your own time in your own home … and our analysts will be reading (and responding when appropriate) alongside fellow collectors and dealers.

BASEBALL

1887 - 1980

1887 Allen and Ginter N28

		PrFr 1	GD 2	VG 3	VgEx 4	EX 5	ExMt 6	NM 7	NmMt 8
1	Cap Anson/Baseball	900	1,200	1,800	2,500	3,000	4,000	8,800	12,000
2	Charles Bennett/Baseball	150	225	275	350	800			
3	Robert L. Caruthers/Baseball	150	200	250	300	500	600	1,000	3,200
4	John Clarkson/Baseball	300	400	500	800	1,000	1,500	2,500	9,500
5	Charles Comiskey/Baseball	350	450	600	800	1,200	2,000	3,000	
6	Captain Jack Glasscock/Baseball	150	250	300	400	600	900	1,200	2,000
7	Timothy Keefe/Baseball	325	400	550	750	1,000	1,500	2,500	9,500
8	Mike Kelly/Baseball	350	600	750	1,000	1,200	1,800	3,000	10,500
9	Joseph Mulvey/Baseball	125	175	250	300	400	700	1,000	2,800
10	John M. Ward/Baseball	350	450	600	750	1,200	1,800	2,500	6,000

1887-90 Old Judge N172

		PrFr 1	GD 2	VG 3	VgEx 4	EX 5	ExMt 6	NM 7	NmMt 8
1	Gus Albert	120	150	200	300	350	500		
3	Alexander	100	120	150	250	350	500		
4	Myron Allen	100	120	150	250	350	500		
5	Bob Allen	100	120	150	400	500	600		
6	Uncle Bill Alvord	100	120	150	250	350	500		
7	Varney Anderson	1,200	1,500	2,000	2,500	3,000	4,000		
8	Ed Andrews	100	120	150	250	350	500		
9	Ed Andrews w/B.Hoover	100	120	150	250	350	500		
10	Wally Andrews	100	120	150	250	350	500		
11	Bill Annis	100	120	150	250	350	500		
12B	Cap Anson Street Clothes	2,500	3,000	4,000	5,000	6,000	8,000		
13	Old Hoss Ardner	100	120	150	250	350	500		
14	Tug Arundel	100	120	150	250	350	500		
15	Jersey Bakley	100	120	150	250	350	500		
16	Clarence Baldwin	100	120	150	250	350	500		
17	Mark (Fido) Baldwin	150	120	250	300	500	700		
18	Lady Baldwin	100	120	150	250	350	500		
19	James Banning	100	120	150	250	350	500		
20	Samuel Barkley	100	200	250	300	500	700		
21	Bald Billy Barnie MG	100	120	150	250	350	500		
22	Charles Bassett	100	120	150	250	350	500		
23	Charles Bastian	100	120	300	350	400	500		
24	Charles Bastian w/P.Schriver	100	120	150	250	350	500		
25	Ebenezer Beatin	100	120	150	250	350	500		
26	Jake Beckley	1,000	1,200	1,500	200	2,500	4,000		
28	Charles Bennett	100	120	150	250	350	500		
29	Louis Bierbauer	100	120	150	500	600	800		
30	Louis Bierbauer w/R.Gamble	100	120	150	250	350	500		
31	Bill Bishop	100	120	200	250	350	500		
32	William Blair	100	200	250	300	350	500		
33	Ned Bligh	120	150	200	250	350	500		
34	Bogart	100	120	150	250	350	500		
35	Boyce	100	120	300	350	400	500		
36	Jake Boyd	100	120	150	250	350	500		
37	Honest John Boyle	100	120	150	250	350	500		
38	Handsome Henry Boyle	100	120	300	400	500	600		
39	Nick Bradley	100	120	150	250	350	500		
40	George (Grin) Bradley	400	600	800	1,000	1,200	2,500		
43	Timothy Brosnan Minn	100	120	150	250	400	1,500		
44	Timothy Brosnan Sioux	100	120	200	300	350	500		
45	Cal Broughton	100	120	150	250	350	500		

		PrFr 1	GD 2	VG 3	VgEx 4	EX 5	ExMt 6	NM 7	NmMt 8
46	Dan Brouthers	400	1,200	1,300	1,400	1,500	4,000		
47	Thomas Brown	100	120	250	300				
48	California Brown	100	200	250	300				
50	Charles Brynan	100	120	150	250	350	500		
51	Al Buckenberger MG	100	120	150	250	350	500		
52	Dick Buckley	100	200	250	300	350	500		
53	Charles Buffington	100	120	150	300	400	500		
54	Ernest Burch	100	120	150	300	350	500		
55	Bill Burdick	100	120	150	250	350	500		
56	Black Jack Burdock	100	120	300	350	400	500		
57	Robert Burks	100	120	150	250	350	500		
59	James Burns Omaha	100	120	150	250	400	800		
60	Jimmy Burns KC	100	120	150	250	350	500		
61	Tommy (Oyster) Burns	150	200	350	400	500	800		
62	Thomas E. Burns	100	120	150	300	350	500		
63	Doc Bushong Brooklyn	100	120	150	250	350	500		
64	Doc Bushong Browns Champs	150	200	400	500	800	1,200		
65	Patsy Cahill	100	120	150	900	1,000	1,200		
66	Count Campau	100	120	150	250	350	500		
67	Jimmy Canavan	100	120	150	250	350	500		
68	Bart Cantz	120	150	200	600	800	1,200		
69	Handsome Jack Carney	100	120	150	250	350	500		
70	Hick Carpenter	150	200	250	400	500	800		
71	Cliff Carroll	200	400	600	1,000	1,200	1,500		
72	Scrappy Carroll	100	120	150	250	350	500		
73	Frederick Carroll	100	250	300	400	500	600		
74	Jumbo Cartwright	150	200	250	400				
75	Bob Caruthers Brooklyn	200	250	350	1,800	2,000	2,500		
76	Bob Caruthers Browns Champs	200	300	350	400	500	800		
77	Daniel Casey	100	120	150	250	350	500		
78	Icebox Chamberlain	100	120	150	250	400	500		
79	Cupid Childs	100	120	150	250	350	500		
80	Bob Clark	150	200	300	400	500	800		
81	Owen (Spider) Clark	150	200	250	400	500	800		
83	William (Dad) Clarke	100	120	150	250	500	800		
84	Pete Connell	100	120	150	250	350	500		
85	John Clarkson	500	600	800	1,000	1,200			
86	Jack Clements	100	120	300	400	500	600		
87	Elmer Cleveland	120	150	350	400	450	500		
88	Monk Cline	100	150	200	250	350	500		
89	Mike Cody	100	120	250	300	350	500		
90	John Coleman	100	120	200	250	400	1,000		
91	Bill Collins	120	150	350	600	800	1,200		
92	Hub Collins	100	120	150	250	350	500		
93	Charles Comiskey	500	1,000	1,200	3,000	6,000	8,000		
94	Commy Comiskey Brown's	500	600	800	2,000	2,500	4,000		
95	Roger Connor Script	1,200	1,500	2,000	3,000	4,000	4,000		
96	Roger Connor New York	1,000	1,200	1,500	2,000	2,500	4,000		
97	Richard Conway	100	120	200	250	350	500		
98	Peter Conway	100	120	150	250	350	500		
99	James Conway	100	120	150	250	350	500		
100	Paul Cook	100	120	150	250	350	500		
101	Jimmy Cooney	120	150	200	250	350	500		
102	Larry Corcoran	150	200	250	2,500				
103	Pop Corkhill	100	120	150	250	350	500		
104	Cannon Ball Crane	120	300	350	400	450	500		
105	Samuel Crane	150	200	250	300	400	600		
106	Jack Crogan	100	450	550	650	800	1,000		

We Buy Everything!

Kruk Cards is currently buying complete collections, inventories, and accumulations. At Kruk Cards we sell everything so we have a need to buy everything.

BUYING JUNK WAX BOXES

BASKETBALL FOOTBALL BASEBALL HOCKEY

Any wax product from 1986 thru 1993 our buy prices are SUPER aggressive
Please email George@krukcards.com, we are paying world record prices.

BUYING COMMONS

PER 5,000 COUNT BOX

NFL Pay $30

MLB Pay $10

NHL Pay $20

NBA Pay $13

For commons from the year 2000 to present we will pay a premium.

We have great shipping rates for groups of 500,000 and up.
Please call or email for the details.

We Specialize in buying large accumulations!!

So if your collection is spread out between your basement, your attic, a storage shed, and a mini warehouse, we can make you an offer on the entire lot.
Call today and ask for George to discuss the details on selling your merchandise.
We could be on a plane and headed your way by tomorrow!
If you have a list please email or send it to us. We will respond to ALL email inquiries.

www.krukcards.com

Check out our website for our available inventory!
We also have over 5,000 auctions updated daily on eBay.
eBay User ID: Krukcards

Sports Collectors Digest / Krause Publications **20** CUSTOMER SERVICE AWARD

ebaY® Power Seller
Dealernet B2B

Kruk Cards
210 Campbell St.
Rochester, MI 48307
Email us:
George@krukcards.com
Hours: 9:30 - 5:30PM EST
Phone: (248) 656-8803 • Fax: (248) 656-6547

#	Name	PrFr 1	GD 2	VG 3	VgEx 4	EX 5	ExMt 6	NM 7	NmMt 8
107	John Crooks	100	200	250	300	350	500		
108	Lave Cross	100	120	150	250	350	500		
109	Bill Crossley	100	120	150	250	350	500		
111	Joe Crotty	120	150	200	250	350	500		
112	Billy Crowell	100	120	150	250	350	500		
113	Jim Cudworth	100	120	150	250	350	500		
114	Bert Cunningham	100	120	150	250	350	500		
115	Tacks Curtis	100	120	150	250	350	500		
117	Ed Cushman	1,200	1,500	2,400	3,000	3,600	5,000		
118	Tony Cusick	1,200	1,500	2,000	2,500	3,000	4,000		
120	Edward Dailey Phi-Wash	100	150	200	250	350	500		
121	Edward Dailey Columbus	150	200	250	400	500	800		
122	Bill Daley	100	120	150	250	350	500		
123	Con Daley	100	200	250	300	350	500		
124	Abner Dalrymple	100	120	150	350	400	500		
125	Tom Daly	120	200	250	300	350	500		
126	James Daly	100	120	150	250	350	500		
127	Law Daniels	120	150	200	300	400	600		
128	Dell Darling	100	200	250	300	350	500		
129	William Darnbrough	100	120	150	250	350	500		
130	D.J. Davin	400	500	600	1,000	1,200	1,500		
131	Jumbo Davis	100	120	150	300	350	500		
132	Pat Dealey	100	120	300	400	500	600		
133	Thomas Deasley Throwing	100	120	150	250	400	500		
134	Thomas Deasley Fielding	120	150	200	400	500	600		
135	Edward Decker	100	120	200	250	350	500		
136	Ed Delahanty	3,000	7,500	9,000					
137	Jeremiah Denny	100	120	300	350	400	500		
138	James Devlin	100	120	200	250	350	500		
139	Thomas Dolan	100	120	150	250	350	500		
142	James Donahue	120	150	200	250	350	500		
143	James Donnelly	150	200	250	400	500	800		
146	Mike Dorgan	150	200	300	400	500	600		
148	Home Run Duffe	150	200	250	300	350	500		
149	Hugh Duffy	400	700	1,000	1,500	2,000	3,000		
150	Dan Dugdale	100	120	150	250	350	500		
151	Duck Duke	100	120	150	250	350	500		
152	Sure Shot Dunlap	150	200	250	300	350	500		
153	J. Dunn	150	200	250	400	500	800		
154	Jesse (Cyclone) Duryea	100	120	200	800	1,000	1,200		
155	John Dwyer	100	120	200	800	1,000	1,200		
156	Billy Earle	100	120	150	250	400	1,000		
157	Buck Ebright	100	120	150	250	350	500		
158	Red Ehret	100	120	150	250	350	500		
159	R. Emmerke	120	150	200	250	350	500		
160	Dude Esterbrook	100	120	150	1,500	2,000	2,800		
161	Henry Esterday	100	120	150	250	350	500		
162	Long John Ewing	100	120	150	250	350	500		
163	Buck Ewing	800	1,000	1,600	2,000	3,000	4,000		
164	Buck Ewing w/Mascot	800	1,000	2,000	4,000	6,000	8,000		
165	Jay Faatz	100	120	250	300	350	500		
166	Clinkgers Fagan	100	200	250	300	350	500		
167	William Farmer	100	150	200	250	350	500		
168	Sidney Farrar	120	150	200	250	300	500		
169	Jack (Moose) Farrell	150	150	200	300	400	600		
170	Charles(Duke) Farrell	100	120	150	250	350	500		
171	Frank Fennelly	100	150	200	250	350	500		
172	Charlie Ferguson	100	120	200	250	350	600		
173	Colonel Ferson	100	120	150	250	350	500		
175	Jocko Fields	120	250	300	400	500	600		
176	Fischer - Maroons	100	120	150	250	350	500		
177	Thomas Flanigan	100	120	150	250	350	500		
178	Silver Flint	120	200	250	300	400	1,000		
179	Thomas Flood	100	120	150	250	350	500		
180	Jocko Flynn Omaha	400	500	800	1,000	1,200	1,500		
181	James Fogarty	150	200	250	300	400	1,500		
182	Frank (Monkey) Foreman	100	120	150	250	350	500		
183	Thomas Forster	100	120	150	250	350	500		
185	Elmer Foster NY-Chi	100	120	150	400	600	800		
187	Scissors Foutz Brown's	120	300	400	500	600	800		
188	Scissors Foutz Brooklyn	100	120	150	250	350	600		
189	Julie Freeman	100	120	250	300	350	500		
190	Will Fry	100	120	150	250	350	500		
192	William Fuller	100	300	350	400	450	500		
193	Shorty Fuller	100	200	300	400	500	600		
194	Christopher Fullmer	100	120	150	300	400	500		
195	Christopher Fullmer w/T.Tucker	100	120	150	250	350	500		
196	Honest John Gaffney MG	120	150	200	300	400	600		
197	Pud Galvin	1,000	1,800	5,700	6,200				
198	Robert Gamble	100	250	300	400	500	600		
199	Charles Ganzel	120	150	200	250	350	500		
200	Gid Gardner	100	120	150	250	350	600		
201	Gid Gardner w/M.Murray	100	120	150	250	350	500		
202	Hank Gastreich	100	120	150	400	500	600		
203	Emil Geiss	100	120	150	250	350	500		
204	Frenchy Genins	100	120	300	400	500	600		
205	William George	100	150	200	250	350	500		
206	Joe Gerhardt	100	120	150	250	350	500		
207	Pretzels Getzein	100	150	200	250	350	500		
208	Lee Gibson	100	120	150	250	350	500		
209	Robert Gilks	100	150	200	400	500	600		
210	Pete Gillespie	100	250	300	350	400	800		
211	Barney Gilligan	100	120	150	250	350	500		
212	Frank Gilmore	100	120	150	250	350	500		
213	Pebbly Jack Glasscock	350	400	450	550	800	1,000		
214	Kid Gleason	120	150	200	500	600	1,500		
215	Brother Bill Gleason	200	250	300	500	800	1,000		
216	William Bill Gleason	120	200	300	400	500	600		
217	Mouse Glenn	100	150	200	250	350	500		
218	Michael Goodfellow	100	120	150	250	350	500		
219	George (Piano Legs) Gore	150	250	300	350	400	500		
220	Frank Graves	100	120	150	250	350	500		
221	William Greenwood	100	120	150	250	350	500		
222	Michael Greer	100	120	150	250	350	500		
223	Mike Griffin	250	300	400					
224	Clark Griffith	600	800	1,000	1,200	2,500	3,000		
225	Henry Gruber	100	120	200	250	350	500		
226	Addison Gumbert	100	120	150	250	350	500		
227	Thomas Gunning	100	120	150	250	350	500		
228	Joseph Gunson	100	120	150	250	350	500		
229	George Haddock	100	120	300	350	400	500		
230	William Hafner	100	120	150	250	350	600		
231	Willie Hahm Mascot	100	120	150	250	350	500		
232	William Hallman	100	120	200	250	350	500		
233	Billy Hamilton	600	800	1,000	1,200	2,000	1,000		
234	Willie Hamm w/N.Williamson	120	150	200	300	400	600		
237	Ned Hanlon	400	500	1,000	1,200	2,000	3,000		
238	William Hanrahan	100	120	150	250	350	500		
240	Pa Harkins	100	150	200	1,200	1,500	2,000		
241	William Hart	100	120	150	250	350	500		
242	William (Bill) Hasamdear	100	120	150	250	350	500		
243	Colonel Hatfield	120	150	200	250	350	675		
244	Egyptian Healey Wash-Ind	100	150	200	250	400	500		
245	Egyptian Healey Washington	100	120	150	250	350	500		
246	J.C. Healy	100	120	150	250	400	1,000		
247	Guy Hecker	100	120	150	250	350	500		
248	Tony Hellman	100	120	200	250	350	500		
249	Hardie Henderson	100	120	150	250	350	500		
250	Hardie Henderson w/M.Greer	100	120	150	250	350	500		
251	Moxie Hengle	100	120	150	250	350	500		
252	John Henry	100	120	150	250	350	500		
253	Edward Herr	150	200	250	300	350	500		
254	Hunkey Hines	100	120	150	250	350	500		
255	Paul Hines	100	120	150	250	350	500		
256	Texas Wonder Hoffman	100	120	150	250	350	500		
257	Eddie Hogan	100	120	150	250	350	500		

#	Name	PrFr 1	GD 2	VG 3	VgEx 4	EX 5	ExMt 6	NM 7	NmMt 8
259	William Holbert	100	120	800	1,000	1,200	1,500		
260	James (Bugs) Holliday	100	120	200	250	400	500		
261	Charles Hoover	100	120	150	250	350	500		
262	Buster Hoover	100	120	150	250	350	500		
263	Jack Horner	300	500	700	900	1,200	5,000		
264	Jack Horner w/E.Warner	100	120	150	250	350	500		
265	Michael Hornung	100	120	300	400	500	800		
266	Pete Hotaling	100	120	150	250	350	500		
267	William Howes	100	120	200	250	350	500		
268	Dummy Hoy	1,200	1,500	2,000	2,500	3,000	4,000	6,000	
269	Nat Hudson Brown's	120	150	300	400	600	800		
270	Nat Hudson St. Louis	100	120	150	250	350	500		
271	Mickey Hughes	100	120	150	250	350	500		
272	Hungler	100	120	200	250	350	500		
273	Wild Bill Hutchinson	100	120	150	250	350	500		
274	John Irwin	100	120	150	250	350	500		
275	Arthur (Cut Rate) Irwin	100	120	150	250	350	600		
276	A.C. Jantzen	100	120	300	350	400	500		
277	Frederick Jevne	100	120	600	800	1,000	1,200		
278	John Johnson	120	150	200	250	350	500		
279	Richard Johnston	100	120	250	300	400	500		
280	Jordan	800	1,000	2,000					
281	Heinie Kappell	100	120	250	300	350	500		
282	Timothy Keefe	600	800	1,000	1,200	1,500	2,500		
283	Tim Keefe w/D.Richardson	500	600	800	1,000	2,300	2,500		
284	George Keefe	100	120	150	250	350	500		
285	James Keenan	100	120	150	250	350	500		
286	Mike (King) Kelly	1,500	2,400	3,000	3,500	4,000	5,000		
287	Honest John Kelly MGR	350	400	450	550	800	1,000		
288	Kelly UMP	100	120	150	250	350	500		
289	Charles Kelly	200	250	1,000	1,100	1,200	1,500		
290	Kelly and Powell UMP-MGR	100	120	150	250	350	500		
291	Rudolph Kemmler Brown's	120	150	400	800	1,000	1,200		
292	Rudolph Kemmler St. Paul	100	120	150	250	350	500		
293	Theodore Kennedy	100	120	150	250	400	500		
294	J.J. Kenyon	100	120	150	250	350	500		
295	John Kerins	100	250	300	400	500	600		
296	Matthew Kilroy	100	120	150	250	350	500		
298	August Kloff	200	400	1,000	1,200	1,500	2,000		
299	William Klusman	100	120	150	250	350	500		
300	Phillip Knell	100	120	150	250	350	500		
301	Fred Knouf	100	150	200	300	350	500		
303	William Krieg	100	200	250	300	350	500		
304	William Krieg w/A.Kloff	100	120	150	250	350	500		
305	Gus Krock	120	200	350	400	450	600		
306	Willie Kuehne	100	120	150	250	350	500		
307	Frederick Lange	100	120	150	250	350	500		
308	Ted Larkin	100	120	150	250	350	500		
309	Arlie Latham Brown's	200	300	350	500	600	1,000		
310	Arlie Latham Stl-Chi	120	150	200	300	400	600		
311	John Lauer	100	120	150	250	350	500		
312	John Leighton	200	250	300	350	450	600		
314	Tom Loftus MGR	100	400	450	500	550	650		
315	Herman (Germany) Long	120	150	200	300	400	600		
317	Tom Lovett	100	120	150	250	350	500		
318	Bobby (Link) Lowe	120	150	200	300	400	600		
321	Dennis Lyons	100	120	150	250	350	500		
322	Harry Lyons	120	150	200	250	350	500		
323	Connie Mack	2,000	2,500	3,000	4,000	5,000	6,000		
324	Joe (Reddie) Mack	100	120	150	250	350	500		
325	James (Little Mack) Macullar	100	120	150	250	350	500		
326	Kid Madden	100	120	400	600	800	1,200		
327	Daniel Mahoney	100	120	150	250	350	500		
328	Willard (Grasshopper) Maines	100	120	150	250	350	500		
329	Fred Mann	100	120	150	400	500	700		
330	Jimmy Manning	100	120	150	250	350	500		
331	Charles (Lefty) Marr	100	120	150	250	350	500		
332	Mascot (Willie) Breslin	100	120	150	250	350	500		

#	Name	PrFr 1	GD 2	VG 3	VgEx 4	EX 5	ExMt 6	NM 7	NmMt 8
333	Samuel Maskery	100	120	150	250	350	500		
335	Michael Mattimore	200	250	300	350	600	800		
336	Albert Maul	100	120	150	250	350	500		
338	Albert Mays	100	120	150	300	350	500		
339	James McAleer	100	120	150	250	350	500		
340	Tommy McCarthy	300	600	800	1,500	2,000	2,500		
341	John McCarthy	100	120	150	250	350	700		
342	James McCauley	100	120	150	250	350	500		
343	William McClellan	100	120	150	250	400	1,000		
344	John McCormack	150	200	250	350	450	600		
345	Big Jim McCormick	100	120	150	300	1,000	1,200		
346	McCreachery MGR	300	400	500	800	1,000	1,200		
347	James (Chippy) McGarr	100	120	150	250	350	500		
348	Jack McGeachy	100	150	200	350	450	600		
349	John McGlone	100	120	150	250	350	500		
350	James (Deacon) McGuire	200	250	300	400	500	600		
351	Bill McGunnigle MGR	120	200	250	300	400	500		
352	Ed McKean	100	120	150	250	350	500		
353	Alex McKinnon	100	250	300	350	400	500		
355	Bid McPhee	3,000	6,000	7,000	8,000	10,000	10,000		
356	James McQuaid	100	120	150	250	350	500		
357	John McQuaid UMP	100	120	150	250	350	500		
358	Jame McTamany	175	200	250	400	500	800		
359	George McVey	100	120	150	250	350	500		
362	George (Doggie) Miller	100	120	250	300	350	500		
363	Joseph Miller	100	120	150	250	350	500		
364	Jocko Milligan	100	120	200	250	350	500		
365	E.L. Mills	100	120	150	250	350	600		
366	Daniel Minnehan	100	120	150	250	350	500		
367	Samuel Moffet	100	120	150	250	350	500		
368	Honest Morrell	150	200	250	400	500	800		
369	Ed Morris	120	150	200	250	350	500		
370	Morrisey	100	120	150	250	350	500		
371	Tony (Count) Mullane	120	150	200	500	600	800		
372	Joseph Mulvey	100	120	300	400	500	700		
373	P.L. Murphy	100	120	150	250	350	500		
374	Pat J. Murphy	100	120	150	250	350	500		
375	Miah Murray	100	120	150	250	350	500		
376	Truthful Mutrie MGR	350	400	450	500	800	1,000		
377	George Myers	100	200	250	300	350	500		
378	Al (Cod) Myers	120	200	250	300	600	800		
379	Thomas Nagle	100	120	150	250	350	500		
380	Billy Nash	200	250	300	400	500	800		
382	Kid Nichols	1,500	2,000	2,500	3,000	6,000	8,000		
383	Samuel Nichols	100	120	150	250	350	500		
384	J.W. Nicholson	100	120	150	250	350	500		
385	Tom Nicholson (Parson)	150	200	250	300	350	500		
386	Nick Nicholl Brown's	120	250	350	450	600	600		
387	Hugh Nicol	100	120	150	250	350	500		
388	Hugh Nicol w/J.Reilly	100	120	150	250	350	500		
389	Frederick Nyce	100	120	150	250	350	500		
390	Doc Oberlander	120	150	200	300	400	600		
391	Jack O'Brien	150	200	250					
392	Billy O'Brien	100	120	150	250	350	500		
393	Billy O'Brien w/J.Irwin	100	120	150	250	350	500		
394	Darby O'Brien	100	200	250	350	450	500		
395	John O'Brien	120	150	200	250	400	500		
396	P.J. O'Connell	100	120	150	250	400	500		
398	Hank O'Day	300	800	1,000	1,100	1,200	1,500		
399	O'Day	100	120	150	250	400	500		
400	James O'Neil Stl-Chi	120	150	200	250	500	800		
401	James O'Neil Brown's	120	150	200	400	500	600		
403	Jim O'Rourke	600	1,200	1,500	2,000	2,500	3,000		
404	Thomas O'Rourke	100	120	200	250	350	500		
406	David Orr	100	120	250	300	400	500		
407	Parsons	100	120	150	250	400	800		
408	Owen Patton	100	120	150	300	400	500		
409	James Peeples	100	120	150	250	400	500		

#	Name	PrFr 1	GD 2	VG 3	VgEx 4	EX 5	ExMt 6	NM 7	NmMt 8
10	James Peeples w/H.Henderson	100	120	150	250	350	500		
12	Patrick Pettee	100	500	600	700	800	1,000		
13	Patrick Pettee w/B.Lowe	100	120	150	250	350	500		
14	Dandelion Pfeffer	150	200	250	500	600	800		
15	Dick Phelan	100	120	250	500	800	1,000		
16	William Phillips	100	120	200	250	350	500		
18	George Pinkney	100	120	250	300	350	500		
19	Thomas Poorman	100	200	250	300	350	500		
20	Henry Porter	250	300	400	450	600	800		
21	James Powell	100	150	200	300	400	500		
23	Bill (Blondie) Purcell	100	120	300	350	400	500		
24	Thomas Quinn	100	150	200	250	350	500		
25	Joseph Quinn	100	150	200	350	400	500		
26	Old Hoss Radbourne Portrait	1,200	2,000	2,200	2,500	4,000	5,000		
27	Old Hoss Radbourne In Action	1,200	2,000	2,200	2,500	3,000	4,000		
28	Shorty Radford	100	120	150	300	350	500		
29	Tom Ramsey	100	120	150	250	350	500		
30	Rehse	100	120	150	250	350	500		
31	Long John Reilly	100	120	150	250	600	800		
32	Charles (Princeton) Reilly	100	120	150	250	350	500		
33	Charles Reynolds	100	120	150	250	350	500		
34	Hardie Richardson	100	120	150	250	350	500		
35	Danny Richardson	100	200	250	350	450	600		
37	John Roach	100	200	250	400	500	600		
38	Wilbert Robinson	1,000	1,200	1,500	2,000	2,500	3,000		
39	M.C. Robinson	100	120	150	300	350	500		
40	Yank Robinson Stl	100	120	150	250	350	500		
41	Yank Robinson Brown's	200	250	300	500	600	800		
42	George Rooks	100	120	150	250	350	500		
45	Jack Rowe	100	120	150	250	350	500		
46	Amos Rusie	1,500	2,000	2,500	3,000				
47	Amos Rusie New York	1,500	2,000	3,000	4,000				
48	James Ryan	120	150	250	300	400	600		
49	Henry Sage	100	120	150	250	350	500		
50	Henry Sage w/W.Van Dyke	100	120	150	250	350	500		
51	Sanders	100	120	150	250	350	500		
52	Al (Ben) Sanders	100	120	200	250	350	500		
53	Frank Scheibeck	100	120	150	250	350	500		
54	Albert Schellhase	100	120	150	250	350	500		
55	William Schenkle	100	120	150	250	400	500		
56	Bill Schildknecht	100	120	150	250	350	500		
57	Gus Schmelz MG	100	120	150	250	350	500		
58	Lewis (Jumbo) Schoeneck	100	120	150	350	450	600		
59	Pop Schriver	100	150	200	250	350	600		
60	John Seery	100	120	200	250	350	500		
61	William Serad	100	120	150	250	350	500		
62	Edward Seward	120	150	200	250	350	500		
63	George (Orator) Shafer	100	120	150	250	350	500		
64	Frank Shafer	100	120	150	250	350	500		
65	Daniel Shannon	100	120	150	250	350	500		
66	William Sharsig	100	120	150	250	350	500		
67	Samuel Shaw	100	120	150	250	350	500		
68	John Shaw	100	120	150	250	600	800		
69	William Shindle	100	120	150	250	350	500		
70	George Shoch	175	250	350	450	550	800		
71	Otto Shomberg	100	120	150	250	500	600		
72	Lev Shrev	100	250	350	450	550	700		
73	Ed (Baldy) Silch	100	150	200	250	350	500		
74	Michael Slattery	100	120	250	300	350	500		
75	Sam (Sky Rocket) Smith	100	120	150	800	1,000	1,200		
76	John Smith Portrait	400	500	600	1,500	2,000	2,500		
77	John Smith Non-Portrait	120	150	200	300	400	600		
78	Elmer Smith	100	120	150	250	350	500		
79	Fred (Sam) Smith	100	120	150	250	350	500		
80	George (Germany) Smith	100	120	150	250	350	500		
81	Pop Smith	100	120	150	250	800	1,000		
82	Nick Smith	100	120	200	250	350	500		
83	P.T. Somers	100	120	150	250	350	500		
484	Joe Sommer	100	120	150	300	350	500		
485	Pete Sommers	100	120	200	250	350	500		
486	William Sowders	120	150	200	250	350	500		
487	John Sowders	100	120	150	600	800	1,000		
488	Charles Sprague	100	120	150	250	350	500		
489	Edward Sproat	100	150	200	250	350	500		
490	Harry Staley	150	200	250	300	400	500		
491	Daniel Stearns	120	150	200	250	400	600		
492	Billy (Cannonball) Stemmyer	100	200	300	400	500	700		
493	B.F. Stephens	100	120	150	250	350	500		
494	John C. Sterling	100	120	150	250	350	500		
496	Harry Stovey	200	300	900	1,000	1,200	1,500		
497	C. Scott Stratton	100	120	500	600	800	1,200		
498	Joseph Straus	100	120	150	250	350	500		
499	John (Cub) Stricker	100	120	150	250	350	500		
500	Marty Sullivan	100	120	300	400	500	700		
501	Michael Sullivan	100	200	250	350	450	600		
502	Billy Sunday	500	800	1,000	2,000	2,500	6,000		
503	Sy Sutcliffe	100	120	150	250	350	500		
504	Ezra Sutton	100	400	450	500	600	800		
505	Ed Cyrus Swartwood	150	200	250	400	500	800		
506	Parke Swartzel	100	120	150	250	350	500		
507	Peter Sweeney	100	120	150	250	350	500		
509	Ed (Dimples) Tate	100	200	250	300	350	500		
510	Patsy Tebeau	120	150	200	300	400	600		
511	John Tener	100	120	150	425	550	800		
512	Bill (Adonis) Terry	100	120	150	250	350	500		
513	Sam Thompson	1,200	1,400	1,800	2,000	5,000	5,000		
514	Silent Mike Tiernan	120	200	250	300	400	600		
515	Ledell Titcomb	100	250	300	400	500	700		
516	Phillip Tomney	100	120	150	250	350	500		
517	Stephen Toole	150	200	250	400	500	600		
518	George Townsend	100	250	350	450	550	700		
519	William Traffley	100	120	150	250	500	1,000		
520	George Treadway	100	200	250	300	350	500		
521	Samuel Trott	100	120	150	250	800	1,000		
522	Samuel Trott w/T.Burns	100	120	150	250	800	1,000		
523	Tom (Foghorn) Tucker	100	120	150	250	350	500		
524	William Tuckerman	150	200	250	300	400	500		
525	George Turner	100	120	150	250	350	500		
526	Lawrence Twitchell	300	350	400	450	500	600		
527	James Tyng	100	120	150	250	350	500		
529	George (Rip) Van Haltren	150	200	250	400	500	800		
530	Farmer Harry Vaughn	100	120	150	250	350	500		
531	Peek-a-Boo Veach St. Paul	150	200	250	400	500	800		
533	Leon Viau	100	120	200	250	350	600		
534	William Vinton	100	120	150	250	350	500		
535	Joseph Visner	100	120	150	250	350	500		
537	Joseph Walsh	100	120	150	250	350	500		
538	John M. Ward	1,000	1,200	1,500	2,000	2,500	4,000		
539	E.H. Warner	150	200	250	400	500	800		
540	William Watkins MGR	100	300	400	500	600	800		
541	Farmer Bill Weaver	100	250	300	400	500	650		
542	Charles Weber	150	200	250	300	400	500		
543	George (Stump) Weidman	150	200	250	350	450	800		
544	William Widner	100	120	150	250	350	500		
545	Curtis Welch Brown's	120	250	350	450	600	800		
546	Curtis Welch A's	100	120	150	400	500	600		
547	Curtis Welch w/B.Gleason	120	150	200	300	400	600		
548	Smilin Mickey Welch	1,000	1,500	1,800	2,000	4,000	5,000		
549	Jake Wells	100	120	150	250	350	500		
550	Frank Wells	100	120	150	250	350	500		
551	Joseph Werrick	100	120	150	250	350	500		
552	Milton (Buck) West	100	120	150	250	350	500		
553	Gus (Cannonball) Weyhing	100	120	150	250	350	500		
554	John Weyhing	100	120	150	300	400	500		
555	Bobby Wheelock	100	200	250	300	350	500		
556	Whitacre	100	120	150	250	400	500		

		PrFr 1	GD 2	VG 3	VgEx 4	EX 5	ExMt 6	NM 7	NmMt 8
557	Pat Whitaker	100	120	150	250	350	500		
558	Deacon White	1,000	2,000	3,000	5,000	6,000	8,000		
559	William White	100	120	150	250	350	500		
560	Jim (Grasshopper) Whitney	120	150	200	300	400	600		
561	Arthur Whitney	120	150	500	600	800	1,000		
562	G. Whitney	100	120	150	250	350	500		
563	James Williams MG	100	120	150	2,500	3,000	5,000		
564	Ned Williamson	120	200	300	400	500	700		
565	Williamson and Mascot	100	120	150	250	350	500		
566	C.H. Willis	100	120	400	500	600	700		
567	Walt Wilmot	100	120	150	500	800	1,000		
568	George Winkleman Hartford	250	300	400	600	5,000	7,000		
569	Samuel Wise	100	300	400	500	600	800		
570	William (Chicken) Wolf	100	120	150	250	350	500		
571	George (Dandy) Wood	120	200	300	400	600	800		
572	Peter Wood	200	250	300	400	500	650		
573	Harry Wright	2,500	3,000	4,000	5,000	6,000	10,000		
574	Charles (Chief) Zimmer	100	120	150	250	350	500		
575	Frank Zinn	100	150	200	250	350	500		

— Many subjects within the N172 Old Judge set appear in multiple poses and/or text variations. Listed prices refer to all variations unless noted.

— Jake Beckley SGC 88 (NmMt) sold for $15,829 (Goodwin; 5/14)

— Ed Delahanty Hands at Waist SGC 84 (NM) sold for $16,440 (Goodwin; 7/13)

— John Doran SGC 30 (Good) sold for $50,000 (Legendary; 11/12)

— John McQuaid UMP PSA 3.5 (VG+) sold for $16,035 (Goodwin; 7/13)

— John McQuaid UMP PSA 3.5 (VG+) sold for $8,030 (Goodwin; 6/12)

— Jim O'Rourke #403 SGC 88 (NmMt) sold for $6,032 (Goodwin; 6/12)

— Amos Rusie SGC 60 (EX) sold for $6,500 (REA; 05/12)

— Arthur Whitney #561 SGC 70 (EX+) sold for $5,729 (Goodwin; 8/12)

1888 Allen and Ginter N29

		PrFr 1	GD 2	VG 3	VgEx 4	EX 5	ExMt 6	NM 7	NmMt 8
1	Buck Ewing/Baseball	600	800	1,000	1,200	1,500	2,500	3,000	6,000

1888 Goodwin Champions N162

		PrFr 1	GD 2	VG 3	VgEx 4	EX 5	ExMt 6	NM 7	NmMt 8
1	Ed Andrews (Baseball)	400	600	800	1,000	1,200	2,500		
2	Cap Anson (Baseball)	2,000	2,500	3,000	4,000	6,000	12,000		
3	Dan Brouthers (Baseball)	800	1,000	1,200	1,500	2,500	4,000		
4	Bob Caruthers (Baseball)	400	600	800	1,000	1,500	2,500	3,000	
5	Fred Dunlap (Baseball)	400	600	800	1,000	1,500	2,500		
6	Jack Glasscock (Baseball)	400	600	800	1,000	1,500	3,000		
7	Tim Keefe (Baseball)	600	800	1,000	1,800	2,500			
8	King Kelly (Baseball)	1,000	1,500	2,000	3,000	5,000	8,000		

1895 Mayo's Cut Plug N300

		PrFr 1	GD 2	VG 3	VgEx 4	EX 5	ExMt 6	NM 7	NmMt 8
1	Charlie Abbey	350	500	650	700	1,000			
2	Cap Anson	2,000	2,500	4,000	6,000	8,000			
3	Jimmy Bannon	200	300	400	500	800			
4A	Dan Brouthers Baltimore	1,200	2,000	2,500	3,000	4,000			
4B	Dan Brouthers Louisville	1,200	2,000	2,500	3,000	4,000			
5	Ed Cartwright	200	300	450	500	800			
6	John Clarkson	500	800	1,200	1,500	2,500	4,000		
7	Tommy Corcoran	200	300	400	500				
8	Lave Cross	200	300	400	500	800			
9	William Dahlen	300	400	1,000	1,200				
10	Tom Daly	200	300	400	500	800			
11	Ed Delahanty UER	1,500	2,800	3,000	4,000	6,000			
12	Hugh Duffy	500	800	1,500	2,500				
13A	Buck Ewing Cincinnati	1,200	2,000	2,500	3,000	5,000			
13B	Buck Ewing Cleveland	1,200	2,200	2,500	3,000	5,000			
14	Dave Foutz	200	300	400	500	800			
15	Bill Joyce	200	250	400	600	800			
16	Charlie Ganzel	200	300	400	500	800			
17A	Jack Glasscock Louisville	200	300	400	500	800			
17B	Jack Glasscock Pittsburgh	300	500	800	1,000				

		PrFr 1	GD 2	VG 3	VgEx 4	EX 5	ExMt 6	NM 7	NmMt 8
18	Mike Griffin	200	300	400	500	800			
19A	George Haddock No Team	400	700	1,200					
19B	George Haddock Philadelphia	200	300	400	500	800			
20	Bill Hallman	200	300	500	500	1,000			
21	Billy Hamilton	600	1,000	1,600	2,000	3,300			
22	Brickyard Kennedy	250	400	500	700	1,000			
23A	Tom Kinslow No Team	400	600	1,000					
23B	Tom Kinslow Pittsburgh	300	500	800	1,000	1,200			
24	Arlie Latham	200	350	400	500	800			
25	Herman Long	200	300	400	500	800			
26	Tom Lovett	200	300	400	500	800			
27	Link Lowe	200	300	400	500	800			
28	Tommy McCarthy	500	800	1,200	1,500	2,000			
29	Yale Murphy	250	400	500	700	1,000			
30	Billy Nash	200	350	400	500	800			
31	Kid Nichols	1,500	2,500	3,000	4,000	7,500			
32A	Fred Pfeffer 2nd Base	250	400	500	700	1,000			
32B	Fred Pfeffer Retired	250	400	500	700	1,000			
33	Wilbert Robinson	1,000	1,500	2,000	2,500	4,000			
34A	Amos Rusie COR	800	2,000	2,500	3,000	5,000			
34B	Amos Russie ERR	1,000	1,500	2,000	2,500	4,000			
35	Jimmy Ryan	200	300	400	500	800			
36	Bill Shindle	200	300	400	500	800			
37	Germany Smith	200	300	400	500	800			
38	Otis Stockdale UER	200	300	400	500	800			
39	Tommy Tucker	200	300	400	500	800			
40A	John Ward 2nd Base	1,000	1,500	2,500	3,000	4,000			
40B	John Ward Retired	1,000	1,500	2,000	2,500	4,000			

— Buck Ewing Cleveland #13B SGC 84 (NrMt) sold for $9,960 (Greg Bussineau; 7/12)

— Buck Ewing Cleveland SGC 7 (Nm) sold for $9,400 (REA; 05/11)

— Kid Nichols PSA 8 (NmMt) sold for $16,450 (REA; 05/11)

1903-04 Breisch-Williams E107

— Tommy Corcoran SGC 10 (Poor) sold for $11,000 (Legendary; 8/13)

— Ed Delahanty SGC 10 (Poor) sold for $23,700 (REA; 5/13)

— Ed Delahanty SGC 10 (Poor) sold for $17,000 (Legendary; 8/13)

— Addie Joss SGC 45 (VG+) sold for $14,220 (REA; 5/13)

— Willie Keeler SGC 20 (Fair) sold for $10,665 (REA; 5/13)

— Christy Mathewson SGC 20 (Fair) sold for $67,500 (Legendary; 11/13)

— Eddie Plank #120 SGC 10 (Poor) sold for $6,115 (Goodwin; 7/12)

— Rube Waddell #148 SGC 20 (Fair) sold for $5,558 (Goodwin; 7/12)

1906 Fan Craze AL WG2

		GD 2	VG 3	VgEx 4	EX 5	ExMt 6	NM 7	NmMt 8	MT 9
1	Nick Altrock	30	40	50	60	80	120	200	400
2	Jim Barrett	25	30	40	50	60	80	120	400
3	Harry Bay	25	30	40	50	60	80	120	300
4	Chief Bender	100	120	150	200	250	400	600	1,200
5	Bill Bernhardt	25	30	40	50	60	80	120	300
6	Bill Bradley	25	30	40	50	60	80	120	300
7	Jack Chesbro	100	120	150	200	400	600	800	1,200
8	Jimmy Collins	80	100	120	150	200	300	500	1,000
9	Sam Crawford	120	150	200	250	300	500	800	1,500
10	Lou Criger	25	30	40	50	60	80	120	300
11	Lave Cross	25	30	40	50	60	80	120	300
12	Monty Cross	25	30	40	50	60	80	120	300
13	Harry Davis	25	30	40	50	60	80	120	300
14	Bill Dineen	25	30	40	50	60	80	120	300
15	Pat Donovan	25	30	40	50	60	80	120	300
16	Pat Dougherty	25	30	40	50	60	80	120	300
17	Norman Elberfeld	25	30	40	50	60	80	120	300
18	Hobe Ferris	25	30	40	50	60	80	120	300
19	Elmer Flick	80	100	120	150	200	300	500	1,000
20	Buck Freeman	25	30	40	50	60	80	120	300
21	Fred Glade	25	30	40	50	60	80	120	300
22	Clark Griffith	80	100	120	150	200	300	500	1,000
23	Charles Hickman	25	30	40	50	60	80	120	300

		GD 2	VG 3	VgEx 4	EX 5	ExMt 6	NM 7	NmMt 8	MT 9
24	William Holmes	25	30	40	50	60	80	120	300
25	Harry Howell	25	30	40	50	60	80	120	300
26	Frank Isbell	25	30	40	50	60	80	120	300
27	Albert Jacobson	25	30	40	50	60	80	120	300
28	Ban Johnson PRES	120	150	200	250	300	500	800	1,500
29	Fielder Jones	25	30	40	50	60	80	120	300
30	Adrian Joss	120	150	200	250	300	500	800	1,500
31	Willie Keeler	100	120	150	200	250	400	600	1,200
32	Nap Lajoie	120	150	200	250	300	500	800	1,500
33	Connie Mack MG	150	200	200	250	300	500	800	2,000
34	Jimmy McAleer	25	30	40	50	60	80	120	300
35	Jim McGuire	25	30	40	50	60	100	120	300
36	Earl Moore	25	30	40	50	60	80	120	300
37	George Mullen	40	50	60	80	100	120	200	500
38	Billy Owen	25	30	40	50	60	80	120	300
39	Fred Parent	25	30	40	50	60	80	120	300
40	Case Patten	25	30	40	50	80	100	120	300
41	Eddie Plank	150	200	250	300	400	500	800	1,500
42	Ossie Schreckengost	25	30	40	50	80	100	120	300
43	Jake Stahl	30	40	50	60	80	120	200	400
44	Fred Stone	25	40	50	60	80	100	120	300
45	William Sudhoff	25	30	40	50	60	80	120	300
46	Roy Turner	25	30	40	80	100	120	120	300
47	Rube Waddell	80	100	120	150	200	300	500	1,000
48	Bob Wallace	60	80	100	120	150	250	400	800
49	G. Harris White	25	30	40	50	60	80	120	300
50	George Winter	25	30	40	50	60	80	120	300
51	Cy Young	250	300	600	700	800	1,500	2,000	

1906 Fan Craze NL WG3

		GD 2	VG 3	VgEx 4	EX 5	ExMt 6	NM 7	NmMt 8	MT 9
1	Red Ames	25	30	40	50	60	80	120	300
2	Ginger Beaumont	25	30	40	50	60	80	120	300
3	Jake Beckley	100	120	150	200	250	400	600	1,200
4	Billy Bergen	25	30	40	50	60	80	120	300
5	Roger Bresnahan	100	120	150	200	250	400	600	1,200
6	George Brown	25	30	40	60	80	100	120	300
7	Mordacai Brown (Mordecai)	100	120	150	200	250	400	600	1,200
8	Doc Casey	25	30	40	50	60	80	120	300
9	Frank Chance	80	100	120	150	200	300	500	1,000
10	Fred Clarke	80	100	120	150	200	300	500	1,000
11	Tommy Corcoran	25	30	40	50	60	80	200	300
12	Bill Dahlen	30	60	80	100	120	150	200	400
13	Mike Donlin	25	30	40	50	60	80	120	300
14	Charley Dooin	25	30	40	50	60	80	120	300
15	Mickey Doolin (Doolan)	25	30	40	50	60	80	120	300
16	Hugh Duffy	80	100	120	150	200	300	500	1,000
17	John E. Dunleavy	25	30	40	50	60	80	120	300
18	Bob Ewing	25	30	40	50	60	80	120	350
19	Chick Fraser	25	30	40	50	60	80	120	300
20	Ned Hanlon MG	80	100	120	150	300	400	500	1,000
21	Del Howard	25	30	40	50	60	80	120	300
22	Miller Huggins	80	100	120	150	200	300	500	1,000
23	Joe Kelley	80	100	120	150	200	300	500	1,300
24	John Kling	25	30	40	50	60	80	150	300
25	Tommy Leach	25	30	40	50	60	80	120	300
26	Harry Lumley	25	30	40		60	80	120	300
27	Carl Lundgren	25	30	40	50	60	80	120	300
28	Bill Maloney	25	30	40	50	60	80	120	800
29	Dan McGann	25	30	40	50	60	80	120	300
30	Joe McGinnity	80	100	120	150	200	300	500	1,000
31	John McGraw MG	80	100	120	150	200	300	500	1,000
32	Harry McIntire	25	30	40	50	60	80	120	300
33	Kid Nichols	50	60	80	300	400	500	700	1,200
34	Mike O'Neil	25	30	40	50	60	80	120	350
35	Orval Overall	25	30	40	50	80	100	120	300
36	Frank Pfeffer	25	30	40	50	60	80	120	300

		GD 2	VG 3	VgEx 4	EX 5	ExMt 6	NM 7	NmMt 8	MT 9
37	Deacon Philippe	25	30	40	50	60	80	120	300
38	Charley Pittinger	25	30	40	50	60	80	120	350
39	Harry C. Pulliam PRES	25	30	40	50	60	80	120	300
40	Ed Reulbach	25	30	40	50	60	80	120	350
41	Claude Ritchey	25	30	40	60	80	100	120	350
42	Cy Seymour	25	30	40	50	60	80	120	800
43	Jim Sheckard	25	30	40	50	60	80	120	300
44	Jack Taylor	25	30	40	60	80	100	120	300
45	Dummy Taylor	25	30	40	100	120	150	200	1,000
46	Fred Tenny (Tenney)	25	30	40	50	60	80	120	300
47	Harry Theilman	25	30	40	50	80	100	120	300
48	Roy Thomas	25	30	40	50	60	80	120	300
49	Honus Wagner	800	1,500	1,800	2,000	2,500	3,000	4,000	
50	Jake Weimer	25	30	40	50	60	80	120	350
51	Bob Wicker	25	30	40	50	60	80	120	300
52	Vic Willis	80	100	120	150	200	300	500	1,000
53	Lew Wiltsie	25	30	40	50	60	80	400	600
54	Irving Young	25	30	40	60	80	100	120	300

1909 E92-1 Dockman and Sons

		PrFr 1	GD 2	VG 3	VgEx 4	EX 5	ExMt 6	NM 7	NmMt 8
1	Harry Bemis	30	60	100	200	350	500		
2	Chief Bender	80	200	250	400				
3	Bill Bergen	30	120	150	200	350	500		
4	Bob Bescher	30	120	150	200	350	500		
5	Al Bridwell	30	60	150	200	350	600		
6	Joe Casey	30	60	100	200	350	500		
7	Frank Chance	100	250	350	600	800			
8	Hal Chase	60	120	200	300	500	800		
9	Sam Crawford	150	200	350	600	1,000			
10	Harry Davis	30	100	120	200	350	500		
11	Art Devlin	30	60	150	200	350	500		
12	Bill Donovan	30	60	100	200	350	500		
13	Mickey Doolan	30	60	100	200	350	500		
14	Patsy Dougherty	30	60	100	200	350	500		
15	Larry Doyle Batting	30	60	120	200	350	500		
16	Larry Doyle Throwing	30	60	150	200	350	500		
17	George Gibson	30	60	150	200	500	800		
18	Topsy Hartsel	30	60	100	200	350	500		
19	Hugh Jennings	100	250	350	600	1,000	1,200		
20	Red Kleinow	30	120	150	200	350	1,000		
21	Nap Lajoie	200	300	500	800	1,200			
22	Hans Lobert	30	60	100	200	350	500		
23	Sherry Magee	30	60	100	200	350	500		
24	Christy Matthewson	400	800	1,200	2,000	3,000	5,000		
25	John McGraw	100	250	350	600	1,000			
26	Larry McLean	30	120	150	200	350	500		
27	Dots Miller Batting	30	60	100	200	350	500		
28	Danny Murphy	30	60	100	120	350	500		
29	Bill O'Hara	30	80	100	200	350	500		
30	Germany Schaefer	30	80	100	500	550	600		
31	Admiral Schlei	30	150	200	250	350	500		
32	Boss Schmidt	30	80	100	200	350	600		
33	John Siegle	60	100	150	250	350	1,500		
34	Dave Shean	30	60	150	200	350	500		
35	Frank Smith	30	60	100	200	350	500		
36	Joe Tinker	100	250	350	600	1,000			
37	Honus Wagner Batting	1,000	1,500	2,800	4,000				
38	Honus Wagner Throwing	1,000	2,000	2,800	3,500	5,000			
39	Cy Young Cleveland	400	800	1,100	1,500	2,500			
40	Heinie Zimmerman	35	60	100	200	350	500		

— Christy Matthewson SGC 86 (NrMt+) sold for $14,034 (Goodwin; 10/12)

— Christy Matthewson SGC 86 (NrMt+) sold for $11,212 (Goodwin; 5/14)

— Honus Wagner Throwing #38 PSA 6 (ExMt) sold for $6,462 (Huggins and Scott; 8/12)

1909 E92-2 Croft's Candy

		PrFr 1	GD 2	VG 3	VgEx 4	EX 5	ExMt 6	NM 7	NmMt 8
1	Jack Barry	50	100	150	200	350	500		
2	Harry Bemis	50	100	120	300	350	500		
3	Chief Bender Striped Cap	100	250	350	600	1,000			
4	Chief Bender White Cap	100	250	350	600	1,000			
5	Bill Bergen	50	100	120	200	350	500		
6	Bob Bescher	50	100	120	200	350	500		
7	Al Bridwell	50	100	120	200	350	500		
8	Doc Casey	50	100	120	200	350	500		
9	Frank Chance	100	300	350	600	1,000			
10	Hal Chase	80	150	200	300	500	800		
11	Ty Cobb	2,000	3,000	4,000	14,000				
12	Eddie Collins	100	250	350	725	1,000			
13	Sam Crawford	100	250	350	600	1,000			
14	Harry Davis	50	100	120	200	350	500		
15	Art Devlin	50	100	120	200	350	500		
16	Bill Donovan	50	100	120	200	350	500		
17	Red Dooin	50	100	120	200	350	500		
18	Mickey Doolan	50	100	120	200	350	500		
19	Patsy Dougherty	50	100	120	200	350	500		
20	Larry Doyle Batting	50	300	400	500	600	800		
21	Larry Doyle Throwing	50	100	120	200	350	500		
22	Johnny Evers	100	250	350	600	1,000			
23	George Gibson	50	100	120	200	350	500		
24	Topsy Hartsel	50	100	120	200	350	500		
25	Fred Jacklitsch	50	100	120	200	350	500		
26	Hugh Jennings	50	100	120	200	350	950		
27	Red Kleinow	50	100	120	200	350	500		
28	Otto Knabe	50	100	120	200	350	500		
29	John Knight	50	100	120	200	350	500		
30	Nap Lajoie	120	300	500	800	1,200			
31	Hans Lobert	50	100	120	200	350	500		
32	Sherry Magee	50	100	120	200	350	500		
33	Christy Matthewson	600	1,000	1,200	3,000				
34	John McGraw	100	250	350	600	1,000			
35	Larry McLean	50	100	120	200	350	500		
36	Dots Miller Batting	50	100	120	200	350	500		
37	Dots Miller Fielding	50	100	120	200	350	500		
38	Danny Murphy	50	100	120	200	350	500		
39	Bill O'Hara	50	100	120	200	350	500		
40	Germany Schaefer	50	100	120	200	350	500		
41	Admiral Schlei	50	100	120	200	350	500		
42	Boss Schmidt	50	100	120	200	350	500		
43	Dave Shean	50	150	200	250	350	500		
44	John Siegle	50	100	120	200	350	500		
45	Frank Smith	50	100	120	200	350	500		
46	Joe Tinker	100	250	350	600	1,000			
47	Honus Wagner Batting	1,000	1,500	2,500	4,000				
48	Honus Wagner Throwing	1,400	1,800	2,000	3,000				
49	Cy Young	500	800	1,000	1,500	2,500			
50	Heinie Zimmerman	50	100	120	200	350	500		

1909 E92-3 Croft's Cocoa

		PrFr 1	GD 2	VG 3	VgEx 4	EX 5	ExMt 6	NM 7	NmMt 8
1	Jack Barry	50	150	200	250	350	500		
2	Harry Bemis	50	100	120	200	350	500		
3	Chief Bender Striped Cap	100	250	350	600	1,000			
4	Chief Bender White Cap	100	250	350	600	1,000			
5	Bill Bergen	50	100	120	200	350	500		
6	Bob Bescher	50	100	120	200	350	500		
7	Al Bridwell	50	150	200	250	400	500		
8	Doc Casey	50	100	120	200	350	500		
9	Frank Chance	100	500	600	700	1,000			
10	Hal Chase	80	150	200	500	600	800		
11	Ty Cobb	2,000	3,000	4,000	6,000	10,000			
12	Eddie Collins	100	250	350	600	1,000			
13	Sam Crawford	100	250	350	600	1,000			
14	Harry Davis	50	100	120	200	350	500		
15	Art Devlin	50	100	120	200	350	500		
16	Bill Donovan	50	200	250	350	450	600		
17	Red Dooin	50	100	150	200	350	500		
18	Mickey Doolan	50	100	200	300	400	550		
19	Patsy Dougherty	50	100	120	200	350	500		
20	Larry Doyle Batting	50	100	120	200	350	500		
21	Larry Doyle Throwing	50	100	120	200	350	500		
22	Johnny Evers	100	250	350	600	1,000			
23	George Gibson	50	100	120	200	350	500		
24	Topsy Hartsel	50	100	120	200	350	500		
25	Fred Jacklitsch	50	100	120	200	350	500		
26	Hugh Jennings	100	250	400	600	1,000	1,200		
27	Red Kleinow	50	100	120	200	350	500		
28	Otto Knabe	50	100	120	200	350	500		
29	Jack Knight	50	100	120	200	350	500		
30	Nap Lajoie	120	300	600	800	1,200			
31	Hans Lobert	50	100	120	200	350	500		
32	Sherry Magee	50	100	120	200	350	500		
33	Christy Matthewson	600	1,000	2,000	3,000	3,500	5,000		
34	John McGraw	100	250	350	600	1,000			
35	Larry McLean	50	100	250	350	450	600		
36	Dots Miller Batting	50	100	120	200	350	500		
37	Dots Miller Fielding	50	150	200	250	350	500		
38	Danny Murphy	50	100	120	200	350	500		
39	Bill O'Hara	50	100	120	200	350	500		
40	Germany Schaefer	50	100	120	200	350	500		
41	Admiral Schlei	50	100	120	200	350	500		
42	Boss Schmidt	50	200	250	350	450	600		
43	Dave Shean	50	100	120	200	350	500		
44	John Siegle	50	100	120	200	350	500		
45	Frank Smith	50	100	120	200	350	500		
46	Joe Tinker	100	250	350	600	1,500			
47	Honus Wagner Batting	1,000	1,500	2,500	4,000				
48	Honus Wagner Throwing	1,000	1,500	3,300	4,300				
49	Cy Young Cleveland	500	800	1,200	1,700	2,800			
50	Heinie Zimmerman	50	100	120	200	350	500		

1909 E92-4 Nadja Caramel

		PrFr 1	GD 2	VG 3	VgEx 4	EX 5	ExMt 6	NM 7	NmMt 8
1	Bill Bailey	50	100	150	200	350	500		
2	Jack Barry	50	100	120	200	350	500		
3	Harry Bemis	50	100	120	200	350	500		
4	Chief Bender Striped Cap	100	800	1,000	1,200	1,500			
5	Chief Bender White Cap	100	250	400	600	1,000			
6	Bill Bergen	50	100	120	200	350	500		
7	Bob Bescher	50	100	120	200	350	500		
8	Roger Bresnahan	100	200	250	300	500			
9	Al Bridwell	50	100	120	200	350	500		
10	Doc Casey	50	100	120	200	350	500		
11	Frank Chance	100	250	350	600	1,000			
12	Hal Chase	80	150	200	300	500	800		
13	Ty Cobb	2,000	3,000	4,000	6,000				
14	Eddie Collins	100	250	350	600	1,000			
15	Sam Crawford	100	250	350	600	1,000			
16	Harry Davis	50	100	120	200	350	500		
17	Art Devlin	50	100	120	200	350	500		
18	Bill Donovan	50	100	120	200	350	500		
19	Red Dooin	50	100	120	200	350	500		
20	Mickey Doolan	50	100	120	200	350	500		
21	Patsy Dougherty	50	100	120	200	350	500		
22	Larry Doyle Batting	50	100	120	200	350	500		
23	Larry Doyle Throwing	50	100	120	200	350	500		
24	Rube Ellis	50	100	120	200	350	500		
25	Johnny Evers	100	250	350	600	1,000			

		PrFr 1	GD 2	VG 3	VgEx 4	EX 5	ExMt 6	NM 7	NmMt 8
26	George Gibson	50	100	120	200	350	500		
27	Topsy Hartsel	50	100	120	200	350	500		
28	Roy Hartzell Batting	50	100	120	200	300	500		
29	Roy Hartzell Fielding	50	80	100	120	250	500		
30	Harry Howell Follow Through	50	100	120	200	300	500		
31	Harry Howell Ready to Pitch	50	120	150	200	250	500		
32	Fred Jacklitsch	50	100	120	200	350	500		
33	Hugh Jennings	100	250	350	600	1,000	500		
34	Red Kleinow	50	100	120	200	350	500		
35	Otto Knabe	50	100	120	200	350	500		
36	Jack Knight	50	100	120	200	350	500		
37	Nap Lajoie	120	300	500	800	1,200			
38	Hans Lobert	50	100	120	200	350	500		
39	Sherry Magee	60	100	120	200	350	500		
40	Christy Matthewson	600	1,000	1,200	2,000	3,000	5,000		
41	John McGraw	100	250	350	600	1,000	1,200		
42	Larry McLean	50	100	120	200	350	500		
43	Dots Miller Batting	60	100	120	300	400	500		
44	Dots Miller Fielding	50	100	120	200	350	500		
45	Danny Murphy	50	100	120	200	350	500		
46	Rebel Oakes	120	150	200	250	300	500		
47	Bill O'Hara	50	100	120	200	350	500		
48	Ed Phelps	50	100	120	200	350	500		
49	Germany Schaefer	50	100	120	200	350	500		
50	Admiral Schlei	50	100	120	200	350	500		
51	Boss Schmidt	50	100	120	200	350	500		
52	Dave Shean	50	100	120	200	350	500		
53	Johnny Seigle (Siegle)	50	100	120	200	350	500		
54	Frank Smith	50	100	120	200	350	500		
55	George Stone Blue Back	50	100	120	200	250	500		
56	George Stone Green Back	50	100	120	200	300	500		
57	Joe Tinker	100	250	350	600	1,000			
58	Honus Wagner Batting	1,000	1,500	6,000	8,000				
59	Honus Wagner Throwing	1,000	1,500	2,000	3,000				
60	Bobby Wallace	80	150	250	400	600	1,000		
71	Cy Young	500	800	1,000	1,500	2,500			
72	Heinie Zimmerman	50	100	120	200	350	500		

1909 Philadelphia Caramel E95

		PrFr 1	GD 2	VG 3	VgEx 4	EX 5	ExMt 6	NM 7	NmMt 8
	Chief Bender	150	200	400	600	1,000			
	Bill Carrigan	40	80	100	200	300	600		
	Frank Chance	150	200	300	500	800			
	Ed Cicotte	150	300	550	850	1,400			
	Ty Cobb	1,000	1,500	2,500	4,000	6,000	10,000		
	Eddie Collins	120	200	300	500	800			
	Sam Crawford	120	200	300	500	800			
	Art Devlin	40	60	100	200	300	600		
	Larry Doyle	40	60	100	200	300	600		
10	Johnny Evers	120	300	400	550	800			
11	Solly Hoffman	40	60	100	200	300	600		
12	Harry Krause	40	60	100	200	300	600		
13	Tommy Leach	40	80	100	350	450	1,000		
14	Harry Lord	40	60	100	200	300	600		
15	Nick Maddox	40	80	100	120	575	1,100		
16	Christy Mathewson	400	500	1,000	1,500	3,000	5,000		
17	Matty McIntyre	40	60	100	300	400	600		
18	Fred Merkle	60	100	150	250	400	800		
19	Cy Morgan	40	80	120	200	300	600		
20	Eddie Plank	800	1,000	1,200	2,000				
21	Ed Reulbach	40	120	150	200	300	600		
22	Honus Wagner	1,200	2,000	2,500	3,500	5,500	9,000		
23	Ed Willetts (Willett)	60	80	100	200	300	900		
24	Vic Willis	120	200	250	300	800	2,000		
25	Hooks Wiltse	50	60	100	200	300	600		

1909 Ramly T204

		PrFr 1	GD 2	VG 3	VgEx 4	EX 5	ExMt 6	NM 7	NmMt 8
1	Whitey Alperman	120	200	250	300	500			
2	John J. Anderson	80	120	200	250	500			
3	Jimmy Archer	80	120	150	250	500			
4	Frank Arrelanes (Arellanes)	120	200	250	400	800			
5	Jim Ball	80	150	200	250	500			
6	Neal Ball	80	150	200	250	500			
7	Frank Bancroft	100	150	275	350	600			
8	Johnny Bates	120	150	200	250	500			
9	Fred Beebe	80	150	200	250	500			
10	George Bell	80	120	150	250	500			
11	Chief Bender	400	500	600	1,000	3,600			
12	Walter Blair	80	120	150	250	500			
13	Cliff Blankenship	80	120	150	250	500			
14	Frank Bowerman	80	120	150	250	500			
15	Kitty Bransfield	120	200	250	400	800			
16	Roger Bresnahan	250	400	800	1,500	2,000			
17	Al Bridwell	80	120	150	250	500			
18	Mordecai Brown	300	500	800	1,200	2,900			
19	Fred Burchell	80	120	200	850	1,600			
20	Jesse Burkett	1,600	2,500	4,300	5,000	7,000			
21	Bobby Byrnes (Byrne)	80	120	150	250	500			
22	Bill Carrigan	80	120	150	250	750			
23	Frank Chance	250	400	700	900	1,500			
24	Charles Chech	100	150	250	350	600			
25	Eddie Cicolte	250	400	500	800	1,500			
26	Otis Clymer	80	120	150	250	500			
27	Andrew Coakley	80	120	150	250	500			
28	Eddie Collins	300	500	800	1,200	2,000			
29	Jimmy Collins	250	400	600	1,000	1,500			
30	Wid Conroy	80	120	150	250	500			
31	Jack Coombs	120	200	250	400	800			
32	Doc Crandall	80	120	250	350	500			
33	Lou Criger	80	120	150	250	500			
34	Harry Davis	80	120	150	250	1,000			
35	Art Devlin	80	120	150	250	500			
36	Bill Dineen (Dineen)	80	120	150	275	500			
37	Pat Donahue	80	120	200	250	500			
38	Mike Donlin	80	120	150	250	500			
39	Bill Donovan	100	150	250	300	600			
40	Gus Dorner	80	120	200	250	500			
41	Joe Dunn	80	120	150	250	500			
42	Kid Elberfield	80	120	150	1,000	1,500			
43	Johnny Evers	300	600	1,000	2,000				
44	Bob Ewing	80	120	150	250	500			
45	George Ferguson	80	120	150	250	500			
46	Hobe Ferris	80	120	150	250	500			
47	Jerry Freeman	80	120	150	250	500			
48	Art Fromme	100	120	200	250	500			
49	Bob Ganley	80	120	150	250	500			
50	Doc Gessler	80	120	150	250	500			
51	Peaches Graham	80	120	150	250	500			
52	Clark Griffith	250	400	600	1,000	2,000			
53	Roy Hartzell (Topsy Hartsel Pictured)		80	120	150	250	500		
54	Charlie Hemphill	80	120	150	300	500			
55	Dick Hoblitzel (Hoblitzell)	80	120	150	250	500			
56	George Howard	80	120	325	425	600			
57	Harry Howell	80	120	150	250	500			
58	Miller Huggins	250	400	500	800	2,000			
59	John Hummel	80	120	150	250	500			
60	Walter Johnson	3,500	6,000	10,000	18,000	25,000			
61	Tom Jones	80	150	200	250	500			
62	Mike Kahoe	80	150	200	250	500			
63	Ed Kargar (Karger)	100	150	300	400	600			
64	Willie Keeler	400	600	1,200	1,500	2,200			

BASEBALL

		PrFr 1	GD 2	VG 3	VgEx 4	EX 5	ExMt 6	NM 7	NmMt 8
65	Red Kleinon (Kleinow)	80	120	150	300	500			
66	John Knight	80	120	250	300	500			
67	Ed Konetchey (Konetchy)	80	120	150	250	500			
68	Vive Lindaman	80	120	200	250	500			
69	Hans Loebert (Lobert)	80	120	250	350	500			
70	Harry Lord	80	150	200	250	500			
71	Harry Lumley	80	120	150	250	500			
72	Ernie Lush	80	120	150	250	500			
73	Rube Manning	80	120	150	300	500			
74	Jimmy McAleer	80	120	150	250	500			
75	Amby McConnell	80	120	150	250	500			
76	Moose McCormick	80	120	150	250	500			
77	Matty McIntyre	80	120	250	300	500			
78	Larry McLean	80	120	150	250	500			
79	Fred Merkle	120	200	250	400	800			
80	Clyde Milan	80	120	150	250	500			
81	Mike Mitchell	80	120	150	250	500			
82	Pat Moran	200	250	300	350	500			
83	Cy Morgan	120	150	200	300	500			
84	Tim Murname (Murnane)	100	150	200	300	500			
85	Danny Murphy	80	120	150	275	500			
86	Red Murray	80	120	150	250	500			
87	Doc Newton	80	120	150	250	600			
88	Simon Nichols (Nicholls)	80	120	150	600	700			
89	Harry Niles	80	120	150	250	500			
90	Bill O'Hare (O'Hara)	80	120	150	250	500			
91	Charley O'Leary	80	120	150	400	600			
92	Dode Paskert	80	120	150	250	500			
93	Barney Pelty	120	300	350	500	800			
94	Jack Pfeister (Pfiester)	80	120	150	250	500			
95	Eddie Plank	1,000	1,800	2,800	3,200	10,000			
96	Jack Powell	80	120	150	250	500			
97	Bugs Raymond	80	120	150	250	500			
98	Tom Reilly	80	120	150	250	500			
99	Claude Ritchey	80	120	150	250	500			
100	Nap Rucker	80	150	200	300	500			
101	Ed Ruelbach (Reulbach)	80	120	150	275	500			
102	Slim Sallee	80	120	150	250	500			
103	Germany Schaefer	80	120	150	250	500			
104	Jimmy Schekard (Sheckard)	80	120	150	250	500			
105	Admiral Schlei	80	120	150	250	500			
106	Wildfire Schulte	80	120	150	250	500			
107	Jimmy Sebring	80	120	150	250	500			
108	Bill Shipke	80	120	150	250	500			
109	Charlie Smith	80	120	250	350	500			
110	Tubby Spencer	80	120	150	250	500			
111	Jake Stahl	120	200	250	400	800			
112	Jim Stephens	80	120	200	250	500			
113	Harry Stienfeldt (Steinfeldt)	120	200	250	400	800			
114	Gabby Street	80	120	150	250	500			
115	Bill Sweeney	80	120	200	250	500			
116	Fred Tenney	80	120	400	600	800			
117	Ira Thomas	80	120	150	250	500			
118	Joe Tinker	400	600	800	2,400	2,500			
119	Bob Unglane (Unglaub)	80	120	150	250	500			
120	Heinie Wagner	80	120	250	500	700			
121	Bobby Wallace	250	400	500	800	1,500			

— Eddie Collins #28 PSA 8 (NmMt) sold for $16,286 (Mile High; 1/13)
— Eddie Collins #28 PSA 8 (NmMt) sold for $13,080 (Goodwin; 8/12)
— Walter Johnson SGC 9 (Mint) sold for $59,250 (REA; Spring '14)
— Walter Johnson SGC 7 (NM) sold for $42,000 (REA; Spring '15)
— Walter Johnson PSA 6 (ExMt) sold for $29,718 (Mile High; 10/13)
— Walter Johnson SGC 80 (ExMt) sold for $21,330 (REA; Spring '14)
— Eddie Plank #95 PSA 8 (NmMt) sold for $40,825 (Mile High; 1/12)

1909-11 Colgan's Chips E254

		PrFr 1	GD 2	VG 3	VgEx 4	EX 5	ExMt 6	NM 7	NmMt 8
1	Ed Abbaticchio	8	10	15	20	25	30		
2	Fred Abbott	8	10	15	20	25	30		
3A	Bill Abstein Pittsburg	8	10	15	20	25	30		
3B	Bill Abstein Jersey City	8	10	15	20	25	30		
4	Babe Adams	8	10	15	20	25	30		
5	Merle (Doc) Adkins	8	10	15	20	25	30		
6	Joe Agler	8	10	15	20	25	30		
7	Alperman	8	10	15	20	25	30		
8A	Dave Altizer Cincinnati	8	10	15	20	25	30		
8B	Dave Altizer Minneapolis	8	10	15	20	25	30		
9	Nick Altrock	8	10	15	20	25	30		
10A	Red Ames Cincinnati	8	10	15	20	25	30		
10B	Red Ames New York	8	10	15	20	25	30		
11	Jimmy Archer	8	10	15	20	25	30		
12A	Atkins Atlanta	8	10	15	20	25	30		
12B	Atkins Fort Wayne	8	10	15	20	25	30		
13	Jake Atz	8	10	15	20	25	30		
14A	Jimmy Austin New York	8	10	15	20	25	30		
14B	Jimmy Austin St. Louis	8	10	15	20	25	30		
15A	Charlie Babb Memphis	8	10	15	20	25	30		
15B	Charlie Babb Norfolk	8	10	15	20	25	30		
16	Rudolph Baerwald	8	10	15	20	25	30		
17	Bill Bailey	8	10	15	20	25	30		
18	Frank Baker	30	40	60	80	150	200		
19	Jack Barry	8	10	15	20	25	30		
20	Bill Bartley	8	10	15	20	25	30		
21A	Johnny Bates Cincinnati	8	10	15	20	25	30		
21B	Johnny Bates Philadelphia	8	10	15	20	25	30		
22	Dick Bayless	8	10	15	20	25	30		
23A	Ginger Beaumont Boston	8	10	15	20	25	30		
23B	Ginger Beaumont Chicago	8	10	15	20	25	30		
23C	Ginger Beaumont St. Paul	8	10	15	20	25	30		
24	Beals Becker	8	10	15	20	25	40		
25	Fred Beebe	8	10	15	20	25	30		
26	George Bell	8	10	15	20	25	30		
27A	Harry Bemis Cleveland	8	10	15	20	25	30		
27B	Harry Bemis Columbus	8	10	15	20	25	30		
28A	Heinie Berger Cleveland	8	10	15	20	25	30		
28B	Heinie Berger Columbus	8	10	15	20	25	30		
29	Bob Bescher	8	10	15	20	25	30		
30	Beumiller	8	10	15	20	25	30		
31	Joe Birmingham	8	10	15	20	25	30		
32	Kitty Bransfield	8	10	15	20	25	30		
33A	Roger Bresnahan St. Louis	30	40	60	80	100	120		
33B	Roger Bresnahan Chicago	30	40	60	80	100	120		
34	Al Bridwell	8	10	15	20	25	30		
35	Lew Brockett	8	10	15	20	25	30		
36	Brown	8	10	15	20	25	30		
37A	Al Burch Brooklyn	8	10	15	20	25	30		
37B	Burch Louisville	8	10	15	20	25	30		
38A	William Burke Ft. Wayne	8	10	15	20	25	30		
38B	William Burke Indianapolis	8	10	15	20	25	30		
39	Burns	8	10	15	20	25	30		
40	Donie Bush	8	10	15	20	25	30		
41	Bill Byers	8	10	15	20	25	30		
42	Bobby Byrne	8	10	15	20	25	30		
43	Callahan	8	10	15	20	25	30		
44	Howie Camnitz	8	10	15	20	25	30		
45	Campbell	8	10	15	20	25	30		
46A	Charlie Carr Indianapolis	8	10	15	20	25	30		
46B	Charlie Carr Utica	8	10	15	20	25	30		
46C	Charlie Carr Kansas City	8	10	15	20	25	30		
47	Cashion Washington	8	10	15	20	25	30		
48A	Frank Chance	30	40	60	80	100	120		

		PrFr 1	GD 2	VG 3	VgEx 4	EX 5	ExMt 6	NM 7	NmMt 8
48B	Frank Chance New York	8	10	15	20	25	30		
49	Hal Chase	20	50	80	100	150	200		
50	Eddie Cicotte	8	10	15	20	25	30		
51	Clancy	8	10	15	20	25	30		
52	Nig Clarke	12	15	25	30	40	50		
53	Fred Clarke	25	30	50	60	80	100		
54	Clarke	8	10	15	20	25	30		
55	Clemons	8	10	15	20	25	30		
56	Otis Clymer	8	10	15	20	25	30		
57A	Ty Cobb w/Name	200	300	400	900	1,200	1,600		
57B	Ty Cobb w/o Name	200	250	500	600	800	1,000		
58	Eddie Collins	30	40	60	80	100	120		
59A	Buck Congalton Columbus	8	10	15	20	25	30		
59B	Buck Congalton Omaha	8	10	15	20	25	30		
59C	Buck Congalton Toledo	8	10	15	20	25	30		
60	Wid Conroy	8	10	15	20	50	60		
61	Cook	8	10	15	20	25	30		
62	Coombs	8	10	15	20	25	30		
63	Corcoran	8	10	15	20	25	30		
64	Courtney	8	10	15	20	25	30		
65A	Harry Coveleski	8	10	15	20	25	30		
65B	Stan Coveleski	12	15	25	30	40	50		
66	Doc Crandall	8	10	15	20	25	30		
67	Gavvy Cravath	8	10	15	20	25	30		
68	Sam Crawford	8	10	15	20	25	30		
69	Dode Criss	8	10	15	20	25	30		
70	Bill Dahlen	8	10	15	20	25	30		
71	Bernard Daniels	8	10	15	20	25	30		
72A	Jake Daubert Memphis	8	10	15	20	25	30		
72B	Jake Daubert Brooklyn	8	10	15	20	25	30		
73	Harry Davis	8	10	15	20	25	30		
74	George Davis	12	15	25	30	40	50		
75	Jim Delahanty	8	10	15	20	25	30		
76A	Ray Demmett New York	8	10	15	20	25	30		
76B	Ray Demmett Montreal	8	10	15	20	25	30		
76C	Ray Demmett St. Louis	8	10	15	20	25	30		
77	Art Devlin	8	10	15	20	25	30		
78A	Joshua Devore Cincinnati	8	10	15	20	25	30		
78B	Joshua Devore New York	8	10	15	20	25	30		
79	Turkey Mike Donlin	8	10	15	20	25	30		
80	Bill Donovan	8	10	15	20	25	30		
81	Charles Dooin	8	10	15	20	25	30		
82	Mickey Doolan	8	10	15	20	25	30		
83	Patsy Dougherty	8	10	15	20	25	30		
84	Tom Downey	8	10	15	20	25	30		
85	Larry Doyle	8	10	15	20	25	30		
86	Drake	8	10	15	20	25	30		
87	Jack Dunn	8	10	15	20	25	30		
88	Charles Eagan	8	10	15	20	25	30		
89A	Kid Elberfield Washington	8	10	15	20	25	30		
89B	Kid Elberfield Chattanooga	8	10	15	20	25	30		
89C	Kid Elberfield New York	8	10	15	20	25	30		
90	Roy Ellam	8	10	15	20	25	30		
91	Elliott	8	10	15	20	25	30		
92	Rube Ellis	8	10	15	20	25	30		
93	Elwert	8	10	15	20	25	30		
94A	Clyde Engle New York	8	10	15	20	25	30		
94B	Clyde Engle Boston	8	10	15	20	25	30		
95	James Esmond	8	10	15	20	25	30		
96	Steve Evans	8	10	15	20	25	30		
97	Johnny Evers	30	40	60	80	100	120		
98	George Ferguson	8	10	15	20	25	30		
99	Hobe Ferris	8	10	15	20	25	30		
100	James Field	8	10	15	20	25	30		
101	Fisher	8	10	15	20	25	30		
102	Matthew Fitzgerald	8	10	15	20	25	30		
103A	Patrick Flaherty Kansas City	8	10	15	20	25	30		
103B	Patrick Flaherty Atlanta	8	10	15	20	25	30		
104	John Flater	8	10	15	20	25	30		
105A	Elmer Flick Cleveland	25	30	50	60	80	100		
105B	Elmer Flick Toledo	25	30	50	60	80	100		
106	Russ Ford	8	10	15	20	25	30		
107	George Foster	8	10	15	20	25	30		
108A	Freck Balt	8	10	15	20	25	30		
108B	Freck Tor	8	10	15	20	25	30		
109	Freeman	8	10	15	20	25	30		
110	Bill Friel	8	10	15	20	25	30		
111	John Frill	8	10	15	20	25	30		
112	Art Fromme	8	10	15	20	25	30		
113A	Larry Gardner Boston	8	10	15	20	25	30		
113B	Larry Gardner New York	8	10	15	20	25	30		
114	Harry Gaspar	8	10	15	20	25	30		
115A	Gus Getz Boston	8	10	15	20	25	30		
115B	Gus Getz Pittsburgh	8	10	15	20	25	30		
116	George Gibson	8	10	15	20	25	30		
117	Graham	8	10	15	20	25	30		
118A	Ed Grant Cincinnati	8	10	15	20	25	30		
118B	Ed Grant New York	8	10	15	20	25	30		
119	Grief	8	10	15	20	25	30		
120A	Moose Grimshaw Toronto	8	10	15	20	25	30		
120B	Moose Grimshaw Louisville	8	10	15	20	25	30		
121	Bob Groom	8	10	15	20	25	30		
122	Noodles Hahn	8	10	15	20	25	30		
123	John Halla	8	10	15	20	25	30		
124	Hally	8	10	15	20	25	30		
125	Charles Hanford	8	10	15	20	25	30		
126A	Topsy Hartsel Philadelphia	8	10	15	20	25	30		
126B	Topsy Hartsel Toledo	8	10	15	20	25	30		
127A	Roy Hartzel St. Louis	8	10	15	20	25	30		
127B	Roy Hartzell New York	8	10	15	20	25	30		
128	Weldon Henley	8	10	15	20	25	30		
129	Harry Hinchman	8	10	15	20	25	30		
130	Richard Hoblitzell	8	10	15	20	25	30		
131	Solly Hofman	8	10	15	20	25	30		
132	William Hogan	8	10	15	20	25	30		
133A	Harry Hooper Boston AL	25	30	150	200	250	300		
133B	Harry Hooper Boston NL	25	30	80	100	120	150		
134	Del Howard	8	10	15	20	25	30		
135	Miller Huggins	8	10	15	20	25	30		
136A	Thomas Hughes Milwaukee	8	10	15	20	25	30		
136B	Thomas Hughes Louisville	8	10	15	20	25	30		
136C	Thomas Hughes Louisville C	8	10	15	20	25	30		
137	Thomas Hughes Rochester	8	10	15	20	25	30		
138A	Rudy Hulswitt St. Louis	8	10	15	20	25	30		
138B	Rudy Hulswitt Chattanooga	8	10	15	20	25	30		
138C	Rudy Hulswitt Louisville	8	10	15	20	25	30		
139	John Hummel	8	10	15	20	25	30		
140	George Hunter	8	10	15	20	25	30		
142	Hugh Jennings	25	50	60	80	100	120		
143	Johns	8	10	15	20	25	30		
144	Davy Jones	8	10	15	40	50	60		
145	Tom Jones	8	10	15	20	25	30		
146A	Jordon Toronto	8	10	15	20	25	30		
146B	Jordon Atlanta	8	10	15	20	25	30		
146C	Jordon Atlanta	8	10	15	20	25	30		
146D	Jordon Louisville	8	10	15	20	25	30		
147	Addie Joss	25	30	50	60	250	300		
148	Kaiser Louisville	8	10	15	20	25	30		
149	Keefe Rochester	8	10	15	20	25	30		
150	Willie Keeler	25	30	50	60	80	100		
151A	Kelly Jersey City	8	10	15	20	25	30		
151B	Kelly Toronto	8	10	15	20	25	30		
152A	William Killefer St. Louis	8	10	15	20	25	30		
152B	William Killefer Philadelphia	8	10	15	20	25	30		
153A	Ed Killian Detroit	8	10	15	20	25	30		
153B	Ed Killian Toronto	8	10	15	20	25	30		

#	Name	PrFr 1	GD 2	VG 3	VgEx 4	EX 5	ExMt 6	NM 7	NmMt 8
154	Johnny Kling	8	10	15	20	25	30		
155	Klipfer	8	10	15	20	25	30		
156	Otto Knabe	8	10	15	20	25	30		
157A	John Knight New York	8	10	15	20	25	30		
157B	John Knight Jersey City	8	10	15	20	25	30		
158	Ed Konetchy	8	10	15	20	25	30		
159	Paul Krichell St. Louis	8	10	15	20	25	30		
160	Rube Kroh	8	10	15	20	25	30		
161A	Doc Lafitte Rochester	8	10	15	20	25	30		
161B	Doc Lafitte Providence	8	10	15	20	25	30		
162	Nap Lajoie	40	50	80	100	120	150		
163	Lakoff	8	10	15	20	25	30		
164	Frank Lange	8	10	15	20	25	30		
165A	Frank LaPorte St. Louis	8	10	15	20	25	30		
165B	Frank LaPorte New York	8	10	15	20	25	30		
166	Tommy Leach	8	10	15	20	25	30		
167	Lee	8	10	15	20	25	30		
168	William Lelivelt	8	10	15	20	25	30		
169A	Lewis Milwaukee	8	10	15	20	25	30		
169B	Lewis Indianapolis	8	10	15	20	25	30		
170A	Vivian Lindaman Boston	8	10	15	20	25	30		
170B	Vivian Lindaman Louisville	8	10	15	20	25	30		
170C	Vivian Lindaman Indianapolis	8	10	15	20	25	30		
171	Bris Lord	8	10	15	20	25	30		
172A	Harry Lord Boston	8	10	15	20	25	30		
172B	Harry Lord Chicago	8	10	15	20	25	30		
173A	William Ludwig Milwaukee	8	10	15	20	25	80		
173B	William Ludwig St. Louis	8	10	15	20	25	30		
174	Lush Toronto	8	10	15	20	25	30		
175	Thomas Madden	8	10	15	20	25	30		
176A	Nick Maddox Pittsburg	8	10	15	20	25	30		
176B	Nick Maddox Louisville	8	10	15	20	25	30		
177A	Manser Jersey City	8	10	15	20	25	30		
177B	Manser Rochester	8	10	15	20	25	30		
178	Rube Marquard	25	30	50	60	80	100		
179	Al Mattern	8	10	15	20	25	30		
180	Matthews Atlanta	8	10	15	20	25	30		
181	McAllister Atlanta	8	10	15	20	25	30		
182	George McBride	8	10	15	20	25	30		
183	Alex McCarthy	8	10	15	20	25	30		
184	Ambrose McConnell Rochester	8	10	15	20	25	30		
185	Ambrose McConnell Toronto	8	10	15	20	25	30		
186	Moose McCormick	8	10	15	20	25	30		
187	Dennis McGann	8	10	15	20	25	30		
188	James McGinley	8	10	15	20	25	30		
189	Joe McGinnity	25	30	50	60	80	100		
190A	Matty McIntyre Detroit	8	10	15	20	25	30		
190B	Matty McIntyre Chicago	8	10	15	20	25	30		
191A	Larry McLean Cincinnati	8	10	15	20	25	30		
191B	Larry McLean St. Louis	8	10	15	20	25	30		
192	Fred Merkle	8	10	15	20	25	30		
193A	George Merritt Buffalo	8	10	15	20	25	30		
193B	George Merritt Jersey City	8	10	15	20	25	30		
194	Lee Meyer	8	10	15	20	25	30		
195	Chief Meyers	8	10	15	20	25	30		
196	Clyde Milan	8	10	15	20	25	30		
197	Dots Miller	8	10	15	20	25	30		
198	Miller Columbus	8	10	15	20	25	30		
199A	Mike Mitchell Cincinnati	8	10	15	20	25	30		
199B	Mike Mitchell Chicago	8	10	15	20	25	30		
200	Mitchell Providence	8	10	15	20	25	30		
201	Albert Mitchell	8	10	15	20	25	30		
202	Carlton Molesworth	8	10	15	20	25	30		
203	Joseph H. Moran	8	10	15	20	80	100		
204	Pat Moran	8	10	15	20	25	30		
205	George Moriarty Detroit	8	10	15	20	25	30		
206A	George Moriarty Louisville	8	10	15	20	25	30		
206B	George Moriarty Omaha	8	10	15	20	25	30		
207	George Mullin	8	10	15	20	25	30		
208A	Simmy Murch Chattanooga	8	10	15	20	25	30		
208B	Simmy Murch Indianapolis	8	10	15	20	25	30		
209	Danny Murphy	8	10	15	20	25	30		
210A	Red Murray	8	10	15	20	25	30		
210B	Red Murray	8	10	15	20	25	30		
211	Murray Buffalo	8	10	15	20	25	30		
212	Bill Nattress	8	10	15	20	25	30		
213A	Red Nelson St. Louis	8	10	15	20	25	30		
213B	Red Nelson Toledo	8	10	15	20	25	30		
214	George Northrop	8	10	15	20	25	30		
215	Rebel Oakes	8	10	15	20	25	30		
216	Frederick Odwell	8	10	15	20	25	30		
217	Rube Oldring	8	10	15	20	25	30		
218	Steve O'Neill	8	10	15	20	25	30		
219A	O'Rourke St. Paul	8	10	15	20	25	30		
219B	O'Rourke Columbus	8	10	15	20	25	30		
220A	Al Orth New York	8	10	15	20	25	30		
220B	Al Orth Indianapolis	8	10	15	20	25	30		
221	Wilfred Osborn	8	10	15	20	25	30		
222	Orvie Overall	8	10	15	20	25	30		
223	Frank Owens	8	10	15	20	25	30		
224	Lawrence Pape	8	10	15	20	25	30		
225A	Freddie Parent	8	10	15	20	25	30		
225B	Freddy Parent	8	10	15	20	25	30		
226A	Dode Paskert Cincinnati	8	10	15	20	25	30		
226B	Dode Paskert Philadelphia	8	10	15	20	25	30		
227	Heinie Peitz	8	10	15	20	25	30		
228	Perry Providence	8	10	15	20	25	30		
229	Robert A. Peterson	8	10	15	20	25	60		
230	John Pfeister	8	10	15	20	25	30		
231	Deacon Phillipe	8	10	15	20	25	30		
232A	Oliver Pickering Louisville	8	10	15	20	25	30		
232B	Oliver Pickering Minneapolis	8	10	15	20	25	30		
232C	Oliver Pickering Omaha	8	10	15	20	25	30		
233A	Billy Purtell Chicago	8	10	15	20	25	30		
233B	Billy Purtell Boston	8	10	15	20	25	30		
233C	Billy Purtell Jersey City	8	10	15	20	25	30		
234	Bill Rariden	8	10	15	20	25	30		
235	Morrie Rath	8	10	15	20	25	30		
236	Bugs Raymond	8	10	15	20	25	30		
237	Michael Regan	8	10	15	20	25	30		
238	Thomas Reilly Chicago	8	10	15	20	25	30		
239	Thomas Reilly Louisville	8	10	15	20	25	30		
240	Ed Reulbach	8	10	15	20	25	30		
241	Claude Ritchey	8	10	15	20	25	30		
242	Lou Ritter	8	10	15	20	25	30		
243	Clyde Robinson	8	10	15	20	25	30		
244	Royal Rock	8	10	15	20	25	30		
245A	Jack Rowan Cin	8	10	15	20	25	30		
245B	Jack Rowan Phil	8	10	15	20	25	30		
246	Nap Rucker	8	10	15	20	25	30		
247A	Dick Rudolph New York	8	10	15	20	25	30		
247B	Dick Rudolph Toronto	8	10	15	20	25	30		
248	Buddy Ryan St. Paul	8	10	15	20	25	30		
249	Buddy Ryan Cleveland	8	10	15	20	25	30		
250	Slim Sallee	8	10	15	20	25	30		
251	Ray Schalk	8	10	15	20	25	30		
252A	Bill Schardt Birmingham	8	10	15	20	25	30		
252B	Bill Schardt Milwaukee	8	10	15	20	25	30		
253	Jimmy Sheckard (Scheckard)	8	10	15	20	25	30		
254A	George Schirm Birmingham	8	10	15	20	25	30		
254B	George Schirm Buffalo	8	10	15	20	25	30		
255	Larry Schlafly	8	10	15	20	25	30		
256	Frank Schulte	8	10	15	20	25	30		
257A	James Seabaugh Nashville	8	10	15	20	25	30		
258	Selby Louisville	8	10	15	20	25	30		
259A	Cy Seymour New York	8	10	15	20	25	30		

		PrFr 1	GD 2	VG 3	VgEx 4	EX 5	ExMt 6	NM 7	NmMt 8
59B	Cy Seymour Baltimore	8	10	15	20	25	30		
60	Bob Shawkey	8	10	15	20	25	30		
61	Shelton Columbus	8	10	15	20	25	30		
62	Hosea Siner	8	10	15	20	25	30		
63A	Smith Atlanta	8	10	15	20	25	30		
63B	Smith Buffalo	8	10	15	20	25	30		
64	Smith Newark	8	10	15	20	25	30		
65	George Henry Smith	8	10	15	20	25	30		
66	Fred Snodgrass	8	10	15	20	25	30		
67A	Robert Spade Cincinnati	8	10	15	20	25	30		
67B	Robert Spade Newark	8	10	15	20	25	30		
68A	Tully Sparks Philadelphia	8	10	15	20	25	30		
68B	Tully Sparks Richmond	8	10	15	20	25	30		
69A	Tris Speaker Boston AL	40	50	80	100	120	150		
69B	Tris Speaker Boston NL	40	50	80	100	120	150		
70	Tubby Spencer	8	10	15	20	25	30		
71	Jake Stahl	8	10	15	20	25	30		
72	Stansberry Louisville	8	10	15	20	25	30		
73	Harry Steinfeldt	8	10	15	20	25	30		
74	George Stone	8	10	15	20	25	30		
75	George Stovall	8	10	15	20	25	30		
76	Gabby Street	8	10	15	20	25	30		
77	Amos Strunk	8	10	15	20	25	30		
78A	Billy Sullivan Louisville	8	10	15	20	25	30		
78B	Billy Sullivan Omaha	8	10	15	20	25	30		
79	Billy Sullivan Indianapolis	8	10	15	20	25	30		
80	J. Sullivan Louisville	8	10	15	20	25	30		
81	Ed Summers	8	10	15	20	25	30		
82	Swacina Newark	8	10	15	20	25	30		
83	Jeff Sweeney	8	10	15	20	25	30		
84	Bill Sweeney	8	10	15	20	25	30		
85	Lee Tannehill	8	10	15	20	25	30		
86	John Taylor Kansas City	8	10	15	20	25	30		
87	John Taylor Montreal	8	10	15	20	25	30		
88	Jim Thorpe	8	10	15	20	25	30		
89A	Joe Tinker	30	40	80	100	120	150		
89B	Joe Tinker Cincinnati	8	10	15	20	25	30		
90A	John Titus Philadelphia	8	10	15	20	25	30		
90B	John Titus Boston	8	10	15	20	25	30		
91	Terry Turner	8	10	15	20	25	30		
92A	Bob Unglaub Washington	8	10	15	20	25	30		
92B	Bob Unglaub Lincoln	8	10	15	20	25	30		
92C	Bob Unglaub Minneapolis	8	10	15	20	25	30		
93	Viebahn Jersey City	8	10	15	20	25	30		
94A	Rube Waddell St. Louis	25	30	50	100	120	150		
94B	Rube Waddell Minneapolis	25	30	50	60	80	100		
94C	Rube Waddell Newark	25	30	50	60	80	100		
95	Honus Wagner	200	250	600	700	1,200	1,500		
96	Walker Atlanta	8	10	15	20	25	30		
97	Bobby Wallace	8	10	15	20	25	30		
98	Waller Jersey City	8	10	15	20	25	30		
99	Ed Walsh	8	10	15	20	25	30		
100	Jack Warhop	8	10	15	20	25	30		
101	Wauner Memphis	8	10	15	20	25	30		
102	Wiesman Nashville	8	10	15	20	25	30		
103	Zach Wheat	8	10	15	20	25	30		
104	White Buffalo	8	10	15	20	25	30		
105	Kirby White	8	10	15	20	25	30		
106	Kaiser Wilhelm	8	10	15	20	25	30		
107	Ed Willett	8	10	15	20	25	30		
108A	Williams Indianapolis	8	10	15	20	25	30		
108B	Williams Minneapolis	8	10	15	20	25	30		
109	Owen Wilson	8	10	15	20	25	30		
110	Hooks Wiltse	8	10	15	20	25	30		
111	Joe Wood Boston	8	10	15	20	25	30		
112A	Orville Woodruff Indianapolis	8	10	15	20	25	30		
112B	Orville Woodruff Louisville	8	10	15	20	25	30		
113	Walter Woods Buffalo	8	10	15	20	25	30		

		PrFr 1	GD 2	VG 3	VgEx 4	EX 5	ExMt 6	NM 7	NmMt 8
314	Joseph Yeager	8	10	15	20	25	30		
315	Cy Young	100	120	200	250	300	400		
316	Heinie Zimmerman Chicago	12	15	25	30	40	50		
317A	Heinie Zimmerman Newark	12	15	25	30	40	50		
317B	Zimmerman Newark	8	10	15	20	25	30		

1909-11 American Caramel E90-1

		PrFr 1	GD 2	VG 3	VgEx 4	EX 5	ExMt 6	NM 7	NmMt 8
1	Bill Bailey	25	50	80	120	200	400		
2	Home Run Baker	80	150	400	500	800	1,800		
3	Jack Barry	25	50	120	150	200	400		
4	George Bell	25	50	100	150	200	400		
5	Harry Bemis	150	200	250	300	400			
6	Chief Bender	80	150	250	300	800	1,800		
7	Bob Bescher	50	100	150	250	400			
8	Cliff Blankenship	25	50	80	150	200	400		
9	John Bliss	25	50	80	120	200	400		
10	Bill Bradley	25	100	120	150	300	500		
11	Kitty Bransfield P on Shirt	25	50	80	150	250	400		
12	Kitty Bransfield No P on Shirt	30	100	150	250	400	600		
13	Roger Bresnahan	70	135	250	400	1,200			
14	Al Bridwell	25	50	80	120	200	400		
15	Buster Brown Horizontal	50	120	200	250	400	800		
16	Mordecai Brown	150	250	400	800				
17	Donie Bush	25	50	80	120	250	400		
18	John Butler	25	50	80	150	200	400		
19	Howie Camnitz	25	50	80	120	250	400		
20	Frank Chance	80	150	250	400	600	1,500		
21	Hal Chase	50	200	250	350	500	1,200		
22	Fred Clarke Philadelphia	80	150	250	400	800			
23	Fred Clarke Pittsburgh	300	400	600	1,000				
24	Wally Clement	30	60	100	150	400	1,200		
25	Ty Cobb	800	1,200	2,000	3,000	6,000			
26	Eddie Collins	80	150	300	400	800			
27	Frank Corridon	25	50	80	120	200	400		
28	Sam Crawford	80	150	250	500	600	1,500		
29	Lou Criger	25	50	80	120	200	600		
30	George Davis	100	200	300	500	800			
31	Jasper Davis	25	50	80	120	200	400		
32	Ray Demmitt	50	100	150	250	400			
33	Mike Donlin	40	80	120	200	300	600		
34	Wild Bill Donovan	30	60	100	200	250	500		
35	Red Dooin	25	50	100	120	200	400		
36	Patsy Dougherty	150	250	350	500	600	800		
37	Hugh Duffy	300	600	1,200	2,000				
38	Jimmy Dygert	25	80	100	120	200	400		
39	Rube Ellis	25	80	100	150	250	400		
40	Clyde Engle	25	50	80	150	300	500		
41	Art Fromme	50	100	150	250	400			
42	George Gibson Back View	50	100	350	450	700			
43	George Gibson Front View	25	100	120	200	250	400		
44	George Graham	250	400	800	2,000				
45	Eddie Grant	30	60	100	150	250	500		
46	Dolly Gray	30	80	100	150	250	500		
47	Bob Groom	25	80	100	120	200	400		
48	Charles Hall Horizontal	30	50	100	150	250	500		
49	Roy Hartzell Fielding	25	50	80	150	200	400		
50	Roy Hartzell Batting	40	80	120	200	300	600		
51	William Heitmuller	25	80	100	120	200			
52	Harry Howell Follow Through	25	50	80	120	200	400		
53	Harry Howell Wind Up	30	60	100	150	250	600		
54	Tex Irwin (Erwin)	25	50	80	150	250	400		
55	Frank Isbell	25	50	80	150	200	400		
56	Joe Jackson	12,000	20,000	25,000	30,000				
57	Hughie Jennings	80	120	200	250	300			
58	Tim Jordan	25	50	80	150	200	400		
59	Addie Joss Pitching	100	400	600	1,000				

		PrFr 1	GD 2	VG 3	VgEx 4	EX 5	ExMt 6	NM 7	NmMt 8
60	Addie Joss Portrait	150	250	600	800	1,200	3,000		
61	Ed Karger	150	400	500	800				
62	Willie Keeler Portrait Pink	100	200	400	700	1,200	2,000		
63	Willie Keeler Portrait Red	300	600	1,000	1,500				
64	Willie Keeler Throwing	250	600	1,000	1,500	2,500			
65	John Knight	25	50	150	250	400	800		
66	Harry Krause	25	50	80	150	250			
67	Nap Lajoie	200	350	500	800	1,500	2,500		
68	Tommy Leach Batting	30	60	120	150	300	500		
69	Tommy Leach Throwing	30	60	100	150	250	500		
70	Sam Leever	25	50	100	120	200	400		
71	Hans Lobert	50	300	400	500	600			
72	Harry Lumley	25	50	120	150	200	400		
73	Rube Marquard	80	200	250	400	800			
74	Christy Mathewson	375	500	800	1,500	3,000	5,000		
75	Stuffy McInnes (McInnis)	40	80	100	150	250	500		
76	Harry McIntyre	25	50	80	120	200	400		
77	Larry McLean	175	250	350	450	600			
78	George McQuillan	25	50	80	120	350	500		
79	Dots Miller/w/o sunset in background	25	50	100	120	200	400		
81	Mike Mitchell	2,000	3,000	4,000	5,000				
82	Fred Mitchell	25	50	80	200	400	600		
83	George Mullin	30	60	100	150	250	500		
84	Rebel Oakes	80	150	300	400	500	600		
85	Patrick O'Connor	30	60	100	150	250			
86	Charley O'Leary	25	50	80	120	200	400		
87	Orval Overall	60	120	250	300	600			
88	Jim Pastorius	25	80	150	200	300	400		
89	Ed Phelps	25	50	100	120	200	400		
90	Eddie Plank	250	500	600	1,000	1,500	4,000		
91	Lew Richie	25	50	80	120	200	400		
92	Germany Schaefer	30	60	120	150	250			
93	Victor Schlitzer	30	120	250	300	400	600		
94	Johnny Siegle	50	100	150	250	400			
95	Dave Shean	50	100	250	350	500			
96	Jimmy Sheckard	30	60	100	150	250	500		
97	Tris Speaker	1,400	1,600	3,000					
98	Jake Stahl	250	500	800	1,200				
99	Oscar Stanage	25	60	80	150	200	400		
100	George Stone Left Hand	25	250	400	600	1,000	2,000		
101	George Stone No Hands	25	60	80	150	200	400		
102	George Stovall	25	50	150	200	250	400		
103	Ed Summers	25	50	80	120	200	1,500		
104	Bill Sweeney	300	600	1,000	1,500				
105	Jeff Sweeney	25	50	80	120	200	400		
106	Jesse Tannehill	25	50	80	120	200	400		
107	Lee Tannehill	25	50	120	150	200	400		
108	Fred Tenney	40	80	120	200	300	600		
109	Ira Thomas	30	60	100	150	250	500		
110	Roy Thomas	25	50	80	120	200	400		
111	Joe Tinker	100	150	300	400	500			
112	Bob Unglaub	30	50	80	120	300	800		
113	Jerry Upp	120	250	400	600	1,000			
114	Honus Wagner Batting	800	1,500	2,000					
115	Honus Wagner Throwing	800	1,200	2,000					
116	Bobby Wallace	50	100	150	300	500			
117	Ed Walsh	500	800	1,500					
118	Vic Willis	100	200	300	500	1,000			
119	Hooks Wiltse	40	80	120	200	300	600		
120	Cy Young Boston	400	800	1,600	2,000	3,500	6,000		
121	Cy Young Cleveland	400	800	1,200	2,000				

— Joe Jackson PSA 8 (NmMt) sold for $667,189 (SCP; 8/16)

— Joe Jackson PSA 2.5 (G/VG) sold for $23,448 (Goodwin; 12/11)

— Joe Jackson PSA 2.5 (G/VG) sold for $18,800 (eBay; 1/13)

— Joe Jackson SGC 20 (Fair) sold for $10,280 (Goodwin; 2/14)

1909-11 T206

		PrFr 1	GD 2	VG 3	VgEx 4	EX 5	ExMt 6	NM 7	NmMt 8
1	Ed Abbaticchio Blue Sleeves	25	30	100	120	400	600		
2	Ed Abbaticchio Brown Sleeves	25	30	50	100	200	300	800	
3	Fred Abbott ML	50	80	100	150	250	500	600	
4	Bill Abstein	20	50	80	120	200	300	500	
5	Doc Adkins ML	40	50	100	200	400	500		
6	Whitey Alperman	40	60	100	120	200	300	600	
7	Red Ames Hands at Chest	30	40	80	120	400	600		
8	Red Ames Hands over Head	20	25	60	100	250	300		
9	Red Ames Portrait	20	30	50	100	200	400	500	
10	John Anderson ML	40	60	100	150	250	400	600	
11	Frank Arellanes	40	60	100	150	250	400	600	
12	Herman Armbruster ML	20	40	60	120	150	350		
13	Harry Arndt ML	30	50	80	120	200	300	1,000	
14	Jake Atz	20	25	40	100	200	300	400	
15	Home Run Baker	80	150	400	500	800	1,400	2,500	
16	Neal Ball Cleveland	20	25	40	80	120	200	500	
17	Neal Ball New York	30	40	60	100	200	250	400	
18	Jap Barbeau	30	50	80	120	200	400	500	
19	Cy Barger ML	30	50	80	120	250	300		
20	Jack Barry	50	80	120	200	250	400	600	
21	Shad Barry ML	50	60	80	150	200	250	800	
22	Jack Bastian SL	40	80	150	300	500	600		
23	Emil Batch ML	25	40	60	100	200	400		
24	Johnny Bates	30	50	60	100	250	300	500	
25	Harry Bay SL	100	150	250	300	600	800		
26	Ginger Beaumont	30	60	80	150	200	400	800	
27	Fred Beck	40	60	100	150	250	300	500	
28	Beals Becker	30	50	80	120	250	300	400	
29	Jake Beckley ML	100	150	250	400	800	1,200	2,000	
30	George Bell Follow Through	20	25	60	120	150	300		
31	George Bell Hands above Head	20	25	40	50	150	250		
32	Chief Bender Pitching No Trees	60	100	200	250	600	1,000	2,700	
33	Chief Bender Pitching Trees	100	120	150	250	350	800	1,900	
34	Chief Bender Portrait	120	150	200	300	600	1,200	2,000	
35	Bill Bergen Batting	20	30	40	60	100	250	500	
36	Bill Bergen Catching	20	25	60	120	150	200	500	
37	Heinie Berger	30	50	80	120	250	300	500	
38	Bill Bernhard SL	50	80	300	400	500	800		
39	Bob Bescher Hands in Air	20	25	50	100	150	300	400	
40	Bob Bescher Portrait	20	25	120	150	200	250	400	
41	Joe Birmingham Horizontal	50	80	120	150	250	300		
42	Lena Blackburne ML	20	50	60	120	200	400	500	
43	Jack Bliss	20	25	50	120	150	400	500	
44	Frank Bowerman	50	80	120	200	300	500	800	
45	Bill Bradley with Bat	25	30	60	100	200	250	600	
46	Bill Bradley Portrait	50	80	100	120	150	300	500	
47	Dave Brain ML	40	60	80	100	200	400	600	
48	Kitty Bransfield	40	60	80	100	120	400	1,000	
49	Roy Brashear ML	50	80	120	200	300	500	800	
50	Ted Breitenstein SL	80	120	250	400	500	600	1,200	
51	Roger Bresnahan Portrait	80	120	150	250	350	1,000	1,800	
52	Roger Bresnahan with Bat	60	100	150	250	400	600	1,500	
53	Al Bridwell No Cap	20	25	50	100	120	200	500	
54	Al Bridwell with Cap	20	25	50	100	150	250	400	
55	George Brown Chicago	30	40	80	120	200	500		
56	George Brown Washington	80	120	200	500	600	1,200	3,600	
57	Mordecai Brown Chicago Shirt	120	150	200	400	500	800	2,500	
58	Mordecai Brown Cubs Shirt	100	150	250	400	500	1,500	2,500	
59	Mordecai Brown Portrait	120	150	250	400	600	1,400	2,000	
60	Al Burch Batting	40	50	80	120	350	500		
61	Al Burch Fielding	20	25	40	100	150	200	400	
62	Fred Burchell ML	30	50	80	120	200	300	500	
63	Jimmy Burke ML	20	25	40	50	120	200	400	
64	Bill Burns	20	60	100	120	250	400		

#		PrFr 1	GD 2	VG 3	VgEx 4	EX 5	ExMt 6	NM 7	NmMt 8
65	Donie Bush	20	25	50	100	150	250		
66	John Butler ML	20	25	40	120	200	250	500	
67	Bobby Byrne	20	25	50	150	200	300	400	
68	Howie Camnitz Arm at Side	60	80	100	125	200	350	600	
69	Howie Camnitz Arms Folded	20	30	60	100	150	200	600	
70	Howie Camnitz Hands above Head	25	30	40	150	200	400	500	
71	Billy Campbell	20	25	40	100	150	250	500	
72	Scoops Carey SL	40	50	100	300	500	800	2,500	
73	Charley Carr ML	20	25	40	80	200	250	500	
74	Bill Carrigan	30	40	60	120	150	250		
75	Doc Casey ML	20	25	50	100	120	250	400	
76	Peter Cassidy ML	50	80	120	200	300	500	800	
77	Frank Chance Batting	60	100	300	400	500	100	2,000	
78	Frank Chance Portrait Red	100	200	300	400	1,000	1,200	2,500	
79	Frank Chance Portrait Yellow	80	120	200	350	600	1,500	2,000	
80	Bill Chappelle ML	20	30	60	80	120	200	425	
81	Chappie Charles	25	30	50	80	150	200	400	
82	Hal Chase Throwing Dark Cap	25	30	100	150	250	450	1,000	
83	Hal Chase Holding Trophy	30	80	120	300	400	800		
84	Hal Chase Portrait Blue	30	50	120	200	300	400	800	
85	Hal Chase Portrait Pink	50	80	100	300	400	1,200		
86	Hal Chase Throwing White Cap	30	40	100	150	300	400	1,200	
87	Jack Chesbro	120	200	400	500	800	1,200	2,500	
88	Ed Cicotte	100	150	250	400	600	1,000		
89	Bill Clancy (Clancey) ML	20	25	50	60	300	400	600	
90	Fred Clarke Holding Bat	50	100	150	300	400	600	1,500	
91	Fred Clarke Portrait	60	100	150	250	400	600	2,000	
92	Josh Clark (Clarke) ML	20	25	60	80	150	200	600	
93	J.J. (Nig) Clarke	20	25	40	150	200	250	400	
94	Bill Clymer ML	40	60	100	150	250	400	600	
95	Ty Cobb Bat off Shoulder	1,000	1,500	2,000	4,000	6,000	8,000	15,000	
96	Ty Cobb Bat on Shoulder	1,000	2,000	2,500	4,000	6,000	8,000	15,000	
97	Ty Cobb Portrait Green	1,500	4,000	5,000	8,000	10,000	25,000		
98	Ty Cobb Portrait Red	1,200	2,000	3,000	5,000	6,000	10,000	15,000	
99	Cad Coles SL	20	25	120	200	300	600	3,000	
00	Eddie Collins Philadelphia	300	500	800	1,200	2,000	3,000	5,000	
01	Jimmy Collins Minneapolis ML	120	200	300	500	800	1,200	2,000	
02	Bunk Congalton ML	20	25	40	100	200	250	1,200	
03	Wid Conroy Fielding	20	25	40	100	150	250	800	
04	Wid Conroy with Bat	20	25	40	60	100	250	500	
05	Harry Covaleski	40	50	120	150	200	300	800	
06	Doc Crandall No Cap	20	25	60	80	200	250	400	
07	Doc Crandall with Cap	20	25	60	120	150	200	500	
08	Bill Cranston SL	50	60	100	150	500	600		
09	Gavvy Cravath ML	20	25	100	120	150	300	800	
10	Sam Crawford Throwing	60	100	200	300	600	1,200	1,500	
11	Sam Crawford with Bat	60	120	200	250	600	600	20,000	
12	Birdie Cree	25	30	50	150	200	250		
13	Lou Criger	20	40	60	80	250	300		
14	Dode Criss UER	40	60	100	150	250	400	600	
15	Monte Cross ML	20	25	40	60	120	200	400	
16	Bill Dahlen Boston	20	50	80	150	200	250	800	
17	Bill Dahlen Brooklyn	100	120	400	800	2,000	5,000	8,000	
18	Paul Davidson ML	30	50	80	120	200	400	600	
19	George Davis	150	250	400	600	1,000	1,500	2,500	
20	Harry Davis (Davis on Front)	20	25	40	120	150	200	500	
21	Harry Davis (H.Davis on Front)	20	25	40	50	150	200	500	
22	Frank Delehanty (Delahanty) ML	20	40	60	120	200	250	500	
23	Jim Delehanty	20	25	80	120	200	800		
24	Ray Demmitt New York	25	30	50	100	150	300	600	
25	Ray Demmitt St. Louis	1,500	2,000	2,500	8,000				
26	Rube Dessau ML	20	30	40	60	175	300	600	
27	Art Devlin	20	25	40	60	150	250	400	
28	Josh Devore	20	50	60	120	150	200	600	
29	Bill Dineen	25	30	40	60	150	200	800	
30	Mike Donlin Fielding	40	50	80	120	200	400		
31	Mike Donlin Seated	20	25	40	60	120	350	500	
32	Mike Donlin with Bat	20	25	60	120	300	350	400	
133	Jiggs Donahue (Donohue)	20	25	40	50	100	200	1,000	
134	Wild Bill Donovan Portrait	30	40	60	100	150	250	1,000	
135	Wild Bill Donovan Throwing	20	25	80	100	200	275	600	
136	Red Dooin	20	25	40	80	150	200	500	
137	Mickey Doolan Batting	30	40	60	120	150	250	500	
138	Mickey Doolan Fielding	20	25	100	120	150	200	400	
139	Mickey Doolin Portrait	20	25	40	50	200	300	400	
140	Gus Dorner ML	20	25	60	80	120	300	400	
143	Patsy Dougherty Portrait	20	25	40	200	250	300	400	
144	Tom Downey Batting	30	40	60	80	150	250		
145	Tom Downey Fielding	20	30	40	80	120	200	400	
146	Jerry Downs ML	30	40	60	100	120	400	600	
147	Joe Doyle Hands Above Head	150	200	250	500	800			
149	Larry Doyle Portrait	20	25	40	60	300	350		
150	Larry Doyle Throwing	20	25	60	100	200	300		
151	Larry Doyle with Bat	30	40	50	80	250	300	400	
152	Jean Dubuc	50	80	100	120	250	200	500	
153	Hugh Duffy	150	250	400	600	1,000	1,500	2,500	
154	Jack Dunn Baltimore ML	20	25	60	120	300	400	500	
155	Joe Dunn Brooklyn	20	25	120	150	200	250	700	
156	Bull Durham	25	30	50	200	400	600		
157	Jimmy Dygert	20	25	40	50	120	250	400	
158	Ted Easterly	20	30	40	100	150	200	600	
159	Dick Egan	20	30	40	100	120	250	800	
160	Kid Elberfeld Fielding	50	60	100	120	200	300		
161	Kid Elberfeld Portrait New York	25	30	50	150	300	400		
162	Kid Elberfeld Portrait Wash	300	400	600	1,000	2,500			
163	Roy Ellam SL	60	100	120	500	600	800		
164	Clyde Engle	20	25	40	80	150	250	500	
165	Steve Evans	30	40	60	100	120	300	500	
166	Johnny Evers Portrait	120	200	300	400	800	1,500	2,500	
167	Johnny Evers w/Bat Chi Shirt	80	120	150	400	500	1,500	2,000	
168	Johnny Evers w/Bat Cubs Shirt	150	200	300	500	1,000	2,000		
169	Bob Ewing	20	25	60	120	150	250	800	
170	Cecil Ferguson	20	25	40	100	120	250	500	
171	Hobe Ferris	20	25	120	150	200	250	500	
172	Lou Fiene Portrait	30	40	60	120	300	500	600	
173	Lou Fiene Throwing	20	25	50	80	150	250	400	
174	Steamer Flanagan ML	20	25	60	80	200	300	500	
175	Art Fletcher	20	25	40	80	120	200	400	
176	Elmer Flick	100	200	300	500	800	1,200	2,000	
177	Russ Ford	20	50	80	120	250	300	500	
178	Ed Foster SL	50	60	250	500	600			
179	Jerry Freeman ML	20	25	80	120	250	400	600	
180	John Frill	20	60	100	120	150	200	500	
181	Charlie Fritz SL	40	80	100	200	400	1,200		
182	Art Fromme	40	60	100	150	250	400	600	
183	Chick Gandil	60	120	200	300	400	1,000	1,500	
184	Bob Ganley	25	30	100	120	200	400		
185	John Ganzel ML	30	50	80	120	200	300	500	
186	Harry Gasper (Gaspar)	20	30	60	200	250	300	400	
187	Rube Geyer	20	40	60	80	120	300	500	
188	George Gibson	25	60	80	120	150	250	500	
189	Billy Gilbert	20	40	50	100	120	200	500	
190	Wilbur Goode	40	60	100	150	250	400	600	
191	Bill Graham St. Louis	20	25	40	80	150	300	400	
192	Peaches Graham Boston	30	50	80	100	120	300	600	
193	Dolly Gray	20	25	40	60	200	250	500	
194	Ed Greminger SL	50	60	100	300	400	800	1,500	
195	Clark Griffith Batting	50	60	100	250	350	500	2,000	
196	Clark Griffith Portrait	50	100	120	200	400	800	2,000	
197	Moose Grimshaw ML	30	50	80	120	200	300	500	
198	Bob Groom	25	40	60	80	200	300	500	
199	Tom Guiheen SL	80	120	200	300	500	800	3,000	
200	Ed Hahn	50	80	120	200	300	500	800	
201	Bob Hall ML	20	25	40	80	120	400		
202	Bill Hallman ML	25	30	40	60	150	250		
203	Jack Hannifan (Hannifin) ML	20	25	50	80	100	200	400	

#	Name	PrFr 1	GD 2	VG 3	VgEx 4	EX 5	ExMt 6	NM 7	NmMt 8
204	Bill Hart Little Rock SL	40	50	120	200	300	850	1,200	
205	Jimmy Hart Montgomery SL	50	60	100	200	400	700		
206	Topsy Hartsel	30	40	60	80	150	200		
207	Jack Hayden ML	20	25	40	120	150	200	500	
208	J.Ross Helm SL	40	50	120	250	400	800	1,500	
209	Charlie Hemphill	20	25	40	50	150	250	500	
210	Buck Herzog Boston	20	25	60	120	250	400	800	
211	Buck Herzog New York	20	25	50	100	150	250		
212	Gordon Hickman SL	80	120	200	300	500	600	3,000	
213	Bill Hinchman Cleveland	20	25	40	50	150	200	500	
214	Harry Hinchman Toledo ML	50	80	120	200	300	500	800	
215	Dick Hoblitzell	20	25	50	100	150	200	400	
216	Danny Hoffman St. Louis	40	60	100	150	250	400	600	
217	Izzy Hoffman Providence ML	20	30	50	100	150	250		
218	Solly Hofman	20	25	40	60	250	300	400	
219	Bock Hooker SL	100	150	200	250	400	650		
220	Del Howard Chicago	20	25	50	100	200	300		
221	Ernie Howard Savannah SL	50	80	120	200	400	800		
222	Harry Howell Hand at Waist	20	25	40	120	200	250	500	
223	Harry Howell Portrait	30	40	120	150	200	250	400	
224	Miller Huggins Hands at Mouth	100	120	150	200	500	600	1,500	
225	Miller Huggins Portrait	50	60	200	250	400	600	1,500	
226	Rudy Hulswitt	30	60	80	120	200	300	400	
227	John Hummel	20	25	100	120	250	400	800	
228	George Hunter	50	80	120	200	300	500	800	
229	Frank Isbell	50	80	120	200	300	500		
230	Fred Jacklitsch	30	50	80	120	200	300	500	
231	Jimmy Jackson ML	20	30	60	100	150	300	500	
232	Hughie Jennings Both Hands	60	120	200	250	500	600	1,500	
233	Hughie Jennings One Hand	80	100	120	200	600	800	2,000	
234	Hughie Jennings Portrait	80	150	200	250	500	600	2,000	
235	Walter Johnson Hands at Chest	200	500	800	1,200	2,500	4,000	10,000	
236	Walter Johnson Portrait	500	600	1,200	2,000	3,000	5,000	20,000	
237	Davy Jones Detroit	25	30	40	100	120	250	800	
238	Fielder Jones Hands at Hips	20	25	40	100	150	250		
239	Fielder Jones Portrait	20	25	40	80	120	500	800	
240	Tom Jones St. Louis	20	25	40	80	100			
241	Dutch Jordan Atlanta SL	40	50	100	300	500	600		
242	Tim Jordan Brooklyn Batting	20	25	40	80	250	350	500	
243	Tim Jordan Brooklyn Portrait	20	25	40	50	150	200	400	
244	Addie Joss Pitching	60	100	200	300	600	700	2,000	
245	Addie Joss Portrait	80	200	250	300	500	1,200	4,000	
246	Ed Karger	20	25	50	80	100	300	500	
247	Willie Keeler Portrait	100	200	250	500	600	1,000	4,000	
248	Willie Keeler with Bat	100	150	200	400	600	2,000	3,000	
249	Joe Kelley ML	120	200	300	500	800	1,200		
250	J.F. Kiernan SL	80	100	150	400	500			
251	Ed Killian Pitching	20	25	40	60	150	200	400	
252	Ed Killian Portrait	20	25	40	120	200	250	400	
253	Frank King SL	60	80	200	400	500	600		
254	Rube Kisinger (Kissinger) ML	25	30	40	60	150	400		
255	Red Kleinow Boston	80	100	200	300	500	800	2,500	
256	Red Kleinow New York Catching	25	30	120	150	250	500	600	
257	Red Kleinow New York with Bat	30	40	60	80	150	300	400	
258	Johnny Kling	20	25	60	80	200	250		
259	Otto Knabe	20	25	40	60	120	200	400	
260	Jack Knight Portrait	20	25	50	100	150	250		
261	Jack Knight with Bat	20	25	40	100	250	300	500	
262	Ed Konetchy Glove Near Ground	30	40	60	120	200	300	600	
263	Ed Konetchy Glove Above Head	20	25	40	120	150	250	500	
264	Harry Krause Pitching	20	25	50	120	150	200	400	
265	Harry Krause Portrait	30	40	60	80	150	250	400	
266	Rube Kroh	20	25	40	50	100	200	500	
267	Otto Kruger (Krueger) ML	20	25	40	60	250	350	800	
268	James LaFitte SL	150	250	400	600	1,000	1,500		
269	Nap Lajoie Portrait	120	300	400	600	1,000	2,000	6,000	
270	Nap Lajoie Throwing	120	200	300	400	600	1,000	2,000	
271	Nap Lajoie with Bat	120	250	400	600	800	1,200	3,000	
272	Joe Lake New York	30	40	80	100	150	250		
273	Joe Lake St. Louis No Ball	20	25	40	80	120	200	400	
274	Joe Lake St. Louis with Ball	20	25	40	80	150	500		
275	Frank LaPorte	30	50	80	120	200	400	800	
276	Arlie Latham	20	25	50	100	200	300	800	
277	Bill Lattimore ML	20	30	40	60	100	200	400	
278	Jimmy Lavender ML	20	25	60	150	200	250	500	
279	Tommy Leach Bending Over	20	25	60	80	150	300	500	
280	Tommy Leach Portrait	20	25	60	100	150	250		
281	Lefty Leifield Batting	30	40	50	100	200	300	400	
282	Lefty Leifield Pitching	20	30	60	80	200	300		
283	Ed Lennox	20	25	40	80	120	200	400	
284	Harry Lentz (Sentz) SL	80	120	200	300	500	1,500		
285	Glenn Liebhardt	40	60	100	150	250	400	600	
286	Vive Lindaman	20	25	40	50	150	300		
287	Perry Lipe SL	40	80	150	400	500	800		
288	Paddy Livingstone	40	60	80	100	150	300	400	
289	Hans Lobert	20	25	100	150	200	300	500	
290	Harry Lord	25	50	80	120	250	300	400	
291	Harry Lumley	30	50	80	120	200	400	600	
292	Carl Lundgren Chicago	120	200	300	500	800	2,500		
293	Carl Lundgren Kansas City ML	25	30	100	200	250	800		
294	Nick Maddox	20	25	40	50	100	200	400	
294	Sherry Magie Portrait (Magee)	10,000	15,000	25,000	40,000				
295	Sherry Magee with Bat	20	25	60	120	250	450	500	
296	Sherry Magee Portrait	40	60	200	300	400	500		
298	Bill Malarkey ML	20	25	40	80	100	250	800	
299	Billy Maloney ML	20	30	40	80	120	400	600	
300	George Manion SL	50	60	150	250	500	600		
301	Rube Manning Batting	20	25	50	80	120	200	400	
302	Rube Manning Pitching	20	25	50	80	200	250		
303	Rube Marquard Follow Through	50	80	120	250	600	800	1,700	
304	Rube Marquard Hands at Thighs	80	100	200	250	400	500	1,700	
305	Rube Marquard Portrait	80	100	150	250	500	1,200	2,000	
306	Doc Marshall	20	25	40	80	120	200	400	
307	Christy Mathewson Dark Cap	300	400	500	1,000	2,000	3,000	6,000	
308	Christy Mathewson Portrait	250	400	800	2,000	2,500	4,000	8,000	
309	Christy Mathewson White Cap	300	400	600	1,000	2,000	2,500	5,000	
310	Al Mattern	40	50	60	100	150	250	400	
311	John McAleese	30	50	60	100	120	200	500	
312	George McBride	40	50	60	120	250	300	400	
313	Pat McCauley SL	120	200	300	500	800	1,200	4,000	
314	Moose McCormick	25	30	60	80	150	200	400	
315	Pryor McElveen	50	80	120	200	300	500	800	
316	Dan McGann ML	20	25	40	60	120	200	400	
317	Jim McGinley ML	20	25	40	60	100	250	400	
318	Iron Man McGinnity ML	60	80	120	200	450	600	2,000	
319	Stoney McGlynn ML	30	40	60	80	150	200	500	
320	John McGraw Finger in Air	60	100	150	250	500	600	2,000	
321	John McGraw Glove at Hip	100	120	200	300	500	800	2,000	
322	John McGraw Portrait No Cap	60	100	200	300	500	800	1,500	
323	John McGraw Portrait with Cap	60	80	200	300	400	600	1,500	
324	Harry McIntyre Brooklyn	20	25	40	80	150	200	400	
325	Harry McIntyre Brooklyn-Chicago	20	25	40	60	100	200	400	
326	Matty McIntyre Detroit	20	25	40	80	150	350		
327	Larry McLean	20	25	40	60	150	200	400	
328	George McQuillan Ball in Hand	20	25	50	80	150	300	500	
329	George McQuillan with Bat	30	40	60	120	250	300	800	
330	Fred Merkle Portrait	25	100	120	150	250	300	800	
331	Fred Merkle Throwing	25	30	60	150	250	500		
332	George Merritt ML	50	80	120	200	300	500	800	
333	Chief Meyers	20	25	40	80	200	400	600	
334	Chief Myers Batting (Meyers)	20	25	40	80	120	250		
335	Chief Myers Fielding (Meyers)	20	25	40	120	300	400	800	
336	Clyde Milan	30	50	80	120	200	400	500	
337	Molly Miller Dallas SL	40	50	200	300	400	600		
338	Dots Miller Pittsburgh	30	40	60	150	250	500		
339	Bill Milligan ML	20	25	40	100	150	250		

#	Player	PrFr 1	GD 2	VG 3	VgEx 4	EX 5	ExMt 6	NM 7	NmMt 8
340	Fred Mitchell Toronto ML	40	60	100	150	250	400		
341	Mike Mitchell Cincinnati	20	25	40	80	150	250	600	
342	Dan Moeller ML	20	25	50	80	100	200	600	
343	Carleton Molesworth SL	100	150	250	400	600	1,000		
344	Herbie Moran Providence ML	20	25	40	60	120	200	500	
345	Pat Moran Chicago	40	60	100	150	250	400		
346	George Moriarty	40	60	100	150	250	400	600	
347	Mike Mowrey	20	25	40	60	150	200	400	
348	Dom Mullaney SL	40	80	150	300	500	700	1,200	
349	George Mullen (Mullin)	30	40	80	100	150	250	500	
350	George Mullin with Bat	20	25	40	80	100	250		
351	George Mullin Throwing	25	30	100	150	200	300		
352	Danny Murphy Batting	20	25	40	100	200	250		
353	Danny Murphy Throwing	25	30	60	100	150	250	800	
354	Red Murray Batting	20	25	40	80	150	200	400	
355	Red Murray Portrait	20	25	40	80	150	200	400	
356	Billy Nattress ML	20	25	40	60	200	250	500	
357	Tom Needham	30	40	60	100	200	300		
358	Simon Nicholls Hands on Knees	20	25	40	120	200	250	800	
359	Simon Nichols Batting (Nicholls)	20	25	60	80	300	500		
360	Harry Niles	20	50	60	100	250	300	400	
361	Rebel Oakes	20	25	60	80	120	250		
362	Frank Oberlin ML	40	50	60	100	200	400	500	
363	Peter O'Brien ML	40	50	60	120	150	250		
364	Bill O'Hara New York	20	25	40	120	150	300		
365	Bill O'Hara St. Louis	1,500	2,000	4,000	8,000				
366	Rube Oldring Batting	20	25	60	80	120	300	400	
367	Rube Oldring Fielding	20	25	40	80	120	200	500	
368	Charley O'Leary Hands on Knees	20	25	40	60	120	200	400	
369	Charley O'Leary Portrait	30	40	60	100	150	200	600	
370	William O'Neil ML	25	40	100	120	200	500		
371	Al Orth SL	40	50	100	300	350	600	1,200	
372	William Otey SL	50	100	200	400	500	1,000		
373	Orval Overall Hand at Face	20	30	50	100	150	200	400	
374	Orval Overall Hands at Waist	20	25	60	100	200	250		
375	Orval Overall Portrait	20	25	50	80	150	250	500	
376	Frank Owen (Owens)	20	40	60	80	150	300	400	
377	George Paige SL	50	60	150	400	500	800	2,500	
378	Fred Parent	20	25	50	80	150	200	600	
379	Dode Paskert	20	25	40	100	120	200	700	
380	Jim Pastorius	20	25	40	100	120	250		
381	Harry Pattee	100	150	250	400	600	1,000	2,000	
382	Fred Payne	20	25	50	80	300	400	600	
383	Barney Pelty Horizontal	30	80	200	250	300	500	1,200	
384	Barney Pelty Vertical	20	25	50	120	250	800	1,000	
385	Hub Perdue SL	40	50	150	250	600	800	1,500	
386	George Perring	30	50	80	120	200	300	500	
387	Arch Persons SL	40	50	150	200	450	600		
388	Francis Pfeffer	30	40	60	100	200	250	600	
389	Jeff Pfeffer ERR/Chicaco								
390	Jake Pfeister Seated (Pfiester)	30	40	60	120	150	200	400	
391	Jake Pfeister Throwing (Pfiester)	20	25	50	100	200	300		
392	Jimmy Phelan ML	20	25	40	80	150	250		
393	Eddie Phelps	20	25	40	80	150	200	400	
394	Deacon Phillippe	20	40	100	150	200	450		
395	Ollie Pickering ML	20	25	50	80	100	250		
396	Eddie Plank	60,000	80,000						
397	Phil Poland ML	20	25	40	120	150	200		
398	Jack Powell	25	30	100	120	200	250	1,000	
399	Mike Powers	25	60	80	200	250	500		
400	Billy Purtell	20	30	40	50	200	300	500	
401	Ambrose Puttman (Puttmann) ML	40	60	100	150	250	400		
402	Lee Quillen (Quillin) ML	20	25	40	100	150	250	400	
403	Jack Quinn	30	40	50	60	200	300	400	
404	Newt Randall ML	20	25	50	60	120	200	1,000	
405	Bugs Raymond	20	25	40	80	200	250	500	
406	Ed Reagan SL	40	50	100	250	400	800		
407	Ed Reulbach Glove Showing	30	60	80	150	300	400		
408	Ed Reulbach No Glove	25	30	60	100	250	350	500	
409	Dutch Revelle SL	40	50	80	150	400	1,000	1,200	
410	Bob Rhoades Hands at Chest	20	25	40	60	100	300	500	
411	Bob Rhoades Right Arm Out	30	40	60	100	150	200	500	
412	Charlie Rhodes	20	25	150	200	250	300	400	
413	Claude Ritchey	30	50	80	150	250	400		
414	Lou Ritter ML	20	25	40	60	120	300		
415	Ike Rockenfeld SL	40	60	100	200	500	600		
416	Claude Rossman	30	50	80	120	300	400	500	
417	Nap Rucker Portrait	25	30	40	120	150	200	600	
418	Nap Rucker Throwing	30	40	50	100	250	500	700	
419	Dick Rudolph ML	20	30	80	150	300	400	500	
420	Ray Ryan SL	60	100	250	300	500	1,000		
421	Germany Schaefer Detroit	20	50	60	150	300	400	500	
422	Germany Schaefer Washington	30	40	60	80	150	200	500	
423	George Schirm ML	30	50	60	80	150	400		
424	Larry Schlafly ML	20	25	40	100	120	250	400	
425	Admiral Schlei Batting	20	25	40	60	150	200	500	
426	Admiral Schlei Catching	20	40	60	100	300	500		
427	Admiral Schlei Portrait	40	50	60	120	200	350	1,200	
428	Boss Schmidt Portrait	20	25	40	60	150	200	400	
429	Boss Schmidt Throwing	20	25	40	80	150	250	400	
430	Ossee Schreck (Schreckengost) ML	20	25	40	80	200	250		850
431	Wildfire Schulte Back View	20	30	40	120	150	400	500	
432	Wildfire Schulte Front View	30	50	80	150	600			
433	Jim Scott	25	40	60	100	150	250	600	
434	Charles Seitz SL	100	150	250	400	600	1,000		
435	Cy Seymour Batting	20	25	40	120	200	400		
436	Cy Seymour Portrait	20	25	40	60	150	200	500	
437	Cy Seymour Throwing	20	25	40	120	200	400	500	
438	Spike Shannon ML	20	25	40	60	150	200	1,000	
439	Bud Sharpe ML	20	25	40	50	150	250	400	
440	Bud Shappe (Sharpe) ML	300	500	800					
441	Shag Shaughnessy SL	100	150	400	450	1,000	1,200		
442	Al Shaw St. Louis	20	50	60	120	150	250		
443	Hunky Shaw Providence ML	20	25	40	50	200	250		
444	Jimmy Sheckard Glove Showing	20	25	40	150	300	600		
445	Jimmy Sheckard No Glove	30	40	80	100	120	200	500	
446	Bill Shipke	20	25	40	60	200	300	500	
447	Jimmy Slagle ML	25	30	40	60	150	200		
448	Carlos Smith Shreveport SL	50	80	150	250	600	1,000		
449	Frank Smith Chicago-Boston	100	120	150	250	600			
450	Frank Smith Chicago F.Smith	40	50	60	120	200	500		
451	Frank Smith Chicago White Cap	25	30	40	150	250	400		
452	Heinie Smith Buffalo ML	25	30	60	150	200	400	500	
453	Happy Smith Brooklyn	20	25	40	100	150	200	800	
454	Sid Smith Atlanta SL	40	60	120	250	500	1,500		
455	Fred Snodgrass Batting	30	40	60	100	200	600		
456	Fred nodgrass (Snodgrass) Batting	400	600	1,000					
457	Fred Snodgrass Catching	20	25	50	120	200	250	500	
458	Bob Spade	20	25	40	80	120	300	500	
459	Tris Speaker	500	800	1,200	2,000	3,000	4,000	5,000	
460	Tubby Spencer	20	25	60	80	150	350		
461	Jake Stahl Glove Shows	20	40	60	80	150	300		
462	Jake Stahl No Glove Shows	20	25	60	120	150		400	
463	Oscar Stanage	40	60	100	150	250	400	600	
464	Dolly Stark SL	60	80	150	200	300	600		
465	Charlie Starr	20	25	40	120	200	300	600	
466	Harry Steinfeldt with Bat	20	25	50	80	150	200	600	
467	Harry Steinfeldt Portrait	30	40	60	100	150	250	600	
468	Jim Stephens	20	25	40	80	120	200	500	
469	George Stone	30	60	80	120	400	500	800	
470	George Stovall Batting	20	25	40	80	150	400	800	
471	George Stovall Portrait	20	25	40	80	150	200	500	
472	Sam Strang ML	20	25	40	80	150	250	400	
473	Gabby Street Catching	20	25	60	100	200	250	400	
474	Gabby Street Portrait	30	40	60	100	200	250	500	

		PrFr 1	GD 2	VG 3	VgEx 4	EX 5	ExMt 6	NM 7	NmMt 8
475	Billy Sullivan	20	25	50	80	150	250	800	
476	Ed Summers	20	40	50	80	120	250	600	
477	Bill Sweeney Boston	20	25	50	80	120	300	600	
478	Jeff Sweeney New York	40	50	80	150	300	400	600	
479	Jesse Tannehill Washington	50	80	120	200	300	500	800	
480	Lee Tannehill Chicago L.Tannehill	20	25	40	80	120	250	600	
481	Lee Tannehill Chicago Tannehill	20	25	40	80	120	250	1,000	
482	Dummy Taylor ML	25	50	80	100	300	400	1,000	
483	Fred Tenney	25	50	100	150	400	500	600	
484	Tony Thebo SL	60	80	120	250	400	1,200		
485	Jake Thielman ML	20	25	40	80	200	250	600	
486	Ira Thomas	50	80	120	200	300	500	800	
487	Woodie Thornton SL	50	120	150	250	500	800	1,200	
488	Joe Tinker Bat off Shoulder	80	100	250	300	800	1,200	3,000	
489	Joe Tinker Bat on Shoulder	100	120	200	300	500	1,000	2,000	
490	Joe Tinker Hands on Knees	80	120	200	400	700	1,200	6,000	
491	Joe Tinker Portrait	100	200	300	500	600	3,000	4,000	
492	John Titus	100	200	250	400	600			
493	Terry Turner	20	50	60	120	200	300	800	
494	Bob Unglaub	20	25	40	80	150	400	600	
495	Juan Violat (Viola) SL	50	60	200	250	400	1,000		
496	Rube Waddell Portrait	80	120	250	400	500	800	2,000	
497	Rube Waddell Throwing	50	120	200	500	600	1,000	2,500	
498	Heinie Wagner Bat on Left	25	30	50	120	150	250	600	
499	Heinie Wagner Bat on Right	25	30	60	200	250	300		
500	Honus Wagner	1,500,000	2,500,000						
501	Bobby Wallace	50	120	150	250	400	600	2,000	
502	Ed Walsh	150	200	250	500	800	1,500	2,000	
503	Jack Warhop	20	25	50	80	150	200	600	
504	Jake Weimer	20	25	40	80	150	250	400	
505	James Westlake SL	80	120	200	300	500	800		
506	Zack Wheat	80	150	200	600	800	1,000	2,000	
507	Doc White Chicago Pitching	20	25	50	80	120	300	800	
508	Doc White Chicago Portrait	40	50	80	100	120	200	400	
509	Foley White Houston SL	80	120	150	300	400	600		
510	Jack White Buffalo ML	20	25	40	60	120	200	400	
511	Kaiser Wilhelm Hands at Chest	25	30	40	120	200	300	500	
512	Kaiser Wilhelm with Bat	25	30	40	120	200	250	500	
513	Ed Willett with Bat	20	25	60	100	200	250	500	
514	Ed Willetts Throwing	20	25	40	50	200	300	500	
515	Jimmy Williams	20	25	60	80	150	200	400	
516	Vic Willis Pittsburgh Portrait	80	120	200	300	500	1,200	1,500	
517	Vic Willis St. Louis Throwing	50	80	120	200	500	800	1,500	
518	Vic Willis St. Louis with Bat	50	80	150	200	400	600	2,000	
519	Owen Wilson	25	30	80	120	150	250	400	
520	Hooks Wiltse Pitching	25	30	40	120	150	250	400	
521	Hooks Wiltse Portrait No Cap	40	50	60	100	150	300		
522	Hooks Wiltse Portrait with Cap	20	25	40	150	200	400	2,000	
523	Lucky Wright ML	20	25	40	80	150	250	400	
524	Cy Young Bare Hand Shows	250	600	800	1,500	2,000	2,500	6,000	
525	Cy Young Glove Shows	500	600	800	1,500	2,000	2,500	4,000	
526	Cy Young Portrait	400	800	1,500	2,500	5,000	6,000	8,000	
527	Irv Young Minneapolis ML	50	60	80	120	200	400		
528	Heinie Zimmerman	40	60	100	150	200	250	400	

— Prices listed above pertain to Piedmont and Sweet Caporal backs. The scarcer backs command premium values.

— ML and SL notations signify Minor Leaguers and Southern Leaguers.

— Jake Beckley ML PSA 8 (NmMt) sold for $33,958 (Goodwin; 10/12)

— Chief Bender Pitching No Trees PSA 8 (NmMt) sold for $14,103 (Goodwin; 4/11)

— Chief Bender Portrait PSA 9 (Mint) sold for $30,090 (Goodwin; 6/12)

— Jake Beckley PSA 8 (NmMt) sold for $33,958 (Goodwin; 9/12)

— Mordecai Brown Chicago Shirt (Red Hindu) SGC 4 (VG/EX) sold for $13,252 (Goodwin; 09/11)

— Mordecai Brown Cubs Shirt PSA 2 (Good) (Black Lennox) sold for $7,770 (Goodwin; 6/12)

— Al Burch Fielding (Brown Lenox) PSA 4 (VG/Ex) sold for $12,334 (Goodwin; 09/11)

— Hal Chase Portrait Pink PSA 7 (NM) sold for $5,117 (Goodwin; 03/12)

— Frank Chance Batting SGC 96 (Mint) sold for $10,809 (Goodwin; 10/12)

— Frank Chance Portrait Yellow PSA 7 (NM) sold for $5,207 (Mile High; 05/11)

— Frank Chance Portrait Yellow (Lenox Back) PSA 4 (VgEx) sold for $7,500 (REA; 05/12)

— Frank Chance Portrait Yellow (Red Hindu Back) PSA 3 (VG) sold for $16,980 (SCP; 12/12)

— Jack Chesbro PSA 8 (NmMt) sold for $7,477 (Goodwin; 8/12)

— Fred Clarke Holding Bat PSA 8 (NmMt) sold for $6,177 (Goodwin; 8/12)

— Fred Clarke Portrait PSA 8 (NmMt) sold for $8,908 (SCP; 5/12)

— Ty Cobb Bat off Shoulder PSA 9 (Mint) sold for $488,425 (SCP; 8/16)

— Ty Cobb Bat off Shoulder PSA 8 (NmMt) sold for $29,625 (REA; 5/13)

— Ty Cobb Bat on Shoulder PSA 8 (NmMt) sold for $24,619 (Goodwin; 4/11)

— Ty Cobb Bat off Shoulder (Uzit) PSA 2 (Good) sold for $17,775 (REA; 5/13)

— Ty Cobb Bat off Shoulder (Uzit) SGC 1.5 (Fair) sold for $14,403 (Mile High; 10/11)

— Ty Cobb Portrait Green PSA 8 (NmMt) sold for $64,506 (Goodwin; 2/11)

— Ty Cobb Portrait Green PSA 7 (NM) sold for $32,588 (REA; 5/13)

— Ty Cobb Portrait Red PSA 8 (NmMt) sold for $27,584 (SCP; 12/14)

— Ty Cobb Portrait Red PSA 8 (NmMt) sold for $26,663 (REA; 5/13)

— Ty Cobb Portrait Red PSA 8 (NmMt) sold for $18,800 (REA; 05/11)

— Ty Cobb Portrait Red (Hindu Red) PSA 3 (VG) sold for $45,510 (SCP; 12/12)

— Ty Cobb Portrait Red (Lennox) PSA 3 (VG) sold for $27,000 (REA; Spring '15)

— Ty Cobb Portrait Red (Cobb Back) SGC 30 (Good) sold for $132,000 (REA; Spring '15)

— Ty Cobb Portrait Red (Blank Back) SGC A (Authentic) sold for $15,654 (Goodwin; 09/11)

— Ty Cobb Portrait Red (Hindu Red) PSA 1 (Poor) sold for $29,336 (SCP; 4/13)

— Eddie Collins Philadelphia PSA 8 (NmMt) sold for $7,500 (REA; 05/12)

— Sam Crawford with Bat (Uzit) PSA 8 (NmMt) sold for $57,159 (Goodwin; 12/11)

— Ray Demmitt St. Louis SGC 60 (Ex) sold for $9,718 (Goodwin; 04/12)

— Ray Demmitt St. Louis SGC 60 (EX) sold for $5,000 (REA; 05/12)

— Gus Dorner Dopner PSA 2 (Good) sold for $5,500 (REA; 05/12)

— Joe Doyle Hands Above Head Nat'l PSA 3 (Vg) sold for $350,000 (REA; 05/12)

— Larry Doyle with Bat PSA 2 (Good) (Drum) sold for $5,362 (Goodwin; 6/12)

— Hugh Duffy PSA 8 (NmMt) sold for $6,797 (Goodwin; 6/12)

— Johnny Evers Portrait PSA 8 (NmMt) sold for $12,440 (Goodwin; 8/12)

— Johnny Evers Portrait PSA 8 (NmMt) sold for $10,690 (Goodwin; 7/14)

— Johnny Evers w/Bat Cubs Shirt PSA 4.5 (Vg/Ex+) (Hindu) sold for $9,306 (SCP; 5/12)

— Hobe Ferris PSA 8 (NmMt) sold for $12,936 (Goodwin; 2/11)

— Lou Fiene Throwing SGC 40 (VG) (Drum) sold for $5,484 (Goodwin; 10/12)

— Elmer Flick PSA 8 (NmMt) sold for $7,477 (Goodwin; 8/12)

— Clark Griffith Batting PSA 4 (Vg/Ex) (Drum) sold for $8,755 (Goodwin; 10/12)

— Miller Huggins Hands at Mouth (Drum) SGC 40 (VG) sold for $14,578 (Goodwin; 6/13)

— Miller Huggins Portrait PSA 8 (NmMt) sold for $6,177 (Goodwin; 8/12)

— Hughie Jennings Both Hands PSA 8 (NmMt) sold for $8,225 (Goodwin; 8/12)

— Walter Johnson Hands at Chest PSA 8 (NmMt) sold for $10,280 (Goodwin; 7/13)

— Walter Johnson Hands at Chest (Hindu Red) SGC 55 (VgEx+) sold for $10,073 (REA; 5/13)

— Walter Johnson Hands at Chest (Hindu Red) SGC 4 (VgEx) sold for $11,000 (REA; 05/12)

— Walter Johnson Hands at Chest (Hindu Red) PSA 4 (VgEx) sold for $10,780 (SCP; 4/13)

— Walter Johnson Hands at Chest (Hindu Red) PSA 4 (VgEx) sold for $9,799 (SCP; 12/12)

— Walter Johnson Portrait PSA 8 (NmMt) sold for $23,971 (Goodwin; 3/15)

— Walter Johnson Portrait PSA 8 (NmMt) sold for $22,440 (Bussineau; 7/13)

— Addie Joss Portrait PSA 9 (MT) sold for $35,202 (Goodwin; 2/11)

— Addie Joss Portrait PSA 8 (NmMt) sold for $5,801 (Goodwin; 8/12)

— Addie Joss Portrait PSA 8 (NmMt) sold for $5,273 (Goodwin; 10/12)

— Willie Keeler Portrait PSA 8 (NmMt) sold for $19,404 (Goodwin; 6/12)

— Willie Keeler with Bat PSA 8 (NmMt) sold for $5,801 (Goodwin; 8/12)

— Rube Kisinger ML PSA 8 (NmMt) sold for $8,550 (Goodwin; 10/12)

— Red Kleinow Boston SGC 30 (Good) (Broad Leaf 460) sold for $5,425 (Memory Lane; 8/12)

— Ed Konetchy Glove Near Ground (Drum) PSA 1 (Poor) sold for $10,347 (Goodwin; 3/13)

— Nap Lajoie Portrait PSA 8 (NmMt) sold for $8,495 (Goodwin; 6/12)

— Nap Lajoie Throwing PSA 8 (NmMt) sold for $6,032 (Mile High; 5/12)

— Nap Lajoie Throwing PSA 8 (NmMt) sold for $5,616 (Goodwin; 11/12)

— Nap Lajoie Throwing PSA 8 (NmMt) sold for $5,105 (Goodwin; 10/12)

— Nap Lajoie with Bat PSA 8 (NmMt) sold for $8,495 (Goodwin; 6/12)

— Sherry Magie Portrait (Magee) PSA 8 (NmMt) sold for $27,660 (Greg Bussineau; 12/15)

— Sherry Magie Portrait (Magee) SGC 80 (ExMt) sold for $80,077 (Goodwin; 04/12)

— Sherry Magie Portrait (Magee) SGC 60 (EX) sold for $30,600 (Greg Bussineau; 12/12)

— Sherry Magie Portrait (Magee) PSA 2.5 (G+) sold for $15,000 (REA; 05/12)

— Sherry Magie Portrait (Magee) SGC 20 (Fair) sold for $8,215 (Goodwin; 8/12)

— Sherry Magee Portrait PSA 2.5 (G+) sold for $7,848 (Memory Lane; 8/12)

— Christy Mathewson Dark Cap PSA 8.5 (NmMt+) sold for $34,693 (Mile High; 10/13)

— Christy Mathewson Portrait PSA 8 (NmMt) sold for $32,588 (REA; 5/13)

— Christy Mathewson Portrait PSA 8 (NmMt) sold for $29,339 (Goodwin; 6/12)

— Christy Mathewson Dark Cap PSA 8 (NmMt) sold for $35,502 (Goodwin; 8/12)

– John McGraw Glove at Hip PSA 8 (NmMt) sold for $5,801 (Goodwin; 10/12)

– George McQuillan with Bat PSA 1 (Poor) (Brown Lennox) sold for $5,484 (Goodwin; 8/12)

– Danny Murphy Batting PSA 2 (Red Hindu Back) (Good) sold for $31,328 (SCP; 12/12)

– Bill O'Hara St. Louis PSA 7 (NM) sold for $44,325 (Mile High; 10/11)

– Eddie Plank PSA 6 (ExMt) sold for $239,000 (Heritage; 7/16)

– Eddie Plank PSA 6 (ExMt) sold for $193,767 (Goodwin; 4/11)

– Eddie Plank SGC 70 (Ex+) (Piedmont 150 Back) sold for $330,826 (Goodwin; 04/12)

– Eddie Plank SGC 60 (EX) sold for $106,650 (REA; 5/13)

– Eddie Plank PSA 5 (EX) sold for $85,237 (Lelands; 12/12)

– Eddie Plank PSA 5 (EX) sold for $78,959 (Mile High; 10/13)

– Eddie Plank PSA 5 (EX) sold for $75,600 (Bussineau; 7/13)

– Eddie Plank PSA 4.5 (VgEx+) sold for $66,000 (REA; Spring '15)

– Eddie Plank PSA 4 (VgEx) sold for $94,000 (REA; 05/11)

– Eddie Plank PSA 4 (VgEx) sold for $88,875 (REA; 5/13)

– Eddie Plank PSA 4 (VgEx) sold for $83,300 (Memory Lane; 5/12)

– Eddie Plank PSA 4 (VgEx) sold for $80,000 (REA; 05/12)

– Eddie Plank SGC 2.5 (G/VG) sold for $42,000 (REA; Spring '15)

– Eddie Plank PSA Authentic (Missing Color) sold for $92,762 (Goodwin; 1/13)

– Germany Schaefer Detroit PSA 9 (Mint) sold for $5,558 (Memory Lane; 8/12)

– Charles Seitz PSA 8 (NmMt) sold for $11,759 (Goodwin; 2/11)

– Cy Seymour Throwing (Drum) PSA 1 (Poor) sold for $24,406 (Goodwin; 3/13)

– Sid Smith Atlanta SL SGC A (Authentic) (Old Mill Brown) sold for $24,000 (REA; Fall '14)

– Tris Speaker PSA 8 (NmMt) sold for $22,041 (Goodwin; 4/11)

– Tris Speaker PSA 8 (NmMt) sold for $12,720 (Greg Bussineau; 12/12)

– Gabby Street Catching SGC 40 (Vg) (Broadleaf 460) sold for $15,307 (Goodwin; 01/12)

– Cy Seymour Throwing (Red Hindu Back) PSA 3 (VG) sold for $12,173 (SCP; 12/12)

– Joe Tinker Bat off Shoulder PSA 8 (NmMt) (EPDG) sold for $15,054 (Goodwin; 8/12)

– Rube Waddell Portrait PSA 8 (NmMt) sold for $13,252 (Goodwin; 8/12)

– Rube Waddell Throwing PSA 9 (Mint) sold for $23,520 (Greg Bussineau; 4/12)

– Honus Wagner PSA 8 (NmMt) sold privately by SCP for $2.8M in September, 2007

– Honus Wagner PSA 8 (NmMt) purchased for $2.35M in March, 2007 by SCP

– Honus Wagner PSA 8 (NmMt) purchased for $1.265M on eBay in 2000 by B.Seigel

– Honus Wagner PSA 8 (NmMt) purchased for $640K at Christy's, 1996 by M.Gidwitz

– Honus Wagner PSA 8 (NmMt) sold by Gretzky for $500,000 to Treat Ent. in 1995

– Honus Wagner PSA 8 (NmMt) purchased for $451,000 in 1991 by Gretzky & McNall

– Honus Wagner PSA 5 MC (EX, Miscut) sold for $2.10M (Goldin; 4/13)

– Honus Wagner PSA 3 (Vg) sold for $1,320,000 (REA; Spring '15)

– Honus Wagner SGC 40 (Vg) sold for $1,232,466 (Goodwin; 04/12)

– Honus Wagner PSA 2 (Good) sold for $654,500 (Memory Lane; 5/12)

– Honus Wagner PSA 2 (Good) sold for $651,150 (REA; 5/12)

– Honus Wagner PSA 1 (Poor) sold for $402,900 (REA; 5/13)

– Honus Wagner SGC Authentic sold for $198,850 (Goodwin; 8/12)

– Honus Wagner PSA Authentic sold for $188,000 (REA; 5/11)

– Vic Willis St. Louis with Bat PSA 8 (NmMt) sold for $7,477 (Goodwin; 8/12)

– Cy Young Bare Hand Shows PSA 9 (MT) sold for $61,885 (Goodwin; 4/11)

– Cy Young Glove Shows PSA 8 (NmMt) sold for $28,373 (Goodwin; 4/11)

– Cy Young Portrait PSA 8 (NmMt) sold for $35,225 (Goodwin; 3/15)

– Cy Young Portrait PSA 8 (NmMt) sold for $27,240 (Bussineau; 7/13)

910 American Caramel Pirates E90-2

		PrFr 1	GD 2	VG 3	VgEx 4	EX 5	ExMt 6	NM 7	NmMt 8
	Babe Adams	120	200	250	800				
	Fred Clarke	120	250	400	800				
	George Gibson	120	200	400	500				
	Ham Hyatt	120	200	400	800				
	Tommy Leach	120	200	300	800				
	Sam Leever	120	200	400	800				
	Nick Maddox	120	200	400	800				
	Dots Miller	120	200	400	800				
	Deacon Phillippe	120	200	300	800				
	Honus Wagner	2,500	4,000	6,000	9,000	10,000			
	Chief Wilson	120	200	400	800				

– Honus Wagner PSA 3.5 (VG+) sold for $6,420 (Goodwin; 12/11)

1910 E98 Set of 30

		PrFr 1	GD 2	VG 3	VgEx 4	EX 5	ExMt 6	NM 7	NmMt 8
1	Chief Bender	120	250	400	800	1,500			
2	Roger Bresnahan	150	300	400	800	1,500			
3	Al Bridwell	150	200	250	500	1,000			
4	Miner Brown	150	500	600	1,000	1,500			
5	Frank Chance	120	400	500	800	1,500			
6	Hal Chase	150	400	500	1,000				
7	Fred Clarke	120	400	500	800	1,500			
8	Ty Cobb	1,500	2,000	3,000	6,000				
9	Eddie Collins	120	300	400	800	3,000			
10	Jack Coombs	100	150	250	500	1,000			
11	Bill Dahlen	100	150	250	500	1,000			
12	Harry Davis	100	150	250	500	1,000			
13	Red Dooin	100	150	400	500	1,000			
14	Johnny Evers	150	300	400	800	1,500			
15	Russ Ford	80	200	500	1,000				
16	Hughey Jennings	150	300	400	800	1,500			
17	Johnny Kling	80	150	250	600	1,000			
18	Nap Lajoie	200	400	600	1,200	2,500			
19	Connie Mack	150	600	1,000	1,500	3,000			
20	Christy Mathewson	800	2,500	3,000					
21	John McGraw	150	250	400	800	1,500			
22	Larry McLean	80	150	250	500	1,000			
23	Chief Meyers	100	150	300	500	1,000			
24	George Mullin	80	200	250	500	1,000			
25	Fred Tenney	80	150	250	500	1,000			
26	Joe Tinker	120	250	400					
27	Hippo Vaughn	120	250	500					
28	Hans Wagner	1,000	1,600	2,500	6,500				
29	Ed Walsh	250	300	600	800	1,500			
30	Cy Young	600	1,200	2,000	3,000				

— Hans Wagner SGC 5.5 (Ex+) sold for $5,435 (Goodwin; 09/11)

— Cy Young #30 PSA 8 (NmMt) sold for $5,273 (Mile High; 1/13)

1910 Old Mill T210

— Joe Jackson SGC 40 (VG) sold for $168,000 (REA; Spring '15)

— Joe Jackson SGC 30 (Good) sold for $118,500 (REA; 5/13)

— Joe Jackson PSA 2 (Good) sold for $96,631 (SCP; 12/12)

— Joe Jackson SGC 30 (Good) sold for $80,000 (Legendary; 11/13)

— Joe Jackson PSA 1.5 (Fair) sold for $77,820 (SCP; 4/13)

— Joe Jackson SGC Authentic sold for $57,500 (Lgendary ; 5/14)

— Joe Jackson PSA Authentic sold for $56,028 (Goodwin; 11/15)

— Casey Stengel SGC 5 (Ex) sold for $27,000 (REA; Sping '15)

1910 Philadelphia Caramel E96

		PrFr 1	GD 2	VG 3	VgEx 4	EX 5	ExMt 6	NM 7	NmMt 8
1	Babe Adams	60	120	200	300				
2	Red Ames	60	120	200	300				
3	Frank Arellanes	60	120	200	300	1,500			
4	Home Run Baker	200	300	400	800				
5	Mordecai Brown	100	200	600	800				
6	Fred Clark (Clarke)	100	200	300	500				
7	Harry Davis	60	120	200	300	600			
8	Jim Delehanty	60	120	200	300				
9	Bill Donovan	60	150	200	300				
10	Red Dooin	60	120	200	300				
11	George Gibson	60	120	200	500				
12	Buck Herzog	60	120	200	300				
13	Hugh Jennings MG	80	150	250	400				
14	Ed Karger	60	120	200	300	600			
15	Johnny Kling	60	120	200	300				
16	Ed Konetchy	60	120	200	300				
17	Napoleon Lajoie	325	400	800	1,000				
18	Connie Mack MG	300	800	1,000	1,200				

		PrFr 1	GD 2	VG 3	VgEx 4	EX 5	ExMt 6	NM 7	NmMt 8
19	Rube Marquard	100	250	400	400				
20	George McQuillan	60	150	200	300				
21	Chief Meyers	60	120	200	300	600			
22	Mike Mowrey	60	120	200	300	600			
23	George Mullin	60	120	200	300				
24	Red Murray	60	120	200	300	600			
25	Jack Pfeister (Pfiester)	60	120	200	300				
26	Claude Rossman	60	120	150	300				
27	Nap Rucker	60	120	250	300				
28	Tubby Spencer	60	120	200	300				
29	Ira Thomas	60	120	300	350				
30	Joe Tinker	100	200	300	800				

— Home Run Baker PSA 6.5 (ExMt+) sold for $5,307 (Mile High; 05/11)
— Bill Donovan PSA 6 (ExMt) sold for $9,068 (Goodwin; 09/11)
— Claude Rossman PSA 6 (ExMt) sold for $9,068 (Goodwin; 09/11)

1910 Standard Caramel E93

		PrFr 1	GD 2	VG 3	VgEx 4	EX 5	ExMt 6	NM 7	NmMt 8
1	Red Ames	60	80	100	120	650	1,200		
2	Chief Bender	120	200	350	400	600	800		
3	Mordecai Brown	200	300	500	800	1,500	2,500		
4	Frank Chance	175	250	350	600	1,200	2,000		
5	Hal Chase	100	150	200	250	600	1,500		
6	Ty Cobb	800	1,500	2,500	4,000	6,000	8,000		
7	Eddie Collins	100	150	300	500	800	1,000		
8	Harry Coveleskie (Coveleski)	50	80	150	400	800	1,500		
9	Fred Clarke	100	150	250	500	800	1,500		
10	Jim Delehanty	50	80	200	250	350	400		
11	Bill Donovan	50	80	150	400	800			
12	Red Dooin	50	80	150	250	350	1,200		
13	Johnny Evers	150	250	400	600	1,500	2,500		
14	George Gibson	50	80	150	300	500	800		
15	Clark Griffith	100	150	250	500	600	1,500		
16	Hugh Jennings	100	150	250	500	1,000	1,500		
17	Davy Jones	50	80	150	325	500	1,200		
18	Addie Joss	150	250	400	600	1,000	2,500		
19	Napoleon Lajoie	200	300	500	800	2,000	3,000		
20	Tommy Leach	50	80	150	300	500	3,600		
21	Christy Mathewson	600	1,000	1,500	2,500	4,000	6,000		
22	John McGraw	100	150	200	300	1,000	1,500		
23	Jim Pastorius	50	80	150	300	500	1,300		
24	Deacon Phillippe	50	80	200	300	500	800		
25	Eddie Plank	250	500	550	600	1,000	3,000		
26	Joe Tinker	100	150	300	500	1,000	1,500		
27	Rube Waddell	120	200	400	600	1,200			
28	Honus Wagner	1,200	2,000	2,500	3,500	6,000	8,000		
29	Hooks Wiltse	50	80	150	250	300	1,500		
30	Cy Young	500	800	1,200	2,000	3,500	6,000		

— Christy Mathewson PSA 8 (NM) sold for $24,000 (REA; Fall '14)
— Honus Wagner SGC 88 (NmMt) sold for $17,101 (Mile High; 1/12)
— Honus Wagner SGC 88 (NmMt) sold for $16,440 (Goodwin; 6/12)
— Honus Wagner SGC 7 (NM) sold for $7,050 (REA; 05/11)

1910-11 Sporting Life M116

		PrFr 1	GD 2	VG 3	VgEx 4	EX 5	ExMt 6	NM 7	NmMt 8
1	Ed Abbaticchio	25	30	40	50	80	120	150	400
2A	Babe Adams Black Back	25	30	40	50	80	120	200	400
2B	Babe Adams Blue Back	25	30	40	50	80	120	200	400
3	Red Ames	25	30	40	60	80	120	200	400
4	Jimmy Archer	25	30	40	50	80	120	200	400
5	Frank Arellanes	25	30	40	50	80	120	200	400
6	Tommy Atkins	25	30	40	50	80	120	200	400
7	Jimmy Austin	25	30	40	50	80	120	200	400
8	Les Bachman	25	30	40	50	80	120	200	400
9	Bill Bailey	25	30	40	50	80	120	200	400
10A	Frank Baker Black Back	120	150	200	250	300	400	600	1,200
10B	Frank Baker Blue Back	100	120	150	350	450	600	800	1,000
11	Cy Barger	25	30	40	50	80	120	200	400
12	Jack Barry	25	30	40	50	80	120	200	400
13A	Johnny Bates Philadelphia	25	30	40	50	80	120	200	400
14	Ginger Beaumont	25	30	40	50	80	120	200	400
15	Fred Beck	25	30	40	50	80	120	200	400
16	Heine Beckendorf	25	30	40	50	80	120	200	400
17	Fred Beebe	25	30	40	50	80	120	200	400
18	George Bell	25	30	40	50	80	120	200	400
19	Harry Bemis	25	30	40	50	80	120	200	400
20A	Chief Bender Blue	120	150	200	250	300	500	900	1,500
20B	Chief Bender Pastel	100	120	150	200	250	400	600	1,000
21	Bill Bergen	25	30	40	50	80	120	200	400
22	Charles Berger	25	30	40	50	80	120	200	400
23	Bob Bescher	25	30	40	50	80	120	200	400
24	Joseph Birmingham	25	30	40	50	80	120	200	400
25	Lena Blackburn	25	30	40	50	80	120	200	400
26	Jack Bliss	25	30	40	50	80	120	200	400
27	James J. Block	25	30	40	50	80	120	200	400
28	Hugh Bradley	25	30	40	50	80	120	200	400
29	Kitty Bransfield	25	30	40	50	100	120	200	400
30A	Roger Bresnahan Blue	120	150	200	250	300	500	800	1,500
30B	Roger Bresnahan Pastel	100	120	150	200	400	500	700	1,000
31	Al Bridwell	25	30	40	50	80	120	200	400
32	Buster Brown	25	30	40	50	80	120	200	400
33A	Mordecai Brown Blue	120	150	200	350	400	600	800	1,500
33B	Mordecai Brown Pastel	120	150	200	350	400	600	850	1,000
34	Al Burch	25	30	40	50	80	120	200	400
35	Donie Bush	25	30	40	50	80	120	200	400
36	Bobby Byrne	25	30	40	50	80	120	200	400
37	Howie Camnitz	25	30	40	50	80	120	200	400
38	Vin Campbell	25	30	40	50	80	120	200	400
39	Bill Carrigan	25	30	40	50	100	120	200	400
40A	Frank Chance Blue	120	150	200	250	300	500	900	1,500
40B	Frank Chance Pastel	100	120	200	250	300	400	600	1,000
41	Chappy Charles	25	30	40	50	80	120	200	400
42A	Hal Chase Blue	80	100	120	150	200	300	600	1,200
42B	Hal Chase Pastel	80	100	120	150	200	300	600	1,000
43	Ed Cicotte	100	120	150	200	300	400	800	1,200
44A	Fred Clarke Black Back	100	120	150	200	250	400	600	1,000
44B	Fred Clarke Blue Back	100	120	150	200	250	400	600	1,000
45	Nig Clarke	25	30	40	50	80	120	200	400
46	Tommy Clarke	25	30	40	50	80	120	200	400
47A	Ty Cobb Blue	1,000	1,500	2,500	3,500	4,000	5,000	6,000	
47B	Ty Cobb Pastel	800	1,000	1,500	2,000	2,500	3,000	5,000	
48A	Eddie Collins Blue	150	200	250	300	500	600	1,000	2,500
48B	Eddie Collins Pastel	120	150	200	250	300	500	800	1,200
49	Ray Collins	25	30	40	50	80	120	200	400
50	Wid Conroy	25	30	40	50	80	120	200	400
51	Jack Coombs	25	30	40	50	80	120	200	400
52	Frank Corridon	25	30	40	50	80	120	200	400
53	Harry Coveleski ML	30	40	50	60	100	150	250	500
54	Doc Crandall	25	30	40	50	80	120	200	400
55A	Sam Crawford Blue	120	150	200	250	400	500	800	1,500
55B	Sam Crawford Pastel	100	120	150	200	300	400	600	1,000
56	Birdie Cree	25	30	40	50	80	120	200	625
57	Lou Criger	25	30	40	50	80	120	200	400
58	Dode Criss	25	30	40	50	80	120	200	400
59	Cliff Curtis	25	30	40	50	80	120	200	400
60	Bill Dahlen MG	25	30	40	50	80	120	200	400
61	William Davidson	25	30	40	50	80	120	200	400
62A	Harry Davis Blue	30	40	50	60	150	200	250	500
62B	Harry Davis Pastel	25	30	40	50	80	120	200	400
63	Jim Delehanty	25	30	40	50	80	120	200	400
64	Ray Demmitt	25	30	40	50	80	120	200	400
65	Frank Dessau	25	30	40	50	80	120	200	400
66A	Art Devlin Black Back	25	30	40	50	80	120	200	400
66B	Art Devlin Blue Back	25	30	40	50	80	120	200	400

		PrFr 1	GD 2	VG 3	VgEx 4	EX 5	ExMt 6	NM 7	NmMt 8
67	Josh Devore	25	30	40	50	80	120	200	400
68	Pat Donahue	25	30	40	50	80	120	200	400
69	Patsy Donovan MG	25	30	40	50	80	120	200	400
70A	Bill Donovan Blue	25	30	40	50	100	120	200	400
70B	Bill Donovan Pastel	25	30	40	50	100	120	200	400
71A	Red Dooin Blue	30	40	50	100	150	200	250	500
71B	Red Dooin Pastel	25	30	40	50	80	120	200	400
72	Mickey Doolan	25	30	40	50	80	120	200	400
73	Patsy Dougherty	25	30	40	50	80	120	200	400
74	Tom Downey	25	30	40	50	80	120	200	400
75	Jim Doyle	25	30	40	50	80	120	200	400
76A	Larry Doyle Blue	30	40	50	60	100	150	250	500
76B	Larry Doyle Pastel	25	30	40	50	80	120	200	400
77	Hugh Duffy MG	100	120	250	300	350	400	600	1,000
78	Jimmy Dygert	25	30	40	50	80	120	150	400
79	Dick Eagan	25	30	40	50	80	120	200	400
80	Kid Elberfeld	25	30	40	50	80	120	200	400
81	Rube Ellis	25	30	40	50	80	120	200	400
82	Clyde Engle	25	30	40	50	80	120	200	400
83	Tex Erwin	25	30	40	50	80	120	300	400
84	Steve Evans	25	30	40	50	80	120	200	400
85A	Johnny Evers Black Back	120	150	200	250	300	500	800	1,500
85B	Johnny Evers Blue Back	120	150	200	250	300	500	800	1,200
86	Bob Ewing	25	30	40	50	80	120	200	400
87	Cy Falkenberg	25	30	40	80	100	120	150	400
88	George Ferguson	25	30	40	50	80	120	200	400
89	Art Fletcher	25	30	40	50	80	120	200	400
90	Elmer Flick	100	120	150	200	250	400	600	1,000
91	John Flynn	25	30	40	50	80	120	200	400
92	Russ Ford	25	30	40	50	80	120	200	400
93	Ed Foster ML	25	30	40	50	120	200	300	400
94	Bill Foxen	25	30	40	50	80	120	200	400
95	John Frill ML	25	30	40	50	80	120	200	400
96	Samuel Frock	25	30	40	50	80	120	200	400
97	Art Fromme	25	30	40	50	80	120	200	400
98	Earle Gardner New York	25	30	40	50	80	120	200	400
99	Larry Gardner Boston	25	30	40	80	120	200	300	400
100	Harry Gaspar	25	30	40	50	80	120	200	400
101	Doc Gessler	25	30	40	50	80	120	150	400
102A	George Gibson Blue	30	40	50	60	150	250		
102B	George Gibson Pastel	25	30	40	60	150	250		
103	Bert Graham	25	30	40	50	80	120	200	400
104	Peaches Graham	25	30	40	50	80	120	200	400
105	Eddie Grant	25	30	40	50	80	120	200	400
106	Clark Griffith MG	100	120	150	200	300	400	600	1,000
107	Ed Hahn	25	30	40	50	80	150	250	
108	Charles Hall	25	30	40	50	80	120	200	400
109	Bob Harmon	25	30	40	50	80	120	200	400
110	Topsy Hartsel	25	30	40	50	80	120	200	400
111	Roy Hartzell	25	30	40	50	80	120	200	400
112	Heinie Heitmuller	25	30	40	50	80	120	200	400
113	Buck Herzog	25	30	40	50	80	120	200	400
114	Doc Hoblitzel	25	30	40	50	80	120	200	400
115	Danny Hoffman	25	30	40	50	80	120	200	400
116	Solly Hofman	25	30	40	50	80	120	200	400
117	Harry Hooper	100	120	150	200	250	400	600	1,500
118	Harry Howell	25	30	40	50	80	120	200	400
119	Miller Huggins	100	120	150	200	250	400	600	1,200
120	Tom Hughes ML	25	30	40	50	80	120	200	400
121	Rudy Hulswitt	25	30	40	50	80	120	200	400
122	John Hummel	25	30	40	50	80	120	200	400
123	George Hunter	25	30	40	50	80	120	200	400
124	Ham Hyatt	25	30	40	50	80	120	200	400
125	Fred Jacklitsch	25	30	50	60	80	120	200	400
126A	Hugh Jennings MG Blue	120	150	200	250	400	500	800	1,500
126B	Hugh Jennings MG Pastel	100	120	150	200	250	400	600	1,000
127	Walter Johnson	500	600	800	1,000	1,800	2,000	4,000	5,000
128A	Davy Jones Blue	30	40	50	60	100	150	250	1,500
128B	Davy Jones Pastel	25	30	40	50	80	120	200	400
129	Tom Jones	25	30	40	50	80	120	200	400
130A	Tim Jordan Blue	30	40	50	60	100	150	250	500
130B	Tim Jordan Pastel	25	30	40	50	80	120	200	400
131	Addie Joss	100	120	200	250	300	1,100	1,800	
132	John Kane	25	30	40	50	80	120	200	400
133	Edwin Karge	25	30	40	50	80	120	200	400
134	Red Killifer	25	30	40	50	120	120	200	625
135	Johnny Kling	25	30	40	50	80	120	200	400
136	Otto Knabe	25	30	40	50	80	120	200	400
137	John Knight	25	30	40	50	80	120	200	400
138	Ed Konetchy	25	30	40	50	80	120	200	400
139	Harry Krause	25	30	40	50	80	120	200	400
140	Rube Kroh	25	30	40	50	80	120	200	400
141	Otto Krueger ML	25	30	40	50	80	120	200	400
142A	Nap Lajoie Blue	300	400	500	600	800	1,000	1,500	
142B	Nap Lajoie Pastel	200	300	400	500	600	800	1,200	
143	Joe Lake	25	30	40	50	80	120	200	400
144	Fred Lake MG	25	30	40	50	80	120	200	400
145	Frank LaPorte	25	30	40	50	80	120	200	400
146	Jack Lapp	25	30	40	80	120	200	300	400
147	Chick Lathers	25	30	40	50	80	120	200	400
148A	Tommy Leach Blue	30	40	50	120	150	200	300	500
148B	Tommy Leach Pastel	25	30	40	50	80	120	200	400
149	Sam Leever	25	30	40	50	80	120	200	400
150	Lefty Leifield	25	30	40	50	80	120	200	400
151	Ed Lennox	25	30	40	50	80	120	200	400
152	Frederick Link	25	30	40	50	80	120	200	400
153	Paddy Livingstone	25	30	40	50	80	120	200	400
154	Hans Lobert	25	30	40	50	80	120	200	400
155	Bris Lord	25	30	40	50	80	120	200	400
156A	Harry Lord Blue	30	40	50	60	100	150	250	500
156B	Harry Lord Pastel	25	30	40	50	80	120	200	400
157	Johnny Lush	25	30	40	50	80	100	120	400
158	Connie Mack MG	150	200	250	300	400	700		
159	Thomas Madden	25	30	40	50	80	120	200	400
160	Nick Maddox	25	30	40	50	80	120	200	400
161	Sherry Magee	25	30	40	50	80	120	200	400
162A	Christy Mathewson Blue	500	600	800	1,000	1,200	1,500	2,500	
162B	Christy Mathewson Pastel	500	600	800	1,000	1,200	1,500	2,500	5,000
163	Al Mattern	25	30	40	60	80	120	200	400
164	Jimmy McAleer MG	25	30	40	50	80	120	200	400
165	George McBride	25	30	40	50	80	120	200	400
166A	Amby McConnell Boston	25	30	40	50	80	120	200	400
167	Pryor McElveen	25	30	40	50	80	120	200	400
168	John McGraw MG	80	100	200	250	300	500	800	1,200
169	Deacon McGuire MG	25	30	40	50	80	120	200	400
170	Stuffy McInnis	25	30	40	50	80	120	200	400
171	Harry McIntire	25	30	40	50	80	120	200	400
172	Matty McIntyre	25	30	40	50	80	120	250	
173	Larry McLean	25	30	40	50	80	120	200	400
174	Tommy McMillan	25	30	40	50	80	120	200	400
175B	George McQuillan Phil Blue	30	40	50	80	100	150	250	500
175C	George McQuillan Phil Pastel	25	30	40	50	80	120	200	400
176	Paul Meloan	25	30	40	80	120	200	300	400
177	Fred Merkle	25	30	40	50	80	120	200	400
178	Chief Meyers	25	30	40	50	120	150	200	400
179	Clyde Milan	25	30	40	50	80	120	200	400
180	Dots Miller	25	30	40	50	80	120	200	400
181	Warren Miller	25	30	40	50	80	120	200	750
182	Fred Mitchell ML	25	30	40	50	80	120	200	400
183	Mike Mitchell	25	30	40	50	80	120	200	400
184	Earl Moore	25	30	40	50	80	120	200	400
185	Pat Moran	25	30	40	50	80	120	200	400
186A	Lew Moren Black Back	25	30	40	50	80	120	200	400
186B	Lew Moren Blue Back	30	40	50	60	100	150	250	500

		PrFr 1	GD 2	VG 3	VgEx 4	EX 5	ExMt 6	NM 7	NmMt 8
187	Cy Morgan	25	30	40	50	80	120	200	400
188	George Moriarty	25	30	40	50	80	120	200	400
189	Mike Mowery	25	30	40	50	80	120	200	400
190A	George Mullin Black Back	25	30	40	50	80	120	200	400
190B	George Mullin Blue Back	30	40	50	60	100	150	250	500
191	Danny Murphy	25	30	40	50	80	120	200	400
192	Red Murray	25	30	40	50	80	175	200	400
193	Tom Needham	25	30	40	50	80	120	200	400
194	Harry Niles	25	30	40	50	80	120	200	400
195	Rebel Oakes	25	30	40	80	100	120	300	400
196	Jack O'Connor	25	30	40	50	80	120	200	400
197	Paddy O'Connor	25	30	40	50	80	120	150	400
198	Bill O'Hara ML	25	30	40	50	80	120	200	400
199	Rube Oldring	25	30	40	50	80	120	200	400
200	Charley O'Leary	25	30	40	50	80	150	200	400
201	Orval Overall	25	30	40	50	80	120	200	400
202	Fred Parent	25	30	40	60	80	120	200	400
203	Dode Paskert	25	30	40	50	80	120	200	400
204	Frederick Payne	25	30	40	50	80	120	200	400
205	Barney Pelty	25	30	40	50	80	120	200	400
206	Hub Pernoll	25	30	40	80	120	200	300	
207	George Perring ML	25	30	40	50	80	300	400	
208	Big Jeff Pfeffer	25	30	40	50	80	120	200	400
209	Jack Pfiester	25	30	40	50	80	120	200	400
210	Art Phelan	25	30	40	50	120	200	300	400
211	Ed Phelps	25	30	40	50	80	120	200	400
212	Deacon Phillipe	25	30	40	50	80	120	200	400
213	Eddie Plank	400	500	600	800	1,000	1,200	2,000	
214	Jack Powell	25	30	40	50	80	120	200	400
215	Billy (William) Purtell	25	30	40	50	80	120	200	400
216	Farmer Ray ML	25	30	40	50	80	120	200	500
217	Bugs Raymond	25	30	40	50	450	500	600	400
218	Doc Reisling	25	30	40	50	80	120	200	400
219	Ed Reulbach	25	30	40	50	80	120	200	
220	Lew Richie	25	30	40	50	80	120	200	400
221	Jack Rowan	25	30	40	50	80	120	200	400
222A	Nap Rucker Black Back	25	30	40	50	80	120	200	400
222B	Nap Rucker Blue Back	25	30	60	80	100	120	200	400
223	Slim Sallee	25	30	40	50	80	120	200	400
224	Doc Scanlon	25	30	40	60	80	120	200	400
225	Germany Schaefer	25	30	40	50	80	120	200	400
226	Lou Schettler	25	30	40	50	80	150	200	400
227	Admiral Schlei	25	30	40	50	80	120	200	400
228	Boss Schmidt	25	30	40	50	80	120	200	400
229	Wildfire Schulte	25	30	40	50	80	120	200	400
230	Al Schweitzer	25	30	40	50	80	120	200	400
231	James Scott	25	30	40	50	80	120	200	400
232	James Seymour	25	30	40	50	80	120	200	400
233	Tillie Shafer	25	30	40	50	80	120	200	400
234	David Shean	25	30	40	50	80	120	200	400
235	Bayard Sharpe	25	30	40	50	80	120	200	400
236	Jimmy Sheckard	25	30	40	50	80	120	200	400
237	Mike Simon	25	30	40	50	80	120	200	400
238	Charlie Smith	25	30	40	50	80	120	200	400
239	Frank Smith	25	30	40	50	80	120	200	675
240	Harry Smith	25	30	40	50	80	120	200	400
241	Fred Snodgrass	25	30	40	50	80	120	200	400
242	Bob Spade UER	25	30	40	50	80	120	200	400
243	Tully Sparks	25	30	40	50	80	120	200	400
244	Tris Speaker	500	600	800	1,000	1,200	2,000	3,000	5,000
245	Jake Stahl	25	30	40	50	120	200	200	400
246	George Stallings MG	25	30	40	50	80	120	200	400
247	Oscar Stanage	25	30	40	50	80	120	200	400
248	Harry Steinfeldt	25	30	40	50	80	120	200	400
249	Jim Stephens	25	30	40	50	80	120	200	400
250	George Stone	25	30	40	50	80	120	200	400
251	George Stovall	25	30	40	80	100	120	200	400

		PrFr 1	GD 2	VG 3	VgEx 4	EX 5	ExMt 6	NM 7	NmMt 8
252	Gabby Street	25	30	40	50	80	120	150	400
253	Sailor Stroud	25	30	40	50	80	120	200	400
254	Amos Strunk	25	30	40	50	80	120	200	400
255	George Suggs	25	30	40	50	80	120	200	525
256	Billy Sullivan	25	30	40	50	80	120	150	400
257A	Ed Summers Black Back	25	30	40	50	80	120	200	400
257B	Ed Summers Blue Back	25	30	40	50	80	120	200	400
258	Bill Sweeney	25	30	40	50	80	120	200	400
259	Jeff Sweeney	25	30	40	50	80	120	200	400
260	Lee Tannehill	25	30	40	50	80	120	200	400
261A	Fred Tenney Blue	30	40	50	60	250	300	400	600
262B	Fred Tenney Pastel	25	30	40	50	100	120	200	400
262A	Ira Thomas Blue	30	40	50	80	100	250	400	600
262B	Ira Thomas Pastel	25	30	40	50	80	120	200	400
263	John Thoney	25	30	40	50	80	120	200	400
264A	Joe Tinker Black Back	120	150	200	250	300	500	800	1,500
264B	Joe Tinker Blue Back	100	120	150	200	250	400	1,400	2,200
265	John Titus	25	30	40	50	80	120	200	400
266	Terry Turner	25	30	40	50	80	120	200	400
267	Bob Unglaub	25	30	40	50	80	120	200	400
268A	Rube Waddell Black Back	120	200	250	300	300	500	800	1,500
268B	Rube Waddell Blue Back	100	120	150	300	350	400	600	1,000
269A	Hans Wagner Blue	2,000	3,000	4,000	5,000	6,000	8,000		
269B	Hans Wagner Pastel	1,200	1,500	3,000	4,000	5,000	6,000	12,000	
270	Heinie Wagner	25	30	40	50	80	120	200	400
271	Bobby Wallace	80	100	120	150	200	300	500	1,000
272	Ed Walsh	100	120	150	250	300	400	900	1,500
273	Jimmy Walsh Gray	60	80	100	120	150	250	500	800
274	Jimmy Walsh White	80	100	120	150	250	300	600	1,000
275	Doc White	25	30	40	50	80	120	200	400
276	Kaiser Wilhelm	25	30	40	50	80	120	200	400
277	Ed Willett	25	30	40	50	80	120	200	400
278	Vic Willis	100	120	150	200	250	400	600	1,500
279	Art Wilson	25	30	40	50	80	200	200	400
280	Chief Wilson	25	30	40	50	80	120	200	400
281	Hooks Wiltse	25	30	40	50	80	120	200	400
282	Harry Wolter	25	30	40	50	80	120	200	400
283	Joe Wood	300	400	500	800	1,200	2,800		
284	Ralph Works	25	30	40	50	80	120	200	400
285A	Cy Young Black Back	500	600	800	1,000	1,200	1,500	2,500	4,000
285B	Cy Young Blue Back	500	600	800	1,000	1,200	1,500	2,500	
286	Irv Young	25	30	40	50	80	120	200	400
287	Heinie Zimmerman	25	30	40	50	80	120	200	400
288	Dutch Zwilling	25	30	40	50	80	200	250	400

1910-12 Sweet Caporal Pins P2

		PrFr 1	GD 2	VG 3	VgEx 4	EX 5	ExMt 6	NM 7	NmMt 8
1	Ed Abbaticchio	6	8	10	12	20	25	40	60
2	Red Ames	6	8	10	12	20	25	40	60
3A	Jimmy Archer Small Letters	6	8	10	12	20	25	40	60
3B	Jimmy Archer Large Letters	8	10	12	15	20	30	50	80
4A	Jimmy Austin Small Letters	6	8	10	12	20	25	40	80
4B	Jimmy Austin Large Letters	8	10	12	15	20	30	50	80
5	Home Run Baker	12	15	20	25	30	80	100	200
6	Neal Ball	6	8	10	12	20	25	40	60
7	Cy Barger	6	8	10	12	20	25	40	60
8	Jack Barry	6	8	10	12	20	25	40	60
9	Johnny Bates	6	8	10	12	20	25	40	60
10	Beals Becker	6	8	10	12	20	25	40	60
11	Fred Beebe	6	8	10	12	20	25	40	60
12A	George Bell Small Letters	6	8	10	12	20	25	40	60
12B	George Bell Large Letters	8	10	12	15	20	30	50	80
13A	Chief Bender Small Letters	12	15	20	25	30	50	80	150
13B	Chief Bender Large Letters	20	25	30	40	50	80	120	300
14	Bill Bergen	6	8	10	12	20	25	40	60
15	Bob Bescher	6	8	10	12	20	25	40	60
16	Joe Birmingham	6	8	10	12	20	25	40	60

	PrFr 1	GD 2	VG 3	VgEx 4	EX 5	ExMt 6	NM 7	NmMt 8
Kitty Bransfield	6	8	10	12	15	50	60	80
A R.Bresnahan Mouth Closed Sm Ltr	12	15	20	25	30	50	80	200
B R.Bresnahan Mouth Closed Lg Ltr	20	25	30	40	60	80	120	400
Al Bridwell	6	8	10	12	20	25	40	60
A Mordecai Brown Small Letters	12	15	20	25	30	50	80	120
B Mordecai Brown Large Letters	20	25	30	40	80	100	175	250
Bobby Byrne	6	8	10	12	20	25	40	60
Nixey Callahan	6	8	10	12	20	25	40	
A Howie Camnitz Small Letters	6	8	10	12	20	25	40	60
B Howie Camnitz Large Letters	8	10	12	15	20	30	50	80
A Bill Carrigan Small Letters	6	8	10	12	20	25	40	60
B Bill Carrigan Large Letters	8	10	12	15	20	30	50	80
A Frank Chance Small Letters	20	25	30	40	80	250	300	500
B Frank Chance Large Letters	12	15	20	25	60	250	300	500
A Hal Chase Small Letters	12	15	20	25	30	80	100	120
B Hal Chase Large Letters	12	15	20	25	30	50	80	120
Ed Cicotte	12	15	20	25	80	100	120	200
A Fred Clarke Small Letters	12	15	20	25	30	50	80	120
B Fred Clarke Large Letters	20	25	30	40	50	100	120	200
A Ty Cobb Small Letters	150	200	250	300	400	600	800	1,200
B Ty Cobb Large Letters	200	250	300	400	500	700	1,000	
A Eddie Collins Small Letters	12	15	20	25	80	100	120	150
B Eddie Collins Large Letters	20	25	30	40	50	80	120	200
Doc Crandall	6	8	10	12	20	25	40	60
A Birdie Cree	6	8	10	12	20	25	40	60
B Bill Dahlen Large Letters	6	8	10	12	20	25	40	60
Jim Delahanty	6	8	10	12	20	25	40	60
Art Devlin	6	8	10	12	20	25	40	60
Josh Devore	6	8	10	12	20	25	40	60
Bill Donovan	6	8	10	12	20	25	40	60
A Red Dooin Small Letters	6	8	10	12	20	25	40	60
B Red Dooin Large Letters	8	10	12	15	20	30	50	80
A Mickey Doolan Small Letters	6	8	10	12	20	25	40	60
B Mickey Doolan Large Letters	8	10	12	15	20	30	50	80
Patsy Dougherty	6	8	10	12	20	25	40	60
Tom Downey Small Letters	6	8	10	12	20	25	40	80
Tom Downey Large Letters	8	10	12	15	20	30	50	80
Larry Doyle Small Letters	6	8	10	12	20	25	40	60
Larry Doyle Large Letters	8	10	12	15	20	30	50	80
Louis Drucke	6	8	10	12	20	25	40	60
Hugh Duffy Small Letters	12	15	20	25	30	50	80	200
Hugh Duffy Large Letters	20	25	30	40	50	100	120	200
Jimmy Dygert	6	8	10	12	20	25	80	120
Kid Elberfeld Small Letters	6	8	10	12	20	25	40	60
Kid Elberfeld Large Letters	8	10	12	15	20	30	50	80
Clyde Engle Small Letters	6	8	10	12	20	25	40	60
Clyde Engle Large Letters	8	10	12	15	20	30	50	80
Tex Erwin	6	8	10	12	20	25	40	60
Steve Evans	6	8	10	12	20	25	40	60
Johnny Evers	12	15	20	25	100	120	150	250
Cecil Ferguson	6	8	10	12	20	25	40	60
John Flynn	6	8	10	12	20	25	40	60
Russ Ford Small Letters	6	8	10	12	20	25	40	60
Russ Ford Large Letters	8	10	12	15	20	30	50	80
Art Fromme	6	8	10	12	20	25	40	60
Harry Gaspar	6	8	10	12	20	25	40	60
George Gibson	6	8	10	12	20	25	60	80
Eddie Grant	6	8	10	12	20	25	40	60
Dolly Gray	6	8	10	12	20	25	40	60
Clark Griffith Small Letters	12	15	20	25	30	50	80	120
Clark Griffith Large Letters	20	25	30	40	50	80	120	200
Bob Groom	6	8	10	12	20	25	40	60
Bob Harmon	6	8	10	12	20	25	40	60
Topsy Hartsel	6	8	10	12	20	25	40	60
Arnold Hauser	6	8	10	12	15	80	100	60
Ira Hemphill	6	8	10	12	20	25	40	60
Buck Herzog Large Letters	6	8	10	12	20	25	40	60

		PrFr 1	GD 2	VG 3	VgEx 4	EX 5	ExMt 6	NM 7	NmMt 8
65	Buck Herzog Small Letters	6	8	10	12	20	25	40	60
66	Dick Hoblitzell	6	8	10	12	20	25	60	80
67	Danny Hoffman	6	8	10	12	20	25	40	60
68	Harry Hooper	12	15	20	25	30	80	100	120
69A	Miller Huggins Small Letters	12	15	20	25	30	50	150	200
69B	Miller Huggins Large Letters	20	25	30	40	60	100	120	200
70	John Hummel	6	8	10	12	20	25	40	80
71A	Hugh Jennings Small Letters	12	15	20	25	30	50	200	250
71B	Hugh Jennings Large Letters	20	25	30	40	50	120	150	200
72A	Walter Johnson Small Letters	50	60	80	150	200	250	400	500
72B	Walter Johnson Large Letters	100	120	150	200	250	300	400	600
73	Tom Jones	6	8	10	12	20	25	40	60
74	Ed Karger	6	8	10	12	20	25	40	60
75	Ed Killian	6	8	10	12	20	25	50	60
76A	Jack Knight Small Letters	6	8	10	12	20	25	40	60
76B	Jack Knight Large Letters	8	10	12	15	20	30	50	80
77	Ed Konetchy	6	8	10	12	20	25	40	60
78	Harry Krause	6	8	10	12	20	25	40	60
79	Rube Kroh	6	8	10	12	20	25	40	60
80	Nap Lajoie	30	40	50	60	120	150	250	300
81A	Frank LaPorte Small Letters	6	8	10	12	20	25	40	60
81B	Frank LaPorte Large Letters	8	10	12	15	20	30	50	80
82	Arlie Latham	6	8	10	12	20	25	40	60
83A	Tommy Leach Small Letters	6	8	10	12	20	25	40	60
83B	Tommy Leach Large Letters	8	10	12	15	20	30	50	80
84	Sam Leever	6	8	10	12	20	25	40	60
85	Lefty Leifield	6	8	10	12	20	25	40	60
86	Paddy Livingston	6	8	10	12	20	25	40	60
87	Hans Lobert	6	8	10	12	20	25	40	60
88A	Harry Lord Small Letters	6	8	10	12	20	25	40	60
88B	Harry Lord Large Letters	8	10	12	15	20	30	50	120
89	Nick Maddox	6	8	10	12	20	25	40	60
90	Sherry Magee	6	8	10	12	15	30	40	80
91	Rube Marquard	25	30	40	50	60	100	150	
92A	Christy Mathewson Small Ltr	50	60	80	120	150	300	350	500
92B	Christy Mathewson Large Ltr	60	80	100	120	200	250	400	600
93A	Al Mattern Small Letters	6	8	10	12	20	25	40	60
93B	Al Mattern Large Letters	8	10	12	15	20	30	50	80
94	George McBride	6	8	10	12	20	25	40	60
95A	John McGraw Small Letters	12	15	20	25	30	50	80	300
95B	John McGraw Large Letters	20	25	30	40	50	150	200	400
96	Harry McIntire	6	8	10	12	20	25	40	60
97A	Matty McIntyre Small Letters	6	8	10	12	20	25	120	200
97B	Matty McIntyre Large Letters	8	10	12	15	20	30	50	80
98A	Larry McLean Small Letters	6	8	10	12	20	25	40	60
98B	Larry McLean Large Letters	8	10	12	15	20	30	50	175
99	Fred Merkle	6	8	10	12	20	25	60	80
100	Chief Meyers	6	8	10	12	15	60	80	100
101	Clyde Milan	6	8	10	12	20	25	40	60
102	Dots Miller	6	8	10	12	20	25	40	60
103	Mike Mitchell	6	8	10	12	20	25	40	60
104	Pat Moran	6	8	10	12	20	25	40	60
105A	George Mullen (Mullin) Small Ltr	6	8	10	12	20	25	40	60
105B	George Mullen (Mullin) Large Ltr	8	10	12	15	20	30	60	80
106	Danny Murphy	6	8	10	12	20	25	40	60
107	Red Murray	6	8	10	12	20	25	40	60
108	Tom Needham	6	8	10	12	15	60	80	100
109A	Rebel Oakes Small Letters	6	8	10	12	20	25	40	300
109B	Rebel Oakes Large Letters	8	10	12	15	20	30	50	350
110	Rube Oldring	6	8	10	12	20	25	40	60
111	Charley O'Leary	6	8	10	12	20	25	40	60
112	Orval Overall	6	8	10	12	20	25	40	60
113	Fred Parent	6	8	10	12	20	25	40	80
114A	Dode Paskert Small Letters	6	8	10	12	20	25	40	60
114B	Dode Paskert Large Letters	8	10	12	15	20	30	50	80
115	Barney Pelty	6	8	10	60	80	100	120	150
116	Jake Pfiester	6	8	10	12	20	25	40	60

#	Player	PrFr 1	GD 2	VG 3	VgEx 4	EX 5	ExMt 6	NM 7	NmMt 8
117	Eddie Phelps	6	8	10	12	15	25	40	60
118	Deacon Phillippe	6	8	10	12	20	25	40	60
119	Jack Quinn	6	8	10	12	20	25	40	60
120	Ed Reulbach	6	8	10	12	20	25	40	60
121	Lew Richie	6	8	10	12	20	25	40	60
122	Jack Rowan	6	8	10	12	20	25	40	60
123A	Nap Rucker Small Letters	6	8	10	12	20	25	40	60
123B	Nap Rucker Large Letters	8	10	12	15	20	30	50	80
124	Doc Scanlon	6	8	10	12	20	25	40	60
125	Herman Schaefer	6	8	10	12	20	25	40	80
126A	Boss Schmidt Small Letters	6	8	10	12	20	25	40	60
126B	Boss Schmidt Large Letters	12	15	20	25	30	60	80	120
127	Wildfire Schulte	6	8	10	12	20	25	40	60
128	Jimmy Sheckard	6	8	10	12	20	25	40	60
129	Hap Smith	6	8	10	12	20	25	40	60
130A	Tris Speaker Small Letters	30	40	50	60	100	120	200	300
130B	Tris Speaker Large Letters	40	50	60	80	120	150	250	400
131	Oscar Stanage	6	8	10	12	20	25	40	
132	Harry Steinfeldt	6	8	10	12	20	25	40	60
133	George Stone	6	8	10	12	15	60	80	100
134A	George Stovall Small Letters	6	8	10	12	20	25	40	60
134B	George Stovall Large Letters	8	10	12	15	20	30	50	80
135A	Gabby Street Small Letters	6	8	10	12	20	25	40	60
135B	Gabby Street Large Letters	8	10	12	15	20	30	50	80
136	George Suggs	6	8	10	12	20	25	40	
137A	Ira Thomas Small Letters	6	8	10	12	20	25	40	80
137B	Ira Thomas Large Letters	8	10	12	15	20	30	50	80
138A	Joe Tinker Small Letters	12	15	20	25	30	80	100	120
138B	Joe Tinker Large Letters	20	25	30	40	50	80	120	200
139A	John Titus Small Letters	6	8	10	12	20	25	40	60
139B	John Titus Large Letters	8	10	12	15	20	30	50	80
140	Terry Turner	6	8	10	12	20	25	80	100
141	Heinie Wagner	6	8	10	12	20	25	40	60
142A	Bobby Wallace w/Cap Small Ltr	8	10	12	15	20	30	50	80
142B	Bobby Wallace w/Cap Large Ltr	12	15	20	25	30	50	80	120
143	Bobby Wallace without Cap	12	15	20	25	30	40	50	80
144	Ed Walsh	12	15	20	25	30	50	100	120
145	Jack Warhop	6	8	10	12	20	25	60	80
146B	Zach Wheat Large Letters	20	25	30	40	50	100	120	200
146A	Zach Wheat Small Letters	20	25	30	40	50	100	120	300
147	Doc White	6	8	10	12	20	25	40	60
148A	Art Wilson Small Letters	6	8	10	12	20	25	40	60
148B	Art Wilson Large Letters	8	10	12	15	20	30	50	80
149	Owen Wilson	6	8	10	12	20	25	40	60
150	Hooks Wiltse	6	8	10	12	20	25	40	60
151	Harry Wolter	6	8	10	12	20	25	40	60
152A	Cy Young C on Cap	50	60	100	120	150	300	400	600
152B	Old Cy Young Plain Cap	50	60	100	120	150	300	400	600

1911 Close Candy E94

#	Player	PrFr 1	GD 2	VG 3	VgEx 4	EX 5	ExMt 6	NM 7	NmMt 8
1	Jimmy Austin	100	250	500	700				
2	Johnny Bates	100	350	500	1,200	1,800			
3	Bob Bescher	120	250	350	400				
4	Bobby Byrne	100	250	500	1,100				
5	Frank Chance	250	600	900					
6	Eddie Cicotte	250	500	1,200	1,300	2,000			
7	Ty Cobb	300	3,500	8,200	8,500	12,000			
8	Sam Crawford	250	550	925	1,200				
9	Harry Davis	100	250	350					
10	Art Devlin	100	250	400	700				
11	Josh Devore	120	250	350					
12	Mickey Doolan	120	250	350	500				
13	Patsy Dougherty	100	250	700					
14	Johnny Evers	250	500	800					
15	Eddie Grant	100	250	500					

#	Player	PrFr 1	GD 2	VG 3	VgEx 4	EX 5	ExMt 6	NM 7	NmMt 8
16	Hugh Jennings	200	450	600					
17	Red Kleinow	100	250	500					
18	Napoleon Lajoie	250	500	800	1,500				
19	Joe Lake	100	250	450	600				
20	Tommy Leach	100	250	350	600	1,000			
21	Hans Lobert	100	250	350					
22	Harry Lord	100	250	800					
23	Sherry Magee	100	300	500	700	1,500			
24	John McGraw	250	500	1,000	1,200				
25	Earl Moore	120	400	500	600				
26	Red Murray	100	250	350	850				
27	Tris Speaker	700	1,000	1,800	2,000				
28	Terry Turner	100	250	500	1,400				
29	Honus Wagner	2,000	2,500	4,800	6,000	10,400			
30	Cy Young	1,000	2,500	3,800					

— Frank Chance #5 PSA 8 (NmMt) sold for $11,212 (Goodwin; 6/12)

1911 Mecca Double Folders T201

#	Player	PrFr 1	GD 2	VG 3	VgEx 4	EX 5	ExMt 6	NM 7	NmMt 8
1	Abstein/Butler	25	40	100	150	250	300	400	1,00
2	Baker/Downie	25	30	50	100	120	150	400	80
3	Barrett/McGlyn	25	30	40	60	120	200	300	80
4	Bender/Oldring	50	60	120	150	175	250	400	1,50
5	Brown/Hofman	60	80	100	150	200	250	400	1,20
6	Chase/Sweeney	30	40	50	80	120	200	500	80
7	Cicotte/Thoney	30	60	80	100	120	250	500	1,20
8	Clarke/Byrne	30	40	60	80	150	250	400	80
9	Collins/Baker	50	80	100	120	250	300	800	1,50
10	Crawford/Cobb	250	400	500	700	1,200	2,000	2,500	8,00
11	Donovan/Stroud	25	30	40	60	100	150	350	80
12	Downs/Odell	25	30	50	60	100	150	300	80
13	Doyle/Meyers	25	30	40	60	100	150	250	80
14	Evers/Chance	60	80	120	200	250	400	700	2,00
15	Ford/Johnson	25	30	40	60	100	150	300	80
16	Foster/Ward	25	30	40	60	100	150	300	80
17	Gaspar/Clarke	25	30	40	60	100	150	300	80
18	Grant/McLean	25	30	60	80	100	150	300	80
19	Hartzell/Blair	25	30	40	60	100	150	300	80
20	Hickman/Hinchman	25	30	40	60	100	200	300	1,00
21	Huggins/Bresnahan	50	60	100	120	200	300	600	1,50
22	Johnson/Street	120	150	200	300	500	700	1,500	4,00
23	Killian/Fitzpatrick	25	30	40	60	100	250	350	80
24	Kling/Cole	25	30	60	80	100	150	300	80
25	Lajoie/Falkenberg	120	150	200	250	600	700	800	2,00
26	Lake/Wallace	30	60	80	100	150	200	400	1,30
27	LaPorte/Stephens	25	30	40	60	100	150	250	80
28	Lapp/Barry	25	30	40	60	100	200	300	80
29	Leach/Gibson	25	30	40	80	100	150	300	80
30	Leifield/Simon	25	30	50	60	100	150	300	80
31	Lobert/Moore	25	30	50	60	100	150	300	80
32	Lord/Dougherty	40	50	60	100	200	400	500	1,50
33	Lush/Hauser	25	30	40	60	100	150	300	80
34	Mattern/Graham	25	30	40	60	100	150	300	80
35	Mathewson/Bridwell UER	120	150	300	350	600	800	1,800	4,00
36	McBride/Elberfeld	25	40	50	60	100	150	300	80
37	McCabe/Starr	25	30	40	60	100	150	300	80
38	McGinnity/McCarty	30	60	80	100	200	300	500	1,20
39	Miller/Herzog	25	30	40	60	100	150	300	80
40	Rucker/Daubert	25	30	40	80	100	150	300	80
41	Seymour/Dygert	25	30	40	60	100	150	300	80
42	Speaker/Gardner	60	80	150	200	400	450	800	2,00
43	Summers/Jennings	30	40	50	80	150	200	400	1,20
44	Thomas/Coombs	25	30	40	60	100	150	300	80
45	Titus/Dooin	25	30	40	60	100	150		
46	Turner/Stovall	25	30	40	60	120	150	300	80
47	Walsh/Payne	40	50	60	100	150	200	400	1,20

	PrFr 1	GD 2	VG 3	VgEx 4	EX 5	ExMt 6	NM 7	NmMt 8
8 Wheat/Bergen	30	80	100	150	200	250	400	1,200
9 Wiltse/Merkle	25	30	40	80	100	150	300	800
0 Woodruff/Williams	25	30	40	80	100	150	150	800

1911 T205 Gold Border

	PrFr 1	GD 2	VG 3	VgEx 4	EX 5	ExMt 6	NM 7	NmMt 8
Ed Abbaticchio	15	25	30	50	120	250		
Doc Adkins	30	50	80	200	250	500		
Leon K. Ames	15	25	30	60	200	300		
Jas. P. Archer	15	25	60	80	120	300		
Jimmy Austin	30	50	80	120	200	300		
Bill Bailey	15	25	30	80	100	250		
Home Run Baker	100	150	200	250	500	800		
Neal Ball	15	25	30	50	100	250		
E.B. Barger Full B on Cap	15	25	30	80	120	400		
E.B. Barger Partial B on Cap	60	100	120	250	500	800		
Jack Barry	15	25	30	50	120	250		
Emil Batch	40	60	100	150	250			
John W. Bates	30	50	80	120	200	300		
Fred Beck	25	40	60	100	150	250		
Beals Becker	15	25	30	50	150	300		
George Bell	15	25	30	60	100	300		
Chas. Bender	60	100	150	200	400	800		
William Bergen	15	25	50	60	120	250		
Bob Bescher	15	25	50	100	200	300		
Joe Birmingham	15	25	30	80	100	300		
Lena Blackburne	20	30	50	80	120	250		
William Bransfield	25	40	50	80	150	300		
Roger Bresnahan Mouth Closed	60	100	200	250	300	600		
Roger Bresnahan Mouth Open	80	120	300	400	600	1,000		
A.H. Bridwell	15	25	30	80	120	200		
Mordecai Brown	120	200	300	500	800	1,200		
Robt. Byrne	25	40	60	100	150	250		
Hick Cady	30	50	60	120	300	600		
Howie Camnitz	15	25	40	80	150	200		
Bill Carrigan	25	40	60	100	150	250		
Frank Chance	80	120	200	300	500	800		
Hal Chase Both Border Ends	30	50	80	120	300	600		
Hal Chase Both Border Extends	30	50	60	200	350	600		
Hal Chase Left Ear	60	120	200	300	400	1,000		
Ed Cicotte	100	150	250	400	600	1,000		
Fred Clarke	80	120	200	300	500	800		
Ty Cobb	600	1,200	1,500	2,000	4,000	10,000		
Eddie Collins Mouth Closed	50	100	150	300	400	1,000		
Eddie Collins Mouth Open	120	200	300	500	600	1,800		
Jimmy Collins	60	120	225	350	500	800		
Frank Corridon	15	25	50	120	150	200		
Otis Crandall T Crossed	20	30	40	80	250			
Otis Crandall T Not Crossed	20	30	40	60	200			
Lou Criger	15	25	40	60	120	250		
W.F. Dahlen	60	100	120	300	400			
Jake Daubert	15	25	30	50	100	250		
Jim Delahanty	15	25	30	60	120	250		
Art Devlin	50	80	120	200	300	500		
Josh Devore	15	25	30	80	120	200		
W.R. Dickson	15	25	30	50	200	300		
Jiggs Donohue (Donahue)	60	100	150	250	400	800		
Chas. S. Dooin	30	50	80	120	200	300		
Michael J. Doolan	15	25	30	50	100	250		
Patsy Dougherty Red Sock	30	50	100	150	350			
Patsy Dougherty White Sock	30	50	80	100	300	700		
Thomas Downey	15	25	30	50	100	250		
Larry Doyle	15	25	40	80	150	250		
Hugh Duffy	80	120	200	300	500	800		
Jack Dunn	50	80	100	150	400	500		
Jimmy Dygert	15	40	50	80	120	200		

	PrFr 1	GD 2	VG 3	VgEx 4	EX 5	ExMt 6	NM 7	NmMt 8
58 R. Egan	25	40	60	100	150	300		
59 Kid Elberfeld	15	25	40	50	100	250		
60 Clyde Engle	15	25	30	50	150	250		
61 Louis Evans	30	50	80	120	200	300		
62 John J. Evers	80	120	150	350	500	1,000		
63 Bob Ewing	25	40	50	80	120	300		
64 G.C. Ferguson	15	25	50	60	100	250		
65 Ray Fisher	40	100	120	150	300	900		
66 Arthur Fletcher	15	25	30	50	200	300		
67 John Flynn	20	25	30	50	100	200		
68 Russ Ford Black Cap	15	25	60	80	120	250		
69 Russ Ford White Cap	60	80	120	150	400			
70 Wm. A. Foxen	15	25	50	80	120	250		
71 Jimmy Frick	30	50	60	150				
72 Arthur Fromme	15	25	40	50	100	250		
73 Earl Gardner	30	50	80	120	200	300		
74 H.L. Gaspar	15	25	40	60	120	200		
75 George Gibson	30	50	80	120	200	300		
76 William Goode (Good)	15	50	60	80	150	250		
77 George Graham Cubs	60	100	150	250	500	1,000		
78 George Graham Rustlers	15	25	40	50	120	350		
79 Edward L. Grant	50	150	350	450	800	1,200		
80A Dolly Gray No Stats on Back	40	60	100	120	250	500		
80B Dolly Gray Stats on Back	200	300	400	800	1,000	3,500		
81 Clark Griffith	50	80	120	150	300	800		
82 Bob Groom	15	25	30	50	120	250		
83 Charlie Hanford	30	50	60	100	250			
84 Bob Harmon Both Ears	15	25	30	60	120	200		
85 Bob Harmon Left Ear	50	80	120	200	475	800		
86 Topsy Hartsel	15	25	30	50	100	250		
87 Arnold J. Hauser	15	25	30	80	120	400		
88 Charlie Hemphill	30	50	60	80	125	200		
89 C.L. Herzog	30	50	80	120	200	300		
90A R.Hoblitzell No Stats on Back	6,000	8,000	10,000	12,000				
90B R.Hoblitzell Cin. after 1908	25	40	60	120	450	600		
90C R.Hoblitzel Name Incorrect	100	150	200	300	600	1,200		
90D R.Hoblitzell No Cin. after 1908	100	150	200	800				
91 Danny Hoffman	15	40	50	80	120	600		
92 Miller J. Huggins	50	80	120	200	500	800		
93 John Hummell	15	25	30	60	100	250		
94 Fred Jacklitsch	15	25	30	50	120	250		
95 Hughie Jennings	80	100	120	150	300	1,000		
96 Walter Johnson	250	400	700	1,000	1,500	5,500		
97 David Jones	20	30	50	80	150	250		
98 Tom Jones	25	40	60	100	150	300		
99 Addie Joss	400	500	1,200	1,500	2,000			
100 Ed Karger	50	80	150	200	400	1,000		
101 Ed Killian	15	25	30	50	150			
102 Red Kleinow	60	100	120	200	400	800		
103 John G. Kling	15	25	30	50	100	300		
104 Jack Knight	15	30	40	80	120	200		
105 Ed Konetchy	20	30	50	80	120	300		
106 Harry Krause	30	50	80	120	200	300		
107 Floyd M. Kroh	15	25	40	60	100	200		
108 Frank Lang	15	25	30	50	100	200		
109 Frank LaPorte	15	25	40	60	120			
110A Arlie Latham A.Latham	25	40	50	80	300	400		
110B Arlie Latham W.A. Latham	60	120	150	400	500			
111 Thomas W. Leach	25	40	60	100	150	250		
112 Wyatt Lee	25	40	60	120	200	400		
113 Sam Leever	15	25	40	60	250	400		
114A A. Leifield A. on Front	40	60	80	120	400	800		
114B A.P. Leifield A.P. on Front	40	60	80	135	400			
115 Edgar Lennox	15	25	50	80	120	600		
116 Paddy Livingston	15	25	30	50	150	200		
117 John B. Lobert	15	25	40	80	120	250		
118 Briscoe Lord	15	25	40	60	175	250		

#	Player	PrFr 1	GD 2	VG 3	VgEx 4	EX 5	ExMt 6	NM 7	NmMt 8
119	Harry Lord	15	25	30	50	100	200		
120	John Lush	15	25	30	60	150	250		
121	Nick Maddox	15	25	30	50	120	300		
122	Sherwood R. Magee	25	40	60	100	150	400		
123	R.W. Marquard	50	100	120	150	300	1,000		
124	Christy Mathewson	600	1,000	1,500	2,000	3,000	5,000		
125	A.A. Mattern	15	25	30	60	120			
126	Lewis McAllister	25	40	80	100	200			
127	George McBride	15	25	40	60	120	250		
128	Amby McConnell	15	25	50	80	120			
129	Pryor McElveen	15	25	30	50	200	250		
130	J.J. McGraw	100	150	250	400	600	1,000		
131	Harry McIntire	15	25	30	80	100	200		
132	Matty McIntyre	15	25	30	50	100	225		
133	M.A. McLean	15	25	30	60	150	300		
134	Fred Merkle	15	25	30	80	120	500		
135	George Merritt	30	50	60	100	250	500		
136	J.T. Meyers	15	20	30	50	120	200		
137	Clyde Milan	15	20	30	50	120	400		
138	J.D. Miller	15	25	40	80	100	250		
139	M.F. Mitchell	15	25	30	50	150	200		
140A	Pat Moran Stray Line	400	600	1,200	1,500	4,000			
140B	Pat Moran No Stray Line	15	25	30	60	120	300		
141	George Moriarty	15	25	30	60	150	300		
142	George Mullin	25	40	60	100	150	250		
143	Danny Murphy	15	25	30	50	100	250		
144	Jack Murray	15	25	30	50	200	400		
145	John Nee	40	60	100	150	400			
146	Thos. J. Needham	25	40	60	100	150	600		
147	Rebel Oakes	15	50	60	100	150	250		
148	Rube Oldring	15	25	40	50	150	250		
149	Charley O'Leary	20	30	50	80	200	300		
150	Fred Olmstead	20	30	50	80	200	300		
151	Orval Overall	30	50	80	120	200	600		
152	Freddy Parent	15	30	40	50	100	200		
153	George Paskert	15	25	30	50	100	300		
154	Fred Payne	15	25	30	60	120	200		
155	Barney Pelty	15	25	40	60	120	200		
156	John Pfiester	15	25	30	50	120	250		
157	Jimmy Phelan	30	50	60	100	250	800		
158	E.J. Phelps	15	25	50	80	100	250		
159	Charles Phillippe	15	25	30	50	100	200		
160	Jack Quinn	30	60	80	100	200	400		
161	Bugs Raymond	60	100	120	200	400	800		
162	E.M. Reulbach	15	25	40	80	120	250		
163	Lewis Richie	20	30	50	80	120	200		
164	John A. Rowan	40	60	100	120	250	600		
165	Geo N. Rucker	15	25	30	50	100	250		
166	W.D. Scanlan	50	80	100	200	400	1,000		
167	Germany Schaefer	15	25	30	50	100	200		
168	Admiral Schlei	15	40	50	60	120	200		
169	Boss Schmidt	20	30	50	80	120	200		
170	F.M. Schulte	15	25	40	60	150	300		
171	Jim Scott	15	25	30	60	120	250		
172	B.H. Sharpe	15	25	30	60	120	200		
173	David Shean Cubs	40	60	80	150	400	800		
174	David Shean Rustlers	15	25	40	100	150	250		
175	Jas. T. Sheckard	15	25	30	80	120	350		
176	Hack Simmons	15	25	30	80	120	400		
177	Tony Smith	15	30	40	50	100	300		
178	Fred Snodgrass	15	25	40	60	100	250		
179	Tris Speaker	120	250	350	500	1,000	1,500		
180	Jake Stahl	15	25	30	50	120	400		
181	Oscar Stanage	20	30	50	80	200	300		
182	Harry Steinfeldt	25	40	60	100	150	250		
183	George Stone	20	30	50	80	200	300		
184	George Stovall	15	25	40	60	250	400		

#	Player	PrFr 1	GD 2	VG 3	VgEx 4	EX 5	ExMt 6	NM 7	NmMt 8
185	Gabby Street	15	25	30	50	100	300		
186	George Suggs	60	100	120	200	500	800		
187	Ed Summers	15	25	30	60	200	300		
188	Jeff Sweeney	50	80	100	200	450			
189	Lee Tannehill	15	25	30	50	100	200		
190	Ira Thomas	15	25	30	60	120	250		
191	Joe Tinker	100	150	250	400	600	1,000		
192	John Titus	15	25	30	50	200	250		
193	Terry Turner	50	80	100	200	400	800		
194	James Vaughn	60	100	120	200	500			
195	Heinie Wagner	50	100	120	200	300	800		
196	Bobby Wallace with Cap	40	80	100	250	400	600		
197A	Bobby Wallace No Cap 1 Line	500	800	1,000	1,500	2,400			
197B	Bobby Wallace No Cap 2 Lines	150	300	400	750	1,200			
198	Ed Walsh	100	150	200	350	800	1,500		
199	Z.D. Wheat	60	100	200	250	300	1,200		
200	Doc White	15	25	30	50	120	800		
201	Kirb White	50	80	100	200	400			
202A	Irvin K. Wilhelm	100	150	200	300	600	1,200		
202B	Irvin K. Wilhelm Suffe ed in Bio	150	200	350	800				
203	Ed Willett	15	25	30	50	120	300		
204	J. Owen Wilson	15	25	40	50	120	300		
205	George R. Wiltse Both Ears	15	25	40	80	120	250		
206	George R. Wiltse Right Ear	40	60	80	150	400	800		
207	Harry Wolter	15	25	30	80	150	250		
208	Cy Young	300	500	1,000	1,200	1,800	4,000		

— Frank Chance #31 PSA 8 (NmMt) sold for $6,000 (Greg Bussineau; 7/12)
— Ty Cobb PSA 7 (NM) sold for $14,220 (REA; Fall '13)
— Ty Cobb SGC 84 (NM) sold for $10,665 (REA; Spring '14)
— Eddie Collins Mouth Open PSA 8 (NmMt) sold for $10,665 (REA; Fall '13)
— Clark Griffith #81 PSA 8 (NmMt) sold for $9,049 (Goodwin; 8/12)
— Richard Hoblitzell No Stats PSA 5 (EX) sold for $11,309 (Mile High; 1/13)
— Richard Hoblitzell No Stats SGC 60 (EX) sold for $10,280 (Mile High; 12/13)
— Walter Johnson SGC 92 (NmMt+) sold for $28,063 (Goodwin; 9/13)
— Addie Joss PSA 6 (ExMt) sold for $6,420 (Mile High; 1/13)
— Addie Joss PSA 6 (ExMt) sold for $5,040 (Greg Bussineau; 7/12)
— Christy Mathewson PSA 8 (NmMt) sold for $24,720 (Greg Bussineau; 4/15)
— Christy Mathewson PSA 8 (NmMt) sold for $23,700 (REA; Fall '13)
— Tris Speaker PSA 8 (NmMt) sold for $10,280 (Mile High; 6/13)
— Tris Speaker #179 PSA 8 (NmMt) sold for $10,440 (Greg Bussineau; 7/12)
— Irvin K. Wilhelm #202B PSA 5 (EX) sold for $5,094 (Memory Lane; 5/12)
— Cy Young PSA 8 (NmMt) sold for $17,775 (REA; Fall '13)

1910-11 Turkey Red T3

#	Player	PrFr 1	GD 2	VG 3	VgEx 4	EX 5	ExMt 6
1	Mordecai Brown	400	600	1,000	1,500	2,500	
4	Roger Bresnahan	200	300	500	1,000	1,750	
5	Sam Crawford	300	500	800	1,200	2,000	
6	Hal Chase	200	300	500	800	1,500	
8	Fred Clarke	300	400	600	1,000	2,000	
9	Ty Cobb	2,500	4,000	5,000	8,000	20,000	30,000
16	Johnny Evers	300	500	800	1,200	2,300	
17	Clark Griffith	250	400	600	1,000	1,750	
18	Hughie Jennings	300	500	800	1,200	2,000	
19	Addie Joss	400	600	1,000	1,500	2,500	
23	Napoleon Lajoie	500	800	1,200	2,000	3,000	
26	John McGraw	300	400	600	1,200	2,000	
27	Christy Mathewson	1,000	2,000	3,000	6,000	12,000	18,000
35	Joe Tinker	300	400	600	1,200	2,500	
36	Tris Speaker	500	800	1,500	2,500	4,000	6,000
39	Rube Waddell	200	400	600	1,000	2,000	
40	Vic Willis	200	300	500	800	1,500	3,500
42	Cy Young	1,000	1,500	2,700	4,000	6,000	
47	Frank Chance At Bat	400	600	1,000	1,500	3,000	
48	Jack Murray At Bat	150	200	500	800	2,000	
49	Close Play At Second	150	200	500	800		
50	Chief Myers At Bat UER	150	200	675	800		

	PrFr 1	GD 2	VG 3	VgEx 4	EX 5	ExMt 6
Frank Baker	120	300	500	800	2,000	
Chief Bender	300	500	800	1,200	2,500	
Eddie Collins	300	400	600	1,000	2,500	
Walter Johnson	1,000	1,500	2,500	4,000	10,600	
Willie Keeler	300	500	800	1,200	2,500	
Bob Rhoads	600	800	1,000	1,500	2,500	
Fred Tenney	500	800	1,200	2,000	3,000	
Bobby Wallace	250	300	500	800	1,500	3,000
Ed Walsh	250	400	600	1,000	2,000	
Chief Wilson	200	300	500	1,000		

912 Hassan Triple Folders T202

	PrFr 1	GD 2	VG 3	VgEx 4	EX 5	ExMt 6	NM 7	NmMt 8
A Close Play (Wallace, LaPorte)	60	80	100	150	250	400	1,000	
A Close Play (Wallace, Pelty)	60	80	100	150	250	400	800	
A Desperate (O'Leary, Cobb)	300	450	600	1,000	1,750	3,500		
A Great Batsman (Barger, Bergen)	30	40	60	100	150	300	800	
A Great Batsman (Rucker, Bergen)	30	50	60	100	150	250	600	
A Wide Throw (Mullin, Stanage)	30	40	60	120	150	250	600	
Ambrose McCon (Blair, Quinn)	30	40	60	100	150	250	800	
Baker Gets His (Collins, Baker)	100	120	150	250	400	800	1,500	
Birmingham Gets (Johnson, Street)	150	200	300	400	700	900		1,200
Birmingham's HR (Birm, Turner)	60	80	100	150	250	400	1,000	
Bush Just (Moran, Magee)	30	40	60	100	150	300	600	
Carrigan (Gaspar, McLean)	30	40	60	100	150	250	600	
Carrigan (Wagner, Carrigan)	30	50	60	100	200	250	600	
Catching (Oakes, Bresnahan)	60	80	100	150	250	500	1,000	
Caught (Bresnahan, Harmon)	60	80	100	150	250	400	1,000	
Chance Beats (Chance, Foxen)	60	80	100	150	250	400	1,000	
Chance Beats (McIntire, Archer)	30	40	60	120	200	250	800	
Chance Beats (Overall, Archer)	30	40	60	100	200	250	800	
Chance Beats (Rowan, Archer)	30	40	60	100	200	250	600	
Chance Beats (Shean, Chance)	60	80	100	150	250	400	1,000	
Chase Dives (Chase, Wolter)	30	40	60	100	200	250	600	
Chase Dives (Gibson, Clarke)	60	80	100	150	250	400	1,000	
Chase Dives (Phillippe, Gibson)	30	40	60	100	150	250	600	
Chase Gets (Egan, Mitchell)	30	40	60	100	200	250	600	
Chase Gets (Wolter, Chase)	30	40	60	200	250	300	600	
Chase Guard (Chase, Wolter)	30	40	80	100	200	400	900	
Chase Guard (Gibson, Clarke)	30	40	60	120	200	250	1,200	
Chase Guard (Leifield, Gibson)	30	40	60	100	200	250	600	
Chase Ready (Paskert, Magee)	30	40	60	100	150	450	600	
Chase Safe (Barry, Baker)	80	100	120	200	500			
Chief Bender (Bender, Thomas)	60	100	120	200	250	400	1,000	
Clarke Hikes (Bridwell, Kling)	30	40	80	100	150	400	1,800	
Close at First (Ball, Stovall)	30	40	60	100	150	250	600	
Close at the Plate (Payne, White)	30	40	80	120	150	400	800	
Close at the Plate (Walsh, Payne)	60	80	120	200	250	450	800	
Close at Third (Carrigan, Wagner)	30	40	60	100	200	250	600	
Close at Third (Wood, Speaker)	200	250	300	350	500	1,200		
Collins Easily (Byrne, Clarke)	60	80	100	150	250	450	1,000	
Collins Easily (Collins, Baker)	100	120	200	250	400	700	1,800	
Collins Easily (Collins, Murphy)	60	80	100	150	300	400	1,000	
Crawford (Stanage, Summers)	30	40	60	100	150	250	600	
Cree Rolls (Daubert, Hummel)	30	40	60	100	150	250	600	
Davy Jones (Delahanty, Jones)	30	40	60	120	150	250	800	
Devlin (Devlin G, Mathewson)	150	300	800	1,000	1,200			
Devlin (Devlin R, Mathewson)	120	150	250	350	700	1,400	2,500	
Devlin (Fletcher, Mathewson)	120	150	250	350	500	1,500		
Devlin (Meyers, Mathewson)	150	200	250	350	500	1,000	2,000	
Donlin Out (Camnitz, Gibson)	30	40	60	100	150	300	600	
Donlin Out (Dooin, Magee)	30	40	60	100	150	250	600	
Donlin Out (Doyle, Merkle)	30	40	60	100	150	250	900	
Donlin Out (Gibson, Phillippe)	30	40	60	100	150	250	600	
Donlin Out (Leach, Wilson)	30	40	60	100	150	400	600	
Dooin Gets (Dooin, Doolan)	30	40	80	100	200	250	600	
Dooin Gets (Dooin, Lobert)	30	40	60	100	150	300	1,200	

		PrFr 1	GD 2	VG 3	VgEx 4	EX 5	ExMt 6	NM 7	NmMt 8
55	Dooin Gets (Dooin, Titus)	30	40	60	100	200	250	800	
56	Easy for Larry (Doyle, Merkle)	30	40	60	100	200	300	1,000	
57	Elberfeld Beats (Elberfeld, Milan)	30	40	60	100	150	300	600	
58	Elberfeld Gets (Elberfeld, Milan)	30	40	60	100	150	250	600	
59	Engle in a (Speaker, Engle)	80	100	200	250	350	500	1,200	
60	Evers Makes (Archer, Evers)	60	80	100	150	250	450	1,000	
61	Evers Makes (Archer, Overall)	30	40	100	120	150	250	1,000	
62	Evers Makes (Archer, Ruelbach)	30	40	60	100	200	400	600	
63	Evers Makes (Chance, Evers)	100	120	150	400	500	800		
64	Evers Makes (Tinker, Chance)	200	300	300	500	700	1,200	3,000	
65	Fast Work (O'Leary, Cobb)	400	450	600	1,000	1,700	2,500	4,000	
66	Ford Putting (Ford, Sweeney)	30	40	60	150	200	250	800	
67	Ford Putting (Ford, Vaughn)	30	40	60	120	200	250	800	
68	Good Play (Moriarty, Cobb)	300	500	600	800	1,800	3,000		
69	Grant Gets (Grant, Hoblitzell)	40	80	100	120	150	300	600	
70	Hal Chase (McConnell, McIntyre)	30	40	60	100	200	400	700	
71	Hal Chase (McLean, Suggs)	30	40	60	100	150	300	600	
72	Harry Lord at (Lennox, Tinker)	60	80	120	150	275	400	1,000	
73	Hartsel Strikes (Gray, Groom)	30	40	60	100	200	400	1,200	
74	Hartzell (Dahlen, Scanlan)	30	40	60	100	150	300	600	
75	Held at Third (Lord, Tannehill)	30	40	60	100	200	250	600	
76	Jake Stahl (Cicotte, Stahl)	30	40	80	120	200	250	600	
77	Jim Delahanty (Delahanty, Jones)	30	40	80	100	200	350	1,000	
78	Just Before (Ames, Meyers)	30	40	60	150	200	400	600	
79	Just Before (Becker, Devore)	30	40	60	120	200	250	600	
80	Just Before (Bresnahan, McGraw)	100	120	150	250	400	600	1,500	
81	Just Before (Crandall, Meyers)	30	40	60	100	150	250	600	
82	Just Before (Fletcher, Mathewson)	150	200	250	400	600	1,500		
83	Just Before (Marquard, Meyers)	60	80	100	250	300	600		
84	Just Before (McGraw, Jennings)	80	100	120	200	400	600	1,500	
85	Just Before (Meyers, Mathewson)	120	150	200	500	700	800	1,800	
86	Just Before (Meyers, Wiltse)	30	40	80	150	250	300	600	
87	Just Before (Murray, Snodgrass)	30	40	60	200	250	300	600	
88	Knight Catches (Knight, Johnson)	150	200	250	400	600	1,000	1,500	
89	Lobert Almost (Bridwell, Kling)	30	40	60	100	200	250	600	
90	Lobert Almost (Kling, Steinfeldt)	30	40	60	100	150	250	600	
91	Lobert Almost (Kling, Young)	150	300	350	400	600	1,000		
92	Lobert Almost (Kling, Mattern)	30	40	60	100	150	250	600	
93	Lobert Gets (Dooin, Lobert)	30	40	60	100	150	250	600	
94	Lobert Catches (Lord, Tannehill)	30	40	60	100	150	500		
95	McConnell (Needham, Richie)	30	40	60	100	150	250	600	
96	McIntyre (McConnell, McIntyre)	30	40	60	100	150	250	900	
97	Moriarty Spiked (Stanage, Willett)	30	40	60	100	200	250	600	
98	Nearly Caught (Bates, Bescher)	30	40	60	100	150	250	800	
99	Oldring Almost (Lord, Oldring)	30	40	60	120	150	300	900	
100	Schaefer On (McBride, Milan)	30	40	60	100	150	250	600	
101	Schaefer Steals (McBride, Griffith)	30	40	60	100	200	250	600	
102	Scoring From (Lord, Oldring)	30	40	60	100	150	250	650	
103	Scrambling (Barger, Bergen)	30	40	60	100	250	350	600	
104	Scrambling (Chase, Wolter)	30	40	80	100	150	400	600	
105	Speaker Almost (Miller, Clarke)	60	80	120	150	250	400	1,000	
106	Speaker Round (Wood, Speaker)	200	250	300	500	600	1,200		
107	Speaker Scores (Speaker, Engle)	120	200	250	300	500	1,000		
108	Stahl Safe (Austin, Stovall)	30	40	60	100	150	250	600	
109	Stone About (Schulte, Sheckard)	30	40	60	100	150	250	600	
110	Sullivan Puts (Evans, Huggins)	60	80	100	150	250	400		
111	Sullivan Puts (Gray, Groom)	30	40	60	120	150	250	800	
112	Sweeney Gets (Ford, Sweeney)	30	40	60	100	200	250	600	
113	Sweeney Gets (Ford, Vaughn)	30	40	60	100	150	400	1,200	
114	Tenney Lands (Latham, Raymond)	30	40	60	300	400	500	600	
115	The Athletic (Barry, Baker)	80	100	150	200	300	500		
116	The Athletic (Brown, Graham)	60	80	100	150	300	400	800	
117	The Athletic (Hauser, Konetchy)	30	40	60	100	150	250	600	
118	The Athletic (Krause, Thomas)	30	40	80	100	150	250	600	
119	The Pinch Hitter (Egan, Hoblitzell)	30	40	60	100	200	250	600	
120	The Scissors (Birmingham, Turner)	30	40	80	100	200	250		600
121	Tom Jones (Fromme, McLean)	30	40	60	150	200	250	600	
122	Tom Jones (Gaspar, McLean)	30	40	60	100	150	250	600	

#	Name	PrFr 1	GD 2	VG 3	VgEx 4	EX 5	ExMt 6	NM 7	NmMt 8
123	Too Late (Ames, Meyers)	30	40	60	100	150	250		1,200
124	Too Late (Crandall, Meyers)	30	50	60	100	250	300		600
125	Too Late (Devlin G, Mathewson)	250	300	400	825	1,200			
126	Too Late (Devlin R, Mathewson)	300	400	500	800	1,500			
127	Too Late (Marquard, Meyers)	60	80	100	200	400			
128	Too Late (Meyers, Wiltse)	30	40	60	100	150	300		600
129	Ty Cobb Steals (Jennings, Cobb)	400	600	800	1,400	2,000	3,200		6,400
130	Ty Cobb Steals (Moriarty, Cobb)	350	450	750	1,000	1,750	3,000		
131	Ty Cobb Steals (Stovall, Austin)	200	250	400	600	1,000	1,500		3,000
132	Wheat Strikes (Dahlen, Wheat)	60	80	100	200	300	400		1,000

— A Desperate (O'Leary, Cobb) #3 PSA 7 (NrMt) sold for $7,800 (Greg Bussineau; 4/12)
— Ty Cobb Steals (Jennings/Cobb) PSA 8 (NmMt) sold for $10,192 (Goodwin; 9/14)
— Devlin (Fletcher, Mathewson) PSA 8 (NmMt) sold for $12,521 (Goodwin; 12/11)
— Good Play (Moriarty/Cobb) PSA 8 (NmMt) sold for $,920 (Bussineau; 7/14)

1912 T207 Brown Background

#	Name	PrFr 1	GD 2	VG 3	VgEx 4	EX 5	ExMt 6	NM 7	NmMt 8
2	Eddie Ainsmith	25	40	50	60	100			
4	Jimmy Austin Insignia	25	40	50	60	100			
5	Jimmy Austin No Insignia	40	60	80	100	150			
6	Neal Ball	40	60	80	100	150			
7	Eros Barger	25	40	50	80	100	200		
8	Jack Barry	40	60	80					
10	Beals Becker	25	40	50	80	100	200		
11	Chief Bender	60	80	120	200	350	500		
13	Robert Bescher	25	40	50	60	120	200		
15	Lena Blackburne	80	120	150	250				
18	Ping Bodie	25	40	50	80	100			
19	Hugh Bradley	25	40	150	200	250	300		
20	Roger Bresnahan	50	80	120	200	325	500		
23	Robert M. Byrne	25	40	50	80	120			
24	Nixey Callahan	25	40	50	60	100			
25	Howie Camnitz	25	40	100	120	200	250		
26	Max Carey	100	150	200	400	500	750		
28	Bill Carrigan Wagner Back	40	60	80	100	150			
29	George Chalmers	25	40	50	60	100	200		
30	Frank Chance	50	80	120	200	350	500		
31	Eddie Cicotte	150	250	300	500	1,000			
32	Tommy Clarke	25	40	50	120	150			
33	King Cole	25	40	50	60	100	200		
34	John Collins	40	60	80					
35	Robert Coulson	25	40	50	60	100	200		
36	Tex Covington	25	40	50	60	100	200		
37	Otis Crandall	25	40	50	60	150	200		
39	Dave Danforth	25	80	100	120	150			
40	Bert Daniels	25	40	50	60	100	200		
41	Jake Daubert	40	60	80	100	150			
42	Harry Davis	25	40	50	100	200			
43	Jim Delahanty	25	40	50	60	100	200		
44	Claud Derrick	25	40	50	60	120	200		
45	Art Devlin	25	40	50	60	120	200		
46	Joshua Devore	25	40	50	60	100	250		
49	Red Dooin	25	40	50	60	100	200		
51	Lawrence Doyle	25	40	50	60	120	200		
52	Dellos Drake	25	40	50	120	150			
56	Tex Erwin	25	40	50	150	200	250		
57	Steve Evans	25	40	50	60	120			
58	John Ferry	25	40	50	60	100	200		
59	Ray Fisher Blue Cap	25	40	200	200	250	300		
60	Ray Fisher White Cap	40	60	80	250	300			
61	Art Fletcher	25	40	50	60	120	200		
63	Art Fromme	25	40	50	60	100			
64	Del Gainor	25	40	50	60	100			
65	Larry Gardner	25	40	50	60	150	250		
67	Roy Golden	25	40	50	80	100	200		
68	Hank Gowdy	25	60	80	150				
69	Peaches Graham	40	60	80	100	150			
70	Jack Graney	25	40	50	150	200	250		
71	Vean Gregg	80	150	400	450	500			
73	Sea Lion Hall	25	40	50	60	250			
74	Ed Hallinan	40	60	80	100	200			
75	Earl Hamilton	25	40	50	60	100			
76	Robert Harmon	25	40	50	120	150	200		
78	Olaf Henriksen	25	40	50	60	100	250		
79	John Henry	40	60	80	100	250			
80	Buck Herzog	60	100	120	150	250			
83	Willie Hogan	25	40	60	100				
84	Harry Hooper	150	250	300	500				
87	Walter Johnson	200	350	500	600	1,000	2,500		
88	George Kaler (Kahler)	25	40	50	60	100			
89	Billy Kelly	40	80	100	120	150			
90	Jay Kirke	60	100	150					
92	Otto Knabe	25	40	50	60	100	200		
94	Ed Konetchy	25	40	50	60	100	250		
95	Harry Krause	25	40	50	60	120			
99	Jack Lapp	25	40	50	60	100			
100	Arlie Latham	25	40	50	60	100	200		
101	Tommy Leach	25	40	50	350	400			
102	Lefty Leifield	25	40	50	60				
103	Ed Lennox	25	40	50	60	120			
104	Duffy Lewis Boston	80	120	250	300				
105A	Irving Lewis Emblem	1,500	2,500	4,000	6,000				
105B	Irving Lewis No Emblem	1,500	2,500	14,000	16,000				
106	Jack Lively	25	40	50	60	250	300		
107	Paddy Livingston A on Shirt	40	60	100	200				
109	Paddy Livingston Small C	40	60	100					
110	Bris Lord Philadelphia	25	40	50	60	100			
111	Harry Lord Chicago	25	40	50	60	100			
112	Louis Lowdermilk	1,000	1,500	2,800	3,500				
113	Richard Marquard	50	80	100	200	300	500		
114	Armando Marsans	40	60	150	200	250			
115	George McBride	25	40	50	60	100	200		
117	Ed McDonald	25	40	120	150	200			
118	John McGraw	50	100	120	150	200			
119	Harry McIntire	25	40	50	60	100	200		
120	Matty McIntyre	25	40	50	60	150			
121	Bill McKechnie	150	250	300	600				
122	Larry McLean	25	40	60	80	100			
123	Clyde Milan	25	40	50	60	100	250		
124	Doc Miller Boston	80	120	300	400				
125	Dots Miller Pittsburgh	25	40	50	60	100	200		
127	Ward Miller Chicago	800	1,400	1,500	2,000				
128	Mike Mitchell Cincinnati	25	40	50	60	100			
129	Willie Mitchell Cleveland	25	40	50	60	100			
132	Pat Moran	25	40	60	60	100	200		
133	Cy Morgan Philadelphia	30	50	60	80	120			
134	Ray Morgan Washington	40	60	80					
135	George Moriarty	60	100	300					
136	George Mullin D Cap	40	60	80	100	150			
137	George Mullin No D on Cap	40	60	80	100	250	350		
138	Tom Needham	25	40	50	60	150			
140	Hub Northen	25	40	50					
141	Les Nunamaker	25	40	50	150	250			
142	Rebel Oakes	25	40	50	60	100	200		
143	Buck O'Brien	25	40	100	120	200	300		
144	Rube Oldring	25	40	50	60	100	200		
145	Ivy Olson	25	40	150	200	250	300		
146	Martin J. O'Toole	25	40	50	60	100	200		
147	George Paskart (Paskert)	25	40	50	60	100	200		
149	Hub Perdue	25	40	80					
152	Jack Quinn	25	40	50	200	250	300		
153	Pat Ragan	100	150	200	300				
154	Arthur Rasmussen	100	250	300	350				
156	Ed Reulbach	25	40	50	80				

	PrFr 1	GD 2	VG 3	VgEx 4	EX 5	ExMt 6	NM 7	NmMt 8
57 Nap Rucker	40	100	200					
99 Vic Saier	400	500	1,200					
0 Doc Scanlon (Scanlan)	25	40	50	60	120	200		
1 Germany Schaefer	25	40	50	60	100	200		
2 Bill Schardt	30	50	60	80	120			
3 Frank Schulte	30	50	60	80	120			
4 Jim Scott	30	50						
5 Hank Severeid	25	40	50	60	100	200		
6 Mike Simon	25	40	50	60	100	200		
7 Frank Smith Cincinnati	30	50	120					
8 Wallace Smith St. Louis	30	50	60					
9 Fred Snodgrass	25	40	50	60	100			
0 Tris Speaker	250	400	700	1,200	1,800	2,200		
Harry Spratt	25	40	50	80	100			
Eddie Stack	25	40	50	100	120	200		
Oscar Stanage	25	40	50	80	150			
Bill Steele	60	100	150					
Harry Steinfeldt	25	40	100	120	150	250		
George Stovall	30	50	120					
Gabby Street	25	40	50	60	100			
Amos Strunk	25	40	50	60	100	200		
Billy Sullivan	25	40	50					
Lee Tannehill	25	40	50	60	100			
Joe Tinker	60	100	200	250	350	500		
Bert Tooley	25	40	50	60	100			
Terry Turner	25	40	50	60	150	200		
Lefty Tyler	250	400	500	600				
Hippo Vaughn	40	60	80	100	200			
Heine Wagner	40	200	250	300	400			
Dixie Walker	25	40	50	60	150	200		
Bobby Wallace	80	120	150					
Jack Warhop	25	40	50	250	400			
Buck Weaver	500	800	1,000	2,000	3,000			
Zack Wheat	80	120	150	250	400			
Dewey Wilie	25	40	50	60	120	200		
Bob Williams	30	50	60	80	120			
Art Wilson New York	25	40	50	60	100	200		
Chief Wilson Pittsburgh	25	40	50	60	100			
George Wiltse	25	40	50	80	100	200		
Harry Wolverton	25	40	50	60	120	200		
Joe Wood	300	600	800	1,000				
Ralph Works	200	300	400	500				
Steve Yerkes	40	60	80					

...ving Lewis (No Emblem) PSA 2.5 (GVg) sold for $12,936 (Goodwin; 2/14)
...ving Lewis (Emblem) SGC 60 (EX) sold for $9,345 (Goodwin; 12/12)
...uis Lowdermilk PSA 7 (NM) sold for $15,405 (REA; 5/13)
...uis Lowdermilk Red Cross SGC 40 (VG) sold for $16,590 (REA; 5/13)
...ard Miller Chicago PSA 8 (NmMt) sold for $13,035 (REA; Spring '14)

13 Tom Barker Game WG6

	PrFr 1	GD 2	VG 3	VgEx 4	EX 5	ExMt 6	NM 7	NmMt 8
Grover Alexander	120	150	200	250	300	400	500	600
Chief Bender	15	20	25	30	40	60	80	100
Bob Bescher	8	10	12	15	20	25	30	50
Joe Birmingham	8	10	12	15	20	25	30	50
Roger Bresnahan	20	25	30	40	50	60	80	120
Nixey Callahan	8	10	12	15	20	25	30	50
Bill Carrigan	8	10	12	15	20	25	30	50
Frank Chance	20	25	30	40	50	60	80	120
Hal Chase	10	12	15	20	25	30	40	60
Fred Clarke	15	20	25	30	40	50	60	100
Ty Cobb	120	250	300	350	400	425	600	1,000
Sam Crawford	20	25	30	40	50	60	80	120
Jake Daubert	8	10	12	15	20	25	30	50
Red Dooin	8	10	12	15	20	25	30	50

	PrFr 1	GD 2	VG 3	VgEx 4	EX 5	ExMt 6	NM 7	NmMt 8
16 Johnny Evers	20	25	30	40	50	60	100	150
17 Vean Gregg	8	10	12	15	20	25	30	50
18 Clark Griffith	15	20	25	30	40	50	60	100
19 Dick Hoblitzel	8	10	12	15	20	25	30	50
20 Miller Huggins	15	20	25	30	40	50	60	100
21 Joe Jackson	500	600	750	1,000	1,200	1,500	2,000	2,500
22 Hugh Jennings	15	20	25	30	40	50	60	100
23 Walter Johnson	50	60	80	100	120	150	200	350
24 Ed Konetchy	8	10	12	15	20	25	30	50
25 Nap Lajoie	25	30	40	50	60	80	100	150
26 Connie Mack	20	25	30	40	50	60	100	200
27 Rube Marquard	15	20	25	30	60	80	100	100
28 Christy Mathewson	50	60	80	100	120	250	400	500
29 John McGraw	20	25	30	40	50	60	80	120
30 Chief Meyers	8	10	12	15	20	25	30	50
31 Clyde Milan	8	10	12	15	20	25	30	50
32 Marty O'Toole	8	10	12	15	20	25	30	50
33 Nap Rucker	8	10	12	15	20	25	30	50
34 Tris Speaker	25	30	40	50	80	150	200	250
35 George Stallings	8	10	12	15	20	25	30	50
36 Bill Sweeney	8	10	12	15	20	25	30	50
37 Joe Tinker	20	25	30	40	50	60	80	120
38 Honus Wagner	120	150	200	250	300	400	500	800
40 Zack Wheat	15	20	30	40	50	60	80	120
42 Joe Wood	15	20	25	30	100	120	150	200
43 Cy Young	50	60	80	100	120	150	200	350

1913 National Game WG5

		PrFr 1	GD 2	VG 3	VgEx 4	EX 5	ExMt 6	NM 7	NmMt 8
1	Grover Alexander	100	120	150	200	250	300	400	500
2	Frank Baker	20	25	30	40	50	60	80	200
3	Chief Bender	15	20	25	30	40	50	60	150
4	Bob Bescher	8	10	12	15	20	25	30	50
5	Joe Birmingham	8	10	12	15	20	25	30	120
6	Roger Bresnahan	20	25	30	40	50	60	80	150
7	Nixey Callahan	8	10	12	15	20	25	30	60
8	Frank Chance	20	25	30	40	50	60	80	120
9	Hal Chase	10	12	15	20	25	30	40	60
10	Fred Clarke	15	20	25	30	40	50	60	100
11	Ty Cobb	120	150	200	250	400	700	800	1,000
12	Sam Crawford	20	25	30	40	50	60	100	120
13	Bill Dahlen	8	10	12	15	20	25	30	150
14	Jake Daubert	8	10	12	15	20	25	30	80
15	Red Dooin	8	10	12	15	20	25	30	120
16	Johnny Evers	20	25	30	120	150	200	250	200
17	Vean Gregg	8	10	12	15	20	25	30	120
18	Clark Griffith MG	15	20	25	30	40	50	60	150
19	Dick Hoblitzel	8	10	12	15	20	25	30	120
20	Miller Huggins	15	20	25	30	40	50	60	100
21	Joe Jackson	500	600	700	800	1,000	1,200	1,500	2,500
22	Hugh Jennings MG	15	20	25	30	40	50	60	100
23	Walter Johnson	40	50	150	200	250	300	400	500
24	Ed Konetchy	8	10	12	15	20	25	30	50
25	Nap Lajoie	25	30	40	50	120	150	200	200
26	Connie Mack MG	20	25	30	40	50	80	120	200
27	Rube Marquard	15	20	25	30	40	50	80	100
28	Christy Mathewson	40	50	60	120	150	200	250	300
29	John McGraw MG	20	25	30	40	50	60	80	120
30	Larry McLean	8	10	12	15	20	25	30	50
31	Clyde Milan	8	10	12	15	20	25	30	120
32	Marty O'Toole	8	10	12	15	20	25	30	120
33	Nap Rucker	8	10	12	15	20	25	30	100
34	Tris Speaker	25	30	40	50	60	80	120	150
35	Jake Stahl	8	10	12	15	20	25	30	50

#		PrFr 1	GD 2	VG 3	VgEx 4	EX 5	ExMt 6	NM 7	NmMt 8
36	George Stallings MG	8	10	12	15	20	25	30	50
37	George Stovall	8	10	12	15	20	25	30	50
39	Joe Tinker	20	25	50	60	80	100	120	150
40	Honus Wagner	120	150	250	300	350	500	600	800
42	Joe Wood	15	20	25	30	40	50	100	150
43	Cy Young	50	60	80	100	200	250	300	400

1913 Fatima Teams T200

#		PrFr 1	GD 2	VG 3	VgEx 4	EX 5	ExMt 6	NM 7	NmMt 8
1	Boston Americans	150	250	350	550	950			
2	Chicago Americans	150	250	300	500	800			
3	Cleveland Americans	500	600	800	1,000	1,800			
4	Detroit Americans	300	600	800	1,200	2,000			
5	New York Americans	400	600	800	1,200				
6	Philadelphia Americans	100	150	300	400	600			
7	St. Louis Americans	300	500	600	1,000	1,500			
8	Washington Americans	200	250	400	500	900			
9	Boston Nationals	600	1,000						
10	Brooklyn Nationals	150	250	300	500	800			
11	Chicago Nationals	120	200	250	400	600			
12	Cincinnati Nationals	100	150	200	400	500			
13	New York Nationals	200	300	400	600	1,200			
14	Philadelphia Nationals	150	200	250	300	500			
15	Pittsburgh Nationals	200	300	400	650	800			
16	St. Louis Nationals	150	250	300	700	1,000			

— Cleveland Americans PSA 8 (NmMt) sold for $11,850 (REA; Spring '14)

1914 Cracker Jack

#		PrFr 1	GD 2	VG 3	VgEx 4	EX 5	ExMt 6	NM 7	NmMt 8
1	Otto Knabe	150	500	600	800				
2	Frank Baker	300	400	800	1,000	1,400	1,800		
3	Joe Tinker	250	300	800	1,200	1,500	2,200		
4	Larry Doyle	80	120	200	300	500			
5	Ward Miller	80	100	200	200	600	800		
6	Eddie Plank	250	600	900	1,300	2,200			
7	Eddie Collins	300	500	800	1,000	1,500	2,000		
8	Rube Oldring	80	100	250	400	1,000			
9	Artie Hoffman (Hofman)	150	250	400	600	1,000			
10	John McInnis	100	150	200	400	500	600		
11	George Stovall	100	100	300	400	600	800		
12	Connie Mack MG	150	250	600	1,000	1,500	2,000		
13	Art Wilson	80	100	250	300	400	400		
14	Sam Crawford	150	300	800	1,200	2,000	3,000		
15	Reb Russell	60	100	200	300	600			
16	Howie Camnitz	80	250	300	400	600	800		
17	Roger Bresnahan	250	600	1,200	1,500	2,000	2,500		
17B	Roger Bresnahan NNO	1,000	1,500	2,000	2,500	3,500			
18	Johnny Evers	300	500	1,000	1,500	2,000	2,500		
19	Chief Bender	150	450	500	1,500	2,000	2,500		
20	Cy Falkenberg	100	200	250	300	400			
21	Heinie Zimmerman	60	120	300	400	500			
22	Joe Wood	400	700	2,000	2,500	3,000			
23	Charles Comiskey	250	500	800	1,000	1,200	1,500		
24	George Mullen (Mullin)	100	200	250	400	500	2,000		
25	Michael Simon	120	200	300	500	800	1,200		
26	James Scott	120	200	400	600	800	1,000		
27	Bill Carrigan	80	300	600	800	1,000			
28	Jack Barry	120	200	300	500	800			
29	Vean Gregg	100	250	300	500	600			
30	Ty Cobb	5,000	6,000	15,000	20,000	30,000	40,000		
31	Heinie Wagner	60	200	300	500	600	700		
32	Mordecai Brown	300	400	1,000	1,200	1,500			
33	Amos Strunk	100	120	250	300	450	400		
34	Ira Thomas	60	120	150	250	600	1,000		

#		PrFr 1	GD 2	VG 3	VgEx 4	EX 5	ExMt 6	NM 7	NmM...
35	Harry Hooper	150	250	800	2,000	3,000	5,000		
36	Ed Walsh	300	500	600	1,000	1,200	1,500		
37	Grover C. Alexander	1,200	1,500	2,500	4,000				
38	Red Dooin	120	250	600	800	1,000			
39	Chick Gandil	800	1,200	2,000	3,000	5,000			
40	Jimmy Austin	120	250	500	600	1,500			
41	Tommy Leach	100	200	300	400	1,000			
42	Al Bridwell	120	250	400	600	800	1,000		
43	Rube Marquard	400	600	800	1,000	1,500	2,500		
44	Charles Tesreau	120	250	300	400	600			
45	Fred Luderus	100	150	250	400	500			
46	Bob Groom	80	200	250	400	500	600		
47	Josh Devore	60	120	250	400	600	1,000		
48	Harry Lord	60	100	400	500	600	800		
49	John Miller	60	300	400	500	600			
50	John Hummell (Hummel)	60	200	300	500	600	800		
51	Nap Rucker	100	120	150	300	350	400		
52	Zach Wheat	150	250	700	1,000	1,500	2,000		
53	Otto Miller	120	250	400	600	800			
54	Marty O'Toole	150	250	400	600	800	1,000		
55	Dick Hoblitzel (Hoblitzell)	120	250	400	600	800	1,000		
56	Clyde Milan	120	250	400	600	800	1,000		
57	Walter Johnson	1,500	3,000	4,000	6,000	8,000			
58	Wally Schang	120	250	400	600	800	1,000		
59	Harry Gessler	80	250	300	600	800	1,000		
60	Rollie Zeider	100	200	300	500	800	1,000		
61	Ray Schalk	300	500	600	1,200	1,500	2,000		
62	Jay Cashion	150	200	400	500	600	1,000		
63	Babe Adams	100	200	250	400	600	800		
64	Jimmy Archer	60	120	400	500	600			
65	Tris Speaker	500	1,000	1,500	2,000	3,000			
66	Napoleon Lajoie	800	1,200	2,000	3,000	5,000			
67	Otis Crandall	150	300	400	500	600	800		
68	Honus Wagner	2,000	2,500	4,000	6,000	10,000			
69	John McGraw	500	800	1,200	2,000	3,000	5,000		
70	Fred Clarke	250	400	600	700	1,200	1,500		
71	Chief Meyers	80	120	250	400	1,500			
72	John Boehling	150	250	400	600	1,000			
73	Max Carey	200	300	500	1,200	2,500	3,000		
74	Frank Owens	60	300	400	1,800	2,000			
75	Miller Huggins	200	300	800	1,000	1,500	2,500		
76	Claude Hendrix	60	100	150	200	300			
77	Hughie Jennings MG	200	300	600	800	1,500	2,500		
78	Fred Merkle	60	300	400	1,000	1,200			
79	Ping Bodie	100	150	400	800	1,000			
80	Ed Ruelbach	60	100	250	300	400			
81	Jim Delahanty	60	120	200	250	300	400		
82	Gavvy Cravath	150	200	400	600	800	1,000		
83	Russ Ford	60	100	150	600	800			
84	Elmer E. Knetzer	60	100	300	400	600			
85	Buck Herzog	80	150	200	250	600			
86	Burt Shotton	60	100	150	200	300			
87	Forrest Cady	100	150	250	300	500			
88	Christy Mathewson	30,000	50,000	80,000	100,000				
89	Lawrence Cheney	120	250	400	1,000	1,500	2,500		
90	Frank Smith	300	500	3,000	4,000	5,000			
91	Roger Peckinpaugh	60	100	600	800	1,000	1,200		
92	Al Demaree	400	600	800	2,000				
93	Del Pratt	5,000	8,000						
94	Eddie Cicotte	300	500	2,000	2,500				
95	Ray Keating	100	150	250	300				
96	Beals Becker	60	100	2,000	3,000	4,000			
97	Rube Benton	80	100	400	600	800			
98	Frank LaPorte	60	200	400	600	800			
99	Frank Chance	500	800	1,200	2,500	4,000			

	PrFr 1	GD 2	VG 3	VgEx 4	EX 5	ExMt 6	NM 7	NmMt 8
) Thomas Seaton	150	300	500	600	800	1,000		
1 Frank Schulte	60	100	300	500	800			
2 Ray Fisher	60	100	150	400	500	600		
3 Joe Jackson	20,000	30,000	50,000	80,000	120,000			
4 Vic Saier	200	250	400	600	800	1,000		
5 James Lavender	60	100	400	500	600	1,500		
6 Joe Birmingham	120	250	400	1,200	2,000			
Tom Downey	100	150	250	400	600	1,200		
Sherry Magee	120	250	1,200	2,000	3,000			
Fred Blanding	60	100	150	300	600	800		
Bob Bescher	60	400	500	600	800			
Jim Callahan	60	100	150	200	300			
Ed Sweeney	60	100	400	500	600			
George Suggs	60	100	150	400	600			
George Moriarity (Moriarty)	60	200	300	400	600	1,200		
Addison Brennan	60	100	150	200	300	400		
Rollie Zeider	80	120	300	400	600	800		
Ted Easterly	80	100	300	500	800			
Ed Konetchy	120	300	400	500	800			
George Perring	60	100	500	800	1,000			
Mike Doolan	60	100	200	200	400			
Hub Perdue	60	100	400	500	1,500	2,500		
Owen Bush	60	100	150	600	800	2,000		
Slim Sallee	60	100	150	250	300	400		
Earl Moore	200	300	500	800	1,000	1,500		
Bert Niehoff	200	300	400	600	800	1,200		
Walter Blair	60	100	300	400	600	800		
Butch Schmidt	60	100	150	500	800			
Steve Evans	60	150	400	500	800	1,000		
Ray Caldwell	60	100	120	400	600			
Ivy Wingo	100	200	300	1,000				
George Baumgardner	60	400	500	600	800	1,000		
Les Nunamaker	60	150	200	400	600	800		
Branch Rickey MG	400	800	3,000	4,000				
Armando Marsans	120	400	500	600	800	1,200		
Bill Killefer	250	300	400	500				
Rabbit Maranville	400	800	1,200	2,000				
William Rariden	120	300	400	600	800			
Hank Gowdy	60	100	200	250	300	400		
Rebel Oakes	80	150	200	200	600			
Danny Murphy	120	300	400	600	800			
Cy Barger	100	200	200	800	1,000			
Eugene Packard	100	200	300	400	500			
Jake Daubert	60	100	800	1,000	1,200			
James C. Walsh	250	300	400	600	800			

ver C. Alexander #37 SGC 60 (EX) sold for $5,500 (Legendary; 8/12)

rdecai Brown #32 SGC 7 (Nm) sold for $6,032 (Goodwin; 11/11)

l Pratt #93 PSA 4 (VgEx) sold for $17,625 (Mile High; 6/13)

Cobb #30 PSA 8.5 (NmMt+) sold for $106,650 (REA; Spring '14)

Cobb #30 PSA 8.5 (NmMt+) sold for $75,000 (REA; 05/12)

n Crawford #14 PSA 8 (NmMt) sold for $6,032 (Mile High; 05/11)

nny Evers #18 PSA 8 (NmMt) sold for $6,032 (Mile High; 05/11)

Jackson #103 PSA 7 (NM) sold for $54,848 (Mile High; 05/11)

Jackson #103 SGC 7 (NM) sold for $46,575 (Mile High; 10/11)

Jackson #103 SGC 70 (EX+) sold for $44,057 (Goodwin; 12/12)

ter Johnson #57 SGC 80 (ExMt) sold for $5,838 (Goodwin; 11/12)

ter Johnson #57 SGC 80 (ExMt) sold for $5,581 (REA; 05/11)

sty Mathewson #88 SGC 9 Mint sold for $35,000 (REA; 05/12)

sty Mathewson #88 PSA 5 (EX) sold for $67,798 (Goodwin; 11/12)

sty Mathewson #88 SGC 20 (Fair) sold for $18,062 (Goodwin; 12/12)

Pratt #93 SGC 80 (ExMt) sold for $24,659 (Goodwin; 12/12)

us Wagner #68 SGC 84 (NM) sold for $28,539 (Mile High; 10/12)

1914 Polo Grounds Game WG4

		GD 2	VG 3	VgEx 4	EX 5	ExMt 6	NM 7	NmMt 8	MT 9
1	Jimmy Archer	8	10	12	15	25	40	80	200
2	Frank Baker	20	25	30	40	60	80	150	400
3	Frank Chance	15	20	25	30	50	80	150	400
4	Larry Cheney	8	10	12	15	25	40	80	200
5	Ty Cobb	120	250	300	400	500	600	800	1,500
6	Eddie Collins	20	25	30	40	60	80	150	400
7	Larry Doyle	8	10	12	15	25	40	80	200
8	Art Fletcher	8	10	12	15	25	40	80	200
9	Claude Hendrix	8	10	12	15	25	40	80	200
10	Joe Jackson	300	400	500	600	800	1,400	1,800	2,500
11	Hugh Jennings MG	20	25	30	40	60	80	150	400
12	Nap Lajoie	25	30	40	50	80	175	225	500
13	Jimmy Lavender	8	10	12	15	25	40	80	200
14	Fritz Maisel	8	10	12	15	25	40	80	200
15	Rabbit Maranville	20	25	30	50	60	80	200	400
16	Rube Marquard	20	25	30	40	60	80	150	400
17	Christy Mathewson	50	60	80	100	150	200	400	800
18	John McGraw MG	20	25	30	40	60	100	150	400
19	Stuffy McInnis	8	10	12	15	25	40	80	200
20	Chief Meyers	8	10	12	15	25	40	80	200
21	Red Murray	8	10	12	15	25	40	80	200
22	Eddie Plank	20	25	30	40	60	80	150	400
23	Nap Rucker	8	10	12	15	25	40	80	200
24	Reb Russell	8	10	12	15	25	40	80	200
25	Frank Schulte	8	10	12	15	25	40	80	200
26	Jim Scott	8	10	12	15	25	40	80	200
27	Tris Speaker	25	30	40	50	80	100	250	500
28	Honus Wagner	80	100	120	150	250	800	1,000	1,200
29	Ed Walsh	20	25	30	40	60	80	150	400
30	Joe Wood	20	25	30	40	60	100	150	400

— Joe Jackson PSA 10 (Gem) sold for $5,288 (REA; 05/11)

1915 American Caramel E106

		PrFr 1	GD 2	VG 3	VgEx 4	EX 5	ExMt 6	NM 7	NmMt 8
1	Jack Barry	60	150	250	300				
2A	Chief Bender Striped Hat	120	300	600					
2B	Chief Bender White Hat	100	250	400					
3	Bob Bescher	60	150	250	300				
4	Roger Bresnahan	100	250	400	800				
5	Al Bridwell	60	150	250	300				
6	Donie Bush	60	150	250	300				
7A	Hal Chase Portrait	100	200	400					
7B	Hal Chase Catching	100	250	400					
8A	Ty Cobb Batting Front	800	2,500	4,000					
8B	Ty Cobb Batting Side	800	2,500	4,000					
9	Eddie Collins	100	250	400	800				
10	Sam Crawford	150	300	500	800				
11	Ray Demmitt	60	150	250	300				
12	Bill Donovan	60	150	250	300				
13	Red Dooin	60	150	250	300				
14	Mickey Doolan	60	150	250	300				
15	Larry Doyle	60	150	250	300				
16	Clyde Engle	60	150	250	300				
17	Johnny Evers	100	500	600	800				
18	Art Fromme	60	150	250	300				
19A	George Gibson Back	60	150	250	300				
19B	George Gibson Front	60	150	250	300				
20	Topsy Hartzell	60	150	250	300				
21	Fred Jacklitsch	60	150	250	300				
22	Hugh Jennings MG	150	300	500					
23	Otto Knabe	60	150	250	300				
24	Nap Lajoie	250	600	1,000					
25	Hans Lobert	60	150	250	300				
26	Rube Marquard	150	300	500					

#	Player	PrFr 1	GD 2	VG 3	VgEx 4	EX 5	ExMt 6	NM 7	NmMt 8
27	Christy Mathewson	500	1,200	2,000					
28	John McGraw MG	150	300	500					
29	George McQuillan	60	150	250	300				
30	Dots Miller	60	150	300	400				
31	Danny Murphy	60	150	250	300				
32	Rebel Oakes	60	150	250	300				
33	Eddie Plank	250	600	1,000					
34	Germany Schaefer	60	150	250	300				
35	Tris Speaker	300	800	1,500					
36	Oscar Stanage	60	150	250	300				
37	George Stovall	60	150	250	300				
38	Jeff Sweeney	60	150	250	300				
39A	Joe Tinker Batting	150	300	500					
39B	Joe Tinker Portrait	150	300	600	1,000				
40A	Honus Wagner Batting	1,200	2,500	4,000					
40B	Honus Wagner Throwing	1,200	2,500	4,000					
41	Hooks Wiltse	60	150	250	300				
42	Heinie Zimmerman	60	150	250	300				

— Honus Wagner Batting PSA 5 (EX) sold for $5,880 (Greg Bussineau; 12/12)

1915 Cracker Jack

#	Player	PrFr 1	GD 2	VG 3	VgEx 4	EX 5	ExMt 6	NM 7	NmMt 8
1	Otto Knabe	80	100	120	150	250	1,500	3,000	
2	Frank Baker	200	500	800	1,000	1,200	1,500	2,000	6,000
3	Joe Tinker	200	300	500	800	1,200	2,000	3,000	8,000
4	Larry Doyle	60	100	150	250	400	600	1,000	
5	Ward Miller	40	120	250	300	400	500	600	1,500
6	Eddie Plank	600	800	1,200	1,500	2,500	3,000	4,000	20,000
7	Eddie Collins	200	400	600	800	1,000	1,800	2,000	4,000
8	Rube Oldring	40	50	60	150	200	250	300	600
9	Artie Hoffman	40	50	60	150	200	250	300	
10	John McInnis	40	120	150	200	250	300	400	1,000
11	George Stovall	40	50	60	120	150	200	300	500
12	Connie Mack MG	250	500	600	800	1,000	1,200	1,500	4,000
13	Art Wilson	40	80	100	200	250	300	500	800
14	Sam Crawford	250	500	600	800	1,000	1,200	1,500	5,000
15	Reb Russell	40	50	120	120	150	200	300	600
16	Howie Camnitz	40	50	60	150	200	250	300	1,000
17	Roger Bresnahan	150	300	500	600	800	1,000	1,200	2,500
18	Johnny Evers	200	300	400	500	600	800	2,000	5,000
19	Chief Bender	200	400	500	600	800	1,000	1,200	6,000
20	Cy Falkenberg	40	100	120	150	200	250	600	600
21	Heinie Zimmerman	40	80	100	150	200	300	500	1,000
22	Joe Wood	250	300	400	850	1,000	1,200	1,500	2,000
23	Charles Comiskey	250	300	500	600	800	1,000	1,500	8,000
24	George Mullen	40	50	60	120	150	200	300	1,000
25	Michael Simon	40	50	60	100	300	400	500	800
26	James Scott	40	50	60	150	200	500	800	
27	Bill Carrigan	40	50	100	150	200	300	500	
28	Jack Barry	50	100	120	150	300	500		
29	Vean Gregg	40	50	60	150	300	400	600	800
30	Ty Cobb	3,000	6,000	8,000	12,000	15,000	20,000	25,000	30,000
31	Heinie Wagner	40	50	60	100	250	300	500	2,500
32	Mordecai Brown	200	250	500	600	800	1,200	2,500	
33	Amos Strunk	50	100	200	300	500	600	800	2,500
34	Ira Thomas	40	80	120	150	175	200	300	1,000
35	Harry Hooper	150	200	250	400	500	600	1,000	4,000
36	Ed Walsh	200	250	400	500	600	800	1,500	6,000
37	Grover C. Alexander	800	1,000	2,000	2,500	3,000	4,000	6,000	8,000
38	Red Dooin	40	50	60	100	200	250	600	800
39	Chick Gandil	200	300	400	500	600	800	1,200	5,000
40	Jimmy Austin	50	60	80	120	200	250	400	800
41	Tommy Leach	40	50	60	100	120	200	300	800
42	Al Bridwell	40	60	80	150	200	250	300	1,000
43	Rube Marquard	300	400	500	600	800	1,000	2,500	4,000
44	Jeff (Charles) Tesreau	40	50	80	100	200	350	400	1,000

#	Player	PrFr 1	GD 2	VG 3	VgEx 4	EX 5	ExMt 6	NM 7	NmMt 8
45	Fred Luderus	40	50	60	150	200	250	300	1,00
46	Bob Groom	40	150	200	300	400	500	600	2,00
47	Josh Devore	40	50	60	300	400	500	600	80
48	Steve O'Neill	40	50	80	120	150	200	400	80
49	John Miller	50	80	120	200	300	500	800	1,20
50	John Hummell	40	80	200	250	300	400	500	80
51	Nap Rucker	40	60	80	100	120	200	400	80
52	Zach Wheat	200	250	300	400	1,000	2,000	2,000	4,00
53	Otto Miller	40	50	60	120	150	200	300	45
54	Marty O'Toole	50	60	150	200	300	400	600	80
55	Dick Hoblitzel	40	50	60	100	120	200	300	80
56	Clyde Milan	40	80	100	120	150	200	400	1,00
57	Walter Johnson	2,000	4,000	5,000	6,000	8,000	10,000	12,000	20,00
58	Wally Schang	40	50	60	200	250	300	400	80
59	Harry Gessler	40	50	60	100	120	200	300	8
60	Oscar Dugey	60	150	200	250	300	400	600	8
61	Ray Schalk	200	250	500	600	800	1,000	1,200	4,0
62	Willie Mitchell	40	50	60	100	120	200	400	8
63	Babe Adams	40	50	60	100	120	200	300	9
64	Jimmy Archer	40	100	120	200	250	300	350	7
65	Tris Speaker	600	800	1,000	1,200	2,000	3,000	4,000	5,0
66	Napoleon Lajoie	300	600	800	1,000	1,200	1,500	2,000	8,0
67	Otis Crandall	50	100	200	300	400	500	600	8
68	Honus Wagner	2,500	3,000	4,000	5,000	10,000	12,000	15,000	20,0
69	John McGraw MG	200	250	300	450	500	800	1,200	6,0
70	Fred Clarke	200	400	450	500	600	800	1,300	
71	Chief Meyers	50	60	100	120	150	250	400	1,2
72	John Boehling	40	60	80	120	150	200	300	
73	Max Carey	200	250	300	400	500	800	1,200	4,0
74	Frank Owens	40	50	60	250	400	600	800	1,0
75	Miller Huggins	200	250	300	400	600	800	1,000	2,5
76	Claude Hendrix	40	50	80	100	150	200	300	6
77	Hughie Jennings MG	200	300	400	500	600	800	1,200	3,0
78	Fred Merkle	40	50	60	100	300	400	600	1,0
79	Ping Bodie	100	150	250	400	600	1,000	1,500	2,5
80	Ed Ruelbach	40	50	60	100	200	250	400	
81	Jim Delahanty	40	50	60	150	200	250	300	
82	Gavvy Cravath	40	50	60	120	150	200	450	1,
83	Russ Ford	40	50	100	120	150	200	400	
84	Elmer E. Knetzer	50	80	120	200	300	500	800	1,
85	Buck Herzog	40	50	60	100	120	300	350	1,
86	Burt Shotton	40	50	60	200	250	300	350	
87	Forrest Cady	50	80	120	200	300	500	800	1,
88	Christy Mathewson	1,200	2,500	3,000	4,000	5,000	6,000	8,000	15,
89	Lawrence Cheney	50	60	80	120	150	200	400	
90	Frank Smith	40	50	60	100	120	200	300	1,
91	Roger Peckinpaugh	40	60	80	100	120	800	1,000	2,
92	Al Demaree	80	300	400	500	600	800	1,000	1,
93	Del Pratt	80	150	200	250	300	400	500	1,
94	Eddie Cicotte	300	500	800	1,000	1,200	1,500	2,000	4
95	Ray Keating	80	250	300	400	500	600	800	1
96	Beals Becker	150	250	300	400	500	800	1,200	2
97	John (Rube) Benton	40	50	60	200	250	800	1,000	1
98	Frank LaPorte	40	50	80	200	250	300	400	
99	Hal Chase	100	120	200	300	400	400	800	2
100	Thomas Seaton	40	50	60	100	120	200	300	
101	Frank Schulte	40	50	200	300	400	500	600	1
102	Ray Fisher	40	100	120	150	200	250	500	
103	Joe Jackson	10,000	12,000	20,000	25,000	30,000	40,000	50,000	60
104	Vic Saier	40	50	120	150	300	400	600	1
105	James Lavender	80	150	300	400	500	600	800	1
106	Joe Birmingham	40	50	60	120	150	200	400	
107	Thomas Downey	40	50	60	200	250	300	400	
108	Sherry Magee	100	150	250	400	600	1,000	1,500	2
109	Fred Blanding	50	60	120	250	300	400	500	
110	Bob Bescher	80	150	200	250	300	400	600	2

		PrFr 1	GD 2	VG 3	VgEx 4	EX 5	ExMt 6	NM 7	NmMt 8
111	Herbie Moran	40	50	120	200	300	400	500	1,000
112	Ed Sweeney	40	50	60	150	200	400	600	1,000
113	George Suggs	40	50	60	200	250	300	400	1,200
114	George Moriarity	40	50	200	300	400	500	600	800
15	Addison Brennan	40	80	100	150	200	400	500	800
16	Rollie Zeider	40	50	60	100	150	250	350	1,000
17	Ted Easterly	50	80	120	200	300	500	800	1,200
18	Ed Konetchy	40	50	250	300	400	500	600	1,000
19	George Perring	40	50	60	200	250	300	400	1,000
20	Mike Doolan	40	200	250	300	400	500	600	1,200
21	Hub Perdue	40	50	60	250	300	400	500	3,000
22	Owen Bush	40	50	60	100	120	200	300	800
23	Slim Sallee	50	80	150	200	250	400	500	600
24	Earl Moore	40	50	60	150	200	250	300	1,000
25	Bert Niehoff	40	120	150	200	250	300	400	2,000
26	Walter Blair	40	150	200	300	400	500	600	1,000
27	Butch Schmidt	40	50	60	100	120	200	300	2,500
28	Steve Evans	50	60	80	250	400	500	600	2,500
29	Ray Caldwell	40	50	60	100	120	200	400	800
30	Ivy Wingo	50	100	120	150	200	250	300	400
31	Geo. Baumgardner	40	100	120	150	200	400	600	4,000
32	Les Nunamaker	60	120	250	300	400	500	800	1,200
33	Branch Rickey MG	250	500	1,000	1,200	1,500	2,000	3,000	5,000
34	Armando Marsans	100	200	250	300	400	500	600	1,500
35	William Killefer	80	150	200	250	300	400	500	1,000
36	Rabbit Maranville	250	400	600	1,000	1,500	2,500	4,000	6,000
37	William Rariden	40	50	60	100	120	200	300	1,500
38	Hank Gowdy	40	50	60	100	200	300	400	1,100
49	Rebel Oakes	40	80	150	200	250	300	400	1,500
0	Danny Murphy	60	100	150	250	400	600	1,000	1,500
1	Cy Barger	40	50	60	150	200	250	300	1,200
2	Eugene Packard	80	150	250	400	500	600	800	1,500
3	Jake Daubert	80	150	200	250	300	400	500	1,000
4	James C. Walsh	40	100	120	150	200	250	300	1,000
5	Ted Cather	40	50	100	120	150	200	300	600
6	George Tyler	40	80	150	250	300	400	500	800
7	Lee Magee	40	50	100	120	150	200	500	800
8	Owen Wilson	40	50	60	200	250	300	400	800
9	Hal Janvrin	40	50	60	100	120	200	350	500
	Doc Johnston	40	50	100	120	300	400	500	800
	George Whitted	40	80	100	150	200	250	400	600
	George McQuillen	40	50	80	120	150	200	350	1,500
	Bill James	40	150	200	300	400	500	600	800
	Dick Rudolph	40	100	120	150	200	250	400	800
	Joe Connolly	40	50	60	200	250	400	500	3,000
	Jean Dubuc	40	50	60	100	120	200	300	1,000
	George Kaiserling	80	100	120	150	200	300	400	2,000
	Fritz Maisel	100	150	250	400	600	1,000	1,500	2,500
	Heinie Groh	80	120	250	300	400	500	600	1,200
	Benny Kauff	50	60	80	120	150	200	300	1,500
	Edd Roush	250	500	1,000	1,200	1,500	2,000	2,500	4,000
	George Stallings MG	50	100	200	250	300	400	500	800
	Bert Whaling	40	50	80	100	120	250	400	800
	Bob Shawkey	40	50	100	120	150	500	600	1,200
	Eddie Murphy	50	60	150	200	250	300	400	600
	Joe Bush	40	50	100	200	250	300	400	1,000
	Clark Griffith	150	250	300	350	400	600	1,000	4,000
	Vin Campbell	50	100	120	150	200	250	400	2,500
	Raymond Collins	40	50	60	100	120	200	300	750
	Hans Lobert	80	100	120	200	400	500	600	1,000
	Earl Hamilton	100	120	150	200	250	300	400	800
	Erskine Mayer	50	100	200	250	300	400	1,000	
	Tilly Walker	100	150	250	400	600	1,000	1,500	3,000
	Robert Veach	80	100	120	150	200	250	300	2,000
	Joseph Benz	40	50	60	100	120	200	1,500	2,000
	Hippo Vaughn	120	100	120	150	300	600		

— Roger Bresnahan #17 PSA 9 (MT) sold for $8,932 (Goodwin; 9/12)
— Grover Alexander #37 SGC 92 (NmMt+) sold for $15,405 (REA; 5/13)
— Eddie Cicotte #94 PSA 9 (MT) sold for $10,440 (Bussineau; Fall '13)
— Ty Cobb #30 SGC 92 (NmMt+) sold for $25,000 (REA; 05/12)
— Ty Cobb #30 SGC 86 (NrMt+) sold for $17,362 (Mile High; 1/13)
— Ty Cobb #30 SGC 86 (NrMt+) sold for $10,361 (eBay; 9/12)
— Ty Cobb #30 SGC 7.5 (NM+) sold for $10,000 (REA; 05/12)
— Joe Jackson #103 PSA 8 (NmMt) sold for $60,000 (Memory Lane; Private Sale - 2007)
— Joe Jackson #103 SGC 92 (NmMt+) sold for $38,267 (Goodwin; 9/12)
— Joe Jackson #103 SGC 92 (NmMt+) sold for $38,267 (Goodwin; 10/12)
— Walter Johnson #57 SGC 86 (NrMt+) sold for $5,271 (Memory Lane; 5/12)
— Christy Mathewson #88 SGC 92 (NmMt+) sold for $13,920 (Greg Bussineau; 7/12)
— Christy Mathewson #88 SGC 92 (NmMt+) sold for $12,545 (SCP; 9/12)
— Christy Mathewson #88 SGC 86 (NrMt+) sold for $5,616 (Goodwin; 7/12)
— Honus Wagner #68 SGC 92 (NmMt+) sold for $14,299 (Mile High; 12/13)

1916 M101-4 Blank Back

		PrFr 1	GD 2	VG 3	VgEx 4	EX 5	ExMt 6	NM 7	NmMt 8
2	Sam Agnew Red Sox	20	25	30	50	60	80	120	200
8	H. D. Baird C.F.	20	25	30	50	60	80	120	200
9	J. Franklin Baker	60	80	150	200	250	300	400	800
10	Dave Bancroft	60	120	150	200	250	300	550	800
11	Jack Barry	20	25	30	50	60	80	120	200
12	Zinn Beck	20	25	30	50	60	80	120	200
13	Chief Bender	60	80	100	150	200	250	300	400
14	Joe Benz	20	25	30	50	60	80	120	200
15	Bob Bescher	20	25	30	50	60	80	120	200
16	Al Betzel 2nd B.	20	25	30	50	60	80	120	200
17	Mordecai Brown	60	80	100	150	200	250	400	800
18	Eddie Burns	20	25	30	50	60	80	120	200
19	George Burns	20	25	30	50	60	80	120	200
20	Geo. J. Burns	20	25	50	60	80	100	120	200
21	Joe Bush	20	25	30	50	60	80	120	200
22	Donie Bush	20	25	50	80	100	120	120	200
23	Art Butler	20	25	30	50	60	80	120	200
24	Bobbie Byrne	20	25	30	50	60	80	120	200
25	Forrest Cady	20	25	30	50	60	80	120	200
26	Jimmy Callahan	20	25	30	50	60	80	120	200
27	Ray Caldwell	20	25	30	50	60	80	120	200
28	Max Carey	60	80	120	150	200	250	400	800
29	George Chalmers	20	25	30	50	60	80	120	200
30	Ray Chapman	20	25	30	50	60	80	120	200
31	Larry Cheney	20	25	30	50	80	100	120	200
32	Eddie Cicotte	60	80	100	150	200	250	400	800
33	Tom Clarke	20	25	30	50	60	80	120	200
34	Eddie Collins	60	80	100	150	200	250	400	800
35	Shauno Collins	20	25	30	50	60	80	250	300
36	Charles Comiskey	60	80	100	150	200	250	400	800
37	Joe Connolly	20	25	30	50	60	80	120	200
38	Ty Cobb	1,000	1,200	1,500	2,000	2,500	3,000	8,000	
39	Harry Coveleskie (Coveleski)	20	25	30	50	60	80	120	200
40	Gavvy Cravath	20	25	30	50	60	80	120	200
41	Sam Crawford	60	80	100	150	200	250	400	800
42	Jean Dale	20	25	30	50	60	80	120	200
43	Jake Daubert	20	25	30	50	60	80	120	200
44	Charles Deal	20	25	30	50	60	80	120	200
45	Al Demaree	20	25	30	50	60	80	120	200
46	Josh Devore	20	25	30	50	60	80	120	200
47	William Doak	20	25	30	50	60	80	120	200
48	Bill Donovan	20	25	30	50	60	80	120	200
49	Charles Dooin	20	25	30	50	60	80	120	200
50	Mike Doolan	20	25	30	50	60	80	120	200
51	Larry Doyle	20	25	30	50	60	80	120	200
52	Jean Dubuc	20	25	30	50	60	80	120	200
53	Oscar Dugey	20	25	30	50	60	80	120	200
54	Johnny Evers	60	80	100	150	200	250	400	800

#	Player	PrFr 1	GD 2	VG 3	VgEx 4	EX 5	ExMt 6	NM 7	NmMt 8
55	Urban Faber	50	60	80	120	150	200	300	500
56	Hap Felsch C.F.	40	50	60	700	800	900	1,000	1,200
57	Bill Fischer	20	25	30	50	60	80	120	200
58	Ray Fisher Pitching	20	25	30	50	60	80	120	200
59	Max Flack	20	25	30	50	60	80	150	200
60	Art Fletcher	20	25	30	50	60	80	120	200
61	Eddie Foster	20	25	30	50	60	80	120	200
62	Jacques Fournier	20	25	30	50	60	80	120	200
63	Del Gainer (Gainor)	20	25	30	50	60	80	120	200
64	Chick Gandil	20	25	30	50	60	80	120	200
68	Geo. Gibson (eo Missing)	20	25	30	50	60	80	120	200
72	Clark Griffith	50	60	100	120	150	200	300	500
73	Tom Griffith	20	25	30	50	60	80	120	200
74	Heinie Groh	20	25	30	50	60	80	120	200
75	Earl Hamilton	20	25	30	50	60	80	120	200
76	Bob Harmon	20	25	30	50	60	80	120	200
77	Roy Hartzell Americans	20	25	30	50	80	100	120	200
78	Claude Hendrix	20	25	30	50	60	80	120	200
79	Olaf Henriksen	20	25	30	50	60	80	120	200
80	John Henry	20	25	30	50	60	80	120	200
81	Buck Herzog	20	25	30	50	60	80	120	200
82	Hugh High	20	25	30	50	60	80	120	200
83	Dick Hoblitzell	20	25	30	50	60	80	120	200
84	Harry Hooper	50	60	80	120	150	200	300	500
85	Ivan Howard 3rd B.	20	25	30	50	60	80	120	200
86	Miller Huggins	50	60	80	120	150	200	300	500
87	Joe Jackson	2,000	2,500	3,000	4,200	5,000	8,000	10,000	25,000
88	William James	20	25	30	50	60	80	120	200
89	Harold Janvrin	20	25	30	50	60	80	120	200
90	Hughie Jennings	50	60	80	120	150	200	300	500
91	Walter Johnson	200	250	300	500	800	1,000	1,500	
92	Fielder Jones	20	25	30	50	60	80	120	200
93	Joe Judge	20	25	30	50	60	80	120	200
94	Benny Kauff	20	25	30	50	60	80	120	200
95	Wm. Killefer Jr.	20	25	30	50	60	80	120	200
96	Ed. Konetchy	20	25	30	50	60	80	120	200
97	Napoleon Lajoie	100	200	250	300	400	500	600	1,200
98	Jack Lapp	20	25	30	50	60	80	120	200
99	John Lavan	20	25	30	50	60	80	120	200
100	Jimmy Lavender	20	25	30	50	60	80	120	200
101	Nemo Leibold	20	25	30	50	60	80	120	200
102	H. B. Leonard	20	25	30	50	60	80	120	200
103	Duffy Lewis	20	25	30	50	60	80	120	200
104	Hans Lobert	20	25	30	50	60	80	120	200
105	Tom Long	20	25	30	50	60	80	120	200
106	Fred Luderus	20	25	30	50	60	80	120	200
107	Connie Mack	80	100	120	200	250	300	500	1,000
108	Lee Magee L.F.	20	25	30	50	60	80	120	200
109	Sherwood Magee	20	25	30	50	60	80	120	200
110	Al. Mamaux	20	25	30	50	60	80	120	200
111	Leslie Mann L.F.	20	25	30	50	60	80	120	200
112	Rabbit Maranville	60	80	100	150	200	250	400	
113	Rube Marquard	60	80	100	150	200	250	400	800
114	J. Erskine Mayer	20	25	30	50	60	80	120	200
115	George McBride	20	25	30	50	60	80	120	200
116	John J. McGraw	60	80	100	150	200	250	400	800
117	Jack McInnis	20	25	30	80	100	120	150	200
118	Fred Merkle	20	25	30	50	60	200	250	300
119	Chief Meyers	20	25	30	50	60	80	120	200
120	Clyde Milan	20	25	30	50	60	80	120	200
121	John Miller	20	25	30	50	60	80	120	200
122	Otto Miller	20	25	30	50	80	100	120	200
123	Willie Mitchell	20	25	30	50	60	80	120	200
124	Fred Mollwitz	20	25	30	50	60	80	120	200
125	Pat Moran	20	25	30	50	60	80	120	200
126	Ray Morgan	20	25	30	50	60	80	120	200

#	Player	PrFr 1	GD 2	VG 3	VgEx 4	EX 5	ExMt 6	NM 7	NmMt 8
127	Geo. Moriarty	20	25	30	50	60	80	120	200
128	Guy Morton	20	25	30	50	60	80	250	300
129	Mike Mowrey	20	25	30	50	60	80	120	200
130	Ed. Murphy	20	25	30	50	60	80	120	200
131	Hy Myers	20	25	30	50	60	80	120	200
132	J. A. Niehoff	20	25	30	50	60	80	120	200
133	Rube Oldring	20	25	30	50	60	80	120	200
134	Oliver O'Mara	20	25	30	50	60	80	120	200
135	Steve O'Neill	20	25	30	50	60	80	120	200
136	Dode Paskert C.F.	20	25	30	50	60	80	120	200
137	Roger Peckinpaugh	20	25	30	50	60	80	120	200
138	Wally Pipp	20	25	30	50	60	80	120	200
139	Derril Pratt (Derrill)	20	25	30	50	60	80	120	200
140	Pat Ragan	20	25	30	50	60	80	120	200
145	Bob Roth R.F.	20	25	30	50	60	80	120	200
146	Ed. Rousch R.F. (Roush)	60	80	100	150	200	250	400	800
154	Ray Schalk	50	60	80	120	150	200	300	500
155	Walter Schang	20	25	30	50	60	80	120	200
156	Frank Schulte	20	25	30	50	60	80	120	200
157	Everett Scott	20	25	30	50	60	80	120	200
158	Jim Scott	20	25	30	50	60	80	120	200
159	Tom Seaton	20	25	30	50	60	80	120	200
160	Howard Shanks	20	25	30	50	60	80	120	200
161	Bob Shawkey	20	25	30	50	60	80	120	200
162	Ernie Shore	20	25	30	50	60	80	120	200
163	Burt Shotton	20	25	30	50	60	80	120	200
164	Geo. Sisler 1st B.	60	80	100	150	200	250	400	800
165	J. Carlisle Smith	20	25	30	50	60	80	120	200
166	Fred Snodgrass	20	25	30	50	60	80	120	200
167	Geo. Stallings	20	25	30	50	60	80	120	200
168A	Oscar Stanage Portrait SP	20	25	30	50	60	80	120	200
168B	Oscar Stanage Catching								
169	Charles Stengel	200	250	300	500	600	800	1,200	2,000
170	Milton Stock	20	25	30	50	60	80	120	200
171	Amos Strunk	20	25	30	50	60	80	120	200
172	Billy Sullivan	20	25	30	50	60	80	120	200
173	Jeff Tesreau	20	25	30	50	60	80	120	200
174	Joe Tinker	60	80	100	150	200	250	400	800
175	Fred Toney	20	25	30	50	60	80	120	200
176	Terry Turner 2nd B.	20	25	30	50	60	80	120	200
177	George Tyler	20	25	30	50	60	80	120	200
178	Jim Vaughn	20	25	30	50	60	80	120	200
179	Bob Veach	20	25	30	50	60	80	120	200
180	James Viox 3rd B.	20	25	30	50	60	80	120	200
181	Oscar Vitt	20	25	30	50	60	80	120	200
182	Hans Wagner	900	1,000	1,100	1,200	1,800	2,000	3,000	
183	Clarence Walker Red Sox	20	25	30	50	60	80	120	200
184	Ed. Walsh	60	80	100	150	200	250	400	800
185	W. Wambsganss UER Photo	20	25	30	50	60	80	120	200
186	Buck Weaver 3rd B.	60	80	100	150	200	250	400	800
187	Carl Weilman	20	25	30	50	60	80	120	200
188	Zach Wheat	60	80	100	150	200	250	400	800
189	Geo. Whitted Nationals	20	25	30	50	60	80	120	200
190	Fred Williams	20	25	30	50	60	80	120	200
191	Art Wilson	20	25	30	50	60	80	120	200
192	J. Owen Wilson	20	25	30	50	60	80	120	200
193	Ivy Wingo	20	25	30	50	60	80	120	200
194	Mel Wolfgang	20	25	30	50	60	80	120	200
195	Joe Wood	80	100	120	200	250	300	500	1,000
196	Steve Yerkes	20	25	30	50	60	80	120	200
197	Pep Young	20	25	30	50	60	80	120	200

1916 M101-4 Sporting News

		PrFr 1	GD 2	VG 3	VgEx 4	EX 5	ExMt 6	NM 7	NmMt 8
151	Babe Ruth	35,000	50,000	60,000	65,000	90,000	200,000	300,000	

— Joe Jackson SGC 50 (Vg/Ex) sold for $6,422 (Goodwin; 3/12)
— Babe Ruth PSA 1 (Poor) sold for $30,343 (SCP; 5/12)
— Babe Ruth PSA 3 (VG) sold for $27,500 (Legendary; 3/11)

1916 M101-5 Blank Back

		PrFr 1	GD 2	VG 3	VgEx 4	EX 5	ExMt 6	NM 7	NmMt 8
1	Babe Adams *	20	25	30	50	60	80	120	200
2	Sam Agnew Browns	20	25	30	50	60	80	120	200
3	Ed Ainsmith *	20	25	30	50	60	80	120	200
4	Grover Alexander *	100	120	150	650				
5	Leon Ames *	20	25	30	50	60	80	120	200
6	Jimmy Archer *	20	25	30	50	60	80	120	200
7	Jimmy Austin *	20	25	30	50	60	80	120	200
8	J. Franklin Baker	60	80	100	150	200	250	400	800
9	Dave Bancroft	60	80	100	150	200	250	400	900
10	Jack Barry	20	25	30	50	60	80	175	250
11	Zinn Beck	20	25	30	50	60	80	120	200
12B	Lute Boone *	20	25	30	50	60	80	120	200
13	Joe Benz	20	25	30	50	60	80	120	200
14	Bob Bescher	20	25	30	50	60	80	120	200
15	Al Betzel 3rd B.	20	25	30	50	60	80	120	200
16	Roger Bresnahan	60	80	100	150	200	250	400	800
17	Eddie Burns	20	25	30	50	60	80	120	200
18	Geo. J. Burns	20	25	30	50	60	80	120	200
19	Joe Bush	20	25	30	50	60	80	120	200
20	Owen J. Bush	20	25	30	50	60	80	120	200
21	Art Butler	20	25	30	50	60	80	120	200
22	Bobby Byrne	20	25	30	50	60	80	120	200
23A	Mordecai Brown	60	80	100	150	200	250	1,100	2,000
24	Jimmy Callahan	20	25	30	50	60	80	120	200
25	Ray Caldwell	20	25	30	50	60	80	120	200
26	Max Carey	60	80	100	150	200	250	400	800
27	George Chalmers	20	25	30	50	60	80	120	200
28	Frank Chance	60	80	100	150	200	250	400	800
29	Ray Chapman	20	25	30	50	60	80	120	200
30	Larry Cheney	20	25	30	50	60	80	120	200
31	Eddie Cicotte	60	80	100	150	200	250	400	800
32	Tom Clarke	20	25	30	50	60	80	120	200
33	Eddie Collins	60	80	100	150	200	250	400	800
34	Shauno Collins	20	25	30	50	60	80	120	200
35	Charles Comisky (Comiskey)	60	80	100	150	200	250	400	800
36	Joe Connolly	20	25	30	50	60	80	120	200
37	Luther Cook	20	25	30	50	60	80	120	200
38	Jack Coombs	40	50	60	100	120	150	250	400
39	Dan Costello	20	25	30	50	60	80	120	200
40	Harry Coveleskie (Coveleski)	20	25	30	50	60	80	120	200
41	Gavvy Cravath	20	25	30	50	60	80	120	200
42	Sam Crawford	60	80	100	150	200	250	400	800
43	Jean Dale	20	25	30	50	60	80	120	200
44	Jake Daubert	20	25	30	50	60	80	120	200
45	Geo. A. Davis Jr.	20	25	30	50	60	80	120	200
46	Charles Deal	20	25	30	50	60	80	120	200
47	Al Demaree	20	25	30	50	60	80	120	200
48	William Doak	20	25	30	50	60	80	120	200
49	Bill Donovan	20	25	30	50	60	80	120	200
50	Charles Dooin	20	25	30	50	60	80	120	200
51	Mike Doolan	20	25	30	50	60	80	120	200
52	Larry Doyle	20	25	30	50	60	80	120	200
53	Jean Dubuc	20	25	30	50	60	80	120	200
54	Oscar Dugey	20	25	30	50	60	80	120	200
55	Johnny Evers	60	80	100	150	200	250	400	800
56	Urban Faber	50	60	80	120	150	200	300	500

		PrFr 1	GD 2	VG 3	VgEx 4	EX 5	ExMt 6	NM 7	NmMt 8
57	Hap Felsch R.F.	40	50	60	100	120	150	1,000	1,200
58	Bill Fischer	20	25	30	50	60	80	120	200
59	Ray Fisher Hands Over Head	20	25	30	50	60	80	120	200
60	Max Flack	20	25	30	50	60	80	120	200
61	Art Fletcher	20	25	30	50	60	80	120	200
62	Eddie Foster	20	25	30	50	60	80	120	200
63	Jacques Fournier	20	25	30	50	60	80	120	200
64	Del Gainer (Gainor)	20	25	30	50	60	80	120	200
65	Larry Gardner *	20	25	30	50	60	80	120	200
66	Joe Gedeon *	20	25	30	50	60	80	120	200
67	Gus Getz *	20	25	30	50	60	80	120	200
68	Geo. Gibson (eo Not Missing)	20	25	30	50	60	80	120	200
69	Wilbur Good *	20	25	30	50	60	80	120	200
70	Hank Gowdy *	20	25	30	50	60	80	120	200
71	Jack Graney *	20	25	30	50	60	80	120	200
72	Tom Griffith	20	25	30	50	60	80	120	200
73	Heinie Groh	20	25	30	50	60	80	120	200
74	Earl Hamilton	20	25	30	50	60	80	120	200
75	Bob Harmon	20	25	30	50	60	80	120	200
76	Roy Hartzell Am.	20	25	30	50	60	80	120	200
77	Claude Hendrix	20	25	30	50	60	80	120	200
78	Olaf Henriksen	20	25	30	50	60	80	120	200
79	John Henry	20	25	30	50	60	80	120	200
80	Buck Herzog	20	25	30	50	60	80	120	200
81	Hugh High	20	25	30	50	60	80	120	200
82	Dick Hoblitzell	20	25	30	50	60	80	120	200
83	Harry Hooper	50	60	80	120	150	200	300	500
84	Ivan Howard 1st B.	20	25	30	50	60	80	120	200
85	Miller Huggins	50	60	80	120	150	200	300	500
86	Joe Jackson	2,000	2,500	3,000	5,000	6,000	10,000	12,000	20,000
87	William James	20	25	30	50	60	80	120	200
88	Harold Janvrin	20	25	30	50	60	80	120	200
89	Hughie Jennings	50	60	80	120	150	200	300	500
90	Walter Johnson	200	250	300	500	800	1,200	4,200	
91	Fielder Jones	20	25	30	50	60	80	120	200
92	Benny Kauff	20	25	30	50	60	80	120	200
93	Wm. Killefer Jr.	20	25	30	50	60	80	120	200
94	Ed. Konetchy	20	25	30	50	60	80	120	200
95	Napoleon Lajoie	100	120	150	250	300	400	600	1,200
96	Jack Lapp	20	25	30	50	60	80	120	200
97	John Lavan	20	25	30	50	60	80	120	200
98	Jimmy Lavender	20	25	30	50	60	80	120	200
99	Nemo Leibold	20	25	30	50	60	80	120	200
100	H. B. Leonard	20	25	30	50	60	80	120	200
101	Duffy Lewis	20	25	30	50	60	80	120	200
102	Hans Lobert	20	25	30	50	60	80	120	200
103	Tom Long	20	25	30	50	60	80	120	200
104	Fred Luderus	20	25	30	50	60	80	120	200
105	Connie Mack	80	100	120	200	250	300	500	1,000
106	Lee Magee 2nd B.	20	25	30	50	60	80	120	200
107	Al. Mamaux	20	25	30	50	60	80	120	200
108	Leslie Mann C.F.	20	25	30	50	60	80	120	200
109	Rabbit Maranville	60	80	100	150	200	250	400	800
110	Rube Marquard	60	80	100	150	200	425	600	800
111	Armando Marsans	20	25	30	50	60	80	120	200
112	J. Erskine Mayer	20	25	30	50	60	80	120	200
113	George McBride	20	25	30	50	60	80	120	200
114	John J. McGraw	60	80	100	150	200	250	400	800
115	Jack McInnis	20	25	30	50	60	80	120	250
116	Fred Merkle	20	25	30	50	60	80	120	200
117	Chief Meyers	20	25	30	50	60	80	120	200
118	Clyde Milan	20	25	30	50	60	80	120	200
119	Otto Miller	20	25	30	50	60	80	120	200
120	Willie Mitchel (Mitchell)	20	25	30	50	60	80	120	200
121	Fred Mollwitz	20	25	30	50	60	80	120	200
122	J. Herbert Moran	20	25	30	50	60	80	120	200

#	Player	PrFr 1	GD 2	VG 3	VgEx 4	EX 5	ExMt 6	NM 7	NmMt 8
123	Pat Moran	20	25	30	50	60	80	120	200
124	Ray Morgan	20	25	30	50	60	80	120	200
125	Geo. Moriarty	20	25	30	50	60	80	120	200
126	Guy Morton	20	25	30	50	60	80	120	200
127	Ed. Murphy UER Photo	20	25	30	50	60	80	120	200
128	John Murray	20	25	30	50	60	80	120	200
129	Hy Myers	20	25	30	50	60	80	120	200
130	J. A. Niehoff	20	25	30	50	60	80	120	200
131	Leslie Nunamaker	20	25	30	50	60	80	120	300
132	Rube Oldring	20	25	30	50	60	80	120	200
133	Oliver O'Mara	20	25	30	50	60	80	120	200
134	Steve O'Neill	20	25	30	50	60	80	120	200
135	Dode Paskert C.	20	25	30	50	60	80	120	200
136	Roger Peckinpaugh UER Photo	20	25	30	50	60	80	120	200
137	E. J. Pfeffer	20	25	30	50	60	80	120	200
138	Geo. Pierce (Pearce)	20	25	30	50	60	80	120	200
139	Wally Pipp	20	25	30	50	60	80	120	200
140	Derril Pratt (Derrill)	20	25	30	50	60	80	120	200
141	Bill Rariden *	20	25	30	50	60	80	120	200
142	Eppa Rixey *	50	60	80	120	150	200	300	500
143	Davey Robertson *	20	25	30	50	60	80	120	200
144	Wilbert Robinson *	50	60	80	120	150	475	600	800
145	Bob Roth C.F.	20	25	30	50	60	80	120	200
146	Ed. Roush C.F.	60	80	100	150	200	250	400	800
147	Clarence Rowland *	20	25	30	50	60	80	120	200
148	Nap Rucker *	20	25	30	50	60	80	120	200
149	Dick Rudolph *	20	25	30	50	60	80	120	200
150	Reb Russell *	20	25	30	50	60	80	120	200
151	Babe Ruth *	35,000	50,000	60,000	65,000	80,000	120,000	200,000	
152	Vic Saier *	20	25	30	50	60	80	120	200
153	Slim Sallee *	20	25	30	50	60	80	120	200
154	Germany Schaefer	20	25	30	50	60	80	120	250
155	Ray Schalk	50	60	80	120	150	200	300	500
156	Walter Schang	20	25	30	50	60	80	120	200
157	Chas. Schmidt	20	25	30	50	60	80	120	200
158	Frank Schulte	20	25	30	50	60	80	120	200
159	Jim Scott	20	25	30	50	60	80	120	200
160	Everett Scott	20	25	30	50	60	80	120	200
161	Tom Seaton	20	25	30	50	60	80	120	200
162	Howard Shanks	20	25	30	50	60	80	120	200
163	Bob Shawkey UER Photo	20	25	30	50	60	80	120	200
164	Ernie Shore	20	25	30	50	60	80	120	200
165	Burt Shotton	20	25	30	50	60	80	120	200
166	Geo. Sisler P	60	80	100	150	200	250	1,200	1,600
167	J. Carlisle Smith	20	25	30	50	60	80	120	200
168	Fred Snodgrass	20	25	30	50	60	80	120	200
169	Geo. Stallings	20	25	30	50	60	80	120	200
170	Oscar Stanage UER Photo	20	25	30	50	60	80	120	200
171	Charles Stengel	200	250	300	500	1,400	1,600	2,000	2,600
172	Milton Stock	20	25	30	50	60	80	120	200
173	Amos Strunk UER Photo	20	25	30	50	60	80	120	200
174	Billy Sullivan	20	25	30	50	60	80	120	200
175	Jeff Tesreau	20	25	30	50	60	80	120	200
176	Jim Thorpe	2,500	3,000	4,000	5,000				
177	Joe Tinker	60	80	100	150	200	250	400	800
178	Fred Toney	20	25	30	50	60	80	120	200
179	Terry Turner 3rd B.	20	25	30	50	60	80	120	200
180	Jim Vaughn	20	25	30	50	60	80	120	200
181	Bob Veach	20	25	30	50	60	80	120	300
182	James Viox 2nd B.	20	25	30	50	60	80	120	200
183	Oscar Vitt	20	25	30	50	60	80	120	200
184	Hans Wagner	600	800	1,000	1,200	1,500	2,000	3,000	
185	Clarence Walker Browns UER Photo	20	25	30	50	60	80	120	200
186A	Zach Wheat	60	80	100	150	200	250	400	800
187	Ed. Walsh	60	80	100	150	200	250	400	800

#	Player	PrFr 1	GD 2	VG 3	VgEx 4	EX 5	ExMt 6	NM 7	NmMt 8
188	Buck Weaver S.S.	120	150	250	400	600			
189	Carl Weilman	20	25	30	50	60	80	120	200
190	Geo. Whitted Nat'ls	20	25	30	50	60	80	120	200
191	Fred Williams	20	25	30	50	60	80	120	200
192	Art Wilson	20	25	30	50	60	80	120	200
193	J. Owen Wilson	20	25	30	50	60	80	120	200
194	Ivy Wingo	20	25	30	50	60	80	120	200
195	Mel Wolfgang	20	25	30	50	60	80	120	200
196	Joe Wood	80	100	120	200	250	300	500	1,000
197	Steve Yerkes	20	25	30	50	60	80	120	200
198	Rollie Zeider *	20	25	30	50	60	80	120	200
199	Heiny Zimmerman *	20	25	30	50	60	80	120	200
200	Ed. Zwilling *	20	25	30	50	60	80	120	200

— Babe Ruth #151 PSA 7 (NrMt) sold for $200,169 (Goodwin; 1/12)

— Babe Ruth #151 SGC 5.5 (Ex+) sold for $84,000 (REA; Fall '14)

— George Sisler P #166 PSA 9 (MT) sold for $18,336 (Goodwin; 09/11)

— Jim Thorpe #176 PSA 6 (ExMt) sold for $11,511 (Goodwin; 03/12)

— Jim Thorpe #176 PSA 6 (ExMt) sold for $11,511 (Goodwin; 3/12)

1919-21 W514

#	Player	PrFr 1	GD 2	VG 3	VgEx 4	EX 5	ExMt 6	NM 7	NmMt 8
2	Babe Ruth	800	1,000	1,200	1,500	1,800	2,200		
15	Joe Jackson	800	1,000	2,000	2,200	2,500	3,000		
43	Ty Cobb	200	250	300	400	500	.800		
56	Rogers Hornsby	100	120	200	250	300	500		
72	Christy Mathewson	120	150	200	250	300	500		
94	Walter Johnson	100	120	300	350	400	600		

— Joe Jackson PSA 8 (NmMt) sold for $5,280 (Greg Bussineau; 12/12)

1921 E121 American Caramel Series of 80

#	Player	PrFr 1	GD 2	VG 3	VgEx 4	EX 5	ExMt 6	NM 7	NmMt
1A	G.C. Alexander Arms Above	200	250	300	500	800	1,200		
1B	Grover Alexander Arm Forward	200	250	300	500	800	1,200		
11A	Ty Cobb Look Ahead	300	500	600	1,000	1,200			
11B	Ty Cobb Look Right Manager	400	500	600	1,000	1,200			
11C	Ty Cobb Look Right Mgr.	300	500	600	1,000	2,000			
38	Rogers Hornsby	250	300	400	500	1,200			
43A	Walter Johnson Throwing	250	350	500	800	1,000			
43B	Walter Johnson Hands at Chest	250	350	500	800	1,000			
82A	Babe Ruth	2,500	8,000	10,000	12,000	10,000	12,000		
82B	Babe Ruth Babe in Quotations	2,000	4,000	10,000	12,000				
82C	George Ruth	1,500	2,000	25,000					
94A	Tris Speaker Manager Large	100	120	150	200	400			
94B	Tris Speaker Manager Small	100	120	150	200				
94C	Tris Speaker Mgr.	100	120	150	200	400			

— Ty Cobb #11C PSA 8 (NmMt) sold for $9,049 (Goodwin; 8/12)

— Babe Ruth SGC 86 (NM+) sold for $31,755 (Goodwin; 3/14)

1921 W551

#	Player	PrFr 1	GD 2	VG 3	VgEx 4	EX 5	ExMt 6	NM 7	NmM
4	Ty Cobb	200	250	350	400	500	800		
7	Babe Ruth	200	250	300	800	1,200			

— Babe Ruth PSA 9 (MT) sold for $8,075 (eBay; 2/13)

1922 E120 American Caramel Series of 240

#	Player	PrFr 1	GD 2	VG 3	VgEx 4	EX 5	ExMt 6	NM 7	NmM
42	Tris Speaker	100	120	150	300	400	500		
48	Ty Cobb	250	350	600	1,000	1,200	2,000		
71	Babe Ruth	1,500	3,000	5,000	8,000				
110	Walter Johnson	150	200	400	500	800	1,000		
152	Grover C. Alexander	150	200	300	500	600	1,000		
232	Rogers Hornsby	150	200	300	500	600			

1922 E121 American Caramel Series of 120

		PrFr 1	GD 2	VG 3	VgEx 4	EX 5	ExMt 6	NM 7	NmMt 8
2	Grover C. Alexander	120	150	200	350	500	800		
10A	Ty Cobb Batting	500	1,000	1,200	1,500	2,000			
10B	Ty Cobb Throwing	500	1,000	1,200	1,500	2,000			
45	Rogers Hornsby	150	250	450	600	800	1,200		
48	Walter Johnson	200	350	400	600	1,000	1,500		
36A	Babe Ruth Montage	1,000	1,500	3,000	4,000	5,000	6,000		
36B	Babe Ruth Montage (Quotations)	1,000	2,000	3,000	4,000	5,000	6,000		
36C	Babe Ruth Bird	600	1,000	2,000	2,500	4,000	5,000		
36D	Babe Ruth Bird (Quotations)	600	1,000	2,000	2,500	4,000	5,000		
36E	Babe Ruth Holding Ball	1,000	1,500	2,000	3,000	5,000	6,000		
102A	Tris Speaker Large Projection	120	150	200	300	500	800		
102B	Tris Speaker Small Projection	120	150	200	300	500	800		

1922 E122 American Caramel Series of 80

		PrFr 1	GD 2	VG 3	VgEx 4	EX 5	ExMt 6	NM 7	NmMt 8
	Grover C. Alexander	120	150	200	300	500	800		
1	Ty Cobb	300	400	500	800	1,200	2,000		
0	Rogers Hornsby	120	150	200	300	500	800		
2	Walter Johnson	150	200	250	400	600	1,000		
7	Babe Ruth	1,000	1,500	4,500					
7	Tris Speaker	120	150	200	300	500	800		

1923 W515-1

		PrFr 1	GD 2	VG 3	VgEx 4	EX 5	ExMt 6	NM 7	NmMt 8
	Babe Ruth	400	500	600	700	800	900	1,100	
7	Babe Ruth	400	500	600	700	800	900	1,100	

1925 Exhibits

		PrFr 1	GD 2	VG 3	VgEx 4	EX 5	ExMt 6	NM 7	NmMt 8
	Tyrus Cobb	80	120	200	300	500	800		
	Lou Gehrig	10,000	25,000	30,000	35,000	80,000			
0	Babe Ruth	800	1,200	1,500	2,500	4,000			

— Lou Gehrig #97 PSA 6 (ExMt) sold for $12,000 (Legendary; 8/12)

1927 W560 Black

		GD 2	VG 3	VgEx 4	EX 5	ExMt 6	NM 7	NmMt 8	MT 9
	Lou Gehrig	120	150	200	300	400	500	600	1,000
K	Babe Ruth	100	120	150	250	300	400	500	800

1932 U.S. Caramel

	PrFr 1	GD 2	VG 3	VgEx 4	EX 5	ExMt 6	NM 7	NmMt 8
Eddie Collins	150	200	250	300	400	600	1,200	5,000
Paul Waner	150	200	250	300	400	600	1,000	4,000
Bill Terry	150	200	250	300	400	600	1,700	
Earl Combs	200	250	300	400	500	600	1,000	
Bill Dickey	200	250	300	400	500	800	1,200	3,000
Joe Cronin	150	200	250	300	400	600	1,000	2,500
Chick Hafey	150	200	250	300	400	600	1,000	2,500
Rabbit Maranville	150	200	250	300	400	600	1,000	3,000
Rogers Hornsby	600	800	1,000	1,200	1,500	2,000	4,000	
Mickey Cochrane	200	250	300	400	500	800	1,200	3,000
Lloyd Waner	150	200	250	300	400	600	1,000	4,000
Ty Cobb	800	1,000	1,200	1,500	2,000	3,000	5,000	12,000
Al Simmons	150	200	250	400	500	800	1,200	3,000
Tony Lazzeri	200	250	300	400	500	800	1,200	3,000
Wally Berger	80	100	120	150	200	300	800	1,200
Red Ruffing	150	200	250	300	400	600	1,000	
Chuck Klein	150	200	250	300	400	600	1,000	4,500
Jimmie Foxx	400	600	800	1,000	1,200	2,500	4,000	5,000
Lefty O'Doul	120	150	200	250	350	500	800	1,500

		PrFr 1	GD 2	VG 3	VgEx 4	EX 5	ExMt 6	NM 7	NmMt 8
26	Lou Gehrig	2,000	2,500	3,000	5,000	8,000	10,000	15,000	20,000
27	Lefty Grove	500	600	800	1,000	1,200	1,500		
30	Frankie Frisch	200	250	300	400	500	800	1,200	3,000
31	Lefty Gomez	200	250	300	400	500	800	1,200	
32	Babe Ruth	2,000	2,500	5,000	8,000	10,000	12,000	15,000	25,000

— Cards are labeled by most grading companies as a 1932 release, but research indicates the set was most likely released in early 1933.

1933 DeLong

		PrFr 1	GD 2	VG 3	VgEx 4	EX 5	ExMt 6	NM 7	NmMt 8
1	Marty McManus	50	80	120	200	300	500	800	4,000
2	Al Simmons	100	150	200	250	400	500	1,500	4,000
3	Oscar Melillo	50	80	120	200	300	500	1,000	
4	Bill Terry	80	100	300	400	500	600	1,500	3,000
5	Charlie Gehringer	80	120	200	300	500	800	1,500	4,000
6	Mickey Cochrane	150	250	400	600	1,000	1,500	2,500	
7	Lou Gehrig	1,000	2,000	2,500	3,000	5,000	8,000	20,000	60,000
8	Kiki Cuyler	100	120	200	500	600	800	1,500	
9	Bill Urbanski	50	80	120	200	300	500	800	
10	Lefty O'Doul	80	100	150	200	250	500	800	3,000
11	Fred Lindstrom	80	100	120	200	500	600	1,500	8,000
12	Pie Traynor	80	150	200	300	500	800	1,500	2,500
13	Rabbit Maranville	120	200	300	500	800	1,200	2,000	4,000
14	Lefty Gomez	100	150	400	500	600	800	1,000	2,500
15	Riggs Stephenson	60	80	100	150	250	400	1,000	
16	Lon Warneke	60	80	100	200	250	400	1,000	
17	Pepper Martin	80	120	200	300	500	800	1,200	2,000
18	Jimmy Dykes	50	60	120	150	300	400	600	2,000
19	Chick Hafey	80	100	200	250	400	1,000	1,200	20,000
20	Joe Vosmik	50	60	150	200	250	400	1,000	
21	Jimmie Foxx	150	200	300	600	800	1,500	3,000	10,000
22	Chuck Klein	80	100	150	200	400	600	1,200	2,500
23	Lefty Grove	250	400	600	1,000	1,500	2,500	4,000	6,000
24	Goose Goslin	120	150	200	300	500	800	2,500	

— Lou Gehrig #7 SGC 7.5 (Nm+) sold for $12,925 (REA; 05/11)

1933 Goudey

		PrFr 1	GD 2	VG 3	VgEx 4	EX 5	ExMt 6	NM 7	NmMt 8
1	Benny Bengough	300	500	800	1,200	2,000	3,000	10,000	
2	Dazzy Vance	120	200	300	600	1,000	1,500	7,000	15,000
3	Hugh Critz Batting	25	40	60	100	150	250	1,000	8,000
4	Heinie Schuble	30	50	80	100	150	300	600	
5	Babe Herman	50	80	120	250	300	400		
6	Jimmy Dykes	30	50	80	120	200	300	500	
7	Ted Lyons	60	100	150	250	400	600	1,000	2,000
8	Roy Johnson	20	30	50	80	100	250	500	
9	Dave Harris	20	30	50	100	120	150	300	2,500
10	Glenn Myatt	25	40	60	100	250	400		
11	Billy Rogell	25	40	60	100	150	250	400	1,500
12	George Pipgras	40	60	100	150	250	400	800	
13	Lafayette Thompson	30	50	80	120	200	300	500	4,000
14	Henry Johnson	25	40	60	100	150	250	400	1,200
15	Victor Sorrell	25	40	60	100	120	150	600	
16	George Blaeholder	20	30	50	80	150	200	400	1,000
17	Watson Clark	20	30	50	100	120	150	800	
18	Muddy Ruel	20	30	50	80	120	150	400	
19	Bill Dickey	200	300	500	800	1,200	2,000	3,000	5,000
20	Bill Terry Throwing	60	100	150	250	400	500	800	3,000
21	Phil Collins	25	40	60	100	150	250	400	1,500
22	Pie Traynor	120	200	300	500	800	1,200	2,000	5,000
23	Kiki Cuyler	100	150	200	300	500	800	1,200	3,000
24	Horace Ford	30	50	80	120	200	300	500	
25	Paul Waner	150	250	400	600	1,000	1,500	2,500	8,000
26	Chalmer Cissell	15	25	40	60	100	150	500	
27	George Connally	25	40	60	100	150	250	400	2,000
28	Dick Bartell	25	40	60	100	120	200	500	
29	Jimmie Foxx	400	600	1,000	1,500	2,500	3,000	5,000	50,000

#	Player	PrFr 1	GD 2	VG 3	VgEx 4	EX 5	ExMt 6	NM 7	NmMt 8
30	Frank Hogan	15	25	40	60	120	200	500	3,000
31	Tony Lazzeri	150	250	400	600	1,000	1,500	2,000	6,000
32	Bud Clancy	25	40	60	100	150	250	400	2,000
33	Ralph Kress	20	30	50	80	100	200	300	
34	Bob O'Farrell	15	25	40	100	150	200	600	
35	Al Simmons	80	120	200	300	500	800	1,200	2,500
36	Tommy Thevenow	25	40	60	100	100	300	1,000	4,000
37	Jimmy Wilson	20	30	50	80	120	200	300	2,000
38	Fred Brickell	25	40	60	100	150	250	400	2,500
39	Mark Koenig	25	40	60	100	150	250	800	
40	Taylor Douthit	20	30	50	80	120	150	300	1,000
41	Gus Mancuso Catching	20	30	50	80	120	200	300	800
42	Eddie Collins	60	100	150	250	400	600	1,000	2,500
43	Lew Fonseca	25	40	60	100	150	250	400	600
44	Jim Bottomley	60	100	150	250	400	600	1,000	2,000
45	Larry Benton	20	30	50	80	120	200	400	4,000
46	Ethan Allen	20	30	50	80	150	200	400	800
47	Heinie Manush Batting	50	80	120	150	300	600	800	4,000
48	Marty McManus	25	40	60	100	150	250	400	
49	Frankie Frisch	120	200	300	500	800	1,200	2,000	20,000
50	Ed Brandt	20	30	50	80	100	200	300	800
51	Charlie Grimm	12	20	30	80	150	300	400	1,200
52	Andy Cohen	15	25	40	80	100	300		
53	Babe Ruth w/Bat Yellow	10,000	15,000	25,000	40,000	60,000	80,000	100,000	200,000
54	Ray Kremer	15	25	40	60	80	100	250	500
55	Pat Malone	20	30	50	60	100	150	600	
56	Red Ruffing	80	120	200	300	500	800	1,200	2,000
57	Earl Clark	15	25	40	60	80	120	250	800
58	Lefty O'Doul	20	30	50	120	150	200	300	1,000
59	Bing Miller	25	40	60	100	150	250	400	600
60	Waite Hoyt	60	100	150	250	400	600	1,000	1,500
61	Max Bishop	20	30	50	80	120	200	300	500
62	Pepper Martin	25	40	60	100	150	250	400	1,000
63	Joe Cronin w/Bat	50	80	120	200	300	500	800	2,000
64	Burleigh Grimes	60	100	150	250	400	600	1,000	1,500
65	Milt Gaston	15	25	40	50	100	120	200	400
66	George Grantham	10	15	25	50	80	120	200	600
67	Guy Bush	20	30	50	80	120	200	300	600
68	Horace Lisenbee	15	25	40	60	80	120	200	400
69	Randy Moore	12	20	30	60	100	120	200	800
70	Floyd (Pete) Scott	15	25	40	60	100	150	250	400
71	Robert J. Burke	15	25	40	80	100	150	200	800
72	Owen Carroll	15	25	40	60	100	150	250	800
73	Jesse Haines	60	100	150	250	400	600	1,000	1,500
74	Eppa Rixey	60	100	150	250	400	600	1,000	1,500
75	Willie Kamm	15	25	40	60	100	150	250	600
76	Mickey Cochrane	100	150	250	400	600	1,000	1,500	2,500
77	Adam Comorosky	20	30	50	80	120	200	300	600
78	Jack Quinn	20	30	50	60	100	150	250	600
79	Red Faber	40	80	120	200	300	500	800	1,200
80	Clyde Manion	10	15	25	50	100	120	250	800
81	Sam Jones	20	30	50	60	100	120	200	600
82	Dibrell Williams	10	15	25	50	80	100	200	800
83	Pete Jablonowski	25	40	50	60	100	120	200	1,500
84	Glenn Spencer	20	30	50	80	120	300	500	
85	Heinie Sand	10	15	25	50	120	200	300	600
86	Phil Todt	20	30	50	80	120	200	300	800
87	Frank O'Rourke	15	25	40	50	100	120	200	600
88	Russell Rollings	12	20	30	60	80	100	200	800
89	Tris Speaker	120	200	300	500	800	1,200	1,500	5,000
90	Jess Petty	25	40	60	100	150	250	400	1,000
91	Tom Zachary	20	30	50	60	80	120	200	500
92	Lou Gehrig	2,500	4,000	6,000	10,000	15,000	25,000	50,000	100,000
93	John Welch	25	40	60	100	150	250	400	600
94	Bill Walker	25	40	50	80	120	200	300	600
95	Alvin Crowder	20	30	50	80	120	200	300	500
96	Willis Hudlin	10	15	25	60	100	120	250	800
97	Joe Morrissey	15	25	40	60	80	100	250	1,200
98	Walter Berger	12	20	30	100	120	150	500	1,500
99	Tony Cuccinello	12	20	30	50	80	200	250	1,200
100	George Uhle	15	25	40	60	150	250	400	1,000
101	Richard Coffman	15	25	40	60	100	150	250	800
102	Travis Jackson	60	100	150	250	400	600	1,000	2,000
103	Earle Combs	60	100	150	250	400	600	1,000	2,000
104	Fred Marberry	30	50	80	120	200	300	500	800
105	Bernie Friberg	15	25	40	60	100	120	200	400
106	Napoleon Lajoie SP	15,000	25,000	40,000	50,000	60,000	80,000	100,000	150,000
107	Heinie Manush	40	60	100	120	250	300	400	1,500
108	Joe Kuhel	25	40	60	100	150	250	400	600
109	Joe Cronin w/Glove	40	60	100	120	200	300	600	1,500
110	Goose Goslin	40	60	100	150	200	250	500	2,000
111	Monte Weaver	20	30	50	80	120	250	400	600
112	Fred Schulte	15	25	40	80	100	200	250	500
113	Oswald Bluege Portrait	20	30	50	80	120	200	300	800
114	Luke Sewell Fieldin	20	30	50	60	120	200	300	800
115	Cliff Heathcote	25	40	60	100	150	250	400	600
116	Eddie Morgan	12	20	30	50	100	120	200	2,000
117	Rabbit Maranville	60	100	150	250	400	600	1,000	2,000
118	Val Picinich	30	50	80	120	200	300	500	1,000
119	Rogers Hornsby Fielding	200	300	500	600	1,000	1,200	2,000	12,000
120	Carl Reynolds	20	30	50	80	120	200	300	800
121	Walter Stewart	15	25	40	50	80	120	150	600
122	Alvin Crowder	10	15	25	80	100	120	200	500
123	Jack Russell	20	30	50	80	100	120	200	500
124	Earl Whitehill	15	25	40	60	120	150	200	1,000
125	Bill Terry	30	50	80	150	250	300	600	2,000
126	Joe Moore Batting	20	30	50	80	120	200	300	500
127	Melvin Ott Portrait	250	400	600	1,000	1,500	2,500	4,000	10,000
128	Chuck Klein	60	100	150	250	400	600	1,000	2,000
129	Harold Schumacher Pitching	25	40	60	100	150	250	400	1,000
130	Fred Fitzsimmons Portrait	15	25	40	60	100	120	250	1,200
131	Fred Frankhouse	25	40	60	100	150	250	400	600
132	Jim Elliott	20	30	50	80	120	200	300	1,200
133	Fred Lindstrom	60	100	150	250	400	600	1,000	2,000
134	Sam Rice	60	100	150	250	400	600	1,000	1,200
135	Woody English	10	15	25	50	100	120	300	800
136	Flint Rhem	25	30	50	80	120	200	300	800
137	Fred (Red) Lucas	20	30	50	60	120	200	250	800
138	Herb Pennock	80	120	200	300	500	800	1,200	2,000
139	Ben Cantwell	20	30	50	80	100	120	300	800
140	Bump Hadley	25	40	60	100	150	250	400	1,000
141	Ray Benge	15	25	40	60	100	150	300	1,500
142	Paul Richards	15	25	40	60	80	120	250	1,000
143	Glenn Wright	25	40	60	100	150	250	400	600
144	Babe Ruth Batting DP	6,000	10,000	15,000	25,000	40,000	60,000	80,000	300,000
145	George Walberg	12	20	30	60	100	120	300	800
146	Walter Stewart Pitching	15	325	40	60	100	150	300	1,500
147	Leo Durocher	50	80	120	150	250	500	600	1,500
148	Eddie Farrell	12	20	30	80	100	120	300	
149	Babe Ruth w/Bat Red	8,000	12,000	20,000	30,000	40,000	50,000	120,000	200,000
150	Ray Kolp	20	30	50	80	120	200	300	600
151	Jake Flowers	20	30	50	80	120	200	300	600
152	James (Zack) Taylor	15	25	40	50	100	120	200	800
153	Buddy Myer	15	25	40	50	100	200	400	
154	Jimmie Foxx	400	600	1,000	1,500	2,500	4,000	8,000	60,000
155	Joe Judge	30	50	80	120	200	300	500	800
156	Danny MacFayden	20	30	50	80	120	200	300	600
157	Sam Byrd	20	30	50	100	120	150	200	600
158	Moe Berg	250	400	600	800	1,000	1,200	1,500	2,500
159	Oswald Bluege Fielding	15	25	40	60	100	150	250	
160	Lou Gehrig	3,000	5,000	8,000	12,000	20,000	30,000	50,000	80,000
161	Al Spohrer	25	45	60	100	150	250	400	600
162	Leo Mangum	30	50	80	120	200	300	500	1,500
163	Luke Sewell Portrait	15	25	40	50	100	120	200	600
164	Lloyd Waner	150	250	400	600	1,000	1,500	2,500	4,000
165	Joe Sewell	50	80	120	200	250	400	500	1,500

#	Player	PrFr 1	GD 2	VG 3	VgEx 4	EX 5	ExMt 6	NM 7	NmMt 8
166	Sam West	25	40	60	100	150	250	400	1,000
167	Jack Russell	10	15	25	50	100	120	250	800
168	Goose Goslin	60	100	150	250	300	500	600	1,500
169	Al Thomas	15	25	40	60	80	100	200	500
170	Harry McCurdy	15	25	40	50	100	120	200	1,000
171	Charlie Jamieson	20	30	50	80	120	200	300	800
172	Billy Hargrave	12	20	30	50	80	120	250	500
173	Roscoe Holm	20	30	50	80	120	200	300	800
174	Warren (Curley) Ogden	15	25	40	60	100	150	250	800
175	Dan Howley MG	25	40	60	100	150	250	400	600
176	John Ogden	20	30	50	80	120	200	300	800
177	Walter French	20	30	50	80	120	200	300	1,000
178	Jackie Warner	15	25	40	60	100	150	250	1,500
179	Fred Leach	12	20	30	50	80	150	250	500
180	Eddie Moore	15	25	40	60	100	150	250	600
181	Babe Ruth Portrait Green	6,000	12,000	20,000	30,000	50,000	60,000	80,000	120,000
182	Andy High	25	40	60	100	150	250	400	600
183	George Walberg	15	25	40	60	80	120	250	600
184	Charley Berry	25	40	60	100	150	250	400	500
185	Bob Smith	20	30	50	80	120	200	300	600
186	John Schulte	20	30	50	80	120	200	300	800
187	Heinie Manush	40	60	100	150	200	250	500	1,200
188	Rogers Hornsby Pointing	120	200	300	500	600	1,200	1,500	3,500
189	Joe Cronin	40	60	100	200	250	300	800	2,500
190	Fred Schulte	10	15	25	50	80	120	200	600
191	Ben Chapman	15	25	40	60	100	150	250	1,000
192	Walter Brown	15	25	40	50	100	150	200	400
193	Lynford Lary	20	30	50	80	120	150	250	1,200
194	Earl Averill	60	100	150	250	400	600	1,000	1,200
195	Evar Swanson	12	20	30	80	100	120	300	1,500
196	Leroy Mahaffey	20	30	50	80	120	200	300	800
197	Rick Ferrell	80	120	200	300	500	800	1,200	2,000
198	Jack Burns	15	25	40	60	100	150	250	500
199	Tom Bridges	25	40	60	100	150	250	400	1,000
200	Bill Hallahan	25	40	60	100	150	250	400	600
201	Ernie Orsatti	25	40	60	100	150	250	400	600
202	Gabby Hartnett	60	100	150	250	300	400	800	3,000
203	Lon Warneke	15	25	40	50	80	150	250	800
204	Riggs Stephenson	10	15	25	60	100	150	200	400
205	Heinie Meine	20	30	50	80	120	200	300	500
206	Gus Suhr	10	15	25	60	80	120	300	600
207	Melvin Ott w/Bat	100	150	250	500	600	800	1,500	6,000
208	Bernie James	20	30	50	80	120	200	300	500
209	Adolfo Luque	15	25	40	60	80	120	300	1,000
210	Spud Davis	15	25	40	60	100	120	600	800
211	Hack Wilson	200	300	500	800	1,200	2,000	3,000	5,000
212	Billy Urbanski	25	40	60	100	150	250	400	600
213	Earl Adams	20	30	50	80	120	200	300	1,000
214	John Kerr	15	25	40	60	100	150	250	600
215	Russell Van Atta	15	25	40	60	100	150	250	600
216	Vernon Gomez	80	120	200	300	500	800	1,200	2,500
217	Frank Crosetti	40	60	100	150	250	400	600	2,000
218	Wes Ferrell	25	40	60	100	150	250	400	800
219	Mule Haas UER	10	15	25	60	150	200	250	800
220	Lefty Grove	200	300	500	800	1,200	2,000	3,000	5,000
221	Dale Alexander	10	15	25	60	100	120	300	2,000
222	Charley Gehringer	120	200	300	500	800	1,200	2,000	4,000
223	Dizzy Dean	300	500	800	1,200	2,000	3,000	5,000	8,000
224	Frank Demaree	20	30	50	80	120	200	300	600
225	Bill Jurges	10	15	25	50	100	120	250	600
226	Charley Root	50	80	120	200	300	500	800	1,200
227	Bill Herman	80	120	200	300	500	800	1,200	3,000
228	Tony Piet	15	25	40	60	80	120	400	600
229	Arky Vaughan	60	100	150	250	400	600	1,000	4,000
230	Carl Hubbell Pitching	80	120	200	300	500	600	1,200	4,000
231	Joe Moore w/Glove	12	20	30	60	100	150		
232	Lefty O'Doul	40	60	100	150	250	400	600	1,000
233	Johnny Vergez	20	30	50	80	120	200	300	1,500
234	Carl Hubbell Portrait	100	150	250	300	600	800	1,000	2,000
235	Fred Fitzsimmons Pitching	15	25	40	60	100	150	250	600
236	George Davis	20	30	50	80	120	200	300	1,000
237	Gus Mancuso Fielding	25	40	60	100	150	250	400	600
238	Hugh Critz Fielding	10	15	25	60	100	120	200	500
239	Leroy Parmelee	12	15	25	50	100	120	200	600
240	Harold Schumacher	20	30	50	80	120	200	500	2,000

— Ray Benge #141 PSA 9 (Mint) sold for $5,899 (Goodwin; 8/12)
— Benny Bengough #1 PSA 8 (NmMt) sold for $26,663 (REA; 5/13)
— Robert Burke #71 SGC 88 (NmMt) sold for $61,793 (Mile High; 10/12)
— Eddie Farrell #148 PSA 8.5 (NmMt+) sold for $6,302 (Mile High; 05/11)
— Lou Gehrig #92 PSA 9 (MT) sold for $50,000 (Memory Lane; Private Sale - 2007)
— Lou Gehrig #92 SGC 92 (NmMt+) sold for $17,000 (Legendary; 3/11)
— Lou Gehrig #92 SGC 92 (NmMt+) sold for $14,975 (Lelands; 12/12)
— Nap Lajoie #106 PSA 9 (MT) sold for $103,137 (Lelands; 12/12)
— Nap Lajoie #106 PSA 9 (MT) sold for $100,000 (REA; 05/12)
— Babe Ruth #53 SGC 86 (NM+) sold for $21,883 (Goodwin; 7/14)
— Babe Ruth #144 PSA 9 (MT) sold for $75,000 (Memory Lane; Private Sale - 2004)
— Babe Ruth #181 PSA 9 (MT) sold for $100,000 (Memory Lane; Private Sale - 2006)
— Babe Ruth #181 PSA 7.5 (NmMt+) sold for $10,073 (REA; 5/13)
— Al Simmons #35 PSA 8.5 (NmMt+) sold for $7,299 (Mile High; 05/11)

1933 Sport Kings

#	Player	PrFr 1	GD 2	VG 3	VgEx 4	EX 5	ExMt 6	NM 7	NmMt 8
1	Ty Cobb BB	500	1,000	1,200	2,000	3,000	4,000	6,000	12,000
2	Babe Ruth BB	1,200	2,500	3,000	4,000	8,000	10,000	12,000	40,000
42	Carl Hubbell BB	100	150	200	300	500	600	1,000	2,000

— Ed Wachter #5 PSA 8 (NmMt) sold for $2,100 (Bussineau; 7/13)

1933 Tattoo Orbit

#	Player	PrFr 1	GD 2	VG 3	VgEx 4	EX 5	ExMt 6	NM 7
1	Dale Alexander	30	40	50	100	150	300	
2	Ivy Andrews SP	60	80	100	150	250	400	
3	Earl Averill	60	80	100	150	250	400	600
4	Dick Bartell	20	30	40	60	100	150	300
5	Wally Berger	20	30	40	60	100	150	300
6	George Blaeholder SP	50	60	80	120	200	300	
7	Irving Burns	20	30	40	60	100	150	
8	Guy Bush	20	30	40	80	100	150	
9	Bruce Campbell	20	30	40	60	100	150	300
10	Chalmers Cissell	20	30	40	60	100	150	200
11	Watson Clark	20	30	40	80	100	150	
12	Mickey Cochrane	100	120	150	250	350	500	1,000
13	Phil Collins	20	30	40	60	100	150	
14	Kiki Cuyler	40	50	60	200	300	400	600
15	Dizzy Dean	120	150	200	500	600	800	1,500
16	Jimmy Dykes	20	30	40	60	100	150	300
17	George Earnshaw	30	40	50	60	100	150	300
18	Woody English	20	30	40	60	100	150	250
19	Lou Fonseca	20	30	40	60	100	150	250
20	Jimmy Foxx	120	150	200	400	500	800	2,000
21	Burleigh Grimes	40	50	60	100	150	250	600
22	Charlie Grimm	20	30	40	60	100	150	
23	Lefty Grove	80	100	150	200	300	400	800
24	Frank Grube	20	30	40	60	100	150	250
25	George Haas	20	30	40	60	100	150	300
26	Bump Hadley SP	60	80	100	150	250	400	
27	Chick Hafey	40	50	80		175	250	700
28	Jess Haines	40	50	60	100	150	250	500
29	Bill Hallahan	20	30	40	60	120	150	300
30	Mel Harder	20	30	40	60	100	150	300
31	Gabby Hartnett	40	60	100	150	250	400	800
32	Babe Herman	20	30	40	60	100	175	
33	Billy Herman	40	50	80	120	200	300	
34	Rogers Hornsby	120	150	200	350	400	600	1,500
35	Roy Johnson	20	30	40	80	100	200	
36	Smead Jolley	20	30	40	60	100	150	300

#	Player	PrFr 1	GD 2	VG 3	VgEx 4	EX 5	ExMt 6	NM 7	NmMt 8
37	Billy Jurges	20	30	40	60	100	150	300	
38	Willie Kamm	20	30	40	60	100	150		
39	Mark Koenig	20	30	40	60	100	150	300	
40	Jim Levey	20	30	40	60	100	200		
41	Ernie Lombardi	60	80	100	250	400	600	1,000	
42	Red Lucas	20	30	40	60	100	150	300	
43	Ted Lyons	40	50	100	120	200	250	400	
44	Connie Mack MG	100	120	150	250	300	500	800	
45	Pat Malone	30	40	50	60	100	150	300	
46	Pepper Martin	20	30	40	60	100	150		
47	Marty McManus	20	30	40	60	100	150	300	
48	Lefty O'Doul	20	30	40	60	100	150	450	
49	Dick Porter	20	30	40	60	100	150	300	
50	Carl N. Reynolds	20	30	40	80	100	150	300	
51	Charlie Root	20	30	40	60	100	150	300	
52	Bob Seeds	20	30	40	60	150	200	300	
53	Al Simmons	50	60	100	120	200	300	500	
54	Riggs Stephenson	30	40	50	60	100	150		
55	Lyle Tinning	20	30	40	60	100	150	300	
56	Joe Vosmik	20	30	40	60	100	150	300	
57	Rube Walberg	20	30	40	60	100	150	300	
58	Paul Waner	40	50	60	100	150	400	600	
59	Lon Warneke	20	30	40	60	100	150	300	
60	Arthur Whitney	20	30	40	60	80	120	300	

1934 Goudey

#	Player	PrFr 1	GD 2	VG 3	VgEx 4	EX 5	ExMt 6	NM 7	NmMt 8
1	Jimmie Foxx	400	600	1,000	1,500	2,500	4,000	6,000	12,000
2	Mickey Cochrane	80	120	200	300	500	800	1,200	4,000
3	Charlie Grimm	12	15	25	50	60	200	250	1,200
4	Woody English	12	15	20	30	60	120	250	1,200
5	Ed Brandt	10	12	15	30	80	100	150	
6	Dizzy Dean	200	300	500	800	1,200	2,000	3,000	5,000
7	Leo Durocher	60	100	150	250	400	600	1,000	2,500
8	Tony Piet	10	15	25	50	60	150	250	600
9	Ben Chapman	20	30	50	80	120	200	300	600
10	Chuck Klein	40	60	100	150	250	400	600	2,000
11	Paul Waner	50	80	100	120	200	250	600	1,500
12	Carl Hubbell	80	120	200	250	400	600	1,000	2,000
13	Frankie Frisch	50	80	120	200	300	500	800	1,000
14	Willie Kamm	12	20	30	50	80	100	200	600
15	Alvin Crowder	12	20	30	50	60	100	200	600
16	Joe Kuhel	10	15	25	40	60	100	150	500
17	Hugh Critz	10	12	15	60	80	150	200	400
18	Heinie Manush	30	50	80	120	200	300	500	1,200
19	Lefty Grove	150	250	400	600	1,000	1,500	2,500	5,000
20	Frank Hogan	10	12	15	50	60	80	150	600
21	Bill Terry	50	80	120	200	300	500	800	1,500
22	Arky Vaughan	30	50	80	120	200	300	500	1,000
23	Charley Gehringer	50	80	120	200	300	500	1,200	2,000
24	Ray Benge	10	12	15	60	80	120	250	
25	Roger Cramer	10	12	15	40	60	80	300	500
26	Gerald Walker	10	15	25	40	60	100	150	500
27	Luke Appling	60	100	150	250	300	500	600	5,000
28	Ed Coleman	10	15	25	40	60	100	200	500
29	Larry French	10	15	25	40	60	100	150	600
30	Julius Solters	10	15	25	40	60	100	150	500
31	Baxter Jordan	10	12	25	40	60	80	200	500
32	Blondy Ryan	10	12	20	40	60	80	200	650
33	Don Hurst	10	15	25	40	60	100	200	500
34	Chick Hafey	30	50	80	120	200	300	500	1,200
35	Ernie Lombardi	50	80	120	200	250	400	600	1,200
36	Walter Betts	12	20	30	50	80	120	200	500
37	Lou Gehrig	3,000	5,000	8,000	12,000	20,000	30,000	50,000	80,000
38	Oral Hildebrand	20	25	30	50	80	120	200	500
39	Fred Walker	10	12	15	60	80	100	150	500
40	John Stone	12	20	30	50	80	120	200	600

#	Player	PrFr 1	GD 2	VG 3	VgEx 4	EX 5	ExMt 6	NM 7	NmMt 8
41	George Earnshaw	12	20	30	50	80	120	200	600
42	John Allen	10	12	25	40	60	80	200	600
43	Dick Porter	10	12	20	30	80	100	250	
44	Tom Bridges	10	15	25	40	60	80	200	800
45	Oscar Melillo	15	25	40	60	100	150	250	500
46	Joe Stripp	10	12	15	40	80	100	200	800
47	John Frederick	12	20	30	50		120	250	2,000
48	Tex Carleton	15	20	40	50	80	100	300	1,000
49	Sam Leslie	10	25	40	60	80	100	200	600
50	Walter Beck	10	15	25	40	60	100	200	
51	Rip Collins	12	20	30	40	60	80	150	500
52	Herman Bell	10	15	25	40	60	80	150	500
53	George Watkins	20	30	50	80	120	200	300	
54	Wesley Schulmerich	12	20	30	50	80	120	200	500
55	Ed Holley	12	15	40	60	80		175	500
56	Mark Koenig	10	15	25	40	60	100	200	400
57	Bill Swift	12	20	30	50	80	120	200	500
58	Earl Grace	10	15	25	40	60	80	200	500
59	Joe Mowry	12	15	20	50	60	80	225	600
60	Lynn Nelson	10	15	25	40	60	100	150	500
61	Lou Gehrig	2,000	3,000	5,000	8,000	12,000	20,000	30,000	50,000
62	Hank Greenberg	500	800	1,200	2,000	3,000	5,000	10,000	15,000
63	Minter Hayes	15	25	50	60	80	100	120	500
64	Frank Grube	12	20	30	50	80	100	200	
65	Cliff Bolton	15	25	50	60	80	100	200	500
66	Mel Harder	12	15	20	60	80	150	300	600
67	Bob Weiland	12	20	30	50	80	120	200	
68	Bob Johnson	15	25	40	60	100	150	250	1,000
69	John Marcum	12	15	20	40	60	80	150	500
70	Pete Fox	10	15	25	40	60	100	300	800
71	Lyle Tinning	12	20	30	50	80	120	250	800
72	Arndt Jorgens	10	15	25	40	60	120	200	300
73	Ed Wells	15	25	40	60	120	200	300	600
74	Bob Boken	20	30	40	60	100	150	250	600
75	Bill Werber	20	30	50	80	120	200	300	800
76	Hal Trosky	25	60	100	120	200	250	300	800
77	Joe Vosmik	20	30	50	80	120	200	300	800
78	Pinky Higgins	20	30	50	80	120	200	300	800
79	Eddie Durham	20	30	50	80	120	200	300	600
80	Marty McManus	20	30	40	60	200	250	300	800
81	Bob Brown	30	50	80	120	200	300	500	800
82	Bill Hallahan	20	30	50	80	120	200	250	600
83	Jim Mooney	20	30	40	80	120	150	250	600
84	Paul Derringer	20	30	40	60	150	200	400	600
85	Adam Comorosky	25	40	60	100	150	250	400	600
86	Lloyd Johnson	15	25	40	60	100	200	300	600
87	George Darrow	20	30	50	100	120	200	250	600
88	Homer Peel	20	30	50	80	120	200	250	600
89	Linus Frey	50	60	80	100	120	150	250	600
90	KiKi Cuyler	100	150	250	400	600	1,000	1,500	2,500
91	Dolph Camilli	25	40	60	100	150	250	400	600
92	Steve Larkin	30	50	80	120	200	300	500	
93	Fred Ostermueller	20	30	50	80	120	250	400	600
94	Red Rolfe	30	50	80	120	200	300	500	1,000
95	Myril Hoag	15	25	40	80	150	200	300	1,200
96	James DeShong	60	100	150	250	400	600	1,000	1,500

— Lou Gehrig #37 SGC 98 (Gem) sold for $125,332 (SCP; 8/13)
— Lou Gehrig #37 SGC 96 (MT) sold for $54,609 (Goodwin; 03/12)
— Lou Gehrig #37 SGC 96 (Mint) sold for $54,609 (Goodwin; 3/12)
— Lou Gehrig #61 PSA 9 (MT) sold for $50,000 (Memory Lane; Private Sale - 2007)
— Lou Gehrig #37 PSA 6.5 (ExMt+) sold for $7,299 (Goodwin; 6/12)
— Joe Kuhel #16 PSA 9 (MT) sold for $5,836 (Goodwin; 03/12)
— Joe Kuhel #16 PSA 9 (Mint) sold for $5,836 (Goodwin; 3/12)

1934-36 Batter-Up

		PrFr 1	GD 2	VG 3	VgEx 4	EX 5	ExMt 6	NM 7	NmMt 8
1	Wally Berger	10	12	15	25	50	100	200	
2	Ed Brandt	10	12	15	25	40	60	150	
3	Al Lopez	15	20	25	40	60	120	250	
4	Dick Bartell	10	12	15	25	40	60	150	
5	Carl Hubbell	30	40	50	80	100	200	400	
6	Bill Terry	25	30	40	60	100	200	400	
7	Pepper Martin	10	12	15	25	40	60	150	
8	Jim Bottomley	15	20	25	40	60	120	250	
9	Tommy Bridges	10	12	15	25	40	60	150	
10	Rick Ferrell	15	20	25	40	60	120	250	
11	Ray Benge	10	12	15	25	40	60	150	
12	Wes Ferrell	10	12	15	25	40	60	150	
13	Chalmer Cissell	10	12	15	25	40	60	150	
14	Pie Traynor	25	30	40	60	100	200	400	
15	Leroy Mahaffey	10	12	15	25	40	60	150	
16	Chick Hafey	15	20	25	40	60	120	250	
17	Lloyd Waner	15	20	25	40	60	120	250	
18	Jack Burns	10	12	15	25	40	60	150	
19	Buddy Myer	10	12	15	25	40	60	150	
20	Bob Johnson	10	12	15	25	40	60	150	
21	Arky Vaughan	15	20	25	40	60	120	250	
22	Red Rolfe	10	12	15	25	40	60	150	
23	Lefty Gomez	25	30	40	80	100	200	500	
24	Earl Averill	25	30	40	60	80	150	250	
25	Mickey Cochrane	25	30	40	60	100	200	400	
26	Van Lingle Mungo	10	12	15	25	40	60	150	
27	Mel Ott	40	50	80	100	200	300	600	
28	Jimmie Foxx	60	80	100	150	250	500	800	
29	Jimmy Dykes	10	12	15	25	40	60	150	
30	Bill Dickey	40	50	80	100	150	250	500	
31	Lefty Grove	40	60	80	100	150	250	500	
32	Joe Cronin	25	30	40	60	100	200	400	
33	Frankie Frisch	25	30	40	60	100	200	400	
34	Al Simmons	25	30	40	60	100	200	400	
35	Rogers Hornsby	60	80	150	200	250	500	800	
36	Ted Lyons	15	20	25	40	60	120	250	
37	Rabbit Maranville	15	20	25	60	60	120	325	
38	Jimmy Wilson	10	12	15	25	40	60	150	
39	Willie Kamm	10	12	15	25	40	60	150	
40	Bill Hallahan	10	12	15	25	40	60	150	
41	Gus Suhr	10	12	15	25	40	60	150	
42	Charley Gehringer	25	30	40	60	150	300	500	
43	Joe Heving	10	12	15	25	40	60	150	
44	Adam Comorosky	10	12	15	25	40	60	150	
45	Tony Lazzeri	25	30	40	60	150	300	500	
46	Sam Leslie	10	12	15	25	40	60	150	
47	Bob Smith	10	12	15	25	40	60	150	
48	Willis Hudlin	10	12	15	25	40	60	150	
49	Carl Reynolds	10	12	15	25	40	60	150	
50	Fred Schulte	10	12	15	25	40	60	150	
51	Cookie Lavagetto	10	12	15	25	40	60	150	
52	Hal Schumacher	10	12	15	25	40	60	150	
53	Roger Cramer	10	12	15	25	40	60	150	
54	Sylvester Johnson	10	12	15	25	40	60	150	
55	Ollie Bejma	10	12	15	25	40	60	150	
56	Sam Byrd	10	12	15	25	40	60	150	
57	Hank Greenberg	80	100	120	200	400	900	1,200	
58	Bill Knickerbocker	10	12	15	25	40	60	150	
59	Bill Urbanski	10	12	15	25	40	60	150	
60	Eddie Morgan	10	12	15	25	40	60	150	
61	Rabbit McNair	10	12	15	25	40	60	150	
62	Ben Chapman	10	12	15	25	40	100		
63	Roy Johnson	10	12	15	25	40	80	150	
64	Dizzy Dean	60	80	120	150	250	500	800	
65	Zeke Bonura	10	12	15	25	40	60	150	
66	Fred Marberry	10	12	15	25	40	60	150	
67	Gus Mancuso	10	12	15	25	40	60	150	
68	Joe Vosmik	10	12	15	25	40	60	150	
69	Earl Grace RC	10	12	15	25	40	60	150	
70	Tony Piet	10	12	15	25	40	60	150	
71	Rollie Hemsley	10	12	15	25	40	60	150	
72	Fred Fitzsimmons	10	12	15	25	50	80	150	
73	Hack Wilson	25	30	40	80	100	250	400	
74	Chick Fullis	10	12	15	25	40	60	150	
75	Fred Frankhouse	10	12	15	25	40	60	150	
76	Ethan Allen	10	12	15	25	40	60	150	
77	Heinie Manush	15	20	25	40	60	120	250	
78	Rip Collins	10	12	15	25	40	60	150	
79	Tony Cuccinello	10	12	15	25	40	60	150	
80	Joe Kuhel	10	12	15	25	40	60	150	
81	Tommy Bridges	20	25	30	100	120	150	250	
82	Clint Brown	20	25	30	50	80	150	250	
83	Albert Blanche	20	25	30	50	80	150	250	
84	Boze Berger	20	25	30	50	80	150	250	
85	Goose Goslin	25	30	40	60	100	200	400	
86	Lefty Gomez	30	40	50	80	120	250	500	
87	Joe Glenn	20	25	30	50	80	150	250	
88	Cy Blanton	20	25	30	50	80	150	250	
89	Tom Carey	20	25	30	50	80	150	250	
90	Ralph Birkofer	20	25	30	50	80	150	250	
91	Fred Gabler	20	25	30	50	80	150	250	
92	Dick Coffman	20	25	30	50	80	150	250	
93	Ollie Bejma	20	25	30	50	80	150	250	
94	Leroy Parmelee	20	25	30	50	80	150	250	
95	Carl Reynolds	20	25	30	50	80	150	250	
96	Ben Cantwell	20	25	30	50	80	150	250	
97	Curtis Davis	20	25	30	50	100	150	250	
98	E. Webb/W. Moses	20	25	30	50	80	150	250	
99	Ray Benge	20	25	30	50	80	150	250	
100	Pie Traynor	25	30	40	60	100	200	400	
101	Phil Cavarretta	20	25	30	50	80	150	250	
102	Pep Young	20	25	30	50	80	150	250	
103	Willis Hudlin	20	25	30	50	80	150	425	
104	Mickey Haslin	20	25	30	50	80	150	250	
105	Ossie Bluege	20	25	30	50	80	150	250	
106	Paul Andrews	20	25	30	50	80	150	250	
107	Ed Brandt	20	25	30	50	80	150	250	
108	Don Taylor	20	25	30	50	80	200	300	
109	Thornton Lee	20	25	30	50	80	150	250	
110	Hal Schumacher	20	25	30	50	80	150	250	
111	F.Hayes/T.Lyons	25	30	40	60	100	250		
112	Odell Hale	20	25	30	50	80	150	250	
113	Earl Averill	25	30	40	60	120	200	400	
114	Italo Chelini	20	25	30	50	80	150	250	
115	I.Andrews/J.Bottomley	25	30	40	60	100	200	400	
116	Bill Walker	20	25	30	50	100	150	250	
117	Bill Dickey	80	100	120	175	250	500	1,000	
118	Gerald Walker	20	25	30	60	80	150	250	
119	Ted Lyons	25	30	40	60	100	200	400	
120	Eldon Auker	20	25	30	50	80	100	250	
121	Bill Hallahan	20	25	30	50	80	150	250	
122	Fred Lindstrom	25	30	40	60	100	200	400	
123	Oral Hildebrand	20	25	30	50	80	150	250	
124	Luke Appling	40	50	100	200	250	300	600	
125	Pepper Martin	20	25	30	50	80	150	250	
126	Rick Ferrell	25	30	40	60	100	200	400	
127	Ival Goodman	20	25	30	50	80	150	250	
128	Joe Kuhel	20	25	30	50	80	150	250	
129	Ernie Lombardi	25	30	40	60	100	200	400	

#	Name	PrFr 1	GD 2	VG 3	VgEx 4	EX 5	ExMt 6	NM 7	NmMt 8
130	Charley Gehringer	40	50	60	100	150	300	600	
131	Van Lingle Mungo	20	25	30	50	80	150	250	
132	Larry French	20	25	30	50	80	150	250	
133	Buddy Myer	20	25	30	50	80	150	250	
134	Mel Harder	20	25	30	50	100	150	250	
135	Augie Galan	20	25	30	50	80	150	525	
136	Gabby Hartnett	25	30	40	60	100	200	400	
137	Stan Hack	20	25	30	50	80	150	250	
138	Billy Herman	25	30	40	100	120	200	400	
139	Bill Jurges	20	25	30	50	80	150	250	
140	Bill Lee	20	25	30	50	80	150	250	
141	Zeke Bonura	20	25	30	50	80	150	250	
142	Tony Piet	20	25	30	50	80	150	250	
143	Paul Dean	25	30	40	100	150	200	400	
144	Jimmie Foxx	80	100	120	200	300	500	1,000	
145	Joe Medwick	30	50	60	80	120	250	500	
146	Rip Collins	20	25	30	50	80	150	250	
147	Mel Almada	20	25	30	50	80	150	250	
148	Allan Cooke	20	25	30	50	80	150	250	
149	Moe Berg	100	120	150	250	400	600	1,600	
150	Dolph Camilli	20	25	30	50	80	150	250	
151	Oscar Melillo	20	25	30	60	100	150	250	
152	Bruce Campbell	20	25	30	50	80	150	250	
153	Lefty Grove	60	100	120	200	250	400	950	
154	Johnny Murphy	20	25	30	50	80	150	250	
155	Luke Sewell	20	25	30	50	80	150	250	
156	Leo Durocher	25	30	40	60	100	200	400	
157	Lloyd Waner	25	30	40	80	100	200	500	
158	Guy Bush	20	25	30	50	100	150	250	
159	Jimmy Dykes	20	25	30	50	80	150	250	
160	Steve O'Neill	20	25	30	50	80	150	300	
161	General Crowder	20	25	30	50	80	150	250	
162	Joe Cascarella	20	25	30	80	100	150	250	
163	Daniel Hafey	20	25	30	50	80	150	250	
164	Gilly Campbell	20	25	30	50	80	150	250	
165	Ray Hayworth	20	25	30	50	120	150	275	
166	Frank Demaree	20	25	30	50	80	150	250	
167	John Babich	20	25	30	50	100	150	300	
168	Marvin Owen	20	25	30	50	80	150	250	
169	Ralph Kress	20	25	30	50	80	150	250	
170	Mule Haas	20	25	30	50	80	150	250	
171	Frank Higgins	20	25	50	60	80	150	250	
172	Wally Berger	20	25	30	100	120	150	250	
173	Frankie Frisch	40	50	60	100	150	300	600	
174	Wes Ferrell	20	25	30	50	80	150	250	
175	Pete Fox	20	25	30	50	80	150	250	
176	John Vergez	20	25	30	50	80	150	250	
177	Billy Rogell	20	25	30	50	80	150	300	
178	Don Brennan	20	25	30	50	80	150	250	
179	Jim Bottomley	25	30	40	60	100	200	400	
180	Travis Jackson	25	30	40	60	100	200	400	
181	Red Rolfe	20	25	30	50	80	150	250	
182	Frank Crosetti	25	30	40	60	100	200	400	
183	Joe Cronin	25	30	40	60	100	200	400	
184	Schoolboy Rowe	20	25	30	60	80	150	300	
185	Chuck Klein	30	40	50	150	200	250	500	
186	Lon Warneke	20	25	30	50	80	150	250	
187	Gus Suhr	20	25	30	50	80	150	250	
188	Ben Chapman	20	25	30	50	80	150	275	
189	Clint Brown	20	25	30	50	80	150	250	
190	Paul Derringer	20	25	30	50	80	150	250	
191	John Burns	20	25	30	50	80	150	250	500
192	John Broaca	25	30	40	60	100	200	400	

1934-36 Diamond Stars

#	Name	PrFr 1	GD 2	VG 3	VgEx 4	EX 5	ExMt 6	NM 7	NmMt 8
1	Lefty Grove	100	250	500	800	1,200	1,500	5,000	20,000
2A	Al Simmons Sox Insignia	30	40	80	100	120	200	500	
2B	Al Simmons No Insignia	30	40	50	80	120	200	600	
3	Rabbit Maranville	30	40	60	100	150	200	500	1,200
4	Buddy Myer	10	12	15	25	80	120	300	800
5	Tom Bridges	10	12	15	25	150	250	350	600
6	Max Bishop	10	12	15	25	60	80	150	500
7	Lew Fonseca	12	15	20	40	50	80	200	850
8	Joe Vosmik	8	10	12	20	35	80	150	300
9	Mickey Cochrane	30	40	80	150	200	400	600	1,200
10A	Roy Mahaffey A's Insignia	8	10	12	20	35	80	200	300
11	Bill Dickey	40	80	80	100	300	400	500	1,200
12A	Dixie Walker 1934 Green Back	8	10	12	20	35	60	120	400
12B	Dixie Walker 1935 Green Back	8	10	12	20	35	60	150	
13	George Blaeholder	12	15	20	30	50	80	200	1,500
14	Bill Terry	30	40	80	150	200	250	600	2,000
15A	Dick Bartell Phillies on Back	10	12	15	25	60	100	250	
16	Lloyd Waner	20	30	60	80	100	250	500	800
17	Frankie Frisch	25	40	50	80	100	300	400	1,000
18	Chick Hafey	20	25	30	80	100	200	300	1,500
19	Van Mungo	15	20	25	60	100	150	300	1,200
20	Shanty Hogan	8	10	12	20	35	60	120	400
21A	Johnny Vergez Giants on back	8	10	12	25	35	100	250	
22	Jimmy Wilson	8	10	12	20	35	60	120	400
23	Bill Hallahan	8	10	12	20	35	60	200	
24	Sparky Adams	8	10	12	20	35	100	120	400
25	Wally Berger	8	10	12	20	35	50	120	300
26	Pepper Martin	12	15	20	60	120	150	200	350
27	Pie Traynor	25	30	40	80	120	200	350	600
28	Al Lopez	12	15	20	60	100	120	200	650
29	Robert Rolfe	10	12	15	25	40	60	100	300
30A	Heinie Manush W on Sleeve	15	20	25	60	100	120	250	600
31A	Kiki Cuyler Cubs	15	20	25	50	100	150	200	500
31B	Kiki Cuyler Reds	15	20	25	40	100	150	200	500
32	Sam Rice	12	15	20	40	80	120	200	400
33	Schoolboy Rowe	6	8	10	15	30	100	120	250
34	Stanley Hack	6	8	10	15	25	80	150	250
35	Earle Averill	12	15	20	60	80	120	200	400
36A	Earnie Lombardi ERR	20	25	30	80	120	150	350	700
36B	Ernie Lombardi COR	20	25	30	50	80	150	250	
37	Billy Urbanski	6	8	10	20	30	50	100	150
38	Ben Chapman	6	8	10	30	50	60	150	250
39	Carl Hubbell	30	40	50	100	120	200	300	700
40	Blondy Ryan	6	8	10	15	25	40	80	225
41	Harvey Hendrick	6	8	10	15	25	40	80	200
42	Jimmy Dykes	6	8	10	30	60	80	120	400
43	Ted Lyons	12	15	30	40	80	120	200	500
44	Rogers Hornsby	80	100	150	200	250	300	500	1,200
45	Jo Jo White	15	20	25	40	50	60	80	120
46	Red Lucas	6	8	10	15	25	40	80	200
47	Bob Bolton	6	8	10	15	25	60	100	150
48	Rick Ferrell	12	15	20	30	100	150	200	500
49	Buck Jordan	6	8	10	15	25	60	100	200
50	Mel Ott	60	80	120	150	200	300	800	1,000
51	Burgess Whitehead	6	8	10	15	25	80	80	200
52	George Stainback	6	8	10	15	25	40	100	200
53	Oscar Melillo	6	8	10	15	25	40	100	200
54A	Hank Greenburg ERR	120	150	200	500	800	1,200	1,500	
54B	Hank Greenberg COR	80	100	150	200	250	600	800	2,000
55	Tony Cuccinello	12	15	20	30	50	100	150	250
56	Gus Suhr	10	12	15	40	60	80	120	300
57	Cy Blanton	6	8	10	15	25	40	80	200
58	Glenn Myatt	8	10	12	20	30	50	120	300
59	Jim Bottomley	20	25	30	40	80	100	150	500

		PrFr 1	GD 2	VG 3	VgEx 4	EX 5	ExMt 6	NM 7	NmMt 8
60	Red Ruffing	20	25	30	60	100	200	250	600
61	Bill Werber	6	8	10	15	25	60	100	300
62	Fred Frankhouse	6	8	10	15	25	60	150	300
63	Stonewall Jackson	15	20	25	40	80	100	150	500
64	Jimmie Foxx	60	80	150	200	300	500	600	1,200
65	Zeke Bonura	6	8	10	15	25	40	80	300
66	Ducky Medwick	60	80	100	120	250	300	350	800
67	Marvin Owen	6	8	10	15	25	80	100	300
68	Sam Leslie	6	8	10	15	25	40	100	250
69	Earl Grace	6	8	10	15	25	40	80	200
70	Hal Trosky	6	8	10	15	50	60	100	500
71	Ossie Bluege	6	8	10	15	25	60	80	200
72	Tony Piet	6	8	10	15	25	40	100	200
73	Fritz Ostermueller	6	8	10	15	30	60	80	200
74	Tony Lazzeri	30	40	50	120	200	300	400	800
75	Irving Burns	10	12	15	25	40	80	120	200
76	Billy Rogell	6	8	10	15	25	50	80	250
77	Charlie Gehringer	40	80	100	120	150	300	400	1,000
78	Joe Kuhel	6	8	10	15	40	60	120	200
79	Willis Hudlin	6	8	10	15	50	80	100	300
80	Lou Chiozza	6	8	10	15	30	60	120	200
81	Bill Delancey	10	12	15	25	40	60	150	300
82A	John Babich Dodgers Insignia	6	8	10	15	25	80	120	200
82B	John Babich No Insignia	6	8	10	15	25	40	80	200
83	Paul Waner	25	30	40	80	150	300	500	800
84	Sam Byrd	12	15	20	30	50	80	100	
85	Julius Solters	12	15	20	40	60	80	150	400
86	Frank Crosetti	20	25	50	60	80	200	300	800
87	Steve O'Neil MG	12	15	20	30	50	80	150	300
88	George Selkirk	12	15	20	40	60	120	150	400
89	Joe Stripp	12	15	20	30	60	120	150	400
90	Ray Hayworth	12	15	20	30	50	80	150	400
91	Bucky Harris MG	25	30	60	80	100	200	400	1,000
92	Ethan Allen	12	15	20	30	50	100	200	400
93	Alvin Crowder	12	15	20	40	80	100	150	400
94	Wes Ferrell	12	15	20	30	60	80	150	500
95	Luke Appling	30	40	50	80	120	300	400	1,200
96	Lew Riggs	12	15	20	50	80	100	250	400
97	Al Lopez	60	80	100	150	250	500	800	2,000
98	Schoolboy Rowe	50	60	80	150	200	300	500	1,500
99	Pie Traynor	60	80	120	150	300	400	800	2,600
100	Earle Averill	60	80	100	150	250	400	800	1,600
101	Dick Bartell	40	50	60	100	200	400	500	1,000
102	Van Mungo	40	50	60	120	200	300	500	1,500
103	Bill Dickey	150	200	250	300	450	600	1,200	
104	Robert Rolfe	40	50	60	120	150	250	500	1,000
105	Ernie Lombardi	60	80	100	250	350	400	700	2,700
106	Red Lucas	50	60	80	120	200	400	700	1,500
107	Stanley Hack	50	60	80	120	200	300	600	
108	Wallter Berger	50	60	80	300	350	400	800	2,500

— Jimmie Foxx #64 PSA 9 (MT) sold for $17,456 (Goodwin; 7/13)

1935 Goudey 4-in-1

	PrFr 1	GD 2	VG 3	VgEx 4	EX 5	ExMt 6	NM 7	NmMt 8
-Jan Berry/Burk/Kres/Vance 2C SP	20	25	30	50	80	150	300	
-Jan Berry/Burk/Kres/Vance 4C	15	20	25	40	60	150	6,000	
-Jan Berry/Burk/Kres/Vance 7C	15	20	25	50	60	120	300	
-Feb Burns/Hems/Grub/Weil 8C	15	20	25	40	60	120		
-Feb Burns/Hems/Grub/Weil 9C	15	20	25	40	60	120		
-Mar Campbell/Mey/Good/Kamp 8D	15	20	25	40	60	120		
-Mar Campbell/Mey/Good/Kamp 9D	15	20	25	40	60	120		
-Apr Cochrane/Gehr/Brid/Rog 1D	25	30	40	80	100	250	600	
-Apr Cochrane/Gehr/Brid/Rog 2D	25	30	40	60	100	250	600	
-Apr Cochrane/Gehr/Brid/Rog 6D SP	30	40	50	80	120	300	800	
-Apr Cochrane/Gehr/Brid/Rog 7D SP	40	40	50	80	120	300	800	
-May Critz/Bartell/Ott/Manc 2A SP	30	40	50	80	150	250	2,000	
-May Critz/Bartell/Ott/Manc 4A	25	30	40	80	120	200	600	
7-May Critz/Bartell/Ott/Manc 7A	25	30	40	60	120	200	600	
1-Jun Cronin/Reyn/Bish/Ciss 1G SP	20	25	30	50	100	250		
3-Jun Cronin/Reyn/Bish/Ciss 3E SP	20	25	30	50	100	200		
5-Jun Cronin/Reyn/Bish/Ciss 5E SP	20	25	30	50	100	200		
6-Jun Cronin/Reyn/Bish/Ciss 6E	15	20	25	40	100	120		
8-Jul DeShong/Allen/Rolfe/Walk 8E	15	20	25	40	60	120		
9-Jul DeShong/Allen/Rolfe/Walk 9E	15	20	25	40	60	120		
1-Aug Earn/Dyk/Sew/Appling 1I	15	20	25	40	60	120	400	
2-Aug Earn/Dyk/Sew/Appling 2F	15	20	25	40	60	120	600	
6-Aug Earn/Dyk/Sew/Appling 6F SP	20	25	30	50	100	200	500	
7-Aug Earn/Dyk/Sew/Appling 7F SP	20	25	30	50	100	200	500	
8-Sep Fox/Greenberg/Walk/Rowe 8F	50	60	80	100	250	400	1,000	
9-Sep Fox/Greenberg/Walk/Rowe 9F	50	60	80	100	250	400	1,000	
1-Oct Frisch/Dean/Ors/Carl 1A	50	80	100	150	200	400	2,000	
2-Oct Frisch/Dean/Ors/Carl 2A	50	60	80	100	200	400	1,000	
6-Oct Frisch/Dean/Ors/Carl 6A SP	60	80	100	120	250	500	1,500	
7-Oct Frisch/Dean/Ors/Carl 7A SP	60	80	100	120	250	500	1,500	
1-Nov Grimes/Klein/Cuyl/Eng 1F	25	30	40	80	120	250	600	
3-Nov Grimes/Klein/Cuyl/Eng 3D	25	30	40	60	120	250	600	
4-Nov Grimes/Klein/Cuyl/Eng 4D SP	30	40	50	80	150	300	800	
5-Nov Grimes/Klein/Cuyl/Eng 5D SP	30	40	50	80	150	300	800	
8-Dec Hayes/Lyons/Haas/Bon 8B	15	20	25	40	80	120	300	
9-Dec Hayes/Lyons/Haas/Bon 9B	15	20	25	40	60	120	300	
13-8 Herman/Suhr/Padd/Blant 8K	15	20	25	40	60	120		
13-9 Herman/Suhr/Padd/Blant 9K	15	20	25	40	60	120		
14-1 Hudlin/Myatt/Com/Bottomley 1K SP	20	25	30	50	80	150		
14-3 Hudlin/Myatt/Com/Bottomley 3B SP	20	25	30	50	80	150		
14-5 Hudlin/Myatt/Com/Bottomley 5B	15	20	25	40	60	120		
14-6 Hudlin/Myatt/Com/Bottomley 6B	15	20	25	40	60	150		
15-8 Johnson/Cole/Marc/Cramer 8J	15	20	25	40	60	120	300	
15-9 Johnson/Cole/Marc/Cramer 9J	15	20	25	40	60	120	400	
16-1 Kamm/Hild/Averill/Tro 1L	15	20	25	40	80	200	500	
16-2 Kamm/Hild/Averill/Tro 2E	15	20	25	50	60	200	500	
16-6 Kamm/Hild/Averill/Tro 6E SP	20	25	30	50	80	250	600	
16-7 Kamm/Hild/Averill/Tro 7E SP	20	25	30	50	80	250	600	
17-8 Koenig/Fitz/Benge/Zach 8A	15	20	25	40	60	120		
17-8 Koenig/Fitz/Benge/Zach 8M	15	20	25	40	60	120		
18-8 Kuhel/White/Myer/Stone 8H	15	20	25	40	60	120		
18-9 Kuhel/White/Myer/Stone 9H	15	20	25	40	60	120		
19-1 Leslie/Frey/Stripp/Clark 1G	15	20	25	40	80	120		
19-3 Leslie/Frey/Stripp/Clark 3E	15	20	25	40	60	120	300	
19-4 Leslie/Frey/Stripp/Clark 4E SP	20	25	30	50	80	150	400	
19-5 Leslie/Frey/Stripp/Clark 5E	15	20	25	40	60	120	300	
20-1 Mahaffey/Foxx/Will/Hig 1B	30	40	80	100	150	300	800	
20-2 Mahaffey/Foxx/Will/Hig 2B	30	40	50	120	150	300	2,000	
20-6 Mahaffey/Foxx/Will/Hig 6B SP	50	60	80	100	200	400	1,000	
20-7 Mahaffey/Foxx/Will/Hig 7B SP	50	60	80	100	200	400	1,000	
21-1 Manush/Lary/Weav/Had 1C	15	20	25	40	60	120	500	
21-2 Manush/Lary/Weav/Had 2C	15	20	25	60	60	120	500	
21-6 Manush/Lary/Weav/Had 6C SP	20	25	30	50	80	150	600	
21-7 Manush/Lary/Weav/Had 7C SP	20	25	30	50	80	150	600	
22-2 Martin/O'Far/Byrd/Mac 2F SP	20	25	30	50	80	150		
22-4 Martin/O'Far/Byrd/Mac 4F	15	20	25	40	60	120		
22-7 Martin/O'Far/Byrd/Mac 7F	15	20	25	40	60	120		
23-2 Moore/Hogan/Frank/Bran 2E SP	20	25	30	50	80	150	400	
23-4 Moore/Hogan/Frank/Bran 4E	15	20	25	40	60	120		
23-7 Moore/Hogan/Frank/Bran 7E	15	20	25	40	60	120	300	
24-1 Piet/Com/Bottomley/Adam 1H	15	20	25	40	60	120	1,000	
24-3 Piet/Com/Bottomley/Adam 3F	15	20	25	40	60	120	300	
24-4 Piet/Com/Bottomley/Adam 4F SP	20	25	30	50	80	150	400	
24-5 Piet/Com/Bottomley/Adam 5F SP	20	25	30	50	80	150	400	
25-1 Ruel/Simmons/Kam/Coch 1J SP	30	40	50	80	150	300	800	
25-3 Ruel/Simmons/Kam/Coch 3A SP	30	40	50	80	150	300	800	
25-5 Ruel/Simmons/Kam/Coch 5A	25	30	40	60	120	250	600	
25-6 Ruel/Simmons/Kam/Coch 6A	25	30	40	60	120	250	600	
26-2 Ruff/Mal/Lazzeri/Dickey 2D SP	40	50	60	100	200	400	1,000	
26-4 Ruff/Mal/Lazzeri/Dickey 4D	30	40	50	80	200	300	800	
26-7 Ruff/Mal/Lazzeri/Dickey 7D	30	40	50	80	150	300	800	

		PrFr 1	GD 2	VG 3	VgEx 4	EX 5	ExMt 6	NM 7	NmMt 8
27-1	Ruth/McM/Bran/Maran 1J	400	500	600	800	1,000	1,500	4,000	
27-3	Ruth/McM/Bran/Maran 3A	300	400	600	800	1,000	1,500	4,000	
27-4	Ruth/McM/Bran/Maran 4A SP	400	500	600	1,000	1,200	2,500	5,000	
27-5	Ruth/McM/Bran/Maran 5A SP	400	500	600	1,000	1,200	2,500	5,000	
28-1	Schuble/Marb/Goslin/Crow 1H SP20	25	30	50	80	150	500		
28-3	Schuble/Marb/Goslin/Crow 3F SP20	25	30	50	80	150	400		
28-5	Schuble/Marb/Goslin/Crow 5F	15	20	25	40	80	150	300	
28-6	Schuble/Marb/Goslin/Crow 6F	15	20	25	40	60	120	300	
29-8	Spohrer/Rhem/Cant/Bent 8L	15	20	25	40	60	120		
29-9	Spohrer/Rhem/Cant/Bent 9L	20	25	25	40	60	120		
30-1	Terry/Schu/Man/Jackson 1K	25	30	40	60	120	250		
30-3	Terry/Schu/Man/Jackson 3B	25	30	40	60	120	250		
30-4	Terry/Schu/Man/Jackson 4B SP	30	40	50	80	150	300		
30-5	Terry/Schu/Man/Jackson 5B SP	30	40	50	80	150	300		
31-2	Traynor/Luc/Thev/Wright 2B SP	20	25	30	50	80	150	400	
31-4	Traynor/Luc/Thev/Wright 4B	15	20	25	60	80	120	300	
31-7	Traynor/Luc/Thev/Wright 7B	15	20	25	40	80	120	300	
32-8	Vosmik/Knick/Hard/Stew 8I	15	20	25	40	60	120	500	
32-9	Vosmik/Knick/Hard/Stew 9I	15	20	25	40	60	120	1,200	
33-1	Waner/Bush/Hoyt/Waner 1E	25	30	40	60	100	250	600	
33-3	Waner/Bush/Hoyt/Waner 3C	25	30	40	60	100	250	600	
33-4	Waner/Bush/Hoyt/Waner 5C	25	30	40	60	100	250	600	
33-5	Waner/Bush/Hoyt/Waner 4C SP	30	40	50	80	150	300	1,000	
34-8	Werber/Ferrell/Ferrell/Ost 8G	15	20	25	40	60	200	300	
34-9	Werber/Ferrell/Ferrell/Ost 9G	15	20	25	40	60	250	300	
35-1	West/Melillo/Blae/Coff 1F SP	20	25	30	50	80	150	400	
35-3	West/Melillo/Blae/Coff 3D SP	20	25	30	50	80	150	400	
35-5	West/Melillo/Blae/Coff 5D	15	20	25	40	60	120		
35-6	West/Melillo/Blae/Coff 6D	15	20	25	40	60	120	300	
36-1	Wilson/Allen/Jonnard/Brick 1E SP20	25	30	50	80	150			
36-3	Wilson/Allen/Jonnard/Brick 3C SP20	25	30	60	80	150			
36-5	Wilson/Allen/Jonnard/Brick 5C SP20	25	30	50	80	150			
36-6	Wilson/Allen/Jonnard/Brick 6C	15	20	25	40	60	120		

1936 Goudey Black and White

		PrFr 1	GD 2	VG 3	VgEx 4	EX 5	ExMt 6	NM 7	NmMt 8
1	Wally Berger	12	15	20	30	50	60	150	300
2	Zeke Bonura	10	12	15	25	40	50	120	250
3	Frenchy Bordagaray	10	12	15	25	40	50	100	250
4	Bill Brubaker	10	12	20	30	50	80	100	250
5	Dolph Camilli	10	12	15	25	40	50	100	250
6	Clyde Castleman	10	12	15	25	40	50	120	
7	Mickey Cochrane	25	40	60	100	150	250	600	1,200
8	Joe Coscarart	10	12	15	25	40	50	100	250
9	Frank Crosetti	15	25	40	60	100	150	250	400
10	Kiki Cuyler	12	15	25	40	60	80	150	400
11	Paul Derringer	10	12	15	25	40	50	120	
12	Jimmy Dykes	10	12	15	25	40	50	100	250
13	Rick Ferrell	12	20	30	50	80	120	200	500
14	Lefty Gomez	25	40	60	100	150	250	400	800
15	Hank Greenberg	60	100	150	250	400	600	1,000	
16	Bucky Harris	12	15	25	40	60	80	200	400
17	Rollie Hemsley	10	12	15	25	40	50	100	250
18	Pinky Higgins	10	12	15	25	40	50	100	250
19	Oral Hildebrand	10	12	15	25	40	50	100	250
20	Chuck Klein	25	40	60	100	150	250	400	1,000
21	Pepper Martin	12	15	25	40	60	100	250	400
22	Bobo Newsom	10	12	15	25	40	50	100	250
23	Joe Vosmik	10	12	15	25	40	50	100	250
24	Paul Waner	25	40	60	100	150	250	400	600
25	Bill Werber	10	12	15	25	40	50	150	

1938 Goudey Heads-Up

		PrFr 1	GD 2	VG 3	VgEx 4	EX 5	ExMt 6	NM 7	NmMt 8
241	Charley Gehringer	80	100	120	200	400	500	800	3,000
242	Pete Fox	20	30	40	60	100	150	500	800
243	Joe Kuhel	20	30	40	60	100	150	400	800

		PrFr 1	GD 2	VG 3	VgEx 4	EX 5	ExMt 6	NM 7	NmMt 8
244	Frank Demaree	20	30	40	60	100	200	300	800
245	Frank Pytlak	20	30	40	60	100	250	400	800
246	Ernie Lombardi	50	80	120	300	400	600	800	1,500
247	Joe Vosmik	20	30	40	80	100	150	300	800
248	Dick Bartell	20	30	40	60	100	200	300	1,000
249	Jimmie Foxx	120	150	200	300	400	600	1,200	4,000
250	Joe DiMaggio	1,000	1,500	2,500	3,000	4,000	5,000	6,000	15,000
251	Bump Hadley	30	40	50	60	100	200	300	800
252	Zeke Bonura	20	30	40	60	100	150	600	800
253	Hank Greenberg	120	150	200	600	800	1,000	1,500	3,000
254	Van Lingle Mungo	20	30	40	60	100	250	400	
255	Moose Solters	20	30	40	60	100	150	300	800
256	Vernon Kennedy	20	30	50	60	80	100	400	800
257	Al Lopez	40	50	60	100	200	300	500	1,200
258	Bobby Doerr	60	100	200	250	300	500	800	2,000
259	Billy Werber	20	30	40	60	100	150	500	800
260	Rudy York	20	30	40	80	150	200	400	1,000
261	Rip Radcliff	20	30	40	50	80	120	300	1,000
262	Joe Medwick	60	80	100	150	300	400	800	2,000
263	Marvin Owen	20	30	40	60	100	150	300	800
264	Bob Feller	250	400	500	600	800	1,500	2,000	5,000
265	Charley Gehringer	80	100	120	200	300	500	800	2,000
266	Pete Fox	40	50	60	100	150	250		
267	Joe Kuhel	20	30	40	60	100	150	300	800
268	Frank Demaree	20	30	40	60	100	150	300	800
269	Frank Pytlak	20	30	40	60	100	150	300	800
270	Ernie Lombardi	50	60	80	200	300	500	600	1,200
271	Joe Vosmik	20	30	40	60	100	150	400	800
272	Dick Bartell	20	30	40	60	100	150	300	800
273	Jimmie Foxx	120	200	250	400	500	800	2,000	4,000
274	Joe DiMaggio	800	1,200	1,400	2,000	2,500	5,000	15,000	20,000
275	Bump Hadley	20	30	40	60	100	150	300	800
276	Zeke Bonura	20	30	40	60	100	200	300	800
277	Hank Greenberg	120	150	200	400	600	1,000	1,500	5,000
278	Van Lingle Mungo	20	30	60	80	100	150	300	800
279	Moose Solters	20	30	40	60	100	150	300	1,200
280	Vernon Kennedy	20	30	40	60	100	150	300	800
281	Al Lopez	40	50	80	100	200	400	500	1,500
282	Bobby Doerr	60	150	200	250	500	600	800	2,000
283	Billy Werber	20	30	40	60	100	150	300	1,000
284	Rudy York	20	30	40	60	150	250	400	1,000
285	Rip Radcliff	20	30	40	60	100	200	300	800
286	Joe Medwick	60	80	100	200	250	400	800	
287	Marvin Owen	20	30	40	60	100	150	400	800
288	Bob Feller	250	300	600	800	1,000	1,500	2,500	

— Joe DiMaggio #274 SGC 7.5 (Nm+) sold for $9,400 (REA; 05/11)
— Joe DiMaggio #274 PSA 7.5 (Nm+) sold for $7,320 (Greg Bussineau; 12/12)
— Joe DiMaggio #274 SGC 86 (NrMt+) sold for $6,115 (Mile High; 5/12)
— Bob Feller #288 PSA 8 (NmMt) sold for $6,500 (REA; 05/12)

1939 Play Ball

		PrFr 1	GD 2	VG 3	VgEx 4	EX 5	ExMt 6	NM 7	NmMt 8
1	Jake Powell	12	15	20	25	40	60		
2	Lee Grissom	6	8	10	12	15	25	60	150
3	Red Ruffing	20	30	50	80	120	200	300	500
4	Eldon Auker	6	10	15	25	40	60	150	
5	Luke Sewell	6	8	10	12	15	25	60	100
6	Leo Durocher	15	25	50	60	100	150	250	400
7	Bobby Doerr	20	25	60	100	150	250	400	600
8	Henry Pippen	6	8	10	12	15	25	60	
9	James Tobin	6	8	10	12	15	25	40	
10	James DeShong	6	8	10	12	20	30	50	100
11	Johnny Rizzo	6	8	10	12	15	25	40	100
12	Hershel Martin	6	8	10	12	15	25	40	100
13	Luke Hamlin	6	8	10	15	25	40	50	150
14	Jim Tabor	6	8	10	20	20	30	80	120
15	Paul Derringer	8	10	12	15	20	30	40	120

	PrFr 1	GD 2	VG 3	VgEx 4	EX 5	ExMt 6	NM 7	NmMt 8
John Peacock	6	8	10	12	15	25	40	100
Emerson Dickman	6	8	10	15	15	25	60	100
Harry Danning	6	8	10	12	15	25	50	100
Paul Dean	12	15	20	20	30	50	120	250
Joe Heving	6	6	10	15	25	40	60	
Dutch Leonard	8	10	12	15	25	40	60	200
Bucky Walters	8	10	12	15	20	30	80	200
Burgess Whitehead	6	8	10	20	20	30	40	150
Richard Coffman	6	8	10	12	15	25	60	
George Selkirk	8	12	20	30	50	80	120	200
Joe DiMaggio	1,200	1,500	2,000	2,500	4,000	6,000	8,000	15,000
Fred Ostermueller	6	8	10	12	15	25	40	120
Sylvester Johnson	6	8	10	12	20	30	40	100
Jack Wilson	5	5	8	12	20	30	50	100
Bill Dickey	30	60	80	60	100	150	300	800
Sam West	6	6	10	15	25	40	60	100
Bob Seeds	5	8	12	20	30	50	80	100
Del Young	6	8	10	12	15	25	40	100
Frank Demaree	6	8	10	12	15	25	50	100
Bill Jurges	6	8	10	12	15	25	40	
Frank McCormick	6	8	10	12	15	25	60	150
Virgil Davis	6	8	10	12	15	25	40	100
Billy Myers	6	8	10	12	15	25	40	100
Rick Ferrell	12	20	30	40	60	100	150	400
James Bagby Jr.	6	8	10	12	15	25	60	
Lon Warneke	6	8	10	12	15	25	40	100
Arndt Jorgens	6	8	10	12	15	25	40	100
Melo Almada	6	8	10	12	15	25	60	
Don Heffner	6	8	10	12	15	25	40	
Merrill May	6	8	10	12	15	25	40	100
Morris Arnovich	6	8	10	12	15	25	40	100
Buddy Lewis	6	10	15	25	40	60	80	120
Lefty Gomez	25	30	50	80	120	200	250	400
Eddie Miller	6	6	8	12	20	30	50	150
Charley Gehringer	40	60	100	150	250	400	600	1,000
Mel Ott	20	30	60	100	150	250	300	600
Tommy Henrich	5	8	12	20	30	50	150	300
Carl Hubbell	40	60	100	150	250	400	600	1,000
Harry Gumpert	6	6	10	15	25	40	60	150
Arky Vaughan	10	15	25	40	60	100	120	500
Hank Greenberg	60	100	150	250	400	600	1,000	2,000
Buddy Hassett	6	8	10	12	15	25	40	
Lou Chiozza	6	8	10	12	15	25	60	
Ken Chase	6	8	10	12	15	25	40	100
Schoolboy Rowe	8	10	12	25	40	60	80	150
Tony Cuccinello	8	12	15	25	40	60	100	
Tom Carey	5	5	8	12	20	30	50	100
Emmett Mueller	5	5	8	12	20	30	50	100
Wally Moses	6	8	10	12	15	25	40	120
Harry Craft	6	8	10	12	20	30	50	100
Jimmy Ripple	6	8	10	12	15	25	60	
Ed Joost	6	8	10	20	30	50	80	150
Fred Sington	6	6	10	15	25	40	60	100
Elbie Fletcher	6	8	10	12	15	25	40	150
Fred Frankhouse	6	8	10	12	20	30	50	100
Monte Pearson	8	10	12	15	20	30	100	150
Debs Garms	6	6	8	12	20	30	50	100
Hal Schumacher	6	8	10	12	15	25	40	120
Cookie Lavagetto	6	8	12	20	30	50	80	1,000
Stan Bordagaray	6	6	10	15	25	40	60	150
Goody Rosen	5	8	12	20	30	50	80	120
Lew Riggs	5	5	8	12	20	30	50	100
Julius Solters	6	8	10	12	15	25	40	100
Jo Jo Moore	6	6	10	15	25	40	60	150
Pete Fox	5	5	8	12	20	30	50	100
Babe Dahlgren	8	10	12	15	20	30	50	150
Chuck Klein	12	20	30	50	80	120	150	400
Gus Suhr	6	8	10	12	15	25	50	

		PrFr 1	GD 2	VG 3	VgEx 4	EX 5	ExMt 6	NM 7	NmMt 8
84	Skeeter Newsom	6	8	10	12	15	25	40	120
85	Johnny Cooney	6	8	10	12	15	25	40	100
86	Dolph Camilli	6	8	10	12	15	25	40	120
87	Milburn Shoffner	6	8	10	12	15	25	60	
88	Charlie Keller	12	15	20	20	30	50	80	200
89	Lloyd Waner	25	40	60	100	150	250	400	600
90	Robert Klinger	5	6	10	15	25	40	60	100
91	John Knott	5	6	10	15	25	40	60	100
92	Ted Williams	1,500	2,500	4,000	6,000	10,000	15,000	40,000	60,000
93	Charles Gelbert	6	8	10	12	15	25	40	100
94	Heinie Manush	12	20	30	50	80	120	200	300
95	Whit Wyatt	5	5	8	12	20	30	50	100
96	Babe Phelps	5	6	10	15	25	40	60	100
97	Bob Johnson	6	8	12	20	30	50	80	150
98	Pinky Whitney	6	8	12	20	30	50	80	120
99	Wally Berger	5	8	12	20	30	50	80	200
100	Buddy Myer	5	8	12	20	30	50	80	120
101	Roger Cramer	6	10	12	25	40	60	100	150
102	Lem (Pep) Young	5	8	12	20	30	50	80	150
103	Moe Berg	40	60	100	150	250	400	600	1,000
104	Tom Bridges	6	8	10	12	15	25	40	120
105	Rabbit McNair	6	8	10	12	20	30	40	100
106	Dolly Stark Umpire	8	10	12	20	30	50	80	250
107	Joe Vosmik	5	8	12	20	30	50	80	100
108	Frank Hayes	6	8	10	12	15	25	40	100
109	Myril Hoag	6	8	10	15	25	40	50	100
110	Fred Fitzsimmons	6	8	10	20	30	50	80	120
111	Van Lingle Mungo	6	8	8	12	20	30	50	100
112	Paul Waner	10	15	25	40	60	100	120	400
113	Al Schacht	5	6	10	15	25	40	80	200
114	Cecil Travis	6	8	10	15	25	40	80	
115	Ralph Kress	5	5	6	10	15	25	60	
116	Gene Desautels	6	10	15	30	50	80	150	
117	Wayne Ambler	6	10	15	25	40	60	100	250
118	Lynn Nelson	6	10	15	25	40	60	150	
119	Will Hershberger	10	15	25	40	60	100	200	500
120	Rabbit Warstler	8	12	20	30	50	80	150	250
121	Bill Posedel	10	12	15	25	40	60	150	
122	George McQuinn	10	12	15	25	40	60	100	250
123	Ray T. Davis	10	12	15	25	40	60	100	250
124	Walter Brown	10	12	15	25	40	60	100	250
125	Cliff Melton	10	15	25	40	60	100	120	250
127	Gil Brack	10	12	15	25	40	60	150	
128	Joe Bowman	10	12	15	25	40	60	100	
129	Bill Swift	10	12	15	25	40	60	150	
130	Bill Brubaker	10	12	15	30	50	80	100	250
131	Mort Cooper	10	12	15	30	50	80	120	
132	Jim Brown	10	12	15	30	50	80	100	300
133	Lynn Myers	10	12	15	25	40	60	100	250
134	Tot Presnell	10	12	15	25	40	60	100	
135	Mickey Owen	10	15	25	40	60	100	150	400
136	Roy Bell	10	12	15	25	40	60	100	250
137	Pete Appleton	10	12	15	25	40	60	100	250
138	George Case	10	12	15	30	50	80	150	
139	Vito Tamulis	10	12	15	30	50	80	100	300
140	Ray Hayworth	10	12	15	25	40	60	100	
141	Pete Coscarart	10	12	15	25	40	60	100	250
142	Ira Hutchinson	10	12	15	25	40	60	100	
143	Earl Averill	25	30	50	80	120	200	250	600
144	Zeke Bonura	10	12	15	25	40	60	120	300
145	Hugh Mulcahy	10	15	25	40	60	100	150	
146	Tom Sunkel	8	12	20	30	50	80	150	
147	George Coffman	10	12	15	25	40	60	100	250
148	Bill Trotter	10	12	15	25	40	60	100	250
149	Max West	10	12	15	25	40	60	100	250
150	James Walkup	10	12	15	25	40	60	100	250
151	Hugh Casey	10	12	15	25	40	60	120	400
152	Roy Weatherly	10	12	15	25	40	60	100	250

#		PrFr 1	GD 2	VG 3	VgEx 4	EX 5	ExMt 6	NM 7	NmMt 8
153	Dizzy Trout	12	15	20	30	50	80	150	500
154	Johnny Hudson	10	15	25	40	60	100	150	
155	Jimmy Outlaw	10	12	15	25	40	60	100	200
156	Ray Berres	10	12	15	25	40	60	100	
157	Don Padgett	10	12	15	30	50	80	200	
158	Bud Thomas	10	12	15	20	50	80	100	
159	Red Evans	10	12	15	25	40	60	100	250
160	Gene Moore	10	12	15	25	40	60	150	
161	Lonnie Frey	10	12	15	25	40	60	150	
162	Whitey Moore	25	30	50	80	120	200	400	

— Joe DiMaggio #26 PSA 9 (MT) sold for $10,665 (REA; Spring '14)

— Joe DiMaggio #26 SGC 96 (Mint) sold for $6,463 (Huggins and Scott; 6/12)

— Joe DiMaggio #26 SGC 96 (MT) sold for $6,600 (Greg Bussineau; 12/12)

— Whitey Moore #162 PSA 8 (NmMt) sold for $6,192 (Goodwin; 09/11)

— Ted Williams #92 GAI 9 (MT) sold for $5,040 (Mile High; 10/11)

— Ted Williams #92 SGC 92 (NmMt+) sold for $8,463 (Mile High; 10/11)

1940 Play Ball

#		PrFr 1	GD 2	VG 3	VgEx 4	EX 5	ExMt 6	NM 7	NmMt 8
1	Joe DiMaggio	800	1,000	1,200	2,000	3,000	5,000	8,000	40,000
2	Art Jorgens	8	10	12	15	20	50	150	
3	Babe Dahlgren	8	10	12	15	20	25	80	
4	Tommy Henrich	10	12	15	20	25	60	150	
5	Monte Pearson	8	10	12	15	20	50	100	
6	Lefty Gomez	25	60	80	100	120	150	200	600
7	Bill Dickey	25	30	40	60	150	200	400	800
8	George Selkirk	8	10	12	15	20	40	150	250
9	Charlie Keller	10	12	15	20	25	40	80	500
10	Red Ruffing	20	40	50	60	80	100	150	500
11	Jake Powell	8	10	12	15	20	25	40	250
12	Johnny Schulte	8	10	12	15	20	30	40	300
13	Jack Knott	8	10	12	15	25	40	120	
14	Rabbit McNair	8	10	12	25	30	40	80	
15	George Case	8	10	12	15	20	25	50	250
16	Cecil Travis	8	10	12	15	20	40	60	250
17	Buddy Myer	8	8	10	15	25	40	60	300
18	Charlie Gelbert	5	8	12	20	30	50	80	250
19	Ken Chase	8	10	12	15	20	25	80	
20	Buddy Lewis	8	10	12	15	20	25	40	250
21	Rick Ferrell	12	20	30	50	80	100	150	800
22	Sammy West	8	10	12	15	20	25	60	
23	Dutch Leonard	8	10	12	25	30	40	60	
24	Frank Hayes	8	10	12	15	20	25	60	150
25	Bob Johnson	10	12	15	20	25	50	60	
26	Wally Moses	5	8	12	20	30	50	80	200
27	Ted Williams	400	600	1,000	1,500	2,500	4,000	6,000	8,000
28	Gene Desautels	8	10	12	15	20	30	60	150
29	Doc Cramer	8	10	12	15	20	25	60	500
30	Moe Berg	40	50	60	100	200	250	300	600
31	Jack Wilson	8	8	10	15	25	40	60	250
32	Jim Bagby	8	10	12	15	20	25	50	250
33	Fritz Ostermueller	8	10	12	15	20	25	40	120
34	John Peacock	8	10	12	15	20	25	40	150
35	Joe Heving	8	10	12	15	20	25	60	150
36	Jim Tabor	8	10	12	15	20	25	50	150
37	Emerson Dickman	8	10	12	15	20	25	50	
38	Bobby Doerr	10	15	25	40	60	100	200	500
39	Tom Carey	8	10	12	15	20	25	40	150
40	Hank Greenberg	60	100	150	250	400	600	1,500	2,500
41	Charley Gehringer	50	80	120	200	300	500	800	1,200
42	Bud Thomas	8	10	12	15	20	25	60	150
43	Pete Fox	8	10	12	15	20	25	100	200
44	Dizzy Trout	8	10	12	15	30	40	100	
45	Red Kress	8	10	12	15	20	25	50	
46	Earl Averill	15	20	25	60	80	100	150	400
47	Oscar Vitt RC	8	10	12	15	20	25	50	300
48	Luke Sewell	8	10	12	15	20	50	60	150

#		PrFr 1	GD 2	VG 3	VgEx 4	EX 5	ExMt 6	NM 7	NmMt 8
49	Stormy Weatherly	8	10	12	15	20	25	60	
50	Hal Trosky	8	10	12	15	20	25	40	250
51	Don Heffner	8	10	12	15	20	25	40	200
52	Myril Hoag	8	10	12	15	20	25	40	150
53	George McQuinn	8	10	12	15	20	25	40	150
54	Bill Trotter	8	10	12	15	20	25	50	
55	Slick Coffman	8	10	12	15	20	25	40	150
56	Eddie Miller RC	8	10	12	15	20	25	60	200
57	Max West	8	10	12	15	20	25	40	100
58	Bill Posedel	8	10	12	15	20	25	50	250
59	Rabbit Warstler	8	10	12	15	20	25	50	100
60	John Cooney	8	10	12	25	30	40	50	150
61	Tony Cuccinello	8	10	12	15	20	25	40	150
62	Buddy Hassett	8	10	12	15	20	25	40	150
63	Pete Coscarart	8	10	12	15	20	25	40	
64	Van Lingle Mungo	8	10	12	15	20	30	40	150
65	Fred Fitzsimmons	8	10	12	20	30	40	50	100
66	Babe Phelps	8	10	12	15	20	25	40	250
67	Whit Wyatt	8	10	12	15	20	25	40	150
68	Dolph Camilli	8	10	12	20	25	40	60	
69	Cookie Lavagetto	8	10	12	15	20	25	40	
70	Luke Hamlin	8	10	12	15	20	25	80	150
71	Mel Almada	8	10	12	15	20	25	80	
72	Chuck Dressen RC	8	10	12	15	20	25	40	150
73	Bucky Walters	8	10	12	15	25	50	80	200
74	Duke Derringer	8	10	12	15	20	40	80	120
75	Buck McCormick	8	10	12	15	20	25	40	150
76	Lonny Frey	8	10	12	15	20	25	40	300
77	Willard Hershberger	8	10	12	15	30	40	80	150
78	Lew Riggs	8	10	12	15	20	40	60	100
79	Harry Craft	8	10	12	15	20	25	60	
80	Billy Myers	8	10	12	15	20	25	40	300
81	Wally Berger	8	10	12	15	20	25	40	25
82	Hank Gowdy CO	8	10	12	15	20	25	50	10
83	Cliff Melton	8	10	12	15	20	30	50	120
84	Jo Jo Moore	8	10	12	15	20	25	50	200
85	Hal Schumacher	8	10	12	15	20	25	80	
86	Harry Gumbert	8	10	12	15	20	25	40	10
87	Carl Hubbell	30	50	80	120	200	300	500	80
88	Mel Ott	60	100	150	250	400	600	1,000	1,50
89	Bill Jurges	8	10	12	15	20	25	100	25
90	Frank Demaree	8	10	12	15	20	25	40	25
91	Bob Seeds	8	10	12	15	20	25	60	12
92	Whitey Whitehead	8	10	12	15	25	40	60	25
93	Harry Danning	8	10	12	15	20	25	60	
94	Gus Suhr	8	10	12	15	20	25	60	10
95	Hugh Mulcahy	8	10	12	15	20	25	60	30
96	Heinie Mueller	8	10	12	15	20	25	40	15
97	Morry Arnovich	8	10	12	15	20	25	50	25
98	Pinky May	8	10	12	15	20	25	40	25
99	Syl Johnson	8	10	15	25	40	60	100	15
100	Hersh Martin	8	10	12	15	20	25	40	12
101	Del Young	8	10	12	15	25	50	80	12
102	Chuck Klein	12	20	30	50	80	100	150	60
103	Elbie Fletcher	8	10	12	15	20	25	40	10
104	Paul Waner	25	40	60	100	150	250	400	60
105	Lloyd Waner	15	20	25	80	100	120	150	60
106	Pep Young	8	10	12	15	20	25	40	12
107	Arky Vaughan	15	20	25	30	40	80	120	40
108	Johnny Rizzo	8	10	12	15	20	25	50	
109	Don Padgett	8	10	12	15	20	25	60	10
110	Tom Sunkel	8	10	12	15	20	25	60	
111	Mickey Owen	8	10	12	15	50	60	80	
112	Jimmy Brown	8	10	12	15	20	40	100	
113	Mort Cooper	8	10	12	15	20	40	150	
114	Lon Warneke	8	10	12	15	20	25	80	25
115	Mike Gonzalez CO	8	10	12	15	20	25	60	25
116	Al Schacht	10	12	15	20	25	80	150	

		PrFr 1	GD 2	VG 3	VgEx 4	EX 5	ExMt 6	NM 7	NmMt 8
17	Dolly Stark UMP	8	10	12	20	40	60	80	300
18	Waite Hoyt	15	20	30	50	80	120	200	500
19	Grover C. Alexander	50	80	120	200	300	500	800	1,200
20	Walter Johnson	60	100	150	250	400	600	1,000	1,500
21	Atley Donald RC	8	10	12	15	20	25	60	
22	Sandy Sundra RC	8	10	12	15	20	40	100	
23	Hildy Hildebrand	8	10	12	15	20	25	40	100
24	Earle Combs	12	15	20	25	60	100	150	200
25	Art Fletcher RC	8	10	12	15	20	25	60	
26	Jake Solters	8	10	12	15	20	25	80	
27	Muddy Ruel	8	10	12	15	20	25	50	120
28	Pete Appleton	8	10	12	25	30	40	50	120
29	Bucky Harris MG	15	20	25	30	40	100	120	400
30	Clyde Milan RC	8	10	12	15	20	25	40	120
31	Zeke Bonura	8	10	12	20	30	50	80	120
32	Connie Mack MG	25	40	60	100	150	250	400	800
33	Jimmie Foxx	60	100	150	250	400	600	1,000	1,500
34	Joe Cronin	20	30	50	80	120	200	300	
35	Line Drive Nelson	8	10	12	15	20	25	50	100
36	Cotton Pippen	8	10	12	15	20	25	40	100
37	Bing Miller	8	10	12	15	20	25	40	120
38	Beau Bell	8	10	12	15	20	25	60	100
39	Elden Auker	8	10	12	15	20	25	40	120
40	Dick Coffman	8	10	12	15	20	25	40	120
41	Casey Stengel MG	40	60	100	150	250	400	600	1,000
42	George Kelly RC	15	20	25	30	40	100	150	600
43	Gene Moore	8	10	12	15	20	25	50	150
44	Joe Vosmik	8	10	12	15	20	25	40	300
45	Vito Tamulis	8	10	12	15	20	25	80	150
46	Tot Pressnell	8	10	12	15	20	25	60	150
47	Johnny Hudson	8	10	12	15	20	25	60	150
48	Hugh Casey	8	10	12	15	20	25	100	
49	Pinky Shoffner	8	10	12	15	25	30	40	
50	Whitey Moore	8	10	12	15	30	40	50	150
51	Edwin Joost	8	10	12	25	30	40	50	120
52	Jimmy Wilson	8	10	12	15	25	40	60	120
53	Bill McKechnie MG	15	20	25	30	40	100	120	300
54	Jumbo Brown	8	10	12	15	20	25	40	100
55	Ray Hayworth	8	10	12	15	20	25	50	150
56	Daffy Dean	8	12	20	30	50	80	120	600
57	Lou Chiozza	8	10	12	15	25	60	80	120
58	Travis Jackson	15	20	25	30	60	80	120	400
59	Pancho Snyder	8	10	12	15	20	30	50	450
60	Hans Lobert CO	8	10	12	15	20	25	50	250
61	Debs Garms	8	10	12	15	20	25	40	150
62	Joe Bowman	8	10	12	15	20	40	80	
63	Spud Davis	8	10	12	15	20	25	50	300
64	Ray Berres	8	10	12	15	20	40	60	250
65	Bob Klinger	8	10	12	15	20	25	40	150
66	Bill Brubaker	8	10	12	20	30	50	120	
67	Frankie Frisch MG	15	25	40	60	100	150	250	600
68	Honus Wagner CO	60	100	150	250	300	400	500	1,500
69	Gabby Street	6	10	12	15	25	30	40	100
70	Tris Speaker	25	40	60	100	150	250	400	800
71	Harry Heilmann	15	20	25	60	80	100	150	500
72	Chief Bender	15	20	25	40	50	100	150	400
73	Napoleon Lajoie	50	80	120	200	300	500	800	1,200
74	Johnny Evers	10	15	25	40	60	100	150	400
75	Christy Mathewson	50	80	120	200	300	500	800	1,200
76	Heinie Manush	15	20	25	40	60	100	120	400
77	Frank Baker	20	25	30	80	100	120	150	400
78	Max Carey	15	20	25	30	50	60	150	
79	George Sisler	20	25	40	80	100	120	200	500
80	Mickey Cochrane	25	30	40	80	120	150	300	
81	Spud Chandler	10	12	15	20	25	80	300	
82	Knick Knickerbocker	10	12	15	20	25	50	150	400
83	Marvin Breuer	10	12	15	20	25	40	120	200
84	Mule Haas	10	12	15	20	25	40	80	300

		PrFr 1	GD 2	VG 3	VgEx 4	EX 5	ExMt 6	NM 7	NmMt 8
185	Joe Kuhel	10	12	15	20	30	50	200	
186	Taft Wright	10	12	15	20	25	50	150	400
187	Jimmy Dykes MG	10	12	15	20	25	50	100	
188	Joe Krakauskas	10	12	15	20	50	60	150	300
189	Jim Bloodworth	10	12	15	20	25	60	200	
190	Charley Berry	10	12	15	30	50	60	100	400
191	John Babich	10	12	15	20	25	40	200	300
192	Dick Siebert	10	12	15	20	25	50	200	400
193	Chubby Dean	10	12	15	20	50	80	120	300
194	Sam Chapman	10	12	15	20	25	40	60	250
195	Dee Miles	10	12	15	20	25	50	150	
196	Red Nonnenkamp	10	12	15	20	40	60	150	300
197	Lou Finney	10	12	15	20	25	40	80	150
198	Denny Galehouse	10	12	15	20	25	40	60	150
199	Pinky Higgins	10	12	15	20	25	40	80	150
200	Soup Campbell	10	12	15	20	25	50	150	300
201	Barney McCosky	10	12	15	20	25	40	60	250
202	Al Milnar	10	12	15	20	25	50	80	300
203	Bad News Hale	10	12	15	20	40	80	120	400
204	Harry Eisenstat	10	12	15	60	80	100	120	300
205	Rollie Hemsley	10	12	15	20	25	40	150	
206	Chet Laabs	10	12	15	20	25	80	200	
207	Gus Mancuso	10	12	15	20	25	40	80	450
208	Lee Gamble	10	12	15	25	40	100	200	
209	Hy Vandenberg	10	12	15	20	25	50	150	
210	Bill Lohrman	10	12	15	20	25	80	120	
211	Pop Joiner	10	12	15	20	25	50	200	450
212	Babe Young	10	12	15	20	30	50	150	
213	John Rucker	10	12	15	25	40	60	100	250
214	Ken O'Dea	10	12	15	20	25	80	150	300
215	Johnnie McCarthy	10	12	15	20	25	50	80	250
216	Joe Marty	10	12	15	20	40	50	60	250
217	Walter Beck	10	12	15	20	30	40	80	250
218	Wally Millies	10	12	15	20	25	60	100	
219	Russ Bauers	10	12	15	20	25	60	100	250
220	Mace Brown	10	12	15	25	40	60	100	300
221	Lee Handley	10	12	15	20	25	60	100	300
222	Max Butcher	10	12	15	20	25	50	100	
223	Hughie Jennings	25	30	40	60	80	100	200	600
224	Pie Traynor	25	30	50	60	80	100	200	1,200
225	Joe Jackson	1,000	1,200	1,500	2,000	2,500	4,000	5,000	15,000
226	Harry Hooper	25	30	40	50	100	120	250	600
227	Jesse Haines	15	25	40	60	100	150	200	600
228	Charlie Grimm	10	12	15	20	25	80	100	250
229	Buck Herzog	10	12	15	20	25	80	100	300
230	Red Faber	25	30	40	50	60	120	250	600
231	Dolf Luque	10	12	15	20	50	100	500	
232	Goose Goslin	25	30	40	50	60	150	250	600
233	George Earnshaw	10	12	15	20	25	60	200	
234	Frank Chance	25	30	40	50	100	150	200	600
235	John McGraw	20	30	50	80	120	300	400	800
236	Jim Bottomley	25	30	40	50	80	200	250	600
237	Willie Keeler	30	40	50	60	120	150	400	800
238	Tony Lazzeri	20	30	50	80	120	200	400	600
239	George Uhle	10	12	15	20	25	40	300	500
240	Bill Atwood	10	15	25	40	60	100	300	

— Charlie Gelbert #18 SGC 96 (Mint) sold for $5,273 (Goodwin; 3/12)

1941 Double Play

		PrFr 1	GD 2	VG 3	VgEx 4	EX 5	ExMt 6	NM 7	NmMt 8
1	L.French/V.Page	10	12	15	20	25	40	100	250
3	B.Herman/S.Hack	10	12	15	50	60	80	100	150
5	L.Frey/J.VanderMeer	6	8	10	12	15	25	40	100
7	P.Derringer/B.Walters	6	8	10	12	15	25	40	100
9	F.McCormick/B.Werber	6	8	10	12	15	25	40	100
11	J.Ripple/E.Lombardi	10	12	15	20	25	40	80	
13	A.Kampouris/W.Wyatt	6	8	10	12	15	25	50	100

#	Player	PrFr 1	GD 2	VG 3	VgEx 4	EX 5	ExMt 6	NM 7	NmMt 8
15	M.Owen/P.Waner	10	12	15	20	40	60	100	150
17	C.Lavagetto/P.Reiser	6	8	10	12	15	25	100	
19	J.Wasdell/D.Camilli	6	8	10	12	15	25	50	100
21	D.Walker/J.Medwick	10	12	15	20	25	80	100	150
23	P.Reese/K.Higbe	40	60	100	150	250	400	600	800
25	H.Danning/C.Melton	6	8	10	12	15	25	40	150
27	H.Gumbert/B.Whitehead	6	8	10	12	15	25	40	100
29	J.Orengo/J.Moore	6	8	10	12	15	50	80	200
31	M.Ott/N.Young	25	30	40	50	80	120	250	400
33	L.Handley/A.Vaughan	10	12	15	20	25	40	60	150
35	B.Klinger/S.Brown	6	8	10	12	15	25	50	100
37	T.Moore/G.Mancuso	6	8	10	12	15	25	40	100
39	J.Mize/E.Slaughter	25	30	40	50	150	200	300	400
41	J.Cooney/S.Sisti	6	8	10	12	15	25	40	100
43	M.West/C.Rowell	6	8	10	12	15	25	40	100
45	D.Litwhiler/M.May	6	8	10	12	15	25	40	100
47	F.Hayes/A.Brancato	6	8	10	12	15	25	40	100
49	B.Johnson/B.Nagel	6	8	10	12	15	25	40	100
51	B.Newsom/H.Greenberg	30	40	80	100	120	150	200	600
53	B.McCosky/C.Gehringer	20	25	30	40	50	80	120	300
55	P.Higgins/D.Bartell	6	8	10	12	15	25	40	100
57	T.Williams/J.Tabor	100	120	150	300	400	500	750	1,500
59	J.Cronin/J.Foxx	40	50	60	80	100	200	300	600
61	L.Gomez/P.Rizzuto	50	60	80	100	300	400	500	800
63	J.DiMaggio/C.Keller	250	400	500	600	800	1,200	2,000	3,000
65	R.Rolfe/B.Dickey	25	30	40	50	60	100	200	400
67	J.Gordon/R.Ruffing	15	20	25	30	40	60	250	400
69	M.Tresh/L.Appling	10	12	15	20	25	80	150	200
71	M.Solters/J.Rigney	6	8	10	12	15	25	40	100
73	B.Meyer/B.Chapman	10	12	15	20	25	40	60	150
75	C.Travis/G.Case	6	8	10	12	15	25	40	100
77	J.Krakauskas/B.Feller	30	40	50	60	150	200	325	600
79	K.Keltner/H.Trosky	6	8	10	12	15	25	40	100
81	T.Williams/J.Cronin	125	200	200	250	350	500	800	2,000
83	J.Gordon/C.Keller	30	40	50	60	80	150	200	400
85	H.Greenberg/R.Ruffing	40	50	80	100	120	150	300	600
87	H.Trosky/G.Case	6	8	10	12	15	25	40	100
89	M.Ott/B.Whitehead	25	30	40	50	60	150	225	800
91	H.Danning/H.Gumbert	6	8	10	12	15	25	40	200
93	N.Young/C.Melton	6	8	10	12	15	25	40	100
95	J.Ripple/B.Walters	6	8	10	12	15	25	40	200
97	S.Hack/B.Klinger	6	8	10	12	30	50	100	120
99	J.Mize/D.Litwhiler	15	20	25	30	40	80	100	250
101	D.Dallesandro/A.Galan	8	10	12	20	30	50	80	120
103	B.Lee/P.Cavarretta	8	10	12	15	20	30	100	120
105	L.Grove/B.Doerr	40	50	60	100	150	200	250	600
107	F.Pytlak/D.DiMaggio	15	20	25	30	60	80	100	300
109	J.Priddy/J.Murphy	8	10	12	15	20	30	80	120
111	T.Henrich/M.Russo	25	30	40	50	60	80	100	150
113	F.Crosetti/J.Sturm	10	12	15	20	25	40	60	250
115	I.Goodman/M.McCormick	8	10	12	15	20	30	50	120
117	E.Joost/E.Koy	8	10	12	15	20	40	50	120
119	L.Waner/H.Majeski	20	25	30	40	50	80	120	300
121	B.Hassett/E.Moore	8	10	12	15	20	30	50	200
123	N.Etten/J.Rizzo	8	10	12	15	20	40	50	150
125	S.Chapman/W.Moses	8	10	12	15	20	30	50	120
127	J.Babich/D.Siebert	8	10	12	15	20	30	50	120
129	N.Potter/B.McCoy	8	10	12	15	20	30	50	120
131	C.Campbell/L.Boudreau	20	25	30	40	50	80	120	300
133	R.Hemsley/M.Harder	8	10	12	15	20	30	60	120
135	G.Walker/J.Heving	8	10	12	15	20	30	50	200
137	J.Rucker/A.Adams	8	10	12	15	20	30	60	200
139	M.Arnovich/C.Hubbell	40	50	60	80	100	150	250	600
141	L.Riggs/L.Durocher	12	15	20	25	30	40	60	120
143	F.Fitzsimmons/J.Vosmik	8	10	12	15	20	30	50	120
145	F.Crespi/J.Brown	8	10	12	15	20	30	50	120
147	D.Heffner/H.Clift	8	10	12	15	20	30	50	120
149	D.Garms/E.Fletcher	8	10	12	15	20	30	50	120

1941 Play Ball

#	Player	PrFr 1	GD 2	VG 3	VgEx 4	EX 5	ExMt 6	NM 7	NmMt 8
1	Eddie Miller	20	30	50	80	120	200	300	1,200
2	Max West	15	20	25	30	50	120	200	1,200
3	Bucky Walters	12	20	30	50	60	100	200	1,200
4	Paul Derringer	12	20	30	50	80	120	150	500
5	Frank (Buck) McCormick	10	15	20	25	60	80	200	600
6	Carl Hubbell	40	60	100	150	250	400	600	1,000
7	Harry Danning	12	20	30	50	80	100	150	300
8	Mel Ott	80	120	200	300	500	800	1,200	2,000
9	Pinky May	6	10	15	25	40	80	120	300
10	Arky Vaughan	25	40	60	80	120	200	300	800
11	Debs Garms	6	10	15	25	40	60	150	500
12	Jimmy Brown	8	12	20	30	50	80	120	300
13	Jimmie Foxx	150	250	40	500	800	1,000	1,500	2,500
14	Ted Williams	400	600	1,000	1,500	2,500	4,000	6,000	20,000
15	Joe Cronin	30	50	80	120	200	300	500	800
16	Hal Trosky	6	10	15	40	80	100	120	300
17	Roy Weatherly	6	10	15	20	50	50	150	400
18	Hank Greenberg	80	100	120	200	300	500	800	1,200
19	Charley Gehringer	40	60	100	150	250	400	600	1,200
20	Red Ruffing	30	50	80	120	200	300	500	800
21	Charlie Keller	20	25	30	40	60	100	150	600
22	Bob Johnson	12	20	30	50	80	120	150	400
23	George McQuinn	12	20	30	50	80	120	200	400
24	Dutch Leonard	10	15	25	40	60	100	120	400
25	Gene Moore	6	10	15	25	40	60	100	300
26	Harry Gumpert	6	10	15	25	40	100	150	500
27	Babe Young	6	10	15	20	60	80	120	500
28	Joe Marty	6	10	15	25	40	50	150	600
29	Jack Wilson	6	10	15	20	50	80	120	300
30	Lou Finney	12	20	30	50	80	120	200	300
31	Joe Kuhel	6	10	15	25	40	60	200	300
32	Taft Wright	6	10	15	25	40	60	120	500
33	Al Milnar	6	10	15	25	40	50	120	400
34	Rollie Hemsley	8	12	20	30	50	80	150	400
35	Pinky Higgins	6	10	15	20	50	80	150	300
36	Barney McCosky	6	10	15	25	40	50	120	200
37	Bruce Campbell	6	10	15	25	40	80	200	500
38	Atley Donald	6	10	15	25	40	120	150	400
39	Tommy Henrich	15	25	40	60	100	150	300	600
40	John Babich	6	10	15	25	40	60	100	300
41	Blimp Hayes	8	12	20	30	50	80	150	400
42	Wally Moses	6	10	15	25	40	80	120	500
43	Al Brancato	6	10	15	20	50	80	120	400
44	Sam Chapman	6	10	15	25	40	80	100	300
45	Eldon Auker	6	10	15	25	40	60	100	300
46	Sid Hudson	6	10	15	25	40	80	120	500
47	Buddy Lewis	6	10	15	25	40	80	120	300
48	Cecil Travis	10	15	25	40	60	100	200	500
49	Babe Dahlgren	6	10	15	25	40	80	150	400
50	Johnny Cooney	6	10	15	25	40	60	150	500
51	Dolph Camilli	10	20	25	50	80	120	200	400
52	Kirby Higbe	10	15	20	25	50	80	150	600
53	Luke Hamlin	8	12	20	30	50	100	200	400
54	Pee Wee Reese	200	300	500	800	1,200	2,000	3,000	10,000
55	Whit Wyatt	6	10	15	25	60	100	200	600
56	Johnny VanderMeer	30	50	80	120	200	300	500	800
57	Moe Arnovich	10	15	20	25	50	100	200	600
58	Frank Demaree	6	10	15	25	40	100	200	800
59	Bill Jurges	6	10	15	25	40	80	120	400
60	Chuck Klein	30	40	60	100	150	250	400	1,000
61	Vince DiMaggio	30	50	80	120	200	300	500	1,200
62	Elbie Fletcher	6	10	15	25	40	60	200	800
63	Dom DiMaggio	30	50	80	120	200	300	500	1,200
64	Bobby Doerr	40	60	100	150	250	400	600	1,000

		PrFr 1	GD 2	VG 3	VgEx 4	EX 5	ExMt 6	NM 7	NmMt 8
65	Tommy Bridges	10	15	20	25	50	60	200	800
66	Harland Clift	6	10	15	25	40	80	200	400
67	Walt Judnich	8	12	20	30	50	80	150	400
68	John Knott	6	10	15	25	40	60	100	300
69	George Case	6	10	15	25	40	60	200	600
70	Bill Dickey	80	120	200	250	300	400	600	2,000
71	Joe DiMaggio	1,000	1,500	2,500	4,000	6,000	10,000	20,000	60,000
72	Lefty Gomez	80	100	150	250	400	500	800	1,500

— Hank Greenberg #18 SGC 96 (MT) sold for $5,273 (Goodwin; 03/12)
— Hank Greenberg #18 SGC 96 (MT) sold for $5,105 (Mile High; 05/11)
— Bob Johnson #22 PSA 9 (MT) sold for $5,117 (Mile High; 10/11)

1948 Bowman

		GD 2	VG 3	VgEx 4	EX 5	ExMt 6	NM 7	NmMt 8	MT 9
1	Bob Elliott RC	10	20	40	50	100	200	400	2,000
2	Ewell Blackwell RC	12	20	30	50	80	80	250	800
3	Ralph Kiner RC	60	100	150	250	400	600	1,000	5,000
4	Johnny Mize RC	30	50	80	120	200	300	500	1,200
5	Bob Feller RC	150	200	250	300	400	600	1,000	2,000
6	Yogi Berra RC	400	500	600	800	1,000	2,000	4,000	8,000
7	Pete Reiser SP RC	20	30	50	80	100	250	600	1,500
8	Phil Rizzuto SP RC	100	150	250	300	500	600	1,200	2,500
9	Walker Cooper RC	15	25	40	60	100	150	250	1,200
10	Buddy Rosar RC	8	12	20	30	50	80	150	800
11	Johnny Lindell RC	5	6	10	25	50	60	200	1,000
12	Johnny Sain RC	6	12	20	40	50	100	250	1,200
13	Willard Marshall SP RC	5	8	12	50	60	100	200	800
14	Allie Reynolds RC	6	12	40	60	80	120	300	1,200
15	Eddie Joost	10	15	25	40	60	100	150	600
16	Jack Lohrke SP RC	5	10	15	30	50	100	400	1,000
17	Enos Slaughter RC	30	50	80	100	150	300	500	1,200
18	Warren Spahn RC	150	250	400	500	600	800	2,000	4,000
19	Tommy Henrich	12	20	30	50	80	120	250	1,000
20	Buddy Kerr SP RC	5	10	15	25	40	120	250	800
21	Ferris Fain RC	10	15	25	40	60	100	150	1,500
22	Floyd Bevens SP RC	12	20	40	50	100	120	250	800
23	Larry Jansen RC	8	12	20	30	50	80	120	500
24	Dutch Leonard SP	10	15	25	40	60	100	300	600
25	Barney McCosky	8	12	20	30	50	60	150	500
26	Frank Shea SP RC	8	12	20	30	60	150	300	
27	Sid Gordon RC	5	6	20	25	50	120	250	1,000
28	Emil Verban SP RC	5	10	15	25	80	100	200	1,200
29	Joe Page SP RC	12	20	30	50	60	120	300	800
30	Whitey Lockman SP RC	6	12	30	50	80	120	250	600
31	Bill McCahan RC	5	6	15	20	25	60	150	500
32	Bill Rigney RC	6	10	15	30	50	80	100	500
33	Bill Johnson RC	5	10	20	30	40	60	150	500
34	Sheldon Jones SP RC	5	15	20	40	60	100	250	800
35	Snuffy Stirnweiss RC	15	25	40	60	100	150	250	1,200
36	Stan Musial RC	600	800	1,000	1,200	2,000	3,000	12,000	25,000
37	Clint Hartung RC	5	10	15	25	100	120	250	1,400
38	Red Schoendienst RC	60	120	200	250	400	600	1,500	5,000
39	Augie Galan RC	5	10	15	25	40	100	200	1,000
40	Marty Marion RC	15	30	50	80	150	250	500	1,500
41	Rex Barney RC	10	15	25	40	60	150	300	1,000
42	Ray Poat RC	5	10	20	30	50	100	200	1,000
43	Bruce Edwards RC	12	20	30	50	80	150	300	1,000
44	Johnny Wyrostek RC	10	15	25	40	60	120	500	1,000
45	Hank Sauer RC	10	20	30	60	80	200	600	1,500
46	Herman Wehmeier RC	5	10	15	30	50	100	300	2,500
47	Bobby Thomson RC	20	40	60	100	150	300	600	3,000
48	Dave Koslo RC	10	20	30	50	60	200	600	1,800

— Stan Musial #36 PSA 10 (Gem) (Young Collection) sold for $129,850 (SCP; 5/12)
— Stan Musial #36 PSA 10 (Gem) sold for $50,000 (Memory Lane; Private Sale - 2006)

1949 Bowman

		GD 2	VG 3	VgEx 4	EX 5	ExMt 6	NM 7	NmMt 8	MT 9
1	Vern Bickford RC	10	15	30	40	60	120	400	
2	Whitey Lockman	5	10	15	20	30	60	200	
3	Bob Porterfield RC	5	8	12	20	30	60	120	
4A	Jerry Priddy NNOF RC	5	6	10	15	20	40	250	
4B	Jerry Priddy NOF	10	15	25	30	50	100	150	
5	Hank Sauer	6	10	15	25	40	60	150	
6	Phil Cavarretta RC	5	8	12	20	25	50	120	
7	Joe Dobson RC	5	6	10	15	20	50	120	
8	Murry Dickson RC	5	6	10	15	20	40	80	
9	Ferris Fain	5	8	12	25	30	50	120	
10	Ted Gray RC	5	8	12	20	25	40	80	
11	Lou Boudreau MG RC	6	10	30	50	60	100	300	
12	Cass Michaels RC	5	6	10	15	20	50	80	
13	Bob Chesnes RC	5	6	10	15	20	50	100	
14	Curt Simmons RC	10	15	25	40	60	80	150	
15	Ned Garver RC	5	6	10	15	20	40	80	
16	Al Kozar RC	5	6	10	15	20	40	80	
17	Earl Torgeson RC	5	6	10	15	25	50	100	
18	Bobby Thomson	10	15	40	50	80	120	200	
19	Bobby Brown RC	8	12	20	40	50	60	300	
20	Gene Hermanski RC	5	8	12	20	30	50	100	
21	Frank Baumholtz RC	5	6	10	20	25	30	100	
22	Peanuts Lowrey RC	5	6	10	20	25	40	120	
23	Bobby Doerr	20	30	50	80	100	200	250	
24	Stan Musial	200	250	300	500	800	1,200	2,000	8,000
25	Carl Scheib RC	5	6	10	15	20	50	120	
26	George Kell RC	10	50	80	120	200	300	400	
27	Bob Feller	20	100	120	150	250	300	800	1,200
28	Don Kolloway RC	5	6	10	15	30	50	80	
29	Ralph Kiner	25	40	60	80	100	250	400	
30	Andy Seminick	5	8	12	20	30	50	80	
31	Dick Kokos RC	5	6	10	15	20	50	80	
32	Eddie Yost RC	5	8	12	20	30	50	80	
33	Warren Spahn	60	100	150	250	400	500	1,000	
34	Dave Koslo	5	6	10	15	20	50	120	
35	Vic Raschi RC	8	12	20	30	60	100	800	
36	Pee Wee Reese	60	100	120	150	250	400	800	3,000
37	Johnny Wyrostek	6	10	15	25	30	40	60	
38	Emil Verban	5	6	10	15	20	50	100	
39	Billy Goodman RC	5	6	10	15	40	50	80	
40	George Munger RC	5	6	10	15	20	80	150	
41	Lou Brissie RC	5	6	10	15	20	50	80	
42	Hoot Evers RC	5	6	10	15	20	50	80	
43	Dale Mitchell RC	5	8	15	20	50	60	120	
44	Dave Philley RC	5	6	10	15	20	40	200	
45	Wally Westlake RC	5	6	10	15	20	50	200	
46	Robin Roberts RC	120	250	300	400	500	600	1,000	3,000
47	Johnny Sain	15	25	40	50	60	100	200	
48	Willard Marshall	5	6	10	15	20	50	100	
49	Frank Shea	5	6	10	15	20	50	300	
50	Jackie Robinson RC	2,000	2,000	2,500	4,000	5,000	6,000	8,000	30,000
51	Herman Wehmeier	5	6	10	15	25	40	120	
52	Johnny Schmitz RC	5	6	10	15	40	50	100	
53	Jack Kramer RC	5	6	10	15	20	60	100	
54	Marty Marion	6	10	25	30	40	100	300	
55	Eddie Joost	5	6	10	15	30	40	80	
56	Pat Mullin RC	5	6	10	15	20	40	100	
57	Gene Bearden RC	5	8	12	20	25	40	120	
58	Bob Elliott	5	6	10	20	25	50	120	
59	Jack Lohrke	5	6	10	20	25	50	100	
60	Yogi Berra	200	300	500	600	1,000	1,200	2,000	4,000
61	Rex Barney	5	8	12	20	25	50	100	
62	Grady Hatton RC	5	6	10	15	20	35	120	
63	Andy Pafko RC	5	10	15	20	50	60	150	

#	Player	GD 2	VG 3	VgEx 4	EX 5	ExMt 6	NM 7	NmMt 8	MT 9
64	Dom DiMaggio	10	15	25	50	100	120	200	
65	Enos Slaughter	25	40	60	100	150	250	400	
66	Elmer Valo RC	5	6	10	20	30	50	100	
67	Alvin Dark RC	5	8	12	20	40	100	150	
68	Sheldon Jones	5	6	10	15	20	40	100	
69	Tommy Henrich	5	10	20	40	50	80	150	
70	Carl Furillo RC	12	20	60	80	120	200	400	
71	Vern Stephens RC	5	6	10	20	40	60	150	
72	Tommy Holmes RC	5	10	15	20	30	80	250	
73	Billy Cox RC	6	10	20	25	40	60	200	
74	Tom McBride RC	5	6	10	15	20	40	80	
75	Eddie Mayo RC	5	6	10	20	25	50	100	
76	Bill Nicholson RC	5	6	10	15	20	60	120	
77	Ernie Bonham RC	5	6	10	15	20	35	80	
78A	Sam Zoldak NNOF RC	5	6	10	15	20	40	80	
78B	Sam Zoldak NOF	10	15	25	30	50	80	400	
79	Ron Northey RC	5	6	10	15	25	50	200	
80	Bill McCahan	5	6	10	15	25	50	120	
81	Virgil Stallcup RC	5	6	10	15	20	40	100	
82	Joe Page	6	10	20	25	40	80	150	
83A	Bob Scheffing NNOF RC	5	6	10	15	20	40	80	
83B	Bob Scheffing NOF	10	15	25	30	50	80	120	
84	Roy Campanella RC	500	600	800	1,000	1,200	1,500	3,000	20,000
85A	Johnny Mize NNOF	10	20	30	40	80	120	250	1,000
85B	Johnny Mize NOF	15	25	40	60	100	150	400	
86	Johnny Pesky RC	6	10	20	40	60	100	250	
87	Randy Gumpert RC	5	8	12	20	30	50	100	
88A	Bill Salkeld NNOF RC	5	6	10	15	20	35	80	
88B	Bill Salkeld NOF	10	15	25	30	50	80	200	
89	Mizell Platt RC	5	6	10	15	20	40	80	
90	Gil Coan RC	5	6	10	15	25	40	100	
91	Dick Wakefield RC	5	6	10	15	20	40	80	
92	Willie Jones RC	5	8	12	20	25	60	100	
93	Ed Stevens RC	5	6	10	15	20	40	120	
94	Mickey Vernon RC	5	10	20	25	30	50	200	
95	Howie Pollet RC	5	6	10	20	25	50	150	
96	Taft Wright	5	6	10	15	20	35	120	
97	Danny Litwhiler RC	5	6	10	15	25	35	80	
98A	Phil Rizzuto NNOF	20	35	80	100	150	250	500	2,500
98B	Phil Rizzuto NOF	30	50	80	150	200	350	600	3,000
99	Frank Gustine RC	6	10	15	25	40	60	200	
100	Gil Hodges RC	60	100	150	200	300	500	800	4,000
101	Sid Gordon	5	6	10	15	20	30	120	
102	Stan Spence RC	5	6	10	15	20	50	120	
103	Joe Tipton RC	5	6	15	20	30	50	80	
104	Eddie Stanky RC	5	8	20	25	30	60	150	
105	Bill Kennedy RC	5	6	10	15	20	80	100	
106	Jake Early RC	5	6	10	15	20	35	60	
107	Eddie Lake RC	5	6	10	15	20	35	60	
108	Ken Heintzelman RC	5	6	10	15	30	50	150	
109A	Ed Fitzgerald Script Name RC	5	6	10	15	20	35	80	
109B	Ed Fitzgerald Print Name	10	15	25	30	50	80	250	
110	Early Wynn RC	60	100	150	250	300	500	600	3,000
111	Red Schoendienst	15	25	40	50	80	150	250	
112	Sam Chapman	6	10	15	25	30	50	100	
113	Ray LaManno RC	5	6	10	15	25	50	80	
114	Allie Reynolds	6	10	20	25	50	60	150	
115	Dutch Leonard	5	6	10	15	20	50	100	
116	Joe Hatten RC	5	6	10	15	30	60	200	
117	Walker Cooper	5	6	10	15	20	40	150	
118	Sam Mele RC	5	6	10	15	30	40	100	
119	Floyd Baker RC	5	6	10	15	20	30	100	
120	Cliff Fannin RC	5	6	10	20	25	30	100	
121	Mark Christman RC	5	6	10	20	25	40	120	
122	George Vico RC	5	6	10	15	25	40	80	
123	Johnny Blatnick	5	6	10	15	20	40	120	
124A	Danny Murtaugh Script Name RC	5	8	12	20	25	40	80	
124B	Danny Murtaugh Print Name	10	15	25	30	50	80	150	
125	Ken Keltner RC	5	6	10	15	20	60	100	
126A	Al Brazle Script Name RC	5	6	10	15	20	40	100	
126B	Al Brazle Print Name	10	15	25	30	50	80	150	
127A	Hank Majeski Script Name RC	5	6	10	15	20	40	60	
127B	Hank Majeski Print Name	10	15	25	30	50	80	250	
128	Johnny VanderMeer	12	20	30	40	50	80	200	
129	Bill Johnson	5	8	12	20	25	50	150	
130	Harry Walker RC	5	6	10	15	20	60	120	
131	Paul Lehner RC	5	8	12	20	30	50	80	
132A	Al Evans Script Name RC	5	6	10	15	20	40	120	
132B	Al Evans Print Name	10	15	25	30	50	80	100	
133	Aaron Robinson RC	5	6	10	15	20	40	60	
134	Hank Borowy RC	6	10	15	25	40	60	100	
135	Stan Rojek RC	5	6	10	15	20	40	100	
136	Hank Edwards RC	5	6	10	20	25	50	80	
137	Ted Wilks RC	5	6	10	15	20	40	80	
138	Buddy Rosar	5	6	10	15	20	40	80	
139	Hank Arft RC	5	6	10	20	25	50	80	
140	Ray Scarborough RC	5	6	10	15	20	40	60	
141	Tony Lupien RC	5	6	15	20	25	30	100	
142	Eddie Waitkus RC	8	12	20	30	40	50	120	
143A	Bob Dillinger Script Name RC	5	6	10	20	25	100	400	
143B	Bob Dillinger Print Name	10	15	25	30	50	80	200	
144	Mickey Haefner RC	5	6	10	15	20	50	200	
145	Blix Donnelly RC	5	10	15	25	40	100	300	
146	Mike McCormick RC	5	8	12	20	50	80	120	
147	Bert Singleton RC	5	8	12	20	50	120	200	
148	Bob Swift RC	5	8	12	20	30	40	300	
149	Roy Partee RC	5	8	12	20	40	80	250	
150	Allie Clark RC	5	8	12	20	25	50	120	
151	Mickey Harris RC	5	8	12	40	50	120	250	
152	Clarence Maddern RC	5	8	12	20	25	100	200	
153	Phil Masi RC	5	8	12	20	25	150	300	
154	Clint Hartung	5	8	12	20	25	80	150	
155	Mickey Guerra RC	5	8	12	20	40	60	120	
156	Al Zarilla RC	5	8	12	20	25	100	150	
157	Walt Masterson RC	5	8	12	20	25	100	250	
158	Harry Brecheen RC	5	8	12	20	25	80	250	
159	Glen Moulder RC	5	8	12	20	40	50	120	
160	Jim Blackburn RC	5	8	12	20	40	80	200	
161	Jocko Thompson RC	5	8	12	20	25	50	150	
162	Preacher Roe RC	15	25	80	100	150	200	600	
163	Clyde McCullough RC	5	8	12	20	25	100	200	
164	Vic Wertz RC	12	20	30	50	80	120	200	
165	Snuffy Stirnweiss	5	8	12	20	25	80	250	
166	Mike Tresh RC	12	20	30	50	80	150	600	
167	Babe Martin RC	5	8	12	30	40	60	150	
168	Doyle Lade RC	5	8	12	20	30	80	150	
169	Jeff Heath RC	5	8	12	20	40	100	200	
170	Bill Rigney	5	8	12	20	25	80	400	
171	Dick Fowler RC	5	8	12	20	50	100	300	
172	Eddie Pellagrini RC	5	8	12	20	25	50	200	
173	Eddie Stewart RC	5	8	12	20	30	100	150	
174	Terry Moore RC	10	20	30	50	80	150	600	
175	Luke Appling	15	25	60	80	200	250	500	
176	Ken Raffensberger RC	5	8	20	25	30	80	100	
177	Stan Lopata RC	5	8	12	20	25	60	200	
178	Tommy Brown RC	8	12	20	30	50	100	250	
179	Hugh Casey RC	5	12	25	50	60	150	400	
180	Connie Berry	5	8	12	20	40	150	300	
181	Gus Niarhos RC	5	8	12	30	40	80	300	
182	Hal Peck RC	5	8	12	25	30	60	200	
183	Lou Stringer RC	5	8	12	25	40	50	120	
184	Bob Chipman RC	5	8	12	20	25	50	100	
185	Pete Reiser	5	8	12	40	60	100	200	
186	Buddy Kerr	5	8	12	20	40	50	120	
187	Phil Marchildon RC	5	8	12	20	25	60	120	
188	Karl Drews RC	5	8	12	20	40	150	500	

#		GD 2	VG 3	VgEx 4	EX 5	ExMt 6	NM 7	NmMt 8	MT 9
189	Earl Wooten RC	5	8	12	20	50	200	400	
190	Jim Hearn RC	5	8	25	30	40	100	150	
191	Joe Haynes RC	5	8	12	20	25	50	120	
192	Harry Gumbert	5	8	12	20	25	60	100	
193	Ken Trinkle RC	5	8	12	20	25	80	200	
194	Ralph Branca RC	10	15	25	40	120	200	300	
195	Eddie Bockman RC	5	8	12	20	25	60	150	
196	Fred Hutchinson RC	5	8	12	20	25	50	120	
197	Johnny Lindell	5	8	12	30	40	120		
198	Steve Gromek RC	5	8	12	20	25	50	250	
199	Tex Hughson RC	5	8	12	20	30	60	120	
200	Jess Dobernic RC	5	8	12	20	25	60	150	
201	Sibby Sisti RC	5	8	12	20	50	80	150	
202	Larry Jansen	5	8	12	20	25	50	150	
203	Barney McCosky	5	8	12	20	25	50	150	
204	Bob Savage RC	5	8	12	20	25	60	200	
205	Dick Sisler RC	5	8	12	20	25	80	150	
206	Bruce Edwards	5	8	12	20	40	150		
207	Johnny Hopp RC	10	15	25	40	50	150	500	
208	Dizzy Trout	5	8	12	30	40	60	150	
209	Charlie Keller	15	25	40	60	100	150	300	
210	Joe Gordon RC	12	20	30	50	80	150	400	
211	Boo Ferriss RC	20	30	50	80	200	250	500	
212	Ralph Hamner RC	5	8	12	20	40	50	150	
213	Red Barrett RC	5	8	12	20	25	60	150	
214	Richie Ashburn RC	250	400	500	600	800	1,000	2,500	
215	Kirby Higbe	5	8	12	20	25	80		
216	Schoolboy Rowe	5	8	12	50	60	100	500	
217	Marino Pieretti RC	5	8	12	20	50	80	120	
218	Dick Kryhoski RC	10	15	30	40	50	80	150	
219	Virgil Trucks RC	5	8	12	20	25	50	200	
220	Johnny McCarthy	5	8	12	20	25	200	400	
221	Bob Muncrief RC	5	8	12	20	25	50	150	
222	Alex Kellner RC	5	8	12	20	40	60	120	
223	Bobby Hofman RC	5	8	12	20	25	60	200	
224	Satchel Paige RC	1,500	2,000	2,500	3,000	4,000	5,000	10,000	20,000
225	Jerry Coleman RC	12	20	30	50	80	120	400	
226	Duke Snider RC	600	800	1,000	1,200	2,000	2,500	3,000	10,000
227	Fritz Ostermueller	5	8	12	20	50	60	120	
228	Jackie Mayo RC	5	8	12	20	25	50	200	
229	Ed Lopat RC	10	25	40	50	80	120	300	
230	Augie Galan	5	8	12	20	30	50	120	
231	Earl Johnson RC	5	8	12	20	40	100	120	
232	George McQuinn	5	8	12	20	40	60	150	
233	Larry Doby RC	250	400	500	600	800	1,000	2,000	
234	Rip Sewell RC	5	8	12	20	40	80	200	
235	Jim Russell RC	5	8	12	25	30	60	150	
236	Fred Sanford RC	5	8	12	20	30	50	150	
237	Monte Kennedy RC	5	8	12	20	30	80	150	
238	Bob Lemon RC	150	200	250	400	500	600	1,500	
239	Frank McCormick	5	8	12	20	25	80	150	
240	Babe Young	10	20	30	50	100	200		

— Roy Campanella #84 PSA 10 (Gem) (Young Collection) sold for $44,428 (SCP; 5/12)
— Larry Doby #233 PSA 9 (Mint) sold for $5,180 (Memory Lane; 8/12)
— Sheldon Jones #68 PSA 10 (Gem) sold for $5,899 (Mile High; 5/12)
— Jackie Robinson #50 SGC 92 (NmMt+) sold for $10,073 (REA; Fall '13)

1949 Leaf

#		PrFr 1	GD 2	VG 3	VgEx 4	EX 5	ExMt 6	NM 7	NmMt 8
	Joe DiMaggio	500	800	1,200	2,000	3,000	5,000	8,000	30,000
	Babe Ruth	1,200	2,000	3,000	5,000	8,000	12,000	25,000	60,000
	Stan Musial	600	1,000	1,500	2,500	4,000	6,000	10,000	40,000
	Virgil Trucks SP RC	80	120	200	300	400	500		
	Satchel Paige SP RC	8,000	12,000	20,000	30,000	50,000	100,000	150,000	
0	Paul Trout	5	10	15	20	25	80	150	400
1	Phil Rizzuto	60	80	100	120	200	300	600	1,200
3	Casimer Michaels SP RC	60	100	250	400	500	600	1,500	

#		PrFr 1	GD 2	VG 3	VgEx 4	EX 5	ExMt 6	NM 7	NmMt 8
14	Billy Johnson	5	10	15	20	40	60	150	
17	Frank Overmire RC	5	10	15	20	25	40	100	300
19	John Wyrostek SP	60	100	150	250	400	600	1,200	
20	Hank Sauer SP	100	200	300	400	500	800	1,200	
22	Al Evans RC	5	10	15	20	40	60	100	400
26	Sam Chapman	5	10	15	20	25	40	100	400
27	Mickey Harris RC	5	10	15	20	25	50	100	300
28	Jim Hegan RC	5	10	15	30	40	60	150	600
29	Elmer Valo RC	5	10	15	20	25	50	100	300
30	Billy Goodman SP RC	60	100	150	250	400	600	1,500	
31	Lou Brissie RC	5	10	15	20	25	40	100	300
32	Warren Spahn	120	200	250	400	600	800	1,500	3,000
33	Harry Lowrey SP RC	60	100	150	250	400	600	1,000	
36	Al Zarilla SP	100	150	200	300	400	600		
38	Ted Kluszewski RC	20	40	80	100	200	250	300	800
39	Ewell Blackwell	10	15	25	40	60	80	150	400
42A	Kent Peterson Black Cap RC	5	10	15	20	25	50	150	
42B	Kent Peterson Red Cap	60	100	150	150	400	600		
43	Eddie Stevens SP RC	100	120	150	250	400	600		
45	Ken Keltner SP RC	60	150	200	250	400	600		
46	Johnny Mize	10	15	20	50	80	150	200	800
47	George Vico RC	5	10	20	25	30	40	120	600
48	Johnny Schmitz SP RC	100	120	150	250	400	600	1,000	
49	Del Ennis RC	5	10	15	20	25	50	100	400
50	Dick Wakefield RC	5	10	15	20	40	60	100	300
51	Alvin Dark SP RC	100	150	250	400	600	1,000		
53	John VanderMeer	10	15	25	40	60	100	150	1,000
54	Bobby Adams SP RC	100	150	200	300	400	600	1,000	
55	Tommy Henrich SP	100	250	300	400	600	800	1,500	
56	Larry Jensen	5	10	15	20	25	60	100	300
57	Bob McCall RC	5	10	15	25	30	40	100	400
59	Luke Appling	10	15	40	60	80	120	200	600
61	Jake Early RC	5	10	15	20	25	40	100	400
62	Eddie Joost SP	60	100	150	400	400	600	1,000	1,500
63	Barney McCosky SP	60	100	150	250	400	600	1,000	
65	Bob Elliott	5	10	15	20	25	40	100	300
66	Orval Grove SP RC	60	200	250	300	400	600		
68	Ed Miller SP	60	100	150	250	500	600		
70	Honus Wagner	80	120	200	250	300	500	800	1,200
72	Hank Edwards RC	5	10	15	20	25	40	100	300
73	Pat Seerey RC	5	10	15	20	25	120	250	600
75	Dom DiMaggio SP	100	200	300	500	800	1,200		
76	Ted Williams	300	500	600	800	1,200	1,500	2,000	8,000
77	Roy Smalley RC	5	10	15	20	25	50	120	400
78	Walter Evers SP RC	80	100	150	200	600	800	1,000	
79	Jackie Robinson RC	1,200	2,000	3,000	4,000	6,000	12,000	15,000	25,000
81	George Kurowski SP RC	80	120	200	300	500	800		
82	Johnny Lindell	5	10	15	20	40	60	120	300
83	Bobby Doerr	10	15	25	60	100	120	250	600
84	Sid Hudson	5	10	20	25	30	40	100	300
85	Dave Philley SP RC	60	100	150	250	500	600	1,200	
86	Ralph Weigel RC	5	10	15	30	40	50	100	400
88	Frank Gustine SP RC	80	120	200	300	600	800	1,500	
91	Ralph Kiner	15	25	80	100	150	250	400	1,000
93	Bob Feller SP	800	1,000	1,200	1,500	2,000	2,500		
95	George Stirnweiss	5	10	15	20	25	40	100	300
97	Marty Marion	6	10	20	25	40	100	200	500
98	Hal Newhouser SP RC	300	400	500	1,000	1,500	2,200		
102A	Gene Hermansk ERR	150	250	400	600	1,200			
102B	Gene Hermanski COR RC	10	15	25	40	50	80	200	600
104	Edward Stewart SP RC	100	120	150	250	400	600		
106	Lou Boudreau MG RC	10	15	25	40	80	120	200	600
108	Matthew Batts SP RC	60	120	150	250	400	600	1,000	1,500
111	Gerald Priddy RC	5	10	15	20	25	40	100	300
113	Emil Leonard SP	60	100	150	400	400	600	1,500	
117	Joe Gordon RC	5	10	15	60	80	100	150	600
120	George Kell SP RC	150	250	400	800	1,000	1,200	3,000	
121	Johnny Pesky SP RC	100	150	200	300	500	800		

#	Player	PrFr 1	GD 2	VG 3	VgEx 4	EX 5	ExMt 6	NM 7	NmMt 8
123	Cliff Fannin SP RC	60	100	200	250	400	600	1,200	
125	Andy Pafko RC	5	10	15	20	25	100	120	800
127	Enos Slaughter SP	300	400	500	600	1,000	1,200	2,000	
128	Warren Rosar	5	10	15	20	25	40	100	300
129	Kirby Higbe SP	100	120	150	200	300	600		
131	Sid Gordon SP	60	200	250	300	400	600		
133	Tommy Holmes SP RC	100	150	200	400	600	800		
136A	Cliff Aberson Full Sleeve RC	5	10	15	20	120	150	200	
136B	Cliff Aberson Short Sleeve	15	25	40	60	100	150	1,000	
137	Harry Walker SP RC	60	120	150	200	400	800		
138	Larry Doby SP RC	300	400	600	1,200	1,500	2,500	4,000	
139	Johnny Hopp RC	5	10	15	30	40	60	100	300
142	Danny Murtaugh SP RC	60	120	150	200	250	500		
143	Dick Sisler SP RC	60	120	150	400	400	600	1,000	2,000
144	Bob Dillinger SP RC	60	100	150	250	400	600	1,200	
146	Harold Reiser SP	80	120	200	300	800	800		
149	Henry Majeski SP RC	60	100	150	250	400	1,000		
153	Floyd Baker SP RC	100	150	200	300	500	800		
158	Harry Brecheen SP RC	100	250	300	400	800	1,500		
159	Mizell Platt RC	6	10	20	25	35	50	120	500
160	Bob Scheffing SP RC	60	100	150	250	400	800		
161	Vernon Stephens SP RC	100	150	300	400	500	800		
163	Fred Hutchinson SP RC	100	150	200	300	500	800		
165	Dale Mitchell SP RC	100	150	200	300	400	600	2,000	
168	Phil Cavaretta SP RC	100	150	250	500	800	1,000		

— Harry Brecheen #158 PSA 7 (NM) sold for $8,833 (Goodwin; 11/11)
— Phil Rizzuto #11 SGC 96 (MT) sold for $5,484 (Goodwin; 10/12)
— Jackie Robinson #79 PSA 9 (MT) sold for $45,000 (Memory Lane; Private - 2006)
— Jackie Robinson #79 SGC 92 (NmMt+) sold for $13,035 (REA; 5/13)
— Jackie Robinson #79 SGC 92 (NmMt+) sold for $11,850 (REA; Spring '14)
— Ted Williams #76 SGC 8.5 (NmMt+) sold for $5,253 (Mile High; 10/11)

1950 Bowman

#	Player	GD 2	VG 3	VgEx 4	EX 5	ExMt 6	NM 7	NmMt 8	MT 9
1	Mel Parnell RC	15	25	50	120	400			
2	Vern Stephens	15	20	30	50	80	100	1,000	
3	Dom DiMaggio	25	40	60	100	150	250	1,200	
4	Gus Zernial RC	5	10	15	25	50	80	500	
5	Bob Kuzava RC	5	8	12	25	30	80	250	
6	Bob Feller	▲100	120	150	200	250	800	2,000	
7	Jim Hegan	5	10	15	40	60	200	400	
8	George Kell	10	15	50	60	80	150	400	
9	Vic Wertz	5	10	15	25	40	120		
10	Tommy Henrich	10	30	40	50	100	150	1,000	
11	Phil Rizzuto	50	80	120	200	300	400	1,200	
12	Joe Page	8	12	18	40	50	120	300	
13	Ferris Fain	5	10	15	30	40	200	300	
14	Alex Kellner	5	8	12	20	30	60	100	
15	Al Kozar	6	10	15	25	30	100	200	
16	Roy Sievers RC	8	12	40	50	100	200	500	
17	Sid Hudson	5	8	12	20	30	60	200	
18	Eddie Robinson RC	5	8	12	20	30	80	300	
19	Warren Spahn	60	100	150	200	300	500	1,200	
20	Bob Elliott	6	10	15	25	60	100	200	
21	Pee Wee Reese	▲50	▲80	▲120	▲200	▲300	▲500	1,000	
22	Jackie Robinson	▲2,500	▲3,000	▲4,000	▲5,000	▲8,000	▲12,000	▲15,000	
23	Don Newcombe RC	40	50	60	120	250	400	▲1,200	
24	Johnny Schmitz	5	8	12	20	30	50	150	
25	Hank Sauer	5	10	15	25	50	80	300	
26	Grady Hatton	5	8	12	30	50	60	250	
27	Herman Wehmeier	5	8	12	20	30	60	120	
28	Bobby Thomson	20	30	40	50	80	200	300	
29	Eddie Stanky	5	10	15	25	40	80	300	
30	Eddie Waitkus	5	10	15	25	50	80	200	
31	Del Ennis	8	12	20	30	80	100	500	
32	Robin Roberts	25	50	80	120	200	400	1,200	
33	Ralph Kiner	30	50	80	100	150	250	500	2,000
34	Murry Dickson	5	10	15	25	40	250	500	
35	Enos Slaughter	25	30	50	60	80	250	500	
36	Eddie Kazak RC	8	12	20	30	50	100	1,200	
37	Luke Appling	10	15	40	80	100	200	500	
38	Bill Wight RC	5	8	12	20	30	60	120	
39	Larry Doby	30	50	60	100	150	300	1,000	
40	Bob Lemon	10	15	50	60	80	200	500	
41	Hoot Evers	6	10	15	25	40	60	120	
42	Art Houtteman RC	5	8	12	20	40	60	150	
43	Bobby Doerr	30	40	50	60	120	200	400	
44	Joe Dobson	5	8	12	20	30	50	150	
45	Al Zarilla	5	8	12	20	30	50	200	
46	Yogi Berra	▲200	▲300	▲400	▲500	▲800	▲1,200	2,500	
47	Jerry Coleman	5	10	25	30	50	120	250	
48	Lou Brissie	5	8	12	20	25	50	150	
49	Elmer Valo	6	10	15	25	40	60	250	
50	Dick Kokos	5	8	12	20	30	60	100	
51	Ned Garver	5	10	15	25	40	60	250	
52	Sam Mele	5	8	12	20	30	60	150	
53	Clyde Vollmer RC	5	8	12	20	30	80	100	
54	Gil Coan	5	8	12	20	30	60	120	
55	Buddy Kerr	5	8	12	20	30	50	150	
56	Del Crandall RC	5	10	25	40	50	100	200	
57	Vern Bickford	5	8	12	20	30	50	200	
58	Carl Furillo	10	15	25	60	80	120	300	800
59	Ralph Branca	10	15	25	40	50	100	300	
60	Andy Pafko	5	20	30	40	50	80	200	
61	Bob Rush RC	5	8	12	20	30	60	100	
62	Ted Kluszewski	10	15	25	60	80	150	400	
63	Ewell Blackwell	10	15	25	30	40	80	250	
64	Alvin Dark	5	10	15	25	50	80	200	
65	Dave Koslo	5	8	12	20	30	80	150	
66	Larry Jansen	5	8	12	20	30	50	200	
67	Willie Jones	5	10	15	25	40	100	500	
68	Curt Simmons	6	10	15	25	50	100	200	
69	Wally Westlake	5	8	12	20	30	50	100	
70	Bob Chesnes	5	8	12	20	30	40	200	
71	Red Schoendienst	10	15	50	60	80	120	400	
72	Howie Pollet	5	8	12	20	30	50	200	
73	Willard Marshall	5	8	12	20	30	60	400	
74	Johnny Antonelli RC	5	10	15	25	40	50	200	
75	Roy Campanella	▲80	▲120	▲200	250	400	500	▲1,200	▲10,000
76	Rex Barney	5	5	8	12	15	30	500	
77	Duke Snider	▲80	▲120	▲150	▲200	250	300	1,000	5,000
78	Mickey Owen	5	5	8	20	25	40	100	
79	Johnny VanderMeer	5	10	15	25	50	120	200	
80	Howard Fox RC	5	5	8	12	15	25	80	
81	Ron Northey	5	6	10	12	15	30	150	
82	Whitey Lockman	5	8	12	15	20	40	150	
83	Sheldon Jones	5	5	8	12	25	60		
84	Richie Ashburn	30	40	50	80	120	400	600	
85	Ken Heintzelman	5	5	8	12	15	40	150	
86	Stan Rojek	5	6	10	15	25	40	100	
87	Bill Werle RC	5	5	8	12	20	40	80	
88	Marty Marion	5	8	12	20	50	60	300	
89	George Munger	5	5	8	12	15	40	120	
90	Harry Brecheen	5	5	8	12	15	40	120	
91	Cass Michaels	5	5	8	12	15	40	100	
92	Hank Majeski	5	6	10	12	15	30	150	
93	Gene Bearden	5	5	8	12	25	40	150	
94	Lou Boudreau MG	10	15	25	40	50	100	150	700
95	Aaron Robinson	5	5	8	12	15	25	80	
96	Virgil Trucks	5	5	8	12	30	40	200	
97	Maurice McDermott RC	5	5	8	12	15	25	300	
98	Ted Williams	▲300	▲500	▲600	▲1,000	▲1,500	▲2,500	8,000	10,000
99	Billy Goodman	5	8	12	20	25	40	150	
100	Vic Raschi	5	10	15	25	40	60	250	
101	Bobby Brown	5	10	15	25	40	80	200	

#	Player	GD 2	VG 3	VgEx 4	EX 5	ExMt 6	NM 7	NmMt 8	MT 9
102	Billy Johnson	5	5	8	12	15	60	120	
103	Eddie Joost	5	5	8	12	25	30	60	
104	Sam Chapman	5	6	10	15	20	30	200	
105	Bob Dillinger	5	5	8	12	15	30	80	
106	Cliff Fannin	5	5	8	12	15	40	150	
107	Sam Dente RC	5	5	8	12	15	40	150	
108	Ray Scarborough	5	5	8	12	25	50	200	
109	Sid Gordon	5	5	8	12	15	40	150	
110	Tommy Holmes	5	5	8	20	25	50	60	
111	Walker Cooper	5	5	8	12	15	25	60	
112	Gil Hodges	30	50	80	120	200	300	500	1,000
113	Gene Hermanski	5	5	8	12	15	40	100	
114	Wayne Terwilliger RC	5	5	8	20	25	50	120	
115	Roy Smalley	5	6	10	12	30	50	80	
116	Virgil Stallcup	5	5	8	12	20	30	80	
117	Bill Rigney	5	5	8	12	15	40	80	
118	Clint Hartung	5	6	10	12	25	30	250	
119	Dick Sisler	5	5	8	12	15	60	80	
120	John Thompson	5	5	8	12	15	25	80	
121	Andy Seminick	5	5	8	12	15	80	150	
122	Johnny Hopp	5	6	10	15	25	40	80	
123	Dino Restelli RC	5	6	10	12	15	40	120	
124	Clyde McCullough	5	5	8	12	15	25	80	
125	Del Rice RC	5	5	8	12	15	40	80	
126	Al Brazle	5	5	8	12	15	25	50	
127	Dave Philley	5	6	10	12	20	30	100	
128	Phil Masi	5	5	12	15	20	50	60	
129	Joe Gordon	5	6	10	25	50	80	250	
130	Dale Mitchell	5	6	10	12	15	50	150	
131	Steve Gromek	5	5	12	15	20	40	80	
132	Mickey Vernon	5	5	8	12	15	40	150	
133	Don Kolloway	5	5	8	12	25	30	80	
134	Paul Trout	5	5	8	12	25	30	80	
135	Pat Mullin	5	5	8	12	15	25	80	
136	Buddy Rosar	5	6	10	12	15	30	200	
137	Johnny Pesky	5	8	12	20	60	100	120	
138	Allie Reynolds	5	10	25	30	50	60	150	
139	Johnny Mize	15	25	40	60	100	150	400	
140	Pete Suder RC	5	5	8	12	15	30	50	
141	Joe Coleman RC	5	5	8	25	30	50	80	
142	Sherman Lollar RC	5	8	12	20	25	50	250	
143	Eddie Stewart	5	5	8	12	15	25	50	
144	Al Evans	5	5	8	12	20	30	120	
145	Jack Graham RC	5	5	8	12	15	50	80	
146	Floyd Baker	5	6	10	12	15	40	100	
147	Mike Garcia RC	5	8	12	20	25	40	120	
148	Early Wynn	15	25	40	60	100	150	300	
149	Bob Swift	5	5	8	12	15	25	120	
150	George Vico	5	5	8	12	20	30	50	
151	Fred Hutchinson	5	5	8	12	15	30	150	
152	Ellis Kinder RC	5	5	8	12	25	30	100	
153	Walt Masterson	5	6	10	15	25	40	80	
154	Gus Niarhos	5	5	8	12	25	30	150	
155	Frank Shea	5	5	8	12	20	30	100	
156	Fred Sanford	5	5	8	12	20	50	80	
157	Mike Guerra	5	5	8	20	25	30	80	
158	Paul Lehner	5	5	8	12	15	30	60	
159	Joe Tipton	5	5	8	15	20	30	60	
160	Mickey Harris	5	5	8	12	15	40	100	
161	Sherry Robertson RC	5	5	8	12	20	25	80	
162	Eddie Yost	5	5	8	12	20	30	100	
163	Earl Torgeson	5	5	8	12	25	30	60	
164	Sibby Sisti	5	5	8	12	15	40	80	
165	Bruce Edwards	5	6	10	12	20	30	120	
166	Joe Hatton	5	5	8	12	15	40	80	
167	Preacher Roe	5	10	20	25	40	60	200	1,000
168	Bob Scheffing	5	5	8	20	25	30	80	
169	Hank Edwards	5	5	8	12	15	25	100	
170	Dutch Leonard	5	5	8	12	15	40	60	
171	Harry Gumbert	5	5	8	12	15	25	60	
172	Peanuts Lowrey	5	5	8	12	25	25	80	
173	Lloyd Merriman RC	5	5	8	20	25	30	150	
174	Hank Thompson RC	6	10	15	25	40	60	150	
175	Monte Kennedy	5	5	8	12	15	40	50	
176	Sylvester Donnelly	5	5	8	12	30	60	80	
177	Hank Borowy	5	6	10	15	25	30	80	
178	Ed Fitzgerald	5	5	8	12	15	40	100	
179	Chuck Diering RC	5	5	8	12	20	25	80	
180	Harry Walker	5	5	8	20	25	30	60	
181	Marino Pieretti	5	5	8	12	15	50	100	
182	Sam Zoldak	5	5	8	12	15	40	80	
183	Mickey Haefner	5	5	8	12	20	25	50	
184	Randy Gumpert	5	5	8	12	15	25	100	
185	Howie Judson RC	5	5	8	12	30	50	80	
186	Ken Keltner	5	5	8	12	15	30	120	
187	Lou Stringer	5	5	8	12	15	30	60	
188	Earl Johnson	5	5	8	12	25	50	60	
189	Owen Friend RC	5	8	12	20	30	50	80	
190	Ken Wood RC	5	6	10	15	20	30	100	
191	Dick Starr RC	5	5	8	12	15	30	60	
192	Bob Chipman	5	5	8	12	15	25	60	
193	Pete Reiser	5	8	12	20	25	40	120	
194	Billy Cox	5	8	12	20	30	50	120	600
195	Phil Cavarretta	5	8	12	20	25	40	100	
196	Doyle Lade	5	5	8	12	15	30	80	
197	Johnny Wyrostek	5	5	8	12	15	30	80	
198	Danny Litwhiler	5	5	8	12	15	25	60	
199	Jack Kramer	5	5	8	12	15	40	120	
200	Kirby Higbe	5	5	8	15	20	25	80	
201	Pete Castiglione RC	5	5	8	15	20	40	80	
202	Cliff Chambers RC	5	5	8	12	20	50	80	
203	Danny Murtaugh	5	5	8	12	15	30	60	
204	Granny Hamner RC	5	8	12	20	40	50	100	
205	Mike Goliat RC	5	5	8	12	15	30	80	
206	Stan Lopata	5	5	8	12	25	30	120	
207	Max Lanier RC	5	5	8	12	20	30	80	
208	Jim Hearn	5	5	8	12	15	40	80	
209	Johnny Lindell	5	5	8	12	20	30	100	
210	Ted Gray	5	5	8	12	15	40	80	
211	Charlie Keller	5	8	12	20	25	80	120	
212	Jerry Priddy	5	5	8	15	20	25	60	
213	Carl Scheib	5	5	8	12	20	30	80	
214	Dick Fowler	5	5	8	12	25	30	60	
215	Ed Lopat	5	10	15	25	40	60	150	
216	Bob Porterfield	5	5	8	12	15	40	100	
217	Casey Stengel MG	10	15	50	60	100	120	400	1,000
218	Cliff Mapes RC	5	5	8	30	40	50	80	
219	Hank Bauer RC	8	25	30	50	60	120	250	800
220	Leo Durocher MG	5	10	30	40	60	100	200	800
221	Don Mueller RC	5	8	12	20	25	50	100	
222	Bobby Morgan RC	5	5	8	12	25	50	120	
223	Jim Russell	5	5	8	12	15	40	80	
224	Jack Banta RC	5	5	8	12	15	30	80	
225	Eddie Sawyer MG RC	5	5	8	20	25	50	100	
226	Jim Konstanty RC	5	8	12	20	50	60	150	
227	Bob Miller RC	5	5	8	12	20	30	80	
228	Bill Nicholson	5	8	12	20	30	50	60	
229	Frankie Frisch MG	6	10	15	25	40	80	200	
230	Bill Serena RC	5	5	8	12	15	30	60	
231	Preston Ward RC	5	5	8	12	25	40	60	
232	Al Rosen RC	5	10	40	50	60	80	250	
233	Allie Clark	5	5	8	20	25	40	100	
234	Bobby Shantz RC	5	10	15	25	40	60	250	
235	Harold Gilbert RC	5	5	8	15	20	50	80	
236	Bob Cain RC	5	5	8	12	20	25	100	
237	Bill Salkeld	5	5	8	12	15	25	60	

		GD 2	VG 3	VgEx 4	EX 5	ExMt 6	NM 7	NmMt 8	MT 9
238	Nippy Jones RC	5	5	8	12	20	30	60	
239	Bill Howerton RC	5	5	8	12	15	30	100	
240	Eddie Lake	5	5	8	12	15	30	80	
241	Neil Berry RC	5	5	8	12	30	40	80	
242	Dick Kryhoski	5	5	8	12	25	30	100	
243	Johnny Groth RC	5	5	8	12	15	25	80	
244	Dale Coogan RC	5	5	8	12	15	40	80	
245	Al Papai RC	5	5	8	12	40	60	100	
246	Walt Dropo RC	5	10	12	20	25	80	100	
247	Irv Noren RC	5	5	8	20	30	40	250	
248	Sam Jethroe RC	5	10	15	25	50	80	200	
249	Snuffy Stirnweiss	5	5	8	12	15	30	100	
250	Ray Coleman RC	5	5	8	12	15	50	80	
251	Les Moss RC	5	5	8	12	25	30	150	
252	Billy DeMars RC	10	15	25	40	60	100	400	

— Jackie Robinson #22 PSA 8.5 (NmMt+) sold for $5,969 (Mile High; 1/13)

1950-51 Toleteros

— Joshua Gibson #JG PSA 7 (NrMt) sold for $27,631 (Mile High; 1/12)
— Joshua Gibson #JG PSA 4 (VgEx) sold for $18,330 (Goodwin; 9/13)
— Joshua Gibson #JG PSA 4 (Vg/Ex) sold for $9,076 (Legendary; 6/12)

1951 Bowman

		GD 2	VG 3	VgEx 4	EX 5	ExMt 6	NM 7	NmMt 8	MT 9
1	Whitey Ford RC	500	600	1,000	1,500	3,000	5,000	20,000	
2	Yogi Berra	100	150	250	400	600	1,000	5,000	8,000
3	Robin Roberts	10	30	40	60	100	200	800	2,000
4	Del Ennis	12	15	40	50	50	120	250	1,000
5	Dale Mitchell	5	5	8	12	20	30	120	
6	Don Newcombe	15	25	40	50	80	200	500	
7	Gil Hodges	12	30	50	60	100	150	400	▲5,000
8	Paul Lehner	5	5	8	12	20	40	80	1,000
9	Sam Chapman	5	5	8	25	30	80	250	500
10	Red Schoendienst	12	20	30	50	80	120	250	1,200
11	George Munger	5	5	8	12	20	30	80	500
12	Hank Majeski	5	5	8	20	25	40	60	600
13	Eddie Stanky	5	5	8	12	20	50	100	3,000
14	Alvin Dark	5	5	8	12	25	60	100	1,500
15	Johnny Pesky	5	5	8	12	50	50	250	1,000
16	Maurice McDermott	5	5	8	12	20	40	100	500
17	Pete Castiglione	5	5	8	12	20	40	80	500
18	Gil Coan	5	5	8	12	20	120	200	
19	Sid Gordon	5	8	12	20	25	50	100	1,200
20	Del Crandall	5	5	8	12	20	30	80	800
21	Snuffy Stirnweiss	5	5	8	12	25	40	150	500
22	Hank Sauer	5	5	8	12	40	150	200	
23	Hoot Evers	5	8	12	20	25	60	100	800
24	Ewell Blackwell	5	5	8	20	30	40	80	
25	Vic Raschi	8	12	20	25	30	60	150	800
26	Phil Rizzuto	40	60	100	150	200	250	500	3,000
27	Jim Konstanty	5	6	10	25	30	40	150	
28	Eddie Waitkus	5	5	8	12	20	100	500	400
29	Allie Clark	5	8	12	15	25	40	80	500
30	Bob Feller	▲50	▲80	▲120	▲200	▲300	▲500	600	5,000
31	Roy Campanella	80	120	150	250	300	600	1,200	8,000
32	Duke Snider	60	100	150	250	400	▲800	1,200	
33	Bob Hooper RC	5	5	8	12	40	60	80	
34	Marty Marion MG	5	8	12	20	30	50	200	1,500
35	Al Zarilla	5	5	8	12	20	40	60	
36	Joe Dobson	5	5	8	12	20	40	100	
37	Whitey Lockman	5	5	8	12	20	50	120	
38	Al Evans	5	5	8	12	20	40	100	800
39	Ray Scarborough	5	6	10	15	20	50	80	500
40	Gus Bell RC	5	8	12	20	25	40	150	1,000
41	Eddie Yost	5	6	10	15	25	40	100	800
42	Vern Bickford	5	8	12	20	25	40	80	500
43	Billy DeMars	5	5	8	12	20	40	80	500

		GD 2	VG 3	VgEx 4	EX 5	ExMt 6	NM 7	NmMt 8	MT 9
44	Roy Smalley	5	5	8	12	20	40	100	500
45	Art Houtteman	5	5	8	12	20	40	100	
46	George Kell	12	20	30	50	60	120	250	1,000
47	Grady Hatton	5	5	8	12	20	40	80	500
48	Ken Raffensberger	5	5	8	12	20	40	80	600
49	Jerry Coleman	5	5	8	12	20	60	120	600
50	Johnny Mize	12	20	30	50	80	120	250	1,200
51	Andy Seminick	5	5	8	15	20	40	100	500
52	Dick Sisler	5	5	8	12	20	60	100	1,000
53	Bob Lemon	12	20	30	50	80	120	200	1,000
54	Ray Boone RC	5	6	10	15	25	100	150	
55	Gene Hermanski	5	8	12	20	30	50	150	
56	Ralph Branca	5	10	25	30	50	80	250	
57	Alex Kellner	5	8	12	20	30	50	80	500
58	Enos Slaughter	12	20	30	50	80	▲150	250	800
59	Randy Gumpert	5	6	10	15	25	30	50	600
60	Chico Carrasquel RC	10	15	25	40	60	100	150	2,200
61	Jim Hearn	5	8	12	20	30	50	80	500
62	Lou Boudreau MG	12	20	30	50	80	120	200	1,000
63	Bob Dillinger	5	5	8	12	20	30	100	
64	Bill Werle	5	5	8	12	20	40	60	
65	Mickey Vernon	5	8	12	20	30	50	120	600
66	Bob Elliott	5	5	8	12	20	30	60	1,000
67	Roy Sievers	5	8	12	20	30	50	150	2,500
68	Dick Kokos	5	5	8	12	20	30	60	
69	Johnny Schmitz	5	5	8	12	20	30	50	
70	Ron Northey	5	5	8	12	20	30	50	1,200
71	Jerry Priddy	5	5	8	12	20	25	60	
72	Lloyd Merriman	5	5	8	12	20	50	60	500
73	Tommy Byrne RC	5	6	10	15	25	100		
74	Billy Johnson	5	5	8	12	20	30	150	1,200
75	Russ Meyer RC	5	6	10	15	25	40	100	1,000
76	Stan Lopata	5	8	12	20	25	40	100	400
77	Mike Goliat	5	5	8	12	20	50	80	250
78	Early Wynn	8	12	20	50	60	100	250	600
79	Jim Hegan	5	5	8	12	25	40	80	800
80	Pee Wee Reese	40	60	100	120	200	300	600	10,000
81	Carl Furillo	12	20	30	50	80	120	300	1,000
82	Joe Tipton	5	5	8	12	25	40	60	1,200
83	Carl Scheib	5	8	12	20	30	50	80	400
84	Barney McCosky	5	5	8	12	20	40	80	800
85	Eddie Kazak	5	5	8	12	20	30	60	400
86	Harry Brecheen	5	6	10	15	25	40	60	500
87	Floyd Baker	5	5	8	12	20	40	60	500
88	Eddie Robinson	5	5	8	12	20	40	100	300
89	Hank Thompson	5	5	8	12	25	40	120	400
90	Dave Koslo	6	10	15	25	40	60	100	
91	Clyde Vollmer	5	6	10	15	25	40	80	1,000
92	Vern Stephens	5	5	8	20	30	40	60	500
93	Danny O'Connell RC	5	6	10	15	25	30	60	500
94	Clyde McCullough	5	6	10	15	25	30	80	600
95	Sherry Robertson	5	5	8	12	20	40	60	1,200
96	Sandy Consuegra RC	5	5	8	12	20	30	100	400
97	Bob Kuzava	5	5	8	12	20	30	80	500
98	Willard Marshall	5	5	8	12	20	30	60	400
99	Earl Torgeson	5	5	8	12	20	40	80	500
100	Sherm Lollar	5	5	8	20	30	50	120	
101	Owen Friend	5	5	8	12	20	40	60	1,000
102	Dutch Leonard	6	10	15	25	40	60	100	500
103	Andy Pafko	6	10	15	25	40	60	120	1,000
104	Virgil Trucks	5	5	8	12	30	50	150	800
105	Don Kolloway	5	6	10	15	20	30	120	1,200
106	Pat Mullin	5	5	8	12	20	30	80	500
107	Johnny Wyrostek	5	5	8	12	20	30	100	500
108	Virgil Stallcup	5	5	8	12	20	30	100	
109	Allie Reynolds	8	12	20	30	40	100	200	1,500
110	Bobby Brown	▲8	▲12	▲20	▲30	▲50	▲80	▲120	800
111	Curt Simmons	6	10	15	25	40	50	120	1,000

#	Player	GD 2	VG 3	VgEx 4	EX 5	ExMt 6	NM 7	NmMt 8	MT 9
112	Willie Jones	5	5	8	12	20	50	100	500
113	Bill Nicholson	5	5	8	12	20	50	100	600
114	Sam Zoldak	5	5	8	12	20	30	80	
115	Steve Gromek	5	5	8	12	20	30	80	2,000
116	Bruce Edwards	5	5	8	12	20	30	120	
117	Eddie Miksis RC	5	5	15	12	20	50	250	
118	Preacher Roe	10	15	25	40	60	100	200	800
119	Eddie Joost	5	5	8	12	20	40	80	
120	Joe Coleman	5	5	8	12	20	50	80	400
121	Gerry Staley RC	5	5	8	12	20	40	80	500
122	Joe Garagiola RC	15	25	40	50	80	100	250	800
123	Howie Judson	5	5	8	12	20	30	50	1,000
124	Gus Niarhos	5	5	8	12	20	30	60	400
125	Bill Rigney	5	6	10	15	25	50	80	500
126	Bobby Thomson	15	25	40	60	100	150	250	1,000
127	Sal Maglie RC	5	10	25	30	50	60	250	
128	Ellis Kinder	5	5	8	12	25	50	120	400
129	Matt Batts	5	5	8	12	20	30	120	500
130	Tom Saffell RC	5	5	8	12	20	30	60	600
131	Cliff Chambers	5	5	8	12	20	30	60	500
132	Cass Michaels	5	5	8	12	20	40	60	800
133	Sam Dente	5	5	8	12	25	30	60	400
134	Warren Spahn	50	80	100	120	150	300	800	4,000
135	Walker Cooper	5	5	8	20	25	40	100	
136	Ray Coleman	5	5	8	12	20	30	80	500
137	Dick Starr	5	5	8	12	20	30	100	
138	Phil Cavarretta	5	5	8	12	30	40	100	500
139	Doyle Lade	5	5	8	12	20	40	80	
140	Eddie Lake	5	5	8	12	20	30	80	4,000
141	Fred Hutchinson	5	5	8	12	20	50	80	500
142	Aaron Robinson	5	5	8	12	20	30	60	500
143	Ted Kluszewski	15	25	40	60	100	150	250	1,500
144	Herman Wehmeier	5	5	8	12	20	50	60	500
145	Fred Sanford	5	5	8	12	20	40	80	500
146	Johnny Hopp	5	8	12	20	30	50	120	500
147	Ken Heintzelman	5	5	8	12	20	30	60	500
148	Granny Hamner	5	5	8	12	20	60	80	
149	Bubba Church RC	5	5	8	12	20	50	60	500
150	Mike Garcia	5	5	8	12	20	50	100	400
151	Larry Doby	40	60	100	150	300	500	800	4,000
152	Cal Abrams RC	5	6	10	15	25	40	80	1,200
153	Rex Barney	6	10	15	25	40	60	100	
154	Pete Suder	5	6	10	15	25	30	60	500
155	Lou Brissie	5	5	8	12	20	30	60	400
156	Del Rice	5	5	8	12	25	30	60	600
157	Al Brazle	5	8	12	20	30	50	80	400
158	Chuck Diering	5	5	8	12	20	30	60	1,000
159	Eddie Stewart	5	5	8	15	20	40	60	400
160	Phil Masi	5	5	8	12	20	30	60	800
161	Wes Westrum RC	5	5	8	12	25	40	80	
162	Larry Jansen	5	5	8	12	20	40	80	
163	Monte Kennedy	5	5	8	20	25	30	60	500
164	Bill Wight	5	5	8	12	20	30	80	2,500
165	Ted Williams	▲500	▲600	▲800	▲1,200	▲2,000	2,500	4,000	8,000
166	Stan Rojek	5	5	8	12	20	40	80	400
167	Murry Dickson	5	5	8	12	20	30	60	500
168	Sam Mele	5	5	8	12	20	30	80	500
169	Sid Hudson	5	5	8	12	20	30	80	2,500
170	Sibby Sisti	5	5	8	12	20	30	60	
171	Buddy Kerr	5	5	8	12	20	30	80	400
172	Ned Garver	5	5	8	12	20	30	100	
173	Hank Arft	5	6	10	15	25	40	60	500
174	Mickey Owen	5	5	8	12	20	30	80	
175	Wayne Terwilliger	5	5	8	12	20	30	60	400
176	Vic Wertz	5	5	8	12	25	40	80	800
177	Charlie Keller	5	6	10	15	25	40	60	600
178	Ted Gray	5	5	8	12	20	30	60	400
179	Danny Litwhiler	5	5	8	12	20	30	80	400

#	Player	GD 2	VG 3	VgEx 4	EX 5	ExMt 6	NM 7	NmMt 8	MT 9
180	Howie Fox	5	8	12	20	30	50	80	500
181	Casey Stengel MG	20	30	50	80	120	200	300	2,000
182	Tom Ferrick RC	5	5	8	12	20	30	120	1,000
183	Hank Bauer	8	12	20	30	50	80	250	2,000
184	Eddie Sawyer MG	5	5	8	12	20	30	80	500
185	Jimmy Bloodworth	5	5	8	12	20	30	60	600
186	Richie Ashburn	20	30	50	80	100	150	400	1,200
187	Al Rosen	5	8	12	20	50	80	200	
188	Roberto Avila RC	5	5	8	12	20	50	100	500
189	Erv Palica RC	5	5	8	25	30	40	100	
190	Joe Hatten	5	6	10	15	25	40	80	2,500
191	Billy Hitchcock RC	5	5	8	12	20	25	80	600
192	Hank Wyse RC	5	5	8	12	20	30	60	400
193	Ted Wilks	5	5	8	12	20	30	80	400
194	Peanuts Lowrey	5	6	10	15	25	30	60	
195	Paul Richards MG	5	5	8	12	25	30	60	800
196	Billy Pierce RC	10	15	25	40	60	100	150	600
197	Bob Cain	5	5	8	12	20	30	60	2,500
198	Monte Irvin RC	40	60	100	150	250	500	1,200	
199	Sheldon Jones	5	5	8	12	25	30	80	
200	Jack Kramer	5	6	10	15	20	50	60	400
201	Steve O'Neill MG RC	5	5	8	12	20	30	80	500
202	Mike Guerra	5	5	8	12	20	30	100	400
203	Vern Law RC	6	10	15	25	40	50	120	600
204	Vic Lombardi RC	5	5	8	20	25	30	60	500
205	Mickey Grasso RC	5	5	8	12	20	40	60	800
206	Conrado Marrero RC	5	5	8	12	20	30	60	1,500
207	Billy Southworth MG RC	8	12	20	30	50	80	120	800
208	Blix Donnelly	5	5	8	12	20	30	60	
209	Ken Wood	5	5	8	12	25	30	60	600
210	Les Moss	5	8	12	20	30	50	80	500
211	Hal Jeffcoat RC	5	5	8	12	20	30	60	2,500
212	Bob Rush	5	5	8	12	25	30	80	500
213	Neil Berry	5	6	10	15	25	30	60	600
214	Bob Swift	5	5	8	12	20	30	100	300
215	Ken Peterson	5	5	8	12	25	30	80	400
216	Connie Ryan RC	5	5	8	12	20	30	100	
217	Joe Page	5	5	15	20	25	50	100	
218	Ed Lopat	5	10	15	25	30	50	100	1,200
219	Gene Woodling RC	5	8	15	25	40	60	150	1,500
220	Bob Miller	5	6	10	15	25	40	100	500
221	Dick Whitman RC	5	5	8	12	20	30	60	500
222	Thurman Tucker RC	5	6	10	15	25	30	60	400
223	Johnny VanderMeer	5	8	12	20	30	50	150	800
224	Billy Cox	5	8	12	20	30	50	120	500
225	Dan Bankhead RC	5	5	8	20	40	50	120	600
226	Jimmie Dykes MG	5	8	12	20	30	50	50	1,200
227	Bobby Shantz	5	5	8	12	25	40	80	2,000
228	Cloyd Boyer RC	5	5	8	12	20	40	100	500
229	Bill Howerton	5	5	8	12	20	30	50	500
230	Max Lanier	5	5	8	12	20	40	60	400
231	Luis Aloma RC	5	6	10	15	25	50	80	400
232	Nellie Fox RC	80	120	200	300	400	▲600	1,200	4,000
233	Leo Durocher MG	10	15	25	40	60	100	▲200	800
234	Clint Hartung	5	5	8	12	20	30	80	400
235	Jack Lohrke	5	5	8	20	25	40	60	400
236	Buddy Rosar	5	5	8	12	20	30	50	400
237	Billy Goodman	5	5	8	12	20	40	60	1,500
238	Pete Reiser	5	6	10	15	25	40	80	1,000
239	Bill MacDonald RC	5	5	8	12	20	30	50	800
240	Joe Haynes	5	5	8	12	20	30	60	400
241	Irv Noren	5	5	8	12	20	30	60	500
242	Sam Jethroe	5	5	8	12	20	30	100	500
243	Johnny Antonelli	5	8	12	20	30	50	100	400
244	Cliff Fannin	5	5	8	12	20	40	60	600
245	John Berardino RC	5	6	8	12	20	50	100	3,000
246	Bill Serena	5	5	8	12	20	40	60	500
247	Bob Ramazzotti RC	5	6	10	15	25	30	100	800

		GD 2	VG 3	VgEx 4	EX 5	ExMt 6	NM 7	NmMt 8	MT 9
248	Johnny Klippstein RC	5	5	8	12	20	30	80	600
249	Johnny Groth	5	5	8	12	20	30	50	400
250	Hank Borowy	5	5	8	12	20	30	60	400
251	Willard Ramsdell RC	6	10	15	25	30	40	80	400
252	Dixie Howell RC	5	5	8	12	20	30	80	500
253	Mickey Mantle RC	▼12,000	▼20,000	▼25,000	▼40,000	80,000	120,000	600,000	
254	Jackie Jensen RC	12	20	40	80	80	120	400	5,000
255	Milo Candini RC	5	8	20	25	30	60	200	800
256	Ken Silvestri RC	5	8	12	20	30	60	200	
257	Birdie Tebbetts RC	5	8	12	20	30	50	120	
258	Luke Easter RC	5	10	15	25	40	60	250	800
259	Chuck Dressen MG	5	8	12	20	30	80	200	800
260	Carl Erskine RC	15	25	40	80	120	150	350	2,500
261	Wally Moses	5	8	12	20	30	50	120	600
262	Gus Zernial	5	8	12	20	30	50	150	600
263	Howie Pollet	8	12	20	30	50	60	120	
264	Don Richmond RC	5	8	12	20	30	50	150	
265	Steve Bilko RC	5	8	15	20	50	120	200	1,200
266	Harry Dorish RC	5	8	12	20	30	40	100	
267	Ken Holcombe RC	5	8	12	20	30	50	100	800
268	Don Mueller	5	8	12	20	30	100	120	2,000
269	Ray Noble RC	5	8	12	20	30	60	200	800
270	Willard Nixon RC	6	10	15	25	40	60	200	800
271	Tommy Wright RC	5	10	15	25	40	80	400	
272	Billy Meyer MG RC	5	8	12	20	50	80	300	
273	Danny Murtaugh	6	10	15	25	40	60	500	
274	George Metkovich RC	5	8	12	20	40	60	250	
275	Bucky Harris MG	5	10	15	50	60	100	250	
276	Frank Quinn RC	5	8	12	20	30	80	200	800
277	Roy Hartsfield RC	5	8	15	30	50	60	120	600
278	Norman Roy RC	5	8	12	20	30	80	120	
279	Jim Delsing RC	8	12	20	30	50	80	120	600
280	Frank Overmire	5	8	12	20	30	80	400	
281	Al Widmar RC	5	8	12	20	30	50	120	
282	Frankie Frisch MG	5	10	15	25	80	100	300	
283	Walt Dubiel RC	5	8	12	20	50	80	120	600
284	Gene Bearden	5	8	12	20	30	50	120	
285	Johnny Lipon RC	5	8	12	20	30	50	120	600
286	Bob Usher RC	5	8	12	20	30	60	250	
287	Jim Blackburn RC	5	8	12	20	30	50	150	600
288	Bobby Adams RC	5	8	12	20	30	50	150	600
289	Cliff Mapes	5	8	12	20	30	50		
290	Bill Dickey CO	10	15	25	80	120	200	400	
291	Tommy Henrich CO	8	12	20	40	80	100	300	1,500
292	Eddie Pellagrini	5	8	12	25	30	50	100	800
293	Ken Johnson RC	8	12	20	30	50	80	200	600
294	Jocko Thompson	5	8	12	20	30	50	150	1,200
295	Al Lopez MG RC	20	30	40	50	60	100	200	1,500
296	Bob Kennedy RC	5	8	12	20	30	100	200	600
297	Dave Philley	5	8	12	20	30	60	120	
298	Joe Astroth RC	5	8	12	20	30	60	150	
299	Clyde King RC	8	12	20	30	50	80	150	
300	Hal Rice RC	6	10	15	25	40	50	200	5,000
301	Tommy Glaviano RC	5	8	12	20	30	40	150	1,200
302	Jim Busby RC	5	8	12	20	40	60	150	1,500
303	Marv Rotblatt RC	5	8	12	20	30	60	150	800
304	Al Gettell RC	5	8	12	20	30	50	150	600
305	Willie Mays RC	▼6,000	12,000	15,000	20,000	30,000	100,000	250,000	
306	Jimmy Piersall RC	12	20	30	50	80	150	500	1,200
307	Walt Masterson	8	12	20	30	40	100	120	800
308	Ted Beard RC	5	8	15	20	30	50	150	
309	Mel Queen RC	5	8	12	20	50	60	200	
310	Erv Dusak RC	5	8	12	20	30	60	150	1,300
311	Mickey Harris	5	8	12	20	30	50	100	800
312	Gene Mauch RC	15	25	40	60	80	100	200	
313	Ray Mueller RC	5	8	12	20	30	60	100	2,800
314	Johnny Sain	8	12	20	25	60	120	300	1,200
315	Zack Taylor MG	5	8	12	20	40	50	120	

		GD 2	VG 3	VgEx 4	EX 5	ExMt 6	NM 7	NmMt 8	MT 9
316	Duane Pillette RC	8	12	20	30	50	80	150	600
317	Forrest Burgess RC	5	10	15	25	60	120	250	
318	Warren Hacker RC	5	8	12	20	30	50	150	800
319	Red Rolfe MG	5	10	15	20	40	100	200	800
320	Hal White RC	5	8	12	20	30	80	120	
321	Earl Johnson	5	8	12	20	30	50	150	1,700
322	Luke Sewell MG	5	9	15	25	40	100	250	
323	Joe Adcock RC	8	12	20	30	60	120	400	
324	Johnny Pramesa RC	9	15	25	40	80	150	400	3,500

— Whitey Ford #1 PSA 9 (MT) sold for $75,000 (Memory Lane; Private 2007)
— Nellie Fox #232 PSA 10 (Gem) (Young Collection) sold for $13,344 (SCP; 5/12)
— Vern Law #203 PSA 10 (Gem) (Young Collection) sold for $6,991 (SCP; 5/12)
— Mickey Mantle #253 PSA 9 (MT) sold for $135,000 (Memory Lane - Private 2007)
— Mickey Mantle #253 SGC 96 (MT) sold for $127,810 (Mile High; 10/13)
— Willie Mays #305 PSA 9 (MT) sold for $85,000 (Memory Lane; Private Sale - 2007)
— Willie Mays #305 SGC 92 (NmMt+) sold for $30,822 (Goodwin; 12/14)
— Willie Mays #305 SGC 92 (NmMt+) sold for $22,730 (Mile High; 4/14)
— Sam Zoldak #114 PSA 10 (Gem) sold for $6,610 (eBay; 9/12)

1951 Topps Blue Backs

		GD 2	VG 3	VgEx 4	EX 5	ExMt 6	NM 7	NmMt 8	MT 9
1	Eddie Yost	5	10	15	80	100	200	▲300	▲500
2	Hank Majeski	5	30	40	50	60	80	100	200
3	Richie Ashburn	60	100	150	200	250	300	400	600
4	Del Ennis	40	50	60	80	100	120	150	250
5	Johnny Pesky	5	8	25	60	80	50	100	250
6	Red Schoendienst	12	20	30	40	50	80	150	300
7	Gerry Staley RC	5	8	12	15	20	30	60	150
8	Dick Sisler	5	8	12	15	20	30	80	200
9	Johnny Sain	8	12	20	25	30	50	100	200
10	Joe Page	10	15	25	40	50	60	150	250
11	Johnny Groth	5	8	12	40	50	60	60	200
12	Sam Jethroe	5	10	15	20	50	60	▲120	200
13	Mickey Vernon	5	8	12	15	30	60	80	150
14	George Munger	5	8	12	15	20	60	100	200
15	Eddie Joost	10	15	25	30	40	60	120	200
16	Murry Dickson	5	8	12	15	20	30	▲200	▲300
17	Roy Smalley	5	8	12	15	20	60	120	150
18	Ned Garver	5	8	12	15	20	30	100	200
19	Phil Masi	5	8	12	15	20	30	▲100	150
20	Ralph Branca	5	10	15	20	25	40	100	250
21	Billy Johnson	5	8	12	15	20	30	60	▲300
22	Bob Kuzava	5	8	12	15	50	60	▲100	150
23	Dizzy Trout	5	10	15	20	25	40	120	200
24	Sherman Lollar	5	8	12	15	20	60	80	250
25	Sam Mele	5	8	12	15	20	50	60	100
26	Chico Carrasquel RC	5	8	12	15	20	30	150	▲250
27	Andy Pafko	5	8	12	15	20	30	80	150
28	Harry Brecheen	5	8	12	15	20	30	60	150
29	Granville Hamner	5	8	12	15	20	30	▲120	▲200
30	Enos Slaughter	15	25	40	50	60	100	150	400
31	Lou Brissie	5	8	12	15	20	30	60	150
32	Bob Elliott	5	10	15	20	25	40	80	200
33	Don Lenhardt RC	5	8	12	15	20	30	100	150
34	Earl Torgeson	5	8	12	15	20	30	60	250
35	Tommy Byrne RC	6	10	15	25	40	50	60	150
36	Cliff Fannin	5	8	12	40	50	60	100	200
37	Bobby Doerr	12	20	30	60	80	100	250	400
38	Irv Noren	5	8	12	15	20	30	80	200
39	Ed Lopat	5	10	15	20	25	40	▲100	300
40	Vic Wertz	5	8	12	15	20	30	120	150
41	Johnny Schmitz	5	8	12	15	20	30	▲100	150
42	Bruce Edwards	5	8	12	15	20	30	100	200
43	Willie Jones	5	8	12	15	20	30	60	200
44	Johnny Wyrostek	5	8	12	15	20	30	80	250
45	Billy Pierce RC	5	10	15	20	25	40	100	200
46	Gerry Priddy	5	8	12	15	20	30	80	150

		GD 2	VG 3	VgEx 4	EX 5	ExMt 6	NM 7	NmMt 8	MT 9
7	Herman Wehmeier	5	8	12	15	20	30	80	150
8	Billy Cox	5	10	15	20	25	50	▲150	▲250
9	Hank Sauer	5	10	15	20	60	80	150	
0	Johnny Mize	12	20	30	40	80	100	150	300
1	Eddie Waitkus	5	25	30	40	50	60	300	
2	Sam Chapman	5	10	50	60	80	100	300	400

1951 Topps Connie Mack's All-Stars

	PrFr 1	GD 2	VG 3	VgEx 4	EX 5	ExMt 6	NM 7	NmMt 8
Grover C. Alexander	100	150	250	300	500	600		
Mickey Cochrane	80	100	150	250	300	400		
Eddie Collins	80	100	200	250	400	600		
Jimmy Collins	60	80	120	200	250	450		
Lou Gehrig	300	400	600	1,200	1,500	2,000		
Walter Johnson	200	250	400	500	600	800		
Connie Mack	100	120	200	300	400	800		
Christy Mathewson	150	200	300	400	800	1,000		
Babe Ruth	350	500	800	1,200	2,000	2,800		
Tris Speaker	80	250	300	400	500	600		
Honus Wagner	150	250	300	450	600	800		

- Babe Ruth #9 SGC 92 (NmMt+) sold for $8,927 (Memory Lane; 5/12)

1951 Topps Red Backs

	GD 2	VG 3	VgEx 4	EX 5	ExMt 6	NM 7	NmMt 8	MT 9
Yogi Berra	50	60	100	150	250	300	600	1,000
Sid Gordon	5	5	8	10	12	20	150	250
Ferris Fain	5	5	8	10	12	20	60	120
Vern Stephens	5	5	8	10	40	50	120	200
Phil Rizzuto	15	25	30	50	60	80	250	500
Allie Reynolds	8	12	20	30	50	60	100	200
Howie Pollet	5	5	8	10	12	25	60	120
Early Wynn	12	30	30	50	80	100	150	2,500
Roy Sievers	5	5	8	10	12	20	60	100
Mel Parnell	5	5	8	10	12	20	60	150
Gene Hermanski	5	5	8	10	12	25	60	120
Jim Hegan	5	6	10	15	25	30	50	100
Dale Mitchell	5	5	8	10	12	20	50	100
Wayne Terwilliger	5	5	8	10	12	40	80	120
Ralph Kiner	8	12	20	30	50	80	120	150
Preacher Roe	5	8	12	20	30	50	▲100	200
Gus Bell RC	5	5	8	12	20	30	50	100
Jerry Coleman	5	5	8	12	25	30	60	120
Dick Kokos	5	5	8	12	15	20	50	100
Dom DiMaggio	8	12	20	30	50	80	100	200
Larry Jansen	5	5	8	10	12	25	60	250
Bob Feller	30	50	80	120	150	200	300	400
Ray Boone RC	5	5	8	10	12	20	80	150
Hank Bauer	5	8	12	15	30	50	100	200
Cliff Chambers	5	5	8	10	12	20	50	100
Luke Easter RC	5	5	8	10	12	20	50	150
Wally Westlake	5	5	8	10	12	20	60	120
Elmer Valo	5	5	8	10	12	20	40	120
Bob Kennedy RC	5	5	8	10	12	20	60	100
Warren Spahn	20	30	60	80	100	150	▲300	500
Gil Hodges	10	15	25	40	60	100	▲200	600
Henry Thompson	5	5	6	10	15	25	50	200
William Werle	5	5	8	10	12	20	50	150
Grady Hatton	5	5	8	10	12	20	50	100
Al Rosen	5	6	10	25	30	50	80	150
Gus Zernial Chicago	5	10	15	20	30	50	100	500
Gus Zernial Philadelphia	5	6	10	12	15	25	80	400
Wes Westrum RC	5	5	8	10	12	20	50	200
Duke Snider	12	20	50	60	80	120	▲300	▲600
Ted Kluszewski	5	8	30	40	50	60	100	150
Mike Garcia	5	5	8	12	20	30	50	150
Whitey Lockman	5	5	6	10	15	25	60	120
Ray Scarborough	5	5	8	10	12	20	50	100

		GD 2	VG 3	VgEx 4	EX 5	ExMt 6	NM 7	NmMt 8	MT 9
43	Maurice McDermott	5	5	8	20	25	30	60	120
44	Sid Hudson	5	5	8	12	20	30	60	100
45	Andy Seminick	5	5	8	10	12	20	50	150
46	Billy Goodman	5	6	10	15	25	30	60	100
47	Tommy Glaviano RC	5	5	8	10	12	20	40	100
48	Eddie Stanky	5	5	8	10	12	20	200	250
49	Al Zarilla	5	5	8	10	12	40	60	200
50	Monte Irvin RC	30	40	50	80	100	120	150	250
51	Eddie Robinson	5	5	8	10	12	30	40	200
52A	Tommy Holmes Boston	5	10	15	20	30	60		
52B	Tommy Holmes Hartford	5	8	12	15	20	30	80	

1952 Berk Ross

		GD 2	VG 3	VgEx 4	EX 5	ExMt 6	NM 7	NmMt 8	MT 9
	COMMON CARD	5	6	10	15	20	30	80	
1	Richie Ashburn	6	10	15	25	40	60	200	
2	Hank Bauer	5	6	10	15	20	30	80	
3	Yogi Berra	25	40	60	80	150	250	500	
4	Ewell Blackwell	5	6	10	15	20	30	200	
5	Bobby Brown	5	6	10	15	20	30	80	
6	Jim Busby	5	6	10	15	20	30	100	
7	Roy Campanella	12	20	30	60	80	200	650	
8	Chico Carrasquel	5	6	10	15	20	30	250	
9	Jerry Coleman	5	6	10	15	20	30	80	
10	Joe Collins	5	6	10	15	20	30	80	
11	Alvin Dark	5	6	10	15	20	30	550	
12	Dom DiMaggio	5	6	10	15	20	400	1,000	
13	Joe DiMaggio	120	200	300	500	800	1,000	2,500	
14	Larry Doby	10	15	25	40	60	100	300	
15	Bobby Doerr	5	8	12	20	40	100	200	
16	Bob Elliott	5	6	10	15	20	30	80	
17	Del Ennis	5	6	10	15	20	30	80	
18	Ferris Fain	5	6	10	15	20	30	100	
19	Bob Feller	10	15	25	40	100	120	400	
20	Nellie Fox	6	10	15	25	40	60	150	
21	Ned Garver	5	6	10	15	20	30	120	
22	Clint Hartung	5	6	10	15	20	30	80	
23	Jim Hearn	5	6	10	15	20	30		
24	Gil Hodges	6	10	15	25	40	60	400	
25	Monte Irvin	5	8	12	20	30	50		
26	Larry Jansen	5	6	10	15	20	30	150	
27	Sheldon Jones	5	6	10	15	20		2,000	
28	George Kell	5	6	10	15	20	30	600	
29	Monte Kennedy	5	6	10	15	20	30		
30	Ralph Kiner	5	8	12	20	30	50		
31	Dave Koslo	5	6	10	15	20	80		
32	Bob Kuzava	5	6	10	15	20	30		
33	Bob Lemon	5	8	12	20	30	60		
34	Whitey Lockman	5	6	10	15	20	30		
35	Ed Lopat	5	6	10	15	20	30	80	
36	Sal Maglie	5	6	10	15	20	30		
37	Mickey Mantle	400	450	600	1,200	3,000	5,000		
38	Billy Martin	8	12	20	30	50	80	200	
39	Willie Mays	100	125	175	250	500	750	1,500	
40	Gil McDougald	12	20	30	50	80	200	500	
41	Minnie Minoso	5	6	10	15	20	30		
42	Johnny Mize	5	8	12	20	30	50	120	
43	Tom Morgan	5	6	10	15	20	30		
44	Don Mueller	5	6	10	15	20	30	80	
45	Stan Musial	25	40	80	100	250	400	1,200	
46	Don Newcombe	5	6	10	15	20	30	200	
47	Ray Noble	5	6	10	15	20	30		
48	Joe Ostrowski	5	6	10	15	20	30		
49	Mel Parnell	5	6	10	15	20	30	80	
50	Vic Raschi	5	6	10	15	20	30	80	
51	Pee Wee Reese	10	15	25	40	100	250	400	
52	Allie Reynolds	5	6	10	20	30	50	200	

#	Player	GD 2	VG 3	VgEx 4	EX 5	ExMt 6	NM 7	NmMt 8	MT 9
53	Bill Rigney	5	6	10	15	20	30	150	
54A	Phil Rizzuto Bunting	10	15	25	40	60	80	300	
54B	Phil Rizzuto Swinging	10	15	25	40	80	100		
55	Robin Roberts	5	8	12	20	30	50	200	
56	Eddie Robinson	5	6	10	15	20	30		
57	Jackie Robinson	120	150	200	250	600	1,000	1,500	
58	Preacher Roe	5	6	10	50	60	80	400	
59	Johnny Sain	5	6	10	15	20	120		
60	Red Schoendienst	5	8	12	20	30	50	120	
61	Duke Snider	15	25	40	60	100	200	700	
62	George Spencer	5	6	10	15	20	30	80	
63	Eddie Stanky	5	6	10	15	20	30	100	
64	Hank Thompson	5	6	10	15	20	30	80	
65	Bobby Thomson	5	6	10	15	20	1,000		
66	Vic Wertz	5	6	10	15	20	30	80	
67	Wally Westlake	5	6	10	15	20	30		
68	Wes Westrum	5	6	10	15	20	30		
69	Ted Williams	100	120	200	300	500	800	1,800	
70	Gene Woodling	5	6	10	15	20	30	150	
71	Gus Zernial	5	6	10	15	20	30	80	

— Willie Mays PSA 9 (MT) sold for $5,899 (Goodwin; 03/12)

1952 Bowman

#	Player	GD 2	VG 3	VgEx 4	EX 5	ExMt 6	NM 7	NmMt 8	MT 9
1	Yogi Berra	150	250	400	600	800	1,200	4,000	20,000
2	Bobby Thomson	20	25	30	40	60	150	500	
3	Fred Hutchinson	5	5	8	10	25	50	120	400
4	Robin Roberts	20	30	50	80	120	150	400	1,200
5	Minnie Minoso RC	50	80	120	200	300	500	1,500	2,500
6	Virgil Stallcup	5	5	8	10	30	40	150	
7	Mike Garcia	5	8	12	20	30	50	200	
8	Pee Wee Reese	30	50	80	120	200	300	500	2,500
9	Vern Stephens	6	10	15	25	40	50	120	
10	Bob Hooper	5	5	8	10	15	30	100	
11	Ralph Kiner	20	30	50	60	80	150	300	1,000
12	Max Surkont RC	5	5	8	10	25	40	60	
13	Cliff Mapes	5	5	8	10	15	30	80	250
14	Cliff Chambers	5	5	8	12	20	40	100	400
15	Sam Mele	5	5	8	12	20	40	80	400
16	Turk Lown RC	5	5	8	10	15	25	100	
17	Ed Lopat	5	10	15	20	40	60	120	800
18	Don Mueller	5	5	8	10	15	25	120	
19	Bob Cain	5	8	12	20	30	40	80	
20	Willie Jones	5	5	8	10	15	50	80	250
21	Nellie Fox	20	30	50	60	100	150	▲400	2,500
22	Willard Ramsdell	5	5	8	10	25	60	80	400
23	Bob Lemon	5	10	25	30	50	80	200	1,000
24	Carl Furillo	8	20	25	30	50	80	200	1,000
25	Mickey McDermott	5	5	8	12	20	25	100	
26	Eddie Joost	5	5	8	12	20	40	100	800
27	Joe Garagiola	10	15	25	30	40	80	150	600
28	Roy Hartsfield	5	5	10	15	25	50	150	400
29	Ned Garver	5	5	8	12	20	40	120	
30	Red Schoendienst	12	20	30	50	60	100	300	1,000
31	Eddie Yost	5	6	10	15	25	50	80	
32	Eddie Miksis	5	5	8	12	20	30	100	400
33	Gil McDougald RC	12	20	30	50	60	80	250	1,000
34	Alvin Dark	5	6	10	15	30	50	150	500
35	Granny Hamner	5	6	10	15	25	50	120	
36	Cass Michaels	5	5	8	10	20	50	100	
37	Vic Raschi	5	8	12	15	25	50	200	
38	Whitey Lockman	5	5	8	10	15	50	100	
39	Vic Wertz	5	6	10	12	20	30	120	
40	Bubba Church	5	6	10	15	25	30	80	
41	Chico Carrasquel	5	6	10	12	20	30	80	500
42	Johnny Wyrostek	5	5	8	12	20	30	120	
43	Bob Feller	40	▲60	▲100	▲150	▲250	▲400	800	2,000

#	Player	GD 2	VG 3	VgEx 4	EX 5	ExMt 6	NM 7	NmMt 8	MT 9
44	Roy Campanella	60	80	100	150	200	300	800	4,000
45	Johnny Pesky	10	15	25	40	50	80	250	
46	Carl Scheib	5	5	8	10	25	30	100	
47	Pete Castiglione	5	5	8	10	25	30	60	400
48	Vern Bickford	5	5	8	12	20	30	80	
49	Jim Hearn	5	5	8	10	15	25	60	
50	Gerry Staley	5	6	10	15	25	40	100	
51	Gil Coan	5	6	10	15	25	40	80	400
52	Phil Rizzuto	▲40	▲60	▲80	▲120	▲200	▲300	▲500	2,000
53	Richie Ashburn	20	30	50	60	80	150	▲500	1,500
54	Billy Pierce	5	6	10	12	20	50	100	
55	Ken Raffensberger	5	5	8	10	15	50	60	
56	Clyde King	5	5	8	10	30	40	100	400
57	Clyde Vollmer	5	5	8	15	20	40	80	
58	Hank Majeski	5	5	8	10	25	40	100	
59	Murry Dickson	5	5	8	10	15	40	60	250
60	Sid Gordon	5	5	8	10	25	40	60	
61	Tommy Byrne	5	5	8	12	20	25	80	300
62	Joe Presko RC	5	5	8	10	15	40	80	400
63	Irv Noren	5	5	8	12	20	30	80	400
64	Roy Smalley	5	8	12	20	30	80	120	400
65	Hank Bauer	5	10	20	30	40	100	250	800
66	Sal Maglie	5	5	10	15	25	50	100	400
67	Johnny Groth	5	5	8	10	20	25	80	300
68	Jim Busby	5	5	8	10	30	120		
69	Joe Adcock	5	6	10	15	25	50	100	400
70	Carl Erskine	10	15	25	40	60	100	150	
71	Vern Law	5	6	10	12	20	30	80	
72	Earl Torgeson	5	6	10	15	25	40	200	300
73	Jerry Coleman	6	10	15	25	40	50	250	600
74	Wes Westrum	5	5	8	10	30	40	100	
75	George Kell	12	20	30	40	50	100	200	1,000
76	Del Ennis	5	6	10	15	25	50	150	400
77	Eddie Robinson	5	5	8	10	15	40	80	300
78	Lloyd Merriman	5	5	8	10	25	30	100	400
79	Lou Brissie	5	5	8	10	25	30	60	400
80	Gil Hodges	25	40	60	80	100	150	400	3,000
81	Billy Goodman	5	6	10	15	25	40	100	250
82	Gus Zernial	5	5	8	10	20	50	100	
83	Howie Pollet	5	5	8	10	20	30	60	
84	Sam Jethroe	6	10	15	25	30	50	120	
85	Marty Marion CO	5	6	10	12	25	50	120	
86	Cal Abrams	5	5	8	10	25	30	60	400
87	Mickey Vernon	5	6	10	15	25	40	100	400
88	Bruce Edwards	5	5	6	10	15	30	80	300
89	Billy Hitchcock	5	5	8	12	20	30	60	300
90	Larry Jansen	5	8	12	20	30	40	150	
91	Don Kolloway	5	5	8	10	15	40	100	300
92	Eddie Waitkus	5	5	8	10	25	60	100	400
93	Paul Richards MG	5	5	8	12	20	30	120	400
94	Luke Sewell MG	5	6	10	15	25	50	80	400
95	Luke Easter	5	8	12	20	40	50	150	500
96	Ralph Branca	5	8	12	25	30	80	150	800
97	Willard Marshall	5	5	8	10	15	50	60	
98	Jimmie Dykes MG	5	5	8	10	15	40	80	500
99	Clyde McCullough	5	5	8	10	15	40	80	500
100	Sibby Sisti	5	5	8	10	25	30	40	
101	Mickey Mantle	3,000	4,000	▲6,000	8,000	10,000	▼20,000	40,000	400,00
102	Peanuts Lowrey	5	5	8	10	15	50	60	400
103	Joe Haynes	5	5	8	10	15	40	120	400
104	Hal Jeffcoat	5	5	8	10	15	25	60	300
105	Bobby Brown	6	10	15	25	30	50	150	
106	Randy Gumpert	5	5	8	10	20	30	80	500
107	Del Rice	5	6	10	15	25	40	100	300
108	George Metkovich	5	5	8	10	15	30	100	
109	Tom Morgan RC	6	10	15	25	40	60	150	
110	Max Lanier	5	5	8	10	20	50	60	
111	Hoot Evers	5	5	8	10	15	50	100	

	GD 2	VG 3	VgEx 4	EX 5	ExMt 6	NM 7	NmMt 8	MT 9
Smoky Burgess	5	8	12	20	25	80	150	500
Al Zarilla	5	5	8	12	20	30	120	400
Frank Hiller RC	5	5	8	10	20	40	120	500
Larry Doby	10	15	40	50	60	100	300	
Duke Snider	50	80	120	200	250	300	600	3,000
Bill Wight	5	5	8	10	15	25	60	
Ray Murray RC	5	5	8	12	20	30	120	300
Bill Howerton	5	5	8	10	25	30	50	250
Chet Nichols RC	5	5	8	10	20	30	80	300
Al Corwin RC	5	5	8	10	20	30	60	500
Billy Johnson	5	5	8	10	15	25	60	400
Sid Hudson	5	5	8	10	15	30	60	250
Birdie Tebbetts	5	8	12	20	25	30	120	250
Howie Fox	5	5	8	10	15	25	80	250
Phil Cavarretta	8	12	20	30	50	80	120	400
Dick Sisler	5	5	8	10	15	50	120	400
Don Newcombe	12	20	30	50	60	120	250	1,200
Gus Niarhos	5	5	8	10	15	25	100	
Allie Clark	5	5	8	10	15	25	100	
Bob Swift	5	5	8	10	15	40	80	
Dave Cole RC	5	6	10	15	25	50	80	
Dick Kryhoski	5	6	10	15	25	40	60	
Al Brazle	5	5	8	10	15	25	50	
Mickey Harris	5	5	8	10	15	50	150	
Gene Hermanski	5	5	8	10	15	25	100	
Stan Rojek	5	5	8	10	15	25	100	300
Ted Wilks	5	5	8	10	15	25	60	500
Jerry Priddy	5	5	8	10	15	30	80	250
Ray Scarborough	5	5	8	10	25	50	80	
Hank Edwards	5	6	10	15	25	40	60	
Early Wynn	10	15	25	40	60	120	250	1,000
Sandy Consuegra	5	5	8	10	15	40	100	400
Joe Hatton	5	6	10	15	25	50	80	400
Johnny Mize	15	25	40	50	60	200	300	1,000
Leo Durocher MG	15	25	40	40	50	80	200	800
Marlin Stuart RC	5	5	8	20	25	60	120	
Ken Heintzelman	5	5	8	15	30	50	80	
Howie Judson	5	5	8	10	25	30	80	400
Herman Wehmeier	5	5	8	10	20	50	80	350
Al Rosen	5	8	12	15	40	50	150	1,000
Billy Cox	5	6	10	12	20	30	150	400
Fred Hatfield RC	5	6	10	15	30	40	80	
Ferris Fain	5	6	10	15	25	50	80	
Billy Meyer MG	5	5	8	12	20	50	80	300
Warren Spahn	▲40	▲60	▲100	▲150	▲250	400	600	1,500
Jim Delsing	5	5	8	10	15	40	80	400
Bucky Harris MG	5	8	12	20	30	60	200	600
Dutch Leonard	5	6	10	15	25	30	120	250
Eddie Stanky	5	6	10	15	20	50	120	400
Jackie Jensen	8	12	20	30	50	80	150	800
Monte Irvin	12	20	30	50	80	200	500	800
Johnny Lipon	5	5	8	10	15	25	60	
Connie Ryan	5	6	10	15	25	30	100	
Saul Rogovin RC	5	5	8	10	25	40	100	800
Bobby Adams	5	5	8	10	15	40	50	250
Bobby Avila	5	6	10	12	20	50	100	400
Preacher Roe	5	10	15	20	40	80	200	600
Walt Dropo	5	6	10	15	25	40	120	400
Joe Astroth	5	5	8	10	15	25	80	
Mel Queen	5	5	8	10	25	30	80	
Ebba St.Claire RC	5	5	8	10	25	30	150	300
Gene Bearden	5	5	8	10	40	50	100	300
Mickey Grasso	5	5	8	12	20	25	60	300
Randy Jackson RC	5	6	10	15	25	50	100	300
Harry Brecheen	5	5	8	10	30	50	100	400
Gene Woodling	8	12	20	30	50	80	150	500
Dave Williams RC	5	5	8	10	15	25	120	400
Pete Suder	5	5	8	10	15	30	60	250

		GD 2	VG 3	VgEx 4	EX 5	ExMt 6	NM 7	NmMt 8	MT 9
180	Ed Fitzgerald	5	5	8	10	15	30	150	
181	Joe Collins RC	5	6	10	15	25	40	200	
182	Dave Koslo	5	5	8	12	20	25	60	
183	Pat Mullin	5	6	10	15	25	40	60	
184	Curt Simmons	5	5	8	10	15	30	80	800
185	Eddie Stewart	5	5	8	10	15	30	60	300
186	Frank Smith RC	5	6	10	15	25	40	100	
187	Jim Hegan	5	5	8	10	15	50	100	
188	Chuck Dressen MG	5	5	8	10	15	30	150	500
189	Jimmy Piersall	5	6	10	20	40	60	120	500
190	Dick Fowler	5	5	8	10	15	30	100	
191	Bob Friend RC	5	6	10	15	25	50	120	800
192	John Cusick RC	5	5	8	10	15	25	50	400
193	Bobby Young RC	5	5	8	10	20	50	50	300
194	Bob Porterfield	5	5	8	10	25	40	50	300
195	Frank Baumholtz	5	6	10	15	25	50	60	300
196	Stan Musial	250	400	500	600	▲1,000	▲1,500	▲3,000	4,000
197	Charlie Silvera RC	5	6	10	15	25	50	120	800
198	Chuck Diering	5	5	8	10	15	50	100	
199	Ted Gray	5	5	8	10	25	30	60	
200	Ken Silvestri	5	5	8	10	20	40	50	200
201	Ray Coleman	5	5	8	10	15	25	60	
202	Harry Perkowski RC	5	5	8	12	20	30	60	300
203	Steve Gromek	5	6	10	15	25	40	60	250
204	Andy Pafko	5	6	10	12	40	50	100	500
205	Walt Masterson	5	5	8	10	25	40	60	400
206	Elmer Valo	5	5	8	10	15	40	60	400
207	George Strickland RC	5	5	8	10	25	50	80	500
208	Walker Cooper	5	5	8	10	15	30	100	400
209	Dick Littlefield RC	5	5	8	10	15	30	100	
210	Archie Wilson RC	5	6	10	15	20	25	80	400
211	Paul Minner RC	5	5	8	10	15	25	60	
212	Solly Hemus RC	6	10	15	25	40	60	100	300
213	Monte Kennedy	5	5	8	10	15	30	60	300
214	Ray Boone	5	8	12	20	30	50	60	300
215	Sheldon Jones	5	5	8	12	20	30	80	
216	Matt Batts	5	5	8	10	15	25	100	300
217	Casey Stengel MG	15	30	40	100	120	200	250	600
218	Willie Mays	1,500	2,000	2,500	▲5,000	6,000	10,000	40,000	
219	Neil Berry	5	8	12	15	25	100	120	
220	Russ Meyer	5	8	12	15	30	80	150	
221	Lou Kretlow RC	5	8	12	15	25	50	60	
222	Dixie Howell	5	8	12	15	25	40	120	
223	Harry Simpson RC	5	8	12	15	25	50	▲120	
224	Johnny Schmitz	5	8	12	15	30	50	80	
225	Del Wilber RC	5	6	10	15	25	80	120	800
226	Alex Kellner	5	8	12	15	25	50	120	300
227	Clyde Sukeforth CO RC	5	8	12	25	40	50	120	800
228	Bob Chipman	6	10	15	20	25	80	200	500
229	Hank Arft	5	8	12	15	25	50	60	
230	Frank Shea	5	8	12	15	25	30	150	
231	Dee Fondy RC	5	8	12	15	25	50	80	
232	Enos Slaughter	15	25	40	60	100	150	250	1,200
233	Bob Kuzava	6	10	15	25	40	60	120	800
234	Fred Fitzsimmons CO	5	8	12	15	50	80	80	600
235	Steve Souchock RC	6	10	15	20	25	60	150	600
236	Tommy Brown	5	8	12	15	25	80	150	400
237	Sherm Lollar	5	10	15	20	30	80	150	
238	Roy McMillan RC	5	10	15	20	30	80	150	800
239	Dale Mitchell	8	12	20	25	40	60	200	
240	Billy Loes RC	5	15	20	25	50	80	200	600
241	Mel Parnell	5	10	15	25	50	100	150	
242	Everett Kell RC	5	8	15	20	40	100	120	
243	George Munger	5	8	12	15	25	60	150	
244	Lew Burdette RC	12	20	30	50	100	120	500	1,000
245	George Schmees RC	5	8	12	15	25	120	250	
246	Jerry Snyder RC	5	8	12	15	30	50	150	
247	Johnny Pramesa	6	10	15	20	25	40	100	600

		GD 2	VG 3	VgEx 4	EX 5	ExMt 6	NM 7	NmMt 8	MT 9
248	Bill Werle	5	8	12	15	25	40	100	
249	Hank Thompson	5	8	12	20	25	30	80	400
250	Ike Delock RC	5	8	12	15	25	50	120	500
251	Jack Lohrke	5	8	12	15	25	60	120	
252	Frank Crosetti CO	12	30	40	60	150	300	600	

— Willie Mays #218 SGC 96 (Mint) sold for $20,037 (Goodwin; 7/12)

1952 Red Man

		GD 2	VG 3	VgEx 4	EX 5	ExMt 6	NM 7	NmMt 8	MT 9
AL1	Casey Stengel MG	15	25	40	60	150			
AL2	Bobby Avila	8	12	20	30	50	100	300	
AL3	Yogi Berra	25	40	100	120	200	300	1,000	
AL4	Gil Coan	8	12	20	30	50			
AL5	Dom DiMaggio	10	15	25	40	60	120	400	
AL6	Larry Doby	10	15	25	40	60	120	400	
AL7	Ferris Fain	8	12	20	30	50	120		
AL8	Bob Feller	20	30	50	100	150	250		
AL9	Nellie Fox	10	15	25	40	60	120	400	
AL10	Johnny Groth	8	12	20	30	50	120	300	
AL11	Jim Hegan	8	12	20	30	50	100	300	
AL12	Eddie Joost	8	12	20	30	50	100	300	
AL13	George Kell	10	15	25	50	60	120	500	
AL14	Gil McDougald	10	15	25	40	60	120	400	
AL15	Minnie Minoso	8	12	20	30	50	100	300	
AL16	Billy Pierce	8	12	20	30	50	100	300	
AL17	Bob Porterfield	8	12	20	30	100	175	300	
AL18	Eddie Robinson	8	12	20	30	50	100		
AL19	Saul Rogovin	8	12	20	30	50	100	300	
AL20	Bobby Shantz	8	12	20	30	50	120	600	
AL21	Vern Stephens	8	12	20	30	50	100	300	
AL22	Vic Wertz	8	12	20	30	50	100	300	
AL23	Ted Williams	125	200	300	600	1,000	2,500	8,000	
AL24	Early Wynn	10	15	25	40	100	120	400	
AL25	Eddie Yost	8	12	20	30	50	120	300	
AL26	Gus Zernial	8	12	20	30	50	120	325	
NL1	Leo Durocher MG	10	15	25	40	80	120		
NL2	Richie Ashburn	12	20	30	50	80	250	500	
NL3	Ewell Blackwell	8	12	20	30	50	100	300	
NL4	Cliff Chambers	8	12	20	30	50	100	300	
NL5	Murry Dickson	8	12	20	30	50	100	300	
NL6	Sid Gordon	8	12	20	30	50	100		
NL7	Granny Hamner	8	12	20	30	50	100	350	
NL8	Jim Hearn	8	12	20	30	50	100	300	
NL9	Monte Irvin	10	15	25	40	60	120	600	
NL10	Larry Jansen	8	12	20	30	50	100	300	
NL11	Willie Jones	8	12	20	30	50	120	300	
NL12	Ralph Kiner	10	15	25	40	60	150	400	
NL13	Whitey Lockman	8	12	20	30	50	100	300	
NL14	Sal Maglie	8	12	20	30	50	100	300	
NL15	Willie Mays	50	100	200	250	500	800	2,000	
NL16	Stan Musial	80	100	150	250	600	800	2,500	
NL17	Pee Wee Reese	20	30	50	100	150	350	800	
NL18	Robin Roberts	15	25	40	60	100	150	400	
NL19	Red Schoendienst	10	15	25	40	80	120	400	
NL20	Enos Slaughter	10	15	25	40	60	200	500	
NL21	Duke Snider	25	40	60	120	200	400	1,600	
NL22	Warren Spahn	12	20	30	50	80	250	800	
NL23	Eddie Stanky	8	12	20	30	50	100	300	
NL24	Bobby Thomson	8	12	20	30	50	100		
NL25	Earl Torgeson	8	12	20	30	50	150	300	
NL26	Wes Westrum	8	12	20	30	50	100	300	

— Prices reference cards with tabs

1952 Topps

		GD 2	VG 3	VgEx 4	EX 5	ExMt 6	NM 7	NmMt 8	MT 9
1	Andy Pafko	200	300	500	1,200	5,000			
1A	Andy Pafko Black	200	300	500	800	2,000			
2	Pete Runnels RC	25	40	80	250	500			
2A	Pete Runnels Black RC	25	40	60	120	500			
3	Hank Thompson	12	20	40	80	120	400	2,500	
3A	Hank Thompson Black	12	20	30	50	80	700	3,000	
4	Don Lenhardt	12	20	50	60	150	250	800	
4A	Don Lenhardt Black	8	12	20	40	120	250	600	
5	Larry Jansen	12	20	40	60	120	250	800	
5A	Larry Jansen Black	12	20	40	60	100	250	800	
6	Grady Hatton	8	12	50	60	100	200	800	
6A	Grady Hatton Black	8	12	20	40	80	200	1,500	
7	Wayne Terwilliger	8	15	40	60	120	400		
7A	Wayne Terwilliger Black	8	12	20	40	120	350	1,000	
8	Fred Marsh RC	8	12	30	50	100	200	600	
8A	Fred Marsh Black	8	12	20	40	80	200	500	
9	Bobby Hogue RC	15	25	50	80	200	500		
9A	Bobby Hogue Black	15	25	40	80	150	400		
10	Al Rosen	25	30	80	100	300	600	2,000	
10A	Al Rosen Black	20	30	50	80	200	500	4,000	
11	Phil Rizzuto	80	100	150	300	400	1,000		
11A	Phil Rizzuto Black	40	80	120	250	500	600		
12	Monty Basgall RC	8	12	40	60	200	400		
12A	Monty Basgall Black	8	12	20	50	100	250		
13	Johnny Wyrostek	12	20	30	60	100	200	600	
13A	Johnny Wyrostek Black	8	12	40	50	200	300		
14	Bob Elliott	8	12	30	50	100	200	500	
14A	Bob Elliott Black	8	12	20	40	60	200	500	
15	Johnny Pesky	25	50	60	100	120	250	1,000	
15A	Johnny Pesky Black	12	20	40	80	120	300	1,000	
16	Gene Hermanski	12	20	30	50	100	200		
16A	Gene Hermanski Black	10	15	25	40	100	200	800	
17	Jim Hegan	15	20	40	80	100	250		
17A	Jim Hegan Black	8	12	40	100	300	1,200		
18	Merrill Combs RC	8	12	40	50	100	200	400	
18A	Merrill Combs Black	8	12	20	40	80	200		
19	Johnny Bucha RC	15	25	40	80	150	400		
19A	Johnny Bucha Black	10	15	25	40	120	400	1,500	
20	Billy Loes SP RC	15	25	60	120	300			
20A	Billy Loes Black	15	25	60	150	250			
21	Ferris Fain	8	20	30	50	100	250		
21A	Ferris Fain Black	8	12	20	50	120	150	500	
22	Dom DiMaggio	40	50	60	150	250	500		
22A	Dom DiMaggio Black	15	30	40	80	200	600		
23	Billy Goodman	10	15	25	50	100	250	500	
23A	Billy Goodman Black	8	12	20	40	80	150	500	
24	Luke Easter	10	15	40	50	100	250	600	
24A	Luke Easter Black	10	15	25	40	80	150	600	
25	Johnny Groth	12	20	30	50	120	250	1,000	
25A	Johnny Groth Black	8	12	20	40	50	200	1,000	
26	Monte Irvin	25	40	60	100	200	300		
26A	Monte Irvin Black	15	25	40	60	100	400		
27	Sam Jethroe	10	15	30	50	100	120	500	
27A	Sam Jethroe Black	8	12	20	40	80	250		
28	Jerry Priddy	12	20	30	50	100	200	500	
28A	Jerry Priddy Black	8	12	20	40	80	100	400	
29	Ted Kluszewski	30	40	60	100	200	500	3,000	
29A	Ted Kluszewski Black	15	25	40	60	150	500	2,000	
30	Mel Parnell	25	30	40	80	150	400	1,200	
30A	Mel Parnell Black	10	15	25	60	100	400	2,000	
31	Gus Zernial	12	20	50	60	150	300		
31A	Gus Zernial Black	10	15	25	60	100	200	800	
32	Eddie Robinson	20	25	40	100	150	400		
32A	Eddie Robinson Black	8	12	20	150	100	400		

#	Player	GD 2	VG 3	VgEx 4	EX 5	ExMt 6	NM 7	NmMt 8	MT 9
3	Warren Spahn	80	12	150	200	300	600	3,000	
3A	Warren Spahn Black	25	40	120	150	200	600	1,200	
4	Elmer Valo	8	20	25	50	100	200	400	
4A	Elmer Valo Black	8	12	20	40	80	200	400	
5	Hank Sauer	25	40	50	80	150	250		
5A	Hank Sauer Black	25	40	50	80	150	250	800	
6	Gil Hodges	60	80	100	200	400	600	2,500	
6A	Gil Hodges Black	25	40	120	150	250	500		
7	Duke Snider	80	100	200	250	400	600	2,500	
7A	Duke Snider Black	50	80	120	200	300	600	2,000	
8	Wally Westlake	8	20	30	50	60	150	500	
8A	Wally Westlake Black	8	12	20	40	60	150	500	
	Dizzy Trout	20	30	50	60	100	250		
A	Dizzy Trout Black	20	30	50	60	100	250		
	Irv Noren	8	12	30	60	120	300	800	
A	Irv Noren Black	8	12	20	40	50	400		
	Bob Wellman RC	8	20	30	50	100	250		
A	Bob Wellman Black	8	12	20	50	60	500		
	Lou Kretlow RC	10	15	30	80	120	400		
A	Lou Kretlow Black	10	15	25	40	120	400		
	Ray Scarborough	15	25	30	60	100	250		
A	Ray Scarborough Black	8	12	20	40	150	250	1,000	
	Con Dempsey RC	20	30	50	80	120	200	1,200	
A	Con Dempsey Black	8	12	20	50	60	200	1,000	
	Eddie Joost	12	20	40	50	100	250		
A	Eddie Joost Black	8	12	20	50	100	120	1,200	
	Gordon Goldsberry RC	12	20	30	50	100	250		
A	Gordon Goldsberry Black	8	12	20	40	100	400		
	Willie Jones	8	12	40	50	100	150		
A	Willie Jones Black	8	12	20	40	120	200	1,000	
A	Joe Page Error Sain Bio Black	200	300	600	900	1,000	1,500	5,000	
B	Joe Page Correct Bio Black	12	20	30	100	150	400		
C	Joe Page Correct Bio Red	12	20	30	60	120	250		
A	John Sain Error Page Bio Black	250	300	500	1,000	1,500			
B	John Sain Correct Bio Black	15	25	40	60	200	500		
C	John Sain Correct Bio Red	15	25	40	60	150	800		
	Marv Rickert RC	12	20	30	60	150	250		
A	Marv Rickert Black	8	12	20	40	100	150		
	Jim Russell	10	15	25	50	120	250		
A	Jim Russell Black	8	12	20	40	150	200		
	Don Mueller	10	15	30	50	120	150		
A	Don Mueller Black	8	12	20	40	60	500		
	Chris Van Cuyk RC	12	20	30	60	80	250		
	Chris Van Cuyk Black	8	12	20	40	80	200		
	Leo Kiely RC	10	15	25	50	100	150	400	
A	Leo Kiely Black	8	12	20	40	60	120	400	
	Ray Boone	12	20	40	50	100	200	600	
A	Ray Boone Black	8	12	20	40	80	200		
	Tommy Glaviano	10	15	30	50	80	200		
A	Tommy Glaviano Black	8	12	20	40	50	120	600	
	Ed Lopat	20	30	40	60	100	250	600	
A	Ed Lopat Black	12	25	30	50	100	200	500	
	Bob Mahoney RC	15	25	40	50	80	200	400	
A	Bob Mahoney Black	8	12	20	40	50	120	400	
	Robin Roberts	30	50	80	150	200	500	2,500	
	Robin Roberts Black	30	50	80	150	200	500	2,500	
	Sid Hudson	12	20	30	50	100	250	800	
	Sid Hudson Black	8	12	20	40	60	300		
	Tookie Gilbert	8	12	25	50	100	200		
	Tookie Gilbert Black	8	12	25	50	100	200	800	
	Chuck Stobbs RC	8	12	25	50	100	200		
	Chuck Stobbs Black	8	12	20	40	60	200	1,000	
	Howie Pollet	8	12	25	50	120	250	800	
	Howie Pollet Black	8	12	20	40	80	250	500	
	Roy Sievers	10	15	30	50	80	200	400	
	Roy Sievers Black	8	12	20	40	80	100	600	
	Enos Slaughter	40	50	80	100	200	400	3,000	
	Enos Slaughter Black	20	30	50	80	200	300	1,500	

#	Player	GD 2	VG 3	VgEx 4	EX 5	ExMt 6	NM 7	NmMt 8	MT 9
66	Preacher Roe	25	30	50	60	120	250	1,500	
66A	Preacher Roe Black	12	20	30	80	120	150	800	
67	Allie Reynolds	25	30	40	80	120	250	500	
67A	Allie Reynolds Black	12	20	30	50	120	200	800	
68	Cliff Chambers	12	20	30	40	80	200	400	
68A	Cliff Chambers Black	8	12	20	40	60	120	400	
69	Virgil Stallcup	8	12	25	50	100	250	500	
69A	Virgil Stallcup Black	8	12	20	40	50	200	800	
70	Al Zarilla	8	12	30	50	100	250		
70A	Al Zarilla Black	8	12	20	40	50	800		
71	Tom Upton RC	8	12	30	60	100	300	1,000	
71A	Tom Upton Black	8	12	20	40	60	300	2,500	
72	Karl Olson RC	8	12	25	60	200	500		
72A	Karl Olson Black	8	12	20	80	120	1,500		
73	Bill Werle	8	12	20	60	100	300		
73A	Bill Werle Black	8	12	20	40	50	400	2,000	
74	Andy Hansen RC	10	15	30	50	100	250	500	
74A	Andy Hansen Black	8	12	20	40	60	200		
75	Wes Westrum	15	20	30	50	150	250		
75A	Wes Westrum Black	8	12	20	40	100	300		
76	Eddie Stanky	10	15	40	50	120	250	1,000	
76A	Eddie Stanky Black	10	15	25	40	150	200		
77	Bob Kennedy	12	20	40	50	100	250		
77A	Bob Kennedy Black	8	12	20	40	100	200		
78	Ellis Kinder	20	25	40	50	100	250	800	
78A	Ellis Kinder Black	8	12	20	40	50	250		
79	Gerald Staley	8	20	25	50	120	600		
79A	Gerald Staley Black	8	12	20	40	80	800		
80	Herman Wehmeier	12	20	50	60	300	1,000		
80A	Herman Wehmeier Black	10	15	30	60				
81	Vern Law	12	20	30	60	100	200	800	
82	Duane Pillette	12	20	30	60	100	100	250	
83	Billy Johnson	10	15	25	40	60	80	300	
84	Vern Stephens	12	20	30	40	80	100	300	1,000
85	Bob Kuzava	▲12	▲20	▲30	▲50	▲80	▲120	250	
86	Ted Gray	12	20	30	40	60	100	250	
87	Dale Coogan	8	12	25	30	50	80	200	
88	Bob Feller	120	200	250	400	500	600	1,200	3,000
89	Johnny Lipon	12	20	30	50	80	120	300	
90	Mickey Grasso	6	10	25	30	60	100	400	
91	Red Schoendienst	30	40	60	80	150	400	800	
92	Dale Mitchell	10	15	25	40	60	100	500	
93	Al Sima RC	▼10	▼15	▼25	▼40	60	100	250	
94	Sam Mele	8	12	25	40	60	100	250	1,000
95	Ken Holcombe	6	10	25	30	60	80	150	1,000
96	Willard Marshall	12	20	30	40	60	100	250	
97	Earl Torgeson	▲12	▲20	▲30	▲50	▲80	▲120	250	
98	Bill Pierce	12	20	30	50	80	120	400	
99	Gene Woodling	20	30	50	60	100	150	400	
100	Del Rice	15	25	30	50	80	100	250	
101	Max Lanier	12	20	30	50	80	100	200	
102	Bill Kennedy	6	10	25	50	60	100	300	
103	Cliff Mapes	12	20	30	50	80	120	250	
104	Don Kolloway	▲15	▲25	▲40	▲60	▲100	▲150	250	
105	Johnny Pramesa	▲15	▲25	▲40	▲60	▲100	▲150	▲250	1,000
106	Mickey Vernon	▲8	▲12	▼20	▼30	▼50	100	400	1,000
107	Connie Ryan	▲15	▲25	▲40	▲60	▲100	▲150	250	
108	Jim Konstanty	15	25	40	60	100	150	300	
109	Ted Wilks	12	20	30	50	80	120	250	
110	Dutch Leonard	▲12	▲20	30	▲50	▲80	▲120	400	1,200
111	Peanuts Lowrey	12	15	20	40	50	100	250	
112	Hank Majeski	▲12	▲20	▲30	▲50	▲80	▲120	250	
113	Dick Sisler	15	25	40	50	60	100	250	1,000
114	Willard Ramsdell	10	15	25	40	60	80	250	
115	George Munger	▲12	▲20	▲30	▲50	▲80	▲120	300	1,000
116	Carl Scheib	▲12	▲20	▲30	▲50	▲80	▲120	300	
117	Sherm Lollar	12	20	30	50	80	120	250	
118	Ken Raffensberger	10	15	25	40	60	100	250	

#	Player	GD 2	VG 3	VgEx 4	EX 5	ExMt 6	NM 7	NmMt 8	MT 9
119	Mickey McDermott	10	15	25	30	50	100	250	
120	Bob Chakales RC	10	15	25	40	60	100	250	
121	Gus Niarhos	12	20	30	50	80	120	250	
122	Jack Jensen	▲25	▲40	▲60	▲100	150	250	400	
123	Eddie Yost	10	15	25	40	60	100	250	1,000
124	Monte Kennedy	▲12	▲20	▲30	▲50	▲80	▲120	250	1,000
125	Bill Rigney	▲12	▲20	▲30	▲50	▲80	▲120	250	
126	Fred Hutchinson	12	20	30	40	60	100	250	1,000
127	Paul Minner RC	▲12	▲20	▲30	▲50	▲80	▲120	250	
128	Don Bollweg RC	15	25	30	50	120	200	500	
129	Johnny Mize	50	60	80	120	200	300	600	
130	Sheldon Jones	12	20	30	50	60	80	250	
131	Morrie Martin RC	8	12	25	30	50	80		
132	Clyde Kluttz RC	10	15	25	40	60	80	300	
133	Al Widmar	10	15	25	40	50	80	250	
134	Joe Tipton	10	15	25	30	50	80	250	
135	Dixie Howell	6	10	30	40	50	100	400	
136	Johnny Schmitz	10	15	25	50	60	120		
137	Roy McMillan RC	10	15	30	40	60	100	300	
138	Bill MacDonald	10	15	25	30	50	80	250	
139	Ken Wood	6	10	15	25	50	80	250	
140	Johnny Antonelli	8	20	25	40	50	120		
141	Clint Hartung	6	10	25	30	50	100	800	
142	Harry Perkowski RC	12	20	25	40	60	120	600	
143	Les Moss	6	10	25	40	50	100	250	
144	Ed Blake RC	8	12	20	30	50	80	250	
145	Joe Haynes	6	10	15	30	50	100	300	
146	Frank House RC	6	10	15	50	60	100	250	
147	Bob Young RC	10	15	25	40	50	120	250	
148	Johnny Klippstein	8	12	20	40	50	80	250	
149	Dick Kryhoski	8	12	20	40	50	60	250	
150	Ted Beard	6	10	15	50	60	100	250	
151	Wally Post RC	6	10	15	50	80	150		
152	Al Evans	6	10	25	50	80	120	500	
153	Bob Rush	8	12	25	30	50	100	300	
154	Joe Muir RC	12	20	30	50	60	80	300	
155	Frank Overmire	6	10	25	40	50	100	400	
156	Frank Hiller RC	6	10	25	30	40	80	300	
157	Bob Usher	6	10	15	50	60	80	250	
158	Eddie Waitkus	10	15	25	40	60	120	300	
159	Saul Rogovin RC	10	15	25	50	60	100	250	
160	Owen Friend	6	10	30	40	60	100	300	
161	Bud Byerly RC	▲20	▲30	▲50	▲80	▲120	400		
162	Del Crandall	15	25	40	50	80	250		
163	Stan Rojek	6	10	20	30	50	150	500	
164	Walt Dubiel	10	15	30	40	50	100	400	
165	Eddie Kazak	6	10	15	40	80	200		
166	Paul LaPalme RC	10	15	25	30	60	100	250	
167	Bill Howerton	6	10	15	30	60	80	500	
168	Charlie Silvera RC	12	25	30	50	80	100	300	
169	Howie Judson	6	10	15	50	80	150		
170	Gus Bell	10	15	30	50	80	120	1,200	
171	Ed Erautt RC	6	10	15	50	80	200		
172	Eddie Miksis	6	10	25	50	80	250		
173	Roy Smalley	15	25	40	50	60	250		
174	Clarence Marshall RC	6	10	15	40	80	120	1,000	
175	Billy Martin RC	120	150	200	300	500	800	5,000	
176	Hank Edwards	6	10	15	50	60	80	400	
177	Bill Wight	6	10	15	25	60	150	300	
178	Cass Michaels	6	10	15	50	60	100	400	
179	Frank Smith RC	6	10	15	25	50	120	400	
180	Charlie Maxwell RC	12	20	60	80	400	500		
181	Bob Swift	10	15	25	50	100	250		
182	Billy Hitchcock	6	12	25	50	60	100	250	
183	Erv Dusak	6	10	25	30	60	100	300	
184	Bob Ramazzotti	8	12	25	40	50	100	250	1,200
185	Bill Nicholson	12	25	30	40	100	150	400	
186	Walt Masterson	8	12	25	30	60	100	400	
187	Bob Miller	6	10	15	40	60	100	400	
188	Clarence Podbielan RC	8	12	25	50	60	120	300	1,000
189	Pete Reiser	15	25	40	50	100	200		
190	Don Johnson RC	6	10	15	30	60	150	500	
191	Yogi Berra	▲300	▲400	500	600	800	2,500	10,000	
192	Myron Ginsberg RC	15	25	40	50	80	200		
193	Harry Simpson RC	8	12	30	40	80	150	600	
194	Joe Hatton	▲12	▲20	▲30	▲50	▲80	120	300	
195	Orestes Minoso RC	40	60	120	150	250	500	1,000	3,000
196	Solly Hemus RC	▲15	▲25	▲40	▲60	▲100	▲150	250	1,000
197	George Strickland RC	6	10	15	30	50	▲120	250	
198	Phil Haugstad RC	6	10	25	40	60	80	250	
199	George Zuverink RC	6	10	15	50	60	120	300	
200	Ralph Houk RC	▲30	▲50	▲80	▲120	▲200	▲300	▲500	
201	Alex Kellner	10	15	25	40	50	100	250	
202	Joe Collins RC	15	25	40	60	100	200	600	
203	Curt Simmons	15	25	40	60	100	150	250	
204	Ron Northey	▲12	▲20	▲30	▲50	▲80	▲120	250	
205	Clyde King	▲15	▲25	▲40	▲60	▲100	▲120	300	1,000
206	Joe Ostrowski RC	12	20	30	50	80	100	250	1,500
207	Mickey Harris	12	20	30	40	50	▲120	250	1,000
208	Marlin Stuart RC	12	20	30	40	60	100	250	
209	Howie Fox	8	12	25	40	60	80	250	
210	Dick Fowler	6	10	15	30	50	100	250	1,000
211	Ray Coleman	10	15	25	40	80	120		
212	Ned Garver	6	10	20	40	80	100		
213	Nippy Jones	12	20	30	50	60	80	250	
214	Johnny Hopp	8	12	30	40	50	120	250	1,200
215	Hank Bauer	▲30	40	60	100	150	250	400	
216	Richie Ashburn	40	60	100	▲150	250	300	600	3,000
217	Snuffy Stirnweiss	6	10	15	25	40	100	250	1,000
218	Clyde McCullough	10	15	25	40	60	100	200	
219	Bobby Shantz	15	25	40	50	80	120	400	
220	Joe Presko RC	6	10	15	40	50	80	200	
221	Granny Hamner	15	25	40	60	100	150	400	
222	Hoot Evers	12	20	30	40	60	80	400	1,000
223	Del Ennis	12	20	30	50	80	120	250	
224	Bruce Edwards	10	15	25	40	60	80	250	
225	Frank Baumholtz	12	20	30	40	50	100	250	1,000
226	Dave Philley	8	12	20	40	50	80	250	
227	Joe Garagiola	20	30	50	▲80	100	200	400	1,500
228	Al Brazle	12	20	30	40	50	80	250	1,200
229	Gene Bearden	6	10	15	30	50	100	250	
230	Matt Batts	▼12	▼20	▼30	▼50	▼80	150	250	
231	Sam Zoldak	10	15	25	40	50	100	300	
232	Billy Cox	15	25	40	60	100	150	400	
233	Bob Friend RC	15	25	40	60	100	150	400	
234	Steve Souchock RC	▲12	▲20	▲30	▲50	▲80	100	200	
235	Walt Dropo	12	20	30	50	80	100	250	
236	Ed Fitzgerald	12	20	30	50	80	120	250	1,000
237	Jerry Coleman	▲15	▲25	▲40	▲60	▲100	150	400	
238	Art Houtteman	8	12	20	30	50	100	200	
239	Rocky Bridges RC	12	20	30	▲50	▲80	120	250	
240	Jack Phillips RC	10	15	25	40	60	100	250	1,000
241	Tommy Byrne	12	20	30	40	60	150	800	
242	Tom Poholsky RC	10	15	30	40	50	100	300	
243	Larry Doby	40	60	100	150	250	400	▲2,500	
244	Vic Wertz	12	20	30	50	80	120	250	
245	Sherry Robertson	▲10	▲15	25	40	▲60	120	250	
246	George Kell	▼30	▼50	▼80	120	200	250	600	
247	Randy Gumpert	10	15	25	40	60	100	250	
248	Frank Shea	12	20	30	50	80	150	400	
249	Bobby Adams	6	10	30	40	50	80	300	
250	Carl Erskine	25	40	60	100	200	300	800	
251	Chico Carrasquel	30	50	80	100	150	250		
252	Vern Bickford	15	25	30	50	60	120	300	
253	Johnny Berardino	12	20	30	50	80	120	300	
254	Joe Dobson	8	12	30	40	60	120	250	

#		GD 2	VG 3	VgEx 4	EX 5	ExMt 6	NM 7	NmMt 8	MT 9
255	Clyde Vollmer	12	20	40	50	60	100	300	
256	Pete Suder	8	12	25	50	60	100	250	1,000
257	Bobby Avila	15	25	40	50	150	250	250	1,000
258	Steve Gromek	15	25	40	60	100	150	300	1,000
259	Bob Addis RC	▲15	▲25	▲40	▲60	▲100	▲150	250	
260	Pete Castiglione	8	12	25	40	50	150	500	
261	Willie Mays	▲8,000	▲10,000	▲12,000	▲15,000	▲20,000	▲25,000	40,000	
262	Virgil Trucks	10	15	40	60	80	120	500	
263	Harry Brecheen	8	12	30	40	80	120	300	1,000
264	Roy Hartsfield	12	20	30	50	80	120	250	1,000
265	Chuck Diering	15	25	40	50	80	120	300	
266	Murry Dickson	8	12	25	40	50	150	300	1,000
267	Sid Gordon	12	20	30	50	60	120	300	
268	Bob Lemon	▲50	▲80	▲120	▲200	▲300	▲500	▲800	▲4,000
269	Willard Nixon	12	20	30	50	80	120	300	
270	Lou Brissie	15	25	40	60	80	120	400	
271	Jim Delsing	8	12	30	40	80	120	400	1,000
272	Mike Garcia	10	25	30	60	80	150	500	
273	Erv Palica	20	30	50	80	150	250	300	
274	Ralph Branca	40	60	100	150	250	400	1,000	
275	Pat Mullin	8	12	20	50	80	150	400	
276	Jim Wilson RC	15	25	40	60	100	150	250	
277	Early Wynn	60	100	150	250	400	600	1,000	2,500
278	Allie Clark	12	20	30	50	80	120	300	
279	Eddie Stewart	8	12	20	40	60	100	250	1,500
280	Cloyd Boyer	12	20	40	100	150	250	500	
281	Tommy Brown SP	15	25	40	60	100	150	300	
282	Birdie Tebbetts SP	10	15	50	80	100	120	300	2,000
283	Phil Masi SP	8	12	30	50	60	100	250	1,200
284	Hank Arft SP	12	20	30	50	80	120	250	1,000
285	Cliff Fannin SP	8	12	40	50	100	120	250	
286	Joe DeMaestri SP RC	12	20	30	50	80	100	250	1,000
287	Steve Bilko SP	25	40	60	100	150	250	400	1,000
288	Chet Nichols SP RC	15	25	40	60	100	150	250	
289	Tommy Holmes MG	20	30	50	80	150	250	400	1,500
290	Joe Astroth SP	15	25	40	60	80	100	300	
291	Gil Coan SP	12	20	40	50	80	120	300	1,000
292	Floyd Baker SP	15	25	40	60	100	150	300	1,200
293	Sibby Sisti SP	8	12	30	50	60	120	300	
294	Walker Cooper SP	15	25	40	60	100	150	250	800
295	Phil Cavarretta	40	60	100	150	250	400	1,000	1,200
296	Red Rolfe MG	25	40	60	100	150	250	500	1,200
297	Andy Seminick SP	15	25	40	60	100	120	200	1,000
298	Bob Ross SP RC	15	25	40	50	100	150	300	1,000
299	Ray Murray SP RC	15	25	40	60	100	150	250	1,200
300	Barney McCosky SP	12	20	40	60	100	150	300	1,200
301	Bob Porterfield	12	20	40	60	80	120	400	
302	Max Surkont RC	20	30	40	60	100	150	300	1,000
303	Harry Dorish	12	20	30	50	80	150	300	1,000
304	Sam Dente	10	15	25	50	80	120	300	
305	Paul Richards MG	10	15	40	60	80	100	300	
306	Lou Sleater RC	10	15	30	50	60	120	300	1,000
307	Frank Campos RC	30	50	80	100	120	200	300	
308	Luis Aloma	20	30	50	60	80	120	250	
309	Jim Busby	20	30	40	50	100	200	400	1,200
310	George Metkovich	15	25	40	80	150	250	600	
311	Mickey Mantle DP	50,000	60,000	80,000	100,000	200,000	250,000	1,200,000	
312	Jackie Robinson DP	10,000	▼12,000	20,000	25,000	30,000	40,000	300,000	
313	Bobby Thomson DP	120	150	200	250	400	800	1,200	3,000
314	Roy Campanella	1,000	▲1,500	▲2,500	▲3,000	▲4,000	▲6,000	▲10,000	
315	Leo Durocher MG	250	300	400	500	800	1,000	2,500	
316	Davey Williams RC	120	150	200	300	400	600		
317	Connie Marrero	100	150	200	300	400	800		
318	Harold Gregg RC	150	200	250	300	400	500	800	
319	Al Walker RC	▲150	▲250	▲400	▲600	▲1,000	▲1,500		
320	John Rutherford RC	200	250	300	400	800	3,000		
321	Joe Black RC	200	250	300	400	500	800	1,500	
322	Randy Jackson RC	120	150	250	300	400	600	1,000	2,500

#		GD 2	VG 3	VgEx 4	EX 5	ExMt 6	NM 7	NmMt 8	MT 9
323	Bubba Church	100	150	250	300	400	500	1,000	
324	Warren Hacker	120	200	300	400	500	600	1,000	2,500
325	Bill Serena	100	150	250	400	600	1,000	1,500	
326	George Shuba RC	150	200	300	500	800	1,200		
327	Al Wilson RC	▲150	▲250	▲300	▲400	▲500	800	▲1,200	
328	Bob Borkowski RC	100	120	150	200	300	400	600	
329	Ike Delock RC	▲120	▲200	▲300	400	600	1,000	1,500	
330	Turk Lown RC	200	250	300	400	500	600	800	
331	Tom Morgan RC	100	150	250	400	600	1,000	2,000	
332	Tony Bartirome RC	600	1,000	1,500	2,500	3,000	6,000	8,000	
333	Pee Wee Reese	▲1,000	▲1,200	▲1,500	▲2,000	▲2,500	▲4,000	▲8,000	
334	Wilmer Mizell RC	100	150	250	400	600	1,000	1,500	2,500
335	Ted Lepcio RC	100	150	250	400	600	1,000	1,500	
336	Dave Koslo	100	150	250	300	400		1,200	
337	Jim Hearn	100	150	250	400	600	1,000	1,500	
338	Sal Yvars RC	120	200	250	400	500	800		
339	Russ Meyer	50	80	150	300	400	500	800	2,500
340	Bob Hooper	100	150	250	400	600	1,000	1,500	
341	Hal Jeffcoat	100	150	250	300	500	800		
342	Clem Labine RC	150	250	400	500	600	1,000	1,500	3,000
343	Dick Gernert RC	100	150	250	400	500	800	1,200	
344	Ewell Blackwell	100	150	250	400	500	1,000	1,500	3,000
345	Sammy White RC	100	150	250	300	400	500	800	2,500
346	George Spencer RC	80	120	200	300	500	600	1,000	
347	Joe Adcock	100	150	250	400	600	1,000	2,000	3,000
348	Robert Kelly RC	▲120	▲200	250	300	400	500	1,000	
349	Bob Cain	100	150	250	400	500	800	1,200	
350	Cal Abrams	100	200	250	300	500	800	1,200	
351	Alvin Dark	120	200	250	300	500	600	1,000	5,500
352	Karl Drews	100	200	250	300	400	500	1,000	3,000
353	Bob Del Greco RC	100	150	250	250	400	600	800	3,500
354	Fred Hatfield RC	▲120	▲200	▲300	▲400	▲500	600	1,000	
355	Bobby Morgan	120	200	300	500	800	1,200		
356	Toby Atwell RC	120	150	250	300	400	▲1,000	▲2,000	
357	Smoky Burgess	150	250	400	500	800	1,200	2,000	
358	John Kucab RC	80	120	200	300	500	800	1,200	
359	Dee Fondy RC	120	200	300	400	600	▲1,500	▲3,000	
360	George Crowe RC	150	200	250	400	500	600	1,500	
361	Bill Posedel CO	80	100	200	250	300	500	800	
362	Ken Heintzelman	120	150	200	300	400	500	1,000	
363	Dick Rozek RC	80	100	200	250	400	600	1,000	1,200
364	Clyde Sukeforth CO RC	100	150	250	300	400	500	800	
365	Cookie Lavagetto CO	120	200	300	400	500	800	1,200	3,000
366	Dave Madison RC	120	150	250	250	300	400	800	
367	Ben Thorpe RC	100	150	250	300	500	800	1,200	
368	Ed Wright RC	80	120	200	300	500	800	1,500	
369	Dick Groat RC	200	300	400	600	1,000	1,500	2,500	5,000
370	Billy Hoeft RC	150	250	400	500	600	800	1,000	
371	Bobby Hofman	120	150	200	250	300	400	800	
372	Gil McDougald RC	▲250	▲400	▲600	▲800	▲1,000	1,200	2,500	5,000
373	Jim Turner CO RC	250	300	400	600	800	1,000		
374	Al Benton RC	150	200	250	400	500	1,000	1,500	2,500
375	John Merson RC	100	150	200	300	500	800	1,200	2,500
376	Faye Throneberry RC	▲150	▲250	▲400	▲500	▲600	▲800	1,200	
377	Chuck Dressen MG	150	250	300	400	600	1,000		
378	Leroy Fusselman RC	150	250	400	500	800	1,200	2,000	
379	Joe Rossi RC	100	150	200	250	300	600		
380	Clem Koshorek RC	120	150	200	250	300	▲600	1,000	
381	Milton Stock CO RC	150	200	250	300	500	800	1,200	
382	Sam Jones RC	120	200	300	500	800	1,000	1,500	
383	Del Wilber RC	100	150	250	300	400	600	1,500	2,500
384	Frank Crosetti CO	▲250	▲300	▲400	▲500	▲600	▲1,200	2,000	5,000
385	Herman Franks CO RC	120	200	300	400	600	1,000	1,500	
386	Ed Yuhas RC	100	150	250	400	600	1,000	1,500	
387	Billy Meyer MG	▲150	▲200	▲250	▲300	400	600	800	2,500
388	Bob Chipman	120	200	250	300	400	800		
389	Ben Wade RC	120	150	250	300	400	500	1,500	
390	Glenn Nelson RC	120	200	250	300	400	1,000		

		GD 2	VG 3	VgEx 4	EX 5	ExMt 6	NM 7	NmMt 8	MT 9
391	Ben Chapman CO UER	120	200	250	300	400	600	1,000	
392	Hoyt Wilhelm RC	800	▲1,200	▲2,000	▲2,500	▲3,000	▲4,000	▲6,000	▲50,000
393	Ebba St.Claire RC	120	200	250	300	400	500	1,200	
394	Billy Herman CO	150	250	400	500	600	800		
395	Jake Pitler CO	100	250	300	500	800	1,200		
396	Dick Williams RC	200	250	300	600	1,000	1,500		
397	Forrest Main RC	▲200	▲250	▲300	400	600	1,000	1,500	
398	Hal Rice	120	200	250	400	500	800		
399	Jim Fridley RC	120	200	250	300	500	800		
400	Bill Dickey CO	500	600	800	1,000	1,500	2,500	4,000	
401	Bob Schultz RC	▲150	▲250	▲300	▲400	400	400	800	3,600
402	Earl Harrist RC	100	120	200	300	400	500	800	
403	Bill Miller RC	150	250	400	500	600	800		
404	Dick Brodowski RC	▲150	▲250	▲400	▲600	▲800	▲1,200	▲2,000	
405	Eddie Pellagrini	120	200	300	500	800	1,200	2,000	
406	Joe Nuxhall RC	300	500	800	1,000	1,500	2,500	2,500	
407	Eddie Mathews RC	4,000	6,000	10,000	15,000	20,000	40,000	100,000	

— Yogi Berra #191 PSA 8.5 (NmMt+) sold for $17,775 (REA; 5/13)
— Yogi Berra #191 PSA 8.5 (NmMt+) sold for $14,220 (REA; Spring '14)
— Frank Campos Black Star #307A PSA 8 (NmMt) sold for $10,207 (Goodwin; 8/12)
— George Crowe #360 PSA 8.5 (NmMt+) sold for $5,207 (Mile High; 10/11)
— Con Dempsey #44 PSA 9 (MT) sold for $9,265 (Goodwin; 03/12)
— Con Dempsey #44 PSA 9 (Mint) sold for $9,265 (Goodwin; 3/12)
— Chuck Dressen MG #377 PSA 9 (MT) sold for $15,439 (Goodwin; 12/11)
— Gil Hodges #36 (Red) PSA 9 (MT) sold for $5,969 (Mile High; 10/12)
— Mickey Mantle #311 PSA 9 (MT) sold for $225,000 (Memory Lane; Private 2006)
— Mickey Mantle #311 PSA 8.5 (NmMt+) sold for $272,550 (REA; 5/13)
— Mickey Mantle #311 PSA 8 (NmMt) sold for $486,100 (eBay; 11/15)
— Mickey Mantle #311 PSA 8 (NmMt) sold for $268,644 (SCP; 12/14)
— Mickey Mantle #311 BGS 8 (NmMt) sold for $81,348 (Goodwin; 9/13)
— Mickey Mantle #311 PSA 8 (NmMt) sold for $75,198 (Mile High; 5/12)
— Mickey Mantle #311 GAI 8 (NmMt) sold for $27,180 (Mile High; 10/12)
— Mickey Mantle #311 SGC 86 (NrMt+) sold for $54,038 (Mile High; 05/11)
— Willie Mays #261 PSA 9 (MT) sold for $478,000 (Heritage; 5/16)
— Willie Mays #261 PSA 9 (MT) sold for $382,400 (Heritage; 8/16)
— Willie Mays #261 PSA 9 (MT) sold for $310,700 (Heritage; 11/16)
— Willie Mays #261 PSA 9 (MT) sold for $40,000 (Memory Lane; Private Sale - 2007)
— Willie Mays #244 PSA 8 (NmMt) sold for $12,684 (Bussineau; 7/13)
— Andy Pafko #1 PSA 10 (Gem) sold for $250,000 (Memory Lane; Private Sale - 2007)
— Andy Pafko #1 PSA 8 (NmMt) sold for $80,000 (Memory Lane; Private Sale - 2007)
— Andy Pafko #1 PSA 7 (NrMt) sold for $14,100 (Huggins and Scott; 8/12)
— Jake Pitler CO #395 PSA 9 (MT) sold for $13,894 (Goodwin; 11/12)
— Hoyt Wilhelm #392 PSA 10 (Gem) (Young Collection) sold for $23,352 (SCP; 5/12)

1953 Bowman Black and White

		PrFr 1	GD 2	VG 3	VgEx 4	EX 5	ExMt 6	NM 7	NmMt 8
1	Gus Bell	10	15	25	40	50	120	600	
2	Willard Nixon	5	6	10	15	20	30	80	200
3	Bill Rigney	5	6	10	15	20	30	80	200
4	Pat Mullin	5	6	10	15	20	30	60	200
5	Dee Fondy	5	6	10	15	20	30	60	300
6	Ray Murray	5	6	10	15	20	30	80	200
7	Andy Seminick	5	6	10	15	20	30	60	200
8	Pete Suder	5	6	10	15	20	30	60	200
9	Walt Masterson	5	6	10	15	40	80	150	
10	Dick Sisler	5	8	12	20	25	40	80	200
11	Dick Gernert	5	6	10	15	20	30	60	200
12	Randy Jackson	5	6	10	15	20	30	80	200
13	Joe Tipton	5	6	10	15	30	40	60	200
14	Bill Nicholson	5	8	12	20	25	40	100	300
15	Johnny Mize	10	15	25	50	60	100	200	350
16	Stu Miller RC	5	8	12	20	25	502	80	300
17	Virgil Trucks	5	8	12	20	30	50	100	500
18	Billy Hoeft	5	6	10	15	50	60	80	200
19	Paul LaPalme	5	6	10	15	30	40	60	200
20	Eddie Robinson	5	6	10	15	20	30	60	200
21	Clarence Podbielan	5	6	10	15	20	30	60	200

		PrFr 1	GD 2	VG 3	VgEx 4	EX 5	ExMt 6	NM 7	NmMt
22	Matt Batts	5	6	10	15	20	30	60	200
23	Wilmer Mizell	5	6	10	15	20	50	100	200
24	Del Wilber	5	6	10	15	20	40	80	200
25	Johnny Sain	8	12	20	30	50	60	150	600
26	Preacher Roe	8	12	20	30	50	60	150	300
27	Bob Lemon	10	15	25	40	50	120	200	600
28	Hoyt Wilhelm	12	20	30	60	100	150	250	500
29	Sid Hudson	5	8	12	20	30	60	100	200
30	Walker Cooper	5	6	10	15	20	30	60	150
31	Gene Woodling	8	12	20	30	40	80	300	500
32	Rocky Bridges	5	6	10	15	20	30	60	200
33	Bob Kuzava	5	8	12	20	25	50	120	250
34	Ebba St.Claire	5	6	10	15	20	30	100	200
35	Johnny Wyrostek	5	6	10	15	20	30	60	200
36	Jimmy Piersall	8	12	20	30	40	80	150	500
37	Hal Jeffcoat	5	8	12	20	25	40	100	500
38	Dave Cole	5	6	10	15	20	30	60	300
39	Casey Stengel MG	50	80	150	200	300	400	600	
40	Larry Jansen	5	8	12	20	25	60		
41	Bob Ramazzotti	5	6	10	15	20	30	60	200
42	Howie Judson	5	6	10	15	20	30	60	200
43	Hal Bevan RC	5	6	10	15	20	40	80	500
44	Jim Delsing	5	6	10	20	25	30	80	250
45	Irv Noren	6	10	15	25	30	50	100	600
46	Bucky Harris MG	8	12	20	30	40	80	120	500
47	Jack Lohrke	5	8	12	20	30	60	150	400
48	Steve Ridzik RC	5	6	10	15	20	50	150	
49	Floyd Baker	5	6	10	15	20	30	80	300
50	Dutch Leonard	5	6	10	15	20	30	60	250
51	Lew Burdette	5	8	12	20	25	50	200	400
52	Ralph Branca	8	12	20	30	40	60	200	
53	Morrie Martin	5	6	10	15	20	30	80	250
54	Bill Miller	5	6	10	15	20	30	120	250
55	Don Johnson	5	6	10	15	25	80		
56	Roy Smalley	8	12	20	30	40	80		
57	Andy Pafko	5	8	12	20	25	40	80	400
58	Jim Konstanty	5	8	12	20	25	40	80	500
59	Duane Pillette	5	6	8	12	20	40	80	200
60	Billy Cox	8	12	20	30	40	80	250	
61	Tom Gorman RC	5	6	10	15	20	30	100	300
62	Keith Thomas RC	5	6	10	15	20	60	150	
63	Steve Gromek	5	6	10	15	20	60		
64	Andy Hansen	10	15	25	40	60	300		

1953 Bowman Color

		GD 2	VG 3	VgEx 4	EX 5	ExMt 6	NM 7	NmMt 8	MT
1	Davey Williams	8	12	20	30	120	500	800	
2	Vic Wertz	6	10	15	20	30	100	250	1,00
3	Sam Jethroe	6	10	15	25	80	120	1,000	
4	Art Houtteman	6	8	12	20	30	60	200	80
5	Sid Gordon	5	8	12	20	40	60	150	60
6	Joe Ginsberg	5	8	12	20	50	80	150	80
7	Harry Chiti RC	6	10	15	25	40	50	150	80
8	Al Rosen	8	12	20	50	60	100	250	80
9	Phil Rizzuto	25	50	60	100	150	▲500	800	
10	Richie Ashburn	▲30	▲50	▲80	100	150	250	800	2,00
11	Bobby Shantz	8	12	20	30	50	100	150	1,00
12	Carl Erskine	6	10	15	25	80	120	250	
13	Gus Zernial	▲8	▲12	▲20	▲30	▲50	▲80	150	1,00
14	Billy Loes	6	10	15	25	40	60	200	
15	Jim Busby	6	10	15	25	40	60	150	80
16	Bob Friend	6	10	15	25	40	60	150	60
17	Gerry Staley	5	8	12	20	30	▲80	300	
18	Nellie Fox	15	25	40	50	100	150	300	2,00
19	Alvin Dark	5	8	12	20	30	50	150	80
20	Don Lenhardt	5	8	12	20	30	50	120	80
21	Joe Garagiola	10	15	25	30	40	100	200	1,00

#	Player	GD 2	VG 3	VgEx 4	EX 5	ExMt 6	NM 7	NmMt 8	MT 9
2	Bob Porterfield	▲6	▲10	▲15	▲25	40	50	150	800
3	Herman Wehmeier	6	10	15	25	40	60	150	800
4	Jackie Jensen	10	15	25	30	40	80	250	
5	Hoot Evers	5	8	12	20	40	60	200	800
6	Roy McMillan	6	10	15	25	40	80	200	600
7	Vic Raschi	8	12	20	30	50	100	300	1,500
8	Smoky Burgess	6	10	15	25	40	80	250	1,000
9	Bobby Avila	5	8	12	20	40	60	250	600
0	Phil Cavarretta	5	8	12	20	40	60	200	1,000
1	Jimmy Dykes MG	5	8	12	20	30	50	200	800
2	Stan Musial	150	250	400	600	1,000	1,500	2,500	4,000
3	Pee Wee Reese	▲300	▲500	▲800	▲1,200	▲1,500	▲2,500	▲4,000	▲6,000
4	Gil Coan	5	8	12	20	30	50	150	600
5	Maurice McDermott	5	8	12	20	30	60	120	600
6	Minnie Minoso	12	20	40	50	80	120	500	1,200
7	Jim Wilson	5	8	12	20	30	80	150	600
8	Harry Byrd RC	5	8	12	20	30	50	150	
9	Paul Richards MG	8	12	20	30	50	80	150	800
0	Larry Doby	30	50	80	120	200	300	1,000	2,000
1	Sammy White	8	12	20	30	40	60	150	800
2	Tommy Brown	5	8	12	20	30	60	150	
3	Mike Garcia	6	10	15	25	40	60	200	1,000
4	Bauer/Berra/Mantle	150	250	400	600	1,000	1,500	3,000	▲50,000
5	Walt Dropo	8	12	20	30	50	80	150	600
6	Roy Campanella	60	100	150	250	400	600	1,000	5,000
7	Ned Garver	6	10	15	30	50	60	200	600
8	Hank Sauer	10	15	25	40	50	120	300	
9	Eddie Stanky MG	5	8	12	20	40	60	150	1,000
0	Lou Kretlow	5	8	12	20	40	60	200	800
1	Monte Irvin	15	25	40	60	100	200	300	1,200
2	Marty Marion MG	8	12	20	30	50	80	200	
3	Del Rice	6	10	15	25	40	60	200	
4	Chico Carrasquel	5	8	12	20	30	80	200	800
5	Leo Durocher MG	10	15	25	40	80	120	300	1,000
6	Bob Cain	5	8	12	25	40	60	150	
7	Lou Boudreau MG	▲12	▲20	▲30	50	60	▲150	250	1,000
8	Willard Marshall	▲8	▲12	▲20	▲30	▲50	80	120	800
9	Mickey Mantle	▲1,500	▲2,000	2,500	▲5,000	6,000	8,000	▼20,000	80,000
0	Granny Hamner	5	8	12	30	40	60	200	800
1	George Kell	15	25	40	60	100	150	300	
2	Ted Kluszewski	20	30	50	60	80	▲200	300	
3	Gil McDougald	10	15	25	50	100	150	400	
4	Curt Simmons	▲10	▲15	▲25	▲40	60	▼120	2,000	
5	Robin Roberts	25	40	60	100	200	400	800	
6	Mel Parnell	6	10	15	25	40	150	800	
7	Mel Clark RC	6	10	15	25	30	60	400	
8	Allie Reynolds	10	15	30	60	100	150	600	
9	Charlie Grimm MG	10	15	25	40	50	150	250	
0	Clint Courtney RC	5	8	12	30	40	100	300	
1	Paul Minner	5	8	12	20	40	60	400	
2	Ted Gray	5	8	12	20	40	60	200	
3	Billy Pierce	6	10	15	25	40	120	250	1,000
4	Don Mueller	6	10	15	25	40	80	250	
5	Saul Rogovin	5	8	12	20	30	60	200	
6	Jim Hearn	5	8	12	20	30	100	200	800
7	Mickey Grasso	6	10	15	30	40	80	250	
8	Carl Furillo	15	25	40	50	80	150	500	
9	Ray Boone	6	10	15	30	50	150	300	1,000
0	Ralph Kiner	15	25	40	60	80	250	500	1,200
1	Enos Slaughter	20	30	50	80	120	200	600	
2	Joe Astroth	5	8	12	20	50	60	200	
3	Jack Daniels RC	5	8	12	20	50	80	300	800
4	Hank Bauer	12	20	25	40	60	150	250	1,200
5	Solly Hemus	8	12	20	30	50	60	250	800
6	Harry Simpson	5	8	12	25	50	120	250	
7	Harry Perkowski	5	8	12	25	50	80	250	800

#	Player	GD 2	VG 3	VgEx 4	EX 5	ExMt 6	NM 7	NmMt 8	MT 9
88	Joe Dobson	5	8	12	20	30	50	120	800
89	Sandy Consuegra	6	10	15	25	50	100	300	
90	Joe Nuxhall	10	15	25	40	60	120	300	
91	Steve Souchock	8	12	20	30	50	80	200	600
92	Gil Hodges	▼30	50	▲80	▲120	250	300	1,000	3,500
93	P.Rizzuto/B.Martin	40	60	100	150	250	400	1,000	6,000
94	Bob Addis	5	8	12	20	40	120	400	
95	Wally Moses CO	6	10	15	25	40	60	200	
96	Sal Maglie	10	15	25	40	60	100	400	
97	Eddie Mathews	50	80	100	200	250	600	1,200	4,000
98	Hector Rodriguez RC	6	10	15	25	60	200		
99	Warren Spahn	▲80	▲120	▲200	▲250	▲400	▲800	1,500	4,000
100	Bill Wight	10	15	25	40	60	120	300	
101	Red Schoendienst	12	20	30	100	150	250	500	
102	Jim Hegan	10	15	25	40	60	250	400	
103	Del Ennis	10	15	25	40	80	250		
104	Luke Easter	15	25	40	60	100			
105	Eddie Joost	6	10	15	25	40	120	500	
106	Ken Raffensberger	5	8	12	25	30	120	400	
107	Alex Kellner	5	8	12	25	40	80	250	
108	Bobby Adams	8	12	20	30	40	80	200	800
109	Ken Wood	6	10	15	30	40	▲120	400	
110	Bob Rush	▲8	▲12	20	25	30	▲150	300	
111	Jim Dyck RC	5	8	12	20	50	120	400	
112	Toby Atwell	8	12	20	30	60	200		
113	Karl Drews	8	12	20	30	100	300		
114	Bob Feller	80	120	200	300	400	800	2,500	5,000
115	Cloyd Boyer	12	20	30	50	80	300	600	
116	Eddie Yost	12	20	30	50	▲120	250	800	
117	Duke Snider	100	150	200	250	500	1,000	2,500	10,000
118	Billy Martin	40	80	100	200	300	600	3,000	6,000
119	Dale Mitchell	10	15	40	60	80	150		
120	Marlin Stuart	10	15	25	80	150	250		
121	Yogi Berra	120	200	300	500	800	▲1,500	3,000	10,000
122	Bill Serena	10	15	25	40	60	200	500	
123	Johnny Lipon	10	15	25	40	100	200	500	2,500
124	Chuck Dressen MG	12	20	30	80	150	250	600	3,000
125	Fred Hatfield	10	15	25	40	▲100	250	800	
126	Al Corwin	10	15	25	40	60	250	1,200	
127	Dick Kryhoski	10	15	25	40	80	300		
128	Whitey Lockman	10	15	25	50	150	600		
129	Russ Meyer	10	15	40	50	100	300		
130	Cass Michaels	8	12	20	40	60	300	800	2,000
131	Connie Ryan	▲12	▲20	▲30	50	60	▲300	800	
132	Fred Hutchinson	8	12	20	30	100	300	800	1,200
133	Willie Jones	▲10	▲15	▲25	▲40	60	250	400	2,000
134	Johnny Pesky	10	15	25	50	120	200	1,000	
135	Bobby Morgan	15	25	40	60	100	250		
136	Jim Brideweser RC	15	25	40	60	100	600		
137	Sam Dente	8	12	20	30	50	250	600	2,500
138	Bubba Church	8	12	20	40	60	200	500	
139	Pete Runnels	12	20	30	50	80	150	1,200	
140	Al Brazle	8	12	20	30	60	150	500	
141	Frank Shea	8	12	20	30	80	200	600	1,500
142	Larry Miggins RC	10	15	25	50	60	300	1,500	
143	Al Lopez MG	10	15	25	80	100	300	2,000	
144	Warren Hacker	10	15	25	40	50	250	1,000	
145	George Shuba	15	25	40	60	150			
146	Early Wynn	25	40	▲60	▲100	▲150	400	1,000	2,500
147	Clem Koshorek	6	10	15	25	60	200	500	1,500
148	Billy Goodman	10	15	25	40	120	300		
149	Al Corwin	8	12	20	50	60	150	600	
150	Carl Scheib	10	15	25	50	100	300		
151	Joe Adcock	10	15	25	60	100	200	1,000	
152	Clyde Vollmer	8	12	20	30	50	120	400	
153	Whitey Ford	▲100	▲150	200	300	500	▲1,500	10,000	

		GD 2	VG 3	VgEx 4	EX 5	ExMt 6	NM 7	NmMt 8	MT 9
154	Turk Lown	8	12	20	40	80	300	1,000	
155	Allie Clark	10	15	25	30	60	250	600	
156	Max Surkont	8	12	20	50	60	300	600	
157	Sherm Lollar	10	15	25	50	80	150	500	2,000
158	Howard Fox	8	12	20	30	60	250	1,000	
159	Mickey Vernon	10	15	25	60	100	250	1,200	
160	Cal Abrams	25	40	60	100	250	500	800	

— Whitey Ford #153 PSA 9 (MT) sold for $75,000 (Memory Lane; Private - 2007)
— Mickey Mantle #59 PSA 10 (Gem) sold for $115,000 (Memory Lane; Private - 2007)

1953 Red Man

		GD 2	VG 3	VgEx 4	EX 5	ExMt 6	NM 7	NmMt 8	MT 9
AL1	Casey Stengel MG	10	15	25	80	100	150		
AL2	Hank Bauer	8	12	20	30	50	100	300	
AL3	Yogi Berra	15	25	50	100	120	250	1,000	
AL4	Walt Dropo	6	10	15	25	40	80	200	
AL5	Nellie Fox	10	15	25	40	60	120	500	
AL6	Jackie Jensen	8	12	20	30	50	100		
AL7	Eddie Joost	6	10	15	25	40	80	200	
AL8	George Kell	10	15	25	40	60	120	500	
AL9	Dale Mitchell	6	10	15	25	40	80	200	
AL10	Phil Rizzuto	15	25	40	60	100	250	800	
AL11	Eddie Robinson	6	10	15	25	40	80		
AL12	Gene Woodling	8	12	20	30	50	100	300	
AL13	Gus Zernial	6	10	15	25	40	80		
AL14	Early Wynn	10	15	25	40	60	120	300	
AL15	Joe Dobson	6	10	15	25	40	80	200	
AL16	Billy Pierce	6	10	15	25	40	80	200	
AL17	Bob Lemon	10	15	25	40	60	120	500	
AL18	Johnny Mize	10	15	25	40	60	120	500	
AL19	Bob Porterfield	6	10	15	25	40	80	250	
AL20	Bobby Shantz	6	10	15	25	40	80		
AL21	Mickey Vernon	6	10	15	25	40	80	200	
AL22	Dom DiMaggio	8	12	20	30	50	100	250	
AL23	Gil McDougald	8	12	20	30	50	100	300	
AL24	Al Rosen	8	12	20	30	50	100	300	
AL25	Mel Parnell	6	10	15	25	40	80	200	
AL26	Bobby Avila	6	10	15	25	40	80	200	
NL1	Charlie Dressen MG	6	10	15	25	40	80		
NL2	Bobby Adams	6	10	15	25	40	80	200	
NL3	Richie Ashburn	10	15	25	40	60	120	500	
NL4	Joe Black	8	12	20	30	60	100	300	
NL5	Roy Campanella	15	25	50	100	120	250	1,000	
NL6	Ted Kluszewski	10	15	25	40	60	120	500	
NL7	Whitey Lockman	6	10	15	25	40	80	300	
NL8	Sal Maglie	6	10	15	25	40	80	200	
NL9	Andy Pafko	6	10	15	25	40	80	200	
NL10	Pee Wee Reese	15	25	40	80	100	200	800	
NL11	Robin Roberts	10	15	25	40	60	120	600	
NL12	Red Schoendienst	10	15	25	40	60	120	500	
NL13	Enos Slaughter	10	15	25	40	60	120	500	
NL14	Duke Snider	15	25	50	80	120	250	1,200	
NL15	Ralph Kiner	8	12	20	30	50	100	300	
NL16	Hank Sauer	6	10	15	25	40	150	200	
NL17	Del Ennis	6	10	15	25	40	80	350	
NL18	Granny Hamner	6	10	15	25	40	80	200	
NL19	Warren Spahn	15	25	40	60	100	200	800	
NL20	Wes Westrum	6	10	15	25	40	80	400	
NL21	Hoyt Wilhelm	10	15	25	40	60	120	500	
NL22	Murry Dickson	6	10	15	25	40	80	250	
NL23	Warren Hacker	6	10	15	25	40	80	200	
NL24	Gerry Staley	6	10	15	25	40	80		
NL25	Bobby Thomson	8	12	20	30	50	100	300	
NL26	Stan Musial	30	50	100	250	350	500		

— Prices reference cards with tabs.
— Duke Snider #NL14 BVG 9 (MT) sold for $1,355 (eBay; 1/0/)

1953 Topps

		GD 2	VG 3	VgEx 4	EX 5	ExMt 6	NM 7	NmMt 8	MT
	COMMON DP (221-280)		15	25	40	60	200		
1	Jackie Robinson DP	▲1,000	▲2,000	▲2,500	▲4,000	5,000	20,000	▲50,000	80,00
2	Luke Easter DP	6	10	15	25	40	100	250	
3	George Crowe	15	25	40	60	100	150	300	
4	Ben Wade	6	10	15	30	50	100	300	
5	Joe Dobson	8	12	20	30	50	80	200	1,20
6	Sam Jones	8	12	20	40	50	80	200	80
7	Bob Borkowski DP	6	10	15	25	40	60	120	1,00
8	Clem Koshorek DP	6	8	12	20	40	50	150	1,00
9	Joe Collins	12	20	30	50	120	200		
10	Smoky Burgess SP	15	25	40	60	100	150	600	
11	Sal Yvars	6	10	15	30	50	100	250	
12	Howie Judson DP	5	6	10	25	30	60	150	
13	Conrado Marrero DP	6	10	15	25	40	60	250	
14	Clem Labine DP	▲15	▲25	▲40	▲60	▲100	▲150	600	
15	Bobo Newsom DP RC	6	10	15	25	40	50	120	
16	Harry Lowrey DP	5	6	10	25	30	60	200	1,50
17	Billy Hitchcock	8	12	20	30	50	80	200	1,50
18	Ted Lepcio DP	5	6	10	15	30	▲60	150	1,20
19	Mel Parnell DP	5	8	12	20	50	50	150	80
20	Hank Thompson	8	12	20	30	50	120	200	1,80
21	Billy Johnson	8	12	20	30	50	80	150	1,20
22	Howie Fox	6	10	15	30	50	60	200	
23	Toby Atwell DP	5	6	10	15	40	50	150	1,00
24	Ferris Fain	8	12	20	30	50	80	250	1,20
25	Ray Boone	6	10	15	30	50	80	250	
26	Dale Mitchell DP	6	10	15	30	50	60	200	
27	Roy Campanella DP	80	120	200	▲300	▲500	600	▲1,200	2,00
28	Eddie Pellagrini	5	8	12	20	40	80	200	1,00
29	Hal Jeffcoat	5	8	12	25	40	60	150	1,20
30	Willard Nixon	8	12	20	30	50	100	400	1,20
31	Ewell Blackwell	8	12	20	40	50	100	300	
32	Clyde Vollmer	6	10	15	25	30	60	200	
33	Bob Kennedy DP	5	8	12	20	30	60	120	80
34	George Shuba	6	10	15	25	50	60	300	
35	Irv Noren DP	10	15	25	40	60	100	120	1,20
36	Johnny Groth DP	5	6	10	15	40	50	150	80
37	Eddie Mathews DP	80	120	200	300	500	800	▲2,000	▲4,00
38	Jim Hearn DP	6	10	15	25	40	60	120	1,20
39	Eddie Miksis	▲8	▲12	▲20	▲30	▲50	▲80	150	1,20
40	John Lipon	5	8	12	20	40	60	200	1,20
41	Enos Slaughter	15	25	50	60	120	250	▲2,000	
42	Gus Zernial DP	6	10	15	25	30	50	150	1,20
43	Gil McDougald	15	25	40	60	100	250		
44	Ellis Kinder SP	8	12	20	30	60	250		
45	Grady Hatton DP	5	6	15	20	30	60	150	
46	Johnny Klippstein DP	5	6	10	15	40	200		
47	Bubba Church DP	5	8	12	20	30	60	150	
48	Bob Del Greco DP	5	6	10	25	30	60	120	
49	Faye Throneberry DP	6	10	15	30	40	60	150	1,20
50	Chuck Dressen DP	10	15	25	30	50	80	200	1,20
51	Frank Campos DP	6	10	15	25	40	50	150	1,20
52	Ted Gray DP	6	10	15	25	30	60	150	1,50
53	Sherm Lollar DP	8	12	20	30	50	80	120	80
54	Bob Feller DP	▲60	▲100	▲120	150	250	300	1,000	4,00
55	Maurice McDermott DP	▲8	▲12	▲20	▲30	▲50	▲80	200	
56	Gerry Staley DP	6	10	15	25	50	80	120	1,20
57	Carl Scheib	6	10	15	25	▲40	▲60	120	
58	George Metkovich	5	8	12	20	40	60	200	1,20
59	Karl Drews DP	6	10	15	25	40	50	120	1,00
60	Cloyd Boyer	6	10	15	25	40	60	200	
61	Early Wynn SP	25	40	60	80	120	200	600	
62	Monte Irvin DP	40	60	100	150	▲300	▲500	800	
63	Gus Niarhos DP	5	6	10	25	30	80	120	1,0

	GD 2	VG 3	VgEx 4	EX 5	ExMt 6	NM 7	NmMt 8	MT 9
Dave Philley	10	15	25	40	60	100	200	
Earl Harrist	10	15	25	30	60	80	200	1,500
Orestes Minoso	20	30	50	100	150	250	400	1,200
Roy Sievers DP	5	6	10	15	30	60	150	800
Del Rice	5	8	12	20	40	60	150	1,200
Dick Brodowski	6	10	15	25	50	80	150	1,000
Ed Yuhas	8	12	20	30	50	80	200	1,200
Tony Bartirome	6	10	15	25	40	80	200	
Fred Hutchinson SP	▲15	▲25	▲40	▲60	▲100	200	400	
Eddie Robinson	5	8	12	20	30	60	150	800
Joe Rossi	8	12	20	30	50	60	200	1,400
Mike Garcia	6	10	15	25	40	80	150	1,200
Pee Wee Reese	▲100	▲150	▲200	250	400	▲800	1,000	4,000
Johnny Mize DP	▲25	▲40	▲60	▲100	▲150	200	400	1,200
Al Schoendienst	20	30	50	80	120	200	1,000	
Johnny Wyrostek	8	12	20	30	50	80	200	1,200
Jim Hegan	6	10	15	25	40	80	150	1,200
Joe Black SP	10	15	25	50	100	200	1,000	
Mickey Mantle	▲4,000	▲5,000	6,000	10,000	▼15,000	40,000	60,000	
Howie Pollet	6	10	15	30	40	100	500	
Bob Hooper DP	5	6	10	15	30	50	150	1,000
Bobby Morgan DP	6	10	15	25	50	120		
Billy Martin	50	80	120	200	300	500	▲2,000	4,000
Ed Lopat	12	20	30	50	100	150	400	
Willie Jones DP	10	15	25	40	60	200	1,200	
Chuck Stobbs DP	▲6	▲10	▲15	▲25	▲40	▲60	150	
Hank Edwards DP	5	8	12	20	30	60	150	
Ebba St.Claire DP	6	10	15	25	40	80	400	1,200
Paul Minner DP	5	6	10	30	40	100	300	
Hal Rice DP	8	12	20	30	60	120		
Bill Kennedy DP	5	8	12	20	30	60	200	1,200
Willard Marshall DP	6	10	15	25	40	80	250	
Virgil Trucks	▲10	▲15	▲25	40	▲60	100	800	
Don Kolloway DP	5	8	12	20	30	60	200	
Cal Abrams DP	8	12	20	30	50	80	250	1,200
Dave Madison	6	10	15	30	40	80	200	
Bill Miller	6	10	25	50	60	200	600	
Ted Wilks	6	10	15	25	50	200	1,200	
Connie Ryan DP	6	10	15	30	40	250	600	
Joe Astroth DP	6	10	15	25	40	60	200	1,200
Yogi Berra	▲150	▲250	▲400	▲600	▲800	▲1,200	4,000	12,000
Joe Nuxhall DP	10	20	30	50	150	500		
Johnny Antonelli	6	10	15	40	60	100	250	
Danny O'Connell DP	5	6	10	15	30	80	400	
Bob Porterfield DP	5	6	15	25	30	50	120	1,400
Alvin Dark	15	25	40	60	100	150	600	
Herman Wehmeier DP	▲8	▲12	▲20	▲30	▲50	▲80	250	1,200
Hank Sauer DP	8	12	20	30	50	100	150	1,800
Ned Garver DP	▲6	▲10	▲15	▲25	▲40	60	250	
Jerry Priddy	5	8	12	20	60	100	400	
Phil Rizzuto	▲80	▲120	▲200	▲300	▲500	▲800	▲1,500	
George Spencer	5	8	25	30	50	60	250	
Frank Smith DP	8	12	20	30	50	80	250	
Sid Gordon DP	5	6	10	15	30	80	300	
Gus Bell DP	6	10	15	25	40	100	250	1,200
Johnny Sain SP	12	20	30	50	100	200	600	
Davey Williams	8	12	20	25	50	60	500	
Walt Dropo	6	10	15	40	50	150	300	
Elmer Valo	8	12	20	30	50	80	250	
Tommy Byrne DP	6	10	15	25	30	60	150	1,200
Sibby Sisti DP	6	10	15	25	40	60	200	
Dick Williams DP	12	20	25	30	80	200	500	
Bill Connelly DP RC	6	10	15	25	40	60	300	
Clint Courtney DP RC	5	6	10	25	40	80	150	
Wilmer Mizell DP	5	6	10	30	50	100	400	
Keith Thomas RC	▲8	▲12	▲20	▲30	▲50	80	300	
Turk Lown DP	8	12	20	30	40	150	800	
Harry Byrd DP RC	6	10	15	25	40	50	120	

		GD 2	VG 3	VgEx 4	EX 5	ExMt 6	NM 7	NmMt 8	MT 9
132	Tom Morgan	12	20	30	50	80	200	400	
133	Gil Coan	5	8	12	20	40	80	200	
134	Rube Walker	8	12	20	40	60	100	800	
135	Al Rosen DP	6	10	15	30	60	120	500	
136	Ken Heintzelman DP	5	6	10	25	50	100	150	
137	John Rutherford DP	8	12	25	30	40	60	400	
138	George Kell	15	25	40	60	100	150	400	
139	Sammy White	5	8	12	20	50	80	200	
140	Tommy Glaviano	5	8	25	30	40	120		
141	Allie Reynolds DP	15	25	40	60	100	150		
142	Vic Wertz	8	12	20	30	▲50	100	500	
143	Billy Pierce	15	25	40	60	80	150	500	
144	Bob Schultz DP	5	6	10	25	40	60	250	
145	Harry Dorish DP	5	8	12	25	30	50	150	
146	Granville Hamner	6	10	15	30	60	150		
147	Warren Spahn	▲80	▲120	▲200	▲300	▲500	▲800	▲1,500	
148	Mickey Grasso	5	8	12	20	40	100	200	
149	Dom DiMaggio DP	15	25	40	60	100	150	400	
150	Harry Simpson DP	5	8	12	20	30	60	250	
151	Hoyt Wilhelm	25	40	60	100	120	300	500	
152	Bob Adams DP	10	15	25	40	60	100	400	
153	Andy Seminick DP	6	10	15	25	40	80	300	
154	Dick Groat	20	30	50	80	120			
155	Dutch Leonard	6	10	15	30	40	100	250	
156	Jim Rivera DP RC	8	12	20	30	50	80	120	1,200
157	Bob Addis DP	10	15	25	40	60	100		
158	Johnny Logan RC	12	20	30	50	80	120	400	1,200
159	Wayne Terwilliger DP	6	10	15	30	40	200	600	
160	Bob Young	6	10	15	25	40	80	150	1,200
161	Vern Bickford DP	5	6	10	30	50	150	300	
162	Ted Kluszewski	10	15	40	80	100	200	400	
163	Fred Hatfield DP	5	8	12	20	30	60	300	1,500
164	Frank Shea DP	5	6	10	15	50	150		
165	Billy Hoeft	5	8	12	40	50	200	400	
166	Billy Hunter RC	8	12	20	30	50	80	200	
167	Art Schult RC	10	15	25	40	60	100	200	1,200
168	Willard Schmidt RC	6	10	15	25	40	60	120	
169	Dizzy Trout	5	6	10	25	40	60	250	1,200
170	Bill Werle	6	10	15	25	40	60	200	1,200
171	Bill Glynn RC	5	6	10	25	30	50	200	
172	Rip Repulski RC	5	6	10	15	50	100	800	
173	Preston Ward	▼6	▼10	▼15	25	▲40	60	120	1,200
174	Billy Loes	10	15	25	30	40	100	400	
175	Ron Kline RC	6	10	15	25	50	100		
176	Don Hoak RC	▲8	▲12	▲20	▲30	▲50	▲80	200	1,800
177	Jim Dyck RC	6	10	15	25	40	100		
178	Jim Waugh RC	5	6	10	25	30	60	200	1,500
179	Gene Hermanski	6	10	15	25	50	60	250	
180	Virgil Stallcup	10	15	25	40	60	100	150	1,200
181	Al Zarilla	▲6	▲10	▲15	▲25	▲40	80	250	1,200
182	Bobby Hofman	6	10	15	25	40	60	120	
183	Stu Miller RC	6	10	15	25	40	60	300	
184	Hal Brown RC	6	10	15	25	40	60	250	1,200
185	Jim Pendleton RC	6	10	15	25	30	50	120	
186	Charlie Bishop RC	6	10	15	25	40	50	150	1,200
187	Jim Fridley	5	6	15	25	30	50	200	1,200
188	Andy Carey RC	15	25	40	60	100	150	400	
189	Ray Jablonski RC	5	6	10	25	40	60	150	1,200
190	Dixie Walker CO	5	6	10	25	40	60	200	
191	Ralph Kiner	20	30	40	50	150	250	500	
192	Wally Westlake	5	▲8	▼12	20	30	▲100	200	1,200
193	Mike Clark RC	6	10	15	25	30	50	200	
194	Eddie Kazak	6	10	15	25	40	50	150	
195	Ed McGhee RC	▲6	▲10	▲15	▲25	▲40	▲60	150	
196	Bob Keegan RC	5	8	12	20	40	50	150	1,200
197	Del Crandall	10	15	25	40	60	100	300	
198	Forrest Main	6	10	15	25	30	50	150	
199	Marion Fricano RC	▲8	▲12	▲20	▲30	▲50	▲80	200	

#	Player	GD 2	VG 3	VgEx 4	EX 5	ExMt 6	NM 7	NmMt 8	MT 9
200	Gordon Goldsberry	5	8	12	20	40	60	150	1,200
201	Paul LaPalme	6	10	15	25	40	50	300	
202	Carl Sawatski RC	5	8	12	30	40	60	200	1,200
203	Cliff Fannin	10	15	25	40	60	100	250	
204	Dick Bokelman RC	5	6	10	15	30	▲60	150	2,000
205	Vern Benson RC	8	12	20	25	30	60	250	
206	Ed Bailey RC	8	12	20	30	50	80	200	
207	Whitey Ford	60	100	150	250	400	600	▲2,500	4,000
208	Jim Wilson	▲6	▲10	▲15	▲25	▲40	60	120	1,200
209	Jim Greengrass RC	6	10	15	25	40	60	200	1,200
210	Bob Cerv RC	12	20	30	50	80	150	600	
211	J.W. Porter RC	8	12	20	▲30	▲50	▲80	150	150
212	Jack Dittmer RC	6	10	15	25	40	60		
213	Ray Scarborough	10	15	25	40	60	100	400	
214	Bill Bruton RC	5	6	10	25	30	60	150	
215	Gene Conley RC	6	10	15	25	50	100	400	
216	Jim Hughes RC	8	12	20	30	40	80	300	
217	Murray Wall RC	6	10	15	25	50	60	250	
218	Les Fusselman	5	6	20	25	50	120	200	
219	Pete Runnels	8	12	20	30	50	80	200	
220	Satchel Paige	600	1,000	1,500	2,500	▼3,000	6,000	15,000	40,000
221	Bob Milliken RC	8	12	20	60	80	200	500	
222	Vic Janowicz DP RC	20	30	50	60	80	300		
223	Johnny O'Brien DP RC	6	10	15	40	50	100	300	
224	Lou Sleater DP	6	10	25	30	80	100	400	
225	Bobby Shantz	12	20	30	60	120	150	400	
226	Ed Erautt	8	12	20	50	60	100	400	
227	Morris Martin	8	12	20	50	60	150	400	
228	Hal Newhouser	50	80	120	200	300	500	800	
229	Rocky Krsnich RC	8	12	20	50	100	200	500	
230	Johnny Lindell DP	▲12	▲20	▲30	50	60	▲150	500	1,200
231	Solly Hemus DP	6	10	15	30	60	100	500	
232	Dick Kokos	15	25	40	60	100	200	400	
233	Al Aber RC	8	12	20	30	80	250	600	
234	Ray Murray DP	6	10	25	40	50	100	250	1,200
235	John Hetki DP RC	6	10	15	40	50	150	400	
236	Harry Perkowski DP	8	12	20	50	80	150	800	
237	Clarence Podbielan DP	10	15	25	40	60	200	500	
238	Cal Hogue DP RC	10	15	25	50	80	150	500	
239	Jim Delsing	12	20	30	50	60	150	400	
240	Freddie Marsh	12	20	30	50	80	250	500	
241	Al Sima DP	10	15	25	30	50	80	200	2,000
242	Charlie Silvera	10	15	25	40	100	200	500	
243	Carlos Bernier DP RC	10	15	30	50	60	120	500	
244	Willie Mays	▲2,500	3,000	5,000	8,000	▼10,000	20,000		
245	Bill Norman CO	10	15	25	50	100	▲250		
246	Roy Face DP RC	20	30	50	80	120	▲400	800	
247	Mike Sandlock DP RC	12	20	25	30	50	120	300	
248	Gene Stephens DP RC	8	12	20	30	60	100	500	
249	Eddie O'Brien RC	▲12	▲20	▲30	▲50	80	200	3,000	1,200
250	Bob Wilson RC	25	40	60	100	150	250	600	
251	Sid Hudson	20	30	50	80	200	250		
252	Henry Foiles RC	10	15	25	60	100	200	600	
254	Preacher Roe DP	10	15	50	60	120	300	500	
255	Dixie Howell	20	30	50	100	120	200	800	
256	Les Peden RC	20	30	50	80	120	200	500	
257	Bob Boyd RC	15	25	40	100	120	200	400	
258	Jim Gilliam RC	100	150	250	400	500	800	2,500	
259	Roy McMillan DP	12	20	30	50	80	200		
260	Sam Calderone RC	12	20	30	50	100	300		
262	Bob Oldis RC	8	12	20	60	80	300	600	
263	Johnny Podres RC	60	100	120	250	400	1,000	2,000	
264	Gene Woodling DP	15	25	40	60	80	250	600	
265	Jackie Jensen	12	20	50	80	100	250	500	
266	Bob Cain	8	12	20	60	80	200	600	
269	Duane Pillette	15	25	40	50	100	300	500	
270	Vern Stephens	▲20	▲30	▲50	▲80	▲120	200	400	
272	Bill Antonello RC	10	15	40	50	80	300	500	

#	Player	GD 2	VG 3	VgEx 4	EX 5	ExMt 6	NM 7	NmMt 8	MT 9
273	Harvey Haddix RC	50	80	120	200	300	500		
274	John Riddle CO	10	15	25	100	150	500		
276	Ken Raffensberger	15	25	50	60	▲250	▲400	800	
277	Don Lund RC	20	30	50	60	120	250	500	
278	Willie Miranda RC	15	25	50	120	200	600		
279	Joe Coleman DP	10	15	25	40	60	120	400	
280	Milt Bolling RC	40	60	100	200	400			

— Mickey Mantle #82 PSA 9 (MT) sold for $80,000 (Memory Lane; Private Sale - 2007)

— Mickey Mantle #82 PSA 8.5 (NmMt+) sold for $23,640 (Greg Bussineau; 7/12)

— Willie Mays #244 PSA 9 (MT) sold for $135,000 (Memory Lane; Private Sale - 2007)

1954 Bowman

#	Player	GD 2	VG 3	VgEx 4	EX 5	ExMt 6	NM 7	NmMt 8	MT 9
1	Phil Rizzuto	25	40	60	100	120	250	800	
2	Jackie Jensen	5	6	10	15	25	60	300	
3	Marion Fricano	5	5	5	8	12	20	120	
4	Bob Hooper	5	5	5	8	12	15	60	300
5	Billy Hunter	5	5	5	8	12	15	50	
6	Nellie Fox	▲12	20	▲30	▲50	▲80	100	300	
7	Walter Dropo	5	5	6	10	15	40	60	
8	Jim Busby	5	5	5	8	12	25	80	
9	Dave Williams	5	5	5	8	12	30	60	
10	Carl Erskine	▲6	▲10	▲15	▲25	▲40	50	▲200	
11	Sid Gordon	5	5	5	8	12	20	50	350
12A	Roy McMillan 551/1290 At Bat	5	5	5	8	12	15	50	250
12B	Roy McMillan 557/1296 At Bat	5	5	6	10	15	25	150	
13	Paul Minner	5	5	5	8	12	20	50	300
14	Gerry Staley	5	5	5	8	12	25	50	
15	Richie Ashburn	▲20	▲30	▲50	▲80	100	150	250	
16	Jim Wilson	5	5	5	8	12	25	80	
17	Tom Gorman	5	5	5	8	12	25	50	35
18	Hoot Evers	5	5	5	8	12	30	80	300
19	Bobby Shantz	5	5	5	8	12	20	50	
20	Art Houtteman	5	5	5	8	12	25	50	300
21	Vic Wertz	5	5	5	8	12	30	80	
22A	Sam Mele 213/1661 Putouts	5	5	5	8	12	15	50	350
22B	Sam Mele 217/1665 Putouts	5	5	6	10	15	25	200	
23	Harvey Kuenn RC	6	10	15	25	40	60	100	500
24	Bob Porterfield	5	5	5	8	12	25	50	
25A	Wes Westrum 1.000/.987	5	5	6	10	15	30		
25B	Wes Westrum .982/.986	5	5	8	12	20	40		
26A	Billy Cox 1.000/.960	5	5	6	10	15	30	150	
26B	Billy Cox .972/.960	5	5	8	12	20	40	150	
27	Dick Cole RC	5	5	5	8	12	30	60	25
28A	Jim Greengrass Addison, NJ	5	5	5	8	12	15	50	25
28B	Jim Greengrass Addison, NY	5	5	5	8	12	15	50	
29	Johnny Klippstein	5	5	6	10	15	20	50	35
30	Del Rice	5	5	5	8	12	25	30	300
31	Smoky Burgess	5	5	8	12	20	30	50	30
32	Del Crandall	5	5	5	8	12	20	60	30
33A	Vic Raschi No Trade	5	5	8	12	20	50	150	
33B	Vic Raschi Traded to St.Louis	5	6	10	15	25	80	600	
34	Sammy White	5	5	5	8	12	25	50	40
35A	Eddie Joost Quiz Answer is 8	5	5	5	8	12	15	50	30
35B	Eddie Joost Quiz Answer is 33	5	5	6	10	15	25		
36	George Strickland	5	5	6	10	15	25	50	25
37	Dick Kokos	5	5	5	8	12	20	50	25
38A	Minnie Minoso .895/.961	5	5	8	12	20	30	80	50
38B	Minnie Minoso .963/.963	5	6	10	15	25	40	250	
39	Ned Garver	5	5	5	8	12	20	50	30
40	Gil Coan	5	5	5	8	12	25	50	
41A	Alvin Dark .986/960	5	5	5	8	12	25	80	40
41B	Alvin Dark .968/.960	5	5	6	10	15	30		
42	Billy Loes	5	5	5	8	12	30	80	40
43A	Bob Friend 20 Shutouts in Quiz	5	5	5	8	12	25	80	
43B	Bob Friend 16 Shutouts in Quiz	5	5	6	10	15	40	120	
44	Harry Perkowski	5	5	5	8	12	25	50	30

#	Player	GD 2	VG 3	VgEx 4	EX 5	ExMt 6	NM 7	NmMt 8	MT 9
45	Ralph Kiner	10	15	25	40	60	120	200	
46	Rip Repulski	5	5	8	12	20	25	50	300
47A	Granny Hamner .970/.953	5	5	5	8	12	15	60	300
47B	Granny Hamner .953/.951	5	5	8	12	20	30	120	
48	Jack Dittmer	5	5	5	8	12	25	80	
49	Harry Byrd	5	6	10	15	25	40	60	
50	George Kell	6	10	15	25	40	50	▲150	400
51	Alex Kellner	5	5	5	8	12	25	50	300
52	Joe Ginsberg	5	5	5	8	12	20	50	350
53A	Don Lenhardt .969/.984	5	5	5	8	12	15	50	300
53B	Don Lenhardt .966/.983	5	5	5	8	12	25	60	
54	Chico Carrasquel	5	5	5	8	12	25	50	300
55	Jim Delsing	5	5	5	8	12	25	50	250
56	Maurice McDermott	5	5	5	8	12	20	50	
57	Hoyt Wilhelm	8	12	20	30	50	▼60	150	500
58	Pee Wee Reese	25	40	60	100	150	250	400	2,000
59	Bob Schultz	5	5	5	8	12	25	50	300
60	Fred Baczewski RC	5	5	6	10	15	25	50	250
61A	Eddie Miksis .954/.962	5	5	5	8	12	15	50	300
61B	Eddie Miksis .954/.961	5	5	6	10	15	25	120	
62	Enos Slaughter	8	12	20	30	50	80	150	600
63	Earl Torgeson	5	5	5	8	12	15	50	250
64	Eddie Mathews	▲40	▲60	▲100	▲150	200	300	500	2,000
65	Mickey Mantle	▲1,000	1,200	2,000	▼2,500	▼4,000	8,000	15,000	25,000
66A	Ted Williams	▲1,200	▲2,000	▲2,500	▲3,000	▲5,000	▲8,000	▲15,000	
66B	Jimmy Piersall	6	10	15	25	60	100	250	
67A	Carl Scheib .306 Pct. Two Lines	5	5	5	8	12	40	200	
67B	Carl Scheib .306 Pct. One Line	5	5	6	10	15	60	300	
67C	Carl Scheib .300 Pct.	5	5	6	10	15	50	200	
68	Bobby Avila	5	5	5	8	12	30	80	
69	Clint Courtney	5	5	5	8	12	15	50	300
70	Willard Marshall	5	5	6	10	15	25	50	250
71	Ted Gray	5	5	6	10	15	30	50	300
72	Eddie Yost	5	5	5	8	12	30	60	300
73	Don Mueller	5	5	5	8	12	20	50	300
74	Jim Gilliam	5	6	10	15	25	60	120	500
75	Max Surkont	5	5	5	8	12	20	50	
76	Joe Nuxhall	5	5	5	8	12	40	60	250
77	Bob Rush	5	5	5	8	12	25	50	300
78	Sal Yvars	5	5	5	8	12	25	50	300
79	Curt Simmons	5	5	5	8	12	25	50	
80A	Johnny Logan 106 Runs	5	5	5	8	12	25	60	
80B	Johnny Logan 100 Runs	5	5	6	10	15	25	150	
81A	Jerry Coleman 1.000/.975	5	5	8	12	20	40	500	
81B	Jerry Coleman .952/.975	5	6	10	15	25	60	500	
82A	Bill Goodman .965/.986	5	5	6	10	15	30	80	400
82B	Bill Goodman .972/.985	5	5	8	12	20	40	120	
83	Ray Murray	5	5	5	8	12	30	50	300
84	Larry Doby	10	15	25	40	50	80	200	600
85A	Jim Dyck .926/.956	5	5	5	8	12	15	60	
85B	Jim Dyck .947/.960	5	5	6	10	15	25	100	
86	Harry Dorish	5	5	5	8	12	40	50	300
87	Don Lund	5	5	5	8	12	20	50	300
88	Tom Umphlett RC	5	5	5	8	12	15	50	
89	Willie Mays	▼400	▼600	▼1,000	▼1,200	▼2,000	5,000	8,000	12,000
90	Roy Campanella	25	40	60	100	150	250	600	800
91	Cal Abrams	5	5	5	8	12	25	50	300
92	Ken Raffensberger	5	5	5	8	12	15	50	300
93A	Bill Serena .983/.966	5	5	5	8	12	15	60	300
93B	Bill Serena .977/.966	5	5	6	10	15	25	120	
94A	Solly Hemus 476/1343	5	5	5	8	12	15	50	300
94B	Solly Hemus 477/1343	5	5	6	10	15	25	150	
95	Robin Roberts	12	20	30	50	▲80	▲120	250	800
96	Joe Adcock	5	5	8	12	20	30	100	
97	Gil McDougald	5	8	12	20	30	▲50	120	500
98	Ellis Kinder	5	5	8	12	20	25	60	400
99A	Peter Suder .985/.974	5	5	5	8	12	15	50	300
99B	Peter Suder .978/.974	5	5	6	10	15	40	200	

#	Player	GD 2	VG 3	VgEx 4	EX 5	ExMt 6	NM 7	NmMt 8	MT 9
100	Mike Garcia	5	5	8	12	20	25	50	
101	Don Larsen RC	15	25	40	60	100	150	250	600
102	Billy Pierce	5	5	8	12	20	40	60	300
103A	Stephen Souchock 144/1192	5	5	5	8	12	15	50	250
103B	Stephen Souchock 147/1195	5	5	6	10	15	25	120	
104	Frank Shea	5	5	5	8	12	25	50	300
105A	Sal Maglie Quiz Answer is 8	5	5	5	8	12	25	150	
105B	Sal Maglie Quiz Answer is 1904	5	5	8	12	20	30		
106	Clem Labine	5	6	10	15	25	40	80	400
107	Paul LaPalme	5	5	5	8	12	25	50	300
108	Bobby Adams	5	5	5	8	12	25	50	300
109	Roy Smalley	5	5	6	10	15	30	50	300
110	Red Schoendienst	6	8	12	20	30	80	150	
111	Murry Dickson	5	5	8	12	20	25	50	
112	Andy Pafko	5	5	8	12	20	30	60	
113	Allie Reynolds	8	12	20	30	50	80	120	600
114	Willard Nixon	5	5	5	8	12	15	50	300
115	Don Bollweg	5	5	5	8	12	25	50	250
116	Luke Easter	5	5	5	8	12	30	100	
117	Dick Kryhoski	5	5	6	10	15	25	50	350
118	Bob Boyd	5	5	5	8	12	15	50	350
119	Fred Hatfield	5	5	6	10	15	25	40	350
120	Mel Hoderlein RC	5	5	5	8	12	20	50	200
121	Ray Katt RC	5	5	5	8	12	15	60	
122	Carl Furillo	8	8	12	20	30	60	150	600
123	Toby Atwell	5	5	5	8	12	15	50	350
124A	Gus Bell 15/27 Errors	5	5	5	8	12	15	50	450
124B	Gus Bell 11/26 Errors	5	5	6	10	15	25	120	
125	Warren Hacker	5	5	5	8	12	15	50	250
126	Cliff Chambers	5	5	5	8	12	25	50	400
127	Del Ennis	5	5	8	12	20	25	50	
128	Ebba St.Claire	5	5	5	8	12	30	50	350
129	Hank Bauer	▲12	▲20	▲30	▲50	▲80	120	1,200	
130	Milt Bolling	5	5	5	8	12	40	150	
131	Joe Astroth	5	5	5	8	12	25	200	
132	Bob Feller	30	50	80	120	200	300	600	
133	Duane Pillette	5	5	5	8	12	30	50	
134	Luis Aloma	5	5	5	8	12	25	60	
135	Johnny Pesky	5	5	5	8	12	30	80	
136	Clyde Vollmer	5	5	5	8	12	15	60	300
137	Al Corwin	5	5	5	8	12	80		
138A	Gil Hodges .993/.991	10	15	25	40	60	100	600	
138B	Gil Hodges .992/.991	10	15	25	40	60	100	600	
139A	Preston Ward .961/.992	5	5	5	8	12	40	300	
139B	Preston Ward .990/.992	5	5	6	10	15	60		
140A	Saul Rogovin 7-12 W-L 2 K's	5	8	12	20	30	80		
140B	Saul Rogovin 7-12 W-L 62 K's	5	8	12	20	30			
140C	Saul Rogovin 8-12 W-L	5	8	12	20	30	80	150	
141	Joe Garagiola	6	10	15	25	50	60	150	
142	Al Brazle	5	5	5	8	12	20	60	
143	Willie Jones	5	5	5	8	12	40	150	350
144	Ernie Johnson RC	5	5	8	12	20	30	250	
145A	Billy Martin .985/.983	10	15	25	40	60	100	400	
145B	Billy Martin .983/.982	10	15	25	40	60	120	400	
146	Dick Gernert	5	5	5	8	12	25	60	300
147	Joe DeMaestri	5	5	5	8	12	25	80	
148	Dale Mitchell	5	5	6	10	15	30	100	
149	Bob Young	5	5	5	8	12	25	200	
150	Cass Michaels	5	5	5	8	12	25	150	
151	Pat Mullin	5	5	5	8	12	25	150	
152	Mickey Vernon	5	6	10	15	25	100		
153A	Whitey Lockman 100/331	5	6	10	15	25			
153B	Whitey Lockman 102/333	5	8	12	20	30			
154	Don Newcombe	5	6	10	15	50	150	400	
155	Frank Thomas RC	5	6	10	15	40	120		
156A	Rocky Bridges 320/467	5	5	8	12	40	150		
156B	Rocky Bridges 328/475	5	6	10	15	40	300		
157	Omar Lown	5	5	8	12	30	250		

#	Player	GD 2	VG 3	VgEx 4	EX 5	ExMt 6	NM 7	NmMt 8	MT 9
158	Stu Miller	5	5	5	8	12	30	400	
159	John Lindell	5	5	5	8	12	50	450	
160	Danny O'Connell	5	5	6	10	15	150		
161	Yogi Berra	▲60	▲100	▲150	▲250	300	500	800	2,000
162	Ted Lepcio	5	5	8	12	20	25	60	300
163A	Dave Philley No Trade 152 Games	5	5	6	10	15	40	120	
163B	Dave Philley Traded 152 Games	5	5	8	12	20	50	150	
163C	Dave Philley Traded 157 Games	5	6	10	15	25	50	150	
164	Early Wynn	8	12	20	▲30	50	▲120	150	
165	Johnny Groth	5	5	5	8	12	30	50	250
166	Sandy Consuegra	5	5	5	8	12	15	50	
167	Billy Hoeft	5	5	5	8	12	25	60	350
168	Ed Fitzgerald	5	5	5	8	12	25	60	
169	Larry Jansen	5	5	5	8	12	25	60	350
170	Duke Snider	40	60	100	120	▲200	▲300	600	1,200
171	Carlos Bernier	5	5	5	8	12	25	50	250
172	Andy Seminick	5	5	5	8	12	20	50	250
173	Dee Fondy	5	5	5	8	12	25	50	300
174A	Pete Castiglione .966/.959	5	5	5	8	12	15	60	300
174B	Pete Castiglione .970/.959	5	5	5	8	12	25	80	
175	Mel Clark	5	5	5	8	12	25	60	350
176	Vern Bickford	5	5	5	8	12	25	80	350
177	Whitey Ford	▲40	▲60	▲100	▲150	▲250	▲400	▲600	2,500
178	Del Wilber	5	5	6	10	15	25	50	
179A	Morris Martin 44 ERA	5	5	5	8	12	15	50	
179B	Morris Martin 4.44 ERA	5	5	5	8	12	25	80	
180	Joe Tipton	5	5	5	8	12	25	50	250
181	Les Moss	5	5	5	8	12	25	50	350
182	Sherm Lollar	5	5	6	10	15	25	50	
183	Matt Batts	5	5	5	8	12	25	50	300
184	Mickey Grasso	5	5	8	12	20	25	60	
185A	Daryl Spencer .941/.944 RC	5	5	5	8	12	15	50	300
185B	Daryl Spencer .933/.936	5	5	6	10	15	25		
186	Russ Meyer	5	5	8	12	20	30	80	
187	Vern Law	5	5	10	15	25	30	80	
188	Frank Smith	5	5	6	10	15	20	50	350
189	Randy Jackson	5	5	5	8	12	25	50	350
190	Joe Presko	5	5	5	8	12	25	50	350
191	Karl Drews	5	5	5	8	12	25	50	250
192	Lew Burdette	5	5	8	12	20	30	120	500
193	Eddie Robinson	5	6	10	15	25	120	200	
194	Sid Hudson	5	5	8	12	20	30	100	
195	Bob Cain	5	5	8	12	20	25	50	250
196	Bob Lemon	8	8	12	20	30	60	120	500
197	Lou Kretlow	5	5	5	8	12	25	50	250
198	Virgil Trucks	5	5	8	12	20	25	50	300
199	Steve Gromek	5	5	5	8	12	30	60	250
200	Conrado Marrero	5	5	5	8	12	25	60	300
201	Bob Thomson	5	5	8	12	20	40	175	
202	George Shuba	5	5	6	10	15	40	120	
203	Vic Janowicz	5	5	5	8	12	30	100	
204	Jack Collum RC	5	5	5	8	12	15	60	300
205	Hal Jeffcoat	5	5	5	8	12	30	50	
206	Steve Bilko	5	5	8	12	20	25	60	250
207	Stan Lopata	5	5	5	8	12	25	50	250
208	Johnny Antonelli	5	5	5	8	12	15	60	300
209	Gene Woodling	▲6	▲10	▲15	▲25	▲40	▲60	200	
210	Jimmy Piersall	6	10	15	25	40	60	120	
211	Al Robertson RC	5	5	5	8	12	15	60	350
212A	Owen Friend .964/.957	5	5	5	8	12	25	80	300
212B	Owen Friend .967/.958	5	5	6	10	15	30	100	350
213	Dick Littlefield	5	5	5	8	12	25	50	350
214	Ferris Fain	5	5	5	8	12	20	50	250
215	Johnny Bucha	5	5	5	8	12	15	60	300
216A	Jerry Snyder .988/.988	5	5	5	8	12	25	80	300
216B	Jerry Snyder .968/.968	5	5	5	8	12	25	80	
217A	Henry Thompson .956/.951	5	6	10	15	25	60	350	
217B	Henry Thompson .958/.952	5	8	12	20	30	80	450	
218	Preacher Roe	5	6	10	15	25	60	150	
219	Hal Rice	5	5	5	8	12	25	50	350
220	Hobie Landrith RC	5	5	5	8	12	15	60	
221	Frank Baumholtz	5	5	5	8	12	25	50	400
222	Memo Luna RC	5	5	5	8	12	40	80	250
223	Steve Ridzik	5	5	5	8	12	20	80	250
224	Bill Bruton	5	6	10	15	25	80	300	

— Ted Williams #66A SGC 92 (NmMt+) sold for $7,080 (Greg Bussineau; 7/12)

— Ted Williams #66A SGC 92 (NmMt+) sold for $6,382 (Mile High; 10/12)

1954 Braves Johnston Cookies

#	Player	GD 2	VG 3	VgEx 4	EX 5	ExMt 6	NM 7	NmMt 8	MT 9
	COMMON CARD	5	8	12	15	20	30	60	200
1	Del Crandall	5	8	12	15	20	30	100	
3	Jim Pendleton	5	8	12	15	20	40	60	
4	Danny O'Connell	5	8	12	15	20	30	100	200
5	Hank Aaron	250	300	350	600	1,200	2,500	3,000	
6	Jack Dittmer	5	8	12	15	20	30	80	
9	Joe Adcock	5	8	12	15	20	30	60	
10	Bob Buhl	5	8	12	15	20	30	80	200
11	Phil Paine	5	8	12	15	20	30	100	200
12	Ben Johnson	5	8	12	15	20	30	60	
13	Sibbi Sisti	5	8	12	15	20	30	60	
15	Charles Gorin	5	8	12	15	20	30	60	
16	Chet Nichols	5	8	12	15	20	30	60	
17	Dave Jolly	5	8	12	15	20	30	120	
19	Jim Wilson	5	8	12	15	20	30	100	
20	Ray Crone	5	8	12	15	20	30		
21	Warren Spahn	15	25	35	50	100	150	350	
22	Gene Conley	5	8	12	15	20	30	80	
23	Johnny Logan	5	8	12	15	20	30		
24	Charlie White	5	8	12	15	20	30	120	
27	George Metkovich	5	8	12	15	20	30	80	
28	Johnny Cooney CO	5	8	12	15	20	30	60	
29	Paul Burris	5	8	12	15	20	30	60	200
31	Bucky Walters CO	5	8	12	15	20	30	60	200
32	Ernie Johnson	5	8	12	15	20	30	60	
33	Lou Burdette	5	8	12	15	20	30	100	
34	Bobby Thomson SP	50	75	100	150	300	400		
35	Bob Keely	5	8	12	15	20	30		
38	Bill Bruton	5	8	12	15	20	30	60	
40	Charlie Grimm MG	5	8	12	15	20	30	60	200
41	Eddie Mathews	15	25	35	50	80	300		
42	Sam Calderone	5	8	12	15	20	30	60	200
47	Joey Jay	5	8	12	15	20	30	80	
48	Andy Pafko	5	8	12	15	20	30	100	
49	Dr. Charles Lacks (Unnumbered)	5	8	12	15	20	30	60	
50	Joseph F. Taylor (Unnumbered)	5	8	12	15	20	30	80	

1954 Dan-Dee

#	Player	GD 2	VG 3	VgEx 4	EX 5	ExMt 6	NM 7	NmMt 8	MT 9
1	Bobby Avila	10	15	25	40	60	150	450	
2	Hank Bauer	15	25	40	80	150	250	600	
3	Walker Cooper SP	30	150	300	350	400	450		
4	Larry Doby	20	30	50	80	120	250	800	
5	Luke Easter	10	15	25	120	150	250	300	
6	Bob Feller	30	100	150	200	250	400	1,500	
7	Bob Friend	10	15	25	40	150	200	400	
8	Mike Garcia	10	15	25	40	60	150	300	
9	Sid Gordon	10	15	25	40	60	150	500	
10	Jim Hegan	10	15	25	40	60	150	300	
11	Gil Hodges	30	100	120	150	200	300	1,200	
12	Art Houtteman	10	15	25	40	60	150	400	
13	Monte Irvin	15	25	40	80	100	300	500	
14	Paul LaPalme	10	15	25	60	80	300	400	
15	Bob Lemon	15	25	40	60	100	225	500	
16	Al Lopez MG	10	15	25	40	60	200		

		GD 2	VG 3	VgEx 4	EX 5	ExMt 6	NM 7	NmMt 8	MT 9
17	Mickey Mantle	▲1,200	▲2,000	▲3,000	▲5,000	▲8,000	▲12,000	▲20,000	
18	Dale Mitchell	10	15	25	40	80	150	300	
19	Phil Rizzuto	25	60	100	120	150	400		
20	Curt Roberts	10	15	25	40	60	150	500	
21	Al Rosen	12	20	30	50	60	175	400	
22	Red Schoendienst	15	25	40	80	120	250	600	
23	Paul Smith SP	30	50	80	120	200	300	800	
24	Duke Snider	50	100	120	200	375	600	1,500	
25	George Strickland	10	15	25	40	60	150	300	
26	Max Surkont	10	15	25	40	60	150	500	
27	Frank Thomas	12	20	30	50	80	200	500	
28	Wally Westlake	10	15	25	40	60	150	300	
29	Early Wynn	15	25	40	60	150	225	500	

— Mickey Mantle PSA 9 (MT) sold for $15,405 (REA; Spring '14)
— Mickey Mantle PSA 9 (MT) sold for $16,286 (Mile High; 10/13)
— Mickey Mantle #17 PSA 8.5 (NmMt+) sold for $9,037 (Goodwin; 12/11)
— Mickey Mantle #17 PSA 8.5 (NmMt+) sold for $6,840 (Greg Bussineau; 12/12)
— Mickey Mantle #17 PSA 8.5 (NmMt+) sold for $6,791 (Memory Lane; 5/12)

1954 Red Heart

		GD 2	VG 3	VgEx 4	EX 5	ExMt 6	NM 7	NmMt 8	MT 9
	COMMON CARD	5	8	12	20	30	50	120	500
1	Richie Ashburn SP	15	25	40	60	100	150	500	
2	Frank Baumholtz SP	5	8	12	20	30	100	150	
3	Gus Bell	5	8	12	20	30	50	250	700
4	Billy Cox	5	8	12	20	40	50	150	500
5	Alvin Dark	5	8	12	20	30	50	150	
6	Carl Erskine SP	10	15	25	40	120	200	500	
7	Ferris Fain	5	8	12	20	30	50	200	
8	Dee Fondy	5	8	12	20	30	150	200	
9	Nellie Fox	12	20	30	50	80	200	250	
10	Jim Gilliam	6	10	15	25	40	80	150	800
11	Jim Hegan SP	5	8	12	20	30	80	225	
12	George Kell	6	10	15	25	40	60	150	
13	Ralph Kiner SP	8	12	20	30	50	150	300	
14	Ted Kluszewski SP	8	12	20	100	120	150	300	1,000
15	Harvey Kuenn	5	8	12	20	30	50	150	500
16	Bob Lemon SP	8	12	20	30	50	100	400	
17	Sherman Lollar	5	8	12	20	30	50	135	
18	Mickey Mantle	▲800	▲1,000	▲1,200	▲1,500	▲2,500	▲4,000	▲5,000	▲20,000
19	Billy Martin	8	12	20	30	100	150	400	1,000
20	Gil McDougald SP	6	10	15	25	50	80	250	800
21	Roy McMillan	5	8	12	20	30	60	120	500
22	Minnie Minoso	6	10	15	25	40	80	300	600
23	Stan Musial SP	▲100	150	▲250	▲400	▲600	▲1,000	2,000	7,000
24	Billy Pierce	5	8	12	20	30	50	200	600
25	Al Rosen SP	6	10	15	25	40	100	300	
26	Hank Sauer	5	8	12	20	30	50	150	500
27	Red Schoendienst SP	12	20	30	50	100	200	300	
28	Enos Slaughter	6	10	15	25	40	150	250	800
29	Duke Snider	15	25	40	100	100	250	800	
30	Warren Spahn	10	15	25	40	60	120	350	
31	Sammy White	5	8	12	20	30	50	250	700
32	Eddie Yost	5	8	12	20	30	50	250	500
33	Gus Zernial	5	8	12	20	30	100	300	

1954 Red Man

		GD 2	VG 3	VgEx 4	EX 5	ExMt 6	NM 7	NmMt 8	MT 9
1	Bobby Avila	5	8	12	20	30	60	250	
2	Jim Busby	5	8	12	20	30	60	150	
3	Nellie Fox	10	15	25	40	60	120	400	
4	George Kell Boston	10	15	25	40	60	120	400	
4	George Kell Chicago	12	20	30	50	80	150		
5	Sherman Lollar	5	8	12	20	30	60	150	
6	Sam Mele Baltimore	6	10	15	25	40	80	200	
6	Sam Mele Chicago	10	15	25	40	60	120		
7	Minnie Minoso	6	10	15	25	40	80		

		GD 2	VG 3	VgEx 4	EX 5	ExMt 6	NM 7	NmMt 8	MT 9
AL8	Mel Parnell	5	8	12	20	30	60	150	
AL9	Dave Philley Cleveland	6	10	15	25	40	80	200	
AL9	Dave Philley Philadelphia	10	15	25	40	60	120	300	
AL10	Billy Pierce	5	8	12	20	30	60	150	
AL11	Jimmy Piersall	6	10	15	25	40	80	200	
AL12	Al Rosen	6	10	15	25	40	80	200	
AL13	Mickey Vernon	5	8	12	20	30	60	150	
AL14	Sammy White	5	8	12	20	30	60	150	
AL15	Gene Woodling	6	10	15	25	40	80	200	
AL16	Whitey Ford	15	25	40	60	80	200	500	
AL17	Phil Rizzuto	12	20	30	50	80	150	500	
AL18	Bob Porterfield	5	8	12	20	30	60	150	
AL19	Chico Carrasquel	5	8	12	20	30	60	150	
AL20	Yogi Berra	15	25	40	80	100	200	600	
AL21	Bob Lemon	6	10	15	25	40	80	200	
AL22	Ferris Fain	5	8	12	20	30	60	150	
AL23	Hank Bauer	6	10	15	25	40	80	200	
AL24	Jim Delsing	5	8	12	20	30	60	150	
AL25	Gil McDougald	6	10	15	25	40	80	250	
NL1	Richie Ashburn	10	15	25	40	60	120	400	
NL2	Billy Cox	6	10	15	25	40	80	200	
NL3	Del Crandall	5	8	12	20	30	60	150	
NL4	Carl Erskine	6	10	15	25	40	80	250	
NL5	Monte Irvin	6	10	15	25	40	80	200	
NL6	Ted Kluszewski	8	12	20	30	50	100	250	
NL7	Don Mueller	5	8	12	20	30	60	175	
NL8	Andy Pafko	5	8	12	20	30	60	150	
NL9	Del Rice	5	8	12	20	30	60	150	
NL10	Red Schoendienst	6	10	15	25	40	80	200	
NL11	Warren Spahn	12	20	30	50	80	150		
NL12	Curt Simmons	5	8	12	20	30	60	150	
NL13	Roy Campanella	15	25	40	80	150	250	800	
NL14	Jim Gilliam	6	10	15	25	40	80	250	
NL15	Pee Wee Reese	12	20	30	50	80	150	500	
NL16	Duke Snider	12	20	30	80	100	200	600	
NL17	Rip Repulski	5	8	12	20	30	60	150	
NL18	Robin Roberts	6	10	15	25	40	80	225	
NL19	Enos Slaughter	12	20	30	50	80	150	500	
NL19	Gus Bell	10	15	25	40	60	120	400	
NL20	Johnny Logan	5	8	12	20	30	60	150	
NL21	John Antonelli	5	8	12	20	30	60	150	
NL22	Gil Hodges	10	15	25	40	60	150	400	
NL23	Eddie Mathews	12	20	30	50	100	150	400	
NL24	Lew Burdette	5	8	12	20	30	60	150	
NL25	Willie Mays	30	50	100	120	250	400	1,200	

— Prices reference cards with tabs.

1954 Topps

		GD 2	VG 3	VgEx 4	EX 5	ExMt 6	NM 7	NmMt 8	MT 9
1	Ted Williams	400	600	1,000	1,500	2,500	5,000	▲12,000	
2	Gus Zernial	5	5	8	12	20	50	250	
3	Monte Irvin	12	25	30	50	80	100	400	
4	Hank Sauer	▲8	▲12	▲20	▲30	▲50	▲80	120	
5	Ed Lopat	5	8	12	20	30	50	250	
6	Pete Runnels	5	8	12	20	30	40	200	800
7	Ted Kluszewski	6	10	20	30	40	80	200	1,500
8	Bob Young	5	5	8	20	25	40	100	800
9	Harvey Haddix	5	6	10	15	30	40	100	800
10	Jackie Robinson	400	600	1,000	1,500	2,500	5,000	12,000	
11	Paul Leslie Smith RC	5	5	8	12	20	40	60	400
12	Del Crandall	▲6	▲10	▲15	▲25	▲40	▲60	100	1,200
13	Billy Martin	25	40	50	60	100	200	400	
14	Preacher Roe	5	6	20	25	30	50	200	
15	Al Rosen	5	6	10	25	40	50	150	800
16	Vic Janowicz	5	6	10	15	25	50	100	
17	Phil Rizzuto	25	40	50	80	100	150	400	2,000
18	Walt Dropo	5	6	10	15	30	50	80	600

		GD 2	VG 3	VgEx 4	EX 5	ExMt 6	NM 7	NmMt 8	MT 9
19	Johnny Lipon	5	6	10	15	25	30	100	800
20	Warren Spahn	25	50	60	80	120	250	600	1,500
21	Bobby Shantz	5	6	10	15	25	50	100	
22	Jim Greengrass	5	5	8	12	20	40	120	
23	Luke Easter	6	10	15	25	40	60	150	1,000
24	Granny Hamner	5	5	8	25	30	50	60	
25	Harvey Kuenn RC	5	12	15	25	40	60	150	
26	Ray Jablonski	5	5	8	12	25	40	150	
27	Ferris Fain	5	6	10	15	25	40	60	
28	Paul Minner	5	5	8	12	20	30	60	800
29	Jim Hegan	5	5	8	12	20	30	120	1,000
30	Eddie Mathews	25	40	50	80	120	250	500	2,000
31	Johnny Klippstein	5	5	8	12	25	30	80	800
32	Duke Snider	30	50	60	100	120	250	500	2,500
33	Johnny Schmitz	5	5	8	12	20	40	80	800
34	Jim Rivera	5	5	8	20	25	30	80	
35	Jim Gilliam	6	10	15	25	50	80	200	
36	Hoyt Wilhelm	6	10	25	40	60	80	250	1,500
37	Whitey Ford	30	50	60	80	150	250	▲1,500	▲4,000
38	Eddie Stanky MG	5	6	10	20	25	40	80	
39	Sherm Lollar	5	5	8	12	20	50	100	
40	Mel Parnell	5	5	12	15	20	40	60	600
41	Willie Jones	5	5	8	12	25	30	60	600
42	Don Mueller	5	5	8	12	20	40	80	600
43	Dick Groat	5	6	10	15	25	50	100	
44	Ned Garver	5	5	8	12	25	50	120	
45	Richie Ashburn	10	25	30	50	80	120	250	1,500
46	Ken Raffensberger	5	5	8	12	25	40	120	
47	Ellis Kinder	5	5	8	15	20	30	80	400
48	Billy Hunter	5	8	12	20	30	50	100	800
49	Ray Murray	5	5	8	12	20	25	60	
50	Yogi Berra	60	100	150	250	400	600	▲2,500	4,000
51	Johnny Lindell	5	6	10	20	25	60	150	
52	Vic Power RC	5	8	12	30	40	60	200	
53	Jack Dittmer	5	6	10	15	30	60	200	
54	Vern Stephens	5	8	12	20	40	60	150	
55	Phil Cavarretta MG	6	10	15	25	40	80	150	1,200
56	Willie Miranda	5	6	10	15	25	80	100	
57	Luis Aloma	▲8	▲12	▲20	▲30	▲50	▲80	▲120	600
58	Bob Wilson	5	8	12	20	30	50	100	600
59	Gene Conley	5	8	12	20	30	80	150	
60	Frank Baumholtz	5	6	10	15	30	50	150	
61	Bob Cain	5	6	10	15	30	40	120	1,200
62	Eddie Robinson	8	12	20	30	50	100	250	1,200
63	Johnny Pesky	12	20	30	50	80	120	200	800
64	Hank Thompson	5	6	10	30	40	120	800	
65	Bob Swift CO	5	6	10	15	25	60	120	
66	Ted Lepcio	▲10	▲15	▲20	▲30	▲50	▲80	▲120	
67	Jim Willis RC	5	6	10	20	25	40	100	600
68	Sam Calderone	6	10	15	25	40	60	100	1,200
69	Bud Podbielan	5	6	10	15	25	50	150	1,000
70	Larry Doby	▲50	▲80	▲120	▲200	▲300	▲500	▲1,200	▲3,000
71	Frank Smith	5	▲8	▲12	▲20	▲30	50	▲200	
72	Preston Ward	5	8	12	20	40	60	250	1,200
73	Wayne Terwilliger	5	8	12	20	30	50	120	
74	Bill Taylor RC	5	6	10	15	25	50	120	
75	Fred Haney MG RC	▲8	▲12	20	30	50	▲200	500	
76	Bob Scheffing CO	5	8	12	20	30	50	120	800
77	Ray Boone	5	6	10	15	25	40	80	500
78	Ted Kazanski RC	5	5	8	12	20	50	120	
79	Andy Pafko	5	8	12	20	30	80	200	
80	Jackie Jensen	5	8	15	25	40	60	250	1,200
81	Dave Hoskins RC	5	8	12	20	25	100	150	600
82	Milt Bolling	5	8	12	20	30	50	80	600
83	Joe Collins	8	12	20	30	40	60	120	1,000
84	Dick Cole RC	5	6	10	15	25	60	120	
85	Bob Turley RC	8	12	20	30	50	80	150	1,000
86	Billy Herman CO	8	12	20	30	50	80	250	800

		GD 2	VG 3	VgEx 4	EX 5	ExMt 6	NM 7	NmMt 8	MT 9
87	Roy Face	5	8	12	20	30	50	120	500
88	Matt Batts	5	8	12	20	30	40	120	600
89	Howie Pollet	5	5	8	12	20	40	60	600
90	Willie Mays	▲500	▲800	1,000	1,500	▼2,000	▼3,000	12,000	20,000
91	Bob Oldis	5	5	8	12	25	30	▲120	600
92	Wally Westlake	5	5	8	25	30	40	100	600
93	Sid Hudson	5	5	8	12	20	40	100	800
94	Ernie Banks RC	1,000	▼1,200	2,500	4,000	6,000	12,000	40,000	40,000
95	Hal Rice	5	8	12	20	30	50	120	
96	Charlie Silvera	▲8	▲12	▲20	▲30	▲50	▲80	120	1,000
97	Hal Lane RC	5	5	8	12	20	50	120	500
98	Joe Black	15	25	40	60	100	150	300	
99	Bobby Hofman	5	5	8	12	20	50	80	
100	Bob Keegan	5	5	8	25	30	50	100	
101	Gene Woodling	6	10	15	25	60	150	500	2,500
102	Gil Hodges	25	40	▲80	100	150	▲400	▲1,000	
103	Jim Lemon RC	5	5	8	25	30	50	150	500
104	Mike Sandlock	5	6	10	15	25	50	▲100	600
105	Andy Carey	6	10	15	25	40	100	200	
106	Dick Kokos	5	5	8	12	30	50	150	
107	Duane Pillette	5	8	12	20	30	50	80	800
108	Thornton Kipper RC	▲6	▲10	▲15	▲25	▲40	▲60	100	800
109	Bill Bruton	5	8	12	20	30	60	120	
110	Harry Dorish	5	5	8	12	20	50	100	400
111	Jim Delsing	5	5	8	12	30	60	120	800
112	Bill Renna RC	5	5	8	12	20	40	80	600
113	Bob Boyd	5	5	8	12	20	50	80	600
114	Dean Stone RC	5	5	8	12	25	40	80	
115	Rip Repulski	6	10	15	25	40	60	▲300	
116	Steve Bilko	5	8	12	20	30	80	250	
117	Solly Hemus	5	5	8	12	20	50	100	400
118	Carl Scheib	5	5	8	12	20	30	80	
119	Johnny Antonelli	6	10	15	25	40	60	100	600
120	Roy McMillan	5	5	8	12	20	40	200	
121	Clem Labine	5	6	20	25	30	100	400	
122	Johnny Logan	5	6	10	20	25	40	100	
123	Bobby Adams	6	10	15	25	40	60	▲150	800
124	Marion Fricano	5	6	10	15	25	40	100	800
125	Harry Perkowski	5	6	10	15	25	50	150	
126	Ben Wade	10	15	25	40	60	400		
127	Steve O'Neill MG	5	▲8	▲12	▲20	30	▲50	▲80	400
128	Hank Aaron RC	▼3,000	▼4,000	▼5,000	▼8,000	▼10,000	▼25,000	▼80,000	800,000
129	Forrest Jacobs RC	5	5	8	12	20	40	100	500
130	Hank Bauer	10	15	25	40	60	100	800	
131	Reno Bertoia RC	5	6	10	15	25	40	80	400
132	Tommy Lasorda RC	200	250	300	400	500	▼600	2,500	6,000
133	Del Baker CO	5	▲6	▲10	▲15	25	40	▲100	400
134	Cal Hogue	5	8	12	20	30	80	300	800
135	Joe Presko	5	6	10	15	25	40	150	
136	Connie Ryan	5	8	12	20	30	50	▲100	400
137	Wally Moon RC	10	15	25	40	60	100	150	800
138	Bob Borkowski	5	8	12	20	30	50	80	400
139	J.O'Brien/E.O'Brien	15	25	40	60	100	150	600	1,500
140	Tom Wright	5	5	8	12	20	30	80	300
141	Joey Jay RC	6	10	15	25	40	60	250	1,000
142	Tom Poholsky	5	8	12	20	30	50	80	500
143	Rollie Hemsley CO	5	6	10	15	25	40	60	600
144	Bill Werle	5	6	10	15	25	40	60	400
145	Elmer Valo	▲6	▲10	▲15	▲25	▲40	▲60	120	400
146	Don Johnson	5	6	10	15	▲30	▲50	80	400
147	Johnny Riddle CO	5	8	12	20	30	50	▲100	
148	Bob Trice RC	5	8	12	20	30	50	80	600
149	Al Robertson	5	5	8	12	20	40	200	
150	Dick Kryhoski	5	5	8	12	30	60	100	800
151	Alex Grammas RC	5	5	8	20	25	▲80	▲120	1,000
152	Michael Blyzka RC	5	8	12	20	30	50	150	
153	Rube Walker	5	6	10	15	40	50	120	▲1,500
154	Mike Fornieles RC	5	5	8	20	30	50	80	

#	Name	GD 2	VG 3	VgEx 4	EX 5	ExMt 6	NM 7	NmMt 8	MT 9
155	Bob Kennedy	5	5	8	12	20	50	150	
156	Joe Coleman	5	8	12	20	30	50	250	
157	Don Lenhardt	6	10	15	25	40	80	300	
158	Peanuts Lowrey	5	8	12	20	30	50	100	600
159	Dave Philley	5	5	8	12	30	50	120	
160	Ralph Kress CO	5	5	8	30	40	50	150	
161	John Hetki	5	5	8	12	20	40	100	800
162	Herman Wehmeier	5	5	8	12	30	50	100	
163	Frank House	5	5	8	12	20	80	120	
164	Stu Miller	5	6	10	15	25	50	▲150	
165	Jim Pendleton	5	▲8	▲12	▲20	30	▲80	120	
166	Johnny Podres	10	15	25	40	60	▲150	300	
167	Don Lund	5	5	8	12	20	60	150	
168	Morrie Martin	6	10	15	25	40	60	100	
169	Jim Hughes	5	8	12	20	30	80	300	
170	Dusty Rhodes RC	5	8	12	20	30	80	300	
171	Leo Kiely	5	6	10	15	25	50	100	
172	Hal Brown RC	5	5	8	12	20	50	150	1,200
173	Jack Harshman RC	5	5	8	12	20	60	100	600
174	Tom Qualters RC	5	5	8	12	40	50	200	1,200
175	Frank Leja RC	8	12	20	30	50	80	1,000	
176	Robert Keely CO	5	8	12	20	30	50	120	600
177	Bob Milliken	5	6	10	15	25	40	▲100	500
178	Bill Glynn UER	5	8	12	20	30	50	80	400
179	Gair Allie RC	5	6	10	15	25	40	100	400
180	Wes Westrum	5	5	8	12	20	40	100	600
181	Mel Roach RC	5	5	8	12	25	30	60	400
182	Chuck Harmon RC	5	5	8	20	30	200	600	
183	Earle Combs CO	▲8	▲12	▲20	▲30	▲50	▲80	▲120	
184	Ed Bailey	5	6	10	15	25	40	100	500
185	Chuck Stobbs	5	5	8	12	20	30	80	500
186	Karl Olson	5	5	8	12	30	40	80	400
187	Heinie Manush CO	6	10	15	25	40	60	200	600
188	Dave Jolly RC	6	10	15	25	40	60	120	400
189	Bob Ross	5	8	12	20	30	50	120	500
190	Ray Herbert RC	5	8	12	20	30	50	150	
191	Dick Schofield RC	5	6	10	25	30	60	80	1,000
192	Ellis Deal CO	5	6	10	15	25	40	60	400
193	Johnny Hopp CO	5	8	12	20	30	50	120	600
194	Bill Sarni RC	▲6	▲10	▲15	▲25	▲40	▲60	▲100	600
195	Billy Consolo RC	5	5	8	12	20	50	120	
196	Stan Jok RC	5	8	12	20	30	50	80	800
197	Lynwood Rowe CO	5	8	12	20	30	60	150	600
198	Carl Sawatski	5	▲8	▲12	▲20	▲30	▲50	▲80	▲1,000
199	Glenn (Rocky) Nelson	5	5	8	12	20	30	80	500
200	Larry Jansen	5	5	8	25	30	80	250	1,000
201	Al Kaline RC	500	600	▼800	1,500	2,500	4,000	8,000	40,000
202	Bob Purkey RC	5	8	12	20	25	▲60	▲100	▲800
203	Harry Brecheen CO	5	5	8	12	25	40	120	1,200
204	Angel Scull RC	5	6	10	15	25	60	100	400
205	Johnny Sain	6	10	15	25	50	100	120	800
206	Ray Crone RC	5	5	8	12	25	40	80	
207	Tom Oliver CO RC	5	5	8	12	20	60	100	
208	Grady Hatton	5	8	12	20	30	50	▲120	400
209	Chuck Thompson RC	5	8	12	20	30	50	100	400
210	Bob Buhl RC	5	8	12	20	30	50	100	600
211	Don Hoak	8	12	20	30	50	80	250	400
212	Bob Micelotta RC	5	5	8	12	20	40	60	400
213	Johnny Fitzpatrick CO RC	5	5	8	12	30	50	▲250	
214	Arnie Portocarrero RC	5	8	12	20	30	50	100	600
215	Ed McGhee	5	8	12	20	30	50	80	400
216	Al Sima	5	5	8	12	30	40	80	800
217	Paul Schreiber CO RC	5	6	10	15	25	40	120	500
218	Fred Marsh	5	8	12	20	30	50	100	400
219	Chuck Kress RC	5	6	10	15	25	40	120	800
220	Ruben Gomez RC	5	8	12	20	30	50	120	300
221	Dick Brodowski	6	10	15	25	40	60	100	400
222	Bill Wilson RC	5	8	12	20	30	50	100	800

#	Name	GD 2	VG 3	VgEx 4	EX 5	ExMt 6	NM 7	NmMt 8	MT 9
223	Joe Haynes CO	5	6	10	15	25	40	120	800
224	Dick Weik RC	5	5	8	12	20	40	100	
225	Don Liddle RC	5	6	10	15	25	40	100	400
226	Jehosie Heard RC	5	8	12	20	30	40	100	500
227	Buster Mills CO RC	5	8	12	20	50	250		
228	Gene Hermanski	5	8	12	20	30	50	80	400
229	Bob Talbot RC	5	5	8	12	20	60		400
230	Bob Kuzava	6	10	15	25	40	60	100	500
231	Roy Smalley	5	5	8	12	20	60	120	
232	Lou Limmer RC	▲6	▲10	▲15	▲25	▲40	▲60	▲100	400
233	Augie Galan CO	5	6	10	15	25	40	60	
234	Jerry Lynch RC	5	6	10	15	25	40	150	
235	Vern Law	▲8	▲12	▲20	▲30	▲50	▲80	150	600
236	Paul Penson RC	8	12	20	30	50	80	150	
237	Mike Ryba CO RC	5	5	8	12	30	50	80	500
238	Al Aber	5	5	8	12	20	40	100	800
239	Bill Skowron RC	15	25	40	60	▲100	▲150	▲500	▲2,500
240	Sam Mele	5	8	12	20	30	50	100	
241	Robert Miller RC	5	5	8	12	30	50	100	
242	Curt Roberts RC	5	5	8	12	20	40	150	600
243	Ray Blades CO RC	5	5	8	12	25	60	100	
244	Leroy Wheat RC	5	6	10	15	25	40	100	600
245	Roy Sievers	5	5	8	12	30	200	600	
246	Howie Fox	5	5	8	12	25	40	120	800
247	Ed Mayo CO	5	5	8	12	25	80	80	800
248	Al Smith RC	▲8	▲12	▲20	▲30	▲50	▲80	300	1,200
249	Wilmer Mizell	5	5	8	12	30	60	150	
250	Ted Williams	400	600	1,000	1,500	2,500	4,000	15,000	25,000

— Hank Aaron #128 PSA 10 (Gem) (Young Collection) sold for $357,594 (SCP; 5/12)
— Hank Aaron #128 PSA 10 (Gem) sold for $110,000 (Memory Lane; Private Sale - 2006)
— Hank Aaron #128 SGC 92 (NmMt+) sold for $21,856 (Goodwin; 12/14)
— Hank Aaron #128 SGC 92 (NmMt+) sold for $17,775 (Huggins and Scott; 8/14)
— Hank Aaron #128 PSA 8.5 (NmMt+) sold for $9,718 (Goodwin; 1/13)
— Ernie Banks #94 PSA 10 (Gem) (Young Collection) sold for $142,836 (SCP; 5/12)
— Bob Borkowski #138 PSA 10 (Gem) sold for $68,112 (Mile High; 10/11)
— Al Kaline #201 PSA 10 (Gem) (Young Collection) sold for $88,688 (SCP; 5/12)
— Bill Skowron #239 PSA 10 (Gem) (Young Collection) sold for $9,799 (SCP; 5/12)
— Ted Williams #1 SGC 96 (Mint) sold for $12,000 (Greg Bussineau; 4/12)
— Ted Williams #1 PSA 8.5 (NmMt+) sold for $5,314 (Memory Lane; 8/12)

1954 Wilson Franks

#	Name	PrFr 1	GD 2	VG 3	VgEx 4	EX 5	ExMt 6	NM 7	NmMt 8
1	Roy Campanella	300	▲500	▲800	▲1,200	▲2,000	▲3,000	▲5,000	
2	Del Ennis	100	150	200	400	300	500		
3	Carl Erskine	80	120	150	200	400	450	800	
4	Ferris Fain	80	120	150	200	300	400		
5	Bob Feller	150	250	300	450	600	800	1,500	
6	Nellie Fox	150	250	300	500	600	1,000		
7	Johnny Groth	80	120	150	200	400			
8	Stan Hack MG	80	120	175	300				
9	Gil Hodges	150	250	300	500	600	1,200		
10	Ray Jablonski	200	300	475	550	650			
11	Harvey Kuenn	80	120	150	250				
12	Roy McMillan	60	100	120	200	250	300	500	
13	Andy Pafko	60	100	120	150	200	400	500	
14	Paul Richards MG	60	100	150	250				
15	Hank Sauer	60	100	120	150	200	600	650	
16	Red Schoendienst	100	150	250	300	500			
17	Enos Slaughter	100	150	200	250	500			
18	Vern Stephens	60	100	120	150	200			
19	Sammy White	60	100	120	150	200	500	500	
20	Ted Williams	▲2,500	▲4,000	▲6,000	▲8,000	▲12,000	▲20,000		

— Roy Campanella #1 PSA 8 (NmMt) sold for $6,268 (Memory Lane; 8/12)
— Ted Williams #20 SGC 84 (NrMt) sold for $11,228 (Goodwin; 8/12)
— Ted Williams #20 PSA 7 (NrMt) sold for $17,261 (Memory Lane; 8/12)

1955 Bowman

#		GD 2	VG 3	VgEx 4	EX 5	ExMt 6	NM 7	NmMt 8	MT 9
1	Hoyt Wilhelm	8	12	20	50	80	120	500	
2	Alvin Dark	5	5	6	8	15	25	60	
3	Joe Coleman	5	5	6	8	12	20	80	
4	Eddie Waitkus	5	5	5	6	10	15	50	
5	Jim Robertson	5	5	5	6	10	15	50	
6	Pete Suder	5	5	5	6	10	30	100	
7	Gene Baker RC	5	5	5	6	10	25	100	
8	Warren Hacker	5	5	5	6	10	30	80	
9	Gil McDougald	8	12	20	30	50	80	120	500
10	Phil Rizzuto	20	40	50	80	100	120	250	1,200
11	Bill Bruton	5	5	6	8	12	25	50	
12	Andy Pafko	5	5	6	8	12	20	50	300
13	Clyde Vollmer	5	5	5	6	20	25	50	250
14	Gus Keriazakos RC	5	5	5	6	10	15	40	
15	Frank Sullivan RC	5	5	5	6	20	25	50	300
16	Jimmy Piersall	5	5	6	15	30	50	120	300
17	Del Ennis	5	5	6	8	20	25	80	
18	Stan Lopata	5	5	5	6	10	15	50	350
19	Bobby Avila	5	5	6	8	12	20	150	
20	Al Smith	5	5	5	6	10	30	50	250
21	Don Hoak	5	5	8	12	20	25	80	250
22	Roy Campanella	40	▲60	▲80	▲100	120	200	500	
23	Al Kaline	30	50	80	▲120	150	250	400	2,500
24	Al Aber	5	5	5	6	10	15	40	
25	Minnie Minoso	8	12	20	30	40	120	150	
26	Virgil Trucks	5	5	5	6	10	20	60	
27	Preston Ward	5	5	5	6	10	20	80	350
28	Dick Cole	5	5	5	6	10	25	50	
29	Red Schoendienst	5	8	12	30	40	80	100	400
30	Bill Sarni	5	5	5	6	10	20	60	
31	Johnny Temple RC	5	5	6	8	25	30	50	
32	Wally Post	5	5	6	8	12	30	50	250
33	Nellie Fox	6	10	15	30	50	80	200	
34	Clint Courtney	5	5	5	6	10	25	60	350
35	Bill Tuttle RC	5	5	5	6	10	25	40	
36	Wayne Belardi RC	5	5	5	6	10	20	60	
37	Pee Wee Reese	20	30	50	60	100	120	250	
38	Early Wynn	8	12	20	30	50	▲80	120	600
39	Bob Darnell RC	5	5	6	8	25	40	200	400
40	Vic Wertz	5	5	6	8	20	40	100	
41	Mel Clark	5	5	5	6	10	25	50	
42	Bob Greenwood RC	5	6	10	15	25	30	50	300
43	Bob Buhl	5	5	5	6	12	30	60	250
44	Danny O'Connell	5	5	5	6	10	25	50	200
45	Tom Umphlett	5	5	8	12	20	25	60	300
46	Mickey Vernon	5	5	6	10	15	25	200	
47	Sammy White	5	5	5	6	15	20	50	300
48A	Milt Bolling ERR Frank on Back	5	5	6	8	12	40	100	
48B	Milt Bolling COR Milt on Back	5	5	6	8	12	25		
49	Jim Greengrass	5	5	5	6	12	25	50	
50	Hobie Landrith	5	5	5	6	10	15	50	250
51	Elvin Tappe RC	5	5	5	6	15	25	40	250
52	Hal Rice	5	5	5	6	10	25	40	250
53	Alex Kellner	5	5	5	6	12	20	50	300
54	Don Bollweg	5	5	6	10	15	30	60	300
55	Cal Abrams	5	5	5	6	10	30	50	200
56	Billy Cox	5	5	5	6	20	25	50	
57	Bob Friend	5	5	6	8	12	30	80	
58	Frank Thomas	5	5	6	8	15	25	50	
59	Whitey Ford	25	40	60	80	120	250	400	2,000
60	Enos Slaughter	8	12	20	25	40	▲100	120	500
61	Paul LaPalme	5	5	5	6	10	30	50	
62	Royce Lint RC	5	5	5	6	10	25	60	
63	Irv Noren	5	5	6	8	12	20	60	300
64	Curt Simmons	5	5	6	8	20	25	60	
65	Don Zimmer RC	6	10	25	30	50	100	200	500
66	George Shuba	5	5	6	8	12	25		
67	Don Larsen	6	10	15	25	60	80	200	
68	Elston Howard RC	▲25	▲40	▲60	▲100	▲150	250	500	800
69	Billy Hunter	5	5	6	8	12	40	150	
70	Lew Burdette	5	5	6	10	20	40	100	
71	Dave Jolly	5	5	5	6	10	40	50	300
72	Chet Nichols	5	5	5	6	10	20	120	
73	Eddie Yost	5	5	6	8	12	25	80	400
74	Jerry Snyder	5	5	5	6	10	30	50	
75	Brooks Lawrence RC	5	5	6	8	25	50	150	300
76	Tom Poholsky	5	5	5	6	10	30	150	
77	Jim McDonald RC	5	5	5	6	10	15	80	
78	Gil Coan	5	5	8	12	20	25	80	300
79	Willie Miranda	5	5	5	6	10	50	80	
80	Lou Limmer	5	5	5	6	10	20	250	
81	Bobby Morgan	5	5	5	6	10	20	80	
82	Lee Walls RC	5	5	5	6	20	50	80	300
83	Max Surkont	5	5	5	6	10	20	100	400
84	George Freese RC	5	5	5	6	10	30	80	
85	Cass Michaels	5	5	8	12	20	30	60	
86	Ted Gray	5	5	5	6	10	25	80	
87	Randy Jackson	5	5	5	6	10	15	100	300
88	Steve Bilko	5	5	5	6	12	25	300	
89	Lou Boudreau MG	5	12	20	25	40	60	120	
90	Art Ditmar RC	5	5	5	6	15	20	60	
91	Dick Marlowe RC	5	5	5	6	12	25	120	
92	George Zuverink	5	5	5	6	10	40	50	
93	Andy Seminick	5	5	5	6	10	25	80	
94	Hank Thompson	5	5	6	8	12	30	80	
95	Sal Maglie	5	5	8	10	30	40	100	
96	Ray Narleski RC	5	5	5	6	25	30	150	
97	Johnny Podres	8	12	20	30	50	▲100	▲150	
98	Jim Gilliam	5	6	10	12	30	60	200	
99	Jerry Coleman	5	5	6	8	30	50	100	
100	Tom Morgan	5	5	6	8	20	30	200	
101A	Don Johnson ERR Ernie on Front	5	5	6	8	12	40	150	
101B	Don Johnson COR Don on Front	5	5	6	8	12	25	60	
102	Bobby Thomson	5	5	8	10	25	50	80	
103	Eddie Mathews	25	40	60	80	120	250	500	
104	Bob Porterfield	5	5	5	6	15	20	60	
105	Johnny Schmitz	5	5	5	6	10	30	60	
106	Del Rice	5	5	5	6	20	25	120	400
107	Solly Hemus	5	5	5	6	10	15	80	
108	Lou Kretlow	5	5	5	6	10	15	80	
109	Vern Stephens	5	5	6	8	10	25	100	250
110	Bob Miller	5	5	5	6	10	15	60	
111	Steve Ridzik	5	5	5	6	10	30	60	
112	Granny Hamner	5	5	6	8	12	25	100	
113	Bob Hall RC	5	5	5	6	10	15	60	
114	Vic Janowicz	5	5	6	8	15	20	120	
115	Roger Bowman RC	5	5	6	8	20	25	50	
116	Sandy Consuegra	5	5	5	6	10	15	60	
117	Johnny Groth	5	5	5	6	10	15	50	
118	Bobby Adams	5	5	5	6	10	15	100	
119	Joe Astroth	5	5	5	6	15	25	80	
120	Ed Burtschy RC	5	5	5	6	10	15	50	
121	Rufus Crawford RC	5	5	5	6	15	30	60	
122	Al Corwin	5	5	5	6	10	20	100	
123	Marv Grissom RC	5	5	5	6	15	25	40	
124	Johnny Antonelli	5	8	12	20	30	40	60	
125	Paul Giel RC	5	5	5	6	20	25	60	
126	Billy Goodman	5	5	5	6	15	20	60	
127	Hank Majeski	5	5	5	6	20	30	100	

#	Player	GD 2	VG 3	VgEx 4	EX 5	ExMt 6	NM 7	NmMt 8	MT 9
3	Mike Garcia	5	5	6	8	12	30	80	
9	Hal Naragon RC	5	5	5	6	10	20	60	
0	Richie Ashburn	10	15	25	30	60	100	400	
1	Willard Marshall	5	5	6	10	15	20	60	
2A	Harvey Kueen ERR	5	5	8	10	15	25	100	
2B	Harvey Kuenn COR	5	8	12	15	25	40		
3	Charles King RC	5	5	5	12	15	25	60	300
4	Bob Feller	30	50	80	▲120	▲200	▲300	▲600	
	Lloyd Merriman	5	5	5	6	10	15	50	
	Rocky Bridges	5	5	5	6	10	20	80	
	Bob Talbot	5	5	5	6	10	15	100	350
	Davey Williams	5	5	6	8	20	25	80	
	B.Shantz/B.Shantz	5	5	6	8	20	40	200	
	Bobby Shantz	5	5	6	8	12	30	120	
	Wes Westrum	5	5	6	10	10	25	60	
	Rudy Regalado RC	5	5	5	6	10	15	100	
	Don Newcombe	▲10	▲15	▲25	▲40	▲60	▲100	▲300	
	Art Houteman	5	5	5	6	10	25	80	
	Bob Nieman RC	5	5	5	6	10	30		
	Don Liddle	5	5	6	10	15	30	150	
	Sam Mele	5	5	5	6	10	20	100	
	Bob Chakales	5	5	5	6	20	25	60	300
	Cloyd Boyer	5	5	5	6	20	30	50	300
	Billy Klaus RC	5	5	5	6	10	15	50	
	Jim Brideweser	5	5	6	10	15	25	60	
	Johnny Klippstein	5	5	5	6	10	20	100	
	Eddie Robinson	5	5	6	8	20	50		
	Frank Lary RC	5	5	8	12	20	40		
	Gerry Staley	5	5	5	6	10	20	150	
	Jim Hughes	5	5	6	10	25	30	100	
	Ernie Johnson ERR Don on Front	5	5	6	8	12	40	225	
	Ernie Johnson COR Ernie on Front	5	5	6	8	12	25		
	Gil Hodges	15	25	40	50	▲80	▲120	400	
	Harry Byrd	5	5	5	6	10	25	80	
	Bill Skowron	8	12	20	30	50	100	200	
	Matt Batts	5	5	5	6	10	15	60	300
	Charlie Maxwell	5	5	5	6	10	15	150	350
	Sid Gordon	5	5	5	6	10	30	50	400
	Toby Atwell	5	5	5	6	20	25	60	
	Maurice McDermott	5	5	8	12	20	30	50	
	Jim Busby	5	6	10	15	25	30	50	
	Bob Grim RC	5	▲6	▲10	▲15	▲25	▲40	80	
	Yogi Berra	80	100	120	150	250	500	1,000	
	Carl Furillo	5	8	12	15	40	60	150	800
	Carl Erskine	5	6	15	20	40	50	200	
	Robin Roberts	12	20	30	50	60	80	▲250	
	Willie Jones	5	5	6	10	15	25	60	300
	Chico Carrasquel	5	5	5	6	10	25	80	250
	Sherm Lollar	5	5	6	8	20	30	60	400
	Wilmer Shantz RC	5	5	5	6	20	25	60	
	Joe DeMaestri	5	5	6	10	15	30	100	
	Willard Nixon	5	5	5	6	20	25	60	350
	Tom Brewer RC	5	5	5	6	25	30	60	
	Hank Aaron	▲200	▲300	▲500	▲600	1,000	▲2,000	▲6,000	
	Johnny Logan	5	5	6	8	20	50	80	
	Eddie Miksis	5	5	5	6	15	30	50	
	Bob Rush	5	5	5	6	10	30	50	
	Ray Katt	5	5	5	6	15	20	50	300
	Willie Mays	120	200	400	500	600	▲2,500	▲6,000	
	Vic Raschi	5	5	5	6	10	15	50	
	Alex Grammas	5	5	5	6	10	15	100	
	Fred Hatfield	5	5	5	6	10	25	60	
	Ned Garver	5	5	5	6	10	30	80	
	Jack Collum	5	5	5	6	10	15	50	
	Fred Baczewski	5	5	5	6	10	30	50	
	Bob Lemon	8	12	20	30	50	80	150	500

#	Player	GD 2	VG 3	VgEx 4	EX 5	ExMt 6	NM 7	NmMt 8	MT 9
192	George Strickland	5	5	6	8	20	30	150	
193	Howie Judson	5	5	5	6	10	25	60	300
194	Joe Nuxhall	5	5	6	8	20	30	50	
195A	Erv Palica No Trade	5	5	6	8	12	20	80	
195B	Erv Palica Trade	6	10	15	20	30	50	150	
196	Russ Meyer	5	5	6	8	12	50	100	
197	Ralph Kiner	10	15	25	40	60	100	150	600
198	Dave Pope RC	5	5	5	6	10	15	80	
199	Vern Law	5	5	8	12	20	30	60	
200	Dick Littlefield	5	5	6	8	12	30	60	
201	Allie Reynolds	6	10	15	25	40	50	100	400
202	Mickey Mantle	▲800	▲1,000	▲1,500	▲2,500	▲3,000	5,000	▲15,000	▲350,000
203	Steve Gromek	5	5	5	6	10	15	50	
204A	Frank Bolling ERR								
	Milt on Back RC	5	5	6	8	12	40		
204B	Frank Bolling COR								
	Frank on Back	5	5	6	8	12	25		
205	Rip Repulski	5	5	6	6	10	20	100	
206	Ralph Beard RC	5	5	6	20	40	60		
207	Frank Shea	5	5	8	12	20	30	80	
208	Ed Fitzgerald	5	5	5	6	10	40	80	300
209	Smoky Burgess	5	5	6	10	15	25	200	
210	Earl Torgeson	5	5	5	6	25	30	200	
211	Sonny Dixon RC	5	5	5	6	10	50	60	
212	Jack Dittmer	5	5	5	6	10	15	50	
213	George Kell	5	6	10	20	30	80	150	
214	Billy Pierce	5	5	6	8	20	30	60	300
215	Bob Kuzava	5	5	5	6	10	15	60	
216	Preacher Roe	5	5	8	10	25	40	120	
217	Del Crandall	5	5	6	8	20	30	100	
218	Joe Adcock	5	5	6	8	20	50	100	
219	Whitey Lockman	5	5	8	12	20	30	60	
220	Jim Hearn	5	5	5	6	10	30	50	
221	Hector Brown	5	5	5	6	10	15	50	
222	Russ Kemmerer RC	5	5	5	6	10	40	60	
223	Hal Jeffcoat	5	5	5	6	10	25	100	350
224	Dee Fondy	5	5	5	6	20	30	100	
225	Paul Richards MG	5	6	10	12	25	60	300	
226	Bill McKinley UMP	5	6	10	12	20	80	250	
227	Frank Baumholtz	5	5	8	10	30	50	100	
228	John Phillips RC	5	5	8	10	15	40	100	
229	Jim Brosnan RC	5	5	6	10	15	40	150	500
230	Al Brazle	5	5	5	6	10	25	100	
231	Jim Konstanty	▲8	▲12	▲20	▲30	▲50	▲80	200	500
232	Birdie Tebbetts MG	6	10	15	20	30	60	300	
233	Bill Serena	5	5	8	10	15	50	300	
234	Dick Bartell CO	5	5	8	10	25	40	120	
235	Joe Paparella UMP	5	6	10	12	30	40	120	
236	Murry Dickson	5	5	8	10	30	40	250	
237	Johnny Wyrostek	5	5	8	10	15	40	80	
238	Eddie Stanky MG	5	6	10	12	20	30	250	500
239	Edwin Rommel UMP	5	6	10	12	30	60	120	
240	Billy Loes	5	8	12	15	50	100		
241	Johnny Pesky	5	6	10	12	20	40		
242	Ernie Banks	▲120	▲200	▲300	▲400	500	1,500	3,000	
243	Gus Bell	5	5	8	10	15	60	100	500
244	Duane Pillette	5	5	8	10	15	60	200	
245	Bill Miller	5	5	8	10	15	40	100	400
246	Hank Bauer	8	12	20	40	60	80	200	500
247	Dutch Leonard CO	8	12	20	30	50	60	120	400
248	Harry Dorish	5	5	8	10	15	40	150	
249	Billy Gardner RC	5	5	8	10	15	40	400	
250	Larry Napp UMP	5	6	10	12	40	60	250	
251	Stan Jok	5	5	8	10	20	25	80	
252	Roy Smalley	5	5	8	10	15	25	100	400
253	Jim Wilson	5	5	8	10	15	40	250	

		GD 2	VG 3	VgEx 4	EX 5	ExMt 6	NM 7	NmMt 8	MT 9
254	Bennett Flowers RC	5	5	8	10	25	40	120	400
255	Pete Runnels	5	5	8	10	15	50	100	
256	Owen Friend	5	5	8	10	25	50	100	
257	Tom Alston RC	5	5	8	10	15	50	80	400
258	John Stevens UMP	5	6	10	12	25	30	100	
259	Don Mossi RC	5	8	12	15	25	50	120	500
260	Edwin Hurley UMP	5	6	10	12	20	40	150	
261	Walt Moryn RC	5	6	10	12	25	80	250	
262	Jim Lemon	5	5	8	20	25	30	100	
263	Eddie Joost	5	5	8	20	25	40	80	
264	Bill Henry RC	5	5	6	10	15	50	200	
265	Al Barlick UMP	15	25	40	60	80	100	250	
266	Mike Fornieles	5	5	8	10	15	25	200	
267	Jim Honochick UMP	6	10	15	25	40	60	120	500
268	Roy Lee Hawes RC	5	5	8	10	25	40	120	
269	Joe Amalfitano RC	5	8	12	15	50	60	120	
270	Chico Fernandez RC	5	6	10	12	50	60	250	
271	Bob Hooper	5	5	8	10	15	25	100	500
272	John Flaherty UMP	5	6	10	12	20	80	150	
273	Bubba Church	5	5	8	10	15	25	100	
274	Jim Delsing	5	5	8	25	30	50	150	
275	William Grieve UMP	5	6	10	12	20	40	120	
276	Ike Delock	5	5	8	10	15	50	120	
277	Ed Runge UMP	5	6	10	25	30	50	150	
278	Charlie Neal RC	8	12	20	40	50	100	600	
279	Hank Soar UMP	6	10	15	20	25	60	150	
280	Clyde McCullough	5	5	8	10	20	50	400	
281	Charles Berry UMP	5	6	10	12	25	30	120	
282	Phil Cavarretta MG	5	8	12	15	25	80	250	
283	Nestor Chylak UMP	8	12	20	40	80	80	500	
284	Bill Jackowski UMP	5	6	10	12	20	50	200	
285	Walt Dropo	5	5	8	15	20	80	100	
286	Frank Secory UMP	▲6	▲10	▲15	▲25	▲40	60	150	400
287	Ron Mrozinski RC	5	5	8	10	25	80	250	
288	Dick Smith RC	5	5	8	10	15	60	200	
289	Arthur Gore UMP	5	6	10	12	20	120	150	400
290	Hershell Freeman RC	5	5	8	10	15	25	100	
291	Frank Dascoli UMP	5	6	10	12	20	80	120	
292	Marv Blaylock RC	5	5	8	10	25	60	300	500
293	Thomas Gorman UMP	5	6	10	12	30	50	100	
294	Wally Moses CO	5	5	8	10	15	25	80	500
295	Lee Ballanfant UMP	5	8	12	20	30	60	150	
296	Bill Virdon RC	6	10	15	30	40	120	200	
297	Dusty Boggess UMP	5	6	10	12	20	80	250	
298	Charlie Grimm	5	5	8	10	30	40		
299	Lon Warneke UMP	5	8	12	20	30	80	200	
300	Tommy Byrne	5	8	12	20	40	120		
301	William Engeln UMP	5	6	10	12	30	30	150	
302	Frank Malzone RC	5	8	12	15	50	80	300	
303	Jocko Conlan UMP	▲12	▲20	▲30	▲50	80	▲250	▲400	1,000
304	Harry Chiti	5	5	8	10	15	30	150	
305	Frank Umont UMP	5	6	10	12	25	30	250	
306	Bob Cerv	5	8	15	20	60	100	400	
307	Babe Pinelli UMP	5	6	10	12	30	100	120	
308	Al Lopez MG	6	10	25	30	40	150	300	
309	Hal Dixon UMP	5	6	10	12	20	50	100	
310	Ken Lehman RC	5	5	8	10	15	80		
311	Lawrence Goetz UMP	5	6	10	12	25	30	100	
312	Bill Wight	5	5	8	10	20	40	120	
313	Augie Donatelli UMP	5	8	12	15	25	50	120	
314	Dale Mitchell	5	6	10	25	30	150		
315	Cal Hubbard UMP	6	10	15	40	60	100	250	
316	Marion Fricano	5	5	8	10	15	25	100	
317	William Summers UMP	5	6	10	12	30	60		
318	Sid Hudson	5	5	8	10	15	50	120	
319	Al Schroll RC	5	5	8	10	20	40		
320	George Susce RC	8	12	25	30	50	120		

1955 Red Man

		GD 2	VG 3	VgEx 4	EX 5	ExMt 6	NM 7	NmMt 8	MT
AL1	Ray Boone	5	8	12	20	35	100	200	
AL2	Jim Busby	5	8	12	20	35	60	200	
AL3	Whitey Ford	12	20	30	50	80	120	500	
AL4	Nellie Fox	8	12	20	30	50	80	250	
AL5	Bob Grim	5	8	12	20	35	80	200	5
AL6	Jack Harshman	5	8	12	20	35	80	200	5
AL7	Jim Hegan	5	8	12	20	35	60	200	
AL8	Bob Lemon	8	12	20	30	50	80	250	
AL9	Irv Noren	5	8	12	20	35	60	200	
AL10	Bob Porterfield	5	8	12	20	35	60	200	
AL11	Al Rosen	5	8	12	20	35	60	200	
AL12	Mickey Vernon	5	8	12	20	35	60	200	
AL13	Vic Wertz	5	8	12	20	35	60	200	
AL14	Early Wynn	8	12	20	30	50	80	250	
AL15	Bobby Avila	5	8	12	20	35	60	200	
AL16	Yogi Berra	20	30	40	60	120	150	600	
AL17	Joe Coleman	5	8	12	20	35	60	200	5
AL18	Larry Doby	8	12	20	30	50	80	200	
AL19	Jackie Jensen	5	8	12	20	35	60	200	
AL20	Pete Runnels	5	8	12	20	35	60		
AL21	Jimmy Piersall	5	8	12	20	35	60	200	
AL22	Hank Bauer	5	8	12	20	35	60	200	8
AL23	Chico Carrasquel	5	8	12	20	35	60	200	
AL24	Minnie Minoso	5	8	12	20	35	60	200	
AL25	Sandy Consuegra	5	8	12	20	35	60	200	5
NL1	Richie Ashburn	10	15	25	40	60	100	400	
NL2	Del Crandall	5	8	12	20	35	60	200	5
NL3	Gil Hodges	10	15	25	40	80	100	400	
NL4	Brooks Lawrence	5	8	12	20	35	60	200	5
NL5	Johnny Logan	5	8	12	20	35	60	200	5
NL6	Sal Maglie	5	8	12	20	35	60	200	
NL7	Willie Mays	40	60	80	120	300	400	1,200	
NL8	Don Mueller	5	8	12	20	35	60	200	
NL9	Bill Sarni	5	8	12	20	35	60	200	
NL10	Warren Spahn	12	20	30	50	80	120	500	
NL11	Hank Thompson	5	8	12	20	35	60	200	
NL12	Hoyt Wilhelm	8	12	20	30	50	80	250	
NL13	John Antonelli	5	8	12	20	35	60	200	
NL14	Carl Erskine	5	8	12	20	35	60	200	
NL15	Granny Hamner	5	8	12	20	35	60	200	
NL16	Ted Kluszewski	8	12	20	30	50	80	250	
NL17	Pee Wee Reese	12	20	30	50	80	120	500	
NL18	Red Schoendienst	8	12	20	30	50	80	250	
NL19	Duke Snider	20	30	40	60	100	150	600	
NL20	Frank Thomas	5	8	12	20	35	60	200	
NL21	Ray Jablonski	5	8	12	20	35	60	200	
NL22	Dusty Rhodes	5	8	12	20	35	80	300	
NL23	Gus Bell	5	8	12	20	35	60	200	
NL24	Curt Simmons	5	8	12	20	35	60		
NL25	Marv Grissom	5	8	12	20	35	80	250	

— Prices reference cards with tabs.

1955 Topps

		GD 2	VG 3	VgEx 4	EX 5	ExMt 6	NM 7	NmMt 8	M
1	Dusty Rhodes	5	15	20	30	60	150	300	4
2	Ted Williams	250	300	500	▲800	▲1,200	▲2,500	▲8,000	▲15
3	Art Fowler RC	8	12	20	30	50	100	800	
4	Al Kaline	▲120	▲150	▲200	250	400	▲1,000	▲2,000	
5	Jim Gilliam	15	25	40	60	100	250	500	
6	Stan Hack MG RC	5	5	8	12	25	50	120	
7	Jim Hegan	5	5	6	15	60	200	1,000	
8	Hal Smith RC	5	5	6	10	40	80	600	
9	Bob Miller	5	5	6	10	15	30	100	1
10	Bob Keegan	5	5	6	10	25	120	800	

	GD 2	VG 3	VgEx 4	EX 5	ExMt 6	NM 7	NmMt 8	MT 9
Ferris Fain	5	5	8	12	25	80	400	
Jake Thies RC	5	5	6	10	15	30	100	600
Fred Marsh	5	5	6	10	20	50	100	500
Jim Finigan RC	5	5	6	10	30	50	200	
Jim Pendleton	5	5	6	10	15	50	80	400
Roy Sievers	5	5	6	10	30	100	250	
Bobby Hofman	5	5	6	10	15	40	80	600
Russ Kemmerer RC	5	5	6	10	30	80	200	
Billy Herman CO	10	15	25	40	50	100	500	
Andy Carey	5	6	10	15	30	150	1,200	
Alex Grammas	5	5	6	15	20	50	100	
Bill Skowron	8	12	20	30	50	80	▲250	1,500
Jack Parks RC	6	10	15	25	40	60	600	
Hal Newhouser	15	25	40	60	100	150	1,200	
Johnny Podres	15	25	40	▲60	▲100	150	▲2,000	
Dick Groat	12	20	30	50	80	▲300	1,200	
Billy Gardner RC	5	8	12	20	30	50	60	
Ernie Banks	▲120	▲150	250	▲400	▲600	1,000	▼3,000	12,000
Herman Wehmeier	5	5	6	10	30	60	120	
Vic Power	5	5	8	15	25	100	250	
Warren Spahn	▲60	▲80	▲100	▲150	▲250	500	1,000	
Ed McGhee RC	5	5	6	10	25	50	250	
Tom Qualters	6	10	15	25	40	80	400	
Wayne Terwilliger	5	5	6	10	25	50	300	
Dave Jolly	5	8	12	20	30	50	80	400
Leo Kiely	6	10	15	25	40	60	250	
Joe Cunningham RC	5	5	8	12	25	50	100	1,000
Bob Turley	5	5	8	25	30	50	150	1,200
Bill Glynn	5	5	6	10	25	80	250	
Don Hoak	5	6	20	30	40	60	300	
Chuck Stobbs	5	6	10	15	25	40	100	600
Windy McCall RC	5	8	12	20	30	50	100	600
Harvey Haddix	6	10	15	25	40	50	80	500
Harold Valentine RC	5	5	6	10	25	40	80	
Hank Sauer	5	5	8	12	25	50	100	600
Ted Kazanski	5	5	6	20	25	40	100	600
Hank Aaron	▲500	600	▼800	▼1,200	2,000	3,000	6,000	15,000
Bob Kennedy	5	5	6	10	25	30	100	500
J.W. Porter	10	12	15	20	25	60	400	
Jackie Robinson	▲500	▲600	▲800	▲1,200	▲2,500	▲4,000	▲10,000	▲20,000
Jim Hughes	5	5	8	12	40	80	120	
Bill Tremel RC	5	5	6	10	15	40	80	500
Bill Taylor	5	5	6	10	15	30	100	600
Lou Limmer	5	5	6	15	25	60	120	800
Rip Repulski	5	5	6	10	25	50	100	
Ray Jablonski	5	5	6	15	25	50	120	800
Billy O'Dell RC	5	5	6	10	15	60	400	
Jim Rivera	6	10	15	25	40	100	400	
Gair Allie	6	10	15	25	30	40	150	
Dean Stone	5	5	8	12	20	30	60	600
Spook Jacobs	5	5	8	12	20	60	100	
Thornton Kipper	5	5	6	10	30	80	100	
Joe Collins	6	10	15	25	50	150		
Gus Triandos RC	6	10	15	25	30	▲100	300	
Ray Boone	5	5	6	10	30	50	120	
Ron Jackson RC	5	5	6	10	50	80	250	
Wally Moon	5	5	6	20	30	50	150	
Jim Davis RC	5	5	6	10	25	50	120	600
Ed Bailey	5	5	6	10	60	80		
Al Rosen	5	8	12	20	30	80	500	
Ruben Gomez	5	5	6	25	30	40	100	400
Karl Olson	8	12	20	30	50	120	250	
Jack Shepard RC	5	5	6	10	15	40	80	600
Bob Borkowski	5	5	6	10	25	50	100	500
Sandy Amoros RC	15	25	40	50	60	150	400	
Howie Pollet	5	5	6	10	15	40	80	400
Arnie Portocarrero	5	5	6	10	25	40	400	
Gordon Jones RC	5	5	6	10	30	50	300	

		GD 2	VG 3	VgEx 4	EX 5	ExMt 6	NM 7	NmMt 8	MT 9
79	Danny Schell RC	5	5	6	15	20	40	100	600
80	Bob Grim RC	8	12	20	30	50	120	400	1,500
81	Gene Conley	6	10	15	25	50	80	300	
82	Chuck Harmon	5	5	6	10	25	80	200	600
83	Tom Brewer RC	5		6	15	20	60	150	
84	Camilo Pascual RC	6	10	15	25	40	▲100	▲500	
85	Don Mossi RC	5	5	6	10	30	60	100	1,200
86	Bill Wilson	5	5	10	12	25	30	80	
87	Frank House	5	6	10	15	20	40	80	800
88	Bob Skinner RC	6	10	15	25	30	80	150	
89	Joe Frazier RC	5	5	6	10	25	60	250	
90	Karl Spooner RC	5	5	20	25	30	60	100	
91	Milt Bolling	5	5	6	20	30	50	100	800
92	Don Zimmer RC	30	50	60	80	▲120	300	▲1,500	
93	Steve Bilko	5	5	6	10	25	50	80	
94	Reno Bertoia	5	5	6	10	30	50	▲120	600
95	Preston Ward	5	5	6	10	30	▲50	100	600
96	Chuck Bishop	5	5	6	10	25	60	100	600
97	Carlos Paula RC	5	5	6	10	20	40	80	600
98	John Riddle CO	5	6	10	15	25	40	80	800
99	Frank Leja	5	5	6	10	20	60	150	
100	Monte Irvin	▲25	▲40	▲60	▲80	▲120	▲400		
101	Johnny Gray RC	5	5	6	10	25	60	250	
102	Wally Westlake	5	6	10	15	50	100	1,200	
103	Chuck White RC	5	5	6	15	20	40	80	500
104	Jack Harshman	5	8	12	20	30	50	120	800
105	Chuck Diering	5	5	6	10	20	50	100	
106	Frank Sullivan RC	6	10	15	25	40	60		
107	Curt Roberts	5	8	12	20	25	40	120	500
108	Rube Walker	6	10	15	25	40	80	120	800
109	Ed Lopat	6	10	15	25	40	120	400	
110	Gus Zernial	5	6	10	15	25	▲100	200	
111	Bob Milliken	5	6	10	15	30	50	100	
112	Nelson King RC	5	5	6	10	30	40		500
113	Harry Brecheen CO	5	5	6	15	25	40	100	600
114	Lou Ortiz RC	5	5	6	10	20	40	100	500
115	Ellis Kinder	5	▲8	▲12	▲20	▲30	50	▲100	500
116	Tom Hurd RC	5	5	6	10	15	30	100	800
117	Mel Roach	5	5	6	10	25	40	100	1,000
118	Bob Purkey	5	8	12	20	30	40	▲120	600
119	Bob Lennon RC	5	5	6	10	25	40	100	
120	Ted Kluszewski	15	25	30	40	50	▲120	300	2,000
121	Bill Renna	5	6	10	15	25	40	100	500
122	Carl Sawatski	5	5	6	10	15	50	80	600
123	Sandy Koufax RC	1,000	1,500	▼2,000	▼2,500	▼5,000	▼10,000	▼25,000	100,000
124	Harmon Killebrew RC	▲250	▲300	▲400	500	800	▼1,200	▲5,000	12,000
125	Ken Boyer RC	▲20	▲30	▲50	80	100	▲300	500	
126	Dick Hall RC	5	5	6	10	15	40	80	600
127	Dale Long RC	5	5	8	12	20	40	100	500
128	Ted Lepcio	5	6	10	15	25	30	120	600
129	Elvin Tappe	5	5	6	15	20	40	100	600
130	Mayo Smith MG RC	5	5	6	10	25	50	100	400
131	Grady Hatton	5	6	10	15	25	40	100	500
132	Bob Trice	5	5	6	20	25	60	120	400
133	Dave Hoskins	5	8	12	20	30	80	100	
134	Joey Jay	5	6	10	15	25	40	100	600
135	Johnny O'Brien	5	5	6	10	30	40	100	
136	Bunky Stewart RC	5	8	12	20	30	50	100	600
137	Harry Elliott RC	5	5	10	12	30	50	150	
138	Ray Herbert	▲8	▲12	▲20	▲30	▲50	▲80	▲120	600
139	Steve Kraly RC	5	5	6	12	20	50	100	800
140	Mel Parnell	5	5	6	10	25	50	80	
141	Tom Wright	5	6	10	15	25	40	100	600
142	Jerry Lynch	5	5	6	15	25	40	100	500
143	Dick Schofield	5	5	6	12	30	50	200	1,200
144	Joe Amalfitano RC	5	5	8	12	20	50	100	
145	Elmer Valo	5	6	10	15	25	80	120	800
146	Dick Donovan RC	5	5	6	10	25	60	100	500

#	Player	GD 2	VG 3	VgEx 4	EX 5	ExMt 6	NM 7	NmMt 8	MT 9
147	Hugh Pepper RC	5	5	6	10	15	40	100	
148	Hal Brown	5	6	10	15	25	50	100	500
149	Ray Crone	5	6	10	15	25	40	▲100	400
150	Mike Higgins MG	5	5	6	10	25	40	100	700
151	Red Kress CO	5	5	6	10	30	50	120	700
152	Harry Agganis RC	20	30	50	80	120	400	600	
153	Bud Podbielan	▲6	▲10	▲15	▲25	40	▲60	▲150	600
154	Willie Miranda	8	12	20	25	40	50	150	
155	Eddie Mathews	30	50	80	120	150	400	800	2,000
156	Joe Black	10	15	25	50	100	200	500	1,000
157	Robert Miller	6	10	15	25	▲40	▲60	120	600
158	Tom Carroll RC	5	6	10	15	40	80	400	800
159	Johnny Schmitz	5	5	8	12	25	▲80	120	
160	Ray Narleski RC	5	5	8	12	25	60	100	
161	Chuck Tanner RC	▲10	▲15	▲25	▲40	60	▲100	250	
162	Joe Coleman	▲10	▲15	▲25	▲40	▲60	▲100	250	
163	Faye Throneberry	5	6	10	15	40	100	250	
164	Roberto Clemente RC	▲2,000	▲3,000	▲4,000	▲5,000	▲8,000	▲25,000	▲100,000	
165	Don Johnson	5	6	10	15	40	80	200	
166	Hank Bauer	15	25	50	60	100	250	600	
167	Tom Casagrande RC	5	6	10	15	50	100	300	
168	Duane Pillette	5	6	10	25	40	80	250	800
169	Bob Oldis	5	8	12	20	40	60	300	800
170	Jim Pearce DP RC	5	5	8	12	25	60	120	
171	Dick Brodowski	▲10	▲15	25	▲40	▲60	▲100	▲200	800
172	Frank Baumholtz DP	5	5	8	15	30	60	150	600
173	Bob Kline RC	8	12	20	30	50	60	200	
174	Rudy Minarcin RC	5	6	10	25	30	50	200	600
176	Norm Zauchin RC	5	8	12	25	60	250	600	
177	Jim Robertson	5	6	10	25	30	80	250	1,000
178	Bobby Adams	10	15	25	40	60	100	200	
179	Jim Bolger RC	5	6	10	30	60	120	250	
180	Clem Labine	6	10	15	50	100	200	400	
181	Roy McMillan	5	8	12	30	50	100	250	
182	Humberto Robinson RC	5	6	10	15	40	120	▲300	
183	Tony Jacobs RC	▲12	▲20	▲30	▲50	▼80	▲250	▲1,000	
184	Harry Perkowski DP	5	6	10	15	40	60	200	800
185	Don Ferrarese RC	5	6	10	15	50	80	200	800
187	Gil Hodges	▲50	▲80	▲120	▲150	▲200	300	1,000	4,000
188	Charlie Silvera DP	6	10	15	25	30	80	200	
189	Phil Rizzuto	60	100	120	150	250	500	1,000	
190	Gene Woodling	5	8	12	40	60	100	300	
191	Ed Stanky MG	▲8	▲12	▲20	▲30	50	200	▲400	
192	Jim Delsing	▲10	▲15	▲25	▲40	60	200	▲600	
193	Johnny Sain	▲12	▲20	▲30	▲50	80	▲200	▲400	
194	Willie Mays	▲400	▲600	▲800	▲1,200	▲2,000	▲4,000	8,000	
195	Ed Roebuck RC	15	25	40	60	100	400	▲2,000	
196	Gale Wade RC	▲8	▲12	▲20	▲30	50	120	300	
197	Al Smith	6	10	15	25	60	150	500	
198	Yogi Berra	▲150	▲250	▲400	▲500	600	1,000	▲2,500	8,000
199	Bert Hamric RC	▲6	▲10	▲15	25	50	100	▲300	
200	Jackie Jensen	▲12	▲20	▲30	50	60	▲200	400	
201	Sherman Lollar	6	10	15	25	80	200	1,000	
202	Jim Owens RC	▲12	▲20	▲30	▲50	80	▲400	▲1,000	
204	Frank Smith	5	6	10	30	60	120	500	
205	Gene Freese RC	▲15	▲25	▲40	60	150	400	▲2,500	
206	Pete Daley RC	▲12	▲20	▲30	50	120	200	▲1,000	
207	Bill Consolo	▲15	▲25	▲40	▲60	100	400	▲1,500	
208	Ray Moore RC	6	10	15	25	80	300	600	
210	Duke Snider	▲120	▲200	▲300	500	▲800	▲1,500	▲6,000	

— Roberto Clemente #164 PSA 10 (Gem) (Young Collection) sold for $432,690 (SCP; 5/12)

— Roberto Clemente #164 PSA 9 (MT) sold for $478,000 (Heritage; 2/16)

— Roberto Clemente #164 PSA 9 (MT) sold for $310,700 (Heritage; 7/15)

— Harmon Killebrew #124 PSA 10 (Gem) (Young Collection) sold for $59,135 (SCP; 5/12)

— Sandy Koufax #123 PSA 10 (Gem) sold for $100,000 (Memory Lane; Private 2006)

1955 Topps Double Header

#	Player	GD 2	VG 3	VgEx 4	EX 5	ExMt 6	NM 7	NmMt 8	MT
1	A.Rosen/C.Diering	15	25	40	80	150	1,200		
3	M.Irvin/R.Kemmerer	8	12	20	30	50	100	250	
5	T.Kazanski/G.Jones	5	8	12	20	40	80	150	
7	B.Taylor/B.O'Dell	5	8	12	20	40	60	100	
9	J.Porter/T.Kipper	8	12	20	30	50	80	150	
11	C.Roberts/A.Portocarrero	5	8	12	20	40	60	200	
13	W.Westlake/F.House	5	8	12	20	40	60	150	
15	R.Walker/L.Limmer	5	8	12	20	40	80	150	
17	D.Stone/C.White	5	8	12	20	40	60	100	
19	K.Spooner/J.Hughes	5	8	12	20	40	60	150	
21	B.Skowron/F.Sullivan	6	10	15	25	40	80	250	
23	J.Shepard/S.Hack	5	8	12	20	40	60	150	
25	J.Robinson/D.Hoak	40	60	80	250	300	500	1,200	
27	D.Rhodes/J.Davis	5	8	12	20	50	60	150	
29	V.Power/E.Bailey	5	8	12	20	40	60	150	
31	H.Pollet/E.Banks	20	30	50	100	250	300	400	
33	J.Pendleton/G.Conley	5	8	12	20	40	100	300	
35	K.Olson/A.Carey	5	8	12	20	50	60	225	
37	W.Moon/J.Cunningham	5	8	12	20	40	60	150	
39	F.Marsh/V.Thies	5	8	12	20	40	60	150	
41	E.Lopat/H.Haddix	5	8	12	20	40	100	150	
43	L.Kiely/C.Stobbs	5	8	12	20	40	60	150	
45	A.Kaline/H.Valentine	20	30	50	100	60	300		
47	F.Jacobs/J.Gray	5	8	12	20	60	80	250	
49	R.Jackson/J.Finigan	5	8	12	20	60	80	225	
51	R.Jablonski/B.Keegan	5	8	12	20	60	80	150	
53	B.Herman/S.Amoros	6	10	15	25	80	100	300	
55	C.Harmon/B.Skinner	5	8	12	20	40	60	150	
57	D.Hall/B.Grim	5	8	12	20	40	80	200	
59	B.Glynn/B.Miller	5	8	12	20	40	60	150	
61	B.Gardner/J.Hetki	5	8	12	20	40	60	150	
63	B.Borkowski/B.Turley	5	8	12	20	40	60	150	
65	J.Collins/J.Harshman	5	8	12	20	40	60	200	
67	J.Hegan/J.Parks	5	8	12	20	40	60	150	
69	T.Williams/M.Smith	80	100	120	400	600	1,000	2,500	
71	G.Allie/G.Hatton	8	12	20	30	50	80	150	
73	J.Lynch/H.Brecheen	5	8	12	20	30	60	150	
75	T.Wright/V.Stewart	5	8	12	20	40	80		
77	D.Hoskins/W.McGhee	5	8	12	20	40	80	150	
79	R.Sievers/A.Fowler	5	8	12	20	40	60	150	
81	D.Schell/G.Triandos	5	8	12	20	60	80	200	
83	J.Frazier/D.Mossi	5	8	12	20	40	60		
85	E.Valo/H.Brown	5	8	12	20	40	80		
87	B.Kennedy/W.McCall	5	8	12	20	60	60	150	
89	R.Gomez/J.Rivera	5	8	12	20	40	60	300	
91	L.Ortiz/M.Bolling	5	8	12	20	40	60	150	
93	C.Sawatski/E.Tappe	5	8	12	20	40	60	150	
95	D.Jolly/B.Hofman	5	8	12	20	40	60	150	
97	P.Ward/D.Zimmer	5	8	12	20	40	80	150	
99	B.Renna/D.Groat	5	8	12	20	30	60	200	
101	B.Wilson/B.Tremel	5	8	12	20	30	80	150	
103	H.Sauer/C.Pascual	5	8	12	20	60	120	200	
105	H.Aaron/R.Herbert	50	80	150	200	250	600	2,000	
107	A.Grammas/T.Qualters	5	8	12	20	30	80	150	
109	H.Newhouser/C.Bishop	8	12	20	30	50	100	250	
111	H.Killebrew/J.Podres	20	30	50	120	250	400	800	
113	R.Boone/B.Purkey	5	8	12	20	30	60	150	
115	D.Long/F.Fain	5	8	12	20	30	60	150	
117	S.Bilko/B.Milliken	5	8	12	20	30	80	150	
119	M.Parnell/T.Hurd	5	8	12	20	40	80	250	
121	T.Kluszewski/J.Owens	10	15	25	40	80	120	500	
123	G.Zernial/B.Trice	5	8	12	20	30	60		

	GD 2	VG 3	VgEx 4	EX 5	ExMt 6	NM 7	NmMt 8	MT 9
25 R.Repulski/T.Lepcio	5	8	12	20	50	60	150	
27 W.Spahn/T.Brewer	15	25	50	60	100	300		
29 J.Gilliam/E.Kinder	6	10	15	25	80	200		
31 H.Wehmeier/W.Terwilliger	5	8	12	20	100	120		

1956 Topps

	GD 2	VG 3	VgEx 4	EX 5	ExMt 6	NM 7	NmMt 8	MT 9
Will Harridge PRES	12	15	30	40	80	200	800	
Warren Giles PRES DP	8	12	20	30	40	100	200	
Elmer Valo	5	5	6	10	30	50	200	500
Carlos Paula	5	5	6	10	25	60	120	
Ted Williams	120	200	250	400	500	1,000	2,500	6,000
Ray Boone	5	6	8	12	25	40	60	500
Ron Negray RC	5	5	6	10	15	30	60	
Walter Alston MG RC	6	8	10	20	40	80	150	
Ruben Gomez DP	5	5	6	10	20	25	50	500
Warren Spahn	20	30	50	60	100	150	400	
A Chicago Cubs TC Center	10	12	15	25	40	100	350	
B Chicago Cubs TC Dated 55	12	15	25	30	60	150		
C Chicago Cubs TC Left	10	12	15	25	40	135	600	
Andy Carey	5	6	8	12	20	40	100	400
Roy Face	5	6	8	12	20	50	80	500
Ken Boyer DP	5	6	8	20	30	50	100	1,000
Ernie Banks DP	30	50	▲80	120	200	400	▲2,000	12,000
Hector Lopez RC	5	5	6	10	20	30	60	500
Gene Conley	5	5	6	10	15	25	60	500
Dick Donovan	5	5	6	15	20	30	50	400
Chuck Diering DP	5	5	6	10	15	25	50	500
Al Kaline	30	40	50	80	120	250	600	4,000
Joe Collins DP	5	5	6	10	20	40	60	400
Jim Finigan	5	5	6	10	15	30	60	
Fred Marsh	5	5	6	10	15	30	50	400
Dick Groat	5	6	8	12	25	50	100	500
Ted Kluszewski	8	10	12	30	50	80	250	800
Grady Hatton	5	5	6	10	15	30	60	500
Nelson Burbrink DP RC	5	5	6	10	15	25	50	400
Bobby Hofman	5	5	6	15	20	30	50	400
Jack Harshman	5	5	6	15	25	30	60	
Jackie Robinson DP	▲250	▲400	▲600	▲1,000	▲1,500	▲2,500	▲8,000	▲15,000
Hank Aaron DP	100	120	200	250	400	2,000	▲4,000	▲8,000
Frank House	5	5	6	10	15	30	60	500
Roberto Clemente	150	250	300	500	2,000	5,000	8,000	25,000
Tom Brewer DP	5	5	6	10	15	30	50	
Al Rosen	5	6	8	25	30	50	80	
Rudy Minarcin	5	5	6	10	20	40	80	
Alex Grammas	5	5	6	20	25	30	50	400
Bob Kennedy	5	5	6	10	20	25	50	300
Don Mossi	5	5	6	10	25	30	60	400
Bob Turley	5	6	12	20	30	50	100	600
Hank Sauer	5	6	8	12	20	30	60	
Sandy Amoros	5	6	8	25	50	60	120	
Ray Moore	5	5	6	10	15	25	60	
Windy McCall	5	5	6	15	25	30	60	500
Gus Zernial	5	5	6	10	20	30	80	600
Gene Freese DP	5	5	6	10	20	25	50	300
Art Fowler	5	5	6	10	20	25	60	400
Jim Hegan	5	8	12	20	30	40	60	500
Pedro Ramos RC	5	5	6	10	20	30	60	300
Dusty Rhodes DP	5	5	6	10	20	25	60	
Ernie Oravetz RC	5	5	6	10	20	30	50	500
Bob Grim DP	5	6	8	12	30	40	80	
Arnie Portocarrero	5	5	6	10	15	30	60	
Bob Keegan	5	5	6	10	15	25	60	
Wally Moon	5	5	6	10	25	40	60	500
Dale Long	5	5	6	10	20	40	80	
Duke Maas RC	5	5	6	10	15	25	50	400
Ed Roebuck	5	5	6	15	20	40	80	500

	GD 2	VG 3	VgEx 4	EX 5	ExMt 6	NM 7	NmMt 8	MT 9
59 Jose Santiago RC	5	5	6	10	15	30	60	400
60 Mayo Smith MG DP	5	5	6	10	20	30	50	400
61 Bill Skowron	8	12	20	30	50	80	300	
62 Hal Smith	5	5	6	10	15	30	50	500
63 Roger Craig RC	5	6	20	25	40	60	120	800
64 Luis Arroyo RC	5	5	6	10	20	30	60	400
65 Johnny O'Brien	5	5	6	10	25	50	60	600
66 Bob Speake DP RC	5	5	6	10	15	25	60	300
67 Vic Power	5	6	8	12	20	30	80	500
68 Chuck Stobbs	5	5	6	10	15	25	50	500
69 Chuck Tanner	5	5	6	10	15	40	60	400
70 Jim Rivera	5	5	6	15	20	50	60	800
71 Frank Sullivan	5	5	6	10	20	40	60	500
72A Philadelphia Phillies TC Center	6	8	10	15	25	50		
72B Philadelphia Phillies TC Dated 5510	12	15	25	80	100	600		
72C Philadelphia Phillies TC Left DP	6	8	10	15	25	80	750	
73 Wayne Terwilliger	5	5	6	15	20	30	50	300
74 Jim King RC	5	5	6	10	20	30	50	400
75 Roy Sievers DP	5	5	6	10	15	25	60	400
76 Ray Crone	5	5	6	10	25	50	60	500
77 Harvey Haddix	5	6	8	20	30	60	400	
78 Herman Wehmeier	5	5	6	10	20	25	60	500
79 Sandy Koufax	120	150	200	250	400	▲1,500	▲5,000	▲10,000
80 Gus Triandos DP	5	5	6	10	15	25	50	
81 Wally Westlake	5	5	6	10	15	25	50	400
82 Bill Renna DP	5	5	6	10	20	30	50	
83 Karl Spooner	5	6	8	12	25	40	60	500
84 Babe Birrer RC	5	5	6	10	20	30	50	250
85A Cleveland Indians TC Center	8	10	12	20	30	60	250	
85B Cleveland Indians TC Dated 55	12	15	20	30	50	100	450	
85C Cleveland Indians TC Left	8	10	12	20	30	60	400	
86 Ray Jablonski DP	5	5	6	10	15	30	50	250
87 Dean Stone	5	5	6	20	25	30	50	500
88 Johnny Kucks RC	5	6	10	15	25	50	80	
89 Norm Zauchin	5	5	6	12	25	30	50	300
90A Cincinnati Reds TC Center	8	10	12	20	40	80	300	
90B Cincinnati Reds TC Dated 55	12	15	20	30	50	135	600	
90C Cincinnati Reds TC Left	8	10	12	20	40	100	600	
91 Gail Harris RC	5	5	6	10	20	25	60	
92 Bob (Red) Wilson	5	5	6	10	40	60		500
93 George Susce	5	5	6	10	20	30	80	
94 Ron Kline	5	5	6	10	15	40	60	300
95A Milwaukee Braves TC Center	10	12	15	25	40	150	600	
95B Milwaukee Braves TC Dated 55	12	15	20	40	100	250	1,000	
95C Milwaukee Braves TC Left	10	12	15	25	50	200	600	
96 Bill Tremel	5	5	6	10	25	30	50	500
97 Jerry Lynch	5	5	6	10	20	30	60	
98 Camilo Pascual	5	5	6	10	20	25	80	500
99 Don Zimmer	6	8	15	30	40	60	150	1,000
100A Baltimore Orioles TC Center	10	12	15	25	60	200		
100B Baltimore Orioles TC Dated 55	12	15	20	30	80	400	600	
100C Baltimore Orioles TC Left	10	12	15	25	60	300		
101 Roy Campanella	40	50	60	100	150	300	600	
102 Jim Davis	5	5	6	10	20	25	60	400
103 Willie Miranda	5	5	6	10	25	50	60	
104 Bob Lennon	5	5	6	10	15	30	60	400
105 Al Smith	5	5	6	20	25	30	50	
106 Joe Astroth	5	5	20	25	30	40	50	500
107 Eddie Mathews	▲20	▲30	▲50	▲80	▲120	200	400	1,500
108 Laurin Pepper	5	5	6	25	30	60	80	400
109 Enos Slaughter	8	12	15	25	50	80	150	1,200
110 Yogi Berra	60	80	100	150	300	400	1,000	3,000
111 Boston Red Sox TC	8	10	12	25	50	80	250	
112 Dee Fondy	5	10	15	20	25	30	50	400
113 Phil Rizzuto	25	30	60	80	120	250	500	1,200
114 Jim Owens	5	5	6	20	25	30	80	300
115 Jackie Jensen	5	6	8	25	30	40	80	500
116 Eddie O'Brien	5	5	6	10	15	25	80	500

#		GD 2	VG 3	VgEx 4	EX 5	ExMt 6	NM 7	NmMt 8	MT 9
117	Virgil Trucks	5	5	6	10	25	40	100	
118	Nellie Fox	▼10	▼15	▼25	40	▲60	100	250	▲1,500
119	Larry Jackson RC	5	5	8	12	20	30	50	400
120	Richie Ashburn	10	15	25	40	60	100	200	1,000
121	Pittsburgh Pirates TC	10	12	20	60	100	200	500	1,500
122	Willard Nixon	5	6	10	15	25	40	50	300
123	Roy McMillan	5	5	6	10	20	40	80	500
124	Don Kaiser	5	5	6	10	25	40	80	500
125	Minnie Minoso	6	8	25	30	50	100	200	
126	Jim Brady RC	5	5	6	10	25	50	100	500
127	Willie Jones	5	6	10	15	25	50	60	1,800
128	Eddie Yost	5	5	6	10	20	50	150	400
129	Jake Martin RC	5	5	6	20	25	30	50	400
130	Willie Mays	120	150	200	300	500	800	5,000	8,000
131	Bob Roselli RC	5	5	6	10	15	30	60	
132	Bobby Avila	5	5	6	10	25	40	60	
133	Ray Narleski	5	5	6	10	15	30	50	400
134	St. Louis Cardinals TC	8	10	12	25	40	80	200	
135	Mickey Mantle	▲1,500	▲2,000	▲2,500	▲4,000	▲5,000	▲6,000	▲25,000	▲200,000
136	Johnny Logan	5	5	6	10	15	25	60	
137	Al Silvera RC	5	5	6	10	15	40	50	
138	Johnny Antonelli	5	5	6	12	20	40	60	300
139	Tommy Carroll	5	6	8	12	30	50	80	
140	Herb Score RC	8	10	30	40	50	80	150	
141	Joe Frazier	5	5	6	10	25	30	60	400
142	Gene Baker	5	5	6	15	20	30	50	300
143	Jim Piersall	5	6	8	12	25	40	80	
144	Leroy Powell RC	5	5	6	10	15	30	60	300
145	Gil Hodges	15	25	40	50	80	150	400	1,500
146	Washington Nationals TC	8	10	30	40	80	100	250	
147	Earl Torgeson	5	5	6	10	20	30	60	400
148	Alvin Dark	5	6	8	12	30	40	60	300
149	Dixie Howell	5	5	6	10	25	50	80	
150	Duke Snider	50	80	120	150	200	300	500	2,000
151	Spook Jacobs	5	5	6	10	15	30	60	250
152	Billy Hoeft	5	5	6	20	25	30	60	400
153	Frank Thomas	5	5	6	10	25	40	100	
154	Dave Pope	5	5	6	10	15	40	50	300
155	Harvey Kuenn	5	6	8	15	40	50	80	500
156	Wes Westrum	5	5	6	10	30	40	50	
157	Dick Brodowski	5	5	6	10	15	25	50	500
158	Wally Post	5	5	6	10	20	30	60	400
159	Clint Courtney	5	5	6	10	15	40	250	
160	Billy Pierce	5	6	15	20	25	40	80	
161	Joe DeMaestri	5	6	10	15	25	40	80	400
162	Dave (Gus) Bell	5	5	8	12	20	30	80	
163	Gene Woodling	5	5	6	20	25	30	60	400
164	Harmon Killebrew	25	50	60	100	120	200	600	
165	Red Schoendienst	6	10	20	30	60	100	150	1,000
166	Brooklyn Dodgers TC	40	60	100	120	150	300	500	
167	Harry Dorish	5	5	6	10	15	25	60	300
168	Sammy White	5	5	6	10	25	30	50	500
169	Bob Nelson RC	5	5	6	15	20	40	50	500
170	Bill Virdon	5	6	8	12	20	30	60	500
171	Jim Wilson	5	5	6	10	25	30	50	
172	Frank Torre RC	5	5	6	25	30	40	60	300
173	Johnny Podres	6	8	25	30	50	60	150	
174	Glen Gorbous RC	5	5	6	20	25	40	80	500
175	Del Crandall	5	5	6	10	15	30	50	500
176	Alex Kellner	5	5	6	10	15	30	50	300
177	Hank Bauer	6	10	15	25	40	60	150	
178	Joe Black	5	6	8	12	20	30	80	
179	Harry Chiti	5	5	6	10	25	30	60	
180	Robin Roberts	8	12	25	40	50	80	200	800
181	Billy Martin	▲25	▲40	▲60	80	100	250	400	1,000
182	Paul Minner	5	8	12	20	30	60	100	500
183	Stan Lopata	5	5	6	10	20	30	60	
184	Don Bessent RC	5	8	12	20	30	60	100	

#		GD 2	VG 3	VgEx 4	EX 5	ExMt 6	NM 7	NmMt 8	MT
185	Bill Bruton	5	5	6	20	25	40	120	
186	Ron Jackson	5	5	6	10	25	50	100	50
187	Early Wynn	▲15	▲25	▲40	▲60	100	▲150	400	
188	Chicago White Sox TC	10	12	20	30	80	200	500	
189	Ned Garver	5	5	6	10	20	30	60	30
190	Carl Furillo	▲15	▲25	▲40	▲60	▲100	▲150	300	
191	Frank Lary	5	6	10	15	25	40	100	50
192	Smoky Burgess	5	5	6	10	30	50	80	40
193	Wilmer Mizell	5	5	6	10	20	60	100	
194	Monte Irvin	15	25	40	60	100	120	▲500	80
195	George Kell	10	15	25	40	60	50	150	60
196	Tom Poholsky	5	6	10	15	25	50	100	
197	Granny Hamner	5	5	6	10	25	40	80	50
198	Ed Fitzgerald	5	5	6	10	25	30	100	
199	Hank Thompson	5	5	6	10	25	40	100	
200	Bob Feller	▲80	▲100	▲120	150	▲250	400	1,000	1,2..
201	Rip Repulski	5	5	6	10	20	30	60	50
202	Jim Hearn	5	8	12	20	30	50	80	40
203	Bill Tuttle	5	8	12	20	30	50	60	
204	Art Swanson RC	5	6	10	15	25	40	80	40
205	Whitey Lockman	5	8	12	20	30	40	100	50
206	Erv Palica	5	6	10	15	25	40	80	30
207	Jim Small RC	5	5	6	10	25	30	60	50
208	Elston Howard	12	20	30	50	▲80	120	400	1,00
209	Max Surkont	5	8	12	20	30	50	50	5
210	Mike Garcia	5	5	6	10	25	40	100	
211	Murry Dickson	5	8	12	20	30	50	80	4
212	Johnny Temple	5	5	6	10	20	50	80	1
213	Detroit Tigers TC	8	10	12	30	50	120	500	
214	Bob Rush	5	5	6	10	25	40	80	4
215	Tommy Byrne	5	8	12	20	30	60	100	
216	Jerry Schoonmaker RC	5	6	10	15	25	40	80	5
217	Billy Klaus	5	6	10	15	25	40	80	4
218	Joe Nuxhall	5	5	6	10	25	60	100	6
219	Lew Burdette	5	5	6	10	30	60	250	
220	Del Ennis	5	5	6	10	25	40	80	
221	Bob Friend	6	10	15	25	40	60	100	3
222	Dave Philley	5	5	6	10	25	30	60	
223	Randy Jackson	5	6	10	15	25	50	100	
224	Bud Podbielan	5	5	6	10	15	30	100	
225	Gil McDougald	8	12	20	30	50	80	▲400	▲8
226	New York Giants TC	10	15	25	30	60	100	400	1,0
227	Russ Meyer	5	5	6	10	15	50	80	5
228	Mickey Vernon	▲6	▲10	▲15	▲25	▲40	▲60	120	
229	Harry Brecheen CO	▲6	▲10	▲15	▲25	▲40	▲60	▲100	4
230	Chico Carrasquel	5	5	6	10	25	30	80	6
231	Bob Hale RC	5	5	6	10	25	40	80	5
232	Toby Atwell	5	5	6	10	25	50	120	
233	Carl Erskine	12	20	30	50	60	80	200	
234	Pete Runnels	5	5	6	12	30	50	60	5
235	Don Newcombe	20	30	50	80	120	300	1,000	
236	Kansas City Athletics TC	6	10	15	25	40	60	250	
237	Jose Valdivielso RC	5	5	6	10	15	40	100	
238	Walt Dropo	5	5	6	10	25	50	80	
239	Harry Simpson	5	8	12	20	30	50	120	
240	Whitey Ford	50	▲80	▲120	▲150	200	500	1,000	4,
241	Don Mueller	5	5	6	10	15	30	120	
242	Hershell Freeman	6	10	15	25	40	60	120	
243	Sherm Lollar	5	▲8	▲12	▲20	▲30	▲50	▲100	
244	Bob Buhl	6	10	15	25	40	60	100	
245	Billy Goodman	5	6	10	15	25	60	100	
246	Tom Gorman	5	5	6	10	25	50	80	
247	Bill Sarni	5	5	6	10	15	50	80	
248	Bob Porterfield	5	5	6	10	25	40	80	
249	Johnny Klippstein	5	8	12	20	30	50	80	
250	Larry Doby	▲25	▲40	▲60	▲100	▲150	▲250	400	1
251	New York Yankees TC	40	60	80	120	200	600	2,500	3,
252	Vern Law	5	5	6	10	25	50	100	

#		GD 2	VG 3	VgEx 4	EX 5	ExMt 6	NM 7	NmMt 8	MT 9
253	Irv Noren	6	8	10	15	50	120	600	
254	George Crowe	5	5	6	10	25	80	200	
255	Bob Lemon	▲12	▲20	▲30	▲50	▲80	▲120	▲250	1,000
256	Tom Hurd	5	▲6	▲10	▲15	25	60	80	500
257	Bobby Thomson	5	▲8	▲12	▲20	30	40	150	
258	Art Ditmar	▲6	▲10	▲15	▲25	▲40	60	100	
259	Sam Jones	5	5	6	10	15	40	100	
260	Pee Wee Reese	50	80	120	200	250	400	1,200	
261	Bobby Shantz	5	8	12	20	30	50	100	500
262	Howie Pollet	5	5	6	20	25	40	80	500
263	Bob Miller	5	5	6	10	15	40	120	
264	Ray Monzant RC	5	8	12	20	30	50	80	400
265	Sandy Consuegra	5	6	10	15	25	40	60	
266	Don Ferrarese	5	5	6	10	25	30	80	
267	Bob Nieman	5	5	6	10	15	50	80	400
268	Dale Mitchell	5	6	8	15	60	200	800	
269	Jack Meyer RC	5	6	10	15	20	30	60	500
270	Billy Loes	5	8	12	20	30	50	60	500
271	Foster Castleman RC	5	5	6	8	12	50	100	
272	Danny O'Connell	5	5	6	10	20	30	60	250
273	Walker Cooper	5	5	6	10	20	30	80	500
274	Frank Baumholtz	5	6	10	15	25	50	60	500
275	Jim Greengrass	5	6	10	15	25	40	80	400
276	George Zuverink	5	5	6	10	30	50	150	
277	Daryl Spencer	5	5	6	10	20	60	100	500
278	Chet Nichols	5	6	10	15	25	50	100	500
279	Johnny Groth	5	5	6	15	25	30	60	250
280	Jim Gilliam	10	15	25	30	40	100	200	600
281	Art Houtteman	5	5	6	10	25	30	60	400
282	Warren Hacker	5	6	10	15	25	40	60	300
283	Hal R.Smith RC	5	6	10	15	25	40	60	
284	Ike Delock	5	5	6	10	20	40	60	500
285	Eddie Miksis	5	5	6	10	15	50	80	400
286	Bill Wight	5	5	6	15	20	25	60	
287	Bobby Adams	5	5	6	10	20	40	60	300
288	Bob Cerv	10	15	25	40	▲60	▲100	▲150	600
289	Hal Jeffcoat	5	5	6	10	25	30	50	300
290	Curt Simmons	5	6	10	15	25	40	▲150	400
291	Frank Kellert RC	5	5	6	15	25	30	80	400
292	Luis Aparicio RC	▲60	▲100	▲150	▲250	▲400	500	▲2,000	
293	Stu Miller	▲8	▲12	▲20	▲30	▲50	▲80	▲120	800
294	Ernie Johnson	5	5	6	10	20	30	60	400
295	Clem Labine	▲8	▲12	▲20	30	▲50	▲80	120	600
296	Andy Seminick	5	5	6	10	20	30	80	500
297	Bob Skinner	5	8	12	20	30	50	60	500
298	Johnny Schmitz	5	6	10	15	25	40	60	250
299	Charlie Neal	10	15	25	40	60	80	200	1,000
300	Vic Wertz	5	8	12	20	30	50	80	800
301	Marv Grissom	5	5	6	10	20	30	80	300
302	Eddie Robinson	5	6	8	12	25	60	300	500
303	Jim Dyck	5	5	6	10	15	30	100	
304	Frank Malzone	5	6	10	15	25	50	120	
305	Brooks Lawrence	5	6	10	15	25	40	60	500
306	Curt Roberts	5	5	10	15	25	60	120	600
307	Hoyt Wilhelm	10	15	25	40	60	100	▲300	800
308	Chuck Harmon	5	5	6	10	15	50	120	500
309	Don Blasingame RC	5	▲8	▲12	▲20	▲30	▲50	80	400
310	Steve Gromek	5	6	10	15	25	40	60	300
311	Hal Naragon	5	5	6	15	25	40	80	
312	Andy Pafko	5	6	8	12	25	30	100	400
313	Gene Stephens	5	5	6	10	20	40	60	500
314	Hobie Landrith	5	5	6	10	20	30	80	300
315	Milt Bolling	5	6	10	15	25	40	60	250
316	Jerry Coleman	5	6	8	20	25	40	120	800
317	Al Aber	5	5	6	10	20	25	50	
318	Fred Hatfield	5	5	6	10	15	30	80	
319	Jack Crimian RC	5	6	10	15	25	30	80	
320	Joe Adcock	6	10	15	25	40	60	100	600

#		GD 2	VG 3	VgEx 4	EX 5	ExMt 6	NM 7	NmMt 8	MT 9
321	Jim Konstanty	5	6	8	15	30	40	60	500
322	Karl Olson	5	6	10	15	25	40	60	
323	Willard Schmidt	5	5	6	10	15	30	80	300
324	Rocky Bridges	5	6	10	15	25	40	60	
325	Don Liddle	5	5	6	10	15	40	80	400
326	Connie Johnson RC	5	5	6	10	15	80	250	
327	Bob Wiesler RC	5	5	6	10	15	40	80	300
328	Preston Ward	5	5	6	20	25	40	80	
329	Lou Berberet RC	5	5	6	10	20	40	60	400
330	Jim Busby	5	8	12	20	30	50	▲100	400
331	Dick Hall	5	6	10	15	25	40	60	400
332	Don Larsen	20	30	50	80	120	200	500	
333	Rube Walker	5	8	12	20	30	50	120	500
334	Bob Miller	6	10	15	25	30	60	120	800
335	Don Hoak	5	6	10	15	25	50	80	400
336	Ellis Kinder	5	5	6	20	25	40	80	
337	Bobby Morgan	5	8	12	20	30	50	▲120	
338	Jim Delsing	5	5	6	10	20	40	80	
339	Rance Pless RC	5	5	6	10	20	60	300	
340	Mickey McDermott	8	12	20	30	50	150	500	
CL1	Checklist 1/3	30	40	60	100	150	300	800	
CL2	Checklist 2/4	30	40	60	100	150	300	800	2,000

— Luis Aparicio #292 PSA 10 (Gem) (Young Collection) sold for $11,028 (SCP; 5/12)
— Boston Red Sox TC #111 PSA 10 (Gem) sold for $6,000 (Legendary; 5/12)
— Harmon Killebrew #164 PSA 9 (MT) sold for $5,460 (Greg Bussineau; 12/12)
— Mickey Mantle #135 PSA 10 (Gem) sold for $382,400 (Heritage; 8/16)
— Mickey Mantle #135 PSA 10 (Gem) sold for $50,000 (Memory Lane; Private 2006)
— Rudy Minarcin #36 PSA 10 (Gem) sold for $5,106 (Memory Lane; 8/12)
— Rip Repulski #201 PSA 10 (Gem) sold for $2,228 (eBay; 1/13)

1957 Topps

#		GD 2	VG 3	VgEx 4	EX 5	ExMt 6	NM 7	NmMt 8	MT 9
1	Ted Williams	200	250	300	▲500	▲600	▲1,200	▲5,000	▼1,000
2	Yogi Berra	40	60	100	120	150	250	500	3,000
3	Dale Long	5	5	6	10	25	30	100	
4	Johnny Logan	5	6	10	15	25	60	250	
5	Sal Maglie	6	8	12	20	30	50	120	400
6	Hector Lopez	5	6	10	15	25	40	100	
7	Luis Aparicio	▼10	▼15	▼25	40	▲60	▲100	300	1,200
8	Don Mossi	5	5	5	8	20	25	100	
9	Johnny Temple	5	5	8	12	20	30	150	500
10	Willie Mays	▲150	▲250	▲400	▲600	▲1,000	▲2,000	▼4,000	▲8,000
11	George Zuverink	5	5	5	6	15	25	50	400
12	Dick Groat	5	5	10	15	25	60	150	
13	Wally Burnette RC	5	5	5	6	10	15	40	
14	Bob Nieman	5	6	10	15	25	40	80	
15	Robin Roberts	8	12	20	30	50	100	400	1,200
16	Walt Moryn	5	5	5	8	12	25	60	400
17	Billy Gardner	5	5	5	6	10	25	50	
18	Don Drysdale RC	▼80	120	▲200	▲300	▲500	▲1,000	▲3,000	15,000
19	Bob Wilson	5	5	5	6	10	20	50	400
20	Hank Aaron	200	250	400	▲600	▼1,000	▲1,500	▼5,000	15,000
21	Frank Sullivan	5	5	5	6	10	20	50	300
22	Jerry Snyder	5	5	5	6	10	20	80	400
23	Sherm Lollar	5	5	5	6	10	25	60	
24	Bill Mazeroski RC	▲40	▲60	▲100	▲150	▲200	▲300	600	3,000
25	Whitey Ford	▲30	▲50	60	100	150	300	1,000	▼3,000
26	Bob Boyd	5	5	5	6	10	20	50	
27	Ted Kazanski	5	5	5	6	10	25	50	300
28	Gene Conley	5	5	5	8	15	30	200	
29	Whitey Herzog RC	▲12	▲20	▲30	▲50	▲80	▲120	▲300	600
30	Pee Wee Reese	25	40	60	100	120	300	600	▲3,000
31	Ron Northey	5	5	5	6	10	25	50	
32	Hershell Freeman	5	5	5	6	10	20	50	250
33	Jim Small	5	5	5	6	10	30	100	
34	Tom Sturdivant RC	5	5	5	8	12	25	60	250
35	Frank Robinson RC	▲200	250	400	500	1,000	▲2,000	5,000	

#	Player	GD 2	VG 3	VgEx 4	EX 5	ExMt 6	NM 7	NmMt 8	MT 9
36	Bob Grim	5	5	6	10	15	50	100	
37	Frank Torre	5	5	5	8	20	30	80	
38	Nellie Fox	15	25	40	50	▲80	▲120	250	1,000
39	Al Worthington RC	5	5	5	6	12	30	50	
40	Early Wynn	5	6	10	15	25	80	200	1,000
41	Hal W. Smith	5	5	5	6	10	15	50	250
42	Dee Fondy	5	5	5	6	10	25	50	250
43	Connie Johnson	5	5	5	6	10	25	40	250
44	Joe DeMaestri	5	5	5	6	10	25	80	
45	Carl Furillo	6	10	15	25	50	80	400	
46	Robert J. Miller	5	5	5	6	10	20	50	200
47	Don Blasingame	5	5	5	6	10	25	60	500
48	Bill Bruton	5	5	5	8	12	30	100	400
49	Daryl Spencer	5	5	5	6	10	25	100	
50	Herb Score	5	6	8	20	30	40	100	
51	Clint Courtney	5	5	5	8	12	30	50	
52	Lee Walls	5	5	5	6	15	25	50	300
53	Clem Labine	5	8	12	20	30	50	60	250
54	Elmer Valo	5	5	5	8	15	40	60	400
55	Ernie Banks	▲100	▲120	▲150	▲250	▲300	500	▲1,200	8,000
56	Dave Sisler RC	5	5	5	6	10	25	80	
57	Jim Lemon	5	5	8	12	20	25	50	400
58	Ruben Gomez	5	5	5	8	12	25	60	
59	Dick Williams	5	5	5	6	10	30	80	250
60	Billy Hoeft	5	5	5	6	10	25	60	
61	Dusty Rhodes	5	5	5	6	25	30	80	
62	Billy Martin	▲30	▲40	▲50	60	80	100	300	▲2,000
63	Ike Delock	5	5	5	6	12	25	50	300
64	Pete Runnels	5	5	5	6	10	25	50	250
65	Wally Moon	5	5	5	8	12	30	80	
66	Brooks Lawrence	5	5	5	6	10	25	60	
67	Chico Carrasquel	5	5	5	6	10	30	60	
68	Ray Crone	5	5	5	6	15	25	250	
69	Roy McMillan	5	5	5	8	20	25	120	
70	Richie Ashburn	12	20	30	50	60	100	200	▲1,000
71	Murry Dickson	5	5	5	6	12	25	40	300
72	Bill Tuttle	5	5	5	6	10	25	50	250
73	George Crowe	5	5	5	6	15	25	50	
74	Vito Valentinetti RC	5	5	8	12	20	30	50	400
75	Jimmy Piersall	5	5	5	8	12	25	60	400
76	Roberto Clemente	120	200	▲300	▲500	▲800	▲1,200	▲3,000	8,000
77	Paul Foytack RC	5	5	5	8	12	20	60	
78	Vic Wertz	5	5	5	8	12	25	80	400
79	Lindy McDaniel RC	5	▼5	▼8	▼12	▼20	30	▲100	500
80	Gil Hodges	12	20	30	50	80	100	250	1,500
81	Herman Wehmeier	5	5	5	6	10	20	40	250
82	Elston Howard	6	8	12	20	40	60	150	1,000
83	Lou Skizas RC	5	5	5	6	10	20	50	400
84	Moe Drabowsky RC	5	5	8	12	20	30	80	300
85	Larry Doby	12	20	30	50	80	150	500	
86	Bill Sarni	5	5	6	10	15	20	60	400
87	Tom Gorman	5	5	5	8	12	25	40	300
88	Harvey Kuenn	5	5	5	8	12	30	120	500
89	Roy Sievers	5	5	5	6	10	40	60	
90	Warren Spahn	25	40	50	60	▲150	▲250	▲300	▲2,000
91	Mack Burk RC	5	5	5	6	10	20	50	
92	Mickey Vernon	5	5	5	8	15	30	50	
93	Hal Jeffcoat	5	5	5	6	10	20	40	
94	Bobby Del Greco	5	5	5	6	10	15	60	400
95	Mickey Mantle	▲400	▲600	▲1,000	▲1,200	▲2,000	▲5,000	▲12,000	▲200,000
96	Hank Aguirre RC	5	5	5	6	10	25	60	300
97	New York Yankees TC	15	20	25	50	80	200	300	1,000
98	Alvin Dark	5	5	8	12	20	30	60	200
99	Bob Keegan	5	5	5	6	10	25	60	400
100	League Presidents	5	8	12	20	25	50	200	
101	Chuck Stobbs	5	5	5	6	10	20	50	
102	Ray Boone	5	6	10	15	25	40	80	400
103	Joe Nuxhall	5	5	6	10	15	50	100	

#	Player	GD 2	VG 3	VgEx 4	EX 5	ExMt 6	NM 7	NmMt 8	MT 9
104	Hank Foiles	5	5	5	6	10	30	50	
105	Johnny Antonelli	5	5	5	8	12	25	60	
106	Ray Moore	5	5	5	6	10	25	50	
107	Jim Rivera	5	5	5	6	10	20	50	200
108	Tommy Byrne	5	5	5	8	25	50	150	
109	Hank Thompson	5	5	8	12	20	30	50	250
110	Bill Virdon	5	5	5	8	12	25	50	250
111	Hal R. Smith	5	5	6	10	15	25	50	
112	Tom Brewer	5	5	5	6	10	25	80	
113	Wilmer Mizell	5	5	6	10	15	25	50	400
114	Milwaukee Braves TC	5	8	12	20	30	40	120	500
115	Jim Gilliam	8	12	20	30	50	80	150	
116	Mike Fornieles	5	5	5	6	10	25	50	400
117	Joe Adcock	5	6	8	12	15	50	120	
118	Bob Porterfield	5	5	5	6	10	25	40	
119	Stan Lopata	5	5	5	6	10	25	50	
120	Bob Lemon	▲12	▲20	▲30	▲50	▲80	▲120	200	1,500
121	Clete Boyer RC	5	6	8	20	25	60	150	
122	Ken Boyer	6	10	15	25	40	60	150	
123	Steve Ridzik	5	5	5	6	10	30	60	
124	Dave Philley	5	5	5	6	10	15	50	
125	Al Kaline	30	50	80	100	120	▲300	500	3,00…
126	Bob Wiesler	5	5	5	6	10	25	50	1,00…
127	Bob Buhl	5	5	6	10	15	30	80	
128	Ed Bailey	5	5	5	8	12	30	60	
129	Saul Rogovin	5	5	5	6	10	25	50	25…
130	Don Newcombe	5	6	8	25	30	100	150	60…
131	Milt Bolling	5	5	5	6	10	20	50	30…
132	Art Ditmar	5	5	5	8	12	30	50	30…
133	Del Crandall	5	5	6	10	15	30	100	60…
134	Don Kaiser	5	5	5	6	10	20	40	35…
135	Bill Skowron	5	6	8	12	40	60	▲150	60…
136	Jim Hegan	5	5	8	12	20	40	60	20…
137	Bob Rush	5	5	6	10	15	25	50	30…
138	Minnie Minoso	5	6	8	20	25	50	120	50…
139	Lou Kretlow	5	5	5	6	10	25	200	
140	Frank Thomas	5	5	5	6	10	25	50	40…
141	Al Aber	5	5	5	6	10	15	40	40…
142	Charley Thompson	5	5	5	6	10	20	40	40…
143	Andy Pafko	5	6	10	15	25	40	60	30…
144	Ray Narleski	5	5	8	12	20	30	50	25…
145	Al Smith	5	5	5	6	10	25	50	20…
146	Don Ferrarese	5	5	5	6	10	25	50	25…
147	Al Walker	5	5	6	10	20	30	100	
148	Don Mueller	5	5	5	6	10	20	50	25…
149	Bob Kennedy	5	5	5	8	12	25	80	
150	Bob Friend	5	5	5	8	12	20	60	2…
151	Willie Miranda	5	5	5	6	10	25	40	30…
152	Jack Harshman	5	5	5	6	10	20	40	30…
153	Karl Olson	5	5	6	10	15	25	40	4…
154	Red Schoendienst	5	6	8	20	30	50	250	6…
155	Jim Brosnan	5	5	5	6	10	25	60	
156	Gus Triandos	5	5	5	6	10	25	50	
157	Wally Post	5	5	5	8	12	25	60	2…
158	Curt Simmons	5	5	5	8	12	40	80	
159	Solly Drake RC	5	5	5	6	10	20	50	4…
160	Billy Pierce	5	5	6	10	15	25	100	4…
161	Pittsburgh Pirates TC	5	5	6	20	25	50	200	
162	Jack Meyer	5	5	6	10	25	50		2…
163	Sammy White	5	5	5	6	10	20	50	3…
164	Tommy Carroll	5	5	6	10	15	30	60	4…
165	Ted Kluszewski	▲25	▲40	▲60	80	120	200	400	3,0…
166	Roy Face	5	5	5	8	15	25	80	4…
167	Vic Power	5	5	6	10	15	25	50	3…
168	Frank Lary	5	5	5	8	12	20	50	2…
169	Herb Plews RC	5	5	5	6	10	25	40	
170	Duke Snider	30	50	80	▲120	▲200	▲300	800	
171	Boston Red Sox TC	6	8	10	15	25	80	150	

#	Player	GD 2	VG 3	VgEx 4	EX 5	ExMt 6	NM 7	NmMt 8	MT 9
172	Gene Woodling	5	5	5	8	12	30	50	300
173	Roger Craig	5	5	5	15	20	30	50	400
174	Willie Jones	5	5	5	6	10	20	50	400
175	Don Larsen	8	10	12	30	40	80	150	
176A	Gene Bakep ERR (Baker)	150	200	250	300	400			
176B	Gene Baker COR	5	5	5	6	10	15	80	
177	Eddie Yost	5	5	5	8	15	40	120	
178	Don Bessent	5	5	5	8	15	50	200	
179	Ernie Oravetz	5	5	5	6	10	20	40	500
180	Gus Bell	5	8	12	20	30	50	120	
181	Dick Donovan	5	5	6	10	15	25	40	300
182	Hobie Landrith	5	5	5	6	10	25	50	400
183	Chicago Cubs TC	5	5	6	10	25	40	100	
184	Tito Francona RC	5	5	5	8	12	40	250	
185	Johnny Kucks	5	5	6	10	15	25	60	400
186	Jim King	5	5	5	6	10	25	50	250
187	Virgil Trucks	5	5	8	12	20	30	50	250
188	Felix Mantilla RC	5	5	5	6	10	30	60	200
189	Willard Nixon	5	5	6	10	15	20	40	250
190	Randy Jackson	5	5	8	12	20	30	50	250
191	Joe Margoneri RC	5	5	5	6	10	20	50	500
192	Jerry Coleman	5	5	5	8	12	50	80	300
193	Del Rice	5	5	5	6	10	20	60	250
194	Hal Brown	5	5	5	6	10	25	50	300
195	Bobby Avila	5	5	6	10	15	25	80	
196	Larry Jackson	5	5	5	6	15	25	60	200
197	Hank Sauer	5	5	5	6	15	25	50	400
198	Detroit Tigers TC	5	5	6	10	15	50	100	400
199	Vern Law	5	5	5	6	10	20	60	250
200	Gil McDougald	▲6	▲10	▲15	▲25	▲40	▲60	▲120	500
201	Sandy Amoros	6	10	15	25	30	60	150	
202	Dick Gernert	5	6	10	15	25	40	60	400
203	Hoyt Wilhelm	6	10	15	25	40	60	120	600
204	Kansas City Athletics TC	5	5	6	10	25	40	80	250
205	Charlie Maxwell	5	5	5	8	12	25	80	400
206	Willard Schmidt	5	5	5	6	10	20	40	250
207	Gordon (Billy) Hunter	5	5	5	6	10	15	50	250
208	Lew Burdette	5	5	6	10	15	40	120	400
209	Bob Skinner	5	5	5	6	10	25	50	250
210	Roy Campanella	25	40	50	60	100	150	300	1,200
211	Camilo Pascual	5	5	5	6	10	25	50	200
212	Rocky Colavito RC	25	40	60	80	▲120	▲200	300	1,500
213	Les Moss	5	5	5	6	10	25	40	250
214	Philadelphia Phillies TC	5	5	6	10	15	30	80	400
215	Enos Slaughter	▲10	▲15	▲25	▲40	▲60	▲100	▲250	600
216	Marv Grissom	5	5	5	6	10	25	40	300
217	Gene Stephens	5	5	5	6	10	25	50	250
218	Ray Jablonski	5	5	5	6	10	25	40	150
219	Tom Acker RC	5	5	5	6	10	15	40	250
220	Jackie Jensen	5	5	6	10	15	50	80	500
221	Dixie Howell	5	5	5	6	10	20	40	250
222	Alex Grammas	5	5	5	6	10	15	50	250
223	Frank House	5	5	5	6	10	25	50	300
224	Marv Blaylock	5	5	5	6	10	25	60	250
225	Harry Simpson	5	5	6	10	15	25	50	200
226	Preston Ward	5	5	5	6	10	20	50	200
227	Gerry Staley	5	5	5	6	10	25	40	300
228	Smoky Burgess	5	6	10	15	25	40	80	250
229	George Susce	5	5	5	6	10	25	50	250
230	George Kell	▲6	▲10	▲15	▲25	▲40	▲60	120	400
231	Solly Hemus	5	5	5	6	10	25	40	250
232	Whitey Lockman	5	5	5	6	10	25	60	300
233	Art Fowler	5	5	5	6	10	25	50	200
234	Dick Cole	5	5	5	6	10	15	40	300
235	Tom Poholsky	5	5	5	6	10	20	50	300
236	Joe Ginsberg	5	5	5	6	10	25	40	250
237	Foster Castleman	5	5	8	12	20	30	50	250
238	Eddie Robinson	5	5	5	6	10	25	50	250

#	Player	GD 2	VG 3	VgEx 4	EX 5	ExMt 6	NM 7	NmMt 8	MT 9
239	Tom Morgan	5	5	5	6	10	20	40	200
240	Hank Bauer	6	8	10	15	50	60	250	
241	Joe Lonnett RC	5	5	5	6	10	20	40	300
242	Charlie Neal	5	5	6	8	15	30	50	200
243	St. Louis Cardinals TC	5	8	12	20	30	50	120	300
244	Billy Loes	5	5	6	10	20	40		300
245	Rip Repulski	5	5	5	6	10	15	50	300
246	Jose Valdivielso	5	5	8	12	20	30	50	250
247	Turk Lown	5	5	5	6	10	25	40	250
248	Jim Finigan	5	5	5	6	10	20	50	200
249	Dave Pope	5	5	5	6	10	25	50	300
250	Eddie Mathews	20	30	50	80	▲120	▲200	▲500	2,000
251	Baltimore Orioles TC	5	5	6	10	25	60	100	300
252	Carl Erskine	5	8	12	20	30	60	▲150	800
253	Gus Zernial	5	5	5	6	15	20	60	200
254	Ron Negray	5	5	5	6	10	20	40	250
255	Charlie Silvera	5	5	8	12	20	30	50	200
256	Ron Kline	5	5	5	6	10	25	40	250
257	Walt Dropo	5	5	8	12	20	30	50	200
258	Steve Gromek	5	5	5	6	15	25	50	300
259	Eddie O'Brien	5	5	5	6	10	20	40	300
260	Del Ennis	5	5	5	8	12	20	60	300
261	Bob Chakales	5	5	5	6	10	20	40	300
262	Bobby Thomson	5	5	5	20	25	40	80	
263	George Strickland	5	5	5	6	10	15	60	300
264	Bob Turley	5	5	6	10	15	30	100	400
265	Harvey Haddix DP	5	6	8	12	25	60	150	
266	Ken Kuhn DP RC	5	5	6	10	25	40	100	
267	Danny Kravitz RC	5	5	6	10	15	30	80	
268	Jack Collum	5	5	6	10	20	40	80	
269	Bob Cerv	5	5	6	10	25	40	80	
270	Washington Senators TC	6	10	15	25	50	150	800	
271	Danny O'Connell DP	5	5	6	10	15	60	150	
272	Bobby Shantz	8	12	20	30	50	80	150	600
273	Jim Davis	5	5	6	10	15	30	100	500
274	Don Hoak	5	5	6	10	15	40	100	
275	Cleveland Indians TC	10	15	25	40	60	100	300	
276	Jim Pyburn RC	5	6	10	15	25	50	300	
277	Johnny Podres DP	10	15	25	40	60	100	▲300	800
278	Fred Hatfield DP	5	6	10	15	25	40	60	
279	Bob Thurman RC	5	5	6	10	20	50	250	
280	Alex Kellner	5	5	6	20	25	50	250	
281	Gail Harris	5	5	6	10	15	30	60	
282	Jack Dittmer DP	5	6	8	12	20	30	80	
283	Wes Covington DP RC	5	6	8	12	20	60	200	1,000
284	Don Zimmer	8	12	20	40	50	100	200	2,000
285	Ned Garver	5	5	6	10	15	30	60	400
286	Bobby Richardson RC	▲40	▲60	▲100	▲120	▲150	▲250	500	
287	Sam Jones	5	5	6	10	30	50	250	
288	Ted Lepcio	5	5	6	10	15	40	80	
289	Jim Bolger DP	5	5	6	10	15	30	50	
290	Andy Carey DP	6	8	10	25	30	100	500	
291	Windy McCall	5	6	10	15	25	40	250	
292	Billy Klaus	5	5	6	10	15	60	200	
293	Ted Abernathy RC	5	5	6	10	15	30	50	
294	Rocky Bridges DP	5	5	6	10	30	40	100	
295	Joe Collins DP	6	8	10	15	40	80	200	
296	Johnny Klippstein	5	6	10	15	20	30	120	
297	Jack Crimian	5	5	6	10	25	30	150	
298	Irv Noren DP	5	5	6	10	20	50	600	
299	Chuck Harmon	5	5	6	10	25	40	200	
300	Mike Garcia	6	10	15	25	40	120	1,000	
301	Sammy Esposito DP RC	5	5	6	10	15	40	100	400
302	Sandy Koufax DP	▲150	▲250	▲400	▲500	600	1,000	▲5,000	
303	Billy Goodman	5	6	8	15	40	120	400	
304	Joe Cunningham	5	5	6	10	15	30	60	500
305	Chico Fernandez	5	5	6	10	25	40	100	
306	Darrell Johnson DP RC	5	6	8	20	30	40	80	400

		GD 2	VG 3	VgEx 4	EX 5	ExMt 6	NM 7	NmMt 8	MT 9
307	Jack D. Phillips DP	5	5	6	10	25	50	500	
308	Dick Hall	5	5	6	10	15	50	80	
309	Jim Busby DP	5	5	6	10	20	40	120	
310	Max Surkont DP	6	10	15	25	30	100	2,000	
311	Al Pilarcik DP RC	5	5	6	10	15	30	100	500
312	Tony Kubek DP RC	▲30	▲50	▲80	100	120	200	300	800
313	Mel Parnell	5	5	6	10	25	50	150	
314	Ed Bouchee DP RC	5	5	6	10	25	50	120	
315	Lou Berberet DP	5	6	10	15	25	40	150	
316	Billy O'Dell	5	5	6	10	15	40	100	
317	New York Giants TC	12	20	30	50	80	150	300	
318	Mickey McDermott	5	5	6	10	25	40	100	
319	Gino Cimoli RC	8	12	20	30	50	100	1,000	
320	Neil Chrisley RC	5	6	10	15	25	40	80	400
321	John (Red) Murff RC	5	5	6	10	30	40	100	
322	Cincinnati Reds TC	8	10	12	20	50	100	400	
323	Wes Westrum	5	5	6	10	15	50	100	
324	Brooklyn Dodgers TC	25	40	60	100	120	300	500	2,500
325	Frank Bolling	6	10	15	25	40	60	120	
326	Pedro Ramos	5	5	6	10	15	30	80	
327	Jim Pendleton	5	5	8	12	20	40	100	
328	Brooks Robinson RC	▲400	▲600	▲800	1,000	▲1,500	▲2,500	5,000	20,000
329	Chicago White Sox TC	8	10	12	20	50	80	250	
330	Jim Wilson	5	5	6	10	20	25	80	
331	Ray Katt	5	5	6	10	25	40	150	
332	Bob Bowman RC	5	5	6	10	20	40	120	
333	Ernie Johnson	5	6	8	12	50	100	300	
334	Jerry Schoonmaker	5	5	6	10	20	30	100	
335	Granny Hamner	5	6	10	15	25	50	600	
336	Haywood Sullivan RC	5	5	6	10	30	40	80	
337	Rene Valdes RC	5	6	8	12	25	50	100	600
338	Jim Bunning RC	▲50	▲80	▲120	▲200	▲300	400	800	2,000
339	Bob Speake	5	6	10	15	25	40	80	400
340	Bill Wight	5	5	6	10	25	60	200	
341	Don Gross RC	5	5	6	10	15	30	100	
342	Gene Mauch	5	5	6	10	20	50	200	
343	Taylor Phillips RC	5	5	6	10	25	100	500	
344	Paul LaPalme	5	5	8	12	20	40	100	
345	Paul Smith	5	5	6	10	15	50	60	250
346	Dick Littlefield	5	5	6	10	15	30	120	500
347	Hal Naragon	5	5	6	10	15	50	300	
348	Jim Hearn	5	5	6	10	20	30	80	
349	Nelson King	5	5	6	10	20	40	100	
350	Eddie Miksis	5	5	6	10	25	60	400	
351	Dave Hillman RC	5	5	6	10	15	50	80	400
352	Ellis Kinder	5	5	6	10	20	50	150	
353	Cal Neeman RC	5	5	5	6	10	25	50	300
354	Rip Coleman RC	5	5	5	6	10	25	50	
355	Frank Malzone	5	5	5	8	12	25	50	250
356	Faye Throneberry	5	5	5	6	10	30	50	
357	Earl Torgeson	5	5	8	12	20	30	60	
358	Jerry Lynch	5	5	5	6	10	20	60	
359	Tom Cheney RC	5	5	5	6	10	20	50	
360	Johnny Groth	5	5	5	6	10	20	60	250
361	Curt Barclay RC	5	5	5	6	12	25	80	
362	Roman Mejias RC	5	5	5	6	10	20	50	
363	Eddie Kasko RC	5	5	5	6	10	20	50	400
364	Cal McLish RC	5	5	5	6	10	25	60	300
365	Ozzie Virgil RC	5	5	5	6	10	30	60	400
366	Ken Lehman	5	5	8	12	20	30	50	
367	Ed Fitzgerald	5	5	5	6	10	20	40	
368	Bob Purkey	5	5	6	10	15	25	50	
369	Milt Graff RC	5	5	5	6	10	25	60	
370	Warren Hacker	5	5	5	6	10	15	60	400
371	Bob Lennon	5	5	5	6	10	15	40	
372	Norm Zauchin	5	5	5	8	12	20	50	250
373	Pete Whisenant RC	5	5	5	6	10	20	50	350
374	Don Cardwell RC	5	5	6	10	15	25	50	
375	Jim Landis RC	5	5	5	8	12	20	100	
376	Don Elston RC	5	5	5	8	12	30	60	
377	Andre Rodgers RC	5	5	8	12	20	30	60	
378	Elmer Singleton	5	5	5	6	10	25	60	
379	Don Lee RC	5	5	5	6	10	25	50	
380	Walker Cooper	5	5	5	6	10	20	50	
381	Dean Stone	5	5	5	6	10	25	50	
382	Jim Brideweser	5	5	5	6	10	20	50	400
383	Juan Pizarro RC	5	5	5	6	10	40	80	
384	Bobby G. Smith RC	5	5	5	6	10	20	60	
385	Art Houtteman	5	5	5	6	10	20	40	
386	Lyle Luttrell RC	5	5	5	6	10	25	50	400
387	Jack Sanford RC	5	5	6	10	15	30	50	
388	Pete Daley	5	5	5	6	10	25	50	400
389	Dave Jolly	5	5	5	6	10	20	50	
390	Reno Bertoia	5	5	5	6	10	25	50	200
391	Ralph Terry RC	5	6	8	12	30	60	150	500
392	Chuck Tanner	5	5	8	12	20	30	200	
393	Raul Sanchez RC	5	5	5	6	10	25	50	
394	Luis Arroyo	5	5	6	10	15	50	50	500
395	Bubba Phillips	5	5	5	6	10	25	60	
396	Casey Wise RC	5	5	5	6	10	25	50	400
397	Roy Smalley	5	5	5	6	10	25	50	400
398	Al Cicotte RC	5	5	5	8	12	30	100	
399	Billy Consolo	5	5	5	6	10	20	50	200
400	Dodgers Sluggers	30	50	80	120	150	400	800	
401	Earl Battey RC	5	5	5	8	12	20	60	300
402	Jim Pisoni RC	5	5	5	6	10	20	50	
403	Dick Hyde RC	5	5	6	10	15	25	50	
404	Harry Anderson RC	5	5	5	8	12	20	50	
405	Duke Maas	5	5	5	6	15	25	50	400
406	Bob Hale	5	5	5	8	15	30	120	
407	Yankees Power Hitters	▲150	▲250	▲400	▲600	▲1,000	▲1,500	▲5,000	
CC1	Contest May 4th	15	20	25	40	60	150		
CC2	Contest May 25th	15	20	25	40	60	150		
CC3	Contest June 22nd	20	25	30	50	100	200		
CC4	Contest July 19th	20	25	30	50	80	250		
NNO	Checklist 1/2 Bazooka	60	80	100	150	200	400		
NNO	Checklist 1/2 Big Blony	60	80	100	135	200	600		
NNO	Checklist 2/3 Bazooka	60	80	100	150	250			
NNO	Checklist 2/3 Big Blony	60	80	100	200				
NNO	Checklist 3/4 Bazooka	150	200	250	400	600			
NNO	Checklist 3/4 Big Blony	120	150	200	300	500			
NNO	Checklist 4/5 Bazooka	200	300	400	500				
NNO	Checklist 4/5 Big Blony	300	400	500	800				
NNO	Lucky Penny Card	50	60	80	120	200			

— Ernie Banks #55 PSA 10 (Gem) sold for $10,073 (REA; Spring '14)
— Ernie Banks #55 PSA 8.5 (NmMt+) sold for $10,665 (REA; Spring '14)
— Rocky Colavito #212 PSA 10 (Gem) (Young Collection) sold for $7,352 (SCP; 5/12)
— Bill Mazeroski #24 PSA 10 (Gem) sold for $21,762 (Mile High; 12/14)
— Bobby Richardson #286 PSA 9 (MT) sold for $5,117 (Goodwin; 03/12)
— Bobby Richardson #286 PSA 9 (Mint) sold for $5,117 (Goodwin; 3/12)
— Brooks Robinson #328 PSA 10 (Gem) (Young Collection) sold for $47,251 (SCP; 5/12)
— Frank Robinson RC #35 PSA 9 (MT) sold for $6,840 (Greg Bussineau; 12/12)
— Frank Robinson #35 PSA 9 (Mint) sold for $9,718 (Mile High; 5/12)

1958 Hires Root Beer

		GD 2	VG 3	VgEx 4	EX 5	ExMt 6	NM 7	NmMt 8	MT
10	Richie Ashburn	8	12	20	30	50	150	1,000	
11	Chico Carrasquel	5	5	8	12	20	30	60	
12	Dave Philley	5	5	8	12	20	30	60	
13	Don Newcombe	5	8	12	20	30	50	100	
14	Wally Post	5	5	8	12	20	30	60	
15	Rip Repulski	5	5	8	12	20	30	60	
16	Chico Fernandez	5	5	8	12	20	30	60	
17	Larry Doby	6	10	15	25	40	60	120	
18	Hector Brown	5	5	8	12	20	30	60	

#	Player	GD 2	VG 3	VgEx 4	EX 5	ExMt 6	NM 7	NmMt 8	MT 9
19	Danny O'Connell	5	5	8	12	20	30	60	
20	Granny Hamner	5	5	8	12	20	30	60	
21	Dick Groat	5	5	8	12	20	30	60	
22	Ray Narleski	5	5	8	12	20	30	60	
23	Pee Wee Reese	8	12	20	30	50	120	150	
24	Bob Friend	5	5	8	12	20	30	60	
25	Willie Mays	40	60	80	200	400	800	1,000	
26	Bob Nieman	5	5	8	12	20	30	60	
27	Frank Thomas	5	5	8	12	20	30	60	
28	Curt Simmons	5	5	8	12	20	30	60	
29	Stan Lopata	5	5	8	12	20	30	60	
30	Bob Skinner	5	5	8	12	20	30	60	
31	Ron Kline	5	5	8	12	20	30	80	
32	Willie Miranda	5	5	8	12	20	30	60	
33	Bobby Avila	5	5	8	12	20	30	60	
34	Clem Labine	5	6	10	15	25	40	80	
35	Ray Jablonski	5	5	8	12	20	30	60	
36	Bill Mazeroski	6	10	15	25	80	120	150	
37	Billy Gardner	5	5	8	50	80	120	250	
38	Pete Runnels	5	5	8	12	20	30	60	
39	Jack Sanford	5	5	8	12	20	30	60	
40	Dave Sisler	5	5	8	12	20	30	60	
41	Don Zimmer	5	8	12	20	30	50	100	
42	Johnny Podres	5	8	12	20	30	50	100	
43	Dick Farrell	5	5	8	12	20	30	60	
44	Hank Aaron	40	60	80	150	550	700	1,500	
45	Bill Virdon	5	5	8	12	20	30	60	
46	Bobby Thomson	5	8	12	20	30	50	120	
47	Willard Nixon	5	5	8	12	20	30	60	
48	Billy Loes	5	5	8	12	20	30	60	
49	Hank Sauer	5	5	8	12	20	30	100	
50	Johnny Antonelli	5	5	8	12	20	30	60	
51	Daryl Spencer	5	5	8	12	20	30	60	
52	Ken Lehman	5	5	8	12	20	30	60	
53	Sammy White	5	5	8	12	20	30	60	
54	Charley Neal	5	5	8	12	20	30	60	
55	Don Drysdale	8	12	20	30	50	80	300	
56	Jackie Jensen	5	5	8	12	20	30	60	
57	Ray Katt	5	5	8	12	20	30	120	
58	Frank Sullivan	5	5	8	12	20	30	60	
59	Roy Face	5	5	8	12	20	30	80	
60	Willie Jones	5	5	8	12	20	30	60	
61	Duke Snider	15	25	60	80	100	150	300	
62	Whitey Lockman	5	5	8	12	20	30	80	
63	Gino Cimoli	5	5	8	12	20	30	60	
64	Marv Grissom	5	5	8	12	20	30	60	
65	Gene Baker	5	5	8	12	20	30	60	
66	George Zuverink	5	5	8	12	20	30	60	
67	Ted Kluszewski	6	10	15	25	40	80	150	
68	Jim Busby	5	5	8	12	20	30	60	
69	Curt Barclay	5	5	8	12	20	30	80	
70	Hank Foiles	5	5	8	12	20	30	60	
71	Gene Stephens	5	5	8	12	20	30	80	
72	Al Worthington	5	5	8	12	20	30	60	
73	Al Walker	5	5	8	12	20	30	60	
74	Bob Boyd	5	5	8	12	20	30	60	
75	Al Pilarcik	5	5	8	12	20	30	60	

1958 Topps

	Player	GD 2	VG 3	VgEx 4	EX 5	ExMt 6	NM 7	NmMt 8	MT 9
	Ted Williams	100	120	150	250	400	600	▲6,000	
	Bob Lemon	5	6	10	15	25	40	200	
	Bob Lemon YT	10	15	25	40	80			
	Alex Kellner	5	5	5	8	20	40	60	
	Hank Foiles	5	5	5	8	12	20	60	
	Willie Mays	60	80	100	150	300	▲2,000	▲6,000	
	George Zuverink	5	5	5	8	12	40	60	250

#	Player	GD 2	VG 3	VgEx 4	EX 5	ExMt 6	NM 7	NmMt 8	MT 9
7	Dale Long	5	5	8	12		50	120	
8A	Eddie Kasko	5	5	5	8	12	30	200	
8B	Eddie Kasko YN	6	10	15	25	60	200		
9	Hank Bauer	8	12	20	30	50	80	120	
10	Lou Burdette	5	5	8	12	30	60	150	
11A	Jim Rivera	5	5	6	10	15	40	400	
11B	Jim Rivera YT	6	10	15	25	50	150		
12	George Crowe	5	5	5	8	12	20	50	
13A	Billy Hoeft	5	5	5	8	12	30	250	
13B	Billy Hoeft YN	6	10	15	25	40	80		
14	Rip Repulski	5	5	5	8	12	30	60	200
15	Jim Lemon	5	5	5	8	12	30	40	
16	Charlie Neal	5	5	6	10	30	50	300	
17	Felix Mantilla	5	5	5	8	15	50	250	
18	Frank Sullivan	5	5	5	8	12	20	50	
19	San Francisco Giants TC	5	6	10	15	50	100	400	
20A	Gil McDougald	5	6	10	15	25	40	200	
20B	Gil McDougald YN	10	15	25	40	60	200	600	
21	Curt Barclay	5	5	5	8	12	25	60	
22	Hal Naragon	5	5	5	8	12	30	60	
23A	Bill Tuttle	5	5	5	8	12	30		
23B	Bill Tuttle YN	6	10	15	30	40	150		
24A	Hobie Landrith	5	5	5	8	12	25	80	
24B	Hobie Landrith YN	6	10	15	30	60	100		
25	Don Drysdale	20	30	▲50	60	100	200	600	
26	Ron Jackson	5	5	5	8	12	20	50	300
27	Bud Freeman	5	5	5	8	12	25	30	300
28	Jim Busby	5	5	5	8	12	30	50	400
29	Ted Lepcio	5	5	5	8	12	20	50	
30A	Hank Aaron	20	50	80	150	200	400	▲5,000	
30B	Hank Aaron YN	50	120	150	200	300	500	▲6,000	
31	Tex Clevenger RC	5	5	5	8	12	25	50	300
32A	J.W. Porter	5	5	5	8	12	40	150	
32B	J.W. Porter YN	6	10	15	25	40	120	400	
33A	Cal Neeman	5	5	5	8	12	20	50	
33B	Cal Neeman YT	6	10	15	25	40	150	500	
34	Bob Thurman	5	5	5	8	12	20	50	250
35A	Don Mossi	5	5	6	10	15	25	150	
35B	Don Mossi YT	6	10	15	25	40	80	300	
36	Ted Kazanski	5	5	5	8	12	25	50	
37	Mike McCormick RC	5	5	6	10	25	60		
38	Dick Gernert	5	5	5	8	20	30	50	
39	Bob Martyn RC	5	5	5	8	12	20	100	250
40	George Kell	5	5	8	20	30	50	150	
41	Dave Hillman	5	5	5	8	12	25	30	300
42	John Roseboro RC	12	20	30	50	80	200	600	
43	Sal Maglie	5	5	6	10	25	50	100	250
44	Washington Senators TC	5	5	6	10	50	150	800	
45	Dick Groat	5	5	6	10	15	40	60	
46A	Lou Sleater	5	5	5	8	12	25	250	
46B	Lou Sleater YN	6	10	15	25	40	150	500	
47	Roger Maris RC	250	▲400	▲500	▲600	▲1,200	1,500	4,000	15,000
48	Chuck Harmon	5	5	5	8	12	20	40	400
49	Smoky Burgess	5	5	6	10	15	30	100	
50A	Billy Pierce	5	5	5	8	12	20	50	
50B	Billy Pierce YT	6	10	15	25	40	80	250	
51	Del Rice	5	5	5	8	12	20	120	
52A	Roberto Clemente	40	60	100	150	200	500	200	800
52B	Roberto Clemente YT	50	80	100	200	300	800	400	
53A	Morrie Martin	5	5	5	8	12	20	100	
53B	Morrie Martin YN	6	10	15	25	40	80	300	
54	Norm Siebern RC	5	5	6	10	15	40	120	400
55	Chico Carrasquel	5	5	5	8	12	20	50	500
56	Bill Fischer RC	5	5	5	8	12	30	50	250
57A	Tim Thompson	5	5	5	8	12	20	50	
57B	Tim Thompson YN	6	10	15	25	40	100	400	
58A	Art Schult	5	5	5	8	12	20	80	
58B	Art Schult YT	12	20	30	60	100	120	100	

#	Player	GD 2	VG 3	VgEx 4	EX 5	ExMt 6	NM 7	NmMt 8	MT 9
59	Dave Sisler	5	5	5	8	12	50	150	
60A	Del Ennis	5	5	5	8	12	20	50	
60B	Del Ennis YN	6	10	15	25	40	80	300	
61A	Darrell Johnson	5	5	6	10	15	25	100	
61B	Darrell Johnson YN	6	10	15	25	40	100		
62	Joe DeMaestri	5	5	5	8	12	20	60	250
63	Joe Nuxhall	5	6	10	15	25	40	60	
64	Joe Lonnett	5	5	5	8	12	40	120	
65A	Von McDaniel RC	5	5	5	8	12	25	135	
65B	Von McDaniel YN	6	10	15	25	50	100		
66	Lee Walls	5	5	5	8	12	20	50	500
67	Joe Ginsberg	5	5	5	8	12	20	80	
68	Daryl Spencer	5	5	5	8	12	25	80	
69	Wally Burnette	5	5	5	8	12	20	40	
70A	Al Kaline	10	15	25	40	100	150	300	1,000
70B	Al Kaline YN	20	30	80	120	200	300	1,000	
71	Los Angeles Dodgers TC	6	10	15	40	60	200	1,000	
72	Bud Byerly	5	5	5	8	12	20	60	
73	Pete Daley	5	5	5	8	25	30	120	
74	Roy Face	5	5	6	10	15	25	60	500
75	Gus Bell	5	5	8	12	20	30	50	
76A	Dick Farrell RC	5	5	5	8	12	20	80	
76B	Dick Farrell YT	6	10	15	25	80	200		
77A	Don Zimmer	5	5	6	10	15	40	100	
77B	Don Zimmer YT	10	15	25	40	60	250	1,000	
78A	Ernie Johnson	5	5	5	8	12	250	400	
78B	Ernie Johnson YN	6	10	15	25	50	150		
79A	Dick Williams	5	5	5	8	12	25	50	
79B	Dick Williams YT	6	10	15	25	50	100	300	
80	Dick Drott RC	5	5	5	8	12	20	40	250
81A	Steve Boros RC	5	5	5	8	12	30	200	
81B	Steve Boros YT	6	10	15	25	60	150		
82	Ron Kline	5	5	5	8	12	15	40	
83	Bob Hazle RC	5	5	5	8	12	30	120	
84	Billy O'Dell	5	5	5	8	12	20	40	300
85A	Luis Aparicio	5	6	10	15	25	40	200	
85B	Luis Aparicio YT	15	25	40	60	100	250		
86	Valmy Thomas RC	5	5	5	8	12	20	40	250
87	Johnny Kucks	5	5	6	10	15	100	200	
88	Duke Snider	▲20	▲30	▲50	▲60	▲100	▲200	400	
89	Billy Klaus	5	5	5	8	12	30	200	
90	Robin Roberts	8	12	20	30	40	100	250	
91	Chuck Tanner	5	5	6	10	15	50	250	
92A	Clint Courtney	5	5	5	8	12	20	40	500
92B	Clint Courtney YN	5	6	10	15	25	40	200	
93	Sandy Amoros	5	6	10	15	25	40	80	
94	Bob Skinner	5	5	5	8	12	25	40	300
95	Frank Bolling	5	5	5	8	12	30	50	
96	Joe Durham RC	5	5	5	8	12	20	40	800
97A	Larry Jackson	5	5	5	8	12	20	100	400
97B	Larry Jackson YN	6	10	15	25	60	80	675	
98A	Billy Hunter	5	5	5	8	12	20	50	
98B	Billy Hunter YN	6	10	15	25	40	100		
99	Bobby Adams	5	5	5	8	12	20	50	400
100A	Early Wynn	5	5	8	12	20	40	100	500
100B	Early Wynn YT	10	15	25	40	60	100	200	
101A	Bobby Richardson	5	8	12	20	30	60	150	
101B	Bobby Richardson YN	10	15	25	40	80	120		
102	George Strickland	5	5	5	8	12	30	50	
103	Jerry Lynch	5	5	5	8	12	20	50	400
104	Jim Pendleton	5	5	5	8	12	30	60	
105	Billy Gardner	5	5	5	8	12	40	250	
106	Dick Schofield	5	5	5	8	12	20	40	300
107	Ossie Virgil	5	5	5	8	12	60	250	
108A	Jim Landis	5	5	5	8	12	25	80	
108B	Jim Landis YT	6	10	15	25	40	100	400	
109	Herb Plews	5	5	6	10	15	25	40	300
110	Johnny Logan	5	6	10	15	25	40	80	
111	Stu Miller	5	5	5	6	10	25	50	
112	Gus Zernial	5	5	5	6	10	25	40	300
113	Jerry Walker RC	5	5	5	6	10	15	40	
114	Irv Noren	5	5	5	6	10	25	40	
115	Jim Bunning	▲6	▲10	▲15	25	▲40	▲60	▲150	400
116	Dave Philley	5	5	5	6	10	15	60	
117	Frank Torre	5	5	5	6	10	25	50	300
118	Harvey Haddix	5	5	5	6	10	25	50	300
119	Harry Chiti	5	5	5	6	10	15	30	200
120	Johnny Podres	5	5	6	10	25	30	60	400
121	Eddie Miksis	5	5	5	6	10	15	30	500
122	Walt Moryn	5	5	5	6	10	15	40	150
123	Dick Tomanek RC	5	5	5	8	12	20	40	250
124	Bobby Usher	5	5	5	6	10	15	30	200
125	Alvin Dark	5	5	5	6	10	15	40	300
126	Stan Palys RC	5	5	5	6	10	15	40	
127	Tom Sturdivant	5	6	10	15	25	40	50	300
128	Willie Kirkland RC	5	5	6	10	15	25	50	275
129	Jim Derrington RC	5	5	5	6	10	15	50	
130	Jackie Jensen	5	5	5	8	12	25	60	250
131	Bob Henrich RC	5	5	5	6	10	20	30	500
132	Vern Law	5	5	5	6	10	20	40	150
133	Russ Nixon RC	5	5	5	6	10	15	40	400
134	Philadelphia Phillies TC	5	5	6	10	25	50	60	300
135	Mike Drabowsky	5	5	5	6	10	15	40	400
136	Jim Finigan	5	5	5	6	10	30	40	300
137	Russ Kemmerer	5	5	5	6	10	15	40	
138	Earl Torgeson	5	5	5	6	10	15	40	400
139	George Brunet RC	5	5	5	6	10	15	30	300
140	Wes Covington	5	5	5	6	10	15	50	
141	Ken Lehman	5	5	5	6	10	15	50	400
142	Enos Slaughter	8	12	20	30	50	80	▲150	250
143	Billy Muffett RC	5	5	5	6	10	15	30	200
144	Bobby Morgan	5	5	5	6	10	15	40	400
146	Dick Gray RC	5	5	5	6	10	25	50	250
147	Don McMahon RC	5	5	5	6	10	15	40	
148	Billy Consolo	5	5	5	6	10	15	40	
149	Tom Acker	5	5	5	6	10	15	30	200
150	Mickey Mantle	▲300	▲500	▲800	▲1,200	▲2,000	▲3,000	▲12,000	
151	Buddy Pritchard RC	5	5	5	6	15	60	250	
152	Johnny Antonelli	5	5	5	6	10	15	40	400
153	Les Moss	5	5	5	6	10	15	40	300
154	Harry Byrd	5	5	5	6	10	15	80	
155	Hector Lopez	5	5	5	6	10	20	40	200
156	Dick Hyde	5	5	5	6	10	15	60	
157	Dee Fondy	5	5	5	6	10	15	50	400
158	Cleveland Indians TC	5	5	6	10	25	50	150	
159	Taylor Phillips	5	5	6	10	15	25	30	300
160	Don Hoak	5	5	5	6	10	25	40	250
161	Don Larsen	8	12	20	30	50	60	▲120	500
162	Gil Hodges	10	15	25	40	50	80	150	600
163	Jim Wilson	5	5	5	6	10	15	30	150
164	Bob Taylor RC	5	5	5	6	10	30	200	
165	Bob Nieman	5	5	5	6	10	15	40	
166	Danny O'Connell	5	5	5	6	10	15	30	200
167	Frank Baumann RC	5	5	5	6	10	15	30	150
168	Joe Cunningham	5	5	5	6	10	15	50	
169	Ralph Terry	5	5	5	8	12	20	60	
170	Vic Wertz	5	5	5	6	10	20	40	200
171	Harry Anderson	5	5	5	6	10	15	40	
172	Don Gross	5	5	5	6	10	15	50	
173	Eddie Yost	5	5	5	6	10	15	50	400
174	Kansas City Athletics TC	5	5	6	10	15	50	100	
175	Marv Throneberry RC	5	5	8	12	50	80	150	
176	Bob Buhl	5	5	5	6	10	25	50	
177	Al Smith	5	5	5	6	10	25	50	300
178	Ted Kluszewski	5	5	8	12	25	50	80	800
179	Willie Miranda	5	5	5	6	10	15	40	

		GD 2	VG 3	VgEx 4	EX 5	ExMt 6	NM 7	NmMt 8	MT 9
180	Lindy McDaniel	5	5	8	12	20	30	50	200
181	Willie Jones	5	5	5	6	10	15	50	300
182	Joe Caffie RC	5	5	5	6	10	15	50	400
183	Dave Jolly	5	5	5	6	10	15	40	300
184	Elvin Tappe	5	5	5	6	10	20	50	
185	Ray Boone	5	5	5	6	10	20	40	
186	Jack Meyer	5	5	5	6	10	25	60	250
187	Sandy Koufax	80	▲120	150	250	300	600	▲1,500	6,000
188	Milt Bolling	5	5	5	6	10	15	40	
189	George Susce	5	5	5	6	10	15	40	
190	Red Schoendienst	6	10	15	25	40	80	150	
191	Art Ceccarelli RC	5	5	5	6	10	15	80	
192	Milt Graff	5	5	5	6	10	20	40	300
193	Jerry Lumpe RC	5	5	5	8	12	30	60	500
194	Roger Craig	5	5	5	6	10	30	60	
195	Whitey Lockman	5	5	5	6	10	15	60	300
196	Mike Garcia	5	5	5	6	10	25	40	200
197	Haywood Sullivan	5	5	5	6	10	15	40	200
198	Bill Virdon	5	5	5	6	10	25	60	
199	Don Blasingame	5	5	5	6	10	15	60	
200	Bob Keegan	5	5	5	6	10	25	40	
201	Jim Bolger	5	5	5	6	10	20	30	
202	Woody Held RC	5	5	5	6	10	20	50	300
203	Al Walker	5	5	5	6	10	15	30	300
204	Leo Kiely	5	5	5	6	10	15	60	
205	Johnny Temple	5	5	5	6	10	25	40	300
206	Bob Shaw RC	5	5	5	6	10	15	60	
207	Solly Hemus	5	5	5	6	15	30	300	
208	Cal McLish	5	5	5	6	10	25	60	
209	Bob Anderson RC	5	5	5	6	10	25	50	
210	Wally Moon	5	5	5	6	10	30	80	
211	Pete Burnside RC	5	5	5	6	10	15	30	
212	Bubba Phillips	5	5	5	6	10	20	100	
213	Red Wilson	5	5	5	6	10	15	40	
214	Willard Schmidt	5	5	5	6	10	20	40	
215	Jim Gilliam	5	5	5	8	20	30	80	
216	St. Louis Cardinals TC	5	5	6	10	25	60	120	
217	Jack Harshman	5	5	5	6	10	15	60	
218	Dick Rand RC	5	5	5	6	10	25	100	
219	Camilo Pascual	5	5	5	6	10	15	40	
220	Tom Brewer	5	5	5	6	10	20	40	300
221	Jerry Kindall RC	5	5	6	10	15	25	40	300
222	Bud Daley RC	5	5	5	6	10	20	30	400
223	Andy Pafko	5	5	5	8	25	40	100	
224	Bob Grim	5	5	5	8	12	25	50	300
225	Billy Goodman	5	5	5	6	10	25	50	
226	Bob Smith RC	5	5	5	6	10	15	40	150
227	Gene Stephens	5	5	5	6	10	15	40	
228	Duke Maas	5	5	5	6	10	15	40	300
229	Frank Zupo RC	5	5	5	6	10	20	40	300
230	Richie Ashburn	10	15	25	40	60	80	▲250	
231	Lloyd Merritt RC	5	5	5	6	10	25	50	
232	Reno Bertoia	5	5	5	6	10	15	40	300
233	Mickey Vernon	5	5	5	6	20	25	50	
234	Carl Sawatski	5	5	5	6	10	20	50	400
235	Tom Gorman	5	5	5	6	10	15	40	300
236	Ed Fitzgerald	5	5	5	6	10	15	50	
237	Bill Wight	5	5	5	6	10	15	50	250
238	Bill Mazeroski	10	15	25	40	60	120	600	
239	Chuck Stobbs	5	5	5	6	10	25	80	
240	Bill Skowron	6	10	15	25	40	50	150	600
241	Dick Littlefield	5	5	5	6	10	15	50	
242	Johnny Klippstein	5	5	5	6	10	20	60	400
243	Larry Raines RC	5	5	5	6	10	25	50	400
244	Don Demeter RC	5	5	5	6	10	15	50	
245	Frank Lary	5	5	5	6	10	25	50	300
246	New York Yankees TC	10	20	40	60	80	300	1,200	
247	Casey Wise	5	5	5	6	10	20	50	
248	Herman Wehmeier	5	5	5	6	10	25	80	
249	Ray Moore	5	5	5	6	10	15	60	
250	Roy Sievers	5	5	5	6	10	25	50	300
251	Warren Hacker	5	5	5	6	10	15	50	
252	Bob Trowbridge RC	5	5	5	6	10	20	60	
253	Don Mueller	5	5	5	6	10	25	40	300
254	Alex Grammas	5	5	5	6	10	15	50	
255	Bob Turley	5	5	6	10	30	40	120	
256	Chicago White Sox TC	5	5	6	10	40	80	400	
257	Hal Smith	5	5	5	6	10	15	70	
258	Carl Erskine	5	5	5	8	20	40	80	400
259	Al Pilarcik	5	5	5	6	10	25	50	400
260	Frank Malzone	5	5	5	6	10	30	60	
261	Turk Lown	5	5	5	6	10	15	60	400
262	Johnny Groth	5	5	5	6	10	15	60	400
263	Eddie Bressoud RC	5	5	5	6	10	25	40	
264	Jack Sanford	5	5	5	6	10	15	40	200
265	Pete Runnels	5	5	5	6	10	25	120	
266	Connie Johnson	5	5	5	6	10	15	40	
267	Sherm Lollar	5	5	5	6	10	20	60	400
268	Granny Hamner	5	5	5	6	10	15	60	
269	Paul Smith	5	5	5	6	10	15	40	300
270	Warren Spahn	8	25	30	40	80	120	500	
271	Billy Martin	6	10	15	25	40	60	100	800
272	Ray Crone	5	5	5	6	10	15	50	200
273	Hal Smith	5	5	5	6	10	15	50	200
274	Rocky Bridges	5	5	5	6	10	15	40	400
275	Elston Howard	8	12	20	30	40	60	300	
276	Bobby Avila	5	5	5	8	12	20	50	
277	Virgil Trucks	5	5	5	6	10	25	80	300
278	Mack Burk	5	5	5	6	10	15	40	
279	Bob Boyd	5	5	5	6	10	25	50	300
280	Jim Piersall	5	5	5	8	12	50	100	
281	Sammy Taylor RC	5	5	5	6	10	15	60	
282	Paul Foytack	5	5	5	6	10	15	30	200
283	Ray Shearer RC	5	5	5	6	10	30	120	300
284	Ray Katt	5	5	6	10	15	25	40	300
285	Frank Robinson	15	20	40	50	100	150	500	
286	Gino Cimoli	5	5	5	6	10	30	120	
287	Sam Jones	5	5	5	6	10	25	150	400
288	Harmon Killebrew	25	40	60	80	120	200	400	2,000
289	Series Hurling Rivals	5	5	6	10	15	60	400	
290	Dick Donovan	5	5	5	6	10	15	40	400
291	Don Landrum RC	5	5	5	6	10	25	100	
292	Ned Garver	5	5	5	6	10	15	50	200
293	Gene Freese	5	5	5	6	10	15	50	300
294	Hal Jeffcoat	5	5	5	6	10	15	50	
295	Minnie Minoso	5	5	12	15	20	50	100	400
296	Ryne Duren RC	8	12	20	30	50	150	500	
297	Don Buddin RC	5	5	5	6	10	15	50	
298	Jim Hearn	5	5	5	6	10	15	50	
299	Harry Simpson	5	5	5	6	10	20	80	300
300	League Presidents	5	5	6	10	15	30	80	
301	Randy Jackson	5	5	5	6	10	20	60	300
302	Mike Baxes RC	5	5	5	6	10	25	150	
303	Neil Chrisley	5	5	5	6	10	25	40	300
304	Tigers Big Bats	5	6	10	15	50	80	200	
305	Clem Labine	5	6	10	15	25	40	60	300
306	Whammy Douglas RC	5	5	5	6	10	20	40	500
307	Brooks Robinson	50	80	100	▲150	▲300	500	▲1,200	
308	Paul Giel	5	5	5	6	10	15	40	
309	Gail Harris	5	5	5	6	10	15	40	400
310	Ernie Banks	10	30	60	100	120	300	600	3,000
311	Bob Purkey	5	5	5	6	10	15	60	
312	Boston Red Sox TC	6	10	15	25	30	200	800	
313	Bob Rush	5	5	5	6	10	30	80	
314	Dodgers Boss and Power	10	15	25	40	60	80	200	
315	Bob Friend	5	5	5	6	10	15	80	400

#	Name	GD 2	VG 3	VgEx 4	EX 5	ExMt 6	NM 7	NmMt 8	MT 9
316	Tito Francona	5	5	5	6	10	25	80	400
317	Albie Pearson RC	5	5	5	6	10	15	100	
318	Frank House	5	5	5	6	10	15	50	
319	Lou Skizas	5	5	5	6	10	15	50	400
320	Whitey Ford	25	50	60	80	120	300	600	2,000
321	Sluggers Supreme	10	15	30	50	60	120	300	2,000
322	Harding Peterson RC	5	5	5	6	10	15	60	
323	Elmer Valo	5	5	5	6	10	25	80	
324	Hoyt Wilhelm	5	5	8	12	25	60	150	600
325	Joe Adcock	5	5	5	6	15	25	100	300
326	Bob Miller	5	5	5	10	15	25	40	
327	Chicago Cubs TC	5	5	8	12	25	80	400	
328	Ike Delock	5	5	5	6	10	30	60	
329	Bob Cerv	5	5	5	6	10	25	50	250
330	Ed Bailey	5	5	5	6	10	15	50	
331	Pedro Ramos	5	5	6	10	15	25	100	400
332	Jim King	5	5	5	6	10	20	60	
333	Andy Carey	5	5	5	8	12	25	60	600
334	Mound Aces	5	5	5	6	10	20	60	
335	Ruben Gomez	5	5	6	10	15	25	60	
336	Bert Hamric	5	5	5	6	10	15	40	
337	Hank Aguirre	5	5	5	6	10	15	40	200
338	Walt Dropo	5	5	5	6	10	15	60	400
339	Fred Hatfield	5	5	5	6	10	15	40	
340	Don Newcombe	6	10	15	25	40	50	120	
341	Pittsburgh Pirates TC	5	5	8	12	25	60	400	
342	Jim Brosnan	5	5	5	6	10	25	60	
343	Orlando Cepeda RC	▲60	▲100	▲150	▲200	▲300	400	▲1,200	3,000
344	Bob Porterfield	5	5	5	6	10	15	50	300
345	Jim Hegan	5	5	5	6	10	15	50	
346	Steve Bilko	5	5	5	6	10	20	80	
347	Don Rudolph RC	5	5	5	6	10	20	40	
348	Chico Fernandez	5	5	5	6	10	20	60	400
349	Murry Dickson	5	5	5	6	10	20		
350	Ken Boyer	5	5	8	12	20	60	200	
351	Braves Fence Busters	20	30	50	80	100	150	600	2,000
352	Herb Score	5	5	5	8	20	40	100	
353	Stan Lopata	5	5	5	6	10	15	60	
354	Art Ditmar	5	5	5	8	12	50	150	400
355	Bill Bruton	5	5	5	8	12	60	250	500
356	Bob Malkmus RC	5	5	5	6	10	15	60	
357	Danny McDevitt RC	5	5	5	6	10	20	80	
358	Gene Baker	5	5	5	6	10	15	50	
359	Billy Loes	5	5	5	6	10	15	50	
360	Roy McMillan	5	5	5	6	10	25	50	250
361	Mike Fornieles	5	5	5	6	10	15	50	
362	Ray Jablonski	5	5	5	6	10	15	80	
363	Don Elston	5	5	5	6	10	20	50	300
364	Earl Battey	5	5	5	6	10	15	50	200
365	Tom Morgan	5	5	5	6	10	15	40	
366	Gene Green RC	5	5	5	6	10	15	60	
367	Jack Urban RC	5	5	5	6	10	15	40	300
368	Rocky Colavito	6	10	15	25	60	100	300	1,500
369	Ralph Lumenti RC	5	5	5	6	10	15	50	200
370	Yogi Berra	60	80	100	120	150	250	600	2,000
371	Marty Keough RC	5	5	5	6	10	15	40	
372	Don Cardwell	5	5	5	6	10	15	60	
373	Joe Pignatano RC	5	5	5	6	10	20	80	400
374	Brooks Lawrence	5	5	5	6	10	40	120	
375	Pee Wee Reese	▲30	▲50	▲60	▲80	▲120	▲200	▲300	800
376	Charley Rabe RC	5	5	5	6	10	15	80	300
377A	Milwaukee Braves TC Alpha	5	5	8	12	20	30	120	
377B	Milwaukee Braves TC Num	10	15	25	40	80			
378	Hank Sauer	5	5	5	15	20	25	50	400
379	Ray Herbert	5	5	5	6	10	15	50	300
380	Charlie Maxwell	5	5	5	6	10	25	60	400
381	Hal Brown	5	5	5	6	10	15	60	
382	Al Cicotte	5	5	5	6	10	25	50	300

#	Name	GD 2	VG 3	VgEx 4	EX 5	ExMt 6	NM 7	NmMt 8	MT 9
383	Lou Berberet	5	5	5	6	10	15	30	
384	John Goryl RC	5	5	5	6	10	25	50	
385	Wilmer Mizell	5	5	5	6	10	20	50	250
386	Birdie's Young Sluggers	6	10	15	25	40	60	200	
387	Wally Post	5	5	5	6	10	25	60	300
388	Billy Moran RC	5	5	5	6	10	15	30	300
389	Bill Taylor	5	5	5	6	10	15	30	250
390	Del Crandall	5	5	5	6	15	25	60	400
391	Dave Melton RC	5	5	5	6	10	15	60	
392	Bennie Daniels RC	5	5	5	6	15	80	400	
393	Tony Kubek	6	10	15	25	▲40	▲60	100	400
394	Jim Grant RC	5	5	5	6	20	30	150	
395	Willard Nixon	5	5	5	6	10	15	80	
396	Dutch Dotterer RC	5	5	5	6	10	15	30	250
397A	Detroit Tigers TC Alpha	5	5	6	10	15	25	80	
397B	Detroit Tigers TC Num	10	15	25	40	60			
398	Gene Woodling	5	5	5	6	10	25	60	
399	Marv Grissom	5	5	5	6	10	15	40	300
400	Nellie Fox	8	12	20	25	30	50	150	500
401	Don Bessent	5	5	5	6	10	15	30	300
402	Bobby Gene Smith	5	5	5	6	10	15	50	
403	Steve Korcheck RC	5	5	5	6	10	15	30	300
404	Curt Simmons	5	5	8	12	20	30	50	
405	Ken Aspromonte RC	5	5	5	6	10	25	40	250
406	Vic Power	5	5	5	6	10	15	40	
407	Carlton Willey RC	5	5	8	12	20	30	50	250
408A	Baltimore Orioles TC Alpha	5	5	6	10	15	25	80	
408B	Baltimore Orioles TC Num	10	15	25	40	80			
409	Frank Thomas	5	5	5	8	15	80	600	
410	Murray Wall	5	5	5	6	10	15	30	
411	Tony Taylor RC	5	5	5	6	10	20	60	300
412	Gerry Staley	5	5	5	6	10	20	40	
413	Jim Davenport RC	5	5	5	6	10	15	40	
414	Sammy White	5	5	5	6	10	25	40	
415	Bob Bowman	5	5	5	6	10	15	30	200
416	Foster Castleman	5	5	5	6	10	25	50	
417	Carl Furillo	5	8	12	20	25	30	100	400
418	World Series Batting Foes	80	120	200	250	300	800	▲4,000	20,000
419	Bobby Shantz	5	5	5	8	12	25	120	500
420	Vada Pinson RC	12	20	30	50	60	100	250	
421	Dixie Howell	5	5	5	6	10	15	40	
422	Norm Zauchin	5	5	5	6	10	15	80	
423	Phil Clark RC	5	5	6	10	15	25	30	
424	Larry Doby	10	15	25	40	50	100	150	
425	Sammy Esposito	5	5	5	6	10	15	40	
426	Johnny O'Brien	5	5	5	6	10	15	40	250
427	Al Worthington	5	5	5	6	15	20	60	300
428A	Cincinnati Reds TC Alpha	5	5	6	10	15	25	120	
428B	Cincinnati Reds TC Num	8	12	20	30	50	80		
429	Gus Triandos	5	5	5	6	10	40	100	
430	Bobby Thomson	5	5	5	8	12	30	50	250
431	Gene Conley	5	5	5	6	20	100	250	
432	John Powers RC	5	5	5	6	10	15	50	
433A	Pancho Herrera COR RC	5	5	5	6	10	15	60	300
433B	Pancho Herrer ERR (No a)	1,200	2,000	3,000	4,000	5,000	8,000	20,000	
434	Harvey Kuenn	5	5	5	8	12	30	50	
435	Ed Roebuck	5	5	5	6	10	20	40	250
436	Rival Fence Busters	20	30	50	60	80	250	800	
437	Bob Speake	5	5	5	6	10	15	50	400
438	Whitey Herzog	5	5	5	6	10	30	50	300
439	Ray Narleski	5	5	5	6	10	25	50	
440	Eddie Mathews	10	15	25	50	60	250	500	
441	Jim Marshall RC	5	5	5	6	10	25	60	
442	Phil Paine RC	5	5	5	6	10	15	30	
443	Billy Harrell SP RC	5	5	5	6	10	30	150	
444	Danny Kravitz	5	5	5	6	10	25	30	300
445	Bob Smith RC	5	5	5	6	10	15	40	500
446	Carroll Hardy SP RC	5	5	8	12	20	30	80	

BASELINE

#	Player	GD 2	VG 3	VgEx 4	EX 5	ExMt 6	NM 7	NmMt 8	MT 9
447	Ray Monzant	5	5	5	6	10	15	40	
448	Charley Lau RC	5	5	5	8	12	30	200	
449	Gene Fodge RC	5	5	5	6	10	20	30	600
450	Preston Ward SP	5	5	5	6	10	50	80	
451	Joe Taylor RC	5	5	5	6	10	25	50	
452	Roman Mejias	5	5	6	10	15	25	40	250
453	Tom Qualters	5	5	5	6	10	15	40	150
454	Harry Hanebrink RC	5	5	5	6	10	20	40	400
455	Hal Griggs RC	5	5	5	6	10	15	30	
456	Dick Brown RC	5	5	5	6	10	15	30	150
457	Milt Pappas RC	5	5	5	8	20	25	80	
458	Julio Becquer RC	5	5	5	6	10	15	40	
459	Ron Blackburn RC	5	5	5	6	10	15	40	200
460	Chuck Essegian RC	5	5	5	6	10	15	40	300
461	Ed Mayer RC	5	5	5	6	10	15	40	300
462	Gary Geiger SP RC	5	5	5	8	20	30	100	
463	Vito Valentinetti	5	5	5	6	10	15	60	
464	Curt Flood RC	15	25	30	50	60	80	250	
465	Arnie Portocarrero	5	5	5	6	10	15	50	400
466	Pete Whisenant	5	5	5	6	10	15	50	400
467	Glen Hobbie RC	5	5	5	6	10	15	40	200
468	Bob Schmidt RC	5	5	5	6	10	15	40	400
469	Don Ferrarese	5	5	5	6	10	15	30	300
470	R.C. Stevens RC	5	5	5	6	10	15	50	250
471	Lenny Green RC	5	5	6	10	15	25	40	
472	Joey Jay	5	5	5	6	10	60	120	
473	Bill Renna	5	5	5	6	10	15	30	400
474	Roman Semproch RC	5	5	5	6	10	30	50	
475	All-Star Managers	10	15	25	30	40	80	300	
476	Stan Musial AS TP	25	40	50	60	▲100	120	300	1,200
477	Bill Skowron AS	5	5	15	20	30	50	80	600
478	Johnny Temple AS	5	5	5	6	10	15	50	400
479	Nellie Fox AS	5	5	15	20	25	40	80	600
480	Eddie Mathews AS	5	8	25	30	40	60	200	
481	Frank Malzone AS	5	5	5	6	10	25	100	
482	Ernie Banks AS	10	15	25	40	60	80	150	1,000
483	Luis Aparicio AS	5	5	6	10	25	40	80	
484	Frank Robinson AS	12	20	30	50	60	80	150	1,500
485	Ted Williams AS	40	50	60	100	120	200	400	1,500
486	Willie Mays AS	20	30	50	80	100	250	500	3,000
487	Mickey Mantle AS TP	▲80	▲120	▲200	▲200	▲500	▲800	▼120	▲4,000
488	Hank Aaron AS	25	30	40	60	80	150	400	5,000
489	Jackie Jensen AS	5	5	5	6	10	50	120	
490	Ed Bailey AS	5	5	5	6	10	15	80	
491	Sherm Lollar AS	5	5	5	6	10	15	60	
492	Bob Friend AS	5	8	12	20	25	40	120	
493	Bob Turley AS	5	5	5	6	25	50	120	
494	Warren Spahn AS	10	15	20	25	40	60	250	1,500
495	Herb Score AS	5	5	6	10	25	50	300	
NO	Contest Card July 8th	5	8	12	20	30	150		
NO	Felt Emblem Insert	5	8	12	20	30	60	500	

– Gus Bell #75 PSA 10 (Gem) sold for $7,114 (eBay; 10/12)
– Sandy Koufax #187 PSA 10 (Gem) sold for $40,000 (Memory Lane; Private 2007)
– Mickey Mantle #150 PSA 10 (MT) sold for $15,692 (Memory Lane; Winter '13)
– Mickey Mantle #150 PSA 9 (MT) sold for $15,405 (REA; Spring '14)
– Mickey Mantle #150 PSA 9 (MT) sold for $13,458 (Memory Lane; 8/12)
– Mickey Mantle #150 PSA 9 (MT) sold for $13,062 (Mile High; 4/14)
– Mickey Mantle #150 PSA 9 (MT) sold for $12,866 (SCP; 8/13)
– Mickey Mantle #150 PSA 9 (MT) sold for $12,440 (Mile High; 5/12)
– Mickey Mantle #150 PSA 9 (MT) sold for $7,638 (REA; 05/11)
– Bob Martyn RC #39 PSA 10 (Gem) sold for $2,560 (eBay; 9/12)
– Mike McCormick RC #37 PSA 9 (MT) sold for $5,609 (eBay; 8/12)
– Robin Roberts #90 PSA 9 (MT) sold for $4,836 (eBay; 02/12)
– Bobby Thomson #430 PSA 10 (Gem) sold for $4,893 (eBay; 12/12)
– Bobby Thomson #430 PSA 10 (Gem) sold for $3,000 (Legendary; 11/12)

1959 Fleer Ted Williams

#	Card	GD 2	VG 3	VgEx 4	EX 5	ExMt 6	NM 7	NmMt 8	MT 9
1	The Early Years	6	10	15	25	60	100	400	
2	Ted's Idol Babe Ruth	8	12	20	80	100	150	300	600
3	Practice Makes Perfect	5	5	8	12	20	30	80	150
4	Learns Fine Points	5	5	5	8	12	20	50	200
5	Ted's Fame Spreads	5	5	5	8	12	20	40	120
6	Ted Turns Professional	5	5	6	10	15	25	50	250
7	From Mound to Plate	5	5	5	8	12	20	40	150
8	1937 First Full Season	5	5	5	8	20	30	50	250
9	First Step to the Majors w/Collins	5	5	6	10	15	25	50	200
10	Gunning as Pastime	5	5	5	8	12	20	40	200
11	First Spring Training w/Foxx	5	5	8	12	20	50	120	200
12	Burning Up Minors	5	5	5	8	12	20	40	200
13	1939 Shows Will Stay	5	5	5	8	12	20	40	150
14	Outstanding Rookie '39	5	5	5	8	12	25	60	200
15	Licks Sophomore Jinx	5	5	5	8	12	20	40	120
16	Williams' Greatest Year	5	5	5	8	15	30	50	120
17	How Ted Hit .400	5	6	10	15	25	50	100	300
18	1941 All Star Hero	5	5	5	8	12	20	40	120
19	Ted Wins Triple Crown	5	5	5	8	12	20	40	150
20	On to Naval Training	5	5	5	8	12	20	40	150
21	Honors for Williams	5	5	5	8	12	20	40	
22	1944 Ted Solos	5	5	5	8	12	20	40	150
23	Williams Wins His Wings	5	5	5	8	12	20	40	175
24	1945 Sharpshooter	5	5	5	8	12	20	25	100
25	1945 Ted Discharged	5	5	5	8	12	20	40	100
26	Off to Flying Start	5	5	5	8	12	20	30	150
27	7/9/46 One Man Show	5	5	5	8	12	30	50	150
28	The Williams Shift	5	5	5	8	12	20	40	120
29	Ted Hits for Cycle	5	5	5	8	12	20	40	120
30	Beating The Williams Shift	5	5	5	8	12	20	50	80
31	Sox Lose Series	5	5	5	8	12	25	40	100
32	Most Valuable Player	5	5	5	8	15	20	40	150
33	Another Triple Crown	5	5	5	8	12	20	40	80
34	Runs Scored Record	5	5	5	8	12	20	40	150
35	Sox Miss Pennant	5	5	5	8	12	20	40	100
36	Banner Year for Ted	5	5	5	8	12	20	40	150
37	1949 Sox Miss Again	5	5	5	8	12	20	40	120
38	1949 Power Rampage	5	5	5	8	12	20	40	120
39	1950 Great Start	5	5	5	8	12	20	40	100
40	Ted Crashes into Wall	5	5	5	8	12	20	50	250
41	1950 Ted Recovers	5	5	5	8	12	20	25	120
42	Williams/Tom Yawkey	5	5	5	8	12	20	40	120
43	Double Play Lead	5	5	5	8	12	20	40	120
44	Back to Marines	5	5	5	8	12	20	40	150
45	Farewell to Baseball	5	5	5	8	12	20	40	100
46	Ready for Combat	5	5	5	8	12	20	30	100
47	Ted Crash Lands Jet	5	5	5	8	12	20	40	100
48	1953 Ted Returns	5	5	5	8	12	20	40	120
49	Smash Return	5	5	5	8	12	20	40	100
50	1954 Spring Injury	5	5	5	8	12	20	30	150
51	Ted is Patched Up	5	5	5	8	12	20	25	150
52	1954 Ted's Comeback	5	5	5	8	12	30	50	100
53	Comeback is Success	5	5	5	8	12	20	40	120
54	Ted Hooks Big One	5	5	5	8	12	20	40	80
55	Retirement No Go	5	5	5	8	12	20	40	150
56	2,000th Hit 8/11/55	5	5	5	8	12	20	30	120
57	Ted Reaches 400th Homer	5	5	5	8	12	20	40	150
58	Williams Hits .388	5	5	5	8	12	20	40	100
59	Hot September for Ted	5	5	5	8	12	20	40	120
60	More Records for Ted	5	5	5	8	12	20	40	100
61	1957 Outfielder Ted	5	5	5	8	12	20	40	175
62	1958 Sixth Batting Title	5	5	5	8	12	20	40	100
63	All-Star Record w/facsimile Auto	8	12	20	30	50	80	100	300
64	Daughter and Daddy	5	5	5	8	12	20	40	100

#		GD 2	VG 3	VgEx 4	EX 5	ExMt 6	NM 7	NmMt 8	MT 9
65	1958 August 30	5	5	5	8	12	20	40	80
66	1958 Powerhouse	5	5	5	8	12	20	40	100
67	Two Famous Fishermen w/Snead	5	5	8	12	20	30	60	120
68	Ted Signs for 1959 SP	250	300	500	500	800	1,000	1,200	2,000
69	A Future Ted Williams	5	5	5	8	12	20	40	100
70	Ted Williams and Jim Thorpe	5	5	8	12	20	40	50	250
71	Hitting Fundamental 1	5	5	5	8	12	20	25	120
72	Hitting Fundamental 2	5	5	5	8	12	20	40	120
73	Hitting Fundamental 3	5	5	5	8	12	20	30	120
74	Here's How	5	5	5	8	12	20	40	200
75	Williams' Value to Sox w/Ruth	5	5	8	12	20	50	80	300
76	On Base Record	5	5	5	8	12	20	40	100
77	Ted Relaxes	5	5	5	8	12	20	25	150
78	Honors for Williams	5	5	5	8	12	20	40	175
79	Where Ted Stands	5	5	5	8	12	20	50	250
80	Ted's Goals for 1959	5	6	10	15	25	50	150	

1959 Topps

#		GD 2	VG 3	VgEx 4	EX 5	ExMt 6	NM 7	NmMt 8	MT 9
1	Ford Frick COMM	15	25	40	60	100	200	600	
2	Eddie Yost	5	5	5	5	8	25	100	500
3	Don McMahon	5	5	5	6	10	20	60	
4	Albie Pearson	5	5	6	10	15	25	60	400
5	Dick Donovan	5	5	5	5	8	15	50	400
6	Alex Grammas	5	5	5	5	8	15	50	300
7	Al Pilarcik	5	5	5	5	8	15	40	250
8	Philadelphia Phillies CL	6	10	25	50	100	150	400	
9	Paul Giel	5	5	5	5	8	20	60	
10	Mickey Mantle	▲300	▲500	▲800	▲1,200	▲2,000	▲2,500	▲10,000	▲100,000
11	Billy Hunter	5	5	5	8	25	80	150	
12	Vern Law	5	5	5	8	12	50	80	400
13	Dick Gernert	5	5	5	5	8	15	50	300
14	Pete Whisenant	5	5	5	5	8	15	40	150
15	Dick Drott	5	5	5	5	8	30	50	
16	Joe Pignatano	5	5	5	5	8	15	40	400
17	Danny's All-Stars	5	5	5	8	12	25	50	
18	Jack Urban	5	5	5	5	8	15	30	200
19	Eddie Bressoud	5	5	6	10	15	25	40	300
20	Duke Snider	10	15	25	40	60	80	250	1,200
21	Connie Johnson	5	5	5	5	8	15	40	250
22	Al Smith	5	5	5	5	8	25	30	
23	Murry Dickson	5	5	6	10	15	25	80	300
24	Red Wilson	5	5	5	5	8	15	30	200
25	Don Hoak	5	5	5	8	12	40	60	
26	Chuck Stobbs	5	5	5	5	8	20	40	200
27	Andy Pafko	5	5	5	5	8	20	40	300
28	Al Worthington	5	5	5	5	8	15	25	200
29	Jim Bolger	5	5	5	5	8	15	30	150
30	Nellie Fox	5	5	8	12	30	50	120	500
31	Ken Lehman	5	5	5	5	8	15	30	150
32	Don Buddin	5	5	5	5	8	15	50	300
33	Ed Fitzgerald	5	5	5	5	10	30	60	
34	Pitchers Beware	5	8	12	20	30	60	120	400
35	Ted Kluszewski	5	5	5	8	25	40	80	400
36	Hank Aguirre	5	5	5	5	8	30	50	250
37	Gene Green	5	5	5	5	8	15	50	
38	Morrie Martin	5	5	5	5	8	30	60	400
39	Ed Bouchee	5	5	5	5	8	25	40	
40A	Warren Spahn 1931 Clear 3	10	15	25	40	60	150		
40B	Warren Spahn 1931 Obscured 3	8	12	20	30	50	120	400	
40C	Warren Spahn 1921	6	10	15	25	40	100	250	
41	Bob Martyn	5	5	5	5	8	15	40	150
42	Murray Wall	5	5	5	5	8	15	30	200
43	Steve Bilko	5	5	5	5	8	25	40	250
44	Vito Valentinetti	5	5	5	5	8	15	40	120
45	Andy Carey	5	5	6	10	15	50	150	
46	Bill R. Henry	5	5	5	5	8	15	40	
47	Jim Finigan	5	5	5	5	8	30	120	
48	Baltimore Orioles CL	5	5	6	10	15	40	100	400
49	Bill Hall RC	5	5	5	5	8	15	50	250
50	Willie Mays	50	60	100	150	250	500	▲2,500	6,000
51	Rip Coleman	5	5	5	5	8	15	50	
52	Coot Veal RC	5	5	5	5	8	15	80	300
53	Stan Williams RC	5	5	6	10	15	25	50	300
54	Mel Roach	5	5	5	5	8	15	40	250
55	Tom Brewer	5	5	5	5	8	15	30	150
56	Carl Sawatski	5	5	5	5	8	25	80	400
57	Al Cicotte	5	5	5	5	8	15	40	300
58	Eddie Miksis	5	5	5	5	8	15	40	150
59	Irv Noren	5	5	5	5	8	15	50	350
60	Bob Turley	5	5	6	10	15	30	80	
61	Dick Brown	5	5	5	5	10	30	60	
62	Tony Taylor	5	5	5	8	20	40	200	
63	Jim Hearn	5	5	5	5	8	15	40	150
64	Joe DeMaestri	5	5	5	5	8	15	30	150
65	Frank Torre	5	5	6	10	15	25	40	300
66	Joe Ginsberg	5	5	6	10	15	25	250	
67	Brooks Lawrence	5	5	5	5	8	15	30	150
68	Dick Schofield	5	5	5	5	8	20	40	
69	San Francisco Giants CL	5	6	10	15	25	60	120	500
70	Harvey Kuenn	5	5	5	5	8	25	40	300
71	Don Bessent	5	5	6	10	15	40	150	
72	Bill Renna	5	5	5	5	8	15	40	150
73	Ron Jackson	5	5	5	5	8	15	40	200
74	Directing the Power	5	5	5	8	12	30	80	
75	Sam Jones	5	5	5	5	8	15	30	400
76	Bobby Richardson	5	8	12	20	30	60	150	500
77	John Goryl	5	5	5	5	8	25	80	
78	Pedro Ramos	5	5	5	5	8	15	30	200
79	Harry Chiti	5	5	5	5	8	12	30	150
80	Minnie Minoso	5	6	10	15	25	50	100	
81	Hal Jeffcoat	5	5	5	5	8	25	40	200
82	Bob Boyd	5	5	5	5	8	15	40	
83	Bob Smith	5	5	5	5	8	15	30	200
84	Reno Bertoia	5	5	5	5	8	25	40	300
85	Harry Anderson	5	5	5	5	8	15	30	300
86	Bob Keegan	5	5	5	5	8	15	40	250
87	Danny O'Connell	5	5	5	5	8	15	30	150
88	Herb Score	5	5	5	8	12	25	80	
89	Billy Gardner	5	5	5	5	8	15	50	250
90	Bill Skowron	5	5	8	12	20	50	120	
91	Herb Moford RC	5	5	5	10	15	25	40	200
92	Dave Philley	5	5	5	5	8	30	80	
93	Julio Becquer	5	5	5	5	8	20	60	250
94	Chicago White Sox CL	5	6	10	15	25	80	100	400
95	Carl Willey	5	5	5	5	8	15	50	250
96	Lou Berberet	5	5	5	5	8	15	25	120
97	Jerry Lynch	5	5	5	5	8	15	40	
98	Arnie Portocarrero	5	5	5	5	8	15	25	300
99	Ted Kazanski	5	5	5	5	8	15	40	200
100	Bob Cerv	5	5	5	5	8	15	40	150
101	Alex Kellner	5	5	5	8	12	20	30	200
102	Felipe Alou RC	5	8	12	20	30	80	120	500
103	Billy Goodman	5	5	5	5	8	25	50	
104	Del Rice	5	5	8	12	50	80	250	
105	Lee Walls	5	5	5	5	8	30	150	
106	Hal Woodeshick RC	5	5	5	5	8	50	80	
107	Norm Larker RC	5	5	5	5	8	15	40	250
108	Zack Monroe RC	5	5	5	5	8	20	100	
109	Bob Schmidt	5	5	5	5	8	25	120	
110	George Witt RC	5	5	5	6	10	15	30	200
111	Cincinnati Redlegs CL	5	5	5	6	10	60	300	
112	Billy Consolo	5	5	5	5	6	12	40	250
113	Taylor Phillips	5	5	5	5	6	12	30	
114	Earl Battey	5	5	5	5	8	20	50	

#	Player	GD 2	VG 3	VgEx 4	EX 5	ExMt 6	NM 7	NmMt 8	MT 9
15	Mickey Vernon	5	5	5	5	8	40	200	
16	Bob Allison RS RC	5	5	5	6	10	40	60	400
17	John Blanchard RS RC	5	5	5	6	10	30	80	400
18	John Buzhardt RS RC	5	5	5	5	6	12	30	150
19	Johnny Callison RS RC	5	5	5	6	10	40	80	
20	Chuck Coles RS RC	5	5	5	5	6	15	50	200
21	Bob Conley RS RC	5	5	5	5	6	12	50	250
22	Bennie Daniels RS	5	5	5	5	6	20	40	150
23	Don Dillard RS RC	5	5	5	5	6	12	25	200
24	Dan Dobbek RS RC	5	5	5	5	6	12	50	200
25	Ron Fairly RS RC	5	5	5	6	10	25	60	500
26	Eddie Haas RS RC	5	5	5	5	6	12	30	250
27	Kent Hadley RS RC	5	5	5	5	6	12	30	200
28	Bob Hartman RS RC	5	5	5	5	6	30	50	
29	Frank Herrera RS	5	5	5	5	6	20	40	250
30	Lou Jackson RS RC	5	5	5	5	6	20	60	
31	Deron Johnson RS RC	5	5	5	8	12	25	100	
32	Don Lee RS	5	5	5	5	6	12	40	250
33	Bob Lillis RS RC	5	5	5	5	6	15	50	120
34	Jim McDaniel RS RC	5	5	5	5	6	25	40	
35	Gene Oliver RS RC	5	5	5	5	6	20	30	200
36	Jim O'Toole RS RC	5	5	5	5	6	12	50	
37	Dick Ricketts RS RC	5	5	5	5	6	20	40	250
38	John Romano RS RC	5	5	5	5	6	20	50	
39	Ed Sadowski RS RC	5	5	5	5	6	15	60	150
40	Charlie Secrest RS RC	5	5	5	5	6	12	30	250
41	Joe Shipley RS RC	5	5	5	5	6	12	40	200
42	Dick Stigman RS RC	5	5	5	5	6	15	50	
43	Willie Tasby RS RC	5	5	5	5	6	12	30	200
44	Jerry Walker RS	5	5	5	5	6	12	50	250
45	Dom Zanni RS RC	5	5	5	5	6	15	30	200
46	Jerry Zimmerman RS RC	5	5	5	5	6	20	60	
47	Cubs Clubbers	5	5	6	20	25	50	100	300
48	Mike McCormick	5	5	5	5	6	12	40	250
49	Jim Bunning	5	8	12	20	30	50	150	
50	Stan Musial	40	50	60	100	150	250	▲1,200	2,000
51	Bob Malkmus	5	5	5	5	6	12	30	150
52	Johnny Klippstein	5	5	5	5	6	12	30	200
53	Jim Marshall	5	5	5	5	6	12	40	250
54	Ray Herbert	5	5	5	5	6	12	25	250
55	Enos Slaughter	▲6	▲10	▲15	▲25	▲40	▲60	120	500
56	Ace Hurlers	5	5	5	8	20	40	80	300
57	Felix Mantilla	5	5	5	5	6	12	30	150
58	Walt Dropo	5	5	5	5	6	15	30	200
59	Bob Shaw	5	5	5	5	6	25	60	300
60	Dick Groat	5	5	5	5	8	25	60	250
61	Frank Baumann	5	5	5	5	6	12	40	
62	Bobby G. Smith	5	5	5	5	6	12	30	150
63	Sandy Koufax	▲80	▲120	▲150	▲250	▲400	▲600	1,200	8,000
64	Johnny Groth	5	5	5	5	6	12	40	250
65	Bill Bruton	5	5	5	5	6	12	40	250
66	Destruction Crew	5	5	6	20	25	50	80	500
67	Duke Maas	5	5	5	6	10	25	120	
68	Carroll Hardy	5	5	5	5	6	12	30	120
69	Ted Abernathy	5	5	5	5	6	15	40	250
70	Gene Woodling	5	5	5	5	6	12	40	150
71	Willard Schmidt	5	5	5	5	6	12	40	
72	Kansas City Athletics CL	5	6	10	15	25	40	80	300
73	Bill Monbouquette RC	5	5	5	5	6	20	60	300
74	Jim Pendleton	5	5	5	5	6	15	40	300
75	Dick Farrell	5	5	5	5	6	12	30	150
76	Preston Ward	5	5	5	5	6	12	30	150
77	John Briggs RC	5	5	5	5	6	12	30	200
78	Ruben Amaro RC	5	5	5	5	8	20	40	300
79	Don Rudolph	5	5	5	5	8	25	60	
80	Yogi Berra	▲50	60	▲100	▲120	▲150	▲300	▲800	2,000
81	Bob Porterfield	5	5	5	5	6	15	25	150
82	Milt Graff	5	5	5	5	6	20	120	

#	Player	GD 2	VG 3	VgEx 4	EX 5	ExMt 6	NM 7	NmMt 8	MT 9
183	Stu Miller	5	5	5	5	8	40	150	
184	Harvey Haddix	5	5	5	5	6	20	30	200
185	Jim Busby	5	5	5	5	6	12	40	200
186	Mudcat Grant	5	`5	5	5	8	15	30	250
187	Bubba Phillips	5	5	5	5	6	12	20	
188	Juan Pizarro	5	5	5	5	6	12	40	250
189	Neil Chrisley	5	5	5	5	6	12	60	
190	Bill Virdon	5	5	5	5	8	15	50	450
191	Russ Kemmerer	5	5	5	5	6	12	30	150
192	Charlie Beamon RC	5	5	5	5	6	12	30	300
193	Sammy Taylor	5	5	5	5	6	12	30	200
194	Jim Brosnan	5	5	5	5	6	15	25	150
195	Rip Repulski	5	5	5	5	8	40	100	
196	Billy Moran	5	5	5	5	6	12	40	200
197	Ray Semproch	5	5	5	5	6	20	100	
198	Jim Davenport	5	5	5	5	6	20	80	
199	Leo Kiely	5	5	5	5	6	30	200	
200	Warren Giles NL PRES	5	5	5	8	12	25	60	300
201	Tom Acker	5	5	5	5	6	15	60	
202	Roger Maris	30	50	60	80	120	200	400	2,500
203	Ossie Virgil	5	5	5	5	6	12	30	250
204	Casey Wise	5	5	5	5	6	15	80	
205	Don Larsen	5	5	8	12	25	30	100	
206	Carl Furillo	5	5	6	10	15	30	80	400
207	George Strickland	5	5	5	5	6	12	50	150
208	Willie Jones	5	5	5	5	6	12	25	250
209	Lenny Green	5	5	5	5	6	12	40	200
210	Ed Bailey	5	5	5	5	6	12	40	200
211	Bob Blaylock RC	5	5	5	5	6	12	40	300
212	Fence Busters	15	20	25	40	80	▲120	250	1,000
213	Jim Rivera	5	5	5	5	6	20	30	200
214	Marcelino Solis RC	5	5	5	5	6	12	50	
215	Jim Lemon	5	5	5	5	6	25	30	200
216	Andre Rodgers	5	5	5	5	6	12	40	250
217	Carl Erskine	5	5	5	6	10	25	60	200
218	Roman Mejias	5	5	5	5	6	20	40	250
219	George Zuverink	5	5	5	5	6	15	60	150
220	Frank Malzone	5	5	5	5	6	20	40	
221	Bob Bowman	5	5	5	5	6	40	200	
222	Bobby Shantz	5	5	6	10	25	40	400	
223	St. Louis Cardinals CL	5	5	6	10	15	100	250	
224	Claude Osteen RC	5	5	6	10	20	50	400	
225	Johnny Logan	5	5	5	5	8	25	80	300
226	Art Ceccarelli	5	5	5	5	6	12	30	200
227	Hal W. Smith	5	5	5	5	6	12	40	200
228	Don Gross	5	5	5	5	6	12	25	200
229	Vic Power	5	5	5	5	8	30	100	
230	Bill Fischer	5	5	5	5	6	12	30	150
231	Ellis Burton RC	5	5	5	5	6	15	60	250
232	Eddie Kasko	5	5	5	5	6	15	50	250
233	Paul Foytack	5	5	5	5	6	15	40	250
234	Chuck Tanner	5	5	5	5	6	12	30	120
235	Valmy Thomas	5	5	5	5	6	12	25	150
236	Ted Bowsfield RC	5	5	5	5	6	12	30	200
237	Run Preventers	5	5	6	10	15	30	100	
238	Gene Baker	5	5	5	5	6	40	100	400
239	Bob Trowbridge	5	5	5	5	6	12	30	150
240	Hank Bauer	5	5	6	10	15	30	60	
241	Billy Muffett	5	5	5	5	6	12	30	150
242	Ron Samford RC	5	5	5	5	6	12	25	200
243	Marv Grissom	5	5	5	5	6	12	25	150
244	Dick Gray	5	5	5	5	6	12	30	250
245	Ned Garver	5	5	5	5	6	12	25	250
246	J.W. Porter	5	5	5	5	6	12	25	150
247	Don Ferrarese	5	5	5	5	6	12	25	200
248	Boston Red Sox CL	5	5	6	10	25	40	80	300
249	Bobby Adams	5	5	5	5	6	15	40	
250	Billy O'Dell	5	5	5	6	10	70	300	

#	Player	GD 2	VG 3	VgEx 4	EX 5	ExMt 6	NM 7	NmMt 8	MT 9
251	Clete Boyer	5	5	6	10	25	30	100	500
252	Ray Boone	5	5	5	5	8	15	50	250
253	Seth Morehead RC	5	5	5	5	6	20	30	150
254	Zeke Bella RC	5	5	5	5	6	20	30	150
255	Del Ennis	5	5	5	5	6	12	30	200
256	Jerry Davie RC	5	5	5	5	6	12	30	150
257	Leon Wagner RC	5	5	5	5	8	15	50	200
258	Fred Kipp RC	5	5	5	5	8	15	50	250
259	Jim Pisoni	5	5	5	5	6	20	40	300
260	Early Wynn	5	5	5	8	25	50	100	500
261	Gene Stephens	5	5	5	5	6	12	25	300
262	Hitters Foes	10	12	15	25	30	50	100	400
263	Bud Daley	5	5	5	5	6	12	30	250
264	Chico Carrasquel	5	5	5	5	6	12	60	250
265	Ron Kline	5	5	5	5	6	12	25	120
266	Woody Held	5	5	5	5	8	25	50	
267	John Romonosky RC	5	5	5	5	6	12	30	200
268	Tito Francona	5	5	5	5	6	12	40	200
269	Jack Meyer	5	5	5	5	6	12	25	150
270	Gil Hodges	5	5	8	20	30	50	100	550
271	Orlando Pena RC	5	5	5	5	6	25	60	
272	Jerry Lumpe	5	5	5	5	8	15	50	
273	Joey Jay	5	5	5	5	6	25	30	100
274	Jerry Kindall	5	5	5	5	6	12	25	120
275	Jack Sanford	5	5	5	5	6	15	50	200
276	Pete Daley	5	5	5	5	6	12	25	150
277	Turk Lown	5	5	5	5	6	12	30	200
278	Chuck Essegian	5	5	5	5	6	12	30	250
279	Ernie Johnson	5	5	5	5	6	12	25	120
280	Frank Bolling	5	5	5	5	6	12	175	400
281	Walt Craddock RC	5	5	5	5	6	12	30	200
282	R.C. Stevens	5	5	5	6	12	30	200	
283	Russ Heman RC	5	5	5	5	6	12	25	150
284	Steve Korcheck	5	5	5	5	6	12	30	200
285	Joe Cunningham	5	5	5	5	6	20	200	250
286	Dean Stone	5	5	5	5	6	20	250	
287	Don Zimmer	5	6	10	15	25	40	100	
288	Dutch Dotterer	5	5	5	5	6	12	30	200
289	Johnny Kucks	5	5	5	5	8	20	40	250
290	Wes Covington	5	5	5	5	6	12	40	200
291	Pitching Partners	5	5	5	5	8	15	30	200
292	Dick Williams	5	5	5	5	6	12	25	200
293	Ray Moore	5	5	5	5	6	20	80	
294	Hank Foiles	5	5	5	5	6	12	25	120
295	Billy Martin	6	10	15	25	40	60	100	
296	Ernie Broglio RC	5	5	5	5	6	12	20	150
297	Jackie Brandt RC	5	5	5	5	6	12	30	250
298	Tex Clevenger	5	5	5	5	6	12	25	150
299	Billy Klaus	5	5	5	5	6	12	40	250
300	Richie Ashburn	6	10	15	25	40	80	300	
301	Earl Averill Jr. RC	5	5	5	5	6	12	25	150
302	Don Mossi	5	5	5	5	6	25	50	
303	Marty Keough	5	5	5	5	6	12	30	250
304	Chicago Cubs CL	5	5	6	10	15	40	80	500
305	Curt Raydon RC	5	5	5	5	6	12	25	200
306	Jim Gilliam	5	5	5	6	10	25	50	250
307	Curt Barclay	5	5	5	5	6	20	40	
308	Norm Siebern	5	5	5	5	6	25	50	
309	Sal Maglie	5	5	5	5	8	15	40	300
310	Luis Aparicio	5	10	12	15	30	50	200	
311	Norm Zauchin	5	5	5	5	6	15	25	250
312	Don Newcombe	5	6	10	15	25	40	60	300
313	Frank House	5	5	5	5	6	12	30	200
314	Don Cardwell	5	5	5	5	6	12	25	150
315	Joe Adcock	5	5	5	5	8	15	30	200
316A	Ralph Lumenti Option	5	5	5	5	6	12	30	
316B	Ralph Lumenti No Option ERR	12	20	30	50	80			
317	NL Hitting Kings	10	20	30	40	50	80	150	800

#	Player	GD 2	VG 3	VgEx 4	EX 5	ExMt 6	NM 7	NmMt 8	MT 9
318	Rocky Bridges	5	5	5	5	6	20	25	200
319	Dave Hillman	5	5	5	5	6	15	50	250
320	Bob Skinner	5	5	5	5	10	20	60	250
321A	Bob Giallombardo Option RC	5	5	5	5	6	20	30	
321B	Bob Giallombardo No Option ERR	10	15	25	40	80	120		
322A	Harry Hanebrink Trade	5	5	5	5	6	15	80	
322B	Harry Hanebrink No Trade ERR	40	60	100	150	250			
323	Frank Sullivan	5	5	5	5	6	12	25	150
324	Don Demeter	5	5	5	5	6	15	60	300
325	Ken Boyer	5	5	5	6	20	30	80	
326	Marv Throneberry	5	5	5	5	8	25	50	300
327	Gary Bell RC	5	5	5	5	6	20	30	150
328	Lou Skizas	5	5	5	5	6	15	30	250
329	Detroit Tigers CL	5	5	6	10	15	50	60	200
330	Gus Triandos	5	5	5	5	6	25	250	
331	Steve Boros	5	5	5	5	6	12	30	250
332	Ray Monzant	5	5	5	5	6	12	25	120
333	Harry Simpson	5	5	5	5	6	12	40	250
334	Glen Hobbie	5	5	5	5	6	12	25	150
335	Johnny Temple	5	5	5	5	8	15	50	300
336A	Billy Loes Trade	5	5	5	5	6	12	40	300
336B	Billy Loes No Trade ERR	12	20	30	50	120	300		
337	George Crowe	5	5	5	5	6	20	40	200
338	Sparky Anderson RC	15	25	40	50	60	100	▲250	600
339	Roy Face	5	5	5	5	6	12	25	200
340	Roy Sievers	5	5	5	5	6	20	50	300
341	Tom Qualters	5	5	5	5	6	12	40	250
342	Ray Jablonski	5	5	5	5	6	12	25	150
343	Billy Hoeft	5	5	5	5	6	15	50	150
344	Russ Nixon	5	5	5	5	6	12	30	250
345	Gil McDougald	5	5	6	10	15	30	100	
346	Batter Bafflers	5	5	5	5	8	20	30	200
347	Bob Buhl	5	5	5	5	8	20	80	
348	Ted Lepcio	5	5	5	5	6	12	25	150
349	Hoyt Wilhelm	5	8	12	20	30	50	100	300
350	Ernie Banks	25	40	50	80	100	200	400	▲2,000
351	Earl Torgeson	5	5	5	5	6	15	40	
352	Robin Roberts	▼6	▼10	▼15	25	▲40	▲60	100	500
353	Curt Flood	5	5	8	12	20	30	100	200
354	Pete Burnside	5	5	5	5	6	12	30	200
355	Jimmy Piersall	5	5	5	5	8	25	80	
356	Bob Mabe RC	5	5	5	5	6	12	25	150
357	Dick Stuart RC	5	5	6	10	15	25	40	150
358	Ralph Terry	5	5	5	5	6	12	40	300
359	Bill White RC	5	5	8	12	20	30	50	250
360	Al Kaline	10	25	30	50	60	100	250	1,800
361	Willard Nixon	5	5	5	5	6	12	25	120
362A	Dolan Nichols Option RC	5	5	5	5	6	12	30	
362B	Dolan Nichols No Option ERR	12	20	30	50	80	275		
363	Bobby Avila	5	5	5	6	10	30	150	
364	Danny McDevitt	5	5	5	5	6	12	30	150
365	Gus Bell	5	5	6	10	15	25	40	200
366	Humberto Robinson	5	5	5	5	6	15	40	200
367	Cal Neeman	5	5	5	5	6	12	25	200
368	Don Mueller	5	5	5	5	6	25	40	200
369	Dick Tomanek	5	5	5	5	6	12	25	250
370	Pete Runnels	5	5	5	5	6	20	30	
371	Dick Brodowski	5	5	5	5	6	12	25	150
372	Jim Hegan	5	5	5	5	8	30	400	
373	Herb Plews	5	5	5	5	6	12	30	
374	Art Ditmar	5	5	5	5	8	25	100	
375	Bob Nieman	5	5	5	5	6	15	25	250
376	Hal Naragon	5	5	5	5	6	12	25	120
377	John Antonelli	5	5	5	5	6	12	30	150
378	Gail Harris	5	5	5	5	6	12	25	120
379	Bob Miller	5	5	5	5	6	12	25	120
380	Hank Aaron	50	60	100	150	200	500	▲2,000	6,000
381	Mike Baxes	5	5	5	5	6	12	25	150

	GD 2	VG 3	VgEx 4	EX 5	ExMt 6	NM 7	NmMt 8	MT 9
32 Curt Simmons	5	5	5	5	6	12	30	120
33 Words of Wisdom	5	5	5	8	20	40	100	300
34 Dave Sisler	5	5	5	5	6	12	25	150
35 Sherm Lollar	5	5	5	8	12	20	30	120
36 Jim Delsing	5	5	5	5	6	12	30	250
37 Don Drysdale	6	10	15	25	40	60	120	500
38 Bob Will RC	5	5	5	5	6	12	25	120
39 Joe Nuxhall	5	5	6	10	15	25	80	150
40 Orlando Cepeda	5	10	12	15	30	60	100	400
41 Milt Pappas	5	5	6	10	15	25	40	200
42 Whitey Herzog	5	5	6	10	15	25	40	120
43 Frank Lary	5	5	5	5	6	15	30	150
44 Randy Jackson	5	5	5	5	6	12	25	150
45 Elston Howard	5	8	12	20	30	50	▲120	300
46 Bob Rush	5	5	5	5	6	12	25	250
47 Washington Senators CL	5	5	6	10	15	25	40	150
48 Wally Post	5	5	5	8	12	20	30	120
49 Larry Jackson	5	5	5	5	6	12	25	120
50 Jackie Jensen	5	5	5	5	8	30	60	400
51 Ron Blackburn	5	5	5	5	6	12	30	120
52 Hector Lopez	5	5	5	8	12	20	30	120
53 Clem Labine	5	5	5	5	6	12	30	200
54 Hank Sauer	5	5	5	5	6	12	30	200
55 Roy McMillan	5	5	5	5	6	12	25	120
56 Solly Drake	5	5	5	5	6	12	25	120
57 Moe Drabowsky	5	5	5	5	6	15	25	120
58 Keystone Combo	5	5	5	8	25	40	80	300
59 Gus Zernial	5	5	5	8	12	20	30	100
60 Billy Pierce	5	5	5	5	8	15	40	200
61 Whitey Lockman	5	5	5	5	6	12	25	120
62 Stan Lopata	5	5	5	5	6	12	25	150
63 Camilo Pascual	5	5	5	5	6	12	30	200
64 Dale Long	5	5	5	5	6	12	25	120
65 Bill Mazeroski	5	5	5	20	25	50	80	250
66 Haywood Sullivan	5	5	20	25	30	50	100	500
67 Virgil Trucks	5	5	5	5	6	15	30	100
68 Gino Cimoli	5	5	5	5	6	12	25	120
69 Milwaukee Braves CL	5	5	5	6	10	25	60	200
70 Rocky Colavito	5	8	12	20	30	40	100	300
71 Herman Wehmeier	5	5	5	5	6	12	25	120
72 Hobie Landrith	5	5	5	5	6	12	25	150
73 Bob Grim	5	5	5	5	6	15	25	120
74 Ken Aspromonte	5	5	5	5	6	12	25	80
75 Del Crandall	5	5	5	5	6	20	30	120
76 Gerry Staley	5	5	5	5	6	15	30	120
77 Charlie Neal	5	5	5	5	8	25	50	300
78 Buc Hill Aces	5	5	5	5	6	20	25	150
79 Bobby Thomson	5	5	5	8	12	30	50	150
80 Whitey Ford	20	30	50	60	▲100	120	300	1,000
81 Whammy Douglas	5	5	5	5	6	12	30	200
82 Smoky Burgess	5	5	5	5	6	20	40	200
83 Billy Harrell	5	5	5	5	6	12	25	120
84 Hal Griggs	5	5	5	5	6	12	20	80
85 Frank Robinson	▲30	▲50	▲80	▲100	▲120	▲200	300	1,000
86 Granny Hamner	5	5	5	5	6	15	25	120
87 Ike Delock	5	5	5	5	6	12	25	120
88 Sammy Esposito	5	5	5	5	6	12	25	150
89 Brooks Robinson	▲30	▲50	▲60	▲80	100	120	300	1,500
90 Lew Burdette	5	6	10	15	25	40	60	250
91 John Roseboro	5	5	5	5	8	25	50	300
92 Ray Narleski	5	5	5	5	6	15	40	
93 Daryl Spencer	5	5	5	5	8	25	120	
94 Ron Hansen RC	5	5	5	5	6	12	40	150
95 Cal McLish	5	5	5	5	8	60	450	
96 Rocky Nelson	5	5	5	5	6	12	30	150
97 Bob Anderson	5	5	5	5	6	12	25	150
98 Vada Pinson	5	6	10	15	25	30	60	250
99 Tom Gorman	5	5	5	5	6	12	80	250

	GD 2	VG 3	VgEx 4	EX 5	ExMt 6	NM 7	NmMt 8	MT 9
450 Eddie Mathews	8	20	30	40	60	200	600	
451 Jimmy Constable RC	5	5	5	5	6	12	30	250
452 Chico Fernandez	5	5	5	5	6	15	30	120
453 Les Moss	5	5	5	5	6	12	30	150
454 Phil Clark	5	5	5	5	6	12	40	250
455 Larry Doby	6	10	15	25	40	60	150	800
456 Jerry Casale RC	5	5	5	5	6	12	30	200
457 Los Angeles Dodgers CL	5	5	5	8	30	50	120	500
458 Gordon Jones	5	5	5	5	6	12	25	200
459 Bill Tuttle	5	5	5	5	6	15	30	200
460 Bob Friend	5	5	5	5	8	20	40	
461 Mickey Mantle BT	40	50	60	100	120	200	500	1,200
462 Rocky Colavito BT	5	5	8	12	20	30	60	250
463 Al Kaline BT	6	10	15	25	40	60	100	250
464 Willie Mays BT	15	25	30	50	60	100	300	▲4,000
465 Roy Sievers BT	5	5	5	5	6	15	50	300
466 Billy Pierce BT	5	5	5	5	6	15	60	300
467 Hank Aaron BT	10	15	25	40	50	80	250	600
468 Duke Snider BT	5	5	5	10	15	20	60	300
469 Ernie Banks BT	8	12	20	30	50	60	100	300
470 Stan Musial BT	8	12	20	30	50	60	120	600
471 Tom Sturdivant	5	5	5	5	8	25	120	
472 Gene Freese	5	5	5	5	6	20	80	250
473 Mike Fornieles	5	5	5	5	6	15	30	
474 Moe Thacker RC	5	5	5	5	6	15	50	250
475 Jack Harshman	5	5	5	5	6	15	100	
476 Cleveland Indians CL	5	5	5	6	20	25	100	300
477 Barry Latman RC	5	5	5	5	6	12	25	150
478 Roberto Clemente	50	80	120	200	300	600	▲1,500	5,000
479 Lindy McDaniel	5	5	5	5	6	25	200	300
480 Red Schoendienst	5	5	15	25	40	100	300	
481 Charlie Maxwell	5	5	5	5	6	25	120	
482 Russ Meyer	5	5	5	5	6	12	30	250
483 Clint Courtney	5	5	5	5	6	12	25	150
484 Willie Kirkland	5	5	5	5	6	12	40	200
485 Ryne Duren	5	5	5	5	8	20	60	250
486 Sammy White	5	5	5	5	6	12	25	120
487 Hal Brown	5	5	5	5	6	12	80	300
488 Walt Moryn	5	5	5	5	6	12	60	150
489 John Powers	5	5	5	5	6	12	40	
490 Frank Thomas	5	5	5	5	6	20	30	
491 Don Blasingame	5	5	5	5	6	12	30	250
492 Gene Conley	5	5	5	5	6	12	25	150
493 Jim Landis	5	5	5	5	6	12	40	200
494 Don Pavletich RC	5	5	5	5	6	15	30	300
495 Johnny Podres	5	5	8	12	20	30	50	250
496 Wayne Terwilliger	5	5	5	5	6	25	30	250
497 Hal R. Smith	5	5	5	5	6	15	30	150
498 Dick Hyde	5	5	5	5	6	12	50	250
499 Johnny O'Brien	5	5	5	5	6	15	60	
500 Vic Wertz	5	5	5	5	10	30	300	
501 Bob Tiefenauer RC	5	5	5	5	6	12	25	250
502 Alvin Dark	5	5	5	5	6	15	50	200
503 Jim Owens	5	5	5	5	6	15	80	
504 Ossie Alvarez RC	5	5	5	5	6	20	80	250
505 Tony Kubek	5	5	6	10	25	50	120	400
506 Bob Purkey	5	5	5	5	6	15	60	200
507 Bob Hale	5	5	5	6	25	30	60	
508 Art Fowler	5	6	10	15	25	30	60	
509 Norm Cash RC	15	25	40	50	80	120	300	
510 New York Yankees CL	20	30	50	80	120	200	400	1,200
511 George Susce	5	5	5	6	25	30	80	300
512 George Altman RC	5	5	5	6	10	40	60	300
513 Tommy Carroll	5	5	5	6	10	20	40	200
514 Bob Gibson RC	500	600	800	1,000	▲1,500	▲3,000	▲8,000	▲30,000
515 Harmon Killebrew	▲30	▲50	▲80	▲120	▲200	▲300	500	5,000
516 Mike Garcia	5	5	6	10	15	30	80	300
517 Joe Koppe RC	5	5	5	6	10	30	60	

#		GD 2	VG 3	VgEx 4	EX 5	ExMt 6	NM 7	NmMt 8	MT 9
518	Mike Cuellar RC	6	10	15	25	40	60	150	600
519	Infield Power	5	5	8	12	20	80	400	
520	Don Elston	5	5	5	6	10	40	80	250
521	Gary Geiger	5	5	5	6	20	30	50	
522	Gene Snyder RC	5	5	5	6	20	50	60	250
523	Harry Bright RC	5	5	5	6	10	25	50	300
524	Larry Osborne RC	5	5	5	6	10	25	60	
525	Jim Coates RC	5	5	6	10	15	40	100	400
526	Bob Speake	5	5	5	6	10	20	60	
527	Solly Hemus	5	5	5	6	10	25	60	250
528	Pittsburgh Pirates CL	5	8	12	20	50	100	150	600
529	George Bamberger RC	5	5	5	6	25	30	80	250
530	Wally Moon	5	5	8	12	30	50	120	
531	Ray Webster RC	5	5	5	6	10	25	50	200
532	Mark Freeman RC	5	5	5	6	10	20	50	250
533	Darrell Johnson	5	5	6	10	15	▲80	▲120	
534	Faye Throneberry	5	5	5	6	10	25	100	400
535	Ruben Gomez	5	5	5	6	20	30	60	250
536	Danny Kravitz	5	5	5	6	10	20	50	
537	Rodolfo Arias RC	5	5	5	6	10	30	120	500
538	Chick King	5	5	5	6	25	30	80	400
539	Gary Blaylock RC	5	5	5	6	10	40	200	400
540	Willie Miranda	5	6	10	15	25	40	60	
541	Bob Thurman	5	5	5	6	10	20	60	200
542	Jim Perry RC	5	5	8	12	20	60	100	500
543	Corsair Trio	5	15	40	50	60	100	200	1,000
544	Lee Tate RC	5	5	6	10	15	25	60	200
545	Tom Morgan	5	5	5	6	10	30	40	
546	Al Schroll	5	5	5	6	10	20	50	250
547	Jim Baxes RC	5	5	5	8	12	40	120	
548	Elmer Singleton	5	5	5	8	25	50	300	
549	Howie Nunn RC	5	5	5	6	10	30	50	200
550	Roy Campanella Courage	25	40	60	100	150	300	1,000	2,500
551	Fred Haney AS MG	5	5	5	8	12	25	80	400
552	Casey Stengel AS MG	5	6	10	15	25	60	150	
553	Orlando Cepeda AS	5	15	20	25	40	60	150	
554	Bill Skowron AS	5	6	10	15	30	40	250	
555	Bill Mazeroski AS	5	5	8	12	40	50	100	400
556	Nellie Fox AS	5	6	10	20	25	50	150	
557	Ken Boyer AS	5	5	8	25	30	50	100	500
558	Frank Malzone AS	5	5	5	6	15	30	80	250
559	Ernie Banks AS	5	20	30	40	60	100	250	2,000
560	Luis Aparicio AS	5	6	10	15	30	50	200	
561	Hank Aaron AS	30	40	60	80	100	150	400	
562	Al Kaline AS	5	8	12	30	50	80	200	600
563	Willie Mays AS	25	40	50	60	100	150	400	1,200
564	Mickey Mantle AS	100	120	150	200	300	400	▲1,500	3,000
565	Wes Covington AS	5	5	5	6	10	40	80	250
566	Roy Sievers AS	5	5	5	6	10	40	80	300
567	Del Crandall AS	5	5	5	6	20	30	150	
568	Gus Triandos AS	5	5	5	6	10	30	120	200
569	Bob Friend AS	5	5	5	6	12	80	200	
570	Bob Turley AS	5	5	6	10	15	40	150	
571	Warren Spahn AS	5	8	12	20	50	80	150	1,000
572	Billy Pierce AS	5	5	8	30	100	250		

— Hank Aaron #380 PSA 10 (Gem) sold for $27,126 (Goodwin; 11/12)
— Norm Cash #509 PSA 10 (Gem) (Young Collection) sold for $6,544 (SCP; 5/12)
— Bob Gibson #514 PSA 10 (Gem) (Young Collection) sold for $53,759 (SCP; 5/12)
— Elston Howard #395 PSA 10 (Gem) sold for $4,158 (eBay; 8/12)
— Warren Spahn 1921 #40C PSA 10 (Gem) sold for $4,613 (eBay; 9/12)

1960 Fleer

#		GD 2	VG 3	VgEx 4	EX 5	ExMt 6	NM 7	NmMt 8	MT 9
1	Napoleon Lajoie DP	6	6	8	20	25	40	150	
2	Christy Mathewson	5	5	8	12	20	40	60	
3	Babe Ruth	50	50	80	100	200	250	500	600
4	Carl Hubbell	5	5	5	5	8	15	40	200

#		GD 2	VG 3	VgEx 4	EX 5	ExMt 6	NM 7	NmMt 8	MT 9
5	Grover C. Alexander	5	5	5	5	8	15	60	700
6	Walter Johnson DP	5	5	5	8	15	40	60	150
7	Chief Bender	5	5	5	5	6	12	20	175
8	Roger Bresnahan	8	8	8	8	10	20	30	135
9	Mordecai Brown	8	8	8	8	10	20	30	350
10	Tris Speaker	5	5	5	5	6	12	30	200
11	Arky Vaughan DP	5	5	5	5	6	12	25	
12	Zach Wheat	6	6	6	8	15	25	150	
13	George Sisler	6	6	6	8	15	20	120	
14	Connie Mack	5	5	5	5	10	20	40	
15	Clark Griffith	5	5	5	5	6	12	40	
16	Lou Boudreau DP	5	5	5	5	6	12	40	
17	Ernie Lombardi	6	6	6	6	8	15	25	80
18	Heinie Manush	6	6	6	6	8	15	30	200
19	Marty Marion	5	5	5	5	6	12	25	
20	Eddie Collins DP	5	5	5	5	6	12	20	80
21	Rabbit Maranville DP	6	6	6	6	8	15	20	200
22	Joe Medwick	5	5	5	5	6	12	25	100
23	Ed Barrow	5	5	5	5	6	12	25	
24	Mickey Cochrane	5	5	5	6	12	20	30	
25	Jimmy Collins	5	5	5	5	6	12	30	300
26	Bob Feller DP	6	6	6	10	20	30	60	150
27	Luke Appling	5	5	5	5	6	12	25	120
28	Lou Gehrig	▲15	▲25	30	50	80	120	200	600
29	Gabby Hartnett	6	6	6	6	8	15	20	80
30	Chuck Klein	5	5	5	5	6	12	20	100
31	Tony Lazzeri DP	6	6	6	6	8	15	40	135
32	Al Simmons	6	6	6	6	8	15	40	120
33	Wilbert Robinson	6	6	6	6	8	15	40	150
34	Sam Rice	5	5	5	5	6	12	20	150
35	Herb Pennock	5	5	5	5	6	12	20	200
36	Mel Ott DP	5	5	5	8	12	20	60	150
37	Lefty O'Doul	5	5	5	5	6	12	20	200
38	Johnny Mize	5	5	6	10	15	25	50	135
39	Bing Miller	6	6	6	6	8	15	20	120
40	Joe Tinker	5	5	5	5	6	12	20	120
41	Frank Baker DP	5	5	5	5	6	12	40	200
42	Ty Cobb	▲12	▲20	▲30	▲50	▲80	▲120	▲200	▼250
43	Paul Derringer	5	5	5	5	6	12	30	150
44	Cap Anson	5	5	5	5	10	20	40	200
45	Jim Bottomley	5	5	5	5	6	12	25	150
46	Eddie Plank DP	6	6	6	6	8	15	25	100
47	Cy Young	6	8	12	20	30	40	80	200
48	Hack Wilson	5	5	5	5	6	20	25	50
49	Ed Walsh	5	5	5	5	6	12	20	100
50	Frank Chance	6	6	6	6	8	15	20	100
51	Dazzy Vance DP	6	6	6	6	8	15	20	150
52	Bill Terry	5	5	5	5	6	12	25	120
53	Jimmie Foxx	▼5	▼5	6	▲10	15	30	100	▲200
54	Lefty Gomez	▼5	▼5	▼5	8	▲12	20	25	120
55	Branch Rickey	6	6	6	6	8	15	25	175
56	Ray Schalk DP	5	5	5	5	6	12	25	150
57	Johnny Evers	5	5	5	5	6	12	25	100
58	Charley Gehringer	6	6	6	6	8	25	30	150
59	Burleigh Grimes	6	6	6	6	10	20	25	150
60	Lefty Grove	6	6	6	6	8	15	40	150
61	Rube Waddell DP	5	5	5	5	6	12	25	
62	Honus Wagner	▲8	▲12	▲20	▲30	▲50	▲80	▲200	300
63	Red Ruffing	5	5	5	5	8	15	30	80
64	Kenesaw M. Landis	5	5	5	5	6	12	20	150
65	Harry Heilmann	6	6	6	6	8	15	25	150
66	John McGraw DP	5	5	5	5	6	12	20	150
67	Hughie Jennings	5	5	5	5	6	12	20	150
68	Hal Newhouser	5	5	5	5	6	12	25	200
69	Waite Hoyt	5	5	5	5	6	12	25	150
70	Bobo Newsom	6	6	6	6	8	15	25	
71	Earl Averill DP	6	6	6	6	8	15	40	250
72	Ted Williams	▲40	▲60	▲80	▲100	▲120	200	▲400	100

	GD 2	VG 3	VgEx 4	EX 5	ExMt 6	NM 7	NmMt 8	MT 9
3 Warren Giles	5	5	5	5	6	12	25	150
4 Ford Frick	5	5	5	5	6	12	30	250
5 Kiki Cuyler	5	5	5	5	6	12	20	625
6 Paul Waner DP	5	5	5	5	6	12	25	225
7 Pie Traynor	5	5	5	5	6	12	40	200
8 Lloyd Waner	5	5	5	5	6	12	30	200
9 Ralph Kiner	5	5	5	5	6	15	80	

1960 Leaf

	GD 2	VG 3	VgEx 4	EX 5	ExMt 6	NM 7	NmMt 8	MT 9
7 Brooks Robinson	5	8	12	20	60	100	200	
7 Duke Snider	5	6	10	15	40	50	100	
25 Sparky Anderson	8	12	20	30	50	250	400	
28 Orlando Cepeda	6	10	15	25	40	60	120	
44 Jim Bunning	6	10	15	25	40	60	135	

1960 Topps

	GD 2	VG 3	VgEx 4	EX 5	ExMt 6	NM 7	NmMt 8	MT 9
Early Wynn	5	5	12	25	50	200	600	
Roman Mejias	5	5	5	6	10	50	150	
Joe Adcock	5	5	6	10	15	25	40	
Bob Purkey	5	5	5	6	10	20	30	100
Wally Moon	5	5	5	5	6	15	50	
Lou Berberet	5	5	5	5	5	20		
Master and Mentor	5	15	20	25	30	40	80	500
Bud Daley	5	5	5	5	5	15	25	150
Faye Throneberry	5	5	5	5	8	15	40	
Ernie Banks	25	40	50	60	100	250	500	
Norm Siebern	5	5	5	6	10	15	30	150
Milt Pappas	5	5	5	6	10	15	30	150
Wally Post	5	5	5	8	12	20	30	
Jim Grant	5	5	6	10	15	25	200	
Pete Runnels	5	5	5	5	5	15	25	150
Ernie Broglio	5	5	5	6	10	15	30	120
Johnny Callison	5	5	5	8	12	20	30	150
Los Angeles Dodgers CL	5	6	10	15	25	60	250	
Felix Mantilla	5	5	5	5	8	25	120	
Roy Face	5	5	5	8	12	20	30	200
Dutch Dotterer	5	5	5	5	8	25	200	
Rocky Bridges	5	5	5	5	5	15	25	150
Eddie Fisher RC	5	5	5	6	10	15	80	
Dick Gray	5	5	5	5	5	15	40	150
Roy Sievers	5	5	5	5	5	15	30	
Wayne Terwilliger	5	5	5	5	8	30	200	
Dick Drott	5	5	5	5	8	40	120	
Brooks Robinson	10	20	30	60	80	▲200	400	2,500
Clem Labine	5	5	5	6	10	15	30	
Tito Francona	5	5	5	8	12	30	80	150
Sammy Esposito	5	5	5	5	5	15	25	150
Sophomore Stalwarts	5	5	5	5	6	15	50	200
Tom Morgan	5	5	5	5	8	25	120	300
Sparky Anderson	5	5	8	12	20	30	250	
Whitey Ford	25	40	▲60	▲100	▲120	▲200	300	800
Russ Nixon	5	5	5	6	10	15	25	150
Bill Bruton	5	5	5	5	5	15	25	
Jerry Casale	5	5	5	5	5	15	80	
Earl Averill Jr.	5	5	5	8	12	20	25	150
Joe Cunningham	5	5	5	6	10	15	25	150
Barry Latman	5	5	5	5	5	15	30	
Hobie Landrith	5	5	5	5	8	15	25	
Washington Senators CL	5	5	5	8	15	250	400	
Bobby Locke RC	5	5	5	6	10	20	250	400
Roy McMillan	5	5	5	5	6	12	25	150
Jack Fisher RC	5	5	5	5	5	15	40	150
Don Zimmer	5	5	5	8	15	25	40	250
Hal W. Smith	5	5	5	5	5	15	30	175
Curt Raydon	5	5	5	5	5	15	60	200

	GD 2	VG 3	VgEx 4	EX 5	ExMt 6	NM 7	NmMt 8	MT 9
50 Al Kaline	20	25	30	50	60	120	400	
51 Jim Coates	5	5	5	5	10	20	40	200
52 Dave Philley	5	5	5	5	5	15	120	
53 Jackie Brandt	5	5	5	5	5	15	25	150
54 Mike Fornieles	5	5	5	5	5	15	30	150
55 Bill Mazeroski	10	15	25	40	60	▲120	400	1,200
56 Steve Korcheck	5	5	5	5	5	15	25	150
57 Win Savers	5	5	5	5	8	15	60	150
58 Gino Cimoli	5	5	5	5	5	15	30	200
59 Juan Pizarro	5	5	5	5	8	15	25	100
60 Gus Triandos	5	5	5	5	5	15	25	120
61 Eddie Kasko	5	5	5	5	5	15	30	150
62 Roger Craig	5	5	5	8	12	20	30	150
63 George Strickland	5	5	5	5	5	15	25	100
64 Jack Meyer	5	5	5	5	5	15	60	120
65 Elston Howard	5	5	5	8	20	40	80	350
66 Bob Trowbridge	5	5	5	5	5	15	40	150
67 Jose Pagan RC	5	5	5	6	10	15	30	120
68 Dave Hillman	5	5	5	5	5	15	25	120
69 Billy Goodman	5	5	5	5	5	15	20	
70 Lew Burdette	5	5	5	6	10	15	30	200
71 Marty Keough	5	5	5	5	5	15	25	150
72 Detroit Tigers CL	5	5	6	10	15	60	120	400
73 Bob Gibson	30	50	60	120	150	▲400	1,000	6,000
74 Walt Moryn	5	5	5	5	5	15	25	100
75 Vic Power	5	5	5	5	6	15	40	150
76 Bill Fischer	5	5	5	5	5	15	30	150
77 Hank Foiles	5	5	5	5	5	15	25	120
78 Bob Grim	5	5	5	5	5	15	150	250
79 Walt Dropo	5	5	5	5	5	15	25	
80 Johnny Antonelli	5	5	5	5	6	15	25	120
81 Russ Snyder RC	5	5	5	5	5	15	25	150
82 Ruben Gomez	5	5	5	5	6	15	30	120
83 Tony Kubek	5	5	6	15	20	50	300	
84 Hal R. Smith	5	5	5	5	5	15	30	100
85 Frank Lary	5	5	5	5	5	15	25	100
86 Dick Gernert	5	5	5	5	5	25	80	120
87 John Romonosky	5	5	5	5	5	15	25	
88 John Roseboro	5	5	5	5	6	15	30	
89 Hal Brown	5	5	5	8	12	20	50	
90 Bobby Avila	5	5	5	6	10	15	40	
91 Bennie Daniels	5	5	5	5	5	25	80	120
92 Whitey Herzog	5	5	6	10	15	25	30	150
93 Art Schult	5	5	5	6	10	15	25	100
94 Leo Kiely	5	5	5	5	8	20	120	
95 Frank Thomas	5	5	5	6	10	15	25	175
96 Ralph Terry	5	5	5	5	8	20	50	300
97 Ted Lepcio	5	5	5	5	5	15	50	200
98 Gordon Jones	5	5	5	5	5	15	80	
99 Lenny Green	5	5	5	6	10	15	25	200
100 Nellie Fox	5	10	15	25	40	50	100	500
101 Bob Miller RC	5	5	5	5	5	15	25	150
102 Kent Hadley	5	5	5	5	5	15	100	
103 Dick Farrell	5	5	5	5	5	15	50	150
104 Dick Schofield	5	5	5	5	5	15	50	200
105 Larry Sherry RC	5	5	5	5	8	15	25	
106 Billy Gardner	5	5	5	5	5	15	150	
107 Carlton Willey	5	5	5	5	5	15	25	
108 Pete Daley	5	5	5	5	5	15	25	100
109 Clete Boyer	5	5	▲8	▲12	20	40	▲150	400
110 Cal McLish	5	5	5	5	5	15	100	
111 Vic Wertz	5	5	5	5	8	30	400	
112 Jack Harshman	5	5	5	5	5	15	20	
113 Bob Skinner	5	5	5	5	5	15	40	100
114 Ken Aspromonte	5	5	5	5	5	15	150	
115 Fork and Knuckler	5	5	5	6	10	15	30	200
116 Jim Rivera	5	5	5	8	12	30	600	
117 Tom Borland RS	5	5	5	5	5	15	25	100

#	Player	GD 2	VG 3	VgEx 4	EX 5	ExMt 6	NM 7	NmMt 8	MT 9
118	Bob Bruce RS RC	5	5	5	5	5	15	25	150
119	Chico Cardenas RS RC	5	5	5	5	10	25	30	120
120	Duke Carmel RS RC	5	5	5	5	8	15	25	
121	Camilo Carreon RS RC	5	5	5	5	5	15	25	120
122	Don Dillard RS	5	5	5	5	5	15	20	100
123	Dan Dobbek RS	5	5	5	5	5	15	25	150
124	Jim Donohue RS RC	5	5	5	5	5	15	25	100
125	Dick Ellsworth RS RC	5	5	5	5	5	15	25	150
126	Chuck Estrada RS RC	5	5	5	6	10	15	25	200
127	Ron Hansen RS	5	5	5	5	5	15	25	100
128	Bill Harris RS RC	5	5	5	5	5	15	25	100
129	Bob Hartman RS	5	5	5	5	5	15	25	100
130	Frank Herrera RS	5	5	5	5	5	15	25	150
131	Ed Hobaugh RS RC	5	5	5	5	5	15	25	100
132	Frank Howard RS RC	6	10	15	25	40	100	200	
133	Julian Javier RS RC	5	5	5	5	6	15	30	120
134	Deron Johnson RS	5	5	5	5	6	15	30	120
135	Ken Johnson RS RC	5	5	5	5	5	15	25	100
136	Jim Kaat RS RC	▲20	▲30	50	▲80	▲120	▲250	▲600	
137	Lou Klimchock RS RC	5	5	5	5	5	15	25	120
138	Art Mahaffey RS RC	5	5	5	5	5	15	25	100
139	Carl Mathias RS RC	5	5	5	5	5	15	25	120
140	Julio Navarro RS RC	5	5	5	5	5	10	25	100
141	Jim Proctor RS RC	5	5	5	5	5	10	25	120
142	Bill Short RS RC	5	5	5	5	6	15	30	250
143	Al Spangler RS RC	5	5	5	5	5	15	25	150
144	Al Stieglitz RS RC	5	5	5	5	6	15	40	150
145	Jim Umbricht RS RC	5	5	5	5	8	15	25	200
146	Ted Wieand RS RC	5	5	5	5	5	15	25	100
147	Bob Will RS	5	5	5	6	10	15	40	150
148	Carl Yastrzemski RS RC	200	250	▲400	▲500	600	▲1,200	3,000	20,000
149	Bob Nieman	5	5	5	5	5	10	20	120
150	Billy Pierce	5	5	5	5	6	20	50	175
151	San Francisco Giants CL	5	5	5	5	25	30	400	800
152	Gail Harris	5	5	5	5	5	15	30	150
153	Bobby Thomson	5	5	6	10	15	25	50	200
154	Jim Davenport	5	5	5	6	10	15	120	
155	Charlie Neal	5	5	5	5	6	20	30	200
156	Art Ceccarelli	5	5	5	5	5	10	25	120
157	Rocky Nelson	5	5	5	5	5	15	30	150
158	Wes Covington	5	5	5	5	5	15	30	
159	Jim Piersall	5	5	5	8	12	20	60	120
160	Rival All-Stars	30	50	60	80	100	200	400	800
161	Ray Narleski	5	5	5	5	5	15	25	200
162	Sammy Taylor	5	5	5	5	5	15	40	
163	Hector Lopez	5	5	5	5	20	25	200	250
164	Cincinnati Reds CL	5	5	5	8	12	20	40	150
165	Jack Sanford	5	5	6	10	15	25	40	100
166	Chuck Essegian	5	5	5	5	5	12	25	
167	Valmy Thomas	5	5	5	5	5	15	25	120
168	Alex Grammas	5	5	5	5	5	15	25	125
169	Jake Striker RC	5	5	5	5	5	15	25	150
170	Del Crandall	5	5	5	8	12	40	150	
171	Johnny Groth	5	5	5	5	5	12	25	100
172	Willie Kirkland	5	5	5	5	5	15	20	150
173	Billy Martin	5	6	10	15	25	50	80	250
174	Cleveland Indians CL	5	5	5	5	6	25	60	200
175	Pedro Ramos	5	5	5	5	5	15	25	120
176	Vada Pinson	5	5	6	10	15	25	300	
177	Johnny Kucks	5	5	5	5	5	15	100	
178	Woody Held	5	5	5	6	10	15	25	100
179	Rip Coleman	5	5	5	5	5	15	25	100
180	Harry Simpson	5	5	5	5	5	15	25	120
181	Billy Loes	5	5	5	5	8	15	25	120
182	Glen Hobbie	5	5	5	5	5	15	25	150
183	Eli Grba RC	5	5	5	5	6	15	30	200
184	Gary Geiger	5	5	5	5	5	15	25	100
185	Jim Owens	5	5	5	5	5	15	100	150

#	Player	GD 2	VG 3	VgEx 4	EX 5	ExMt 6	NM 7	NmMt 8	MT 9
186	Dave Sisler	5	5	5	5	5	15	25	
187	Jay Hook RC	5	5	5	5	5	15	25	150
188	Dick Williams	5	5	5	5	5	15	25	100
189	Don McMahon	5	5	5	5	5	15	25	150
190	Gene Woodling	5	5	5	5	5	15	25	
191	Johnny Klippstein	5	5	5	6	10	15	60	
192	Danny O'Connell	5	5	5	5	5	15	25	100
193	Dick Hyde	5	5	5	5	5	15	25	100
194	Bobby Gene Smith	5	5	5	5	5	20	80	
195	Lindy McDaniel	5	5	5	5	5	15	25	100
196	Andy Carey	5	5	5	5	6	30	60	
197	Ron Kline	5	5	5	5	5	15	40	120
198	Jerry Lynch	5	5	5	5	5	15	25	100
199	Dick Donovan	5	5	5	5	5	15	40	200
200	Willie Mays	50	60	80	120	200	300	▲2,500	▲12,000
201	Larry Osborne	5	5	5	5	5	15	25	100
202	Fred Kipp	5	5	5	5	5	15	25	150
203	Sammy White	5	5	5	5	5	15	25	120
204	Ryne Duren	5	6	10	15	25	50		
205	Johnny Logan	5	5	5	5	5	20	25	200
206	Claude Osteen	5	5	5	5	5	15	40	
207	Bob Boyd	5	5	5	5	5	15	25	80
208	Chicago White Sox CL	5	5	5	5	8	15	80	200
209	Ron Blackburn	5	5	5	5	5	15	25	150
210	Harmon Killebrew	15	25	50	60	80	150	300	
211	Taylor Phillips	5	5	5	5	5	15	25	150
212	Walter Alston MG	5	5	6	10	20	25	50	150
213	Chuck Dressen MG	5	5	5	5	5	15	50	
214	Jimmy Dykes MG	5	5	5	5	8	15	20	
215	Bob Elliott MG	5	5	5	5	5	15	25	100
216	Joe Gordon MG	5	5	5	5	6	20	30	120
217	Charlie Grimm MG	5	5	5	5	5	15	25	120
218	Solly Hemus MG	5	5	5	5	5	15	25	150
219	Fred Hutchinson MG	5	5	5	5	5	20	30	120
220	Billy Jurges MG	5	5	5	5	8	80	300	
221	Cookie Lavagetto MG	5	5	5	5	5	15	25	120
222	Al Lopez MG	5	5	5	5	15	30	80	250
223	Danny Murtaugh MG	5	5	8	12	20	100		
224	Paul Richards MG	5	5	5	5	5	15	200	500
225	Bill Rigney MG	5	5	5	5	5	15	25	120
226	Eddie Sawyer MG	5	5	5	5	5	15	40	150
227	Casey Stengel MG	6	10	15	25	40	60	200	
228	Ernie Johnson	5	5	5	5	6	15	30	200
229	Joe M. Morgan RC	5	5	5	5	5	15	20	100
230	Mound Magicians	5	5	10	12	20	50	120	300
231	Hal Naragon	5	5	5	5	5	15	25	120
232	Jim Busby	5	5	5	5	5	10	15	175
233	Don Elston	5	5	5	5	5	15	25	120
234	Don Demeter	5	5	5	5	5	20	25	120
235	Gus Bell	5	5	5	5	5	15	30	
236	Dick Ricketts	5	5	5	5	5	15	25	150
237	Elmer Valo	5	5	5	5	10	30	250	
238	Danny Kravitz	5	5	5	5	5	15	25	200
239	Joe Shipley	5	5	5	5	5	15	80	
240	Luis Aparicio	5	5	15	20	30	50	150	500
241	Albie Pearson	5	5	5	5	5	15	25	150
242	St. Louis Cardinals CL	5	5	5	5	8	30	100	
243	Bubba Phillips	5	5	5	5	5	15	25	100
244	Hal Griggs	5	5	5	5	5	15	25	150
245	Eddie Yost	5	5	5	5	6	15	80	
246	Lee Maye RC	5	5	5	5	8	20	80	200
247	Gil McDougald	5	5	5	6	10	25	50	250
248	Del Rice	5	5	5	5	5	15	25	120
249	Earl Wilson RC	5	5	5	5	5	15	30	120
250	Stan Musial	30	50	100	120	150	300	500	2,500
251	Bob Malkmus	5	5	5	5	5	15	25	120
252	Ray Herbert	5	5	5	5	5	15	25	150
253	Eddie Bressoud	5	5	5	5	5	15	25	100

#	Player	GD 2	VG 3	VgEx 4	EX 5	ExMt 6	NM 7	NmMt 8	MT 9
254	Arnie Portocarrero	5	5	5			15	25	150
255	Jim Gilliam	5	5	6	10	15	25	60	200
256	Dick Brown	5	5	5	5	5	15	50	150
257	Gordy Coleman RC	5	5	6	10	15	25	150	150
258	Dick Groat	5	5	5	8	12	25	50	250
259	George Altman	5	5	5	5	5	15	25	120
260	Power Plus	5	5	5	8	12	25	60	250
261	Pete Burnside	5	5	5	5	5	15	60	
262	Hank Bauer	5	5	5	5	8	15	300	
263	Darrell Johnson	5	5	5	5	5	15	25	120
264	Robin Roberts	5	5	6	12	30	40	80	
265	Rip Repulski	5	5	5	5	5	15	20	100
266	Joey Jay	5	5	5	5	5	20	30	150
267	Jim Marshall	5	5	5	5	5	15	30	120
268	Al Worthington	5	5	5	5	5	15	25	200
269	Gene Green	5	5	5	5	5	15	25	120
270	Bob Turley	5	5	5	5	8	25	30	200
271	Julio Becquer	5	5	5	5	5	15	15	150
272	Fred Green RC	5	5	5	5	5	15	30	120
273	Neil Chrisley	5	5	5	5	5	15	30	
274	Tom Acker	5	5	5	5	5	15	30	
275	Curt Flood	5	5	8	15	20	40	60	200
276	Ken McBride RC	5	5	5	5	5	15	25	100
277	Harry Bright	5	5	5	5	5	15	25	100
278	Stan Williams	5	5	5	5	5	15	25	120
279	Chuck Tanner	5	5	5	5	5	15	25	150
280	Frank Sullivan	5	5	5	5	5	15	25	120
281	Ray Boone	5	5	5	6	10	15	40	
282	Joe Nuxhall	5	5	5	5	6	15	40	200
283	Johnny Blanchard	5	5	5	5	8	15	40	
284	Don Gross	5	5	5	5	5	20	60	150
285	Harry Anderson	5	5	5	5	5	20	25	120
286	Ray Semproch	5	5	8	12	20	30	150	
287	Felipe Alou	5	5	5	8	12	40	400	
288	Bob Mabe	5	5	5	5	5	15	30	
289	Willie Jones	5	5	5	6	10	15	25	200
290	Jerry Lumpe	5	5	5	5	5	15	50	
291	Bob Keegan	5	5	5	6	10	15	25	
292	Dodger Backstops	5	5	5	5	6	15	80	150
293	Gene Conley	5	5	5	5	5	15	40	150
294	Tony Taylor	5	5	5	5	5	25	40	150
295	Gil Hodges	5	10	12	15	30	40	80	500
296	Nelson Chittum RC	5	5	5	5	5	15	30	
297	Reno Bertoia	5	5	5	5	5	15	25	150
298	George Witt	5	5	5	5	5	15	50	150
299	Earl Torgeson	5	5	5	5	5	15	40	200
300	Hank Aaron	50	80	120	200	250	500	2,000	
301	Jerry Davie	5	5	5	5	5	15	25	
302	Philadelphia Phillies CL	5	5	5	8	12	20	80	
303	Billy O'Dell	5	5	5	5	5	15	25	120
304	Joe Ginsberg	5	5	5	5	6	15	200	300
305	Richie Ashburn	5	8	12	25	30	50	200	300
306	Frank Baumann	5	5	5	5	5	15	25	120
307	Gene Oliver	5	5	5	5	5	15	25	120
308	Dick Hall	5	5	5	5	5	15	30	100
309	Bob Hale	5	5	5	5	5	15	50	120
310	Frank Malzone	5	5	5	8	12	20	80	
311	Raul Sanchez	5	5	5	5	5	15	30	200
312	Charley Lau	5	5	5	5	5	15	25	150
313	Turk Lown	5	5	5	5	5	15	25	120
314	Chico Fernandez	5	5	5	5	5	15	25	100
315	Bobby Shantz	5	5	6	15	20	25	300	
316	Willie McCovey ASR RC	60	80	120	200	250	500	▲3,000	▲40,000
317	Pumpsie Green ASR RC	5	5	5	6	10	50	100	
318	Jim Baxes ASR	5	5	5	5	5	15	60	
319	Joe Koppe ASR	5	5	5	5	5	15	50	150
320	Bob Allison ASR	5	5	5	5	5	15	50	500
321	Ron Fairly ASR	5	5	5	5	6	20	60	200

#	Player	GD 2	VG 3	VgEx 4	EX 5	ExMt 6	NM 7	NmMt 8	MT 9
322	Willie Tasby ASR	5	5	5	5	8	15	40	250
323	John Romano ASR	5	5	5	5	5	15	40	200
324	Jim Perry ASR	5	5	5	6	10	25	200	
325	Jim O'Toole ASR	5	5	5	6	10	20	30	
326	Roberto Clemente	100	120	200	▲300	▲500	▲800	▲2,000	8,000
327	Ray Sadecki RC	5	5	5	5	5	15	25	100
328	Earl Battey	5	5	5	5	5	15	50	200
329	Zack Monroe	5	5	5	5	6	15	30	150
330	Harvey Kuenn	5	5	5	5	8	30	40	
331	Henry Mason RC	5	5	5	5	5	15	25	100
332	New York Yankees CL	10	15	25	30	50	80	250	400
333	Danny McDevitt	5	5	5	6	10	15	120	250
334	Ted Abernathy	5	5	5	6	10	15	25	100
335	Red Schoendienst	5	5	6	10	25	30	80	250
336	Ike Delock	5	5	5	5	5	15	25	100
337	Cal Neeman	5	5	5	5	5	15	100	
338	Ray Monzant	5	5	5	5	5	15	25	120
339	Harry Chiti	5	5	5	5	5	15	25	200
340	Harvey Haddix	5	5	5	5	8	20	80	150
341	Carroll Hardy	5	5	5	5	5	15	40	150
342	Casey Wise	5	5	5	6	10	15	30	200
343	Sandy Koufax	80	▲120	150	200	▲300	▲500	1,000	3,000
344	Clint Courtney	5	5	5	5	5	15	25	120
345	Don Newcombe	5	5	5	6	10	25	50	120
346	J.C. Martin RC	5	5	5	8	12	20	40	150
347	Ed Bouchee	5	5	5	5	5	15	25	120
348	Barry Shetrone RC	5	5	5	5	5	15	25	150
349	Moe Drabowsky	5	5	5	5	8	15	30	120
350	Mickey Mantle	▲300	▲500	▲800	▲1,000	▲1,500	▲2,500	▲10,000	60,000
351	Don Nottebart RC	5	5	5	5	5	15	40	200
352	Cincy Clouters	5	5	5	6	10	40	60	500
353	Don Larsen	5	▲8	▲12	▲20	▲30	▲50	▲80	250
354	Bob Lillis	5	5	5	5	6	15	80	120
355	Bill White	5	5	5	5	8	40	120	200
356	Joe Amalfitano	5	5	5	5	5	15	25	
357	Al Schroll	5	5	5	5	5	15	25	250
358	Joe DeMaestri	5	5	5	5	8	20	150	
359	Buddy Gilbert RC	5	5	5	5	5	15	25	120
360	Herb Score	5	5	5	5	6	15	150	250
361	Bob Oldis	5	5	5	8	12	20	150	200
362	Russ Kemmerer	5	5	5	5	5	15	100	
363	Gene Stephens	5	5	5	6	10	15	40	120
364	Paul Foytack	5	5	5	5	8	15	50	200
365	Minnie Minoso	5	6	10	15	25	40	100	175
366	Dallas Green RC	5	5	5	15	20	30	60	300
367	Bill Tuttle	5	5	5	5	5	15	40	
368	Daryl Spencer	5	5	5	5	5	15	25	150
369	Billy Hoeft	5	5	5	5	5	15	25	200
370	Bill Skowron	5	5	8	12	25	50		
371	Bud Byerly	5	5	5	5	5	15	25	150
372	Frank House	5	5	5	5	5	15	25	120
373	Don Hoak	5	5	5	5	5	20	50	120
374	Bob Buhl	5	5	5	6	10	15	40	200
375	Dale Long	5	5	5	6	10	25	60	
376	John Briggs	5	5	5	5	5	10	25	225
377	Roger Maris	40	▲60	▲100	▲150	▲250	▲400	▲800	▲5,000
378	Stu Miller	5	5	5	5	5	15	25	150
379	Red Wilson	5	5	5	8	12	20	60	150
380	Bob Shaw	5	5	5	5	5	10	25	150
381	Milwaukee Braves CL	5	5	5	5	8	15	50	150
382	Ted Bowsfield	5	5	5	5	5	10	25	
383	Leon Wagner	5	5	5	5	5	10	25	120
384	Don Cardwell	5	5	5	5	5	10	80	150
385	Charlie Neal WS1	5	5	5	5	8	40	50	300
386	Charlie Neal WS2	5	5	5	5	8	15	40	250
387	Carl Furillo WS3	5	5	5	5	12	15	40	300
388	Gil Hodges WS4	5	▲6	▲10	▲15	▲25	▲60	200	500
389	L.Aparicio/M.Wills WS 5	5	6	10	15	25	50	150	

#	Player	GD 2	VG 3	VgEx 4	EX 5	ExMt 6	NM 7	NmMt 8	MT 9
390	Scrambling After Ball WS6	5	5	5	5	8	20	60	250
391	Champs Celebrate WS	5	5	5	6	10	50	250	
392	Tex Clevenger	5	5	5	5	5	15	25	100
393	Smoky Burgess	5	5	5	5	8	30	80	200
394	Norm Larker	5	5	5	5	6	15	30	150
395	Hoyt Wilhelm	5	5	5	8	20	40	60	200
396	Steve Bilko	5	5	5	5	6	15	50	150
397	Don Blasingame	5	5	5	5	5	10	40	200
398	Mike Cuellar	5	5	5	8	12	20	30	120
399	Young Hill Stars	5	5	5	5	6	20	50	200
400	Rocky Colavito	▲6	▲10	▲15	▲25	▲40	60	120	800
401	Bob Duliba RC	5	5	5	8	12	20	80	
402	Dick Stuart	5	5	5	5	8	25	50	
403	Ed Sadowski	5	5	5	5	5	10	25	100
404	Bob Rush	5	5	5	5	5	10	25	100
405	Bobby Richardson	5	8	12	20	25	80	120	
406	Billy Klaus	5	5	5	5	5	10	25	150
407	Gary Peters RC	5	5	5	5	6	12	40	150
408	Carl Furillo	5	5	5	5	6	25	40	150
409	Ron Samford	5	5	5	5	5	15	25	100
410	Sam Jones	5	5	5	5	5	15	25	120
411	Ed Bailey	5	5	5	5	5	15	25	120
412	Bob Anderson	5	5	5	5	5	15	40	
413	Kansas City Athletics CL	5	5	5	10	15	25	40	100
414	Don Williams RC	5	5	5	5	8	25	60	
415	Bob Cerv	5	5	5	5	8	12	25	100
416	Humberto Robinson	5	5	5	5	5	10	25	150
417	Chuck Cottier RC	5	5	5	6	10	15	25	100
418	Don Mossi	5	5	5	5	5	10	30	
419	George Crowe	5	5	5	5	8	20	60	200
420	Eddie Mathews	12	20	25	30	50	80	200	1,000
421	Duke Maas	5	5	5	5	8	15	40	175
422	John Powers	5	5	5	5	5	10	30	100
423	Ed Fitzgerald	5	5	5	5	5	10	25	120
424	Pete Whisenant	5	5	5	5	5	10	25	150
425	Johnny Podres	5	5	5	5	6	20	30	150
426	Ron Jackson	5	5	5	5	5	15	25	120
427	Al Grunwald RC	5	5	5	5	5	15	30	250
428	Al Smith	5	5	5	5	5	15	30	175
429	American League Kings	5	5	5	6	15	25	80	
430	Art Ditmar	5	5	5	5	8	15	40	200
431	Andre Rodgers	5	5	5	5	5	10	40	200
432	Chuck Stobbs	5	5	5	5	5	10	25	200
433	Irv Noren	5	5	5	5	5	15	25	150
434	Brooks Lawrence	5	5	5	5	5	10	25	
435	Gene Freese	5	5	5	5	5	10	25	150
436	Marv Throneberry	5	5	5	5	5	10	25	150
437	Bob Friend	5	5	5	5	6	20	25	150
438	Jim Coker RC	5	5	5	5	8	25	150	300
439	Tom Brewer	5	5	5	5	5	15	25	120
440	Jim Lemon	5	5	5	5	5	15	40	150
441	Gary Bell	5	5	5	6	10	15	30	300
442	Joe Pignatano	5	5	5	5	6	20	120	300
443	Charlie Maxwell	5	5	5	5	6	15	30	150
444	Jerry Kindall	5	5	5	5	6	15	30	120
445	Warren Spahn	25	30	40	50	80	▲200	300	800
446	Ellis Burton	5	5	5	5	6	40	800	
447	Ray Moore	5	5	5	5	6	20	100	
448	Jim Gentile RC	5	5	6	10	20	60	80	
449	Jim Brosnan	5	5	5	6	10	12	25	150
450	Orlando Cepeda	12	20	30	50	80	120	400	800
451	Curt Simmons	5	6	10	15	25	80	500	
452	Ray Webster	5	5	5	5	6	20	60	
453	Vern Law	5	5	5	5	8	25	60	300
454	Hal Woodeshick	5	5	5	5	6	15	50	
455	Baltimore Coaches	5	5	5	5	6	15	40	250
456	Red Sox Coaches	5	5	5	8	12	30	120	
457	Cubs Coaches	5	5	5	5	6	15	30	
458	White Sox Coaches	5	5	5	6	10	25	30	150
459	Reds Coaches	5	5	5	5	6	15	40	150
460	Indians Coaches	5	5	5	5	6	20	80	150
461	Tigers Coaches	5	5	5	6	10	40	50	
462	Athletics Coaches	5	5	5	6	10	15	25	150
463	Dodgers Coaches	5	5	5	5	8	15	80	300
464	Braves Coaches	5	5	5	5	6	15	40	
465	Yankees Coaches	▲6	▲10	▲15	▲25	▲40	▲60	100	250
466	Phillies Coaches	5	5	5	5	6	15	30	200
467	Pirates Coaches	5	5	5	8	12	20	30	200
468	Cardinals Coaches	5	5	5	5	8	20	60	150
469	Giants Coaches	5	5	5	5	6	15	100	250
470	Senators Coaches	5	5	5	6	10	15	40	150
471	Ned Garver	5	5	5	5	6	20	400	
472	Alvin Dark	5	5	5	5	6	12	30	120
473	Al Cicotte	5	5	5	5	6	20	60	
474	Haywood Sullivan	5	5	5	5	6	12	30	200
475	Don Drysdale	6	10	25	30	60	80	200	400
476	Lou Johnson RC	5	5	5	5	8	30	80	
477	Don Ferrarese	5	5	5	5	6	15	120	
478	Frank Torre	5	5	5	5	6	15	25	500
479	Georges Maranda RC	5	5	5	5	6	15	40	120
480	Yogi Berra	50	60	100	120	▲200	300	800	1,500
481	Wes Stock RC	5	5	5	5	8	12	50	120
482	Frank Bolling	5	5	5	5	6	20	30	120
483	Camilo Pascual	5	5	5	5	6	20	30	120
484	Pittsburgh Pirates CL	5	5	8	12	20	50	150	800
485	Ken Boyer	5	5	▲8	▲12	▲20	30	▲150	200
486	Bobby Del Greco	5	5	5	5	6	15	30	200
487	Tom Sturdivant	5	5	5	5	6	12	30	100
488	Norm Cash	5	5	8	12	25	80		
489	Steve Ridzik	5	6	10	15	25	40	300	
490	Frank Robinson	20	25	30	40	60	100	▲400	
491	Mel Roach	5	5	5	5	6	12	80	
492	Larry Jackson	5	5	5	5	6	12	40	120
493	Duke Snider	▼20	▼30	50	▲80	▲120	▲200	▼300	800
494	Baltimore Orioles CL	5	5	5	8	12	▲80	▲150	
495	Sherm Lollar	5	5	5	5	8	15	120	
496	Bill Virdon	5	5	5	5	25	30	500	
497	John Tsitouris	5	5	5	8	12	20	80	
498	Al Pilarcik	5	5	5	5	6	25	400	
499	Johnny James RC	5	5	5	5	8	▲30	50	
500	Johnny Temple	5	5	5	6	10	15	30	250
501	Bob Schmidt	5	5	5	5	6	15	120	
502	Jim Bunning	8	12	20	30	50	80	200	
503	Don Lee	5	5	5	5	6	15	30	
504	Seth Morehead	5	5	5	5	6	15	40	200
505	Ted Kluszewski	5	5	6	10	25	60	120	250
506	Lee Walls	5	5	5	5	6	15	25	200
507	Dick Stigman	5	5	5	5	8	25	60	200
508	Billy Consolo	5	5	5	5	8	30	▲60	
509	Tommy Davis RC	5	5	8	12	50	150	500	
510	Gerry Staley	5	5	5	5	8	15	60	200
511	Ken Walters RC	5	5	5	5	8	25	120	500
512	Joe Gibbon RC	5	5	5	5	8	30	100	200
513	Chicago Cubs CL	5	6	10	15	30	50	80	300
514	Steve Barber RC	5	5	5	5	8	20	60	
515	Stan Lopata	5	5	5	5	8	20	100	120
516	Marty Kutyna RC	5	5	5	5	8	25	120	
517	Charlie James RC	5	5	5	5	8	25	40	250
518	Tony Gonzalez RC	5	5	5	5	8	25	60	150
519	Ed Roebuck	5	5	5	5	15	20	50	
520	Don Buddin	5	5	5	5	8	30	50	200
521	Mike Lee RC	5	5	5	8	12	25	40	150
522	Ken Hunt RC	5	5	5	10	25	50	100	
523	Clay Dalrymple RC	5	5	5	5	8	20	▲60	200
524	Bill Henry	5	5	5	5	8	25	50	120
525	Marv Breeding RC	5	5	5	8	12	15	60	250

#	Player	GD 2	VG 3	VgEx 4	EX 5	ExMt 6	NM 7	NmMt 8	MT 9
526	Paul Giel	5	5	5	6	10	30	60	
527	Jose Valdivielso	5	5	▲6	▲10	▲15	▲25	40	100
528	Ben Johnson RC	5	5	5	6	10	60	150	
529	Norm Sherry RC	5	5	5	6	10	40	50	200
530	Mike McCormick	5	5	▲8	▲12	▲20	30	80	400
531	Sandy Amoros	5	▲6	▲10	▲15	25	40	250	
532	Mike Garcia	5	5	▲6	▲10	▲15	25	50	
533	Lu Clinton RC	5	5	▲6	▲10	▲15	▲25	40	200
534	Ken MacKenzie RC	5	5	5	6	10	15	50	300
535	Whitey Lockman	5	5	5	6	10	15	60	200
536	Wynn Hawkins RC	5	5	5	6	10	15	50	150
537	Boston Red Sox CL	5	5	6	10	15	50	▲150	300
538	Frank Barnes RC	5	5	5	6	10	20	40	120
539	Gene Baker	5	▲6	▲10	▲15	25	100	400	
540	Jerry Walker	5	5	5	▲8	▲12	20	50	120
541	Tony Curry RC	5	5	▲6	▲10	▲15	25	▲60	120
542	Ken Hamlin RC	5	5	5	▲8	▲12	20	50	150
543	Elio Chacon RC	5	5	▲6	▲10	▲15	25	60	
544	Bill Monbouquette	5	5	▲6	▲10	▲15	25	60	
545	Carl Sawatski	5	5	▲6	▲10	▲15	25	40	
546	Hank Aguirre	5	5	5	▲8	▲12	20	80	
547	Bob Aspromonte RC	5	5	▲8	▲12	▲20	30	▲80	150
548	Don Mincher RC	5	5	5	▲6	▲10	15	60	300
549	John Buzhardt	5	5	5	▲8	▲12	▲20	40	120
550	Jim Landis	5	5	5	8	12	25	80	150
551	Ed Rakow RC	5	5	6	10	15	25	▲80	
552	Walt Bond RC	5	5	5	5	8	25	40	150
553	Bill Skowron AS	▲6	▲10	▲15	25	30	40	80	400
554	Willie McCovey AS	15	20	30	40	80	120	250	800
555	Nellie Fox AS	5	5	8	12	25	50	100	400
556	Charlie Neal AS	5	5	5	8	12	30	80	250
557	Frank Malzone AS	5	5	6	10	15	40	150	300
558	Eddie Mathews AS	▲10	▲15	25	30	40	60	120	
559	Luis Aparicio AS	5	▲8	▲12	20	30	50	100	300
560	Ernie Banks AS	6	20	25	40	80	120	200	500
561	Al Kaline AS	▲12	20	25	30	50	60	200	500
562	Joe Cunningham AS	5	5	5	▲8	▲12	20	80	150
563	Mickey Mantle AS	100	120	200	250	300	500	600	▲3,000
564	Willie Mays AS	▲30	50	60	80	120	200	400	
565	Roger Maris AS	▲20	30	60	80	100	▲200	300	
566	Hank Aaron AS	▲25	40	60	80	100	200	300	1,200
567	Sherm Lollar AS	5	5	▲6	▲10	▲15	▲40	60	150
568	Del Crandall AS	5	▲6	▲10	▲15	▲25	40	50	250
569	Camilo Pascual AS	5	5	▲8	▲12	▲20	30	100	
570	Don Drysdale AS	▲10	▲15	▲25	▲40	60	80	250	800
571	Billy Pierce AS	5	5	▲8	▲12	▲20	30	60	200
572	Johnny Antonelli AS	5	▲6	▲10	▲15	▲25	40	100	

— Hank Aaron #300 PSA 8.5 (NmMt+) sold for $2,492 (eBay; 08/12)
— Ernie Banks #10 PSA 9 (MT) sold for $4,386 (eBay; 12/12)
— Mickey Mantle #350 PSA 8.5 (NmMt+) sold for $3,270 (Greg Bussineau; 12/12)
— Carl Yastrzemski #148 PSA 10 (Gem) (Young Collection) sold for $83,813 (SCP; 5/12)

1961 Fleer

#	Player	GD 2	VG 3	VgEx 4	EX 5	ExMt 6	NM 7	NmMt 8	MT 9
1	Baker/Cobb/Wheat CL	5	6	10	15	30	80	250	
2	Grover C. Alexander	5	5	5	5	6	15	60	
3	Nick Altrock	5	5	5	5	5	12	30	
4	Cap Anson	5	5	5	5	5	10	30	
5	Earl Averill	5	5	5	5	5	8	25	
6	Frank Baker	5	5	5	5	5	8	20	
7	Dave Bancroft	5	5	5	5	8	10	30	60
8	Chief Bender	5	5	5	5	5	8	15	80
9	Jim Bottomley	5	5	5	5	5	8	20	60
10	Roger Bresnahan	5	5	5	5	5	8	25	
11	Mordecai Brown	5	5	5	5	5	8	20	
12	Max Carey	5	5	5	5	5	8	40	
13	Jack Chesbro	5	5	5	5	5	10	20	60
14	Ty Cobb	5	6	10	20	50	60	80	250
15	Mickey Cochrane	5	5	5	5	5	10	20	60
16	Eddie Collins	5	5	5	5	5	8	15	60
17	Earle Combs	5	5	5	5	5	8	30	
18	Charles Comiskey	5	5	5	5	5	10	30	
19	Kiki Cuyler	5	5	5	5	5	8	15	50
20	Paul Derringer	5	5	5	5	5	8	20	100
21	Howard Ehmke	5	5	5	5	5	8	15	50
22	Billy Evans UMP	5	5	5	5	5	10	20	50
23	Johnny Evers	5	5	5	5	5	8	15	50
24	Red Faber	5	5	5	5	5	8	15	50
25	Bob Feller	5	5	5	6	10	20	50	200
26	Wes Ferrell	5	5	5	5	8	10	20	50
27	Lew Fonseca	5	5	5	5	5	8	15	60
28	Jimmie Foxx	5	5	5	6	10	15	50	120
29	Ford Frick	5	5	5	5	5	8	15	80
30	Frankie Frisch	5	5	5	6	10	20	25	60
31	Lou Gehrig	15	25	40	60	100	120	150	400
32	Charley Gehringer	5	5	5	5	5	8	15	50
33	Warren Giles	5	5	5	5	5	10	25	
34	Lefty Gomez	5	5	5	5	5	10	20	60
35	Goose Goslin	5	5	5	5	5	8	15	50
36	Clark Griffith	5	5	5	5	5	8	15	50
37	Burleigh Grimes	5	5	5	5	5	8	15	50
38	Lefty Grove	5	5	5	5	5	10	25	50
39	Chick Hafey	5	5	5	5	5	8	15	60
40	Jesse Haines	5	5	5	5	8	10	20	50
41	Gabby Hartnett	5	5	5	5	5	8	15	60
42	Harry Heilmann	5	5	5	5	5	8	15	60
43	Rogers Hornsby	5	5	5	6	10	15	40	150
44	Waite Hoyt	5	5	5	5	5	8	15	60
45	Carl Hubbell	5	5	5	5	8	15	25	80
46	Miller Huggins	5	5	5	5	8	15	25	80
47	Hughie Jennings	5	5	5	5	5	8	15	50
48	Ban Johnson	5	5	5	5	5	10	20	50
49	Walter Johnson	5	5	5	8	12	25	40	150
50	Ralph Kiner	5	5	5	8	10	20	40	60
51	Chuck Klein	5	5	5	5	8	10	20	60
52	Johnny Kling	5	5	5	5	5	8	15	50
53	Kenesaw M. Landis	5	5	5	5	5	8	15	50
54	Tony Lazzeri	5	5	5	5	5	8	15	60
55	Ernie Lombardi	5	5	5	5	5	8	15	50
56	Dolf Luque	5	5	5	5	5	8	15	60
57	Heinie Manush	5	5	5	5	8	10	15	25
58	Marty Marion	5	5	5	5	5	8	15	60
59	Christy Mathewson	5	▲6	▲10	▲15	▲25	▲40	50	300
60	John McGraw	5	5	5	5	5	8	10	20
61	Joe Medwick	5	5	5	5	5	8	15	50
62	Bing Miller	5	5	5	5	5	8	15	50
63	Johnny Mize	5	5	5	5	5	8	15	50
64	John Mostil	5	5	5	5	5	8	15	50
65	Art Nehf	5	5	5	8	10	15	25	
66	Hal Newhouser	5	5	5	5	5	8	15	50
67	Bobo Newsom	5	5	5	5	5	8	15	50
68	Mel Ott	5	5	5	8	10	15	25	60
69	Allie Reynolds	5	5	5	5	5	8	15	50
70	Sam Rice	5	5	5	5	8	10	20	50
71	Eppa Rixey	5	5	5	5	5	8	15	50
72	Edd Roush	5	5	5	8	10	15	25	60
73	Schoolboy Rowe	5	5	5	5	5	8	20	50
74	Red Ruffing	5	5	5	5	5	10	20	50
75	Babe Ruth	30	50	80	150	250	300	500	600
76	Joe Sewell	5	5	5	5	5	8	12	30
77	Al Simmons	5	5	5	5	5	8	15	50
78	George Sisler	5	5	5	5	5	8	15	50
79	Tris Speaker	5	5	5	5	8	10	15	60
80	Fred Toney	5	5	5	5	8	10	15	25
81	Dazzy Vance	5	5	5	5	5	8	25	

#	Name	GD 2	VG 3	VgEx 4	EX 5	ExMt 6	NM 7	NmMt 8	MT 9
82	Jim Vaughn	5	5	5	8	10	15	25	60
83	Ed Walsh	5	5	5	8	10	15	25	60
84	Lloyd Waner	5	5	5	8	10	15	25	60
85	Paul Waner	5	5	5	8	10	15	25	80
86	Zack Wheat	5	5	5	5	5	8	15	100
87	Hack Wilson	5	5	5	5	5	10	25	80
88	Jimmy Wilson	5	5	5	5	5	8	20	100
89	G.Sisler/P.Traynor CL	8	10	15	25	40	80	150	
90	Babe Adams	5	5	5	5	5	10	25	
91	Dale Alexander	5	5	5	5	5	10	30	
92	Jim Bagby	5	5	5	5	5	10		
93	Ossie Bluege	5	5	5	5	5	10	20	
94	Lou Boudreau	5	5	5	5	5	10	50	
95	Tommy Bridges	5	5	5	5	5	10	80	
96	Donie Bush	5	5	5	5	5	10	20	120
97	Dolph Camilli	5	5	5	5	5	10	25	150
98	Frank Chance	5	5	5	5	5	10	40	60
99	Jimmy Collins	5	5	5	5	5	10	25	
100	Stan Coveleskie	5	5	5	5	5	10	150	
101	Hugh Critz	5	5	5	5	5	10	20	60
102	Alvin Crowder	5	5	5	5	5	10	20	60
103	Joe Dugan	5	5	5	5	5	10	20	60
104	Bibb Falk	5	5	5	5	5	10	25	60
105	Rick Ferrell	5	5	5	5	8	15	30	80
106	Art Fletcher	5	5	5	5	5	10	20	150
107	Dennis Galehouse	5	5	5	5	5	10	20	60
108	Chick Galloway	5	5	5	5	5	10	20	60
109	Mule Haas	5	5	5	5	5	10	20	150
110	Stan Hack	5	5	5	5	5	10	20	150
111	Bump Hadley	5	5	5	8	10	15	30	60
112	Billy Hamilton	5	5	5	5	5	10	20	
113	Joe Hauser	5	5	5	8	10	15	30	60
114	Babe Herman	5	5	5	8	10	15	30	60
115	Travis Jackson	5	5	5	▲6	▲10	▲15	▲60	
116	Eddie Joost	5	5	5	5	5	10	20	80
117	Addie Joss	5	5	5	8	10	20	40	100
118	Joe Judge	5	5	5	5	5	10	20	
119	Joe Kuhel	5	5	5	8	10	15	30	60
120	Napoleon Lajoie	5	5	▲8	▲12	▲20	▲30	40	
121	Dutch Leonard	5	5	5	5	5	10	40	
122	Ted Lyons	5	5	8	10	15	30	60	
123	Connie Mack	5	5	5	5	8	15	60	150
124	Rabbit Maranville	5	5	5	5	5	10	20	
125	Fred Marberry	5	5	5	5	5	10	20	100
126	Joe McGinnity	5	5	5	5	5	10	30	60
127	Oscar Melillo	5	5	5	8	12	20	40	80
128	Ray Mueller	5	5	5	5	5	10	20	60
129	Kid Nichols	5	5	5	5	5	10	20	60
130	Lefty O'Doul	5	5	5	5	5	10	20	60
131	Bob O'Farrell	5	5	5	5	5	10	20	60
132	Roger Peckinpaugh	5	5	5	5	5	10	20	80
133	Herb Pennock	5	5	5	8	12	25	50	
134	George Pipgras	5	5	5	5	5	10	100	200
135	Eddie Plank	5	5	5	8	12	25	50	80
136	Ray Schalk	5	5	5	5	5	10	20	60
137	Hal Schumacher	5	5	5	5	5	10	20	60
138	Luke Sewell	5	5	5	5	5	10	20	60
139	Bob Shawkey	5	5	5	5	5	10	20	60
140	Riggs Stephenson	5	5	5	5	5	15	20	60
141	Billy Sullivan	5	5	5	5	5	10	20	60
142	Bill Terry	5	5	5	5	8	12	40	100
143	Joe Tinker	5	5	5	5	5	10	20	60
144	Pie Traynor	5	5	5	5	5	10	40	
145	Hal Trosky	5	5	5	5	5	10	30	200
146	George Uhle	5	5	5	5	5	10	20	60
147	Johnny VanderMeer	5	5	5	5	5	10	20	60
148	Arky Vaughan	5	5	5	5	5	10	40	80
149	Rube Waddell	5	5	5	5	5	10	100	150
150	Honus Wagner	5	8	12	20	50	60	150	300
151	Dixie Walker	5	5	5	5	5	10	60	
152	Ted Williams	15	25	40	100	120	250	300	800
153	Cy Young	5	▲8	▲12	▲20	▲30	50	100	250
154	Ross Youngs	5	5	5	6	12	30	200	

1961 Golden Press

#	Name	VG 3	VgEx 4	EX 5	ExMt 6	NM 7	NmMt 8	MT 9	Gem 9.5/10
1	Mel Ott	5	5	6	10	40	80	250	
2	Grover C. Alexander	5	5	5	8	15	50	250	
3	Babe Ruth	10	12	40	50	100	250	500	
4	Hank Greenberg	5	5	5	5	8	15	50	200
5	Bill Terry	5	5	5	5	8	15	40	250
6	Carl Hubbell	5	5	5	5	10	20	40	
7	Rogers Hornsby	5	5	6	10	15	25	80	
8	Dizzy Dean	5	5	8	12	20	60	▲120	
9	Joe DiMaggio	8	10	12	20	35	100	300	
10	Charlie Gehringer	5	5	5	5	8	15	40	150
11	Gabby Hartnett	5	5	5	5	8	15	40	
12	Mickey Cochrane	5	5	5	5	8	15	40	
13	George Sisler	5	5	5	5	8	15	40	200
14	Joe Cronin	5	5	5	5	8	30	40	200
15	Pie Traynor	5	5	5	5	8	15	40	150
16	Lou Gehrig	6	10	15	25	30	100	400	
17	Lefty Grove	5	5	5	5	8	15	40	250
18	Chief Bender	5	5	5	5	8	15	40	200
19	Frankie Frisch	5	5	5	5	8	15	40	200
20	Al Simmons	5	5	5	5	8	15	40	200
21	Home Run Baker	5	5	5	5	8	15	50	200
22	Jimmy Foxx	5	5	6	10	15	40	60	
23	John McGraw	5	5	5	5	8	15	40	200
24	Christy Mathewson	5	5	6	10	15	25	50	
25	Ty Cobb	6	8	10	15	25	100	150	300
26	Dazzy Vance	5	5	5	5	8	15	40	
27	Bill Dickey	5	5	5	5	8	15	40	
28	Eddie Collins	5	5	5	5	8	40	120	
29	Walter Johnson	5	▲8	▲12	▲20	▲30	80	400	
30	Tris Speaker	5	5	6	10	15	25	150	
31	Nap Lajoie	5	5	5	8	12	40	120	
32	Honus Wagner	8	10	10	25	60	80	200	
33	Cy Young	4	5	10	15	25	60	300	

1961 Topps

#	Name	GD 2	VG 3	VgEx 4	EX 5	ExMt 6	NM 7	NmMt 8	MT 9
1	Dick Groat	5	5	5	10	25	40	150	300
2	Roger Maris	40	60	80	100	150	300	600	8,000
3	John Buzhardt	5	5	5	5	5	10	20	80
4	Lenny Green	5	5	5	5	5	10	20	80
5	John Romano	5	5	5	5	5	10	25	
6	Ed Roebuck	5	5	5	5	8	12	20	80
7	Chicago White Sox TC	5	5	5	5	6	12	30	100
8	Dick Williams	5	5	5	6	10	15	40	120
9	Bob Purkey	5	5	5	5	5	10	20	60
10	Brooks Robinson	10	15	25	30	40	80	100	500
11	Curt Simmons	5	5	5	5	5	10	25	80
12	Moe Thacker	5	5	5	5	5	10	20	50
13	Chuck Cottier	5	5	5	5	5	10	20	50
14	Don Mossi	5	5	5	5	5	10	20	50
15	Willie Kirkland	5	5	5	5	5	10	30	
16	Billy Muffett	5	5	5	5	5	10	20	80
17	Checklist 1	5	5	5	5	6	12	25	100
18	Jim Grant	5	5	5	5	5	10	20	80
19	Clete Boyer	5	5	5	8	12	40	100	
20	Robin Roberts	5	5	8	12	25	30	60	▲400
21	Zoilo Versalles RC	5	5	5	5	8	12	30	100
22	Clem Labine	5	5	5	5	8	12	30	80
23	Don Demeter	5	5	5	5	6	12	25	150

#	Name	GD 2	VG 3	VgEx 4	EX 5	ExMt 6	NM 7	NmMt 8	MT 9
24	Ken Johnson	5	5	5	5	5	10	20	80
25	Reds Heavy Artillery	5	5	5	8	12	25	50	120
26	Wes Stock	5	5	5	5	10	20	100	
27	Jerry Kindall	5	5	5	5	5	10	25	80
28	Hector Lopez	5	5	5	5	8	12	30	150
29	Don Nottebart	5	5	5	5	5	10	20	60
30	Nellie Fox	5	5	6	10	25	30	60	250
31	Bob Schmidt	5	5	5	5	5	10	20	80
32	Ray Sadecki	5	5	5	5	5	10	20	80
33	Gary Geiger	5	5	5	5	5	10	20	50
34	Wynn Hawkins	5	5	5	5	5	10	15	50
35	Ron Santo RC	▲30	▲50	▲80	100	▲150	▲250	▲500	1,500
36	Jack Kralick RC	5	5	5	5	5	10	20	60
37	Charley Maxwell	5	5	5	5	6	12	30	100
38	Bob Lillis	5	5	5	5	5	10	20	40
39	Leo Posada RC	5	5	5	5	5	10	20	60
40	Bob Turley	5	5	5	5	8	15	50	120
41	NL Batting Leaders	8	12	15	20	25	50	80	250
42	AL Batting Leaders	5	5	5	6	10	15	30	100
43	NL Home Run Leaders	5	5	15	20	25	40	80	300
44	AL Home Run Leaders	15	25	40	50	60	120	200	800
45	NL ERA Leaders	5	5	5	5	8	15	30	80
46	AL ERA Leaders	5	5	5	5	6	12	25	120
47	NL Pitching Leaders	5	5	5	5	8	20	40	300
48	AL Pitching Leaders	5	5	5	6	10	15	25	100
49	NL Strikeout Leaders	5	5	6	10	20	30	80	300
50	AL Strikeout Leaders	5	5	5	5	8	15	40	200
51	Detroit Tigers TC	5	5	5	5	6	12	30	150
52	George Crowe	5	5	5	5	5	10	20	60
53	Russ Nixon	5	5	5	5	5	10	20	80
54	Earl Francis RC	5	5	5	5	5	10	20	150
55	Jim Davenport	5	5	5	5	5	10	20	60
56	Russ Kemmerer	5	5	5	5	5	10	20	80
57	Marv Throneberry	5	5	5	5	6	12	20	80
58	Joe Schaffernoth RC	5	5	5	5	5	10	20	80
59	Jim Woods	5	5	5	5	5	10	20	80
60	Woody Held	5	5	5	5	5	10	20	80
61	Ron Piche RC	5	5	5	5	5	10	20	120
62	Al Pilarcik	5	5	5	5	5	10	20	60
63	Jim Kaat	5	5	6	10	15	25	40	250
64	Alex Grammas	5	5	5	5	5	10	20	60
65	Ted Kluszewski	5	5	5	5	8	20	40	200
66	Bill Henry	5	5	5	5	5	10	20	80
67	Ossie Virgil	5	5	5	5	5	12	50	
68	Deron Johnson	5	5	5	6	10	15	25	60
69	Earl Wilson	5	5	5	5	5	10	25	80
70	Bill Virdon	5	5	5	5	8	15	50	150
71	Jerry Adair	5	5	5	5	5	10	15	80
72	Stu Miller	5	5	5	5	5	10	20	100
73	Al Spangler	5	5	5	5	5	10	20	80
74	Joe Pignatano	5	5	5	5	5	10	20	80
75	Lindy Shows Larry	5	5	5	5	6	12	25	80
76	Harry Anderson	5	5	5	5	5	10	20	60
77	Dick Stigman	5	5	5	5	5	10	20	80
78	Lee Walls	5	5	5	5	5	10	20	80
79	Joe Ginsberg	5	5	5	5	5	10	20	80
80	Harmon Killebrew	▲15	▲25	▲40	▲60	▲100	▲150	▲300	
81	Tracy Stallard RC	5	5	5	5	5	10	20	80
82	Joe Christopher RC	5	5	5	5	5	10	20	80
83	Bob Bruce	5	5	5	5	5	10	20	80
84	Lee Maye	5	5	5	5	5	10	20	100
85	Jerry Walker	5	5	5	5	5	10	20	50
86	Los Angeles Dodgers TC	5	5	6	10	15	25	40	250
87	Joe Amalfitano	5	5	5	5	5	10	20	60
88	Richie Ashburn	5	5	6	10	15	25	50	▲250
89	Billy Martin	5	▲8	▲12	▲20	▲30	▲50	100	
90	Gerry Staley	5	5	5	5	5	10	20	100
91	Walt Moryn	5	5	5	5	5	10	20	100

#	Name	GD 2	VG 3	VgEx 4	EX 5	ExMt 6	NM 7	NmMt 8	MT 9
92	Hal Naragon	5	5	5	5	5	10	20	80
93	Tony Gonzalez	5	5	5	5	5	10	20	100
94	Johnny Kucks	5	5	5	5	5	10	20	80
95	Norm Cash	5	5	5	6	25	40	120	
96	Billy O'Dell	5	5	5	5	6	12	80	100
97	Jerry Lynch	5	5	5	5	5	10	15	50
98A	Checklist 2 Red	5	5	5	5	15	60	150	
98B	Checklist 2 Yellow w/White 98	5	5	5	5	6	12	50	
98C	Checklist 2 Yellow w/Black 98	5	5	5	5	6	12	30	
99	Don Buddin	5	5	5	5	5	10	20	80
100	Harvey Haddix	5	5	5	5	6	12	20	80
101	Bubba Phillips	5	5	5	5	5	10	20	100
102	Gene Stephens	5	5	5	5	5	10	20	80
103	Ruben Amaro	5	5	5	5	5	10	20	120
104	John Blanchard	5	5	5	5	8	15	25	80
105	Carl Willey	5	5	5	6	10	15	20	80
106	Whitey Herzog	5	5	5	5	5	10	20	80
107	Seth Morehead	5	5	5	5	5	10	20	80
108	Dan Dobbek	5	5	5	5	5	10	20	100
109	Johnny Podres	5	5	5	5	6	12	30	100
110	Vada Pinson	5	5	5	8	12	30	50	
111	Jack Meyer	5	5	5	5	5	10	20	150
112	Chico Fernandez	5	5	5	5	5	10	20	
113	Mike Fornieles	5	5	5	5	5	10	80	
114	Hobie Landrith	5	5	5	5	5	12	30	
115	Johnny Antonelli	5	5	5	5	5	10	25	
116	Joe DeMaestri	5	5	5	5	6	12	25	120
117	Dale Long	5	5	5	5	5	10	20	120
118	Chris Cannizzaro RC	5	5	5	5	5	10	25	
119	A's Big Armor	5	5	5	5	6	12	100	200
120	Eddie Mathews	20	25	30	40	50	100	150	▲800
121	Eli Grba	5	5	5	5	10	12	25	
122	Chicago Cubs TC	5	5	5	5	6	12	30	
123	Billy Gardner	5	5	5	5	5	10	30	
124	J.C. Martin	5	5	5	5	5	10	20	
125	Steve Barber	5	5	5	5	5	10	20	100
126	Dick Stuart	5	5	5	8	12	20	100	400
127	Ron Kline	5	5	5	5	5	10	20	80
128	Rip Repulski	5	5	5	5	5	10	60	
129	Ed Hobaugh	5	5	5	5	5	8	15	50
130	Norm Larker	5	5	5	5	5	10	20	100
131	Paul Richards MG	5	5	5	5	5	10	20	
132	Al Lopez MG	5	5	5	5	6	25	60	
133	Ralph Houk MG	5	5	5	8	12	20	400	
134	Mickey Vernon MG	5	5	5	5	6	12	25	150
135	Fred Hutchinson MG	5	5	5	5	8	15	30	
136	Walter Alston MG	5	5	5	5	8	20	60	
137	Chuck Dressen MG	5	5	5	5	6	15	150	
138	Danny Murtaugh MG	5	5	5	5	6	12	30	
139	Solly Hemus MG	5	5	5	5	5	10	25	
140	Gus Triandos	5	5	5	5	6	12	25	500
141	Billy Williams RC	▲25	▲40	▲60	▲100	▲150	▲250	500	▲5,000
142	Luis Arroyo	5	5	5	5	6	12	25	100
143	Russ Snyder	5	5	5	6	10	15	60	
144	Jim Coker	5	5	5	5	5	10	20	100
145	Bob Buhl	5	5	5	5	6	12	25	150
146	Marty Keough	5	5	5	5	5	10	20	150
147	Ed Rakow	5	5	5	5	5	10	20	100
148	Julian Javier	5	5	5	5	6	15	50	
149	Bob Oldis	5	5	5	5	5	10	20	100
150	Willie Mays	▲50	▲80	▲120	▲200	▲300	▲500	▲2,000	▲15,000
151	Jim Donohue	5	5	5	5	5	10	30	
152	Earl Torgeson	5	5	5	5	5	10	20	100
153	Don Lee	5	5	5	5	5	12	80	
154	Bobby Del Greco	5	5	5	5	5	10	50	150
155	Johnny Temple	5	5	5	5	8	12	20	
156	Ken Hunt	5	5	5	8	12	20	30	
157	Cal McLish	5	5	5	5	5	10	20	200

#	Player	GD 2	VG 3	VgEx 4	EX 5	ExMt 6	NM 7	NmMt 8	MT 9
158	Pete Daley	5	5	5	5	5	10	20	100
159	Baltimore Orioles TC	5	5	5	5	6	12	25	250
160	Whitey Ford	15	20	25	30	50	80	400	
161	Sherman Jones RC	5	5	5	5	5	10	20	150
162	Jay Hook	5	5	5	5	5	10	20	120
163	Ed Sadowski	5	5	5	5	5	10	20	100
164	Felix Mantilla	5	5	5	5	5	10	20	100
165	Gino Cimoli	5	5	5	5	5	10	25	100
166	Danny Kravitz	5	5	5	5	5	10	20	80
167	San Francisco Giants TC	5	5	5	5	6	12	60	100
168	Tommy Davis	5	5	5	6	10	15	50	120
169	Don Elston	5	5	5	5	5	10	20	80
170	Al Smith	5	5	5	5	5	12	40	
171	Paul Foytack	5	5	5	5	5	12	80	
172	Don Dillard	5	5	5	5	5	8	15	100
173	Beantown Bombers	5	5	5	5	6	25	50	
174	Ray Semproch	5	5	5	5	5	10	25	
175	Gene Freese	5	5	5	5	6	15	60	
176	Ken Aspromonte	5	5	5	5	5	10	20	80
177	Don Larsen	5	5	5	5	8	12	60	250
178	Bob Nieman	5	5	5	5	5	10	20	100
179	Joe Koppe	5	5	5	5	5	10	20	
180	Bobby Richardson	5	5	6	12	20	50	100	600
181	Fred Green	5	5	5	5	5	10	20	150
182	Dave Nicholson RC	5	5	5	5	5	12	150	
183	Andre Rodgers	5	5	5	5	5	10	20	120
184	Steve Bilko	5	5	5	6	10	15	25	80
185	Herb Score	5	5	5	5	6	25	60	
186	Elmer Valo	5	5	5	5	5	10	30	
187	Billy Klaus	5	5	5	5	5	10	20	100
188	Jim Marshall	5	5	5	5	5	10	20	
189A	Checklist 3 Copyright at 263	5	5	5	5	6	12	25	
189B	Checklist 3 Copyright at 264	5	5	5	5	8	15		
190	Stan Williams	5	5	5	6	10	15	25	60
191	Mike de la Hoz RC	5	5	5	5	5	10	20	
192	Dick Brown	5	5	5	5	5	10	25	
193	Gene Conley	5	5	5	5	5	10	20	80
194	Gordy Coleman	5	5	5	5	5	10	20	80
195	Jerry Casale	5	5	5	5	5	10	30	
196	Ed Bouchee	5	5	5	5	5	10	20	100
197	Dick Hall	5	5	5	5	5	10	20	80
198	Carl Sawatski	5	5	5	5	5	10	20	80
199	Bob Boyd	5	5	5	5	5	10	20	80
200	Warren Spahn	5	10	20	30	40	50	120	600
201	Pete Whisenant	5	5	5	5	8	10	15	120
202	Al Neiger RC	5	5	5	5	8	10	15	100
203	Eddie Bressoud	5	5	5	5	5	10	20	80
204	Bob Skinner	5	5	5	5	6	12	40	▲200
205	Billy Pierce	5	5	5	5	5	10	20	80
206	Gene Green	5	5	5	5	5	10	20	60
207	Dodger Southpaws	▲6	▲10	▲15	25	40	60	120	▲1,500
208	Larry Osborne	5	5	5	5	5	10	20	80
209	Ken McBride	5	5	5	5	5	10	20	60
210	Pete Runnels	5	5	5	5	5	10	30	150
211	Bob Gibson	30	40	50	80	▲120	▲200	▲400	▲2,000
212	Haywood Sullivan	5	5	5	5	5	10	20	80
213	Bill Stafford RC	5	5	6	10	15	25	30	100
214	Danny Murphy RC	5	5	5	5	5	10	25	120
215	Gus Bell	5	5	5	5	5	10	25	80
216	Ted Bowsfield	5	5	5	5	5	10	20	60
217	Mel Roach	5	5	5	5	5	10	20	60
218	Hal Brown	5	5	5	5	5	10	20	100
219	Gene Mauch MG	5	5	5	5	5	10	20	80
220	Alvin Dark MG	5	5	5	5	6	12	20	80
221	Mike Higgins MG	5	5	5	5	5	8	15	140
222	Jimmy Dykes MG	5	5	5	5	5	10	20	80
223	Bob Scheffing MG	5	5	5	5	6	12	30	100
224	Joe Gordon MG	5	5	5	5	5	12	25	80

#	Player	GD 2	VG 3	VgEx 4	EX 5	ExMt 6	NM 7	NmMt 8	MT 9
225	Bill Rigney MG	5	5	5	5	5	10	25	80
226	Cookie Lavagetto MG	5	5	5	5	5	10	25	100
227	Juan Pizarro	5	5	5	5	5	10	20	80
228	New York Yankees TC	▲15	▲25	▲40	▲50	▲60	▲100	150	▲1,000
229	Rudy Hernandez RC	5	5	5	5	5	10	20	80
230	Don Hoak	5	5	5	5	5	12	40	200
231	Dick Drott	5	5	5	5	5	10	20	
232	Bill White	5	5	5	5	8	15	50	
233	Joey Jay	5	5	5	5	5	10	20	100
234	Ted Lepcio	5	5	5	5	5	12	60	150
235	Camilo Pascual	5	5	5	5	5	10	25	80
236	Don Gile RC	5	5	5	5	5	10	20	100
237	Billy Loes	5	5	5	5	5	10	20	80
238	Jim Gilliam	5	5	5	5	6	12	25	100
239	Dave Sisler	5	5	5	5	5	10	20	60
240	Ron Hansen	5	5	5	5	5	12	60	150
241	Al Cicotte	5	5	5	5	5	10	20	60
242	Hal Smith	5	5	5	12	25	50	100	150
243	Frank Lary	5	5	5	5	5	10	60	150
244	Chico Cardenas	5	5	5	5	5	10	25	100
245	Joe Adcock	5	5	5	5	6	15	25	
246	Bob Davis RC	5	5	5	5	5	10	20	80
247	Billy Goodman	5	5	5	5	8	15	80	
248	Ed Keegan RC	5	5	5	5	5	10	15	60
249	Cincinnati Reds TC	5	5	5	8	12	20	50	250
250	Buc Hill Aces	5	5	5	5	6	12	50	150
251	Bill Bruton	5	5	5	5	5	12	40	
252	Bill Short	5	5	5	5	5	10	25	200
253	Sammy Taylor	5	5	5	5	5	8	15	80
254	Ted Sadowski RC	5	5	5	5	8	10	20	80
255	Vic Power	5	5	5	6	8	12	25	100
256	Billy Hoeft	5	5	5	6	8	12	25	100
257	Carroll Hardy	5	5	5	6	8	12	25	100
258	Jack Sanford	5	5	6	8	10	15	30	120
259	John Schaive RC	5	5	5	5	5	10	20	80
260	Don Drysdale	10	15	25	40	50	▲80	100	400
261	Charlie Lau	5	5	5	5	5	10	20	80
262	Tony Curry	5	5	5	5	5	10	20	80
263	Ken Hamlin	5	5	5	5	5	10	20	80
264	Glen Hobbie	5	5	5	5	5	10	20	
265	Tony Kubek	5	6	8	12	25	60	150	
266	Lindy McDaniel	5	5	5	5	5	8	15	80
267	Norm Siebern	5	5	5	5	5	10	20	120
268	Ike Delock	5	5	5	5	5	10	20	80
269	Harry Chiti	5	5	5	5	5	10	20	80
270	Bob Friend	5	5	5	5	8	12	40	200
271	Jim Landis	5	5	5	5	5	10	20	100
272	Tom Morgan	5	5	5	5	5	10	20	80
273A	Checklist 4 Copyright at 336	5	5	5	5	8	15		
273B	Checklist 4 Copyright at 339	5	5	5	6	12	30		
274	Gary Bell	5	5	5	5	5	8	15	100
275	Gene Woodling	5	5	5	5	5	10	25	60
276	Ray Rippelmeyer RC	5	5	5	5	5	10	20	80
277	Hank Foiles	5	5	5	5	5	10	20	60
278	Don McMahon	5	5	5	5	5	10	20	80
279	Jose Pagan	5	5	5	5	5	12	40	
280	Frank Howard	5	6	8	10	12	20	60	120
281	Frank Sullivan	5	5	6	10	15	25	60	
282	Faye Throneberry	5	5	5	5	5	10	20	100
283	Bob Anderson	5	5	5	5	5	10	20	60
284	Dick Gernert	5	5	5	5	5	8	15	60
285	Sherm Lollar	5	5	5	5	6	12	25	80
286	George Witt	5	5	5	5	5	10	20	120
287	Carl Yastrzemski	▲50	▲80	▲120	▲150	▲250	400	600	3,000
288	Albie Pearson	5	5	5	5	5	10	25	
289	Ray Moore	5	5	5	5	5	10	25	
290	Stan Musial	▲30	▲50	▲80	100	120	200	400	▲2,500
291	Tex Clevenger	5	5	5	5	5	12	50	

		GD 2	VG 3	VgEx 4	EX 5	ExMt 6	NM 7	NmMt 8	MT 9
292	Jim Baumer RC	5	5	5	5	5	10	25	100
293	Tom Sturdivant	5	5	5	5	5	12	60	
294	Don Blasingame	5	5	5	5	6	15	80	
295	Milt Pappas	5	5	5	5	5	10	25	100
296	Wes Covington	5	5	6	10	15	25	40	80
297	Kansas City Athletics TC	5	5	5	5	6	12	30	
298	Jim Golden RC	5	5	5	5	5	10	20	100
299	Clay Dalrymple	5	5	5	5	5	10	20	200
300	Mickey Mantle	▲250	▲400	▲600	▲1,000	▲1,500	2,000	▲8,000	20,000
301	Chet Nichols	5	5	5	5	5	15	80	150
302	Al Heist RC	5	5	5	5	5	10	60	
303	Gary Peters	5	5	5	5	5	12	30	150
304	Rocky Nelson	5	5	5	5	6	12	25	100
305	Mike McCormick	5	5	5	5	6	12	25	150
306	Bill Virdon WS1	5	5	5	5	15	80	500	
307	Mickey Mantle WS2	30	50	60	100	120	▲200	▲300	800
308	Bobby Richardson WS3	5	5	5	5	12	40	120	
309	Gino Cimoli WS4	5	5	5	5	12	30	80	
310	Roy Face WS5	5	5	8	12	20	30	120	500
311	Whitey Ford WS6	5	5	6	10	15	30	60	▲1,500
312	Bill Mazeroski WS7	5	6	10	15	50	100	400	
313	The Winners Celebrate WS	5	5	6	10	15	25	80	
314	Bob Miller	5	5	5	5	5	10	20	80
315	Earl Battey	5	5	5	5	5	10	50	100
316	Bobby Gene Smith	5	5	5	5	5	10	25	
317	Jim Brewer RC	5	5	5	5	5	10	20	60
318	Danny O'Connell	5	5	5	5	5	10	20	100
319	Valmy Thomas	5	5	5	5	5	10	20	100
320	Lou Burdette	5	5	5	5	6	12	50	150
321	Marv Breeding	5	5	5	5	5	10	20	80
322	Bill Kunkel RC	5	5	5	5	5	10	20	
323	Sammy Esposito	5	5	5	5	5	10	20	
324	Hank Aguirre	5	5	5	5	5	10	30	300
325	Wally Moon	5	5	5	5	6	12	30	250
326	Dave Hillman	5	5	5	5	5	10	20	100
327	Matty Alou RC	5	5	6	8	20	25	60	200
328	Jim O'Toole	5	5	5	5	5	10	25	80
329	Julio Becquer	5	5	5	5	5	10	20	100
330	Rocky Colavito	5	8	10	15	20	40	60	500
331	Ned Garver	5	5	5	5	5	10	30	
332	Dutch Dotterer	5	5	5	5	5	10	20	50
333	Fritz Brickell RC	5	5	5	5	6	12	25	100
334	Walt Bond	5	5	5	5	5	10	20	80
335	Frank Bolling	5	5	5	5	5	10	20	120
336	Don Mincher	5	5	5	5	5	10	30	80
337	Al's Aces	5	5	5	5	8	20	80	
338	Don Landrum	5	5	5	5	5	15	80	
339	Gene Baker	5	5	5	5	5	10	20	80
340	Vic Wertz	5	5	5	5	5	20	25	80
341	Jim Owens	5	5	5	5	5	10	20	100
342	Clint Courtney	5	5	5	5	6	12	40	100
343	Earl Robinson RC	5	5	5	5	5	10	20	80
344	Sandy Koufax	30	50	60	80	100	150	▲1,000	▲5,000
345	Jimmy Piersall	5	5	5	5	8	30	60	250
346	Howie Nunn	5	5	5	5	5	10	20	80
347	St. Louis Cardinals TC	5	5	5	5	8	12	20	100
348	Steve Boros	5	5	5	5	6	12	50	200
349	Danny McDevitt	5	5	6	10	15	25	40	
350	Ernie Banks	▲12	▲20	30	40	50	80	200	▲1,200
351	Jim King	5	5	5	5	5	10	30	
352	Bob Shaw	5	5	5	5	6	12	40	
353	Howie Bedell RC	5	5	5	5	5	10	20	100
354	Billy Harrell	5	5	5	5	5	10	20	
355	Bob Allison	5	5	5	5	6	8	40	60
356	Ryne Duren	5	5	5	5	8	25	80	300
357	Daryl Spencer	5	5	5	5	5	10	20	80
358	Earl Averill Jr.	5	5	5	5	8	12	30	100
359	Dallas Green	5	5	5	5	6	12	25	120
360	Frank Robinson	5	10	30	40	50	60	200	400
361A	Checklist 5 Black Topps	5	5	5	5	6	12	50	200
361B	Checklist 5 Yelllow Topps	5	5	5	5	8	15	120	
362	Frank Funk RC	5	5	5	5	5	10	20	
363	John Roseboro	5	5	5	5	6	12	25	80
364	Moe Drabowsky	5	5	5	5	5	10	25	60
365	Jerry Lumpe	5	5	5	5	5	10	30	
366	Eddie Fisher	5	5	5	5	5	8	20	80
367	Jim Rivera	5	5	5	5	5	10	25	150
368	Bennie Daniels	5	5	5	5	5	10	30	200
369	Dave Philley	5	5	5	5	5	10	80	100
370	Roy Face	5	5	5	5	6	12	40	250
371	Bill Skowron SP	5	6	10	15	30	50	80	200
372	Bob Hendley RC	5	5	5	5	5	10	20	
373	Boston Red Sox TC	5	5	5	8	15	40		
374	Paul Giel	5	5	5	5	5	10	20	80
375	Ken Boyer	5	5	5	8	10	25	80	
376	Mike Roarke RC	5	5	5	5	5	10	20	100
377	Ruben Gomez	5	5	5	5	6	12	25	80
378	Wally Post	5	5	5	5	6	12	25	80
379	Bobby Shantz	5	5	5	5	8	15	50	200
380	Minnie Minoso	5	5	5	5	6	12	40	150
381	Dave Wickersham RC	5	5	5	5	6	12	25	80
382	Frank Thomas	5	5	5	5	5	20	40	120
383	Frisco First Liners	5	5	5	5	8	25	80	
384	Chuck Essegian	5	5	5	5	5	10	20	80
385	Jim Perry	5	5	5	5	5	10	25	50
386	Joe Hicks	5	5	5	5	5	10	20	100
387	Duke Maas	5	5	5	5	6	12	25	100
388	Roberto Clemente	50	80	100	120	200	300	1,000	1,500
389	Ralph Terry	5	5	5	6	15	40	150	
390	Del Crandall	5	5	5	5	5	10	25	80
391	Winston Brown RC	5	5	5	5	5	10	20	80
392	Reno Bertoia	5	5	5	5	5	10	20	80
393	Batter Bafflers	5	5	5	5	6	12	25	120
394	Ken Walters	5	5	5	5	5	10	60	80
395	Chuck Estrada	5	5	5	5	5	20	30	
396	Bob Aspromonte	5	5	5	5	6	12	40	80
397	Hal Woodeshick	5	5	5	5	5	10	20	80
398	Hank Bauer	5	5	5	5	6	12	40	
399	Cliff Cook RC	5	5	5	5	5	10	20	80
400	Vern Law	5	5	5	5	6	12	40	150
401	Babe Ruth 60th HR	30	40	50	60	100	200	250	600
402	Don Larsen Perfect SP	5	6	10	15	25	40	150	200
403	26 Inning Tire	5	5	5	5	6	15	30	100
404	Rogers Hornsby .424	5	5	5	8	12	20	60	120
405	Lou Gehrig Streak	20	25	30	50	60	80	120	250
406	Mickey Mantle 565 HR	▲20	▲30	▲50	▲80	100	120	200	500
407	Jack Chesbro Wins 41	5	5	6	10	12	20	30	200
408	Christy Mathewson K's SP	6	8	12	15	20	40	60	
409	Walter Johnson Shutout	5	5	6	10	20	40	100	
410	Harvey Haddix 12 Perfect	5	5	5	6	8	20	30	80
411	Tony Taylor	5	5	5	5	5	10	20	50
412	Larry Sherry	5	5	5	5	5	10	25	100
413	Eddie Yost	5	5	5	5	5	10	25	100
414	Dick Donovan	5	5	5	5	5	10	20	80
415	Hank Aaron	40	60	80	100	200	300	▲2,000	▲4,000
416	Dick Howser RC	5	5	5	5	6	20	80	200
417	Juan Marichal SP RC	▲80	▲120	▲200	300	▲500	▲800	▲1,200	4,000
418	Ed Bailey	5	5	5	5	5	10	20	60
419	Tom Borland	5	5	5	5	6	12	40	
420	Ernie Broglio	5	5	5	5	5	10	20	80
421	Ty Cline SP RC	5	5	5	8	12	20	30	120
422	Bud Daley	5	5	5	5	5	10	20	350
423	Charlie Neal SP	5	5	5	8	12	25	40	100
424	Turk Lown	5	5	5	5	6	12	25	
425	Yogi Berra	20	30	50	60	100	200	400	2,000
426	Milwaukee Braves TC UER 463	5	5	5	5	8	15	40	150

#	Player	GD 2	VG 3	VgEx 4	EX 5	ExMt 6	NM 7	NmMt 8	MT 9
427	Dick Ellsworth	5	5	5	5	5	10	25	80
428	Ray Barker SP RC	5	5	▲8	▲12	▲20	30	▲50	80
429	Al Kaline	6	10	15	25	40	80	200	
430	Bill Mazeroski SP	▲8	▲12	▲20	▲30	▲50	▲80	▲120	500
431	Chuck Stobbs	5	5	5	5	5	10	30	100
432	Coot Veal	5	5	5	5	5	10	30	60
433	Art Mahaffey	5	5	5	5	5	10	20	80
434	Tom Brewer	5	5	5	5	5	10	20	80
435	Orlando Cepeda	5	8	12	20	30	50	80	
436	Jim Maloney SP RC	5	5	5	8	12	50	100	250
437A	Checklist 6 440 is Louis	5	5	5	5	6	12	60	100
437B	Checklist 6 440 is Luis	5	5	5	5	6	12	25	150
438	Curt Flood	5	5	6	10	15	25	60	
439	Phil Regan RC	5	5	5	5	8	15	30	100
440	Luis Aparicio	5	5	6	10	20	30	60	120
441	Dick Bertell RC	5	5	5	5	5	10	20	60
442	Gordon Jones	5	5	5	5	5	10	20	100
443	Duke Snider	10	15	30	40	50	60	150	500
444	Joe Nuxhall	5	5	5	5	6	12	25	80
445	Frank Malzone	5	5	5	5	6	10	25	200
446	Bob Taylor	5	5	5	5	8	20	50	
447	Harry Bright	5	5	5	5	6	12	20	
448	Del Rice	5	5	5	8	12	20	30	100
449	Bob Bolin RC	5	5	5	5	6	12	25	80
450	Jim Lemon	5	5	5	5	6	12	40	120
451	Power for Ernie	5	5	5	5	8	15	30	100
452	Bob Allen RC	5	5	5	5	6	10	25	80
453	Dick Schofield	5	5	5	5	6	12	25	80
454	Pumpsie Green	5	5	5	5	6	12	30	80
455	Early Wynn	5	▲6	▲10	▲15	▲25	▲40	▲60	▲300
456	Hal Bevan	5	5	5	5	6	12	25	100
457	Johnny James	5	5	5	5	8	15	40	150
458	Willie Tasby	5	5	5	5	6	10	20	60
459	Terry Fox RC	5	5	5	5	6	12	25	80
460	Gil Hodges	5	5	6	15	25	50	▲120	250
461	Smoky Burgess	5	5	5	8	15	50	▲250	
462	Lou Klimchock	5	5	5	5	6	12	20	80
463	Jack Fisher	5	5	6	8	10	25	100	150
464	Lee Thomas RC	5	5	5	5	6	12	40	120
465	Roy McMillan	5	5	5	5	6	12	30	100
466	Ron Moeller RC	5	5	5	5	6	12	25	80
467	Cleveland Indians TC	5	5	5	5	8	20	40	150
468	John Callison	5	5	5	5	6	20	40	80
469	Ralph Lumenti	5	5	5	5	6	12	20	80
470	Roy Sievers	5	5	5	5	12	15	25	
471	Phil Rizzuto MVP	▲6	▲10	▲15	▲25	▲40	▲100	150	
472	Yogi Berra MVP SP	12	20	30	50	60	100	250	1,500
473	Bob Shantz MVP	5	5	5	5	▲8	12	30	
474	Al Rosen MVP	5	5	5	▲8	▲12	20	40	▲250
475	Mickey Mantle MVP	80	▲120	▲200	▲300	▲500	▲800	▲1,200	▲3,000
476	Jackie Jensen MVP	5	5	5	10	20	50	100	
477	Nellie Fox MVP	5	5	5	8	15	50	60	300
478	Roger Maris MVP	10	25	40	50	60	80	250	▲2,500
479	Jim Konstanty MVP	5	5	5	5	6	25	60	
480	Roy Campanella MVP	6	▲10	▼15	25	40	60	▲250	800
481	Hank Sauer MVP	5	5	5	5	5	10	15	120
482	Willie Mays MVP	▲25	▲40	▲60	▲100	▲120	▲150	250	▲4,000
483	Don Newcombe MVP	5	5	5	5	12	25	50	100
484	Hank Aaron MVP	▲25	▲40	▲60	▲100	▲120	▲200	▲400	▲1,200
485	Ernie Banks MVP	8	12	20	30	50	80	300	1,000
486	Dick Groat MVP	5	5	5	8	12	20	50	300
487	Gene Oliver	5	5	5	5	6	12	25	100
488	Joe McClain RC	5	5	5	6	10	15	25	60
489	Walt Dropo	5	5	5	5	8	25	60	
490	Jim Bunning	5	5	5	8	15	25	80	300
491	Philadelphia Phillies TC	5	5	5	5	8	20	40	▲250
492A	Ron Fairly White	5	5	5	5	8	15	60	
493	Don Zimmer	5	5	5	5	12	25	40	150
494	Tom Cheney	5	5	5	6	10	20	50	200
495	Elston Howard	5	▲8	▲12	▲20	▲30	▲50	▲100	250
496	Ken MacKenzie	5	5	5	5	6	12	30	100
497	Willie Jones	5	5	5	5	6	12	30	80
498	Ray Herbert	5	5	5	5	6	12	50	100
499	Chuck Schilling RC	5	5	5	5	10	12	25	80
500	Harvey Kuenn	5	5	▲6	▲10	15	25	▲80	
501	John DeMerit RC	5	5	5	5	6	12	40	100
502	Choo Choo Coleman RC	5	5	5	5	6	12	30	100
503	Tito Francona	5	5	5	5	6	12	30	100
504	Billy Consolo	5	5	5	5	6	20	25	60
505	Red Schoendienst	5	5	▲6	▲10	▼15	25	▲100	400
506	Willie Davis RC	5	6	8	12	20	30	80	
507	Pete Burnside	5	5	5	6	8	10	25	60
508	Rocky Bridges	5	5	5	5	6	12	25	80
509	Camilo Carreon	5	5	5	5	6	12	40	
510	Art Ditmar	5	5	5	5	8	15	40	80
511	Joe M. Morgan	5	5	5	5	6	15	30	100
512	Bob Will	5	5	5	5	6	12	25	80
513	Jim Brosnan	5	5	5	5	6	12	25	80
514	Jake Wood RC	5	5	5	5	6	12	25	80
515	Jackie Brandt	5	5	5	8	12	20	40	600
516A	Checklist 7	5	5	5	5	8	15	100	
516B	Checklist 7								
	(C on front fully above Braves cap)								
517	Willie McCovey	▲15	▲25	40	▲60	▲100	▲150	250	▲1,200
518	Andy Carey	5	5	5	5	6	12	25	80
519	Jim Pagliaroni RC	5	5	5	5	6	12	30	100
520	Joe Cunningham	5	5	5	8	12	20	80	
521	Brother Battery	5	5	5	8	12	20	30	80
522	Dick Farrell	5	5	5	8	12	20	30	100
523	Joe Gibbon	5	6	10	15	40	▲120	300	
524	Johnny Logan	5	6	10	15	40	50	▲80	300
525	Ron Perranoski RC	▲10	▲15	▲25	▲40	▲60	▲100	▲150	▲300
526	R.C. Stevens	5	▲6	▲10	▲15	▲25	▲60	▲100	
527	Gene Leek RC	5	5	8	12	20	30	60	▲200
528	Pedro Ramos	5	6	8	12	20	50	80	
529	Bob Roselli	5	5	6	15	20	30	50	120
530	Bob Malkmus	5	▲6	▲10	▲15	▲25	40	▲100	
531	Jim Coates	▲10	▲15	▲25	40	▲60	▲100	150	
532	Bob Hale	5	5	6	10	15	40	50	150
533	Jack Curtis RC	5	5	8	12	20	40	60	
534	Eddie Kasko	5	5	8	12	20	30	100	600
535	Larry Jackson	5	8	12	20	30	50	60	
536	Bill Tuttle	5	5	6	8	12	50	▲100	▲200
537	Bobby Locke	5	5	8	12	20	40	50	150
538	Chuck Hiller RC	5	5	8	15	20	50	60	250
539	Johnny Klippstein	5	5	8	12	25	40	60	200
540	Jackie Jensen	5	6	8	12	25	30	80	200
541	Rollie Sheldon RC	6	10	15	50	60	100	▲200	
542	Minnesota Twins TC	6	10	15	25	40	80	150	800
543	Roger Craig	▲6	▲10	▲15	25	▲40	▲60	100	250
544	George Thomas RC	5	6	8	12	25	50	60	150
545	Hoyt Wilhelm	5	10	30	40	60	80	150	300
546	Marty Kutyna	5	5	8	12	25	50	80	
547	Leon Wagner	5	8	12	20	30	40	60	150
548	Ted Wills	5	6	10	15	25	50	120	
549	Hal R. Smith	5	5	6	10	15	40	60	▲100
550	Frank Baumann	5	5	8	12	20	30	50	150
551	George Altman	5	6	8	12	20	40	60	150
552	Jim Archer RC	5	6	10	15	25	40	▲80	
553	Bill Fischer	5	5	8	12	20	50	80	
554	Pittsburgh Pirates TC	15	20	50	60	80	120	250	
555	Sam Jones	5	6	10	15	25	50	100	250
556	Ken R. Hunt RC	5	5	8	12	20	40	80	250
557	Jose Valdivielso	5	5	8	12	25	50	80	150
558	Don Ferrarese	5	5	8	12	20	40	60	▲200
559	Jim Gentile	15	▲25	▲40	60	80	200	600	

#	Player	GD 2	VG 3	VgEx 4	EX 5	ExMt 6	NM 7	NmMt 8	MT 9
60	Barry Latman	5	▲6	▲10	▲15	▲25	▼40	▲60	120
61	Charley James	5	5	8	12	20	50	80	100
62	Bill Monbouquette	5	5	8	12	20	40	50	
63	Bob Cerv	12	20	40	60	100	200	600	
64	Don Cardwell	5	5	8	12	20	50	80	
65	Felipe Alou	5	6	8	12	▲50	▲80	▲120	▲250
66	Paul Richards AS MG	5	5	8	12	20	50	60	150
67	Danny Murtaugh AS MG	5	5	8	12	20	40	100	250
68	Bill Skowron AS	5	5	8	12	30	60	80	150
69	Frank Herrera AS	5	5	8	12	25	30	80	250
70	Nellie Fox AS	5	6	8	12	40	60	80	150
71	Bill Mazeroski AS	5	8	12	40	50	60	120	300
72	Brooks Robinson AS	6	10	15	25	60	▲120	250	400
73	Ken Boyer AS	8	8	12	30	40	50	60	120
74	Luis Aparicio AS	6	8	12	20	30	60	80	150
75	Ernie Banks AS	8	12	30	60	80	100	200	600
76	Roger Maris AS	25	30	60	80	120	200	250	500
77	Hank Aaron AS	20	25	50	100	120	200	300	600
78	Mickey Mantle AS	▲250	▲300	▲500	▲600	▲800	▲1,200	▲1,500	▲3,000
79	Willie Mays AS	▲30	▲50	▲80	▲120	▲200	▲300	▲800	1,200
80	Al Kaline AS	6	10	15	40	50	100	250	400
81	Frank Robinson AS	25	30	40	50	60	80	200	400
82	Earl Battey AS	5	5	8	25	30	40	60	120
83	Del Crandall AS	5	5	8	12	20	40	80	200
84	Jim Perry AS	5	5	8	12	25	40	80	200
85	Bob Friend AS	5	5	8	12	25	40	80	200
86	Whitey Ford AS	8	12	20	40	60	80	120	500
89	Warren Spahn AS	6	10	15	40	80	100	200	500

- Whitey Ford #160 PSA 9 (MT) sold for $3,518 (Mile High; 05/11)
- Juan Marichal SP #417 PSA 10 (Gem) (Young Collection) sold for $7,691 (SCP; 5/12)
- Ron Santo #35 PSA 10 (Gem) (Young Collection) sold for $5,948 (SCP; 5/12)
- Billy Williams #141 PSA 10 (Gem) (Young Collection) sold for $6,738 (SCP; 5/12)

1962 Topps

Player	GD 2	VG 3	VgEx 4	EX 5	ExMt 6	NM 7	NmMt 8	MT 9
Roger Maris	50	60	100	120	250	800	▲5,000	
Jim Brosnan	5	5	5	8	15	30	100	
Pete Runnels	5	5	6	10	15	25	450	
John DeMerit	5	5	5	5	6	12	25	
Sandy Koufax	▲50	80	▲120	▲200	▲300	▲800	2,000	
Marv Breeding	5	5	5	5	6	25	300	
Frank Thomas	5	5	5	5	6	20	60	
Ray Herbert	5	5	5	5	6	20	60	
Jim Davenport	5	5	5	5	6	15	40	
Roberto Clemente	60	▲100	▲150	▲250	▲400	600	▲2,500	8,000
Tom Morgan	5	5	5	5	6	12	25	
Harry Craft MG	5	5	5	5	6	15	80	
Dick Howser	5	5	5	5	6	12	30	
Bill White	5	5	5	5	8	15	120	
Dick Donovan	5	5	5	5	6	12	25	
Darrell Johnson	5	5	5	5	6	12	25	
Johnny Callison	5	5	5	5	8	15	150	
Managers Dream	50	60	100	120	150	400	1,200	
Ray Washburn RC	5	5	5	5	6	12	25	
Rocky Colavito	5	6	10	15	25	40	80	
Jim Kaat	5	5	6	8	12	20	40	200
Checklist 1 ERR 121-176	5	5	5	5	6	12	25	150
Checklist 1 COR 33-88	5	5	5	8	12	25	100	
Norm Larker	5	5	5	5	6	12	20	80
Detroit Tigers TC	5	5	5	5	8	15	30	300
Ernie Banks	20	50	60	80	120	200	600	6,000
Chris Cannizzaro	8	12	25	5	6	12	30	
Chuck Cottier	5	5	5	5	6	12	25	
Minnie Minoso	5	5	5	6	20	30	80	
Casey Stengel MG	5	6	10	15	25	50	80	
Eddie Mathews	8	12	40	50	60	100	500	
Tom Tresh RC	5	8	12	20	30	50	60	400

#	Player	GD 2	VG 3	VgEx 4	EX 5	ExMt 6	NM 7	NmMt 8	MT 9
32	John Roseboro	5	5	5	5	8	15	80	
33	Don Larsen	5	5	5	5	8	15	30	200
34	Johnny Temple	5	5	5	5	6	12	25	200
35	Don Schwall RC	5	5	5	5	8	20	50	400
36	Don Leppert RC	5	5	5	5	6	12	25	
37	Tribe Hill Trio	5	5	5	5	8	15	30	
38	Gene Stephens	5	5	5	5	6	12	80	
39	Joe Koppe	5	5	5	5	6	12	25	200
40	Orlando Cepeda	5	5	8	12	25	100	300	
41	Cliff Cook	5	5	5	5	6	12	25	
42	Jim King	5	5	5	5	6	12	25	
43	Los Angeles Dodgers TC	5	5	5	6	10	20	40	325
44	Don Taussig RC	5	5	5	5	6	12	25	250
45	Brooks Robinson	8	15	20	30	50	80	300	
46	Jack Baldschun RC	5	5	5	6	8	15	30	
47	Bob Will	5	5	5	5	6	12	25	
48	Ralph Terry	5	5	6	10	15	25	60	
49	Hal Jones RC	5	5	5	5	6	12	25	
50	Stan Musial	20	30	40	60	80	120	250	2,000
51	AL Batting Leaders	5	5	5	5	8	20	60	
52	NL Batting Leaders	8	12	15	20	25	50	120	500
53	AL Home Run Leaders	10	30	40	60	80	120	400	800
54	NL Home Run Leaders	5	5	6	20	25	40	80	600
55	AL ERA Leaders	5	5	5	5	8	15	30	200
56	NL ERA Leaders	5	5	5	5	8	15	40	300
57	AL Win Leaders	5	5	6	10	15	25	50	300
58	NL Win Leaders	5	5	5	6	10	25	80	
59	AL Strikeout Leaders	5	5	5	5	8	20	30	250
60	NL Strikeout Leaders	5	5	6	8	30	40	100	575
61	St. Louis Cardinals TC	5	5	5	5	8	15	40	250
62	Steve Boros	5	5	5	5	6	12	25	
63	Tony Cloninger RC	5	5	5	5	6	12	25	350
64	Russ Snyder	5	5	5	5	6	12	25	250
65	Bobby Richardson	5	5	5	12	15	50	120	
66	Cuno Barragan RC	5	5	5	5	6	12	25	150
67	Harvey Haddix	5	5	5	6	10	15	25	
68	Ken Hunt	5	5	5	5	6	12	30	
69	Phil Ortega RC	5	5	5	5	6	12	25	150
70	Harmon Killebrew	5	8	20	30	40	80	400	4,000
71	Dick LeMay RC	5	5	5	5	6	12	25	200
72	Bob's Pupils	5	5	5	5	6	12	30	300
73	Nellie Fox	5	5	12	15	25	50	250	500
74	Bob Lillis	5	5	5	5	6	12	25	
75	Milt Pappas	5	5	5	5	6	20	80	
76	Howie Bedell	5	5	5	5	6	12	25	
77	Tony Taylor	5	5	5	5	6	25	60	
78	Gene Green	5	5	5	5	6	12	50	150
79	Ed Hobaugh	5	5	5	5	6	12	25	200
80	Vada Pinson	5	5	5	5	8	20	50	250
81	Jim Pagliaroni	5	5	5	5	6	12	25	
82	Deron Johnson	5	5	5	5	6	15	25	200
83	Larry Jackson	5	5	5	5	6	12	40	
84	Lenny Green	5	5	5	5	6	20	100	
85	Gil Hodges	5	6	10	15	40	50	100	
86	Donn Clendenon RC	5	5	5	5	8	15	40	250
87	Mike Roarke	5	5	5	5	6	12	30	
88	Ralph Houk MG	5	5	5	5	8	15	60	
89	Barney Schultz RC	5	5	5	5	6	12	25	175
90	Jimmy Piersall	5	5	5	5	8	20	30	
91	J.C. Martin	5	5	5	5	6	12	200	
92	Sam Jones	5	5	5	5	6	25	30	
93	John Blanchard	5	5	5	5	8	50	500	
94	Jay Hook	5	5	5	5	6	12	25	250
95	Don Hoak	5	5	5	5	6	15	50	
96	Eli Grba	5	5	5	5	6	12	25	
97	Tito Francona	5	5	5	5	6	12	40	
98	Checklist 2	5	5	5	5	6	12	25	100
99	Boog Powell RC	8	12	20	30	40	60	120	

#	Name	GD 2	VG 3	VgEx 4	EX 5	ExMt 6	NM 7	NmMt 8	MT 9
100	Warren Spahn	12	15	20	30	40	100	400	
101	Carroll Hardy	5	5	5	5	6	12	25	150
102	Al Schroll	5	5	5	5	6	12	25	
103	Don Blasingame	5	5	5	5	6	12	80	
104	Ted Savage RC	5	5	5	6	10	15	30	120
105	Don Mossi	5	5	5	5	6	15	25	
106	Carl Sawatski	5	5	5	6	10	15	25	150
107	Mike McCormick	5	5	5	5	6	20	30	
108	Willie Davis	5	5	5	5	8	20	30	
109	Bob Shaw	5	5	5	5	6	12	30	
110	Bill Skowron	5	5	5	6	10	40	200	500
111	Dallas Green	5	5	5	5	8	30	135	
112	Hank Foiles	5	5	5	5	6	12	30	
113	Chicago White Sox TC	5	5	5	5	8	15	50	200
114	Howie Koplitz RC	5	5	5	5	6	12	30	200
115	Bob Skinner	5	5	5	5	10	50	200	
116	Herb Score	5	5	5	5	8	40	10	
117	Gary Geiger	5	5	5	5	6	15	120	
118	Julian Javier	5	5	5	6	12	60	300	
119	Danny Murphy	5	5	5	5	6	12	30	200
120	Bob Purkey	5	5	5	5	6	25	200	
121	Billy Hitchcock MG	5	5	5	5	6	15	40	
122	Norm Bass RC	5	5	5	5	6	20	30	
123	Mike de la Hoz	5	5	5	5	6	12	40	
124	Bill Pleis RC	5	5	5	5	6	12	30	
125	Gene Woodling	5	5	5	5	6	12	30	
126	Al Cicotte	5	5	5	5	6	12	30	200
127	Pride of A's	5	5	5	5	8	15	40	200
128	Art Fowler	5	5	5	5	6	12	40	
129A	Lee Walls Face Right, Plain Jsy	5	5	5	5	6	15	80	
129B	Lee Walls Face Left, Striped Jsy	5	5	5	8	12	30	100	
130	Frank Bolling	5	5	5	5	6	30	250	
131	Pete Richert RC	5	5	5	5	6	10	40	
132A	Los Angeles Angels TC No Inset	5	5	5	5	8	15	40	
132B	Los Angeles Angels TC With Inset	5	5	6	10	15	25	60	
133	Felipe Alou	5	5	5	5	8	15	50	300
134A	Billy Hoeft Blue Sky	5	5	6	10	15	60		
135	Babe as a Boy	5	5	8	12	25	50	250	800
136	Babe Joins Yanks	5	5	6	10	30	50	100	
137	Babe with Mgr. Huggins	5	5	15	20	25	30	100	800
138	The Famous Slugger	5	5	6	10	40	50	120	800
139A1	Babe Hits 60 (Pole)	5	6	10	30	50	100		
139A2	Babe Hits 60 (No Pole)	5	6	10	30	50	80	1,000	
139B	Hal Reniff Portrait	5	5	5	8	15	50	250	
139C	Hal Reniff Pitching	6	10	15	25	40	100	400	
140	Gehrig and Ruth	5	8	12	40	50	80	250	800
141	Twilight Years	10	12	15	25	30	40	120	600
142	Coaching the Dodgers	5	5	8	15	40	50	120	800
143	Greatest Sports Hero	5	15	20	25	30	40	100	600
144	Farewell Speech	5	5	8	25	30	60	150	800
145	Barry Latman	5	5	5	5	8	15	30	150
146	Don Demeter	5	5	5	5	6	12	25	
147A	Bill Kunkel Portrait	5	5	5	8	12	20	100	
147B	Bill Kunkel Pitching	5	5	6	10	15	25	100	
148	Wally Post	5	5	5	5	12	20	60	400
149	Bob Duliba	5	5	5	5	6	12	25	200
150	Al Kaline	10	20	25	30	50	80	400	2,700
151	Johnny Klippstein	5	5	5	5	6	12	30	150
152	Mickey Vernon MG	5	5	5	6	10	15	30	150
153	Pumpsie Green	5	5	5	5	8	15	30	225
154	Lee Thomas	5	5	5	5	6	25	60	
155	Stu Miller	5	5	5	5	6	12	40	150
156	Merritt Ranew RC	5	5	6	8	12	20	40	150
157	Wes Covington	5	5	5	5	8	20	30	
158	Milwaukee Braves TC	5	5	5	5	8	15	30	200
159	Hal Reniff RC	5	5	5	6	12	40	200	
160	Dick Stuart	5	5	5	5	8	30	200	
161	Frank Baumann	5	5	5	5	6	25	30	
162	Sammy Drake RC	5	5	5	5	8	15	40	200
163	Hot Corner Guardians	5	5	5	8	12	20	80	300
164	Hal Naragon	5	5	5	5	6	12	25	150
165	Jackie Brandt	5	5	5	5	6	15	50	
166	Don Lee	5	5	5	5	6	12	50	400
167	Tim McCarver RC	5	5	20	25	40	50	150	600
168	Leo Posada	5	5	5	5	6	12	25	
169	Bob Cerv	5	5	5	6	10	40	120	300
170	Ron Santo	5	5	15	25	30	60	200	900
171	Dave Sisler	5	5	5	5	8	15	40	
172	Fred Hutchinson MG	5	5	5	5	6	12	30	150
173	Chico Fernandez	5	5	5	5	6	12	100	
174A	Carl Willey w/o Cap	5	5	5	8	12	30	175	
174B	Carl Willey w/Cap	5	6	10	15	25	60	150	
175	Frank Howard	5	5	5	5	20	25	80	
176A	Eddie Yost Portrait	5	5	5	5	6	15	100	
176B	Eddie Yost Batting	5	5	8	12	20	40	150	
177	Bobby Shantz	5	5	5	5	8	15	40	
178	Camilo Carreon	5	5	5	5	6	12	40	
179	Tom Sturdivant	5	5	5	5	6	12	40	
180	Bob Allison	5	5	5	5	8	30	60	250
181	Paul Brown RC	5	5	5	5	6	12	25	100
182	Bob Nieman	5	5	5	5	6	15	150	
183	Roger Craig	5	5	5	5	8	15	30	200
184	Haywood Sullivan	5	5	5	5	6	12	40	150
185	Roland Sheldon	5	5	5	5	8	15	50	
186	Mack Jones RC	5	5	5	5	6	12	80	
187	Gene Conley	5	5	5	5	8	15	30	200
188	Chuck Hiller	5	5	5	6	10	15	25	200
189	Dick Hall	5	5	5	5	6	12	80	
190A	Wally Moon No Cap	5	5	5	5	8	30	200	
190B	Wally Moon w/Cap	5	5	6	10	15	50	250	
191	Jim Brewer	5	5	5	8	12	20	40	
192A	Checklist 3 192 No Comma	5	5	5	5	6	12	30	
192B	Checklist 3 192 with Comma	5	5	5	5	6	12	40	150
193	Eddie Kasko	5	5	5	5	6	12	30	
194	Dean Chance RC	5	5	5	6	10	50	200	
195	Joe Cunningham	5	5	5	5	6	12	50	
196	Terry Fox	5	5	5	5	6	15	120	
197	Daryl Spencer	5	5	5	5	6	15	60	300
198	Johnny Keane MG	5	5	5	5	6	12	30	
199	Gaylord Perry RC	40	60	▲100	▲150	▲250	▲500	1,000	
200	Mickey Mantle	▲250	▲400	▲600	▲1,000	▲1,500	▲2,500	8,000	▲150,000
201	Ike Delock	5	5	5	5	6	12	60	
202	Carl Warwick RC	5	5	5	5	6	12	25	150
203	Jack Fisher	5	5	5	5	6	12	25	
204	Johnny Weekly RC	5	5	5	5	6	12	25	200
205	Gene Freese	5	5	5	5	6	12	30	
206	Washington Senators TC	5	5	5	5	8	25	30	200
207	Pete Burnside	5	5	5	5	6	15	120	
208	Billy Martin	5	5	8	12	30	40	120	
209	Jim Fregosi RC	5	5	5	8	12	50	100	1,000
210	Roy Face	5	5	5	5	8	25	80	
211	Midway Masters	5	5	5	5	8	15	40	250
212	Jim Owens	5	5	5	5	6	12	30	
213	Richie Ashburn	5	5	6	10	15	40	100	300
214	Dom Zanni	5	5	5	5	6	15	40	
215	Woody Held	5	5	5	5	6	12	40	
216	Ron Kline	5	5	5	5	6	12	40	200
217	Walter Alston MG	5	5	5	5	8	25	50	
218	Joe Torre RC	▲40	▲60	▲100	▲150	▲250	▲400	▲1,000	
219	Al Downing RC	5	5	8	12	20	40	80	
220	Roy Sievers	5	5	5	5	6	12	30	
221	Bill Short	5	5	5	5	6	15	200	
222	Jerry Zimmerman	5	5	5	5	6	12	25	
223	Alex Grammas	5	5	5	5	6	12	50	
224	Don Rudolph	5	5	5	5	6	15	60	
225	Frank Malzone	5	5	5	5	8	15	100	

		GD 2	VG 3	VgEx 4	EX 5	ExMt 6	NM 7	NmMt 8	MT 9
26	San Francisco Giants TC	5	5	5	5	8	15	50	300
27	Bob Tiefenauer	5	5	5	5	6	12	25	200
28	Dale Long	5	5	5	5	6	12	40	
29	Jesus McFarlane RC	5	5	5	5	6	12	30	
30	Camilo Pascual	5	5	5	5	6	15	60	
31	Ernie Bowman RC	5	5	5	5	6	12	25	
32	Yanks Win Opener WS1	5	5	5	6	10	30	▲100	300
33	Joey Jay WS2	5	8	12	20	30	▲150	▲300	
34	Roger Maris WS3	5	5	8	30	40	120	150	400
35	Whitey Ford WS4	5	5	5	6	25	60	80	
36	Yanks Crush Reds WS5	5	6	10	15	25	60	250	
37	Yanks Celebrate WS	5	6	10	15	25	40	80	400
38	Norm Sherry	5	5	5	5	6	12	25	
39	Cecil Butler RC	5	5	5	5	6	12	25	
40	George Altman	5	5	5	5	6	12	40	
41	Johnny Kucks	5	5	5	5	6	12	40	
42	Mel McGaha MG RC	5	5	5	5	6	12	30	
43	Robin Roberts	5	5	6	10	25	40	100	900
44	Don Gile	5	5	5	5	6	12	25	200
45	Ron Hansen	5	5	5	5	6	12	25	150
46	Art Ditmar	5	5	5	5	6	12	25	
47	Joe Pignatano	5	5	5	5	8	15	30	200
48	Bob Aspromonte	5	5	5	5	6	12	25	200
49	Ed Keegan	5	5	5	5	6	12	30	
50	Norm Cash	5	5	5	6	10	25	60	
51	New York Yankees TC	5	8	12	40	50	60	200	700
52	Earl Francis	5	5	5	5	6	12	60	200
53	Harry Chiti CO	5	5	5	5	6	12	25	
54	Gordon Windhorn RC	5	5	5	5	6	12	50	250
55	Juan Pizarro	5	5	5	5	6	10	30	
56	Elio Chacon	5	5	5	5	6	15	60	
57	Jack Spring RC	5	5	5	5	6	12	25	200
58	Marty Keough	5	5	5	5	6	10	25	150
59	Lou Klimchock	5	5	5	5	6	12	30	150
60	Billy Pierce	5	5	5	5	6	12	40	
61	George Alusik RC	5	5	5	5	6	12	25	
62	Bob Schmidt	5	5	5	5	6	12	25	150
63	The Right Pitch	5	5	5	5	6	12	40	200
64	Dick Ellsworth	5	5	5	5	6	10	20	
65	Joe Adcock	5	5	5	5	8	20	150	
66	John Anderson RC	5	5	5	5	6	20	80	150
67	Dan Dobbek	5	5	5	5	6	10	20	
68	Ken McBride	5	5	5	5	6	12	30	
69	Bob Oldis	5	5	5	5	6	12	25	200
70	Dick Groat	5	5	5	5	8	15	60	250
71	Ray Rippelmeyer	5	5	5	5	6	12	30	
72	Earl Robinson	5	5	5	5	6	12	30	
73	Gary Bell	5	5	5	5	6	12	40	
74	Sammy Taylor	5	5	5	5	6	12	25	
75	Norm Siebern	5	5	5	5	6	12	40	250
76	Hal Kolstad RC	5	5	5	5	6	12	25	200
77	Checklist 4	5	5	5	5	15	20	25	
78	Ken Johnson	5	5	5	5	6	12	50	
79	Hobie Landrith	5	5	5	5	6	12	25	
80	Johnny Podres	5	5	5	5	8	20	80	
81	Jake Gibbs RC	5	5	6	8	12	25	60	
82	Dave Hillman	5	5	5	5	6	12	25	200
83	Charlie Smith RC	5	5	5	5	8	15	30	
84	Ruben Amaro	5	5	5	5	6	20	250	
85	Curt Simmons	5	5	5	5	8	30	200	
86	Al Lopez MG	5	5	5	5	8	25	50	250
87	George Witt	5	5	6	10	15	100		
88	Billy Williams	15	25	40	60	100	500	2,000	
89	Mike Krsnich RC	5	5	5	6	8	15	50	
90	Jim Gentile	5	5	5	5	8	30	300	
91	Hal Stowe RC	5	5	5	8	12	20	200	
92	Jerry Kindall	5	5	5	5	6	12	40	250
93	Bob Miller	5	5	5	5	6	15	60	

		GD 2	VG 3	VgEx 4	EX 5	ExMt 6	NM 7	NmMt 8	MT 9
294	Philadelphia Phillies TC	5	5	5	5	8	25	30	
295	Vern Law	5	5	5	5	8	50	400	
296	Ken Hamlin	5	5	5	5	6	15	80	
297	Ron Perranoski	5	5	5	5	6	25	200	
298	Bill Tuttle	5	5	5	5	8	30	300	
299	Don Wert RC	5	5	5	5	8	40	300	
300	Willie Mays	▲80	▲120	▲200	▲300	▲500	1,500	2,000	▲8,000
301	Galen Cisco RC	5	5	5	5	6	25	400	
302	Johnny Edwards RC	5	5	5	5	6	15	60	
303	Frank Torre	5	5	5	5	6	25	50	
304	Dick Farrell	5	5	5	5	6	25	40	
305	Jerry Lumpe	5	5	5	5	6	12	80	
306	Redbird Rippers	5	5	5	5	6	15	80	
307	Jim Grant	5	5	5	5	6	25	60	
308	Neil Chrisley	5	5	5	5	6	15	80	300
309	Moe Morhardt RC	5	5	5	5	6	15	60	
310	Whitey Ford	15	25	30	40	50	100	400	1,800
311	Tony Kubek IA	5	5	5	8	20	50	150	
312	Warren Spahn IA	5	5	5	8	20	50	100	
313	Roger Maris IA	8	12	20	40	60	150	300	
314	Rocky Colavito IA	5	5	5	8	25	30	60	
315	Whitey Ford IA	5	6	10	15	30	40	80	500
316	Harmon Killebrew IA	5	5	15	20	25	50	150	
317	Stan Musial IA	5	6	10	25	30	50	120	400
318	Mickey Mantle IA	30	40	60	80	100	250	1,200	▲20,000
319	Mike McCormick IA	5	5	5	5	6	12	50	
320	Hank Aaron	▲60	▲100	▲150	▲250	▲400	▲600	▲2,500	10,000
321	Lee Stange RC	5	5	5	5	8	15	40	
322	Alvin Dark MG	5	5	5	5	6	15	100	
323	Don Landrum	5	5	5	5	8	60		
324	Joe McClain	5	5	5	5	6	15	80	
325	Luis Aparicio	5	5	5	8	25	40	400	
326	Tom Parsons RC	5	5	5	5	8	15	80	
327	Ozzie Virgil	5	5	5	5	6	15	40	
328	Ken Walters	5	5	5	5	6	12	25	200
329	Bob Bolin	5	5	5	5	6	15	300	
330	John Romano	5	5	5	5	6	25	60	
331	Moe Drabowsky	5	5	5	5	8	15	100	400
332	Don Buddin	5	5	5	5	6	15	80	
333	Frank Cipriani RC	5	5	5	5	6	12	30	
334	Boston Red Sox TC	5	5	5	5	20	30	60	
335	Bill Bruton	5	5	5	5	8	25	60	
336	Billy Muffett	5	5	5	5	6	30	120	
337	Jim Marshall	5	5	5	5	8	40	300	
338	Billy Gardner	5	5	5	5	6	15	60	250
339	Jose Valdivielso	5	5	5	5	6	12	60	200
340	Don Drysdale	▲10	15	25	30	40	▲120	▲500	1,000
341	Mike Hershberger RC	5	5	5	5	6	15	30	250
342	Ed Rakow	5	5	5	5	6	12	60	
343	Albie Pearson	5	5	5	5	8	25	200	
344	Ed Bauta RC	5	5	5	5	6	15	60	
345	Chuck Schilling	5	5	5	5	6	15	50	300
346	Jack Kralick	5	5	5	5	6	12	25	
347	Chuck Hinton RC	5	5	5	5	6	12	30	
348	Larry Burright RC	5	5	5	5	6	15	120	
349	Paul Foytack	5	5	5	8	12	100		
350	Frank Robinson	6	10	20	40	80	300	3,000	
351	Braves Backstops	5	5	5	5	6	30	100	
352	Frank Sullivan	5	5	5	5	6	30	150	
353	Bill Mazeroski	5	5	8	25	40	50	400	
354	Roman Mejias	5	5	5	5	6	12	40	150
355	Steve Barber	5	5	5	5	6	15	100	
356	Tom Haller RC	5	5	5	5	6	15	120	
357	Jerry Walker	5	5	5	5	6	12	30	
358	Tommy Davis	5	5	6	10	15	25	60	200
359	Bobby Locke	5	5	5	5	6	30	250	
360	Yogi Berra	▲25	40	▲60	▲100	▲150	▲250	400	▲10,000
361	Bob Hendley	5	5	5	5	6	15	150	

#	Player	GD 2	VG 3	VgEx 4	EX 5	ExMt 6	NM 7	NmMt 8	MT 9
362	Ty Cline	5	5	5	5	6	15	60	
363	Bob Roselli	5	5	5	5	6	15	40	
364	Ken Hunt	5	5	5	5	6	12	40	
365	Charlie Neal	5	5	5	5	8	40	250	
366	Phil Regan	5	5	5	5	6	12	40	
367	Checklist 5	5	5	5	5	6	25	30	300
368	Bob Tillman RC	5	5	5	5	6	12	25	
369	Ted Bowsfield	5	5	5	5	6	12	30	
370	Ken Boyer	5	▲6	▲10	▲15	▲25	50	200	
371	Earl Battey	5	5	▲8	▲12	▲20	▲30	100	
372	Jack Curtis	5	5	5	5	6	12	25	200
373	Al Heist	5	5	5	5	6	12	25	325
374	Gene Mauch MG	5	5	▲8	▲12	▲20	▲30	▲50	200
375	Ron Fairly	5	5	5	5	8	25	30	300
376	Bud Daley	5	5	5	5	6	12	40	
377	John Orsino RC	5	5	5	5	6	12	25	
378	Bennie Daniels	5	5	5	5	6	12	30	
379	Chuck Essegian	5	5	5	5	6	12	25	250
380	Lew Burdette	5	5	5	5	8	20	80	200
381	Chico Cardenas	5	5	5	5	6	12	40	
382	Dick Williams	5	5	5	5	6	25	40	
383	Ray Sadecki	5	5	5	5	8	15	30	
384	Kansas City Athletics TC	5	5	5	5	8	15	40	250
385	Early Wynn	5	▲6	▲10	▲15	▲25	▲40	60	500
386	Don Mincher	5	5	5	5	6	12	25	
387	Lou Brock RC	120	200	250	▲400	▲600	1,000	3,000	15,000
388	Ryne Duren	5	5	5	5	8	15	150	
389	Smoky Burgess	5	5	5	5	8	25	80	
390	Orlando Cepeda AS	5	▲6	▲10	▲15	▲25	▲40	80	
391	Bill Mazeroski AS	5	5	5	5	15	25	50	200
392	Ken Boyer AS	5	5	5	5	8	15	120	
393	Roy McMillan AS	5	5	5	5	6	12	40	
394	Hank Aaron AS	12	20	30	40	60	80	300	
395	Willie Mays AS	10	15	25	40	50	80	200	800
396	Frank Robinson AS	5	6	10	15	25	40	100	1,200
397	John Roseboro AS	5	5	5	5	8	12	30	200
398	Don Drysdale AS	5	5	10	12	15	30	60	300
399	Warren Spahn AS	5	5	12	15	20	40	60	300
400	Elston Howard	▲6	▲10	▲15	▲25	▲40	80	150	
401	AL and NL Homer Kings	10	15	25	30	40	120	250	1,000
402	Gino Cimoli	5	5	5	5	6	12	30	
403	Chet Nichols	5	5	5	5	6	12	25	150
404	Tim Harkness RC	5	5	5	5	6	12	30	250
405	Jim Perry	5	5	5	5	6	15	100	
406	Bob Taylor	5	5	5	5	6	12	40	200
407	Hank Aguirre	5	5	5	5	6	12	30	
408	Gus Bell	5	5	5	5	6	25	50	
409	Pittsburgh Pirates TC	5	5	5	5	8	15	30	300
410	Al Smith	5	5	5	5	6	12	40	
411	Danny O'Connell	5	5	5	5	6	12	25	200
412	Charlie James	5	5	5	5	6	12	25	
413	Matty Alou	5	5	6	10	15	25	80	
414	Joe Gaines RC	5	5	5	5	6	12	25	150
415	Bill Virdon	5	5	5	5	6	12	50	
416	Bob Scheffing MG	5	5	5	5	6	12	30	200
417	Joe Azcue RC	5	5	5	5	6	12	40	
418	Andy Carey	5	5	5	5	6	12	25	
419	Bob Bruce	5	5	5	5	6	12	25	
420	Gus Triandos	5	5	5	5	6	15	120	
421	Ken MacKenzie	5	5	5	5	6	12	25	
422	Steve Bilko	5	5	5	5	6	12	30	200
423	Rival League Relief Aces	5	5	5	5	8	15	80	
424	Al McBean RC	5	5	5	5	6	12	30	300
425	Carl Yastrzemski	▲25	▲40	▲60	▲100	▲150	250	1,000	1,200
426	Bob Farley RC	5	5	5	5	8	20	40	200
427	Jake Wood	5	5	5	5	6	12	30	200
428	Joe Hicks	5	5	5	5	6	12	40	
429	Billy O'Dell	5	5	5	5	6	15	40	
430	Tony Kubek	5	6	10	15	20	60	250	
431	Bob Rodgers RC	5	5	5	5	6	25	40	200
432	Jim Pendleton	5	5	5	5	6	12	25	
433	Jim Archer	5	5	5	5	6	12	25	
434	Clay Dalrymple	5	5	5	5	6	15	50	
435	Larry Sherry	5	5	5	5	8	30	250	
436	Felix Mantilla	5	5	5	5	6	20	25	
437	Ray Moore	5	5	5	5	6	12	30	250
438	Dick Brown	5	5	5	5	6	12	25	250
439	Jerry Buchek RC	5	5	5	5	6	20	30	150
440	Joey Jay	5	5	5	5	6	12	25	250
441	Checklist 6	5	5	5	5	15	30	300	
442	Wes Stock	5	5	5	5	6	12	25	
443	Del Crandall	5	5	5	5	8	15	30	200
444	Ted Wills	5	5	5	5	6	12	25	
445	Vic Power	5	5	5	5	8	25	80	
446	Don Elston	5	5	5	5	6	12	25	200
447	Willie Kirkland	5	5	5	5	8	15	30	
448	Joe Gibbon	5	5	5	▲8	▲12	▲20	30	
449	Jerry Adair	5	5	5	5	8	15	50	300
450	Jim O'Toole	5	5	5	5	8	25	60	
451	Jose Tartabull RC	5	5	5	5	15	20	30	350
452	Earl Averill Jr.	5	5	5	5	8	20	80	
453	Cal McLish	5	5	5	5	8	25	80	
454	Floyd Robinson RC	5	5	5	5	8	20	120	
455	Luis Arroyo	5	5	5	5	20	25	50	
456	Joe Amalfitano	5	5	5	5	8	15	30	
457	Lou Clinton	5	5	5	5	8	15	30	200
458A	Bob Buhl M on Cap	5	5	5	5	8	30	150	
458B	Bob Buhl Plain Cap	5	6	10	15	25	40	120	
459	Ed Bailey	5	5	5	5	10	25	120	200
460	Jim Bunning	5	6	8	12	20	60	100	
461	Ken Hubbs RC	5	▲6	▲10	▲15	▲25	50	120	600
462A	Willie Tasby W on Cap	5	5	5	5	8	30	150	
462B	Willie Tasby Plain Cap	5	6	10	15	25	40	80	250
463	Hank Bauer MG	5	5	5	6	10	20	25	200
464	Al Jackson RC	5	5	5	10	15	80	300	
465	Cincinnati Reds TC	5	5	5	5	8	15	50	300
466	Norm Cash AS	5	5	5	6	15	30	120	
467	Chuck Schilling AS	5	5	5	5	8	30	40	250
468	Brooks Robinson AS	▲6	▲10	▲15	▲25	▲40	▲60	▲100	400
469	Luis Aparicio AS	5	5	5	6	15	25	50	300
470	Al Kaline AS	5	6	8	12	50	60	300	
471	Mickey Mantle AS	60	100	120	▲200	▲300	600	800	▲25,000
472	Rocky Colavito AS	5	5	5	6	20	25	50	400
473	Elston Howard AS	5	5	5	6	10	30	80	300
474	Frank Lary AS	5	5	5	5	8	25	60	300
475	Whitey Ford AS	5	8	12	20	40	50	100	
476	Baltimore Orioles TC	5	5	5	5	8	25	50	300
477	Andre Rodgers	5	5	5	5	8	15	40	
478	Don Zimmer	5	▲8	▲12	▲20	▲30	▲50	100	300
479	Joel Horlen RC	5	5	▲6	▲10	▲15	▲25	40	
480	Harvey Kuenn	5	5	5	5	8	20	40	150
481	Vic Wertz	5	5	5	5	8	15	40	200
482	Sam Mele MG	5	5	5	5	8	15	30	150
483	Don McMahon	5	5	5	5	8	15	40	
484	Dick Schofield	5	5	5	5	8	15	80	
485	Pedro Ramos	5	5	▲6	▲10	▲15	25	30	
486	Jim Gilliam	5	5	5	▲8	▲12	20	80	
487	Jerry Lynch	5	5	5	▲8	▲12	20	40	250
488	Hal Brown	5	5	▲6	▲10	▲15	25	60	
489	Julio Gotay RC	5	5	▲6	▲10	▲15	▲25	40	325
490	Clete Boyer	5	8	12	20	25	▲50	120	
491	Leon Wagner	5	5	5	6	10	25	50	
492	Hal W. Smith	5	5	5	5	12	20	30	150
493	Danny McDevitt	5	5	5	5	8	15	50	
494	Sammy White	5	5	5	▲8	▲12	▲20	50	
495	Don Cardwell	5	5	5	▲8	▲12	20	40	

		GD 2	VG 3	VgEx 4	EX 5	ExMt 6	NM 7	NmMt 8	MT 9
6	Wayne Causey RC	5	5	5	▲8	▲12	20	40	200
7	Ed Bouchee	5	5	▲6	▲10	▲15	25	▲60	250
8	Jim Donohue	5	5	▲6	▲10	▲15	25	30	150
9	Zoilo Versalles	5	5	5	▲6	▲10	15	100	250
0	Duke Snider	▲10	▲15	25	▲40	▲60	100	▲600	1,200
1	Claude Osteen	5	5	5	5	15	20	30	200
2	Hector Lopez	5	5	5	6	10	20	80	250
3	Danny Murtaugh MG	5	5	5	5	12	20	40	
4	Eddie Bressoud	5	5	5	5	8	20	40	
5	Juan Marichal	▲12	▲20	▲30	▲50	▲80	▲120	▲200	
6	Charlie Maxwell	5	5	5	5	8	25	50	
7	Ernie Broglio	5	5	5	5	8	25	▲60	
8	Gordy Coleman	5	5	5	5	6	25	40	
9	Dave Giusti RC	5	5	5	5	8	25	50	
0	Jim Lemon	5	5	6	10	15	25	40	
1	Bubba Phillips	5	5	5	5	8	15	80	
2	Mike Fornieles	5	5	6	8	12	30	50	150
3	Whitey Herzog	5	5	5	10	12	25	50	300
4	Sherm Lollar	5	5	5	6	10	25	80	
5	Stan Williams	5	5	5	5	8	15	30	250
6A	Checklist 7 White Boxes	5	5	5	5	8	15	30	
6B	Checklist 7 Yellow Boxes	5	5	5	5	8			
7	Dave Wickersham	5	5	5	5	6	15	50	
8	Lee Maye	5	5	5	5	8	25	40	150
9	Bob Johnson RC	5	5	5	5	8	15	60	
0	Bob Friend	5	5	6	10	15	25	80	
1	Jacke Davis RC	5	5	5	5	8	25	50	200
2	Lindy McDaniel	5	5	5	5	8	15	30	
3	Russ Nixon SP	5	5	5	8	12	20	60	
4	Howie Nunn SP	5	▲6	▲10	▲15	▲25	40	60	
5	George Thomas	5	5	▲6	▲10	▲15	▲25	40	150
6	Hal Woodeshick SP	5	5	▲6	▲10	▲15	25	60	200
7	Dick McAuliffe RC	5	5	6	10	15	40	▲120	
8	Turk Lown	5	5	5	▲8	▲12	25	40	800
9	John Schaive SP	5	5	5	8	12	25	60	120
0	Bob Gibson SP	60	100	150	▲250	▲400	600	2,500	
1	Bobby G. Smith	5	5	8	12	20	25	40	
2	Dick Stigman	5	5	6	6	10	15	40	
3	Charley Lau SP	5	5	6	10	15	25	60	250
4	Tony Gonzalez SP	5	6	8	10	20	30	50	500
5	Ed Roebuck	5	5	5	8	20	25	40	250
6	Dick Gernert	5	5	6	8	12	20	50	300
7	Cleveland Indians TC	5	5	5	6	25	30	50	150
8	Jack Sanford	5	5	5	6	8	20	40	150
9	Billy Moran	5	5	5	6	8	25	40	150
0	Jim Landis SP	5	5	6	8	12	30	50	
1	Don Nottebart SP	5	5	5	8	12	30	50	200
2	Dave Philley	5	5	5	6	8	20	50	
3	Bob Allen SP	5	5	5	8	25	30	60	200
4	Willie McCovey SP	▲50	▲80	▲120	200	250	▲500	800	1,500
5	Hoyt Wilhelm SP	8	10	15	30	50	100	300	
6	Moe Thacker SP	5	5	6	8	15	30	60	200
7	Don Ferrarese	5	5	6	▲10	▲15	▲25	40	200
8	Bobby Del Greco	5	5	6	8	12	20	30	200
9	Bill Rigney MG SP	5	▲6	▲10	▲15	▲25	▲40	80	
0	Art Mahaffey SP	5	5	6	10	15	40	60	250
1	Harry Bright	5	5	6	8	12	20	40	200
2	Chicago Cubs TC SP	5	6	8	12	40	50	100	400
3	Jim Coates	5	5	5	8	12	30	60	250
4	Bubba Morton SP RC	5	6	8	12	20	40	80	250
5	John Buzhardt SP	5	5	▲8	▲12	▼20	▲30	120	
6	Al Spangler	5	5	5	6	6	15	50	250
7	Bob Anderson SP	5	5	5	8	25	30	50	120
8	John Goryl	5	5	5	6	8	25	40	100
9	Mike Higgins MG	5	5	5	6	8	25	50	
0	Chuck Estrada SP	5	5	5	8	12	25	40	200
1	Gene Oliver SP	5	5	5	8	10	40	80	200
2	Bill Henry	5	5	5	6	8	20	40	120

		GD 2	VG 3	VgEx 4	EX 5	ExMt 6	NM 7	NmMt 8	MT 9
563	Ken Aspromonte	5	5	▲6	▲10	▲15	▲25	▲40	80
564	Bob Grim	5	5	5	6	10	20	50	150
565	Jose Pagan	5	5	5	6	8	25	40	150
566	Marty Kutyna SP	5	5	5	8	10	30	60	200
567	Tracy Stallard SP	5	5	5	8	10	30	40	200
568	Jim Golden	5	5	5	6	10	20	60	150
569	Ed Sadowski SP	5	5	5	8	12	30	50	
570	Bill Stafford SP	5	5	6	25	40	50	150	
571	Billy Klaus SP	5	5	5	8	10	30	60	200
572	Bob G.Miller SP	5	5	5	8	12	25	60	350
573	Johnny Logan	5	5	5	6	10	20	40	250
574	Dean Stone	5	5	5	8	10	20	50	150
575	Red Schoendienst SP	8	12	20	40	60	80	150	
576	Russ Kemmerer SP	5	5	5	8	12	30	80	200
577	Dave Nicholson SP	5	5	5	8	12	40	60	300
578	Jim Duffalo RC	5	5	5	8	8	25	40	350
579	Jim Schaffer SP RC	5	▲8	▲12	▲20	▲30	▲50	120	
580	Bill Monbouquette	5	5	6	10	15	30	40	250
581	Mel Roach	5	5	5	6	8	20	40	
582	Ron Piche	5	5	8	10	12	25	40	150
583	Larry Osborne	5	6	8	10	12	25	40	150
584	Minnesota Twins TC SP	5	8	12	20	40	80	100	
585	Glen Hobbie SP	5	5	5	8	12	20	50	
586	Sammy Esposito SP	5	5	5	8	12	25	60	200
587	Frank Funk SP	5	5	5	8	12	30	60	200
588	Birdie Tebbetts MG	5	5	5	8	12	20	50	150
589	Bob Turley	5	5	8	12	40	50	60	300
590	Curt Flood	5	5	6	10	15	60	150	500
591	Sam McDowell SP RC	25	40	50	100	120	150	300	
592	Jim Bouton SP RC	▲20	▲30	▲50	▲80	▲120	▲150	▲250	500
593	Bob Veale SP RC	5	8	40	60	80	100	200	
594	Bob Uecker SP RC	40	60	100	250	200	500	600	
595	Rookie Infielders SP	5	8	12	20	60	80	120	250
596	Joe Pepitone SP RC	▲25	▲40	▲60	▲100	▲150	▲250	▲400	
597	Rookie Infielders SP	5	8	12	20	80	▲120	250	
598	Rookie Outfielders SP	▲25	▲40	60	▲100	▲150	250	1,200	

— Lou Brock #387 PSA 10 (Gem) (Young Collection) sold for $32,545 (SCP; 5/12)
— Sandy Koufax #5 SGC 96 (MT) sold for $11,309 (Goodwin; 9/13)
— Sandy Koufax #5 SGC 96 (MT) sold for $4,320 (Mile High; 10/11)
— Juan Marichal #505 PSA 9 (MT) sold for $3,505 (eBay; 12/12)
— Roger Maris #1 PSA 9 (Mint) sold for $27,171 (Mile High; 12/13)
— Roger Maris #1 SGC 92 (NmMt+) sold for $2,065 (Mile High; 10/12)
— Ron Santo #170 PSA 10 (Gem) sold for $5,899 (Goodwin; 09/11)
— Joe Torre #218 PSA 10 (Gem) (Young Collection) sold for $10,780 (SCP; 5/12)

1963 Fleer

		GD 2	VG 3	VgEx 4	EX 5	ExMt 6	NM 7	NmMt 8	MT 9
1	Steve Barber	▲8	▲12	▲20	▲30	▲50	80	250	
2	Ron Hansen	5	5	5	6	12	25	60	
3	Milt Pappas	5	5	5	10	12	30	80	200
4	Brooks Robinson	12	20	30	50	80	▲120	▲250	600
5	Willie Mays	▲50	▲80	▲120	▲200	▲300	▲500	▲1,000	3,000
6	Lou Clinton	5	5	▲8	▲12	20	▲50	▲80	150
7	Bill Monbouquette	5	5	▲8	▲12	▲20	▲50	▲80	150
8	Carl Yastrzemski	12	20	30	50	60	150	▲300	800
9	Ray Herbert	5	5	5	6	12	20	30	100
10	Jim Landis	5	5	5	6	12	20	40	150
11	Dick Donovan	5	5	5	6	12	20	40	
12	Tito Francona	5	5	5	6	12	20	40	
13	Jerry Kindall	5	5	5	6	12	20	▲50	200
14	Frank Lary	5	5	5	6	12	20	40	150
15	Dick Howser	5	5	5	6	10	15	40	120
16	Jerry Lumpe	5	5	5	6	12	20	30	200
17	Norm Siebern	5	5	5	6	10	15	30	
18	Don Lee	5	5	5	6	12	20	40	150
19	Albie Pearson	5	5	5	6	12	20	40	200
20	Bob Rodgers	5	5	5	6	12	20	40	▲200

		GD 2	VG 3	VgEx 4	EX 5	ExMt 6	NM 7	NmMt 8	MT 9
21	Leon Wagner	5	5	5	6	12	25	50	100
22	Jim Kaat	5	5	6	15	20	25	50	250
23	Vic Power	5	5	5	6	20	25	40	200
24	Rich Rollins	5	5	5	6	10	15	40	200
25	Bobby Richardson	5	5	8	12	20	30	60	400
26	Ralph Terry	5	5	▲8	▲12	▲20	▲30	50	150
27	Tom Cheney	5	5	5	6	12	20	40	150
28	Chuck Cottier	5	5	▲6	▲10	▲15	25	▲40	100
29	Jimmy Piersall	5	5	6	8	12	15	40	200
30	Dave Stenhouse	5	5	6	12	20	40	40	200
31	Glen Hobbie	5	5	5	6	10	15	30	150
32	Ron Santo	6	10	15	25	40	60	120	250
33	Gene Freese	5	5	5	6	12	20	40	150
34	Vada Pinson	5	5	6	10	15	25	50	150
35	Bob Purkey	5	5	5	6	10	15	40	200
36	Joe Amalfitano	5	5	5	6	12	25	40	150
37	Bob Aspromonte	5	5	5	6	10	25	30	200
38	Dick Farrell	5	5	5	6	10	15	30	120
39	Al Spangler	5	5	5	6	10	15	40	150
40	Tommy Davis	5	5	6	10	15	25	▲80	300
41	Don Drysdale	12	20	30	40	50	100	▲250	500
42	Sandy Koufax	▲40	▲60	80	100	120	250	▲600	2,000
43	Maury Wills RC	▲20	▲30	▲50	▲80	100	150	250	1,000
44	Frank Bolling	5	5	▲8	▲12	▲20	30	40	120
45	Warren Spahn	10	15	25	30	60	80	120	300
46	Joe Adcock SP	12	▼20	▼30	50	▲80	120	250	1,000
47	Roger Craig	5	5	▲6	▲10	▲15	25	40	150
48	Al Jackson	5	5	6	8	15	25	50	200
49	Rod Kanehl	5	5	5	8	15	25	50	200
50	Ruben Amaro	5	5	5	8	15	25	50	150
51	Johnny Callison	5	5	5	8	15	25	60	200
52	Clay Dalrymple	5	5	5	6	12	30	50	150
53	Don Demeter	5	5	▲6	▲10	▲15	▲25	▲60	250
54	Art Mahaffey	5	5	5	6	12	20	40	250
55	Smoky Burgess	5	5	5	6	10	25	60	200
56	Roberto Clemente	▲50	▲80	▲120	▲200	▲250	▲400	800	1,500
57	Roy Face	5	5	5	▲8	12	25	40	200
58	Vern Law	5	5	▲8	▲12	▲20	▲30	▲50	200
59	Bill Mazeroski	5	5	8	12	20	50	60	
60	Ken Boyer	5	5	6	10	15	25	▲80	
61	Bob Gibson	12	20	30	50	60	100	200	600
62	Gene Oliver	5	5	▲6	▲10	▲15	▲25	40	150
63	Bill White	5	5	6	15	25	40	80	200
64	Orlando Cepeda	5	8	12	20	30	80	150	600
65	Jim Davenport	5	5	5	6	12	25	50	
66	Billy O'Dell	5	5	6	10	15	30	120	
NNO	Checklist SP	75	100	150	200	250	400	600	800

1963 Topps

		GD 2	VG 3	VgEx 4	EX 5	ExMt 6	NM 7	NmMt 8	MT 9
1	NL Batting Leaders	5	6	10	15	25	100	800	
2	AL Batting Leaders	15	25	30	40	50	80	150	800
3	NL Home Run Leaders	5	8	12	20	50	80	400	
4	AL Home Run Leaders	5	6	10	15	25	50	80	
5	NL ERA Leaders	5	6	10	15	25	50	200	
6	AL ERA Leaders	5	5	8	12	20	30	60	600
7	NL Pitching Leaders	5	5	5	8	12	30	80	
8	AL Pitching Leaders	5	5	5	8	12	20	40	
9	NL Strikeout Leaders	5	8	12	20	30	40	60	400
10	AL Strikeout Leaders	5	5	5	8	12	30	80	
11	Lee Walls	5	5	5	8	12	20	40	
12	Steve Barber	5	5	5	5	6	10	20	100
13	Philadelphia Phillies TC	5	5	5	6	10	15	120	250
14	Pedro Ramos	5	6	10	15	30	60	120	
15	Ken Hubbs NPO	5	5	5	5	8	30	80	
16	Al Smith	5	5	5	5	6	10	20	
17	Ryne Duren	5	5	5	5	6	10	50	200

		GD 2	VG 3	VgEx 4	EX 5	ExMt 6	NM 7	NmMt 8	MT 9
18	Buc Blasters	8	12	20	30	50	80	150	1,000
19	Pete Burnside	5	5	5	5	6	10	20	
20	Tony Kubek	5	5	▲8	▲12	20	▲50	120	500
21	Marty Keough	5	5	5	8	12	20	200	
22	Curt Simmons	5	5	5	8	12	20	120	
23	Ed Lopat MG	5	5	5	5	6	10	30	
24	Bob Bruce	5	5	5	5	6	10	20	
25	Al Kaline	20	30	50	60	100	120	400	
26	Ray Moore	5	5	5	5	6	10	40	
27	Choo Choo Coleman	5	5	5	6	10	15	80	
28	Mike Fornieles	5	5	5	5	6	10	50	
29A	1962 Rookie Stars	5	5	5	6	10	15	30	
29B	1963 Rookie Stars	5	5	5	5	6	10	25	
30	Harvey Kuenn	5	5	5	8	12	20	60	
31	Cal Koonce RC	5	5	5	5	6	10	25	
32	Tony Gonzalez	5	5	5	5	6	10	20	
33	Bo Belinsky	5	5	5	5	6	10	20	15
34	Dick Schofield	5	5	6	10	15	25	400	
35	John Buzhardt	5	5	5	5	6	10	25	
36	Jerry Kindall	5	5	5	5	6	10	30	
37	Jerry Lynch	5	5	5	5	6	10	40	
38	Bud Daley	5	5	5	5	8	12	25	12
39	Los Angeles Angels TC	5	5	5	5	8	12	25	12
40	Vic Power	5	5	5	6	10	15	60	
41	Charley Lau	5	5	5	5	8	12	25	
42	Stan Williams	5	5	5	8	12	25	50	
43	Veteran Masters	5	5	5	8	12	20	100	
44	Terry Fox	5	5	5	5	6	10	30	
45	Bob Aspromonte	5	5	5	5	6	10	20	10
46	Tommie Aaron RC	5	5	5	5	6	10	30	
47	Don Lock RC	5	5	5	8	12	25	50	10
48	Birdie Tebbetts MG	5	5	5	5	6	10	30	
49	Dal Maxvill RC	5	5	5	8	12	20	40	
50	Billy Pierce	5	5	5	5	6	10	50	15
51	George Alusik	5	5	5	5	6	10	20	15
52	Chuck Schilling	5	5	5	5	6	10	25	
53	Joe Moeller RC	5	5	5	5	6	10	30	12
54A	Dave DeBusschere 1962	5	5	6	10	15	25	50	40
54B	Dave DeBusschere 1963 RC	5	5	6	10	15	25	50	
55	Bill Virdon	5	5	5	8	12	20	40	
56	Dennis Bennett RC	5	5	5	8	12	20	40	
57	Billy Moran	5	5	5	8	12	20	40	8
58	Bob Will	5	5	5	8	12	20	40	
59	Craig Anderson	5	5	5	5	6	10	20	15
60	Elston Howard	5	5	5	8	12	60	80	
61	Ernie Bowman	5	5	6	10	15	30	60	
62	Bob Hendley	5	5	5	5	6	10	20	8
63	Cincinnati Reds TC	5	5	5	8	12	50	50	32
64	Dick McAuliffe	5	5	5	6	10	15	50	
65	Jackie Brandt	5	5	5	5	6	10	20	10
66	Mike Joyce RC	5	5	5	5	6	10	25	
67	Ed Charles	5	5	5	5	6	10	20	
68	Friendly Foes	5	6	10	15	25	50	80	2,00
69	Bud Zipfel RC	5	5	5	5	6	10	20	
70	Jim O'Toole	5	5	5	6	10	15	30	
71	Bobby Wine RC	5	5	5	5	6	10	20	15
72	Johnny Romano	5	5	5	5	6	10	40	
73	Bobby Bragan MG RC	5	5	5	5	6	10	20	10
74	Denny Lemaster RC	5	5	5	5	6	10	20	12
75	Bob Allison	5	5	5	6	10	15	50	
76	Earl Wilson	5	5	5	5	8	12	40	
77	Al Spangler	5	5	5	5	6	10	20	
78	Marv Throneberry	5	5	5	6	10	15	60	15
79	Checklist 1	5	5	5	6	10	20	30	12
80	Jim Gilliam	5	5	5	6	10	15	30	
81	Jim Schaffer	5	5	5	5	6	10	20	
82	Ed Rakow	5	5	5	5	6	10	20	
83	Charley James	5	5	5	5	6	10	20	10

	GD 2	VG 3	VgEx 4	EX 5	ExMt 6	NM 7	NmMt 8	MT 9
Ron Kline	5	5	5	6	10	15	60	
Tom Haller	5	5	5	5	6	10	30	80
Charley Maxwell	5	5	5	5	6	10	20	300
Bob Veale	5	5	5	5	6	10	30	
Ron Hansen	5	5	5	5	6	10	20	150
Dick Stigman	5	5	5	5	8	12	80	
Gordy Coleman	5	5	5	5	6	10	30	
Dallas Green	5	5	5	5	6	10	20	120
Hector Lopez	5	5	5	8	12	20	25	
Galen Cisco	5	5	5	5	6	10	20	80
Bob Schmidt	5	5	5	5	6	10	25	
Larry Jackson	5	5	5	5	6	10	30	80
Lou Clinton	5	5	5	5	6	10	40	
Bob Duliba	5	5	5	5	6	10	20	150
George Thomas	5	5	5	5	6	10	20	
Jim Umbricht	5	5	5	5	6	10	20	
Joe Cunningham	5	5	5	8	12	20	150	
Joe Gibbon	5	5	5	5	8	12	30	
Checklist 2 Red/Yellow	5	5	5	5	6	10	25	
Checklist 2 White/Red	5	5	5	5	6	10	25	120
Chuck Essegian	5	5	5	5	6	10	20	200
Lew Krausse RC	5	5	5	5	6	10	30	150
Ron Fairly	5	5	5	8	12	20	120	250
Bobby Bolin	5	5	5	5	6	10	20	120
Jim Hickman	5	5	5	5	6	10	50	
Hoyt Wilhelm	5	▲6	▲10	▲15	▲25	▲40	▲60	200
Lee Maye	5	5	5	5	8	12	30	
Rich Rollins	5	5	5	5	6	10	20	
Al Jackson	5	5	5	5	6	10	20	
Dick Brown	5	5	5	5	6	10	30	80
Don Landrum	5	5	5	5	6	10	25	
Dan Osinski RC	5	5	5	6	10	15	30	150
Carl Yastrzemski	20	30	50	▲80	▲120	▲200	500	
Jim Brosnan	5	5	5	6	10	15	25	80
Jacke Davis	5	5	5	5	6	10	30	
Sherm Lollar	5	5	5	5	6	10	20	
Bob Lillis	5	5	5	5	6	10	20	120
Roger Maris	30	40	60	80	100	150	600	
Jim Hannan RC	5	5	5	5	6	10	20	
Julio Gotay	5	5	5	5	6	10	25	150
Frank Howard	5	5	5	5	8	25	100	150
Dick Howser	5	5	5	5	6	10	20	120
Robin Roberts	5	5	8	12	20	30	100	
Bob Uecker	▲15	▲25	▲40	▲60	▲100	▲150	▲250	
Bill Tuttle	5	5	5	5	6	10	20	
Matty Alou	5	5	5	5	8	12	25	100
Gary Bell	5	5	5	5	6	10	20	
Dick Groat	5	5	5	5	8	12	25	150
Washington Senators TC	5	5	5	5	8	12	50	150
Jack Hamilton	5	5	5	5	6	10	20	60
Gene Freese	5	5	5	5	6	10	25	150
Bob Scheffing MG	5	5	5	5	6	10	30	150
Richie Ashburn	▲6	▲10	▲15	▲25	▲40	▲60	100	
Ike Delock	5	5	5	5	6	10	20	150
Mack Jones	5	5	5	5	6	10	20	80
Pride of NL	▲15	25	▲40	50	100	120	200	▲1,000
Earl Averill Jr.	5	5	5	5	6	10	20	100
Frank Lary	5	5	5	6	10	15	50	200
Manny Mota RC	5	5	5	5	8	12	50	150
Whitey Ford WS1	5	5	8	12	20	50	120	500
Jack Sanford WS2	5	5	5	5	6	30	50	175
Roger Maris WS3	5	6	10	15	25	30	200	
Chuck Hiller WS4	5	5	5	5	8	12	40	150
Tom Tresh WS5	5	5	5	6	10	15	120	
Billy Pierce WS6	5	5	5	5	8	12	60	
Ralph Terry WS7	5	5	5	8	12	20	150	
Marv Breeding	5	5	5	5	8	12	40	
Johnny Podres	5	5	5	6	10	15	25	400

		GD 2	VG 3	VgEx 4	EX 5	ExMt 6	NM 7	NmMt 8	MT 9
151	Pittsburgh Pirates TC	5	5	5	5	8	12	40	150
152	Ron Nischwitz	5	5	5	5	6	10	20	150
153	Hal Smith	5	5	5	5	6	10	20	100
154	Walter Alston MG	5	5	5	5	8	12	30	150
155	Bill Stafford	5	5	5	6	10	15	120	
156	Roy McMillan	5	5	5	5	6	10	20	
157	Diego Segui RC	5	5	5	5	6	10	30	80
158	Tommy Harper RC	5	5	5	8	12	20	40	150
159	Jim Pagliaroni	5	5	5	5	6	10	30	
160	Juan Pizarro	5	5	5	5	6	10	20	120
161	Frank Torre	5	5	5	5	8	12	25	100
162	Minnesota Twins TC	5	5	5	5	8	25	80	
163	Don Larsen	5	5	5	5	8	12	30	135
164	Bubba Morton	5	5	5	5	6	10	20	200
165	Jim Kaat	5	5	5	8	12	20	25	150
166	Johnny Keane MG	5	5	5	5	8	12	40	
167	Jim Fregosi	5	5	5	5	6	10	40	150
168	Russ Nixon	5	5	5	5	6	10	40	
169	Gaylord Perry	5	6	10	15	25	60	100	300
170	Joe Adcock	5	5	5	5	8	12	30	100
171	Steve Hamilton RC	5	5	5	5	6	10	20	80
172	Gene Oliver	5	5	5	5	6	10	20	
173	Bomber's Best	40	60	80	▲120	▲200	▲300	500	1,000
174	Larry Burright	5	5	5	5	8	12	40	
175	Bob Buhl	5	5	5	5	6	10	25	
176	Jim King	5	5	5	5	6	10	25	
177	Bubba Phillips	5	5	5	5	6	10	20	120
178	Johnny Edwards	5	5	5	5	6	10	20	150
179	Ron Piche	5	5	5	5	6	10	20	150
180	Bill Skowron	5	5	5	5	8	12	25	120
181	Sammy Esposito	5	5	5	5	6	10	20	80
182	Albie Pearson	5	5	5	5	6	10	20	80
183	Joe Pepitone	5	5	5	8	12	20	40	150
184	Vern Law	5	5	5	6	10	15	50	200
185	Chuck Hiller	5	5	5	5	6	10	20	150
186	Jerry Zimmerman	5	5	5	5	6	10	20	
187	Willie Kirkland	5	5	5	5	6	10	20	200
188	Eddie Bressoud	5	5	5	5	6	10	20	
189	Dave Giusti	5	5	5	5	6	10	25	150
190	Minnie Minoso	5	5	5	5	8	25	150	
191	Checklist 3	5	5	5	5	8	12	30	150
192	Clay Dalrymple	5	5	5	5	6	10	20	80
193	Andre Rodgers	5	5	5	5	6	10	20	150
194	Joe Nuxhall	5	5	5	5	8	12	40	
195	Manny Jimenez	5	5	5	5	6	10	20	
196	Doug Camilli	5	5	5	5	6	10	20	120
197	Roger Craig	5	5	5	5	6	10	20	200
198	Lenny Green	5	5	5	5	6	10	20	100
199	Joe Amalfitano	5	5	5	5	6	10	20	
200	Mickey Mantle	200	▲300	▲500	▲600	▲1,000	▲2,500	6,000	▲80,000
201	Cecil Butler	5	5	5	8	12	20	25	150
202	Boston Red Sox TC	5	5	5	5	8	12	40	150
203	Chico Cardenas	5	5	5	5	6	10	20	80
204	Don Nottebart	5	5	5	5	6	10	25	150
205	Luis Aparicio	5	5	8	12	20	25	50	200
206	Ray Washburn	5	5	5	5	8	12	20	200
207	Ken Hunt	5	5	5	8	12	20	30	150
208	1963 Rookie Stars	5	5	5	5	8	60	100	
209	Hobie Landrith	5	5	5	5	6	10	20	200
210	Sandy Koufax	▲60	▲100	▲150	▲200	▲250	500	1,000	4,000
211	Fred Whitfield RC	5	5	5	5	6	10	30	
212	Glen Hobbie	5	5	5	5	6	10	25	150
213	Billy Hitchcock MG	5	5	5	5	6	10	20	100
214	Orlando Pena	5	5	5	6	10	15	25	80
215	Bob Skinner	5	5	5	5	6	10	20	100
216	Gene Conley	5	5	5	5	6	10	30	100
217	Joe Christopher	5	5	5	5	6	10	60	
218	Tiger Twirlers	5	5	5	8	12	20	80	120

#	Player	GD 2	VG 3	VgEx 4	EX 5	ExMt 6	NM 7	NmMt 8	MT 9
219	Chuck Cottier	5	5	5	5	6	10	25	60
220	Camilo Pascual	5	5	5	5	8	12	60	
221	Cookie Rojas RC	5	5	5	8	12	20	60	
222	Chicago Cubs TC	5	5	5	8	12	20	100	
223	Eddie Fisher	5	5	5	6	10	15	25	80
224	Mike Roarke	5	5	5	5	8	12	60	
225	Joey Jay	5	5	5	5	6	10	25	
226	Julian Javier	5	5	5	5	6	10	40	150
227	Jim Grant	5	5	5	8	12	20	60	
228	Tony Oliva RC	12	20	30	50	100	▲250	500	
229	Willie Davis	5	5	5	5	8	12	40	150
230	Pete Runnels	5	5	5	5	6	10	50	
231	Eli Grba	5	5	5	6	10	15	20	80
232	Frank Malzone	5	5	5	5	6	10	50	120
233	Casey Stengel MG	5	5	8	12	20	25	80	200
234	Dave Nicholson	5	5	5	5	6	10	20	80
235	Billy O'Dell	5	5	5	5	6	10	20	80
236	Bill Bryan RC	5	5	5	5	8	12	40	
237	Jim Coates	5	5	5	5	5	25	120	
238	Lou Johnson	5	5	5	5	6	10	20	100
239	Harvey Haddix	5	5	5	5	8	12	40	100
240	Rocky Colavito	5	5	6	10	15	30	100	
241	Billy Smith RC	5	5	5	5	6	10	30	80
242	Power Plus	15	25	40	50	120	200	300	▲2,500
243	Don Leppert	5	5	5	5	6	10	20	50
244	John Tsitouris	5	5	5	5	6	10	30	100
245	Gil Hodges	5	5	8	12	20	30	100	200
246	Lee Stange	5	5	5	5	6	10	20	150
247	New York Yankees TC	▲10	▲15	▲25	40	60	120	600	
248	Tito Francona	5	5	5	5	6	10	40	200
249	Leo Burke RC	5	5	5	5	6	10	20	100
250	Stan Musial	15	25	50	60	100	150	400	2,000
251	Jack Lamabe	5	5	5	5	6	10	20	200
252	Ron Santo	5	6	10	15	30	50	▲200	500
253	1963 Rookie Stars	5	5	5	5	6	10	40	120
254	Mike Hershberger	5	5	5	5	6	10	40	150
255	Bob Shaw	5	5	5	5	6	10	20	80
256	Jerry Lumpe	5	5	5	5	8	12	40	
257	Hank Aguirre	5	5	5	5	6	10	20	100
258	Alvin Dark MG	5	5	5	5	6	10	25	80
259	Johnny Logan	5	5	5	5	6	10	20	300
260	Jim Gentile	5	5	5	5	8	12	40	
261	Bob Miller	5	5	5	6	10	15	80	
262	Ellis Burton	5	5	5	5	8	12	40	
263	Dave Stenhouse	5	5	5	5	6	10	30	100
264	Phil Linz	5	5	5	6	10	15	80	
265	Vada Pinson	5	5	5	5	8	12	60	
266	Bob Allen	5	5	5	5	6	10	30	150
267	Carl Sawatski	5	5	5	5	6	10	20	100
268	Don Demeter	5	5	5	5	6	10	30	
269	Don Mincher	5	5	5	5	6	10	20	200
270	Felipe Alou	5	5	5	8	12	20	50	200
271	Dean Stone	5	5	5	5	6	10	40	
272	Danny Murphy	5	5	5	5	6	10	50	150
273	Sammy Taylor	5	5	5	5	6	10	30	80
274	Checklist 4	5	5	5	5	6	10	40	150
275	Eddie Mathews	▲10	▲15	▲25	▼40	60	▲100	▲250	500
276	Barry Shetrone	5	5	5	5	6	10	20	80
277	Dick Farrell	5	5	5	5	8	12	40	
278	Chico Fernandez	5	5	5	5	6	10	30	150
279	Wally Moon	5	5	5	5	8	12	50	
280	Bob Rodgers	5	5	5	5	6	10	30	150
281	Tom Sturdivant	5	5	5	5	6	10	20	80
282	Bobby Del Greco	5	5	5	5	6	10	25	80
283	Roy Sievers	5	5	5	6	10	15	300	300
284	Dave Sisler	5	5	5	5	8	12	50	150
285	Dick Stuart	5	5	8	12	20	30	100	
286	Stu Miller	5	5	5	5	6	10	50	200

#	Player	GD 2	VG 3	VgEx 4	EX 5	ExMt 6	NM 7	NmMt 8	MT
287	Dick Bertell	5	5	5	5	6	10	20	12
288	Chicago White Sox TC	5	5	5	6	10	15	50	12
289	Hal Brown	5	5	5	8	12	20	200	
290	Bill White	5	5	5	5	8	12	40	12
291	Don Rudolph	5	5	5	6	10	15	80	
292	Pumpsie Green	5	5	5	5	8	12	50	
293	Bill Pleis	5	5	5	5	8	12	100	
294	Bill Rigney MG	5	5	5	5	6	10	40	
295	Ed Roebuck	5	5	5	5	6	10	40	15
296	Doc Edwards	5	5	5	5	6	10	20	8
297	Jim Golden	5	5	5	5	6	10	40	
298	Don Dillard	5	5	5	5	6	10	100	20
299	1963 Rookie Stars	5	5	5	6	10	15	120	20
300	Willie Mays	▲80	▲120	▲200	▲300	▲500	▲800	▲1,500	3,00
301	Bill Fischer	5	5	5	5	6	10	40	
302	Whitey Herzog	5	5	5	5	5	50	200	
303	Earl Francis	5	5	5	5	6	10	25	12
304	Harry Bright	5	5	5	5	6	10	30	15
305	Don Hoak	5	5	5	5	8	12	80	15
306	Star Receivers	5	5	8	12	20	30	100	50
307	Chet Nichols	5	5	5	5	6	10	50	
308	Camilo Carreon	5	5	5	5	6	10	40	20
309	Jim Brewer	5	5	5	6	10	15	100	
310	Tommy Davis	5	5	5	5	8	40	150	
311	Joe McClain	5	5	5	5	6	10	40	12
312	Houston Colts TC	5	6	10	15	25	30	100	15
313	Ernie Broglio	5	5	5	6	10	15	50	
314	John Goryl	5	5	5	6	10	15	60	
315	Ralph Terry	5	5	5	8	12	20	200	
316	Norm Sherry	5	5	5	5	6	10	50	15
317	Sam McDowell	5	5	6	10	15	25	30	20
318	Gene Mauch MG	5	5	5	5	6	10	25	
319	Joe Gaines	5	5	5	5	8	12	80	
320	Warren Spahn	12	20	30	60	80	120	400	
321	Gino Cimoli	5	5	5	5	6	10	50	30
322	Bob Turley	5	5	5	5	6	10	40	15
323	Bill Mazeroski	8	12	20	30	50	60	300	
324	Vic Davalillo RC	5	5	5	5	8	25	120	25
325	Jack Sanford	5	5	6	10	15	25	100	
326	Hank Foiles	5	5	5	5	5	10	80	
327	Paul Foytack	5	5	5	5	6	10	40	
328	Dick Williams	5	5	5	5	8	25	300	
329	Lindy McDaniel	5	5	5	5	6	10	30	15
330	Chuck Hinton	5	5	5	5	6	10	30	15
331	Series Foes	5	5	8	12	20	30	60	35
332	Joel Horlen	5	5	5	5	6	10	40	15
333	Carl Warwick	5	5	5	6	10	15	120	
334	Wynn Hawkins	5	5	5	5	6	10	50	10
335	Leon Wagner	5	5	5	6	10	15	120	
336	Ed Bauta	5	5	5	5	6	10	60	
337	Los Angeles Dodgers TC	5	5	8	12	20	30	200	
338	Russ Kemmerer	5	5	5	5	8	12	50	
339	Ted Bowsfield	5	5	5	5	6	10	25	15
340	Yogi Berra	25	40	80	100	120	300	2,000	
341	Jack Baldschun	5	5	5	6	10	15	60	
342	Gene Woodling	5	5	5	6	10	15	25	15
343	Johnny Pesky MG	5	5	5	6	10	15	80	20
344	Don Schwall	5	5	5	5	6	10	30	
345	Brooks Robinson	▲20	▲30	▲50	▲80	▲120	▲200	300	8
346	Billy Hoeft	5	5	5	5	6	10	30	10
347	Joe Torre	▲6	▲10	▲15	▲25	▲40	60	120	
348	Vic Wertz	5	5	5	5	6	10	50	20
349	Zoilo Versalles	5	5	5	5	6	10	60	15
350	Bob Purkey	5	5	5	5	6	10	40	15
351	Al Luplow	5	5	5	5	8	12	20	80
352	Ken Johnson	5	5	5	5	6	10	40	20
353	Billy Williams	▲12	▲20	▲30	▲50	▲80	▲120	▲200	
354	Dom Zanni	5	5	5	5	6	10	15	80

#	Player	GD 2	VG 3	VgEx 4	EX 5	ExMt 6	NM 7	NmMt 8	MT 9
55	Dean Chance	5	5	5	6	10	15	80	250
56	John Schaive	5	5	5	5	6	10	200	
57	George Altman	5	5	5	5	6	10	20	100
58	Milt Pappas	5	5	5	5	6	10	60	
59	Haywood Sullivan	5	5	5	5	6	10	60	
60	Don Drysdale	10	15	25	40	50	100	250	
61	Clete Boyer	▲8	▲12	▲20	▲30	▲50	▲80	120	
62	Checklist 5	5	5	5	6	10	15	▲150	
63	Dick Radatz	5	5	5	8	12	20	80	
64	Howie Goss	5	5	5	5	6	10	25	
65	Jim Bunning	5	5	8	12	20	50	120	
66	Tony Taylor	5	5	5	5	6	10	60	150
67	Tony Cloninger	5	5	5	5	6	10	30	120
68	Ed Bailey	5	5	5	5	6	10	40	150
69	Jim Lemon	5	5	5	5	8	12	50	
70	Dick Donovan	5	5	5	5	6	10	30	150
71	Rod Kanehl	5	5	5	5	6	10	20	100
72	Don Lee	5	5	5	5	6	10	20	100
73	Jim Campbell RC	5	5	5	5	6	10	20	80
74	Claude Osteen	5	5	5	5	6	10	25	120
75	Ken Boyer	5	5	6	10	15	50	100	150
76	John Wyatt RC	5	5	5	5	6	10	20	80
77	Baltimore Orioles TC	5	5	8	12	20	25	40	150
78	Bill Henry	5	5	5	8	12	20	30	80
79	Bob Anderson	5	5	5	5	6	10	20	120
80	Ernie Banks	▲25	▲40	▲60	▲100	▲150	▲250	800	2,500
81	Frank Baumann	5	5	5	5	6	10	25	100
82	Ralph Houk MG	5	6	10	15	25	30	150	400
83	Pete Richert	5	5	5	5	6	10	100	
84	Bob Tillman	5	5	5	5	6	10	40	
85	Art Mahaffey	5	5	5	5	6	10	20	150
86	1963 Rookie Stars	5	5	5	5	8	12	50	
87	Al McBean	5	5	5	5	6	10	40	120
88	Jim Davenport	5	5	5	5	8	12	25	80
89	Frank Sullivan	5	5	5	6	10	15	25	100
90	Hank Aaron	▲40	60	100	▲150	▲250	400	▲3,000	▲6,000
91	Bill Dailey RC	5	5	5	5	6	10	20	150
92	Tribe Thumpers	5	5	5	5	8	12	50	250
93	Ken MacKenzie	5	5	5	6	10	15	50	
94	Tim McCarver	5	5	6	10	15	30	80	120
95	Don McMahon	5	5	5	6	10	15	25	120
96	Joe Koppe	5	5	5	5	6	10	20	120
97	Kansas City Athletics TC	5	5	5	6	10	15	80	120
98	Boog Powell	6	10	15	25	40	50	120	
99	Dick Ellsworth	5	5	5	5	6	10	40	100
100	Frank Robinson	20	30	50	60	100	150	▲400	2,000
101	Jim Bouton	6	10	15	25	40	60	120	1,200
102	Mickey Vernon MG	5	5	5	5	8	12	25	150
103	Ron Perranoski	5	5	5	5	6	10	30	100
104	Bob Oldis	5	5	5	5	6	10	20	150
105	Floyd Robinson	5	5	5	5	6	10	20	80
106	Howie Koplitz	5	5	5	5	8	12	30	
107	1963 Rookie Stars	5	5	5	5	6	10	40	
108	Billy Gardner	5	5	5	5	6	10	50	
109	Roy Face	5	5	5	5	8	12	30	
110	Earl Battey	5	5	5	5	6	10	30	200
111	Jim Constable	5	5	5	5	6	10	20	
112	Dodgers Big Three	8	12	20	30	80	120	300	800
113	Jerry Walker	5	5	5	6	10	15	25	150
114	Ty Cline	5	5	5	5	6	10	20	
115	Bob Gibson	30	▲50	▲80	▲120	▲200	300	800	2,000
116	Alex Grammas	5	5	5	5	6	10	20	
117	San Francisco Giants TC	5	5	5	5	5	25	100	
118	John Orsino	5	5	5	5	6	10	20	150
119	Tracy Stallard	5	5	5	5	6	10	20	80
120	Bobby Richardson	5	10	15	25	30	40	100	200
121	Tom Morgan	5	5	5	5	6	10	30	
122	Fred Hutchinson MG	5	5	5	5	6	10	20	135

#	Player	GD 2	VG 3	VgEx 4	EX 5	ExMt 6	NM 7	NmMt 8	MT 9
423	Ed Hobaugh	5	5	5	5	6	10	25	100
424	Charlie Smith	5	5	5	5	6	10	20	100
425	Smoky Burgess	5	5	5	5	8	12	30	150
426	Barry Latman	5	5	5	5	6	10	20	120
427	Bernie Allen	5	5	5	5	6	10	25	80
428	Carl Boles RC	5	5	5	5	6	10	25	
429	Lew Burdette	5	5	5	5	8	12	40	
430	Norm Siebern	5	5	5	5	6	10	20	
431A	Checklist 6 White/Red	5	5	5	6	10	15	100	
431B	Checklist 6 Black/Orange	5	5	5	6	10	15	40	200
432	Roman Mejias	5	5	5	5	6	10	20	100
433	Denis Menke	5	5	5	6	10	15	40	80
434	John Callison	5	5	5	5	8	12	60	200
435	Woody Held	5	5	5	5	6	10	20	120
436	Tim Harkness	5	5	5	5	6	10	20	120
437	Bill Bruton	5	5	5	5	6	10	20	
438	Wes Stock	5	5	5	5	6	10	20	80
439	Don Zimmer	5	5	5	5	8	12	30	120
440	Juan Marichal	8	12	20	50	60	80	▲250	400
441	Lee Thomas	5	5	5	5	6	10	25	
442	J.C. Hartman RC	5	5	5	5	6	10	30	150
443	Jimmy Piersall	5	5	5	8	12	20	60	
444	Jim Maloney	5	5	5	5	6	10	50	120
445	Norm Cash	5	5	5	8	12	30	40	
446	Whitey Ford	8	12	30	40	50	80	300	
447	Felix Mantilla	5	5	5	6	10	15	40	80
448	Jack Kralick	5	5	5	6	10	15	30	120
449	Jose Tartabull	5	5	5	8	12	20	60	
450	Bob Friend	5	5	▲6	▲10	▲15	▲25	▲40	80
451	Cleveland Indians TC	5	5	6	10	15	25	50	
452	Barney Schultz	5	5	5	6	10	15	40	150
453	Jake Wood	5	5	5	6	10	15	30	
454A	Art Fowler White Card No.	5	5	5	6	10	60	100	200
454B	Art Fowler Orange Card No.	5	5	5	6	10	15	25	120
455	Ruben Amaro	5	5	5	6	10	15	80	
456	Jim Coker	5	5	5	6	10	15	50	100
457	Tex Clevenger	5	5	5	8	12	20	60	200
458	Al Lopez MG	5	5	8	12	20	30	80	
459	Dick LeMay	5	5	5	6	10	15	60	120
460	Del Crandall	5	5	5	8	12	20	60	
461	Norm Bass	5	5	5	6	10	15	40	100
462	Wally Post	5	5	5	6	10	15	50	150
463	Joe Schaffernoth	5	5	5	6	10	15	40	100
464	Ken Aspromonte	5	5	5	6	10	25	60	
465	Chuck Estrada	5	5	▲8	▲12	▲20	▲30	▲50	100
466	Bill Freehan SP RC	▲12	▲20	▲30	▲50	▲80	▲120	▲250	▲400
467	Phil Ortega	5	5	5	6	10	15	80	
468	Carroll Hardy	5	5	▲8	▲12	▲20	▲30	▲40	200
469	Jay Hook	5	5	5	8	12	30	60	
470	Tom Tresh SP	6	10	15	25	30	80	120	400
471	Ken Retzer	5	5	5	6	10	15	30	80
472	Lou Brock	25	40	100	120	200	250	800	
473	New York Mets TC	6	10	15	25	40	50	150	800
474	Jack Fisher	5	5	5	▲8	▲12	▲20	40	100
475	Gus Triandos	5	5	5	8	12	20	50	
476	Frank Funk	5	5	5	6	10	15	50	120
477	Donn Clendenon	5	5	5	8	12	25	60	
478	Paul Brown	5	5	5	6	10	25	80	150
479	Ed Brinkman RC	5	5	5	6	10	15	50	
480	Bill Monbouquette	5	5	5	6	10	40	80	150
481	Bob Taylor	5	5	5	6	10	15	50	100
482	Felix Torres	5	5	5	6	10	15	30	100
483	Jim Owens	5	5	5	6	10	15	50	275
484	Dale Long SP	5	6	10	15	25	40	60	550
485	Jim Landis	5	5	5	6	10	15	50	100
486	Ray Sadecki	5	5	5	8	12	20	40	100
487	John Roseboro	5	5	5	8	12	20	80	250
488	Jerry Adair	5	5	5	6	10	30	40	150

#	Player	GD 2	VG 3	VgEx 4	EX 5	ExMt 6	NM 7	NmMt 8	MT 9
489	Paul Toth RC	5	5	5	▲8	▲12	▲20	30	120
490	Willie McCovey	▲25	▲40	60	▲100	▲120	▲200	▲400	800
491	Harry Craft MG	5	5	5	6	10	25	40	60
492	Dave Wickersham	5	5	5	6	10	15	30	150
493	Walt Bond	5	5	5	6	10	15	50	120
494	Phil Regan	5	5	5	6	10	15	30	100
495	Frank Thomas SP	5	▲8	▲12	▲20	▲30	▲50	150	
496	1963 Rookie Stars	5	5	60	80	100	120	1,000	
497	Bennie Daniels	5	5	5	6	10	15	30	120
498	Eddie Kasko	5	5	5	6	10	15	30	100
499	J.C. Martin	5	5	5	6	10	15	40	100
500	Harmon Killebrew SP	▲25	▲40	▲60	▲100	▲150	▲250	400	1,500
501	Joe Azcue	5	5	5	6	10	15	▲150	
502	Daryl Spencer	5	5	5	6	10	15	50	80
503	Milwaukee Braves TC	5	5	5	8	12	30	▲80	120
504	Bob Johnson	5	5	5	6	10	15	40	150
505	Curt Flood	▲8	▲12	▲20	▲30	▲50	▲80	150	250
506	Gene Green	5	5	5	6	10	15	40	
507	Roland Sheldon	5	5	8	12	20	25	50	100
508	Ted Savage	5	5	5	6	10	25	40	200
509A	Checklist 7 Copyright Centered	5	5	5	8	12	20	30	
509B	Checklist 7 Copyright to Right	5	5	5	8	12	20	40	
510	Ken McBride	5	5	5	6	10	15	40	100
511	Charlie Neal	5	5	5	8	12	20	50	
512	Cal McLish	5	5	5	6	10	15	50	
513	Gary Geiger	5	5	5	6	10	15	50	150
514	Larry Osborne	5	5	5	6	10	15	40	100
515	Don Elston	5	5	5	6	10	15	25	120
516	Purnell Goldy RC	5	5	5	6	10	30	60	
517	Hal Woodeshick	5	5	5	6	10	15	50	
518	Don Blasingame	5	5	5	6	10	15	30	80
519	Claude Raymond RC	5	5	5	6	10	25	40	150
520	Orlando Cepeda	5	8	12	20	30	80	300	500
521	Dan Pfister	5	5	5	6	20	25	40	100
522	1963 Rookie Stars	5	5	5	8	12	20	100	
523	Bill Kunkel	5	5	5	5	8	25	60	
524	St. Louis Cardinals TC	5	5	5	8	12	20	60	200
525	Nellie Fox	6	10	15	25	40	60	100	300
526	Dick Hall	5	5	5	8	12	20	100	
527	Ed Sadowski	5	5	5	8	12	20	30	80
528	Carl Willey	5	5	5	5	8	12	30	80
529	Wes Covington	5	5	5	5	8	12	60	
530	Don Mossi	5	5	5	5	8	12	60	100
531	Sam Mele MG	5	5	5	8	12	20	30	120
532	Steve Boros	5	5	5	5	8	12	40	100
533	Bobby Shantz	5	5	5	5	6	25	30	80
534	Ken Walters	5	5	5	5	8	12	30	
535	Jim Perry	5	5	▲8	▲12	▲20	▲30	60	
536	Norm Larker	5	5	5	5	8	12	40	
537	Pete Rose RC	600	▲1,000	▲1,500	▲2,500	▲3,000	▲6,000	▲15,000	▲125,000
538	George Brunet	5	5	5	5	8	12	25	100
539	Wayne Causey	5	5	5	5	8	12	▲50	100
540	Roberto Clemente	80	120	200	300	400	600	1,500	3,000
541	Ron Moeller	5	5	5	5	8	12	40	80
542	Lou Klimchock	5	5	5	▲6	▲10	▲15	▲30	100
543	Russ Snyder	5	5	5	5	8	12	30	100
544	Rusty Staub RC	12	20	30	60	80	120	250	600
545	Jose Pagan	5	5	5	5	8	12	40	100
546	Hal Reniff	5	5	▲8	▲12	▲20	▲30	▲50	
547	Gus Bell	5	5	5	5	8	12	30	135
548	Tom Satriano RC	5	5	5	5	8	12	100	
549	1963 Rookie Stars	5	5	5	6	10	25	250	
550	Duke Snider	10	15	25	40	▲60	▲80	▲250	800
551	Billy Klaus	5	5	5	5	8	12	25	80
552	Detroit Tigers TC	5	6	10	15	25	40	100	▲800
553	Willie Stargell RC	120	200	250	300	500	600	2,000	8,000
554	Hank Fischer RC	5	5	5	▲8	▲12	▲20	40	150
555	John Blanchard	5	5	5	6	10	30	50	
556	Al Worthington	5	5	5	5	8	12	50	100
557	Cuno Barragan	5	5	5	5	8	12	25	▲600
558	Ron Hunt RC	5	8	12	20	30	50	▲120	150
559	Danny Murtaugh MG	5	5	5	5	8	12	60	
560	Ray Herbert	5	5	5	6	10	15	30	80
561	Mike De La Hoz	5	5	5	5	8	12	50	
562	Dave McNally RC	6	10	15	25	40	60	120	300
563	Mike McCormick	5	5	5	5	8	12	30	80
564	George Banks RC	5	5	5	6	10	15	40	
565	Larry Sherry	5	5	5	5	6	30	60	
566	Cliff Cook	5	5	5	▲6	▲10	▲15	40	100
567	Jim Duffalo	5	5	5	5	8	12	50	
568	Bob Sadowski	5	5	5	5	8	12	30	150
569	Luis Arroyo	5	5	5	5	8	25	60	200
570	Frank Bolling	5	5	5	5	8	12	40	
571	Johnny Klippstein	5	5	5	5	8	12	25	▲80
572	Jack Spring	5	5	5	5	8	12	25	60
573	Coot Veal	5	5	5	5	6	25	100	150
574	Hal Kolstad	5	5	5	6	10	15	80	
575	Don Cardwell	5	5	5	6	10	15	100	200
576	Johnny Temple	5	5	5	5	8	25	50	200

— Roger Maris #120 PSA 9 (MT) sold for $2,670 (Mile High; 05/11)
— Roger Maris #120 PSA 9 (MT) sold for $2,177 (eBay; 01/12)
— Pete Rose #537 PSA 10 (Gem) sold for $717,000 (Heritage; 8/16)
— Pete Rose #537 PSA 10 (Gem) (Young Collection) sold for $157,366 (SCP; 5/12)
— Pete Rose RC #537 PSA 8.5 (NmMt+) sold for $5,005 (eBay; 12/12)
— Pete Rose #537 PSA 8.5 (NmMt+) sold for $3,660 (Goodwin; 11/11)
— Willie Stargell #553 PSA 10 (Gem) (Young Collection) sold for $12,131 (SCP; 5/12)

1963 Topps Peel-Offs

#	Player	GD 2	VG 3	VgEx 4	EX 5	ExMt 6	NM 7	NmMt 8	MT
1	Hank Aaron	5	8	10	12	20	100	200	300
2	Luis Aparicio	5	5	5	5	5	10	20	60
3	Richie Ashburn	5	5	5	5	8	12	40	
4	Bob Aspromonte	5	5	5	5	5	8	15	
5	Ernie Banks	5	5	5	6	10	15	50	
6	Ken Boyer	5	5	5	5	5	8	15	5
7	Jim Bunning	5	5	5	5	5	10	25	6
8	Johnny Callison	5	5	5	5	5	8	15	5
9	Roberto Clemente	5	8	12	15	25	120	250	
10	Orlando Cepeda	5	5	5	5	5	10	20	6
11	Rocky Colavito	5	5	5	5	8	12	80	
12	Tommy Davis	5	5	5	5	5	8	15	
13	Dick Donovan	5	5	5	5	5	8	15	6
14	Don Drysdale	5	5	5	5	8	12	40	8
15	Dick Farrell	5	5	5	5	5	8	15	5
16	Jim Gentile	5	5	5	5	5	8	15	
17	Ray Herbert	5	5	5	5	5	8	15	5
18	Chuck Hinton	5	5	5	5	5	8	15	
19	Ken Hubbs	5	5	5	5	5	10	30	6
20	Al Jackson	5	5	5	5	5	8	15	5
21	Al Kaline	5	5	5	6	10	15	150	
22	Harmon Killebrew	5	5	5	6	10	15	60	8
23	Sandy Koufax	5	8	12	15	60	80	200	
24	Jerry Lumpe	5	5	5	5	8	12	30	
25	Art Mahaffey	5	5	5	5	5	8	15	
26	Mickey Mantle	15	20	25	100	120	150	500	
27	Willie Mays	5	5	8	10	15	30	60	
28	Bill Mazeroski	5	5	5	5	8	12	80	15
29	Bill Monbouquette	5	5	5	5	5	8	15	5
30	Stan Musial	5	5	8	10	15	50	120	
31	Camilo Pascual	5	5	5	5	5	8	15	
32	Bob Purkey	5	5	5	5	5	8	15	6
33	Bobby Richardson	5	5	5	5	5	10	40	6
34	Brooks Robinson	5	5	5	6	10	15	50	10
35	Floyd Robinson	5	5	5	5	5	8	15	6
36	Frank Robinson	5	5	5	6	10	15	50	6

	GD 2	VG 3	VgEx 4	EX 5	ExMt 6	NM 7	NmMt 8	MT 9
47 Bob Rodgers	5	5	5	5	5	8	15	60
48 Johnny Romano	5	5	5	5	5	8	15	
49 Jack Sanford	5	5	5	5	5	8	15	
50 Norm Siebern	5	5	5	5	5	8	15	50
51 Warren Spahn	5	5	5	6	10	15	50	100
52 Dave Stenhouse	5	5	5	5	5	8	15	
53 Ralph Terry	5	5	5	5	5	8	15	
54 Lee Thomas	5	5	5	5	5	8	15	60
55 Bill White	5	5	5	5	5	8	15	
56 Carl Yastrzemski	5	5	8	10	40	60	200	

1964 Topps

	GD 2	VG 3	VgEx 4	EX 5	ExMt 6	NM 7	NmMt 8	MT 9
NL ERA Leaders	5	5	8	12	30	50	250	
AL ERA Leaders	5	5	5	6	10	15	120	
NL Pitching Leaders	5	5	8	12	20	120		
AL Pitching Leaders	5	5	5	8	12	40	100	500
NL Strikeout Leaders	5	5	6	10	12	30	60	400
AL Strikeout Leaders	5	5	5	5	8	30	80	300
NL Batting Leaders	5	6	10	15	25	50	100	500
AL Batting Leaders	5	5	6	10	25	40	500	
NL Home Run Leaders	5	6	10	30	50	60	150	500
AL Home Run Leaders	5	5	5	6	10	15	80	500
NL RBI Leaders	5	5	6	15	25	30	80	500
AL RBI Leaders	5	5	5	6	10	15	100	600
Hoyt Wilhelm	5	▲8	▲12	▲20	▲30	▲50	100	400
D.Nen RC/N.Willhite RC	5	5	5	5	5	8	15	100
Zoilo Versalles	5	5	5	5	6	15	40	
John Boozer	5	5	5	5	5	8	15	50
Willie Kirkland	5	5	5	5	5	8	15	50
Billy O'Dell	5	5	5	5	5	8	15	50
Don Wert	5	5	5	5	5	8	15	100
Bob Friend	5	5	5	5	5	15	20	
Yogi Berra MG	▲15	▲25	▼40	60	80	120	300	600
Jerry Adair	5	5	5	5	5	8	20	150
Chris Zachary RC	5	5	5	5	5	8	30	100
Carl Sawatski	5	5	5	5	5	8	15	50
Bill Monbouquette	5	5	5	5	5	8	25	80
Gino Cimoli	5	5	5	5	5	8	15	50
New York Mets TC	5	5	5	5	8	15	30	100
Claude Osteen	5	5	5	5	5	15	50	80
Lou Brock	▲25	▲40	▲60	▲100	▲150	▲250	▲400	▲1,000
Ron Perranoski	5	5	5	5	5	8	20	80
Dave Nicholson	5	5	5	5	5	8	15	800
Dean Chance	5	5	5	5	5	10	20	80
S.Ellis/M.Queen	5	5	5	5	5	8	25	
Jim Perry	5	5	5	5	5	10	50	80
Eddie Mathews	5	6	10	40	50	100	250	800
Hal Reniff	5	5	5	5	6	15	50	
Smoky Burgess	5	5	5	5	6	15	40	
Jim Wynn RC	5	8	12	20	30	50	100	150
Hank Aguirre	5	5	5	5	5	8	15	50
Dick Groat	5	5	5	5	8	25	60	
Friendly Foes	5	5	5	8	12	20	40	
Moe Drabowsky	5	5	5	5	5	8	20	
Roy Sievers	5	5	5	5	5	10	20	100
Duke Carmel	5	5	5	5	5	8	15	100
Milt Pappas	5	5	5	5	5	8	15	100
Ed Brinkman	5	5	5	5	5	8	15	50
J.Alou RC/R.Herbel	5	5	5	5	5	10	20	80
Bob Perry RC	5	5	5	5	5	8	25	120
Bill Henry	5	5	5	5	5	8	20	
Mickey Mantle	200	▲300	▲400	500	600	▲2,000	▲5,000	▲60,000
Pete Richert	5	5	5	5	5	8	20	50
Chuck Hinton	5	5	5	5	5	8	15	50
Denis Menke	5	5	5	5	5	8	25	80
Sam Mele MG	5	5	5	5	5	8	15	60

	GD 2	VG 3	VgEx 4	EX 5	ExMt 6	NM 7	NmMt 8	MT 9
55 Ernie Banks	15	25	50	60	100	250	400	▲2,500
56 Hal Brown	5	5	5	5	5	8	15	60
57 Tim Harkness	5	5	5	5	5	8	15	80
58 Don Demeter	5	5	5	5	5	8	25	
59 Ernie Broglio	5	5	5	5	5	8	25	100
60 Frank Malzone	5	5	5	5	5	10	30	80
61 Angel Backstops	5	5	5	5	5	8	15	50
62 Ted Savage	5	5	5	5	5	8	15	50
63 John Orsino	5	5	5	5	5	8	15	50
64 Ted Abernathy	5	5	5	5	5	8	25	
65 Felipe Alou	5	5	5	5	5	10	20	80
66 Eddie Fisher	5	5	5	5	5	8	20	
67 Detroit Tigers TC	5	5	5	5	6	12	25	200
68 Willie Davis	5	5	5	6	10	15	25	50
69 Clete Boyer	5	5	5	5	5	15	60	200
70 Joe Torre	5	5	5	8	12	30	100	250
71 Jack Spring	5	5	5	5	6	12	30	100
72 Chico Cardenas	5	5	5	5	5	15	50	
73 Jimmie Hall RC	5	5	5	5	5	15	50	100
74 B.Priddy RC/T.Butters	5	5	5	5	5	8	25	100
75 Wayne Causey	5	5	5	5	5	8	25	
76 Checklist 1	5	5	5	5	5	10	20	80
77 Jerry Walker	5	5	5	5	5	8	25	100
78 Merritt Ranew	5	5	5	5	5	8	15	50
79 Bob Heffner RC	5	5	5	5	5	8	25	100
80 Vada Pinson	5	5	5	5	5	10	80	150
81 All-Star Vets	5	5	5	8	12	20	60	200
82 Jim Davenport	5	5	5	5	5	10	20	80
83 Gus Triandos	5	5	5	5	5	8	15	80
84 Carl Willey	5	5	5	5	5	8	15	50
85 Pete Ward	5	5	5	5	5	8	15	50
86 Al Downing	5	5	5	5	5	10	30	150
87 St. Louis Cardinals TC	5	5	5	5	5	10	20	100
88 John Roseboro	5	5	5	5	5	10	20	100
89 Boog Powell	5	5	5	5	5	10	80	200
90 Earl Battey	5	5	5	5	5	8	15	150
91 Bob Bailey	5	5	5	5	5	8	25	
92 Steve Ridzik	5	5	5	5	5	8	25	100
93 Gary Geiger	5	5	5	5	5	8	25	
94 J.Britton RC/L.Maxie RC	5	5	5	5	5	8	20	
95 George Altman	5	5	5	5	5	8	15	50
96 Bob Buhl	5	5	5	5	5	8	15	100
97 Jim Fregosi	5	5	5	5	5	10	20	60
98 Bill Bruton	5	5	5	5	5	10	20	120
99 Al Stanek RC	5	5	5	5	5	8	25	80
100 Elston Howard	5	5	5	8	12	20	40	200
101 Walt Alston MG	5	5	5	5	5	10	20	80
102 Checklist 2	5	5	5	5	5	8	15	50
103 Curt Flood	6	10	15	25	40	100	300	
104 Art Mahaffey	5	5	5	5	5	8	20	120
105 Woody Held	5	5	5	5	5	8	15	60
106 Joe Nuxhall	5	5	5	5	5	10	25	
107 B.Howard RC/F.Kruetzer RC	5	5	5	5	5	8	15	50
108 John Wyatt	5	5	5	5	5	8	25	
109 Rusty Staub	5	5	5	5	8	25	30	150
110 Albie Pearson	5	5	5	5	5	12	25	
111 Don Elston	5	5	5	5	5	8	15	50
112 Bob Tillman	5	5	5	5	5	8	15	50
113 Grover Powell RC	5	5	5	5	5	8	15	50
114 Don Lock	5	5	5	5	5	8	30	60
115 Frank Bolling	5	5	5	5	5	8	15	80
116 J.Ward RC/T.Oliva	5	6	10	15	25	60	▲100	300
117 Earl Francis	5	5	5	5	5	8	15	80
118 John Blanchard	5	5	5	5	6	20	50	
119 Gary Kolb RC	5	5	5	5	5	8	15	50
120 Don Drysdale	6	10	15	25	40	60	120	400
121 Pete Runnels	5	5	5	5	5	10	40	
122 Don McMahon	5	5	5	5	5	8	15	50

#	Player	GD 2	VG 3	VgEx 4	EX 5	ExMt 6	NM 7	NmMt 8	MT 9
123	Jose Pagan	5	5	5	5	5	8	15	50
124	Orlando Pena	5	5	5	5	5	8	15	50
125	Pete Rose	▲200	▲300	▲500	▲600	800	▲1,500	▲5,000	▲12,000
126	Russ Snyder	5	5	5	5	5	8	15	50
127	A.Gatewood RC/D.Simpson	5	5	5	5	5	8	15	50
128	Mickey Lolich RC	6	10	15	25	40	60	▲200	400
129	Amado Samuel	5	5	5	5	5	8	15	50
130	Gary Peters	5	5	5	5	5	8	20	100
131	Steve Boros	5	5	5	5	5	8	15	50
132	Milwaukee Braves TC	5	5	5	5	5	10	20	70
133	Jim Grant	5	5	5	5	5	8	25	80
134	Don Zimmer	5	5	5	5	5	10	25	80
135	Johnny Callison	5	5	5	5	5	10	25	80
136	Sandy Koufax WS1	6	10	15	25	40	80	400	
137	Willie Davis WS2	5	5	5	5	8	15	40	150
138	Ron Fairly WS3	5	5	5	5	8	15	40	120
139	Frank Howard WS4	5	5	5	5	8	15	50	650
140	Dodgers Celebrate WS	5	5	5	5	8	15	30	120
141	Danny Murtaugh MG	5	5	5	5	5	8	25	50
142	John Bateman	5	5	5	5	5	10	30	120
143	Bubba Phillips	5	5	5	5	5	8	15	50
144	Al Worthington	5	5	5	5	5	8	15	50
145	Norm Siebern	5	5	5	5	5	8	15	80
146	T.John RC/B.Chance RC	6	10	15	50	60	80	200	800
147	Ray Sadecki	5	5	5	5	5	8	30	120
148	J.C. Martin	5	5	5	5	5	10	40	100
149	Paul Foytack	5	5	5	5	5	8	15	50
150	Willie Mays	40	50	60	100	150	250	▲1,500	▲4,000
151	Kansas City Athletics TC	5	5	5	5	5	10	20	80
152	Denny Lemaster	5	5	5	5	5	8	15	50
153	Dick Williams	5	5	5	5	5	8	25	50
154	Dick Tracewski RC	5	5	5	5	5	10	20	60
155	Duke Snider	6	10	15	25	40	60	120	400
156	Bill Dailey	5	5	5	5	5	8	15	60
157	Gene Mauch MG	5	5	5	5	5	8	15	100
158	Ken Johnson	5	5	5	5	5	8	15	50
159	Charlie Dees RC	5	5	5	5	5	8	50	80
160	Ken Boyer	5	5	5	5	8	20	60	200
161	Dave McNally	5	5	5	5	5	10	25	60
162	Hitting Area	5	5	5	5	5	8	30	
163	Donn Clendenon	5	5	5	5	5	10	20	80
164	Bud Daley	5	5	5	5	5	8	15	50
165	Jerry Lumpe	5	5	5	5	5	8	15	50
166	Marty Keough	5	5	5	5	5	8	15	50
167	M.Brumley RC/L.Piniella RC	6	10	15	25	40	60	120	1,000
168	Al Weis	5	5	5	5	5	8	15	60
169	Del Crandall	5	5	5	5	5	10	20	80
170	Dick Radatz	5	5	5	5	5	15	40	100
171	Ty Cline	5	5	5	5	5	8	15	50
172	Cleveland Indians TC	5	5	5	5	5	10	20	80
173	Ryne Duren	5	5	5	5	5	8	15	60
174	Doc Edwards	5	5	5	5	5	8	15	50
175	Billy Williams	5	6	10	15	25	60	250	
176	Tracy Stallard	5	5	5	5	5	8	15	50
177	Harmon Killebrew	▲8	▲12	▲20	▲30	▲50	▲80	200	1,000
178	Hank Bauer MG	5	5	5	5	5	10	20	60
179	Carl Warwick	5	5	5	5	5	8	20	50
180	Tommy Davis	5	5	5	5	5	10	25	80
181	Dave Wickersham	5	5	5	5	5	8	15	50
182	Sox Sockers	5	5	5	8	15	40	80	200
183	Ron Taylor	5	5	5	5	5	8	15	450
184	Al Luplow	5	5	5	5	5	8	15	50
185	Jim O'Toole	5	5	5	5	5	8	15	50
186	Roman Mejias	5	5	5	5	5	8	25	
187	Ed Roebuck	5	5	5	5	5	8	15	50
188	Checklist 3	5	5	5	5	5	8	25	80
189	Bob Hendley	5	5	5	5	5	8	15	175
190	Bobby Richardson	5	5	5	6	10	20	80	300

#	Player	GD 2	VG 3	VgEx 4	EX 5	ExMt 6	NM 7	NmMt 8	MT
191	Clay Dalrymple	5	5	5	5	5	8	15	50
192	J.Boccabella RC/B.Cowan RC	5	5	5	5	5	8	15	50
193	Jerry Lynch	5	5	5	5	5	8	15	120
194	John Goryl	5	5	5	5	5	8	15	50
195	Floyd Robinson	5	5	5	5	5	8	15	50
196	Jim Gentile	5	5	5	5	5	8	20	
197	Frank Lary	5	5	5	5	5	8	15	100
198	Len Gabrielson	5	5	5	5	6	12	30	100
199	Joe Azcue	5	5	5	5	5	8	15	50
200	Sandy Koufax	25	40	60	80	100	200	400	1,200
201	S.Bowens RC/W.Bunker RC	5	5	5	5	5	8	15	400
202	Galen Cisco	5	5	5	5	5	8	25	50
203	John Kennedy RC	5	5	5	5	5	8	20	50
204	Matty Alou	5	5	5	6	10	15	40	80
205	Nellie Fox	5	5	5	8	20	25	40	150
206	Steve Hamilton	5	5	5	5	5	8	15	50
207	Fred Hutchinson MG	5	5	5	5	5	8	15	50
208	Wes Covington	5	5	5	5	5	10	30	
209	Bob Allen	5	5	5	5	6	12	30	80
210	Carl Yastrzemski	▲12	20	25	30	50	▲200	▲300	▲1,500
211	Jim Coker	5	5	5	5	5	8	15	50
212	Pete Lovrich	5	5	5	5	5	8	15	50
213	Los Angeles Angels TC	5	5	5	5	5	10	20	80
214	Ken McMullen	5	5	5	5	5	8	25	50
215	Ray Herbert	5	5	5	5	5	8	25	80
216	Mike de la Hoz	5	5	5	5	5	8	15	50
217	Jim King	5	5	5	5	5	8	15	50
218	Hank Fischer	5	5	5	5	5	8	15	80
219	Young Aces	5	5	5	5	5	10	30	120
220	Dick Ellsworth	5	5	5	5	5	8	15	50
221	Bob Saverine	5	5	5	5	5	8	15	50
222	Billy Pierce	5	5	5	5	5	8	25	50
223	George Banks	5	5	5	5	5	8	15	60
224	Tommie Sisk	5	5	5	5	5	8	15	80
225	Roger Maris	▲25	▲40	60	▲100	▲150	▲200	400	1,000
226	J.Grote RC/L.Yellen RC	5	5	5	5	5	8	15	50
227	Barry Latman	5	5	5	5	5	8	15	50
228	Felix Mantilla	5	5	5	5	5	8	15	80
229	Charley Lau	5	5	5	5	5	8	15	50
230	Brooks Robinson	▲8	▲12	▲20	▲30	▲50	▲80	200	500
231	Dick Calmus RC	5	5	5	5	5	8	15	50
232	Al Lopez MG	5	5	5	5	5	10	20	80
233	Hal Smith	5	5	5	5	5	8	15	50
234	Gary Bell	5	5	5	5	5	10	20	60
235	Ron Hunt	5	5	5	5	5	8	15	60
236	Bill Faul	5	5	5	5	5	8	15	80
237	Chicago Cubs TC	5	5	5	5	5	10	25	100
238	Roy McMillan	5	5	5	5	5	8	20	50
239	Herm Starrette RC	5	5	5	5	5	8	25	80
240	Bill White	5	5	5	5	8	15	40	120
241	Jim Owens	5	5	5	5	5	8	15	50
242	Harvey Kuenn	5	5	5	5	5	8	15	50
243	R.Allen RC/J.Hernstein	5	12	20	▲30	▲50	▲80	200	▲1,200
244	Tony LaRussa RC	▲6	▲10	▲15	▲25	40	▼60	▼100	300
245	Dick Stigman	5	5	5	5	5	8	15	50
246	Manny Mota	5	5	5	5	5	10	20	80
247	Dave DeBusschere	5	5	5	5	5	10	40	150
248	Johnny Pesky MG	5	5	5	5	5	10	30	80
249	Doug Camilli	5	5	5	5	5	8	20	50
250	Al Kaline	20	25	30	40	50	▲80	120	500
251	Choo Choo Coleman	5	5	5	5	5	10	20	60
252	Ken Aspromonte	5	5	5	5	5	8	25	
253	Wally Post	5	5	5	5	5	8	25	80
254	Don Hoak	5	5	5	5	5	8	15	50
255	Lee Thomas	5	5	5	5	5	8	15	100
256	Johnny Weekly	5	5	5	5	5	8	25	80
257	San Francisco Giants TC	5	5	5	5	5	8	25	80
258	Garry Roggenburk	5	5	5	5	5	10	20	80

#	Player	GD 2	VG 3	VgEx 4	EX 5	ExMt 6	NM 7	NmMt 8	MT 9
259	Harry Bright	5	5	5	5	5	10	20	80
260	Frank Robinson	12	▼20	30	▲50	▲80	100	200	500
261	Jim Hannan	5	5	5	5	5	8	15	50
262	M.Shannon RC/H.Fanok	5	5	5	5	8	15	50	100
263	Chuck Estrada	5	5	5	5	5	8	15	50
264	Jim Landis	5	5	5	5	5	8	15	50
265	Jim Bunning	5	5	5	8	12	20	50	120
266	Gene Freese	5	5	5	5	5	8	15	50
267	Wilbur Wood RC	5	5	5	5	6	12	25	100
268	Bill's Got It	5	5	5	5	6	12	40	100
269	Ellis Burton	5	5	5	5	5	8	15	50
270	Rich Rollins	5	5	5	5	5	8	15	50
271	Bob Sadowski	5	5	5	5	5	8	15	50
272	Jake Wood	5	5	5	5	5	8	15	150
273	Mel Nelson	5	5	5	5	5	8	15	50
274	Checklist 4	5	5	5	5	▲8	▲12	25	50
275	John Tsitouris	5	5	5	5	5	10	30	100
276	Jose Tartabull	5	5	5	5	5	8	20	50
277	Ken Retzer	5	5	5	5	5	10	30	100
278	Bobby Shantz	5	5	5	5	5	8	25	50
279	Joe Koppe	5	5	5	5	5	8	15	50
280	Juan Marichal	▲6	▲10	▲15	▲25	▲40	▲100	200	350
281	J.,Gibbs/T.Metcalf RC	5	5	5	5	5	10	25	120
282	Bob Bruce	5	5	5	5	5	8	15	50
283	Tom McCraw RC	5	5	5	5	5	8	15	50
284	Dick Schofield	5	5	5	5	5	8	15	80
285	Robin Roberts	5	5	5	8	12	20	60	100
286	Don Landrum	5	5	5	5	5	8	15	50
287	Tony Conigliaro RC	10	15	25	40	60	80	150	500
288	Al Moran	5	5	5	5	5	8	15	50
289	Frank Funk	5	5	5	5	5	8	15	50
290	Bob Allison	5	5	5	5	5	10	20	80
291	Phil Ortega	5	5	5	5	5	8	15	50
292	Mike Roarke	5	5	5	5	5	8	15	50
293	Philadelphia Phillies TC	5	5	5	5	5	10	20	120
294	Ken L. Hunt	5	5	5	5	5	8	15	30
295	Roger Craig	5	5	5	5	5	8	25	100
296	Ed Kirkpatrick	5	5	5	5	5	8	15	50
297	Ken MacKenzie	5	5	5	5	5	8	15	50
298	Harry Craft MG	5	5	5	5	5	8	15	50
299	Bill Stafford	5	5	5	5	5	12	60	100
300	Hank Aaron	25	50	80	100	150	250	▲1,000	3,000
301	Larry Brown RC	5	5	5	5	5	8	15	50
302	Dan Pfister	5	5	5	5	5	8	15	60
303	Jim Campbell	5	5	5	5	5	8	15	50
304	Bob Johnson	5	5	5	5	5	8	15	50
305	Jack Lamabe	5	5	5	5	5	8	15	50
306	Giant Gunners	8	12	20	30	▲50	▲80	100	500
307	Joe Gibbon	5	5	5	5	5	8	15	50
308	Gene Stephens	5	5	5	5	5	8	15	50
309	Paul Toth	5	5	5	5	6	12	30	100
310	Jim Gilliam	5	5	5	5	6	12	30	50
311	Tom W. Brown RC	5	5	5	5	5	8	15	50
312	F.Fisher RC/F.Gladding RC	5	5	5	5	5	8	15	50
313	Chuck Hiller	5	5	5	5	5	8	15	50
314	Jerry Buchek	5	5	5	5	5	8	15	50
315	Bo Belinsky	5	5	5	5	5	8	15	50
316	Gene Oliver	5	5	5	5	5	8	15	50
317	Al Smith	5	5	5	5	5	8	15	50
318	Minnesota Twins TC	5	5	5	5	6	12	25	120
319	Paul Brown	5	5	5	5	5	8	15	50
320	Rocky Colavito	5	5	5	8	12	20	50	300
321	Bob Lillis	5	5	5	5	5	8	15	50
322	George Brunet	5	5	5	5	5	8	15	50
323	John Buzhardt	5	5	5	5	5	8	15	50
324	Casey Stengel MG	5	▲8	▲12	▲20	▲30	▲50	▲80	250
325	Hector Lopez	5	5	5	5	5	10	30	80
326	Ron Brand RC	5	5	5	5	5	8	15	50
327	Don Blasingame	5	5	5	5	5	8	15	50
328	Bob Shaw	5	5	5	5	5	8	15	50
329	Russ Nixon	5	5	5	5	5	8	15	60
330	Tommy Harper	5	5	5	5	8	20	60	120
331	AL Bombers	▲80	▲120	▲150	▲200	▲300	▲500	▲800	▲2,500
332	Ray Washburn	5	5	5	5	6	12	30	150
333	Billy Moran	5	5	5	5	5	8	15	50
334	Lew Krausse	5	5	5	5	5	8	15	50
335	Don Mossi	5	5	5	5	5	10	25	80
336	Andre Rodgers	5	5	5	5	5	8	15	50
337	A.Ferrara RC/J.Torborg RC	5	5	5	5	5	8	25	50
338	Jack Kralick	5	5	5	5	5	8	15	50
339	Walt Bond	5	5	5	5	5	8	15	50
340	Joe Cunningham	5	5	5	5	5	8	15	50
341	Jim Roland	5	5	5	5	5	8	15	50
342	Willie Stargell	▲20	▲30	▲50	▲80	▲120	▲200	▲300	▲2,000
343	Washington Senators TC	5	5	5	5	5	10	20	80
344	Phil Linz	5	5	5	5	5	10	25	80
345	Frank Thomas	5	5	5	5	5	10	25	80
346	Joey Jay	5	5	5	5	5	8	15	50
347	Bobby Wine	5	5	5	5	5	8	15	50
348	Ed Lopat MG	5	5	5	5	5	10	20	50
349	Art Fowler	5	5	5	5	5	8	15	50
350	Willie McCovey	▲8	▲12	20	▲30	▲50	▲80	100	400
351	Dan Schneider	5	5	5	5	5	8	15	50
352	Eddie Bressoud	5	5	5	5	5	8	15	50
353	Wally Moon	5	5	5	5	5	10	60	80
354	Dave Giusti	5	5	5	5	5	8	15	50
355	Vic Power	5	5	5	5	5	10	25	50
356	B.McCool RC/C.Ruiz	5	5	5	5	5	8	15	50
357	Charley James	5	5	5	5	5	8	15	60
358	Ron Kline	5	5	5	5	5	8	15	50
359	Jim Schaffer	5	5	5	5	5	8	15	50
360	Joe Pepitone	5	5	5	5	8	25	40	100
361	Jay Hook	5	5	5	5	5	8	15	50
362	Checklist 5	5	5	5	▲6	▲10	15	▲40	60
363	Dick McAuliffe	5	5	5	▲6	▲10	15	25	50
364	Joe Gaines	5	5	5	5	5	8	15	50
365	Cal McLish	5	5	5	5	5	8	15	50
366	Nelson Mathews	5	5	5	5	5	8	15	50
367	Fred Whitfield	5	5	5	5	5	8	15	50
368	F.Ackley RC/D.Buford RC	5	5	5	5	5	8	20	100
369	Jerry Zimmerman	5	5	5	5	5	8	15	50
370	Hal Woodeshick	5	5	5	5	5	8	15	50
371	Frank Howard	5	5	5	10	15	30	60	150
372	Howie Koplitz	5	5	5	5	5	10	25	60
373	Pittsburgh Pirates TC	5	5	5	5	6	15	60	100
374	Bobby Bolin	5	5	5	5	5	10	20	60
375	Ron Santo	▲6	▲10	▲15	25	▲40	▲120	300	600
376	Dave Morehead	5	5	5	5	5	10	25	60
377	Bob Skinner	5	5	5	5	5	10	20	100
378	W.Woodward RC/J.Smith	5	5	5	5	5	10	25	60
379	Tony Gonzalez	5	5	5	5	5	15	30	120
380	Whitey Ford	6	10	15	30	60	120	150	600
381	Bob Taylor	5	5	5	5	5	10	30	60
382	Wes Stock	5	5	5	5	5	20	30	60
383	Bill Rigney MG	5	5	5	5	5	15	25	60
384	Ron Hansen	5	5	5	5	5	15	40	80
385	Curt Simmons	5	5	5	5	6	12	30	150
386	Lenny Green	5	5	5	5	5	10	25	60
387	Terry Fox	5	5	5	5	5	10	25	60
388	J.O'Donoghue RC/G.Williams	5	5	5	5	5	10	25	80
389	Jim Umbricht	5	5	5	5	5	10	20	▲80
390	Orlando Cepeda	5	8	12	20	25	50	100	250
391	Sam McDowell	5	5	5	▲8	▲12	▲20	40	80
392	Jim Pagliaroni	5	5	5	5	5	10	25	60
393	Casey Teaches	5	5	5	6	15	20	30	120
394	Bob Miller	5	5	5	5	5	10	20	60

#	Player	GD 2	VG 3	VgEx 4	EX 5	ExMt 6	NM 7	NmMt 8	MT 9
395	Tom Tresh	5	5	5	6	10	30	100	150
396	Dennis Bennett	5	5	5	5	5	10	20	60
397	Chuck Cottier	5	5	5	5	5	10	25	60
398	B.Haas/D.Smith	5	5	5	5	6	15	60	80
399	Jackie Brandt	5	5	5	5	5	10	25	120
400	Warren Spahn	5	8	12	30	50	60	150	400
401	Charlie Maxwell	5	5	5	5	5	15	80	100
402	Tom Sturdivant	5	5	5	5	5	10	20	60
403	Cincinnati Reds TC	5	5	5	5	6	12	60	150
404	Tony Martinez	5	5	5	5	5	10	20	60
405	Ken McBride	5	5	5	5	5	10	20	60
406	Al Spangler	5	5	5	5	5	10	25	100
407	Bill Freehan	5	5	5	8	12	40	50	150
408	J.Stewart RC/F.Burdette RC	5	5	5	5	5	10	25	60
409	Bill Fischer	5	5	5	5	5	10	20	60
410	Dick Stuart	5	5	5	5	5	10	▲40	120
411	Lee Walls	5	5	5	5	5	10	20	60
412	Ray Culp	5	5	6	8	12	20	50	80
413	Johnny Keane MG	5	5	5	5	5	10	20	80
414	Jack Sanford	5	5	5	5	5	15	30	100
415	Tony Kubek	5	8	12	20	25	40	60	250
416	Lee Maye	5	5	5	5	5	10	40	80
417	Don Cardwell	5	5	5	5	5	10	25	60
418	D.Knowles RC/B.Narum RC	5	5	5	5	5	10	30	60
419	Ken Harrelson RC	5	5	6	10	15	25	60	100
420	Jim Maloney	5	5	5	5	20	25	30	60
421	Camilo Carreon	5	5	5	5	5	10	20	60
422	Jack Fisher	5	5	5	5	5	10	25	60
423	Tops in NL	▲30	▲50	▲80	▲120	▲200	▲300	▲500	▲1,200
424	Dick Bertell	5	5	5	5	5	10	20	60
425	Norm Cash	5	5	5	8	12	20	40	100
426	Bob Rodgers	5	5	5	5	5	10	30	50
427	Don Rudolph	5	5	5	6	10	15	25	60
428	A.Skeen RC/P.Smith RC	5	5	5	5	5	10	25	60
429	Tim McCarver	5	5	5	5	20	25	60	250
430	Juan Pizarro	5	5	5	5	5	20		
431	George Alusik	5	5	5	5	5	10	20	60
432	Ruben Amaro	5	5	5	5	5	10	25	60
433	New York Yankees TC	5	8	12	20	30	50	150	400
434	Don Nottebart	5	5	5	5	5	10	20	60
435	Vic Davalillo	5	5	5	5	8	30	80	400
436	Charlie Neal	5	5	5	5	6	12	30	80
437	Ed Bailey	5	5	5	5	5	10	30	80
438	Checklist 6	5	5	5	5	8	15	30	100
439	Harvey Haddix	5	5	5	5	6	15	▲80	▲120
440	Roberto Clemente	▲120	▲200	▲300	▲400	▲500	▲1,000	▲2,000	3,000
441	Bob Duliba	5	5	5	5	5	10	20	60
442	Pumpsie Green	5	5	5	5	6	15	40	100
443	Chuck Dressen MG	5	5	5	5	6	20	30	80
444	Larry Jackson	5	5	5	5	5	10	20	150
445	Bill Skowron	5	5	5	5	6	12	30	80
446	Julian Javier	5	5	6	10	15	25	150	
447	Ted Bowsfield	5	5	5	5	5	10	20	60
448	Cookie Rojas	5	5	5	5	6	20	25	80
449	Deron Johnson	5	5	5	▲6	▲10	▲15	25	100
450	Steve Barber	5	5	5	5	8	20	50	100
451	Joe Amalfitano	5	5	5	5	5	10	20	60
452	G.Garrido RC/J.Hart RC	5	5	▲6	▲10	▲15	▲25	40	80
453	Frank Baumann	5	5	5	5	5	15	40	80
454	Tommie Aaron	5	5	5	5	6	12	25	60
455	Bernie Allen	5	5	5	5	5	10	25	60
456	W.Parker RC/J.Werhas RC	5	5	5	5	6	25	50	100
457	Jesse Gonder	5	5	5	5	5	10	25	60
458	Ralph Terry	5	5	6	10	15	25	50	150
459	P.Charton RC/D.Jones RC	5	5	5	5	5	10	20	60
460	Bob Gibson	20	30	50	60	80	200	300	1,000
461	George Thomas	5	5	5	5	5	15	40	80
462	Birdie Tebbetts MG	5	5	5	5	5	15	40	100
463	Don Leppert	5	5	5	5	5	10	25	80
464	Dallas Green	5	5	5	8	15	20	80	120
465	Mike Hershberger	5	5	5	5	5	15	100	
466	D.Green RC/A.Monteagudo RC	5	5	5	5	6	20	60	80
467	Bob Aspromonte	5	5	5	5	5	10	20	60
468	Gaylord Perry	6	10	15	25	40	80	120	500
469	F.Norman RC/S.Slaughter RC	5	5	5	5	6	20	50	120
470	Jim Bouton	5	5	5	8	12	30	50	120
471	Gates Brown RC	5	5	5	8	12	20	50	
472	Vern Law	5	5	5	▲8	▲12	20	▲80	▲120
473	Baltimore Orioles TC	▲30	▲50	▲60	▲80	▲120	▲250	800	
474	Larry Sherry	5	5	5	5	6	12	60	100
475	Ed Charles	5	5	5	5	5	10	20	60
476	R.Carty RC/D.Kelley RC	5	5	5	5	10	40	120	200
477	Mike Joyce	5	5	5	5	5	15	50	50
478	Dick Howser	5	5	5	5	5		30	120
479	D.Bakenhaster RC/J.Lewis RC	5	5	5	5	5	10	25	60
480	Bob Purkey	5	5	5	5	5	10	25	60
481	Chuck Schilling	5	5	5	5	5	10	30	80
482	J.Briggs RC/D.Cater RC	5	5	5	5	10	20	80	150
483	Fred Valentine RC	5	5	5	5	5	10	20	60
484	Bill Pleis	5	5	5	5	5	10	20	60
485	Tom Haller	5	5	5	5	5	10	20	60
486	Bob Kennedy MG	5	5	5	5	5	10	25	60
487	Mike McCormick	5	5	5	5	6	25	40	
488	P.Mikkelsen RC/B.Meyer RC	5	5	5	5	5	12	50	800
489	Julio Navarro	5	5	5	5	5	10	40	60
490	Ron Fairly	5	5	5	5	6	12	40	80
491	Ed Rakow	5	5	5	5	5	10	30	60
492	J.Beauchamp RC/M.White RC	5	5	5	5	5	10	25	60
493	Don Lee	5	5	5	5	5	10	20	40
494	Al Jackson	5	5	5	5	5	10	25	60
495	Bill Virdon	5	5	5	5	6	15	50	120
496	Chicago White Sox TC	5	5	5	5	6	12	25	80
497	Jeoff Long RC	5	5	5	5	5	10	20	60
498	Dave Stenhouse	5	5	5	5	5	10	20	60
499	C.Slamon RC/G.Seyfried RC	5	5	5	5	8	15	30	100
500	Camilo Pascual	5	5	5	5	6	40	100	
501	Bob Veale	5	5	5	5	5	10	150	
502	B.Knoop RC/B.Lee RC	5	5	5	5	5	10	20	60
503	Earl Wilson	5	5	5	5	5	12	40	100
504	Claude Raymond	5	5	5	5	5	10	25	60
505	Stan Williams	5	5	6	10	15	25	60	120
506	Bobby Bragan MG	5	5	5	5	5	10	30	100
507	Johnny Edwards	5	5	5	5	5	10	25	50
508	Diego Segui	5	5	5	5	5	10	25	
509	G.Alley RC/O.McFarlane RC	5	5	5	5	8	25	100	400
510	Lindy McDaniel	5	5	5	5	6	12	30	80
511	Lou Jackson	5	5	5	5	5	20	25	80
512	W.Horton RC/J.Sparma RC	5	5	6	10	15	25	100	300
513	Don Larsen	5	5	5	▲6	▲10	15	▲80	120
514	Jim Hickman	5	5	5	8	12	20	▲80	150
515	Johnny Romano	5	5	5	5	5	10	60	
516	J.Arrigo RC/D.Siebler RC	5	5	5	5	5	10	30	
517A	Checklist 7 Incorrect Numbering	5	5	6	10	15	25	40	150
517B	Checklist 7 Correct Numbering	5	5	6	10	15	40	100	
518	Carl Bouldin	5	5	5	5	5	10	20	60
519	Charlie Smith	5	5	5	5	5	10	20	60
520	Jack Baldschun	5	5	5	5	5	10	60	100
521	Tom Satriano	5	5	5	5	5	15	60	100
522	Bob Tiefenauer	5	5	5	5	5	10	25	60
523	Lou Burdette	5	5	5	5	8	15	50	▲150
524	J.Dickson RC/B.Klaus RC	5	5	5	5	8	15	40	
525	Al McBean	5	5	5	5	8	15	30	80
526	Lou Clinton	5	5	5	5	8	20	30	80
527	Larry Bearnarth	5	5	5	5	8	15	40	120
528	D.Duncan RC/T.Reynolds RC	5	5	5	5	8	15	30	
529	Alvin Dark MG	5	5	5	5	8	15	30	80

		GD 2	VG 3	VgEx 4	EX 5	ExMt 6	NM 7	NmMt 8	MT 9
530	Leon Wagner	5	5	5	5	8	15	50	120
531	Los Angeles Dodgers TC	5	▲8	▲12	▲20	▲30	▲50	120	500
532	B.Bloomfield RC/J.Nossek RC	5	5	5	5	8	15	60	150
533	Johnny Klippstein	5	5	5	5	8	15	30	80
534	Gus Bell	5	5	5	▲8	▲12	▲20	40	
535	Phil Regan	5	5	5	5	8	20	30	80
536	L.Elliot/J.Stephenson RC	5	5	5	5	8	15	▲40	
537	Dan Osinski	5	5	5	5	8	15	30	80
538	Minnie Minoso	5	5	8	12	20	80	200	
539	Roy Face	5	5	5	5	8	15	40	120
540	Luis Aparicio	5	6	10	15	25	60	500	
541	P.Roof/P.Niekro RC	▲60	100	120	150	200	▲400	600	▲1,500
542	Don Mincher	5	5	5	▲6	▲10	15	30	100
543	Bob Uecker	5	6	10	15	50	100	200	400
544	S.Hertz RC/J.Hoerner RC	5	5	5	▲6	▲10	15	50	
545	Max Alvis	5	5	5	▲6	▲10	15	▲50	80
546	Joe Christopher	5	5	5	▲6	▲10	15	▲60	150
547	Gil Hodges MG	5	5	6	10	15	25	80	250
548	W.Schurr RC/P.Speckenbach RC	5	5	5	▲8	▲12	▲20	▲30	80
549	Joe Moeller	5	5	5	5	8	15	30	80
550	Ken Hubbs MEM	5	6	10	15	25	80	100	300
551	Billy Hoeft	5	5	5	5	8	25	40	80
552	T.Kelley RC/S.Siebert RC	5	5	5	5	8	20	25	150
553	Jim Brewer	5	5	5	5	8	15	30	120
554	Hank Foiles	5	5	5	5	8	15	25	80
555	Lee Stange	5	5	5	5	8	15	▲60	100
556	S.Dillon RC/R.Locke RC	5	5	5	5	8	15	50	
557	Leo Burke	5	5	5	5	8	15	25	80
558	Don Schwall	5	5	5	5	8	15	40	
559	Dick Phillips	5	5	5	5	8	15	30	80
560	Dick Farrell	5	5	5	5	8	15	30	80
561	D.Bennett RC/R.Wise RC	5	5	6	12	20	30	50	150
562	Pedro Ramos	5	5	5	8	10	20	▲50	80
563	Dal Maxvill	5	5	5	5	8	25	60	120
564	J.McCabe RC/J.McNertney RC	5	5	5	5	8	15	40	80
565	Stu Miller	5	5	5	5	8	15	50	80
566	Ed Kranepool	5	5	5	▲8	▲12	20	40	100
567	Jim Kaat	5	6	10	15	25	40	50	120
568	P.Gagliano RC/C.Peterson RC	5	5	5	8	12	20	30	80
569	Fred Newman	5	5	▲6	▲10	▲15	▲25	▲40	80
570	Bill Mazeroski	8	12	30	40	50	60	100	250
571	Gene Conley	5	5	5	5	8	15	30	80
572	D.Gray RC/D.Egan	5	5	5	5	8	15	50	
573	Jim Duffalo	5	5	5	▲8	▲12	▲20	▲30	80
574	Manny Jimenez	5	5	5	5	8	15	25	50
575	Tony Cloninger	5	5	5	5	8	15	30	60
576	J.Hinsley RC/B.Wakefield RC	5	5	5	5	8	20	40	200
577	Gordy Coleman	5	5	5	5	8	15	60	200
578	Glen Hobbie	5	5	5	5	8	15	50	80
579	Boston Red Sox TC	5	▲8	▲12	▲20	▲30	▲50	▲80	▲400
580	Johnny Podres	5	5	5	6	10	25	▲60	100
581	P.Gonzalez/A.Moore RC	5	5	5	8	15	50	200	
582	Rod Kanehl	5	5	5	5	8	20	▲60	100
583	Tito Francona	5	5	5	5	8	20	50	300
584	Joel Horlen	5	5	5	5	10	25	100	200
585	Tony Taylor	5	5	5	5	8	25	80	
586	Jimmy Piersall	5	6	10	15	25	40	60	150
587	Bennie Daniels	5	5	5	6	10	25	60	

– Chicago Cubs TC #237 PSA 10 (Gem) sold for $2,670 (Greg Bussineau; 12/12)

– P.Roof/P.Niekro #541 PSA 10 (Gem) (Young Collection) sold for $8,711 (SCP; 5/12)

1964 Topps Giants

		VG 3	VgEx 4	EX 5	ExMt 6	NM 7	NmMt 8	MT 9	Gem 9.5/10
	Gary Peters	5	5	5	5	8	30	120	
	Ken Johnson	5	5	5	5	8	25	100	
	Sandy Koufax SP	30	80	120	150	250	400	2,500	
	Bob Bailey	5	5	5	5	8	15	60	

		VG 3	VgEx 4	EX 5	ExMt 6	NM 7	NmMt 8	MT 9	Gem 9.5/10
5	Milt Pappas	5	5	5	5	8	15	30	400
6	Ron Hunt	5	5	5	5	8	15	40	250
7	Whitey Ford	5	8	12	30	40	60	80	
8	Roy McMillan	5	5	5	5	8	20	40	300
9	Rocky Colavito	5	5	5	5	8	15	60	300
10	Jim Bunning	5	5	5	6	10	30	200	300
11	Roberto Clemente	15	25	50	60	▲200	▲300	▲800	
12	Al Kaline	5	8	12	20	30	50	60	400
13	Nellie Fox	5	5	5	5	25	40	▲60	400
14	Tony Gonzalez	5	5	5	5	8	30	80	
15	Jim Gentile	5	5	5	5	8	40	60	
16	Dean Chance	5	5	5	5	8	20	60	
17	Dick Ellsworth	5	5	5	5	8	15	40	
18	Jim Fregosi	5	5	5	6	15	50		
19	Dick Groat	5	5	5	5	8	15	50	350
20	Chuck Hinton	5	5	5	5	8	15	40	450
21	Elston Howard	5	5	5	6	15	80	150	
22	Dick Farrell	5	5	5	5	8	15	40	150
23	Albie Pearson	5	5	5	5	8	15	30	150
24	Frank Howard	5	5	5	5	8	15	40	300
25	Mickey Mantle	80	100	▲150	▲200	250	▲400	▲1,500	
26	Joe Torre	5	5	5	5	8	15	40	500
27	Eddie Brinkman	5	5	5	5	8	40	60	
28	Bob Friend SP	▲8	▲12	▲20	▲30	▲50	▲60	120	
29	Frank Robinson	5	6	10	25	40	80	200	1,200
30	Bill Freehan	5	5	5	6	15	50	300	
31	Warren Spahn	5	6	10	15	30	50	60	300
32	Camilo Pascual	5	5	5	8	15	30		300
33	Pete Ward	5	5	5	5	8	15	30	
34	Jim Maloney	5	5	5	5	8	40	60	300
35	Dave Wickersham	5	5	5	5	8	15	60	500
36	Johnny Callison	5	5	5	5	8	15	30	250
37	Juan Marichal	5	5	5	6	10	20	50	
38	Harmon Killebrew	▲8	▲12	▲20	▲30	▲50	▲60	▲100	400
39	Luis Aparicio	5	5	5	6	10	20	60	
40	Dick Radatz	5	5	5	5	8	15	30	200
41	Bob Gibson	8	12	20	30	▲80	▲120	250	
42	Dick Stuart SP	5	5	8	12	20	50	80	
43	Tommy Davis	5	5	5	5	8	15	60	200
44	Tony Oliva	5	5	5	6	10	20	40	400
45	Wayne Causey SP	▲6	▲10	▲15	25	▲40	▲60	▲120	
46	Max Alvis	5	5	5	5	8	15	40	
47	Galen Cisco SP	6	10	15	25	30	50	100	
48	Carl Yastrzemski	5	8	12	20	40	60	100	
49	Hank Aaron	▲25	▲40	▲60	100	120	▲250	▲400	
50	Brooks Robinson	▲8	▲12	▲20	▲30	▲50	▲80	▲200	600
51	Willie Mays SP	▲50	▲80	▲120	▲200	250	400	600	
52	Billy Williams	5	5	5	6	10	25	200	
53	Juan Pizarro	5	5	5	8	12	20	30	250
54	Leon Wagner	5	5	5	5	8	15	30	250
55	Orlando Cepeda	5	5	5	8	12	20	25	200
56	Vada Pinson	5	5	5	5	8	15	30	400
57	Ken Boyer	5	6	10	15	25	200		
58	Ron Santo	5	5	6	10	15	20	100	
59	John Romano	5	5	5	5	8	20	80	
60	Bill Skowron SP	5	6	15	30	40	150		

— Bill Freehan #30 PSA 10 (Gem) sold for $2,030 (eBay; 1/13)

1964 Topps Stand-Ups

		GD 2	VG 3	VgEx 4	EX 5	ExMt 6	NM 7	NmMt 8	MT 9
1	Hank Aaron	20	30	40	80	150	200	▲1,000	2,500
2	Hank Aguirre	5	5	5	5	20	25	50	300
3	George Altman	5	5	5	5	10	30	200	
4	Max Alvis	5	5	6	10	15	25	60	
5	Bob Aspromonte	5	5	5	5	10	15	50	300
6	Jack Baldschun SP	5	5	8	12	20	200		
7	Ernie Banks	8	12	20	40	80	150	300	

		GD 2	VG 3	VgEx 4	EX 5	ExMt 6	NM 7	NmMt 8	MT 9
8	Steve Barber	5	5	5	5	10	20	300	
9	Earl Battey	5	5	5	5	10	20	200	
10	Ken Boyer	5	5	5	8	15	30	120	
11	Ernie Broglio	5	5	5	8	12	20	100	
12	John Callison	5	5	5	8	12	20	100	
13	Norm Cash SP	6	10	15	25	40	120	300	
14	Wayne Causey	5	5	5	5	10	15	80	
15	Orlando Cepeda	5	5	5	8	15	60	200	
16	Ed Charles	5	5	5	5	10	15	40	250
17	Roberto Clemente	25	50	60	150	200	350	600	
18	Donn Clendenon SP	5	5	8	12	20	30	80	300
19	Rocky Colavito	5	5	5	8	15	30	80	
20	Ray Culp SP	5	5	8	12	20	40	200	
21	Tommy Davis	5	5	5	5	10	20	120	
22	Don Drysdale SP	10	15	40	50	100	120	300	
23	Dick Ellsworth	5	5	5	5	10	15	40	250
24	Dick Farrell	5	5	5	5	10	15	40	300
25	Jim Fregosi	5	5	5	5	10	20	200	
26	Bob Friend	5	5	5	5	10	15	100	
27	Jim Gentile	5	5	5	5	10	15	60	
28	Jesse Gonder SP	5	5	8	12	20	100	200	
29	Tony Gonzalez SP	5	5	8	12	20	100	200	
30	Dick Groat	5	5	5	6	12	25	200	
31	Woody Held	5	5	5	5	10	15	120	
32	Chuck Hinton	5	5	5	5	10	15	40	400
33	Elston Howard	5	5	5	8	15	30	120	
34	Frank Howard SP	5	8	12	20	30	80	150	
35	Ron Hunt	5	5	5	5	10	20		
36	Al Jackson	5	5	5	5	10	15	80	
37	Ken Johnson	5	5	5	5	10	20	120	
38	Al Kaline	10	15	25	40	80	100	200	
39	Harmon Killebrew	5	8	12	20	30	100	200	
40	Sandy Koufax	20	30	40	100	150	200	600	
41	Don Lock SP	5	5	8	12	20	40	100	
42	Jerry Lumpe SP	5	5	8	12	20	40	200	
43	Jim Maloney	5	5	5	5	10	15	80	
44	Frank Malzone	5	5	5	5	10	15	80	
45	Mickey Mantle	80	120	200	250	400	800	1,500	5,000
46	Juan Marichal SP	8	12	20	30	50	100	250	800
47	Eddie Mathews SP	10	15	25	40	60	120	300	1,200
48	Willie Mays	25	40	50	80	150	300	1,500	
49	Bill Mazeroski	5	5	5	10	15	50	150	
50	Ken McBride	5	5	5	5	10	15	50	
51	Willie McCovey SP	8	12	20	30	50	200	400	
52	Claude Osteen	5	5	5	5	10	20	60	
53	Jim O'Toole	5	5	5	5	10	15	50	
54	Camilo Pascual	5	5	5	5	10	15	80	
55	Albie Pearson SP	5	5	8	12	20	35	70	
56	Gary Peters	5	5	5	5	10	15	100	
57	Vada Pinson	5	5	5	5	10	20	100	
58	Juan Pizarro	5	5	5	5	10	15	40	150
59	Boog Powell	5	5	5	8	15	30	120	
60	Bobby Richardson	5	5	5	8	15	30	150	300
61	Brooks Robinson	6	10	15	25	60	100	250	700
62	Floyd Robinson	5	5	5	5	10	30	80	
63	Frank Robinson	6	10	15	25	80	100	400	
64	Ed Roebuck SP	5	5	8	12	20	35	100	
65	Rich Rollins	5	5	5	5	10	20		
66	John Romano	5	5	5	5	10	15	50	200
67	Ron Santo SP	6	10	15	25	50	200	350	
68	Norm Siebern	5	5	5	5	10	15	80	
69	Warren Spahn SP	10	15	25	40	60	150	350	1,200
70	Dick Stuart SP	5	8	12	20	30	80	200	
71	Lee Thomas	5	5	5	8	12	20	50	
72	Joe Torre	5	5	8	12	20	60	250	
73	Pete Ward	5	5	5	5	10	15	120	

		GD 2	VG 3	VgEx 4	EX 5	ExMt 6	NM 7	NmMt 8	MT 9
74	Bill White SP	5	6	10	15	25	50	135	400
75	Billy Williams SP	8	12	20	30	50	300	500	
76	Hal Woodeshick SP	5	5	8	12	30	50		
77	Carl Yastrzemski SP	25	40	80	200	250	500	1,000	

1965 Topps

		GD 2	VG 3	VgEx 4	EX 5	ExMt 6	NM 7	NmMt 8	MT 9
	COMMON SP (371-598)	5	5	8	5	8	15	25	60
1	AL Batting Leaders	5	5	8	12	20	30	120	500
2	NL Batting Leaders	5	6	10	15	50	80	150	700
3	AL Home Run Leaders	6	30	40	50	60	80	120	600
4	NL Home Run Leaders	5	5	8	12	20	50	120	600
5	AL RBI Leaders	6	10	15	25	60	80	200	500
6	NL RBI Leaders	5	5	8	12	20	40	80	500
7	AL ERA Leaders	5	5	5	5	6	10	30	100
8	NL ERA Leaders	6	10	15	25	30	60	120	500
9	AL Pitching Leaders	5	5	5	8	12	20	80	150
10	NL Pitching Leaders	5	5	5	8	12	20	50	120
11	AL Strikeout Leaders	5	5	5	10	15	25	100	300
12	NL Strikeout Leaders	5	5	5	8	12	20	60	300
13	Pedro Ramos	5	5	5	5	6	10	25	80
14	Len Gabrielson	5	5	5	5	8	30	200	
15	Robin Roberts	5	5	8	10	20	25	60	150
16	Joe Morgan DP RC	80	100	120	200	300	400	1,200	4,000
17	Johnny Romano	5	5	5	5	5	8	20	60
18	Bill McCool	5	5	5	5	5	8	20	30
19	Gates Brown	5	5	5	10	15	25	80	
20	Jim Bunning	5	5	5	10	15	25	50	300
21	Don Blasingame	5	5	5	6	10	15	100	
22	Charlie Smith	5	5	8	12	20	30	250	
23	Bob Tiefenauer	5	5	5	5	5	8	20	60
24	Minnesota Twins TC	5	5	5	8	12	20	80	175
25	Al McBean	5	5	5	5	5	8	40	80
26	Bobby Knoop	5	5	5	5	5	8	25	
27	Dick Bertell	5	5	5	5	5	8	20	50
28	Barney Schultz	5	5	5	5	5	8	20	60
29	Felix Mantilla	5	5	5	5	5	8	20	60
30	Jim Bouton	5	5	5	6	10	15	50	150
31	Mike White	5	5	5	5	5	8	20	100
32	Herman Franks MG	5	5	5	5	5	8	20	60
33	Jackie Brandt	5	5	5	5	5	8	20	60
34	Cal Koonce	5	5	5	5	5	8	20	80
35	Ed Charles	5	5	5	5	5	8	20	80
36	Bobby Wine	5	5	5	5	5	8	20	60
37	Fred Gladding	5	5	5	5	5	8	20	60
38	Jim King	5	5	5	5	5	8	20	60
39	Gerry Arrigo	5	5	5	5	5	8	20	80
40	Frank Howard	5	5	5	6	10	15	50	120
41	B.Howard/M.Staehle RC	5	5	5	5	5	8	20	60
42	Earl Wilson	5	5	5	5	6	10	30	80
43	Mike Shannon	5	5	5	5	5	8	20	60
44	Wade Blasingame RC	5	5	5	5	6	10	40	80
45	Roy McMillan	5	5	5	5	5	8	20	60
46	Bob Lee	5	5	5	6	10	15	25	225
47	Tommy Harper	5	5	5	5	5	8	20	60
48	Claude Raymond	5	5	5	5	5	8	20	50
49	C.Blefary RC/J.Miller	5	5	5	5	5	8	20	50
50	Juan Marichal	5	6	10	15	25	60	120	500
51	Bill Bryan	5	5	5	5	5	8	20	60
52	Ed Roebuck	5	5	5	5	5	8	25	150
53	Dick McAuliffe	5	5	5	5	6	10	30	200
54	Joe Gibbon	5	5	5	5	5	8	20	60
55	Tony Conigliaro	5	▲8	▲12	▲20	▲30	50	▼80	
56	Ron Kline	5	5	5	5	5	8	20	60
57	St. Louis Cardinals TC	5	5	5	5	6	10	25	80
58	Fred Talbot RC	5	5	5	5	5	8	20	60
59	Nate Oliver	5	5	5	5	5	8	20	150

#	Name	GD 2	VG 3	VgEx 4	EX 5	ExMt 6	NM 7	NmMt 8	MT 9
60	Jim O'Toole	5	5	5	5	5	8	20	120
61	Chris Cannizzaro	5	5	5	5	5	8	25	60
62	Jim Kaat DP	5	5	6	10	15	25	40	100
63	Ty Cline	5	5	5	5	5	8	20	60
64	Lou Burdette	5	5	5	5	5	8	20	60
65	Tony Kubek	5	5	6	10	15	30	60	200
66	Bill Rigney MG	5	5	5	5	5	8	20	60
67	Harvey Haddix	5	5	5	5	6	10	25	150
68	Del Crandall	5	5	5	5	5	8	20	60
69	Bill Virdon	5	5	5	5	5	8	25	60
70	Bill Skowron	5	5	5	5	6	10	25	80
71	John O'Donoghue	5	5	5	5	5	8	40	80
72	Tony Gonzalez	5	5	5	5	5	8	20	60
73	Dennis Ribant RC	5	5	5	5	5	8	20	60
74	Rico Petrocelli RC	5	6	10	15	25	30	60	120
75	Deron Johnson	5	5	5	5	5	8	20	150
76	Sam McDowell	5	5	5	5	6	10	40	120
77	Doug Camilli	5	5	5	5	6	10	30	60
78	Dal Maxvill	5	5	5	5	5	8	20	60
79A	Checklist 1 Cannizzaro	5	5	5	5	5	8	150	
79B	Checklist 1 C.Cannizzaro	5	5	5	5	5	8	30	
80	Turk Farrell	5	5	5	5	5	8	20	60
81	Don Buford	5	5	5	5	5	8	20	50
82	S.Alomar RC/J.Braun RC	5	5	5	5	6	10	25	150
83	George Thomas	5	5	5	5	5	8	20	100
84	Ron Herbel	5	5	5	5	5	8	20	80
85	Willie Smith RC	5	5	5	5	5	8	25	120
86	Buster Narum	5	5	5	5	5	8	20	80
87	Nelson Mathews	5	5	5	5	5	8	20	60
88	Jack Lamabe	5	5	5	5	5	8	20	80
89	Mike Hershberger	5	5	5	5	5	8	25	80
90	Rich Rollins	5	5	5	5	5	8	20	60
91	Chicago Cubs TC	5	5	5	8	12	20	30	80
92	Dick Howser	5	5	5	5	6	10	40	
93	Jack Fisher	5	5	5	5	5	8	20	80
94	Charlie Lau	5	5	5	5	5	8	60	
95	Bill Mazeroski DP	5	6	10	15	25	40	60	200
96	Sonny Siebert	5	5	5	6	10	15	150	
97	Pedro Gonzalez	5	5	5	5	5	8	20	50
98	Bob Miller	5	5	5	5	5	8	30	60
99	Gil Hodges MG	5	5	5	6	10	15	40	150
100	Ken Boyer	5	5	5	6	10	30	80	
101	Fred Newman	5	5	5	5	5	8	20	60
102	Steve Boros	5	5	5	5	5	8	20	80
103	Harvey Kuenn	5	5	5	5	5	8	20	60
104	Checklist 2	5	5	5	5	5	8	20	80
105	Chico Salmon	5	5	5	5	5	8	20	50
106	Gene Oliver	5	5	5	5	5	8	20	50
107	P.Corrales RC/C.Shockley RC	5	5	5	5	5	8	40	150
108	Don Mincher	5	5	5	5	5	8	20	80
109	Walt Bond	5	5	5	5	6	10	60	150
110	Ron Santo	5	6	10	15	25	50	100	400
111	Lee Thomas	5	5	5	5	5	8	20	60
112	Derrell Griffith RC	5	5	5	5	5	8	20	60
113	Steve Barber	5	5	5	5	5	8	20	60
114	Jim Hickman	5	5	5	5	6	10	40	175
115	Bobby Richardson	5	5	8	12	20	▲80	200	
116	D.Dowling RC/B.Tolan RC	5	5	5	5	5	8	20	50
117	Wes Stock	5	5	5	5	5	8	25	100
118	Hal Lanier RC	5	5	5	5	5	8	20	60
119	John Kennedy	5	5	5	5	5	8	20	60
120	Frank Robinson	▲20	▲30	50	60	▲100	▲150	▲300	2,000
121	Gene Alley	5	5	5	5	5	8	20	60
122	Bill Pleis	5	5	5	5	5	8	20	60
123	Frank Thomas	5	5	5	5	5	8	20	80
124	Tom Satriano	5	5	5	5	5	8	20	60
125	Juan Pizarro	5	5	5	5	5	8	20	60
126	Los Angeles Dodgers TC	5	5	5	6	10	15	60	150

#	Name	GD 2	VG 3	VgEx 4	EX 5	ExMt 6	NM 7	NmMt 8	MT 9
127	Frank Lary	5	5	5	5	5	8	25	
128	Vic Davalillo	5	5	5	5	5	8	20	60
129	Bennie Daniels	5	5	5	5	5	8	20	50
130	Al Kaline	8	15	30	40	80	100	150	1,000
131	Johnny Keane MG	5	5	5	5	5	8	40	
132	Cards Take Opener WS1	5	5	5	6	10	15	80	150
133	Mel Stottlemyre WS2	5	5	5	5	6	10	40	250
134	Mickey Mantle WS3	25	50	60	80	100	200	250	▲1,000
135	Ken Boyer WS4	5	5	5	8	12	20	60	150
136	Tim McCarver WS5	5	5	5	5	6	10	30	80
137	Jim Bouton WS6	5	5	5	5	6	10	30	100
138	Bob Gibson WS7	5	5	5	8	12	20	40	200
139	Cards Celebrate WS	5	5	5	5	6	10	30	100
140	Dean Chance	5	5	5	5	5	8	20	60
141	Charlie James	5	5	5	5	5	8	20	60
142	Bill Monbouquette	5	5	5	5	5	8	20	80
143	J.Gelnar RC/J.May RC	5	5	5	5	5	8	20	60
144	Ed Kranepool	5	5	5	5	5	8	30	60
145	Luis Tiant RC	▲12	▲20	▲30	▲50	▲80	▲150	▲250	400
146	Ron Hansen	5	5	5	5	5	8	20	60
147	Dennis Bennett	5	5	5	5	5	8	20	60
148	Willie Kirkland	5	5	5	5	5	8	25	80
149	Wayne Schurr	5	5	5	5	5	8	20	50
150	Brooks Robinson	8	12	20	40	50	60	120	600
151	Kansas City Athletics TC	5	5	5	5	6	10	25	80
152	Phil Ortega	5	5	5	5	5	8	20	50
153	Norm Cash	5	6	10	15	25	30	▲60	250
154	Bob Humphreys RC	5	5	5	5	5	8	20	50
155	Roger Maris	▲30	▲50	▲60	▲80	▲120	200	250	1,200
156	Bob Sadowski	5	5	5	5	5	8	20	50
157	Zoilo Versalles	5	5	5	5	6	10	40	100
158	Dick Sisler	5	5	5	5	5	8	20	60
159	Jim Duffalo	5	5	5	5	5	8	20	80
160	Roberto Clemente	▲60	▲100	▲150	▲250	▲300	400	1,200	6,000
161	Frank Baumann	5	5	5	5	5	8	20	60
162	Russ Nixon	5	5	5	5	5	8	20	60
163	Johnny Briggs	5	5	5	5	5	8	20	60
164	Al Spangler	5	5	5	5	5	8	25	80
165	Dick Ellsworth	5	5	5	5	5	8	20	50
166	G.Culver RC/T.Agee RC	5	5	5	5	5	8	20	60
167	Bill Wakefield	5	5	5	5	5	8	20	50
168	Dick Green	5	5	5	5	5	8	25	50
169	Dave Vineyard RC	5	5	5	5	5	8	20	50
170	Hank Aaron	30	50	60	100	200	250	▲1,500	5,000
171	Jim Roland	5	5	5	5	5	8	20	80
172	Jimmy Piersall	5	5	5	5	6	10	30	80
173	Detroit Tigers TC	5	5	5	6	10	15	25	100
174	Joey Jay	5	5	5	5	5	8	20	80
175	Bob Aspromonte	5	5	5	5	5	8	20	80
176	Willie McCovey	▼10	▼15	25	▲40	▲60	▲100	200	400
177	Pete Mikkelsen	5	5	5	5	6	10	25	100
178	Dalton Jones	5	5	5	5	5	8	20	60
179	Hal Woodeshick	5	5	5	5	5	8	20	50
180	Bob Allison	5	5	5	5	5	8	30	100
181	D.Loun RC/J.McCabe	5	5	5	5	5	8	20	50
182	Mike de la Hoz	5	5	5	5	5	8	20	50
183	Dave Nicholson	5	5	5	5	5	8	20	60
184	John Boozer	5	5	5	5	5	8	20	50
185	Max Alvis	5	5	5	5	5	8	20	50
186	Billy Cowan	5	5	5	5	5	8	25	100
187	Casey Stengel MG	6	6	10	15	25	30	80	200
188	Sam Bowens	5	5	5	5	5	8	20	50
189	Checklist 3	5	5	5	5	6	10	40	60
190	Bill White	5	5	5	5	6	10	15	100
191	Phil Regan	5	5	5	5	5	8	20	100
192	Jim Coker	5	5	5	5	5	8	20	60
193	Gaylord Perry	6	6	10	15	25	30	▲80	150
194	B.Kelso RC/R.Reichardt RC	5	5	5	5	5	8	20	50

#	Player	GD 2	VG 3	VgEx 4	EX 5	ExMt 6	NM 7	NmMt 8	MT 9
195	Bob Veale	5	5	5	5	5	8	20	60
196	Ron Fairly	5	5	5	5	8	12	40	120
197	Diego Segui	5	5	5	5	5	8	30	
198	Smoky Burgess	5	5	5	5	8	12	40	150
199	Bob Heffner	5	5	5	5	5	8	20	60
200	Joe Torre	5	5	5	6	10	30	100	300
201	S.Valdespino RC/C.Tovar RC	5	5	5	5	5	8	25	
202	Leo Burke	5	5		5	5	8	20	60
203	Dallas Green	5	5	5	5	5	8	40	60
204	Russ Snyder	5	5	5	5	5	8	20	50
205	Warren Spahn	▲8	▲12	▲20	▲30	▲50	▲80	120	400
206	Willie Horton	5	5	5	8	12	20	120	150
207	Pete Rose	60	100	▲150	▲200	▲300	▲600	▲2,000	▼5,000
208	Tommy John	5	5	5	8	12	30	120	150
209	Pittsburgh Pirates TC	5	5	5	8	12	20	120	
210	Jim Fregosi	5	5	5	5	5	8	20	80
211	Steve Ridzik	5	5	5	5	5	8	20	80
212	Ron Brand	5	5	5	5	5	8	20	60
213	Jim Davenport	5	5	5	5	5	8	30	100
214	Bob Purkey	5	5	5	5	5	8	20	300
215	Pete Ward	5	5	5	5	5	8	25	200
216	Al Worthington	5	5	5	5	5	8	20	80
217	Walter Alston MG	5	5	5	5	6	10	30	80
218	Dick Schofield	5	5	5	6	10	15	60	150
219	Bob Meyer	5	5	5	5	5	8	25	100
220	Billy Williams	10	15	25	40	60	100	200	
221	John Tsitouris	5	5	5	5	5	8	20	50
222	Bob Tillman	5	5	5	5	5	8	20	60
223	Dan Osinski	5	5	5	6	10	15	30	80
224	Bob Chance	5	5	5	5	5	8	25	80
225	Bo Belinsky	5	5	5	5	5	8	20	60
226	E.Jimenez RC/J.Gibbs	5	5	5	5	6	10	40	100
227	Bobby Klaus	5	5	5	5	5	8	20	80
228	Jack Sanford	5	5	5	5	5	8	20	60
229	Lou Clinton	5	5	5	5	5	8	20	60
230	Ray Sadecki	5	5	5	5	5	8	20	60
231	Jerry Adair	5	5	5	5	5	8	20	80
232	Steve Blass RC	5	5	5	5	5	8	30	80
233	Don Zimmer	5	5	5	5	6	10	25	100
234	Chicago White Sox TC	5	5	5	5	6	10	25	100
235	Chuck Hinton	5	5	5	5	5	8	20	60
236	Denny McLain RC	10	15	40	50	60	80	120	600
237	Bernie Allen	5	5	5	5	5	8	20	80
238	Joe Moeller	5	5	5	5	5	8	40	80
239	Doc Edwards	5	5	5	5	5	8	20	80
240	Bob Bruce	5	5	5	5	5	8	25	50
241	Mack Jones	5	5	5	5	5	8	20	60
242	George Brunet	5	5	5	5	5	8	25	
243	T.Davidson RC/T.Helms RC	5	5	5	5	6	10	30	100
244	Lindy McDaniel	5	5	5	5	5	8	20	50
245	Joe Pepitone	5	5	5	6	10	30	250	
246	Tom Butters	5	5	5	5	5	8	20	80
247	Wally Moon	5	5	5	5	6	10	25	80
248	Gus Triandos	5	5	5	5	5	8	20	80
249	Dave McNally	5	5	5	5	6	10	25	100
250	Willie Mays	▲60	▲100	▲150	▲250	▲400	▲600	▲1,000	▲4,000
251	Billy Herman MG	5	5	5	5	5	8	20	80
252	Pete Richert	5	5	5	5	5	8	20	80
253	Danny Cater	5	5	5	5	5	8	20	100
254	Roland Sheldon	5	5	5	5	6	10	40	200
255	Camilo Pascual	5	5	5	5	6	10	40	200
256	Tito Francona	5	5	5	5	6	10	25	200
257	Jim Wynn	5	5	5	6	10	15	50	
258	Larry Bearnarth	5	5	5	5	5	8	20	150
259	J.Northrup RC/R.Oyler RC	5	5	8	12	20	30	50	250
260	Don Drysdale	6	10	15	25	50	60	100	600
261	Duke Carmel	5	5	5	5	6	10	50	150
262	Bud Daley	5	5	5	5	5	8	20	60
263	Marty Keough	5	5	5	5	5	8	20	60
264	Bob Buhl	5	5	5	5	5	8	25	80
265	Jim Pagliaroni	5	5	5	5	5	8	25	120
266	Bert Campaneris RC	5	▲8	▲12	▲20	▲30	40	▲120	200
267	Washington Senators TC	5	5	5	5	6	10	25	150
268	Ken McBride	5	5	5	5	5	8	20	80
269	Frank Bolling	5	5	5	5	5	8	20	80
270	Milt Pappas	5	5	5	5	5	8	20	60
271	Don Wert	5	5	5	5	8	12	60	250
272	Chuck Schilling	5	5	5	5	5	8	20	150
273	Checklist 4	5	5	5	5	5	8	20	60
274	Lum Harris MG RC	5	5	5	5	5	8	20	60
275	Dick Groat	5	5	5	6	10	15	80	150
276	Hoyt Wilhelm	5	6	10	15	25	40	80	250
277	Johnny Lewis	5	5	5	5	5	8	60	150
278	Ken Retzer	5	5	5	5	5	8	30	80
279	Dick Tracewski	5	5	5	5	5	8	20	80
280	Dick Stuart	5	5	5	5	5	8	25	100
281	Bill Stafford	5	5	5	5	8	12	30	150
282	Masanori Murakami RC	8	12	20	40	60	80	120	250
283	Fred Whitfield	5	5	5	5	5	8	25	80
284	Nick Willhite	5	5	5	5	5	8	20	80
285	Ron Hunt	5	5	5	5	6	10	80	150
286	J.Dickson/A.Monteagudo	5	5	5	5	5	8	20	60
287	Gary Kolb	5	5	5	5	5	8	25	80
288	Jack Hamilton	5	5	5	5	5	8	20	50
289	Gordy Coleman	5	5	5	5	5	8	30	150
290	Wally Bunker	5	5	5	5	5	8	25	120
291	Jerry Lynch	5	5	5	5	6	10	40	
292	Larry Yellen	5	5	5	5	6	10	40	150
293	Los Angeles Angels TC	5	5	5	5	8	12	30	100
294	Tim McCarver	5	5	5	5	8	30	80	150
295	Dick Radatz	5	5	5	5	5	8	20	60
296	Tony Taylor	5	5	5	5	5	8	30	100
297	Dave DeBusschere	5	5	5	8	12	20	30	200
298	Jim Stewart	5	5	5	5	6	10	30	150
299	Jerry Zimmerman	5	5	5	5	5	8	30	120
300	Sandy Koufax	30	50	80	100	200	▲400	▲600	▲12,000
301	Birdie Tebbetts MG	5	5	5	5	6	10	30	150
302	Al Stanek	5	5	5	5	5	8	20	50
303	John Orsino	5	5	5	5	5	8	20	60
304	Dave Stenhouse	5	5	5	5	5	8	20	50
305	Rico Carty	5	5	5	6	10	60	100	
306	Bubba Phillips	5	5	5	6	10	15	80	120
307	Barry Latman	5	5	5	5	5	8	20	50
308	C.Jones RC/T.Parsons	5	5	5	6	10	15	80	120
309	Steve Hamilton	5	5	5	5	6	10	50	
310	Johnny Callison	5	5	5	6	10	15	40	200
311	Orlando Pena	5	5	5	5	5	8	20	100
312	Joe Nuxhall	5	5	5	5	6	10	25	100
313	Jim Schaffer	5	5	5	5	5	8	25	80
314	Sterling Slaughter	5	5	5	5	5	8	30	60
315	Frank Malzone	5	5	5	5	6	10	25	100
316	Cincinnati Reds TC	5	5	5	6	10	15	60	300
317	Don McMahon	5	5	5	5	5	8	20	200
318	Matty Alou	5	5	6	10	15	25	100	150
319	Ken McMullen	5	5	5	5	5	8	20	60
320	Bob Gibson	▲15	▲25	▲40	▲60	▲100	▲150	▲500	1,200
321	Rusty Staub	5	5	▲6	▲10	▲15	▲25	▲60	100
322	Rick Wise	5	5	5	5	6	10	25	80
323	Hank Bauer MG	5	5	5	5	6	10	40	
324	Bobby Locke	5	5	5	5	5	8	20	60
325	Donn Clendenon	5	5	5	5	6	10	30	60
326	Dwight Siebler	5	5	5	5	5	8	60	120
327	Denis Menke	5	5	5	5	5	8	30	80
328	Eddie Fisher	5	5	5	5	5	8	25	120
329	Hawk Taylor RC	5	5	5	5	5	8	20	80
330	Whitey Ford	10	15	25	▲40	▲60	▲120	250	600

#	Player	GD 2	VG 3	VgEx 4	EX 5	ExMt 6	NM 7	NmMt 8	MT 9
1	A.Ferrara/J.Purdin RC	5	5	5	6	10	15	25	100
2	Ted Abernathy	5	5	5	5	5	8	25	
3	Tom Reynolds	5	5	5	5	5	8	20	60
4	Vic Roznovsky RC	5	5	5	5	5	8	30	
5	Mickey Lolich	5	8	12	20	30	50	80	
6	Woody Held	5	5	5	5	5	8	30	150
7	Mike Cuellar	5	5	5	6	10	15	30	
8	Philadelphia Phillies TC	5	5	5	5	6	10	30	120
9	Ryne Duren	5	5	5	8	12	20	60	
10	Tony Oliva	6	10	15	25	50	100	200	
11	Bob Bolin	5	5	5	5	5	8	30	100
12	Bob Rodgers	5	5	5	5	6	10	25	100
13	Mike McCormick	5	5	5	5	5	8	25	80
14	Wes Parker	5	5	5	5	6	10	25	100
15	Floyd Robinson	5	5	5	5	5	8	20	80
16	Bobby Bragan MG	5	5	5	5	5	8	25	100
17	Roy Face	5	5	5	5	6	10	25	100
18	George Banks	5	5	5	5	5	8	30	60
19	Larry Miller RC	5	5	5	5	6	10	40	100
20	Mickey Mantle	200	▲300	▲500	▲800	▲1,500	▲2,500	▲6,000	▲40,000
21	Jim Perry	5	5	5	6	10	15	50	80
22	Alex Johnson RC	5	5	5	5	5	8	60	120
23	Jerry Lumpe	5	5	5	6	10	15	50	
24	B.Ott RC/J.Warner RC	5	5	5	5	5	8	20	60
25	Vada Pinson	5	5	5	5	6	10	60	120
26	Bill Spanswick	5	5	5	5	5	8	20	100
27	Carl Warwick	5	5	5	5	5	8	20	80
28	Albie Pearson	5	5	5	5	5	8	20	60
29	Ken Johnson	5	5	5	5	5	8	20	80
30	Orlando Cepeda	5	6	10	15	25	60	150	500
31	Checklist 5	5	5	5	5	5	8	30	50
32	Don Schwall	5	5	5	6	10	15	40	
33	Bob Johnson	5	5	5	5	5	8	20	80
34	Galen Cisco	5	5	5	5	5	8	20	60
35	Jim Gentile	5	5	5	5	5	8	20	80
36	Dan Schneider	5	5	5	5	5	8	20	80
37	Leon Wagner	5	5	5	5	6	10	60	80
38	K.Berry RC/J.Gibson RC	5	5	5	6	10	15	25	60
39	Phil Linz	5	8	12	20	30	50	80	
40	Tommy Davis	5	5	5	6	10	15	50	80
41	Frank Kreutzer	5	5	5	5	6	10	25	100
42	Clay Dalrymple	5	5	5	6	10	15	25	60
43	Curt Simmons	5	5	5	6	10	15	25	60
44	J.Cardenal RC/D.Simpson	5	5	5	5	6	10	20	60
45	Dave Wickersham	5	5	5	5	6	10	20	50
46	Jim Landis	5	5	5	5	6	10	20	60
47	Willie Stargell	10	15	25	40	60	100	▲300	▲800
48	Chuck Estrada	5	5	5	5	6	10	20	60
49	San Francisco Giants TC	5	5	5	5	8	12	30	100
50	Rocky Colavito	5	5	6	10	15	40	60	200
51	Al Jackson	5	5	5	5	6	10	30	80
52	J.C. Martin	5	5	5	5	6	10	20	60
53	Felipe Alou	5	5	5	8	12	20	100	
54	Johnny Klippstein	5	5	5	5	6	10	20	50
55	Carl Yastrzemski	15	25	40	60	80	150	▲300	800
56	P.Jaeckel RC/F.Norman	5	5	5	5	6	10	20	50
57	Johnny Podres	5	5	5	6	10	15	25	120
58	John Blanchard	5	5	5	8	12	20	80	250
59	Don Larsen	5	5	6	10	15	25	30	50
60	Bill Freehan	5	5	5	6	10	15	100	
61	Mel McGaha MG	5	5	5	5	6	10	20	100
62	Bob Friend	5	5	5	8	12	20	25	80
63	Ed Kirkpatrick	5	5	5	5	6	10	15	40
64	Jim Hannan	5	5	5	5	6	10	20	50
65	Jim Ray Hart	5	5	5	5	8	12	25	80
66	Frank Bertaina RC	5	5	5	5	8	12	50	
67	Jerry Buchek	5	5	5	5	6	10	20	40
68	D.Neville RC/A.Shamsky RC	5	5	5	5	8	12	40	100

#	Player	GD 2	VG 3	VgEx 4	EX 5	ExMt 6	NM 7	NmMt 8	MT 9
399	Ray Herbert	5	5	5	5	6	10	20	60
400	Harmon Killebrew	12	20	30	50	80	120	200	600
401	Carl Willey	5	5	5	5	6	10	20	60
402	Joe Amalfitano	5	5	5	5	8	12	30	200
403	Boston Red Sox TC	5	5	5	6	10	15	30	150
404	Stan Williams	5	5	5	5	6	10	20	60
405	John Roseboro	5	5	5	5	8	12	50	150
406	Ralph Terry	5	5	5	5	8	12	30	80
407	Lee Maye	5	5	5	5	6	10	20	80
408	Larry Sherry	5	5	5	6	10	15	25	80
409	J.Beauchamp RC/L.Dierker RC	5	5	5	6	10	15	30	120
410	Luis Aparicio	5	5	6	10	15	50	60	250
411	Roger Craig	5	5	5	5	5	10	30	50
412	Bob Bailey	5	5	5	5	5	10	30	60
413	Hal Reniff	5	5	5	5	8	12	30	100
414	Al Lopez MG	5	5	5	8	12	20	30	120
415	Curt Flood	5	6	8	12	20	50	100	200
416	Jim Brewer	5	5	5	5	6	10	25	60
417	Ed Brinkman	5	5	5	5	6	10	20	40
418	Johnny Edwards	5	5	5	5	6	10	20	60
419	Ruben Amaro	5	5	5	5	6	10	30	60
420	Larry Jackson	5	5	5	5	6	10	40	80
421	G.Dotter RC/J.Ward	5	5	5	5	6	10	20	50
422	Aubrey Gatewood	5	5	5	5	6	10	20	50
423	Jesse Gonder	5	5	5	5	6	10	25	60
424	Gary Bell	5	5	5	5	6	10	20	60
425	Wayne Causey	5	5	5	5	6	10	25	60
426	Milwaukee Braves TC	5	5	5	5	8	12	50	100
427	Bob Saverine	5	5	5	5	6	10	20	60
428	Bob Shaw	5	5	5	5	6	10	50	150
429	Don Demeter	5	5	5	5	5	10	20	60
430	Gary Peters	5	5	5	5	8	12	30	80
431	N.Briles RC/W.Spiezio RC	5	5	5	5	8	12	50	120
432	Jim Grant	5	5	5	5	8	12	▲50	80
433	John Bateman	5	5	5	5	8	12	30	150
434	Dave Morehead	5	5	5	5	6	10	30	60
435	Willie Davis	5	5	5	10	15	25	40	100
436	Don Elston	5	5	5	5	6	10	20	50
437	Chico Cardenas	5	5	5	5	6	10	25	60
438	Harry Walker MG	5	5	5	5	6	10	30	50
439	Moe Drabowsky	5	5	5	5	6	10	▲40	▲60
440	Tom Tresh	5	5	5	6	10	15	▲60	
441	Denny Lemaster	5	5	5	5	6	10	20	60
442	Vic Power	5	5	5	5	6	10	20	80
443	Checklist 6	5	5	5	5	8	12	▲40	80
444	Bob Hendley	5	5	5	5	6	10	20	80
445	Don Lock	5	5	5	5	6	10	20	60
446	Art Mahaffey	5	5	5	5	6	10	25	100
447	Julian Javier	5	5	5	8	12	20	40	150
448	Lee Stange	5	5	5	5	6	10	25	60
449	J.Hinsley/G.Kroll RC	5	5	5	5	8	12	30	80
450	Elston Howard	▲6	▲10	▲15	▲25	▲40	▲60	100	▲250
451	Jim Owens	5	5	5	5	6	10	20	50
452	Gary Geiger	5	5	5	5	6	10	20	40
453	W.Crawford RC/J.Werhas	5	5	5	5	8	12	▲40	60
454	Ed Rakow	5	5	5	5	6	10	20	50
455	Norm Siebern	5	5	5	8	12	20	60	
456	Bill Henry	5	5	5	5	6	10	30	120
457	Bob Kennedy MG	5	5	5	5	6	10	▲40	120
458	John Buzhardt	5	5	5	5	6	10	25	40
459	Frank Kostro	5	5	5	5	6	10	20	60
460	Richie Allen	6	10	15	25	40	120	200	500
461	C.Carroll RC/P.Niekro	15	25	30	40	100	120	▲200	400
462	Lew Krausse	5	5	5	5	6	10	25	150
463	Manny Mota	5	5	5	▲8	▲12	▲20	▲30	50
464	Ron Piche	5	5	5	5	6	10	20	50
465	Tom Haller	5	5	5	5	6	10	20	80
466	P.Craig RC/D.Nen	5	5	5	5	6	10	20	50

#	Player	GD 2	VG 3	VgEx 4	EX 5	ExMt 6	NM 7	NmMt 8	MT 9
467	Ray Washburn	5	5	6	10	15	25	40	80
468	Larry Brown	5	5	5	5	6	10	25	60
469	Don Nottebart	5	5	5	5	6	10	20	50
470	Yogi Berra P/CO	▲12	▲20	▲30	▲50	80	100	▲250	400
471	Billy Hoeft	5	5	5	5	6	10	30	
472	Don Pavletich	5	5	5	5	6	10	20	80
473	P.Blair RC/D.Johnson RC	5	5	8	12	20	80	150	
474	Cookie Rojas	5	5	5	5	8	25	40	60
475	Clete Boyer	5	5	6	10	15	25	40	60
476	Billy O'Dell	5	5	5	5	6	10	20	50
477	Steve Carlton RC	100	150	200	250	300	▲600	1,000	4,000
478	Wilbur Wood	5	5	5	5	8	12	30	60
479	Ken Harrelson	5	5	5	5	6	10	▲40	▲60
480	Joel Horlen	5	5	5	5	6	10	25	80
481	Cleveland Indians TC	5	5	5	5	8	12	▲50	100
482	Bob Priddy	5	5	5	5	6	10	30	80
483	George Smith RC	5	5	5	5	6	10	25	120
484	Ron Perranoski	5	5	5	5	8	12	30	300
485	Nellie Fox	5	▲6	▲10	▲15	▲25	▲40	▲60	▲200
486	T.Egan/P.Rogan RC	5	5	5	5	6	10	20	50
487	Woody Woodward	5	5	5	5	6	10	20	100
488	Ted Wills	5	5	5	5	8	12	40	150
489	Gene Mauch MG	5	5	5	5	8	12	▲80	▲150
490	Earl Battey	5	5	5	5	8	12	40	80
491	Tracy Stallard	5	5	5	5	6	10	20	60
492	Gene Freese	5	5	5	5	6	10	25	50
493	B.Roman RC/B.Brubaker RC	5	5	5	5	6	10	20	60
494	Jay Ritchie RC	5	5	5	5	6	10	30	50
495	Joe Christopher	5	5	5	5	6	10	30	60
496	Joe Cunningham	5	5	5	5	6	10	20	50
497	K.Henderson RC/J.Hiatt RC	5	5	5	5	6	10	25	80
498	Gene Stephens	5	5	5	5	6	10	20	30
499	Stu Miller	5	5	5	5	8	12	30	40
500	Eddie Mathews	▲20	▲30	▲50	▲80	▲120	▲200	▲300	1,000
501	R.Gagliano RC/J.Rittwage RC	5	5	5	5	6	10	20	50
502	Don Cardwell	5	5	5	5	6	10	20	80
503	Phil Gagliano	5	5	5	5	6	10	20	50
504	Jerry Grote	5	5	5	5	8	12	30	60
505	Ray Culp	5	5	5	5	8	12	25	100
506	Sam Mele MG	5	5	5	5	6	10	25	80
507	Sammy Ellis	5	5	5	5	8	12	20	50
508	Checklist 7	5	5	5	5	8	12	60	50
509	B.Guindon RC/G.Vezendy RC	5	5	5	5	6	10	25	60
510	Ernie Banks	30	▲50	▲80	▲100	▲120	250	▲400	▲2,000
511	Ron Locke	5	5	5	5	6	10	25	60
512	Cap Peterson	5	5	5	5	6	10	20	60
513	New York Yankees TC	▲8	▲12	▲20	▲30	▲50	▲80	▲120	▲400
514	Joe Azcue	5	5	5	5	6	10	20	50
515	Vern Law	5	5	5	5	8	12	▲40	80
516	Al Weis	5	5	5	5	6	10	25	50
517	P.Schaal RC/J.Warner	5	5	5	5	6	10	▲25	50
518	Ken Rowe	5	5	5	5	6	10	20	60
519	Bob Uecker	8	12	20	30	50	60	▲200	▲400
520	Tony Cloninger	5	5	5	5	6	10	25	60
521	D.Bennett/M.Steevens RC	5	5	5	5	6	10	25	80
522	Hank Aguirre	5	5	5	5	6	10	20	50
523	Mike Brumley SP	5	5	5	6	10	15	25	100
524	Dave Giusti SP	5	5	5	6	10	15	20	60
525	Eddie Bressoud	5	5	5	5	6	10	20	50
526	J.Odom/J.Hunter SP RC	40	50	80	120	200	250	400	2,500
527	Jeff Torborg SP	5	5	▲8	▲12	▲20	▲30	▲50	80
528	George Altman	5	5	5	5	6	10	20	80
529	Jerry Fosnow SP RC	5	5	5	6	10	15	30	200
530	Jim Maloney	5	5	5	5	6	10	▲40	120
531	Chuck Hiller	5	5	5	5	6	10	20	50
532	Hector Lopez	5	5	5	8	12	20	30	50
533	R.Swoboda RC/T.McGraw RC SP	6	10	15	40	50	80	100	250
534	John Herrnstein	5	5	5	5	6	10	20	50

#	Player	GD 2	VG 3	VgEx 4	EX 5	ExMt 6	NM 7	NmMt 8	MT (cut off)
535	Jack Kralick SP	5	5	▲8	▲12	▲20	▲30	▲50	8
536	Andre Rodgers SP	5	5	5	6	10	15	25	12
537	Lopez/Roof/May RC	5	5	5	5	6	10	25	6
538	Chuck Dressen MG SP	5	5	5	6	10	15	25	8
539	Herm Starrette	5	5	5	5	6	10	20	
540	Lou Brock SP	▲30	▲50	▲80	▲100	▲150	▲200	▲400	8
541	G.Bollo RC/B.Locker RC	5	5	5	5	6	10	20	4
542	Lou Klimchock	5	5	5	5	6	10	20	
543	Ed Connolly SP RC	5	5	5	6	10	15	25	12
544	Howie Reed RC	5	5	5	5	6	10	40	
545	Jesus Alou SP	5	6	10	15	25	50	60	20
546	Davis/Hed/Bark/Weav RC	5	5	5	5	8	12	25	
547	Jake Wood SP	5	5	5	6	10	15	40	1
548	Dick Stigman	5	5	5	5	6	10	20	
549	R.Pena RC/G.Beckert RC	5	5	▲6	▲10	▲15	▲25	80	▲1
550	Mel Stottlemyre SP RC	▲8	▲12	▲20	▲30	50	80	▲120	6
551	New York Mets TC SP	5	5	5	8	12	30	40	1
552	Julio Gotay	5	5	5	5	6	10	20	
553	Coombs/Ratliff/McClure RC	5	5	5	5	6	10	20	
554	Chico Ruiz SP	5	5	5	6	10	15	50	
555	Jack Baldschun SP	5	5	5	10	15	25	50	1
556	Red Schoendienst SP	5	5	5	8	12	30	50	2
557	Jose Santiago RC	5	5	5	5	6	10	30	
558	Tommie Sisk	5	5	5	5	6	10	20	
559	Ed Bailey SP	5	5	5	6	10	15	25	1
560	Boog Powell SP	5	5	8	12	20	30	▲100	▲2
561	Dab/Kek/Valle/Lefebvre RC	5	5	▲6	▲10	▲15	▲25	▲40	1
562	Billy Moran	5	5	5	5	6	10	20	
563	Julio Navarro	5	5	5	5	6	10	20	
564	Mel Nelson	5	5	5	5	6	10	20	
565	Ernie Broglio SP	5	▲6	▲10	▲15	▲25	▲40	▲60	1
566	Blanco RC/Mosch RC/Lopez RC	5	5	▲6	▲10	▲15	▲25	▲40	
567	Tommie Aaron	5	5	5	5	6	10	30	
568	Ron Taylor SP	5	5	5	10	15	25	50	
569	Gino Cimoli SP	5	▲6	▲10	▲15	▲25	▲40	▲60	▲1
570	Claude Osteen SP	5	5	5	6	10	15	40	
571	Ossie Virgil SP	5	5	5	▲8	▲12	▲20	30	
572	Baltimore Orioles TC SP	5	5	▲8	▲12	▲20	▲30	50	
573	Jim Lonborg SP RC	▲8	▲12	▲20	▲30	▲50	▲80	▲120	▲2
574	Roy Sievers	5	5	5	8	12	20	30	
575	Jose Pagan	5	5	5	5	8	12	25	
576	Terry Fox SP	5	5	5	▲8	▲12	▲20	30	
577	Knowles/Buschhorn RC Schein RC	5	5	▲6	▲10	▲15	▲25	▲40	
578	Camilo Carreon SP	5	5	▲6	▲10	▲15	25	▲40	
579	Dick Smith SP	5	5	5	6	10	15	40	
580	Jimmie Hall SP	5	5	5	6	10	20	25	
581	Tony Perez SP RC	40	80	100	120	▲200	300	▲600	2,
582	Bob Schmidt SP	5	5	▲8	▲12	▲20	▲30	▲50	
583	Wes Covington SP	5	5	5	6	10	15	▲30	
584	Harry Bright	5	5	5	5	6	10	25	
585	Hank Fischer	5	5	5	5	6	10	20	
586	Tom McCraw SP	5	5	5	5	6	10	15	30
587	Joe Sparma	5	5	5	5	6	10	15	
588	Lenny Green	5	5	5	5	6	10	25	
589	F.Linzy RC/B.Schroder RC	5	5	5	8	12	20	30	
590	John Wyatt	5	5	5	5	6	10	25	
591	Bob Skinner SP	5	5	5	6	10	15	30	
592	Frank Bork SP RC	5	5	5	6	10	15	40	
593	J.Sullivan RC/J.Moore RC SP	5	5	5	6	10	15	50	
594	Joe Gaines	5	5	5	5	6	10	25	
595	Don Lee	5	5	5	5	6	10	15	
596	Don Landrum SP	5	5	5	5	8	12	40	
597	Nossek/Sevcik/Reese RC	5	6	10	15	30	80	150	
598	Al Downing SP	5	5	8	12	20	50	120	

— Steve Carlton #477 PSA 10 (Gem) (Young Collection) sold for $12,756 (SCP; 5/12)
— Len Gabrielson #14 PSA 9 (MT) sold for $2,862 (Mile High; 10/12)
— Jim Hunter #526 PSA 10 (Gem) (Young Collection) sold for $11,596 (SCP; 5/12)

– Joe Morgan #16 PSA 10 (Gem) (Young Collection) sold for $8,897 (SCP; 5/12)
– NL Strikeout Leaders #12 PSA 10 (Gem) sold for $2,000 (eBay; 10/12)
– Tony Oliva #340 PSA 9 (MT) sold for $3,055 (eBay; 08/12)
– Tony Perez SP #581 PSA 10 (Gem) (Young Collection) sold for $7,919 (SCP; 5/12)

1965 Topps Embossed

	GD 2	VG 3	VgEx 4	EX 5	ExMt 6	NM 7	NmMt 8	MT 9
Sandy Koufax	6	10	15	40	50	60	150	
Mickey Mantle	▲40	▲60	▲80	▲100	▲150	▲250	1,000	
Roberto Clemente	15	25	40	60	100	150	500	
Willie Mays	5	5	8	12	25	40		
Hank Aaron	5	5	8	20	40	80	120	

1966 Topps

	GD 2	VG 3	VgEx 4	EX 5	ExMt 6	NM 7	NmMt 8	MT 9
Willie Mays	40	60	80	120	250	▲1,000	2,000	5,000
Ted Abernathy	5	6	5	5	5	12	30	
Sam Mele MG	5	5	5	5	5	10	50	
Ray Culp	5	5	5	5	5	10	30	
Jim Fregosi	5	5	5	5	5	20	30	
Chuck Schilling	5	5	5	5	5	8	20	200
Tracy Stallard	5	5	5	5	5	8	20	
Floyd Robinson	5	5	5	5	5	8	15	60
Clete Boyer	5	5	5	5	8	15	50	
Tony Cloninger	5	5	5	5	5	10	25	150
B.Alyea RC/P.Craig	5	5	5	5	5	8	25	
John Tsitouris	5	5	5	5	5	8	25	
Lou Johnson	5	5	5	5	5	8	25	
Norm Siebern	5	5	5	5	5	8	20	60
Vern Law	5	5	5	5	5	8	15	60
Larry Brown	5	5	5	5	5	8	15	50
John Stephenson	5	5	5	5	5	8	15	100
Roland Sheldon	5	5	5	5	5	8	20	
San Francisco Giants TC	5	5	5	5	5	10	40	
Willie Horton	5	5	5	5	6	15	50	
Don Nottebart	5	5	5	5	5	8	15	50
Joe Nossek	5	5	5	5	5	8	20	60
Jack Sanford	5	5	5	5	5	8	20	100
Don Kessinger RC	5	5	5	5	5	12	40	
Pete Ward	5	5	5	5	5	8	30	
Ray Sadecki	5	5	5	5	5	8	25	60
D.Knowles/A.Etchebarren RC	5	5	5	5	5	10	30	80
Phil Niekro	▲8	▲12	▲20	▲30	▲50	▲80	▲120	
Mike Brumley	5	5	5	5	5	8	25	60
Pete Rose DP	40	▲60	▲100	▲150	▲250	▲400	800	▲5,000
Jack Cullen	5	5	5	5	5	10	25	
Adolfo Phillips RC	5	5	5	5	5	8	15	80
Jim Pagliaroni	5	5	5	5	5	8	15	50
Checklist 1	5	5	5	5	5	8	25	
Ron Swoboda	5	5	5	5	8	15	40	
Jim Hunter DP	5	6	10	15	25	30	80	500
Billy Herman MG	5	5	5	5	5	8	15	50
Ron Nischwitz	5	5	5	5	5	8	20	80
Ken Henderson	5	5	5	5	5	8	20	100
Jim Grant	5	5	5	5	5	8	15	80
Don LeJohn RC	5	5	5	5	5	8	20	100
Aubrey Gatewood	5	5	5	5	5	8	25	100
Don Landrum Full Button	5	5	5	5	6	12	40	
Don Landrum Partial Button	5	5	6	10	15	25		
Don Landrum No Button	5	5	5	5	6	12	40	
B.Davis/T.Kelley	5	5	5	5	5	8	20	70
Jim Gentile	5	5	5	5	5	8	15	60
Howie Koplitz	5	5	5	5	5	8	15	50
J.C. Martin	5	5	5	5	5	8	20	80
Paul Blair	5	5	5	5	5	10	40	
Woody Woodward	5	5	5	5	5	8	15	
Mickey Mantle DP	▲250	▲300	400	500	▲800	▲1,500	4,000	▲25,000

		GD 2	VG 3	VgEx 4	EX 5	ExMt 6	NM 7	NmMt 8	MT 9
51	Gordon Richardson RC	5	5	5	5	5	8	20	60
52	Power Plus	5	5	5	5	5	10	20	100
53	Bob Duliba	5	5	5	5	5	8	20	
54	Jose Pagan	5	5	5	5	5	8	20	100
55	Ken Harrelson	5	5	5	5	5	8	30	100
56	Sandy Valdespino	5	5	5	5	5	8	30	
57	Jim Lefebvre	5	5	5	5	5	8	20	100
58	Dave Wickersham	5	5	5	5	5	8	15	60
59	Cincinnati Reds TC	5	5	5	5	5	10	40	80
60	Curt Flood	5	5	5	5	5	10	40	
61	Bob Bolin	5	5	5	5	5	8	15	60
62A	Merritt Ranew Sold Line	5	5	5	5	5	8	25	80
62B	Merritt Ranew No Sold Line	5	6	10	15	25	40		
63	Jim Stewart	5	5	5	5	5	8	20	60
64	Bob Bruce	5	5	5	5	5	8	25	80
65	Leon Wagner	5	5	5	5	5	8	20	60
66	Al Weis	5	5	5	5	5	8	15	50
67	C.Jones/D.Selma RC	5	5	5	5	5	10	40	120
68	Hal Reniff	5	5	5	5	5	8	20	300
69	Ken Hamlin	5	5	5	5	5	8	20	60
70	Carl Yastrzemski	▲15	25	40	50	▲80	100	250	800
71	Frank Carpin RC	5	5	5	5	5	8	25	120
72	Tony Perez	▲20	▲30	▲50	▲80	▲120	▲200	400	
73	Jerry Zimmerman	5	5	5	5	5	8	20	60
74	Don Mossi	5	5	5	5	5	8	15	60
75	Tommy Davis	5	5	5	5	5	8	60	
76	Red Schoendienst MG	5	5	5	5	8	15	30	
77	Johnny Orsino	5	5	5	5	5	8	15	50
78	Frank Linzy	5	5	5	5	5	8	15	60
79	Joe Pepitone	5	5	5	5	6	12	30	
80	Richie Allen	5	5	5	5	8	20	60	
81	Ray Oyler	5	5	5	5	5	8	30	100
82	Bob Hendley	5	5	5	5	5	8	15	60
83	Albie Pearson	5	5	5	5	5	8	20	60
84	J.Beauchamp/D.Kelley	5	5	5	5	5	8	15	50
85	Eddie Fisher	5	5	5	5	5	8	20	60
86	John Bateman	5	5	5	5	5	8	20	80
87	Dan Napoleon	5	5	5	5	5	8	20	100
88	Fred Whitfield	5	5	5	5	5	8	20	60
89	Ted Davidson	5	5	5	5	5	8	20	60
90	Luis Aparicio DP	5	5	8	12	20	30	60	200
91A	Bob Uecker Trade Line	5	5	6	10	15	50	200	
91B	Bob Uecker No Trade Line	12	20	30	50	60	150		
92	New York Yankees TC	5	5	6	10	15	25	100	
93	Jim Lonborg DP	5	5	5	5	5	8	20	60
94	Matty Alou	5	5	5	5	5	8	25	80
95	Pete Richert	5	5	5	5	5	8	15	50
96	Felipe Alou	5	5	5	5	5	10	30	
97	Jim Merritt RC	5	5	5	5	5	8	25	100
98	Don Demeter	5	5	5	5	5	10	30	
99	Buc Belters	5	5	5	5	8	20	40	
100	Sandy Koufax DP	30	50	60	80	100	200	500	5,000
101A	Checklist 2 Spahn 115 ERR	5	5	5	5	5	8	30	
101B	Cheklist 2 Henry 115 COR	5	5	5	5	5	8	30	
102	Ed Kirkpatrick	5	5	5	5	5	8	20	100
103A	Dick Groat Trade Line	5	5	5	5	5	10	25	60
103B	Dick Groat No Trade Line	5	6	10	15	25	40		
104A	Alex Johnson Trade Line	5	5	5	5	5	8	20	100
104B	Alex Johnson No Trade Line	5	6	10	15	25	40		
105	Milt Pappas	5	5	5	5	5	12	40	
106	Rusty Staub	5	5	5	5	5	10	30	
107	L.Stahl RC/R.Tompkins RC	5	5	5	5	5	8	20	100
108	Bobby Klaus	5	5	5	5	5	8	25	
109	Ralph Terry	5	5	5	5	5	8	25	200
110	Ernie Banks	▲20	30	▲50	80	100	120	300	▲2,500
111	Gary Peters	5	5	5	5	5	12	40	100
112	Manny Mota	5	5	5	5	5	8	30	
113	Hank Aguirre	5	5	5	5	5	8	20	60

#	Player	GD 2	VG 3	VgEx 4	EX 5	ExMt 6	NM 7	NmMt 8	MT 9
114	Jim Gosger	5	5	5	5	5	8	20	80
115	Bill Henry	5	5	5	5	5	8	25	
116	Walter Alston MG	5	5	5	5	5	10	30	
117	Jake Gibbs	5	5	5	5	5	10	40	
118	Mike McCormick	5	5	5	5	5	8	20	60
119	Art Shamsky	5	5	5	5	5	8	20	60
120	Harmon Killebrew	8	12	20	30	50	80	100	800
121	Ray Herbert	5	5	5	5	5	8	25	100
122	Joe Gaines	5	5	5	5	5	8	25	
123	F.Bork/J.May	5	5	5	5	5	8	20	
124	Tug McGraw	5	5	5	5	5	10	25	
125	Lou Brock	15	25	40	▲60	▲100	▲150	▲300	1,200
126	Jim Palmer UER RC	▲40	▲60	▲100	▲150	▲250	400	▲1,000	3,000
127	Ken Berry	5	5	5	5	5	8	25	120
128	Jim Landis	5	5	5	5	5	8	25	100
129	Jack Kralick	5	5	5	5	5	8	30	100
130	Joe Torre	5	5	6	10	15	25	40	120
131	California Angels TC	5	5	5	5	5	10	20	80
132	Orlando Cepeda	5	5	6	10	15	25	80	200
133	Don McMahon	5	5	5	5	5	8	20	60
134	Wes Parker	5	5	5	5	5	10	25	60
135	Dave Morehead	5	5	5	5	5	8	20	
136	Woody Held	5	5	5	5	5	8	20	80
137	Pat Corrales	5	5	5	5	5	8	20	
138	Roger Repoz RC	5	5	5	5	5	12	50	
139	B.Browne RC/D.Young RC	5	5	5	5	5	8	15	50
140	Jim Maloney	5	5	5	5	5	12	60	
141	Tom McCraw	5	5	5	5	5	8	15	60
142	Don Dennis RC	5	5	5	5	5	8	40	
143	Jose Tartabull	5	5	5	5	5	8	25	
144	Don Schwall	5	5	5	5	5	8	15	100
145	Bill Freehan	5	5	5	5	8	15	40	
146	George Altman	5	5	5	5	5	8	25	60
147	Lum Harris MG	5	5	5	5	5	8	20	100
148	Bob Johnson	5	5	5	5	5	8	20	100
149	Dick Nen	5	5	5	5	5	8	20	60
150	Rocky Colavito	5	5	6	10	15	25	80	400
151	Gary Wagner RC	5	5	5	5	5	8	25	60
152	Frank Malzone	5	5	5	5	5	8	20	
153	Rico Carty	5	5	5	5	5	10	25	80
154	Chuck Hiller	5	5	5	5	5	8	25	
155	Marcelino Lopez	5	5	5	5	5	8	15	50
156	DP Combo	5	5	5	5	5	8	20	100
157	Rene Lachemann	5	5	5	5	5	8	25	60
158	Jim Brewer	5	5	5	5	5	8	15	60
159	Chico Ruiz	5	5	5	5	5	8	20	60
160	Whitey Ford	▲10	15	▲25	▲40	50	100	200	600
161	Jerry Lumpe	5	5	5	5	10	30	80	
162	Lee Maye	5	5	5	5	5	8	20	120
163	Tito Francona	5	5	5	5	5	8	25	80
164	T.Agee/M.Staehle	5	5	5	5	5	10	25	80
165	Don Lock	5	5	5	5	5	8	15	50
166	Chris Krug RC	5	5	5	5	5	8	20	60
167	Boog Powell	5	5	5	5	5	20	50	
168	Dan Osinski	5	5	5	5	5	8	20	60
169	Duke Sims RC	5	5	5	5	5	8	20	
170	Cookie Rojas	5	5	5	5	5	10	25	
171	Nick Willhite	5	5	5	5	5	8	40	80
172	New York Mets TC	5	5	5	5	8	15	30	60
173	Al Spangler	5	5	5	5	5	8	15	60
174	Ron Taylor	5	5	5	5	5	8	15	80
175	Bert Campaneris	5	5	5	5	5	10	40	
176	Jim Davenport	5	5	5	5	5	8	20	100
177	Hector Lopez	5	5	5	5	5	10	30	80
178	Bob Tillman	5	5	5	5	5	8	25	100
179	D.Aust RC/B.Tolan	5	5	5	5	5	10	30	
180	Vada Pinson	5	5	5	5	5	10	25	80
181	Al Worthington	5	5	5	5	5	8	20	50

#	Player	GD 2	VG 3	VgEx 4	EX 5	ExMt 6	NM 7	NmMt 8	MT
182	Jerry Lynch	5	5	5	5	5	8	20	6
183A	Checklist 3 Large Print	5	5	5	5	5	8	25	6
183B	Checklist 3 Small Print	5	5	5	5	5	8	25	6
184	Denis Menke	5	5	5	5	5	8	20	5
185	Bob Buhl	5	5	5	5	5	8	25	
186	Ruben Amaro	5	5	5	5	5	15	50	
187	Chuck Dressen MG	5	5	5	6	10	15	50	10
188	Al Luplow	5	5	5	5	5	8	25	6
189	John Roseboro	5	5	5	5	5	10	20	8
190	Jimmie Hall	5	5	5	5	5	8	15	5
191	Darrell Sutherland RC	5	5	5	5	5	8	15	6
192	Vic Power	5	5	5	5	5	8	20	6
193	Dave McNally	5	5	5	5	5	10	20	20
194	Washington Senators TC	5	5	5	5	5	10	20	8
195	Joe Morgan	▲25	▲40	▲60	▲100	▲150	250	500	1,50
196	Don Pavletich	5	5	5	5	5	8	25	
197	Sonny Siebert	5	5	5	5	5	8	15	8
198	Mickey Stanley RC	5	5	6	10	15	25	50	12
199	ChiSox Clubbers	5	5	5	5	5	10	20	6
200	Eddie Mathews	▲10	▲15	▲25	▲40	▲60	▲100	▲150	40
201	Jim Dickson	5	5	5	5	5	8	15	5
202	Clay Dalrymple	5	5	5	5	5	8	30	8
203	Jose Santiago	5	5	5	5	5	8	15	5
204	Chicago Cubs TC	5	5	5	5	5	10	20	6
205	Tom Tresh	5	5	5	5	8	15	50	25
206	Al Jackson	5	5	5	5	5	8	15	5
207	Frank Quilici RC	5	5	5	5	5	8	15	5
208	Bob Miller	5	5	5	5	5	8	20	
209	F.Fisher/J.Hiller RC	5	5	5	5	5	10	20	1
210	Bill Mazeroski	5	6	10	15	25	40	60	20
211	Frank Kreutzer	5	5	5	5	5	8	20	10
212	Ed Kranepool	5	5	5	5	5	10	25	
213	Fred Newman	5	5	5	5	5	8	15	
214	Tommy Harper	5	5	5	5	5	10	20	
215	NL Batting Leaders	▲50	▲80	▲120	▲200	▲300	▲500	▲1,000	
216	AL Batting Leaders	5	6	10	15	25	40	250	
217	NL Home Run Leaders	5	6	10	15	20	50	100	4
218	AL Home Run Leaders	5	5	5	6	10	20	60	2
219	NL RBI Leaders	5	8	12	20	25	40	100	
220	AL RBI Leaders	5	5	5	5	8	15	60	
221	NL ERA Leaders	5	5	6	10	15	30	120	
222	AL ERA Leaders	5	5	5	5	8	15	50	
223	NL Pitching Leaders	5	15	20	25	30	40	100	
224	AL Pitching Leaders	5	5	5	5	8	20	120	
225	NL Strikeout Leaders	5	12	15	20	30	50	80	4
226	AL Strikeout Leaders	5	5	5	5	8	15	50	
227	Russ Nixon	5	5	5	5	5	8	20	
228	Larry Dierker	5	5	5	5	5	8	15	
229	Hank Bauer MG	5	5	5	5	5	8	20	
230	Johnny Callison	5	5	5	5	5	10	30	1
231	Floyd Weaver	5	5	5	5	5	8	20	
232	Glenn Beckert	5	5	5	5	5	8	25	
233	Dom Zanni	5	5	5	5	5	8	20	
234	R.Beck RC/R.White RC	5	5	5	5	5	10	40	
235	Don Cardwell	5	5	5	5	5	8	15	
236	Mike Hershberger	5	5	5	5	5	8	20	
237	Billy O'Dell	5	5	5	5	5	8	20	
238	Los Angeles Dodgers TC	5	5	5	5	8	15	40	2
239	Orlando Pena	5	5	5	5	5	8	15	1
240	Earl Battey	5	5	5	5	5	8	20	
241	Dennis Ribant	5	5	5	5	5	8	20	
242	Jesus Alou	5	5	5	5	5	8	20	
243	Nelson Briles	5	5	5	5	5	8	15	
244	C.Harrison RC//S.Jackson	5	5	5	5	5	8	15	
245	John Buzhardt	5	5	5	5	5	8	15	
246	Ed Bailey	5	5	5	5	5	8	15	
247	Carl Warwick	5	5	5	5	5	8	15	
248	Pete Mikkelsen	5	5	5	5	5	8	15	

Left table:

	GD 2	VG 3	VgEx 4	EX 5	ExMt 6	NM 7	NmMt 8	MT 9
Bill Rigney MG	5	5	5	5	5	8	20	50
Sammy Ellis	5	5	5	5	5	8	20	60
Ed Brinkman	5	5	5	5	5	8	20	50
Denny Lemaster	5	5	5	5	5	8	15	50
Don Wert	5	5	5	5	5	8	15	125
Fergie Jenkins RC	▲30	50	▲80	▲120	▲200	▲300	500	▲2,500
Willie Stargell	5	6	10	15	40	50	120	1,000
Lew Krausse	5	5	5	5	5	8	20	60
Jeff Torborg	5	5	5	5	5	8	20	80
Dave Giusti	5	5	5	5	5	8	15	50
Boston Red Sox TC	5	5	5	5	6	12	30	300
Bob Shaw	5	5	5	5	5	8	20	60
Ron Hansen	5	5	5	5	5	8	15	50
Jack Hamilton	5	5	5	5	5	8	15	50
Tom Egan	5	5	5	5	5	8	15	50
A.Kosco RC/T.Uhlaender RC	5	5	5	5	5	8	20	60
Stu Miller	5	5	5	5	5	8	20	60
Pedro Gonzalez	5	5	5	5	5	8	15	50
Joe Sparma	5	5	5	5	5	8	15	80
John Blanchard	5	5	5	5	5	8	15	80
Don Heffner MG	5	5	5	5	5	8	20	80
Claude Osteen	5	5	5	5	5	10	20	60
Hal Lanier	5	5	5	5	5	8	20	60
Jack Baldschun	5	5	5	5	5	8	15	50
Astro Aces	5	5	5	5	5	10	25	120
Buster Narum	5	5	5	5	5	8	20	60
Tim McCarver	5	5	5	5	6	12	30	100
Jim Bouton	5	5	5	5	5	10	20	60
George Thomas	5	5	5	5	5	8	15	50
Cal Koonce	5	5	5	5	5	8	15	60
Checklist 4 Black Cap	5	5	5	5	5	10	20	120
Checklist 4 Red Cap	5	5	5	5	5	8	25	
Bobby Knoop	5	5	5	5	5	8	15	50
Bruce Howard	5	5	5	5	5	8	20	60
Johnny Lewis	5	5	5	5	5	8	15	60
Jim Perry	5	5	5	5	5	8	20	80
Bobby Wine	5	5	5	5	5	8	40	
Luis Tiant	5	5	5	5	5	10	40	80
Gary Geiger	5	5	5	5	5	8	20	200
Jack Aker RC	5	5	5	5	5	8	40	100
Don Sutton RC	25	40	60	80	120	250	400	1,500
Larry Sherry	5	5	5	5	5	8	20	80
Ron Santo	5	5	6	10	15	40	120	250
Moe Drabowsky	5	5	5	5	5	10	30	
Jim Coker	5	5	5	5	5	8	25	60
Mike Shannon	5	5	5	5	8	15	30	
Steve Ridzik	5	5	5	5	5	8	20	60
Jim Ray Hart	5	5	5	5	5	8	25	80
Johnny Keane MG	5	5	5	5	5	10	25	
Jim Owens	5	5	5	5	5	8	15	60
Rico Petrocelli	5	5	5	8	12	30	100	300
Lou Burdette	5	5	5	8	10	20	40	
Roberto Clemente	▼40	▼60	100	▲150	▲250	▲400	1,500	3,000
Greg Bollo	5	5	5	5	5	8	20	60
Ernie Bowman	5	5	5	5	5	8	40	
Cleveland Indians TC	5	5	5	5	5	8	25	80
John Herrnstein	5	5	5	5	5	8	20	60
Camilo Pascual	5	5	5	5	5	8	25	150
Ty Cline	5	5	5	5	5	8	20	60
Clay Carroll	5	5	5	5	5	8	40	
Tom Haller	5	5	5	5	5	8	40	
Diego Segui	5	5	5	5	5	8	25	60
Frank Robinson	5	20	25	30	50	100	120	800
T.Helms/D.Simpson	5	5	5	5	5	8	25	60
Bob Saverine	5	5	5	5	5	8	20	60
Chris Zachary	5	5	5	5	5	8	25	100
Hector Valle	5	5	5	5	5	8	20	150
Norm Cash	5	5	5	8	12	25	150	

Right table:

		GD 2	VG 3	VgEx 4	EX 5	ExMt 6	NM 7	NmMt 8	MT 9
316	Jack Fisher	5	5	5	5	5	8	20	120
317	Dalton Jones	5	5	5	5	5	8	15	60
318	Harry Walker MG	5	5	5	5	5	8	30	80
319	Gene Freese	5	5	5	5	5	8	25	100
320	Bob Gibson	15	20	30	40	50	100	300	1,200
321	Rick Reichardt	5	5	5	5	5	5	20	100
322	Bill Faul	5	5	5	5	5	5	15	60
323	Ray Barker	5	5	5	5	5	12	40	120
324	John Boozer	5	5	5	5	5	8	20	
325	Vic Davalillo	5	5	5	5	5	8	25	
326	Atlanta Braves TC	5	5	5	5	5	10	30	
327	Bernie Allen	5	5	5	5	5	8	20	60
328	Jerry Grote	5	5	5	5	5	10	25	
329	Pete Charton	5	5	5	5	5	8	20	60
330	Ron Fairly	5	5	5	5	5	20	60	
331	Ron Herbel	5	5	5	5	5	12	40	100
332	Bill Bryan	5	5	5	5	5	8	25	100
333	J.Coleman RC/J.French RC	5	5	5	5	5	8	20	80
334	Marty Keough	5	5	5	5	5	10	30	150
335	Juan Pizarro	5	5	5	5	5	8	20	60
336	Gene Alley	5	5	5	5	5	10	30	80
337	Fred Gladding	5	5	5	5	5	8	20	60
338	Dal Maxvill	5	5	5	5	5	8	30	100
339	Del Crandall	5	5	5	5	5	10	20	80
340	Dean Chance	5	5	5	6	10	15	25	100
341	Wes Westrum MG	5	5	5	5	5	10	25	60
342	Bob Humphreys	5	5	5	5	5	8	25	
343	Joe Christopher	5	5	5	5	5	8	15	60
344	Steve Blass	5	5	5	5	5	8	15	120
345	Bob Allison	5	5	5	5	5	10	120	
346	Mike de la Hoz	5	5	5	5	5	8	20	50
347	Phil Regan	5	5	5	5	5	8	20	60
348	Baltimore Orioles TC	5	5	5	5	6	12	120	200
349	Cap Peterson	5	5	5	5	5	8	20	60
350	Mel Stottlemyre	5	5	5	5	8	40	120	
351	Fred Valentine	5	5	5	5	5	8	20	
352	Bob Aspromonte	5	5	5	5	5	8	25	80
353	Al McBean	5	5	5	5	5	8	20	120
354	Smoky Burgess	5	5	5	5	5	10	25	80
355	Wade Blasingame	5	5	5	5	5	8	20	60
356	O.Johnson RC/K.Sanders RC	5	5	5	5	5	12	80	100
357	Gerry Arrigo	5	5	5	5	5	8	20	60
358	Charlie Smith	5	5	5	5	5	8	15	60
359	Johnny Briggs	5	5	5	5	5	8	20	100
360	Ron Hunt	5	5	5	5	5	10	30	200
361	Tom Satriano	5	5	5	5	5	8	20	60
362	Gates Brown	5	5	5	5	6	15	40	100
363	Checklist 5	5	5	5	5	5	8	25	
364	Nate Oliver	5	5	5	5	5	8	20	60
365	Roger Maris	30	▲50	▲80	▲120	▲200	▲300	▲500	1,200
366	Wayne Causey	5	5	5	5	5	8	25	
367	Mel Nelson	5	5	5	5	5	8	25	100
368	Charlie Lau	5	5	5	5	5	8	20	60
369	Jim King	5	5	5	5	5	8	15	60
370	Chico Cardenas	5	5	5	5	5	8	40	60
371	Lee Stange	5	5	5	5	6	10	15	50
372	Harvey Kuenn	5	5	5	5	8	12	20	50
373	J.Hiatt/D.Estelle	5	5	5	6	10	15	25	60
374	Bob Locker	5	5	5	5	6	10	15	50
375	Donn Clendenon	5	5	5	5	6	10	20	60
376	Paul Schaal	5	5	5	5	6	10	15	50
377	Turk Farrell	5	5	5	5	5	8	20	50
378	Dick Tracewski	5	5	5	5	5	8	30	80
379	St. Louis Cardinals TC	5	5	5	5	6	12	25	150
380	Tony Conigliaro	5	5	5	8	15	25	80	200
381	Hank Fischer	5	5	5	5	5	8	20	60
382	Phil Roof	5	5	5	5	6	10	20	60
383	Jackie Brandt	5	5	5	5	6	10	15	50

BASEBALL

#	Player	GD 2	VG 3	VgEx 4	EX 5	ExMt 6	NM 7	NmMt 8	MT 9
384	Al Downing	5	5	5	5	8	12	20	80
385	Ken Boyer	5	5	▲6	▲10	▲15	▲25	50	80
386	Gil Hodges MG	5	5	5	8	12	20	40	120
387	Howie Reed	5	5	5	5	6	10	15	50
388	Don Mincher	5	5	5	5	6	10	20	
389	Jim O'Toole	5	5	5	5	6	10	20	60
390	Brooks Robinson	▲10	▲15	▲25	▲40	▲60	▲100	200	600
391	Chuck Hinton	5	5	5	5	6	10	20	120
392	B.Hands RC/R.Hundley RC	5	5	5	6	10	15	40	200
393	George Brunet	5	5	5	5	6	10	15	50
394	Ron Brand	5	5	5	5	6	10	15	50
395	Len Gabrielson	5	5	5	5	6	10	15	60
396	Jerry Stephenson	5	5	5	6	10	15	25	100
397	Bill White	5	5	5	5	8	12	20	60
398	Danny Cater	5	5	5	5	6	10	20	60
399	Ray Washburn	5	5	5	5	6	12	20	60
400	Zoilo Versalles	5	5	5	5	6	10	25	50
401	Ken McMullen	5	5	5	5	6	12	20	50
402	Jim Hickman	5	5	5	5	6	10	20	100
403	Fred Talbot	5	5	5	5	6	10	15	50
404	Pittsburgh Pirates TC	5	5	8	12	20	25	60	150
405	Elston Howard	5	5	5	6	10	15	120	250
406	Joey Jay	5	5	5	5	6	10	20	80
407	John Kennedy	5	5	5	5	6	10	15	50
408	Lee Thomas	5	5	5	5	6	10	15	50
409	Billy Hoeft	5	5	5	5	6	10	15	60
410	Al Kaline	5	15	20	25	40	100	250	
411	Gene Mauch MG	5	5	5	5	6	10	15	60
412	Sam Bowens	5	5	5	5	6	10	20	50
413	Johnny Romano	5	5	5	5	6	10	20	60
414	Dan Coombs	5	5	5	5	10	15	25	50
415	Max Alvis	5	5	5	5	6	10	20	80
416	Phil Ortega	5	5	5	5	6	10	15	60
417	J.McGlothlin RC/E.Sukla RC	5	5	5	5	6	10	15	50
418	Phil Gagliano	5	5	5	5	6	12	20	50
419	Mike Ryan	5	5	5	5	6	10	20	
420	Juan Marichal	▲8	▲12	▲20	▲30	▲50	▲80	150	500
421	Roy McMillan	5	5	5	5	6	10	20	
422	Ed Charles	5	5	5	5	6	10	15	50
423	Ernie Broglio	5	5	5	5	6	10	20	60
424	L.May RC/D.Osteen RC	5	5	5	6	10	15	25	120
425	Bob Veale	5	5	5	5	6	10	20	100
426	Chicago White Sox TC	5	5	5	5	8	12	50	300
427	John Miller	5	5	5	5	6	10	15	80
428	Sandy Alomar	5	5	5	5	6	10	15	60
429	Bill Monbouquette	5	5	5	5	8	12	30	
430	Don Drysdale	5	8	12	20	30	60	150	600
431	Walt Bond	5	5	5	5	6	10	20	
432	Bob Heffner	5	5	5	5	6	10	15	50
433	Alvin Dark MG	5	5	5	5	6	10	15	50
434	Willie Kirkland	5	5	5	5	6	10	15	50
435	Jim Bunning	▲6	▲10	▲15	▲25	▲40	▲100	200	
436	Julian Javier	5	5	5	5	6	10	60	200
437	Al Stanek	5	5	5	5	6	10	15	50
438	Willie Smith	5	5	5	5	6	10	15	60
439	Pedro Ramos	5	5	5	5	8	12	20	60
440	Deron Johnson	5	5	5	5	6	10	25	100
441	Tommie Sisk	5	5	5	5	8	12	20	50
442	E.Barnowski RC/E.Watt RC	5	5	5	5	8	25	200	
443	Bill Wakefield	5	5	5	5	6	10	20	60
444	Checklist 6 R.Sox	5	5	5	5	6	10	30	60
445	Jim Kaat	5	5	5	▲8	▲12	▲20	▲30	100
446	Mack Jones	5	5	5	5	6	10	20	50
447	Dick Ellsworth (Hubbs Photo)	5	5	5	5	8	20	30	200
448	Eddie Stanky MG	5	5	5	5	8	12	20	80
449	Joe Moeller	5	5	5	5	10	25	80	
450	Tony Oliva	5	5	6	10	40	50	100	400
451	Barry Latman	5	5	5	5	8	12	20	60

#	Player	GD 2	VG 3	VgEx 4	EX 5	ExMt 6	NM 7	NmMt 8	MT
452	Joe Azcue	5	5	5	5	8	12	20	
453	Ron Kline	5	5	5	6	10	15	25	
454	Jerry Buchek	5	5	5	5	8	12	20	
455	Mickey Lolich	5	5	5	6	10	25	40	
456	D.Brandon RC/J.Foy RC	5	5	5	5	8	20	25	
457	Joe Gibbon	5	5	5	▲6	▲10	▲15	▲25	
458	Manny Jiminez	5	5	5	5	8	12	20	
459	Bill McCool	5	5	5	5	8	12	20	
460	Curt Blefary	5	5	5	6	10	25	30	
461	Roy Face	5	5	5	5	6	10	20	
462	Bob Rodgers	5	5	5	5	8	12	20	
463	Philadelphia Phillies TC	5	5	5	5	8	12	30	
464	Larry Bearnarth	5	5	5	5	8	12	25	
465	Don Buford	5	5	5	▲8	▲12	▲20	30	
466	Ken Johnson	5	5	5	5	8	12	20	
467	Vic Roznovsky	5	5	5	6	10	15	25	
468	Johnny Podres	5	5	5	6	10	15	40	
469	Bobby Murcer RC	▲8	▲12	▲20	▲30	▲50	▼80	150	
470	Sam McDowell	5	5	5	6	10	15	60	
471	Bob Skinner	5	5	5	5	10	25	60	
472	Terry Fox	5	5	5	5	10	25	100	
473	Rich Rollins	5	5	5	5	8	12	20	
474	Dick Schofield	5	5	5	5	8	12	20	
475	Dick Radatz	5	5	5	5	8	12	25	
476	Bobby Bragan MG	5	5	5	5	8	12	20	
477	Steve Barber	5	5	5	5	8	12	30	
478	Tony Gonzalez	5	5	5	5	8	20	50	
479	Jim Hannan	5	5	5	▲8	▲12	▲20	▲30	
480	Dick Stuart	5	5	5	5	8	12	30	
481	Bob Lee	5	5	5	▲6	▲10	▲15	▲25	
482	J.Boccabella/D.Dowling	5	5	5	6	15	50	200	
483	Joe Nuxhall	5	5	5	5	8	12	60	
484	Wes Covington	5	5	▲6	▲10	▲15	▲25	▲40	
485	Bob Bailey	5	5	5	5	8	12	25	
486	Tommy John	5	5	5	6	10	40	60	
487	Al Ferrara	5	5	5	5	8	12	25	
488	George Banks	5	5	5	▲6	▲10	▲15	▲25	
489	Curt Simmons	5	5	5	5	8	12	20	
490	Bobby Richardson	5	6	10	15	25	40	80	
491	Dennis Bennett	5	5	5	5	8	20	25	
492	Kansas City Athletics TC	5	5	5	5	8	12	25	
493	Johnny Klippstein	5	5	5	5	8	12	20	
494	Gordy Coleman	5	5	5	5	8	12	25	
495	Dick McAuliffe	5	5	5	6	10	15	25	
496	Lindy McDaniel	5	5	5	5	8	12	25	
497	Chris Cannizzaro	5	5	5	▲6	▲10	▲15	▲25	
498	L.Walker RC/W.Fryman RC	5	5	5	5	8	12	25	
499	Wally Bunker	5	5	5	5	8	12	60	
500	Hank Aaron	▲60	▲100	▲150	▲250	▲400	▲600	▲1,200	▲4,
501	John O'Donoghue	5	5	5	5	8	12	20	
502	Lenny Green	5	5	5	▲6	▲10	▲15	▲25	
503	Steve Hamilton	5	5	5	6	10	15	40	
504	Grady Hatton MG	5	5	5	5	8	12	20	
505	Jose Cardenal	5	5	5	5	8	12	30	
506	Bo Belinsky	5	5	5	6	10	15	25	
507	Johnny Edwards	5	5	5	5	8	20	100	
508	Steve Hargan RC	5	5	5	5	8	12	20	
509	Jake Wood	5	5	5	5	10	25	80	
510	Hoyt Wilhelm	5	▲8	▲12	▲20	▲30	▲50	▲80	
511	B.Barton RC/T.Fuentes RC	5	5	5	6	15	40	200	
512	Dick Stigman	5	5	5	▲8	▲12	▲20	▲30	
513	Camilo Carreon	5	5	5	5	8	12	30	80
514	Hal Woodeshick	5	5	5	▲6	▲10	▲15	▲25	
515	Frank Howard	5	5	5	6	10	15	40	
516	Eddie Bressoud	5	5	5	5	8	12	30	
517A	Checklist 7 529 is White Sox	5	5	5	6	10	15	40	
517B	Checklist 7 529 is W.Sox	5	5	5	6	10	15	50	
518	H.Hippauf RC/A.Umbach RC	5	5	5	5	8	12	30	

#	Player	GD 2	VG 3	VgEx 4	EX 5	ExMt 6	NM 7	NmMt 8	MT 9
19	Bob Friend	5	5	5	5	8	15	80	250
20	Jim Wynn	5	5	5	6	10	15	50	60
21	John Wyatt	5	5	5	▲8	▲12	▲20	▲30	60
22	Phil Linz	5	5	5	5	8	12	20	60
23	Bob Sadowski	5	5	5	6	10	15	40	100
24	O.Brown RC/D.Mason RC SP	5	5	8	12	50	60	100	500
25	Gary Bell SP	5	6	10	15	25	40	100	250
26	Minnesota Twins TC SP	▲20	▲30	▲50	▲80	▲120	▲200	▲300	▲500
27	Julio Navarro	5	▲8	▲12	▲20	▲30	50	80	200
28	Jesse Gonder SP	5	▲8	▲12	▲20	30	50	▲100	▲250
29	Elia/Higgins/Voss RC	5	5	5	6	10	15	40	80
30	Robin Roberts	▲10	▲15	▲25	▲40	▲60	▲100	▲200	▲400
31	Joe Cunningham	5	5	5	6	10	25	30	▲80
32	Aurelio Monteagudo SP	5	5	6	10	15	40	60	200
33	Jerry Adair SP	5	5	6	10	15	30	60	250
34	D.Eilers RC/R.Gardner RC	5	5	5	6	15	25	50	60
35	Willie Davis SP	5	6	10	15	40	100	120	300
36	Dick Egan	5	5	5	6	10	15	30	60
37	Herman Franks MG	5	5	8	12	20	25	80	
38	Bob Allen SP	5	5	5	8	15	40	50	100
39	B.Heath RC/C.Sembera RC	5	5	5	8	12	50	100	
40	Denny McLain SP	▲20	▲30	50	80	100	120	300	500
41	Gene Oliver SP	5	6	10	15	25	40	60	100
42	George Smith	5	5	5	6	10	15	30	60
43	Roger Craig SP	5	8	10	15	25	▲80	▲120	▲250
44	Cardinals Rookies SP RC	5	8	12	20	30	250	500	
45	Dick Green SP	5	5	6	10	20	30	60	200
46	Dwight Siebler	5	5	5	8	12	40	50	100
47	Horace Clarke SP RC	30	50	80	120	200	250	400	600
48	Gary Kroll SP	5	5	6	10	15	25	50	100
49	A.Closter RC/C.Cox RC	5	5	▲8	▲12	▲20	▲30	▲50	100
50	Willie McCovey SP	8	25	60	80	100	150	250	▲1,200
51	Bob Purkey SP	5	▲8	▲12	▲20	30	50	▲80	150
52	Birdie Tebbetts MG SP	5	5	▲8	▲12	▲20	60	100	150
53	P.Garrett RC/J.Warner	5	5	5	8	12	30	40	100
54	Jim Northrup SP	5	6	10	15	25	40	80	200
55	Ron Perranoski SP	5	8	12	20	40	120	250	
56	Mel Queen SP	5	5	10	15	50	100	200	
57	Felix Mantilla SP	5	5	8	12	20	60	100	250
58	Grilli/Magrini/Scott RC	5	5	8	12	25	80	100	250
59	Roberto Pena SP	5	5	8	12	20	50	120	
60	Joel Horlen	5	5	5	6	10	25	50	150
61	Choo Choo Coleman SP	50	60	80	100	120	▲250	▲500	
62	Russ Snyder	5	6	10	15	▲100	▲150	400	
63	P.Cimino RC/C.Tovar RC	5	5	5	8	12	50	120	200
64	Bob Chance SP	5	5	6	10	30	40	80	200
65	Jimmy Piersall SP	5	6	10	15	40	50	100	500
66	Mike Cuellar SP	5	8	12	20	30	50	80	150
67	Dick Howser SP	▲6	▲10	▲15	▲25	40	60	80	300
68	P.Lindblad RC/R.Stone RC	5	5	▲6	▲10	▲15	▲25	60	100
69	Orlando McFarlane SP	5	5	6	10	15	60	80	▲150
70	Art Mahaffey SP	5	5	6	10	15	60	120	
71	Dave Roberts SP	5	5	6	10	20	30	50	100
72	Bob Priddy	5	5	5	6	10	20	40	60
73	Derrell Griffith	5	5	5	6	10	25	40	60
74	B.Hepler RC/B.Murphy RC	5	5	5	6	10	30	50	80
75	Earl Wilson	5	5	5	8	12	20	50	100
76	Dave Nicholson SP	5	5	8	12	30	50	60	400
77	Jack Lamabe SP	5	5	6	10	15	40	60	100
78	Chi Chi Olivo SP RC	5	5	6	10	15	25	60	120
79	Bertaina/Brabender/Johnson RC	5	5	8	10	25	50	80	200
80	Billy Williams SP	▲12	▲20	▲30	▲50	▲80	120	400	800
81	Tony Martinez	5	5	▲8	▲12	▲20	▲30	▲50	80
82	Garry Roggenburk	5	5	5	6	10	15	30	80
83	Detroit Tigers TC SP	▲30	▲50	▲80	▲120	▲150	▲200	300	600
84	F.Fernandez RC/F.Peterson RC	5	5	6	10	20	40	50	150
85	Tony Taylor	5	5	5	6	10	50	60	
86	Claude Raymond SP	5	5	6	10	15	80	120	200

#	Player	GD 2	VG 3	VgEx 4	EX 5	ExMt 6	NM 7	NmMt 8	MT 9
587	Dick Bertell	5	5	5	6	10	15	50	▲120
588	C.Dobson RC/K.Suarez RC	5	5	5	6	10	50	60	120
589	Lou Klimchock SP	5	6	10	15	25	60	100	200
590	Bill Skowron SP	5	6	10	40	50	80	100	250
591	Grant Jackson SP RC	150	200	250	300	400	500	600	
592	Andre Rodgers	5	5	5	6	10	20	50	80
593	Doug Camilli SP	5	5	6	10	15	25	50	150
594	Chico Salmon	5	5	5	6	10	20	100	100
595	Larry Jackson	5	5	▲6	▲10	▲15	▲25	40	80
596	N.Colbert RC/G.Sims RC SP	5	6	10	15	25	50	100	300
597	John Sullivan	5	5	5	8	12	▲60	▲100	▲200
598	Gaylord Perry SP	20	25	60	100	150	▲300	600	1,000

— Don Sutton #288 PSA 10 (Gem) (Young Collection) sold for $7,919 (SCP; 5/12)

1966 Topps Rub-Offs

#	Player	GD 2	VG 3	VgEx 4	EX 5	ExMt 6	NM 7	NmMt 8	MT 9
1	Hank Aaron	5	5	6	10	20			
18	Roberto Clemente	5	6	10	15	25			
47	Sandy Koufax	5	6	10	15	25	40	80	150
57	Mickey Mantle	10	15	25	40	100	120	150	500
60	Willie Mays	5	5	6	10	15	25	100	150
83	Pete Rose	5	6	8	12	30	100	250	
100	Carl Yastrzemski	5	5	6	10	15	60	80	

— Roberto Clemente #18 PSA 10 (Gem) sold for $7,014 (eBay; 1/13)

1967 Topps

#	Player	GD 2	VG 3	VgEx 4	EX 5	ExMt 6	NM 7	NmMt 8	MT 9
1	The Champs	5	5	6	15	40	60	150	1,000
2	Jack Hamilton	5	5	5	5	5	40		
3	Duke Sims	5	5	5	6	10	25	150	
4	Hal Lanier	5	5	5	5	5	30	200	
5	Whitey Ford	▲12	▲20	▲30	▲50	▲80	▲120	200	400
6	Dick Simpson	5	5	5	5	5	50	200	
7	Don McMahon	5	5	5	5	8	20	200	
8	Chuck Harrison	5	5	5	5	5	8	20	80
9	Ron Hansen	5	5	5	5	8	15	80	
10	Matty Alou	5	5	5	5	6	15	100	200
11	Barry Moore RC	5	5	5	5	8	20	80	
12	J.Campanis RC/B.Singer	5	5	5	5	5	40	80	
13	Joe Sparma	5	5	5	5	6	15	60	200
14	Phil Linz	5	5	5	5	8	25	300	
15	Earl Battey	5	5	5	5	5	15	60	
16	Bill Hands	5	5	5	6	15	50		
17	Jim Gosger	5	5	5	5	8	15	80	
18	Gene Oliver	5	5	5	5	5	20	100	
19	Jim McGlothlin	5	5	5	5	5	20	60	
20	Orlando Cepeda	5	5	5	6	30	60	200	1,000
21	Dave Bristol MG RC	5	5	5	5	6	15	80	200
22	Gene Brabender	5	5	5	5	8	20	50	
23	Larry Elliot	5	5	5	5	5	25	100	
24	Bob Allen	5	5	5	5	5	20	80	
25	Elston Howard	5	5	5	5	10	25	80	
26A	Bob Priddy No Trade Line	5	6	10	15	25	60	25	
26B	Bob Priddy Trade Line	5	5	5	6	15	60	150	
27	Bob Saverine	5	5	5	5	8	15	80	
28	Barry Latman	5	5	5	5	5	20	100	
29	Tom McCraw	5	5	5	5	5	20	80	
30	Al Kaline DP	5	5	20	25	30	50	80	600
31	Jim Brewer	5	5	5	5	5	15	80	
32	Bob Bailey	5	5	5	5	6	20	100	
33	S.Bando RC/R.Schwartz RC	5	5	5	5	6	15	100	
34	Pete Cimino	5	5	5	5	8	15	80	
35	Rico Carty	5	5	5	5	8	25	120	
36	Bob Tillman	5	5	5	5	5	20	200	
37	Rick Wise	5	5	5	5	6	15	100	250
38	Bob Johnson	5	5	5	5	5	8	30	100
39	Curt Simmons	5	5	5	5	5	8	15	80

#	Player	GD 2	VG 3	VgEx 4	EX 5	ExMt 6	NM 7	NmMt 8	MT 9
40	Rick Reichardt	5	5	5	5	8	15		100
41	Joe Hoerner	5	5	5	5	6	15	60	150
42	New York Mets TC	5	5	5	5	8	15	40	300
43	Chico Salmon	5	5	5	5	6	15	50	400
44	Joe Nuxhall	5	5	5	5	5	8	25	100
45	Roger Maris Cardinals	5	8	25	40	60	100	200	
46	Lindy McDaniel	5	5	5	5	5	8	15	60
47	Ken McMullen	5	5	5	5	5	8	15	80
48	Bill Freehan	5	5	5	5	8	15	30	300
49	Roy Face	5	5	5	5	5	10	15	150
50	Tony Oliva	5	5	5	5	8	15	80	150
51	D.Adlesh RC/W.Bales RC	5	5	5	5	5	8	15	60
52	Dennis Higgins	5	5	5	5	5	8	30	100
53	Clay Dalrymple	5	5	5	5	5	8	15	80
54	Dick Green	5	5	5	5	5	8	25	150
55	Don Drysdale	▲10	▲15	▲25	▲40	▲60	▲100	150	600
56	Jose Tartabull	5	5	5	5	5	8	50	150
57	Pat Jarvis RC	5	5	5	5	5	8	25	100
58A	Paul Schaal Green Bat	5	5	6	10	15	25	60	250
58B	Paul Schaal Natural Bat	5	5	5	5	5	8	15	80
59	Ralph Terry	5	5	5	5	5	8	15	80
60	Luis Aparicio	5	5	8	12	20	30	80	
61	Gordy Coleman	5	5	5	5	5	8	15	80
62	Frank Robinson CL1	5	5	5	5	8	15	80	
63	Cards Clubbers	5	5	5	8	12	30	100	
64	Fred Valentine	5	5	5	5	5	8	15	80
65	Tom Haller	5	5	5	5	5	8	15	50
66	Manny Mota	5	5	5	5	5	8	15	60
67	Ken Berry	5	5	5	5	5	8	15	120
68	Bob Buhl	5	5	5	5	5	8	25	100
69	Vic Davalillo	5	5	5	5	5	8	60	200
70	Ron Santo	6	10	15	25	40	60	120	250
71	Camilo Pascual	5	5	5	5	5	8	15	100
72	G.Korince RC/T.Matchick RC	5	5	5	5	6	20	80	400
73	Rusty Staub	5	5	5	5	6	15	50	150
74	Wes Stock	5	5	5	5	5	8	20	100
75	George Scott	5	5	5	5	5	10	25	100
76	Jim Barbieri RC	5	5	5	5	5	8	15	80
77	Dooley Womack	5	5	5	5	5	8	15	80
78	Pat Corrales	5	5	5	5	5	8	15	80
79	Bubba Morton	5	5	5	5	5	8	15	100
80	Jim Maloney	5	5	5	5	6	12	25	150
81	Eddie Stanky MG	5	5	5	5	5	8	15	50
82	Steve Barber	5	5	5	5	6	15	120	
83	Ollie Brown	5	5	5	5	5	8	25	100
84	Tommie Sisk	5	5	5	5	5	8	15	50
85	Johnny Callison	5	5	5	5	6	15	80	200
86A	Mike McCormick No Trade Line	5	6	10	15	25	40		
86B	Mike McCormick Trade Line	5	5	5	5	8	15		150
87	George Altman	5	5	5	5	5	8	15	50
88	Mickey Lolich	5	5	5	5	5	10	25	
89	Felix Millan RC	5	5	5	5	5	8	15	60
90	Jim Nash RC	5	5	5	5	6	25	80	
91	Johnny Lewis	5	5	5	5	5	10	20	60
92	Ray Washburn	5	5	5	5	5	8	25	150
93	S.Bahnsen RC/B.Murcer	5	5	5	5	8	30	40	200
94	Ron Fairly	5	5	5	5	5	8	15	60
95	Sonny Siebert	5	5	5	5	6	12	25	100
96	Art Shamsky	5	5	5	5	5	8	15	60
97	Mike Cuellar	5	5	5	5	5	10	20	80
98	Rich Rollins	5	5	5	5	6	15	40	135
99	Lee Stange	5	5	5	5	5	8	20	150
100	Frank Robinson DP	5	5	15	20	40	50	200	300
101	Ken Johnson	5	5	5	5	5	8	15	50
102	Philadelphia Phillies TC	5	5	5	5	5	8	15	50
103A	Mickey Mantle / CL2 DP D.McAuliffe	5	5	6	10	15	25	60	200
103B	Mickey Mantle								

#	Player	GD 2	VG 3	VgEx 4	EX 5	ExMt 6	NM 7	NmMt 8	MT 9
	CL2 DP D McAuliffe	5	5	8	12	20	30		
104	Minnie Rojas RC	5	5	5	5	5	8	25	100
105	Ken Boyer	5	5	5	5	6	12	40	200
106	Randy Hundley	5	5	5	5	6	12	25	150
107	Joel Horlen	5	5	5	5	5	8	20	80
108	Alex Johnson	5	5	5	5	5	10	30	300
109	Tribe Thumpers	5	5	5	5	5	10	30	60
110	Jack Aker	5	5	5	5	5	8	15	50
111	John Kennedy	5	5	5	5	5	8	40	150
112	Dave Wickersham	5	5	5	5	5	8	20	100
113	Dave Nicholson	5	5	5	5	5	8	15	80
114	Jack Baldschun	5	5	5	5	5	8	15	150
115	Paul Casanova RC	5	5	5	5	6	15	60	200
116	Herman Franks MG	5	5	5	5	5	8	15	60
117	Darrell Brandon	5	5	5	5	5	8	15	120
118	Bernie Allen	5	5	5	5	5	8	15	80
119	Wade Blasingame	5	5	5	5	5	8	15	50
120	Floyd Robinson	5	5	5	5	5	8	20	80
121	Eddie Bressoud	5	5	5	5	5	8	25	120
122	George Brunet	5	5	5	5	5	8	15	60
123	J.Price RC/L.Walker	5	5	5	5	5	8	15	100
124	Jim Stewart	5	5	5	5	5	8	15	100
125	Moe Drabowsky	5	5	5	5	6	15	30	100
126	Tony Taylor	5	5	5	5	6	15	50	150
127	John O'Donoghue	5	5	5	5	5	8	30	120
128A	Ed Spiezio RC	5	5	5	5	5	8	25	120
129	Phil Roof	5	5	5	5	5	8	15	50
130	Phil Regan	5	5	5	5	5	10	25	120
131	New York Yankees TC	5	5	5	15	20	▲40	800	200
132	Ozzie Virgil	5	5	5	5	5	8	20	100
133	Ron Kline	5	5	5	5	5	8	15	60
134	Gates Brown	5	5	5	5	6	12	60	
135	Deron Johnson	5	5	5	5	6	15	40	120
136	Carroll Sembera	5	5	5	5	5	8	40	120
137	R.Clark RC/J.Ollum	5	5	5	5	5	8	15	60
138	Dick Kelley	5	5	5	5	5	8	20	80
139	Dalton Jones	5	5	5	5	5	10	20	10
140	Willie Stargell	▲10	▲15	▲25	▲40	▲60	▲120	▲250	1,00
141	John Miller	5	5	5	5	5	10	50	10
142	Jackie Brandt	5	5	5	5	5	8	15	8
143	Sox Sockers	5	5	5	5	5	10	25	15
144	Bill Hepler	5	5	5	5	5	8	30	
145	Larry Brown	5	5	5	5	6	15	40	20
146	Steve Carlton	15	20	30	50	80	100	300	1,50
147	Tom Egan	5	5	5	5	5	8	15	8
148	Adolfo Phillips	5	5	5	5	5	8	15	8
149	Joe Moeller	5	5	5	5	5	8	50	10
150	Mickey Mantle	120	▲200	▲300	▲400	▲800	▲2,000	▲4,000	12,00
151	Moe Drabowsky WS1	5	5	5	5	5	10	40	20
152	Jim Palmer WS2	5	5	5	5	8	20	100	25
153	Paul Blair WS3	5	5	5	5	5	10	30	8
154	B.Robinson/D.McNally WS4	5	5	5	5	6	12	30	
155	Orioles Celebrate WS	5	5	5	5	6	12	50	8
156	Ron Herbel	5	5	5	5	5	8	20	10
157	Danny Cater	5	5	5	5	5	8	15	10
158	Jimmie Coker	5	5	5	5	5	8	15	8
159	Bruce Howard	5	5	5	5	5	8	15	8
160	Willie Davis	5	5	5	5	5	10	20	8
161	Dick Williams MG	5	5	5	5	6	15	50	25
162	Billy O'Dell	5	5	5	5	5	8	20	8
163	Vic Roznovsky	5	5	5	5	6	20	50	20
164	Dwight Siebler	5	5	5	5	5	8	20	10
165	Cleon Jones	5	5	5	5	6	12	30	20
166	Eddie Mathews	5	▲8	▲12	▲20	▲30	▲50	▲80	▲
167	J.Coleman RC/T.Cullen RC	5	5	5	5	5	8	25	15
168	Ray Culp	5	5	5	5	5	8	20	8
169	Horace Clarke	5	5	5	5	6	12	25	15
170	Dick McAuliffe	5	5	5	5	6	15	60	

#	Player	GD 2	VG 3	VgEx 4	EX 5	ExMt 6	NM 7	NmMt 8	MT 9
1	Cal Koonce	5	5	5	5	5	8	20	60
2	Bill Heath	5	5	5	5	5	8	20	80
3	St. Louis Cardinals TC	5	5	5	5	6	12	30	120
4	Dick Radatz	5	5	5	5	5	8	15	60
5	Bobby Knoop	5	5	5	5	5	8	15	80
6	Sammy Ellis	5	5	5	5	5	8	30	120
7	Tito Fuentes	5	5	5	5	5	8	15	80
8	John Buzhardt	5	5	5	5	5	8	20	80
9	C.Vaughan RC/C.Epshaw RC	5	5	5	5	5	8	20	120
10	Curt Blefary	5	5	5	5	5	8	20	100
11	Terry Fox	5	5	5	5	5	8	25	150
12	Ed Charles	5	5	5	5	5	8	20	200
13	Jim Pagliaroni	5	5	5	5	5	8	15	80
14	George Thomas	5	5	5	5	5	8	30	250
15	Ken Holtzman RC	5	5	5	5	6	10	40	100
16	Mets Maulers	5	5	5	5	6	15	70	250
17	Pedro Ramos	5	5	5	5	5	8	15	80
18	Ken Harrelson	5	5	5	5	5	8	25	120
19	Chuck Hinton	5	5	5	5	6	15	40	120
20	Turk Farrell	5	5	5	5	5	8	20	135
21A	Willie Mays CL3 214 is Tom	5	5	5	5	5	10	30	150
21B	Willie Mays CL3 214 is Dick	5	5	5	5	5	10	25	80
22	Fred Gladding	5	5	5	5	5	8	15	135
23	Jose Cardenal	5	5	5	5	5	8	15	60
24	Bob Allison	5	5	5	5	5	10	25	60
25	Al Jackson	5	5	5	5	5	8	30	200
26	Johnny Romano	5	5	5	5	5	12	150	
27	Ron Perranoski	5	5	5	5	5	10	20	80
28	Chuck Hiller	5	5	5	5	5	8	20	80
29	Billy Hitchcock MG	5	5	5	5	5	8	15	50
30	Willie Mays	25	40	60	80	120	150	▲1,500	▲5,000
31	Hal Reniff	5	5	5	5	5	10	25	150
32	Johnny Edwards	5	5	5	5	5	8	15	50
33	Al McBean	5	5	5	5	5	8	15	60
34	M.Epstein RC/T.Phoebus RC	5	5	5	5	5	8	20	80
35	Dick Groat	5	5	5	5	5	10	20	50
36	Dennis Bennett	5	5	5	5	5	8	20	60
37	John Orsino	5	5	5	5	5	8	15	80
38	Jack Lamabe	5	5	5	5	5	8	15	50
39	Joe Nossek	5	5	5	5	5	8	15	80
40	Bob Gibson	8	12	20	30	40	100	250	800
41	Minnesota Twins TC	5	5	5	5	5	8	15	60
42	Chris Zachary	5	5	5	5	5	8	15	50
43	Jay Johnstone RC	5	5	5	5	5	8	15	50
44	Tom Kelley	5	5	5	5	5	8	15	60
45	Ernie Banks	▲30	50	60	▲100	▲120	▲200	400	1,000
46	Bengal Belters	5	5	6	10	20	50	100	250
47	Rob Gardner	5	5	5	5	5	8	15	80
48	Wes Parker	5	5	5	5	6	15	40	200
49	Clay Carroll	5	5	5	5	5	8	15	50
50	Jim Ray Hart	5	5	5	5	5	8	15	60
51	Woody Fryman	5	5	5	5	5	8	15	50
52	D.Osteen/L.May	5	5	5	5	5	8	25	50
53	Mike Ryan	5	5	5	5	5	10	60	150
54	Walt Bond	5	5	5	5	5	8	15	50
55	Mel Stottlemyre	5	5	5	5	6	12	40	150
56	Julian Javier	5	5	5	5	5	8	15	60
57	Paul Lindblad	5	5	5	5	5	8	15	80
58	Gil Hodges MG	5	5	5	5	6	12	25	100
59	Larry Jackson	5	5	5	5	5	8	20	120
60	Boog Powell	5	5	5	5	5	10	40	
61	John Bateman	5	5	5	5	5	8	15	50
62	Don Buford	5	5	5	5	5	8	20	100
63	AL ERA Leaders	5	5	5	5	5	8	25	100
64	NL ERA Leaders	5	▲8	▲12	20	25	▲40	80	300
65	AL Pitching Leaders	5	5	5	5	5	10	25	200
66	NL Pitching Leaders	▲10	▲15	▲25	▲40	▲60	▲100	▲150	300
67	AL Strikeout Leaders	5	5	5	5	5	10	80	100
238	NL Strikeout Leaders	▲8	12	▲20	▲30	▲50	▲80	▲120	▲250
239	AL Batting Leaders	5	5	▲8	▲12	▲20	▲30	▼50	400
240	NL Batting Leaders	5	5	5	5	8	15	50	120
241	AL RBI Leaders	5	5	5	5	8	25	50	200
242	NL RBI Leaders	▲8	▲12	20	▲30	50	▲80	▲200	500
243	AL Home Run Leaders	5	5	5	5	8	25	60	200
244	NL Home Run Leaders	5	5	15	20	30	50	100	400
245	Curt Flood	5	5	5	5	6	12	40	150
246	Jim Perry	5	5	5	5	5	10	25	120
247	Jerry Lumpe	5	5	5	5	5	8	20	100
248	Gene Mauch MG	5	5	5	5	5	8	20	100
249	Nick Willhite	5	5	5	5	5	8	15	50
250	Hank Aaron	▲30	50	60	80	120	▲500	▲1,200	4,000
251	Woody Held	5	5	5	5	5	8	30	80
252	Bob Bolin	5	5	5	5	5	8	20	50
253	B.Davis/G.Gil RC	5	5	5	5	5	8	15	50
254	Milt Pappas	5	5	5	5	5	8	15	50
255	Frank Howard	5	5	5	5	5	10	30	60
256	Bob Hendley	5	5	5	5	5	8	15	50
257	Charlie Smith	5	5	5	5	5	8	15	100
258	Lee Maye	5	5	5	5	5	8	15	50
259	Don Dennis	5	5	5	5	5	8	15	50
260	Jim Lefebvre	5	5	5	5	5	8	20	80
261	John Wyatt	5	5	5	5	5	8	15	50
262	Kansas City Athletics TC	5	5	5	5	5	8	20	60
263	Hank Aguirre	5	5	5	5	5	8	15	50
264	Ron Swoboda	5	5	5	5	5	10	25	
265	Lou Burdette	5	5	5	5	5	8	15	50
266	Pitt Power	5	5	5	5	8	15	40	150
267	Don Schwall	5	5	5	5	5	8	15	50
268	Johnny Briggs	5	5	5	5	5	8	15	60
269	Don Nottebart	5	5	5	5	5	8	20	80
270	Zoilo Versalles	5	5	5	5	5	8	15	80
271	Eddie Watt	5	5	5	5	5	8	20	80
272	B.Connors RC/D.Dowling	5	5	5	5	5	8	15	50
273	Dick Lines RC	5	5	5	5	5	8	15	120
274	Bob Aspromonte	5	5	5	5	5	8	20	80
275	Fred Whitfield	5	5	5	5	5	8	30	100
276	Bruce Brubaker	5	5	5	5	5	8	15	50
277	Steve Whitaker RC	5	5	5	5	5	10	20	60
278	Jim Kaat CL4	5	5	5	6	10	15	40	250
279	Frank Linzy	5	5	5	5	5	8	15	60
280	Tony Conigliaro	5	5	5	5	8	12	40	60	250
281	Bob Rodgers	5	5	5	5	5	8	15	100
282	John Odom	5	5	5	5	5	8	15	60
283	Gene Alley	5	5	5	5	5	8	15	100
284	Johnny Podres	5	5	5	5	6	10	20	80
285	Lou Brock	8	12	20	30	40	80	120	800
286	Wayne Causey	5	5	5	5	5	8	15	60
287	G.Goosen RC/B.Shirley	5	5	5	5	5	8	30	100
288	Denny Lemaster	5	5	5	5	5	8	20	50
289	Tom Tresh	5	5	5	5	5	10	25	50
290	Bill White	5	5	5	5	5	10	30	100
291	Jim Hannan	5	5	5	5	5	8	15	80
292	Don Pavletich	5	5	5	5	5	10	20	100
293	Ed Kirkpatrick	5	5	5	5	5	8	15	50
294	Walter Alston MG	5	5	5	5	5	10	50	120
295	Sam McDowell	5	5	5	5	5	10	50	150
296	Glenn Beckert	5	5	5	5	5	10	40	80
297	Dave Morehead	5	5	5	5	5	8	20	50
298	Ron Davis RC	5	5	5	5	5	8	15	50
299	Norm Siebern	5	5	5	5	6	15	40	200
300	Jim Kaat	5	5	5	5	8	15	50	150
301	Jesse Gonder	5	5	5	5	5	10	20	80
302	Baltimore Orioles TC	5	5	5	5	5	8	25	80
303	Gil Blanco	5	5	5	5	5	8	25	120
304	Phil Gagliano	5	5	5	5	5	8	20	80
305	Earl Wilson	5	5	5	5	5	12	25	80

#	Player	GD 2	VG 3	VgEx 4	EX 5	ExMt 6	NM 7	NmMt 8	MT 9
306	Bud Harrelson RC	5	5	5	8	12	20	50	60
307	Jim Beauchamp	5	5	5	5	5	8	15	50
308	Al Downing	5	5	5	5	5	8	40	80
309	Hurlers Beware	5	5	5	5	10	25	80	150
310	Gary Peters	5	5	5	5	5	8	20	80
311	Ed Brinkman	5	5	5	5	5	8	15	60
312	Don Mincher	5	5	5	5	5	8	15	60
313	Bob Lee	5	5	5	5	5	8	20	80
314	M.Andrews RC/R.Smith RC	5	5	5	5	6	12	50	300
315	Billy Williams	6	10	15	25	40	50	▲120	400
316	Jack Kralick	5	5	5	5	6	15	50	200
317	Cesar Tovar	5	5	5	5	5	8	20	80
318	Dave Giusti	5	5	5	5	5	8	15	100
319	Paul Blair	5	5	5	6	10	15	40	100
320	Gaylord Perry	5	5	▲6	▲10	▲15	▲25	▲100	▲250
321	Mayo Smith MG	5	5	5	5	5	10	20	120
322	Jose Pagan	5	5	5	5	5	8	15	50
323	Mike Hershberger	5	5	5	5	5	8	15	60
324	Hal Woodeshick	5	5	5	5	5	8	30	200
325	Chico Cardenas	5	5	5	5	5	8	15	50
326	Bob Uecker	5	▲6	▲10	▲15	25	80	▲120	300
327	California Angels TC	5	5	5	5	5	8	20	40
328	Clete Boyer	5	5	5	5	▲6	10	25	60
329	Charlie Lau	5	5	5	5	5	8	15	30
330	Claude Osteen	5	5	5	5	5	8	15	50
331	Joe Foy	5	5	5	5	5	8	40	100
332	Jesus Alou	5	5	5	5	5	8	15	60
333	Fergie Jenkins	▲6	▲10	▲15	▲25	40	50	▲200	400
334	Twin Terrors	5	▲6	▲10	▲15	▲25	40	▲60	200
335	Bob Veale	5	5	5	5	5	8	15	60
336	Joe Azcue	5	5	5	5	5	8	15	60
337	Joe Morgan	6	10	15	25	40	60	▲150	500
338	Bob Locker	5	5	5	5	5	8	15	80
339	Chico Ruiz	5	5	5	5	5	8	25	80
340	Joe Pepitone	5	5	5	5	6	12	40	80
341	D.Dietz RC/B.Sorrell	5	5	5	5	5	8	15	60
342	Hank Fischer	5	5	5.	5	5	8	20	60
343	Tom Satriano	5	5	5	5	5	8	15	50
344	Ossie Chavarria RC	5	5	5	5	5	8	20	50
345	Stu Miller	5	5	5	5	5	8	25	50
346	Jim Hickman	5	5	5	5	5	8	15	50
347	Grady Hatton MG	5	5	5	5	5	8	15	50
348	Tug McGraw	5	5	5	8	12	20	40	80
349	Bob Chance	5	5	5	5	5	8	15	80
350	Joe Torre	5	6	10	15	25	50	80	250
351	Vern Law	5	5	5	5	6	15	60	200
352	Ray Oyler	5	5	5	5	5	10	20	80
353	Bill McCool	5	5	5	5	5	8	15	50
354	Chicago Cubs TC	5	5	5	5	5	12	40	
355	Carl Yastrzemski	15	25	▲40	▲60	▲100	250	300	1,200
356	Larry Jaster RC	5	5	5	5	5	8	15	50
357	Bill Skowron	5	5	5	6	10	15	25	50
358	Ruben Amaro	5	5	5	5	5	8	15	60
359	Dick Ellsworth	5	5	5	5	5	8	15	50
360	Leon Wagner	5	5	5	5	5	10	20	100
361	Roberto Clemente CL5	5	5	▲8	▲12	20	▲30	▲50	120
362	Darold Knowles	5	5	5	5	5	8	30	200
363	Davey Johnson	5	5	5	5	6	12	80	150
364	Claude Raymond	5	5	5	5	5	8	15	60
365	John Roseboro	5	5	5	6	10	15	25	60
366	Andy Kosco	5	5	5	5	5	8	15	50
367	B.Kelso/D.Wallace RC	5	5	5	5	5	8	15	40
368	Jack Hiatt	5	5	5	5	5	8	15	60
369	Jim Hunter	▲8	▲12	20	▲30	▲50	▲80	▲120	400
370	Tommy Davis	5	5	5	5	5	10	20	50
371	Jim Lonborg	5	5	5	5	6	20	100	600
372	Mike de la Hoz	5	5	5	5	5	8	20	100
373	D.Josephson RC/F.Klages RC DP	5	5	5	5	5	8	20	100

#	Player	GD 2	VG 3	VgEx 4	EX 5	ExMt 6	NM 7	NmMt 8	MT
374A	Mel Queen Partial Line	5	5	6	10	15	25		
374B	Mel Queen Complete Line DP	5	5	5	5	6	15	60	35
375	Jake Gibbs	5	5	5	5	5	8	30	8
376	Don Lock DP	5	5	5	5	5	8	30	20
377	Luis Tiant	5	5	5	8	20	80		40
378	Detroit Tigers TC	5	5	5	5	8	20	60	
379	Jerry May DP	5	5	5	5	5	8	15	8
380	Dean Chance DP	5	5	5	5	5	10	25	10
381	Dick Schofield DP	5	5	5	5	5	8	15	6
382	Dave McNally	5	5	5	6	10	15	80	25
383	Ken Henderson DP	5	5	5	5	5	8	30	8
384	J.Cosman RC/D.Hughes RC	5	5	5	5	5	8	15	10
385	Jim Fregosi	5	5	5	5	5	8	20	8
386	Dick Selma DP	5	5	5	5	5	10	30	12
387	Cap Peterson DP	5	5	5	5	5	8	15	8
388	Arnold Earley DP	5	5	5	5	5	8	30	30
389	Alvin Dark MG DP	5	5	5	6	10	15	25	5
390	Jim Wynn DP	5	5	5	5	5	8	20	6
391	Wilbur Wood DP	5	5	5	5	5	10	25	10
392	Tommy Harper DP	5	5	5	5	6	15	40	15
393	Jim Bouton DP	5	5	5	5	5	12	50	
394	Jake Wood DP	5	5	5	5	5	12	30	2
395	Chris Short RC	5	5	5	5	5	10	50	1
396	Atlanta Aces	5	5	5	5	8	20	80	2
397	Willie Smith DP	5	5	5	5	5	8	30	20
398	Jeff Torborg	5	5	5	6	10	15	25	5
399	Al Worthington DP	5	5	5	5	6	15	60	25
400	Roberto Clemente DP	30	50	60	80	120	250	1,000	▲6,0
401	Jim Coates	5	5	5	5	5	5	15	
402A	G.Jackson/B.Wilson Partial	5	5	6	10	15			
402B	G.Jackson B.Wilson Complete RC DP	5	5	5	5	6	15	40	1
403	Dick Nen	5	5	5	6	15	30		5
404	Nelson Briles	5	5	5	5	5	8	30	
405	Russ Snyder	5	5	5	5	5	8	15	
406	Lee Elia DP	5	5	5	5	5	8	20	1
407	Cincinnati Reds TC	5	5	5	5	5	20	40	1
408	Jim Northrup DP	5	5	5	8	12	20	100	3
409	Ray Sadecki	5	5	5	5	5	8	15	1
410	Lou Johnson DP	5	5	5	5	5	8	30	1
411	Dick Howser DP	5	5	5	5	5	10	25	
412	N.Miller RC/D.Rader RC	5	5	5	5	5	10	40	
413	Jerry Grote	5	5	5	5	6	12	40	1
414	Casey Cox	5	5	5	5	5	8	30	
415	Sonny Jackson	5	5	5	5	5	8	25	1
416	Roger Repoz	5	5	5	5	5	10	30	1
417A	Bob Bruce ERR Rbaves	5	5	6	10	15	25	120	
417B	Bob Bruce COR Braves DP	5	5	5	5	8	40		2
418	Sam Mele MG	5	5	5	5	6	15	50	
419	Don Kessinger DP	5	5	5	5	5	8	25	
420	Denny McLain	5	5	5	5	8	25	60	1
421	Dal Maxvill DP	5	5	5	5	5	12	35	
422	Hoyt Wilhelm	5	5	▲8	▲12	▲20	▲30	50	
423	Fence Busters	5	6	10	30	60	▲250	▲500	
424	Pedro Gonzalez	5	5	5	5	6	15	50	
425	Pete Mikkelsen	5	5	5	5	5	15	50	1
426	Lou Clinton	5	5	5	5	5	10	25	2
427A	Ruben Gomez Partial	5	5	6	10	25			
427B	Ruben Gomez Complete DP	5	5	5	5	6	15	40	
428	T.Hutton RC/G.Michael RC DP	5	5	5	5	6	15	80	
429	Garry Roggenburk DP	5	5	5	5	5	6	15	80
430	Pete Rose	40	▲60	100	▲150	▲200	400	800	3,0
431	Ted Uhlaender	5	5	5	5	5	8	25	
432	Jimmie Hall DP	5	5	5	5	5	8	15	
433	Al Luplow DP	5	5	5	5	5	8	30	
434	Eddie Fisher DP	5	5	5	5	5	8	20	
435	Mack Jones DP	5	5	5	5	5	8	15	
436	Pete Ward	5	5	5	5	5	10	30	

#	Player	GD 2	VG 3	VgEx 4	EX 5	ExMt 6	NM 7	NmMt 8	MT 9
437	Washington Senators TC	5	5	5	5	5	8	15	80
438	Chuck Dobson	5	5	5	5	5	8	15	80
439	Byron Browne	5	5	5	5	5	8	25	100
440	Steve Hargan	5	5	5	5	5	8	15	60
441	Jim Davenport	5	5	5	5	5	10	20	80
442	B.Robinson RC/J.Verbanic RC DP	5	5	6	10	15	40	200	
443	Tito Francona DP	5	5	5	5	5	8	25	100
444	George Smith	5	5	5	5	5	10	20	80
445	Don Sutton	▲10	▲15	▲25	▲40	▲60	▲100	250	500
446	Russ Nixon DP	5	5	5	5	5	8	20	120
447A	Bo Belinsky Partial	5	5	6	10	15			
447B	Bo Belinsky Complete DP	5	5	5	▲6	▲10	▲15	25	250
448	Harry Walker MG DP	5	5	▲6	▲10	▲15	▲25	40	300
449	Orlando Pena	5	5	5	▲6	▲10	▲15	25	150
450	Richie Allen	5	5	5	▲6	▲10	15	120	200
451	Fred Newman DP	5	5	5	5	5	8	15	60
452	Ed Kranepool	5	5	5	5	6	15	40	150
453	Aurelio Monteagudo DP	5	5	5	5	5	8	40	250
454A	Juan Marichal CL6 No Left Ear DP	5	5	5	5	8	30	150	
454B	Juan Marichal CL6 Left Ear DP	5	5	5	5	8	30	150	
455	Tommie Agee	5	5	5	5	5	10	30	150
456	Phil Niekro UER ERA incorrect as .288	6	10	15	25	30	50	120	▲400
457	Andy Etchebarren DP	5	5	6	10	25	50	200	300
458	Lee Thomas	5	5	5	5	5	10	20	60
459	D.Bosman RC/P.Craig	5	5	5	5	5	10	20	80
460	Harmon Killebrew	▲8	▲12	▲20	30	40	▲120	▲200	800
461	Bob Miller	5	5	5	5	6	15	80	120
462	Bob Barton	5	5	5	5	5	10	40	100
463	Hill Aces	5	5	5	5	6	12	40	120
464	Dan Coombs	5	5	5	5	5	10	30	80
465	Willie Horton	5	▲6	▲10	▲15	▲25	▲40	100	250
466	Bobby Wine	5	5	5	5	20	25	60	300
467	Jim O'Toole	5	5	5	5	5	10	20	80
468	Ralph Houk MG	5	5	5	5	6	15	40	150
469	Len Gabrielson	5	5	5	6	10	15	25	80
470	Bob Shaw	5	5	5	5	6	15	60	
471	Rene Lachemann	5	5	5	5	5	10	40	80
472	J.Gelnar/G.Spriggs RC	5	5	5	5	8	25	60	
473	Jose Santiago	5	5	5	5	5	10	50	100
474	Bob Tolan	5	5	▲6	▲10	▲15	25	▲100	200
475	Jim Palmer	5	8	25	30	50	80	250	
476	Tony Perez SP	6	10	30	40	60	120	▲400	1,000
477	Atlanta Braves TC	5	5	5	5	6	30	50	150
478	Bob Humphreys	5	5	5	5	5	10	25	80
479	Gary Bell	5	5	5	5	5	12	60	150
480	Willie McCovey	▲8	12	20	▲30	▲50	▲80	150	300
481	Leo Durocher MG	5	5	5	5	8	40	60	120
482	Bill Monbouquette	5	5	5	10	15	30	80	
483	Jim Landis	5	5	5	5	5	10	20	200
484	Jerry Adair	5	5	5	5	5	10	40	
485	Tim McCarver	5	5	5	25	30	80	250	
486	R.Reese RC/B.Whitby RC	5	5	5	5	5	10	50	100
487	Tommie Reynolds	5	5	5	5	5	10	30	100
488	Gerry Arrigo	5	5	5	5	5	10	40	80
489	Doug Clemens RC	5	5	5	5	5	10	50	150
490	Tony Cloninger	5	5	5	5	5	10	20	80
491	Sam Bowens	5	5	5	5	5	10	20	80
492	Pittsburgh Pirates TC	5	5	6	10	15	80	▲200	
493	Phil Ortega	5	5	5	5	5	10	25	150
494	Bill Rigney MG	5	5	5	5	5	10	20	80
495	Fritz Peterson	5	5	5	5	6	15	60	
496	Orlando McFarlane	5	5	5	5	5	10	20	50
497	Ron Campbell RC	5	5	5	5	6	25	80	200
498	Larry Dierker	5	5	5	▲6	▲10	▲15	40	100
499	G.Culver/J.Vidal RC	5	5	5	5	5	10	20	80
500	Juan Marichal	5	5	10	25	40	50	80	200
501	Jerry Zimmerman	5	5	5	5	6	15	50	

#	Player	GD 2	VG 3	VgEx 4	EX 5	ExMt 6	NM 7	NmMt 8	MT 9
502	Derrell Griffith	5	5	5	5	5	10	30	100
503	Los Angeles Dodgers TC	5	5	5	8	12	20	40	150
504	Orlando Martinez RC	5	5	5	5	5	10	20	120
505	Tommy Helms	5	6	10	15	25	40	100	400
506	Smoky Burgess	5	5	5	5	5	10	30	100
507	E.Barnowski/L.Haney RC	5	5	5	5	5	10	20	80
508	Dick Hall	5	5	5	5	15	30	80	120
509	Jim King	5	5	5	5	5	10	25	100
510	Bill Mazeroski	5	▲8	▲12	▲20	▲30	▲50	▲80	200
511	Don Wert	5	5	5	5	6	15	30	150
512	Red Schoendienst MG	5	5	6	10	15	60	100	250
513	Marcelino Lopez	5	5	5	5	5	10	25	100
514	John Werhas	5	5	5	5	10	20	50	100
515	Bert Campaneris	5	5	5	8	10	20	50	120
516	San Francisco Giants TC	5	5	5	5	6	30	100	200
517	Fred Talbot	5	5	5	5	5	10	25	
518	Denis Menke	5	5	5	5	5	10	20	80
519	Ted Davidson	5	5	5	5	5	10	30	100
520	Max Alvis	5	5	5	5	5	10	25	80
521	Bird Bombers	5	5	5	5	6	30	100	200
522	John Stephenson	5	5	5	5	5	10	30	60
523	Jim Merritt	5	5	5	5	5	10	40	80
524	Felix Mantilla	5	5	5	5	6	15	50	150
525	Ron Hunt	5	5	5	5	6	10	15	25
526	P.Dobson RC/G.Korince RC	5	5	5	5	6	15	40	175
527	Dennis Ribant	5	5	5	5	5	15	50	100
528	Rico Petrocelli	5	5	8	12	20	60	120	300
529	Gary Wagner	5	5	5	5	5	10	50	200
530	Felipe Alou	5	5	5	5	6	40	50	200
531	Brooks Robinson CL7 DP	5	5	6	10	20	100	300	1,200
532	Jim Hicks RC	5	5	5	5	5	10	30	80
533	Jack Fisher	5	5	5	5	6	15	80	300
534	Hank Bauer MG DP	5	5	5	6	10	25	40	150
535	Donn Clendenon	5	8	12	20	60	100	200	600
536	J.Niekro RC/P.Popovich RC	15	25	40	60	100	150	200	600
537	Chuck Estrada DP	5	5	6	10	15	25	30	80
538	J.C. Martin	5	5	6	10	15	30	▲80	120
539	Dick Egan DP	5	5	5	6	10	15	30	100
540	Norm Cash	6	10	15	25	60	100	200	400
541	Joe Gibbon	5	5	6	10	15	60	100	150
542	R.Monday RC/T.Pierce RC DP	5	6	10	15	25	30	100	▲200
543	Dan Schneider	5	▲6	▲10	▲15	▲25	40	▲80	250
544	Cleveland Indians TC	▲12	▲20	▲30	▲50	80	▲120	▲200	300
545	Jim Grant	▲10	▲15	▲25	▲40	▲60	100	▲150	300
546	Woody Woodward	5	5	6	10	15	40	50	200
547	R.Gibson RC/B.Rohr RC DP	5	5	5	6	10	20	60	100
548	Tony Gonzalez DP	5	5	5	6	10	15	30	100
549	Jack Sanford	5	5	6	10	15	30	80	
550	Vada Pinson DP	5	6	10	15	25	50	100	300
551	Doug Camilli DP	5	5	5	8	12	20	30	60
552	Ted Savage	6	10	15	25	40	50	100	150
553	M.Hegan RC/T.Tillotson	5	5	6	12	50	60	150	300
554	Andre Rodgers DP	5	5	5	6	10	15	50	
555	Don Cardwell	6	10	15	25	40	50	100	100
556	Al Weis DP	5	5	5	10	15	25	30	80
557	Al Ferrara	5	5	6	10	15	50	80	200
558	M.Belanger RC/B.Dillman RC	6	10	25	80	150	200	300	800
559	Dick Tracewski DP	5	5	5	6	10	25	30	120
560	Jim Bunning	10	40	50	80	100	150	250	600
561	Sandy Alomar	5	6	10	15	50	60	150	200
562	Steve Blass DP	5	5	5	6	10	30	50	300
563	Joe Adcock MG	5	5	8	12	20	100	150	250
564	A.Harris RC/A.Pointer RC DP	5	5	5	6	10	20	40	80
565	Lew Krausse	5	5	6	10	15	25	50	120
566	Gary Geiger DP	5	5	5	▲8	12	20	50	100
567	Steve Hamilton	▲6	▲10	▲15	▲25	▲40	▲60	120	150
568	John Sullivan	6	10	15	25	40	60	150	200
569	Rod Carew DP RC	▲300	▲500	500	600	800	▲1,500	▲3,000	▲15,000

		GD 2	VG 3	VgEx 4	EX 5	ExMt 6	NM 7	NmMt 8	MT 9
570	Maury Wills	15	25	40	60	80	200	300	1,000
571	Larry Sherry	5	5	8	12	20	50	▲100	
572	Don Demeter	5	8	12	20	30	100	150	
573	Chicago White Sox TC	5	5	8	15	20	50	100	150
574	Jerry Buchek	5	5	8	12	50	60	100	120
575	Dave Boswell RC	5	5	6	10	15	60	120	300
576	R.Hernandez RC/N.Gigon RC	5	8	12	20	40	100	200	250
577	Bill Short	5	5	8	12	20	50	120	
578	John Boccabella	5	5	6	10	15	40	80	150
579	Bill Henry	5	5	6	10	15	25	60	120
580	Rocky Colavito	12	20	100	120	150	200	300	500
581	Tom Seaver RC	800	1,000	1,200	1,500	2,000	3,000	6,000	25,000
582	Jim Owens DP	5	5	5	6	10	15	25	150
583	Ray Barker	5	6	10	15	25	60	80	
584	Jimmy Piersall	5	5	6	10	25	50	▲80	150
585	Wally Bunker	5	5	6	10	15	60	150	
586	Manny Jimenez	5	5	8	12	20	40	120	300
587	D.Shaw RC/G.Sutherland RC	5	8	12	20	80	100	120	200
588	Johnny Klippstein DP	5	5	5	6	10	15	40	150
589	Dave Ricketts DP	5	5	5	6	10	15	50	150
590	Pete Richert	5	5	▲8	▲12	▲20	▲30	▲80	150
591	Ty Cline	5	5	6	10	25	40	60	120
592	J.Shellenback RC/R.Willis RC	8	12	20	30	100	150	300	
593	Wes Westrum MG	▲8	▲12	▲20	▲30	▲50	80	120	150
594	Dan Osinski	5	6	10	15	25	50	100	300
595	Cookie Rojas	5	6	10	15	25	80	120	200
596	Galen Cisco DP	5	5	5	6	10	25	100	400
597	Ted Abernathy	5	6	10	15	25	50	100	150
598	W.Williams RC/E.Stroud RC	5	6	10	15	25	40	80	▲120
599	Bob Duliba DP	5	5	5	6	10	15	30	80
600	Brooks Robinson	80	100	200	250	400	500	1,000	3,000
601	Bill Bryan DP	5	5	5	6	10	15	60	
602	Juan Pizarro	5	5	8	12	50	60	100	200
603	T.Talton RC/R.Webster RC	6	10	15	25	40	60	▲120	200
604	Boston Red Sox TC	▲40	▲60	▲100	▲150	▲250	▲400	▲800	
605	Mike Shannon	▲20	▲30	▲50	80	120	250	▲500	▲1,000
606	Ron Taylor	5	5	8	12	40	60	100	
607	Mickey Stanley	8	12	25	50	100	120	300	
608	R.Nye RC/J.Upham RC DP	5	5	5	6	10	15	50	
609	Tommy John	▲30	▲50	80	100	▲150	▲250	400	1,500

— Rod Carew #569 PSA 10 (Gem) (Young Collection) sold for $95,294 (Mile High; 12/14)

— Rod Carew #569 PSA 10 (Gem) (SCP; 5/12) sold for $40,388 (SCP; 5/12)

— Mickey Mantle #150 PSA 10 (Gem) sold for $68,676 (Mile High; 10/13)

— Tom Seaver #581 PSA 10 (Gem) (Young Collection) sold for $24,450 (SCP; 5/12)

1967 Topps Who Am I

		GD 2	VG 3	VgEx 4	EX 5	ExMt 6	NM 7	NmMt 8	MT 9
12	Babe Ruth	40	60	80	100	150	200	400	
22	Mickey Mantle	40	50	60	100	150	400	600	
33	Willie Mays	15	20	30	50	80	120	300	
41	Sandy Koufax	▲20	▲30	▲50	80	100	150	400	

1968 Topps

		GD 2	VG 3	VgEx 4	EX 5	ExMt 6	NM 7	NmMt 8	MT 9
1	NL Batting Leaders	5	5	6	15	25	50	80	
2	AL Batting Leaders	5	5	5	8	30	60	150	
3	NL RBI Leaders	5	5	20	25	40	60	200	
4	AL RBI Leaders	5	5	5	6	10	30	60	200
5	NL Home Run Leaders	5	5	6	10	30	50	250	
6	AL Home Run Leaders	5	5	5	5	6	10	60	200
7	NL ERA Leaders	5	5	5	5	6	15	25	250
8	AL ERA Leaders	5	5	5	5	5	8	15	50
9	NL Pitching Leaders	5	5	5	5	6	10	30	200
10A	AL Pitching Leaders ERR Lonborg	5	5	5	5	6	15	80	
10B	AL Pitching Leaders COR Lonborg	5	5	5	5	6	15	120	
11	NL Strikeout Leaders	5	5	5	5	6	10	30	80
12	AL Strikeout Leaders/Jim Lonborg/Sam McDowell								

		GD 2	VG 3	VgEx 4	EX 5	ExMt 6	NM 7	NmMt 8	MT 9
	Dean Chance	5	5	5	5	6	10	40	200
13	Chuck Hartenstein RC	5	5	5	5	5	5	15	120
14	Jerry McNertney	5	5	5	5	5	5	10	30
15	Ron Hunt	5	5	5	5	5	6	12	30
16	L.Piniella/R.Scheinblum	5	5	5	5	6	10	30	300
17	Dick Hall	5	5	5	5	5	5	10	25
18	Mike Hershberger	5	5	5	5	5	5	10	30
19	Juan Pizarro	5	5	5	5	5	6	20	150
20	Brooks Robinson	5	5	6	10	30	50	80	200
21	Ron Davis	5	5	5	5	8	25	80	
22	Pat Dobson	5	5	5	5	6	15	50	250
23	Chico Cardenas	5	5	5	5	6	15	40	
24	Bobby Locke	5	5	5	5	5	5	10	60
25	Julian Javier	5	5	5	5	6	15	80	
26	Darrell Brandon	5	5	5	5	5	5	10	60
27	Gil Hodges MG	5	▲6	▲10	▲15	▲25	▲40	▲60	▲120
28	Ted Uhlaender	5	5	5	5	5	5	10	▲80
29	Joe Verbanic	5	5	5	5	5	5	10	30
30	Joe Torre	5	5	5	5	10	20	60	150
31	Ed Stroud	5	5	5	5	5	5	15	50
32	Joe Gibbon	5	5	5	5	5	5	10	25
33	Pete Ward	5	5	5	5	5	5	15	80
34	Al Ferrara	5	5	5	5	5	5	10	50
35	Steve Hargan	5	5	5	5	5	5	10	30
36	B.Moose RC/B.Robertson RC	5	5	5	5	5	6	12	30
37	Billy Williams	5	6	10	15	25	40	80	200
38	Tony Pierce	5	5	5	5	5	5	10	25
39	Cookie Rojas	5	5	5	5	5	5	15	80
40	Denny McLain	5	6	10	15	25	50	100	200
41	Julio Gotay	5	5	5	5	5	5	12	40
42	Larry Haney	5	5	5	5	5	5	15	10
43	Gary Bell	5	5	5	5	5	5	10	2
44	Frank Kostro	5	5	5	5	5	5	10	2
45	Tom Seaver DP	▲40	60	▲100	120	150	300	▲1,200	▲6,000
46	Dave Ricketts	5	5	5	5	5	5	10	25
47	Ralph Houk MG	5	5	5	5	5	6	12	30
48	Ted Davidson	5	5	5	5	5	5	20	60
49A	Ed Brinkman White Team	5	5	5	5	5	5	10	25
49B	Ed Brinkman Yellow Team	8	12	20	30	100	150	450	
50	Willie Mays	▲50	▲80	▲120	▲200	▲300	400	600	1,500
51	Bob Locker	5	5	5	5	5	5	10	60
52	Hawk Taylor	5	5	5	5	5	5	10	2
53	Gene Alley	5	5	5	5	5	5	10	2
54	Stan Williams	5	5	5	5	5	5	10	2
55	Felipe Alou	5	5	5	5	5	6	12	3
56	D.Leonhard RC/D.May RC	5	5	5	5	5	6	20	10
57	Dan Schneider	5	5	5	5	5	5	10	2
58	Eddie Mathews	5	8	12	20	30	50	▲150	▲40
59	Don Lock	5	5	5	5	5	5	10	2
60	Ken Holtzman	5	5	5	5	5	6	12	3
61	Reggie Smith	5	5	5	5	5	6	12	3
62	Chuck Dobson	5	5	5	5	5	5	10	2
63	Dick Kenworthy RC	5	5	5	5	5	5	25	6
64	Jim Merritt	5	5	5	5	5	5	10	2
65	John Roseboro	5	5	5	5	5	6	12	3
66A	Casey Cox White Team	5	5	5	5	5	5	10	2
66B	Casey Cox Yellow Team	8	12	20	30	50	80	120	
67	Checklist 1/Kaat	5	5	5	5	5	5	10	3
68	Ron Willis	5	5	5	5	5	5	10	12
69	Tom Tresh	5	5	5	5	5	8	15	5
70	Bob Veale	5	5	5	5	10	60	15	
71	Vern Fuller RC	5	5	5	5	5	5	10	3
72	Tommy John	5	5	5	5	8	12	20	3
73	Jim Ray Hart	5	5	5	5	5	6	15	4
74	Milt Pappas	5	5	5	5	5	6	15	8
75	Don Mincher	5	5	5	5	5	6	20	8
76	J.Britton/R.Reed RC	5	5	5	5	5	8	25	15
77	Don Wilson RC	5	5	5	5	5	5	10	3

#	Player	GD 2	VG 3	VgEx 4	EX 5	ExMt 6	NM 7	NmMt 8	MT 9
78	Jim Northrup	5	5	5	5	5	8	15	60
79	Ted Kubiak RC	5	5	5	5	5	5	10	25
80	Rod Carew	5	6	10	15	30	150	250	800
81	Larry Jackson	5	5	5	5	5	5	10	30
82	Sam Bowens	5	5	5	5	5	5	10	50
83	John Stephenson	5	5	5	5	5	5	10	25
84	Bob Tolan	5	5	5	5	5	5	10	60
85	Gaylord Perry	5	▲6	▲10	▲15	▲25	▲40	▲60	▲120
86	Willie Stargell	▲8	▲12	▲20	30	▲50	80	▲200	▲400
87	Dick Williams MG	5	5	5	5	5	5	10	25
88	Phil Regan	5	5	5	5	5	5	10	25
89	Jake Gibbs	5	5	5	5	5	6	12	30
90	Vada Pinson	5	5	5	5	5	6	12	30
91	Jim Ollom RC	5	5	5	5	5	5	10	25
92	Ed Kranepool	5	5	5	5	5	6	12	40
93	Tony Cloninger	5	5	5	5	5	5	10	25
94	Lee Maye	5	5	5	5	5	5	10	25
95	Bob Aspromonte	5	5	5	5	5	6	12	30
96	F.Coggins RC/D.Nold	5	5	5	5	5	5	15	120
97	Tom Phoebus	5	5	5	5	5	5	10	25
98	Gary Sutherland	5	5	5	5	5	5	10	25
99	Rocky Colavito	5	5	5	8	12	20	30	50
100	Bob Gibson	5	5	6	10	50	60	150	400
101	Glenn Beckert	5	5	5	5	5	6	12	50
102	Jose Cardenal	5	5	5	5	5	8	30	100
103	Don Sutton	5	5	5	5	10	15	30	100
104	Dick Dietz	5	5	5	5	5	5	10	25
105	Al Downing	5	5	5	5	5	6	15	30
106	Dalton Jones	5	5	5	5	5	5	10	25
107A	Checklist 2/Marichal Wide Mesh	5	5	5	5	5	12	30	150
107B	Checklist 2/Marichal Fine Mesh	5	5	5	5	5	12	30	200
108	Don Pavletich	5	5	5	5	5	5	10	25
109	Bert Campaneris	5	5	5	5	5	6	15	40
110	Hank Aaron	6	20	25	60	100	150	300	2,500
111	Rich Reese	5	5	5	5	5	5	10	25
112	Woody Fryman	5	5	5	5	5	5	10	40
113	T.Matchick/D.Patterson RC	5	5	5	5	6	10	25	100
114	Ron Swoboda	5	5	5	5	5	8	15	40
115	Sam McDowell	5	5	5	5	5	6	12	40
116	Ken McMullen	5	5	5	5	5	5	10	25
117	Larry Jaster	5	5	5	5	5	5	10	25
118	Mark Belanger	5	5	5	5	5	6	12	40
119	Ted Savage	5	5	5	5	5	5	10	25
120	Mel Stottlemyre	5	5	5	5	5	6	15	40
121	Jimmie Hall	5	5	5	5	5	5	10	30
122	Gene Mauch MG	5	5	5	5	5	5	15	80
123	Jose Santiago	5	5	5	5	5	5	10	25
124	Nate Oliver	5	5	5	5	5	5	10	40
125	Joel Horlen	5	5	5	5	5	5	10	40
126	Bobby Etheridge RC	5	5	5	5	5	6	20	80
127	Paul Lindblad	5	5	5	5	5	6	15	80
128	T.Dukes RC/A.Harris	5	5	5	5	5	8	30	150
129	Mickey Stanley	5	5	5	5	5	8	20	60
130	Tony Perez	5	5	5	5	25	40	150	250
131	Frank Bertaina	5	5	5	5	5	5	10	25
132	Bud Harrelson	5	5	5	5	5	8	15	40
133	Fred Whitfield	5	5	5	5	5	5	10	25
134	Pat Jarvis	5	5	5	5	5	5	10	25
135	Paul Blair	5	5	5	5	5	8	20	135
136	Randy Hundley	5	5	5	5	5	5	15	60
137	Minnesota Twins TC	5	5	5	5	5	6	15	40
138	Ruben Amaro	5	5	5	5	5	5	10	30
139	Chris Short	5	5	5	5	5	5	10	30
140	Tony Conigliaro	5	5	5	5	6	15	25	120
141	Dal Maxvill	5	5	5	5	5	6	12	50
142	B.Bradford RC/B.Voss	5	5	5	5	5	5	10	40
143	Pete Cimino	5	5	5	5	5	5	15	80
144	Joe Morgan	5	5	10	12	20	30	60	150

#	Player	GD 2	VG 3	VgEx 4	EX 5	ExMt 6	NM 7	NmMt 8	MT 9
145	Don Drysdale	▲10	▲15	▲25	▲40	▲60	▲100	▲200	▲300
146	Sal Bando	5	5	5	5	5	6	12	60
147	Frank Linzy	5	5	5	5	5	5	10	40
148	Dave Bristol MG	5	5	5	5	5	5	10	25
149	Bob Saverine	5	5	5	5	5	5	10	25
150	Roberto Clemente	▼30	▼50	80	▲120	▲200	▲300	▲800	3,000
151	Lou Brock WS1	5	5	5	▲8	▲12	20	40	80
152	Carl Yastrzemski WS2	5	5	▲6	▲10	▲15	25	60	150
153	Nelson Briles WS3	5	5	5	5	5	6	20	30
154	Bob Gibson WS4	5	5	5	▲8	▲12	20	▲50	▲100
155	Jim Lonborg WS5	5	5	5	5	5	6	12	30
156	Rico Petrocelli WS6	5	5	5	5	5	6	12	40
157	St. Louis Wins It WS7	5	5	5	5	5	6	20	40
158	Cardinals Celebrate WS	5	5	5	5	5	12	25	50
159	Don Kessinger	5	5	5	5	5	8	15	80
160	Earl Wilson	5	5	5	5	8	12	30	100
161	Norm Miller	5	5	5	5	5	5	30	120
162	H.Gilson RC/M.Torrez RC	5	5	5	5	5	6	12	40
163	Gene Brabender	5	5	5	5	5	5	10	60
164	Ramon Webster	5	5	5	5	5	5	10	50
165	Tony Oliva	5	5	5	5	8	15	60	225
166	Claude Raymond	5	5	5	5	5	6	20	80
167	Elston Howard	5	5	5	5	5	8	25	60
168	Los Angeles Dodgers TC	5	5	5	5	5	8	12	30
169	Bob Bolin	5	5	5	5	5	5	10	50
170	Jim Fregosi	5	5	5	5	5	6	12	40
171	Don Nottebart	5	5	5	5	5	5	10	30
172	Walt Williams	5	5	5	8	12	20	30	135
173	John Boozer	5	5	5	5	5	5	10	50
174	Bob Tillman	5	5	5	5	5	5	10	30
175	Maury Wills	5	5	5	5	5	8	20	150
176	Bob Allen	5	5	5	5	5	5	10	50
177	N.Ryan RC/J.Koosman RC	600	▲1,000	▲1,200	▲2,000	▲2,500	4,000	▲12,000	▲120,000
178	Don Wert	5	5	5	5	6	15	60	250
179	Bill Stoneman RC	5	5	5	5	5	5	10	30
180	Curt Flood	5	5	5	5	5	8	15	40
181	Jerry Zimmerman	5	5	5	5	5	5	15	50
182	Dave Giusti	5	5	5	5	5	5	10	25
183	Bob Kennedy MG	5	5	5	5	5	5	12	120
184	Lou Johnson	5	5	5	5	5	5	10	30
185	Tom Haller	5	5	5	5	5	5	10	60
186	Eddie Watt	5	5	5	5	5	5	10	30
187	Sonny Jackson	5	5	5	5	5	5	10	40
188	Cap Peterson	5	5	5	5	5	5	10	60
189	Bill Landis RC	5	5	5	5	5	5	10	50
190	Bill White	5	5	5	5	5	6	15	50
191	Dan Frisella RC	5	5	5	5	5	5	12	80
192A	Checklist 3/Yaz Spec. BB	5	5	5	5	8	12	40	
192B	Checklist 3 Yaz Spec. BB Play Card	5	5	5	5	8	12	30	
193	Jack Hamilton	5	5	5	5	5	5	15	100
194	Don Buford	5	5	5	5	5	6	12	50
195	Joe Pepitone	5	5	5	5	5	6	12	50
196	Gary Nolan RC	5	5	5	5	6	10	25	135
197	Larry Brown	5	5	5	5	5	5	10	40
198	Roy Face	5	5	5	5	5	6	12	50
199	R.Rodriguez RC/D.Osteen	5	5	5	5	5	5	15	100
200	Orlando Cepeda	5	5	5	10	25	30	80	150
201	Mike Marshall RC	5	5	5	5	5	8	15	120
202	Adolfo Phillips	5	5	5	5	5	5	10	25
203	Dick Kelley	5	5	5	5	5	5	10	25
204	Andy Etchebarren	5	5	5	5	5	5	10	25
205	Juan Marichal	5	5	5	5	8	12	30	150
206	Cal Ermer MG RC	5	5	5	5	5	5	10	25
207	Carroll Sembera	5	5	5	5	5	5	10	25
208	Willie Davis	5	5	5	5	5	5	10	25
209	Tim Cullen	5	5	5	5	5	5	10	25
210	Gary Peters	5	5	5	5	5	5	10	25

#	Name	GD 2	VG 3	VgEx 4	EX 5	ExMt 6	NM 7	NmMt 8	MT 9
211	J.C. Martin	5	5	5	5	5	5	10	25
212	Dave Morehead	5	5	5	5	5	5	10	25
213	Chico Ruiz	5	5	5	5	5	5	10	30
214	S.Bahnsen/F.Fernandez	5	5	5	5	5	6	15	175
215	Jim Bunning	5	5	5	5	5	8	25	50
216	Bubba Morton	5	5	5	5	5	5	10	25
217	Dick Farrell	5	5	5	5	5	5	10	25
218	Ken Suarez	5	5	5	5	5	5	10	30
219	Rob Gardner	5	5	5	5	5	5	10	40
220	Harmon Killebrew	5	5	15	25	30	50	80	250
221	Atlanta Braves TC	5	5	5	5	5	6	12	30
222	Jim Hardin RC	5	5	5	5	5	5	10	25
223	Ollie Brown	5	5	5	5	5	5	15	
224	Jack Aker	5	5	5	5	5	5	12	50
225	Richie Allen	5	5	5	5	5	8	15	60
226	Jimmie Price	5	5	5	5	5	8	15	40
227	Joe Hoerner	5	5	5	5	5	5	10	50
228	J.Billingham RC/J.Fairey RC	5	5	5	5	5	6	12	40
229	Fred Klages	5	5	5	5	5	5	10	25
230	Pete Rose	40	50	60	80	120	250	500	▲2,500
231	Dave Baldwin RC	5	5	5	5	5	5	10	25
232	Denis Menke	5	5	5	5	5	5	10	25
233	George Scott	5	5	5	5	5	6	12	40
234	Bill Monbouquette	5	5	5	5	5	5	10	30
235	Ron Santo	5	5	5	8	12	25	40	150
236	Tug McGraw	5	5	5	5	5	8	30	50
237	Alvin Dark MG	5	5	5	5	5	6	15	
238	Tom Satriano	5	5	5	5	5	6	20	200
239	Bill Henry	5	5	5	5	5	5	10	25
240	Al Kaline	▲10	15	▲25	▲40	▲60	▲100	▲300	▲1,000
241	Felix Millan	5	5	5	5	5	5	10	25
242	Moe Drabowsky	5	5	5	5	5	8	20	100
243	Rich Rollins	5	5	5	5	5	5	10	60
244	John Donaldson RC	5	5	5	5	5	5	10	25
245	Tony Gonzalez	5	5	5	5	5	5	10	40
246	Fritz Peterson	5	5	5	5	5	6	12	80
247A	Rookie Stars/Johnny Bench RC								
	Ron Tompkins	120	150	200	250	400	600	▲2,500	▲6,000
247B	Rookie Stars/Johnny Bench RC/Ron Tompkins UER the is								
	Misspelled in First Line								
248	Fred Valentine	5	5	5	5	5	5	10	25
249	Bill Singer	5	5	5	5	5	5	10	25
250	Carl Yastrzemski	▼10	▼15	25	▲40	▲60	▲100	▲150	▲600
251	Manny Sanguillen RC	5	5	6	10	15	25	50	150
252	California Angels TC	5	5	5	5	5	6	12	40
253	Dick Hughes	5	5	5	5	5	5	10	40
254	Cleon Jones	5	5	5	5	5	8	20	100
255	Dean Chance	5	5	5	5	5	5	10	30
256	Norm Cash	5	5	8	12	20	40	100	200
257	Phil Niekro	5	▲6	▲10	▲15	▲25	▲40	▲60	▲150
258	J.Arcia RC/B.Schlesinger	5	5	5	5	5	5	15	80
259	Ken Boyer	5	5	5	5	6	10	30	100
260	Jim Wynn	5	5	5	5	5	6	12	40
261	Dave Duncan	5	5	5	5	5	5	10	30
262	Rick Wise	5	5	5	5	5	5	10	30
263	Horace Clarke	5	5	5	5	5	5	15	
264	Ted Abernathy	5	5	5	5	5	5	10	50
265	Tommy Davis	5	5	5	5	5	6	15	120
266	Paul Popovich	5	5	5	5	5	5	10	50
267	Herman Franks MG	5	5	5	5	5	5	10	40
268	Bob Humphreys	5	5	5	5	5	5	15	50
269	Bob Tiefenauer	5	5	5	5	5	5	10	40
270	Matty Alou	5	5	5	5	5	6	15	120
271	Bobby Knoop	5	5	5	5	5	5	15	80
272	Ray Culp	5	5	5	5	5	5	10	25
273	Dave Johnson	5	5	5	5	5	6	12	40
274	Mike Cuellar	5	5	5	5	5	6	12	40
275	Tim McCarver	5	5	5	5	8	12	40	150
276	Jim Roland	5	5	5	5	5	5	10	40
277	Jerry Buchek	5	5	5	5	5	5	12	40
278	Checklist 4/Cepeda	5	5	5	5	5	8	25	80
279	Bill Hands	5	5	5	5	5	5	15	60
280	Mickey Mantle	▲250	▲300	▲400	▲500	600	1,000	▲2,500	20,000
281	Jim Campanis	5	5	5	5	5	5	15	150
282	Rick Monday	5	5	5	5	5	6	15	165
283	Mel Queen	5	5	5	5	5	5	10	25
284	Johnny Briggs	5	5	5	5	5	5	10	40
285	Dick McAuliffe	5	5	5	8	12	20	30	80
286	Cecil Upshaw	5	5	5	5	5	5	15	80
287	M.Abarbanel RC/C.Carlos RC	5	5	5	5	5	5	10	25
288	Dave Wickersham	5	5	5	5	5	5	10	25
289	Woody Held	5	5	5	5	5	5	10	25
290	Willie McCovey	6	10	15	30	50	80	120	▲400
291	Dick Lines	5	5	5	5	5	5	10	40
292	Art Shamsky	5	5	5	5	5	5	10	25
293	Bruce Howard	5	5	5	5	5	5	10	25
294	Red Schoendienst MG	5	5	6	10	15	25	50	100
295	Sonny Siebert	5	5	5	5	5	5	10	40
296	Byron Browne	5	5	5	5	5	5	10	40
297	Russ Gibson	5	5	5	5	5	5	10	25
298	Jim Brewer	5	5	5	5	5	5	10	30
299	Gene Michael	5	5	5	5	5	5	10	25
300	Rusty Staub	5	5	5	5	8	12	40	100
301	G.Mitterwald RC/R.Renick RC	5	5	5	5	5	5	10	40
302	Gerry Arrigo	5	5	5	5	5	5	10	25
303	Dick Green	5	5	5	5	5	5	10	25
304	Sandy Valdespino	5	5	5	5	5	5	10	25
305	Minnie Rojas	5	5	5	5	5	5	10	25
306	Mike Ryan	5	5	5	5	5	5	10	30
307	John Hiller	5	5	5	5	5	8	25	120
308	Pittsburgh Pirates TC	5	5	5	5	5	5	20	80
309	Ken Henderson	5	5	5	5	5	6	12	50
310	Luis Aparicio	5	5	6	10	15	25	▲50	80
311	Jack Lamabe	5	5	5	5	5	5	10	25
312	Curt Blefary	5	5	5	5	5	5	10	60
313	Al Weis	5	5	5	5	5	6	12	30
314	B.Rohr/G.Spriggs	5	5	5	5	5	5	15	120
315	Zoilo Versalles	5	5	5	5	5	5	10	30
316	Steve Barber	5	5	5	5	5	6	12	30
317	Ron Brand	5	5	5	5	5	5	10	25
318	Chico Salmon	5	5	5	5	5	5	10	30
319	George Culver	5	5	5	5	5	5	10	25
320	Frank Howard	5	5	5	5	5	6	12	50
321	Leo Durocher MG	5	5	5	5	5	5	40	60
322	Dave Boswell	5	5	5	5	5	5	10	40
323	Deron Johnson	5	5	5	5	5	5	10	30
324	Jim Nash	5	5	5	5	5	5	10	50
325	Manny Mota	5	5	5	5	5	8	25	120
326	Dennis Ribant	5	5	5	5	5	8	15	100
327	Tony Taylor	5	5	5	5	5	6	12	50
328	C.Vinson RC/J.Weaver RC	5	5	5	5	5	5	10	30
329	Duane Josephson	5	5	5	5	5	5	10	30
330	Roger Maris	▲30	▲40	▲50	▲60	▲80	120	150	▲500
331	Dan Osinski	5	5	5	5	5	5	10	40
332	Doug Rader	5	5	5	5	5	6	12	50
333	Ron Herbel	5	5	5	5	5	5	10	40
334	Baltimore Orioles TC	5	5	5	5	5	6	12	40
335	Bob Allison	5	5	5	5	5	6	12	50
336	John Purdin	5	5	5	5	5	5	10	25
337	Bill Robinson	5	5	5	5	5	6	12	40
338	Bob Johnson	5	5	5	5	5	5	10	25
339	Rich Nye	5	5	5	5	5	5	10	25
340	Max Alvis	5	5	5	5	5	5	10	25
341	Jim Lemon MG	5	5	5	5	5	5	10	25
342	Ken Johnson	5	5	5	5	5	5	10	30
343	Jim Gosger	5	5	5	5	5	5	10	25

Card #	Player	GD 2	VG 3	VgEx 4	EX 5	ExMt 6	NM 7	NmMt 8	MT 9
344	Donn Clendenon	5	5	5	5	5	6	12	40
345	Bob Hendley	5	5	5	5	5	6	12	30
346	Jerry Adair	5	5	5	5	5	5	10	30
347	George Brunet	5	5	5	5	5	5	10	25
348	L.Colton RC/D.Thoenen RC	5	5	5	5	5	5	10	30
349	Ed Spiezio	5	5	5	5	5	5	10	25
350	Hoyt Wilhelm	5	5	5	8	12	20	▲40	▲120
351	Bob Barton	5	5	5	5	5	5	10	25
352	Jackie Hernandez RC	5	5	5	5	5	5	10	25
353	Mack Jones	5	5	5	5	5	6	12	30
354	Pete Richert	5	5	5	5	5	5	10	25
355	Ernie Banks	▲25	▲40	▲50	▲60	▲100	▲120	▲250	▲600
356A	Checklist 5/Holtzman Center	5	5	5	5	5	8	25	
356B	Checklist 5/Holtzman Right	5	5	5	5	5	8	20	80
357	Len Gabrielson	5	5	5	5	5	5	10	40
358	Mike Epstein	5	5	5	5	5	5	10	30
359	Joe Moeller	5	5	5	5	5	5	10	30
360	Willie Horton	5	5	5	5	8	15	40	150
361	Harmon Killebrew AS	5	5	5	5	20	25	50	100
362	Orlando Cepeda AS	5	5	5	5	5	6	25	60
363	Rod Carew AS	5	5	5	5	6	25	50	100
364	Joe Morgan AS	5	5	5	5	6	20	30	80
365	Brooks Robinson AS	5	5	5	5	15	25	50	100
366	Ron Santo AS	5	5	5	5	5	10	15	80
367	Jim Fregosi AS	5	5	5	5	5	5	10	25
368	Gene Alley AS	5	5	5	5	5	5	15	80
369	Carl Yastrzemski AS	5	5	15	20	25	30	60	100
370	Hank Aaron AS	8	12	20	30	50	60	80	250
371	Tony Oliva AS	5	5	5	5	5	6	25	60
372	Lou Brock AS	5	5	8	12	20	30	50	100
373	Frank Robinson AS	5	5	5	5	8	25	50	100
374	Roberto Clemente AS	12	20	25	30	80	100	250	600
375	Bill Freehan AS	5	5	5	5	5	8	25	80
376	Tim McCarver AS	5	5	5	5	5	6	12	40
377	Joel Horlen AS	5	5	5	5	5	5	10	25
378	Bob Gibson AS	5	5	5	5	8	20	50	100
379	Gary Peters AS	5	5	5	5	5	6	15	30
380	Ken Holtzman AS	5	5	5	5	5	6	15	30
381	Boog Powell	5	5	5	5	6	10	25	100
382	Ramon Hernandez	5	5	5	5	5	5	10	60
383	Steve Whitaker	5	5	5	5	5	6	15	30
384	B.Henry/H.McRae RC	5	5	5	5	5	8	20	120
385	Jim Hunter	5	5	8	12	20	30	60	150
386	Greg Goossen	5	5	5	5	5	5	12	30
387	Joe Foy	5	5	5	5	5	6	15	30
388	Ray Washburn	5	5	5	5	5	5	10	25
389	Jay Johnstone	5	5	5	5	5	5	10	40
390	Bill Mazeroski	5	▲6	▲10	▲15	▲25	▲40	60	120
391	Bob Priddy	5	5	5	5	5	5	10	25
392	Grady Hatton MG	5	5	5	5	5	6	20	120
393	Jim Perry	5	5	5	5	5	5	10	25
394	Tommie Aaron	5	5	5	5	5	5	10	25
395	Camilo Pascual	5	5	5	5	5	6	15	60
396	Bobby Wine	5	5	5	5	5	5	10	25
397	Vic Davalillo	5	5	5	5	5	5	15	25
398	Jim Grant	5	5	5	5	5	5	10	30
399	Ray Oyler	5	5	5	5	5	8	20	60
400A	Mike McCormick Yellow Team	5	5	5	5	5	5	10	25
401	Mets Team	5	5	5	5	5	5	20	40
402	Mike Hegan	5	5	5	5	5	5	10	25
403	John Buzhardt	5	5	5	5	5	5	10	25
404	Floyd Robinson	5	5	5	5	5	5	10	25
405	Tommy Helms	5	5	5	5	5	5	15	80
406	Dick Ellsworth	5	5	5	5	5	5	10	60
407	Gary Kolb	5	5	5	5	5	5	10	25
408	Steve Carlton	▲12	▲20	30	40	▲60	▲100	▲150	400
409	F.Peters RC/R.Stone	5	5	5	5	5	5	10	25
410	Ferguson Jenkins	5	5	6	10	15	30	80	300
411	Ron Hansen	5	5	5	5	5	5	10	25
412	Clay Carroll	5	5	5	5	5	5	10	25
413	Tom McCraw	5	5	5	5	5	5	10	25
414	Mickey Lolich	5	5	5	5	6	10	30	150
415	Johnny Callison	5	5	5	5	5	6	12	40
416	Bill Rigney MG	5	5	5	5	5	5	10	25
417	Willie Crawford	5	5	5	5	5	5	10	25
418	Eddie Fisher	5	5	5	5	5	5	10	25
419	Jack Hiatt	5	5	5	5	5	5	12	40
420	Cesar Tovar	5	5	5	5	5	5	8	25
421	Ron Taylor	5	5	5	5	5	5	25	100
422	Rene Lachemann	5	5	5	5	5	5	10	25
423	Fred Gladding	5	5	5	5	5	5	10	25
424	Chicago White Sox TC	5	5	5	5	5	6	20	80
425	Jim Maloney	5	5	5	5	5	5	12	40
426	Hank Allen	5	5	5	5	5	5	10	25
427	Dick Calmus	5	5	5	5	5	5	10	25
428	Vic Roznovsky	5	5	5	5	5	5	10	60
429	Tommie Sisk	5	5	5	5	5	5	10	25
430	Rico Petrocelli	5	5	5	5	6	10	30	150
431	Dooley Womack	5	5	5	5	5	5	12	60
432	B.Davis/J.Vidal	5	5	5	5	5	5	10	50
433	Bob Rodgers	5	5	5	5	5	5	10	25
434	Ricardo Joseph RC	5	5	5	5	5	5	10	80
435	Ron Perranoski	5	5	5	5	5	5	12	60
436	Hal Lanier	5	5	5	5	5	5	10	60
437	Don Cardwell	5	5	5	5	5	5	40	120
438	Lee Thomas	5	5	5	5	5	5	10	25
439	Lum Harris MG	5	5	5	5	5	5	10	25
440	Claude Osteen	5	5	5	5	5	5	10	30
441	Alex Johnson	5	5	5	5	5	8	30	135
442	Dick Bosman	5	5	5	5	5	5	10	50
443	Joe Azcue	5	5	5	5	5	5	10	25
444	Jack Fisher	5	5	5	5	5	5	10	25
445	Mike Shannon	5	5	5	5	5	5	15	50
446	Ron Kline	5	5	5	5	5	5	10	40
447	G.Korince/F.Lasher RC	5	5	5	5	5	8	30	200
448	Gary Wagner	5	5	5	5	5	5	10	25
449	Gene Oliver	5	5	5	5	5	5	15	60
450	Jim Kaat	5	5	5	5	6	10	20	60
451	Al Spangler	5	5	5	5	5	5	10	25
452	Jesus Alou	5	5	5	5	5	6	12	60
453	Sammy Ellis	5	5	5	5	5	8	30	250
454A	Checklist 6/F.Rob Cap Complete	5	5	5	5	5	5	12	60
454B	Checklist 6/F.Rob Cap Partial	5	5	5	5	5	5	12	60
455	Rico Carty	5	5	5	5	5	6	15	80
456	John O'Donoghue	5	5	5	5	5	5	10	25
457	Jim Lefebvre	5	5	5	5	5	5	10	30
458	Lew Krausse	5	5	5	5	5	5	10	25
459	Dick Simpson	5	5	5	5	5	5	10	25
460	Jim Lonborg	5	5	5	5	5	5	15	30
461	Chuck Hiller	5	5	5	5	5	5	10	25
462	Barry Moore	5	5	5	5	5	5	10	25
463	Jim Schaffer	5	5	5	5	5	5	10	25
464	Don McMahon	5	5	5	5	5	8	40	135
465	Tommie Agee	5	5	5	5	5	6	30	60
466	Bill Dillman	5	5	5	5	5	5	10	25
467	Dick Howser	5	5	5	5	5	5	25	40
468	Larry Sherry	5	5	5	5	5	5	10	25
469	Ty Cline	5	5	5	5	5	5	10	30
470	Bill Freehan	5	5	5	6	10	15	50	80
471	Orlando Pena	5	5	5	5	5	5	10	25
472	Walter Alston MG	5	5	5	5	5	5	20	40
473	Al Worthington	5	5	5	5	5	5	10	25
474	Paul Schaal	5	5	5	5	5	5	6	15
475	Joe Niekro	5	5	5	5	6	10	15	30
476	Woody Woodward	5	5	5	5	5	5	10	25
477	Philadelphia Phillies TC	5	5	5	5	5	5	10	30

#	Player	GD 2	VG 3	VgEx 4	EX 5	ExMt 6	NM 7	NmMt 8	MT 9
478	Dave McNally	5	5	5	6	10	15	25	60
479	Phil Gagliano	5	5	5	5	5	5	10	25
480	Manager's Dream	▲40	▲50	▲60	▲80	▲100	▲150	200	▲500
481	John Wyatt	5	5	5	5	5	5	10	25
482	Jose Pagan	5	5	5	5	5	5	10	25
483	Darold Knowles	5	5	5	5	5	5	10	30
484	Phil Roof	5	5	5	5	5	5	8	20
485	Ken Berry	5	5	5	5	5	5	10	25
486	Cal Koonce	5	5	5	5	5	6	15	30
487	Lee May	5	5	5	25	30	50	80	250
488	Dick Tracewski	5	5	5	6	8	10	20	80
489	Wally Bunker	5	5	5	5	5	5	10	25
490	Super Stars	60	100	150	250	400	600	1,000	2,500
491	Denny Lemaster	5	5	5	5	5	5	10	25
492	Jeff Torborg	5	5	5	5	5	5	10	80
493	Jim McGlothlin	5	5	5	5	5	5	6	15
494	Ray Sadecki	5	5	5	5	5	5	6	15
495	Leon Wagner	5	5	5	5	5	8	60	120
496	Steve Hamilton	5	5	5	5	5	6	15	50
497	St. Louis Cardinals TC	5	5	5	5	8	12	40	80
498	Bill Bryan	5	5	5	5	5	8	40	80
499	Steve Blass	5	5	5	5	5	5	10	25
500	Frank Robinson	5	5	6	20	30	60	100	250
501	John Odom	5	6	10	15	25	100	200	500
502	Mike Andrews	5	5	5	5	5	5	10	30
503	Al Jackson	5	5	5	5	6	8	12	50
504	Russ Snyder	5	5	5	5	5	5	10	40
505	Joe Sparma	5	5	5	6	25	50	60	120
506	Clarence Jones RC	5	5	5	5	5	5	10	25
507	Wade Blasingame	5	5	5	5	5	5	10	25
508	Duke Sims	5	5	5	5	5	5	10	25
509	Dennis Higgins	5	5	5	5	5	5	10	25
510	Ron Fairly	5	5	5	5	5	6	20	40
511	Bill Kelso	5	5	5	5	5	6	8	20
512	Grant Jackson	5	5	5	5	5	5	10	25
513	Hank Bauer MG	5	5	5	5	8	12	20	30
514	Al McBean	5	5	5	5	5	5	10	25
515	Russ Nixon	5	5	5	5	5	5	10	25
516	Pete Mikkelsen	5	5	5	5	5	5	10	25
517	Diego Segui	5	5	5	5	5	5	10	25
518A	Checklist 7/Boyer ERR AL	5	5	5	5	5	5	15	25
518B	Checklist 7/Boyer COR ML	5	5	5	5	5	5	10	25
519	Jerry Stephenson	5	5	5	5	5	5	10	25
520	Lou Brock	▲10	▲15	▲25	▲40	▲60	▲100	▲150	▲400
521	Don Shaw	5	5	5	5	5	5	10	25
522	Wayne Causey	5	5	5	5	5	5	10	25
523	John Tsitouris	5	5	5	5	5	6	30	60
524	Andy Kosco	5	5	5	5	5	6	12	80
525	Jim Davenport	5	5	5	5	5	5	10	50
526	Bill Denehy	5	5	5	5	5	6	15	80
527	Tito Francona	5	5	5	5	5	5	10	50
528	Detroit Tigers TC	5	6	10	20	50	60	120	300
529	Bruce Von Hoff RC	5	5	5	5	5	6	20	80
530	Bird Belters	5	5	8	30	40	50	120	250
531	Chuck Hinton	5	5	5	5	5	5	10	30
532	Luis Tiant	5	5	5	5	8	12	50	100
533	Wes Parker	5	5	5	5	5	8	25	60
534	Bob Miller	5	5	5	5	5	5	12	40
535	Danny Cater	5	5	5	5	5	5	12	20
536	Bill Short	5	5	5	5	6	8	10	25
537	Norm Siebern	5	5	5	5	5	5	20	30
538	Manny Jimenez	5	5	5	5	5	5	10	30
539	J.Ray RC/M.Ferraro RC	5	5	5	5	5	5	10	50
540	Nelson Briles	5	5	5	5	5	5	25	40
541	Sandy Alomar	5	5	5	5	5	5	12	25
542	John Boccabella	5	5	5	5	5	5	10	25
543	Bob Lee	5	5	5	5	5	5	12	40
544	Mayo Smith MG	5	5	6	10	15	25	40	100

#	Player	GD 2	VG 3	VgEx 4	EX 5	ExMt 6	NM 7	NmMt 8	MT 9
545	Lindy McDaniel	5	5	5	5	5	5	20	40
546	Roy White	5	5	5	8	12	20	40	60
547	Dan Coombs	5	5	5	5	5	5	10	25
548	Bernie Allen	5	5	5	5	5	5	10	25
549	C.Motton RC/R.Nelson RC	5	5	5	5	5	5	10	40
550	Clete Boyer	5	5	5	5	5	6	12	40
551	Darrell Sutherland	5	5	5	5	5	5	10	25
552	Ed Kirkpatrick	5	5	5	5	5	5	10	40
553	Hank Aguirre	5	5	5	5	5	5	10	25
554	Oakland Athletics TC	5	5	5	5	5	8	40	120
555	Jose Tartabull	5	5	5	5	5	5	10	25
556	Dick Selma	5	5	5	5	5	6	30	80
557	Frank Quilici	5	5	5	5	8	12	20	50
558	Johnny Edwards	5	5	5	5	5	5	10	50
559	C.Taylor RC/L.Walker	5	5	5	5	5	6	15	100
560	Paul Casanova	5	5	5	5	5	5	10	40
561	Lee Elia	5	5	5	5	5	5	10	25
562	Jim Bouton	5	5	8	12	20	▲30	▲50	▲120
563	Ed Charles	5	5	5	5	5	6	20	100
564	Eddie Stanky MG	5	5	5	5	5	8	40	150
565	Larry Dierker	5	5	5	5	5	5	15	40
566	Ken Harrelson	5	5	5	8	12	20	30	40
567	Clay Dalrymple	5	5	5	5	5	6	15	60
568	Willie Smith	5	5	5	5	5	5	10	25
569	I.Murrell RC/L.Rohr RC	5	5	5	5	5	5	15	80
570	Rick Reichardt	5	5	5	5	5	5	10	25
571	Tony LaRussa	5	5	5	5	5	8	30	60
572	Don Bosch RC	5	5	5	5	5	5	12	30
573	Joe Coleman	5	5	5	5	5	5	10	25
574	Cincinnati Reds TC	5	5	5	5	5	6	30	80
575	Jim Palmer	▲10	▲15	▲25	▲40	▲60	80	100	▲400
576	Dave Adlesh	5	5	5	5	5	5	10	25
577	Fred Talbot	5	5	5	5	5	5	10	25
578	Orlando Martinez	5	5	5	5	5	5	10	25
579	L.Hisle RC/M.Lum RC	5	5	8	12	20	30	60	150
580	Bob Bailey	5	5	5	5	▲8	▲12	20	50
581	Garry Roggenburk	5	5	5	5	5	5	▼8	25
582	Jerry Grote	5	5	5	▲6	▲10	▲15	▲25	▲80
583	Gates Brown	5	5	8	15	30	80	200	
584	Larry Shepard MG RC	5	5	5	5	5	5	10	30
585	Wilbur Wood	5	5	5	8	12	20	30	
586	Jim Pagliaroni	5	5	5	5	5	5	10	40
587	Roger Repoz	5	5	5	5	5	5	10	25
588	Dick Schofield	5	5	5	5	5	6	12	30
589	R.Clark/M.Ogier RC	5	5	5	5	5	6	15	100
590	Tommy Harper	5	5	5	5	5	5	10	30
591	Dick Nen	5	5	5	5	5	5	10	25
592	John Bateman	5	5	5	5	5	5	10	25
593	Lee Stange	5	5	5	5	5	5	10	25
594	Phil Linz	5	5	5	5	5	5	10	40
595	Phil Ortega	5	5	5	5	5	5	10	40
596	Charlie Smith	5	5	5	5	5	5	10	30
597	Bill McCool	5	5	5	5	5	6	20	50
598	Jerry May	5	5	5	8	12	20	30	100

— Johnny Bench #247 PSA 10 (Gem) (Young Collection) sold for $8,711 (SCP; 5/12)

— Rod Carew #80 PSA 10 (Gem) sold for $2,607 (eBay; 02/12)

— Nolan Ryan #177 PSA 10 (Gem) sold for $612,360 (Heritage; 8/27)

1968 Topps 3-D

— Roberto Clemente PSA 10 (Gem) sold for $30,000 (REA; 05/12)

— Roberto Clemente SGC 96 (MT) sold for $15,569 (SCP; 5/12)

— Roberto Clemente PSA 9 (MT) sold for $25,000 (REA; 05/12)

— Roberto Clemente #1 PSA 6 (ExMt) sold for $8,000 (Legendary; 5/12)

1968 Topps Game

#	Player	GD 2	VG 3	VgEx 4	EX 5	ExMt 6	NM 7	NmMt 8	MT 9
1	Matty Alou	5	5	5	5	6	10	50	
2	Mickey Mantle	▲40	60	▲100	▲150	▲250	▲300	▲500	▲1,000
3	Carl Yastrzemski	5	6	10	15	30	50	80	300
4	Hank Aaron	▲12	▲20	▲30	▲50	▲80	▲120	▲150	▲500
5	Harmon Killebrew	5	5	8	12	20	25	50	150
6	Roberto Clemente	8	12	20	40	60	100	250	400
7	Frank Robinson	5	▲8	▲12	▲20	30	▲50	▲80	▲150
8	Willie Mays	▲10	▲15	▲25	40	▲60	▲100	▲120	400
9	Brooks Robinson	5	5	8	12	20	25	▲80	▲200
10	Tommy Davis	5	5	5	5	5	6	15	50
11	Bill Freehan	5	5	5	5	5	8	20	60
12	Claude Osteen	5	5	5	5	5	6	20	120
13	Gary Peters	5	5	5	5	5	6	15	60
14	Jim Lonborg	5	5	5	5	5	6	15	80
15	Steve Hargan	5	5	5	5	5	6	15	60
16	Dean Chance	5	5	5	5	5	6	15	50
17	Mike McCormick	5	5	5	5	5	6	15	50
18	Tim McCarver	5	5	5	5	5	6	15	50
19	Ron Santo	5	5	5	5	5	8	20	80
20	Tony Gonzalez	5	5	5	5	5	6	15	100
21	Frank Howard	5	5	5	5	5	8	20	100
22	George Scott	5	5	5	5	5	6	30	200
23	Richie Allen	5	5	5	5	5	6	15	100
24	Jim Wynn	5	5	5	5	5	6	25	80
25	Gene Alley	5	5	5	5	5	6	15	80
26	Rick Monday	5	5	5	5	5	8	25	120
27	Al Kaline	5	5	6	10	15	30	30	▲250
28	Rusty Staub	5	5	5	5	5	6	25	60
29	Rod Carew	5	5	6	10	15	20	30	200
30	Pete Rose	8	12	20	30	50	60	100	200
31	Joe Torre	5	5	5	5	5	6	20	80
32	Orlando Cepeda	5	5	5	5	5	8	20	120
33	Jim Fregosi	5	5	5	5	6	10	40	300

1969 Topps

#	Player	GD 2	VG 3	VgEx 4	EX 5	ExMt 6	NM 7	NmMt 8	MT 9
1	AL Batting Leaders	5	5	6	10	25	30	80	150
2	NL Batting Leaders	5	5	5	8	20	40	120	250
3	AL RBI Leaders	5	5	5	5	5	8	20	30
4	NL RBI Leaders	5	5	5	5	5	8	15	80
5	AL Home Run Leaders	5	5	5	5	5	8	25	60
6	NL Home Run Leaders	5	5	5	5	6	15	60	100
7	AL ERA Leaders	5	5	5	5	5	6	12	25
8	NL ERA Leaders	5	5	5	6	10	20	120	
9	AL Pitching Leaders	5	5	5	5	5	6	25	60
10	NL Pitching Leaders	5	5	5	5	5	8	25	50
11	AL Strikeout Leaders	5	5	5	5	5	6	12	30
12	NL Strikeout Leaders	5	5	5	5	6	10	25	50
13	Mickey Stanley	5	5	5	5	6	10	25	50
14	Al McBean	5	5	5	5	5	5	10	25
15	Boog Powell	5	5	5	6	10	15	25	60
16	C.Gutierrez RC/R.Robertson RC	5	5	5	5	5	5	25	40
17	Mike Marshall	5	5	5	5	5	6	12	25
18	Dick Schofield	5	5	5	5	5	5	10	25
19	Ken Suarez	5	5	5	5	5	6	12	30
20	Ernie Banks	▲12	▲20	▲30	▲50	▲80	▲100	▲250	▲500
21	Jose Santiago	5	5	5	5	5	8	20	150
22	Jesus Alou	5	5	5	5	5	6	12	30
23	Lew Krausse	5	5	5	5	5	5	20	40
24	Walt Alston MG	5	5	5	5	5	8	20	40
25	Roy White	5	5	5	5	6	15	40	150
26	Clay Carroll	5	5	5	5	5	5	10	25
27	Bernie Allen	5	5	5	5	5	5	10	25
28	Mike Ryan	5	5	5	5	5	8	15	25
29	Dave Morehead	5	5	5	5	5	5	10	25
30	Bob Allison	5	5	5	5	5	8	15	30
31	G.Gentry RC/A.Otis RC	5	5	5	5	5	8	20	40
32	Sammy Ellis	5	5	5	5	5	8	15	60
33	Wayne Causey	5	5	5	5	5	8	15	25
34	Gary Peters	5	5	5	5	5	8	15	80
35	Joe Morgan	▲8	▲12	▲20	▲30	▲50	▲80	▲120	250
36	Luke Walker	5	5	5	5	5	8	15	25
37	Curt Motton	5	5	5	5	5	8	15	50
38	Zoilo Versalles	5	5	5	5	5	8	15	30
39	Dick Hughes	5	5	5	5	5	5	10	25
40	Mayo Smith MG	5	5	5	6	10	15	25	100
41	Bob Barton	5	5	5	5	5	5	12	40
42	Tommy Harper	5	5	5	5	5	5	10	30
43	Joe Niekro	5	5	5	5	8	20	40	
44	Danny Cater	5	5	5	5	5	5	15	30
45	Maury Wills	5	5	5	5	5	6	15	30
46	Fritz Peterson	5	5	5	5	8	15	40	
47A	Paul Popovich No C Thick Airbrush	5	5	5	5	5	5	10	25
47B	Paul Popovich No C Light Airbrush	5	5	5	5	5	5	10	25
47C	Paul Popovich C on Helmet	5	5	5	6	10	15	25	
48	Brant Alyea	5	5	5	5	5	8	20	120
49A	S.Jones/E.Rodriguez ERR	5	5	5	6	10	30	40	
49B	S.Jones RC/E.Rodriguez RC	5	5	5	5	5	5	10	25
50	Roberto Clemente	▲60	▲80	▲100	▲120	150	250	▲800	2,000
51	Woody Fryman	5	5	5	5	5	5	10	25
52	Mike Andrews	5	5	5	5	6	15	60	
53	Sonny Jackson	5	5	5	5	5	5	10	25
54	Cisco Carlos	5	5	5	5	5	5	60	175
55	Jerry Grote	5	5	5	5	5	8	15	30
56	Rich Reese	5	5	5	5	5	8	40	60
57	Checklist 1/McLain	5	5	5	5	5	8	15	30
58	Fred Gladding	5	5	5	5	5	5	10	25
59	Jay Johnstone	5	5	5	5	5	6	15	80
60	Nelson Briles	5	5	5	5	6	15	25	200
61	Jimmie Hall	5	5	5	5	5	5	10	30
62	Chico Salmon	5	5	5	5	5	5	10	25
63	Jim Hickman	5	5	5	5	6	25	40	150
64	Bill Monbouquette	5	5	5	5	5	5	10	25
65	Willie Davis	5	5	5	5	5	8	15	120
66	M.Adamson RC/M.Rettenmund RC	5	5	5	5	5	5	10	50
67	Bill Stoneman	5	5	5	5	5	5	12	60
68	Dave Duncan	5	5	5	5	8	20	200	
69	Steve Hamilton	5	5	5	5	8	30	300	
70	Tommy Helms	5	5	5	5	6	10	50	120
71	Steve Whitaker	5	5	5	5	5	8	40	100
72	Ron Taylor	5	5	5	5	6	10	40	200
73	Johnny Briggs	5	5	5	5	5	5	10	25
74	Preston Gomez MG	5	5	5	5	5	5	10	25
75	Luis Aparicio	5	5	5	5	5	12	30	50
76	Norm Miller	5	5	5	5	5	5	10	80
77A	Ron Perranoski No LA on Cap	5	5	5	5	5	8	20	50
77B	Ron Perranoski LA on Cap	5	5	5	6	10	15	25	150
78	Tom Satriano	5	5	5	5	5	20	80	
79	Milt Pappas	5	5	5	5	5	5	12	25
80	Norm Cash	5	5	5	8	12	20	25	120
81	Mel Queen	5	5	5	5	5	5	12	25
82	R.Hebner RC/A.Oliver RC	5	5	5	5	8	50	80	250
83	Mike Ferraro	5	5	5	5	6	15	100	
84	Bob Humphreys	5	5	5	5	5	5	10	25
85	Lou Brock	6	10	12	25	40	100	800	
86	Pete Richert	5	5	5	5	5	5	15	50
87	Horace Clarke	5	5	5	5	5	10	30	200
88	Rich Nye	5	5	5	5	5	5	10	25
89	Russ Gibson	5	5	5	5	5	5	10	30
90	Jerry Koosman	5	5	5	5	8	15	40	200

#	Player	GD 2	VG 3	VgEx 4	EX 5	ExMt 6	NM 7	NmMt 8	MT 9
91	Alvin Dark MG	5	5	5	5	5	5	10	25
92	Jack Billingham	5	5	5	5	5	5	12	30
93	Joe Foy	5	5	5	5	5	6	40	
94	Hank Aguirre	5	5	5	5	5	5	15	40
95	Johnny Bench	40	60	80	120	150	250	500	2,000
96	Denny Lemaster	5	5	5	5	5	5	10	30
97	Buddy Bradford	5	5	5	5	5	5	12	40
98	Dave Giusti	5	5	5	5	5	5	12	60
99A	D.Morris RC G.Nettles RC No Loop	5	5	5	8	12	20	200	
99B	D.Morris/G.Nettles Black Loop	5	5	5	8	12	20	60	
100	Hank Aaron	▲50	▲80	▲100	▲150	▲250	300	600	3,000
101	Daryl Patterson	5	5	5	5	5	12	50	
102	Jim Davenport	5	5	5	5	6	15	150	
103	Roger Repoz	5	5	5	5	5	5	10	30
104	Steve Blass	5	5	5	5	6	15	50	
105	Rick Monday	5	5	5	5	5	8	50	
106	Jim Hannan	5	5	5	5	5	5	25	50
107A	Checklist 2 Gibson ERR 161 is Jim	5	5	5	5	5	6	20	40
107B	Checklist 2 Gibson COR 161 is John	5	5	5	5	5	6	20	50
108	Tony Taylor	5	5	5	5	5	8	30	135
109	Jim Lonborg	5	5	5	5	6	10	25	60
110	Mike Shannon	5	5	5	6	15	30	150	
111	John Morris RC	5	5	5	5	5	6	15	80
112	J.C. Martin	5	5	5	5	6	10	25	50
113	Dave May	5	5	5	5	5	5	12	50
114	A.Closter/J.Cumberland RC	5	5	5	5	5	6	25	100
115	Bill Hands	5	5	5	5	5	6	25	120
116	Chuck Harrison	5	5	5	5	8	12	40	60
117	Jim Fairey	5	5	5	5	5	5	15	30
118	Stan Williams	5	5	5	5	5	5	10	25
119	Doug Rader	5	5	5	5	5	5	10	40
120	Pete Rose	15	25	40	50	60	100	200	1,000
121	Joe Grzenda RC	5	5	5	5	5	8	25	
122	Ron Fairly	5	5	5	5	5	6	12	40
123	Wilbur Wood	5	5	5	5	5	5	10	25
124	Hank Bauer MG	5	5	5	5	5	5	10	40
125	Ray Sadecki	5	5	5	5	5	5	10	30
126	Dick Tracewski	5	5	5	5	5	6	15	50
127	Kevin Collins	5	5	5	5	6	15	50	200
128	Tommie Aaron	5	5	5	5	5	5	10	30
129	Bill McCool	5	5	5	5	5	5	10	40
130	Carl Yastrzemski	5	10	20	25	50	80	250	2,000
131	Chris Cannizzaro	5	5	5	5	5	6	20	80
132	Dave Baldwin	5	5	5	5	5	5	15	40
133	Johnny Callison	5	5	5	5	6	15	60	150
134	Jim Weaver	5	5	5	5	5	5	10	40
135	Tommy Davis	5	5	5	5	5	8	20	60
136	S.Huntz RC/M.Torrez	5	5	5	5	5	6	15	50
137	Wally Bunker	5	5	5	5	5	6	15	30
138	John Bateman	5	5	5	5	5	6	15	80
139	Andy Kosco	5	5	5	5	5	6	20	
140	Jim Lefebvre	5	5	5	5	5	6	12	50
141	Bill Dillman	5	5	5	5	8	12	30	135
142	Woody Woodward	5	5	5	5	5	5	10	25
143	Joe Nossek	5	5	5	5	5	6	20	
144	Bob Hendley	5	5	5	5	6	10	60	100
145	Max Alvis	5	5	5	5	5	8	25	60
146	Jim Perry	5	5	5	5	5	8	25	60
147	Leo Durocher MG	5	5	5	5	5	6	20	60
148	Lee Stange	5	5	5	5	5	5	15	40
149	Ollie Brown	5	5	5	5	5	5	10	25
150	Denny McLain	5	5	5	5	8	25	50	300
151A	Clay Dalrymple Orioles	5	5	5	▲8	▲12	▲20	▲30	▲80
151B	Clay Dalrymple Phillies	5	5	5	6	10	15	60	
152	Tommie Sisk	5	5	5	5	5	8	30	80
153	Ed Brinkman	5	5	5	5	5	6	25	60
154	Jim Britton	5	5	5	5	5	5	10	40
155	Pete Ward	5	5	5	5	5	5	30	60
156	H.Gilson/L.McFadden RC	5	5	5	5	5	6	15	25
157	Bob Rodgers	5	5	5	5	5	6	25	80
158	Joe Gibbon	5	5	5	5	5	5	10	50
159	Jerry Adair	5	5	5	5	5	5	15	40
160	Vada Pinson	5	5	5	5	5	6	15	60
161	John Purdin	5	5	5	5	5	5	20	60
162	Bob Gibson WS1	5	5	5	5	10	20	80	300
163	Willie Horton WS2	5	5	5	5	5	6	30	50
164	T.McCarver w/Maris WS3	5	5	5	5	5	8	20	50
165	Lou Brock WS4	5	5	5	5	6	10	40	100
166	Al Kaline WS5	5	5	5	10	15	30	80	400
167	Jim Northrup WS6	5	5	5	5	5	8	15	60
168	M.Lolich/B.Gibson WS7	5	5	5	6	10	15	30	100
169	Tigers Celebrate WS	5	5	5	5	6	15	40	150
170	Frank Howard	5	5	5	5	5	6	15	60
171	Glenn Beckert	5	5	5	5	8	12	20	200
172	Jerry Stephenson	5	5	5	5	5	5	15	50
1/3	B.Christian RC/G.Nyman RC	5	5	5	5	5	5	15	60
174	Grant Jackson	5	5	5	5	5	5	15	40
175	Jim Bunning	5	5	5	5	6	10	25	100
176	Joe Azcue	5	5	5	5	5	5	10	80
177	Ron Reed	5	5	5	5	5	5	10	40
178	Ray Oyler	5	5	5	5	6	15	30	
179	Don Pavletich	5	5	5	5	5	5	10	25
180	Willie Horton	5	5	5	5	8	12	40	300
181	Mel Nelson	5	5	5	5	5	8	20	60
182	Bill Rigney MG	5	5	5	5	5	8	40	150
183	Don Shaw	5	5	5	5	5	5	15	50
184	Roberto Pena	5	5	5	5	5	5	12	50
185	Tom Phoebus	5	5	5	5	5	8	25	60
186	Johnny Edwards	5	5	5	5	5	5	15	80
187	Leon Wagner	5	5	5	5	5	6	15	150
188	Rick Wise	5	5	5	5	5	5	10	60
189	J.Lahoud RC/J.Thibodeau RC	5	5	5	5	5	6	15	80
190	Willie Mays	▲60	▲100	▲150	▲250	▲400	▲600	▲800	▲4,000
191	Lindy McDaniel	5	5	5	5	8	25	250	
192	Jose Pagan	5	5	5	5	8	25	50	
193	Don Cardwell	5	5	5	5	5	8	15	80
194	Ted Uhlaender	5	5	5	5	5	5	15	50
195	John Odom	5	5	5	5	5	5	12	25
196	Lum Harris MG	5	5	5	5	5	5	12	40
197	Dick Selma	5	5	5	5	5	5	15	40
198	Willie Smith	5	5	5	5	5	8	20	100
199	Jim French	5	5	5	5	5	5	15	40
200	Bob Gibson	5	5	20	30	60	80	250	800
201	Russ Snyder	5	5	5	5	5	8	20	80
202	Don Wilson	5	5	5	5	5	5	20	50
203	Dave Johnson	5	5	5	5	5	6	12	40
204	Jack Hiatt	5	5	5	5	5	6	15	80
205	Rick Reichardt	5	5	5	5	5	6	20	60
206	L.Hisle/B.Lersch RC	5	5	5	5	5	5	12	25
207	Roy Face	5	5	5	5	6	15	30	150
208A	Donn Clendenon Houston	5	5	5	5	5	5	40	150
208B	Donn Clendenon Expos	5	5	6	10	15	40	100	400
209	Larry Haney	5	5	5	5	5	6	15	60
210	Felix Millan	5	5	5	5	5	5	25	100
211	Galen Cisco	5	5	5	5	5	6	20	200
212	Tom Tresh	5	5	5	6	10	15	40	200
213	Gerry Arrigo	5	5	5	5	5	5	15	60
214	Checklist 3	5	5	5	5	5	8	20	60
215	Rico Petrocelli	5	5	5	5	8	12	30	200
216	Don Sutton DP	5	5	5	6	10	15	50	175
217	John Donaldson	5	5	5	5	5	8	20	150
218	John Roseboro	5	5	5	5	5	8	20	40
219	Fred Patek RC	5	5	5	5	5	6	15	60

	GD 2	VG 3	VgEx 4	EX 5	ExMt 6	NM 7	NmMt 8	MT 9
Sam McDowell	5	5	5	5	6	15	80	200
Art Shamsky	5	5	5	5	6	15	60	300
Duane Josephson	5	5	5	5	5	6	15	60
Tom Dukes	5	5	5	5	5	6	15	50
B.Harrelson RC/S.Kealey RC	5	5	5	5	5	5	10	30
Don Kessinger	5	5	5	5	6	15	40	
Bruce Howard	5	5	5	5	5	8	30	80
Frank Johnson RC	5	5	5	5	5	5	10	50
Dave Leonhard	5	5	5	5	5	6	12	25
Don Lock	5	5	5	5	5	8	30	100
Rusty Staub	5	5	5	5	5	6	15	175
Pat Dobson	5	5	5	5	5	8	30	120
Dave Ricketts	5	5	5	5	6	15	30	150
Steve Barber	5	5	5	5	5	12	30	80
Dave Bristol MG	5	5	5	5	5	6	15	60
Jim Hunter	5	5	5	8	15	30	60	
Manny Mota	5	5	5	5	5	8	40	
Bobby Cox RC	15	25	40	60	100	150	200	500
Ken Johnson	5	5	5	5	5	5	25	100
Bob Taylor	5	5	5	5	5	8	60	200
Ken Harrelson	5	5	5	5	6	10	50	150
Jim Brewer	5	5	5	5	5	5	12	40
Frank Kostro	5	5	5	5	5	5	10	60
Ron Kline	5	5	5	5	6	15	25	
R.Fosse RC/G.Woodson RC	5	5	5	5	5	8	25	100
Ed Charles	5	5	5	5	8	25	60	
Joe Coleman	5	5	5	5	5	6	20	50
Gene Oliver	5	5	5	5	5	6	15	60
Bob Priddy	5	5	5	5	8	12	40	
Ed Spiezio	5	5	5	5	5	6	15	80
Frank Robinson	▲12	▲20	▲30	▲50	▲80	▲120	250	1,000
Ron Herbel	5	5	5	5	5	5	10	30
Chuck Cottier	5	5	5	5	5	8	20	80
Jerry Johnson RC	5	5	5	5	5	5	10	40
Joe Schultz MG RC	5	5	5	5	6	15	40	80
Steve Carlton	10	15	▲25	▲40	▲60	▲100	▲200	500
Gates Brown	5	5	5	6	10	15	60	120
Jim Ray	5	5	5	5	5	5	10	40
Jackie Hernandez	5	5	5	5	5	6	30	
Bill Short	5	5	5	5	5	6	20	100
Reggie Jackson RC	150	200	300	400	600	▲1,500	▲5,000	▲80,000
Bob Johnson	5	5	5	5	5	5	10	25
Mike Kekich	5	5	5	5	8	40	150	
Jerry May	5	5	5	5	5	8	30	100
Bill Landis	5	5	5	5	5	5	10	40
Chico Cardenas	5	5	5	5	6	25	50	
T.Hutton/A.Foster RC	5	5	5	5	5	12	40	
Vicente Romo RC	5	5	5	5	6	10	40	150
Al Spangler	5	5	5	5	6	15	30	60
Al Weis	5	5	5	5	8	30	60	200
Mickey Lolich	5	5	5	6	10	25	60	300
Larry Stahl	5	5	5	5	5	8	20	80
Ed Stroud	5	5	5	5	5	5	10	25
Ron Willis	5	5	5	5	6	15	100	250
Clyde King MG	5	5	5	5	5	5	25	60
Vic Davalillo	5	5	5	5	5	8	30	60
Gary Wagner	5	5	5	5	5	5	15	40
Rod Hendricks RC	5	5	5	5	6	10	30	100
Gary Geiger	5	5	5	5	5	5	20	120
Roger Nelson	5	5	5	5	5	6	12	50
Alex Johnson	5	5	5	5	5	6	15	80
Ted Kubiak	5	5	5	5	5	6	15	80
Pat Jarvis	5	5	5	5	5	8	25	120
Sandy Alomar	5	5	5	5	5	8	25	80
J.Robertson RC/M.Wegener RC	5	5	5	5	5	5	12	50
Don Mincher	5	5	5	5	5	6	20	
Dock Ellis RC	5	5	5	5	8	12	100	200
Jose Tartabull	5	5	5	5	5	8	25	

	GD 2	VG 3	VgEx 4	EX 5	ExMt 6	NM 7	NmMt 8	MT 9
288 Ken Holtzman	5	5	5	5	8	20	80	
289 Bart Shirley	5	5	5	5	5	5	20	100
290 Jim Kaat	5	5	5	5	6	10	60	200
291 Vern Fuller	5	5	5	5	5	8	30	120
292 Al Downing	5	5	5	5	6	15	40	120
293 Dick Dietz	5	5	5	5	5	6	15	50
294 Jim Lemon MG	5	5	5	5	5	12	50	
295 Tony Perez	▲6	▲10	▲15	▲25	▲40	▲60	100	400
296 Andy Messersmith RC	5	5	5	5	5	6	25	120
297 Deron Johnson	5	5	5	5	5	5	30	100
298 Dave Nicholson	5	5	5	5	5	5	15	60
299 Mark Belanger	5	5	5	5	5	6	10	30
300 Felipe Alou	5	5	5	5	8	15	60	
301 Darrell Brandon	5	5	5	5	5	5	10	30
302 Jim Pagliaroni	5	5	5	5	5	5	8	30	120
303 Cal Koonce	5	5	5	5	5	6	15	100
304 B.Davis/C.Gaston RC	5	5	5	5	5	6	12	30
305 Dick McAuliffe	5	5	5	5	6	10	30	
306 Jim Grant	5	5	5	5	5	6	15	80
307 Gary Kolb	5	5	5	5	5	5	20	80
308 Wade Blasingame	5	5	5	5	5	5	20	
309 Walt Williams	5	5	5	5	5	5	10	30
310 Tom Haller	5	5	5	5	5	5	10	50
311 Sparky Lyle RC	5	5	5	5	5	8	50	▲200
312 Lee Elia	5	5	5	5	6	15	25	
313 Bill Robinson	5	5	5	5	8	25	80	
314 Checklist 4/Drysdale	5	5	5	5	8	12	30	150
315 Eddie Fisher	5	5	5	5	5	8	30	100
316 Hal Lanier	5	5	5	5	5	6	15	60
317 Bruce Look RC	5	5	5	5	5	5	12	50
318 Jack Fisher	5	5	5	5	5	5	10	30
319 Ken McMullen	5	5	5	5	5	5	10	50
320 Dal Maxvill	5	5	5	5	5	6	15	80
321 Jim McAndrew RC	5	5	5	5	5	5	25	80
322 Jose Vidal	5	5	5	5	5	5	10	25
323 Larry Miller	5	5	5	5	5	5	10	40
324 L.Cain RC/D.Campbell RC	5	5	5	5	5	6	12	40
325 Jose Cardenal	5	5	5	5	5	6	12	40
326 Gary Sutherland	5	5	5	5	5	5	40	100
327 Willie Crawford	5	5	5	5	5	5	10	25
328 Joel Horlen	5	5	5	5	5	8	30	120
329 Rick Joseph	5	5	5	5	5	5	10	25
330 Tony Conigliaro	5	5	5	5	8	12	30	120
331 G.Garrido/T.House RC	5	5	5	5	5	5	10	40
332 Fred Talbot	5	5	5	5	5	5	15	50
333 Ivan Murrell	5	5	5	5	5	5	10	40
334 Phil Roof	5	5	5	5	5	5	15	50
335 Bill Mazeroski	5	5	5	8	12	20	60	150
336 Jim Roland	5	5	5	5	5	6	15	80
337 Marty Martinez RC	5	5	5	5	5	5	10	25
338 Del Unser RC	5	5	5	5	5	5	15	50
339 S.Mingori RC/J.Pena RC	5	5	5	5	5	5	10	25
340 Dave McNally	5	5	5	5	5	8	20	100
341 Dave Adlesh	5	5	5	5	5	5	15	40
342 Bubba Morton	5	5	5	5	5	5	25	120
343 Dan Frisella	5	5	5	5	5	8	20	60
344 Tom Matchick	5	5	5	5	5	5	10	40
345 Frank Linzy	5	5	5	5	5	5	10	60
346 Wayne Comer RC	5	5	5	5	5	6	20	50
347 Randy Hundley	5	5	5	5	5	8	25	50
348 Steve Hargan	5	5	5	5	5	5	10	25
349 Dick Williams MG	5	5	5	5	5	5	15	60
350 Richie Allen	5	5	5	5	5	8	25	200
351 Carroll Sembera	5	5	5	5	5	5	10	30
352 Paul Schaal	5	5	5	5	5	5	10	25
353 Jeff Torborg	5	5	5	5	5	5	12	60
354 Nate Oliver	5	5	5	5	5	5	10	30
355 Phil Niekro	5	5	5	5	25	40	50	150

#	Player	GD 2	VG 3	VgEx 4	EX 5	ExMt 6	NM 7	NmMt 8	MT 9
356	Frank Quilici	5	5	5	5	5	6	15	60
357	Carl Taylor	5	5	5	5	5	6	15	60
358	G.Lauzerique RC/R.Rodriguez	5	5	5	5	5	5	10	25
359	Dick Kelley	5	5	5	5	5	5	15	60
360	Jim Wynn	5	5	5	5	5	6	12	30
361	Gary Holman RC	5	5	5	5	5	5	10	25
362	Jim Maloney	5	5	5	5	5	5	15	40
363	Russ Nixon	5	5	5	5	5	5	10	25
364	Tommie Agee	5	5	5	5	6	10	20	150
365	Jim Fregosi	5	5	5	5	5	6	15	40
366	Bo Belinsky	5	5	5	5	5	5	15	25
367	Lou Johnson	5	5	5	5	5	6	20	40
368	Vic Roznovsky	5	5	5	5	5	5	10	30
369	Bob Skinner MG	5	5	5	5	5	5	12	40
370	Juan Marichal	5	5	5	6	12	40	50	400
371	Sal Bando	5	5	5	5	5	8	20	80
372	Adolfo Phillips	5	5	5	5	5	8	25	
373	Fred Lasher	5	5	5	5	5	5	12	40
374	Bob Tillman	5	5	5	5	5	5	10	40
375	Harmon Killebrew	10	15	25	40	60	100	120	500
376	M.Fiore RC/J.Rooker RC	5	5	5	5	5	5	15	40
377	Gary Bell	5	5	5	5	5	5	15	50
378	Jose Herrera RC	5	5	5	5	5	5	10	30
379	Ken Boyer	5	5	5	5	5	8	15	40
380	Stan Bahnsen	5	5	5	5	8	20	30	120
381	Ed Kranepool	5	5	5	8	12	30	100	300
382	Pat Corrales	5	5	5	5	5	6	15	40
383	Casey Cox	5	5	5	5	5	5	15	40
384	Larry Shepard MG	5	5	5	5	5	5	20	30
385	Orlando Cepeda	5	5	5	5	8	15	30	100
386	Jim McGlothlin	5	5	5	5	5	5	12	80
387	Bobby Klaus	5	5	5	5	5	5	10	60
388	Tom McCraw	5	5	5	5	5	5	25	60
389	Dan Coombs	5	5	5	5	5	5	25	60
390	Bill Freehan	5	5	5	6	10	25	50	150
391	Ray Culp	5	5	5	5	5	8	20	80
392	Bob Burda RC	5	5	5	5	5	6	15	60
393	Gene Brabender	5	5	5	5	5	6	15	40
394	L.Piniella/M.Staehle	5	5	5	5	8	12	40	
395	Chris Short	5	5	5	5	5	6	15	50
396	Jim Campanis	5	5	5	5	5	5	10	40
397	Chuck Dobson	5	5	5	5	5	6	15	60
398	Tito Francona	5	5	5	5	6	25	100	
399	Bob Bailey	5	5	5	5	5	5	15	40
400	Don Drysdale	▲8	▲12	▲20	▲30	▲50	▲80	▲120	▲400
401	Jake Gibbs	5	5	5	5	5	6	15	40
402	Ken Boswell RC	5	5	5	8	12	20	50	120
403	Bob Miller	5	5	5	5	5	5	12	40
404	V.LaRose RC/G.Ross RC	5	5	5	5	5	5	20	80
405	Lee May	5	5	5	5	5	6	30	100
406	Phil Ortega	5	5	5	5	5	5	10	40
407	Tom Egan	5	5	5	5	5	5	10	60
408	Nate Colbert	5	5	5	5	5	5	10	40
409	Bob Moose	5	5	5	5	5	6	15	40
410	Al Kaline	▲8	12	▲20	▲30	▲50	▲80	▲120	
411	Larry Dierker	5	5	5	5	5	5	10	50
412	Checklist 5/Mantle DP	▲8	▲12	20	▲30	▲50	▲80	▲120	▲300
413	Roland Sheldon	5	5	5	5	5	6	15	50
414	Duke Sims	5	5	5	5	5	5	10	40
415	Ray Washburn	5	5	5	5	5	6	20	125
416	Willie McCovey AS	5	5	5	5	8	15	60	300
417	Ken Harrelson AS	5	5	5	5	5	6	20	
418	Tommy Helms AS	5	5	5	5	5	6	25	100
419	Rod Carew AS	5	5	5	6	15	20	50	200
420	Ron Santo AS	5	5	5	5	5	8	20	60
421	Brooks Robinson AS	5	5	5	6	10	15	40	150
422	Don Kessinger AS	5	5	5	5	5	6	20	
423	Bert Campaneris AS	5	5	5	5	5	6	25	80

#	Player	GD 2	VG 3	VgEx 4	EX 5	ExMt 6	NM 7	NmMt 8	MT 9
424	Pete Rose AS	▼5	▼6	▼10	15	25	▲60	100	250
425	Carl Yastrzemski AS	5	▲6	▲10	▲15	25	▲40	▲60	350
426	Curt Flood AS	5	5	5	5	8	25	100	300
427	Tony Oliva AS	5	5	5	5	5	8	50	175
428	Lou Brock AS	5	5	5	6	10	25	40	
429	Willie Horton AS	5	5	5	5	6	15	25	150
430	Johnny Bench AS	5	5	6	25	50	60	100	400
431	Bill Freehan AS	5	5	5	5	8	20	60	200
432	Bob Gibson AS	5	5	5	6	15	20	60	350
433	Denny McLain AS	5	5	5	5	6	15	50	150
434	Jerry Koosman AS	5	5	5	5	6	15	40	150
435	Sam McDowell AS	5	5	5	5	6	30		80
436	Gene Alley	5	5	5	5	5	6	15	100
437	Luis Alcaraz RC	5	5	5	5	5	6	15	80
438	Gary Waslewski RC	5	5	5	5	5	6	15	40
439	E.Herrmann RC/D.Lazar RC	5	5	5	5	5	5	12	50
440A	Willie McCovey	5	5	6	10	15	25	120	
440B	Willie McCovey WL	12	20	30	40	60	150	500	
441A	Dennis Higgins	5	5	5	5	5	5	15	30
441B	Dennis Higgins WL	5	8	12	20	30	80	200	
442	Ty Cline	5	5	5	5	5	5	15	40
443	Don Wert	5	5	5	5	12	20	30	
444A	Joe Moeller	5	5	5	5	5	5	15	30
444B	Joe Moeller WL	5	8	12	20	30	60		
445	Bobby Knoop	5	5	5	5	5	5	15	50
446	Claude Raymond	5	5	5	5	5	6	15	80
447A	Ralph Houk MG	5	5	5	5	5	6	25	100
447B	Ralph Houk MG WL	6	10	15	25	40	80	250	
448	Bob Tolan	5	5	5	5	5	6	15	
449	Paul Lindblad	5	5	5	5	5	8	20	80
450	Billy Williams	▲6	▲10	▲15	▲25	▲40	▲60	150	
451A	Rich Rollins	5	5	5	5	6	15	100	
451B	Rich Rollins WL	5	8	12	20	30	60		
452A	Al Ferrara	5	5	5	5	5	5	15	80
452B	Al Ferrara WL	5	8	12	20	30	80	200	
453	Mike Cuellar	5	5	5	5	6	10	25	150
454A	L.Colton/D.Money RC	5	5	5	5	5	5	15	30
454B	L.Colton/D.Money WL	5	8	12	20	30	150	350	
455	Sonny Siebert	5	5	5	5	5	6	15	60
456	Bud Harrelson	5	5	5	5	8	20	80	
457	Dalton Jones	5	5	5	5	5	6	15	60
458	Curt Blefary	5	5	5	5	5	6	20	
459	Dave Boswell	5	5	5	5	5	5	30	80
460	Joe Torre	5	5	5	5	8	12	30	
461A	Mike Epstein	5	5	5	5	5	5	20	
461B	Mike Epstein WL	5	8	12	20	30	100	200	
462	Red Schoendienst MG	5	5	5	5	6	15	50	
463	Dennis Ribant	5	5	5	5	5	5	10	50
464A	Dave Marshall RC	5	5	5	5	5	5	25	
464B	Dave Marshall WL	5	8	12	20	30	120		
465	Tommy John	5	5	5	5	8	12	30	150
466	John Boccabella	5	5	5	6	10	15	60	150
467	Tommie Reynolds	5	5	5	5	5	6	20	150
468A	B.Dal Canton RC/B.Robertson	5	5	5	5	5	5	15	30
468B	B.Dal Canton/B.Robertson WL	5	8	12	20	30	60	200	
469	Chico Ruiz	5	5	5	5	5	8	60	100
470A	Mel Stottlemyre	5	5	5	5	8	12	25	200
470B	Mel Stottlemyre WL	6	10	15	25	40	80	250	
471A	Ted Savage	5	5	5	5	5	5	12	50
471B	Ted Savage WL	5	8	12	20	30	60	200	
472	Jim Price	5	5	5	5	5	5	25	120
473A	Jose Arcia	5	5	5	5	5	5	15	30
473B	Jose Arcia WL	5	8	12	20	50	60	200	
474	Tom Murphy RC	5	5	5	5	5	6	15	100
475	Tim McCarver	5	5	5	5	6	15	50	200
476A	K.Brett RC/G.Moses	5	5	5	5	5	12	40	
476B	K.Brett/G.Moses WL	5	8	12	20	30	60		
477	Jeff James RC	5	5	5	5	5	5	15	100

#	Player	GD 2	VG 3	VgEx 4	EX 5	ExMt 6	NM 7	NmMt 8	MT 9
478	Don Buford	5	5	5	5	5	6	15	100
479	Richie Scheinblum	5	5	5	5	5	5	20	60
480	Tom Seaver	▲20	30	50	▲80	▲120	250	600	
481	Bill Melton RC	5	5	5	5	5	6	15	50
482A	Jim Gosger	5	5	5	5	5	5	15	50
482B	Jim Gosger WL	5	8	12	20	30	100	200	
483	Ted Abernathy	5	5	5	5	6	20	150	
484	Joe Gordon MG	5	5	5	5	5	6	20	100
485A	Gaylord Perry	5	5	5	5	8	12	40	300
485B	Gaylord Perry WL	6	10	15	25	40	150	300	
486A	Paul Casanova	5	5	5	5	5	5	15	50
486B	Paul Casanova WL	5	8	12	20	30	100		
487	Denis Menke	5	5	5	5	5	6	25	
488	Joe Sparma	5	5	5	5	5	8	25	80
489	Clete Boyer	5	5	5	5	6	15	50	
490	Matty Alou	5	5	5	5	5	6	20	100
491A	J.Crider RC/G.Mitterwald	5	5	5	5	5	5	15	50
491B	J.Crider/G.Mitterwald WL	5	8	12	20	30	60	250	
492	Tony Cloninger	5	5	5	5	5	5	15	60
493A	Wes Parker	5	5	5	5	5	8	15	80
493B	Wes Parker WL	8	12	20	30	50	100	400	
494	Ken Berry	5	5	5	5	5	8	40	100
495	Bert Campaneris	5	5	5	5	6	10	40	120
496	Larry Jaster	5	5	5	5	5	6	15	100
497	Julian Javier	5	5	5	5	5	6	15	80
498	Juan Pizarro	5	5	5	5	5	5	15	50
499	D.Bryant RC/S.Shea RC	5	5	5	5	5	6	12	25
500A	Mickey Mantle	▲100	▲150	▲250	▲400	▲600	▲1,500	▲5,000	▲30,000
500B	Mickey Mantle WL	▲1,000	▲1,500	▲2,000	▲2,500	▲4,000	▲8,000	▲12,000	
501A	Tony Gonzalez	5	5	5	5	5	6	25	50
501B	Tony Gonzalez WL	6	10	15	25	40	100	200	
502	Minnie Rojas	5	5	5	5	5	12	30	
503	Larry Brown	5	5	5	5	5	6	15	150
504	Checklist 6/B.Robinson	5	5	5	5	5	6	20	80
505A	Bobby Bolin	5	5	5	5	5	5	15	30
505B	Bobby Bolin WL	5	8	12	20	50	60		
506	Paul Blair	5	5	5	5	5	8	30	80
507	Cookie Rojas	5	5	5	5	5	5	15	80
508	Moe Drabowsky	5	5	5	5	5	6	15	60
509	Manny Sanguillen	5	5	5	5	6	10	25	150
510	Rod Carew	8	12	20	25	40	50	150	500
511A	Diego Segui	5	5	5	5	5	5	10	120
511B	Diego Segui WL	5	8	12	20	30	60	200	
512	Cleon Jones	5	5	6	10	15	30	150	400
513	Camilo Pascual	5	5	5	5	5	5	12	25
514	Mike Lum	5	5	5	5	5	5	10	25
515	Dick Green	5	5	5	5	5	5	12	40
516	Earl Weaver MG RC	5	5	▲8	▲12	▲20	30	▲80	250
517	Mike McCormick	5	5	5	5	5	5	10	30
518	Fred Whitfield	5	5	5	5	5	5	10	25
519	J.Kenney RC/L.Boehmer RC	5	5	5	5	5	5	10	25
520	Bob Veale	5	5	5	5	5	5	10	25
521	George Thomas	5	5	5	5	5	5	15	40
522	Joe Hoerner	5	5	5	5	5	6	20	50
523	Bob Chance	5	5	5	5	5	5	10	25
524	J.Laboy RC/F.Wicker RC	5	5	5	5	5	5	10	25
525	Earl Wilson	5	5	5	5	5	6	12	30
526	Hector Torres RC	5	5	5	5	5	5	10	25
527	Al Lopez MG	5	5	5	5	5	5	12	40
528	Claude Osteen	5	5	5	5	5	6	12	30
529	Ed Kirkpatrick	5	5	5	5	5	5	10	25
530	Cesar Tovar	5	5	5	5	5	5	10	40
531	Dick Farrell	5	5	5	5	5	5	10	25
532	Bird Hill Aces	5	5	5	5	5	6	12	30
533	Nolan Ryan	▲200	250	▲400	▲500	600	▲1,000	▲2,500	6,000
534	Jerry McNertney	5	5	5	5	5	5	10	25
535	Phil Regan	5	5	5	5	5	6	12	40
536	D.Breeden RC/D.Roberts RC	5	5	5	5	5	5	10	25

#	Player	GD 2	VG 3	VgEx 4	EX 5	ExMt 6	NM 7	NmMt 8	MT 9
537	Mike Paul RC	5	5	5	5	5	5	10	25
538	Charlie Smith	5	5	5	5	5	5	10	40
539	Ted Shows How	5	5	5	6	20	25	30	100
540	Curt Flood	5	5	5	5	5	8	20	80
541	Joe Verbanic	5	5	5	5	5	5	10	25
542	Bob Aspromonte	5	5	5	5	5	5	10	25
543	Fred Newman	5	5	5	5	5	5	10	30
544	M.Kilkenny RC/R.Woods RC	5	5	5	5	5	5	10	25
545	Willie Stargell	▲8	▲12	▲20	▲30	▲50	▲80	▲120	▲300
546	Jim Nash	5	5	5	5	5	5	10	30
547	Billy Martin MG	5	5	5	5	5	8	25	80
548	Bob Locker	5	5	5	5	5	5	10	25
549	Ron Brand	5	5	5	5	5	5	10	25
550	Brooks Robinson	▲6	▲10	▲15	▲25	▲40	▲60	▲100	250
551	Wayne Granger RC	5	5	5	5	5	5	10	25
552	T.Sizemore RC/B.Sudakis RC	5	5	5	5	5	6	12	50
553	Ron Davis	5	5	5	5	5	5	10	25
554	Frank Bertaina	5	5	5	5	5	5	10	30
555	Jim Ray Hart	5	5	5	5	5	5	10	25
556	A's Stars	5	5	5	5	5	5	15	25
557	Frank Fernandez	5	5	5	5	5	5	10	30
558	Tom Burgmeier RC	5	5	5	5	5	5	15	30
559	J.Hague RC/J.Hicks	5	5	5	5	5	5	10	25
560	Luis Tiant	5	5	5	5	5	8	20	40
561	Ron Clark	5	5	5	5	5	5	10	25
562	Bob Watson RC	5	5	5	5	5	5	20	30
563	Marty Pattin RC	5	5	5	5	5	5	10	25
564	Gil Hodges MG	5	5	6	10	15	25	80	150
565	Hoyt Wilhelm	5	5	5	5	5	12	25	60
566	Ron Hansen	5	5	5	5	5	5	10	25
567	E.Jimenez/J.Shellenback	5	5	5	5	5	5	10	25
568	Cecil Upshaw	5	5	5	5	5	5	10	40
569	Billy Harris	5	5	5	5	5	5	10	40
570	Ron Santo	5	5	6	15	20	40	50	150
571	Cap Peterson	5	5	5	5	5	5	10	25
572	Giants Heroes	5	5	5	8	15	25	60	200
573	Jim Palmer	▲12	▲20	30	40	50	▲80	▲150	▲300
574	George Scott	5	5	5	5	5	6	12	30
575	Bill Singer	5	5	5	5	5	5	10	25
576	R.Stone/B.Wilson	5	5	5	5	5	5	10	25
577	Mike Hegan	5	5	5	5	5	5	10	25
578	Don Bosch	5	5	5	5	5	5	10	25
579	Dave Nelson RC	5	5	5	5	5	5	10	25
580	Jim Northrup	5	5	5	5	5	6	12	30
581	Gary Nolan	5	5	5	5	5	6	12	30
582A	Checklist 7/Oliva White Circle	5	5	5	5	5	6	15	40
582B	Checklist 7/Oliva Red Circle	5	5	5	5	5	6	15	40
583	Clyde Wright RC	5	5	5	5	5	5	15	30
584	Don Mason	5	5	5	5	5	5	10	25
585	Ron Swoboda	5	5	5	5	5	6	15	40
586	Tim Cullen	5	5	5	5	5	5	10	25
587	Joe Rudi RC	5	5	5	5	5	5	30	60
588	Bill White	5	5	5	5	5	5	10	25
589	Joe Pepitone	5	5	5	5	5	6	20	50
590	Rico Carty	5	5	5	5	5	8	20	60
591	Mike Hedlund	5	5	5	5	5	5	12	30
592	R.Robles RC/A.Santorini RC	5	5	5	5	5	6	12	40
593	Don Nottebart	5	5	5	5	5	5	12	30
594	Dooley Womack	5	5	5	5	5	5	12	25
595	Lee Maye	5	5	5	5	5	6	12	30
596	Chuck Hartenstein	5	5	5	5	5	5	12	30
597	Rollie Fingers RC	▲30	▲50	▲80	▲120	▲200	▲250	▲400	▲2,000
598	Ruben Amaro	5	5	5	5	5	6	15	100
599	John Boozer	5	5	5	5	5	6	12	25
600	Tony Oliva	5	5	5	5	8	15	50	200
601	Tug McGraw SP	5	5	5	5	6	15	50	100
602	Distaso/Young/Qualls RC	5	5	5	5	6	10	40	100
603	Joe Keough RC	5	5	5	5	5	6	12	40

		GD 2	VG 3	VgEx 4	EX 5	ExMt 6	NM 7	NmMt 8	MT 9
604	Bobby Etheridge	5	5	5	5	5	6	12	40
605	Dick Ellsworth	5	5	5	5	5	6	20	60
606	Gene Mauch MG	5	5	5	5	5	6	12	20
607	Dick Bosman	5	5	5	5	5	6	12	30
608	Dick Simpson	5	5	5	5	5	6	12	30
609	Phil Gagliano	5	5	5	5	6	15	50	120
610	Jim Hardin	5	5	5	5	5	5	10	25
611	Didier/Hriniak/Niebauer RC	5	5	5	5	5	6	12	30
612	Jack Aker	5	5	5	5	5	6	12	30
613	Jim Beauchamp	5	5	5	5	5	6	12	30
614	T.Griffin RC/S.Guinn RC	5	5	5	5	5	6	12	40
615	Len Gabrielson	5	5	5	5	5	6	12	30
616	Don McMahon	5	5	5	5	5	8	20	30
617	Jesse Gonder	5	5	5	5	5	6	15	60
618	Ramon Webster	5	5	5	5	5	6	15	80
619	Butler/Kelly/Rios RC	5	5	5	5	5	6	12	30
620	Dean Chance	5	5	5	6	10	15	30	60
621	Bill Voss	5	5	5	5	5	6	12	40
622	Dan Osinski	5	5	5	5	5	6	12	40
623	Hank Allen	5	5	5	5	5	6	12	40
624	Chaney/Dyer/Harmon RC	5	5	5	5	5	8	15	30
625	Mack Jones	5	5	5	5	5	6	12	40
626	Gene Michael	5	5	5	5	5	8	25	50
627	George Stone RC	5	5	5	5	5	8	25	60
628	Conigliaro/O'Brien/Wenz RC	5	5	5	5	5	6	20	40
629	Jack Hamilton	5	5	5	5	5	6	12	30
630	Bobby Bonds RC	▲10	▲15	▲25	▲40	▲60	▲100	▲150	▲400
631	John Kennedy	5	5	5	5	5	6	12	30
632	Jon Warden RC	5	5	5	5	5	6	15	30
633	Harry Walker MG	5	5	5	5	5	6	12	30
634	Andy Etchebarren	5	5	5	5	5	6	15	30
635	George Culver	5	5	5	5	5	6	12	30
636	Woody Held	5	5	5	5	5	6	12	40
637	DaVanon/Reberger/Kirby RC	5	5	5	5	5	6	12	30
638	Ed Sprague RC	5	5	5	5	5	6	10	25
639	Barry Moore	5	5	5	5	5	6	12	25
640	Ferguson Jenkins	▲6	▲10	▲15	▲25	▲40	▲60	▲100	▲250
641	Darwin/Miller/Dean RC	5	5	5	5	5	6	12	30
642	John Hiller	5	5	5	5	5	8	20	50
643	Billy Cowan	5	5	5	5	5	8	40	50
644	Chuck Hinton	5	5	5	5	5	6	12	30
645	George Brunet	5	5	5	5	5	6	12	30
646	D.McGinn RC/C.Morton RC	5	5	5	5	5	6	12	30
647	Dave Wickersham	5	5	5	5	5	6	12	40
648	Bobby Wine	5	5	5	5	5	6	12	40
649	Al Jackson	5	5	5	5	6	10	25	80
650	Ted Williams MG	5	▲8	▲12	20	25	50	▲80	250
651	Gus Gil	5	5	5	5	5	6	15	100
652	Eddie Watt	5	5	5	5	5	6	12	30
653	Aurelio Rodriguez RC	5	5	5	5	5	6	15	50
654	May/Secrist/Morales RC	5	5	5	5	5	6	15	40
655	Mike Hershberger	5	5	5	5	5	8	40	100
656	Dan Schneider	5	5	5	5	5	6	10	25
657	Bobby Murcer	5	5	5	6	12	30	40	120
658	Hall/Burbach/Miles RC	5	5	5	5	5	6	12	30
659	Johnny Podres	5	5	5	5	6	10	12	30
660	Reggie Smith	5	5	5	5	6	10	25	100
661	Jim Merritt	5	5	5	5	5	6	12	30
662	Drago/Spriggs/Oliver RC	5	5	5	5	5	8	30	
663	Dick Radatz	5	5	5	5	5	8	25	50
664	Ron Hunt	5	5	5	5	6	10	20	120

— Johnny Bench #95 PSA 10 (Gem) sold for $2,749 (Mile High; 10/11)

— Steve Carlton #255 PSA 10 (Gem) sold for $3,823 (eBay; 09/12)

— Rollie Fingers #597 PSA 10 (Gem) (Young Collection) sold for $5,329 (SCP; 5/12)

— Reggie Jackson #260 PSA 10 (Gem) (Young Collection) sold for $115,242 (SCP; 5/12)

— Dave Marshall WL #464B PSA 8 (NmMt) sold for $3,029 (eBay; 08/12)

— Nolan Ryan #533 PSA 10 (Gem) sold for $20,100 (Mile High; 10/12)

— Tom Seaver #480 PSA 9 (MT) sold for $6,933 (Mile High; 05/11)

— Tom Seaver #480 PSA 9 (MT) sold for $3,936 (eBay; 11/12)

— Tom Seaver #480 PSA 9 (MT) sold for $2,900 (eBay; 1/13)

— Ted Williams #650 PSA 10 (Gem) sold for $1,056 (Madec; 5/0)

1969 Topps Decals

		VG 3	VgEx 4	EX 5	ExMt 6	NM 7	NmMt 8	MT 9	Gem 9.5/10
1	Hank Aaron	5	5	8	12	20	30	100	
2	Richie Allen	5	5	5	5	6	10	30	
3	Felipe Alou	5	5	5	5	5	10	40	
4	Matty Alou	5	5	5	5	5	10	30	
5	Luis Aparicio	5	5	5	5	6	10	40	60
6	Roberto Clemente	5	6	10	15	25	120	200	
7	Donn Clendenon	5	5	5	5	5	10	30	
8	Tommy Davis	5	5	5	5	5	8	15	40
9	Don Drysdale	5	5	5	6	10	15	25	50
10	Joe Foy	5	5	5	5	5	8	15	30
11	Jim Fregosi	5	5	5	5	5	8	15	60
12	Bob Gibson	5	5	5	8	12	50	120	
13	Tony Gonzalez	5	5	5	5	5	10	40	
14	Tom Haller	5	5	5	5	5	8	15	
15	Ken Harrelson	5	5	5	5	5	8	20	
16	Tommy Helms	5	5	5	5	5	8	15	40
17	Willie Horton	5	5	5	5	5	8	15	50
18	Frank Howard	5	5	5	5	5	8	15	
19	Reggie Jackson	5	6	10	15	25	60	120	500
20	Ferguson Jenkins	5	5	5	5	6	10	40	80
21	Harmon Killebrew	5	5	5	6	10	15	50	100
22	Jerry Koosman	5	5	5	5	5	8	15	40
23	Mickey Mantle	▲40	▲60	▲100	▲150	▲250	▲400	▲1,000	
24	Willie Mays	5	5	20	25	30	40	100	500
25	Tim McCarver	5	5	5	5	5	8	15	
26	Willie McCovey	5	5	5	6	10	15	40	
27	Sam McDowell	5	5	5	5	5	8	15	50
28	Denny McLain	5	5	5	5	5	8	15	100
29	Dave McNally	5	5	5	5	5	8	15	100
30	Don Mincher	5	5	5	5	5	8	15	
31	Rick Monday	5	5	5	5	5	8	15	
32	Tony Oliva	5	5	5	5	5	8	25	40
33	Camilo Pascual	5	5	5	5	5	10	40	
34	Rick Reichardt	5	5	5	5	5	8	15	40
35	Frank Robinson	5	5	5	▲8	▲12	▲20	▲40	50
36	Pete Rose	5	5	6	25	30	40	80	200
37	Ron Santo	5	5	5	5	8	12	30	100
38	Tom Seaver	5	5	5	8	12	50	80	
39	Dick Selma	5	5	5	5	5	8	15	40
40	Chris Short	5	5	5	5	5	8	15	40
41	Rusty Staub	5	5	5	5	5	10	40	
42	Mel Stottlemyre	5	5	5	5	5	10	30	
43	Luis Tiant	5	5	5	5	5	8	15	40
44	Pete Ward	5	5	5	5	5	10	40	
45	Hoyt Wilhelm	5	5	5	5	5	8	15	30
46	Maury Wills	5	5	5	5	5	8	15	30
47	Jim Wynn	5	5	5	5	5	10	40	
48	Carl Yastrzemski	5	5	5	20	25	30	50	250

1969 Topps Deckle Edge

		GD 2	VG 3	VgEx 4	EX 5	ExMt 6	NM 7	NmMt 8	MT 9
1	Brooks Robinson	5	5	5	6	10	20	80	
2	Boog Powell	5	5	5	5	8	15	50	
3	Ken Harrelson	5	5	5	5	6	12	60	
4	Carl Yastrzemski	5	5	5	6	10	50	80	
5	Jim Fregosi	5	5	5	5	6	15	80	
6	Luis Aparicio	5	5	5	5	8	20	80	
7	Luis Tiant	5	5	5	5	6	12	50	
8	Denny McLain	5	5	5	5	8	20	60	

		GD 2	VG 3	VgEx 4	EX 5	ExMt 6	NM 7	NmMt 8	MT 9
	Willie Horton	5	5	5	5	6	12	60	
0	Bill Freehan	5	5	5	5	6	12	80	
1A	Hoyt Wilhelm	5	5	5	5	8	15		
1B	Jim Wynn	5	5	5	6	10	30	80	
2	Rod Carew	5	5	5	6	10	20	80	
3	Mel Stottlemyre	5	5	5	5	6	12	50	
4	Rick Monday	5	5	5	5	6	12	30	
5	Tommy Davis	5	5	5	5	6	12	60	
6	Frank Howard	5	5	5	5	6	12	50	
7	Felipe Alou	5	5	5	5	6	15	150	
8	Don Kessinger	5	5	5	5	6	12	50	
9	Ron Santo	5	5	5	5	8	15	50	
0	Tommy Helms	5	5	5	5	6	12	80	
1	Pete Rose	5	5	8	10	60	100	200	
2A	Rusty Staub	5	5	5	5	6	12		
2B	Joe Foy	5	5	5	8	12	30	150	
3	Tom Haller	5	5	5	5	6	15	60	
4	Maury Wills	5	5	5	5	6	12	50	
5	Jerry Koosman	5	5	5	5	6	12	30	
6	Richie Allen	5	5	5	5	8	15	120	
7	Roberto Clemente	▲25	▲40	▲60	100	▲150	250	500	
8	Curt Flood	5	5	5	5	6	12	50	
9	Bob Gibson	5	5	5	6	10	50	175	
0	Al Ferrara	5	5	5	5	6	12	40	
1	Willie McCovey	5	5	5	6	10	20	50	
2	Juan Marichal	5	5	5	5	8	15	150	
3	Willie Mays	5	6	15	50	80	100		

1969 Topps Super

		VG 3	VgEx 4	EX 5	ExMt 6	NM 7	NmMt 8	MT 9	Gem 9.5/10
	Dave McNally	12	20	30	50	80	200		
	Frank Robinson	10	15	25	60	80	100	250	500
	Brooks Robinson	15	25	40	60	100	200	500	
	Ken Harrelson	5	5	6	10	15	30	80	120
	Carl Yastrzemski	20	30	50	80	120	300	400	
	Ray Culp	5	5	6	10	15	30	▲60	100
	Jim Fregosi	5	5	6	10	15	30	80	120
	Rick Reichardt	5	5	6	10	15	30	50	100
	Vic Davalillo	5	5	6	10	15	30	50	250
	Luis Aparicio	8	12	20	30	50	▲100	▲200	250
	Pete Ward	5	5	6	10	15	30	80	150
	Joel Horlen	5	5	6	10	15	30	100	120
	Luis Tiant	5	5	6	10	15	30	80	200
	Sam McDowell	5	5	8	12	20	40	100	400
	Jose Cardenal	5	5	6	10	15	▲50	▲100	300
	Willie Horton	5	5	6	10	15	30	80	120
	Denny McLain	5	8	12	20	30	50	120	150
	Bill Freehan	5	5	6	10	15	30	50	▲200
	Harmon Killebrew	12	20	30	50	80	150	250	600
	Tony Oliva	5	8	12	20	30	50	120	200
	Dean Chance	5	5	6	10	15	30	50	400
	Joe Foy	5	5	6	10	15	30	50	120
	Roger Nelson	5	5	6	10	15	▲40	100	▲200
	Mickey Mantle	200	250	400	500	900	1,200	▲4,000	
	Mel Stottlemyre	5	5	6	10	15	30	120	▲250
	Roy White	5	5	6	10	15	40	80	300
	Rick Monday	5	5	6	10	15	30	50	120
	Reggie Jackson	40	60	100	150	250	600	1,500	
	Bert Campaneris	5	5	6	10	15	30	50	100
	Frank Howard	5	5	6	10	15	30	80	150
	Camilo Pascual	5	5	6	10	15	30	50	120
	Tommy Davis	5	5	6	10	15	▲50	▲100	250
	Don Mincher	5	5	6	10	15	30	100	150
	Hank Aaron	25	40	60	100	150	200	800	▲1,500
	Felipe Alou	5	5	6	10	15	30	200	▲400
	Joe Torre	5	6	10	15	25	▲100	▲200	▲400
	Ferguson Jenkins	6	10	15	25	40	60	120	300

		VG 3	VgEx 4	EX 5	ExMt 6	NM 7	NmMt 8	MT 9	Gem 9.5/10
38	Ron Santo	6	10	15	25	40	60	200	250
39	Billy Williams	6	10	15	25	40	60	200	
40	Tommy Helms	5	5	6	10	15	30	60	
41	Pete Rose	30	50	80	120	200	300	800	1,200
42	Joe Morgan	10	15	25	40	60	250	400	300
43	Jim Wynn	5	5	6	10	15	30	60	120
44	Curt Blefary	5	5	6	10	15	30	50	100
45	Willie Davis	5	5	6	10	15	30	60	200
46	Don Drysdale	10	15	25	40	60	100	150	500
47	Tom Haller	5	5	6	10	15	▲40	▲100	▲200
48	Rusty Staub	5	5	6	10	15	30	60	120
49	Maury Wills	5	5	6	10	15	30	60	
50	Cleon Jones	5	6	10	15	25	40	150	200
51	Jerry Koosman	5	5	6	10	15	30	60	400
52	Tom Seaver	25	40	60	100	150	300	600	
53	Richie Allen	5	5	6	10	15	30	60	400
54	Chris Short	5	5	6	10	15	30	100	150
55	Cookie Rojas	5	5	6	10	15	30	60	150
56	Matty Alou	5	5	6	10	15	30	120	150
57	Steve Blass	5	5	6	10	15	50	80	150
58	Roberto Clemente	50	80	120	200	300	800	1,500	
59	Curt Flood	5	5	6	10	15	30	100	200
60	Bob Gibson	12	20	30	50	80	150	400	
61	Tim McCarver	5	6	10	15	25	40	80	250
62	Dick Selma	5	5	6	10	15	30	50	150
63	Ollie Brown	5	5	6	10	15	▲50	▲100	▲200
64	Juan Marichal	10	15	25	40	60	150	250	
65	Willie Mays	30	50	80	120	200	800	1,000	
66	Willie McCovey	12	20	30	50	80	250	500	

1970 Kellogg's

		VG 3	VgEx 4	EX 5	ExMt 6	NM 7	NmMt 8	MT 9	Gem 9.5/10
1	Ed Kranepool	4	4	4	5	10	15	70	250
2	Pete Rose	4	4	10	12	15	20	60	250
3	Cleon Jones	4	4	4	4	5	8	15	100
4	Willie McCovey	4	4	4	5	6	10	20	100
5	Mel Stottlemyre	4	4	4	4	5	8	12	30
6	Frank Howard	4	4	4	4	5	8	12	50
7	Tom Seaver	4	4	6	8	10	15	30	120
8	Don Sutton	4	4	4	5	6	10	20	80
9	Jim Wynn	4	4	4	4	5	8	12	40
10	Jim Maloney	4	4	4	4	5	8	12	40
11	Tommie Agee	4	4	4	4	5	8	15	100
12	Willie Mays	4	4	10	12	15	20	50	150
13	Juan Marichal	4	4	4	5	6	10	25	60
14	Dave McNally	4	4	4	4	5	8	15	40
15	Frank Robinson	4	4	5	6	8	12	25	80
16	Carlos May	4	4	4	4	5	8	100	
17	Bill Singer	4	4	4	4	5	8	50	250
18	Rick Reichardt	4	4	4	4	5	8	150	
19	Boog Powell	4	4	4	4	5	8	25	
20	Gaylord Perry	4	4	4	5	6	10	30	120
21	Brooks Robinson	4	4	6	8	10	15	30	250
22	Luis Aparicio	4	4	4	5	6	10	20	80
23	Joel Horlen	4	4	4	4	5	8	12	80
24	Mike Epstein	4	4	4	4	5	8	15	
25	Tom Haller	4	4	4	4	5	8	50	
26	Willie Crawford	4	4	4	4	5	8	12	
27	Roberto Clemente	4	8	25	30	40	80	120	500
28	Matty Alou	4	4	4	4	5	8	15	120
29	Willie Stargell	4	4	5	6	8	25	60	200
30	Tim Cullen	4	4	4	4	5	8	80	200
31	Randy Hundley	4	4	4	4	5	8	15	50
32	Reggie Jackson	4	4	6	8	10	15	40	150
33	Rich Allen	4	4	4	4	5	8	15	175
34	Tim McCarver	4	4	4	4	5	8	25	50
35	Ray Culp	4	4	4	4	5	8	12	50

#	Player	VG 3	VgEx 4	EX 5	ExMt 6	NM 7	NmMt 8	MT 9	Gem 9.5/10
36	Jim Fregosi	4	4	4	4	5	8	12	100
37	Billy Williams	4	4	4	5	6	10	25	80
38	Johnny Odom	4	4	4	4	5	8	12	80
39	Bert Campaneris	4	4	4	4	5	8	12	60
40	Ernie Banks	4	4	6	8	10	15	50	120
41	Chris Short	4	4	4	4	5	8	15	60
42	Ron Santo	4	4	4	5	6	10	20	
43	Glenn Beckert	4	4	4	4	5	8	12	40
44	Lou Brock	4	4	4	5	6	10	20	60
45	Larry Hisle	4	4	4	4	5	8	15	50
46	Reggie Smith	4	4	4	4	5	8	15	200
47	Rod Carew	4	4	4	5	6	10	20	80
48	Curt Flood	4	4	4	4	5	8	15	
49	Jim Lonborg	4	4	4	4	5	8	15	200
50	Sam McDowell	4	4	4	4	5	8	15	60
51	Sal Bando	4	4	4	4	5	8	30	60
52	Al Kaline	4	4	5	6	8	12	25	80
53	Gary Nolan	4	4	4	4	5	8	20	120
54	Rico Petrocelli	4	4	4	4	5	8	12	50
55	Ollie Brown	4	4	4	4	5	8	30	
56	Luis Tiant	4	4	4	4	5	8	12	80
57	Bill Freehan	4	4	4	4	5	8	15	150
58	Johnny Bench	4	4	6	8	10	15	50	200
59	Joe Pepitone	4	4	4	4	5	8	20	80
60	Bobby Murcer	4	4	5	6	8	12	40	100
61	Harmon Killebrew	4	4	5	6	8	12	25	120
62	Don Wilson	4	4	4	4	5	8	12	40
63	Tony Oliva	4	4	4	4	5	8	15	60
64	Jim Perry	4	4	4	4	5	8	12	30
65	Mickey Lolich	4	4	4	4	5	8	15	30
66	Jose Laboy	4	4	4	4	5	8	12	40
67	Dean Chance	4	4	4	4	5	8	12	40
68	Ken Harrelson	4	4	4	4	5	8	12	50
69	Willie Horton	4	4	4	4	5	8	25	60
70	Wally Bunker	4	4	4	4	5	8	12	50
71A	Bob Gibson ERR 1959 IP Blank	4	4	4	5	6	10	20	
71B	Bob Gibson COR 1959 IP 76	4	4	5	6	8	12	60	120
72	Joe Morgan	4	4	4	5	6	10	25	150
73	Denny McLain	4	4	4	4	5	8	15	80
74	Tommy Harper	4	4	4	4	5	8	15	80
75	Don Mincher	4	4	4	4	5	8	20	300

1970 Topps

#	Player	VG 3	VgEx 4	EX 5	ExMt 6	NM 7	NmMt 8	NmMt+ 8.5	MT 9
1	New York Mets TC	5	10	20	25	50	100		
2	Diego Segui	4	8	15	20	40	80		
3	Darrel Chaney	4	4	8	10	20	50		
4	Tom Egan	4	4	4	5	10	20	25	50
5	Wes Parker	4	4	8	10	20	40	80	100
6	Grant Jackson	4	4	4	5	10	20	25	50
7	G.Boyd RC/R.Nagelson RC	4	6	12	15	30	80		
8	Jose Martinez RC	4	4	4	5	10	20	25	50
9	Checklist 1	4	8	15	20	40	80		
10	Carl Yastrzemski	6	15	20	30	50	100	150	400
11	Nate Colbert	4	4	4	5	10	20	25	50
12	John Hiller	4	4	5	6	12	25	30	80
13	Jack Hiatt	4	6	12	15	30	60		
14	Hank Allen	4	4	4	4	10	20	15	30
15	Larry Dierker	4	4	4	5	10	20	25	80
16	Charlie Metro MG RC	4	4	4	5	10	20	25	100
17	Hoyt Wilhelm	4	4	6	8	15	50		
18	Carlos May	4	4	6	8	15	30		
19	John Boccabella	4	4	4	5	10	20	25	80
20	Dave McNally	4	4	4	5	10	20		
21	V.Blue RC/G.Tenace RC	4	6	12	15	30	100		
22	Ray Washburn	4	4	4	4	6	15	15	30
23	Bill Robinson	4	4	4	4	8	15	20	
24	Dick Selma	4	4	4	4	5	15	15	25
25	Cesar Tovar	4	4	4	5	10	20	30	50
26	Tug McGraw	6	12	20	25	30	40	150	250
27	Chuck Hinton	4	4	4	5	10	12	25	50
28	Billy Wilson	4	4	4	4	6	12	15	40
29	Sandy Alomar	4	4	4	4	6	12	15	30
30	Matty Alou	4	4	4	5	10	20	25	
31	Marty Pattin	4	4	4	5	10	20	30	50
32	Harry Walker MG	4	4	4	4	6	12	15	30
33	Don Wert	4	4	4	4	6	12	15	25
34	Willie Crawford	4	4	4	5	10	12	25	
35	Joel Horlen	4	4	4	5	10	12	25	
36	D.Breeden/B.Carbo RC	4	4	4	5	10	12	25	
37	Dick Drago	4	4	4	4	6	15	20	30
38	Mack Jones	4	4	4	5	10	12	25	
39	Mike Nagy RC	4	4	4	5	10	20	25	100
40	Richie Allen	4	4	6	8	15	30		
41	George Lauzerique	4	4	4	4	8	15	20	
42	Tito Fuentes	4	4	4	5	10	12	25	
43	Jack Aker	4	4	4	4	8	30	40	50
44	Roberto Pena	4	4	6	8	15	30	40	80
45	Dave Johnson	4	4	5	6	12	25	30	60
46	Ken Rudolph RC	4	4	4	4	6	12	15	60
47	Bob Miller	4	4	4	5	10	12	25	
48	Gil Garrido	4	4	4	4	6	12	15	40
49	Tim Cullen	4	4	4	5	10	12	25	
50	Tommie Agee	4	8	15	20	40	50		
51	Bob Christian	4	4	4	4	8	15	20	40
52	Bruce Dal Canton	4	4	5	6	12	25	60	100
53	John Kennedy	4	4	5	6	8	12	30	60
54	Jeff Torborg	4	4	4	5	10	20	25	80
55	John Odom	4	4	4	6	10	15	40	80
56	J.Lis RC/S.Reid RC	4	4	4	5	10	12	25	
57	Pat Kelly	4	4	4	5	10	12	30	
58	Dave Marshall	4	4	4	5	10	12	30	
59	Dick Ellsworth	4	4	4	8	20	30		
60	Jim Wynn	4	4	4	4	6	12	15	60
61	NL Batting Leaders	12	15	30	40	60	150	200	500
62	AL Batting Leaders	6	12	25	30	50	60	150	300
63	NL RBI Leaders	4	4	8	10	20	40	60	
64	AL RBI Leaders	4	4	8	10	15	25	50	150
65	NL Home Run Leaders	4	8	12	15	20	50	60	120
66	AL Home Run Leaders	4	4	6	8	15	30		
67	NL ERA Leaders	4	4	8	10	20	50		
68	AL ERA Leaders	4	6	12	15	25	30	80	150
69	NL Pitching Leaders	4	5	6	8	12	30	60	120
70	AL Pitching Leaders	4	5	10	12	25	50		
71	NL Strikeout Leaders	4	5	10	12	20	25	80	150
72	AL Strikeout Leaders	4	4	8	10	20	40	50	150
73	Wayne Granger	4	4	4	5	10	20	25	60
74	G.Washburn RC/W.Wolf	4	4	4	4	6	12	15	30
75	Jim Kaat	4	4	5	6	12	20	25	100
76	Carl Taylor	4	4	8	10	20	40	50	
77	Frank Linzy	4	5	10	12	25	50	60	150
78	Joe Lahoud	4	4	5	6	12	15	20	60
79	Clay Kirby	4	4	4	4	6	12	15	30
80	Don Kessinger	4	4	4	4	8	20	30	
81	Dave May	4	4	4	4	6	12	15	60
82	Frank Fernandez	4	4	4	4	8	15	20	30
83	Don Cardwell	4	4	4	4	8	15	20	40
84	Paul Casanova	4	4	6	8	15	30	40	120
85	Max Alvis	4	4	4	4	5	10	12	50
86	Lum Harris MG	4	4	4	4	8	15	20	60
87	Steve Renko RC	4	4	4	4	8	15	20	50
88	M.Fuentes RC/D.Baney RC	4	4	4	4	6	12	15	30
89	Juan Rios	4	4	4	5	10	25	30	60
90	Tim McCarver	4	4	6	8	15	30	40	80
91	Rich Morales	4	4	4	4	8	15	20	50

#	Player	VG 3	VgEx 4	EX 5	ExMt 6	NM 7	NmMt 8	NmMt+ 8.5	MT 9
2	George Culver	4	4	4	4	8	15	20	
3	Rick Renick	4	4	4	4	6	12	15	40
4	Freddie Patek	4	4	5	6	12	25	30	60
5	Earl Wilson	4	4	4	4	8	15	20	40
6	L.Lee RC/J.Reuss RC	4	4	6	8	15	30	50	100
7	Joe Moeller	4	4	4	4	8	15	20	
8	Gates Brown	4	4	4	4	6	15	20	30
9	Bobby Pfeil RC	4	4	6	8	15	30		
00	Mel Stottlemyre	4	4	4	4	8	15	20	100
01	Bobby Floyd	4	4	4	4	8	15	20	
02	Joe Rudi	4	4	4	4	8	15	20	
03	Frank Reberger	4	4	4	4	6	12	15	40
04	Gerry Moses	4	4	4	4	6	15	25	
05	Tony Gonzalez	4	4	4	4	6	12	15	100
06	Darold Knowles	4	4	4	5	10	20	25	60
07	Bobby Etheridge	4	4	4	4	6	12	20	60
08	Tom Burgmeier	4	4	4	5	10	20	25	60
09	G.Jestadt RC/C.Morton	4	4	4	4	8	15	20	80
10	Bob Moose	4	4	4	4	5	10	12	100
11	Mike Hegan	4	4	6	8	15	30		
12	Dave Nelson	4	4	4	4	8	15	20	40
13	Jim Ray	4	4	4	4	8	15	20	
14	Gene Michael	4	6	8	10	20	30	40	150
15	Alex Johnson	6	12	25	30	50	60	200	250
16	Sparky Lyle	4	4	5	6	12	25	30	150
17	Don Young	4	4	4	4	8	15	20	40
18	George Mitterwald	4	4	4	6	10	15	20	50
19	Chuck Taylor RC	4	4	4	4	8	15	20	100
20	Sal Bando	4	4	5	6	12	25	30	100
21	F.Beene RC/T.Crowley RC	4	4	8	10	20	40	50	
22	George Stone	4	4	4	4	6	12	15	30
23	Don Gutteridge MG RC	4	4	6	8	15	30	40	80
24	Larry Jaster	4	4	4	4	5	10	12	30
25	Deron Johnson	4	4	8	10	20	80		
26	Marty Martinez	4	6	12	15	30	60	80	200
27	Joe Coleman	4	4	4	4	5	10	12	25
28A	Checklist 2 R Perranoski	4	4	5	6	12	25		
28B	Checklist 2 R. Perranoski	4	4	5	6	12	30		
29	Jimmie Price	4	4	4	4	6	15	20	50
30	Ollie Brown	4	4	4	5	10	20	25	50
31	R.Lamb RC/B.Stinson RC	4	4	4	5	10	20	25	60
32	Jim McGlothlin	4	4	4	4	8	20	25	60
33	Clay Carroll	4	4	6	8	15	30	40	80
34	Danny Walton RC	4	4	4	4	5	10	12	40
35	Dick Dietz	4	6	12	15	30	60	80	100
36	Steve Hargan	4	4	4	4	6	10	12	80
37	Art Shamsky	4	5	10	12	25	30	40	250
38	Joe Foy	4	4	6	8	15	30	40	150
39	Rich Nye	4	4	4	4	5	10	12	25
40	Reggie Jackson	25	30	40	50	80	250	500	1,500
41	D.Cash RC/J.Jeter RC	4	4	4	5	10	20	25	50
42	Fritz Peterson	4	4	8	10	20	40	50	150
43	Phil Gagliano	4	4	4	5	10	20	25	50
44	Ray Culp	4	5	10	12	20	25	30	
45	Rico Carty	4	4	4	5	10	20	25	100
46	Danny Murphy	4	4	4	5	10	20	25	50
47	Angel Hermoso RC	4	4	4	4	6	12	15	30
48	Earl Weaver MG	4	4	8	10	20	25	30	80
49	Billy Champion RC	4	4	4	5	10	20	25	40
50	Harmon Killebrew	10	15	25	30	50	200	250	300
51	Dave Roberts	4	4	4	4	6	12	15	40
52	Ike Brown RC	4	4	4	4	6	12	15	60
53	Gary Gentry	4	4	4	4	5	10	12	25
54	J.Miles/J.Dukes RC	4	4	5	6	12	30	40	60
55	Denis Menke	4	4	4	4	8	15	20	
56	Eddie Fisher	4	4	4	4	5	10	12	25
57	Manny Mota	4	4	5	6	12	15	20	50
58	Jerry McNertney	4	4	4	5	10	20	25	50
159	Tommy Helms	4	4	4	4	6	12	15	60
160	Phil Niekro	4	5	10	12	20	50	60	200
161	Richie Scheinblum	4	4	5	6	12	25	30	60
162	Jerry Johnson	4	4	4	5	10	12	15	25
163	Syd O'Brien	4	4	4	4	8	15	20	40
164	Ty Cline	4	4	4	4	6	8	10	15
165	Ed Kirkpatrick	4	4	4	5	10	12	15	50
166	Al Oliver	4	4	5	6	12	25		
167	Bill Burbach	4	4	4	5	10	12	15	50
168	Dave Watkins RC	4	4	5	6	12	25	30	60
169	Tom Hall	4	4	4	4	8	15	20	40
170	Billy Williams	5	8	12	20	30	50	60	120
171	Jim Nash	4	4	4	5	10	12	15	40
172	G.Hill RC/R.Garr RC	4	4	4	4	6	12	15	80
173	Jim Hicks	4	4	5	6	10	12	15	60
174	Ted Sizemore	4	4	5	6	10	12	15	60
175	Dick Bosman	4	4	4	4	8	15	20	80
176	Jim Ray Hart	4	4	8	10	20	25	30	120
177	Jim Northrup	4	4	4	5	10	15	20	80
178	Denny Lemaster	4	4	4	4	6	10	25	50
179	Ivan Murrell	4	4	5	6	12	25	30	60
180	Tommy John	4	4	6	8	15	25	40	60
181	Sparky Anderson MG	4	6	10	15	25	50	60	
182	Dick Hall	4	4	4	4	8	15	20	80
183	Jerry Grote	4	4	4	4	6	12	15	30
184	Ray Fosse	4	4	8	10	20	25	30	100
185	Don Mincher	4	4	4	4	8	15	20	30
186	Rick Joseph	4	4	5	6	12	15	20	60
187	Mike Hedlund	4	4	4	4	5	10	12	20
188	Manny Sanguillen	4	4	6	8	15	30	40	150
189	Thurman Munson RC	50	80	120	200	400	800	1,200	3,000
190	Joe Torre	4	4	8	10	30	60	80	200
191	Vicente Romo	4	4	4	4	8	15	20	60
192	Jim Qualls	4	4	5	6	12	25	30	60
193	Mike Wegener	4	4	4	4	8	15	20	40
194	Chuck Manuel RC	4	4	4	4	5	10	12	80
195	Tom Seaver NLCS1	6	10	15	25	40	60	80	250
196	Ken Boswell NLCS2	4	8	15	20	25	80	100	200
197	Nolan Ryan NLCS3	4	6	12	20	50	150	100	300
198	Mets Celebrate NLCS w/Ryan	4	6	12	25	30	80	100	500
199	Mike Cuellar ALCS1	4	4	6	8	15	30		
200	Boog Powell ALCS2	4	8	15	20	40	80		
201	B.Powell/A.Etchebarren ALCS3	4	4	8	10	20	25	50	150
202	Orioles Celebrate ALCS	4	4	4	5	10	25		50
203	Rudy May	4	4	4	4	8	15	20	40
204	Len Gabrielson	4	4	4	4	6	12	15	30
205	Bert Campaneris	4	4	6	8	15	30	40	150
206	Clete Boyer	4	4	4	4	6	12	15	30
207	N.McRae RC/B.Reed RC	4	4	5	6	12	25	30	60
208	Fred Gladding	4	4	4	5	10	12		25
209	Ken Suarez	4	4	4	5	10	12		25
210	Juan Marichal	6	8	10	15	25	40		
211	Ted Williams MG	10	15	25	40	60	100	120	300
212	Al Santorini	4	4	4	4	6	10	12	25
213	Andy Etchebarren	4	4	4	4	6	12	15	50
214	Ken Boswell	4	4	4	5	10	20	25	120
215	Reggie Smith	4	4	4	4	6	15	20	60
216	Chuck Hartenstein	4	4	4	4	6	12	15	60
217	Ron Hansen	4	4	4	4	6	12	15	40
218	Ron Stone	4	4	4	4	5	10	12	30
219	Jerry Kenney	4	4	4	4	6	20	25	30
220	Steve Carlton	8	12	20	25	40	100	120	400
221	Ron Brand	4	4	4	4	6	12	25	80
222	Jim Rooker	4	4	4	5	10	20	25	50
223	Nate Oliver	4	4	5	6	8	15	20	40
224	Steve Barber	4	4	4	4	5	10	12	50
225	Lee May	4	4	4	4	8	20	25	80
226	Ron Perranoski	4	4	4	4	8	15	20	50

#	Player	VG 3	VgEx 4	EX 5	ExMt 6	NM 7	NmMt 8	NmMt+ 8.5	MT 9
227	J.Mayberry RC/B.Watkins RC	4	4	4	4	8	15		
228	Aurelio Rodriguez	4	4	4	4	5	10	12	25
229	Rich Robertson	4	4	4	4	8	20	25	40
230	Brooks Robinson	4	8	15	20	▲50	60	80	300
231	Luis Tiant	4	4	5	6	12	15	20	80
232	Bob Didier	4	4	4	4	8	60	30	
233	Lew Krausse	4	4	4	4	5	10	12	50
234	Tommy Dean	4	4	4	4	8	20	25	
235	Mike Epstein	4	4	4	4	8	15	20	100
236	Bob Veale	4	4	4	5	10	20	25	50
237	Russ Gibson	4	4	4	4	6	12	15	30
238	Jose Laboy	4	4	4	4	5	10	12	50
239	Ken Berry	4	4	4	5	10	20	25	100
240	Ferguson Jenkins	4	5	10	12	25	40	50	120
241	A.Fitzmorris RC/S.Northey RC	4	4	5	6	12	25	30	60
242	Walt Alston MG	4	4	4	4	8	15	20	60
243	Joe Sparma	4	4	4	5	10	20	25	100
244A	Checklist 3 Red Bat	4	4	5	6	12	40		
244B	Checklist 3 Brown Bat	4	8	15	20	40	80		
245	Leo Cardenas	4	4	4	5	10	12	15	60
246	Jim McAndrew	4	4	8	10	20	40	50	100
247	Lou Klimchock	4	4	4	4	8	15	20	80
248	Jesus Alou	4	4	4	4	8	15	20	40
249	Bob Locker	4	4	4	4	8	15	20	100
250	Willie McCovey	4	8	15	20	50	80	100	500
251	Dick Schofield	4	4	4	5	10	20	25	30
252	Lowell Palmer RC	4	4	4	5	10	20	25	50
253	Ron Woods	4	4	4	4	8	15		
254	Camilo Pascual	4	4	4	4	6	12	15	30
255	Jim Spencer RC	4	4	4	4	5	10	12	25
256	Vic Davalillo	4	4	4	5	10	20	25	50
257	Dennis Higgins	4	4	4	5	10	20	25	60
258	Paul Popovich	4	4	4	4	6	12	15	30
259	Tommie Reynolds	4	4	4	4	8	15	20	60
260	Claude Osteen	4	4	4	4	6	12	15	30
261	Curt Motton	4	4	4	4	8	25	40	50
262	J.Morales RC/J.Williams RC	4	4	4	5	10	30	40	50
263	Duane Josephson	4	4	4	5	10	20		
264	Rich Hebner	4	4	4	5	10	80		
265	Randy Hundley	4	4	4	4	5	10	12	25
266	Wally Bunker	4	4	4	4	5	10	12	25
267	H.Hill RC/P.Ratliff	4	4	4	4	5	10	12	20
268	Claude Raymond	4	4	4	4	4	6	8	12
269	Cesar Gutierrez	4	4	4	4	5	10	12	15
270	Chris Short	4	4	4	4	6	12	15	30
271	Greg Goossen	4	4	4	4	5	10	12	25
272	Hector Torres	4	4	4	4	8	15		
273	Ralph Houk MG	4	4	4	5	10	20		
274	Gerry Arrigo	4	4	4	4	8	10	12	20
275	Duke Sims	4	4	4	4	8	15	20	40
276	Ron Hunt	4	4	4	4	4	6	10	15
277	Paul Doyle RC	4	4	4	4	4	6	10	15
278	Tommie Aaron	4	4	4	4	5	10	12	20
279	Bill Lee RC	4	4	8	10	20	40	50	80
280	Donn Clendenon	4	5	10	12	25	50		
281	Casey Cox	4	4	4	4	6	12	15	30
282	Steve Huntz	4	4	4	4	6	12	15	30
283	Angel Bravo RC	4	4	4	4	4	6	8	12
284	Jack Baldschun	4	4	4	4	5	10	12	25
285	Paul Blair	4	4	4	4	5	10	12	25
286	Bill Buckner RC	▲8	▲12	▲20	▲25	40	▲60	▲80	▲150
287	Fred Talbot	4	4	4	4	8	10	12	50
288	Larry Hisle	4	4	4	4	4	8	10	15
289	Gene Brabender	4	4	6	8	15	30	40	80
290	Rod Carew	6	10	20	25	40	80	80	400
291	Leo Durocher MG	4	4	4	4	6	12	15	30
292	Eddie Leon RC	4	4	4	4	5	10	12	25
293	Bob Bailey	4	4	4	4	5	10	12	25
294	Jose Azcue	4	4	4	4	5	10	12	25
295	Cecil Upshaw	4	4	4	4	4	8	10	15
296	Woody Woodward	4	4	4	5	10	12	15	50
297	Curt Blefary	4	4	4	4	5	10	12	25
298	Ken Henderson	4	4	4	4	5	10	12	20
299	Buddy Bradford	4	4	4	4	6	12	15	30
300	Tom Seaver	8	20	25	30	50	80	150	600
301	Chico Salmon	4	4	4	4	6	12	15	30
302	Jeff James	4	4	4	4	5	10	12	25
303	Brant Alyea	4	4	4	4	6	12	15	30
304	Bill Russell RC	4	4	4	4	8	20	25	60
305	Don Buford WS1	4	4	4	4	6	12	15	30
306	Donn Clendenon WS2	4	4	4	4	8	20	25	60
307	Tommie Agee WS3	4	8	15	20	40	60	80	200
308	J.C. Martin WS4	4	4	5	6	12	25	30	80
309	Jerry Koosman WS5	4	4	4	4	5	10	12	25
310	Mets Celebrate WS	4	4	4	5	10	30	40	80
311	Dick Green	4	4	4	4	4	8	10	15
312	Mike Torrez	4	4	4	5	10	12	15	50
313	Mayo Smith MG	4	4	4	4	5	10	12	25
314	Bill McCool	4	4	4	4	6	12	15	30
315	Luis Aparicio	4	6	10	15	25	40	50	100
316	Skip Guinn	4	4	4	4	5	10	12	25
317	B.Conigliaro/L.Alvarado RC	4	4	4	4	8	15		
318	Willie Smith	4	4	4	4	6	12	15	30
319	Clay Dalrymple	4	4	4	4	5	10	12	20
320	Jim Maloney	4	4	4	5	10	30		
321	Lou Piniella	4	4	4	4	8	15	20	80
322	Luke Walker	4	4	4	4	4	8	10	15
323	Wayne Comer	4	4	4	4	6	12	15	40
324	Tony Taylor	4	4	4	4	6	12	15	30
325	Dave Boswell	4	4	4	4	8	15	20	40
326	Bill Voss	4	4	4	4	4	8	10	15
327	Hal King RC	4	4	4	4	5	10	12	25
328	George Brunet	4	4	4	4	4	8	10	15
329	Chris Cannizzaro	4	4	4	4	6	12	15	80
330	Lou Brock	▲10	▲15	▲25	▲40	▲60	80	100	200
331	Chuck Dobson	4	4	4	4	6	12	15	30
332	Bobby Wine	4	4	4	4	4	8	10	15
333	Bobby Murcer	4	4	5	6	12	25	30	100
334	Phil Regan	4	4	4	4	5	10	12	30
335	Bill Freehan	4	4	4	4	8	15	20	50
336	Del Unser	4	4	4	4	8	15		
337	Mike McCormick	4	4	4	4	6	12	15	30
338	Paul Schaal	4	4	4	4	6	12	15	30
339	Johnny Edwards	4	4	4	4	5	10	12	25
340	Tony Conigliaro	6	12	25	30	50	80	150	150
341	Bill Sudakis	4	4	4	4	6	12	15	30
342	Wilbur Wood	4	4	4	4	5	10	12	20
343A	Checklist 4 Red Bat	4	4	6	8	15	50		
343B	Checklist 4 Brown Bat	4	4	5	6	12	25		
344	Marcelino Lopez	4	4	4	4	6	12	15	50
345	Al Ferrara	4	4	4	4	4	8	10	15
346	Red Schoendienst MG	4	4	4	4	8	15		
347	Russ Snyder	4	4	4	5	10	12		25
348	M.Jorgensen RC/J.Hudson RC	4	4	4	4	8	15	20	40
349	Steve Hamilton	4	4	4	4	6	12	15	30
350	Roberto Clemente	▲50	▲80	▲120	▲150	▲300	▲600	800	▲6,000
351	Tom Murphy	4	4	4	4	6	12	15	30
352	Bob Barton	4	4	4	4	5	10	12	20
353	Stan Williams	4	4	4	4	6	12	15	30
354	Amos Otis	4	4	4	5	10	20	25	50
355	Doug Rader	4	4	4	4	5	10	12	25
356	Fred Lasher	4	4	4	4	4	8	10	15
357	Bob Burda	4	4	4	4	6	12	15	30
358	Pedro Borbon RC	4	4	4	4	5	10	12	25
359	Phil Roof	4	4	4	4	6	12	15	30
360	Curt Flood	4	4	4	4	8	15	20	60

#	Player	VG 3	VgEx 4	EX 5	ExMt 6	NM 7	NmMt 8	NmMt+ 8.5	MT 9
61	Ray Jarvis	4	4	4	4	5	10	12	25
62	Joe Hague	4	4	4	4	5	10	12	25
63	Tom Shopay RC	4	4	4	4	5	10	12	25
64	Dan McGinn	4	4	4	4	5	10	12	20
65	Zoilo Versalles	4	4	4	4	5	10	12	80
66	Barry Moore	4	4	4	4	5	10	12	25
67	Mike Lum	4	4	4	4	5	10	12	30
68	Ed Herrmann	4	4	4	4	6	12	15	30
69	Alan Foster	4	4	4	4	8	15		
70	Tommy Harper	4	4	4	4	8	15	20	40
71	Rod Gaspar RC	4	4	4	4	5	10	12	25
72	Dave Giusti	4	4	4	4	6	12	15	30
73	Roy White	4	4	4	5	10	20	25	100
74	Tommie Sisk	4	4	4	4	6	12	15	30
75	Johnny Callison	4	4	4	4	8	15	20	80
76	Lefty Phillips MG RC	4	4	4	4	8	15	20	25
77	Bill Butler	4	4	4	4	8	15		
78	Jim Davenport	4	4	4	4	6	12	15	30
79	Tom Tischinski RC	4	4	5	6	12	25		
80	Tony Perez	4	5	10	12	30	100		
81	B.Brooks RC/M.Olivo RC	4	4	4	4	6	12	15	25
82	Jack DiLauro RC	4	4	4	5	10	12		50
83	Mickey Stanley	4	4	4	5	10	20	25	120
84	Gary Neibauer	4	4	4	4	8	15		
85	George Scott	4	4	5	6	12	25	30	60
86	Bill Dillman	4	4	4	4	6	12	15	50
87	Baltimore Orioles TC	4	4	8	10	20	30		
88	Byron Browne	4	4	4	4	6	12	15	30
89	Jim Shellenback	4	4	4	4	6	15	20	30
90	Willie Davis	4	4	4	4	8	20	25	80
91	Larry Brown	4	4	4	4	6	12	15	30
92	Walt Hriniak	4	4	4	4	8	15		
93	John Gelnar	4	4	4	4	6	12	15	50
94	Gil Hodges MG	4	5	10	12	25	50		
95	Walt Williams	4	4	4	4	8	15	20	80
96	Steve Blass	4	4	5	6	12	25	30	100
97	Roger Repoz	4	4	4	4	8	15		
98	Bill Stoneman	4	4	4	4	6	12	15	25
99	New York Yankees TC	4	6	12	15	20	30	40	150
00	Denny McLain	4	6	12	15	30	80	150	250
01	J.Harrell RC/B.Williams RC	4	4	4	5	10	20	25	100
02	Ellie Rodriguez	4	4	4	4	6	12	15	30
03	Jim Bunning	4	5	8	12	20	30	40	80
04	Rich Reese	4	4	4	4	6	12	15	50
05	Bill Hands	4	4	4	4	5	20	25	40
06	Mike Andrews	4	4	4	4	6	12	15	30
07	Bob Watson	4	4	4	4	6	12	15	60
08	Paul Lindblad	4	4	6	8	15	30	40	120
09	Bob Tolan	4	4	4	4	5	10	12	30
10	Boog Powell	4	4	5	6	12	25	30	120
11	Los Angeles Dodgers TC	4	4	4	4	6	12	15	40
12	Larry Burchart	4	4	6	8	15	30	40	80
13	Sonny Jackson	4	4	4	4	6	12	15	30
14	Paul Edmondson RC	4	4	4	4	5	10	12	25
15	Julian Javier	4	4	4	5	10	20	25	50
16	Joe Verbanic	4	4	4	4	6	12	15	60
17	John Bateman	4	4	4	4	8	15		
18	John Donaldson	4	4	5	6	12	25	30	80
19	Ron Taylor	4	4	6	8	15	30	40	100
20	Ken McMullen	4	4	4	4	8	15	20	50
21	Pat Dobson	4	4	5	6	12	25	30	60
22	Kansas City Royals TC	4	4	4	4	5	10	12	20
23	Jerry May	4	6	12	15	30	60	80	150
24	Mike Kilkenny	4	4	6	8	15	30	40	120
25	Bobby Bonds	4	5	10	10	20	25	60	120
26	Bill Rigney MG	4	4	6	8	15	30	40	80
27	Fred Norman	4	4	4	4	6	12	15	30
28	Don Buford	4	4	4	4	6	12	15	50
429	R.Bobb RC/J.Cosman	4	4	4	5	10	20	25	80
430	Andy Messersmith	4	4	4	4	8	80		
431	Ron Swoboda	4	4	4	4	6	12	15	25
432A	Checklist 5 Yellow Letters	4	4	5	6	12	40		
432B	Checklist 5 White Letters	4	4	5	6	12	25		
433	Ron Bryant RC	4	4	4	4	8	15	20	60
434	Felipe Alou	4	4	4	4	6	12	15	100
435	Nelson Briles	4	4	4	4	6	12	15	30
436	Philadelphia Phillies TC	4	4	4	4	6	12	15	40
437	Danny Cater	4	4	4	4	6	12	15	60
438	Pat Jarvis	4	4	4	4	6	12	15	100
439	Lee Maye	4	4	4	4	5	10	12	30
440	Bill Mazeroski	4	4	5	15	25	30	50	60
441	John O'Donoghue	4	4	4	4	5	10	12	40
442	Gene Mauch MG	4	4	4	5	10	20	25	30
443	Al Jackson	4	4	4	4	5	10	12	30
444	B.Farmer RC/J.Matias RC	4	4	4	4	6	12	15	60
445	Vada Pinson	4	4	5	6	12	40		100
446	Billy Grabarkewitz RC	4	4	4	4	5	10	12	60
447	Lee Stange	4	4	4	4	6	20	25	30
448	Houston Astros TC	4	4	4	4	5	10	12	30
449	Jim Palmer	▲12	▲20	▲30	▲50	▲60	▲100	▲120	400
450	Willie McCovey AS	6	10	15	25	40	60	80	120
451	Boog Powell AS	4	4	6	8	15	50		
452	Felix Millan AS	4	4	4	5	10	20	25	50
453	Rod Carew AS	4	6	8	10	20	40	100	200
454	Ron Santo AS	4	4	5	6	12	50		
455	Brooks Robinson AS	4	5	10	20	30	150		
456	Don Kessinger AS	4	4	4	5	10	25		60
457	Rico Petrocelli AS	4	4	6	8	15	30	50	80
458	Pete Rose AS	10	15	25	30	80	300		
459	Reggie Jackson AS	4	10	12	25	60	250		
460	Matty Alou AS	4	6	12	15	30	100		
461	Carl Yastrzemski AS	4	10	20	30	60	250		
462	Hank Aaron AS	12	25	30	50	80	500		
463	Frank Robinson AS	▲8	▲12	20	▲30	▲50	▲80	▲100	500
464	Johnny Bench AS	▲12	20	▲30	▲50	100	▲500		
465	Bill Freehan AS	4	6	12	15	30	60	80	175
466	Juan Marichal AS	4	6	12	15	30	60	80	150
467	Denny McLain AS	4	4	5	6	12	50		
468	Jerry Koosman AS	4	6	12	15	30	80		
469	Sam McDowell AS	4	8	15	20	40	200		
470	Willie Stargell	▲12	▲20	▲30	▲50	80	▲200		
471	Chris Zachary	4	4	4	4	6	12	15	80
472	Atlanta Braves TC	4	4	4	4	5	10	12	80
473	Don Bryant	4	4	4	4	6	12	15	100
474	Dick Kelley	4	4	4	4	6	12	15	80
475	Dick McAuliffe	4	4	5	6	12	25	30	60
476	Don Shaw	4	4	4	5	10	20	25	50
477	A.Severinsen RC/R.Freed RC	4	4	5	6	12	25	60	100
478	Bobby Heise RC	4	4	4	4	8	20		
479	Dick Woodson RC	4	4	5	6	12	25		
480	Glenn Beckert	4	4	6	8	15	30	40	200
481	Jose Tartabull	4	4	4	5	10	20	30	60
482	Tom Hilgendorf RC	4	4	4	4	6	12	15	25
483	Gail Hopkins RC	4	4	4	4	8	15		
484	Gary Nolan	5	6	8	10	20	80	100	150
485	Jay Johnstone	4	5	6	8	10	20	25	60
486	Terry Harmon	4	4	5	6	12	40		
487	Cisco Carlos	4	4	4	4	8	15		
488	J.C. Martin	4	4	6	8	15	30	40	80
489	Eddie Kasko MG	4	4	4	5	10	20	25	50
490	Bill Singer	4	4	4	5	10	20	25	100
491	Graig Nettles	4	4	4	8	15	30	40	120
492	K.Lampard RC/S.Spinks RC	4	4	4	4	6	12	15	30
493	Lindy McDaniel	4	4	4	4	8	20	25	50
494	Larry Stahl	4	4	4	4	8	15	20	60
495	Dave Morehead	4	4	4	5	10	20	25	50

#	Player	VG 3	VgEx 4	EX 5	ExMt 6	NM 7	NmMt 8	NmMt+ 8.5	MT 9
496	Steve Whitaker	4	4	4	5	10	20	25	
497	Eddie Watt	4	4	8	10	20	40	50	100
498	Al Weis	4	4	4	4	5	10	12	60
499	Skip Lockwood	4	4	5	6	12	25	30	120
500	Hank Aaron	▲60	▲100	▲120	▲250	▲300	▲600	▲800	▲1,500
501	Chicago White Sox TC	4	4	4	4	8	15	20	60
502	Rollie Fingers	10	15	25	40	▲60	▲100	▲120	150
503	Dal Maxvill	4	4	4	4	8	15	20	100
504	Don Pavletich	4	4	4	4	6	12	15	80
505	Ken Holtzman	4	4	5	6	12	25	30	150
506	Ed Stroud	4	4	4	5	10	20	25	80
507	Pat Corrales	6	8	10	12	25	40		
508	Joe Niekro	4	4	4	4	8	15	30	50
509	Montreal Expos TC	4	4	4	5	10	20	25	
510	Tony Oliva	6	8	10	12	25	120		
511	Joe Hoerner	4	4	4	4	8	15	20	80
512	Billy Harris	4	4	4	4	6	12	15	50
513	Preston Gomez MG	4	4	4	4	5	10	12	25
514	Steve Hovley RC	4	4	4	4	5	10	12	25
515	Don Wilson	4	4	4	5	10	20	25	80
516	J.Ellis RC/J.Lyttle RC	4	5	10	12	25	50		
517	Joe Gibbon	4	4	4	4	5	10	12	25
518	Bill Melton	4	4	4	5	10	20	25	
519	Don McMahon	4	4	4	4	8	15		
520	Willie Horton	8	10	12	15	30	80		
521	Cal Koonce	5	6	8	10	20	40		
522	California Angels TC	4	4	5	6	12	25	30	60
523	Jose Pena	4	4	5	6	12	100		
524	Alvin Dark MG	4	4	4	4	6	12	15	25
525	Jerry Adair	4	4	6	8	15	30	50	80
526	Ron Herbel	4	4	4	5	10	20	25	
527	Don Bosch	4	4	4	4	8	15	20	40
528	Elrod Hendricks	4	4	5	6	12	25	30	200
529	Bob Aspromonte	4	4	4	4	6	12	15	30
530	Bob Gibson	▲15	▲25	▲40	▲60	▲100	▲200	▲250	▲600
531	Ron Clark	4	4	4	5	10	20	25	
532	Danny Murtaugh MG	4	4	5	6	12	25	30	80
533	Buzz Stephen RC	4	4	4	4	8	15	20	50
534	Minnesota Twins TC	4	4	5	6	12	25	30	60
535	Andy Kosco	4	4	4	4	8	15	20	25
536	Mike Kekich	4	5	10	12	25	50		
537	Joe Morgan	10	15	25	▲40	▲80	▲120	▲150	400
538	Bob Humphreys	4	4	4	5	10	20	25	60
539	D.Doyle RC/L.Bowa RC	6	8	15	20	30	60		
540	Gary Peters	4	4	6	8	15	30	40	
541	Bill Heath	4	4	4	4	5	10	12	40
542A	Checklist 6 Brown Bat	4	4	6	8	15	30	40	80
542B	Checklist 6 Gray Bat	4	4	5	6	12	25		
543	Clyde Wright	4	4	4	5	10	60	80	
544	Cincinnati Reds TC	4	4	5	6	12	25	30	150
545	Ken Harrelson	4	4	4	5	10	50	60	100
546	Ron Reed	4	4	4	4	6	12	15	30
547	Rick Monday	4	4	4	4	6	20	25	100
548	Howie Reed	4	4	4	4	5	10	12	40
549	St. Louis Cardinals TC	4	4	4	4	6	20	30	100
550	Frank Howard	4	4	4	4	8	40	50	60
551	Dock Ellis	4	4	4	5	10	20	25	30
552	O'Riley/Paepke/Rico RC	4	4	4	4	8	15	20	60
553	Jim Lefebvre	4	4	4	4	5	10	12	25
554	Tom Timmermann RC	4	4	4	4	5	10	12	30
555	Orlando Cepeda	4	5	15	20	30	80	100	300
556	Dave Bristol MG	4	4	4	4	6	12	15	40
557	Ed Kranepool	4	5	10	12	25	50	60	150
558	Vern Fuller	4	4	4	4	5	10	12	25
559	Tommy Davis	4	5	4	4	8	12	15	80
560	Gaylord Perry	4	6	10	15	30	50	60	100
561	Tom McCraw	4	4	4	4	6	12	15	30
562	Ted Abernathy	4	4	4	4	5	10	12	20

#	Player	VG 3	VgEx 4	EX 5	ExMt 6	NM 7	NmMt 8	NmMt+ 8.5	MT 9
563	Boston Red Sox TC	4	4	5	6	12	25	30	50
564	Johnny Briggs	4	4	4	5	6	12	15	25
565	Jim Hunter	8	12	20	30	40	60	80	120
566	Gene Alley	4	4	4	4	6	15	20	25
567	Bob Oliver	4	4	4	4	5	10	12	20
568	Stan Bahnsen	4	4	4	4	5	15	20	25
569	Cookie Rojas	4	4	4	4	5	15	20	25
570	Jim Fregosi	4	4	4	4	6	12	15	30
571	Jim Brewer	4	4	4	4	5	10	12	30
572	Frank Quilici	4	4	4	4	4	8	10	15
573	Corkins/Robles/Slocum RC	4	4	4	4	5	10	12	20
574	Bobby Bolin	4	4	4	4	5	10	12	25
575	Cleon Jones	4	4	4	4	5	30	40	50
576	Milt Pappas	4	4	4	4	5	10	12	25
577	Bernie Allen	4	4	4	4	5	10	12	25
578	Tom Griffin	4	4	4	4	8	15	20	30
579	Detroit Tigers TC	4	4	4	4	8	30	50	100
580	Pete Rose	▲30	▲50	▲80	▲120	▲200	▲500	▲600	▲2,500
581	Tom Satriano	4	4	4	4	6	12	15	25
582	Mike Paul	4	4	4	4	5	10	12	25
583	Hal Lanier	4	4	4	4	5	10	12	25
584	Al Downing	4	4	4	4	6	12	15	50
585	Rusty Staub	4	4	5	6	12	25	30	80
586	Rickey Clark RC	4	4	6	8	15	30	40	80
587	Jose Arcia	4	4	4	4	5	10	12	25
588A	Checklist 7 666 is Adolfo	4	4	5	6	12	25		
588B	Checklist 7 666 is Adolpho	4	4	5	6	12	25		
589	Joe Keough	4	4	4	4	5	10	12	20
590	Mike Cuellar	4	4	5	6	12	25	30	80
591	Mike Ryan	4	4	4	4	5	10	12	25
592	Daryl Patterson	4	4	4	4	5	10	12	20
593	Chicago Cubs TC	4	4	4	5	10	20	25	40
594	Jake Gibbs	4	4	4	4	8	15	20	80
595	Maury Wills	▲6	▲10	▲15	▲25	▲40	50	60	120
596	Mike Hershberger	4	4	4	4	4	8	15	25
597	Sonny Siebert	4	4	4	4	5	10	12	25
598	Joe Pepitone	4	4	4	5	8	12	20	40
599	Stelmaszek/Martin/Such RC	4	4	4	4	6	12	15	25
600	Willie Mays	50	▲80	▲120	▲200	300	▲800	▲1,000	2,000
601	Pete Richert	4	4	4	4	5	10	12	20
602	Ted Savage	4	4	4	4	5	10	12	25
603	Ray Oyler	4	4	4	4	5	10	12	25
604	Cito Gaston	4	4	5	8	12	20	25	50
605	Rick Wise	4	4	4	4	5	10	12	25
606	Chico Ruiz	4	4	4	4	5	10	12	25
607	Gary Waslewski	4	4	4	4	4	8	10	15
608	Pittsburgh Pirates TC	4	4	4	5	10	20	25	80
609	Buck Martinez RC	4	4	4	4	8	15	20	30
610	Jerry Koosman	4	4	5	6	8	15	20	40
611	Norm Cash	4	5	6	12	15	30	40	200
612	Jim Hickman	4	4	4	4	8	15	20	50
613	Dave Baldwin	4	4	4	4	5	15	20	25
614	Mike Shannon	4	4	4	4	6	12	15	60
615	Mark Belanger	4	4	4	4	6	15	20	30
616	Jim Merritt	4	4	4	4	6	12	15	25
617	Jim French	4	4	4	4	4	8	10	15
618	Billy Wynne RC	4	4	4	4	5	10	12	25
619	Norm Miller	4	4	4	4	5	10	12	25
620	Jim Perry	4	4	5	8	12	20	25	50
621	McQueen/Evans/Kester RC	4	6	10	15	40	50	60	▲250
622	Don Sutton	▲8	▲12	▲20	▲30	▲50	▲80	▲100	▲150
623	Horace Clarke	4	4	4	4	6	12	15	25
624	Clyde King MG	4	4	4	4	4	8	10	15
625	Dean Chance	4	4	4	4	5	10	12	20
626	Dave Ricketts	4	4	4	4	5	10	12	30
627	Gary Wagner	4	4	4	4	5	10	12	20
628	Wayne Garrett RC	4	4	4	5	10	20	25	200
629	Merv Rettenmund	4	4	4	4	8	15	20	40

		VG 3	VgEx 4	EX 5	ExMt 6	NM 7	NmMt 8	NmMt+ 8.5	MT 9
630	Ernie Banks	25	40	▲60	▲100	▲150	200	250	▲800
631	Oakland Athletics TC	4	4	6	8	15	30	40	80
632	Gary Sutherland	4	4	4	4	5	10	12	20
633	Roger Nelson	4	4	4	4	4	8	10	15
634	Bud Harrelson	5	10	20	25	50	100		
635	Bob Allison	4	4	4	5	20	25	30	80
636	Jim Stewart	4	4	4	4	6	15	20	60
637	Cleveland Indians TC	4	4	4	4	8	25	30	50
638	Frank Bertaina	4	4	4	5	10	30	40	
639	Dave Campbell	4	4	4	4	6	20	25	50
640	Al Kaline	▼15	▼25	▼40	60	100	▲150	▲200	▲400
641	Al McBean	4	4	4	4	6	15	25	50
642	Garrett/Lund/Tatum RC	4	4	4	4	8	25	30	50
643	Jose Pagan	4	4	4	5	10	20	25	80
644	Gerry Nyman	4	4	4	5	10	20	25	80
645	Don Money	4	4	4	5	10	20	30	40
646	Jim Britton	4	4	4	4	6	12	20	40
647	Tom Matchick	4	4	4	4	6	25	30	50
648	Larry Haney	4	4	4	4	6	15	20	30
649	Jimmie Hall	4	4	4	4	6	15	20	40
650	Sam McDowell	4	4	4	6	12	25	30	60
651	Jim Gosger	4	4	4	4	10	20	25	40
652	Rich Rollins	4	4	6	10	15	25	30	60
653	Moe Drabowsky	4	4	4	4	6	12	25	40
654	Oscar Gamble RC	4	4	10	20	50	100	150	300
655	John Roseboro	4	▲6	▲10	▲15	▲25	▲40	▲50	▲100
656	Jim Hardin	4	4	4	4	8	20	25	60
657	San Diego Padres TC	4	4	4	4	6	20	25	40
658	Ken Tatum RC	4	4	4	4	6	20	25	50
659	Pete Ward	4	4	5	10	20	40	50	80
660	Johnny Bench	▲80	▲120	▲200	▲250	▲400	▲600	▲800	▲1,500
661	Jerry Robertson	4	4	4	6	12	25	40	60
662	Frank Lucchesi MG RC	4	4	4	6	12	40	50	80
663	Tito Francona	4	4	6	10	15	25	30	60
664	Bob Robertson	4	5	8	12	20	30	40	100
665	Jim Lonborg	4	4	4	5	10	20	25	50
666	Adolpho Phillips	4	4	4	5	10	20	25	50
667	Bob Meyer	4	4	4	4	8	25	30	50
668	Bob Tillman	4	4	4	4	8	15		
669	Johnson/Lazar/Scott RC	4	4	4	4	8	25	30	80
670	Ron Santo	4	8	15	30	50	120	100	500
671	Jim Campanis	4	4	4	4	5	8	12	30
672	Leon McFadden	4	4	4	4	6	15	20	40
673	Ted Uhlaender	4	4	6	10	15	25	25	30
674	Dave Leonhard	4	4	4	4	6	12	15	40
675	Jose Cardenal	4	4	4	4	6	15	20	30
676	Washington Senators TC	4	4	5	6	10	15	25	50
677	Woodie Fryman	4	▲5	▲6	▲10	▲15	▲25	▲30	▲60
678	Dave Duncan	4	4	▲5	▲8	▲12	▲20	▲25	▲50
679	Ray Sadecki	4	4	4	4	6	20	25	80
680	Rico Petrocelli	4	5	10	12	25	30	60	120
681	Bob Garibaldi RC	4	4	4	5	10	20	25	100
682	Dalton Jones	4	4	4	5	10	25	25	50
683	Geishart/McRae/Simpson RC	4	6	12	15	40	50	100	300
684	Jack Fisher	4	4	4	4	6	20	25	50
685	Tom Haller	4	4	4	5	10	20	25	50
686	Jackie Hernandez	4	4	4	4	6	12	15	50
687	Bob Priddy	4	4	4	4	6	12	15	40
688	Ted Kubiak	4	4	4	4	8	15	20	40
689	Frank Tepedino RC	4	4	4	5	10	25	30	60
690	Ron Fairly	4	4	5	6	12	25	30	80
691	Joe Grzenda	4	4	4	4	6	12	15	30
692	Duffy Dyer	4	4	5	6	12	25	30	100
693	Bob Johnson	4	4	4	4	6	15	20	40
694	Gary Ross	4	4	4	4	6	20	25	40
695	Bobby Knoop	4	4	4	4	8	25	30	80
696	San Francisco Giants TC	4	4	5	6	12	50	60	120
697	Jim Hannan	4	4	4	4	8	25	30	60

		VG 3	VgEx 4	EX 5	ExMt 6	NM 7	NmMt 8	NmMt+ 8.5	MT 9
698	Tom Tresh	4	6	12	15	30	40	80	250
699	Hank Aguirre	4	4	4	4	6	15	20	40
700	Frank Robinson	6	25	30	50	60	80	150	400
701	Jack Billingham	4	4	4	4	8	15	20	80
702	Johnson/Klimkowski/Zepp RC	4	4	5	6	25	80	100	300
703	Lou Marone RC	4	4	4	4	8	15	20	150
704	Frank Baker RC	4	4	5	6	12	25	30	80
705	Tony Cloninger	4	4	4	4	6	20	25	80
706	John McNamara MG RC	4	4	4	4	6	12	15	40
707	Kevin Collins	4	4	4	4	8	15	20	80
708	Jose Santiago	4	4	4	4	6	12	15	25
709	Mike Fiore	4	4	4	4	6	15	20	40
710	Felix Millan	4	4	4	5	15	20		40
711	Ed Brinkman	4	4	4	4	6	20	25	40
712	Nolan Ryan	▲150	▲250	▲400	▲500	▲800	▲1,500	▲2,000	8,000
713	Seattle Pilots TC	5	6	12	15	30	120	150	300
714	Al Spangler	4	4	▲5	▲8	12	▼20	▼25	▲50
715	Mickey Lolich	4	8	15	20	40	50	80	300
716	Campisi/Cleveland/Guzman RC	4	4	4	4	8	25	30	40
717	Tom Phoebus	4	4	4	4	8	20	25	30
718	Ed Spiezio	4	4	4	▲6	▲10	15	20	▲40
719	Jim Roland	4	4	4	4	6	20	25	40
720	Rick Reichardt	4	4	5	6	12	40	60	80

— Hank Aaron AS #462 PSA 9 (MT) sold for $2,005 (Mile High; 05/11)
— Thurman Munson #189 PSA 10 (Gem) (Young Collection) sold for $13,045 (SCP; 5/12)
— Pete Rose #580 PSA 10 (Gem) sold for $2,499 (Mile High; 05/11)
— Pete Rose AS #458 PSA 9 (MT) sold for $1,478 (eBay; 01/12)
— Tom Seaver #300 PSA 10 (Gem) sold for $10,645 (Memory Lane; 5/13)

1970 Topps Super

		GD 2	VG 3	VgEx 4	EX 5	ExMt 6	NM 7	NmMt 8	MT 9
1	Claude Osteen SP	▲5	▲8	▲12	▲20	▲30	▲50	▲80	
2	Sal Bando SP	▲5	▲8	▲12	▲20	▲30	▲50	▲80	▲250
3	Luis Aparicio SP	▲6	▲10	▲15	▲25	▲40	▲60	▲100	▲300
4	Harmon Killebrew	▲6	▲10	▲15	▲25	▲40	▲60	▲100	▲300
5	Tom Seaver SP	▲10	▲15	▲25	▲40	▲60	▲100	▲150	▲2,000
6	Larry Dierker	4	4	4	4	4	8	15	40
7	Bill Freehan	4	4	4	6	8	15	60	120
8	Johnny Bench	▲20	▲30	▲50	▲80	▲120	▲200	▲300	▲1,200
9	Tommy Harper	4	4	▲5	▲8	▲12	▲20	▲30	▲100
10	Sam McDowell	▲6	▲10	▲15	▲25	▲40	▲60	▲100	▲300
11	Lou Brock	▲6	▲10	▲15	▲25	▲40	▲60	▲100	▲300
12	Roberto Clemente	▲40	▲60	▲100	▲150	▲250	▲400	▲600	▲1,500
13	Willie McCovey	▲12	▲20	▲30	▲50	▲80	▲120	▲200	▲600
14	Rico Petrocelli	4	4	▲6	▲10	▲15	▲25	▲40	▲120
15	Phil Niekro	4	▲6	▲10	▲15	▲25	▲40	▲60	▲200
16	Frank Howard	4	▲5	▲8	▲12	▲20	▲30	▲50	▲150
17	Denny McLain	4	▲5	▲8	▲12	▲20	▲30	▲50	▲150
18	Willie Mays	▲12	▲20	▲30	▲50	▲80	▲120	200	▲600
19	Willie Stargell	▲6	▲10	▲15	▲25	▲40	▲60	▲100	▲300
20	Joel Horlen	4	▲5	▲8	▲12	▲20	▲30	▲50	▲150
21	Ron Santo	4	▲6	▲10	▲15	▲25	▲40	▲60	▲200
22	Dick Bosman	▲6	▲10	▲15	▲25	▲40	▲60	▲100	▲300
23	Tim McCarver	4	▲5	▲8	▲12	▲20	▲30	▲50	▲150
24	Hank Aaron	▲15	▲25	▲40	60	▲100	▲150	▲250	▲800
25	Andy Messersmith	4	▲5	▲8	▲12	▲20	▲30	▲50	▲150
26	Tony Oliva	4	▲5	▲8	▲12	▲20	▲30	▲50	▲150
27	Mel Stottlemyre	4	▲5	▲8	▲12	▲20	▲30	▲50	▲150
28	Reggie Jackson	▲12	▲20	▲30	▲50	80	120	▲200	▲600
29	Carl Yastrzemski	▲10	▲15	▲25	▲40	▲60	▲100	▲150	▲500
30	Jim Fregosi	4	▲5	▲8	▲12	▲20	▲30	▲50	▲150
31	Vada Pinson	4	▲6	▲10	▲15	▲25	▲40	▲60	▲200
32	Lou Piniella	4	▲5	▲8	▲12	▲20	▲30	▲50	▲150
33	Bob Gibson	▲8	▲12	▲20	▲30	▲50	▲80	▲120	▲400
34	Pete Rose	▲25	▲30	▲50	▲80	▲120	▲200	▲300	▲2,000
35	Jim Wynn	4	▲5	▲8	▲12	▲20	▲30	▲50	▲150
36	Ollie Brown SP	▲5	▲8	▲12	▲20	▲30	▲50	▲80	▲250

		GD 2	VG 3	VgEx 4	EX 5	ExMt 6	NM 7	NmMt 8	MT 9
37	Frank Robinson SP	▲6	▲10	▲15	25	40	▲60	▲100	▲800
38	Boog Powell SP	▲15	▲25	▲40	▲60	▲100	▲150	▲250	
39	Willie Davis SP	4	▲5	▲8	▲12	▲20	▲30	▲50	▲150
40	Billy Williams SP	▲8	▲12	▲20	▲30	▲50	▲80	▲120	
41	Rusty Staub	4	4	▲6	▲10	▲15	▲25	▲40	▲120
42	Tommie Agee	4	4	▲5	▲8	▲12	▲20	▲30	▲100

1971 Kellogg's

		GD 2	VG 3	VgEx 4	EX 5	ExMt 6	NM 7	NmMt 8	MT 9
1A	Wayne Simpson 119 SO	4	4	4	5	6	12	120	
1B	Wayne Simpson 120 SO	4	4	4	5	6	12	25	
2	Tom Seaver	4	4	8	10	20	40	80	200
3A	Jim Perry 2238 IP	4	4	4	4	5	10	20	40
3B	Jim Perry 2239 IP	4	4	4	4	6	12	25	
4A	Bob Robertson 94 RBI	4	4	6	8	15	30	60	150
4B	Bob Robertson 95 RBI	4	4	4	6	12	25	50	
5	Roberto Clemente	4	5	10	20	50	80	150	400
6A	Gaylord Perry 2014 IP	4	4	4	8	10	20	40	100
6B	Gaylord Perry 2015 IP	4	4	4	8	10	20	40	100
7A	Felipe Alou Oakland NL	4	4	4	8	10	20	40	
7B	Felipe Alou Oakland AL	4	4	4	8	10	20	40	60
8	Denis Menke	4	4	4	8	10	20	40	60
9B	Don Kessinger 1970, 849 Hits	4	4	4	5	6	12	25	60
9C	Don Kessinger 1970, 850 Hits	4	4	4	5	6	12	25	50
10	Willie Mays	4	4	4	8	15	30	60	150
11	Jim Hickman	4	4	4	4	5	10	20	60
12	Tony Oliva	4	4	4	5	10	20	40	60
13	Manny Sanguillen	4	4	4	5	6	12	25	60
14A	Frank Howard Washington NL	4	4	4	6	12	25	50	80
14B	Frank Howard Washington AL	4	4	4	8	10	20	40	
15	Frank Robinson	4	4	4	6	8	15	30	150
16	Willie Davis	4	4	4	4	5	10	20	40
17	Lou Brock	4	4	4	6	8	15	30	100
18	Cesar Tovar	4	4	4	4	5	10	20	50
19	Luis Aparicio	4	4	4	5	6	12	25	80
20	Boog Powell	4	4	4	5	6	12	25	50
21A	Dick Selma 584 SO	4	4	4	4	5	10	20	40
21B	Dick Selma 587 SO	4	4	4	5	6	12	25	50
22	Danny Walton	4	4	4	4	5	10	20	60
23	Carl Morton	4	4	4	4	5	10	20	40
24A	Sonny Siebert 1054 SO	4	4	4	4	5	10	20	40
24B	Sonny Siebert 1055 SO	4	4	4	6	8	15	30	50
25	Jim Merritt	4	4	4	4	5	10	20	40
26A	Jose Cardenal 828 Hits	4	4	4	4	5	10	20	40
26B	Jose Cardenal 829 Hits	4	4	4	5	6	12	25	50
27	Don Mincher	4	4	4	4	5	10	20	40
28B	Clyde Wright No 1970, Cal	4	4	4	4	5	10	20	50
28C	Clyde Wright 1970, Cal	4	4	4	4	5	10	20	60
29	Les Cain	4	4	4	5	6	12	25	50
30	Danny Cater	4	4	4	4	5	10	20	60
31	Don Sutton	4	4	4	5	6	12	25	60
32	Chuck Dobson	4	4	4	4	5	10	20	60
33	Willie McCovey	4	4	4	6	12	25	50	120
34	Mike Epstein	4	4	4	4	5	10	50	70
35A	Paul Blair 386 Runs	4	4	4	4	5	10	20	100
35B	Paul Blair 385 Runs	4	4	4	5	6	12	25	
36B	Gary Nolan 1970, 577 SO	4	4	4	4	5	10	20	50
36C	Gary Nolan 1970, 581 SO	4	4	4	4	5	10	20	100
37	Sam McDowell	4	4	4	5	6	12	25	60
38	Amos Otis	4	4	4	4	5	10	20	50
39A	Ray Fosse 69 RBI	4	4	4	4	5	10	20	40
39B	Ray Fosse 70 RBI	4	4	4	5	6	12	25	50
40	Mel Stottlemyre	4	4	4	5	6	12	25	50
41	Clarence Gaston	4	4	4	4	5	10	20	50
42	Dick Dietz	4	4	4	4	5	10	20	50
43	Roy White	4	4	4	4	5	10	20	50
44	Al Kaline	4	4	4	8	10	20	40	120
45	Carlos May	4	4	4	4	5	10	20	60
46A	Tommie Agee 313 RBI	4	4	4	5	6	12	25	100
46B	Tommie Agee 314 RBI	4	4	6	12	25	50	100	
47	Tommy Harper	4	4	4	4	5	10	20	40
48	Larry Dierker	4	4	4	4	5	10	20	60
49	Mike Cuellar	4	4	4	5	6	12	25	50
50	Ernie Banks	4	4	8	10	20	40	100	
51	Bob Gibson	4	4	8	15	30	120		
52	Reggie Smith	4	4	4	4	5	10	20	60
53A	Matty Alou 273 RBI	4	4	4	4	5	10	20	100
53B	Matty Alou 274 RBI	4	4	4	5	6	12	25	
54A	Alex Johnson No 1970, Angels	4	4	4	4	5	10	20	50
54B	Alex Johnson No 1970, Cal	4	4	4	4	5	10	20	100
55	Harmon Killebrew	4	4	4	8	10	20	40	100
56	Bill Grabarkewitz	4	4	4	4	5	10	20	40
57	Richie Allen	4	4	4	5	6	12	25	50
58	Tony Perez	4	4	4	8	15	30	60	100
59A	Dave McNally 1065 SO	4	4	4	5	6	12	25	80
59B	Dave McNally 1067 SO	4	5	10	20	40	80	150	
60A	Jim Palmer 564 SO	4	4	4	6	8	15	30	120
60B	Jim Palmer 567 SO	4	4	4	8	10	20	40	
61	Billy Williams	4	4	4	8	10	20	40	80
62	Joe Torre	4	4	4	6	8	15	30	80
63A	Jim Northrup 2773 AB	4	4	4	4	5	10	20	
63B	Jim Northrup 2772 AB	4	4	6	12	25	50	100	
64A	Jim Fregosi No 1970, Angels	4	4	4	6	8	15	30	
64C	Jim Fregosi 1970, Cal, 1326 Hits	4	4	4	4	5	10	20	40
64D	Jim Fregosi 1970, Cal, 1327 Hits	4	4	4	5	6	12	25	
65	Pete Rose	4	4	8	15	30	60	200	300
66B	Bud Harrelson 1970, 112 RBI	4	4	4	5	6	12	25	50
66C	Bud Harrelson 1970, 113 RBI	4	4	4	5	6	12	25	60
67	Tony Taylor	4	4	4	4	5	10	20	50
68	Willie Stargell	4	4	4	8	10	20	50	100
69	Tony Horton	4	4	4	4	5	10	20	100
70A	Claude Osteen No 1970, No #	4	4	4	6	8	15	30	
70C	Claude Osteen 1970, No. 70	4	4	4	4	5	10	20	60
71	Glenn Beckert	4	4	4	8	10	20	40	80
72	Nate Colbert	4	4	4	4	5	10	20	60
73B	Rick Monday 1970, 1705 AB	4	4	4	4	5	10	20	
73C	Rick Monday 1970, 1704 AB	4	4	4	6	8	15	30	
74A	Tommy John 444 BB	4	4	4	8	10	20	40	80
74B	Tommy John 443 BB	4	4	4	6	8	15	30	
75	Chris Short	4	4	4	8	10	20	40	150

1971 O-Pee-Chee

— Pete Rose #100 SGC 96 (MT) sold for $2,386 (eBay; 09/12)

1971 Topps

		VG 3	VgEx 4	EX 5	ExMt 6	NM 7	NmMt 8	NmMt+ 8.5	MT 9
1	Baltimore Orioles TC	5	10	20	25	50	150		
2	Dock Ellis	4	4	8	10	20	60		
3	Dick McAuliffe	4	5	10	12	25	60		
4	Vic Davalillo	4	4	6	8	15	30	50	200
5	Thurman Munson	40	50	60	120	400	3,000		
6	Ed Spiezio	4	4	6	8	15	30	100	325
7	Jim Holt RC	4	4	5	6	12	60	80	150
8	Mike McQueen	4	4	4	5	10	20	25	200
9	George Scott	5	10	20	25	50	100	120	200
10	Claude Osteen	4	5	10	12	25	50		
11	Elliott Maddox RC	4	4	6	8	15	30	80	200
12	Johnny Callison	4	5	10	12	25	60		
13	C.Brinkman RC/D.Moloney RC	4	4	4	4	8	30	40	120
14	Dave Concepcion RC	▲40	▲50	▲60	▲80	200	400	500	1,000
15	Andy Messersmith	4	4	8	10	20	60	80	275
16	Ken Singleton RC	4	4	6	8	15	30		
17	Billy Sorrell	4	4	4	4	8	15	40	120
18	Norm Miller	4	4	4	4	8	20	100	150

#		VG 3	VgEx 4	EX 5	ExMt 6	NM 7	NmMt 8	NmMt+ 8.5	MT 9
9	Skip Pitlock RC	4	4	4	4	8	30	100	120
0	Reggie Jackson	30	40	▲60	100	▲400	2,000		
1	Dan McGinn	4	4	4	5	10	20		
2	Phil Roof	4	4	4	6	12	25	50	175
3	Oscar Gamble	4	4	8	10	20	40		
4	Rich Hand RC	4	4	4	4	8	25		
5	Cito Gaston	4	4	8	10	30	80		
6	Bert Blyleven RC	25	40	60	100	▼250	1,200		
7	F.Cambria RC/G.Clines RC	4	4	6	8	25	30		
8	Ron Klimkowski	4	5	10	12	25	80		
9	Don Buford	4	4	4	4	8	20	40	175
0	Phil Niekro	5	8	12	20	30	80		
1	Eddie Kasko MG	4	4	5	6	12	30		
2	Jerry DaVanon	4	4	6	8	15	30	50	200
3	Del Unser	4	4	6	8	15	30		
4	Sandy Vance RC	4	8	15	20	40	100		
5	Lou Piniella	4	4	5	10	20	40		
6	Dean Chance	4	4	8	10	20	40		
7	Rich McKinney RC	4	4	8	10	20	40		
8	Jim Colborn RC	4	4	4	5	10	20	40	500
9	L.LaGrow RC/G.Lamont RC	4	4	5	6	12	30	60	400
0	Lee May	4	4	8	10	20	40	60	150
1	Rick Austin RC	4	4	4	4	8	15	30	
2	Boots Day	4	4	4	4	8	15	40	150
3	Steve Kealey	4	4	4	4	8	15	25	100
4	Johnny Edwards	4	4	5	6	12	25	30	150
5	Jim Hunter	4	6	10	15	25	100	150	400
6	Dave Campbell	4	4	4	4	8	15	40	500
7	Johnny Jeter	4	4	4	4	8	25	40	150
8	Dave Baldwin	4	4	4	4	8	15	25	150
9	Don Money	4	6	12	15	30	60		
0	Willie McCovey	4	10	15	40	50	150	300	500
1	Steve Kline RC	4	4	4	4	8	20	40	150
2	O.Brown RC/E.Williams RC	4	4	4	4	8	15	25	200
3	Paul Blair	4	4	6	8	15	30	50	200
	Checklist 1	4	6	12	15	30	60		
	Steve Carlton	12	20	30	50	60	250		
	Duane Josephson	4	4	6	8	15	30		
	Von Joshua RC	4	4	4	5	10	20		
	Bill Lee	4	4	6	8	15	40		
	Gene Mauch MG	4	4	4	4	8	20	40	150
	Dick Bosman	4	8	15	20	40	100		
	AL Batting Leaders	4	6	12	15	30	80		
	NL Batting Leaders	4	4	6	8	15	30	50	150
	AL RBI Leaders	4	4	5	6	12	25		
	NL RBI Leaders	4	4	8	15	30	60	120	400
	AL Home Run Leaders	4	5	10	12	25	50	60	300
	NL Home Run Leaders	4	4	6	12	40	100	120	300
	AL ERA Leaders	4	4	8	10	20	40	80	250
	NL ERA Leaders	4	4	8	10	20	50	80	225
	AL Pitching Leaders	4	4	8	10	20	50		
	NL Pitching Leaders	4	4	6	12	25	80	100	200
	AL Strikeout Leaders	4	4	6	8	15	30	60	300
	NL Strikeout Leaders	4	4	8	10	20	40	80	400
	George Brunet	4	4	4	4	8	15	40	150
	P.Hamm RC/J.Nettles RC	4	4	4	5	10	20		
	Gary Nolan	4	4	4	5	10	50	80	150
	Ted Savage	4	4	5	6	12	30		
	Mike Compton RC	4	4	4	5	10	25		
	Jim Spencer	4	4	4	4	8	15		
	Wade Blasingame	4	6	12	15	30	50		
	Bill Melton	4	4	4	5	10	20		
	Felix Millan	4	4	4	5	10	20		
	Casey Cox	4	4	5	6	12	25		
	T.Foli RC/R.Bobb RC	4	8	15	20	40	120		
	Marcel Lachemann RC	4	4	5	6	12	30		
	Billy Grabarkewitz	4	4	▲5	6	▲12	50	40	300
	Mike Kilkenny	4	4	4	4	8	20		

#		VG 3	VgEx 4	EX 5	ExMt 6	NM 7	NmMt 8	NmMt+ 8.5	MT 9
87	Jack Heidemann RC	4	4	4	5	10	20		
88	Hal King	4	4	4	4	8	15	40	200
89	Ken Brett	4	4	6	8	15	40		
90	Joe Pepitone	4	4	4	5	10	25	50	250
91	Bob Lemon MG	4	4	4	6	12	25		
92	Fred Wenz	4	6	12	15	30	80		
93	N.McRae/D.Riddleberger	4	4	4	5	10	25		
94	Don Hahn RC	4	4	4	5	10	20		
95	Luis Tiant	4	4	8	10	20	40		
96	Joe Hague	4	4	6	8	15	30		
97	Floyd Wicker	4	4	4	4	8	15	50	150
98	Joe Decker RC	4	4	4	4	8	15		
99	Mark Belanger	4	4	4	5	10	30	80	450
100	Pete Rose	25	30	40	60	250	1,200		
101	Les Cain	4	4	4	5	10	20		
102	K.Forsch RC/L.Howard RC	4	4	4	5	10	25	60	250
103	Rich Severson RC	4	4	4	4	8	15		
104	Dan Frisella	4	4	6	8	15	30		300
105	Tony Conigliaro	4	4	4	4	8	15	25	200
106	Tom Dukes	4	4	4	4	8	15	40	120
107	Roy Foster RC	4	8	15	20	40	80	40	120
108	John Cumberland	4	4	4	4	8	15	50	200
109	Steve Hovley	4	4	4	5	10	20	40	120
110	Bill Mazeroski	6	10	15	25	40	80	100	300
111	L.Colson RC/B.Mitchell RC	4	8	15	20	40	80		
112	Manny Mota	4	4	5	6	12	25	80	200
113	Jerry Crider	4	4	4	4	8	20	40	120
114	Billy Conigliaro	4	6	12	15	40	60		
115	Donn Clendenon	4	4	6	8	15	30		
116	Ken Sanders	4	4	4	6	12	25	40	150
117	Ted Simmons RC	▲50	80	▲120	▲200	300	1,000	1,000	2,000
118	Cookie Rojas	4	4	4	5	10	25		
119	Frank Lucchesi MG	4	4	4	6	12	20	40	120
120	Willie Horton	4	4	4	5	10	25	50	200
121	J.Dunegan/R.Skidmore RC	4	4	4	5	10	20		
122	Eddie Watt	4	4	8	10	20	40	80	▲250
123A	Checklist 2 Bottom Right	4	5	10	12	25	50		
123B	Checklist 2 Centered	4	6	12	15	30	60		
124	Don Gullett RC	4	4	4	8	15	20	50	200
125	Ray Fosse	4	4	4	5	10	20	50	150
126	Danny Coombs	4	4	4	4	8	15	40	120
127	Danny Thompson RC	4	4	4	6	12	25		
128	Frank Johnson	4	4	4	5	10	20	25	200
129	Aurelio Monteagudo	4	4	4	5	10	20		
130	Denis Menke	4	4	4	5	10	20	40	120
131	Curt Blefary	4	5	10	12	25	50		
132	Jose Laboy	4	5	10	12	25	50		
133	Mickey Lolich	4	5	10	20	40	80		
134	Jose Arcia	4	4	4	5	10	30		
135	Rick Monday	5	10	20	25	50	100		
136	Duffy Dyer	4	4	4	5	10	20	40	275
137	Marcelino Lopez	4	4	8	10	20	40		
138	J.Lis/W.Montanez RC	5	10	20	25	50	100		
139	Paul Casanova	4	4	4	4	8	15		
140	Gaylord Perry	4	4	5	10	25	80		
141	Frank Quilici	4	4	4	5	10	20		
142	Mack Jones	4	4	5	10	20	40		
143	Steve Blass	4	4	4	5	10	30		
144	Jackie Hernandez	4	4	4	5	10	20	50	200
145	Bill Singer	4	4	6	8	12	25		
146	Ralph Houk MG	4	4	6	8	15	50		
147	Bob Priddy	4	4	4	4	8	15		
148	John Mayberry	4	4	6	8	10	20	50	
149	Mike Hershberger	4	4	4	5	10	20		
150	Sam McDowell	4	4	4	8	15	30	50	150
151	Tommy Davis	4	4	4	5	10	20		
152	L.Allen RC/W.Llenas RC	4	4	4	5	10	20		
153	Gary Ross	4	6	12	15	30	60		

#	Player	VG 3	VgEx 4	EX 5	ExMt 6	NM 7	NmMt 8	NmMt+ 8.5	MT 9
154	Cesar Gutierrez	4	4	4	4	8	20	40	150
155	Ken Henderson	4	4	4	5	10	20	40	120
156	Bart Johnson	4	6	12	15	30	100		
157	Bob Bailey	4	4	4	4	8	15	40	120
158	Jerry Reuss	4	4	4	6	12	25	60	150
159	Jarvis Tatum	4	4	4	4	8	15	50	150
160	Tom Seaver	15	25	30	40	▲120	300		
161	Coin Checklist	4	▲6	▲10	▲15	▲25	▲40	▲50	120
162	Jack Billingham	4	4	4	4	8	15		
163	Buck Martinez	4	4	4	6	12	25		
164	F.Duffy RC/M.Wilcox RC	4	4	4	8	15	30		
165	Cesar Tovar	4	4	6	8	15	30		
166	Joe Hoerner	4	4	5	6	12	25		
167	Tom Grieve RC	4	4	4	4	5	20	60	200
168	Bruce Dal Canton	4	4	6	8	15	30	40	150
169	Ed Herrmann	4	4	5	6	12	25		
170	Mike Cuellar	4	4	4	8	15	30	60	250
171	Bobby Wine	4	5	10	12	25	50		
172	Duke Sims	4	4	5	6	12	25	60	275
173	Gil Garrido	4	5	10	12	25	80		
174	Dave LaRoche RC	4	4	4	5	10	20		
175	Jim Hickman	4	4	4	5	10	25	30	400
176	B.Montgomery RC/D.Griffin RC	4	4	8	10	20	50		
177	Hal McRae	4	4	4	5	10	25	50	200
178	Dave Duncan	4	4	4	5	10	80	100	200
179	Mike Corkins	4	4	4	4	8	15	40	120
180	Al Kaline	12	20	30	50	80	300	400	3,000
181	Hal Lanier	4	4	4	5	10	20		
182	Al Downing	4	4	4	5	10	20	50	150
183	Gil Hodges MG	4	4	6	8	15	30		
184	Stan Bahnsen	4	4	4	4	8	20	100	250
185	Julian Javier	4	4	8	10	20	40		
186	Bob Spence RC	4	4	4	4	8	15		
187	Ted Abernathy	4	4	4	4	8	15	40	150
188	Bobby Valentine RC	5	6	10	15	25	60		
189	George Mitterwald	4	4	4	5	10	50	60	150
190	Bob Tolan	4	4	6	12	25	50		
191	Mike Andrews	4	4	4	5	10	25		
192	Billy Wilson	4	4	6	8	15	30		
193	Bob Grich RC	4	4	6	8	15	30		
194	Mike Lum	4	4	6	8	15	30	40	120
195	Boog Powell ALCS	4	4	6	8	15	40		
196	Dave McNally ALCS	4	4	4	6	12	25		
197	Jim Palmer ALCS	4	4	8	15	30	200		
198	Orioles Celebrate ALCS	4	6	12	15	30	120		
199	Ty Cline NLCS	5	10	20	25	50	120		
200	Bobby Tolan NLCS	4	6	12	15	30	100		
201	Ty Cline NLCS	4	4	5	10	20	40	80	150
202	Reds Celebrate NLCS	4	4	5	10	20	80		
203	Larry Gura RC	4	4	4	6	12	25	50	250
204	B.Smith RC/G.Kopacz RC	4	4	4	4	8	20		
205	Gerry Moses	4	4	4	4	8	15	40	120
206	Checklist 3 Orange Helmet	5	6	10	15	25	40	50	150
207	Alan Foster	4	4	4	5	10	30		
208	Billy Martin MG	4	4	5	6	12	30	80	300
209	Steve Renko	4	4	4	4	8	15		
210	Rod Carew	12	20	▲30	▲50	100	300	400	1,000
211	Phil Hennigan RC	4	4	4	4	8	15	40	120
212	Rich Hebner	4	4	4	4	8	25	40	120
213	Frank Baker RC	4	4	4	5	10	25		
214	Al Ferrara	4	4	4	4	8	15	40	150
215	Diego Segui	4	4	4	5	10	25	40	250
216	R.Cleveland/L.Melendez RC	4	5	10	12	25	50		
217	Ed Stroud	4	4	4	5	10	20	40	120
218	Tony Cloninger	4	4	4	5	10	20	40	150
219	Elrod Hendricks	4	4	4	4	8	15	40	150
220	Ron Santo	6	12	25	30	50	150		
221	Dave Morehead	4	4	4	5	10	20	50	150
222	Bob Watson	4	4	4	5	10	30		
223	Cecil Upshaw	4	4	4	5	10	20	40	120
224	Alan Gallagher RC	4	4	4	4	8	15		
225	Gary Peters	4	4	8	10	20	40	100	200
226	Bill Russell	4	4	8	10	20	40		
227	Floyd Weaver	4	4	4	4	8	15	40	100
228	Wayne Garrett	4	4	4	6	12	25	80	300
229	Jim Hannan	4	4	8	10	20	40	60	250
230	Willie Stargell	▲15	▲25	▲40	▲60	▲100	▲300	▲400	1,000
231	V.Colbert RC/J.Lowenstein RC	4	4	4	8	15	60		
232	John Strohmayer RC	4	4	5	6	12	30	40	150
233	Larry Bowa	4	4	5	10	20	40		
234	Jim Lyttle	4	4	4	8	15	100		
235	Nate Colbert	4	4	4	5	10	20		
236	Bob Humphreys	4	4	4	5	10	20	40	150
237	Cesar Cedeno RC	4	4	8	15	30	60		
238	Chuck Dobson	4	4	4	6	12	25	50	120
239	Red Schoendienst MG	4	4	4	8	15	25	60	150
240	Clyde Wright	4	4	4	5	10	20	40	150
241	Dave Nelson	4	4	4	4	8	15	50	150
242	Jim Ray	4	4	4	5	10	20	40	120
243	Carlos May	4	4	5	10	20	40	60	250
244	Bob Tillman	4	4	4	5	10	20	40	100
245	Jim Kaat	4	4	4	8	15	30	60	200
246	Tony Taylor	5	10	20	25	50	100		
247	J.Cram RC/P.Splittorff RC	4	4	4	5	10	20	50	150
248	Hoyt Wilhelm	4	4	8	10	20	80	15	300
249	Chico Salmon	4	4	4	5	10	20		
250	Johnny Bench	10	25	50	60	200	▲2,000		
251	Frank Reberger	4	4	4	5	10	20		
252	Eddie Leon	4	4	5	10	20	30	50	150
253	Bill Sudakis	4	4	8	10	20	120		
254	Cal Koonce	4	4	4	5	10	20		
255	Bob Robertson	4	4	4	6	12	25	40	150
256	Tony Gonzalez	4	4	4	5	10	20	30	120
257	Nelson Briles	4	4	4	4	8	20		
258	Dick Green	5	10	20	25	50	200		
259	Dave Marshall	4	4	4	4	8	15		
260	Tommy Harper	4	4	8	10	20	100		
261	Darold Knowles	4	4	8	10	20	120		
262	J.Williams/D.Robinson RC	4	4	4	5	10	20	30	150
263	John Ellis	4	8	15	20	40	80		
264	Joe Morgan	8	12	20	40	50	500		
265	Jim Northrup	4	4	4	5	10	40	60	200
266	Bill Stoneman	4	4	4	4	8	15	40	120
267	Rich Morales	4	4	4	5	10	20	40	200
268	Philadelphia Phillies TC	4	4	4	6	12	20	40	150
269	Gail Hopkins	4	4	4	5	10	20		
270	Rico Carty	5	6	12	15	30	200		
271	Bill Zepp	4	4	4	5	10	20	40	200
272	Tommy Helms	4	4	5	10	20	40	60	120
273	Pete Richert	4	4	4	8	15	40	100	150
274	Ron Slocum	4	4	4	8	15	50		
275	Vada Pinson	5	10	20	25	50	100		
276	M.Davison RC/G.Foster RC	10	15	25	50	80	120		
277	Gary Waslewski	4	8	15	20	40	100		
278	Jerry Grote	4	5	10	12	25	80		
279	Lefty Phillips MG	4	4	4	5	10	20		
280	Ferguson Jenkins	4	6	12	20	50	150		
281	Danny Walton	4	4	6	8	15	30		
282	Jose Pagan	4	4	5	6	12	30	60	150
283	Dick Such	4	4	4	6	12	25	40	150
284	Jim Gosger	4	4	4	4	8	15	40	150
285	Sal Bando	4	4	4	5	10	20	80	350
286	Jerry McNertney	4	4	4	5	10	20	40	100
287	Mike Fiore	5	10	20	25	50	60		
288	Joe Moeller	4	5	10	12	25	80		
289	Chicago White Sox TC	4	4	4	5	10	20		

#	Player	VG 3	VgEx 4	EX 5	ExMt 6	NM 7	NmMt 8	NmMt+ 8.5	MT 9
290	Tony Oliva	4	6	12	25	50	80		
291	George Culver	4	4	4	4	8	15	40	150
292	Jay Johnstone	4	4	4	5	10	20		
293	Pat Corrales	4	4	4	4	8	15	40	100
294	Steve Dunning RC	6	12	25	30	60	80		
295	Bobby Bonds	4	4	5	6	12	50	60	200
296	Tom Timmermann	4	4	5	6	12	25	50	200
297	Johnny Briggs	4	4	4	6	12	25	50	175
298	Jim Nelson RC	4	4	4	6	12	25	40	150
299	Ed Kirkpatrick	4	6	12	15	30	60		
300	Brooks Robinson	8	15	30	50	120	800		
301	Earl Wilson	4	4	4	5	10	20	80	200
302	Phil Gagliano	4	4	5	6	12	25		
303	Lindy McDaniel	4	4	4	8	15	50		
304	Ron Brand	4	4	4	4	8	15	80	300
305	Reggie Smith	4	4	8	10	20	40		
306	Jim Nash	4	4	4	4	8	20	40	100
307	Don Wert	4	4	4	4	8	15		
308	St. Louis Cardinals TC	4	4	5	6	12	25	40	120
309	Dick Ellsworth	4	6	12	15	30	60		
310	Tommie Agee	4	4	5	10	20	40	50	175
311	Lee Stange	4	4	4	5	10	20	40	120
312	Harry Walker MG	4	4	4	5	10	20		
313	Tom Hall	4	4	4	4	8	15	40	300
314	Jeff Torborg	4	4	8	15	30	60		
315	Ron Fairly	4	4	4	4	8	15	40	150
316	Fred Scherman RC	4	4	4	5	10	20	40	100
317	J.Driscoll RC/A.Mangual	4	4	4	5	10	20		
318	Rudy May	4	4	5	6	12	25	60	200
319	Ty Cline	4	4	4	5	10	20	50	120
320	Dave McNally	4	4	6	8	15	100		
321	Tom Matchick	4	4	4	4	8	15	40	120
322	Jim Beauchamp	4	4	5	6	12	25		
323	Billy Champion	4	4	4	4	8	15		
324	Graig Nettles	4	4	5	10	20	60	200	575
325	Juan Marichal	10	15	25	▲40	▲60	▲200		
326	Richie Scheinblum	4	4	4	4	8	15	40	120
327	Boog Powell WS	4	4	4	8	15	30		
328	Don Buford WS	4	4	5	10	20	50	100	250
329	Frank Robinson WS	4	4	5	6	12	30	60	200
330	Reds Stay Alive WS	4	4	4	5	10	25	50	300
331	Brooks Robinson WS	4	4	4	8	15	30	60	200
332	Orioles Celebrate WS	4	4	6	12	25	50		
333	Clay Kirby	4	4	4	6	12	25		
334	Roberto Pena	4	4	5	6	12	60		
335	Jerry Koosman	4	4	4	8	15	30	80	200
336	Detroit Tigers TC	4	4	4	6	12	25	50	200
337	Jesus Alou	4	4	6	8	15	60		
338	Gene Tenace	4	4	4	6	12	60		
339	Wayne Simpson	4	4	4	5	10	20	60	300
340	Rico Petrocelli	4	4	4	6	12	25		
341	Steve Garvey RC	30	50	60	100	250	500	600	3,000
342	Frank Tepedino	4	4	4	5	10	25		
343	E.Acosta RC/M.May RC	4	4	4	5	10	20	50	100
344	Ellie Rodriguez	4	4	4	4	8	15	50	120
345	Joel Horlen	4	4	4	5	10	20	40	100
346	Lum Harris MG	4	4	6	8	15	50		
347	Ted Uhlaender	4	4	4	4	8	15	30	80
348	Fred Norman	4	4	4	5	10	20		
349	Rich Reese	4	4	5	10	20	40		
350	Billy Williams	4	5	10	15	40	100		
351	Jim Shellenback	12	25	50	60	120	400		
352	Denny Doyle	4	4	5	10	20	50		
353	Carl Taylor	4	4	4	5	10	20	40	150
354	Don McMahon	4	4	4	5	10	20		
355	Bud Harrelson w/Ryan	4	4	8	10	20	60		
356	Bob Locker	4	4	4	4	8	15	40	100
357	Cincinnati Reds TC	4	4	6	8	15	40	60	250

#	Player	VG 3	VgEx 4	EX 5	ExMt 6	NM 7	NmMt 8	NmMt+ 8.5	MT 9
358	Danny Cater	4	4	8	15	30	40	100	150
359	Ron Reed	4	4	4	4	8	15	40	120
360	Jim Fregosi	4	4	5	6	12	80		
361	Don Sutton	▲10	▲15	▲25	▲40	▲60	▲200		
362	M.Adamson/R.Freed	4	4	4	5	10	25		
363	Mike Nagy	4	4	4	8	15	60		
364	Tommy Dean	4	4	4	4	8	15	40	80
365	Bob Johnson	4	4	8	10	20	40		
366	Ron Stone	4	4	4	5	10	20		
367	Dalton Jones	4	4	4	4	8	25		
368	Bob Veale	4	4	4	5	10	20	50	200
369	Checklist 4	4	4	6	10	20	30		
370	Joe Torre	4	5	10	12	25	100	120	300
371	Jack Hiatt	4	4	4	4	8	15	50	120
372	Lew Krausse	4	4	4	5	10	20	40	120
373	Tom McCraw	4	5	10	12	25	60		
374	Clete Boyer	4	4	4	5	10	20		
375	Steve Hargan	4	4	4	5	10	20	40	120
376	C.Mashore RC/E.McAnally RC	4	4	4	4	8	15	40	100
377	Greg Garrett	4	4	4	8	15	30		
378	Tito Fuentes	4	4	4	4	8	100	150	250
379	Wayne Granger	4	5	10	12	25	50		
380	Ted Williams MG	4	5	15	25	60	120		
381	Fred Gladding	4	4	4	8	15	80		
382	Jake Gibbs	5	10	20	25	50	100		
383	Rod Gaspar	4	4	4	8	15	30		
384	Rollie Fingers	10	15	25	50	200	800		
385	Maury Wills	4	4	4	8	15	120		
386	Boston Red Sox TC	4	4	4	8	15	30	50	150
387	Ron Herbel	4	4	4	4	8	15	40	120
388	Al Oliver	4	4	4	8	15	30		
389	Ed Brinkman	4	4	4	4	8	20		
390	Glenn Beckert	4	6	12	15	30	60		
391	S.Brye RC/C.Nash RC	4	4	4	6	12	25		
392	Grant Jackson	4	4	5	6	12	40		
393	Merv Rettenmund	4	4	4	8	15	40		
394	Clay Carroll	4	4	4	8	15	30	50	300
395	Roy White	4	6	12	15	30	60	60	250
396	Dick Schofield	4	4	4	5	10	25		
397	Alvin Dark MG	4	4	4	5	10	40		
398	Howie Reed	4	8	15	20	40	100		
399	Jim French	4	4	4	5	10	25	40	120
400	Hank Aaron	▲60	▲100	▲150	▲250	▲400	▲1,000	▲1,200	4,000
401	Tom Murphy	4	4	4	4	8	15	40	150
402	Los Angeles Dodgers TC	4	4	4	8	15	30	50	200
403	Joe Coleman	4	4	5	6	12	25		
404	B.Harris RC/R.Metzger RC	4	4	4	6	12	20	100	250
405	Leo Cardenas	4	4	4	4	8	15	80	120
406	Ray Sadecki	4	4	4	4	8	15	50	450
407	Joe Rudi	4	4	8	10	20	40	80	250
408	Rafael Robles	4	4	4	6	12	25		
409	Don Pavletich	4	4	4	5	10	50		
410	Ken Holtzman	4	4	4	5	10	20	60	120
411	George Spriggs	4	4	4	4	8	25		
412	Jerry Johnson	4	4	4	5	10	20		
413	Pat Kelly	4	4	8	10	20	40		
414	Woodie Fryman	4	4	4	4	8	20	40	200
415	Mike Hegan	4	4	8	10	20	40		
416	Gene Alley	4	4	4	5	10	20	50	120
417	Dick Hall	4	4	4	8	15	30		
418	Adolfo Phillips	4	4	4	6	12	25		
419	Ron Hansen	4	4	4	5	10	20		
420	Jim Merritt	4	4	4	6	12	25	40	150
421	John Stephenson	4	4	4	8	15	40		120
422	Frank Bertaina	4	5	10	12	25	50		
423	D.Saunders/T.Marting RC	4	4	4	5	10	25	50	150
424	Roberto Rodriquez	4	4	4	4	8	15		
425	Doug Rader	4	4	4	5	10	20	50	150

#	Player	VG 3	VgEx 4	EX 5	ExMt 6	NM 7	NmMt 8	NmMt+ 8.5	MT 9
426	Chris Cannizzaro	4	4	4	4	6	12	40	150
427	Bernie Allen	4	4	4	4	8	15	40	200
428	Jim McAndrew	4	4	4	6	12	25		
429	Chuck Hinton	4	4	8	10	20	40		
430	Wes Parker	4	4	4	5	10	20	50	200
431	Tom Burgmeier	4	4	4	5	10	20		
432	Bob Didier	4	4	4	5	10	20		
433	Skip Lockwood	4	4	4	4	8	25		
434	Gary Sutherland	8	15	30	40	60	120		
435	Jose Cardenal	4	4	4	6	12	25	40	150
436	Wilbur Wood	4	4	4	5	10	25		
437	Danny Murtaugh MG	4	4	5	6	12	25		
438	Mike McCormick	4	4	4	5	10	20		
439	Greg Luzinski RC	5	8	12	20	30	80	100	200
440	Bert Campaneris	4	4	4	6	12	25	50	250
441	Milt Pappas	4	4	4	5	10	20		
442	California Angels TC	4	4	4	5	10	20	40	120
443	Rich Robertson	4	4	4	4	8	20	40	120
444	Jimmie Price	4	4	4	4	8	60	100	150
445	Art Shamsky	4	4	8	10	20	50	100	375
446	Bobby Bolin	4	4	4	5	10	20	50	150
447	Cesar Geronimo RC	4	4	5	10	20	50		
448	Dave Roberts	4	4	4	4	8	15	40	120
449	Brant Alyea	4	4	4	4	8	20	40	200
450	Bob Gibson	12	20	30	50	100	200	350	1,200
451	Joe Keough	4	4	4	4	8	15	40	120
452	John Boccabella	4	4	4	4	8	20	40	120
453	Terry Crowley	4	4	4	6	12	25	50	300
454	Mike Paul	4	4	4	5	10	20	40	200
455	Don Kessinger	4	4	4	5	10	25	60	400
456	Bob Meyer	4	4	4	4	8	15	40	120
457	Willie Smith	4	4	4	5	10	20	50	120
458	R.Lolich RC/D.Lemonds RC	4	4	4	4	8	15	40	120
459	Jim Lefebvre	4	4	8	10	20	120	150	200
460	Fritz Peterson	4	4	4	6	12	25	40	120
461	Jim Ray Hart	4	4	4	4	8	15		
462	Washington Senators TC	4	4	4	6	12	25	50	200
463	Tom Kelley	4	4	4	4	8	15	50	80
464	Aurelio Rodriguez	4	4	4	4	6	12	40	100
465	Tim McCarver	4	4	4	5	10	20	60	120
466	Ken Berry	4	4	4	5	10	20	50	350
467	Al Santorini	4	4	4	5	10	20	40	120
468	Frank Fernandez	4	4	4	4	8	15	40	100
469	Bob Aspromonte	4	4	4	5	10	20	60	100
470	Bob Oliver	4	4	4	5	10	20	40	150
471	Tom Griffin	4	4	4	5	10	20	40	150
472	Ken Rudolph	4	4	4	5	10	20		
473	Gary Wagner	4	8	15	20	40	50		
474	Jim Fairey	4	4	4	4	8	15	40	100
475	Ron Perranoski	4	4	4	5	10	20	80	250
476	Dal Maxvill	4	4	5	6	12	40		
477	Earl Weaver MG	4	4	4	6	12	30	80	200
478	Bernie Carbo	4	5	10	12	25	80	120	200
479	Dennis Higgins	4	4	4	4	8	15	40	120
480	Manny Sanguillen	4	4	6	8	15	30	60	150
481	Daryl Patterson	4	4	4	4	6	12	40	120
482	San Diego Padres TC	4	4	4	4	8	20	40	120
483	Gene Michael	4	4	4	4	8	20	40	200
484	Don Wilson	4	4	4	6	12	25		
485	Ken McMullen	4	4	4	4	8	15	40	120
486	Steve Huntz	4	4	4	4	8	15	60	150
487	Paul Schaal	4	4	4	6	12	25	40	100
488	Jerry Stephenson	4	4	6	8	15	40		
489	Luis Alvarado	4	4	4	4	8	20	40	200
490	Deron Johnson	4	5	10	12	25	50		
491	Jim Hardin	4	4	4	5	10	25		
492	Ken Boswell	4	6	12	15	30	60	100	150
493	Dave May	4	4	4	5	10	20	40	100
494	R.Garr/R.Kester	4	4	4	5	10	20	40	200
495	Felipe Alou	4	4	5	6	12	30	50	150
496	Woody Woodward	4	4	6	8	15	30	80	200
497	Horacio Pina RC	4	4	4	4	8	20		
498	John Kennedy	4	4	4	5	10	20		
499	Checklist 5	4	4	4	6	12	25	80	500
500	Jim Perry	4	4	4	5	10	20	120	200
501	Andy Etchebarren	4	4	6	8	15	30	120	400
502	Chicago Cubs TC	4	5	8	12	20	60	150	600
503	Gates Brown	4	4	5	10	20	50	60	200
504	Ken Wright RC	4	4	4	5	10	20		
505	Ollie Brown	4	4	4	4	8	15		
506	Bobby Knoop	4	4	4	4	8	20	80	120
507	George Stone	4	4	4	5	10	20	40	120
508	Roger Repoz	4	4	4	4	8	15	50	120
509	Jim Grant	4	4	4	4	8	15		
510	Ken Harrelson	4	4	4	4	8	20	40	150
511	Chris Short w/Rose	4	4	4	8	15	30		
512	D.Mills RC/M.Garman RC	4	4	4	4	8	15	40	100
513	Nolan Ryan	▲60	▲100	▲150	▲250	▲500	800		
514	Ron Woods	4	4	4	5	10	20		
515	Carl Morton	4	4	4	8	15	30		
516	Ted Kubiak	4	4	4	6	12	25	40	150
517	Charlie Fox MG RC	4	4	4	4	8	15	25	200
518	Joe Grzenda	4	4	4	5	10	20	40	100
519	Willie Crawford	4	4	6	8	15	80		
520	Tommy John	4	4	5	10	25	50	80	450
521	Leron Lee	4	4	4	5	10	20	40	150
522	Minnesota Twins TC	4	4	4	5	10	20	50	200
523	John Odom	4	4	4	5	10	20	50	120
524	Mickey Stanley	4	4	5	6	12	40	50	200
525	Ernie Banks	40	▲60	▲100	▲150	▲200	▲1,000		
526	Ray Jarvis	4	4	4	4	8	15	40	100
527	Cleon Jones	4	4	4	8	15	80	120	250
528	Wally Bunker	4	4	4	4	8	15	40	120
529	Hernandez/Buckner/Perez RC	4	4	6	15	30	80	100	200
530	Carl Yastrzemski	▲15	▲25	▲40	60	80	▲500		
531	Mike Torrez	4	4	4	5	10	20	50	150
532	Bill Rigney MG	4	4	4	4	8	15	40	100
533	Mike Ryan	4	4	4	6	12	25	40	120
534	Luke Walker	4	4	4	4	8	15	40	80
535	Curt Flood	4	4	5	10	20	25	60	150
536	Claude Raymond	8	15	30	40	100			
537	Tom Egan	4	4	4	4	8	15	40	100
538	Angel Bravo	4	4	5	6	12	25		
539	Larry Brown	10	20	40	50	100	200		
540	Larry Dierker	4	4	4	4	15	20	40	100
541	Bob Burda	4	5	10	12	25	50		
542	Bob Miller	4	4	4	4	8	25		
543	New York Yankees TC	4	4	5	10	25	60		400
544	Vida Blue	4	8	15	25	80	150	200	300
545	Dick Dietz	4	4	4	5	10	20	40	300
546	John Matias	4	4	4	4	8	15	40	150
547	Pat Dobson	4	5	8	12	20	30	50	200
548	Don Mason	4	4	4	4	8	15	40	120
549	Jim Brewer	12	25	40	60	80	500		
550	Harmon Killebrew	▲20	▲30	▲50	▲80	▲120	▲250	▲300	▲1,000
551	Frank Linzy	6	12	25	30	60	150	200	250
552	Buddy Bradford	4	4	4	4	8	20	40	100
553	Kevin Collins	4	4	4	5	10	20		
554	Lowell Palmer	4	4	4	6	12	25		
555	Walt Williams	4	4	5	10	12	40	40	250
556	Jim McGlothlin	4	4	4	5	10	20	40	120
557	Tom Satriano	4	4	8	10	20	120	150	500
558	Hector Torres	4	4	4	4	8	15	40	150
559	Cox/Gogolewsk/Jones RC	4	4	6	12	25	50	60	150
560	Rusty Staub	4	4	5	6	12	50	80	200
561	Syd O'Brien	4	4	8	10	20	60		

	VG 3	VgEx 4	EX 5	ExMt 6	NM 7	NmMt 8	NmMt+ 8.5	MT 9
2 Dave Giusti	4	4	4	8	15	30		
3 San Francisco Giants TC	4	4	4	8	15	30		
4 Al Fitzmorris	6	12	25	30	60	150		
5 Jim Wynn	4	4	4	8	20	25		
6 Tim Cullen	4	4	4	4	8	15	40	250
7 Walt Alston MG	4	6	10	15	25	40	50	▲200
8 Sal Campisi	4	4	6	8	15	40		
9 Ivan Murrell	4	4	4	8	15	30		
0 Jim Palmer	▲15	▲25	▲40	▲60	▲200	▲300	▲400	1,000
1 Ted Sizemore	4	4	4	6	12	25	40	200
2 Jerry Kenney	4	4	6	8	15	30	50	120
3 Ed Kranepool	4	6	12	15	30	80	120	300
4 Jim Bunning	4	4	6	8	30	50	80	200
5 Bill Freehan	4	5	10	12	25	120		
6 Garrett/Davis/Jestadt RC	4	4	4	5	10	40	50	500
7 Jim Lonborg	8	15	30	40	80	150		
8 Ron Hunt	4	4	4	4	8	15	40	100
9 Marty Pattin	4	4	12	15	20	100	150	200
0 Tony Perez	6	12	15	50	60	250	300	500
1 Roger Nelson	4	4	6	8	15	100	120	300
2 Dave Cash	4	4	6	12	25	50		
3 Ron Cook RC	4	4	4	5	10	20		
4 Cleveland Indians TC	4	4	4	4	8	20	40	120
5 Willie Davis	4	8	15	30	60	250		
6 Dick Woodson	4	4	4	8	15	30		
7 Sonny Jackson	4	4	4	4	8	20		
8 Tom Bradley RC	4	8	15	20	30	80		
9 Bob Barton	4	4	4	5	10	20	40	150
0 Alex Johnson	4	4	4	6	12	25	50	120
1 Jackie Brown RC	4	4	4	6	12	25	40	150
2 Randy Hundley	4	4	8	10	20	40	60	250
3 Jack Aker	4	4	4	4	8	15	40	120
4 Chlupsa/Stinson/Hrabosky RC	4	4	6	12	25	50		
5 Dave Johnson	4	4	4	6	12	25	60	300
6 Mike Jorgensen	6	12	25	30	60	100		
7 Ken Suarez	4	4	4	6	12	25		
8 Rick Wise	4	4	4	4	8	20	40	120
9 Norm Cash	4	4	4	8	15	30	60	150
0 Willie Mays	▲100	▲150	▲250	▲400	▲800	▲2,000		
1 Ken Tatum	4	4	4	4	8	15	40	120
2 Marty Martinez	4	4	4	4	8	15	25	150
3 Pittsburgh Pirates TC	4	4	6	12	25	50	80	200
4 John Gelnar	4	4	6	8	15	40		
5 Orlando Cepeda	▲12	▲20	▲30	▲50	▲120	▲200		
6 Chuck Taylor	4	4	4	5	10	20	50	120
7 Paul Ratliff	4	4	4	4	8	15		
8 Mike Wegener	15	25	30	40	50	200		
9 Leo Durocher MG	4	4	8	10	25	80		
0 Amos Otis	4	4	6	8	20	50	60	500
1 Tom Phoebus	4	4	6	8	15	30	50	120
2 Camilli/Ford/Mingori RC	4	4	5	6	12	25		
3 Pedro Borbon	4	4	4	5	10	20	40	300
4 Billy Cowan	4	4	5	6	12	30	40	150
5 Mel Stottlemyre	4	4	6	12	25	50		
6 Larry Hisle	4	4	6	10	15	25	40	100
7 Clay Dalrymple	4	4	8	10	20	40	60	150
8 Tug McGraw	4	4	4	6	12	40	50	200
A Checklist 6 No Copyright No Line	4	4	5	6	12	50		
3 Checklist 6 Copyright w/Line	4	4	5	6	12	50		
Frank Howard	4	4	4	6	25	30	50	150
Ron Bryant	4	4	4	4	8	15	40	150
Joe Lahoud	4	4	5	6	12	25	40	200
Pat Jarvis	4	4	4	5	10	20		
Oakland Athletics TC	4	4	5	10	20	60	100	250
Lou Brock	12	20	40	60	150	250	300	2,500
Freddie Patek	4	4	4	6	15	30		
Steve Hamilton	4	4	4	5	10	20	40	150
John Bateman	4	4	6	8	15	60		

	VG 3	VgEx 4	EX 5	ExMt 6	NM 7	NmMt 8	NmMt+ 8.5	MT 9
629 John Hiller	4	4	4	6	12	25	50	200
630 Roberto Clemente	▲120	▲200	▲300	▲500	▲1,000	▲2,500		
631 Eddie Fisher	4	4	4	5	10	20	50	120
632 Darrel Chaney	4	4	4	5	10	20	40	120
633 Brooks/Koegel/Northey RC	4	4	4	4	8	20	40	120
634 Phil Regan	4	8	15	20	40	300		
635 Bobby Murcer	15	30	60	80	100	600		
636 Denny Lemaster	4	4	8	10	20	60	80	150
637 Dave Bristol MG	4	4	5	10	20	25	50	200
638 Stan Williams	4	4	4	6	12	25	40	
639 Tom Haller	4	5	10	12	40	120		
640 Frank Robinson	▲12	▲20	▲30	▼30	100	250	300	1,200
641 New York Mets TC	4	4	4	5	25	50	50	200
642 Jim Roland	4	4	5	6	12	25	50	150
643 Rick Reichardt	4	4	4	6	12	25	40	120
644 Jim Stewart SP	10	20	30	40	50	100		
645 Jim Maloney SP	▲8	▲12	▲20	▲30	▲404	60		
646 Bobby Floyd SP	8	15	20	25	30	60		
647 Juan Pizarro	4	6	12	15	30	60		
648 Folkers/Martinez/Matlack RC	6	12	25	30	50	200		
649 Sparky Lyle SP	12	20	25	40	100	200		
650 Richie Allen SP	▲80	▲120	▲200	▲300	▲600	▲1,200		
651 Jerry Robertson SP	▲8	▲12	▲20	▲30	50	▲150		
652 Atlanta Braves TC	▲5	▲8	▲12	▲20	▲40	50	80	300
653 Russ Snyder SP	4	8	15	20	30	80		
654 Don Shaw SP	4	▲5	▲8	▲12	20	▲60		
655 Mike Epstein SP	4	5	10	20	50	150		
656 Gerry Nyman SP	5	8	10	15	25	80		
657 Jose Azcue	4	4	4	8	15	25		
658 Paul Lindblad SP	4	▲6	▲10	▲15	25	▲80		
659 Byron Browne SP	4	▲6	10	▲15	25	▲250		
660 Ray Culp	4	4	4	8	15	30		
661 Chuck Tanner MG SP	▲6	▲10	▲15	▲25	▲40	▲80		
662 Mike Hedlund SP	▲10	▲15	▲25	▲40	▼60	300		
663 Marv Staehle	4	5	10	12	25	50		
664 Reynolds/Reynolds/Reynolds RC	▲8	▲12	20	30	80	200		
665 Ron Swoboda SP	▲6	▲10	▲15	25	60	▲400		
666 Gene Brabender SP	4	4	6	12	25	60		
667 Pete Ward	4	4	6	12	30	80		
668 Gary Neibauer	4	4	4	5	12	30		
669 Ike Brown SP	▲8	▲12	20	▲30	▲50	▲200		
670 Bill Hands	4	4	4	8	15	40		
671 Bill Voss SP	5	10	20	25	30	200		
672 Ed Crosby SP RC	▲6	▲10	▲15	▲25	▲40	▲100		
673 Gerry Janeski SP RC	▲8	▲12	▲20	▲30	50	▲200		
674 Montreal Expos TC	4	4	5	6	12	40	80	200
675 Dave Boswell	4	4	4	6	12	30	60	200
676 Tommie Reynolds	4	6	8	10	15	40		
677 Jack DiLauro SP	4	▲6	▲10	▲15	▲25	▲80		
678 George Thomas	4	4	5	8	15	30		
679 Don O'Riley	4	4	5	6	12	25	60	200
680 Don Mincher SP	4	4	6	12	25	50		
681 Bill Butler	4	4	4	▲6	10	20		
682 Terry Harmon	4	▲5	▲8	▲12	20	40		
683 Bill Burbach SP	4	▲5	▲8	▲12	20	▲50		
684 Curt Motton	4	4	4	8	15	40		
685 Moe Drabowsky	6	10	20	30	40	60		
686 Chico Ruiz SP	4	4	8	10	20	60		
687 Ron Taylor SP	6	10	15	25	▲40	▲100		
688 Sparky Anderson MG SP	▲10	▲15	▲25	▲40	60	▲250		
689 Frank Baker	8	10	20	25	40	50		
690 Bob Moose	4	4	4	8	15	30		
691 Bobby Heise	4	4	5	5	20	25		
692 Haydel/Moret/Twitchell RC	4	4	5	10	40	50	60	200
693 Jose Pena SP	▲8	▲12	▲20	▲30	▲50	▲200		
694 Rick Renick SP	4	4	6	12	20	80		
695 Joe Niekro	4	▲6	▲10	▲15	▲25	▲100	▲120	400
696 Jerry Morales	4	4	6	▲10	15	30		

BASEBALL

#	Player	VG 3	VgEx 4	EX 5	ExMt 6	NM 7	NmMt 8	NmMt+ 8.5	MT 9
697	Rickey Clark SP	▲5	▲8	▲12	▲20	30	▲80		
698	Milwaukee Brewers TC SP	▲5	▲8	▲12	20	30	▲80		
699	Jim Britton	4	4	5	10	20	30		
700	Boog Powell SP	5	15	30	50	120	200		
701	Bob Garibaldi	4	4	4	8	15	50		
702	Milt Ramirez RC	4	4	4	8	15	50		
703	Mike Kekich	4	4	4	8	15	40		
704	J.C. Martin SP	4	15	20	25	50	150		
705	Dick Selma SP	4	4	5	6	12	50		
706	Joe Foy SP	4	6	12	15	30	120		
707	Fred Lasher	4	4	8	10	20	40		
708	Russ Nagelson SP	▲10	▲15	▲25	▲40	▲60	▲200		
709	Baker/Baylor/Paciorek SP RC	▲60	▲100	▲120	▲200	▲400	▲2,000		
710	Sonny Siebert	4	4	5	10	30	40	150	250
711	Larry Stahl SP	4	5	10	12	20	40		
712	Jose Martinez	5	8	12	20	30	50		
713	Mike Marshall SP	4	▲6	▲10	▲15	▲25	▲120		
714	Dick Williams MG SP	8	12	20	30	60	80		
715	Horace Clarke SP	▲5	▲8	▲12	▲20	▲30	▲80		
716	Dave Leonhard	4	4	5	6	12	30	60	250
717	Tommie Aaron SP	4	4	5	15	30	50		
718	Billy Wynne	4	5	10	12	25	60		
719	Jerry May SP	4	▲6	▲10	▲15	▲50	▲80		
720	Matty Alou	4	4	4	12	15	30		
721	John Morris	4	4	5	6	20	25	60	250
722	Houston Astros TC SP	6	12	25	25	60	150		
723	Vicente Romo SP	4	6	12	15	50	200		
724	Tom Tischinski SP	4	5	10	12	30	60		
725	Gary Gentry SP	4	4	6	12	25	80		
726	Paul Popovich	4	4	6	8	15	30	80	200
727	Ray Lamb SP	4	4	5	10	20	80		
728	Redmond/Lampard/Williams RC	4	4	5	10	20	30	60	120
729	Dick Billings RC	4	4	5	8	25	30		
730	Jim Rooker	4	4	5	10	20	40		
731	Jim Qualls SP	12	20	30	50	100	200		
732	Bob Reed	4	4	4	5	10	20	60	150
733	Lee Maye SP	12	15	20	25	40	300		
734	Rob Gardner SP	4	4	8	15	40	50		
735	Mike Shannon SP	5	8	12	20	40	60		
736	Mel Queen SP	4	▲6	▲10	▲15	▲25	▲50		
737	Preston Gomez MG SP	4	6	12	15	20	50		
738	Russ Gibson SP	4	4	8	10	25	60		
739	Barry Lersch SP	4	▲6	▲10	▲15	25	▲60	80	200
740	Luis Aparicio SP	▲12	▲20	▲30	▲50	▲80	120	150	500
741	Skip Guinn	4	4	4	6	12	30		
742	Kansas City Royals TC	4	4	5	10	20	40	60	150
743	John O'Donoghue SP	8	▼12	▼20	▼30	▼50	150		
744	Chuck Manuel SP	▲8	▲12	▲20	▲30	▲50	▲100	▲120	▲250
745	Sandy Alomar SP	8	15	25	30	60	80		
746	Andy Kosco	4	4	4	5	10	30	60	250
747	Severinsen/Spinks/Moore RC	4	4	5	6	25	50	60	350
748	John Purdin SP	8	12	15	20	50	400		
749	Ken Szotkiewicz RC	5	8	12	20	30	100		
750	Denny McLain SP	12	20	25	30	100	250		
751	Al Weis SP	▼6	▼10	15	▲25	▲80	▲150		
752	Dick Drago	4	4	8	10	25	50		

— Bert Blyleven #26 PSA 10 (Gem) (Young Collection) sold for $15,052 (SCP; 5/12)
— Bert Blyleven RC #26 PSA 9 (MT) sold for $3,080 (eBay; 1/13)
— Roberto Clemente #630 PSA 9 (MT) sold for $4,700 (REA; 05/11)
— Roberto Clemente #630 PSA 9 (MT) sold for $4,652 (Mile High; 05/11)
— Steve Garvey #341 PSA 10 (Gem) (Young Collection) sold for $25,393 (SCP; 5/12)
— Tommy John #520 PSA 10 (Gem) sold for $1,085 (eBay; 02/12)
— Willie Mays #600 PSA 9 (MT) sold for $3,000 (eBay; 10/12)
— Thurman Munson #5 BGS 9 (MT) sold for $2,111 (eBay; 11/11)
— Brooks Robinson #300 PSA 9 (MT) sold for $4,051 (eBay; 11/11)
— Brooks Robinson #300 PSA 9 (MT) sold for $3,454 (eBay; 1/13)
— Brooks Robinson #300 PSA 9 (MT) sold for $3,160 (eBay; 02/12)
— Tom Seaver #160 PSA 9 (MT) sold for $5,700 (eBay; 11/11)

footer:

1971 Topps Greatest Moments

#	Player	GD 2	VG 3	VgEx 4	EX 5	ExMt 6	NM 7	NmMt 8	MT 9
1	Thurman Munson DP	▲60	▲100	▲150	▲250	▲400			
2	Hoyt Wilhelm	▲40	▲60	▲100	▲150	250			
3	Rico Carty	▲25	▲40	▲60	▲100	150	400	500	
4	Carl Morton DP	▲12	▲20	▲30	▲50	80	150		
5	Sal Bando DP	▲10	▲15	▲25	▼40	60	80	200	
6	Bert Campaneris DP	▲6	▲10	▲15	▲25	40	120		
7	Jim Kaat	▲15	▲25	▲40	▲60	100	200	250	
8	Harmon Killebrew	▲80	▲120	▲200	▲300	▲500	800		
9	Brooks Robinson	▲15	▲25	▲40	▲60	100	400	1,000	
10	Jim Perry	▲50	▲80	▲120	▲200	300			
11	Tony Oliva	▲25	▲40	▲60	▲100	150	250	300	
12	Vada Pinson	▲20	▲30	▲50	▲80	120	300	500	
13	Johnny Bench	▲30	▲50	▲80	▲120	200	600	800	
14	Tony Perez	▲25	▲40	▲60	▲100	150	500		
15	Pete Rose DP	▲80	▲120	▲200	▲300	▲500	▲600	▲1,500	
16	Jim Fregosi DP	▲8	▲12	▲20	▲30	50			
17	Alex Johnson DP	▲6	▲10	▲15	▲25	40			
18	Clyde Wright DP	▲6	▲10	▲15	▲25	▲40			
19	Al Kaline DP	▲15	▲25	▲40	▼60	100	200	400	
20	Denny McLain DP	▲12	▲20	▲30	▲50	80	150	500	
21	Jim Northrup	▲10	▲15	▲25	▲40	60	120	400	
22	Bill Freehan	▲8	▲12	▲20	▲30	50	120	400	
23	Mickey Lolich	▲25	▲40	▲60	▲100	▲150	▲400	▲800	
24	Bob Gibson DP	▲15	▲25	▲40	▲60	100	250	500	
25	Tim McCarver DP	▲6	▲10	▲15	▲25	40	120	200	
26	Orlando Cepeda DP	▲12	▲20	▲30	▲50	80	200	250	
27	Lou Brock DP	▲15	▲25	▲40	▲60	100			
28	Nate Colbert DP	▲6	▲10	▲15	25	40	80	150	
29	Maury Wills	▲20	▲30	▲50	▲80	120	150		
30	Wes Parker	▲12	▲20	▲30	▲50	80	150	250	
31	Jim Wynn	▲15	▲25	▲40	▲60	100	120	200	
32	Larry Dierker	▲10	▲15	▲25	▲40	60	200		
33	Bill Melton	▲6	▲10	▲15	▲25	40	80		
34	Joe Morgan	▲20	▲30	▲50	▲80	120	150		
35	Rusty Staub	▲10	▲15	▲25	▲40	60	150	250	
36	Ernie Banks DP	▲40	▲60	▲100	▲150	250	300	400	
37	Billy Williams	▲15	▲25	▲40	▲60	100	200	400	
38	Lou Piniella	▲12	▲20	▲30	▲50	80	150	250	
39	Rico Petrocelli DP	▲8	▲12	▲20	▲30	50	120	300	
40	Carl Yastrzemski DP	▲30	▲50	▲80	▲120	200	300	800	
41	Willie Mays DP	▲25	▲40	▲60	▲100	150	400	1,000	
42	Tommy Harper	▲10	▲15	▲25	▲40	60	120	250	
43	Jim Bunning DP	▲8	▲12	▲20	▲30	50	100	300	
44	Fritz Peterson	▲8	▲12	▲20	▲30	50	150	200	
45	Roy White	▲12	▲20	▲30	▲50	80	400		
46	Bobby Murcer	▲50	▲80	▲120	▲200	300	500	800	
47	Reggie Jackson	▲100	▲150	▲250	▲400	600			
48	Frank Howard	▲25	▲40	▲60	▲100	150			
49	Dick Bosman	▲8	▲12	▲20	▲30	50	200	200	
50	Sam McDowell DP	▲6	▲10	▲15	▼25	40	100	250	
51	Luis Aparicio DP	▲8	▲12	▲20	▲30	50	120	500	
52	Willie McCovey DP	▲12	▲20	▲30	▲50	80	120	350	
53	Joe Pepitone	▲15	▲25	▲40	▲60	100	175		
54	Jerry Grote	▲12	▲20	▲30	▲50	80	150	300	
55	Bud Harrelson	▲25	▲40	▲60	▲100	150			

1971 Topps Super

#	Player	GD 2	VG 3	VgEx 4	EX 5	ExMt 6	NM 7	NmMt 8	MT 9
1	Reggie Smith	4	4	4	4	4	6	12	5
2	Gaylord Perry	4	4	4	4	4	6	12	8
3	Ted Savage	4	4	4	4	4	5	10	2
4	Donn Clendenon	4	4	4	4	4	6	12	25
5	Boog Powell	4	4	4	4	4	6	12	30
6	Tony Perez	4	4	4	4	4	6	12	60

	GD 2	VG 3	VgEx 4	EX 5	ExMt 6	NM 7	NmMt 8	MT 9
Dick Bosman	4	4	4	4	4	5	10	20
Alex Johnson	4	4	4	4	4	5	10	25
Rusty Staub	4	4	4	4	4	8	15	100
Mel Stottlemyre	4	4	4	4	4	5	10	60
Tony Oliva	4	4	4	4	4	6	12	40
Bill Freehan	4	4	4	4	4	5	10	20
Fritz Peterson	4	4	4	4	4	5	10	20
Wes Parker	4	4	4	4	4	5	10	25
Cesar Cedeno	4	4	4	4	4	5	10	25
Sam McDowell	4	4	4	4	4	5	10	20
Frank Howard	4	4	4	4	4	5	10	20
Dave McNally	4	4	4	4	4	5	10	20
Rico Petrocelli	4	4	4	4	4	5	10	20
Pete Rose	4	4	6	12	15	80	250	400
Luke Walker	4	4	4	4	4	5	10	20
Nate Colbert	4	4	4	4	4	5	10	20
Luis Aparicio	4	4	4	4	4	8	15	
Jim Perry	4	4	4	4	4	5	10	40
Lou Brock	4	4	4	5	6	12	25	150
Roy White	4	4	4	4	4	5	10	20
Claude Osteen	4	4	4	4	4	5	10	25
Carl Morton	4	4	4	4	4	5	10	20
Rico Carty	4	4	4	4	4	5	10	20
Larry Dierker	4	4	4	4	4	5	10	80
Bert Campaneris	4	4	4	4	4	6	12	80
Johnny Bench	4	4	4	8	10	20	60	300
Felix Millan	4	4	4	4	4	6	12	150
Tim McCarver	4	4	4	4	4	5	10	120
Ron Santo	4	4	4	5	6	12	40	120
Tommie Agee	4	4	4	4	4	5	10	40
Roberto Clemente	▲20	▲30	▲50	▲80	▲120	▲200	500	800
Reggie Jackson	4	4	8	15	20	40	60	200
Clyde Wright	4	4	4	4	4	5	10	80
Rich Allen	4	4	4	4	4	5	10	20
Curt Flood	4	4	4	4	4	5	10	50
Ferguson Jenkins	4	4	4	4	4	6	12	60
Willie Stargell	4	4	4	4	4	8	20	120
Hank Aaron	▲12	▲20	▲30	▲50	▲80	▲120	▲200	200
Amos Otis	4	4	4	4	4	5	10	40
Willie McCovey	4	4	4	5	6	12	25	60
Bill Melton	4	4	4	4	4	5	10	25
Bob Gibson	4	4	6	10	20	30	60	120
Carl Yastrzemski	4	4	4	5	6	12	80	300
Glenn Beckert	4	4	4	4	4	5	10	25
Ray Fosse	4	4	4	4	4	5	10	20
Cito Gaston	4	4	4	4	4	5	10	20
Tom Seaver	4	4	4	6	8	60	150	250
Al Kaline	4	4	4	5	6	12	80	150
Jim Northrup	4	4	4	4	4	5	10	80
Willie Mays	4	5	10	25	50	60	100	400
Sal Bando	4	4	4	4	4	5	10	50
Deron Johnson	4	4	4	4	4	5	10	40
Brooks Robinson	4	4	4	5	6	12	25	100
Harmon Killebrew	4	4	4	8	10	20	40	100
Joe Torre	4	4	4	4	4	6	12	60
Lou Piniella	4	4	4	4	4	5	10	30
Tommy Harper	4	4	4	4	4	6	12	30

972 Kellogg's

	VG 3	VgEx 4	EX 5	ExMt 6	NM 7	NmMt 8	MT 9	Gem 9.5/10
Tom Seaver ERA 2.85	4	4	4	4	8	15	135	
Tom Seaver ERA 2.81	4	4	4	4	6	12	100	
Amos Otis	4	4	4	4	4	4	10	60
Willie Davis Runs 842	4	4	4	4	4	4	10	
Willie Davis Runs 841	4	4	4	4	4	4	10	60
Wilbur Wood	4	4	4	4	4	4	10	40
Bill Parsons	4	4	4	4	4	4	10	

		VG 3	VgEx 4	EX 5	ExMt 6	NM 7	NmMt 8	MT 9	Gem 9.5/10
6	Pete Rose	4	4	4	4	8	15	40	
7A	Willie McCovey HR 360	4	4	4	4	4	6	15	
7B	Willie McCovey HR 370	4	4	4	4	4	6	15	
8	Ferguson Jenkins	4	4	4	4	4	6	15	30
9A	Vida Blue ERA 2.35	4	4	4	4	4	4	15	
9B	Vida Blue ERA 2.31	4	4	4	4	4	4	10	60
10	Joe Torre	4	4	4	4	4	4	10	
11	Merv Rettenmund	4	4	4	4	4	4	10	
12	Bill Melton	4	4	4	4	4	4	10	30
13A	Jim Palmer Games 170	4	4	4	4	4	6	25	
13B	Jim Palmer Games 168	4	4	4	4	4	6	15	60
14	Doug Rader	4	4	4	4	4	4	20	30
15B	Dave Roberts NL Leader	4	4	4	4	4	4	10	60
16	Bobby Murcer	4	4	4	4	4	6	15	80
17	Wes Parker	4	4	4	4	4	4	10	25
18A	Joe Coleman BB 394	4	4	4	4	4	4	10	
18B	Joe Coleman BB 393	4	4	4	4	4	4	10	25
19	Manny Sanguillen	4	4	4	4	4	4	10	60
20	Reggie Jackson	4	4	4	4	5	10	25	
21	Ralph Garr	4	4	4	4	4	4	10	50
22	Jim Hunter	4	4	4	4	4	6	15	
23	Rick Wise	4	4	4	4	4	4	10	
24	Glenn Beckert	4	4	4	4	4	4	10	25
25	Tony Oliva	4	4	4	4	4	4	10	50
26A	Bob Gibson SO 2577	4	4	4	4	4	6	15	
26B	Bob Gibson SO 2578	4	4	4	4	4	6	15	
27A	Mike Cuellar ERA 3.80	4	4	4	4	4	4	25	
27B	Mike Cuellar ERA 3.08	4	4	4	4	4	4	10	
28	Chris Speier	4	4	4	4	4	4	10	
29A	Dave McNally ERA 3.18	4	4	4	4	4	4	10	
29B	Dave McNally ERA 3.15	4	4	4	4	4	4	10	
30	Leo Cardenas	4	4	4	4	4	4	10	
31A	Bill Freehan Runs 497	4	4	4	4	4	4	10	
32A	Bud Harrelson Hits 634	4	4	4	4	4	4	10	
32B	Bud Harrelson Hits 624	4	4	4	4	4	4	10	
33B	Sam McDowell Less than 225	4	4	4	4	4	4	10	50
34B	Claude Osteen ERA 3.51	4	4	4	4	4	4	10	
35	Reggie Smith	4	4	4	4	4	4	10	25
36	Sonny Siebert	4	4	4	4	4	4	10	25
37	Lee May	4	4	4	4	4	4	10	60
38	Mickey Lolich	4	4	4	4	4	4	10	
39A	Cookie Rojas 2B 149	4	4	4	4	4	4	10	
39B	Cookie Rojas 2B 150	4	4	4	4	4	4	10	30
40A	Dick Drago Poyals	4	4	4	4	4	4	10	
40B	Dick Drago Royals	4	4	4	4	4	4	10	25
41	Nate Colbert	4	4	4	4	4	4	10	25
42	Andy Messersmith	4	4	4	4	4	4	10	25
43B	Dave Johnson Avg .264	4	4	4	4	4	4	10	60
44	Steve Blass	4	4	4	4	4	4	10	
45	Bob Robertson	4	4	4	4	4	4	10	
46A	Billy Williams Missed Only 1	4	4	4	4	4	6	15	
46B	Billy Williams Phrase Omitted	4	4	4	4	4	6	15	40
47	Juan Marichal	4	4	4	4	4	6	15	60
48	Lou Brock	4	4	4	4	4	6	15	
49	Roberto Clemente	4	4	6	8	15	30	100	300
50	Mel Stottlemyre	4	4	4	4	4	4	10	25
51	Don Wilson	4	4	4	4	4	4	10	30
52A	Sal Bando RBI 355	4	4	4	4	4	4	10	
52B	Sal Bando RBI 356	4	4	4	4	4	4	10	
53A	Willie Stargell 2B 197	4	4	4	4	4	6	60	
53B	Willie Stargell 2B 196	4	4	4	4	4	6	20	50
54A	Willie Mays RBI 1855	4	4	4	4	8	15	80	
54B	Willie Mays RBI 1856	4	4	4	4	8	15	50	

1972 Kellogg's ATG

		VG 3	VgEx 4	EX 5	ExMt 6	NM 7	NmMt 8	MT 9	Gem 9.5/10
1	Walter Johnson	4	4	4	4	5	10	30	
2	Rogers Hornsby	4	4	4	4	4	8	15	60
3	John McGraw	4	4	4	4	4	8	15	40
4	Mickey Cochrane	4	4	4	4	4	8	15	
5	George Sisler	4	4	4	4	4	8	15	60
6	Babe Ruth	4	4	4	4	8	15	30	200
7	Lefty Grove	4	4	4	4	4	8	15	
8	Pie Traynor	4	4	4	4	4	8	15	60
9	Honus Wagner	4	4	4	4	6	12	25	100
10	Eddie Collins	4	4	4	4	4	8	15	50
11	Tris Speaker	4	4	4	4	4	8	15	60
12	Cy Young	4	4	4	4	5	10	20	60
13	Lou Gehrig	4	4	4	4	6	12	25	100
14	Babe Ruth	4	4	4	4	8	15	50	120
15	Ty Cobb	4	4	4	4	6	12	25	

1972 Topps

		VG 3	VgEx 4	EX 5	ExMt 6	NM 7	NmMt 8	NmMt+ 8.5	MT 9
1	Pittsburgh Pirates TC	4	5	10	20	40	100	150	250
2	Ray Culp	4	5	10	12	25	80	100	200
3	Bob Tolan	4	4	4	4	8	15	20	30
4	Checklist 1-132	4	4	4	4	6	12	20	200
5	John Bateman	4	4	4	4	6	12	20	80
6	Fred Scherman	4	4	4	4	5	10	12	30
7	Enzo Hernandez	4	4	4	4	5	10	12	20
8	Ron Swoboda	4	4	4	4	8	15	20	150
9	Stan Williams	4	4	4	4	5	10	12	25
10	Amos Otis	4	4	4	4	5	10	12	25
11	Bobby Valentine	4	4	4	4	5	10	12	25
12	Jose Cardenal	4	4	4	4	5	10	15	40
13	Joe Grzenda	4	4	4	4	6	12	40	150
14	Koegel/Anderson/Twitchell RC	4	4	4	4	8	15		
15	Walt Williams	4	4	4	4	5	10	12	30
16	Mike Jorgensen	4	4	4	4	5	10	15	80
17	Dave Duncan	4	4	4	4	5	10	15	50
18A	Juan Pizarro Yellow	4	4	4	4	5	10	15	60
18B	Juan Pizarro Green	4	4	4	4	5	10	15	60
19	Billy Cowan	4	4	4	4	5	10	12	20
20	Don Wilson	4	4	4	4	5	10	12	20
21	Atlanta Braves TC	4	4	4	4	5	10	12	20
22	Rob Gardner	4	4	5	6	12	25	40	250
23	Ted Kubiak	4	4	4	4	5	10	12	80
24	Ted Ford	4	4	4	4	5	10	12	40
25	Bill Singer	4	4	4	4	5	10	12	50
26	Andy Etchebarren	4	4	4	4	6	12	20	60
27	Bob Johnson	4	4	4	4	5	10	12	200
28	Gebhard/Brye/Haydel RC	4	4	4	4	5	10	12	25
29A	Bill Bonham Yellow RC	4	4	4	4	5	10	15	50
29B	Bill Bonham Green	4	4	4	4	5	10	15	40
30	Rico Petrocelli	4	4	4	4	8	15	20	30
31	Cleon Jones	4	4	4	4	5	10	12	25
32	Cleon Jones IA	4	4	4	5	10	20	30	100
33	Billy Martin MG	4	4	4	6	12	25	30	150
34	Billy Martin IA	4	4	4	4	8	15	25	120
35	Jerry Johnson	4	4	4	4	5	10	12	20
36	Jerry Johnson IA	4	4	4	4	8	15	25	100
37	Carl Yastrzemski	6	10	20	25	30	60	80	200
38	Carl Yastrzemski IA	4	4	12	15	20	30	40	100
39	Bob Barton	4	4	4	4	4	10	12	25
40	Bob Barton IA	4	5	10	12	30	50	100	200
41	Tommy Davis	4	4	4	4	5	10	12	25
42	Tommy Davis IA	4	4	4	4	5	10	12	25
43	Rick Wise	4	4	4	4	5	10	12	25
44	Rick Wise IA	4	4	4	4	8	15	25	150
45A	Glenn Beckert Yellow	4	4	4	4	5	10	12	2
45B	Glenn Beckert Green	4	4	4	4	5	10	12	6
46	Glenn Beckert IA	4	4	4	4	5	10	12	6
47	John Ellis	4	4	4	4	5	10	12	6
48	John Ellis IA	4	4	4	4	8	15	25	12
49	Willie Mays	20	25	40	50	80	120	200	50
50	Willie Mays IA	12	15	20	25	60	250		
51	Harmon Killebrew	4	4	5	15	30	40	50	12
52	Harmon Killebrew IA	4	4	4	5	10	20	30	10
53	Bud Harrelson	4	4	4	4	5	10	15	4
54	Bud Harrelson IA	4	4	4	4	6	12	20	10
55	Clyde Wright	4	4	4	4	5	10	12	4
56	Rich Chiles RC	4	4	4	4	5	10	12	2
57	Bob Oliver	4	4	4	4	5	10	12	2
58	Ernie McAnally	4	4	4	4	5	10	12	2
59	Fred Stanley RC	4	4	4	4	5	10	12	2
60	Manny Sanguillen	4	4	4	4	5	10	12	3
61	Burt Hooten RC	4	4	4	4	5	10	15	6
62	Angel Mangual	4	4	4	4	5	10	12	2
63	Duke Sims	4	4	4	4	5	10	12	2
64	Pete Broberg RC	4	4	4	4	5	10	12	3
65	Cesar Cedeno	4	4	4	4	5	10	12	2
66	Ray Corbin RC	4	4	4	4	5	10	12	2
67	Red Schoendienst MG	4	4	4	4	8	15	20	3
68	Jim York RC	4	4	4	4	5	10	12	4
69	Roger Freed	4	4	4	4	6	12	20	15
70	Mike Cuellar	4	4	4	4	5	10	15	2
71	California Angels TC	4	4	4	4	5	10	12	2
72	Bruce Kison RC	4	4	4	4	6	12	15	2
73	Steve Huntz	4	4	4	4	5	10	12	2
74	Cecil Upshaw	4	4	4	4	5	10	12	3
75	Bert Campaneris	4	4	4	4	8	15	20	3
76	Don Carrithers RC	4	4	4	4	5	10	12	4
77	Ron Theobald RC	4	4	4	4	5	10	12	2
78	Steve Arlin RC	4	4	4	4	5	10	12	2
79	C.Fisk RC/C.Cooper RC	30	40	▲60	▲100	▲200	▲500	▲600	2,50
80	Tony Perez	4	4	5	6	12	25	30	10
81	Mike Hedlund	4	4	4	4	5	10	12	2
82	Ron Woods	4	4	4	4	5	10	12	6
83	Dalton Jones	4	4	4	4	5	10	12	2
84	Vince Colbert	4	4	4	4	5	10	12	3
85	NL Batting Leaders	4	4	4	4	6	12	20	20
86	AL Batting Leaders	4	4	4	4	6	12	20	8
87	NL RBI Leaders	4	4	5	8	12	50	60	10
88	AL RBI Leaders	4	4	4	4	8	15	25	8
89	NL Home Run Leaders	4	4	4	8	20	30	40	10
90	AL Home Run Leaders	4	4	4	4	6	12	15	4
91	NL ERA Leaders	4	4	4	4	6	12	20	5
92	AL ERA Leaders	4	4	4	4	6	12	15	3
93	NL Pitching Leaders	4	4	4	4	8	15	30	10
94	AL Pitching Leaders	4	4	4	4	8	15	25	15
95	NL Strikeout Leaders	4	4	4	5	10	20	25	12
96	AL Strikeout Leaders	4	4	4	4	8	15	25	6
97	Tom Kelley	4	4	4	4	4	6	8	1
98	Chuck Tanner MG	4	4	4	4	5	10	12	3
99	Ross Grimsley RC	4	4	4	4	5	10	12	5
100	Frank Robinson	4	4	6	10	20	30	40	10
101	J.R. Richard RC	4	4	4	4	6	12	15	5
102	Lloyd Allen	4	4	4	4	5	10	15	20
103	Checklist 133-263	4	4	4	4	5	10	12	2
104	Toby Harrah RC	4	4	4	4	5	10	15	
105	Gary Gentry	4	4	4	4	5	10	12	2
106	Milwaukee Brewers TC	4	4	4	4	5	10	12	2
107	Jose Cruz RC	4	4	4	4	5	10	15	
108	Gary Waslewski	4	4	4	4	5	10	12	2
109	Jerry May	4	4	4	4	5	10	12	2
110	Ron Hunt	4	4	4	4	5	10	12	12
111	Jim Grant	4	4	4	4	5	10	12	

#	Player	VG 3	VgEx 4	EX 5	ExMt 6	NM 7	NmMt 8	NmMt+ 8.5	MT 9
112	Greg Luzinski	4	4	4	4	5	10	12	25
113	Rogelio Moret	4	4	4	4	6	12	15	80
114	Bill Buckner	4	4	4	6	12	25	30	60
115	Jim Fregosi	4	4	4	4	5	10	12	20
116	Ed Farmer RC	4	4	4	4	5	10	12	20
117A	Cleo James Yellow RC	4	4	4	4	5	10	15	80
117B	Cleo James Green	4	4	4	4	8	15	25	250
118	Skip Lockwood	4	4	4	4	5	10	12	30
119	Marty Perez	4	4	4	4	5	10	12	25
120	Bill Freehan	4	4	4	4	6	12	20	50
121	Ed Sprague	4	4	4	4	5	10	12	20
122	Larry Biittner RC	4	4	4	4	5	10	12	50
123	Ed Acosta	4	4	4	4	5	10	12	60
124	Closter/Torres/Hambright RC	4	4	4	4	5	10	12	20
125	Dave Cash	4	4	4	4	8	15	25	80
126	Bart Johnson	4	4	4	4	5	10	12	20
127	Duffy Dyer	4	4	4	4	5	10	12	30
128	Eddie Watt	4	4	4	4	5	10	12	25
129	Charlie Fox MG	4	4	4	4	5	10	12	25
130	Bob Gibson	▲8	▲12	▲20	▲30	▲60	120	150	500
131	Jim Nettles	4	4	4	4	5	10	12	20
132	Joe Morgan	4	4	4	8	15	40	50	200
133	Joe Keough	4	4	4	4	5	10	12	60
134	Carl Morton	4	4	4	4	5	10	12	20
135	Vada Pinson	4	4	4	4	5	10	12	60
136	Darrel Chaney	4	4	4	4	5	10	12	20
137	Dick Williams MG	4	4	4	4	8	15	20	60
138	Mike Kekich	4	4	4	4	8	15	25	300
139	Tim McCarver	4	4	4	4	5	10	15	40
140	Pat Dobson	4	4	4	4	5	10	12	25
141	Capra/Stanton/Matlack RC	4	4	4	4	5	10	12	25
142	Chris Chambliss RC	4	4	4	4	6	12	15	30
143	Garry Jestadt	4	4	4	4	5	10	12	100
144	Marty Pattin	4	5	10	12	25	30		
145	Don Kessinger	4	4	4	4	5	10	12	20
146	Steve Kealey	4	4	4	4	5	10	12	20
147	Dave Kingman RC	4	4	4	15	20	30	40	120
148	Dick Billings	4	4	4	4	5	10	12	20
149	Gary Neibauer	4	4	4	4	5	10	15	50
150	Norm Cash	4	6	12	15	30	60		
151	Jim Brewer	4	4	4	4	8	15	20	150
152	Gene Clines	4	4	4	4	5	10	12	20
153	Rick Auerbach RC	4	4	4	4	5	10	12	30
154	Ted Simmons	4	4	4	4	5	10	12	200
155	Larry Dierker	4	4	4	4	5	10	12	25
156	Minnesota Twins TC	4	4	4	4	5	10	12	25
157	Don Gullett	4	4	4	4	5	10	12	30
158	Jerry Kenney	4	4	4	4	5	10	12	25
159	John Boccabella	4	4	4	4	4	8	10	15
160	Andy Messersmith	4	4	4	4	5	10	12	25
161	Brock Davis	4	4	4	4	5	10	15	40
162	Bell/Porter/Reynolds RC	4	4	4	4	5	10	12	30
163	Tug McGraw	4	4	4	4	5	10	12	40
164	Tug McGraw IA	4	4	4	4	5	10	12	100
165	Chris Speier RC	4	4	4	4	5	10	12	25
166	Chris Speier IA	4	4	4	4	5	10	12	25
167	Deron Johnson	4	4	4	4	5	10	12	20
168	Deron Johnson IA	4	4	4	4	8	15	20	80
169	Vida Blue	4	4	4	4	6	12	15	100
170	Vida Blue IA	6	12	25	30	60	120	135	400
171	Darrell Evans	4	4	4	4	5	10	12	25
172	Darrell Evans IA	4	4	4	4	5	10	12	80
173	Clay Kirby	4	4	4	4	5	10	12	20
174	Clay Kirby IA	4	4	4	4	5	10	12	40
175	Tom Haller	4	4	4	4	5	10	12	20
176	Tom Haller IA	4	4	4	4	5	10	12	40
177	Paul Schaal	4	4	4	4	5	10	12	20
178	Paul Schaal IA	4	4	6	8	15	30	50	250
179	Dock Ellis	4	4	4	4	5	10	12	100
180	Dock Ellis IA	4	4	4	4	6	12	15	80
181	Ed Kranepool	4	4	4	4	6	12	15	25
182	Ed Kranepool IA	4	4	4	5	10	20	25	120
183	Bill Melton	4	4	4	4	5	10	12	40
184	Bill Melton IA	4	4	4	4	5	10	12	25
185	Ron Bryant	4	4	4	4	5	10	12	20
186	Ron Bryant IA	4	4	4	4	5	10	12	20
187	Gates Brown	4	4	4	4	5	10	12	20
188	Frank Lucchesi MG	4	4	4	4	5	10	12	20
189	Gene Tenace	4	4	4	4	6	12	15	25
190	Dave Giusti	4	4	4	4	5	10	12	50
191	Jeff Burroughs RC	4	4	4	4	6	12	20	100
192	Chicago Cubs TC	4	4	4	4	5	10	12	60
193	Kurt Bevacqua RC	4	4	4	4	5	10	12	40
194	Fred Norman	4	4	4	4	5	10	12	20
195	Orlando Cepeda	4	6	10	15	25	40	50	100
196	Mel Queen	4	4	4	4	5	10	12	20
197	Johnny Briggs	4	4	4	4	5	10	12	20
198	Charlie Hough RC	4	4	6	10	25	30	40	150
199	Mike Fiore	4	4	4	4	5	10	12	20
200	Lou Brock	▲8	▲12	▲20	▲30	▲50	▲100	▲120	▲250
201	Phil Roof	4	4	4	4	5	10	12	20
202	Scipio Spinks	4	4	4	4	5	10	12	20
203	Ron Blomberg RC	4	4	4	4	5	10	12	25
204	Tommy Helms	4	4	4	4	5	10	12	80
205	Dick Drago	4	4	4	4	5	10	12	20
206	Dal Maxvill	4	4	4	4	5	10	12	20
207	Tom Egan	4	4	4	4	5	10	12	20
208	Milt Pappas	4	4	4	4	6	12	15	25
209	Joe Rudi	4	4	4	4	5	10	12	100
210	Denny McLain	4	4	4	4	5	10	12	30
211	Gary Sutherland	4	4	4	4	5	10	12	25
212	Grant Jackson	4	4	4	4	5	10	12	20
213	Parker/Kusnyer/Silverio RC	4	4	4	4	5	10	12	40
214	Mike McQueen	4	4	4	4	5	10	12	20
215	Alex Johnson	4	4	4	4	5	10	12	20
216	Joe Niekro	4	4	4	4	6	12	15	30
217	Roger Metzger	4	4	4	4	5	10	12	30
218	Eddie Kasko MG	4	4	4	4	5	10	12	100
219	Rennie Stennett RC	4	4	4	4	6	12	20	80
220	Jim Perry	4	4	4	4	5	10	12	20
221	NL Playoffs Bucs	4	4	4	4	8	15	20	120
222	AL Playoffs B.Robinson	4	4	4	4	6	12	15	40
223	Dave McNally WS1	4	4	4	4	8	15	25	100
224	D.Johnson/M.Belanger WS2	4	4	4	6	12	25	30	350
225	Manny Sanguillen WS3	4	4	4	4	6	12	15	80
226	Roberto Clemente WS4	4	4	5	10	30	50	60	200
227	Nellie Briles WS5	4	4	4	4	5	10	12	25
228	F.Robinson/M.Sanguillen WS6	4	6	12	15	30	60	100	250
229	Steve Blass WS7	4	4	4	5	10	20	30	200
230	Pirates Celebrate WS	4	5	6	12	25	50	80	200
231	Casey Cox	4	4	4	4	5	10	12	80
232	Arnold/Barr/Rader RC	4	4	4	4	5	10	12	20
233	Jay Johnstone	4	4	4	4	5	10	12	25
234	Ron Taylor	4	4	4	4	5	10	12	50
235	Merv Rettenmund	4	4	4	4	5	10	12	20
236	Jim McGlothlin	4	4	4	4	5	10	12	20
237	New York Yankees TC	4	4	4	4	6	12	15	30
238	Leron Lee	4	4	4	4	5	10	12	20
239	Tom Timmermann	4	4	4	4	6	12	20	150
240	Richie Allen	4	4	4	4	5	10	12	30
241	Rollie Fingers	4	5	8	12	20	50	60	100
242	Don Mincher	4	4	4	4	5	10	12	40
243	Frank Linzy	4	4	4	4	5	10	12	80
244	Steve Braun RC	4	4	4	4	5	10	12	20
245	Tommie Agee	4	4	4	4	6	12	15	80
246	Tom Burgmeier	4	4	4	4	5	10	12	20

#	Player	VG 3	VgEx 4	EX 5	ExMt 6	NM 7	NmMt 8	NmMt+ 8.5	MT 9
247	Milt May	4	4	4	4	5	10	12	20
248	Tom Bradley	4	4	4	4	5	10	12	20
249	Harry Walker MG	4	4	4	4	5	10	12	20
250	Boog Powell	4	4	5	6	12	25	30	100
251	Checklist 264-394	4	4	4	4	6	12	15	80
252	Ken Reynolds	4	4	4	4	5	10	12	20
253	Sandy Alomar	4	4	4	4	5	10	12	25
254	Boots Day	4	4	4	4	5	10	12	20
255	Jim Lonborg	4	4	4	4	5	10	12	25
256	George Foster	4	4	4	4	6	12	15	40
257	Foor/Hosley/Jata RC	4	4	4	4	6	12	20	60
258	Randy Hundley	4	4	4	4	5	10	12	20
259	Sparky Lyle	4	4	4	4	5	10	12	20
260	Ralph Garr	4	4	4	4	5	10	12	20
261	Steve Mingori	4	4	4	4	5	10	12	20
262	San Diego Padres TC	4	4	4	4	5	10	12	40
263	Felipe Alou	4	6	12	15	30	80	100	200
264	Tommy John	4	4	4	4	6	12	15	30
265	Wes Parker	4	4	4	4	5	10	12	20
266	Bobby Bolin	4	4	4	4	5	10	12	20
267	Dave Concepcion	4	4	4	5	10	20	25	100
268	D.Anderson RC/C.Floethe RC	4	4	4	4	4	8	10	15
269	Don Hahn	4	4	4	4	5	10	12	20
270	Jim Palmer	▲5	▲8	▲12	▲20	▲30	50	60	▲200
271	Ken Rudolph	4	4	4	4	5	10	12	20
272	Mickey Rivers RC	4	4	4	4	5	10	12	25
273	Bobby Floyd	4	4	4	4	5	10	12	20
274	Al Severinsen	4	4	4	4	4	8	10	15
275	Cesar Tovar	4	4	4	4	5	10	12	25
276	Gene Mauch MG	4	4	4	4	4	8	10	15
277	Elliott Maddox	4	4	4	4	5	10	12	25
278	Dennis Higgins	4	4	4	4	5	10	12	20
279	Larry Brown	4	4	4	4	5	10	12	20
280	Willie McCovey	4	4	4	8	15	40	50	120
281	Bill Parsons RC	4	4	4	4	5	10	12	20
282	Houston Astros TC	4	4	4	4	5	10	12	20
283	Darrell Brandon	4	4	4	4	5	10	12	20
284	Ike Brown	4	4	4	4	5	10	12	20
285	Gaylord Perry	4	4	4	4	8	15	20	40
286	Gene Alley	4	4	4	4	5	10	12	25
287	Jim Hardin	4	4	4	4	5	10	12	20
288	Johnny Jeter	4	4	4	4	5	10	12	20
289	Syd O'Brien	4	4	4	4	4	8	10	15
290	Sonny Siebert	4	4	4	4	5	10	12	20
291	Hal McRae	4	4	4	4	5	10	12	30
292	Hal McRae IA	8	15	30	40	80	100		
293	Dan Frisella	4	4	4	4	8	15	25	120
294	Dan Frisella IA	4	4	4	4	5	10	12	30
295	Dick Dietz	4	4	4	4	5	10	12	50
296	Dick Dietz IA	4	5	10	12	25	50	60	200
297	Claude Osteen	4	4	4	4	5	10	12	25
298	Claude Osteen IA	4	4	4	5	10	20	25	80
299	Hank Aaron	15	25	50	60	100	250	400	1,200
300	Hank Aaron IA	12	15	20	30	80	250		
301	George Mitterwald	4	4	4	4	5	10	12	40
302	George Mitterwald IA	4	4	4	4	5	10	12	50
303	Joe Pepitone	4	4	4	4	5	10	12	25
304	Joe Pepitone IA	4	4	4	4	5	10	12	30
305	Ken Boswell	4	4	4	4	5	10	12	20
306	Ken Boswell IA	4	4	5	6	12	25	30	100
307	Steve Renko	4	4	4	4	5	10	12	20
308	Steve Renko IA	4	4	4	5	10	20	25	60
309	Roberto Clemente	▲40	▲60	▲100	▲150	▲250	▲500	▲600	▲1,000
310	Roberto Clemente IA	4	4	25	30	50	150	200	300
311	Clay Carroll	4	4	4	4	5	10	12	20
312	Clay Carroll IA	4	4	4	4	6	12	15	100
313	Luis Aparicio	4	4	4	5	10	30	40	80
314	Luis Aparicio IA	4	4	4	4	6	12	15	40

#	Player	VG 3	VgEx 4	EX 5	ExMt 6	NM 7	NmMt 8	NmMt+ 8.5	MT 9
315	Paul Splittorff	4	4	4	4	5	10	12	25
316	Bibby/Roque/Guzman RC	4	4	4	4	5	10	12	20
317	Rich Hand	4	4	4	4	5	10	12	20
318	Sonny Jackson	4	4	4	4	4	8	10	15
319	Aurelio Rodriguez	4	4	4	4	5	10	12	25
320	Steve Blass	4	4	4	4	8	15	20	100
321	Joe Lahoud	4	4	4	4	5	10	12	25
322	Jose Pena	4	4	4	4	8	15	25	80
323	Earl Weaver MG	4	4	4	4	6	15	20	80
324	Mike Ryan	4	4	4	4	5	10	12	20
325	Mel Stottlemyre	4	4	4	4	5	10	12	20
326	Pat Kelly	4	4	4	4	4	8	10	15
327	Steve Stone RC	4	4	4	4	5	10	12	60
328	Boston Red Sox TC	4	4	4	4	8	15	25	150
329	Roy Foster	4	4	4	4	5	10	12	20
330	Jim Hunter	4	4	6	8	15	30	40	200
331	Stan Swanson RC	4	4	4	4	5	10	12	20
332	Buck Martinez	4	4	4	4	5	10	12	20
333	Steve Barber	4	4	4	4	5	10	12	20
334	Fahey/Mason Ragland RC	4	4	4	4	5	10	12	20
335	Bill Hands	4	4	4	4	5	10	12	20
336	Marty Martinez	4	4	4	4	6	12	20	120
337	Mike Kilkenny	4	4	4	4	5	10	12	20
338	Bob Grich	4	4	4	4	5	10	12	25
339	Ron Cook	4	4	4	4	5	10	12	20
340	Roy White	4	4	4	4	8	15	20	30
341	Joe Torre KP	4	4	4	4	5	10	12	20
342	Wilbur Wood KP	4	4	4	4	5	10	12	50
343	Willie Stargell KP	4	4	4	4	6	12	15	50
344	Dave McNally KP	4	4	4	4	5	10	12	50
345	Rick Wise KP	4	4	4	4	5	10	12	20
346	Jim Fregosi KP	4	4	5	6	8	15	20	100
347	Tom Seaver KP	4	4	4	4	8	15	20	50
348	Sal Bando KP	4	4	5	4	8	15	20	100
349	Al Fitzmorris	4	4	4	4	5	10	12	25
350	Frank Howard	4	4	4	4	5	10	12	25
351	House/Kester/Britton	4	4	4	4	5	10	12	20
352	Dave LaRoche	4	4	4	4	5	10	12	20
353	Art Shamsky	4	4	4	4	5	10	12	20
354	Tom Murphy	4	4	4	4	5	10	12	20
355	Bob Watson	4	4	4	4	4	8	10	15
356	Gerry Moses	4	4	4	4	5	10	12	20
357	Woody Fryman	4	4	4	4	5	10	12	20
358	Sparky Anderson MG	4	4	4	5	10	20	25	50
359	Don Pavletich	4	4	4	4	5	10	12	20
360	Dave Roberts	4	4	4	4	5	10	12	20
361	Mike Andrews	4	4	4	4	5	10	12	20
362	New York Mets TC	4	4	4	4	6	12	15	40
363	Ron Klimkowski	4	4	4	4	5	10	12	20
364	Johnny Callison	4	4	4	4	5	10	12	30
365	Dick Bosman	4	4	4	4	5	10	12	20
366	Jimmy Rosario RC	4	4	4	4	8	15	25	100
367	Ron Perranoski	4	4	4	4	5	10	12	25
368	Danny Thompson	4	4	4	4	4	8	10	15
369	Jim Lefebvre	4	4	4	4	6	12	15	30
370	Don Buford	4	4	4	4	5	10	12	30
371	Denny Lemaster	4	4	4	4	5	10	12	20
372	L.Clemons RC/M.Montgomery RC4	4	4	4	5	10	12		20
373	John Mayberry	4	4	4	4	4	8	10	40
374	Jack Heidemann	4	4	4	4	5	10	12	20
375	Reggie Cleveland	4	4	4	4	4	8	10	15
376	Andy Kosco	4	4	4	4	5	10	12	25
377	Terry Harmon	4	4	6	8	15	30		
378	Checklist 395-525	4	4	4	4	5	10	12	20
379	Ken Berry	4	4	4	4	5	10	12	30
380	Earl Williams	4	4	4	4	5	10	12	20
381	Chicago White Sox TC	4	4	4	4	5	10	12	25
382	Joe Gibbon	4	4	4	4	5	10	12	25

#	Name	VG 3	VgEx 4	EX 5	ExMt 6	NM 7	NmMt 8	NmMt+ 8.5	MT 9
383	Brant Alyea	4	4	4	4	5	10	12	25
384	Dave Campbell	4	4	4	4	5	10	12	20
385	Mickey Stanley	4	4	4	4	8	15	20	80
386	Jim Colborn	4	4	4	4	5	10	12	20
387	Horace Clarke	4	4	4	4	5	10	12	25
388	Charlie Williams RC	4	4	4	4	4	8	10	15
389	Bill Rigney MG	4	4	4	4	5	10	12	20
390	Willie Davis	4	4	4	4	5	10	12	30
391	Ken Sanders	4	4	4	4	5	10	12	20
392	F.Cambria/R.Zisk RC	4	4	4	4	6	12	15	30
393	Curt Motton	4	4	4	4	5	10	12	20
394	Ken Forsch	4	4	4	4	5	10	12	20
395	Matty Alou	4	4	8	15	30	60	80	200
396	Paul Lindblad	4	4	4	4	5	10	12	30
397	Philadelphia Phillies TC	4	4	4	4	8	15	20	80
398	Larry Hisle	4	4	4	5	10	20	25	200
399	Milt Wilcox	4	4	4	4	8	15	20	40
400	Tony Oliva	4	4	4	6	12	25	30	100
401	Jim Nash	4	4	4	4	8	15	20	50
402	Bobby Heise	4	4	4	4	5	10	15	80
403	John Cumberland	4	4	4	4	5	10	12	20
404	Jeff Torborg	4	4	4	4	5	10	12	40
405	Ron Fairly	4	4	4	4	6	12	20	50
406	George Hendrick RC	4	4	4	4	5	10	15	40
407	Chuck Taylor	4	4	4	4	5	10	12	50
408	Jim Northrup	4	4	4	5	10	20	25	50
409	Frank Baker	4	4	4	4	5	10	15	50
410	Ferguson Jenkins	4	4	4	5	10	30	40	60
411	Bob Montgomery	4	4	4	4	8	15	20	80
412	Dick Kelley	4	4	4	4	8	15	20	40
413	D.Eddy RC/D.Lemonds	4	4	4	4	8	15	20	60
414	Bob Miller	4	4	4	4	8	15	20	40
415	Cookie Rojas	4	4	4	4	6	12	15	40
416	Johnny Edwards	4	4	4	4	5	10	12	25
417	Tom Hall	4	4	4	4	5	10	12	20
418	Tom Shopay	4	4	4	4	5	10	12	20
419	Jim Spencer	4	4	4	4	5	10	12	40
420	Steve Carlton	▲5	▲8	▲12	▲20	▲30	50	50	150
421	Ellie Rodriguez	4	4	4	4	5	10	12	25
422	Ray Lamb	4	4	4	4	5	10	12	20
423	Oscar Gamble	4	4	4	4	5	10	12	20
424	Bill Gogolewski	4	4	4	4	5	10	12	20
425	Ken Singleton	4	4	4	5	10	20	25	80
426	Ken Singleton IA	4	4	4	4	8	15	20	40
427	Tito Fuentes	4	4	4	6	12	25	30	50
428	Tito Fuentes IA	4	4	4	4	5	10	12	25
429	Bob Robertson	4	4	4	5	10	20	25	50
430	Bob Robertson IA	4	4	4	4	8	15	20	30
431	Cito Gaston	4	4	4	4	5	10	12	20
432	Cito Gaston IA	4	4	4	4	5	10	12	20
433	Johnny Bench	▲15	▲25	▲40	▲60	▲150	▲300	▲400	▲1,200
434	Johnny Bench IA	4	4	12	20	50	100	120	600
435	Reggie Jackson	▲15	▲25	▲40	▲60	▲100	▲200	▲400	▲1,200
436	Reggie Jackson IA	4	5	8	15	30	80	100	300
437	Maury Wills	4	4	4	4	6	12	15	50
438	Maury Wills IA	4	4	5	10	20	40	50	300
439	Billy Williams	4	4	4	5	10	50	60	80
440	Billy Williams IA	4	4	4	4	6	12	15	40
441	Thurman Munson	10	15	25	30	40	80	100	250
442	Thurman Munson IA	4	4	6	12	25	40	60	200
443	Ken Henderson	4	6	12	25	50	60		
444	Ken Henderson IA	4	4	4	4	5	10	12	20
445	Tom Seaver	10	15	25	50	60	150	200	600
446	Tom Seaver IA	6	10	15	20	25	60	80	300
447	Willie Stargell	4	4	5	10	30	50	60	200
448	Willie Stargell IA	4	4	6	8	15	50	60	300
449	Bob Lemon MG	4	4	4	4	8	15	20	40
450	Mickey Lolich	4	4	4	5	10	20	25	50

#	Name	VG 3	VgEx 4	EX 5	ExMt 6	NM 7	NmMt 8	NmMt+ 8.5	MT 9
451	Tony LaRussa	4	4	4	4	8	15	20	50
452	Ed Herrmann	4	4	4	4	5	10	12	25
453	Barry Lersch	4	4	4	4	8	15	20	40
454	Oakland Athletics TC	4	4	4	5	10	20	25	80
455	Tommy Harper	4	4	4	4	5	10	12	30
456	Mark Belanger	4	4	4	5	10	20	25	50
457	Fast/Thomas/Ivie RC	4	4	4	4	6	12	20	150
458	Aurelio Monteagudo	4	4	4	4	5	10	12	20
459	Rick Renick	4	4	4	4	5	10	12	20
460	Al Downing	4	4	4	4	5	10	12	50
461	Tim Cullen	4	4	4	4	5	10	12	20
462	Rickey Clark	4	4	4	4	5	10	12	25
463	Bernie Carbo	4	4	4	8	15	30	40	80
464	Jim Roland	4	4	4	4	5	10	12	25
465	Gil Hodges MG	4	4	5	10	20	40		
466	Norm Miller	4	4	4	4	5	10	12	20
467	Steve Kline	4	4	4	4	5	10	15	120
468	Richie Scheinblum	4	4	4	4	5	10	12	25
469	Ron Herbel	4	4	4	4	5	10	12	20
470	Ray Fosse	4	4	4	4	5	10	12	50
471	Luke Walker	4	4	4	4	5	10	12	20
472	Phil Gagliano	4	4	4	4	5	10	12	20
473	Dan McGinn	4	4	4	4	5	10	12	20
474	Baylor/Harrison/Oates RC	4	6	10	15	25	40	50	80
475	Gary Nolan	4	4	4	4	5	10	12	25
476	Lee Richard RC	4	4	4	4	5	10	12	20
477	Tom Phoebus	4	4	4	4	5	10	12	20
478	Checklist 526-656	4	4	4	4	5	10	12	120
479	Don Shaw	4	4	4	4	5	10	12	20
480	Lee May	4	4	4	4	5	10	12	20
481	Billy Conigliaro	4	4	4	4	4	8	10	15
482	Joe Hoerner	4	4	4	4	8	15	20	40
483	Ken Suarez	4	4	4	4	5	10	12	20
484	Lum Harris MG	4	4	4	4	5	10	12	20
485	Phil Regan	4	4	4	4	5	10	12	40
486	John Lowenstein	4	4	4	4	5	10	12	25
487	Detroit Tigers TC	4	4	4	4	8	15	20	40
488	Mike Nagy	4	4	4	4	5	10	12	20
489	T.Humphrey RC/K.Lampard	4	4	4	5	10	20	25	250
490	Dave McNally	4	4	4	4	6	12	15	120
491	Lou Piniella KP	4	4	4	4	5	10	12	25
492	Mel Stottlemyre KP	4	4	4	4	6	12	15	25
493	Bob Bailey KP	4	4	5	6	12	25	30	50
494	Willie Horton KP	4	4	4	4	6	12	15	30
495	Bill Melton KP	4	4	4	4	8	15	20	40
496	Bud Harrelson KP	4	4	4	5	10	20	25	100
497	Jim Perry KP	4	4	4	4	5	10	15	50
498	Brooks Robinson KP	4	4	4	4	8	15	20	80
499	Vicente Romo	4	4	4	4	5	10	12	20
500	Joe Torre	4	4	4	5	10	20	25	120
501	Pete Hamm	4	4	4	4	8	15	20	40
502	Jackie Hernandez	4	4	4	4	5	10	12	20
503	Gary Peters	4	4	4	4	8	15	20	50
504	Ed Spiezio	4	4	4	4	6	12	20	120
505	Mike Marshall	4	4	4	4	5	10	12	30
506	Ley/Moyer/Tidrow RC	4	4	4	4	8	15	20	80
507	Fred Gladding	4	4	4	4	5	10	12	25
508	Elrod Hendricks	4	4	4	4	5	10	12	60
509	Don McMahon	4	4	4	4	5	10	12	25
510	Ted Williams MG	▲8	▲12	▲20	▲30	▲50	▲60	80	▲400
511	Tony Taylor	4	4	4	4	5	10	12	25
512	Paul Popovich	4	4	4	4	5	10	12	80
513	Lindy McDaniel	4	4	4	4	5	10	12	30
514	Ted Sizemore	4	4	4	4	5	10	12	50
515	Bert Blyleven	4	4	4	4	6	12	15	120
516	Oscar Brown	4	4	4	4	5	10	12	20
517	Ken Brett	4	4	4	4	8	20	25	60
518	Wayne Garrett	8	15	30	40	80	100		

#	Player	VG 3	VgEx 4	EX 5	ExMt 6	NM 7	NmMt 8	NmMt+ 8.5	MT 9
519	Ted Abernathy	4	4	4	4	6	12	20	120
520	Larry Bowa	4	4	4	4	6	12	20	150
521	Alan Foster	4	4	4	4	5	10	12	25
522	Los Angeles Dodgers TC	4	4	4	4	5	10	15	60
523	Chuck Dobson	4	4	4	4	5	10	15	60
524	E.Armbrister RC/M.Behney RC	4	5	10	12	25	80		
525	Carlos May	4	4	8	10	20	40		
526	Bob Bailey	4	4	4	4	5	10	15	40
527	Dave Leonhard	4	4	4	4	5	10	15	100
528	Ron Stone	4	4	4	4	6	12	15	40
529	Dave Nelson	4	4	4	4	5	10	12	20
530	Don Sutton	4	4	4	6	12	50	60	80
531	Freddie Patek	4	4	4	6	10	15	12	20
532	Fred Kendall RC	5	10	20	25	50	150		
533	Ralph Houk MG	4	6	12	15	30	60	100	250
534	Jim Hickman	4	4	4	4	5	10	12	20
535	Ed Brinkman	4	4	4	4	5	10	12	25
536	Doug Rader	4	4	4	4	5	10	12	150
537	Bob Locker	4	4	4	4	5	10	12	30
538	Charlie Sands RC	4	4	4	4	5	10	12	80
539	Terry Forster RC	4	4	4	4	5	10	12	20
540	Felix Millan	4	4	4	4	6	12	15	30
541	Roger Repoz	4	4	4	4	5	10	12	20
542	Jack Billingham	4	4	4	4	8	15	20	40
543	Duane Josephson	4	4	4	4	5	10	12	20
544	Ted Martinez	4	4	4	4	5	10	12	30
545	Wayne Granger	4	4	4	4	5	10	12	20
546	Joe Hague	4	4	4	4	5	10	12	20
547	Cleveland Indians TC	4	4	4	4	5	10	12	20
548	Frank Reberger	4	4	4	4	5	10	12	20
549	Dave May	4	4	4	4	5	10	12	50
550	Brooks Robinson	4	10	12	20	30	50	80	250
551	Ollie Brown	4	4	4	4	6	12	15	40
552	Ollie Brown IA	4	4	4	4	6	12	15	40
553	Wilbur Wood	4	4	4	4	5	10	12	20
554	Wilbur Wood IA	4	4	4	4	5	10	12	20
555	Ron Santo	4	4	5	6	25	50	60	100
556	Ron Santo IA	4	4	8	10	20	40	50	120
557	John Odom	4	4	4	4	5	10	12	20
558	John Odom IA	4	4	4	4	5	10	15	50
559	Pete Rose	▲25	▲40	▲60	▲100	▲200	▲300	400	▲1,500
560	Pete Rose IA	10	20	25	25	50	80	100	500
561	Leo Cardenas	4	4	4	4	5	10	12	25
562	Leo Cardenas IA	4	4	4	4	5	10	12	20
563	Ray Sadecki	4	4	4	4	6	12	20	150
564	Ray Sadecki IA	4	4	4	4	5	10	12	30
565	Reggie Smith	4	4	4	4	8	15	20	100
566	Reggie Smith IA	4	4	4	4	5	10	12	30
567	Juan Marichal	4	6	12	15	30	40	80	200
568	Juan Marichal IA	4	4	5	10	30	40	50	150
569	Ed Kirkpatrick	4	4	4	4	5	10	12	20
570	Ed Kirkpatrick IA	4	4	4	4	5	10	15	80
571	Nate Colbert	4	4	4	4	5	10	12	20
572	Nate Colbert IA	4	4	4	4	6	12	20	120
573	Fritz Peterson	4	4	4	4	5	10	12	20
574	Fritz Peterson IA	4	4	4	4	5	10	15	40
575	Al Oliver	4	4	4	4	5	15	20	30
576	Leo Durocher MG	4	4	4	5	15	25	30	80
577	Mike Paul	4	4	4	4	5	10	12	20
578	Billy Grabarkewitz	4	4	4	4	5	10	12	20
579	Doyle Alexander RC	4	4	4	4	6	20	25	30
580	Lou Piniella	4	4	4	4	8	15	20	30
581	Wade Blasingame	4	4	4	4	5	10	12	25
582	Montreal Expos TC	5	8	10	15	60	120		
583	Darold Knowles	4	4	4	4	5	10	12	20
584	Jerry McNertney	4	4	4	4	5	10	12	20
585	George Scott	4	4	4	4	6	12	15	60
586	Denis Menke	4	4	4	4	5	10	12	25
587	Billy Wilson	4	4	4	4	5	10	12	20
588	Jim Holt	4	4	4	4	5	10	12	120
589	Hal Lanier	4	4	4	4	5	10	12	30
590	Graig Nettles	4	4	4	5	8	12	20	40
591	Paul Casanova	4	4	4	4	5	10	12	20
592	Lew Krausse	4	4	4	4	5	10	12	20
593	Rich Morales	4	4	4	4	5	10	12	20
594	Jim Beauchamp	4	4	4	4	5	10	12	20
595	Nolan Ryan	50	80	▲120	▲200	▲300	▲800	▲1,000	2,500
596	Manny Mota	4	4	4	4	8	15	20	80
597	Jim Magnuson RC	4	4	4	4	5	10	12	20
598	Hal King	4	4	4	4	5	10	12	30
599	Billy Champion	4	4	4	4	5	10	12	20
600	Al Kaline	8	20	25	30	80	100	120	300
601	George Stone	4	4	4	4	5	10	12	20
602	Dave Bristol MG	4	4	4	4	5	10	15	60
603	Jim Ray	4	4	4	4	5	10	12	20
604A	Checklist								
	657-787 Copyright on Right	4	4	4	4	6	12	15	30
604B	Checklist								
	657-787 Copyright on Left	4	4	4	4	6	12	15	30
605	Nelson Briles	4	4	4	4	5	10	12	50
606	Luis Melendez	4	4	4	4	5	10	12	20
607	Frank Duffy	4	4	4	4	5	10	12	20
608	Mike Corkins	4	4	4	4	5	10	12	20
609	Tom Grieve	4	4	4	4	5	10	12	20
610	Bill Stoneman	4	4	4	4	5	10	12	25
611	Rich Reese	4	4	4	4	5	10	12	20
612	Joe Decker	4	4	4	4	6	12	15	60
613	Mike Ferraro	4	4	4	4	5	10	12	20
614	Ted Uhlaender	4	4	4	4	5	10	12	50
615	Steve Hargan	4	4	4	4	5	10	12	20
616	Joe Ferguson RC	4	4	4	4	6	12	15	40
617	Kansas City Royals TC	4	4	4	4	8	12	20	20
618	Rich Robertson	4	4	4	4	5	10	12	20
619	Rich McKinney	4	4	4	5	10	20	25	250
620	Phil Niekro	5	8	15	20	30	100	120	50
621	Commish Award	4	4	4	4	5	10	12	5
622	MVP Award	4	4	4	4	6	12	15	3
623	Cy Young Award	4	4	4	6	15	20	30	4
624	Minor Lg POY Award	4	4	4	4	8	15		
625	Rookie of the Year	4	4	5	8	12	25	30	5
626	Babe Ruth Award	4	6	8	10	15	25	40	6
627	Moe Drabowsky	4	4	5	6	12	25		
628	Terry Crowley	4	4	4	4	5	10	12	2
629	Paul Doyle	4	4	4	4	5	10	12	2
630	Rich Hebner	4	4	4	4	6	12	15	4
631	John Strohmayer	4	4	4	4	5	10	12	3
632	Mike Hegan	4	4	4	4	5	10	15	6
633	Jack Hiatt	4	4	4	4	5	10	12	2
634	Dick Woodson	4	4	4	4	5	10	12	2
635	Don Money	4	4	4	4	5	15	20	5
636	Bill Lee	4	4	4	4	5	10	20	6
637	Preston Gomez MG	4	4	4	4	5	10	12	3
638	Ken Wright	4	4	4	4	5	10	15	4
639	J.C. Martin	4	4	4	4	5	10	12	4
640	Joe Coleman	4	4	4	4	5	10	12	2
641	Mike Lum	4	4	4	6	12	25	30	8
642	Dennis Riddleberger RC	4	4	4	4	5	10	12	2
643	Russ Gibson	4	4	4	4	5	10	12	6
644	Bernie Allen	4	4	4	4	5	10	12	6
645	Jim Maloney	4	4	4	4	6	12	20	5
646	Chico Salmon	4	4	4	4	5	10	12	20
647	Bob Moose	4	4	4	4	6	12	15	6
648	Jim Lyttle	4	4	4	4	5	10	12	2
649	Pete Richert	4	4	4	4	5	10	12	2
650	Sal Bando	4	4	4	4	5	20	40	6
651	Cincinnati Reds TC	4	4	4	4	6	15	20	10

#	Player	VG 3	VgEx 4	EX 5	ExMt 6	NM 7	NmMt 8	NmMt+ 8.5	MT 9
652	Marcelino Lopez	4	4	4	4	5	10	12	20
653	Jim Fairey	4	4	4	4	5	10	12	30
654	Horacio Pina	4	4	4	4	5	10	12	60
655	Jerry Grote	4	8	15	20	40	80		
656	Rudy May	4	4	4	4	5	10	12	25
657	Bobby Wine	4	4	4	4	8	25	30	40
658	Steve Dunning	4	4	8	10	20	50	60	300
659	Bob Aspromonte	4	4	4	4	8	15	20	50
660	Paul Blair	4	4	4	6	15	20	40	60
661	Bill Virdon MG	4	4	6	8	15	50	60	100
662	Stan Bahnsen	4	4	4	5	10	20	30	80
663	Fran Healy RC	4	4	5	8	25	30	40	50
664	Bobby Knoop	4	▲5	▲8	▲12	▲20	▲30	▲40	▲80
665	Chris Short	4	4	5	6	12	30	30	50
666	Hector Torres	4	4	4	5	10	25	30	50
667	Ray Newman RC	4	4	5	6	12	40	50	120
668	Texas Rangers TC	4	5	8	10	20	30	50	60
669	Willie Crawford	4	4	4	5	10	30	40	50
670	Ken Holtzman	4	5	▼8	12	25	60		
671	Donn Clendenon	4	▲6	▲10	▲15	▲25	▲40	▲50	▲120
672	Archie Reynolds	4	4	4	5	10	20	40	50
673	Dave Marshall	4	5	10	12	25	50		
674	John Kennedy	4	4	4	5	10	20	30	80
675	Pat Jarvis	4	4	4	4	8	20	25	30
676	Danny Cater	4	4	5	6	12	25	30	150
677	Ivan Murrell	4	4	4	4	8	25	30	50
678	Steve Luebber RC	4	4	4	4	8	15	30	40
679	B.Fenwick RC/B.Stinson	4	4	4	4	8	15	25	30
680	Dave Johnson	4	4	4	4	10	25	30	50
681	Bobby Pfeil	4	4	4	5	10	25	25	100
682	Mike McCormick	4	4	4	5	10	30	40	80
683	Steve Hovley	4	4	6	8	15	30		
684	Hal Breeden RC	4	4	4	4	8	20	25	30
685	Joel Horlen	4	4	4	4	8	15	20	30
686	Steve Garvey	15	25	40	▲60	100	▲200	▲250	▲800
687	Del Unser	4	5	6	8	12	30		
688	St. Louis Cardinals TC	4	4	5	8	12	25	30	▲100
689	Eddie Fisher	4	4	4	4	8	25	30	50
690	Willie Montanez	4	4	4	6	12	25	30	50
691	Curt Blefary	4	4	4	5	10	20	30	100
692	Curt Blefary IA	4	4	4	5	10	30	40	120
693	Alan Gallagher	4	5	8	12	20	30		
694	Alan Gallagher IA	4	4	5	6	12	25	30	75
695	Rod Carew	▲25	▲40	▲60	▲100	▲200	▲300	▲400	▲1,000
696	Rod Carew IA	▲8	▲12	▲20	30	40	▲120	▲150	500
697	Jerry Koosman	4	4	5	6	12	25	30	80
698	Jerry Koosman IA	4	4	8	10	20	50		
699	Bobby Murcer	4	4	8	15	50	80	100	150
700	Bobby Murcer IA	4	4	8	10	30	50	60	200
701	Jose Pagan	4	4	4	4	8	20	25	50
702	Jose Pagan IA	4	4	5	8	12	40	60	100
703	Doug Griffin	4	4	4	4	8	25	30	▲60
704	Doug Griffin IA	4	4	4	5	10	25	30	150
705	Pat Corrales	4	4	4	15	20	25	30	▲60
706	Pat Corrales IA	4	4	4	6	12	30	40	80
707	Tim Foli	4	4	4	5	10	20	25	40
708	Tim Foli IA	6	12	25	30	60	150		
709	Jim Kaat	4	4	4	6	12	40	50	60
710	Jim Kaat IA	4	4	6	8	25	30	40	80
711	Bobby Bonds	4	4	5	6	12	30	40	50
712	Bobby Bonds IA	4	4	5	6	12	30	40	60
713	Gene Michael	4	4	8	10	20	40	50	200
714	Gene Michael IA	4	4	8	15	30	50	80	300
715	Mike Epstein	4	▲6	▲10	▲15	▲25	50	60	100
716	Jesus Alou	4	4	5	6	12	50		
717	Bruce Dal Canton	4	4	4	5	10	25	30	100
718	Del Rice MG	4	4	4	4	8	15	20	60
719	Cesar Geronimo	4	4	4	5	10	40	50	80
720	Sam McDowell	4	4	4	4	10	30	40	50
721	Eddie Leon	4	4	4	4	8	20	25	40
722	Bill Sudakis	4	▲6	▲10	▲15	▲25	▲40	▲50	80
723	Al Santorini	4	4	8	10	20	40	60	350
724	Curtis/Hinton/Scott RC	4	4	8	10	20	40	50	60
725	Dick McAuliffe	4	4	4	4	8	25	30	60
726	Dick Selma	4	4	4	4	8	25	30	40
727	Jose Laboy	4	4	4	5	10	20	25	40
728	Gail Hopkins	4	4	4	6	12	30	40	250
729	Bob Veale	4	4	4	5	10	30	40	50
730	Rick Monday	4	4	6	8	15	50	60	120
731	Baltimore Orioles TC	4	5	6	8	15	40	50	▲100
732	George Culver	4	4	4	4	8	15	20	50
733	Jim Ray Hart	4	4	4	4	8	25	30	50
734	Bob Burda	4	4	4	8	15	30	40	200
735	Diego Segui	4	4	4	4	8	25	30	40
736	Bill Russell	4	4	4	5	8	30	40	60
737	Len Randle RC	▲6	▲10	▲15	▲25	▲40	▲100	▲120	300
738	Jim Merritt	4	4	4	4	8	25	30	40
739	Don Mason	4	4	4	4	8	25	30	40
740	Rico Carty	4	4	6	8	15	30	40	150
741	Hutton/Milner/Miller RC	4	4	4	8	15	30	40	▲80
742	Jim Rooker	4	4	4	4	8	25	30	50
743	Cesar Gutierrez	4	4	4	4	12	20	25	30
744	Jim Slaton RC	4	▲5	▲8	▲12	▲20	▲30	▲40	▲60
745	Julian Javier	4	4	4	5	10	20	25	80
746	Lowell Palmer	4	4	4	4	8	20	25	50
747	Jim Stewart	4	4	4	4	8	25	30	60
748	Phil Hennigan	4	4	4	4	8	15	20	30
749	Walt Alston MG	4	4	5	10	20	30	40	60
750	Willie Horton	4	4	4	6	12	25	30	60
751	Steve Carlton TR	8	12	20	40	50	60	80	250
752	Joe Morgan TR	▲25	▲40	▲60	▲100	▲150	▲300	▲400	▲1,000
753	Denny McLain TR	4	4	4	12	15	40	50	60
754	Frank Robinson TR	4	4	8	25	50	60	80	200
755	Jim Fregosi TR	4	4	4	10	20	30	50	100
756	Rick Wise TR	4	4	4	5	10	30	40	60
757	Jose Cardenal TR	4	6	12	15	30	80	120	450
758	Gil Garrido	4	4	4	5	10	25	40	120
759	Chris Cannizzaro	4	4	4	5	10	25	30	40
760	Bill Mazeroski	▲10	▲15	▲25	▲40	▲60	100	120	▲250
761	Oglivie/Cey/Williams RC	12	20	30	50	100	120	150	250
762	Wayne Simpson	4	4	4	4	10	25	30	40
763	Ron Hansen	4	4	4	5	10	20	40	100
764	Dusty Baker	4	4	5	6	30	40	50	150
765	Ken McMullen	4	4	4	4	8	25	30	40
766	Steve Hamilton	4	4	5	6	12	25	40	350
767	Tom McCraw	4	4	4	5	10	30	40	60
768	Denny Doyle	4	4	4	4	8	30	40	50
769	Jack Aker	4	4	4	4	8	30	40	50
770	Jim Wynn	4	4	4	4	10	40	50	150
771	San Francisco Giants TC	4	4	4	5	10	30	40	50
772	Ken Tatum	4	4	4	4	8	25	30	▲50
773	Ron Brand	4	4	4	4	8	20	25	40
774	Luis Alvarado	4	▲6	▲10	▲15	▲15	▲25	▲30	▲50
775	Jerry Reuss	4	4	4	6	10	20	25	50
776	Bill Voss	4	4	4	5	10	30	40	100
777	Hoyt Wilhelm	4	4	4	20	25	40	50	▲100
778	Rick Dempsey RC	4	4	8	10	30	40	50	100
779	Tony Cloninger	4	4	4	4	8	25	30	40
780	Dick Green	4	4	4	4	8	30	40	50
781	Jim McAndrew	4	4	6	10	15	30	40	50
782	Larry Stahl	4	5	6	8	15	40	50	150
783	Les Cain	4	▲5	▲8	▲12	▲20	▲30	▲40	▲60
784	Ken Aspromonte	4	4	4	5	10	40	50	60
785	Vic Davalillo	4	4	4	6	10	20	50	80
786	Chuck Brinkman	4	5	6	8	15	30	40	100
787	Ron Reed	4	5	10	12	25	80	120	200

— Hank Aaron #299 PSA 10 (Gem) sold for $20,655 (Mile High; 10/13)
— Roberto Clemente #309 PSA 10 (Gem) sold for $3,888 (eBay; 09/12)
— C.Fisk/C.Cooper #79 PSA 10 (Gem) (Young Collection) sold for $10,855 (SCP; 5/12)
— Steve Garvey #686 PSA 10 (Gem) sold for $2,003 (eBay; 1/13)

1973 O-Pee-Chee

		GD 2	VG 3	VgEx 4	EX 5	ExMt 6	NM 7	NmMt 8	MT 9
615	Mike Schmidt RC	▲100	▲150	▲250	▲400	▲600	▲1,000	▲1,500	▲4,000

1973 Kellogg's

		VG 3	VgEx 4	EX 5	ExMt 6	NM 7	NmMt 8	MT 9	Gem 9.5/10
1	Amos Otis	4	4	4	4	4	5	8	40
2	Ellie Rodriguez	4	4	4	4	4	5	8	25
3	Mickey Lolich	4	4	4	4	4	5	8	25
4	Tony Oliva	4	4	4	4	4	5	8	20
5	Don Sutton	4	4	4	4	4	5	8	20
6	Pete Rose	4	4	4	4	6	12	25	100
7	Steve Carlton	4	4	4	4	4	5	10	25
8	Bobby Bonds	4	4	4	4	4	5	8	20
9	Wilbur Wood	4	4	4	4	4	5	8	25
10	Billy Williams	4	4	4	4	4	5	10	25
11	Steve Blass	4	4	4	4	4	5	8	25
12	Jon Matlack	4	4	4	4	4	5	8	25
13	Cesar Cedeno	4	4	4	4	4	5	8	40
14	Bob Gibson	4	4	4	4	4	5	10	30
15	Sparky Lyle	4	4	4	4	4	5	8	60
16	Nolan Ryan	4	4	4	5	10	20	50	120
17	Jim Palmer	4	4	4	4	4	5	10	25
18	Ray Fosse	4	4	4	4	4	5	8	20
19	Bobby Murcer	4	4	4	4	4	5	10	25
20	Jim Hunter	4	4	4	4	4	5	10	25
21	Tug McGraw	4	4	4	4	4	5	8	25
22	Reggie Jackson	4	4	4	4	4	8	15	40
23	Bill Stoneman	4	4	4	4	4	5	8	60
24	Lou Piniella	4	4	4	4	4	5	8	50
25	Willie Stargell	4	4	4	4	4	5	10	25
26	Dick Allen	4	4	4	4	4	5	10	25
27	Carlton Fisk	4	4	4	4	4	6	50	60
28	Ferguson Jenkins	4	4	4	4	4	5	10	60
29	Phil Niekro	4	4	4	4	4	5	10	25
30	Gary Nolan	4	4	4	4	4	5	8	25
31	Joe Torre	4	4	4	4	4	5	8	20
32	Bobby Tolan	4	4	4	4	4	5	8	20
33	Nate Colbert	4	4	4	4	4	5	8	60
34	Joe Morgan	4	4	4	4	4	5	10	25
35	Bert Blyleven	4	4	4	4	4	5	8	20
36	Joe Rudi	4	4	4	4	4	5	8	25
37	Ralph Garr	4	4	4	4	4	5	8	40
38	Gaylord Perry	4	4	4	4	4	5	10	50
39	Bobby Grich	4	4	4	4	4	5	8	40
40	Lou Brock	4	4	4	4	4	5	10	150
41	Pete Broberg	4	4	4	4	4	5	8	25
42	Manny Sanguillen	4	4	4	4	4	5	8	20
43	Willie Davis	4	4	4	4	4	5	8	20
44	Dave Kingman	4	4	4	4	4	5	8	20
45	Carlos May	4	4	4	4	4	5	8	20
46	Tom Seaver	4	4	4	4	4	8	15	30
47	Mike Cuellar	4	4	4	4	4	5	8	60
48	Joe Coleman	4	4	4	4	4	5	8	20
49	Claude Osteen	4	4	4	4	4	5	8	25
50	Steve Kline	4	4	4	4	4	5	8	20
51	Rod Carew	4	4	4	4	4	5	10	50
52	Al Kaline	4	4	4	4	4	6	15	30
53	Larry Dierker	4	4	4	4	4	5	8	20
54	Ron Santo	4	4	4	4	4	5	10	25

1973 Topps

		VG 3	VgEx 4	EX 5	ExMt 6	NM 7	NmMt 8	NmMt+ 8.5	MT 9
1	Ruth/Aaron/Mays HR	20	25	30	60	80	250	200	600
2	Rich Hebner	4	4	4	4	4	8	10	30
3	Jim Lonborg	4	4	4	4	6	8		20
4	John Milner	4	4	4	4	6	8		60
5	Ed Brinkman	4	4	4	4	6	8		20
6	Mac Scarce RC	4	4	4	4	6	8		20
7	Texas Rangers TC	4	4	4	4	6	8		20
8	Tom Hall	4	4	4	4	6	8		15
9	Johnny Oates	4	4	4	4	6	8		15
10	Don Sutton	4	4	4	4	5	10	12	40
11	Chris Chambliss	4	4	4	4	4	8	10	30
12A	Don Zimmer MG Podres w/o Ear	4	4	4	4	4	6	8	20
12B	Don Zimmer MG Podres w/Ear	4	4	4	4	4	6	8	20
13	George Hendrick	4	4	4	4	4	6	8	20
14	Sonny Siebert	4	4	4	4	4	6	8	20
15	Ralph Garr	4	4	4	4	4	6	8	20
16	Steve Braun	4	4	4	4	4	6	8	20
17	Fred Gladding	4	4	4	4	4	6	8	25
18	Leroy Stanton	4	4	4	4	4	6	8	40
19	Tim Foli	4	4	4	4	4	6	8	12
20	Stan Bahnsen	4	4	4	4	4	6	8	20
21	Randy Hundley	4	4	4	4	4	6	8	20
22	Ted Abernathy	4	4	4	4	4	6	8	20
23	Dave Kingman	4	4	4	4	4	8	10	40
24	Al Santorini	4	4	4	4	4	6	8	20
25	Roy White	4	4	4	4	4	8	10	30
26	Pittsburgh Pirates TC	4	4	4	4	4	6	8	20
27	Bill Gogolewski	4	4	4	4	4	6	8	20
28	Hal McRae	4	4	4	4	4	8	10	25
29	Tony Taylor	4	4	4	4	4	6	8	20
30	Tug McGraw	4	4	4	4	4	8	10	25
31	Buddy Bell RC	4	4	4	4	8	15	20	120
32	Fred Norman	4	4	4	4	4	6	8	20
33	Jim Breazeale RC	4	4	4	4	4	6	8	20
34	Pat Dobson	4	4	4	4	4	6	8	20
35	Willie Davis	4	4	4	4	4	6	8	20
36	Steve Barber	4	4	4	4	4	6	8	20
37	Bill Robinson	4	4	4	4	4	6	8	20
38	Mike Epstein	4	4	4	4	4	6	8	20
39	Dave Roberts	4	4	4	4	4	6	8	20
40	Reggie Smith	4	4	4	4	4	8	10	50
41	Tom Walker RC	4	4	4	4	4	6	8	25
42	Mike Andrews	4	4	4	4	4	6	8	12
43	Randy Moffitt RC	4	4	4	4	4	6	8	20
44	Rick Monday	4	4	4	4	4	6	8	30
45	Ellie Rodriguez	4	4	4	4	4	6	8	20
46	Lindy McDaniel	4	4	4	4	4	6	8	20
47	Luis Melendez	4	4	4	4	4	6	8	20
48	Paul Splittorff	4	4	4	4	4	6	8	50
49A	Frank Quilici MG Solid	4	4	4	4	4	6	8	40
49B	Frank Quilici MG Natural	4	4	4	4	4	6	8	20
50	Roberto Clemente	50	60	80	▲120	▲200	400	400	1,500
51	Chuck Seelbach RC	4	4	4	4	4	6	8	20
52	Denis Menke	4	4	4	4	4	6	8	20
53	Steve Dunning	4	4	4	4	4	6	8	20
54	Checklist 1-132	4	4	4	4	8	20	25	40
55	Jon Matlack	4	4	4	4	4	6	8	20
56	Merv Rettenmund	4	4	4	4	4	6	8	20
57	Derrel Thomas	4	4	4	4	4	6	8	20
58	Mike Paul	4	4	4	4	4	6	8	15

#	Player	VG 3	VgEx 4	EX 5	ExMt 6	NM 7	NmMt 8	NmMt+ 8.5	MT 9
9	Steve Yeager RC	4	4	4	4	5	10	12	30
0	Ken Holtzman	4	4	4	4	4	6	8	30
1	Batting Leaders	4	4	4	4	4	8	10	30
2	Home Run Leaders	4	4	4	4	4	8	10	25
3	RBI Leaders	4	4	4	4	5	10	12	50
4	Stolen Base Leaders	4	4	4	4	4	8	10	25
5	ERA Leaders	4	4	4	4	4	8	10	25
6	Victory Leaders	4	4	4	4	4	8	10	25
7	Strikeout Leaders	4	6	10	15	40	50	60	150
8	Leading Firemen	4	4	4	4	4	8	10	25
9	Phil Gagliano	4	4	4	4	4	6	8	20
0	Milt Pappas	4	4	4	4	4	6	8	15
1	Johnny Briggs	4	4	4	4	4	6	8	12
2	Ron Reed	4	4	4	4	4	6	8	15
3	Ed Herrmann	4	4	4	4	4	5	6	10
4	Billy Champion	4	4	4	4	4	5	6	10
5	Vada Pinson	4	4	4	4	4	6	8	20
6	Doug Rader	4	4	4	4	4	6	8	15
7	Mike Torrez	4	4	4	4	4	6	8	20
8	Richie Scheinblum	4	4	4	4	4	6	8	12
9	Jim Willoughby RC	4	4	4	4	4	6	8	12
0	Tony Oliva	4	4	4	4	5	10	12	250
A	W.Lockman MG w/Banks Solid	4	4	4	4	4	8	10	60
B	W.Lockman MG w/Banks Natural	4	4	4	4	4	8	10	25
2	Fritz Peterson	4	4	4	4	4	6	8	20
	Leron Lee	4	4	4	4	4	6	8	15
	Rollie Fingers	4	4	5	6	12	25	30	150
	Ted Simmons	4	4	4	4	4	8	10	30
	Tom McCraw	4	4	4	4	4	6	8	15
	Ken Boswell	4	4	4	4	4	6	8	20
	Mickey Stanley	4	4	4	4	4	6	8	20
	Jack Billingham	4	4	4	4	4	6	8	20
	Brooks Robinson	▲10	▲15	▲25	▲40	▲60	▲100	▲120	▲250
	Los Angeles Dodgers TC	4	4	4	4	4	8	10	25
	Jerry Bell	4	4	4	4	4	6	8	20
	Jesus Alou	4	4	4	4	4	6	8	20
	Dick Billings	4	4	4	4	4	6	8	20
	Steve Blass	4	4	4	4	4	6	8	20
	Doug Griffin	4	4	4	4	4	6	8	20
	Willie Montanez	4	4	4	4	4	6	8	20
	Dick Woodson	4	4	4	4	4	6	8	20
	Carl Taylor	4	4	4	4	4	6	8	20
0	Hank Aaron	25	30	40	50	60	120	200	▲1,500
1	Ken Henderson	4	4	4	4	4	6	8	20
2	Rudy May	4	4	4	4	4	6	8	20
3	Celerino Sanchez RC	4	4	4	4	4	6	8	20
4	Reggie Cleveland	4	4	4	4	4	6	8	12
5	Carlos May	4	4	4	4	4	6	8	20
6	Terry Humphrey	4	4	4	4	4	6	8	20
7	Phil Hennigan	4	4	4	4	4	6	8	20
8	Bill Russell	4	4	4	4	4	8	10	25
9	Doyle Alexander	4	4	4	4	4	6	8	20
	Bob Watson	4	4	4	4	4	6	8	20
	Dave Nelson	4	4	4	4	4	6	8	20
2	Gary Ross	4	4	4	4	4	6	8	20
	Jerry Grote	4	4	4	4	4	5	6	10
	Lynn McGlothen RC	4	4	4	4	4	6	8	12
	Ron Santo	4	4	4	4	8	15	20	30
A	Ralph Houk MG Solid	4	4	4	4	4	6	8	120
B	Ralph Houk MG Natural	4	4	4	4	4	6	8	20
	Ramon Hernandez	4	4	4	4	4	6	8	20
	John Mayberry	4	4	4	4	4	6	8	20
	Larry Bowa	4	4	4	4	4	8	10	25
	Joe Coleman	4	4	4	4	4	6	8	20
	Dave Rader	4	4	4	4	4	6	8	20
	Jim Strickland	4	4	4	4	4	6	8	20
	Sandy Alomar	4	4	4	4	4	8	10	25
	Jim Hardin	4	4	4	4	4	6	8	20

#	Player	VG 3	VgEx 4	EX 5	ExMt 6	NM 7	NmMt 8	NmMt+ 8.5	MT 9
125	Ron Fairly	4	4	4	4	4	6	8	20
126	Jim Brewer	4	4	4	4	4	6	8	20
127	Milwaukee Brewers TC	4	4	4	4	4	6	8	25
128	Ted Sizemore	4	4	4	4	4	6	8	60
129	Terry Forster	4	4	4	4	4	8	10	25
130	Pete Rose	▲15	25	▲40	▲60	▲100	150	200	▲1,500
131A	Eddie Kasko MG Popowski w/oEar	4	4	4	4	4	60	80	400
131B	Eddie Kasko MG Popowski w/Ear	4	4	4	4	4	6	8	25
132	Matty Alou	4	4	4	4	4	6	8	20
133	Dave Roberts RC	4	4	4	4	4	6	8	25
134	Milt Wilcox	4	4	4	4	4	6	8	25
135	Lee May	4	4	4	4	4	6	8	20
136A	Earl Weaver MG Orange	4	4	4	4	5	10	12	60
136B	Earl Weaver MG Brown	4	4	4	4	4	8	10	400
137	Jim Beauchamp	4	4	4	4	4	6	8	25
138	Horacio Pina	4	4	4	4	4	6	8	40
139	Carmen Fanzone RC	4	4	4	4	4	6	8	20
140	Lou Piniella	4	4	4	4	4	8	10	25
141	Bruce Kison	4	4	4	4	4	6	8	150
142	Thurman Munson	▲10	▲15	▲25	▲40	▲60	▲200	▲250	600
143	John Curtis	4	4	4	4	4	6	8	25
144	Marty Perez	4	4	4	4	4	6	8	10
145	Bobby Bonds	4	4	4	4	4	8	10	80
146	Woodie Fryman	4	4	4	4	4		15	20
147	Mike Anderson	4	4	4	4	4	6	8	20
148	Dave Goltz RC	4	4	4	4	4	6	8	20
149	Ron Hunt	4	4	4	4	4	6	8	25
150	Wilbur Wood	4	4	4	4	4	8	10	25
151	Wes Parker	4	4	4	4	4	8	10	25
152	Dave May	4	4	4	4	4	6	8	20
153	Al Hrabosky	4	4	4	4	4	8	10	25
154	Jeff Torborg	4	4	4	4	4	6	8	20
155	Sal Bando	4	4	4	4	4	8	10	30
156	Cesar Geronimo	4	4	4	4	4	6	8	50
157	Denny Riddleberger	4	4	4	4	4	6	8	200
158	Houston Astros TC	4	4	4	4	4	6	8	20
159	Cito Gaston	4	4	4	4	4	6	8	20
160	Jim Palmer	4	4	4	4	8	30	40	200
161	Ted Martinez	4	4	4	4	4	6	8	20
162	Pete Broberg	4	4	4	4	4	6	8	12
163	Vic Davalillo	4	4	4	4	4		10	
164	Monty Montgomery	4	4	4	4	4	6	8	20
165	Luis Aparicio	4	4	4	4	5	15	20	30
166	Terry Harmon	4	4	4	4	4	6	8	20
167	Steve Stone	4	4	4	4	4	6	8	20
168	Jim Northrup	4	4	4	4	4	8	10	25
169	Ron Schueler RC	4	4	4	4	4	6	8	250
170	Harmon Killebrew	4	4	6	15	30	▲100	▲120	200
171	Bernie Carbo	4	4	4	4	4	6	8	25
172	Steve Kline	4	4	4	4	4	6	8	20
173	Hal Breeden	4	4	4	5	10	40		
174	Rich Gossage RC	▲20	▲30	▲50	▲80	▲100	▲250	▲300	600
175	Frank Robinson	5	8	12	20	40	60	60	150
176	Chuck Taylor	4	4	4	4	4	6	8	20
177	Bill Plummer RC	4	4	4	4	4	6	8	20
178	Don Rose RC	4	4	4	4	4	6	8	80
179A	Dick Williams MG Hoscheit w/Ear	4	4	4	4	4	6	8	30
179B	Dick Williams MG Hoscheit w/o Ear	4	4	4	4	4	6	8	20
180	Ferguson Jenkins	4	4	4	4	5	10	12	50
181	Jack Brohamer RC	4	4	4	4	4	6	8	25
182	Mike Caldwell RC	4	4	4	4	4	8	10	30
183	Don Buford	4	4	4	4	4		10	
184	Jerry Koosman	4	4	4	4	4	8	10	25
185	Jim Wynn	4	4	4	4	4	8	10	25
186	Bill Fahey	4	4	4	4	4	6	8	40
187	Luke Walker	4	4	4	4	4	6	8	15
188	Cookie Rojas	4	4	4	4	4	6	8	20

#	Player	VG 3	VgEx 4	EX 5	ExMt 6	NM 7	NmMt 8	NmMt+ 8.5	MT 9
189	Greg Luzinski	4	4	4	4	4	8	10	50
190	Bob Gibson	▲15	25	30	50	▲80	▲150	▲200	400
191	Detroit Tigers TC	4	4	4	4	4	8	10	50
192	Pat Jarvis	4	4	4	4	4	6	8	25
193	Carlton Fisk	▲12	▲20	▲30	▲50	▲80	▲200	▲250	400
194	Jorge Orta RC	4	4	4	4	4	6	8	50
195	Clay Carroll	4	4	4	4	4	15	20	100
196	Ken McMullen	4	4	4	4	4	6	8	20
197	Ed Goodson RC	4	4	4	4	4	6	8	25
198	Horace Clarke	4	4	4	4	4	6	8	30
199	Bert Blyleven	4	4	4	4	4	8	10	60
200	Billy Williams	4	4	4	4	6	20	25	80
201	George Hendrick ALCS	4	4	4	4	4	8	10	30
202	George Foster NLCS	4	4	4	4	4	15	20	150
203	Gene Tenace WS1	4	4	4	4	4	8	10	25
204	A's Two Straight WS2	4	4	4	4	4	8	10	30
205	Tony Perez WS3	4	4	4	4	4	8	10	30
206	Gene Tenace WS4	4	4	4	4	4	8	10	40
207	Blue Moon Odom WS5	4	4	4	4	4	8	10	50
208	Johnny Bench WS6	4	4	4	5	8	12	20	25
209	Bert Campaneris WS7	4	4	4	4	4	8	10	30
210	A's Win WS	4	4	4	4	4	6	8	80
211	Balor Moore	4	4	4	4	4	6	8	40
212	Joe Lahoud	4	4	4	4	4	6	8	20
213	Steve Garvey	▲6	▲10	▲15	▲25	▲40	▲60	▲80	100
214	Dave Hamilton RC	4	4	4	4	4	6	8	25
215	Dusty Baker	4	4	4	4	4	8	10	25
216	Toby Harrah	4	4	4	4	4	6	8	20
217	Don Wilson	4	4	4	6	12	25	30	900
218	Aurelio Rodriguez	4	4	4	4	4	6	8	25
219	St. Louis Cardinals TC	4	4	4	4	4	8	10	80
220	Nolan Ryan	▲20	▲30	▲50	▲80	▲150	▲400	600	1,500
221	Fred Kendall	4	4	4	4	4	6	8	20
222	Rob Gardner	4	4	4	4	5	10	12	25
223	Bud Harrelson	4	4	4	4	5	10	12	60
224	Bill Lee	4	4	4	4	4	8	10	30
225	Al Oliver	4	4	4	4	4	8	10	25
226	Ray Fosse	4	4	4	4	4	6	8	20
227	Wayne Twitchell	4	4	4	4	4	12	15	60
228	Bobby Darwin	4	4	4	4	4	6	8	20
229	Roric Harrison	4	4	4	4	4	6	8	60
230	Joe Morgan	▲8	▲12	▲20	▲30	▲50	150		
231	Bill Parsons	4	4	4	4	4	6	8	20
232	Ken Singleton	4	4	4	4	4	8	10	25
233	Ed Kirkpatrick	4	4	4	4	4	6	8	25
234	Bill North RC	4	4	4	4	4	6	8	50
235	Jim Hunter	4	4	5	6	12	25	30	60
236	Tito Fuentes	4	4	4	4	4	6	8	15
237A	Eddie Mathews MG Burdette w/Ear	4	4	4	4	5	10	12	700
237B	Eddie Mathews MG Burdette w/o Ear	4	4	4	4	5	10	12	300
238	Tony Muser RC	4	4	4	4	4	6	8	20
239	Pete Richert	4	4	4	4	5	10	15	
240	Bobby Murcer	4	4	4	4	8	15	20	50
241	Dwain Anderson	4	4	4	4	5	10	12	20
242	George Culver	4	4	4	4	4	6	8	20
243	California Angels TC	4	4	4	4	4	6	8	25
244	Ed Acosta	4	4	4	4	4	6	8	20
245	Carl Yastrzemski	8	12	20	25	60	120		
246	Ken Sanders	4	4	4	4	4	6	8	20
247	Del Unser	4	4	4	4	5	10	15	
248	Jerry Johnson	4	4	4	4	4	6	8	20
249	Larry Biittner	4	4	4	4	4	6	8	20
250	Manny Sanguillen	4	4	4	4	4	8	10	50
251	Roger Nelson	4	4	4	4	4	6	8	15
252A	Charlie Fox MG Orange	4	4	4	4	4	6	8	60
252B	Charlie Fox MG Brown	4	4	4	4	4	6	8	20
253	Mark Belanger	4	4	4	4	4	8	10	25
254	Bill Stoneman	4	4	4	4	4	6	8	12

#	Player	VG 3	VgEx 4	EX 5	ExMt 6	NM 7	NmMt 8	NmMt+ 8.5	MT 9
255	Reggie Jackson	▲12	▲20	30	▲50	▲80	150	200	1,000
256	Chris Zachary	4	4	4	4	4	6	8	15
257A	Yogi Berra MG Orange	4	4	4	4	5	15	20	80
257B	Yogi Berra MG Brown	4	4	4	4	5	15	20	60
258	Tommy John	4	4	4	4	4	8	10	50
259	Jim Holt	4	4	4	4	5	10	15	
260	Gary Nolan	4	4	4	4	4	6	8	20
261	Pat Kelly	4	4	4	4	4	6	8	25
262	Jack Aker	4	4	4	4	4	6	8	20
263	George Scott	4	4	4	4	4	6	8	20
264	Checklist 133-264	4	4	4	4	8	60	80	100
265	Gene Michael	4	4	4	4	4	6	8	50
266	Mike Lum	4	4	4	4	4	6	8	25
267	Lloyd Allen	4	4	4	4	4	6	8	20
268	Jerry Morales	4	4	4	4	4	6	8	20
269	Tim McCarver	4	4	4	4	4	8	10	25
270	Luis Tiant	4	4	4	4	4	8	10	25
271	Tom Hutton	4	4	4	4	4	6	8	20
272	Ed Farmer	4	4	4	4	4	6	8	25
273	Chris Speier	4	4	4	4	4	6	8	20
274	Darold Knowles	4	4	4	4	4	6	8	25
275	Tony Perez	4	4	4	4	8	60	80	200
276	Joe Lovitto RC	4	4	4	4	4	6	8	20
277	Bob Miller	4	4	4	4	4	6	8	20
278	Baltimore Orioles TC	4	4	4	4	6	12	15	100
279	Mike Strahler	4	4	4	4	4	6	8	50
280	Al Kaline	5	8	12	25	40	100	120	250
281	Mike Jorgensen	4	4	4	4	4	6	8	80
282	Steve Hovley	4	4	4	4	4	6	8	80
283	Ray Sadecki	4	4	4	4	4	6	8	120
284	Glenn Borgmann RC	4	4	4	4	4	6	8	20
285	Don Kessinger	4	4	4	4	4	6	8	120
286	Frank Linzy	4	4	4	4	4	6	8	20
287	Eddie Leon	4	4	4	4	4	6	8	20
288	Gary Gentry	4	4	4	4	4	6	8	120
289	Bob Oliver	4	4	4	4	4	6	8	20
290	Cesar Cedeno	4	4	4	4	4	6	10	50
291	Rogelio Moret	4	4	4	4	4	6	8	10
292	Jose Cruz	4	4	4	4	4	6	10	20
293	Bernie Allen	4	4	4	4	4	6	8	20
294	Steve Arlin	4	4	4	4	4	6	8	20
295	Bert Campaneris	4	4	4	4	4	6	8	20
296	Sparky Anderson MG	4	4	4	4	6	12	15	60
297	Walt Williams	4	4	4	4	4	6	8	20
298	Ron Bryant	4	4	4	4	4	6	8	50
299	Ted Ford	4	4	4	4	4	6	8	30
300	Steve Carlton	4	6	10	15	25	60	80	200
301	Billy Grabarkewitz	4	4	4	4	4	6	8	10
302	Terry Crowley	4	4	4	4	4	6	8	10
303	Nelson Briles	4	4	4	4	4	6	8	20
304	Duke Sims	4	4	4	4	4	6	8	20
305	Willie Mays	▲40	▲60	▲100	▲120	▲300	▲400	▲500	▲1,500
306	Tom Burgmeier	4	4	4	4	4	6	8	
307	Boots Day	4	4	4	4	4	6	8	
308	Skip Lockwood	4	4	4	4	4	6	8	
309	Paul Popovich	4	4	4	4	4	6	8	
310	Dick Allen	4	4	4	5	10	20	25	
311	Joe Decker	4	4	4	4	4	6	8	
312	Oscar Brown	4	4	4	4	4	6	8	
313	Jim Ray	4	4	4	4	4	6	8	
314	Ron Swoboda	4	4	4	4	5	10	15	
315	John Odom	4	4	4	4	4	6	8	
316	San Diego Padres TC	4	4	4	4	4	6	8	
317	Danny Cater	4	4	4	4	4	6	8	
318	Jim McGlothlin	4	4	4	4	4	6	8	
319	Jim Spencer	4	4	4	4	4	6	8	
320	Lou Brock	4	4	5	10	20	40	50	100
321	Rich Hinton	4	4	4	4	4	6	8	
322	Garry Maddox RC	4	4	4	4	4	8	10	

#		VG 3	VgEx 4	EX 5	ExMt 6	NM 7	NmMt 8	NmMt+ 8.5	MT 9
323	Billy Martin MG	4	4	4	4	6	12	15	80
324	Al Downing	4	4	4	4	4	6	8	50
325	Boog Powell	4	4	5	6	8	15	20	50
326	Darrell Brandon	4	4	4	4	4	6	8	25
327	John Lowenstein	4	4	4	4	4	6	8	30
328	Bill Bonham	4	4	4	4	4	6	8	80
329	Ed Kranepool	4	4	4	4	4	6	8	20
330	Rod Carew	4	4	5	15	25	50	80	500
331	Carl Morton	4	4	4	4	4	6	8	25
332	John Felske RC	4	4	4	4	4	6	8	25
333	Gene Clines	4	4	4	4	4	6	8	60
334	Freddie Patek	4	4	4	4	4	6	8	30
335	Bob Tolan	4	4	4	4	4	6	8	25
336	Tom Bradley	4	4	4	4	4	6	8	20
337	Dave Duncan	4	4	4	4	4	6	8	20
338	Checklist 265-396	4	4	4	4	8	15	20	100
339	Dick Tidrow	4	4	4	4	4	6	8	80
340	Nate Colbert	4	4	4	4	4	6	8	20
341	Jim Palmer KP	4	4	4	4	4	8	10	30
342	Sam McDowell KP	4	4	4	4	4	6	8	50
343	Bobby Murcer KP	4	4	4	4	4	6	8	20
344	Jim Hunter KP	4	4	4	4	4	8	10	25
345	Chris Speier KP	4	4	4	4	4	6	8	30
346	Gaylord Perry KP	4	4	4	4	4	8	10	30
347	Kansas City Royals TC	4	4	4	4	4	6	8	100
348	Rennie Stennett	4	4	4	4	4	6	8	60
349	Dick McAuliffe	4	4	4	4	4	6	8	25
350	Tom Seaver	▲15	▲25	▲40	▲60	▲100	▲200	▲250	500
351	Jimmy Stewart	4	4	4	4	4	6	8	25
352	Don Stanhouse RC	4	4	4	4	4	6	8	20
353	Steve Brye	4	4	4	4	4	6	8	20
354	Billy Parker	4	4	4	4	4	6	8	20
355	Mike Marshall	4	4	4	4	4	8	10	150
356	Chuck Tanner MG	4	4	4	4	4	6	8	50
357	Ross Grimsley	4	4	4	4	4	6	8	15
358	Jim Nettles	4	4	4	4	4	6	8	15
359	Cecil Upshaw	4	4	4	4	4	6	8	30
360	Joe Rudi	4	4	4	4	4	8	10	50
361	Fran Healy	4	4	4	4	4	6	8	25
362	Eddie Watt	4	4	4	4	4	6	8	25
363	Jackie Hernandez	4	4	4	4	4	6	8	60
364	Rick Wise	4	4	4	4	4	6	8	25
365	Rico Petrocelli	4	4	4	4	4	8	10	25
366	Brock Davis	4	4	4	4	4	6	8	20
367	Burt Hooton	4	4	4	4	4	6	8	25
368	Bill Buckner	4	4	4	4	4	8	10	50
369	Lerrin LaGrow	4	4	4	4	4	6	8	20
370	Willie Stargell	5	6	8	10	25	40	50	150
371	Mike Kekich	4	4	4	4	4	6	8	20
372	Oscar Gamble	4	4	4	4	4	6	8	20
373	Clyde Wright	4	4	4	4	4	6	8	50
374	Darrell Evans	4	4	4	4	4	8	10	25
375	Larry Dierker	4	4	4	4	4	6	8	20
376	Frank Duffy	4	4	4	4	4	6	8	25
377	Gene Mauch MG	4	4	4	4	4	6	8	30
378	Len Randle	4	4	4	4	4	6	8	80
379	Cy Acosta RC	4	4	4	4	4	6	8	40
380	Johnny Bench	12	15	20	25	50	▲150	▲200	1,000
381	Vicente Romo	4	4	4	4	4	6	8	120
382	Mike Hegan	4	4	4	4	4	20	25	
383	Diego Segui	4	4	4	4	4	6	8	30
384	Don Baylor	4	4	4	4	4	8	10	50
385	Jim Perry	4	4	4	4	6	12	15	50
386	Don Money	4	4	4	4	4	6	8	20
387	Jim Barr	4	4	4	4	4	6	8	20
388	Ben Oglivie	4	4	4	4	4	8	10	30
389	New York Mets TC	4	4	4	4	8	15	20	60
390	Mickey Lolich	4	4	4	4	4	8	10	25
391	Lee Lacy RC	4	4	4	4	4	8	10	25

#		VG 3	VgEx 4	EX 5	ExMt 6	NM 7	NmMt 8	NmMt+ 8.5	MT 9
392	Dick Drago	4	4	4	4	4	6	8	40
393	Jose Cardenal	4	4	4	4	4	6	8	20
394	Sparky Lyle	4	4	4	4	5	10	12	30
395	Roger Metzger	4	4	4	4	4	6	8	20
396	Grant Jackson	4	4	4	4	4	6	8	80
397	Dave Cash	4	4	4	4	4	6	8	50
398	Rich Hand	4	4	4	4	4	6	8	20
399	George Foster	4	4	4	4	5	10	12	200
400	Gaylord Perry	4	5	6	8	15	30	40	150
401	Clyde Mashore	4	4	4	4	4	6	8	20
402	Jack Hiatt	4	4	4	4	4	6	8	20
403	Sonny Jackson	4	4	4	4	4	6	8	20
404	Chuck Brinkman	4	4	4	4	4	6	8	30
405	Cesar Tovar	4	4	4	4	4	6	8	20
406	Paul Lindblad	4	4	4	4	4	6	8	80
407	Felix Millan	4	4	4	4	4	6	8	20
408	Jim Colborn	4	4	4	4	4	6	8	20
409	Ivan Murrell	4	4	4	4	4	6	8	20
410	Willie McCovey	4	4	5	6	20	30	40	120
411	Ray Corbin	4	4	4	4	4	6	8	40
412	Manny Mota	4	4	4	4	4	6	8	30
413	Tom Timmermann	4	4	4	4	4	6	8	20
414	Ken Rudolph	4	4	4	4	4	6	8	20
415	Marty Pattin	4	4	4	4	4	6	8	20
416	Paul Schaal	4	4	4	4	4	6	8	30
417	Scipio Spinks	4	4	4	4	4	6	8	25
418	Bob Grich	4	4	4	4	4	8	10	
419	Casey Cox	4	4	4	4	4	6	8	50
420	Tommie Agee	4	4	4	4	4	6	8	120
421A	Bobby Winkles MG Orange RC	4	4	4	4	4	6	8	30
421B	Bobby Winkles MG Brown	4	4	4	4	4	6	8	100
422	Bob Robertson	4	4	4	4	4	6	8	30
423	Johnny Jeter	4	4	4	4	4	6	8	20
424	Denny Doyle	4	4	4	4	4	6	8	60
425	Alex Johnson	4	4	4	4	4	6	8	20
426	Dave LaRoche	4	4	4	4	4	6	8	20
427	Rick Auerbach	4	4	4	4	4	6	8	30
428	Wayne Simpson	4	4	4	4	4	6	8	60
429	Jim Fairey	4	4	4	4	4	6	8	20
430	Vida Blue	4	4	4	4	8	15	20	50
431	Gerry Moses	4	4	4	4	4	6	8	30
432	Dan Frisella	4	4	4	4	4	6	8	60
433	Willie Horton	4	4	4	4	5	10	12	50
434	San Francisco Giants TC	4	4	4	4	4	6	8	20
435	Rico Carty	4	4	4	4	4	6	8	20
436	Jim McAndrew	4	4	4	4	4	6	8	30
437	John Kennedy	4	4	4	4	4	6	8	20
438	Enzo Hernandez	4	4	4	4	4	6	8	20
439	Eddie Fisher	4	4	4	4	4	6	8	20
440	Glenn Beckert	4	4	4	4	4	6	8	80
441	Gail Hopkins	4	4	4	4	4	6	8	100
442	Dick Dietz	4	4	4	4	4	6	8	20
443	Danny Thompson	4	4	4	4	4	6	8	20
444	Ken Brett	4	4	4	4	4	6	8	25
445	Ken Berry	4	4	4	4	4	6	8	20
446	Jerry Reuss	4	4	4	4	4	6	8	50
447	Joe Hague	4	4	4	4	4	6	8	25
448	John Hiller	4	4	4	4	4	6	8	20
449A	Ken Aspromonte MG Spahn Ear Pointed	4	4	4	4	4	8	10	25
449B	Ken Aspromonte MG Spahn Ear Round	4	4	4	4	4	8	10	40
450	Joe Torre	4	4	4	4	8	15	20	30
451	John Vukovich RC	4	4	4	4	4	6	8	20
452	Paul Casanova	4	4	4	4	4	6	8	25
453	Checklist 397-528	4	4	4	4	8	15	20	150
454	Tom Haller	4	4	4	4	4	6	8	20
455	Bill Melton	4	4	4	4	4	6	8	25
456	Dick Green	4	4	4	4	4	6	8	30

#	Player	VG 3	VgEx 4	EX 5	ExMt 6	NM 7	NmMt 8	NmMt+ 8.5	MT 9
457	John Strohmayer	4	4	4	4	4	6	8	25
458	Jim Mason	4	4	4	4	4	6	8	20
459	Jimmy Howarth RC	4	4	4	4	4	6	8	20
460	Bill Freehan	4	4	4	4	4	8	10	80
461	Mike Corkins	4	4	4	4	4	6	8	20
462	Ron Blomberg	4	4	4	4	4	6	8	20
463	Ken Tatum	4	4	4	4	4	6	8	20
464	Chicago Cubs TC	4	4	4	4	4	8	10	80
465	Dave Giusti	4	4	4	4	4	6	8	20
466	Jose Arcia	4	4	4	4	4	8	10	
467	Mike Ryan	4	4	4	4	4	6	8	15
468	Tom Griffin	4	4	4	4	4	6	8	40
469	Dan Monzon RC	4	4	4	4	4	6	8	20
470	Mike Cuellar	4	4	4	4	8	15	20	120
471	Ty Cobb LDR	4	4	4	12	15	40	60	250
472	Lou Gehrig LDR	4	4	6	12	25	50	60	120
473	Hank Aaron LDR	4	5	10	20	30	60	100	350
474	Babe Ruth LDR	12	15	20	▲30	▲50	▲80	100	200
475	Ty Cobb LDR	4	4	4	15	25	50	60	150
476	Walter Johnson LDR	4	4	4	4	8	15	20	80
477	Cy Young LDR	4	4	5	6	12	40		
478	Walter Johnson LDR	4	4	4	5	10	20	25	100
479	Hal Lanier	4	4	4	4	4	6	8	20
480	Juan Marichal	4	4	4	6	12	30	40	120
481	Chicago White Sox TC	4	4	4	4	4	6	8	50
482	Rick Reuschel RC	4	4	4	4	5	10	12	40
483	Dal Maxvill	4	4	4	4	4	6	8	25
484	Ernie McAnally	4	4	4	4	4	6	8	20
485	Norm Cash	4	4	4	4	5	10	12	40
486A	Danny Ozark MG Orange RC	4	4	4	4	4	6	8	60
486B	Danny Ozark MG Brown	4	4	4	4	4	6	8	25
487	Bruce Dal Canton	4	4	4	4	4	6	8	30
488	Dave Campbell	4	4	4	4	4	8	10	25
489	Jeff Burroughs	4	4	4	4	4	8	10	25
490	Claude Osteen	4	4	4	4	4	6	8	20
491	Bob Montgomery	4	4	4	4	4	6	8	20
492	Pedro Borbon	4	4	4	4	4	6	8	25
493	Duffy Dyer	4	4	4	4	4	6	8	25
494	Rich Morales	4	4	4	4	4	6	8	20
495	Tommy Helms	4	4	4	4	4	6	8	20
496	Ray Lamb	4	4	4	4	4	6	8	100
497A	Red Schoendienst MG Orange	4	4	4	4	4	8	10	60
497B	Red Schoendienst MG Brown	4	4	4	4	4	8	10	25
498	Graig Nettles	4	4	4	4	8	15	20	200
499	Bob Moose	4	4	4	4	4	6	8	80
500	Oakland Athletics TC	4	4	4	4	4	8	10	20
501	Larry Gura	4	4	4	4	4	6	8	20
502	Bobby Valentine	4	4	4	4	4	8	10	25
503	Phil Niekro	4	4	4	4	8	15	20	120
504	Earl Williams	4	4	4	4	4	6	8	50
505	Bob Bailey	4	4	4	4	4	6	8	20
506	Bart Johnson	4	4	4	4	4	6	8	20
507	Darrel Chaney	4	4	4	4	4	6	8	25
508	Gates Brown	4	4	4	4	4	6	8	20
509	Jim Nash	4	4	4	4	4	6	8	20
510	Amos Otis	4	4	4	4	4	8	10	40
511	Sam McDowell	4	4	4	4	4	8	10	40
512	Dalton Jones	4	4	4	4	4	6	8	20
513	Dave Marshall	4	4	4	4	4	6	8	20
514	Jerry Kenney	4	4	4	4	4	6	8	25
515	Andy Messersmith	4	4	4	4	4	8	10	15
516	Danny Walton	4	4	4	4	5	10	12	20
517A	Bill Virdon MG Mazeroski w/o Ear	4	4	4	4	4	6	8	60
517B	Bill Virdon MG Mazeroski w/Ear	4	4	4	4	4	6	8	60
518	Bob Veale	4	4	4	4	4	6	8	20
519	Johnny Edwards	4	4	4	4	4	6	8	15
520	Mel Stottlemyre	4	4	4	4	6	12	15	25
521	Atlanta Braves TC	4	4	4	4	4	6	8	20

#	Player	VG 3	VgEx 4	EX 5	ExMt 6	NM 7	NmMt 8	NmMt+ 8.5	MT 9
522	Leo Cardenas	4	4	4	4	4	6	8	20
523	Wayne Granger	4	4	4	4	4	6	8	20
524	Gene Tenace	4	4	4	4	4	8	10	200
525	Jim Fregosi	4	4	4	4	4	8	10	25
526	Ollie Brown	4	4	4	4	4	6	8	25
527	Dan McGinn	4	4	4	4	4	6	8	25
528	Paul Blair	4	4	4	4	4	8	10	100
529	Milt May	4	4	4	4	5	10	12	25
530	Jim Kaat	4	4	6	12	25	30	60	100
531	Ron Woods	4	4	4	4	5	10	12	30
532	Steve Mingori	4	4	4	4	5	10	12	25
533	Larry Stahl	4	4	4	4	5	10	12	25
534	Dave Lemonds	4	4	4	4	8	15	25	
535	Johnny Callison	4	4	5	8	12	20	25	100
536	Philadelphia Phillies TC	4	4	4	4	6	12	15	40
537	Bill Slayback RC	4	4	4	4	5	10	12	30
538	Jim Ray Hart	4	4	4	4	5	10	12	50
539	Tom Murphy	4	4	4	4	5	10	12	80
540	Cleon Jones	4	4	4	4	6	12	15	50
541	Bob Bolin	4	4	4	4	5	10	12	25
542	Pat Corrales	4	4	4	4	5	10	12	40
543	Alan Foster	4	4	4	4	5	10	12	25
544	Von Joshua	4	4	4	4	5	10	12	25
545	Orlando Cepeda	4	4	4	8	12	20	30	80
546	Jim York	4	4	4	4	5	10	12	25
547	Bobby Heise	5	6	8	10	20	40	50	
548	Don Durham RC	4	4	4	4	5	10	12	80
549	Whitey Herzog MG	4	4	4	4	30	80		
550	Dave Johnson	4	4	4	4	10	25		
551	Mike Kilkenny	4	4	4	4	8	15	25	
552	J.C. Martin	4	4	4	4	5	10	12	40
553	Mickey Scott	4	4	4	4	8	15	25	
554	Dave Concepcion	4	4	5	8	15	40	50	150
555	Bill Hands	4	4	4	4	5	10	12	400
556	New York Yankees TC	5	6	8	10	15	20	50	120
557	Bernie Williams	4	4	4	4	5	10	12	50
558	Jerry May	4	4	4	4	5	10	12	40
559	Barry Lersch	4	4	4	4	5	10	12	50
560	Frank Howard	5	6	8	10	20	30		
561	Jim Geddes RC	4	4	4	4	8	25	30	
562	Wayne Garrett	4	4	4	4	5	10	12	50
563	Larry Haney	4	4	4	4	5	10	12	120
564	Mike Thompson RC	4	4	4	4	5	10	12	25
565	Jim Hickman	4	4	4	4	5	10	12	50
566	Lew Krausse	4	4	4	4	5	10	12	80
567	Bob Fenwick	4	4	4	4	5	10	12	40
568	Ray Newman	4	4	4	4	5	10	12	30
569	Walt Alston MG	4	4	4	5	6	12	25	120
570	Bill Singer	4	4	4	4	5	10	12	20
571	Rusty Torres	4	4	4	4	6	12	15	20
572	Gary Sutherland	4	4	4	4	6	12	15	30
573	Fred Beene	4	4	4	4	5	10	12	80
574	Bob Didier	4	4	4	5	10	20	25	200
575	Dock Ellis	4	4	4	4	5	10	12	50
576	Montreal Expos TC	4	4	4	4	4	6	10	10
577	Eric Soderholm RC	4	4	4	4	5	10	12	20
578	Ken Wright	4	4	4	4	5	10	12	60
579	Tom Grieve	4	4	4	4	5	10	12	20
580	Joe Pepitone	4	4	4	4	6	12	15	40
581	Steve Kealey	4	4	4	4	8	15	25	
582	Darrell Porter	4	4	4	4	8	15	20	50
583	Bill Grief	4	4	4	4	5	10	12	20
584	Chris Arnold	4	4	4	4	8	15	20	150
585	Joe Niekro	4	4	4	4	5	10	12	
586	Bill Sudakis	4	4	4	4	5	10	12	
587	Rich McKinney	4	4	4	4	5	10	12	50
588	Checklist 529-660	4	8	15	20	40	100	150	40
589	Ken Forsch	4	4	4	4	5	10	12	80

#	Name	VG 3	VgEx 4	EX 5	ExMt 6	NM 7	NmMt 8	NmMt+ 8.5	MT 9
90	Deron Johnson	4	4	5	6	12	25	30	200
91	Mike Hedlund	4	4	4	4	5	10	12	25
92	John Boccabella	4	4	4	4	5	10	12	60
93	Jack McKeon MG RC	4	4	4	4	8	100	120	300
94	Vic Harris RC	4	4	4	4	8	15	25	
95	Don Gullett	4	4	4	4	5	10	12	80
96	Boston Red Sox TC	4	4	4	4	8	15	20	150
97	Mickey Rivers	4	4	4	4	6	12	15	40
98	Phil Roof	4	4	4	4	5	10	12	60
99	Ed Crosby	4	4	4	4	5	10	12	100
00	Dave McNally	4	4	4	4	6	30	40	100
1	Rookie Catchers	4	4	4	5	10	20	25	150
2	Rookie Pitchers	4	4	4	4	8	15	20	250
3	Rookie Third Basemen	4	4	4	4	8	40	60	450
4	Rookie Pitchers	4	4	4	6	12	20	30	100
5	Rookie First Basemen	4	4	4	5	10	25	30	100
6	Gary Matthews RC	4	4	4	5	10	20	25	100
7	Rookie Shortstops	4	4	4	5	10	20	30	100
8	Rookie Pitchers	4	4	4	8	15	30	40	500
9	Davey Lopes RC	4	6	10	15	25	60		
0	Rookie Pitchers	4	5	8	12	20	30	40	120
1	Rookie Outfielders	4	4	4	5	10	20	25	60
2	Rookie Pitchers	4	4	4	4	6	12	15	40
3	Bob Boone RC	8	10	12	15	20	30	50	150
4	Dwight Evans RC	20	30	60	100	150	250	300	600
5	Mike Schmidt RC	150	250	300	400	600	1,500	▲2,500	▲15,000
6	Rookie Pitchers	4	4	4	5	10	25	30	150
7	Rich Chiles	4	4	4	4	5	10	12	50
8	Andy Etchebarren	4	4	4	4	5	10	12	50
9	Billy Wilson	4	4	4	4	5	10	12	20
0	Tommy Harper	4	4	4	4	6	12	15	100
	Joe Ferguson	4	4	4	4	5	12	20	50
	Larry Hisle	4	4	4	5	8	15	20	200
	Steve Renko	4	4	4	4	8	15	20	50
	Leo Durocher MG	4	4	4	5	8	20	25	50
	Angel Mangual	4	4	4	5	8	15	20	25
	Bob Barton	4	4	4	4	5	10	12	25
	Luis Alvarado	4	4	4	4	6	12	15	25
	Jim Slaton	4	4	4	4	5	10	12	50
	Cleveland Indians TC	4	4	4	4	5	10	12	25
	Denny McLain	4	4	4	5	8	15	25	80
	Tom Matchick	4	4	4	4	5	10	12	100
	Dick Selma	4	4	4	4	5	10	12	80
	Ike Brown	4	4	4	4	5	10	12	80
	Alan Closter	4	4	4	4	5	10	12	40
	Gene Alley	4	4	4	4	5	10	12	80
	Rickey Clark	4	4	4	4	5	10	12	25
	Norm Miller	4	4	4	4	5	10	12	25
	Ken Reynolds	4	4	4	4	5	10	12	50
	Willie Crawford	4	4	4	4	5	10	12	30
	Dick Bosman	4	4	4	4	5	10	12	25
	Cincinnati Reds TC	4	5	6	8	15	60	80	150
	Jose Laboy	4	4	4	4	5	10	12	30
	Al Fitzmorris	4	4	4	4	5	10	12	80
	Jack Heidemann	4	4	4	4	5	10	12	25
	Bob Locker	4	4	4	4	5	10	12	250
	Del Crandall MG	4	4	4	4	6	12	15	50
	George Stone	4	4	4	4	5	10	12	25
	Tom Egan	4	4	4	5	8	15	20	50
	Rich Folkers	4	4	4	4	5	10	12	60
	Felipe Alou	4	4	4	4	8	15	20	80
	Don Carrithers	4	4	4	4	5	10	12	25
	Ted Kubiak	4	4	4	4	5	10	12	25
	Joe Hoerner	4	4	8	10	20	25		
	Minnesota Twins TC	4	5	6	8	15	30	40	150
	Clay Kirby	4	4	4	4	5	10	12	150
	John Ellis	4	4	4	4	5	10	12	50
	Bob Johnson	4	4	4	4	5	10	12	60

#	Name	VG 3	VgEx 4	EX 5	ExMt 6	NM 7	NmMt 8	NmMt+ 8.5	MT 9
658	Elliott Maddox	4	4	4	4	5	10	12	60
659	Jose Pagan	4	4	4	4	5	10	12	25
660	Fred Scherman	4	4	6	10	15	40	60	100

— Nolan Ryan #220 PSA 10 (Gem) sold for $10,573 (Memory Lane; 8/12)

— Mike Schmidt #615 PSA 10 (Gem) (Young Collection) sold for $15,766 (SCP; 5/12)

1974 Kellogg's

#	Name	VG 3	VgEx 4	EX 5	ExMt 6	NM 7	NmMt 8	MT 9	Gem 9.5/10
1	Bob Gibson	4	4	4	4	4	5		
2	Rick Monday	4	4	4	4	4	5		
3	Joe Coleman	4	4	4	4	4	5	10	25
4	Bert Campaneris	4	4	4	4	4	8	15	50
5	Carlton Fisk	4	4	4	4	4	8	15	80
6	Jim Palmer	4	4	4	4	4	5	10	30
7A	Ron Santo Cubs	4	4	4	4	5	10	20	
7B	Ron Santo White Sox	4	4	4	4	4	8	15	
8	Nolan Ryan	4	4	4	5	10	20	40	200
9	Greg Luzinski	4	4	4	4	4	5	10	40
10A	Buddy Bell 134 Runs	4	4	4	4	4	5	10	
10B	Buddy Bell 135 Runs	4	4	4	4	4	5	10	
11	Bob Watson	4	4	4	4	4	5	10	25
12	Bill Singer	4	4	4	4	4	5	10	20
13	Dave May	4	4	4	4	4	5	10	20
14	Jim Brewer	4	4	4	4	4	5	10	25
15	Manny Sanguillen	4	4	4	4	4	5	10	20
16	Jeff Burroughs	4	4	4	4	4	5	10	20
17	Amos Otis	4	4	4	4	4	5	10	25
18	Ed Goodson	4	4	4	4	4	5	10	20
19	Nate Colbert	4	4	4	4	4	5	10	20
20	Reggie Jackson	4	4	4	4	4	8	15	40
21	Ted Simmons	4	4	4	4	4	5	10	20
22	Bobby Murcer	4	4	4	4	4	5	10	25
23	Willie Horton	4	4	4	4	4	5	10	20
24	Orlando Cepeda	4	4	4	4	4	5	10	20
25	Ron Hunt	4	4	4	4	4	5	10	20
26	Wayne Twitchell	4	4	4	4	4	5	10	20
27	Ron Fairly	4	4	4	4	4	5	10	20
28	Johnny Bench	4	4	4	4	4	8	15	40
29	John Mayberry	4	4	4	4	4	5	10	20
30	Rod Carew	4	4	4	4	4	5	10	80
31	Ken Holtzman	4	4	4	4	4	5	10	20
32	Billy Williams	4	4	4	4	4	5	10	30
33	Dick Allen	4	4	4	4	4	5	10	40
34A	Wilbur Wood SO 959	4	4	4	4	4	5	10	
34B	Wilbur Wood SO 960	4	4	4	4	4	5	10	25
35	Danny Thompson	4	4	4	4	4	5	10	20
36	Joe Morgan	4	4	4	4	4	5	10	30
37	Willie Stargell	4	4	4	4	4	5	10	30
38	Pete Rose	4	4	4	4	5	10	20	80
39	Bobby Bonds	4	4	4	4	4	5	10	20
40	Chris Speier	4	4	4	4	4	5	10	20
41	Sparky Lyle	4	4	4	4	4	5	10	20
42	Cookie Rojas	4	4	4	4	4	5	10	20
43	Tommy Davis	4	4	4	4	4	5	10	20
44	Jim Hunter	4	4	4	4	4	5	10	30
45	Willie Davis	4	4	4	4	4	5	10	20
46	Bert Blyleven	4	4	4	4	4	5	10	25
47	Pat Kelly	4	4	4	4	4	5	10	25
48	Ken Singleton	4	4	4	4	4	5	10	20
49	Manny Mota	4	4	4	4	4	5	10	20
50	Dave Johnson	4	4	4	4	4	5	10	20
51	Sal Bando	4	4	4	4	4	5	10	20
52	Tom Seaver	4	4	4	4	4	8	15	40
53	Felix Millan	4	4	4	4	4	5	10	20
54	Ron Blomberg	4	4	4	4	4	5	10	25

1974 Topps

#	Player	GD 2	VG 3	EX 5	ExMt 6	NM 7	NmMt 8	NmMt+ 8.5	MT 9
1	Hank Aaron 715	8	12	30	40	100	200	250	▲3,000
2	Aaron Special 54-57	4	4	15	20	25	80	80	150
3	Aaron Special 58-61	4	4	15	20	25	50	60	120
4	Aaron Special 62-65	4	4	10	15	25	50	60	120
5	Aaron Special 66-69	4	4	15	20	25	40	50	120
6	Aaron Special 70-73	4	4	5	8	20	40	50	120
7	Jim Hunter	4	4	4	6	12	25	30	150
8	George Theodore RC	4	4	4	4	8	15	20	120
9	Mickey Lolich	4	4	4	4	4	5	6	20
10	Johnny Bench	4	4	15	20	30	80	80	300
11	Jim Bibby	4	4	4	4	4	5	6	15
12	Dave May	4	4	4	4	4	5	6	15
13	Tom Hilgendorf	4	4	4	4	4	5	6	15
14	Paul Popovich	4	4	4	4	4	8	10	40
15	Joe Torre	4	4	4	4	4	6	8	20
16	Baltimore Orioles TC	4	4	4	4	4	6	10	150
17	Doug Bird RC	4	4	4	4	4	5	6	15
18	Gary Thomasson RC	4	4	4	4	4	5	6	15
19	Gerry Moses	4	4	4	4	4	5	6	20
20	Nolan Ryan	12	15	25	30	50	100	250	600
21	Bob Gallagher RC	4	4	4	4	4	5	6	15
22	Cy Acosta	4	4	4	4	4	5	6	20
23	Craig Robinson RC	4	4	4	4	4	5	6	15
24	John Hiller	4	4	4	4	4	5	6	15
25	Ken Singleton	4	4	4	4	4	5	6	15
26	Bill Campbell RC	4	4	4	4	4	5	6	25
27	George Scott	4	4	4	4	4	5	6	15
28	Manny Sanguillen	4	4	4	4	4	5	6	15
29	Phil Niekro	4	4	4	4	4	8	10	80
30	Bobby Bonds	4	4	4	4	4	5	6	15
31	Preston Gomez MG	4	4	4	4	4	5	6	20
32A	Johnny Grubb SD RC	4	4	4	4	4	5	6	15
32B	Johnny Grubb WASH	4	4	5	6	12	25	30	100
33	Don Newhauser RC	4	4	4	4	4	5	6	15
34	Andy Kosco	4	4	4	4	4	5	6	15
35	Gaylord Perry	4	4	4	4	4	6	8	20
36	St. Louis Cardinals TC	4	4	4	4	4	5	6	15
37	Dave Sells RC	4	4	4	4	4	5	6	15
38	Don Kessinger	4	4	4	4	4	5	6	15
39	Ken Suarez	4	4	4	4	4	5	6	20
40	Jim Palmer	4	4	4	4	12	40	50	150
41	Bobby Floyd	4	4	4	4	4	5	6	15
42	Claude Osteen	4	4	4	4	4	5	6	15
43	Jim Wynn	4	4	4	4	4	5	6	15
44	Mel Stottlemyre	4	4	4	4	4	5	6	15
45	Dave Johnson	4	4	4	4	4	5	6	15
46	Pat Kelly	4	4	4	4	4	5	6	15
47	Dick Ruthven RC	4	4	4	4	4	5	6	20
48	Dick Sharon RC	4	4	4	4	4	5	6	15
49	Steve Renko	4	4	4	4	4	5	6	15
50	Rod Carew	4	4	4	15	20	30	40	100
51	Bobby Heise	4	4	4	4	4	5	6	15
52	Al Oliver	4	4	4	4	4	5	6	20
53A	Fred Kendall SD	4	4	4	4	4	5	6	60
53B	Fred Kendall WASH	4	4	5	6	12	25	30	120
54	Elias Sosa RC	4	4	4	4	4	5	6	20
55	Frank Robinson	4	▲5	▲12	▲20	▲30	▲50	▲60	60
56	New York Mets TC	4	4	4	4	4	5	6	15
57	Darold Knowles	4	4	4	4	4	5	6	15
58	Charlie Spikes	4	4	4	4	4	5	6	25
59	Ross Grimsley	4	4	4	4	4	5	6	15
60	Lou Brock	4	4	4	5	12	30	40	80
61	Luis Aparicio	4	4	4	4	5	10	15	60
62	Bob Locker	4	4	4	4	4	5	6	15
63	Bill Sudakis	4	4	4	4	4	5	6	1
64	Doug Rau	4	4	4	4	4	5	6	1
65	Amos Otis	4	4	4	4	4	8	10	10
66	Sparky Lyle	4	4	4	4	4	5	6	3
67	Tommy Helms	4	4	4	4	4	5	6	1
68	Grant Jackson	4	4	4	4	4	5	6	2
69	Del Unser	4	4	4	4	4	8	12	8
70	Dick Allen	4	4	4	4	4	8	10	2
71	Dan Frisella	4	4	4	4	4	5	6	1
72	Aurelio Rodriguez	4	4	4	4	4	5	6	1
73	Mike Marshall	4	4	4	4	4	5	6	1
74	Minnesota Twins TC	4	4	4	4	4	5	6	1
75	Jim Colborn	4	4	4	4	4	5	6	1
76	Mickey Rivers	4	4	4	4	4	5	6	2
77A	Rich Troedson SD	4	4	4	4	4	5	6	2
77B	Rich Troedson WASH	4	4	5	6	12	25	30	8
78	Charlie Fox MG	4	4	4	4	4	5	6	2
79	Gene Tenace	4	4	4	4	4	5	6	1
80	Tom Seaver	▲10	▲15	▲40	▲60	▲100	▲200	▲250	▲1,0
81	Frank Duffy	4	4	4	4	4	5	6	
82	Dave Giusti	4	4	4	4	4	5	6	
83	Orlando Cepeda	4	4	4	4	8	12	15	5
84	Rick Wise	4	4	4	4	4	5	6	
85	Joe Morgan	4	4	4	5	15	25	30	1.
86	Joe Ferguson	4	4	4	4	4	5	6	
87	Fergie Jenkins	4	4	4	4	6	12	15	
88	Freddie Patek	4	4	4	4	4	5	6	
89	Jackie Brown	4	4	4	4	4	5	6	1
90	Bobby Murcer	4	4	4	4	5	10	15	
91	Ken Forsch	4	4	4	4	4	5	6	
92	Paul Blair	4	4	4	4	4	5	6	
93	Rod Gilbreath RC	4	4	4	4	4	5	6	
94	Detroit Tigers TC	4	4	4	4	4	8	10	
95	Steve Carlton	4	4	4	8	20	25	30	2
96	Jerry Hairston RC	4	4	4	4	4	5	6	
97	Bob Bailey	4	4	4	4	4	5	6	
98	Bert Blyleven	4	4	4	4	4	6	8	
99	Del Crandall MG	4	4	4	4	4	5	6	
100	Willie Stargell	4	4	4	6	12	30	40	1
101	Bobby Valentine	4	4	4	4	4	5	6	
102A	Bill Greif SD	4	4	4	4	4	6	10	
102B	Bill Greif WASH	4	4	4	4	8	15	20	
103	Sal Bando	4	4	4	4	4	5	6	
104	Ron Bryant	4	4	4	4	4	5	6	
105	Carlton Fisk	5	6	10	12	25	50	60	5
106	Harry Parker RC	4	4	4	4	4	5	6	
107	Alex Johnson	4	4	4	4	4	5	6	
108	Al Hrabosky	4	4	4	4	4	5	6	
109	Bob Grich	4	4	4	4	4	5	6	
110	Billy Williams	4	4	4	4	5	10	15	
111	Clay Carroll	4	4	4	4	6	12	15	
112	Davey Lopes	4	4	4	4	4	6	8	
113	Dick Drago	4	4	4	4	4	5	6	
114	California Angels TC	4	4	4	4	4	5	6	
115	Willie Horton	4	4	4	4	4	5	6	
116	Jerry Reuss	4	4	4	4	4	5	6	
117	Ron Blomberg	4	4	4	4	4	5	6	
118	Bill Lee	4	4	4	4	4	5	6	
119	Danny Ozark MG	4	4	4	4	4	5	6	
120	Wilbur Wood	4	4	4	4	5	10	12	
121	Larry Lintz RC	4	4	4	4	4	5	6	
122	Jim Holt	4	4	4	4	4	5	6	
123	Nelson Briles	4	4	4	4	4	5	6	
124	Bobby Coluccio RC	4	4	4	4	4	5	6	
125A	Nate Colbert SD	4	4	4	4	4	6	10	
125B	Nate Colbert WASH	4	4	5	6	12	25	30	
126	Checklist 1-132	4	4	4	4	4	6	8	
127	Tom Paciorek	4	4	4	4	4	5	6	

#	Player	GD 2	VG 3	EX 5	ExMt 6	NM 7	NmMt 8	NmMt+ 8.5	MT 9
28	John Ellis	4	4	4	4	4	5	6	15
29	Chris Speier	4	4	4	4	4	5	6	15
30	Reggie Jackson	8	10	15	20	30	60	200	800
31	Bob Boone	4	4	4	4	4	5	6	15
32	Felix Millan	4	4	4	4	4	8	10	200
33	David Clyde RC	4	4	4	4	4	5	6	15
34	Denis Menke	4	4	4	4	4	5	6	15
35	Roy White	4	4	4	4	4	6	10	80
36	Rick Reuschel	4	4	4	4	4	5	6	15
37	Al Bumbry	4	4	4	4	4	5	6	15
38	Eddie Brinkman	4	4	4	4	4	5	6	15
39	Aurelio Monteagudo	4	4	4	4	4	5	6	15
40	Darrell Evans	4	4	4	4	4	5	6	15
41	Pat Bourque	4	4	4	4	4	5	6	15
42	Pedro Garcia	4	4	4	4	4	5	6	20
43	Dick Woodson	4	4	4	4	4	5	6	15
44	Walter Alston MG	4	4	4	4	4	6	8	20
45	Dock Ellis	4	4	4	4	4	5	6	15
46	Ron Fairly	4	4	4	4	4	5	6	20
47	Bart Johnson	4	4	4	4	4	5	6	20
48A	Dave Hilton SD	4	4	4	4	4	5	6	15
48B	Dave Hilton WASH	4	4	5	6	12	25	30	100
49	Mac Scarce	4	4	4	4	4	5	6	15
50	John Mayberry	4	4	4	4	4	5	6	40
51	Diego Segui	4	4	4	4	4	5	6	15
52	Oscar Gamble	4	4	4	4	4	5	6	15
53	Jon Matlack	4	4	4	4	4	5	6	15
54	Houston Astros TC	4	4	4	4	4	5	6	15
55	Bert Campaneris	4	4	4	4	4	5	6	15
56	Randy Moffitt	4	4	4	4	4	5	6	15
57	Vic Harris	4	4	4	4	4	5	6	15
58	Jack Billingham	4	4	4	4	4	5	6	20
59	Jim Ray Hart	4	4	4	4	4	5	6	15
60	Brooks Robinson	4	4	4	15	20	30	40	100
61	Ray Burris RC	4	4	4	4	4	5	6	15
62	Bill Freehan	4	4	4	4	4	5	6	15
63	Ken Berry	4	4	4	4	4	5	6	15
64	Tom House	4	4	4	4	4	5	6	20
65	Willie Davis	4	4	4	4	4	5	6	60
66	Jack McKeon MG	4	4	4	4	4	5	6	20
67	Luis Tiant	4	4	4	4	4	5	6	15
68	Danny Thompson	4	4	4	4	4	5	6	15
69	Steve Rogers RC	4	4	4	4	4	5	6	15
70	Bill Melton	4	4	4	4	4	5	6	60
71	Eduardo Rodriguez RC	4	4	4	4	4	5	6	15
72	Gene Clines	4	4	4	4	4	5	6	20
73A	Randy Jones SD RC	4	4	4	4	4	6	10	200
73B	Randy Jones WASH	4	4	6	8	15	30	40	120
74	Bill Robinson	4	4	4	4	4	5	6	20
75	Reggie Cleveland	4	4	4	4	4	5	6	15
76	John Lowenstein	4	4	4	4	4	5	6	15
77	Dave Roberts	4	4	4	4	4	5	6	15
78	Garry Maddox	4	4	4	4	4	5	6	15
79	Yogi Berra MG	4	4	4	4	5	10	15	100
80	Ken Holtzman	4	4	4	4	4	5	6	15
81	Cesar Geronimo	4	4	4	4	4	5	6	20
82	Lindy McDaniel	4	4	4	4	4	5	6	12
83	Johnny Oates	4	4	4	4	4	5	6	15
84	Texas Rangers TC	4	4	4	4	4	5	6	15
85	Jose Cardenal	4	4	4	4	4	5	6	15
86	Fred Scherman	4	4	4	4	4	5	6	15
87	Don Baylor	4	4	4	4	4	5	6	15
88	Rudy Meoli RC	4	4	4	4	4	5	6	15
89	Jim Brewer	4	4	4	4	4	5	6	15
90	Tony Oliva	4	4	4	4	6	12	15	40
91	Al Fitzmorris	4	4	4	4	4	5	6	15
92	Mario Guerrero	4	4	4	4	4	5	6	10
93	Tom Walker	4	4	4	4	4	5	6	20
194	Darrell Porter	4	4	4	4	4	5	6	15
195	Carlos May	4	4	4	4	4	5	6	20
196	Jim Fregosi	4	4	4	4	4	5	6	15
197A	Vicente Romo SD	4	4	4	4	4	5	6	50
197B	Vicente Romo WASH	4	4	5	6	12	25	30	100
198	Dave Cash	4	4	4	4	4	5	6	15
199	Mike Kekich	4	4	4	4	4	5	6	25
200	Cesar Cedeno	4	4	4	4	4	5	6	15
201	Batting Leaders	4	4	4	4	8	25	30	60
202	Home Run Leaders	4	4	4	4	6	12	15	40
203	RBI Leaders	4	4	4	4	6	20	25	150
204	Stolen Base Leaders	4	4	4	4	4	5	6	15
205	Victory Leaders	4	4	4	4	4	5	6	15
206	ERA Leaders	4	4	4	4	6	12	15	50
207	Strikeout Leaders	4	4	4	5	25	50	60	120
208	Leading Firemen	4	4	4	4	4	5	6	15
209	Ted Sizemore	4	4	4	4	4	5	6	15
210	Bill Singer	4	4	4	4	4	5	6	15
211	Chicago Cubs TC	4	4	4	4	4	5	6	15
212	Rollie Fingers	4	4	4	4	6	12	15	30
213	Dave Rader	4	4	4	4	4	6	8	120
214	Billy Grabarkewitz	4	4	4	4	4	5	6	15
215	Al Kaline	4	4	4	25	30	80	100	400
216	Ray Sadecki	4	4	4	4	4	5	6	15
217	Tim Foli	4	4	4	4	4	5	6	15
218	Johnny Briggs	4	4	4	4	4	5	6	20
219	Doug Griffin	4	4	4	4	4	5	6	20
220	Don Sutton	4	4	4	4	4	6	8	25
221	Chuck Tanner MG	4	4	4	4	4	5	6	30
222	Ramon Hernandez	4	4	4	4	4	5	6	20
223	Jeff Burroughs	4	4	4	4	4	5	6	15
224	Roger Metzger	4	4	4	4	4	5	6	15
225	Paul Splittorff	4	4	4	4	4	5	6	20
226A	San Diego Padres TC SD	4	4	4	4	4	6	8	60
226B	San Diego Padres TC WASH	4	4	5	8	15	30	40	300
227	Mike Lum	4	4	4	4	4	5	6	15
228	Ted Kubiak	4	4	4	4	4	5	6	15
229	Fritz Peterson	4	4	4	4	4	5	6	200
230	Tony Perez	4	4	4	4	8	15	20	80
231	Dick Tidrow	4	4	4	4	4	5	6	15
232	Steve Brye	4	4	4	4	4	5	6	25
233	Jim Barr	4	4	4	4	4	5	6	30
234	John Milner	4	4	4	4	4	5	6	12
235	Dave McNally	4	4	4	4	4	6	8	15
236	Red Schoendienst MG	4	4	4	4	4	6	8	20
237	Ken Brett	4	4	4	4	4	5	6	20
238	F.Healy w/Munson	4	4	4	4	4	5	6	80
239	Bill Russell	4	4	4	4	4	5	6	20
240	Joe Coleman	4	4	4	4	4	5	6	15
241A	Glenn Beckert SD	4	4	4	4	4	5	6	25
241B	Glenn Beckert WASH	4	4	5	6	12	25	30	150
242	Bill Gogolewski	4	4	4	4	4	5	6	15
243	Bob Oliver	4	4	4	4	4	5	6	20
244	Carl Morton	4	4	4	4	4	5	6	15
245	Cleon Jones	4	4	4	4	4	5	6	25
246	Oakland Athletics TC	4	4	4	4	4	5	6	15
247	Rick Miller	4	4	4	4	4	5	6	15
248	Tom Hall	4	4	4	4	4	5	6	15
249	George Mitterwald	4	4	4	4	4	5	6	50
250A	Willie McCovey SD	4	4	4	4	8	25	30	80
250B	Willie McCovey WASH	4	4	8	10	20	50	60	200
251	Graig Nettles	4	4	4	4	6	12	15	120
252	Dave Parker RC	▲12	▲20	40	50	100	▲250	▲300	500
253	John Boccabella	4	4	4	4	4	5	6	15
254	Stan Bahnsen	4	4	4	4	4	5	6	15
255	Larry Bowa	4	4	4	4	4	5	6	20
256	Tom Griffin	4	4	4	4	4	5	6	15
257	Buddy Bell	4	4	4	4	4	5	6	15

BASEBALL

#	Player	GD 2	VG 3	EX 5	ExMt 6	NM 7	NmMt 8	NmMt+ 8.5	MT 9
258	Jerry Morales	4	4	4	4	4	5	6	15
259	Bob Reynolds	4	4	4	4	4	5	6	20
260	Ted Simmons	4	4	4	4	4	6	8	25
261	Jerry Bell	4	4	4	4	4	5	6	20
262	Ed Kirkpatrick	4	4	4	4	4	6	8	80
263	Checklist 133-264	4	4	4	4	4	5	6	50
264	Joe Rudi	4	4	4	4	4	5	6	15
265	Tug McGraw	4	4	4	4	4	5	6	15
266	Jim Northrup	4	4	4	4	4	5	6	15
267	Andy Messersmith	4	4	4	4	4	5	6	15
268	Tom Grieve	4	4	4	4	4	5	6	15
269	Bob Johnson	4	4	4	4	4	5	6	15
270	Ron Santo	4	4	4	4	4	8	10	50
271	Bill Hands	4	4	4	4	4	5	6	15
272	Paul Casanova	4	4	4	4	4	5	6	15
273	Checklist 265-396	4	4	4	4	4	8	10	100
274	Fred Beene	4	4	4	4	4	5	6	15
275	Ron Hunt	4	4	4	4	4	5	6	15
276	Bobby Winkles MG	4	4	4	4	4	5	6	10
277	Gary Nolan	4	4	4	4	4	8	10	120
278	Cookie Rojas	4	4	4	4	4	5	6	15
279	Jim Crawford RC	4	4	4	4	4	5	6	15
280	Carl Yastrzemski	▲5	▲8	▲20	▲30	50	▲80	▲100	▲200
281	San Francisco Giants TC	4	4	4	4	4	5	6	15
282	Doyle Alexander	4	4	4	4	4	5	6	10
283	Mike Schmidt	15	25	50	60	100	250	400	▲1,200
284	Dave Duncan	4	4	4	4	4	5	6	15
285	Reggie Smith	4	4	4	4	4	5	6	15
286	Tony Muser	4	4	4	4	4	5	6	15
287	Clay Kirby	4	4	4	4	4	5	6	12
288	Gorman Thomas RC	4	4	4	4	4	5	6	15
289	Rick Auerbach	4	4	4	4	4	5	6	100
290	Vida Blue	4	4	4	4	4	5	6	30
291	Don Hahn	4	4	4	4	4	5	6	15
292	Chuck Seelbach	4	4	4	4	4	5	6	15
293	Milt May	4	4	4	4	4	5	6	15
294	Steve Foucault RC	4	4	4	4	4	5	6	15
295	Rick Monday	4	4	4	4	4	5	6	15
296	Ray Corbin	4	4	4	4	4	5	6	15
297	Hal Breeden	4	4	4	4	4	5	6	15
298	Roric Harrison	4	4	4	4	4	5	6	15
299	Gene Michael	4	4	4	4	4	5	6	15
300	Pete Rose	10	▲15	▲40	▲60	▲100	▲200	▲250	▲1,000
301	Bob Montgomery	4	4	4	4	4	5	6	25
302	Rudy May	4	4	4	4	4	5	6	10
303	George Hendrick	4	4	4	4	4	5	6	15
304	Don Wilson	4	4	4	4	4	5	6	15
305	Tito Fuentes	4	4	4	4	4	5	6	15
306	Earl Weaver MG	4	4	4	4	4	5	6	10
307	Luis Melendez	4	4	4	4	4	5	6	15
308	Bruce Dal Canton	4	4	4	4	4	5	6	15
309A	Dave Roberts SD	4	4	4	4	4	5	6	20
309B	Dave Roberts WASH	4	4	6	8	15	60	80	120
310	Terry Forster	4	4	4	4	4	5	6	15
311	Jerry Grote	4	4	4	4	4	6	8	50
312	Deron Johnson	4	4	4	4	4	5	6	60
313	Barry Lersch	4	4	4	4	4	5	6	15
314	Milwaukee Brewers TC	4	4	4	4	4	5	6	15
315	Ron Cey	4	4	4	4	4	5	6	15
316	Jim Perry	4	4	4	4	4	5	6	15
317	Richie Zisk	4	4	4	4	4	5	6	40
318	Jim Merritt	4	4	4	4	4	5	6	15
319	Randy Hundley	4	4	4	4	4	5	6	200
320	Dusty Baker	4	4	4	4	4	6	8	20
321	Steve Braun	4	4	4	4	4	5	6	300
322	Ernie McAnally	4	4	4	4	4	5	6	15
323	Richie Scheinblum	4	4	4	4	4	5	6	150
324	Steve Kline	4	4	4	4	4	5	6	15

#	Player	GD 2	VG 3	EX 5	ExMt 6	NM 7	NmMt 8	NmMt+ 8.5	MT
325	Tommy Harper	4	4	4	4	4	5	6	15
326	Sparky Anderson MG	4	4	4	4	4	8	10	8
327	Tom Timmerman	4	4	4	4	4	5	6	2
328	Skip Jutze	4	4	4	4	4	5	6	1
329	Mark Belanger	4	4	4	4	4	5	6	1
330	Juan Marichal	4	4	4	8	15	20	6	
331	C.Fisk/J.Bench AS	4	4	4	4	10	30	40	8
332	D.Allen/H.Aaron AS	4	4	4	5	10	25	30	6
333	R.Carew/J.Morgan AS	4	4	4	5	10	20	25	15
334	B.Robinson/R.Santo AS	4	4	4	4	4	8	10	3
335	B.Campaneris/C.Speier AS	4	4	4	4	4	5	6	1
336	B.Murcer/P.Rose AS	4	4	4	8	15	20	8	
337	A.Otis/C.Cedeno AS	4	4	4	4	4	5	6	1
338	R.Jackson/B.Williams AS	4	4	4	4	6	15	20	2
339	J.Hunter/R.Wise AS	4	4	4	4	4	6	8	5
340	Thurman Munson	▲5	▲8	▲20	▲30	▲50	▲100	▲120	▲25
341	Dan Driessen RC	4	4	4	4	4	5	6	
342	Jim Lonborg	4	4	4	4	4	5	6	
343	Kansas City Royals TC	4	4	4	4	4	5	6	
344	Mike Caldwell	4	4	4	4	4	5	6	10
345	Bill North	4	4	4	4	4	5	6	
346	Ron Reed	4	4	4	4	4	5	6	
347	Sandy Alomar	4	4	4	4	4	5	6	2
348	Pete Richert	4	4	4	4	4	5	6	1
349	John Vukovich	4	4	4	4	4	5	6	2
350	Bob Gibson	4	▲6	▲15	▲25	▲40	▲100	120	▲3
351	Dwight Evans	4	4	4	4	6	12	15	
352	Bill Stoneman	4	4	4	4	4	5	6	
353	Rich Coggins	4	4	4	4	4	5	6	
354	Whitey Lockman MG	4	4	4	4	4	5	6	
355	Dave Nelson	4	4	4	4	4	5	6	5
356	Jerry Koosman	4	4	4	4	4	5	6	
357	Buddy Bradford	4	4	4	4	4	5	6	
358	Dal Maxvill	4	4	4	4	4	5	6	
359	Brent Strom	4	4	4	4	4	5	6	
360	Greg Luzinski	4	4	4	4	4	5	6	
361	Don Carrithers	4	4	4	4	4	5	6	
362	Hal King	4	4	4	4	4	6	8	
363	New York Yankees TC	4	4	4	4	4	5	6	
364A	Cito Gaston SD	4	4	4	4	8	15	20	2
364B	Cito Gaston WASH	4	4	12	15	30	60	80	4
365	Steve Busby	4	4	4	4	4	5	6	
366	Larry Hisle	4	4	4	4	4	5	6	
367	Norm Cash	4	4	4	4	4	8	10	
368	Manny Mota	4	4	4	4	4	5	6	
369	Paul Lindblad	4	4	4	4	4	8	10	
370	Bob Watson	4	4	4	4	4	5	6	
371	Jim Slaton	4	4	4	4	4	5	6	
372	Ken Reitz	4	4	4	4	4	5	6	
373	John Curtis	4	4	4	4	4	5	6	
374	Marty Perez	4	4	4	4	4	5	6	
375	Earl Williams	4	4	4	4	4	5	6	
376	Jorge Orta	4	4	4	4	4	5	6	
377	Ron Woods	4	4	4	4	4	5	6	
378	Burt Hooton	4	4	4	4	4	5	6	
379	Billy Martin MG	4	4	4	4	4	6	8	
380	Bud Harrelson	4	4	4	4	4	5	6	
381	Charlie Sands	4	4	4	4	4	5	6	
382	Bob Moose	4	4	4	4	4	5	6	
383	Philadelphia Phillies TC	4	4	4	4	4	5	6	
384	Chris Chambliss	4	4	4	4	4	5	6	
385	Don Gullett	4	4	4	4	4	5	6	
386	Gary Matthews	4	4	4	4	4	5	6	
387A	Rich Morales SD	4	4	4	4	4	5	6	
387B	Rich Morales WASH	4	4	8	10	20	40	60	
388	Phil Roof	4	4	4	4	4	5	6	
389	Gates Brown	4	4	4	4	4	5	6	
390	Lou Piniella	4	4	4	4	4	5	6	

	GD 2	VG 3	EX 5	ExMt 6	NM 7	NmMt 8	NmMt+ 8.5	MT 9
91 Billy Champion	4	4	4	4	4	5	6	15
92 Dick Green	4	4	4	4	4	5	6	15
93 Orlando Pena	4	4	4	4	4	5	6	15
94 Ken Henderson	4	4	4	4	4	5	6	25
95 Doug Rader	4	4	4	4	4	5	6	15
96 Tommy Davis	4	4	4	4	4	5	6	15
97 George Stone	4	4	4	4	4	5	6	20
98 Duke Sims	4	4	4	4	4	5	6	15
99 Mike Paul	4	4	4	4	4	5	6	20
00 Harmon Killebrew	4	▲6	▲15	▲25	▲40	▲60	▲80	▲250
01 Elliott Maddox	4	4	4	4	4	5	6	15
02 Jim Rooker	4	4	4	4	4	5	6	15
03 Darrell Johnson MG	4	4	4	4	4	5	6	15
04 Jim Howarth	4	4	4	4	4	5	6	15
05 Ellie Rodriguez	4	4	4	4	4	5	6	25
06 Steve Arlin	4	4	4	4	4	5	6	25
07 Jim Wohlford	4	4	4	4	4	5	6	15
08 Charlie Hough	4	4	4	4	4	5	6	15
09 Ike Brown	4	4	4	4	4	5	6	20
10 Pedro Borbon	4	4	4	4	4	5	6	15
11 Frank Baker	4	4	4	4	4	5	6	12
12 Chuck Taylor	4	4	4	4	4	5	6	15
13 Don Money	4	4	4	4	4	5	6	15
14 Checklist 397-528	4	4	4	4	5	10	12	50
15 Gary Gentry	4	4	4	4	4	5	6	15
16 Chicago White Sox TC	4	4	4	4	4	5	6	12
17 Rich Folkers	4	4	4	4	4	5	6	20
18 Walt Williams	4	4	4	4	4	5	6	15
19 Wayne Twitchell	4	4	4	4	4	5	6	15
20 Ray Fosse	4	4	4	4	4	5	6	15
21 Dan Fife RC	4	4	4	4	4	5	6	15
22 Gonzalo Marquez	4	4	4	4	4	5	6	15
23 Fred Stanley	4	4	4	4	4	5	6	15
24 Jim Beauchamp	4	4	4	4	4	5	6	15
25 Pete Broberg	4	4	4	4	4	5	6	15
26 Rennie Stennett	4	4	4	4	4	5	6	20
27 Bobby Bolin	4	4	4	4	4	5	6	15
28 Gary Sutherland	4	4	4	4	4	5	6	15
29 Dick Lange RC	4	4	4	4	4	5	6	15
30 Matty Alou	4	4	4	4	4	6	8	80
31 Gene Garber RC	4	4	4	4	4	5	6	15
32 Chris Arnold	4	4	4	4	4	5	6	15
33 Lerrin LaGrow	4	4	4	4	4	5	6	15
34 Ken McMullen	4	4	4	4	4	5	6	15
35 Dave Concepcion	4	4	4	4	4	8	10	50
36 Don Hood RC	4	4	4	4	4	5	6	15
37 Jim Lyttle	4	4	4	4	4	5	6	15
38 Ed Herrmann	4	4	4	4	4	5	6	15
39 Norm Miller	4	4	4	4	4	5	6	15
40 Jim Kaat	4	4	4	4	4	8	12	200
41 Tom Ragland	4	4	4	4	4	5	6	15
42 Alan Foster	4	4	4	4	4	5	6	25
43 Tom Hutton	4	4	4	4	4	5	6	15
44 Vic Davalillo	4	4	4	4	4	5	6	15
45 George Medich	4	4	4	4	4	5	6	15
46 Len Randle	4	4	4	4	4	5	6	15
47 Frank Quilici MG	4	4	4	4	4	5	6	15
48 Ron Hodges RC	4	4	4	4	4	5	6	15
49 Tom McCraw	4	4	4	4	4	5	6	15
50 Rich Hebner	4	4	4	4	4	5	6	20
51 Tommy John	4	4	4	4	4	5	6	15
52 Gene Hiser	4	4	4	4	4	5	6	25
53 Balor Moore	4	4	4	4	4	5	6	15
54 Kurt Bevacqua	4	4	4	4	4	5	6	40
55 Tom Bradley	4	4	4	4	4	5	6	20
56 Dave Winfield RC	▼15	▼25	▲60	▲100	▲150	▲400	▲500	▲2,500
57 Chuck Goggin RC	4	4	4	4	4	5	6	15
58 Jim Ray	4	4	4	4	4	5	6	15

	GD 2	VG 3	EX 5	ExMt 6	NM 7	NmMt 8	NmMt+ 8.5	MT 9
459 Cincinnati Reds TC	4	4	4	4	4	8	10	30
460 Boog Powell	4	4	4	4	5	10	12	30
461 John Odom	4	4	4	4	4	5	6	50
462 Luis Alvarado	4	4	4	4	4	5	6	15
463 Pat Dobson	4	4	4	4	4	5	6	15
464 Jose Cruz	4	4	4	4	4	5	6	15
465 Dick Bosman	4	4	4	4	4	5	6	20
466 Dick Billings	4	4	4	4	4	5	6	10
467 Winston Llenas	4	4	4	4	4	5	6	15
468 Pepe Frias	4	4	4	4	4	5	6	12
469 Joe Decker	4	4	4	4	4	5	6	15
470 Reggie Jackson ALCS	4	4	4	4	4	12	20	30
471 Jon Matlack NLCS	4	4	4	4	4	5	6	15
472 Darold Knowles WS1	4	4	4	4	4	5	6	15
473 Willie Mays WS	6	8	12	15	20	80	100	120
474 Bert Campaneris WS3	4	4	4	4	4	8	10	150
475 Rusty Staub WS4	4	4	4	4	4	5	6	15
476 Cleon Jones WS5	4	4	4	4	4	5	6	12
477 Reggie Jackson WS	4	4	4	4	6	10	15	30
478 Bert Campaneris WS7	4	4	4	4	4	5	6	12
479 A's Celebrate WS	4	4	4	4	4	5	6	15
480 Willie Crawford	4	4	4	4	4	5	6	50
481 Jerry Terrell RC	4	4	4	4	4	5	6	15
482 Bob Didier	4	4	4	4	4	5	6	15
483 Atlanta Braves TC	4	4	4	4	4	5	6	10
484 Carmen Fanzone	4	4	4	4	4	5	6	15
485 Felipe Alou	4	4	4	4	4	5	6	10
486 Steve Stone	4	4	4	4	4	5	6	15
487 Ted Martinez	4	4	4	4	4	5	6	20
488 Andy Etchebarren	4	4	4	4	4	5	6	15
489 Danny Murtaugh MG	4	4	4	4	4	5	6	15
490 Vada Pinson	4	4	4	4	4	6	8	40
491 Roger Nelson	4	4	4	4	4	5	6	15
492 Mike Rogodzinski RC	4	4	4	4	6	12	15	100
493 Joe Hoerner	4	4	4	4	4	5	6	20
494 Ed Goodson	4	4	4	4	4	5	6	15
495 Dick McAuliffe	4	4	4	4	4	5	6	15
496 Tom Murphy	4	4	4	4	4	5	6	15
497 Bobby Mitchell	4	4	4	4	4	5	6	15
498 Pat Corrales	4	4	4	4	4	5	6	15
499 Rusty Torres	4	4	4	4	4	5	6	20
500 Lee May	4	4	4	4	4	5	6	12
501 Eddie Leon	4	4	4	4	4	5	6	20
502 Dave LaRoche	4	4	4	4	4	5	6	15
503 Eric Soderholm	4	4	4	4	4	5	6	15
504 Joe Niekro	4	4	4	4	4	5	6	15
505 Bill Buckner	4	4	4	4	4	5	6	15
506 Ed Farmer	4	4	4	4	4	5	6	15
507 Larry Stahl	4	4	4	4	4	5	6	15
508 Montreal Expos TC	4	4	4	4	4	5	6	15
509 Jesse Jefferson	4	4	4	4	4	5	6	15
510 Wayne Garrett	4	4	4	4	4	5	6	10
511 Toby Harrah	4	4	4	4	4	5	6	15
512 Joe Lahoud	4	4	4	4	4	5	6	15
513 Jim Campanis	4	4	4	4	4	5	6	15
514 Paul Schaal	4	4	4	4	4	5	6	15
515 Willie Montanez	4	4	4	4	4	5	6	20
516 Horacio Pina	4	4	4	4	4	5	6	15
517 Mike Hegan	4	4	4	4	4	5	6	15
518 Derrel Thomas	4	4	4	4	4	5	6	15
519 Bill Sharp RC	4	4	4	4	4	5	6	15
520 Tim McCarver	4	4	4	4	4	5	6	15
521 Ken Aspromonte MG	4	4	4	4	4	5	6	15
522 J.R. Richard	4	4	4	4	4	5	6	15
523 Cecil Cooper	4	4	4	4	4	5	6	15
524 Bill Plummer	4	4	4	4	4	5	6	15
525 Clyde Wright	4	4	4	4	4	5	6	15
526 Frank Tepedino	4	4	4	4	4	5	6	15

#	Player	GD 2	VG 3	EX 5	ExMt 6	NM 7	NmMt 8	NmMt+ 8.5	MT 9
527	Bobby Darwin	4	4	4	4	4	5	6	20
528	Bill Bonham	4	4	4	4	4	5	6	15
529	Horace Clarke	4	4	4	4	4	5	6	15
530	Mickey Stanley	4	4	4	4	4	5	6	15
531	Gene Mauch MG	4	4	4	4	4	5	6	15
532	Skip Lockwood	4	4	4	4	4	5	6	15
533	Mike Phillips RC	4	4	4	4	4	5	6	25
534	Eddie Watt	4	4	4	4	4	5	6	15
535	Bob Tolan	4	4	4	4	4	5	6	15
536	Duffy Dyer	4	4	4	4	4	5	6	15
537	Steve Mingori	4	4	4	4	4	5	6	15
538	Cesar Tovar	4	4	4	4	4	5	6	15
539	Lloyd Allen	4	4	4	4	4	5	6	15
540	Bob Robertson	4	4	4	4	4	5	6	15
541	Cleveland Indians TC	4	4	4	4	4	5	6	15
542	Goose Gossage	4	4	4	4	8	15	20	50
543	Danny Cater	4	4	4	4	4	5	6	15
544	Ron Schueler	4	4	4	4	4	5	6	15
545	Billy Conigliaro	4	4	4	4	4	5	6	15
546	Mike Corkins	4	4	4	4	4	5	6	15
547	Glenn Borgmann	4	4	4	4	4	5	6	15
548	Sonny Siebert	4	4	4	4	4	5	6	15
549	Mike Jorgensen	4	4	4	4	4	5	6	15
550	Sam McDowell	4	4	4	4	4	5	6	15
551	Von Joshua	4	4	4	4	4	5	6	20
552	Denny Doyle	4	4	4	4	4	5	6	15
553	Jim Willoughby	4	4	4	4	4	5	6	15
554	Tim Johnson RC	4	4	4	4	4	5	6	15
555	Woodie Fryman	4	4	4	4	4	5	6	15
556	Dave Campbell	4	4	4	4	4	5	6	15
557	Jim McGlothlin	4	4	4	4	4	5	6	15
558	Bill Fahey	4	4	4	4	4	5	6	15
559	Darrel Chaney	4	4	4	4	4	5	6	15
560	Mike Cuellar	4	4	4	4	4	5	6	15
561	Ed Kranepool	4	4	4	4	4	5	6	15
562	Jack Aker	4	4	4	4	4	5	6	20
563	Hal McRae	4	4	4	4	4	5	6	12
564	Mike Ryan	4	4	4	4	4	5	6	15
565	Milt Wilcox	4	4	4	4	4	5	6	15
566	Jackie Hernandez	4	4	4	4	4	5	6	15
567	Boston Red Sox TC	4	4	4	4	4	5	6	15
568	Mike Torrez	4	4	4	4	4	5	6	15
569	Rick Dempsey	4	4	4	4	4	5	6	15
570	Ralph Garr	4	4	4	4	4	5	6	15
571	Rich Hand	4	4	4	4	4	5	6	15
572	Enzo Hernandez	4	4	4	4	4	5	6	15
573	Mike Adams RC	4	4	4	4	4	5	6	15
574	Bill Parsons	4	4	4	4	4	5	6	15
575	Steve Garvey	4	4	4	5	10	25	30	300
576	Scipio Spinks	4	4	4	4	4	5	6	15
577	Mike Sadek RC	4	4	4	4	4	5	6	15
578	Ralph Houk MG	4	4	4	4	4	5	6	15
579	Cecil Upshaw	4	4	4	4	4	5	6	15
580	Jim Spencer	4	4	4	4	4	5	6	15
581	Fred Norman	4	4	4	4	4	5	6	15
582	Bucky Dent RC	4	4	5	8	12	20	40	400
583	Marty Pattin	4	4	4	4	4	5	6	15
584	Ken Rudolph	4	4	4	4	4	5	6	15
585	Merv Rettenmund	4	4	4	4	4	5	6	15
586	Jack Brohamer	4	4	4	4	4	5	6	15
587	Larry Christenson RC	4	4	4	4	4	5	6	15
588	Hal Lanier	4	4	4	4	4	5	6	15
589	Boots Day	4	4	4	4	4	5	6	15
590	Roger Moret	4	4	4	4	4	5	6	15
591	Sonny Jackson	4	4	4	4	4	5	6	15
592	Ed Bane RC	4	4	4	4	4	5	6	15
593	Steve Yeager	4	4	4	4	4	5	6	15
594	Leroy Stanton	4	4	4	4	4	5	6	15

#	Player	GD 2	VG 3	EX 5	ExMt 6	NM 7	NmMt 8	NmMt+ 8.5	MT 9
595	Steve Blass	4	4	4	4	4	5	6	20
596	Rookie Pitchers	4	4	4	4	4	5	6	15
597	Rookie Infielders	4	4	4	4	4	6	8	80
598	Ken Griffey RC	8	10	15	20	25	40	50	80
599A	Rookie Pitchers WASH	4	4	4	4	8	15	20	30
599B	Rookie Pitchers SD Large	4	4	4	4	8	15	20	100
599C	Rookie Pitchers SD Small	4	5	20	25				
600	Bill Madlock RC	4	4	4	5	10	30	40	60
601	Rookie Outfielders	4	4	4	4	5	10	15	80
602	Rookie Pitchers	4	4	4	4	4	5	6	120
603	Rookie Catchers	4	4	4	4	4	5	6	30
604	A.Thornton RC/F.White RC	4	4	4	4	8	15	25	60
605	Frank Tanana RC	4	4	4	4	4	8	10	40
606	Rookie Outfielders	4	4	4	4	4	5	6	80
607	Rookie Shortstops	4	4	4	4	4	5	6	15
608A	Rookie Pitchers ERR Apodaco	4	4	4	4	4	8	10	40
608B	Rookie Pitchers COR Apodaca	4	4	4	4	5	10	12	60
609	Rico Petrocelli	4	4	4	4	4	5	6	15
610	Dave Kingman	4	4	4	4	4	6	8	20
611	Rich Stelmaszek	4	4	4	4	4	5	6	15
612	Luke Walker	4	4	4	4	4	5	6	15
613	Dan Monzon	4	4	4	4	4	5	6	15
614	Adrian Devine RC	4	4	4	4	4	5	6	
615	Johnny Jeter	4	4	4	4	4	5	6	
616	Larry Gura	4	4	4	4	4	5	6	
617	Ted Ford	4	4	4	4	4	5	6	
618	Jim Mason	4	4	4	4	4	5	6	
619	Mike Anderson	4	4	4	4	4	5	6	
620	Al Downing	4	4	4	4	4	5	6	
621	Bernie Carbo	4	4	4	4	4	5	6	
622	Phil Gagliano	4	4	4	4	4	5	6	
623	Celerino Sanchez	4	4	4	4	4	5	6	
624	Bob Miller	4	4	4	4	4	5	6	
625	Ollie Brown	4	4	4	4	4	5	6	
626	Pittsburgh Pirates TC	4	4	4	4	4	5	6	
627	Carl Taylor	4	4	4	4	4	5	6	
628	Ivan Murrell	4	4	4	4	4	5	6	
629	Rusty Staub	4	4	4	4	4	8	10	
630	Tommie Agee	4	4	4	4	4	5	6	
631	Steve Barber	4	4	4	4	4	5	6	
632	George Culver	4	4	4	4	4	5	6	
633	Dave Hamilton	4	4	4	4	4	5	6	
634	Eddie Mathews MG	4	4	4	4	4	6	8	
635	Johnny Edwards	4	4	4	4	4	5	6	
636	Dave Goltz	4	4	4	4	4	5	6	
637	Checklist 529-660	4	4	4	4	4	8	10	
638	Ken Sanders	4	4	4	4	4	5	6	
639	Joe Lovitto	4	4	4	4	4	5	6	
640	Milt Pappas	4	4	4	4	4	5	6	
641	Chuck Brinkman	4	4	4	4	4	5	6	
642	Terry Harmon	4	4	4	4	4	5	6	
643	Los Angeles Dodgers TC	4	4	4	4	4	5	6	
644	Wayne Granger	4	4	4	4	4	5	6	
645	Ken Boswell	4	4	4	4	4	5	6	3
646	George Foster	4	4	4	4	6	12	15	
647	Juan Beniquez RC	4	4	4	4	4	5	6	
648	Terry Crowley	4	4	4	4	4	5	6	
649	Fernando Gonzalez RC	4	4	4	4	4	5	6	
650	Mike Epstein	4	4	4	4	4	5	6	
651	Leron Lee	4	4	4	4	4	5	6	
652	Gail Hopkins	4	4	4	4	4	5	6	
653	Bob Stinson	4	4	4	4	4	5	6	
654A	Jesus Alou ERR No Position	4	4	4	4	4	6	8	
654B	Jesus Alou COR Outfield	4	4	4	4	4	5	6	
655	Mike Tyson RC	4	4	4	4	4	5	6	
656	Adrian Garrett	4	4	4	4	4	5	6	
657	Jim Shellenback	4	4	4	4	4	5	6	
658	Lee Lacy	4	4	4	4	4	5	6	

		GD 2	VG 3	EX 5	ExMt 6	NM 7	NmMt 8	NmMt+ 8.5	MT 9
659	Joe Lis	4	4	4	6	8	15	20	150
660	Larry Dierker	4	4	4	4	4	5	6	15

— Hank Aaron 715 #1 PSA 10 (Gem) sold for $9,677 (Memory Lane; 5/12)
— Dave Parker #252 PSA 10 (Gem) sold for $2,028 (eBay; 01/12)
— Frank Robinson #55 PSA 10 (Gem) sold for $1,028 (eBay; 01/12)
— Tom Seaver #80 PSA 10 (Gem) sold for $1,380 (eBay; 01/12)
— Dave Winfield #456 PSA 10 (Gem) (Young Collection) sold for $5,020 (SCP; 5/12)

1974 Topps Traded

		GD 2	VG 3	EX 5	ExMt 6	NM 7	NmMt 8	NmMt+ 8.5	MT 9
23T	Craig Robinson	4	4	4	4	4	5	6	
42T	Claude Osteen	4	4	4	4	4	5	6	
43T	Jim Wynn	4	4	4	4	5	10	12	
1T	Bobby Heise	4	4	4	4	4	5	6	20
9T	Ross Grimsley	4	4	4	4	4	6	8	
2T	Bob Locker	4	4	4	4	4	6	8	25
3T	Bill Sudakis	4	4	4	4	4	6	8	
3T	Mike Marshall	4	4	4	4	5	10	12	
23T	Nelson Briles	4	4	4	4	4	6	8	80
39T	Aurelio Monteagudo	4	4	4	4	4	5	6	
51T	Diego Segui	4	4	4	4	4	5	6	
65T	Willie Davis	4	4	4	4	4	6	8	25
75T	Reggie Cleveland	4	4	4	4	4	5	6	20
82T	Lindy McDaniel	4	4	4	4	4	5	6	20
86T	Fred Scherman	4	4	4	4	4	5	6	
49T	George Mitterwald	4	4	4	4	4	5	6	15
62T	Ed Kirkpatrick	4	4	4	4	4	5	6	15
69T	Bob Johnson	4	4	4	4	4	6	8	25
70T	Ron Santo	4	4	4	4	8	10	12	25
73T	Barry Lersch	4	4	4	4	4	6	8	25
79T	Randy Hundley	4	4	4	4	8	8	10	40
80T	Juan Marichal	4	4	4	4	5	10	12	25
8T	Pete Richert	4	4	4	4	4	5	6	20
3T	John Curtis	4	4	4	4	4	6	8	
0T	Lou Piniella	4	4	4	4	5	10	12	40
8T	Gary Sutherland	4	4	4	4	4	8	10	40
4T	Kurt Bevacqua	4	4	4	4	4	6	8	25
8T	Jim Ray	4	4	4	4	4	6	8	25
5T	Felipe Alou	4	4	4	4	4	6	8	
6T	Steve Stone	4	4	4	4	4	8	10	
6T	Tom Murphy	4	4	4	4	4	5	6	15
6T	Horacio Pina	4	4	4	4	4	5	6	15
4T	Eddie Watt	4	4	4	4	4	6	8	25
3T	Cesar Tovar	4	4	4	4	4	5	6	15
1T	Ron Schueler	4	4	4	4	4	5	6	20
9T	Cecil Upshaw	4	4	4	4	4	5	6	15
9T	Merv Rettenmund	4	4	4	4	4	5	6	20
2T	Luke Walker	4	4	4	4	4	5	6	
9T	Larry Gura	4	4	4	4	4	6	8	
9T	Jim Mason	4	4	4	4	4	5	6	80
9T	Tommie Agee	4	4	4	4	4	6	8	120
9T	Terry Crowley	4	4	4	4	4	6	8	25
9T	Fernando Gonzalez	4	4	4	4	4	5	6	20
0	Traded Checklist	4	4	4	8	15	30	100	

1975 Kellogg's

		VG 3	VgEx 4	EX 5	ExMt 6	NM 7	NmMt 8	MT 9	Gem 9.5/10
	Roy White	4	4	4	4	4	8		
	Ross Grimsley	4	4	4	4	4	6	12	
	Reggie Smith	4	4	4	4	4	6	40	
	Bob Grich 1973 Work	4	4	4	4	4	6	12	
	Bob Grich Because	4	4	4					
	Greg Gross	4	4					12	
	Bob Watson	4	4	4	4	4	6	12	
	Johnny Bench	4	4	4	4	8	15	50	
	Jeff Burroughs	4	4	4	4	4	6	12	
	Elliott Maddox	4	4	4	4	4	6	12	

		GD 2	VG 3	EX 5	ExMt 6	NM 7	NmMt 8	NmMt+ 8.5	MT 9
10	Jon Matlack	4	4	4	4	4	6	25	
11	Pete Rose	4	4	6	8	15	30	80	
12	Lee Stanton	4	4	4	4	4	6	15	
13	Bake McBride	4	4	4	4	4	6	12	40
14	Jorge Orta	4	4	4	4	4	6	12	25
15	Al Oliver	4	4	4	4	4	6	12	50
16	John Briggs	4	4	4	4	4	6	12	
17	Steve Garvey	4	4	4	4	4	8	15	50
18	Brooks Robinson	4	4	4	4	5	10	20	
19	John Hiller	4	4	4	4	4	6	12	
20	Lynn McGlothen	4	4	4	4	4	6	12	
21	Cleon Jones	4	4	4	4	4	6	12	
22	Fergie Jenkins	4	4	4	4	4	8	15	
23	Bill North	4	4	4	4	4	6	12	
24	Steve Busby	4	4	4	4	4	6	12	
25	Richie Zisk	4	4	4	4	4	6	12	25
26	Nolan Ryan	4	4	6	8	15	30	80	
27	Joe Morgan	4	4	4	4	5	10	20	60
28	Joe Rudi	4	4	4	4	4	6	12	
29	Jose Cardenal	4	4	4	4	4	6	12	40
30	Andy Messersmith	4	4	4	4	4	6	12	
31	Willie Montanez	4	4	4	4	4	6	12	25
32	Bill Buckner	4	4	4	4	4	6	12	40
33	Rod Carew	4	4	4	4	5	10	25	
34	Lou Piniella	4	4	4	4	4	6	12	
35	Ralph Garr	4	4	4	4	4	6	12	
36	Mike Marshall	4	4	4	4	4	6	12	
37	Garry Maddox	4	4	4	4	4	6	12	
38	Dwight Evans	4	4	4	4	4	8	20	
39	Lou Brock	4	4	4	4	5	10	100	
40	Ken Singleton	4	4	4	4	4	6	12	60
41	Steve Braun	4	4	4	4	4	6	12	
42	Rich Allen	4	4	4	4	4	6	15	40
43	John Grubb	4	4	4	4	4	6	12	25
44A	Jim Hunter Oakland	4	4	4	4	4	8	15	
44B	Jim Hunter New York	4	4	4	4	4	8	40	
45	Gaylord Perry	4	4	4	4	4	8	15	
46	George Hendrick	4	4	4	4	4	6	12	
47	Sparky Lyle	4	4	4	4	4	6	20	
48	Dave Cash	4	4	4	4	4	6	12	
49	Luis Tiant	4	4	4	4	4	6	12	40
50	Cesar Geronimo	4	4	4	4	4	6	12	25
51	Carl Yastrzemski	4	4	4	8	15	40		
52	Ken Brett	4	4	4	4	4	6	12	25
53	Hal McRae	4	4	4	4	4	6	12	
54	Reggie Jackson	4	4	4	4	8	15	30	
55	Rollie Fingers	4	4	4	4	5	10		
56	Mike Schmidt	4	4	4	4	8	15	50	
57	Richie Hebner	4	4	4	4	5	10		

1975 Topps

		VG 3	VgEx 4	EX 5	ExMt 6	NM 7	NmMt 8	NmMt+ 8.5	MT 9
1	Hank Aaron HL	12	15	25	30	50	200	250	800
2	Lou Brock HL	4	4	4	5	10	50	80	400
3	Bob Gibson HL	4	4	4	5	10	40	50	250
4	Al Kaline HL	4	6	10	15	25	30	40	▲250
5	Nolan Ryan HL	4	8	12	15	20	50	100	300
6	Mike Marshall HL	4	4	5	6	12	25	80	400
7	Ryan/Busby/Bosman HL	4	4	4	5	10	25	30	100
8	Rogelio Moret	4	4	4	4	5	10	12	25
9	Frank Tepedino	4	4	4	4	5	10	12	25
10	Willie Davis	4	4	4	4	5	10	12	25
11	Bill Melton	4	4	4	4	5	10	12	25
12	David Clyde	4	4	4	4	5	10	12	25
13	Gene Locklear RC	4	4	4	4	6	12	15	30
14	Milt Wilcox	4	4	4	4	5	10	12	30
15	Jose Cardenal	4	4	4	6	12	20	120	

BASEBALL

#	Player	VG 3	VgEx 4	EX 5	ExMt 6	NM 7	NmMt 8	NmMt+ 8.5	MT 9
16	Frank Tanana	4	6	12	15	30	60	80	250
17	Dave Concepcion	4	4	4	4	8	15	20	40
18	Detroit Tigers CL/Houk	4	4	4	4	6	12	15	50
19	Jerry Koosman	4	4	4	4	5	10	12	25
20	Thurman Munson	6	10	25	30	50	120	150	2,500
21	Rollie Fingers	4	4	4	4	8	15	20	150
22	Dave Cash	4	4	4	4	6	12	15	60
23	Bill Russell	4	4	4	4	6	12	20	80
24	Al Fitzmorris	4	4	4	4	5	10	12	25
25	Lee May	4	4	4	4	4	8	10	15
26	Dave McNally	4	4	4	4	5	10	12	30
27	Ken Reitz	4	4	4	4	5	10	15	60
28	Tom Murphy	4	4	4	4	5	10	12	25
29	Dave Parker	4	4	4	4	8	15	20	100
30	Bert Blyleven	4	4	4	6	12	25	30	400
31	Dave Rader	4	4	4	4	5	10	12	25
32	Reggie Cleveland	4	4	4	4	5	10	12	60
33	Dusty Baker	4	4	4	4	6	12	15	60
34	Steve Renko	4	4	4	4	4	8	10	15
35	Ron Santo	4	4	4	4	6	12	15	30
36	Joe Lovitto	4	4	4	4	8	15	20	50
37	Dave Freisleben	4	4	4	4	5	10	15	120
38	Buddy Bell	4	4	4	4	5	10	12	25
39	Andre Thornton	4	4	4	4	5	10	12	50
40	Bill Singer	4	4	4	4	5	10	12	25
41	Cesar Geronimo	4	4	4	4	8	15	20	80
42	Joe Coleman	4	4	4	4	5	10	12	25
43	Cleon Jones	4	4	4	4	6	12	15	40
44	Pat Dobson	4	4	4	4	5	10	12	25
45	Joe Rudi	4	4	4	4	6	12	15	30
46	Philadelphia Phillies CL/Ozark	4	4	4	4	5	10	12	40
47	Tommy John	4	4	4	4	8	20	25	200
48	Freddie Patek	4	4	4	4	5	10	12	25
49	Larry Dierker	4	4	4	4	5	10	12	25
50	Brooks Robinson	4	4	4	6	15	50	60	150
51	Bob Forsch RC	4	4	4	4	6	12	15	30
52	Darrell Porter	4	4	4	4	5	10	12	25
53	Dave Giusti	4	4	5	6	12	25	40	500
54	Eric Soderholm	4	4	4	4	6	12	15	80
55	Bobby Bonds	4	4	4	4	6	12	20	80
56	Rick Wise	4	4	5	6	12	25	40	120
57	Dave Johnson	4	4	4	4	5	10	12	25
58	Chuck Taylor	4	4	4	4	5	10	12	30
59	Ken Henderson	4	4	4	4	5	10	12	25
60	Fergie Jenkins	4	4	4	4	8	15	20	60
61	Dave Winfield	▲6	▲10	▲15	▲25	▲60	▲100	▲120	▲500
62	Fritz Peterson	4	4	4	4	5	10	12	25
63	Steve Swisher RC	4	4	4	4	5	10	12	30
64	Dave Chalk	4	4	4	4	5	10	12	25
65	Don Gullett	4	4	4	6	12	25	30	150
66	Willie Horton	4	4	4	4	6	12	15	30
67	Tug McGraw	4	4	4	4	6	12	15	30
68	Ron Blomberg	4	4	4	4	5	10	12	25
69	John Odom	4	4	4	4	5	10	12	20
70	Mike Schmidt	▼6	10	▲15	▲25	▲80	▲120	▲150	▲1,500
71	Charlie Hough	4	4	4	4	6	12	15	30
72	Kansas City Royals CL/McKeon	4	4	4	4	5	10	12	40
73	J.R. Richard	4	4	4	4	6	12	15	60
74	Mark Belanger	4	4	4	4	6	12	20	80
75	Ted Simmons	4	4	4	4	8	15	60	350
76	Ed Sprague	4	4	4	4	5	10	12	25
77	Richie Zisk	4	4	4	4	5	10	15	100
78	Ray Corbin	4	4	4	4	5	10	12	25
79	Gary Matthews	4	4	4	4	6	12	15	30
80	Carlton Fisk	▲8	▲12	▲20	▲30	▲50	▲100	▲120	▲300
81	Ron Reed	4	4	4	4	5	10	12	25
82	Pat Kelly	4	4	4	4	8	15	25	120
83	Jim Merritt	4	4	4	4	5	10	12	20

#	Player	VG 3	VgEx 4	EX 5	ExMt 6	NM 7	NmMt 8	NmMt+ 8.5	MT 9
84	Enzo Hernandez	4	4	4	4	4	8	10	15
85	Bill Bonham	4	4	4	4	6	12	15	60
86	Joe Lis	4	4	4	4	8	15	20	120
87	George Foster	4	4	4	6	12	25	30	50
88	Tom Egan	4	4	4	4	5	10	12	25
89	Jim Ray	4	4	4	4	4	8	10	15
90	Rusty Staub	4	4	4	4	8	25	30	500
91	Dick Green	4	4	4	4	5	10	12	25
92	Cecil Upshaw	4	4	4	4	5	10	12	40
93	Davey Lopes	4	4	4	4	6	12	15	60
94	Jim Lonborg	4	4	4	4	5	10	12	60
95	John Mayberry	4	4	4	4	5	10	12	25
96	Mike Cosgrove RC	4	4	4	4	5	10	12	25
97	Earl Williams	4	4	4	4	5	10	15	40
98	Rich Folkers	4	4	4	4	5	10	12	25
99	Mike Hegan	4	4	4	4	5	10	12	25
100	Willie Stargell	4	4	5	6	12	25	40	100
101	Montreal Expos CL/Mauch	4	4	4	5	10	20	40	100
102	Joe Decker	4	4	4	4	5	10	12	25
103	Rick Miller	4	5	10	12	25	50	60	150
104	Bill Madlock	4	4	4	5	10	20	25	150
105	Buzz Capra	4	4	4	4	5	10	12	60
106	Mike Hargrove RC	4	4	4	4	8	15	25	120
107	Jim Barr	4	4	4	4	5	10	12	25
108	Tom Hall	4	4	4	4	5	10	12	25
109	George Hendrick	4	4	4	4	5	10	12	25
110	Wilbur Wood	4	4	4	4	5	10	12	25
111	Wayne Garrett	4	4	4	4	6	12	15	100
112	Larry Hardy RC	4	4	4	4	5	10	12	25
113	Elliott Maddox	4	4	4	4	5	10	12	25
114	Dick Lange	4	4	4	4	5	10	12	25
115	Joe Ferguson	4	4	4	4	5	10	12	60
116	Lerrin LaGrow	4	4	4	4	5	10	12	25
117	Baltimore Orioles CL/Weaver	4	4	5	10	20	40	50	650
118	Mike Anderson	4	4	4	4	5	10	12	25
119	Tommy Helms	4	4	4	4	4	8	10	15
120	Steve Busby	4	4	4	4	5	10	15	100
121	Bill North	4	4	4	4	5	10	12	25
122	Al Hrabosky	4	4	4	4	6	12	15	25
123	Johnny Briggs	4	4	4	4	5	10	12	25
124	Jerry Reuss	4	4	4	4	5	10	12	25
125	Ken Singleton	4	4	4	4	6	12	20	15
126	Checklist 1-132	4	4	4	4	5	10	15	5
127	Glenn Borgmann	4	4	4	4	6	12	15	12
128	Bill Lee	4	4	4	4	6	12	15	3
129	Rick Monday	4	4	4	5	10	20	25	15
130	Phil Niekro	4	4	4	4	8	15	20	5
131	Toby Harrah	4	4	4	4	5	10	12	6
132	Randy Moffitt	4	4	4	4	5	10	15	6
133	Dan Driessen	4	5	6	12	25	50	60	20
134	Ron Hodges	4	4	4	4	5	10	12	2
135	Charlie Spikes	4	4	4	4	5	10	12	6
136	Jim Mason	4	4	4	4	5	10	12	6
137	Terry Forster	4	4	4	4	6	12	15	3
138	Del Unser	4	4	4	4	4	8	10	
139	Horacio Pina	4	4	4	4	5	10	15	10
140	Steve Garvey	4	4	4	6	12	25	30	10
141	Mickey Stanley	4	4	4	4	5	10	15	8
142	Bob Reynolds	4	4	4	4	5	10	12	2
143	Cliff Johnson RC	4	4	4	4	5	10	15	15
144	Jim Wohlford	4	4	4	4	5	10	12	3
145	Ken Holtzman	4	4	4	4	5	10	12	2
146	San Diego Padres CL/McNamara	4	4	4	4	5	10	12	2
147	Pedro Garcia	4	4	4	4	5	10	12	2

#	Player	VG 3	VgEx 4	EX 5	ExMt 6	NM 7	NmMt 8	NmMt+ 8.5	MT 9
148	Jim Rooker	4	4	4	4	5	10	12	2
149	Tim Foli	4	4	4	4	5	10	12	2
150	Bob Gibson	4	4	8	10	20	80	100	50
151	Steve Brye	4	4	4	4	5	10	12	

#	Player	VG 3	VgEx 4	EX 5	ExMt 6	NM 7	NmMt 8	NmMt+ 8.5	MT 9
152	Mario Guerrero	4	4	4	4	5	10	12	25
153	Rick Reuschel	4	4	4	4	5	10	12	30
154	Mike Lum	4	4	4	4	4	8	10	15
155	Jim Bibby	4	4	4	4	5	10	12	25
156	Dave Kingman	4	4	4	4	5	10	12	50
157	Pedro Borbon	4	4	4	4	5	10	12	20
158	Jerry Grote	4	4	4	4	5	10	12	25
159	Steve Arlin	4	4	4	4	5	10	12	25
160	Graig Nettles	4	4	4	4	8	15	20	30
161	Stan Bahnsen	4	4	4	4	5	10	12	25
162	Willie Montanez	4	4	4	4	5	10	12	25
163	Jim Brewer	4	4	4	4	5	10	12	25
164	Mickey Rivers	4	4	4	4	6	12	15	30
165	Doug Rader	4	4	4	4	5	10	12	25
166	Woodie Fryman	4	4	4	4	5	10	12	25
167	Rich Coggins	4	4	4	4	5	10	12	25
168	Bill Greif	4	4	4	4	5	10	15	150
169	Cookie Rojas	4	4	4	4	5	10	12	40
170	Bert Campaneris	4	4	4	4	6	12	15	80
171	Ed Kirkpatrick	4	4	4	4	5	10	15	80
172	Boston Red Sox CL/Johnson	4	4	4	4	8	15	20	40
173	Steve Rogers	4	4	4	4	5	10	15	80
174	Bake McBride	4	4	4	4	5	10	12	25
175	Don Money	4	4	4	4	5	10	15	150
176	Burt Hooton	4	4	4	4	5	10	12	30
177	Vic Correll RC	4	4	4	4	5	10	12	25
178	Cesar Tovar	4	4	4	6	12	25	30	150
179	Tom Bradley	4	4	4	4	5	10	12	25
180	Joe Morgan	▲10	▲15	▲25	▲40	▲60	▲100	▲120	▲250
181	Fred Beene	4	4	4	4	5	10	12	25
182	Don Hahn	4	4	4	4	5	10	12	80
183	Mel Stottlemyre	4	4	4	4	8	15	20	40
184	Jorge Orta	4	4	4	4	5	10	12	40
185	Steve Carlton	4	4	4	6	15	30	40	200
186	Willie Crawford	4	4	4	4	5	10	12	25
187	Denny Doyle	4	4	4	4	5	10	15	40
188	Tom Griffin	4	4	4	4	5	10	12	25
189	Y.Berra/Campanella MVP	4	4	4	4	6	12	15	50
190	B.Shantz/H.Sauer MVP	4	4	4	4	5	10	12	50
191	Al Rosen/Campanella MVP	4	4	4	4	8	15	20	80
192	Y.Berra/W.Mays MVP	4	4	4	5	10	20	25	400
193	Y.Berra/Campanella MVP	4	4	4	4	6	12	15	40
194	M.Mantle/D.Newcombe MVP	4	4	4	6	20	25	30	100
195	M.Mantle/H.Aaron MVP	4	4	6	8	20	50	80	150
196	J.Jensen/E.Banks MVP	4	4	4	4	6	20	25	200
197	N.Fox/E.Banks MVP	4	4	4	4	5	10	12	25
198	R.Maris/D.Groat MVP	4	4	4	4	6	12	15	60
199	R.Maris/F.Robinson MVP	4	4	4	4	6	12	15	40
200	M.Mantle/M.Wills MVP	4	4	4	6	12	30	40	200
201	E.Howard/S.Koufax MVP	4	4	4	4	5	10	12	20
202	B.Robinson/K.Boyer MVP	4	4	4	4	6	12	20	100
203	Z.Versailes/W.Mays MVP	4	4	4	4	6	12	15	40
204	F.Robinson/B.Clemente MVP	4	5	8	12	20	30	40	80
205	C.Yastrzemski/O.Cepeda MVP	4	4	4	4	6	12	15	50
206	D.McLain/B.Gibson MVP	4	4	4	4	6	12	15	25
207	H.Killebrew/W.McCovey MVP	4	4	4	4	6	12	15	40
208	B.Powell/J.Bench MVP	4	4	4	4	6	12	50	275
209	V.Blue/J.Torre MVP	4	4	4	4	5	10	12	30
210	R.Allen/J.Bench MVP	4	4	4	4	8	15	20	60
211	R.Jackson/P.Rose MVP	4	4	4	4	8	15	25	100
212	J.Burroughs/S.Garvey MVP	4	4	4	4	5	10	12	40
213	Oscar Gamble	4	4	4	4	6	12	15	25
214	Harry Parker	4	4	4	4	5	10	12	25
215	Bobby Valentine	4	4	4	4	6	12	20	50
216	San Francisco Giants CL/Westrum	4	4	4	4	5	10	12	25
217	Lou Piniella	4	4	4	4	6	12	15	40
218	Jerry Johnson	4	4	4	4	4	8	10	15
219	Ed Herrmann	4	4	4	4	5	60	80	150

#	Player	VG 3	VgEx 4	EX 5	ExMt 6	NM 7	NmMt 8	NmMt+ 8.5	MT 9
220	Don Sutton	4	4	4	4	6	12	15	40
221	Aurelio Rodriguez	4	4	4	4	5	10	12	25
222	Dan Spillner RC	4	4	4	4	5	10	12	25
223	Robin Yount RC	▼30	▼50	80	▼120	▼200	500	600	▲4,000
224	Ramon Hernandez	4	4	4	4	5	10	12	25
225	Bob Grich	4	4	4	4	6	12	20	80
226	Bill Campbell	4	4	4	4	5	10	12	25
227	Bob Watson	4	4	4	4	5	10	12	25
228	George Brett RC	100	120	150	▲250	400	▲1,200	▲1,500	▲8,000
229	Barry Foote	4	4	4	4	5	10	12	60
230	Jim Hunter	4	4	4	4	8	15	20	80
231	Mike Tyson	4	4	4	4	5	10	12	25
232	Diego Segui	4	4	4	4	4	8	10	15
233	Billy Grabarkewitz	4	4	4	4	5	10	12	50
234	Tom Grieve	4	4	4	4	4	8	10	15
235	Jack Billingham	4	4	4	4	5	10	12	40
236	California Angels CL/Williams	4	4	4	4	5	10	12	60
237	Carl Morton	4	4	4	4	5	10	12	25
238	Dave Duncan	4	4	4	4	5	10	15	80
239	George Stone	4	4	4	4	4	8	10	15
240	Garry Maddox	4	4	4	4	6	12	15	30
241	Dick Tidrow	4	4	4	4	5	10	12	25
242	Jay Johnstone	4	4	4	4	5	10	12	25
243	Jim Kaat	4	4	4	4	6	12	15	30
244	Bill Buckner	4	4	4	4	6	12	15	40
245	Mickey Lolich	4	4	4	4	6	12	15	60
246	St. Louis Cardinals CL/Schoen	4	4	4	4	5	10	12	50
247	Enos Cabell	4	4	4	4	5	10	12	25
248	Randy Jones	4	4	4	4	6	12	15	30
249	Danny Thompson	4	4	4	4	5	10	15	60
250	Ken Brett	4	4	4	5	10	20	30	200
251	Fran Healy	4	4	4	4	6	12	20	60
252	Fred Scherman	4	4	4	4	5	10	12	30
253	Jesus Alou	4	4	4	4	8	15	25	100
254	Mike Torrez	4	4	4	4	8	15	20	40
255	Dwight Evans	4	4	4	4	8	15	20	80
256	Billy Champion	4	4	4	4	5	10	15	40
257	Checklist: 133-264	4	4	4	4	5	10	15	40
258	Dave LaRoche	4	4	4	4	5	10	12	25
259	Len Randle	4	4	4	5	10	20	30	100
260	Johnny Bench	4	5	12	25	30	60	100	300
261	Andy Hassler RC	4	4	4	4	5	10	12	25
262	Rowland Office RC	4	4	4	4	5	10	15	30
263	Jim Perry	4	4	4	4	5	10	15	40
264	John Milner	4	4	4	4	5	10	12	25
265	Ron Bryant	4	4	4	4	5	10	12	25
266	Sandy Alomar	4	4	4	4	6	12	15	30
267	Dick Ruthven	4	4	4	4	5	10	12	25
268	Hal McRae	4	4	4	4	6	12	20	150
269	Doug Rau	4	4	4	4	5	10	12	25
270	Ron Fairly	4	4	4	4	6	12	15	30
271	Gerry Moses	4	4	4	4	5	10	12	25
272	Lynn McGlothen	4	4	4	4	5	10	12	25
273	Steve Braun	4	4	4	4	5	10	12	30
274	Vicente Romo	4	4	4	4	5	10	12	25
275	Paul Blair	4	4	4	4	6	12	15	30
276	Chicago White Sox CL/Tanner	4	4	4	4	5	10	12	30
277	Frank Taveras	4	4	4	4	5	10	12	50
278	Paul Lindblad	4	4	4	4	5	10	12	25
279	Milt May	4	4	4	4	4	8	10	15
280	Carl Yastrzemski	6	8	10	12	25	40	40	120
281	Jim Slaton	4	4	4	4	5	10	12	25
282	Jerry Morales	4	4	4	4	5	10	12	25
283	Steve Foucault	4	4	4	4	5	10	12	25
284	Ken Griffey Sr.	4	4	4	5	10	20	25	120
285	Ellie Rodriguez	4	4	4	4	5	10	12	25
286	Mike Jorgensen	4	4	4	4	5	10	12	25
287	Roric Harrison	4	4	4	4	4	8	10	15

#	Player	VG 3 (4)	VgEx 4 (4)	EX 5 (4)	ExMt 6 (4)	NM 7	NmMt 8	NmMt+ 8.5	MT 9
288	Bruce Ellingsen RC	4	4	4	4	4	8	10	15
289	Ken Rudolph	4	4	4	4	4	8	10	15
290	Jon Matlack	4	4	4	4	5	10	12	80
291	Bill Sudakis	4	4	4	4	5	10	12	25
292	Ron Schueler	4	4	4	4	5	10	12	25
293	Dick Sharon	4	4	4	4	5	10	12	25
294	Geoff Zahn RC	4	4	4	4	5	10	12	25
295	Vada Pinson	4	4	4	4	5	10	12	50
296	Alan Foster	4	4	4	4	5	10	12	25
297	Craig Kusick RC	4	4	5	6	12	25	30	60
298	Johnny Grubb	4	4	4	4	5	10	12	25
299	Bucky Dent	4	4	4	4	5	10	12	20
300	Reggie Jackson	4	4	6	12	30	80	100	500
301	Dave Roberts	4	4	4	4	5	10	12	500
302	Rick Burleson RC	4	4	4	4	8	15	25	150
303	Grant Jackson	4	4	4	4	4	8	10	15
304	Pittsburgh Pirates CL/Murtaugh	4	4	4	4	5	10	12	30
305	Jim Colborn	4	4	4	4	5	10	12	25
306	Batting Leaders	4	4	4	4	6	12	15	30
307	Home Run Leaders	4	4	4	4	6	12	15	30
308	RBI Leaders	4	4	4	4	6	12	15	60
309	Stolen Base Leaders	4	4	4	4	6	12	15	80
310	Victory Leaders	4	4	4	4	6	12	15	50
311	ERA Leaders	4	4	4	4	6	12	15	30
312	Strikeout Leaders	4	4	4	5	12	30	40	80
313	Leading Firemen	4	4	4	4	6	12	15	50
314	Buck Martinez	4	4	4	4	5	10	12	25
315	Don Kessinger	4	4	4	4	5	10	12	100
316	Jackie Brown	4	4	4	4	5	10	12	25
317	Joe Lahoud	4	4	4	4	5	10	12	25
318	Ernie McAnally	4	4	4	4	4	8	10	15
319	Johnny Oates	4	4	4	4	5	10	12	25
320	Pete Rose	6	10	15	30	40	80	100	300
321	Rudy May	4	4	4	4	5	10	12	20
322	Ed Goodson	4	4	4	4	5	10	15	50
323	Fred Holdsworth	4	4	4	4	4	8	10	15
324	Ed Kranepool	4	4	4	4	4	8	10	15
325	Tony Oliva	4	4	4	4	6	12	15	40
326	Wayne Twitchell	4	4	4	4	5	10	12	40
327	Jerry Hairston	4	4	4	4	4	8	10	15
328	Sonny Siebert	4	4	4	4	4	8	10	15
329	Ted Kubiak	4	4	4	4	5	10	12	25
330	Mike Marshall	4	4	4	4	6	12	15	25
331	Cleveland Indians CL/Robinson	4	4	4	4	6	12	15	60
332	Fred Kendall	4	4	4	4	5	10	12	25
333	Dick Drago	4	4	4	4	5	10	12	25
334	Greg Gross RC	4	4	4	4	4	8	10	15
335	Jim Palmer	4	4	4	6	12	25	30	400
336	Rennie Stennett	4	4	4	5	10	20	25	100
337	Kevin Kobel	4	4	4	4	5	10	12	25
338	Rich Stelmaszek	4	4	4	4	5	10	12	80
339	Jim Fregosi	4	4	4	4	5	10	12	25
340	Paul Splittorff	4	4	4	4	6	12	20	150
341	Hal Breeden	4	4	4	4	4	8	10	15
342	Leroy Stanton	4	4	4	4	4	8	10	15
343	Danny Frisella	4	4	4	4	8	15	25	80
344	Ben Oglivie	4	4	4	4	6	12	15	30
345	Clay Carroll	4	4	4	4	5	10	12	25
346	Bobby Darwin	4	4	4	4	5	10	12	25
347	Mike Caldwell	4	4	4	4	5	10	12	25
348	Tony Muser	4	4	4	4	5	10	12	25
349	Ray Sadecki	4	4	4	4	5	10	12	25
350	Bobby Murcer	4	4	4	4	6	12	15	30
351	Bob Boone	4	4	4	4	5	10	12	20
352	Darold Knowles	4	4	4	4	5	10	12	25
353	Luis Melendez	4	4	4	4	5	10	12	25
354	Dick Bosman	4	4	4	4	5	10	12	25
355	Chris Cannizzaro	4	4	4	4	4	8	10	15

#	Player	VG 3 (4)	VgEx 4 (4)	EX 5 (4)	ExMt 6 (4)	NM 7	NmMt 8	NmMt+ 8.5	MT 9
356	Rico Petrocelli	4	4	4	4	6	12	15	30
357	Ken Forsch	4	4	4	4	5	10	12	25
358	Al Bumbry	4	4	4	4	6	12	15	30
359	Paul Popovich	4	4	4	4	5	10	12	25
360	George Scott	4	4	4	4	5	10	12	25
361	Los Angeles Dodgers CL/Alston	4	4	4	4	6	12	15	30
362	Steve Hargan	4	4	4	4	5	10	12	25
363	Carmen Fanzone	4	4	4	4	5	10	12	25
364	Doug Bird	4	4	4	4	5	10	12	25
365	Bob Bailey	4	4	4	4	5	10	12	25
366	Ken Sanders	4	4	4	4	5	10	12	25
367	Craig Robinson	4	4	4	4	5	10	12	25
368	Vic Albury	4	4	4	4	5	10	12	20
369	Merv Rettenmund	4	4	4	4	5	10	12	25
370	Tom Seaver	▲10	▲15	▲25	▲40	▲60	▲120	▲150	300
371	Gates Brown	4	4	4	4	6	12	15	80
372	John D'Acquisto	4	4	4	4	5	10	15	25
373	Bill Sharp	4	4	4	4	4	8	10	15
374	Eddie Watt	4	4	4	4	4	8	10	15
375	Roy White	4	4	4	4	5	10	12	25
376	Steve Yeager	4	4	4	4	6	12	15	80
377	Tom Hilgendorf	4	4	4	4	5	10	12	50
378	Derrel Thomas	4	4	4	4	5	10	15	40
379	Bernie Carbo	4	4	4	4	5	10	12	25
380	Sal Bando	4	4	4	4	6	12	20	250
381	John Curtis	4	4	4	4	5	10	12	25
382	Don Baylor	4	4	4	4	6	12	15	40
383	Jim York	4	4	4	4	5	10	12	20
384	Milwaukee Brewers CL/Crandall	4	4	4	4	5	10	12	25
385	Dock Ellis	4	4	4	4	4	8	10	15
386	Checklist: 265-396	4	4	4	4	5	10	12	4
387	Jim Spencer	4	4	4	4	5	10	12	2
388	Steve Stone	4	4	4	4	5	10	12	2
389	Tony Solaita RC	4	4	4	4	5	10	12	2
390	Ron Cey	4	4	4	4	5	10	12	3
391	Don DeMola RC	4	4	4	4	5	10	12	2
392	Bruce Bochte RC	4	4	4	4	5	10	12	12
393	Gary Gentry	4	4	4	4	4	8	10	1
394	Larvell Blanks	4	4	4	4	5	10	12	2
395	Bud Harrelson	4	4	4	4	5	10	12	4
396	Fred Norman	4	4	4	4	6	12	15	10
397	Bill Freehan	4	4	4	4	6	12	15	4
398	Elias Sosa	4	4	4	4	4	8	10	1
399	Terry Harmon	4	4	4	4	5	10	12	2
400	Dick Allen	4	4	4	4	6	12	15	6
401	Mike Wallace	4	4	4	4	5	10	12	2
402	Bob Tolan	4	4	4	4	6	12	25	50
403	Tom Buskey RC	4	4	4	4	5	10	12	2
404	Ted Sizemore	4	4	4	4	5	10	12	2
405	John Montague RC	4	4	4	4	6	12	20	25
406	Bob Gallagher	4	4	4	4	5	10	12	4
407	Herb Washington RC	4	4	4	4	8	15	30	15
408	Clyde Wright	4	4	4	4	5	10	12	2
409	Bob Robertson	4	4	4	4	5	10	15	8
410	Mike Cuellar	4	4	4	4	6	12	20	6
411	George Mitterwald	4	4	4	4	5	10	12	2
412	Bill Hands	4	4	4	4	5	10	12	2
413	Marty Pattin	4	4	4	4	5	10	12	2
414	Manny Mota	4	4	4	4	5	10	12	2
415	John Hiller	4	4	4	4	5	10	12	2
416	Larry Lintz	4	4	4	4	5	10	12	2
417	Skip Lockwood	4	4	4	4	5	10	15	12
418	Leo Foster	4	4	4	4	5	10	12	2
419	Dave Goltz	4	4	4	4	5	10	12	2
420	Larry Bowa	4	4	4	4	6	12	15	2
421	New York Mets CL/Berra	4	4	4	4	6	12	15	2
422	Brian Downing	4	4	4	4	5	10	12	
423	Clay Kirby	4	4	4	4	5	10	12	

#	Player	VG 3	VgEx 4	EX 5	ExMt 6	NM 7	NmMt 8	NmMt+ 8.5	MT 9
424	John Lowenstein	4	4	4	4	5	10	12	25
425	Tito Fuentes	4	4	4	4	5	10	12	25
426	George Medich	4	4	4	4	5	10	12	25
427	Clarence Gaston	4	4	4	4	5	10	15	40
428	Dave Hamilton	4	4	4	4	5	10	12	60
429	Jim Dwyer RC	4	4	4	4	5	10	12	25
430	Luis Tiant	4	4	4	4	6	12	15	60
431	Rod Gilbreath	4	4	4	4	5	10	12	25
432	Ken Berry	4	4	4	4	5	10	12	25
433	Larry Demery RC	4	4	4	4	5	10	15	40
434	Bob Locker	4	4	4	4	5	10	15	50
435	Dave Nelson	4	4	4	4	5	10	15	50
436	Ken Frailing	4	4	4	4	5	10	15	60
437	Al Cowens RC	4	4	4	4	6	12	15	30
438	Don Carrithers	4	4	4	4	8	15	25	80
439	Ed Brinkman	4	4	4	4	5	10	12	25
440	Andy Messersmith	4	4	4	4	6	12	15	60
441	Bobby Heise	4	4	4	4	6	12	15	50
442	Maximino Leon RC	4	4	4	4	6	12	15	80
443	Minnesota Twins CL/Quilici	4	4	4	4	5	10	12	25
444	Gene Garber	4	4	4	4	5	10	15	40
445	Felix Millan	4	4	4	4	6	12	15	100
446	Bart Johnson	4	4	4	4	6	12	15	100
447	Terry Crowley	4	4	4	4	5	10	12	50
448	Frank Duffy	4	4	4	4	4	8	10	15
449	Charlie Williams	4	4	4	4	5	10	12	25
450	Willie McCovey	4	4	4	5	20	30	40	60
451	Rick Dempsey	4	4	4	4	5	10	12	25
452	Angel Mangual	4	4	4	4	6	12	15	50
453	Claude Osteen	4	4	4	4	5	10	12	25
454	Doug Griffin	4	4	4	4	5	10	12	25
455	Don Wilson	4	4	4	4	5	10	12	25
456	Bob Coluccio	4	4	4	4	5	10	12	25
457	Mario Mendoza RC	4	4	4	4	5	10	12	25
458	Ross Grimsley	4	4	4	4	8	15	25	150
459	1974 AL Championships	4	4	4	4	8	15		
460	1974 NL Championships	4	4	4	4	6	12	20	150
461	Reggie Jackson WS1	4	4	4	4	6	12	15	40
462	W.Alston/J.Ferguson WS2	4	4	4	4	6	12	15	30
463	Rollie Fingers WS3	4	4	4	4	6	12	15	30
464	A's Batter WS4	4	4	4	4	6	12	15	50
465	Joe Rudi WS5	4	4	4	4	6	12	15	30
466	A's Do it Again WS	4	4	4	4	6	12	15	50
467	Ed Halicki RC	4	4	4	4	5	10	15	150
468	Bobby Mitchell	4	4	4	4	5	10	12	25
469	Tom Dettore RC	4	4	4	4	5	10	12	25
470	Jeff Burroughs	4	4	4	4	6	12	15	30
471	Bob Stinson	4	4	4	4	5	10	12	150
472	Bruce Dal Canton	4	4	4	4	5	10	15	80
473	Ken McMullen	4	4	4	4	6	12	15	25
474	Luke Walker	4	4	4	4	5	10	12	25
475	Darrell Evans	4	4	5	5	10	20		
476	Ed Figueroa RC	4	4	4	4	5	10	15	40
477	Tom Hutton	4	4	4	4	5	10	15	80
478	Tom Burgmeier	4	4	4	4	5	10	12	25
479	Ken Boswell	4	4	4	4	5	10	12	25
480	Carlos May	4	4	4	4	5	10	12	25
481	Will McEnaney RC	4	4	8	15	30	60	80	800
482	Tom McCraw	4	4	4	4	5	10	12	25
483	Steve Ontiveros	4	4	4	4	5	10	12	50
484	Glenn Beckert	4	4	4	4	5	10	15	50
485	Sparky Lyle	4	4	4	4	8	15	20	200
486	Ray Fosse	4	4	4	4	5	10	12	30
487	Houston Astros CL/Gomez	4	4	4	4	5	10	12	40
488	Bill Travers RC	4	4	4	4	6	12	15	30
489	Cecil Cooper	4	4	4	4	6	12	20	80
490	Reggie Smith	4	4	4	4	6	12	20	100
491	Doyle Alexander	4	4	4	4	5	10	12	20
492	Rich Hebner	4	4	4	4	5	10	12	40
493	Don Stanhouse	4	4	4	4	4	8	10	15
494	Pete LaCock RC	4	4	4	4	5	10	15	50
495	Nelson Briles	4	4	4	4	5	10	12	25
496	Pepe Frias	4	4	4	4	5	10	12	25
497	Jim Nettles	4	4	4	4	5	10	15	50
498	Al Downing	4	4	4	4	5	10	12	25
499	Marty Perez	4	4	4	6	12	25	30	120
500	Nolan Ryan	5	15	25	50	100	300	800	2,500
501	Bill Robinson	4	4	4	4	5	10	12	25
502	Pat Bourque	4	4	4	4	4	8	10	15
503	Fred Stanley	4	4	4	4	5	10	15	200
504	Buddy Bradford	4	4	4	4	6	12	20	50
505	Chris Speier	4	4	4	4	5	10	15	50
506	Leron Lee	4	4	4	4	5	10	12	25
507	Tom Carroll RC	4	4	4	4	5	10	12	25
508	Bob Hansen RC	4	4	4	4	5	10	12	50
509	Dave Hilton	4	4	4	4	5	10	12	25
510	Vida Blue	4	4	4	4	8	15	20	100
511	Texas Rangers CL/Martin	4	4	4	4	4	8	10	15
512	Larry Milbourne RC	4	4	4	4	5	10	12	80
513	Dick Pole	4	4	4	4	5	10	15	80
514	Jose Cruz	4	4	4	4	6	12	20	100
515	Manny Sanguillen	4	4	4	4	6	12	15	40
516	Don Hood	4	4	4	4	5	10	12	25
517	Checklist: 397-528	4	4	4	4	5	10	13	30
518	Leo Cardenas	4	4	4	4	5	10	12	25
519	Jim Todd RC	4	4	4	4	5	10	12	50
520	Amos Otis	4	4	4	4	6	12	20	200
521	Dennis Blair RC	4	4	4	4	5	10	15	80
522	Gary Sutherland	4	4	4	4	5	10	15	25
523	Tom Paciorek	4	4	4	4	5	10	15	50
524	John Doherty RC	4	4	4	4	5	10	12	25
525	Tom House	4	4	4	4	5	10	12	25
526	Larry Hisle	4	4	4	4	5	10	12	30
527	Mac Scarce	4	4	4	4	5	10	15	50
528	Eddie Leon	4	4	4	4	5	10	12	50
529	Gary Thomasson	4	4	4	4	5	10	15	60
530	Gaylord Perry	4	4	4	4	8	15	30	150
531	Cincinnati Reds CL/Anderson	4	4	4	6	12	20	30	80
532	Gorman Thomas	4	4	4	4	5	10	15	30
533	Rudy Meoli	4	4	4	4	5	10	12	25
534	Alex Johnson	4	4	4	4	6	12	15	60
535	Gene Tenace	4	4	4	4	6	12	15	40
536	Bob Moose	4	4	4	5	10	20	25	300
537	Tommy Harper	4	4	4	4	5	10	12	25
538	Duffy Dyer	4	4	4	4	5	10	15	60
539	Jesse Jefferson	4	4	4	4	6	12	15	30
540	Lou Brock	4	4	4	6	12	20	30	80
541	Roger Metzger	4	4	4	4	5	10	12	25
542	Pete Broberg	4	4	4	4	5	10	12	25
543	Larry Biittner	4	4	4	4	5	10	12	25
544	Steve Mingori	4	4	4	4	5	10	15	80
545	Billy Williams	4	4	4	4	8	15	20	50
546	John Knox	4	4	4	4	4	8	10	15
547	Von Joshua	4	4	5	6	12	25	30	120
548	Charlie Sands	4	4	4	4	5	10	15	80
549	Bill Butler	4	4	4	4	5	10	12	30
550	Ralph Garr	4	4	4	4	5	10	15	50
551	Larry Christenson	4	4	4	4	6	12	20	275
552	Jack Brohamer	4	4	4	4	4	8	10	15
553	John Boccabella	4	4	4	4	5	10	12	30
554	Rich Gossage	4	4	4	5	10	20	25	80
555	Al Oliver	4	4	4	4	6	12	20	150
556	Tim Johnson	4	4	4	4	5	10	15	60
557	Larry Gura	4	4	4	4	5	10	12	25
558	Dave Roberts	4	4	4	4	5	10	12	25
559	Bob Montgomery	4	4	4	4	5	10	12	25

#	Player	VG 3	VgEx 4	EX 5	ExMt 6	NM 7	NmMt 8	NmMt+ 8.5	MT 9
560	Tony Perez	4	4	4	4	6	12	15	40
561	Oakland Athletics CL/Dark	4	4	4	4	6	12	15	50
562	Gary Nolan	4	4	4	4	5	10	12	25
563	Wilbur Howard	4	4	4	4	4	8	10	15
564	Tommy Davis	4	6	12	15	30	60	90	500
565	Joe Torre	4	4	4	4	6	12	20	60
566	Ray Burris	4	4	4	4	5	10	12	25
567	Jim Sundberg RC	4	4	4	4	6	12	15	40
568	Dale Murray RC	4	4	4	4	5	10	12	50
569	Frank White	4	4	4	4	5	10	15	20
570	Jim Wynn	4	4	4	4	6	12	15	30
571	Dave Lemanczyk RC	4	4	4	4	5	10	12	25
572	Roger Nelson	4	4	4	4	5	10	12	25
573	Orlando Pena	4	4	4	4	4	8	10	15
574	Tony Taylor	4	4	4	4	5	10	60	30
575	Gene Clines	4	4	4	4	5	10	15	50
576	Phil Roof	4	4	4	4	5	10	12	25
577	John Morris	4	4	4	4	5	10	12	25
578	Dave Tomlin RC	4	4	4	4	5	10	12	25
579	Skip Pitlock	4	4	4	4	5	10	12	25
580	Frank Robinson	4	4	4	5	12	40	50	150
581	Darrel Chaney	4	4	4	4	8	15	20	40
582	Eduardo Rodriguez	4	4	4	4	5	10	12	40
583	Andy Etchebarren	4	4	4	5	10	20	40	350
584	Mike Garman	4	4	4	4	5	10	15	80
585	Chris Chambliss	4	4	4	4	8	15	20	60
586	Tim McCarver	4	4	4	4	6	12	15	60
587	Chris Ward RC	4	4	4	4	4	8	10	15
588	Rick Auerbach	4	4	4	4	5	10	15	80
589	Atlanta Braves CL/King	4	4	4	4	5	10	12	30
590	Cesar Cedeno	4	4	4	4	6	12	20	80
591	Glenn Abbott	4	4	4	4	5	10	12	25
592	Balor Moore	4	4	4	4	5	10	12	20
593	Gene Lamont	4	4	4	4	4	8	10	15
594	Jim Fuller	4	4	4	4	5	10	12	25
595	Joe Niekro	4	4	4	4	6	12	15	60
596	Ollie Brown	4	4	4	4	5	10	12	60
597	Winston Llenas	4	4	4	4	5	10	12	25
598	Bruce Kison	4	4	4	4	5	10	12	30
599	Nate Colbert	4	4	4	4	5	10	12	25
600	Rod Carew	4	4	5	10	20	40	50	300
601	Juan Beniquez	4	4	6	8	15	30	60	400
602	John Vukovich	4	4	4	4	8	15	20	50
603	Lew Krausse	4	4	4	4	5	10	12	100
604	Oscar Zamora RC	4	4	4	4	6	12	15	30
605	John Ellis	4	4	4	4	5	10	12	25
606	Bruce Miller RC	4	4	4	4	5	10	12	25
607	Jim Holt	4	4	4	4	6	12	15	40
608	Gene Michael	4	4	4	4	5	10	8	60
609	Elrod Hendricks	4	4	4	4	5	10	12	40
610	Ron Hunt	4	4	4	4	5	10	12	25
611	New York Yankees CL/Virdon	4	4	4	4	6	12	15	50
612	Terry Hughes	4	4	4	4	6	15	15	150
613	Bill Parsons	4	4	4	4	5	10	12	25
614	Rookie Pitchers	4	4	4	4	5	10	12	25
615	Rookie Pitchers	4	4	4	4	6	12	15	40
616	Jim Rice RC	12	25	30	50	100	200	250	800
617	Rookie Infielders	4	4	4	4	6	12	15	50
618	Rookie Pitchers	4	4	4	4	6	12	15	120
619	Rookie Outfielders	4	4	4	4	5	10	12	25
620	Gary Carter RC	▲15	▲25	40	▲60	100	▲250	▲300	▲1,500
621	Rookie Pitchers	4	4	4	4	6	12	15	30
622	Fred Lynn RC	4	6	10	15	25	40	50	120
623	K.Hernandez/P.Garner RC	4	4	4	8	40	50	60	150
624	Rookie Pitchers	4	4	4	4	5	10	15	60
625	Boog Powell	4	4	4	5	10	20	25	250
626	Larry Haney	4	4	4	4	5	10	12	25
627	Tom Walker	4	4	4	4	5	10	15	30

#	Player	VG 3	VgEx 4	EX 5	ExMt 6	NM 7	NmMt 8	NmMt+ 8.5	MT 9
628	Ron LeFlore RC	4	4	4	4	8	15	30	100
629	Joe Hoerner	4	4	4	4	4	8	10	15
630	Greg Luzinski	4	4	4	4	6	12	15	25
631	Lee Lacy	4	4	4	4	6	12	20	80
632	Morris Nettles RC	4	4	4	4	5	10	12	25
633	Paul Casanova	4	4	4	4	5	10	15	60
634	Cy Acosta	4	4	4	4	6	12	20	120
635	Chuck Dobson	4	4	4	4	5	10	12	25
636	Charlie Moore	4	4	4	4	5	10	12	25
637	Ted Martinez	4	4	4	4	5	10	15	250
638	Chicago Cubs CL/Marshall	4	4	8	10	20	40	50	250
639	Steve Kline	4	4	4	4	5	10	15	80
640	Harmon Killebrew	4	4	5	10	20	30	40	200
641	Jim Northrup	4	4	4	4	6	12	15	50
642	Mike Phillips	4	4	4	4	8	15	40	350
643	Brent Strom	4	4	4	4	5	10	15	100
644	Bill Fahey	4	4	4	4	4	8	10	15
645	Danny Cater	4	4	4	4	5	10	15	40
646	Checklist: 529-660	4	4	4	4	5	10	15	40
647	Claudell Washington RC	4	4	5	6	12	150	200	500
648	Dave Pagan RC	4	4	4	4	5	10	12	60
649	Jack Heidemann	4	4	4	4	8	15	20	80
650	Dave May	4	4	4	4	5	10	15	50
651	John Morlan RC	4	5	10	12	25	50	60	80
652	Lindy McDaniel	4	4	4	4	5	10	15	50
653	Lee Richard	4	4	4	4	4	8	10	15
654	Jerry Terrell	4	4	4	4	5	10	15	60
655	Rico Carty	4	4	4	4	5	10	15	30
656	Bill Plummer	4	4	4	4	6	12	15	30
657	Bob Oliver	4	4	4	4	5	10	15	60
658	Vic Harris	4	4	4	5	10	20	25	60
659	Bob Apodaca	4	4	4	4	8	15	20	250
660	Hank Aaron	4	8	25	50	80	250		

— George Brett #228 PSA 10 (Gem) (Young Collection) sold for $11,596 (SCP; 5/12)
— Gary Carter #620 PSA 10 (Gem) (Young Collection) sold for $9,144 (SCP; 5/12)
— Gary Carter #620 PSA 10 (Gem) sold for $6,933 (Mile High; 1/13)
— Gary Carter #620 PSA 10 (Gem) sold for $4,060 (eBay; 09/12)
— Gary Carter #620 PSA 10 (Gem) sold for $3,736 (eBay; 11/12)
— Larry Lintz #416 PSA 10 (Gem) sold for $2,958 (eBay; 08/12)
— Jim Rice #616 PSA 10 (Gem) (Young Collection) sold for $5,676 (SCP; 5/12)
— Brooks Robinson #50 PSA 10 (Gem) sold for $1,133 (eBay; 02/12)
— Frank Robinson #580 PSA 10 (Gem) sold for $1,682 (eBay; 02/12)
— Pete Rose #320 PSA 10 (Gem) sold for $2,328 (eBay; 08/12)
— Robin Yount #223 PSA 10 (Gem) (Young Collection) sold for $22,602 (SCP; 5/12)
— Robin Yount #223 PSA 10 (Gem) sold for $19,799 (Mile High; 4/14)

1975 Topps Mini

#	Player	GD 2	VG 3	VgEx 4	EX 5	ExMt 6	NM 7	NmMt 8	MT 9
1	Hank Aaron HL	4	4	8	12	25	50	200	600
2	Lou Brock HL	4	4	4	4	5	10	25	150
3	Bob Gibson HL	4	4	4	4	8	15	30	200
4	Al Kaline HL	4	4	5	8	10	20	50	100
5	Nolan Ryan HL	6	8	10	12	15	25	60	500
6	Mike Marshall HL	4	4	4	4	4	6	12	120
7	Ryan/Busby/Bosman HL	4	4	4	4	6	20	25	250
8	Rogelio Moret	4	4	4	4	5	10		
9	Frank Tepedino	4	4	4	4	5	10		30
10	Willie Davis	4	4	4	4	5	10		25
11	Bill Melton	4	4	4	4	5	10		25
12	David Clyde	4	4	4	4	5	10		
13	Gene Locklear	4	4	4	4	5	10		25
14	Milt Wilcox	4	4	4	4	5	10		60
15	Jose Cardenal	4	4	4	4	5	10		50
16	Frank Tanana	4	4	4	6	8	15	80	
17	Dave Concepcion	4	4	4	5	6	12	25	
18	Detroit Tigers CL/Houk	4	4	4	4	8	15		55
19	Jerry Koosman	4	4	4	4	6	12		30

#	Name	GD 2	VG 3	VgEx 4	EX 5	ExMt 6	NM 7	NmMt 8	MT 9
20	Thurman Munson	5	6	8	10	12	25	80	250
21	Rollie Fingers	4	4	4	4	4	8	25	150
22	Dave Cash	4	4	4	4	4	5	10	25
23	Bill Russell	4	4	4	4	4	6	12	60
24	Al Fitzmorris	4	4	4	4	4	5	10	25
25	Lee May	4	4	4	4	4	5	10	100
26	Dave McNally	4	4	4	4	4	6	12	40
27	Ken Reitz	4	4	4	4	4	5	10	150
28	Tom Murphy	4	4	4	4	4	6	12	50
29	Dave Parker	4	4	4	4	4	8	15	60
30	Bert Blyleven	4	4	8	15	20	40	80	
31	Dave Rader	4	4	4	4	4	8	15	
32	Reggie Cleveland	4	4	4	4	4	5	10	30
33	Dusty Baker	4	4	4	4	4	6	12	60
34	Steve Renko	4	4	4	4	4	5	10	25
35	Ron Santo	4	4	4	4	4	6	12	25
36	Joe Lovitto	4	4	4	4	4	5	10	25
37	Dave Freisleben	4	4	4	4	4	5	10	50
38	Buddy Bell	4	4	4	4	4	6	12	50
39	Andre Thornton	4	4	4	4	4	8	15	60
40	Bill Singer	4	4	4	4	4	5	10	25
41	Cesar Geronimo	4	4	4	4	4	6	12	
42	Joe Coleman	4	4	4	4	4	5	10	25
43	Cleon Jones	4	4	4	4	4	6	12	30
44	Pat Dobson	4	4	4	4	4	8	15	
45	Joe Rudi	4	4	4	4	4	6	12	30
46	Philadelphia Phillies CL/Ozark	4	4	4	4	4	6	12	30
47	Tommy John	4	4	4	4	4	8	15	
48	Freddie Patek	4	4	4	4	4	8	15	
49	Larry Dierker	4	4	4	4	4	5	10	25
50	Brooks Robinson	4	4	5	6	10	25	80	800
51	Bob Forsch	4	4	4	4	4	5	10	25
52	Darrell Porter	4	4	4	4	4	5	10	25
53	Dave Giusti	4	4	4	5	6	12	60	
54	Eric Soderholm	4	4	4	4	5	6	12	30
55	Bobby Bonds	4	4	4	6	8	15	30	
56	Rick Wise	4	4	4	4	4	8	15	
57	Dave Johnson	4	4	4	4	4	5	10	40
58	Chuck Taylor	4	4	4	6	8	15	30	
59	Ken Henderson	4	4	4	4	4	5	10	25
60	Fergie Jenkins	4	4	4	4	4	12	20	100
61	Dave Winfield	4	▲6	▲10	▲15	▲25	▲40	▲80	300
62	Fritz Peterson	4	4	4	4	4	5	10	100
63	Steve Swisher	4	4	4	4	4	8	15	
64	Dave Chalk	4	4	4	4	4	8	15	135
65	Don Gullett	4	4	4	4	4	6	12	80
66	Willie Horton	4	4	4	4	4	6	12	80
67	Tug McGraw	4	4	4	4	4	6	12	30
68	Ron Blomberg	4	4	4	4	4	5	10	25
69	John Odom	4	4	4	4	4	6	12	40
70	Mike Schmidt	4	4	6	12	15	25	60	▲1,200
71	Charlie Hough	4	4	4	4	4	6	12	30
72	Kansas City Royals CL/McKeon	4	4	4	4	4	6	12	40
73	J.R. Richard	4	4	4	4	4	6	12	30
74	Mark Belanger	4	4	4	5	6	8	15	80
75	Ted Simmons	4	4	4	8	10	12	25	120
76	Ed Sprague	4	4	4	4	4	8	15	
77	Richie Zisk	4	4	4	4	4	8	15	
78	Ray Corbin	4	4	4	4	4	5	10	25
79	Gary Matthews	4	4	4	4	4	6	12	30
80	Carlton Fisk	4	4	4	5	10	20	50	120
81	Ron Reed	4	4	4	4	4	8	15	
82	Pat Kelly	4	4	4	4	4	5	10	100
83	Jim Merritt	4	4	4	4	4	5	10	25
84	Enzo Hernandez	4	4	4	4	4	5	10	50
85	Bill Bonham	4	4	4	4	4	5	10	50
86	Joe Lis	4	4	4	5	6	12	25	
87	George Foster	4	4	4	4	4	6	12	50

#	Name	GD 2	VG 3	VgEx 4	EX 5	ExMt 6	NM 7	NmMt 8	MT 9
88	Tom Egan	4	4	4	4	4	5	10	25
89	Jim Ray	4	4	4	4	4	5	10	25
90	Rusty Staub	4	4	4	4	5	10	20	200
91	Dick Green	4	4	4	6	8	15	30	
92	Cecil Upshaw	4	4	4	4	4	6	12	30
93	Davey Lopes	4	4	4	4	4	6	12	30
94	Jim Lonborg	4	4	4	4	4	8	15	60
95	John Mayberry	4	4	4	4	4	5	10	40
96	Mike Cosgrove	4	4	4	6	8	15	30	
97	Earl Williams	4	4	4	4	4	5	10	60
98	Rich Folkers	4	4	4	4	4	5	10	25
99	Mike Hegan	4	5	10	20	25	50	100	
100	Willie Stargell	4	4	4	4	5	20	25	80
101	Montreal Expos CL/Mauch	4	4	4	5	6	12	25	
102	Joe Decker	4	4	4	4	4	5	10	25
103	Rick Miller	4	4	4	4	4	8	15	
104	Bill Madlock	4	4	4	5	6	12	25	200
105	Buzz Capra	4	4	4	4	4	5	10	30
106	Mike Hargrove	4	4	4	4	4	6	12	40
107	Jim Barr	4	4	4	4	4	5	10	25
108	Tom Hall	4	4	4	4	4	5	10	25
109	George Hendrick	4	4	4	4	4	8	15	
110	Wilbur Wood	4	4	4	4	4	5	10	25
111	Wayne Garrett	4	4	4	4	4	8	15	
112	Larry Hardy	4	4	4	4	4	5	10	25
113	Elliott Maddox	4	4	4	4	4	5	10	25
114	Dick Lange	4	4	4	4	4	5	10	25
115	Joe Ferguson	4	4	4	4	4	5	10	25
116	Lerrin LaGrow	4	4	4	4	4	5	10	100
117	Baltimore Orioles CL/Weaver	4	4	4	4	4	6	12	50
118	Mike Anderson	4	4	4	4	4	5	10	25
119	Tommy Helms	4	4	4	4	4	5	10	25
120	Steve Busby	4	4	4	4	4	6	12	100
121	Bill North	4	4	4	4	4	5	10	30
122	Al Hrabosky	4	4	4	4	4	8	15	
123	Johnny Briggs	4	4	4	4	4	5	10	25
124	Jerry Reuss	4	4	4	4	4	5	10	25
125	Ken Singleton	4	4	4	5	6	12	50	
126	Checklist 1-132	4	4	4	4	4	6	12	50
127	Glenn Borgmann	4	4	4	4	5	10	80	
128	Bill Lee	4	4	4	4	4	6	12	40
129	Rick Monday	4	4	4	4	4	6	12	50
130	Phil Niekro	4	4	4	4	4	6	12	100
131	Toby Harrah	4	4	4	6	8	15	30	
132	Randy Moffitt	4	4	4	4	4	5	10	25
133	Dan Driessen	4	4	4	5	6	12	80	
134	Ron Hodges	4	4	4	4	4	5	10	25
135	Charlie Spikes	4	4	4	4	4	5	10	50
136	Jim Mason	4	4	4	5	6	12	25	
137	Terry Forster	4	4	4	4	4	6	12	40
138	Del Unser	4	4	4	4	4	5	10	25
139	Horacio Pina	4	4	4	5	6	12	25	
140	Steve Garvey	4	4	4	8	10	20	50	
141	Mickey Stanley	4	4	4	4	4	8	15	
142	Bob Reynolds	4	4	4	4	4	5	10	30
143	Cliff Johnson	4	4	4	4	5	10	50	
144	Jim Wohlford	4	4	4	4	4	5	10	25
145	Ken Holtzman	4	4	4	4	4	5	10	30
146	San Diego Padres CL/McNamara	4	4	4	4	4	6	12	40
147	Pedro Garcia	4	4	4	4	4	5	10	25
148	Jim Rooker	4	4	4	4	4	5	10	25
149	Tim Foli	4	4	4	4	4	8	15	
150	Bob Gibson	4	5	8	10	20	25	60	300
151	Steve Brye	4	4	4	4	4	5	10	25
152	Mario Guerrero	4	4	4	4	4	5	10	80
153	Rick Reuschel	4	4	4	4	4	5	10	30
154	Mike Lum	4	4	4	4	4	6	12	30
155	Jim Bibby	4	4	4	4	4	5	10	80

#	Player	GD 2	VG 3	VgEx 4	EX 5	ExMt 6	NM 7	NmMt 8	MT 9
156	Dave Kingman	4	4	4	4	4	6	12	60
157	Pedro Borbon	4	4	4	4	4	8	30	
158	Jerry Grote	4	4	4	4	4	8	15	175
159	Steve Arlin	4	4	4	4	4	5	10	25
160	Graig Nettles	4	4	4	4	4	6	12	120
161	Stan Bahnsen	4	4	4	6	8	15	30	
162	Willie Montanez	4	4	4	4	4	8	15	
163	Jim Brewer	4	4	4	4	4	8	15	
164	Mickey Rivers	4	4	4	4	4	8	15	
165	Doug Rader	4	4	4	4	4	5	10	25
166	Woodie Fryman	4	4	4	4	4	5	10	25
167	Rich Coggins	4	4	4	4	4	5	10	25
168	Bill Greif	4	4	5	10	12	25	60	
169	Cookie Rojas	4	4	4	4	4	8	15	50
170	Bert Campaneris	4	4	4	5	6	12	25	
171	Ed Kirkpatrick	4	4	4	4	4	5	10	30
172	Boston Red Sox CL/Johnson	4	4	4	4	4	6	12	50
173	Steve Rogers	4	4	4	5	6	12	25	
174	Bake McBride	4	4	4	4	4	6	12	30
175	Don Money	4	4	4	4	4	5	10	40
176	Burt Hooton	4	4	4	4	4	5	10	60
177	Vic Correll	4	4	4	4	4	5	10	80
178	Cesar Tovar	4	4	4	4	4	5	10	100
179	Tom Bradley	4	4	4	4	4	6	12	25
180	Joe Morgan	4	4	6	10	15	25	50	120
181	Fred Beene	4	4	4	4	4	5	10	25
182	Don Hahn	4	4	4	4	4	5	10	50
183	Mel Stottlemyre	4	4	4	4	4	8	15	80
184	Jorge Orta	4	4	4	4	4	5	10	25
185	Steve Carlton	4	4	4	5	6	15	30	80
186	Willie Crawford	4	4	4	4	4	5	10	25
187	Denny Doyle	4	4	4	5	6	12	40	
188	Tom Griffin	4	4	4	4	4	5	10	25
189	Y.Berra/Campanella MVP	4	4	4	4	4	6	15	30
190	B.Shantz/H.Sauer MVP	4	4	4	4	4	6	12	30
191	Al Rosen/Campanella MVP	4	4	4	4	4	6	12	30
192	Y.Berra/W.Mays MVP	4	4	4	4	4	8	25	80
193	Y.Berra/Campanella MVP	4	4	4	4	4	5	10	25
194	M.Mantle/D.Newcombe MVP	4	4	4	5	5	20	30	100
195	M.Mantle/H.Aaron MVP	6	8	10	12	15	20	40	250
196	J.Jensen/E.Banks MVP	4	4	4	4	4	6	12	60
197	N.Fox/E.Banks MVP	4	4	4	4	4	5	10	50
198	R.Maris/D.Groat MVP	4	4	4	4	4	8	15	40
199	R.Maris/F.Robinson MVP	4	4	4	4	4	8	10	25
200	M.Mantle/M.Wills MVP	4	4	4	5	6	12	30	80
201	E.Howard/S.Koufax MVP	4	4	4	4	4	6	12	40
202	B.Robinson/K.Boyer MVP	4	4	4	4	4	6	12	80
203	Z.Versalles/W.Mays MVP	4	4	4	4	4	8	15	25
204	F.Robinson/B.Clemente MVP	4	4	4	4	5	10	20	100
205	C.Yastrzemski/O.Cepeda MVP	4	4	4	4	4	8	15	50
206	D.McLain/B.Gibson MVP	4	4	4	4	4	6	12	40
207	H.Killebrew/W.McCovey MVP	4	4	4	4	4	6	12	30
208	B.Powell/J.Bench MVP	4	4	4	4	4	6	12	60
209	V.Blue/J.Torre MVP	4	4	4	4	4	6	12	60
210	R.Allen/J.Bench MVP	4	4	4	4	5	10	20	50
211	R.Jackson/P.Rose MVP	4	4	4	4	5	10	20	150
212	J.Burroughs/S.Garvey MVP	4	4	4	4	4	6	12	50
213	Oscar Gamble	4	4	4	4	4		8	15
214	Harry Parker	4	4	4	4	4	5	10	25
215	Bobby Valentine	4	4	4	4	4	6	12	40
216	San Francisco Giants CL/Westrum	4	4	4	4	4	6	12	40
217	Lou Piniella	4	4	4	4	4	6	12	40
218	Jerry Johnson	4	4	4	4	4	5	10	25
219	Ed Herrmann	4	4	4	4	4	8	15	
220	Don Sutton	4	4	4	5	6	12	25	80
221	Aurelio Rodriguez	4	4	4	4	4	5	10	25
222	Dan Spillner	4	4	4	4	5	10	20	
223	Robin Yount	20	30	50	80	100	150	400	1,500
224	Ramon Hernandez	4	4	4	4	4	5	10	25
225	Bob Grich	4	4	4	4	4	8	15	
226	Bill Campbell	4	4	4	4	4	8	15	
227	Bob Watson	4	4	4	4	4	8	15	150
228	George Brett	▲40	▲60	100	150	▲250	▲400	▲1,000	4,000
229	Barry Foote	4	4	4	4	4	8	15	
230	Jim Hunter	4	4	4	4	4	8	25	80
231	Mike Tyson	4	4	4	4	4	5	10	25
232	Diego Segui	4	4	4	5	6	12	25	100
233	Billy Grabarkewitz	4	4	4	6	8	15	30	
234	Tom Grieve	4	4	4	4	4	5	10	25
235	Jack Billingham	4	4	4	4	4	6	12	30
236	California Angels CL/Williams	4	4	4	4	4	6	12	60
237	Carl Morton	4	4	4	4	4	8	15	
238	Dave Duncan	4	4	4	4	4	5	10	80
239	George Stone	4	4	4	4	4	5	10	25
240	Garry Maddox	4	4	4	4	4	6	12	40
241	Dick Tidrow	4	4	4	4	4	5	10	50
242	Jay Johnstone	4	4	4	4	4	5	10	30
243	Jim Kaat	4	4	6	12	15	30	60	
244	Bill Buckner	4	4	4	4	4	8	15	
245	Mickey Lolich	4	4	4	4	5	10	20	300
246	St. Louis Cardinals CL/Schoen	4	4	5	10	20	40	80	150
247	Enos Cabell	4	4	4	4	4	5	10	25
248	Randy Jones	4	4	4	4	4	8	15	
249	Danny Thompson	4	4	4	4	4	8	15	
250	Ken Brett	4	4	4	4	4	8	15	60
251	Fran Healy	4	4	4	4	4	8	15	
252	Fred Scherman	4	4	4	4	4	5	10	25
253	Jesus Alou	4	8	15	30	40	80	150	
254	Mike Torrez	4	4	4	4	4	5	10	30
255	Dwight Evans	4	4	4	4	4	6	12	50
256	Billy Champion	4	4	4	4	4	8	15	
257	Checklist: 133-264	4	4	4	4	4	6	12	40
258	Dave LaRoche	4	4	4	4	4	8	15	100
259	Len Randle	4	4	4	4	4	8	15	
260	Johnny Bench	4	4	5	10	12	30	60	300
261	Andy Hassler	4	4	4	4	4	5	10	25
262	Rowland Office	4	4	4	4	4	8	15	100
263	Jim Perry	4	4	4	4	4	5	10	25
264	John Milner	4	4	4	4	4	8	15	
265	Ron Bryant	4	4	4	4	4	5	10	25
266	Sandy Alomar	4	4	4	4	4	6	12	40
267	Dick Ruthven	4	4	4	4	4	5	10	25
268	Hal McRae	4	4	4	4	4	8	15	120
269	Doug Rau	4	4	4	4	4	5	10	25
270	Ron Fairly	4	4	4	4	4	5	10	25
271	Gerry Moses	4	4	4	4	4	8	15	
272	Lynn McGlothen	4	4	4	4	4	5	10	25
273	Steve Braun	4	4	4	4	4	5	10	25
274	Vicente Romo	4	4	4	4	4	5	10	20
275	Paul Blair	4	4	4	4	4	6	12	50
276	Chicago White Sox CL/Tanner	4	4	4	4	4	6	12	40
277	Frank Taveras	4	4	4	4	4	8	15	
278	Paul Lindblad	4	4	4	4	4	8	15	
279	Milt May	4	4	4	4	4	5	10	25
280	Carl Yastrzemski	8	10	15	20	25	30	50	250
281	Jim Slaton	4	4	4	4	4	5	10	25
282	Jerry Morales	4	4	4	4	4	5	10	25
283	Steve Foucault	4	4	4	4	4	5	10	25
284	Ken Griffey Sr.	4	4	4	4	4	8	25	80
285	Ellie Rodriguez	4	4	4	4	4	5	10	25
286	Mike Jorgensen	4	4	4	4	4	5	10	25
287	Roric Harrison	4	4	4	4	4	8	15	50
288	Bruce Ellingsen	4	4	4	4	4	5	10	25
289	Ken Rudolph	4	4	4	4	4	8	15	50
290	Jon Matlack	4	4	4	4	4	8	15	
291	Bill Sudakis	4	4	4	4	4	5	10	25

#	Player	GD 2	VG 3	VgEx 4	EX 5	ExMt 6	NM 7	NmMt 8	MT 9
292	Ron Schueler	4	4	4	4	4	5	10	25
293	Dick Sharon	4	4	4	4	4	5	10	25
294	Geoff Zahn	4	4	4	4	4	5	10	25
295	Vada Pinson	4	4	4	4	4	6	12	120
296	Alan Foster	4	4	4	4	4	8	15	
297	Craig Kusick	4	4	4	4	4		50	
298	Johnny Grubb	4	4	4	4	4	5	10	25
299	Bucky Dent	4	4	4	4	4	6	12	40
300	Reggie Jackson	4	4	4	6	12	25	50	400
301	Dave Roberts	4	4	6	12	15	30	60	
302	Rick Burleson	6	12	15	30	40	80	150	
303	Grant Jackson	4	4	4	4	4	8	15	100
304	Pittsburgh Pirates CL/Murtaugh	4	4	4	4	4	6	12	80
305	Jim Colborn	4	4	4	4	4	5	10	25
306	Batting Leaders	4	4	4	4	4	6	12	30
307	Home Run Leaders	4	4	4	4	4	6	12	60
308	RBI Leaders	4	4	4	4	4	6	12	30
309	Stolen Base Leaders	4	4	4	4	4	6	12	40
310	Victory Leaders	4	4	4	4	4	8	15	
311	ERA Leaders	4	4	4	4	4	6	12	30
312	Strikeout Leaders	4	4	4	6	8	15	25	100
313	Leading Firemen	4	4	4	4	4	6	12	40
314	Buck Martinez	4	4	4	4	4	8	15	
315	Don Kessinger	4	4	5	10	12	25	50	
316	Jackie Brown	4	4	4	4	4	5	10	25
317	Joe Lahoud	4	4	4	4	4	5	10	80
318	Ernie McAnally	4	4	4	4	4	5	10	25
319	Johnny Oates	4	4	4	4	4	8	15	
320	Pete Rose	▼5	▼8	▼12	20	▲30	▲50	80	500
321	Rudy May	4	4	4	4	4	5	10	25
322	Ed Goodson	4	4	4	4	4	8	15	
323	Fred Holdsworth	4	4	4	4	4	5	10	50
324	Ed Kranepool	4	4	4	4	4	6	12	30
325	Tony Oliva	4	4	4	4	4	6	12	50
326	Wayne Twitchell	4	4	4	4	4	8	60	
327	Jerry Hairston	4	4	4	4	4	5	10	20
328	Sonny Siebert	4	4	4	4	4	5	10	25
329	Ted Kubiak	4	4	4	4	4	5	10	25
330	Mike Marshall	4	4	4	4	4	6	12	40
331	Cleveland Indians CL/Robinson	4	4	4	4	4	8	15	
332	Fred Kendall	4	4	4	4	4	5	10	25
333	Dick Drago	4	4	4	4	4	5	10	30
334	Greg Gross	4	4	4	4	4	5	10	25
335	Jim Palmer	4	4	4	4	8	25	40	300
336	Rennie Stennett	4	4	4	8	10	20	40	
337	Kevin Kobel	4	4	4	4	4	8	15	
338	Rich Stelmaszek	4	4	4	4	4	8	15	
339	Jim Fregosi	4	4	4	5	6	12	50	
340	Paul Splittorff	4	4	4	4	4	8	15	
341	Hal Breeden	4	4	4	4	4	5	10	25
342	Leroy Stanton	4	4	4	4	4	5	10	25
343	Danny Frisella	4	4	4	4	4	8	15	
344	Ben Oglivie	4	4	4	5	6	12	25	
345	Clay Carroll	4	4	4	4	4	6	12	80
346	Bobby Darwin	4	4	4	4	4	8	15	
347	Mike Caldwell	4	4	4	4	4	5	10	25
348	Tony Muser	4	4	4	4	4	5	10	25
349	Ray Sadecki	4	4	4	4	4	5	10	25
350	Bobby Murcer	4	4	4	4	4	8	15	80
351	Bob Boone	4	4	4	4	4	6	12	30
352	Darold Knowles	4	4	4	4	4	5	10	50
353	Luis Melendez	4	4	4	4	4	5	10	25
354	Dick Bosman	4	4	4	4	4	5	10	50
355	Chris Cannizzaro	4	4	4	4	4	5	10	25
356	Rico Petrocelli	4	4	4	4	4	6	12	40
357	Ken Forsch	4	4	4	4	4	5	10	25
358	Al Bumbry	4	4	4	4	4	5	10	30
359	Paul Popovich	4	4	4	4	4	5	10	25
360	George Scott	4	4	4	4	4	5	10	30
361	Los Angeles Dodgers CL/Alston	4	4	4	4	4	6	12	30
362	Steve Hargan	4	4	4	4	4	8	15	
363	Carmen Fanzone	4	4	4	4	4	5	10	25
364	Doug Bird	4	4	4	4	4	8	15	
365	Bob Bailey	4	4	4	4	4	5	10	25
366	Ken Sanders	4	4	4	4	4	8	15	
367	Craig Robinson	4	4	4	4	4	5	10	25
368	Vic Albury	4	4	4	4	4	5	10	25
369	Merv Rettenmund	4	4	4	4	4	8	15	
370	Tom Seaver	▲6	▲10	▲15	▲25	▲40	▲60	▲100	▲300
371	Gates Brown	4	4	5	10	12	25	60	
372	John D'Acquisto	4	4	4	4	4	8	15	
373	Bill Sharp	4	4	4	4	4	5	10	25
374	Eddie Watt	4	4	4	4	4	5	10	25
375	Roy White	4	4	4	4	4	8	15	
376	Steve Yeager	4	4	4	4	4	8	15	
377	Tom Hilgendorf	4	4	4	4	4	5	10	25
378	Derrel Thomas	4	4	4	4	4	5	10	60
379	Bernie Carbo	4	4	4	4	4	5	10	60
380	Sal Bando	4	4	4	8	10	20	50	
381	John Curtis	4	4	4	4	4	5	10	25
382	Don Baylor	4	4	4	4	4	6	12	40
383	Jim York	4	4	4	4	4	5	10	25
384	Milwaukee Brewers CL/Crandall	4	4	4	4	4	6	12	60
385	Dock Ellis	4	4	4	4	4	5	10	25
386	Checklist: 265-396	4	4	4	4	4	6	12	30
387	Jim Spencer	4	4	4	4	4	5	10	25
388	Steve Stone	4	4	4	4	4	5	10	25
389	Tony Solaita	4	4	4	4	4	5	10	25
390	Ron Cey	4	4	4	5	6	12	25	
391	Don DeMola	4	4	4	4	4	5	10	25
392	Bruce Bochte	4	4	4	6	8	15	30	
393	Gary Gentry	4	4	4	4	4	5	10	25
394	Larvell Blanks	4	4	4	4	4	5	10	25
395	Bud Harrelson	4	4	4	4	4	5	10	30
396	Fred Norman	4	4	4	4	4	5	10	25
397	Bill Freehan	4	4	4	4	4	6	12	40
398	Elias Sosa	4	4	4	4	4	5	10	25
399	Terry Harmon	4	4	4	4	4	5	10	25
400	Dick Allen	4	4	4	4	4	8	15	
401	Mike Wallace	4	4	4	4	4	8	15	
402	Bob Tolan	4	4	4	5	6	12	25	
403	Tom Buskey	4	4	4	4	4	5	10	25
404	Ted Sizemore	4	4	4	4	4	5	10	25
405	John Montague	4	4	4	8	10	20	40	
406	Bob Gallagher	4	4	4	4	4	5	10	25
407	Herb Washington	4	4	4	4	4	6	12	120
408	Clyde Wright	4	4	4	4	4	5	10	25
409	Bob Robertson	4	4	4	4	4	8	15	
410	Mike Cuellar	4	4	4	4	4	8	15	
411	George Mitterwald	4	4	4	4	4	5	10	25
412	Bill Hands	4	4	4	4	4	5	10	25
413	Marty Pattin	4	4	4	4	4	5	10	25
414	Manny Mota	4	4	4	4	4	5	10	50
415	John Hiller	4	4	4	4	4	5	10	30
416	Larry Lintz	4	4	4	4	4	5	10	25
417	Skip Lockwood	4	4	4	8	10	20	40	
418	Leo Foster	4	4	4	4	4	5	10	25
419	Dave Goltz	4	4	4	4	4	5	10	25
420	Larry Bowa	4	4	4	4	4	6	12	30
421	New York Mets CL/Berra	4	4	4	4	4	8	15	
422	Brian Downing	4	4	4	4	4	6	12	40
423	Clay Kirby	4	4	4	4	4	5	10	30
424	John Lowenstein	4	4	4	4	4	5	10	25
425	Tito Fuentes	4	4	4	4	4	4	8	15
426	George Medich	4	4	4	4	4	5	10	50
427	Clarence Gaston	4	4	4	4	4	5	10	30

#	Player	GD 2	VG 3	VgEx 4	EX 5	ExMt 6	NM 7	NmMt 8	MT 9
428	Dave Hamilton	4	4	4	4	4	5	10	25
429	Jim Dwyer	4	4	4	4	4	5	10	25
430	Luis Tiant	4	4	4	4	4	6	12	100
431	Rod Gilbreath	4	4	4	4	4	8	15	
432	Ken Berry	4	4	4	4	4	5	10	25
433	Larry Demery	4	4	4	4	4	8	15	
434	Bob Locker	4	4	4	4	4	5	10	25
435	Dave Nelson	4	4	4	4	4	5	10	150
436	Ken Frailing	4	4	4	4	4	5	10	40
437	Al Cowens	4	4	4	4	4	5	10	25
438	Don Carrithers	4	4	4	4	4	5	10	60
439	Ed Brinkman	4	4	4	4	4	5	10	25
440	Andy Messersmith	4	4	4	4	4	5	10	60
441	Bobby Heise	4	4	4	4	4	5	10	80
442	Maximino Leon	4	4	4	4	5	10	20	
443	Minnesota Twins CL/Quilici	4	4	4	4	4	6	12	40
444	Gene Garber	4	4	4	4	5	10	20	
445	Felix Millan	4	4	4	4	4	8	15	
446	Bart Johnson	4	4	4	4	4	8	15	
447	Terry Crowley	4	4	4	4	4	5	10	25
448	Frank Duffy	4	4	4	4	4	5	10	25
449	Charlie Williams	4	4	4	4	4	5	10	50
450	Willie McCovey	▼4	▼5	8	▲12	▲20	▲30	▲50	▲100
451	Rick Dempsey	4	4	4	4	4	5	10	25
452	Angel Mangual	4	4	4	4	4	5	10	25
453	Claude Osteen	4	4	4	4	4	8	15	
454	Doug Griffin	4	4	4	4	4	5	10	25
455	Don Wilson	4	4	4	4	4	5	10	25
456	Bob Coluccio	4	4	4	4	4	5	10	25
457	Mario Mendoza	4	4	4	4	4	5	10	25
458	Ross Grimsley	4	5	10	20	25	50	100	
459	1974 AL Championships	4	4	5	10	12	25	50	
460	1974 NL Championships	4	4	4	8	10	20	40	
461	Reggie Jackson WS1	4	4	4	4	4	8	15	50
462	W.Alston/J.Ferguson WS2	4	4	4	4	4	6	12	40
463	Rollie Fingers WS3	4	4	4	5	6	12	25	
464	A's Batter WS4	4	4	4	4	4	8	15	
465	Joe Rudi WS5	4	4	4	4	5	10	20	
466	A's Do it Again WS	4	4	4	4	4	6	12	40
467	Ed Halicki	4	4	4	4	4	5	10	25
468	Bobby Mitchell	4	4	4	4	4	8	15	
469	Tom Dettore	4	4	4	4	4	5	10	25
470	Jeff Burroughs	4	4	4	4	4	5	10	50
471	Bob Stinson	4	4	4	4	4	5	10	150
472	Bruce Dal Canton	4	4	4	4	4	5	10	40
473	Ken McMullen	4	4	4	4	4	5	10	25
474	Luke Walker	4	4	4	4	4	5	10	25
475	Darrell Evans	4	4	4	4	4	8	15	
476	Ed Figueroa	4	4	4	4	4	8	15	
477	Tom Hutton	4	4	4	4	4	8	15	
478	Tom Burgmeier	4	4	4	4	4	5	10	40
479	Ken Boswell	4	4	4	4	4	5	10	25
480	Carlos May	4	4	4	4	4	5	10	120
481	Will McEnaney	4	4	4	4	5	10	20	
482	Tom McCraw	4	4	4	4	4	8	15	
483	Steve Ontiveros	4	4	4	4	5	6	12	25
484	Glenn Beckert	4	4	4	4	4	5	10	25
485	Sparky Lyle	4	4	4	4	4	6	12	40
486	Ray Fosse	4	4	4	4	4	5	10	25
487	Houston Astros CL/Gomez	4	4	4	4	4	8	15	40
488	Bill Travers	4	4	4	4	4	5	10	40
489	Cecil Cooper	4	4	4	4	4	8	15	
490	Reggie Smith	4	4	4	4	4	8	15	
491	Doyle Alexander	4	4	4	4	4	5	10	25
492	Rich Hebner	4	4	4	4	4	8	15	50
493	Don Stanhouse	4	4	4	4	4	5	10	30
494	Pete LaCock	4	4	4	4	4	5	10	25
495	Nelson Briles	4	4	4	4	4	5	10	30
496	Pepe Frias	4	4	4	4	4	5	10	25
497	Jim Nettles	4	4	4	4	4	5	10	25
498	Al Downing	4	4	4	4	4	5	10	25
499	Marty Perez	4	4	4	4	4	8	15	
500	Nolan Ryan	4	6	12	25	40	60	250	1,000
501	Bill Robinson	4	4	4	4	4	5	10	60
502	Pat Bourque	4	4	4	4	4	5	10	25
503	Fred Stanley	4	5	10	20	25	50	100	
504	Buddy Bradford	4	4	4	4	4	8	15	
505	Chris Speier	4	4	4	4	4	8	15	
506	Leron Lee	4	4	4	4	4	5	10	25
507	Tom Carroll	4	4	4	4	4	5	10	25
508	Bob Hansen	4	4	4	4	4	5	10	80
509	Dave Hilton	4	4	4	4	4	5	10	25
510	Vida Blue	4	4	4	4	4	8	15	60
511	Texas Rangers CL/Martin	4	4	4	4	4	6	12	30
512	Larry Milbourne	4	4	4	8	10	20	100	
513	Dick Pole	4	4	4	4	4	8	15	
514	Jose Cruz	4	4	4	6	8	15	30	
515	Manny Sanguillen	4	4	4	4	4	8	15	
516	Don Hood	4	4	4	4	4	5	10	25
517	Checklist: 397-528	4	4	4	4	4	8	15	
518	Leo Cardenas	4	4	4	4	4	5	10	25
519	Jim Todd	4	4	4	4	4	8	15	100
520	Amos Otis	4	4	4	4	4	5	10	50
521	Dennis Blair	4	4	4	4	4	5	10	30
522	Gary Sutherland	4	4	4	4	4	5	10	25
523	Tom Paciorek	4	4	4	4	4	5	10	80
524	John Doherty	4	4	4	4	4	5	10	25
525	Tom House	4	4	4	4	4	8	15	
526	Larry Hisle	4	4	4	4	4	5	10	25
527	Mac Scarce	4	4	4	4	4	8	15	
528	Eddie Leon	4	4	4	4	4	5	10	25
529	Gary Thomasson	4	4	4	4	4	5	10	25
530	Gaylord Perry	4	4	4	4	5	10	20	150
531	Cincinnati Reds CL/Anderson	4	4	4	4	6	12	25	50
532	Gorman Thomas	4	4	4	4	4	6	12	40
533	Rudy Meoli	4	4	4	4	4	5	10	25
534	Alex Johnson	4	4	4	4	4	6	12	40
535	Gene Tenace	4	4	4	4	4	8	15	
536	Bob Moose	4	4	4	4	4	5	10	40
537	Tommy Harper	4	4	4	4	4	8	15	
538	Duffy Dyer	4	4	4	4	4	5	10	40
539	Jesse Jefferson	4	4	4	4	4	8	15	
540	Lou Brock	4	4	4	4	10	15	30	80
541	Roger Metzger	4	4	4	4	4	5	10	25
542	Pete Broberg	4	4	4	4	4	8	15	
543	Larry Biittner	4	4	4	4	4	5	10	25
544	Steve Mingori	4	4	4	5	6	12	25	
545	Billy Williams	4	4	4	4	4	8	15	200
546	John Knox	4	4	4	4	4	5	10	25
547	Von Joshua	4	4	4	4	4	5	10	50
548	Charlie Sands	4	4	4	4	4	5	10	25
549	Bill Butler	4	4	4	4	4	5	10	25
550	Ralph Garr	4	4	4	4	4	5	10	120
551	Larry Christenson	4	4	4	4	4	8	15	
552	Jack Brohamer	4	4	4	4	4	5	10	25
553	John Boccabella	4	4	4	4	4	5	10	60
554	Goose Gossage	4	4	4	4	4	8	15	50
555	Al Oliver	4	4	4	4	4	6	12	100
556	Tim Johnson	4	4	4	4	4	8	15	
557	Larry Gura	4	4	4	4	4	5	10	60
558	Dave Roberts	4	4	4	4	4	5	10	40
559	Bob Montgomery	4	4	4	4	4	5	10	25
560	Tony Perez	4	4	4	4	5	10	20	50
561	Oakland Athletics CL/Dark	4	4	4	5	6	12	25	120
562	Gary Nolan	4	4	4	4	4	8	15	
563	Wilbur Howard	4	4	4	4	4	5	10	25

#	Player	GD 2	VG 3	VgEx 4	EX 5	ExMt 6	NM 7	NmMt 8	MT 9
564	Tommy Davis	4	4	4	4	8	15	150	
565	Joe Torre	4	4	4	4	4	6	12	40
566	Ray Burris	4	4	4	4	5	10	25	
567	Jim Sundberg	4	4	4	4	4	6	12	30
568	Dale Murray	4	4	4	4	4	5	10	60
569	Frank White	4	4	4	4	4	6	12	30
570	Jim Wynn	4	4	4	4	4	6	12	30
571	Dave Lemanczyk	4	4	4	4	4	5	10	25
572	Roger Nelson	4	4	4	4	4	8	15	
573	Orlando Pena	4	4	4	4	4	5	10	25
574	Tony Taylor	4	4	4	4	4	8	15	
575	Gene Clines	4	4	4	4	4	5	10	25
576	Phil Roof	4	4	4	4	4	5	10	25
577	John Morris	4	4	4	4	4	5	10	50
578	Dave Tomlin	4	4	4	4	4	5	10	25
579	Skip Pitlock	4	4	4	4	4	5	10	25
580	Frank Robinson	4	4	8	10	12	20	30	250
581	Darrel Chaney	4	4	4	4	4	5	10	
582	Eduardo Rodriguez	4	4	4	4	4	5	10	60
583	Andy Etchebarren	4	4	4	5	6	12	25	
584	Mike Garman	4	4	4	4	4	5	10	25
585	Chris Chambliss	4	4	4	4	4	6	12	30
586	Tim McCarver	4	4	4	4	4	8	15	30
587	Chris Ward	4	4	4	4	4	5	10	25
588	Rick Auerbach	4	4	4	4	4	8	15	
589	Atlanta Braves CL/King	4	4	4	4	4	8	15	
590	Cesar Cedeno	4	4	4	5	6	12	25	
591	Glenn Abbott	4	4	4	4	4	5	10	25
592	Balor Moore	4	4	4	4	4	5	10	40
593	Gene Lamont	4	4	4	4	4	5	10	25
594	Jim Fuller	4	4	4	4	4	5	10	25
595	Joe Niekro	4	4	4	4	4	5	10	60
596	Ollie Brown	4	4	4	4	4	8	15	
597	Winston Llenas	4	4	4	4	4	5	10	25
598	Bruce Kison	4	4	4	4	4	5	10	80
599	Nate Colbert	4	4	4	4	4	5	10	25
600	Rod Carew	4	4	4	4	8	25	40	500
601	Juan Beniquez	4	4	4	4	4	8	15	
602	John Vukovich	4	4	4	4	4	5	10	80
603	Lew Krausse	4	4	5	10	12	25	50	
604	Oscar Zamora	4	4	4	4	4	5	10	25
605	John Ellis	4	4	4	4	4	5	10	25
606	Bruce Miller	4	4	4	4	4	6	12	25
607	Jim Holt	4	4	4	4	4	8	15	
608	Gene Michael	4	4	4	4	4	5	10	25
609	Elrod Hendricks	4	4	4	4	4	5	10	30
610	Ron Hunt	4	4	4	4	4	5	10	25
611	New York Yankees CL/Virdon	4	4	4	4	4	8	15	80
612	Terry Hughes	4	4	4	4	4	5	10	300
613	Bill Parsons	4	4	4	4	4	5	10	25
614	Rookie Pitchers	4	4	4	4	4	5	10	25
615	Rookie Pitchers	4	4	4	4	4	6	12	30
616	Jim Rice	▲8	▲12	▲20	▲30	▲50	▲80	▲120	▲400
617	Rookie Infielders	4	4	4	4	4	6	12	30
618	Rookie Pitchers	4	4	4	4	4	6	12	50
619	Rookie Outfielders	4	4	4	4	4	5	10	25
620	Gary Carter	4	6	10	15	25	60	▲150	500
621	Rookie Pitchers	4	4	4	4	4	6	12	30
622	Fred Lynn	4	4	4	4	8	15	25	60
623	K.Hernandez/P.Garner	4	4	4	4	8	15	40	200
624	Rookie Pitchers	4	4	4	5	6	12	25	
625	Boog Powell	4	4	4	4	6	12	25	200
626	Larry Haney	4	4	4	8	10	20	40	
627	Tom Walker	4	4	4	4	4	5	10	25
628	Ron LeFlore	4	4	4	4	4	5	10	40
629	Joe Hoerner	4	4	4	4	4	5	10	40
630	Greg Luzinski	4	4	4	4	4	6	12	30
631	Lee Lacy	4	4	4	4	4	8	15	

#	Player	GD 2	VG 3	VgEx 4	EX 5	ExMt 6	NM 7	NmMt 8	MT 9
632	Morris Nettles	4	4	4	4	4	5	10	25
633	Paul Casanova	4	4	4	4	4	5	10	50
634	Cy Acosta	4	4	4	4	8	15	40	
635	Chuck Dobson	4	4	4	4	4	5	10	25
636	Charlie Moore	4	4	4	4	5	10	20	
637	Ted Martinez	4	4	4	4	4	8	15	
638	Chicago Cubs CL/Marshall	4	4	4	8	10	20	40	
639	Steve Kline	4	4	4	4	4	5	10	25
640	Harmon Killebrew	4	4	4	6	8	25	30	200
641	Jim Northrup	4	4	4	4	4	6	12	30
642	Mike Phillips	4	4	4	4	4	8	15	
643	Brent Strom	4	4	4	4	4	5	10	25
644	Bill Fahey	4	4	4	4	4	5	10	25
645	Danny Cater	4	4	4	4	4	5	10	25
646	Checklist: 529-660	4	4	4	4	4	8	15	
647	Claudell Washington	4	4	5	10	12	25		
648	Dave Pagan	4	4	4	4	4	5	10	25
649	Jack Heidemann	4	4	4	4	4	8	15	
650	Dave May	4	4	4	4	4	5	10	60
651	John Morlan	4	4	4	4	4	8	15	
652	Lindy McDaniel	4	4	4	4	4	5	10	60
653	Lee Richard	4	4	4	4	4	5	10	20
654	Jerry Terrell	4	4	4	4	4	5	10	60
655	Rico Carty	4	4	4	4	4	5	10	25
656	Bill Plummer	4	4	4	4	4	5	10	25
657	Bob Oliver	4	4	4	4	4	8	15	
658	Vic Harris	4	4	4	4	4	5	10	25
659	Bob Apodaca	4	4	4	4	4	8	15	150
660	Hank Aaron	8	10	12	25	40	60	200	800

— George Brett #228 PSA 10 (Gem) (Young Collection) sold for $5,948 (SCP; 5/12)
— Gary Carter #620 PSA 10 (Gem) sold for $3,315 (eBay; 09/12)

1976 Kellogg's

#	Player	VG 3	VgEx 4	EX 5	ExMt 6	NM 7	NmMt 8	MT 9	Gem 9.5/10
1	Steve Hargan SP	4	4	4	4	8	15	30	
2	Claudell Washington SP	4	4	4	4	6	12	25	60
3	Don Gullett SP	4	4	4	4	6	12	25	120
4	Randy Jones	4	4	4	4	4	4	8	20
5	Jim Hunter	4	4	4	4	4	5	10	25
6A	Clay Carroll Reds Logo	4	4	4	4	4	4	8	
6B	Clay Carroll White Sox Logo	4	4	4	4	4	4	8	
7	Joe Rudi	4	4	4	4	4	4	8	20
8	Reggie Jackson	4	4	4	4	4	8	15	50
9	Felix Millan	4	4	4	4	4	4	8	25
10	Jim Rice	4	4	4	4	4	6	12	40
11	Bert Blyleven	4	4	4	4	4	4	8	25
12	Ken Singleton	4	4	4	4	4	4	8	25
13	Don Sutton	4	4	4	4	4	5	10	25
14	Joe Morgan	4	4	4	4	4	5	10	25
15	Dave Parker	4	4	4	4	4	5	10	60
16	Dave Cash	4	4	4	4	4	4	8	25
17	Ron LeFlore	4	4	4	4	4	4	8	25
18	Greg Luzinski	4	4	4	4	4	4	8	25
19	Dennis Eckersley	4	4	4	4	4	8	15	60
20	Bill Madlock	4	4	4	4	4	4	8	25
21	George Scott	4	4	4	4	4	4	8	3
22	Willie Stargell	4	4	4	4	4	5	10	25
23	Al Hrabosky	4	4	4	4	4	4	8	25
24	Carl Yastrzemski	4	4	4	4	4	8	15	40
25A	Jim Kaat White Sox Logo	4	4	4	4	4	4	8	30
25B	Jim Kaat Phillies Logo	4	4	4	4	4	4	8	
26	Marty Perez	4	4	4	4	4	4	8	15
27	Bob Watson	4	4	4	4	4	4	8	25
28	Eric Soderholm	4	4	4	4	4	4	8	25
29	Bill Lee	4	4	4	4	4	4	8	20
30A	Frank Tanana 1975 ERA 2.63	4	4	4	4	4	4	8	25
31	Fred Lynn	4	4	4	4	4	5	10	40

		VG 3	VgEx 4	EX 5	ExMt 6	NM 7	NmMt 8	MT 9	Gem 9.5/10
32A	Tom Seaver Pct. 552 No Decimal	4	4	4	4	4	8	15	40
32B	Tom Seaver Pct. .552 w/Decimal	4	4	4	4	4	8		
33	Steve Busby	4	4	4	4	4	4	8	25
34	Gary Carter	4	4	4	4	4	5	10	25
35	Rick Wise	4	4	4	4	4	4	8	15
36	Johnny Bench	4	4	4	4	4	8	15	60
37	Jim Palmer	4	4	4	4	4	5	10	25
38	Bobby Murcer	4	4	4	4	4	4	8	25
39	Von Joshua	4	4	4	4	4	4	8	25
40	Lou Brock	4	4	4	4	4	5	10	25
41A	Mickey Rivers No Last Line	4	4	4	4	4	4	8	25
42	Manny Sanguillen	4	4	4	4	4	4	8	25
43	Jerry Reuss	4	4	4	4	4	4	8	15
44	Ken Griffey	4	4	4	4	4	4	8	15
45B	Jorge Orta AB 1616	4	4	4	4	4	4	8	15
46	John Mayberry	4	4	4	4	4	4	8	25
47A	Vida Blue Struck Out More	4	4	4	4	4	4	8	20
47B	Vida Blue Pitched More	4	4	4	4	4	4	8	25
48	Rod Carew	4	4	4	4	4	5	10	25
49B	Jon Matlack ER 86	4	4	4	4	4	4	8	25
50	Boog Powell	4	4	4	4	4	4	8	20
51B	Mike Hargrove AB 934	4	4	4	4	4	4	8	25
52A	Paul Lindblad ERA 2.73	4	4	4	4	4	4	8	20
53	Thurman Munson	4	4	4	4	4	8	15	50
54	Steve Garvey	4	4	4	4	4	5	10	25
55	Pete Rose	4	4	4	4	5	10	20	60
56A	Greg Gross Games 334	4	4	4	4	4	4	8	25
57	Ted Simmons	4	4	4	4	4	4	8	25

1976 Topps

		VG 3	VgEx 4	EX 5	ExMt 6	NM 7	NmMt 8	NmMt+ 8.5	MT 9
1	Hank Aaron RB	8	10	12	20	25	60	100	250
2	Bobby Bonds RB	4	4	4	4	4	6	15	80
3	Mickey Lolich RB	4	4	4	4	4	6	10	200
4	Dave Lopes RB	4	4	4	4	4	6	8	25
5	Tom Seaver RB	4	4	4	4	5	20	25	30
6	Rennie Stennett RB	4	4	4	4	4	6	8	200
7	Jim Umbarger RC	4	4	4	4	4	6	8	150
8	Tito Fuentes	4	4	4	4	4	5	8	50
9	Paul Lindblad	4	4	4	4	4	5	6	15
10	Lou Brock	4	4	4	4	8	15	20	50
11	Jim Hughes	4	4	4	4	4	6	8	60
12	Richie Zisk	4	4	4	4	4	6	8	25
13	John Wockenfuss RC	4	4	4	4	4	5	6	15
14	Gene Garber	4	4	4	4	4	5	6	10
15	George Scott	4	4	4	4	4	5	6	20
16	Bob Apodaca	4	4	4	4	4	5	6	10
17	New York Yankees CL/Martin	4	4	4	4	4	6	8	25
18	Dale Murray	4	4	4	4	4	5	6	12
19	George Brett	▲20	▲30	▲40	▲80	150	▲800	1,000	
20	Bob Watson	4	4	4	4	4	5	6	15
21	Dave LaRoche	4	4	4	4	4	5	8	30
22	Bill Russell	4	4	4	4	4	5	6	15
23	Brian Downing	4	4	4	4	4	5	8	25
24	Cesar Geronimo	4	4	4	4	4	5	6	20
25	Mike Torrez	4	4	4	4	4	5	6	15
26	Andre Thornton	4	4	4	4	4	5	6	10
27	Ed Figueroa	4	4	4	4	4	5	6	15
28	Dusty Baker	4	4	4	4	4	5	8	20
29	Rick Burleson	4	4	4	4	4	5	6	15
30	John Montefusco RC	4	4	4	4	4	6	8	20
31	Len Randle	4	4	4	4	4	5	6	12
32	Danny Frisella	4	4	4	4	4	6	8	20
33	Bill North	4	4	4	4	4	5	6	20
34	Mike Garman	4	4	4	4	4	5	6	15
35	Tony Oliva	4	4	4	4	4	25	30	400
36	Frank Taveras	4	4	4	4	4	5	8	40
37	John Hiller	4	4	4	4	4	5	6	10
38	Garry Maddox	4	4	4	4	4	5	6	15
39	Pete Broberg	4	4	4	4	4	5	6	15
40	Dave Kingman	4	4	4	4	4	6	8	20
41	Tippy Martinez RC	4	4	4	4	4	5	6	30
42	Barry Foote	4	4	4	4	4	5	6	10
43	Paul Splittorff	4	4	4	4	4	5	6	15
44	Doug Rader	4	4	4	4	4	5	6	10
45	Boog Powell	4	4	4	4	4	6	8	40
46	Los Angeles Dodgers CL/Alston	4	4	4	4	4	5	6	15
47	Jesse Jefferson	4	4	4	4	4	6	8	60
48	Dave Concepcion	4	4	4	4	4	8	10	50
49	Dave Duncan	4	4	4	4	4	5	6	15
50	Fred Lynn	4	4	4	4	5	10	15	50
51	Ray Burris	4	4	4	4	4	6	8	40
52	Dave Chalk	4	4	4	4	4	5	6	10
53	Mike Beard RC	4	4	4	4	4	5	6	15
54	Dave Rader	4	4	4	4	4	5	6	15
55	Gaylord Perry	4	4	4	4	4	10	12	100
56	Bob Tolan	4	4	4	4	4	5	6	10
57	Phil Garner	4	4	4	4	4	5	6	15
58	Ron Reed	4	4	4	4	4	5	6	15
59	Larry Hisle	4	4	4	4	4	5	6	10
60	Jerry Reuss	4	4	4	4	4	5	6	15
61	Ron LeFlore	4	4	4	4	4	5	6	15
62	Johnny Oates	4	4	4	4	4	5	6	15
63	Bobby Darwin	4	4	4	4	4	5	6	15
64	Jerry Koosman	4	4	4	4	4	5	6	15
65	Chris Chambliss	4	4	4	4	4	5	6	40
66	Gus/Buddy Bell FS	4	4	4	4	4	5	6	15
67	Bob/Ray Boone FS	4	4	4	4	4	5	6	15
68	Joe/Joe Jr. Coleman FS	4	4	4	4	4	5	6	15
69	Jim/Mike Hegan FS	4	4	4	4	4	5	6	15
70	Roy/Roy Jr. Smalley FS	4	4	4	4	4	5	6	30
71	Steve Rogers	4	4	4	4	4	5	6	15
72	Hal McRae	4	4	4	4	4	5	6	15
73	Baltimore Orioles CL/Weaver	4	4	4	4	4	5	6	12
74	Oscar Gamble	4	4	4	4	4	5	6	15
75	Larry Dierker	4	4	4	4	4	5	8	25
76	Willie Crawford	4	4	4	4	4	6	8	50
77	Pedro Borbon	4	4	4	4	4	5	6	20
78	Cecil Cooper	4	4	4	4	4	5	6	25
79	Jerry Morales	4	4	4	4	4	5	6	15
80	Jim Kaat	4	4	4	4	4	6	8	20
81	Darrell Evans	4	4	4	4	4	5	6	15
82	Von Joshua	4	4	4	4	4	5	6	10
83	Jim Spencer	4	4	4	4	4	5	6	10
84	Brent Strom	4	4	4	4	4	5	6	10
85	Mickey Rivers	4	4	4	4	4	5	6	20
86	Mike Tyson	4	4	4	4	4	5	6	10
87	Tom Burgmeier	4	4	4	4	4	5	6	15
88	Duffy Dyer	4	4	4	4	4	5	6	15
89	Vern Ruhle	4	4	4	4	4	5	6	30
90	Sal Bando	4	4	4	4	4	5	6	25
91	Tom Hutton	4	4	4	4	4	5	6	15
92	Eduardo Rodriguez	4	4	4	4	4	5	6	15
93	Mike Phillips	4	4	4	4	4	5	6	15
94	Jim Dwyer	4	4	4	4	4	5	6	15
95	Brooks Robinson	▲6	▲10	▲15	25	▲40	▲60	▲80	▲250
96	Doug Bird	4	4	4	4	4	5	6	15
97	Wilbur Howard	4	4	4	4	4	5	6	15
98	Dennis Eckersley RC	▲15	▲25	40	60	▲120	200	250	▲2,000
99	Lee Lacy	4	4	4	4	4	5	8	80
100	Jim Hunter	4	4	4	4	8	15	25	120
101	Pete LaCock	4	4	4	4	4	5	6	15
102	Jim Willoughby	4	4	4	4	4	5	6	15
103	Biff Pocoroba RC	4	4	4	4	4	5	6	15
104	Cincinnati Reds CL/Anderson	4	4	4	4	4	5	10	12	40

#	Player	VG 3	VgEx 4	EX 5	ExMt 6	NM 7	NmMt 8	NmMt+ 8.5	MT 9
105	Gary Lavelle	4	4	4	4	4	5	6	12
106	Tom Grieve	4	4	4	4	4	5	6	12
107	Dave Roberts	4	4	4	4	4	5	6	10
108	Don Kirkwood RC	4	4	4	4	4	5	6	12
109	Larry Lintz	4	4	4	4	4	5	6	15
110	Carlos May	4	4	4	4	4	5	6	15
111	Danny Thompson	4	4	4	4	4	5	6	10
112	Kent Tekulve RC	4	4	4	4	4	8	10	25
113	Gary Sutherland	4	4	4	4	4	5	6	15
114	Jay Johnstone	4	4	4	4	4	5	6	15
115	Ken Holtzman	4	4	4	4	4	5	6	15
116	Charlie Moore	4	4	4	4	4	5	6	12
117	Mike Jorgensen	4	4	4	4	4	5	6	10
118	Boston Red Sox CL/Johnson	4	4	4	4	4	6	8	15
119	Checklist 1-132	4	4	4	4	4	6	8	80
120	Rusty Staub	4	4	4	4	4	5	6	15
121	Tony Solaita	4	4	4	4	4	5	6	15
122	Mike Cosgrove	4	4	4	4	4	5	6	15
123	Walt Williams	4	4	4	4	4	5	6	60
124	Doug Rau	4	4	4	4	4	5	6	15
125	Don Baylor	4	4	4	4	4	6	8	20
126	Tom Dettore	4	4	4	4	4	6	8	200
127	Larvell Blanks	4	4	4	4	4	5	6	15
128	Ken Griffey Sr.	4	4	4	4	4	6	8	25
129	Andy Etchebarren	4	4	4	4	4	5	6	15
130	Luis Tiant	4	4	4	4	4	6	8	25
131	Bill Stein RC	4	4	4	4	4	5	6	15
132	Don Hood	4	4	4	4	4	5	6	15
133	Gary Matthews	4	4	4	4	4	5	6	25
134	Mike Ivie	4	4	4	4	4	5	8	50
135	Bake McBride	4	4	4	4	4	5	6	15
136	Dave Goltz	4	4	4	4	4	5	6	12
137	Bill Robinson	4	4	4	4	4	5	8	80
138	Lerrin LaGrow	4	4	4	4	4	5	6	12
139	Gorman Thomas	4	4	4	4	4	5	6	15
140	Vida Blue	4	4	4	4	4	6	8	40
141	Larry Parrish RC	4	4	4	4	4	6	8	25
142	Dick Drago	4	4	4	4	4	5	8	25
143	Jerry Grote	4	4	4	4	4	5	6	20
144	Al Fitzmorris	4	4	4	4	4	5	6	15
145	Larry Bowa	4	4	4	4	4	5	6	15
146	George Medich	4	4	4	4	4	5	6	15
147	Houston Astros CL/Virdon	4	4	4	4	4	5	6	15
148	Stan Thomas RC	4	4	4	4	4	5	6	15
149	Tommy Davis	4	4	4	4	4	5	6	15
150	Steve Garvey	4	4	4	4	5	10	15	50
151	Bill Bonham	4	4	4	4	4	5	6	15
152	Leroy Stanton	4	4	4	4	4	6	8	30
153	Buzz Capra	4	4	4	4	4	5	6	15
154	Bucky Dent	4	4	4	4	4	5	6	10
155	Jack Billingham	4	4	4	4	4	5	6	15
156	Rico Carty	4	4	4	4	4	5	6	15
157	Mike Caldwell	4	4	4	4	4	5	8	25
158	Ken Reitz	4	4	4	4	4	5	6	50
159	Jerry Terrell	4	4	4	4	4	5	6	15
160	Dave Winfield	▲5	▲8	▲12	▲20	▲50	▲80	▲100	▲200
161	Bruce Kison	4	4	4	4	4	6	8	150
162	Jack Pierce RC	4	4	4	4	4	5	6	30
163	Jim Slaton	4	4	4	4	4	6	8	100
164	Pepe Mangual	4	4	4	4	4	5	6	15
165	Gene Tenace	4	4	4	4	4	5	6	15
166	Skip Lockwood	4	4	4	4	4	5	6	12
167	Freddie Patek	4	4	4	4	4	5	6	10
168	Tom Hilgendorf	4	4	4	4	4	5	8	25
169	Graig Nettles	4	4	4	4	4	8	10	30
170	Rick Wise	4	4	4	4	4	5	8	25
171	Greg Gross	4	4	4	4	4	5	6	15
172	Texas Rangers CL/Lucchesi	4	4	4	4	4	5	6	12

#	Player	VG 3	VgEx 4	EX 5	ExMt 6	NM 7	NmMt 8	NmMt+ 8.5	MT 9
173	Steve Swisher	4	4	4	4	4	5	6	15
174	Charlie Hough	4	4	4	4	4	6	8	40
175	Ken Singleton	4	4	4	4	4	5	6	15
176	Dick Lange	4	4	4	4	4	6	8	80
177	Marty Perez	4	4	4	4	4	5	6	15
178	Tom Buskey	4	4	4	4	4	5	6	15
179	George Foster	4	4	4	4	4	8	10	25
180	Goose Gossage	4	4	4	4	4	8	10	25
181	Willie Montanez	4	4	4	4	4	5	6	15
182	Harry Rasmussen	4	4	4	4	4	5	8	25
183	Steve Braun	4	4	4	4	4	5	6	25
184	Bill Greif	4	4	4	4	4	5	6	15
185	Dave Parker	4	4	4	4	4	12	15	25
186	Tom Walker	4	4	4	4	4	5	6	15
187	Pedro Garcia	4	4	4	4	4	5	6	15
188	Fred Scherman	4	4	4	4	4	5	6	10
189	Claudell Washington	4	4	4	4	4	5	6	10
190	Jon Matlack	4	4	4	4	4	5	6	15
191	NL Batting Leaders	4	4	4	4	4	5	6	15
192	AL Batting Leaders	4	4	4	4	4	6	8	20
193	NL Home Run Leaders	4	4	4	4	4	10	12	15
194	AL Home Run Leaders	4	4	4	4	4	6	8	20
195	NL RBI Leaders	4	4	4	4	4	6	8	15
196	AL RBI Leaders	4	4	4	4	4	5	6	15
197	NL Stolen Base Leaders	4	4	4	4	4	6	8	15
198	AL Stolen Base Leaders	4	4	4	4	4	6	8	20
199	NL Victory Leaders	4	4	4	4	4	6	8	20
200	AL Victory Leaders	4	4	4	4	4	6	8	20
201	NL ERA Leaders	4	4	4	4	4	6	8	20
202	AL ERA Leaders	4	4	4	4	4	6	8	15
203	NL Strikeout Leaders	4	4	4	4	4	6	8	20
204	AL Strikeout Leaders	4	4	4	4	4	5	6	15
205	NL/AL Leading Firemen	4	4	4	4	4	5	6	20
206	Manny Trillo	4	4	4	4	4	8	10	80
207	Andy Hassler	4	4	4	4	4	5	6	15
208	Mike Lum	4	4	4	4	4	5	6	12
209	Alan Ashby RC	4	4	4	4	4	5	6	15
210	Lee May	4	4	4	4	4	5	6	15
211	Clay Carroll	4	4	4	4	4	5	6	15
212	Pat Kelly	4	4	4	4	4	5	6	10
213	Dave Heaverlo RC	4	4	4	4	4	5	6	15
214	Eric Soderholm	4	4	4	4	4	5	6	15
215	Reggie Smith	4	4	4	4	4	5	6	15
216	Montreal Expos CL/Kuehl	4	4	4	4	4	5	6	10
217	Dave Freisleben	4	4	4	4	4	5	6	15
218	John Knox	4	4	4	4	4	5	8	25
219	Tom Murphy	4	4	4	4	4	5	8	25
220	Manny Sanguillen	4	4	4	4	4	5	6	20
221	Jim Todd	4	4	4	4	4	5	6	10
222	Wayne Garrett	4	4	4	4	4	5	6	10
223	Ollie Brown	4	4	4	4	4	5	6	15
224	Jim York	4	4	4	4	4	5	6	15
225	Roy White	4	4	4	4	4	5	6	20
226	Jim Sundberg	4	4	4	4	4	5	6	15
227	Oscar Zamora	4	4	4	4	4	5	6	15
228	John Hale RC	4	4	4	4	4	5	6	15
229	Jerry Remy RC	4	4	4	4	4	5	6	60
230	Carl Yastrzemski	6	10	15	25	40	80	100	150
231	Tom House	4	4	4	4	4	5	6	15
232	Frank Duffy	4	4	4	4	4	5	6	15
233	Grant Jackson	4	4	4	4	4	5	6	15
234	Mike Sadek	4	4	4	4	4	5	6	15
235	Bert Blyleven	4	4	4	4	4	6	8	60
236	Kansas City Royals CL/Herzog	4	4	4	4	4	5	6	15
237	Dave Hamilton	4	4	4	4	4	5	6	15
238	Larry Biittner	4	4	4	4	4	5	6	10
239	John Curtis	4	4	4	4	4	5	6	15
240	Pete Rose	15	20	25	60	▲120	250	300	▲1,500

#	Name	VG 3	VgEx 4	EX 5	ExMt 6	NM 7	NmMt 8	NmMt+ 8.5	MT 9
241	Hector Torres	4	4	4	4	4	5	6	15
242	Dan Meyer	4	4	4	4	4	5	6	10
243	Jim Rooker	4	4	4	4	4	5	6	10
244	Bill Sharp	4	4	4	4	4	5	6	25
245	Felix Millan	4	4	4	4	4	5	6	15
246	Cesar Tovar	4	4	4	4	4	5	6	15
247	Terry Harmon	4	4	4	4	4	5	6	15
248	Dick Tidrow	4	4	4	4	4	5	6	15
249	Cliff Johnson	4	4	4	4	4	5	6	15
250	Fergie Jenkins	4	4	4	4	4	6	8	25
251	Rick Monday	4	4	4	4	4	5	6	15
252	Tim Nordbrook RC	4	4	4	4	4	5	6	15
253	Bill Buckner	4	4	4	4	4	5	6	15
254	Rudy Meoli	4	4	4	4	4	5	8	10
255	Fritz Peterson	4	4	4	4	4	5	6	10
256	Rowland Office	4	4	4	4	4	5	6	15
257	Ross Grimsley	4	4	4	4	4	5	6	15
258	Nyls Nyman	4	4	4	4	4	5	6	10
259	Darrel Chaney	4	4	4	4	4	5	6	15
260	Steve Busby	4	4	4	4	4	5	6	15
261	Gary Thomasson	4	4	4	4	4	5	8	40
262	Checklist 133-264	4	4	4	4	4	6	8	40
263	Lyman Bostock RC	4	4	4	4	4	8	10	40
264	Steve Renko	4	4	4	4	4	5	6	4
265	Willie Davis	4	4	4	4	4	5	6	50
266	Alan Foster	4	4	4	4	4	5	8	25
267	Aurelio Rodriguez	4	4	4	4	4	5	6	15
268	Del Unser	4	4	4	4	4	5	8	25
269	Rick Austin	4	4	4	4	4	5	6	15
270	Willie Stargell	4	4	4	4	8	15	20	60
271	Jim Lonborg	4	4	4	4	4	5	6	15
272	Rick Dempsey	4	4	4	4	4	5	6	15
273	Joe Niekro	4	4	4	4	4	5	6	15
274	Tommy Harper	4	4	4	4	4	5	6	15
275	Rick Manning RC	4	4	4	4	4	5	6	20
276	Mickey Scott	4	4	4	4	4	5	6	25
277	Chicago Cubs CL/Marshall	4	4	4	4	4	5	6	15
278	Bernie Carbo	4	4	4	4	4	5	8	80
279	Roy Howell RC	4	4	4	4	4	5	6	15
280	Burt Hooton	4	4	4	4	4	5	6	15
281	Dave May	4	4	4	4	4	5	6	15
282	Dan Osborn RC	4	4	4	4	4	5	6	10
283	Merv Rettenmund	4	4	4	4	4	5	6	12
284	Steve Ontiveros	4	4	4	4	4	5	6	15
285	Mike Cuellar	4	4	4	4	4	5	8	100
286	Jim Wohlford	4	4	4	4	4	5	6	15
287	Pete Mackanin	4	4	4	4	4	5	6	15
288	Bill Campbell	4	4	4	4	4	5	6	15
289	Enzo Hernandez	4	4	4	4	4	5	6	15
290	Ted Simmons	4	4	4	4	4	8	10	50
291	Ken Sanders	4	4	4	4	4	5	6	10
292	Leon Roberts	4	4	4	4	4	5	6	15
293	Bill Castro RC	4	4	4	4	4	5	6	15
294	Ed Kirkpatrick	4	4	4	4	4	5	8	60
295	Dave Cash	4	4	4	4	4	6	8	100
296	Pat Dobson	4	4	4	4	4	5	6	10
297	Roger Metzger	4	4	4	4	4	5	6	10
298	Dick Bosman	4	4	4	4	4	5	6	12
299	Champ Summers RC	4	4	4	4	4	5	6	15
300	Johnny Bench	▲15	▲25	▲40	▲60	▲120	▲250	▲300	▲500
301	Jackie Brown	4	4	4	4	4	5	6	15
302	Rick Miller	4	4	4	4	4	6	8	40
303	Steve Foucault	4	4	4	4	4	5	6	15
304	California Angels CL/Williams	4	4	4	4	4	5	6	10
305	Andy Messersmith	4	4	4	4	4	5	6	15
306	Rod Gilbreath	4	4	4	4	4	5	6	10
307	Al Bumbry	4	4	4	4	4	5	6	15
308	Jim Barr	4	4	4	4	4	5	8	80
309	Bill Melton	4	4	4	4	4	5	6	15
310	Randy Jones	4	4	4	4	4	5	6	10
311	Cookie Rojas	4	4	4	4	4	5	6	15
312	Don Carrithers	4	4	4	4	4	5	6	15
313	Dan Ford RC	4	4	4	4	4	5	8	150
314	Ed Kranepool	4	4	4	4	4	5	6	15
315	Al Hrabosky	4	4	4	4	4	8	10	200
316	Robin Yount	▲8	▲12	▲20	▲25	▲50	▲60	▲80	150
317	John Candelaria RC	4	4	4	4	4	8	10	30
318	Bob Boone	4	4	4	4	4	6	8	25
319	Larry Gura	4	4	4	4	4	5	6	15
320	Willie Horton	4	4	4	4	4	6	8	60
321	Jose Cruz	4	4	4	4	4	5	6	15
322	Glenn Abbott	4	4	4	4	4	5	6	15
323	Rob Sperring RC	4	4	4	4	4	5	6	25
324	Jim Bibby	4	4	4	4	4	5	6	12
325	Tony Perez	4	4	4	4	4	8	10	40
326	Dick Pole	4	4	4	4	4	5	6	15
327	Dave Moates RC	4	4	4	4	4	5	6	10
328	Carl Morton	4	4	4	4	4	5	6	15
329	Joe Ferguson	4	4	4	4	4	5	8	15
330	Nolan Ryan	▲15	25	▲40	▲60	▲80	▲200	▲250	1,200
331	San Diego Padres CL/McNamara	4	4	4	4	4	5	6	15
332	Charlie Williams	4	4	4	4	4	5	6	15
333	Bob Coluccio	4	4	4	4	4	5	6	10
334	Dennis Leonard	4	4	4	4	4	5	6	15
335	Bob Grich	4	4	4	4	4	5	6	15
336	Vic Albury	4	4	4	4	4	5	6	10
337	Bud Harrelson	4	4	4	4	4	5	6	20
338	Bob Bailey	4	4	4	4	4	5	6	15
339	John Denny	4	4	4	4	4	5	6	15
340	Jim Rice	6	10	20	30	50	100	120	300
341	Lou Gehrig ATG	4	5	8	12	20	▲50	▲60	▲120
342	Rogers Hornsby ATG	4	4	4	4	4	6	8	30
343	Pie Traynor ATG	4	4	4	4	4	6	8	80
344	Honus Wagner ATG	4	4	4	4	5	8	12	15	30
345	Babe Ruth ATG	▲10	▲15	▲25	▲40	▲60	▲100	▲120	▲250
346	Ty Cobb ATG	4	▲6	▲10	▲15	▲25	40	50	▲120
347	Ted Williams ATG	4	4	6	10	15	25	▲50	▲100
348	Mickey Cochrane ATG	4	4	4	4	4	6	8	20
349	Walter Johnson ATG	4	4	4	4	4	6	8	40
350	Lefty Grove ATG	4	4	4	4	4	6	10	60
351	Randy Hundley	4	4	4	4	4	5	6	10
352	Dave Giusti	4	4	4	4	4	5	6	12
353	Sixto Lezcano RC	4	4	4	4	4	5	6	10
354	Ron Blomberg	4	4	4	4	4	5	6	20
355	Steve Carlton	4	▲5	▲8	▲12	▲20	▲30	▲40	▲120
356	Ted Martinez	4	4	4	4	4	5	6	15
357	Ken Forsch	4	4	4	4	4	6	8	30
358	Buddy Bell	4	4	4	4	4	5	6	15
359	Rick Reuschel	4	4	4	4	4	5	6	15
360	Jeff Burroughs	4	4	4	4	4	5	6	15
361	Detroit Tigers CL/Houk	4	4	4	4	4	5	6	15
362	Will McEnaney	4	4	4	4	4	5	6	15
363	Dave Collins RC	4	4	4	4	4	5	6	10
364	Elias Sosa	4	4	4	4	4	5	6	15
365	Carlton Fisk	4	4	4	5	10	25	30	100
366	Bobby Valentine	4	4	4	4	4	5	6	15
367	Bruce Miller	4	4	4	4	4	5	6	15
368	Wilbur Wood	4	4	4	4	4	5	8	25
369	Frank White	4	4	4	4	4	5	6	20
370	Ron Cey	4	4	4	4	4	6	8	20
371	Elrod Hendricks	4	4	4	4	4	5	6	15
372	Rick Baldwin RC	4	4	4	4	4	5	6	12
373	Johnny Briggs	4	4	4	4	8	15	25	
374	Dan Warthen RC	4	4	4	4	4	5	6	15
375	Ron Fairly	4	4	4	4	4	5	6	10
376	Rich Hebner	4	4	4	4	4	5	6	15

#	Player	VG 3	VgEx 4	EX 5	ExMt 6	NM 7	NmMt 8	NmMt+ 8.5	MT 9
377	Mike Hegan	4	4	4	4	4	5	6	20
378	Steve Stone	4	4	4	4	4	5	6	15
379	Ken Boswell	4	4	4	4	4	5	6	15
380	Bobby Bonds	4	4	4	4	4	6	8	25
381	Denny Doyle	4	4	4	4	4	5	8	25
382	Matt Alexander RC	4	4	4	4	4	5	6	15
383	John Ellis	4	4	4	4	4	6	8	50
384	Philadelphia Phillies CL/Ozark	4	4	4	4	4	5	6	15
385	Mickey Lolich	4	4	4	4	4	6	8	30
386	Ed Goodson	4	4	4	4	4	5	6	15
387	Mike Miley RC	4	4	4	4	4	5	6	15
388	Stan Perzanowski RC	4	4	4	4	4	5	6	15
389	Glenn Adams RC	4	4	4	4	4	5	8	25
390	Don Gullett	4	4	4	4	4	5	6	20
391	Jerry Hairston	4	4	4	4	4	5	6	15
392	Checklist 265-396	4	4	4	4	4	6	8	
393	Paul Mitchell RC	4	4	4	4	4	5	6	15
394	Fran Healy	4	4	4	4	4	5	6	10
395	Jim Wynn	4	4	4	4	4	5	6	15
396	Bill Lee	4	4	4	4	4	5	6	25
397	Tim Foli	4	4	4	4	4	5	6	10
398	Dave Tomlin	4	4	4	4	4	5	6	10
399	Luis Melendez	4	4	4	4	4	5	6	15
400	Rod Carew	4	4	4	6	15	20	25	100
401	Ken Brett	4	4	4	4	4	5	6	15
402	Don Money	4	4	4	4	4	5	6	15
403	Geoff Zahn	4	4	4	4	4	5	6	15
404	Enos Cabell	4	4	4	4	4	5	8	50
405	Rollie Fingers	4	4	4	4	4	6	8	25
406	Ed Herrmann	4	4	4	4	4	5	6	12
407	Tom Underwood	4	4	4	4	4	5	6	10
408	Charlie Spikes	4	4	4	4	4	5	6	10
409	Dave Lemanczyk	4	4	4	4	4	5	6	15
410	Ralph Garr	4	4	4	4	4	5	8	25
411	Bill Singer	4	4	4	4	4	5	6	15
412	Toby Harrah	4	4	4	4	4	5	6	15
413	Pete Varney RC	4	4	4	4	4	5	6	15
414	Wayne Garland	4	4	4	4	4	5	6	15
415	Vada Pinson	4	4	4	4	4	5	6	15
416	Tommy John	4	4	4	4	4	5	6	15
417	Gene Clines	4	4	4	4	4	5	6	20
418	Jose Morales RC	4	4	4	4	4	5	6	15
419	Reggie Cleveland	4	4	4	4	4	5	6	20
420	Joe Morgan	5	8	12	20	25	60	80	▲200
421	Oakland Athletics CL	4	4	4	4	4	5	6	15
422	Johnny Grubb	4	4	4	4	4	5	8	25
423	Ed Halicki	4	4	4	4	4	5	6	10
424	Phil Roof	4	4	4	4	4	5	6	10
425	Rennie Stennett	4	4	4	4	4	5	8	60
426	Bob Forsch	4	4	4	4	4	5	6	15
427	Kurt Bevacqua	4	4	4	4	4	5	6	20
428	Jim Crawford	4	4	4	4	4	5	6	10
429	Fred Stanley	4	4	4	4	4	5	6	15
430	Jose Cardenal	4	4	4	4	4	5	6	15
431	Dick Ruthven	4	4	4	4	4	5	6	10
432	Tom Veryzer	4	4	4	4	4	5	6	25
433	Rick Waits RC	4	4	4	4	4	5	6	15
434	Morris Nettles	4	4	4	4	4	5	6	15
435	Phil Niekro	4	4	4	4	4	8	10	25
436	Bill Fahey	4	4	4	4	4	5	6	15
437	Terry Forster	4	4	4	4	4	5	6	10
438	Doug DeCinces	4	4	4	4	4	5	6	20
439	Rick Rhoden	4	4	4	4	4	5	6	15
440	John Mayberry	4	4	4	4	4	5	6	120
441	Gary Carter	4	4	4	6	12	25	30	50
442	Hank Webb	4	4	4	4	4	5	6	15
443	San Francisco Giants CL	4	4	4	4	4	5	6	15
444	Gary Nolan	4	4	4	4	4	5	6	12
445	Rico Petrocelli	4	4	4	4	4	6	8	30
446	Larry Haney	4	4	4	4	4	5	8	10
447	Gene Locklear	4	4	4	4	4	5	6	10
448	Tom Johnson	4	4	4	4	4	5	6	12
449	Bob Robertson	4	4	4	4	4	6	8	40
450	Jim Palmer	4	4	4	4	8	15	25	60
451	Buddy Bradford	4	4	4	4	4	5	8	15
452	Tom Hausman RC	4	4	4	4	4	5	6	15
453	Lou Piniella	4	4	4	4	5	10	12	50
454	Tom Griffin	4	4	4	4	4	5	8	25
455	Dick Allen	4	4	4	4	4	6	8	20
456	Joe Coleman	4	4	4	4	4	5	6	15
457	Ed Crosby	4	4	4	4	4	5	6	15
458	Earl Williams	4	4	4	4	4	5	6	15
459	Jim Brewer	4	4	4	4	4	5	8	25
460	Cesar Cedeno	4	4	4	4	4	5	6	15
461	NL/AL Champs	4	4	4	4	4	5	6	25
462	1975 WS/Reds Champs	4	4	4	4	5	10	12	30
463	Steve Hargan	4	4	4	4	4	5	6	10
464	Ken Henderson	4	4	4	4	4	5	6	10
465	Mike Marshall	4	4	4	4	4	5	6	30
466	Bob Stinson	4	4	4	4	4	5	6	12
467	Woodie Fryman	4	4	4	4	4	5	6	10
468	Jesus Alou	4	4	4	4	4	5	6	10
469	Rawly Eastwick	4	4	4	4	4	5	6	15
470	Bobby Murcer	4	4	4	4	4	5	6	30
471	Jim Burton	4	4	4	4	4	5	6	15
472	Bob Davis RC	4	4	4	4	4	5	6	15
473	Paul Blair	4	4	4	4	4	5	6	15
474	Ray Corbin	4	4	4	4	4	5	6	15
475	Joe Rudi	4	4	4	4	4	6	8	80
476	Bob Moose	4	4	4	4	4	5	6	15
477	Cleveland Indians CL/Robinson	4	4	4	4	4	5	6	10
478	Lynn McGlothen	4	4	4	4	4	5	6	15
479	Bobby Mitchell	4	4	4	4	4	5	6	15
480	Mike Schmidt	▲6	▲10	▲15	25	▲60	▲100	▲120	▲600
481	Rudy May	4	4	4	4	4	5	6	25
482	Tim Hosley	4	4	4	4	4	5	6	15
483	Mickey Stanley	4	4	4	4	4	5	6	15
484	Eric Raich RC	4	4	4	4	4	5	6	15
485	Mike Hargrove	4	4	4	4	4	5	6	15
486	Bruce Dal Canton	4	4	4	4	4	5	6	15
487	Leron Lee	4	4	4	4	4	5	6	15
488	Claude Osteen	4	4	4	4	4	5	6	15
489	Skip Jutze	4	4	4	4	4	5	6	10
490	Frank Tanana	4	4	4	4	4	5	6	15
491	Terry Crowley	4	4	4	4	4	5	6	15
492	Marty Pattin	4	4	4	4	4	5	6	12
493	Derrel Thomas	4	4	4	4	4	5	6	10
494	Craig Swan	4	4	4	4	4	5	6	15
495	Nate Colbert	4	4	4	4	4	5	6	10
496	Juan Beniquez	4	4	4	4	4	5	6	20
497	Joe McIntosh RC	4	4	4	4	4	5	6	15
498	Glenn Borgmann	4	4	4	4	4	5	6	10
499	Mario Guerrero	4	4	4	4	4	5	6	15
500	Reggie Jackson	4	6	10	15	25	120	150	300
501	Billy Champion	4	4	4	4	4	5	6	15
502	Tim McCarver	4	4	4	4	4	6	8	20
503	Elliott Maddox	4	4	4	4	4	5	6	10
504	Pittsburgh Pirates CL/Murtaugh	4	4	4	4	4	5	6	20
505	Mark Belanger	4	4	4	4	4	5	6	15
506	George Mitterwald	4	4	4	4	4	5	6	15
507	Ray Bare RC	4	4	4	4	4	5	6	15
508	Duane Kuiper RC	4	4	4	4	4	5	6	15
509	Bill Hands	4	4	4	4	4	5	6	15
510	Amos Otis	4	4	4	4	4	5	6	15
511	Jamie Easterley	4	4	4	4	4	5	6	15
512	Ellie Rodriguez	4	4	4	4	4	5	6	15

	VG 3	VgEx 4	EX 5	ExMt 6	NM 7	NmMt 8	NmMt+ 8.5	MT 9
513 Bart Johnson	4	4	4	4	4	5	6	15
514 Dan Driessen	4	4	4	4	4	5	6	15
515 Steve Yeager	4	4	4	4	4	5	6	15
516 Wayne Granger	4	4	4	4	4	5	6	15
517 John Milner	4	4	4	4	4	5	6	15
518 Doug Flynn RC	4	4	4	4	4	5	6	60
519 Steve Brye	4	4	4	4	4	5	6	15
520 Willie McCovey	4	5	8	15	20	40	50	60
521 Jim Colborn	4	4	4	4	4	5	6	10
522 Ted Sizemore	4	4	4	4	4	5	6	10
523 Bob Montgomery	4	4	4	4	4	5	6	15
524 Pete Falcone RC	4	4	4	4	4	5	6	15
525 Billy Williams	4	4	4	4	4	6	8	30
526 Checklist 397-528	4	4	4	4	4	6	8	12
527 Mike Anderson	4	4	4	4	4	5	6	10
528 Dock Ellis	4	4	4	4	4	5	6	15
529 Deron Johnson	4	4	4	4	4	5	6	20
530 Don Sutton	4	4	4	4	4	6	8	25
531 New York Mets CL/Frazier	4	4	4	4	4	5	6	12
532 Milt May	4	4	4	4	4	5	6	10
533 Lee Richard	4	4	4	4	4	5	6	15
534 Stan Bahnsen	4	4	4	4	4	5	6	10
535 Dave Nelson	4	4	4	4	4	5	8	25
536 Mike Thompson	4	4	4	4	4	5	6	10
537 Tony Muser	4	4	4	4	4	5	6	10
538 Pat Darcy	4	4	4	4	4	5	6	15
539 John Balaz RC	4	4	4	4	4	5	6	15
540 Bill Freehan	4	4	4	4	4	5	6	20
541 Steve Mingori	4	4	4	4	4	5	8	25
542 Keith Hernandez	4	4	4	4	4	8	10	40
543 Wayne Twitchell	4	4	4	4	4	5	6	15
544 Pepe Frias	4	4	4	4	4	5	6	15
545 Sparky Lyle	4	4	4	4	4	5	6	15
546 Dave Rosello	4	4	4	4	4	5	6	10
547 Roric Harrison	4	4	4	4	4	5	6	15
548 Manny Mota	4	4	4	4	4	5	6	15
549 Randy Tate RC	4	4	4	4	4	5	6	15
550 Hank Aaron	15	20	25	40	80	150	250	1,000
551 Jerry DaVanon	4	4	4	4	4	5	6	15
552 Terry Humphrey	4	4	4	4	4	5	6	15
553 Randy Moffitt	4	4	4	4	4	5	6	15
554 Ray Fosse	4	4	4	4	4	5	6	15
555 Dyar Miller	4	4	4	4	4	5	6	15
556 Minnesota Twins CL/Mauch	4	4	4	4	4	5	6	15
557 Dan Spillner	4	4	4	4	4	5	6	15
558 Clarence Gaston	4	4	4	4	4	5	6	15
559 Clyde Wright	4	4	4	4	4	5	6	15
560 Jorge Orta	4	4	4	4	4	5	6	15
561 Tom Carroll	4	4	4	4	4	5	6	40
562 Adrian Garrett	4	4	4	4	4	5	6	15
563 Larry Demery	4	4	4	4	4	5	6	15
564 Kurt Bevacqua GUM	4	4	4	4	4	5	6	50
565 Tug McGraw	4	4	4	4	4	5	6	15
566 Ken McMullen	4	4	4	4	4	5	6	15
567 George Stone	4	4	4	4	4	5	6	15
568 Rob Andrews RC	4	4	4	4	4	5	6	15
569 Nelson Briles	4	4	4	4	4	5	6	15
570 George Hendrick	4	4	4	4	4	5	6	15
571 Don DeMola	4	4	4	4	4	5	6	10
572 Rich Coggins	4	4	4	4	4	5	6	15
573 Bill Travers	4	4	4	4	4	5	8	25
574 Don Kessinger	4	4	4	4	4	5	6	10
575 Dwight Evans	4	4	4	4	4	6	8	25
576 Maximino Leon	4	4	4	4	4	5	6	15
577 Marc Hill	4	4	4	4	4	5	6	15
578 Ted Kubiak	4	4	4	4	4	5	6	25
579 Clay Kirby	4	4	4	4	4	5	6	15
580 Bert Campaneris	4	4	4	4	4	5	6	15

	VG 3	VgEx 4	EX 5	ExMt 6	NM 7	NmMt 8	NmMt+ 8.5	MT 9
581 St. Louis Cardinals CL Schoendienst	4	4	4	4	4	5	6	20
582 Mike Kekich	4	4	4	4	4	5	6	15
583 Tommy Helms	4	4	4	4	4	5	8	40
584 Stan Wall RC	4	4	4	4	4	5	6	15
585 Joe Torre	4	4	4	4	8	15	25	120
586 Ron Schueler	4	4	4	4	4	5	6	15
587 Leo Cardenas	4	4	4	4	4	5	6	10
588 Kevin Kobel	4	4	4	4	4	5	6	15
589 Rookie Pitchers	4	4	4	4	4	8	10	30
590 Rookie Outfielders	4	4	4	4	4	8	10	25
591 Rookie Pitchers	4	4	4	4	4	6	8	25
592 Willie Randolph RC	4	4	4	4	12	25	30	60
593 Rookie Pitchers	4	4	4	4	4	6	8	25
594 Rookie Catchers and Outfielders	4	4	4	4	4	5	6	15
595 Rookie Pitchers	4	4	4	4	4	5	6	15
596 Rookie Infielders	4	4	4	4	4	5	6	15
597 Rookie Pitchers	4	4	4	4	4	5	6	15
598 Rookie Outfielders	4	4	4	4	4	5	6	15
599 Ron Guidry RC	4	5	8	12	20	30	40	300
600 Tom Seaver	8	10	12	15	25	40	40	120
601 Ken Rudolph	4	4	4	4	4	5	6	15
602 Doug Konieczny	4	4	4	4	4	5	6	15
603 Jim Holt	4	4	4	4	4	5	6	15
604 Joe Lovitto	4	4	4	4	4	5	6	15
605 Al Downing	4	4	4	4	4	5	6	15
606 Milwaukee Brewers CL/Grammas	4	4	4	4	4	5	6	15
607 Rich Hinton	4	4	4	4	4	5	6	15
608 Vic Correll	4	4	4	4	4	5	6	15
609 Fred Norman	4	4	4	4	4	5	8	25
610 Greg Luzinski	4	4	4	4	4	6	15	60
611 Rich Folkers	4	4	4	4	4	5	6	15
612 Joe Lahoud	4	4	4	4	4	5	6	10
613 Tim Johnson	4	4	4	4	4	6	8	40
614 Fernando Arroyo RC	4	4	4	4	4	5	8	25
615 Mike Cubbage	4	4	4	4	4	5	6	15
616 Buck Martinez	4	4	4	4	4	5	6	10
617 Darold Knowles	4	4	4	4	4	5	6	12
618 Jack Brohamer	4	4	4	4	4	5	6	15
619 Bill Butler	4	4	4	4	4	6	8	80
620 Al Oliver	4	4	4	4	4	5	6	15
621 Tom Hall	4	4	4	4	4	5	8	25
622 Rick Auerbach	4	4	4	4	4	5	6	10
623 Bob Allietta RC	4	4	4	4	4	5	6	15
624 Tony Taylor	4	4	4	4	4	6	8	60
625 J.R. Richard	4	4	4	4	8	10		30
626 Bob Sheldon	4	4	4	4	4	5	6	10
627 Bill Plummer	4	4	4	4	4	5	6	15
628 John D'Acquisto	4	4	4	4	4	5	6	10
629 Sandy Alomar	4	4	4	4	4	6	8	30
630 Chris Speier	4	4	4	4	4	5	6	15
631 Atlanta Braves CL/Bristol	4	4	4	4	4	5	6	12
632 Rogelio Moret	4	4	4	4	4	5	6	15
633 John Stearns RC	4	4	4	4	4	5	6	15
634 Larry Christenson	4	4	4	4	4	5	8	60
635 Jim Fregosi	4	4	4	4	4	5	6	15
636 Joe Decker	4	4	4	4	4	5	6	15
637 Bruce Bochte	4	4	4	4	4	5	6	10
638 Doyle Alexander	4	4	4	4	4	5	6	15
639 Fred Kendall	4	4	4	4	4	5	6	15
640 Bill Madlock	4	4	4	4	4	8	10	20
641 Tom Paciorek	4	4	4	4	4	5	6	15
642 Dennis Blair	4	4	4	4	4	5	6	10
643 Checklist 529-660	4	4	4	4	4	6	8	25
644 Tom Bradley	4	4	4	4	4	5	6	15
645 Darrell Porter	4	4	4	4	4	5	6	15
646 John Lowenstein	4	4	4	4	4	5	6	15
647 Ramon Hernandez	4	4	4	4	4	5	15	150

	VG 3	VgEx 4	EX 5	ExMt 6	NM 7	NmMt 8	NmMt+ 8.5	MT 9
648	Al Cowens	4	4	4	4	4	6	8	
649	Dave Roberts	4	4	4	4	4	5	6	15
650	Thurman Munson	▲8	▲12	▲20	▲30	▲50	100	120	▲200
651	John Odom	4	4	4	4	4	5	6	30
652	Ed Armbrister	4	4	4	4	4	5	6	15
653	Mike Norris RC	4	4	4	4	4	5	6	15
654	Doug Griffin	4	4	4	4	4	5	6	15
655	Mike Vail RC	4	4	4	4	4	5	8	25
656	Chicago White Sox CL/Tanner	4	4	4	4	4	5	6	15
657	Roy Smalley RC	4	4	4	4	4	5	8	25
658	Jerry Johnson	4	4	4	4	4	5	6	10
659	Ben Oglivie	4	4	4	4	4	6	8	20
660	Davey Lopes	4	4	4	4	4	6	10	50

— George Brett #19 PSA 9 (MT) sold for $3,685 (eBay; 12/12)
— George Brett #19 PSA 9 (MT) sold for $3,200 (eBay; 11/12)
— Dennis Eckersley #98 PSA 10 (Gem) (Young Collection) sold for $6,684 (SCP; 5/12)
— Nolan Ryan #330 PSA 10 (Gem) sold for $3,119 (eBay; 08/12)
— Nolan Ryan #330 PSA 10 (Gem) sold for $2,984 (eBay; 11/12)

1976 Topps Traded

		GD 2	VG 3	VgEx 4	EX 5	ExMt 6	NM 7	NmMt 8	MT 9
27T	Ed Figueroa	4	4	4	4	4	4	5	20
28T	Dusty Baker	4	4	4	4	4	4	8	40
44T	Doug Rader	4	4	4	4	4	4	5	15
58T	Ron Reed	4	4	4	4	4	4	5	15
74T	Oscar Gamble	4	4	4	4	4	4	6	25
80T	Jim Kaat	4	4	4	4	4	4	6	25
83T	Jim Spencer	4	4	4	4	4	4	5	15
85T	Mickey Rivers	4	4	4	4	4	4	5	25
99T	Lee Lacy	4	4	4	4	4	4	5	100
120T	Rusty Staub	4	4	4	4	4	4	6	25
127T	Larvell Blanks	4	4	4	4	4	4	5	80
146T	George Medich	4	4	4	4	4	4	5	15
158T	Ken Reitz	4	4	4	4	4	4	5	20
208T	Mike Lum	4	4	4	4	4	4	5	20
211T	Clay Carroll	4	4	4	4	4	4	5	20
231T	Tom House	4	4	4	4	4	4	5	25
250T	Fergie Jenkins	4	4	4	4	4	5	10	50
259T	Darrel Chaney	4	4	4	4	4	4	5	20
292T	Leon Roberts	4	4	4	4	4	4	5	15
296T	Pat Dobson	4	4	4	4	4	4	5	25
309T	Bill Melton	4	4	4	4	4	4	5	15
338T	Bob Bailey	4	4	4	4	4	4	5	25
380T	Bobby Bonds	4	4	4	4	4	4	8	25
383T	John Ellis	4	4	4	4	4	4	5	15
385T	Mickey Lolich	4	4	4	4	4	4	6	20
401T	Ken Brett	4	4	4	4	4	4	5	15
410T	Ralph Garr	4	4	4	4	4	4	5	15
411T	Bill Singer	4	4	4	4	4	4	5	10
428T	Jim Crawford	4	4	4	4	4	4	5	80
434T	Morris Nettles	4	4	4	4	4	4	5	15
464T	Ken Henderson	4	4	4	4	4	4	5	15
497T	Joe McIntosh	4	4	4	4	4	4	5	15
524T	Pete Falcone	4	4	4	4	4	4	5	20
527T	Mike Anderson	4	4	4	4	4	4	5	12
528T	Dock Ellis	4	4	4	4	4	4	5	25
532T	Milt May	4	4	4	4	4	4	5	
534T	Ray Fosse	4	4	4	4	4	4	5	
579T	Clay Kirby	4	4	4	4	4	4	5	15
583T	Tommy Helms	4	4	4	4	4	4	5	15
592T	Willie Randolph	4	4	4	4	4	6	12	25
618T	Jack Brohamer	4	4	4	4	4	4	5	15
642T	Rogelio Moret	4	4	4	4	4	4	5	20
649T	Dave Roberts	4	4	4	4	4	4	5	
740T	Traded Checklist	▲4	▲8	▲12	▲20	▲30	4	6	25

1977 Topps

		VgEx 4	EX 5	ExMt 6	NM 7	NmMt 8	NmMt+ 8.5	MT 9	Gem 9.5/10
1	Batting Leaders	4	4	4	4	8	12	50	
2	Home Run Leaders	4	4	4	4	6	8	25	
3	RBI Leaders	4	4	4	4	5	6	15	100
4	Stolen Base Leaders	4	4	4	4	5	6	15	
5	Victory Leaders	4	4	4	4	5	6	15	
6	Strikeout Leaders	4	6	10	15	25	30	40	
7	ERA Leaders	4	4	4	4	6	8	50	
8	Leading Firemen	4	4	4	4	5	6	15	
9	Doug Rader	4	4	4	4	5	6	15	
10	Reggie Jackson	10	15	25	▲40	▼12	▲150	300	
11	Rob Dressler	4	4	4	4	5	6	15	
12	Larry Haney	4	4	4	4	5	6	15	
13	Luis Gomez RC	4	4	4	4	5	6	15	
14	Tommy Smith	4	4	4	4	6	8	20	
15	Don Gullett	4	4	4	4	5	6	15	
16	Bob Jones RC	4	4	4	4	5	6	15	
17	Steve Stone	4	4	4	4	5	8		
18	Cleveland Indians CL/Robinson	4	4	4	4	5	6	15	
19	John D'Acquisto	4	4	4	4	5	6	15	
20	Graig Nettles	4	4	4	4	6	8	25	100
21	Ken Forsch	4	4	4	4	5	6	15	
22	Bill Freehan	4	4	4	4	5	6	15	60
23	Dan Driessen	4	4	4	4	5	6	15	60
24	Carl Morton	4	4	4	4	5	6	60	50
25	Dwight Evans	4	4	4	4	6	10		
26	Ray Sadecki	4	4	4	4	5	6	15	100
27	Bill Buckner	4	4	4	4	5	6	15	
28	Woodie Fryman	4	4	4	4	5	6	15	50
29	Bucky Dent	4	4	4	4	6	8	30	
30	Greg Luzinski	4	4	4	4	6	8	15	100
31	Jim Todd	4	4	4	4	5	6	15	
32	Checklist 1-132	4	4	4	4	5	6	15	
33	Wayne Garland	4	4	4	4	5	6	15	50
34	California Angels CL/Sherry	4	4	4	4	5	6	30	50
35	Rennie Stennett	4	4	4	4	5	6	15	
36	John Ellis	4	4	4	4	5	6	15	
37	Steve Hargan	4	4	4	4	5	6	15	100
38	Craig Kusick	4	4	4	4	5	6	15	50
39	Tom Griffin	4	4	4	4	5	6	15	
40	Bobby Murcer	4	4	4	4	5	6	15	
41	Jim Kern	4	4	4	4	5	6	15	50
42	Jose Cruz	4	4	4	4	5	6	20	50
43	Ray Bare	4	4	4	4	5	6	15	
44	Bud Harrelson	4	4	4	4	5	6	15	50
45	Rawly Eastwick	4	4	4	4	5	6	20	
46	Buck Martinez	4	4	4	4	5	6	15	50
47	Lynn McGlothen	4	4	4	4	5	6	15	50
48	Tom Paciorek	4	4	4	4	5	6	15	
49	Grant Jackson	4	4	4	4	5	6	15	
50	Ron Cey	4	4	4	4	5	6	15	
51	Milwaukee Brewers CL/Grammas	4	4	4	4	5	6	15	100
52	Ellis Valentine	4	4	4	4	5	6	15	
53	Paul Mitchell	4	4	4	4	5	6	15	
54	Sandy Alomar	4	4	4	4	5	6	15	
55	Jeff Burroughs	4	4	4	4	5	6		
56	Rudy May	4	4	4	4	5	6	100	
57	Marc Hill	4	4	4	4	5	6	15	
58	Chet Lemon	4	4	4	4	5	6	20	
59	Larry Christenson	4	4	4	4	5	6	15	
60	Jim Rice	4	4	4	4	8	10	30	
61	Manny Sanguillen	4	4	4	4	5	6	15	
62	Eric Raich	4	4	4	4	5	6	15	50
63	Tito Fuentes	4	4	4	4	5	6	10	50
64	Larry Biittner	4	4	4	4	5	6	15	50

#	Player	VgEx 4	EX 5	ExMt 6	NM 7	NmMt 8	NmMt+ 8.5	MT 9	Gem 9.5/10
65	Skip Lockwood	4	4	4	4	5	6	15	50
66	Roy Smalley	4	4	4	4	5	6	15	50
67	Joaquin Andujar RC	4	4	4	4	5	6	15	120
68	Bruce Bochte	4	4	4	4	5	6	15	60
69	Jim Crawford	4	4	4	4	5	6	15	
70	Johnny Bench	8	10	15	20	40	40	100	
71	Dock Ellis	4	4	4	4	5	6	15	80
72	Mike Anderson	4	4	4	4	5	6	15	50
73	Charlie Williams	4	4	4	4	5	6	15	
74	Oakland Athletics CL/McKeon	4	4	4	4	5	6	15	
75	Dennis Leonard	4	4	4	4	5	6	50	
76	Tim Foli	4	4	4	4	5	6	15	
77	Dyar Miller	4	4	4	4	5	6	15	
78	Bob Davis	4	4	4	4	5	6	15	
79	Don Money	4	4	4	4	5	6	15	
80	Andy Messersmith	4	4	4	4	5	6	15	
81	Juan Beniquez	4	4	4	4	5	8		
82	Jim Rooker	4	4	4	4	5	6	15	50
83	Kevin Bell RC	4	4	4	4	5	6	60	
84	Ollie Brown	4	4	4	4	5	6	15	
85	Duane Kuiper	4	4	4	4	5	6	20	
86	Pat Zachry	4	4	4	4	5	6	60	
87	Glenn Borgmann	4	4	4	4	5	6	15	50
88	Stan Wall	4	4	4	4	5	6	15	50
89	Butch Hobson RC	4	4	4	4	6	8	60	
90	Cesar Cedeno	4	4	4	4	5	6	15	50
91	John Verhoeven RC	4	4	4	4	5	6	15	50
92	Dave Rosello	4	4	4	4	5	6	15	
93	Tom Poquette	4	4	4	4	5	6	15	50
94	Craig Swan	4	4	4	4	5	6	15	
95	Keith Hernandez	4	4	4	4	8	12	40	
96	Lou Piniella	4	4	4	4	5	6	15	60
97	Dave Heaverlo	4	4	4	4	5	6	15	
98	Milt May	4	4	4	4	5	6	20	
99	Tom Hausman	4	4	4	4	5	6	15	
100	Joe Morgan	4	4	4	8	15	20	50	
101	Dick Bosman	4	4	4	4	5	6	15	
102	Jose Morales	4	4	4	4	5	6	15	50
103	Mike Bacsik RC	4	4	4	4	5	8		
104	Omar Moreno RC	4	4	4	4	5	6	15	
105	Steve Yeager	4	4	4	4	5	6	15	
106	Mike Flanagan	4	4	4	4	5	6	12	
107	Bill Melton	4	4	4	4	5	6	10	50
108	Alan Foster	4	4	4	4	5	6	15	
109	Jorge Orta	4	4	4	4	5	6	15	
110	Steve Carlton	4	6	10	15	30	40	80	300
111	Rico Petrocelli	4	4	4	4	5	6	15	100
112	Bill Greif	4	4	4	4	5	6	15	
113	Toronto Blue Jays CL/Hartsfield	4	4	4	4	5	6	15	
114	Bruce Dal Canton	4	4	4	4	5	6	15	
115	Rick Manning	4	4	4	4	5	6	15	
116	Joe Niekro	4	4	4	4	5	6	15	
117	Frank White	4	4	4	4	5	6	15	
118	Rick Jones RC	4	4	4	4	5	6	15	
119	John Stearns	4	4	4	4	5	6	15	100
120	Rod Carew	4	6	10	25	50	60	120	
121	Gary Nolan	4	4	4	4	5	6	15	
122	Ben Oglivie	4	4	4	4	5	6	15	
123	Fred Stanley	4	4	4	4	5	6	15	
124	George Mitterwald	4	4	4	4	5	6	15	50
125	Bill Travers	4	4	4	4	5	6	15	
126	Rod Gilbreath	4	4	4	4	5	6	15	
127	Ron Fairly	4	4	4	4	5	6	15	50
128	Tommy John	4	4	4	4	5	6	15	
129	Mike Sadek	4	4	4	4	5	6	15	50
130	Al Oliver	4	4	4	4	5	6	15	
131	Orlando Ramirez RC	4	4	4	4	5	6	15	
132	Chip Lang RC	4	4	4	4	5	6	15	

#	Player	VgEx 4	EX 5	ExMt 6	NM 7	NmMt 8	NmMt+ 8.5	MT 9	Gem 9.5/10
133	Ralph Garr	4	4	4	4	5	6	15	
134	San Diego Padres CL/McNamara	4	4	4	4	5	6	15	
135	Mark Belanger	4	4	4	4	5	6	40	
136	Jerry Mumphrey RC	4	4	4	4	5	6	10	
137	Jeff Terpko RC	4	4	4	4	5	6	15	50
138	Bob Stinson	4	4	4	4	5	6	15	
139	Fred Norman	4	4	4	4	5	6	10	50
140	Mike Schmidt	4	4	8	12	30	30	80	
141	Mark Littell	4	4	4	4	5	6	150	
142	Steve Dillard RC	4	4	4	4	5	6	15	50
143	Ed Herrmann	4	4	4	4	5	6	15	50
144	Bruce Sutter RC	▲25	▲40	▲50	▲60	▲120	▲150	300	1,200
145	Tom Veryzer	4	4	4	4	5	6	15	
146	Dusty Baker	4	4	4	4	5	6	15	
147	Jackie Brown	4	4	4	4	5	6	15	
148	Fran Healy	4	4	4	4	5	6	15	
149	Mike Cubbage	4	4	4	4	5	6	250	
150	Tom Seaver	4	4	5	20	50	60	500	
151	Johnny LeMaster	4	4	4	4	5	6	15	
152	Gaylord Perry	4	4	4	4	6	8	20	
153	Ron Jackson RC	4	4	4	4	5	6	15	50
154	Dave Giusti	4	4	4	4	5	6	15	
155	Joe Rudi	4	4	4	4	5	6	15	60
156	Pete Mackanin	4	4	4	4	5	6	15	
157	Ken Brett	4	4	4	4	5	6	15	
158	Ted Kubiak	4	4	4	4	5	6	15	
159	Bernie Carbo	4	4	4	4	5	6	15	
160	Will McEnaney	4	4	4	4	5	6	25	80
161	Garry Templeton RC	4	4	4	4	8	10	20	
162	Mike Cuellar	4	4	4	4	5	6	15	
163	Dave Hilton	4	4	4	4	5	6	15	
164	Tug McGraw	4	4	4	4	5	6	15	
165	Jim Wynn	4	4	4	4	5	6	15	50
166	Bill Campbell	4	4	4	4	5	6	15	
167	Rich Hebner	4	4	4	4	5	6	15	50
168	Charlie Spikes	4	4	4	4	5	6	15	50
169	Darold Knowles	4	4	4	4	5	6	15	50
170	Thurman Munson	▲20	▲30	▲50	▲80	▲120	▲150	300	
171	Ken Sanders	4	4	4	4	5	6	15	50
172	John Milner	4	4	4	4	5	6	15	50
173	Chuck Scrivener RC	4	4	4	4	5	6	15	
174	Nelson Briles	4	4	4	4	5	6	15	50
175	Butch Wynegar RC	4	4	4	4	5	6	15	
176	Bob Robertson	4	4	4	4	5	6	15	
177	Bart Johnson	4	4	4	4	5	6	15	
178	Bombo Rivera RC	4	4	4	4	5	6	15	
179	Paul Hartzell RC	4	4	4	4	5	6	10	
180	Dave Lopes	4	4	4	4	5	6	20	
181	Ken McMullen	4	4	4	4	5	6	15	
182	Dan Spillner	4	4	4	4	5	6	15	
183	St.Louis Cardinals CL/V.Rapp	4	4	4	4	5	6	15	100
184	Bo McLaughlin RC	4	4	4	4	5	6	15	
185	Sixto Lezcano	4	4	4	4	5	6	10	50
186	Doug Flynn	4	4	4	4	5	6	15	
187	Dick Pole	4	4	4	4	5	8		
188	Bob Tolan	4	4	4	4	5	6	10	
189	Rick Dempsey	4	4	4	4	5	6	10	
190	Ray Burris	4	4	4	4	5	6	10	100
191	Doug Griffin	4	4	4	4	5	6	15	
192	Clarence Gaston	4	4	4	4	5	6	15	50
193	Larry Gura	4	4	4	4	5	6	10	50
194	Gary Matthews	4	4	4	4	5	6	15	
195	Ed Figueroa	4	4	4	4	5	6	15	50
196	Len Randle	4	4	4	4	5	6	15	
197	Ed Ott	4	4	4	4	5	6	15	50
198	Wilbur Wood	4	4	4	4	5	6	15	
199	Pepe Frias	4	4	4	4	5	8		
200	Frank Tanana	4	4	4	4	5	6	20	60

#	Name	VgEx 4	EX 5	ExMt 6	NM 7	NmMt 8	NmMt+ 8.5	MT 9	Gem 9.5/10
201	Ed Kranepool	4	4	4	4	5	6	30	
202	Tom Johnson	4	4	4	4	5	6	15	
203	Ed Armbrister	4	4	4	4	5	6	15	50
204	Jeff Newman RC	4	4	4	4	5	6	60	
205	Pete Falcone	4	4	4	4	5	6	15	50
206	Boog Powell	4	4	4	4	5	6	10	150
207	Glenn Abbott	4	4	4	4	5	8		
208	Checklist 133-264	4	4	4	4	5	8	25	80
209	Rob Andrews	4	4	4	4	5	6	15	
210	Fred Lynn	4	4	4	5	10	12	30	
211	San Francisco Giants CL/Altobelli	4	4	4	4	5	6	15	50
212	Jim Mason	4	4	4	4	5	6	10	
213	Maximino Leon	4	4	4	4	5	6	15	50
214	Darrell Porter	4	4	4	4	5	6	10	
215	Butch Metzger	4	4	4	4	5	6	15	
216	Doug DeCinces	4	4	4	4	5	6	15	
217	Tom Underwood	4	4	4	4	5	6	15	
218	John Wathan RC	4	4	4	4	5	6	15	
219	Joe Coleman	4	4	4	4	5	6	15	
220	Chris Chambliss	4	4	4	4	6	8	20	
221	Bob Bailey	4	4	4	4	5	6	15	
222	Francisco Barrios RC	4	4	4	4	5	6	15	
223	Earl Williams	4	4	4	4	5	6	15	
224	Rusty Torres	4	4	4	4	5	6	15	
225	Bob Apodaca	4	4	4	4	5	6	15	
226	Leroy Stanton	4	4	4	4	5	6	15	
227	Joe Sambito RC	4	4	4	4	5	6	15	
228	Minnesota Twins CL/Mauch	4	4	4	4	5	6	15	50
229	Don Kessinger	4	4	4	4	5	6	15	
230	Vida Blue	4	4	4	4	6	8	25	
231	George Brett RB	4	4	4	5	15	20	25	
232	Minnie Minoso RB	4	4	4	4	5	6	15	100
233	Jose Morales RB	4	4	4	4	5	6	12	
234	Nolan Ryan RB	8	10	12	20	25	30	50	
235	Cecil Cooper	4	4	4	4	5	6	10	
236	Tom Buskey	4	4	4	4	5	6	15	
237	Gene Clines	4	4	4	4	5	6	15	
238	Tippy Martinez	4	4	4	4	5	6	10	
239	Bill Plummer	4	4	4	4	5	6	15	
240	Ron LeFlore	4	4	4	4	6	8	20	120
241	Dave Tomlin	4	4	4	4	5	6	15	
242	Ken Henderson	4	4	4	4	5	6	15	
243	Ron Reed	4	4	4	4	5	6	15	50
244	John Mayberry	4	4	4	4	5	6	15	
245	Rick Rhoden	4	4	4	4	5	6	15	50
246	Mike Vail	4	4	4	4	5	6	15	60
247	Chris Knapp RC	4	4	4	4	5	6	15	
248	Wilbur Howard	4	4	4	4	5	6	15	50
249	Pete Redfern RC	4	4	4	4	5	6	15	
250	Bill Madlock	4	4	4	4	5	6	15	200
251	Tony Muser	4	4	4	4	5	6	10	50
252	Dale Murray	4	4	4	4	5	6	15	
253	John Hale	4	4	4	4	5	6	25	
254	Doyle Alexander	4	4	4	4	5	6	10	
255	George Scott	4	4	4	4	5	8		
256	Joe Hoerner	4	4	4	4	5	6	15	60
257	Mike Miley	4	4	4	4	5	6	15	
258	Luis Tiant	4	4	4	4	6	8	15	
259	New York Mets CL/Frazier	4	4	4	4	5	6	15	
260	J.R. Richard	4	4	4	4	5	6	15	100
261	Phil Garner	4	4	4	4	5	6	15	
262	Al Cowens	4	4	4	4	5	6	15	50
263	Mike Marshall	4	4	4	4	6	8	20	
264	Tom Hutton	4	4	4	4	5	6	15	
265	Mark Fidrych RC	4	5	10	20	30	40	250	
266	Derrel Thomas	4	4	4	4	5	6	15	80
267	Ray Fosse	4	4	4	4	5	6	15	
268	Rick Sawyer RC	4	4	4	4	5	6	15	50
269	Joe Lis	4	4	4	4	5	6	25	50
270	Dave Parker	4	4	4	4	6	8	50	
271	Terry Forster	4	4	4	4	5	6	15	
272	Lee Lacy	4	4	4	4	5	6	15	
273	Eric Soderholm	4	4	4	4	5	6	15	60
274	Don Stanhouse	4	4	4	4	5	6	15	50
275	Mike Hargrove	4	4	4	4	5	6	15	
276	Chris Chambliss ALCS	4	4	4	4	5	6	15	
277	Pete Rose NLCS	4	4	4	4	8	10	25	200
278	Danny Frisella	4	4	4	4	5	6	15	50
279	Joe Wallis	4	4	4	4	5	6	15	
280	Jim Hunter	4	4	5	10	20	30	150	
281	Roy Staiger	4	4	4	4	5	6	15	
282	Sid Monge	4	4	4	4	5	6	15	50
283	Jerry DaVanon	4	4	4	4	5	6	15	
284	Mike Norris	4	4	4	4	5	6	15	50
285	Brooks Robinson	▲8	▲12	20	▲30	▲50	▲60	▲120	
286	Johnny Grubb	4	4	4	4	5	6	15	
287	Cincinnati Reds CL/Anderson	4	4	4	4	6	8	50	
288	Bob Montgomery	4	4	4	4	5	6	15	
289	Gene Garber	4	4	4	4	5	6	60	
290	Amos Otis	4	4	4	4	5	6	15	120
291	Jason Thompson RC	4	4	4	4	6	8	50	
292	Rogelio Moret	4	4	4	4	5	6	15	
293	Jack Brohamer	4	4	4	4	5	6	15	
294	George Medich	4	4	4	4	5	6	15	
295	Gary Carter	4	4	5	10	20	25	30	200
296	Don Hood	4	4	4	4	5	6	10	50
297	Ken Reitz	4	4	4	4	5	6	15	
298	Charlie Hough	4	4	4	4	5	6	15	
299	Otto Velez	4	4	4	4	5	6	10	
300	Jerry Koosman	4	4	4	4	5	6	15	
301	Toby Harrah	4	4	4	4	6	8	25	
302	Mike Garman	4	4	4	4	5	6	15	50
303	Gene Tenace	4	4	4	4	5	6	15	
304	Jim Hughes	4	4	4	4	5	6	15	
305	Mickey Rivers	4	4	4	4	5	6	15	
306	Rick Waits	4	4	4	4	5	6	15	
307	Gary Sutherland	4	4	4	4	5	6	10	50
308	Gene Pentz RC	4	4	4	4	5	6	15	
309	Boston Red Sox CL/Zimmer	4	4	4	6	12	15	25	
310	Larry Bowa	4	4	4	4	5	6	15	100
311	Vern Ruhle	4	4	4	4	5	6	15	
312	Rob Belloir RC	4	4	4	4	5	6	15	
313	Paul Blair	4	4	4	4	5	6	15	
314	Steve Mingori	4	4	4	4	5	6	15	50
315	Dave Chalk	4	4	4	4	5	8		
316	Steve Rogers	4	4	4	4	5	6	15	
317	Kurt Bevacqua	4	4	4	4	5	6	10	
318	Duffy Dyer	4	4	4	4	5	6	15	
319	Goose Gossage	4	4	4	4	8	12	40	
320	Ken Griffey Sr.	4	4	4	4	6	8	20	
321	Dave Goltz	4	4	4	4	5	6	15	
322	Bill Russell	4	4	4	4	5	6	15	
323	Larry Lintz	4	4	4	4	5	6	15	
324	John Curtis	4	4	4	4	5	6	15	50
325	Mike Ivie	4	4	4	4	5	6	20	
326	Jesse Jefferson	4	4	4	4	5	6	15	
327	Houston Astros CL/Virdon	4	4	4	4	5	6	15	120
328	Tommy Boggs RC	4	4	4	4	5	6	15	100
329	Ron Hodges	4	4	4	4	5	6	15	
330	George Hendrick	4	4	4	4	5	6	15	
331	Jim Colborn	4	4	4	4	5	6	15	50
332	Elliott Maddox	4	4	4	4	5	6	15	
333	Paul Reuschel RC	4	4	4	4	5	6	20	50
334	Bill Stein	4	4	4	4	5	6	15	
335	Bill Robinson	4	4	4	4	5	6	15	
336	Denny Doyle	4	4	4	4	5	6	15	50

#	Name	VgEx 4	EX 5	ExMt 6	NM 7	NmMt 8	NmMt+ 8.5	MT 9	Gem 9.5/10
337	Ron Schueler	4	4	4	4	5	6	10	
338	Dave Duncan	4	4	4	4	5	6	15	
339	Adrian Devine	4	4	4	4	5	6	15	120
340	Hal McRae	4	4	4	4	5	6	15	60
341	Joe Kerrigan RC	4	4	4	4	5	6	15	80
342	Jerry Remy	4	4	4	4	5	6	15	50
343	Ed Halicki	4	4	4	4	5	6	15	50
344	Brian Downing	4	4	4	4	5	8		
345	Reggie Smith	4	4	4	4	5	6	15	50
346	Bill Singer	4	4	4	4	5	8		
347	George Foster	4	4	4	4	8	10	25	
348	Brent Strom	4	4	4	4	5	6	15	60
349	Jim Holt	4	4	4	4	5	6	15	
350	Larry Dierker	4	4	4	4	5	6	15	
351	Jim Sundberg	4	4	4	4	5	6	15	
352	Mike Phillips	4	4	4	4	5	6	15	
353	Stan Thomas	4	4	4	4	5	6	15	
354	Pittsburgh Pirates CL/Tanner	4	4	4	4	5	6	15	
355	Lou Brock	4	4	4	5	10	15	30	
356	Checklist 265-396	4	4	4	4	5	6	15	
357	Tim McCarver	4	4	4	4	5	6	15	
358	Tom House	4	4	4	4	5	6	15	
359	Willie Randolph	4	4	4	4	6	8	20	
360	Rick Monday	4	4	4	4	5	6	15	
361	Eduardo Rodriguez	4	4	4	4	5	6	15	
362	Tommy Davis	4	4	4	4	5	6	15	80
363	Dave Roberts	4	4	4	4	5	6	15	
364	Vic Correll	4	4	4	4	5	6	15	50
365	Mike Torrez	4	4	4	4	5	6	20	50
366	Ted Sizemore	4	4	4	4	5	6	15	50
367	Dave Hamilton	4	4	4	4	5	6	15	
368	Mike Jorgensen	4	4	4	4	5	6	15	
369	Terry Humphrey	4	4	4	4	5	6	15	50
370	John Montefusco	4	4	4	4	5	6	15	50
371	Kansas City Royals CL/Herzog	4	4	4	4	5	6	15	50
372	Rich Folkers	4	4	4	4	5	6	10	
373	Bert Campaneris	4	4	4	4	5	6	10	
374	Kent Tekulve	4	4	4	4	6	8	25	
375	Larry Hisle	4	4	4	4	5	6	15	
376	Nino Espinosa RC	4	4	4	4	5	6	15	
377	Dave McKay	4	4	4	4	5	6	10	50
378	Jim Umbarger	4	4	4	4	5	6	15	50
379	Larry Cox RC	4	4	4	4	5	6	15	
380	Lee May	4	4	4	4	5	6	15	80
381	Bob Forsch	4	4	4	4	5	6	15	50
382	Charlie Moore	4	4	4	4	5	6	15	60
383	Stan Bahnsen	4	4	4	4	5	8		
384	Darrel Chaney	4	4	4	4	5	6	15	50
385	Dave LaRoche	4	4	4	4	5	6	15	
386	Manny Mota	4	4	4	4	5	6	20	
387	New York Yankees CL/Martin	4	4	4	6	20	25	200	
388	Terry Harmon	4	4	4	4	5	8		
389	Ken Kravec RC	4	4	4	4	5	6	15	50
390	Dave Winfield	6	10	15	25	50	60	120	
391	Dan Warthen	4	4	4	4	5	6	15	50
392	Phil Roof	4	4	4	4	5	6	15	
393	John Lowenstein	4	4	4	4	5	6	15	
394	Bill Laxton RC	4	4	4	4	5	6	15	50
395	Manny Trillo	4	4	4	4	5	6	20	
396	Tom Murphy	4	4	4	4	5	6	15	50
397	Larry Herndon RC	4	4	4	4	5	6	15	
398	Tom Burgmeier	4	4	4	4	5	6	15	
399	Bruce Boisclair RC	4	4	4	4	5	6	20	
400	Steve Garvey	4	4	5	10	20	25	60	
401	Mickey Scott	4	4	4	4	5	6	20	
402	Tommy Helms	4	4	4	4	5	6	15	
403	Tom Grieve	4	4	4	4	5	6	15	
404	Eric Rasmussen RC	4	4	4	4	5	6	15	
405	Claudell Washington	4	4	4	4	5	6	15	
406	Tim Johnson	4	4	4	4	5	6	10	50
407	Dave Freisleben	4	4	4	4	5	6	15	
408	Cesar Tovar	4	4	4	4	5	6	15	50
409	Pete Broberg	4	4	4	4	5	6	15	100
410	Willie Montanez	4	4	4	4	5	6	15	
411	J.Morgan/J.Bench WS	4	4	4	4	6	8	20	
412	Johnny Bench WS	4	4	4	4	6	8	20	
413	Cincy Wins WS	4	4	4	4	5	6	15	60
414	Tommy Harper	4	4	4	4	5	6	15	50
415	Jay Johnstone	4	4	4	4	5	6	15	
416	Chuck Hartenstein	4	4	4	4	5	6	25	
417	Wayne Garrett	4	4	4	4	5	6	15	
418	Chicago White Sox CL/Lemon	4	4	4	4	6	8	30	
419	Steve Swisher	4	4	4	4	5	6	15	
420	Rusty Staub	4	4	4	4	5	6	30	
421	Doug Rau	4	4	4	4	5	6	15	
422	Freddie Patek	4	4	4	4	5	6	15	
423	Gary Lavelle	4	4	4	4	5	6	15	
424	Steve Brye	4	4	4	4	5	6	15	50
425	Joe Torre	4	4	4	4	6	8	20	60
426	Dick Drago	4	4	4	4	5	6	15	50
427	Dave Rader	4	4	4	4	5	6	15	
428	Texas Rangers CL/Lucchesi	4	4	4	4	5	6	15	
429	Ken Boswell	4	4	4	4	5	6	15	
430	Fergie Jenkins	4	4	4	4	6	8	10	
431	Dave Collins	4	4	4	4	5	8		
432	Buzz Capra	4	4	4	4	5	6	10	
433	Nate Colbert TBC	4	4	4	4	5	6	15	
434	Carl Yastrzemski TBC	4	4	4	4	5	6	10	
435	Maury Wills TBC	4	4	4	4	5	6	15	
436	Bob Keegan TBC	4	4	4	4	5	6	15	
437	Ralph Kiner TBC	4	4	4	4	5	6	15	
438	Marty Perez	4	4	4	4	5	6	15	50
439	Gorman Thomas	4	4	4	4	5	6	15	
440	Jon Matlack	4	4	4	4	5	6	15	60
441	Larvell Blanks	4	4	4	4	5	6	15	50
442	Atlanta Braves CL/Bristol	4	4	4	4	5	6	20	
443	Lamar Johnson	4	4	4	4	5	6	15	120
444	Wayne Twitchell	4	4	4	4	5	6	15	50
445	Ken Singleton	4	4	4	4	5	6	15	100
446	Bill Bonham	4	4	4	4	5	6	15	
447	Jerry Turner	4	4	4	4	5	6	15	
448	Ellie Rodriguez	4	4	4	4	5	6	15	50
449	Al Fitzmorris	4	4	4	4	5	6	15	
450	Pete Rose	▲10	▲15	▲25	▲40	▲60	▲100	▲250	2,500
451	Checklist 397-528	4	4	4	4	5	6	15	80
452	Mike Caldwell	4	4	4	4	5	6	15	
453	Pedro Garcia	4	4	4	4	5	6	15	
454	Andy Etchebarren	4	4	4	4	5	6	15	
455	Rick Wise	4	4	4	4	5	6	25	
456	Leon Roberts	4	4	4	4	5	8		
457	Steve Luebber	4	4	4	4	5	8		
458	Leo Foster	4	4	4	4	5	6	15	
459	Steve Foucault	4	4	4	4	5	6	15	50
460	Willie Stargell	4	4	5	6	12	15	50	
461	Dick Tidrow	4	4	4	4	5	6	15	120
462	Don Baylor	4	4	4	4	6	8	20	
463	Jamie Quirk	4	4	4	4	5	6	15	
464	Randy Moffitt	4	4	4	4	5	6	15	
465	Rico Carty	4	4	4	4	5	6	15	
466	Fred Holdsworth	4	4	4	4	5	6	15	
467	Philadelphia Phillies CL/Ozark	4	4	4	4	5	6	15	50
468	Ramon Hernandez	4	4	4	4	5	6	15	
469	Pat Kelly	4	4	4	4	5	6	15	
470	Ted Simmons	4	4	4	4	5	6	20	200
471	Del Unser	4	4	4	4	5	6	15	
472	Rookie Pitchers	4	4	4	4	5	6	15	

#	Player	VgEx 4	EX 5	ExMt 6	NM 7	NmMt 8	NmMt+ 8.5	MT 9	Gem 9.5/10
473	Andre Dawson RC	▲30	▲50	60	▲100	▲200	▲250	500	2,500
474	Rookie Shortstops	4	4	4	4	5	6	15	60
475	Rookie Pitchers	4	4	4	5	10	15		
476	Dale Murphy RC	▲25	▲40	▲60	80	▲120	▲150	▲500	1,000
477	Rookie Infielders	4	4	4	4	5	6	15	60
478	Rookie Pitchers	4	4	4	4	5	6	15	60
479	Rookie Outfielders	4	4	4	4	5	6	15	
480	Carl Yastrzemski	4	4	5	25	30	40	80	
481	Roger Metzger	4	4	4	4	5	6	15	
482	Tony Solaita	4	4	4	4	5	6	25	
483	Richie Zisk	4	4	4	4	5	6	15	
484	Burt Hooton	4	4	4	4	5	6	15	
485	Roy White	4	4	4	4	5	6	15	60
486	Ed Bane	4	4	4	4	5	6	15	50
487	Rookie Pitchers	4	4	4	4	5	6	15	60
488	J.Clark RC/L.Mazzilli RC	4	4	4	6	12	15	30	
489	Rookie Pitchers	4	4	4	4	6	8	20	60
490	Rookie Shortstops	4	4	4	4	5	6	25	
491	Dennis Martinez RC	4	4	4	5	10	12	25	150
492	Rookie Outfielders	4	4	4	4	5	6	15	
493	Rookie Pitchers	4	4	4	4	5	6	15	
494	Rookie Infielders	4	4	4	4	5	6	15	
495	Al Hrabosky	4	4	4	4	5	6	80	
496	Gary Thomasson	4	4	4	4	5	6	30	50
497	Clay Carroll	4	4	4	4	5	6	15	50
498	Sal Bando	4	4	4	4	5	6	15	
499	Pablo Torrealba	4	4	4	4	5	6	15	
500	Dave Kingman	4	4	4	4	6	8	40	
501	Jim Bibby	4	4	4	4	5	6	15	50
502	Randy Hundley	4	4	4	4	5	6	15	50
503	Bill Lee	4	4	4	4	5	6	15	50
504	Los Angeles Dodgers CL/Lasorda	4	4	4	4	5	6	10	60
505	Oscar Gamble	4	4	4	4	5	6	15	
506	Steve Grilli	4	4	4	4	5	6	15	50
507	Mike Hegan	4	4	4	4	5	6	15	50
508	Dave Pagan	4	4	4	4	5	8		
509	Cookie Rojas	4	4	4	4	5	6	15	50
510	John Candelaria	4	4	4	4	5	6	20	
511	Bill Fahey	4	4	4	4	5	6	15	50
512	Jack Billingham	4	4	4	4	5	6	15	
513	Jerry Terrell	4	4	4	4	5	6	15	
514	Cliff Johnson	4	4	4	4	5	6	15	
515	Chris Speier	4	4	4	4	5	6	15	
516	Bake McBride	4	4	4	4	5	6	15	
517	Pete Vuckovich RC	4	4	4	4	5	6	100	
518	Chicago Cubs CL/Franks	4	4	4	4	6	8	12	
519	Don Kirkwood	4	4	4		5	6	15	
520	Garry Maddox	4	4	4	4	5	6	15	
521	Bob Grich	4	4	4	4	5	6	20	
522	Enzo Hernandez	4	4	4	4	5	6	15	
523	Rollie Fingers	4	4	4	4	6	8	20	
524	Rowland Office	4	4	4	4	5	6	15	
525	Dennis Eckersley	4	6	10	25	40	40	▲120	300
526	Larry Parrish	4	4	4	4	5	6	15	80
527	Dan Meyer	4	4	4	4	5	6	15	
528	Bill Castro	4	4	4	4	5	6	15	50
529	Jim Essian RC	4	4	4	4	5	6	15	
530	Rick Reuschel	4	4	4	4	5	6	15	
531	Lyman Bostock	4	4	4	4	5	6	50	80
532	Jim Willoughby	4	4	4	4	5	6	15	100
533	Mickey Stanley	4	4	4	4	5	6	15	
534	Paul Splittorff	4	4	4	4	5	6	15	
535	Cesar Geronimo	4	4	4	4	5	6	15	60
536	Vic Albury	4	4	4	4	5	6	12	
537	Dave Roberts	4	4	4	4	5	6	15	
538	Frank Taveras	4	▲50	4	4	5	6	15	
539	Mike Wallace	4	4	4	4	5	6	10	50
540	Bob Watson	4	4	4	4	5	6	15	
541	John Denny	4	4	4	4	5	6	15	80
542	Frank Duffy	4	4	4	4	5	6	15	
543	Ron Blomberg	4	4	4	4	5	6	15	50
544	Gary Ross	4	4	4	4	5	6	15	50
545	Bob Boone	4	4	4	4	5	6	15	
546	Baltimore Orioles CL/Weaver	4	4	4	4	5	6	15	60
547	Willie McCovey	4	4	4	5	10	12	25	
548	Joel Youngblood RC	4	4	4	4	5	6	15	
549	Jerry Royster	4	4	4	4	5	8		
550	Randy Jones	4	4	4	4	6	8	30	
551	Bill North	4	4	4	4	5	6	15	50
552	Pepe Mangual	4	4	4	4	5	6	15	50
553	Jack Heidemann	4	4	4	4	5	6	15	
554	Bruce Kimm RC	4	4	4	4	5	6	15	
555	Dan Ford	4	4	4	4	5	6	15	50
556	Doug Bird	4	4	4	4	5	6	15	
557	Jerry White	4	4	4	4	5	6	15	
558	Elias Sosa	4	4	4	4	5	6	15	
559	Alan Bannister RC	4	4	4	4	5	6	15	50
560	Dave Concepcion	4	4	4	4	6	8	30	
561	Pete LaCock	4	4	4	4	6	8	20	
562	Checklist 529-660	4	4	4	4	5	6	15	60
563	Bruce Kison	4	4	4	4	5	6	15	120
564	Alan Ashby	4	4	4	4	5	6	15	
565	Mickey Lolich	4	4	4	4	6	8	20	80
566	Rick Miller	4	4	4	4	5	6	15	80
567	Enos Cabell	4	4	4	4	5	6	15	
568	Carlos May	4	4	4	4	5	6	15	
569	Jim Lonborg	4	4	4	4	5	6	15	
570	Bobby Bonds	4	4	4	4	6	8	20	
571	Darrell Evans	4	4	4	4	5	6	15	100
572	Ross Grimsley	4	4	4	4	5	5	10	50
573	Joe Ferguson	4	4	4	4	5	6	15	
574	Aurelio Rodriguez	4	4	4	4	5	6	15	50
575	Dick Ruthven	4	4	4	4	5	8		
576	Fred Kendall	4	4	4	4	5	6	15	
577	Jerry Augustine RC	4	4	4	4	5	6	10	
578	Bob Randall RC	4	4	4	4	5	6	15	
579	Don Carrithers	4	4	4	4	5	6	15	50
580	George Brett	12	15	20	25	50	60	200	1,500
581	Pedro Borbon	4	4	4	4	5	6	15	50
582	Ed Kirkpatrick	4	4	4	4	5	6	50	
583	Paul Lindblad	4	4	4	4	5	6	15	
584	Ed Goodson	4	4	4	4	5	6	10	
585	Rick Burleson	4	4	4	4	5	6	15	
586	Steve Renko	4	4	4	4	5	6	15	
587	Rick Baldwin	4	4	4	4	5	6	15	
588	Dave Moates	4	4	4	4	5	6	15	
589	Mike Cosgrove	4	4	4	4	5	6	15	50
590	Buddy Bell	4	4	4	4	5	6	10	50
591	Chris Arnold	4	4	4	4	5	6	15	
592	Dan Briggs RC	4	4	4	4	5	6	15	
593	Dennis Blair	4	4	4	4	5	6	15	
594	Biff Pocoroba	4	4	4	4	5	6	15	
595	John Hiller	4	4	4	4	5	6	15	50
596	Jerry Martin RC	4	4	4	4	5	8		
597	Seattle Mariners CL/Johnson	4	4	4	4	5	6	15	50
598	Sparky Lyle	4	4	4	4	6	8	20	
599	Mike Tyson	4	4	4	4	5	6	15	
600	Jim Palmer	4	4	4	8	15	20	100	
601	Mike Lum	4	4	4	4	5	6	15	
602	Andy Hassler	4	4	4	4	5	6	100	
603	Willie Davis	4	4	4	4	5	8		
604	Jim Slaton	4	4	4	4	5	6	15	
605	Felix Millan	4	4	4	4	5	6	10	
606	Steve Braun	4	4	4	4	5	6	15	
607	Larry Demery	4	4	4	4	5	6	15	
608	Roy Howell	4	4	4	4	5	6	15	

#	Player	VgEx 4	EX 5	ExMt 6	NM 7	NmMt 8	NmMt+ 8.5	MT 9	Gem 9.5/10
609	Jim Barr	4	4	4	4			20	
610	Jose Cardenal	4	4	4	4	5	8		
611	Dave Lemanczyk	4	4	4	4	5	6	15	
612	Barry Foote	4	4	4	4	5	6	15	
613	Reggie Cleveland	4	4	4	4	5	6	15	80
614	Greg Gross	4	4	4	4	5	6	15	50
615	Phil Niekro	4	4	4	4	8	10	40	
616	Tommy Sandt RC	4	4	4	4	5	6	15	80
617	Bobby Darwin	4	4	4	4	5	6	15	50
618	Pat Dobson	4	4	4	4	5	6	15	50
619	Johnny Oates	4	4	4	4	5	6	15	
620	Don Sutton	4	4	4	4	8	10	25	
621	Detroit Tigers CL/Houk	4	4	4	4	6	8	20	
622	Jim Wohlford	4	4	4	4	5	8		
623	Jack Kucek	4	4	4	4	5	8		
624	Hector Cruz	4	4	4	4	5	6	15	
625	Ken Holtzman	4	4	4	4	5	6	15	80
626	Al Bumbry	4	4	4	4	5	6	15	150
627	Bob Myrick RC	4	4	4	4	5	6	15	50
628	Mario Guerrero	4	4	4	4	5	6	15	80
629	Bobby Valentine	4	4	4	4	5	8		
630	Bert Blyleven	4	4	4	4	6	8		80
631	Brett Brothers	4	4	4	5	10	15		80
632	Forsch Brothers	4	4	4	4	5	8		
633	May Brothers	4	4	4	4	5	6	15	
634	Reuschel Brothers	4	4	4	4	5	6	20	
635	Robin Yount	4	4	6	12	50	60	350	
636	Santo Alcala	4	4	4	4	5	6	15	50
637	Alex Johnson	4	4	4	4	5	6	15	
638	Jim Kaat	4	4	4	4	5	6	15	80
639	Jerry Morales	4	4	4	4	5	6	15	
640	Carlton Fisk	4	4	6	20	25	30	100	
641	Dan Larson RC	4	4	4	4	5	6	15	50
642	Willie Crawford	4	4	4	4	5	6	15	50
643	Mike Pazik	4	4	4	4	5	8		
644	Matt Alexander	4	4	4	4	5	6	15	
645	Jerry Reuss	4	4	4	4	5	6	15	
646	Andres Mora RC	4	4	4	4	5	6	15	
647	Montreal Expos CL/Williams	4	4	4	4	5	6	15	
648	Jim Spencer	4	4	4	4	5	6	15	
649	Dave Cash	4	4	4	4	5	6	15	50
650	Nolan Ryan	12	20	30	50	120	150	600	
651	Von Joshua	4	4	4	4	5	6	40	
652	Tom Walker	4	4	4	4	5	6	15	50
653	Diego Segui	4	4	4	4	5	6	15	50
654	Ron Pruitt RC	4	4	4	4	5	6	15	
655	Tony Perez	4	4	4	6	12	15	40	
656	Ron Guidry	4	4	5	10	20	25		
657	Mick Kelleher RC	4	4	4	4	5	6	15	
658	Marty Pattin	4	4	4	4	5	6		
659	Merv Rettenmund	4	4	4	4	5	6	15	
660	Willie Horton	4	4	4	4	6	8	25	

— Tom Seaver #150 PSA 10 (Gem) sold for $1,368 (eBay; 02/12)

— Robin Yount #635 PSA 10 (Gem) sold for $1,813 (eBay; 01/12)

1977 Topps Cloth Stickers

#	Player	VG 3	VgEx 4	EX 5	ExMt 6	NM 7	NmMt 8	MT 9	Gem 9.5/10
1	Alan Ashby	4	4	4	4	5	6	12	80
2	Buddy Bell SP	4	4	4	4	5	6	12	
3	Johnny Bench	4	4	5	6	8	12	25	100
4	Vida Blue	4	4	4	4	5	6	12	
5	Bert Blyleven	4	4	4	4	5	6	12	40
6	Steve Braun SP	4	4	4	4	5	6	12	
7	George Brett	4	5	6	8	10	25	40	
8	Lou Brock	4	4	4	4	5	8	15	40
9	Jose Cardenal	4	4	4	4	5	6	12	
10	Rod Carew SP	4	4	4	5	6	10	25	100

#	Player	VG 3	VgEx 4	EX 5	ExMt 6	NM 7	NmMt 8	MT 9	Gem 9.5/10
11	Steve Carlton	4	4	4	4	5	8	15	80
12	Dave Cash	4	4	4	4	5	6	12	40
13	Cesar Cedeno SP	4	4	4	4	5	6	12	40
14	Ron Cey	4	4	4	4	5	6	15	50
15	Mark Fidrych	4	4	4	4	8	10	30	100
16	Dan Ford	4	4	4	4	5	6	12	30
17	Wayne Garland	4	4	4	4	5	6	12	50
18	Ralph Garr	4	4	4	4	5	6	12	40
19	Steve Garvey	4	4	4	4	5	8	15	50
20	Mike Hargrove	4	4	4	4	5	6	12	40
21	Jim Hunter	4	4	4	4	5	8	15	
22	Reggie Jackson	4	4	5	6	8	15	25	150
23	Randy Jones	4	4	4	4	5	6	15	
24	Dave Kingman SP	4	4	4	4	5	6	12	40
25	Bill Madlock	4	4	4	4	5	6	12	30
26	Lee May SP	4	4	4	4	5	6	12	40
27	John Mayberry	4	4	4	4	5	6	12	30
28	Andy Messersmith	4	4	4	4	5	6	12	50
29	Willie Montanez	4	4	4	4	5	6	12	30
30	John Montefusco SP	4	4	4	4	5	6	12	
31	Joe Morgan	4	4	4	4	5	8	15	50
32	Thurman Munson	4	4	5	6	8	12	50	100
33	Bobby Murcer	4	4	4	4	5	6	12	
34	Al Oliver SP	4	4	4	4	5	6	12	50
35	Dave Pagan	4	4	4	4	5	6	12	
36	Jim Palmer SP	4	4	4	4	5	8	15	200
37	Tony Perez	4	4	4	4	5	8	15	40
38	Pete Rose SP	8	10	12	15	20	40	▲250	
39	Joe Rudi	4	4	4	4	5	6	12	
40	Nolan Ryan SP	8	10	15	20	25	50	▲300	
41	Mike Schmidt	4	4	5	6	8	12	50	250
42	Tom Seaver	4	4	4	5	6	10	25	
43	Ted Simmons	4	4	4	4	5	6	12	50
44	Bill Singer	4	4	4	4	5	6	12	
45	Willie Stargell	4	4	4	4	5	8	30	40
46	Rusty Staub	4	4	4	4	5	6	12	100
47	Don Sutton	4	4	4	4	5	8	15	60
48	Luis Tiant	4	4	4	4	5	6	12	30
49	Bill Travers	4	4	4	4	5	6	12	
50	Claudell Washington	4	4	4	4	5	6	12	
51	Bob Watson	4	4	4	4	5	6	12	
52	Dave Winfield	4	4	4	4	8	15	30	100
53	Carl Yastrzemski	4	4	4	4	8	15	30	120
54	Robin Yount	4	4	4	5	6	10	25	100
55	Richie Zisk	4	4	4	4	5	6	12	40

1978 Kellogg's

#	Player	VG 3	VgEx 4	EX 5	ExMt 6	NM 7	NmMt 8	MT 9	Gem 9.5/10
1	Steve Carlton	4	4	4	4	4	5	10	30
2	Bucky Dent	4	4	4	4	4	4	8	25
3	Mike Schmidt	4	4	4	4	4	8	15	50
4	Ken Griffey	4	4	4	4	4	4	8	25
5	Al Cowens	4	4	4	4	4	4	8	25
6	George Brett	4	4	5	10	20	40	80	
7	Lou Brock	4	4	4	4	4	5	10	30
8	Goose Gossage	4	4	4	4	4	4	8	30
9	Tom Johnson	4	4	4	4	4	4	8	
10	George Foster	4	4	4	4	4	4	8	30
11	Dave Winfield	4	4	4	4	4	5	10	30
12	Dan Meyer	4	4	4	4	4	4	8	25
13	Chris Chambliss	4	4	4	4	4	4	8	25
14	Paul Dade	4	4	4	4	4	4	8	
15	Jeff Burroughs	4	4	4	4	4	4	8	
16	Jose Cruz	4	4	4	4	4	4	8	
17	Mickey Rivers	4	4	4	4	4	4	8	
18	John Candelaria	4	4	4	4	4	4	8	50
19	Ellis Valentine	4	4	4	4	4	4	8	25

		VG 3	VgEx 4	EX 5	ExMt 6	NM 7	NmMt 8	MT 9	Gem 9.5/10
20	Hal McRae	4	4	4	4	4	4	8	
21	Dave Rozema	4	4	4	4	4	4	8	
22	Lenny Randle	4	4	4	4	4	4	8	
23	Willie McCovey	4	4	4	4	4	5	10	
24	Ron Cey	4	4	4	4	4	4	8	30
25	Eddie Murray	4	4	4	5	10	20	40	
26	Larry Bowa	4	4	4	4	4	4	8	25
27	Tom Seaver	4	4	4	4	4	6	12	
28	Garry Maddox	4	4	4	4	4	4	8	
29	Rod Carew	4	4	4	4	4	5	10	
30	Thurman Munson	4	4	4	4	5	10	20	
31	Garry Templeton	4	4	4	4	4	4	8	30
32	Eric Soderholm	4	4	4	4	4	4	8	
33	Greg Luzinski	4	4	4	4	4	4	8	25
34	Reggie Smith	4	4	4	4	4	4	8	25
35	Dave Goltz	4	4	4	4	4	4	8	25
36	Tommy John	4	4	4	4	4	4	8	25
37	Ralph Garr	4	4	4	4	4	4	8	
38	Alan Bannister	4	4	4	4	4	4	8	25
39	Bob Bailor	4	4	4	4	4	4	8	
40	Reggie Jackson	4	4	4	4	4	8	15	50
41	Cecil Cooper	4	4	4	4	4	4	8	30
42	Burt Hooton	4	4	4	4	4	4	8	25
43	Sparky Lyle	4	4	4	4	4	4	8	30
44	Steve Ontiveros	4	4	4	4	4	4	8	25
45	Rick Reuschel	4	4	4	4	4	4	8	25
46	Lyman Bostock	4	4	4	4	4	4	8	
47	Mitchell Page	4	4	4	4	4	4	8	25
48	Bruce Sutter	4	4	4	4	4	4	8	
49	Jim Rice	4	4	4	4	4	4	8	25
50	Ken Forsch	4	4	4	4	4	4	8	25
51	Nolan Ryan	4	4	4	4	8	15	30	100
52	Dave Parker	4	4	4	4	4	4	8	30
53	Bert Blyleven	4	4	4	4	4	4	8	25
54	Frank Tanana	4	4	4	4	4	4	8	25
55	Ken Singleton	4	4	4	4	4	4	8	25
56	Mike Hargrove	4	4	4	4	4	4	8	
57	Don Sutton	4	4	4	4	4	4	8	30

1978 O-Pee-Chee

		GD 2	VG 3	VgEx 4	EX 5	ExMt 6	NM 7	NmMt 8	MT 9
154	Eddie Murray RC	4	4	4	8	15	50	150	800

— Milt May #115 PSA 10 (Gem) sold for $4,546 (eBay; 10/12)

— Eddie Murray #154 PSA 10 (Gem) sold for $2,385 (Mile High; 10/12)

1978 Tigers Burger King

		GD 2	VG 3	VgEx 4	EX 5	ExMt 6	NM 7	NmMt 8	MT 9
3	Jack Morris *	4	4	4	5	6	8	15	
13	Lou Whitaker *	4	4	4	5	6	8	15	
15	Alan Trammell *	4	4	5	6	8	15	30	120

— Cards produced by Topps and feature same design as basic 1978 Topps set (but photos are different).

1978 Topps

		VgEx 4	EX 5	ExMt 6	NM 7	NmMt 8	NmMt+ 8.5	MT 9	Gem 9.5/10
	Lou Brock RB	4	4	4	4	8	10	25	500
	Sparky Lyle RB	4	4	4	4	8	10	15	
	Willie McCovey RB	4	4	4	4	8	10	15	
	Brooks Robinson RB	4	8	10	20	40	50	80	
	Pete Rose RB	4	4	4	6	12	15	30	150
	Nolan Ryan RB	8	10	12	20	25	25	50	
	Reggie Jackson RB	4	4	4	5	10	12	20	
	Mike Sadek	4	4	4	4	4	5	8	
	Doug DeCinces	4	4	4	4	4	5	8	40
0	Phil Niekro	4	4	4	4	5	6	10	200
1	Rick Manning	4	4	4	4	4	5	8	50
2	Don Aase	4	4	4	4	4	5	8	40
3	Art Howe RC	4	4	4	4	8	10	15	

		VgEx 4	EX 5	ExMt 6	NM 7	NmMt 8	NmMt+ 8.5	MT 9	Gem 9.5/10
14	Lerrin LaGrow	4	4	4	4	4	5	8	50
15	Tony Perez DP	4	4	4	4	5	6	10	80
16	Roy White	4	4	4	4	4	6	10	80
17	Mike Krukow	4	4	4	4	4	5	8	40
18	Bob Grich	4	4	4	4	4	5	8	40
19	Darrell Porter	4	4	4	4	4	5	8	40
20	Pete Rose DP	8	10	12	15	▲25	▲30	80	300
21	Steve Kemp	4	4	4	4	4	5	8	
22	Charlie Hough	4	4	4	4	4	5	8	40
23	Bump Wills	4	4	4	4	4	5	8	40
24	Don Money DP	4	4	4	4	4	5	8	40
25	Jon Matlack	4	4	4	4	4	5	8	50
26	Rich Hebner	4	4	4	4	4	5	8	
27	Geoff Zahn	4	4	4	4	4	5	8	50
28	Ed Ott	4	4	4	4	4	5	8	50
29	Bob Lacey RC	4	4	4	4	4	5	8	
30	George Hendrick	4	4	4	4	4	5	8	40
31	Glenn Abbott	4	4	4	4	4	5	8	50
32	Garry Templeton	4	4	4	4	4	5	8	
33	Dave Lemanczyk	4	4	4	4	4	5	8	50
34	Willie McCovey	4	4	4	5	10	12	50	
35	Sparky Lyle	4	4	4	4	8	10	15	
36	Eddie Murray RC	40	50	60	100	300	400	1,500	▲50,000
37	Rick Waits	4	4	4	4	4	5	8	50
38	Willie Montanez	4	4	4	4	8	10	15	
39	Floyd Bannister RC	4	4	4	4	4	5	8	
40	Carl Yastrzemski	▲6	▲10	▲15	▲25	▲50	▲60	120	
41	Burt Hooton	4	4	4	4	4	5	8	40
42	Jorge Orta	4	4	4	4	4	5	8	50
43	Bill Atkinson RC	4	4	4	4	4	5	8	60
44	Toby Harrah	4	4	4	4	4	5	8	
45	Mark Fidrych	4	4	4	4	8	10	15	200
46	Al Cowens	4	4	4	4	4	5	8	
47	Jack Billingham	4	4	4	4	4	5	8	40
48	Don Baylor	4	4	4	4	5	6	10	50
49	Ed Kranepool	4	4	4	4	4	5	8	40
50	Rick Reuschel	4	4	4	4	4	5	8	60
51	Charlie Moore DP	4	4	4	4	4	5	8	40
52	Jim Lonborg	4	4	4	4	4	5	8	
53	Phil Garner DP	4	4	4	4	4	5	8	40
54	Tom Johnson	4	4	4	4	4	5	8	50
55	Mitchell Page RC	4	4	4	4	4	5	8	50
56	Randy Jones	4	4	4	4	4	5	8	
57	Dan Meyer	4	4	4	4	4	5	8	40
58	Bob Forsch	4	4	4	4	4	5	8	40
59	Otto Velez	4	4	4	4	4	5	8	50
60	Thurman Munson	4	4	5	10	20	25	50	
61	Larvell Blanks	4	4	4	4	4	5	8	40
62	Jim Barr	4	4	4	4	4	5	8	40
63	Don Zimmer MG	4	4	4	4	4	5	8	40
64	Gene Pentz	4	4	4	4	4	5	8	
65	Ken Singleton	4	4	4	4	4	5	8	40
66	Chicago White Sox CL	4	4	4	4	8	10	80	
67	Claudell Washington	4	4	4	4	4	5	8	40
68	Steve Foucault DP	4	4	4	4	4	5	8	40
69	Mike Vail	4	4	4	4	4	5	8	40
70	Goose Gossage	4	4	4	4	8	10	15	250
71	Terry Humphrey	4	4	4	4	4	5	8	
72	Andre Dawson	4	4	4	8	15	20	30	300
73	Andy Hassler	4	4	4	4	8	10	15	
74	Checklist 1-121	4	4	4	4	4	5	8	60
75	Dick Ruthven	4	4	4	4	4	5	8	50
76	Steve Ontiveros	4	4	4	4	4	5	8	50
77	Ed Kirkpatrick	4	4	4	4	4	5	8	60
78	Pablo Torrealba	4	4	4	4	4	5	8	60
79	Darrell Johnson MG DP	4	4	4	4	4	5	8	60
80	Ken Griffey Sr.	4	4	4	4	5	6	10	80
81	Pete Redfern	4	4	4	4	4	5	8	40

#	Player	VgEx 4	EX 5	ExMt 6	NM 7	NmMt 8	NmMt+ 8.5	MT 9	Gem 9.5/10
82	San Francisco Giants CL	4	4	4	4	8	10	15	
83	Bob Montgomery	4	4	4	4	4	5	8	100
84	Kent Tekulve	4	4	4	4	4	5	8	40
85	Ron Fairly	4	4	4	4	4	5	8	50
86	Dave Tomlin	4	4	4	4	4	5	8	40
87	John Lowenstein	4	4	4	4	8	10	15	
88	Mike Phillips	4	4	4	4	4	5	8	60
89	Ken Clay RC	4	4	4	4	8	10	15	120
90	Larry Bowa	4	4	4	4	4	5	8	40
91	Oscar Zamora	4	4	4	4	8	10	15	
92	Adrian Devine	4	4	4	4	4	5	8	40
93	Bobby Cox DP	4	4	4	4	4	5	8	40
94	Chuck Scrivener	4	4	4	4	4	5	8	
95	Jamie Quirk	4	4	4	4	4	5	8	40
96	Baltimore Orioles CL	4	4	4	8	15	20	30	40
97	Stan Bahnsen	4	4	4	4	8	10	15	
98	Jim Essian	4	4	4	4	4	5	8	
99	Willie Hernandez RC	4	4	5	10	20	25	40	80
100	George Brett	8	12	20	30	▲60	▲80	300	
101	Sid Monge	4	4	4	4	8	10	15	
102	Matt Alexander	4	4	4	4	8	10	15	
103	Tom Murphy	4	4	5	10	20	25	40	
104	Lee Lacy	4	4	4	4	4	5	8	40
105	Reggie Cleveland	4	4	4	4	4	5	8	40
106	Bill Plummer	4	4	4	4	8	10	15	
107	Ed Halicki	4	4	4	4	4	5	8	
108	Von Joshua	4	4	4	4	4	5	8	40
109	Joe Torre MG	4	4	4	4	5	6	12	50
110	Richie Zisk	4	4	4	6	12	15	25	
111	Mike Tyson	4	4	4	4	8	10	15	
112	Houston Astros CL	4	4	4	4	8	10	15	
113	Don Carrithers	4	4	4	4	4	5	8	
114	Paul Blair	4	4	4	4	5	6	10	
115	Gary Nolan	4	4	4	4	8	10	15	
116	Tucker Ashford RC	4	4	4	4	4	5	8	60
117	John Montague	4	4	4	4	4	5	8	40
118	Terry Harmon	4	4	4	4	4	5	8	40
119	Dennis Martinez	4	4	4	4	4	5	8	40
120	Gary Carter	4	4	4	4	8	10	15	350
121	Alvis Woods	4	4	4	4	8	10	15	60
122	Dennis Eckersley	4	4	4	4	8	10	15	100
123	Manny Trillo	4	4	4	4	4	5	8	40
124	Dave Rozema RC	4	4	4	4	4	5	8	40
125	George Scott	4	4	4	4	8	10	15	
126	Paul Moskau RC	4	4	4	4	4	5	10	40
127	Chet Lemon	4	4	4	4	4	5	8	40
128	Bill Russell	4	4	4	4	4	5	8	40
129	Jim Colborn	4	4	4	4	4	5	8	40
130	Jeff Burroughs	4	4	4	4	4	5	8	
131	Bert Blyleven	4	4	4	4	5	6	10	80
132	Enos Cabell	4	4	4	4	4	5	8	
133	Jerry Augustine	4	4	4	4	4	5	8	
134	Steve Henderson RC	4	4	4	4	4	5	8	100
135	Ron Guidry DP	4	4	4	4	8	10	15	100
136	Ted Sizemore	4	4	4	4	4	5	8	40
137	Craig Kusick	4	4	4	4	8	10	10	
138	Larry Demery	4	4	4	4	4	5	8	60
139	Wayne Gross	4	4	4	4	4	5	8	40
140	Rollie Fingers	4	4	4	4	5	6	10	100
141	Ruppert Jones	4	4	4	4	8	10	15	
142	John Montefusco	4	4	4	4	4	5	8	
143	Keith Hernandez	4	4	4	4	4	5	8	40
144	Jesse Jefferson	4	4	4	4	4	5	8	40
145	Rick Monday	4	4	4	4	4	5	8	
146	Doyle Alexander	4	4	4	4	4	5	8	40
147	Lee Mazzilli	4	4	4	4	4	5	8	40
148	Andre Thornton	4	4	4	4	8	10	15	
149	Dale Murray	4	4	4	4	4	5	8	40
150	Bobby Bonds	4	4	4	4	4	5	8	
151	Milt Wilcox	4	4	4	4	4	5	8	
152	Ivan DeJesus RC	4	4	4	4	4	5	8	60
153	Steve Stone	4	4	4	4	4	5	8	60
154	Cecil Cooper DP	4	4	4	4	4	5	8	
155	Butch Hobson	4	4	4	4	4	5	8	40
156	Andy Messersmith	4	4	4	4	4	5	8	100
157	Pete LaCock DP	4	4	4	4	4	5	8	40
158	Joaquin Andujar	4	4	5	10	20	25	40	
159	Lou Piniella	4	4	4	4	5	6	10	
160	Jim Palmer	4	4	4	4	8	10	15	200
161	Bob Boone	4	4	4	4	4	5	8	60
162	Paul Thormodsgard RC	4	4	4	4	4	5	8	50
163	Bill North	4	4	4	4	4	5	8	
164	Bob Owchinko RC	4	4	4	4	4	5	8	60
165	Rennie Stennett	4	8	10	20	40	50	80	
166	Carlos Lopez	4	4	4	4	4	5	8	40
167	Tim Foli	4	4	4	4	4	5	8	
168	Reggie Smith	4	4	4	4	4	5	8	
169	Jerry Johnson	4	4	4	4	8	10	15	50
170	Lou Brock	4	4	4	4	8	10	15	80
171	Pat Zachry	4	4	4	4	4	5	8	40
172	Mike Hargrove	4	4	4	4	8	10	15	
173	Robin Yount	▲6	▲10	15	20	▲30	▲40	▲80	300
174	Wayne Garland	4	4	4	4	4	5	8	60
175	Jerry Morales	4	4	4	4	4	5	8	60
176	Milt May	4	4	4	4	4	5	8	50
177	Gene Garber DP	4	4	4	4	4	5	8	40
178	Dave Chalk	4	4	4	4	8	10	15	
179	Dick Tidrow	4	4	4	4	6	8	12	
180	Dave Concepcion	4	4	4	4	5	6	10	80
181	Ken Forsch	4	4	4	4	4	5	8	
182	Jim Spencer	4	4	4	4	4	5	8	60
183	Doug Bird	4	4	4	4	8	10	60	
184	Checklist 122-242	4	4	4	4	4	5	8	60
185	Ellis Valentine	4	4	4	4	8	10	100	
186	Bob Stanley DP RC	4	4	4	4	4	5	8	
187	Jerry Royster DP	4	4	4	4	4	5	8	40
188	Al Bumbry	4	4	4	4	4	5	8	
189	Tom Lasorda MG DP	4	4	4	4	8	10	15	100
190	John Candelaria	4	4	4	4	4	5	8	80
191	Rodney Scott RC	4	4	4	4	4	5	8	
192	San Diego Padres CL	4	4	4	4	4	5	8	
193	Rich Chiles	4	4	4	4	4	5	8	
194	Derrel Thomas	4	4	4	4	4	5	8	60
195	Larry Dierker	4	4	4	4	4	5	8	
196	Bob Bailor	4	4	4	4	8	10	15	150
197	Nino Espinosa	4	4	4	4	4	5	8	
198	Ron Pruitt	4	4	4	4	4	5	8	40
199	Craig Reynolds	4	4	4	4	4	5	8	60
200	Reggie Jackson	4	4	5	20	40	50	120	
201	Batting Leaders	4	4	4	4	5	6	10	80
202	Home Run Leaders DP	4	4	4	4	6	8	12	100
203	RBI Leaders	4	4	4	4	4	5	8	50
204	Stolen Base Leaders DP	4	4	4	4	4	5	8	60
205	Victory Leaders	4	4	4	4	6	8	12	50
206	Strikeout Leaders DP	4	4	5	15	20	30	150	
207	ERA Leaders DP	4	4	4	4	5	6	10	40
208	Leading Firemen	4	4	4	4	6	8	12	
209	Dock Ellis	4	4	4	4	4	5	8	60
210	Jose Cardenal	4	4	4	4	4	5	8	
211	Earl Weaver MG DP	4	4	4	4	5	6	10	60
212	Mike Caldwell	4	4	4	4	4	5	8	
213	Alan Bannister	4	4	4	4	4	5	8	60
214	California Angels CL	4	4	4	4	4	5	8	200
215	Darrell Evans	4	4	4	4	4	5	8	50
216	Mike Paxton RC	4	4	4	4	4	5	8	40
217	Rod Gilbreath	4	4	4	4	4	5	8	60

#	Player	VgEx 4	EX 5	ExMt 6	NM 7	NmMt 8	NmMt+ 8.5	MT 9	Gem 9.5/10
218	Marty Pattin	4	4	4	4	4	5	8	40
219	Mike Cubbage	4	4	4	4	4	5	8	60
220	Pedro Borbon	4	4	4	4	4	5	8	60
221	Chris Speier	4	4	5	10	20	25	40	
222	Jerry Martin	4	4	4	4	4	5	8	40
223	Bruce Kison	4	4	4	4	4	5	8	60
224	Jerry Tabb RC	4	4	4	4	4	5	8	40
225	Don Gullett DP	4	4	4	4	5	6	10	50
226	Joe Ferguson	4	4	4	4	4	5	8	60
227	Al Fitzmorris	4	4	4	4	4	5	8	40
228	Manny Mota DP	4	4	4	4	4	5	8	40
229	Leo Foster	4	4	4	4	4	5	8	40
230	Al Hrabosky	4	4	4	4	4	5	8	
231	Wayne Nordhagen RC	4	4	4	4	8	10	15	
232	Mickey Stanley	4	4	4	4	4	5	8	60
233	Dick Pole	4	4	4	4	4	5	8	
234	Herman Franks MG	4	4	4	4	8	10	15	40
235	Tim McCarver	4	4	4	4	8	10	15	
236	Terry Whitfield	4	4	4	4	4	5	8	
237	Rich Dauer	4	4	4	4	8	10	15	50
238	Juan Beniquez	4	4	4	4	4	5	8	40
239	Dyar Miller	4	4	4	4	4	5	8	40
240	Gene Tenace	4	4	4	4	4	5	8	50
241	Pete Vuckovich	4	4	4	4	4	5	8	40
242	Barry Bonnell DP RC	4	4	4	4	4	5	8	
243	Bob McClure	4	4	4	4	4	5	8	60
244	Montreal Expos CL DP	4	4	4	4	4	5	8	40
245	Rick Burleson	4	4	5	10	20	25	250	
246	Dan Driessen	4	4	4	4	4	5	8	
247	Larry Christenson	4	4	4	4	4	5	8	40
248	Frank White DP	4	4	4	4	4	5	8	40
249	Dave Goltz DP	4	4	4	4	4	5	8	40
250	Graig Nettles DP	4	4	4	5	10	12	20	100
251	Don Kirkwood	4	4	4	4	4	5	8	40
252	Steve Swisher DP	4	4	4	4	4	5	8	40
253	Jim Kern	4	4	4	4	4	5	8	40
254	Dave Collins	4	4	4	4	4	5	8	50
255	Jerry Reuss	4	4	4	4	4	5	8	40
256	Joe Altobelli MG RC	4	4	4	6	12	15	25	80
257	Hector Cruz	4	4	4	4	4	5	8	60
258	John Hiller	4	4	4	4	8	10	15	200
259	Los Angeles Dodgers CL	4	4	5	10	20	25	40	
260	Bert Campaneris	4	4	4	4	4	5	8	40
261	Tim Hosley	4	4	4	4	4	5	8	40
262	Rudy May	4	4	4	4	4	5	8	60
263	Danny Walton	4	4	4	4	8	10	15	
264	Jamie Easterly	4	4	4	4	8	10	15	60
265	Sal Bando DP	4	4	4	4	4	5	8	40
266	Bob Shirley RC	4	4	4	4	4	5	8	40
267	Doug Ault	4	4	4	4	4	5	8	50
268	Gil Flores RC	4	4	4	4	4	5	8	
269	Wayne Twitchell	4	4	4	4	4	5	8	40
270	Carlton Fisk	4	4	4	4	8	10	20	200
271	Randy Lerch DP	4	4	4	4	4	5	8	40
272	Royle Stillman	4	4	4	4	8	10	15	60
273	Fred Norman	4	4	4	4	4	5	8	40
274	Freddie Patek	4	4	4	4	4	5	8	40
275	Dan Ford	4	4	4	4	4	5	8	
276	Bill Bonham DP	4	4	4	4	4	5	8	40
277	Bruce Boisclair	4	4	4	4	4	5	8	60
278	Enrique Romo RC	4	4	4	4	4	5	8	40
279	Bill Virdon MG	4	4	4	4	8	10	15	80
280	Buddy Bell	4	4	4	4	4	5	8	40
281	Eric Rasmussen DP	4	4	4	4	4	5	8	60
282	New York Yankees CL	4	6	8	15	30	40	200	
283	Omar Moreno	4	4	4	4	4	5	8	
284	Randy Moffitt	4	4	4	4	4	5	8	
285	Steve Yeager DP	4	4	4	4	4	5	8	40
286	Ben Oglivie	4	4	4	4	4	5	8	50
287	Kiko Garcia	4	4	4	4	4	5	8	60
288	Dave Hamilton	4	4	4	4	4	5	8	40
289	Checklist 243-363	4	4	4	4	4	5	8	40
290	Willie Horton	4	4	4	4	4	5	8	
291	Gary Ross	4	4	4	4	4	5	8	
292	Gene Richards	4	4	4	4	4	5	8	40
293	Mike Willis	4	4	4	4	4	5	8	40
294	Larry Parrish	4	4	4	4	4	5	8	50
295	Bill Lee	4	4	4	4	4	5	8	50
296	Biff Pocoroba	4	4	4	4	4	5	8	40
297	Warren Brusstar DP RC	4	4	4	4	4	5	8	40
298	Tony Armas	4	4	4	4	8	10	15	
299	Whitey Herzog MG	4	4	4	4	4	5	8	
300	Joe Morgan	4	4	4	5	10	12	20	200
301	Buddy Schultz RC	4	4	4	4	4	5	8	60
302	Chicago Cubs CL	4	4	4	4	8	10	50	
303	Sam Hinds RC	4	4	4	4	4	5	8	40
304	John Milner	4	4	4	4	4	5	8	80
305	Rico Carty	4	4	4	4	4	5	8	40
306	Joe Niekro	4	4	4	4	4	5	8	
307	Glenn Borgmann	4	4	4	4	4	5	8	40
308	Jim Rooker	4	4	4	4	4	5	8	40
309	Cliff Johnson	4	4	4	4	5	6	10	60
310	Don Sutton	4	4	4	4	5	6	10	100
311	Jose Baez DP RC	4	4	4	4	4	5	8	40
312	Greg Minton	4	4	4	4	4	5	8	80
313	Andy Etchebarren	4	4	4	4	4	5	8	
314	Paul Lindblad	4	4	4	4	4	5	8	
315	Mark Belanger	4	4	4	4	4	5	8	50
316	Henry Cruz DP	4	4	4	4	4	5	8	40
317	Dave Johnson	4	4	4	4	4	5	8	40
318	Tom Griffin	4	4	4	4	4	5	8	40
319	Alan Ashby	4	4	4	4	8	10	15	
320	Fred Lynn	4	4	4	4	6	8	12	
321	Santo Alcala	4	4	4	4	4	5	8	
322	Tom Paciorek	4	4	4	4	5	6	10	
323	Jim Fregosi DP	4	4	4	4	4	5	8	40
324	Vern Rapp MG RC	4	4	4	4	4	5	8	
325	Bruce Sutter	4	4	4	4	8	10	15	100
326	Mike Lum DP	4	4	4	4	4	5	8	40
327	Rick Langford DP RC	4	4	4	4	4	5	8	60
328	Milwaukee Brewers CL	4	4	5	10	20	25	40	
329	John Verhoeven	4	4	4	4	4	5	8	
330	Bob Watson	4	8	10	20	40	50	250	
331	Mark Littell	4	4	4	4	4	5	8	40
332	Duane Kuiper	4	4	4	4	4	5	8	
333	Jim Todd	4	4	4	4	8	10	15	
334	John Stearns	4	4	4	4	4	5	8	60
335	Bucky Dent	4	4	4	4	8	10	15	100
336	Steve Busby	4	4	4	4	4	5	8	60
337	Tom Grieve	4	4	4	4	4	5	8	50
338	Dave Heaverlo	4	4	4	4	8	10	15	
339	Mario Guerrero	4	4	4	4	4	5	8	40
340	Bake McBride	4	4	4	4	4	5	8	50
341	Mike Flanagan	4	4	4	4	4	5	15	100
342	Aurelio Rodriguez	4	4	4	4	4	5	8	60
343	John Wathan DP	4	4	4	4	4	5	8	25
344	Sam Ewing RC	4	4	4	4	8	10	15	
345	Luis Tiant	4	4	4	4	4	5	8	50
346	Larry Biittner	4	4	4	4	8	10	15	
347	Terry Forster	5	10	12	25	50	60	100	
348	Del Unser	4	4	4	4	4	5	8	
349	Rick Camp DP	4	4	4	4	8	10	15	
350	Steve Garvey	4	4	4	4	8	10	15	100
351	Jeff Torborg	4	4	4	4	8	10	15	60
352	Tony Scott RC	4	4	4	4	4	5	8	40
353	Doug Bair RC	4	4	4	4	4	5	8	

#	Player	VgEx 4	EX 5	ExMt 6	NM 7	NmMt 8	NmMt+ 8.5	MT 9	Gem 9.5/10
354	Cesar Geronimo	4	4	4	4	4	5	8	150
355	Bill Travers	4	4	4	4	4	5	8	40
356	New York Mets CL	4	4	4	4	8	10	20	50
357	Tom Poquette	4	4	4	4	4	5	8	
358	Mark Lemongello	4	4	4	4	4	5	8	40
359	Marc Hill	4	4	4	4	4	5	8	
360	Mike Schmidt	▲6	▲10	▲15	▲25	▲40	▲50	▲100	500
361	Chris Knapp	4	4	4	4	8	10	15	60
362	Dave May	4	4	4	4	4	5	8	40
363	Bob Randall	4	4	4	4	6	8	12	
364	Jerry Turner	4	4	4	4	4	5	8	
365	Ed Figueroa	4	4	4	4	8	10	10	
366	Larry Milbourne DP	4	4	4	4	8	10	15	
367	Rick Dempsey	4	4	4	4	4	5	8	40
368	Balor Moore	4	4	4	4	4	5	8	
369	Tim Nordbrook	4	4	4	4	8	10	15	
370	Rusty Staub	4	4	4	4	8	10	15	40
371	Ray Burris	4	4	4	4	4	5	8	
372	Brian Asselstine	4	4	4	4	4	5	8	40
373	Jim Willoughby	4	4	4	4	8	10	15	
374A	Jose Morales	4	4	4	4	4	5	8	
375	Tommy John	4	4	4	4	4	5	8	40
376	Jim Wohlford	4	4	4	4	8	10	15	60
377	Manny Sarmiento	4	4	4	4	4	5	8	60
378	Bobby Winkles MG	4	4	4	4	4	5	8	40
379	Skip Lockwood	4	4	4	4	8	10	15	60
380	Ted Simmons	4	4	4	4	5	6	10	50
381	Philadelphia Phillies CL	4	4	4	4	4	5	8	40
382	Joe Lahoud	4	4	4	4	4	5	8	60
383	Mario Mendoza	4	4	4	4	4	5	8	40
384	Jack Clark	4	4	4	4	5	6	10	80
385	Tito Fuentes	4	4	4	4	5	6	10	
386	Bob Gorinski RC	4	4	4	4	8	10	15	
387	Ken Holtzman	4	4	4	4	5	6	10	
388	Bill Fahey DP	4	4	4	4	4	5	8	40
389	Julio Gonzalez RC	4	4	4	4	4	5	8	
390	Oscar Gamble	4	4	4	4	4	5	8	
391	Larry Haney	4	4	4	4	4	5	8	40
392	Billy Almon	4	4	4	4	4	5	8	40
393	Tippy Martinez	4	4	4	4	4	5	8	
394	Roy Howell DP	4	4	4	4	4	5	8	40
395	Jim Hughes	4	4	4	5	10	12	20	
396	Bob Stinson DP	4	4	4	4	4	5	8	40
397	Greg Gross	4	4	4	4	4	5	8	
398	Don Hood	4	4	4	4	4	5	8	40
399	Pete Mackanin	4	4	4	4	4	5	8	
400	Nolan Ryan	12	15	25	30	80	80	▲2,500	
401	Sparky Anderson MG	4	4	4	4	5	6	10	80
402	Dave Campbell	4	4	5	10	20	25	40	
403	Bud Harrelson	4	4	4	4	4	5	8	40
404	Detroit Tigers CL	4	4	4	4	5	6	10	80
405	Rawly Eastwick	4	4	4	4	4	5	8	
406	Mike Jorgensen	4	4	4	4	4	5	8	
407	Odell Jones RC	4	4	4	4	4	5	8	40
408	Joe Zdeb RC	4	4	4	4	4	5	8	
409	Ron Schueler	4	4	4	4	4	5	8	
410	Bill Madlock	4	4	4	4	4	5	8	
411	Mickey Rivers ALCS	4	4	4	4	5	6	10	80
412	Davey Lopes NLCS	4	4	4	4	8	10	15	120
413	Reggie Jackson WS	4	4	4	5	10	12	25	
414	Darold Knowles DP	4	4	4	4	4	5	8	
415	Ray Fosse	4	4	4	4	4	5	8	
416	Jack Brohamer	4	4	4	4	4	5	8	
417	Mike Garman DP	4	4	4	4	4	5	8	40
418	Tony Muser	4	4	4	4	4	5	8	60
419	Jerry Garvin RC	4	4	4	4	8	10	15	
420	Greg Luzinski	4	4	4	4	4	5	8	60
421	Junior Moore RC	4	4	4	4	4	5	8	40
422	Steve Braun	4	4	4	4	4	5	8	40
423	Dave Rosello	4	4	4	4	4	5	8	60
424	Boston Red Sox CL	4	4	4	4	8	10	15	60
425	Steve Rogers DP	4	4	4	4	4	5	8	40
426	Fred Kendall	4	4	4	4	4	5	8	60
427	Mario Soto RC	4	4	4	4	4	5	8	100
428	Joel Youngblood	4	4	4	4	4	5	8	60
429	Mike Barlow RC	4	4	4	4	4	5	8	40
430	Al Oliver	4	4	4	4	4	5	8	50
431	Butch Metzger	4	4	4	4	4	5	8	
432	Terry Bulling RC	4	4	4	4	4	5	8	
433	Fernando Gonzalez	4	4	4	4	4	5	8	
434	Mike Norris	4	4	4	4	4	5	8	100
435	Checklist 364-484	4	4	4	4	4	5	8	60
436	Vic Harris DP	4	4	4	4	4	5	8	60
437	Bo McLaughlin	4	4	4	4	4	5	8	60
438	John Ellis	4	4	4	4	4	5	8	40
439	Ken Kravec	4	4	4	4	4	5	8	40
440	Dave Lopes	4	4	4	4	4	5	8	
441	Larry Gura	4	4	4	4	4	5	8	40
442	Elliott Maddox	4	4	4	4	4	5	8	
443	Darrel Chaney	4	4	4	4	4	5	8	
444	Roy Hartsfield MG	4	4	5	10	20	25	40	
445	Mike Ivie	4	4	4	4	4	5	8	40
446	Tug McGraw	4	4	4	4	4	5	8	60
447	Leroy Stanton	4	4	4	4	4	5	8	40
448	Bill Castro	4	4	4	4	4	5	8	60
449	Tim Blackwell DP RC	4	4	4	4	4	5	8	40
450	Tom Seaver	4	5	8	12	20	25	50	200
451	Minnesota Twins CL	4	4	4	4	8	10	15	
452	Jerry Mumphrey	4	4	4	4	4	5	8	60
453	Doug Flynn	4	4	4	4	4	5	8	40
454	Dave LaRoche	4	4	4	4	4	5	8	40
455	Bill Robinson	4	4	4	4	4	5	8	50
456	Vern Ruhle	4	4	5	10	20	25	50	
457	Bob Bailey	4	4	4	4	4	5	8	
458	Jeff Newman	4	4	4	4	4	5	8	40
459	Charlie Spikes	4	4	4	4	4	5	8	40
460	Jim Hunter	4	4	4	4	8	10	15	120
461	Rob Andrews DP	4	4	4	4	4	5	8	
462	Rogelio Moret	4	4	4	4	4	5	8	40
463	Kevin Bell	4	4	4	4	4	5	8	
464	Jerry Grote	4	4	4	4	4	5	8	
465	Hal McRae	4	4	4	4	4	5	8	
466	Dennis Blair	4	6	8	15	30	40	60	
467	Alvin Dark MG	4	4	4	4	4	5	8	50
468	Warren Cromartie RC	4	4	4	4	4	5	8	40
469	Rick Cerone	4	4	4	4	4	5	8	40
470	J.R. Richard	4	4	4	4	4	5	8	50
471	Roy Smalley	4	4	4	4	4	5	8	
472	Ron Reed	4	4	4	4	4	5	8	40
473	Bill Buckner	4	4	4	4	4	5	8	40
474	Jim Slaton	4	4	4	4	4	5	8	40
475	Gary Matthews	4	4	4	4	4	5	8	40
476	Bill Stein	4	4	4	4	4	5	8	40
477	Doug Capilla RC	4	4	4	4	4	5	8	
478	Jerry Remy	4	4	4	4	4	5	8	60
479	St. Louis Cardinals CL	4	4	4	4	4	5	8	
480	Ron LeFlore	4	4	4	4	4	5	8	40
481	Jackson Todd RC	4	4	4	4	8	10		
482	Rick Miller	4	4	4	4	8	10	15	
483	Ken Macha RC	4	4	4	4	4	5	8	
484	Jim Norris RC	4	4	4	4	8	10	15	
485	Chris Chambliss	4	4	4	4	5	6	10	60
486	John Curtis	4	4	4	4	4	5	8	60
487	Jim Tyrone	4	4	4	4	4	5	8	
488	Dan Spillner	4	4	4	4	4	5	8	40
489	Rudy Meoli	4	4	5	10	20	25	40	

#	Player	VgEx 4	EX 5	ExMt 6	NM 7	NmMt 8	NmMt+ 8.5	MT 9	Gem 9.5/10
90	Amos Otis	4	4	4	4	4	5	8	50
91	Scott McGregor	4	4	4	4	5	6	10	60
92	Jim Sundberg	4	4	4	4	4	5	8	50
93	Steve Renko	4	4	4	4	5	40		
94	Chuck Tanner MG	4	4	4	4	4	5	8	40
95	Dave Cash	4	4	4	4	4	5	8	60
96	Jim Clancy DP RC	4	4	4	4	4	5	8	40
97	Glenn Adams	4	4	4	4	4	5	8	40
98	Joe Sambito	4	4	4	4	4	5	8	40
99	Seattle Mariners CL	4	4	4	4	4	5	8	40
00	George Foster	4	4	4	4	8	10	15	150
01	Dave Roberts	4	4	4	4	4	5	8	60
02	Pat Rockett RC	4	4	4	4	4	5	8	60
03	Ike Hampton RC	4	4	4	4	4	5	8	
04	Roger Freed	4	4	4	6	12	15	25	
05	Felix Millan	4	4	4	4	4	5	8	
06	Ron Blomberg	4	4	5	10	20	25	40	
07	Willie Crawford	4	4	4	4	4	5	8	
08	Johnny Oates	4	4	4	8	15	20	30	
09	Brent Strom	4	4	4	4	8	10	15	
10	Willie Stargell	4	4	4	4	8	10	15	100
11	Frank Duffy	4	4	4	4	4	5	8	40
12	Larry Herndon	4	4	4	4	8	10	15	
13	Barry Foote	4	4	4	4	4	5	8	
14	Rob Sperring	4	4	4	4	4	5	8	60
15	Tim Corcoran RC	4	4	4	4	8	10	15	
16	Gary Beare RC	4	4	4	4	8	10	15	
17	Andres Mora	4	4	4	4	8	10	15	
18	Tommy Boggs DP	4	4	4	4	4	5	8	50
19	Brian Downing	4	4	4	4	4	5	8	
20	Larry Hisle	4	4	4	4	4	5	8	80
21	Steve Staggs RC	4	4	4	4	4	5	8	60
22	Dick Williams MG	4	4	4	4	8	10	80	
23	Donnie Moore RC	4	4	4	4	4	5	8	
24	Bernie Carbo	4	4	4	4	4	5	8	40
25	Jerry Terrell	4	4	4	4	8	10	15	60
26	Cincinnati Reds CL	4	5	6	12	25	30	150	
27	Vic Correll	4	4	4	4	4	5	8	
28	Rob Picciolo RC	4	4	4	4	4	5	8	100
29	Paul Hartzell	4	4	4	4	4	5	8	40
30	Dave Winfield	4	4	4	6	12	15	30	200
31	Tom Underwood	4	4	4	4	8	10	15	
32	Skip Jutze	4	4	4	4	4	5	8	
33	Sandy Alomar	4	4	4	4	8	10	15	
34	Wilbur Howard	4	4	5	10	20	25	40	
35	Checklist 485-605	4	4	4	4	4	5	8	
36	Roric Harrison	4	4	4	4	4	5	8	
37	Bruce Bochte	4	4	4	4	4	5	8	40
38	Johnny LeMaster	4	4	4	4	8	10		
39	Vic Davalillo DP	4	4	4	4	4	5	8	50
40	Steve Carlton	4	4	4	4	8	10	15	200
41	Larry Cox	4	4	4	4	4	5	8	
42	Tim Johnson	4	4	4	4	8	10	15	
43	Larry Harlow DP RC	4	4	4	4	4	5	8	50
44	Len Randle DP	4	4	4	4	4	5	8	40
45	Bill Campbell	4	4	4	4	4	5	8	40
46	Ted Martinez	4	4	4	4	4	5	8	40
47	John Scott	4	4	4	4	4	5	8	40
48	Billy Hunter MG DP	4	4	4	4	4	5	8	40
49	Joe Kerrigan	4	4	4	4	4	5	8	
50	John Mayberry	4	4	4	4	4	5	8	50
51	Atlanta Braves CL	4	4	4	4	4	5	8	
52	Francisco Barrios	4	4	4	4	4	5	8	50
53	Terry Puhl RC	4	4	4	4	4	5	8	80
54	Joe Coleman	4	4	4	4	4	5	8	
55	Butch Wynegar	4	4	4	4	8	10	15	
56	Ed Armbrister	4	4	4	4	8	10	15	
57	Tony Solaita	4	4	4	4	4	5	8	40

#	Player	VgEx 4	EX 5	ExMt 6	NM 7	NmMt 8	NmMt+ 8.5	MT 9	Gem 9.5/10
558	Paul Mitchell	4	4	4	4	4	5	8	
559	Phil Mankowski	4	4	5	10	20	25	80	
560	Dave Parker	4	4	6	12	25	30	120	
561	Charlie Williams	4	4	4	4	4	5	8	
562	Glenn Burke RC	4	4	5	10	20	25	60	
563	Dave Rader	4	5	6	12	25	30	50	
564	Mick Kelleher	4	4	4	4	4	5	8	60
565	Jerry Koosman	4	4	4	4	4	5	8	50
566	Merv Rettenmund	4	4	4	4	4	5	8	60
567	Dick Drago	4	4	4	4	4	5	8	
568	Tom Hutton	4	4	4	4	4	5	8	60
569	Lary Sorensen RC	4	4	4	4	4	5	8	
570	Dave Kingman	4	4	4	4	5	6	10	60
571	Buck Martinez	4	4	4	4	4	5	8	40
572	Rick Wise	4	4	5	10	20	25	40	
573	Luis Gomez	4	4	4	6	12	15	25	
574	Bob Lemon MG	4	4	4	6	12	15	25	
575	Pat Dobson	4	4	4	4	4	5	8	40
576	Sam Mejias	4	4	4	4	8	10	100	
577	Oakland Athletics CL	4	4	4	4	4	5	8	40
578	Buzz Capra	4	4	4	4	4	5	8	
579	Rance Mulliniks RC	4	4	4	4	4	5	8	
580	Rod Carew	4	4	4	8	15	20	80	
581	Lynn McGlothen	4	4	4	4	4	5	8	40
582	Fran Healy	4	4	4	4	8	10	15	
583	George Medich	4	4	4	4	4	5	8	40
584	John Hale	4	4	4	4	8	10	15	60
585	Woodie Fryman DP	4	4	4	4	4	5	8	40
586	Ed Goodson	4	4	4	4	8	10	15	60
587	John Urrea RC	4	4	4	4	4	5	8	
588	Jim Mason	4	4	4	4	4	5	8	
589	Bob Knepper RC	4	4	4	4	4	5	8	
590	Bobby Murcer	4	4	4	5	10	12	20	
591	George Zeber RC	4	4	4	4	5	6	10	80
592	Bob Apodaca	4	4	4	4	8	10	15	
593	Dave Skaggs RC	4	4	4	4	4	5	8	60
594	Dave Freisleben	4	4	4	4	4	5	8	50
595	Sixto Lezcano	4	4	4	4	4	5	8	40
596	Gary Wheelock	4	4	4	4	4	5	8	40
597	Steve Dillard	4	4	4	4	8	10	15	
598	Eddie Solomon	4	4	4	4	4	5	8	
599	Gary Woods	4	4	4	4	4	5	8	
600	Frank Tanana	4	4	4	4	4	5	8	
601	Gene Mauch MG	4	4	4	4	8	10	15	
602	Eric Soderholm	4	4	4	4	4	5	8	80
603	Will McEnaney	4	4	4	4	4	5	8	
604	Earl Williams	4	4	4	4	4	5	8	40
605	Rick Rhoden	4	4	4	4	4	5	8	50
606	Pittsburgh Pirates CL	4	4	4	4	8	10	15	
607	Fernando Arroyo	4	4	4	4	8	10	15	
608	Johnny Grubb	4	4	4	4	8	10	15	
609	John Denny	4	4	4	4	8	10	60	
610	Garry Maddox	4	4	4	4	8	10	15	50
611	Pat Scanlon RC	4	4	4	4	4	5	8	
612	Ken Henderson	4	4	4	4	4	5	8	
613	Marty Perez	4	4	4	4	4	5	8	40
614	Joe Wallis	4	4	4	4	4	5	8	
615	Clay Carroll	4	4	4	4	4	5	8	
616	Pat Kelly	4	4	4	4	4	5	8	
617	Joe Nolan RC	4	4	4	4	4	5	8	
618	Tommy Helms	4	4	4	4	8	10	60	60
619	Thad Bosley DP RC	4	4	4	4	4	5	8	
620	Willie Randolph	4	4	4	4	8	10	15	100
621	Craig Swan DP	4	4	4	4	4	5	8	40
622	Champ Summers	4	4	4	4	4	5	8	
623	Eduardo Rodriguez	4	4	4	4	4	5	8	
624	Gary Alexander DP	4	4	4	4	4	5	8	
625	Jose Cruz	4	4	4	4	4	5	8	40

#	Name	VgEx 4	EX 5	ExMt 6	NM 7	NmMt 8	NmMt+ 8.5	MT 9	Gem 9.5/10
626	Toronto Blue Jays CL DP	4	4	4	4	4	5	8	40
627	David Johnson	4	4	4	4	4	5	8	50
628	Ralph Garr	4	4	4	4	4	5	8	
629	Don Stanhouse	4	4	4	4	4	5	8	40
630	Ron Cey	4	6	8	15	30	40	60	
631	Danny Ozark MG	4	4	4	4	4	5	8	60
632	Rowland Office	4	4	4	4	4	5	8	60
633	Tom Veryzer	4	4	4	4	4	5	8	60
634	Len Barker	4	4	4	4	4	5	8	
635	Joe Rudi	4	4	4	4	4	5	8	40
636	Jim Bibby	4	4	4	4	8	10	15	
637	Duffy Dyer	4	4	4	4	4	5	8	40
638	Paul Splittorff	4	4	4	4	4	5	8	
639	Gene Clines	4	4	4	4	4	5	8	
640	Lee May DP	4	4	4	4	4	5	8	60
641	Doug Rau	4	4	4	4	4	5	8	40
642	Denny Doyle	4	4	5	10	20	25	120	
643	Tom House	4	4	4	4	4	5	8	
644	Jim Dwyer	4	4	4	4	4	5	8	
645	Mike Torrez	4	4	4	4	8	10	15	
646	Rick Auerbach DP	4	4	4	4	4	5	8	50
647	Steve Dunning	4	4	4	4	4	5	8	40
648	Gary Thomasson	4	4	4	4	4	5	8	
649	Moose Haas RC	4	4	4	4	4	5	8	
650	Cesar Cedeno	4	4	4	4	4	5	8	
651	Doug Rader	4	4	4	4	8	10	15	
652	Checklist 606-726	4	4	4	4	5	6	10	50
653	Ron Hodges DP	4	4	4	4	4	5	8	40
654	Pepe Frias	4	4	4	4	4	5	8	
655	Lyman Bostock	4	4	4	4	4	5	8	40
656	Dave Garcia MG RC	4	4	4	4	4	5	8	
657	Bombo Rivera	4	4	4	4	4	5	8	
658	Manny Sanguillen	4	4	4	4	4	5	8	
659	Texas Rangers CL	4	4	4	4	4	5	8	40
660	Jason Thompson	4	4	4	4	4	5	8	60
661	Grant Jackson	4	4	4	4	4	5	8	40
662	Paul Dade RC	4	4	4	4	4	5	8	
663	Paul Reuschel	4	4	4	4	4	5	8	40
664	Fred Stanley	4	4	4	6	12	15	25	
665	Dennis Leonard	4	4	4	4	8	10	15	
666	Billy Smith RC	4	4	4	4	4	5	8	80
667	Jeff Byrd RC	4	4	4	4	4	5	8	60
668	Dusty Baker	4	4	4	4	4	5	8	50
669	Pete Falcone	4	4	4	4	4	5	8	60
670	Jim Rice	4	4	4	6	12	15	25	175
671	Gary Lavelle	4	4	4	4	4	5	8	
672	Don Kessinger	4	4	4	4	4	5	8	
673	Steve Brye	4	4	4	4	8	10	60	
674	Ray Knight RC	4	4	4	4	5	6	10	80
675	Jay Johnstone	4	4	4	4	8	10	15	80
676	Bob Myrick	4	4	4	4	4	5	8	40
677	Ed Herrmann	4	4	4	4	4	5	8	
678	Tom Burgmeier	4	4	4	4	4	5	8	40
679	Wayne Garrett	4	4	4	4	4	5	8	40
680	Vida Blue	4	4	4	4	4	5	8	50
681	Rob Belloir	4	4	4	4	8	10	15	
682	Ken Brett	4	4	4	4	8	10	15	
683	Mike Champion	4	4	4	4	4	5	8	60
684	Ralph Houk MG	4	4	4	4	8	10	15	60
685	Frank Taveras	4	4	4	4	4	5	8	60
686	Gaylord Perry	4	4	4	4	5	6	10	
687	Julio Cruz RC	4	4	4	4	4	5	8	60
688	George Mitterwald	4	4	4	4	4	5	8	
689	Cleveland Indians CL	4	4	4	4	8	10	15	
690	Mickey Rivers	5	10	12	25	50	60	120	
691	Ross Grimsley	4	4	4	4	4	5	8	
692	Ken Reitz	4	4	4	4	4	5	8	60
693	Lamar Johnson	4	4	4	4	8	10	15	
694	Elias Sosa	4	4	4	4	4	5	8	40
695	Dwight Evans	4	4	4	6	12	15	25	
696	Steve Mingori	4	4	4	4	4	5	8	40
697	Roger Metzger	4	4	4	4	4	5	8	40
698	Juan Bernhardt	4	4	4	4	4	5	8	40
699	Jackie Brown	4	4	4	4	4	5	8	40
700	Johnny Bench	▲8	▲12	20	▲30	▲80	▲100	▲150	600
701	Rookie Pitchers	4	4	4	4	4	5	8	
702	Rookie Catchers	4	4	4	4	8	10	15	60
703	Jack Morris DP RC	6	15	25	▲40	▲50	▲60	▲150	1,200
704	Lou Whitaker RC	10	15	25	50	80	100	250	1,000
705	Rookie Outfielders	4	4	4	4	4	5	8	
706	Rookie 1st Basemen	4	4	4	4	5	6	10	60
707	P.Molitor RC/A.Trammell RC	25	30	60	▲120	250	250	▲2,500	12,000
708	D.Murphy/L.Parrish RC	4	4	6	12	20	25	40	450
709	Rookie Pitchers	4	4	4	4	4	5	8	40
710	Rookie Outfielders	4	8	10	20	40	50	80	
711	Rookie Pitchers	4	4	4	4	4	5	8	60
712	Bobby Valentine	4	4	4	4	4	5	8	
713	Bob Davis	4	4	4	4	4	5	8	
714	Mike Anderson	4	4	4	4	4	5	8	60
715	Jim Kaat	4	4	4	4	5	6	10	
716	Clarence Gaston	4	4	4	4	4	5	8	
717	Nelson Briles	4	4	4	4	8	10	15	
718	Ron Jackson	4	4	4	4	4	5	8	60
719	Randy Elliott RC	4	4	4	4	8	10	15	
720	Fergie Jenkins	4	4	4	5	10	12	20	250
721	Billy Martin MG	4	4	4	4	8	8	15	100
722	Pete Broberg	4	4	4	4	4	5	8	60
723	John Wockenfuss	4	4	4	4	8	10	15	60
724	Kansas City Royals CL	4	4	5	10	20	25	40	
725	Kurt Bevacqua	4	4	5	10	20	25	50	
726	Wilbur Wood	4	4	4	4	6	8	12	50

1979 Kellogg's

#	Name	VG 3	VgEx 4	EX 5	ExMt 6	NM 7	NmMt 8	MT 9	Gem 9.5/10
1	Bruce Sutter	4	4	4	4	4	5	10	30
2	Ted Simmons	4	4	4	4	4	4	8	
3	Ross Grimsley	4	4	4	4	4	4	8	
4	Wayne Nordhagen	4	4	4	4	4	4	8	25
5B	Jim Palmer Pct. .650	4	4	4	4	4	5	10	
6	John Henry Johnson	4	4	4	4	4	5	10	
7	Jason Thompson	4	4	4	4	4	4	8	
8	Pat Zachry	4	4	4	4	4	4	8	25
9	Dennis Eckersley	4	4	4	4	4	5	10	
10B	Paul Splittorff IP 1666	4	4	4	4	4	4	8	25
11B	Ron Guidry Hits 396	4	4	4	4	4	5	10	
12	Jeff Burroughs	4	4	4	4	4	4	8	
13	Rod Carew	4	4	4	4	4	5	10	
14A	Buddy Bell No Trade	4	4	4	4	4	4	8	
15	Jim Rice	4	4	4	4	4	5	10	
16	Garry Maddox	4	4	4	4	4	4	8	
17	Willie McCovey	4	4	4	4	4	5	10	40
18	Steve Carlton	4	4	4	4	4	5	10	
19B	J.R. Richard Stats Begin 1971	4	4	4	4	4	4	8	
20	Paul Molitor	4	4	4	4	4	8	15	
21B	Dave Parker Avg. 318	4	4	4	4	4	5	10	
22A	Pete Rose 1978 3B 3	4	4	4	4	5	10	20	80
23B	Vida Blue Runs 818	4	4	4	4	4	4	8	
24	Richie Zisk	4	4	4	4	4	4	8	
25B	Darrell Porter 2B 111	4	4	4	4	4	4	8	25
26A	Dan Driessen Games 742	4	4	4	4	4	4	8	
27B	Geoff Zahn 1978 Minnesota	4	4	4	4	4	8	15	
28	Phil Niekro	4	4	4	4	4	5	10	
29	Tom Seaver	4	4	4	4	4	8	15	
30	Fred Lynn	4	4	4	4	4	5	10	
31	Bill Bonham	4	4	4	4	4	4	8	

		VG 3	VgEx 4	EX 5	ExMt 6	NM 7	NmMt 8	MT 9	Gem 9.5/10
	George Foster	4	4	4	4	4	5	10	
B	John Candelaria Age 25	4	4	4	4	4	4	8	
	Bob Knepper	4	4	4	4	4	4	8	25
	Fred Patek	4	4	4	4	4	4	8	
	Chris Chambliss	4	4	4	4	4	4	8	25
B	Bob Forsch 1977 Games 35	4	4	4	4	4	4	8	
	Jack Clark	4	4	4	4	4	4	8	
B	Dwight Evans 1978 Hits 123	4	4	4	4	4	5	10	
	Lee Mazzilli	4	4	4	4	4	4	8	
	Mario Guerrero	4	4	4	4	4	4	8	25
	Larry Bowa	4	4	4	4	4	4	8	
A	Carl Yastrzemski AB 9930 SP	4	4	4	4	5	10	20	
3	Carl Yastrzemski AB 9929	4	4	4	4	4	8	15	
3	Reggie Jackson 1978 Games 1394	4	4	4	4	4	8	15	
	Rick Reuschel	4	4	4	4	4	4	8	
3	Mike Flanagan 1976 SO 56	4	4	4	4	4	4	8	
A	Gaylord Perry 1973 Hits 315	4	4	4	4	4	5	10	
	George Brett	4	4	4	4	4	8	15	
3	Craig Reynolds In Those	4	4	4	4	4	4	8	
	Dave Lopes	4	4	4	4	4	4	8	
3	Bill Almon 2B 41	4	4	4	4	4	4	8	
	Roy Howell	4	4	4	4	4	4	8	
	Frank Tanana	4	4	4	4	4	4	8	25
3	Doug Rau 1978 Pct. .625	4	4	4	4	4	8	15	
	Jon Matlack	4	4	4	4	4	4	8	
3	Ron Jackson The Twins	4	4	4	4	4	4	8	
	Jim Sundberg	4	4	4	4	4	5	10	

979 Ogden A's TCMA

	VG 3	VgEx 4	EX 5	ExMt 6	NM 7	NmMt 8	MT 9	Gem 9.5/10
Rickey Henderson	4	6	8	12	20	120	300	

979 O-Pee-Chee

	GD 2	VG 3	VgEx 4	EX 5	ExMt 6	NM 7	NmMt 8	MT 9
Nolan Ryan	4	4	4	6	10	15	60	250
Ozzie Smith RC	4	5	15	20	40	100	200	800

Steve Stone #115 PSA 10 (Gem) sold for $3,174 (eBay; 1/13)

979 Topps

	VgEx 4	EX 5	ExMt 6	NM 7	NmMt 8	NmMt+ 8.5	MT 9	Gem 9.5/10
Batting Leaders	4	4	4	6	12	15	25	
Home Run Leaders	4	6	8	15	30	40	60	
RBI Leaders	4	4	4	4	8	10	15	
Stolen Base Leaders	4	4	4	4	5	6	10	
Victory Leaders	4	4	4	4	5	6	10	
Strikeout Leaders	4	4	4	4	8	10	20	100
ERA Leaders	4	4	5	10	20	25	40	
Leading Firemen	4	4	4	4	5	6	10	
Dave Campbell	4	4	4	4	5	6	10	
Lee May	4	4	4	4	5	6	10	
Marc Hill	4	4	4	4	8	10	15	
Dick Drago	4	4	4	4	5	6	10	
Paul Dade	4	4	4	4	8	10	15	
Rafael Landestoy RC	4	4	4	4	5	6	10	
Ross Grimsley	4	4	4	4	5	6	10	
Fred Stanley	4	4	4	4	5	6	10	
Donnie Moore	4	4	4	4	5	6	10	
Tony Solaita	4	4	4	4	5	6	10	
Larry Gura DP	4	4	4	4	5	6	10	
Joe Morgan DP	4	4	4	5	10	12	20	150
Kevin Kobel	4	4	4	4	5	6	10	
Mike Jorgensen	4	4	4	4	5	6	10	
Terry Forster	4	4	4	4	5	6	10	
Paul Molitor	6	12	25	▲40	50	60	▲500	
Steve Carlton	4	4	4	4	8	10	20	200
Jamie Quirk	4	4	4	4	8	10	50	
Dave Goltz	4	4	4	4	8	10	15	

		VgEx 4	EX 5	ExMt 6	NM 7	NmMt 8	NmMt+ 8.5	MT 9	Gem 9.5/10
28	Steve Brye	4	4	4	6	10	15		
29	Rick Langford	4	4	4	4	8	10	15	
30	Dave Winfield	6	8	10	20	40	50	80	
31	Tom House DP	4	4	4	4	8	10	15	
32	Jerry Mumphrey	4	4	4	4	5	6	10	
33	Dave Rozema	4	4	4	4	5	6	10	
34	Rob Andrews	4	4	4	4	8	10	15	
35	Ed Figueroa	4	4	4	4	5		50	
36	Alan Ashby	4	4	4	4	8	10	15	
37	Joe Kerrigan DP	4	4	4	4	5	6	10	
38	Bernie Carbo	4	4	4	4	8	10	15	40
39	Dale Murphy	4	4	4	8	15	20	40	
40	Dennis Eckersley	4	4	4	8	15	20	60	
41	Minnesota Twins CL/Mauch	4	4	4	4	8	10	15	
42	Ron Blomberg	4	4	4	4	5	6	10	50
43	Wayne Twitchell	4	4	4	4	5	6	10	
44	Kurt Bevacqua	4	4	4	4	5	6	10	
45	Al Hrabosky	4	4	4	4	5	6	10	
46	Ron Hodges	4	4	4	4	8	10	15	
47	Fred Norman	4	4	4	4	5	6	10	
48	Merv Rettenmund	4	4	4	4	5	6	10	
49	Vern Ruhle	4	4	4	4	5	6	10	
50	Steve Garvey DP	4	4	4	4	8	10	15	200
51	Ray Fosse DP	4	4	4	4	5	6	10	
52	Randy Lerch	4	4	4	4	5	6	10	
53	Mick Kelleher	4	4	4	4	8	10	15	
54	Dell Alston DP	4	4	4	4	5	6	10	40
55	Willie Stargell	4	5	10	20	40	50	400	
56	John Hale	4	4	4	4	5	6	10	
57	Eric Rasmussen	4	4	4	6	10	15		
58	Bob Randall DP	4	4	4	4	5	6	10	40
59	John Denny DP	4	4	4	4	5	6	10	40
60	Mickey Rivers	4	4	4	4	6	8	12	50
61	Bo Diaz	4	4	4	4	5	6	10	
62	Randy Moffitt	4	4	4	4	5	6	10	
63	Jack Brohamer	4	4	4	4	5	6	10	
64	Tom Underwood	4	4	4	4	8	10	15	
65	Mark Belanger	4	4	4	4	5	6	10	80
66	Detroit Tigers CL/Moss	4	4	4	4	8	10	15	
67	Jim Mason DP	4	4	4	4	5	6	10	
68	Joe Niekro DP	4	4	4	4	5	6	10	
69	Elliott Maddox	4	4	4	4	5	6	10	
70	John Candelaria	4	4	4	4	8	10	15	50
71	Brian Downing	4	4	4	4	5	6	10	
72	Steve Mingori	4	4	4	4	5	6	10	
73	Ken Henderson	4	4	4	4	8	10	15	
74	Shane Rawley RC	4	4	4	4	8	10	15	
75	Steve Yeager	4	4	4	4	5	6	10	
76	Warren Cromartie	4	4	4	4	5	6	10	
77	Dan Briggs DP	4	4	4	4	8	10	15	
78	Elias Sosa	4	4	4	4	8	10	15	
79	Ted Cox	4	4	4	4	8	10	15	
80	Jason Thompson	4	4	4	4	5	6	10	
81	Roger Erickson RC	4	4	4	4	5	6	10	40
82	New York Mets CL/Torre	4	4	4	5	10	12	50	
83	Fred Kendall	4	4	4	4	8	10	15	
84	Greg Minton	4	4	4	4	8	10	15	
85	Gary Matthews	4	4	4	4	5	6	10	
86	Rodney Scott	4	4	4	4	5	6	10	
87	Pete Falcone	4	4	4	4	5	6	10	
88	Bob Molinaro RC	4	4	4	4	5	6	10	40
89	Dick Tidrow	4	4	4	4	5	6	10	
90	Bob Boone	4	4	4	4	8	10	15	
91	Terry Crowley	4	4	4	4	8	10	60	
92	Jim Bibby	4	4	4	4	8	10	15	
93	Phil Mankowski	4	4	4	4	5	6	10	
94	Len Barker	4	4	4	4	5	6	10	40
95	Robin Yount	4	4	4	5	12	15	30	

#	Player	VgEx 4	EX 5	ExMt 6	NM 7	NmMt 8	NmMt+ 8.5	MT 9	Gem 9.5/10
96	Cleveland Indians CL/Torborg	4	4	4	4	5	6	10	
97	Sam Mejias	4	4	4	6	10	15		
98	Ray Burris	4	4	4	4	5	6	10	
99	John Wathan	4	4	4	4	5	6	10	
100	Tom Seaver DP	4	4	4	4	8	10	20	300
101	Roy Howell	4	4	4	4	5	6	10	
102	Mike Anderson	4	4	4	6	10	15		
103	Jim Todd	4	4	4	4	5	6	10	
104	Johnny Oates DP	4	4	4	4	5	6	10	40
105	Rick Camp DP	4	4	4	6	10	15		
106	Frank Duffy	4	4	4	4	5	6	10	
107	Jesus Alou DP	4	4	4	4	5	6	10	
108	Eduardo Rodriguez	4	4	4	4	5	6	10	
109	Joel Youngblood	4	4	4	4	5	6	10	
110	Vida Blue	4	4	4	4	5	6	10	
111	Roger Freed	4	4	4	4	8	10	15	
112	Philadelphia Phillies CL/Ozark	4	4	4	4	8	10	15	
113	Pete Redfern	4	4	4	4	8	10	15	
114	Cliff Johnson	4	4	4	4	8	10	15	
115	Nolan Ryan	▲10	▲15	▲25	▲50	▲80	100	▲250	
116	Ozzie Smith RC	60	80	▲120	200	500	800	4,000	
117	Grant Jackson	4	4	4	4	5	6	10	
118	Bud Harrelson	4	4	4	4	8	10	15	
119	Don Stanhouse	4	4	4	4	8	10	15	
120	Jim Sundberg	4	4	4	4	5	6	10	
121	Checklist 1-121 DP	4	4	4	4	5	6	10	
122	Mike Paxton	4	4	4	4	5	6	10	
123	Lou Whitaker	4	4	4	4	8	10	15	
124	Dan Schatzeder	4	4	4	4	8	10	15	
125	Rick Burleson	4	4	4	4	5	6	10	
126	Doug Bair	4	4	4	4	5	6	10	
127	Thad Bosley	4	4	4	4	5	6	10	50
128	Ted Martinez	4	4	4	4	8	10	15	
129	Marty Pattin DP	4	4	4	4	5	6	10	
130	Bob Watson DP	4	4	4	4	5	6	10	40
131	Jim Clancy	4	4	4	4	5	6	10	
132	Rowland Office	4	4	4	4	5	6	10	40
133	Bill Castro	4	4	4	4	8	10	15	
134	Alan Bannister	4	4	4	4	5	6	10	
135	Bobby Murcer	4	4	4	4	5	6	10	80
136	Jim Kaat	4	4	4	4	6	8	12	
137	Larry Wolfe DP RC	4	4	4	4	5	6	10	
138	Mark Lee RC	4	4	4	4	8	10	15	
139	Luis Pujols RC	4	4	4	4	5	6	10	
140	Don Gullett	4	4	4	4	5	6	10	
141	Tom Paciorek	4	4	4	4	5	6	10	
142	Charlie Williams	4	4	4	4	5	6	10	
143	Tony Scott	4	4	4	4	8	10	15	
144	Sandy Alomar	4	4	4	4	8	10	15	
145	Rick Rhoden	4	4	4	4	5	6	10	
146	Duane Kuiper	4	4	4	4	5	6	10	40
147	Dave Hamilton	4	4	4	4	5	6	10	
148	Bruce Boisclair	4	4	4	4	5	6	10	
149	Manny Sarmiento	4	4	4	4	5	6	10	
150	Wayne Cage	4	4	4	4	8	10	15	
151	John Hiller	4	4	4	4	5	6	10	
152	Rick Cerone	4	4	4	4	5	6	10	40
153	Dennis Lamp	4	4	4	4	5	6	10	
154	Jim Gantner DP	4	4	4	4	5	6	10	
155	Dwight Evans	4	4	4	4	5	6	10	120
156	Buddy Solomon RC	4	4	4	4	5	6	10	
157	U.L. Washington	4	4	4	6	10	15		
158	Joe Sambito	4	4	4	4	8	10	15	
159	Roy White	4	4	4	4	8	10	15	
160	Mike Flanagan	4	4	4	4	5	6	10	
161	Barry Foote	4	4	4	4	5	6	10	
162	Tom Johnson	4	4	4	4	5	6	10	
163	Glenn Burke	4	4	4	4	5	6	10	
164	Mickey Lolich	4	4	4	4	8	10	15	
165	Frank Taveras	4	4	4	4	5	6	10	
166	Leon Roberts	4	4	4	4	5	6	10	
167	Roger Metzger DP	4	4	5	10	20	25	40	80
168	Dave Freisleben	4	4	4	6	10	15		
169	Bill Nahorodny	4	4	4	4	8	10	15	
170	Don Sutton	4	4	4	4	5	6	10	
171	Gene Clines	4	4	4	4	5	6	10	
172	Mike Bruhert RC	4	4	4	4	8	10	15	
173	John Lowenstein	4	4	4	4	5	6	10	
174	Rick Auerbach	4	4	4	4	5	6	10	
175	George Hendrick	4	4	4	4	5	6	10	
176	Aurelio Rodriguez	4	4	4	4	8	10	15	40
177	Ron Reed	4	4	4	4	5	6	10	
178	Alvis Woods	4	4	4	4	5	6	10	
179	Jim Beattie DP RC	4	4	4	4	5	6	10	40
180	Larry Hisle	4	4	4	4	8	10	15	
181	Mike Garman	4	4	4	4	5	6	10	
182	Tim Johnson	4	4	4	4	5	6	10	
183	Paul Splittorff	4	4	4	4	8	10	15	
184	Darrel Chaney	4	4	4	4	5	6	10	
185	Mike Torrez	4	4	4	4	5	6	10	
186	Eric Soderholm	4	4	4	4	5	6	10	
187	Mark Lemongello	4	4	4	6	10	15		
188	Pat Kelly	4	4	4	4	5	6	10	
189	Ed Whitson RC	4	4	4	4	5	6	10	
190	Ron Cey	4	4	4	4	6	8	12	
191	Mike Norris	4	4	4	4	5	6	10	
192	St. Louis Cardinals CL/Boyer	4	4	4	4	8	10	15	
193	Glenn Adams	4	4	4	4	5	6	10	
194	Randy Jones	4	4	4	4	5	6	10	
195	Bill Madlock	4	4	4	4	8	10	15	
196	Steve Kemp DP	4	4	4	4	5	6	10	40
197	Bob Apodaca	4	4	4	4	5	6	10	40
198	Johnny Grubb	4	4	4	4	5	6	10	
199	Larry Milbourne	4	4	4	4	5	6	10	
200	Johnny Bench DP	4	4	6	10	15	20	50	150
201	Mike Edwards RB	4	4	4	4	5	6	10	
202	Ron Guidry RB	4	4	4	4	5	6	10	
203	J.R. Richard RB	4	4	4	4	5	6	10	
204	Pete Rose RB	4	4	4	5	12	15	20	150
205	John Stearns RB	4	4	4	4	5	6	10	
206	Sammy Stewart RB	4	4	4	4	5	6	10	40
207	Dave Lemanczyk	4	4	4	4	5	6	10	
208	Clarence Gaston	4	4	4	4	5	6	10	
209	Reggie Cleveland	4	4	4	4	5	6	10	
210	Larry Bowa	4	4	4	4	5	6	10	40
211	Dennis Martinez	4	4	4	4	5	6	10	
212	Carney Lansford RC	4	4	4	4	8	10	15	
213	Bill Travers	4	4	4	6	10	15		
214	Boston Red Sox CL/Zimmer	4	4	4	4	5	6	10	
215	Willie McCovey	4	4	4	6	12	15	25	
216	Wilbur Wood	4	4	4	4	5	6	10	
217	Steve Dillard	4	4	4	4	5	6	10	
218	Dennis Leonard	4	4	4	4	5	6	10	
219	Roy Smalley	4	4	4	4	5	6	10	40
220	Cesar Geronimo	4	4	4	4	5	6	10	
221	Jesse Jefferson	4	4	4	6	10	15		
222	Bob Beall RC	4	4	4	4	5	6	10	40
223	Kent Tekulve	4	4	4	4	5	6	10	
224	Dave Revering	4	4	4	4	5	6	10	
225	Goose Gossage	4	4	4	4	8	10	15	60
226	Ron Pruitt	4	4	4	4	8	10	15	
227	Steve Stone	4	4	4	4	5	6	10	
228	Vic Davalillo	4	4	4	4	5	6	10	
229	Doug Flynn	4	4	4	4	5	6	10	
230	Bob Forsch	4	4	4	4	5	6	10	
231	John Wockenfuss	4	4	4	4	5	6	10	

#	Player	VgEx 4	EX 5	ExMt 6	NM 7	NmMt 8	NmMt+ 8.5	MT 9	Gem 9.5/10
32	Jimmy Sexton RC	4	4	4	4	5	6	10	
33	Paul Mitchell	4	4	4	4	5	6	10	
34	Toby Harrah	4	4	4	4	5	6	10	40
35	Steve Rogers	4	4	4	4	5	6	10	
36	Jim Dwyer	4	4	4	6	10	15		
37	Billy Smith	4	4	4	4	8	10	15	
38	Balor Moore	4	4	4	4	5	6	10	
39	Willie Horton	4	4	4	4	5	6	10	
40	Rick Reuschel	4	4	4	4	8	10	15	
41	Checklist 122-242 DP	4	4	4	4	8	10	15	
42	Pablo Torrealba	4	4	4	4	8	10	15	
43	Buck Martinez DP	4	4	4	4	5	6	10	40
44	Pittsburgh Pirates CL/Tanner	4	4	4	4	8	10	15	
45	Jeff Burroughs	4	4	4	4	5	6	10	40
46	Darrell Jackson RC	4	4	4	4	8	10	15	
47	Tucker Ashford DP	4	4	4	4	5	6	10	40
48	Pete LaCock	4	4	4	4	5	6	10	
49	Paul Thormodsgard	4	4	4	4	8	10	15	
50	Willie Randolph	4	4	4	4	5	6	10	100
51	Jack Morris	4	4	4	4	5	6	10	
52	Bob Stinson	4	4	4	4	5	6	10	
53	Rick Wise	4	4	4	4	5	6	10	
54	Luis Gomez	4	4	4	4	8	10	15	
55	Tommy John	4	4	4	4	5	6	10	60
56	Mike Sadek	4	4	4	4	5	6	10	
57	Adrian Devine	4	4	4	4	8	10	15	
58	Mike Phillips	4	4	4	6	10	15		
59	Cincinnati Reds CL/Anderson	4	4	4	4	5	6		
60	Richie Zisk	4	4	4	4	5	6	10	
61	Mario Guerrero	4	4	4	4	5	6	10	
62	Nelson Briles	4	4	4	4	5	6	10	
63	Oscar Gamble	4	4	4	4	5	6	10	40
64	Don Robinson RC	4	4	4	4	5	6	10	40
65	Don Money	4	4	4	4	5	6	10	
66	Jim Willoughby	4	4	4	4	5	6	10	
67	Joe Rudi	4	4	4	4	5	6	10	
68	Julio Gonzalez	4	4	4	4	5	6	10	
69	Woodie Fryman	4	4	4	4	5	6	10	
70	Butch Hobson	4	4	4	4	8	10	15	
71	Rawly Eastwick	4	4	4	4	5	6	10	
72	Tim Corcoran	4	4	4	4	5	6	10	
73	Jerry Terrell	4	4	4	6	10	15		
74	Willie Norwood	4	4	4	4	5	6		
75	Junior Moore	4	4	4	4	5	6	10	
76	Jim Colborn	4	4	4	4	8	10	15	
77	Tom Grieve	4	4	4	4	5	6	10	40
78	Andy Messersmith	4	4	4	4	5	6	10	
79	Jerry Grote DP	4	4	4	4	5	6	10	
80	Andre Thornton	4	4	4	4	5	6	10	
81	Vic Correll DP	4	4	4	4	5	6	10	
82	Toronto Blue Jays CL/Hartsfield	4	4	4	4	8	10	15	
83	Ken Kravec	4	4	4	4	5	6	10	
84	Johnnie LeMaster	4	4	4	6	10	15		
85	Bobby Bonds	4	4	4	4	5	6	10	
86	Duffy Dyer	4	4	4	4	5	6	10	
87	Andres Mora	4	4	4	4	8	10	15	
88	Milt Wilcox	4	4	4	4	5	6	10	
89	Jose Cruz	4	4	4	4	5	6	10	
90	Dave Lopes	4	4	4	4	5	6	10	
91	Tom Griffin	4	4	4	4	5	6	10	
92	Don Reynolds RC	4	4	4	4	5	6	10	40
93	Jerry Garvin	4	4	4	4	5	6	10	
94	Pepe Frias	4	4	4	4	8	10	15	
95	Mitchell Page	4	4	4	4	8	10	15	
96	Preston Hanna RC	4	4	4	4	5	6	10	
97	Ted Sizemore	4	4	4	4	5	6	10	40
98	Rich Gale RC	4	4	4	6	10	15		
99	Steve Ontiveros	4	4	4	4	5	6	10	

#	Player	VgEx 4	EX 5	ExMt 6	NM 7	NmMt 8	NmMt+ 8.5	MT 9	Gem 9.5/10
300	Rod Carew	4	4	4	5	10	12	25	200
301	Tom Hume	4	4	4	4	5	6	10	
302	Atlanta Braves CL/Cox	4	4	5	8	12	20		
303	Lary Sorensen DP	4	4	4	4	5	6	10	
304	Steve Swisher	4	4	4	4	5	6	10	
305	Willie Montanez	4	4	4	4	5	6	10	50
306	Floyd Bannister	4	4	4	4	5	6	10	
307	Larvell Blanks	4	4	4	4	5	6	10	
308	Bert Blyleven	4	4	4	4	8	10	15	
309	Ralph Garr	4	4	4	4	5	6	10	
310	Thurman Munson	4	4	5	10	15	20	50	
311	Gary Lavelle	4	4	4	4	5	6	10	
312	Bob Robertson	4	4	4	4	5	6	10	
313	Dyar Miller	4	4	4	4	5	6	10	
314	Larry Harlow	4	4	4	4	5	6	10	
315	Jon Matlack	4	4	4	4	5	6	10	
316	Milt May	4	4	4	4	5	6	10	
317	Jose Cardenal	4	4	4	4	5	6	10	
318	Bob Welch RC	4	4	4	4	8	10	25	
319	Wayne Garrett	4	4	4	6	10	15		
320	Carl Yastrzemski	4	4	4	6	15	20	60	
321	Gaylord Perry	4	4	4	4	6	8	12	
322	Danny Goodwin RC	4	4	4	4	8	10	60	
323	Lynn McGlothen	4	4	4	4	5	6	10	
324	Mike Tyson	4	4	4	4	5	6	10	40
325	Cecil Cooper	4	4	5	8	12	20		
326	Pedro Borbon	4	4	4	4	5	6	10	
327	Art Howe DP	4	4	4	4	8	10	15	
328	Oakland Athletics CL/McKeon	4	4	4	4	5	6	10	
329	Joe Coleman	4	4	4	4	8	10	15	
330	George Brett	▼8	▼12	20	▲30	▲60	▲80	100	
331	Mickey Mahler	4	4	4	4	8	10	50	
332	Gary Alexander	4	4	4	4	5	6	10	
333	Chet Lemon	4	4	4	4	5	6	10	
334	Craig Swan	4	4	4	4	8	10	15	
335	Chris Chambliss	4	4	4	4	6	8	12	
336	Bobby Thompson RC	4	4	4	4	5	6	10	
337	John Montague	4	4	4	4	5	6	10	
338	Vic Harris	4	4	4	4	8	10	15	
339	Ron Jackson	4	4	4	4	5	6	10	
340	Jim Palmer	4	4	4	6	12	15	80	
341	Willie Upshaw RC	4	4	4	4	8	10	15	
342	Dave Roberts	4	4	4	4	5	6	10	
343	Ed Glynn	4	4	4	4	5	6	10	40
344	Jerry Royster	4	4	4	4	5	6	10	
345	Tug McGraw	4	4	4	4	5	6	10	50
346	Bill Buckner	4	4	4	4	5	6	10	
347	Doug Rau	4	4	4	4	5	6	10	
348	Andre Dawson	4	4	4	5	10	12	20	
349	Jim Wright RC	4	4	4	4	5	6	10	
350	Garry Templeton	4	4	4	4	5	6	10	
351	Wayne Nordhagen DP	4	4	4	4	5	6	10	
352	Steve Renko	4	4	4	4	5	6	10	
353	Checklist 243-363	4	4	4	4	5	6	10	
354	Bill Bonham	4	4	4	4	5	6	10	
355	Lee Mazzilli	4	4	4	4	5	6	10	40
356	San Francisco Giants CL/Altobelli	4	4	5	8	12	20		
357	Jerry Augustine	4	4	4	4	5	6	10	
358	Alan Trammell	4	4	4	4	5	6	10	
359	Dan Spillner DP	4	4	4	4	5	6	10	40
360	Amos Otis	4	4	4	4	5	6	10	
361	Tom Dixon RC	4	4	4	4	8	10	15	
362	Mike Cubbage	4	4	4	4	8	10	15	
363	Craig Skok RC	4	4	4	4	5	6	10	
364	Gene Richards	4	4	4	6	10	15		
365	Sparky Lyle	4	4	4	4	5	6	10	120
366	Juan Bernhardt	4	4	4	4	5	6	10	
367	Dave Skaggs	4	4	4	6	10	15		

#	Player	VgEx 4	EX 5	ExMt 6	NM 7	NmMt 8	NmMt+ 8.5	MT 9	Gem 9.5/10
368	Don Aase	4	4	4	4	5	6	10	
369A	Bump Wills ERR Blue Jays	4	4	4	4	8	10	15	
369B	Bump Wills COR Rangers	4	4	4	4	6	8	12	
370	Dave Kingman	4	4	4	4	5	6	10	
371	Jeff Holly RC	4	4	4	4	5	6	10	
372	Lamar Johnson	4	4	4	4	5	6	10	
373	Lance Rautzhan	4	4	4	4	5	6	10	
374	Ed Herrmann	4	4	4	4	5	6	10	
375	Bill Campbell	4	4	4	4	5	6	10	40
376	Gorman Thomas	4	4	4	4	5	6	10	
377	Paul Moskau	4	4	4	4	8	10	15	
378	Rob Picciolo DP	4	4	4	4	5	6	10	
379	Dale Murray	4	4	4	4	5	6	10	40
380	John Mayberry	4	4	4	4	5	6	10	
381	Houston Astros CL/Virdon	4	4	4	4	8	10	15	
382	Jerry Martin	4	4	4	4	5	6	10	
383	Phil Garner	4	4	4	4	5	6	10	
384	Tommy Boggs	4	4	4	4	5	6	10	
385	Dan Ford	4	4	4	4	5	6	10	40
386	Francisco Barrios	4	4	4	4	5	6	10	
387	Gary Thomasson	4	4	4	4	8	10	15	40
388	Jack Billingham	4	4	4	6	10	15		
389	Joe Zdeb	4	4	4	4	8	10	15	
390	Rollie Fingers	4	4	4	5	50	80	100	
391	Al Oliver	4	4	4	4	5	6	10	
392	Doug Ault	4	4	4	4	5	6	10	
393	Scott McGregor	4	4	4	4	8	10	15	
394	Randy Stein RC	4	4	4	4	5	6	10	
395	Dave Cash	4	4	4	4	5	6	10	
396	Bill Plummer	4	4	4	4	5	6	10	
397	Sergio Ferrer RC	4	4	4	4	5	6	10	
398	Ivan DeJesus	4	4	4	4	5	6	10	
399	David Clyde	4	4	4	4	8	10	15	
400	Jim Rice	4	4	4	5	10	12	25	
401	Ray Knight	4	4	4	4	5	6	10	
402	Paul Hartzell	4	4	4	4	5	6	10	
403	Tim Foli	4	4	4	4	8	10	15	
404	Chicago White Sox CL/Kessinger	4	4	4	4	5	6	10	
405	Butch Wynegar DP	4	4	4	4	5	6	10	40
406	Joe Wallis DP	4	4	4	4	5	6	10	
407	Pete Vuckovich	4	4	4	4	5	6	10	
408	Charlie Moore DP	4	4	4	4	5	6	10	40
409	Willie Wilson RC	4	4	4	8	15	20	50	
410	Darrell Evans	4	4	4	4	5	6	10	
411	G.Sisler/T.Cobb ATL	4	4	4	4	5	6	10	40
412	H.Wilson/H.Aaron ATL	4	4	4	4	6	8	12	60
413	R.Maris/H.Aaron ATL	4	4	4	4	8	10	15	60
414	R.Hornsby/T.Cobb ATL	4	4	4	4	5	6	10	
415	L.Brock/L.Brock ATL	4	4	4	4	5	6	10	40
416	J.Chesbro/C.Young ATL	4	4	4	4	5	6	10	40
417	N.Ryan/W.Johnson ATL DP	4	4	5	8	12	15	20	100
418	D.Leonard/W.Johnson ATL DP	4	4	4	4	5	6	10	40
419	Dick Ruthven	4	4	4	4	5	6	10	
420	Ken Griffey Sr.	4	4	4	4	5	6	10	
421	Doug DeCinces	4	4	4	4	5	6	10	
422	Ruppert Jones	4	4	4	4	8	10	15	
423	Bob Montgomery	4	4	4	4	5	6	10	
424	California Angels CL/Fregosi	4	4	4	4	5	6	10	
425	Rick Manning	4	4	4	4	5	6	10	
426	Chris Speier	4	4	4	4	5	6	10	
427	Andy Replogle RC	4	4	4	4	8	10	15	
428	Bobby Valentine	4	4	4	4	5	6	10	
429	John Urrea DP	4	4	4	4	5	6	10	40
430	Dave Parker	4	4	4	4	8	10	15	120
431	Glenn Borgmann	4	4	4	4	5	6	10	
432	Dave Heaverlo	4	4	4	4	5	6	10	
433	Larry Biittner	4	4	4	4	8	10	15	
434	Ken Clay	4	4	4	4	5	6	10	40
435	Gene Tenace	4	4	4	4	5	6	10	
436	Hector Cruz	4	4	4	4	8	10	15	
437	Rick Williams RC	4	4	4	4	8	10	15	
438	Horace Speed RC	4	4	4	4	5	6	10	
439	Frank White	4	4	4	4	5	6	10	
440	Rusty Staub	4	4	4	4	5	6	10	5
441	Lee Lacy	4	4	4	4	5	6	10	
442	Doyle Alexander	4	4	4	4	5	6	10	
443	Bruce Bochte	4	4	4	6	10	15		
444	Aurelio Lopez RC	4	4	4	4	8	10	15	
445	Steve Henderson	4	4	4	4	5	6	10	
446	Jim Lonborg	4	4	4	4	5	6	10	
447	Manny Sanguillen	4	4	4	4	5	6	10	
448	Moose Haas	4	4	4	4	5	6	10	
449	Bombo Rivera	4	4	4	4	8	10	15	
450	Dave Concepcion	4	4	4	4	8	10	60	
451	Kansas City Royals CL/Herzog	4	4	4	4	8	10	15	
452	Jerry Morales	4	4	4	4	5	6	10	4
453	Chris Knapp	4	4	4	4	8	10	15	
454	Len Randle	4	4	4	4	5	6	10	
455	Bill Lee DP	4	4	4	4	5	6	10	5
456	Chuck Baker RC	4	4	4	4	5	6	10	4
457	Bruce Sutter	4	4	4	5	10	12	20	
458	Jim Essian	4	4	4	4	5	6	10	
459	Sid Monge	4	4	4	4	5	6	10	
460	Graig Nettles	4	4	4	4	6	8	12	
461	Jim Barr DP	4	4	4	4	5	6	10	4
462	Otto Velez	4	4	4	4	5	6	10	
463	Steve Comer RC	4	4	4	4	8	10	15	
464	Joe Nolan	4	4	4	4	5	6	10	
465	Reggie Smith	4	4	4	4	5	6	10	
466	Mark Littell	4	4	4	4	5	6	10	
467	Don Kessinger DP	4	4	4	4	5	6	10	
468	Stan Bahnsen DP	4	4	4	4	5	6	10	
469	Lance Parrish	4	4	4	4	5	6	10	
470	Garry Maddox DP	4	4	4	4	5	6	10	4
471	Joaquin Andujar	4	4	4	4	8	10	15	
472	Craig Kusick	4	4	4	4	5	6	10	
473	Dave Roberts	4	4	4	4	5	6	10	
474	Dick Davis RC	4	4	4	4	8	10	15	
475	Dan Driessen	4	4	4	4	8	10	15	
476	Tom Poquette	4	4	4	4	8	10	15	
477	Bob Grich	4	4	4	4	5	6	10	
478	Juan Beniquez	4	4	4	4	8	10	15	
479	San Diego Padres CL/Craig	4	4	4	4	5	6	10	
480	Fred Lynn	4	4	4	4	5	6	10	15
481	Skip Lockwood	4	4	4	4	5	6	10	5
482	Craig Reynolds	4	4	4	4	5	6	10	
483	Checklist 364-484 DP	4	4	4	4	5	6	10	
484	Rick Waits	4	4	4	4	8	10	15	
485	Bucky Dent	4	4	4	4	5	6	10	5
486	Bob Knepper	4	4	4	4	8	10	15	
487	Miguel Dilone	4	4	4	4	5	6	10	
488	Bob Owchinko	4	4	4	4	5	6	10	
489	Larry Cox	4	4	4	4	5	6	10	4
490	Al Cowens	4	4	4	4	8	10	15	
491	Tippy Martinez	4	4	4	6	10	15		
492	Bob Bailor	4	4	4	4	5	6	10	4
493	Larry Christenson	4	4	4	4	5	6	10	4
494	Jerry White	4	4	4	4	5	6	10	
495	Tony Perez	4	4	4	4	5	6	10	
496	Barry Bonnell DP	4	4	4	4	5	6	10	
497	Glenn Abbott	4	4	4	4	5	6	10	
498	Rich Chiles	4	4	4	6	10	15		
499	Texas Rangers CL/Corrrales	4	4	4	4	8	10	15	
500	Ron Guidry	4	4	4	4	8	10	15	8
501	Junior Kennedy RC	4	4	4	6	10	15		
502	Steve Braun	4	4	4	4	5	6	10	

		VgEx 4	EX 5	ExMt 6	NM 7	NmMt 8	NmMt+ 8.5	MT 9	Gem 9.5/10
503	Terry Humphrey	4	4	4	4	8	10	15	
504	Larry McWilliams RC	4	4	4	4	5	6	10	
505	Ed Kranepool	4	4	4	4	5	6	10	
506	John D'Acquisto	4	4	4	4	5	6	10	
507	Tony Armas	4	4	4	4	5	6	10	40
508	Charlie Hough	4	4	4	4	5	6	10	
509	Mario Mendoza	4	4	4	4	5	6	10	40
510	Ted Simmons	4	4	4	4	5	6	10	
511	Paul Reuschel DP	4	4	4	4	5	6	10	
512	Jack Clark	4	4	4	4	5	6	10	
513	Dave Johnson	4	4	4	4	5	6	10	
514	Mike Proly RC	4	4	4	4	8	10	15	
515	Enos Cabell	4	4	4	4	5	6	10	
516	Champ Summers DP	4	4	4	4	5	6	10	40
517	Al Bumbry	4	4	5		12	20		
518	Jim Umbarger	4	4	4	4	5	6	10	
519	Ben Oglivie	4	4	5		12	20		
520	Gary Carter	4	4	4	5	10	12	20	
521	Sam Ewing	4	4	4	4	8	10	15	
522	Ken Holtzman	4	4	4	4	5	6	10	
523	John Milner	4	4	4	4	5	6	10	
524	Tom Burgmeier	4	4	4	4	5	6	10	40
525	Freddie Patek	4	4	4	4	5	6	10	100
526	Los Angeles Dodgers CL/Lasorda	4	4	4	4	5	6	10	
527	Lerrin LaGrow	4	4	4	6	10	15		
528	Wayne Gross DP	4	4	4	4	5	6	10	
529	Brian Asselstine	4	4	4	4	5	6	10	
530	Frank Tanana	4	4	4	4	8	10	15	
531	Fernando Gonzalez	4	4	4	4	8	10	15	
532	Buddy Schultz	4	4	4	4	5	6	10	
533	Leroy Stanton	4	4	4	4	5	6	10	
534	Ken Forsch	4	4	4	4	8	10	15	
535	Ellis Valentine	4	4	4	4	5	6	10	60
536	Jerry Reuss	4	4	4	4	8	10	15	
537	Tom Veryzer	4	4	4	4	5	6	10	
538	Mike Ivie DP	4	4	4	4	5	6	10	
539	John Ellis	4	4	4	4	5	6	10	40
540	Greg Luzinski	4	4	4	4	6	8	12	
541	Jim Slaton	4	4	4	4	8	10	15	
542	Rick Bosetti	4	4	4	4	5	6	10	
543	Kiko Garcia	4	4	4	6	10	15		
544	Fergie Jenkins	4	4	4	4	8	10	15	
545	John Stearns	4	4	4	4	5	6	10	
546	Bill Russell	4	4	4	4	5	6	10	
547	Clint Hurdle	4	4	4	4	5	6	10	
548	Enrique Romo	4	4	4	4	8	10	15	
549	Bob Bailey	4	4	4	4	5	6	10	
550	Sal Bando	4	4	4	4	5	6	10	40
551	Chicago Cubs CL/Franks	4	4	4	8	15	20	30	
552	Jose Morales	4	4	4	4	5	6	10	
553	Denny Walling	4	4	4	4	8	10	15	
554	Matt Keough	4	4	4	4	8	10	15	
555	Biff Pocoroba	4	4	4	4	5	6	10	
556	Mike Lum	4	4	4	4	5	6	10	
557	Ken Brett	4	4	4	4	8	10	15	
558	Jay Johnstone	4	4	4	4	5	6	10	
559	Greg Pryor RC	4	4	4	4	8	10	15	
560	John Montefusco	4	4	4	4	5	6	10	
561	Ed Ott	4	4	4	4	5	6	10	40
562	Dusty Baker	4	4	4	4	5	6	10	
563	Roy Thomas	4	4	4	4	8	10	15	
564	Jerry Turner	4	4	4	6	10	15		
565	Rico Carty	4	4	4	4	5	6	10	
566	Nino Espinosa	4	4	4	4	5	6	10	
567	Richie Hebner	4	4	4	4	5	6	10	
568	Carlos Lopez	4	4	4	4	8	10	15	
569	Bob Sykes	4	4	4	4	8	10	15	
570	Cesar Cedeno	4	4	4	4	8	10	15	
571	Darrell Porter	4	4	4	4	5	6	10	
572	Rod Gilbreath	4	4	4	4	5	6	10	40
573	Jim Kern	4	4	4	4	5	6	10	
574	Claudell Washington	4	4	4	4	5	6	10	
575	Luis Tiant	4	4	4	4	5	6	10	
576	Mike Parrott RC	4	4	4	4	8	10	15	40
577	Milwaukee Brewers CL/Bamberger	4	4	4	4	5	6	10	
578	Pete Broberg	4	4	4	4	5	6	10	
579	Greg Gross	4	4	4	4	5	6	10	40
580	Ron Fairly	4	4	4	4	5	6	10	
581	Darold Knowles	4	4	4	4	5	6	10	
582	Paul Blair	4	4	4	4	5	6	10	
583	Julio Cruz	4	4	4	4	5	6	10	40
584	Jim Rooker	4	4	4	4	8	10	60	
585	Hal McRae	4	4	4	4	5	6	10	
586	Bob Horner RC	4	4	4	6	12	15	25	
587	Ken Reitz	4	4	4	4	5	6	10	
588	Tom Murphy	4	4	4	4	5	6	10	
589	Terry Whitfield	4	4	4	4	5	6	10	40
590	J.R. Richard	4	4	4	4	5	6	10	
591	Mike Hargrove	4	4	4	4	5	6	10	
592	Mike Krukow	4	4	4	4	5	6	10	
593	Rick Dempsey	4	4	4	4	8	10	15	
594	Bob Shirley	4	4	4	4	5	6	10	
595	Phil Niekro	4	4	4	5	10	12	20	
596	Jim Wohlford	4	4	4	4	5	6	10	
597	Bob Stanley	4	4	4	4	5	6	10	
598	Mark Wagner	4	4	4	4	5	6	10	
599	Jim Spencer	4	4	4	4	8	10	15	
600	George Foster	4	4	4	4	8	10	15	
601	Dave LaRoche	4	4	4	4	5	6	10	
602	Checklist 485-605	4	4	4	4	8	10	15	
603	Rudy May	4	4	4	4	5	6	10	
604	Jeff Newman	4	4	4	4	5	6	10	40
605	Rick Monday DP	4	4	4	4	5	6	10	
606	Montreal Expos CL/Williams	4	4	4	4	5	6	10	
607	Omar Moreno	4	4	4	4	5	6	10	
608	Dave McKay	4	4	4	4	5	6	10	
609	Silvio Martinez RC	4	4	4	4	5	6	10	
610	Mike Schmidt	4	6	15	25	30	40	100	400
611	Jim Norris	4	4	4	6	10	15		
612	Rick Honeycutt RC	4	4	4	4	5	6	10	
613	Mike Edwards RC	4	4	4	4	8	10	15	
614	Willie Hernandez	4	4	4	4	5	6	10	
615	Ken Singleton	4	4	4	4	5	6	10	
616	Billy Almon	4	4	4	4	5	6	10	
617	Terry Puhl	4	4	4	4	5	6	10	
618	Jerry Remy	4	4	4	4	5	6	10	
619	Ken Landreaux RC	4	4	5		12	20		
620	Bert Campaneris	4	4	4	4	5	6	10	
621	Pat Zachry	4	4	4	4	5	6	10	
622	Dave Collins	4	4	4	4	5	6	10	80
623	Bob McClure	4	4	4	4	5	6	10	
624	Larry Herndon	4	4	4	4	8	10	15	
625	Mark Fidrych	4	4	4	4	5	6	10	
626	New York Yankees CL/Lemon	4	4	4	4	8	10	20	60
627	Gary Serum RC	4	4	4	4	8	10	15	
628	Del Unser	4	4	4	4	5	6	10	
629	Gene Garber	4	4	4	4	8	10	15	
630	Bake McBride	4	4	4	4	5	6	10	
631	Jorge Orta	4	4	4	4	5	6	10	
632	Don Kirkwood	4	4	4	4	5	6	10	
633	Rob Wilfong DP RC	4	4	4	4	5	6	10	
634	Paul Lindblad	4	4	4	4	5	6	10	
635	Don Baylor	4	4	4	4	5	6	10	
636	Wayne Garland	4	4	4	4	8	10	15	
637	Bill Robinson	4	4	4	4	5	6	10	
638	Al Fitzmorris	4	4	4	6	10	15		

#	Player	VgEx 4	EX 5	ExMt 6	NM 7	NmMt 8	NmMt+ 8.5	MT 9	Gem 9.5/10
639	Manny Trillo	4	4	4	4	5	6	10	
640	Eddie Murray	▲8	▲12	▲20	▲30	▲40	▲50	▲120	600
641	Bobby Castillo RC	4	4	4	6	10			
642	Wilbur Howard DP	4	4	4	4	5	6	10	
643	Tom Hausman	4	4	4	4	5	6	10	40
644	Manny Mota	4	4	4	4	5	6	10	80
645	George Scott DP	4	4	4	4	5	6	10	50
646	Rick Sweet	4	4	4	4	5	6	10	40
647	Bob Lacey	4	4	4	4	5	6	10	
648	Lou Piniella	4	4	4	4	6	8	12	
649	John Curtis	4	4	4	4	5	6	10	
650	Pete Rose	10	12	15	20	30	40	250	
651	Mike Caldwell	4	4	4	4	8	10	15	
652	Stan Papi RC	4	4	4	4	8	10	15	
653	Warren Brusstar DP	4	4	4	4	5	6	10	
654	Rick Miller	4	4	4	4	5	6	10	
655	Jerry Koosman	4	4	4	4	5	6	10	40
656	Hosken Powell RC	4	4	4	4	5	6	10	
657	George Medich	4	4	4	4	8	10	15	
658	Taylor Duncan RC	4	4	4	4	8	10	15	
659	Seattle Mariners CL/Johnson	4	4	4	4	8	10	15	
660	Ron LeFlore DP	4	4	4	4	5	6	10	
661	Bruce Kison	4	4	4	4	8	10	15	
662	Kevin Bell	4	4	4	4	5	6	10	
663	Mike Vail	4	4	4	4	5	6	10	
664	Doug Bird	4	4	4	4	5	6	10	
665	Lou Brock	4	4	4	6	12	15	25	
666	Rich Dauer	4	4	4	4	5	6	10	
667	Don Hood	4	4	4	4	5	6	10	
668	Bill North	4	4	4	4	8	10	15	
669	Checklist 606-726	4	4	4	4	5	6	10	
670	Jim Hunter DP	4	4	4	4	6	8	12	80
671	Joe Ferguson DP	4	4	4	4	5	6	10	40
672	Ed Halicki	4	4	4	4	5	6	10	
673	Tom Hutton	4	4	4	4	5	6	10	
674	Dave Tomlin	4	4	4	4	5	6	10	
675	Tim McCarver	4	4	4	4	5	6	10	
676	Johnny Sutton RC	4	4	4	4	5	6	10	
677	Larry Parrish	4	4	4	4	5	6	10	
678	Geoff Zahn	4	4	4	4	5	6	10	
679	Derrel Thomas	4	4	4	4	5	6	10	
680	Carlton Fisk	4	4	4	5	10	12	25	200
681	John Henry Johnson RC	4	4	4	4	5	6	10	40
682	Dave Chalk	4	4	4	4	5	6	10	40
683	Dan Meyer DP	4	4	4	4	5	6	10	
684	Jamie Easterly DP	4	4	4	4	5	6	10	
685	Sixto Lezcano	4	4	4	4	5	6	10	
686	Ron Schueler DP	4	4	4	4	5	6	10	
687	Rennie Stennett	4	4	4	4	5	6	10	
688	Mike Willis	4	4	4	4	8	10	15	
689	Baltimore Orioles CL/Weaver	4	4	4	4	5	6	10	
690	Buddy Bell DP	4	4	4	4	5	6	10	
691	Dock Ellis DP	4	4	4	4	5	6	10	
692	Mickey Stanley	4	4	4	4	5	6	10	
693	Dave Rader	4	4	4	4	5	6	10	
694	Burt Hooton	4	4	4	4	5	6	10	
695	Keith Hernandez	4	4	4	4	6	8	12	50
696	Andy Hassler	4	4	4	4	8	10	15	
697	Dave Bergman	4	4	4	4	8	10	15	
698	Bill Stein	4	4	4	4	5	6	10	
699	Hal Dues RC	4	4	4	4	5	6	10	
700	Reggie Jackson DP	▲8	▲12	▲20	▲30	▲50	▲60	▲120	▲1,200
701	Corey/Flinn/Stewart RC	4	4	4	4	5	6	10	
702	Finch/Hancock/Ripley RC	4	4	4	4	5	6	10	
703	Anderson/Frost/Slater RC	4	4	4	4	5	6	10	40
704	Baumgarten/Colborn/Squires RC	4	4	4	4	5	6	10	
705	Griffin/Norrid/Oliver RC	4	4	4	4	5	6	10	50
706	Stegman/Tobik/Young RC	4	4	4	4	5	6	10	
707	Bass/Gaudet/McGilberry RC	4	4	4	4	5	6	10	40
708	Bass/Romero/Yost RC	4	4	4	4	5	6	10	40
709	Perlozzo/Sofield/Stanfield RC	4	4	4	4	5	6	10	
710	Doyle/Heath/Rajisch RC	4	4	4	4	5	6	10	40
711	Murphy/Robinson/Wirth RC	4	4	4	4	5	6	10	
712	Anderson/Biercevicz/McLaughlin RC	4	4	4	4	5	6	10	
713	Darwin/Putnam/Sample RC	4	4	4	4	5	6	10	
714	Cruz/Kelly/Whitt RC	4	4	4	4	5	6	10	60
715	Benedict/Hubbard/Whisenton RC	4	4	4	4	5	6	10	
716	Geisel/Pagel/Thompson RC	4	4	4	4	5	6	10	
717	LaCoss/Oester/Spilman RC	4	4	4	4	5	6	10	
718	Bochy/Fischlin/Pisker RC	4	4	4	4	25	30	50	150
719	Guerrero/Law/Simpson RC	4	4	4	4	6	8	12	50
720	Fry/Pirtle/Sanderson RC	4	4	4	4	5	6	10	
721	Berenguer/Bernard/Norman RC	4	4	4	4	5	6	10	40
722	Morrison/Smith/Wright RC	4	4	4	4	5	6	10	50
723	Berra/Cotes/Wiltbank RC	4	4	4	4	5	6	10	40
724	Bruno/Frazier/Kennedy RC	4	4	4	4	5	6	10	
725	Beswick/Mura/Perkins RC	4	4	4	4	5	6	10	40
726	Johnston/Strain/Tamargo RC	4	4	4	4	5		10	40

— Ozzie Smith #116 PSA 10 (Gem) sold for $20,852 (Mile High; 1/12)
— Ozzie Smith #116 PSA 10 (Gem) (Young Collection) sold for $19,567 (SCP; 5/12)

1980 Topps

#	Player	VgEx 4	EX 5	ExMt 6	NM 7	NmMt 8	NmMt+ 8.5	MT 9	Gem 9.5/10
1	L.Brock/C.Yastrzemski HL	4	4	4	6	12	20	40	
2	Willie McCovey HL	4	4	4	4	5	6	10	100
3	Manny Mota HL	4	4	4	4	5	6	10	
4	Pete Rose HL	4	4	4	4	8	10	20	
5	Garry Templeton HL	4	4	4	4	5	6	10	50
6	Del Unser HL	4	4	4	4	5	6	10	
7	Mike Lum	4	4	4	4	5	6	10	40
8	Craig Swan	4	4	4	4	5	6	10	40
9	Steve Braun	4	4	4	4	5	6	10	
10	Dennis Martinez	4	4	4	6	12	15	25	30
11	Jimmy Sexton	4	4	4	4	5	6	10	25
12	John Curtis DP	4	4	4	4	5	6	10	40
13	Ron Pruitt	4	4	4	4	5	6	10	
14	Dave Cash	4	4	4	4	5	6	10	
15	Bill Campbell	4	4	4	4	5	6	10	40
16	Jerry Narron RC	4	4	4	4	5	10	20	50
17	Bruce Sutter	4	4	4	8	15	15	20	80
18	Ron Jackson	4	4	4	4	5	6	10	
19	Balor Moore	4	4	4	4	5	6	10	40
20	Dan Ford	4	4	4	4	5	6	10	
21	Manny Sarmiento	4	4	4	4	5	6	10	
22	Pat Putnam	4	4	4	4	5	6	10	
23	Derrel Thomas	4	4	4	4	5	6	10	
24	Jim Slaton	4	4	4	4	5	6	10	25
25	Lee Mazzilli	4	4	4	4	6	8	12	
26	Marty Pattin	4	4	4	6	12	15	25	
27	Del Unser	4	4	4	4	5	6	10	40
28	Bruce Kison	4	4	4	4	5	6	10	
29	Mark Wagner	4	4	4	4	5	6	10	
30	Vida Blue	4	4	4	4	5	6	10	4
31	Jay Johnstone	4	4	4	4	5	6	10	4
32	Julio Cruz DP	4	4	4	4	5	6	10	4
33	Tony Scott	4	4	4	4	5	6	10	
34	Jeff Newman DP	4	4	4	4	5	6	10	4
35	Luis Tiant	4	4	4	4	5	6	10	8
36	Rusty Torres	4	4	4	4	5	6	10	
37	Kiko Garcia	4	4	4	4	5	6	10	
38	Dan Spillner DP	4	4	4	4	5	6	10	4
39	Rowland Office	4	4	4	4	5	6	10	
40	Carlton Fisk	4	4	4	4	8	10	15	8
41	Texas Rangers CL/Corrrales	4	4	4	4	5	6	10	

#	Player	VgEx 4	EX 5	ExMt 6	NM 7	NmMt 8	NmMt+ 8.5	MT 9	Gem 9.5/10
2	David Palmer RC	4	4	4	4	5	6	10	40
3	Bombo Rivera	4	4	4	4	5	6	10	
4	Bill Fahey	4	4	4	4	5	6	10	
5	Frank White	4	4	4	4	5	6	30	
6	Rico Carty	4	4	4	4	5	6	10	
7	Bill Bonham DP	4	4	4	4	5	6	10	
8	Rick Miller	4	4	4	4	5	6	10	
9	Mario Guerrero	4	4	4	4	5	6	10	
10	J.R. Richard	4	4	4	4	5	6	10	40
11	Joe Ferguson DP	4	4	4	4	5	6	10	40
12	Warren Brusstar	4	4	4	4	5	6	10	
13	Ben Oglivie	4	4	4	4	5	6	10	40
14	Dennis Lamp	4	4	4	4	5	6	10	
15	Bill Madlock	4	4	4	4	5	6	10	40
16	Bobby Valentine	4	4	4	4	5	6	10	
17	Pete Vuckovich	4	4	4	4	5	6	10	50
18	Doug Flynn	4	4	4	4	5	6	10	40
19	Eddy Putman RC	4	4	4	4	5	6	10	
20	Bucky Dent	4	4	4	4	5	6	10	40
21	Gary Serum	4	4	4	4	5	6	10	
22	Mike Ivie	4	4	4	4	5	6	10	40
23	Bob Stanley	4	4	4	4	5	6	10	
24	Joe Nolan	4	4	4	4	5	6	10	
25	Al Bumbry	4	4	4	4	5	6	10	
26	Kansas City Royals CL/Frey	4	4	4	4	8	10	15	
27	Doyle Alexander	4	4	4	4	6	8	12	
28	Larry Harlow	4	4	4	4	6	8	12	
29	Rick Williams	4	4	4	4	5	6	10	
30	Gary Carter	4	4	4	4	6	8	20	100
31	John Milner DP	4	4	4	4	5	6	10	
32	Fred Howard DP RC	4	4	4	4	5	6	10	25
33	Dave Collins	4	4	4	4	5	6	10	
34	Sid Monge	4	4	4	4	5	6	10	
35	Bill Russell	4	4	4	4	5	6	15	25
36	John Stearns	4	4	4	4	5	6	10	40
37	Dave Stieb RC	4	4	4	4	6	10	15	150
38	Ruppert Jones	4	4	4	4	5	6	10	
39	Bob Owchinko	4	4	4	4	5	6	10	
40	Ron LeFlore	4	4	4	4	5	6	10	
41	Ted Sizemore	4	4	4	4	5	8	12	
42	Houston Astros CL/Virdon	4	4	4	4	8	10	15	
43	Steve Trout RC	4	4	4	4	5	6	10	25
44	Gary Lavelle	4	4	4	4	5	6	10	40
45	Ted Simmons	4	4	4	5	10	12	20	200
46	Dave Hamilton	4	4	4	4	5	6	10	40
47	Pepe Frias	4	4	4	4	5	6	10	
48	Ken Landreaux	4	4	4	4	5	6	10	
49	Don Hood	4	4	4	4	5	6	15	60
50	Manny Trillo	4	4	4	4	5	6	10	
51	Rick Dempsey	4	4	4	4	5	6	10	40
52	Rick Rhoden	4	4	4	4	5	6	10	
53	Dave Roberts DP	4	4	4	4	5	6	10	25
54	Neil Allen RC	4	4	4	4	5	6	10	40
55	Cecil Cooper	4	4	4	4	5	6	10	30
56	Oakland Athletics CL/Marshall	4	4	4	4	5	6	10	50
57	Bill Lee	4	4	4	4	5	6	10	40
58	Jerry Terrell	4	4	4	4	5	6	10	
59	Victor Cruz	4	4	4	4	5	6	10	25
60	Johnny Bench	4	4	4	4	8	15	25	150
61	Aurelio Lopez	4	4	4	4	5	6	10	
62	Rich Dauer	4	4	4	4	5	6	15	
63	Bill Caudill RC	4	4	4	4	5	6	10	
64	Manny Mota	4	4	4	4	5	8	15	40
65	Frank Tanana	4	4	4	4	5	6	10	40
66	Jeff Leonard RC	4	4	4	4	6	8	12	
67	Francisco Barrios	4	4	4	4	5	6	10	
68	Bob Horner	4	4	4	4	5	6	10	30
69	Bill Travers	4	4	4	4	5	6	10	

#	Player	VgEx 4	EX 5	ExMt 6	NM 7	NmMt 8	NmMt+ 8.5	MT 9	Gem 9.5/10
110	Fred Lynn DP	4	4	4	5	8	10	15	60
111	Bob Knepper	4	4	4	4	5	6	10	
112	Chicago White Sox CL/LaRussa	4	4	4	4	6	8	12	
113	Geoff Zahn	4	4	4	4	5	6	10	40
114	Juan Beniquez	4	4	4	4	5	6	10	
115	Sparky Lyle	4	4	4	4	5	6	10	
116	Larry Cox	4	4	4	4	5	6	10	40
117	Dock Ellis	4	4	4	4	5	6	10	40
118	Phil Garner	4	4	4	4	5	6	10	40
119	Sammy Stewart	4	4	4	4	5	6	10	
120	Greg Luzinski	4	4	4	4	5	6	10	30
121	Checklist 1-121	4	4	4	4	5	8	15	
122	Dave Rosello DP	4	4	4	4	5	6	10	25
123	Lynn Jones RC	4	4	4	4	5	6	10	40
124	Dave Lemanczyk	4	4	4	4	5	6	10	
125	Tony Perez	4	4	4	4	5	10	20	50
126	Dave Tomlin	4	4	4	4	5	6	10	
127	Gary Thomasson	4	4	4	4	5	6	10	
128	Tom Burgmeier	4	4	4	4	5	8	12	
129	Craig Reynolds	4	4	4	4	5	6	10	40
130	Amos Otis	4	4	4	4	5	6	10	
131	Paul Mitchell	4	4	4	4	5	6	10	60
132	Biff Pocoroba	4	4	4	4	5	6	10	40
133	Jerry Turner	4	4	4	4	5	6	10	
134	Matt Keough	4	4	4	4	5	6	10	
135	Bill Buckner	4	4	4	4	5	6	10	25
136	Dick Ruthven	4	4	4	4	5	6	10	
137	John Castino RC	4	4	4	4	5	6	10	
138	Ross Baumgarten	4	4	4	4	5	8	12	
139	Dane Iorg RC	4	4	4	4	5	6	10	30
140	Rich Gossage	4	4	4	4	5	6	30	100
141	Gary Alexander	4	4	4	4	5	6	10	
142	Phil Huffman RC	4	4	4	4	5	6	10	40
143	Bruce Bochte DP	4	4	4	4	5	6	10	25
144	Steve Comer	4	4	4	4	5	6	10	
145	Darrell Evans	4	4	4	4	5	6	10	
146	Bob Welch	4	4	4	4	5	6	10	
147	Terry Puhl	4	4	4	4	5	6	10	
148	Manny Sanguillen	4	4	4	4	5	6	10	40
149	Tom Hume	4	4	4	4	5	6	10	
150	Jason Thompson	4	4	4	4	5	6	10	40
151	Tom Hausman DP	4	4	4	4	5	6	10	
152	John Fulgham RC	4	4	4	4	5	6	10	40
153	Tim Blackwell	4	4	4	4	5	6	10	
154	Lary Sorensen	4	4	4	4	5	6	10	
155	Jerry Remy	4	4	4	4	5	6	10	
156	Tony Brizzolara RC	4	4	4	4	5	6	10	
157	Willie Wilson DP	4	4	4	4	5	6	10	40
158	Rob Picciolo DP	4	4	4	4	5	6	10	
159	Ken Clay	4	4	4	4	5	6	10	30
160	Eddie Murray	4	4	▲6	▲10	▲50	▲50	▲120	▲500
161	Larry Christenson	4	4	4	4	5	6	10	40
162	Bob Randall	4	4	4	4	5	6	10	
163	Steve Swisher	4	4	4	4	5	6	10	25
164	Greg Pryor	4	4	4	4	6	8	12	
165	Omar Moreno	4	4	4	4	5	6	10	20
166	Glenn Abbott	4	4	4	4	5	6	10	
167	Jack Clark	4	4	4	4	5	6	10	40
168	Rick Waits	4	4	4	4	5	6	10	40
169	Luis Gomez	4	4	4	4	5	6	10	40
170	Burt Hooton	4	4	4	4	5	6	10	40
171	Fernando Gonzalez	4	4	4	4	5	6	10	
172	Ron Hodges	4	4	4	4	5	6	10	40
173	John Henry Johnson	4	4	4	4	5	6	10	
174	Ray Knight	4	4	4	4	5	6	10	25
175	Rick Reuschel	4	4	4	4	6	8	12	
176	Champ Summers	4	4	4	4	5	6	10	
177	Dave Heaverlo	4	4	4	4	5	6	10	40

#	Player	VgEx 4	EX 5	ExMt 6	NM 7	NmMt 8	NmMt+ 8.5	MT 9	Gem 9.5/10
178	Tim McCarver	4	4	4	4	5	6	10	40
179	Ron Davis RC	4	4	4	4	6	8	12	50
180	Warren Cromartie	4	4	4	4	5	6	10	40
181	Moose Haas	4	4	4	4	5	6	10	40
182	Ken Reitz	4	4	4	4	5	8	15	40
183	Jim Anderson DP	4	4	4	4	5	6	10	15
184	Steve Renko DP	4	4	4	4	5	6	10	
185	Hal McRae	4	4	4	4	5	6	10	40
186	Junior Moore	4	4	4	4	5	6	10	
187	Alan Ashby	4	4	4	4	5	6	10	
188	Terry Crowley	4	4	4	4	5	6	10	40
189	Kevin Kobel	4	4	4	4	5	8	12	
190	Buddy Bell	4	4	4	4	5	6	10	50
191	Ted Martinez	4	4	4	4	5	6	10	
192	Atlanta Braves CL/Cox	4	4	4	4	5	6	10	
193	Dave Goltz	4	4	4	4	5	6	10	
194	Mike Easler	4	4	4	4	5	10	20	
195	John Montefusco	4	4	4	4	5	6	10	
196	Lance Parrish	4	4	4	4	5	8	12	
197	Byron McLaughlin	4	4	4	4	5	6	10	20
198	Dell Alston DP	4	4	4	4	5	6	10	
199	Mike LaCoss	4	4	4	4	5	6	10	
200	Jim Rice	4	4	5	10	12	15	20	150
201	Batting Leaders	4	4	4	4	5	6	10	40
202	Home Run Leaders	4	4	4	4	6	8	12	80
203	RBI Leaders	4	4	4	4	5	6	10	30
204	Stolen Base Leaders	4	4	4	4	5	10	20	40
205	Victory Leaders	4	4	4	4	5	6	10	25
206	Strikeout Leaders	4	4	4	4	8	12	15	100
207	ERA Leaders	4	4	4	5	10	12	20	40
208	Wayne Cage	4	4	4	4	5	6	10	30
209	Von Joshua	4	4	4	4	5	6	10	25
210	Steve Carlton	4	4	4	5	8	10	15	200
211	Dave Skaggs DP	4	4	4	4	5	6	10	
212	Dave Roberts	4	4	4	4	5	6	10	30
213	Mike Jorgensen DP	4	4	4	4	5	6	10	40
214	California Angels CL/Fregosi	4	4	4	4	8	10	15	
215	Sixto Lezcano	4	4	4	4	5	6	10	40
216	Phil Mankowski	4	4	4	4	5	6	10	
217	Ed Halicki	4	4	4	4	5	6	10	
218	Jose Morales	4	4	4	4	5	6	10	40
219	Steve Mingori	4	4	4	4	5	6	10	
220	Dave Concepcion	4	4	4	4	5	6	10	40
221	Joe Cannon RC	4	4	4	4	5	6	10	
222	Ron Hassey RC	4	4	4	4	5	6	10	
223	Bob Sykes	4	4	4	4	5	6	10	
224	Willie Montanez	4	4	4	4	5	6	10	
225	Lou Piniella	4	4	4	4	5	6	10	50
226	Bill Stein	4	4	4	4	5	6	10	
227	Len Barker	4	4	4	4	5	6	10	
228	Johnny Oates	4	4	4	4	5	6	10	30
229	Jim Bibby	4	4	4	4	8	10	20	
230	Dave Winfield	4	4	4	4	8	10	15	
231	Steve McCatty	4	4	4	4	5	6	10	
232	Alan Trammell	4	4	4	5	10	12	20	100
233	LaRue Washington RC	4	4	4	4	5	6	10	40
234	Vern Ruhle	4	4	4	4	5	6	10	40
235	Andre Dawson	4	4	4	4	8	10	15	120
236	Marc Hill	4	4	4	4	5	6	10	
237	Scott McGregor	4	4	4	4	5	6	10	
238	Rob Wilfong	4	4	4	4	5	6	10	
239	Don Aase	4	4	4	4	5	6	10	25
240	Dave Kingman	4	4	4	4	5	6	10	40
241	Checklist 122-242	4	4	4	4	5	6	10	
242	Lamar Johnson	4	4	4	4	5	6	10	
243	Jerry Augustine	4	4	4	4	5	6	10	40
244	St. Louis Cardinals CL/Boyer	4	4	4	4	5	8	12	
245	Phil Niekro	4	4	4	4	6	8	12	120
246	Tim Foli DP	4	4	4	4	5	6	10	40
247	Frank Riccelli	4	4	4	4	5	6	10	40
248	Jamie Quirk	4	4	4	4	5	6	10	40
249	Jim Clancy	4	4	4	4	5	6	10	40
250	Jim Kaat	4	4	4	4	5	6	10	60
251	Kip Young	4	4	4	4	5	6	10	40
252	Ted Cox	4	4	4	4	5	6	10	
253	John Montague	4	4	4	4	6	8	12	
254	Paul Dade DP	4	4	4	4	5	6	10	25
255	Dusty Baker DP	4	4	4	4	5	6	10	80
256	Roger Erickson	4	4	4	4	5	6	10	40
257	Larry Herndon	4	4	4	4	5	6	10	
258	Paul Moskau	4	4	4	4	5	6	10	40
259	New York Mets CL/Torre	4	4	4	4	6	8	12	40
260	Al Oliver	4	4	4	4	5	6	10	40
261	Dave Chalk	4	4	4	4	5	6	10	40
262	Benny Ayala	4	4	4	4	5	6	10	
263	Dave LaRoche DP	4	4	4	4	5	6	10	40
264	Bill Robinson	4	4	4	4	5	6	10	30
265	Robin Yount	4	4	4	4	8	12	25	150
266	Bernie Carbo	4	4	4	4	5	6	10	
267	Dan Schatzeder	4	4	4	4	5	6	10	
268	Rafael Landestoy	4	4	4	4	5	6	10	40
269	Dave Tobik	4	4	4	4	5	6	10	40
270	Mike Schmidt DP	4	4	4	5	10	12	20	150
271	Dick Drago DP	4	4	4	4	5	6	10	40
272	Ralph Garr	4	4	4	4	5	6	10	
273	Eduardo Rodriguez	4	4	4	4	5	6	10	
274	Dale Murphy	4	4	4	4	6	8	15	60
275	Jerry Koosman	4	4	4	4	5	6	10	25
276	Tom Veryzer	4	4	4	4	5	6	10	30
277	Rick Bosetti	4	4	4	4	5	6	10	25
278	Jim Spencer	4	4	4	4	5	6	10	40
279	Rob Andrews	4	4	4	4	5	6	10	
280	Gaylord Perry	4	4	4	4	5	6	10	50
281	Paul Blair	4	4	4	4	5	6	10	40
282	Seattle Mariners CL/Johnson	4	4	4	4	8	10	15	50
283	John Ellis	4	4	4	4	5	6	10	
284	Larry Murray DP RC	4	4	4	4	5	6	10	40
285	Don Baylor	4	4	4	4	5	10	20	25
286	Darold Knowles DP	4	4	4	4	5	6	10	40
287	John Lowenstein	4	4	4	4	5	6	10	40
288	Dave Rozema	4	4	4	4	5	6	10	40
289	Bruce Bochy	4	4	4	4	5	6	10	
290	Steve Garvey	4	4	4	4	6	8	12	120
291	Randy Scarberry RC	4	4	4	4	5	6	10	
292	Dale Berra	4	4	4	4	5	6	10	
293	Elias Sosa	4	4	4	4	5	6	10	
294	Charlie Spikes	4	4	4	4	5	8	15	
295	Larry Gura	4	4	4	4	5	6	10	30
296	Dave Rader	4	4	4	4	5	6	10	
297	Tim Johnson	4	4	4	4	5	6	10	40
298	Ken Holtzman	4	4	4	4	5	6	10	40
299	Steve Henderson	4	4	4	4	5	6	10	40
300	Ron Guidry	4	4	4	4	5	6	10	40
301	Mike Edwards	4	4	4	4	5	6	10	
302	Los Angeles Dodgers CL/Lasorda	4	4	4	4	6	8	12	50
303	Bill Castro	4	4	4	4	5	6	10	30
304	Butch Wynegar	4	4	4	4	5	6	10	40
305	Randy Jones	4	4	4	4	5	6	10	
306	Denny Walling	4	4	4	4	5	6	10	25
307	Rick Honeycutt	4	4	4	4	5	6	10	
308	Mike Hargrove	4	4	4	4	5	6	10	
309	Larry McWilliams	4	4	4	4	5	6	10	
310	Dave Parker	4	4	4	6	12	15	25	150
311	Roger Metzger	4	4	4	4	5	8	15	
312	Mike Barlow	4	4	4	4	5	6	10	
313	Johnny Grubb	4	4	4	4	5	6	10	

#	Player	VgEx 4	EX 5	ExMt 6	NM 7	NmMt 8	NmMt+ 8.5	MT 9	Gem 9.5/10
314	Tim Stoddard RC	4	4	4	4	5	6	10	40
315	Steve Kemp	4	4	4	4	5	6	10	
316	Bob Lacey	4	4	4	4	5	6	10	
317	Mike Anderson DP	4	4	4	4	5	6	10	40
318	Jerry Reuss	4	4	4	4	5	6	10	
319	Chris Speier	4	4	4	4	5	6	10	25
320	Dennis Eckersley	4	4	4	4	8	10	15	80
321	Keith Hernandez	4	4	4	4	5	8	15	40
322	Claudell Washington	4	4	4	4	5	6	10	
323	Mick Kelleher	4	4	4	4	5	6	10	25
324	Tom Underwood	4	4	4	4	5	6	10	40
325	Dan Driessen	4	4	4	4	5	6	10	
326	Bo McLaughlin	4	4	4	4	5	6	10	40
327	Ray Fosse DP	4	4	4	4	5	6	10	40
328	Minnesota Twins CL/Mauch	4	4	4	4	5	6	10	40
329	Bert Roberge RC	4	4	4	4	5	6	10	
330	Al Cowens	4	4	4	4	5	6	10	
331	Richie Hebner	4	4	4	4	5	6	10	
332	Enrique Romo	4	4	4	4	5	6	10	
333	Jim Norris DP	4	4	4	4	5	6	10	25
334	Jim Beattie	4	4	4	4	5	6	10	40
335	Willie McCovey	4	4	4	4	8	12	20	120
336	George Medich	4	4	4	4	5	6	10	
337	Carney Lansford	4	4	4	4	5	6	10	40
338	John Wockenfuss	4	4	4	4	5	6	10	
339	John D'Acquisto	4	4	4	4	5	6	10	
340	Ken Singleton	4	4	4	4	5	6	10	
341	Jim Essian	4	4	4	4	5	6	10	40
342	Odell Jones	4	4	4	4	5	6	10	
343	Mike Vail	4	4	4	4	5	6	10	
344	Randy Lerch	4	4	4	4	5	6	10	
345	Larry Parrish	4	4	4	4	5	6	10	25
346	Buddy Solomon	4	4	4	4	5	6	10	
347	Harry Chappas RC	4	4	4	4	5	6	10	
348	Checklist 243-363	4	4	4	4	5	12	25	
349	Jack Brohamer	4	4	4	4	5	6	10	
350	George Hendrick	4	4	4	4	5	6	10	
351	Bob Davis	4	4	4	4	5	6	10	
352	Dan Briggs	4	4	4	4	5	6	10	40
353	Andy Hassler	4	4	4	4	5	6	10	40
354	Rick Auerbach	4	4	4	4	5	6	10	25
355	Gary Matthews	4	4	4	4	5	6	10	40
356	San Diego Padres CL/Coleman	4	4	4	4	5	6	10	40
357	Bob McClure	4	4	4	4	5	6	10	40
358	Lou Whitaker	4	4	4	4	5	6	10	50
359	Randy Moffitt	4	4	4	4	5	6	10	25
360	Darrell Porter DP	4	4	4	4	5	6	10	25
361	Wayne Garland	4	4	4	4	5	10	20	40
362	Danny Goodwin	4	4	4	4	5	6	10	
363	Wayne Gross	4	4	4	4	5	6	10	25
364	Ray Burris	4	4	4	4	5	6	10	
365	Bobby Murcer	4	4	4	4	5	6	10	100
366	Rob Dressler	4	4	4	4	5	6	10	
367	Billy Smith	4	4	4	4	5	6	10	
368	Willie Aikens RC	4	4	4	4	5	6	10	
369	Jim Kern	4	4	4	4	5	6	10	
370	Cesar Cedeno	4	4	4	4	5	6	10	40
371	Jack Morris	4	4	4	4	5	6	10	
372	Joel Youngblood	4	4	4	4	5	6	10	
373	Dan Petry DP RC	4	4	4	4	5	6	10	50
374	Jim Gantner	4	4	4	4	5	6	10	
375	Ross Grimsley	4	4	4	4	5	6	10	40
376	Gary Allenson RC	4	4	4	4	5	8	15	
377	Junior Kennedy	4	4	4	4	5	6	10	
378	Jerry Mumphrey	4	4	4	4	5	6	10	
379	Kevin Bell	4	4	4	4	5	6	10	40
380	Garry Maddox	4	4	4	4	5	6	10	
381	Chicago Cubs CL/Gomez	4	4	4	5	10	12	20	

#	Player	VgEx 4	EX 5	ExMt 6	NM 7	NmMt 8	NmMt+ 8.5	MT 9	Gem 9.5/10
382	Dave Freisleben	4	4	4	4	5	6	10	
383	Ed Ott	4	4	4	4	5	6	10	40
384	Joey McLaughlin RC	4	4	4	4	5	6	10	
385	Enos Cabell	4	4	4	4	5	6	10	
386	Darrell Jackson	4	4	4	4	5	12	25	40
387A	Fred Stanley Yellow Name	4	4	4	4	6	8	12	50
388	Mike Paxton	4	4	4	4	5	6	10	
389	Pete LaCock	4	4	4	4	5	6	10	
390	Fergie Jenkins	4	4	4	4	5	6	10	50
391	Tony Armas DP	4	4	4	4	5	6	10	
392	Milt Wilcox	4	4	4	4	5	6	10	
393	Ozzie Smith	▼8	12	▲20	▲30	50	▼50	▲150	▲1,000
394	Reggie Cleveland	4	4	4	4	5	6	10	40
395	Ellis Valentine	4	4	4	4	5	6	10	
396	Dan Meyer	4	4	4	4	5	6	10	
397	Roy Thomas DP	4	4	4	4	5	6	10	40
398	Barry Foote	4	4	4	4	5	6	10	
399	Mike Proly DP	4	4	4	4	5	6	10	
400	George Foster	4	4	4	4	6	8	15	
401	Pete Falcone	4	4	4	4	8	10	15	
402	Merv Rettenmund	4	4	4	4	5	6	10	20
403	Pete Redfern DP	4	4	4	4	5	6	10	
404	Baltimore Orioles CL/Weaver	4	4	4	4	5	8	12	40
405	Dwight Evans	4	4	4	4	5	8	15	
406	Paul Molitor	4	4	4	4	8	10	15	80
407	Tony Solaita	4	4	4	4	5	6	10	40
408	Bill North	4	4	4	4	5	6	10	40
409	Paul Splittorff	4	4	4	4	5	6	10	40
410	Bobby Bonds	4	4	4	4	6	8	12	
411	Frank LaCorte	4	4	4	4	5	6	10	40
412	Thad Bosley	4	4	4	4	5	6	10	
413	Allen Ripley	4	4	4	4	5	6	10	30
414	George Scott	4	4	4	4	5	6	10	40
415	Bill Atkinson	4	4	4	4	5	6	10	30
416	Tom Brookens RC	4	4	4	4	5	6	10	
417	Craig Chamberlain DP RC	4	4	4	4	5	6	10	25
418	Roger Freed DP	4	4	4	4	5	6	10	20
419	Vic Correll	4	4	4	4	5	6	10	40
420	Butch Hobson	4	4	4	4	6	8	12	
421	Doug Bird	4	4	4	4	5	6	10	40
422	Larry Milbourne	4	4	4	4	5	6	10	
423	Dave Frost	4	4	4	4	5	6	10	40
424	New York Yankees CL/Howser	4	4	4	5	10	12	20	80
425	Mark Belanger	4	4	4	4	5	6	10	40
426	Grant Jackson	4	4	4	4	5	6	10	
427	Tom Hutton DP	4	4	4	4	5	6	10	30
428	Pat Zachry	4	4	4	4	5	6	10	
429	Duane Kuiper	4	4	4	4	5	6	10	25
430	Larry Hisle DP	4	4	4	4	5	6	10	40
431	Mike Krukow	4	4	4	4	5	6	10	40
432	Willie Norwood	4	4	4	4	5	6	10	
433	Rich Gale	4	4	4	4	5	6	10	40
434	Johnnie LeMaster	4	4	4	4	5	6	10	40
435	Don Gullett	4	4	4	4	5	6	10	
436	Billy Almon	4	4	4	4	5	6	10	40
437	Joe Niekro	4	4	4	4	5	6	10	
438	Dave Revering	4	4	4	4	5	6	10	
439	Mike Phillips	4	4	4	4	5	6	10	
440	Don Sutton	4	4	4	4	5	6	10	40
441	Eric Soderholm	4	4	4	4	5	6	10	40
442	Jorge Orta	4	4	4	4	5	6	10	40
443	Mike Parrott	4	4	4	4	5	6	10	
444	Alvis Woods	4	4	4	4	5	6	10	
445	Mark Fidrych	4	4	4	4	6	8	12	50
446	Duffy Dyer	4	4	4	4	5	6	10	
447	Nino Espinosa	4	4	4	4	5	6	10	
448	Jim Wohlford	4	4	4	4	5	6	10	25
449	Doug Bair	4	4	4	4	5	6	10	
450	George Brett	▲6	▲10	▲15	▲25	▲40	▲50	▲120	▲2,000

#	Player	VgEx 4	EX 5	ExMt 6	NM 7	NmMt 8	NmMt+ 8.5	MT 9	Gem 9.5/10
451	Cleveland Indians CL/Garcia	4	4	4	4	6	8	12	
452	Steve Dillard	4	4	4	4	5	6	10	
453	Mike Bacsik	4	4	4	4	5	6	10	
454	Tom Donohue RC	4	4	4	4	5	6	10	40
455	Mike Torrez	4	4	4	4	5	6	10	
456	Frank Taveras	4	4	4	4	5	6	10	
457	Bert Blyleven	4	4	4	4	5	10	20	30
458	Billy Sample	4	4	4	4	5	6	10	30
459	Mickey Lolich DP	4	4	4	4	5	6	10	80
460	Willie Randolph	4	4	4	5	10	12	20	
461	Dwayne Murphy	4	4	4	4	5	6	10	
462	Mike Sadek DP	4	4	4	4	5	6	10	
463	Jerry Royster	4	4	4	4	5	6	10	40
464	John Denny	4	4	4	4	5	6	10	40
465	Rick Monday	4	4	4	4	5	6	10	40
466	Mike Squires	4	4	4	8	15	20	30	
467	Jesse Jefferson	4	4	4	4	5	6	10	
468	Aurelio Rodriguez	4	4	4	4	5	6	10	40
469	Randy Niemann DP RC	4	4	4	4	5	6	10	40
470	Bob Boone	4	4	4	4	5	6	10	30
471	Hosken Powell DP	4	4	4	4	5	6	10	25
472	Willie Hernandez	4	4	4	4	5	6	10	40
473	Bump Wills	4	4	4	4	5	6	10	40
474	Steve Busby	4	4	4	4	5	6	10	40
475	Cesar Geronimo	4	4	4	4	5	6	10	
476	Bob Shirley	4	4	4	4	5	6	10	40
477	Buck Martinez	4	4	4	4	5	6	10	
478	Gil Flores	4	4	4	4	5	6	10	
479	Montreal Expos CL/Williams	4	4	4	4	8	10	15	50
480	Bob Watson	4	4	4	4	5	6	10	40
481	Tom Paciorek	4	4	4	4	5	6	10	40
482	Rickey Henderson RC	80	100	120	250	▼400	▼400	▲2,500	▲150,000
483	Bo Diaz	4	4	4	4	5	6	10	
484	Checklist 364-484	4	4	4	4	5	6	10	30
485	Mickey Rivers	4	4	4	4	5	6	10	40
486	Mike Tyson DP	4	4	4	4	5	6	10	25
487	Wayne Nordhagen	4	4	4	4	5	6	10	
488	Roy Howell	4	4	4	4	5	6	10	40
489	Preston Hanna DP	4	4	4	4	5	15	30	
490	Lee May	4	4	4	4	5	6	10	
491	Steve Mura DP	4	4	4	4	5	6	10	
492	Todd Cruz RC	4	4	4	4	5	6	10	40
493	Jerry Martin	4	4	4	4	5	6	10	
494	Craig Minetto RC	4	4	4	4	5	6	10	
495	Bake McBride	4	4	4	4	5	6	10	
496	Silvio Martinez	4	4	4	4	5	6	10	
497	Jim Mason	4	4	4	4	5	6	10	
498	Danny Darwin	4	4	4	4	5	6	10	500
499	San Francisco Giants CL/Bristol	4	4	4	4	8	10	15	50
500	Tom Seaver	4	4	4	6	8	10	15	150
501	Rennie Stennett	4	4	4	4	5	6	10	
502	Rich Wortham DP RC	4	4	4	4	5	6	10	25
503	Mike Cubbage	4	4	4	4	5	6	10	40
504	Gene Garber	4	4	4	4	5	6	10	
505	Bert Campaneris	4	4	4	4	5	6	10	
506	Tom Buskey	4	4	4	4	5	6	10	
507	Leon Roberts	4	4	4	4	5	6	10	
508	U.L. Washington	4	4	4	4	5	6	10	
509	Ed Glynn	4	4	4	4	5	6	10	
510	Ron Cey	4	4	4	4	5	6	10	40
511	Eric Wilkins RC	4	4	4	4	5	6	10	40
512	Jose Cardenal	4	4	4	4	5	6	10	40
513	Tom Dixon DP	4	4	4	4	5	6	10	25
514	Steve Ontiveros	4	4	4	4	5	6	10	40
515	Mike Caldwell	4	4	4	4	5	6	10	25
516	Hector Cruz	4	4	4	4	5	6	10	
517	Don Stanhouse	4	4	4	4	5	6	10	40
518	Nelson Norman RC	4	4	4	4	5	6	10	30
519	Steve Nicosia RC	4	4	4	4	5	6	10	40
520	Steve Rogers	4	4	4	4	5	6	10	
521	Ken Brett	4	4	4	4	5	6	10	40
522	Jim Morrison	4	4	4	4	5	6	10	40
523	Ken Henderson	4	4	4	4	5	6	10	40
524	Jim Wright DP	4	4	4	4	5	6	10	
525	Clint Hurdle	4	4	4	4	5	6	10	40
526	Philadelphia Phillies CL/Green	4	4	4	6	12	20	50	
527	Doug Rau DP	4	4	4	4	5	6	10	25
528	Adrian Devine	4	4	4	4	5	6	10	40
529	Jim Barr	4	4	4	4	5	6	10	30
530	Jim Sundberg DP	4	4	4	4	5	6	10	
531	Eric Rasmussen	4	4	4	4	5	6	10	40
532	Willie Horton	4	4	4	4	5	6	10	
533	Checklist 485-605	4	4	4	4	8	10	15	50
534	Andre Thornton	4	4	4	4	5	6	10	
535	Bob Forsch	4	4	4	4	5	6	10	
536	Lee Lacy	4	4	4	4	5	6	10	
537	Alex Trevino RC	4	4	4	4	5	6	10	
538	Joe Strain	4	4	4	4	5	6	10	
539	Rudy May	4	4	4	4	5	6	10	
540	Pete Rose	5	6	8	10	▲50	▲60	▲100	400
541	Miguel Dilone	4	4	4	4	5	12	25	
542	Joe Coleman	4	4	4	4	5	6	10	30
543	Pat Kelly	4	4	4	4	5	6	10	
544	Rick Sutcliffe RC	4	4	4	4	6	8	12	40
545	Jeff Burroughs	4	4	4	4	5	6	10	30
546	Rick Langford	4	4	4	4	5	6	10	40
547	John Wathan	4	4	4	4	5	6	10	40
548	Dave Rajsich	4	4	4	4	5	6	10	25
549	Larry Wolfe	4	4	5	10	20	25	40	
550	Ken Griffey Sr.	4	4	4	4	5	6	10	
551	Pittsburgh Pirates CL/Tanner	4	4	5	10	12	15	25	60
552	Bill Nahorodny	4	4	4	4	5	6	10	40
553	Dick Davis	4	4	4	4	5	6	10	
554	Art Howe	4	4	4	4	5	6	10	40
555	Ed Figueroa	4	4	4	4	5	6	10	
556	Joe Rudi	4	4	4	4	5	6	10	
557	Mark Lee	4	4	4	4	5	6	10	30
558	Alfredo Griffin	4	4	4	4	5	6	10	40
559	Dale Murray	4	4	4	4	5	6	10	
560	Dave Lopes	4	4	4	4	5	6	10	
561	Eddie Whitson	4	4	4	4	5	6	10	
562	Joe Wallis	4	4	4	4	5	6	10	40
563	Will McEnaney	4	4	4	4	5	6	10	40
564	Rick Manning	4	4	4	4	5	6	10	40
565	Dennis Leonard	4	4	4	4	5	6	10	
566	Bud Harrelson	4	4	4	4	5	6	10	
567	Skip Lockwood	4	4	4	4	5	6	10	
568	Gary Roenicke RC	4	4	4	4	5	6	10	
569	Terry Kennedy	4	4	4	4	5	6	10	
570	Roy Smalley	4	4	4	6	12	15	25	80
571	Joe Sambito	4	4	4	4	5	6	10	40
572	Jerry Morales DP	4	4	4	4	5	6	10	40
573	Kent Tekulve	4	4	4	4	5	6	10	30
574	Scot Thompson	4	4	4	4	5	6	10	40
575	Ken Kravec	4	4	4	4	5	6	10	40
576	Jim Dwyer	4	4	4	4	5	6	10	
577	Toronto Blue Jays CL/Matlick	4	4	4	4	5	6	10	
578	Scott Sanderson	4	4	4	4	5	6	10	
579	Charlie Moore	4	4	4	4	5	6	10	40
580	Nolan Ryan	▲12	▲20	▲30	▲50	80	120	▼300	▲5,000
581	Bob Bailor	4	4	4	4	5	6	10	25
582	Brian Doyle	4	4	4	4	5	6	10	40
583	Bob Stinson	4	4	4	4	6	8	12	
584	Kurt Bevacqua	4	4	4	4	5	6	10	40
585	Al Hrabosky	4	4	4	4	5	6	10	40
586	Mitchell Page	4	4	4	4	5	6	10	40
587	Garry Templeton	4	4	4	4	5	6	10	
588	Greg Minton	4	4	4	4	5	6	10	40

#	Name	VgEx 4	EX 5	ExMt 6	NM 7	NmMt 8	NmMt+ 8.5	MT 9	Gem 9.5/10
589	Chet Lemon	4	4	4		5	6	10	
590	Jim Palmer	4	4	4	8	15	20	40	
591	Rick Cerone	4	4	4	4	5	6	10	
592	Jon Matlack	4	4	4	4	5	6	10	
593	Jesus Alou	4	4	4	4	5	6	10	40
594	Dick Tidrow	4	4	4	4	5	6	10	
595	Don Money	4	4	4	4	5	6	10	40
596	Rick Matula RC	4	4	4	4	5	6	10	
597	Tom Poquette	4	4	4	4	5	6	10	
598	Fred Kendall DP	4	4	4	4	5	6	10	20
599	Mike Norris	4	4	4	4	5	6	10	
600	Reggie Jackson	4	4	4	6	12	15	25	150
601	Buddy Schultz	4	4	4	4	5	6	10	
602	Brian Downing	4	4	4	4	5	6	10	
603	Jack Billingham DP	4	4	4	4	5	6	10	40
604	Glenn Adams	4	4	4	4	5	6	10	40
605	Terry Forster	4	4	4	4	5	6	10	
606	Cincinnati Reds CL/McNamara	4	4	4	5	10	15	30	50
607	Woodie Fryman	4	4	4	4	5	6	10	40
608	Alan Bannister	4	4	4	4	5	6	10	40
609	Ron Reed	4	4	4	4	5	6	10	
610	Willie Stargell	4	4	4	6	12	15	25	
611	Jerry Garvin DP	4	4	4	4	5	6	10	40
612	Cliff Johnson	4	4	4	4	5	6	10	
613	Randy Stein	4	4	4	4	5	6	10	40
614	John Hiller	4	4	4	4	5	6	10	40
615	Doug DeCinces	4	4	4	4	5	6	10	
616	Gene Richards	4	4	4	4	5	6	10	40
617	Joaquin Andujar	4	4	4	4	5	6	10	
618	Bob Montgomery DP	4	4	4	4	5	6	10	30
619	Sergio Ferrer	4	4	4	4	5	6	10	
620	Richie Zisk	4	4	4	4	6	8	12	
621	Bob Grich	4	4	4	4	5	6	10	
622	Mario Soto	4	4	4	4	5	6	10	40
623	Gorman Thomas	4	4	4	4	5	8	12	30
624	Lerrin LaGrow	4	4	4	4	5	6	10	40
625	Chris Chambliss	4	4	4	4	6	8	12	40
626	Detroit Tigers CL/Anderson	4	4	4	6	12	15	25	
627	Pedro Borbon	4	4	4	4	5	6	10	
628	Doug Capilla	4	4	4	4	5	6	10	
629	Jim Todd	4	4	4	4	5	6	10	40
630	Larry Bowa	4	4	4	4	5	6	10	40
631	Mark Littell	4	4	4	4	5	6	10	25
632	Barry Bonnell	4	4	4	4	5	6	10	40
633	Bob Apodaca	4	4	4	4	5	6	10	40
634	Glenn Borgmann DP	4	4	4	4	5	6	10	40
635	John Candelaria	4	4	4	4	5	10	20	
636	Toby Harrah	4	4	4	4	5	6	10	40
637	Joe Simpson	4	4	4	4	5	6	10	
638	Mark Clear RC	4	4	4	4	5	6	10	
639	Larry Biittner	4	4	4	4	5	8	15	
640	Mike Flanagan	4	4	4	4	5	6	10	
641	Ed Kranepool	4	4	4	4	5	6	10	
642	Ken Forsch DP	4	4	4	4	5	6	10	40
643	John Mayberry	4	4	4	4	5	6	10	
644	Charlie Hough	4	4	4	4	5	6	10	40
645	Rick Burleson	4	4	4	4	5	6	10	
646	Checklist 606-726	4	4	4	4	5	6	10	40
647	Milt May	4	4	4	4	5	6	10	40
648	Roy White	4	4	4	4	5	6	10	60
649	Tom Griffin	4	4	4	4	5	6	10	
650	Joe Morgan	4	4	4	4	6	8	12	100
651	Rollie Fingers	4	4	4	4	5	6	10	50
652	Mario Mendoza	4	4	4	4	5	6	10	
653	Stan Bahnsen	4	4	4	4	5	6	10	25
654	Bruce Boisclair DP	4	4	4	4	5	6	10	
655	Tug McGraw	4	4	4	4	5	6	10	40
656	Larvell Blanks	4	4	4	4	5	6	10	40
657	Dave Edwards RC	4	4	4	4	5	6	10	
658	Chris Knapp	4	4	4	4	5	6	10	60
659	Milwaukee Brewers CL/Bamberger	4	4	4	4	5	6	10	40
660	Rusty Staub	4	4	4	4	5	6	10	25
661	Corey/Ford/Krenchiki RC	4	4	4	4	5	6	10	
662	Finch/O'Berry/Rainey RC	4	4	4	4	5	8	15	
663	Botting/Clark/Thon RC	4	4	4	4	5	8	15	
664	Colbern/Hoffman/Robinson RC	4	4	4	4	5	6	10	40
665	Andersen/Cuellar/Wihtol RC	4	4	4	4	5	6	10	
666	Chris/Greene/Robbins RC	4	4	4	4	5	6	10	
667	Mart/Pasch/Quisenberry RC	4	4	4	4	8	10	15	60
668	Boitano/Mueller/Sakata RC	4	4	4	4	5	6	10	25
669	Graham/Sofield/Ward RC	4	4	4	4	5	6	10	40
670	Brown/Gulden/Jones RC	4	4	4	4	5	6	10	
671	Bryant/Kingman/Morgan RC	4	4	4	4	5	6	10	
672	Beamon/Craig/Vasquez RC	4	4	4	4	5	6	10	
673	Allard/Gleaton/Mahlberg RC	4	4	4	4	5	6	10	
674	Edge/Kelly/Wilborn RC	4	4	4	4	5	6	10	
675	Benedict/Bradford/Miller RC	4	4	4	4	5	6	10	40
676	Geisel/Macko/Pagel RC	4	4	4	4	5	6	10	40
677	DeFreites/Pastore/Spilman RC	4	4	4	4	5	6	10	
678	Baldwin/Knicely/Ladd RC	4	4	4	4	5	6	10	
679	Beckwith/Hatcher/Patterson RC	4	4	4	4	5	6	10	
680	Bernazard/Miller/Tamargo RC	4	4	4	4	8	10	15	
681	Norman/Orosco/Scott RC	4	4	4	4	6	8	12	
682	Aviles/Noles/Saucier RC	4	4	4	4	6	8	12	
683	Boyland/Lois/Saferight RC	4	4	4	4	5	8	15	
684	Frazier/Herr/O'Brien RC	4	4	4	4	5	8	15	
685	Flannery/Greer/Wilhelm RC	4	4	4	4	5	6	10	25
686	Johnston/Littlejohn/Nastu RC	4	4	4	4	5	6	10	
687	Mike Heath DP	4	4	4	4	5	6	10	40
688	Steve Stone	4	4	4	4	5	6	10	
689	Boston Red Sox CL/Zimmer	4	4	4	4	8	10	15	60
690	Tommy John	4	4	4	4	5	6	10	40
691	Ivan DeJesus	4	4	4	4	5	6	10	
692	Rawly Eastwick DP	4	4	4	4	5	6	10	
693	Craig Kusick	4	4	4	4	5	6	10	40
694	Jim Rooker	4	4	4	4	5	6	10	40
695	Reggie Smith	4	4	4	4	5	6	10	
696	Julio Gonzalez	4	4	4	4	5	6	10	
697	David Clyde	4	4	4	4	5	6	10	
698	Oscar Gamble	4	4	4	4	5	6	10	
699	Floyd Bannister	4	4	4	4	5	6	10	
700	Rod Carew DP	4	4	4	4	6	8	12	120
701	Ken Oberkfell RC	4	4	4	4	5	6	10	
702	Ed Farmer	4	4	4	4	5	6	10	
703	Otto Velez	4	4	4	4	5	6	10	
704	Gene Tenace	4	4	4	4	5	6	10	40
705	Freddie Patek	4	4	4	4	5	6	10	
706	Tippy Martinez	4	4	4	6	12	15	25	
707	Elliott Maddox	4	4	4	4	5	6	10	
708	Bob Tolan	4	4	4	4	5	6	10	
709	Pat Underwood RC	4	4	4	4	5	6	10	
710	Graig Nettles	4	4	4	5	10	15	20	50
711	Bob Galasso RC	4	4	4	4	5	6	10	25
712	Rodney Scott	4	4	4	4	5	6	10	
713	Terry Whitfield	4	4	4	4	5	6	10	40
714	Fred Norman	4	4	4	4	5	6	10	
715	Sal Bando	4	4	4	4	5	6	10	40
716	Lynn McGlothen	4	4	4	4	5	6	10	30
717	Mickey Klutts DP	4	4	4	4	5	6	10	50
718	Greg Gross	4	4	4	4	5	6	10	40
719	Don Robinson	4	4	4	4	5	6	10	40
720	Carl Yastrzemski DP	4	4	5	10	12	15	20	120
721	Paul Hartzell	4	4	4	4	5	6	10	40
722	Jose Cruz	4	4	4	4	5	6	10	40
723	Shane Rawley	4	4	4	4	5	6	10	
724	Jerry White	4	4	4	4	5	6	10	50
725	Rick Wise	4	4	4	4	5	6	10	25
726	Steve Yeager	4	4	4	4	5	6	10	

1981 Rochester Red Wings TCMA

		NmMt 8	NmMt+ 8.5	MT 9	Gem 9.5/10
15	Cal Ripken Jr.	250	300	350	700

1981 Topps

		NmMt 8	NmMt+ 8.5	MT 9	Gem 9.5/10
180	Pete Rose	15	20	40	1,500
240	Nolan Ryan	▲50	▲60	80	1,500
254	Ozzie Smith	10	15	20	80
261	Rickey Henderson	20	25	50	500
302	F.Valenzuela/M.Scioscia RC	▲60	▲60	▲250	
315	Kirk Gibson RC	▲60	▲80	▲200	▲2,500
347	Harold Baines RC	8	10	15	400
479	Tim Raines RC	15	20	25	250

1981 Topps Traded

		NmMt 8	NmMt+ 8.5	MT 9	Gem 9.5/10
727	Danny Ainge XRC	▲20	▲25	30	150
816	Tim Raines	▲50	▲60	▲120	600
850	Fernando Valenzuela	▲80	▲100	▲250	

1982 Donruss

		NmMt 8	NmMt+ 8.5	MT 9	Gem 9.5/10
168	Pete Rose	6	8	12	60
405	Cal Ripken RC	60	▼60	▲150	600
419	Nolan Ryan	5	6	10	40

1982 Fleer

		NmMt 8	NmMt+ 8.5	MT 9	Gem 9.5/10
176	Cal Ripken RC	60	60	▲150	▲2,000
229	Nolan Ryan	10	15	25	40

1982 Topps

		NmMt 8	NmMt+ 8.5	MT 9	Gem 9.5/10
21	Cal Ripken RC	▲80	▲100	▲200	▲2,000
90	Nolan Ryan	15	20	30	300
780	Pete Rose	10	12	20	120

1982 Topps Traded

		NmMt 8	NmMt+ 8.5	MT 9	Gem 9.5/10
98T	Cal Ripken	300	400	▲800	▲6,000
109T	Ozzie Smith	30	40	80	150

1983 Donruss

		NmMt 8	NmMt+ 8.5	MT 9	Gem 9.5/10
42	Pete Rose	5	8	15	40
118	Nolan Ryan	6	8	12	30
277	Ryne Sandberg RC	▲50	▲60	80	250
279	Cal Ripken	▲12	▲15	▲50	80
525	Julio Franco RC	6	8	12	40
586	Wade Boggs RC	30	40	60	▲120
598	Tony Gwynn RC	40	50	▲100	250

1983 Fleer

		NmMt 8	NmMt+ 8.5	MT 9	Gem 9.5/10
70	Cal Ripken	6	8	▲30	80
171	Pete Rose	5	6	12	40
179	Wade Boggs RC	30	40	▲60	120
360	Tony Gwynn RC	40	▼40	▲80	250
463	Nolan Ryan	5	6	10	80
507	Ryne Sandberg RC	▲40	▲40	60	▲200

1983 Topps

		NmMt 8	NmMt+ 8.5	MT 9	Gem 9.5/10
83	Ryne Sandberg RC	30	40	60	▲1,500
100	Pete Rose	8	10	15	50
163	Cal Ripken	25	30	▲60	120
180	Rickey Henderson	6	8	12	50
360	Nolan Ryan	10	12	25	120
482	Tony Gwynn RC	▲80	▲100	▲250	▲4,000
498	Wade Boggs RC	50	60	▲150	▲3,000

1984 Donruss

		NmMt 8	NmMt+ 8.5	MT 9	Gem 9.5/10
41	Joe Carter RC	40	50	▲100	200
60	Nolan Ryan	▲25	25	50	100
61	Pete Rose	8	10	▲50	60
68	Darryl Strawberry RC	40	40	60	100
106	Cal Ripken	▲25	▲25	▲50	50
248	Don Mattingly RC	▼100	▼120	300	▲4,000
311	Ryne Sandberg	20	25	▼40	60

1984 Fleer

		NmMt 8	NmMt+ 8.5	MT 9	Gem 9.5/10
17	Cal Ripken	15	20	▲40	▲80
46	Pete Rose	5	6	10	30
131	Don Mattingly RC	60	60	100	600
239	Nolan Ryan	▲20	20	▲50	▲120
504	Ryne Sandberg	6	8	15	50
599	Darryl Strawberry RC	▲30	▲40	▲60	▲200

1984 Fleer Update

		NmMt 8	NmMt+ 8.5	MT 9	Gem 9.5/10
U27	Roger Clemens XRC	▲300	300	500	▲2,500
U43	Dwight Gooden XRC	▲120	▲150	▲250	400
U93	Kirby Puckett XRC	▼250	300	500	▲1,500
U102	Pete Rose	12	15	25	80

1984 Topps

		NmMt 8	NmMt+ 8.5	MT 9	Gem 9.5/10
8	Don Mattingly RC	50	60	120	▲1,500
182	Darryl Strawberry RC	8	10	15	50
300	Pete Rose	6	8	12	50
470	Nolan Ryan	8	10	15	100
490	Cal Ripken	6	8	12	50
596	Ryne Sandberg	5	6	12	60

1984 Topps Traded Tiffany

		NmMt 8	NmMt+ 8.5	MT 9	Gem 9.5/10
104T	Bret Saberhagen	12	15	25	80

1985 Donruss

		NmMt 8	NmMt+ 8.5	MT 9	Gem 9.5/10
60	Nolan Ryan	8	10	20	80
169	Cal Ripken	5	6	15	50
190	Dwight Gooden RC	5	6	12	50
254	Pete Rose Fxpos	6	8	15	50
273	Roger Clemens RC	40	40	100	300
438	Kirby Puckett RC	▲50	▲60	100	▲5,000
581	Orel Hershiser RC	5	6	10	80
641	Pete Rose	5	6	12	60

1985 Fleer

		NmMt 8	NmMt+ 8.5	MT 9	Gem 9.5/10
155	Roger Clemens RC	40	50	▲100	500
187	Cal Ripken	5	6	15	50
286	Kirby Puckett RC	50	50	100	250
359	Nolan Ryan	5	6	10	100
550	Pete Rose	6	8	12	40

1985 Topps

		NmMt 8	NmMt+ 8.5	MT 9	Gem 9.5/10
30	Cal Ripken	5	6	12	600
181	Roger Clemens RC	▲40	40	100	▲1,500
401	Mark McGwire OLY RC	▼50	▼60	▼150	▲2,500
493	Orel Hershiser RC	20	20	25	100
536	Kirby Puckett RC	50	50	100	250
600	Pete Rose	5	6	12	50
620	Dwight Gooden RC	10	12	20	80
760	Nolan Ryan	8	10	20	120

1986 Donruss

		NmMt 8	NmMt+ 8.5	MT 9	Gem 9.5/10
28	Fred McGriff RC	▼25	▼30	▼60	500
33A	Andres Galarraga RC	5	6	8	25
37	Paul O'Neill RC	5	5	10	30
39	Jose Canseco RC	50	60	▼80	▲500
258	Nolan Ryan	5	6	12	50
512	Cecil Fielder RC	8	10	15	

1986 Donruss Rookies

		NmMt 8	NmMt+ 8.5	MT 9	Gem 9.5/10
11	Barry Bonds XRC	▲30	40	▼50	200
22	Jose Canseco	5	5	8	25
32	Will Clark XRC	5	5	6	25
38	Bo Jackson XRC	5	6	▲40	50

1986 Fleer Update

		NmMt 8	NmMt+ 8.5	MT 9	Gem 9.5/10
U14	Barry Bonds XRC	30	▼30	▲80	300
U20	Jose Canseco	5	6	12	40
U25	Will Clark XRC	10	12	25	80

1986 Sportflics Rookies

		NmMt 8	NmMt+ 8.5	MT 9	Gem 9.5/10
13	Barry Bonds	▲25	▲25	▲50	100
34	Barry Larkin	4	6	12	20

1986 Topps Traded

		NmMt 8	NmMt+ 8.5	MT 9	Gem 9.5/10
11T	Barry Bonds XRC	▼30	40	▼60	500
20T	Jose Canseco XRC	▲25	▲25	40	120
24T	Will Clark XRC	▲25	▲25	30	80
50T	Bo Jackson XRC	40	50	▲100	▲2,000

1986 Topps Traded Tiffany

		NmMt 8	NmMt+ 8.5	MT 9	Gem 9.5/10
11T	Barry Bonds	800	1,000	▲2,000	▲10,000
20T	Jose Canseco	50	60	100	600
24T	Will Clark	50	60	100	400
50T	Bo Jackson	400	500	600	▲10,000

1987 Donruss

		NmMt 8	NmMt+ 8.5	MT 9	Gem 9.5/10
35	Bo Jackson RC	30	40	60	200
36	Greg Maddux RC	25	30	50	▲250
43	Rafael Palmeiro RC	4	5	8	20
46	Mark McGwire	20	20	▼25	60
66	Will Clark	5	5	8	20
361	Barry Bonds RC	▲25	25	▼40	150
492	Barry Larkin RC	6	8	12	30
502	David Cone RC	5	5	6	25

1987 Fleer

		NmMt 8	NmMt+ 8.5	MT 9	Gem 9.5/10
204	Barry Larkin RC	▲25	▲25	▲40	120
269	Will Clark RC	5	6	12	30
369	Bo Jackson RC	▲25	25	▲50	300
604	Barry Bonds RC	25	▼25	50	600

1987 Fleer Update

		NmMt 8	NmMt+ 8.5	MT 9	Gem 9.5/10
U68	Greg Maddux XRC	25	25	▼30	300
U76	Mark McGwire	▲15	▲15	▲25	▲50

1987 Topps

		NmMt 8	NmMt+ 8.5	MT 9	Gem 9.5/10
170	Bo Jackson RC	25	30	50	150
320	Barry Bonds RC	25	30	50	300
366	Mark McGwire	5	6	10	20
420	Will Clark	5	5	6	20
634	Rafael Palmeiro RC	5	6	10	20
648	Barry Larkin RC	4	10	15	30

1987 Topps Glossy Send-Ins

		NmMt 8	NmMt+ 8.5	MT 9	Gem 9.5/10
30	Barry Bonds	20	20	▼25	▼60

1987 Topps Traded

		NmMt 8	NmMt+ 8.5	MT 9	Gem 9.5/10
70T	Greg Maddux XRC	25	25	▲50	200

1988 Fleer Glossy

		NmMt 8	NmMt+ 8.5	MT 9	Gem 9.5/10
378	Edgar Martinez			50	200
539	Tom Glavine	▲12	▲15	▲25	50

1988 Fleer Update

		NmMt 8	NmMt+ 8.5	MT 9	Gem 9.5/10
U69	David Wells XRC	5	5	8	20
U74	John Smoltz XRC	20	20	30	250
U89	Craig Biggio XRC	20	20	30	100
U122	Roberto Alomar XRC	5	5	8	20

1988 Fleer Update Glossy

		NmMt 8	NmMt+ 8.5	MT 9	Gem 9.5/10
U74	John Smoltz	▲25	25	▲40	150
U89	Craig Biggio	▲15	15	▲50	100

1988 Score Rookie/Traded

		NmMt 8	NmMt+ 8.5	MT 9	Gem 9.5/10
80T	Mark Grace XRC	8	10	12	25
103T	Craig Biggio XRC	12	15	20	50
105T	Roberto Alomar XRC	10	12	15	40

1988 Score Rookie/Traded Glossy

		NmMt 8	NmMt+ 8.5	MT 9	Gem 9.5/10
80T	Mark Grace	10	15	20	60
103T	Craig Biggio	60	80	150	400
105T	Roberto Alomar	30	40	80	400

1989 Bowman

		NmMt 8	NmMt+ 8.5	MT 9	Gem 9.5/10
142	Gary Sheffield RC	5	5	8	40
220	Ken Griffey Jr. RC	12	15	25	120
266	John Smoltz RC	6	8	12	25

1989 Donruss

		NmMt 8	NmMt+ 8.5	MT 9	Gem 9.5/10
31	Gary Sheffield RC	12	12	20	80
33	Ken Griffey Jr. RC	25	30	▲60	▼250
42	Randy Johnson RC	5	5	8	30
561	Craig Biggio RC	5	5	10	20
635	Curt Schilling RC	5	5	10	25
642	John Smoltz RC	5	5	6	20

1989 Fleer

		NmMt 8	NmMt+ 8.5	MT 9	Gem 9.5/10
96	Gary Sheffield RC	5	5	6	30
353	Craig Biggio RC	5	6	10	40
381	Randy Johnson RC	6	8	12	40
548	Ken Griffey Jr. RC	25	25	50	200
602	John Smoltz RC	5	5	10	30
616A	Bill Ripken ERR/Rick Face written/on knob of bat	12	15	50	100

1989 Score Rookie/Traded

		NmMt 8	NmMt+ 8.5	MT 9	Gem 9.5/10
87T	Randy Johnson	5	5	5	25
100T	Ken Griffey Jr. RC	25	25	40	200

1989 Topps

		NmMt 8	NmMt+ 8.5	MT 9	Gem 9.5/10
49	Craig Biggio RC	5	5	6	30
343	Gary Sheffield RC	6	8	10	20
382	John Smoltz RC	6	8	10	30
647	Randy Johnson RC	6	8	10	30

1989 Topps Traded

		NmMt 8	NmMt+ 8.5	MT 9	Gem 9.5/10
41T	Ken Griffey Jr. RC	▲30	▲30	50	300
57T	Randy Johnson	4	5	8	15
104T	Kenny Rogers RC	5	5	8	15
122T	Omar Vizquel RC	5	5	5	25

1989 Upper Deck

		NmMt 8	NmMt+ 8.5	MT 9	Gem 9.5/10
1	Ken Griffey Jr. RC	120	150	▲300	▼3,000
13	Gary Sheffield RC	10	10	20	30
	John Smoltz RC	▲25	▲25	▲30	100
	Randy Johnson RC	25	▼25	40	250
273	Craig Biggio RC	▲10	▲12	20	▲50
17	Omar Vizquel RC	8	8	12	30

1990 Leaf

		NmMt 8	NmMt+ 8.5	MT 9	Gem 9.5/10
	Sammy Sosa RC	12	15	25	150
	John Olerud RC	4	5	8	25
	Ken Griffey Jr.	▲20	▲20	30	▲250
	David Justice RC	6	8	12	20
	Frank Thomas RC	▼30	▼30	60	▼250
	Larry Walker RC	12	15	30	200

1990 Topps

		NmMt 8	NmMt+ 8.5	MT 9	Gem 9.5/10
	Juan Gonzalez RC	5	5	6	15
414A	FrankThomas NNOF	2,000	2,500	4,500	
414B	Frank Thomas RC	5	6	10	30
	Sammy Sosa RC	5	5	5	25

		NmMt 8	NmMt+ 8.5	MT 9	Gem 9.5/10
701	Bernie Williams RC	5	5	6	25
757	Larry Walker RC	5	5	6	20
USA1	George Bush PRES	1,500	2,000		

1991 Bowman

		NmMt 8	NmMt+ 8.5	MT 9	Gem 9.5/10
68	Jim Thome RC	15	20	25	100
183	Jeff Bagwell RC	5	6	10	60
272	Ivan Rodriguez RC	6	8	12	60
569	Chipper Jones RC	20	25	▼30	▼150

1991 Fleer Update

		NmMt 8	NmMt+ 8.5	MT 9	Gem 9.5/10
U62	Ivan Rodriguez RC	5	5	8	25
U87	Jeff Bagwell RC	5	6	10	20

1991 Stadium Club

		NmMt 8	NmMt+ 8.5	MT 9	Gem 9.5/10
388	Jeff Bagwell RC	8	10	15	25
576	Luis Gonzalez RC	5	6	10	50

1991 Topps

		NmMt 8	NmMt+ 8.5	MT 9	Gem 9.5/10
333	Chipper Jones RC	25	30	40	150

1991 Upper Deck

		NmMt 8	NmMt+ 8.5	MT 9	Gem 9.5/10
55	Chipper Jones RC	12	15	20	40
65	Mike Mussina RC	4	5	8	15
567	Luis Gonzalez RC	4	4	5	10
755	Jeff Bagwell RC	5	5	8	20
SP1	Michael Jordan	60	80	150	▼600

1991 Upper Deck Final Edition

		NmMt 8	NmMt+ 8.5	MT 9	Gem 9.5/10
2F	Pedro Martinez RC	▲15	▲20	30	80
17F	Jim Thome RC	15	20	25	50
55F	Ivan Rodriguez RC	5	5	6	20

1992 Bowman

		NmMt 8	NmMt+ 8.5	MT 9	Gem 9.5/10
11	Trevor Hoffman RC	20	25	▲60	▲250
28	Chipper Jones	20	25	30	50
82	Pedro Martinez	▼15	▼20	50	120
127	Carlos Delgado RC	6	8	12	50
298	Garret Anderson RC	5	6	10	30
302	Mariano Rivera RC	▲150	▲200	250	800
460	Jim Thome	6	8	10	30
461	Mike Piazza RC	▼40	▼50	80	▲300
532	Manny Ramirez RC	8	8	12	30
676	Manny Ramirez FOIL	10	12	15	30

1992 Fleer Update

		NmMt 8	NmMt+ 8.5	MT 9	Gem 9.5/10
92	Mike Piazza RC	80	80	120	250
104	Jeff Kent RC	25	30	50	150

1992 Upper Deck Minors

		NmMt 8	NmMt+ 8.5	MT 9	Gem 9.5/10
5	Derek Jeter FDP	40	▲50	▲60	150

1993 Bowman

		NmMt 8	NmMt+ 8.5	MT 9	Gem 9.5/10
103	Andy Pettitte RC	▼15	▼15	▼50	100
327	Mariano Rivera	25	▼20	▲60	120
511	Derek Jeter RC	50	▼60	▼120	500

1993 Pinnacle

		NmMt 8	NmMt+ 8.5	MT 9	Gem 9.5/10
457	Derek Jeter RC	▼60	▼80	▼120	▲600

1993 Select

		NmMt 8	NmMt+ 8.5	MT 9	Gem 9.5/10
360	Derek Jeter RC	50	50	▼60	▲300

1993 SP

		NmMt 8	NmMt+ 8.5	MT 9	Gem 9.5/10
273	Johnny Damon FOIL RC	10	12	20	200
279	Derek Jeter FOIL RC	▼800	▼1,200	3,000	▲25,000

— Derek Jeter #279 PSA 10 (Gem Mt) sold for $138,000 (Heritage; 12/19)
— Derek Jeter #279 PSA 10 (Gem Mt) sold for $168,000 (REA; 12/19)
— Derek Jeter #279 PSA 10 (Gem Mt) sold for $140,400 (eBay; 3/20)
— Derek Jeter #279 PSA 10 (Gem Mt) sold for $166,712.70 (Mile High; 5/20)
— Derek Jeter #279 PSA 10 (Gem Mt) sold for $468,000 (Heritage; 4/21)
— Derek Jeter #279 PSA 10 (Gem Mt) sold for $492,000 (Goldin; 5/21)
— Derek Jeter #279 PSA 10 (Gem Mt) sold for $396,000 (Heritage; 8/21)

1993 Stadium Club Murphy

		NmMt 8	NmMt+ 8.5	MT 9	Gem 9.5/10
93	Nomar Garciaparra USA	5	6	15	30
117	Derek Jeter RC	▼150	▼200	▼300	▼600

1993 Topps

		NmMt 8	NmMt+ 8.5	MT 9	Gem 9.5/10
98	Derek Jeter RC	▼50	▼60	▼120	▲500
799	Jim Edmonds RC	5	5	8	25

1993 Topps Inaugural Marlins

		NmMt 8	NmMt+ 8.5	MT 9	Gem 9.5/10
98	Derek Jeter	120	200	300	1,200

1993 Topps Inaugural Rockies

		NmMt 8	NmMt+ 8.5	MT 9	Gem 9.5/10
98	Derek Jeter	120	150	500	1,500

1993 Topps Traded

		NmMt 8	NmMt+ 8.5	MT 9	Gem 9.5/10
19T	Todd Helton USA RC	6	8	12	50

1993 Upper Deck

		NmMt 8	NmMt+ 8.5	MT 9	Gem 9.5/10
449	Derek Jeter RC	▼30	▼30	▼80	400

1994 Bowman

		NmMt 8	NmMt+ 8.5	MT 9	Gem 9.5/10
38	Jorge Posada RC	8	10	20	100
94	Edgar Renteria RC	5	6	8	25
104	Torii Hunter RC	8	10	15	40
232	Derrek Lee RC	8	10	15	20
433	Jermaine Dye RC	5	6	10	20
594	Paul LoDuca RC	5	5	8	15

1994 Bowman's Best

		NmMt 8	NmMt+ 8.5	MT 9	Gem 9.5/10
B19	Billy Wagner RC	5	5	8	12
B29	Jorge Posada RC	10	12	20	40
B63	Edgar Renteria RC	6	6	8	12

1994 Flair

		NmMt 8	NmMt+ 8.5	MT 9	Gem 9.5/10
340	Alex Rodriguez RC	25	30	40	80

1994 Flair Wave of the Future

		NmMt 8	NmMt+ 8.5	MT 9	Gem 9.5/10
B8	Alex Rodriguez	▲20	▲25	▲30	▲100

1994 Fleer Update

		NmMt 8	NmMt+ 8.5	MT 9	Gem 9.5/10
U86	Alex Rodriguez	▼15	▼20	30	60

1994 Leaf Limited Rookies Phenoms

		NmMt 8	NmMt+ 8.5	MT 9	Gem 9.5/10
10	Alex Rodriguez	100	▲250	▲300	600

1994 Score Rookie/Traded

		NmMt 8	NmMt+ 8.5	MT 9	Gem 9.5/10
HC1	Alex Rodriguez CU	120	150	▲300	

1994 SP

		NmMt 8	NmMt+ 8.5	MT 9	Gem 9.5/10
10	Derek Lee FOIL RC	10	12	50	150
15	Alex Rodriguez FOIL RC	▲80	120	300	▲1,000

1994 SP Holoviews

		NmMt 8	NmMt+ 8.5	MT 9	Gem 9.5/10
33	Alex Rodriguez	25	30	40	150

1994 SP Holoviews Die Cuts

		NmMt 8	NmMt+ 8.5	MT 9	Gem 9.5/10
16	Michael Jordan	120	150	200	800
33	Alex Rodriguez	200	200	250	1,000

1994 Upper Deck

		NmMt 8	NmMt+ 8.5	MT 9	Gem 9.5/10
19	Michael Jordan RC	20	25	30	60
24	Alex Rodriguez RC	12	15	20	60
298	Alex Rodriguez UDCA	5	6	10	30
A298	Alex Rodriguez AU	100	100	120	300

1995 Bowman's Best

		NmMt 8	NmMt+ 8.5	MT 9	Gem 9.5/10
B2	Vladimir Guerrero RC	▲80	▲80	▲120	1,000
B3	Bob Abreu RC	6	8	10	40
B7	Andruw Jones RC	▲30	▲30	▲40	▲250
B10	Richie Sexson RC	8	10	25	40
B73	Bartolo Colon RC	8	10	12	50
B74	Chris Carpenter RC	8	10	12	20
B87	Scott Rolen RC	8	10	20	25
X5	C.Beltran/J.Gonzalez UER	5	6	8	20

1997 Bowman

		NmMt 8	NmMt+ 8.5	MT 9	Gem 9.5/10
194	Adrian Beltre RC	20	40	100	300
196	Kerry Wood RC	5	6	8	15
308	Roy Halladay RC	15	30	60	300

(top table, continued)

		NmMt 8	NmMt+ 8.5	MT 9	Gem 9.5/10
411	Miguel Tejada RC	8	10	15	30
424	Vernon Wells RC	5	5	6	10
438	Lance Berkman RC	8	10	15	40

1997 Bowman Chrome

		NmMt 8	NmMt+ 8.5	MT 9	Gem 9.5/10
182	Adrian Beltre RC	▲60	▲80	▲150	250
183	Kerry Wood RC	5	6	12	30
192	Eric Chavez RC	5	5	6	15
212	Roy Halladay RC	80	80	▼100	400
214	Aramis Ramirez RC	5	6	10	15
273	Miguel Tejada RC	5	5	15	20
284	Vernon Wells RC	6	8	10	30
287	Jon Garland RC	6	8	12	40

1997 Bowman's Best

		NmMt 8	NmMt+ 8.5	MT 9	Gem 9.5/10
114	Miguel Tejada RC	6	8	12	25
117	Adrian Beltre RC	12	20	25	100
134	Roy Halladay RC	20	25	▲50	120
154	Kerry Wood RC	5	5	8	20

1997 Fleer

		NmMt 8	NmMt+ 8.5	MT 9	Gem 9.5/10
512	David Arias-Ortiz RC	▲120	▲120	▲200	▲400

1997 Ultra

		NmMt 8	NmMt+ 8.5	MT 9	Gem 9.5/10
518	David Arias-Ortiz RC	50	60	150	400

1998 Bowman Chrome

		NmMt 8	NmMt+ 8.5	MT 9	Gem 9.5/10
85	Mike Lowell RC	5	6	10	15
91	Kevin Millwood RC	5	5	8	12
134	Troy Glaus RC	4	5	8	12
181	Jimmy Rollins RC	5	6	10	40
185	Magglio Ordonez RC	6	6	15	20
221	Orlando Hernandez RC	5	6	8	25
428	Carlos Lee RC	8	10	15	25

1999 Bowman Chrome

		NmMt 8	NmMt+ 8.5	MT 9	Gem 9.5/10
175	Pat Burrell RC	4	5	8	12
200	Austin Kearns RC	8	10	15	25
344	C.C. Sabathia RC	8	10	▲40	100
350	Alfonso Soriano RC	6	8	15	▼30
355	Mark Mulder RC	5	6	10	20
364	Rafael Furcal RC	5	6	10	20
369	Adam Dunn RC	5	6	10	15
375	Tim Hudson RC	5	6	10	30
400	Matt Holliday RC	5	5	8	20
421	David Eckstein RC	6	8	12	25
431	Josh Hamilton RC	6	8	15	20
440	Carl Crawford RC	4	5	8	12

1999 Bowman's Best

		NmMt 8	NmMt+ 8.5	MT 9	Gem 9.5/10
171	C.C. Sabathia RC	5	6	12	40

1999 Finest

		NmMt 8	NmMt+ 8.5	MT 9	Gem 9.5/10
294	C.C. Sabathia RC	6	8	12	30

1999 Fleer Tradition Update

		NmMt 8	NmMt+ 8.5	MT 9	Gem 9.5/10
U3	Pat Burrell RC	5	5	8	20
U5	Alfonso Soriano RC	5	6	10	25
U42	Eric Gagne RC	5	5	8	25
U122	Josh Beckett RC	10	12	15	25

1999 Topps Traded Autographs

		NmMt 8	NmMt+ 8.5	MT 9	Gem 9.5/10
T33	C.C. Sabathia	30	40	50	120
T50	Adam Dunn	15	20	25	50
T51	Austin Kearns	6	8	10	25
T65	Alfonso Soriano	25	30	▲50	▲120
T66	Josh Hamilton	25	40	50	120

1999 Topps Chrome Traded

		NmMt 8	NmMt+ 8.5	MT 9	Gem 9.5/10
T33	C.C. Sabathia	6	6	12	50

2000 Bowman Draft

		NmMt 8	NmMt+ 8.5	MT 9	Gem 9.5/10
69	Mark Buehrle RC	5	5	8	12
86	Adrian Gonzalez RC	6	8	12	20
93	Adam Wainwright RC	5	5	6	12
109	Grady Sizemore RC	5	5	6	10

2000 Bowman Chrome

		NmMt 8	NmMt+ 8.5	MT 9	Gem 9.5/10
321	Francisco Rodriguez RC	6	8	20	40
395	Roy Oswalt RC	8	10	12	25
419	Barry Zito RC	5	5	12	20

2000 Bowman Chrome Draft

		NmMt 8	NmMt+ 8.5	MT 9	Gem 9.5/10
4	Barry Zito RC	5	5	15	30
69	Mark Buehrle RC	10	15	20	40
86	Adrian Gonzalez RC	10	▼10	▼12	▲40
93	Adam Wainwright RC	5	6	10	20

2000 Topps Traded

		NmMt 8	NmMt+ 8.5	MT 9	Gem 9.5/10
T38	Francisco Rodriguez RC	8	10	15	40
T40	Miguel Cabrera RC	▲150	▲200	▲250	▼600
T46	Mike Young RC	6	8	10	20

2000 Topps Traded Autographs

		NmMt 8	NmMt+ 8.5	MT 9	Gem 9.5/10
TTA29	Carlos Zambrano	12	15	25	150
TTA38	Francisco Rodriguez	15	20	25	60
TTA40	Miguel Cabrera	▲1,200	▲1,200	2,500	▲6,000
TTA46	Mike Young	40	50	100	250

2000 Topps Chrome Traded

		NmMt 8	NmMt+ 8.5	MT 9	Gem 9.5/10
T40	Miguel Cabrera RC	▲200	▲200	▲400	▼100
T46	Mike Young RC	6	8	12	25
T81	Adrian Gonzalez RC	8	10	▲25	▲30
T88	Adam Wainwright RC	5	8	12	30

2001 Bowman

		NmMt 8	NmMt+ 8.5	MT 9	Gem 9.5/10
264	Albert Pujols RC	▼150	▼150	▼250	800

2001 Bowman Autographs

		NmMt 8	NmMt+ 8.5	MT 9	Gem 9.5/10
BAAP	Albert Pujols	300	400	800	3,000

2001 Bowman Draft

		NmMt 8	NmMt+ 8.5	MT 9	Gem 9.5/10
BDP69	Chase Utley RC	▲50	▲50	100	150
BDP84	Ichiro Suzuki RC	80	100	120	▲600
BDP88	Bobby Crosby RC	5	5	10	30

2001 Bowman Chrome

		NmMt 8	NmMt+ 8.5	MT 9	Gem 9.5/10
164	Jose Reyes RC	10	10	12	40
169	Justin Morneau RC	12	15	20	30
183	Jake Peavy RC	15	20	25	40
340	Albert Pujols AU RC	▲12,000	▲12,000	▲20,000	▲60,000
351A	Ichiro Suzuki English RC	100	120	200	300
351B	Ichiro Suzuki Japan RC	100	120	200	300

— Albert Pujols #340 PSA 10 (Gem Mt) sold for $168,000 (Heritage; 12/20)

2001 Bowman Heritage

		NmMt 8	NmMt+ 8.5	MT 9	Gem 9.5/10
304	Chase Utley RC	10	12	25	40
351	Albert Pujols SP RC	60	80	100	250
352	Ichiro Suzuki SP RC	12	15	25	120

2001 Bowman's Best

		NmMt 8	NmMt+ 8.5	MT 9	Gem 9.5/10
162	Ichiro Suzuki RC	40	50	120	250
166	Justin Morneau RC	5	6	10	25
174	Albert Pujols RC	80	100	250	500

2001 Donruss Rookies

		NmMt 8	NmMt+ 8.5	MT 9	Gem 9.5/10
R97	Albert Pujols UPD	▲50	▲60	▲100	▲250

2001 Donruss Elite

		NmMt 8	NmMt+ 8.5	MT 9	Gem 9.5/10
156	Albert Pujols SP RC	150	200	200	1,200
195	Ichiro Suzuki SP RC	50	60	150	400
206	Victor Martinez/410 XRC	30	40	120	200
250	Mark Teixeira/543 XRC	20	25	50	200

2001 E-X

		NmMt 8	NmMt+ 8.5	MT 9	Gem 9.5/10
105	Ichiro Suzuki/1999 RC	30	40	100	200
131	Albert Pujols/499 RC	150	200	250	600

2001 Finest

		NmMt 8	NmMt+ 8.5	MT 9	Gem 9.5/10
134	Jose Reyes PROS RC	20	25	30	50

2001 Fleer Authority

		NmMt 8	NmMt+ 8.5	MT 9	Gem 9.5/10
101	Ichiro Suzuki RC	▲25	▲50	▼100	▲250
102	Albert Pujols RC	▲100	▲150	▲200	▲500
146	Mark Teixeira RC	5	5	8	20

2001 Fleer Platinum

		NmMt 8	NmMt+ 8.5	MT 9	Gem 9.5/10
301	Albert Pujols/1500 RC	25	30	50	150

2001 Fleer Premium

		NmMt 8	NmMt+ 8.5	MT 9	Gem 9.5/10
233	Albert Pujols RC	30	40	100	300

2001 Fleer Tradition

		NmMt 8	NmMt+ 8.5	MT 9	Gem 9.5/10
451	Albert Pujols RC	▲80	▲100	▲150	▲250

2001 Fleer Triple Crown

		NmMt 8	NmMt+ 8.5	MT 9	Gem 9.5/10
309	Albert Pujols/2999 RC	30	30	60	150

2001 Leaf Rookies and Stars

		NmMt 8	NmMt+ 8.5	MT 9	Gem 9.5/10
205	Albert Pujols RC	▲150	▲200	▲400	▲1,000
221	Mark Teixeira RC	20	25	40	100
273	Mark Prior RC	20	25	50	120

2001 SP Authentic

		NmMt 8	NmMt+ 8.5	MT 9	Gem 9.5/10
91	Ichiro Suzuki FW RC	150	200	500	1,000
95	Travis Hafner FW RC	30	40	50	200
126	Albert Pujols FW RC	1,200	2,500	4,000	8,000
211	Mark Prior FW RC	▼8	▼10	▼12	▼25
212	Mark Teixeira FW RC	15	20	25	50
234	Brian Roberts FW RC	5	6	8	20

2001 SPx

		NmMt 8	NmMt+ 8.5	MT 9	Gem 9.5/10
150	Ichiro Suzuki Jsy AU RC	1,000	1,200	2,500	4,000
206	Albert Pujols YS AU RC	400	500	600	1,500
207	Mark Teixeira YS AU RC	12	15	20	40
208	Mark Prior YS AU RC	10	12	20	40

2001 Sweet Spot

		NmMt 8	NmMt+ 8.5	MT 9	Gem 9.5/10
62	Ichiro Suzuki SB RC	100	120	150	300
121	Albert Pujols SB RC	50	60	100	250
138	Mark Teixeira SB RC	10	12	15	30
139	Mark Prior SB RC	5	6	8	12

2001 Topps

		NmMt 8	NmMt+ 8.5	MT 9	Gem 9.5/10
726	Ichiro Suzuki RC	100	120	300	1,000

2001 Topps Traded

		NmMt 8	NmMt+ 8.5	MT 9	Gem 9.5/10
T99	I.Suzuki/A.Pujols ROY	40	50	80	250
T235	Justin Morneau RC	6	8	15	40
T242	Jose Reyes RC	8	10	15	40
T247	Albert Pujols RC	50	60	120	300

2001 Topps Chrome

		NmMt 8	NmMt+ 8.5	MT 9	Gem 9.5/10
596	Albert Pujols RC	▼250	▼400	▼600	▼2,500

2001 Topps Chrome Traded

		NmMt 8	NmMt+ 8.5	MT 9	Gem 9.5/10
T99	I.Suzuki/A.Pujols ROY	250	300	1,500	2,000
T214	Hank Blalock RC	5	6	15	80
T235	Justin Morneau RC	5	6	10	15
T242	Jose Reyes RC	8	10	15	30
T247	Albert Pujols	250	300	1,500	1,500
T266	Ichiro Suzuki RC	300	400	2,000	250

2001 Topps Gallery

		NmMt 8	NmMt+ 8.5	MT 9	Gem 9.5/10
135	Albert Pujols RC	80	▼80	▼100	▼250
151A	Ichiro Suzuki English RC	12	15	25	60
151B	Ichiro Suzuki Japan RC	12	15	25	60

2001 Topps Stars

		NmMt 8	NmMt+ 8.5	MT 9	Gem 9.5/10
198	Albert Pujols RC	20	25	▲100	▲300

2001 UD Reserve

		NmMt 8	NmMt+ 8.5	MT 9	Gem 9.5/10
181	Ichiro Suzuki SP RC	15	20	30	50
204	Albert Pujols SP RC	60	80	100	250

2001 Upper Deck Ovation

		NmMt 8	NmMt+ 8.5	MT 9	Gem 9.5/10
76	Ichiro Suzuki WP RC	12	15	120	150

2001 Upper Deck Victory

		NmMt 8	NmMt+ 8.5	MT 9	Gem 9.5/10
564	Ichiro Suzuki RC	6	8	12	25

2001 Upper Deck Vintage

		NmMt 8	NmMt+ 8.5	MT 9	Gem 9.5/10
346	Ichiro Suzuki RC	6	8	12	25

2002 Bowman Chrome

		NmMt 8	NmMt+ 8.5	MT 9	Gem 9.5/10
65	Rich Harden SP RC	5	6	10	15
48	Jose Bautista SP RC	12	15	25	60
35	David Wright AU A RC	60	80	100	200
91	Joe Mauer AU A RC	80	100	120	300

2002 Bowman Chrome Draft

		NmMt 8	NmMt+ 8.5	MT 9	Gem 9.5/10
	Zack Greinke RC	10	12	20	30
	Nick Swisher RC	5	5	6	15
	Cole Hamels RC	12	15	▲25	▲100
	Jeff Francoeur RC	5	5	6	15
	Matt Cain RC	8	10	15	20
	Joey Votto RC	30	▲80	▲200	▲500
	Curtis Granderson RC	10	12	15	25
	B.J. Upton RC	5	5	5	12

2002 Bowman's Best

		NmMt 8	NmMt+ 8.5	MT 9	Gem 9.5/10
	Joe Mauer AU A RC	40	50	60	100
	Francisco Liriano AU A RC	10	12	15	30

2002 Topps

		NmMt 8	NmMt+ 8.5	MT 9	Gem 9.5/10
	Joe Mauer RC	10	12	25	100

2002 Upper Deck Prospect Premieres

		NmMt 8	NmMt+ 8.5	MT 9	Gem 9.5/10
	Jon Lester XRC	6	8	20	40
	Curtis Granderson XRC	5	5	8	12
	Francisco Liriano XRC	5	5	8	12
	Prince Fielder AU XRC	20	20	25	30
	Zack Greinke AU XRC	30	40	50	80
	Scott Kazmir AU XRC	6	8	12	20
	B.J. Upton AU XRC	6	8	12	20

2003 Bowman Chrome

		NmMt 8	NmMt+ 8.5	MT 9	Gem 9.5/10
	Brian McCann AU A RC	12	15	20	50
	Hanley Ramirez AU A RC	15	20	40	80
	Kevin Youkilis AU A RC	10	12	15	40

2003 Bowman Chrome Draft

		NmMt 8	NmMt+ 8.5	MT 9	Gem 9.5/10
	Jon Papelbon RC	5	6	10	20
	Robinson Cano RC	15	20	25	100
	Ryan Howard RC	8	10	12	20
	Nick Markakis AU RC	40	50	60	100

2003 Bowman Heritage Signs of Greatness

		NmMt 8	NmMt+ 8.5	MT 9	Gem 9.5/10
	Robinson Cano	50	60	100	250

2003 SP Authentic

		NmMt 8	NmMt+ 8.5	MT 9	Gem 9.5/10
	Hid Matsui FW AU RC	150	200	250	400
	Delmon Young FW AU RC	12	15	20	60

2003 SPx

		NmMt 8	NmMt+ 8.5	MT 9	Gem 9.5/10
	Hideki Matsui AU Jsy RC	150	200	250	400
	Delm Young AU Jsy RC	20	25	30	60

2003 Upper Deck Prospect Premieres

		NmMt 8	NmMt+ 8.5	MT 9	Gem 9.5/10
	Adam Jones XRC	5	6	10	15
	Andre Ethier XRC	8	10	15	30
	Carlos Quentin XRC	6	8	12	25
	Chad Billingsley XRC	6	8	12	25
	Conor Jackson XRC	5	6	10	25
	Jarrod Saltalamacchia XRC	5	5	10	25
	Lastings Milledge XRC	5	5	10	25
	Brandon Wood XRC	5	6	10	25
	Nick Markakis XRC	5	5	10	25
	Delmon Young XRC	8	10	15	30

2003 Upper Deck Prospect Premieres Autographs

		NmMt 8	NmMt+ 8.5	MT 9	Gem 9.5/10
	Adam Jones	50	60	80	200

2003 USA Baseball National Team

		NmMt 8	NmMt+ 8.5	MT 9	Gem 9.5/10
	Justin Verlander	10	12	25	60

2004 Bowman Signs of the Future

		NmMt 8	NmMt+ 8.5	MT 9	Gem 9.5/10
	Joey Votto A	80	100	120	250

2004 Bowman Chrome

		NmMt 8	NmMt+ 8.5	MT 9	Gem 9.5/10
	Yadier Molina RC	30	40	80	300
	Felix Hernandez AU RC	50	60	80	150

2004 Bowman Chrome Draft

		NmMt 8	NmMt+ 8.5	MT 9	Gem 9.5/10
166	Matt Bush AU RC	6	8	10	15
170	Homer Bailey AU RC	10	12	15	25
174	Philip Hughes AU RC	8	10	12	▲30

2004 Bowman Chrome Draft AFLAC

		NmMt 8	NmMt+ 8.5	MT 9	Gem 9.5/10
5	Andrew McCutchen	8	10	15	25

2004 Bowman Heritage

		NmMt 8	NmMt+ 8.5	MT 9	Gem 9.5/10
30	Yadier Molina FY RC	10	12	50	200

2004 Bowman Sterling

		NmMt 8	NmMt+ 8.5	MT 9	Gem 9.5/10
DW	David Wright AU Jsy	15	20	25	40
FH	Felix Hernandez FY AU	15	20	25	40

2004 Bowman's Best

		NmMt 8	NmMt+ 8.5	MT 9	Gem 9.5/10
FH	Felix Hernandez FY AU RC	30	30	▲50	▲250
YM	Yadier Molina FY AU RC	200	250	500	600

2004 SP Prospects

		NmMt 8	NmMt+ 8.5	MT 9	Gem 9.5/10
339	Hunter Pence AU 600/RC	30	40	50	120
340	Dustin Pedroia AU 400/RC	40	50	▼80	250

2004 Topps

		NmMt 8	NmMt+ 8.5	MT 9	Gem 9.5/10
324	Yadier Molina FY RC	▲100	▲100	▲120	▲600

2004 Topps Traded

		NmMt 8	NmMt+ 8.5	MT 9	Gem 9.5/10
T144	Felix Hernandez FY RC	5	6	10	30

2004 Topps Chrome

		NmMt 8	NmMt+ 8.5	MT 9	Gem 9.5/10
219	Yadier Molina FY RC	120	150	250	600

2004 Topps Chrome Traded

		NmMt 8	NmMt+ 8.5	MT 9	Gem 9.5/10
T144	Felix Hernandez FY RC	8	10	15	50

2005 Bowman Chrome

		NmMt 8	NmMt+ 8.5	MT 9	Gem 9.5/10
171	Ian Kinsler RC	5	5	5	40
331	Justin Verlander AU RC	200	250	▲500	▲1,000
349	Matthew Kemp AU RC	20	30	40	100

2005 Bowman Chrome Draft

		NmMt 8	NmMt+ 8.5	MT 9	Gem 9.5/10
32	Jay Bruce FY RC	5	6	8	12
63	Andrew McCutchen FY RC	12	15	20	40
105	Troy Tulowitzki FY RC	10	12	15	25
129	Justin Verlander FY	8	10	25	40
167	Jered Weaver AU A RC	15	20	25	40
168	Ryan Braun AU B RC	30	40	50	80
178	Ryan Zimmerman AU B RC	25	30	▲100	▲200

2005 Bowman Sterling

		NmMt 8	NmMt+ 8.5	MT 9	Gem 9.5/10
AM	Andrew McCutchen AU Jsy D RC	40	40	▲80	120
DP	Dustin Pedroia AU Jsy A	30	40	50	100
JB	Jay Bruce AU Jsy D RC	8	10	12	30
JV	J.Verlander AU Jsy A RC	100	120	150	300
RB	Ryan Braun AU Jsy B	15	20	25	60
RM	Russ Martin AU Jsy F RC	8	10	12	30
RZ	Ryan Zimmerman RC	6	8	10	20
TT	Troy Tulowitzki RC	10	12	15	30

2005 SP Authentic

		NmMt 8	NmMt+ 8.5	MT 9	Gem 9.5/10
137	Justin Verlander AU RC	80	100	120	600
152	Nelson Cruz AU RC	50	60	80	120
159	Prince Fielder AU RC	25	30	40	100

2005 SPx

		NmMt 8	NmMt+ 8.5	MT 9	Gem 9.5/10
135	Justin Verlander AU RC	60	80	100	200
147	Nelson Cruz AU RC	30	40	50	100
153	Prince Fielder AU RC	20	25	30	60
169	Ubaldo Jimenez AU RC	15	20	25	50
173	Ryan Zimmerman AU RC	40	50	60	120

2005 Topps

		NmMt 8	NmMt+ 8.5	MT 9	Gem 9.5/10
677	Justin Verlander FY RC	50	60	120	250

2005 Topps Chrome

		NmMt 8	NmMt+ 8.5	MT 9	Gem 9.5/10
214	Ian Kinsler FY RC	6	8	10	25
242	Justin Verlander FY AU RC	120	200	300	500

2005 Topps Chrome Update

		NmMt 8	NmMt+ 8.5	MT 9	Gem 9.5/10
169	Matthew Kemp FY RC	5	6	8	20
198	Ryan Braun FY RC	8	10	15	25
202	Jacoby Ellsbury FY RC	8	10	15	25
208	Ryan Zimmerman FY RC	8	10	12	15
222	Jay Bruce FY AU A RC	10	12	15	25
234	A.McCutchen FY AU B RC	50	60	80	120

2005-06 USA Baseball Junior National Team

		NmMt 8	NmMt+ 8.5	MT 9	Gem 9.5/10
86	Clayton Kershaw	8	10	15	60

2005-06 USA Baseball National Team

		NmMt 8	NmMt+ 8.5	MT 9	Gem 9.5/10
56	Max Scherzer	8	12	25	100

2006 Bowman Chrome

		NmMt 8	NmMt+ 8.5	MT 9	Gem 9.5/10
221	Prince Fielder AU (RC)	20	20	40	50

2006 Bowman Chrome Prospects

		NmMt 8	NmMt+ 8.5	MT 9	Gem 9.5/10
BC1	Alex Gordon	5	5	8	15
BC122	Elvis Andrus	5	5	8	15
BC129	Hunter Pence	5	5	8	15

2006 Bowman Chrome Draft Draft Picks

		NmMt 8	NmMt+ 8.5	MT 9	Gem 9.5/10
66	Evan Longoria AU	15	20	▲40	▲120
84	Clayton Kershaw AU	▲500	▲500	▲1,200	▲2,000

2006 Bowman Heritage Prospects

		NmMt 8	NmMt+ 8.5	MT 9	Gem 9.5/10
85	Clayton Kershaw	▼25	40	▲80	▲200

2006 Bowman Sterling Prospects

		NmMt 8	NmMt+ 8.5	MT 9	Gem 9.5/10
CK	Clayton Kershaw AU A	150	200	500	800
EL	Evan Longoria AU B	12	15	20	30
JU	Justin Upton AU B	10	12	15	30

2007 Bowman Draft Draft Picks

		NmMt 8	NmMt+ 8.5	MT 9	Gem 9.5/10
BDPP54	Jason Heyward	5	6	20	30

2007 Bowman Draft Future's Game Prospects

		NmMt 8	NmMt+ 8.5	MT 9	Gem 9.5/10
BDPP77	Clayton Kershaw	20	25	30	80

2007 Bowman Chrome

		NmMt 8	NmMt+ 8.5	MT 9	Gem 9.5/10
210	Daisuke Matsuzaka RC	6	8	15	25
217	Tim Lincecum RC	5	6	10	15

2007 Bowman Chrome Prospects

		NmMt 8	NmMt+ 8.5	MT 9	Gem 9.5/10
BC181	Daniel Murphy	10	12	20	50
BC238	Tim Lincecum AU	▲60	▲60	▲80	▲200
BC248	Hunter Pence AU	12	15	20	40

2007 Bowman Chrome Draft

		NmMt 8	NmMt+ 8.5	MT 9	Gem 9.5/10
BDP3	Justin Upton RC	6	8	12	30
BDP11	Tim Lincecum RC	8	10	15	40
BDP54	Mark Reynolds RC	5	6	10	20

2007 Bowman Chrome Draft Draft Picks

		NmMt 8	NmMt+ 8.5	MT 9	Gem 9.5/10
BDPP54	Jason Heyward	5	5	8	15
BDPP55	David Price	5	5	8	15
BDPP61	Madison Bumgarner	8	10	20	40

2007 Bowman Chrome Draft Future's Game Prospects

		NmMt 8	NmMt+ 8.5	MT 9	Gem 9.5/10
BDPP77	Clayton Kershaw	15	20	30	100

2007 Bowman Sterling

		NmMt 8	NmMt+ 8.5	MT 9	Gem 9.5/10
TL	Tim Lincecum AU RC	20	25	30	40

2007 Bowman Sterling Prospects

		NmMt 8	NmMt+ 8.5	MT 9	Gem 9.5/10
CK	Clayton Kershaw Jsy AU	80	100	120	300
DPP	David Price AU	15	20	25	▼30
EL	Evan Longoria Jsy AU	12	15	20	30
JV	Joey Votto Jsy AU	25	30	40	60
MBB	Madison Bumgarner AU	▼40	▼50	▼80	▼100
SP	Steve Pearce Jsy AU	15	20	25	40

2007 Bowman's Best

		NmMt 8	NmMt+ 8.5	MT 9	Gem 9.5/10
93	Tim Lincecum AU RC UER	30	40	50	100

2007 Donruss Elite Extra Edition

		NmMt 8	NmMt+ 8.5	MT 9	Gem 9.5/10
106	Jason Heyward AU/750	20	25	30	50
117	Madison Bumgarner AU/794	50	60	80	120

2007 SPx

		NmMt 8	NmMt+ 8.5	MT 9	Gem 9.5/10
106	Tim Lincecum AU RC	40	50	60	150
120	Ryan Braun AU (RC)	15	20	25	50
128	Daisuke Matsuzaka AU RC	30	40	50	120

2007 Topps

		NmMt 8	NmMt+ 8.5	MT 9	Gem 9.5/10
40a	Derek Jeter w/Mantle/Bush	12	15	20	150

2008 Bowman Chrome Prospects

		NmMt 8	NmMt+ 8.5	MT 9	Gem 9.5/10
BCP111	David Price AU	20	25	30	50
BCP120	Madison Bumgarner AU	60	80	100	120
BCP121	Jason Heyward AU	12	15	20	▲50

2008 Bowman Chrome Draft

		NmMt 8	NmMt+ 8.5	MT 9	Gem 9.5/10
BDP26a	Clayton Kershaw RC	12	15	30	80
BDP26b	Clayton Kershaw AU	150	200	250	500
BDP33	Max Scherzer RC	12	15	25	100

2008 Bowman Chrome Draft Prospects

		NmMt 8	NmMt+ 8.5	MT 9	Gem 9.5/10
BDPP115	Michael Stanton AU	▼120	▼150	▼200	500
BDPP128	Buster Posey AU	120	150	200	300

2008 Bowman Sterling Prospects

		NmMt 8	NmMt+ 8.5	MT 9	Gem 9.5/10
BP	Buster Posey AU	50	60	100	150
CB	Charlie Blackmon AU	20	25	30	50
JA	Jake Arrieta Jsy AU	20	25	30	50

2008 Donruss Elite Extra Edition

		NmMt 8	NmMt+ 8.5	MT 9	Gem 9.5/10
121	Dominic Brown AU/996	25	30	40	80
123	Gordon Beckham AU/710	8	10	12	30
156	Rick Porcello AU/1299	10	12	15	30
177	Buster Posey AU/934	60	80	100	150

2008 Playoff Contenders

		NmMt 8	NmMt+ 8.5	MT 9	Gem 9.5/10
63	Buster Posey AU	50	60	80	100
66	Chris Davis AU	15	20	25	50
117	Rick Porcello AU	10	12	15	30

2008 SPx

		NmMt 8	NmMt+ 8.5	MT 9	Gem 9.5/10
150	Max Scherzer AU RC	120	150	200	500

2008 Topps Update

		NmMt 8	NmMt+ 8.5	MT 9	Gem 9.5/10
UH240	Clayton Kershaw RC	▲150	▲150	▼300	▲800
UH280	Max Scherzer RC	▲150	▲150	▲250	▲600

2008 Topps Allen and Ginter

		NmMt 8	NmMt+ 8.5	MT 9	Gem 9.5/10
72	Clayton Kershaw RC	▲80	▲80	▲100	▲150
297	Max Scherzer RC	8	10	20	30

2008 Topps Chrome

		NmMt 8	NmMt+ 8.5	MT 9	Gem 9.5/10
193	Evan Longoria RC	6	8	12	25

2009 Bowman AFLAC

		NmMt 8	NmMt+ 8.5	MT 9	Gem 9.5/10
BH	Bryce Harper	120	150	200	400
KB2	Kris Bryant	60	80	100	250

2009 Bowman Chrome Prospects

		NmMt 8	NmMt+ 8.5	MT 9	Gem 9.5/10
BCP101	Freddie Freeman AU	▲300	▲300	▲400	▲1,000
BCP108	Carlos Santana AU	▲20	▲25	▲30	▲50
BCP115	Lance Lynn AU	15	20	25	40
BCP121	Charlie Blackmon AU	▲80	▲100	▲120	▲200

2009 Bowman Chrome WBC Prospects

		NmMt 8	NmMt+ 8.5	MT 9	Gem 9.5/10
BCW1	Yu Darvish	6	8	10	20
BCW12	Aroldis Chapman	4	5	8	20
BCW30	Masahiro Tanaka	8	10	15	30
BCW49	Yoennis Cespedes	5	6	10	25

2009 Bowman Chrome Draft Prospects

		NmMt 8	NmMt+ 8.5	MT 9	Gem 9.5/10
BDPP85	Steve Matz AU	▼15	▼20	▼25	40
BDPP86	Zack Wheeler AU	▼20	▼25	▼30	▼50
BDPP89	Mike Trout AU	▼1,000	▼1,200	▼12,000	▲30,000
BDPP93	Tyler Matzek AU	25	30	40	60

— Mike Trout AU #236 PSA 10 (Gem Mt) sold for $16,800 (Heritage; 7/19)
— Mike Trout AU #236 PSA 10 (Gem Mt) sold for $35,000 (eBay; 8/20)
— Mike Trout AU #236 BGS 9.5 (Gem Mt) sold for $28,800 (Goldin; 4/21)
— Mike Trout AU #236 BGS 9.5 (Gem Mt) sold for $25,475 (eBay; 6/21)
— Mike Trout AU #236 BGS 9.5 (Gem Mt) sold for $22,627 (eBay; 9/21)
— Mike Trout AU #236 BGS 9.5 (Gem Mt) sold for $26,400 (Goldin; 10/21)
— Mike Trout AU #236 BGS 9.5 (Gem Mt) sold for $18,000 (Goldin; 10/21)
— Mike Trout AU #236 BGS 9.5 (Gem Mt) sold for $16,800 (Goldin; 10/21)

2009 Bowman Chrome Draft WBC Prospects

		NmMt 8	NmMt+ 8.5	MT 9	Gem 9.5/10
BDPW2	Yu Darvish	6	8	12	30

2009 Bowman Sterling Prospects

		NmMt 8	NmMt+ 8.5	MT 9	Gem 9.5/10
MT	Mike Trout AU	1,500	2,000	▼2,500	▼5,000

2009 Donruss Elite Extra Edition

		NmMt 8	NmMt+ 8.5	MT 9	Gem 9.5/10
57	Mike Trout AU/495	1,500	2,000	2,500	5,000

2009 Donruss Elite Extra Edition Signature Turn of the Century

		NmMt 8	NmMt+ 8.5	MT 9	Gem 9.5/10
6	Nolan Arenado AU/844	50	60	100	200
57	Mike Trout AU/149	300	400	500	1,000
90	Randal Grichuk AU/50	50	60	80	150
150	Aroldis Chapman AU/149	40	50	60	120

2009 TRISTAR Prospects Plus

		NmMt 8	NmMt+ 8.5	MT 9	Gem 9.5/10
20	Michael Trout	15	20	30	80

2009 Upper Deck Signature Stars USA Star Prospects

		NmMt 8	NmMt+ 8.5	MT 9	Gem 9.5/10
USA8	Bryce Harper	12	15	20	60

2010 Bowman

		NmMt 8	NmMt+ 8.5	MT 9	Gem 9.5/10
200	Jason Heyward RC	5	6	10	15
208	Buster Posey RC	8	10	15	25

2010 Bowman Prospects

		NmMt 8	NmMt+ 8.5	MT 9	Gem 9.5/10
BP1a	Stephen Strasburg	6	8	12	25
BP1b	Stephen Strasburg AU	80	▲100	▲120	150

2010 Bowman Draft

		NmMt 8	NmMt+ 8.5	MT 9	Gem 9.5/10
BDP1	Stephen Strasburg RC	5	6	10	20

2010 Bowman Draft Prospects

		NmMt 8	NmMt+ 8.5	MT 9	Gem 9.5/10
BDPP47	Russell Wilson	▲20	▲30	▲50	▲120
BDPP80	Manny Machado	8	10	15	20
BDPP84	Matt Harvey	4	5	10	20

2010 Bowman Chrome

		NmMt 8	NmMt+ 8.5	MT 9	Gem 9.5/10
198B	Mike Stanton RC	▲25	▲25	▲40	▲60
200A	Jason Heyward AU	10	12	15	25
205A	Stephen Strasburg RC	10	12	20	40
205B	Stephen Strasburg AU	50	60	100	150

2010 Bowman Chrome 18U USA Baseball

		NmMt 8	NmMt+ 8.5	MT 9	Gem 9.5/10
18BC8	Bryce Harper	▲50	▲60	▲80	▲150

2010 Bowman Chrome 18U USA Baseball Autographs

		NmMt 8	NmMt+ 8.5	MT 9	Gem 9.5/10
FL	Francisco Lindor	80	100	120	200

2010 Bowman Chrome Prospects

		NmMt 8	NmMt+ 8.5	MT 9	Gem 9.5/10
BCP1	Stephen Strasburg	15	20	40	50
BCP91B	Nolan Arenado AU	250	300	400	600
BCP100B	Starlin Castro AU	12	15	20	30
BCP101B	Anthony Rizzo AU	100	120	150	250
BCP113B	Josh Donaldson AU	30	40	50	80
BCP117B	Wil Myers AU	25	30	40	▼50
BCP124	Salvador Perez UER Dodgers logo on front	50	60	120	300
BCP137	Jose Altuve	▼15	▼20	50	▲150
BCP165	J.D. Martinez	12	15	25	100
BCP195B	Kyle Seager AU	10	12	15	25
BCP199B	Aroldis Chapman AU	20	25	30	60
BCP203B	Max Kepler AU	▲15	▲20	▲30	▲50
BCP205B	Miguel Sano AU	▼15	▼20	▼25	▲80
BCP207B	Gary Sanchez AU	▼60	▼80	▼120	400

2010 Bowman Chrome Draft

		NmMt 8	NmMt+ 8.5	MT 9	Gem 9.5/10
BDP1A	Stephen Strasburg RC	5	6	10	50
BDP1B	Stephen Strasburg AU	150	200	250	400
BDP30	Mike Stanton RC	8	10	30	60
BDP61	Buster Posey RC	5	6	10	50

2010 Bowman Chrome Draft Prospect Autographs

		NmMt 8	NmMt+ 8.5	MT 9	Gem 9.5/10
BDPP78	Christian Yelich	▼80	▼100	▼120	▼150
BDPP80	Manny Machado	150	200	250	▼400
BDPP92	Chris Sale	100	120	150	▼250

2010 Bowman Chrome Draft Prospects

		NmMt 8	NmMt+ 8.5	MT 9	Gem 9.5/10
BDPP47	Russell Wilson	10	12	20	50
BDPP80	Manny Machado	12	15	25	50
BDPP108	Corey Seager	12	15	25	50

2010 Bowman Chrome Draft USA Baseball Autographs

		NmMt 8	NmMt+ 8.5	MT 9	Gem 9.5/10
USAA5	Alex Bregman	50	60	80	▼120
USAA14	Matt Olson	▲50	▲60	▲80	▲120
USAA18	Corey Seager	▼80	▼100	▼120	▼200

2010 Bowman Platinum

		NmMt 8	NmMt+ 8.5	MT 9	Gem 9.5/10
1	Stephen Strasburg RC	5	6	8	25
18	Buster Posey RC	▲40	▲40	▲60	▲200
73	Madison Bumgarner RC	6	8	12	20
86	Mike Stanton RC	▲10	▲12	▲25	▲50

2010 Bowman Platinum Prospect Autographs Refractors

		NmMt 8	NmMt+ 8.5	MT 9	Gem 9.5/10
ACH	Aroldis Chapman	20	25	30	50
FF	Freddie Freeman	25	30	40	60
JDM	J.D. Martinez	▼30	▼40	▼80	150
MS	Miguel Sano	▼12	▼15	▼20	▼25
MT	Mike Trout	▲1,500	▲1,500	▲2,000	4,000
PG	Paul Goldschmidt	30	40	80	150

2010 Bowman Platinum Prospects

		NmMt 8	NmMt+ 8.5	MT 9	Gem 9.5/10
PP5	Mike Trout	120	150	▼200	▼400

2010 Bowman Sterling Prospect Autographs

		NmMt 8	NmMt+ 8.5	MT 9	Gem 9.5/10
CS	Chris Sale	▲30	▲40	▲50	▲80
CY	Christian Yelich	▼50	▼60	▼120	▼150

2010 Bowman Sterling Rookie Autographs

		NmMt 8	NmMt+ 8.5	MT 9	Gem 9.5/10
1	Stephen Strasburg	▲50	▲60	▼80	▼120

2010 Donruss Elite Extra Edition

		NmMt 8	NmMt+ 8.5	MT 9	Gem 9.5/10
103	Chris Sale AU/655	30	40	80	120
113	Noah Syndergaard AU/809	25	30	40	80
132	Manny Machado AU/425	40	50	60	100
147	Christian Yelich AU/815	40	50	▼60	200
191	Paul Goldschmidt AU/820	50	60	100	120

2010 Donruss Elite Extra Edition Franchise Futures Signatures

		NmMt 8	NmMt+ 8.5	MT 9	Gem 9.5/10
34	Gary Sanchez/669	100	120	150	250
46	Matt Harvey/149	80	100	120	200

2010 Topps

		NmMt 8	NmMt+ 8.5	MT 9	Gem 9.5/10
2	Buster Posey RC	▲50	▲50	▲100	▲250
105	Madison Bumgarner RC	6	8	12	30
661A	Stephen Strasburg Million Card Giveaway	15	20	25	40

2010 Topps Red Hot Rookie Redemption

		NmMt 8	NmMt+ 8.5	MT 9	Gem 9.5/10
RHR8	Stephen Strasburg	15	20	25	40

2010 Topps 206

		NmMt 8	NmMt+ 8.5	MT 9	Gem 9.5/10
55	Stephen Strasburg RC	6	8	12	30

2010 Topps Allen and Ginter

		NmMt 8	NmMt+ 8.5	MT 9	Gem 9.5/10
6	Madison Bumgarner RC	4	5	20	40
294	Buster Posey RC	8	10	20	30

2010 Topps Chrome

		NmMt 8	NmMt+ 8.5	MT 9	Gem 9.5/10
212	Stephen Strasburg RC	5	6	10	20

2010 Topps Chrome Rookie Autographs

		NmMt 8	NmMt+ 8.5	MT 9	Gem 9.5/10
190	Mike Stanton	▲150	▲150	▲200	250
212	Stephen Strasburg	50	60	80	▼120

2010 Topps Chrome Wrapper Redemption Refractors

		NmMt 8	NmMt+ 8.5	MT 9	Gem 9.5/10
190	Mike Stanton	25	30	60	150
212	Stephen Strasburg	-12	12	15	40
221	Buster Posey	▲150	▲200	▲300	▲500

2010 Topps Pro Debut

		NmMt 8	NmMt+ 8.5	MT 9	Gem 9.5/10
181	Mike Trout	300	400	500	800

2010 Upper Deck

		NmMt 8	NmMt+ 8.5	MT 9	Gem 9.5/10
28	Buster Posey RC	▲25	▲30	▲50	▲120

2011 Bowman Bowman's Best Prospects

		NmMt 8	NmMt+ 8.5	MT 9	Gem 9.5/10
BBP1	Bryce Harper	8	10	25	60
BBP9	Mike Trout	150	200	250	500
BBP51	Bryce Harper	8	10	12	50
BBP55	Manny Machado	5	6	10	25

2011 Bowman Prospect Autographs

		NmMt 8	NmMt+ 8.5	MT 9	Gem 9.5/10
MM	Manny Machado	40	50	60	120

2011 Bowman Prospects

		NmMt 8	NmMt+ 8.5	MT 9	Gem 9.5/10
BP1A	Bryce Harper	5	6	12	30
BP1B	Bryce Harper AU	250	300	400	500

2011 Bowman Chrome

		NmMt 8	NmMt+ 8.5	MT 9	Gem 9.5/10
175	Mike Trout RC	400	500	▼800	▲3,000
185	Freddie Freeman RC	50	60	80	300

2011 Bowman Chrome 18U USA National Team Autographs Refractors

		NmMt 8	NmMt+ 8.5	MT 9	Gem 9.5/10
18U2	Alex Bregman	50	60	80	120
18U28	Jesse Winker	50	60	80	120

2011 Bowman Chrome Bryce Harper Retail Exclusive

		NmMt 8	NmMt+ 8.5	MT 9	Gem 9.5/10
CE1G	Bryce Harper Gold	15	20	25	50
CE1R	Bryce Harper Red	6	8	12	25
CE1S	Bryce Harper Silver	6	8	12	25

2011 Bowman Chrome Prospect Autographs

		NmMt 8	NmMt+ 8.5	MT 9	Gem 9.5/10
CP92	J.D. Martinez	▲50	▲60	▲80	▼100
CP99	Paul Goldschmidt	▼80	▼100	▼120	▼200
CP111B	Bryce Harper	▲500	▲600	▲1,000	▲1,500

2011 Bowman Chrome Prospects

		NmMt 8	NmMt+ 8.5	MT 9	Gem 9.5/10
CP1	Bryce Harper	15	30	40	60
CP111	Bryce Harper	15	20	25	60

2011 Bowman Chrome Rookie Autographs

		NmMt 8	NmMt+ 8.5	MT 9	Gem 9.5/10
5	Freddie Freeman	▲200	▲250	▲300	▲600

2011 Bowman Chrome Draft

		NmMt 8	NmMt+ 8.5	MT 9	Gem 9.5/10
	Jose Altuve RC	20	25	40	80
1	Mike Trout RC	400	500	1,000	1,500
8	Paul Goldschmidt RC	10	12	20	50

2011 Bowman Chrome Draft Prospects

		NmMt 8	NmMt+ 8.5	MT 9	Gem 9.5/10
PP18	Dylan Bundy	5	6	10	20
PP29	Jose Fernandez	6	8	12	25

2011 Bowman Chrome Draft Prospect Autographs

		NmMt 8	NmMt+ 8.5	MT 9	Gem 9.5/10
N	Blake Snell	40	50	60	▼100
	Francisco Lindor	250	300	400	▼600
	George Springer	▼60	▼80	▼100	▼120
A	Javier Baez	250	300	400	▼600
	Trevor Bauer	▼80	▼100	▼120	▼200
	Trevor Story	▲120	▲150	▲200	300

2011 Bowman Draft

		NmMt 8	NmMt+ 8.5	MT 9	Gem 9.5/10
	Mike Trout RC	▼400	500	600	1,000

2011 Bowman Draft Bryce Harper Green Border Autograph

		NmMt 8	NmMt+ 8.5	MT 9	Gem 9.5/10
	Bryce Harper	250	300	400	500

2011 Bowman Platinum

		NmMt 8	NmMt+ 8.5	MT 9	Gem 9.5/10
57	Freddie Freeman RC	50	60	80	200

2011 Bowman Platinum Prospect Autograph Refractors

		NmMt 8	NmMt+ 8.5	MT 9	Gem 9.5/10
BH	Bryce Harper	150	200	▼200	400
MH	Matt Harvey	15	20	25	40
MM	Manny Machado	40	50	▲80	120

2011 Bowman Sterling

		NmMt 8	NmMt+ 8.5	MT 9	Gem 9.5/10
15	Jose Altuve RC	▼50	▼60	▼80	▼120
22	Mike Trout RC	600	800	1,200	3,000
27	Paul Goldschmidt RC	30	40	50	80

2011 Bowman Sterling Prospect Autographs

		NmMt 8	NmMt+ 8.5	MT 9	Gem 9.5/10
BS	Blake Snell	15	20	25	40
FL	Francisco Lindor	▼40	▼50	▼60	150
GS	George Springer	▼20	▼25	▼40	▼120
JB	Javier Baez	50	60	80	120
TB	Trevor Bauer	30	40	50	80
TS	Trevor Story	▲60	▲80	▲100	▲150

2011 Bowman Sterling Rookie Autographs

		NmMt 8	NmMt+ 8.5	MT 9	Gem 9.5/10
4	Anthony Rizzo	▼30	▼40	▼50	80
6	Eric Hosmer	30	40	50	80
7	Freddie Freeman	▲50	▲60	▲80	▲120
13	Mike Moustakas	20	25	30	50

2011 Donruss Elite Extra Edition Prospects

		NmMt 8	NmMt+ 8.5	MT 9	Gem 9.5/10
P4	Dylan Bundy AU/435	50	60	80	100

2011 Finest

		NmMt 8	NmMt+ 8.5	MT 9	Gem 9.5/10
94	Mike Trout RC	▼200	▼250	▼500	▼1,000

2011 Finest Rookie Autographs Refractors

		NmMt 8	NmMt+ 8.5	MT 9	Gem 9.5/10
84	Mike Trout	1,000	2,000	2,500	3,000

2011 Playoff Contenders

		NmMt 8	NmMt+ 8.5	MT 9	Gem 9.5/10
17	Mike Trout RC	150	200	250	500

2011 Topps Update

		NmMt 8	NmMt+ 8.5	MT 9	Gem 9.5/10
US47	Paul Goldschmidt RC	▲25	▲30	40	▲80
US55	Anthony Rizzo RC	▲25	▲30	▲40	▲120
US132	Jose Altuve RC	25	30	50	80
US175	Mike Trout RC	▼1,000	▼1,200	▼1,500	▼3,000
US186	J.D. Martinez RC	15	20	25	60

2011 Topps Chrome Rookie Autographs

		NmMt 8	NmMt+ 8.5	MT 9	Gem 9.5/10
170	Eric Hosmer	▲50	▲60	▲80	120
171	Tsuyoshi Nishioka EXCH	60	80	100	▼150
173	Freddie Freeman	▲250	▲300	▲400	▲600
195	Craig Kimbrel	▲30	▲40	▲50	80
205	Chris Sale	▲50	▲60	▲80	▲120

2011 Topps Heritage Minors

		NmMt 8	NmMt+ 8.5	MT 9	Gem 9.5/10
44	Mike Trout	150	200	250	400

2011 Topps Pro Debut

		NmMt 8	NmMt+ 8.5	MT 9	Gem 9.5/10
62	Joc Pederson	5	6	10	15
196	Bryce Harper	▲20	▲25	▲40	▲60
263	Mike Trout	120	150	250	500

2011 USA Baseball Autographs

		NmMt 8	NmMt+ 8.5	MT 9	Gem 9.5/10
A51	Joey Gallo	30	40	50	80

2012 Bowman

		NmMt 8	NmMt+ 8.5	MT 9	Gem 9.5/10
209A	Yu Darvish RC	8	10	15	30

2012 Bowman Prospects

		NmMt 8	NmMt+ 8.5	MT 9	Gem 9.5/10
BP10	Bryce Harper	12	15	30	50

2012 Bowman Chrome

		NmMt 8	NmMt+ 8.5	MT 9	Gem 9.5/10
84	Yu Darvish RC	8	10	15	25
157	Mike Trout	50	60	80	200
214	Bryce Harper RC	20	25	60	▲150

2012 Bowman Chrome Prospect Autographs

		NmMt 8	NmMt+ 8.5	MT 9	Gem 9.5/10
MO	Marcell Ozuna	40	50	60	▲100
NC	Nick Castellanos	▲60	▲80	▲100	▲150
JSO	Jorge Soler	▲40	▲50	▲60	▲100
BCP9	Eddie Rosario	▲40	▲50	▲60	▲150
BCP79	Josh Bell	▼30	▼40	▼50	▼60
BCP86	Gerrit Cole	▼100	▼120	▼150	▼250
BCP88	Anthony Rendon	▼60	▼80	▼100	▼120
BCP104	Joc Pederson	▼30	▼40	▼50	▼100
BCP105	Xander Bogaerts	▲120	▲150	▲200	▲500

2012 Bowman Chrome Prospects

		NmMt 8	NmMt+ 8.5	MT 9	Gem 9.5/10
BCP10	Bryce Harper	▲15	▲20	▼25	▲80
BCP105	Xander Bogaerts	8	10	15	25
BCP120	Jorge Soler	8	10	15	25
BCP182	Gregory Polanco	10	12	20	30
BCP217	Manny Machado	8	10	15	25

2012 Bowman Chrome Rookie Autographs

		NmMt 8	NmMt+ 8.5	MT 9	Gem 9.5/10
BH	Bryce Harper	200	250	300	▼500
TB	Trevor Bauer	30	40	50	▼80
YD	Yu Darvish	120	150	200	▼300
209	Yu Darvish	120	150	200	▼300

2012 Bowman Chrome Draft

		NmMt 8	NmMt+ 8.5	MT 9	Gem 9.5/10
10	Bryce Harper RC	▲30	▲40	▲60	▲120
50	Yu Darvish RC	5	6	10	25

2012 Bowman Chrome Draft Draft Pick Autographs

		NmMt 8	NmMt+ 8.5	MT 9	Gem 9.5/10
AR	Addison Russell	40	50	60	▼100
CS	Corey Seager	▼120	▼150	▼200	▼150
DD	David Dahl	30	40	50	▼80
JG	Joey Gallo	40	50	60	▼100
MF	Max Fried	▼30	▼40	▼50	▼80
MS	Marcus Stroman	30	40	50	▼80
TN	Tyler Naquin	30	40	50	▼80

2012 Bowman Chrome Draft Rookie Autographs

		NmMt 8	NmMt+ 8.5	MT 9	Gem 9.5/10
BH	Bryce Harper	200	250	300	▼500
YD	Yu Darvish EXCH	120	▲150	200	▼300

2012 Bowman Draft

		NmMt 8	NmMt+ 8.5	MT 9	Gem 9.5/10
10	Bryce Harper RC	8	15	30	80
50	Yu Darvish RC	5	6	10	25

2012 Bowman Platinum

		NmMt 8	NmMt+ 8.5	MT 9	Gem 9.5/10
9	Yu Darvish RC	8	10	15	25
16	Mike Trout	▼40	▼50	▼80	600
56	Bryce Harper RC	▼25	30	▼40	200

2012 Bowman Platinum Prospect Autographs

		NmMt 8	NmMt+ 8.5	MT 9	Gem 9.5/10
AR	Anthony Rendon	15	20	25	40
GB	Greg Bird	30	40	60	100
YC	Yoenis Cespedes	25	30	50	80
YD	Yu Darvish	60	80	120	200

2012 Bowman Sterling Prospect Autographs

		NmMt 8	NmMt+ 8.5	MT 9	Gem 9.5/10
CS	Corey Seager	▼15	▲60	▲80	▲150
FL	Francisco Lindor	▲40	▲50	60	100
GCO	Gerrit Cole	30	40	50	80
JGA	Joey Gallo	▲15	▲20	▲25	▲40
JWI	Jesse Winker	25	30	40	60
MF	Max Fried	25	30	40	60
NC	Nick Castellanos	15	20	25	40
PW	Patrick Wisdom	20	25	30	50

2012 Bowman Sterling Rookie Autographs

		NmMt 8	NmMt+ 8.5	MT 9	Gem 9.5/10
BH	Bryce Harper	100	120	150	250
MT	Mike Trout	600	800	1,000	1,500
SM	Starling Marte	15	20	25	40
TB	Trevor Bauer	15	20	25	40
YC	Yoenis Cespedes	25	30	40	60
YD	Yu Darvish	100	120	150	250

2012 Elite Extra Edition

		NmMt 8	NmMt+ 8.5	MT 9	Gem 9.5/10
101	Carlos Correa AU/470	50	60	80	100
102	Byron Buxton AU/599	20	25	30	60
113	Corey Seager AU/330	60	80	100	120

2012 Finest

		NmMt 8	NmMt+ 8.5	MT 9	Gem 9.5/10
35	Yu Darvish RC	6	8	15	30
73	Bryce Harper RC	20	25	25	50

2012 Panini Prizm

		NmMt 8	NmMt+ 8.5	MT 9	Gem 9.5/10
50	Mike Trout	50	120	300	
151	Yu Darvish RC	4	5	6	15
152	Bryce Harper RC	▲30	▲40	▲50	100

2012 Panini Prizm Rookie Autographs

		NmMt 8	NmMt+ 8.5	MT 9	Gem 9.5/10
RMH	Matt Harvey	30	40	50	100

2012 Topps

		NmMt 8	NmMt+ 8.5	MT 9	Gem 9.5/10
446	Mike Trout	▲30	▲40	▼50	▼120
660A	Yu Darvish RC	5	6	10	30

2012 Topps Update

		NmMt 8	NmMt+ 8.5	MT 9	Gem 9.5/10
US183	Bryce Harper RC	25	30	40	80
US299A	Bryce Harper	10	12	20	30

2012 Topps Allen and Ginter

		NmMt 8	NmMt+ 8.5	MT 9	Gem 9.5/10
4	Yu Darvish RC	8	10	15	25
12	Bryce Harper RC	10	12	15	40

2012 Topps Archives

		NmMt 8	NmMt+ 8.5	MT 9	Gem 9.5/10
119	Yu Darvish RC	5	6	10	25

2012 Topps Chrome

		NmMt 8	NmMt+ 8.5	MT 9	Gem 9.5/10
151A	Yu Darvish Arm Back RC	6	8	12	25
196A	Bryce Harper Hitting RC	8	10	15	50

2012 Topps Chrome Rookie Autographs

		NmMt 8	NmMt+ 8.5	MT 9	Gem 9.5/10
BH	Bryce Harper	▼200	▼250	▲500	▲1,500
151	Yu Darvish	30	40	50	▼80

2012 Topps Heritage

		NmMt 8	NmMt+ 8.5	MT 9	Gem 9.5/10
207	Mike Trout	▼120	▼120	▼200	▼500
H650	Bryce Harper RC	400	500	600	1,000

2013 Bowman

		NmMt 8	NmMt+ 8.5	MT 9	Gem 9.5/10
215	Manny Machado RC	5	6	10	20

2013 Bowman Prospects

		NmMt 8	NmMt+ 8.5	MT 9	Gem 9.5/10
BP1	Byron Buxton	5	6	10	30
BP100	Carlos Correa	10	12	15	25

2013 Bowman Top 100 Prospects

		NmMt 8	NmMt+ 8.5	MT 9	Gem 9.5/10
BTP58	Yasiel Puig	15	20	25	50

2013 Bowman Chrome

		NmMt 8	NmMt+ 8.5	MT 9	Gem 9.5/10
78	Yasiel Puig RC	5	6	12	20
147	Didi Gregorius RC	4	5	8	15
205	Manny Machado RC	5	6	12	30

2013 Bowman Chrome Prospect Autographs

		NmMt 8	NmMt+ 8.5	MT 9	Gem 9.5/10
BB	Byron Buxton	▲100	▲120	▲150	▼250
CC	Carlos Correa	100	120	150	▲400
LG	Lucas Giolito	▼25	▼30	50	▲120
MO	Matt Olson	▲40	▲50	▲60	▲150
PW	Patrick Wisdom	40	50	60	100
TG	Tyler Glasnow	40	50	60	150
YP	Yasiel Puig	▼30	▼40	▼50	▼80

2013 Bowman Chrome Prospects

		NmMt 8	NmMt+ 8.5	MT 9	Gem 9.5/10
BCP100	Carlos Correa	8	10	15	25

2013 Bowman Chrome Rookie Autographs

		NmMt 8	NmMt+ 8.5	MT 9	Gem 9.5/10
EG	Evan Gattis	30	40	50	▼80
HJR	Hyun-Jin Ryu	80	100	120	▼200
MM	Manny Machado	40	50	60	▼100
WM	Wil Myers	▲30	40	50	▼80

2013 Bowman Chrome Draft

		NmMt 8	NmMt+ 8.5	MT 9	Gem 9.5/10
1	Yasiel Puig RC	6	8	10	20

2013 Bowman Chrome Draft Draft Pick Autographs

		NmMt 8	NmMt+ 8.5	MT 9	Gem 9.5/10
AJ	Aaron Judge	500	600	800	▼1,000
KB	Kris Bryant	250	300	400	▼500
TA	Tim Anderson	80	100	120	▼200

2013 Bowman Chrome Draft Draft Picks

		NmMt 8	NmMt+ 8.5	MT 9	Gem 9.5/10
BDPP19	Aaron Judge	40	50	▲100	▲200

2013 Bowman Chrome Draft Rookie Autographs

		NmMt 8	NmMt+ 8.5	MT 9	Gem 9.5/10
YP	Yasiel Puig	150	200	250	▼400

2013 Bowman Chrome Draft Top Prospects

		NmMt 8	NmMt+ 8.5	MT 9	Gem 9.5/10
TP10	Carlos Correa	8	10	15	20

2013 Bowman Chrome Mini

		NmMt 8	NmMt+ 8.5	MT 9	Gem 9.5/10
311	Aaron Judge	15	20	25	80

2013 Bowman Draft

		NmMt 8	NmMt+ 8.5	MT 9	Gem 9.5/10
1	Yasiel Puig RC	5	6	10	20

2013 Bowman Draft Draft Picks

		NmMt 8	NmMt+ 8.5	MT 9	Gem 9.5/10
BDPP19	Aaron Judge	20	25	40	100

2013 Bowman Draft Top Prospects

		NmMt 8	NmMt+ 8.5	MT 9	Gem 9.5/10
TP10	Carlos Correa	6	8	12	25

2013 Bowman Platinum Prospect Autographs

		NmMt 8	NmMt+ 8.5	MT 9	Gem 9.5/10
AR	Addison Russell	15	20	25	40
BB	Byron Buxton	20	25	30	50
CC	Carlos Correa	50	60	50	200

2013 Bowman Sterling

		NmMt 8	NmMt+ 8.5	MT 9	Gem 9.5/10
32	Yasiel Puig RC	10	12	25	40

2013 Bowman Sterling Prospect Autographs

		NmMt 8	NmMt+ 8.5	MT 9	Gem 9.5/10
AJ	Aaron Judge	150	200	250	▲500
CC	Carlos Correa	▲30	▲40	▲50	▲100
JS	Jorge Soler	15	20	25	40
JU	Julio Urias	▲40	▲60	▲80	▲120
NS	Noah Syndergaard	15	20	25	40
RMM	Ryan McMahon	20	25	30	50
TA	Tim Anderson	30	40	50	80

2013 Bowman Sterling Prospects

		NmMt 8	NmMt+ 8.5	MT 9	Gem 9.5/10
11	Kris Bryant	15	20	▲30	▲50

2013 Bowman Sterling Rookie Autographs

		NmMt 8	NmMt+ 8.5	MT 9	Gem 9.5/10
JF	Jose Fernandez	30	40	50	80
NA	Nolan Arenado	100	120	150	250
YP	Yasiel Puig	100	120	150	250

2013 Elite Extra Edition

		NmMt 8	NmMt+ 8.5	MT 9	Gem 9.5/10
102	Kris Bryant AU/324	80	100	120	150
107	Austin Meadows AU/322	15	20	25	80
111	J.P. Crawford AU/411	15	20	25	40
116	Alex Gonzalez AU/420	15	20	25	40
122	Aaron Judge AU/599	120	150	200	400
158	Cody Bellinger AU/673	150	200	250	400
185	Rosell Herrera AU/174 EXCH	20	25	30	50

2013 Elite Extra Edition Franchise Futures Signatures

		NmMt 8	NmMt+ 8.5	MT 9	Gem 9.5/10
71	Gleyber Torres/250	100	120	150	250

2013 Finest

		NmMt 8	NmMt+ 8.5	MT 9	Gem 9.5/10
80	Manny Machado RC	5	5	8	25
91	Yasiel Puig RC	5	6	10	20

2013 Topps

		NmMt 8	NmMt+ 8.5	MT 9	Gem 9.5/10
270A	Manny Machado RC	5	6	10	25

2013 Topps Update

		NmMt 8	NmMt+ 8.5	MT 9	Gem 9.5/10
US250A	Yasiel Puig RC	5	6	10	20
US259	Nolan Arenado RC	▼30	▼40	▼60	▼120
US290	Christian Yelich RC	40	50	▼80	▼120

2013 Topps Allen and Ginter

		NmMt 8	NmMt+ 8.5	MT 9	Gem 9.5/10
44	Yasiel Puig RC	6	8	15	30

2013 Topps Chrome

		NmMt 8	NmMt+ 8.5	MT 9	Gem 9.5/10
12	Manny Machado RC	8	12	20	50
78	Nolan Arenado RC	50	60	80	▼200
128	Anthony Rendon RC	20	25	30	80
138A	Yasiel Puig RC	6	8	12	25

2013 Topps Chrome Rookie Autographs

		NmMt 8	NmMt+ 8.5	MT 9	Gem 9.5/10
CY	Christian Yelich	▼80	▼100	▼120	▼250
GC	Gerrit Cole	60	80	100	▼150
YP	Yasiel Puig	40	50	60	▼100
12	Manny Machado	100	120	150	▼250
25	Hyun-Jin Ryu	60	80	100	▼150
32	Jose Fernandez	▲30	▲40	▲50	▲100
78	Nolan Arenado	150	200	250	▼400
128	Anthony Rendon	▼40	▼50	▼60	▼120

2013 Topps Heritage

		NmMt 8	NmMt+ 8.5	MT 9	Gem 9.5/10
201	Manny Machado RC				
	Dylan Bundy RC	6	8	12	25
H509	Anthony Rendon RC	▼12	▼15	▼20	50
H519	Nolan Arenado RC	30	50	▲100	▲150
H536	Christian Yelich RC	▼25	▼30	▼40	▼60
H584	Yasiel Puig RC	6	8	12	20
H596	Gerrit Cole RC	12	15	30	50

2013 Topps Pro Debut

		NmMt 8	NmMt+ 8.5	MT 9	Gem 9.5/10
35A	Yasiel Puig	6	8	12	30

2014 Bowman Prospects

		NmMt 8	NmMt+ 8.5	MT 9	Gem 9.5/10
BP17	Jose Abreu	5	6	10	15
BP25	Kris Bryant	▲12	▲15	▲20	▼30
BP73	Jacob deGrom	10	12	20	50

2014 Bowman Chrome Mini

		NmMt 8	NmMt+ 8.5	MT 9	Gem 9.5/10
MCKB	Kris Bryant	12	15	25	40

2014 Bowman Chrome Prospect Autographs

		NmMt 8	NmMt+ 8.5	MT 9	Gem 9.5/10
BCAPCT	Chris Taylor	40	50	60	100
BCAPJAB	Jose Abreu	▼40	▼50	▼80	▼150
BCAPJU	Julio Urias	▲80	▲100	▲120	▲200
BCAPJW	Jesse Winker	30	40	60	120
BCAPKB	Kris Bryant	▲150	▲200	▲250	400
BCAPKM	Ketel Marte	▼30	▼40	▼50	▼80
BCAPMB	Mookie Betts	▼600	▼800	▼1,000	▼2,000

2014 Bowman Chrome Prospects

		NmMt 8	NmMt+ 8.5	MT 9	Gem 9.5/10
BCP17	Jose Abreu	5	6	10	15
BCP25	Kris Bryant	▲25	▲30	▲40	▲80
BCP73	Jacob deGrom	▲50	▲80	▲120	▲400
BCP109	Mookie Betts	▼40	50	▼120	▼300

2014 Bowman Chrome Rookie Autographs

		NmMt 8	NmMt+ 8.5	MT 9	Gem 9.5/10
BCARJA	Jose Abreu	60	80	100	▼150

2014 Bowman Chrome Draft

		NmMt 8	NmMt+ 8.5	MT 9	Gem 9.5/10
CDP2	Kyle Schwarber	6	8	20	50
CDP122	Rhys Hoskins	8	10	12	40

2014 Bowman Chrome Draft Draft Pick Autographs

		NmMt 8	NmMt+ 8.5	MT 9	Gem 9.5/10
BCAAV	Alex Verdugo	▲40	▲50	▲60	▼100
BCAJF	Jack Flaherty	▲40	▲50	▲60	▼100
BCAKS	Kyle Schwarber	▲40	▲50	▲60	100
BCAMCH	Matt Chapman	▼40	▼50	▼60	▼100
BCAMK	Michael Kopech	30	40	50	▼80
BCAMC	Michael Conforto	▼30	▼40	▼50	▼80
BCATT	Trea Turner	▲120	▲150	▲200	▲300

2014 Bowman Chrome Draft Top Prospects

		NmMt 8	NmMt+ 8.5	MT 9	Gem 9.5/10
CTP33	Eloy Jimenez	10	12	30	50
CTP39	Aaron Judge	12	15	20	40
CTP62	Kris Bryant	8	10	12	25

2014 Bowman Draft

		NmMt 8	NmMt+ 8.5	MT 9	Gem 9.5/10
DP2	Kyle Schwarber	8	10	15	30

2014 Bowman Draft Top Prospects

	NmMt 8	NmMt+ 8.5	MT 9	Gem 9.5/10
TP37 Rafael Devers	▲20	▲30	▲40	▲80
TP39 Aaron Judge	10	12	20	40
TP62 Kris Bryant	8	10	15	25

2014 Bowman Platinum Prospect Autographs

	NmMt 8	NmMt+ 8.5	MT 9	Gem 9.5/10
APCCO Carlos Correa	25	25	30	50
APCFR Clint Frazier	20	25	30	50
APCT Chris Taylor	20	25	30	50
APJBA Javier Baez	40	50	60	100
APKB Kris Bryant	250	300	350	500

2014 Bowman Sterling Prospect Autographs

	NmMt 8	NmMt+ 8.5	MT 9	Gem 9.5/10
SPACC Carlos Correa	▼25	▼30	50	80
SPAERO Eddie Rosario	15	20	25	40
SPAFL Francisco Lindor	▲30	▲40	▲50	▲80
SPAGS Gary Sanchez	▼25	▼30	▼40	▼60
SPAJBA Javier Baez	▼10	▲50	60	▲120
SPAJF Jack Flaherty	20	25	30	50
SPALS Luis Severino	15	20	25	40
SPAMC Michael Conforto	20	25	30	50

2014 Bowman Sterling Rookie Autographs

	NmMt 8	NmMt+ 8.5	MT 9	Gem 9.5/10
SRAGS George Springer	20	25	30	50
SRAMB Mookie Betts	150	200	250	400
SRANC Nick Castellanos	25	30	40	60

2014 Topps Update

	NmMt 8	NmMt+ 8.5	MT 9	Gem 9.5/10
26A Mookie Betts RC	120	200	400	800
50A Jacob deGrom RC	200	250	300	800

2014 Topps Chrome Rookie Autographs

	NmMt 8	NmMt+ 8.5	MT 9	Gem 9.5/10
Nick Castellanos	30	40	50	80
Jose Ramirez	▲80	▲100	▲120	▲200
George Springer	▲50	▲60	▲80	▲120
Jose Abreu	▼60	▼80	▼120	▼200

2014 Topps Heritage

	NmMt 8	NmMt+ 8.5	MT 9	Gem 9.5/10
19 Randal Grichuk RC	8	10	15	30
49 Jacob deGrom RC	▼120	▼150	▼200	▼500
58 Mookie Betts RC	▼100	▼120	▼150	▼400
90 Jose Ramirez RC	10	12	15	25

2015 Bowman Chrome

	NmMt 8	NmMt+ 8.5	MT 9	Gem 9.5/10
Francisco Lindor RC	20	25	50	150
Carlos Correa RC	▲20	▲25	▲40	▲60
Kris Bryant RC	▲15	▲20	▲30	▲40

2015 Bowman Chrome Prospect Autographs

	NmMt 8	NmMt+ 8.5	MT 9	Gem 9.5/10
APCBE Cody Bellinger	▼200	▼250	▼400	▼800
APGT Gleyber Torres	▼120	▼150	▼200	▼300
APLS Luis Severino	30	40	50	▼80
APMY Mike Yastrzemski	▼30	▼40	▼50	▼80
APOAL Ozhaino Albies	120	150	▼150	▼250
APRD Rafael Devers	150	200	250	▼400
APTH Teoscar Hernandez	▼30	▼40	▼50	▼80
APWA Willy Adames	▲30	▲40	▲50	▲80

2015 Bowman Chrome Prospects

	NmMt 8	NmMt+ 8.5	MT 9	Gem 9.5/10
71 Ozhaino Albies	25	30	50	100
138 Mike Yastrzemski	20	25	30	50

2015 Bowman Chrome Rookie Autographs

	NmMt 8	NmMt+ 8.5	MT 9	Gem 9.5/10
RBB Byron Buxton	▲80	▲100	▲120	▲200
RFL Francisco Lindor	40	50	60	▼100
RJB Javier Baez	50	60	80	▼120
RKB Kris Bryant	100	120	150	▼250
RNS Noah Syndergaard	30	40	50	▼80

2015 Bowman Chrome Draft

	NmMt 8	NmMt+ 8.5	MT 9	Gem 9.5/10
Walker Buehler	30	30	40	80
Kyle Tucker	25	30	40	100
Ryan Mountcastle	30	40	50	120
Ke'Bryan Hayes	30	40	50	150
Aaron Judge	▲15	▲25	▲30	▼60
Austin Riley	30	40	60	150
Andrew Benintendi	8	10	12	▼30

2015 Bowman Chrome Draft Draft Pick Autographs

	NmMt 8	NmMt+ 8.5	MT 9	Gem 9.5/10
BCAARI Austin Riley	▲150	▲200	▲250	▲400
BCABR Brendan Rodgers	30	40	50	▼80
BCADS Dansby Swanson	▲60	▲80	▲100	▲200
BCAKHA Ke'Bryan Hayes	▼120	▼150	▼250	▼400
BCAKT Kyle Tucker	▲100	▲120	150	400
BCAMS Michael Soroka	▼40	▼50	80	▼120
BCARMO Ryan Mountcastle	120	150	200	400
BCAWB Walker Buehler	▲150	▲200	▲250	400

2015 Bowman's Best Best of '15 Autographs

	NmMt 8	NmMt+ 8.5	MT 9	Gem 9.5/10
B15ANB Andrew Benintendi	20	25	30	50
B15BSN Blake Snell	20	25	30	50
B15DS Dansby Swanson	15	20	25	50
B15FL Francisco Lindor	50	60	80	120
B15TT Trea Turner	20	25	30	60
B15WB Walker Buehler	40	50	80	120

2015 Finest

	NmMt 8	NmMt+ 8.5	MT 9	Gem 9.5/10
111 Kris Bryant SP RC	60	80	100	150

2015 Stadium Club

	NmMt 8	NmMt+ 8.5	MT 9	Gem 9.5/10
300 Kris Bryant RC	▲25	▲30	▲40	▲100

2015 Topps

	NmMt 8	NmMt+ 8.5	MT 9	Gem 9.5/10
616A Kris Bryant RC	10	12	20	60

2015 Topps Update

	NmMt 8	NmMt+ 8.5	MT 9	Gem 9.5/10
US78 Kris Bryant RC	10	12	20	40
US242 Kris Bryant	10	12	20	40

2015 Topps Update Chrome

	NmMt 8	NmMt+ 8.5	MT 9	Gem 9.5/10
US174 Carlos Correa RC	12	15	20	40

2015 Topps Allen and Ginter

	NmMt 8	NmMt+ 8.5	MT 9	Gem 9.5/10
85 Kris Bryant RC	10	12	20	40

2015 Topps Chrome

	NmMt 8	NmMt+ 8.5	MT 9	Gem 9.5/10
89 Javier Baez RC	▼30	▼40	▼50	▼100
112 Kris Bryant RC	20	25	50	100
202 Francisco Lindor SP RC	▼120	▼150	▼200	▼400
205 Carlos Correa SP RC	▲30	▲40	▲50	▲120

2015 Topps Chrome Rookie Autographs

	NmMt 8	NmMt+ 8.5	MT 9	Gem 9.5/10
ARARU Addison Russell EXCH	150	200	250	▼400
ARBBN Byron Buxton	▲100	▲120	▲150	▲250
ARCC Carlos Correa	▲80	▲100	▲120	▲200
ARFL Francisco Lindor	200	250	300	▼500
ARJB Javier Baez	▲80	▲100	▲120	▲200
ARKB Kris Bryant	150	200	250	▼300

2016 Bowman Prospects

	NmMt 8	NmMt+ 8.5	MT 9	Gem 9.5/10
BP17 Fernando Tatis Jr.	▼50	▼60	▼80	▼250
BP55 Vladimir Guerrero Jr.	20	▲25	▲80	▲200

2016 Bowman Chrome Prospect Autographs

	NmMt 8	NmMt+ 8.5	MT 9	Gem 9.5/10
BCAPOC Oneal Cruz	▲100	▲120	▲150	▲300
CPAAB Alex Bregman	▼80	▼100	▼120	▼250
CPADAS Dansby Swanson	30	40	50	▼80
CPAFT Fernando Tatis Jr.	▼1,500	▼2,000	▼2,500	▼4,000
CPAHB Harrison Bader	▲40	▲50	▲60	▲100
CPAJS Juan Soto	▼2,000	▼2,500	▼3,000	▼6,000
CPATM Trey Mancini	▲60	▲80	▲120	▼60
CPATO Tyler O'Neill	▲50	▲60	▲80	▲120
CPAVG Vladimir Guerrero Jr.	▲1,000	▲1,200	▲1,500	▲3,000
CPAWC Willson Contreras	▼40	▼50	▼60	▼120
CPAYM Yoan Moncada	▼100	▼120	▼150	▼250

2016 Bowman Chrome Prospects

	NmMt 8	NmMt+ 8.5	MT 9	Gem 9.5/10
BCP17 Fernando Tatis Jr.	▼150	▼200	▼250	▼600
BCP55 Vladimir Guerrero Jr.	▲100	▲120	▲150	▲400
BCP148 Yoan Moncada	▼20	▼25	▼30	▼80
BCP182 Cody Bellinger	25	30	▼40	100
BCP236 Gleyber Torres	15	20	25	50

2016 Bowman Chrome Rookie Autographs

	NmMt 8	NmMt+ 8.5	MT 9	Gem 9.5/10
CRATT Trea Turner	▲60	▲80	▲100	▲150

2016 Bowman Chrome Draft

	NmMt 8	NmMt+ 8.5	MT 9	Gem 9.5/10
BDC3 Dylan Carlson	▼25	▼30	▼40	▼100
BDC60 Kyle Lewis	15	20	40	50
BDC67 Gavin Lux	▼12	▼15	▼20	▼60
BDC68 Shane Bieber	15	20	25	80
BDC74 Bo Bichette	▼30	▼40	▼80	▼200
BDC90 Alex Kirilloff	30	40	60	▼150
BDC92 Pete Alonso	20	25	50	▼100
BDC143 Gleyber Torres	8	10	25	▼50

2016 Bowman Chrome Draft Draft Pick Autographs

	NmMt 8	NmMt+ 8.5	MT 9	Gem 9.5/10
CDAAK Alex Kirilloff	▼60	▼80	▼100	▼200
CDABD Bobby Dalbec	▼100	▼120	▼150	▼300
CDABOB Bo Bichette	▼250	▼300	▼400	▼1,000
CDABRR Bryan Reynolds	▲60	▲80	▲100	▲200
CDACB Cavan Biggio	▼30	▼40	▼50	▼80
CDADC Dylan Carlson	▼100	▼120	▼150	▼250
CDAGL Gavin Lux	▼80	▼100	▼120	▼400
CDAIA Ian Anderson	60	80	100	▼150
CDAJL Joshua Lowe	▲30	▲40	▲50	▲120
CDAKL Kyle Lewis	▼50	▼60	▼80	▼200
CDAMM Matt Manning	▲30	▲40	▲50	80
CDAPA Pete Alonso	▼120	▼150	▼200	▼500
CDAWS Will Smith	▼50	▼60	▼80	▼120

2016 Topps Chrome

	NmMt 8	NmMt+ 8.5	MT 9	Gem 9.5/10
32 Trea Turner RC	20	25	30	80
143 Gary Sanchez RC	15	20	25	60
150 Corey Seager RC	30	40	60	▼200

2016 Topps Chrome Rookie Autographs

	NmMt 8	NmMt+ 8.5	MT 9	Gem 9.5/10
RACS Corey Seager	▼120	▼150	▼200	▼300
RAJU Julio Urias	▲60	▲80	▲100	▲150
RAKM Ketel Marte	30	40	50	▼80
RAMC Michael Conforto	50	60	80	▼120
RATA Tim Anderson	▼60	▼80	▼100	▼200
RATS Trevor Story	80	100	120	▼200
RATTU Trea Turner	▲50	▲60	▲80	120

2017 Bowman

	NmMt 8	NmMt+ 8.5	MT 9	Gem 9.5/10
32 Aaron Judge RC	▲20	▲25	▲30	▲60

2017 Bowman Prospects

	NmMt 8	NmMt+ 8.5	MT 9	Gem 9.5/10
BP127 Ronald Acuna	▼30	▼40	▼50	▼150

2017 Bowman Chrome

	NmMt 8	NmMt+ 8.5	MT 9	Gem 9.5/10
27 Cody Bellinger RC	▼20	▼25	▼30	▼60
56A Aaron Judge RC	25	30	40	80

2017 Bowman Chrome Prospect Autographs

	NmMt 8	NmMt+ 8.5	MT 9	Gem 9.5/10
CPAEJ Eloy Jimenez	200	250	300	▼500
CPAFP Freddy Peralta	▲30	▲40	▲50	▲80
CPAGT Gleyber Torres	▼60	▼80	▼100	▼150
CPAJC Jazz Chisholm	▼80	▼100	▼120	▼300
CPAJS Jesus Sanchez	60	80	100	200
CPALA Luis Arraez	▼30	▼40	▼50	▼80
CPARA Ronald Acuna	1,500	2,000	2,500	▼4,000
CPASS Sixto Sanchez	▼40	▼50	▼60	▼150

2017 Bowman Chrome Prospects

	NmMt 8	NmMt+ 8.5	MT 9	Gem 9.5/10
BCP32 Vladimir Guerrero Jr.	▲25	▲30	▲40	▲80
BCP127 Ronald Acuna	▼80	▼100	▼120	▼300
BCP160 Fernando Tatis Jr.	40	50	60	▼80
BCP180 Juan Soto	▼40	▼50	▼60	▼200
BCP207 Jazz Chisholm	30	40	50	150

2017 Bowman Chrome Rookie Autographs

	NmMt 8	NmMt+ 8.5	MT 9	Gem 9.5/10
BCARAB Alex Bregman	30	40	50	▼80
BCARCB Cody Bellinger	▼120	▼150	▼200	▼250
BCARYM Yoan Moncada	40	50	60	▼100
CRAAB Alex Bregman	30	40	50	▼80
CRAAJ Aaron Judge	▼150	▼200	▼250	▼500
CRADS Dansby Swanson	30	40	50	▼80
CRAYM Yoan Moncada	60	80	100	▼150

2017 Bowman Chrome Draft

	NmMt 8	NmMt+ 8.5	MT 9	Gem 9.5/10
BDC39 Ronald Acuna	25	30	60	200
BDC71 Fernando Tatis Jr.	60	80	100	200
BDC95 Jo Adell	30	40	50	120
BDC150 Vladimir Guerrero Jr.	▲25	▲30	▲40	▲80
BDC162 Juan Soto	25	30	▲80	▼150

2017 Bowman Chrome Draft Autographs

		NmMt 8	NmMt+ 8.5	MT 9	Gem 9.5/10
CDADW	Drew Waters	60	80	100	▼150
CDAGS	Gavin Sheets	30	40	50	100
CDAHR	Heliot Ramos	▼50	▼60	▼80	▼200
CDAJA	Jo Adell	▼200	▼250	▼300	▼600
CDAJD	Jeter Downs	▼40	▼50	▼60	▼100
CDAKH	Keston Hiura	▼30	▼40	▼50	▼80
CDAMG	MacKenzie Gore	▼60	▼80	▼100	▼150
CDAMJM	MJ Melendez	40	50	60	100
CDAMV	Mark Vientos	▲60	▲80	▲100	▲200
CDANP	Nick Pratto	50	60	80	200
CDANPE	Nate Pearson	▼50	▼60	▼80	▼120
CDAPS	Pavin Smith				
CDARL	Royce Lewis	▼80	▼100	▼120	▼200
CDASB	Shane Baz	▲30	▲40	▲50	▲80
CDATH	Tanner Houck	30	40	50	▲150
CDATR	Trevor Rogers	30	40	50	▼80

2017 Bowman Chrome Mega Box Prospects Refractors

		NmMt 8	NmMt+ 8.5	MT 9	Gem 9.5/10
BCP31	Shohei Otani UER/Ohtani	50	60	80	120
BCP127	Ronald Acuna	100	120	150	600

2017 Bowman Chrome Mini Prospects

		NmMt 8	NmMt+ 8.5	MT 9	Gem 9.5/10
BCP32	Vladimir Guerrero Jr.	12	15	20	60
BCP127	Ronald Acuna	▼80	▼100	▼120	300
BCP160	Fernando Tatis Jr.	30	40	50	150
BCP180	Juan Soto	30	40	50	80

2017 Bowman Draft

		NmMt 8	NmMt+ 8.5	MT 9	Gem 9.5/10
BD39	Ronald Acuna	25	30	40	80
BD162	Juan Soto	25	30	▼50	100

2017 Bowman Platinum

		NmMt 8	NmMt+ 8.5	MT 9	Gem 9.5/10
76	Cody Bellinger RC	15	20	25	50
91	Aaron Judge RC	▼20	▼25	▼30	▼60

2017 Bowman Platinum Top Prospects Autographs

		NmMt 8	NmMt+ 8.5	MT 9	Gem 9.5/10
TPAR	Amed Rosario	30	30	40	60
TPEJ	Eloy Jimenez	50	50	60	100
TPGT	Gleyber Torres	60	60	80	120
TPIH	Ian Happ	30	30	40	60
TPJG	Jason Groome	15	20	25	40
TPJS	Juan Soto	250	250	300	500
TPMM	Mickey Moniak	15	20	25	40
TPNS	Nick Senzel	50	50	60	100

2017 Bowman's Best Best of '17 Autographs

		NmMt 8	NmMt+ 8.5	MT 9	Gem 9.5/10
B17GT	Gleyber Torres	50	60	100	150
B17JA	Jo Adell	50	60	100	150
B17RA	Ronald Acuna	150	200	250	500
B17RL	Royce Lewis	20	25	40	80

2017 Donruss Optic

		NmMt 8	NmMt+ 8.5	MT 9	Gem 9.5/10
38	Aaron Judge RR RC	▼15	▼20	▼20	▼50
65	Cody Bellinger RR RC	15	20	25	60

2017 Finest

		NmMt 8	NmMt+ 8.5	MT 9	Gem 9.5/10
2	Aaron Judge RC	15	20	25	50

2017 Topps Update

		NmMt 8	NmMt+ 8.5	MT 9	Gem 9.5/10
US4	Matt Chapman RC	▼10	▼12	▼15	▼25
US50A	Cody Bellinger RC	25	30	40	100

2017 Topps Allen and Ginter

		NmMt 8	NmMt+ 8.5	MT 9	Gem 9.5/10
172	Aaron Judge RC	15	20	25	50

2017 Topps Archives

		NmMt 8	NmMt+ 8.5	MT 9	Gem 9.5/10
62	Aaron Judge RC	25	30	60	100

2017 Topps Chrome

		NmMt 8	NmMt+ 8.5	MT 9	Gem 9.5/10
79	Cody Bellinger RC	▼25	▼30	▼40	▼80
169A	Aaron Judge RC	▲30	▲40	▲50	▲150

2017 Topps Chrome Rookie Autographs

		NmMt 8	NmMt+ 8.5	MT 9	Gem 9.5/10
RAAB	Alex Bregman	▼60	▼80	▼100	▼150
RAAJ	Aaron Judge	250	300	400	▼600
RACB	Cody Bellinger	▼150	▼200	▼250	▼500
RAJW	Jesse Winker	25	50	60	150
RAMO	Matt Olson	▲30	▲40	▲50	80
RAYM	Yoan Moncada	▼40	▼50	▼60	▼100

2018 Bowman

		NmMt 8	NmMt+ 8.5	MT 9	Gem 9.5/10
49	Shohei Ohtani RC	▲50	▲60	▲100	▲300

2018 Bowman Prospects

		NmMt 8	NmMt+ 8.5	MT 9	Gem 9.5/10
BP21	Luis Robert	▼25	30	▼40	▼100

2018 Bowman Chrome

		NmMt 8	NmMt+ 8.5	MT 9	Gem 9.5/10
1	Shohei Ohtani RC	▲150	▲200	▲250	▲600
40	Ronald Acuna Jr. RC	▼40	▲60	▲100	▼200
83	Gleyber Torres RC	▼10	▼12	▼15	▼50

2018 Bowman Chrome Prospect Autographs

		NmMt 8	NmMt+ 8.5	MT 9	Gem 9.5/10
BCPAAB	Akil Baddoo	▼60	▼80	▼100	▼250
CPABW	Jose Adolis Garcia	60	80	100	120
CPACB	Corbin Burnes	40	50	60	200
CPACM	Cedric Mullins	50	60	100	200
CPACP	Cristian Pache	▼60	▼80	▼100	▼150
CPAEF	Estevan Florial	▲40	▲50	▲60	100
CPAHG	Hunter Greene	▲80	▲100	▲120	200
CPAKR	Keibert Ruiz	▲50	▲60	▲80	▲150
CPALR	Luis Robert	▼300	▼600	1,200	▼2,000
CPAYA	Yordan Alvarez	▼150	▼200	▼250	▼500
BCPABM	Brandon Marsh	40	50	60	120
BCPADM	Dustin May	▲50	▲60	▲80	▲150
BCPAJLO	Jonathan Loaisiga	30	40	50	100
BCPAKR	Kristian Robinson	▼50	▼60	▼80	▼200
BCPALGA	Luis Garcia	▼40	▼50	▼60	▼100
BCPARW	Russell Wilson	300	400	500	▼800
BCPASB	Shane Bieber	▼60	▼80	▼100	▼200

2018 Bowman Chrome Prospects

		NmMt 8	NmMt+ 8.5	MT 9	Gem 9.5/10
BCP21	Luis Robert	▼50	▼60	▼80	▼200
BCP52	Juan Soto	▲30	▲40	▲50	▼100

2018 Bowman Chrome Rookie Autographs

		NmMt 8	NmMt+ 8.5	MT 9	Gem 9.5/10
CRAJF	Jack Flaherty	30	40	50	80
CRARD	Rafael Devers	▲100	▲120	▲150	▲250
CRARH	Rhys Hoskins	▼40	▼50	▼60	▼100
CRASO	Shohei Ohtani/Pitching	▲2,500	▲3,000	▲4,000	▲6,000
CRAWB	Walker Buehler	▲120	▲150	▲200	▲300
BCRAGT	Gleyber Torres	120	150	200	▼300
BCRAJF	Jack Flaherty	30	40	50	80
BCRAOA	Ozzie Albies	60	80	100	▼150
BCRARA	Ronald Acuna	▼300	▼400	▼500	▲8,000
BCRARD	Rafael Devers	▲100	▲120	▲150	▲250
BCRASO	Shohei Ohtani/Batting	▲2,500	▲3,000	▲4,000	▲6,000

2018 Bowman Chrome Draft

		NmMt 8	NmMt+ 8.5	MT 9	Gem 9.5/10
BDC6	Jarred Kelenic	▼30	▼40	▼50	▼120
BDC25	Alec Bohm	▼15	▼20	▼25	▼60
BDC38	Nick Madrigal	15	20	25	50
BDC47	Brennen Davis	25	30	40	120
BDC112	Jonathan India	40	50	60	150
BDC117	Nolan Gorman	20	25	30	80
BDC171	Triston Casas	20	25	40	120
BDC188	Luis Robert	25	30	40	100

2018 Bowman Chrome Draft Autographs

		NmMt 8	NmMt+ 8.5	MT 9	Gem 9.5/10
CDAAB	Alec Bohm	▼80	▼100	▼120	▼200
CDAAT	Alek Thomas	▲60	▲80	▲100	▲250
CDACM	Casey Mize	80	100	120	250
CDAGR	Grayson Rodriguez	▲80	▲100	▲120	▲300
CDAJG	Jordan Groshans	▲80	▲100	▲120	▲200
CDAJI	Jonathan India	▲100	▲120	▲150	▲300
CDAJJ	Jeremiah Jackson	▼30	▼40	▼50	▼80
CDAJK	Jarred Kelenic	▼250	▼300	▼400	▼800
CDALG	Logan Gilbert	40	50	60	120
CDANG	Nolan Gorman	100	120	150	300
CDANH	Nico Hoerner	▼30	▼40	▼50	▼80
CDANM	Nick Madrigal	60	80	100	▼120
CDASWR	Simeon Woods-Richardson	30	40	50	100
CDATC	Triston Casas	▲120	▲150	▲200	▲400

2018 Bowman Chrome Mega Box Prospects Refractors

		NmMt 8	NmMt+ 8.5	MT 9	Gem 9.5/10
BCP21	Luis Robert	100	120	150	500

2018 Bowman Platinum Top Prospect Autographs

		NmMt 8	NmMt+ 8.5	MT 9	Gem 9.5/10
TOP2	Ronald Acuna	120	150	200	300
TOP3	Gleyber Torres	50	80	100	150
TOP4	Hunter Greene	40	50	60	100
TOP5	Royce Lewis	30	40	50	80
TOP8	Luis Robert	▼120	▼150	▼200	▼600
TOP11	Jo Adell	20	25	30	80
TOP15	Peter Alonso	60	80	120	200
TOP80	Shane Bieber	80	100	150	250

2018 Bowman's Best

		NmMt 8	NmMt+ 8.5	MT 9	Gem 9.5/10
1	Shohei Ohtani RC	▲60	▲80	▲100	▲150
29	Juan Soto RC	▼30	▼40	▼50	▼120
50	Gleyber Torres RC	15	20	25	50
51	Ronald Acuna Jr. RC	30	40	50	▲120

2018 Bowman's Best Best of '18 Autographs

		NmMt 8	NmMt+ 8.5	MT 9	Gem 9.5/10
B18ABO	Alec Bohm	▼40	▼50	▼60	▼120
B18AJ	Aaron Judge	▲120	▲150	▲200	▲300
B18AR	Anthony Rizzo	30	40	50	80
B18CM	Casey Mize	30	40	50	80
B18EF	Estevan Florial	30	40	50	80
B18FT	Fernando Tatis Jr.	▲250	▲300	▲400	▲600
B18GR	Grayson Rodriguez	40	50	60	120
B18HG	Hunter Greene	30	40	50	80
B18HR	Heliot Ramos	30	40	50	120
B18JAD	Jo Adell	▲40	▲50	▲60	▼100
B18JI	Jonathan India	60	80	100	200
B18JKE	Jarred Kelenic	▼40	▼50	▼60	▼100
B18JSO	Juan Soto	▲600	▲800	▲1,000	▲1,500
B18KB	Kris Bryant	50	60	80	▲120
B18LR	Luis Robert	150	200	250	▲600
B18MT	Mike Trout	▲400	▲500	▲600	▲1,000
B18NG	Nolan Gorman	▲40	▲50	▲60	▲120
B18NM	Nick Madrigal	40	50	60	100
B18OA	Ozzie Albies	50	60	100	200
B18RA	Ronald Acuna Jr.	▲250	▲300	▲400	▲600
B18SO	Shohei Ohtani	▲1,200	▲1,500	▲2,000	▲3,000
B18TC	Triston Casas	40	50	60	150
B18YA	Yordan Alvarez	▲60	▲80	▼100	▼150

2018 Donruss Optic

		NmMt 8	NmMt+ 8.5	MT 9	Gem 9.5/10
56	Shohei Ohtani RR RC	▲50	▲60	▲80	▲200
63	Ronald Acuna Jr. RR RC	▲30	▲40	▲50	▲200
65	Gleyber Torres RR RC	15	20	40	

2018 Donruss Optic Rated Rookies Signatures

		NmMt 8	NmMt+ 8.5	MT 9	Gem 9.5/10
RRSSO	Shohei Ohtani	800	1,000	1,200	2,500
RRSVG	Vladimir Guerrero Jr	600	800	1,000	1,200

2018 Finest

		NmMt 8	NmMt+ 8.5	MT 9	Gem 9.5/10
100	Shohei Ohtani RC	▲40	▲60	▲100	▲300

2018 Topps

		NmMt 8	NmMt+ 8.5	MT 9	Gem 9.5/10
700	Shohei Ohtani RC	▲60	▲80	▲100	▲250

2018 Topps Update

		NmMt 8	NmMt+ 8.5	MT 9	Gem 9.5/10
US1	Shohei Ohtani RC	40	50	80	250
US198	Shane Bieber RC	20	25	40	120
US200	Gleyber Torres RC	15	20	25	80
US250	Ronald Acuna Jr. RC	60	80	100	300
US300	Juan Soto RC	60	80	100	300

2018 Topps Allen and Ginter

		NmMt 8	NmMt+ 8.5	MT 9	Gem 9.5/10
100	Shohei Ohtani RC	50	60	80	200
207	Ronald Acuna Jr. RC	25	30	40	▲100
240	Gleyber Torres RC	8	10	12	25

2018 Topps Archives

		NmMt 8	NmMt+ 8.5	MT 9	Gem 9.5/10
50	Shohei Ohtani RC	▲50	▲60	▲80	▲200
73	Juan Soto RC	30	40	50	▼120
164	Gleyber Torres RC	15	20	25	40
212	Ronald Acuna Jr. RC	25	30	50	200

2018 Topps Chrome

		NmMt 8	NmMt+ 8.5	MT 9	Gem 9.5/10
25	Rafael Devers RC	30	40	▲80	120
31	Gleyber Torres RC	▼25	▼30	▼40	▼60
71	Walker Buehler RC	20	25	30	80
150	Shohei Ohtani RC	▲100	▲120	▲150	▲300
193	Ronald Acuna RC	▼50	▼60	▼80	▼250

2018 Topps Chrome Rookie Autographs

		NmMt 8	NmMt+ 8.5	MT 9	Gem 9.5/10
RAGT	Gleyber Torres	▼60	▼80	▼100	▼150
RAJF	Jack Flaherty	▲30	▲40	▲50	80
RAMF	Max Fried	▲80	▲100	▲120	▲200

	NmMt 8	NmMt+ 8.5	MT 9	Gem 9.5/10
RAMS Mike Soroka	▲50	▲60	▲80	▲150
RAOA Ozzie Albies	▲80	▲100	▲120	▲200
RARA Ronald Acuna	▲800	▲1,000	▲1,200	▲2,000
RARD Rafael Devers	▲150	▲200	▲250	400
RASO Shohei Ohtani	▲1,500	▲2,000	▲2,500	▲5,000
RAWB Walker Buehler	▼50	▼60	▼100	250

2018 Topps Chrome Update

	NmMt 8	NmMt+ 8.5	MT 9	Gem 9.5/10
HMT1 Shohei Ohtani RC	▲60	▲80	▲100	▲250
HMT9 Gleyber Torres RC	12	15	20	60
HMT19 Walker Buehler RC	▲15	▲20	▲25	▲80
HMT25 Ronald Acuna Jr. RC	60	80	100	250
HMT26 Gleyber Torres RC	8	10	20	40
HMT55 Juan Soto RC	▼100	▼120	▼150	▼40
HMT59 Shane Bieber RC	▼12	▼15	▼20	▼60

2018 Topps Heritage

	NmMt 8	NmMt+ 8.5	MT 9	Gem 9.5/10
502 Juan Soto RC	▼25	▼30	▼50	▼150
580 Ronald Acuna Jr. RC	30	40	▼50	▼120
600 Shohei Ohtani RC	▲30	▲40	▲80	▲250
603 Gleyber Torres RC	▲20	▲25	▲30	50

2018 Topps Heritage Real One Autographs

	NmMt 8	NmMt+ 8.5	MT 9	Gem 9.5/10
ROASO Shohei Ohtani	1,000	1,200	1,600	3,000

2018 Topps Opening Day

	NmMt 8	NmMt+ 8.5	MT 9	Gem 9.5/10
200 Shohei Ohtani RC	8	10	15	30

2019 Bowman Prospects

	NmMt 8	NmMt+ 8.5	MT 9	Gem 9.5/10
BP100 Wander Franco	40	50	60	▼100

2019 Bowman Chrome

	NmMt 8	NmMt+ 8.5	MT 9	Gem 9.5/10
26 Fernando Tatis Jr. RC	25	30	▲120	400
48 Pete Alonso RC	15	20	▼25	60
73 Vladimir Guerrero Jr. RC	30	▲40	▲100	▲250

2019 Bowman Chrome Prospect Autographs

	NmMt 8	NmMt+ 8.5	MT 9	Gem 9.5/10
CPAAB Alec Bohm	▼40	▼50	▼60	▼100
CPAAC Alexander Canario	▼40	▼50	▼60	▼120
CPAAK Alejandro Kirk	▼30	▼40	▼50	▼120
CPAAT Abraham Toro	30	40	50	80
CPABM Brailyn Marquez	▼30	▼40	▼50	▼100
CPABR Brayan Rocchio	▲40	▲50	▲80	▲150
CPACM Casey Mize	30	40	50	▼80
CPADCA Diego Cartaya	▲80	▲100	▲120	▲300
CPAEC Edward Cabrera	▲40	▲50	▲60	▲100
CPAEJ Eloy Jimenez	60	80	100	▼150
CPAEM Elehuris Montero	▲30	▲40	▲60	▲120
CPAJB Joey Bart	▼100	▼120	▼150	▼300
CPAJRO Julio Rodriguez	▲500	▲600	▲800	▲1,500
CPALGI Luis Gil	▲50	▲60	▲80	▲200
CPALW Logan Webb	60	80	120	300
CPAML Marco Luciano	▼300	▼400	▼500	▼1,000
CPAMMA Mason Martin	40	50	60	▼100
CPANM Nick Madrigal	30	40	50	▼80
CPANMA Noelvi Marte	▲250	▲300	▲400	600
CPAOM Orelvis Martinez	▲150	▲200	▲250	▲500
CPARM Ronny Mauricio	100	120	150	▼250
CPAVGJ Vladimir Guerrero Jr.	▲150	▲200	▲250	400
CPAWF Wander Franco	1,000	1,200	1,500	▼2,500

2019 Bowman Chrome Prospects

	NmMt 8	NmMt+ 8.5	MT 9	Gem 9.5/10
CP33 Julio Rodriguez	15	20	40	60
CP50 Joey Bart	12	15	20	40
CP69 Orelvis Martinez	40	50	60	120
CP82 Marco Luciano	▼25	▼30	▼40	▼120
CP97 Noelvi Marte	25	30	40	150
CP100 Wander Franco	▼60	▼80	▼100	▼250
CP123 Yordan Alvarez	12	15	20	50

2019 Bowman Chrome Draft

	NmMt 8	NmMt+ 8.5	MT 9	Gem 9.5/10
C1 Adley Rutschman	▲30	▲40	▲80	▼150
C50 Riley Greene	▲30	▲40	▲50	150
C85 CJ Abrams	25	30	40	150
C93 Wander Franco	▲40	▲50	▲60	▲200
C100 Andrew Vaughn	▼15	▼20	▼30	▼60

2019 Bowman Chrome Draft Autographs

	NmMt 8	NmMt+ 8.5	MT 9	Gem 9.5/10
AAM Alek Manoah	▲80	▲100	▲120	▲200
AAR Adley Rutschman	300	400	500	1,000
AAV Andrew Vaughn	▼150	▼200	▼250	▼400

	NmMt 8	NmMt+ 8.5	MT 9	Gem 9.5/10
CDABB Brett Baty	▼80	▼100	▼120	▲300
CDABS Bryson Stott	▲50	▲60	▲80	120
CDACA CJ Abrams	▼200	▼250	▼300	▼600
CDACC Corbin Carroll	▼120	▼150	▼200	300
CDAGH Gunnar Henderson	▼60	▼80	▼100	▲200
CDAGK George Kirby	▲50	▲60	▲120	▲300
CDAHB Hunter Bishop	▼60	▼80	▼100	▼150
CDAJJ Josh Jung	▼120	▼150	▼200	300
CDAJJB J.J. Bleday	▼100	▼120	▼150	▼250
CDAJS Josh Smith	50	60	80	120
CDAKC Keoni Cavaco	30	40	50	▼80
CDAKH Kody Hoese	30	40	50	▼80
CDAKP Kyren Paris	▲30	▲40	▲50	80
CDAMB Michael Busch	▼30	▼40	▼50	120
CDANL Nick Lodolo	▲40	▲50	▲60	▲100
CDAPB Peyton Burdick	▼50	▼60	▼80	▼120
CDAQP Quinn Priester	40	50	60	▼100
CDARG Riley Greene	250	300	400	800
CDARH Rece Hinds	40	50	▲80	▲150
CDASL Shea Langeliers	▼60	▼80	▼100	▼150

2019 Bowman Chrome Mega Box Prospects Refractors

	NmMt 8	NmMt+ 8.5	MT 9	Gem 9.5/10
BCP1 Vladimir Guerrero Jr.	15	20	25	50
BCP25 Fernando Tatis Jr.	15	20	25	50
BCP44 Luis Robert	40	50	80	120
BCP100 Wander Franco	100	120	200	400
BCP123 Yordan Alvarez	15	20	20	80

2019 Bowman Sterling Prospect Autographs

	NmMt 8	NmMt+ 8.5	MT 9	Gem 9.5/10
BSPAAB Akil Baddoo	30	40	50	80
BSPAABO Alec Bohm	30	40	50	▼80
BSPACM Casey Mize	50	60	80	120
BSPADM Dustin May	15	20	25	40
BSPAGR Grayson Rodriguez	25	30	40	60
BSPAJB Joey Bart	25	30	40	60
BSPAJI Jonathan India	40	50	80	150
BSPAJR Julio Rodriguez	80	100	120	200
BSPAKR Keibert Ruiz	15	20	25	40
BSPAMLU Marco Luciano	▼60	▼80	120	▼200
BSPANMA Noelvi Marte	▲50	▲60	▲80	▲200
BSPAOM Orelvis Martinez	30	40	50	80
BSPARM Ronny Mauricio	40	50	80	150
BSPAWF Wander Franco	▲250	▲300	▲400	▲800

2019 Bowman Sterling Rookie Autographs

	NmMt 8	NmMt+ 8.5	MT 9	Gem 9.5/10
BSRABL Brandon Lowe	15	20	25	40
BSRACB Corbin Burnes	30	40	50	80
BSRACM Cedric Mullins	30	40	60	100

2019 Bowman's Best Best of '19 Autographs

	NmMt 8	NmMt+ 8.5	MT 9	Gem 9.5/10
B19AR Adley Rutschman	100	120	150	250
B19ARI Austin Riley	100	120	150	250
B19BH Bryce Harper	120	150	200	300
B19CJA CJ Abrams	50	60	80	200
B19EJ Eloy Jimenez	50	60	80	200
B19FTJ Fernando Tatis Jr.	150	200	250	400
B19JI Jonathan India	100	120	150	300
B19JK Jarred Kelenic	60	80	100	150
B19JR Julio Rodriguez	80	100	120	300
B19MT Mike Trout	300	400	500	800
B19PA Pete Alonso	80	100	120	200
B19RG Riley Greene	50	60	80	200
B19SO Shohei Ohtani	▲500	▲600	▲800	▲1,500
B19VGJ Vladimir Guerrero Jr.	▲120	▲150	▲200	▲400
B19WF Wander Franco	▲200	▲250	▲300	▲600

2019 Donruss Optic

	NmMt 8	NmMt+ 8.5	MT 9	Gem 9.5/10
64 Vladimir Guerrero Jr. RR RC	30	40	50	120
84 Fernando Tatis Jr. RR RC	▲40	▲50	▲60	150

2019 Finest

	NmMt 8	NmMt+ 8.5	MT 9	Gem 9.5/10
44 Pete Alonso RC	15	20	25	50
85 Fernando Tatis Jr. RC	50	60	80	▼150
101 Vladimir Guerrero Jr. RC	▲40	▲50	▲60	▲150

2019 Topps

	NmMt 8	NmMt+ 8.5	MT 9	Gem 9.5/10
410 Fernando Tatis Jr. RC	▼50	60	▼80	▼150
475 Pete Alonso RC	▼12	▼15	▼20	▼40
670 Eloy Jimenez RC	▼10	▼12	▼15	▼30
NNO Vladimir Guerrero Jr SP	▲50	▲60	▲100	▼250

2019 Topps Update

	NmMt 8	NmMt+ 8.5	MT 9	Gem 9.5/10
US56 Fernando Tatis Jr. RD	▼20	▼25	▼30	▼80

2019 Topps Allen and Ginter

	NmMt 8	NmMt+ 8.5	MT 9	Gem 9.5/10
183 Fernando Tatis Jr. RC	50	60	100	200

2019 Topps Chrome

	NmMt 8	NmMt+ 8.5	MT 9	Gem 9.5/10
201 Vladimir Guerrero Jr. RC	▲50	▲60	80	▼200
202 Eloy Jimenez RC	▼12	▼15	▼20	▼50
203 Fernando Tatis Jr. RC	▼60	▼80	▼100	▼200
204 Pete Alonso RC	▼12	▼15	▼20	▼50

2019 Topps Chrome Rookie Autographs

	NmMt 8	NmMt+ 8.5	MT 9	Gem 9.5/10
RAAG Adolis Garcia	30	40	50	80
RAAR Austin Riley	▲150	▲200	▲250	▲500
RABL Brandon Lowe	▲30	▲40	▲50	80
RACB Corbin Burnes	30	40	50	80
RACM Cedric Mullins	40	50	60	120
RAEJ Eloy Jimenez	▲100	▲120	▲150	▲300
RAFT Fernando Tatis Jr.	▲800	▲1,000	▲1,200	▼2,000
RAPA Peter Alonso	120	150	200	▼300
RAVGJ Vladimir Guerrero Jr.	▲400	▲500	▲600	1,000
RAWS Will Smith	50	60	80	▼120

2019 Topps Chrome Update

	NmMt 8	NmMt+ 8.5	MT 9	Gem 9.5/10
54 Fernando Tatis Jr. RD	▼30	▼40	▼50	▼100

2019 Topps Chrome Update Rookie Autograph Refractors

	NmMt 8	NmMt+ 8.5	MT 9	Gem 9.5/10
RDAFT Fernando Tatis Jr.	500	600	800	1,500
RDAPA Pete Alonso	80	100	120	300

2019 Topps Heritage

	NmMt 8	NmMt+ 8.5	MT 9	Gem 9.5/10
504 Vladimir Guerrero Jr. RC	▲25	▲30	▲50	▲100
517 Fernando Tatis Jr. RC	▼30	▼40	▼50	▼120
519 Pete Alonso RC	10	12	20	40

2019 Topps Gallery

	NmMt 8	NmMt+ 8.5	MT 9	Gem 9.5/10
56 Fernando Tatis Jr. RC	40	50	80	200
98 Vladimir Guerrero Jr. RC	40	50	60	120

2020 Bowman Prospects

	NmMt 8	NmMt+ 8.5	MT 9	Gem 9.5/10
BP8 Jasson Dominguez	▼20	▼25	▼30	▼50
BP25 Bobby Witt Jr.	▼20	▼25	▼30	▼80

2020 Bowman 1st Edition

	NmMt 8	NmMt+ 8.5	MT 9	Gem 9.5/10
BFE8 Jasson Dominguez	▼40	▼50	▼60	▼200
BFE25 Bobby Witt Jr.	▼40	▼50	▼60	▼200

2020 Bowman Chrome

	NmMt 8	NmMt+ 8.5	MT 9	Gem 9.5/10
8 Luis Robert RC	20	25	30	80
11 Randy Arozarena RC	20	25	30	60
50 Bo Bichette RC	20	25	30	60

2020 Bowman Chrome Prospect Autographs

	NmMt 8	NmMt+ 8.5	MT 9	Gem 9.5/10
CPAAA Aaron Ashby	40	50	60	100
CPAAG Anthony Garcia	▲40	▲50	▲60	▲120
CPAAP Andy Pages	▲80	▲100	▲150	▲400
CPAAR Adley Rutschman	▼80	▼100	▼120	▼250
CPAAV Anthony Volpe	▲400	▲500	▲600	▲1,200
CPAAVA Andrew Vaughn	▼60	▼80	▼100	▼150
CPABBA Bryce Ball	▼40	▼50	▼60	200
CPABD Brennen Davis	▲150	▲200	▲250	▲400
CPABL Bayron Lora	▼60	▼80	▼100	▼250
CPABWJ Bobby Witt Jr.	600	800	1,000	2,000
CPAED Ezequiel Duran	▲30	▲40	▲50	▲120
CPAEP Everson Pereira	▲100	▲120	▲150	▲400
CPAEPE Erick Pena	▼50	▼60	▼80	▼200
CPAFA Francisco Alvarez	▲200	▲250	▲300	▲600
CPAGJ Gilberto Jimenez	▼50	▼60	▼80	▼120
CPAGM Gabriel Moreno	▲100	▲120	▲150	▲250
CPAIH Ivan Herrera	▼30	▼40	▼50	▼80
CPAJD Jarren Duran	▼100	▼120	▼150	400
CPAJDI Jhon Diaz	50	60	80	▼120
CPAJDO Jasson Dominguez	▼600	▼800	▼1,000	▼2,000
CPAJJB J.J. Bleday	30	40	50	▼80
CPAJP Jeremy Pena	30	40	50	▼80
CPALA Luisangel Acuna	150	200	250	▼400
CPALM Luis Matos	150	200	250	500
CPALP Luis Patino	▼40	▼50	▼60	▼120
CPAMH Michael Harris	▼120	▼150	▼200	▼300
CPAMV Miguel Vargas	▲60	▲80	▲100	▲250

		NmMt 8	NmMt+ 8.5	MT 9	Gem 9.5/10
CPAOP	Oswald Peraza	▲100	▲120	▲150	▲400
CPARC	Ruben Cardenas	30	40	50	100
CPARG	Riley Greene	▲80	▲100	▲120	▲300
CPARP	Robert Puason	▼60	▼80	▼100	▼250
CPARPE	Ryan Pepiot	▲30	▲40	▲50	▲100
CPASH	Sam Huff	▼30	▼40	▼50	▲150
CPATS	Tarik Skubal	▲40	▲50	▲60	▲150
CPAVB	Vidal Brujan	60	80	100	▲250
CPAVG	Vaughn Grissom	▲40	▲50	▲60	▲150
CPAXE	Xavier Edwards	▼30	▼40	▼50	120

2020 Bowman Chrome Prospects

		NmMt 8	NmMt+ 8.5	MT 9	Gem 9.5/10
BCP8	Jasson Dominguez	▼30	▼40	▼60	▼200
BCP25	Bobby Witt Jr.	▲40	▲50	▲60	200
BCP139	Anthony Volpe	30	40	50	150
BCP145	Robert Puason	▼15	▼20	▼25	▼60

2020 Bowman Chrome Rookie Autographs

		NmMt 8	NmMt+ 8.5	MT 9	Gem 9.5/10
CRADM	Dustin May	▼40	▼50	▼60	150
CRAGL	Gavin Lux	▼50	▼60	▼80	▼150
CRAKL	Kyle Lewis	▼60	▼80	▼100	▼250
CRALR	Luis Robert/Facing Left	400	500	600	▼1,000
CRALR	Luis Robert/Facing Right	400	500	600	▼1,000
CRANH	Nico Hoerner	30	40	50	▼80
CRATG	Trent Grisham	▼30	▼40	▼50	▼80
CRAYA	Yordan Alvarez	80	100	120	▼200
CRAYT	Yoshi Tsutsugo	40	50	60	▼100

2020 Bowman Chrome Mega Box Prospects Refractors

		NmMt 8	NmMt+ 8.5	MT 9	Gem 9.5/10
BCP8	Jasson Dominguez	150	200	250	600
BCP25	Bobby Witt Jr.	40	50	60	300

2020 Bowman Chrome Sapphire Prospects

		NmMt 8	NmMt+ 8.5	MT 9	Gem 9.5/10
BCP8	Jasson Dominguez	▼100	▼120	▼150	▼500
BCP25	Bobby Witt Jr.	▼120	▼150	250	800

2020 Bowman Chrome Draft

		NmMt 8	NmMt+ 8.5	MT 9	Gem 9.5/10
BD34	Austin Hendrick	20	25	30	60
BD39	Robert Hassell	25	30	40	100
BD57	Jordan Walker	50	60	80	150
BD81	Nick Gonzales	25	30	40	80
BD107	Zac Veen	40	50	60	100
BD118	Garrett Mitchell	25	30	40	100
BD119	Tyler Soderstrom	80	100	120	200
BD121	Spencer Torkelson	60	80	100	300

2020 Bowman Chrome Draft Autographs

		NmMt 8	NmMt+ 8.5	MT 9	Gem 9.5/10
CDAAB	Alec Burleson	▲50	▲60	▲80	▲120
CDAAH	Austin Hendrick	▼120	▼150	▼200	▼300
CDAAL	Asa Lacy	100	120	150	▼250
CDAAV	AJ Vukovich	40	50	60	▼100
CDAAWE	Austin Wells	▼60	▼80	▼100	▼150
CDABM	Bobby Miller	40	50	60	▼100
CDACM	Casey Martin	▼30	▼40	▼50	▼80
CDACT	Carson Tucker	▼30	▼40	▼50	▼80
CDADD	Dillon Dingler	▲50	▲60	▲80	▲120
CDAEC	Evan Carter	30	40	50	▼80
CDAEH	Ed Howard	▼80	▼100	▼120	▼250
CDAEHA	Emerson Hancock	▲60	▲80	▲100	150
CDAGC	Garrett Crochet	▼50	▼60	▼80	▼120
CDAGM	Garrett Mitchell	▼150	▼200	▼250	▼400
CDAHK	Heston Kjerstad	▼80	▼100	▼120	▼200
CDAIG	Isaiah Greene	▲40	▲50	▲60	100
CDAJF	Justin Foscue	▲100	▲120	▲150	▲250
CDAJFR	Jesse Franklin V	▲50	▲60	▲80	▲120
CDAJW	Jordan Walker	▲300	▲400	▲500	▲800
CDAMM	Max Meyer	▲60	▲80	▲100	150
CDANGO	Nick Gonzales	120	150	200	▼300
CDANY	Nick Yorke	▲200	▲250	▲300	▲500
CDAOC	Owen Caissie	▲60	▲80	▲100	▲150
CDAPC	Pete Crow-Armstrong	120	150	200	▼300
CDAPH	Petey Halpin	▲30	▲40	▲50	▲100
CDARD	Reid Detmers	▼30	▼40	▼50	▼80
CDARHA	Robert Hassell	150	200	250	▼400
CDAST	Spencer Torkelson	▼500	▼600	▼800	▼1,200
CDATH	Trevor Hauver	▲40	▲50	▲60	▲100
CDATS	Tyler Soderstrom	▲120	▲150	▲200	▲300
CDAZD	Zach DeLoach	30	40	50	▼80
CDAZV	Zac Veen	200	250	300	▼500

2020 Bowman Draft

		NmMt 8	NmMt+ 8.5	MT 9	Gem 9.5/10
BD121	Spencer Torkelson	30	40	50	120

2020 Bowman Sterling Prospect Autographs

		NmMt 8	NmMt+ 8.5	MT 9	Gem 9.5/10
BSPAAM	Alek Manoah	60	80	100	150
BSPAAP	Andy Pages	30	40	50	80
BSPAAR	Adley Rutschman	80	100	120	250
BSPAAV	Anthony Volpe	100	120	150	300
BSPAAVA	Andrew Vaughn	30	40	50	120
BSPABB	Brett Baty	25	30	40	60
BSPABD	Brennen Davis	50	60	80	120
BSPABS	Bryson Stott	15	20	25	40
BSPABWJ	Bobby Witt Jr.	120	150	200	400
BSPAJD	Jasson Dominguez	120	150	200	300
BSPAJDU	Jarren Duran	40	50	60	120
BSPAJJB	JJ Bleday	20	25	30	50
BSPAJJU	Josh Jung	25	30	40	60
BSPAJRY	Joe Ryan	20	25	40	60
BSPAMV	Miguel Vargas	20	25	30	50
BSPANL	Nick Lodolo	15	20	25	40
BSPARG	Riley Greene	50	60	80	120
BSPAXE	Xavier Edwards	15	20	25	40

2020 Bowman Sterling Rookie Autographs

		NmMt 8	NmMt+ 8.5	MT 9	Gem 9.5/10
BSRADC	Dylan Cease	15	20	25	40
BSRADM	Dustin May	25	30	40	60
BSRAGL	Gavin Lux	25	30	40	60
BSRAKL	Kyle Lewis	25	30	40	60
BSRALR	Luis Robert	200	250	300	500
BSRANH	Nico Hoerner	20	25	30	50
BSRAYA	Yordan Alvarez	50	60	80	120

2020 Bowman's Best Best of '20 Autographs

		NmMt 8	NmMt+ 8.5	MT 9	Gem 9.5/10
B20BW	Bobby Witt Jr.	150	200	250	600
B20JD	Jasson Dominguez	150	200	250	500
B20RH	Robert Hassell	40	50	60	100

2020 Finest

		NmMt 8	NmMt+ 8.5	MT 9	Gem 9.5/10
27	Bo Bichette RC	▼12	▼15	▼20	▼50
50	Yordan Alvarez RC	▼15	▼20	▼25	▼40
97	Luis Robert RC	▼12	▼15	▼20	▼50

2020 Finest Flashbacks

		NmMt 8	NmMt+ 8.5	MT 9	Gem 9.5/10
18	Gavin Lux RC	▼10	▼12	▼15	▼40
40	Yordan Alvarez RC	▼20	▼25	▼30	▼80
59	Luis Robert RC	▼40	▼50	▼60	▼150
133	Kyle Lewis RC	▼12	▼15	▼20	▼40
190	Bo Bichette RC	▼30	▼40	▼100	

2020 Topps

		NmMt 8	NmMt+ 8.5	MT 9	Gem 9.5/10
392	Luis Robert RC	▼12	▼15	▼20	▼50

2020 Topps Chrome

		NmMt 8	NmMt+ 8.5	MT 9	Gem 9.5/10
60	Luis Robert RC	▼25	▼30	▼40	▼80
150	Bo Bichette RC	▼15	▼20	▼25	▼60
186	Kyle Lewis RC	▼12	▼15	▼20	▼40
200	Yordan Alvarez RC	▼12	▼15	▼20	▼50

2020 Topps Chrome Rookie Autographs

		NmMt 8	NmMt+ 8.5	MT 9	Gem 9.5/10
RABBI	Bo Bichette	▼250	▼300	▼400	▼600
RADCE	Dylan Cease	30	40	50	120
RADM	Dustin May	40	50	60	▼100
RAGL	Gavin Lux	▼50	▼60	▼80	▼150
RAKL	Kyle Lewis	▼50	▼60	▼80	▼150
RALR	Luis Robert	300	400	500	▼800
RALW	Logan Webb	80	100	120	300
RANH	Nico Hoerner	30	40	▼50	100
RARAR	Randy Arozarena	▼100	▼120	▼150	▼400
RATGR	Trent Grisham	50	60	80	▼120
RAYA	Yordan Alvarez	▼100	▼120	▼150	▼300

2020 Topps Opening Day

		NmMt 8	NmMt+ 8.5	MT 9	Gem 9.5/10
201	Luis Robert SP RC	100	120	500	2,000

2021 Bowman Chrome Prospect Autographs

		NmMt 8	NmMt+ 8.5	MT 9	Gem 9.5/10
CPAAC	Armando Cruz	40	50	60	100
CPAAS	Aaron Sabato	50	60	80	120
CPABJ	Blaze Jordan	150	200	250	400
CPACC	Carlos Colmenarez	120	150	200	300
CPACH	Cristian Hernandez	300	400	500	800
CPACS	Cristian Santana	50	60	80	120
CPAGA	Gabriel Arias	30	40	50	80
CPAHH	Heriberto Hernandez	30	40	50	80
CPAHK	Heston Kjerstad	30	40	50	80
CPAHP	Hedbert Perez	120	150	200	300
CPAJP	Jairo Pomares	80	100	120	200
CPAJR	Johan Rojas	40	50	60	100
CPAJS	Jose Salas	60	80	100	150
CPAJV	Jake Vogel	30	40	50	80
CPAKA	Kevin Alcantara	80	100	120	200
CPALP	Liover Peguero	60	80	100	150
CPALR	Luis Rodriguez	200	250	300	500
CPAMA	Maximo Acosta	60	80	100	150
CPAPL	Pedro Leon	100	120	150	250
CPAPP	Pedro Pineda	40	50	60	100
CPARH	Robert Hassell	30	40	50	80
CPASP	Shalin Polanco	40	50	60	100
CPAST	Spencer Torkelson	200	250	300	500
CPAVA	Victor Acosta	60	80	100	150
CPAWD	Wilman Diaz	100	120	150	250
CPAYC	Yiddi Cappe	40	50	60	100
CPAYC	Yoelqui Cespedes	80	100	120	200
CPAZV	Zac Veen	30	40	50	80
CPAARA	Alexander Ramirez	40	50	60	100
CPAAVE	Arol Vera	40	50	60	100
CPACMA	Coby Mayo	60	80	100	150
CPAEHO	Ed Howard	30	40	50	80
CPAERO	Emmanuel Rodriguez	30	40	50	80
CPAETO	Ezequiel Tovar	30	40	50	80
CPAJCO	JC Correa	30	40	50	80
CPAJDL	Jeremy De La Rosa	30	40	50	80
CPAJRO	Jose Rodriguez	30	40	50	80
CPAMAB	Mick Abel	30	40	50	80
CPAMBL	Miguel Bleis	60	80	100	150
CPARDC	Brayan Buelvas	30	40	50	80
CPARPR	Reginald Preciado	80	100	120	200

2021 Bowman Chrome Rookie Autographs

		NmMt 8	NmMt+ 8.5	MT 9	Gem 9.5/10
CRAAB	Alec Bohm	120	150	200	300
CRACM	Casey Mize	40	50	60	100
CRACP	Cristian Pache	100	120	150	250
CRADC	Dylan Carlson	60	80	100	150
CRAJA	Jo Adell	80	100	120	200
CRAJB	Joey Bart	30	40	50	80
CRAJCR	Jake Cronenworth	60	80	100	150
CRAKH	Ke'Bryan Hayes	100	120	150	250
CRANM	Nick Madrigal	30	40	50	80
CRARM	Ryan Mountcastle	60	80	100	150
CRASS	Sixto Sanchez	40	50	60	100
BCRAJC	Jazz Chisholm	40	50	60	100
BCRAJG	Jose Garcia	30	40	50	80
BCRANM	Nick Madrigal	30	40	50	80
BCRATH	Tanner Houck	30	40	50	80

2021 Bowman Sterling Prospect Autographs

		NmMt 8	NmMt+ 8.5	MT 9	Gem 9.5/10
BSPAAM	Austin Martin	40	50	60	100
BSPABJ	Blaze Jordan	60	80	100	150
BSPAHK	Heston Kjerstad	20	25	30	50
BSPAHP	Hedbert Perez	30	40	50	80
BSPAJW	Jordan Walker	25	30	40	60
BSPAKA	Kevin Alcantara	20	25	30	50
BSPAMA	Mick Abel	15	20	25	40
BSPANG	Nick Gonzales	20	25	30	50
BSPANY	Nick Yorke	25	30	40	60
BSPARH	Robert Hassell	25	30	40	60
BSPAST	Spencer Torkelson	80	100	120	200
BSPAYC	Yoelqui Cespedes	25	30	40	60
BSPAZV	Zac Veen	25	30	40	60
BSPACMA	Coby Mayo	15	20	25	40

2021 Bowman Sterling Rookie Autographs

		NmMt 8	NmMt+ 8.5	MT 9	Gem 9.5/10
BSRAAB	Alec Bohm	30	40	50	80
BSRACM	Casey Mize	20	25	30	50
BSRAJB	Joey Bart	20	25	30	50
BSRAJC	Jazz Chisholm	25	30	40	60
BSRAKH	Ke'Bryan Hayes	50	60	80	120
BSRATH	Tanner Houck	20	25	30	50

2021 Topps Chrome Rookie Autographs

		NmMt 8	NmMt+ 8.5	MT 9	Gem 9.5/10
RAAK	Alex Kirilloff	60	80	100	150
RABD	Bobby Dalbec	60	80	100	150
RACM	Casey Mize	60	80	100	150
RACP	Cristian Pache	50	60	80	120
RADC	Dylan Carlson	120	150	200	300
RAJB	Joey Bart	50	60	80	120
RAJC	Jake Cronenworth	80	100	120	200
RAJG	Jose Garcia	50	60	80	120
RAKH	Ke'Bryan Hayes	120	150	200	300
RATH	Tanner Houck	30	40	50	80
RATS	Tyler Stephenson	40	50	60	100
RAJCH	Jazz Chisholm	50	60	80	120
RASHU	Sam Huff	30	40	50	80

BASKETBALL
1933 -1989/90

1933 Sport Kings

	PrFr 1	GD 2	VG 3	VgEx 4	EX 5	ExMt 6	NM 7	NmMt 8
Nat Holman BK	▲200	▲300	▲450	▲600	▲800	▲1,000		
Ed Wachter BK	▲100	▲150	▲250	▲300	▲500	275		
Joe Lapchick BK	▲150	▲200	▲300	▲400	▲600	▲1,000		
Eddie Burke BK	▲150	▲200	▲300	▲400	▲600	▲1,000		

— Red Grange #4 PSA 8 (NmMt) sold for $13,394.40 (Mastro Auctions; 12/07)
— Red Grange #4 SGC 8 (NmMt) sold for $3,704 (Mile High Auctions; 11/10)
— Carl Hubbell #42 PSA 9 (MT) sold for $7,929 (Mastro; 12/05)
— Babe Ruth #2 SGC 92 (NmMt+) sold for $64,417 (Mastro; 4/07)
— Babe Ruth #2 GAI 7.5 (NM+) sold for $5,541 (Mile High; 8/07)
— Jim Thorpe #6 PSA 8 (NmMt) sold for $7,200.00 (Mastro Auctions; 5/08)
— Ed Wachter #5 PSA 8 (NmMt) sold for $2,100 (Bussineau; 7/13)

1948 Bowman

	PrFr 1	GD 2	VG 3	VgEx 4	EX 5	ExMt 6	NM 7	NmMt 8
Ernie Calverley RC	▲25	▲50	▲100	▲200	▲300	▲400	▲500	▲800
Ralph Hamilton	10	15	20	▲30	▲50	▲60	▲100	▲300
Gale Bishop	10	20	25	30	50	60	100	▲300
Fred Lewis RC	10	12	20	30	40	60	80	150
Single Cut Off Post	10	12	20	30	40	50	80	200
Bob Feerick RC	10	12	20	30	40	60	150	250
John Logan	10	12	15	20	40	50	60	120
Mel Riebe	10	12	20	30	40	60	80	200
Andy Phillip RC	15	25	50	80	100	125	300	600
Bob Davies RC	15	30	60	80	100	▲150	▲250	▲500
Single Cut With	10	12	20	25	40	▲60	80	200
Kenny Sailors RC	10	12	20	30	50	80	120	350
Paul Armstrong	10	12	20	25	40	50	75	200
Howard Dallmar RC	10	15	30	50	80	120	150	▲300
Bruce Hale RC	10	12	25	30	40	60	80	200
Sid Hertzberg	10	12	20	25	40	50	80	200
Single Cut Using	10	12	25	30	40	50	80	225
Red Rocha	10	12	25	30	40	50	120	200
Eddie Ehlers	10	12	20	30	40	▲60	▲100	▲250
Ellis (Gene) Vance	10	12	15	20	30	50	80	200
Fuzzy Levane RC	10	12	25	30	40	80	100	200
Earl Shannon	10	12	20	25	40	60	100	250
Double Cut Off Post	10	12	20	25	40	60	100	250
Leo(Crystal) Klier	10	12	20	25	40	50	80	150
George Senesky	10	12	20	25	40	60	80	200
Price Brookfield	10	12	25	30	40	50	80	200
John Norlander	10	12	25	30	40	60	80	200
Don Putman	10	12	20	30	40	60	▲100	▲200
Double Post	10	12	25	30	▲50	▲80	▲200	▲300
Jack Garfinkel	10	12	20	25	40	60	120	250
Chuck Gilmur	10	12	15	20	30	40	80	250
Red Holzman RC	25	30	60	80	120	200	350	600
Jack Smiley	10	12	20	25	▲40	▲80	▲150	▲300
Joe Fulks RC	20	30	50	▲100	▲200	▲300	400	600
Screen Play	10	12	20	30	40	▲60	▲150	▲400
Hal Tidrick	10	▲20	▲40	▲80	▲150	▲200	▲300	▲500
Don (Swede) Carlson	10	25	40	50	▲80	▲200	▲300	▲600
Buddy Jeanette CO RC	20	40	80	100	200	300	450	1,000
Ray Kuka	15	25	40	60	80	100	200	600
Stan Miasek	15	20	30	50	60	120	300	600

	PrFr 1	GD 2	VG 3	VgEx 4	EX 5	ExMt 6	NM 7	NmMt 8
41	Double Screen With	15	25	40	60	100	125	200	375
42	George Nostrand	20	30	50	60	80	120	200	500
43	Chuck Halbert RC	20	30	50	60	80	100	200	400
44	Arnie Johnson	10	12	25	40	60	80	120	400
45	Bob Doll	15	25	30	40	60	100	150	500
46	Bones McKinney RC	15	25	40	50	80	200	250	400
47	Out Of Bounds	10	15	30	60	80	125	200	400
48	Ed Sadowski	20	30	50	75	100	150	250	500
49	Bob Kinney	15	25	40	50	80	150	300	
50	Charles (Hawk) Black	10	15	30	40	60	100	200	500
51	Jack Dwan	▲30	▲50	▲100	▲120	▲200	▲300	▲400	▲800
52	Connie Simmons RC	20	30	50	60	100	125	200	400
53	Out Of Bounds Play	15	25	40	50	100	150	200	300
54	Bud Palmer RC	15	25	40	60	▲120	▲250	▲400	600
55	Max Zaslofsky RC	30	50	60	80	100	150	400	800
56	Lee Roy Robbins	15	25	40	60	100	150	▼300	700
57	Arthur Spector	15	25	50	80	100	150	200	400
58	Arnie Risen RC	25	▲50	▲100	▲150	▲300	▲400	▲500	▲800
59	Out Of Bounds Play	10	12	20	30	50	100	200	350
60	Ariel Maughan	10	12	25	40	60	80	200	500
61	Dick O'Keefe	15	25	40	50	60	60	200	400
62	Herman Schaefer	10	15	30	40	50	100	200	400
63	John Mahnken	20	25	50	60	80	120	200	400
64	Tommy Byrnes	10	15	30	▲50	▲80	▲150	▲300	▲600
65	Held Ball Play	15	25	40	60	80	150	200	500
66	Jim Pollard RC	50	100	300	500	600	800	1,000	2,000
67	Lee Mogus	12	20	40	60	80	150	200	500
68	Lee Knorek	12	20	40	60	80	150	300	700
69	George Mikan RC	▲4,000	▲5,000	▲6,000	▲12,000	▲20,000	▲30,000	40,000	
70	Walter Budko	10	12	30	50	60	150	200	400
71	Guards Down Play	20	30	50	60	120	200	400	600
72	Carl Braun RC	▲80	▲150	▲250	▲400	▲600	700	1,000	4,000

— Max Zaslofsky #55 PSA 9 (MT) sold for $2,953 (Mile High; 1/10)
— Jim Pollard #66 PSA 9 (MT) sold for $8,520 (Greg Bussineau; Fall 2012
— Jim Pollard #66 PSA 8 (NmMt) sold for $1,704 (Memory Lane; 5/13)
— Jim Pollard #66 PSA 8 (NmMt) sold for $1,059 (eBay; 12/12)
— George Mikan #69 PSA 10 (Gem Mt) sold for $403,664 (SCP; 12/15)
— George Mikan #69 SGC 96 (Mint) sold for $35,850 (Heritage; 11/15)
— George Mikan #69 PSA 7 (NM) sold for $4,877 (Mile High; 6/10)

1957-58 Topps

	PrFr 1	GD 2	VG 3	VgEx 4	EX 5	ExMt 6	NM 7	NmMt 8
1	Nat Clifton DP RC	35	▲60	▲120	▲250	▲400	600	2,000	
2	George Yardley DP RC	10	▲20	▲40	▲80	▲150	▲300	▲600	4,000
3	Neil Johnston DP RC	10	12	20	30	60	150	400	2,000
4	Carl Braun DP	10	12	20	▲50	▲80	▲150	300	800
5	Bill Sharman DP RC	15	25	30	▲80	▲150	▲300	▲500	1,000
6	George King DP RC	8	10	15	25	30	50	125	400
7	Kenny Sears DP RC	10	12	20	25	30	50	150	500
8	Dick Ricketts DP RC	10	12	20	30	40	50	150	400
9	Jack Nichols DP	8	▲12	▲25	▲50	▲100	▲200	▲300	▲500
10	Paul Arizin DP RC	20	25	▲40	▲80	▲150	▲300	400	800
11	Chuck Noble DP	10	12	20	30	50	80	200	400
12	Slater Martin DP RC	15	30	50	80	▲150	▲300	▲600	▲1,200
13	Dolph Schayes DP RC	15	25	▲40	▲80	▲150	▲300	▲500	1,000
14	Dick Atha DP	8	10	15	30	50	80	150	500
15	Frank Ramsey DP RC	15	25	40	▲80	▲150	▲300	▲500	▲800

#	Player	PrFr 1	GD 2	VG 3	VgEx 4	EX 5	ExMt 6	NM 7	NmMt 8
16	Dick McGuire DP RC	10	15	30	▲50	▲80	▲150	▲400	▲800
17	Bob Cousy DP RC	100	200	1,000	2,000	3,000	4,000	6,000	25,000
18	Larry Foust DP RC	8	10	15	25	40	80	200	500
19	Tom Heinsohn RC	50	60	▲120	▲250	▲400	▲600	▲1,200	▲2,500
20	Bill Thieben DP	▲10	▲15	▲30	▲60	▲80	▲150	300	1,500
21	Don Meineke DP RC	8	10	15	25	40	60	100	600
22	Tom Marshall	10	12	20	25	40	50	100	450
23	Dick Garmaker	10	12	▲25	▲50	▲100	▲200	▲300	600
24	Bob Pettit DP RC	▲25	▲50	▲100	▲200	400	600	800	3,000
25	Jim Krebs DP RC	10	12	20	25	40	60	120	500
26	Gene Shue DP RC	10	15	25	30	40	50	100	500
27	Ed Macauley DP RC	12	20	25	30	60	120	300	1,000
28	Vern Mikkelsen RC	12	20	30	50	80	120	400	2,000
29	Willie Naulls RC	10	12	15	20	40	60	200	500
30	Walter Dukes DP RC	10	15	25	▲40	▲60	▲100	▲250	▲400
31	Dave Piontek DP	8	10	15	20	30	50	100	300
32	John (Red) Kerr RC	15	25	40	50	60	100	300	600
33	Larry Costello DP RC	10	12	20	25	40	60	200	500
34	Woody Sauldsberry DP RC	10	15	25	30	40	50	125	400
35	Ray Felix RC	10	12	20	25	30	40	150	500
36	Ernie Beck	8	10	20	30	40	60	200	3,000
37	Cliff Hagan RC	▲25	▲50	▲100	▲200	300	400	600	1,000
38	Guy Sparrow DP	10	12	20	25	40	60	120	400
39	Jim Loscutoff RC	10	▲20	▲40	▲80	▲150	▲300	▲500	1,200
40	Arnie Risen DP	10	▲20	▲40	▲80	▲150	▲300	▲400	▲800
41	Joe Graboski	10	12	20	25	40	80	120	500
42	Maurice Stokes DP RC	12	20	25	40	▲80	▲150	▲300	500
43	Rod Hundley DP RC	12	20	30	40	80	100	250	500
44	Tom Gola DP RC	15	25	30	50	80	120	400	1,500
45	Med Park RC	10	12	20	40	60	80	150	450
46	Mel Hutchins DP	8	10	20	30	50	80	300	800
47	Larry Friend DP	8	10	15	20	30	50	80	800
48	Len Rosenbluth DP RC	10	▲20	▲40	▲80	▲150	▲300	▲400	▲600
49	Walt Davis	10	12	20	25	30	40	150	600
50	Richie Regan RC	10	12	20	30	50	80	200	500
51	Frank Selvy DP RC	12	20	25	▲40	▲80	▲150	▲300	▲500
52	Art Spoelstra DP	8	10	15	20	30	60	120	400
53	Bob Hopkins RC	8	10	▲20	▲40	▲80	▲150	▲300	600
54	Earl Lloyd RC	▲20	▲40	▲80	▲150	▲300	▲600	▲1,200	▲2,500
55	Phil Jordan DP	8	10	▲20	▲40	▲80	▲150	▲300	▲700
56	Bob Houbregs DP RC	10	12	20	25	30	50	150	500
57	Lou Tsioropoulos DP	10	12	20	30	40	80	120	400
58	Ed Conlin RC	10	12	20	40	60	100	300	700
59	Al Bianchi RC	10	12	20	▲30	▲60	▲120	300	800
60	George Dempsey RC	10	12	15	20	30	60	120	300
61	Chuck Share	8	10	12	20	40	80	200	500
62	Harry Gallatin DP RC	10	15	25	40	80	150	450	600
63	Bob Harrison	10	15	25	30	40	60	200	600
64	Bob Burrow DP	8	10	15	25	30	60	125	400
65	Win Wilfong DP	8	10	15	25	40	60	125	300
66	Jack McMahon DP RC	8	10	15	25	40	60	150	450
67	Jack George	8	10	15	20	30	40	200	400
68	Charlie Tyra DP	10	12	20	25	30	60	200	750
69	Ron Sobie	10	15	20	25	30	60	150	450
70	Jack Coleman	10	12	20	25	40	60	125	450
71	Jack Twyman DP RC	12	20	30	▲60	▲100	▲250	▲500	▲1,000
72	Paul Seymour RC	10	12	20	25	40	80	200	600
73	Jim Paxson DP RC	10	12	25	40	60	80	150	400
74	Bob Leonard RC	10	12	▲25	▲50	▲100	▲250	▲400	▲600
75	Andy Phillip	12	20	25	30	50	100	450	700
76	Joe Holup	10	12	20	30	50	80	200	400
77	Bill Russell RC	5,000	8,000	▼10,000	15,000	30,000	40,000	80,000	200,000
78	Clyde Lovellette DP RC	15	▲30	▲60	▲100	▲200	▲300	▲500	1,000
79	Ed Fleming DP	10	▲15	▲30	▲60	▲120	▲250	▲500	
80	Dick Schnittker RC	15	20	30	40	80	▲200	500	3,500

— Nat Clifton #1 PSA 8 (NMMT) sold for $3,081 (eBay; 12/10)
— Tom Heinsohn #19 PSA 8 (NMMT) sold for $822 (Mile High; 6/10)

— Phil Jordan #55 PSA 9 (MT) sold for $2,225 (eBay; 2/12)
— Bob Houbregs #56 PSA 9 (MT) sold for $4,062 (eBay; 4/12)
— Lou Tsioropoulos #57 PSA 9 (MT) sold for $3,950 (eBay; 4/12)
— Jack McMahon #66 PSA 9 (MT) sold for $2,948 (eBay; 4/12)
— Bill Russell #77 PSA 7 (NM) sold for $2,218 (Mile High; 10/09)
— Bill Russell #77 SGC 70 (EX+) sold for $1,304 (Huggins & Scott; 4/13)
— Clyde Lovellette #78 PSA 8 (NMMT) sold for $910 (Mile High; 6/10)
— Ed Flemming #79 PSA 8 (NMMT) sold for $4,057 (eBay; 3/12)
— Dick Schnittker #80 PSA 8 (NMMT) sold for $2,901 (Goodwin; 6/10)

1961-62 Fleer

#	Player	GD 2	VG 3	VgEx 4	EX 5	ExMt 6	NM 7	NmMt 8	MT 9
1	Al Attles RC	30	80	150	300	400	600	1,200	4,000
2	Paul Arizin	10	15	30	60	100	250	1,000	2,000
3	Elgin Baylor RC	200	300	400	800	2,500	4,000	10,000	30,000
4	Walt Bellamy RC	30	60	100	200	400	800	2,000	6,000
5	Arlen Bockhorn	▲10	▲20	▲40	▲60	▲80	▲150	▲300	1,500
6	Bob Boozer RC	▲6	▲10	▲20	▲40	▲80	▲150	400	2,000
7	Carl Braun	5	8	10	20	40	80	200	800
8	Wilt Chamberlain RC	3,000	6,000	10,000	15,000	20,000	30,000		
9	Larry Costello	5	8	10	20	25	50	80	500
10	Bob Cousy	40	50	▲100	200	400	800	2,200	
11	Walter Dukes	▲6	▲12	▲25	▲50	▲80	▲150	▲300	▲800
12	Wayne Embry RC	5	8	10	15	30	80	150	
13	Dave Gambee	5	8	12	20	30	40	120	500
14	Tom Gola	▲6	8	▲15	▲30	▲60	▲120	▲250	600
15	Sihugo Green RC	5	8	12	▲25	▲50	▲100	▲200	500
16	Hal Greer RC	20	40	80	120	▲200	300	500	1,200
17	Richie Guerin RC	5	8	10	20	40	80	150	500
18	Cliff Hagan	8	12	20	25	50	80	200	650
19	Tom Heinsohn	10	15	30	50	80	120	250	800
20	Bailey Howell RC	8	12	20	100	150	300	500	1,000
21	Rod Hundley	8	12	▲25	▲50	▲100	▲200	▲350	800
22	K.C. Jones RC	15	40	50	60	120	200	600	2,000
23	Sam Jones RC	▲20	▲40	▲80	▲150	▲250	▲400	▲800	2,000
24	Phil Jordan	5	8	12	▲20	▲40	▲80	200	1,000
25	John/Red Kerr	▲6	▲10	▲20	▲40	▲80	▲150	▲300	800
26	Rudy LaRusso RC	5	8	10	15	30	60	120	600
27	George Lee	5	8	10	20	25	50	120	550
28	Bob Leonard	5	8	12	20	30	60	150	450
29	Clyde Lovellette	▲6	▲10	▲20	▲40	▲80	▲150	▲300	850
30	John McCarthy	5	6	8	10	15	40	100	400
31	Tom Meschery RC	▲10	▲20	▲40	▲80	▲150	▲300	▲500	800
32	Willie Naulls	▲10	▲20	▲40	▲60	▲100	▲200	▲400	1,000
33	Don Ohl RC	5	10	15	20	30	60	300	1,800
34	Bob Pettit	10	20	▲40	▲80	▲150	▲300	▲600	▲2,000
35	Frank Ramsey	5	10	15	20	50	100	250	1,800
36	Oscar Robertson RC	1,000	1,500	2,000	3,500	5,000	10,000	20,000	
37	Guy Rodgers RC	8	10	20	40	80	120	200	800
38	Bill Russell	▲200	▲400	▲800	▲1,500	▲2,000	▲3,000	▲4,000	▲6,000
39	Dolph Schayes	5	10	15	20	40	60	150	800
40	Frank Selvy	5	8	10	15	30	60	150	1,000
41	Gene Shue	5	10	15	20	30	60	150	800
42	Jack Twyman	8	12	20	25	▲40	▲100	▲200	900
43	Jerry West RC	1,000	1,500	2,000	3,500	5,000	10,000	20,000	
44	Len Wilkens RC	▲25	▲50	▲100	▲200	▲300	▲400	▲600	▲2,000
45	Paul Arizin IA	6	8	10	15	25	40	100	800
46	Elgin Baylor IA	▲12	▲25	▲50	▲100	▲200	▲400	▲600	1,200
47	Wilt Chamberlain IA	600	800	1,000	1,500	2,000	3,000	5,000	
48	Larry Costello IA	5	8	12	15	20	50	100	55
49	Bob Cousy IA	▲25	▲50	▲100	▲200	▲300	▲400	500	1,000
50	Walter Dukes IA	5	8	10	15	30	40	80	50
51	Tom Gola IA	8	8	10	15	25	50	100	50
52	Richie Guerin IA	5	8	10	15	30	40	80	52
53	Cliff Hagan IA	8	10	15	20	30	50	120	50
54	Tom Heinsohn IA	10	15	25	30	50	80	150	55

#		GD 2	VG 3	VgEx 4	EX 5	ExMt 6	NM 7	NmMt 8	MT 9
55	Bailey Howell IA	5	8	12	15	40	60	100	600
56	John/Red Kerr IA	8	12	20	25	30	50	100	500
57	Rudy LaRusso IA	5	8	▲15	▲30	▲60	▲100	▲250	
58	Clyde Lovellette IA	5	10	15	▲30	▲60	▲100	▲200	600
59	Bob Pettit IA	8	12	▲25	▲50	▲80	▲150	▲300	700
60	Frank Ramsey IA	5	8	12	15	25	50	100	600
61	Oscar Robertson IA	100	200	400	600	800	2,000	4,000	
62	Bill Russell IA	300	400	600	800	1,500	3,000		
63	Dolph Schayes IA	5	8	15	20	40	60	300	800
64	Gene Shue IA	5	8	12	20	25	50	200	
65	Jack Twyman IA	5	10	15	20	25	60	120	500
66	Jerry West IA	100	200	400	600	800	2,000	4,000	

— Elgin Baylor #3 PSA 9 (Mint) sold for $3,730 (eBay, 2/10)

— Wilt Chamberlain #8 PSA 9 (Mint) sold for $7,240 (eBay, 4/12)

— Wayne Embry #12 PSA 9 (MT) sold for $1,118 (SCP; 4/13)

— Sam Jones #23 PSA 10 (Gem Mt) sold for $10,157 (Heritage; 8/16)

— Jerry West #43 PSA 9 (Mint) sold for $6,932 (Goodwin; 2/11)

— Jerry West #43 PSA 8.5 (NmMt+) sold for $17,788 (Goodwin; 8/16)

— Len Wilkens #44 PSA 10 (Gem Mt) sold for $10,157 (Heritage; 8/16)

1969-70 Topps

#		GD 2	VG 3	VgEx 4	EX 5	ExMt 6	NM 7	NmMt 8	MT 9
1	Wilt Chamberlain	200	300	400	600	1,000	2,000	6,000	15,000
2	Gail Goodrich RC	▲10	▲20	▲40	▲80	▲150	▲300	▲600	1,500
3	Cazzie Russell RC	5	8	10	12	50	100	250	500
4	Darrall Imhoff RC	5	8	10	12	15	20	50	350
5	Bailey Howell	5	5	8	10	12	20	60	200
6	Lucius Allen RC	5	8	▲12	▲25	▲50	▲100	▲300	
7	Tom Boerwinkle RC	5	5	6	8	12	30	120	
8	Jimmy Walker RC	5	5	8	10	15	25	80	
9	John Block RC	5	5	6	8	10	15	60	425
10	Nate Thurmond RC	5	12	20	30	120	200	500	1,000
11	Gary Gregor	5	5	8	10	15	▲30	▲80	400
12	Gus Johnson RC	5	10	15	20	25	50	150	
13	Luther Rackley	5	5	6	8	▲15	▲30	▲80	
14	Jon McGlocklin RC	5	5	12	15	20	50	125	250
15	Connie Hawkins RC	▲20	▲40	▲60	▲100	▲200	▲400	600	1,000
16	Johnny Egan	5	5	6	8	▲15	▲30	▲60	150
17	Jim Washington	5	5	6	8	10	▲20	▲40	150
18	Dick Barnett RC	5	6	8	▲12	▲30	80	150	300
19	Tom Meschery	5	5	8	12	20	40	200	
20	John Havlicek RC	80	150	300	400	600	1,000	2,500	12,000
21	Eddie Miles	5	5	8	10	12	15	50	200
22	Walt Wesley	5	8	10	12	20	40	80	225
23	Rick Adelman RC	5	▲8	▲15	▲30	▲60	▲120	▲200	▲400
24	Al Attles	5	▲6	▲10	▲20	▲40	▲80	▲150	300
25	Lew Alcindor RC	1,000	▼1,500	3,000	5,000	8,000	15,000	20,000	50,000
26	Jack Marin RC	5	5	8	10	12	25	50	225
27	Walt Hazzard RC	5	8	10	12	15	30	80	400
28	Connie Dierking	5	5	8	12	▲20	▲40	▲80	
29	Keith Erickson RC	5	8	10	12	▲25	▲40	▲80	300
30	Bob Rule RC	5	8	10	12	20	40	80	200
31	Dick Van Arsdale RC	5	8	10	12	15	30	60	400
32	Archie Clark RC	5	8	10	12	25	50	80	300
33	Terry Dischinger RC	5	5	6	8	▲12	20	60	200
34	Henry Finkel RC	5	5	6	8	▲12	▲20	▲50	▲200
35	Elgin Baylor	8	12	50	60	80	150	400	1,000
36	Ron Williams	5	5	6	10	15	30	50	150
37	Loy Petersen	5	5	6	▲10	▲20	▲50	▲100	300
38	Guy Rodgers	5	8	10	12	15	20	50	250
39	Toby Kimball	5	5	6	▲10	▲20	▲40	100	300
40	Billy Cunningham RC	▲6	12	20	▲40	▲80	▲150	300	800
41	Joe Caldwell RC	5	8	10	12	15	25	50	
42	Leroy Ellis RC	5	5	6	10	12	20	40	150
43	Bill Bradley RC	10	15	30	50	60	▲120	300	1,200
44	Len Wilkens	5	10	15	20	30	40	100	800

#		GD 2	VG 3	VgEx 4	EX 5	ExMt 6	NM 7	NmMt 8	MT 9
45	Jerry Lucas RC	5	10	15	25	40	80	200	700
46	Neal Walk RC	5	8	10	12	15	20	60	200
47	Emmette Bryant RC	5	10	12	15	30	100	350	600
48	Bob Kauffman RC	5	5	8	10	12	20	40	
49	Mel Counts RC	5	5	8	10	12	▲25	▲50	200
50	Oscar Robertson	▲10	▲20	▲40	▲80	▲200	▲350	▲500	1,000
51	Jim Barnett RC	5	5	8	10	12	20	80	400
52	Don Smith	5	5	6	8	10	15	80	400
53	Jim Davis	5	5	8	10	12	▲25	▲80	350
54	Wally Jones RC	5	5	6	8	10	20	▲50	300
55	Dave Bing RC	8	12	20	40	80	▲150	▲300	800
56	Wes Unseld RC	▲8	▲12	▲20	▲40	▲80	▲150	▲300	800
57	Joe Ellis	5	5	8	12	▲20	▲40	▲80	
58	John Tresvant	5	5	6	8	10	20	40	500
59	Larry Siegfried RC	5	5	6	8	▲12	▲25	50	200
60	Willis Reed RC	10	25	50	100	250	500	800	2,000
61	Paul Silas RC	5	8	12	15	25	40	120	400
62	Bob Weiss RC	5	8	12	15	▲25	▲50	▲100	300
63	Willie McCarter RC	5	5	6	8	10	12	60	300
64	Don Kojis RC	5	5	6	8	10	20	30	125
65	Lou Hudson RC	5	10	15	▲25	▲50	▲100	▲250	500
66	Jim King	5	5	6	▲10	▲20	▲40	▲80	200
67	Luke Jackson RC	5	5	6	8	12	20	60	200
68	Len Chappell RC	5	5	6	8	10	15	25	50
69	Ray Scott	5	5	8	10	▲20	▲40	▲80	
70	Jeff Mullins RC	5	5	6	8	10	12	25	60
71	Howie Komives	5	5	6	▲10	▲20	▲40	▲80	200
72	Tom Sanders RC	5	8	10	15	▲30	▲80	▲200	600
73	Dick Snyder	5	5	6	8	10	20	35	
74	Dave Stallworth RC	5	5	6	10	15	30	60	
75	Elvin Hayes RC	25	50	▲100	▲200	300	500	2,000	4,000
76	Art Harris	5	5	6	8	10	20	50	200
77	Don Ohl	5	5	6	8	12	20	40	
78	Bob Love RC	5	8	▲15	▲30	▲60	▲150	▲450	▲600
79	Tom Van Arsdale RC	5	8	10	12	▲20	▲40	150	
80	Earl Monroe RC	▲20	▲40	▲80	▲150	▲200	▲350	▲500	800
81	Greg Smith	5	5	6	8	▲15	▲30	▲60	325
82	Don Nelson RC	8	12	20	30	50	▲100	▲300	600
83	Happy Hairston RC	5	5	8	10	15	30	50	300
84	Hal Greer	5	▲10	▲15	▲30	80	120	300	600
85	Dave DeBusschere RC	5	10	15	20	▲60	▲120	▲300	
86	Bill Bridges RC	5	5	8	10	▲15	▲30	▲80	200
87	Herm Gilliam RC	5	5	6	8	▲15	▲40	▲80	
88	Jim Fox	5	5	6	8	10	20	50	550
89	Bob Boozer	5	5	6	8	15	20	100	
90	Jerry West	▲80	▲120	▲200	▲300	▲400	500	1,000	4,000
91	Chet Walker RC	5	10	15	20	25	40	150	400
92	Flynn Robinson RC	5	8	12	15	20	25	60	400
93	Clyde Lee	5	5	6	8	12	20	40	175
94	Kevin Loughery RC	5	5	8	10	15	30	60	400
95	Walt Bellamy	5	5	10	15	20	30	60	
96	Art Williams	5	5	6	8	10	15	20	40
97	Adrian Smith RC	5	5	8	10	15	20	50	225
98	Walt Frazier RC	▲15	▲30	▲60	▲120	▲300	▲600	800	4,000
99	Checklist 1-99	40	60	▲120	250	500	1,000	2,500	10,000

— Rick Adelman #23 PSA 10 (Gem MT) sold for $2,025 (eBay; 3/12)

— Lew Alcindor #25 PSA 10 (Gem MT) sold for $501,900 (Heritage; 8/16)

— Lew Alcindor #25 BSG 10 (Pristine) sold for $12,245 (eBay; 3/11)

— John Havlicek #20 PSA 10 (Gem MT) sold for $25,273 (Mile High; 12/13)

— John Havlicek #20 PSA 9 (MT) sold for $3,696 (Mile High; 10/09)

1970-71 Topps

#		GD 2	VG 3	VgEx 4	EX 5	ExMt 6	NM 7	NmMt 8	MT 9
1	Alcind/West/Hayes LL	5	5	10	12	30	50	200	
2	West/Alcin/Hayes LL SP	5	5	10	12	30	60	250	800
3	Green/Imhoff/Hudson LL	5	5	8	10	▲15	▲30	▲60	125

#	Player	GD 2	VG 3	VgEx 4	EX 5	ExMt 6	NM 7	NmMt 8	MT 9
4	Rob/Walker/Mull LL SP	5	5	8	10	12	200	500	
5	Hayes/Uns/Alcindor LL	5	5	8	10	25	40	100	300
6	Wilkens/Fraz/Hask LL SP	5	5	10	12	15	30	80	
7	Bill Bradley	5	5	10	▲20	▲40	▲80	▲150	300
8	Ron Williams	5	5	6	8	10	15	40	300
9	Otto Moore	5	5	6	8	10	12	▲25	▲50
10	John Havlicek SP	5	10	15	25	80	150	350	500
11	George Wilson RC	5	5	6	8	10	12	20	50
12	John Trapp	5	5	6	8	10	12	20	50
13	Pat Riley RC	15	25	50	80	120	200	400	1,000
14	Jim Washington	5	5	5	▲6	▲8	▲15	▲30	▲80
15	Bob Rule	5	5	5	6	8	10	15	200
16	Bob Weiss	5	5	5	6	8	10	12	100
17	Neil Johnson	5	5	5	6	8	12	25	150
18	Walt Bellamy	5	5	5	6	10	20	50	200
19	McCoy McLemore	5	5	5	5	6	▲15	▲30	60
20	Earl Monroe	6	8	10	20	40	80	200	900
21	Wally Anderzunas	5	5	5	5	6	8	12	50
22	Guy Rodgers	5	5	5	6	10	15	40	200
23	Rick Roberson	5	5	5	6	8	10	12	50
24	Checklist 1-110	5	5	8	10	12	20	60	300
25	Jimmy Walker	5	5	5	5	6	8	20	50
26	Mike Riordan RC	5	5	6	8	10	12	25	150
27	Henry Finkel	5	5	5	5	6	10	20	80
28	Joe Ellis	5	5	5	6	8	10	20	60
29	Mike Davis	5	5	5	6	8	10	12	60
30	Lou Hudson	5	5	8	10	12	15	25	80
31	Lucius Allen SP	5	5	8	10	12	80	150	
32	Toby Kimball SP	5	5	6	15	20	30	150	
33	Luke Jackson SP	5	5	6	8	10	15	80	250
34	Johnny Egan	5	5	6	8	10	15	80	200
35	Leroy Ellis SP	5	5	6	8	12	30	150	300
36	Jack Marin SP	5	5	6	8	12	30	120	
37	Joe Caldwell SP	5	5	6	8	15	30	120	
38	Keith Erickson	5	5	6	8	10	▲15	▲30	80
39	Don Smith	5	5	5	5	6	10	40	
40	Flynn Robinson	5	5	5	6	8	12	25	120
41	Bob Boozer	5	5	5	5	6	10	20	
42	Howie Komives	5	5	5	5	6	8	12	40
43	Dick Barnett	5	5	6	8	10	12	15	100
44	Stu Lantz RC	5	5	6	8	10	12	25	150
45	Dick Van Arsdale	5	5	6	8	10	12	25	150
46	Jerry Lucas	5	5	8	10	15	30	60	400
47	Don Chaney RC	5	5	8	10	12	20	60	200
48	Ray Scott	5	5	5	5	6	10	20	60
49	Dick Cunningham SP	5	5	6	10	25	60	350	
50	Wilt Chamberlain	80	100	120	▲250	▲500	▲1,000	▲2,000	▲5,000
51	Kevin Loughery	5	5	5	6	8	10	20	70
52	Stan McKenzie	5	5	5	6	8	10	15	60
53	Fred Foster	5	5	5	6	8	10	15	40
54	Jim Davis	5	5	5	6	8	10	12	40
55	Walt Wesley	5	5	5	6	8	10	15	50
56	Bill Hewitt	5	5	5	6	8	10	12	50
57	Darrall Imhoff	5	5	5	6	8	10	15	35
58	John Block	5	5	5	6	8	10	15	
59	Al Attles SP	5	5	6	8	12	30	200	
60	Chet Walker	5	5	6	8	▲12	▲20	▲40	100
61	Luther Rackley	5	5	5	6	8	10	15	60
62	Jerry Chambers SP RC	5	6	8	10	25	60	150	300
63	Bob Dandridge RC	6	8	10	20	50	150	300	600
64	Dick Snyder	5	5	5	5	6	8	12	40
65	Elgin Baylor	5	5	10	15	30	60	150	500
66	Connie Dierking	5	5	5	5	8	10	15	50
67	Steve Kuberski RC	5	5	6	8	10	20	40	400
68	Tom Boerwinkle	5	5	5	5	6	8	10	60
69	Paul Silas	5	5	6	8	15	20	30	200
70	Elvin Hayes	5	5	10	15	▲30	▲60	▲120	▲250
71	Bill Bridges	5	5	5	6	8	10	20	75
72	Wes Unseld	5	6	8	10	20	40	80	250
73	Herm Gilliam	5	5	5	5	6	8	20	80
74	Bobby Smith SP RC	5	5	6	8	10	60	150	
75	Lew Alcindor	▲60	▲120	▲150	▲300	▲400	▲500	▲800	5,000
76	Jeff Mullins	5	5	5	6	8	▲12	▲25	▲80
77	Happy Hairston	5	5	5	6	8	10	20	60
78	Dave Stallworth SP	5	5	6	8	15	25	80	300
79	Fred Hetzel	5	5	5	6	8	10	15	50
80	Len Wilkens SP	5	5	10	12	30	60	120	
81	Johnny Green RC	5	5	6	8	10	15	25	
82	Erwin Mueller	5	5	5	5	6	8	12	
83	Wally Jones	5	5	5	6	8	▲12	▲25	▲80
84	Bob Love	5	▲6	▲10	▲12	▲20	▲40	▲80	▲200
85	Dick Garrett RC	5	5	5	5	6	10	15	50
86	Don Nelson SP	5	8	12	15	20	30	80	250
87	Neal Walk SP	5	5	6	8	10	30	100	
88	Larry Siegfried	5	5	5	6	8	▲15	▲30	80
89	Gary Gregor	5	5	5	5	6	8	12	50
90	Nate Thurmond	5	▲6	▲8	▲12	▲20	▲40	100	200
91	John Warren	5	5	6	8	10	12	20	150
92	Gus Johnson	5	5	6	8	10	12	30	125
93	Gail Goodrich	5	5	8	10	15	20	30	100
94	Dorrie Murrey	5	5	5	▲6	▲8	▲15	▲30	60
95	Cazzie Russell SP	5	8	12	15	20	60	300	
96	Terry Dischinger	5	5	5	5	6	8	12	50
97	Norm Van Lier SP RC	5	5	10	12	20	120	450	
98	Jim Fox	5	5	5	▲6	▲10	▲15	▲30	60
99	Tom Meschery	5	5	5	5	6	8	12	100
100	Oscar Robertson	5	5	10	25	80	150	300	600
101A	Checklist 111-175	5	5	8	12	20	25	60	
101B	Checklist 111-175	5	10	15	20	25	30	40	250
102	Rich Johnson	5	5	5	5	6	8	12	75
103	Mel Counts	5	5	5	6	8	10	15	100
104	Bill Hosket SP RC	5	10	15	40	50	80	200	
105	Archie Clark	5	5	5	6	8	10	20	80
106	Walt Frazier AS	5	5	10	15	25	50	100	500
107	Jerry West AS	▲6	▲10	▲20	▲40	80	120	300	600
108	Billy Cunningham AS SP	5	5	8	10	15	20	120	
109	Connie Hawkins AS	5	5	6	8	10	12	40	
110	Willis Reed AS	5	5	6	8	12	15	30	150
111	Nate Thurmond AS	5	5	6	8	12	15	25	80
112	John Havlicek AS	5	5	10	▲20	▲40	▲80	▲200	400
113	Elgin Baylor AS	5	5	8	▲15	▲30	▲60	▲150	▲300
114	Oscar Robertson AS	5	▲6	▲10	▲20	▲40	▲80	▲200	▲400
115	Lou Hudson AS	5	5	5	6	8	10	100	200
116	Emmette Bryant	5	5	5	6	8	10	30	60
117	Greg Howard	5	5	5	5	6	8	15	80
118	Rick Adelman	5	5	6	8	10	12	15	50
119	Barry Clemens	5	5	5	5	6	8	20	60
120	Walt Frazier	5	10	15	20	40	80	200	1,000
121	Jim Barnes RC	5	5	5	5	6	8	15	60
122	Bernie Williams	5	5	5	5	6	10	15	125
123	Pete Maravich RC	200	250	500	1,500	2,000	3,000	8,000	25,000
124	Matt Guokas RC	5	5	6	8	10	▲20	▲40	80
125	Dave Bing	5	5	8	10	12	15	25	120
126	John Tresvant	5	5	5	5	6	▲12	▲25	▲60
127	Shaler Halimon	5	5	5	6	8	10	15	50
128	Don Ohl	5	5	5	5	6	8	12	50
129	Fred Carter RC	5	5	6	8	10	12	20	60
130	Connie Hawkins	5	5	10	12	15	20	30	120
131	Jim King	5	5	5	5	6	8	15	50
132	Ed Manning RC	5	5	6	8	10	▲15	▲30	80
133	Adrian Smith	5	5	5	5	6	8	15	30
134	Walt Hazzard	5	5	6	8	10	12	20	150
135	Dave DeBusschere	5	5	8	10	12	30	40	250
136	Don Kojis	5	5	5	6	8	10	15	50

#	Player	GD 2	VG 3	VgEx 4	EX 5	ExMt 6	NM 7	NmMt 8	MT 9
137	Calvin Murphy RC	5	8	12	15	30	60	150	600
138	Nate Bowman	5	5	5	5	▲10	▲15	▲30	▲60
139	Jon McGlocklin	5	5	5	6	8	12	25	60
140	Billy Cunningham	5	5	8	10	12	25	60	200
141	Willie McCarter	5	5	5	5	6	8	12	50
142	Jim Barnett	5	5	5	5	6	8	12	60
143	Jo Jo White RC	▲6	▲8	▲15	▲30	▲60	▲120	▲200	▲400
144	Clyde Lee	5	5	5	5	8	10	15	30
145	Tom Van Arsdale	5	5	5	8	10	15	40	250
146	Len Chappell	5	5	5	5	6	8	12	30
147	Lee Winfield	5	5	5	5	6	8	15	50
148	Jerry Sloan RC	5	6	12	20	30	50	80	200
149	Art Harris	5	5	5	5	6	10	20	60
150	Willis Reed	5	5	8	15	20	40	150	500
151	Art Williams	5	5	5	5	6	8	12	50
152	Don May	5	5	5	5	6	8	12	50
153	Loy Petersen	5	5	5	5	6	10	25	70
154	Dave Gambee	5	5	5	5	6	8	12	50
155	Hal Greer	5	5	8	8	12	20	40	80
156	Dave Newmark	5	5	5	5	6	10	25	60
157	Jimmy Collins	5	5	5	5	6	8	15	50
158	Bill Turner	5	5	5	5	6	8	15	50
159	Eddie Miles	5	5	5	5	6	8	15	50
160	Jerry West	▲6	▲12	▲25	▲50	▲100	▲150	▲300	700
162	Fred Crawford	5	5	5	5	6	8	15	40
163	Tom Sanders	5	5	6	8	10	15	40	125
164	Dale Schlueter	5	5	5	5	6	8	12	50
165	Clem Haskins RC	5	5	8	10	12	15	20	50
166	Greg Smith	5	5	5	5	6	8	15	50
167	Rod Thorn RC	5	5	6	8	10	12	25	80
168	Playoff G1/W.Reed	5	5	8	10	12	20	50	100
169	Playoff G2/D.Garnett	5	5	5	6	8	10	25	150
170	Playoff G3/DeBussch	5	5	8	10	12	15	30	
171	Playoff G4/J.West	5	8	12	15	20	30	50	300
172	Playoff G5/Bradley	5	5	8	10	12	15	25	
173	Playoff G6/Wilt	5	8	12	15	30	50	100	300
174	Playoff G7/Frazier	5	5	8	10	15	20	80	
175	Knicks Celebrate	5	6	10	12	▲20	▲40	80	150

— Wally Anderzunas #21 PSA 10 (Gem MT) sold for $2,615 (eBay; 9/12)

— Al Attles #59 PSA 9 (Mint) sold for $459 (eBay; 9/12)

— Connie Hawkins #130 PSA 10 (Gem MT) sold for 1,502 (eBay; 6/11)

— Pete Maravich #123 PSA 8 (NMMT) sold for $470 (Goodwin; 9/11)

— Pete Maravich #123 PSA 9 (MT) sold for $2,987 (eBay; 12/11)

— Oscar Robertson #114 PSA 10 (Gem MT) sold for $3,232 (Goodwin; 2012)

1971-72 Topps

#	Player	GD 2	VG 3	VgEx 4	EX 5	ExMt 6	NM 7	NmMt 8	MT 9
1	Oscar Robertson	10	15	30	60	120	200	400	1,000
2	Bill Bradley	4	5	8	10	▲15	▲30	▲60	200
3	Jim Fox	4	4	4	4	5	8	20	80
4	John Johnson RC	4	4	4	4	5	6	8	30
5	Luke Jackson	4	4	4	4	5	6	8	40
6	Don May DP	4	4	4	4	5	6	10	40
7	Kevin Loughery	4	4	4	▲5	▲8	▲15	▲30	▲80
8	Terry Dischinger	4	4	4	4	5	8	20	
9	Neal Walk	4	4	4	4	5	6	20	50
10	Elgin Baylor	5	6	12	25	50	120	350	600
11	Rick Adelman	4	4	4	4	5	6	15	50
12	Clyde Lee	4	4	4	▲5	▲8	▲15	▲30	▲60
13	Jerry Chambers	4	4	4	4	5	6	15	30
14	Fred Carter	4	4	4	▲5	▲6	▲12	▲25	80
15	Tom Boerwinkle DP	4	4	4	4	5	6	8	50
16	John Block	4	4	4	4	5	6	50	
17	Dick Barnett	4	4	4	4	5	6	12	40
18	Henry Finkel	4	4	4	4	5	6	15	
19	Norm Van Lier	4	4	4	4	5	8	12	60
20	Spencer Haywood RC	10	20	40	80	120	200	400	600
21	George Johnson	4	4	4	4	5	6	20	40
22	Bobby Lewis	4	4	4	4	5	6	12	40
23	Bill Hewitt	4	4	▲5	▲8	▲15	▲30	▲60	▲120
24	Walt Hazzard	4	4	4	4	5	8	15	50
25	Happy Hairston	4	4	4	4	5	10	40	80
26	George Wilson	4	4	4	4	5	8	25	60
27	Lucius Allen	4	4	4	4	5	6	20	40
28	Jim Washington	4	4	4	4	5	8	12	60
29	Nate Archibald RC	10	15	20	40	100	300	600	2,200
30	Willis Reed	4	4	6	8	15	20	60	200
31	Erwin Mueller	4	4	4	4	5	8	15	75
32	Art Harris	4	4	4	4	5	6	8	40
33	Pete Cross	4	4	4	4	5	6	10	40
34	Geoff Petrie RC	4	4	4	4	5	8	20	50
35	John Havlicek	▲5	▲6	▲10	▲15	▲30	▲60	▲120	▲300
36	Larry Siegfried	4	4	4	4	5	8	20	80
37	John Tresvant DP	4	4	4	▲5	▲6	▲12	▲25	50
38	Ron Williams	4	4	4	4	5	6	10	40
39	Lamar Green DP	4	4	4	4	5	6	8	25
40	Bob Rule DP	4	4	4	4	5	6	20	40
41	Jim McMillian RC	4	4	4	5	8	12	20	50
42	Wally Jones	4	4	4	▲5	▲8	▲15	▲30	▲60
43	Bob Boozer	4	4	4	4	5	6	15	65
44	Eddie Miles	4	4	4	4	5	6	8	40
45	Bob Love DP	4	4	4	4	5	6	10	30
46	Claude English	4	4	4	4	5	6	10	60
47	Dave Cowens RC	4	5	10	20	60	100	250	1,500
48	Emmette Bryant	4	4	4	4	5	6	8	40
49	Dave Stallworth	4	4	4	4	5	12	30	125
50	Jerry West	5	8	12	20	40	100	250	500
51	Joe Ellis	4	4	4	4	5	6	8	40
52	Walt Wesley DP	4	4	4	4	5	6	8	25
53	Howie Komives	4	4	▲5	▲8	▲15	▲40	▲80	▲150
54	Paul Silas	4	4	4	4	5	8	12	50
55	Pete Maravich DP	▲8	▲15	▲30	▲60	▼120	▼150	500	800
56	Gary Gregor	4	4	4	4	5	6	8	40
57	Sam Lacey RC	4	4	4	4	5	8	10	50
58	Calvin Murphy DP	4	4	▲5	▲6	▲10	▲15	▲30	▲60
59	Bob Dandridge	4	4	4	▲5	▲8	▲15	▲30	60
60	Hal Greer	4	4	4	4	5	10	15	80
61	Keith Erickson	4	4	4	4	6	10	20	120
62	Joe Cooke	4	4	4	4	5	8	12	35
63	Bob Lanier RC	6	8	15	30	60	120	400	1,500
64	Don Kojis	4	4	4	5	6	8	10	30
65	Walt Frazier	▲5	▲6	▲12	▲25	▲50	▲100	▲200	▲400
66	Chet Walker DP	4	4	4	4	5	6	10	25
67	Dick Garrett	4	4	4	5	6	8	20	50
68	John Trapp	4	4	4	4	5	6	8	50
69	Jo Jo White	4	▲5	▲6	▲12	▲25	▲50	▲100	▲200
70	Wilt Chamberlain	25	50	100	▲200	▲400	500	2,000	10,000
71	Dave Sorenson	4	4	4	4	5	8	15	80
72	Jim King	4	4	4	4	5	6	15	60
73	Cazzie Russell	4	4	4	4	5	8	15	70
74	Jon McGlocklin	4	4	4	4	5	6	8	40
75	Tom Van Arsdale	4	4	4	4	5	6	8	50
76	Dale Schlueter	4	4	4	4	5	6	40	
77	Gus Johnson DP	4	4	4	4	5	8	12	40
78	Dave Bing	4	4	4	4	6	10	40	200
79	Billy Cunningham	4	4	6	8	▲12	▲25	▲50	▲120
80	Len Wilkens	4	4	4	6	10	12	40	150
81	Jerry Lucas DP	4	4	4	4	5	6	15	25
82	Don Chaney	4	4	4	4	5	8	15	60
83	McCoy McLemore	4	4	4	4	5	6	8	40
84	Bob Kauffman DP	4	4	4	4	5	6	8	20
85	Dick Van Arsdale	4	4	4	4	5	8	10	
86	Johnny Green	4	4	4	4	5	6	8	50

#	Player	GD 2	VG 3	VgEx 4	EX 5	ExMt 6	NM 7	NmMt 8	MT 9
87	Jerry Sloan	4	4	4	6	8	12	20	80
88	Luther Rackley DP	4	4	4	4	5	6	8	20
89	Shaler Halimon	4	4	4	4	5	6	8	
90	Jimmy Walker	4	4	4	4	5	6	10	40
91	Rudy Tomjanovich RC	4	4	6	8	40	80	150	300
92	Levi Fontaine	4	4	4	4	5	6	10	20
93	Bobby Smith	4	4	4	4	5	6	20	60
94	Bob Arnzen	4	4	4	4	5	6	12	30
95	Wes Unseld DP	4	4	▲6	▲8	▲15	▲30	▲60	▲120
96	Clem Haskins DP	4	4	4	4	5	8	10	20
97	Jim Davis	4	4	4	4	5	6	8	
98	Steve Kuberski	4	4	4	4	5	6	8	100
99	Mike Davis DP	4	4	4	4	5	6	10	40
100	Lew Alcindor	12	30	60	150	300	600	800	2,000
101	Willie McCarter	4	4	4	4	5	6	8	40
102	Charlie Paulk	4	4	4	4	5	6	8	50
103	Lee Winfield	4	4	4	4	5	6	15	75
104	Jim Barnett	4	4	4	4	5	6	8	20
105	Connie Hawkins DP	4	4	4	5	6	15	25	80
106	Archie Clark DP	4	4	4	4	5	6	8	20
107	Dave DeBusschere	4	4	5	6	10	20	40	▲80
108	Stu Lantz DP	4	4	4	4	5	6	8	40
109	Don Smith	4	4	4	4	5	8	15	60
110	Lou Hudson	4	4	4	4	5	8	10	50
111	Leroy Ellis	4	4	4	4	5	8	25	
112	Jack Marin	4	4	4	4	5	6	15	60
113	Matt Guokas	4	4	4	4	5	6	15	80
114	Don Nelson	4	4	6	8	10	15	20	80
115	Jeff Mullins DP	4	4	4	4	5	6	10	40
116	Walt Bellamy	4	4	5	6	8	12	25	60
117	Bob Quick	4	4	4	5	6	8	20	120
118	John Warren	4	4	4	4	5	6	20	60
119	Barry Clemens	4	4	4	4	5	6	12	60
120	Elvin Hayes DP	4	4	6	8	10	12	20	50
121	Gail Goodrich	4	4	4	5	25	40	100	300
122	Ed Manning	4	4	4	4	5	6	8	40
123	Herm Gilliam DP	4	4	4	4	5	6	8	20
124	Dennis Awtrey RC	4	4	4	4	5	8	15	50
125	John Hummer DP	4	4	4	4	5	6	8	20
126	Mike Riordan	4	4	4	▲5	▲10	▲20	▲40	
127	Mel Counts	4	4	4	4	5	6	8	20
128	Bob Weiss DP	4	4	4	4	5	6	8	20
129	Greg Smith DP	4	4	4	4	5	6	8	20
130	Earl Monroe	4	▲5	▲8	▲15	▲30	▲60	▲120	▲300
131	Nate Thurmond DP	4	4	4	5	6	10	15	40
132	Bill Bridges DP	4	4	4	4	5	6	8	30
133	Playoffs G1/Alcindor	4	4	▲6	▲12	25	50	100	300
134	NBA Playoffs G2	4	4	4	4	6	12	20	60
135	NBA Playoffs G3	4	4	4	4	5	8	12	75
136	Playoffs G4/Oscar	4	4	4	4	5	8	20	50
137	NBA Champs/Oscar	4	4	6	8	10	15	25	50
138	Alcind/Hayes/Havl LL	▲5	▲6	▲12	▲25	▲50	▲100	▲200	
139	Alcind/Havl/Hayes LL	▲5	▲6	▲12	▲25	▲50	▲100	▲200	
140	Green/Alcind/Wilt LL	4	▲6	▲10	▲15	▲30	▲60	▲120	▲250
141	Walker/Oscar/Williams LL	4	4	4	4	5	8	10	
142	Wilt/Hayes/Alcind LL	4	▲6	▲10	▲15	▲30	▲60	▲120	▲250
143	Van Lier/Oscar/West LL	4	▲6	▲10	▲15	▲30	▲60	▲120	▲250
144A	NBA Checklist 1-144	4	4	6	8	10	12	15	60
144B	NBA Checklist 1-144	4	4	6	8	10	12	15	60
145	ABA Checklist 145-233	4	4	5	6	▲10	▲15	▲30	60
146	Issel/Brisker/Scott LL	4	4	6	8	10	15	25	60
147	Issel/Barry/Brisker LL	4	4	6	8	10	15	25	80
148	ABA 2pt FG Pct Leaders	4	4	4	4	5	8	12	50
149	Barry/Carrier/Keller LL	4	4	6	8	10	12	20	80
150	ABA Rebound Leaders	4	4	4	4	5	10	15	80
151	ABA Assist Leaders	4	4	5	6	8	15	30	75
152	Larry Brown RC	6	10	20	30	40	60	120	300

#	Player	GD 2	VG 3	VgEx 4	EX 5	ExMt 6	NM 7	NmMt 8	MT 9
153	Bob Bedell	4	4	4	4	5	6	10	50
154	Merv Jackson	4	4	4	4	5	6	10	50
155	Joe Caldwell	4	4	4	5	6	8	12	60
156	Billy Paultz RC	4	4	4	5	6	10	30	80
157	Les Hunter	4	4	4	5	6	8	10	35
158	Charlie Williams	4	4	4	4	5	6	10	40
159	Stew Johnson	4	4	4	4	6	12	25	50
160	Mack Calvin RC	4	4	4	4	8	12	40	150
161	Don Sidle	4	4	4	5	6	8	10	50
162	Mike Barrett	4	4	4	4	5	6	10	65
163	Tom Workman	4	4	4	4	5	6	10	50
164	Joe Hamilton	4	4	4	4	5	6	12	50
165	Zelmo Beaty RC	4	4	4	10	20	60	150	
166	Dan Hester	4	4	4	4	5	6	12	40
167	Bob Verga	4	4	4	4	5	6	12	50
168	Wilbert Jones	4	4	4	4	5	8	20	100
169	Skeeter Swift	4	4	4	4	5	6	12	50
170	Rick Barry RC	▲8	▲15	▲30	▲60	▲150	▲400	600	1,000
171	Billy Keller RC	4	4	4	4	5	8	15	60
172	Ron Franz	4	4	4	4	5	6	10	60
173	Roland Taylor RC	4	4	4	4	5	6	10	60
174	Julian Hammond	4	4	4	4	8	12	30	
175	Steve Jones RC	4	4	4	5	6	10	12	40
176	Gerald Govan	4	4	4	4	5	8	25	
177	Darrell Carrier RC	4	4	4	4	5	8	12	50
178	Ron Boone RC	4	4	4	4	5	10	20	50
179	George Peeples	4	4	4	4	5	6	8	50
180	John Brisker	4	▲5	▲6	▲10	▲20	▲50	▲100	▲200
181	Doug Moe RC	4	4	4	5	6	10	20	60
182	Ollie Taylor	4	4	4	4	5	6	8	40
183	Bob Netolicky RC	4	4	4	4	5	6	12	50
184	Sam Robinson	4	4	4	4	5	6	8	50
185	James Jones	4	4	4	4	5	6	8	40
186	Julius Keye	4	4	4	4	5	6	8	40
187	Wayne Hightower	4	4	▲5	▲8	▲15	▲30	▲60	▲120
188	Warren Armstrong RC	4	4	4	4	6	10	20	50
189	Mike Lewis	4	4	4	4	5	6	10	50
190	Charlie Scott RC	4	4	6	12	150	200	400	700
191	Jim Ard	4	4	4	4	5	6	10	50
192	George Lehmann	4	4	4	4	5	6	10	30
193	Ira Harge	4	4	4	4	5	6	10	40
194	Willie Wise RC	4	4	4	4	5	10	20	80
195	Mel Daniels RC	4	4	6	15	40	80	200	400
196	Larry Cannon	4	4	4	4	5	6	10	60
197	Jim Eakins	4	4	4	4	5	8	15	60
198	Rich Jones	4	4	4	5	6	8	12	60
199	Bill Melchionni RC	4	4	4	4	5	8	10	40
200	Dan Issel RC	▲5	▲6	▲12	▲25	▲50	▲100	▲200	400
201	George Stone	4	4	4	4	5	6	12	75
202	George Thompson	4	4	4	4	5	6	8	
203	Craig Raymond	4	4	4	4	5	8	20	100
204	Freddie Lewis RC	4	4	4	4	5	6	8	50
205	George Carter	4	4	4	4	5	6	10	40
206	Lonnie Wright	4	4	4	4	5	6	8	40
207	Cincy Powell	4	4	4	4	5	6	10	50
208	Larry Miller	4	4	4	5	6	8	12	30
209	Sonny Dove	4	4	4	4	5	6	10	50
210	Byron Beck RC	4	4	4	4	5	6	15	70
211	John Beasley	4	4	4	4	5	6	15	100
212	Lee Davis	4	4	4	4	5	6	8	30
213	Rick Mount RC	4	4	4	6	10	15	40	80
214	Walt Simon	4	4	4	4	5	6	10	30
215	Glen Combs	4	4	4	4	5	6	8	30
216	Neil Johnson	4	4	4	4	5	6	12	
217	Manny Leaks	4	4	4	4	5	6	15	50
218	Chuck Williams	4	4	4	4	5	6	10	50
219	Warren Davis	4	4	4	4	5	6	12	100

	GD 2	VG 3	VgEx 4	EX 5	ExMt 6	NM 7	NmMt 8	MT 9
Donnie Freeman RC	4	4	5	6	8	10	15	80
Randy Mahaffey	4	4	4	4	5	6	8	50
John Barnhill	4	4	4	▲5	▲8	▲20	▲40	▲100
Al Cueto	4	4	4	4	5	6	8	40
Louie Dampier RC	4	4	4	12	25	80	120	500
Roger Brown RC	4	4	5	12	30	60	120	300
Joe DePre	4	4	4	4	5	6	10	30
Ray Scott	4	4	4	4	5	6	12	50
Arvesta Kelly	4	4	4	4	5	6	10	40
Vann Williford	4	4	4	4	5	6	20	
Larry Jones	4	4	4	4	5	8	12	50
Gene Moore	4	4	4	4	5	6	15	40
Ralph Simpson RC	4	4	4	4	5	6	10	
Red Robbins RC	4	4	4	6	10	30	60	200

— Oscar Robertson #1 PSA 9 (MT) sold for $1,219 (eBay; 4/12)

— Pete Maravich #55 PSA 10 (Gem MT) sold for $2,397 (Mile High; 6/10)

— Pete Maravich #55 PSA 10 (Gem MT) sold for $1,937 (eBay; 4/12)

— Walt Frazier #65 PSA 10 (Gem MT) sold for $640 (eBay; 1/13)

— Lew Alcindor #100 PSA 10 (Gem MT) sold for $3,070 (eBay; 4/12)

— Rick Barry #170 PSA 10 (Gem MT) sold for $2,117 (eBay; 4/12)

1971-72 Topps Trios

	GD 2	VG 3	VgEx 4	EX 5	ExMt 6	NM 7	NmMt 8	MT 9
Hudson/Rule/Murphy	5	5	6	10	12	20	60	300
Jones/Wise/Issel SP	5	5	8	12	15	20	60	250
Wesley/White/Dand	5	5	6	10	12	15	50	
Calvin/Brown/Verga SP	5	5	6	10	12	20	40	200
Thurm/Monroe/Hay	5	▲6	▲8	▲15	▲30	▲60	▲120	▲250
Melch/Daniels/Freem SP	5	5	6	10	12	20	40	125
DeBuss/Lanier/Van Ars	5	5	8	12	15	20	60	250
Cald/Dampier/Lewis SP	5	5	8	12	20	30	80	
Greer/Green/Hayes	5	5	8	12	20	40	150	425
Barry/Jones/Keye SP	5	5	8	12	15	25	60	
Walker/May/Clark	5	5	8	10	▲15	▲30	▲60	200
Cannon/Beaty/Scott SP	5	5	6	10	12	15	60	175
Hairston/Ellis/Sloan	5	5	6	10	▲20	▲30	60	150
Jones/Carter/Brisk SP	5	5	8	12	15	20	60	250
Maravich/Kauf/Hav	8	12	20	30	60	150	300	600
ABA Team DP	5	5	6	15	20	40	50	275
ABA Team SP	5	5	8	15	20	40	60	
ABA Team SP	5	5	8	15	20	40	80	
Frazier/Van Arsd/Bing	5	5	8	15	20	25	60	300
Love/Williams/Cowens	5	5	8	12	▲25	▲50	▲120	▲350
West/Reed/Walker	5	8	10	25	30	80	300	
Rober/Unsel/Smith SP	5	▲6	▲10	▲20	▲40	80	200	
Hawk/Mullins/Alcin	5	10	20	40	100	150	300	600
Cunn/Bellamy/Petrie SP	5	5	8	12	15	30	70	225
Cham/Johns/Van L SP	5	10	20	40	100	150	300	
NBA Team QP	5	5	6	10	12	15	30	100

— ABA Team SP #24 A PSA 10 (Gem MT) sold for $1,137 (eBay; 4/07)

— Cannon/Beaty/Scott #16A PSA 10 (Gem MT) sold for $750 (eBay; 12/06)

— Walker/May/Clark #16 PSA 10 (Gem MT) sold for $1,425 (eBay; 3/07)

1972-73 Icee Bear

	VG 3	VgEx 4	EX 5	ExMt 6	NM 7	NmMt 8	MT 9	Gem 9.5/10
Kareem Abdul-Jabbar	12	20	40	80	▲200	400	650	
Dennis Awtrey	4	4	4	4	8	20	50	
Tom Boerwinkle	4	4	8	10	15	20	60	
Austin Carr SP	4	4	5	6	8	15	40	120
Wilt Chamberlain	12	20	40	80	▲200	400		
Archie Clark SP	4	6	8	12	20	40	100	
Dave DeBusschere	4	4	6	8	12	20	40	100
Walt Frazier SP	4	6	8	▲15	▲40	100	▼250	
John Havlicek	5	10	20	40	100	250	400	
Connie Hawkins	4	6	12	25	60	120		
Bob Love	4	4	4	5	▲8	▲15	▲40	▲150

	VG 3	VgEx 4	EX 5	ExMt 6	NM 7	NmMt 8	MT 9	Gem 9.5/10
12 Jerry Lucas	4	5	6	10	25	60	200	
13 Pete Maravich SP	10	20	40	80	150	400	800	
14 Calvin Murphy	4	4	4	5	6	15	40	150
15 Oscar Robertson	▲6	▲10	▲20	▲40	▲80	▲150	▲300	
16 Jerry Sloan	4	4	4	6	12	30	100	
17 Wes Unseld	4	4	6	12	30	80	200	
18 Dick Van Arsdale	4	4	6	12	30	80	200	
19 Jerry West	8	▲15	▲30	▲60	150	▼250	400	
20 Sidney Wicks	4	4	5	8	20	60		

— Pete Maravich #13 PSA 10 (Gem MT) sold for $1,084 (eBay; 4/12)

— Oscar Robertson #15 PSA 10 (Gem MT) sold for $810 (eBay; 4/07)

— Jerry West #19 PSA 10 (Gem MT) sold for $802 (eBay; 7/07)

— Sidney Wicks #20 PSA 10 (Gem MT) sold for $356 (eBay; 11/06)

1972-73 Topps

		VG 3	VgEx 4	EX 5	ExMt 6	NM 7	NmMt 8	MT 9	Gem 9.5/10
1	Wilt Chamberlain	50	100	200	300	500	800		
2	Stan Love	4	4	4	5	6	20	40	
3	Geoff Petrie	4	5	6	8	10	12	25	
4	Curtis Perry RC	4	4	4	5	6	10	25	
5	Pete Maravich	▲20	▲40	▲80	▲150	▲300	▲600		
6	Gus Johnson	4	4	4	5	6	10	20	100
7	Dave Cowens	4	6	8	12	25	40	80	
8	Randy Smith RC	4	5	6	8	10	20	25	225
9	Matt Guokas	4	4	4	5	6	8	15	
10	Spencer Haywood	4	4	5	6	8	12	40	150
11	Jerry Sloan	4	4	4	5	8	20	30	125
12	Dave Sorenson	4	4	4	5	6	8	15	
13	Howie Komives	4	4	4	5	6	8	15	
14	Joe Ellis	4	4	4	5	6	8	15	
15	Jerry Lucas	4	4	5	6	8	25	50	
16	Stu Lantz	4	4	4	5	6	8	15	100
17	Bill Bridges	4	4	4	5	6	8	15	
18	Leroy Ellis	4	4	4	5	6	8	20	
19	Art Williams	4	4	4	5	6	8	15	125
20	Sidney Wicks RC	4	4	5	6	8	15	50	300
21	Wes Unseld	4	4	4	5	6	8	15	50
22	Jim Washington	4	4	4	5	6	8	20	
23	Fred Hilton	4	4	4	5	6	10	50	
24	Curtis Rowe RC	4	4	4	5	6	8	15	120
25	Oscar Robertson	▲8	▲15	▲30	60	150	400	800	
26	Larry Steele RC	4	4	4	5	8	15	30	
27	Charlie Davis	4	4	4	5	6	8	15	60
28	Nate Thurmond	4	4	5	6	8	12	30	
29	Fred Carter	4	4	4	5	6	8	15	80
30	Connie Hawkins	4	4	5	6	10	15	75	
31	Calvin Murphy	4	▲5	▲8	▲15	▲40	▲80	▲200	
32	Phil Jackson RC	40	80	150	250	400	600	800	
33	Lee Winfield	4	4	4	5	6	8	15	
34	Jim Fox	4	4	4	5	6	8	20	100
35	Dave Bing	4	4	5	6	8	12	30	250
36	Gary Gregor	4	4	4	5	6	8	20	
37	Mike Riordan	4	4	4	5	6	8	30	100
38	George Trapp	4	4	5	6	8	12	25	
39	Mike Davis	4	4	4	5	6	8	15	
40	Bob Rule	4	4	4	5	6	8	15	100
41	John Block	4	4	4	5	6	10	20	
42	Bob Dandridge	4	4	4	5	6	8	10	35
43	John Johnson	4	4	4	5	6	8	20	
44	Rick Barry	5	8	10	12	15	40	250	
45	Jo Jo White	4	4	4	6	8	15	50	100
46	Cliff Meely	4	4	5	6	8	12	40	
47	Charlie Scott	4	4	4	5	6	8	25	
48	Johnny Green	4	4	4	5	6	8	25	125
49	Pete Cross	4	4	4	5	6	8	15	
50	Gail Goodrich	4	4	6	8	10	15	50	

#	Player	VG 3	VgEx 4	EX 5	ExMt 6	NM 7	NmMt 8	MT 9	Gem 9.5/10
51	Jim Davis	4	4	4	5	6	8	15	100
52	Dick Barnett	4	4	4	5	6	8	15	100
53	Bob Christian	4	4	4	5	6	8	15	100
54	Jon McGlocklin	4	4	4	5	8	12	30	150
55	Paul Silas	4	4	4	5	6	10	25	100
56	Hal Greer	4	4	4	5	6	10	20	
57	Barry Clemens	4	4	4	5	6	10	25	
58	Nick Jones	4	4	4	5	8	12	30	150
59	Cornell Warner	4	4	4	5	6	8	15	100
60	Walt Frazier	4	4	6	12	30	60	200	
61	Dorie Murrey	4	4	4	5	6	8	15	100
62	Dick Cunningham	4	4	4	5	6	8	20	100
63	Sam Lacey	4	4	4	5	6	8	20	80
64	John Warren	4	4	4	5	6	8	15	100
65	Tom Boerwinkle	4	4	4	5	6	8	15	100
66	Fred Foster	4	4	4	5	6	8	20	
67	Mel Counts	4	4	4	5	6	10	20	80
68	Toby Kimball	4	4	4	5	6	8	15	
69	Dale Schlueter	4	4	4	5	6	8	15	100
70	Jack Marin	4	4	4	5	6	8	15	125
71	Jim Barnett	4	4	4	5	6	8	15	
72	Clem Haskins	4	4	4	5	6	8	15	
73	Earl Monroe	4	5	6	8	10	25	60	
74	Tom Sanders	4	4	4	5	6	10	20	
75	Jerry West	5	8	15	30	80	200	600	
76	Elmore Smith RC	4	4	4	5	6	10	20	200
77	Don Adams	4	4	4	5	6	8	15	80
78	Wally Jones	4	4	4	5	6	8	15	
79	Tom Van Arsdale	4	4	4	5	6	8	15	80
80	Bob Lanier	5	8	10	15	20	30	60	200
81	Len Wilkens	4	4	4	5	8	12	50	
82	Neal Walk	4	4	4	5	6	8	15	
83	Kevin Loughery	4	4	4	5	6	8	15	80
84	Stan McKenzie	4	4	4	5	6	8	15	
85	Jeff Mullins	4	4	4	5	6	8	15	80
86	Otto Moore	4	4	4	5	6	8	20	80
87	John Tresvant	4	4	4	5	6	8	15	
88	Dean Meminger RC	4	4	4	5	8	20	80	
89	Jim McMillian	4	4	4	5	6	8	15	
90	Austin Carr RC	4	4	5	6	8	15	60	
91	Clifford Ray RC	4	4	4	5	6	10	20	
92	Don Nelson	4	4	5	6	8	10	20	
93	Mahdi Abdul-Rahman	4	4	4	5	6	8	15	100
94	Willie Norwood	4	4	4	5	6	8	20	
95	Dick Van Arsdale	4	4	4	5	6	8	20	125
96	Don May	4	4	4	5	6	10	30	
97	Walt Bellamy	4	4	5	6	8	10	50	
98	Garfield Heard RC	4	4	5	6	8	12	50	
99	Dave Wohl	4	4	4	5	6	8	15	
100	Kareem Abdul-Jabbar	▲30	▲60	▲125	250	400	600		
101	Ron Knight	4	4	4	5	8	25	50	
102	Phil Chenier RC	4	4	5	6	8	10	20	
103	Rudy Tomjanovich	4	4	5	6	8	12	15	
104	Flynn Robinson	4	4	4	5	6	8	40	
105	Dave DeBusschere	4	4	5	6	8	12	50	
106	Dennis Layton	4	4	4	5	6	8	20	
107	Bill Hewitt	4	4	4	5	6	10	30	
108	Dick Garrett	4	4	4	5	6	8	20	
109	Walt Wesley	4	4	4	5	6	8	15	
110	John Havlicek	▲6	▲10	▲20	40	80	200	400	800
111	Norm Van Lier	4	4	4	5	6	8	15	
112	Cazzie Russell	4	4	4	5	6	8	20	100
113	Herm Gilliam	4	4	4	5	6	8	15	
114	Greg Smith	4	4	4	5	6	8	25	100
115	Nate Archibald	4	4	5	6	12	50	300	
116	Don Kojis	4	4	4	5	6	8	15	
117	Rick Adelman	4	4	4	5	6	8	20	100
118	Luke Jackson	4	4	4	5	6	8	20	
119	Lamar Green	4	4	4	5	6	8	15	60
120	Archie Clark	4	4	4	5	6	8	25	
121	Happy Hairston	4	4	4	5	6	8	20	
122	Bill Bradley	4	6	8	10	15	25	60	
123	Ron Williams	4	4	4	5	6	8	20	
124	Jimmy Walker	4	4	4	5	6	8	15	
125	Bob Kauffman	4	4	4	5	6	8	30	100
126	Rick Roberson	4	4	4	5	6	8	25	
127	Howard Porter RC	4	4	4	5	6	8	20	
128	Mike Newlin RC	4	4	4	5	6	8	20	125
129	Willis Reed	4	5	6	8	15	30	100	
130	Lou Hudson	4	4	4	5	6	8	20	
131	Don Chaney	4	4	4	5	8	10	25	
132	Dave Stallworth	4	4	4	5	6	8	15	
133	Charlie Yelverton	4	4	4	5	6	8	15	
134	Ken Durrett	4	6	10	15	30	200	400	
135	John Brisker	4	4	4	5	6	8	15	
136	Dick Snyder	4	4	4	5	6	8	50	
137	Jim McDaniels	4	4	4	5	6	8	50	
138	Clyde Lee	4	4	4	5	6	8	70	
139	Dennis Awtrey	4	4	4	5	6	8	40	
140	Keith Erickson	4	4	4	5	6	10	60	
141	Bob Weiss	4	4	4	5	8	15	120	
142	Butch Beard RC	4	4	4	5	6	10	75	
143	Terry Dischinger	4	4	4	8	20	50	100	
144	Pat Riley	5	8	10	15	25	40	100	
145	Lucius Allen	4	4	4	5	6	8	40	
146	John Mengelt RC	4	4	4	5	8	25	150	
147	John Hummer	4	4	4	5	6	8	40	
148	Bob Love	4	5	6	8	10	15	75	
149	Bobby Smith	4	4	4	5	8	15	100	
150	Elvin Hayes	4	▲5	▲10	▲20	▲40	▲80	▲200	
151	Nate Williams	4	4	4	5	6	8	80	
152	Chet Walker	4	4	4	5	10	25	100	
153	Steve Kuberski	4	4	4	5	6	8	20	
154	Playoffs G1/Monroe	4	4	4	5	8	20		
155	NBA Playoffs G2	4	4	4	5	10	20	125	
156	NBA Playoffs G3	4	4	4	6	12	25	80	
157	NBA Playoffs G4	4	4	4	5	6	10	60	
158	Playoffs G5/J.West	4	4	5	6	20	60	225	
159	Champs Lakers/Wilt	4	5	6	8	12	20	80	
160	NBA Checklist 1-176	4	5	6	10	12	40	175	
161	John Havlicek AS	4	5	6	8	10	30	75	
162	Spencer Haywood AS	4	4	4	5	6	8	50	
163	Kareem Abdul-Jabbar AS	▲10	▲20	▲40	▲80	▲150	▲300		
164	Jerry West AS	▲6	▲12	▲25	▲50	▲100	▲200	▲500	
165	Walt Frazier AS	4	4	5	6	8	15	60	
166	Bob Love AS	4	4	4	5	6	30	100	
167	Billy Cunningham AS	4	4	5	6	8	15	30	
168	Wilt Chamberlain AS	▲8	▲15	▲30	▲60	▲120	▲250	▲500	
169	Nate Archibald AS	4	4	5	6	8	20	50	
170	Archie Clark AS	4	4	5	6	6	8	70	
171	Jabbar/Havl/Arch LL	4	6	8	10	15	50	200	
172	Jabbar/Arch/Havl LL	4	5	6	10	15	50	200	
173	Wilt/Jabbar/Bell LL	▲5	▲8	▲15	▲30	▲60	▲120	▲400	
174	Marin/Murphy/Goodr LL	4	4	4	5	6	8	50	
175	Wilt/Jabbar/Unseld LL	5	8	10	15	30	80	300	
176	Wilkens/West/Arch LL	4	4	6	8	10	20	225	
177	Roland Taylor	4	4	4	5	6	8	20	
178	Art Becker	4	4	4	5	6	10	30	
179	Mack Calvin	4	4	4	5	6	8	30	
180	Artis Gilmore RC	20	40	80	120	200	400		
181	Collis Jones	4	4	4	5	6	12	125	
182	John Roche RC	4	4	4	5	6	8	100	
183	George McGinnis RC	▲12	▲25	▲50	▲100	▲200	500	1,000	
184	Johnny Neumann	4	4	4	5	6	8	15	

		VG 3	VgEx 4	EX 5	ExMt 6	NM 7	NmMt 8	MT 9	Gem 9.5/10
185	Willie Wise	4	4	4	5	6	8	25	
186	Bernie Williams	4	4	4	5	6	8	40	
187	Byron Beck	4	4	4	5	6	8	15	
188	Larry Miller	4	4	4	5	6	8	40	
189	Cincy Powell	4	4	4	5	6	8	60	
190	Donnie Freeman	4	4	4	5	6	12	60	
191	John Baum	4	4	4	5	6	12	20	
192	Billy Keller	4	4	4	5	6	8	15	125
193	Wilbert Jones	4	4	4	5	6	8	75	
194	Glen Combs	4	4	4	5	6	8	15	
195	Julius Erving RC	600	700	800	1,500	4,000	8,000	20,000	
196	Al Smith	4	4	4	5	6	8	50	
197	George Carter	4	4	4	5	6	8	15	
198	Louie Dampier	4	4	4	6	8	10	20	
199	Rich Jones	4	4	4	5	6	8	15	
200	Mel Daniels	4	4	4	5	8	12	30	
201	Gene Moore	4	4	4	5	6	8	15	100
202	Randy Denton	4	4	4	5	6	8	50	
203	Larry Jones	4	4	4	5	6	8	15	
204	Jim Ligon	4	4	4	5	10	50	150	
205	Warren Jabali	4	4	4	5	6	8	15	
206	Joe Caldwell	4	4	4	6	8	10	25	100
207	Darrell Carrier	4	4	4	5	6	8	15	
208	Gene Kennedy	4	4	4	5	6	8	60	
209	Ollie Taylor	4	4	4	5	6	8	20	
210	Roger Brown	4	4	4	5	6	8	40	
211	George Lehmann	4	4	4	5	8	12	30	
212	Red Robbins	4	4	4	5	6	8	30	
213	Jim Eakins	4	4	4	5	8	15	30	
214	Willie Long	4	4	4	5	6	8	15	
215	Billy Cunningham	4	4	4	6	8	15	80	
216	Steve Jones	4	4	4	5	6	8	15	
217	Les Hunter	4	4	4	5	6	8	50	
218	Billy Paultz	4	4	4	5	6	8	30	
219	Freddie Lewis	4	4	4	6	10	15	30	125
220	Zelmo Beaty	4	4	4	5	6	10	25	
221	George Thompson	4	4	4	5	6	8	15	
222	Neil Johnson	4	4	4	5	6	8	30	80
223	Dave Robisch RC	4	4	4	5	6	8	50	
224	Walt Simon	4	4	4	5	6	8	30	125
225	Bill Melchionni	4	4	4	5	6	8	30	
226	Wendell Ladner RC	4	4	4	6	10	60		
227	Joe Hamilton	4	4	4	5	6	10	30	
228	Bob Netolicky	4	4	4	5	6	8	15	
229	James Jones	4	4	4	5	6	8	15	
230	Dan Issel	4	5	8	10	12	20	60	
231	Charlie Williams	4	4	4	5	6	8	25	
232	Willie Sojourner	4	4	4	5	6	8	15	
233	Merv Jackson	4	4	4	5	8	12	30	
234	Mike Lewis	4	4	4	5	6	8	15	125
235	Ralph Simpson	4	4	4	5	6	8	15	125
236	Darnell Hillman	4	4	5	8	10	12	40	
237	Rick Mount	4	4	4	5	10	50		
238	Gerald Govan	4	4	4	5	6	10	40	
239	Ron Boone	4	4	5	8	10	30		
240	Tom Washington	4	4	4	5	6	8	15	
241	ABA Playoffs G1	4	4	4	5	6	8	20	100
242	Playoffs G2/Barry	4	4	4	6	8	15	50	150
243	Playoffs G3/McGinnis	4	4	4	6	8	10	160	
244	Playoffs G4/Barry	4	4	4	6	8	10	30	
245	ABA Playoffs G5	4	4	4	6	6	10	25	
246	ABA Playoffs G6	4	4	4	6	6	8	20	
247	ABA Champs: Pacers	4	4	4	6	6	8	30	
248	ABA Checklist 177-264	4	5	10	12	20	40	200	
249	Dan Issel AS	4	4	4	6	10	20	40	
250	Rick Barry AS	4	4	4	6	10	25	100	
251	Artis Gilmore AS	4	4	4	6	10	25	80	

		VG 3	VgEx 4	EX 5	ExMt 6	NM 7	NmMt 8	MT 9	Gem 9.5/10
252	Donnie Freeman AS	4	4	4	5	6	10	40	150
253	Bill Melchionni AS	4	4	4	5	6	10	25	
254	Willie Wise AS	4	4	4	5	8	15	60	
255	Julius Erving AS	▲25	▲50	100	150	300	700	1,500	
256	Zelmo Beaty AS	4	4	4	5	6	10	25	
257	Ralph Simpson AS	4	4	4	5	6	10	50	
258	Charlie Scott AS	4	4	4	5	6	10	60	150
259	Scott/Barry/Issel LL	4	4	4	6	8	12	50	
260	Gilmore/Wash/Jones LL	4	4	4	6	8	12	100	
261	ABA 3pt FG Pct.	4	4	4	5	6	10	100	
262	Barry/Calvin/Jones LL	4	4	4	6	8	15	150	
263	Gilmore/Erving/Dan LL	▲6	▲10	▲20	▲40	▲80	▲150	▲300	
264	Melch/Brown/Damp LL!	4	4	4	6	10	60	150	

— Kareem Abdul-Jabbar #100 PSA 10 (Gem MT) sold for $2,040 (eBay; 1/11)
— Artis Gilmore #180 PSA 10 (Gem MT) sold for $618 (Goodwin; 11/12)
— Julius Erving #195 BGS 9.5 (Gem MT) sold for $3,057 (eBay; 8/12)
— Julius Erving #195 BGS 9.5 (Gem MT) sold for $2,638 (eBay; 1/13)

1973-74 Topps

		GD 2	VG 3	VgEx 4	EX 5	ExMt 6	NM 7	NmMt 8	MT 9
	COM. NBA CARD (1-176)	4	4	4	4	4	4	5	15
1	Nate Archibald	4	4	5	6	8	10	100	
4	Jim McMillian	4	4	4	5	6	8	20	
5	Nate Thurmond	4	4	4	5	8	15	30	
10	Walt Frazier	4	4	4	6	▲12	▲30	▲60	200
13	Calvin Murphy	4	4	4	5	6	8	120	
20	John Havlicek	4	4	5	8	10	20	80	
21	Pat Riley	4	4	4	8	10	12	20	50
30	Dave DeBusschere	4	4	4	5	6	15	30	
34	Leroy Ellis	4	4	4	5	8	15	50	
40	Dave Cowens	4	4	4	6	8	10	20	100
41	Cazzie Russell	4	4	4	5	6	10	20	
43	Connie Hawkins	4	4	4	5	6	10	50	
45	Chet Walker	4	4	4	5	6	10	25	
50	Kareem Abdul-Jabbar	▲5	▲8	▲15	▲30	▲80	150	300	600
53	Kevin Porter RC	4	4	4	5	▲10	▲20	▲50	
57	Don Chaney	4	4	4	5	6	12	40	
60	Bob Love	4	4	4	5	6	12	25	
64	Western Semis/Wilt	4	4	4	5	6	12	30	80
65	NBA Western Semis	4	4	4	5	6	8	30	
68	Knicks Champs/Frazier	4	4	4	5	6	8	25	
70	Oscar Robertson	▲5	▲6	▲12	▲25	▲50	▲80	▲150	300
71	Phil Jackson	4	4	5	8	10	20	40	120
80	Wilt Chamberlain	▲6	▲12	▲25	▲50	▲100	150	300	600
82	Bill Bradley	4	4	4	6	8	10	15	40
86	Dick Snyder	4	4	4	4	4	4	5	50
90	Rick Barry	4	4	▲5	▲6	▲12	▲30	▲60	120
95	Elvin Hayes	4	4	4	6	8	20	80	
100	Jerry West	▲5	▲8	▲15	▲30	▲60	▲100	▲200	▲400
103	Fred Brown RC	4	4	4	4	6	20	100	
105	Willis Reed	4	4	4	5	8	12	30	
110	Bob Lanier	4	4	5	8	15	30	60	120
119	Steve Bracey	4	4	4	4	4	4	5	20
120	Spencer Haywood	4	4	4	4	4	6	8	30
121	NBA Checklist 1-176	4	4	4	6	8	10	15	30
122	Jack Marin	4	4	4	4	4	6	8	20
125	Jerry Lucas	4	4	4	4	4	8	10	20
126	Paul Westphal RC	4	4	6	8	12	15	50	150
130	Pete Maravich	5	8	12	▲25	▲50	▲100	▲150	▲300
131	Don May	4	4	4	4	4	4	5	20
134	Dick Cunningham	4	4	4	4	4	8	10	40
135	Bob McAdoo RC	5	8	12	30	60	150	350	600
142	Earl Monroe	4	4	4	5	8	12	50	
143	Clyde Lee	4	4	4	4	4	4	5	60
144	Rick Roberson	4	4	4	4	4	4	5	40
145	Rudy Tomjanovich	4	4	4	4	6	8	12	25

#	Player	GD 2	VG 3	VgEx 4	EX 5	ExMt 6	NM 7	NmMt 8	MT 9
147	Art Williams	4	4	4	4	4	4	5	20
153	Arch/Jabbar/Hayw LL	4	4	4	8	10	25	80	300
154	Arch/Jabbar/Hayw LL	4	4	4	8	10	25	80	300
155	Wilt/Guokas/Jabbar LL	4	4	5	8	10	25	80	300
156	Barry/Murphy/Newlin LL	4	4	4	4	4	6	8	50
157	Wilt/Thurm/Cowens LL	4	4	4	4	6	12	50	200
158	Arch/Wilkens/Bing LL	4	4	4	4	4	6	8	40
165	Len Wilkens	4	4	4	4	6	8	12	20
168	Jo Jo White	4	4	4	4	▲5	▲10	▲20	▲40
170	Dave Bing	4	4	4	4	▲6	▲12	▲25	▲50
175	Geoff Petrie	4	4	4	4	4	6	8	20
176	Wes Unseld	4	4	4	4	4	8	10	40
190	Ralph Simpson AS2	4	4	4	4	4	6	▲15	50
200	Billy Cunningham	4	4	4	4	▲6	▲10	▲15	▲40
201	John Roche	4	4	4	4	4	6	8	20
202	ABA Western Semis	4	4	4	4	4	6	8	20
203	ABA Western Semis	4	4	4	4	4	6	8	20
204	ABA Eastern Semis	4	4	4	4	4	6	8	20
205	ABA Eastern Semis	4	4	4	4	4	6	8	30
206	ABA Western Finals	4	4	4	4	4	6	8	20
207	Eastern Finals/Gilmore	4	4	4	4	4	6	8	20
208	ABA Championship	4	4	4	4	4	6	8	20
210	Dan Issel	4	4	4	4	6	8	▲15	▲40
222	Don Buse RC	4	4	4	4	4	6	8	▲20
234	Erving/McG/Issel LL	4	4	4	▲5	▲8	▲12	▲30	▲80
240	Julius Erving	10	12	30	50	100	▼150	▼300	600
242	ABA Checklist 177-264	4	4	4	6	8	12	20	40
243	Johnny Neumann	4	4	4	4	4	6	8	20
250	Artis Gilmore	4	4	4	▲5	▲8	▲15	▲30	▲60
263	Les Hunter	4	4	4	4	4	6	▲10	▲30
264	Billy Keller	4	4	4	4	▲6	▲10	▲20	▲50

1974-75 Topps

#	Player	GD 2	VG 3	VgEx 4	EX 5	ExMt 6	NM 7	NmMt 8	MT 9
	COM. NBA CARD (1-176)	4	4	4	4	4	4	5	15
1	Kareem Abdul-Jabbar	10	20	40	80	200	300	500	1,000
6	Jim Chones	4	4	4	4	4	6	8	20
10	Pete Maravich	▲5	▲6	▲10	▲20	▲40	▲80	▲200	▲500
25	Earl Monroe	4	4	4	4	4	6	8	20
27	Jo Jo White	4	4	4	4	4	6	8	25
28	Rudy Tomjanovich	4	4	4	4	5	8	12	20
30	Elvin Hayes	4	4	4	4	5	8	15	40
31	Pat Riley	4	4	4	4	5	8	12	25
39	Bill Walton RC	8	▲15	▲40	▲80	▲150	▲250	500	2,500
50	Rick Barry	4	4	4	4	5	8	15	100
51	Jerry Sloan	4	4	4	4	4	6	15	30
55	Oscar Robertson	4	4	4	4	8	12	30	80
64	Paul Westphal	4	4	4	4	4	6	8	25
70	Spencer Haywood	4	4	4	4	4	6	10	60
80	Bob McAdoo	4	4	4	4	5	8	15	30
81	Hawks TL/Maravich/Bell	4	4	4	4	4	6	8	40
82	Celtics TL/Havlicek	4	4	4	4	4	8	12	40
83	Buffalo Braves TL	4	4	4	4	4	6	8	20
84	Bulls TL/Love/Walker	4	4	4	4	4	6	8	20
87	Warriors TL/Barry	4	4	4	4	4	6	8	40
91	Bucks TL/Jabbar/Oscar	4	4	▲6	▲12	▲25	▲50	▲100	▲200
93	Knicks TL/Fraz/Brad/DeB	4	4	▲6	▲12	▲25	▲50	▲100	▲200
100	John Havlicek	4	4	4	5	8	12	40	450
105	Nate Thurmond	4	4	4	4	4	6	8	50
113	Bill Bradley	4	4	4	4	5	8	15	40
120	Gail Goodrich	4	4	4	4	4	6	10	20
123	Jeff Mullins	4	4	4	4	4	6	8	40
129	Doug Collins RC	4	4	4	6	8	15	30	60
131	Bob Lanier	4	4	4	4	4	6	10	80
132	Phil Jackson	4	4	4	6	8	15	25	50
135	Ernie DiGregorio RC	4	4	4	4	5	10	15	30
141	NBA Checklist 1-176	4	4	4	4	6	10	15	30

#	Player	GD 2	VG 3	VgEx 4	EX 5	ExMt 6	NM 7	NmMt 8	MT 9
144	McAd/Jabbar/Marav LL	4	4	▲10	▲20	▲40	▲80	▲150	▲300
145	McAd/Marav/Jabbar LL	4	▲5	▲10	▲20	▲40	▲80	▲150	300
146	McAd/Jabbar/Tomjan LL	4	4	▲6	▲12	▲25	▲50	▲100	▲200
148	Hayes/Cowens/McAd LL	4	4	4	4	4	6	10	20
150	Walt Frazier	4	4	4	4	4	8	20	60
155	Dave Cowens	4	4	4	4	6	8	15	150
170	Nate Archibald	4	4	4	4	4	6	8	10
175	Sidney Wicks	4	4	4	4	4	6	8	30
176	Jerry West	5	8	12	20	40	80	200	400
178	George Carter	4	4	4	4	4	6	8	25
180	Artis Gilmore	4	4	4	4	4	6	10	40
186	James Silas RC	4	4	4	4	4	6	8	30
187	Caldwell Jones RC	4	4	4	4	4	6	8	30
190	Dan Issel	4	4	4	4	5	8	10	
196	George Gervin RC	4	10	25	60	120	300	800	
200	Julius Erving	▲10	▲20	▲40	▲80	▲120	▲250	▲500	800
203	ABA Checklist 177-264	4	4	4	4	6	10	15	
207	Erving/McG/Issel LL	4	4	4	4	6	10	20	60
220	George McGinnis	4	4	4	4	▲6	▲12	▲30	▲60
224	Colonels TL/Issel	4	4	4	4	4	6	8	30
226	Nets TL/Erving	4	4	▲5	▲6	▲10	▲12	▲25	▲50
227	Spurs TL/Gervin	4	4	4	4	4	8	12	40
248	ABA Div. Finals	4	4	4	4	6	10	12	
249	ABA Championships/Dr.J.	4	4	4	▲6	▲12	▲20	40	80
250	Wilt Chamberlain CO	▲8	▲15	▲30	▲60	▲100	▲150	▲300	▲600
257	George Karl RC	4	4	4	5	8	15	25	50

1975-76 Topps

#	Player	GD 2	VG 3	VgEx 4	EX 5	ExMt 6	NM 7	NmMt 8	MT 9
	COM. NBA CARD (1-220)	4	4	4	4	4	4	5	15
1	McAd/Barry/Jabbar LL	4	4	▲5	6	▲12	▲25	▲60	▲120
2	Nelson/Beard/Tomj LL	4	4	4	4	4	6	8	40
3	Barry/Murphy/Bradley LL	4	4	4	4	6	8	10	30
4	Unseld/Cowens/Lacey LL	4	4	4	4	4	6	8	30
7	Tom Van Arsdale	4	4	4	4	4	6	8	30
9	Jerry Sloan	4	4	4	4	4	6	8	30
10	Bob McAdoo	4	4	4	4	6	8	10	60
20	Billy Cunningham	4	4	4	4	4	6	8	30
30	Bob Lanier	4	4	4	4	6	8	12	50
34	Cazzie Russell	4	4	4	4	4	6	8	25
37	Bill Bradley	4	4	4	4	6	12	15	50
38	Fred Carter	4	4	4	4	4	6	8	20
42	Rowland Garrett	4	4	4	4	4	4	5	25
50	Keith/Jamaal Wilkes RC	6	10	20	40	80	150	300	600
55	Walt Frazier	4	4	5	6	12	15	40	120
57	Nate Hawthorne	4	4	4	4	4	4	5	25
60	Elvin Hayes	4	4	4	4	4	6	12	30
61	Checklist 1-110	4	4	4	4	6	8	12	
63	Randy Smith	4	4	4	4	4	6	8	60
65	Charlie Scott	4	4	4	4	8	20	50	200
67	Rick Adelman	4	4	4	4	4	6	8	20
70	Rudy Tomjanovich	4	4	4	4	4	6	10	20
71	Pat Riley	4	4	4	4	6	8	10	20
73	Earl Monroe	4	4	4	4	4	6	12	30
74	Allan Bristow RC	4	4	4	4	4	6	8	20
75	Pete Maravich DP	4	▲6	▲8	▲15	▲30	▲60	▲120	▲300
77	Bill Walton	4	4	6	8	12	20	50	150
80	John Havlicek	4	4	▲10	▲15	▲30	▲60	▲100	▲250
85	Nate Thurmond	4	4	4	4	4	6	8	40
90	Kareem Abdul-Jabbar	▲8	▲15	▲30	▲60	▲120	▲300	▲600	▲2,000
97	Mike Bantom	4	4	4	4	4	4	5	40
99	Kevin Stacom RC	4	4	4	4	4	6	8	25
100	Rick Barry	4	4	4	4	6	8	10	30
105	Austin Carr	4	4	4	4	4	6	8	25
110	Gail Goodrich	4	4	4	4	6	8	20	80
111	Phil Jackson	4	4	4	▲5	▲6	▲12	▲25	▲80
115	Wes Unseld	4	4	4	4	4	6	8	30
126	Kareem Abdul-Jabbar TL	4	4	4	4	6	8	12	40

#	Player	GD 2	VG 3	VgEx 4	EX 5	ExMt 6	NM 7	NmMt 8	MT 9
27	Pete Maravich TL	4	4	4	4	6	10	25	80
34	John Drew RC	4	4	4	4	4	8	15	60
35	Jo Jo White	4	4	4	4	4	8	15	60
43	Brian Winters RC	4	4	4	4	4	6	8	20
51	Leonard Robinson RC	4	4	4	4	4	8	15	60
56	Campy Russell RC	4	4	4	4	6	10	20	80
70	Dave Cowens	4	4	4	▲6	▲10	▲30	▲80	▲300
77	Zelmo Beaty	4	4	4	4	4	6	8	25
81	Checklist 111-220 DP	4	4	4	4	4	8	12	40
85	Connie Hawkins DP	4	4	4	4	4	6	8	30
90	Spencer Haywood	4	4	4	4	4	6	8	30
93	Atlanta Hawks	4	4	4	4	4	6	8	20
104	Celtics Team CL	4	4	4	4	4	6	8	20
106	Bulls Team CL	4	4	4	4	6	8	10	25
113	Milwaukee Bucks	4	4	4	4	4	6	8	30
115	New York Knicks	4	4	4	4	4	6	8	30
119	Sonics Team/B.Russell	4	4	4	4	6	10	20	60
121	McGin/Erving/Boone LL	4	4	4	4	4	6	10	30
122	Jones/Gilmore/Malone LL	4	4	4	4	6	10	15	30
125	ABA Rebounds Leaders	4	4	4	4	4	6	8	30
133	George Gervin	4	▲5	▲6	8	▲20	▲40	▲100	▲250
137	Kevin Joyce RC	4	4	4	4	4	6	8	40
140	Artis Gilmore	4	▲5	▲6	▲8	▲15	▲30	▲60	▲150
144	Moses Malone RC	10	15	30	60	120	▼200	▼600	1,200
147	Checklist 221-330	4	4	4	4	4	8	15	25
150	Dan Issel	4	4	4	4	5	8	10	50
152	Julius Erving TL	4	4	5	6	10	15	20	40
153	Fly Williams RC	4	4	4	4	4	6	8	20
155	Red Robbins	4	4	4	4	4	6	8	25
158	Bobby Jones RC	4	▲5	▲6	▲12	▲25	▲50	▲120	300
160	Julius Erving	8	15	30	50	100	200	300	600
161	Billy Shepherd	4	4	4	4	4	6	8	20
162	Maurice Lucas RC	4	4	4	4	6	8	10	40
163	George Karl	4	4	4	4	6	8	10	20
165	Artis Gilmore PO	4	4	4	4	4	6	8	20
171	Denver Nuggets	4	4	4	4	4	6	8	50
174	Memphis Sounds	4	4	4	4	4	6	8	20
178	San Diego Sails	4	4	4	4	4	6	8	40

Pete Maravich #75 PSA 10 (Gem MT) sold for $1,732 (Memory Lane; 7/12)

Moses Malone #254 PSA 10 (Gem MT) sold for $1,540 (eBay; 4/12)

Maurice Lucas #302 PSA 10 (Gem MT) sold for $248 (eBay; 1/13)

1976-77 Topps

Player	VG 3	VgEx 4	EX 5	ExMt 6	NM 7	NmMt 8	MT 9	Gem 9.5/10
COMMON CARD (1-144)	4	4	4	4	5	8	20	
Julius Erving	12	20	40	80	200	400	800	
Paul Silas	4	4	4	4	5	8	25	
Keith Erickson	4	4	4	4	6	25	60	
Wes Unseld	4	4	4	5	6	8	60	200
Jim McMillian	4	4	4	4	5	8	60	
Bob Lanier	4	4	4	5	6	12	30	100
Junior Bridgeman RC	4	4	4	4	5	8	30	
Billy Keller	4	4	4	4	6	10	60	200
Nate Archibald	4	4	▲6	▲12	▲25	▲50	▲150	
Ralph Simpson	4	4	4	4	5	8	25	
Campy Russell	4	4	4	4	8	50	80	
Charlie Scott	4	4	4	4	6	10	60	
Artis Gilmore	4	4	4	5	8	15	80	
Dick Van Arsdale	4	4	4	4	5	8	50	
Chris Ford	4	4	4	4	6	10	25	
Dave Cowens	4	▲6	▲8	▲15	▲30	▲60	▲150	
Lucius Allen	4	4	4	6	8	12	60	
Henry Bibby	4	4	4	4	5	8	80	
Doug Collins	4	4	4	6	10	12	80	
Garfield Heard	4	4	4	4	5	8	30	
Randy Smith	4	4	4	4	5	8	25	
Dave Twardzik	4	4	4	4	5	8	25	
Bill Bradley	4	4	6	8	12	15	25	100

#	Player	VG 3	VgEx 4	EX 5	ExMt 6	NM 7	NmMt 8	MT 9	Gem 9.5/10
44	Calvin Murphy	4	4	4	4	6	10	25	175
46	Brian Winters	4	4	4	4	5	8	50	
48	Checklist 1-144	5	8	12	15	20	25	80	
49	Bird Averitt	4	4	4	4	5	8	40	
50	Rick Barry	4	4	4	4	8	12	20	80
53	Austin Carr	4	4	4	4	5	8	80	
56	Mike Riordan	4	4	4	4	5	8	25	
57	Bill Walton	4	▲6	▲12	▲25	▲50	▲80	▲200	
58	Eric Money RC	4	4	4	4	5	8	30	
60	Pete Maravich	6	10	▲20	▲40	▲80	▲150	▲300	600
61	John Shumate RC	4	4	4	5	8	12	30	200
64	Walt Frazier	4	▲6	▲8	▲15	▲30	▲80	200	
65	Elmore Smith	4	4	4	4	6	8	15	80
66	Rudy Tomjanovich	4	4	4	4	6	12	25	
67	Sam Lacey	4	4	4	4	6	10	30	125
68	George Gervin	6	8	▲15	▲30	▲60	150	▲400	
69	Gus Williams RC	4	5	8	▲15	▲40	▲80		
70	George McGinnis	4	4	4	4	5	8	30	
71	Len Elmore	4	4	4	4	5	8	25	
75	Alvan Adams RC	4	4	4	▲6	▲12	▲25	▲60	
76	Dave Bing	4	4	4	5	6	10	30	225
77	Phil Jackson	5	6	▲10	▲20	▲50	▲100	▲600	
82	Ernie DiGregorio	4	▲6	▲10	▲20	▲40	▲80	▲250	
90	John Havlicek	5	6	▲15	▲30	▲60	▲150		
91	Kevin Kunnert	4	4	4	4	5	10	50	
92	Jimmy Walker	4	4	4	6	10	20		
93	Billy Cunningham	4	4	4	6	8	20	80	
94	Dan Issel	5	6	8	15	25	50	150	500
98	Earl Monroe	▲5	▲6	▲8	▲15	▲25	▲50	▲200	
100	Kareem Abdul-Jabbar	▲20	▲40	▲80	▲150	▲300	▲600	▲1,500	
101	Moses Malone	▲6	▲8	▲15	▲30	▲60	▲120	▲300	
106	Otto Moore	4	4	4	4	5	8	25	60
107	Maurice Lucas	4	4	4	4	5	8	25	60
108	Norm Van Lier	4	4	4	4	5	8	25	
109	Clifford Ray	4	4	4	4	5	8	40	
110	David Thompson RC	8	▲15	▲30	▲60	▲120	250	▲700	
114	Bobby Smith	4	4	4	4	5	8	25	150
115	Jo Jo White	4	4	4	4	5	8	40	
118	Curtis Rowe	4	4	4	4	5	8	25	
120	Elvin Hayes	4	▲5	▲6	▲10	▲20	▲50	▲120	
123	Jerry Sloan	4	4	▲6	▲8	▲15	▲40	▲80	▲300
124	Billy Knight	4	4	4	4	5	10	80	
126	K. Abdul-Jabbar AS	6	10	20	▲50	▲100	200	500	
127	Julius Erving AS	6	10	20	40	80	200	500	
128	George McGinnis AS	4	4	4	6	12	30	80	
130	Pete Maravich AS	6	10	20	40	80	200	500	
131	Dave Cowens AS	4	▲5	▲6	▲10	▲20	▲40	▲120	
132	Rick Barry AS	4	4	6	▲20	▲50	▲150	300	
133	Elvin Hayes AS	4	4	4	5	6	10	40	200
134	James Silas AS	4	4	4	4	5	8	30	
139	Mike Newlin	4	4	4	4	5	8	80	
140	Bob McAdoo	4	▲5	▲6	▲10	▲20	▲50	80	
141	Mike Gale	4	4	4	4	5	8	25	
142	Scott Wedman	4	4	4	4	5	8	30	125
143	Lloyd Free RC	▲6	▲10	▲20	▲50	▲80	200	400	
144	Bobby Jones	4	4	4	6	10	12	80	

— David Thompson #110 PSA 10 (Gem MT) sold for $404 (eBay; 12/12)

1977-78 Topps

#	Player	VG 3	VgEx 4	EX 5	ExMt 6	NM 7	NmMt 8	MT 9	Gem 9.5/10
	COMMON CARD (1-132)	4	4	4	4	4	5	10	
1	Kareem Abdul-Jabbar	8	15	30	60	120	300	600	
6	Earl Monroe	4	4	4	4	6	8	15	40
7	Leonard Gray	4	4	4	4	4	5	15	
9	Jim Brewer	4	4	4	4	4	5	15	
10	Paul Westphal	4	4	4	4	6	10	15	30
11	Bob Gross RC	4	4	4	4	4	5	15	
15	Rudy Tomjanovich	4	4	4	4	6	8	12	

#	Player	VG 3	VgEx 4	EX 5	ExMt 6	NM 7	NmMt 8	MT 9	Gem 9.5/10
16	Kevin Porter	4	4	4	4	4	5	20	
18	Lloyd Free	4	4	4	4	8	15	40	
20	Pete Maravich	4	6	15	30	80	200		
23	Kevin Grevey RC	4	4	4	4	6	8	12	
28	Larry Kenon	4	4	4	4	4	5	15	
29	Checklist 1-132	4	4	4	4	6	8	15	
33	Keith/Jamaal Wilkes	4	4	4	4	4	5	15	
35	Jo Jo White	4	4	4	4	4	5	15	
36	Scott May RC	4	4	4	4	6	8	25	
40	Elvin Hayes	4	4	4	4	6	8	15	
41	Dan Issel	4	4	4	4	6	10	20	
42	Ricky Sobers	4	4	4	4	4	5	12	
43	Don Ford	4	4	4	4	4	5	12	
45	Bob McAdoo	4	4	4	4	6	8	20	
49	Sam Lacey	4	4	4	4	4	5	12	
50	George McGinnis	4	4	4	4	4	5	12	30
56	Adrian Dantley RC	4	4	6	12	30	100		
57	Jim Chones	4	4	4	4	4	5	20	
58	John Lucas RC	4	4	4	4	6	8	20	
59	Cazzie Russell	4	4	4	4	4	8	12	
60	David Thompson	4	4	4	4	6	20	50	
61	Bob Lanier	4	4	4	4	6	8	15	
65	Doug Collins	4	4	4	4	6	8	12	
66	Tom McMillen RC	4	4	4	4	6	8	12	
68	Mike Bantom	4	4	4	4	4	5	12	
70	John Havlicek	4	4	6	10	15	25	60	
71	Marvin Webster RC	4	4	4	4	4	5	12	
73	George Gervin	4	4	4	4	8	12	20	
75	Wes Unseld	4	4	4	4	6	8	30	
78	Richard Washington RC	4	4	4	4	4	5	50	
84	Kevin Kunnert	4	4	4	4	4	5	12	
85	Lou Hudson	4	4	4	4	4	5	12	
87	Lucius Allen	4	4	4	4	4	5	30	
88	Spencer Haywood	4	4	4	4	6	8	20	
93	Tom Henderson	4	4	4	4	4	5	15	
100	Julius Erving	6	10	20	40	100	250	700	1,000
103	Billy Paultz	4	4	4	4	5	10	25	
105	Calvin Murphy	4	4	4	4	6	8	20	
107	Jim McMillian	4	4	4	4	4	5	12	20
111	Robert Parish RC	8	10	20	40	80	200	450	
113	Bruce Seals	4	4	4	4	8	10	20	
116	Steve Mix	4	4	4	4	4	5	12	25
120	Bill Walton	4	4	6	12	25	60	150	400
124	Moses Malone	4	4	4	6	▲10	▲20	▲50	
127	Nate Archibald	4	4	4	4	6	8	15	30
128	Mitch Kupchak RC	4	4	4	4	6	8	12	
129	Walt Frazier	4	4	▲6	▲12	▲25	▲50		
130	Rick Barry	4	4	4	4	6	10	20	60
131	Ernie DiGregorio	4	4	4	4	4	5	15	
132	Darryl Dawkins RC	4	4	6	12	30	80		

1978-79 Topps

#	Player	VG 3	VgEx 4	EX 5	ExMt 6	NM 7	NmMt 8	MT 9	Gem 9.5/10
	COMMON CARD (1-132)	4	4	4	4	5	6	10	
1	Bill Walton	4	4	▲5	▲10	▲15	30	120	
5	Bob McAdoo	4	4	4	4	6	8	12	30
7	Wes Unseld	4	4	4	4	6	8	12	60
9	Austin Carr	4	4	4	4	5	6	12	40
10	Walter Davis RC	4	4	4	6	8	12	30	
14	Bobby Jones	4	4	4	4	5	8	12	30
20	George Gervin	4	4	4	6	8	10	60	
25	Elvin Hayes	4	4	▲5	▲6	▲12	▲25	▲50	
27	James Edwards RC	4	4	4	4	▲8	▲20	▲50	
28	Howard Porter	4	4	4	4	5	6	15	
29	Quinn Buckner RC	4	4	4	4	▲8	▲20	▲50	
32	Campy Russell	4	4	4	4	5	6	15	50
39	Gus Williams	4	4	4	4	5	6	15	
40	Dave Cowens	4	4	4	4	6	8	12	60

#	Player	VG 3	VgEx 4	EX 5	ExMt 6	NM 7	NmMt 8	MT 9	Gem 9.5/10
42	Wilbert Jones	4	4	4	4	5	6	15	
43	Charlie Scott	4	4	4	4	5	8	20	
45	Earl Monroe	4	4	4	4	6	8	12	
51	Louie Dampier	4	4	4	4	5	8	12	40
61	Dave Bing	4	4	4	4	6	10	15	
63	Norm Nixon RC	4	4	4	6	▲12	30	▲60	
67	Checklist 1-132	4	4	4	4	6	10	15	60
75	Bernard King RC	8	10	20	40	80	▼200	▼400	
78	Dennis Johnson RC	6	10	25	50	80	150	400	
79	Scott Wedman	4	4	4	4	6	8	12	40
80	Pete Maravich	4	6	8	15	30	80	250	
81	Dan Issel	4	4	4	4	6	8	12	
83	Walt Frazier	4	4	4	4	6	10	15	
85	Jo Jo White	4	4	4	4	5	10	15	
86	Robert Parish	4	4	4	4	6	10	15	40
95	Gail Goodrich	4	4	▲5	▲8	▲15	▲30	▲60	
100	David Thompson	4	4	4	▲5	▲10	▲20	▲40	
110	Kareem Abdul-Jabbar	6	10	20	40	80	150	400	
117	Jack Sikma RC	4	4	▲5	▲8	▲20	▲60		
126	Marques Johnson RC	4	4	▲5	▲8	▲15	▲30	▲80	
128	Cedric Maxwell RC	4	4	▲5	▲8	▲12	25	60	
130	Julius Erving	6	10	20	40	80	120	300	
132	Adrian Dantley	4	4	4	4	▲8	▲15	▲30	

1979-80 Topps

#	Player	GD 2	VG 3	VgEx 4	EX 5	ExMt 6	NM 7	NmMt 8	MT 9
	COMMON CARD (1-132)	4	4	4	4	4	4	5	10
1	George Gervin	4	4	▲5	▲6	12	▲25	▲50	150
3	Henry Bibby	4	4	4	4	4	4	5	12
6	Dennis Johnson	4	4	4	4	4	5	8	25
10	Kareem Abdul-Jabbar	4	4	6	▲12	▼40	100	200	400
13	Kevin Porter	4	4	4	4	4	4	5	15
14	Bernard King	4	4	4	4	4	5	6	40
17	Dan Issel	4	4	4	4	4	4	6	15
20	Julius Erving	4	4	6	10	40	80	200	300
23	Cedric Maxwell	4	4	4	4	4	4	5	20
25	Artis Gilmore	4	4	4	4	4	4	5	15
31	Alex English RC	4	6	8	15	30	60	150	400
32	Gail Goodrich	4	4	4	4	4	4	8	12
33	Caldwell Jones	4	4	4	4	4	4	5	12
41	Rudy Tomjanovich	4	4	4	4	4	5	6	12
42	Foots Walker	4	4	4	4	4	4	5	20
44	Reggie Theus RC	4	4	4	4	6	8	20	60
45	Bill Walton	4	4	▲5	▲8	▲12	25	60	
54	Adrian Dantley	4	4	4	4	4	5	6	20
58	Bob Lanier	4	4	4	4	4	5	10	15
60	Pete Maravich	4	▲5	6	▲12	▲25	▲50	100	300
62	Robert Reid RC	4	4	4	4	4	4	10	30
63	Mychal Thompson RC	4	4	4	4	4	5	6	12
64	Doug Collins	4	4	4	4	4	5	6	10
65	Wes Unseld	4	4	4	4	4	5	6	10
67	Bobby Wilkerson	4	4	4	4	4	4	5	12
73	Tim Bassett	4	4	4	4	4	4	6	15
75	Bob McAdoo	4	4	▲5	▲6	▲10	▲20	▲40	▲80
93	Robert Parish	4	4	4	4	4	6	10	15
100	Moses Malone	4	4	▲5	▲6	▲10	▲20	▲40	
101	Checklist 1-132	4	4	4	4	4	5	6	12
105	Darryl Dawkins	4	4	4	4	4	5	6	12
130	Bob Dandridge AS2	4	4	4	4	4	4	6	15
132	Bobby Jones	4	4	4	4	4	5	8	50

1980-81 Topps

#	Player	GD 2	VG 3	VgEx 4	EX 5	ExMt 6	NM 7	NmMt 8	MT 9
6	Bird/Erving/Magic	.600	800	1,000	1,200	▼1,500	▼3,000	8,000	20,000
8	Maravich/Free/Johnson	4	4	5	6	8	15	30	100
48	Bird/Marques/Sikma	10	20	50	100	200	300	400	600
49	Bridgeman/Bird/Brewer	10	20	50	100	200	300	400	600

BASKETBALL

		GD 2	VG 3	VgEx 4	EX 5	ExMt 6	NM 7	NmMt 8	MT 9
66	Cheeks/Johnson/Boone	10	20	50	100	200	300	400	600
94	Bird/Cartwright/Drew	6	10	20	40	80	200	400	1,000
98	May/Bird/Sikma	6	8	12	25	50	100	250	500
111	Long/Johnson/Boone	10	20	50	100	200	300	400	600
146	Kloff/Erving/Johnson	25	50	100	200	400	500	600	1,000
165	Brown/Bird/Brewer	4	4	6	10	20	40	100	300

— Bird/Erving/Magic #6 BGS 10 (Pristine) sold for $60,667 (SCP; 8/13)

— Bird/Erving/Magic #6 PSA 10 (Gem MT) sold for $14,467 (eBay; 9/12)

1981-82 Topps

		VG 3	VgEx 4	EX 5	ExMt 6	NM 7	NmMt 8	MT 9	Gem 9.5/10
4	Larry Bird	25	50	100	200	400	600	2,000	
6	Robert Parish	4	4	4	4	6	10	30	
14	Moses Malone	4	4	4	4	6	10	30	
20	Kareem Abdul-Jabbar	4	▲8	▲15	▲30	▲60	▲120	▲300	
21	Magic Johnson	25	50	100	200	400	600	2,000	
30	Julius Erving	4	6	8	10	15	40		
37	George Gervin	4	4	4	4	4	6	15	40
45	Celtics TL/Bird/Arch	4	4	4	4	4	6	12	150
55	Lakers TL/Jabbar	4	4	4	4	4	6	8	40
59	76ers TL/Erving	4	4	4	4	4	6	8	50
E75	Kevin McHale RC	5	6	8	15	30	60	200	600
E101	Larry Bird SA	6	10	20	40	80	200	500	
E104	Julius Erving SA	4	6	8	15	30	100		
W68	Alex English	4	4	4	4	4	4	8	50
W87	Jim Paxson RC	4	4	4	4	4	4	5	15
W106	Kareem Abdul-Jabbar SA	4	6	10	20	40	100		
W109	Magic Johnson SA	6	10	20	40	80	200	500	
MW74	Bill Laimbeer RC	4	4	6	8	▲15	30	80	

— Larry Bird #4 PSA 10 (Gem MT) sold for $518 (Mile High; 5/11)

— Magic Johnson #21 PSA 10 (Gem MT) sold for $285 (Mile High; 5/11)

1983 Star All-Star Game

		VgEx 4	EX 5	ExMt 6	NM 7	NmMt 8	NmMt+ 8.5	MT 9	Gem 9.5/10
2	Larry Bird	5	6	12	▲50	▲80	▲150	▲400	▲800
4	Julius Erving	5	5	▲8	▲15	▲30	▲40	▲80	▲200
11	Isiah Thomas	5	6	10	12	20	40	100	
14	Kareem Abdul-Jabbar	5	5	6	10	14	30	60	120
18	Magic Johnson	▲10	▲20	▲40	▲80	▲150	▲200	▲450	▲800
26	Julius Erving MVP	5	5	▲15	▲30	▲50	▲60	▲100	▲200

1983-84 Star

		VgEx 4	EX 5	ExMt 6	NM 7	NmMt 8	NmMt+ 8.5	MT 9	Gem 9.5/10
1	Julius Erving SP !	▲8	▲15	▲30	▲50	▲80	▲100	▲200	▲500
2	Maurice Cheeks SP	5	5	5	6	10	25	60	
13	Magic Johnson SP !	▲25	▲50	▲100	▲200	▲300	▲400	▲800	
14	Kareem Abdul-Jabbar SP	10	20	40	100	200	350	600	
21	Kurt Rambis SP XRC	5	5	6	10	15	20	60	
22	Byron Scott SP XRC	5	5	6	10	15	25	60	
25	James Worthy SP XRC	10	20	40	100	200	250	500	1,200
27	Danny Ainge SP XRC	5	6	8	12	25	40	80	250
35	Robert Parish SP !	5	5	6	10	15	25	60	
49	Mark Aguirre SP XRC	5	6	8	12	30	60	120	
51	Pat Cummings SP	5	5	5	6	10	15	25	
52	Brad Davis SP XRC	5	6	8	12	15	25	40	80
94	Isiah Thomas XRC	20	40	80	200	400	600	1,000	3,000
100	Clyde Drexler XRC	30	40	80	200	400	600	1,000	2,500
263	Dominique Wilkins XRC	30	▲50	▲100	200	400	600	1,200	3,000
271	Doc Rivers XRC	6	10	20	30	60	80	150	400

— Larry Bird #26 BGS 9.5 (Gem MT) sold for $487 (eBay; 4/13)

— Clyde Drexler #100 BGS 10 (Pristine) sold for $1,549 (Memory Lane; 5/13)

1983-84 Star All-Rookies

		VgEx 4	EX 5	ExMt 6	NM 7	NmMt 8	NmMt+ 8.5	MT 9	Gem 9.5/10
3	Dominique Wilkins !	5	▲8	▲15	▲30	▲60	▲80	▲200	▲400
10	James Worthy	5	▲8	▲15	▲30	▲60	▲80	▲200	▲400

1984-85 Star

		VG 3	VgEx 4	EX 5	ExMt 6	NM 7	NmMt 8	NmMt+ 8.5	MT 9
1	Larry Bird	10	15	30	50	100			
101	Michael Jordan XRC	4,000	6,000	8,000	▼12,000	▼15,000	40,000	60,000	100,000
172	Magic Johnson !	8	15	30	60	100	150	200	500
195	Michael Jordan OLY !	▲500	▲600	▲700	▲800	▲1,500	4,000		
202	Charles Barkley XRC	▲200	▲300	▲400	▲500	▲700	▲1,000	▲1,500	▲2,500
204	Julius Erving	5	8	10	15	20	30	60	
235	John Stockton XRC	▲100	▲200	▲300	▲400	▲600	▲800	▲1,000	▲2,000
237	Hakeem Olajuwon XRC !	▲150	▲300	▲400	▲600	▲800	▲1,500	▲2,000	▲3,000
261	Isiah Thomas	8	15	30	60	80	150	200	400
288	Michael Jordan SPEC !	▲600	▲800	▲1,000	▲2,000	▲3,000	▲6,000	▲8,000	

— Michael Jordan #101 BGS 9.5 (Gem Mt) sold for $52,500 (Beckett Auctions; 3/15)

— Michael Jordan #101 BGS 9 (Mint) sold for $9,531 (eBay; 3/13)

— Michael Jordan #101 BGS 9 (Mint) sold for $6,102 (eBay; 2/14)

— Michael Jordan #101 BGS 8.5 (NMMT+) sold for $3,200 [eBay; 9/11]

— Michael Jordan #101 BGS 8.5 (NMMT+) sold for $2,225 [eBay; 9/11]

— Charles Barkley #202 BGS 9.5 (Gem MT) sold for $1,038 (eBay; 10/12)

— Hakeem Olajuwon #237 BGS 9 (Mint) sold for $1,825 (eBay; 4/13)

1984-85 Star Court Kings 5x7

		VgEx 4	EX 5	ExMt 6	NM 7	NmMt 8	NmMt+ 8.5	MT 9	Gem 9.5/10
26	Michael Jordan	▲800	▲1,000	▲1,500	2,000	3,000	5,000	10,000	
47	Hakeem Olajuwon	10	20	40	80	150	400	800	

1985 Star Gatorade Slam Dunk

		VgEx 4	EX 5	ExMt 6	NM 7	NmMt 8	NmMt+ 8.5	MT 9	Gem 9.5/10
7	Michael Jordan	▲500	▲600	▲800	▲1,000	▲1,500	▲2,000	▲5,000	
NNO	Charles Barkley SP	▲30	▲40	▲60	▲80	▲100	▲150	▲300	▲500

1985-86 Star

		VgEx 4	EX 5	ExMt 6	NM 7	NmMt 8	NmMt+ 8.5	MT 9	Gem 9.5/10
106	Clyde Drexler !	8	10	15	20	30	80	200	500
117	Michael Jordan !	▲200	▲250	▲500	▲800	▲1,500	▲2,200	▲3,000	▲6,000
144	John Stockton	10	15	25	40	60	▲120	▲250	500
166	Patrick Ewing XRC	40	50	80	▲150	▲300	▲450	▲700	2,000

1985-86 Star All-Rookie Team

		VgEx 4	EX 5	ExMt 6	NM 7	NmMt 8	NmMt+ 8.5	MT 9	Gem 9.5/10
1	Hakeem Olajuwon	▲60	▲100	▲150	▲300	▲400	▲600	▲1,200	
2	Michael Jordan	150	200	300	▲800	▲1,000	▲1,500	▲6,000	
8	John Stockton	6	10	20	40	80	150	300	

1986-87 Fleer

		VgEx 4	EX 5	ExMt 6	NM 7	NmMt 8	NmMt+ 8.5	MT 9	Gem 9.5/10
1	Kareem Abdul-Jabbar	▲10	▲20	▲40	▲60	▲120	▲250	500	1,000
2	Alvan Adams	4	4	4	6	25	30	120	800
3	Mark Aguirre RC	4	▲6	▲15	▲40	▲60	▲80	▲200	400
4	Danny Ainge RC	4	4	5	10	20	30	50	200
5	John Bagley RC	4	4	4	8	15	20	30	150
6	Thurl Bailey RC	4	4	4	8	15	20	30	80
7	Charles Barkley RC	40	80	150	300	600	700	▼1,500	4,000
8	Benoit Benjamin RC	4	4	4	5	15	20	30	300
9	Larry Bird	6	15	▲80	▲150	▲250	▲400	▲700	▲1,500
10	Otis Birdsong	4	4	4	4	15	20	60	400
11	Rolando Blackman RC	4	4	6	10	25	30	120	300
12	Manute Bol RC	4	▲6	▲12	▲30	▲80	▲100	▲250	500
13	Sam Bowie RC	4	▲6	▲8	▲20	▲40	▲60	▲100	▲300
14	Joe Barry Carroll	4	4	4	6	▲12	▲20	▲50	
15	Tom Chambers RC	4	4	6	12	20	50	200	
16	Maurice Cheeks	4	4	4	6	10	15	30	80
17	Michael Cooper	4	4	4	4	15	20	25	100
18	Wayne Cooper	4	4	4	4	12	15	25	50
19	Pat Cummings	4	4	4	4	12	15	30	80
20	Terry Cummings RC	4	4	4	6	12	25	60	200

#	Player	VgEx 4	EX 5	ExMt 6	NM 7	NmMt 8	NmMt+ 8.5	MT 9	Gem 9.5/10
21	Adrian Dantley	4	4	4	5	15	20	30	150
22	Brad Davis RC	4	4	6	15	30	60	250	
23	Walter Davis	4	4	4	6	15	20	25	80
24	Darryl Dawkins	4	4	▲6	▲8	15	▲30	▲100	
25	Larry Drew	4	▲6	▲8	▲20	▲50	▲60	▲120	▲250
26	Clyde Drexler RC	8	12	20	40	80	200	500	1,000
27	Joe Dumars RC	▲6	▲10	▲20	▲40	▲80	▲120	300	600
28	Mark Eaton RC	4	4	4	6	15	20	30	80
29	James Edwards	4	4	4	4	6	12	25	60
30	Alex English	4	▲6	▲8	▲15	▲40	▲50	▲100	▲300
31	Julius Erving	▲10	▲20	▲40	▲80	▲150	▲250	▲500	▲1,000
32	Patrick Ewing RC	▲15	▲30	▲60	▲120	▲250	▲300	700	1,200
33	Vern Fleming RC	4	4	4	10	20	▲30	▲60	▲250
34	Sleepy Floyd RC	4	4	4	6	20	25	40	120
35	World B. Free	4	4	4	6	12	15	25	60
36	George Gervin	4	4	4	6	12	15	25	80
37	Artis Gilmore	4	4	4	6	▲50	▲60	▲100	80
38	Mike Gminski	4	4	▲6	▲12	▲25	▲30	▲80	
39	Rickey Green	4	4	▲6	▲12	▲30	▲40	▲80	▲200
40	Sidney Green	4	▲6	▲8	▲20	▲50	▲60	▲100	▲250
41	David Greenwood	4	4	4	4	15	20	25	60
42	Darrell Griffith	4	4	4	4	15	20	25	100
43	Bill Hanzlik	4	4	4	4	10	15	30	300
44	Derek Harper RC	4	4	4	▲25	▲40	▲50	▲120	
45	Gerald Henderson	4	4	4	5	10	15	25	80
46	Roy Hinson	4	4	4	4	12	15	25	80
47	Craig Hodges RC	4	4	▲6	▲10	▲25	▲40	▲150	
48	Phil Hubbard	4	4	4	4	▲40	▲60	▲100	▲250
49	Jay Humphries RC	4	4	4	4	10	15	25	60
50	Dennis Johnson	4	4	4	5	10	15	30	100
51	Eddie Johnson RC	4	4	4	▲6	▲15	▲25	▲80	
52	Frank Johnson RC	4	4	4	4	15	20	25	120
53	Magic Johnson	4	8	15	30	150	200	400	1,000
54	Marques Johnson	4	4	4	5	10	20	50	400
55	Steve Johnson	4	4	4	8	20	25	100	300
56	Vinnie Johnson	4	4	▲8	▲15	▲30	▲50	▲100	300
57	Michael Jordan RC	4,000	5,000	▼6,000	▼8,000	▼10,000	▼12,000	▼25,000	▼60,000
58	Clark Kellogg RC	4	4	▲6	▲8	▲20	▲30	▲100	
59	Albert King	4	4	4	▲6	15	▲25	▲80	
60	Bernard King	4	4	▲6	▲8	20	25	▲50	
61	Bill Laimbeer	4	4	4	6	12	15	40	150
62	Allen Leavell	4	4	▲6	▲8	▲20	▲30	▲80	
63	Fat Lever RC	4	4	▲6	▲12	▲25	▲40	▲120	
64	Alton Lister	4	4	4	4	15	20	40	300
65	Lewis Lloyd	4	4	▲6	▲8	▲20	▲40	▲200	500
66	Maurice Lucas	4	▲6	▲8	▲20	▲60	▲80	▲200	500
67	Jeff Malone RC	4	4	▲8	▲20	▲40	▲120	▲300	
68	Karl Malone RC	12	20	40	80	220	300	800	2,000
69	Moses Malone	4	4	4	5	10	20	25	120
70	Cedric Maxwell	4	4	4	4	15	20	25	150
71	Rodney McCray RC	4	4	4	5	10	15	25	200
72	Xavier McDaniel RC	4	4	▲6	▲10	▲20	▲30	▲120	
73	Kevin McHale	6	8	10	20	40	50	120	300
74	Mike Mitchell	4	4	4	4	10	12	25	200
75	Sidney Moncrief	4	4	4	5	15	20	30	200
76	Johnny Moore	4	4	4	8	20	50	150	600
77	Chris Mullin RC	6	10	20	40	80	150	500	800
78	Larry Nance RC	4	▲6	▲12	▲30	▲50	▲60	▲120	300
79	Calvin Natt	4	4	4	5	15	20	25	120
80	Norm Nixon	4	4	4	▲6	▲15	▲25	▲80	
81	Charles Oakley RC	4	4	6	10	20	30	80	200
82	Hakeem Olajuwon RC	20	50	100	250	400	600	1,500	4,000
83	Louis Orr	4	4	4	5	10	15	25	80
84	Robert Parish	4	4	4	6	15	20	30	150
85	Jim Paxson	4	4	4	4	15	20	25	100
86	Sam Perkins RC	4	▲6	▲12	▲30	▲50	▲60	▲120	▲300
87	Ricky Pierce RC	4	▲6	▲12	▲30	▲50	▲60	▲120	
88	Paul Pressey RC	4	4	4	5	12	20	60	250
89	Kurt Rambis RC	4	4	4	5	10	20	50	250
90	Robert Reid	4	4	4	5	12	15	25	60
91	Doc Rivers RC	4	▲6	▲10	▲20	▲50	▲80	▲150	▲300
92	Alvin Robertson RC	4	4	4	4	10	12	25	80
93	Cliff Robinson	4	4	▲6	▲15	▲25	▲80		
94	Tree Rollins	4	4	▲6	▲10	▲30	▲40	▲80	▲150
95	Dan Roundfield	4	4	4	4	15	20	25	60
96	Jeff Ruland	4	▲6	▲10	▲25	▲40	▲50	▲120	▲500
97	Ralph Sampson RC	4	4	4	5	12	15	40	120
98	Danny Schayes RC	4	4	4	4	15	20	30	120
99	Byron Scott RC	4	4	6	10	30	40	120	250
100	Purvis Short	4	4	4	6	15	20	30	100
101	Jerry Sichting	4	4	4	4	12	15	25	150
102	Jack Sikma	4	4	4	4	15	20	25	60
103	Derek Smith	4	4	4	▲6	10	▲20	▲60	
104	Larry Smith	4	4	4	▲6	▲12	▲25	▲80	
105	Rory Sparrow	4	4	4	4	10	15	25	80
106	Steve Stipanovich	4	4	4	4	10	15	25	80
107	Terry Teagle	4	4	4	4	10	15	30	80
108	Reggie Theus	4	4	4	5	10	20	30	60
109	Isiah Thomas RC	▲40	▲50	▲60	▲100	▲150	▲300	▲800	▲2,000
110	LaSalle Thompson RC	4	4	4	6	25	30	60	200
111	Mychal Thompson	4	4	▲6	▲8	▲15	▲30	▲100	
112	Sedale Threatt RC	4	4	4	5	12	15	25	80
113	Wayman Tisdale RC	4	4	4	8	20	30	80	250
114	Andrew Toney	4	4	▲6	▲15	▲40	▲60	▲120	▲250
115	Kelly Tripucka RC	4	4	4	4	15	20	25	80
116	Mel Turpin	4	4	▲8	▲25	▲25	▲50	▲150	
117	Kiki Vandeweghe RC	4	4	4	8	10	15	25	120
118	Jay Vincent	4	4	4	4	10	15	30	100
119	Bill Walton	4	4	4	8	▲50	▲60	▲100	▲250
120	Spud Webb RC	6	8	12	25	50	80	150	350
121	Dominique Wilkins RC	▲30	▲50	▲100	▲200	▲400	▲500	1,000	3,000
122	Gerald Wilkins RC	4	4	4	5	12	15	30	200
123	Buck Williams RC	4	4	4	5	12	15	30	120
124	Gus Williams	4	▲6	▲8	▲20	▲40	▲50	▲80	▲200
125	Herb Williams RC	4	4	4	4	15	20	25	80
126	Kevin Willis RC	4	▲6	▲8	▲20	▲50	▲60	▲120	▲250
127	Randy Wittman	4	▲6	▲8	▲15	▲40	▲50	▲120	
128	Al Wood	4	4	4	6	15	20	25	120
129	Mike Woodson	4	4	4	4	10	15	30	60
130	Orlando Woolridge RC	4	4	6	8	15	20	50	200
131	James Worthy RC	8	20	40	100	200	300	600	
132	Checklist 1-132	8	15	30	60	150	400	800	2,000

— Charles Barkley #7 PSA 10 (Gem MT) sold for $455 (eBay; 10/11)

— Magic Johnson #53 PSA 10 (Gem MT) sold for $346 (Mile High; 5/11)

— Michael Jordan #57 BGS 10 (Pristine) sold for $8,025 (eBay; 10/12)

— Michael Jordan #57 in PSA 10 (Gem MT) typically sell for $14,000-$18,000

— Michael Jordan #57 BGS 9.5 (Gem MT) sold for $6,500 (eBay; 10/11)

— Karl Malone #68 PSA 10 (Gem MT) sold for $471 (Mile High; 5/11)

— Hakeem Olajuwon #82 PSA 10 (Gem MT) sold for $510 (Mile High; 5/11)

— Dominique Wilkins #121 BGS 10 (Pristine) sold for $3,859 (eBay; 4/14)

1986-87 Fleer Stickers

#	Player	VgEx 4	EX 5	ExMt 6	NM 7	NmMt 8	NmMt+ 8.5	MT 9	Gem 9.5/10
1	Kareem Abdul-Jabbar	▲45	▲60	▲120	▲250	▲500	▲800	2,500	
2	Larry Bird	30	40	50	▲100	▲200	▲250	▲400	2,000
3	Adrian Dantley	8	15	▲50	▲80	▲120	150	300	
4	Alex English	▲15	▲30	▲60	▲80	▲200	▲250	▲500	▲2,000
5	Julius Erving	30	40	▲60	80	▲200	▲250	▲500	2,000
6	Patrick Ewing	30	40	50	60	▲120	▲200	▲400	1,200
7	Magic Johnson	40	50	▲80	▲120	▲200	▲300	▲600	
8	Michael Jordan	500	600	1,500	▼2,000	▼3,000	▼5,000	▼10,000	▲40,000
9	Hakeem Olajuwon	40	60	80	150	300	400	600	2,000
10	Isiah Thomas	▲20	▲30	▲50	▲80	▲150	▲200	▲500	1,500
11	Dominique Wilkins	30	40	50	▲120	▲300	▲400	▲500	2,000

1987-88 Fleer

#	Player	VgEx 4	EX 5	ExMt 6	NM 7	NmMt 8	NmMt+ 8.5	MT 9	Gem 9.5/10
1	Kareem Abdul-Jabbar	4	▲6	▲8	▲20	▲40	▲50	▲80	350
2	Alvan Adams	4	4	4	5	10	15	25	
3	Mark Aguirre	4	4	4	4	6	8	15	
4	Danny Ainge	4	4	4	6	12	15	35	
5	John Bagley	4	4	4	5	8	12	50	
6	Thurl Bailey	4	4	4	4	6	8	15	
7	Greg Ballard	4	4	4	5	8	10	60	
8	Gene Banks	4	4	4	6	10	15	25	
9	Charles Barkley	4	4	▲8	▲15	▲25	50	▲200	
10	Benoit Benjamin	4	4	4	5	8	10	20	
11	Larry Bird	4	4	8	▲15	▲25	▲50	▲200	
12	Rolando Blackman	4	4	4	4	4	8	12	40
13	Manute Bol	4	4	4	5	6	15	30	
14	Tony Brown	4	4	4	5	10	15	25	
15	Michael Cage RC	4	4	4	5	6	15	40	150
16	Joe Barry Carroll	4	4	4	4	6	8	12	
17	Bill Cartwright	4	4	4	4	6	8	20	
18	Terry Catledge RC	4	4	4	5	10	15	25	
19	Tom Chambers	4	4	4	4	4	8	25	
20	Maurice Cheeks	4	4	4	4	6	8	15	50
21	Michael Cooper	4	4	4	4	6	8	15	
22	Dave Corzine	4	4	4	4	8	10	20	
23	Terry Cummings	4	4	4	4	6	8	15	
24	Adrian Dantley	4	4	4	4	6	8	15	
25	Brad Daugherty RC	4	4	4	5	6	8	20	100
26	Walter Davis	4	4	4	4	6	8	15	
27	Johnny Dawkins RC	4	4	4	5	10	15	30	100
28	James Donaldson	4	4	4	4	5	8	10	
29	Larry Drew	4	4	4	4	5	8	10	30
30	Clyde Drexler	4	4	4	8	10	15	25	
31	Joe Dumars	4	4	4	5	6	8	10	40
32	Mark Eaton	4	4	4	4	6	8	15	
33	Dale Ellis RC	4	4	4	5	8	12	50	
34	Alex English	4	4	4	4	6	8	12	
35	Julius Erving	4	4	4	8	12	15	25	150
36	Mike Evans	4	4	4	4	6	8	10	
37	Patrick Ewing	4	4	4	4	8	12	20	
38	Vern Fleming	4	4	4	4	6	8	10	25
39	Sleepy Floyd	4	4	4	4	6	8	12	
40	Artis Gilmore	4	4	4	4	6	8	12	40
41	Mike Gminski	4	4	4	4	6	8	15	30
42	A.C.Green RC	4	4	4	4	6	8	▲15	80
43	Rickey Green	4	4	4	4	5	8	10	
44	Sidney Green	4	4	4	4	5	8	10	
45	David Greenwood	4	4	4	4	5	8	10	40
46	Darrell Griffith	4	4	4	4	6	8	12	40
47	Bill Hanzlik	4	4	4	4	4	6	8	20
48	Derek Harper	4	4	4	4	6	8	10	40
49	Ron Harper RC	4	4	4	4	6	10	20	100
50	Gerald Henderson	4	4	4	4	4	5	6	
51	Roy Hinson	4	4	4	4	4	6	8	30
52	Craig Hodges	4	4	4	4	4	6	8	30
53	Phil Hubbard	4	4	4	4	6	8	12	
54	Dennis Johnson	4	4	4	4	6	8	12	60
55	Eddie Johnson	4	4	4	4	6	8	10	25
56	Magic Johnson	4	4	10	12	15	25	50	400
57	Steve Johnson	4	4	4	4	6	8	10	
58	Vinnie Johnson	4	4	4	5	8	10	12	50
59	Michael Jordan	120	250	400	600	▲1,000	▲1,500	▲4,000	6,000
60	Jerome Kersey RC	4	4	4	4	8	10	12	50
61	Bill Laimbeer	4	4	4	5	8	10	12	
62	Lafayette Lever	4	4	4	4	6	8	20	80
63	Cliff Levingston RC	4	4	4	4	6	8	12	
64	Alton Lister	4	4	4	6	8	12	25	
65	John Long	4	4	4	5	8	10	20	100
66	John Lucas	4	4	4	5	8	10	12	
67	Jeff Malone	4	4	4	4	6	8	12	40
68	Karl Malone	4	6	8	15	30	40	120	400
69	Moses Malone	4	4	4	4	6	8	10	80
70	Cedric Maxwell	4	4	4	4	4	6	8	50
71	Tim McCormick	4	4	4	4	4	6	8	
72	Rodney McCray	4	4	4	4	6	8	10	25
73	Xavier McDaniel	4	4	4	4	6	8	10	25
74	Kevin McHale	4	4	4	4	6	8	10	50
75	Nate McMillan RC	4	4	4	4	6	10	15	
76	Sidney Moncrief	4	4	4	4	4	6	8	
77	Chris Mullin	4	4	4	4	6	8	12	60
78	Larry Nance	4	4	4	5	6		10	100
79	Charles Oakley	4	4	4	4	5	8	12	30
80	Hakeem Olajuwon	4	4	4	8	10	15	25	150
81	Robert Parish	4	4	4	5	10	12	15	100
82	Jim Paxson	4	4	4	4	6	8	12	
83	John Paxson RC	4	4	4		▲20	▲25	▲40	80
84	Sam Perkins	4	4	4	4	6	8	10	50
85	Chuck Person RC	4	4	4		▲10	▲15	▲25	60
86	Jim Petersen	4	4	4	4	4	6	8	25
87	Ricky Pierce	4	4	4	4	4	6	8	25
88	Ed Pinckney RC	4	4	4	4	8	10	15	
89	Terry Porter RC	4	4	4	4	8	12	15	50
90	Paul Pressey	4	4	4	4	6	8	10	25
91	Robert Reid	4	4	4	4	5	8	10	25
92	Doc Rivers	4	4	4	4	4	6	8	50
93	Alvin Robertson	4	4	4	4	4	6	8	30
94	Tree Rollins	4	4	4	4	4	6	8	25
95	Ralph Sampson	4	4	4	4	6	8	10	30
96	Mike Sanders	4	4	4	5	8	10	12	60
97	Detlef Schrempf RC	4	4	4	6	10	20	40	120
98	Byron Scott	4	4	4	4	6	8	▲15	▲40
99	Jerry Sichting	4	4	4	4	6	8	10	25
100	Jack Sikma	4	4	4	4	▲10	▲15	▲25	▲50
101	Larry Smith	4	4	4	4	6	8	10	25
102	Rory Sparrow	4	4	4	4	4	6	8	25
103	Steve Stipanovich	4	4	4	4	4	6	8	25
104	Jon Sundvold	4	4	4	4	6	8	10	25
105	Reggie Theus	4	4	4	4	6	8	10	30
106	Isiah Thomas	4	4	4	4	6	8	15	40
107	LaSalle Thompson	4	4	4	4	4	6	▲12	▲30
108	Mychal Thompson	4	4	4	4	6	8	▲12	▲30
109	Otis Thorpe RC	4	4	4	4	8	10	15	40
110	Sedale Threatt	4	4	4	4	4	6	8	25
111	Wayman Tisdale	4	4	4	5	8	10	15	
112	Kelly Tripucka	4	4	4	4	4	5	6	30
113	Trent Tucker RC	4	4	4	4	4	6	8	25
114	Terry Tyler	4	4	4	4	6	8	12	40
115	Darnell Valentine	4	4	4	4	4	6	8	25
116	Kiki Vandeweghe	4	4	4	4	4	6	10	25
117	Darrell Walker RC	4	4	4	4	4	6	8	▲40
118	Dominique Wilkins	4	4	6	8	10	20	50	200
119	Gerald Wilkins	4	4	4	4	6	▲10	▲30	
120	Buck Williams	4	4	4	4	6	8	10	25
121	Herb Williams	4	4	4	4	6	8	10	25
122	John Williams RC	4	4	4	6	10	15	25	
123	Hot Rod Williams RC	4	4	4	▲6	▲8	▲15	▲50	
124	Kevin Willis	4	4	4	4	4	6	10	25
125	David Wingate RC	4	4	4	4	6	8	10	30
126	Randy Wittman	4	4	4	4	6	8	10	25
127	Leon Wood	4	4	4	4	4	6	10	40

#		VgEx 4	EX 5	ExMt 6	NM 7	NmMt 8	NmMt+ 8.5	MT 9	Gem 9.5/10
128	Mike Woodson	4	4	4	5	8	10	15	50
129	Orlando Woolridge	4	4	4	4	4	6	8	40
130	James Worthy	4	4	4	4	10	12	25	150
131	Danny Young RC	4	4	4	6	8	10	12	
132	Checklist 1-132	4	4	4	5	8	10	15	80

1987-88 Fleer Stickers

#		VgEx 4	EX 5	ExMt 6	NM 7	NmMt 8	NmMt+ 8.5	MT 9	Gem 9.5/10
1	Magic Johnson	4	6	▲10	▲20	▲50	▲100	▲300	
2	Michael Jordan	▲60	100	200	250	400	600	▲2,000	
3	Hakeem Olajuwon	4	6	10	20	50	80	200	
4	Larry Bird	4	6	10	20	50	80	200	
5	Kevin McHale	4	4	6	▲10	20	▲30	▲100	
6	Charles Barkley	4	6	8	15	40	60	200	
7	Dominique Wilkins	4	6	10	20	50	80	200	
8	Kareem Abdul-Jabbar	4	6	8	20	50	80	200	
9	Mark Aguirre	4	4	4	▲8	20	▲30	▲80	
10	Chuck Person	4	4	4	▲8	20	▲30	▲100	
11	Alex English	4	4	4	6	20	30	150	

— Larry Bird #4 BGS 9.5 (Gem MT) sold for $650 (eBay; 10/11)

1988-89 Fleer

#		VgEx 4	EX 5	ExMt 6	NM 7	NmMt 8	NmMt+ 8.5	MT 9	Gem 9.5/10
	COMMON CARD (1-132)	4	4	4	4	4	6	8	20
1	Antoine Carr RC	4	4	4	4	6	8	10	50
5	Dominique Wilkins	4	4	4	4	6	8	10	30
8	Danny Ainge	4	4	4	4	6	8	12	25
9	Larry Bird	4	4	4	6	8	10	15	50
11	Kevin McHale	4	4	4	4	4	6	10	30
13	Muggsy Bogues RC	4	4	4	4	6	8	12	40
14	Dell Curry RC	4	4	4	4	6	8	10	30
16	Horace Grant RC	4	4	4	▲6	8	▲15	▲40	▲100
17	Michael Jordan	12	25	50	100	250	400	800	3,000
20	Scottie Pippen RC	▼20	▼30	▼50	▼80	▼150	▼200	▼400	2,000
25	Mark Price RC	4	4	4	5	6	8	12	60
32	Roy Tarpley RC	4	4	4	4	6	8	10	60
33	Michael Adams RC	4	4	4	4	6	8	10	50
39	Adrian Dantley	4	4	4	4	5	6	10	30
40	Joe Dumars	4	4	4	4	4	6	12	30
43	Dennis Rodman RC	▼15	▼20	▼40	▼60	▼100	▼150	▼300	800
44	John Salley RC	4	4	4	4	10	15	30	60
45	Isiah Thomas	4	4	4	4	6	10	20	50
53	Hakeem Olajuwon	4	4	▲8	▲10	▲12	▲15	▲30	▲60
57	Reggie Miller RC	8	10	20	40	100	150	400	800
58	Chuck Person	4	4	4	4	6	8	12	30
61	Benoit Benjamin	4	4	4	4	4	5	8	30
64	Kareem Abdul-Jabbar	4	4	4	4	6	8	12	30
67	Magic Johnson	4	4	4	5	8	10	15	100
70	James Worthy	4	4	4	4	6	8	10	25
76	Jack Sikma	4	4	4	4	6	8	10	30
80	Patrick Ewing	4	4	4	4	6	8	15	40
82	Mark Jackson RC	4	4	4	4	4	6	10	25
83	Kenny Walker RC	4	4	4	4	4	6	10	40
84	Gerald Wilkins	4	4	4	4	4	6	10	25
85	Charles Barkley	4	4	4	4	6	8	20	60
86	Maurice Cheeks	4	4	4	4	4	6	10	25
88	Cliff Robinson	4	4	4	4	5	6	10	25
92	Clyde Drexler	4	4	4	4	5	8	12	
93	Kevin Duckworth RC	4	4	4	4	5	8	12	30
94	Steve Johnson	4	4	4	4	4	5	12	50
98	Reggie Theus	4	4	4	4	5	6		25
99	Otis Thorpe	4	4	4	4	5	8		40
100	Kenny Smith RC	4	4	4	4	5	6	10	50
102	Walter Berry RC	4	4	4	4	4	5	6	25
103	Frank Brickowski RC	4	4	4	4	4	6	8	25
105	Alvin Robertson	4	4	4	4	4	5	6	25

#		VgEx 4	EX 5	ExMt 6	NM 7	NmMt 8	NmMt+ 8.5	MT 9	Gem 9.5/10
106	Tom Chambers	4	4	4	4	5	6	8	25
108	Xavier McDaniel	4	4	4	4	4	5	6	25
112	Mark Eaton	4	4	4	4	4	5	6	25
114	Karl Malone	4	4	4	5	6	8	12	40
115	John Stockton RC	4	5	6	10	30	50	150	400
116	Bernard King	4	4	4	4	5	6	10	80
118	Moses Malone	4	4	4	4	5	8		40
120	Michael Jordan AS	20	40	80	150	300	400	▼800	4,000
123	Magic Johnson AS	4	4	4	4	5	8	10	40
124	Larry Bird AS	4	4	4	4	5	8	10	40
125	Dominique Wilkins AS	4	4	4	4	4	5	10	40
126	Hakeem Olajuwon AS	4	4	4	4	5	6	8	30
127	John Stockton AS	4	4	4	4	6	8	12	60
129	Charles Barkley AS	4	4	4	4	6	8	10	40
130	Patrick Ewing AS	4	4	4	4	5	6	8	30
132	Checklist 1-132	4	4	4	4	4	5	6	60

— Dennis Rodman #43 PSA 10 (Gem MT) sold for $200 (eBay; 9/11)
— Reggie Miller #57 PSA 10 (Gem MT) sold for $222 (eBay; 10/11)

1988-89 Fleer Stickers

#		VgEx 4	EX 5	ExMt 6	NM 7	NmMt 8	NmMt+ 8.5	MT 9	Gem 9.5/10
1	Mark Aguirre	4	4	4	4	10			
2	Larry Bird	6	10	15	20	40	100	700	
3	Clyde Drexler	4	4	4	8	20	80	250	
4	Alex English	4	4	4	4	6	8		
5	Patrick Ewing	4	4	6	10	20	80	300	
6	Magic Johnson	6	10	15	20	40	100	400	
7	Michael Jordan	25	40	60	200	300	500	2,000	
8	Karl Malone	6	8	10	20	40	80	200	
9	Kevin McHale	4	4	6	8	15	30	100	
10	Isiah Thomas	4	4	4	10	20	80	300	
11	Dominique Wilkins	4	4	4	6	15	60	200	

— Clyde Drexler #3 PSA 10 (Gem MT) sold for $475 (eBay; 12/06)
— Magic Johnson #6 PSA 10 (Gem MT) sold for $763 (eBay; 4/13)

1989-90 Fleer

#		VgEx 4	EX 5	ExMt 6	NM 7	NmMt 8	NmMt+ 8.5	MT 9	Gem 9.5/10
21	Michael Jordan	5	6	20	30	50	80	200	1,200
22	John Paxson	4	4	4	4	5	6	8	20
23	Scottie Pippen	4	4	4	8	20		60	300
49	Dennis Rodman	4	4	4	8	15		40	150
55	Chris Mullin	4	4	4	4	4	6	8	12
56	Mitch Richmond RC	4	4	4	6	12		30	150
61	Hakeem Olajuwon	4	4	4	6	12		30	120
65	Reggie Miller	4	4	4	6	12		30	150
77	Magic Johnson	4	4	4	6	12		30	100
113	Charles Barkley	4	4	4	6	12		30	100
121	Jeff Hornacek RC	4	4	4	8	12		30	
123	Kevin Johnson RC				8	15		40	120
124	Dan Majerle RC				6	10		25	80

1989-90 Fleer Stickers

#		VgEx 4	EX 5	ExMt 6	NM 7	NmMt 8	NmMt+ 8.5	MT 9	Gem 9.5/10
3	Michael Jordan	4	5	6	30	60	100	300	1,000
10	Larry Bird	4	4	4	5	25	40	120	

— Michael Jordan #3 BGS 10 (Pristine) sold for $2,985 (Mile High; 1/10)

1989-90 Hoops

#		VgEx 4	EX 5	ExMt 6	NM 7	NmMt 8	NmMt+ 8.5	MT 9	Gem 9.5/10
21	Michael Jordan AS	4	6	10	25	30	50	80	250
138	David Robinson SP RC	4	4	4	6	▼20	▼40	▼100	400
200	Michael Jordan	4	4	6	8	15	30	80	200
266	Phil Jackson CO	4	4	4	4	8	15	40	120
310	David Robinson IA	4	4	4	4	8	15	40	▼120
351	Steve Kerr RC	4	4	4	8	15	25	60	120

BASKETBALL

1990/91 - Present

1990-91 Fleer

		NmMt 8	NmMt+ 8.5	MT 9	Gem 9.5/10
8	Larry Bird	20	30	50	120
26	Michael Jordan	▼15	▼30	▼60	▼200
93	Magic Johnson	20	30	50	120
139	Charles Barkley UER	6	10	30	100
172	David Robinson	4	6	12	40
178	Shawn Kemp RC	6	10	25	80
189	John Stockton	4	6	12	40

1990-91 Fleer All-Stars

		NmMt 8	NmMt+ 8.5	MT 9	Gem 9.5/10
1	Charles Barkley	4	8	20	80
2	Larry Bird	6	10	30	120
3	Hakeem Olajuwon	4	8	20	80
4	Magic Johnson	6	10	30	120
5	Michael Jordan	▼25	▼40	▼80	400
10	David Robinson	6	10	30	120
12	Patrick Ewing	4	8	20	80

1990-91 Fleer Rookie Sensations

		NmMt 8	NmMt+ 8.5	MT 9	Gem 9.5/10
1	David Robinson	10	20	50	150
8	Tim Hardaway	10	12	30	80

1990-91 Fleer Update

		NmMt 8	NmMt+ 8.5	MT 9	Gem 9.5/10
U81	Drazen Petrovic RC	10	15	40	120
U92	Gary Payton RC	25	30	60	300

1990-91 Hoops

		NmMt 8	NmMt+ 8.5	MT 9	Gem 9.5/10
5	Michael Jordan AS SP	15	30	80	150
65	Michael Jordan	15	30	80	150
205	Mark Jackson/Lyle and Erik Menendez in background	12	20	40	
248	Drazen Petrovic RC	8	12	30	60
391	Gary Payton RC	4	6	15	40

1990-91 SkyBox

		NmMt 8	NmMt+ 8.5	MT 9	Gem 9.5/10
41	Michael Jordan	20	40	80	250
268	Shawn Kemp RC	10	15	30	60
365	Gary Payton RC	10	150	30	60

1991-92 Fleer

		NmMt 8	NmMt+ 8.5	MT 9	Gem 9.5/10
29	Michael Jordan	12	20	50	▲250
211	Michael Jordan AS	▲10	▲20	▲40	▲120

1991-92 Fleer Pro-Visions

		NmMt 8	NmMt+ 8.5	MT 9	Gem 9.5/10
2	Michael Jordan	25	40	80	200

1991-92 Hoops

		NmMt 8	NmMt+ 8.5	MT 9	Gem 9.5/10
30	Michael Jordan	20	30	60	120
253	Michael Jordan AS	10	15	30	60
455	Michael Jordan SC	12	15	30	60
579	Michael Jordan USA	15	30	60	120

1991-92 Hoops All-Star MVP's

		NmMt 8	NmMt+ 8.5	MT 9	Gem 9.5/10
9	Michael Jordan	25	40	80	200

1991-92 Hoops Slam Dunk

		NmMt 8	NmMt+ 8.5	MT 9	Gem 9.5/10
4	Michael Jordan	25	40	80	250

1991-92 SkyBox

		NmMt 8	NmMt+ 8.5	MT 9	Gem 9.5/10
39	Michael Jordan	10	20	40	100
534	Michael Jordan USA	15	30	80	150
572	Michael Jordan SAL	10	20	40	100

1991-92 Upper Deck

		NmMt 8	NmMt+ 8.5	MT 9	Gem 9.5/10
34	M.Johnson/M.Jordan CC	20	30	60	120
44	Michael Jordan	20	30	60	120
48	Michael Jordan AS CL	15	25	50	100
452	Michael Jordan AS	20	30	60	120

1991-92 Upper Deck Award Winner Holograms

		NmMt 8	NmMt+ 8.5	MT 9	Gem 9.5/10
AW1	Michael Jordan	25	40	100	200
AW4	Michael Jordan	25	40	100	200

1992 Classic

		NmMt 8	NmMt+ 8.5	MT 9	Gem 9.5/10
1	Shaquille O'Neal	10	20	40	80

1992-93 Fleer

		NmMt 8	NmMt+ 8.5	MT 9	Gem 9.5/10
32	Michael Jordan	25	40	80	200
238	Michael Jordan LL	20	25	50	100
298	Shaquille O'Neal SD	15	20	40	80
401	Shaquille O'Neal RC	25	40	80	200

1992-93 Fleer All-Stars

		NmMt 8	NmMt+ 8.5	MT 9	Gem 9.5/10
6	Michael Jordan	100	150	300	1,500

1992-93 Fleer Team Leaders

		NmMt 8	NmMt+ 8.5	MT 9	Gem 9.5/10
4	Michael Jordan	400	500	800	2,000

1992-93 Fleer Total D

		NmMt 8	NmMt+ 8.5	MT 9	Gem 9.5/10
5	Michael Jordan	200	300	600	2,000

1992-93 Hoops

		NmMt 8	NmMt+ 8.5	MT 9	Gem 9.5/10
30	Michael Jordan	15	20	40	100
442	Shaquille O'Neal RC	25	40	80	200

1992-93 Hoops Draft Redemption

		NmMt 8	NmMt+ 8.5	MT 9	Gem 9.5/10
A	Shaquille O'Neal	100	150	250	500
B	Alonzo Mourning	12	20	40	100

1992-93 Hoops Magic's All-Rookies

		NmMt 8	NmMt+ 8.5	MT 9	Gem 9.5/10
1	Shaquille O'Neal	100	120	250	500
2	Alonzo Mourning	30	40	80	200

1992-93 Hoops Supreme Court

		NmMt 8	NmMt+ 8.5	MT 9	Gem 9.5/10
SC1	Michael Jordan	20	30	60	150

1992-93 SkyBox

		NmMt 8	NmMt+ 8.5	MT 9	Gem 9.5/10
31	Michael Jordan	▲20	▲25	▲50	▲120
314	Michael Jordan MVP	▲20	▲25	▲50	▲120
382	Shaquille O'Neal SP RC	▼20	▼30	▼60	▼150

1992-93 SkyBox Draft Picks

		NmMt 8	NmMt+ 8.5	MT 9	Gem 9.5/10
DP1	Shaquille O'Neal	20	40	80	200

1992-93 SkyBox Olympic Team

		NmMt 8	NmMt+ 8.5	MT 9	Gem 9.5/10
USA11	Michael Jordan	25	40	80	200

1992-93 Stadium Club

		NmMt 8	NmMt+ 8.5	MT 9	Gem 9.5/10
1	Michael Jordan	25	40	80	200
201	Shaquille O'Neal MC	15	20	40	100
210	Michael Jordan MC	20	30	60	150
247	Shaquille O'Neal RC	30	40	80	200

1992-93 Stadium Club Beam Team

		NmMt 8	NmMt+ 8.5	MT 9	Gem 9.5/10
1	Michael Jordan	250	400	800	1,500
21	Shaquille O'Neal	400	600	1,200	3,000

1992-93 Topps

		NmMt 8	NmMt+ 8.5	MT 9	Gem 9.5/10
115	Michael Jordan AS	20	30	60	120
141	Michael Jordan	20	30	60	120
205	Michael Jordan 50P	20	30	60	120
362	Shaquille O'Neal RC	30	60	120	400

1992-93 Topps Gold

		NmMt 8	NmMt+ 8.5	MT 9	Gem 9.5/10
141	Michael Jordan	40	60	100	300
362	Shaquille O'Neal	120	200	400	1,000

1992-93 Ultra

		NmMt 8	NmMt+ 8.5	MT 9	Gem 9.5/10
27	Michael Jordan	15	20	40	100
328	Shaquille O'Neal RC	20	25	50	150

1992-93 Ultra All-NBA

		NmMt 8	NmMt+ 8.5	MT 9	Gem 9.5/10
4	Michael Jordan	25	40	80	200

1992-93 Ultra All-Rookies

		NmMt 8	NmMt+ 8.5	MT 9	Gem 9.5/10
6	Alonzo Mourning	8	10	15	40
7	Shaquille O'Neal	25	40	80	200

1992-93 Ultra Award Winners

		NmMt 8	NmMt+ 8.5	MT 9	Gem 9.5/10
1	Michael Jordan	25	40	80	200

1992-93 Ultra Rejectors

		NmMt 8	NmMt+ 8.5	MT 9	Gem 9.5/10
4	Shaquille O'Neal	15	25	50	120

1992-93 Upper Deck

		NmMt 8	NmMt+ 8.5	MT 9	Gem 9.5/10
1	Shaquille O'Neal SP RC	▼40	▼60	▼200	800
1B	Shaquille O'Neal TRADE	25	40	150	600
23	Michael Jordan	20	25	60	150
67	Michael Jordan MVP	12	15	30	100
453A	M.Jordan FACE 85 ERR	15	30	80	200
474	Shaquille O'Neal TP	12	15	30	60

1992-93 Upper Deck All-Division

		NmMt 8	NmMt+ 8.5	MT 9	Gem 9.5/10
AD1	Shaquille O'Neal	10	12	25	60
AD9	Michael Jordan	10	12	25	60

1992-93 Upper Deck Award Winner Holograms

		NmMt 8	NmMt+ 8.5	MT 9	Gem 9.5/10
AW9	Michael Jordan	15	25	50	100

1992-93 Upper Deck 15000 Point Club

		NmMt 8	NmMt+ 8.5	MT 9	Gem 9.5/10
PC4	Michael Jordan	15	25	50	120

1992-93 Upper Deck Rookie Standouts

		NmMt 8	NmMt+ 8.5	MT 9	Gem 9.5/10
RS15	Shaquille O'Neal	15	25	50	120

1992-93 Upper Deck Team MVPs

		NmMt 8	NmMt+ 8.5	MT 9	Gem 9.5/10
TM1	Michael Jordan CL	15	20	40	100
TM5	Michael Jordan	20	30	80	200

1993-94 Finest

		NmMt 8	NmMt+ 8.5	MT 9	Gem 9.5/10
1	Michael Jordan	100	200	350	600
189	Anfernee Hardaway RC	20	25	50	120
212	Chris Webber RC	25	40	100	200

1993-94 Finest Refractors

		NmMt 8	NmMt+ 8.5	MT 9	Gem 9.5/10
1	Michael Jordan	1,200	2,000	3,000	8,000
3	Shaquille O'Neal SP !				
189	Anfernee Hardaway				
212	Chris Webber SP !				

1993-94 Fleer

		NmMt 8	NmMt+ 8.5	MT 9	Gem 9.5/10
28	Michael Jordan	12	15	30	100
224	Michael Jordan LL	10	12	20	50

1993-94 Fleer All-Stars

		NmMt 8	NmMt+ 8.5	MT 9	Gem 9.5/10
5	Michael Jordan	25	40	100	

1993-94 Fleer Living Legends

		NmMt 8	NmMt+ 8.5	MT 9	Gem 9.5/10
4	Michael Jordan	60	100	200	600

1993-94 Fleer NBA Superstars

		NmMt 8	NmMt+ 8.5	MT 9	Gem 9.5/10
7	Michael Jordan	12	20	40	120

1993-94 Fleer Sharpshooters

		NmMt 8	NmMt+ 8.5	MT 9	Gem 9.5/10
3	Michael Jordan	25	40	80	200

1993-94 Hoops

		NmMt 8	NmMt+ 8.5	MT 9	Gem 9.5/10
28	Michael Jordan	10	15	25	60
257	Michael Jordan AS	10	15	25	60

1993-94 Hoops Fifth Anniversary Gold

		NmMt 8	NmMt+ 8.5	MT 9	Gem 9.5/10
28	Michael Jordan	25	60	120	

1993-94 Hoops Draft Redemption

		NmMt 8	NmMt+ 8.5	MT 9	Gem 9.5/10
LP1	Chris Webber	10	15	30	100
LP3	Anfernee Hardaway	10	15	20	50

1993-94 Hoops Supreme Court

		NmMt 8	NmMt+ 8.5	MT 9	Gem 9.5/10
SC11	Michael Jordan	15	25	50	150

1993-94 SkyBox Premium

		NmMt 8	NmMt+ 8.5	MT 9	Gem 9.5/10
14	Michael Jordan PO	10	12	20	50
45	Michael Jordan	10	12	20	50
227	Chris Webber RC	4	6	10	20

1993-94 SkyBox Premium Center Stage

		NmMt 8	NmMt+ 8.5	MT 9	Gem 9.5/10
CS1	Michael Jordan	40	60	120	400

1993-94 SkyBox Premium Draft Picks

		NmMt 8	NmMt+ 8.5	MT 9	Gem 9.5/10
DP1	Chris Webber	8	10	15	30

1993-94 SkyBox Premium Dynamic Dunks

		NmMt 8	NmMt+ 8.5	MT 9	Gem 9.5/10
D4	Michael Jordan	30	60	150	400

1993-94 SkyBox Premium Showdown Series

		NmMt 8	NmMt+ 8.5	MT 9	Gem 9.5/10
SS11	C.Drexler/M.Jordan	10	15	30	80

1993-94 Stadium Club

		NmMt 8	NmMt+ 8.5	MT 9	Gem 9.5/10
169	Michael Jordan	12	15	30	80

1993-94 Stadium Club First Day Issue

		NmMt 8	NmMt+ 8.5	MT 9	Gem 9.5/10
1	Michael Jordan TD	100	150	300	600

1993-94 Stadium Club Beam Team

		NmMt 8	NmMt+ 8.5	MT 9	Gem 9.5/10
4	Michael Jordan	60	120	350	

1993-94 Topps

		NmMt 8	NmMt+ 8.5	MT 9	Gem 9.5/10
224	Chris Webber RC	5	8	20	

1993-94 Ultra

		NmMt 8	NmMt+ 8.5	MT 9	Gem 9.5/10
30	Michael Jordan	15	20	40	100

1993-94 Ultra All-Defensive

		NmMt 8	NmMt+ 8.5	MT 9	Gem 9.5/10
2	Michael Jordan	100	150	250	500

1993-94 Ultra All-NBA

		NmMt 8	NmMt+ 8.5	MT 9	Gem 9.5/10
2	Michael Jordan	25	40	80	200

1993-94 Ultra Famous Nicknames

		NmMt 8	NmMt+ 8.5	MT 9	Gem 9.5/10
7	Michael Jordan	40	60	150	500

1993-94 Ultra Inside/Outside

		NmMt 8	NmMt+ 8.5	MT 9	Gem 9.5/10
4	Michael Jordan	80	120	250	500

1993-94 Ultra Power In The Key

		NmMt 8	NmMt+ 8.5	MT 9	Gem 9.5/10
	Michael Jordan	400	600	1,500	5,000

1993-94 Ultra Scoring Kings

		NmMt 8	NmMt+ 8.5	MT 9	Gem 9.5/10
	Michael Jordan	1,000	1,500	3,000	6,000
	Shaquille O'Neal	100	150	300	600

1993-94 Upper Deck

		NmMt 8	NmMt+ 8.5	MT 9	Gem 9.5/10
A	Michael Jordan	12	20	40	120

1993-94 Upper Deck All-NBA

		NmMt 8	NmMt+ 8.5	MT 9	Gem 9.5/10
N4	Michael Jordan	25	30	60	150
N15	Michael Jordan CL	25	30	60	150

1993-94 Upper Deck SE Behind the Glass

		NmMt 8	NmMt+ 8.5	MT 9	Gem 9.5/10
1	Michael Jordan	100	150	300	600

1994-95 Emotion

		NmMt 8	NmMt+ 8.5	MT 9	Gem 9.5/10
	Jason Kidd RC	8	12	25	50
0	Michael Jordan	20	30	60	150

1994-95 Emotion N-Tense

		NmMt 8	NmMt+ 8.5	MT 9	Gem 9.5/10
	Michael Jordan	150	200	400	800
	Shaquille O'Neal	60	80	150	300

1994-95 Finest

		NmMt 8	NmMt+ 8.5	MT 9	Gem 9.5/10
	Grant Hill CB	20	25	50	100
	Grant Hill RC	20	25	50	100
	Jason Kidd RC	20	25	50	100
	Michael Jordan	80	100	▼250	600

1994-95 Finest Refractors

		NmMt 8	NmMt+ 8.5	MT 9	Gem 9.5/10
	Grant Hill	200	250	500	800
	Jason Kidd	200	250	500	800
	Michael Jordan	1,000	1,200	2,500	5,000

1994-95 Flair

		NmMt 8	NmMt+ 8.5	MT 9	Gem 9.5/10
	Michael Jordan	15	25	50	120

1994-95 SP

		NmMt 8	NmMt+ 8.5	MT 9	Gem 9.5/10
	Jason Kidd FOIL RC	▼10	▼15	▼40	▼100
	Grant Hill FOIL RC	▼10	▼15	▼40	▼100
1RM.	Jordan Red	25	40	100	250

1994-95 SP Die Cuts

		NmMt 8	NmMt+ 8.5	MT 9	Gem 9.5/10
	Jason Kidd	10	15	▲40	100

1994-95 SP Championship Playoff Heroes

		NmMt 8	NmMt+ 8.5	MT 9	Gem 9.5/10
P2	Michael Jordan	30	40	80	200

1994-95 SP Championship Playoff Heroes Die Cuts

		NmMt 8	NmMt+ 8.5	MT 9	Gem 9.5/10
P2	Michael Jordan	100	120	200	400

1994-95 Topps

		NmMt 8	NmMt+ 8.5	MT 9	Gem 9.5/10
37	Jason Kidd RC	▼10	▼15	▼30	▼80
211	Grant Hill RC	▼10	▼15	▼30	▼80

1994-95 Upper Deck

		NmMt 8	NmMt+ 8.5	MT 9	Gem 9.5/10
157	Grant Hill RC	10	15	30	60
160	Jason Kidd RC	10	15	30	60

1995-96 Collector's Choice

		NmMt 8	NmMt+ 8.5	MT 9	Gem 9.5/10
275	Kevin Garnett RC	8	12	30	80

1995-96 E-XL

		NmMt 8	NmMt+ 8.5	MT 9	Gem 9.5/10
10	Michael Jordan	20	30	60	150
49	Kevin Garnett RC	20	30	60	150

1995-96 E-XL Blue

		NmMt 8	NmMt+ 8.5	MT 9	Gem 9.5/10
10	Michael Jordan	40	60	120	300
49	Kevin Garnett RC	40	60	120	300

1995-96 E-XL Natural Born Thrillers

		NmMt 8	NmMt+ 8.5	MT 9	Gem 9.5/10
1	Michael Jordan	800	1,000	2,000	5,000
5	Kevin Garnett	200	300	500	1,000

1995-96 E-XL No Boundaries

		NmMt 8	NmMt+ 8.5	MT 9	Gem 9.5/10
1	Michael Jordan	80	120	250	500

1995-96 Finest

		NmMt 8	NmMt+ 8.5	MT 9	Gem 9.5/10
115	Kevin Garnett RC	▼50	▼80	▼150	▼400
229	Michael Jordan	60	80	120	300

1995-96 Finest Refractors

		NmMt 8	NmMt+ 8.5	MT 9	Gem 9.5/10
229	Michael Jordan	1,000	1,200	2,000	4,000

1995-96 Finest Hot Stuff

		NmMt 8	NmMt+ 8.5	MT 9	Gem 9.5/10
HS1	Michael Jordan	80	100	150	300

1995-96 Finest Mystery

		NmMt 8	NmMt+ 8.5	MT 9	Gem 9.5/10
M1	Michael Jordan	80	120	250	500

1995-96 Finest Veteran/Rookie

		NmMt 8	NmMt+ 8.5	MT 9	Gem 9.5/10
RV5	K.Garnett/T.Gugliotta	60	80	150	300
RV20	J.Caffey/M.Jordan	100	120	250	500

1995-96 Flair

		NmMt 8	NmMt+ 8.5	MT 9	Gem 9.5/10
15	Michael Jordan	25	40	80	200
206	Kevin Garnett RC	25	40	80	200

1995-96 Flair Anticipation

		NmMt 8	NmMt+ 8.5	MT 9	Gem 9.5/10
2	Michael Jordan	200	250	500	1,000

1995-96 Flair Class of '95

		NmMt 8	NmMt+ 8.5	MT 9	Gem 9.5/10
R2	Kevin Garnett	20	30	60	150

1995-96 Flair Hot Numbers

		NmMt 8	NmMt+ 8.5	MT 9	Gem 9.5/10
4	Michael Jordan	600	800	1,200	2,500
11	Shaquille O'Neal	200	250	500	800

1995-96 Flair New Heights

		NmMt 8	NmMt+ 8.5	MT 9	Gem 9.5/10
4	Michael Jordan	200	250	500	1,000

1995-96 Flair Wave of the Future

		NmMt 8	NmMt+ 8.5	MT 9	Gem 9.5/10
3	Kevin Garnett	40	60	120	300

1995-96 Fleer

		NmMt 8	NmMt+ 8.5	MT 9	Gem 9.5/10
22	Michael Jordan	10	12	30	100

1995-96 Fleer Flair Hardwood Leaders

		NmMt 8	NmMt+ 8.5	MT 9	Gem 9.5/10
4	Michael Jordan	40	60	120	300

1995-96 Hoops Hot List

		NmMt 8	NmMt+ 8.5	MT 9	Gem 9.5/10
1	Michael Jordan	150	200	400	800

1995-96 Hoops SkyView

		NmMt 8	NmMt+ 8.5	MT 9	Gem 9.5/10
SV1	Michael Jordan	300	400	800	1,500

1995-96 Metal

		NmMt 8	NmMt+ 8.5	MT 9	Gem 9.5/10
167	Kevin Garnett RC	20	30	60	150
212	Michael Jordan NB	20	30	60	120

1995-96 Metal Maximum Metal

		NmMt 8	NmMt+ 8.5	MT 9	Gem 9.5/10
4	Michael Jordan	100	150	300	600

1995-96 Metal Scoring Magnets

		NmMt 8	NmMt+ 8.5	MT 9	Gem 9.5/10
4	Michael Jordan	150	200	300	600

1995-96 Metal Slick Silver

		NmMt 8	NmMt+ 8.5	MT 9	Gem 9.5/10
3	Michael Jordan	100	120	250	500

BASKETBALL

1995-96 SkyBox Premium Larger Than Life

		NmMt 8	NmMt+ 8.5	MT 9	Gem 9.5/10
L1	Michael Jordan	400	600	1,200	

1995-96 SkyBox Premium Meltdown

		NmMt 8	NmMt+ 8.5	MT 9	Gem 9.5/10
M1	Michael Jordan	500	800	2,000	

1995-96 SP

		NmMt 8	NmMt+ 8.5	MT 9	Gem 9.5/10
23	Michael Jordan	20	30	50	150
159	Kevin Garnett RC	12	20	40	120

1995-96 SP All-Stars

		NmMt 8	NmMt+ 8.5	MT 9	Gem 9.5/10
AS2	Michael Jordan	40	60	120	300
AS28	Kevin Garnett	12	20	40	100

1995-96 SP All-Stars Gold

		NmMt 8	NmMt+ 8.5	MT 9	Gem 9.5/10
AS2	Michael Jordan	250	300	600	1,200

1995-96 SP Holoviews

		NmMt 8	NmMt+ 8.5	MT 9	Gem 9.5/10
PC5	Michael Jordan	80	120	300	600

1995-96 Stadium Club

		NmMt 8	NmMt+ 8.5	MT 9	Gem 9.5/10
1	Michael Jordan	20	30	60	120
343	Kevin Garnett RC	30	50	100	200

1995-96 Stadium Club Beam Team

		NmMt 8	NmMt+ 8.5	MT 9	Gem 9.5/10
B14	Michael Jordan	250	400	800	2,000

1995-96 Stadium Club Warp Speed

		NmMt 8	NmMt+ 8.5	MT 9	Gem 9.5/10
WS1	Michael Jordan	250	300	600	1,200

1995-96 Topps

		NmMt 8	NmMt+ 8.5	MT 9	Gem 9.5/10
237	Kevin Garnett RC	50	60	150	300

1995-96 Topps Draft Redemption

		NmMt 8	NmMt+ 8.5	MT 9	Gem 9.5/10
5	Kevin Garnett	100	150	300	500

1995-96 Topps Power Boosters

		NmMt 8	NmMt+ 8.5	MT 9	Gem 9.5/10
277	Michael Jordan	250	300	600	1,200

1995-96 Topps Spark Plugs

		NmMt 8	NmMt+ 8.5	MT 9	Gem 9.5/10
SP2	Michael Jordan	50	80	200	400

1995-96 Topps Top Flight

		NmMt 8	NmMt+ 8.5	MT 9	Gem 9.5/10
TF1	Michael Jordan	60	100	200	400

1995-96 Ultra

		NmMt 8	NmMt+ 8.5	MT 9	Gem 9.5/10
274	Kevin Garnett RC	25	40	80	200

1995-96 Ultra Gold Medallion

		NmMt 8	NmMt+ 8.5	MT 9	Gem 9.5/10
25	Michael Jordan	100	150	300	600

1995-96 Ultra Double Trouble

		NmMt 8	NmMt+ 8.5	MT 9	Gem 9.5/10
3	Michael Jordan	25	40	80	200

1995-96 Upper Deck

		NmMt 8	NmMt+ 8.5	MT 9	Gem 9.5/10
23	Michael Jordan	15	30	60	120
273	Kevin Garnett RC	20	30	60	120

1995-96 Upper Deck Special Edition

		NmMt 8	NmMt+ 8.5	MT 9	Gem 9.5/10
100	Michael Jordan	60	100	250	500

1996 SPx

		NmMt 8	NmMt+ 8.5	MT 9	Gem 9.5/10
8	Michael Jordan	50	80	150	300
R1	Michael Jordan RB	12	20	30	80

1996 SPx Gold

		NmMt 8	NmMt+ 8.5	MT 9	Gem 9.5/10
8	Michael Jordan	120	150	300	600

1996 SPx Holoview Heroes

		NmMt 8	NmMt+ 8.5	MT 9	Gem 9.5/10
H1	Michael Jordan	120	150	300	600

1996-97 Bowman's Best

		NmMt 8	NmMt+ 8.5	MT 9	Gem 9.5/10
80	Michael Jordan	25	50	100	300
R1	Allen Iverson RC	40	80	150	300
R5	Ray Allen RC	8	15	30	80
R18	Steve Nash RC	20	40	80	150
R23	Kobe Bryant RC	250	300	600	1,000

1996-97 Bowman's Best Refractors

		NmMt 8	NmMt+ 8.5	MT 9	Gem 9.5/10
80	Michael Jordan	400	500	1,000	
R1	Allen Iverson	400	500	1,000	
R18	Steve Nash	400	500	800	1,200
R23	Kobe Bryant	2,500	3,000	6,000	

1996-97 Bowman's Best Honor Roll

		NmMt 8	NmMt+ 8.5	MT 9	Gem 9.5/10
HR2	M.Jordan/H.Olajuwon	40	50	80	200

1996-97 Bowman's Best Honor Roll Refractors

		NmMt 8	NmMt+ 8.5	MT 9	Gem 9.5/10
HR2	M.Jordan/H.Olajuwon	500	600	1,000	

1996-97 Bowman's Best Picks

		NmMt 8	NmMt+ 8.5	MT 9	Gem 9.5/10
BP10	Kobe Bryant	200	300	500	800

1996-97 Bowman's Best Picks Refractors

		NmMt 8	NmMt+ 8.5	MT 9	Gem 9.5/10
BP10	Kobe Bryant	3,000	4,000	5,000	

1996-97 Bowman's Best Shots

		NmMt 8	NmMt+ 8.5	MT 9	Gem 9.5/10
BS6	Michael Jordan	40	60	120	300

1996-97 Bowman's Best Shots Refractors

		NmMt 8	NmMt+ 8.5	MT 9	Gem 9.5/10
BS6	Michael Jordan	120	150	300	600

1996-97 Collector's Choice

		NmMt 8	NmMt+ 8.5	MT 9	Gem 9.5/10
267	Kobe Bryant RC	40	60	150	400
301	Allen Iverson RC	20	30	60	150

1996-97 E-X2000

		NmMt 8	NmMt+ 8.5	MT 9	Gem 9.5/10
9	Michael Jordan	100	120	250	500
30	Kobe Bryant RC	400	500	2,500	6,000
37	Ray Allen RC	20	40	100	
53	Allen Iverson RC	100	200	500	

1996-97 E-X2000 A Cut Above

		NmMt 8	NmMt+ 8.5	MT 9	Gem 9.5/10
5	Michael Jordan	4,000	5,000	10,000	

1996-97 E-X2000 Net Assets

		NmMt 8	NmMt+ 8.5	MT 9	Gem 9.5/10
8	Michael Jordan	800	1,000	2,000	4,000

1996-97 E-X2000 Star Date 2000

		NmMt 8	NmMt+ 8.5	MT 9	Gem 9.5/10
3	Kobe Bryant	2,000	3,000	5,000	10,000
7	Allen Iverson	600	800	1,500	3,000

1996-97 Finest

		NmMt 8	NmMt+ 8.5	MT 9	Gem 9.5/10
50	Michael Jordan B	20	40	100	300
69	Allen Iverson B RC	30	50	100	200
74	Kobe Bryant B RC	200	300	600	1,500
75	Steve Nash B RC	20	40	80	150
127	Michael Jordan S	20	40	100	300
269	Kobe Bryant G	1,500	2,500	5,000	10,000
291	Michael Jordan G	300	400	600	

1996-97 Finest Refractors

		NmMt 8	NmMt+ 8.5	MT 9	Gem 9.5/10
69	Allen Iverson B	800	1,000	2,000	
74	Kobe Bryant B	8,000	10,000	15,000	
75	Steve Nash B	300	400	800	
269	Kobe Bryant G	12,000	15,000	25,000	40,000

1996-97 Flair Showcase Row 2

		NmMt 8	NmMt+ 8.5	MT 9	Gem 9.5/10
3	Allen Iverson RC	100	150	300	600
23	Michael Jordan	100	120	250	500
31	Kobe Bryant RC	600	800	1,500	3,000

252 www.beckett.com/price-guide

1996-97 Flair Showcase Row 1

		NmMt 8	NmMt+ 8.5	MT 9	Gem 9.5/10
23	Michael Jordan	100	200	400	
31	Kobe Bryant	500	600	1,000	2,000

1996-97 Flair Showcase Row 0

		NmMt 8	NmMt+ 8.5	MT 9	Gem 9.5/10
23	Michael Jordan	1,000	1,500	3,000	
31	Kobe Bryant	2,000	3,000	6,000	
35	Ray Allen	40	80	150	300

1996-97 Flair Showcase Class of '96

		NmMt 8	NmMt+ 8.5	MT 9	Gem 9.5/10
1	Kobe Bryant	200	250	500	1,000
10	Allen Iverson	60	100	200	400
15	Steve Nash	40	80	150	300

1996-97 Flair Showcase Hot Shots

		NmMt 8	NmMt+ 8.5	MT 9	Gem 9.5/10
	Michael Jordan	3,000	4,000	6,000	10,000

1996-97 Fleer

		NmMt 8	NmMt+ 8.5	MT 9	Gem 9.5/10
203	Kobe Bryant RC	40	60	150	400
235	Allen Iverson RC	20	30	60	150
239	Steve Nash RC	20	30	60	150

1996-97 Fleer Decade of Excellence

		NmMt 8	NmMt+ 8.5	MT 9	Gem 9.5/10
	Michael Jordan	40	60	150	300

1996-97 Fleer Game Breakers

		NmMt 8	NmMt+ 8.5	MT 9	Gem 9.5/10
	M.Jordan/S.Pippen	100	150	300	

1996-97 Fleer Lucky 13

		NmMt 8	NmMt+ 8.5	MT 9	Gem 9.5/10
	Allen Iverson	15	20	50	150
	Ray Allen	10	15	30	60
3	Kobe Bryant	250	300	600	1,200

1996-97 Fleer Rookie Sensations

		NmMt 8	NmMt+ 8.5	MT 9	Gem 9.5/10
	Kobe Bryant	600	800	1,500	3,000
	Allen Iverson	100	150	300	600

1996-97 Fleer Total O

		NmMt 8	NmMt+ 8.5	MT 9	Gem 9.5/10
	Michael Jordan	100	150	300	600

1996-97 Hoops

		NmMt 8	NmMt+ 8.5	MT 9	Gem 9.5/10
281	Kobe Bryant RC	30	60	150	400
295	Allen Iverson RC	15	20	40	80
304	Steve Nash RC	15	20	40	80

1996-97 Hoops Hot List

		NmMt 8	NmMt+ 8.5	MT 9	Gem 9.5/10
	Michael Jordan	200	300	600	1,000

1996-97 Hoops Rookies

		NmMt 8	NmMt+ 8.5	MT 9	Gem 9.5/10
3	Kobe Bryant	150	200	400	800

1996-97 Hoops Superfeats

		NmMt 8	NmMt+ 8.5	MT 9	Gem 9.5/10
1	Michael Jordan	50	80	150	300

1996-97 Metal

		NmMt 8	NmMt+ 8.5	MT 9	Gem 9.5/10
11	Michael Jordan	10	20	40	100
137	Kobe Bryant FF RC	100	150	300	600
181	Kobe Bryant	100	150	300	600
201	Allen Iverson RC	25	40	80	150
241	Michael Jordan MS	40	50	80	200

1996-97 Metal Cyber-Metal

		NmMt 8	NmMt+ 8.5	MT 9	Gem 9.5/10
5	Kobe Bryant	60	100	300	600

1996-97 Metal Decade of Excellence

		NmMt 8	NmMt+ 8.5	MT 9	Gem 9.5/10
M4	Michael Jordan	120	250	500	

1996-97 Metal Freshly Forged

		NmMt 8	NmMt+ 8.5	MT 9	Gem 9.5/10
3	Kobe Bryant	150	200	500	1,200

1996-97 Metal Maximum Metal

		NmMt 8	NmMt+ 8.5	MT 9	Gem 9.5/10
4	Michael Jordan	▲800	▲1,000	▲2,000	▲4,000

1996-97 Metal Metal Edge

		NmMt 8	NmMt+ 8.5	MT 9	Gem 9.5/10
15	Kobe Bryant	100	120	300	2,000

1996-97 Metal Molten Metal

		NmMt 8	NmMt+ 8.5	MT 9	Gem 9.5/10
18	Michael Jordan	600	800	1,500	

1996-97 Metal Net-Rageous

		NmMt 8	NmMt+ 8.5	MT 9	Gem 9.5/10
5	Michael Jordan	1,000	2,000	4,000	

1996-97 Metal Platinum Portraits

		NmMt 8	NmMt+ 8.5	MT 9	Gem 9.5/10
5	Michael Jordan	500	800	1,500	3,000

1996-97 Metal Steel Slammin'

		NmMt 8	NmMt+ 8.5	MT 9	Gem 9.5/10
6	Michael Jordan	▲400	▲500	▲1,000	

1996-97 SkyBox Premium

		NmMt 8	NmMt+ 8.5	MT 9	Gem 9.5/10
16	Michael Jordan	10	15	30	60
55	Kobe Bryant RC	80	120	300	600
85	Allen Iverson RC	10	15	30	60
91	Steve Nash RC	10	15	30	60
203	Kobe Bryant ROO	40	60	150	400

1996-97 SkyBox Premium Rubies

		NmMt 8	NmMt+ 8.5	MT 9	Gem 9.5/10
55	Kobe Bryant	5,000	6,000		
203	Kobe Bryant ROO	5,000	6,000		

1996-97 SkyBox Premium Golden Touch

		NmMt 8	NmMt+ 8.5	MT 9	Gem 9.5/10
5	Michael Jordan	1,500	2,000	3,000	

1996-97 SkyBox Premium New Editions

		NmMt 8	NmMt+ 8.5	MT 9	Gem 9.5/10
3	Kobe Bryant	▲500	▲600	▲1,200	▲4,000

1996-97 SkyBox Premium Rookie Prevue

		NmMt 8	NmMt+ 8.5	MT 9	Gem 9.5/10
R3	Kobe Bryant	250	300	600	

1996-97 SP

		NmMt 8	NmMt+ 8.5	MT 9	Gem 9.5/10
134	Kobe Bryant RC	40	60	150	400
136	Ray Allen RC	8	12	25	50
141	Allen Iverson RC	15	20	40	80
142	Steve Nash RC	15	20	40	80

1996-97 SP Holoviews

		NmMt 8	NmMt+ 8.5	MT 9	Gem 9.5/10
PC5	Michael Jordan	150	200	400	800
PC18	Kobe Bryant	600	800	1,500	

1996-97 Stadium Club

		NmMt 8	NmMt+ 8.5	MT 9	Gem 9.5/10
101	Michael Jordan	15	20	40	100

1996-97 Stadium Club Rookie Showcase

		NmMt 8	NmMt+ 8.5	MT 9	Gem 9.5/10
RS11	Kobe Bryant	150	200	400	800

1996-97 Stadium Club Rookies 1

		NmMt 8	NmMt+ 8.5	MT 9	Gem 9.5/10
R12	Kobe Bryant	60	100	250	500

1996-97 Stadium Club Rookies 2

		NmMt 8	NmMt+ 8.5	MT 9	Gem 9.5/10
R9	Kobe Bryant	60	100	250	500

1996-97 Stadium Club Top Crop

		NmMt 8	NmMt+ 8.5	MT 9	Gem 9.5/10
TC9	M.Jordan/G.Payton	40	80	150	400

1996-97 Topps

		NmMt 8	NmMt+ 8.5	MT 9	Gem 9.5/10
138	Kobe Bryant RC	▼200	▼300	▼600	▼1,200
139	Michael Jordan	30	50	100	200
171	Allen Iverson RC	40	60	100	300
182	Steve Nash RC	40	60	100	300

1996-97 Topps NBA at 50

		NmMt 8	NmMt+ 8.5	MT 9	Gem 9.5/10
138	Kobe Bryant	▼600	▼1,000	▼2,000	4,000

1996-97 Topps Draft Redemption

		NmMt 8	NmMt+ 8.5	MT 9	Gem 9.5/10
DP1	Allen Iverson	80	150	300	600
DP13	Kobe Bryant	800	1,000	2,000	4,000

1996-97 Topps Holding Court Refractors

		NmMt 8	NmMt+ 8.5	MT 9	Gem 9.5/10
HC2	Michael Jordan	250	300	600	1,200

1996-97 Topps Pro Files

		NmMt 8	NmMt+ 8.5	MT 9	Gem 9.5/10
PF3	Michael Jordan	15	25	50	200

1996-97 Topps Season's Best

		NmMt 8	NmMt+ 8.5	MT 9	Gem 9.5/10
SB1	Michael Jordan	80	120	250	500
SB18	Michael Jordan	80	120	250	500

1996-97 Topps Youthquake

		NmMt 8	NmMt+ 8.5	MT 9	Gem 9.5/10
YQ1	Allen Iverson	60	150	300	600
YQ15	Kobe Bryant	500	600	1,200	3,000

1996-97 Topps Chrome

		NmMt 8	NmMt+ 8.5	MT 9	Gem 9.5/10
138	Kobe Bryant RC	▼2,500	▼4,000	▼6,000	▼10,000
139	Michael Jordan	200	300	600	1,000
171	Allen Iverson RC	▼150	▼300	▼500	▼1,000
182	Steve Nash RC	▼100	▼200	▼400	▼800
217	Ray Allen RC	60	120	300	600

1996-97 Topps Chrome Refractors

		NmMt 8	NmMt+ 8.5	MT 9	Gem 9.5/10
138	Kobe Bryant	▼20,000	▼30,000	▼40,000	▼60,000
139	Michael Jordan	8,000	10,000	15,000	25,000
171	Allen Iverson	▼4,000	▼6,000	▼10,000	
182	Steve Nash	▼1,500	▼2,500	▼5,000	
217	Ray Allen	1,000	1,500	3,000	

1996-97 Topps Chrome Youthquake

		NmMt 8	NmMt+ 8.5	MT 9	Gem 9.5/10
YQ1	Allen Iverson	60	100	300	
YQ15	Kobe Bryant	400	600	1,000	3,000

1996-97 UD3

		NmMt 8	NmMt+ 8.5	MT 9	Gem 9.5/10
19	Kobe Bryant RC	80	120	250	500
43	Kobe Bryant	40	80	200	500

1996-97 Ultra

		NmMt 8	NmMt+ 8.5	MT 9	Gem 9.5/10
52	Kobe Bryant RC	120	200	600	2,000
60	Ray Allen RC	12	20	50	150
82	Allen Iverson RC	15	30	150	
87	Steve Nash RC	15	30	150	

1996-97 Ultra Gold Medallion

		NmMt 8	NmMt+ 8.5	MT 9	Gem 9.5/10
G52	Kobe Bryant	800	1,200		

1996-97 Ultra All-Rookies

		NmMt 8	NmMt+ 8.5	MT 9	Gem 9.5/10
3	Kobe Bryant	80	150	500	2,000

1996-97 Ultra Court Masters

		NmMt 8	NmMt+ 8.5	MT 9	Gem 9.5/10
2	Michael Jordan	800	1,000	1,500	3,000

1996-97 Ultra Fresh Faces

		NmMt 8	NmMt+ 8.5	MT 9	Gem 9.5/10
3	Kobe Bryant	600	1,000	2,000	5,000

1996-97 Ultra Full Court Trap

		NmMt 8	NmMt+ 8.5	MT 9	Gem 9.5/10
1	Michael Jordan	60	100	200	500

1996-97 Ultra Scoring Kings

		NmMt 8	NmMt+ 8.5	MT 9	Gem 9.5/10
4	Michael Jordan	600	800	1,500	3,000

1996-97 Upper Deck

		NmMt 8	NmMt+ 8.5	MT 9	Gem 9.5/10
16	Michael Jordan	12	20	40	100
58	Kobe Bryant RC	50	80	200	600
91	Allen Iverson RC	12	20	40	150
280	Steve Nash RC	8	12	30	80

1996-97 Upper Deck Fast Break Connections

		NmMt 8	NmMt+ 8.5	MT 9	Gem 9.5/10
FB23	Michael Jordan	20	40	80	200

1996-97 Upper Deck Rookie Exclusives

		NmMt 8	NmMt+ 8.5	MT 9	Gem 9.5/10
R1	Allen Iverson	10	15	30	100
R7	Ray Allen	8	10	15	40
R10	Kobe Bryant	50	80	150	400

1996-97 Upper Deck Smooth Grooves

		NmMt 8	NmMt+ 8.5	MT 9	Gem 9.5/10
SG8	Michael Jordan	250	300	600	1,200

1996-97 Z-Force

		NmMt 8	NmMt+ 8.5	MT 9	Gem 9.5/10
142	Kobe Bryant RC	60	100	200	500

1996-97 Z-Force Slam Cam

		NmMt 8	NmMt+ 8.5	MT 9	Gem 9.5/10
SC5	Michael Jordan	2,000	2,500	5,000	

1996-97 Z-Force Zebut

		NmMt 8	NmMt+ 8.5	MT 9	Gem 9.5/10
3	Kobe Bryant	400	500	1,000	3,000

1996-97 Z-Force Zebut Z-peat

		NmMt 8	NmMt+ 8.5	MT 9	Gem 9.5/10
3	Kobe Bryant	1,000	2,000	4,000	8,000

1997 SPx

		NmMt 8	NmMt+ 8.5	MT 9	Gem 9.5/10
22	Kobe Bryant	150	300	600	1,200

1997 SPx Gold

		NmMt 8	NmMt+ 8.5	MT 9	Gem 9.5/10
22	Kobe Bryant	500	600	1,200	

1997-98 Bowman's Best

		NmMt 8	NmMt+ 8.5	MT 9	Gem 9.5/10
60	Michael Jordan	25	40	80	200
96	Michael Jordan BP	30	40	80	200
106	Tim Duncan RC	15	30	60	120
111	Tracy McGrady RC	10	20	40	80

1997-98 Bowman's Best Refractors

		NmMt 8	NmMt+ 8.5	MT 9	Gem 9.5/10
60	Michael Jordan	200	250	400	800
106	Tim Duncan	200	250	400	800
111	Tracy McGrady	100	120	250	500

1997-98 Bowman's Best Techniques

		NmMt 8	NmMt+ 8.5	MT 9	Gem 9.5/10
T2	Michael Jordan	15	30	60	120

1997-98 Bowman's Best Techniques Refractors

		NmMt 8	NmMt+ 8.5	MT 9	Gem 9.5/10
T2	Michael Jordan	150	200	400	800

1997-98 Collector's Choice StarQuest

		NmMt 8	NmMt+ 8.5	MT 9	Gem 9.5/10
83	Michael Jordan	60	80	200	400

1997-98 E-X2001

		NmMt 8	NmMt+ 8.5	MT 9	Gem 9.5/10
9	Michael Jordan	150	200	400	
75	Tim Duncan RC	60	80	150	400
79	Tracy McGrady RC	25	40	80	200

1997-98 Finest

		NmMt 8	NmMt+ 8.5	MT 9	Gem 9.5/10
101	Tim Duncan B RC	30	40	80	150
103	Chauncey Billups B RC	6	10	20	40
107	Tracy McGrady B RC	8	15	30	60
137	Kobe Bryant S	60	80	150	300
154	Michael Jordan G	60	80	200	400
262	Kobe Bryant B	60	80	150	300
271	Michael Jordan B	10	15	30	60
287	Michael Jordan S	20	40	80	200
294	Tracy McGrady S	10	15	30	60
306	Tim Duncan S	15	30	60	150
316	Tracy McGrady G	15	20	40	80
325	Tim Duncan G	40	80	150	300

1997-98 Finest Refractors

		NmMt 8	NmMt+ 8.5	MT 9	Gem 9.5/10
101	Tim Duncan B	150	300	600	1,200
107	Tracy McGrady B	60	120	250	500
137	Kobe Bryant S	400	500	800	
271	Michael Jordan B	600	800	1,200	
287	Michael Jordan S	600	800	1,500	4,000

1997-98 Flair Showcase Row 3

		NmMt 8	NmMt+ 8.5	MT 9	Gem 9.5/10
1	Michael Jordan	30	40	80	200
5	Tim Duncan RC	30	40	80	200

1997-98 Flair Showcase Row 2

	NmMt 8	NmMt+ 8.5	MT 9	Gem 9.5/10
Tim Duncan	20	40	80	200
Kobe Bryant	50	80	150	300

1997-98 Flair Showcase Row 1

	NmMt 8	NmMt+ 8.5	MT 9	Gem 9.5/10
Michael Jordan	200	250	500	
Tim Duncan	80	100	300	600
Kobe Bryant	200	250	500	

1997-98 Flair Showcase Row 0

	NmMt 8	NmMt+ 8.5	MT 9	Gem 9.5/10
Kobe Bryant	800	1,000	2,000	4,000

1997-98 Fleer

	NmMt 8	NmMt+ 8.5	MT 9	Gem 9.5/10
Michael Jordan	6	8	15	40
Tim Duncan RC	12	15	30	60
Tracy McGrady RC	6	8	15	30

1997-98 Fleer Tiffany Collection

	NmMt 8	NmMt+ 8.5	MT 9	Gem 9.5/10
Michael Jordan	500	600	1,200	3,000

1997-98 Fleer Decade of Excellence

	NmMt 8	NmMt+ 8.5	MT 9	Gem 9.5/10
Michael Jordan	100	150	300	600

1997-98 Fleer Soaring Stars

	NmMt 8	NmMt+ 8.5	MT 9	Gem 9.5/10
Michael Jordan	100	120	250	500

1997-98 Fleer Thrill Seekers

	NmMt 8	NmMt+ 8.5	MT 9	Gem 9.5/10
Michael Jordan	1,500	2,000	4,000	

1997-98 Hoops

	NmMt 8	NmMt+ 8.5	MT 9	Gem 9.5/10
Tim Duncan RC	20	30	60	120
Tracy McGrady RC	10	15	30	60

1997-98 Hoops Frequent Flyer Club

	NmMt 8	NmMt+ 8.5	MT 9	Gem 9.5/10
Michael Jordan	100	150	300	500

1997-98 Hoops Frequent Flyer Club Upgrade

	NmMt 8	NmMt+ 8.5	MT 9	Gem 9.5/10
Michael Jordan	1,500	2,000	3,000	

1997-98 Hoops HOOPerstars

	NmMt 8	NmMt+ 8.5	MT 9	Gem 9.5/10
Michael Jordan	400	500	800	2,000

1997-98 Metal Universe

	NmMt 8	NmMt+ 8.5	MT 9	Gem 9.5/10
Michael Jordan	200	250	400	800
Tracy McGrady RC	20	30	60	150
Tim Duncan RC	40	60	120	300

1997-98 Metal Universe Planet Metal

		NmMt 8	NmMt+ 8.5	MT 9	Gem 9.5/10
1	Michael Jordan	800	1,000	2,000	

1997-98 Metal Universe Titanium

		NmMt 8	NmMt+ 8.5	MT 9	Gem 9.5/10
1	Michael Jordan	1,000	1,500	3,000	5,000
3	Kobe Bryant	1,000	1,200	2,000	4,000

1997-98 Metal Universe Championship

		NmMt 8	NmMt+ 8.5	MT 9	Gem 9.5/10
23	Michael Jordan	60	80	200	400
36	Tracy McGrady RC	8	10	20	50
72	Tim Duncan RC	20	30	60	150

1997-98 Metal Universe Championship Championship Galaxy

		NmMt 8	NmMt+ 8.5	MT 9	Gem 9.5/10
1	Michael Jordan	2,000	3,000	4,000	8,000
3	Kobe Bryant/UER front Kobe, Bryant	1,000	1,500	3,000	6,000

1997-98 SkyBox Premium

		NmMt 8	NmMt+ 8.5	MT 9	Gem 9.5/10
79	Tracy McGrady RC	8	10	20	40
112	Tim Duncan RC	10	15	30	60

1997-98 SkyBox Premium Competitive Advantage

		NmMt 8	NmMt+ 8.5	MT 9	Gem 9.5/10
CA2	Kobe Bryant	500	600	1,000	2,000
CA3	Michael Jordan	600	800	1,500	3,000

1997-98 SkyBox Premium Premium Players

		NmMt 8	NmMt+ 8.5	MT 9	Gem 9.5/10
1	Michael Jordan	2,000	3,000	4,000	8,000
3	Kobe Bryant	1,000	1,500	3,000	6,000

1997-98 SP Authentic

		NmMt 8	NmMt+ 8.5	MT 9	Gem 9.5/10
128	Tim Duncan RC	60	80	150	300
166	Tracy McGrady FW RC	30	40	100	200

1997-98 SPx

		NmMt 8	NmMt+ 8.5	MT 9	Gem 9.5/10
37	Tim Duncan RC	30	40	80	200
42	Tracy McGrady RC	20	30	60	120

1997-98 Stadium Club

		NmMt 8	NmMt+ 8.5	MT 9	Gem 9.5/10
201	Tim Duncan RC	20	30	60	150
217	Tracy McGrady RC	15	20	40	100

1997-98 Stadium Club Hardcourt Heroics

		NmMt 8	NmMt+ 8.5	MT 9	Gem 9.5/10
H1	Michael Jordan	100	150	300	600

1997-98 Stadium Club Hardwood Hopefuls

		NmMt 8	NmMt+ 8.5	MT 9	Gem 9.5/10
HH4	Tim Duncan	10	15	30	60

1997-98 Stadium Club Triumvirate

		NmMt 8	NmMt+ 8.5	MT 9	Gem 9.5/10
T1B	Michael Jordan	400	600	1,000	
T9B	Michael Jordan	400	600	1,000	

1997-98 Topps

		NmMt 8	NmMt+ 8.5	MT 9	Gem 9.5/10
115	Tim Duncan RC	20	30	60	200
123	Michael Jordan	20	30	60	150
125	Tracy McGrady RC	15	20	40	80
171	Kobe Bryant	25	40	80	300

1997-98 Topps Draft Redemption

		NmMt 8	NmMt+ 8.5	MT 9	Gem 9.5/10
DP1	Tim Duncan	60	80	200	400

1997-98 Topps Generations

		NmMt 8	NmMt+ 8.5	MT 9	Gem 9.5/10
G2	Michael Jordan	150	200	400	800

1997-98 Topps Generations Refractors

		NmMt 8	NmMt+ 8.5	MT 9	Gem 9.5/10
G2	Michael Jordan	600	800	1,500	3,000
G24	Kobe Bryant	600	800	1,500	3,000

1997-98 Topps Rock Stars

		NmMt 8	NmMt+ 8.5	MT 9	Gem 9.5/10
RS1	Michael Jordan	150	200	400	800

1997-98 Topps Rock Stars Refractors

		NmMt 8	NmMt+ 8.5	MT 9	Gem 9.5/10
RS1	Michael Jordan	600	800	1,200	3,000

1997-98 Topps Chrome

		NmMt 8	NmMt+ 8.5	MT 9	Gem 9.5/10
115	Tim Duncan RC	▼80	▼120	▼250	▼600
123	Michael Jordan	100	120	250	500
125	Tracy McGrady RC	▼15	▼25	▼50	▼150
171	Kobe Bryant	▼150	▼250	▼400	800
181	Chauncey Billups RC	8	10	20	50

1997-98 Topps Chrome Refractors

		NmMt 8	NmMt+ 8.5	MT 9	Gem 9.5/10
51	CL/Bulls - Team of the 90s	600	800	1,500	3,000
115	Tim Duncan	▼1,500	▼2,500	▼4,000	▼8,000
123	Michael Jordan	1,000	1,500	3,000	6,000
125	Tracy McGrady	▲400	▲500	▲800	▲2,000
171	Kobe Bryant	3,000	5,000	8,000	15,000

1997-98 Topps Chrome Destiny Refractors

		NmMt 8	NmMt+ 8.5	MT 9	Gem 9.5/10
D5	Kobe Bryant	250	300	600	1,200
D8	Tim Duncan	60	80	200	400

1997-98 Topps Chrome Season's Best

		NmMt 8	NmMt+ 8.5	MT 9	Gem 9.5/10
SB6	Michael Jordan	100	150	250	500

1997-98 Topps Chrome Season's Best Refractors

		NmMt 8	NmMt+ 8.5	MT 9	Gem 9.5/10
SB6	Michael Jordan	400	500	800	2,000

1997-98 Topps Chrome Topps 40

		NmMt 8	NmMt+ 8.5	MT 9	Gem 9.5/10
T5	Michael Jordan	80	120	300	600

1997-98 Topps Chrome Topps 40 Refractors

		NmMt 8	NmMt+ 8.5	MT 9	Gem 9.5/10
T5	Michael Jordan	600	800	1,500	3,000

1997-98 Ultra

		NmMt 8	NmMt+ 8.5	MT 9	Gem 9.5/10
131	Tim Duncan RC	15	30	120	
138	Tracy McGrady RC	12	15	50	

1997-98 Ultra Gold Medallion

		NmMt 8	NmMt+ 8.5	MT 9	Gem 9.5/10
131G	Tim Duncan	15	30	60	250

1997-98 Ultra Big Shots

		NmMt 8	NmMt+ 8.5	MT 9	Gem 9.5/10
1	Michael Jordan	40	60	▲150	▲400

1997-98 Ultra Court Masters

		NmMt 8	NmMt+ 8.5	MT 9	Gem 9.5/10
CM1	Michael Jordan	▲1,500	▲3,000	▲6,000	

1997-98 Ultra Star Power

		NmMt 8	NmMt+ 8.5	MT 9	Gem 9.5/10
SP1	Michael Jordan	▲80	▲120	▲250	▲500

1997-98 Ultra Star Power Plus

		NmMt 8	NmMt+ 8.5	MT 9	Gem 9.5/10
SPP1	Michael Jordan	▲300	▲400	▲800	▲2,000

1997-98 Ultra Stars

		NmMt 8	NmMt+ 8.5	MT 9	Gem 9.5/10
1	Michael Jordan	▲2,000	▲3,000	▲4,000	▲6,000

1997-98 Upper Deck

		NmMt 8	NmMt+ 8.5	MT 9	Gem 9.5/10
114	Tim Duncan RC	8	10	15	40
300	Tracy McGrady RC	4	6	10	25

1997-98 Upper Deck Rookie Discovery 1

		NmMt 8	NmMt+ 8.5	MT 9	Gem 9.5/10
R1	Tim Duncan	6	10	20	40

1997-98 Z-Force

		NmMt 8	NmMt+ 8.5	MT 9	Gem 9.5/10
111	Tim Duncan RC	6	10	20	40

1997-98 Z-Force Big Men on Court

		NmMt 8	NmMt+ 8.5	MT 9	Gem 9.5/10
2	Kobe Bryant	1,500	2,000	3,000	5,000
9	Michael Jordan	2,000	3,000	4,000	8,000

1997-98 Z-Force Slam Cam

		NmMt 8	NmMt+ 8.5	MT 9	Gem 9.5/10
1	Kobe Bryant	100	150	300	600
5	Michael Jordan	150	200	400	800

1998-99 Black Diamond

		NmMt 8	NmMt+ 8.5	MT 9	Gem 9.5/10
22	Michael Jordan	6	10	20	40
92	Dirk Nowitzki RC	20	30	60	120
101	Paul Pierce RC	10	12	25	50
120	Vince Carter RC	15	25	50	100

1998-99 Bowman's Best

		NmMt 8	NmMt+ 8.5	MT 9	Gem 9.5/10
105	Vince Carter RC	30	40	80	200
109	Dirk Nowitzki RC	40	60	150	300
110	Paul Pierce RC	20	25	50	100

1998-99 Bowman's Best Refractors

		NmMt 8	NmMt+ 8.5	MT 9	Gem 9.5/10
105	Vince Carter	300	400	800	
109	Dirk Nowitzki	400	500	1,000	
110	Paul Pierce	150	200	400	

1998-99 Bowman's Best Autographs Refractors

		NmMt 8	NmMt+ 8.5	MT 9	Gem 9.5/10
A9	Vince Carter	800	1,000	2,000	

1998-99 E-X Century

		NmMt 8	NmMt+ 8.5	MT 9	Gem 9.5/10
68	Dirk Nowitzki RC	25	40	100	300
82	Paul Pierce RC	10	12	25	60
89	Vince Carter RC	20	40	80	250

1998-99 E-X Century Dunk 'N Go Nuts

		NmMt 8	NmMt+ 8.5	MT 9	Gem 9.5/10
6	Kobe Bryant	1,000	1,500	2,500	5,000
15	Michael Jordan	1,500	2,000	▲4,000	▲8,000

1998-99 Finest

		NmMt 8	NmMt+ 8.5	MT 9	Gem 9.5/10
81	Michael Jordan	6	8	15	40
230	Vince Carter RC	12	20	40	100
234	Dirk Nowitzki RC	15	25	50	200
235	Paul Pierce RC	12	20	40	100

1998-99 Finest No Protectors

		NmMt 8	NmMt+ 8.5	MT 9	Gem 9.5/10
234	Dirk Nowitzki	20	30	60	250

1998-99 Finest Refractors

		NmMt 8	NmMt+ 8.5	MT 9	Gem 9.5/10
230	Vince Carter	200	300	500	1,000
234	Dirk Nowitzki	500	600	1,000	2,000
235	Paul Pierce	100	150	300	600

1998-99 Finest Arena Stars

		NmMt 8	NmMt+ 8.5	MT 9	Gem 9.5/10
AS19	Michael Jordan	300	400	800	1,500

1998-99 Flair Showcase takeit2.net

		NmMt 8	NmMt+ 8.5	MT 9	Gem 9.5/10
5	Kobe Bryant	2,000	3,000	4,000	8,000
13	Michael Jordan	3,000	4,000	6,000	10,000

1998-99 Fleer Electrifying

		NmMt 8	NmMt+ 8.5	MT 9	Gem 9.5/10
1	Kobe Bryant	600	800	1,500	3,000
6	Michael Jordan	1,000	1,200	2,500	5,000

1998-99 Fleer Lucky 13

		NmMt 8	NmMt+ 8.5	MT 9	Gem 9.5/10
5	Vince Carter	50	60	120	300

1998-99 Fleer Brilliants

		NmMt 8	NmMt+ 8.5	MT 9	Gem 9.5/10
105	Vince Carter RC	15	20	40	80
109	Dirk Nowitzki RC	20	30	60	150

1998-99 Metal Universe Linchpins

		NmMt 8	NmMt+ 8.5	MT 9	Gem 9.5/10
2	Kobe Bryant	2,000	3,000	5,000	8,000
8	Michael Jordan	▲4,000	▲5,000	▲8,000	▲12,000

1998-99 SkyBox Molten Metal

		NmMt 8	NmMt+ 8.5	MT 9	Gem 9.5/10
35	Dirk Nowitzki RC	10	15	40	100
91	Paul Pierce RC	6	8	20	50
134	Vince Carter RC	10	12	30	80

1998-99 SkyBox Molten Metal Xplosion

		NmMt 8	NmMt+ 8.5	MT 9	Gem 9.5/10
141	Michael Jordan	▲400	▲600	▲1,200	▲2,500

1998-99 SkyBox Premium

		NmMt 8	NmMt+ 8.5	MT 9	Gem 9.5/10
234	Vince Carter RC	12	15	30	100
255	Dirk Nowitzki RC	20	25	50	120

1998-99 SkyBox Premium 3D's

		NmMt 8	NmMt+ 8.5	MT 9	Gem 9.5/10
1	Kobe Bryant	800	1,000	2,000	
4	Michael Jordan	▲1,500	2,000	3,000	6,000

1998-99 SkyBox Thunder Noyz Boyz

		NmMt 8	NmMt+ 8.5	MT 9	Gem 9.5/10
3	Kobe Bryant	4,000	5,000	6,000	10,000
9	Michael Jordan	6,000	8,000	10,000	15,000

1998-99 SP Authentic

		NmMt 8	NmMt+ 8.5	MT 9	Gem 9.5/10
95	Vince Carter RC	▼250	▼300	▼500	1,000
97	Jason Williams RC	30	40	80	200
99	Dirk Nowitzki RC	300	400	600	▲1,500
100	Paul Pierce RC	▼100	▼150	▼250	▼500

1998-99 SP Authentic First Class

		NmMt 8	NmMt+ 8.5	MT 9	Gem 9.5/10
FC1	Michael Jordan	25	40	80	200
FC14	Kobe Bryant	20	30	60	150

1998-99 SP Authentic Sign of the Times Gold

		NmMt 8	NmMt+ 8.5	MT 9	Gem 9.5/10
MJ	Michael Jordan	25,000	30,000	50,000	

1998-99 SP Authentic Sign of the Times Silver

		NmMt 8	NmMt+ 8.5	MT 9	Gem 9.5/10
VC	Vince Carter	200	250	500	800

1998-99 SPx Finite

		NmMt 8	NmMt+ 8.5	MT 9	Gem 9.5/10
215	Vince Carter RC	120	200	400	800
219	Dirk Nowitzki RC	120	200	400	800

1998-99 Stadium Club

		NmMt 8	NmMt+ 8.5	MT 9	Gem 9.5/10
62	Michael Jordan	20	30	60	120
105	Vince Carter RC	20	30	60	200
109	Dirk Nowitzki RC	25	40	80	250

1998-99 Topps

		NmMt 8	NmMt+ 8.5	MT 9	Gem 9.5/10
154	Dirk Nowitzki RC	▼25	▼40	▼80	300
199	Vince Carter RC	25	40	80	200

1998-99 Topps Draft Redemption

		NmMt 8	NmMt+ 8.5	MT 9	Gem 9.5/10
9	Dirk Nowitzki	100	150	300	600

1998-99 Topps East/West

		NmMt 8	NmMt+ 8.5	MT 9	Gem 9.5/10
EW5	M.Jordan/K.Bryant	600	800	1,500	3,000

1998-99 Topps East/West Refractors

		NmMt 8	NmMt+ 8.5	MT 9	Gem 9.5/10
EW5	M.Jordan/K.Bryant	3,000	4,000	6,000	10,000

1998-99 Topps Gold Label

		NmMt 8	NmMt+ 8.5	MT 9	Gem 9.5/10
GL1	Michael Jordan	25	50	100	300

1998-99 Topps Legacies

		NmMt 8	NmMt+ 8.5	MT 9	Gem 9.5/10
15	Michael Jordan	250	300	600	1,200

1998-99 Topps Roundball Royalty

		NmMt 8	NmMt+ 8.5	MT 9	Gem 9.5/10
1	Michael Jordan	60	80	200	400

1998-99 Topps Roundball Royalty Refractors

		NmMt 8	NmMt+ 8.5	MT 9	Gem 9.5/10
1	Michael Jordan	600	800	1,500	3,000

1998-99 Topps Chrome

		NmMt 8	NmMt+ 8.5	MT 9	Gem 9.5/10
35	Paul Pierce RC	▼30	▼50	▼120	400
54	Dirk Nowitzki RC	▼100	▼200	▼400	1,000
199	Vince Carter RC	▼80	▼100	▼200	▼500

1998-99 Topps Chrome Refractors

		NmMt 8	NmMt+ 8.5	MT 9	Gem 9.5/10
35	Paul Pierce	600	1,000	2,000	4,000
54	Dirk Nowitzki	1,500	2,500	4,000	8,000
199	Vince Carter	1,000	1,500	3,000	6,000

1998-99 Topps Chrome Back 2 Back

		NmMt 8	NmMt+ 8.5	MT 9	Gem 9.5/10
B1	Michael Jordan	15	30	60	200

1998-99 Topps Chrome Champion Spirit

		NmMt 8	NmMt+ 8.5	MT 9	Gem 9.5/10
CS1	Michael Jordan	25	50	100	300

1998-99 UD Ionix

		NmMt 8	NmMt+ 8.5	MT 9	Gem 9.5/10
65	Vince Carter RC	10	20	40	80
69	Dirk Nowitzki RC	15	25	50	100
70	Paul Pierce RC	10	15	30	60

1998-99 UD Ionix Warp Zone

		NmMt 8	NmMt+ 8.5	MT 9	Gem 9.5/10
Z1	Michael Jordan	800	1,000	2,000	4,000

1998-99 Ultra

		NmMt 8	NmMt+ 8.5	MT 9	Gem 9.5/10
85	Michael Jordan	8	10	15	40
106	Vince Carter RC	10	15	40	150
118	Dirk Nowitzki RC	10	15	40	150

1998-99 Upper Deck

		NmMt 8	NmMt+ 8.5	MT 9	Gem 9.5/10
316	Vince Carter RC	12	25	50	120
320	Dirk Nowitzki RC	12	25	50	120

1998-99 Upper Deck Ovation

		NmMt 8	NmMt+ 8.5	MT 9	Gem 9.5/10
7	Michael Jordan	20	30	60	150
75	Vince Carter RC	▲12	▲20	▲40	100
79	Dirk Nowitzki RC	▲20	▲30	▲60	▲120
80	Paul Pierce RC	8	10	▲20	▲50

1998-99 Upper Deck Ovation Gold

		NmMt 8	NmMt+ 8.5	MT 9	Gem 9.5/10
79	Dirk Nowitzki	▲100	▲200	▲400	▲600

1999-00 SPx

		NmMt 8	NmMt+ 8.5	MT 9	Gem 9.5/10
92	Steve Francis AU/500 RC	20	30	60	
93	Baron Davis AU/500 RC	30	40	80	

1999-00 Upper Deck Retro Inkredible

		NmMt 8	NmMt+ 8.5	MT 9	Gem 9.5/10
JW	Jerry West	30	40	60	120

2000-01 Ultimate Collection

		NmMt 8	NmMt+ 8.5	MT 9	Gem 9.5/10
8	Michael Jordan	400	500	800	1,500

2001-02 SP Authentic

		NmMt 8	NmMt+ 8.5	MT 9	Gem 9.5/10
90	Michael Jordan	▲15	▲25	▲50	▲120
138	Tony Parker AU RC	120	150	▲300	▲600

2001-02 SPx

		NmMt 8	NmMt+ 8.5	MT 9	Gem 9.5/10
90	Michael Jordan	15	20	30	60
91A	Tony Parker JSY AU RC	40	60	100	250
91B	Tony Parker JSY AU RC	40	60	100	250
91C	Tony Parker JSY AU RC	40	60	100	250
140	Pau Gasol RC	8	12	25	50

2001-02 Topps Chrome

		NmMt 8	NmMt+ 8.5	MT 9	Gem 9.5/10
95	Michael Jordan	20	40	100	300
131	Pau Gasol RC	30	50	100	250
155	Tony Parker RC	30	50	100	250

2001-02 Topps Chrome Refractors

		NmMt 8	NmMt+ 8.5	MT 9	Gem 9.5/10
95	Michael Jordan	250	300	500	800
131	Pau Gasol	100	150	300	600
155	Tony Parker	100	150	300	600

2001-02 Topps Chrome Fast and Furious

		NmMt 8	NmMt+ 8.5	MT 9	Gem 9.5/10
FF5	Michael Jordan	12	20	40	100

2001-02 Topps Chrome Fast and Furious Refractors

		NmMt 8	NmMt+ 8.5	MT 9	Gem 9.5/10
FF5	Michael Jordan	120	150	300	600

2001-02 Topps Pristine

		NmMt 8	NmMt+ 8.5	MT 9	Gem 9.5/10
6	Michael Jordan	25	40	80	150

2001-02 Ultimate Collection

		NmMt 8	NmMt+ 8.5	MT 9	Gem 9.5/10
60	Michael Jordan	40	60	120	300
64	Tony Parker RC	25	40	80	200

2001-02 Upper Deck

		NmMt 8	NmMt+ 8.5	MT 9	Gem 9.5/10
403	Michael Jordan	12	15	25	50

2002-03 Bowman Signature Edition

		NmMt 8	NmMt+ 8.5	MT 9	Gem 9.5/10
SEEG	Manu Ginobili AU RC	200	250	400	800
SEYM	Yao Ming AU RC	400	500	1,000	2,000

2002-03 Finest

		NmMt 8	NmMt+ 8.5	MT 9	Gem 9.5/10
100	Michael Jordan	6	8	12	30
178	LeBron James XRC	1,200	1,500	2,000	4,000
180	Carmelo Anthony XRC	8	10	15	25
182	Dwyane Wade XRC	12	15	20	50

2002-03 Finest Refractors

		NmMt 8	NmMt+ 8.5	MT 9	Gem 9.5/10
100	Michael Jordan	300	400	600	1,000
178	LeBron James	8,000	10,000	15,000	25,000
182	Dwyane Wade	500	600	1,000	3,000

2002-03 Hoops Hot Prospects

		NmMt 8	NmMt+ 8.5	MT 9	Gem 9.5/10
81	Yao Ming JSY RC	40	50	60	

2002-03 SP Authentic

		NmMt 8	NmMt+ 8.5	MT 9	Gem 9.5/10
143	Yao Ming AU RC	300	400	600	1,200
172	M.Ginobili AU RC	80	120	250	500

2002-03 SP Game Used

		NmMt 8	NmMt+ 8.5	MT 9	Gem 9.5/10
142	Manu Ginobili RC	30	40	80	200

2002-03 SPx

		NmMt 8	NmMt+ 8.5	MT 9	Gem 9.5/10
132	Yao Ming JSY AU RC	200	300	600	1,200
155	Manu Ginobili RC	20	30	60	150

2002-03 Topps Chrome

		NmMt 8	NmMt+ 8.5	MT 9	Gem 9.5/10
124A	Manu Ginobili RC	40	60	▼120	300
124B	Manu Ginobili RC	40	60	▼120	300
146A	Yao Ming RC	50	80	▼150	400
146B	Yao Ming RC	50	80	▼150	400

2002-03 Topps Chrome Refractors

		NmMt 8	NmMt+ 8.5	MT 9	Gem 9.5/10
10	Michael Jordan	250	300	600	1,200
124A	Manu Ginobili	200	300	500	1,000
124B	Manu Ginobili	200	300	500	1,000
146A	Yao Ming	500	600	1,200	2,500
146B	Yao Ming	500	600	1,200	2,500

2002-03 Topps Chrome Coast to Coast

		NmMt 8	NmMt+ 8.5	MT 9	Gem 9.5/10
CC8	Michael Jordan	20	30	60	120

2002-03 Topps Chrome Coast to Coast Refractors

		NmMt 8	NmMt+ 8.5	MT 9	Gem 9.5/10
CC8	Michael Jordan	250	300	500	1,000

2002-03 Topps Chrome Zone Busters

		NmMt 8	NmMt+ 8.5	MT 9	Gem 9.5/10
ZB13	Michael Jordan	20	30	60	120

2002-03 Topps Chrome Zone Busters Refractors

		NmMt 8	NmMt+ 8.5	MT 9	Gem 9.5/10
ZB13	Michael Jordan	250	300	500	1,000

2002-03 Topps Pristine

		NmMt 8	NmMt+ 8.5	MT 9	Gem 9.5/10
4	Michael Jordan	20	25	50	120
51	Yao Ming C RC	25	30	60	150

2002-03 Ultimate Collection

		NmMt 8	NmMt+ 8.5	MT 9	Gem 9.5/10
79	Yao Ming AU RC	1,000	1,500	3,000	

2002-03 Ultimate Collection Signatures

		NmMt 8	NmMt+ 8.5	MT 9	Gem 9.5/10
BRS	Bill Russell	600	1,000	2,000	
KBS	Kobe Bryant	3,000	4,000	6,000	10,000
LBS	Larry Bird	400	600	1,000	
MJS	Michael Jordan	3,000	4,000	6,000	10,000
YMS	Yao Ming	600	800	1,200	

2002-03 Ultra

		NmMt 8	NmMt+ 8.5	MT 9	Gem 9.5/10
181	Yao Ming RC	20	30	60	150
204	Manu Ginobili RC	20	30	60	150

2002-03 Upper Deck

		NmMt 8	NmMt+ 8.5	MT 9	Gem 9.5/10
210	Yao Ming RC	20	30	60	150
392	Manu Ginobili RC	20	30	60	150

2002-03 Upper Deck Inspirations

		NmMt 8	NmMt+ 8.5	MT 9	Gem 9.5/10
156	LeBron James XRC	1,500	2,000	4,000	

2003-04 Bazooka

		NmMt 8	NmMt+ 8.5	MT 9	Gem 9.5/10
223A	LeBron James RC	150	250	400	800
223B	LeBron James RC	150	250	400	800
252A	Dwyane Wade Dribble RC	60	80	150	300
252B	Dwyane Wade Layup RC	60	80	150	300
276	LeBron James BAZ	250	300	600	1,000
280	Dwyane Wade BAZ	40	80	150	300

2003-04 Bazooka Comics

		NmMt 8	NmMt+ 8.5	MT 9	Gem 9.5/10
8	Kobe Bryant	▼60	▼80	▼150	▼300
15	LeBron James	▼200	▼250	▼400	▼800
17	Carmelo Anthony	12	20	40	80

2003-04 Black Diamond

		NmMt 8	NmMt+ 8.5	MT 9	Gem 9.5/10
148	Dwyane Wade RC	40	80	200	400
184	LeBron James RC	500	600	1,200	3,000
186	Carmelo Anthony RC	30	40	80	200

2003-04 Bowman

		NmMt 8	NmMt+ 8.5	MT 9	Gem 9.5/10
123	LeBron James RC	400	600	1,000	2,500
140	Carmelo Anthony RC	20	30	60	150
149	Dwyane Wade AU RC	150	200	400	800

2003-04 Bowman Chrome

		NmMt 8	NmMt+ 8.5	MT 9	Gem 9.5/10
123	LeBron James RC	1,000	1,200	2,000	4,000
140	Carmelo Anthony RC	40	60	150	300
149	Dwyane Wade AU RC	200	250	400	800

2003-04 Bowman Chrome Refractors

		NmMt 8	NmMt+ 8.5	MT 9	Gem 9.5/10
123	LeBron James	▼10,000	▼15,000	▼20,000	

2003-04 E-X

		NmMt 8	NmMt+ 8.5	MT 9	Gem 9.5/10
73	Carmelo Anthony RC	50	80	150	300
90	Dwyane Wade RC	100	150	300	600
102	LeBron James RC	1,500	3,000	4,000	6,000

2003-04 E-X Buzzer Beaters Autographs

		NmMt 8	NmMt+ 8.5	MT 9	Gem 9.5/10
10	Dwyane Wade/299	300	400	600	

2003-04 Finest

		NmMt 8	NmMt+ 8.5	MT 9	Gem 9.5/10
133	LeBron James RC	4,000	6,000	10,000	20,000
158	Dwyane Wade AU RC	500	600	1,000	
163	Carmelo Anthony AU RC	100	120	250	500

2003-04 Finest Refractors

		NmMt 8	NmMt+ 8.5	MT 9	Gem 9.5/10
133	LeBron James	15,000	20,000	30,000	

2003-04 Flair

		NmMt 8	NmMt+ 8.5	MT 9	Gem 9.5/10
94	LeBron James RC	1,000	1,500	3,000	

2003-04 Fleer Focus

		NmMt 8	NmMt+ 8.5	MT 9	Gem 9.5/10
137	LeBron James RC	800	1,000	2,000	4,000
148	Dwyane Wade RC	40	60	120	300

2003-04 Fleer Mystique

		NmMt 8	NmMt+ 8.5	MT 9	Gem 9.5/10
99	LeBron James RC	1,000	1,200	2,000	4,000
119	Dwyane Wade RC	20	30	60	150

2003-04 Fleer Mystique Die Cut

		NmMt 8	NmMt+ 8.5	MT 9	Gem 9.5/10
99	LeBron James	1,000	1,200	2,000	4,000
119	Dwyane Wade	40	60	150	400

2003-04 Fleer Showcase

		NmMt 8	NmMt+ 8.5	MT 9	Gem 9.5/10
130	LeBron James RC	600	800	1,500	3,000

2003-04 Fleer Tradition

		NmMt 8	NmMt+ 8.5	MT 9	Gem 9.5/10
261	LeBron James RC	400	500	800	2,000
263	Carmelo Anthony RC	25	40	80	200
265	Dwyane Wade RC	40	60	120	300
291	James/Darko/Melo	100	150	300	600
300	LeBron/Melo/Wade	600	800	1,500	3,000

2003-04 Hoops Hot Prospects Cream of the Crop

		NmMt 8	NmMt+ 8.5	MT 9	Gem 9.5/10
1	LeBron James	80	120	250	500
8	Carmelo Anthony	10	15	30	80

2003-04 SkyBox Autographics

		NmMt 8	NmMt+ 8.5	MT 9	Gem 9.5/10
77	LeBron James RC	300	400	600	1,200

2003-04 SkyBox Autographics Rookies Affirmed

		NmMt 8	NmMt+ 8.5	MT 9	Gem 9.5/10
12	L.James/K.Bryant	400	600	1,000	2,000

2003-04 SkyBox LE Sky's the Limit

		NmMt 8	NmMt+ 8.5	MT 9	Gem 9.5/10
16	LeBron James	100	150	300	600

2003-04 SP Authentic

		NmMt 8	NmMt+ 8.5	MT 9	Gem 9.5/10
148	LeBron James AU RC	25,000	30,000	40,000	100,000
150	Carmelo Anthony AU RC	600	1,000	2,000	
152	Dwyane Wade AU RC	1,200	2,500	5,000	

2003-04 SP Authentic Signatures

		NmMt 8	NmMt+ 8.5	MT 9	Gem 9.5/10
YA	Dwyane Wade	500	600	1,000	2,000
JA	LeBron James SP	15,000	20,000	30,000	

2003-04 SP Game Used

		NmMt 8	NmMt+ 8.5	MT 9	Gem 9.5/10
07	Lebron James RC	600	800	1,500	4,000
09	Carmelo Anthony RC	30	40	80	200
11	Dwyane Wade RC	50	80	200	400

2003-04 SP Signature Edition

		NmMt 8	NmMt+ 8.5	MT 9	Gem 9.5/10
01	LeBron James RC	1,000	1,200	2,500	5,000

2003-04 SP Signature Edition Rookie INKorporated

	NmMt 8	NmMt+ 8.5	MT 9	Gem 9.5/10
LeBron James	15,000	20,000	30,000	

2003-04 SP Signature Edition Signatures

		NmMt 8	NmMt+ 8.5	MT 9	Gem 9.5/10
Y	Dwyane Wade	400	500	1,000	2,000
3	Kobe Bryant	1,000	2,000	3,000	6,000
	LeBron James	12,000	15,000	20,000	30,000

2003-04 SPx

		NmMt 8	NmMt+ 8.5	MT 9	Gem 9.5/10
	Michael Jordan	25	40	80	200
1	LeBron James JSY AU RC	10,000	15,000	20,000	30,000
3	Carmelo Anthony JSY AU RC	250	300	600	1,000
5	Dwyane Wade JSY AU RC	600	800	1,500	3,000

2003-04 Sweet Shot

	NmMt 8	NmMt+ 8.5	MT 9	Gem 9.5/10
LeBron James RC	800	1,000	1,500	3,000
Dwyane Wade RC	40	80	150	300

2003-04 Topps

		NmMt 8	NmMt+ 8.5	MT 9	Gem 9.5/10
1	LeBron James RC	▼400	▼500	▼1,000	▼3,000
3	Carmelo Anthony RC	▲40	▲60	▲100	▲250
5	Dwyane Wade RC	40	▼60	▼100	▼250

2003-04 Topps First Edition

		NmMt 8	NmMt+ 8.5	MT 9	Gem 9.5/10
1	LeBron James	▲2,000	▲3,000	▲5,000	▲8,000

2003-04 Topps Collection

		NmMt 8	NmMt+ 8.5	MT 9	Gem 9.5/10
	LeBron James RC	▼600	▼800	▼1,500	▼3,000

2003-04 Topps Chrome

	NmMt 8	NmMt+ 8.5	MT 9	Gem 9.5/10
Lebron James RC	▼2,000	▼2,500	▼4,000	▼10,000
Carmelo Anthony RC	80	100	▼200	▼400
Dwyane Wade RC	▼150	▼200	▼400	▼800

2003-04 Topps Chrome Refractors

	NmMt 8	NmMt+ 8.5	MT 9	Gem 9.5/10
LeBron James	▼15,000	▼20,000	▼30,000	▼40,000
Carmelo Anthony	▼400	▼600	▼1,000	▼2,000
Dwyane Wade	▼600	▼800	▼1,200	▼2,500

2003-04 Topps Contemporary Collection

		NmMt 8	NmMt+ 8.5	MT 9	Gem 9.5/10
1	LeBron James RC	1,200	2,000	4,000	
4	Dwyane Wade RC	80	120	300	

2003-04 Topps Jersey Edition

		NmMt 8	NmMt+ 8.5	MT 9	Gem 9.5/10
DW	Dwyane Wade SS RC	200	300	600	1,000
LJ	LeBron James SS RC	2,500	3,000	5,000	8,000

2003-04 Topps Pristine

		NmMt 8	NmMt+ 8.5	MT 9	Gem 9.5/10
101	LeBron James C RC	500	600	800	2,000
102	LeBron James U	500	600	800	2,000
103	LeBron James R	800	1,000	1,500	3,000
107	Carmelo Anthony C RC	20	40	80	200
108	Carmelo Anthony U	20	40	80	200
109	Carmelo Anthony R	20	40	80	200
113	Dwyane Wade C RC	50	80	150	300
114	Dwyane Wade U	50	80	150	300
115	Dwyane Wade R	50	80	150	300

2003-04 Topps Pristine Refractors

		NmMt 8	NmMt+ 8.5	MT 9	Gem 9.5/10
102	LeBron James U	1,500	2,000	4,000	8,000
103	LeBron James R	2,000	3,000	5,000	10,000
107	Carmelo Anthony C	40	80	200	400
108	Carmelo Anthony U	40	80	200	400
109	Carmelo Anthony R	40	80	200	400
113	Dwyane Wade C	100	150	300	600
114	Dwyane Wade U	100	150	300	600
115	Dwyane Wade R	100	150	300	600

2003-04 Topps Pristine Minis

		NmMt 8	NmMt+ 8.5	MT 9	Gem 9.5/10
PM21	LeBron James	300	400	600	1,200
PM23	Carmelo Anthony	20	30	60	150

2003-04 Topps Pristine Personal Endorsements

		NmMt 8	NmMt+ 8.5	MT 9	Gem 9.5/10
DWA	Dwyane Wade C	100	200	400	800

2003-04 Topps Rookie Matrix

		NmMt 8	NmMt+ 8.5	MT 9	Gem 9.5/10
WJB	Wade/LeBron/Bosh	200	300	600	1,500

2003-04 Topps Rookie Matrix Rookie Frames

		NmMt 8	NmMt+ 8.5	MT 9	Gem 9.5/10
111	LeBron James	150	300	600	1,000

2003-04 UD Top Prospects

		NmMt 8	NmMt+ 8.5	MT 9	Gem 9.5/10
3	LeBron James	15	20	50	▼150
55	LeBron James	15	20	50	▼150
60	LeBron James	15	20	50	▼150

2003-04 UD Top Prospects Signs of Success

		NmMt 8	NmMt+ 8.5	MT 9	Gem 9.5/10
SSCA	Carmelo Anthony	40	80	150	300
SSLJ	LeBron James	3,000	4,000	8,000	15,000

2003-04 Ultra

		NmMt 8	NmMt+ 8.5	MT 9	Gem 9.5/10
171	LeBron James L13 RC	1,000	1,500	3,000	6,000

2003-04 Ultra Gold Medallion

		NmMt 8	NmMt+ 8.5	MT 9	Gem 9.5/10
171	LeBron James L13	800	1,000	2,000	4,000

2003-04 Ultra Roundball Discs

		NmMt 8	NmMt+ 8.5	MT 9	Gem 9.5/10
31	LeBron James	150	200	300	600

2003-04 Upper Deck

		NmMt 8	NmMt+ 8.5	MT 9	Gem 9.5/10
301	LeBron James RC	500	700	1,000	3,000
303	Carmelo Anthony RC	15	30	60	120
305	Dwyane Wade RC	40	80	150	300

2003-04 Upper Deck Air Academy

		NmMt 8	NmMt+ 8.5	MT 9	Gem 9.5/10
AA3	LeBron James	100	200	400	800

2003-04 Upper Deck Black Diamond Rookies F/X

		NmMt 8	NmMt+ 8.5	MT 9	Gem 9.5/10
BD1	LeBron James	1,200	2,000	4,000	

2003-04 Upper Deck SE Die Cut Future All-Stars

		NmMt 8	NmMt+ 8.5	MT 9	Gem 9.5/10
E11	Dwyane Wade	80	120	250	500
E15	LeBron James	500	600	1,000	2,000

2003-04 Upper Deck Finite

		NmMt 8	NmMt+ 8.5	MT 9	Gem 9.5/10
242	LeBron James RC	3,000	4,000	6,000	

2003-04 Upper Deck Finite Elements Jerseys

		NmMt 8	NmMt+ 8.5	MT 9	Gem 9.5/10
FJ18	LeBron James	250	300	600	1,000

2003-04 Upper Deck Finite Signatures

		NmMt 8	NmMt+ 8.5	MT 9	Gem 9.5/10
CA	Carmelo Anthony	60	80	120	250
DW	Dwyane Wade	100	150	250	500

2003-04 Upper Deck Hardcourt

		NmMt 8	NmMt+ 8.5	MT 9	Gem 9.5/10
132	LeBron James RC	500	600	1,200	2,500

2003-04 Upper Deck Legends

		NmMt 8	NmMt+ 8.5	MT 9	Gem 9.5/10
131	Dwyane Wade RC	60	100	250	500
133	Carmelo Anthony RC	25	40	80	200
135	LeBron James RC	600	800	1,500	3,000

2003-04 Upper Deck Legends Legendary Signatures

		NmMt 8	NmMt+ 8.5	MT 9	Gem 9.5/10
MJ	Michael Jordan SP	6,000	8,000	12,000	20,000

2003-04 Upper Deck MVP

		NmMt 8	NmMt+ 8.5	MT 9	Gem 9.5/10
201	LeBron James RC	250	300	600	1,200
203	Carmelo Anthony RC	20	30	60	150
205	Dwyane Wade RC	50	80	150	300

2003-04 Upper Deck MVP Rising to the Occasion

		NmMt 8	NmMt+ 8.5	MT 9	Gem 9.5/10
RO2	LeBron James	120	150	300	600

2003-04 Upper Deck Rookie Exclusives

		NmMt 8	NmMt+ 8.5	MT 9	Gem 9.5/10
1	LeBron James RC	150	250	400	800
5	Dwyane Wade RC	25	40	80	200

2003-04 Upper Deck Rookie Exclusives Jerseys

		NmMt 8	NmMt+ 8.5	MT 9	Gem 9.5/10
J1	LeBron James	250	300	500	800

2003-04 Upper Deck Standing O

		NmMt 8	NmMt+ 8.5	MT 9	Gem 9.5/10
85	LeBron James RC	200	300	500	800

2003-04 Upper Deck Triple Dimensions Reflections

		NmMt 8	NmMt+ 8.5	MT 9	Gem 9.5/10
10	LeBron James	200	300	600	1,000

2003-04 Upper Deck Victory

		NmMt 8	NmMt+ 8.5	MT 9	Gem 9.5/10
100	Michael Jordan	20	30	60	120
101	Lebron James SP RC	80	100	250	500
103	Carmelo Anthony RC	15	25	50	100

2004-05 Bowman Chrome

		NmMt 8	NmMt+ 8.5	MT 9	Gem 9.5/10
23	LeBron James	100	150	300	600
129	Dwight Howard RC	15	25	50	100

2004-05 Exquisite Collection

		NmMt 8	NmMt+ 8.5	MT 9	Gem 9.5/10
90	Dwight Howard JSY AU RC	800	1,000	2,000	4,000

2004-05 Finest

		NmMt 8	NmMt+ 8.5	MT 9	Gem 9.5/10
159	Dwight Howard RC	20	30	60	120
194	Chris Paul XRC	40	80	200	400

2004-05 Finest Refractors

		NmMt 8	NmMt+ 8.5	MT 9	Gem 9.5/10
194	Chris Paul	150	200	400	800

2004-05 Fleer Tradition

		NmMt 8	NmMt+ 8.5	MT 9	Gem 9.5/10
221	Dwight Howard RC	6	10	15	40

2004-05 SP Authentic

		NmMt 8	NmMt+ 8.5	MT 9	Gem 9.5/10
14	LeBron James	25	40	80	200
186	Dwight Howard AU RC	50	60	150	300

2004-05 SP Authentic Limited

		NmMt 8	NmMt+ 8.5	MT 9	Gem 9.5/10
186	Dwight Howard AU	50	80	150	300

2004-05 SP Authentic Signatures

		NmMt 8	NmMt+ 8.5	MT 9	Gem 9.5/10
DH	Dwight Howard	25	40	80	200

2004-05 SP Game Used SIGnificance

		NmMt 8	NmMt+ 8.5	MT 9	Gem 9.5/10
MJ	Michael Jordan	6,000	8,000	12,000	

2004-05 SPx

		NmMt 8	NmMt+ 8.5	MT 9	Gem 9.5/10
147	Dwight Howard JSY AU RC	40	60	120	300

2004-05 Topps

		NmMt 8	NmMt+ 8.5	MT 9	Gem 9.5/10
221	Dwight Howard RC	8	12	25	50

2004-05 Topps Chrome

		NmMt 8	NmMt+ 8.5	MT 9	Gem 9.5/10
23	LeBron James	100	150	300	600
166	Dwight Howard RC	15	20	40	80

2004-05 Topps Chrome Refractors

		NmMt 8	NmMt+ 8.5	MT 9	Gem 9.5/10
23	LeBron James	1,500	▼2,000	▼3,000	▼6,000
166	Dwight Howard	60	80	150	300

2004-05 Topps Pristine

		NmMt 8	NmMt+ 8.5	MT 9	Gem 9.5/10
101	Dwight Howard C RC	15	20	40	80

2004-05 Ultimate Collection

		NmMt 8	NmMt+ 8.5	MT 9	Gem 9.5/10
127	Dwight Howard AU RC	40	60	120	250

2004-05 Upper Deck

		NmMt 8	NmMt+ 8.5	MT 9	Gem 9.5/10
224	Dwight Howard SP RC	8	12	25	50

2004-05 Upper Deck Trilogy

		NmMt 8	NmMt+ 8.5	MT 9	Gem 9.5/10
141	Dwight Howard RC	20	25	50	100

2005-06 Bowman

		NmMt 8	NmMt+ 8.5	MT 9	Gem 9.5/10
111	Chris Paul RC	12	20	40	80

2005-06 Bowman Chrome

		NmMt 8	NmMt+ 8.5	MT 9	Gem 9.5/10
111	Chris Paul RC	▼25	▼40	▼80	▼200

2005-06 Bowman Chrome Refractors

		NmMt 8	NmMt+ 8.5	MT 9	Gem 9.5/10
111	Chris Paul	▼200	▼300	▼500	▼800

2005-06 Exquisite Collection

		NmMt 8	NmMt+ 8.5	MT 9	Gem 9.5/10
46	Chris Paul JSY AU RC/99	5,000	8,000	12,000	

2005-06 Finest

		NmMt 8	NmMt+ 8.5	MT 9	Gem 9.5/10
106	Chris Paul RC	▼60	▼100	▼200	▼400

2005-06 Finest Refractors

		NmMt 8	NmMt+ 8.5	MT 9	Gem 9.5/10
106	Chris Paul	150	200	400	800

2005-06 Greats of the Game

		NmMt 8	NmMt+ 8.5	MT 9	Gem 9.5/10
113	Chris Paul AU RC	150	200	400	800

2005-06 SP Authentic

		NmMt 8	NmMt+ 8.5	MT 9	Gem 9.5/10
94	Chris Paul AU RC	150	300	600	1,200

2005-06 SP Game Used

		NmMt 8	NmMt+ 8.5	MT 9	Gem 9.5/10
149	Chris Paul RC	60	100	200	400

2005-06 SPx

		NmMt 8	NmMt+ 8.5	MT 9	Gem 9.5/10
153	Chris Paul JSY AU RC	200	250	500	1,000

2005-06 Topps

		NmMt 8	NmMt+ 8.5	MT 9	Gem 9.5/10
224	Chris Paul RC	▼30	▼50	▼100	▼250

2005-06 Topps Chrome

		NmMt 8	NmMt+ 8.5	MT 9	Gem 9.5/10
168	Chris Paul RC	▼100	▼150	▼300	▼600

2005-06 Topps Chrome Refractors

		NmMt 8	NmMt+ 8.5	MT 9	Gem 9.5/10
168	Chris Paul	▼400	▼500	▼800	▼2,500

2005-06 Topps Chrome Refractors Black

		NmMt 8	NmMt+ 8.5	MT 9	Gem 9.5/10
168	Chris Paul	1,000	▼1,200	▼2,500	▼4,000

2005-06 Topps Style

		NmMt 8	NmMt+ 8.5	MT 9	Gem 9.5/10
154	Chris Paul RC	15	25	50	100

2005-06 Ultimate Collection

		NmMt 8	NmMt+ 8.5	MT 9	Gem 9.5/10
146	Chris Paul AU RC	800	1,000	2,000	4,000

2005-06 Ultimate Collection Rookie Autographs Gold

		NmMt 8	NmMt+ 8.5	MT 9	Gem 9.5/10
146	Chris Paul	400	600	1,000	

2005-06 Ultimate Collection Signatures

		NmMt 8	NmMt+ 8.5	MT 9	Gem 9.5/10
USCP	Chris Paul	200	250	500	1,000

2005-06 Upper Deck

		NmMt 8	NmMt+ 8.5	MT 9	Gem 9.5/10
230	Chris Paul SP RC	50	80	150	300

2005-06 Upper Deck Rookie Debut

		NmMt 8	NmMt+ 8.5	MT 9	Gem 9.5/10
03	Chris Paul RC	20	40	80	200

2005-06 Upper Deck Slam

		NmMt 8	NmMt+ 8.5	MT 9	Gem 9.5/10
3	Chris Paul RC	15	30	60	150

2005-06 Upper Deck Trilogy

		NmMt 8	NmMt+ 8.5	MT 9	Gem 9.5/10
37	Chris Paul RC	50	80	150	300

2005-06 Upper Deck Trilogy Auto Focus

		NmMt 8	NmMt+ 8.5	MT 9	Gem 9.5/10
P	Chris Paul	150	200	400	800

2006-07 Bowman Chrome

		NmMt 8	NmMt+ 8.5	MT 9	Gem 9.5/10
53	Rajon Rondo B AU RC	25	40	80	200

2006-07 E-X

		NmMt 8	NmMt+ 8.5	MT 9	Gem 9.5/10
	Michael Jordan	100	150	300	600
	LeBron James	80	100	250	500
	LaMarcus Aldridge				
	199 AU RC	15	25	40	60

2006-07 Exquisite Collection

		NmMt 8	NmMt+ 8.5	MT 9	Gem 9.5/10
	Rajon Rondo JSY AU RC	150	200	300	

2006-07 Finest

		NmMt 8	NmMt+ 8.5	MT 9	Gem 9.5/10
	Rajon Rondo RC	5	6	8	15
	LaMarcus Aldridge RC	6	8	10	20
2	Kevin Durant XRC	150	250	500	1,000

2006-07 Finest Refractors

		NmMt 8	NmMt+ 8.5	MT 9	Gem 9.5/10
	LeBron James	200	250	500	
2	Kevin Durant	200	350	600	1,200

2006-07 Fleer

		NmMt 8	NmMt+ 8.5	MT 9	Gem 9.5/10
	Michael Jordan	15	20	40	100

2006-07 Fleer 1986-87 20th Anniversary

		NmMt 8	NmMt+ 8.5	MT 9	Gem 9.5/10
	Michael Jordan	200	300	600	1,000
	LeBron James	60	100	200	400

2006-07 SP Authentic

		NmMt 8	NmMt+ 8.5	MT 9	Gem 9.5/10
	Rajon Rondo AU RC	▲25	▲40	▲80	▲200

2006-07 Topps

		NmMt 8	NmMt+ 8.5	MT 9	Gem 9.5/10
A	LaMarcus Aldridge RC	▲6	▲8	▲15	▲40
B	LaMarcus Aldridge Draft RC	▲6	▲8	▲15	▲40

2006-07 Topps Chrome

		NmMt 8	NmMt+ 8.5	MT 9	Gem 9.5/10
183	LaMarcus Aldridge RC	10	20	40	80
201	Rajon Rondo RC	20	25	50	100

2006-07 Topps Chrome Autographs Refractors Black

		NmMt 8	NmMt+ 8.5	MT 9	Gem 9.5/10
201	Rajon Rondo C	▲150	▲200	▲400	▲600

2006-07 Ultimate Collection

		NmMt 8	NmMt+ 8.5	MT 9	Gem 9.5/10
209	Rajon Rondo AU RC	25	40	80	200

2007-08 Bowman Chrome

		NmMt 8	NmMt+ 8.5	MT 9	Gem 9.5/10
111	Kevin Durant RC	▼300	▼400	▼700	▼1,500

2007-08 Bowman Chrome Refractors

		NmMt 8	NmMt+ 8.5	MT 9	Gem 9.5/10
111	Kevin Durant	2,000	2,500	4,000	8,000

2007-08 Bowman Elevation

		NmMt 8	NmMt+ 8.5	MT 9	Gem 9.5/10
71	Kevin Durant RC	150	▲250	▲500	▲1,000

2007-08 Bowman Sterling

		NmMt 8	NmMt+ 8.5	MT 9	Gem 9.5/10
KD	Kevin Durant RC	▼60	▼100	▼200	500

2007-08 Bowman Sterling Refractors

		NmMt 8	NmMt+ 8.5	MT 9	Gem 9.5/10
KD	Kevin Durant/399	600	800	1,500	3,000

2007-08 Finest

		NmMt 8	NmMt+ 8.5	MT 9	Gem 9.5/10
71	Kevin Durant RC	▲120	150	300	600
101	Derrick Rose XRC	40	▼60	▼120	▼250
104	Russell Westbrook XRC	▼80	▼120	▼250	▼500

2007-08 Finest Refractors

		NmMt 8	NmMt+ 8.5	MT 9	Gem 9.5/10
71	Kevin Durant	600	800	1,500	3,000

2007-08 Fleer

		NmMt 8	NmMt+ 8.5	MT 9	Gem 9.5/10
212	Kevin Durant RC	▼40	▼80	▼150	▼400

2007-08 Fleer 1986-87 Rookies

		NmMt 8	NmMt+ 8.5	MT 9	Gem 9.5/10
143	Kevin Durant	▼150	▼250	▼400	▼800

2007-08 Fleer Rookie Sensations

		NmMt 8	NmMt+ 8.5	MT 9	Gem 9.5/10
RS2	Kevin Durant	40	▼60	▼120	▼300

2007-08 Fleer Rookie Sensations Glossy

		NmMt 8	NmMt+ 8.5	MT 9	Gem 9.5/10
RS2	Kevin Durant	▲60	100	▼200	▼400

2007-08 Fleer Hot Prospects

		NmMt 8	NmMt+ 8.5	MT 9	Gem 9.5/10
123	Kevin Durant JSY AU RC	800	1,200	2,500	5,000

2007-08 Fleer Hot Prospects Notable Newcomers

		NmMt 8	NmMt+ 8.5	MT 9	Gem 9.5/10
NN-1	Kevin Durant	40	80	150	300

2007-08 SP Authentic

		NmMt 8	NmMt+ 8.5	MT 9	Gem 9.5/10
152	Kevin Durant				
	JSY AU/299 RC	▲5,000	▲6,000	8,000	15,000

2007-08 SP Authentic Profiles

		NmMt 8	NmMt+ 8.5	MT 9	Gem 9.5/10
AP13	Kevin Durant	30	50	100	300

2007-08 SP Authentic Retail Rookie Autographs

		NmMt 8	NmMt+ 8.5	MT 9	Gem 9.5/10
152	Kevin Durant/399	1,500	2,000	3,000	6,000

2007-08 SP Game Used

		NmMt 8	NmMt+ 8.5	MT 9	Gem 9.5/10
142	Kevin Durant RC	40	80	150	300

2007-08 SP Rookie Edition

		NmMt 8	NmMt+ 8.5	MT 9	Gem 9.5/10
61	Kevin Durant RC	60	100	200	400
106	Kevin Durant 96-97	50	80	200	400

2007-08 SP Rookie Edition Rookie Autographs

		NmMt 8	NmMt+ 8.5	MT 9	Gem 9.5/10
61	Kevin Durant	400	600	1,000	2,000

2007-08 SP Rookie Threads

		NmMt 8	NmMt+ 8.5	MT 9	Gem 9.5/10
49	Kevin Durant JSY AU RC	1,500	2,000	3,000	6,000

2007-08 SPx

		NmMt 8	NmMt+ 8.5	MT 9	Gem 9.5/10
101	Kevin Durant JSY AU RC	800	1,200	2,500	5,000

2007-08 SPx Endorsements

		NmMt 8	NmMt+ 8.5	MT 9	Gem 9.5/10
KD	Kevin Durant	400	600	1,000	2,000

2007-08 SPx Super Scripts

		NmMt 8	NmMt+ 8.5	MT 9	Gem 9.5/10
KD	Kevin Durant	400	600	1,000	2,000

2007-08 Stadium Club

		NmMt 8	NmMt+ 8.5	MT 9	Gem 9.5/10
102	Kevin Durant RC	80	120	250	500

2007-08 Stadium Club Chrome Rookie Refractors

		NmMt 8	NmMt+ 8.5	MT 9	Gem 9.5/10
102	Kevin Durant	400	600	1,000	3,000

2007-08 Topps

		NmMt 8	NmMt+ 8.5	MT 9	Gem 9.5/10
112	Kevin Durant RC	▼120	▼250	▼500	▲1,500

2007-08 Topps 1957-58 Variations

		NmMt 8	NmMt+ 8.5	MT 9	Gem 9.5/10
112	Kevin Durant	▼60	▼80	▼150	500

2007-08 Topps Rookie Set

		NmMt 8	NmMt+ 8.5	MT 9	Gem 9.5/10
2	Kevin Durant	▼80	▼120	▼250	▼600

2007-08 Topps Chrome

		NmMt 8	NmMt+ 8.5	MT 9	Gem 9.5/10
23	LeBron James	50	80	120	300
131	Kevin Durant RC	▼600	▼800	▼1,200	▼2,500

2007-08 Topps Chrome Refractors

		NmMt 8	NmMt+ 8.5	MT 9	Gem 9.5/10
131	Kevin Durant	▼4,000	▼5,000	▼8,000	▼15,000

2007-08 Topps Echelon

		NmMt 8	NmMt+ 8.5	MT 9	Gem 9.5/10
74	Kevin Durant RC	300	400	600	1,200

2007-08 Ultra SE

		NmMt 8	NmMt+ 8.5	MT 9	Gem 9.5/10
232	Kevin Durant L13 RC	50	80	200	500

2007-08 Upper Deck

		NmMt 8	NmMt+ 8.5	MT 9	Gem 9.5/10
234	Kevin Durant SP RC	30	40	80	200

2007-08 Upper Deck First Edition

		NmMt 8	NmMt+ 8.5	MT 9	Gem 9.5/10
202	Kevin Durant RC	30	40	80	200

2007-08 Upper Deck NBA Rookie Box Set

		NmMt 8	NmMt+ 8.5	MT 9	Gem 9.5/10
11	Kevin Durant	50	80	150	300

2008-09 Bowman

		NmMt 8	NmMt+ 8.5	MT 9	Gem 9.5/10
111	Derrick Rose RC	15	25	50	100
114	Russell Westbrook RC	60	80	150	300
115	Kevin Love RC	5	6	8	15

2008-09 Bowman Chrome

		NmMt 8	NmMt+ 8.5	MT 9	Gem 9.5/10
111	Derrick Rose RC	25	40	80	200
114	Russell Westbrook RC	80	120	250	500
115	Kevin Love RC	10	12	20	30

2008-09 Bowman Chrome Refractors

		NmMt 8	NmMt+ 8.5	MT 9	Gem 9.5/10
111	Derrick Rose	60	80	200	400
114	Russell Westbrook	200	300	500	800

2008-09 Bowman Chrome X-Fractors

		NmMt 8	NmMt+ 8.5	MT 9	Gem 9.5/10
111	Derrick Rose	80	100	250	500
114	Russell Westbrook	250	300	600	1,000

2008-09 Exquisite Collection

		NmMt 8	NmMt+ 8.5	MT 9	Gem 9.5/10
61	Kevin Love JSY AU RC	100	150	300	500
92	Derrick Rose JSY AU/99 RC	500	800	2,000	
93	R.Westbrook JSY AU RC	2,000	4,000	8,000	15,000

2008-09 Fleer

		NmMt 8	NmMt+ 8.5	MT 9	Gem 9.5/10
201	Derrick Rose RC	8	12	25	50
204	Russell Westbrook RC	25	40	80	200

2008-09 Fleer 1986-87 Rookies

		NmMt 8	NmMt+ 8.5	MT 9	Gem 9.5/10
86R163	Derrick Rose	10	20	40	80
86R166	Russell Westbrook	80	100	200	400
86R167	Kevin Love	4	6	8	20

2008-09 SkyBox

		NmMt 8	NmMt+ 8.5	MT 9	Gem 9.5/10
201	Derrick Rose RC	▼8	▼12	▼25	▼60
204	Russell Westbrook RC	▼20	▼30	▼60	▼120

2008-09 SkyBox Metal Universe

		NmMt 8	NmMt+ 8.5	MT 9	Gem 9.5/10
71	Derrick Rose	▼20	▼30	▼60	▼150
74	Russell Westbrook	▼40	▼60	▼120	▼300

2008-09 SP Authentic

		NmMt 8	NmMt+ 8.5	MT 9	Gem 9.5/10
126	Kevin Love JSY AU/299 RC	40	60	150	300
130	D.Rose JSY AU/299 RC	200	400	600	1,000
139	R.Westbrook JSY AU/299 RC	400	600	1,000	2,000

2008-09 SP Authentic Destination Stardom

		NmMt 8	NmMt+ 8.5	MT 9	Gem 9.5/10
DS1	Derrick Rose	▼6	▼10	▼15	▼40
DS4	Russell Westbrook	▼15	▼20	▼40	▼80

2008-09 SP Authentic Profiles

		NmMt 8	NmMt+ 8.5	MT 9	Gem 9.5/10
AP46	Derrick Rose	▼5	▼6	▼10	▼25
AP49	Russell Westbrook	▼8	▼12	▼25	▼50

2008-09 SP Rookie Threads

		NmMt 8	NmMt+ 8.5	MT 9	Gem 9.5/10
67	Russell Westbrook JSY AU RC	▼300	▼500	▼800	▼1,500
95	Derrick Rose JSY AU RC	▼100	▼120	▼250	▼400

2008-09 SPx

		NmMt 8	NmMt+ 8.5	MT 9	Gem 9.5/10
111	Derrick Rose JSY AU RC	▼100	▼150	▼300	▼500
114	Russell Westbrook JSY AU RC	200	▼250	▼500	▼800
121	Derrick Rose JSY AU RC	▼100	▼150	▼300	▼500
124	Russell Westbrook JSY AU RC	200	▼250	▼500	▼800
125	Kevin Love JSY AU RC	▼15	▼30	▼60	▼120

2008-09 Topps

		NmMt 8	NmMt+ 8.5	MT 9	Gem 9.5/10
23	LeBron James	▼100	▼150	▼300	▼600
24	Kobe Bryant	200	300	600	1,000
196	Derrick Rose RC	▼8	▼12	▼25	▼50
199	Russell Westbrook RC	▼30	▼50	▼100	▼250

2008-09 Topps 1958-59 Variations

		NmMt 8	NmMt+ 8.5	MT 9	Gem 9.5/10
196	Derrick Rose	6	10	20	40
199	Russell Westbrook	▼15	▼25	▼50	▼120

2008-09 Topps Chrome

		NmMt 8	NmMt+ 8.5	MT 9	Gem 9.5/10
23	LeBron James	▼150	▼200	▼400	▼800
24	Kobe Bryant	▼300	▼400	▼600	▼1,200
156	Kevin Durant	▼40	▼80	▼150	▼300
181	Derrick Rose RC	▼20	▼30	▼60	▼150
184	Russell Westbrook RC	▼100	▼120	▼250	▼500

2008-09 Topps Chrome Refractors

		NmMt 8	NmMt+ 8.5	MT 9	Gem 9.5/10
23	LeBron James	▼1,000	▼1,500	▼3,000	▼5,000
24	Kobe Bryant	1,500	2,000	4,000	6,000
156	Kevin Durant	300	400	800	1,500
181	Derrick Rose	150	200	400	▼800
184	Russell Westbrook	▼500	▼600	▼1,000	▼2,000

2008-09 Topps Chrome Refractors Orange

		NmMt 8	NmMt+ 8.5	MT 9	Gem 9.5/10
184	Russell Westbrook	800	1,000	▼1,500	▼3,000

2008-09 Topps Signature

		NmMt 8	NmMt+ 8.5	MT 9	Gem 9.5/10
TSDR	Derrick Rose RC	▼6	▼10	▼20	▼40
TSRW	Russell Westbrook RC	▼20	▼30	▼60	▼120

2008-09 Upper Deck

		NmMt 8	NmMt+ 8.5	MT 9	Gem 9.5/10
259	Derrick Rose RC	▼4	▼6	▼12	▼30
262	Russell Westbrook RC	▼15	▼30	▼60	▼150

2008-09 Upper Deck First Edition

		NmMt 8	NmMt+ 8.5	MT 9	Gem 9.5/10
259	Derrick Rose	▼4	▼6	▼12	▼30
262	Russell Westbrook	▼15	▼30	▼60	▼150

2008-09 Upper Deck MVP

		NmMt 8	NmMt+ 8.5	MT 9	Gem 9.5/10
201	Derrick Rose RC	▼4	▼6	▼12	▼30
204	Russell Westbrook RC	▼15	▼25	▼50	▼120

2008-09 Upper Deck Radiance

		NmMt 8	NmMt+ 8.5	MT 9	Gem 9.5/10
89RC	Derrick Rose AU RC	▼80	▼120	▼250	▼500
90RC	Russell Westbrook AU RC	▼250	▼300	▼600	▼1,000

2009-10 Absolute Memorabilia

		NmMt 8	NmMt+ 8.5	MT 9	Gem 9.5/10
144	Stephen Curry JSY AU/499 RC	▲3,000	▲5,000	8,000	15,000

#	Player	NmMt 8	NmMt+ 8.5	MT 9	Gem 9.5/10
146	James Harden JSY AU/499 RC	▼300	▼500	▼800	▼1,500
172	Blake Griffin JSY AU/499 RC50	80	150	300	

2009-10 Adrenalyn XL

#	Player	NmMt 8	NmMt+ 8.5	MT 9	Gem 9.5/10
67	Stephen Curry RC	150	200	400	800

2009-10 Bowman 48

#	Player	NmMt 8	NmMt+ 8.5	MT 9	Gem 9.5/10
101	Blake Griffin RC	30	40	80	150
104	James Harden RC	200	250	500	▼800
106	Stephen Curry RC	▲800	▲1,200	▲2,500	▲5,000

2009-10 Certified

#	Player	NmMt 8	NmMt+ 8.5	MT 9	Gem 9.5/10
173	James Harden JSY AU RC	▲300	▲400	600	1,200
176	Stephen Curry JSY AU RC	▲1,200	▲1,500	▲2,500	▲5,000

2009-10 Classics

#	Player	NmMt 8	NmMt+ 8.5	MT 9	Gem 9.5/10
161	Blake Griffin AU/499 RC	40	60	150	300
163	James Harden AU/499 RC	▼400	▼600	▼1,000	▼2,000
166	Stephen Curry AU/499 RC	1,500	2,000	4,000	8,000

2009-10 Court Kings

#	Player	NmMt 8	NmMt+ 8.5	MT 9	Gem 9.5/10
129	Stephen Curry AU RC	1,000	1,200	2,500	5,000
145	James Harden AU RC	400	600	1,000	2,000
150	Blake Griffin AU RC	40	60	150	300

2009-10 Crown Royale

#	Player	NmMt 8	NmMt+ 8.5	MT 9	Gem 9.5/10
103	Stephen Curry AU/399 RC	2,000	2,500	4,000	8,000
104	James Harden AU/599 RC	500	600	1,000	2,000
108	Blake Griffin AU/399 RC	30	50	100	250

2009-10 Donruss Elite

#	Player	NmMt 8	NmMt+ 8.5	MT 9	Gem 9.5/10
161	Blake Griffin AU RC	25	40	60	120
163	James Harden/479 AU RC	250	300	600	1,200
166	Stephen Curry AU RC	1,000	1,200	2,500	5,000

2009-10 Limited

#	Player	NmMt 8	NmMt+ 8.5	MT 9	Gem 9.5/10
153	James Harden JSY AU RC	500	600	1,000	2,000
156	Stephen Curry JSY AU RC	1,500	2,000	3,000	5,000

2009-10 Panini

#	Player	NmMt 8	NmMt+ 8.5	MT 9	Gem 9.5/10
303	James Harden RC	▼40	▼60	▼100	▼200
307	Stephen Curry RC	100	150	300	600
353	James Harden RC	▼40	▼60	▼100	▼200
357	Stephen Curry RC	100	150	300	600
372	Stephen Curry RC	100	150	300	600
400	James Harden RC	▼40	▼60	▼100	▼200

2009-10 Playoff Contenders

#	Player	NmMt 8	NmMt+ 8.5	MT 9	Gem 9.5/10
101	Blake Griffin SP AU RC	50	80	150	300
103	James Harden SP AU RC	600	800	1,500	3,000
106	Stephen Curry SP AU RC	5,000	6,000	10,000	15,000

2009-10 Prestige

#	Player	NmMt 8	NmMt+ 8.5	MT 9	Gem 9.5/10
157	Stephen Curry RC	100	150	300	600
207	Stephen Curry RC	100	150	300	600
230	Stephen Curry Davidson RC100	150	300	600	

2009-10 Rookies and Stars

#	Player	NmMt 8	NmMt+ 8.5	MT 9	Gem 9.5/10
131	Blake Griffin AU/449 RC	25	40	80	200
133	James Harden AU/449 RC	600	800	1,500	3,000
136	Stephen Curry AU/449 RC	2,000	2,500	4,000	8,000

2009-10 Studio

#	Player	NmMt 8	NmMt+ 8.5	MT 9	Gem 9.5/10
129	Stephen Curry RC	80	120	250	500
135	James Harden RC	40	60	150	300

2009-10 Topps

#	Player	NmMt 8	NmMt+ 8.5	MT 9	Gem 9.5/10
319	James Harden RC	▼150	▼250	▼400	▼800
321	Stephen Curry RC	▲1,000	▲1,500	3,000	6,000

2009-10 Topps Chrome

#	Player	NmMt 8	NmMt+ 8.5	MT 9	Gem 9.5/10
99	James Harden RC	▼800	▼1,200	▼2,500	▼5,000
101	Stephen Curry RC	▲8,000	▲10,000	▲15,000	▲30,000

2009-10 Topps Chrome Refractors

#	Player	NmMt 8	NmMt+ 8.5	MT 9	Gem 9.5/10
99	James Harden	▼3,000	▼4,000	▼8,000	▼15,000
101	Stephen Curry	▲20,000	▲30,000	▲40,000	▲60,000

2009-10 Upper Deck

#	Player	NmMt 8	NmMt+ 8.5	MT 9	Gem 9.5/10
227	James Harden SP RC	40	80	150	300
234	Stephen Curry SP RC	150	200	400	800

2009-10 Upper Deck Draft Edition

#	Player	NmMt 8	NmMt+ 8.5	MT 9	Gem 9.5/10
34	Stephen Curry SP	50	80	150	400
40	James Harden	20	30	60	120

2009-10 Upper Deck First Edition

#	Player	NmMt 8	NmMt+ 8.5	MT 9	Gem 9.5/10
188	James Harden RC	40	80	150	300
196	Stephen Curry RC	250	300	600	1,200

2010-11 Classics

#	Player	NmMt 8	NmMt+ 8.5	MT 9	Gem 9.5/10
155	John Wall/199 AU RC	30	60	120	250
163	Gordon Hayward/449 AU RC12	25	50	120	
164	Paul George/449 AU RC	60	80	200	500

2010-11 Donruss

#	Player	NmMt 8	NmMt+ 8.5	MT 9	Gem 9.5/10
228	John Wall RC	▼6	▼8	▼15	▼40
237	Paul George RC	▼25	▼40	▼80	▼200

2010-11 Panini Gold Standard

#	Player	NmMt 8	NmMt+ 8.5	MT 9	Gem 9.5/10
213	John Wall AU RC	▼20	▼30	▼60	▼150
222	Paul George AU RC	80	100	250	500

2010-11 Playoff Contenders Patches

#	Player	NmMt 8	NmMt+ 8.5	MT 9	Gem 9.5/10
151	John Wall AU SP	▼30	▼50	▼100	▼250
160	Paul George AU SP	▲150	▲200	▲400	▲800

2010-11 Playoff National Treasures

#	Player	NmMt 8	NmMt+ 8.5	MT 9	Gem 9.5/10
201	John Wall JSY AU/99 RC	500	600	1,000	2,000
210	Paul George JSY AU/99 RC	1,000	1,200	2,000	3,000

2010-11 Rookies and Stars

#	Player	NmMt 8	NmMt+ 8.5	MT 9	Gem 9.5/10
140	Paul George AU/455 RC	60	100	200	400
170	John Wall AU/454 RC	40	60	120	250

2011-12 SP Authentic

#	Player	NmMt 8	NmMt+ 8.5	MT 9	Gem 9.5/10
23	Klay Thompson	30	40	80	200
27	Kawhi Leonard	30	40	80	200

2011-12 SP Authentic Autographs

#	Player	NmMt 8	NmMt+ 8.5	MT 9	Gem 9.5/10
23	Klay Thompson	▼150	300	▼500	▼800
27	Kawhi Leonard	▼150	300	▼500	▼800

2012-13 Hoops

#	Player	NmMt 8	NmMt+ 8.5	MT 9	Gem 9.5/10
223	Kyrie Irving RC	▼10	▼12	▼30	▼60
232	Klay Thompson RC	▼20	▼30	▼60	▼120
236	Kawhi Leonard RC	▼20	▼30	▼60	▼120
249	Jimmy Butler RC	▼8	▼12	▼25	▼50
275	Anthony Davis RC	▼15	▼20	▼40	▼80
280	Damian Lillard RC	▼15	▼20	▼40	▼80

2012-13 Immaculate Collection

#	Player	NmMt 8	NmMt+ 8.5	MT 9	Gem 9.5/10
112	Kawhi Leonard JSY AU RC	1,500	2,500	5,000	
134	Anthony Davis JSY AU RC	1,500	2,500	5,000	

2012-13 Panini Contenders

#	Player	NmMt 8	NmMt+ 8.5	MT 9	Gem 9.5/10
201	Anthony Davis AU RC	150	300	600	1,200
203	Bradley Beal AU RC	60	80	150	400
233	Draymond Green AU RC	20	30	60	150
250	Kyrie Irving AU RC	150	300	500	800
254	Jimmy Butler AU RC	80	120	250	500
263	Kawhi Leonard AU RC	400	500	800	1,500
271	Klay Thompson AU RC	100	200	400	800

2012-13 Panini Past and Present

#	Player	NmMt 8	NmMt+ 8.5	MT 9	Gem 9.5/10
193	Kawhi Leonard RC	▼15	▼25	▼50	▼120
214	Jimmy Butler RC	▼6	▼10	▼20	▼50
219	Bradley Beal RC	▼8	▼10	▼20	▼40
237	Anthony Davis RC	▼15	▼25	▼50	▼120
249	Damian Lillard RC	▼15	▼25	▼50	▼120

2012-13 Panini Prizm

#	Player	NmMt 8	NmMt+ 8.5	MT 9	Gem 9.5/10
1	LeBron James	▼100	▼200	▼400	▼800
24	Kobe Bryant	▼50	▼80	▼150	▼400

		NmMt 8	NmMt+ 8.5	MT 9	Gem 9.5/10
72	Stephen Curry	100	150	300	600
201	Kyrie Irving RC	▼30	▼50	▼100	▼220
203	Klay Thompson RC	▼100	▼120	▼250	▼500
205	Jimmy Butler RC	▼30	▼50	▼100	▼220
209	Kawhi Leonard RC	▼100	▼120	▼250	▼500
236	Anthony Davis RC	▼100	▼120	▼250	▼500
238	Bradley Beal RC	▼60	▼80	▼120	▼300
245	Damian Lillard RC	▼100	▼120	▼250	▲500
267	Nikola Vucevic RC	20	30	60	120
282	Draymond Green RC	▼40	60	▼100	▼200
285	Khris Middleton RC	▼20	▼30	▼60	▼150

2012-13 Prestige

		NmMt 8	NmMt+ 8.5	MT 9	Gem 9.5/10
151	Kyrie Irving RC	▼10	▼20	▼40	▼80
155	Klay Thompson RC	20	30	60	150
162	Kawhi Leonard RC	▼25	▼40	▼80	▼200
199	Jimmy Butler RC	▼8	▼12	▼25	▼60
201	Anthony Davis RC	▼15	▼25	▼50	▼120
212	Bradley Beal RC	8	15	30	60
214	Damian Lillard RC	▼15	▼25	▼50	▼120
237	Draymond Green RC	▼6	▼10	▼20	▼40

2012-13 Select

		NmMt 8	NmMt+ 8.5	MT 9	Gem 9.5/10
150	Damian Lillard RC	▼40	▼80	▼150	▼300
151	Kyrie Irving AU/149 RC	▼100	▼150	▼300	▼600
152	Anthony Davis AU/149 RC	▼200	▼300	▼500	▼800
170	Klay Thompson AU/149	120	200	400	800
178	Kawhi Leonard AU/199	▼200	▼300	▼500	▼800
246	Klay Thompson JSY AU/199 RC	400	▼500	▼800	▼1,500
250	Kawhi Leonard JSY AU/249 RC	▼400	▼500	▼800	▼1,500
270	Anthony Davis JSY AU/149 RC	▼200	▼300	▼500	▼800

2012-13 Totally Certified

		NmMt 8	NmMt+ 8.5	MT 9	Gem 9.5/10
11	Kawhi Leonard RC	▼15	▼25	▼50	▼120
12	Kyrie Irving RC	▼8	▼12	▼25	▼50
29	Anthony Davis RC	20	25	50	100
70	Damian Lillard RC	▼15	▼25	▼50	▼100

2013-14 Elite

		NmMt 8	NmMt+ 8.5	MT 9	Gem 9.5/10
229	Giannis Antetokounmpo RC	200	250	400	800

2013-14 Hoops

		NmMt 8	NmMt+ 8.5	MT 9	Gem 9.5/10
275	Giannis Antetokounmpo RC	▼80	▼100	▼200	▼400

2013-14 Panini Crusade

		NmMt 8	NmMt+ 8.5	MT 9	Gem 9.5/10
122	Giannis Antetokounmpo RC	60	100	200	400

2013-14 Panini Gold Standard

		NmMt 8	NmMt+ 8.5	MT 9	Gem 9.5/10
231	G.Antetokounmpo JSY AU RC	1,500	2,000	4,000	8,000

2013-14 Panini Prizm

		NmMt 8	NmMt+ 8.5	MT 9	Gem 9.5/10
1	Kobe Bryant	▼12	▼15	▼30	▼80
65	LeBron James	▼15	▼20	▼40	▼100
290	Giannis Antetokounmpo RC	▼300	▼400	▼800	▼2,000

2013-14 Panini Prizm Autographs

		NmMt 8	NmMt+ 8.5	MT 9	Gem 9.5/10
33	Giannis Antetokounmpo	1,500	2,000	3,000	6,000

2013-14 Panini Spectra

		NmMt 8	NmMt+ 8.5	MT 9	Gem 9.5/10
120	Giannis Antetokounmpo JSY AU RC	1,000	1,500	2,500	5,000

2013-14 Pinnacle

		NmMt 8	NmMt+ 8.5	MT 9	Gem 9.5/10
5	Giannis Antetokounmpo RC	60	100	200	400

2013-14 Prestige

		NmMt 8	NmMt+ 8.5	MT 9	Gem 9.5/10
175	Giannis Antetokounmpo RC	▲80	▲120	▲250	▲500

2013-14 Select

		NmMt 8	NmMt+ 8.5	MT 9	Gem 9.5/10
178	Giannis Antetokounmpo RC	300	500	800	1,500

2014-15 Donruss

		NmMt 8	NmMt+ 8.5	MT 9	Gem 9.5/10
203	Joel Embiid RC	▼25	▼40	▼80	▼200
221	Zach LaVine RC	▲15	20	40	▲100
224	Julius Randle RC	▼8	▼10	▼25	▼60

2014-15 Hoops

		NmMt 8	NmMt+ 8.5	MT 9	Gem 9.5/10
263	Joel Embiid RC	▼12	▼20	▼40	▼100
267	Julius Randle RC	6	▼8	▼15	▼40
272	Zach LaVine RC	▼10	▼15	▼30	▼80

2014-15 Panini Prizm

		NmMt 8	NmMt+ 8.5	MT 9	Gem 9.5/10
48	LeBron James	▼10	▼15	▼30	▼80
73	Giannis Antetokounmpo	▼12	▼20	▼40	▼100
251	Andrew Wiggins RC	▼10	▼12	▼30	▼60
253	Joel Embiid RC	▼40	▼60	▼120	▼300
257	Julius Randle RC	▼12	▼15	▼30	▼80
262	Zach LaVine RC	40	▼60	▼120	300

2014-15 Panini Prizm Prizms

		NmMt 8	NmMt+ 8.5	MT 9	Gem 9.5/10
251	Andrew Wiggins	40	60	▲120	▲250
253	Joel Embiid	▼200	▼250	▼400	▼800
257	Julius Randle	60	▼80	▼150	▼300
262	Zach LaVine	▲120	150	300	600

2014-15 Select

		NmMt 8	NmMt+ 8.5	MT 9	Gem 9.5/10
84	Zach LaVine CON RC	30	40	80	200
90	Joel Embiid CON RC	▲30	▲40	▲80	▲200
100	Andrew Wiggins CON RC	▲6	▲8	▲15	▲40

2015-16 Donruss

		NmMt 8	NmMt+ 8.5	MT 9	Gem 9.5/10
208	Karl-Anthony Towns RC	10	15	30	60
215	Nikola Jokic RC	▼60	▼80	▼150	▼300
223	Devin Booker RC	60	▼80	150	300
238	Christian Wood RC	15	25	50	120

2015-16 Panini Prizm

		NmMt 8	NmMt+ 8.5	MT 9	Gem 9.5/10
308	Devin Booker RC	▼120	▼150	▼300	▼600
328	Karl-Anthony Towns RC	25	40	80	200
335	Nikola Jokic RC	▼100	▼150	▼300	▼600
348	Kristaps Porzingis RC	▼10	▼15	▼30	▼60

2015-16 Panini Prizm Prizms Silver

		NmMt 8	NmMt+ 8.5	MT 9	Gem 9.5/10
308	Devin Booker	▼400	▼600	▼1,000	▼2,000
328	Karl-Anthony Towns	▲120	▲200	300	500
335	Nikola Jokic	▼400	▼600	▼1,000	▼2,000
348	Kristaps Porzingis	▼40	▼60	▼120	▼250

2015-16 Select

		NmMt 8	NmMt+ 8.5	MT 9	Gem 9.5/10
16	Karl-Anthony Towns CON RC	▼12	▼25	▼50	▼100
17	Kristaps Porzingis CON RC	▼6	▼10	▼20	▼40
128	Nikola Jokic PRE RC	▼40	▼60	▼120	▼300
136	Karl-Anthony Towns PRE	▼15	▼25	▼50	▼120
196	Kristaps Porzingis PRE	▼8	▼12	▼20	▼40
203	Devin Booker COU RC	▼100	▼150	▼300	▼600

2016-17 Absolute Memorabilia

		NmMt 8	NmMt+ 8.5	MT 9	Gem 9.5/10
200	Ben Simmons RC	20	30	60	120

2016-17 Donruss Optic

		NmMt 8	NmMt+ 8.5	MT 9	Gem 9.5/10
5	Giannis Antetokounmpo	▼6	▼10	▼20	▼50
15	LeBron James	▼20	▼30	▼60	▼120
151	Ben Simmons RC	▼8	▼12	▼30	▼60
152	Brandon Ingram RC	▼8	▼12	▼30	▼60
153	Jaylen Brown RC	▼15	▼25	▼50	▼100
171	Pascal Siakam RC	▼6	▼8	▼15	▼40
173	Dejounte Murray RC	10	12	30	60

2016-17 Panini Prizm

		NmMt 8	NmMt+ 8.5	MT 9	Gem 9.5/10
1	Ben Simmons RC	▼20	▼30	▼60	▼120
44	Jaylen Brown RC	40	60	120	250
131	Brandon Ingram RC	▼15	▼25	▼50	▼100
175	Jamal Murray RC	▼20	▼30	▼60	▼120
220	Pascal Siakam RC	▼10	▼15	▼30	▼60
236	Dejounte Murray RC	15	25	50	120

2016-17 Panini Prizm Prizms Silver

		NmMt 8	NmMt+ 8.5	MT 9	Gem 9.5/10
1	Ben Simmons	▼80	▼120	▼250	▼500
44	Jaylen Brown	▼100	▼150	▼300	▼600
131	Brandon Ingram	▼80	▼120	▼250	▼500

#	Player	NmMt 8	NmMt+ 8.5	MT 9	Gem 9.5/10
175	Jamal Murray	80	▼100	▼200	▼400
220	Pascal Siakam	▼25	▼40	▼80	▼150
236	Dejounte Murray	50	80	120	300

2016-17 Panini Spectra

#	Player	NmMt 8	NmMt+ 8.5	MT 9	Gem 9.5/10
60	Ben Simmons RC	▼15	▼30	▼60	▼150

2016-17 Select

#	Player	NmMt 8	NmMt+ 8.5	MT 9	Gem 9.5/10
50	Ben Simmons RC	▼8	▼12	▼25	▼60
91	Brandon Ingram RC	▼8	▼12	▼25	▼60
101	Brandon Ingram	▼10	▼15	▼30	▼80
141	Ben Simmons	▼8	▼12	▼25	▼60

2017-18 Donruss Optic

#	Player	NmMt 8	NmMt+ 8.5	MT 9	Gem 9.5/10
187	Bam Adebayo RR RC	6	10	20	50
188	Donovan Mitchell RR RC	▼15	▼25	▼50	▼100
196	De'Aaron Fox RR RC	▼6	▼10	▼20	▼50
198	Jayson Tatum RR RC	▼20	▼30	▼60	▼120

2017-18 Hoops

#	Player	NmMt 8	NmMt+ 8.5	MT 9	Gem 9.5/10
53	Jayson Tatum RC	▼12	▼15	▼40	▼100
63	Donovan Mitchell RC	▼8	▼12	▼30	▼60

2017-18 Panini Prizm

#	Player	NmMt 8	NmMt+ 8.5	MT 9	Gem 9.5/10
5	Jayson Tatum RC	▼40	▼60	▼120	▼300
4	De'Aaron Fox RC	▼8	▼12	▼30	▼60
1	Bam Adebayo RC	▼10	▼15	▼30	▼80
17	Donovan Mitchell RC	▼25	▼40	▼80	▼200

2017-18 Panini Prizm Prizms Silver

#	Player	NmMt 8	NmMt+ 8.5	MT 9	Gem 9.5/10
5	Jayson Tatum	300	400	800	▼1,500
4	De'Aaron Fox	▼40	▼60	▼120	▼300
1	Bam Adebayo	▼40	▼60	▼120	▼300
17	Donovan Mitchell	▼120	▼200	▼400	▼600

2017-18 Select

#	Player	NmMt 8	NmMt+ 8.5	MT 9	Gem 9.5/10
	Donovan Mitchell RC	▼25	▼40	▼80	▼200
	De'Aaron Fox RC	▼12	20	▼40	▼80
	Jayson Tatum RC	▼20	▼30	▼60	▼150
6	Jayson Tatum	▼30	▼40	▼80	▼200
75	De'Aaron Fox	▼15	▼20	▼40	▼80

2018-19 Absolute Memorabilia

#	Player	NmMt 8	NmMt+ 8.5	MT 9	Gem 9.5/10
	Luka Doncic RC	500	600	1,000	2,500

2018-19 Donruss Optic

#	Player	NmMt 8	NmMt+ 8.5	MT 9	Gem 9.5/10
	LeBron James	12	20	40	100
7	Luka Doncic RR RC	▼100	▼120	▼250	▼500
8	Trae Young RR RC	▼20	▼25	▼60	▼120

2018-19 Hoops

#	Player	NmMt 8	NmMt+ 8.5	MT 9	Gem 9.5/10
250	Trae Young RC	▼10	▼15	▼30	▼60
268	Luka Doncic RC	▼30	▼40	▼80	▼200

2018-19 Panini Contenders

#	Player	NmMt 8	NmMt+ 8.5	MT 9	Gem 9.5/10
122	Luka Doncic AU RC	2,500	3,000	5,000	8,000
142	Trae Young AU RC	▲600	▲800	▲1,500	▲3,000

2018-19 Panini Contenders Draft Picks

#	Player	NmMt 8	NmMt+ 8.5	MT 9	Gem 9.5/10
126	Luka Doncic AU RC	▲1,200	▲1,500	▲2,500	▲4,000

2018-19 Panini Prizm

#	Player	NmMt 8	NmMt+ 8.5	MT 9	Gem 9.5/10
32	Michael Porter Jr. RC	▼8	▼12	▼25	▼60
78	Trae Young RC	40	50	150	300
280	Luka Doncic RC	▼120	▼150	▼300	▼600

2018-19 Panini Prizm Prizms Silver

#	Player	NmMt 8	NmMt+ 8.5	MT 9	Gem 9.5/10
78	Trae Young	200	300	500	1,000
280	Luka Doncic	▼800	▼1,000	▼2,000	4,000

2018-19 Select

#	Player	NmMt 8	NmMt+ 8.5	MT 9	Gem 9.5/10
25	Luka Doncic RC	▼60	▼100	▼200	▼500
45	Trae Young RC	40	60	120	300
122	Luka Doncic	▼80	▼120	▼250	▼500
142	Trae Young	40	60	120	300

2019-20 Donruss

#	Player	NmMt 8	NmMt+ 8.5	MT 9	Gem 9.5/10
201	Zion Williamson RR RC	▼6	▼10	▼20	▼50
202	Ja Morant RR RC	▼6	▼10	▼20	▼50

2019-20 Donruss Optic

#	Player	NmMt 8	NmMt+ 8.5	MT 9	Gem 9.5/10
158	Zion Williamson RR RC	▼15	▼25	▼50	▼120
168	Ja Morant RR RC	▼15	▼25	▼50	120

2019-20 Donruss Optic Holo

#	Player	NmMt 8	NmMt+ 8.5	MT 9	Gem 9.5/10
158	Zion Williamson RR	▼100	▼150	▼300	▼600
168	Ja Morant RR	80	120	250	500

2019-20 Hoops

#	Player	NmMt 8	NmMt+ 8.5	MT 9	Gem 9.5/10
258	Zion Williamson RC	▼8	▼12	▼25	▼50
259	Ja Morant RC	▼8	12	▼25	▼50

2019-20 Hoops Premium Stock

#	Player	NmMt 8	NmMt+ 8.5	MT 9	Gem 9.5/10
258	Zion Williamson RC	▼12	▼15	▼30	▼60
259	Ja Morant RC	▼12	▼15	▼30	▼60

2019-20 Panini Mosaic

#	Player	NmMt 8	NmMt+ 8.5	MT 9	Gem 9.5/10
209	Zion Williamson RC	▼10	▼15	▼30	▼60
219	Ja Morant RC	▼10	▼15	▼30	▼60

2019-20 Panini Prizm

#	Player	NmMt 8	NmMt+ 8.5	MT 9	Gem 9.5/10
75	Luka Doncic	▼6	▼8	▼15	▼30
129	LeBron James	▼6	▼10	▼20	▼40
248	Zion Williamson RC	▼30	▼50	▼100	▼200
249	Ja Morant RC	▼30	50	100	▼200
250	RJ Barrett RC	▼6	▼8	▼15	▼30
259	Tyler Herro RC	12	15	40	80

2019-20 Panini Prizm Prizms Silver

#	Player	NmMt 8	NmMt+ 8.5	MT 9	Gem 9.5/10
75	Luka Doncic	▼20	▼30	▼60	▼120
129	LeBron James	▼20	▼30	▼60	▼120
248	Zion Williamson	▼300	▼400	▼600	▼1,200
249	Ja Morant	150	250	400	800
259	Tyler Herro	▲50	▲80	▲150	▼300

2019-20 Panini Revolution

#	Player	NmMt 8	NmMt+ 8.5	MT 9	Gem 9.5/10
101	Zion Williamson RC	▼12	▼20	▼40	▼120
102	Ja Morant RC	▼12	▼20	▼40	▼120

2019-20 Select

#	Player	NmMt 8	NmMt+ 8.5	MT 9	Gem 9.5/10
1	Zion Williamson RC	▼20	▼30	▼60	▼120
72	Ja Morant RC	20	30	60	120

2020-21 Certified

#	Player	NmMt 8	NmMt+ 8.5	MT 9	Gem 9.5/10
198	LaMelo Ball RC	▼15	▼25	▼50	▼120

2020-21 Donruss

#	Player	NmMt 8	NmMt+ 8.5	MT 9	Gem 9.5/10
201	Anthony Edwards RR RC	▼6	▼10	▼20	▼50
202	LaMelo Ball RR RC	▼10	▼20	▼40	▼80

2020-21 Hoops

#	Player	NmMt 8	NmMt+ 8.5	MT 9	Gem 9.5/10
216	Anthony Edwards RC	▼6	▼10	▼20	▼50
223	LaMelo Ball RC	▼12	▼20	▼40	▼80

2020-21 Panini Prizm

#	Player	NmMt 8	NmMt+ 8.5	MT 9	Gem 9.5/10
1	LeBron James	▼15	▼30	▼60	▼150
258	Anthony Edwards RC	▼20	▼40	▼80	▼200
278	LaMelo Ball RC	▼40	▼60	▼150	▼400

2000 Ultra WNBA

#	Player	NmMt 8	NmMt+ 8.5	MT 9	Gem 9.5/10
21	Becky Hammon RC	30	50	100	300

2016 WNBA

#	Player	NmMt 8	NmMt+ 8.5	MT 9	Gem 9.5/10
95	Breanna Stewart RC	▲800	▲1,000	▲2,000	

2020 Panini Prizm WNBA

#	Player	NmMt 8	NmMt+ 8.5	MT 9	Gem 9.5/10
89	Sabrina Ionescu	▼20	▼40	▼60	▼120

FOOTBALL

1888 Goodwin Champions N162

		PrFr 1	GD 2	VG 3	VgEx 4	EX 5	ExMt 6	NM 7	NmMt 8
12	Harry Beecher (Football)	1,500	3,000	6,000					

— Ed Andrews PSA 7 (NM) sold for $6,600 (Mastro; 5/08)
— Ed Andrews PSA 7 (NM) sold for $3,884 (Heritage; 10/07)
— Cap Anson PSA 7 (NM) sold for $25,831 (Memory Lane; 5/08)
— Cap Anson PSA 7 (NM) sold for $23,184 (Goodwin; 3/09)
— Cap Anson PSA 7 (NM) sold for $10,443 (Mastro; 12/05)
— Cap Anson SGC 80 (ExMt) sold for $13,698 (Mastro; 4/07)
— Dan Brouthers PSA 7 (NM) sold for $11,596 (Mastro; 4/07)
— Dan Brouthers PSA 7 (NM) sold for $6,600 (Mastro; 4/07)
— Fred Dunlap PSA 7.5 (NM+) sold for $9,000 (mastro; 5/08)
— Tim Keefe PSA 8 (NmMt) sold for $18,448 (Goodwin; 11/07)
— Tim Keefe PSA 7 (NM) sold for $13,394 (Mastro; 4/07)
— Tim Keefe SGC 80 (ExMt) sold for $7,050 (REA; 5/08)
— Tim Keefe PSA 6 (ExMt) sold for $3,680 (Superior; 3/05)
— King Kelly PSA 8 (NmMt) sold for $66,337 (SCP; 7/08)
— King Kelly PSA 8 (NmMt) sold for $18,975 (SCP Sotheby's 8/03)
— King Kelly PSA 7 (NM) sold for $12,000 (Mastro; 5/08)

1894 Mayo

— George Adee #2 PSA 8 (NM/MT) sold for $2400 (Legendary; 8/12)
— H.W.Barnett #4 PSA 8 (NM/MT) sold for $2100 (Legendary; 8/12)
— Anson Beard #6 SGC 5 (EXC) sold for $1057.5 (Huggins&Scott; 10/12)
— Charles Brewer #7 SGC 7.5 (Near MT+) sold for $1600 (Legendary; 8/12)
— H.D.Brown #8 PSA 8 (NM/MT) sold for $2200 (Legendary; 8/12)
— C.D. Burt #9 PSA 6 (EX-MT) sold for $1300 (Legendary; 8/12)
— Frank Butterworth #10 SGC 7 (Near MT) sold for $950 (Legendary; 8/12)
— Anonymous John Dunlop SGC 1 (Poor) sold for $12,659 (Goodiwn; 7/09)
— Anonymous John Dunlop #35 PSA 1 (Poor) sold for $9000 (Legendary; 8/12)
— Madison Gonterman #13 PSA 7 (Near MT) sold for $1000 (Legendary; 8/12)
— George Gray PSA 5 (Ex) sold for $1,035 (Huggins&Scott; 4/08)
— George Gray #14 PSA 7 (Near MT) sold for $900 (Legendary; 8/12)
— John Greenway SGC 4 (VgEx) sold for $794 (Memory Lane; 8/06)
— Frank Hinkey PSA 6 (ExMt) sold for $1,645 (Robert Edward Auction; 4/07)
— William Hickok #16 PSA 6 (EX-MT) sold for $1200 (Legendary; 8/12)
— Augustus Holly #18 SGC 4 (VgEx) sold for $655 (Memory Lane; 8/06)
— Langdon Lea #19 PSA 7 (Near MT) sold for $1200 (Legendary; 8/12)
— William Mackie #20 PSA 7 (Near MT) sold for $1400 (Legendary; 8/12)
— Tom Manahan #21 PSA 7 (Near MT) sold for $2000 (Legendary; 8/12)
— Fred Murphy #24 PSA 7 (Near MT) sold for $950 (Legendary; 8/12)
— Neilson Poe #25 PSA 3 (VG) sold for $1,406 (Barry Sloate Auction; 9/07)
— Neilson Poe #25 PSA 7 (Near MT) sold for $3750 (Legendary; 8/12)
— Dudley Riggs #26 PSA 8 (NM/MT) sold for $2300 (Legendary; 8/12)
— Phillip Stillman #27 PSA 8 (NM/MT) sold for $2200 (Legendary; 8/12)
— Knox Taylor #28 PSA 8 (NM/MT) sold for $2500 (Legendary; 8/12)
— T.Trenchard #30 SGC 7 (Near MT) sold for $2100 (Legendary; 8/12)
— William Ward #31 PSA 7 (Near MT) sold for $1600 (Legendary; 8/12)
— Bert Waters #32 PSA 8 (NM/MT) sold for $2200 (Legendary; 8/12)
— A. Wheeler #33 PSA 7 (Near MT) sold for $1300 (Legendary; 8/12)
— Edgar Wrightington #34 PSA 7 (Near MT) sold for $1200 (Legendary; 8/12)

1933 Sport Kings

		PrFr 1	GD 2	VG 3	VgEx 4	EX 5	ExMt 6	NM 7	NmMt 8
4	Red Grange RC FB	250	300	400	550	700	1,200	2,500	
6	Jim Thorpe RC FB	▲1,200	▲2,000	▲3,000	▲4,000	▲6,000	▲8,000		
35	Knute Rockne RC FB		200	250	450	600	800	1,200	4,000

— Red Grange #4 PSA 8 (NmMt) sold for $13,394.40 (Mastro Auctions; 12/07)
— Red Grange #4 SGC 8 (NmMt) sold for $3,704 (Mile High Auctions; 11/10)
— Carl Hubbell #42 PSA 9 (MT) sold for $7,929 (Mastro; 12/05)
— Babe Ruth #2 SGC 92 (NmMt+) sold for $64,417 (Mastro; 4/08)
— Babe Ruth #2 GAI 7.5 (NM+) sold for $5,541 (Mile High; 8/07)
— Jim Thorpe #6 PSA 8 (NmMt) sold for $7,200.00 (Mastro Auctions; 5/08)
— Ed Wachter #5 PSA 8 (NmMt) sold for $2,100 (Bussineau; 7/13)

1935 National Chicle

		PrFr 1	GD 2	VG 3	VgEx 4	EX 5	ExMt 6	NM 7	NmMt 8
1A	Dutch Clark RC	150	200	250	400	600	1,000	2,500	3,500
2A	Bo Molenda RC	30	50	60	100	150	250	600	3,000
3A	George Kenneally RC	30	50	60	100	150	200	800	1,500
4A	Ed Matesic RC	30	50	60	100	125	200	600	1,500
5A	Glenn Presnell RC	30	50	60	100	150	225	500	1,800
6A	Pug Rentner RC	30	50	60	100	125	200	400	1,000
7A	Ken Strong RC	60	80	125	200	350	400	1,000	2,500
8A	Jim Zyntell RC	30	50	60	100	125	175	400	900
9A	Knute Rockne CO	250	350	450	600	1,200	2,000	4,000	8,000
10A	Cliff Battles RC	80	120	150	250	400	600	1,000	2,500
11A	Turk Edwards RC	80	120	150	250	400	600	1,200	4,000
12A	Tom Hupke RC	30	50	60	100	125	175	400	900
13A	Homer Griffiths RC	30	50	60	100	125	175	400	900
14A	Phil Sarboe RC	30	50	60	100	125	175	400	900
15A	Ben Ciccone RC	30	50	60	100	125	175	400	900
16A	Ben Smith RC	30	50	60	100	125	175	400	900
17A	Tom Jones RC	30	50	60	100	125	175	400	900
18A	Mike Mikulak RC	30	50	60	100	125	200	400	900
19	Ralph Kercheval RC	30	50	60	100	125	200	400	900
20A	Warren Heller RC	30	50	60	100	125	175	400	900
21A	Cliff Montgomery RC	30	50	60	100	125	175	400	900
22A	Shipwreck Kelly RC	30	50	60	100	125	175	400	900
23A	Beattie Feathers RC	40	60	90	150	200	300	600	1,200
24A	Clarke Hinkle RC	120	150	200	350	500	700	1,500	3,500
25	Dale Burnett RC	175	250	300	400	500	750	1,200	
26	John Dell Isola RC	175	250	400	400	500	750	1,200	
27	Bull Tosi RC	300	600	900	1,500	2,500	4,000	12,000	
28	Stan Kostka RC	175	250	300	500	600	750	1,200	
29	Jim MacMurdo RC	175	250	300	400	500	750	1,200	
30	Ernie Caddel RC	175	250	300	400	500	750	1,200	
31	Nic Niccola RC	175	250	300	400	500	1,200	1,500	
32	Swede Johnston RC	175	250	300	400	500	750	1,200	
33	Ernie Smith RC	175	250	300	400	500	750	2,000	
34	Bronko Nagurski RC	3,000	3,500	4,000	10,000	15,000	20,000	25,000	
35	Luke Johnsos RC	175	250	300	400	600	1,000	1,500	
36	Bernie Masterson RC	175	250	300	450	600	1,000	3,000	

— Dale Burnett #25 PSA 8 (NmMt) sold for $2,550 (eBay; 1/05)
— Ernie Caddel #30 SGC 96 (Mint) sold for $5,000 (Robert Edward; 5/09)
— Ernie Caddel #30 PSA 8 (NmMt) sold for $2,360 (Love of the Game Winter; 2/14)
— John Dell Isola #26 SGC 96 (Mint) sold for $3,500 (Robert Edward; 5/09)
— John Dell Isola #26 PSA 8 (NmMt) sold for $1,912 (Heritage; 10/06)
— Beattie Feathers #23 PSA 9 (Mint) sold for $2,496 (Mile High; 11/09)
— Homer Griffiths #13 PSA 9 (Mint) sold for $1,912 (Heritage; 10/06)
— Warren Heller #20 PSA 9 (Mint) sold for $3,287 (Mastro; 12/03)
— Luke Johnsos #35 PSA 8 (NmMt) sold for $2,988 (Mastro; 4/04)
— Swede Johnston #32 PSA 8 (NmMt) sold for $2,490 (Heritage; 5/06)
— Swede Johnston #32 PSA 8 (NmMt) sold for $2,950 (Love of the Game Winter; 2/14)
— Tom Jones #17 PSA 9 (Mint) sold for $3,884 (Heritage; 5/06)
— Shipwreck Kelly #22 PSA 9 (Mint) sold for $1,400 (Robert Edward; 5/09)
— Ralph Kercheval #19 PSA 9 (Mint) sold for $2,495 (eBay; 6/04)
— Stan Kostka #28 PSA 8 (NmMt) sold for $3,300 (Mastro; 5/08)
— Bernie Masterson #36 PSA 8 (NmMt) sold for $14,340 (Heritage; 5/06)
— Jim MacMurdo #36 PSA 8 (NmMt) sold for $3,650 (Memory Lane; 6/08)
— Jim MacMurdo #36 PSA 8 (NmMt) sold for $2,478 (Love of the Game Winter; 2/14)
— Mike Mikulak #18 PSA 9 (Mint) sold for $4,050 (eBay; 11/07)
— Mike Mikulak #18 SGC 96 (Mint) sold for $1,526 (eBay; 5/05)
— Bronko Nagurski #34 SGC 96 (Mint) private sale $240,000 (SGC reported; 7/06)
— Bronko Nagurski #34 SGC 96 (Mint) sold for $80,000 (eBay; 6/03)
— Bronko Nagurski #34 PSA 8 (NmMt) sold for $58,417 (Memory Lane; 12/06)
— Bronko Nagurski #34 PSA 8 (NmMt) sold for $66,354 (SCP Auctions; 7/08)
— Bronko Nagurski #34 PSA 8 (NmMt) sold for $23,148 (Memory Lane; 5/13)
— Nic Niccola #31 PSA 9 (Mint) sold for $7,200 (Mastro; 4/08)
— Nic Niccola #31 PSA 8 (NmMt) sold for $2,616 (eBay; 4/07)
— Nic Niccola #31 PSA 8 (NmMt) sold for $4,050 (eBay; 3/05)

— Knute Rockne #9 SGC 8.5 (NmMt+) sold for $6,019 (Mastro; 12/07)
— Knute Rockne #9 PSA 8 (NmMt) sold for $6,114 (SCP Auctions; 7/08)
— Ken Strong #7 PSA 9 (Mint) sold for $11,352 (Heritage; 5/06)
— Bull Tosi #27 PSA 8 (NmMt) sold for $5,826 (Mastro; 4/04)
— Jim Zyntell #8 PSA 9 (Mint) sold for $2,987 (Heritage; 5/06)

1948 Bowman

		PrFr 1	GD 2	VG 3	VgEx 4	EX 5	ExMt 6	NM 7	NmMt 8
1	Joe Tereshinski RC	20	30	25	30	40	100	200	700
2	Larry Olsonoski	6	8	10	15	25	35	60	250
3	Johnny Lujack SP RC	30	50	80	125	175	250	450	1,000
4	Ray Poole	5	6	8	12	20	30	50	150
5	Bill DeCorrevont RC	6	8	10	15	25	35	50	175
6	Paul Briggs SP	10	15	25	30	50	75	100	250
7	Steve Van Buren RC	20	30	50	60	100	150	300	1,000
8	Kenny Washington RC	10	15	20	40	50	60	120	150
9	Nolan Luhn SP	10	15	25	30	60	100	175	400
10	Chris Iversen	5	6	8	12	20	30	50	150
11	Jack Wiley	6	8	10	15	25	35	50	175
12	Charley Conerly SP RC	30	50	80	100	150	200	350	500
13	Hugh Taylor RC	5	6	8	12	20	30	50	175
14	Frank Seno	6	8	10	15	50	60	80	150
15	Gil Bouley SP	10	15	25	30	50	75	100	300
16	Tommy Thompson RC	5	6	8	12	20	30	50	200
17	Charley Trippi RC	10	15	20	30	60	75	125	400
18	Vince Banonis SP	10	15	25	30	50	75	100	350
19	Art Faircloth	5	6	8	20	25	30	50	150
20	Clyde Goodnight	6	8	10	15	25	35	50	150
21	Bill Chipley SP	10	15	25	30	50	75	100	300
22	Sammy Baugh RC	60	100	250	300	500	600	800	1,500
23	Don Kindt	5	6	8	10	15	25	35	175
24	John Koniszewski SP	10	15	25	30	50	75	150	300
25	Pat McHugh	5	6	8	12	20	30	50	200
26	Bob Waterfield RC	20	30	40	60	80	125	250	500
27	Tony Compagno SP	10	15	25	30	50	80	100	350
28	Paul Governali RC	5	6	8	12	20	30	50	175
29	Pat Harder RC	8	12	15	20	35	50	80	200
30	Vic Lindskog SP	10	15	25	30	50	75	150	300
31	Salvatore Rosato	5	6	8	12	20	30	50	175
32	John Mastrangelo	6	8	10	15	25	40	50	175
33	Fred Gehrke SP	10	15	25	30	50	75	100	300
34	Bosh Pritchard	5	6	8	12	20	30	50	150
35	Mike Micka	6	8	10	15	25	35	50	175
36	Bulldog Turner SP RC	30	50	60	100	150	250	600	2,000
37	Len Younce	5	6	8	20	25	30	50	175
38	Pat West	6	8	10	15	25	35	50	175
39	Russ Thomas SP	10	15	25	30	40	50	60	350
40	James Peebles	5	6	8	12	20	30	50	150
41	Bob Skoglund	6	8	10	15	25	35	50	175
42	Walt Stickle SP	10	15	25	30	50	75	100	300
43	Whitey Wistert RC	5	6	8	12	20	30	60	175
44	Paul Christman RC	8	12	15	20	35	50	80	200
45	Jay Rhodemyre SP	10	15	25	30	50	75	100	350
46	Tony Minisi	5	6	8	12	30	40	50	150
47	Bob Mann	6	8	10	25	30	40	50	175
48	Mal Kutner SP RC	10	15	25	30	50	75	100	300
49	Dick Poillon	5	6	8	12	20	30	50	175
50	Charles Cherundolo	6	8	10	15	25	35	50	175
51	Gerald Cowhig SP	10	15	25	30	40	75	100	300
52	Neill Armstrong RC	5	6	8	12	20	30	50	200
53	Frank Maznicki	6	8	10	15	25	35	50	175
54	John Sanchez SP	10	15	25	30	50	75	100	300
55	Frank Reagan	5	6	8	12	20	30	60	200
56	Jim Hardy	6	8	10	15	25	35	80	150
57	John Badaczewski SP	10	15	25	30	50	75	100	350
58	Robert Nussbaumer	5	6	8	12	20	30	50	175
59	Marvin Pregulman	6	8	10	15	25	35	50	125
60	Elbie Nickel SP RC	12	20	30	40	75	100	150	350
61	Alex Wojciechowicz RC	20	30	40	60	80	100	200	600
62	Walt Schlinkman	6	8	10	15	25	35	50	150
63	Pete Pihos SP RC	30	50	60	125	200	250	350	1,200
64	Joseph Sulaitis	5	6	8	12	20	30	50	125
65	Mike Holovak RC	6	8	10	15	25	35	50	175
66	Cy Souders SP RC	10	15	25	30	50	75	100	300
67	Paul McKee	5	6	8	12	20	30	50	150
68	Bill Moore	6	8	10	15	25	35	50	175
69	Frank Minini SP	10	15	25	30	50	75	125	300
70	Jack Ferrante	5	6	8	12	20	30	50	175

		PrFr 1	GD 2	VG 3	VgEx 4	EX 5	ExMt 6	NM 7	NmMt 8
71	Les Horvath RC	6	10	12	25	30	50	125	200
72	Ted Fritsch Sr. SP RC	12	20	30	35	60	80	200	350
73	Tex Coulter RC	5	6	8	12	20	30	50	200
74	Boley Dancewicz	6	8	10	15	25	35	50	150
75	Dante Mangani SP	10	15	25	30	50	75	100	300
76	James Hefti	5	6	8	12	30	40	50	150
77	Paul Sarringhaus	6	8	20	25	30	40	50	150
78	Joe Scott SP	10	15	25	30	50	75	100	200
79	Bucko Kilroy RC	5	6	8	12	20	30	80	300
80	Bill Dudley RC	12	20	30	80	100	125	150	350
81	Mar. Goldberg SP RC	10	15	25	40	60	100	225	400
82	John Cannady	5	6	8	12	20	30	50	175
83	Perry Moss	6	8	10	15	25	35	50	200
84	Harold Crisler SP RC	10	15	25	30	50	75	100	400
85	Bill Gray	5	6	8	12	20	30	50	175
86	John Clement	6	8	10	15	25	35	50	175
87	Dan Sandifer SP	10	15	25	30	50	75	100	600
88	Ben Kish	5	6	8	20	25	30	50	175
89	Herbert Banta	6	8	10	15	25	35	50	175
90	Bill Garnaas SP	10	15	25	30	50	100	150	
91	Jim White RC	8	12	15	25	50	80	150	200
92	Frank Barzilauskas	6	8	10	15	25	50	60	175
93	Vic Sears SP	10	15	25	30	50	75	125	300
94	John Adams	5	6	8	12	20	30	50	250
95	George McAfee RC	15	25	35	50	80	100	150	500
96	Ralph Heywood SP	10	15	25	30	40	50	150	300
97	Joe Muha	5	6	8	12	20	30	50	175
98	Fred Enke	6	8	10	15	25	35	50	175
99	Harry Gilmer SP RC	25	40	50	60	80	100	300	500
100	Bill Miklich	5	6	8	12	20	30	60	125
101	Joe Gottlieb	6	8	10	15	25	35	60	200
102	Bud Angsman SP RC	10	15	25	30	50	75	100	400
103	Tom Farmer	5	6	8	25	30	40	50	
104	Bruce Smith RC	12	20	30	40	100	300	400	800
105	Bob Cifers SP	10	15	25	30	50	75	100	400
106	Ernie Steele	5	6	8	12	25	60	150	
107	Sid Luckman RC	25	40	50	100	150	175	400	800
108	Buford Ray SP RC	30	50	60	150	225	350	500	1,200

— Bud Angsman #102 PSA 9 (Mint) sold for $1,478.56 (Ebay; 1/14)
— Sammy Baugh #22 SGC 9 (Mint) sold for $2640 (Ebay; 9/14)
— Sammy Baugh #22 PSA 9 (Mint) sold for $6917 (Ebay; 4/15)
— John Cannady #82 PSA 9 (Mint) sold for $1,477.98 (Goodwin; 8/12)
— John Clement #86 PSA 9 (Mint) sold for $464 (eBay; 6/12)
— Paul Christman #44 PSA 9 (Mint) sold for $1,533 (eBay; 2/14)
— Harold Crisler #84 PSA 9 (MT) sold for $1,475 (REA; 4/07)
— Gerald Cowhig SP #51 PSA 9 (Mint) sold for $1633 (eBay; 8/12)
— Bill Dudley #80 PSA 9 (MT) sold for $3,285 (Goodwin; 7/09)
— Boley Dancewicz #74 PSA 9 (MT) sold for $1,170 (eBay; 8/08)
— Art Faircloth #19 PSA 9 (MT) sold for $810 (REA; 4/07)
— Harry Gilmer #99 PSA 8.5 (NmMt+) sold for $3,253.50 (Ebay; 3/14)
— Jim Hardy #56 PSA 9 (MT) sold for $761(eBay; 4/14)
— John Mastrangelo #32 PSA 9 (Mint) sold for $1,076 (Memory Lane; 8/12)
— Mar. Goldberg #81 PSA 9 (Mint) sold for $3,546.95 (Ebay; 2/14)
— Marvin Pregulman #59 PSA 9 (MT) sold for $1,261 (Goodwin;01/13)
— Frank Reagan #55 PSA 9 (MT) sold for $895 (REA; 4/07)
— John Sanchez #54 PSA 9 (MT) sold for $961 (eBay; 11/07)
— Ernie Steele #54 PSA 8 (NmMt) sold for $1,075 (eBay; 11/07)
— Joe Tereshinksi #1 PSA 9 (MT) sold for $2,448 (Mastro; 12/06)
— Charley Trippi #17 PSA 9 (MT) sold for $1,853 (Goodwin; 2/10)
— Charley Trippi #17 PSA 9 (MT) sold for $1,373 (eBay; 4/07)
— Charley Trippi #17 PSA 9 (MT) sold for $1,229 (eBay; 9/14)
— Bob Waterfield #26 PSA 9 (MT) sold for $1,833 (Memory Lane; 12/06)
— Pat West #38 PSA 9 (MT) sold for $1,767 (Goodwin; 2/10)
— Alex Wojciechowicz #38 PSA 9 (MT) sold for $2,042 (Mile High; 11/10)

1948 Leaf

		PrFr 1	GD 2	VG 3	VgEx 4	EX 5	ExMt 6	NM 7	NmMt 8
1A	Sid Luckman Yell.Bkgrd RC	100	125	200	250	450	1,600		
2	Steve Suhey	6	10	12	20	30	50	150	
3A	Bulldog Turner Red Bkgrd RC	20	35	40	60	100	250	600	
3C	Bulldog Turner Wht.Bkgrd RC	20	30	40	60	125	200		
4A	Doak Walker RC	30	50	75	135	175	800	1,600	
5A	Levi Jackson Blu Jsy RC	6	10	12	20	30	50	150	
5B	Levi Jackson Wht Jsy RC	10	15	20	30	50	75		
6A	Bobby Layne Yell.Pants RC	80	125	150	225	300	700	4,000	
6B	Bobby Layne Red Pants RC	100	125	150	225	400	600		
7A	Bill Fischer Red Bkgrd RC	6	10	12	20	30	50	350	
7C	Bill Fischer Wht.Bkgrd RC	10	15	20	30	50	75		

#	Player	PrFr 1	GD 2	VG 3	VgEx 4	EX 5	ExMt 6	NM 7	NmMt 8
8A	Vince Banonis Blk Name RC	6	10	12	20	30	50	150	
8B	Vince Banonis Wht Name RC	10	15	20	30	50	75		
9A	Tommy Thompson Yell.#'s RC	6	10	12	20	30	60	250	
9B	Tommy Thompson Blu #'s RC	10	15	20	30	50	75		
10A	Perry Moss	6	10	15	30	50	75	200	
11A	Terry Brennan RC	6	10	12	20	30	50	150	
12A	Bill Swiacki Blk Name RC	6	10	12	20	30	50	150	
12B	Bill Swiacki Wht Name RC	10	15	20	30	50	75		
13A	Johnny Lujack RC	25	40	50	75	100	200	600	
13B	Johnny Lujack RC ERR	125	200	300	400	500	750		
14A	Mal Kutner BL RC	6	10	12	20	30	50	150	
14B	Mal Kutner WL RC	10	15	20	30	50	75		
15	Charlie Justice RC	10	15	20	35	60	100	350	
16A	Pete Pihos Yell.#'s RC	20	30	35	60	100	175	600	
16B	Pete Pihos Blu #'s RC	30	50	60	80	100	300		
17A	Ken Washington Blk Name RC	6	10	12	20	30	50	150	
17B	Ken Washington Wht Name RC	10	15	20	30	50	80		
18A	Harry Gilmer RC	6	10	12	20	30	50	150	
19A	George McAfee RC	15	25	30	50	100	250	600	
19B	Gorgeous George McAfee RC	80	60	80	100	200	350		
20A	George Taliaferro Yell.Bkgrd RC	6	10	12	20	30	80	150	
20B	George Taliaferro Wht.Bkgrd RC	10	15	20	30	50	75		
21	Paul Christman RC	6	10	12	20	35	60	150	
22A	Steve Van Buren Green Jsy RC	30	50	60	100	150	300	1,000	
22B	Steve Van Buren Yell.Jsy RC	40	60	90	150	250	400		
22C	S.Van Buren Grn Jsy Blu Sck RC	80	100	125	175	300			
23A	Ken Kavanaugh YS RC	6	10	12	20	30	50	150	
24A	Jim Martin Red Bkgrd RC	6	10	12	20	30	75	175	
24C	Jim Martin Wht.Bkgrd RC	10	15	20	30	50	75		
25A	Bud Angsman Blk Name RC	6	10	12	20	30	50	150	
25B	Bud Angsman Wht Name RC	10	15	20	30	50	75		
26A	Bob Waterfield Blk Name RC	30	50	60	100	175	300	1,000	
26B	Bob Waterfield Wht Name RC	40	60	90	150	250	450		
27A	Fred Davis Yell.Bkgrd	6	10	12	20	30	50	600	
27B	Fred Davis Wht.Bkgrd	10	15	20	30	50	75		
28A	Whitey Wistert Yell.Jsy RC	8	12	15	30	40	100	250	
28B	Whitey Wistert Green Jsy RC	12	20	25	40	60	150		
29	Charley Trippi RC	10	15	20	40	100	225	500	2,000
30A	P.Governali RC dark tan hlmt	6	10	12	20	30	50	150	
31A	Tom McWilliams Maroon Jsy RC	6	10	12	20	30	50	150	
31B	Tom McWilliams Red Jsy RC	6	15	20	30	50	75		
32A	Leroy Zimmerman	6	10	12	20	30	50	150	
33	Pat Harder RC	6	10	12	20	60	80	150	
34A	Sammy Baugh RC maroon	100	125	200	300	500	1,500	8,000	
35A	Ted Fritsch Sr. RC	6	10	12	20	40	80	300	
36	Bill Dudley RC	12	20	35	60	100	200	600	
37A	George Connor RC	6	10	15	25	35	80	150	400
38A	F.Dancewicz RC green num	6	10	12	20	30	50	150	
39	Billy Dewell	6	10	12	20	30	50	150	
40A	John Nolan RC green numbr	6	10	12	20	30	50	150	
41A	H.Szulborski Orng Pants RC	6	10	12	20	30	50	150	
41B	Harry Szulborski Yell.Pants RC	10	15	20	30	50	75		
42	Tex Coulter RC	6	10	12	20	30	50	200	
43A	R.Nussbaumer Maroon RC	6	10	12	20	30	50	200	
43B	R.Nussbaumer Red Jsy RC	10	15	20	30	50	75		
44	Bob Mann	6	10	12	25	30	40	150	
45A	Jim White RC	20	30	35	60	80	125	400	
46A	Jack Jacobs Jsy # RC	6	10	12	20	30	50	300	
46B	Jack Jacobs No Jsy # RC	12	20	25	40	60	100		
47A	John Clement RC brown FB	6	10	12	20	30	50	150	
48	Frank Reagan	6	10	12	20	30	50	200	
49	Frank Tripucka RC	8	12	15	25	40	100	300	
50	John Rauch RC	20	30	40	60	120	200	800	
51A	Mike Dimitro	20	30	40	60	120	200	800	
52A	Nomellini Blu Bkg Maroon RC	125	150	200	300	500	1,000	2,000	
52B	Nomellini Blu Bkg Red Jsy RC	100	125	150	250	500	1,200		
53	Charley Conerly RC	100	125	150	250	400	800		
54A	Chuck Bednarik Yell Bkgrd RC	150	225	350	500	800	2,000	3,500	
55	Chick Jagade	20	30	40	60	120	250		
56A	Bob Folsom RC	20	30	40	60	120	300		
57	Gene Rossides RC	20	30	40	60	80	300		
58	Art Weiner	20	30	40	60	▼100	150	800	
59	Alex Sarkistian	20	30	40	60	100	200	800	
60	Dick Harris Texas	20	30	40	60	100	250		
61	Len Younce	20	30	40	60	100	150		
62	Gene Derricotte	20	30	40	60	100	200		
63A	Roy Rebel Steiner Red Jsy RC	20	30	40	60	120	250		
64A	Frank Seno	20	30	40	60	100	250		
65A	Bob Hendren RC	20	30	40	60	120	200	600	
66A	Jack Cloud Blue Bkgrd RC	20	30	40	60	120	200	600	
67	Harrell Collins	20	30	40	50	120	200	800	
68A	Clyde LeForce Red Bkgrd RC	20	30	40	60	100	200	400	
69	Larry Joe	20	30	40	60	100	200	300	
70	Phil O'Reilly	20	30	40	60	100	150		
71	Paul Campbell	20	30	40	▼50	▼100	150	500	
72A	Ray Evans	20	30	40	60	120	400	800	
73A	Jackie Jensen Red Bkgrd RC	60	80	100	175	250	400	800	
74	Russ Steger	20	30	40	60	100	120	400	
75	Tony Minisi	20	30	40	60	100	200	500	
76A	Clayton Tonnemaker	20	30	40	60	120	200	1,000	
77A	George Savitsky Grn Strps RC	20	30	40	60	120	200	800	
78	Clarence Self	20	30	40	60	▼100	250	300	
79	Rod Franz	20	30	40	60	120	200	800	
80A	Jim Youle Red Bkgrd RC	20	30	40	60	120	250		
81A	B.Bye Yell.Pants Maroon Jsy RC	20	30	40	60	120	200	800	
82	Fred Enke	20	30	40	60	100	200	500	
83A	Fred Folger Gray Jsy RC	20	30	40	60	120	250		
84	Jug Girard RC	20	30	40	100	120	200	400	
85	Joe Scott	20	30	40	60	100	150	200	
86A	Bob Demoss	20	30	60	80	150	400	1,000	
87	Dave Templeton	20	30	40	60	120	200	800	
88A	Herb Siegert	20	30	40	60	120	200	800	
89A	Bucky O'Conner RC blu jsy	20	30	40	60	120	200	800	
90	Joe Whisler	20	30	40	60	120	200	500	
91	Leon Hart RC	60	80	100	200	300	500		
92	Earl Banks	20	30	40	60	100	250	800	
93A	Frank Aschenbrenner	20	30	40	60	120	200	800	
94	John Goldsberry RC	20	30	40	60	100	250		
95	Porter Payne	20	30	40	60	100	150	800	
96A	Pete Perini	20	30	40	60	120	250		
97A	Jay Rhodemyre	20	30	40	60	120	250		
98A	Al DiMarco	30	50	60	100	200	300		

— Al DiMarco #98A PSA 7 (NrMt) sold for $5,121 (eBay; 7/13)
— Sammy Baugh #34 SGC 9 (NmMt) sold for $37,950 (Hunt; 3/08)
— Sammy Baugh #34 SGC 9 (NmMt) sold for $14,998 (eBay; 01/13)
— Sammy Baugh #34 PSA 8 (NmMt) sold for $12,925 (REA; 4/07)
— Sammy Baugh #34 PSA 8 (NmMt) sold for $9121 (eBay; 9/14)
— Sammy Baugh #34 PSA 8 (NmMt) sold for $7,000 (Legendary; 8/13)
— Sammy Baugh #34 SGC 8.5 (NmMt) sold for $12,000 (Hunt; 3/09)
— Sammy Baugh #34 PSA 8 (NmMt) sold for $8,833 (Goodwin; 2/11)
— Sammy Baugh #34 PSA 8 (NmMt) sold for $8,495 (Mile High; 5/11)
— Sammy Baugh #34 SGC 8 (NmMt) sold for $4,500 (Mastro; 5/08)
— Sammy Baugh #34 PSA 8 (NmMt) sold for $7,000 (Legendary; 8/13)
— Chuck Bednarik YB #54A PSA 8 (NmMt) sold for $38,561 (Goodwin; 11/07)
— Chuck Bednarik YB #54A PSA 7 (NrMt) sold for $8,159 (Ebay; 11/13)
— Terry Brennan #11 SGC 9 (NmMt) sold for $2,990 (Hunt; 3/08)
— Paul Campbell #71 PSA 8.5 (NmMt+) sold for $9,112 (Goodwin; 9/09)
— Paul Christman #21 PSA 8 (NmMt) sold for $3,815 (REA; 4/07)
— John Clement #47 PSA 8 (NmMt) sold for $1,277 (eBay; 2/09)
— Jack Cloud Blue Bkgrd #66A PSA 8 (NmMt) sold for $1,012 (eBay; 4/12)
— Charley Conerly RC #53 PSA 8 (NM/MT) sold for $11227.65 (Goodwin; 9/12)
— Charley Conerly RC #53 PSA 7 (NM) sold for $3080 (eBay; 6/16)
— George Connor #37 SGC 8 (NmMt) sold for $2,185 (Hunt; 3/08)
— George Connor #37 PSA 8 (NmMt) sold for $2,450 (eBay; 11/07)
— George Connor #37 PSA 8 (NmMt) sold for $1,367 (Goodwin; 2/11)
— Frank Dancewicz #38A PSA 9 (Mt) sold for $3,327 (Goodwin; 9/11)
— Bill Dudley #36 PSA 8 (NmMt) sold for $4,150 (eBay; 11/06)
— Bill Dudley #36 PSA 8 (NMMT) sold for $3163.07 (eBay; 6/12)
— Bill Dudley #36 SGC 8 (NmMt) sold for $2,226 (Mile High; 11/09)
— Fred Enke #82 PSA 8 (NmMt) sold for $2,851 (Goodwin; 11/07)
— Ray Evans #72 PSA 8 (NM/MT) sold for $2805.99 (eBay; 6/12)
— Ted Fritsch #35 SGC 8.5 (NmMt+) sold for $1,840 (Hunt; 3/08)
— Jug Girard #84 PSA 8 (NmMt) sold for $1,828 (eBay; 4/11)
— John Goldsberry #94 PSA 7.5 (NrMt+) sold for $1,928 (eBay; 10/11)
— Jug Girard RC #84 PSA 8 (NM/MT) sold for $1488.69 (Goodwin; 2/12)
— Pat Harder #33 PSA 9 (Mt) sold for $1,979 (Goodwin; 11/09)
— Pat Harder #33 SGC 8.5 (NmMt+) sold for $1,092 (Hunt; 3/08)
— Bob Hendren #65 PSA 9 (Mt) sold for $2,021 (eBay; 11/07)
— Bob Hendren #65 PSA 8 (NmMt) sold for $1,012 (eBay; 12/12)
— Jack Jacobs #46A PSA 9 (Mt) sold for $5,362 (Goodwin; 2/11)
— Jack Jacobs #46A PSA 8.5 (NmMt+) sold for $1,955 (Hunt; 3/08)
— Levi Jackson BL JSY #5A PSA 8.5 (NmMt+) sold for $1,626 (Goodwin; 11/12)
— Jackie Jensen RB #73A PSA 8.5 (NmMt+) sold for $15,114 (Goodwin; 9/09)
— Jackie Jensen RB #73A PSA 8 (NmMt) sold for $3,862 (Mile High; 6/10)
— Charlie Justice #15 PSA 8.5 (NmMt+) sold for $5,295 (Goodwin; 6/10)
— Charlie Justice #15 SGC 8 (NmMt) sold for $5,142 (Hunt; 3/08)
— Sid Luckman YB #1A PSA 8 (NmMt) sold for $71,836 (Goodwin; 9/09)
— Sid Luckman YB #1A PSA 7 (NrMt) sold for $11,239 (Goodwin; 2/10)

— Sid Luckman YB #1A PSA 7 (NmMt) sold for $5605 (eBay; 10/14)
— Sid Luckman YB #1A PSA 7 (Near MT) sold for $5483.52 (Goodwin; 6/12)
— Sid Luckman YB #1A PSA 7 (NrMt) sold for $9,717 (Goodwin;01/13)
— Sid Luckman YB #1A PSA 7 (NrMt) sold for $6,933 (Goodwin;06/13)
— Johnny Lujack #13 PSA 9 (Mt) sold for $10,701 (Goodwin; 5/08)
— Johnny Lujack #13 SGC 9 (Mt) sold for $8,912 (Hunt; 3/08)
— Johnny Lujack #13 SGC 8 (NmMt) sold for $2,760 (Hunt; 3/08)
— Bob Mann #44 SGC 9 (Mt) sold for $3,105 (Hunt; 3/08)
— Perry Moss #10 PSA 9 (Mt) sold for $4,027 (Goodwin; 2/11)
— George McAfee #19A PSA 8 (NmMt) sold for $1,980 (Goodwin; 2/10)
— George McAfee #19A PSA 8 (NmMt) sold for $1,504 (Goodwin; 2/11)
— Leo Nomellini Blu Bkg Maroon RC #52A PSA 8 (NM/MT) sold for $10539.83 (Memory Lane; 5/12)
— Porter Payne #95 PSA 8 (NmMt) sold for $5,052 (Goodwin; 2/09)
— Pete Perini #96 PSA 7 (NrMt) sold for $1,057 (eBay; 9/07)
— Pete Pihos #16A PSA 8.5 (NmMt+) sold for $4,813 (Goodwin; 6/10)
— Frank Reagan #48 PSA 8 (NmMt) sold for $1,955 (eBay; 11/07)
— Clarence Self #78 PSA 7 (NM) sold for $1,780 (eBay; 1/07)
— Russ Steger #74 PSA 8 (NmMt) sold for $6,846 (Goodwin; 2/10)
— Roy Steiner #63 PSA 9 (Mt) sold for $19,160 (Goodwin; 9/09)
— Bill Swiacki #12A PSA 9 (Mt) sold for $4,922 (Goodwin; 5/08)
— Bill Swiacki #12A SGC 9 (Mt) sold for $3,680 (Hunt; 3/08)
— Harry Szulborski #41A SGC 9 (Mt) sold for $2,185 (Hunt; 3/08)
— Dave Templeton #87 PSA 8 (NmMt) sold for $6,223 (Goodwin; 9/09)
— Charley Trippi #29 SGC 8 (NmMt) sold for $3,220 (Hunt; 3/08)
— Charley Trippi #29 PSA 8 (NmMt) sold for $2,427 (Mile High; 11/10)
— Charley Trippi #29 PSA 8 (NmMt) sold for $1,275 (eBay; 4/11)
— Bulldog Turner RB #3A PSA 9 (Mint) sold for $7,207 (Goodwin; 2/09)
— Bulldog Turner RB #3A PSA 8 (NmMt) sold for $2,196 (eBay; 4/11)
— Bulldog Turner RB #3A PSA 8 (NmMt) sold for $2,140 (Goodwin; 11/09)
— Bulldog Turner RB #3A PSA 8 (NmMt) sold for $2,070 (Hunt; 3/08)
— Steve Van Buren #22A PSA 7.5 (NrMt+) sold for $3,176 (Goodwin; 2/11)
— Steve Van Buren Green Jsy RC #22A PSA 8 (NM/MT) sold for $3427.07 (eBay; 6/12)
— Doak Walker #4 SGC 8.5 (NmMt+) sold for $6,325 (Hunt; 3/08)
— Doak Walker #4 PSA 8 (NmMt) sold for $9,382 (Goodwin; 6/10)
— Doak Walker #4 PSA 8 (NmMt) sold for $8,139 (Goodwin; 11/07)
— Doak Walker #4 PSA 8 (NmMt) sold for $6,489 (Goodwin; 2/11)
— Bob Waterfield #26A PSA 8.5 (NmMt+) sold for $31,598 (Goodwin; 2/10)
— Bob Waterfield Blk Name RC #26A PSA 8 (NM/MT) sold for $2811.97 (Goodwin; 6/12)
— Jim Youle Red Bkgrd RC #80A PSA 7.5 (Near MT+) sold for $1090 (eBay; 6/12)

1949 Leaf

Player	PrFr 1	GD 2	VG 3	VgEx 4	EX 5	ExMt 6	NM 7	NmMt 8
Bob Hendren	10	15	20	30	50	80	175	
Joe Scott	6	10	12	20	30	50	200	
Frank Reagan	6	10	12	20	30	60		
John Rauch	6	10	12	20	30	60	120	
Bill Fischer	6	10	12	20	30	50	120	
Elmer Bud Angsman	6	10	10	15	5	40	100	350
Billy Dewell	6	10	12	20	30	50	120	
Tommy Thompson QB	6	10	12	20	30	60	120	
Sid Luckman	20	30	60	100	125	250	350	500
Charley Trippi	8	12	15	25	35	80	200	
Bob Mann	6	10	12	20	30	80		
Paul Christman	6	10	12	20	50	60	125	
Bill Dudley	8	12	15	50	60	200	300	
Clyde LeForce	6	10	12	20	30	50	120	
Sammy Baugh	50	80	100	150	250	400	600	2,000
Pete Pihos	10	15	40	50	60	80	175	600
Tex Coulter	6	10	12	20	40	50	120	
Mal Kutner	6	10	12	30	40	50	120	350
Whitey Wistert	6	10	12	25	30	50	120	
Ted Fritsch Sr.	6	10	12	20	40	50	120	
Vince Banonis	6	10	12	20	30	60	120	
Jim White	6	10	12	20	30	50	120	
George Connor	8	12	15	25	40	60	125	400
George McAfee	8	12	15	40	100	125	200	
Frank Tripucka	8	12	15	25	40	80	250	
Fred Enke	6	10	12	20	30	80		
Charley Conerly	10	15	25	40	60	100		
Ken Kavanaugh	6	10	12	20	30	50	120	350
Bob Demoss	6	10	12	20	30	60	120	
Johnny Lujack	10	15	25	40	80	120	175	600
Jim Youle	6	10	12	20	30	80		
Harry Gilmer	6	10	12	20	30	50	120	
Robert Nussbaumer	6	10	12	20	30	50	120	
Bobby Layne	25	50	80	100	250	300	400	
Herb Siegert	6	10	12	20	30	50	120	350
Tony Minisi	6	10	12	20	30	80		

#	Player	PrFr 1	GD 2	VG 3	VgEx 4	EX 5	ExMt 6	NM 7	NmMt 8
79	Steve Van Buren	15	25	40	60	80	200	300	800
81	Perry Moss	6	10	12	20	30	50	120	
89	Bob Waterfield	12	20	30	50	75	125	225	600
90	Jack Jacobs	6	10	12	20	30	50	120	
95	Kenny Washington	8	12	15	20	40	60	120	
101	Pat Harder	6	10	12	20	30	50	120	
110	Bill Swiacki	6	10	12	20	30	50	120	
118	Fred Davis	6	10	12	20	30	50	120	350
126	Jay Rhodemyre	6	10	12	20	30	50	120	
127	Frank Seno	6	10	12	20	30	50	120	
134	Chuck Bednarik	20	30	50	100	120	200	350	
144	George Savitsky	6	10	12	20	30	150		
150	Bulldog Turner	25	40	50	90	125	200	300	400

— Chuck Bednarik #134 SGC 8.5 (NmMt+) sold for $1,526 (Memory Lane; 5/08)
— Bob Demoss #52 PSA 8 (NmMt) sold for $1,440 (eBay; 2/08)
— Bob Hendren #1 PSA 8 (NmMt) sold for $1,930 (eBay; 4/07)
— Bob Mann #17 PSA 8 (NmMt) sold for $1,295 (eBay; 12/07)
— Frank Tripucka #43 PSA 8 (NmMt) sold for $822 (Goodwin; 11/07)

1950 Bowman

#	Player	GD 2	VG 3	VgEx 4	EX 5	ExMt 6	NM 7	NmMt 8	MT 9
1	Doak Walker	40	50	80	100	125	800	6,300	
2	John Greene	8	10	12	20	30	80	150	
3	Bob Nowasky	8	10	12	20	25	40	125	
4	Jonathan Jenkins	8	10	12	20	25	50	125	
5	Y.A. Tittle RC	80	100	150	250	600	1,000	2,500	
6	Lou Groza RC	25	30	40	100	250	300	600	
7	Alex Agase RC	8	10	12	20	25	40	150	
8	Mac Speedie RC	8	10	12	20	30	60	300	
9	Tony Canadeo RC	25	35	80	100	150	300	1,000	
10	Larry Craig	8	10	12	20	25	125	250	
11	Ted Fritsch Sr.	8	10	12	20	25	60	300	
12	Joe Golding	8	10	12	20	25	40	100	
13	Martin Ruby	8	10	12	20	25	40	125	
14	George Taliaferro	8	10	12	20	25	40	100	
15	Tank Younger RC	10	12	15	30	60	80	200	1,000
16	Glenn Davis RC	20	25	40	50	75	100	300	
17	Bob Waterfield	20	25	30	50	75	125	300	
18	Val Jansante	8	10	12	20	25	50	100	
19	Joe Geri	8	10	12	20	25	40	100	
20	Jerry Nuzum	8	10	12	20	25	40	100	
21	Elmer Bud Angsman	8	10	12	20	25	40	100	
22	Billy Dewell	8	10	12	20	25	40	100	
23	Steve Van Buren	15	20	25	50	▼100	150	300	
24	Cliff Patton	8	10	12	20	30	60	150	300
25	Bosh Pritchard	8	10	12	20	25	40	100	
26	Johnny Lujack	15	20	25	35	60	100	200	600
27	Sid Luckman	20	25	30	50	125	150	350	1,200
28	Bulldog Turner	10	12	15	25	40	80	250	
29	Bill Dudley	10	12	15	25	50	80	175	
30	Hugh Taylor	8	10	12	20	25	40	100	
31	George Thomas	8	10	12	20	25	40	100	
32	Ray Poole	8	10	12	20	25	40	100	
33	Travis Tidwell	8	10	12	20	25	40	100	
34	Gail Bruce	8	10	12	20	25	40	100	
35	Joe Perry RC	40	50	60	125	150	250	800	2,500
36	Frankie Albert RC	8	10	12	25	40	60	200	
37	Bobby Layne	30	50	60	75	125	150	400	
38	Leon Hart	8	10	12	20	30	50	175	
39	Bob Hoernschemeyer RC	8	10	12	20	25	50	200	
40	Dick Barwegan RC	8	10	12	20	25	50	150	
41	Adrian Burk RC	8	10	12	20	25	40	100	500
42	Barry French	8	10	12	20	25	40	100	
43	Marion Motley RC	40	60	80	300	▲600	▲800	2,000	
44	Jim Martin	8	10	12	20	25	40	100	500
45	Otto Graham RC	150	400	500	800	1,000	1,500	3,000	1,500
46	Al Baldwin	8	10	12	20	25	40	100	800
47	Larry Coutre	8	10	12	20	25	40	100	
48	John Rauch	8	10	12	20	25	40	100	
49	Sam Tamburo	8	10	12	20	25	40	100	500
50	Mike Swistowicz	8	10	12	20	25	40	100	
51	Tom Fears RC	25	60	80	100	125	▲200	400	1,800
52	Elroy Hirsch RC	40	50	60	100	▲400	▲500	800	4,000
53	Dick Huffman	8	10	12	20	25	40	100	300
54	Bob Gage	8	10	12	20	25	40	100	
55	Buddy Tinsley	8	10	12	20	25	40	100	
56	Bill Blackburn	8	10	20	25	30	40	80	
57	John Cochran	8	10	12	20	25	40	100	

		GD 2	VG 3	VgEx 4	EX 5	ExMt 6	NM 7	NmMt 8	MT 9
58	Bill Fischer	8	10	12	20	25	40	100	
59	Whitey Wistert	8	10	12	20	25	40	100	
60	Clyde Scott	8	10	12	20	25	40	100	
61	Walter Barnes	8	10	12	20	25	40	100	
62	Bob Perina	8	10	12	20	25	40	100	
63	Bill Wightkin	8	10	12	20	25	40	100	
64	Bob Goode	8	10	12	20	25	40	100	500
65	Al Demao	8	10	12	20	25	40	100	
66	Harry Gilmer	8	10	12	20	25	40	100	
67	Bill Austin	8	10	12	20	25	40	100	
68	Joe Scott	8	10	12	20	25	40	100	
69	Tex Coulter	8	10	12	20	25	40	100	500
70	Paul Salata	8	10	12	20	25	40	100	
71	Emil Sitko RC	8	10	12	20	25	40	100	
72	Bill Johnson C	8	10	12	20	25	40	100	
73	Don Doll RC	8	10	12	20	25	40	100	
74	Dan Sandifer	8	10	12	20	25	40	100	
75	John Panelli	8	10	12	20	25	40	100	
76	Bill Leonard	8	10	12	20	25	40	100	
77	Bob Kelly	8	10	12	20	25	40	100	400
78	Dante Lavelli RC	25	30	40	60	100	175	400	
79	Tony Adamle	8	10	12	20	25	80	100	
80	Dick Wildung	8	10	12	20	25	40	100	
81	Tobin Rote RC	10	12	15	25	40	60	300	
82	Paul Burris	8	10	12	20	25	40	100	
83	Lowell Tew	8	10	12	20	25	40	100	
84	Barney Poole	8	10	12	20	25	40	100	
85	Fred Naumetz	8	10	12	20	25	40	150	
86	Dick Hoerner	8	10	12	20	25	40	100	
87	Bob Reinhard	8	10	12	20	25	40	100	
88	Howard Hartley RC	8	10	12	20	25	40	100	
89	Darrell Hogan RC	8	10	12	20	25	40	100	
90	Jerry Shipkey	8	10	12	20	25	40	200	
91	Frank Tripucka	8	10	12	20	25	40	100	
92	Buster Ramsey RC	8	10	12	20	25	40	100	
93	Pat Harder	8	10	12	20	25	40	100	500
94	Vic Sears	8	10	12	20	25	40	100	
95	Tommy Thompson QB	8	10	12	20	25	40	100	
96	Bucko Kilroy	8	10	12	20	25	40	100	
97	George Connor	10	12	15	25	35	100	150	
98	Fred Morrison	8	10	12	20	25	40	100	
99	Jim Keane RC	8	10	12	20	25	40	100	
100	Sammy Baugh	50	60	75	150	200	300	600	
101	Harry Ulinski	8	10	12	20	25	40	100	
102	Frank Spaniel	8	10	12	20	25	40	100	
103	Charley Conerly	15	20	25	50	60	100	225	1,000
104	Dick Hensley	8	10	12	20	25	40	100	500
105	Eddie Price	8	10	12	20	25	40	100	400
106	Ed Carr	8	10	12	20	25	40	100	
107	Leo Nomellini	12	15	20	30	50	75	200	800
108	Verl Lillywhite	8	10	12	20	25	40	100	
109	Wallace Triplett	8	10	12	20	25	50	100	
110	Joe Watson	8	10	12	20	25	40	100	400
111	Cloyce Box RC	8	10	12	20	25	40	100	400
112	Billy Stone	8	10	12	20	25	40	100	
113	Earl Murray	8	10	12	20	25	40	100	
114	Chet Mutryn RC	8	10	12	20	25	80	100	400
115	Ken Carpenter	8	10	12	20	25	40	100	
116	Lou Rymkus RC	8	10	12	20	25	40	100	
117	Dub Jones RC	8	10	12	20	40	60	300	
118	Clayton Tonnemaker	8	10	12	20	25	50	100	
119	Walt Schlinkman	8	10	12	20	25	40	200	
120	Billy Grimes	8	10	12	20	25	40	100	
121	George Ratterman RC	8	10	12	20	25	50	100	
122	Bob Mann	8	10	12	20	25	40	125	
123	Buddy Young RC	8	10	12	30	40	50	120	600
124	Jack Zilly	8	10	12	20	25	40	100	500
125	Tom Kalmanir	8	10	12	20	25	40	100	
126	Frank Sinkovitz	8	10	12	20	25	40	100	
127	Elbert Nickel	8	10	12	20	25	40	100	
128	Jim Finks RC	12	15	20	▲60	▲80	▲100	300	
129	Charley Trippi	12	15	20	30	80	100	200	
130	Tom Wham	8	10	12	20	25	40	100	
131	Ventan Yablonski	8	10	12	20	25	40	150	
132	Chuck Bednarik	20	25	30	80	100	125	350	
133	Joe Muha	8	10	12	20	25	40	125	
134	Pete Pihos	12	15	20	30	60	100	200	400
135	Washington Serini	8	10	12	20	25	50	125	
136	George Gulyanics	8	10	12	20	25	40	300	

		GD 2	VG 3	VgEx 4	EX 5	ExMt 6	NM 7	NmMt 8	MT 9
137	Ken Kavanaugh	8	10	12	20	25	40	150	
138	Howie Livingston	8	10	12	20	25	40	100	
139	Joe Tereshinski	8	10	12	20	30	40	200	
140	Jim White	10	15	40	100	200	300	600	
141	Gene Roberts	8	10	12	20	25	40	150	
142	Bill Swiacki	8	10	12	20	25	40	▲200	
143	Norm Standlee	8	10	12	20	25	40	200	
144	Knox Ramsey RC	25	40	60	80	150	300	1,200	

— Chuck Bednarik #132 PSA 9 (MT) sold for $1,410 (eBay; 4/11)
— Chuck Bednarik #132 SGC 98 (Gem MT) sold for $1,004 (eBay; 7/09)
— Tony Canadeo #9 PSA 8.5 (NmMt+) sold for $1,214 (Mile High; 3/09)
— Glenn Davis #16 PSA 9 (MT) sold for $1,526 (Memory Lane; 12/07)
— Jim Finks #128 PSA 9 (Mint) sold for $810.94 (eBay; 5/12)
— Otto Graham #45 PSA 8.5 (NmMt+) sold for $1,853 (Goodwin; 5/08)
— John Greene #2 PSA 9 (Mint) sold for $1,278 (eBay; 12/12)
— Lou Groza #6 PSA 10 (Gem Mint) sold for $4,918 (eBay; 01/13)
— Lou Groza #6 PSA 9 (Mint) sold for $1,444 (eBay; 11/12)
— Lou Groza #6 PSA 9 (Mint) sold for $1,700 (Memory; 05/13)
— Lou Groza #6 PSA 9 (Mint) sold for $4,030 (eBay; 09/16)
— Howard Hartley #88 PSA 9 (Mint) sold for $1,229 (eBay; 08/13)
— Elroy Hirsch #52 PSA 10 (Gem Mt) sold for $4,481 (Legendary; 8/11)
— Elroy Hirsch #52 PSA 9 (MT) sold for $3,976 (Goodwin; 2/09)
— Elroy Hirsch #52 PSA 9 (MT) sold for $2,700 (eBay; 3/05)
— Dub Jones #117 PSA 9 (MT) sold for $791.27 (eBay; 1/14)
— Johnny Lujack #26 PSA 9 (MT) sold for $1,218 (Memory Lane; 12/07)
— Marion Motley #43 PSA 9 (MT) sold for $6,600 (Mastro; 12/08)
— Marion Motley #43 PSA 9 (MT) sold for $2,030 (eBay; 4/11)
— Marion Motley #43 PSA 9 (MT) sold for $2,221 (eBay; 2/12)
— Vic Sears #94 PSA 9 (Mint) sold for $1076.5 (eBay; 7/12)
— Mac Speedie #8 PSA 10 (Gem MT) sold for $3,471 (Mile High; 1/07)
— Billy Stone #112 PSA 9 (MT) sold for $718 (eBay; 11/07)
— George Taliaferro #14 PSA 9 (MT) sold for $1596 (eBay; 08/13)
— Y.A. Tittle #5 SGC 9 (MT) sold for $4,200 (Mastro; 5/08)
— Steve Van Buren #23 PSA 9 (MT) sold for $1,108 (Mastro, 2/07)
— Doak Walker #1 PSA 8 (NmMt) sold for $3,585 (Legendary, 8/11)
— Doak Walker #1 SGC 8.5 (NmMt+) sold for $2,839 (Memory Lane, 5/08)
— Bob Waterfield #17 PSA 9 (MT) sold for $997 (eBay, 11/07)
— Bob Waterfield #17 PSA 9 (Mint) sold for $983.55 (eBay; 9/12)

1949 Topps Felt Backs

		PrFr 1	GD 2	VG 3	VgEx 4	EX 5	ExMt 6	NM 7	NmMt 8
1	Lou Allen	10	15	25	40	60			
2	Morris Bailey	10	15	25	40	50	80		
3	George Bell	10	15	25					
4	Lindy Berry HOR	10	15	25	40	60			
5B	Mike Boldin Yel	25	30	50	60	80	125		
6B	Bernie Botula Yel	25	30	50	60	80	125		
7	Bob Bowlby	10	15	25	40	50	80		
8	Bob Bucher	10	15	25	40	50	80		
9B	Al Burnett Yel	25	30	50	60	80			
10	Don Burson	10	15	25	40	60			
11	Paul Campbell	10	15	25	40	50	80		
12	Herb Carey	10	15	25	40	50	80		
13B	Bimbo Cecconi Yel	25	30	50	60	80	125		
14	Bill Chauncey	10	15	25	40	60			
15	Dick Clark	10	15	25	40	50	80		
16	Tom Coleman	10	15	25	40	50	80		
17	Billy Conn	10	15	25	40	60			
18	John Cox	10	15	25	40	60			
19	Lou Creekmur RC	50	60	100	150	300			
20	Richard Glen Davis RC	15	20	30	50	75			
21	Warren Davis	10	15	25	40	50	80		
22	Bob Deuber	10	15	25	40	50	80		
23	Ray Dooney	10	15	25	40	50	80		
24	Tom Dublinski	15	20	30	50	75			
25	Jeff Fleischman	10	15	25	40	50	80		
26	Jack Friedland	10	15	25	40	60			
27	Bob Fuchs	10	15	25	40	60			
28	Arnold Galiffa RC	15	20	30	50	60	100		
29	Dick Gilman	10	15	25	40	50	80		
30A	Frank Gitschier Brn	25	30	50	60	80	125		
30B	Frank Gitschier Yel	25	30	50	60	80	125		
31	Gene Glick	10	15	25	40	50	80		
32	Bill Gregus	10	15	25	40	50	80		
33	Harold Hagan	10	15	25	40	80			
34	Charles Hall	10	15	25	40	60			
35A	Leon Hart Brn	50	60	100	150	200	350		
35B	Leon Hart Yel	50	60	100	150	200	350		

		PrFr 1	GD 2	VG 3	VgEx 4	EX 5	ExMt 6	NM 7	NmMt 8
36B	Bob Hester Yel	25	30	50	60	80	150		
37	George Hughes	10	15	25	40	60			
38	Levi Jackson	15	20	30	50	60	100		
39A	Jack Jensen Brn	60	80	135	175	250	500		
39B	Jack Jensen Yel	60	80	135	175	250	500		
40	Charlie Justice	30	40	60	80	100			
41	Gary Kerkorian	10	15	25	40	60			
42	Bernie Krueger	10	15	25	40	50	80		
43	Bill Kuhn	10	15	25	40	60			
44	Dean Laun	10	15	25	40	60			
45	Chet Leach	10	15	25	40	50	80		
46B	Bobby Lee Yel	25	30	50	60	80			
47	Roger Lehew	10	15	25	40	50	80		
48	Glenn Lippman	10	15	25	40	50	80		
49	Melvin Lyle	10	15	25	40	50	80		
50	Len Makowski	10	15	25	40	50	80		
51B	Al Malekoff Yel	25	30	50	60	80			
52B	Jim Martin Yel	30	40	60	80	100			
53	Frank Mataya	10	15	25	40	60			
54B	Ray Mathews Yel RC	30	40	60	80	100	150		
55B	Dick McKissack Yel	25	30	50	60	80	125		
56	Frank Miller	10	15	25	40	50	80		
57B	John Miller Yel	25	30	50	60	80	125		
58	Ed Modzelewski RC	15	20	30	50	80	125		
59	Don Mouser	10	15	25	40	60			
60	James Murphy	10	15	25	40	60			
61A	Ray Nagle Brn	25	30	50	60	80	150		
61B	Ray Nagle Yel	25	30	50	60	80	150		
62	Leo Nomellini	60	80	125	200	350	500		
63	James O'Day	10	15	25	40				
64	Joe Paterno RC	400	500	600	800	1,200	2,000		
65	Andy Pavich	10	15	25	40	50	80		
66A	Pete Perini Brn	25	30	50	60	80			
66B	Pete Perini Yel	25	30	50	60	80			
67	Jim Powers	10	15	25	40	60			
68	Dave Rakestraw	10	15	25	40	50	80		
69	Herb Rich	10	15	25	40	50	80		
70	Fran Rogel RC	10	15	25	40	60			
71A	Darrell Royal Brn RC	175	225	350					
71B	Darrell Royal Yel RC	150	200	300	500				
72	Steve Sawle	10	15	25	40	50	80		
73	Nick Sebek	10	15	25	40	60			
74	Herb Seidell	10	15	25	40	50	80		
75B	Charles Shaw Yel	25	30	50	60	80			
76A	Emil Sitko Brn RC	25	30	50	60	80	125		
76B	Emil Sitko Yel RC	25	30	50	60	80	125		
77	Butch Songin RC	15	20	30	50	60	100		
78A	Mariano Stalloni Brn	25	30	50	60	80			
78B	Mariano Stalloni Yel	25	30	50	60	80			
79	Ernie Stautner RC	60	80	125	200	300	400		
80	Don Stehley	10	15	25	40	60			
81	Gil Stevenson	10	15	25	40	50	80		
82	Bishop Strickland	10	15	25	40	50	80		
83	Harry Szulborski	10	15	25	40	60			
84A	Wally Teninga Brn	25	30	50	60	80			
84B	Wally Teninga Yel	25	30	50	60	80			
85	Clayton Tonnemaker	10	15	25	40	50	80		
86A	Dan Towler Brn RC	60	80	125	175	250			
86B	Dan Towler RC Yel	60	80	125	175	250			
87A	Bert Turek Brn	25	30	50	60	80			
87B	Bert Turek Yel	25	30	50	60	80			
88	Harry Ulinski	10	15	25	40	60			
89	Leon Van Billingham	10	15	25	40	60			
90	Langdon Viracola	10	15	25	40	60			
91	Leo Wagner	10	15	25	40	50	80		
92A	Doak Walker Brn	150	200	300					
92B	Doak Walker Yel	125	150	250	350	500			
93	Jim Ward	10	15	25	40	60			
94	Art Weiner	10	15	25	40	50	80		
95	Dick Weiss	10	15	25	40	50	80		
96	Froggie Williams	10	15	25	40	50	80		
97	Robert (Red) Wilson	10	15	25	40	50	80		
98	Roger Red Wilson	10	15	25	40	60	80		
99	Carl Wren	10	15	25	40				
100A	Pete Zinaich Brn	25	30	50	60	80	125		
100B	Pete Zinaich Yel	25	30	50	60	80	125		

Len Makowski PSA 8 (NmMt) sold for $1,035 (Huggins&Scott; 4/08)
Joe Paterno PSA 7 (NrMt) sold for $5,215 (eBay; 10/11)
Joe Paterno PSA 7 (NrMt) sold for $2,714.51 (eBay; 11/13)

— Joe Paterno RC #64 PSA 8 (NM/MT) sold for $9124.8 (SCP; 5/12)
— Darrell Royal Yel PSA 5 (NmMt) sold for $1,265 (Huggins&Scott; 4/08)
— Wally Teninga Yel PSA 7 (NM) sold for $431 (Huggins&Scott; 4/08)
— Dan Towler Yel PSA 8 (NmMt) sold for $1,305 (eBay; 12/08)
— Bert Turek Yel PSA 7 (NM) sold for $431 (Huggins&Scott; 4/08)
— Doak Walker Brn SGC 6 (ExNm) sold for $700 (eBay; 1/08)

1951 Bowman

		GD 2	VG 3	VgEx 4	EX 5	ExMt 6	NM 7	NmMt 8	MT 9
1	Weldon Humble RC	12	20	25	40	60	100	800	
2	Otto Graham	40	50	60	100	200	250	600	
3	Mac Speedie	5	8	10	15	25	40	200	
4	Norm Van Brocklin RC	60	100	125	175	500	600	2,200	
5	Woodley Lewis RC	5	8	10	15	20	30	100	
6	Tom Fears	6	10	12	20	40	80	200	
7	George Musacco	5	8	10	15	20	30	100	
8	George Taliaferro	5	8	10	15	20	30	100	
9	Barney Poole	5	8	10	15	20	30	150	
10	Steve Van Buren	8	12	15	25	40	80	200	
11	Whitey Wistert	5	8	10	15	20	40	100	
12	Chuck Bednarik	10	15	20	40	60	100	200	
13	Bulldog Turner	6	10	12	30	40	80	250	
14	Bob Williams	5	8	10	15	20	30	100	
15	Johnny Lujack	8	12	15	30	40	80	150	
16	Roy Rebel Steiner	5	8	10	15	20	40	100	
17	Jug Girard	5	8	10	15	20	30	100	
18	Bill Neal	5	8	10	15	20	40	100	
19	Travis Tidwell	5	8	10	15	20	30	100	
20	Tom Landry RC	125	150	200	250	400	▲1,000	2,000	4,000
21	Arnie Weinmeister RC	8	12	15	40	80	135	350	
22	Joe Geri	5	8	10	15	20	30	100	
23	Bill Walsh C RC	6	10	12	18	30	50	120	
24	Fran Rogel	5	8	10	15	20	30	100	
25	Doak Walker	8	12	20	60	80	100	150	
26	Leon Hart	5	8	10	15	25	40	120	
27	Thurman McGraw	5	8	10	15	20	30	100	
28	Buster Ramsey	5	8	10	15	20	30	80	
29	Frank Tripucka	5	8	10	15	25	40	80	
30	Don Paul DB	5	8	10	15	20	30	80	
31	Alex Loyd	5	8	10	15	25	40	100	
32	Y.A. Tittle	20	30	35	60	100	135	450	1,500
33	Verl Lillywhite	5	8	10	15	20	50	100	
34	Sammy Baugh	30	40	80	100	125	200	400	
35	Chuck Drazenovich	5	8	10	15	20	30	100	
36	Bob Goode	5	8	20	25	30	40	100	
37	Horace Gillom RC	5	8	10	15	20	30	100	
38	Lou Rymkus	5	8	10	15	20	30	100	
39	Ken Carpenter	5	8	10	15	20	50	250	
40	Bob Waterfield	10	15	20	30	50	75	200	
41	Vitamin Smith RC	5	8	10	15	20	30	80	
42	Glenn Davis	8	12	15	25	40	60	200	
43	Dan Edwards	5	8	10	15	25	40	200	
44	John Rauch	5	8	10	15	20	30	100	
45	Zollie Toth	5	8	10	15	20	40	250	
46	Pete Pihos	8	12	15	25	40	60	200	
47	Russ Craft	5	8	10	15	20	30	100	
48	Walter Barnes	5	8	10	15	20	30	80	
49	Fred Morrison	5	8	10	15	20	30	100	
50	Ray Bray	5	8	10	15	20	30	80	350
51	Ed Sprinkle RC	5	8	10	15	20	35	120	
52	Floyd Reid	5	8	10	15	20	30	100	
53	Billy Grimes	5	8	10	15	20	40	150	
54	Ted Fritsch Sr.	5	8	10	15	20	40	200	
55	Al DeRogatis	5	8	10	15	20	30	100	
56	Charley Conerly	10	15	20	30	50	75	200	800
57	Jon Baker	5	8	10	15	20	30	100	
58	Tom McWilliams	5	8	10	15	20	30	100	
59	Jerry Shipkey	5	8	10	15	20	30	100	
60	Lynn Chandnois RC	5	8	10	20	25	30	100	
61	Don Doll	5	8	10	15	20	30	100	
62	Lou Creekmur	8	12	15	30	60	125	400	
63	Bob Hoernschemeyer	5	8	10	15	20	30	100	
64	Tom Wham	5	8	10	15	20	30	100	
65	Bill Fischer	5	8	10	15	20	40	100	
66	Robert Nussbaumer	5	8	10	15	20	30	80	
67	Gordy Soltau RC	5	8	10	15	20	30	100	
68	Visco Grgich	5	8	10	15	20	50	100	
69	John Strzykalski RC	5	8	10	15	20	30	100	

		GD 2	VG 3	VgEx 4	EX 5	ExMt 6	NM 7	NmMt 8	MT 9
70	Pete Stout	5	8	10	15	20	30	100	
71	Paul Lipscomb	5	8	10	15	20	30	100	
72	Harry Gilmer	5	8	10	15	25	60	120	
73	Dante Lavelli	8	12	15	25	50	100	1,000	
74	Dub Jones	5	8	10	15	20	30	300	
75	Lou Groza	10	15	20	30	50	100	300	
76	Elroy Hirsch	10	15	20	30	60	100	300	
77	Tom Kalmanir	5	8	10	15	20	40	100	
78	Jack Zilly	5	8	10	15	20	30	100	
79	Bruce Alford	5	8	10	15	20	30	100	
80	Art Weiner	5	8	10	15	20	30	100	
81	Brad Ecklund	5	8	10	15	20	40	200	
82	Bosh Pritchard	5	8	10	15	20	30	100	
83	John Green	5	8	10	15	20	30	100	
84	Ebert Van Buren	5	8	10	15	20	30	80	
85	Julie Rykovich	5	8	10	15	20	30	100	
86	Fred Davis	5	8	10	15	20	30	80	
87	John Hoffman RC	5	8	10	15	20	30	100	
88	Tobin Rote	5	8	10	25	30	40	150	
89	Paul Burris	5	8	10	15	20	30	100	
90	Tony Canadeo	6	10	12	30	40	125	400	
91	Emlen Tunnell RC	15	25	30	50	150	300	600	
92	Otto Schnellbacher RC	5	8	10	15	20	30	100	
93	Ray Poole	5	8	10	15	20	30	100	
94	Darrell Hogan	5	8	10	15	20	30	80	
95	Frank Sinkovitz	5	8	10	15	20	30	100	
96	Ernie Stautner	12	20	25	50	80	200	500	
97	Elmer Bud Angsman	5	8	10	15	20	30	100	
98	Jack Jennings	5	8	10	15	20	30	100	
99	Jerry Groom	5	8	10	15	20	30	100	
100	John Prchlik	5	8	10	15	▲30	▲40	100	
101	J. Robert Smith	5	8	10	15	20	30	100	
102	Bobby Layne	20	30	35	50	80	135	350	
103	Frankie Albert	5	8	10	15	25	40	120	
104	Gail Bruce	5	8	10	15	20	30	100	
105	Joe Perry	10	15	20	30	50	80	200	
106	Leon Heath	5	8	10	15	20	30	100	
107	Ed Quirk	5	8	10	15	20	30	100	
108	Hugh Taylor	5	8	10	15	20	50	100	
109	Marion Motley	12	20	25	60	100	135	500	
110	Tony Adamle	5	8	10	15	20	40	120	
111	Alex Agase	5	8	10	15	20	30	100	
112	Tank Younger	5	8	10	15	25	50	150	
113	Bob Boyd	5	8	10	15	20	30	100	
114	Jerry Williams	5	8	10	15	20	30	100	
115	Joe Golding	5	8	10	15	20	30	100	
116	Sherman Howard	5	8	10	15	20	30	100	
117	John Wozniak	5	8	10	15	20	50	150	
118	Frank Reagan	5	8	10	15	30	40	175	
119	Vic Sears	5	8	10	15	20	30	100	
120	Clyde Scott	5	8	10	15	20	30	100	
121	George Gulyanics	5	8	10	15	20	60	100	
122	Bill Wightkin	5	8	10	15	20	30	100	
123	Chuck Hunsinger	5	8	10	15	20	30	100	
124	Jack Cloud	5	8	10	15	20	30	100	
125	Abner Wimberly	5	8	10	15	30	40	200	
126	Dick Wildung	5	8	10	15	20	50	200	
127	Eddie Price	5	8	10	15	20	30	150	
128	Joe Scott	5	8	10	15	20	30	100	
129	Jerry Nuzum	5	8	10	15	20	30	100	
130	Jim Finks	5	8	10	15	50	60	150	
131	Bob Gage	5	8	10	15	20	30	100	
132	Bill Swiacki	5	8	10	15	20	30	100	
133	Joe Watson	5	8	10	15	20	30	100	
134	Ollie Cline	5	8	10	15	20	30	100	
135	Jack Lininger	5	8	10	15	20	50	175	
136	Fran Polsfoot	5	8	10	15	20	50	125	
137	Charley Trippi	6	10	12	20	60	80	250	
138	Ventan Yablonski	5	8	10	15	20	30	150	
139	Emil Sitko	5	8	10	15	20	40	125	
140	Leo Nomellini	8	12	15	25	40	60	250	
141	Norm Standlee	5	8	10	15	20	30	100	
142	Eddie Saenz	5	8	10	15	20	30	125	
143	Al Demao	5	8	10	15	20	30	120	
144	Bill Dudley	20	40	60	100	100	200	1,500	

— Sammy Baugh #34 SGC 96 (MT) sold for $1,440 (Mastro; 5/08)
— Chuck Bednarik #12 PSA 9 (MT) sold for $897 (eBay; 2/10)
— Tony Canadeo #12 PSA 9 (MT) sold for $1,780 (Mile High; 6/10)
— Lou Creekmur #34 PSA 9 (MT) sold for $2,640 (Mastro; 7/08)

— Al DeRogatis #55 PSA 9 (Mint) sold for $747.5 (eBay: 7/12)
— Bill Dudley #144 PSA 9 (MT) sold for $6,087 (Memory Lane; 5/08)
— Bill Dudley #144 PSA 9 (MT) sold for $3,245 (Mile High; 1/07)
— Dan Edwards #43 PSA 9 (MT) sold for $1,225 (eBay; 3/08)
— Elroy Hirsch #76 PSA 9 (MT) sold for $2,520 (eBay; 11/06)
— Weldon Humble #1 PSA 9 (MT) sold for $3,386 (Memory Lane; 12/06)
— Tom Landry #20 PSA 10 (Gem MT) sold for $16,286 (Mile High; 11/10)
— Tom Landry #20 PSA 10 (Gem MT) sold for $22,130 (eBay; 7/16)
— Tom Landry #20 PSA 9 (MT) sold for $5,407 (Mastro; 12/07)
— Tom Landry #20 PSA 9 (Gem MT) sold for $4483 (eBay; 10/14)
— Bobby Layne #102 PSA 9 (MT) sold for $1,350 (eBay; 2/10)
— Woodley Lewis #5 PSA 9 (MT) sold for $1,187 (Memory Lane; 5/08)
— Floyd Reid #52 PSA 9 (MT) sold for $1,148 (eBay; 8/07)
— Ernie Stautner #96 PSA 9 (MT) sold for $3,976 (Goodwin; 2/10)
— Ernie Stautner #96 PSA 9 (MT) sold for $3,900 (eBay; 4/09)
— Ernie Stautner #96 SGC 9 (MT) sold for $1,136 (Mile High; 10/09)
— Norm Van Brocklin #4 PSA 9 (MT) sold for $8063 (eBay; 11/14)
— Norm Van Brocklin #4 SGC 9 (MT) sold for $2,250 (eBay; 11/09)
— Norm Van Brocklin #4 SGC 8.5 (NmMt+) sold for $1,560 (Mastro; 5/08)
— Norm Van Brocklin #4 PSA 8.5 (NmMt+) sold for $2,554.95 (eBay; 2/14)
— Steve Van Buren #10 PSA 9 (MT) sold for $1,614 (eBay; 11/07)
— Arnie Weinmeister #21 PSA 9 (MT) sold for $1,242 (Mile High; 5/11)
— Arnie Weinmeister #21 PSA 9 (MT) sold for $1,481 (eBay; 2/14)

1951 Topps Magic

		PrFr 1	GD 2	VG 3	VgEx 4	EX 5	ExMt 6	NM 7	NmMt 8
1	Jimmy Monahan RC	5	6	8	12	25	50		
2	Bill Wade RC	8	10	12	20	40	75		
3	Bill Reichardt	5	5	5	10	20	40		
4	Babe Parilli RC	8	10	20	20	40	75	350	
5	Billie Burkhalter	5	5	5	10	20	40		
6	Ed Weber	5	5	5	10	20	40		
7	Tom Scott	5	5	6	12	25	50		
8	Frank Guthridge	5	5	5	10	20	40	150	
9	John Karras	5	5	5	10	20	40		
10	Vic Janowicz RC	15	25	40	60	125	200	1,000	
11	Lloyd Hill	5	5	5	10	20	40	150	
12	Jim Weatherall RC	5	5	6	12	25	50	100	
13	Howard Hansen	5	5	5	10	20	40		
14	Lou D'Achille	5	5	5	10	20	40		
15	Johnny Turco	5	5	5	10	20	40		
16	Jerrell Price	5	5	5	10	20	40		
17	John Coatta	5	5	5	10	20	40		
18	Bruce Patton	5	5	5	10	20	40		
19	Marion Campbell RC	6	8	12	20	35	60		
20	Blaine Earon	5	5	5	10	20	40		
21	Dewey McConnell	5	5	5	10	20	40		
22	Ray Beck	5	5	5	10	20	40		
23	Jim Prewett	5	5	5	10	30	40	150	
24	Bob Steele	5	5	5	10	▲50	▲60	150	
25	Art Betts	5	5	5	10	20	40		
26	Walt Trillhaase	5	5	5	10	30	40		
27	Gil Bartosh	5	5	5	10	20	40		
28	Bob Bestwick	5	5	5	10	30	40		
29	Tom Rushing	5	5	5	10	20	30	100	
30	Bert Rechichar RC	6	8	10	15	30	40	50	
31	Bill Owens	5	5	5	10	20	40		
32	Mike Goggins	5	5	5	10	20	40		
33	John Petitbon	5	5	5	10	20	40		
34	Byron Townsend	5	5	5	10	30	40	150	
35	Ed Rotticci	5	5	5	10	20	40		
36	Steve Wadiak	5	5	5	10	20	40		
37	Bobby Marlow RC	5	5	6	12	40	50		
38	Bill Fuchs	5	5	5	10	20	40		
39	Ralph Staub	5	5	5	10	20	40		
40	Bill Vesprini	5	5	5	10	20	40		
41	Zack Jordan	5	5	5	10	20	40		
42	Bob Smith RC	5	5	6	12	25	50		
43	Charles Hanson	5	5	5	10	20	40		
44	Glenn Smith	5	5	5	10	20	40		
45	Armand Kitto	5	5	5	10	20	40		
46	Vinnie Drake	5	5	5	10	20	40	150	
47	Bill Putich RC	5	5	5	10	20	40		
48	George Young RC	6	8	10	15	30	50		
49	Don McRae	5	5	5	10	20	40		
50	Frank Smith RC	5	5	5	10	20	40		
51	Dick Hightower	5	5	5	10	20	40		
52	Clyde Pickard	5	5	5	10	30	40		

	PrFr 1	GD 2	VG 3	VgEx 4	EX 5	ExMt 6	NM 7	NmMt 8
3 Bob Reynolds HB	5	5	6	12	25	50		
4 Dick Gregory	5	5	5	10	20	40		
5 Dale Samuels	5	5	5	10	20	40		
6 Gale Galloway	5	5	5	10	20	40		
7 Vic Pujo		5	5	10	20	40		
8 Dave Waters	5	5	5	10	20	40		
9 Joe Ernest	5	5	5	10	20	40		
Elmer Costa	5	5	5	10	20	40		
Nick Liotta	5	5	5	10	20	40		
John Dottley	5	5	5	10	20	40		
Hi Faubion	5	5	5	10	20	40		
David Harr	5	5	5	10	20	40		
Bill Matthews	5	5	5	10	20	40		
Carroll McDonald	5	5	5	10	20	40		
Dick Dewing	5	5	5	10	30	40		
Joe Johnson RB	5	5	5	10	20	40		
Arnold Burwitz	5	5	5	10	30	40		
Ed Dobrowolski	5	5	5	10	20	40		
Joe Dudeck	5	5	5	10	20	40		
Johnny Bright RC	5	5	6	12	25	50		
Harold Loehlein	5	5	5	10	20	35		
Lawrence Hairston	5	5	5	10	25	40		
Bob Carey RC	5	5	6	12	25	50		

Bill Wade #2 PSA 7 (NrMt) sold for $565 (eBay; 10/07)
Bob Carey #75 PSA 7 (NrMt) sold for $1,260 (eBay; 11/07)

952 Bowman Large

	GD 2	VG 3	VgEx 4	EX 5	ExMt 6	NM 7	NmMt 8	MT 9
Norm Van Brocklin SP	60	150	200	250	400	800	2,800	
Otto Graham	60	80	100	135	▲400	500	1,400	
Doak Walker	10	15	20	35	▲150	▲200	500	
Steve Owen CO RC	10	15	40	50	60	150	500	
Frankie Albert	6	10	12	20	40	60	200	
Laurie Niemi RC	5	8	12	20	40	60	175	
Chuck Hunsinger	5	8	12	20	40	80	200	
Ed Modzelewski	6	10	12	20	40	60	250	
Joe Spencer SP RC	15	25	30	50	75	300		
Chuck Bednarik SP	60	80	100	150	350	500	1,200	
Barney Poole	5	8	12	20	40	60	225	
Charley Trippi	10	15	18	30	60	100	350	
Tom Fears	10	15	20	60	80	125	300	
Paul Brown CO RC	30	50	60	100	200	350	1,000	
Leon Hart	8	12	15	25	40	100	200	
Frank Gifford RC	100	150	200	250	500	1,000	2,500	6,000
Y.A.Tittle	40	60	80	125	175	300	800	
Charlie Justice SP	30	50	▼60	125	250	400	1,500	
George Connor SP	30	50	60	100	150	225	500	
Lynn Chandnois	5	8	12	20	40	60	225	
Billy Howton RC	6	10	12	30	40	100	400	
Kenneth Snyder RC	5	8	12	20	40	60	225	
Gino Marchetti RC	30	50	100	200	250	400	2,000	
John Karras	5	8	12	20	40	60	225	
Tank Younger	6	10	12	20	40	80	350	
Tommy Thompson LB RC	5	8	12	20	40	150	400	
Bob Miller SP RC	80	150	200	250	350	500		
Kyle Rote SP RC	30	50	60	100	150	300	600	
Hugh McElhenny RC	40	60	▲150	▲200	500	600	1,500	
Sammy Baugh	50	80	100	150	200	500	1,200	
Jim Dooley RC	6	10	12	20	40	60	300	
Ray Mathews	5	8	12	20	40	60	200	
Fred Cone RC	5	8	12	20	40	60	225	
Al Pollard RC	5	8	12	20	40	80	400	
Brad Ecklund	5	8	12	20	40	60	250	
John Hancock SP RC	100	150	200	250	400	1,200		
Elroy Hirsch SP	40	50	80	125	300	400	600	
Keever Jankovich RC	5	8	12	20	25	60	175	
Emlen Tunnell	12	20	25	40	80	125	400	
Steve Dowden RC	5	8	12	20	40	60	200	
Claude Hipps RC	5	8	12	20	40	60	200	
Norm Standlee	5	8	12	20	40	60	150	
Dick Todd CO RC	5	8	12	20	40	80	200	
Babe Parilli	6	10	12	25	50	150	400	
Steve Van Buren SP	50	60	80	200	300	500		
Art Donovan SP RC	60	100	125	200	250	500	1,200	
Bill Fischer	5	8	12	20	40	60	175	
George Halas CO RC	100	125	▲200	250	300	400	800	
Jerrell Price	5	8	12	20	40	60	100	
John Sandusky RC	5	8	12	20	40	80	250	

		GD 2	VG 3	VgEx 4	EX 5	ExMt 6	NM 7	NmMt 8	MT 9
51	Ray Beck	5	8	12	20	40	60	175	
52	Jim Martin	6	10	12	20	30	80	200	
53	Joe Bach CO RC	5	8	12	20	40	60	175	
54	Glen Christian SP RC	15	25	30	50	▲200	▲1,200		
55	Andy Davis SP RC	15	25	30	50	80	150	400	
56	Tobin Rote	6	10	12	50	80	100	350	
57	Wayne Millner CO RC	15	25	30	50	80	250	1,000	
58	Zollie Toth	5	8	12	20	40	60	150	
59	Jack Jennings	5	8	12	20	40	60	175	
60	Bill McColl RC	5	8	12	20	40	60	200	
61	Les Richter RC	10	15	20	50	60	250	400	
62	Walt Michaels RC	6	10	12	20	30	80	350	
63	Charley Conerly SP	200	300	400	500	700	1,000	2,500	
64	Howard Hartley SP	15	20	25	50	75	125	400	
65	Jerome Smith RC	5	8	12	20	40	60	200	
66	James Clark RC	5	8	12	20	40	60	300	
67	Dick Logan RC	5	8	12	20	40	80	250	
68	Wayne Robinson RC	5	8	12	20	40	60	300	
69	James Hammond RC	5	8	12	20	40	60	350	
70	Gene Schroeder RC	5	8	12	20	50	60	300	
71	Tex Coulter	6	10	12	20	40	60	250	
72	John Schweder SP RC	125	150	200	450	550	1,200		
73	Vitamin Smith SP	30	50	60	100	125	225	500	
74	Joe Campanella RC	8	12	15	25	40	80	150	
75	Joe Kuharich CO RC	8	12	15	25	40	60	250	
76	Herman Clark RC	8	12	15	25	40	80	250	
77	Dan Edwards	8	12	15	25	40	80	250	
78	Bobby Layne	40	60	80	100	125	150	600	
79	Bob Hoernschemeyer	8	12	15	25	40	80	200	
80	John Carr Blount RC	8	12	15	25	40	80	200	
81	John Kastan SP RC	30	50	60	100	150	250	500	
82	Harry Minarik SP RC	30	50	60	100	125	225	500	
83	Joe Perry	15	25	30	50	75	150	450	
84	Buddy Parker CO RC	8	12	15	25	40	80	150	
85	Andy Robustelli RC	25	40	50	90	150	300	800	
86	Dub Jones	8	12	15	25	40	80	400	
87	Mal Cook RC	8	12	15	25	40	80	200	
88	Billy Stone	8	12	15	25	40	80	200	
89	George Taliaferro	8	12	15	25	40	80	200	
90	Thomas Johnson SP RC	30	100	125	150	200	400	800	
91	Leon Heath SP	20	30	40	60	80	150	300	
92	Pete Pihos	12	20	25	40	75	125	300	
93	Fred Benners RC	8	12	15	25	40	80	200	
94	George Tarasovic RC	12	20	25	40	80	250		
95	Buck Shaw CO RC	8	12	15	25	40	80	200	
96	Bill Wightkin	8	12	15	25	40	80	200	
97	John Wozniak	8	12	15	25	40	80	200	
98	Bobby Dillon RC	8	12	15	25	40	100	1,500	
99	Joe Stydahar SP RC	200	300	350	800	1,000	1,200	3,000	
100	Dick Alban SP RC	30	50	60	100	150	250	600	
101	Arnie Weinmeister	10	15	18	30	40	100	400	
102	Bobby Cross RC	8	12	15	25	40	80	350	
103	Don Paul DB	8	12	15	25	40	80	400	
104	Buddy Young	10	15	18	30	40	80	400	
105	Lou Groza	20	30	40	60	100	200	600	
106	Ray Pelfrey RC	8	12	15	30	80	100	350	
107	Maurice Nipp RC	8	12	15	25	40	80	400	
108	Hubert Johnston SP RC	200	250	300	500	600	800	2,500	
109	Vol.Quinlan SP RC	20	30	40	60	100	250	450	
110	Jack Simmons RC	8	12	15	25	40	80	120	
111	George Ratterman	8	12	15	25	40	80	200	
112	John Badaczewski RC	8	12	15	25	40	80	200	
113	Bill Reichardt	8	12	15	25	40	80	200	
114	Art Weiner	8	12	15	25	40	80	200	
115	Keith Flowers RC	8	12	15	25	40	80	200	
116	Russ Craft	8	12	15	25	40	80	150	
117	Jim O'Donahue SP RC	30	50	60	100	135	250	800	
118	Darrell Hogan SP	20	30	40	60	100	150	500	
119	Frank Ziegler RC	8	12	15	25	40	80	150	
120	Dan Towler	10	15	18	30	40	100	250	
121	Fred Williams RC	8	12	15	25	40	80	200	
122	Jimmy Phelan CO RC	8	12	15	25	40	80	200	
123	Eddie Price	8	12	15	40	50	100	250	
124	Chet Ostrowski RC	8	12	15	25	40	80	200	
125	Leo Nomellini	12	20	40	50	60	150	450	
126	Steve Romanik SP RC	50	60	80	200	300	400	2,000	
127	Ollie Matson SP RC	100	125	150	200	400	800	3,800	
128	Dante Lavelli	12	20	25	40	75	200	350	
129	Jack Christiansen RC	30	50	60	100	175	400	1,000	

#		GD 2	VG 3	VgEx 4	EX 5	ExMt 6	NM 7	NmMt 8	MT 9
130	Dom Moselle RC	8	12	15	25	40	80	500	
131	John Rapacz RC	8	12	15	25	50	125	300	
132	Chuck Ortmann UER RC	8	12	15	25	40	80	200	
133	Bob Williams	8	12	15	25	40	80	200	
134	Chuck Ulrich RC	8	12	15	25	40	125	300	
135	Gene Ronzani CO SP RC	200	450	800	1,000	1,200	1,500	3,000	
136	Bert Rechichar SP	25	40	50	100	200	250	600	
137	Bob Waterfield	15	60	80	100	125	200	600	
138	Bobby Walston RC	8	12	15	25	40	125	200	
139	Jerry Shipkey	8	12	15	25	40	100	600	
140	Yale Lary RC	30	50	60	100	175	400	1,000	
141	Gordy Soltau	8	12	15	25	40	100	200	
142	Tom Landry	125	150	200	250	500	1,000	1,500	5,000
143	John Papit RC	8	12	15	25	40	80	200	
144	Jim Lansford SP RC	400	500	800	1,500	2,000	4,400	10,000	

— Dick Alban #5 PSA 10 (Gem) sold for $3,273 (Memory Lane; 5/13)
— Dick Alban #100 PSA 9 (MT) sold for $1,790 (Mile High; 6/13)
— Frankie Albert #5 PSA 9 (MT) sold for $1,055 (eBay; 12/12)
— Lou Groza #105 PSA 9 (MT) sold for $1,100 (eBay; 11/07)
— Otto Graham #2 PSA 9 (MT) sold for $5,467 (eBay; 5/13)
— Leon Hart #15 PSA 9 (MT) sold for $1,055 (eBay; 1/08)
— George Halas #48 PSA 9 (MT) sold for $3,550 (eBay; 1/07)
— Jim Lansford #144 PSA 8 (NmMt) sold for $10,321 (Andy Madec; 11/09)
— Jim Lansford #144 PSA 9 (Mint) sold for $17,920 (Memory Lane; 5/13)
— Dante Lavelli #128 PSA 9 (MT) sold for $1,446.40 (eBay; 2/14)
— Bobby Layne #78 PSA 9 (MT) sold for $2,247 (Mile High; 6/13)
— Yale Lary #140 PSA 9 (MT) sold for $4,517 (Memory Lane; 5/13)
— Gino Marchetti #23 PSA 9 (Mint) sold for $2,272 (Mile High; 11/10)
— Ray Matthews #32 PSA 9 (Mint) sold for $1,353 (Mile High; 6/13)
— Ollie Matson #127 PSA 7.5 (NrMt+) sold for $1,361 (Mile High; 3/09)
— Leo Nomellini #125 PSA 9 (Mint) sold for $1,375 (eBay; 11/13)
— Joe Perry #83 PSA 10 (Gem) sold for $4,357 (Memory Lane; 5/13)
— Kyle Rote #28 PSA 9 (MT) sold for $2,151 (Legendary; 3/11)
— Joe Spencer #9 PSA 8 (NmMt) sold for $3,912 (Mile High; 6/13)
— John Schweder SP RC #72 SGC 8 (NM/MT) sold for $2249.1 (Goodwin; 9/12)
— Y.A. Tittle #17 PSA 9 (MT) sold for $2,278 (Mastro; 12/06)
— Charley Trippi #12 PSA 9 (MT) sold for $1,243 (eBay; 02/13)
— Chuck Ulrich #134 PSA 9 (MT) sold for $1,620 (REA; 4/07)
— Steve Van Buren #45 PSA 9 (NmMt) sold for $2,140 (eBay; 4/07)
— Steve Van Buren #45 PSA 8 (NmMt) sold for $2,804 (Memory Lane; 5/13)

1952 Bowman Small

#		GD 2	VG 3	VgEx 4	EX 5	ExMt 6	NM 7	NmMt 8	MT 9
1	Norm Van Brocklin	50	60	100	150	350	500	2,500	
2	Otto Graham	25	80	100	125	150	300	550	
3	Doak Walker	8	12	15	25	60	100	300	
4	Steve Owen CO RC	10	15	20	30	60	80	300	
5	Frankie Albert	6	10	12	18	25	50	125	
6	Laurie Niemi	6	8	10	15	25	50	150	
7	Chuck Hunsinger	6	8	10	15	25	50	200	
8	Ed Modzelewski	6	10	12	18	25	60	300	
9	Joe Spencer	6	8	10	15	25	50	300	
10	Chuck Bednarik	10	15	20	30	50	80	300	
11	Barney Poole	6	8	10	15	25	50	125	
12	Charley Trippi	8	12	15	25	40	80	200	
13	Tom Fears	8	12	15	25	35	60	225	
14	Paul Brown CO RC	▲50	▲60	▲80	▲100	125	250	800	
15	Leon Hart	6	10	12	18	25	50	150	
16	Frank Gifford RC	50	60	150	300	400	600	1,000	3,000
17	Y.A. Tittle	20	30	40	60	100	175	500	
18	Charlie Justice	8	12	15	20	30	50	300	
19	George Connor	6	10	12	18	30	50	150	
20	Lynn Chandnois	6	8	10	15	25	50	125	
21	Billy Howton RC	6	10	12	18	80	100	400	
22	Kenneth Snyder	6	8	10	15	25	50	175	
23	Gino Marchetti RC	25	▲60	▲80	▲200	▲250	▲300	550	
24	John Karras	6	8	10	15	25	50	100	
25	Tank Younger	6	10	12	18	25	100	250	
26	Tommy Thompson LB	6	8	10	15	25	60		
27	Bob Miller RC	6	8	10	15	25	50	250	
28	Kyle Rote RC	10	15	20	30	50	100	500	
29	Hugh McElhenny RC	25	40	▲125	▲150	250	300	800	
30	Sammy Baugh	30	40	50	80	100	200	500	
31	Jim Dooley RC	6	8	10	15	25	50	125	
32	Ray Mathews	6	8	10	15	25	50	150	
33	Fred Cone	6	8	10	15	25	50	150	
34	Al Pollard	6	8	10	15	25	50	125	
35	Brad Ecklund	6	8	10	15	25	50	125	

#		GD 2	VG 3	VgEx 4	EX 5	ExMt 6	NM 7	NmMt 8	MT 9
36	John Lee Hancock	6	8	10	15	25	50	125	
37	Elroy Hirsch	10	15	20	60	80	100	250	
38	Keever Jankovich	6	8	10	15	25	60	300	
39	Emlen Tunnell	8	12	15	20	30	60	225	
40	Steve Dowden	6	8	10	15	30	50	125	
41	Claude Hipps	6	8	10	15	25	50	125	
42	Norm Standlee	6	8	10	15	25	50	125	
43	Dick Todd CO	6	8	10	15	25	50	125	
44	Babe Parilli	6	10	12	18	30	60	400	
45	Steve Van Buren	10	15	20	30	50	75	400	
46	Art Donovan RC	25	40	60	75	125	350	800	
47	Bill Fischer	6	8	10	15	25	50	125	
48	George Halas CO RC	30	50	80	100	400	500	700	
49	Jerrell Price	6	8	10	15	25	50	125	
50	John Sandusky RC	6	8	10	15	25	100	150	
51	Ray Beck	6	8	10	15	25	50	125	
52	Jim Martin	6	8	10	15	25	50	200	
53	Joe Bach CO	6	8	10	15	25	50	125	
54	Glen Christian	6	8	10	15	25	75	200	
55	Andy Davis	6	8	10	15	25	50		
56	Tobin Rote	6	10	12	20	30	75		
57	Wayne Millner CO RC	8	12	15	30	100	150	300	
58	Zollie Toth	6	8	10	15	25	50	125	
59	Jack Jennings	6	8	10	15	25	50	125	
60	Bill McColl	6	8	10	15	25	50	200	
61	Les Richter RC	12	15	25	40	60	200	500	
62	Walt Michaels RC	6	8	10	15	25	50	250	
63	Charley Conerly	10	15	20	30	50	80	300	
64	Howard Hartley	6	8	10	15	25	50	125	
65	Jerome Smith	6	8	10	15	25	50	150	
66	James Clark	6	8	10	15	25	50	250	
67	Dick Logan	6	8	10	15	25	50	150	
68	Wayne Robinson	6	8	10	15	25	50	200	
69	James Hammond	6	8	10	15	25	50	125	
70	Gene Schroeder	6	8	10	15	25	50	125	
71	Tex Coulter	6	8	10	15	25	50	100	
72	John Schweder	6	8	10	15	25	125		
73	Vitamin Smith	8	12	15	25	40	225		
74	Joe Campanella RC	6	10	12	20	30	60	400	
75	Joe Kuharich CO RC	6	10	12	18	30	80	200	
76	Herman Clark	6	10	12	18	30	60	300	
77	Dan Edwards	6	10	12	18	30	60	300	
78	Bobby Layne	20	30	40	60	100	175	500	
79	Bob Hoernschemeyer	6	10	12	18	30	60	300	
80	John Carr Blount	6	10	12	18	30	60	250	
81	John Kastan RC	6	10	12	40	50	60	250	
82	Harry Minarik	6	10	12	18	30	60		
83	Joe Perry	10	15	20	30	50	75	450	
84	Buddy Parker CO RC	6	10	12	18	30	60	250	
85	Andy Robustelli RC	15	25	30	60	100	200	500	
86	Dub Jones	6	10	12	18	40	60	350	
87	Mal Cook	6	10	12	18	30	60		
88	Billy Stone	8	12	15	25	40	60	350	
89	George Taliaferro	6	10	12	18	40	60	300	
90	Thomas Johnson RC	6	10	12	18	40	60	300	
91	Leon Heath	6	10	12	25	50	100	600	
92	Pete Pihos	8	12	15	25	35	60	500	
93	Fred Benners	6	10	12	18	40	100		
94	George Tarasovic	6	10	12	18	30	60	300	
95	Buck Shaw CO RC	6	10	12	18	50	60	200	
96	Bill Wightkin	6	10	12	18	30	60	300	
97	John Wozniak	6	10	12	18	30	60	300	
98	Bobby Dillon RC	6	10	12	18	50	60	400	
99	Joe Stydahar CO RC	40	60	60	125	200	400	2,000	
100	Dick Alban RC	6	10	12	18	30	60	300	
101	Arnie Weinmeister	8	12	15	20	35	60	300	
102	Bobby Cross	6	10	12	18	30	60	250	
103	Don Paul DB	6	10	12	18	30	60	250	
104	Buddy Young	8	12	15	20	35	60	300	
105	Lou Groza	10	15	20	50	60	100	300	
106	Ray Pelfrey	6	10	12	18	30	80	600	
107	Maurice Nipp	6	10	12	18	30	60	300	
108	Hubert Johnston	6	10	12	18	30	60	400	
109	Volney Quinlan RC	8	12	15	25	40	80		
110	Jack Simmons	6	10	12	18	30	60	250	
111	George Ratterman	6	10	12	18	30	60	250	
112	John Badaczewski	6	10	12	18	50	60	300	
113	Bill Reichardt	6	10	12	18	30	60	300	
114	Art Weiner	6	10	12	18	30	60	250	

		GD 2	VG 3	VgEx 4	EX 5	ExMt 6	NM 7	NmMt 8	MT 9
115	Keith Flowers	6	10	12	18	30	60	400	
116	Russ Craft	6	10	12	18	30	60	150	
117	Jim O'Donahue RC	6	10	12	25	30	80	300	
118	Darrell Hogan	8	12	15	25	40			
119	Frank Ziegler	6	10	12	30	40	60	1,000	
120	Dan Towler	8	12	15	20	30	60	300	
121	Fred Williams	6	10	12	18	30	60	300	
122	Jimmy Phelan CO	6	10	12	18	30	50	250	
123	Eddie Price	6	10	12	18	30	60	300	
124	Chet Ostrowski	6	10	12	18	30	60	150	
125	Leo Nomellini	10	15	20	30	50	100	300	
126	Steve Romanik	6	10	12	18	30	60	250	
127	Ollie Matson RC	▲40	▲50	▲60	80	200	500		
128	Dante Lavelli	10	15	20	30	50	75	300	
129	Jack Christiansen RC	12	20	25	35	60	150	400	
130	Dom Moselle	6	10	12	18	30	60	800	
131	John Rapacz	6	10	12	18	30	60	250	
132	Chuck Ortmann	6	10	12	18	30	60	250	
133	Bob Williams	6	10	12	18	30	60	250	
134	Chuck Ulrich	6	10	12	18	30	100	300	
135	Gene Ronzani CO RC	6	10	12	18	30	60	300	
136	Bert Rechichar	6	10	12	18	30	60	500	
137	Bob Waterfield	10	15	20	30	60	100	600	
138	Bobby Walston RC	6	10	12	18	40	50	400	
139	Jerry Shipkey	6	10	12	18	30	60	300	
140	Yale Lary RC	12	20	25	40	125	300	600	
141	Gordy Soltau	6	10	12	18	30	60	500	
142	Tom Landry	50	60	100	150	250	400	1,000	
143	John Papit	6	10	12	18	30	60	200	
144	Jim Lansford RC	25	40	50	75	150	200	1,200	

— Mal Cook #87 PSA 8 (NmMt) sold for $2,223 (Mile High; 5/11)
— Mal Cook #87 PSA 8 (NmMt) sold for $1683 (eBay; 12/12)
— Art Donovan #46 PSA 8.5 (NmMt+) sold for $1,367 (Mile High; 11/10)
— Art Donovan #46 PSA 8.5 (NmMt+) sold for $2,310 (Greg Bussineau Fall; Fall 2013)
— Frank Gifford #16 PSA 9 (Mint) sold for $8,500 (eBay; 10/11)
— Frank Gifford #16 PSA 9 (Mint) sold for $3658 (eBay; 11/12)
— Frank Gifford #16 PSA 9 (Mint) sold for $3480 (Memory Lane; 5/13)
— Frank Gifford #16 SGC 8.5 (NmMt+) sold for $1,826 (Mile High; 3/09)
— Darrell Hogan #118 PSA 8 (NmMt) sold for $1,034 (Mile High; 5/11)
— Tom Landry #142 SGC 9 (Mint) sold for $1209 (Memory Lane; 8/12)
— Ollie Matson #118 PSA 9 (NmMt) sold for $999 (Mile High; 5/11)
— Ollie Matson #118 PSA 8 (NmMt) sold for $1,079 (eBay; 12/12)
— Hugh McElhenny #29 PSA 8.5 (NmMt+) sold for $1,969 (Mile High; 11/10)
— Jim O'Donahue #117 PSA 8.5 (NmMt+) sold for $1,099 (Mile High; 5/11)
— Steve Owen #4 PSA 9 (Mint) sold for $1,115 (Mile High; 3/09)
— Buddy Parker #84 PSA 9 (Mint) sold for $1,206 (eBay; 5/09)
— Volney Quinlan #109 PSA 8 (NmMt) sold for $1,034 (Mile High; 5/11)
— Zollie Toth #58 PSA 9 (Mint) sold for $1,015 (eBay; 2/09)
— Emlen Tunnell #39 PSA 9 (Mint) sold for $1106 (eBay; 11/14)
— Chuck Ulrich #134 PSA 9 (Mint) sold for $1,002 (Mile High; 10/09)
— Norm Van Brocklin #1 PSA 8.5 (NmMt+) sold for $2,153 (Goodwin; 5/08)
— Bob Williams #133 PSA 9 (Mint) sold for $1,015 (eBay; 2/09)

953 Bowman

	GD 2	VG 3	VgEx 4	EX 5	ExMt 6	NM 7	NmMt 8	MT 9
Eddie LeBaron RC	15	30	25	50	100	300	2,000	
John Dottley	8	10	12	15	25	60	200	
Babe Parilli	8	10	12	15	25	60	200	
Bucko Kilroy	8	10	12	15	25	80	300	
Joe Tereshinski	8	10	12	15	25	60	175	
Doak Walker	15	20	25	35	60	125	350	
Fran Polsfoot	8	10	12	15	25	60	150	
Sisto Averno RC	8	10	12	15	25	60	175	
Marion Motley	20	30	40	60	100	250	1,000	
Pat Brady RC	8	10	12	15	25	60	175	
Norm Van Brocklin	25	35	40	60	▼80	150	500	
Bill McColl	8	10	12	15	25	60	175	
Jerry Groom	8	10	12	15	25	60	175	
Al Pollard	8	10	12	15	25	60	175	
Dante Lavelli	10	12	15	20	40	80	300	
Eddie Price	8	10	12	15	25	60	175	
Charley Trippi	10	12	15	30	40	60	250	
Elbert Nickel	8	10	12	25	30	60	175	
George Taliaferro	8	10	12	15	25	60	175	
Charley Conerly	15	20	VgEx 25	35	60	80	250	
Bobby Layne	20	30	40	50	75	150	300	
Elroy Hirsch	15	20	25	35	60	100	400	1,000
Jim Finks	8	10	12	15	25	80	250	

		GD 2	VG 3	VgEx 4	EX 5	ExMt 6	NM 7	NmMt 8	MT 9
24	Chuck Bednarik	15	20	25	35	60	100	400	
25	Kyle Rote	8	10	12	15	25	80	150	
26	Otto Graham	25	35	60	80	100	300	800	
27	Harry Gilmer	8	10	12	15	25	60	175	
28	Tobin Rote	8	10	12	15	30	60	200	
29	Billy Stone	8	10	12	15	30	60	125	
30	Buddy Young	8	10	12	15	25	60	200	
31	Leon Hart	8	10	12	15	30	80	300	
32	Hugh McElhenny	12	15	15	30	50	100	450	
33	Dale Samuels	8	10	12	15	30	60		
34	Lou Creekmur	10	12	15	20	30	60		
35	Tom Catlin RC	8	10	12	20	40	80	300	
36	Tom Fears	10	12	15	20	50	100	150	
37	George Connor	8	10	12	15	25	60	175	
38	Bill Walsh C	8	10	12	15	25	60	250	
39	Leo Sanford SP RC	10	12	15	20	40	100	300	
40	Horace Gillom	8	10	12	15	25	60		
41	John Schweder SP	10	12	15	20	40	80	350	
42	Tom O'Connell RC	8	10	12	15	25	60	175	
43	Frank Gifford SP	60	80	100	125	200	300	1,000	
44	Frank Continetti SP RC	10	12	15	20	40	60	250	
45	John Olszewski SP RC	10	12	15	20	40	60	250	
46	Dub Jones	8	10	12	15	25	100	200	
47	Don Paul LB SP RC	10	12	15	20	40	▼80	500	
48	Gerald Weatherly RC	8	10	12	15	25	60	175	
49	Fred Bruney SP RC	10	12	15	20	50	100	450	
50	Jack Scarbath RC	8	10	12	15	50	60	200	
51	John Karras	8	10	12	15	25	60	200	
52	Al Conway RC	8	10	12	15	25	60	125	
53	Emlen Tunnell SP	20	30	40	50	75	150	600	
54	Gern Nagler SP RC	10	12	15	20	35	60	250	
55	Kenneth Snyder SP	10	12	15	20	35	60	250	
56	Y.A.Tittle	25	35	80	100	125	200	600	
57	John Rapacz SP	10	12	15	20	35	100	350	
58	Harley Sewell SP RC	10	12	15	25	40	80	250	
59	Don Bingham RC	8	10	12	15	25	60	150	
60	Darrell Hogan	8	10	12	15	25	60	200	
61	Tony Curcillo RC	8	10	12	15	25	60	175	
62	Ray Renfro SP RC	10	12	15	25	60	80	300	
63	Leon Heath	8	10	12	15	25	60	200	
64	Tex Coulter SP	10	12	15	20	35	60	250	
65	Dewayne Douglas RC	8	10	12	15	25	60		
66	J. Robert Smith SP	10	12	15	20	35	60	300	
67	Bob McChesney SP RC	10	12	15	20	35	60	200	
68	Dick Alban SP	10	12	15	20	35	60	300	
69	Andy Kozar RC	8	10	12	15	25	60	175	
70	Merwin Hodel SP RC	10	12	15	20	35	60	250	
71	Thurman McGraw	8	10	12	15	25	60	150	
72	Cliff Anderson RC	8	10	12	15	25	60	150	
73	Pete Pihos	10	12	15	20	35	80	250	
74	Julie Rykovich	8	10	12	15	25	60	200	
75	John Kreamcheck SP RC	10	12	15	20	35	60	250	
76	Lynn Chandnois	8	10	12	15	25	60	125	
77	Cloyce Box SP	10	12	15	20	35	60	300	
78	Ray Mathews	8	10	12	15	25	60	175	
79	Bobby Walston	8	10	12	15	25	60	200	
80	Jim Dooley	8	10	12	15	25	60	100	
81	Pat Harder SP	10	12	15	20	35	60	400	
82	Jerry Shipkey	8	10	12	15	25	60	175	
83	Bobby Thomason RC	8	10	12	15	25	60	175	
84	Hugh Taylor	8	10	12	15	25	60	175	
85	George Ratterman	8	10	12	15	25	60	175	
86	Don Stonesifer RC	8	10	12	15	25	60	175	
87	John Williams SP RC	10	12	15	20	35	60	200	
88	Leo Nomellini	10	12	15	25	40	100	400	
89	Frank Ziegler	8	10	12	15	25	60	175	
90	Don Paul DB UER	8	10	12	15	25	60	200	
91	Tom Dublinski	8	10	12	15	25	60	150	
92	Ken Carpenter	8	10	12	15	25	60	175	
93	Ted Marchibroda RC	8	10	12	25	50	80	250	
94	Chuck Drazenovich	8	10	12	15	25	60	200	
95	Lou Groza SP	25	35	40	60	150	200	600	
96	William Cross SP RC	15	20	25	30	40	300	800	

— Chuck Bednarik #24 PSA 9 (Mint) sold for $1,510 (eBay; 10/08)
— Cloyce Box #77 PSA 9 (Mint) sold for $1,015 (eBay; 7/07)
— Cloyce Box #77 PSA 9 (Mint) sold for $686 (Mastro; 6/07)
— Lou Creekmur #34 PSA 8 (NmMt) sold for $1,220 (eBay; 3/07)
— William Cross #96 PSA 9 (Mint) sold for $1,975 (Mile High; 12/10)
— William Cross #96 PSA 9 (Mint) sold for $2,247 (Mile High; 6/13)

1954 Bowman

		GD 2	VG 3	VgEx 4	EX 5	ExMt 6	NM 7	NmMt 8	MT 9
1	Ray Mathews	6	8	10	12	30	100	250	1,000
2	John Huzvar	5	5	6	8	12	20	40	
3	Jack Scarbath	5	5	6	8	12	20	40	200
4	Doug Atkins RC	12	15	20	25	50	100	400	800
5	Bill Stits	5	5	6	8	12	20	40	
6	Joe Perry	8	10	12	15	20	30	75	400
7	Kyle Rote	6	8	10	12	15	25	60	
8	Norm Van Brocklin	10	12	15	20	30	50	125	600
9	Pete Pihos	6	8	10	12	15	30	75	
10	Babe Parilli	5	5	6	8	12	20	40	
11	Zeke Bratkowski RC	6	8	10	12	15	30	60	300
12	Ollie Matson	8	10	12	15	20	30	75	400
13	Pat Brady	5	5	6	8	12	20	40	200
14	Fred Enke	5	5	6	8	12	20	80	200
15	Harry Ulinski	5	5	6	8	12	20	40	
16	Bob Garrett	5	5	6	8	12	20	80	200
17	Bill Bowman	5	5	6	8	12	20	80	
18	Leo Rucka	5	5	6	8	12	20	50	
19	John Cannady	5	5	6	8	12	20	40	200
20	Tom Fears	8	10	12	15	25	30	80	200
21	Norm Willey	5	5	6	8	12	20	40	
22	Floyd Reid	5	5	6	8	12	20	40	200
23	George Blanda RC	30	50	80	200	250	300	1,200	1,500
24	Don Doheney	5	5	6	8	12	20	40	200
25	John Schweder	5	5	6	8	12	20	40	200
26	Bert Rechichar	5	5	6	8	12	20	40	200
27	Harry Dowda	5	5	6	8	12	20	40	
28	John Sandusky	5	5	6	8	12	20	40	200
29	Les Bingaman RC	6	8	10	12	15	25	50	250
30	Joe Arenas	5	5	6	8	12	20	40	200
31	Ray Wietecha RC	5	5	6	8	12	20	40	200
32	Elroy Hirsch	8	10	12	15	20	40	100	
33	Harold Giancanelli	5	5	6	8	12	20	40	
34	Billy Howton	5	5	6	8	12	30	80	250
35	Fred Morrison	5	5	6	8	12	20	40	200
36	Bobby Cavazos	5	5	6	8	12	20	40	
37	Darrell Hogan	5	5	6	8	12	20	40	200
38	Buddy Young	5	5	6	8	12	20	40	200
39	Charlie Justice	6	8	10	12	15	25	100	300
40	Otto Graham	15	20	25	60	80	150	225	800
41	Doak Walker	10	12	15	20	25	50	120	
42	Y.A.Tittle	10	12	15	20	40	60	175	800
43	Buford Long	5	5	6	8	12	20	40	200
44	Volney Quinlan	5	5	6	8	12	20	40	200
45	Bobby Thomason	5	5	6	8	12	20	50	200
46	Fred Cone	5	5	6	8	12	20	50	200
47	Gerald Weatherly	5	5	6	8	12	20	40	200
48	Don Stonesifer	5	5	6	8	12	20	40	
49A	L.Chandnois ERR Chadnois back	5	5	6	8	12	20	40	
49B	Lynn Chandnois COR	5	5	6	8	12	20	40	
50	George Taliaferro	5	5	6	8	12	20	40	200
51	Dick Alban	5	5	6	8	12	20	60	200
52	Lou Groza	10	12	15	20	25	40	100	500
53	Bobby Layne	10	12	30	40	50	60	120	1,200
54	Hugh McElhenny	10	12	15	20	25	40	75	400
55	Frank Gifford	15	20	25	35	60	100	150	800
56	Leon McLaughlin	5	5	6	8	12	20	40	
57	Chuck Bednarik	10	12	15	20	25	40	100	
58	Art Hunter	5	5	6	8	12	20	40	
59	Bill McColl	5	5	6	8	12	20	40	200
60	Charley Trippi	8	10	12	15	18	30	75	
61	Jim Finks	6	8	10	12	15	25	60	250
62	Bill Lange G	5	5	6	8	12	20	40	200
63	Laurie Niemi	5	5	6	8	12	20	40	200
64	Ray Renfro	5	5	6	8	12	20	40	
65	Dick Chapman SP	8	10	12	15	25	30	80	
66	Bob Hantla SP	8	10	12	15	20	30	120	

		GD 2	VG 3	VgEx 4	EX 5	ExMt 6	NM 7	NmMt 8	MT 9
67	Ralph Starkey SP	8	10	12	15	20	30	80	250
68	Don Paul LB SP	8	10	12	15	20	30	100	
69	Kenneth Snyder SP	8	10	12	15	20	30	50	250
70	Tobin Rote SP	8	10	12	15	20	30	120	250
71	Art DeCarlo SP	8	10	12	15	20	30	60	250
72	Tom Keane SP	8	10	12	15	20	30	80	
73	Hugh Taylor SP	8	10	12	15	20	30	120	
74	Warren Lahr SP RC	8	10	12	15	20	60	150	
75	Jim Neal SP	8	10	12	15	20	30	80	250
76	Leo Nomellini SP	15	20	25	30	50	80	125	800
77	Dick Yelvington SP	8	10	12	15	20	30	80	250
78	Les Richter SP	8	10	12	15	20	30	80	250
79	Bucko Kilroy SP	8	10	12	15	20	30	80	250
80	John Martinkovic SP	8	10	12	15	20	30	120	250
81	Dale Dodrill SP RC	8	10	12	15	20	30	150	
82	Ken Jackson SP	8	10	12	15	20	30	150	
83	Paul Lipscomb SP	8	10	12	15	20	40	100	
84	John Bauer SP	8	10	12	15	20	30	80	
85	Lou Creekmur SP	12	15	20	25	35	50	80	400
86	Eddie Price SP	8	10	12	15	20	30	80	250
87	Kenneth Farragut SP	8	10	12	15	20	30	80	250
88	Dave Hanner SP RC	8	10	12	15	20	40	200	250
89	Don Boll SP	8	10	12	15	20	30	150	
90	Chet Hanulak SP	8	10	12	15	20	40	125	300
91	Thurman McGraw SP	8	10	12	15	20	30	100	150
92	Don Heinrich SP RC	8	10	12	15	20	30	100	250
93	Dan McKown SP	8	10	12	15	20	30	100	
94	Bob Fleck SP	8	10	12	15	30	50	150	250
95	Jerry Hilgenberg SP	8	10	12	15	20	50	80	200
96	Bill Walsh C SP	8	10	12	15	20	30	80	250
97A	Tom Finnin ERR	15	20	25	40	60	100	300	
97B	Tom Finnan COR	5	5	6	8	12	20	40	200
98	Paul Barry	5	5	6	8	12	20	40	200
99	Chick Jagade	5	5	6	8	12	20	40	200
100	Jack Christiansen	6	8	10	12	30	40	60	400
101	Gordy Soltau	5	5	6	8	12	20	40	200
102A	Emlen Tunnell ERR Tunnel	10	12	15	20	40	75	200	500
102B	Emlen Tunnell COR	6	8	10	12	15	25	75	300
102C	Emlen Tunnell COR	6	8	10	12	15	25	75	300
103	Stan West	5	5	6	8	12	20	40	
104	Jerry Williams	5	5	6	8	12	30	40	
105	Veryl Switzer	5	5	6	8	12	20	30	150
106	Billy Stone	5	5	6	8	12	20	40	200
107	Jerry Watford	5	5	6	8	12	20	40	200
108	Elbert Nickel	5	5	6	8	12	20	40	200
109	Ed Sharkey	5	5	6	8	12	20	40	200
110	Steve Meilinger	5	5	6	8	12	20	40	150
111	Dante Lavelli	6	8	10	12	15	25	60	300
112	Leon Hart	6	8	10	12	15	25	50	
113	Charley Conerly	8	10	12	15	18	30	100	300
114	Richard Lemmon	5	5	6	8	12	20	40	
115	Al Carmichael	5	5	6	8	12	20	50	
116	George Connor	6	8	10	12	15	25	80	
117	John Olszewski	5	5	6	8	12	20	40	150
118	Ernie Stautner	8	10	12	15	20	30	100	
119	Ray Smith	5	5	6	8	12	20	80	
120	Neil Worden	5	5	6	8	12	20	40	
121	Jim Dooley	5	5	6	8	12	20	60	200
122	Arnold Galiffa	5	5	6	8	12	20	60	200
123	Kline Gilbert	5	5	6	8	12	20	40	200
124	Bob Hoernschemeyer	5	5	6	8	12	20	50	
125	Wilford White RC	6	8	10	12	15	30	100	250
126	Art Spinney	5	5	6	8	12	20	80	
127	Joe Koch	5	5	6	8	12	50	100	200
128	John Lattner RC	12	15	20	25	50	150	800	

1955 Bowman

		GD 2	VG 3	VgEx 4	EX 5	ExMt 6	NM 7	NmMt 8	MT 9
1	Doak Walker	10	12	15	25	50	120	400	1,800
2	Mike McCormack RC	8	10	12	▲40	▲50	60	200	600
3	John Olszewski	5	5	6	8	12	20	40	250
4	Dorne Dibble RC	5	5	6	8	12	20	40	250
5	Lindon Crow RC	5	5	6	8	12	20	40	
6	Hugh Taylor UER	5	5	6	8	12	20	40	250
7	Frank Gifford	10	12	15	25	40	60	150	800
8	Alan Ameche RC	8	10	12	15	25	50	150	1,200

FOOTBALL

#	Player	GD 2	VG 3	VgEx 4	EX 5	ExMt 6	NM 7	NmMt 8	MT 9
9	Don Stonesifer	5	5	6	8	12	25	60	
10	Pete Pihos	6	8	10	12	18	30	60	200
11	Bill Austin	5	5	6	8	12	20	40	250
12	Dick Alban	5	5	6	8	12	20	40	250
13	Bobby Walston	5	5	6	8	12	20	50	250
14	Len Ford RC	8	10	12	15	40	50	125	
15	Jug Girard	5	5	6	8	12	20	40	
16	Charley Conerly	8	10	12	15	20	30	80	400
17	Volney Peters RC	5	5	6	8	12	20	40	300
18	Max Boydston RC	5	5	6	8	12	20	40	
19	Leon Hart	6	8	10	12	15	40	50	
20	Bert Rechichar	5	5	6	8	12	20	40	250
21	Lee Riley RC	5	5	6	8	12	20	40	250
22	Johnny Carson RC	5	5	6	8	12	20	40	200
23	Harry Thompson	5	5	6	8	12	20	40	250
24	Ray Wietecha	5	5	6	8	12	20	40	250
25	Ollie Matson	8	10	12	15	20	▲50	▲200	
26	Eddie LeBaron	6	8	10	12	18	30	75	400
27	Jack Simmons	5	5	6	8	12	20	40	
28	Jack Christiansen	6	8	10	12	18	30	60	
29	Bucko Kilroy	5	5	6	8	12	20	50	
30	Tom Keane	5	5	6	8	12	20	50	
31	Dave Leggett RC	5	5	6	8	12	20	40	
32	Norm Van Brocklin	8	10	12	15	25	50	150	1,000
33	Harlon Hill RC	5	5	6	8	12	25	80	200
34	Robert Haner RC	5	5	6	8	12	20	60	200
35	Veryl Switzer	5	5	6	8	12	20	40	250
36	Dick Stanfel RC	6	8	10	12	18	40	200	
37	Lou Groza	8	10	12	15	20	35	75	500
38	Tank Younger	6	8	10	12	15	25	50	300
39	Dick Flanagan RC	5	5	6	8	12	20	40	200
40	Jim Dooley	5	5	6	8	12	20	40	250
41	Ray Collins RC	5	5	6	8	12	20	40	250
42	John Henry Johnson RC	8	12	20	25	60	100	200	1,200
43	Tom Fears	6	8	10	12	▲40	▲50	60	
44	Joe Perry	8	10	12	15	25	35	75	
45	Gene Brito RC	5	5	6	8	12	20	40	
46	Bill Johnson C	5	5	6	8	12	20	40	
47	Dan Towler	6	8	10	12	15	25	50	
48	Dick Moegle RC	5	5	6	8	12	20	40	200
49	Kline Gilbert	5	5	6	8	12	20	40	200
50	Les Gobel RC	5	5	6	8	12	20	40	125
51	Ray Krouse RC	5	5	6	8	12	20	40	250
52	Pat Summerall RC	12	15	18	30	50	75	120	400
53	Ed Brown RC	6	8	10	12	20	30	60	
54	Lynn Chandnois	5	5	6	8	12	20	40	200
55	Joe Heap RC	5	5	6	8	12	20	40	200
56	John Hoffman	5	5	6	8	12	20	40	
57	Howard Ferguson RC	5	5	6	8	12	20	100	300
58	Bobby Watkins RC	5	5	6	8	12	20	40	
59	Charlie Ane RC	5	5	6	8	12	20	40	250
60	Ken MacAfee E RC	5	5	6	8	12	20	40	
61	Ralph Guglielmi RC	5	5	6	8	12	20	40	
62	George Blanda	10	12	15	25	35	80	150	600
63	Kenneth Snyder	5	5	6	8	12	20	50	
64	Chet Ostrowski	5	5	6	8	12	20	40	
65	Buddy Young	8	10	12	15	20	30	80	
66	Gordy Soltau	5	6	8	10	15	30	80	
67	Eddie Bell RC	5	6	8	10	15	30	80	200
68	Ben Agajanian RC	6	8	10	12	15	30	50	200
69	Tom Dahms RC	5	6	8	10	15	30	60	
70	Jim Ringo RC	15	20	30	35	50	125	1,000	
71	Bobby Layne	15	20	25	50	60	75	250	800
72	Y.A.Tittle	15	30	40	50	60	100	250	
73	Bob Gaona RC	5	6	8	10	15	30	100	
74	Tobin Rote	6	8	10	12	15	30	100	
75	Hugh McElhenny	10	12	15	20	25	35	150	400
76	John Kreamcheck	5	6	8	10	15	30	60	
77	Al Dorow RC	6	8	10	12	15	30	60	
78	Bill Wade	8	10	12	15	20	30	60	
79	Dale Dodrill	5	6	8	10	15	30	80	200
80	Chuck Drazenovich	5	6	8	10	15	30	80	
81	Billy Wilson RC	6	8	10	12	20	50	200	
82	Les Richter	6	8	10	12	15	30	80	
83	Pat Brady	5	6	8	10	15	30	80	
84	Bob Hoernschemeyer	6	8	10	12	15	30	80	200
85	Joe Arenas	5	6	8	10	15	30	60	200
86	Len Szafaryn UER RC	5	6	8	10	15	30	100	
87	Rick Casares RC	10	12	15	20	25	35	80	

#	Player	GD 2	VG 3	VgEx 4	EX 5	ExMt 6	NM 7	NmMt 8	MT 9
88	Leon McLaughlin	5	6	8	10	15	30	60	200
89	Charley Toogood RC	5	6	8	10	15	50	250	
90	Tom Bettis RC	5	6	8	10	15	50	125	
91	John Sandusky	5	6	8	10	15	30	80	250
92	Bill Wightkin	5	6	8	10	15	30	80	250
93	Darrel Brewster RC	5	6	8	10	15	30	80	
94	Marion Campbell	8	10	12	15	20	30	60	350
95	Floyd Reid	5	6	8	10	15	30	80	
96	Chick Jagade	5	6	8	10	15	30	60	250
97	George Taliaferro	5	6	8	10	15	25	150	
98	Carlton Massey RC	5	6	8	10	15	30	250	
99	Fran Rogel	5	6	8	10	15	25	150	
100	Alex Sandusky RC	5	6	8	10	15	30	125	
101	Bob St.Clair RC	15	20	25	30	60	200	600	
102	Al Carmichael	5	6	8	10	15	30	200	
103	Carl Taseff RC	5	6	8	10	15	30	125	
104	Leo Nomellini	10	12	15	20	25	35	▲150	
105	Tom Scott	5	6	8	10	15	30	150	
106	Ted Marchibroda	8	10	12	15	20	30	125	
107	Art Spinney	5	6	8	10	15	30	80	
108	Wayne Robinson	5	6	8	10	15	30	80	
109	Jim Ricca RC	5	6	8	10	15	30	50	
110	Lou Ferry RC	5	6	8	10	15	30	80	
111	Roger Zatkoff RC	5	6	8	10	15	30	120	
112	Lou Creekmur	8	10	12	15	20	35	80	
113	Kenny Konz RC	5	6	8	10	15	50	80	
114	Doug Eggers RC	5	6	8	10	15	30	60	
115	Bobby Thomason	5	6	8	10	15	30	80	
116	Bill McPeak RC	5	6	8	10	15	30	100	
117	William Brown RC	5	6	8	10	15	30	60	
118	Royce Womble RC	5	6	8	10	15	30	60	200
119	Frank Gatski RC	10	12	15	30	40	100	▲600	
120	Jim Finks	8	10	12	15	20	60	80	
121	Andy Robustelli	10	12	15	20	25	40	▲200	
122	Bobby Dillon	5	6	8	10	15	30	80	
123	Leo Sanford	5	6	8	10	15	30	60	250
124	Elbert Nickel	6	8	10	12	15	30	▲200	
125	Wayne Hansen RC	5	6	8	10	15	50	60	200
126	Buck Lansford RC	5	6	8	10	15	30	80	
127	Gern Nagler	5	6	8	10	15	25	60	200
128	Jim Salsbury RC	5	6	8	10	15	30	80	
129	Dale Atkeson RC	5	6	8	10	15	30	150	
130	John Schweder	5	6	8	10	15	30	100	
131	Dave Hanner	6	8	10	12	15	30	100	
132	Eddie Price	5	6	8	10	15	30	80	250
133	Vic Janowicz	10	12	15	20	25	35	125	300
134	Ernie Stautner	10	12	15	20	25	35	▲150	
135	James Parmer RC	5	6	8	10	15	25	120	
136	Emlen Tunnell UER	10	12	15	20	25	50	▲250	
137	Kyle Rote	8	10	12	15	25	60	1,200	
138	Norm Willey	5	6	8	10	15	30	135	
139	Charley Trippi	10	12	15	20	25	40	150	
140	Billy Howton	6	8	10	12	15	40	100	
141	Bobby Clatterbuck RC	5	6	8	10	15	30	60	
142	Bob Boyd	5	6	8	10	15	30	150	
143	Bob Toneff RC	6	8	10	12	20	30	300	
144	Jerry Helluin RC	5	6	8	10	15	30	120	
145	Adrian Burk	5	6	8	10	15	30	150	
146	Walt Michaels	6	8	10	12	15	30	80	
147	Zollie Toth	5	6	8	10	15	30	80	
148	Frank Varrichione RC	5	6	8	10	15	30	150	
149	Dick Bielski RC	5	6	8	10	15	30	80	300
150	George Ratterman	6	8	10	12	15	30	200	
151	Mike Jarmoluk RC	5	6	8	10	15	40	400	
152	Tom Landry	60	100	125	150	200	350	1,000	
153	Ray Renfro	6	8	10	12	15	30	100	
154	Zeke Bratkowski	6	8	10	12	15	30	100	
155	Jerry Norton RC	5	6	8	10	15	30	100	
156	Maurice Bassett RC	5	8	10	20	30	60	300	
157	Volney Quinlan	5	6	8	10	15	40	100	
158	Chuck Bednarik	10	12	15	20	25	40	300	
159	Don Colo RC	5	6	8	10	18	60	350	
160	L.G. Dupre RC	6	8	10	20	40	60	300	

— Joe Arenas #85 PSA 9 (Mint) sold for $568.5 (eBay: 4/12)
— Len Ford #14 PSA 9 (Mint) sold for $921 (eBay: 11/14)
— Tom Fears #43 PSA 9 (MT) sold for $990 (Mastro: 10/06)
— Frank Gatski #119 PSA 9 (MT) sold for $940 (eBay: 10/12)
— Les Richter #82 PSA 9 (MT) sold for $714 (eBay: 10/07)
— Y.A.Tittle #72 PSA 9 (Mint) sold for $569.5 (eBay: 5/12)

1955 Topps All American

		GD 2	VG 3	VgEx 4	EX 5	ExMt 6	NM 7	NmMt 8	MT 9
1	Herman Hickman RC	30	35	40	60	80	125	400	2,000
2	John Kimbrough RC	5	6	8	20	25	50	150	
3	Ed Weir RC	5	6	8	12	25	80	500	
4	Erny Pinckert RC	5	6	8	12	20	50	125	
5	Bobby Grayson RC	5	6	8	12	30	40	125	500
6	Nile Kinnick UER RC	30	35	40	60	100	150	400	1,500
7	Andy Bershak RC	5	6	8	12	20	40	125	500
8	George Cafego RC	5	6	8	12	20	40	125	400
9	Tom Hamilton SP RC	6	8	10	15	30	50	125	600
10	Bill Dudley	8	10	12	20	35	60	120	500
11	Bobby Dodd SP RC	6	8	10	15	30	60	125	400
12	Otto Graham	35	40	50	75	200	250	400	1,500
13	Aaron Rosenberg	5	6	8	12	20	40	125	500
14A	Gaynell Tinsley ERR RC	30	35	40	60	100	250	800	
14B	Gaynell Tinsley COR RC	6	8	10	18	30	80	200	
15	Ed Kaw SP	6	8	10	15	25	40	100	600
16	Knute Rockne	50	60	150	200	250	300	800	1,500
17	Bob Reynolds	6	8	10	15	25	80	150	
18	Pudge Heffelfinger SP RC	6	8	10	30	40	50	120	400
19	Bruce Smith	8	10	12	20	60	80	250	800
20	Sammy Baugh	40	50	60	100	150	200	300	1,500
21A	W.White RC SP ERR	60	80	100	150	250	400	800	
21B	W.White RC SP COR	15	20	25	40	75	150	250	1,000
22	Brick Muller RC	5	6	8	12	20	40	125	
23	Dick Kazmaier RC	5	6	8	20	25	40	▲200	
24	Ken Strong	10	12	15	20	35	80	400	800
25	Casimir Myslinski SP RC	6	8	10	15	25	50	120	
26	Larry Kelley SP RC	6	8	10	15	25	50	120	750
27	Red Grange UER	50	125	150	200	250	300	600	2,000
28	Mel Hein SP RC	12	15	20	60	80	100	250	
29	Leo Nomellini SP	12	15	20	40	50	80	150	1,000
30	Wes Fesler RC	5	6	8	12	20	40	125	500
31	George Sauer Sr. RC	5	6	8	25	30	80	125	500
32	Hank Foldberg RC	8	10	25	30	40	60	125	
33	Bob Higgins RC	5	6	8	12	20	40	125	500
34	Davey O'Brien RC	10	12	15	25	40	80	150	500
35	Tom Harmon SP RC	15	20	▲60	▲80	▲100	125	250	1,200
36	Turk Edwards SP	10	12	15	25	40	60	200	800
37	Jim Thorpe	250	300	400	500	800	1,000	1,500	
38	Amos A. Stagg RC	12	15	18	25	50	100	300	1,600
39	Jerome Holland RC	5	6	8	12	20	60	125	1,200
40	Donn Moomaw RC	5	6	8	12	20	40	125	500
41	Joseph Alexander SP RC	6	8	10	15	30	50	175	
42	Eddie Tryon RC	6	8	10	15	25	50	100	750
43	George Savitsky	5	6	8	12	20	40	▲150	500
44	Ed Garbisch RC	5	6	8	12	20	40	100	500
45	Elmer Oliphant RC	5	6	8	12	35	80	200	
46	Arnold Lassman RC	5	6	8	12	20	40	125	
47	Bo McMillin RC	5	6	8	20	30	40	125	500
48	Ed Widseth RC	5	6	8	12	25	50	150	
49	Don Gordon Zimmerman RC	5	6	8	12	30	40	125	500
50	Ken Kavanaugh RC	5	6	8	20	25	40	175	500
51	Duane Purvis SP RC	6	8	10	15	25	50	120	
52	Johnny Lujack	15	20	25	60	80	100	200	1,000
53	John F. Green RC	5	6	8	12	20	40	125	600
54	Edwin Dooley SP RC	6	8	10	15	30	50	150	500
55	Frank Merritt SP RC	6	8	10	25	30	40	100	600
56	Ernie Nevers RC	25	30	35	60	75	125	400	
57	Vic Hanson SP RC	6	8	10	15	25	40	120	500
58	Ed Franco RC	5	6	8	12	20	40	125	500
59	Doc Blanchard RC	12	15	20	30	50	100	250	
60	Dan Hill RC	5	6	8	12	20	40	100	
61	Charles Brickley SP RC	6	8	10	15	25	40	125	600
62	Harry Newman RC	6	8	10	20	30	50	150	600
63	Charlie Justice	8	10	12	18	30	50	150	600
64	Benny Friedman RC	8	10	12	20	40	80	200	
65	Joe Donchess SP RC	6	8	10	15	25	40	120	
66	Bruiser Kinard RC	8	10	15	25	35	▲100	150	600
67	Frankie Albert	8	10	12	18	30	50	225	600
68	Four Horsemen SP RC	80	125	200	250	800	1,000	1,500	5,000
69	Frank Sinkwich RC	8	10	12	20	40	▼60	700	
70	Bill Daddio RC	5	6	8	12	20	40	125	
71	Bobby Wilson RC	6	8	10	15	25	50	175	500
72	Chub Peabody RC	5	6	8	12	20	40	150	
73	Paul Governali RC	5	6	8	12	25	50	125	500
74	Gene McEver RC	5	6	8	12	20	40	▲250	500
75	Hugh Gallarneau RC	5	6	8	12	20	40	125	500
76	Angelo Bertelli RC	6	8	10	20	40	100	200	
77	Bowden Wyatt SP RC	6	8	10	15	25	40	125	750
78	Jay Berwanger RC	8	10	12	20	30	60	150	1,000
79	Pug Lund RC	5	6	8	12	25	40	125	
80	Bennie Oosterbaan RC	6	8	10	15	25	50	250	
81	Cotton Warburton RC	6	8	10	15	25	80	400	
82	Alex Wojciechowicz	8	10	12	20	35	60	400	
83	Ted Coy SP RC	6	8	10	18	30	50	125	750
84	Ace Parker SP RC	12	15	18	35	60	100	300	
85	Sid Luckman	35	40	50	60	80	120	300	
86	Albie Booth SP RC	6	8	10	18	30	50	125	
87	Adolph Schultz SP	6	8	10	15	25	40	175	700
88	Ralph Kercheval	5	6	8	12	20	40	150	600
89	Marshall Goldberg	6	8	10	15	25	50	100	600
90	Charlie O'Rourke RC	5	6	8	12	25	100	600	
91	Bob Odell UER RC	5	6	8	12	30	40	125	600
92	Biggie Munn RC	6	8	10	15	30	50	125	500
93	Willie Heston SP RC	8	10	20	25	35	60	125	750
94	Joe Bernard SP RC	8	10	12	18	30	80	125	
95	Chris Cagle SP RC	8	10	12	20	30	60	120	500
96	Bill Hollenback SP	8	10	12	18	30	60	150	750
97	Don Hutson SP RC	60	80	125	150	225	400	1,000	5,500
98	Beattie Feathers SP	20	25	30	40	60	100	200	1,000
99	Don Whitmire SP RC	8	10	12	18	30	60	200	750
100	Fats Henry SP RC	20	25	30	60	120	300	600	2,500

— Joe Bernard #94 PSA 9 (MT) sold for $960 (eBay; 12/06)
— Otto Graham #12 PSA 10 (Gem Mt) sold for $4,900 (eBay; 11/09)
— Mel Hein SP RC #28 PSA 9 (Mint) sold for $1,478 (Memory Lane; 8/12)
— Mel Hein SP RC #28 PSA 9 (Mint) sold for $1,422 (Robert Edward; Fall 2013)
— Fats Henry SP RC #100 PSA 9 (Mint) sold for $4,444 (Robert Edward; Fall 2013)
— Four Horsemen #68 GAI 9 (MT) sold for $2,082 (Mastro; 4/07)
— Sid Luckman #85 PSA 9 (MT) sold for $2,805 (eBay; 7/08)
— Sid Luckman #85 SGC 9 (Mint) sold for $1504.16 (Goodwin; 2/12)
— Ernie Nevers #56 PSA 9 (MT) sold for $1,549 (eBay; 2/14)
— Charlie O'Rourke #90 PSA 9 (MT) sold for $1,075 (Legendary; 5/11)
— Knute Rockne #16 PSA 10 (Gem Mint) sold for $4680 (SCP; 5/12)
— Jim Thorpe #37 PSA 9 (MT) sold for $11,860 (Memory Lane; 4/07)
— Jim Thorpe #37 PSA 9 (Mint) sold for $6791 (Memory Lane; 5/12)
— Jim Thorpe #37 PSA 8.5 (NrMt) sold for $1946 (eBay; 8/13)

1956 Topps

		GD 2	VG 3	VgEx 4	EX 5	ExMt 6	NM 7	NmMt 8	MT 9
1	Johnny Carson SP	10	12	15	30	80	200	2,000	
2	Gordy Soltau	5	5	5	8	12	50	80	200
3	Frank Varrichione	5	5	5	8	12	40	100	200
4	Eddie Bell	5	5	5	8	12	20	40	200
5	Alex Webster RC	5	6	8	10	15	25	80	250
6	Norm Van Brocklin	8	10	12	40	50	60	200	450
7	Green Bay Packers	8	10	12	18	30	50	100	600
8	Lou Creekmur	5	6	8	10	15	25	60	300
9	Lou Groza	6	8	10	15	20	35	100	550
10	Tom Bienemann SP RC	5	6	8	10	18	25	40	100
11	George Blanda	8	10	12	20	30	50	100	▲500
12	Alan Ameche	5	6	8	10	15	25	60	125
13	Vic Janowicz SP	8	10	▲30	▲50	▲60	▲80	500	
14	Dick Moegle	5	5	5	8	12	20	60	
15	Fran Rogel	5	5	5	8	12	20	40	
16	Harold Giancanelli	5	5	5	8	12	20	40	200
17	Emlen Tunnell	5	6	8	10	15	▲80	▲100	
18	Tank Younger	5	6	8	10	15	25	50	250
19	Billy Howton	5	5	5	8	12	20	40	200
20	Jack Christiansen	5	6	8	10	15	25	60	350
21	Darrel Brewster	5	5	5	8	12	20	40	
22	Chicago Cardinals SP	12	15	18	30	50	80	100	200
23	Ed Brown	5	5	5	8	12	20	40	125
24	Joe Campanella	5	5	5	8	12	20	40	125
25	Leon Heath SP	6	8	10	15	25	50	250	
26	San Francisco 49ers	5	6	8	10	15	25	80	
27	Dick Flanagan RC	5	5	5	8	12	20	40	
28	Chuck Bednarik	6	8	10	15	20	35	100	500
29	Kyle Rote	5	6	8	10	15	25	50	250
30	Les Richter	5	5	5	8	12	20	40	
31	Howard Ferguson	5	5	5	8	12	20	40	200
32	Dorne Dibble	5	5	5	8	12	20	40	
33	Kenny Konz	5	5	5	8	12	20	50	300
34	Dave Mann SP RC	5	6	8	10	18	80	▲600	

		GD 2	VG 3	VgEx 4	EX 5	ExMt 6	NM 7	NmMt 8	MT 9
35	Rick Casares	5	6	8	10	15	25	50	300
36	Art Donovan	8	10	12	18	25	40	80	400
37	Chuck Drazenovich SP	6	8	10	15	25	40	350	
38	Joe Arenas	5	5	5	8	12	20	125	400
39	Lynn Chandnois	5	5	5	8	12	20	30	300
40	Philadelphia Eagles	5	6	8	10	▲40	▲50	60	300
41	Roosevelt Brown RC	8	10	12	18	30	100	200	600
42	Tom Fears	6	8	10	15	20	35	80	400
43	Gary Knafelc RC	5	5	5	8	12	20	40	250
44	Joe Schmidt RC	8	10	12	40	50	80	250	600
45	Cleveland Browns	5	6	8	10	15	25	80	400
46	Len Teeuws SP RC	6	8	10	15	25	40	250	
47	Bill George RC	8	10	12	30	40	60	150	600
48	Baltimore Colts	5	6	8	10	15	25	60	150
49	Eddie LeBaron SP	10	12	15	25	40	175	600	
50	Hugh McElhenny	8	10	12	18	25	80	100	400
51	Ted Marchibroda	5	6	8	10	15	25	60	250
52	Adrian Burk	5	5	5	8	12	20	40	200
53	Frank Gifford	10	12	15	30	50	80	150	500
54	Charley Toogood	5	5	5	8	12	20	40	200
55	Tobin Rote	5	5	5	8	12	20	40	200
56	Bill Stits	5	5	5	8	12	20	60	
57	Don Colo	5	5	5	8	12	20	40	
58	Ollie Matson SP	12	15	18	30	50	60	250	500
59	Harlon Hill	5	5	5	8	12	20	40	
60	Lenny Moore RC	15	20	40	50	100	300	1,200	
61	Wash.Redskins SP	12	15	18	30	60	100	250	
62	Billy Wilson	5	5	5	8	12	20	60	
63	Pittsburgh Steelers	5	6	8	10	15	50	60	300
64	Bob Pellegrini RC	5	5	5	8	12	20	40	
65	Ken MacAfee E	5	5	5	8	12	20	40	
66	Willard Sherman RC	5	5	5	8	12	20	40	200
67	Roger Zatkoff	5	5	5	8	12	20	40	
68	Dave Middleton RC	5	5	5	8	12	20	40	200
69	Ray Renfro	5	5	5	8	12	20	50	
70	Don Stonesifer SP	8	10	12	20	50	150	400	
71	Stan Jones RC	8	10	12	20	30	60	300	
72	Jim Mutscheller RC	5	5	5	8	12	30	50	
73	Volney Peters SP	6	8	10	15	25	50	500	1,000
74	Leo Nomellini	6	8	10	12	18	30	125	300
75	Ray Mathews	5	5	5	8	12	20	50	200
76	Dick Bielski	5	5	5	8	12	20	40	
77	Charley Conerly	6	8	10	15	20	35	100	350
78	Elroy Hirsch	8	10	12	18	40	50	100	
79	Bill Forester RC	5	5	5	8	12	20	50	200
80	Jim Doran RC	5	5	5	8	12	20	40	200
81	Fred Morrison	5	5	5	8	12	20	40	
82	Jack Simmons SP	6	8	10	15	30	40	250	
83	Bill McColl	5	5	5	8	12	20	40	125
84	Bert Rechichar	5	5	5	8	12	20	40	125
85	Joe Scudero SP RC	6	8	10	15	20	40	300	
86	Y.A.Tittle	8	10	12	20	30	50	250	600
87	Ernie Stautner	6	8	10	12	18	30	90	
88	Norm Willey	5	5	5	8	12	20	40	
89	Bob Schnelker RC	5	5	5	8	12	20	40	200
90	Dan Towler	5	6	8	10	15	25	60	
91	John Martinkovic	5	5	5	8	12	20	40	200
92	Detroit Lions	5	6	8	10	15	25	60	300
93	George Ratterman	5	5	5	8	12	20	40	
94	Chuck Ulrich SP	6	8	10	15	20	40	200	
95	Bobby Watkins	5	5	5	8	12	20	50	200
96	Buddy Young	5	6	8	10	15	25	60	250
97	Billy Wells SP RC	6	8	10	15	20	40	250	
98	Bob Toneff	5	5	5	8	12	20	50	200
99	Bill McPeak	5	5	5	8	12	20	50	200
100	Bobby Thomason	5	5	5	8	12	30	40	400
101	Roosevelt Grier RC	12	15	25	30	40	60	175	500
102	Ron Waller RC	5	5	5	8	12	20	50	200
103	Bobby Dillon	5	5	5	8	12	20	50	300
104	Leon Hart	5	6	8	10	15	25	60	250
105	Mike McCormack	5	6	8	10	15	25	80	400
106	John Olszewski SP	6	8	10	15	25	50	500	
107	Bill Wightkin	5	6	8	10	15	40	80	300
108	George Shaw RC	5	5	5	8	12	25	60	250
109	Dale Atkeson SP	6	8	10	15	30	175	1,600	
110	Joe Perry	6	8	10	15	20	35	75	
111	Dale Dodrill	5	5	5	8	12	20	50	
112	Tom Scott	5	5	5	8	12	20	50	
113	New York Giants	5	6	8	10	15	50	80	600

		GD 2	VG 3	VgEx 4	EX 5	ExMt 6	NM 7	NmMt 8	MT 9
114	Los Angeles Rams	5	5	8	10	15	25	60	
115	Al Carmichael	5	5	5	8	12	20	50	
116	Bobby Layne	8	10	15	25	30	50	150	500
117	Ed Modzelewski	5	5	5	8	12	20	40	
118	Lamar McHan RC SP	6	8	10	15	20	20	50	250
119	Chicago Bears	5	6	8	10	15	60	150	500
120	Billy Vessels RC	5	8	10	25	35	60	150	500
NNO	Checklist SP NNO	50	60	100	200	300	500	1,000	
C1	Contest Card 1	20	25	30	50	100	175		
C2	Contest Card 2	25	30	40	75	150	225		
C3	Contest Card 3	25	30	40	75				
CA	Contest Card A	25	30	40	75	150	250		
CB	Contest Card B	25	30	40	75	150	250	400	

— George Blanda #11 PSA 10 (Gem) sold for $940 (eBay; 3/07)
— Stan Jones #71 SGC 9 (Mint) sold for $987 (Mile High; 10/09)
— Dick Moegle #14 PSA 10 (Gem) sold for $1,485 (eBay; 3/07)
— Lenny Moore #60 PSA 9 (Mint) sold for $3,385 (eBay; 12/07)
— Lenny Moore #60 PSA 9 (Mint) sold for $2,201 (eBay; 7/13)
— Lenny Moore #60 PSA 9 (Mint) sold for $5,730 (eBay; 7/16)
— Volney Peters SP #73 PSA 9 (Mint) sold for $1480 (eBay; 9/12)
— Elroy Hirsch #78 PSA 10 (Gem Mint) sold for $3,024 (Mile High; 1/20)

1957 Topps

		GD 2	VG 3	VgEx 4	EX 5	ExMt 6	NM 7	NmMt 8	MT 9
1	Eddie LeBaron	6	8	10	15	25	60	175	800
2	Pete Retzlaff RC	5	5	6	10	25	30	150	
3	Mike McCormack	5	5	6	10	15	25	60	
4	Lou Baldacci	5	5	5	8	12	20	40	
5	Gino Marchetti	5	6	8	12	20	40	80	300
6	Leo Nomellini	5	6	8	12	20	30	60	400
7	Bobby Watkins	5	5	5	8	12	20	40	
8	Dave Middleton	5	5	5	8	12	20	40	250
9	Bobby Dillon	5	5	5	8	12	20	50	300
10	Les Richter	5	5	5	8	12	20	40	
11	Roosevelt Brown	5	6	8	12	20	30	60	
12	Lavern Torgeson RC	5	5	5	8	12	20	50	
13	Dick Bielski	5	5	5	8	12	20	40	
14	Pat Summerall	5	6	8	12	20	30	80	
15	Jack Butler RC	5	5	10	20	35	60	175	300
16	John Henry Johnson	5	5	6	10	15	30	80	
17	Art Spinney	5	5	5	8	12	20	40	
18	Bob St. Clair	5	5	6	10	15	25	50	350
19	Perry Jeter	5	5	5	8	12	20	40	
20	Lou Creekmur	5	5	6	10	15	25	50	400
21	Dave Hanner	5	5	5	8	12	20	40	300
22	Norm Van Brocklin	6	8	10	15	40	50	75	600
23	Don Chandler RC	5	5	6	10	15	25	50	500
24	Al Dorow	5	5	5	8	12	20	35	250
25	Tom Scott	5	5	5	8	12	20	40	
26	Ollie Matson	5	6	8	12	20	25	60	
27	Fran Rogel	5	5	5	8	12	20	40	
28	Lou Groza	6	8	10	15	20	30	75	500
29	Billy Vessels	5	5	5	8	12	30	150	
30	Y.A.Tittle	8	10	12	30	40	50	100	400
31	George Blanda	6	8	10	15	30	50	125	300
32	Bobby Layne	8	10	12	18	30	50	125	400
33	Billy Howton	5	5	5	8	12	20	30	
34	Bill Wade	5	5	6	10	15	25	50	300
35	Emlen Tunnell	5	5	6	10	15	25	50	
36	Leo Elter	5	5	5	8	12	20	35	250
37	Clarence Peaks RC	5	5	5	8	12	20	40	400
38	Don Stonesifer	5	5	5	8	12	20	40	
39	George Tarasovic	5	5	5	8	12	20	40	
40	Darrel Brewster	5	5	5	8	12	20	40	
41	Bert Rechichar	5	5	5	8	12	20	35	250
42	Billy Wilson	5	5	5	8	12	20	40	200
43	Ed Brown	5	5	5	8	12	20	50	250
44	Gene Gedman	5	5	5	8	12	20	35	250
45	Gary Knafelc	5	5	5	8	12	20	35	250
46	Elroy Hirsch	6	8	10	15	25	35	100	600
47	Don Heinrich	5	5	5	8	12	20	40	
48	Gene Brito	5	5	5	8	12	20	35	200
49	Chuck Bednarik	6	8	10	15	20	30	75	
50	Dave Mann	5	5	5	8	12	20	40	
51	Bill McPeak	5	5	5	8	12	20	40	
52	Kenny Konz	5	5	5	8	12	20	40	
53	Alan Ameche	5	6	8	10	15	25	80	600
54	Gordy Soltau	5	5	5	8	12	20	35	350

#	Player	GD 2	VG 3	VgEx 4	EX 5	ExMt 6	NM 7	NmMt 8	MT 9
55	Rick Casares	5	5	5	8	12	20	40	
56	Charlie Ane	5	5	5	8	12	20	40	
57	Al Carmichael	5	5	5	8	12	20	40	
58A	W.Sherman ERR no pos/team	60	80	100	150	200	350	600	
58B	Willard Sherman COR	5	5	5	8	12	20	35	250
59	Kyle Rote	5	5	6	10	15	30	50	500
60	Chuck Drazenovich	5	5	5	8	12	20	35	300
61	Bobby Walston	5	5	5	8	12	20	35	250
62	John Olszewski	5	5	5	8	12	20	35	250
63	Ray Mathews	5	5	5	8	12	20	35	350
64	Maurice Bassett	5	5	5	8	12	20	35	250
65	Art Donovan	6	8	10	15	20	30	60	350
66	Joe Arenas	5	5	5	8	12	20	35	250
67	Harlon Hill	5	5	5	8	12	20	35	250
68	Yale Lary	5	5	6	10	15	25	60	
69	Bill Forester	5	5	5	8	12	20	35	250
70	Bob Boyd	5	5	5	8	12	20	35	250
71	Andy Robustelli	5	6	8	12	20	30	60	
72	Sam Baker RC	5	5	5	8	12	20	35	250
73	Bob Pellegrini	5	5	5	8	12	20	40	
74	Leo Sanford	5	5	5	8	12	20	100	
75	Sid Watson	5	5	5	8	12	20	60	250
76	Ray Renfro	5	5	5	8	12	20	35	250
77	Carl Taseff	5	5	5	8	12	20	50	
78	Clyde Conner	5	5	5	8	12	20	35	250
79	J.C. Caroline	5	5	5	8	12	25	50	
80	Howard Cassady RC	5	5	6	10	15	25	60	400
81	Tobin Rote	5	5	5	8	12	30	40	
82	Ron Waller	5	5	5	8	12	20	35	250
83	Jim Patton RC	5	5	5	8	12	20	50	300
84	Volney Peters	5	5	5	8	12	20	40	250
85	Dick Lane RC	10	12	30	40	60	300	600	
86	Royce Womble	5	5	5	8	12	20	35	200
87	Duane Putnam RC	5	5	5	8	12	20	35	250
88	Frank Gifford	8	10	12	20	35	60	150	400
89	Steve Meilinger	5	6	8	12	20	30	100	
90	Buck Lansford	5	6	8	12	20	30	150	
91	Lindon Crow DP	5	5	5	8	12	25	60	
92	Ernie Stautner DP	5	6	8	12	30	40	200	
93	Preston Carpenter DP RC	5	5	5	8	15	40	80	
94	Raymond Berry RC	40	60	80	150	300	600	5,000	
95	Hugh McElhenny	6	8	10	15	30	60	200	
96	Stan Jones	6	8	10	15	25	35	175	
97	Dorne Dibble	5	6	8	12	20	40	120	
98	Joe Scudero DP	5	5	5	8	12	30	120	
99	Eddie Bell	5	6	8	12	20	30	100	
100	Joe Childress DP	5	5	5	8	12	30	150	
101	Elbert Nickel	5	6	8	12	20	40	350	
102	Walt Michaels	5	6	8	12	20	30	100	
103	Jim Mutscheller DP	5	5	5	8	12	25	250	
104	Earl Morrall RC	8	10	12	25	40	120	500	
105	Larry Strickland	5	6	8	12	20	30	135	
106	Jack Christiansen	5	6	8	12	20	30	100	
107	Fred Cone DP	5	5	5	8	12	25	60	
108	Bud McFadin RC	5	6	8	12	20	30	250	
109	Charley Conerly	6	8	10	30	40	100	150	600
110	Tom Runnels DP	5	5	5	8	12	20	60	
111	Ken Keller DP	5	5	5	8	12	20	60	
112	James Root	5	6	8	12	20	40	150	
113	Ted Marchibroda DP	5	5	6	10	15	30	135	
114	Don Paul DB	5	5	6	10	15	35	125	
115	George Shaw	5	6	8	12	20	40	200	
116	Dick Moegle	5	6	8	12	20	50	100	
117	Don Bingham	5	6	8	12	20	60	175	
118	Leon Hart	5	6	8	12	20	125	250	
119	Bart Starr RC	250	400	1,000	1,500	1,600	2,000	10,000	
120	Paul Miller DP	5	5	5	8	12	20	80	
121	Alex Webster	5	6	8	12	20	30	200	
122	Ray Wietecha DP	5	5	5	8	12	20	120	
123	Johnny Carson	5	6	8	12	20	40	135	
124	Tom. McDonald DP RC	8	10	12	25	40	200	400	
125	Jerry Tubbs RC	5	6	8	12	20	30	80	
126	Jack Scarbath	5	6	8	12	30	40	80	
127	Ed Modzelewski DP	5	5	5	8	12	100	400	
128	Lenny Moore	8	10	12	40	50	80	175	
129	Joe Perry DP	5	6	8	12	25	35	100	
130	Bill Wightkin	5	6	8	12	20	30	80	
131	Jim Doran	5	6	8	12	20	30	80	
132	Howard Ferguson	5	6	8	12	20	30	300	
133	Tom Wilson	5	6	8	12	20	30	135	
134	Dick James	5	6	8	12	20	40	150	
135	Jimmy Harris	5	6	8	12	20	30	100	
136	Chuck Ulrich	6	8	10	20	40	60	200	
137	Lynn Chandnois	5	6	8	12	20	30	80	
138	Johnny Unitas DP RC	400	500	800	1,000	2,200	4,000	8,000	15,000
139	Jim Ridlon DP	5	5	5	8	12	20	60	
140	Zeke Bratkowski DP	5	5	6	10	30	135	1,000	
141	Ray Krouse	5	6	8	12	20	30	150	
142	John Martinkovic	5	6	8	12	30	50	250	
143	Jim Cason DP	5	5	5	8	12	20	60	
144	Ken MacAfee E	5	6	8	12	20	50	200	
145	Sid Youngelman RC	5	6	8	12	20	40	150	
146	Paul Larson	5	6	8	12	30	40	150	
147	Len Ford	6	8	10	15	60	80	250	
148	Bob Toneff DP	5	5	5	8	12	20	60	
149	Ronnie Knox DP	5	5	5	8	12	20	60	
150	Jim David RC	5	6	8	12	20	40	150	
151	Paul Hornung RC	80	120	400	500	600	1,000	6,000	
152	Tank Younger	5	6	8	12	20	40	250	
153	Bill Svoboda DP	5	5	5	8	12	20	200	
154	Fred Morrison	6	8	10	15	80	150	1,500	
CL1	Checklist Card SP#((Bazooka back)	175	250	300	400	600	1,200		
CL2	Checklist Blony SP	175	250	300	400	800			

— Alan Ameche #12 PSA 9 (Mint) sold for $681 (Mile High; 11/10)
— Raymond Berry #94 PSA 8.5 (NmMt+) sold for $3,862 (Mile High; 6/10)
— Raymond Berry #94 PSA 8.5 (NmMt+) sold for $9,009 (eBay; 8/16)
— Jack Christiansen #106 PSA 9 (Mint) sold for $528 (eBay; 6/12)
— Jack Christiansen #106 PSA 9 (Mint) sold for $1,097.50 (eBay; 11/13)
— Charlie Conerly #109 PSA 9 (Mint) sold for $1,497 (Andy Madec; 5/07)
— Howard Ferguson #132 PSA 9 (Mint) sold for $901 (eBay; 12/13)
— Paul Hornung #151 PSA 9 (Mint) sold for $6,552 (Mile High; 6/10)
— Paul Hornung #151 PSA 9 (Mint) sold for $7,300 (Goodwin; 6/13)
— Dick Lane #85 SGC 9 (Mint) sold for $1,833 (Mile High; 10/09)
— Dick Lane #85 SGC 9 (Mint) sold for $825 (Goodwin; 2/11)
— Ollie Matson #26 PSA 9 (Mint) sold for $737 (eBay; 11/14)
— Hugh McElhenny #95 PSA 9 (Mint) sold for $761.5 (eBay; 5/12)
— Walt Michaels #102 PSA 9 (Mint) sold for $715 (eBay; 1/08)
— Dave Middleton #8 PSA 10 (Gem Mt) sold for $904 (Mile High; 10/09)
— Lenny Moore #128 PSA 9 (Mt) sold for $2,949 (eBay; 9/12)
— Pete Retzlaff #2 PSA 9 (Mint) sold for $1,260 (eBay; 3/07)
— Andy Robustelli #71 PSA 9 (Mint) sold for $897 (eBay; 1/08)
— George Shaw #115 PSA 9 (Mint) sold for $810 (eBay; 4/05)
— Willard Sherman ERR #58A SGC 9 (Mint) sold for $1,684 (Mile High; 3/09)
— Bart Starr RC #119 SGC 9 (Mint) sold for $10280.41 (Mile High; 5/12)
— Johnny Unitas #138 PSA 9 (Mint) sold for $15,457 (Goodwin; 11/09)
— Johnny Unitas DP RC #138 PSA 9 (Mint) sold for $27205.78 (Mile High; 1/12)
— Johnny Unitas #138 SGC 8.5 (NmMt+) sold for $2,954 (Mile High; 3/09)
— Johnny Unitas #138 PSA 8.5 (NmMt+) sold for $7,626.71 (Mile High; Dec 2013)
— Royce Womble #86 PSA 10 (Gem Mint) sold for $954 (Ebay; 1/14)

1958 Topps

#	Player	GD 2	VG 3	VgEx 4	EX 5	ExMt 6	NM 7	NmMt 8	MT 9
1	Gene Filipski RC	5	5	6	10	18	40	80	
2	Bobby Layne	6	8	10	15	40	50	150	
3	Joe Schmidt	5	5	6	10	15	30	80	
4	Bill Barnes	5	5	5	8	12	25	80	
5	Milt Plum RC	5	6	8	10	15	30	150	
6	Billy Howton	5	5	5	8	12	30	200	
7	Howard Cassady	5	5	5	8	12	30	80	
8	Jim Dooley	5	5	5	8	12	25	125	
9	Cleveland Browns	5	5	6	8	12	25	150	
10	Lenny Moore	5	6	8	12	20	50	250	
11	Darrel Brewster	5	5	5	8	12	25	100	
12	Alan Ameche	5	6	8	10	12	30	100	
13	Jim David	5	5	5	8	12	25	80	
14	Jim Mutscheller	5	5	5	8	12	25	80	
15	Andy Robustelli	5	5	6	10	15	30	80	
16	Gino Marchetti	5	5	6	10	15	40	150	
17	Ray Renfro	5	5	5	8	12	30	200	500
18	Yale Lary	5	6	8	10	12	30	80	
19	Gary Glick	5	5	5	8	12	30	120	
20	Jon Arnett RC	5	6	8	10	15	30	60	500
21	Bob Boyd	5	5	5	8	12	25	80	
22	Johnny Unitas	30	80	100	125	150	400	3,000	
23	Zeke Bratkowski	5	5	5	8	12	25	80	
24	Sid Youngelman	5	5	5	8	12	25	80	
25	Leo Elter	5	5	5	8	12	25	100	

		GD 2	VG 3	VgEx 4	EX 5	ExMt 6	NM 7	NmMt 8	MT 9
26	Kenny Konz	5	5	5	8	12	25	80	
27	Washington Redskins	5	5	6	8	12	25	80	
28	Carl Brettschneider	5	5	5	8	12	25	80	
29	Chicago Bears	5	5	6	8	12	30	120	
30	Alex Webster	5	5	5	8	12	25	80	
31	Al Carmichael	5	5	5	8	12	25	80	
32	Bobby Dillon	5	5	5	8	12	30	100	
33	Steve Meilinger	5	5	5	8	12	25	80	
34	Sam Baker	5	5	5	8	12	25	60	
35	Chuck Bednarik	5	6	8	12	18	30	100	
36	Bert Vic Zucco	5	5	5	8	12	25	80	
37	George Tarasovic	5	5	5	8	12	25	80	
38	Bill Wade	5	6	8	10	12	30	80	
39	Dick Stanfel	5	5	5	8	12	40	200	
40	Jerry Norton	5	5	5	8	12	25	80	
41	San Francisco 49ers	5	5	6	8	12	25	60	
42	Emlen Tunnell	5	5	6	10	15	30	60	
43	Jim Doran	5	5	5	8	12	25	80	
44	Ted Marchibroda	5	6	8	10	12	30	200	
45	Chet Hanulak	5	5	5	8	12	25	80	
46	Dale Dodrill	5	5	5	8	12	25	80	
47	Johnny Carson	5	5	5	8	12	25	80	
48	Dick Deschaine	5	5	5	8	12	25	80	
49	Billy Wells	5	5	5	8	12	25	80	
50	Larry Morris	5	5	5	8	12	25	80	
51	Jack McClairen	5	5	5	8	12	25	80	
52	Lou Groza	5	6	8	12	18	30	80	
53	Rick Casares	5	5	5	8	12	25	100	
54	Don Chandler	5	5	5	8	12	30	120	
55	Duane Putnam	5	5	5	8	12	25	80	
56	Gary Knafelc	5	5	5	8	12	25	80	
57	Earl Morrall	5	5	6	10	15	30	80	
58	Ron Kramer RC	5	5	5	8	12	25	400	
59	Mike McCormack	5	6	8	10	12	30	80	
60	Gern Nagler	5	5	5	8	12	25	80	
61	New York Giants	5	5	6	8	12	25	80	
62	Jim Brown RC	1,000	1,200	1,500	3,000	4,000	6,000	10,000	20,000
63	Joe Marconi RC	5	5	5	8	12	25	80	
64	R.C. Owens RC	5	5	5	8	12	25	80	
65	Jimmy Carr RC	5	5	5	8	12	30	80	
66	Bart Starr	20	30	40	80	150	400	600	
67	Tom Wilson	5	5	5	8	12	30	80	
68	Lamar McHan	5	5	5	8	12	25	100	
69	Chicago Cardinals	5	5	6	8	12	30	100	
70	Jack Christiansen	5	6	8	10	12	30	80	
71	Don McIlhenny RC	5	5	5	8	12	25	80	
72	Ron Waller	5	5	5	8	12	35	80	
73	Frank Gifford	8	10	25	30	40	60	150	
74	Bert Rechichar	5	5	5	8	12	25	225	
75	John Henry Johnson	5	5	6	10	15	40	350	
76	Jack Butler	5	5	5	8	20	30	80	
77	Frank Varrichione	5	5	5	8	12	30	80	
78	Ray Mathews	5	5	5	8	12	30	80	
79	Marv Matuszak	5	5	5	8	12	25	80	
80	Harlon Hill	5	5	5	8	12	25	80	
81	Lou Creekmur	5	6	8	10	12	30	100	
82	Woodley Lewis	5	5	5	8	12	30	100	
83	Don Heinrich	5	5	5	8	12	25	80	
84	Charley Conerly	5	6	8	12	18	30	80	
85	Los Angeles Rams	5	5	6	8	12	25	80	
86	Y.A. Tittle	5	6	8	12	30	40	125	
87	Bobby Walston	5	5	5	8	12	25	80	
88	Earl Putman	5	5	5	8	12	30	100	
89	Leo Nomellini	5	6	8	12	18	30	80	
90	Sonny Jurgensen RC	15	40	50	100	150	250	600	2,000
91	Don Paul DB	5	5	5	8	12	30	80	
92	Paige Cothren	5	5	5	8	12	30	80	
93	Joe Perry	5	6	8	12	18	30	80	
94	Tobin Rote	5	5	5	8	12	25	80	
95	Billy Wilson	5	5	5	8	12	25	80	
96	Green Bay Packers	5	6	8	12	25	50	300	
97	Lavern Torgeson	5	5	5	8	12	25	80	
98	Milt Davis	5	5	5	8	12	25	80	
99	Larry Strickland	5	5	5	8	12	30	150	
100	Matt Hazeltine RC	5	5	5	8	12	30	200	
101	Walt Yowarsky	5	5	5	8	12	30	125	
102	Roosevelt Brown	5	6	8	10	12	30	400	
103	Jim Ringo	5	5	6	10	15	30	80	400
104	Joe Krupa	5	5	5	8	12	25	80	

		GD 2	VG 3	VgEx 4	EX 5	ExMt 6	NM 7	NmMt 8	MT 9
105	Les Richter	5	5	5	8	12	25	80	
106	Art Donovan	5	6	8	12	18	30	100	
107	John Olszewski	5	5	5	8	12	30	125	
108	Ken Keller	5	5	5	8	12	25	80	
109	Philadelphia Eagles	5	5	6	8	15	30	200	
110	Baltimore Colts	5	5	6	8	12	30	100	
111	Dick Bielski	5	5	5	8	12	25	80	
112	Eddie LeBaron	5	6	8	10	12	30	80	400
113	Gene Brito	5	5	5	8	12	25	80	
114	Willie Galimore RC	5	6	8	10	12	30	300	
115	Detroit Lions	5	5	6	8	12	25	100	
116	Pittsburgh Steelers	5	5	6	8	12	25	80	300
117	L.G. Dupre	5	5	5	8	12	25	80	
118	Babe Parilli	5	5	5	8	12	25	100	
119	Bill George	5	5	6	10	15	30	80	
120	Raymond Berry	6	8	10	15	25	50	150	
121	Jim Podoley	5	5	5	8	12	25	100	
122	Hugh McElhenny	5	6	8	12	18	30	80	
123	Ed Brown	5	5	5	8	12	30	100	
124	Dick Moegle	5	5	5	8	12	30	80	
125	Tom Scott	5	5	5	8	12	25	60	250
126	Tommy McDonald	5	6	10	15	30	80		
127	Ollie Matson	5	6	8	12	18	30	100	
128	Preston Carpenter	5	5	5	8	12	25	80	
129	George Blanda	5	6	8	12	20	50	250	
130	Gordy Soltau	5	5	5	8	12	30	80	
131	Dick Nolan RC	5	5	5	8	12	30	80	
132	Don Bosseler RC	5	6	8	12	20	50	350	1,200
NNO	Free Felt Initial Card	5	6	10	15	30	80		

— Chuck Bednarik #35 PSA 9 (Mint) sold for $700 (eBay; 12/07)
— George Blanda #129 PSA 9 (Mint) sold for $1,277 (Andy Madec; 5/07)
— Gene Brito #113 PSA 9 (Mint) sold for $713 (eBay; 12/12)
— Jim Brown #62 PSA 9 (Mint) sold for $29,257 (Mile High; 11/10)
— Jim Brown #62 SGC 8.5 (NmMt+) sold for $4,474 (Mile High; 3/09)
— Jim Brown #62 PSA 8.5 (NmMt+) sold for $5,377 (eBay; 4/12)
— Rick Casares #53 PSA 9 (Mint) sold for $1,230 (Greg Bussineau; Fall 2013)
— Jack Christiansen #70 PSA 9 (Mint) sold for $630 (eBay 11/14)
— Paige Cothran #28 PSA 10 (Gem Mt) sold for $908 (Mile High; 11/10)
— Bobby Dillon #32 PSA 9 (Mint) sold for $570 (eBay; 10/13)
— Lou Groza #52 PSA 9 (Mint) sold for $831 (Mastro; 2/07)
— Sonny Jurgensen #90 PSA 9 (Mint) sold for $2,180 (eBay; 12/07)
— Bobby Layne #2 PSA 9 (Mint) sold for $1,055 (Andy Madec; 5/07)
— Ted Marchibroda #44 PSA 9 (Mint) sold for $725 (eBay; 9/07)
— Earl Morrall #57 PSA 9 (Mint) sold for $410 (eBay; 6/06)
— Don Owens #47 PSA 10 (Gem Mt) sold for $1,634 (Goodwin; 6/10)
— Babe Parilli #118 PSA 9 (Mint) sold for $549 (eBay 11/14)
— Duane Putnam #55 PSA 10 (Gem Mt) sold for $1,030 (eBay; 3/07)
— Bart Starr #66 PSA 10 (Gem Mint) sold for $9036.86 (Mile High; 1/12)
— Y.A. Tittle #86 PSA 9 (Mint) sold for $1,055 (Andy Madec; 5/07)
— Johnny Unitas #22 PSA 9 (Mint) sold for $5,105 (eBay; 9/08)
— Johnny Unitas #22 PSA 9 (Mint) sold for $7852.81 (Mile High; 1/12)
— Johnny Unitas #22 PSA 9 (Mint) sold for $9239 (eBay; 8/13)
— Johnny Unitas #22 PSA 9 (Mint) sold for $ 4,737 (eBay; 11/13)
— Johnny Unitas #22 PSA 8.5 (Mint) sold for $ 1806 (eBay; 11/14)

1959 Topps

		GD 2	VG 3	VgEx 4	EX 5	ExMt 6	NM 7	NmMt 8	MT 9
1	Johnny Unitas	30	35	80	100	150	▲350	1,800	
2	Gene Brito	5	5	5	6	10	15	60	
3	Detroit Lions CL	5	5	6	8	12	20	60	175
4	Max McGee RC	5	6	8	10	20	50	80	400
5	Hugh McElhenny	5	5	5	8	12	20	50	200
6	Joe Schmidt	5	5	6	8	12	20	40	175
7	Kyle Rote	5	5	5	8	12	25	80	
8	Clarence Peaks	5	5	5	6	10	15	30	
9	Steelers Pennant	5	5	5	6	10	15	30	125
10	Jim Brown	30	60	80	300	400	1,200	1,500	3,000
11	Ray Mathews	5	5	5	6	10	15	30	125
12	Bobby Dillon	5	5	5	6	10	15	30	125
13	Joe Childress	5	5	5	6	10	15	40	125
14	Terry Barr RC	5	5	5	6	10	15	30	125
15	Del Shofner RC	5	5	6	10	15	50	125	
16	Bob Pellegrini UER	5	5	5	6	10	15	30	125
17	Baltimore Colts CL	5	5	6	8	12	20	35	
18	Preston Carpenter	5	5	5	6	10	15	30	
19	Leo Nomellini	5	5	6	8	12	20	40	150
20	Frank Gifford	8	10	25	30	40	50	▲150	250
21	Charlie Ane	5	5	5	6	10	15	30	125

#	Player	GD 2	VG 3	VgEx 4	EX 5	ExMt 6	NM 7	NmMt 8	MT 9
22	Jack Butler	5	5	6		10	25	30	125
23	Bart Starr	15	20	25	40	60	200	400	1,500
24	Cardinals Pennant	5	5	5	6	10	20	60	125
25	Bill Barnes	5	5	5	6	10	15	30	125
26	Walt Michaels	5	5	5	6	10	15	30	125
27	Clyde Conner UER	5	5	5	6	10	15	60	125
28	Paige Cothren	5	5	5	6	10	15	30	125
29	Roosevelt Grier	5	5	6	8	12	20	50	150
30	Alan Ameche	5	5	6	8	12	25	60	200
31	Philadelphia Eagles CL	5	5	6	8	12	20	35	100
32	Dick Nolan	5	5	5	6	10	15	30	
33	R.C. Owens	5	5	5	6	10	15	30	125
34	Dale Dodrill	5	5	5	6	10	15	30	
35	Gene Gedman	5	5	5	6	10	15	30	125
36	Gene Lipscomb RC	5	5	6	8	12	20	60	400
37	Ray Renfro	5	5	5	6	10	15	30	150
38	Browns Pennant	5	5	5	6	10	20	50	125
39	Bill Forester	5	5	5	6	10	15	40	125
40	Bobby Layne	6	8	10	12	18	40	60	250
41	Pat Summerall	5	5	6	8	12	20	100	200
42	Jerry Mertens RC	5	5	5	6	10	15	30	125
43	Steve Myhra RC	5	5	5	6	10	15	30	125
44	John Henry Johnson	5	5	6	8	12	20	35	125
45	Woodley Lewis UER	5	5	5	6	10	15	30	
46	Green Bay Packers CL	5	5	6	8	12	30	60	200
47	Don Owens UER RC	5	5	5	6	10	15	30	125
48	Ed Beatty RC	5	5	5	6	10	15	30	125
49	Don Chandler	5	5	5	6	10	15	40	125
50	Ollie Matson	5	5	6	8	12	20	40	175
51	Sam Huff RC	12	30	40	50	60	80	200	600
52	Tom Miner RC	5	5	5	6	10	15	30	125
53	Giants Pennant	5	5	5	6	10	15	30	125
54	Kenny Konz	5	5	5	6	10	15	30	125
55	Raymond Berry	5	6	8	10	15	25	60	300
56	Howard Ferguson UER	5	5	5	6	10	15	30	125
57	Chuck Ulrich	5	5	5	6	10	15	30	125
58	Bob St.Clair	5	5	6	8	12	20	50	150
59	Don Burroughs RC	5	5	5	6	10	15	30	125
60	Lou Groza	5	5	6	8	12	40	80	125
61	San Francisco 49ers CL	5	5	6	8	12	20	35	100
62	Andy Nelson RC	5	5	5	6	10	15	30	125
63	Harold Bradley RC	5	5	5	6	10	15	40	
64	Dave Hanner	5	5	5	6	10	15	30	150
65	Charley Conerly	5	6	8	10	15	25	60	
66	Gene Cronin RC	5	5	5	6	10	15	30	100
67	Duane Putnam	5	5	5	6	10	15	30	
68	Colts Pennant	5	5	5	6	10	15	80	250
69	Ernie Stautner	5	5	6	8	12	20	50	150
70	Jon Arnett	5	5	5	6	10	15	30	100
71	Ken Panfil RC	5	5	5	6	10	15	50	125
72	Matt Hazeltine	5	5	5	6	10	15	30	125
73	Harley Sewell	5	5	5	6	10	15	30	125
74	Mike McCormack	5	5	6	8	12	20	120	
75	Jim Ringo	5	5	6	8	12	25	80	300
76	Los Angeles Rams CL	5	5	6	8	12	20	50	120
77	Bob Gain RC	5	5	5	6	10	15	60	
78	Buzz Nutter RC	5	5	5	6	10	15	40	125
79	Jerry Norton	5	5	5	6	10	15	30	150
80	Joe Perry	5	5	6	8	12	20	40	150
81	Carl Brettschneider	5	5	5	6	10	15	30	100
82	Paul Hornung	10	12	15	20	50	100	150	800
83	Eagles Pennant	5	5	5	6	10	15	30	125
84	Les Richter	5	5	5	6	10	15	40	
85	Howard Cassady	5	5	5	6	10	15	30	125
86	Art Donovan	5	5	6	8	12	20	50	200
87	Jim Patton	5	5	5	6	10	15	30	120
88	Pete Retzlaff	5	5	5	6	10	15	30	100
89	Jim Mutscheller	5	5	5	5	8	12	50	125
90	Zeke Bratkowski	5	5	5	5	8	12	25	
91	Washington Redskins CL	5	5	5	5	8	12	25	100
92	Art Hunter	5	5	5	5	8	12	25	100
93	Gern Nagler	5	5	5	5	8	12	25	100
94	Chuck Weber RC	5	5	5	5	8	12	30	100
95	Lew Carpenter RC	5	5	5	5	8	12	25	100
96	Stan Jones	5	5	5	6	10	15	30	150
97	Ralph Guglielmi UER	5	5	5	5	8	12	25	100
98	Packers Pennant	5	5	5	5	8	12	25	100
99	Ray Wietecha	5	5	5	5	8	12	25	100
100	Lenny Moore	5	6	8	15	25	30	50	200

#	Player	GD 2	VG 3	VgEx 4	EX 5	ExMt 6	NM 7	NmMt 8	MT 9
101	Jim Ray Smith UER RC	5	5	6	8	10	20	80	250
102	Abe Woodson RC	5	5	5	5	8	12	25	100
103	Alex Karras RC	8	10	12	30	40	60	250	300
104	Chicago Bears CL	5	5	5	5	8	12	25	80
105	John David Crow RC	5	6	8	10	15	25	50	150
106	Joe Fortunato RC	5	5	5	5	8	12	25	100
107	Babe Parilli	5	5	5	5	8	12	25	80
108	Proverb Jacobs RC	5	5	5	5	8	12	30	100
109	Gino Marchetti	5	5	6	8	12	20	50	200
110	Bill Wade	5	5	5	5	8	12	25	
111	49ers Pennant	5	5	5	5	8	12	25	80
112	Karl Rubke RC	5	5	5	5	8	12	25	100
113	Dave Middleton UER	5	5	5	5	8	12	25	80
114	Roosevelt Brown	5	5	5	6	10	15	30	125
115	John Olszewski	5	5	5	5	8	12	25	80
116	Jerry Kramer RC	6	8	10	12	60	100	250	400
117	King Hill RC	5	5	5	5	8	12	25	80
118	Chicago Cardinals CL	5	5	5	5	8	12	25	80
119	Frank Varrichione	5	5	5	5	8	12	25	100
120	Rick Casares	5	5	5	5	8	12	25	
121	George Strugar RC	5	5	5	5	8	12	25	80
122	Bill Glass RC	5	5	5	5	8	12	25	80
123	Don Bosseler	5	5	5	5	8	12	25	80
124	John Reger RC	5	5	5	5	8	12	25	
125	Jim Ninowski RC	5	5	5	5	8	12	50	100
126	Rams Pennant	5	5	5	5	8	12	25	100
127	Willard Sherman	5	5	5	5	8	12	25	100
128	Bob Schnelker	5	5	5	5	8	12	25	80
129	Ollie Spencer RC	5	5	5	5	8	12	25	100
130	Y.A.Tittle	6	8	10	12	40	50	60	200
131	Yale Lary	5	5	5	6	10	15	30	100
132	Jim Parker RC	6	12	15	20	40	50	250	600
133	New York Giants CL	5	5	5	5	8	12	25	80
134	Jim Schrader RC	5	5	5	5	8	12	25	100
135	M.C. Reynolds RC	5	5	5	5	8	12	25	80
136	Mike Sandusky RC	5	5	5	5	8	12	25	150
137	Ed Brown	5	5	5	5	8	12	25	100
138	Al Barry RC	5	5	5	5	8	12	25	100
139	Lions Pennant	5	5	5	5	8	12	25	80
140	Bobby Mitchell RC	6	8	10	12	20	60	100	600
141	Larry Morris	5	5	5	5	8	12	25	100
142	Jim Phillips RC	5	5	5	5	8	12	25	100
143	Jim David	5	5	5	5	8	12	25	80
144	Joe Krupa	5	5	5	5	8	12	25	80
145	Willie Galimore	5	5	5	5	8	12	25	80
146	Pittsburgh Steelers CL	5	5	5	5	8	12	25	80
147	Andy Robustelli	5	5	6	8	12	20	40	200
148	Billy Wilson	5	5	5	5	8	12	25	100
149	Leo Sanford	5	5	5	5	8	12	25	100
150	Eddie LeBaron	5	5	5	6	10	15	30	125
151	Bill McColl	5	5	5	5	8	12	25	100
152	Buck Lansford UER	5	5	5	5	8	12	25	80
153	Bears Pennant	5	5	5	5	8	12	25	100
154	Leo Sugar RC	5	5	5	5	8	12	25	100
155	Jim Taylor UER RC	8	10	12	15	60	100	125	600
156	Lindon Crow	5	5	5	5	8	12	100	
157	Jack McClairen	5	5	5	5	8	12	25	100
158	Vince Costello UER RC	5	5	5	5	8	12	25	100
159	Stan Wallace RC	5	5	5	5	8	12	25	80
160	Mel Triplett RC	5	5	5	5	8	12	25	80
161	Cleveland Browns CL	5	5	5	5	8	12	25	80
162	Dan Currie RC	5	5	5	5	8	15	40	200
163	L.G. Dupre UER	5	5	5	5	8	12	25	80
164	John Morrow UER RC	5	5	5	5	8	12	25	100
165	Jim Podoley	5	5	5	5	8	12	25	80
166	Bruce Bosley RC	5	5	5	5	8	12	25	100
167	Harlon Hill	5	5	5	5	8	12	25	80
168	Redskins Pennant	5	5	5	5	8	12	25	100
169	Junior Wren RC	5	5	5	5	8	12	40	125
170	Tobin Rote	5	5	5	5	8	12	25	100
171	Art Spinney	5	5	5	5	8	12	25	100
172	Chuck Drazenovich UER	5	5	5	5	8	12	25	80
173	Bobby Joe Conrad RC	5	5	5	5	8	12	25	80
174	Jesse Richardson RC	5	5	5	5	8	12	25	80
175	Sam Baker	5	5	5	5	8	12	25	80
176	Tom Tracy RC	5	5	6	8	12	20	50	150

— Jon Arnett #70 PSA 10 (Gem Mint) sold for $1330 (eBay; 11/14)
— Ed Beatty RC #48 PSA 10 (Gem Mint) sold for $870 (Bussineau; 4/12)
— Jack Butler #22 PSA 10 (Gem Mint) sold for $1050 (Bussineau; 4/12)

— Joe Childress #13 PSA 10 (Gem Mint) sold for $628 (eBay 11/14)
— Charley Conerly #65 PSA 9 (Mint) sold for $2,006 (eBay; 1/09)
— Dale Dodrill #34 PSA 10 (Gem Mint) sold for $870 (Bussineau; 4/12)
— Harlon Hill #103 PSA 10 (Gem Mint) sold for $1,280 (eBay; 3/11)
— Alex Karras #103 PSA 10 (Gem Mint) sold for $1,740 (eBay; 1/06)
— Stan Jones #96 PSA 10 (Gem) sold for $1630 (eBay; 11/14)
— Bobby Layne #40 PSA 10 (Gem Mint) sold for $3150 (Bussineau; 4/12)
— Eddie LeBaron #150 PSA 10 (Gem Mint) sold for $1590 (Bussineau; 4/12)
— Ray Mathews #11 PSA 10 (Gem Mint) sold for $810 (Bussineau; 4/12)
— Don Owens UER RC #47 PSA 10 (Gem Mint) sold for $810 (Bussineau; 4/12)
— Ken Panfil RC #71 PSA 10 (Gem Mint) sold for $990 (Bussineau; 4/12)
— Jim Patton RC #87 PSA 10 (Gem Mint) sold for $740 (ebay; 11/14)
— Bob Pellegrini UER #16 PSA 10 (Gem Mint) sold for $930 (Bussineau; 4/12)
— Duane Putnam #67 PSA 10 (Gem Mint) sold for $1,210 (eBay; 1/14)
— Ray Renfro #37 PSA 10 (Gem Mint) sold for $1685 (eBay; 4/12)
— Del Shofner RC #15 PSA 10 (Gem Mint) sold for $1170 (Bussineau; 4/12)
— Bart Starr #23 PSA 10 (Gem Mint) sold for $7260 (Bussineau; 4/12)
— Bart Starr #23 PSA 9 (Mint) sold for $802 (eBay; 11/14)
— Y.A. Tittle #130 PSA 10 (Gem Mint) sold for $3,200 (Mastro; 4/07)
— Billy Wilson #148 PSA 10 (Gem Mint) sold for $1,366 (eBay; 10/12)
— Redskins Pennant #168 PSA 10 (Gem) sold for $2,129.50 (eBay; 2/14)

1960 Fleer

		GD 2	VG 3	VgEx 4	EX 5	ExMt 6	NM 7	NmMt 8	MT 9
1	Harvey White RC	4	4	4	5	8	20	175	
2	Tom Corky Tharp	4	4	4	5	6	20	175	
3	Dan McGrew	4	4	4	5	6	20	200	
4	Bob White	4	4	4	5	6	20	200	
5	Dick Jamieson	4	4	4	5	6	15	150	
6	Sam Salerno	4	4	4	5	6	15	100	
7	Sid Gillman CO RC	5	6	8	12	15	30	175	
8	Ben Preston	4	4	4	5	6	10	25	100
9	George Blanch	4	4	4	5	6	10	50	
10	Bob Stransky	4	4	4	5	6	10	30	150
11	Fran Curci	4	4	4	5	6	10	30	
12	George Shirkey	4	4	4	5	6	10	25	100
13	Paul Larson	4	4	4	5	6	10	25	100
14	John Stolte	4	4	4	5	6	10	30	
15	Serafino Fazio RC	4	4	4	5	6	10	30	
16	Tom Dimitroff	4	4	4	5	6	10	25	
17	Elbert Dubenion RC	4	5	6	8	10	15	40	
18	Hogan Wharton	4	4	4	5	6	10	25	100
19	Tom O'Connell	4	4	4	5	6	10	25	80
20	Sammy Baugh CO	10	12	15	20	25	40	60	150
21	Tony Sardisco	4	4	4	5	6	10	25	100
22	Alan Cann	4	4	4	5	6	10	25	100
23	Mike Hudock	4	4	4	5	6	10	30	
24	Bill Atkins	4	4	4	5	6	10	25	100
25	Charlie Jackson	4	4	4	5	6	10	25	80
26	Frank Tripucka	4	4	4	5	8	12	30	100
27	Tony Teresa	4	4	4	5	6	10	25	100
28	Joe Amstutz	4	4	4	5	6	10	25	100
29	Bob Fee RC	4	4	4	5	6	10	30	
30	Jim Baldwin	4	4	4	5	6	10	25	100
31	Jim Yates	4	4	4	5	6	10	25	100
32	Don Flynn	4	4	4	5	6	10	25	80
33	Ken Adamson	4	4	4	5	6	10	25	100
34	Ron Drzewiecki	4	4	4	5	6	10	25	80
35	J.W. Slack	4	4	4	5	6	10	25	80
36	Bob Yates	4	4	4	5	6	10	30	80
37	Gary Cobb	4	4	4	5	6	10	30	80
38	Jacky Lee RC	4	4	4	5	6	10	25	80
39	Jack Spikes RC	4	4	4	5	6	10	30	
40	Jim Padgett	4	4	4	5	6	10	30	100
41	Jack Larscheid RC	4	4	4	5	6	10	25	100
42	Bob Reifsnyder RC	4	4	4	5	6	10	30	
43	Fran Rogel	4	4	4	5	6	10	25	100
44	Ray Moss	4	4	4	5	6	10	25	80
45	Tony Banfield RC	4	4	4	5	6	10	25	100
46	George Herring	4	4	4	5	6	10	30	100
47	Willie Smith RC	4	4	4	5	6	10	25	100
48	Buddy Allen	4	4	4	5	6	10	35	100
49	Bill Brown LB	4	4	4	5	6	10	25	80
50	Ken Ford RC	4	4	4	5	6	10	25	100
51	Billy Kinard	4	4	4	5	6	10	25	100
52	Buddy Mayfield	4	4	4	5	6	10	25	100
53	Bill Krisher	4	4	4	5	6	10	25	100
54	Frank Bernardi	4	4	4	5	6	10	30	
55	Lou Saban CO RC	4	4	4	5	6	10	25	100

		GD 2	VG 3	VgEx 4	EX 5	ExMt 6	NM 7	NmMt 8	MT 9
56	Gene Cockrell	4	4	4	5	6	10	25	80
57	Sam Sanders	4	4	4	5	6	10	25	100
58	George Blanda	12	15	18	20	30	40	80	250
59	Sherrill Headrick RC	4	4	4	5	6	10	25	100
60	Carl Larpenter	4	4	4	5	6	10	30	
61	Gene Prebola	4	4	4	5	6	10	25	100
62	Dick Chorovich	4	4	4	5	6	10	25	100
63	Bob McNamara	4	4	4	5	6	10	25	
64	Tom Saidock	4	4	4	5	6	10	30	
65	Willie Evans	4	4	4	5	6	10	25	100
66	Billy Cannon RC	5	6	8	10	20	30	125	250
67	Sam McCord	4	4	4	5	6	10	25	100
68	Mike Simmons	4	4	4	5	6	10	25	80
69	Jim Swink RC	4	4	4	5	6	10	25	80
70	Don Hitt	4	4	4	5	6	10	25	80
71	Gerhard Schwedes	4	4	4	5	6	10	30	
72	Thurlow Cooper	4	4	4	5	6	10	30	
73	Abner Haynes RC	5	6	8	10	12	30	40	
74	Billy Shoemake	4	4	4	5	6	10	30	
75	Marv Lasater	4	4	6	10	15	40	100	
76	Paul Lowe RC	5	6	8	10	12	20	200	
77	Bruce Hartman	4	4	4	5	6	10	60	135
78	Blanche Martin	4	4	6	10	15	40	100	
79	Gene Grabosky	4	4	4	5	6	10	30	
80	Lou Rymkus CO	4	4	4	5	6	10	30	80
81	Chris Burford RC	4	4	4	5	8	25	125	
82	Don Allen	4	4	4	5	6	10	150	
83	Bob Nelson C	4	4	4	5	6	10	125	
84	Jim Woodard	4	4	4	5	6	20		
85	Tom Rychlec	4	4	4	5	6	10	25	100
86	Bob Cox	4	4	4	5	6	10	20	80
87	Jerry Cornelison	4	4	4	5	6	10	25	100
88	Jack Work	4	4	4	5	6	10	25	100
89	Sam DeLuca	4	4	4	5	6	10	25	100
90	Rommie Loudd	4	4	4	5	6	10	30	
91	Teddy Edmondson	4	4	4	5	6	10	25	80
92	Buster Ramsey CO	4	4	4	5	6	10	25	80
93	Doug Asad	4	4	4	5	6	10	25	80
94	Jimmy Harris	4	4	4	5	6	10	30	
95	Larry Cundiff	4	4	4	5	6	10	25	80
96	Richie Lucas RC	4	4	4	5	8	12	30	150
97	Don Norwood	4	4	4	5	6	10	25	80
98	Larry Grantham RC	4	4	4	5	6	10	25	100
99	Bill Mathis RC	4	4	4	5	8	12	30	150
100	Mel Branch RC	4	4	4	5	6	10	25	100
101	Marvin Terrell	4	4	4	5	6	10	25	100
102	Charlie Flowers	4	4	4	5	6	10	25	80
103	John McMullan	4	4	4	5	6	10	25	80
104	Charlie Kaaihue	4	4	4	5	6	10	25	100
105	Joe Schaffer	4	4	4	5	6	10	30	
106	Al Day	4	4	4	5	6	10	30	
107	Johnny Carson	4	4	4	5	6	10	30	
108	Alan Goldstein	4	4	4	5	6	10	25	100
109	Doug Cline	4	4	4	5	6	10	30	
110	Al Carmichael	4	4	4	5	6	10	25	100
111	Bob Dee	4	4	4	5	6	10	30	
112	John Bredice	4	4	4	5	6	10	30	
113	Don Floyd	4	4	4	5	6	10	25	100
114	Ronnie Cain	4	4	4	5	6	10	30	
115	Stan Flowers	4	4	4	5	6	10	25	100
116	Hank Stram CO RC	10	12	15	20	30	40	100	350
117	Bob Dougherty	4	4	4	5	6	10	25	100
118	Ron Mix RC	10	12	15	15	25	60	150	800
119	Roger Ellis	4	4	4	5	6	10	25	100
120	Elvin Caldwell	4	4	4	5	6	10	30	100
121	Bill Kimber	4	4	4	5	6	10	30	
122	Jim Matheny	4	4	4	5	6	10	25	80
123	Curley Johnson RC	4	4	4	5	6	10	40	
124	Jack Kemp RC	30	40	50	60	80	100	175	600
125	Ed Denk	4	4	4	5	6	10	25	80
126	Jerry McFarland	4	4	4	5	6	10	30	
127	Dan Lanphear	4	4	4	5	6	15	80	
128	Paul Maguire RC	5	6	8	10	12	20	40	100
129	Ray Collins	4	4	4	5	6	10	20	100
130	Ron Burton RC	4	4	4	5	8	12	30	
131	Eddie Erdelatz CO	4	4	4	5	6	10	30	
132	Ron Beagle RC	4	4	4	5	6	10	40	250

— Jack Kemp RC #124 PSA 10 (Gem Mint) sold for $2850 (eBay; 4/12)
— Paul Maguire #128 PSA 10 (Gem) sold for $2,505 (eBay; 4/08)

1960 Topps

#	Player	GD 2	VG 3	VgEx 4	EX 5	ExMt 6	NM 7	NmMt 8	MT 9
1	Johnny Unitas	20	30	40	50	100	300	1,200	15,000
2	Alan Ameche	4	4	4	6	10	15	300	
3	Lenny Moore	5	5	6	8	12	25	60	
4	Raymond Berry	5	5	6	8	12	25	50	250
5	Jim Parker	4	4	5	6	10	20	40	125
6	George Preas	4	4	4	4	6	12	60	
7	Art Spinney	4	4	4	4	6	12	50	
8	Bill Pellington RC	4	4	4	4	6	12	40	
9	Johnny Sample RC	4	4	4	4	6	12	40	
10	Gene Lipscomb	4	4	4	4	6	12	25	120
11	Baltimore Colts	4	4	4	4	6	12	80	200
12	Ed Brown	4	4	4	4	6	12	30	120
13	Rick Casares	4	4	4	4	6	12	40	
14	Willie Galimore	4	4	4	4	6	12	135	
15	Jim Dooley	4	4	4	4	6	12	40	
16	Harlon Hill	4	4	4	4	6	12	30	120
17	Stan Jones	4	4	4	4	6	12	25	150
18	Bill George	4	4	4	4	6	12	30	150
19	Erich Barnes RC	4	4	4	4	6	12	40	120
20	Doug Atkins	4	4	5	6	10	20	60	
21	Chicago Bears	4	4	4	4	6	12	30	120
22	Milt Plum	4	4	4	4	6	12	25	120
23	Jim Brown	20	125	150	200	250	500	1,500	1,500
24	Sam Baker	4	4	4	4	6	12	60	
25	Bobby Mitchell	5	5	6	8	12	25	50	250
26	Ray Renfro	4	4	4	4	6	12	20	120
27	Billy Howton	4	4	4	4	6	12	40	120
28	Jim Ray Smith	4	4	4	4	6	12	30	120
29	Jim Shofner RC	4	4	4	4	6	12	50	
30	Bob Gain	4	4	4	4	6	12	40	
31	Cleveland Browns	4	4	6	10	15	40	100	
32	Don Heinrich	4	4	4	4	6	12	40	120
33	Ed Modzelewski	4	4	4	4	6	12	40	
34	Fred Cone	4	4	4	4	6	20	40	120
35	L.G. Dupre	4	4	4	4	6	12	25	120
36	Dick Bielski	4	4	4	4	6	12	30	120
37	Charlie Ane	4	4	4	4	6	12	60	
38	Jerry Tubbs	4	4	4	5	8	15	50	200
39	Doyle Nix	4	4	4	4	6	12	20	200
40	Ray Krouse	4	4	4	4	6	12	40	
41	Earl Morrall	4	4	4	5	10	15	60	
42	Howard Cassady	4	4	4	4	6	12	40	
43	Dave Middleton	4	4	4	4	6	12	25	120
44	Jim Gibbons RC	4	4	4	4	6	12	20	175
45	Darris McCord	4	4	4	4	6	12	50	
46	Joe Schmidt	4	4	5	6	10	20	40	
47	Terry Barr	4	4	4	4	6	12	60	
48	Yale Lary	4	4	4	4	6	12	40	
49	Gil Mains	4	4	4	4	6	12	25	120
50	Detroit Lions	4	4	4	4	6	12	40	
51	Bart Starr	10	12	30	50	60	100	400	800
52	Jim Taylor	4	4	5	6	10	20	50	200
53	Lew Carpenter	4	4	4	4	6	12	40	
54	Paul Hornung	8	10	12	30	40	50	100	400
55	Max McGee	4	4	5	6	10	25	125	
56	Forrest Gregg RC	8	10	12	20	30	50	200	1,200
57	Jim Ringo	4	4	5	6	10	20	40	150
58	Bill Forester	4	4	4	4	6	12	40	200
59	Dave Hanner	4	4	4	4	6	12	60	
60	Green Bay Packers	4	4	5	6	10	20	80	
61	Bill Wade	4	4	4	4	6	12	20	120
62	Frank Ryan RC	4	4	4	5	8	15	30	250
63	Ollie Matson	5	5	6	8	12	25	60	200
64	Jon Arnett	4	4	4	4	6	12	20	120
65	Del Shofner	4	4	4	4	6	12	20	120
66	Jim Phillips	4	4	4	4	6	12	20	120
67	Art Hunter	4	4	4	4	6	12	40	
68	Les Richter	4	4	4	4	6	12	50	
69	Lou Michaels RC	4	4	4	4	6	12	80	
70	John Baker	4	4	4	4	6	12	40	200
71	Los Angeles Rams	4	4	4	4	6	12	40	
72	Charley Conerly	4	4	5	6	10	20	40	150
73	Mel Triplett	4	4	4	4	6	12	40	
74	Frank Gifford	6	8	10	25	40	60	100	250
75	Alex Webster	4	4	4	4	6	12	40	150
76	Bob Schnelker	4	4	4	4	6	12	20	120
77	Pat Summerall	5	5	6	8	12	25	60	
78	Roosevelt Brown	4	4	4	4	6	12	30	150
79	Jim Patton	4	4	4	4	6	12	20	120
80	Sam Huff	5	5	6	8	12	25	50	200
81	Andy Robustelli	4	4	4	6	10	20	40	150
82	New York Giants	4	4	4	4	6	12	40	
83	Clarence Peaks	4	4	4	4	6	12	40	
84	Bill Barnes	4	4	4	4	6	12	20	120
85	Pete Retzlaff	4	4	4	4	6	12	20	120
86	Bobby Walston	4	4	4	4	6	12	40	
87	Chuck Bednarik	4	4	5	6	10	20	50	200
88	Bob Pellegrini	4	4	4	4	6	12	20	120
89	Tom Brookshier RC	4	4	4	4	6	15	200	
90	Marion Campbell	4	4	4	4	6	12	30	120
91	Jesse Richardson	4	4	4	4	6	12	20	120
92	Philadelphia Eagles	4	4	4	4	6	12	30	120
93	Bobby Layne	6	8	10	15	20	30	60	250
94	John Henry Johnson	4	4	6	10	15	40	120	
95	Tom Tracy	4	4	4	4	6	12	40	
96	Preston Carpenter	4	4	4	4	6	12	20	120
97	Frank Varrichione	4	4	4	4	6	12	20	
98	John Nisby	4	4	4	4	6	12	40	
99	Dean Derby	4	4	4	4	6	12	40	
100	George Tarasovic	4	4	4	4	6	12	25	120
101	Ernie Stautner	4	4	5	6	10	20	60	200
102	Pittsburgh Steelers	4	4	4	4	6	12	40	
103	King Hill	4	4	4	4	6	12	20	120
104	Mal Hammack	4	4	4	4	6	12	80	175
105	John David Crow	4	4	4	6	10	30	120	
106	Bobby Joe Conrad	4	4	4	4	6	12	20	120
107	Woodley Lewis	4	4	4	4	6	12	20	120
108	Don Gillis	4	4	4	4	6	12	20	120
109	Carl Brettschneider	4	4	4	4	6	12	20	120
110	Leo Sugar	4	4	4	4	6	12	60	
111	Frank Fuller	4	4	4	4	6	12	60	300
112	St. Louis Cardinals	4	4	4	4	6	12	20	120
113	Y.A.Tittle	6	8	10	12	20	40	80	300
114	Joe Perry	4	4	5	6	10	20	60	500
115	J.D.Smith RC	4	4	4	4	6	12	40	
116	Hugh McElhenny	4	4	5	6	10	20	40	200
117	Billy Wilson	4	4	4	4	6	12	25	150
118	Bob St.Clair	4	4	4	4	6	12	30	150
119	Matt Hazeltine	4	4	4	4	6	12	20	120
120	Abe Woodson	4	4	4	4	6	12	20	120
121	Leo Nomellini	4	4	5	6	10	20	40	
122	San Francisco 49ers	4	4	4	4	6	12	50	150
123	Ralph Guglielmi	4	4	4	4	6	12	40	
124	Don Bosseler	4	4	4	4	6	12	20	120
125	John Olszewski	4	4	4	4	6	12	20	120
126	Bill Anderson	4	4	4	4	6	12	20	120
127	Joe Walton RC	4	4	4	4	6	12	25	120
128	Jim Schrader	4	4	4	4	6	12	20	120
129	Ralph Felton	4	4	4	4	6	12	20	120
130	Gary Glick	4	4	4	4	6	20	200	
131	Bob Toneff	4	4	4	4	6	12	40	
132	Redskins Team	5	5	6	8	12	30	50	200

— Cleveland Browns #31 PSA 9 (Mint) sold for $903.5 (eBay: 4/12)
— Forrest Gregg #56 PSA 9 (Mint) sold for $840 (eBay; 3/07)
— John Henry Johnson #94 PSA 9 (Mint) sold for $405.83 (eBay: 4/12)
— Leo Nomellini #121 PSA 10 (Gem Mt) sold for $1,327 (Goodwin; 12/10)
— Bart Starr #51 PSA 10 (Gem Mt) sold for $2400 (Mastro; 12/08)

1961 Fleer

#	Player	GD 2	VG 3	VgEx 4	EX 5	ExMt 6	NM 7	NmMt 8	MT 9
1	Ed Brown	4	5	5	8	12	20	40	
2	Rick Casares	4	5	5	5	6	10	60	
3	Willie Galimore	4	5	5	5	6	10	40	
4	Jim Dooley	4	5	5	5	6	10	25	100
5	Harlon Hill	4	5	5	5	6	10	30	
6	Stan Jones	4	5	5	6	8	12	80	
7	J.C. Caroline	4	5	5	5	6	10	30	
8	Joe Fortunato	4	5	5	5	6	10	30	250
9	Doug Atkins	4	5	5	6	8	12	25	150
10	Milt Plum	4	5	5	5	6	10	20	175
11	Jim Brown	25	60	80	100	200	400	1,200	2,500
12	Bobby Mitchell	4	5	6	8	10	15	50	300
13	Ray Renfro	4	5	5	5	6	10	20	120

#	Player	GD 2	VG 3	VgEx 4	EX 5	ExMt 6	NM 7	NmMt 8	MT 9
14	Gern Nagler	4	5	5	5	6	10	30	
15	Jim Shofner	4	5	5	5	6	10	20	100
16	Vince Costello	4	5	5	5	6	10	20	125
17	Galen Fiss RC	4	5	5	5	6	10	20	100
18	Walt Michaels	4	5	5	5	6	10	30	
19	Bob Gain	4	5	5	5	6	10	30	
20	Mal Hammack	4	5	5	5	6	10	20	100
21	Frank Mestnik RC	4	5	5	5	6	10	20	100
22	Bobby Joe Conrad	4	5	5	5	6	10	30	
23	John David Crow	4	5	5	5	6	10	20	100
24	Sonny Randle RC	4	5	5	5	6	10	25	100
25	Don Gillis	4	5	5	5	6	10	30	
26	Jerry Norton	4	5	5	5	6	10	20	80
27	Bill Stacy RC	4	5	5	5	6	10	50	200
28	Leo Sugar	4	5	5	5	6	10	20	100
29	Frank Fuller	4	5	5	5	6	10	20	100
30	Johnny Unitas	12	20	50	60	80	100	300	600
31	Alan Ameche	4	5	5	6	8	12	30	150
32	Lenny Moore	4	6	8	10	12	20	60	300
33	Raymond Berry	4	6	8	10	12	20	50	200
34	Jim Mutscheller	4	5	5	5	6	10	20	100
35	Jim Parker	4	5	5	6	8	12	25	150
36	Bill Pellington	4	5	5	5	6	10	20	100
37	Gino Marchetti	4	5	6	8	10	25	30	150
38	Gene Lipscomb	4	5	5	6	8	12	35	150
39	Art Donovan	4	6	8	10	12	25	60	250
40	Eddie LeBaron	4	5	5	5	6	10	20	120
41	Don Meredith RC	80	100	125	150	▼200	▼250	▼300	800
42	Don McIlhenny	4	5	5	5	6	10	20	100
43	L.G. Dupre	4	5	5	5	6	10	40	100
44	Fred Dugan RC	4	5	5	5	6	10	20	100
45	Billy Howton	4	5	5	5	6	10	30	100
46	Duane Putnam	4	5	5	5	6	10	20	100
47	Gene Cronin	4	5	5	5	6	15	20	100
48	Jerry Tubbs	4	5	5	5	6	10	40	100
49	Clarence Peaks	4	5	5	5	6	10	20	100
50	Ted Dean RC	4	5	5	5	6	10	20	100
51	Tommy McDonald	4	5	5	6	8	12	30	
52	Bill Barnes	4	5	5	5	6	10	40	
53	Pete Retzlaff	4	5	5	5	6	10	20	100
54	Bobby Walston	4	5	5	5	6	10	40	
55	Chuck Bednarik	4	5	6	8	10	15	30	200
56	Maxie Baughan RC	4	5	5	5	20	60	80	175
57	Bob Pellegrini	4	5	5	5	6	10	20	100
58	Jesse Richardson	4	5	5	5	6	10	30	
59	John Brodie RC	8	12	15	20	30	50	150	500
60	J.D. Smith RB	4	5	5	5	6	10	20	100
61	Ray Norton RC	4	5	5	5	6	10	40	400
62	Monty Stickles RC	4	5	5	5	6	10	30	
63	Bob St.Clair	4	5	5	6	8	12	30	150
64	Dave Baker RC	4	5	5	5	6	10	30	
65	Abe Woodson	4	5	5	5	6	10	20	100
66	Matt Hazeltine	4	5	5	5	6	10	30	120
67	Leo Nomellini	4	5	6	8	10	15	30	
68	Charley Conerly	4	5	6	8	10	18	30	300
69	Kyle Rote	4	5	6	8	12	30		
70	Jack Stroud RC	4	5	5	5	6	10	20	100
71	Roosevelt Brown	4	5	5	6	8	12	25	150
72	Jim Patton	4	5	5	5	6	10	80	
73	Erich Barnes	4	5	5	5	6	10	20	100
74	Sam Huff	4	6	8	10	12	20	60	250
75	Andy Robustelli	4	5	6	8	10	15	25	120
76	Dick Modzelewski RC	4	5	5	5	6	10	50	120
77	Roosevelt Grier	4	5	5	6	8	15	40	
78	Earl Morrall	4	5	5	6	8	12	25	150
79	Jim Ninowski	4	5	5	5	6	10	25	100
80	Nick Pietrosante RC	4	5	5	5	6	10	20	100
81	Howard Cassady	4	5	5	5	6	10	25	100
82	Jim Gibbons	4	5	5	5	6	10	20	100
83	Gail Cogdill RC	4	5	5	5	6	10	20	100
84	Dick Lane	4	5	5	6	8	12	35	
85	Yale Lary	4	5	5	6	8	12	35	
86	Joe Schmidt	4	5	5	6	8	12	25	150
87	Darris McCord	4	5	5	5	6	10	40	
88	Bart Starr	12	20	25	35	80	150	250	600
89	Jim Taylor	8	12	15	25	40	100	125	350
90	Paul Hornung	8	12	15	25	40	▼60	125	500
91	Tom Moore RC	4	5	5	6	8	12	30	150
92	Boyd Dowler RC	4	5	6	8	10	15	60	250
93	Max McGee	4	5	5	6	8	12	50	
94	Forrest Gregg	4	5	5	6	8	30	30	250
95	Jerry Kramer	4	5	6	8	10	15	60	
96	Jim Ringo	4	5	5	6	8	12	40	
97	Bill Forester	4	5	5	5	6	10	40	100
98	Frank Ryan	4	5	5	5	6	10	40	
99	Ollie Matson	4	5	6	8	10	20	30	175
100	Jon Arnett	4	5	5	5	6	10	20	100
101	Dick Bass RC	4	5	5	5	6	10	20	100
102	Jim Phillips	4	5	5	5	6	10	20	100
103	Del Shofner	4	5	5	5	6	10	20	100
104	Art Hunter	4	5	5	5	6	10	30	
105	Lindon Crow	4	5	5	5	6	10	20	100
106	Les Richter	4	5	5	5	6	10	20	100
107	Lou Michaels	4	5	5	5	6	10	20	100
108	Ralph Guglielmi	4	5	5	5	6	10	20	100
109	Don Bosseler	4	5	5	5	6	10	30	
110	John Olszewski	4	5	5	5	6	10	20	100
111	Bill Anderson	4	5	5	5	6	10	20	100
112	Joe Walton	4	5	5	5	6	10	20	100
113	Jim Schrader	4	5	5	5	6	10	20	100
114	Gary Glick	4	5	5	5	6	10	30	
115	Ralph Felton	4	5	5	5	6	10	20	100
116	Bob Toneff	4	5	5	5	6	10	20	100
117	Bobby Layne	5	8	10	15	25	40	80	200
118	John Henry Johnson	4	5	5	6	8	12	30	
119	Tom Tracy	4	5	5	5	6	10	20	60
120	Jimmy Orr RC	4	5	5	6	8	20	40	150
121	John Nisby	4	5	5	5	6	10	20	100
122	Dean Derby	4	5	5	5	6	10	20	100
123	John Reger	4	5	5	5	6	10	20	100
124	George Tarasovic	4	5	5	5	6	10	20	100
125	Ernie Stautner	4	5	6	8	10	15	30	
126	George Shaw	4	5	5	5	6	15	60	250
127	Hugh McElhenny	4	5	6	8	10	15	30	175
128	Dick Haley RC	4	5	5	5	6	10	30	120
129	Dave Middleton	4	5	5	5	6	10	30	
130	Perry Richards RC	4	5	5	5	6	10	20	100
131	Gene Johnson DB RC	4	5	5	5	6	10	40	
132	Don Joyce RC	4	5	5	5	6	10	25	175
133	Johnny Green RC	4	5	5	5	6	10	25	80
134	Wray Carlton RC	4	5	5	5	6	10	30	80
135	Richie Lucas	4	5	5	5	6	10	20	80
136	Elbert Dubenion	4	5	5	5	6	10	20	80
137	Tom Rychlec	4	5	5	5	6	10	20	60
138	Mack Yoho RC	4	5	5	5	6	10	20	60
139	Phil Blazer RC	4	5	5	5	6	10	25	80
140	Dan McGrew	4	5	5	5	6	10	20	60
141	Bill Atkins	4	5	5	5	6	10	20	50
142	Archie Matsos RC	4	5	5	5	6	10	20	60
143	Gene Grabosky	4	5	5	5	6	10	20	50
144	Frank Tripucka	4	5	5	5	6	8	12	25	80
145	Al Carmichael	4	5	5	5	6	10	20	60
146	Bob McNamara	4	5	5	5	6	10	20	60
147	Lionel Taylor RC	4	5	6	8	10	20	50	150
148	Eldon Danenhauer RC	4	5	5	5	6	10	20	60
149	Willie Smith	4	5	5	5	6	10	20	60
150	Carl Larpenter	4	5	5	5	6	10	20	60
151	Ken Adamson	4	5	5	5	6	10	20	60
152	Goose Gonsoulin UER RC	4	5	5	6	8	12	30	80
153	Joe Young RC	4	5	5	5	6	10	20	60
154	Gordy Holz RC	4	5	5	5	6	10	20	50
155	Jack Kemp	12	20	25	30	40	60	100	150
156	Charlie Flowers	4	5	5	5	6	10	20	60
157	Paul Lowe	4	5	5	6	8	12	25	80
158	Don Norton RC	4	5	5	5	6	10	20	80
159	Howard Clark RC	4	5	5	5	6	10	20	60
160	Paul Maguire	4	5	6	8	10	15	30	100
161	Ernie Wright RC	4	5	5	5	6	10	60	
162	Ron Mix	4	5	6	8	10	15	40	100
163	Fred Cole RC	4	5	5	5	6	10	20	60
164	Jim Sears RC	4	5	5	5	6	10	20	60
165	Volney Peters	4	5	5	5	6	10	20	60
166	George Blanda	6	10	12	18	30	50	60	100
167	Jacky Lee	4	5	5	5	6	10	20	60
168	Bob White	4	5	5	5	6	10	60	
169	Doug Cline	4	5	5	5	6	10	20	60
170	Dave Smith RB RC	4	5	5	5	6	10	20	40
171	Billy Cannon	4	5	6	8	10	15	40	80

		GD 2	VG 3	VgEx 4	EX 5	ExMt 6	NM 7	NmMt 8	MT 9
172	Bill Groman RC	4	5	5	5	6	10	20	60
173	Al Jamison RC	4	5	5	5	6	10	20	40
174	Jim Norton RC	4	5	5	5	6	10	20	40
175	Dennit Morris RC	4	5	5	5	6	10	20	60
176	Don Floyd	4	5	5	5	6	15	20	60
177	Butch Songin	4	5	5	5	6	10	20	60
178	Billy Lott RC	4	5	5	5	6	10	20	80
179	Ron Burton	4	5	5	6	8	12	30	80
180	Jim Colclough RC	4	5	5	5	6	10	25	
181	Charley Leo RC	4	5	5	5	6	10	20	60
182	Walt Cudzik RC	4	5	5	5	6	10	20	60
183	Fred Bruney	4	5	5	5	6	10	20	60
184	Ross O'Hanley RC	4	5	5	5	6	10	20	60
185	Tony Sardisco	4	5	5	5	6	10	20	60
186	Harry Jacobs RC	4	5	5	5	6	10	20	80
187	Bob Dee	4	5	5	5	6	10	20	60
188	Tom Flores RC	5	8	10	15	18	30	60	200
189	Jack Larscheid	4	5	5	5	6	10	20	60
190	Dick Christy RC	4	5	5	5	6	10	20	40
191	Alan Miller RC	4	5	5	5	6	10	20	60
192	James Smith	4	5	5	5	6	10	20	60
193	Gerald Burch RC	4	5	5	5	6	10	20	60
194	Gene Prebola	4	5	5	5	6	10	20	60
195	Alan Goldstein	4	5	5	5	6	10	20	60
196	Don Manoukian RC	4	5	5	5	6	10	20	80
197	Jim Otto RC	10	15	20	30	80	150	200	300
198	Wayne Crow	4	5	5	5	6	10	20	80
199	Cotton Davidson RC	4	5	5	5	6	10	20	80
200	Randy Duncan RC	4	5	5	5	6	10	25	
201	Jack Spikes	4	5	5	5	6	10	20	80
202	Johnny Robinson RC	4	6	8	10	80	100	250	400
203	Abner Haynes	4	5	6	8	10	15	30	100
204	Chris Burford	4	5	5	5	6	10	20	80
205	Bill Krisher	4	5	5	5	6	10	20	60
206	Marvin Terrell	4	5	5	5	6	10	20	80
207	Jimmy Harris	4	5	5	5	6	10	20	80
208	Mel Branch	4	5	5	5	6	10	20	80
209	Paul Miller	4	5	5	5	6	10	25	
210	Al Dorow	4	5	5	5	6	10	25	
211	Dick Jamieson	4	5	5	5	6	10	25	
212	Pete Hart RC	4	5	5	5	6	10	20	60
213	Bill Shockley RC	4	5	5	5	6	10	20	60
214	Dewey Bohling RC	4	5	5	5	6	10	20	60
215	Don Maynard RC	12	20	25	35	50	75	200	350
216	Bob Mischak RC	4	5	5	5	6	10	20	80
217	Mike Hudock	4	5	5	5	6	10	20	80
218	Bob Reifsnyder	4	5	5	5	6	10	25	
219	Tom Saidock	4	5	5	5	6	10	25	
220	Sid Youngelman	4	5	6	8	10	20	40	800

— Billy Cannon #171 PSA 10 (Gem Mt) sold for $653 (Mile High; 1/07)
— Jerry Kramer #95 PSA 9 (MT) sold for $899 (ebay; 11/07)
— Dick Lane #84 PSA 10 (Gem Mt) sold for $643 (eBay; 5/11)
— Paul Maguire #160 PSA 10 (Gem Mt) sold for $715 (eBay; 3/07)
— Jim Otto #197 PSA 10 (Gem Mt) sold for $2,843 (eBay; 2/08)
— Jim Otto #197 PSA 10 (Gem Mt) sold for $2,500 (eBay; 4/11)
— Jim Otto #197 PSA 10 (Gem Mt) sold for $2,251 (eBay; 11/09)
— Jim Otto #197 PSA 10 (Gem Mint) sold for $1,080 (Bussineau; 7/12)
— Jim Otto #197 PSA 10 (Gem Mint) sold for $1,206 (eBay; 2/14)
— Gern Nagler #14 PSA 10 (Gem Mt) sold for $755 (eBay; 6/06)

1961 Nu-Card

		VG 3	VgEx 4	EX 5	ExMt 6	NM 7	NmMt 8	MT 9	Gem 9.5/10
	COMMON CARD (101-180)	4	4	5	5	6	10	20	
101	Bob Ferguson	4	4	5	5	8	12	30	
105	Vern Von Sydow	4	4	5	5	6	10	20	80
112	Don Purcell	4	4	5	5	6	10	20	80
116	Bobby Iles	4	4	5	5	6	10	25	
117	John Hadl	6	8	10	12	20	30	60	
118	Charlie Mitchell	4	4	5	5	6	10	25	
120	Bill King	4	4	5	5	6	10	25	
121	Mike Lucci	4	4	5	5	8	12	25	
128	Gary Collins	4	4	5	6	10	15	25	
130	Bobby Dodd Flor.	4	4	5	5	8	12	25	
131	Curtis McClinton	4	4	5	5	6	10	30	
135	Larry Libertore	4	4	4	5	6	10	20	80
136	Stan Sczurek	4	4	5	5	6	10	20	80
138	Jesse Bradford	4	4	5	5	6	10	15	80
140	Walter Doleschal	4	4	5	5	6	10	20	80

		VG 3	VgEx 4	EX 5	ExMt 6	NM 7	NmMt 8	MT 9	Gem 9.5/10
142	Pat Trammell	4	4	5	5	8	12	25	80
143	Ernie Davis	10	12	15	20	35	60	120	
148	Roger Kochman	4	4	5	5	6	10	25	
150	Sherwyn Torson	4	4	5	5	6	10	25	
151	Russ Hepner	4	4	5	5	6	10	20	80
155	Ken Bolin	4	4	5	5	6	10	20	80
159	Dan Celoni G	4	4	5	5	6	10	20	80
166	Roman Gabriel	6	8	10	12	20	30	80	
169	Charles Rieves	4	4	5	5	6	10	20	80
172	Galen Hall	4	4	5	5	8	12	25	
174	Don Kasso	4	4	5	6	15			
175	Bill Miller	4	4	5	5	6	10	20	80
178	Mel Melin UER{(misspelled Mellin)4	4	4	5	5	6	10	15	80
179	Tom Vassell	4	4	5	5	6	10	25	

— Ernie Davis #143 PSA 10 (Gem) sold for $420 (eBay; 2/07)

1961 Topps

		GD 2	VG 3	VgEx 4	EX 5	ExMt 6	NM 7	NmMt 8	MT 9
1	Johnny Unitas	20	25	30	40	60	150	350	1,200
2	Lenny Moore	4	4	5	8	12	25	50	
3	Alan Ameche	4	4	5	5	10	15	60	
4	Raymond Berry	4	4	5	8	12	25	100	
5	Jim Mutscheller	4	4	5	5	6	12	20	100
6	Jim Parker	4	4	5	5	8	15	35	
7	Gino Marchetti	4	4	5	6	10	20	40	175
8	Gene Lipscomb	4	4	5	5	8	12	50	
9	Baltimore Colts	4	4	5	5	6	12	60	
10	Bill Wade	4	4	5	5	6	12	25	
11	Johnny Morris RC	4	4	5	5	8	12	30	150
12	Rick Casares	4	4	5	5	6	12	35	
13	Harlon Hill	4	4	5	5	6	12	25	
14	Stan Jones	4	4	5	5	8	12	25	120
15	Doug Atkins	4	4	5	5	8	40	150	
16	Bill George	4	4	5	5	8	12	25	120
17	J.C. Caroline	4	4	5	5	6	12	100	
18	Chicago Bears	4	4	5	5	6	12	20	150
19	Eddie LeBaron IA	4	4	5	6	10	20	100	
20	Eddie LeBaron	4	4	5	5	6	12	50	
21	Don McIlhenny	4	4	5	5	6	12	40	
22	L.G. Dupre	4	4	5	5	6	12	40	125
23	Jim Doran	4	4	5	5	6	12	35	
24	Billy Howton	4	4	5	5	6	12	40	
25	Buzz Guy	4	4	5	6	12	15	60	
26	Jack Patera RC	4	4	5	5	6	12	40	120
27	Tom Franckhauser RC	4	4	5	5	6	12	40	
28	Cowboys Team	4	5	6	10	15	25	80	
29	Jim Ninowski	4	4	5	5	6	12	25	
30	Dan Lewis RC	4	4	5	5	6	12	20	100
31	Nick Pietrosante RC	4	4	5	5	6	12	25	
32	Gail Cogdill RC	4	4	5	5	6	12	40	
33	Jim Gibbons	4	4	5	5	6	12	25	
34	Jim Martin	4	4	5	5	6	12	20	100
35	Alex Karras	4	5	6	10	15	25	60	
36	Joe Schmidt	4	4	5	5	8	15	40	
37	Detroit Lions	4	4	5	5	6	12	25	
38	Paul Hornung IA	4	5	6	10	15	25	150	
39	Bart Starr	10	12	15	25	50	150	300	600
40	Paul Hornung	6	8	10	15	25	50	100	400
41	Jim Taylor	6	8	10	15	25	40	125	450
42	Max McGee	4	4	5	5	8	12	50	150
43	Boyd Dowler RC	4	4	5	6	10	25	100	
44	Jim Ringo	4	4	5	5	8	15	50	300
45	Hank Jordan RC	6	8	10	20	30	60	300	
46	Bill Forester	4	4	5	5	6	12	30	100
47	Green Bay Packers	4	5	6	10	15	25	60	200
48	Frank Ryan	4	4	5	5	6	12	20	100
49	Jon Arnett	4	4	5	5	6	12	20	100
50	Ollie Matson	4	4	5	6	10	20	40	150
51	Jim Phillips	4	4	5	5	6	12	30	100
52	Del Shofner	4	4	5	5	6	12	25	
53	Art Hunter	4	4	5	5	6	12	25	
54	Gene Brito	4	4	5	5	6	12	25	
55	Lindon Crow	4	4	5	5	6	12	25	
56	Los Angeles Rams	4	4	5	5	6	12	20	100
57	Johnny Unitas IA	6	6	8	12	20	35	150	
58	Y.A. Tittle	5	6	8	12	18	30	80	250
59	John Brodie RC	6	8	10	15	25	40	80	350
60	J.D. Smith	4	4	5	5	6	12	25	

		GD 2	VG 3	VgEx 4	EX 5	ExMt 6	NM 7	NmMt 8	MT 9
61	R.C. Owens	4	4	5	5	6	12	20	100
62	Clyde Conner	4	4	5	5	6	12	25	
63	Bob St.Clair	4	4	5	5	8	12	25	
64	Leo Nomellini	4	4	5	6	10	20	50	
65	Abe Woodson	4	4	5	5	6	12	20	100
66	San Francisco 49ers	4	4	5	5	6	12	20	100
67	Checklist 1	4	5	6	10	15	40	80	
68	Milt Plum	4	4	5	5	6	12	20	100
69	Ray Renfro	4	4	5	5	6	12	30	120
70	Bobby Mitchell	4	5	6	8	15	30	80	200
71	Jim Brown	20	30	50	300	400	500	1,000	1,500
72	Mike McCormack	4	4	5	5	8	12	30	
73	Jim Ray Smith	4	4	5	5	6	12	25	
74	Sam Baker	4	4	5	5	6	12	25	
75	Walt Michaels	4	4	5	5	6	12	20	100
76	Cleveland Browns	4	4	5	5	6	15	25	100
77	Jim Brown IA	8	10	12	15	100	125	225	400
78	George Shaw	4	4	5	5	6	12	25	
79	Hugh McElhenny	4	4	5	6	10	20	40	200
80	Clancy Osborne	4	4	5	5	6	12	30	
81	Dave Middleton	4	4	5	5	6	12	30	
82	Frank Youso	4	4	5	6	12	15	50	
83	Don Joyce	4	4	5	5	6	12	30	
84	Ed Culpepper	4	4	5	5	6	12	30	
85	Charley Conerly	4	4	5	6	10	20	40	150
86	Mel Triplett	4	4	5	5	6	12	20	100
87	Kyle Rote	4	4	5	5	6	12	20	100
88	Roosevelt Brown	4	4	5	5	8	12	25	
89	Ray Wietecha	4	4	5	5	6	12	20	100
90	Andy Robustelli	4	4	5	5	8	15	50	
91	Sam Huff	4	4	5	6	10	20	30	125
92	Jim Patton	4	4	5	5	6	12	20	100
93	New York Giants	4	4	5	5	6	12	50	
94	Charley Conerly IA	4	4	5	6	10	20	50	
95	Sonny Jurgensen	4	5	6	10	15	25	100	250
96	Tommy McDonald	4	4	5	5	8	20	40	
97	Bill Barnes	4	4	5	5	6	12	20	100
98	Bobby Walston	4	4	5	5	6	12	25	
99	Pete Retzlaff	4	4	5	5	6	12	25	
100	Jim McCusker	4	4	5	5	6	12	25	
101	Chuck Bednarik	4	4	5	6	10	20	50	175
102	Tom Brookshier	4	4	5	5	6	12	20	100
103	Philadelphia Eagles	4	4	5	5	6	12	30	100
104	Bobby Layne	5	6	8	12	18	30	50	
105	John Henry Johnson	4	4	5	5	8	12	25	120
106	Tom Tracy	4	4	5	5	6	12	60	
107	Buddy Dial RC	4	4	5	5	6	12	25	
108	Jimmy Orr RC	4	4	5	6	10	20	50	120
109	Mike Sandusky	4	4	5	5	6	12	20	100
110	John Reger	4	4	5	5	6	12	20	100
111	Junior Wren	4	4	5	5	6	12	20	100
112	Pittsburgh Steelers	4	4	5	5	6	15	30	150
113	Bobby Layne IA	4	4	5	8	12	25	50	
114	John Roach	4	4	5	5	6	12	25	
115	Sam Etcheverry RC	4	4	5	5	6	12	20	100
116	John David Crow	4	4	5	5	6	12	25	
117	Mal Hammack	4	4	5	5	6	12	25	
118	Sonny Randle RC	4	4	5	5	6	12	80	
119	Leo Sugar	4	4	5	5	6	12	25	
120	Jerry Norton	4	4	5	5	6	12	20	100
121	St. Louis Cardinals	4	4	5	5	6	12	25	
122	Checklist 2	5	6	8	12	20	50	100	
123	Ralph Guglielmi	4	4	5	5	6	12	25	
124	Dick James	4	4	5	5	6	12	20	100
125	Don Bosseler	4	4	5	5	6	12	20	100
126	Joe Walton	4	4	5	5	6	12	20	100
127	Bill Anderson	4	4	5	5	6	12	20	100
128	Vince Promuto RC	4	4	5	5	6	12	50	
129	Bob Toneff	4	4	5	5	6	12	20	100
130	John Paluck	4	4	5	5	6	12	25	
131	Washington Redskins	4	4	5	5	6	12	60	
132	Milt Plum IA	4	4	5	5	6	12	30	
133	Abner Haynes	4	4	5	5	8	12	25	100
134	Mel Branch	4	4	5	5	6	12	20	80
135	Jerry Cornelison	4	4	5	5	6	12	20	80
136	Bill Krisher	4	4	5	5	6	12	20	80
137	Paul Miller	4	4	5	5	6	12	20	80
138	Jack Spikes	4	4	5	5	6	12	20	80
139	Johnny Robinson RC	4	4	5	5	8	12	25	100

		GD 2	VG 3	VgEx 4	EX 5	ExMt 6	NM 7	NmMt 8	MT 9
140	Cotton Davidson RC	4	4	5	5	6	12	20	80
141	Dave Smith RB	4	4	5	5	6	12	20	80
142	Bill Groman	4	4	5	5	6	12	20	80
143	Rich Michael	4	4	5	5	6	12	20	80
144	Mike Dukes	4	4	5	5	6	12	20	50
145	George Blanda	4	4	5	8	12	25	50	150
146	Billy Cannon	4	4	5	5	6	12	20	80
147	Dennit Morris	4	4	5	5	6	12	20	50
148	Jacky Lee	4	4	5	5	6	12	20	80
149	Al Dorow	4	4	5	5	6	12	20	80
150	Don Maynard RC	10	12	15	40	50	100	150	300
151	Art Powell RC	4	4	5	5	8	12	25	150
152	Sid Youngelman	4	4	5	5	6	12	20	80
153	Bob Mischak	4	4	5	5	6	12	20	80
154	Larry Grantham	4	4	5	5	6	12	20	80
155	Tom Saidock	4	4	5	5	6	12	20	80
156	Roger Donnahoo	4	4	5	5	6	12	20	
157	Laverne Torczon	4	4	5	5	6	12	20	
158	Archie Matsos RC	4	4	5	5	6	12	20	80
159	Elbert Dubenion	4	4	5	5	6	12	20	80
160	Wray Carlton RC	4	4	5	5	6	12	20	80
161	Rich McCabe	4	4	5	5	6	12	20	80
162	Ken Rice	4	4	5	5	6	12	20	80
163	Art Baker RC	4	4	5	5	6	12	20	80
164	Tom Rychlec	4	4	5	5	6	12	20	80
165	Mack Yoho	4	4	5	5	6	12	25	100
166	Jack Kemp	12	20	25	35	40	60	100	300
167	Paul Lowe	4	4	5	5	6	12	20	80
168	Ron Mix	4	4	5	6	10	15	30	
169	Paul Maguire	4	4	5	5	6	12	20	60
170	Volney Peters	4	4	5	5	6	12	20	
171	Ernie Wright RC	4	4	5	5	6	12	20	135
172	Ron Nery RC	4	4	5	5	6	12	20	100
173	Dave Kocourek RC	4	4	5	5	6	12	20	100
174	Jim Colclough	4	4	5	5	6	12	20	80
175	Babe Parilli	4	4	5	5	6	12	20	80
176	Billy Lott	4	4	5	5	6	12	20	
177	Fred Bruney	4	4	5	5	6	12	20	80
178	Ross O'Hanley	4	4	5	5	6	12	20	80
179	Walt Cudzik	4	4	5	5	6	10	20	80
180	Charley Leo	4	4	5	5	6	10	20	80
181	Bob Dee	4	4	5	5	6	10	20	80
182	Jim Otto RC	8	50	60	80	100	150	250	300
183	Eddie Macon	4	4	5	5	6	10	20	80
184	Dick Christy	4	4	5	5	6	10	20	80
185	Alan Miller RC	4	4	5	5	6	10	20	80
186	Tom Flores RC	5	6	8	10	20	30	50	200
187	Joe Cannavino	4	4	5	5	6	10	20	80
188	Don Manoukian	4	4	5	5	6	10	20	80
189	Bob Coolbaugh	4	4	5	5	6	10	20	
190	Lionel Taylor RC	4	4	5	5	8	12	30	
191	Bud McFadin	4	4	5	5	6	10	20	80
192	Goose Gonsoulin RC	4	4	5	5	6	10	20	100
193	Frank Tripucka	4	4	5	5	6	10	20	80
194	Gene Mingo RC	4	4	5	5	6	10	30	100
195	Eldon Danenhauer	4	4	5	5	6	10	20	80
196	Bob McNamara	4	4	5	5	6	10	20	80
197	Dave Rolle	4	4	5	5	6	12	20	80
198	Checklist 3	6	8	10	20	40	50	100	250

— Alan Ameche #2 PSA 9 (MT) sold for $610 (eBay; 2/07)
— Joe Cannavino #187 PSA 10 (Gem Mt) sold for $611 (Mile High; 3/09)
— Paul Hornung IA #38 PSA 9 (MT) sold for $770 (eBay; 4/07)
— Don Joyce #83 PSA 10 (Gem Mint) sold for $464 (eBay: 4/12)
— Jim Parker #6 PSA 9 (Mint) sold for $1,583.50 (eBay: 2/14)
— Vince Promuto #128 PSA 9 (Mint) sold for $725 (eBay: 11/14)

1962 Fleer

		GD 2	VG 3	VgEx 4	EX 5	ExMt 6	NM 7	NmMt 8	MT 9
1	Billy Lott	5	5	5	8	15	35	125	
2	Ron Burton	5	5	5	8	12	18	80	
3	Gino Cappelletti RC	5	5	5	10	15	20	60	
4	Babe Parilli	5	5	5	8	12	18	40	
5	Jim Colclough	5	5	5	6	10	15	40	
6	Tony Sardisco	5	5	5	6	10	15	40	
7	Walt Cudzik	5	5	5	6	10	15	40	
8	Bob Dee	5	5	5	6	10	15	40	
9	Tommy Addison RC	5	5	5	6	10	15	40	
10	Harry Jacobs	5	5	5	6	10	15	40	150

#	Player	GD 2	VG 3	VgEx 4	EX 5	ExMt 6	NM 7	NmMt 8	MT 9
11	Ross O'Hanley	5	5	5	6	10	15	40	
12	Art Baker	5	5	5	6	10	15	40	
13	Johnny Green	5	5	5	6	10	15	40	120
14	Elbert Dubenion	5	5	5	8	12	18	40	
15	Tom Rychlec	5	5	5	6	10	15	80	
16	Billy Shaw RC	15	20	25	60	200	250	500	
17	Ken Rice	5	5	5	6	10	15	40	
18	Bill Atkins	5	5	5	6	10	15	40	
19	Richie Lucas	5	5	5	6	10	15	40	150
20	Archie Matsos	5	5	5	6	10	15	40	
21	Laverne Torczon	5	5	5	6	10	15	40	
22	Warren Rabb RC UER	5	5	5	6	10	15	40	
23	Jack Spikes	5	5	5	6	10	15	40	
24	Cotton Davidson	5	5	5	6	10	15	40	
25	Abner Haynes	5	5	5	8	12	20	50	
26	Jimmy Saxton	5	5	5	6	10	15	40	
27	Chris Burford	5	5	5	6	10	15	40	
28	Bill Miller	5	5	5	6	10	15	40	
29	Sherrill Headrick	5	5	5	6	10	15	40	
30	E.J.Holub RC	5	5	5	6	10	15	40	
31	Jerry Mays RC	5	5	5	8	12	18	40	
32	Mel Branch	5	5	5	6	10	15	40	
33	Paul Rochester RC	5	5	5	6	10	15	40	
34	Frank Tripucka	5	5	5	8	12	18	50	250
35	Gene Mingo	5	5	5	6	10	15	40	
36	Lionel Taylor	5	5	5	8	12	20	50	200
37	Ken Adamson	5	5	5	6	10	15	40	125
38	Eldon Danenhauer	5	5	5	6	10	15	40	
39	Goose Gonsoulin	5	5	5	8	12	18	40	
40	Gordy Holz	5	5	5	6	10	15	40	100
41	Bud McFadin	5	5	5	6	10	15	40	150
42	Jim Stinnette	5	5	5	6	10	15	40	
43	Bob Hudson RC	5	5	5	6	10	15	40	
44	George Herring	5	5	5	6	10	15	40	
45	Charley Tolar RC	5	5	5	6	10	15	40	150
46	George Blanda	10	12	15	20	40	60	100	400
47	Billy Cannon	5	5	5	8	12	20	60	
48	Charlie Hennigan RC	5	5	5	8	12	20	60	
49	Bill Groman	5	5	5	6	10	15	40	
50	Al Jamison	5	5	5	6	10	15	40	
51	Tony Banfield	5	5	5	6	10	15	40	
52	Jim Norton	5	5	5	6	10	15	40	
53	Dennit Morris	5	5	5	6	10	15	40	120
54	Don Floyd	5	5	5	6	10	15	40	
55	Ed Husmann	5	5	5	6	10	15	40	
56	Robert Brooks	5	5	5	6	10	15	40	100
57	Al Dorow	5	5	5	6	10	15	40	
58	Dick Christy	5	5	5	6	10	15	40	
59	Don Maynard	10	12	15	20	30	50	80	500
60	Art Powell	5	5	5	8	12	18	40	
61	Mike Hudock	5	5	5	6	10	15	40	150
62	Bill Mathis	5	5	5	6	10	15	40	150
63	Butch Songin	5	5	5	6	10	15	40	
64	Larry Grantham	5	5	5	6	10	15	40	
65	Nick Mumley	5	5	5	6	10	15	40	
66	Tom Saidock	5	5	5	6	10	15	40	
67	Alan Miller	5	5	5	6	10	15	40	
68	Tom Flores	5	5	5	8	12	20	50	
69	Bob Coolbaugh	5	5	5	6	10	15	40	150
70	George Fleming	5	5	5	6	10	15	40	
71	Wayne Hawkins RC	5	5	5	6	10	25	40	
72	Jim Otto	6	8	10	15	25	40	120	
73	Wayne Crow	5	5	5	6	10	15	40	
74	Fred Williamson RC	5	6	8	20	60	100	150	
75	Tom Louderback	5	5	5	6	10	15	100	
76	Volney Peters	5	5	5	6	10	15	50	
77	Charley Powell	5	5	5	6	10	15	40	225
78	Don Norton	5	5	5	6	10	15	40	
79	Jack Kemp	15	20	30	40	60	60	125	600
80	Paul Lowe	5	5	5	8	12	18	40	
81	Dave Kocourek	5	5	5	6	10	15	40	
82	Ron Mix	5	5	5	8	12	20	50	400
83	Ernie Wright	5	5	5	8	12	20	40	
84	Dick Harris	5	5	5	6	10	15	40	
85	Bill Hudson	5	5	5	6	10	15	40	
86	Ernie Ladd RC	5	5	6	12	30	40	60	300
87	Earl Faison RC	5	5	6	10	20	60	100	
88	Ron Nery	5	5	5	6	15	30	100	

— Gordy Holz #40 PSA 10 (Gem) sold for $500 (eBay; 6/06)
— Bill Hudson #85 PSA 10 (Gem Mt) sold for $987 (Mile High, 10/09)
— Al Jamison #50 PSA 10 (Gem Mt) sold for $1,265 (eBay; 3/07)
— Ron Mix #82 PSA 9 (MT) sold for $1,275 (eBay; 2/07)
— Babe Parilli #4 PSA 10 (Gem Mt) sold for $1,053 (eBay; 11/12)
— Warren Rabb #22 PSA 10 (Gem Mt) sold for $987 (Mile High, 10/09)
— Billy Shaw #16 PSA 9 (MT) sold for $4275 (eBay; 11/07)
— Jack Spikes #23 PSA 10 (Gem) sold for $930 (eBay; 4/06)
— LaVerne Torczon #21 PSA 10 (Gem) sold for $905 (eBay; 1/06)

1962 Topps

#	Player	GD 2	VG 3	VgEx 4	EX 5	ExMt 6	NM 7	NmMt 8	MT 9
1	Johnny Unitas	30	80	100	150	250	600	8,000	
2	Lenny Moore	6	8	10	12	20	80	300	
3	Alex Hawkins SP RC	4	5	6	8	12	60	200	
4	Joe Perry	4	5	6	8	20	150	500	
5	Raymond Berry SP	10	12	15	20	30	50	200	
6	Steve Myhra	4	4	5	6	12	25	80	
7	Tom Gilburg SP	4	5	6	8	12	30	150	
8	Gino Marchetti	4	5	6	8	15	50	125	
9	Bill Pellington	4	4	5	6	12	40	125	
10	Andy Nelson	4	4	5	6	12	25	80	
11	Wendell Harris SP	4	5	6	8	12	30	135	
12	Baltimore Colts	4	4	5	6	12	30	100	
13	Bill Wade SP	4	5	6	8	12	30	135	
14	Willie Galimore	4	4	5	6	12	25	150	
15	Johnny Morris SP	4	5	6	8	12	30	100	
16	Rick Casares	4	4	5	6	12	40	100	
17	Mike Ditka RC	100	250	300	500	1,000	1,000	2,500	
18	Stan Jones	4	4	5	6	12	40	100	
19	Roger LeClerc	4	4	5	6	12	25	100	
20	Angelo Coia	4	4	5	6	12	25	100	
21	Doug Atkins	4	5	6	8	15	25	125	
22	Bill George	4	4	5	6	12	25	350	
23	Richie Petitbon RC	4	4	5	6	12	25	350	
24	Ronnie Bull SP RC	5	6	8	10	15	50	150	
25	Chicago Bears	4	4	5	6	12	25	100	
26	Howard Cassady	4	4	5	6	12	25	80	
27	Ray Renfro SP	4	5	6	8	12	30	175	
28	Jim Brown	40	125	150	250	800	1,000	5,000	
29	Rich Kreitling	4	4	5	6	12	25	135	
30	Jim Ray Smith	4	4	5	6	12	25	80	
31	John Morrow	4	4	5	6	12	25	150	
32	Lou Groza	5	6	8	10	25	30	150	
33	Bob Gain	4	4	5	6	12	25	150	
34	Bernie Parrish	4	4	5	6	12	30	100	
35	Jim Shofner	4	4	5	6	12	40	150	
36	Ernie Davis SP RC	30	150	200	250	400	800	1,000	
37	Cleveland Browns	4	4	5	6	12	35	150	
38	Eddie LeBaron	4	4	5	6	12	25	80	
39	Don Meredith SP	25	30	40	60	100	300	400	
40	J.W. Lockett SP	4	5	6	8	12	30	100	
41	Don Perkins RC	8	10	12	20	60	250	500	
42	Billy Howton	4	4	8	10	20	50	250	
43	Dick Bielski	4	4	5	6	15	25	80	
44	Mike Connelly RC	4	4	5	6	12	40	120	
45	Jerry Tubbs SP	4	5	6	8	12	50	120	
46	Don Bishop SP	4	5	6	10	15	40	200	
47	Dick Moegle	4	4	5	6	12	40	150	
48	Bobby Plummer SP	4	5	6	8	20	60	120	
49	Cowboys Team	6	8	10	12	40	50	150	
50	Milt Plum	4	4	5	6	12	25	80	
51	Dan Lewis	4	4	5	6	12	30	100	
52	Nick Pietrosante SP	4	5	6	8	12	30	125	
53	Gail Cogdill	4	4	5	6	12	25	80	
54	Jim Gibbons	4	4	5	6	12	25	100	
55	Jim Martin	4	4	5	6	12	40	100	
56	Yale Lary	4	4	5	6	12	40	100	
57	Darris McCord	4	4	5	6	12	25	80	
58	Alex Karras	6	8	10	12	20	40	120	
59	Joe Schmidt	4	5	6	8	15	40	100	
60	Dick Lane	4	4	5	6	12	40	120	
61	John Lomakoski SP	4	4	5	6	12	30	100	
62	Detroit Lions SP	6	8	10	12	18	30	125	
63	Bart Starr SP	20	25	35	50	200	400	600	
64	Paul Hornung SP	40	50	60	80	100	400	800	
65	Tom Moore SP	5	6	8	10	15	60	300	
66	Jim Taylor SP	12	15	20	40	60	80	250	

#	Player	GD 2	VG 3	VgEx 4	EX 5	ExMt 6	NM 7	NmMt 8	MT 9
67	Max McGee SP	5	6	8	10	20	50	120	
68	Jim Ringo SP	5	6	8	10	18	30	120	
69	Fuzzy Thurston SP RC	8	10	12	15	30	60	175	
70	Forrest Gregg	4	5	6	8	15	40	150	
71	Boyd Dowler	4	4	5	6	12	40	200	
72	Hank Jordan SP	6	8	10	12	20	60	120	
73	Bill Forester SP	4	5	6	8	12	30	120	
74	Earl Gros SP	4	5	6	8	12	100	150	
75	Packers Team SP	10	12	15	18	30	60	225	
76	Checklist SP	6	8	10	20	50	125	250	
77	Zeke Bratkowski SP	4	5	6	8	12	50	250	
78	Jon Arnett SP	4	5	6	8	12	30	100	
79	Ollie Matson SP	10	12	15	18	25	40	100	
80	Dick Bass SP	4	5	6	8	12	80	225	
81	Jim Phillips	4	4	5	6	12	30	80	
82	Carroll Dale RC	4	4	5	6	12	30	100	
83	Frank Varrichione	4	4	5	6	12	25	100	
84	Art Hunter	4	4	5	6	12	60	300	
85	Danny Villanueva RC	4	4	5	6	12	25	80	
86	Les Richter SP	4	5	6	8	12	30	100	
87	Lindon Crow	4	4	5	6	12	25	80	
88	Roman Gabriel SP RC	12	15	20	40	60	120	250	
89	Los Angeles Rams SP	6	8	10	12	18	40	150	
90	Fran Tarkenton SP RC	100	125	200	250	500	1,200	4,000	
91	Jerry Reichow SP	4	5	6	8	12	30	100	
92	Hugh McElhenny SP	8	10	12	15	25	80	200	
93	Mel Triplett SP	4	5	6	8	12	40	150	
94	Tommy Mason SP RC	5	6	8	12	30	150	350	
95	Dave Middleton SP	4	5	6	8	12	60	120	
96	Frank Youso SP	4	5	6	8	12	30	100	
97	Mike Mercer SP	4	5	6	8	12	60	400	
98	Rip Hawkins SP	4	5	6	8	15	100	400	
99	Cliff Livingston SP	4	5	6	8	12	30	120	
100	Roy Winston SP RC	4	5	6	8	12	40	125	
101	Vikings Team SP	8	10	12	15	20	80	150	
102	Y.A.Tittle	10	12	15	20	30	60	150	
103	Joe Walton	4	4	5	6	12	40	100	
104	Frank Gifford	12	15	20	40	50	80	200	
105	Alex Webster	4	4	5	6	12	25	100	
106	Del Shofner	4	4	5	6	12	40	150	
107	Don Chandler	4	4	5	6	12	25	80	
108	Andy Robustelli	4	5	6	8	15	25	100	
109	Jim Katcavage RC	4	4	5	6	12	25	80	
110	Sam Huff SP	10	12	15	18	25	80	300	
111	Erich Barnes	4	4	5	6	12	25	100	
112	Jim Patton	4	4	5	6	12	30	125	
113	Jerry Hillebrand SP	4	5	6	8	12	40	100	
114	New York Giants	4	4	5	6	12	25	80	
115	Sonny Jurgensen	10	12	15	18	30	50	175	
116	Tommy McDonald	4	5	6	8	15	25	80	
117	Ted Dean SP	4	5	6	12	25	40	250	
118	Clarence Peaks	4	4	5	6	12	25	80	
119	Bobby Walston	4	4	5	6	12	25	125	
120	Pete Retzlaff SP	4	5	6	8	12	30	80	
121	Jim Schrader SP	4	5	6	8	12	30	200	
122	J.D. Smith T	4	4	5	6	12	25	125	
123	King Hill	4	4	5	6	12	30	80	
124	Maxie Baughan	4	4	5	6	12	25	80	
125	Pete Case SP	4	5	6	8	12	30	100	
126	Philadelphia Eagles	4	4	5	6	12	25	100	
127	Bobby Layne	10	12	15	18	30	40	150	
128	Tom Tracy	4	4	5	6	12	40	100	
129	John Henry Johnson	4	4	5	6	12	30	80	
130	Buddy Dial SP	4	5	6	8	12	35	120	
131	Preston Carpenter	4	4	5	6	20	40	225	
132	Lou Michaels SP	4	5	6	8	12	30	100	
133	Gene Lipscomb SP	5	6	8	10	20	80	150	
134	Ernie Stautner SP	6	8	10	12	25	80	150	
135	John Reger SP	4	5	6	8	12	30	100	
136	Myron Pottios RC	4	4	5	6	12	40	300	
137	Bob Ferguson SP	4	5	6	8	12	40	150	
138	Pittsburgh Steelers SP	6	8	10	12	20	50	150	
139	Sam Etcheverry SP	4	4	5	6	12	25	80	
140	John David Crow SP	4	5	6	8	15	30	175	
141	Bobby Joe Conrad SP	4	5	6	8	12	30	100	
142	Prentice Gautt SP RC	4	5	6	8	12	80	250	
143	Frank Mestnik SP	4	4	5	6	12	25	80	
144	Sonny Randle	4	4	5	6	12	25	100	
145	Gerry Perry	4	4	5	6	12	25	150	
146	Jerry Norton	4	4	5	6	12	25	80	
147	Jimmy Hill	4	4	5	6	12	35	175	
148	Bill Stacy	4	4	5	6	12	25	80	
149	Fate Echols SP	4	5	6	8	12	30	100	
150	St. Louis Cardinals	4	4	5	6	12	25	120	
151	Billy Kilmer RC	10	12	15	20	35	60	150	
152	John Brodie	6	8	10	12	20	40	350	
153	J.D. Smith RB	4	4	5	6	12	30	120	
154	C.R. Roberts SP	4	5	6	8	12	40	60	
155	Monty Stickles	4	4	5	6	12	30	80	
156	Clyde Conner	4	4	5	6	12	30	80	
157	Bob St.Clair	4	4	5	6	12	30	80	
158	Tommy Davis RC	4	4	5	6	12	40	80	
159	Leo Nomellini	4	5	6	8	15	40	80	
160	Matt Hazeltine	4	4	5	6	20	25	120	
161	Abe Woodson	4	4	5	6	12	25	80	
162	Dave Baker	4	4	5	6	12	30	100	
163	San Francisco 49ers	4	4	5	6	12	30	200	
164	Norm Snead SP RC	10	12	15	20	30	150	350	
165	Dick James	4	4	5	6	12	80	200	
166	Bobby Mitchell	4	5	6	8	15	40	200	
167	Sam Horner	4	4	5	6	12	25	80	
168	Bill Barnes	4	4	5	6	12	25	80	
169	Bill Anderson	4	4	5	6	12	25	100	
170	Fred Dugan	4	4	5	6	12	25	80	
171	John Aveni SP	4	5	6	8	12	30	100	
172	Bob Toneff	4	4	5	6	12	50	250	
173	Jim Kerr	4	4	5	6	12	100	300	
174	Leroy Jackson SP	4	5	6	8	12	40	150	
175	Washington Redskins	4	4	5	8	15	50	200	
176	Checklist	15	20	40	50	60	125	800	

— Raymond Berry SP #5 PSA 9 (Mint) sold for $2384.76 (Goodwin; 8/12)
— Dick Bielski #43 PSA 9 (eBay) sold for $957.5 (eBay; 7/12)
— Jim Brown #28 PSA 9 (MT) sold for $10,540 (Mastro; 12/06)
— Jim Brown #28 PSA 8.5 (NmMt+) sold for $2,714 (Mile High; 3/09)
— Ronnie Bull #24 PSA 9 (Mt) sold for $1185 (eBay; 11/14)
— Mike Ditka #17 PSA 9 (Mt) sold for $9,132 (eBay; 02/13)
— Bill Forester #73 PSA 9 (MT) sold for $615 (eBay; 1/07)
— Rip Hawkins #98 PSA 9 (MT) sold for $1,459 (Goodwin; 11/09)
— Matt Hazeltine #160 PSA 9 (MT) sold for $1,631 (eBay; 2/14)
— Jim Kerr #173 PSA 9 (Mint) sold for $813.49 (eBay; 8/12)
— Dick Lane #60 PSA 9 (MT) sold for $925 (eBay; 4/07)
— Max Mcgee #67 PSA 9 (MT) sold for $1,240 (eBay; 2/13)
— Hugh McElhenny #92 PSA 9 (MT) sold for $715 (eBay; 9/05)
— Lenny Moore #1 PSA 9 (MT) sold for $635 (eBay; 6/06)
— Johnny Morris #15 PSA 9 (MT) sold for $390 (eBay; 9/05)
— Bernie Parrish #34 PSA 9 (MT) sold for $510 (eBay; 1/06)
— Don Perkins RC #41 PSA 9 (Mint) sold for $890.5 (eBay; 6/12)

1963 Fleer

#	Player	GD 2	VG 3	VgEx 4	EX 5	ExMt 6	NM 7	NmMt 8	MT 9
1	Larry Garron RC	4	5	6	20	25	▲50	400	
2	Babe Parilli	4	5	5	6	10	20	80	
3	Ron Burton	4	5	5	8	12	20	60	
4	Jim Colclough	4	5	5	6	10	15	150	
5	Gino Cappelletti	4	5	5	8	12	20	60	150
6	Charles Long SP RC	25	35	40	50	60	60	80	450
7	Billy Neighbors RC	4	5	5	6	10	20	50	
8	Dick Felt	4	5	5	6	10	15	30	120
9	Tommy Addison	4	5	5	6	10	15	40	
10	Nick Buoniconti RC	12	20	25	35	200	250	400	1,200
11	Larry Eisenhauer RC	4	5	5	6	10	20	35	200
12	Bill Mathis	4	5	5	6	10	15	40	
13	Lee Grosscup RC	4	5	5	6	10	15	30	120
14	Dick Christy	4	5	5	6	10	15	30	150
15	Don Maynard	6	10	12	18	30	▼60	100	250
16	Alex Kroll RC	4	5	5	6	10	15	30	150
17	Bob Mischak	4	5	5	6	10	15	30	100
18	Dainard Paulson	4	5	5	6	10	15	40	
19	Lee Riley	4	5	5	6	10	15	30	100
20	Larry Grantham	4	5	5	6	10	15	25	150
21	Hubert Bobo	4	5	5	6	10	15	30	150
22	Nick Mumley	4	5	5	6	10	15	30	150
23	Cookie Gilchrist RC	10	12	15	30	40	60	200	300
24	Jack Kemp	15	25	30	50	60	80	125	350
25	Wray Carlton	4	5	5	6	10	15	40	100
26	Elbert Dubenion	4	5	5	6	10	15	60	
27	Ernie Warlick RC	4	5	5	6	10	15	30	▲200

#	Player	GD 2	VG 3	VgEx 4	EX 5	ExMt 6	NM 7	NmMt 8	MT 9
28	Billy Shaw	4	5	6	10	15	25	50	150
29	Ken Rice	4	5	5	6	10	15	30	100
30	Booker Edgerson	4	5	5	6	10	15	30	150
31	Ray Abruzzese	4	5	5	6	10	15	30	120
32	Mike Stratton RC	4	5	6	10	15	30	60	150
33	Tom Sestak RC	4	5	5	6	10	20	50	
34	Charley Tolar	4	5	5	6	10	15	40	
35	Dave Smith RB	4	5	5	6	10	15	40	
36	George Blanda	10	12	15	20	35	50	100	350
37	Billy Cannon	4	5	6	10	15	25	40	300
38	Charlie Hennigan	4	5	5	6	10	15	30	150
39	Bob Talamini RC	4	5	5	6	10	15	30	100
40	Jim Norton	4	5	5	6	10	15	25	120
41	Tony Banfield	4	5	5	6	10	15	50	100
42	Doug Cline	4	5	5	6	10	15	40	
43	Don Floyd	4	5	5	6	10	15	40	150
44	Ed Husmann	4	5	5	6	10	15	40	
45	Curtis McClinton RC	4	5	6	10	15	25	40	200
46	Jack Spikes	4	5	5	6	10	15	30	150
47	Len Dawson RC	50	500	600	800	1,000	1,200	1,600	2,000
48	Abner Haynes	4	5	6	10	15	25	40	200
49	Chris Burford	4	5	5	6	10	15	30	120
50	Fred Arbanas RC	4	5	5	8	12	20	40	150
51	Johnny Robinson	4	5	5	6	10	15	40	100
52	E.J. Holub	4	5	5	6	10	15	120	150
53	Sherrill Headrick	4	5	5	6.	10	15	30	100
54	Mel Branch	4	5	5	6	10	15	30	120
55	Jerry Mays	4	5	5	6	10	15	30	150
56	Cotton Davidson	4	5	5	6	10	15	40	100
57	Clem Daniels RC	4	5	6	10	20	30	50	
58	Bo Roberson RC	4	5	5	6	10	15	40	200
59	Art Powell	4	5	5	8	12	20	30	150
60	Bob Coolbaugh	4	5	5	6	10	15	40	100
61	Wayne Hawkins	4	5	5	6	10	20	40	100
62	Jim Otto	4	6	8	12	18	30	80	
63	Fred Williamson	4	5	6	10	15	25	80	
64	Bob Dougherty SP	20	30	35	60	80	100	150	300
65	Dalva Allen	4	5	5	6	10	15	30	80
66	Chuck McMurtry	4	5	5	6	10	15	60	
67	Gerry McDougall RC	4	5	5	6	10	15	30	120
68	Tobin Rote	4	5	5	6	10	20	40	120
69	Paul Lowe	4	5	5	8	12	20	50	200
70	Keith Lincoln RC	5	8	10	15	25	40	80	250
71	Dave Kocourek	4	5	5	6	10	18	40	150
72	Lance Alworth RC	50	80	100	500	600	1,200	1,500	2,200
73	Ron Mix	4	5	6	10	15	25	100	300
74	Charley McNeil RC	4	5	5	6	10	15	30	150
75	Emil Karas	4	5	5	6	10	15	40	80
76	Ernie Ladd	4	5	6	10	15	25	40	120
77	Earl Faison	4	5	5	6	10	15	30	80
78	Jim Stinnette	4	5	5	6	10	15	30	150
79	Frank Tripucka	4	5	5	8	12	20	35	150
80	Don Stone	4	5	5	6	10	15	30	100
81	Bob Scarpitto	4	5	5	6	10	15	40	
82	Lionel Taylor	4	5	5	8	12	20	40	150
83	Jerry Tarr	4	5	5	6	10	15	30	100
84	Eldon Danenhauer	4	5	5	6	10	15	25	150
85	Goose Gonsoulin	4	5	5	6	10	15	25	100
86	Jim Fraser	4	5	5	6	10	15	30	80
87	Chuck Gavin	4	5	5	6	10	15	30	100
88	Bud McFadin	4	5	6	10	15	25	80	
NNO	Checklist SP	60	100	150	200	250	400	1,200	

— Checklist SP #NNO PSA 9 (Mint) sold for $2,747 (Mile High; 10/09)
— Checklist SP #NNO PSA 9 (Mint) sold for $2,182 (Goodwin; 2/11)
— Earl Faison #77 PSA 10 (Gem Mt) sold for $561 (eBay; 11/14)
— Larry Garron #1 PSA 9 (Mint) sold for $1042.03 (eBay; 8/12)
— Ron Mix #73 PSA 10 (Gem Mt) sold for $1,618 (eBay; 6/07)
— Ron Mix #73 PSA 10 (Gem Mt) sold for $1,010 (eBay; 1/06)

1963 Topps

#	Player	GD 2	VG 3	VgEx 4	EX 5	ExMt 6	NM 7	NmMt 8	MT 9
1	Johnny Unitas	20	25	35	60	100	300	1,500	
2	Lenny Moore	4	5	6	10	15	30	100	
3	Jimmy Orr	4	5	5	6	10	40	80	
4	Raymond Berry	4	5	6	10	15	40	60	
5	Jim Parker	4	5	5	8	12	30	50	
6	Alex Sandusky	4	5	5	6	10	15	40	
7	Dick Szymanski RC	4	5	5	6	10	15	40	

#	Player	GD 2	VG 3	VgEx 4	EX 5	ExMt 6	NM 7	NmMt 8	MT 9
8	Gino Marchetti	4	5	5	8	12	20	40	
9	Billy Ray Smith RC	4	5	5	6	10	15	40	
10	Bill Pellington	4	5	5	6	10	30	60	
11	Bob Boyd DB RC	4	5	5	6	10	40	80	
12	Baltimore Colts SP	4	5	5	8	12	40	100	
13	Frank Ryan SP	4	5	5	6	10	60	100	
14	Jim Brown SP	30	40	▲150	200	250	300	800	6,000
15	Ray Renfro SP	4	5	5	8	10	20	40	
16	Rich Kreitling SP	4	5	5	6	10	15	40	
17	Mike McCormack SP	4	5	5	8	12	40	60	
18	Jim Ray Smith SP	4	5	5	8	10	15	40	
19	Lou Groza SP	4	5	6	10	15	25	120	
20	Bill Glass SP	4	5	5	6	10	15	40	
21	Galen Fiss SP	4	5	5	8	10	40	80	
22	Don Fleming SP RC	4	5	5	8	10	40	150	
23	Bob Gain SP	4	5	5	8	10	40	100	
24	Cleveland Browns SP	4	5	5	8	12	50	200	
25	Milt Plum	4	5	5	6	10	30	80	
26	Dan Lewis	4	5	5	6	10	15	40	
27	Nick Pietrosante	4	5	5	6	10	15	50	
28	Gail Cogdill	4	5	5	6	10	15	40	
29	Harley Sewell	4	5	5	6	10	15	40	
30	Jim Gibbons	4	5	5	6	10	15	40	
31	Carl Brettschneider	4	5	5	6	10	15	40	
32	Dick Lane	4	5	5	8	12	20	40	
33	Yale Lary	4	5	5	8	12	20	40	
34	Roger Brown RC	4	5	5	6	10	15	40	
35	Joe Schmidt	4	5	5	8	12	40	80	
36	Detroit Lions SP	4	5	5	6	10	20	40	
37	Roman Gabriel	4	5	6	8	12	30	100	
38	Zeke Bratkowski	4	5	5	6	10	15	30	
39	Dick Bass	4	5	5	6	10	15	40	
40	Jon Arnett	4	5	5	6	10	15	40	300
41	Jim Phillips	4	5	5	6	10	15	30	
42	Frank Varrichione	4	5	5	6	10	15	40	
43	Danny Villanueva	4	5	5	6	10	15	40	
44	Deacon Jones RC	8	12	20	30	40	125	1,000	1,500
45	Lindon Crow	4	5	5	6	10	15	40	
46	Marlin McKeever	4	5	5	6	10	15	30	
47	Ed Meador RC	4	5	5	6	10	40	80	
48	Los Angeles Rams	4	5	5	6	10	15	40	
49	Y.A. Tittle SP	6	10	12	40	50	60	175	
50	Del Shofner SP	4	5	5	8	10	15	80	
51	Alex Webster SP	4	5	5	8	10	20	40	
52	Phil King SP	4	5	5	8	10	15	40	
53	Jack Stroud SP	4	5	5	6	10	40	50	
54	Darrell Dess SP	4	5	5	8	10	15	20	
55	Jim Katcavage SP	4	5	5	8	10	15	40	
56	Roosevelt Grier SP	4	5	5	8	12	20	125	250
57	Erich Barnes SP	4	5	5	8	10	15	40	
58	Jim Patton SP	4	5	5	8	10	15	30	150
59	Sam Huff SP	4	5	6	10	15	30	120	
60	New York Giants	4	5	5	6	10	15	40	
61	Bill Wade	4	5	5	6	10	40	100	
62	Mike Ditka	10	15	20	30	60	80	400	1,000
63	Johnny Morris	4	5	5	6	10	15	40	
64	Roger LeClerc	4	5	5	6	10	15	40	
65	Roger Davis RC	4	5	5	6	10	15	40	
66	Joe Marconi	4	5	5	6	10	15	40	
67	Herman Lee	4	5	5	6	10	15	40	
68	Doug Atkins	4	5	5	8	12	20	40	
69	Joe Fortunato	4	5	5	6	10	15	40	
70	Bill George	4	5	5	8	12	20	40	
71	Richie Petitbon	4	5	5	6	10	40	80	
72	Bears Team SP	4	5	5	20	25	40	80	
73	Eddie LeBaron SP	4	5	5	8	12	40	80	
74	Don Meredith SP	8	12	15	25	35	75	200	
75	Don Perkins SP	4	5	5	8	12	20	80	
76	Amos Marsh SP	4	5	5	6	10	15	40	
77	Billy Howton SP	4	5	5	6	10	15	150	
78	Andy Cvercko SP	4	5	5	6	10	15	50	
79	Sam Baker SP	4	5	5	6	10	15	40	
80	Jerry Tubbs SP	4	5	5	6	10	20	40	
81	Don Bishop SP	4	5	5	8	10	15	50	
82	Bob Lilly SP RC	35	80	▲125	150	400	800	1,000	
83	Jerry Norton SP	4	5	5	6	10	40	120	
84	Cowboys Team SP	4	5	6	10	15	30	80	350
85	Checklist 1	4	5	5	6	10	15	30	80
86	Bart Starr	10	15	20	35	60	150	800	

		GD 2	VG 3	VgEx 4	EX 5	ExMt 6	NM 7	NmMt 8	MT 9
87	Jim Taylor	5	6	8	12	40	60	100	
88	Boyd Dowler	4	5	5	8	12	25	60	
89	Forrest Gregg	4	5	5	8	12	25	60	400
90	Fuzzy Thurston	4	5	6	12	20	30	60	
91	Jim Ringo	4	5	5	8	12	20	50	
92	Ron Kramer	4	5	5	6	10	15	40	
93	Hank Jordan	4	5	5	8	12	20	50	
94	Bill Forester	4	5	5	6	10	15	40	
95	Willie Wood RC	6	10	12	20	60	80	150	1,000
96	Ray Nitschke RC	20	25	40	60	125	250	800	4,200
97	Green Bay Packers	4	5	6	10	20	30	100	
98	Fran Tarkenton	8	12	15	25	60	80	200	
99	Tommy Mason	4	5	5	6	10	15	40	
100	Mel Triplett	4	5	5	6	10	15	40	
101	Jerry Reichow	4	5	5	6	10	15	40	
102	Frank Youso	4	5	5	6	10	15	40	
103	Hugh McElhenny	4	5	6	8	12	20	50	
104	Gerald Huth	4	5	5	6	10	15	40	
105	Ed Sharockman	4	5	5	6	10	15	40	
106	Rip Hawkins	4	5	5	6	10	15	40	
107	Jim Marshall RC	5	8	15	20	25	50	100	
108	Jim Prestel	4	5	5	6	10	15	40	
109	Minnesota Vikings	4	5	5	6	10	15	40	
110	Sonny Jurgensen SP	5	8	10	15	25	50	200	
111	Timmy Brown SP RC	4	5	5	8	12	25	100	
112	Tommy McDonald SP	4	5	6	10	25	40	175	
113	Clarence Peaks SP	4	5	5	8	10	15	40	
114	Pete Retzlaff SP	4	5	5	8	10	15	40	
115	Jim Schrader SP	4	5	5	8	10	15	40	
116	Jim McCusker SP	4	5	5	8	10	15	40	
117	Don Burroughs SP	4	5	5	8	10	15	40	
118	Maxie Baughan SP	4	5	5	8	10	20	40	
119	Riley Gunnels SP	4	5	5	8	10	15	40	
120	Jimmy Carr SP	4	5	5	8	10	40	135	
121	Philadelphia Eagles SP	4	5	5	8	12	20	150	
122	Ed Brown SP	4	5	5	8	12	60		
123	John H.Johnson SP	4	5	6	10	15	80	150	
124	Buddy Dial SP	4	5	5	8	10	40	120	
125	Bill Red Mack SP	4	5	5	8	10	15	50	
126	Preston Carpenter SP	4	5	5	8	10	40	100	
127	Ray Lemek SP	4	5	5	8	10	20	40	
128	Buzz Nutter SP	4	5	5	8	10	40	150	
129	Ernie Stautner SP	4	5	6	10	15	50	80	
130	Lou Michaels SP	4	5	5	8	10	40	135	
131	Clendon Thomas SP RC	4	5	5	8	10	20	50	
132	Tom Bettis SP	4	5	5	8	10	40	135	
133	Pittsburgh Steelers SP	4	5	5	8	12	40	100	
134	John Brodie	4	5	6	8	12	40	135	
135	J.D. Smith	4	5	5	6	10	15	30	
136	Billy Kilmer	4	5	5	8	12	20	40	
137	Bernie Casey RC	4	5	5	6	10	15	40	
138	Tommy Davis	4	5	5	6	10	15	40	
139	Ted Connolly	4	5	5	6	10	15	30	
140	Bob St.Clair	4	5	5	8	12	20	40	
141	Abe Woodson	4	5	5	6	10	15	30	100
142	Matt Hazeltine	4	5	5	6	10	15	40	
143	Leo Nomellini	4	5	5	8	12	20	40	350
144	Dan Colchico	4	5	5	6	10	15	40	
145	San Francisco 49ers SP	4	5	5	8	12	30		
146	Charlie Johnson RC	4	5	6	8	12	20	40	
147	John David Crow	4	5	5	6	10	15	40	400
148	Bobby Joe Conrad	4	5	5	6	10	15	40	
149	Sonny Randle	4	5	5	6	10	15	25	100
150	Prentice Gautt	4	5	5	6	10	15	40	
151	Taz Anderson	4	5	5	6	10	15	30	100
152	Ernie McMillan RC	4	5	5	6	10	15	40	
153	Jimmy Hill	4	5	5	6	10	15	40	150
154	Bill Koman	4	5	5	6	10	15	40	100
155	Larry Wilson RC	4	5	8	12	80	100		
156	Don Owens	4	5	5	6	10	15	40	
157	St. Louis Cardinals SP	4	5	5	8	12	20	50	
158	Norm Snead SP	4	5	5	8	12	20	100	
159	Bobby Mitchell SP	4	5	6	10	15	60	80	
160	Bill Barnes SP	4	5	5	8	10	15	40	
161	Fred Dugan SP	4	5	5	8	10	15	40	
162	Don Bosseler SP	4	5	5	8	10	15	40	300
163	John Nisby SP	4	5	5	8	10	15	40	
164	Riley Mattson SP	4	5	5	8	10	40	100	
165	Bob Toneff SP	4	5	5	8	10	40	100	

		GD 2	VG 3	VgEx 4	EX 5	ExMt 6	NM 7	NmMt 8	MT 9
166	Rod Breedlove SP	4	5	5	8	10	40	150	
167	Dick James SP	4	5	5	8	10	40	100	
168	Claude Crabb SP	4	5	5	8	10	50	250	
169	Washington Redskins SP	4	5	5	8	12	40	200	
170	Checklist 2 UER	6	10	12	20	30	50	80	

— Raymond Berry #4 PSA 10 (Gem Mint) sold for $3,235 (eBay:11/13)
— John Brodie #134 PSA 9 (Mint) sold for $1117.89 (eBay: 7/12)
— Mike Ditka #62 PSA 9 (MT) sold for $2,247 (eBay; 12/07)
— Mike Ditka #62 SGC 9 (MT) sold for $1,095 (eBay; 10/09)
— Mike Ditka #62 PSA 9 (Mile High) sold for $995 (eBay; 10/09)
— Mike Ditka #62 PSA 9 (MT) sold for $1,503 (eBay; 60/16)
— Boyd Dowler #88 PSA 9 (Mint) sold for $865.49 (eBay: 4/12)
— Forrest Gregg #89 PSA 9 (Mint) sold for $570 (eBay; 2/07)
— Rosey Grier #56 PSA 10 (Gem Mt) sold for $1,194 (Mile High; 10/09)
— Sam Huff #59 PSA 9 (Mint) sold for $1,580 (eBay; 4/12)
— Sam Huff SP #59 PSA 9 (Mint) sold for $1580.49 (eBay; 4/12)
— Deacon Jones #44 PSA 9 (MT) sold for $2869 (Mile High; 6/10)
— Deacon Jones #44 PSA 9 (MT) sold for $2,505 (eBay; 4/08)
— Deacon Jones #44 PSA 9 (MT) sold for $2,250 (eBay; 10/11)
— Deacon Jones #44 PSA 9 (MT) sold for $1415 (eBay; 11/14)
— Deacon Jones #44 PSA 9 (MT) sold for $1,312 (eBay; 10/12)
— Deacon Jones #44 PSA 9 (MT) sold for $968 (eBay; 12/12)
— Deacon Jones #44 PSA 9 (MT) sold for $1,216 (eBay; 3/14)
— Sonny Jurgensen #110 PSA 9 (MT) sold for $1,085 (Mastro; 10/06)
— Rich Kreitling #16 PSA 10 (Gem Mint) sold for $1,789 (Memory Lane; Winter 2013)
— Dick Lane #32 PSA 9 (MT) sold for $1230 (eBay; 6/13)
— Dan Lewis #26 PSA 10 (Gem Mt) sold for $1,108 (Mastro; 6/07)
— Bob Lilly #26 PSA 9 (Mt) sold for $7050 (eBay; 11/14)
— Bob Lilly #26 PSA 8.5 (NmMt+) sold for $1,095 (Mile High; 10/09)
— Gino Marchetti #8 PSA 9 (Mint) sold for $1528 (eBay; 11/14)
— Gino Marchetti #8 PSA 9 (Mint) sold for $590.77 (eBay; 7/12)
— Jim Marshall RC #107 PSA 9 (Mint) sold for $767 (eBay; 11/13)
— Riley Mattson SP #164 PSA 9 (Mint) sold for $613.49 (eBay: 7/12)
— Mike McCormack SP #17 PSA 9 (Mint) sold for $901.5 (eBay; 4/12)
— Marlin McKeever #46 PSA 10 (Gem Mint) sold for $1681.5 (eBay; 4/12)
— Minnesota Vikings #109 PSA 9 (Mint) sold for $630 (Bussineau; 4/12)
— Lenny Moore #2 PSA 9 (Mint) sold for $2998 (eBay; 6/13)
— Jim Parker #5 PSA 10 (GemMt) sold for $1033 (eBay; 11/14)
— Jim Ray Smith SP #18 PSA 9 (Mint) sold for $913.5 (eBay; 5/12)
— Ernie Stautner #129 PSA 9 (MT) sold for $1,013 (eBay; 2/10)
— Bart Starr #86 PSA 9 (MT) sold for $1,578 (Mile High; 1/07)
— Fran Tarkenton #98 PSA 9 (Mint) sold for $3750 (Bussineau; 4/12)
— Fuzzy Thurston #90 PSA 9 (Mint) sold for $703.89 (eBay; 6/12)
— Johnny Unitas #1 PSA 9 (MT) sold for $4,340 (Mastro; 4/07)
— Washington Redskins SP #169 PSA 9 (Mint) sold for $902.49 (eBay: 8/12)
— Larry Wilson #551 PSA 9 (MT) sold for $995 (eBay; 5/11)
— Willie Wood #95 PSA 9 (MT) sold for $903 (eBay; 2/10)
— Willie Wood #95 PSA 9 (MT) sold for $961.5 (eBay; 4/12)

1964 Philadelphia

		GD 2	VG 3	VgEx 4	EX 5	ExMt 6	NM 7	NmMt 8	MT 9
1	Raymond Berry	4	5	5	8	12	20	50	100
2	Tom Gilburg	4	5	5	5	8	20	50	
3	John Mackey RC	4	5	6	10	40	80	200	1,000
4	Gino Marchetti	4	5	5	8	12	18	40	125
5	Jim Martin	4	5	5	5	8	12	20	120
6	Tom Matte RC	4	5	5	6	10	15	40	120
7	Jimmy Orr	4	5	5	5	8	12	20	80
8	Jim Parker	4	5	5	6	10	15	25	80
9	Bill Pellington	4	5	5	5	8	12	20	80
10	Alex Sandusky	4	5	5	5	8	12	20	80
11	Dick Szymanski	4	5	5	5	8	12	20	80
12	Johnny Unitas	5	10	15	40	50	100	125	500
13	Baltimore Colts Team	4	5	5	5	8	20	60	
14	Colts Play/Don Shula	4	6	8	12	20	35	50	80
15	Doug Atkins	4	5	5	8	12	18	30	100
16	Ronnie Bull	4	5	5	5	8	20	50	100
17	Mike Ditka	4	6	8	20	30	40	150	400
18	Joe Fortunato	4	5	5	5	8	12	20	60
19	Willie Galimore	4	5	5	5	8	12	20	80
20	Joe Marconi	4	5	5	5	8	12	20	80
21	Bennie McRae RC	4	5	5	5	8	12	20	50
22	Johnny Morris	4	5	5	5	8	12	20	80
23	Richie Petitbon	4	5	5	5	8	12	30	80
24	Mike Pyle	4	5	5	5	8	12	20	80
25	Roosevelt Taylor RC	4	5	5	5	8	12	20	80
26	Bill Wade	4	5	5	5	8	12	20	80
27	Chicago Bears Team	4	5	5	5	8	12	20	80

#	Name	GD 2	VG 3	VgEx 4	EX 5	ExMt 6	NM 7	NmMt 8	MT 9
28	Bears Play/George Halas	4	5	5	8	12	18	30	100
29	Johnny Brewer	4	5	5	5	8	12	20	80
30	Jim Brown	15	30	50	60	200	250	500	2,000
31	Gary Collins RC	4	5	5	5	8	20	50	
32	Vince Costello	4	5	5	5	8	12	20	60
33	Galen Fiss	4	5	5	5	8	12	40	80
34	Bill Glass	4	5	5	5	8	12	20	60
35	Ernie Green RC	4	5	5	5	8	15	150	250
36	Rich Kreitling	4	5	5	5	8	12	20	
37	John Morrow	4	5	5	5	8	12	20	100
38	Frank Ryan	4	5	5	5	8	12	20	·80
39	Charlie Scales RC	4	5	5	5	8	12	20	80
40	Dick Schafrath RC	4	5	5	5	8	12	40	80
41	Cleveland Browns Team	4	5	5	5	8	12	30	100
42	Cleveland Browns Play	4	5	5	5	8	12	20	80
43	Don Bishop	4	5	5	5	8	12	20	80
44	Frank Clarke RC	4	5	5	5	8	12	20	80
45	Mike Connelly	4	5	5	5	8	12	20	80
46	Lee Folkins	4	5	5	5	8	12	20	80
47	Cornell Green RC	4	5	5	5	8	12	40	150
48	Bob Lilly	4	6	8	12	20	80	100	400
49	Amos Marsh	4	5	5	5	8	12	30	
50	Tommy McDonald	4	5	5	8	12	18	30	400
51	Don Meredith	6	8	10	15	25	50	150	500
52	Pettis Norman RC	4	5	5	5	8	12	25	200
53	Don Perkins	4	5	5	6	10	15	25	120
54	Guy Reese	4	5	5	5	8	12	25	80
55	Dallas Cowboys Team	4	5	5	5	8	12	50	
56	Cowboys Play/Landry	4	5	5	8	12	20	30	150
57	Terry Barr	4	5	5	5	8	12	20	80
58	Roger Brown	4	5	5	5	8	12	20	60
59	Gail Cogdill	4	5	5	5	8	12	20	80
60	John Gordy	4	5	5	5	8	12	20	60
61	Dick Lane	4	5	5	6	10	15	25	100
62	Yale Lary	4	5	5	6	10	15	25	
63	Dan Lewis	4	5	5	5	8	12	20	50
64	Darris McCord	4	5	5	5	8	12	20	
65	Earl Morrall	4	5	5	5	8	12	20	80
66	Joe Schmidt	4	5	5	8	12	18	50	
67	Pat Studstill RC	4	5	5	5	8	15	30	80
68	Wayne Walker RC	4	5	5	5	8	15	30	100
69	Detroit Lions Team	4	5	5	5	8	12	20	80
70	Detroit Lions Play	4	5	5	5	8	12	20	80
71	Herb Adderley RC	4	6	8	12	20	50	125	300
72	Willie Davis DE RC	4	6	8	12	40	50	60	300
73	Forrest Gregg	4	5	5	8	12	18	30	80
74	Paul Hornung	4	6	8	12	20	35	80	250
75	Hank Jordan	4	5	5	8	12	18	30	100
76	Jerry Kramer	4	5	5	8	12	18	30	100
77	Tom Moore	4	5	5	5	8	12	20	200
78	Jim Ringo	4	5	5	8	12	18	30	120
79	Bart Starr	8	12	15	25	60	80	250	1,000
80	Jim Taylor	4	5	6	10	15	25	50	▲200
81	Jesse Whittenton RC	4	5	5	5	8	12	20	80
82	Willie Wood	4	5	5	8	12	18	40	150
83	Green Bay Packers Team	4	5	5	8	12	18	40	300
84	Packers Play/Lombardi	4	6	8	12	20	35	60	200
85	Jon Arnett	4	5	5	5	8	12	25	80
86	Pervis Atkins RC	4	5	5	5	8	12	20	80
87	Dick Bass	4	5	5	5	8	12	20	80
88	Carroll Dale	4	5	5	6	10	15	25	120
89	Roman Gabriel	4	5	5	8	12	18	40	200
90	Ed Meador	4	5	5	5	8	12	20	80
91	Merlin Olsen RC	5	8	12	25	35	60	100	300
92	Jack Pardee RC	4	5	5	6	10	15	25	100
93	Jim Phillips	4	5	5	5	8	12	20	60
94	Carver Shannon	4	5	5	5	8	12	20	50
95	Frank Varrichione	4	5	5	5	8	12	20	60
96	Danny Villanueva	4	5	5	5	8	12	20	50
97	Los Angeles Rams Team	4	5	5	5	8	12	20	80
98	Los Angeles Rams Play	4	5	5	5	8	12	20	60
99	Grady Alderman RC	4	5	5	5	8	12	25	120
100	Larry Bowie	4	5	5	5	8	12	20	
101	Bill Brown RC	4	5	5	6	10	15	30	
102	Paul Flatley RC	4	5	5	5	8	12	20	
103	Rip Hawkins	4	5	5	5	8	12	20	80
104	Jim Marshall	4	5	5	8	12	18	30	150
105	Tommy Mason	4	5	5	5	8	12	20	60
106	Jim Prestel	4	5	5	5	8	12	20	80
107	Jerry Reichow	4	5	5	5	8	12	20	80
108	Ed Sharockman	4	5	5	5	8	12	20	80
109	Fran Tarkenton	4	6	8	12	30	40	60	200
110	Mick Tingelhoff RC	4	5	5	6	10	30	80	600
111	Minnesota Vikings Team	4	5	5	5	8	12	25	80
112	Vikings Play/Van Brocklin	4	5	5	5	8	12	20	80
113	Erich Barnes	4	5	5	5	8	12	20	80
114	Roosevelt Brown	4	5	5	6	10	15	25	100
115	Don Chandler	4	5	5	5	8	12	20	80
116	Darrell Dess	4	5	5	5	8	12	20	60
117	Frank Gifford	4	6	8	12	20	35	60	200
118	Dick James	4	5	5	5	8	12	20	80
119	Jim Katcavage	4	5	5	5	8	12	20	80
120	John Lovetere	4	5	5	5	8	12	20	50
121	Dick Lynch RC	4	5	5	5	8	12	20	80
122	Jim Patton	4	5	5	5	8	12	20	
123	Del Shofner	4	5	5	5	8	12	20	60
124	Y.A.Tittle	4	5	5	8	12	20	50	200
125	New York Giants Team	4	5	5	5	8	12	40	50
126	New York Giants Play	4	5	5	5	8	12	20	80
127	Sam Baker	4	5	5	5	8	12	20	60
128	Maxie Baughan	4	5	5	5	8	12	20	60
129	Timmy Brown	4	5	5	5	8	12	20	60
130	Mike Clark	4	5	5	5	8	12	20	60
131	Irv Cross RC	4	5	5	5	8	12	30	60
132	Ted Dean	4	5	5	5	8	12	20	60
133	Ron Goodwin	4	5	5	5	8	12	20	60
134	King Hill	4	5	5	5	8	12	20	80
135	Clarence Peaks	4	5	5	5	8	12	20	80
136	Pete Retzlaff	4	5	5	5	8	12	20	80
137	Jim Schrader	4	5	5	5	8	12	60	
138	Norm Snead	4	5	5	5	8	12	20	80
139	Philadelphia Eagles Team	4	5	5	5	8	12	25	50
140	Philadelphia Eagles Play	4	5	5	5	8	12	20	80
141	Gary Ballman RC	4	5	5	5	8	12	20	
142	Charley Bradshaw RC	4	5	5	5	8	12	20	50
143	Ed Brown	4	5	5	5	8	12	20	80
144	John Henry Johnson	4	5	5	6	10	15	25	80
145	Joe Krupa	4	5	5	5	8	12	30	
146	Bill Mack	4	5	5	5	8	12	20	80
147	Lou Michaels	4	5	5	5	8	12	20	50
148	Buzz Nutter	4	5	5	5	8	12	20	80
149	Myron Pottios	4	5	5	5	8	12	20	50
150	John Reger	4	5	5	5	8	12	50	
151	Mike Sandusky	4	5	5	5	8	12	20	80
152	Clendon Thomas	4	5	5	5	8	12	20	
153	Pittsburgh Steelers Team	4	5	5	5	8	12	40	175
154	Pittsburgh Steelers Play	4	5	5	5	8	12	20	40
155	Kermit Alexander RC	4	5	5	5	8	12	20	80
156	Bernie Casey	4	5	5	5	8	12	20	80
157	Dan Colchico	4	5	5	5	8	12	20	80
158	Clyde Conner	4	5	5	5	8	12	20	50
159	Tommy Davis	4	5	5	5	8	12	20	80
160	Matt Hazeltine	4	5	5	5	8	12	20	80
161	Jim Johnson RC	4	5	6	10	15	35	80	500
162	Don Lisbon RC	4	5	5	5	8	12	20	80
163	Lamar McHan	4	5	5	5	8	12	20	100
164	Bob St.Clair	4	5	5	6	10	15	25	80
165	J.D. Smith	4	5	5	5	8	12	20	100
166	Abe Woodson	4	5	5	5	8	12	20	60
167	San Francisco 49ers Team	4	5	5	5	8	12	20	80
168	San Francisco 49ers Play	4	5	5	5	8	12	20	80
169	Garland Boyette	4	5	5	5	8	12	20	60
170	Bobby Joe Conrad	4	5	5	5	8	12	20	80
171	Bob DeMarco RC	4	5	5	5	8	12	20	80
172	Ken Gray RC	4	5	5	5	8	12	20	80
173	Jimmy Hill	4	5	5	5	8	12	20	80
174	Charlie Johnson	4	5	5	5	8	12	20	80
175	Ernie McMillan	4	5	5	5	8	12	20	80
176	Dale Meinert	4	5	5	5	8	12	20	80
177	Luke Owens	4	5	5	5	8	12	20	80
178	Sonny Randle	4	5	5	5	8	12	20	80
179	Joe Robb	4	5	5	5	8	12	20	80
180	Bill Stacy	4	5	5	5	8	12	20	
181	St. Louis Cardinals Team	4	5	5	5	8	12	20	80
182	St. Louis Cardinals Play	4	5	5	5	8	12	20	50
183	Bill Barnes	4	5	5	5	8	12	40	
184	Don Bosseler	4	5	5	5	8	12	20	60
185	Sam Huff	4	5	5	8	12	18	30	

#	Player	GD 2	VG 3	VgEx 4	EX 5	ExMt 6	NM 7	NmMt 8	MT 9
186	Sonny Jurgensen	4	5	5	8	12	20	50	150
187	Bob Khayat	4	5	5	5	8	12	20	80
188	Riley Mattson	4	5	5	5	8	12	20	
189	Bobby Mitchell	4	5	5	8	12	18	30	150
190	John Nisby	4	5	5	5	8	12	20	80
191	Vince Promuto	4	5	5	5	8	12	20	80
192	Joe Rutgens	4	5	5	5	8	12	20	50
193	Lonnie Sanders	4	5	5	5	8	12	20	
194	Jim Steffen	4	5	5	5	8	12	20	
195	Washington Redskins Team	4	5	5	5	8	15	150	
196	Washington Redskins Play	4	5	5	5	8	12	20	80
197	Checklist 1	4	5	5	8	15	40	200	
198	Checklist 2	4	5	6	10	20	60	120	

— Bobby Mitchell #189 PSA 10 (Gem Mt) sold for $750 (eBay; 12/14)
— Mike Ditka #17 PSA 10 (Gem Mt) sold for $3,353 (eBay; 5/11)
— Mike Ditka #17 PSA 10 (Gem Mt) sold for $3,080 (Mile High; 1/07)
— Paul Hornung #74 PSA 10 (Gem Mt) sold for $2832.2 (Goodwin; 3/12)
— Tommy McDonald #50 PSA 10 (Gem Mt) sold for $970 (eBay; 1/06)
— Merlin Olson #91 PSA 10 (Gem Mt) sold for $1,625 (eBay; 01/13)

1964 Topps

#	Player	GD 2	VG 3	VgEx 4	EX 5	ExMt 6	NM 7	NmMt 8	MT 9
1	Tommy Addison SP	5	6	8	12	18	35	200	
2	Houston Antwine RC	4	5	5	5	8	12	80	
3	Nick Buoniconti	4	5	6	10	15	25	80	
4	Ron Burton SP	4	5	5	6	10	20	60	120
5	Gino Cappelletti	4	5	5	5	8	12	40	
6	Jim Colclough SP	4	5	6	10	15	40	100	
7	Bob Dee SP	4	5	5	6	10	15	150	
8	Larry Eisenhauer	4	5	5	5	8	12	30	80
9	Dick Felt SP	4	5	5	6	10	15	60	
10	Larry Garron	4	5	5	5	8	12	40	120
11	Art Graham	4	5	5	5	8	12	40	
12	Ron Hall DB	4	5	5	5	8	12	30	80
13	Charles Long	4	5	5	5	8	12	30	
14	Don McKinnon	4	5	5	5	8	12	30	175
15	Don Oakes SP	4	5	5	6	10	15	125	
16	Ross O'Hanley SP	4	5	5	6	10	15	60	225
17	Babe Parilli SP	4	5	5	6	10	15	40	225
18	Jesse Richardson SP	4	5	5	6	10	15	100	
19	Jack Rudolph SP	4	5	5	6	10	15	80	
20	Don Webb RC	4	5	5	5	8	12	40	250
21	Boston Patriots Team	4	5	5	6	10	15	40	
22	Ray Abruzzese	4	5	5	5	8	12	30	80
23	Stew Barber RC	4	5	5	5	8	12	30	200
24	Dave Behrman	4	5	5	5	8	12	40	
25	Al Bemiller	4	5	5	5	8	12	40	150
26	Elbert Dubenion SP	4	5	5	6	10	15	125	
27	Jim Dunaway SP RC	4	5	5	6	12	30	225	
28	Booker Edgerson SP	4	5	5	6	10	15	40	
29	Cookie Gilchrist SP	4	5	6	10	15	40	250	
30	Jack Kemp SP	12	15	18	30	40	60	150	400
31	Daryle Lamonica RC	10	12	15	25	40	60	100	350
32	Bill Miller	4	5	5	5	8	12	40	80
33	Herb Paterra RC	4	5	5	5	8	12	40	100
34	Ken Rice SP	4	5	5	6	10	15	60	120
35	Ed Rutkowski	4	5	5	5	8	12	40	120
36	George Saimes RC	4	5	5	5	8	12	30	150
37	Tom Sestak	4	5	5	5	8	12	30	80
38	Billy Shaw SP	4	5	5	8	12	20	100	
39	Mike Stratton	4	5	5	5	8	12	40	
40	Gene Sykes	4	5	5	5	8	12	30	100
41	John Tracey SP	4	5	5	6	10	15	120	
42	Sid Youngelman SP	4	5	5	6	10	15	60	120
43	Buffalo Bills Team	4	5	5	6	10	15	50	
44	Eldon Danenhauer SP	4	5	5	6	10	15	40	120
45	Jim Fraser SP	4	5	5	6	10	15	40	150
46	Chuck Gavin SP	4	5	5	6	10	15	60	
47	Goose Gonsoulin SP	4	5	5	6	10	15	60	
48	Ernie Barnes RC	4	5	5	5	8	12	30	80
49	Tom Janik	4	5	5	5	8	12	25	80
50	Billy Joe RC	4	5	5	5	8	12	40	100
51	Ike Lassiter RC	4	5	5	5	8	12	30	100
52	John McCormick QB SP	4	5	5	6	10	15	40	100
53	Bud McFadin SP	4	5	5	6	10	15	120	
54	Gene Mingo SP	4	5	5	6	10	15	60	
55	Charlie Mitchell	4	5	5	5	8	12	30	80
56	John Nocera SP	4	5	5	6	10	15	40	150

#	Player	GD 2	VG 3	VgEx 4	EX 5	ExMt 6	NM 7	NmMt 8	MT 9
57	Tom Nomina	4	5	5	5	8	12	40	80
58	Harold Olson SP	4	5	6	10	15	40	150	
59	Bob Scarpitto	4	5	5	5	8	12	40	
60	John Sklopan	4	5	5	6	8	12	30	80
61	Mickey Slaughter	4	5	5	5	8	12	60	
62	Don Stone	4	5	5	5	8	12	40	100
63	Jerry Sturm	4	5	5	5	8	12	40	100
64	Lionel Taylor SP	4	5	5	8	12	20	50	
65	Denver Broncos Team SP	4	5	5	8	12	20	175	
66	Scott Appleton RC	4	5	5	5	8	12	40	250
67	Tony Banfield SP	4	5	5	6	10	15	60	
68	George Blanda SP	12	15	18	30	50	80	135	
69	Billy Cannon	4	5	5	6	10	15	60	
70	Doug Cline SP	4	5	5	6	10	15	40	
71	Gary Cutsinger SP	4	5	5	6	10	15	60	
72	Willard Dewveall SP	4	5	5	6	10	15	30	
73	Don Floyd SP	4	5	5	6	10	15	40	
74	Freddy Glick SP	4	5	5	6	10	15	40	100
75	Charlie Hennigan SP	4	5	5	6	10	15	40	
76	Ed Husmann SP	4	5	5	6	10	15	60	
77	Bobby Jancik SP	4	5	5	6	10	15	30	175
78	Jacky Lee SP	4	5	5	6	10	15	80	175
79	Bob McLeod SP	4	5	5	6	10	15	50	
80	Rich Michael SP	4	5	5	6	10	15	60	
81	Larry Onesti RC	4	5	5	5	8	12	40	200
82	Checklist Card 1	5	6	8	15	25	50	80	350
83	Bob Schmidt SP	4	5	5	6	10	15	80	
84	Walt Suggs SP	4	5	5	6	10	15	40	
85	Bob Talamini SP	4	5	5	5	8	12	30	150
86	Charley Tolar SP	4	5	5	6	10	15	100	
87	Don Trull RC	4	5	5	5	8	12	30	120
88	Houston Oilers Team	4	5	5	6	10	15	40	100
89	Fred Arbanas	4	5	5	5	8	12	60	
90	Bobby Bell RC	6	8	10	15	50	60	120	1,300
91	Mel Branch SP	4	5	5	6	10	15	60	
92	Buck Buchanan RC	6	8	10	15	25	▲125	150	800
93	Ed Budde RC	4	5	5	5	8	12	40	
94	Chris Burford SP	4	5	5	6	10	15	60	
95	Walt Corey RC	4	5	5	5	8	12	40	135
96	Len Dawson SP	12	15	18	30	50	75	250	1,200
97	Dave Grayson RC	4	5	5	5	8	12	50	100
98	Abner Haynes	4	5	5	6	10	15	150	
99	Sherrill Headrick SP	4	5	5	6	10	15	120	
100	E.J. Holub	4	5	5	5	8	15	200	
101	Bobby Hunt RC	4	5	5	5	8	12	40	200
102	Frank Jackson SP	4	5	5	6	10	15	40	100
103	Curtis McClinton SP	4	5	5	5	8	12	30	100
104	Jerry Mays SP	4	5	5	6	10	15	60	
105	Johnny Robinson SP	4	5	5	8	12	20	150	
106	Jack Spikes SP	4	5	5	6	10	15	25	120
107	Smokey Stover SP	4	5	5	6	10	20		
108	Jim Tyrer RC	4	5	5	6	20	30	200	
109	Duane Wood SP	4	5	5	5	8	12	80	250
110	Kansas City Chiefs Team	4	5	5	5	8	12	30	80
111	Dick Christy SP	4	5	5	6	10	20	125	
112	Dan Ficca SP	4	5	5	6	10	15	60	200
113	Larry Grantham	4	5	5	5	8	12	40	
114	Curley Johnson SP	4	5	5	6	10	15	100	
115	Gene Heeter	4	5	5	5	8	12	30	100
116	Jack Klotz	4	5	5	5	8	12	30	120
117	Pete Liske RC	4	5	5	5	8	12	30	80
118	Bob McAdam	4	5	5	5	8	12	30	80
119	Dee Mackey SP	4	5	5	6	10	15	80	125
120	Bill Mathis SP	4	5	5	6	10	15	100	
121	Don Maynard	5	6	8	12	20	35	80	300
122	Dainard Paulson SP	4	5	5	6	10	15	40	
123	Gerry Philbin RC	4	5	5	5	8	12	40	120
124	Mark Smolinski SP	4	5	5	6	10	15	40	
125	Matt Snell RC	4	5	5	8	12	20	80	
126	Mike Taliaferro	4	5	5	5	8	12	40	175
127	Bake Turner SP RC	4	5	5	6	10	15	60	
128	Jeff Ware	4	5	5	5	8	12	40	
129	Clyde Washington	4	5	5	5	8	12	60	
130	Dick Wood RC	4	5	5	5	8	12	30	100
131	New York Jets Team	4	5	5	6	10	15	40	150
132	Dalva Allen SP	4	5	5	6	10	15	100	
133	Dan Birdwell	4	5	5	5	8	12	30	80
134	Dave Costa RC	4	5	5	5	8	12	30	80
135	Dobie Craig	4	5	5	5	8	12	40	

		GD 2	VG 3	VgEx 4	EX 5	ExMt 6	NM 7	NmMt 8	MT 9
136	Clem Daniels	4	5	5	5	8	12	40	150
137	Cotton Davidson SP	4	5	5	6	10	15	100	
138	Claude Gibson	4	5	5	5	8	12	40	
139	Tom Flores SP	4	5	6	10	15	40	200	
140	Wayne Hawkins SP	4	5	5	6	10	15	60	
141	Ken Herock	4	5	5	5	8	12	40	
142	Jon Jelacic SP	4	5	5	6	10	15	175	
143	Joe Krakoski	4	5	5	5	8	12	30	80
144	Archie Matsos SP	4	5	5	6	10	15	60	120
145	Mike Mercer	4	5	5	5	8	12	40	
146	Alan Miller SP	4	5	5	6	10	15	60	
147	Bob Mischak SP	4	5	5	6	10	15	60	175
148	Jim Otto SP	5	6	8	12	20	30	125	
149	Clancy Osborne SP	4	5	5	6	10	15	60	
150	Art Powell SP	4	5	5	8	12	25		
151	Bo Roberson	4	5	5	5	8	12	40	
152	Fred Williamson SP	6	8	10	15	25	40	250	
153	Oakland Raiders Team	4	5	5	6	10	15	60	
154	Chuck Allen SP RC	4	5	5	5	8	12	40	150
155	Lance Alworth	8	10	12	25	35	60	100	400
156	George Blair	4	5	5	5	8	12	40	200
157	Earl Faison	4	5	5	5	8	12	30	150
158	Sam Gruneisen	4	5	5	5	8	12	40	
159	John Hadl RC	6	8	10	15	30	50	60	400
160	Dick Harris SP	4	5	5	6	10	15	40	225
161	Emil Karas SP	4	5	5	6	10	20	75	150
162	Dave Kocourek SP	4	5	5	6	10	20	100	
163	Ernie Ladd	4	5	5	6	10	15	40	
164	Keith Lincoln	4	5	5	5	8	12	50	120
165	Paul Lowe SP	4	5	5	6	12	20	60	
166	Charley McNeil	4	5	5	5	8	12	40	
167	Jacque MacKinnon SP RC	4	5	5	6	10	15	60	
168	Ron Mix SP	4	5	5	8	12	50	200	
169	Don Norton SP	4	5	5	6	10	15	80	
170	Don Rogers SP	4	5	5	6	10	15	150	
171	Tobin Rote SP	4	5	5	6	15	20	60	
172	Henry Schmidt SP RC	4	5	5	6	10	15	120	
173	Bud Whitehead	4	5	5	5	8	12	40	
174	Ernie Wright SP	4	5	5	8	12	40	250	
175	San Diego Chargers Team	4	5	5	8	15	30	100	200
176	Checklist Card 2 SP	12	15	20	35	60	150	300	

— Buck Buchanan #92 PSA 10 (Gem) sold for $7,503 (eBay; 1/15)
— Houston Antwine #2 PSA 9 (MT) sold for $515 (eBay; 10/07)
— Ed Budde #93 PSA 9 (MT) sold for $893 (eBay; 5/09)
— Jim Dunaway #27 PSA 8 (NmMt) sold for $1,029 (eBay; 2/10)
— Goose Gonsoulin SP #47 PSA 9 (MT) sold for $1,028.50 (eBay; 10/13)
— E.J. Holub #100 PSA 9 (MT) sold for $559 (eBay; 9/07)
— Frank Jackson #102 PSA 10 (Gem) sold for $1,477 (Mastro; 2/07)
— Daryle Lamonica RC #31 PSA 10 (Gem Mint) sold for $799.95 (eBay; 6/12)
— Don Norton SP #169 PSA 10 (Gem Mint) sold for $1099 (eBay; 11/14)
— Art Powell SP #150 PSA 8 (NM/MT) sold for $598.88 (eBay; 5/12)
— Jack Rudolph SP #19 PSA 9 (Mint) sold for $524.50 (eBay; 2/14)
— Mickey Slaughter #61 PSA 10 (Gem) sold for $1,365 (eBay; 1/07)
— Jim Tyrer RC #108 PSA 9 (Mint) sold for $1,283 (eBay; 11/13)

1965 Philadelphia

		GD 2	VG 3	VgEx 4	EX 5	ExMt 6	NM 7	NmMt 8	MT 9
1	Baltimore Colts Team	4	4	5	8	12	60	135	
2	Raymond Berry	4	4	5	6	10	15	100	
3	Bob Boyd DB	4	4	5	5	8	12	35	120
4	Wendell Harris	4	4	5	5	8	12	20	80
5	Jerry Logan	4	4	5	5	8	12	20	50
6	Tony Lorick	4	4	5	5	8	12	20	60
7	Lou Michaels	4	4	5	5	8	12	20	80
8	Lenny Moore	4	4	5	6	10	15	30	
9	Jimmy Orr	4	4	5	5	8	12	20	40
10	Jim Parker	4	4	5	6	10	15	30	
11	Dick Szymanski	4	4	5	5	8	12	20	80
12	Johnny Unitas	8	10	12	20	30	50	150	400
13	Bob Vogel RC	4	4	5	5	8	12	25	
14	Colts Play/Don Shula	4	4	5	8	12	20	40	
15	Chicago Bears Team	4	4	5	5	8	12	40	
16	Jon Arnett	4	4	5	5	8	12	20	50
17	Doug Atkins	4	4	5	6	10	15	30	80
18	Rudy Bukich RC	4	4	5	5	8	12	20	80
19	Mike Ditka	5	6	8	12	40	50	100	
20	Dick Evey	4	4	5	5	8	12	20	80
21	Joe Fortunato	4	4	5	5	8	12	20	
22	Bobby Joe Green RC	4	4	5	5	8	12	20	80
23	Johnny Morris	4	4	5	5	8	12	50	80
24	Mike Pyle	4	4	5	5	8	12	20	
25	Roosevelt Taylor	4	4	5	5	8	12	20	
26	Bill Wade	4	4	5	5	8	12	20	80
27	Bob Wetoska	4	4	5	5	8	12	20	80
28	Bears Play/George Halas	4	4	5	6	10	15	30	100
29	Cleveland Browns Team	4	4	5	5	8	12	20	
30	Walter Beach	4	4	5	5	8	12	20	100
31	Jim Brown	20	25	30	40	150	200	500	1,200
32	Gary Collins	4	4	5	5	8	12	20	80
33	Bill Glass	4	4	5	5	8	12	20	80
34	Ernie Green	4	4	5	5	8	12	20	80
35	Jim Houston RC	4	4	6	12	40	60	200	
36	Dick Modzelewski	4	4	5	5	8	12	25	
37	Bernie Parrish	4	4	5	5	8	12	15	80
38	Walter Roberts	4	4	5	5	8	12	20	80
39	Frank Ryan	4	4	5	5	8	12	20	
40	Dick Schafrath	4	4	5	5	8	12	30	
41	Paul Warfield RC	12	20	30	50	100	125	600	1,200
42	Cleveland Browns Play	4	4	5	5	8	12	20	80
43	Dallas Cowboys Team	4	4	5	5	8	20	50	
44	Frank Clarke	4	4	5	5	8	12	20	80
45	Mike Connelly	4	4	5	5	8	12	20	
46	Buddy Dial	4	4	5	5	8	12	20	80
47	Bob Lilly	5	6	8	12	20	35	80	450
48	Tony Liscio RC	4	4	5	5	8	12	20	80
49	Tommy McDonald	4	4	5	6	10	15	30	100
50	Don Meredith	4	5	10	15	20	35	60	200
51	Pettis Norman	4	4	5	5	8	12	20	60
52	Don Perkins	4	4	5	6	10	15	25	80
53	Mel Renfro RC	8	10	15	40	50	80	300	1,200
54	Jim Ridlon	4	4	5	5	8	12	20	80
55	Jerry Tubbs	4	4	5	5	8	12	20	80
56	Cowboys Play/T.Landry	4	4	5	6	10	15	40	150
57	Detroit Lions Team	4	4	5	5	8	12	20	
58	Terry Barr	4	4	5	5	8	12	20	
59	Roger Brown	4	4	5	5	8	12	20	80
60	Gail Cogdill	4	4	5	5	8	12	20	80
61	Jim Gibbons	4	4	5	5	8	12	20	80
62	John Gordy	4	4	5	5	8	12	20	80
63	Yale Lary	4	4	5	6	10	15	30	100
64	Dick LeBeau RC	6	8	12	20	60	80	150	400
65	Earl Morrall	4	4	5	5	8	12	20	60
66	Nick Pietrosante	4	4	5	5	8	12	20	80
67	Pat Studstill	4	4	5	5	8	12	20	80
68	Wayne Walker	4	4	5	5	8	12	20	80
69	Tom Watkins	4	4	5	5	8	12	20	60
70	Detroit Lions Play	4	4	5	5	8	12	20	60
71	Green Bay Packers Team	4	4	5	6	10	15	30	200
72	Herb Adderley	4	4	5	6	10	15	40	
73	Willie Davis DE	4	4	5	6	10	20	40	
74	Boyd Dowler	4	4	5	5	8	12	25	80
75	Forrest Gregg	4	4	5	6	10	15	60	
76	Paul Hornung	5	6	8	12	30	▲80	▲100	200
77	Hank Jordan	4	4	5	6	10	15	50	
78	Tom Moore	4	4	5	5	8	12	40	80
79	Ray Nitschke	4	5	6	10	20	30	80	
80	Elijah Pitts RC	4	4	5	6	10	15	30	100
81	Bart Starr	8	10	15	25	35	80	200	600
82	Jim Taylor	4	5	6	10	15	25	60	300
83	Willie Wood	4	4	5	6	10	15	30	150
84	Packers Play/Lombardi	4	5	6	10	15	25	50	150
85	Los Angeles Rams Team	4	4	5	5	8	12	20	80
86	Dick Bass	4	4	5	5	8	12	20	80
87	Roman Gabriel	4	4	5	6	10	15	30	150
88	Roosevelt Grier	4	4	5	6	10	15	30	80
89	Deacon Jones	4	4	5	6	10	15	40	
90	Lamar Lundy RC	4	4	5	6	10	15	30	80
91	Marlin McKeever	4	4	5	5	8	12	20	50
92	Ed Meador	4	4	5	5	8	12	20	50
93	Bill Munson RC	4	4	5	6	10	15	20	80
94	Merlin Olsen	4	4	5	6	10	15	40	120
95	Bobby Smith	4	4	5	5	8	12	20	50
96	Frank Varrichione	4	4	5	5	8	12	20	50
97	Ben Wilson	4	4	5	5	8	12	20	80
98	Los Angeles Rams Play	4	4	5	5	8	12	20	
99	Minnesota Vikings Team	4	4	5	5	8	12	20	
100	Grady Alderman	4	4	5	5	8	12	20	60

#	Player	GD 2	VG 3	VgEx 4	EX 5	ExMt 6	NM 7	NmMt 8	MT 9
101	Hal Bedsole RC	4	4	5	5	8	12	20	50
102	Bill Brown	4	4	5	5	8	12	20	80
103	Bill Butler	4	4	5	5	8	12	20	80
104	Fred Cox RC	4	4	5	5	8	12	20	100
105	Carl Eller RC	6	8	10	20	25	50	100	400
106	Paul Flatley	4	4	5	5	8	12	20	50
107	Jim Marshall	4	4	5	6	10	15	30	
108	Tommy Mason	4	4	5	5	8	12	20	125
109	George Rose	4	4	5	5	8	12	20	80
110	Fran Tarkenton	4	5	6	10	15	30	125	
111	Mick Tingelhoff	4	4	5	5	8	12	20	
112	Vikings Play/Van Brock.	4	4	5	6	10	15	60	
113	New York Giants Team	4	4	5	5	8	12	20	
114	Erich Barnes	4	4	5	5	8	15	150	
115	Roosevelt Brown	4	4	5	6	10	15	40	
116	Clarence Childs	4	4	5	5	8	12	20	50
117	Jerry Hillebrand	4	4	5	5	8	12	20	
118	Greg Larson RC	4	4	5	5	8	12	20	60
119	Dick Lynch	4	4	5	5	8	12	20	80
120	Joe Morrison RC	4	4	5	6	10	15	25	60
121	Lou Slaby	4	4	5	5	8	12	20	
122	Aaron Thomas RC	4	4	5	5	8	12	20	
123	Steve Thurlow	4	4	5	5	8	12	20	
124	Ernie Wheelwright RC	4	4	5	5	8	12	20	80
125	Gary Wood RC	4	4	5	5	8	12	20	80
126	New York Giants Play	4	4	5	5	8	12	20	
127	Philadelphia Eagles Team	4	4	5	5	8	15	40	
128	Sam Baker	4	4	5	5	8	15	120	
129	Maxie Baughan	4	4	5	5	8	12	20	80
130	Timmy Brown	4	4	5	5	8	12	20	80
131	Jack Concannon RC	4	4	5	5	8	12	20	50
132	Irv Cross	4	4	5	5	8	12	20	
133	Earl Gros	4	4	5	5	8	12	20	50
134	Dave Lloyd	4	4	5	5	8	12	20	
135	Floyd Peters RC	4	4	5	5	8	12	20	80
136	Nate Ramsey	4	4	5	5	8	12	20	80
137	Pete Retzlaff	4	4	5	5	8	12	20	80
138	Jim Ringo	4	4	5	6	10	15	40	
139	Norm Snead	4	4	5	6	10	15	40	60
140	Philadelphia Eagles Play	4	4	5	5	8	12	20	80
141	Pittsburgh Steelers Team	4	4	5	5	8	12	40	80
142	John Baker	4	4	5	5	8	12	20	
143	Gary Ballman	4	4	5	5	8	12	20	80
144	Charley Bradshaw	4	4	5	5	8	12	20	80
145	Ed Brown	4	4	5	5	8	12	20	
146	Dick Haley	4	4	5	5	8	15	80	120
147	John Henry Johnson	4	4	5	6	10	15	40	
148	Brady Keys	4	4	5	5	8	12	20	50
149	Ray Lemek	4	4	5	5	8	12	20	80
150	Ben McGee	4	4	5	5	8	12	20	50
151	Clarence Peaks UER	4	4	5	5	8	12	20	50
152	Myron Pottios	4	4	5	5	8	12	20	80
153	Clendon Thomas	4	4	5	5	8	12	20	50
154	Pittsburgh Steelers Play	4	4	5	5	8	12	20	
155	St. Louis Cardinals Team	4	4	5	5	8	12	20	
156	Jim Bakken RC	4	4	5	5	8	15	50	100
157	Joe Childress	4	4	5	5	8	12	20	
158	Bobby Joe Conrad	4	4	5	5	8	12	20	
159	Bob DeMarco	4	4	5	5	8	12	20	80
160	Pat Fischer RC	4	4	5	6	10	15	50	
161	Irv Goode	4	4	5	5	8	12	15	60
162	Ken Gray	4	4	5	5	8	12	20	80
163	Charlie Johnson	4	4	5	5	8	12	20	60
164	Bill Koman	4	4	5	5	8	12	20	
165	Dale Meinert	4	4	5	5	8	12	20	60
166	Jerry Stovall RC	4	4	5	5	8	12	20	80
167	Abe Woodson	4	4	5	5	8	12	20	60
168	St. Louis Cardinals Play	4	4	5	5	8	12	20	80
169	San Francisco 49ers Team	4	4	5	5	8	12	30	80
170	Kermit Alexander	4	4	5	5	8	12	20	80
171	John Brodie	4	4	5	6	10	15	30	150
172	Bernie Casey	4	4	5	5	8	12	20	
173	John David Crow	4	4	5	5	8	12	20	60
174	Tommy Davis	4	4	5	5	8	12	20	80
175	Matt Hazeltine	4	4	5	5	8	12	20	80
176	Jim Johnson	4	4	5	6	10	15	30	100
177	Charlie Krueger RC	4	4	5	5	8	12	20	80
178	Roland Lakes	4	4	5	5	8	12	20	60
179	George Mira RC	4	4	5	5	8	12	20	80
180	Dave Parks RC	4	4	5	5	8	12	20	80
181	John Thomas RC	4	4	5	5	8	12	20	80
182	49ers Play/Christiansen	4	4	5	5	8	12	20	80
183	Washington Redskins Team	4	4	5	5	8	12	20	80
184	Pervis Atkins	4	4	5	5	8	12	20	
185	Preston Carpenter	4	4	5	5	8	12	20	80
186	Angelo Coia	4	4	5	5	8	12	20	80
187	Sam Huff	4	4	5	6	10	15	60	125
188	Sonny Jurgensen	4	4	5	6	10	15	60	
189	Paul Krause RC	6	6	10	15	30	60	150	800
190	Jim Martin	4	4	5	5	8	12	20	
191	Bobby Mitchell	4	4	5	6	10	15	30	80
192	John Nisby	4	4	5	5	8	12	20	
193	John Paluck	4	4	5	5	8	12	20	80
194	Vince Promuto	4	4	5	5	8	12	20	80
195	Charley Taylor RC	6	8	10	25	40	100	200	800
196	Washington Redskins Play	4	4	5	5	8	15	40	
197	Checklist 1	4	5	6	10	15	30	60	150
198	Checklist 2	4	4	5	10	15	25	60	120

— Raymond Berry #2 PSA 9 (MT) sold for $488 (eBay; 1/08)
— Carl Eller #105 PSA 10 (Gem Mt) sold for $8,284 (Mile High; 6/10)
— Deacon Jones #89 PSA 9 (MT) sold for $465 (eBay; 6/06)
— Tommy Mason #108 PSA 10 (Gem) sold for $795 (eBay; 2/07)
— Ray Nitschke #79 PSA 9 (MT) sold for $525 (eBay; 1/08)
— Fran Tarkenton #110 PSA 9 (MT) sold for $1,228 (eBay; 9/09)
— Fran Tarkenton #110 PSA 9 (Mint) sold for $420 (Bussineau; 4/12)
— Charley Taylor #195 PSA 10 (Gem Mt) sold for $8,284 (Mile High; 10/09)
— Paul Warfield #41 PSA 10 (Gem Mt) sold for $11,027 (Mile High; 6/10)

1965 Topps

#	Player	GD 2	VG 3	VgEx 4	EX 5	ExMt 6	NM 7	NmMt 8	MT 9
1	Tommy Addison SP	6	8	10	15	25	40	400	
2	Houston Antwine SP	5	6	8	12	20	50	175	
3	Nick Buoniconti SP	6	8	10	15	30	80	500	
4	Ron Burton SP	6	8	10	15	25	80	250	
5	Gino Cappelletti SP	6	8	10	15	40	50	200	
6	Jim Colclough	5	5	6	8		50	100	
7	Bob Dee SP	5	6	8	12	20	30	60	
8	Larry Eisenhauer	5	5	6	8	15	30	60	
9	J.D. Garrett	5	5	6	8	15	25	60	
10	Larry Garron	5	5	6	8	15	25	80	
11	Art Graham SP	5	6	8	12	20	30	80	
12	Ron Hall DB	5	5	6	8	15	25	125	250
13	Charles Long	5	5	6	8	15	25	50	
14	Jon Morris RC	5	5	6	8	15	25	50	
15	Billy Neighbors SP	5	6	8	12	20	30	60	
16	Ross O'Hanley	5	5	6	8	15	25	100	
17	Babe Parilli SP	6	8	10	15	25	35	150	
18	Tony Romeo SP	5	6	8	12	20	30	60	
19	Jack Rudolph SP	5	6	8	12	20	30	60	
20	Bob Schmidt	5	5	6	8	15	25	60	
21	Don Webb SP	5	6	8	12	20	30	60	
22	Jim Whalen SP	5	6	8	12	20	30	80	
23	Stew Barber	5	5	6	8	15	60	400	
24	Glenn Bass SP	5	6	8	12	20	30	60	
25	Al Bemiller SP	5	6	8	12	20	30	60	
26	Wray Carlton SP	5	6	8	12	30	40	100	
27	Tom Day	5	5	6	8	15	30	80	
28	Elbert Dubenion SP	5	6	8	12	20	30	80	
29	Jim Dunaway	5	5	6	8	15	25	60	
30	Pete Gogolak SP RC	6	8	10	15	30	40	150	
31	Dick Hudson SP	5	6	8	12	20	30	60	
32	Harry Jacobs SP	5	6	8	12	20	30	60	
33	Billy Joe SP	5	6	8	12	20	30	100	
34	Tom Keating SP RC	5	6	8	12	20	40	250	
35	Jack Kemp SP	20	25	40	50	80	125	250	
36	Daryle Lamonica SP	8	10	12	20	▲50	80	150	
37	Paul Maguire SP	6	8	10	15	25	35	150	
38	Ron McDole SP RC	5	6	8	12	20	30	100	
39	George Saimes SP	5	6	8	12	20	30	150	
40	Tom Sestak SP	5	6	8	12	20	30	60	
41	Billy Shaw SP	6	8	10	15	25	100	200	
42	Mike Stratton SP	5	6	8	12	20	30	80	300
43	John Tracey SP	5	6	8	12	20	30	60	
44	Ernie Warlick	5	5	6	8	15	25	50	300
45	Odell Barry	5	5	6	8	15	80		
46	Willie Brown SP RC	20	25	30	50	▲200	300	500	
47	Gerry Bussell SP	5	6	8	12	20	30	60	

#	Player	GD 2	VG 3	VgEx 4	EX 5	ExMt 6	NM 7	NmMt 8	MT 9
48	Eldon Danenhauer SP	5	6	8	12	20	30	60	
49	Al Denson SP	5	6	8	12	20	30	150	
50	Hewritt Dixon SP RC	5	6	8	12	20	30	200	
51	Cookie Gilchrist SP	6	8	10	15	25	60	120	
52	Goose Gonsoulin SP	5	6	8	12	20	30	100	
53	Abner Haynes SP	6	8	10	15	25	35	100	
54	Jerry Hopkins	5	5	6	8	15	60	200	
55	Ray Jacobs SP	5	6	8	12	20	30	60	
56	Jacky Lee SP	5	6	8	20	25	40	200	
57	John McCormick QB	5	5	6	8	15	25	50	
58	Bob McCullough SP	5	6	8	12	20	30	120	
59	John McGeever	5	5	6	8	15	25	50	
60	Charlie Mitchell SP	5	6	8	12	20	30	50	
61	Jim Perkins SP	5	6	8	12	20	30	100	
62	Bob Scarpitto SP	5	6	8	12	20	30	100	
63	Mickey Slaughter SP	5	6	8	12	20	30	100	
64	Jerry Sturm SP	5	6	8	12	20	30	200	
65	Lionel Taylor SP	6	8	10	15	25	40	100	300
66	Scott Appleton SP	5	6	8	12	20	30	60	300
67	Johnny Baker SP	5	6	8	12	20	30	60	
68	Sonny Bishop SP	5	6	8	12	20	30	80	
69	George Blanda SP	15	20	25	40	100	125	400	
70	Sid Blanks SP	5	6	8	12	15	30	60	
71	Ode Burrell SP	5	6	8	12	20	30	80	
72	Doug Cline SP	5	6	8	12	20	25	40	250
73	Willard Dewveall	5	5	6	8	15	25	80	300
74	Larry Elkins RC	5	5	6	8	15	25	50	
75	Don Floyd SP	5	6	8	12	20	30	60	
76	Freddy Glick	5	5	6	8	15	25	50	
77	Tom Goode SP	5	6	8	12	20	30	60	
78	Charlie Hennigan SP	6	8	10	15	25	35	100	
79	Ed Husmann	5	5	6	8	15	25	50	
80	Bobby Jancik SP	5	6	8	12	20	30	60	
81	Bud McFadin SP	5	6	8	12	20	30	80	
82	Bob McLeod SP	5	6	8	12	20	30	80	400
83	Jim Norton SP	5	6	8	12	20	30	400	
84	Walt Suggs SP	5	5	6	8	15	25	60	
85	Bob Talamini	5	5	6	8	15	25	50	
86	Charley Tolar SP	5	6	8	12	20	30	60	250
87	Checklist SP	20	25	35	60	150	200	250	
88	Don Trull SP	5	6	8	12	20	30	80	
89	Fred Arbanas SP	5	6	8	12	20	50	120	
90	Pete Beathard SP RC	5	6	8	12	20	80	200	
91	Bobby Bell SP	6	8	10	15	25	50	120	
92	Mel Branch SP	5	6	8	12	15	30	80	
93	Tommy Brooker SP	5	6	8	12	20	30	60	
94	Buck Buchanan SP	6	8	10	15	25	120		
95	Ed Budde SP	5	6	8	12	20	30	60	
96	Chris Burford SP	5	6	8	12	20	50	120	
97	Walt Corey	5	5	6	8	15	25	50	
98	Jerry Cornelison	5	5	6	8	15	25	50	200
99	Len Dawson SP	15	20	25	40	80	100	400	
100	Jon Gilliam SP	5	6	8	12	20	30	60	
101	Sherrill Headrick SP	5	6	8	12	20	30	150	
102	Dave Hill SP	5	6	8	12	20	30	60	
103	E.J. Holub SP	5	6	8	12	20	30	60	
104	Bobby Hunt SP	5	6	8	12	15	40	80	
105	Frank Jackson SP	5	6	8	12	20	30	300	
106	Jerry Mays SP	5	5	6	8	15	25	50	
107	Curtis McClinton SP	5	6	8	12	20	30	60	
108	Bobby Ply SP	5	6	8	12	15	30	60	
109	Johnny Robinson SP	5	6	8	12	20	30	100	
110	Jim Tyrer SP	5	6	8	12	20	30	80	400
111	Bill Baird SP	5	6	8	12	20	30	60	
112	Ralph Baker SP RC	5	6	8	12	20	30	100	400
113	Sam DeLuca SP	5	6	8	12	20	30	50	
114	Larry Grantham SP	5	6	8	12	20	30	80	
115	Gene Heeter SP	5	6	8	12	20	30	60	
116	Winston Hill SP RC	6	8	10	15	25	40	125	
117	John Huarte SP RC	6	8	10	15	25	50	120	
118	Cosmo Iacavazzi SP	5	6	8	12	20	30	60	
119	Curley Johnson SP	5	6	8	12	20	30	60	
120	Dee Mackey SP	5	5	6	8	15	25	50	300
121	Don Maynard SP	8	10	12	40	80	100	250	
122	Joe Namath SP RC	1,500	▲2,200	3,000	6,000	8,000	10,000	60,000	
123	Dainard Paulson	5	5	6	8	15	25	50	
124	Gerry Philbin SP	5	6	8	12	20	30	80	
125	Sherman Plunkett SP RC	5	6	8	12	20	30	80	
126	Mark Smolinski	5	5	6	8	15	25	50	300

#	Player	GD 2	VG 3	VgEx 4	EX 5	ExMt 6	NM 7	NmMt 8	MT 9
127	Matt Snell SP	6	8	20	25	30	40	100	600
128	Mike Taliaferro SP	5	6	8	20	25	40	60	350
129	Bake Turner SP	5	6	8	12	20	30	150	
130	Clyde Washington SP	5	6	8	20	25	30	60	
131	Verlon Biggs SP RC	5	6	8	12	20	40	100	
132	Dalva Allen	5	5	6	8	15	35	200	
133	Fred Biletnikoff SP RC	40	80	80	500	600	800	1,200	10,000
134	Billy Cannon SP	6	8	10	15	25	50	150	
135	Dave Costa SP	5	6	8	12	20	100	300	
136	Clem Daniels SP	5	6	8	12	30	100	200	
137	Ben Davidson SP RC	10	12	20	50	50	100	400	
138	Cotton Davidson SP	5	6	8	12	20	40	60	
139	Tom Flores SP	6	8	10	15	25	40	100	
140	Claude Gibson	5	5	6	8	15	25	50	
141	Wayne Hawkins	5	6	8	12	35	50	300	
142	Archie Matsos SP	5	6	8	12	20	30	60	
143	Mike Mercer SP	5	6	8	12	20	30	80	
144	Bob Mischak SP	5	6	8	12	20	30	80	
145	Jim Otto	6	8	10	15	40	60	200	
146	Art Powell	5	5	6	8	15	50	120	
147	Warren Powers DB SP	5	6	8	12	20	80	100	
148	Ken Rice SP	5	6	8	12	20	60	175	
149	Bo Roberson SP	5	6	8	12	20	30	200	
150	Harry Schuh RC	5	5	6	8	15	25	50	
151	Larry Todd SP	5	6	8	12	25	35	80	350
152	Fred Williamson SP	6	8	10	15	25	40	120	
153	J.R. Williamson SP	5	5	6	8	15	25	50	
154	Chuck Allen	5	5	6	8	15	40	60	
155	Lance Alworth	12	15	20	30	50	80	300	
156	Frank Buncom	5	5	6	8	15	25	50	
157	Steve DeLong SP RC	5	6	8	12	20	30	60	
158	Earl Faison SP	5	6	8	12	20	40	80	
159	Kenny Graham SP	5	6	8	12	20	30	60	
160	George Gross SP	5	6	8	12	20	30	60	
161	John Hadl SP	6	8	12	20	35	60	135	
162	Emil Karas SP	5	6	8	12	20	30	60	
163	Dave Kocourek SP	5	6	8	12	20	30	150	
164	Ernie Ladd SP	6	8	10	15	25	50	120	
165	Keith Lincoln SP	6	8	10	15	25	40	100	
166	Paul Lowe SP	6	8	10	15	25	35	100	
167	Jacque MacKinnon	5	5	6	8	15	25	50	
168	Ron Mix	6	8	10	15	25	40	100	
169	Don Norton SP	5	6	8	12	20	40	60	
170	Bob Petrich	5	5	6	8	15	25	50	
171	Rick Redman SP	5	6	8	12	20	30	60	250
172	Pat Shea	5	5	6	8	15	30	60	
173	Walt Sweeney SP RC	5	6	8	12	20	50	150	
174	Dick Westmoreland RC	5	5	6	10	30	80	500	
175	Ernie Wright SP	6	8	10	15	25	60	150	
176	Checklist SP	30	40	60	150	200	300	600	

— Tommy Addison #1 PSA 9 (MT) sold for $1,735 (Memory Lane; 4/07)
— Willie Brown #46 PSA 9 (MT) sold for $3215 (eBay; 11/14)
— Checklist #87 PSA 9 (MT) sold for $1,485 (Mile High; 3/09)
— Clem Daniels #136 PSA 9 (MT) sold for $2,555 (eBay; 11/08)
— Sam DeLuca SP #113 PSA 9 (Mint) sold for $500.89 (eBay; 8/12)
— Tom Keating SP RC #34 PSA 9 (Mint) sold for $1042 (eBay; 8/12)
— Joe Namath #122 PSA 8.5 (NmMT+) sold for $15,000 (eBay; 1/14)
— Billy Shaw #41 PSA 9 (MT) sold for $1,004 (eBay; 10/08)
— Jim Whalen SP #22 PSA 9 (Mint) sold for $414.89 (eBay; 8/12)

1966 Philadelphia

#		GD 2	VG 3	VgEx 4	EX 5	ExMt 6	NM 7	NmMt 8	MT 9
1	Atlanta Falcons Logo	4	6	6	8	12	20	50	
2	Larry Benz	4	5	5	5	12	30		
3	Dennis Claridge	4	5	5	5	8	15	50	
4	Perry Lee Dunn	4	5	5	5	8	15	50	
5	Dan Grimm	4	5	5	5	8	15	50	
6	Alex Hawkins	4	5	5	5	8	15	40	
7	Ralph Heck	4	5	5	5	8	15	50	
8	Frank Lasky	4	5	5	5	8	15	50	
9	Guy Reese	4	5	5	5	8	15	50	
10	Bob Richards	4	5	5	5	8	15	50	
11	Ron Smith RC	4	5	5	5	8	15	50	
12	Ernie Wheelwright	4	5	5	5	8	15	30	
13	Atlanta Falcons Roster	4	5	VgEx 5	5	8	15	50	
14	Baltimore Colts Team	4	5	5	5	8	15	50	
15	Raymond Berry	4	5	5	6	10	15	50	200
16	Bob Boyd DB	4	5	5	5	8	12	50	60

		GD 2	VG 3	VgEx 4	EX 5	ExMt 6	NM 7	NmMt 8	MT 9
17	Jerry Logan	4	5	5	5	8	12	50	80
18	John Mackey	4	5	5	6	10	15	50	
19	Tom Matte	4	5	5	5	8	15	60	
20	Lou Michaels	4	5	5	5	8	15	50	
21	Lenny Moore	4	5	5	6	12	20	50	
22	Jimmy Orr	4	5	5	5	8	15	50	
23	Jim Parker	4	5	5	5	8	15	50	
24	Johnny Unitas	12	15	20	25	50	125	250	
25	Bob Vogel	4	5	5	5	8	15	50	
26	Colts Play/Moore/Parker	4	5	5	5	8	15	50	
27	Chicago Bears Team	4	5	5	5	8	12	25	80
28	Doug Atkins	4	5	5	5	8	15	50	
29	Rudy Bukich	4	5	5	5	8	15	50	
30	Ronnie Bull	4	5	5	5	8	15	50	
31	Dick Butkus RC	100	125	200	500	800	1,000	2,000	
32	Mike Ditka	8	12	12	15	25	60	100	400
33	Joe Fortunato	4	5	5	5	8	15	50	
34	Bobby Joe Green	4	5	5	5	8	15	50	
35	Roger LeClerc	4	5	5	5	10	25	100	
36	Johnny Morris	4	5	5	5	8	15	50	
37	Mike Pyle	4	5	5	5	8	15	50	
38	Gale Sayers RC	80	100	150	250	250	500	1,000	3,000
39	Bears Play/G.Sayers	8	10	12	15	25	40	100	300
40	Cleveland Browns Team	4	5	5	5	8	15	80	
41	Jim Brown	20	25	30	50	80	120	600	800
42	Gary Collins	4	5	5	5	8	15	50	
43	Ross Fichtner	4	5	5	5	8	15	60	
44	Ernie Green	4	5	5	5	8	15	50	80
45	Gene Hickerson RC	8	10	12	15	25	40	100	
46	Jim Houston	4	5	5	5	8	15	50	
47	John Morrow	4	5	5	5	8	15	50	100
48	Walter Roberts	4	5	5	5	8	15	50	
49	Frank Ryan	4	5	5	5	8	15	50	
50	Dick Schafrath	4	5	5	5	8	15	50	
51	Paul Wiggin RC	4	5	5	5	8	12	25	100
52	Cleveland Browns Play	4	5	5	5	8	15	50	
53	Dallas Cowboys Team	4	5	5	5	8	15	100	
54	George Andrie RC	4	5	5	6	10	20	120	
55	Frank Clarke	4	5	5	5	8	15	50	
56	Mike Connelly	4	5	5	5	8	15	50	
57	Cornell Green	4	5	5	5	15	40		
58	Bob Hayes RC	20	25	30	100	125	200	250	
59	Chuck Howley RC	6	8	10	20	60	100	250	
60	Bob Lilly	5	6	6	8	12	20	50	
61	Don Meredith	6	8	8	10	15	50	60	
62	Don Perkins	4	5	5	5	15	50		
63	Mel Renfro	5	6	6	8	12	40	50	
64	Danny Villanueva	4	5	5	5	8	15	50	
65	Dallas Cowboys Play	4	5	5	5	8	12	25	80
66	Detroit Lions Team	4	5	5	5	8	15	50	
67	Roger Brown	4	5	5	5	8	15	50	
68	John Gordy	4	5	5	5	15	40		
69	Alex Karras	5	6	6	8	12	30	50	200
70	Dick LeBeau	4	5	5	5	8	15	50	
71	Amos Marsh	4	5	5	5	8	15	50	
72	Milt Plum	4	5	5	5	8	12	25	80
73	Bobby Smith	4	5	5	5	8	15	50	
74	Wayne Rasmussen	4	5	5	5	8	15	50	
75	Pat Studstill	4	5	5	5	8	15	50	
76	Wayne Walker	4	5	5	5	8	15	30	
77	Tom Watkins	4	5	5	5	8	15	30	
78	Detroit Lions Play	4	5	5	5	8	15	30	
79	Green Bay Packers Team	4	5	5	6	10	20	50	
80	Herb Adderley	4	5	5	6	10	15	30	300
81	Lee Roy Caffey RC	4	5	5	5	8	15	60	
82	Don Chandler	4	5	5	5	8	15	80	
83	Willie Davis DE	4	5	5	6	10	25	60	
84	Boyd Dowler	4	5	5	5	8	20	50	
85	Forrest Gregg	4	5	5	5	8	15	50	
86	Tom Moore	4	5	5	5	8	15	50	
87	Ray Nitschke	5	6	6	8	12	40	150	
88	Bart Starr	10	12	15	30	40	100	200	800
89	Jim Taylor	5	6	6	8	12	20	50	
90	Willie Wood	4	5	5	6	10	15	50	
91	Green Bay Packers Play	4	5	5	5	8	20	50	
92	Los Angeles Rams Team	4	5	5	5	8	15	50	
93	Willie Brown WR	4	5	5	5	8	15	50	
94	R.Gabriel/D.Bass	4	5	5	5	8	15	50	
95	Bruce Gossett RC	4	5	5	5	8	15	50	

		GD 2	VG 3	VgEx 4	EX 5	ExMt 6	NM 7	NmMt 8	MT 9
96	Deacon Jones	4	5	5	6	10	15	40	100
97	Tommy McDonald	4	5	5	5	8	12	30	80
98	Marlin McKeever	4	5	5	5	8	15	50	
99	Aaron Martin	4	5	5	5	8	15	50	
100	Ed Meador	4	5	5	5	8	15	50	
101	Bill Munson	4	5	5	5	8	12	25	80
102	Merlin Olsen	4	5	5	6	10	40	150	
103	Jim Stiger	4	5	5	5	8	12	25	80
104	Rams Play/W.Brown	4	5	5	5	8	15	30	
105	Minnesota Vikings Team	4	5	5	5	8	15	50	
106	Grady Alderman	4	5	5	5	8	15	50	
107	Bill Brown	4	5	5	5	8	12	25	100
108	Fred Cox	4	5	5	5	8	15	60	
109	Paul Flatley	4	5	5	5	8	15	50	
110	Rip Hawkins	4	5	5	5	8	15	30	
111	Tommy Mason	4	5	5	5	15	40		
112	Ed Sharockman	4	5	5	5	8	15	50	
113	Gordon Smith	4	5	5	5	8	15	50	
114	Fran Tarkenton	6	8	10	12	18	60	150	
115	Mick Tingelhoff	4	5	5	5	8	15	120	
116	Bobby Walden RC	4	5	5	5	8	15	40	
117	Minnesota Vikings Play	4	5	5	5	8	15	50	
118	New York Giants Team	4	5	5	5	8	12	25	60
119	Roosevelt Brown	4	5	5	5	8	12	25	80
120	Henry Carr RC	4	5	5	5	6	12	30	80
121	Clarence Childs	4	5	5	5	8	15	30	
122	Tucker Frederickson RC	4	5	5	5	8	15	50	
123	Jerry Hillebrand	4	5	5	5	8	15	50	
124	Greg Larson	4	5	5	5	8	15	50	
125	Spider Lockhart RC	4	5	5	5	8	15	60	
126	Dick Lynch	4	5	5	5	8	15	50	
127	E.Morrall/B.Scholtz	4	5	5	5	8	15	50	
128	Joe Morrison	4	5	5	5	8	15	50	
129	Steve Thurlow	4	5	5	5	8	15	60	
130	New York Giants Play	4	5	5	5	8	12	25	50
131	Philadelphia Eagles Team	4	5	5	5	8	12	25	80
132	Sam Baker	4	5	5	5	8	15	50	
133	Maxie Baughan	4	5	5	5	8	15	50	
134	Bob Brown OT RC	5	6	6	8	20	80	250	
135	Timmy Brown	4	5	5	5	8	15	50	
136	Irv Cross	4	5	5	5	15	60		
137	Earl Gros	4	5	5	5	8	15	50	
138	Ray Poage	4	5	5	5	8	15	50	
139	Nate Ramsey	4	5	5	5	8	15	50	
140	Pete Retzlaff	4	5	5	5	8	15	50	
141	Jim Ringo	4	5	5	5	8	15	50	
142	Norm Snead	4	5	5	5	8	15	50	
143	Philadelphia Eagles Play	4	5	5	5	8	15	60	
144	Pittsburgh Steelers Team	4	5	5	5	8	15	50	
145	Gary Ballman	4	5	5	5	8	15	50	
146	Jim Bradshaw	4	5	5	5	15	40		
147	Jim Butler	4	5	5	5	8	15	50	
148	Mike Clark	4	5	5	5	8	15	50	
149	Dick Hoak RC	4	5	5	5	8	15	50	
150	Roy Jefferson RC	4	5	5	5	8	15	50	
151	Frank Lambert	4	5	5	5	8	15	30	
152	Mike Lind	4	5	5	5	8	15	50	
153	Bill Nelsen RC	4	5	5	5	8	15	50	
154	Clarence Peaks	4	5	5	5	8	15	50	
155	Clendon Thomas	4	5	5	5	8	15	50	
156	Pittsburgh Steelers Play	4	5	5	5	8	15	50	
157	St. Louis Cardinals Team	4	5	5	5	8	15	50	
158	Jim Bakken	4	5	5	5	8	15	40	
159	Bobby Joe Conrad	4	5	5	5	8	15	40	80
160	Willis Crenshaw RC	4	5	5	5	8	15	50	
161	Bob DeMarco	4	5	5	5	8	15	50	
162	Pat Fischer	4	5	5	5	8	15	50	
163	Charlie Johnson	4	5	5	5	8	12	25	120
164	Dale Meinert	4	5	5	5	8	15	30	
165	Sonny Randle	4	5	5	5	8	15	50	
166	Sam Silas RC	4	5	5	5	8	15	30	
167	Bill Triplett	4	5	5	5	8	15	50	
168	Larry Wilson	4	5	5	5	8	15	50	
169	St. Louis Cardinals Play	4	5	5	5	8	15	50	
170	San Francisco 49ers Team	4	5	5	5	8	15	50	
171	Kermit Alexander	4	5	5	5	8	15	50	
172	Bruce Bosley	4	5	5	5	8	15	50	
173	John Brodie	4	5	5	6	10	15	50	
174	Bernie Casey	4	5	5	5	8	15	50	

#		GD 2	VG 3	VgEx 4	EX 5	ExMt 6	NM 7	NmMt 8	MT 9
175	John David Crow	4	5	5	5	8	12	25	
176	Tommy Davis	4	5	5	5	8	15	50	
177	Jim Johnson	4	5	5	5	8	15	40	
178	Gary Lewis RC	4	5	5	5	8	15	50	
179	Dave Parks	4	5	5	5	8	15	50	
180	Walter Rock RC	4	5	5	5	8	15	50	
181	Ken Willard RC	4	5	5	5	8	15	50	
182	San Francisco 49ers Play	4	5	5	5	8	12	20	40
183	Washington Redskins Team	4	5	5	5	8	15	50	
184	Rickie Harris	4	5	5	5	8	40		
185	Sonny Jurgensen	4	5	5	6	10	20	50	
186	Paul Krause	4	5	5	6	10	15	50	
187	Bobby Mitchell	4	5	5	6	10	15	60	
188	Vince Promuto	4	5	5	5	8	15	80	
189	Pat Richter RC	4	5	5	5	8	15	50	
190	Joe Rutgens	4	5	5	5	8	15	50	
191	Johnny Sample	4	5	5	5	8	15	50	
192	Lonnie Sanders	4	5	5	5	8	15	50	
193	Jim Steffen	4	5	5	5	8	12	25	100
194	Charley Taylor	5	6	6	8	12	20	40	
195	Washington Redskins Play	4	5	5	5	8	15	50	
196	Referee Signals	4	5	5	5	8	15	50	
197	Checklist 1	6	8	8	10	15	25	60	175
198	Checklist 2 UER	6	8	10	12	25	80	250	

— George Andrie #54 PSA 9 (MT) sold for $925 (eBay; 8/06)
— Sam Baker #132 PSA 9 (MT) sold for $1,003 (eBay; 1/10)
— Baltimore Colts #14 PSA 10 (Gem Mt) sold for $1,195 (Mile High; 3/09)
— Bob Brown #134 PSA 9 (MT) sold for $1,619 (eBay; 6/13)
— Bob Hayes RC #58 PSA 9 (MT) sold for $4,003 (eBay; 12/14)
— Dick Butkus #31 PSA 9 (MT) sold for $11,166 (Goodwin; 5/08)
— Dick Butkus RC #31 SGC 9 (Mint) sold for $4716 (Memory Lane; 8/12)
— Dick Butkus #31 PSA 8.5 (NmMt+) sold for $1,655 (Mile High; 5/11)
— Dick Butkus #31 SGC 9 (Mint) sold for $4,075 (eBay; 11/13)
— Checklist 2 #198 PSA 9 (MT) sold for $3,058 (eBay; 8/13)
— Irv Cross #136 PSA 8 (NmMt) sold for $715 (eBay; 1/10)
— Dallas Cowboys #53 PSA 9 (MT) sold for $1,060 (eBay; 1/10)
— Bob Hayes #58 PSA 9 (MT) sold for $1,500 (eBay; 9/12)
— Gene Hickerson #45 PSA 9 (MT) sold for $1,580 (eBay; 3/07)
— Chuck Howley #59 PSA 9 (MT) sold for $1,855 (eBay; 8/06)
— Philadelphia Eagles Play #143 PSA 9 (Mint) sold for $801 (eBay; 7/12)
— Gale Sayers #38 GAI 8.5 (NmMt+) sold for $800 (eBay; 1/07)
— Norm Snead #142 PSA 10 (Gem Mt) sold for $1,063 (Andy Madec; 12/08)
— Fran Tarkenton #114 PSA 9 (MT) sold for $1,740 (Memory Lane; 4/07)
— Fran Tarkenton #114 PSA 9 (Mint) sold for $690 (Bussineau; 4/12)
— Johnny Unitas #24 PSA 9 (MT) sold for $1,030 (eBay; 9/06)

1966 Topps

#		GD 2	VG 3	VgEx 4	EX 5	ExMt 6	NM 7	NmMt 8	MT 9
1	Tommy Addison	4	5	8	12	30	40	60	
2	Houston Antwine	4	5	5	8	12	18	60	
3	Nick Buoniconti	4	5	6	10	15	20	50	
4	Gino Cappelletti	4	5	5	8	12	18	40	150
5	Bob Dee	4	5	5	8	12	18	60	
6	Larry Garron	4	5	5	8	12	18	40	150
7	Art Graham	4	5	5	8	12	18	40	150
8	Ron Hall DB	4	5	5	8	12	18	40	
9	Charles Long	4	5	5	8	12	18	40	120
10	Jon Morris	4	5	5	8	12	18	40	
11	Don Oakes	4	5	5	8	12	18	40	
12	Babe Parilli	4	5	5	8	12	18	40	150
13	Don Webb	4	5	5	8	12	18	40	
14	Jim Whalen	4	5	5	8	12	18	40	
15	Funny Ring Checklist	50	60	80	100	175	800	1,000	
16	Stew Barber	4	5	5	8	12	18	40	120
17	Glenn Bass	4	5	5	8	12	18	40	120
18	Dave Behrman	4	5	5	8	12	18	40	120
19	Al Bemiller	4	5	5	8	12	18	40	120
20	Butch Byrd RC	4	5	5	8	12	18	40	250
21	Wray Carlton	4	5	5	8	12	18	80	
22	Tom Day	4	5	5	8	12	15	40	150
23	Elbert Dubenion	4	5	5	8	12	18	40	
24	Jim Dunaway	4	5	5	8	12	18	25	150
25	Dick Hudson	4	5	5	8	12	18	40	150
26	Jack Kemp	15	20	25	35	50	60	200	
27	Daryle Lamonica	5	6	8	12	18	25	50	
28	Tom Sestak	4	5	5	8	12	18	40	150
29	Billy Shaw	4	5	6	10	15	20	50	120
30	Mike Stratton	4	5	5	8	12	18	40	150
31	Eldon Danenhauer	4	5	5	8	12	18	40	150
32	Cookie Gilchrist	4	5	6	10	15	20	40	
33	Goose Gonsoulin	4	5	5	8	12	18	40	
34	Wendell Hayes RC	4	5	6	10	15	20	40	200
35	Abner Haynes	4	5	6	10	15	20	40	150
36	Jerry Hopkins	4	5	5	8	12	18	40	
37	Ray Jacobs	4	5	5	8	12	18	30	
38	Charlie Janerette	4	5	5	8	12	18	40	150
39	Ray Kubala	4	5	5	8	12	18	40	200
40	John McCormick QB	4	5	5	8	12	18	80	
41	Leroy Moore	4	5	5	8	12	18	40	120
42	Bob Scarpitto	4	5	5	8	12	15	40	150
43	Mickey Slaughter	4	5	5	8	12	18	40	150
44	Jerry Sturm	4	5	5	8	12	18	40	
45	Lionel Taylor	4	5	6	10	15	20	40	
46	Scott Appleton	4	5	5	8	12	18	40	
47	Johnny Baker	4	5	5	8	12	18	40	
48	George Blanda	8	10	12	18	25	40	80	300
49	Sid Blanks	4	5	5	8	12	18	40	
50	Danny Brabham	4	5	5	8	12	18	40	
51	Ode Burrell	4	5	5	8	12	15	30	120
52	Gary Cutsinger	4	5	5	8	12	18	40	120
53	Larry Elkins	4	5	5	8	12	18	40	
54	Don Floyd	4	5	5	8	12	18	40	
55	Willie Frazier RC	4	5	5	8	12	18	40	
56	Freddy Glick	4	5	5	8	12	15	25	150
57	Charlie Hennigan	4	5	5	8	12	15	25	150
58	Bobby Jancik	4	5	5	8	10	12	25	
59	Rich Michael	4	5	5	8	12	18	40	
60	Don Trull	4	5	5	8	12	18	40	
61	Checklist 1	10	12	15	25	40	80	300	
62	Fred Arbanas	4	5	5	8	12	18	20	200
63	Pete Beathard	4	5	5	8	12	20	40	
64	Bobby Bell	4	5	6	10	15	20	50	200
65	Ed Budde	4	5	5	8	12	18	40	
66	Chris Burford	4	5	5	8	12	18	40	150
67	Len Dawson	10	12	15	20	30	50	120	
68	Jon Gilliam	4	5	5	8	12	18	30	150
69	Sherrill Headrick	4	5	5	8	12	18	30	150
70	E.J. Holub	4	5	5	8	12	18	40	150
71	Bobby Hunt	4	5	5	8	12	15	20	120
72	Curtis McClinton	4	5	5	8	12	18	25	250
73	Jerry Mays	4	5	5	8	12	18	40	150
74	Johnny Robinson	4	5	5	8	12	18	60	
75	Otis Taylor RC	5	6	8	12	18	35	125	350
76	Tom Erlandson	4	5	5	8	12	18	40	
77	Norm Evans RC	4	5	6	10	15	20	50	
78	Tom Goode	4	5	5	8	12	18	40	
79	Mike Hudock	4	5	5	8	12	18	30	200
80	Frank Jackson	4	5	5	8	12	18	60	
81	Billy Joe	4	5	5	8	12	18	35	
82	Dave Kocourek	4	5	5	8	12	18	40	
83	Bo Roberson	4	5	5	8	12	18	40	150
84	Jack Spikes	4	5	5	8	12	18	40	
85	Jim Warren RC	4	5	5	8	12	18	40	200
86	Willie West RC	4	5	5	8	12	18	40	
87	Dick Westmoreland	4	5	5	8	12	18	40	150
88	Eddie Wilson	4	5	5	8	12	18	40	
89	Dick Wood	4	5	5	8	12	18	60	
90	Verlon Biggs	4	5	5	8	12	18	40	120
91	Sam DeLuca	4	5	5	8	12	18	40	
92	Winston Hill	4	5	5	8	12	18	40	
93	Dee Mackey	4	5	5	8	12	18	50	
94	Bill Mathis	4	5	5	8	12	18	40	
95	Don Maynard	6	8	10	15	20	30	60	225
96	Joe Namath	50	60	100	125	400	500	600	2,200
97	Dainard Paulson	4	5	5	8	12	18	40	
98	Gerry Philbin	4	5	5	8	12	18	40	
99	Sherman Plunkett	4	5	5	8	12	18	40	80
100	Paul Rochester	4	5	5	8	12	18	50	200
101	George Sauer Jr. RC	4	5	6	10	15	20	40	
102	Matt Snell	4	5	6	10	15	20	40	
103	Jim Turner RC	4	5	5	8	12	18	40	150
104	Fred Biletnikoff	10	12	25	30	40	60	200	300
105	Bill Budness	4	5	5	8	12	18	40	60
106	Billy Cannon	4	5	5	10	15	20	40	
107	Clem Daniels	4	5	5	8	12	18	40	
108	Ben Davidson	4	5	6	10	15	40	50	
109	Cotton Davidson	4	5	5	8	12	18	40	100

#	Player	GD 2	VG 3	VgEx 4	EX 5	ExMt 6	NM 7	NmMt 8	MT 9
10	Claude Gibson	4	5	5	8	12	18	40	
11	Wayne Hawkins	4	5	5	8	12	18	40	100
12	Ken Herock	4	5	5	8	12	18	50	
13	Bob Mischak	4	5	5	8	12	18	60	
14	Gus Otto	4	5	5	8	12	20	50	125
15	Jim Otto	5	6	8	12	18	25	50	350
16	Art Powell	4	5	6	10	15	20	40	120
17	Harry Schuh	4	5	5	8	12	18	40	
18	Chuck Allen	4	5	5	8	12	18	50	
19	Lance Alworth	10	12	15	20	30	60	150	
20	Frank Buncom	4	5	5	8	12	18	100	
21	Steve DeLong	4	5	5	8	12	18	40	
22	John Farris	4	5	5	8	12	18	40	
23	Kenny Graham	4	5	5	8	12	18	30	
24	Sam Gruneisen	4	5	5	8	12	18	40	
25	John Hadl	4	5	6	10	15	20	40	
26	Walt Sweeney	4	5	5	8	15	30	80	
27	Keith Lincoln	4	5	6	10	15	20	40	200
28	Ron Mix	4	5	6	10	15	20	40	
29	Don Norton	4	5	5	8	12	18	40	200
30	Pat Shea	4	5	5	8	12	18	40	
31	Ernie Wright	4	5	6	10	15	20	100	
32	Checklist 2	25	30	40	75	150	300		

— Tommy Addison #1 PSA 9 (MT) sold for $756 (Mile High; 11/10)
— Bobby Bell #64 PSA 10 (Gem Mt) sold for $1,242 (Mile High; 5/11)
— Fred Biletnikoff #104 PSA 9 (MT) sold for $2,545 (Memory Lane; 4/07)
— Ed Budde #65 PSA 9 (MT) sold for $700 (eBay; 6/11)
— Nick Buoniconti #3 PSA 9 (MT) sold for $425 (eBay; 1/06)
— Len Dawson #67 PSA 9 (MT) sold for $925 (eBay; 9/05)
— Kenny Graham #123 PSA 10 (Gem Mt) sold for $628 (Mile High; 5/11)
— Bobby Hunt #71 PSA 10 (Gem Mt) sold for $1,477 (Mastro; 2/07)
— Bobby Hunt #71 PSA 10 (Gem Mt) sold for $1,214 (eBay; 1/10)
— Don Maynard #95 PSA 10 (Gem Mt) sold for $1,640 (Mastro; 4/07)
— Don Maynard #95 PSA 9 (MT) sold for $795 (eBay; 3/05)
— Joe Namath #96 PSA 10 (Gem Mt) sold for $14,771 (Mile High; 11/10)
— Jim Otto #115 PSA 9 (MT) sold for $790 (eBay; 4/07)
— Willie West RC #86 PSA 10 (Gem Mint) sold for $570 (Bussineau; 7/12)

1967 Philadelphia

#	Player	GD 2	VG 3	VgEx 4	EX 5	ExMt 6	NM 7	NmMt 8	MT 9
1	Atlanta Falcons Team	4	5	5	6	10	20	125	
2	Junior Coffey RC	4	5	5	5	8	15	30	
3	Alex Hawkins	4	5	5	5	8	12	35	
4	Randy Johnson RC	4	5	5	5	8	12	35	80
5	Lou Kirouac	4	5	5	5	8	12	25	80
6	Billy Martin RC	4	5	5	5	8	12	35	80
7	Tommy Nobis RC	5	6	8	10	18	35	150	
8	Jerry Richardson RC	4	5	5	6	10	15	30	
9	Marion Rushing	4	5	5	5	8	12	25	80
10	Ron Smith	4	5	5	5		10	20	
11	Ernie Wheelwright	4	5	5	5		10	20	
12	Atlanta Falcons Logo	4	5	5	5		10	20	
13	Baltimore Colts Team	4	5	5	5	8	12	25	80
14	Raymond Berry	4	5	6	8	12	20	60	
15	Bob Boyd DB	4	5	5	5	8	12	35	80
16	Ordell Braase RC	4	5	5	5	8	12	35	80
17	Alvin Haymond RC	4	5	5	5	8	12	35	250
18	Tony Lorick	4	5	5	5	8	12	35	
19	Lenny Lyles	4	5	5	5	8	15	50	
20	John Mackey	4	5	5	6	10	15	40	120
21	Tom Matte	4	5	5	5		10	25	
22	Lou Michaels	4	5	5	5	8	15	30	
23	Johnny Unitas	15	18	20	25	40	80	600	
24	Baltimore Colts Logo	4	5	5	5		10	20	
25	Chicago Bears Team	4	5	5	5	8	12	35	
26	Rudy Bukich	4	5	5	8	12	25	50	
27	Ronnie Bull	4	5	5	5	8	12	35	
28	Dick Butkus	15	18	20	40	50	150	500	
29	Mike Ditka	8	10	12	15	25	60	100	
30	Dick Gordon RC	4	5	5	5	8	12	40	80
31	Roger LeClerc	4	5	5	5	8	15	100	
32	Bennie McRae	4	5	5	5	8	12	25	
33	Richie Petitbon	4	5	5	5	8	12	30	80
34	Mike Pyle	4	5	5	5	8	12	40	80
35	Gale Sayers	15	20	25	40	60	100	300	1,200
36	Chicago Bears Logo	4	5	5	5	8	12	35	
37	Cleveland Browns Team	4	5	5	5	8	12	35	100
38	Johnny Brewer	4	5	5	5	8	12	35	80

#	Player	GD 2	VG 3	VgEx 4	EX 5	ExMt 6	NM 7	NmMt 8	MT 9
39	Gary Collins	4	5	5	5	8	12	30	
40	Ross Fichtner	4	5	5	5	8	15	25	
41	Ernie Green	4	5	5	5	8	12	40	
42	Gene Hickerson	4	5	5	5	8	15	100	
43	Leroy Kelly RC	15	18	20	25	35	150	800	
44	Frank Ryan	4	5	5	5		10	20	
45	Dick Schafrath	4	5	5	5	8	12	35	
46	Paul Warfield	4	5	6	8	12	20	50	300
47	John Wooten	4	5	5	6		10	50	
48	Cleveland Browns Logo	4	5	5	5	8	12	35	100
49	Dallas Cowboys Team	4	5	5	5	8	12	35	80
50	George Andrie	4	5	5	5	8	20	80	
51	Cornell Green	4	5	5	5	8	12	35	80
52	Bob Hayes	5	6	8	10	15	40	100	250
53	Chuck Howley	4	5	5	6	10	25	35	
54	Lee Roy Jordan RC	4	5	6	8	12	30	80	300
55	Bob Lilly	4	5	6	8	12	20	50	350
56	Dave Manders RC	4	5	5	5	8	15	200	
57	Don Meredith	6	8	10	12	20	40	175	
58	Dan Reeves RC	10	12	15	20	30	50	300	
59	Mel Renfro	4	5	6	10		30	40	
60	Dallas Cowboys Logo	4	5	5	5	8	12	35	100
61	Detroit Lions Team	4	5	5	5	8	15	30	
62	Roger Brown	4	5	5	5	8	12	35	
63	Gail Cogdill	4	5	5	5	8	12	35	250
64	John Gordy	4	5	5	5	8	12	35	
65	Ron Kramer	4	5	5	5	8	12	25	50
66	Dick LeBeau	4	5	5	5	8	12	35	80
67	Mike Lucci RC	4	5	5	6	10	15	35	125
68	Amos Marsh	4	5	5	5	8	12	30	
69	Tom Nowatzke	4	5	5	5	8	12	30	80
70	Pat Studstill	4	5	5	5	8	12	30	
71	Karl Sweetan	4	5	5	5	8	12	30	
72	Detroit Lions Logo	4	5	5	5	8	12	30	80
73	Green Bay Packers Team	4	5	5	6	12	20	500	
74	Herb Adderley	4	5	5	6	10	15	30	100
75	Lee Roy Caffey	4	5	5	5	8	12	80	
76	Willie Davis DE	4	5	5	6	10	15	35	200
77	Forrest Gregg	4	5	5	6	10	15	60	
78	Hank Jordan	4	5	5	6	10	15	35	350
79	Ray Nitschke	4	5	6	8	12	40	60	
80	Dave Robinson RC	12	15	20	30	40	60	175	500
81	Bob Skoronski	4	5	5	5	8	20	100	
82	Bart Starr	15	18	20	50	60	80	300	
83	Willie Wood	4	5	5	6	10	20	100	
84	Green Bay Packers Logo	4	5	5	5	8	12	30	
85	Los Angeles Rams Team	4	5	5	5	8	15	50	
86	Dick Bass	4	5	5	5	8	12	30	40
87	Maxie Baughan	4	5	5	5	8	15	30	
88	Roman Gabriel	4	5	5	6	10	15	25	100
89	Bruce Gossett	4	5	5	5	8	12	30	60
90	Deacon Jones	4	5	5	6	10	15	35	100
91	Tommy McDonald	4	5	5	6	10	15	35	100
92	Marlin McKeever	4	5	5	5	8	15	30	
93	Tom Moore	4	5	5	5	8	12	30	60
94	Merlin Olsen	4	5	5	6	10	15	35	
95	Clancy Williams	4	5	5	5	8	12	30	60
96	Los Angeles Rams Logo	4	5	5	5	8	12	30	80
97	Minnesota Vikings Team	4	5	5	5	8	12	30	80
98	Grady Alderman	4	5	5	5	8	15	30	
99	Bill Brown	4	5	5	5	8	15	30	
100	Fred Cox	4	5	5	5	8	15	30	
101	Paul Flatley	4	5	5	5	8	12	30	80
102	Dale Hackbart RC	4	5	5	5	8	12	30	80
103	Jim Marshall	4	5	5	6	10	15	25	100
104	Tommy Mason	4	5	5	5	8	15	30	
105	Milt Sunde RC	4	5	5	5	8		25	
106	Fran Tarkenton	5	6	8	10	18	50	60	350
107	Mick Tingelhoff	4	5	5	5	8	12	30	
108	Minnesota Vikings Logo	4	5	5	5	8		25	
109	New York Giants Team	4	5	5	5	8	12	30	80
110	Henry Carr	4	5	5	5		10	20	
111	Clarence Childs	4	5	5	5	8	12	30	
112	Allen Jacobs	4	5	5	5	8	15	50	
113	Homer Jones RC	4	5	5	5	8	12	30	80
114	Tom Kennedy	4	5	5	5	8	15	80	
115	Spider Lockhart	4	5	5	5	8	15	30	
116	Joe Morrison	4	5	5	5	8	12	25	80
117	Francis Peay	4	5	5	5	8	12	30	80

#	Player	GD 2	VG 3	VgEx 4	EX 5	ExMt 6	NM 7	NmMt 8	MT 9
118	Jeff Smith LB	4	5	5	5	8	12	30	80
119	Aaron Thomas	4	5	5	5	8	12	25	80
120	New York Giants Logo	4	5	5	5	8	12	40	
121	New Orleans Saints Logo	4	5	5	5	8	12	35	80
122	Charley Bradshaw	4	5	5	5	8	12	20	80
123	Paul Hornung	6	8	15	15	30	40	200	
124	Elbert Kimbrough	4	5	5	5	8	15	80	
125	Earl Leggett RC	4	5	5	5	8	15	30	
126	Obert Logan	4	5	5	5	8	15	30	
127	Riley Mattson	4	5	5	5	8	15	80	
128	John Morrow	4	5	5	5	8	12	30	
129	Bob Scholtz	4	5	5	5	8	12	40	80
130	Dave Whitsell RC	4	5	5	5	8	12	30	80
131	Gary Wood	4	5	5	5	8	12	20	80
132	NO Saints Roster ERR 121	4	5	5	5	8	12	30	
133	Philadelphia Eagles Team	4	5	5	5	8	12	30	80
134	Sam Baker	4	5	5	5	8	12	20	80
135	Bob Brown OT	4	5	5	6	10	20	60	
136	Timmy Brown	4	5	5	5	8	15	50	
137	Earl Gros	4	5	5	5	8	12	30	
138	Dave Lloyd	4	5	5	5	8	12	30	
139	Floyd Peters	4	5	5	5	8	12	30	
140	Pete Retzlaff	4	5	5	5	8	12	30	80
141	Joe Scarpati	4	5	5	5	8	12	30	
142	Norm Snead	4	5	5	5	8	12	35	120
143	Jim Skaggs	4	5	5	5	8	12	30	
144	Philadelphia Eagles Logo	4	5	5	5	8	15	200	
145	Pittsburgh Steelers Team	4	5	5	5	8	15	40	
146	Bill Asbury	4	5	5	5	8	12	30	
147	John Baker	4	5	5	5	8	15	30	
148	Gary Ballman	4	5	5	5	8	12	30	
149	Mike Clark	4	5	5	5	8	12	30	50
150	Riley Gunnels	4	5	5	5	8	15	50	
151	John Hilton	4	5	5	5	8	12	25	60
152	Roy Jefferson	4	5	5	5	8	15	30	
153	Brady Keys	4	5	5	5	8	15	30	
154	Ben McGee	4	5	5	5	8	12	30	
155	Bill Nelsen	4	5	5	5	8	12	30	
156	Pittsburgh Steelers Logo	4	5	5	5	8	12	30	
157	St. Louis Cardinals Team	4	5	5	5	8	12	30	
158	Jim Bakken	4	5	5	5	8	15	30	
159	Bobby Joe Conrad	4	5	5	5	8	15	30	
160	Ken Gray	4	5	5	5	8	12	30	
161	Charlie Johnson	4	5	5	5	8	15	30	
162	Joe Robb	4	5	5	5	8	15	30	
163	Johnny Roland RC	4	5	5	5	8	12	30	80
164	Roy Shivers	4	5	5	5	8	15	25	
165	Jackie Smith RC	6	8	10	12	20	50	▲200	
166	Jerry Stovall	4	5	5	5	8	12	30	
167	Larry Wilson	4	5	5	6	10	15	25	
168	St. Louis Cardinals Logo	4	5	5	5	8	15	30	80
169	San Francisco 49ers Team	4	5	5	5	8	15	30	
170	Kermit Alexander	4	5	5	5	8	12	30	
171	Bruce Bosley	4	5	5	5	8	12	30	
172	John Brodie	4	5	5	6	10	20	50	
173	Bernie Casey	4	5	5	5	8	15	30	
174	Tommy Davis	4	5	5	5	8	15	30	
175	Howard Mudd	4	5	5	6	10	20	100	
176	Dave Parks	4	5	5	5	8	15	30	
177	John Thomas	4	5	5	5	8	15	30	
178	Dave Wilcox RC	5	6	8	10	50	80	150	350
179	Ken Willard	4	5	5	5	8	15	30	
180	San Francisco 49ers Logo	4	5	5	5	8	12	30	
181	Washington Redskins Team	4	5	5	5	8	12	40	
182	Charlie Gogolak RC	4	5	5	5	8	12	25	
183	Chris Hanburger RC	5	6	8	10	40	100	200	
184	Len Hauss RC	4	5	5	5	8	15	50	
185	Sonny Jurgensen	4	5	5	6	10	15	35	175
186	Bobby Mitchell	4	5	5	6	10	15	25	80
187	Brig Owens	4	5	5	5	8	12	30	
188	Jim Shorter	4	5	5	5	8	15	35	
189	Jerry Smith RC	4	5	5	5	8	15	80	
190	Charley Taylor	4	5	6	8	12	20	60	
191	A.D. Whitfield	4	5	5	5	8	12	25	50
192	Washington Redskins Logo	4	5	5	5	8	15	50	
193	Browns Play/Leroy Kelly	4	5	5	5	10	15	30	
194	Giants Play/Joe Morrison	4	5	5	5	8	12	30	
195	Falcons Play/Wheelwright	4	5	5	5	8	12	25	
196	Referee Signals	4	5	5	5	6	10	35	

#	Player	GD 2	VG 3	VgEx 4	EX 5	ExMt 6	NM 7	NmMt 8	MT 9
197	Checklist 1	4	5	6	8	12	20	35	80
198	Checklist 2	8	10	12	15	40	50	80	300

— Bob Lilly #55 PSA 10 (Gem) sold for $1,232 (eBay; 2/14)
— Raymond Berry #14 PSA 10 (Gem) sold for $1,140 (eBay; 2/07)
— Charley Bradshaw #122 PSA 10 (Gem) sold for $892 (Memory Lane; 5/08)
— Junior Coffey #2 PSA 10 (Gem) sold for $795 (eBay; 5/05)
— Willie Davis #76 PSA 10 (Gem) sold for $803 (eBay; 9/13)
— Chris Hanburger #183 PSA 9 (MT) sold for $4497 (eBay; 11/14)
— Hank Jordan #78 PSA 10 (Gem) sold for $818 (eBay; 8/13)
— Tommy Nobis #7 PSA 9 (MT) sold for $435 (eBay; 9/05)
— Merlin Olsen #94 PSA 9 (MT) sold for $365 (eBay; 1/06)
— Dan Reeves #58 PSA 9 (MT) sold for $1,465 (eBay; 2/07)
— Johnny Unitas #23 PSA 9 (Mint) sold for $2909.55 (Memory Lane; 5/12)
— Ken Willard #179 PSA 10 (Gem) sold for $2,544 (Memory Lane; 5/08)

1967 Topps

#	Player	GD 2	VG 3	VgEx 4	EX 5	ExMt 6	NM 7	NmMt 8	MT 9
1	John Huarte	4	5	5	5	10	30	80	200
2	Babe Parilli	4	5	5	5	8	15	100	
3	Gino Cappelletti	4	5	5	5	8	12	25	100
4	Larry Garron	4	5	5	5	8	12	25	80
5	Tommy Addison	4	5	5	5	8	12	25	80
6	Jon Morris	4	5	5	5	8	12	25	80
7	Houston Antwine	4	5	5	5	8	12	35	
8	Don Oakes	4	5	5	5	8	12	35	
9	Larry Eisenhauer	4	5	5	5	8	12	25	
10	Jim Hunt	4	5	5	5	8	12	35	
11	Jim Whalen	4	5	5	5	8	12	25	80
12	Art Graham	4	5	5	5	8	12	25	80
13	Nick Buoniconti	4	5	5	5	10	15	40	
14	Bob Dee	4	5	5	5	8	12	25	80
15	Keith Lincoln	4	5	5	5	8	15	30	100
16	Tom Flores	4	5	5	5	8	15	30	100
17	Art Powell	4	5	5	5	8	12	25	80
18	Stew Barber	4	5	5	5	8	12	25	80
19	Wray Carlton	4	5	5	5	8	12	35	
20	Elbert Dubenion	4	5	5	5	8	12	25	80
21	Jim Dunaway	4	5	5	5	8	12	25	80
22	Dick Hudson	4	5	5	5	8	12	25	80
23	Harry Jacobs	4	5	5	5	8	12	35	
24	Jack Kemp	12	15	20	25	40	50	60	200
25	Ron McDole	4	5	5	5	8	12	25	50
26	George Saimes	4	5	5	5	8	12	25	100
27	Tom Sestak	4	5	5	5	8	12	35	
28	Billy Shaw	4	5	5	5	8	15	30	100
29	Mike Stratton	4	5	5	5	8	12	25	80
30	Nemiah Wilson RC	4	5	5	5	8	12	25	80
31	John McCormick QB	4	5	5	5	8	12	25	80
32	Rex Mirich	4	5	5	5	8	15	50	150
33	Dave Costa	4	5	5	5	8	12	25	80
34	Goose Gonsoulin	4	5	5	5	8	12	25	80
35	Abner Haynes	4	5	5	5	8	12	25	80
36	Wendell Hayes	4	5	5	5	8	12	25	60
37	Archie Matsos	4	5	5	5	8	12	25	80
38	John Bramlett	4	5	5	5	8	12	25	80
39	Jerry Sturm	4	5	5	5	8	12	30	40
40	Max Leetzow	4	5	5	5	8	12	25	80
41	Bob Scarpitto	4	5	5	5	8	12	25	80
42	Lionel Taylor	4	5	5	5	8	15	30	100
43	Al Denson	4	5	5	5	8	12	25	80
44	Miller Farr RC	4	5	5	5	8	12	25	60
45	Don Trull	4	5	5	5	8	12	20	
46	Jacky Lee	4	5	5	5	8	12	20	80
47	Bobby Jancik	4	5	5	5	8	12	25	80
48	Ode Burrell	4	5	5	5	8	12	30	
49	Larry Elkins	4	5	5	5	8	10	30	60
50	W.K. Hicks	4	5	5	5	8	12	25	80
51	Sid Blanks	4	5	5	5	8	12	25	80
52	Jim Norton	4	5	5	5	8	12	25	80
53	Bobby Maples RC	4	5	5	5	8	12	35	100
54	Bob Talamini	4	5	5	5	8	12	35	
55	Walt Suggs	4	5	5	5	8	12	25	80
56	Gary Cutsinger	4	5	5	5	8	12	25	80
57	Danny Brabham	4	5	5	5	5	8	35	80
58	Ernie Ladd	4	5	5	5	8	15	30	100
59	Checklist 1	6	8	10	12	25	50	100	
60	Pete Beathard	4	5	5	5	8	12	25	80
61	Len Dawson	6	8	10	12	18	30	80	300

		GD 2	VG 3	VgEx 4	EX 5	ExMt 6	NM 7	NmMt 8	MT 9
62	Bobby Hunt	4	5	5	5	8	12	25	80
63	Bert Coan	4	5	5	5	8	12	25	80
64	Curtis McClinton	4	5	5	5	8	12	25	80
65	Johnny Robinson	4	5	5	5	8	12	25	80
66	E.J. Holub	4	5	5	5	8	12	25	80
67	Jerry Mays	4	5	5	5	8	12	25	80
68	Jim Tyrer	4	5	5	5	8	12	35	
69	Bobby Bell	4	5	5	5	8	15	40	100
70	Fred Arbanas	4	5	5	5	8	12	35	
71	Buck Buchanan	4	5	5	5	8	15	30	100
72	Chris Burford	4	5	5	5	8	12	50	
73	Otis Taylor	4	5	5	5	8	15	30	100
74	Cookie Gilchrist	4	5	5	6	10	15	30	100
75	Earl Faison	4	5	5	5	8	12	50	80
76	George Wilson Jr.	4	5	5	5	8	12	30	150
77	Rick Norton	4	5	5	5	8	12	25	120
78	Frank Jackson	4	5	5	5	8	12	25	80
79	Joe Auer	4	5	5	5	8	12	40	
80	Willie West	4	5	5	5	8	12	25	80
81	Jim Warren	4	5	5	5	8	12	35	
82	Wahoo McDaniel RC	10	12	15	25	80	100	▲150	250
83	Ernie Park	4	5	5	5	8	12	25	80
84	Billy Neighbors	4	5	5	5	8	12	25	150
85	Norm Evans	4	5	5	5	8	12	40	120
86	Tom Nomina	4	5	5	5	8	12	30	100
87	Rich Zecher	4	5	5	5	8	12	30	100
88	Dave Kocourek	4	5	5	5	8	12	25	80
89	Bill Baird	4	5	5	5	8	12	25	80
90	Ralph Baker	4	5	5	5	8	12	25	80
91	Verlon Biggs	4	5	5	5	8	12	25	80
92	Sam DeLuca	4	5	5	5	8	12	25	80
93	Larry Grantham	4	5	5	5	8	12	25	100
94	Jim Harris	4	5	5	5	8	12	25	80
95	Winston Hill	4	5	5	5	8	12	25	
96	Bill Mathis	4	5	5	5	8	12	25	80
97	Don Maynard	4	5	6	8	12	20	60	
98	Joe Namath	20	30	100	125	150	200	350	800
99	Gerry Philbin	4	5	5	5	8	12	25	50
100	Paul Rochester	4	5	5	5	8	12	30	
101	George Sauer Jr.	4	5	5	5	8	12	30	120
102	Matt Snell	4	5	5	5	8	15	35	
103	Daryle Lamonica	4	5	5	6	10	30	40	150
104	Glenn Bass	4	5	5	5	8	12	25	80
105	Jim Otto	4	5	5	5	8	15	30	120
106	Fred Biletnikoff	6	8	10	12	18	30	80	300
107	Cotton Davidson	4	5	5	5	8	12	30	
108	Larry Todd	4	5	5	5	8	12	30	
109	Billy Cannon	4	5	5	5	8	15	30	
110	Clem Daniels	4	5	5	5	8	12	30	
111	Dave Grayson	4	5	5	5	8	12	25	80
112	Kent McCloughan RC	4	5	5	5	8	12	25	80
113	Bob Svihus	4	5	5	5	8	12	25	80
114	Ike Lassiter	4	5	5	5	8	12	25	80
115	Harry Schuh	4	5	5	5	8	12	25	80
116	Ben Davidson	4	5	5	6	10	15	30	200
117	Tom Day	4	5	5	5	8	12	30	
118	Scott Appleton	4	5	5	5	8	12	25	80
119	Steve Tensi RC	4	5	5	5	8	12	30	
120	John Hadl	4	5	5	5	8	15	30	100
121	Paul Lowe	4	5	5	5	8	12	25	125
122	Jim Allison	4	5	5	5	8	12	25	80
123	Lance Alworth	8	10	12	15	20	35	80	400
124	Jacque MacKinnon	4	5	5	5	8	12	25	80
125	Ron Mix	4	5	5	5	8	15	30	
126	Bob Petrich	4	5	5	5	8	12	25	80
127	Howard Kindig	4	5	5	5	8	12	25	100
128	Steve DeLong	4	5	5	5	8	12	25	80
129	Chuck Allen	4	5	5	5	8	12	35	
130	Frank Buncom	4	5	5	5	8	12	25	80
131	Speedy Duncan RC	4	5	5	6	8	12	80	350
132	Checklist 2	12	15	20	25	40	75	150	

– Don Maynard #97 PSA 10 (Gem Mt) sold for $1,206 (Mile High; 10/09)
– Wahoo McDaniel #82 PSA 9 (Mint) sold for $1,205 (eBay; 3/07)
– Wahoo McDaniel #82 PSA 10 (Gem) sold for $768 (Lelands; 6/13)
– Billy Neighbors #84 PSA 10 (Gem Mint) sold for $515.64 (eBay; 9/12)
– Larry Todd #108 PSA 10 (Gem Mint) sold for $912.5 (eBay; 5/12)

1968 Topps

		GD 2	VG 3	VgEx 4	EX 5	ExMt 6	NM 7	NmMt 8	MT 9
1	Bart Starr	8	10	12	60	80	100	400	1,200
2	Dick Bass	4	5	5	5	6	10	20	80
3	Grady Alderman	4	5	5	5	6	10	40	
4	Obert Logan	4	5	5	5	6	10	20	80
5	Ernie Koy RC	4	5	5	5	6	10	40	100
6	Don Hultz	4	5	5	5	6	15	30	150
7	Earl Gros	4	5	5	5	6	10	20	50
8	Jim Bakken	4	5	5	5	6	10	20	80
9	George Mira	4	5	5	5	6	10	30	100
10	Carl Kammerer	4	5	5	5	6	10	20	60
11	Willie Frazier	4	5	5	5	6	10	20	50
12	Kent McCloughan	4	5	5	5	6	10	60	
13	George Sauer Jr.	4	5	5	5	6	10	20	80
14	Jack Clancy	4	5	5	5	6	10	30	
15	Jim Tyrer	4	5	5	5	6	10	30	150
16	Bobby Maples	4	5	5	5	6	10	20	80
17	Bo Hickey	4	5	5	5	6	10	20	80
18	Frank Buncom	4	5	5	5	6	10	30	
19	Keith Lincoln	4	5	5	5	6	10	20	100
20	Jim Whalen	4	5	5	5	6	10	30	
21	Junior Coffey	4	5	5	5	6	10	30	
22	Billy Ray Smith	4	5	5	5	6	10	25	
23	Johnny Morris	4	5	5	5	6	10	20	50
24	Ernie Green	4	5	5	5	6	10	25	60
25	Don Meredith	5	6	8	10	20	25	80	400
26	Wayne Walker	4	5	5	5	6	10	20	50
27	Carroll Dale	4	5	5	5	6	40	250	
28	Bernie Casey	4	5	5	5	6	10	30	
29	Dave Osborn RC	4	5	5	5	6	10	20	80
30	Ray Poage	4	5	5	5	6	10	20	80
31	Homer Jones	4	5	5	5	6	10	20	80
32	Sam Baker	4	5	5	5	6	10	30	
33	Bill Saul	4	5	5	5	6	10	20	80
34	Ken Willard	4	5	5	5	6	10	30	100
35	Bobby Mitchell	4	5	5	5	6	10	30	100
36	Gary Garrison RC	4	5	5	5	6	10	20	125
37	Billy Cannon	4	5	5	5	6	10	30	100
38	Ralph Baker	4	5	5	5	6	10	20	80
39	Howard Twilley RC	4	5	5	5	6	10	30	120
40	Wendell Hayes	4	5	5	5	6	10	20	80
41	Jim Norton	4	5	5	5	6	10	30	100
42	Tom Beer	4	5	5	5	6	10	30	
43	Chris Burford	4	5	5	5	6	10	30	
44	Stew Barber	4	5	5	5	6	10	40	
45	Leroy Mitchell	4	5	5	5	6	10	60	
46	Dan Grimm	4	5	5	5	6	10	30	
47	Jerry Logan	4	5	5	5	6	10	20	80
48	Andy Livingston	4	5	5	5	6	10	30	100
49	Paul Warfield	4	5	6	8	12	20	50	150
50	Don Perkins	4	5	5	5	6	10	20	80
51	Ron Kramer	4	5	5	5	6	10	20	50
52	Bob Jeter RC	4	5	5	5	6	10	30	
53	Les Josephson RC	4	5	5	5	6	10	20	60
54	Bobby Walden	4	5	5	5	6	10	20	80
55	Checklist 1	4	5	5	6	10	20	30	150
56	Walter Roberts	4	5	5	5	6	10	20	80
57	Henry Carr	4	5	5	5	6	10	30	
58	Gary Ballman	4	5	5	5	6	10	30	
59	J.R. Wilburn	4	5	5	5	6	10	20	80
60	Jim Hart RC	4	5	5	5	8	12	30	100
61	Jim Johnson	4	5	5	5	6	10	20	80
62	Chris Hanburger	4	5	5	5	6	10	25	125
63	John Hadl	4	5	5	5	6	10	25	125
64	Hewritt Dixon	4	5	5	5	6	10	30	
65	Joe Namath	20	25	30	80	150	200	250	800
66	Jim Warren	4	5	5	5	6	10	30	100
67	Curtis McClinton	4	5	5	5	6	10	20	80
68	Bob Talamini	4	5	5	5	6	10	30	
69	Steve Tensi	4	5	5	5	6	10	20	80
70	Dick Van Raaphorst	4	5	5	5	6	10	30	
71	Art Powell	4	5	5	5	6	10	20	80
72	Jim Nance RC	4	5	5	5	6	10	30	200
73	Bob Riggle	4	5	5	5	6	10	20	80
74	John Mackey	4	5	5	5		10	25	60
75	Gale Sayers	10	12	20	25	50	60	300	600

#	Player	GD 2	VG 3	VgEx 4	EX 5	ExMt 6	NM 7	NmMt 8	MT 9
76	Gene Hickerson	4	5	5	5	6	10	30	
77	Dan Reeves	4	5	5	5	8	12	100	
78	Tom Nowatzke	4	5	5	5	6	10	20	80
79	Elijah Pitts	4	5	5	5	6	12	80	
80	Lamar Lundy	4	5	5	5	6	10	30	100
81	Paul Flatley	4	5	5	5	6	10	20	60
82	Dave Whitsell	4	5	5	5	6	10	40	
83	Spider Lockhart	4	5	5	5	6	10	20	80
84	Dave Lloyd	4	5	5	5	6	10	20	80
85	Roy Jefferson	4	5	5	5	6	10	20	80
86	Jackie Smith	4	5	5	5	8	12	40	150
87	John David Crow	4	5	5	5	6	10	30	
88	Sonny Jurgensen	4	5	5	5	8	12	40	
89	Ron Mix	4	5	5	5	6	10	30	
90	Clem Daniels	4	5	5	5	6	10	30	
91	Cornell Gordon	4	5	5	5	6	10	20	60
92	Tom Goode	4	5	5	5	6	10	30	100
93	Bobby Bell	4	5	5	5	6	10	30	150
94	Walt Suggs	4	5	5	5	6	10	40	
95	Eric Crabtree	4	5	5	5	6	10	30	
96	Sherrill Headrick	4	5	5	5	6	10	20	50
97	Wray Carlton	4	5	5	5	6	10	20	80
98	Gino Cappelletti	4	5	5	5	6	10	20	60
99	Tommy McDonald	4	5	5	5	6	10	20	80
100	Johnny Unitas	10	12	15	40	50	100	200	600
101	Richie Petitbon	4	5	5	5	6	10	30	
102	Erich Barnes	4	5	5	5	6	10	30	
103	Bob Hayes	4	5	5	5	8	12	50	
104	Milt Plum	4	5	5	5	6	10	30	80
105	Boyd Dowler	4	5	5	5	6	10	40	
106	Ed Meador	4	5	5	5	6	10	25	100
107	Fred Cox	4	5	5	5	6	10	25	100
108	Steve Stonebreaker RC	4	5	5	5	6	10	20	60
109	Aaron Thomas	4	5	5	5	6	10	20	80
110	Norm Snead	4	5	5	5	6	10	20	60
111	Paul Martha RC	4	5	5	5	10	25	100	
112	Jerry Stovall	4	5	5	5	6	10	20	60
113	Kay McFarland	4	5	5	5	6	10	25	
114	Pat Richter	4	5	5	5	6	10	20	80
115	Rick Redman	4	5	5	5	6	10	30	
116	Tom Keating	4	5	5	5	6	10	20	100
117	Matt Snell	4	5	5	5	6	10	25	100
118	Dick Westmoreland	4	5	5	5	6	10	30	
119	Jerry Mays	4	5	5	5	6	10	30	
120	Sid Blanks	4	5	5	5	6	10	20	80
121	Al Denson	4	5	5	5	6	10	30	
122	Bobby Hunt	4	5	5	5	6	10	30	
123	Mike Mercer	4	5	5	5	6	10	60	
124	Nick Buoniconti	4	5	5	5	6	10	40	
125	Ron Vanderkelen RC	4	5	5	5	6	10	30	
126	Ordell Braase	4	5	5	5	6	10	150	
127	Dick Butkus	10	12	15	20	30	50	100	600
128	Gary Collins	4	5	5	5	6	10	20	80
129	Mel Renfro	4	5	5	5	8	15	40	150
130	Alex Karras	4	5	5	5	6	10	30	150
131	Herb Adderley	4	5	5	5	6	15	80	
132	Roman Gabriel	4	5	5	5	6	10	25	80
133	Bill Brown	4	5	5	5	6	10	20	
134	Kent Kramer	4	5	5	5	6	10	30	
135	Tucker Frederickson	4	5	5	5	6	10	40	
136	Nate Ramsey	4	5	5	5	6	10	20	80
137	Marv Woodson	4	5	5	5	6	10	20	50
138	Ken Gray	4	5	5	5	6	10	20	80
139	John Brodie	4	5	5	5	6	10	20	100
140	Jerry Smith	4	5	5	5	6	10	150	
141	Brad Hubbert	4	5	5	5	6	10	20	50
142	George Blanda	4	5	6	8	12	30	50	150
143	Pete Lammons RC	4	5	5	5	6	10	40	120
144	Doug Moreau	4	5	5	5	6	10	20	80
145	E.J. Holub	4	5	5	5	6	10	20	80
146	Ode Burrell	4	5	5	5	6	10	20	80
147	Bob Scarpitto	4	5	5	5	6	10	20	80
148	Andre White	4	5	5	5	6	10	40	
149	Jack Kemp	8	10	12	15	30	40	60	
150	Art Graham	4	5	5	5	6	10	20	50
151	Tommy Nobis	4	5	5	5	8	12	25	100
152	Willie Richardson RC	4	5	5	5	6	10	30	
153	Jack Concannon	4	5	5	5	6	10	50	
154	Bill Glass	4	5	5	5	6	10	20	60

#	Player	GD 2	VG 3	VgEx 4	EX 5	ExMt 6	NM 7	NmMt 8	MT 9
155	Craig Morton RC	4	5	5	5	8	15	100	200
156	Pat Studstill	4	5	5	5	6	10	20	80
157	Ray Nitschke	4	5	8	15	30	80	150	400
158	Roger Brown	4	5	5	5	6	10	30	
159	Joe Kapp RC	4	5	5	5	6	10	25	125
160	Jim Taylor	5	5	6	8	12	20	40	135
161	Fran Tarkenton	5	6	8	10	15	50	80	200
162	Mike Ditka	6	8	10	12	20	35	100	250
163	Andy Russell RC	4	5	5	6	10	30	100	250
164	Larry Wilson	4	5	5	5	6	10	20	80
165	Tommy Davis	4	5	5	5	6	10	20	80
166	Paul Krause	4	5	5	5	6	10	20	100
167	Speedy Duncan	4	5	5	5	6	10	25	200
168	Fred Biletnikoff	5	6	8	10	15	20	50	200
169	Don Maynard	4	5	5	6	10	15	30	120
170	Frank Emanuel	4	5	5	5	6	10	20	150
171	Len Dawson	5	5	6	8	12	20	60	350
172	Miller Farr	4	5	5	5	6	10	20	80
173	Floyd Little RC	8	10	12	15	30	80	150	
174	Lonnie Wright	4	5	5	5	6	10	30	
175	Paul Costa	4	5	5	5	6	10	20	80
176	Don Trull	4	5	5	5	6	10	40	
177	Jerry Simmons	4	5	5	5	6	10	40	
178	Tom Matte	4	5	5	5	6	10	20	50
179	Bennie McRae	4	5	5	5	6	10	30	120
180	Jim Kanicki	4	5	5	5	6	10	20	100
181	Bob Lilly	5	5	6	8	12	20	80	150
182	Tom Watkins	4	5	5	5	6	10	30	100
183	Jim Grabowski RC	4	5	5	5	8	15	50	
184	Jack Snow RC	4	5	5	5	6	10	30	150
185	Gary Cuozzo RC	4	5	5	5	6	10	20	50
186	Billy Kilmer	4	5	5	5	6	10	30	
187	Jim Katcavage	4	5	5	5	6	10	20	80
188	Floyd Peters	4	5	5	5	6	10	30	50
189	Bill Nelsen	4	5	5	5	6	10	20	50
190	Bobby Joe Conrad	4	5	5	5	6	10	20	80
191	Kermit Alexander	4	5	5	5	6	10	30	100
192	Charley Taylor	4	5	5	5	8	20	25	100
193	Lance Alworth	5	6	8	10	15	25	50	400
194	Daryle Lamonica	4	5	5	5	6	10	50	
195	Al Atkinson	4	5	5	5	6	10	20	80
196	Bob Griese RC	25	30	35	50	100	200	400	1,500
197	Buck Buchanan	4	5	5	5	6	10	20	80
198	Pete Beathard	4	5	5	5	6	10	20	80
199	Nemiah Wilson	4	5	5	5	6	10	20	80
200	Ernie Wright	4	5	5	5	6	10	30	
201	George Saimes	4	5	5	5	6	10	20	50
202	John Charles	4	5	5	5	6	10	20	50
203	Randy Johnson	4	5	5	5	6	10	20	60
204	Tony Lorick	4	5	5	5	6	10	20	60
205	Dick Evey	4	5	5	5	6	10	20	60
206	Leroy Kelly	4	5	5	5	8	30	50	
207	Lee Roy Jordan	4	5	5	5	8	12	40	120
208	Jim Gibbons	4	5	5	5	6	10	20	50
209	Donny Anderson RC	4	5	5	5	6	12	60	175
210	Maxie Baughan	4	5	5	8	20	40	250	
211	Joe Morrison	4	5	5	5	6	10	20	120
212	Jim Snowden	4	5	5	5	6	10	30	
213	Lenny Lyles	4	5	5	5	6	10	20	80
214	Bobby Joe Green	4	5	5	5	6	10	25	100
215	Frank Ryan	4	5	5	5	6	10	40	120
216	Cornell Green	4	5	5	5	6	10	25	120
217	Karl Sweetan	4	5	5	5	6	10	30	
218	Dave Williams	4	5	5	5	6	10	20	60
219A	Checklist Green	5	5	6	8	12	25	100	
219B	Checklist Blue	5	5	6	8	12	25	80	

— Donny Anderson RC #209 PSA 10 (Gem Mint) sold for $451.5 (eBay: 5/12)
— George Blanda #142 PSA 10 (Gem Mint) sold for $758.5 (eBay: 8/12)
— Tommy Davis #165 PSA 10 (Gem) sold for $416 (Mile High; 10/09)
— Carroll Dale #27 PSA 9 (Mt) sold for $1028 (eBay; 11/14)
— Mike Ditka #162 PSA 10 (Gem) sold for $8,246 (eBay; 10/07)
— Roy Jefferson #85 PSA 10 (Gem Mint) sold for $616 (eBay; 4/12)
— Floyd Little #173 PSA 9 (Mt) sold for $2407 (eBay; 11/14)
— Floyd Little #173 PSA 9 (Mt) sold for $1007 (eBay; 11/14)
— Bobby Maples #16 PSA 10 (Gem) sold for $765 (eBay; 12/06)
— George Mira #9 PSA 10 (Gem Mint) sold for $284 (eBay; 4/12)
— Carig Morton #155 PSA 10 (Gem) sold for $680 (eBay; 11/06)
— Dan Reeves #77 PSA 10 (Gem) sold for $715 (eBay; 2/07)
— Frank Ryan #215 PSA 10 (Gem) sold for $740 (Mile High; 10/09)

1968 Topps Stand-Ups Inserts

		GD 2	VG 3	VgEx 4	EX 5	ExMt 6	NM 7	NmMt 8	MT 9
	COMMON CARD (1-22)	4	5	5	8	12	20	80	
	John Brodie	5	6	8	10	15	30	80	
	Jack Concannon	5	5	6	8	12	20	100	
	Roman Gabriel	5	6	8	10	15	30	80	
	Jim Grabowski	5	5	6	8	12	40	80	
	John Hadl	5	5	6	8	12	30	60	
0	Sonny Jurgensen	5	6	8	10	15	40	120	
1	Alex Karras	5	6	8	10	15	30	60	
2	Billy Kilmer	5	6	8	10	15	30	120	
3	Daryle Lamonica	5	6	8	10	15	30	80	
5	Curtis McClinton	5	5	6	8	12	30	60	
6	Don Meredith	8	10	12	15	25	50	150	
7	Joe Namath	15	20	25	35	60	80	400	
0	Willie Richardson	5	5	6	8	12	30	100	

1969 Topps

		GD 2	VG 3	VgEx 4	EX 5	ExMt 6	NM 7	NmMt 8	MT 9
	Leroy Kelly	4	5	6	8	25	30	80	400
	Paul Flatley	4	4	5	6	8	10	20	125
	Jim Cadile	4	4	5	6	8	12	60	
	Erich Barnes	4	4	5	6	8	10	20	80
	Willie Richardson	4	4	5	6	8	10	30	150
	Bob Hayes	4	5	6	8	10	12	50	125
	Bob Jeter	4	4	5	6	8	10	50	175
	Jim Colclough	4	4	5	6	8	10	20	60
	Sherrill Headrick	4	4	5	6	8	10	25	
0	Jim Dunaway	4	4	5	6	8	10	20	
1	Bill Munson	4	4	5	6	8	10	20	80
2	Jack Pardee	4	4	5	6	8	10	20	60
3	Jim Lindsey	4	4	5	6	8	10	25	
4	Dave Whitsell	4	4	5	6	8	10	20	50
5	Tucker Frederickson	4	4	5	6	8	10	25	60
6	Alvin Haymond	4	4	5	6	8	10	25	
7	Andy Russell	4	4	5	6	8	10	20	80
8	Tom Beer	4	4	5	6	8	10	20	50
9	Bobby Maples	4	4	5	6	8	10	20	60
0	Len Dawson	4	5	6	8	20	25	40	200
1	Willis Crenshaw	4	4	5	6	8	10	15	60
2	Tommy Davis	4	4	5	6	8	10	20	60
3	Rickie Harris	4	4	5	6	8	10	20	60
4	Jerry Simmons	4	4	5	6	8	10	20	
5	Johnny Unitas	10	12	15	40	80	100	200	1,000
6	Brian Piccolo RC	20	25	30	50	60	▲200	▲400	1,400
7	Bob Matheson	4	4	5	6	8	10	20	60
	Howard Twilley	4	4	5	6	8	10	20	80
	Jim Turner	4	4	5	6	8	10	20	80
	Pete Banaszak RC	4	4	5	6	8	10	20	80
	Lance Rentzel RC	4	4	5	6	8	10	20	80
	Bill Triplett	4	4	5	6	8	10	20	80
	Boyd Dowler	4	4	5	6	8	10	20	80
	Merlin Olsen	4	5	6	8	10	15	25	100
	Joe Kapp	4	4	5	6	8	10	20	80
	Dan Abramowicz RC	4	4	5	6	8	10	20	80
	Spider Lockhart	4	4	5	6	8	10	20	60
	Tom Day	4	4	5	6	8	10	20	60
	Art Graham	4	4	5	6	8	10	20	60
	Bob Cappadona	4	4	5	6	8	10	20	50
	Gary Ballman	4	4	5	6	8	10	20	60
	Clendon Thomas	4	4	5	6	8	10	20	100
	Jackie Smith	4	5	6	8	10	12	25	100
	Dave Wilcox	4	4	5	6	8	10	20	80
	Jerry Smith	4	4	5	6	8	10	20	80
	Dan Grimm	4	4	5	6	8	10	20	60
	Tom Matte	4	4	5	6	8	10	20	80
	John Stofa	4	4	5	6	8	10	20	80
	Rex Mirich	4	4	5	6	8	10	20	50
	Miller Farr	4	4	5	6	8	10	20	60
	Gale Sayers	10	12	15	20	100	150	▲600	1,500
	Bill Nelsen	4	4	5	6	8	10	20	80

		GD 2	VG 3	VgEx 4	EX 5	ExMt 6	NM 7	NmMt 8	MT 9
53	Bob Lilly	4	5	6	8	10	12	40	200
54	Wayne Walker	4	4	5	6	8	10	25	
55	Ray Nitschke	4	5	6	8	12	30	120	
56	Ed Meador	4	4	5	6	8	10	20	60
57	Lonnie Warwick	4	4	5	6	8	10	20	80
58	Wendell Hayes	4	4	5	6	8	10	20	60
59	Dick Anderson RC	4	5	6	8	10	12	25	100
60	Don Maynard	4	5	6	8	10	12	30	100
61	Tony Lorick	4	4	5	6	8	10	25	100
62	Pete Gogolak	4	4	5	6	8	10	20	80
63	Nate Ramsey	4	4	5	6	8	10	20	80
64	Dick Shiner	4	4	5	6	8	10	20	60
65	Larry Wilson	4	4	5	6	8	10	20	60
66	Ken Willard	4	4	5	6	8	10	20	60
67	Charley Taylor	4	5	6	8	10	12	25	100
68	Billy Cannon	4	4	5	6	8	10	25	
69	Lance Alworth	4	5	6	8	12	20	30	200
70	Jim Nance	4	4	5	6	8	10	20	60
71	Nick Rassas	4	4	5	6	8	10	25	
72	Lenny Lyles	4	4	5	6	8	10	20	60
73	Bennie McRae	4	4	5	6	8	10	20	80
74	Bill Glass	4	4	5	6	8	10	25	
75	Don Meredith	5	6	8	10	15	25	60	200
76	Dick LeBeau	4	4	5	6	8	10	20	80
77	Carroll Dale	4	4	5	6	8	10	20	100
78	Ron McDole	4	4	5	6	8	10	20	50
79	Charley King	4	4	5	6	8	10	20	60
80	Checklist 1	4	4	5	6	10	20	60	125
81	Dick Bass	4	4	5	6	8	10	20	60
82	Roy Winston	4	4	5	6	8	10	20	60
83	Don McCall	4	4	5	6	8	10	20	60
84	Jim Katcavage	4	4	5	6	8	10	20	60
85	Norm Snead	4	4	5	6	8	10	20	60
86	Earl Gros	4	4	5	6	8	10	20	60
87	Don Brumm	4	4	5	6	8	10	20	60
88	Sonny Bishop	4	4	5	6	8	10	20	100
89	Fred Arbanas	4	4	5	6	8	10	20	50
90	Karl Noonan	4	4	5	6	8	10	20	80
91	Dick Witcher	4	4	5	6	8	10	20	60
92	Vince Promuto	4	4	5	6	8	10	20	60
93	Tommy Nobis	4	4	5	6	8	10	20	100
94	Jerry Hill	4	4	5	6	8	10	20	150
95	Ed O'Bradovich RC	4	4	5	6	8	12	30	
96	Ernie Kellerman	4	4	5	6	8	10	20	40
97	Chuck Howley	4	4	5	6	8	10	30	100
98	Hewritt Dixon	4	4	5	6	8	10	20	50
99	Ron Mix	4	4	5	6	8	10	25	100
100	Joe Namath	15	20	▲60	▲80	▲100	200	400	1,000
101	Billy Gambrell	4	4	5	6	8	10	20	50
102	Elijah Pitts	4	4	5	6	8	10	30	150
103	Billy Truax RC	4	4	5	6	8	10	20	60
104	Ed Sharockman	4	4	5	6	8	10	25	50
105	Doug Atkins	4	4	5	6	8	10	25	80
106	Greg Larson	4	4	5	6	8	12	30	
107	Israel Lang	4	4	5	6	8	10	20	60
108	Houston Antwine	4	4	5	6	8	10	20	60
109	Paul Guidry	4	4	5	6	8	10	20	60
110	Al Denson	4	4	5	6	8	10	20	60
111	Roy Jefferson	4	4	5	6	8	10	20	80
112	Chuck Latourette	4	4	5	6	8	10	20	60
113	Jim Johnson	4	4	5	6	8	10	20	40
114	Bobby Mitchell	4	5	6	8	10	12	25	80
115	Randy Johnson	4	4	5	6	8	10	20	60
116	Lou Michaels	4	4	5	6	8	10	20	80
117	Rudy Kuechenberg	4	4	5	6	8	10	20	50
118	Walt Suggs	4	4	5	6	8	10	40	
119	Goldie Sellers	4	4	5	6	8	10	20	60
120	Larry Csonka RC	15	20	50	60	100	200	300	2,500
121	Jim Houston	4	4	5	6	8	10	20	80
122	Craig Baynham	4	4	5	6	8	10	20	80
123	Alex Karras	4	5	6	8	10	12	40	125
124	Jim Grabowski	4	4	5	6	8	10	20	60
125	Roman Gabriel	4	4	5	6	8	10	12	60
126	Larry Bowie	4	4	5	6	8	10	20	60
127	Dave Parks	4	4	5	6	8	10	20	80
128	Ben Davidson	4	5	6	8	10	20	80	
129	Steve DeLong	4	4	5	6	8	10	12	30
130	Fred Hill	4	4	5	6	8	12	40	80
131	Ernie Koy	4	4	5	6	8	12	30	

FOOTBALL

#	Player	GD 2	VG 3	VgEx 4	EX 5	ExMt 6	NM 7	NmMt 8	MT 9
132A	Checklist 2 no border	4	4	5	6	12	25	60	150
132B	Checklist 2 bordered	4	4	5	6	12	25	60	
133	Dick Hoak	4	4	5	6	10	15	80	
134	Larry Stallings RC	4	4	5	6	8	12	80	100
135	Clifton McNeil RC	4	4	5	6	8	12	80	100
136	Walter Rock	4	4	5	6	8	10	30	80
137	Billy Lothridge	4	4	5	6	8	10	30	50
138	Bob Vogel	4	4	5	6	8	10	25	80
139	Dick Butkus	8	10	12	15	25	40	200	800
140	Frank Ryan	4	4	5	6	8	10	35	150
141	Larry Garron	4	4	5	6	8	10	30	80
142	George Saimes	4	4	5	6	8	10	30	80
143	Frank Buncom	4	4	5	6	8	10	25	80
144	Don Perkins	4	5	6	8	10	12	40	150
145	Johnnie Robinson	4	4	5	6	8	10	30	60
146	Lee Roy Caffey	4	4	5	6	8	10	30	100
147	Bernie Casey	4	4	5	6	8	10	30	60
148	Billy Martin E	4	4	5	6	8	12	40	100
149	Gene Howard	4	4	5	6	8	10	30	100
150	Fran Tarkenton	5	6	8	10	15	30	150	300
151	Eric Crabtree	4	4	5	6	8	10	20	100
152	W.K. Hicks	4	4	5	6	8	10	40	80
153	Bobby Bell	4	5	6	8	10	12	30	125
154	Sam Baker	4	4	5	6	8	12	50	100
155	Marv Woodson	4	4	5	6	8	10	30	80
156	Dave Williams	4	4	5	6	8	10	30	80
157	Bruce Bosley	4	4	5	6	8	10	30	100
158	Carl Kammerer	4	4	5	6	8	10	30	100
159	Jim Burson	4	4	5	6	8	10	25	80
160	Roy Hilton	4	4	5	6	8	12	40	150
161	Bob Griese	5	6	8	10	20	30	60	500
162	Bob Talamini	4	4	5	6	8	10	30	60
163	Jim Otto	4	4	5	6	8	20	80	175
164	Ronnie Bull	4	4	5	6	8	10	30	100
165	Walter Johnson RC	4	4	5	6	8	12	50	125
166	Lee Roy Jordan	4	4	5	6	10	12	40	200
167	Mike Lucci	4	4	5	6	8	12	40	
168	Willie Wood	4	5	6	8	10	12	40	150
169	Maxie Baughan	4	4	5	6	8	10	25	
170	Bill Brown	4	4	5	6	8	10	25	80
171	John Hadl	4	4	5	6	8	15	80	175
172	Gino Cappelletti	4	4	5	6	8	10	20	80
173	George Butch Byrd	4	4	5	6	8	10	30	80
174	Steve Stonebreaker	4	4	5	6	8	10	30	60
175	Joe Morrison	4	4	5	6	8	10	30	80
176	Joe Scarpati	4	4	5	6	8	12	40	100
177	Bobby Walden	4	4	5	6	8	10	30	80
178	Roy Shivers	4	4	5	6	8	12	25	80
179	Kermit Alexander	4	4	5	6	8	10	30	80
180	Pat Richter	4	4	5	6	8	10	30	80
181	Pete Perreault	4	4	5	6	8	10	30	80
182	Pete Duranko	4	4	5	6	8	10	30	80
183	Leroy Mitchell	4	4	5	6	8	10	20	80
184	Jim Simon	4	4	5	6	8	10	30	80
185	Billy Ray Smith	4	4	5	6	8	10	30	80
186	Jack Concannon	4	4	5	6	8	12	40	80
187	Ben Davis	4	4	5	6	8	10	25	80
188	Mike Clark	4	4	5	6	8	10	40	120
189	Jim Gibbons	4	4	5	6	8	10	25	80
190	Dave Robinson	4	4	5	8	10	20	60	175
191	Otis Taylor	4	4	5	6	8	10	30	60
192	Nick Buoniconti	4	4	5	6	8	10	35	135
193	Matt Snell	4	4	5	6	8	10	30	80
194	Bruce Gossett	4	4	5	6	8	10	30	80
195	Mick Tingelhoff	4	4	5	6	8	10	30	100
196	Earl Leggett	4	4	5	6	8	10	25	50
197	Pete Case	4	4	5	6	8	10	30	80
198	Tom Woodeshick RC	4	4	5	6	8	10	30	80
199	Ken Kortas	4	4	5	6	8	10	30	80
200	Jim Hart	4	4	5	6	8	10	30	80
201	Fred Biletnikoff	4	5	6	8	12	40	50	250
202	Jacque MacKinnon	4	4	5	6	8	10	40	80
203	Jim Whalen	4	4	5	6	8	10	40	
204	Matt Hazeltine	4	4	5	6	8	10	30	80
205	Charlie Gogolak	4	4	5	6	8	10	25	60
206	Ray Ogden	4	4	5	6	8	10	25	50
207	John Mackey	4	5	6	8	10	12	30	60
208	Roosevelt Taylor	4	4	5	6	8	12	40	125
209	Gene Hickerson	4	4	5	6	8	10	25	100
210	Dave Edwards RC	4	4	5	6	8	10	40	80
211	Tom Sestak	4	4	5	6	8	10	30	80
212	Ernie Wright	4	4	5	6	8	10	25	100
213	Dave Costa	4	4	5	6	8	10	30	50
214	Tom Vaughn	4	4	5	6	8	10	30	80
215	Bart Starr	6	8	10	12	20	100	300	800
216	Les Josephson	4	4	5	6	8	10	30	80
217	Fred Cox	4	4	5	6	8	10	30	80
218	Mike Tilleman	4	4	5	6	8	10	30	80
219	Darrell Dess	4	4	5	6	8	10	30	80
220	Dave Lloyd	4	4	5	6	8	10	30	80
221	Pete Beathard	4	4	5	6	8	10	20	80
222	Buck Buchanan	4	5	6	8	10	12	35	100
223	Frank Emanuel	4	4	5	6	8	10	30	80
224	Paul Martha	4	4	5	6	8	10	30	80
225	Johnny Roland	4	4	5	6	8	10	30	80
226	Gary Lewis	4	4	5	6	8	10	20	80
227	Sonny Jurgensen	4	5	6	8	10	12	30	200
228	Jim Butler	4	4	5	6	8	10	20	60
229	Mike Curtis RC	4	5	6	8	10	12	50	200
230	Richie Petitbon	4	4	5	6	8	10	30	60
231	George Sauer Jr.	4	4	5	6	8	10	30	80
232	George Blanda	4	5	6	8	12	20	50	175
233	Gary Garrison	4	4	5	6	8	10	25	80
234	Gary Collins	4	4	5	6	8	10	30	100
235	Craig Morton	4	4	5	6	8	10	30	175
236	Tom Nowatzke	4	4	5	6	8	10	20	50
237	Donny Anderson	4	4	5	6	8	12	100	200
238	Deacon Jones	4	5	6	8	10	12	50	125
239	Grady Alderman	4	4	5	6	8	10	30	80
240	Billy Kilmer	4	4	5	6	8	10	20	100
241	Mike Taliaferro	4	4	5	6	8	10	30	100
242	Stew Barber	4	4	5	6	8	10	30	80
243	Bobby Hunt	4	4	5	6	8	10	30	60
244	Homer Jones	4	4	5	6	8	10	30	100
245	Bob Brown OT	4	4	5	6	8	15	60	120
246	Bill Asbury	4	4	5	6	8	10	30	100
247	Charlie Johnson	4	4	5	6	8	10	50	80
248	Chris Hanburger	4	4	5	6	8	10	20	80
249	John Brodie	4	5	6	8	15	20	60	250
250	Earl Morrall	4	4	5	6	8	10	40	120
251	Floyd Little	4	5	6	8	10	15	40	150
252	Jerrel Wilson RC	4	4	5	6	8	10	30	100
253	Jim Keyes	4	4	5	6	8	10	30	100
254	Mel Renfro	4	5	6	8	10	12	35	125
255	Herb Adderley	4	5	6	8	10	15	40	150
256	Jack Snow	4	4	5	6	8	10	30	100
257	Charlie Durkee	4	4	5	6	8	10	30	100
258	Charlie Harper	4	4	5	6	8	10	25	80
259	J.R. Wilburn	4	4	5	6	8	10	40	150
260	Charlie Krueger	4	4	5	6	8	10	40	100
261	Pete Jacques	4	4	5	6	8	10	30	80
262	Gerry Philbin	4	4	5	6	10	12	40	100
263	Daryle Lamonica	4	5	6	8	12	20	80	

— John Brodie #249 PSA 10 (Gem Mt) sold for $1,033 (eBay; 2/09)
— Dick Butkus #139 PSA 9 (Mint) sold for $2,007 (eBay; 1/09)
— Dick Butkus #139 PSA 9 (Mint) sold for $1,125 (eBay; 2/10)
— Dick Butkus #139 PSA 9 (Mint) sold for $656 (eBay; 8/12)
— Checklist bordered #132B PSA 9 (Mint) sold for $765 (eBay; 3/08)
— Jim Dunaway #10 PSA 9 (Mint) sold for $1,103 (Mile High; 3/09)
— Wendell Hayes #10 PSA 10 (Gem) sold for $854 (eBay; 11/14)
— Randy Johnson #115 PSA 10 (Gem Mt) sold for $672 (Mile High; 10/09)
— Lou Michaels #116 PSA 10 (Gem Mt) sold for $611 (Mile High; 10/09)
— Leory Mitchell #183 PSA 9 (Mint) sold for $977 (eBay; 10/12)
— Ron Mix #99 PSA 10 (Gem Mt) sold for $1,317 (eBay; 2/13)
— Gayle Sayers #51 PSA 9 (Mint) sold for $1683 (eBay; 8/13)

1969 Topps Four-in-One Inserts

#	Card	GD 2	VG 3	VgEx 4	EX 5	ExMt 6	NM 7	NmMt 8	MT 9
	COMMON CARD (1-66)	4	4	4	5	6	10	20	
1	Aldmn/Je.Smth/Sayrs/LeBeau	4	4	5	6	10	15	50	
3	Alwrth/Mynrd/McDle/Cannon	4	4	4	5	8	12	25	60
4	Andrsn/Talifrro/Biltnikff/O/Tylr	4	4	4	5	6	8	12	25
6	Bllmn/J.Hill/R.Jeffrsn/Dowler	4	4	4	5	6	10	20	60
8	Bishop/Bnask/Guidry/Day	4	4	4	5	6	10	20	60
11	Bnicnti/Saimes/McKinn/Drnko	4	4	4	5	6	10	20	60
13	Carln/Grron/Hicks/Jacques	4	4	4	5	6	10	20	60
15	Dixon/Sell/Namath/Twilley	5	6	8	10	15	25	50	

		GD 2	VG 3	VgEx 4	EX 5	ExMt 6	NM 7	NmMt 8	MT 9
16	Durk/McNeil/Bghn/Tarken	4	4	5	6	10	15	30	80
18	Griese/LeMne/Grysn/Swney	4	4	5	6	10	15	30	100
21	Hickrsn/D.Andrsn/Butks/Luc	4	4	5	6	10	15	30	
25	Howrd/Morrisn/B.Mrtin/B.Dvis	4	4	4	5	6	10	20	60
26	Hwly/Picclo/Hnbrgr/Barnes	5	6	8	10	15	25	50	100
29	W.John/Frdricksn/Lloyd/Wldn	4	4	4	5	6	10	20	60
30	Jurgensen/Bass/Martha/Parks	4	4	4	5	8	12	25	
31	Kelly/Meador/Starr/Ogden	4	4	5	6	10	15	35	120
33	Lamon/Cnninghm/Hunt/Brbr	4	4	4	5	6	10	20	60
34	Lang/Lilly/Butler/Brodie	4	4	4	5	8	12	25	
38	Mrdith/G.Cllins/H.Jnes/Wdsn	4	4	5	6	10	15	30	80
41	Nance/Dunaway/Csonka/Mix	4	4	5	6	10	15	30	100
42	Nlsn/Munson/Ramsey/Curtis	4	4	4	5	6	10	20	60
44	Pard/Snead/Baynham/Jeter	4	4	4	5	6	10	20	60
46	Rass/Mtte/Rntzl/B.Mitchell	4	4	4	5	6	10	20	60
48	Rolnd/Mortn/Bi.Brown/Baker	4	4	4	5	6	10	20	60
49	Rssll/R.Jhnsn/Mthsn/Karras	4	4	4	5	8	12	25	
51	Sestak/Wright/Moreau/Snell	4	4	4	5	6	10	20	60
52	Simmns/B.Hyes/Atkns/Lckhrt	4	4	4	5	6	10	20	60
53	Ja.Smth/Grbw/Ji.Jhnsn/C.Tylr	4	4	4	5	8	12	25	60
55	Strttn/Rshing/Brnnan/Keyes	4	4	4	5	6	10	20	60
56	Suggs/Dwsn/Hedrck/Denson	4	4	4	5	8	12	25	80
57	Talam/Blanda/Whalen/Kemp	4	5	6	8	12	20	40	
59	Trull/Philbin/Garrison/Buchan	4	4	4	5	6	10	20	60
60	Unitas/Josephson/Cox/Renfro	4	4	5	6	10	20	40	100
62	West/Herock/Byrd/Cappell	4	4	4	5	6	10	20	60

— Dixon/Sellers/Namath/Twilley #15 PSA 9 (MT) sold for $400 (eBay; 11/06)
— Dixon/Sell/Namath/Twilley #15 PSA 10 (Gem Mint) sold for $575.96 (Memory Lane; 5/12)

1970 Kellogg's

		VG 3	VgEx 4	EX 5	ExMt 6	NM 7	NmMt 8	MT 9	Gem 9.5/10
	COMMON CARD (1-60)	4	4	5	6	10	12	15	60
	Carl Eller	4	5	5	5	6	12	30	80
	Len Dawson	4	5	5	5	6	12	20	60
10	Dick Butkus	4	5	5	6	8	15	30	350
1	George Sauer Jr.	4	5	5	5	6	12	20	50
3	Alex Karras	4	5	5	5	6	12	18	50
7	Bob Griese	4	5	5	5	6	12	25	100
1	Paul Warfield	4	5	5	5	6	12	20	60
5	Mike Garrett	4	5	5	5	6	10	25	400
7	Carl Garrett	4	5	5	5	6	12	20	175
5	Merlin Olsen	4	5	5	5	6	12	18	60
0	Lance Alworth	4	5	5	5	6	12	30	300
1	Larry Csonka	4	5	5	5	6	12	30	300
2	Bobby Bell	4	5	5	5	6	10	25	
3	George Webster	4	5	5	5	6	10	20	120
6	Bubba Smith	4	5	5	5	6	10	20	60
8	O.J. Simpson	4	5	5	6	8	12	25	50	200
0	Fred Biletnikoff	4	5	5	5	6	12	18	60
2	Gale Sayers	4	5	5	5	6	15	30	100
3	Sonny Jurgensen	4	5	5	5	6	12	20	80
4	Bob Lilly	4	5	5	5	6	12	18	80
5	Johnny Unitas	4	5	6	8	10	20	50	250
9	Don Maynard	4	5	5	5	6	10	20	60

1970 Topps

		VG 3	VgEx 4	EX 5	ExMt 6	NM 7	NmMt 8	MT 9	Gem 9.5/10
	Len Dawson	4	5	6	10	30	60	175	
	Doug Hart	4	5	5	5	8	12	60	
	Verlon Biggs	4	5	5	5	8	12	40	120
	Ralph Neely RC	4	5	5	5	8	20	300	
	Harmon Wages	4	5	5	5	8	12	40	
	Dan Conners	4	5	5	5	8	12	40	
	Gino Cappelletti	4	5	5	5	8	12	150	
	Erich Barnes	4	5	5	5	8	12	150	
	Checklist 1	4	5	5	6	10	30		
	Bob Griese	5	6	8	12	20	40	175	
	Ed Flanagan	4	5	5	5	8	12	40	
	George Seals	4	5	5	5	8	12	50	
	Harry Jacobs	4	5	5	5	8	12	40	
	Mike Haffner	4	5	5	5	8	12	50	
	Bob Vogel	4	5	5	5	8	12	40	
	Bill Peterson	4	5	5	5	8	12	50	
	Spider Lockhart	4	5	5	5	8	12	50	
	Billy Truax	4	5	5	5	8	12	50	
	Jim Beirne	4	5	5	5	8	12	40	
	Leroy Kelly	4	5	5	6	10	20	80	
	Dave Lloyd	4	5	5	5	8	12	40	

		VG 3	VgEx 4	EX 5	ExMt 6	NM 7	NmMt 8	MT 9	Gem 9.5/10
22	Mike Tilleman	4	5	5	5	8	12	40	
23	Gary Garrison	4	5	5	5	8	12	50	
24	Larry Brown RC	4	5	5	8	12	30	100	
25	Jan Stenerud RC	4	5	5	10	15	40	150	
26	Rolf Krueger	4	5	5	5	8	12	50	
27	Roland Lakes	4	5	5	5	8	12	50	
28	Dick Hoak	4	5	5	5	8	12	50	
29	Gene Washington Vik RC	4	5	5	5	10	15	200	
30	Bart Starr	6	8	10	15	50	80	300	
31	Dave Grayson	4	5	5	5	8	12	50	
32	Jerry Rush	4	5	5	5	8	12	50	
33	Len St. Jean	4	5	5	5	8	20		
34	Randy Edmunds	4	5	5	5	8	12	50	
35	Matt Snell	4	5	5	5	8	12	40	
36	Paul Costa	4	5	5	5	8	12	40	
37	Mike Pyle	4	5	5	5	8	12	50	
38	Roy Hilton	4	5	5	5	8	12	50	
39	Steve Tensi	4	5	5	5	8	12	60	
40	Tommy Nobis	4	5	5	6	10	15	50	
41	Pete Case	4	5	5	5	8	12	40	
42	Andy Rice	4	5	5	5	8	12	40	
43	Elvin Bethea RC	4	5	5	8	15	40	150	600
44	Jack Snow	4	5	5	5	8	12	50	
45	Mel Renfro	4	5	5	6	10	20	60	
46	Andy Livingston	4	5	5	5	8	12	30	120
47	Gary Ballman	4	5	5	5	8	12	40	
48	Bob DeMarco	4	5	5	5	8	12	40	
49	Steve DeLong	4	5	5	5	8	25		
50	Daryle Lamonica	4	5	5	6	10	15	60	300
51	Jim Lynch RC	4	5	5	6	12	25	135	
52	Mel Farr RC	4	5	5	5	8	12	40	
53	Bob Long RC	4	5	5	5	8	12	50	
54	John Elliott	4	5	5	5	8	12	50	
55	Ray Nitschke	4	5	5	5	12	30	100	
56	Jim Shorter	4	5	5	5	8	12	50	
57	Dave Wilcox	4	5	5	6	10	15	60	
58	Eric Crabtree	4	5	5	5	8	12	40	
59	Alan Page RC	6	8	12	20	50	125	200	800
60	Jim Nance	4	5	5	5	8	12	40	
61	Glen Ray Hines	4	5	5	5	8	12	40	120
62	John Mackey	4	5	5	6	10	15	60	
63	Ron McDole	4	5	5	5	8	12	40	
64	Tom Beier	4	5	5	5	8	12	40	120
65	Bill Nelsen	4	5	5	5	8	12	80	
66	Paul Flatley	4	5	5	5	8	12	40	
67	Sam Brunelli	4	5	5	5	8	12	40	
68	Jack Pardee	4	5	5	5	8	12	40	
69	Brig Owens	4	5	5	5	8	12	50	
70	Gale Sayers	6	8	10	40	50	80	400	
71	Lee Roy Jordan	4	5	5	6	10	15	80	
72	Harold Jackson RC	4	5	5	6	10	20	50	
73	John Hadl	4	5	5	6	10	15	100	
74	Dave Parks	4	5	5	5	8	12	40	
75	Lem Barney RC	5	6	8	12	40	50	150	
76	Johnny Roland	4	5	5	5	8	12	50	
77	Ed Budde	4	5	5	5	8	12	50	
78	Ben McGee	4	5	5	5	8	12	40	
79	Ken Bowman	4	5	5	5	8	12	40	
80	Fran Tarkenton	4	5	6	10	18	30	100	600
81	G.Washington 49er RC	4	5	5	6	10	20	80	
82	Larry Grantham	4	5	5	5	8	12	50	
83	Bill Brown	4	5	5	5	8	12	50	
84	John Charles	4	5	5	5	8	12	50	
85	Fred Biletnikoff	4	5	5	6	10	25	100	
86	Royce Berry	4	5	5	5	8	12	40	
87	Bob Lilly	4	5	5	5	10	20	60	
88	Earl Morrall	4	5	5	5	8	15	50	
89	Jerry LeVias RC	4	5	5	5	8	12	40	
90	O.J. Simpson RC	50	80	200	300	500	600	1,500	
91	Mike Howell	4	5	5	5	8	12	50	
92	Ken Gray	4	5	5	5	8	12	40	100
93	Chris Hanburger	4	5	5	5	8	12	40	
94	Larry Seiple RC	4	5	5	5	8	12	40	250
95	Rich Jackson RC	4	5	5	5	8	12	200	
96	Rockne Freitas	4	5	5	5	8	12	50	
97	Dick Post RC	4	5	5	5	8	12	50	
98	Ben Hawkins RC	4	5	5	5	8	12	50	
99	Ken Reaves	4	5	5	5	8	12	50	
100	Roman Gabriel	4	5	5	6	10	15	60	

#	Player	VG 3	VgEx 4	EX 5	ExMt 6	NM 7	NmMt 8	MT 9	Gem 9.5/10
101	Dave Rowe	4	5	5	5	8	15		
102	Dave Robinson	4	5	5	5	8	12	40	
103	Otis Taylor	4	5	5	5	8	12	60	
104	Jim Turner	4	5	5	5	8	15		
105	Joe Morrison	4	5	5	5	8	12	50	
106	Dick Evey	4	5	5	5	8	12	50	
107	Ray Mansfield	4	5	5	5	8	12	40	
108	Grady Alderman	4	5	5	5	8	12	50	
109	Bruce Gossett	4	5	5	5	8	12	50	
110	Bob Trumpy RC	4	5	5	6	10	20	80	
111	Jim Hunt	4	5	5	5	8	12	40	
112	Larry Stallings	4	5	5	5	8	12	40	
113A	Lance Rentzel Red	4	5	5	5	8	12	40	
113B	Lance Rentzel Black	4	5	5					
114	Bubba Smith RC	5	6	8	12	30	40	150	800
115	Norm Snead	4	5	5	5	8	12	40	
116	Jim Otto	4	5	5	6	10	15	60	
117	Bo Scott RC	4	5	5	5	8	15	60	
118	Rick Redman	4	5	5	5	8	12	40	150
119	George Butch Byrd	4	5	5	5	8	12	40	
120	George Webster RC	4	5	5	5	8	12	40	
121	Chuck Walton RC	4	5	5	5	8	12	40	
122	Dave Costa	4	5	5	5	8	12	40	
123	Al Dodd	4	5	5	5	8	12	40	
124	Len Hauss	4	5	5	5	8	15		
125	Deacon Jones	4	5	5	6	10	20	100	
126	Randy Johnson	4	5	5	5	8	12	40	
127	Ralph Heck	4	5	5	5	8	12	40	
128	Emerson Boozer RC	4	5	5	5	8	12	40	
129	Johnny Robinson	4	5	5	5	8	12	60	
130	John Brodie	4	5	5	6	10	20	60	
131	Gale Gillingham RC	4	5	5	5	8	12	40	
132	Checklist 2 DP	4	5	5	5	8	15	60	
133	Chuck Walker	4	5	5	5	8	12	80	
134	Bennie McRae	4	5	5	5	8	12	50	
135	Paul Warfield	4	5	5	6	10	20	150	
136	Dan Darragh	4	5	5	5	8	12	50	
137	Paul Robinson RC	4	5	5	5	8	12	50	
138	Ed Philpott	4	5	5	5	8	12	40	
139	Craig Morton	4	5	5	5	8	20	100	
140	Tom Dempsey RC	4	5	5	5	8	12	60	
141	Al Nelson	4	5	5	5	8	12	50	
142	Tom Matte	4	5	5	5	8	12	60	
143	Dick Schafrath	4	5	5	5	8	12	50	
144	Willie Brown	4	5	5	5	8	15	100	
145	Charley Taylor	4	5	5	6	10	20	60	
146	John Huard	4	5	5	5	8	12	50	
147	Dave Osborn	4	5	5	5	8	12	50	
148	Gene Mingo	4	5	5	5	8	12	50	
149	Larry Hand	4	5	5	5	8	12	50	
150	Joe Namath	15	40	50	100	200	400	1,300	
151	Tom Mack RC	4	5	5	8	15	60	200	
152	Kenny Graham	4	5	5	5	8	12	50	
153	Don Herrmann	4	5	5	5	8	12	50	
154	Bobby Bell	4	5	5	5	8	20		
155	Hoyle Granger	4	5	5	5	8	12	60	
156	Claude Humphrey RC	4	5	8	12	50	100	250	
157	Clifton McNeil	4	5	5	5	8	12	50	
158	Mick Tingelhoff	4	5	5	5	8	40	200	
159	Don Horn RC	4	5	5	5	8	12	50	
160	Larry Wilson	4	5	5	6	10	30	300	
161	Tom Neville	4	5	5	5	8	12	50	
162	Larry Csonka	5	6	8	12	40	80	300	
163	Doug Buffone RC	4	5	5	5	8	20	80	
164	Cornell Green	4	5	5	5	8	12	50	
165	Haven Moses RC	4	5	5	5	8	12	40	
166	Billy Kilmer	4	5	5	5	8	15	60	
167	Tim Rossovich RC	4	5	5	5	8	12	50	
168	Bill Bergey RC	4	5	5	5	8	15	150	
169	Gary Collins	4	5	5	5	8	12	50	
170	Floyd Little	4	5	5	5	8	15	200	
171	Tom Keating	4	5	5	5	8	20	100	
172	Pat Fischer	4	5	5	5	8	12	50	
173	Walt Sweeney	4	5	5	5	8	20		
174	Greg Larson	4	5	5	5	8	12	80	
175	Carl Eller	4	5	5	6	10	40	300	
176	George Sauer Jr.	4	5	5	5	8	12	50	
177	Jim Hart	4	5	5	5	8	15	60	
178	Bob Brown OT	4	5	5	5	8	15	100	
179	Mike Garrett RC	4	5	5	5	8	25	60	
180	Johnny Unitas	8	10	12	25	80	▲200	350	
181	Tom Regner	4	5	5	5	8	12	50	
182	Bob Jeter	4	5	5	5	8	12	50	
183	Gail Cogdill	4	5	5	5	8	12	50	
184	Earl Gros	4	5	5	5	8	12	50	
185	Dennis Partee	4	5	5	5	8	12	50	
186	Charlie Krueger	4	5	5	5	8	12	50	
187	Martin Baccaglio	4	5	5	5	8	12	50	
188	Charles Long	4	5	5	5	8	12	50	
189	Bob Hayes	4	5	5	6	12	30		
190	Dick Butkus	8	10	12	30	60	60	250	
191	Al Bemiller	4	5	5	5	8	12	50	
192	Dick Westmoreland	4	5	5	5	8	12	50	
193	Joe Scarpati	4	5	5	5	8	12	50	
194	Ron Snidow	4	5	5	5	8	12	50	
195	Earl McCullouch RC	4	5	5	5	8	12	80	
196	Jake Kupp	4	5	5	5	8	12	50	
197	Bob Lurtsema	4	5	5	5	8	12	50	
198	Mike Current	4	5	5	5	8	12	50	
199	Charlie Smith RB	4	5	5	5	8	12	80	
200	Sonny Jurgensen	4	5	5	6	10	20	100	
201	Mike Curtis	4	5	5	5	8	12	50	
202	Aaron Brown RC	4	5	5	5	8	12	50	
203	Richie Petitbon	4	5	5	5	8	12	50	
204	Walt Suggs	4	5	5	5	8	12	50	
205	Roy Jefferson	4	5	5	5	8	12	100	
206	Russ Washington RC	4	5	5	5	8	12	125	
207	Woody Peoples RC	4	5	5	5	8	12	80	
208	Dave Williams	4	5	5	5	8	12	50	
209	John Zook RC	4	5	5	5	8	12	50	
210	Tom Woodeshick	4	5	5	5	8	12	50	
211	Howard Fest	4	5	5	5	8	12	50	
212	Jack Concannon	4	5	5	5	8	12	50	
213	Jim Marshall	4	5	5	5	8	15	60	
214	Jon Morris	4	5	5	5	8	12	50	
215	Dan Abramowicz	4	5	5	5	8	12	50	
216	Paul Martha	4	5	5	5	8	12	40	
217	Ken Willard	4	5	5	5	8	12	50	
218	Walter Rock	4	5	5	5	8	12	50	
219	Garland Boyette	4	5	5	5	8	12	50	
220	Buck Buchanan	4	5	5	5	8	15	200	
221	Bill Munson	4	5	5	5	10	25	150	
222	David Lee RC	4	5	5	5	8	15		
223	Karl Noonan	4	5	5	5	8	25		
224	Harry Schuh	4	5	5	5	8	12	50	
225	Jackie Smith	4	5	5	5	8	15	60	
226	Gerry Philbin	4	5	5	5	8	12	50	
227	Ernie Koy	4	5	5	5	8	12	50	
228	Chuck Howley	4	5	5	5	8	25	60	
229	Billy Shaw	4	5	5	5	8	15	60	
230	Jerry Hillebrand	4	5	5	5	8	12	50	
231	Bill Thompson RC	4	5	5	5	8	12	50	
232	Carroll Dale	4	5	5	5	8	12	60	
233	Gene Hickerson	4	5	5	5	8	12	50	
234	Jim Butler	4	5	5	5	8	12	50	
235	Greg Cook RC	4	5	5	5	8	12	50	
236	Lee Roy Caffey	4	5	5	5	8	12	50	
237	Merlin Olsen	4	5	5	5	8	25	80	
238	Fred Cox	4	5	5	5	8	12	60	
239	Nate Ramsey	4	5	5	5	8	12	50	
240	Lance Alworth	4	5	5	6	10	25	100	
241	Chuck Hinton	4	5	5	5	8	12	80	
242	Jerry Smith	4	5	5	5	8	12	50	
243	Tony Baker FB	4	5	5	5	8	12	50	
244	Nick Buoniconti	4	5	5	5	8	15	60	
245	Jim Johnson	4	5	5	5	8	15	60	
246	Willie Richardson	4	5	5	5	8	12	100	
247	Fred Dryer RC	4	5	5	8	15	50	200	
248	Bobby Maples	4	5	5	5	8	12	50	
249	Alex Karras	4	5	5	5	8	15	200	
250	Joe Kapp	4	5	5	5	8	12	50	
251	Ben Davidson	4	5	5	5	8	15	60	
252	Mike Stratton	4	5	5	5	8	12	60	
253	Les Josephson	4	5	5	5	8	12	50	
254	Don Maynard	4	5	5	6	10	20	80	
255	Houston Antwine	4	5	5	5	8	25	60	
256	Mac Percival RC	4	5	5	5	8	12	80	
257	George Goeddeke	4	5	5	5	8	12	50	

	VG 3	VgEx 4	EX 5	ExMt 6	NM 7	NmMt 8	MT 9	Gem 9.5/10
58 Homer Jones	4	5	5	5	8	12	50	
59 Bob Berry	4	5	5	5	8	15		
60A Calvin Hill Red RC	4	5	6	10	20	40	150	
60B Calvin Hill RC Black	4	5	10	25	50	100		
61 Willie Wood	4	5	5	5	8	20	80	
62 Ed Weisacosky	4	5	5	5	8	25	300	
63 Jim Tyrer	4	5	5	6	10	30		

- Lem Barney #75 PSA 10 (Gem) sold for $2,011 (eBay; 2/13)
- Lem Barney #75 PSA 10 (Gem) sold for $1440 (eBay; 11/14)
- Elvin Bethea #43 PSA 10 (Gem) sold for $1,280 (eBay; 2/08)
- Elvin Bethea #43 PSA 10 (Gem Mint) sold for $573 (eBay; 6/12)
- Lee Roy Caffey #236 PSA 10 (Gem) sold for $1,252 (Mile High; 10/13)
- Larry Csonka #162 PSA 10 (Gem) sold for $2,055 (eBay; 3/07)
- Larry Csonka #162 PSA 10 (Gem Mint) sold for $1517.67 (eBay; 6/12)
- Larry Csonka #162 PSA 10 (Gem Mint) sold for $2510 (eBay; 6/16)
- Len Dawson #1 PSA 10 (Gem Mint) sold for $832.69 (eBay; 6/12)
- Fred Dryer RC #247 PSA 10 (Gem Mint) sold for $569.33 (eBay; 6/12)
- Don Maynard #254 PSA 10 (Gem Mint) sold for $570.03 (eBay; 6/12)
- Ray Nitschke #55 PSA 10 (Gem) sold for $698 (Andy Madec; 5/07)
- Merlin Olsen #237 PSA 10 (Gem Mint) sold for $560.43 (eBay; 6/12)
- Alan Page #59 PSA 10 (Gem) sold for $790 (eBay; 4/07)
- Bart Starr #30 PSA 10 (Gem) sold for $720 (eBay; 11/12)
- Bart Starr #30 PSA 10 (Gem) sold for $910 (eBay; 2/07)
- Bart Starr #30 PSA 10 (Gem) sold for $913 (eBay; 4/14)

1970 Topps Glossy Inserts

	GD 2	VG 3	VgEx 4	EX 5	ExMt 6	NM 7	NmMt 8	MT 9
COMMON CARD (1-33)	4	4	4	5	6	10	18	80
Tommy Nobis	4	5	5	6	10	15	30	150
Johnny Unitas	6	8	10	12	20	30	50	200
Mac Percival	4	5	5	5	6	10	18	120
Leroy Kelly	4	5	5	5	8	12	20	60
Bob Hayes	4	5	5	5	6	10	18	150
Bart Starr	5	5	6	8	12	20	40	175
Willie Wood	4	5	5	5	8	12	20	80
Dave Osborn	4	5	5	5	6	10	18	120
Fran Tarkenton	4	5	5	5	8	12	40	100
Tom Woodeshick	4	5	5	5	6	10	18	120
Sonny Jurgensen	4	5	5	6	10	15	60	150
Houston Antwine	4	5	5	5	6	10	20	120
O.J. Simpson	4	5	6	8	12	20	40	150
Rich Jackson	4	5	5	5	6	10	18	120
George Webster	4	5	5	5	6	10	18	120
Len Dawson	4	5	5	5	8	12	50	100
Bob Griese	4	5	5	5	8	12	25	100
Joe Namath	8	10	12	15	25	60	80	175
Daryle Lamonica	4	5	5	5	8	12	25	150
Fred Biletnikoff	4	5	5	5	8	12	20	80

1971 Kellogg's

	GD 2	VG 3	VgEx 4	EX 5	ExMt 6	NM 7	NmMt 8	MT 9
COMMON CARD (1-60)	4	4	5	5	6	12	25	60
Tom Barrington	4	4	5	5	6	12	50	150
Chris Hanburger	4	4	5	5	6	15	40	80
Fred Dryer	4	4	5	5	6	12	25	60
Larry Brown	4	4	5	5	6	12	25	100
Joe Greene	4	5	6	8	25	30	50	125
Johnny Unitas	8	10	12	15	25	40	125	250
George Blanda	4	5	6	8	12	18	30	100
Dick Butkus	5	6	8	10	15	25	40	200
John Brodie	4	4	5	5	8	15	30	60
Bob Griese	4	5	6	8	12	20	35	100

Doug Cunningham #58 PSA 10 (Gem) sold for $500 (eBay; 4/07)
Len Dawson #1 PSA 10 (Gem) sold for $384 (Mile High; 10/09)
Gary Garrison #110 PSA 10 (Gem) sold for $460 (eBay; 4/07)

1971 Topps

	GD 2	VG 3	VgEx 4	EX 5	ExMt 6	NM 7	NmMt 8	MT 9
Johnny Unitas	5	8	12	40	50	100	200	1,250
Jim Butler	4	4	5	5	6	12	60	
Marty Schottenheimer RC	4	5	6	8	20	25	50	
Joe O'Donnell	4	4	5	5	6	10	20	
Tom Dempsey	4	4	5	5	6	10	20	200
Chuck Allen	4	4	5	5	6	10	20	
Ernie Kellerman	4	4	5	5	6	10	20	100
Walt Garrison RC	4	4	5	5	6	10	30	150
Bill Van Heusen	4	4	5	5	6	10	20	

	GD 2	VG 3	VgEx 4	EX 5	ExMt 6	NM 7	NmMt 8	MT 9
10 Lance Alworth	4	4	5	5	8	15	25	150
11 Greg Landry RC	4	4	5	5	6	10	20	80
12 Larry Krause	4	4	5	5	6	10	20	80
13 Buck Buchanan	4	4	5	5	6	10	40	
14 Roy Gerela RC	4	4	5	5	6	10	20	80
15 Clifton McNeil	4	4	5	5	6	12	50	
16 Bob Brown OT	4	4	5	5	6	10	20	80
17 Lloyd Mumphord	4	4	5	5	6	10	50	
18 Gary Cuozzo	4	4	5	5	6	12	40	
19 Don Maynard	4	4	5	5	6	12	25	150
20 Larry Wilson	4	4	5	5	6	10	25	
21 Charlie Smith RB	4	4	5	5	6	10	20	80
22 Ken Avery	4	4	5	5	6	10	20	120
23 Billy Walik	4	4	5	5	6	10	20	80
24 Jim Johnson	4	4	5	5	6	10	25	
25 Dick Butkus	5	8	10	12	20	50	125	
26 Charley Taylor	4	4	5	5	6	12	25	100
27 Checklist 1	4	4	5	5	8	30	300	
28 Lionel Aldridge RC	4	4	5	5	6	10	60	150
29 Billy Lothridge	4	4	5	5	6	10	20	80
30 Terry Hanratty RC	4	4	5	5	6	10	20	150
31 Lee Roy Jordan	4	4	5	5	6	10	40	
32 Rick Volk RC	4	4	5	5	6	10	20	
33 Howard Kindig	4	4	5	5	6	10	20	80
34 Carl Garrett RC	4	4	5	5	6	10	20	80
35 Bobby Bell	4	4	5	5	6	20	60	
36 Gene Hickerson	4	4	5	5	6	10	20	100
37 Dave Parks	4	4	5	5	6	10	20	
38 Paul Martha	4	4	5	5	6	10	20	80
39 George Blanda	4	4	5	5	8	15	50	100
40 Tom Woodeshick	4	4	5	5	6	10	20	100
41 Alex Karras	4	4	5	5	6	12	25	100
42 Rick Redman	4	4	5	5	6	10	20	120
43 Zeke Moore	4	4	5	5	6	10	20	
44 Jack Snow	4	4	5	5	6	12	40	120
45 Larry Csonka	4	4	5	6	10	18	80	300
46 Karl Kassulke	4	4	5	5	6	10	20	80
47 Jim Hart	4	4	5	5	6	10	20	80
48 Al Atkinson	4	4	5	5	6	12	100	
49 Horst Muhlmann RC	4	4	5	5	6	10	20	
50 Sonny Jurgensen	4	4	5	5	6	15	30	150
51 Ron Johnson RC	4	4	5	5	6	10	20	
52 Cas Banaszek	4	4	5	5	6	12	60	
53 Bubba Smith	4	4	5	5	6	12	25	150
54 Bobby Douglass RC	4	4	5	5	6	10	20	80
55 Willie Wood	4	4	5	5	6	10	20	
56 Bake Turner	4	4	5	5	6	10	20	
57 Mike Morgan LB	4	4	5	5	6	10	20	
58 George Butch Byrd	4	4	5	5	6	10	40	
59 Don Horn	4	4	5	5	6	12	40	
60 Tommy Nobis	4	4	5	5	6	10	20	135
61 Jan Stenerud	4	4	5	5	6	12	25	100
62 Altie Taylor RC	4	4	5	5	6	10	20	
63 Gary Pettigrew	4	4	5	5	6	10	20	
64 Spike Jones RC	4	4	5	5	6	10	50	
65 Duane Thomas RC	4	4	5	5	6	10	50	
66 Marty Domres RC	4	4	5	5	6	10	20	
67 Dick Anderson	4	4	5	5	6	10	20	150
68 Ken Iman	4	4	5	5	6	10	20	
69 Miller Farr	4	4	5	5	6	12	60	
70 Daryle Lamonica	4	4	5	5	6	12	25	150
71 Alan Page	4	4	5	6	10	▲40	▲50	400
72 Pat Matson	4	4	5	5	6	10	20	80
73 Emerson Boozer	4	4	5	5	6	10	20	80
74 Pat Fischer	4	4	5	5	6	12	60	
75 Gary Collins	4	4	5	5	6	10	20	
76 John Fuqua RC	4	4	5	5	8	15	50	
77 Bruce Gossett	4	4	5	5	6	12	50	
78 Ed O'Bradovich	4	4	5	5	6	10	20	80
79 Bob Tucker RC	4	4	5	5	6	12	30	
80 Mike Curtis	4	4	5	5	6	12	50	
81 Rich Jackson	4	4	5	5	6	10	20	100
82 Tom Janik	4	4	5	5	6	10	20	100
83 Gale Gillingham	4	4	5	5	6	10	20	
84 Jim Mitchell TE	4	4	5	5	6	10	20	
85 Charlie Johnson	4	4	5	5	6	10	20	100
86 Edgar Chandler	4	4	5	5	6	10	20	
87 Cyril Pinder	4	4	5	5	6	10	20	
88 Johnny Robinson	4	4	5	5	6	10	20	

FOOTBALL

#	Name	GD 2	VG 3	VgEx 4	EX 5	ExMt 6	NM 7	NmMt 8	MT 9
89	Ralph Neely	4	4	5	5	6	10	25	
90	Dan Abramowicz	4	4	5	5	6	10	50	
91	Mercury Morris RC	4	4	5	8	12	30	100	
92	Steve DeLong	4	4	5	5	6	10	20	150
93	Larry Stallings	4	4	5	5	6	10	20	
94	Tom Mack	4	4	5	5	6	10	20	
95	Hewritt Dixon	4	4	5	5	6	10	20	120
96	Fred Cox	4	4	5	5	6	12	80	
97	Chris Hanburger	4	4	5	5	6	10	20	
98	Gerry Philbin	4	4	5	5	6	12	30	
99	Ernie Wright	4	4	5	5	6	10	20	
100	John Brodie	4	4	5	5	6	12	40	100
101	Tucker Frederickson	4	4	5	5	6	10	20	
102	Bobby Walden	4	4	5	5	6	10	20	
103	Dick Gordon	4	4	5	5	6	10	25	
104	Walter Johnson	4	4	5	5	6	10	20	
105	Mike Lucci	4	4	5	5	6	10	20	
106	Checklist 2 DP	4	4	5	5	6	10	20	
107	Ron Berger	4	4	5	5	6	10	20	80
108	Dan Sullivan	4	4	5	5	6	10	20	80
109	George Kunz RC	4	4	5	5	6	10	20	80
110	Floyd Little	4	4	5	5	6	12	40	
111	Zeke Bratkowski	4	4	5	5	6	10	40	
112	Haven Moses	4	4	5	5	6	10	20	
113	Ken Houston RC	4	5	6	8	12	20	125	600
114	Willie Lanier RC	4	5	6	8	12	20	80	800
115	Larry Brown	4	4	5	5	6	10	20	120
116	Tim Rossovich	4	4	5	5	6	12	120	
117	Errol Linden	4	4	5	5	6	10	20	
118	Mel Renfro	4	4	5	5	6	10	40	
119	Mike Garrett	4	4	5	5	6	10	40	
120	Fran Tarkenton	4	4	5	6	10	18	50	400
121	Garo Yepremian RC	4	4	5	5	6	10	20	
122	Glen Condren	4	4	5	5	6	10	20	
123	Johnny Roland	4	4	5	5	6	10	30	
124	Dave Herman	4	4	5	5	6	10	20	
125	Merlin Olsen	4	4	5	5	6	12	25	
126	Doug Buffone	4	4	5	5	6	10	30	
127	Earl McCullouch	4	4	5	5	6	10	20	
128	Spider Lockhart	4	4	5	5	6	10	20	100
129	Ken Willard	4	4	5	5	6	10	20	150
130	Gene Washington Vik	4	4	5	5	6	10	20	135
131	Mike Phipps RC	4	4	5	5	6	10	20	150
132	Andy Russell	4	4	5	5	6	12	60	
133	Ray Nitschke	4	4	5	6	8	60	600	
134	Jerry Logan	4	4	5	5	6	12	200	
135	MacArthur Lane RC	4	4	5	5	6	12	80	
136	Jim Turner	4	4	5	5	6	12	175	
137	Kent McCloughan	4	4	5	5	6	12	250	
138	Paul Guidry	4	4	5	5	6	12	150	
139	Otis Taylor	4	4	5	5	6	10	60	
140	Virgil Carter RC	4	4	5	5	6	10	60	
141	Joe Dawkins	4	4	5	5	6	10	25	
142	Steve Preece	4	4	5	5	6	12	30	
143	Mike Bragg RC	4	4	5	5	6	10	50	
144	Bob Lilly	4	4	5	5	6	15	100	
145	Joe Kapp	4	4	5	5	6	10	30	
146	Al Dodd	4	4	5	5	6	12	80	
147	Nick Buoniconti	4	4	5	5	6	10	40	
148	Speedy Duncan	4	4	5	5	6	10	25	
149	Cedrick Hardman RC	4	4	5	5	6	10	150	
150	Gale Sayers	5	8	10	12	20	35	200	800
151	Jim Otto	4	4	5	5	6	10	40	
152	Billy Truax	4	4	5	5	6	10	60	
153	John Elliott	4	4	5	5	6	10	25	
154	Dick LeBeau	4	4	5	5	6	10	60	
155	Bill Bergey	4	4	5	5	6	12	135	
156	Terry Bradshaw RC	300	400	500	600	1,000	1,500	5,000	40,000
157	Leroy Kelly	4	4	5	5	6	12	40	
158	Paul Krause	4	4	5	5	6	15	50	
159	Ted Vactor	4	4	5	5	6	10	20	80
160	Bob Griese	4	4	5	6	10	18	60	500
161	Ernie McMillan	4	4	5	5	6	10	25	
162	Donny Anderson	4	4	5	5	6	10	30	
163	John Pitts	4	4	5	5	6	12	50	
164	Dave Costa	4	4	5	5	6	10	25	
165	Gene Washington 49er	4	4	5	5	6	10	30	
166	John Zook	4	4	5	5	6	10	25	
167	Pete Gogolak	4	4	5	5	6	10	50	

#	Name	GD 2	VG 3	VgEx 4	EX 5	ExMt 6	NM 7	NmMt 8	MT 9
168	Erich Barnes	4	4	5	5	6	12	80	
169	Alvin Reed	4	4	5	5	6	12	50	
170	Jim Nance	4	4	5	5	6	10	30	80
171	Craig Morton	4	4	5	5	6	10	50	
172	Gary Garrison	4	4	5	5	6	10	30	150
173	Joe Scarpati	4	4	5	5	6	10	25	
174	Adrian Young	4	4	5	5	6	12	120	
175	John Mackey	4	4	5	5	6	15	80	
176	Mac Percival	4	4	5	5	6	12	100	
177	Preston Pearson RC	4	4	5	5	6	12	40	
178	Fred Biletnikoff	4	4	5	5	8	20	80	
179	Mike Battle RC	4	4	5	5	6	10	30	
180	Len Dawson	4	4	5	5	8	15	200	
181	Les Josephson	4	4	5	5	6	10	20	120
182	Royce Berry	4	4	5	5	6	10	60	
183	Herman Weaver	4	4	5	5	6	12	100	
184	Norm Snead	4	4	5	5	6	20	40	
185	Sam Brunelli	4	4	5	5	6	10	25	
186	Jim Kiick RC	4	4	5	5	6	12	80	
187	Austin Denney	4	4	5	5	6	10	20	80
188	Roger Wehrli RC	4	4	5	8	12	25	80	
189	Dave Wilcox	4	4	5	5	6	12	50	
190	Bob Hayes	4	4	5	5	6	10	60	
191	Joe Morrison	4	4	5	5	6	10	50	
192	Manny Sistrunk	4	4	5	5	6	10	100	
193	Don Cockroft RC	4	4	5	5	6	10	25	
194	Lee Bouggess	4	4	5	5	6	12	100	
195	Bob Berry	4	4	5	5	6	10	25	125
196	Ron Sellers	4	4	5	5	6	12	30	
197	George Webster	4	4	5	5	6	12	150	
198	Hoyle Granger	4	4	5	5	6	10	20	150
199	Bob Vogel	4	4	5	5	6	10	40	
200	Bart Starr	4	6	8	15	25	80	200	800
201	Mike Mercer	4	4	5	5	6	12	30	
202	Dave Smith WR	4	4	5	5	6	12	100	
203	Lee Roy Caffey	4	4	5	5	6	10	25	
204	Mick Tingelhoff	4	4	5	5	6	12	60	
205	Matt Snell	4	4	5	5	6	10	20	125
206	Jim Tyrer	4	4	5	5	6	12	40	
207	Willie Brown	4	4	5	5	6	10	60	
208	Bob Johnson RC	4	4	5	5	6	10	30	
209	Deacon Jones	4	4	5	5	6	12	80	
210	Charlie Sanders RC	4	5	6	20	25	60	250	
211	Jake Scott RC	4	4	6	10	20	25	80	
212	Bob Anderson RC	4	4	5	5	6	10	25	
213	Charlie Krueger	4	4	5	5	6	10	50	
214	Jim Bakken	4	4	5	5	6	15	100	
215	Harold Jackson	4	4	5	5	6	15	100	
216	Bill Brundige	4	4	5	5	6	10	50	300
217	Calvin Hill	4	4	5	5	6	15	60	
218	Claude Humphrey	4	4	5	5	6	12	150	
219	Glen Ray Hines	4	4	5	5	6	12	30	
220	Bill Nelsen	4	4	5	5	6	10	50	80
221	Roy Hilton	4	4	5	5	6	12	150	
222	Don Herrmann	4	4	5	5	6	10	25	
223	John Bramlett	4	4	5	5	6	12	100	
224	Ken Ellis	4	4	5	5	6	30	250	500
225	Dave Osborn	4	4	5	5	6	10	50	
226	Edd Hargett RC	4	4	5	5	6	12	100	
227	Gene Mingo	4	4	5	5	6	12	50	
228	Larry Grantham	4	4	5	5	6	12	100	
229	Dick Post	4	4	5	5	6	25	150	
230	Roman Gabriel	4	4	5	5	6	10	50	300
231	Mike Eischeid	4	4	5	5	6	20	150	
232	Jim Lynch	4	4	5	5	6	10	50	
233	Lemar Parrish RC	4	4	5	5	6	20	135	
234	Cecil Turner	4	4	5	5	6	12	100	
235	Dennis Shaw RC	4	4	5	5	6	10	40	
236	Mel Farr	4	4	5	5	6	12	100	
237	Curt Knight	4	4	5	5	6	10	25	
238	Chuck Howley	4	4	5	5	6	10	50	
239	Bruce Taylor RC	4	4	5	5	6	10	100	
240	Jerry LeVias	4	4	5	5	6	12	100	
241	Bob Lurtsema	4	4	5	5	6	10	25	
242	Earl Morrall	4	4	5	5	6	12	50	
243	Kermit Alexander	4	4	5	5	6	10	25	150
244	Jackie Smith	4	4	5	5	6	10	50	
245	Joe Greene RC	10	15	▲100	▲125	▲300	400	700	
246	Harmon Wages	4	4	5	5	6	10	50	

	GD 2	VG 3	VgEx 4	EX 5	ExMt 6	NM 7	NmMt 8	MT 9
47 Errol Mann	4	4	5	5	6	20	120	
48 Mike McCoy DT RC	4	4	5	5	6	10	30	
49 Milt Morin RC	4	4	5	5	6	10	25	
50 Joe Namath	6	10	12	25	100	125	500	
51 Jackie Burkett	4	4	5	5	6	10	100	
52 Steve Chomyszak	4	4	5	5	6	10	35	
53 Ed Sharockman	4	4	5	5	6	12	200	
54 Robert Holmes RC	4	4	5	5	6	10	40	100
55 John Hadl	4	4	5	5	6	10	25	
56 Cornell Gordon	4	4	5	5	6	12	30	
57 Mark Moseley RC	4	4	5	5	6	12	30	
58 Gus Otto	4	4	5	5	6	20	300	
59 Mike Taliaferro	4	4	5	5	6	12	30	
60 O.J.Simpson	4	6	15	40	60	▲150	600	
61 Paul Warfield	4	4	5	5	8	20	250	
62 Jack Concannon	4	4	5	5	10	20	100	
63 Tom Matte	4	4	5	5	8	50	150	

- Lance Alworth #10 PSA 9 (MT) sold for $760 (eBay; 1/07)
- Willie Brown #207 PSA 9 (MT) sold for $710 (eBay; 1/08)
- Dick Butkus #25 PSA 9 (MT) sold for $770 (eBay; 7/05)
- Dick Butkus #25 PSA 9 (MT) sold for $1,228 (eBay; 9/13)
- Joe Greene #245 PSA 10 (Gem) sold for $5115 (eBay; 11/14)
- Joe Greene #245 PSA 9 (MT) sold for $2,497 (Mile High; 10/09)
- Joe Greene #245 PSA 9 (MT) sold for $2,613 (eBay; 11/13)
- John Hadl #255 PSA 9 (MT) sold for $565 (eBay; 1/08)
- Ken Houston #113 PSA 10 (Gem Mint) sold for $5,510 (eBay; 2/13)
- Les Josephson #181 PSA 9 (MT) sold for $1,335 (eBay; 6/09)
- Mike Lucci #105 PSA 10 (Gem Mint) sold for $607 (Memory Lane; 8/12)
- John Mackey #175 PSA 9 (MT) sold for $520 (eBay; 10/06)
- Mercury Morris #91 PSA 10 (Gem MT) sold for $2,555 (eBay; 12/11)
- Craig Morton #171 PSA 10 (Gem MT) sold for $1,228.50 (eBay; 2/14)
- Joe Namath #250 PSA 8.5 (NmMT+) sold for $974 (eBay; 12/12)
- Ed O'Bradovich #78 PSA 10 (Gem Mint) sold for $552 (Memory Lane; 8/12)
- Charlie Sanders #210 PSA 9 (MT) sold for $453 (eBay; 12/12)
- Marty Schottenheimer #3 PSA 9 (MT) sold for $550 (eBay; 6/06)
- Altie Taylor RC #62 PSA 10 (Gem Mint) sold for $668 (Memory Lane; 8/12)
- Duane Thomas #65 PSA 9 (MT) sold for $337 (eBay; 2/13)
- Billy Truax #152 PSA 10 (Gem Mint) sold for $889 (Memory Lane; 8/12)
- Johnny Unitas #1 PSA 9 (MT) sold for $1,285 (eBay; 3/07)
- Roger Wehrli #188 PSA 9 (MT) sold for $1,335 (eBay; 6/09)
- Dave Wilcox #189 PSA 10 (Gem Mint) sold for $1,032 (eBay; 7/13)

1971 Topps Game Inserts

	GD 2	VG 3	VgEx 4	EX 5	ExMt 6	NM 7	NmMt 8	MT 9
COMMON CARD (1-53)	4	4	4	5	5	8	15	
Dick Butkus DP	4	4	4	5	6	10	25	
Joe Namath DP	4	4	5	6	8	12	30	100
Mike Curtis	4	4	4	5	5	8	15	80
Jim Nance	4	4	4	5	5	8	12	
O.J. Simpson	4	4	4	5	6	8	12	50	120
Tommy Nobis	4	4	4	5	5	8	10	80
Gale Sayers	4	4	4	5	6	10	30	60
Floyd Little	4	4	4	5	5	10	25	
Sam Brunelli	4	4	4	5	6	12		
Gene Washington 49er	4	4	4	5	5	8	15	80
Willie Wood	4	4	4	5	5	8	15	80
Charley Johnson	4	4	4	5	5	10	25	
Len Dawson	4	4	4	5	6	10	20	
Merlin Olsen	4	4	4	5	5	8	20	
Roman Gabriel	4	4	4	5	5	10	25	
Bob Griese	4	4	4	5	6	10	30	
Larry Csonka	4	4	4	5	6	15	20	100
Dan Abramowicz	4	4	4	5	5	10	25	
Tom Dempsey	4	4	4	5	6	12		
Fran Tarkenton	4	4	4	5	6	10	25	
Johnny Unitas	4	4	5	6	10	15	60	150
Daryle Lamonica	4	4	4	5	5	8	15	80
Terry Bradshaw	4	4	5	8	12	30	40	200
MacArthur Lane	4	4	4	5	5	8	20	100
Lance Alworth	4	4	4	5	6	10	20	80
John Brodie	4	4	4	5	5	8	30	
Bart Starr DP	4	4	4	5	6	10	30	120
Sonny Jurgensen	4	4	4	5	6	10	15	
Larry Brown	4	4	4	5	6	12		

1972 Topps

	VG 3	VgEx 4	EX 5	ExMt 6	NM 7	NmMt 8	MT 9	Gem 9.5/10
1 Csonka/Little/Hubbard LL	4	5	5	8	15	10	500	
2 Brockington/Owens/Ellison LL	4	5	5	5	8	25	60	
3 Griese/Dawson/Carter LL	4	5	5	5	8	20	120	
4 Staubach/Landry/Kilmer LL	4	5	5	6	15	40	150	
5 Biletnikoff/O.Taylor/Vataha LL	4	5	5	5	8	20	80	
6 Tucker/Kwalick/H.Jack./Jeffer.LL	4	5	5	5	8	15	60	
7 Yepremian/Stenerud/O'Brien LL	4	5	5	5	8	15	50	
8 Knight/Mann/Gossett LL	4	5	5	5	8	12	40	
9 Jim Kiick	4	5	5	5	8	15	50	
10 Otis Taylor	4	5	5	5	8	12	40	
11 Bobby Joe Green	4	5	5	5	8	12	40	
12 Ken Ellis	4	5	5	5	8	12	40	
13 John Riggins RC	8	10	12	15	30	60	300	
14 Dave Parks	4	5	5	5	8	12	40	
15 John Hadl	4	5	5	5	8	15	40	
16 Ron Hornsby	4	5	5	5	8	15		
17 Chip Myers RC	4	5	5	5	8	15		
18 Billy Kilmer	4	5	5	5	8	12	40	
19 Fred Hoaglin	4	5	5	5	8	12	40	
20 Carl Eller	4	5	5	5	8	12	40	
21 Steve Zabel	4	5	5	5	8	12	40	
22 Vic Washington RC	4	5	5	5	8	12	40	
23 Len St. Jean	4	5	5	5	8	12	40	
24 Bill Thompson	4	5	5	5	8	12	40	
25 Steve Owens RC	4	5	5	5	10	25	80	
26 Ken Burrough RC	4	5	5	5	8	12	50	
27 Mike Clark	4	5	5	5	8	12	60	
28 Willie Brown	4	5	5	5	8	12	40	
29 Checklist 1	4	5	5	5	10	20	80	
30 Marlin Briscoe RC	4	5	5	5	8	12	40	
31 Jerry Logan	4	5	5	5	8	12	40	
32 Donny Anderson	4	5	5	5	8	12	40	
33 Rich McGeorge	4	5	5	5	8	12	40	
34 Charlie Durkee	4	5	5	5	8	12	40	
35 Willie Lanier	4	5	5	5	8	12	40	
36 Chris Farasopoulos	4	5	5	5	8	12	40	
37 Ron Shanklin RC	4	5	5	5	8	15		
38 Forrest Blue RC	4	5	5	5	8	12	40	
39 Ken Reaves	4	5	5	5	8	12	40	
40 Roman Gabriel	4	5	5	5	8	12	40	
41 Mac Percival	4	5	5	5	8	12	40	
42 Lem Barney	4	5	5	5	8	12	40	
43 Nick Buoniconti	4	5	5	5	8	15	40	
44 Charlie Gogolak	4	5	5	5	8	12	40	
45 Bill Bradley RC	4	5	5	5	8	12	40	
46 Joe Jones DE	4	5	5	5	8	12	40	
47 Dave Williams	4	5	5	5	8	12	40	
48 Pete Athas	4	5	5	5	8	12	40	
49 Virgil Carter	4	5	5	5	8	12	40	
50 Floyd Little	4	5	5	5	8	20	40	
51 Curt Knight	4	5	5	5	8	12	40	
52 Bobby Maples	4	5	5	5	8	12	40	
53 Charlie West	4	5	5	5	8	12	50	
54 Marv Hubbard RC	4	5	5	5	8	12	40	
55 Archie Manning RC	5	6	10	15	25	50	400	750
56 Jim O'Brien RC	4	5	5	5	8	12	40	
57 Wayne Patrick	4	5	5	5	8	12	40	
58 Ken Bowman	4	5	5	5	8	15		
59 Roger Wehrli	4	5	5	5	8	12	40	
60 Charlie Sanders	4	5	5	5	8	12	40	
61 Jan Stenerud	4	5	5	5	8	12	40	
62 Willie Ellison	4	5	5	5	8	12	40	
63 Walt Sweeney	4	5	5	5	8	12	40	
64 Ron Smith	4	5	5	5	8	12	40	
65 Jim Plunkett RC	5	6	8	12	20	▲100	400	
66 Herb Adderley	4	5	5	5	8	12	40	
67 Mike Reid RC	4	5	5	5	8	12	50	
68 Richard Caster RC	4	5	5	5	8	12	40	
69 Dave Wilcox	4	5	5	5	8	12	50	
70 Leroy Kelly	4	5	5	5	8	30	60	
71 Bob Lee RC	4	5	5	5	8	12	50	
72 Verlon Biggs	4	5	5	5	8	12	80	
73 Henry Allison	4	5	5	5	8	12	40	
74 Steve Ramsey	4	5	5	5	8	12	40	
75 Claude Humphrey	4	5	5	5	8	12	40	

#	Player	VG 3	VgEx 4	EX 5	ExMt 6	NM 7	NmMt 8	MT 9	Gem 9.5/10
76	Bob Grim RC	4	5	5	5	8	12	40	
77	John Fuqua	4	5	5	5	8	12	100	
78	Ken Houston	4	5	5	5	8	20	40	
79	Checklist 2 DP	4	5	5	5	8	15	40	
80	Bob Griese	4	5	6	8	15	25	120	
81	Lance Rentzel	4	5	5	5	8	12	40	
82	Ed Podolak RC	4	5	5	5	8	12	40	
83	Ike Hill	4	5	5	5	8	12	40	
84	George Farmer	4	5	5	5	8	12	40	
85	John Brockington RC	4	5	5	5	8	12	40	
86	Jim Otto	4	5	5	5	8	12	40	
87	Richard Neal	4	5	5	5	8	12	40	
88	Jim Hart	4	5	5	5	8	12	40	
89	Bob Babich	4	5	5	5	8	12	40	
90	Gene Washington 49ers	4	5	5	5	8	12	40	
91	John Zook	4	5	5	5	8	12	40	
92	Bobby Duhon	4	5	5	5	8	12	40	
93	Ted Hendricks RC	4	5	5	8	30	60	400	
94	Rockne Freitas	4	5	5	5	8	12	40	
95	Larry Brown	4	5	5	5	8	12	40	
96	Mike Phipps	4	5	5	5	8	12	40	
97	Julius Adams	4	5	5	5	8	12	40	
98	Dick Anderson	4	5	5	5	8	12	40	
99	Fred Willis	4	5	5	5	8	12	40	
100	Joe Namath	10	12	15	50	60	200	250	1,500
101	L.C.Greenwood RC	4	5	6	10	20	80	200	400
102	Mark Nordquist	4	5	5	5	8	12	40	
103	Robert Holmes	4	5	5	5	8	12	40	
104	Ron Yary RC	4	5	6	8	25	50	200	
105	Bob Hayes	4	5	5	5	8	15	50	
106	Lyle Alzado RC	4	5	6	▲15	▲40	▲80	200	
107	Bob Berry	4	5	5	5	8	12	40	
108	Phil Villapiano RC	4	5	5	5	8	12	60	
109	Dave Elmendorf	4	5	5	5	8	12	40	
110	Gale Sayers	5	6	15	20	▲100	▲125	300	
111	Jim Tyrer	4	5	5	5	8	12	40	
112	Mel Gray RC	4	5	5	5	8	12	40	
113	Gerry Philbin	4	5	5	5	8	12	40	
114	Bob James	4	5	5	5	8	12	40	
115	Garo Yepremian	4	5	5	5	8	12	50	
116	Dave Robinson	4	5	5	5	8	12	40	
117	Jeff Queen	4	5	5	5	8	12	40	
118	Norm Snead	4	5	5	5	8	25		
119	Jim Nance IA	4	5	5	5	8	12	40	
120	Terry Bradshaw IA	4	5	6	8	12	25	100	300
121	Jim Kiick IA	4	5	5	5	8	12	40	
122	Roger Staubach IA	5	6	8	12	40	50	250	
123	Bo Scott IA	4	5	5	5	8	12	40	
124	John Brodie IA	4	5	5	5	8	12	40	175
125	Rick Volk IA	4	5	5	5	8	12	40	
126	John Riggins IA	4	5	5	6	10	20	30	250
127	Bubba Smith IA	4	5	5	5	8	12	40	
128	Roman Gabriel IA	4	5	5	5	8	12	40	
129	Calvin Hill IA	4	5	5	5	8	12	40	
130	Bill Nelsen IA	4	5	5	5	8	12	40	
131	Tom Matte IA	4	5	5	5	8	12	40	
132	Bob Griese IA	4	5	5	5	8	20	80	
133	AFC Semi-Final	4	5	5	6	10	30	150	
134	NFC Semi-Final	4	5	5	5	8	12	80	
135	AFC Semi-Final	4	5	5	5	8	12	50	
136	NFC Semi-Final	4	5	5	5	8	12	60	
137	AFC Title Game/Unitas	4	5	5	5	10	20	60	
138	NFC Title Game/Lilly	4	5	5	5	8	25		
139	Super Bowl VI/Staubach	4	5	5	6	10	50	100	
140	Larry Csonka	4	5	5	8	15	50	200	
141	Rick Volk	4	5	5	5	8	12	40	
142	Roy Jefferson	4	5	5	5	8	12	40	
143	Raymond Chester RC	4	5	5	5	8	12	60	
144	Bobby Douglass	4	5	5	5	8	12	40	
145	Bob Lilly	4	5	5	5	8	30	150	
146	Harold Jackson	4	5	5	5	8	12	50	
147	Pete Gogolak	4	5	5	5	8	12	40	
148	Art Malone	4	5	5	5	8	12	40	
149	Ed Flanagan	4	5	5	5	8	12	40	
150	Terry Bradshaw	12	15	20	30	40	150	750	
151	MacArthur Lane	4	5	5	5	8	12	40	
152	Jack Snow	4	5	5	5	8	10	40	
153	Al Beauchamp	4	5	5	5	8	12	40	
154	Bob Anderson	4	5	5	5	8	12	40	
155	Ted Kwalick RC	4	5	5	5	8	12	40	
156	Dan Pastorini RC	4	5	5	5	10	20	60	
157	Emmitt Thomas RC	5	6	8	12	20	▲100	400	
158	Randy Vataha RC	4	5	5	5	8	12	40	
159	Al Atkinson	4	5	5	5	8	12	40	
160	O.J.Simpson	4	5	6	8	25	40	150	
161	Jackie Smith	4	5	5	5	8	12	40	
162	Ernie Kellerman	4	5	5	5	8	15		
163	Dennis Partee	4	5	5	5	8	12	40	
164	Jake Kupp	4	5	5	5	8	12	150	
165	Johnny Unitas	8	10	12	30	40	50	200	
166	Clint Jones RC	4	5	5	5	8	12	40	
167	Paul Warfield	4	5	5	6	10	25	80	
168	Roland McDole	4	5	5	5	8	20	60	
169	Daryle Lamonica	4	5	5	5	8	15	125	
170	Dick Butkus	4	5	6	8	20	50	150	
171	Jim Butler	4	5	5	5	8	12	40	
172	Mike McCoy DT	4	5	5	5	8	12	40	
173	Dave Smith WR	4	5	5	5	8	12	40	
174	Greg Landry	4	5	5	5	8	12	40	
175	Tom Dempsey	4	5	5	5	8	15	50	
176	John Charles	4	5	5	5	8	12	150	
177	Bobby Bell	4	5	5	5	8	12	60	
178	Don Horn	4	5	5	5	8	10	40	
179	Bob Trumpy	4	5	5	5	8	15		
180	Duane Thomas	4	5	5	5	8	12	40	
181	Merlin Olsen	4	5	5	5	8	15	60	
182	Dave Herman	4	5	5	5	8	12	40	
183	Jim Nance	4	5	5	5	8	12	40	
184	Pete Beathard	4	5	5	5	8	12	40	
185	Bob Tucker	4	5	5	5	8	12	40	
186	Gene Upshaw RC	4	5	6	▲20	▲40	50	400	
187	Bo Scott	4	5	5	5	8	12	40	
188	J.D.Hill RC	4	5	5	5	8	12	40	
189	Bruce Gossett	4	5	5	5	8	12	40	
190	Bubba Smith	4	5	5	5	8	15	40	
191	Edd Hargett	4	5	5	5	8	12	40	
192	Gary Garrison	4	5	5	5	8	12	40	
193	Jake Scott	4	5	5	5	8	12	50	
194	Fred Cox	4	5	5	5	8	25		
195	Sonny Jurgensen	4	5	5	5	8	25	80	
196	Greg Brezina RC	4	5	5	5	8	12	50	
197	Ed O'Bradovich	4	5	5	5	8	12	50	
198	John Rowser	4	5	5	5	8	12	50	
199	Altie Taylor	4	5	5	5	8	12	50	
200	Roger Staubach RC	60	80	200	300	500	1,500	10,000	
201	Leroy Keyes RC	4	5	5	5	8	12	40	
202	Garland Boyette	4	5	5	5	8	12	40	
203	Tom Beer	4	5	5	5	8	12	40	
204	Buck Buchanan	4	5	5	5	8	12	40	
205	Larry Wilson	4	5	5	5	8	12	40	
206	Scott Hunter RC	4	5	5	5	8	12	40	
207	Ron Johnson	4	5	5	5	8	12	40	
208	Sam Brunelli	4	5	5	5	8	12	40	
209	Deacon Jones	4	5	5	5	8	12	50	
210	Fred Biletnikoff	4	5	5	6	10	25	80	
211	Bill Nelsen	4	5	5	5	8	20	80	
212	George Nock	4	5	5	5	8	12	40	
213	Dan Abramowicz	4	5	5	5	8	12	40	
214	Irv Goode	4	5	5	5	8	12	40	
215	Isiah Robertson RC	4	5	5	5	8	12	40	
216	Tom Matte	4	5	5	5	8	12	50	
217	Pat Fischer	4	5	5	5	8	15		
218	Gene Washington Vik	4	5	5	5	8	12	50	
219	Paul Robinson	4	5	5	5	8	12	40	
220	John Brodie	4	5	5	5	8	15	50	
221	Manny Fernandez RC	4	5	5	5	8	12	40	
222	Errol Mann	4	5	5	5	8	12	40	
223	Dick Gordon	4	5	5	5	8	12	40	
224	Calvin Hill	4	5	5	5	8	12	120	
225	Fran Tarkenton	4	5	▲12	▲15	25	50	200	
226	Jim Turner	4	5	5	5	8	12	40	
227	Jim Mitchell TE	4	5	5	5	8	12	40	
228	Pete Liske	4	5	5	5	8	12	40	
229	Carl Garrett	4	5	5	5	8	12	40	
230	Joe Greene	5	8	12	20	50	250		
231	Gale Gillingham	4	5	5	5	8	12	40	
232	Norm Bulaich RC	4	5	5	5	8	20	60	
233	Spider Lockhart	4	5	5	5	8	15		

#	Player	VG 3	VgEx 4	EX 5	ExMt 6	NM 7	NmMt 8	MT 9	Gem 9.5/10
234	Ken Willard	4	5	5	8	15	25	80	
235	George Blanda	4	5	6	8	15	25	100	
236	Wayne Mulligan	4	5	5	5	8	12	60	
237	Dave Lewis	4	5	5	5	8	12	60	
238	Dennis Shaw	4	5	5	5	8	12	40	
239	Fair Hooker	4	5	5	5	8	12	40	
240	Larry Little RC	4	5	6	8	15	50	200	
241	Mike Garrett	4	5	5	5	8	12	50	
242	Glen Ray Hines	4	5	5	5	8	15		
243	Myron Pottios	4	5	5	5	8	12	40	
244	Charlie Joiner RC	8	10	12	15	25	▲60	250	
245	Len Dawson	4	5	5	8	12	25	80	
246	W.K. Hicks	4	5	5	5	8	12	40	
247	Les Josephson	4	5	5	5	8	12	40	
248	Lance Alworth	4	5	5	8	12	25	100	
249	Frank Nunley	4	5	5	5	8	12	40	
250	Mel Farr IA	4	5	5	5	8	12	40	
251	Johnny Unitas IA	4	5	5	8	15	40	125	
252	George Farmer IA	4	5	5	5	8	12	40	
253	Duane Thomas IA	4	5	5	5	8	12	40	
254	John Hadl IA	4	5	5	5	8	12	40	
255	Vic Washington IA	4	5	5	5	8	12	40	
256	Don Horn IA	4	5	5	5	8	12	40	
257	L.C. Greenwood IA	4	5	5	6	10	25	125	
258	Bob Lee IA	4	5	5	5	8	12	60	
259	Larry Csonka IA	4	5	5	5	8	15	60	
260	Mike McCoy IA	4	5	5	5	8	12	40	
261	Greg Landry IA	4	5	5	5	8	12	50	
262	Ray May IA	4	5	5	5	8	20	125	
263	Bobby Douglass IA	4	5	5	5	8	12	60	
264	Charlie Sanders AP	8	10	12	15	20	30	60	
265	Ron Yary AP	8	10	12	15	25	35	60	175
266	Rayfield Wright AP	10	12	15	30	60	80	100	250
267	Larry Little AP	8	10	12	15	20	40	75	
268	John Niland AP	6	8	10	15	25	40	75	
269	Forrest Blue AP	6	8	10	12	15	30	50	
270	Otis Taylor AP	6	8	10	12	15	30	50	200
271	Paul Warfield AP	8	10	12	18	30	50	80	300
272	Bob Griese AP	10	12	30	40	40	60	120	600
273	John Brockington AP	6	8	10	12	15	50	60	
274	Floyd Little AP	6	8	10	12	15	40	80	200
275	Garo Yepremian AP	6	8	10	12	15	50	60	
276	Jerrel Wilson AP	6	8	10	12	15	30	50	150
277	Carl Eller AP	6	8	10	12	15	50	60	
278	Bubba Smith AP	8	10	12	15	25	40	80	
279	Alan Page AP	8	10	12	15	40	50	80	
280	Bob Lilly AP	8	10	12	18	30	80	100	
281	Ted Hendricks AP	8	10	12	18	30	50	80	
282	Dave Wilcox AP	6	8	10	12	15	30	50	
283	Willie Lanier AP	8	10	12	15	20	35	60	250
284	Jim Johnson AP	6	8	10	12	15	30	50	200
285	Willie Brown AP	8	10	12	15	20	35	80	
286	Bill Bradley AP	6	8	10	12	15	30	50	200
287	Ken Houston AP	8	10	12	15	20	35	50	250
288	Mel Farr	6	8	10	12	15	30	50	
289	Kermit Alexander	6	8	10	12	15	30	50	
290	John Gilliam RC	6	8	10	12	15	50	120	
291	Steve Spurrier RC	15	20	50	100	125	200	250	
292	Walter Johnson	6	8	10	12	15	30	60	
293	Jack Pardee	6	8	10	12	15	30	60	
294	Checklist 3	8	10	50	60	80	200	200	
295	Winston Hill	6	8	10	12	15	30	60	
296	Hugo Hollas	6	8	10	12	15	30	50	
297	Ray May RC	6	8	10	12	15	50	80	
298	Jim Bakken	6	8	10	12	15	30	50	
299	Larry Carwell	6	8	10	12	15	30	50	
300	Alan Page	8	10	12	18	40	60	200	
301	Walt Garrison	6	8	10	12	15	150	200	
302	Mike Lucci	6	8	10	12	15	40	50	
303	Nemiah Wilson	6	8	10	12	15	50	60	
304	Carroll Dale	6	8	10	12	15	30	50	
305	Jim Kanicki	6	8	10	12	15	30	50	
306	Preston Pearson	8	10	12	15	18	30	80	
307	Lemar Parrish	6	8	10	12	15	▲100	100	
308	Earl Morrall	6	8	10	12	20	40	▲200	
309	Tommy Nobis	6	8	10	12	15	40	60	
310	Rich Jackson	6	8	10	12	15	30	60	
311	Doug Cunningham	6	8	10	12	15	30	50	
312	Jim Marsalis	6	8	10	12	15	▲50	▲125	
313	Jim Beirne	6	8	10	12	15	30	50	
314	Tom McNeill	6	8	10	12	15	30	50	
315	Milt Morin	6	8	10	12	15	30	125	
316	Rayfield Wright RC	12	80	100	125	200	300	400	
317	Jerry LeVias	6	8	10	12	15	30	50	
318	Travis Williams RC	6	8	10	12	15	30	50	
319	Edgar Chandler	6	8	10	12	15	30	50	
320	Bob Wallace	6	8	10	12	15	30	100	
321	Delles Howell	6	8	10	12	15	30	50	
322	Emerson Boozer	6	8	10	12	15	50	60	
323	George Atkinson RC	6	8	10	12	15	30	50	
324	Mike Montler	6	8	10	12	15	30	50	
325	Randy Johnson	6	8	10	12	15	40	50	
326	Mike Curtis	6	8	10	12	15	60	80	
327	Miller Farr	6	8	10	12	15	30	50	
328	Horst Muhlmann	6	8	10	25	30	40	50	
329	John Niland RC	8	10	12	15	100	125	350	
330	Andy Russell	8	10	12	15	20	60	100	
331	Mercury Morris	8	10	12	60	125	150	200	
332	Jim Johnson	8	10	15	18	40	60		
333	Jerrel Wilson	6	8	10	12	15	40	50	
334	Charley Taylor	8	10	12	15	25	80	100	
335	Dick LeBeau	6	8	10	12	15	40	60	
336	Jim Marshall	8	10	12	15	25	60	80	
337	Tom Mack	8	10	12	15	20	40	50	
338	Steve Spurrier IA	10	12	15	20	35	60	100	
339	Floyd Little IA	6	8	10	12	15	50	60	
340	Len Dawson IA	8	10	12	15	25	40	80	
341	Dick Butkus IA	12	15	20	40	80	100	150	
342	Larry Brown IA	6	8	10	12	15	40	60	
343	Joe Namath IA	25	50	80	100	125	200	300	
344	Jim Turner IA	6	8	10	12	15	30	50	
345	Doug Cunningham IA	6	8	10	12	15	30	60	
346	Edd Hargett IA	6	8	10	12	15	30	60	
347	Steve Owens IA	6	8	10	25	30	40	80	
348	George Blanda IA	8	10	12	25	40	60	150	
349	Ed Podolak IA	6	8	10	12	15	30	50	
350	Rich Jackson IA	6	8	10	12	15	30	60	
351	Ken Willard IA	6	8	10	25	40	175	800	

— Csonka/Little Hubbard LL #1 PSA 10 (Gem) sold for $2,205 (eBay; 1/07)
— Yepr/Stenerud/O'Brien LL #7 PSA 10 (Gem) sold for $1,345 (eBay; 11/06)
— Lyle Alzado #106 PSA 10 (Gem) sold for $1411 (eBay; 11/14)
— Dick Anderson #98 PSA 10 (Gem) sold for $1,325 (eBay; 12/07)
— George Blanda IA #348 PSA 10 (Gem) sold for $1,080 (eBay; 9/07)
— Forrest Blue #38 PSA 10 (Gem) sold for $835 (eBay; 12/07)
— Terry Bradshaw #150 PSA 10 (Gem) sold for $1,734 (Mile High; 10/09)
— Nick Buoniconti #43 PSA 10 (Gem) sold for $1,130 (eBay; 4/08)
— Chris Farasopoulis #36 PSA 10 (Gem) sold for $905 (eBay; 4/07)
— Bobby Joe Green #11 PSA 10 (Gem Mint) sold for $717 (eBay: 8/12)
— Bob Griese #272 PSA 10 (Gem) sold for $1,055 (Andy Madec; 10/06)
— Charlie Joiner RC #244 PSA 10 (Gem) sold for $4,059 (eBay 09/14)
— Leroy Kelly #70 PSA 10 (Gem) sold for $563 (eBay; 02/13)
— Floyd Little #50 PSA 10 (Gem) sold for $724 (eBay; 11/14)
— Mercury Morris #331 PSA 10 (Gem) sold for $2,130 (eBay; 3/07)
— Mercury Morris #331 PSA 10 (Gem) sold for $1,025 (eBay; 2/14)
— Joe Namath IA #343 PSA 10 (Gem) sold for $1,535 (eBay; 2/07)
— Joe Namath IA #343 PSA 10 (Gem) sold for $569 (Mile High 10/09)
— Merlin Olsen #181 PSA 10 (Gem) sold for $602 (eBay; 7/07)
— Jim Plunkett #65 PSA 10 (Gem) sold for $1,458 (eBay; 1/09)
— Jim Plunkett #65 PSA 10 (Gem) sold for $1,285 (eBay; 12/07)
— John Riggins #13 PSA 10 (Gem) sold for $4,500 (eBay; 2/07)
— John Riggins #13 PSA 10 (Gem) sold for $4,044 (eBay; 11/14)
— John Riggins #13 PSA 10 (Gem) sold for $1,459 (Mile High; 6/10)
— Charlie Sanders #60 PSA 10 (Gem) sold for $795 (eBay; 4/07)
— Gale Sayers #110 PSA 10 (Gem) sold for $560 (Mile High; 10/09)
— Dennis Shaw #238 PSA 10 (Gem) sold for $835 (eBay; 12/07)
— Steve Spurrier #291 PSA 10 (Gem) sold for $509 (Mile High; 6/10)
— Roger Staubach IA #122 PSA 10 (Gem) sold for $1,225 (eBay; 1/08)
— Roger Staubach IA #122 PSA 10 (Gem) sold for $22,161.37 (Mile High; 12/13)
— Johnny Unitas #165 PSA 10 (Gem) sold for $2,670 (Mile High; 11/10)
— Gene Upshaw #186 PSA 10 (Gem) sold for $3558 (eBay; 11/14)
— Vic Washington #22 PSA 10 (Gem) sold for $1,335 (eBay; 4/07)
— Dave Williams #47 PSA 10 (Gem Mint) sold for $717 (eBay: 8/12)
— Ron Yary #104 PSA 10 (Gem) sold for $2,230 (eBay; 4/08)
— Ron Yary #104 PSA 10 (Gem) sold for $1543 (eBay; 11/14)

FOOTBALL

1973 Topps

#		VgEx 4	EX 5	ExMt 6	NM 7	NmMt 8	NmMt+ 8.5	MT 9	Gem 9.5/10
1	Simpson/L.Brown LL	5	6	8	12	20	30	150	
2	Snea/Morrall LL	5	6	8	10	15	20	30	
3	H.Jackson/Biletnikoff LL	5	6	8	10	15	20	60	
4	Marcol/Howfield LL	5	6	8	10	15	20	30	
5	Bradley/Sensibaugh LL	5	6	8	10	15	25	60	
6	Capple/J.Wilson LL	5	6	8	10	15	20	50	
7	Bob Trumpy	5	6	8	10	15	20	30	
8	Mel Tom	5	6	8	10	15	20	30	
9	Clarence Ellis	5	6	8	10	15	20	30	
10	John Niland	5	6	8	10	15	20	30	
11	Randy Jackson	5	6	8	10	15	20	30	
12	Greg Landry	5	6	8	10	15	20	30	
13	Cid Edwards	5	6	8	10	15	20	30	
14	Phil Olsen	5	6	8	10	15	20	30	
15	Terry Bradshaw	12	30	40	80	100	125	400	
16	Al Cowlings RC	5	6	8	10	20	25		
17	Walker Gillette	5	6	8	10	15	20	30	
18	Bob Atkins	5	6	8	10	15	20	30	
19	Diron Talbert RC	5	6	8	10	15	20	50	
20	Jim Johnson	5	6	8	10	20	25		
21	Howard Twilley	5	6	8	10	15	20	30	
22	Dick Enderle	5	6	8	10	15	20	30	
23	Wayne Colman	5	6	8	10	15	20	30	
24	John Schmitt	5	6	8	10	15	20	30	
25	George Blanda	5	6	8	10	25	30	80	
26	Milt Morin	5	6	8	10	15	20	30	
27	Mike Current	5	6	8	10	15	20	30	
28	Rex Kern RC	5	6	8	10	15	20	25	
29	MacArthur Lane	5	6	8	10	15	20	30	
30	Alan Page	5	6	8	10	15	20	50	
31	Randy Vataha	5	6	8	10	15	20	25	
32	Jim Kearney	5	6	8	10	20	25		
33	Steve Smith T	5	6	8	10	15	20	30	
34	Ken Anderson RC	8	10	12	40	50	60	300	
35	Calvin Hill	5	6	8	10	15	20	30	
36	Andy Maurer	5	6	8	10	15	20	30	
37	Joe Taylor	5	6	8	10	15	20	30	
38	Deacon Jones	5	6	8	10	15	20	30	
39	Mike Weger	5	6	8	10	20	25		
40	Roy Gerela	5	6	8	10	15	20	30	
41	Les Josephson	5	6	8	10	15	20	30	
42	Dave Washington	5	6	8	10	15	20	30	
43	Bill Curry RC	5	6	8	10	15	20	30	
44	Fred Heron	5	6	8	10	15	20	30	
45	John Brodie	5	6	8	10	15	20	35	
46	Roy Winston	5	6	8	10	15	20	30	
47	Mike Bragg	5	6	8	10	15	20	30	
48	Mercury Morris	5	6	8	10	15	20	50	
49	Jim Files	5	6	8	10	15	20	30	
50	Gene Upshaw	5	6	8	10	15	20	40	
51	Hugo Hollas	5	6	8	10	15	20	30	
52	Rod Sherman	5	6	8	10	15	20	30	
53	Ron Snidow	5	6	8	10	15	20	30	
54	Steve Tannen RC	5	6	8	10	15	20	30	
55	Jim Carter RC	5	6	8	10	15	20	30	
56	Lydell Mitchell RC	5	6	8	10	15	20	30	
57	Jack Rudnay RC	5	6	8	10	20	25		
58	Halvor Hagen	5	6	8	10	15	20	30	
59	Tom Dempsey	5	6	8	10	15	20	30	
60	Fran Tarkenton	5	6	8	10	15	20	80	
61	Lance Alworth	5	6	8	10	15	20	50	
62	Vern Holland	5	6	8	10	15	20	30	
63	Steve DeLong	5	6	8	10	15	20	30	
64	Art Malone	5	6	8	10	15	20	30	
65	Isiah Robertson	5	6	8	10	20	25		
66	Jerry Rush	5	6	8	10	15	20	30	
67	Bryant Salter	5	6	8	10	15	20	30	
68	Checklist 1-132	5	6	8	10	15	20	60	
69	J.D. Hill	5	6	8	10	15	20	30	
70	Forrest Blue	5	6	8	10	15	20	30	
71	Myron Pottios	5	6	8	10	15	20	30	
72	Norm Thompson RC	5	6	8	10	15	20	30	
73	Paul Robinson	5	6	8	10	15	20	30	
74	Larry Grantham	5	6	8	10	15	20	30	
75	Manny Fernandez	5	6	8	10	15	20	30	
76	Kent Nix	5	6	8	10	15	20	30	
77	Art Shell RC	8	10	12	20	▲125	▲150	400	
78	George Saimes	5	6	8	10	15	20	30	
79	Don Cockroft	5	6	8	10	15	20	30	
80	Bob Tucker	5	6	8	10	15	20	30	
81	Don McCauley RC	5	6	8	10	15	20	30	
82	Bob Brown DT	5	6	8	10	15	20	30	
83	Larry Carwell	5	6	8	10	15	20	30	
84	Mo Moorman	5	6	8	10	15	20	30	
85	John Gilliam	5	6	8	10	15	20	30	
86	Wade Key	5	6	8	10	15	20	30	
87	Ross Brupbacher	5	6	8	10	15	20	30	
88	Dave Lewis	5	6	8	10	15	20	30	
89	Franco Harris RC	20	30	▲125	200	300	400	2,000	
90	Tom Mack	5	6	8	10	15	20	30	
91	Mike Tilleman	5	6	8	10	15	20	30	
92	Carl Mauck	5	6	8	10	15	20	30	
93	Larry Hand	5	6	8	10	15	20	30	
94	Dave Foley RC	5	6	8	10	15	20	30	
95	Frank Nunley	5	6	8	10	15	20	30	
96	John Charles	5	6	8	10	15	20	30	
97	Jim Bakken	5	6	8	10	15	20	30	
98	Pat Fischer	5	6	8	10	20	25	35	
99	Randy Rasmussen	5	6	8	10	15	20	30	
100	Larry Csonka	5	6	8	10	25	40	175	
101	Mike Siani RC	5	6	8	10	15	20	30	
102	Tom Roussel	5	6	8	10	15	20	30	
103	Clarence Scott RC	5	6	8	10	15	20	30	
104	Charlie Johnson	5	6	8	10	15	20	30	
105	Rick Volk	5	6	8	10	15	20	30	
106	Willie Young	5	6	8	10	15	20	30	
107	Emmitt Thomas	5	6	8	10	15	20	30	
108	Jon Morris	5	6	8	10	15	20	30	
109	Clarence Williams	5	6	8	10	15	20	30	
110	Rayfield Wright	5	6	8	10	15	20	30	
111	Norm Bulaich	5	6	8	10	15	20	30	
112	Mike Eischeid	5	6	8	10	15	20	30	
113	Speedy Thomas	5	6	8	10	20	25		
114	Glen Holloway	5	6	8	10	15	20	30	
115	Jack Ham RC	15	20	25	▲50	100	120	400	
116	Jim Nettles	5	6	8	10	15	20	30	
117	Errol Mann	5	6	8	10	15	20	30	
118	John Mackey	5	6	8	10	15	20	30	
119	George Kunz	5	6	8	10	20	25		
120	Bob James	5	6	8	10	15	20	30	
121	Garland Boyette	5	6	8	10	15	20	30	
122	Mel Phillips	5	6	8	10	15	20	30	
123	Johnny Roland	5	6	8	10	15	20	30	
124	Doug Swift	5	6	8	10	15	20	30	
125	Archie Manning	5	6	8	10	15	20	80	
126	Dave Herman	5	6	8	10	15	20	30	
127	Carleton Oats	5	6	8	10	15	20	30	
128	Bill Van Heusen	5	6	8	10	15	20	30	
129	Rich Jackson	5	6	8	10	15	20	30	
130	Len Hauss	5	6	8	10	15	20	30	
131	Billy Parks RC	5	6	8	10	15	20	30	
132	Ray May	5	6	8	10	15	20	30	
133	NFC Semi/R.Staubach	5	6	8	12	30	50	150	
134	AFC Semi/Immac.Rec.	5	6	8	10	15	20	80	
135	NFC Semi-Final	5	6	8	10	15	20	50	
136	AFC Semi/L.Csonka	5	6	8	10	15	20	40	
137	NFC Title Game/Kilmer	5	6	8	10	15	20	40	
138	AFC Title Game	5	6	8	10	15	20	60	
139	Super Bowl VII	5	6	8	10	15	20	30	
140	Dwight White RC	5	6	8	10	40	50	200	
141	Jim Marsalis	5	6	8	10	15	20	30	
142	Doug Van Horn	5	6	8	10	20	25		
143	Al Matthews	5	6	8	10	15	20	30	
144	Bob Windsor	5	6	8	10	15	20	30	
145	Dave Hampton RC	5	6	8	10	15	20	30	
146	Horst Muhlmann	5	6	8	10	15	20	30	
147	Wally Hilgenberg RC	5	6	8	10	15	20	30	
148	Ron Smith	5	6	8	10	15	20	30	
149	Coy Bacon RC	5	6	8	10	15	20	60	
150	Winston Hill	5	6	8	10	15	20	30	
151	Ron Jessie RC	5	6	8	10	15	20	30	
152	Ken Iman	5	6	8	10	15	20	30	
153	Ron Saul	5	6	8	10	▲15	▲150	30	
154	Jim Braxton RC	5	6	8	10	15	20	30	

#	Player	VgEx 4	EX 5	ExMt 6	NM 7	NmMt 8	NmMt+ 8.5	MT 9	Gem 9.5/10
155	Bubba Smith	5	6	8	10	15	20	35	80
156	Gary Cuozzo	5	6	8	10	15	20	30	
157	Charlie Krueger	5	6	8	10	15	20	30	
158	Tim Foley RC	5	6	8	10	15	20	30	
159	Lee Roy Jordan	5	6	8	10	15	20	30	
160	Bob Brown OT	5	6	8	10	15	20	30	
161	Margene Adkins	5	6	8	10	15	20	30	
162	Ron Widby	5	6	8	10	15	20	30	
163	Jim Houston	5	6	8	10	15	20	30	
164	Joe Dawkins	5	6	8	10	15	20	30	
165	L.C.Greenwood	5	6	8	10	15	20	35	150
166	Richmond Flowers RC	5	6	8	10	15	20	30	
167	Curley Culp RC	8	12	20	50	80	100	150	
168	Len St. Jean	5	6	8	10	20	25		
169	Walter Rock	5	6	8	10	15	20	30	
170	Bill Bradley	5	6	8	10	15	20	30	
171	Ken Riley RC	5	6	8	10	15	20	50	
172	Rich Coady	5	6	8	10	15	20	30	
173	Don Hansen	5	6	8	10	15	20	30	
174	Lionel Aldridge	5	6	8	10	15	20	30	
175	Don Maynard	5	6	8	10	15	20	35	
176	Dave Osborn	5	6	8	10	15	20	30	
177	Jim Bailey	5	6	8	10	15	20	30	
178	John Pitts	5	6	8	10	15	20	30	
179	Dave Parks	5	6	8	10	15	20	30	
180	Chester Marcol RC	5	6	8	10	15	20	30	
181	Len Rohde	5	6	8	10	15	20	30	
182	Jeff Staggs	5	6	8	10	15	20	30	80
183	Gene Hickerson	5	6	8	10	15	20	30	
184	Charlie Evans	5	6	8	10	15	20	30	
185	Mel Renfro	5	6	8	10	15	20	30	
186	Marvin Upshaw	5	6	8	10	15	20	30	
187	George Atkinson	5	6	8	10	15	20	50	
188	Norm Evans	5	6	8	10	15	20	30	
189	Steve Ramsey	5	6	8	10	15	20	30	80
190	Dave Chapple	5	6	8	10	15	20	30	
191	Gerry Mullins	5	6	8	10	15	20	50	
192	John Didion	5	6	8	10	15	20	30	
193	Bob Gladieux	5	6	8	10	15	20	30	
194	Don Hultz	5	6	8	10	15	20	30	
195	Mike Lucci	5	6	8	10	15	20	30	
196	John Wilbur	5	6	8	10	15	20	30	
197	George Farmer	5	6	8	10	15	20	30	
198	Tommy Casanova RC	5	6	8	10	15	20	40	
199	Russ Washington	5	6	8	10	15	20	40	
200	Claude Humphrey	5	6	8	10	15	20	30	
201	Pat Hughes	5	6	8	10	15	20	30	80
202	Zeke Moore	5	6	8	10	15	20	30	
203	Chip Glass	5	6	8	10	15	20	30	
204	Glenn Ressler	5	6	8	10	15	20	30	
205	Willie Ellison	5	6	8	10	15	20	30	
206	John Leypoldt	5	6	8	10	15	20	30	
207	Johnny Fuller	5	6	8	10	15	20	30	
208	Bill Hayhoe	5	6	8	10	15	20	30	
209	Ed Bell	5	6	8	10	15	20	30	
210	Willie Brown	5	6	8	10	15	20	50	
211	Carl Eller	5	6	8	10	15	20	30	80
212	Mark Nordquist	5	6	8	10	15	20	30	
213	Larry Willingham	5	6	8	10	15	20	30	
214	Nick Buoniconti	5	6	8	10	15	20	30	
215	John Hadl	5	6	8	10	15	20	30	80
216	Jethro Pugh RC	5	6	8	10	20	25	50	
217	Leroy Mitchell	5	6	8	10	15	20	30	
218	Billy Newsome	5	6	8	10	15	20	30	
219	John McMakin	5	6	8	10	15	20	30	
220	Larry Brown	5	6	8	10	15	20	30	80
221	Clarence Scott RC	5	6	8	10	15	20	30	
222	Paul Naumoff	5	6	8	10	15	20	30	
223	Ted Fritsch Jr.	5	6	8	10	15	20	30	
224	Checklist 133-264	5	6	8	10	15	20	50	
225	Dan Pastorini	5	6	8	10	15	20	30	80
226	Joe Beauchamp	5	6	8	10	15	20	30	
227	Pat Matson	5	6	8	10	15	20	30	
228	Tony McGee DT	5	6	8	10	15	20	30	80
229	Mike Phipps	5	6	8	10	15	20	30	80
230	Harold Jackson	5	6	8	10	12	20	30	
231	Willie Williams	5	6	8	10	15	20	30	100
232	Spike Jones	5	6	8	10	15	20	30	
233	Jim Tyrer	5	6	8	10	15	20	30	
234	Roy Hilton	5	6	8	10	15	20	30	
235	Phil Villapiano	5	6	8	10	15	20	30	
236	Charley Taylor	5	6	8	10	15	20	35	
237	Malcolm Snider	5	6	8	10	15	20	30	
238	Vic Washington	5	6	8	10	15	20	30	80
239	Grady Alderman	5	6	8	10	15	20	30	
240	Dick Anderson	5	6	8	10	15	20	30	
241	Ron Yankowski	5	6	8	10	15	20	30	
242	Billy Masters	5	6	8	10	15	20	30	
243	Herb Adderley	5	6	8	10	15	20	30	
244	David Ray	5	6	8	10	15	20	40	
245	John Riggins	5	6	8	10	15	20	80	
246	Mike Wagner RC	5	6	8	10	35	30	100	
247	Don Morrison	5	6	8	10	15	20	30	
248	Earl McCullouch	5	6	8	10	20	25	50	
249	Dennis Wirgowski	5	6	8	10	15	20	30	
250	Chris Hanburger	5	6	8	10	12	20	30	
251	Pat Sullivan RC	5	6	8	10	15	20	30	
252	Walt Sweeney	5	6	8	10	15	20	30	
253	Willie Alexander	5	6	8	10	15	20	30	
254	Doug Dressler	5	6	8	10	20	25		
255	Walter Johnson	5	6	8	10	15	20	30	
256	Ron Hornsby	5	6	8	10	15	20	25	
257	Ben Hawkins	5	6	8	10	15	20	30	80
258	Donnie Green RC	5	6	8	10	15	20	30	100
259	Fred Hoaglin	5	6	8	10	15	20	30	
260	Jerrel Wilson	5	6	8	10	15	20	30	
261	Horace Jones	5	6	8	10	15	20	30	
262	Woody Peoples	5	6	8	10	15	20	30	
263	Jim Hill RC	5	6	8	10	15	20	30	
264	John Fuqua	5	6	8	10	15	20	30	
265	Donny Anderson KP	5	6	8	10	15	20	30	
266	Roman Gabriel KP	5	6	8	10	15	20	30	
267	Mike Garrett KP	5	6	8	10	15	20	30	
268	Rufus Mayes RC	5	6	8	10	15	20	60	
269	Chip Myrtle	5	6	8	10	15	20	30	
270	Bill Stanfill RC	5	6	8	10	15	20	30	
271	Clint Jones	5	6	8	10	15	20	30	
272	Miller Farr	5	6	8	10	15	20	30	
273	Harry Schuh	5	6	8	10	15	20	30	80
274	Bob Hayes	5	6	8	10	15	20	30	80
275	Bobby Douglass	5	6	8	10	15	20	30	
276	Gus Hollomon	5	6	8	10	15	20	30	
277	Del Williams	5	6	8	10	15	20	30	
278	Julius Adams	5	6	8	10	12	15	20	80
279	Herman Weaver	5	6	8	10	15	20	30	
280	Joe Greene	5	6	8	10	15	20	100	
281	Wes Chesson	5	6	8	10	15	20	30	
282	Charlie Harraway	5	6	8	10	15	20	30	
283	Paul Guidry	5	6	8	10	15	20	30	80
284	Terry Owens RC	5	6	8	10	15	20	30	
285	Jan Stenerud	5	6	8	10	15	20	30	
286	Pete Athas	5	6	8	10	15	20	30	80
287	Dale Lindsey	5	6	8	10	15	20	30	
288	Jack Tatum RC	6	8	10	20	50	60	100	
289	Floyd Little	5	6	8	10	15	20	30	80
290	Bob Johnson	5	6	8	10	15	20	30	
291	Tommy Hart RC	5	6	8	10	15	20	30	
292	Tom Mitchell	5	6	8	10	15	20	30	
293	Walt Patulski RC	5	6	8	10	15	20	30	
294	Jim Skaggs	5	6	8	10	15	20	30	
295	Bob Griese	5	6	8	10	15	20	50	300
296	Mike McCoy DT	5	6	8	10	15	20	30	
297	Mel Gray	5	6	8	10	15	20	30	80
298	Bobby Bryant	5	6	8	10	15	20	30	
299	Blaine Nye RC	5	6	8	10	15	20	30	
300	Dick Butkus	5	8	10	30	▲60	▲80	150	225
301	Charlie Cowan RC	5	6	8	10	15	20	30	
302	Mark Lomas	5	6	8	10	15	20	30	
303	Josh Ashton	5	6	8	10	15	20	30	
304	Happy Feller	5	6	8	10	15	20	30	
305	Ron Shanklin	5	6	8	10	15	20	30	
306	Wayne Rasmussen	5	6	8	10	15	20	30	
307	Jerry Smith	5	6	8	10	15	20	30	80
308	Ken Reaves	5	6	8	10	15	20	30	
309	Ron East	5	6	8	10	15	20	30	
310	Otis Taylor	5	6	8	10	15	20	30	
311	John Garlington	5	6	8	10	15	20	30	
312	Lyle Alzado	5	6	8	10	15	20	40	

#	Player	VgEx 4	EX 5	ExMt 6	NM 7	NmMt 8	NmMt+ 8.5	MT 9	Gem 9.5/10
313	Remi Prudhomme	5	6	8	10	15	20	30	
314	Cornelius Johnson	5	6	8	10	15	20	30	
315	Lemar Parrish	5	6	8	10	20	25		
316	Jim Kiick	5	6	8	10	15	20	25	
317	Steve Zabel	5	6	8	10	15	20	30	
318	Alden Roche	5	6	8	10	15	20	30	
319	Tom Blanchard	5	6	8	10	15	20	30	
320	Fred Biletnikoff	5	6	8	10	15	20	40	
321	Ralph Neely	5	6	8	10	15	20	30	80
322	Dan Dierdorf RC	8	10	12	20	40	50	175	
323	Richard Caster	5	6	8	10	15	20	30	
324	Gene Howard	5	6	8	10	15	20	30	
325	Elvin Bethea	5	6	8	10	15	20	30	
326	Carl Garrett	5	6	8	10	15	20	30	
327	Ron Billingsley	5	6	8	10	15	20	30	
328	Charlie West	5	6	8	10	15	20	30	
329	Tom Neville	5	6	8	10	15	20	30	
330	Ted Kwalick	5	6	8	10	15	20	30	
331	Rudy Redmond	5	6	8	10	15	20	30	
332	Henry Davis	5	6	8	10	15	20	30	
333	John Zook	5	6	8	10	15	20	30	
334	Jim Turner	5	6	8	10	15	20	30	60
335	Len Dawson	5	6	8	10	15	20	60	
336	Bob Chandler RC	5	6	8	10	15	20	30	
337	Al Beauchamp	5	6	8	10	15	20	30	80
338	Tom Matte	5	6	8	10	15	20	30	80
339	Paul Laaveg	5	6	8	10	15	20	30	
340	Ken Ellis	5	6	8	10	15	20	30	80
341	Jim Langer RC	5	6	8	▲30	▲40	▲50	80	500
342	Ron Porter	5	6	8	10	15	20	30	
343	Jack Youngblood RC	6	8	12	20	▲150	▲200	▲250	
344	Cornell Green	5	6	8	10	15	20	30	80
345	Marv Hubbard	5	6	8	10	15	20	30	80
346	Bruce Taylor	5	6	8	10	15	20	30	
347	Sam Havrilak	5	6	8	10	15	20	30	80
348	Walt Sumner	5	6	8	10	15	20	30	
349	Steve O'Neal	5	6	8	10	15	20	30	80
350	Ron Johnson	5	6	8	10	15	20	30	60
351	Rockne Freitas	5	6	8	10	15	20	30	60
352	Larry Stallings	5	6	8	10	15	20	30	
353	Jim Cadile	5	6	8	10	15	20	30	
354	Ken Burrough	5	6	8	10	15	20	30	60
355	Jim Plunkett	5	6	8	10	15	20	100	
356	Dave Long	5	6	8	10	15	20	30	
357	Ralph Anderson	5	6	8	10	15	20	40	
358	Checklist 265-396	5	6	8	10	15	20	40	
359	Gene Washington Vik	5	6	8	10	15	20	30	
360	Dave Wilcox	5	6	8	10	15	20	30	80
361	Paul Smith	5	6	8	10	15	20	30	
362	Alvin Wyatt	5	6	8	10	15	20	30	
363	Charlie Smith RB	5	6	8	10	15	20	30	
364	Royce Berry	5	6	8	10	15	20	30	80
365	Dave Elmendorf	5	6	8	10	15	20	30	
366	Scott Hunter	5	6	8	10	15	20	30	
367	Bob Kuechenberg RC	5	6	8	10	30	30	50	500
368	Pete Gogolak	5	6	8	10	15	20	30	
369	Dave Edwards	5	6	8	10	15	20	30	
370	Lem Barney	5	6	8	10	15	20	30	
371	Verlon Biggs	5	6	8	10	15	20	30	60
372	John Reaves RC	5	6	8	10	15	20	30	80
373	Ed Podolak	5	6	8	10	15	20	30	
374	Chris Farasopoulos	5	6	8	10	15	20	30	60
375	Gary Garrison	5	6	8	10	15	20	30	
376	Tom Funchess	5	6	8	10	15	20	30	80
377	Bobby Joe Green	5	6	8	10	15	20	30	
378	Don Brumm	5	6	8	10	15	20	30	
379	Jim O'Brien	5	6	8	10	15	20	30	
380	Paul Krause	5	6	8	10	15	20	30	
381	Leroy Kelly	5	6	8	10	15	20	30	
382	Ray Mansfield	5	6	8	10	15	20	30	
383	Dan Abramowicz	5	6	8	10	15	20	30	
384	John Outlaw RC	5	6	8	10	15	20	30	
385	Tommy Nobis	5	6	8	10	15	20	30	
386	Tom Domres	5	6	8	10	15	20	30	
387	Ken Willard	5	6	8	10	15	20	30	
388	Mike Stratton	5	6	8	10	15	20	30	80
389	Fred Dryer	5	6	8	10	15	20	30	
390	Jake Scott	5	6	8	10	15	20	30	
391	Rich Houston	5	6	8	10	15	20	30	
392	Virgil Carter	5	6	8	10	15	20	30	
393	Tody Smith	5	6	8	10	15	20	30	
394	Ernie Calloway	5	6	8	10	15	20	30	60
395	Charlie Sanders	5	6	8	10	15	20	30	
396	Fred Willis	5	6	8	10	15	20	30	80
397	Curt Knight	5	6	8	10	15	20	30	
398	Nemiah Wilson	5	6	8	10	15	20	30	
399	Carroll Dale	5	6	8	10	15	20	30	
400	Joe Namath	12	15	50	▲80	100	125	300	500
401	Wayne Mulligan	5	6	8	10	15	20	30	
402	Jim Harrison	5	6	8	10	15	20	30	
403	Tim Rossovich	5	6	8	10	15	20	30	
404	David Lee	5	6	8	10	15	20	30	
405	Frank Pitts	5	6	8	10	15	20	30	
406	Jim Marshall	5	6	8	10	15	20	30	
407	Bob Brown TE	5	6	8	10	15	20	30	
408	John Rowser	5	6	8	10	15	20	30	
409	Mike Montler	5	6	8	10	20	25		
410	Willie Lanier	5	6	8	10	15	20	30	
411	Bill Bell K	5	6	8	10	15	20	30	
412	Cedrick Hardman	5	6	8	10	15	20	30	80
413	Bob Anderson	5	6	8	10	15	20	30	100
414	Earl Morrall	5	6	8	10	15	20	30	
415	Ken Houston	5	6	8	10	15	20	30	
416	Jack Snow	5	6	8	10	15	20	30	
417	Dick Cunningham	5	6	8	10	15	20	30	
418	Greg Larson	5	6	8	10	15	20	30	
419	Mike Bass	5	6	8	10	15	20	30	80
420	Mike Reid	5	6	8	10	15	20	30	
421	Walt Garrison	5	6	8	10	15	20	30	80
422	Pete Liske	5	6	8	10	15	20	30	
423	Jim Yarbrough	5	6	8	10	15	20	30	
424	Rich McGeorge	5	6	8	10	20	25		
425	Bobby Howfield	5	6	8	10	15	20	30	
426	Pete Banaszak	5	6	8	10	15	20	30	
427	Willie Holman	5	6	8	10	15	20	30	
428	Dale Hackbart	5	6	8	10	15	20	30	
429	Fair Hooker	5	6	8	10	15	20	30	
430	Ted Hendricks	5	6	8	10	15	20	40	
431	Mike Garrett	5	6	8	10	15	20	30	
432	Glen Ray Hines	5	6	8	10	20	25	100	
433	Fred Cox	5	6	8	10	15	20	50	
434	Bobby Walden	5	6	8	10	15	20	30	
435	Bobby Bell	5	6	8	10	15	20	30	
436	Dave Rowe	5	6	8	10	15	20	30	
437	Bob Berry	5	6	8	10	15	20	30	
438	Bill Thompson	5	6	8	10	20	25	100	
439	Jim Beirne	5	6	8	10	15	20	30	
440	Larry Little	5	6	8	10	20	25	80	
441	Rocky Thompson	5	6	8	10	15	20	30	
442	Brig Owens	5	6	8	10	20	25		
443	Richard Neal	5	6	8	10	20	25		
444	Al Nelson	5	6	8	10	15	20	30	
445	Chip Myers	5	6	8	10	15	20	30	
446	Ken Bowman	5	6	8	10	15	20	30	
447	Jim Purnell	5	6	8	10	15	20	30	
448	Altie Taylor	5	6	8	10	15	20	30	
449	Linzy Cole	5	6	8	10	15	20	25	
450	Bob Lilly	5	6	8	10	15	20	40	200
451	Charlie Ford	5	6	8	10	15	20	30	
452	Milt Sunde	5	6	8	10	15	20	30	
453	Doug Wyatt	5	6	8	10	15	20	30	
454	Don Nottingham RC	5	6	8	10	15	20	30	
455	Johnny Unitas	6	8	10	15	35	40	135	
456	Frank Lewis RC	5	6	8	10	15	20	40	
457	Roger Wehrli	5	6	8	10	15	20	30	
458	Jim Cheyunski	5	6	8	10	15	20	30	
459	Jerry Sherk RC	5	6	8	10	15	20	30	
460	Gene Washington 49er	5	6	8	10	15	20	30	
461	Jim Otto	5	6	8	10	15	20	30	
462	Ed Budde	5	6	8	10	15	20	30	
463	Jim Mitchell TE	5	6	8	10	15	20	30	
464	Emerson Boozer	5	6	8	10	15	20	30	
465	Garo Yepremian	5	6	8	10	15	20	40	
466	Pete Duranko	5	6	8	10	15	20	30	
467	Charlie Joiner	5	6	8	10	15	20	60	
468	Spider Lockhart	5	6	8	10	15	20	30	
469	Marty Domres	5	6	8	10	15	20	30	
470	John Brockington	5	6	8	10	15	20	30	

		VgEx 4	EX 5	ExMt 6	NM 7	NmMt 8	NmMt+ 8.5	MT 9	Gem 9.5/10
471	Ed Flanagan	5	6	8	10	15	20	30	
472	Roy Jefferson	5	6	8	10	15	20	30	
473	Julian Fagan	5	6	8	10	15	20	30	
474	Bill Brown	5	6	8	10	15	20	30	80
475	Roger Staubach	12	15	25	40	125	150	350	
476	Jan White RC	5	6	8	10	15	20	40	
477	Pat Holmes	5	6	8	10	15	20	30	
478	Bob DeMarco	5	6	8	10	15	20	30	
479	Merlin Olsen	5	6	8	10	15	20	35	100
480	Andy Russell	5	6	8	10	15	20	80	
481	Steve Spurrier	5	6	8	20	25	30	60	
482	Nate Ramsey	5	6	8	10	20	25		
483	Dennis Partee	5	6	8	10	20	25	30	
484	Jerry Simmons	5	6	8	10	15	20	30	
485	Donny Anderson	5	6	8	10	15	20	30	
486	Ralph Baker	5	6	8	10	15	20	30	
487	Ken Stabler RC	20	50	100	125	▲350	400	▼2,000	
488	Ernie McMillan	5	6	8	10	15	20	30	
489	Ken Burrow	5	6	8	10	15	20	30	
490	Jack Gregory RC	5	6	8	10	15	20	30	
491	Larry Seiple	5	6	8	10	15	20	30	
492	Mick Tingelhoff	5	6	8	10	15	20	50	
493	Craig Morton	5	6	8	10	12	15	20	
494	Cecil Turner	5	6	8	10	15	20	30	
495	Steve Owens	5	6	8	10	15	20	30	
496	Rickie Harris	5	6	8	10	15	20	30	
497	Buck Buchanan	5	6	8	10	15	20	50	
498	Checklist 397-528	5	6	8	10	15	20	50	
499	Billy Kilmer	5	6	8	10	15	20	30	
500	O.J.Simpson	6	8	10	15	40	50	80	
501	Bruce Gossett	5	6	8	10	15	20	30	
502	Art Thoms RC	5	6	8	10	20	25	80	
503	Larry Kaminski	5	6	8	10	15	20	30	
504	Larry Smith RB	5	6	8	10	15	20	30	
505	Bruce Van Dyke	5	6	8	10	15	20	30	
506	Alvin Reed	5	6	8	10	15	20	30	
507	Delles Howell	5	6	8	10	15	20	30	
508	Leroy Keyes	5	6	8	10	15	20	30	
509	Bo Scott	5	6	8	10	15	20	30	
510	Ron Yary	5	6	8	10	15	20	60	
511	Paul Warfield	5	6	8	10	15	20	60	
512	Mac Percival	5	6	8	10	15	20	30	80
513	Essex Johnson	5	6	8	10	15	25	50	
514	Jackie Smith	5	6	8	10	15	20	30	
515	Norm Snead	5	6	8	10	15	20	30	
516	Charlie Stukes	5	6	8	10	15	20	30	100
517	Reggie Rucker RC	5	6	8	10	15	20	30	100
518	Bill Sandeman	5	6	8	10	15	20	30	
519	Mel Farr	5	6	8	10	15	20	30	
520	Raymond Chester	5	6	8	10	15	20	30	
521	Fred Carr RC	5	6	8	10	15	20	30	
522	Jerry LeVias	5	6	8	10	15	20	30	
523	Jim Strong	5	6	8	10	15	20	30	
524	Roland McDole	5	6	8	10	15	20	30	
525	Dennis Shaw	5	6	8	10	15	20	30	
526	Dave Manders	5	6	8	10	15	20	40	
527	Skip Vanderbundt	5	6	8	10	15	20	30	
528	Mike Sensibaugh RC	5	6	8	10	40	50	250	

— Terry Bradshaw #15 BGS 9.5 (Gem) sold for $505 (eBay; 10/07)
— Terry Bradshaw #15 PSA 10 (Gem Mint) sold for $2548.98 (Memory Lane; 5/12)
— Jack Ham #115 PSA 10 (Gem) sold for $2,185 (Mastro; 12/06)
— Jack Ham #115 PSA 10 (Gem) sold for $1,679 (Memory Lane; 5/08)
— Jack Ham RC #115 PSA 10 (Gem Mint) sold for $2057.51 (Memory Lane; 5/12)
— Larry Little #440 PSA 9 (MT) sold for $480 (eBay; 10/07)
— Art Shell RC #77 PSA 10 (Gem Mint) sold for $3158.02 (eBay; 8/12)
— O.J. Simpson #500 PSA 10 (Gem Mint) sold for $1657 (eBay; 10/14)

1974 Topps

	VgEx 4	EX 5	ExMt 6	NM 7	NmMt 8	NmMt+ 8.5	MT 9	Gem 9.5/10
O.J.Simpson RB	5	8	12	25	50	60	125	
Blaine Nye	4	5	6	8	10	12	25	
Don Hansen	4	5	6	8	10	12	25	
Ken Bowman	4	5	6	8	10	12	25	
Carl Eller	4	5	6	8	20			
Jerry Smith	4	5	6	8	20			
Ed Podolak	4	5	6	8	10	12	25	
Mel Gray	4	5	6	8	10	12	25	100
Pat Matson	4	5	6	8	20			

		VgEx 4	EX 5	ExMt 6	NM 7	NmMt 8	NmMt+ 8.5	MT 9	Gem 9.5/10
10	Floyd Little	4	5	6	8	10	12	50	
11	Frank Pitts	4	5	6	8	20			
12	Vern Den Herder RC	4	5	6	8	30	40	100	
13	John Fuqua	4	5	6	8	10	12	60	
14	Jack Tatum	4	5	6	8	10	12	30	
15	Winston Hill	4	5	6	8	10	12	25	
16	John Beasley	4	5	6	8	10	12	25	
17	David Lee	4	5	6	8	10	12	25	
18	Rich Coady	4	5	6	8	10	12	25	
19	Ken Willard	4	5	6	8	10	12	25	
20	Coy Bacon	4	5	6	8	10	12	25	
21	Ben Hawkins	4	5	6	8	10	12	25	
22	Paul Guidry	4	5	6	8	10	12	25	
23	Norm Snead HOR	4	5	6	8	10	12	25	
24	Jim Yarbrough	4	5	6	8	10	12	25	
25	Jack Reynolds RC	4	5	6	8	25			
26	Josh Ashton	4	5	6	8	10	12	25	
27	Donnie Green	4	5	6	8	10	12	20	
28	Bob Hayes	4	5	6	8	12	16	40	
29	John Zook	4	5	6	8	10	12	15	
30	Bobby Bryant	4	5	6	8	10	12	25	
31	Scott Hunter	4	5	6	8	10	12	25	
32	Dan Dierdorf	4	5	6	10	15	20	50	
33	Curt Knight	4	5	6	8	20			
34	Elmo Wright RC	4	5	6	8	10	12	25	
35	Essex Johnson	4	5	6	8	10	12	25	
36	Walt Sumner	4	5	6	8	10	12	25	80
37	Marv Montgomery	4	5	6	8	10	12	25	
38	Tim Foley	4	5	6	8	10	12	15	
39	Mike Siani	4	5	6	8	10	12	25	
40	Joe Greene	4	5	6	10	30	40	200	
41	Bobby Howfield	4	5	6	8	10	12	25	
42	Del Williams	4	5	6	8	10	12	25	100
43	Don McCauley	4	5	6	8	10	12	25	
44	Randy Jackson	4	5	6	8	10	12	25	100
45	Ron Smith	4	5	6	8	10	12	25	
46	Gene Washington 49er	4	5	6	8	10	12	25	
47	Po James	4	5	6	8	10	12	25	
48	Solomon Freelon	4	5	6	8	10	12	25	
49	Bob Windsor HOR	4	5	6	8	10	12	25	
50	John Hadl	4	5	6	8	10	12	25	
51	Greg Larson	4	5	6	8	10	12	15	
52	Steve Owens	4	5	6	8	20			
53	Jim Cheyunski	4	5	6	8	10	12	20	
54	Rayfield Wright	4	5	6	8	10	12	25	
55	Dave Hampton	4	5	6	8	10	12	25	
56	Ron Widby	4	5	6	8	20			
57	Milt Sunde	4	5	6	8	10	12	25	
58	Billy Kilmer	4	5	6	8	10	12	25	
59	Bobby Bell	4	5	6	8	10	12	25	
60	Jim Bakken	4	5	6	8	10	12	25	
61	Rufus Mayes	4	5	6	8	20			
62	Vic Washington	4	5	6	8	20			
63	Gene Washington Vik	4	5	6	8	10	12	25	100
64	Clarence Scott	4	5	6	8	20			
65	Gene Upshaw	4	5	6	8	10	20	80	
66	Larry Seiple	4	5	6	8	10	12	25	
67	John McMakin	4	5	6	8	10	12	25	
68	Ralph Baker	4	5	6	8	10	12	25	
69	Lydell Mitchell	4	5	6	8	10	12	20	
70	Archie Manning	4	5	6	8	10	12	40	
71	George Farmer	4	5	6	8	10	12	25	100
72	Ron East	4	5	6	8	10	12	25	
73	Al Nelson	4	5	6	8	10	12	25	
74	Pat Hughes	4	5	6	8	10	12	25	
75	Fred Willis	4	5	6	8	10	12	25	
76	Larry Walton	4	5	6	8	10	12	25	
77	Tom Neville	4	5	6	8	10	12	25	
78	Ted Kwalick	4	5	6	8	10	12	25	
79	Walt Patulski	4	5	6	8	10	12	20	
80	John Niland	4	5	6	8	10	12	25	
81	Ted Fritsch Jr.	4	5	6	8	10	12	25	
82	Paul Krause	4	5	6	8	10	12	25	
83	Jack Snow	4	5	6	8	15			
84	Mike Bass	4	5	6	8	10	12	25	
85	Jim Tyrer	4	5	6	8	30	50		
86	Ron Yankowski	4	5	6	8	10	12	25	
87	Mike Phipps	4	5	6	8	10	12	25	
88	Al Beauchamp	4	5	6	8	10	12	25	

#	Player	VgEx 4	EX 5	ExMt 6	NM 7	NmMt 8	NmMt+ 8.5	MT 9	Gem 9.5/10
89	Riley Odoms RC	4	5	6	8	15	20	80	
90	MacArthur Lane	4	5	6	8	20			
91	Art Thoms	4	5	6	8	20			
92	Marlin Briscoe	4	5	6	8	10	12	25	60
93	Bruce Van Dyke	4	5	6	8	10	12	25	
94	Tom Myers RC	4	5	6	8	10	12	25	
95	Calvin Hill	4	5	6	8	10	12	25	
96	Bruce Laird	4	5	6	8	10	12	20	60
97	Tony McGee DT	4	5	6	8	10	12	25	
98	Len Rohde	4	5	6	8	10	12	25	100
99	Tom McNeill	4	5	6	8	10	12	25	
100	Delles Howell	4	5	6	8	10	12	25	
101	Gary Garrison	4	5	6	8	10	12	25	
102	Dan Goich	4	5	6	8	10	12	25	
103	Len St. Jean	4	5	6	8	10	12	25	
104	Zeke Moore	4	5	6	8	10	12	25	
105	Ahmad Rashad RC	6	8	20	25	▲80	▲100	▲125	
106	Mel Renfro	4	5	6	8	10	12	25	
107	Jim Mitchell TE	4	5	6	8	10	12	25	100
108	Ed Budde	4	5	6	8	20		50	
109	Harry Schuh	4	5	6	8	10	12	25	
110	Greg Pruitt RC	4	5	6	8	10	15	135	
111	Ed Flanagan	4	5	6	8	10	12	25	
112	Larry Stallings	4	5	6	8	10	12	25	
113	Chuck Foreman RC	4	6	8	15	25	30	80	
114	Royce Berry	4	5	6	8	10	12	25	
115	Gale Gillingham	4	5	6	8	10	12	25	
116	Charlie Johnson HOR	4	5	6	8	20			
117	Checklist 1-132	4	5	6	8	10	12	25	
118	Bill Butler	4	5	6	8	10	12	25	
119	Roy Jefferson	4	5	6	8	20			
120	Bobby Douglass	4	5	6	8	10	12	25	
121	Harold Carmichael RC	4	6	10	30	100	30	125	
122	George Kunz AP	4	5	6	8	10	15	25	
123	Larry Little	4	5	6	8	10	12	25	
124	Forrest Blue AP	4	5	6	8	20			
125	Ron Yary	4	5	6	8	10	12	25	
126	Tom Mack AP	4	5	6	8	10	12	25	
127	Bob Tucker AP	4	5	6	8	10	12	25	
128	Paul Warfield	4	5	6	8	10	15	60	
129	Fran Tarkenton	4	5	6	10	50	60	200	
130	O.J.Simpson	4	6	8	15	50	60	250	
131	Larry Csonka	4	5	6	10	15	30	120	
132	Bruce Gossett AP	4	5	6	8	10	12	25	
133	Bill Stanfill AP	4	5	6	8	10	12	25	
134	Alan Page	4	5	6	8	10	12	30	
135	Paul Smith AP	4	5	6	8	10	12	25	
136	Claude Humphrey AP	4	5	6	8	10	12	25	
137	Jack Ham	4	6	8	12	30	▲50	60	
138	Lee Roy Jordan	4	5	6	8	10	12	40	
139	Phil Villapiano AP	4	5	6	8	10	12	25	
140	Ken Ellis AP	4	5	6	8	10	12	25	80
141	Willie Brown	4	5	6	8	10	12	40	100
142	Dick Anderson AP	4	5	6	8	10	12	25	
143	Bill Bradley AP	4	5	6	8	10	12	25	
144	Jerrel Wilson AP	4	5	6	8	10	12	25	
145	Reggie Rucker	4	5	6	8	20			
146	Marty Domres	4	5	6	8	10	12	25	80
147	Bob Kowalkowski	4	5	6	8	10	12	25	100
148	John Matuszak RC	4	5	6	10	15	20	50	
149	Mike Adamle RC	4	5	6	8	10	12	25	
150	Johnny Unitas	▲10	▲12	▲20	▲40	▲80	▲100	▲125	
151	Charlie Ford	4	5	6	8	10	12	20	
152	Bob Klein RC	4	5	6	8	10	12	25	
153	Jim Merlo	4	5	6	8	10	12	25	
154	Willie Young	4	5	6	8	10	12	25	60
155	Donny Anderson	4	5	6	8	10	12	25	60
156	Brig Owens	4	5	6	8	10	12	25	
157	Bruce Jarvis	4	5	6	8	10	12	25	
158	Ron Carpenter RC	4	5	6	8	10	12	25	60
159	Don Cockroft	4	5	6	8	10	12	25	
160	Tommy Nobis	4	5	6	8	10	12	25	80
161	Craig Morton	4	5	6	8	10	12	25	80
162	Jon Staggers	4	5	6	8	20			
163	Mike Eischeid	4	5	6	8	10	12	25	
164	Jerry Sisemore RC	4	5	6	8	10	12	25	
165	Cedrick Hardman	4	5	6	8	20			
166	Bill Thompson	4	5	6	8	10	12	25	
167	Jim Lynch	4	5	6	8	10	12	20	
168	Bob Moore	4	5	6	8	10	12	25	
169	Glen Edwards	4	5	6	8	10	12	25	100
170	Mercury Morris	4	5	6	8	10	12	25	
171	Julius Adams	4	5	6	8	10	12	20	100
172	Cotton Speyrer	4	5	6	8	10	12	25	100
173	Bill Munson	4	5	6	8	10	12	25	
174	Benny Johnson	4	5	6	8	10	12	25	150
175	Burgess Owens RC	4	5	6	8	10	12	25	80
176	Cid Edwards	4	5	6	8	10	12	25	
177	Doug Buffone	4	5	6	8	10	12	20	100
178	Charlie Cowan	4	5	6	8	10	12	25	60
179	Bob Newland	4	5	6	8	10	12	25	
180	Ron Johnson	4	5	6	8	10	12	25	100
181	Bob Rowe	4	5	6	8	10	12	25	
182	Len Hauss	4	5	6	8	10	12	25	80
183	Joe DeLamielleure RC	6	8	12	15	30	80	60	400
184	Sherman White RC	4	5	6	8	10	12	25	
185	Fair Hooker	4	5	6	8	10	12	20	80
186	Nick Mike-Mayer	4	5	6	8	15			
187	Ralph Neely	4	5	6	8	10	12	20	80
188	Rich McGeorge	4	5	6	8	10	12	25	80
189	Ed Marinaro RC	4	5	6	8	10	12	25	100
190	Dave Wilcox	4	5	6	8	10	12	25	80
191	Joe Owens RC	4	5	6	8	10	12	25	80
192	Bill Van Heusen	4	5	6	8	10	12	25	100
193	Jim Kearney	4	5	6	8	20			
194	Otis Sistrunk RC	4	5	6	8	30	50		
195	Ron Shanklin	4	5	6	8	10	12	25	50
196	Bill Lenkaitis	4	5	6	8	10	12	25	
197	Tom Drougas	4	5	6	8	10	12	15	80
198	Larry Hand	4	5	6	8	10	12	25	80
199	Mack Alston	4	5	6	8	10	12	25	80
200	Bob Griese	4	5	6	10	15	20	80	
201	Earlie Thomas	4	5	6	8	10	12	25	
202	Carl Gersbach	4	5	6	8	10	12	25	80
203	Jim Harrison	4	5	6	8	10	12	25	80
204	Jake Kupp	4	5	6	8	10	12	20	
205	Merlin Olsen	4	5	6	8	10	12	25	
206	Spider Lockhart	4	5	6	8	10	12	25	
207	Walker Gillette	4	5	6	8	10	12	15	100
208	Verlon Biggs	4	5	6	8	10	12	25	100
209	Bob James	4	5	6	8	10	12	25	100
210	Bob Trumpy	4	5	6	8	20			
211	Jerry Sherk	4	5	6	8	10	12	25	80
212	Andy Maurer	4	5	6	8	10	12	25	80
213	Fred Carr	4	5	6	8	10	12	25	100
214	Mick Tingelhoff	4	5	6	8	10	12	25	100
215	Steve Spurrier	4	5	6	20	25	30	40	
216	Richard Harris	4	5	6	8	10	12	25	100
217	Charlie Greer	4	5	6	8	10	12	15	100
218	Buck Buchanan	4	5	6	8	20			
219	Ray Guy RC	8	10	15	50	200	250	500	
220	Franco Harris	5	6	8	12	50	60	100	
221	Darryl Stingley RC	4	5	6	8	10	12	25	
222	Rex Kern	4	5	6	8	10	12	25	80
223	Toni Fritsch	4	5	6	8	10	12	25	80
224	Levi Johnson	4	5	6	8	10	12	25	50
225	Bob Kuechenberg	4	5	6	8	10	12	25	
226	Elvin Bethea	4	5	6	8	10	12	25	100
227	Al Woodall RC	4	5	6	8	10	12	25	
228	Terry Owens	4	5	6	8	10	12	25	80
229	Bivian Lee	4	5	6	8	10	12	25	
230	Dick Butkus	5	6	10	15	40	50	200	
231	Jim Bertelsen RC	4	5	6	8	10	12	25	80
232	John Mendenhall RC	4	5	6	8	15			
233	Conrad Dobler RC	4	5	6	8	10	12	20	100
234	J.D. Hill	4	5	6	8	10	12	25	60
235	Ken Houston	4	5	6	8	10	12	25	
236	Dave Lewis	4	5	6	8	10	12	25	80
237	John Garlington	4	5	6	8	10	12	25	100
238	Bill Sandeman	4	5	6	8	10	12	25	100
239	Alden Roche	4	5	6	8	10	12	25	100
240	John Gilliam	4	5	6	8	10	12	25	80
241	Bruce Taylor	4	5	6	8	10	12	25	
242	Vern Winfield	4	5	6	8	10	12	25	80
243	Bobby Maples	4	5	6	8	10	12	25	100
244	Wendell Hayes	4	5	6	8	10	12	25	
245	George Blanda	4	5	6	10	15	20	50	
246	Dwight White	4	5	6	8	10	12	25	100

#	Player	VgEx 4	EX 5	ExMt 6	NM 7	NmMt 8	NmMt+ 8.5	MT 9	Gem 9.5/10
247	Sandy Durko	4	5	6	8	10	12	25	50
248	Tom Mitchell	4	5	6	8	10	12	25	60
249	Chuck Walton	4	5	6	8	10	12	25	
250	Bob Lilly	4	5	6	8	10	15	50	
251	Doug Swift	4	5	6	8	10	12	25	60
252	Lynn Dickey RC	4	5	6	8	15	20	25	
253	Jerome Barkum RC	4	5	6	8	20			100
254	Clint Jones	4	5	6	8	20			
255	Billy Newsome	4	5	6	8	10	12	25	100
256	Bob Asher	4	5	6	8	10	12	25	
257	Joe Scibelli	4	5	6	8	20		80	
258	Tom Blanchard	4	5	6	8	10	12	25	80
259	Norm Thompson	4	5	6	8	10	12	15	60
260	Larry Brown	4	5	6	8	10	12	25	
261	Paul Seymour	4	5	6	8	10	12	25	80
262	Checklist 133-264	4	5	6	8	10	12	25	80
263	Doug Dieken RC	4	5	6	8	10	12	25	100
264	Lemar Parrish	4	5	6	8	20		50	
265	Bob Lee	4	5	6	8	10	12	25	100
266	Bob Brown DT	4	5	6	8	10	12	25	
267	Roy Winston	4	5	6	8	10	12	25	
268	Randy Beisler	4	5	6	8	10	12	25	100
269	Joe Dawkins	4	5	6	8	10	12	25	
270	Tom Dempsey	4	5	6	8	10	12	25	
271	Jack Rudnay	4	5	6	8	10	12	25	
272	Art Shell	4	5	6	8	12	20	40	
273	Mike Wagner	4	5	6	8	10	12	25	
274	Rick Cash	4	5	6	8	10	12	20	
275	Greg Landry	4	5	6	8	10	12	25	
276	Glenn Ressler	4	5	6	8	10	12	25	100
277	Billy Joe DuPree RC	4	5	6	8	10	12	25	
278	Norm Evans	4	5	6	8	10	12	25	100
279	Billy Parks	4	5	6	8	10	12	25	
280	John Riggins	4	5	6	10	15	20	70	
281	Lionel Aldridge	4	5	6	8	10	12	25	
282	Steve O'Neal	4	5	6	8	10	12	25	
283	Craig Clemons	4	5	6	8	10	12	25	100
284	Willie Williams	4	5	6	8	10	12	25	80
285	Isiah Robertson	4	5	6	8	10	12	25	
286	Dennis Shaw	4	5	6	8	10	12	25	
287	Bill Brundige	4	5	6	8	10	12	25	
288	John Leypoldt	4	5	6	8	10	12	20	
289	John DeMarie	4	5	6	8	10	12	25	
290	Mike Reid	4	5	6	8	10	12	25	
291	Greg Brezina	4	5	6	8	10	12	25	
292	Willie Buchanon RC	4	5	6	8	10	12	25	
293	Dave Osborn	4	5	6	8	10	12	25	
294	Mel Phillips	4	5	6	8	10	12	25	
295	Haven Moses	4	5	6	8	10	12	25	
296	Wade Key	4	5	6	8	10	12	25	50
297	Marvin Upshaw	4	5	6	8	10	12	25	
298	Ray Mansfield	4	5	6	8	10	12	25	
299	Edgar Chandler	4	5	6	8	10	12	25	
300	Marv Hubbard	4	5	6	8	10	12	25	
301	Herman Weaver	4	5	6	8	10	12	25	
302	Jim Bailey	4	5	6	8	10	12	15	80
303	D.D.Lewis RC	4	5	6	8	10	12	25	100
304	Ken Burrough	4	5	6	8	10	12	25	
305	Jake Scott	4	5	6	8	10	12	25	
306	Randy Rasmussen	4	5	6	8	10	12	25	
307	Pettis Norman	4	5	6	8	10	12	15	80
308	Carl Johnson	4	5	6	8	10	12	25	
309	Joe Taylor	4	5	6	8	10	12	15	
310	Pete Gogolak	4	5	6	8	10	12	25	100
311	Tony Baker FB	4	5	6	8	10	12	25	
312	John Richardson	4	5	6	8	10	12	25	
313	Dave Robinson	4	5	6	8	10	12	25	100
314	Reggie McKenzie RC	4	5	6	8	10	12	25	
315	Isaac Curtis RC	4	5	6	8	10	12	25	100
316	Thom Darden	4	5	6	8	10	12	25	
317	Ken Reaves	4	5	6	8	10	12	25	
318	Malcolm Snider	4	5	6	8	10	12	25	
319	Jeff Siemon RC	4	5	6	8	10	12	25	100
320	Dan Abramowicz	4	5	6	8	20			
321	Lyle Alzado	4	5	6	8	10	12	25	
322	John Reaves	4	5	6	8	10	12	25	100
323	Morris Stroud	4	5	6	8	10	12	25	
324	Bobby Walden	4	5	6	8	10	12	25	60
325	Randy Vataha	4	5	6	8	10	12	25	

#	Player	VgEx 4	EX 5	ExMt 6	NM 7	NmMt 8	NmMt+ 8.5	MT 9	Gem 9.5/10
326	Nemiah Wilson	4	5	6	8	20			
327	Paul Naumoff	4	5	6	8	10	12	25	80
328	Simpson/Brockington LL	4	5	6	8	10	12	30	
329	Staubach/Stabler LL	4	5	6	8	20	25	40	
330	Carmichael/Willis LL	4	5	6	8	10	12	25	
331	Gerela/Ray LL	4	5	6	8	10	12	25	
332	Interception Leaders	4	5	6	8	10	12	25	
333	J.Wilson/Wittum LL	4	5	6	8	10	12	25	100
334	Dennis Nelson	4	5	6	8	10	12	25	
335	Walt Garrison	4	5	6	8	10	12	25	100
336	Tody Smith	4	5	6	8	10	12	25	80
337	Ed Bell	4	5	6	8	10	12	25	
338	Bryant Salter	4	5	6	8	10	12	25	
339	Wayne Colman	4	5	6	8	10	12	15	80
340	Garo Yepremian	4	5	6	8	10	12	25	
341	Bob Newton	4	5	6	8	10	12	25	
342	Vince Clements RC	4	5	6	8	10	12	25	
343	Ken Iman	4	5	6	8	10	12	20	
344	Jim Tolbert	4	5	6	8	10	12	25	100
345	Chris Hanburger	4	5	6	8	10	12	25	
346	Dave Foley	4	5	6	8	10	12	20	80
347	Tommy Casanova	4	5	6	8	20			
348	John James	4	5	6	8	10	12	25	100
349	Clarence Williams	4	5	6	8	10	12	25	60
350	Leroy Kelly	4	5	6	8	10	12	25	
351	Stu Voigt RC	4	5	6	8	10	12	25	
352	Skip Vanderbundt	4	5	6	8	10	12	25	
353	Pete Duranko	4	5	6	8	20			
354	John Outlaw	4	5	6	8	10	12	25	100
355	Jan Stenerud	4	5	6	8	10	12	25	
356	Barry Pearson	4	5	6	8	10	12	25	100
357	Brian Dowling RC	4	5	6	8	10	12	25	
358	Dan Conners	4	5	6	8	10	12	25	
359	Bob Bell	4	5	6	8	10	12	25	
360	Rick Volk	4	5	6	8	10	12	25	100
361	Pat Toomay	4	5	6	8	10	12	25	
362	Bob Gresham	4	5	6	8	20			
363	John Schmitt	4	5	6	8	10		25	
364	Mel Rogers	4	5	6	8	10	12	25	100
365	Manny Fernandez	4	5	6	8	10	12	25	60
366	Ernie Jackson	4	5	6	8	10	12	25	50
367	Gary Huff RC	4	5	6	8	10	12	25	
368	Bob Grim	4	5	6	8	20			
369	Ernie McMillan	4	5	6	8	10	12	25	60
370	Dave Elmendorf	4	5	6	8	10	12	25	
371	Mike Bragg	4	5	6	8	10	12	25	100
372	John Skorupan	4	5	6	8	10	12	25	
373	Howard Fest	4	5	6	8	10	12	25	
374	Jerry Tagge RC	4	5	6	8	10	12	25	
375	Art Malone	4	5	6	8	10	12	25	80
376	Bob Babich	4	5	6	8	20			
377	Jim Marshall	4	5	6	8	10	12	25	
378	Bob Hoskins	4	5	6	8	10	12	25	100
379	Don Zimmerman	4	5	6	8	10	12	25	
380	Ray May	4	5	6	8	10	12	20	
381	Emmitt Thomas	4	5	6	8	10	12	25	100
382	Terry Hanratty	4	5	6	8	10	12	25	
383	John Hannah RC	6	8	12	50	200	250	800	
384	George Atkinson	4	5	6	8	10	12	25	
385	Ted Hendricks	4	5	6	8	10	12	25	
386	Jim O'Brien	4	5	6	8	20			
387	Jethro Pugh	4	5	6	8	10	12	30	
388	Elbert Drungo	4	5	6	8	10	12	15	100
389	Richard Caster	4	5	6	8	10	12	25	
390	Deacon Jones	4	5	6	8	10	12	25	
391	Checklist 265-396	4	5	6	8	10	12	25	
392	Jess Phillips	4	5	6	8	10	12	25	
393	Garry Lyle	4	5	6	8	10	12	25	
394	Jim Files	4	5	6	8	10	12	25	100
395	Jim Hart	4	5	6	8	10	12	25	
396	Dave Chapple	4	5	6	8	20			
397	Jim Langer	4	5	6	8	15	20	25	
398	John Wilbur	4	5	6	8	20			
399	Dwight Harrison	4	5	6	8	10	12	25	
400	John Brockington	4	5	6	8	10	12	25	
401	Ken Anderson	4	5	6	10	15	20	50	
402	Mike Tilleman	4	5	6	8	10	12	25	
403	Charlie Hall	4	5	6	8	10	12	25	
404	Tommy Hart	4	5	6	8	10	12	25	100

#	Name	VgEx 4	EX 5	ExMt 6	NM 7	NmMt 8	NmMt+ 8.5	MT 9	Gem 9.5/10
405	Norm Bulaich	4	5	6	8	10	12	25	
406	Jim Turner	4	5	6	8	10	12	25	
407	Mo Moorman	4	5	6	8	10	12	25	
408	Ralph Anderson	4	5	6	8	10	12	25	
409	Jim Otto	4	5	6	8	10	12	25	
410	Andy Russell	4	5	6	8	10	12	25	
411	Glenn Doughty	4	5	6	8	10	12	15	50
412	Altie Taylor	4	5	6	8	10	12	25	
413	Marv Bateman	4	5	6	8	10	12	25	
414	Willie Alexander	4	5	6	8	25			
415	Bill Zapalac RC	4	5	6	8	10	12	25	
416	Russ Washington	4	5	6	8	10	12	25	
417	Joe Federspiel	4	5	6	8	10	12	20	
418	Craig Cotton	4	5	6	8	10	12	25	
419	Randy Johnson	4	5	6	8	10	12	25	
420	Harold Jackson	4	5	6	8	10	12	25	80
421	Roger Wehrli	4	5	6	8	10	12	15	100
422	Charlie Harraway	4	5	6	8	20			
423	Spike Jones	4	5	6	8	10	12	15	
424	Bob Johnson	4	5	6	8	20			
425	Mike McCoy DT	4	5	6	8	10	12	15	
426	Dennis Havig	4	5	6	8	10	12	25	
427	Bob McKay RC	4	5	6	8	10	12	25	
428	Steve Zabel	4	5	6	8	10	12	25	
429	Horace Jones	4	5	6	8	10	12	25	
430	Jim Johnson	4	5	6	8	10	12	30	
431	Roy Gerela	4	5	6	8	10	12	25	
432	Tom Graham RC	4	5	6	8	10	12	20	
433	Curley Culp	4	5	6	10	15	20	40	125
434	Ken Mendenhall	4	5	6	8	10	12	20	
435	Jim Plunkett	4	5	6	8	12	15	30	
436	Julian Fagan	4	5	6	8	10	12	25	
437	Mike Garrett	4	5	6	8	10	12	25	
438	Bobby Joe Green	4	5	6	8	10	12	25	
439	Jack Gregory	4	5	6	8	10	12	25	
440	Charlie Sanders	4	5	6	8	10	12	25	100
441	Bill Curry	4	5	6	8	10	12	25	
442	Bob Pollard	4	5	6	8	20			
443	David Ray	4	5	6	8	10	12	25	
444	Terry Metcalf RC	4	5	6	8	20			
445	Pat Fischer	4	5	6	8	10	12	25	100
446	Bob Chandler	4	5	6	8	10	12	25	
447	Bill Bergey	4	5	6	8	10	12	25	100
448	Walter Johnson	4	5	6	8	10	12	25	
449	Charle Young RC	4	5	6	8	20			
450	Chester Marcol	4	5	6	8	10	12	30	
451	Ken Stabler	6	8	12	20	60	80	200	
452	Preston Pearson	4	5	6	8	10	12	25	
453	Mike Current	4	5	6	8	10	12	25	
454	Ron Bolton	4	5	6	8	20			
455	Mark Lomas	4	5	6	8	10	12	25	
456	Raymond Chester	4	5	6	8	10	12	25	
457	Jerry LeVias	4	5	6	8	10	12	25	
458	Skip Butler	4	5	6	8	10	12	25	80
459	Mike Livingston RC	4	5	6	8	15			
460	AFC Semi-Final	4	5	6	8	20	25	125	
461	NFC Semi-Finals/R.Staubach	4	5	6	8	20	30	150	
462	Playoff Champmships/Stabler	4	5	6	8	12	15	50	
463	SB VIII/L.Csonka	4	5	6	8	10	12	120	
464	Wayne Mulligan	4	5	6	8	10	12	25	60
465	Horst Muhlmann	4	5	6	8	10	12	25	
466	Milt Morin	4	5	6	8	10	12	20	
467	Don Parish	4	5	6	8	10	12	25	
468	Richard Neal	4	5	6	8	10	12	25	
469	Ron Jessie	4	5	6	8	10	12	25	
470	Terry Bradshaw	8	10	15	25	60	80	400	
471	Fred Dryer	4	5	6	8	10	12	25	
472	Jim Carter	4	5	6	8	10	12	25	100
473	Ken Burrow	4	5	6	8	10	12	15	60
474	Wally Chambers RC	4	5	6	8	10	12	25	
475	Dan Pastorini	4	5	6	8	20			
476	Don Morrison	4	5	6	8	10	12	25	
477	Carl Mauck	4	5	6	8	10	12	25	100
478	Larry Cole RC	4	5	6	8	10	12	25	
479	Jim Kiick	4	5	6	8	20		120	
480	Willie Lanier	4	5	6	8	10	12	25	100
481	Don Herrmann	4	5	6	8	10	12	25	
482	George Hunt	4	5	6	8	10	12	25	
483	Bob Howard RC	4	5	6	8	10	12	25	
484	Myron Pottios	4	5	6	8	10	12	25	
485	Jackie Smith	4	5	6	8	10	12	25	100
486	Vern Holland	4	5	6	8	10	12	25	
487	Jim Braxton	4	5	6	8	10	12	20	100
488	Joe Reed	4	5	6	8	20			
489	Wally Hilgenberg	4	5	6	8	10	12	30	
490	Fred Biletnikoff	4	5	6	8	12	15	50	
491	Bob DeMarco	4	5	6	8	20			
492	Mark Nordquist	4	5	6	8	10	12	25	
493	Larry Brooks	4	5	6	8	20			
494	Pete Athas	4	5	6	8	10	12	25	
495	Emerson Boozer	4	5	6	8	10	12	25	
496	L.C.Greenwood	4	5	6	8	10	12	80	
497	Rockne Freitas	4	5	6	8	10	12	25	
498	Checklist 397-528	4	5	6	8	10	12	25	
499	Joe Schmiesing	4	5	6	8	10	12	25	
500	Roger Staubach	8	10	15	25	60	80	400	
501	Al Cowlings	4	5	6	8	10	12	25	100
502	Sam Cunningham RC	4	5	6	8	10	12	25	
503	Dennis Partee	4	5	6	8	10	12	25	
504	John Didion	4	5	6	8	10	12	25	
505	Nick Buoniconti	4	5	6	8	10	12	25	
506	Carl Garrett	4	5	6	8	10	12	25	
507	Doug Van Horn	4	5	6	8	10	12	25	
508	Jamie Rivers	4	5	6	8	10	12	30	
509	Jack Youngblood	4	5	6	8	10	15	40	
510	Charley Taylor	4	5	6	8	20			
511	Ken Riley	4	5	6	8	10	12	25	
512	Joe Ferguson RC	4	5	6	8	10	20	40	
513	Bill Lueck	4	5	6	8	10	12	25	
514	Ray Brown DB RC	4	5	6	8	10	12	25	
515	Fred Cox	4	5	6	8	20			
516	Joe Jones DE	4	5	6	8	10	12	25	
517	Larry Schreiber	4	5	6	8	10	12	25	
518	Dennis Wirgowski	4	5	6	8	10	12	25	
519	Leroy Mitchell	4	5	6	8	10	12	25	
520	Otis Taylor	4	5	6	8	10	12	25	80
521	Henry Davis	4	5	6	8	20			
522	Bruce Barnes	4	5	6	8	20	20		
523	Charlie Smith RB	4	5	6	8	10	12	25	
524	Bert Jones RC	4	5	6	10	40	50	125	
525	Lem Barney	4	5	6	8	10	12	25	
526	John Fitzgerald RC	4	5	6	8	10	12	40	
527	Tom Funchess	4	5	6	8	10	12	25	
528	Steve Tannen	4	5	6	8	10	12	20	

— Dick Butkus #230 PSA 10 (Gem) sold for $1,403.65 (eBay; 12/13)
— Billy Joe Dupree #277 PSA 10 (Gem) sold for $1,237 (Andy Madec; 5/07)
— Chuck Foreman RC #113 PSA 10 (Gem Mint) sold for $300 (Bussineau; 4/12)
— Ray Guy #219 PSA 10 (Gem) sold for $3,755 (eBay; 9/13)
— Franco Harris #220 PSA 10 (Gem) sold for $886 (eBay; 12/07)
— Roger Staubach #500 PSA 10 (Gem) sold for $825 (Goodwin; 2/11)
— Roger Staubach #500 PSA 10 (Gem) sold for $1,220.94 (Mile High; 12/13)

1975 Topps

#	Name	VgEx 4	EX 5	ExMt 6	NM 7	NmMt 8	NmMt+ 8.5	MT 9	Gem 9.5/1
1	McCutcheon/Armstrong LL	4	4	5	6	10	15	60	
2	Jurgensen/K.Anderson LL	4	4	5	5	10	15	60	
3	C.Young/L.Mitchell LL	4	4	5	5	10	12	25	
4	Marcol/Gerela LL	4	4	5	5	10	12	30	
5	R.Brown/E.Thomas LL	4	4	5	5	10	12	25	
6	Blanchard/Guy LL	4	4	5	5	10	12	25	
7	George Blanda HL	4	4	5	6	10	12	25	
8	George Blanda HL	4	4	5	6	10	12	25	80
9	Ralph Baker	4	4	5	5	10	12	25	
10	Don Woods	4	4	5	5	10	12	25	
11	Bob Asher	4	4	5	5	10	12	25	60
12	Mel Blount RC	6	8	▲15	▲50	▲125	▲150	200	1,500
13	Sam Cunningham	4	4	5	5	10	12	25	
14	Jackie Smith	4	4	5	5	10	12	25	80
15	Greg Landry	4	4	5	5	15	20	150	
16	Buck Buchanan	4	4	5	5	10	12	25	60
17	Haven Moses	4	4	5	5	10	12	25	50
18	Clarence Ellis	4	4	5	5	10	12	25	80
19	Jim Carter	4	4	5	5	10	12	25	50
20	Charley Taylor	4	4	5	5	10	12	25	
21	Jess Phillips	4	4	5	5	10	12	25	
22	Larry Seiple	4	4	5	5	10	12	25	
23	Doug Dieken	4	4	5	5	10	12	20	60

#	Player	VgEx 4	EX 5	ExMt 6	NM 7	NmMt 8	NmMt+ 8.5	MT 9	Gem 9.5/10
24	Ron Saul	4	4	5	5	10	12	15	50
25	Isaac Curtis	4	4	5	5	10	12	25	60
26	Gary Larsen RC	4	4	5	5	10	12	25	100
27	Bruce Jarvis	4	4	5	5	10	12	25	60
28	Steve Zabel	4	4	5	5	10	12	20	50
29	John Mendenhall	4	4	5	5	10	12	25	60
30	Rick Volk	4	4	5	5	10	12	25	60
31	Checklist 1-132	4	4	5	5	10	12	25	
32	Dan Abramowicz	4	4	5	5	10	12	20	80
33	Bubba Smith	4	4	5	5	10	12	25	100
34	David Ray	4	4	5	5	10	12	25	60
35	Dan Dierdorf	4	4	5	6	10	12	25	
36	Randy Rasmussen	4	4	5	5	10	12	25	
37	Bob Howard	4	4	5	5	10	12	25	80
38	Gary Huff	4	4	5	5	10	12	20	
39	Rocky Bleier RC	10	12	15	25	40	50	80	
40	Mel Gray	4	4	5	5	10	12	20	60
41	Tony McGee DT	4	4	5	5	10	12	25	
42	Larry Hand	4	4	5	5	10	12	25	60
43	Wendell Hayes	4	4	5	5	10	12	25	60
44	Doug Wilkerson RC	4	4	5	5	10	12	25	60
45	Paul Smith	4	4	5	5	10	12	25	
46	Dave Robinson	4	4	5	5	10	12	25	80
47	Bivian Lee	4	4	5	5	10	12	25	80
48	Jim Mandich RC	4	4	5	5	10	12	80	
49	Greg Pruitt	4	4	5	5	10	12	25	135
50	Dan Pastorini	4	4	5	5	10	12	25	60
51	Ron Pritchard	4	4	5	5	10	12	25	60
52	Dan Conners	4	4	5	5	10	12	25	
53	Fred Cox	4	4	5	5	10	12	25	50
54	Tony Greene	4	4	5	5	10	12	25	
55	Craig Morton	4	4	5	5	10	12	25	200
56	Jerry Sisemore	4	4	5	5	10	12	25	60
57	Glenn Doughty	4	4	5	5	10	12	25	
58	Larry Schreiber	4	4	5	5	10	12	20	60
59	Charlie Waters RC	4	4	5	6	15	20	50	
60	Jack Youngblood	4	4	5	5	10	12	25	80
61	Bill Lenkaitis	4	4	5	5	10	12	25	
62	Greg Brezina	4	4	5	5	10	12	25	
63	Bob Pollard	4	4	5	5	10	12	25	80
64	Mack Alston	4	4	5	5	10	12	25	
65	Drew Pearson RC	6	8	10	15	50	60	150	
66	Charlie Stukes	4	4	5	5	10	12	25	60
67	Emerson Boozer	4	4	5	5	10	12	25	
68	Dennis Partee	4	4	5	5	10	12	20	120
69	Bob Newton	4	4	5	5	10	12	25	80
70	Jack Tatum	4	4	5	5	10	12	25	
71	Frank Lewis	4	4	5	5	10	12	25	
72	Bob Young	4	4	5	5	10	12	25	60
73	Julius Adams	4	4	5	5	40	60	150	
74	Paul Naumoff	4	4	5	5	10	12	25	
75	Otis Taylor	4	4	5	5	10	12	25	
76	Dave Hampton	4	4	5	5	10	12	25	60
77	Mike Current	4	4	5	5	10	12	25	60
78	Brig Owens	4	4	5	5	10	12	25	80
79	Bobby Scott	4	4	5	5	10	12	25	
80	Harold Carmichael	4	4	5	5	10	12	25	
81	Bill Stanfill	4	4	5	5	10	12	25	80
82	Bob Babich	4	4	5	5	10	12	25	
83	Vic Washington	4	4	5	5	10	12	25	
84	Mick Tingelhoff	4	4	5	5	10	12	25	60
85	Bob Trumpy	4	4	5	5	10	12	25	60
86	Earl Edwards	4	4	5	5	10	12	20	60
87	Ron Hornsby	4	4	5	5	10	12	25	
88	Don McCauley	4	4	5	5	10	12	20	80
89	Jim Johnson	4	4	5	5	10	12	25	
90	Andy Russell	4	4	5	5	10	12	25	80
91	Cornell Green	4	4	5	5	10	12	25	
92	Charlie Cowan	4	4	5	5	10	12	15	60
93	Jon Staggers	4	4	5	5	10	12	25	60
94	Billy Newsome	4	4	5	5	10	12	20	
95	Willie Brown	4	4	5	5	10	12	25	60
96	Carl Mauck	4	4	5	5	10	12	20	60
97	Doug Buffone	4	4	5	5	10	12	20	60
98	Preston Pearson	4	4	5	5	15	20	60	
99	Jim Bakken	4	4	5	5	10	12	25	60
100	Bob Griese	4	4	5	6	10	12	25	
101	Bob Windsor	4	4	5	5	10	12	25	
102	Rockne Freitas	4	4	5	5	10	12	25	

#	Player	VgEx 4	EX 5	ExMt 6	NM 7	NmMt 8	NmMt+ 8.5	MT 9	Gem 9.5/10
103	Jim Marsalis	4	4	5	5	10	12	25	
104	Bill Thompson	4	4	5	5	10	12	25	
105	Ken Burrow	4	4	5	5	10	12	20	60
106	Diron Talbert	4	4	5	5	10	12	20	60
107	Joe Federspiel	4	4	5	5	10	12	25	
108	Norm Bulaich	4	4	5	5	10	12	25	50
109	Bob DeMarco	4	4	5	5	10	12	25	50
110	Tom Wittum	4	4	5	5	10	12	25	
111	Larry Hefner	4	4	5	5	10	12	25	80
112	Tody Smith	4	4	5	5	10	12	20	
113	Stu Voigt	4	4	5	5	10	12	25	60
114	Horst Muhlmann	4	4	5	5	10	12	25	60
115	Ahmad Rashad	4	4	5	8	12	15	25	
116	Joe Dawkins	4	4	5	5	10	12	20	
117	George Kunz	4	4	5	5	10	12	25	60
118	D.D.Lewis	4	4	5	5	10	12	25	60
119	Levi Johnson	4	4	5	5	10	12	30	
120	Len Dawson	4	4	5	6	10	15	50	
121	Jim Bertelsen	4	4	5	5	10	12	25	60
122	Ed Bell	4	4	5	5	10	12	25	
123	Art Thoms	4	4	5	5	10	12	25	60
124	Joe Beauchamp	4	4	5	5	10	12	15	60
125	Jack Ham	4	4	5	8	20	30	80	
126	Carl Garrett	4	4	5	5	10	12	25	
127	Roger Finnie	4	4	5	5	10	12	25	
128	Howard Twilley	4	4	5	5	10	12	25	
129	Bruce Barnes	4	4	5	5	10	12	25	
130	Nate Wright	4	4	5	5	10	12	25	
131	Jerry Tagge	4	4	5	5	10	12	25	
132	Floyd Little	4	4	5	5	10	12	25	80
133	John Zook	4	4	5	5	10	12	20	
134	Len Hauss	4	4	5	5	10	12	25	
135	Archie Manning	4	4	5	6	12	15	25	
136	Po James	4	4	5	5	10	12	20	60
137	Walt Sumner	4	4	5	5	10	12	25	
138	Randy Beisler	4	4	5	5	10	12	25	60
139	Willie Alexander	4	4	5	5	10	12	25	
140	Garo Yepremian	4	4	5	5	10	12	20	
141	Chip Myers	4	4	5	5	10	12	25	80
142	Jim Braxton	4	4	5	5	10	12	50	
143	Doug Van Horn	4	4	5	5	10	12	25	
144	Stan White	4	4	5	5	10	12	25	80
145	Roger Staubach	6	8	10	25	50	60	80	800
146	Herman Weaver	4	4	5	5	10	12	25	60
147	Marvin Upshaw	4	4	5	5	10	12	25	
148	Bob Klein	4	4	5	5	10	12	25	
149	Earlie Thomas	4	4	5	5	10	12	25	60
150	John Brockington	4	4	5	5	10	12	25	80
151	Mike Siani	4	4	5	5	10	12	25	
152	Sam Davis RC	4	4	5	5	10	12	25	
153	Mike Wagner	4	4	5	5	10	12	25	
154	Larry Stallings	4	4	5	5	10	12	25	60
155	Wally Chambers	4	4	5	5	10	12	25	60
156	Randy Vataha	4	4	5	5	10	12	25	
157	Jim Marshall	4	4	5	5	10	12	25	
158	Jim Turner	4	4	5	5	10	12	25	60
159	Walt Sweeney	4	4	5	5	10	12	25	
160	Ken Anderson	4	4	5	6	10		35	
161	Ray Brown DB	4	4	5	5	10	12	25	60
162	John Didion	4	4	5	5	10	12	25	
163	Tom Dempsey	4	4	5	5	10	12	15	
164	Clarence Scott	4	4	5	5	10	12	25	60
165	Gene Washington 49er	4	4	5	5	10	12	25	60
166	Willie Rodgers RC	4	4	5	5	10	12	25	80
167	Doug Swift	4	4	5	5	10	12	25	
168	Rufus Mayes	4	4	5	5	10	12	25	80
169	Marv Bateman	4	4	5	5	10	12	25	100
170	Lydell Mitchell	4	4	5	5	10	12	25	60
171	Ron Smith	4	4	5	5	10	12	25	
172	Bill Munson	4	4	5	5	10	12	25	
173	Bob Grim	4	4	5	5	10	12	25	60
174	Ed Budde	4	4	5	5	10	12	15	60
175	Bob Lilly	4	4	5	6	10		35	120
176	Jim Youngblood RC	4	4	5	5	10	12	25	60
177	Steve Tannen	4	4	5	5	10	12	25	60
178	Rich McGeorge	4	4	5	5	10	12	20	60
179	Jim Tyrer	4	4	5	5	10	12	20	
180	Forrest Blue	4	4	5	5	10	12	25	
181	Jerry LeVias	4	4	5	5	10	12	15	60

FOOTBALL

#	Player	VgEx 4	EX 5	ExMt 6	NM 7	NmMt 8	NmMt+ 8.5	MT 9	Gem 9.5/10
182	Joe Gilliam RC	4	4	5	5	10	12	25	60
183	Jim Otis RC	4	4	5	5	10	12	25	
184	Mel Tom	4	4	5	5	10	12	25	60
185	Paul Seymour	4	4	5	5	10	12	20	
186	George Webster	4	4	5	5	10	12	25	50
187	Pete Duranko	4	4	5	5	10	12	20	60
188	Essex Johnson	4	4	5	5	10	12	25	
189	Bob Lee	4	4	5	5	10	12	25	60
190	Gene Upshaw	4	4	5	5	10	12	25	80
191	Tom Myers	4	4	5	5	10	12	25	60
192	Don Zimmerman	4	4	5	5	10	12	25	60
193	John Garlington	4	4	5	5	10	12	25	
194	Skip Butler	4	4	5	5	10	12	25	60
195	Tom Mitchell	4	4	5	5	10	12	25	60
196	Jim Langer	4	4	5	5	10	12	25	
197	Ron Carpenter	4	4	5	5	10	12	25	60
198	Dave Foley	4	4	5	5	10	12	25	
199	Bert Jones	4	4	5	5	10	12	25	80
200	Larry Brown	4	4	5	5	10	12	25	80
201	F.Biletnikoff/C.Taylor AP	4	4	5	5	10	12	25	80
202	R.Wright/R.Washington AP	4	4	5	5	10	12	25	80
203	L.Little/T.Mack AP	4	4	5	5	10	12	25	
204	J.Van Note/J.Rudnay AP	4	4	5	5	10	12	25	60
205	J.Hannah/G.Gillingham AP	4	4	5	5	10	12	25	80
206	D.Dierdorf/W.Hill AP	4	4	5	5	10	12	25	50
207	C.Young/R.Odoms AP	4	4	5	5	10	12	25	
208	F.Tarkenton/K.Stabler AP	4	4	5	6	10	12	35	100
209	O.Simpson/L.McCutchen AP	4	4	5	5	10	12	40	
210	T.Metcalf/O.Armstrong AP	4	4	5	5	10	12	25	
211	M.Gray/I.Curtis AP	4	4	5	5	10	12	25	
212	C.Marcol/R.Gerela AP	4	4	5	5	10	12	25	
213	J.Youngblood/E.Bethea AP	4	4	5	5	10	12	25	
214	A.Page/O.Sistrunk AP	4	4	5	5	10	12	25	
215	M.Olsen/M.Reid AP	4	4	5	5	10	12	25	
216	C.Eller/L.Alzado AP	4	4	5	5	10	12	25	
217	T.Hendricks/P.Villapiano AP	4	4	5	5	10	12	25	
218	W.Lanier/L.Jordan AP	4	4	5	5	10	12	25	60
219	I.Robertson/A.Russell AP	4	4	5	5	10	12	25	
220	N.Wright/E.Thomas AP	4	4	5	5	10	12	25	
221	W.Buchanon/L.Parrish AP	4	4	5	5	10	12	15	80
222	K.Houston/D.Anderson AP	4	4	5	5	10	12	25	80
223	C.Harris/J.Tatum AP	4	4	5	5	10	12	25	80
224	T.Wittum/R.Guy AP	4	4	5	5	10	12	25	
225	T.Metcalf/G.Pruitt AP	4	4	5	5	10	12	20	60
226	Ted Kwalick	4	4	5	5	10	12	20	
227	Spider Lockhart	4	4	5	5	10	12	25	
228	Mike Livingston	4	4	5	5	10	12	25	
229	Larry Cole	4	4	5	5	10	12	25	80
230	Gary Garrison	4	4	5	5	10	12	25	60
231	Larry Brooks	4	4	5	5	10	12	20	60
232	Bobby Howfield	4	4	5	5	10	12	15	60
233	Fred Carr	4	4	5	5	10	12	25	60
234	Norm Evans	4	4	5	5	10	12	20	60
235	Dwight White	4	4	5	5	10	12	40	125
236	Conrad Dobler	4	4	5	5	10	12	25	60
237	Garry Lyle	4	4	5	5	10	12	15	60
238	Darryl Stingley	4	4	5	5	10	12	25	60
239	Tom Graham	4	4	5	5	10	12	25	60
240	Chuck Foreman	4	4	5	5	10	12	50	
241	Ken Riley	4	4	5	5	10	12	30	
242	Don Morrison	4	4	5	5	10	12	25	
243	Lynn Dickey	4	4	5	5	10	12	20	80
244	Don Cockroft	4	4	5	5	10	12	20	
245	Claude Humphrey	4	4	5	5	10	12	50	
246	John Skorupan	4	4	5	5	10	12	25	60
247	Raymond Chester	4	4	5	5	10	12	25	60
248	Cas Banaszek	4	4	5	5	10	12	20	50
249	Art Malone	4	4	5	5	10	12	25	
250	Ed Flanagan	4	4	5	5	10	12	25	60
251	Checklist 133-264	4	4	5	5	10	20	100	
252	Nemiah Wilson	4	4	5	5	10	12	25	60
253	Ron Jessie	4	4	5	5	10	12	25	60
254	Jim Lynch	4	4	5	5	10	12	25	
255	Bob Tucker	4	4	5	5	10	12	25	
256	Terry Owens	4	4	5	5	10	12	25	
257	John Fitzgerald	4	4	5	5	10	12	25	
258	Jack Snow	4	4	5	5	10	12	25	
259	Garry Puetz	4	4	5	5	10	12	25	60
260	Mike Phipps	4	4	5	5	10	12	25	
261	Al Matthews	4	4	5	5	10	12	25	
262	Bob Kuechenberg	4	4	5	5	10	12	20	80
263	Ron Yankowski	4	4	5	5	10	12	25	
264	Ron Shanklin	4	4	5	5	10	12	30	
265	Bobby Douglass	4	4	5	5	10	12	25	
266	Josh Ashton	4	4	5	5	10	12	25	
267	Bill Van Heusen	4	4	5	5	10	12	25	
268	Jeff Siemon	4	4	5	5	10	12	25	60
269	Bob Newland	4	4	5	5	10	12	20	60
270	Gale Gillingham	4	4	5	5	10	12	25	
271	Zeke Moore	4	4	5	5	10	12	25	60
272	Mike Tilleman	4	4	5	5	10	12	25	
273	John Leypoldt	4	4	5	5	10	12	15	60
274	Ken Mendenhall	4	4	5	5	10	12	15	60
275	Norm Snead	4	4	5	5	10	12	25	80
276	Bill Bradley	4	4	5	5	10	12	25	60
277	Jerry Smith	4	4	5	5	10	12	20	60
278	Clarence Davis	4	4	5	5	10	12	25	
279	Jim Yarbrough	4	4	5	5	10	12	15	
280	Lemar Parrish	4	4	5	5	10	12	15	60
281	Bobby Bell	4	4	5	5	10	12	25	80
282	Lynn Swann RC	15	30	40	60	125	250	500	2,000
283	John Hicks	4	4	5	5	10	12	25	60
284	Coy Bacon	4	4	5	5	10	12	40	
285	Lee Roy Jordan	4	4	5	5	10	12	25	80
286	Willie Buchanon	4	4	5	5	10	12	25	
287	Al Woodall	4	4	5	5	10	12	25	
288	Reggie Rucker	4	4	5	5	10	12	25	
289	John Schmitt	4	4	5	5	10	12	25	
290	Carl Eller	4	4	5	5	10	12	25	
291	Jake Scott	4	4	5	5	10	12	25	
292	Donny Anderson	4	4	5	5	10	12	20	
293	Charley Wade	4	4	5	5	10	12	20	60
294	John Tanner	4	4	5	5	10	12	20	60
295	Charlie Johnson	4	4	5	5	10	12	25	
296	Tom Blanchard	4	4	5	5	10	12	15	60
297	Curley Culp	4	4	5	5	10	15	40	60
298	Jeff Van Note RC	4	4	5	5	10	12	25	
299	Bob James	4	4	5	5	10	12	25	60
300	Franco Harris	4	5	6	10	15	20	80	200
301	Tim Berra	4	4	5	5	10	12	20	60
302	Bruce Gossett	4	4	5	5	10	12	20	
303	Verlon Biggs	4	4	5	5	10	12	20	
304	Bob Kowalkowski	4	4	5	5	10	12	25	
305	Marv Hubbard	4	4	5	5	10	12	25	
306	Ken Avery	4	4	5	5	10	12	25	60
307	Mike Adamle	4	4	5	5	10	12	25	60
308	Don Herrmann	4	4	5	5	10	12	25	60
309	Chris Fletcher	4	4	5	5	10	12	25	60
310	Roman Gabriel	4	4	5	5	10	12	25	60
311	Billy Joe DuPree	4	4	5	5	10	12	20	80
312	Fred Dryer	4	4	5	5	10	12	20	
313	John Riggins	4	4	5	6	10	12	35	
314	Bob McKay	4	4	5	5	10	12	25	60
315	Ted Hendricks	4	4	5	5	10	12	35	80
316	Bobby Bryant	4	4	5	5	10	12	25	100
317	Don Nottingham	4	4	5	5	10	12	20	80
318	John Hannah	4	4	5	6	10	12	25	120
319	Rich Coady	4	4	5	5	10	12	30	60
320	Phil Villapiano	4	4	5	5	10	12	25	
321	Jim Plunkett	4	4	5	5	10	12	25	
322	Lyle Alzado	4	4	5	5	10	12	25	
323	Ernie Jackson	4	4	5	5	10	12	25	
324	Billy Parks	4	4	5	5	10	12	25	
325	Willie Lanier	4	4	5	5	10	12	25	
326	John James	4	4	5	5	10	12	25	60
327	Joe Ferguson	4	4	5	5	10	12	25	60
328	Ernie Holmes RC	4	5	6	12	30	40	80	
329	Bruce Laird	4	4	5	5	10	12	80	
330	Chester Marcol	4	4	5	5	10	12	25	60
331	Dave Wilcox	4	4	5	5	10	12	25	80
332	Pat Fischer	4	4	5	5	10	12	20	
333	Steve Owens	4	4	5	5	10	12	25	
334	Royce Berry	4	4	5	5	10	12	30	
335	Russ Washington	4	4	5	5	10	12	40	
336	Walker Gillette	4	4	5	5	10	12	25	80
337	Mark Nordquist	4	4	5	5	10	12	25	60
338	James Harris RC	4	4	5	6	10	12	50	
339	Warren Koegel	4	4	5	5	10	12	25	60

		VgEx 4	EX 5	ExMt 6	NM 7	NmMt 8	NmMt+ 8.5	MT 9	Gem 9.5/10
340	Emmitt Thomas	4	4	5	5	10	12	25	
341	Walt Garrison	4	4	5	5	10	12	25	
342	Thom Darden	4	4	5	5	10	12	25	100
343	Mike Eischeid	4	4	5	5	10	12	25	80
344	Ernie McMillan	4	4	5	5	10	12	20	60
345	Nick Buoniconti	4	4	5	5	10	12	20	
346	George Farmer	4	4	5	5	10	12	25	60
347	Sam Adams OL	4	4	5	5	10	12	25	
348	Larry Cipa	4	4	5	5	10	12	25	80
349	Bob Moore	4	4	5	5	10	12	25	
350	Otis Armstrong RC	4	4	5	5	10	12	25	80
351	George Blanda RB	4	4	5	5	10	12	40	
352	Fred Cox RB	4	4	5	5	10	12	25	60
353	Tom Dempsey RB	4	4	5	5	10	12	25	
354	Ken Houston RB	4	4	5	5	10	12	25	80
355	O.J.Simpson RB	4	4	5	6	15	20	50	
356	Ron Smith RB	4	4	5	5	10	12	25	60
357	Bob Atkins	4	4	5	5	10	12	40	
358	Pat Sullivan	4	4	5	5	10	12	25	80
359	Joe DeLamielleure	4	4	5	5	10	12	25	
360	Lawrence McCutcheon RC	4	4	5	5	10	12	25	100
361	David Lee	4	4	5	5	10	12	50	
362	Mike McCoy DT	4	4	5	5	10	12	20	60
363	Skip Vanderbundt	4	4	5	5	10	12	25	
364	Mark Moseley	4	4	5	5	10	12	25	
365	Lem Barney	4	4	5	5	10	12	25	120
366	Doug Dressler	4	4	5	5	10	12	25	
367	Dan Fouts RC	15	20	▲60	▲125	▲200	▲250	▲500	1,500
368	Bob Hyland	4	4	5	5	10	12	25	
369	John Outlaw	4	4	5	5	10	12	25	60
370	Roy Gerela	4	4	5	5	10	12	25	
371	Isiah Robertson	4	4	5	5	10	12	25	60
372	Jerome Barkum	4	4	5	5	10	12	25	
373	Ed Podolak	4	4	5	5	10	12	25	60
374	Milt Morin	4	4	5	5	10	12	25	60
375	John Niland	4	4	5	5	20	40	60	
376	Checklist 265-396	4	4	5	5	10	12	30	
377	Ken Iman	4	4	5	5	10	12	25	80
378	Manny Fernandez	4	4	5	5	10	12	25	
379	Dave Gallagher	4	4	5	5	10	12	25	60
380	Ken Stabler	5	6	8	15	25	30	50	300
381	Mack Herron	4	4	5	5	10	12	25	
382	Bill McClard	4	4	5	5	10	12	25	60
383	Ray May	4	4	5	5	10	12	25	
384	Don Hansen	4	4	5	5	10	12	25	
385	Elvin Bethea	4	4	5	5	10	12	25	80
386	Joe Scibelli	4	4	5	5	10	12	25	60
387	Neal Craig	4	4	5	5	10	12	25	60
388	Marty Domres	4	4	5	5	10	12	25	60
389	Ken Ellis	4	4	5	5	10	12	25	
390	Charle Young	4	4	5	5	10	12	25	
391	Tommy Hart	4	4	5	5	10	12	25	
392	Moses Denson	4	4	5	5	10	12	25	60
393	Larry Walton	4	4	5	5	10	12	25	60
394	Dave Green	4	4	5	5	10	12	50	
395	Ron Johnson	4	4	5	5	10	12	25	80
396	Ed Bradley RC	4	4	5	5	10	12	25	60
397	J.T. Thomas	4	4	5	5	10	12	30	175
398	Jim Bailey	4	4	5	5	10	12	25	60
399	Barry Pearson	4	4	5	5	10	12	25	
400	Fran Tarkenton	4	5	6	10	15	20	50	400
401	Jack Rudnay	4	4	5	5	10	12	25	60
402	Rayfield Wright	4	4	5	5	10	12	30	
403	Roger Wehrli	4	4	5	5	10	12	40	200
404	Vern Den Herder	4	4	5	5	10	12	25	60
405	Fred Biletnikoff	4	4	5	5	10	12	25	
406	Ken Grandberry	4	4	5	5	10	12	25	
407	Bob Adams	4	4	5	5	10	12	25	60
408	Jim Merlo	4	4	5	5	10	12	25	
409	John Pitts	4	4	5	5	10	12	25	60
410	Dave Osborn	4	4	5	5	10	12	25	60
411	Dennis Havig	4	4	5	5	10	12	25	80
412	Bob Johnson	4	4	5	5	10	12	25	60
413	Ken Burrough	4	4	5	5	10	12	25	80
414	Jim Cheyunski	4	4	5	5	10	12	25	60
415	MacArthur Lane	4	4	5	5	10	12	25	
416	Joe Theismann RC	8	10	12	20	80	100	200	
417	Mike Boryla RC	4	4	5	5	10	12	25	60
418	Bruce Taylor	4	4	5	5	10	12	25	60

		VgEx 4	EX 5	ExMt 6	NM 7	NmMt 8	NmMt+ 8.5	MT 9	Gem 9.5/10
419	Chris Hanburger	4	4	5	5	10	12	30	
420	Tom Mack	4	4	5	5	10	12	25	
421	Errol Mann	4	4	5	5	10	12	25	
422	Jack Gregory	4	4	5	5	10	12	25	60
423	Harrison Davis	4	4	5	5	10	12	25	
424	Burgess Owens	4	4	5	5	10	12	25	60
425	Joe Greene	4	4	8	15	30	50	125	
426	Morris Stroud	4	4	5	5	10	12	25	60
427	John DeMarie	4	4	5	5	10	12	25	60
428	Mel Renfro	4	4	5	5	10	12	50	
429	Cid Edwards	4	4	5	5	10	12	25	80
430	Mike Reid	4	4	5	5	10	12	25	60
431	Jack Mildren RC	4	4	5	5	10	12	25	80
432	Jerry Simmons	4	4	5	5	10	12	25	
433	Ron Yary	4	4	5	5	10	12	60	
434	Howard Stevens	4	4	5	5	10	12	25	
435	Ray Guy	4	4	5	5	10	12	60	
436	Tommy Nobis	4	4	5	5	10	12	25	100
437	Solomon Freelon	4	4	5	5	10	12	25	
438	J.D. Hill	4	4	5	5	10	12	25	60
439	Toni Linhart	4	4	5	5	10	12	50	
440	Dick Anderson	4	4	5	5	10	12	25	
441	Guy Morriss	4	4	5	5	10	12	25	60
442	Bob Hoskins	4	4	5	5	10	12	25	60
443	John Hadl	4	4	5	5	10	12	50	80
444	Roy Jefferson	4	4	5	5	10	12	25	
445	Charlie Sanders	4	4	5	5	10	12	25	80
446	Pat Curran	4	4	5	5	10	12	25	60
447	David Knight	4	4	5	5	10	12	25	60
448	Bob Brown DT	4	4	5	5	10	12	25	
449	Pete Gogolak	4	4	5	5	10	12	25	
450	Terry Metcalf	4	4	5	5	10	12	25	
451	Bill Bergey	4	4	5	5	10	12	25	60
452	Dan Abramowicz HL	4	4	5	5	10	12	25	60
453	Otis Armstrong HL	4	4	5	5	10	12	25	60
454	Cliff Branch HL	4	4	5	5	10	12	25	60
455	John James HL	4	4	5	5	10	12	25	
456	Lydell Mitchell HL	4	4	5	5	10	12	25	60
457	Lemar Parrish HL	4	4	5	5	10	12	25	
458	Ken Stabler HL	4	4	5	6	10	12	25	
459	Lynn Swann HL	4	5	6	10	15	20	40	200
460	Emmitt Thomas HL	4	4	5	5	10	12	25	
461	Terry Bradshaw	8	10	15	20	30	50	80	1,000
462	Jerrel Wilson	4	4	5	5	10	12	25	
463	Walter Johnson	4	4	5	5	10	12	25	
464	Golden Richards	4	4	5	5	10	12	25	
465	Tommy Casanova	4	4	5	5	10	12	25	
466	Randy Jackson	4	4	5	5	10	12	25	
467	Ron Bolton	4	4	5	5	10	12	25	60
468	Joe Owens	4	4	5	5	10	12	25	
469	Wally Hilgenberg	4	4	5	5	10	12	30	
470	Riley Odoms	4	4	5	5	10	12	25	80
471	Otis Sistrunk	4	4	5	5	10	12	25	
472	Eddie Ray	4	4	5	5	10	12	25	60
473	Reggie McKenzie	4	4	5	5	10	12	25	60
474	Elbert Drungo	4	4	5	5	10	12	35	100
475	Mercury Morris	4	4	5	5	10	12	35	
476	Dan Dickel	4	4	5	5	10	12	25	60
477	Merritt Kersey	4	4	5	5	10	12	25	
478	Mike Holmes	4	4	5	5	10	12	25	
479	Clarence Williams	4	4	5	5	10	12	25	60
480	Billy Kilmer	4	4	5	5	10	12	25	
481	Altie Taylor	4	4	5	5	10	12	25	60
482	Dave Elmendorf	4	4	5	5	10	12	25	60
483	Bob Rowe	4	4	5	5	10	12	30	
484	Pete Athas	4	4	5	5	10	12	25	
485	Winston Hill	4	4	5	5	10	12	25	60
486	Bo Matthews	4	4	5	5	10	12	100	
487	Earl Thomas	4	4	5	5	10	12	25	
488	Jan Stenerud	4	4	5	5	10	12	25	
489	Steve Holden	4	4	5	5	10	12	25	
490	Cliff Harris RC	4	5	6	8	80	100	300	
491	Boobie Clark RC	4	4	5	5	10	12	80	
492	Joe Taylor	4	4	5	5	10	12	40	
493	Tom Neville	4	4	5	5	10	12	25	60
494	Wayne Colman	4	4	5	5	10	12	25	
495	Jim Mitchell TE	4	4	5	5	10	12	25	60
496	Paul Krause	4	4	5	5	10	12	25	80
497	Jim Otto	4	4	5	5	10	12	50	

FOOTBALL

#	Player	VgEx 4	EX 5	ExMt 6	NM 7	NmMt 8	NmMt+ 8.5	MT 9	Gem 9.5/10
498	John Rowser	4	4	5	5	10	12	25	60
499	Larry Little	4	4	8	12	25	30	100	
500	O.J.Simpson	5	6	8	12	25	30	100	
501	John Dutton RC	4	4	5	5	10	12	25	
502	Pat Hughes	4	4	5	5	10	12	25	80
503	Malcolm Snider	4	4	5	5	10	12	25	60
504	Fred Willis	4	4	5	5	10	12	25	
505	Harold Jackson	4	4	5	5	10	12	25	
506	Mike Bragg	4	4	5	5	10	12	25	
507	Jerry Sherk	4	4	5	5	10	12	25	
508	Mirro Roder	4	4	5	5	10	12	25	
509	Tom Sullivan	4	4	5	5	10	12	25	60
510	Jim Hart	4	4	5	5	10	12	25	
511	Cedrick Hardman	4	4	5	5	10	12	25	
512	Blaine Nye	4	4	5	5	10	12	30	
513	Elmo Wright	4	4	5	5	10	12	25	60
514	Herb Orvis	4	4	5	5	10	12	60	
515	Richard Caster	4	4	5	5	10	12	25	
516	Doug Kotar RC	4	4	5	5	10	12	30	
517	Checklist 397-528	4	4	5	5	10	12	25	
518	Jesse Freitas	4	4	5	5	10	12	25	
519	Ken Houston	4	4	5	5	10	12	25	
520	Alan Page	4	4	5	5	10	12	40	
521	Tim Foley	4	4	5	5	10	12	25	
522	Bill Olds	4	4	5	5	10	12	25	60
523	Bobby Maples	4	4	5	5	10	12	25	
524	Cliff Branch RC	5	6	8	25	50	60	200	
525	Merlin Olsen	4	4	5	5	10	12	50	
526	AFC Champs/Bradshaw/Harris	4	4	5	6	10	12	80	
527	NFC Champs/Foreman	4	4	5	5	10	15	40	
528	Super Bowl IX/Bradshaw	4	5	6	10	25	40	120	

— AFC Champs/Brad/Harris #526 PSA 10 (Gem) sold for $672 (Mile High; 6/10)
— Rocky Bleier RC #39 PSA 10 (Gem Mint) sold for $590.77 (eBay: 6/12)
— Rocky Bleier RC #39 PSA 10 (Gem Mint) sold for $570 (eBay: 6/12)
— Bob Brown DT #448 PSA 10 (Gem Mint) sold for $505 (eBay: 6/12)
— Dan Fouts #367 PSA 10 (Gem) sold for $3,055 (eBay: 4/07)
— Joe Greene #425 PSA 10 (Gem Mint) sold for $839.02 (eBay: 6/12)
— Drew Pearson #65 PSA 10 (Gem) sold for $1,000 (eBay; 11/07)
— O.J.Simpson #500 PSA 10 (Gem Mint) sold for $543 (eBay: 6/12)
— Super Bowl IX/Bradshaw #528 PSA 10 (Gem Mint) sold for $791 (eBay: 6/12)
— Lynn Swann #282 PSA 10 (Gem) sold for $2,809.99 (eBay; 3/14)
— Lynn Swann #282 PSA 10 (Gem) sold for $2,805 (eBay; 4/07)
— Lynn Swann #282 PSA 10 (Gem) sold for $1,767 (Mile High; 10/09)
— Joe Theismann RC #416 PSA 10 (Gem Mint) sold for $2958 (eBay: 8/12)
— Joe Theismann RC #416 PSA 10 (Gem Mint) sold for $3553 (eBay: 10/14)
— Joe Theismann RC #416 PSA 10 (Gem Mint) sold for $3008 (eBay: 10/14)

1976 Topps

#	Player	VgEx 4	EX 5	ExMt 6	NM 7	NmMt 8	NmMt+ 8.5	MT 9	Gem 9.5/10
1	George Blanda RB	4	4	5	8	10	12	60	175
2	Neal Colzie RB	4	4	5	8	20	25	60	
3	Chuck Foreman RB	4	4	5	8	10	12	30	
4	Jim Marshall RB	4	4	5	8	12	15	40	
5	Terry Metcalf RB	4	4	5	8	10	12	30	
6	O.J.Simpson RB	4	4	5	8	12	15	60	
7	Fran Tarkenton RB	4	4	5	8	10	12	25	
8	Charley Taylor RB	4	4	5	8	10	12	30	100
9	Ernie Holmes	4	4	5	8	10	12	30	
10	Ken Anderson	4	4	5	8	15	20	120	
11	Bobby Bryant	4	4	5	8	10	12	25	60
12	Jerry Smith	4	4	5	8	10	12	30	
13	David Lee	4	4	5	8	10	12	25	
14	Robert Newhouse RC	4	4	5	8	20	25	80	
15	Vern Den Herder	4	4	5	8	10	12	25	60
16	John Hannah	4	4	5	8	10	12	30	
17	J.D. Hill	4	4	5	8	10	12	30	
18	James Harris	4	4	5	8	10	12	30	
19	Willie Buchanon	4	4	5	8	10	12	25	60
20	Charle Young	4	4	5	8	10	12	30	
21	Jim Yarbrough	4	4	5	8	10	12	25	
22	Ronnie Coleman	4	4	5	8	10	12	25	
23	Don Cockroft	4	4	5	8	10	12	25	
24	Willie Lanier	4	4	5	8	10	12	30	
25	Fred Biletnikoff	4	4	5	8	10	12	30	
26	Ron Yankowski	4	4	5	8	10	12	25	80
27	Spider Lockhart	4	4	5	8	10	12	25	
28	Bob Johnson	4	4	5	8	10	12	25	
29	J.T. Thomas	4	4	5	8	10	12	25	60

#	Player	VgEx 4	EX 5	ExMt 6	NM 7	NmMt 8	NmMt+ 8.5	MT 9	Gem 9.5/10
30	Ron Yary	4	4	5	8	10	12	30	
31	Brad Dusek RC	4	4	5	8	10	12	25	
32	Raymond Chester	4	4	5	8	10	12	30	
33	Larry Little	4	4	5	8	10	12	30	
34	Pat Leahy RC	4	4	5	8	10	12	30	
35	Steve Bartkowski RC	4	4	5	8	10	12	40	
36	Tom Myers	4	4	5	8	10	12	25	
37	Bill Van Heusen	4	4	5	8	10	12	25	60
38	Russ Washington	4	4	5	8	10	12	25	
39	Tom Sullivan	4	4	5	8	10	12	25	
40	Curley Culp	4	4	5	8	30	40	100	
41	Johnnie Gray	4	4	5	8	10	12	25	60
42	Bob Klein	4	4	5	8	10	12	25	60
43	Lem Barney	4	4	5	8	10	12	30	
44	Harvey Martin RC	4	4	5	12	20	25	80	
45	Reggie Rucker	4	4	5	8	10	12	30	
46	Neil Clabo	4	4	5	8	10	12	25	
47	Ray Hamilton	4	4	5	8	10	12	25	
48	Joe Ferguson	4	4	5	8	10	12	30	60
49	Ed Podolak	4	4	5	8	10	12	25	
50	Ray Guy	4	4	5	8	10	12	30	
51	Glen Edwards	4	4	5	8	10	12	25	
52	Jim LeClair	4	4	5	8	10	12	25	80
53	Mike Barnes	4	4	5	8	10	12	25	
54	Nat Moore RC	4	4	5	8	10	12	30	
55	Billy Kilmer	4	4	5	8	10	12	30	
56	Larry Stallings	4	4	5	8	10	12	25	60
57	Jack Gregory	4	4	5	8	10	12	25	
58	Steve Mike-Mayer	4	4	5	8	10	12	25	
59	Virgil Livers	4	4	5	8	10	12	25	
60	Jerry Sherk	4	4	5	8	10	12	30	
61	Guy Morriss	4	4	5	8	10	12	25	
62	Barty Smith	4	4	5	8	10	12	25	
63	Jerome Barkum	4	4	5	8	10	12	25	
64	Ira Gordon	4	4	5	8	10	12	25	
65	Paul Krause	4	4	5	8	10	12	30	80
66	John McMakin	4	4	5	8	10	12	25	
67	Checklist 1-132	4	4	5	8	10	12	30	
68	Charlie Johnson	4	4	5	8	10	12	30	60
69	Tommy Nobis	4	4	5	8	10	12	30	80
70	Lydell Mitchell	4	4	5	8	10	12	30	
71	Vern Holland	4	4	5	8	10	12	25	
72	Tim Foley	4	4	5	8	10	12	30	
73	Golden Richards	4	4	5	8	10	12	30	
74	Bryant Salter	4	4	5	5	10	12	25	
75	Terry Bradshaw	6	8	12	20	35	40	150	
76	Ted Hendricks	4	4	5	8	10	12	30	80
77	Rich Saul RC	4	4	5	8	10	12	25	
78	John Smith RC	4	4	5	8	10	12	25	
79	Altie Taylor	4	4	5	8	10	12	25	80
80	Cedrick Hardman	4	4	5	8	10	12	100	
81	Ken Payne	4	4	5	8	10	12	25	
82	Zeke Moore	4	4	5	8	10	12	25	
83	Alvin Maxson	4	4	5	8	10	12	25	
84	Wally Hilgenberg	4	4	5	8	10	12	25	
85	John Niland	4	4	5	8	10	12	25	
86	Mike Sensibaugh	4	4	5	8	10	12	25	
87	Ron Johnson	4	4	5	8	10	12	30	
88	Winston Hill	4	4	5	8	10	12	25	
89	Charlie Joiner	4	4	5	8	10	12	25	100
90	Roger Wehrli	4	4	5	8	10	12	30	
91	Mike Bragg	4	4	5	8	10	12	25	
92	Dan Dickel	4	4	5	8	10	12	25	
93	Earl Morrall	4	4	5	8	10	12	30	
94	Pat Toomay	4	4	5	8	10	12	25	
95	Gary Garrison	4	4	5	8	10	12	25	80
96	Ken Geddes	4	4	5	8	10	12	25	60
97	Mike Current	4	4	5	8	10	12	25	
98	Bob Avellini RC	4	4	5	8	10	12	50	
99	Dave Pureifory	4	4	5	8	10	12	25	
100	Franco Harris	4	4	5	8	15	20	60	
101	Randy Logan	4	4	5	8	10	12	25	
102	John Fitzgerald	4	4	5	8	10	12	25	60
103	Gregg Bingham RC	4	4	5	8	10	12	100	
104	Jim Plunkett	4	4	5	8	10	12	25	
105	Carl Eller	4	4	5	8	10	12	30	
106	Larry Walton	4	4	5	8	10	12	25	
107	Clarence Scott	4	4	5	8	10	12	25	
108	Skip Vanderbundt	4	4	5	8	10	12	25	

#	Player	VgEx 4	EX 5	ExMt 6	NM 7	NmMt 8	NmMt+ 8.5	MT 9	Gem 9.5/10
109	Boobie Clark	4	4	5	8	10	12	30	
110	Tom Mack	4	4	5	8	10	12	30	60
111	Bruce Laird	4	4	5	8	10	12	25	
112	Dave Dalby RC	4	4	5	8	10	12	30	
113	John Leypoldt	4	4	5	8	10	12	25	
114	Barry Pearson	4	4	5	8	10	12	25	
115	Larry Brown	4	4	5	8	10	12	30	
116	Jackie Smith	4	4	5	8	10	12	30	80
117	Pat Hughes	4	4	5	8	10	12	25	
118	Al Woodall	4	4	5	8	10	12	25	80
119	John Zook	4	4	5	8	15	20	25	
120	Jake Scott	4	4	5	8	10	12	30	
121	Rich Glover	4	4	5	8	10	12	25	
122	Ernie Jackson	4	4	5	8	10	12	25	
123	Otis Armstrong	4	4	5	8	10	12	30	
124	Bob Grim	4	4	5	8	10	12	25	60
125	Jeff Siemon	4	4	5	8	10	12	25	
126	Harold Hart	4	4	5	8	10	12	25	
127	John DeMarie	4	4	5	8	10	12	25	
128	Dan Fouts	4	5	6	10	15	20	40	
129	Jim Kearney	4	4	5	8	10	12	25	
130	John Dutton	4	4	5	8	10	12	100	
131	Calvin Hill	4	4	5	8	10	12	30	80
132	Toni Fritsch	4	4	5	8	10	12	25	
133	Ron Jessie	4	4	5	8	10	12	25	60
134	Don Nottingham	4	4	5	8	10	12	25	
135	Lemar Parrish	4	4	5	8	10	12	25	60
136	Russ Francis RC	4	4	5	8	10	12	30	
137	Joe Reed	4	4	5	8	10	12	25	60
138	C.L. Whittington	4	4	5	8	10	12	25	50
139	Otis Sistrunk	4	4	5	8	10	12	30	
140	Lynn Swann	4	6	10	15	30	50	300	
141	Jim Carter	4	4	5	8	10	12	25	
142	Mike Montler	4	4	5	8	10	12	25	100
143	Walter Johnson	4	4	5	8	10	12	25	
144	Doug Kotar	4	4	5	8	10	12	25	
145	Roman Gabriel	4	4	5	8	10	12	30	
146	Billy Newsome	4	4	5	8	10	12	25	80
147	Ed Bradley	4	4	5	8	10	12	25	50
148	Walter Payton RC	▼600	▼800	▼1,000	▼1,500	▼2,000	4,000	12,000	120,000
149	Johnny Fuller	4	4	5	8	10	12	25	
150	Alan Page	4	4	5	8	10	12	30	
151	Frank Grant	4	4	5	8	10	12	25	50
152	Dave Green	4	4	5	8	10	12	25	
153	Nelson Munsey	4	4	5	8	10	12	25	
154	Jim Mandich	4	4	5	8	10	12	25	
155	Lawrence McCutcheon	4	4	5	8	10	12	30	
156	Steve Ramsey	4	4	5	8	10	12	25	
157	Ed Flanagan	4	4	5	8	10	12	25	
158	Randy White RC	5	6	12	25	80	100	400	
159	Gerry Mullins	4	4	5	8	10	12	25	
160	Jan Stenerud	4	4	5	8	10	12	30	
161	Steve Odom	4	4	5	8	10	12	25	60
162	Roger Finnie	4	4	5	8	10	12	25	
163	Norm Snead	4	4	5	8	10	12	30	
164	Jeff Van Note	4	4	5	8	10	12	30	
165	Bill Bergey	4	4	5	8	10	12	30	
166	Allen Carter	4	4	5	8	10	12	25	
167	Steve Holden	4	4	5	8	10	12	25	
168	Sherman White	4	4	5	8	10	12	25	
169	Bob Berry	4	4	5	8	10	12	25	80
170	Ken Houston	4	4	5	8	10	12	25	
171	Bill Olds	4	4	5	8	10	12	25	
172	Larry Seiple	4	4	5	8	10	12	25	
173	Cliff Branch	4	4	5	8	10	12	30	100
174	Reggie McKenzie	4	4	5	8	10	12	30	
175	Dan Pastorini	4	4	5	8	10	12	30	
176	Paul Naumoff	4	4	5	8	10	12	25	
177	Checklist 133-264	4	4	5	8	10	12	30	
178	Durwood Keeton	4	4	5	8	10	12	25	
179	Earl Thomas	4	4	5	8	10	12	25	
180	L.C.Greenwood	4	4	5	10	15	20	50	
181	John Outlaw	4	4	5	8	10	12	25	
182	Frank Nunley	4	4	5	8	10	12	25	
183	Dave Jennings RC	4	4	5	8	10	12	30	
184	MacArthur Lane								
185	Chester Marcol	4	4	5	8	10	12	25	
186	J.J. Jones	4	4	5	8	10	12	25	
187	Tom DeLeone	4	4	5	8	10	12	25	100
188	Steve Zabel	4	4	5	8	10	12	25	
189	Ken Johnson DT	4	4	5	8	10	12	25	
190	Rayfield Wright	4	4	5	8	10	12	40	
191	Brent McClanahan	4	4	5	8	10	12	25	60
192	Pat Fischer	4	4	5	8	10	12	30	
193	Roger Carr RC	4	4	5	8	10	12	30	
194	Manny Fernandez	4	4	5	8	10	12	30	
195	Roy Gerela	4	4	5	8	10	12	25	
196	Dave Elmendorf	4	4	5	8	10	12	25	
197	Bob Kowalkowski	4	4	5	8	10	12	25	
198	Phil Villapiano	4	4	5	8	10	12	30	
199	Will Wynn	4	4	5	8	10	12	25	60
200	Terry Metcalf	4	4	5	8	10	12	30	
201	F.Tarkenton/K.Anderson LL	4	4	5	8	10	12	30	
202	Rucker/Mitchell/Foreman LL	4	4	5	8	10	12	30	80
203	O.Simpson/J.Otis LL	4	4	5	8	10	12	30	
204	O.Simpson/C.Foreman LL	4	4	5	8	10	12	30	
205	M.Blount/P.Krause LL	4	4	5	8	10	12	30	
206	R.Guy/H.Weaver LL	4	4	5	8	10	12	30	
207	Ken Ellis	4	4	5	8	10	12	25	60
208	Ron Saul	4	4	5	8	10	12	25	80
209	Toni Linhart	4	4	5	8	10	12	25	80
210	Jim Langer	4	4	5	8	10	12	30	
211	Jeff Wright S	4	4	5	8	10	12	25	
212	Moses Denson	4	4	5	8	10	12	25	
213	Earl Edwards	4	4	5	8	10	12	25	
214	Walker Gillette	4	4	5	8	10	12	25	60
215	Bob Trumpy	4	4	5	8	10	12	30	
216	Emmitt Thomas	4	4	5	8	10	12	30	
217	Lyle Alzado	4	4	5	8	10	12	30	
218	Carl Garrett	4	4	5	8	10	12	30	
219	Van Green	4	4	5	8	10	12	25	
220	Jack Lambert RC	12	15	50	60	100	300	500	4,000
221	Spike Jones	4	4	5	8	10	12	25	
222	John Hadl	4	4	5	8	10	12	30	
223	Billy Johnson RC	4	4	5	8	12	15	40	
224	Tony McGee DT	4	4	5	8	10	12	25	
225	Preston Pearson	4	4	5	8	10	12	40	
226	Isiah Robertson	4	4	5	8	10	12	30	80
227	Errol Mann	4	4	5	8	10	12	25	
228	Paul Seal	4	4	5	8	10	12	25	60
229	Roland Harper RC	4	4	5	8	10	12	25	
230	Ed White RC	4	4	5	8	10	12	30	
231	Joe Theismann	4	4	5	8	10	12	40	
232	Jim Cheyunski	4	4	5	8	10	12	25	
233	Bill Stanfill	4	4	5	8	10	12	30	
234	Marv Hubbard	4	4	5	8	10	12	25	
235	Tommy Casanova	4	4	5	8	10	12	30	
236	Bob Hyland	4	4	5	8	10	12	25	60
237	Jesse Freitas	4	4	5	8	10	12	25	
238	Norm Thompson	4	4	5	8	10	12	25	
239	Charlie Smith WR	4	4	5	8	10	12	25	
240	John James	4	4	5	8	10	12	25	
241	Alden Roche	4	4	5	8	10	12	25	
242	Gordon Jolley	4	4	5	8	10	12	25	
243	Larry Ely	4	4	5	8	10	12	25	
244	Richard Caster	4	4	5	8	10	12	25	80
245	Joe Greene	4	4	5	8	10	12	50	200
246	Larry Schreiber	4	4	5	8	10	12	25	
247	Terry Schmidt	4	4	5	8	10	12	25	
248	Jerrel Wilson	4	4	5	8	10	12	25	
249	Marty Domres	4	4	5	8	10	12	25	
250	Isaac Curtis	4	4	5	8	10	12	35	
251	Harold McLinton	4	4	5	8	10	12	25	
252	Fred Dryer	4	4	5	8	10	12	30	80
253	Bill Lenkaitis	4	4	5	8	10	12	25	80
254	Don Hardeman	4	4	5	8	10	12	25	
255	Bob Griese	4	4	5	8	10	12	30	
256	Oscar Roan RC	4	4	5	8	10	12	25	
257	Randy Gradishar RC	4	4	5	8	25	30	60	
258	Bob Thomas RC	4	4	5	8	10	12	25	
259	Joe Owens	4	4	5	8	10	12	25	
260	Cliff Harris	4	4	5	8	10	12	30	
261	Frank Lewis	4	4	5	8	10	12	25	
262	Mike McCoy DT	4	4	5	8	10	12	25	60
263	Rickey Young RC	4	4	5	8	10	12	25	60
264	Brian Kelley RC	4	4	5	8	10	12	25	60
265	Charlie Sanders	4	4	5	8	10	12	30	
266	Jim Hart	4	4	5	8	10	12	25	

#	Player	VgEx 4	EX 5	ExMt 6	NM 7	NmMt 8	NmMt+ 8.5	MT 9	Gem 9.5/10
267	Greg Gantt	4	4	5	8	10	12	25	
268	John Ward	4	4	5	8	10	12	25	
269	Al Beauchamp	4	4	5	8	10	12	25	
270	Jack Tatum	4	4	5	8	10	12	30	
271	Jim Lash	4	4	5	8	10	12	25	80
272	Diron Talbert	4	4	5	8	10	12	25	
273	Checklist 265-396	4	4	5	8	10	12	30	
274	Steve Spurrier	4	4	5	8	10	12	30	120
275	Greg Pruitt	4	4	5	8	10	12	30	
276	Jim Mitchell TE	4	4	5	8	10	12	25	
277	Jack Rudnay	4	4	5	8	10	12	25	
278	Freddie Solomon RC	4	4	5	8	10	12	30	
279	Frank LeMaster	4	4	5	8	10	12	25	
280	Wally Chambers	4	4	5	8	10	12	25	
281	Mike Collier	4	4	5	8	10	12	25	
282	Clarence Williams	4	4	5	8	10	12	25	
283	Mitch Hoopes	4	4	5	8	10	12	25	
284	Ron Bolton	4	4	5	8	10	12	25	
285	Harold Jackson	4	4	5	8	10	12	30	
286	Greg Landry	4	4	5	8	10	12	30	
287	Tony Greene	4	4	5	8	10	12	25	
288	Howard Stevens	4	4	5	8	10	12	25	
289	Roy Jefferson	4	4	5	8	10	12	25	
290	Jim Bakken	4	4	5	8	10	12	25	
291	Doug Sutherland	4	4	5	8	10	12	25	
292	Marvin Cobb RC	4	4	5	8	10	12	25	
293	Mack Alston	4	4	5	8	10	12	25	60
294	Rod McNeill	4	4	5	8	10	12	25	80
295	Gene Upshaw	4	4	5	8	10	12	30	
296	Dave Gallagher	4	4	5	8	10	12	25	
297	Larry Ball	4	4	5	8	10	12	25	60
298	Ron Howard	4	4	5	8	10	12	25	
299	Don Strock RC	4	4	5	8	10	12	30	
300	O.J.Simpson	4	4	5	8	30	40	60	
301	Ray Mansfield	4	4	5	20	25	30	40	
302	Larry Marshall	4	4	5	8	10	12	25	
303	Dick Himes	4	4	5	8	10	12	25	
304	Ray Wersching RC	4	4	5	8	10	12	25	
305	John Riggins	4	4	5	8	10	12	30	
306	Bob Parsons	4	4	5	8	10	12	25	
307	Ray Brown DB	4	4	5	8	10	12	25	
308	Len Dawson	4	4	5	8	10	12	30	
309	Andy Maurer	4	4	5	8	10	12	25	60
310	Jack Youngblood	4	4	5	8	10	12	30	80
311	Essex Johnson	4	4	5	8	10	12	25	
312	Stan White	4	4	5	8	10	12	25	
313	Drew Pearson	4	4	5	8	15	20	40	
314	Rockne Freitas	4	4	5	8	10	12	25	60
315	Mercury Morris	4	4	5	8	10	12	30	100
316	Willie Alexander	4	4	5	8	10	12	25	
317	Paul Warfield	4	4	5	8	10	12	30	
318	Bob Chandler	4	4	5	8	10	12	30	
319	Bobby Walden	4	4	5	8	10	12	25	60
320	Riley Odoms	4	4	5	8	10	12	30	
321	Mike Boryla	4	4	5	8	10	12	25	
322	Bruce Van Dyke	4	4	5	8	10	12	25	
323	Pete Banaszak	4	4	5	8	10	12	25	
324	Darryl Stingley	4	4	5	8	10	12	30	60
325	John Mendenhall	4	4	5	8	10	12	40	
326	Dan Dierdorf	4	4	5	8	10	12	30	
327	Bruce Taylor	4	4	5	8	10	12	25	
328	Don McCauley	4	4	5	8	10	12	25	
329	John Reaves	4	4	5	8	10	12	25	100
330	Chris Hanburger	4	4	5	8	10	12	30	
331	NFC Champs/Staubach	4	4	5	8		12	25	
332	AFC Champs/F.Harris	4	4	5	8	10	18	60	
333	Super Bowl X/Bradshaw	4	5	6	12	50	80		
334	Godwin Turk	4	4	5	8	10	12	25	60
335	Dick Anderson	4	4	5	8	10	12	30	
336	Woody Green	4	4	5	8	10	12	25	
337	Pat Curran	4	4	5	8	10	12	25	
338	Council Rudolph	4	4	5	8	10	12	25	60
339	Joe Lavender	4	4	5	8	10	12	25	60
340	John Gilliam	4	4	5	8	10	12	30	80
341	Steve Furness RC	4	4	5	8	10	12	30	
342	D.D. Lewis	4	4	5	8	10	15	60	
343	Duane Carrell	4	4	5	8	10	12	25	
344	Jon Morris	4	4	5	8	10	12	25	
345	John Brockington	4	4	5	8	10	12	30	100

#	Player	VgEx 4	EX 5	ExMt 6	NM 7	NmMt 8	NmMt+ 8.5	MT 9	Gem 9.5/10
346	Mike Phipps	4	4	5	8	10	12	30	
347	Lyle Blackwood RC	4	4	5	8	10	12	25	
348	Julius Adams	4	4	5	8	10	12	25	
349	Terry Hermeling	4	4	5	8	10	12	25	80
350	Rolland Lawrence RC	4	4	5	8	10	12	25	
351	Glenn Doughty	4	4	5	8	10	12	25	
352	Doug Swift	4	4	5	8	10	12	25	
353	Mike Strachan	4	4	5	8	10	12	25	
354	Craig Morton	4	4	5	8	10	12	30	
355	George Blanda	4	4	5	8	10	12	25	150
356	Garry Puetz	4	4	5	8	10	12	25	
357	Carl Mauck	4	4	5	8	10	12	25	
358	Walt Patulski	4	4	5	8	10	12	25	60
359	Stu Voigt	4	4	5	8	10	12	25	60
360	Fred Carr	4	4	5	8	10	12	25	
361	Po James	4	4	5	8	10	12	25	60
362	Otis Taylor	4	4	5	8	10	12	30	
363	Jeff West	4	4	5	8	10	12	30	
364	Gary Huff	4	4	5	8	10	12	30	
365	Dwight White	4	4	5	8	10	12	30	
366	Dan Ryczek	4	4	5	8	10	12	25	
367	Jon Keyworth RC	4	4	5	8	10	12	25	
368	Mel Renfro	4	4	5	8	10	12	30	100
369	Bruce Coslet RC	4	4	5	8	10	12	30	
370	Len Hauss	4	4	5	8	10	12	25	
371	Rick Volk	4	4	5	8	10	12	25	
372	Howard Twilley	4	4	5	8	10	12	30	
373	Cullen Bryant RC	4	4	5	8	10	12	25	
374	Bob Babich	4	4	5	8	10	12	25	
375	Herman Weaver	4	4	5	8	10	12	25	
376	Steve Grogan RC	4	4	5	8	10	15	30	
377	Bubba Smith	4	4	5	8	10	12	30	
378	Burgess Owens	4	4	5	8	10	12	25	
379	Al Matthews	4	4	5	8	10	12	25	80
380	Art Shell	4	4	5	8	10	12	30	
381	Larry Brown	4	4	5	8	10	12	25	
382	Horst Muhlmann	4	4	5	8	10	12	25	
383	Ahmad Rashad	4	4	5	8	10	12	35	
384	Bobby Maples	4	4	5	8	10	12	25	
385	Jim Marshall	4	4	5	8	10	12	30	
386	Joe Dawkins	4	4	5	8	10	12	25	
387	Dennis Partee	4	4	5	8	10	12	25	80
388	Eddie McMillan RC	4	4	5	8	10	12	25	
389	Randy Johnson	4	4	5	8	10	12	25	
390	Bob Kuechenberg	4	4	5	8	10	12	25	
391	Rufus Mayes	4	4	5	8	10	12	25	
392	Lloyd Mumphord	4	4	5	8	10	12	25	60
393	Ike Harris	4	4	5	8	10	12	30	
394	Dave Hampton	4	4	5	8	10	12	25	60
395	Roger Staubach	5	8	12	20	30	35	125	800
396	Doug Buffone	4	4	5	8	10	12	25	
397	Howard Fest	4	4	5	8	10	12	25	
398	Wayne Mulligan	4	4	5	8	10	12	25	
399	Bill Bradley	4	4	5	8	10	12	30	
400	Chuck Foreman	4	4	5	8	10	12	30	
401	Jack Snow	4	4	5	8	10	12	30	
402	Bob Howard	4	4	5	8	10	12	25	60
403	John Matuszak	4	4	5	8	10	12	30	
404	Bill Munson	4	4	5	8	10	12	30	
405	Andy Russell	4	4	5	8	10	12	30	80
406	Skip Butler	4	4	5	8	10	12	25	
407	Hugh McKinnis	4	4	5	8	10	12	25	
408	Bob Penchion	4	4	5	8	10	12	25	
409	Mike Bass	4	4	5	8	10	12	25	60
410	George Kunz	4	4	5	8	10	12	25	
411	Ron Pritchard	4	4	5	8	10	12	25	60
412	Barry Smith	4	4	5	8	10	12	25	
413	Norm Bulaich	4	4	5	8	10	12	25	
414	Marv Bateman	4	4	5	8	10	12	25	
415	Ken Stabler	4	5	6	10	15	20	80	
416	Conrad Dobler	4	4	5	8	10	12	30	
417	Bob Tucker	4	4	5	8	10	12	30	
418	Gene Washington 49er	4	4	5	8	10	12	30	
419	Ed Marinaro	4	4	5	8	10	12	30	60
420	Jack Ham	4	4	5	8	10	12	100	
421	Jim Turner	4	4	5	8	10	12	25	80
422	Chris Fletcher	4	4	5	8	10	12	25	60
423	Carl Barzilauskas	4	4	5	8	10	12	25	
424	Robert Brazile RC	4	4	6	10	15	20	60	

		VgEx 4	EX 5	ExMt 6	NM 7	NmMt 8	NmMt+ 8.5	MT 9	Gem 9.5/10
425	Harold Carmichael	4	4	5	8	10	12	35	
426	Ron Jaworski RC	4	4	5	10	25	30	80	
427	Ed Too Tall Jones RC	▲6	▲10	▲25	▲40	▲80	▲100	▲150	1,000
428	Larry McCarren	4	4	5	8	10	12	30	
429	Mike Thomas RC	4	4	5	8	10	12	25	
430	Joe DeLamielleure	4	4	5	8	10	12	30	80
431	Tom Blanchard	4	4	5	8	10	12	25	
432	Ron Carpenter	4	4	5	8	10	12	25	
433	Levi Johnson	4	4	5	8	10	12	25	60
434	Sam Cunningham	4	4	5	8	10	12	30	
435	Garo Yepremian	4	4	5	8	10	12	25	
436	Mike Livingston	4	4	5	8	10	12	25	
437	Larry Csonka	4	4	5	8	10	12	40	
438	Doug Dieken	4	4	5	8	10	12	30	
439	Bill Lueck	4	4	5	8	10	12	25	80
440	Tom MacLeod	4	4	5	8	10	12	25	
441	Mick Tingelhoff	4	4	5	8	10	12	30	
442	Terry Hanratty	4	4	5	8	10	12	30	
443	Mike Siani	4	4	5	8	10	12	25	
444	Dwight Harrison	4	4	5	8	10	12	25	
445	Jim Otis	4	4	5	8	10	12	30	
446	Jack Reynolds	4	4	5	8	10	12	30	
447	Jean Fugett RC	4	4	5	8	10	12	30	
448	Dave Beverly	4	4	5	8	10	12	25	
449	Bernard Jackson RC	4	4	5	8	10	12	30	
450	Charley Taylor	4	4	5	8	10	12	35	
451	Atlanta Falcons CL	4	4	5	8	10	12	30	
452	Baltimore Colts CL	4	4	5	8	10	12		
453	Buffalo Bills CL	4	4	5	8	12	15	25	
454	Chicago Bears CL	4	4	5	8	10	12	50	
455	Cincinnati Bengals CL	4	4	5	8	10	12		
456	Cleveland Browns CL	4	4	5	8	10	12	30	
457	Dallas Cowboys CL	4	4	5	8	10	12	40	
458	Denver Broncos CL	4	4	5	8	10	12		
459	Detroit Lions CL	4	4	5	8	10	12	25	60
460	Green Bay Packers CL	4	4	5	8	10	12		
461	Houston Oilers CL	4	4	5	8	10	12	25	
462	Kansas City Chiefs CL	4	4	5	8	10	12	30	80
463	Los Angeles Rams CL	4	4	5	8	10	12		
464	Miami Dolphins CL	4	4	5	8	10	12	30	
465	Minnesota Vikings CL	4	4	5	8	10	12		
466	New England Patriots CL	4	4	5	8	10	12		
467	New Orleans Saints CL	4	4	5	8	10	12		
468	New York Giants CL	4	4	5	8	10	12		
469	New York Jets CL	4	4	5	8	10	12	25	
470	Oakland Raiders CL	4	4	5	8	10	12	50	
471	Philadelphia Eagles CL	4	4	5	8	10	12	25	
472	Pittsburgh Steelers CL	4	4	5	8	10	12	40	
473	St. Louis Cardinals CL	4	4	5	8	10	12		
474	San Diego Chargers CL	4	4	5	8	10	12	30	
475	San Francisco 49ers CL	4	4	5	8	10	12	100	
476	Seattle Seahawks CL	4	4	5	8	10	12		
477	Tampa Bay Buccaneers CL	4	4	5	8	10	12	40	
478	Washington Redskins CL	4	4	5	8	10	12	30	
479	Fred Cox	4	4	5	8	10	12	25	60
480	Mel Blount	4	4	5	8	10	12	80	
481	John Bunting RC	4	4	5	8	10	12	25	60
482	Ken Mendenhall	4	4	5	8	10	12	25	
483	Will Harrell	4	4	5	8	10	12	25	
484	Marlin Briscoe	4	4	5	8	10	12	25	
485	Archie Manning	4	4	5	8	10	12	25	
486	Tody Smith	4	4	5	8	10	12	25	
487	George Hunt	4	4	5	8	10	12	25	80
488	Roscoe Word	4	4	5	8	10	12	25	
489	Paul Seymour	4	4	5	8	10	12	25	60
490	Lee Roy Jordan	4	4	5	8	15	20	35	
491	Chip Myers	4	4	5	8	10	12	25	
492	Norm Evans	4	4	5	8	10	12	25	
493	Jim Bertelsen	4	4	5	8	10	12	25	
494	Mark Moseley	4	4	5	8	10	12	25	
495	George Buehler	4	4	5	8	10	12	25	
496	Charlie Hall	4	4	5	8	10	12	25	
497	Marvin Upshaw	4	4	5	8	10	12	25	60
498	Tom Banks RC	4	4	5	8	10	12	80	
499	Randy Vataha	4	4	5	8	10	12	25	
500	Fran Tarkenton	4	4	5	8	15	20	100	
501	Mike Wagner	4	4	5	8	10	12	25	60
502	Art Malone	4	4	5	8	10	12	25	
503	Fred Cook	4	4	5	8	10	12	25	

		VgEx 4	EX 5	ExMt 6	NM 7	NmMt 8	NmMt+ 8.5	MT 9	Gem 9.5/10
504	Rich McGeorge	4	4	5	8	10	12	25	
505	Ken Burrough	4	4	5	8	10	12	25	
506	Nick Mike-Mayer	4	4	5	8	10	12	25	
507	Checklist 397-528	4	4	5	8	10	12	30	
508	Steve Owens	4	4	5	8	10	12	25	
509	Brad Van Pelt RC	4	4	5	8	10	12	25	
510	Ken Riley	4	4	5	8	10	12	25	
511	Art Thoms	4	4	5	8	10	12	25	
512	Ed Bell	4	4	5	8	10	12	25	
513	Tom Wittum	4	4	5	8	10	12	25	60
514	Jim Braxton	4	4	5	8	10	12	25	80
515	Nick Buoniconti	4	4	6	10	10	12	30	
516	Brian Sipe RC	4	4	5	8	35	50	100	
517	Jim Lynch	4	4	5	8	10	12	30	
518	Prentice McCray	4	4	5	8	10	12	25	
519	Tom Dempsey	4	4	5	8	10	12	25	
520	Mel Gray	4	4	5	8	10	12	20	
521	Nate Wright	4	4	5	8	10	12	25	
522	Rocky Bleier	4	4	5	8	10	12	40	
523	Dennis Johnson RC	4	4	5	8	10	12	25	
524	Jerry Sisemore	4	4	5	8	10	12	25	
525	Bert Jones	4	4	5	8	10	12	40	
526	Perry Smith	4	4	5	8	10	12	25	
527	Blaine Nye	4	4	5	8	10	12	25	
528	Bob Moore	4	4	5	5	10	12	25	

— Terry Bradshaw #75 BGS 9.5 (Gem Mint) sold for $435.01 (eBay: 5/12)
— L.C.Greenwood #180 PSA 10 (Gem Mint) sold for $532 (eBay: 8/12)
— Jack Lambert #220 PSA 10 (Gem) sold for $1,179 (eBay: 2/10)
— Jack Lambert #220 PSA 10 (Gem) sold for $1,538.65 (eBay: 11/13)
— Jack Lambert #220 BGS 10 (Gem) sold for $6573 (eBay: 09/14)
— Jack Lambert #220 BGS 9.5 (Gem Mint) sold for $840.01 (eBay: 5/12)
— Walter Payton #148 BVG 10 (Pristine) sold for $11,050 (eBay: 11/07)
— Walter Payton #148 PSA 10 (Gem) sold for $10,230 (eBay: 10/14)
— O.J. Simpson #6 PSA 10 (Gem) sold for $695 (eBay: 10/14)
— Fran Tarkenton #500 PSA 10 (Gem Mint) sold for $540 (Bussineau: 4/12)
— Randy White #158 PSA 10 (Gem) sold for $1,476 (eBay: 9/07)
— Super Bowl X/Bradshaw #333 PSA 10 (Gem) sold for $1,037 (eBay: 7/13)

1977 Topps

		VgEx 4	EX 5	ExMt 6	NM 7	NmMt 8	NmMt+ 8.5	MT 9	Gem 9.5/10
1	K.Stabler/J.Harris LL	4	4	5	5	10	15	40	
2	D.Pearson/M.Lane LL	4	4	5	5	10	12	30	
3	W.Payton/O.Simpson LL	4	4	6	10	40	50	120	
4	M.Moseley/T.Linhart LL	4	4	5	5	10	12	25	60
5	M.Jackson/K.Riley LL	4	4	5	5	10	12	25	
6	J.James/M.Bateman LL	4	4	5	5	10	12	25	
7	Mike Phipps	4	4	5	5	10	12	25	
8	Rick Volk	4	4	5	5	10	12	25	
9	Steve Furness	4	4	5	5	10	12	25	
10	Isaac Curtis	4	4	5	5	10	12	25	
11	Nate Wright	4	4	5	5	10	12	25	
12	Jean Fugett	4	4	5	5	10	12	25	80
13	Ken Mendenhall	4	4	5	5	10	12	25	
14	Sam Adams OL	4	4	5	5	10	12	25	
15	Charlie Waters	4	4	5	5	10	12	25	80
16	Bill Stanfill	4	4	5	5	10	12	25	
17	John Holland	4	4	5	5	10	12	25	
18	Pat Haden RC	4	4	5	5	10	12	25	60
19	Bob Young	4	4	5	5	10	12	25	
20	Wally Chambers	4	4	5	5	10	12	25	
21	Lawrence Gaines	4	4	5	5	10	12	25	
22	Larry McCarren	4	4	5	5	10	12	25	
23	Horst Muhlmann	4	4	5	5	10	12	25	60
24	Phil Villapiano	4	4	5	5	10	12	25	60
25	Greg Pruitt	4	4	5	5	10	12	40	
26	Ron Howard	4	4	5	5	10	12	25	
27	Craig Morton	4	4	5	5	10	12	25	
28	Rufus Mayes	4	4	5	5	10	12	50	
29	Lee Roy Selmon RC	4	5	8	15	25	30	125	
30	Ed White	4	4	5	5	10	12	25	
31	Harold McLinton	4	4	5	5	10	12	25	50
32	Glenn Doughty	4	4	5	5	10	12	25	60
33	Bob Kuechenberg	4	4	5	5	10	12	25	
34	Duane Carrell	4	4	5	5	10	12	25	
35	Riley Odoms	4	4	5	5	10	12	25	
36	Bobby Scott	4	4	5	5	10	12	25	
37	Nick Mike-Mayer	4	4	5	5	10	12	25	
38	Bill Lenkaitis	4	4	5	5	10	12	25	

FOOTBALL

#	Player	VgEx 4	EX 5	ExMt 6	NM 7	NmMt 8	NmMt+ 8.5	MT 9	Gem 9.5/10
39	Roland Harper	4	4	5	5	10	12	25	
40	Tommy Hart	4	4	5	5	10	12	25	
41	Mike Sensibaugh	4	4	5	5	10	12	25	
42	Rusty Jackson	4	4	5	5	10	12	25	
43	Levi Johnson	4	4	5	5	10	12	25	
44	Mike McCoy DT	4	4	5	5	10	12	25	60
45	Roger Staubach	5	8	12	50	60	80	200	
46	Fred Cox	4	4	5	5	10	12	25	
47	Bob Babich	4	4	5	5	10	12	25	
48	Reggie McKenzie	4	4	5	5	10	12	25	
49	Dave Jennings	4	4	5	5	10	12	25	
50	Mike Haynes RC	4	5	8	25	60	80	200	
51	Larry Brown	4	4	5	5	10	12	25	
52	Marvin Cobb	4	4	5	5	10	12	25	
53	Fred Cook	4	4	5	5	10	12	25	
54	Freddie Solomon	4	4	5	5	10	12	25	
55	John Riggins	4	4	5	5	12	15	30	
56	John Bunting	4	4	5	5	10	12	25	
57	Ray Wersching	4	4	5	5	10	12	25	
58	Mike Livingston	4	4	5	5	10	12	25	60
59	Billy Johnson	4	4	5	5	10	12	25	
60	Mike Wagner	4	4	5	5	10	12	25	
61	Waymond Bryant	4	4	5	5	10	12	25	
62	Jim Otis	4	4	5	5	10	12	25	60
63	Ed Galigher	4	4	5	5	10	12	25	60
64	Randy Vataha	4	4	5	5	10	12	25	
65	Jim Zorn RC	4	4	5	8	15	20	40	
66	Jon Keyworth	4	4	5	5	10	12	25	60
67	Checklist 1-132	4	4	5	5	10	12	25	
68	Henry Childs	4	4	5	5	10	12	25	60
69	Thom Darden	4	4	5	5	10	12	25	
70	George Kunz	4	4	5	5	10	12	25	
71	Lenvil Elliott	4	4	5	5	10	12	25	
72	Curtis Johnson	4	4	5	5	10	12	25	
73	Doug Van Horn	4	4	5	5	10	12	20	80
74	Joe Theismann	4	4	5	8	15	20	40	125
75	Dwight White	4	4	5	5	10	12	30	100
76	Scott Laidlaw	4	4	5	5	10	12	25	
77	Monte Johnson	4	4	5	5	10	12	25	
78	Dave Beverly	4	4	5	5	10	12	25	
79	Jim Mitchell TE	4	4	5	5	10	12	25	60
80	Jack Youngblood	4	4	5	5	10	12	25	60
81	Mel Gray	4	4	5	5	10	12	25	
82	Dwight Harrison	4	4	5	5	10	12	25	60
83	John Hadl	4	4	5	5	10	12	25	
84	Matt Blair RC	4	4	5		10	12	100	
85	Charlie Sanders	4	4	5	5	10	12	25	
86	Noah Jackson	4	4	5	5	10	12	25	
87	Ed Marinaro	4	4	5	5	10	12	25	80
88	Bob Howard	4	4	5	5	10	12	25	
89	John McDaniel	4	4	5	5	10	12	25	
90	Dan Dierdorf	4	4	5	5	10	12	40	60
91	Mark Moseley	4	4	5	5	10	12	25	
92	Cleo Miller	4	4	5	5	10	12	25	
93	Andre Tillman	4	4	5	5	10	12	25	60
94	Bruce Taylor	4	4	5	5	10	12	25	60
95	Bert Jones	4	4	5	5	10	12	25	
96	Anthony Davis RC	4	4	5	5	10	12	25	
97	Don Goode	4	4	5	5	10	12	25	
98	Ray Rhodes RC	4	4	5	8	15	20	50	
99	Mike Webster RC	4	5	8	12	50	60	80	700
100	O.J.Simpson	4	4	5	8	20	25	100	300
101	Doug Plank RC	4	4	5	5	10	12	25	
102	Efren Herrera	4	4	5	5	10	12	50	
103	Charlie Smith WR	4	4	5	5	10	12	25	60
104	Carlos Brown RC	4	4	5	5	10	12	25	
105	Jim Marshall	4	4	5	5	10	12	25	80
106	Paul Naumoff	4	4	5	5	10	12	25	60
107	Walter White	4	4	5	5	10	12	25	60
108	John Cappelletti RC	4	4	5	5	10	15	40	
109	Chip Myers	4	4	5	5	10	12	25	
110	Ken Stabler	4	4	6	10	30	50	60	200
111	Joe Ehrmann	4	4	5	5	10	12	25	
112	Rick Engles	4	4	5	5	10	12	25	
113	Jack Dolbin RC	4	4	5	5	10	12	25	60
114	Ron Bolton	4	4	5	5	10	12	25	60
115	Mike Thomas	4	4	5	5	10	12	25	
116	Mike Fuller	4	4	5	5	10	12	25	
117	John Hill	4	4	5	5	10	12	20	
118	Richard Todd RC	4	4	5	5	10	12	30	
119	Duriel Harris RC	4	4	5	5	10	12	30	
120	John James	4	4	5	5	10	12	25	
121	Lionel Antoine	4	4	5	5	10	12	25	
122	John Skorupan	4	4	5	5	10	12	25	
123	Skip Butler	4	4	5	5	10	12	25	
124	Bob Tucker	4	4	5	5	10	12	25	
125	Paul Krause	4	4	5	5	10	12	25	
126	Dave Hampton	4	4	5	5	10	12	25	
127	Tom Wittum	4	4	5	5	10	12	25	60
128	Gary Huff	4	4	5	5	10	12	25	60
129	Emmitt Thomas	4	4	5	5	10	12	25	
130	Drew Pearson	4	4	5	5	10	12	30	
131	Ron Saul	4	4	5	5	10	12	25	
132	Steve Niehaus	4	4	5	5	10	12	25	
133	Fred Carr	4	4	5	5	10	12	25	60
134	Norm Bulaich	4	4	5	5	10	12	25	
135	Bob Trumpy	4	4	5	5	10	12	25	
136	Greg Landry	4	4	5	5	10	12	25	
137	George Buehler	4	4	5	5	10	12	25	
138	Reggie Rucker	4	4	5	5	10	12	25	
139	Julius Adams	4	4	5	5	10	12	25	
140	Jack Ham	4	4	5	5	10	12	80	
141	Wayne Morris RC	4	4	5	5	10	12	25	
142	Marv Bateman	4	4	5	5	10	12	25	
143	Bobby Maples	4	4	5	5	10	12	25	
144	Harold Carmichael	4	4	5	5	10	12	25	
145	Bob Avellini	4	4	5	5	10	12	25	
146	Harry Carson RC	5	8	12	20	50	80	250	
147	Lawrence Pillers	4	4	5	5	10	12	25	60
148	Ed Williams RC	4	4	5	5	10	12	25	
149	Dan Pastorini	4	4	5	5	10	12	25	60
150	Ron Yary	4	4	5	5	10	12	25	
151	Joe Lavender	4	4	5	5	10	12	25	60
152	Pat McInally RC	4	4	5	5	10	12	100	
153	Lloyd Mumphord	4	4	5	5	10	12	25	60
154	Cullen Bryant	4	4	5	5	10	12	25	
155	Willie Lanier	4	4	5	5	10	12	25	60
156	Gene Washington 49er	4	4	5	5	10	12	25	
157	Scott Hunter	4	4	5	5	10	12	25	60
158	Jim Merlo	4	4	5	5	10	12	25	
159	Randy Grossman	4	4	5	5	10	12	30	
160	Blaine Nye	4	4	5	5	10	12	25	
161	Ike Harris	4	4	5	5	10	12	25	
162	Doug Dieken	4	4	5	5	10	12	25	
163	Guy Morriss	4	4	5	5	10	12	25	60
164	Bob Parsons	4	4	5	5	10	12	25	80
165	Steve Grogan	4	4	5	5	10	12	25	
166	John Brockington	4	4	5	5	10	12	25	
167	Charlie Joiner	4	4	5	5	10	12	30	
168	Ron Carpenter	4	4	5	5	10	12	25	
169	Jeff Wright S	4	4	5	5	10	12	25	
170	Chris Hanburger	4	4	5	5	10	12	25	
171	Roosevelt Leaks RC	4	4	5	5	10	12	25	80
172	Larry Little	4	4	5	5	10	12	25	
173	John Matuszak	4	4	5	5	10	12	25	80
174	Joe Ferguson	4	4	5	5	10	12	25	
175	Brad Van Pelt	4	4	5	5	10	12	25	
176	Dexter Bussey RC	4	4	5	5	10	12	25	60
177	Steve Largent RC	12	15	50	80	125	150	500	4,000
178	Dewey Selmon	4	4	5	5	10	12	25	80
179	Randy Gradishar	4	4	5	5	10	12	25	80
180	Mel Blount	4	4	5	5	10	12	30	
181	Dan Neal	4	4	5	5	10	12	25	50
182	Rich Szaro	4	4	5	5	10	12	25	
183	Mike Boryla	4	4	5	5	10	12	25	60
184	Steve Jones	4	4	5	5	10	12	25	60
185	Paul Warfield	4	4	5	5	10	12	30	
186	Greg Buttle RC	4	4	5	5	10	12	25	
187	Rich McGeorge	4	4	5	5	10	12	25	
188	Leon Gray RC	4	4	5	5	10	12	25	
189	John Shinners	4	4	5	5	10	12	25	60
190	Toni Linhart	4	4	5	5	10	12	25	60
191	Robert Miller	4	4	5	5	10	12	25	
192	Jake Scott	4	4	5	5	10	12	25	
193	Jon Morris	4	4	5	5	10	12	25	
194	Randy Crowder	4	4	5	5	10	12	25	
195	Lynn Swann	4	5	8	12	40	50	60	
196	Marsh White	4	4	5	5	10	12	25	

#	Player	VgEx 4	EX 5	ExMt 6	NM 7	NmMt 8	NmMt+ 8.5	MT 9	Gem 9.5/10
197	Rod Perry RC	4	4	5	5	10	12	25	
198	Willie Hall	4	4	5	5	10	12	25	60
199	Mike Hartenstine	4	4	5	5	10	12	25	60
200	Jim Bakken	4	4	5	5	10	12	25	
201	Atlanta Falcons CL	4	4	5	5	10	12	25	
202	Baltimore Colts CL	4	4	5	5	10	12	25	
203	Buffalo Bills CL	4	4	5	5	10	12	25	
204	Chicago Bears CL	4	4	5	5	10	12	25	
205	Cincinnati Bengals CL	4	4	5	5	10	12	25	60
206	Cleveland Browns CL	4	4	5	5	10	12	25	80
207	Dallas Cowboys CL	4	4	5	5	10	12	25	
208	Denver Broncos CL	4	4	5	5	10	12	25	
209	Detroit Lions CL	4	4	5	5	10	12	25	
210	Green Bay Packers CL	4	4	5	5	10	12	25	
211	Houston Oilers CL	4	4	5	5	10	12	25	
212	Kansas City Chiefs CL	4	4	5	5	10	12	60	
213	Los Angeles Rams CL	4	4	5	5	10	12	25	
214	Miami Dolphins CL	4	4	5	5	10	12	25	
215	Minnesota Vikings CL	4	4	5	5	10	12	25	
216	New England Patriots CL	4	4	5	5	10	12	25	
217	New Orleans Saints CL	4	4	5	5	10	12	25	
218	New York Giants CL	4	4	5	5	10	12	25	50
219	New York Jets CL	4	4	5	5	10	12	25	50
220	Oakland Raiders CL	4	4	5	5	10	12	25	80
221	Philadelphia Eagles CL	4	4	5	5	10	12	25	
222	Pittsburgh Steelers CL	4	4	5	5	10	12	25	80
223	St. Louis Cardinals CL	4	4	5	5	10	12	25	
224	San Diego Chargers CL	4	4	5	5	10	12	25	80
225	San Francisco 49ers CL	4	4	5	5	10	12	25	
226	Seattle Seahawks CL	4	4	5	5	10	12	40	
227	Tampa Bay Buccaneers CL	4	4	5	5	10	12	25	
228	Washington Redskins CL	4	4	5	5	10	12	25	
229	Sam Cunningham	4	4	5	5	10	12	25	
230	Alan Page	4	4	5	5	10	12	40	
231	Eddie Brown S	4	4	5	5	10	12	25	
232	Stan White	4	4	5	5	10	12	25	60
233	Vern Den Herder	4	4	5	5	10	12	25	
234	Clarence Davis	4	4	5	5	10	12	25	
235	Ken Anderson	4	4	5	5	8	12	25	60
236	Karl Chandler	4	4	5	5	10	12	25	
237	Will Harrell	4	4	5	5	10	12	25	
238	Clarence Scott	4	4	5	5	10	12	25	
239	Bo Rather	4	4	5	5	10	12	25	50
240	Robert Brazile	4	4	5	5	10	12	25	
241	Bob Bell	4	4	5	5	10	12	25	
242	Rolland Lawrence	4	4	5	5	10	12	25	
243	Tom Sullivan	4	4	5	5	10	12	25	60
244	Larry Brunson	4	4	5	5	10	12	25	60
245	Terry Bradshaw	4	5	8	20	60	80	200	
246	Rich Saul	4	4	5	5	10	12	25	60
247	Cleveland Elam	4	4	5	5	10	12	25	
248	Don Woods	4	4	5	5	10	12	25	
249	Bruce Laird	4	4	5	5	10	12	25	
250	Coy Bacon	4	4	5	5	10	12	25	80
251	Russ Francis	4	4	5	5	10	12	25	
252	Jim Braxton	4	4	5	5	10	12	25	
253	Perry Smith	4	4	5	5	10	12	25	
254	Jerome Barkum	4	4	5	5	10	12	25	50
255	Garo Yepremian	4	4	5	5	10	12	25	
256	Checklist 133-264	4	4	5	5	10	12	25	
257	Tony Galbreath RC	4	4	5	5	10	12	25	
258	Troy Archer	4	4	5	5	10	12	25	
259	Brian Sipe	4	4	5	5	10	12	25	
260	Billy Joe DuPree	4	4	5	5	10	12	25	60
261	Bobby Walden	4	4	5	5	10	12	25	
262	Larry Marshall	4	4	5	5	10	12	25	
263	Ted Fritsch Jr.	4	4	5	5	10	12	25	
264	Larry Hand	4	4	5	5	10	12	25	
265	Tom Mack	4	4	5	5	10	12	25	60
266	Ed Bradley	4	4	5	5	10	12	25	60
267	Pat Leahy	4	4	5	5	10	12	25	
268	Louis Carter	4	4	5	5	8	12	25	
269	Archie Griffin RC	4	4	5	10	20	25	60	
270	Art Shell	4	4	5	5	10	12	25	
271	Stu Voigt	4	4	5	5	10	12	25	
272	Prentice McCray	4	4	5	5	10	12	25	
273	MacArthur Lane	4	4	5	5	10	12	25	
274	Dan Fouts	4	4	5	8	12	20	40	
275	Charle Young	4	4	5	5	10	12	25	50

#	Player	VgEx 4	EX 5	ExMt 6	NM 7	NmMt 8	NmMt+ 8.5	MT 9	Gem 9.5/10
276	Wilbur Jackson RC	4	4	5	5	10	12	25	
277	John Hicks	4	4	5	5	10	12	25	
278	Nat Moore	4	4	5	5	10	12	25	60
279	Virgil Livers	4	4	5	5	10	12	25	
280	Curley Culp	4	4	5	5	10	12	25	
281	Rocky Bleier	4	4	5	5	10	12	30	
282	John Zook	4	4	5	5	10	12	25	60
283	Tom DeLeone	4	4	5	5	10	12	25	
284	Danny White RC	4	4	6	12	25	30	60	400
285	Otis Armstrong	4	4	5	5	10	12	25	
286	Larry Walton	4	4	5	5	10	12	25	60
287	Jim Carter	4	4	5	5	10	12	25	
288	Don McCauley	4	4	5	5	10	12	25	
289	Frank Grant	4	4	5	5	10	12	25	50
290	Roger Wehrli	4	4	5	5	10	12	25	80
291	Mick Tingelhoff	4	4	5	5	10	12	25	60
292	Bernard Jackson	4	4	5	5	10	12	25	
293	Tom Owen RC	4	4	5	5	10	12	25	
294	Mike Esposito	4	4	5	5	10	12	25	60
295	Fred Biletnikoff	4	4	5	5	10	12	30	
296	Revie Sorey RC	4	4	5	5	10	12	25	
297	John McMakin	4	4	5	5	10	12	25	
298	Dan Ryczek	4	4	5	5	10	12	25	
299	Wayne Moore	4	4	5	5	8	12	25	80
300	Franco Harris	4	4	5	8	25	35	175	
301	Rick Upchurch RC	4	4	5	5	10	12	25	80
302	Jim Stienke	4	4	5	5	10	12	25	
303	Charlie Davis	4	4	5	5	10	12	25	
304	Don Cockroft	4	4	5	5	10	12	25	60
305	Ken Burrough	4	4	5	5	10	12	25	
306	Clark Gaines	4	4	5	5	10	12	25	
307	Bobby Douglass	4	4	5	5	10	12	50	
308	Ralph Perretta	4	4	5	5	10	12	25	
309	Wally Hilgenberg	4	4	5	5	10	12	25	
310	Monte Jackson RC	4	4	5	5	10	12	25	60
311	Chris Bahr RC	4	4	5	5	10	12	25	
312	Jim Cheyunski	4	4	5	5	10	12	25	60
313	Mike Patrick	4	4	5	5	8	12	25	
314	Ed Too Tall Jones	4	4	5	8	20	25	50	
315	Bill Bradley	4	4	5	5	10	12	25	
316	Benny Malone	4	4	5	5	10	12	25	
317	Paul Seymour	4	4	5	5	10	12	25	60
318	Jim Laslavic	4	4	5	5	10	12	25	
319	Frank Lewis	4	4	5	5	10	12	25	60
320	Ray Guy	4	4	5	5	10	12	30	
321	Allan Ellis	4	4	5	5	10	12	25	
322	Conrad Dobler	4	4	5	5	10	12	25	
323	Chester Marcol	4	4	5	5	10	12	25	
324	Doug Kotar	4	4	5	5	10	12	25	
325	Lemar Parrish	4	4	5	5	10	12	25	
326	Steve Holden	4	4	5	5	10	12	25	
327	Jeff Van Note	4	4	5	5	10	12	25	
328	Howard Stevens	4	4	5	5	10	12	25	
329	Brad Dusek	4	4	5	5	10	12	25	
330	Joe DeLamielleure	4	4	5	5	10	12	20	
331	Jim Plunkett	4	4	5	5	10	12	30	
332	Checklist 265-396	4	4	5	5	10	12	25	
333	Lou Piccone	4	4	5	5	10	12	25	60
334	Ray Hamilton	4	4	5	5	10	12	25	
335	Jan Stenerud	4	4	5	5	10	12	25	
336	Jeris White	4	4	5	5	10	12	25	
337	Sherman Smith RC	4	4	5	5	10	12	25	
338	Dave Green	4	4	5	5	10	12	25	
339	Terry Schmidt	4	4	5	5	10	12	25	
340	Sammie White RC	4	4	5	5	10	12	50	
341	Jon Kolb RC	4	4	5	5	8	12	25	
342	Randy White	4	4	5	10	20	25	60	175
343	Bob Klein	4	4	5	5	10	12	40	
344	Bob Kowalkowski	4	4	5	5	10	12	25	60
345	Terry Metcalf	4	4	5	5	10	12	25	
346	Joe Danelo	4	4	5	5	10	12	25	60
347	Ken Payne	4	4	5	5	10	12	25	
348	Neal Craig	4	4	5	5	10	12	25	
349	Dennis Johnson	4	4	5	5	10	12	25	
350	Bill Bergey	4	4	5	5	10	12	25	
351	Raymond Chester	4	4	5	5	10	12	25	
352	Bob Matheson	4	4	5	5	10	12	25	60
353	Mike Kadish	4	4	5	5	10	12	25	60
354	Mark Van Eeghen RC	4	4	5	5	10	12	40	

#	Name	VgEx 4	EX 5	ExMt 6	NM 7	NmMt 8	NmMt+ 8.5	MT 9	Gem 9.5/10
355	L.C.Greenwood	4	4	5	5	10	12	25	
356	Sam Hunt	4	4	5	5	10	12	25	
357	Darrell Austin	4	4	5	5	10	12	25	
358	Jim Turner	4	4	5	5	10	12	25	
359	Ahmad Rashad	4	4	5	5	8	12	25	
360	Walter Payton	8	12	25	35	100	125	600	
361	Mark Arneson	4	4	5	5	10	12	25	
362	Jerrel Wilson	4	4	5	5	10	12	25	
363	Steve Bartkowski	4	4	5	5	10	12	25	
364	John Watson	4	4	5	5	10	12	25	
365	Ken Riley	4	4	5	5	10	12	25	
366	Gregg Bingham	4	4	5	5	10	12	25	60
367	Golden Richards	4	4	5	5	10	12	25	
368	Clyde Powers	4	4	5	5	10	12	25	
369	Diron Talbert	4	4	5	5	10	12	25	
370	Lydell Mitchell	4	4	5	5	10	12	25	
371	Bob Jackson	4	4	5	5	10	12	25	
372	Jim Mandich	4	4	5	5	10	12	25	
373	Frank LeMaster	4	4	5	5	10	12	25	
374	Benny Ricardo	4	4	5	5	10	12	25	
375	Lawrence McCutcheon	4	4	5	5	10	12	25	
376	Lynn Dickey	4	4	5	5	10	12	25	
377	Phil Wise	4	4	5	5	10	12	25	
378	Tony McGee DT	4	4	5	5	10	12	25	
379	Norm Thompson	4	4	5	5	8	12	25	
380	Dave Casper RC	4	5	8	15	50	60	300	
381	Glen Edwards	4	4	5	5	10	12	25	
382	Bob Thomas	4	4	5	5	10	12	25	
383	Bob Chandler	4	4	5	5	10	12	25	
384	Rickey Young	4	4	5	5	10	12	25	
385	Carl Eller	4	4	5	5	10	12	25	
386	Lyle Alzado	4	4	5	5	10	12	25	
387	John Leypoldt	4	4	5	5	10	12	25	
388	Gordon Bell	4	4	5	5	10	12	25	60
389	Mike Bragg	4	4	5	5	10	12	25	
390	Jim Langer	4	4	5	5	10	12	25	
391	Vern Holland	4	4	5	5	10	12	25	
392	Nelson Munsey	4	4	5	5	10	12	25	
393	Mack Mitchell	4	4	5	5	10	12	25	
394	Tony Adams RC	4	4	5	5	10	12	25	
395	Preston Pearson	4	4	5	5	10	12	25	
396	Emanuel Zanders	4	4	5	5	8	12	25	
397	Vince Papale RC	5	8	12	15	25	35	60	
398	Joe Fields RC	4	4	5	5	10	12	25	
399	Craig Clemons	4	4	5	5	10	12	25	80
400	Fran Tarkenton	4	4	5	8	15	20	50	
401	Andy Johnson	4	4	5	5	10	12	25	60
402	Willie Buchanon	4	4	5	5	10	12	25	60
403	Pat Curran	4	4	5	5	10	12	25	
404	Ray Jarvis	4	4	5	5	10	12	25	
405	Joe Greene	4	4	5	5	10	12	40	
406	Bill Simpson	4	4	5	5	10	12	25	
407	Ronnie Coleman	4	4	5	5	10	12	25	
408	J.K. McKay RC	4	4	5	5	10	12	25	60
409	Pat Fischer	4	4	5	5	10	12	25	
410	John Dutton	4	4	5	5	10	12	25	
411	Boobie Clark	4	4	5	5	10	12	25	
412	Pat Tilley RC	4	4	5	5	10	12	25	80
413	Don Strock	4	4	5	5	10	12	25	
414	Brian Kelley	4	4	5	5	10	12	25	
415	Gene Upshaw	4	4	5	5	10	12	25	
416	Mike Montler	4	4	5	5	10	12	25	
417	Checklist 397-528	4	4	5	5	10	12	25	
418	John Gilliam	4	4	5	5	10	12	25	60
419	Brent McClanahan	4	4	5	5	10	12	30	
420	Jerry Sherk	4	4	5	5	10	12	30	
421	Roy Gerela	4	4	5	5	10	12	25	60
422	Tim Fox	4	4	5	5	10	12	25	60
423	John Ebersole	4	4	5	5	10	12	25	
424	James Scott RC	4	4	5	5	10	12	25	60
425	Delvin Williams RC	4	4	5	5	10	12	25	
426	Spike Jones	4	4	5	5	10	12	25	
427	Harvey Martin	4	4	5	5	10	12	25	120
428	Don Herrmann	4	4	5	5	10	12	25	60
429	Calvin Hill	4	4	5	5	10	12	25	
430	Isiah Robertson	4	4	5	5	10	12	25	60
431	Tony Greene	4	4	5	5	10	12	25	
432	Bob Johnson	4	4	5	5	10	12	25	
433	Lem Barney	4	4	5	5	10	12	25	80
434	Eric Torkelson	4	4	5	5	10	12	25	
435	John Mendenhall	4	4	5	5	10	12	25	
436	Larry Seiple	4	4	5	5	10	12	25	
437	Art Kuehn	4	4	5	5	10	12	60	
438	John Vella	4	4	5	5	10	12	25	
439	Greg Latta	4	4	5	5	10	12	25	100
440	Roger Carr	4	4	5	5	10	12	25	
441	Doug Sutherland	4	4	5	5	10	12	25	80
442	Mike Kruczek RC	4	4	5	5	10	12	25	60
443	Steve Zabel	4	4	5	5	10	12	25	
444	Mike Pruitt RC	4	4	5	5	10	12	25	
445	Harold Jackson	4	4	5	5	10	12	25	
446	George Jakowenko	4	4	5	5	10	12	25	
447	John Fitzgerald	4	4	5	5	10	12	60	
448	Carey Joyce	4	4	5	5	10	12	25	
449	Jim LeClair	4	4	5	5	10	12	25	
450	Ken Houston	4	4	5	5	10	12	50	
451	Steve Grogan RB	4	4	5	5	10	12	25	50
452	Jim Marshall RB	4	4	5	5	10	12	25	
453	O.J.Simpson RB	4	4	5	5	10	12	30	100
454	Fran Tarkenton RB	4	4	5	5	10	12	30	
455	Jim Zorn RB	4	4	5	5	10	12	25	50
456	Robert Pratt	4	4	5	5	10	12	25	50
457	Walker Gillette	4	4	5	5	10	12	25	60
458	Charlie Hall	4	4	5	5	10	12	25	
459	Robert Newhouse	4	4	5	5	10	12	25	
460	John Hannah	4	4	5	5	10	12	25	
461	Ken Reaves	4	4	5	5	10	12	25	
462	Herman Weaver	4	4	5	5	10	12	25	50
463	James Harris	4	4	5	5	10	12	25	80
464	Howard Twilley	4	4	5	5	10	12	30	
465	Jeff Siemon	4	4	5	5	10	12	25	80
466	John Outlaw	4	4	5	5	10	12	25	
467	Chuck Muncie RC	4	4	5	5	12	15	40	
468	Bob Moore	4	4	5	5	10	12	25	80
469	Robert Woods	4	4	5	5	10	12	25	
470	Cliff Branch	4	4	5	5	10	12	25	100
471	Johnnie Gray	4	4	5	5	10	12	25	50
472	Don Hardeman	4	4	5	5	10	12	25	50
473	Steve Ramsey	4	4	5	5	10	12	25	50
474	Steve Mike-Mayer	4	4	5	5	10	12	25	
475	Gary Garrison	4	4	5	5	10	12	25	
476	Walter Johnson	4	4	5	5	10	12	25	50
477	Neil Clabo	4	4	5	5	8	12	25	
478	Len Hauss	4	4	5	5	10	12	25	
479	Darryl Stingley	4	4	5	5	10	12	30	
480	Jack Lambert	4	4	5	10	20	25	150	
481	Mike Adamle	4	4	5	5	10	12	25	50
482	David Lee	4	4	5	5	10	12	25	
483	Tom Mullen	4	4	5	5	10	12	25	60
484	Claude Humphrey	4	4	5	5	10	12	25	
485	Jim Hart	4	4	5	5	10	12	25	
486	Bobby Thompson RB	4	4	5	5	10	12	25	
487	Jack Rudnay	4	4	5	5	10	12	25	
488	Rich Sowells	4	4	5	5	10	12	25	
489	Reuben Gant	4	4	5	5	10	12	25	
490	Cliff Harris	4	4	5	5	10	12	25	
491	Bob Brown DT	4	4	5	5	10	12	25	
492	Don Nottingham	4	4	5	5	10	12	25	
493	Ron Jessie	4	4	5	5	10	12	25	
494	Otis Sistrunk	4	4	5	5	10	12	25	60
495	Billy Kilmer	4	4	5	5	10	12	25	
496	Oscar Roan	4	4	5	5	10	12	25	
497	Bill Van Heusen	4	4	5	5	10	12	25	
498	Randy Logan	4	4	5	5	10	12	25	
499	John Smith	4	4	5	5	10	12	25	
500	Chuck Foreman	4	4	5	5	10	12	50	
501	J.T. Thomas	4	4	5	5	10	12	25	
502	Steve Schubert	4	4	5	5	10	12	25	
503	Mike Barnes	4	4	5	5	10	12	25	
504	J.V. Cain	4	4	5	5	10	12	25	
505	Larry Csonka	4	4	5	5	10	12	30	135
506	Elvin Bethea	4	4	5	5	10	12	25	
507	Ray Easterling	4	4	5	5	10	12	25	
508	Joe Reed	4	4	5	5	10	12	25	
509	Steve Odom	4	4	5	5	10		25	
510	Tommy Casanova	4	4	5	5	10	12	25	
511	Dave Dalby	4	4	5	5	10	12	25	
512	Richard Caster	4	4	5	5	10	12	25	

		VgEx 4	EX 5	ExMt 6	NM 7	NmMt 8	NmMt+ 8.5	MT 9	Gem 9.5/10
513	Fred Dryer	4	4	5	5	10	12	40	
514	Jeff Kinney	4	4	5	5	10	12	25	
515	Bob Griese	4	4	5	5	10	12	40	
516	Butch Johnson RC	4	4	5	5	10	12	40	
517	Gerald Irons	4	4	5	5	10	12	25	
518	Don Calhoun	4	4	5	5	10	12	25	
519	Jack Gregory	4	4	5	5	10	12	25	
520	Tom Banks	4	4	5	5	10	12	25	
521	Bobby Bryant	4	4	5	5	10	12	25	
522	Reggie Harrison	4	4	5	5	10	12	25	
523	Terry Hermeling	4	4	5	5	10	12	25	
524	David Taylor	4	4	5	5	10	12	25	60
525	Brian Baschnagel RC	4	4	5	5	10	12	25	
526	AFC Champ/Stabler	4	4	5	5	10	12	25	120
527	NFC Championship	4	4	5	5	10	12	35	80
528	Super Bowl XI	4	4	5	5	12	20	50	

— Dave Casper #380 PSA 10 (Gem) sold for $4,275 (eBay; 10/07)
— Joe Greene #405 PSA 10 (Gem) sold for $300 (eBay; 1/08)
— John Hannah #460 PSA 10 (Gem Mint) sold for $421.26 (Goodwin; 3/12)
— Walter Payton #360 PSA 10 (Gem) sold for $4,600 (eBay; 8/08)
— Walter Payton #360 PSA 10 (Gem) sold for $5,661 (eBay; 12/13)
— Walter Payton #360 PSA 10 (Gem Mint) sold for $4110 (Bussineau; 6/12)
— Lee Roy Selmon #29 PSA 10 (Gem Mint) sold for $1,186 (eBay; 2/13)
— Lee Roy Selmon #29 PSA 10 (Gem Mint) sold for $4,059 (eBay; 09/14)
— Mike Webster #99 PSA 10 (Gem) sold for $504 (eBay; 6/08)

1978 Topps

		VgEx 4	EX 5	ExMt 6	NM 7	NmMt 8	NmMt+ 8.5	MT 9	Gem 9.5/10
1	Gary Huff HL	4	4	5	5	8	10	25	50
2	Craig Morton HL	4	4	5	5	8	10	15	50
3	Walter Payton HL	4	4	5	8	25	30	40	200
4	O.J.Simpson HL	4	4	5	5	8	10	20	60
5	Fran Tarkenton HL	4	4	5	5	8	10	20	80
6	Bob Thomas HL	4	4	5	5	8	10	20	
7	Joe Pisarcik	4	4	5	5	8	10	20	
8	Skip Thomas	4	4	5	5	8	10	25	
9	Roosevelt Leaks	4	4	5	5	8	10	20	
10	Ken Houston	4	4	5	5	8	10	20	
11	Tom Blanchard	4	4	5	5	8	10	20	
12	Jim Turner	4	4	5	5	8	10	20	40
13	Tom DeLeone	4	4	5	5	8	10	20	
14	Jim LeClair	4	4	5	5	8	10	20	40
15	Bob Avellini	4	4	5	5	8	10	20	
16	Tony McGee DT	4	4	5	5	8	10	20	50
17	James Harris	4	4	5	5	8	10	20	
18	Terry Nelson	4	4	5	5	8	10	20	
19	Rocky Bleier	4	4	5	5	8	10	20	
20	Joe DeLamielleure	4	4	5	5	8	10	20	
21	Richard Caster	4	4	5	5	8	10	20	
22	A.J.Duhe RC	4	4	5	5	8	10	20	
23	John Outlaw	4	4	5	5	8	10	20	50
24	Danny White	4	4	5	5	8	10	20	80
25	Larry Csonka	4	4	5	6	10	12	25	
26	David Hill RC	4	4	5	5	8	10	20	
27	Mark Arneson	4	4	5	5	8	10	20	50
28	Jack Tatum	4	4	5	5	8	10	20	
29	Norm Thompson	4	4	5	5	8	10	20	50
30	Sammie White	4	4	5	5	8	10	20	50
31	Dennis Johnson	4	4	5	5	8	10	20	
32	Robin Earl	4	4	5	5	8	10	20	40
33	Don Cockroft	4	4	5	5	8	10	20	50
34	Bob Johnson	4	4	5	5	8	10	20	50
35	John Hannah	4	4	5	5	8	10	20	
36	Scott Hunter	4	5	6	15	30	40	50	
37	Ken Burrough	4	4	5	5	8	10	20	
38	Wilbur Jackson	4	4	5	5	8	10	20	50
39	Rich McGeorge	4	4	5	5	8	10	20	60
40	Lyle Alzado	4	4	5	5	8	10	15	60
41	John Ebersole	4	4	5	5	8	10	20	50
42	Gary Green RC	4	4	5	5	8	10	20	
43	Art Kuehn	4	4	5	5	8	10	20	40
44	Glen Edwards	4	4	5	5	8	10	20	40
45	Lawrence McCutcheon	4	4	5	5	8	10	20	50
46	Duriel Harris	4	4	5	5	8	10	20	
47	Rich Szaro	4	4	5	5	8	10	20	50
48	Mike Washington	4	4	5	5	8	10	20	
49	Stan White	4	4	5	5	8	10	20	50
50	Dave Casper	4	4	5	5	8	10	20	

		VgEx 4	EX 5	ExMt 6	NM 7	NmMt 8	NmMt+ 8.5	MT 9	Gem 9.5/10
51	Len Hauss	4	4	5	5	8	10	20	
52	James Scott	4	4	5	5	8	10	20	50
53	Brian Sipe	4	4	5	5	8	10	20	50
54	Gary Shirk	4	4	5	5	8	10	20	50
55	Archie Griffin	4	4	5	5	8	10	15	60
56	Mike Patrick	4	4	5	5	8	10	20	50
57	Mario Clark	4	4	5	5	8	10	20	50
58	Jeff Siemon	4	4	5	5	8	10	20	50
59	Steve Mike-Mayer	4	4	5	5	8	10	20	50
60	Randy White	4	4	5	8	12	15	25	175
61	Darrell Austin	4	4	5	5	8	10	20	50
62	Tom Sullivan	4	4	5	5	8	10	20	40
63	Johnny Rodgers RC	4	4	5	5	15	20	30	
64	Ken Reaves	4	4	5	5	8	10	20	
65	Terry Bradshaw	4	5	5	10	15	20	60	
66	Fred Steinfort	4	4	5	5	8	10	20	
67	Curley Culp	4	4	5	5	8	10	20	50
68	Ted Hendricks	4	4	5	5	8	10	25	
69	Raymond Chester	4	4	5	5	8	10	20	
70	Jim Langer	4	4	5	5	8	10	20	50
71	Calvin Hill	4	4	5	5	8	10	20	50
72	Mike Hartenstine	4	4	5	5	8	10	20	40
73	Gerald Irons	4	4	5	5	8	10	50	
74	Billy Brooks	4	4	5	5	8	10	20	
75	John Mendenhall	4	4	5	5	8	10	20	50
76	Andy Johnson	4	4	5	5	8	10	20	50
77	Tom Wittum	4	4	5	5	8	10	20	
78	Lynn Dickey	4	4	5	5	8	10	20	60
79	Carl Eller	4	4	5	5	8	10	20	
80	Tom Mack	4	4	5	5	8	10	20	50
81	Clark Gaines	4	4	5	5	8	10	20	50
82	Lem Barney	4	4	5	5	8	10	20	50
83	Mike Montler	4	4	5	5	8	10	20	50
84	Jon Kolb	4	4	5	5	8	10	30	
85	Bob Chandler	4	4	5	5	8	10	20	
86	Robert Newhouse	4	4	5	5	8	10	25	
87	Frank LeMaster	4	4	5	5	8	10	25	50
88	Jeff West	4	4	5	5	8	10	20	50
89	Lyle Blackwood	4	4	5	5	8	10	20	
90	Gene Upshaw	4	4	5	5	8	10	40	
91	Frank Grant	4	4	5	5	8	10	20	50
92	Tom Hicks	4	4	5	5	8	10	20	50
93	Mike Pruitt	4	4	5	5	8	10	20	80
94	Chris Bahr	4	4	5	5	8	10	20	50
95	Russ Francis	4	4	5	5	8	10	20	
96	Norris Thomas	4	4	5	5	8	10	20	50
97	Gary Barbaro RC	4	4	5	5	8	10	20	
98	Jim Merlo	4	4	5	5	8	10	20	50
99	Karl Chandler	4	4	5	5	8	10	20	
100	Fran Tarkenton	4	4	5	8	12	15	30	
101	Abdul Salaam	4	4	5	5	8	10	20	50
102	Marv Kellum	4	4	5	5	8	10	20	50
103	Herman Weaver	4	4	5	5	8	10	20	
104	Roy Gerela	4	4	5	5	8	10	20	40
105	Harold Jackson	4	4	5	5	8	10	20	40
106	Dewey Selmon	4	4	5	5	8	10	20	40
107	Checklist 1-132	4	4	5	5	8	10	20	
108	Clarence Davis	4	4	5	5	8	10	20	
109	Robert Pratt	4	4	5	5	8	10	20	50
110	Harvey Martin	4	4	5	5	8	10	20	
111	Brad Dusek	4	4	5	5	8	10	20	50
112	Greg Latta	4	4	5	5	8	10	20	50
113	Tony Peters	4	4	5	5	8	10	20	50
114	Jim Braxton	4	4	5	5	8	10	20	50
115	Ken Riley	4	4	5	5	8	10	20	
116	Steve Nelson	4	4	5	5	8	10	25	50
117	Rick Upchurch	4	4	5	5	8	10	20	60
118	Spike Jones	4	4	5	5	8	10	20	50
119	Doug Kotar	4	4	5	5	8	10	20	60
120	Bob Griese	4	4	5	6	10	12	20	150
121	Burgess Owens	4	4	5	5	8	10	20	
122	Rolf Benirschke RC	4	4	5	5	8	10	20	
123	Haskel Stanback RC	4	4	5	5	8	10	20	
124	J.T. Thomas	4	4	5	5	8	10	20	60
125	Ahmad Rashad	4	4	5	5	8	10	20	50
126	Rick Kane	4	4	5	5	8	10	20	
127	Elvin Bethea	4	4	5	5	8	10	20	
128	Dave Dalby	4	4	5	5	8	10	20	
129	Mike Barnes	4	4	5	5	8	10	20	

#	Player	VgEx 4	EX 5	ExMt 6	NM 7	NmMt 8	NmMt+ 8.5	MT 9	Gem 9.5/10
130	Isiah Robertson	4	4	5	5	8	10	20	
131	Jim Plunkett	4	4	5	5	8	10	20	
132	Allan Ellis	4	4	5	5	8	10	20	40
133	Mike Bragg	4	4	5	5	8	10	20	
134	Bob Jackson	4	4	5	5	8	10	20	50
135	Coy Bacon	4	4	5	5	8	10	20	50
136	John Smith	4	4	5	5	8	10	20	50
137	Chuck Muncie	4	4	5	5	8	10	20	
138	Johnnie Gray	4	4	5	5	8	10	20	50
139	Jimmy Robinson	4	4	5	5	8	10	20	50
140	Tom Banks	4	4	5	5	8	10	20	
141	Marvin Powell RC	4	4	5	5	8	10	20	40
142	Jerrel Wilson	4	4	5	5	8	10	20	
143	Ron Howard	4	4	5	5	8	10	20	
144	Rob Lytle RC	4	4	5	5	8	10	20	50
145	L.C.Greenwood	4	4	5	5	10	12	25	50
146	Morris Owens	4	4	5	5	8	10	20	50
147	Joe Reed	4	4	5	5	8	10	20	
148	Mike Kadish	4	4	5	5	8	10	20	50
149	Phil Villapiano	4	4	5	5	8	10	20	100
150	Lydell Mitchell	4	4	5	5	8	10	20	50
151	Randy Logan	4	4	5	5	8	10	20	60
152	Mike Williams RC	4	4	5	5	8	10	20	
153	Jeff Van Note	4	4	5	5	8	10	20	50
154	Steve Schubert	4	4	5	5	8	10	20	50
155	Billy Kilmer	4	4	5	5	8	10	20	60
156	Boobie Clark	4	4	5	5	8	10	20	
157	Charlie Hall	4	4	5	5	8	10	20	
158	Raymond Clayborn RC	4	4	5	5	8	10	20	
159	Jack Gregory	4	4	5	5	8	10	20	50
160	Cliff Harris	4	4	5	5	8	10	20	50
161	Joe Fields	4	4	5	5	8	10	20	50
162	Don Nottingham	4	4	5	5	8	10	20	
163	Ed White	4	4	5	5	8	10	20	50
164	Toni Fritsch	4	4	5	5	8	10	20	50
165	Jack Lambert	4	4	5	10	12	15	25	150
166	NFC Champs/Staubach	4	4	5	5	8	10	25	
167	AFC Champs/Lytle	4	4	5	5	8	10	50	
168	Super Bowl XII/Dorsett	4	4	5	8	10	12	30	
169	Neal Colzie RC	4	4	5	5	8	10	20	
170	Cleveland Elam	4	4	5	5	8	10	20	
171	David Lee	4	4	5	5	8	10	20	50
172	Jim Otis	4	4	5	5	8	10	20	
173	Archie Manning	4	4	5	5	8	10	20	60
174	Jim Carter	4	4	5	5	8	10	20	50
175	Jean Fugett	4	4	5	5	8	10	20	
176	Willie Parker C	4	4	5	5	8	10	20	50
177	Haven Moses	4	4	5	5	8	10	20	50
178	Horace King RC	4	4	5	5	8	10	20	50
179	Bob Thomas	4	4	5	5	8	10	20	
180	Monte Jackson	4	4	5	5	8	10	20	50
181	Steve Zabel	4	4	5	5	8	10	20	
182	John Fitzgerald	4	4	5	5	8	10	20	
183	Mike Livingston	4	4	5	5	8	10	20	50
184	Larry Poole	4	4	5	5	8	10	20	50
185	Isaac Curtis	4	4	5	5	8	10	20	
186	Chuck Ramsey	4	4	5	5	8	10	20	
187	Bob Klein	4	4	5	5	8	10	20	50
188	Ray Rhodes	4	4	5	5	8	10	20	
189	Otis Sistrunk	4	4	5	5	8	10	20	
190	Bill Bergey	4	4	5	5	8	10	20	
191	Sherman Smith	4	4	5	5	8	10	20	
192	Dave Green	4	4	5	5	8	10	20	
193	Carl Mauck	4	4	5	5	8	10	20	50
194	Reggie Harrison	4	4	5	5	8	10	20	
195	Roger Carr	4	4	5	5	8	10	20	50
196	Steve Bartkowski	4	4	5	5	8	10	20	
197	Ray Wersching	4	4	5	5	8	10	20	60
198	Willie Buchanon	4	4	5	5	8	10	20	
199	Neil Clabo	4	4	5	5	8	10	20	
200	Walter Payton	5	6	12	20	40	50	200	800
201	Sam Adams OL	4	4	5	5	8	10	20	50
202	Larry Gordon	4	4	5	5	8	10	20	50
203	Pat Tilley	4	4	5	5	8	10	20	
204	Mack Mitchell	4	4	5	5	8	10	20	
205	Ken Anderson	4	4	5	5	8	10	30	
206	Scott Dierking	4	4	5	5	8	10	20	50
207	Jack Rudnay	4	4	5	5	8	10	20	
208	Jim Stienke	4	4	5	5	8	10	20	
209	Bill Simpson	4	4	5	5	8	10	20	50
210	Errol Mann	4	4	5	5	8	10	20	80
211	Bucky Dilts	4	4	5	5	8	10	20	50
212	Reuben Gant	4	4	5	5	8	10	20	50
213	Thomas Henderson RC	4	4	5	5	8	10	20	
214	Steve Furness	4	4	5	5	8	10	100	
215	John Riggins	4	4	5	5	8	10	20	
216	Keith Krepfle RC	4	4	5	5	8	10	20	60
217	Fred Dean RC	4	5	6	10	40	50	100	1,500
218	Emanuel Zanders	4	4	5	5	8	10	20	50
219	Don Testerman	4	4	5	5	8	10	20	60
220	George Kunz	4	4	5	5	8	10	20	
221	Darryl Stingley	4	4	5	5	8	10	20	
222	Ken Sanders	4	4	5	5	8	10	20	50
223	Gary Huff	4	4	5	5	8	10	20	40
224	Gregg Bingham	4	4	5	5	8	10	20	
225	Jerry Sherk	4	4	5	5	8	10	20	50
226	Doug Plank	4	4	5	5	8	10	20	40
227	Ed Taylor	4	4	5	5	8	10	20	
228	Emery Moorehead	4	4	5	5	8	10	20	
229	Reggie Williams RC	4	4	5	5	8	10	20	60
230	Claude Humphrey	4	4	5	5	8	10	20	
231	Randy Cross RC	4	4	5	5	10	12	25	
232	Jim Hart	4	4	5	5	8	10	20	50
233	Bobby Bryant	4	4	5	5	8	10	20	
234	Larry Brown	4	4	5	5	8	10	20	40
235	Mark Van Eeghen	4	4	5	5	8	10	20	
236	Terry Hermeling	4	4	5	5	8	10	20	
237	Steve Odom	4	4	5	5	8	10	20	
238	Jan Stenerud	4	4	5	5	8	10	20	
239	Andre Tillman	4	4	5	5	8	10	20	50
240	Tom Jackson RC	4	4	5	8	12	15	30	150
241	Ken Mendenhall	4	4	5	5	8	10	20	
242	Tim Fox	4	4	5	5	8	10	20	60
243	Don Herrmann	4	4	5	5	8	10	20	
244	Eddie McMillan	4	4	5	5	8	10	20	50
245	Greg Pruitt	4	4	5	5	8	10	20	60
246	J.K. McKay	4	4	5	5	8	10	20	40
247	Larry Keller	4	4	5	5	8	10	20	
248	Dave Jennings	4	4	5	5	8	10	20	40
249	Bo Harris	4	4	5	5	8	10	20	40
250	Revie Sorey	4	4	5	5	8	10	20	50
251	Tony Greene	4	4	5	5	8	10	20	
252	Butch Johnson	4	4	5	5	8	10	20	
253	Paul Naumoff	4	4	5	5	8	10	20	50
254	Rickey Young	4	4	5	5	8	10	20	50
255	Dwight White	4	4	5	5	8	10	20	
256	Joe Lavender	4	4	5	5	8	10	20	
257	Checklist 133-264	4	4	5	5	8	10	20	
258	Ronnie Coleman	4	4	5	5	8	10	20	50
259	Charlie Smith WR	4	4	5	5	8	10	20	40
260	Ray Guy	4	4	5	5	8	10	20	
261	David Taylor	4	4	5	5	8	10	20	50
262	Bill Lenkaitis	4	4	5	5	8	10	20	50
263	Jim Mitchell TE	4	4	5	5	8	10	20	50
264	Delvin Williams	4	4	5	5	8	10	20	40
265	Jack Youngblood	4	4	5	5	8	10	20	
266	Chuck Crist	4	4	5	5	8	10	20	50
267	Richard Todd	4	4	5	5	8	10	20	50
268	Dave Logan RC	4	4	5	5	8	10	20	50
269	Rufus Mayes	4	4	5	5	8	10	20	
270	Brad Van Pelt	4	4	5	5	8	10	20	40
271	Chester Marcol	4	4	5	5	8	10	20	40
272	J.V. Cain	4	4	5	5	8	10	20	40
273	Larry Seiple	4	4	5	5	8	10	20	
274	Brent McClanahan	4	4	5	5	8	10	20	
275	Mike Wagner	4	4	5	5	8	10	30	80
276	Diron Talbert	4	4	5	5	8	10	20	
277	Brian Baschnagel	4	4	5	5	8	10	20	40
278	Ed Podolak	4	4	5	5	8	10	20	50
279	Don Goode	4	4	5	5	8	10	20	40
280	John Dutton	4	4	5	5	8	10	20	40
281	Don Calhoun	4	4	5	5	8	10	20	40
282	Monte Johnson	4	4	5	5	8	10	20	
283	Ron Jessie	4	4	5	5	8	10	20	
284	Jon Morris	4	4	5	5	8	10	20	50
285	Riley Odoms	4	4	5	5	8	10	20	50
286	Marv Bateman	4	4	5	5	8	10	20	50
287	Joe Klecko RC	4	4	5	5	8	10	25	

#	Player	VgEx 4	EX 5	ExMt 6	NM 7	NmMt 8	NmMt+ 8.5	MT 9	Gem 9.5/10
288	Oliver Davis	4	4	5	5	8	10	20	
289	John McDaniel	4	4	5	5	8	10	20	
290	Roger Staubach	4	5	6	20	150	200	250	
291	Brian Kelley	4	4	5	5	8	10	20	
292	Mike Hogan	4	4	5	5	8	10	20	
293	John Leypoldt	4	4	5	5	8	10	20	
294	Jack Novak	4	4	5	5	8	10	20	
295	Joe Greene	4	4	5	5	10	12	30	
296	John Hill	4	4	5	5	8	10	20	50
297	Danny Buggs	4	4	5	5	8	10	20	50
298	Ted Albrecht	4	4	5	5	8	10	20	
299	Nelson Munsey	4	4	5	5	8	10	20	
300	Chuck Foreman	4	4	5	5	8	10	20	60
301	Dan Pastorini	4	4	5	5	8	10	20	50
302	Tommy Hart	4	4	5	5	8	10	20	40
303	Dave Beverly	4	4	5	5	8	10	20	60
304	Tony Reed RC	4	4	5	5	8	10	20	50
305	Cliff Branch	4	4	5	5	8	10	20	
306	Clarence Duren	4	4	5	5	8	10	20	40
307	Randy Rasmussen	4	4	5	5	8	10	20	
308	Oscar Roan	4	4	5	5	8	10	20	60
309	Lenvil Elliott	4	4	5	5	8	10	20	50
310	Dan Dierdorf	4	4	5	5	8	10	20	
311	Johnny Perkins	4	4	5	5	8	10	20	
312	Rafael Septien RC	4	4	5	5	8	10	20	50
313	Terry Beeson	4	4	5	5	8	10	20	50
314	Lee Roy Selmon	4	4	5	5	8	10	20	
315	Tony Dorsett RC	10	15	25	60	100	150	500	
316	Greg Landry	4	4	5	5	8	10	20	50
317	Jake Scott	4	4	5	5	8	10	20	40
318	Dan Peiffer	4	4	5	5	8	10	20	
319	John Bunting	4	4	5	5	8	10	20	
320	John Stallworth RC	5	6	8	12	50	60	150	1,000
321	Bob Howard	4	4	5	5	8	10	20	40
322	Larry Little	4	4	5	5	8	10	20	50
323	Reggie McKenzie	4	4	5	5	8	10	20	
324	Duane Carrell	4	4	5	5	8	10	20	
325	Ed Simonini	4	4	5	5	8	10	20	
326	John Vella	4	4	5	5	8	10	20	
327	Wesley Walker RC	4	4	5	6	10	12	25	200
328	Jon Keyworth	4	4	5	5	8	10	20	40
329	Ron Bolton	4	4	5	5	8	10	20	40
330	Tommy Casanova	4	4	5	5	8	10	20	
331	R.Staubach/B.Griese LL	4	4	5	8	12	15	30	
332	A.Rashad/Mitchell LL	4	4	5	5	8	10	30	
333	W.Payton/VanEeghenLL	4	4	5	6	10	12	50	
334	W.Payton/E.Mann LL	4	4	5	6	10	12	40	
335	Interception Leaders	4	4	5	5	8	10	20	
336	Punting Leaders	4	4	5	5	8	10	30	
337	Robert Brazile	4	4	5	5	8	10	20	50
338	Charlie Joiner	4	4	5	5	8	10	20	
339	Joe Ferguson	4	4	5	5	8	10	20	40
340	Bill Thompson	4	4	5	5	8	10	20	40
341	Sam Cunningham	4	4	5	5	8	10	20	50
342	Curtis Johnson	4	4	5	5	8	10	20	
343	Jim Marshall	4	4	5	5	8	10	20	100
344	Charlie Sanders	4	4	5	5	8	10	20	40
345	Willie Hall	4	4	5	5	8	10	20	
346	Pat Haden	4	4	5	5	8	10	20	100
347	Jim Bakken	4	4	5	5	8	10	20	40
348	Bruce Taylor	4	4	5	5	8	10	20	
349	Barty Smith	4	4	5	5	8	10	20	50
350	Drew Pearson	4	4	5	5	8	10	20	
351	Mike Webster	4	4	5	6	10	12	25	
352	Bobby Hammond	4	4	5	5	8	10	20	100
353	Dave Mays	4	4	5	5	8	10	20	40
354	Pat McInally	4	4	5	5	8	10	20	
355	Toni Linhart	4	4	5	5	8	10	20	
356	Larry Hand	4	4	5	5	8	10	20	50
357	Ted Fritsch Jr.	4	4	5	5	8	10	20	
358	Larry Marshall	4	4	5	5	8	10	20	50
359	Waymond Bryant	4	4	5	5	8	10	20	
360	Louie Kelcher RC	4	4	5	5	8	10	20	
361	Stanley Morgan RC	4	4	5	5	8	12	30	200
362	Bruce Harper RC	4	4	5	5	8	10	20	50
363	Bernard Jackson	4	4	5	5	8	10	20	40
364	Walter White	4	4	5	5	8	10	20	50
365	Ken Stabler	4	4	5	8	12	15	25	150
366	Fred Dryer	4	4	5	5	8	10	20	50

#	Player	VgEx 4	EX 5	ExMt 6	NM 7	NmMt 8	NmMt+ 8.5	MT 9	Gem 9.5/10
367	Ike Harris	4	4	5	5	8	10	20	40
368	Norm Bulaich	4	4	5	5	8	10	20	
369	Merv Krakau	4	4	5	5	8	10	20	
370	John James	4	4	5	5	8	10	20	
371	Bennie Cunningham RC	4	4	5	5	8	10	20	
372	Doug Van Horn	4	4	5	5	8	10	20	40
373	Thom Darden	4	4	5	5	8	10	20	40
374	Eddie Edwards RC	4	4	5	5	8	10	20	
375	Mike Thomas	4	4	5	5	8	10	20	
376	Fred Cook	4	4	5	5	8	10	20	50
377	Mike Phipps	4	4	5	5	8	10	20	
378	Paul Krause	4	4	5	5	8	10	20	60
379	Harold Carmichael	4	4	5	5	8	10	20	60
380	Mike Haynes	4	4	5	5	8	10	20	
381	Wayne Morris	4	4	5	5	8	10	20	
382	Greg Buttle	4	4	5	5	8	10	20	50
383	Jim Zorn	4	4	5	5	8	10	20	50
384	Jack Dolbin	4	4	5	5	8	10	20	40
385	Charlie Waters	4	4	5	5	8	10	20	50
386	Dan Ryczek	4	4	5	5	8	10	20	40
387	Joe Washington RC	4	4	5	5	8	10	20	50
388	Checklist 265-396	4	4	5	5	8	10	25	40
389	James Hunter	4	4	5	5	8	10	20	40
390	Billy Johnson	4	4	5	5	8	10	20	
391	Jim Allen RC	4	4	5	5	8	10	20	40
392	George Buehler	4	4	5	5	8	10	20	
393	Harry Carson	4	4	5	5	8	10	20	60
394	Cleo Miller	4	4	5	5	8	10	20	40
395	Gary Burley	4	4	5	5	8	10	20	
396	Mark Moseley	4	4	5	5	8	10	20	
397	Virgil Livers	4	4	5	5	8	10	20	40
398	Joe Ehrmann	4	4	5	5	8	10	20	40
399	Freddie Solomon	4	4	5	5	8	10	20	
400	O.J.Simpson	4	4	5	8	12	15	25	
401	Julius Adams	4	4	5	5	8	10	20	40
402	Artimus Parker	4	4	5	5	8	10	20	40
403	Gene Washington 49er	4	4	5	5	8	10	20	
404	Herman Edwards	4	4	5	5	8	10	20	80
405	Craig Morton	4	4	5	5	8	10	20	60
406	Alan Page	4	4	5	5	8	10	20	50
407	Larry McCarren	4	4	5	5	8	10	20	
408	Tony Galbreath	4	4	5	5	8	10	20	40
409	Roman Gabriel	4	4	5	5	8	10	20	60
410	Efren Herrera	4	4	5	5	8	10	30	60
411	Jim Smith RC	4	4	5	5	8	10	20	50
412	Bill Bryant	4	4	5	5	8	10	20	
413	Doug Dieken	4	4	5	5	8	10	20	50
414	Marvin Cobb	4	4	5	5	8	10	20	40
415	Fred Biletnikoff	4	4	5	5	8	10	20	
416	Joe Theismann	4	4	5	6	10	12	20	80
417	Roland Harper	4	4	5	5	8	10	20	50
418	Derrel Luce	4	4	5	5	8	10	20	50
419	Ralph Perretta	4	4	5	5	8	10	20	40
420	Louis Wright RC	4	4	5	5	8	10	20	
421	Prentice McCray	4	4	5	5	8	10	20	40
422	Garry Puetz	4	4	5	5	8	10	20	40
423	Alfred Jenkins RC	4	4	5	5	8	10	20	
424	Paul Seymour	4	4	5	5	8	10	20	50
425	Garo Yepremian	4	4	5	5	8	10	20	50
426	Emmitt Thomas	4	4	5	5	8	10	15	50
427	Dexter Bussey	4	4	5	5	8	10	20	40
428	John Sanders	4	4	5	5	8	10	20	40
429	Ed Too Tall Jones	4	4	5	5	8	10	40	
430	Ron Yary	4	4	5	5	8	10	20	60
431	Frank Lewis	4	4	5	5	8	10	20	40
432	Jerry Golsteyn	4	4	5	5	8	10	20	
433	Clarence Scott	4	4	5	5	8	10	20	60
434	Pete Johnson RC	4	4	5	5	8	10	20	80
435	Charle Young	4	4	5	5	8	10	20	40
436	Harold McLinton	4	4	5	5	8	10	20	
437	Noah Jackson	4	4	5	5	8	10	20	40
438	Bruce Laird	4	4	5	5	8	10	20	40
439	John Matuszak	4	4	5	5	8	10	20	50
440	Nat Moore	4	4	5	5	8	10	20	125
441	Leon Gray	4	4	5	5	8	10	20	100
442	Jerome Barkum	4	4	5	5	8	10	20	
443	Steve Largent	4	5	6	20	25	30	40	300
444	John Zook	4	4	5	5	8	10	20	60
445	Preston Pearson	4	4	5	5	8	10	20	50

#	Player	VgEx 4	EX 5	ExMt 6	NM 7	NmMt 8	NmMt+ 8.5	MT 9	Gem 9.5/10
446	Conrad Dobler	4	4	5	5	8	10	20	40
447	Wilbur Summers	4	4	5	5	8	10	20	40
448	Lou Piccone	4	4	5	5	8	10	20	50
449	Ron Jaworski	4	4	5	5	8	10	20	60
450	Jack Ham	4	4	5	5	8	10	25	80
451	Mick Tingelhoff	4	4	5	5	8	10	20	
452	Clyde Powers	4	4	5	5	8	10	20	
453	John Cappelletti	4	4	5	5	8	10	20	40
454	Dick Ambrose	4	4	5	5	8	10	20	
455	Lemar Parrish	4	4	5	5	8	10	20	50
456	Ron Saul	4	4	5	5	8	10	20	
457	Bob Parsons	4	4	5	5	8	10	20	50
458	Glenn Doughty	4	4	5	5	8	10	20	
459	Don Woods	4	4	5	5	8	10	20	50
460	Art Shell	4	4	5	5	8	10	25	
461	Sam Hunt	4	4	5	5	8	10	20	40
462	Lawrence Pillers	4	4	5	5	8	10	20	
463	Henry Childs	4	4	5	5	8	10	20	40
464	Roger Wehrli	4	4	5	5	8	10	30	
465	Otis Armstrong	4	4	5	5	8	10	20	80
466	Bob Baumhower RC	4	4	5	5	12	15	25	
467	Ray Jarvis	4	4	5	5	8	10	20	40
468	Guy Morriss	4	4	5	5	8	10	20	40
469	Matt Blair	4	4	5	5	8	10	20	50
470	Billy Joe DuPree	4	4	5	5	8	10	20	
471	Roland Hooks	4	4	5	5	8	10	20	40
472	Joe Danelo	4	4	5	5	8	10	20	
473	Reggie Rucker	4	4	5	5	8	10	20	
474	Vern Holland	4	4	5	5	8	10	20	50
475	Mel Blount	4	4	5	5	8	10	25	
476	Eddie Brown S	4	4	5	5	8	10	20	
477	Bo Rather	4	4	5	5	8	10	20	
478	Don McCauley	4	4	5	5	8	10	20	40
479	Glen Walker	4	4	5	5	8	10	20	40
480	Randy Gradishar	4	4	5	5	8	12	25	50
481	Dave Rowe	4	4	5	5	8	10	20	
482	Pat Leahy	4	4	5	5	8	10	20	50
483	Mike Fuller	4	4	5	5	8	10	20	40
484	David Lewis RC	4	4	5	5	8	10	20	
485	Steve Grogan	4	4	5	5	8	10	20	50
486	Mel Gray	4	4	5	5	8	10	20	
487	Eddie Payton RC	4	4	5	5	8	10	20	
488	Checklist 397-528	4	4	5	5	8	10	20	60
489	Stu Voigt	4	4	5	5	8	10	20	50
490	Rolland Lawrence	4	4	5	5	8	10	20	100
491	Nick Mike-Mayer	4	4	5	5	8	10	20	40
492	Troy Archer	4	4	5	5	8	10	20	50
493	Benny Malone	4	4	5	5	8	10	20	40
494	Golden Richards	4	4	5	5	8	12	80	
495	Chris Hanburger	4	4	5	5	8	10	20	80
496	Dwight Harrison	4	4	5	5	8	10	20	
497	Gary Fencik RC	4	4	5	5	8	10	20	80
498	Rich Saul	4	4	5	5	8	10	20	50
499	Dan Fouts	4	4	5	8	12	15	25	
500	Franco Harris	4	4	5	8	12	15	25	150
501	Atlanta Falcons TL	4	4	5	5	8	10	20	40
502	Baltimore Colts TL	4	4	5	5	8	10	20	
503	Bills TL/O.J.Simpson	4	4	5	5	8	10	25	
504	Bears TL/W.Payton	4	4	5	5	8	10	40	
505	Bengals TL/Reg.Williams	4	4	5	5	8	10	25	
506	Cleveland Browns TL	4	4	5	5	8	10	25	
507	Cowboys TL/T.Dorsett	4	4	5	6	10	12	25	
508	Denver Broncos TL	4	4	5	5	8	10	20	
509	Detroit Lions TL	4	4	5	5	8	10	20	
510	Green Bay Packers TL	4	4	5	5	8	10	20	50
511	Houston Oilers TL	4	4	5	5	8	10	20	50
512	Kansas City Chiefs TL	4	4	5	5	8	10	20	60
513	Los Angeles Rams TL	4	4	5	5	8	10	20	50
514	Miami Dolphins TL	4	4	5	5	8	10	20	50
515	Minnesota Vikings TL	4	4	5	5	8	10	20	60
516	New England Patriots TL	4	4	5	5	8	10	20	50
517	New Orleans Saints TL	4	4	5	5	8	10	20	
518	New York Giants TL	4	4	5	5	8	10	20	60
519	Jets TL/Wesley Walker	4	4	5	5	8	10	20	
520	Oakland Raiders TL	4	4	5	5	8	10	20	60
521	Philadelphia Eagles TL	4	4	5	5	8	10	20	
522	Steelers TL/Harris/Blount	4	4	5	5	8	10	50	
523	St.Louis Cardinals TL	4	4	5	5	8	10	20	40
524	San Diego Chargers TL	4	4	5	5	8	10	20	50
525	San Francisco 49ers TL	4	4	5	5	8	10	20	
526	Seahawks TL/S.Largent	4	4	5	5	8	10	25	
527	Tampa Bay Bucs TL	4	4	5	5	8	10	20	50
528	Redskins TL/Ken Houston	4	4	5	5	12	15	35	60

— Terry Bradshaw #65 PSA 10 (Gem) sold for $577 (Andy Madec; 5/07)
— Terry Bradshaw #65 PSA 10 (Gem) sold for $1,331 (Goodwin; 11/12)
— Fred Dean RC #217 PSA 10 (Gem) sold for $2910 (eBay; 09/14)
— Tony Dorsett #315 PSA 10 (Gem) sold for $4500 (eBay; 1/08)
— Tony Dorsett #315 PSA 10 (Gem) sold for $3825.01 (eBay; 5/12)
— Tony Dorsett #315 PSA 10 (Gem) sold for $6520 (eBay; 09/14)
— Tony Dorsett #315 PSA 10 (Gem) sold for $16,661 (eBay; 07/16)
— Joe Greene #295 PSA 10 (Gem) sold for $575 (eBay; 10/14)
— Roger Staubach #290 PSA 10 (Gem) sold for $812.31 (eBay; 3/14)
— Roger Staubach #290 PSA 10 (Gem) sold for $908 (Mile High; 4/14)

1979 Topps

#	Player	VgEx 4	EX 5	ExMt 6	NM 7	NmMt 8	NmMt+ 8.5	MT 9	Gem 9.5/10
1	Staubach/Bradshaw LL	4	4	5	8	12	15	50	400
2	S.Largent/R.Young LL	4	4	5	5	8	10	20	50
3	E.Campbell/W.Payton LL	4	4	5	6	10	12	30	175
4	F.Corral/P.Leahy LL	4	4	5	5	8	10	20	
5	Buchanon/Stone/Darden LL	4	4	5	5	8	10	20	40
6	T.Skladany/P.McInally LL	4	4	5	5	8	10	20	40
7	Johnny Perkins	4	4	5	5	8	10	20	
8	Charles Phillips	4	4	5	5	8	10	20	
9	Derrel Luce	4	4	5	5	8	10	20	50
10	John Riggins	4	4	5	5	8	10	20	
11	Chester Marcol	4	4	5	5	8	10	20	40
12	Bernard Jackson	4	4	5	5	8	10	20	
13	Dave Logan	4	4	5	5	8	10	20	50
14	Bo Harris	4	4	5	5	8	10	20	
15	Alan Page	4	4	5	5	8	10	20	50
16	John Smith	4	4	5	5	8	10	20	
17	Dwight McDonald	4	4	5	5	8	10	20	40
18	John Cappelletti	4	4	5	5	8	10	20	
19	Steelers TL/Harris/Dungy	4	4	5	8	12	15	25	
20A	Bill Bergey	4	4	5	5	8	10	20	80
21	Jerome Barkum	4	4	5	5	8	10	20	60
22	Larry Csonka	4	4	5	5	8	10	25	80
23	Joe Ferguson	4	4	5	5	8	10	30	50
24	Ed Too Tall Jones	4	4	5	5	8		40	
25	Dave Jennings	4	4	5	5	8	10	20	
26	Horace King	4	4	5	5	8	10	20	40
27	Steve Little	4	4	5	5	8	10	20	50
28	Morris Bradshaw	4	4	5	5	8	10	20	
29	Joe Ehrmann	4	4	5	5	8	10	20	60
30	Ahmad Rashad	4	4	5	5	8	10	20	
31	Joe Lavender	4	4	5	5	8	10	20	50
32	Dan Neal	4	4	5	5	8	10	20	
33	Johnny Evans	4	4	5	5	8	10	20	40
34	Pete Johnson	4	4	5	5	8	10	20	
35	Mike Haynes	4	4	5	5	8	10	20	50
36	Tim Mazzetti	4	4	5	5	8	10	20	40
37	Mike Barber RC	4	4	5	5	8	10	20	
38	49ers TL/O.J.Simpson	4	4	5	5	8	10	20	50
39	Bill Gregory	4	4	5	5	8	10	20	50
40	Randy Gradishar	4	4	5	5	8	10	20	80
41	Richard Todd	4	4	5	5	8	10	20	60
42	Henry Marshall	4	4	5	5	8	10	20	
43	John Hill	4	4	5	5	8	10	20	
44	Sidney Thornton	4	4	5	5	8	10	20	
45	Ron Jessie	4	4	5	5	8	10	20	40
46	Bob Baumhower	4	4	5	5	8	10	30	
47	Johnnie Gray	4	4	5	5	8	10	20	40
48	Doug Williams RC	4	4	5	6	10	12	30	400
49	Don McCauley	4	4	5	5	8	10	20	
50	Ray Guy	4	4	5	5	8	10	20	
51	Bob Klein	4	4	5	5	8	10	20	40
52	Golden Richards	4	4	5	5	8	10	20	
53	Mark Miller QB	4	4	5	5	8	10	20	
54	John Sanders	4	4	5	5	8	10	20	
55	Gary Burley	4	4	5	5	8	10	20	
56	Steve Nelson	4	4	5	5	8	10	20	
57	Buffalo Bills TL	4	4	5	5	8	10	20	40
58	Bobby Bryant	4	4	5	5	8	10	20	
59	Rick Kane	4	4	5	5	8	10	20	
60	Larry Little	4	4	5	5	8	10	20	
61	Ted Fritsch Jr.	4	4	5	5	8	10	20	
62	Larry Mallory	4	4	5	5	8	10	20	

#	Name	VgEx 4	EX 5	ExMt 6	NM 7	NmMt 8	NmMt+ 8.5	MT 9	Gem 9.5/10
63	Marvin Powell	4	4	5	5	8	10	20	
64	Jim Hart	4	4	5	5	8	10	20	40
65	Joe Greene	4	4	5	5	8	10	30	150
66	Walter White	4	4	5	5	8	10	20	40
67	Gregg Bingham	4	4	5	5	8	10	20	40
68	Errol Mann	4	4	5	5	8	10	20	
69	Bruce Laird	4	4	5	5	8	10	20	
70	Drew Pearson	4	4	5	5	8	10	20	60
71	Steve Bartkowski	4	4	5	5	8	10	20	40
72	Ted Albrecht	4	4	5	5	8	10	20	40
73	Charlie Hall	4	4	5	5	8	10	20	40
74	Pat McInally	4	4	5	5	8	10	20	
75	Bubba Baker RC	4	4	5	5	8	10	20	
76	New England Pats TL	4	4	5	5	8	10	20	40
77	Steve DeBerg RC	4	4	5	5	8	10	25	60
78	John Yarno	4	4	5	5	8	10	20	40
79	Stu Voigt	4	4	5	5	8	10	20	
80	Frank Corral AP	4	4	5	5	8	10	20	50
81	Troy Archer	4	4	5	5	8	10	20	
82	Bruce Harper	4	4	5	5	8	10	20	
83	Tom Jackson	4	4	5	5	8	10	20	50
84	Larry Brown	4	4	5	5	8	10	20	
85A	Wilbert Montgomery RC	4	4	5	5	8	10	25	
86	Butch Johnson	4	4	5	5	8	10	20	
87	Mike Kadish	4	4	5	5	8	10	20	40
88	Ralph Perretta	4	4	5	5	8	10	20	40
89	David Lee	4	4	5	5	8	10	20	40
90	Mark Van Eeghen	4	4	5	5	8	10	20	
91	John McDaniel	4	4	5	5	8	10	20	
92	Gary Fencik	4	4	5	5	8	10	20	40
93	Mack Mitchell	4	4	5	5	8	10	20	
94	Cincinnati Bengals TL	4	4	5	5	8	10	20	60
95	Steve Grogan	4	4	5	5	8	10	20	
96	Garo Yepremian	4	4	5	5	8	10	20	40
97	Barty Smith	4	4	5	5	8	10	20	40
98	Frank Reed	4	4	5	5	8	10	20	40
99	Jim Clack	4	4	5	5	8	10	20	
100	Chuck Foreman	4	4	5	5	8	10	20	
101	Joe Klecko	4	4	5	5	8	10	20	
102	Pat Tilley	4	4	5	5	8	10	20	80
103	Conrad Dobler	4	4	5	5	8	10	20	
104	Craig Colquitt	4	4	5	5	8	10	20	
105	Dan Pastorini	4	4	5	5	8	10	20	40
106	Rod Perry AP	4	4	5	5	8	10	20	40
107	Nick Mike-Mayer	4	4	5	5	8	10	20	40
108	John Matuszak	4	4	5	5	8	10	20	
109	David Taylor	4	4	5	5	8	10	20	40
110	Billy Joe DuPree	4	4	5	5	8	10	20	80
111	Harold McLinton	4	4	5	5	8	10	20	
112	Virgil Livers	4	4	5	5	8	10	20	
113	Cleveland Browns TL	4	4	5	5	8	10	20	
114	Checklist 1-132	4	4	5	5	8	10	20	
115	Ken Anderson	4	4	5	5	8	10	20	60
116	Bill Lenkaitis	4	4	5	5	8	10	20	40
117	Bucky Dilts	4	4	5	5	8	10	20	40
118	Tony Greene	4	4	5	5	8	10	20	
119	Bobby Hammond	4	4	5	5	8	10	20	
120	Nat Moore	4	4	5	5	8	10	20	40
121	Pat Leahy	4	4	5	5	8	10	20	
122	James Harris	4	4	5	5	8	10	20	
123	Lee Roy Selmon	4	4	5	5	8	10	20	
124	Bennie Cunningham	4	4	5	5	8	10	20	40
125	Matt Blair AP	4	4	5	5	8	10	20	
126	Jim Allen	4	4	5	5	8	10	20	40
127	Alfred Jenkins	4	4	5	5	8	10	20	
128	Arthur Whittington	4	4	5	5	8	10	20	
129	Norm Thompson	4	4	5	5	8	10	20	
130	Pat Haden	4	4	5	5	8	10	20	40
131	Freddie Solomon	4	4	5	5	8	10	20	40
132	Bears TL/W.Payton	4	4	5	5	8	10	30	
133	Mark Moseley	4	4	5	5	8	10	20	
134	Cleo Miller	4	4	5	5	8	10	20	
135	Ross Browner RC	4	4	5	5	8	10	20	50
136	Don Calhoun	4	4	5	5	8	10	20	40
137	David Whitehurst	4	4	5	5	8	10	20	200
138	Terry Beeson	4	4	5	5	8	10	20	40
139	Ken Stone	4	4	5	5	8	10	20	
140	Brad Van Pelt AP	4	4	5	5	8	10	20	
141	Wesley Walker	4	4	5	5	8	10	20	50
142	Jan Stenerud	4	4	5	5	8	10	20	
143	Henry Childs	4	4	5	5	8	10	20	
144	Otis Armstrong	4	4	5	5	8	10	20	
145	Dwight White	4	4	5	5	8	10	25	
146	Steve Wilson	4	4	5	5	8	10	20	
147	Tom Skladany RC	4	4	5	5	8	10	20	40
148	Lou Piccone	4	4	5	5	8	10	20	40
149	Monte Johnson	4	4	5	5	8	10	30	
150	Joe Washington	4	4	5	5	8	10	20	
151	Eagles TL/W.Montgomery	4	4	5	5	8	10	20	40
152	Fred Dean	4	4	5	5	8	20	50	
153	Rolland Lawrence	4	4	5	5	8	10	20	
154	Brian Baschnagel	4	4	5	5	8	10	20	
155	Joe Theismann	4	4	5	5	8	10	25	80
156	Marvin Cobb	4	4	5	5	8	10	20	
157	Dick Ambrose	4	4	5	5	8	10	20	
158	Mike Patrick	4	4	5	5	8	10	20	
159	Gary Shirk	4	4	5	5	8	10	20	
160	Tony Dorsett	4	5	6	20	30	40	50	250
161	Greg Buttle	4	4	5	5	8	10	20	
162	A.J. Duhe	4	4	5	5	8	10	20	50
163	Mick Tingelhoff	4	4	5	5	8	10	20	
164	Ken Burrough	4	4	5	5	8	10	20	40
165	Mike Wagner	4	4	5	5	8	10	30	
166	AFC Champs/F.Harris	4	4	5	5	8	10	20	60
167	NFC Championship	4	4	5	5	8	10	20	50
168	Super Bowl XIII/Harris	4	4	5	5	8	10	20	100
169	Raiders TL/T.Hendricks	4	4	5	5	8	10	20	40
170	O.J.Simpson	4	4	5	5	8	10	40	120
171	Doug Nettles	4	4	5	5	8	10	20	40
172	Dan Dierdorf	4	4	5	5	8	10	20	
173	Dave Beverly	4	4	5	5	8	10	20	
174	Jim Zorn	4	4	5	5	8	10	20	40
175	Mike Thomas	4	4	5	5	8	10	20	40
176	John Outlaw	4	4	5	5	8	10	20	
177	Jim Turner	4	4	5	5	8	10	20	
178	Freddie Scott	4	4	5	5	8	10	20	50
179	Mike Phipps	4	4	5	5	8	10	20	
180	Jack Youngblood	4	4	5	5	8	10	20	
181	Sam Hunt	4	4	5	5	8	10	20	
182	Tony Hill RC	4	4	5	5	8	12	60	250
183	Gary Barbaro	4	4	5	5	8	10	20	
184	Archie Griffin	4	4	5	5	8	10	20	40
185	Jerry Sherk	4	4	5	5	8	10	20	40
186	Bobby Jackson	4	4	5	5	8	10	20	40
187	Don Woods	4	4	5	5	8	10	20	60
188	New York Giants TL	4	4	5	5	8	10	20	
189	Raymond Chester	4	4	5	5	8	10	20	50
190	Joe DeLamielleure AP	4	4	5	5	8	10	20	50
191	Tony Galbreath	4	4	5	5	8	10	20	
192	Robert Brazile AP	4	4	5	5	8	10	20	
193	Neil O'Donoghue	4	4	5	5	8	10	20	
194	Mike Webster	4	4	5	5	8	10	40	150
195	Ed Simonini	4	4	5	5	8	10	20	40
196	Benny Malone	4	4	5	5	8	10	20	
197	Tom Wittum	4	4	5	5	8	10	20	
198	Steve Largent	4	4	5	6	10	12	25	125
199	Tommy Hart	4	4	5	5	8	10	20	50
200	Fran Tarkenton	4	4	5	5	8	10	25	
201	Leon Gray AP	4	4	5	5	8	10	20	40
202	Leroy Harris	4	4	5	5	8	10	20	40
203	Eric Williams LB	4	4	5	5	8	10	20	
204	Thom Darden AP	4	4	5	5	8	10	20	40
205	Ken Riley	4	4	5	5	8	10	20	
206	Clark Gaines	4	4	5	5	8	10	20	40
207	Kansas City Chiefs TL	4	4	5	5	8	10	20	
208	Joe Danelo	4	4	5	5	8	10	20	
209	Glen Walker	4	4	5	5	8	10	20	
210	Art Shell	4	4	5	5	8	10	40	
211	Jon Keyworth	4	4	5	5	8	10	20	40
212	Herman Edwards	4	4	5	5	8	10	20	40
213	John Fitzgerald	4	4	5	5	8	10	20	
214	Jim Smith	4	4	5	5	8	10	20	60
215	Coy Bacon	4	4	5	5	8	10	20	40
216	Dennis Johnson RC	4	4	5	5	8	10	20	
217	John Jefferson RC	4	4	5	5	8	10	30	
218	Gary Weaver	4	4	5	5	8	10	20	
219	Tom Blanchard	4	4	5	5	8	10	20	
220	Bert Jones	4	4	5	5	8	10	20	
221	Stanley Morgan	4	4	5	5	8	10	20	50
222	James Hunter	4	4	5	5	8	10	20	40

#	Name	VgEx 4	EX 5	ExMt 6	NM 7	NmMt 8	NmMt+ 8.5	MT 9	Gem 9.5/10
223	Jim O'Bradovich	4	4	5	5	8	10	20	40
224	Carl Mauck	4	4	5	5	8	10	20	40
225	Chris Bahr	4	4	5	5	8	10	20	
226	Jets TL/W.Walker	4	4	5	5	8	10	20	60
227	Roland Harper	4	4	5	5	8	10	20	50
228	Randy Dean	4	4	5	5	8	10	20	40
229	Bob Jackson	4	4	5	5	8	10	20	40
230	Sammie White	4	4	5	5	8	10	20	
231	Mike Dawson	4	4	5	5	8	10	20	
232	Checklist 133-264	4	4	5	5	8	10	20	40
233	Ken MacAfee RC	4	4	5	5	8	10	20	
234	Jon Kolb AP	4	4	5	5	8	10	30	80
235	Willie Hall	4	4	5	5	8	10	20	
236	Ron Saul AP	4	4	5	5	8	10	20	
237	Haskel Stanback	4	4	5	5	8	10	20	
238	Zenon Andrusyshyn	4	4	5	5	8	10	20	
239	Norris Thomas	4	4	5	5	8	10	20	
240	Rick Upchurch	4	4	5	5	8	10	20	
241	Robert Pratt	4	4	5	5	8	10	20	40
242	Julius Adams	4	4	5	5	8	10	20	
243	Rich McGeorge	4	4	5	5	8	10	20	40
244	Seahawks TL/S.Largent	4	4	5	5	8	10	20	100
245	Blair Bush RC	4	4	5	5	8	10	20	
246	Billy Johnson	4	4	5	5	8	10	20	40
247	Randy Rasmussen	4	4	5	5	8	10	20	40
248	Brian Kelley	4	4	5	5	8	10	20	40
249	Mike Pruitt	4	4	5	5	8	10	20	100
250	Harold Carmichael	4	4	5	5	8	10	25	50
251	Mike Hartenstine	4	4	5	5	8	10	20	
252	Robert Newhouse	4	4	5	5	8	10	20	
253	Gary Danielson RC	4	4	5	5	8	10	20	50
254	Mike Fuller	4	4	5	5	8	10	20	
255	L.C.Greenwood	4	4	5	5	8	10	20	
256	Lemar Parrish	4	4	5	5	8	10	20	
257	Ike Harris	4	4	5	5	8	10	20	
258	Ricky Bell RC	4	4	5	5	8	10	20	
259	Willie Parker C	4	4	5	5	8	10	20	
260	Gene Upshaw	4	4	5	5	8	10	30	60
261	Glenn Doughty	4	4	5	5	8	10	20	
262	Steve Zabel	4	4	5	5	8	10	30	
263	Atlanta Falcons TL	4	4	5	5	8	10	20	
264	Ray Wersching	4	4	5	5	8	10	20	40
265	Lawrence McCutcheon	4	4	5	5	8	10	20	
266	Willie Buchanon AP	4	4	5	5	8	10	20	40
267	Matt Robinson	4	4	5	5	8	10	20	40
268	Reggie Rucker	4	4	5	5	8	10	20	40
269	Doug Van Horn	4	4	5	5	8	10	20	
270	Lydell Mitchell	4	4	5	5	8	10	20	
271	Vern Holland	4	4	5	5	8	10	20	40
272	Eason Ramson	4	4	5	5	8	10	20	40
273	Steve Towle	4	4	5	5	8	10	20	
274	Jim Marshall	4	4	5	5	8	10	20	40
275	Mel Blount	4	4	5	5	8	10	20	80
276	Bob Kuziel	4	4	5	5	8	10	20	
277	James Scott	4	4	5	5	8	10	20	40
278	Tony Reed	4	4	5	5	8	10	20	40
279	Dave Green	4	4	5	5	8	10	20	40
280	Toni Linhart	4	4	5	5	8	10	20	40
281	Andy Johnson	4	4	5	5	8	10	20	
282	Los Angeles Rams TL	4	4	5	5	8	10	20	40
283	Phil Villapiano	4	4	5	5	8	10	20	
284	Dexter Bussey	4	4	5	5	8	10	20	
285	Craig Morton	4	4	5	5	8	10	20	
286	Guy Morriss	4	4	5	5	8	10	20	40
287	Lawrence Pillers	4	4	5	5	8	10	20	
288	Gerald Irons	4	4	5	5	8	10	20	40
289	Scott Perry	4	4	5	5	8	10	20	40
290	Randy White	4	4	5	5	8	10	50	
291	Jack Gregory	4	4	5	5	8	10	20	
292	Bob Chandler	4	4	5	5	8	10	20	50
293	Rich Szaro	4	4	5	5	8	10	20	40
294	Sherman Smith	4	4	5	5	8	10	20	40
295	Tom Banks AP	4	4	5	5	8	10	20	40
296	Revie Sorey AP	4	4	5	5	8	10	30	
297	Ricky Thompson	4	4	5	5	8	10	20	
298	Ron Yary	4	4	5	5	8	10	20	40
299	Lyle Blackwood	4	4	5	5	8	10	20	
300	Franco Harris	4	4	5	5	8	10	30	200
301	Oilers TL/E.Campbell	4	4	5	5	8	10	25	
302	Scott Bull	4	4	5	5	8	10	40	
303	Dewey Selmon	4	4	5	5	8	10	20	40
304	Jack Rudnay	4	4	5	5	8	10	20	40
305	Fred Biletnikoff	4	4	5	5	8	10	25	
306	Jeff West	4	4	5	5	8	10	20	
307	Shafer Suggs	4	4	5	5	8	10	20	
308	Ozzie Newsome RC	5	6	8	30	50	60	300	400
309	Boobie Clark	4	4	5	5	8	10	20	50
310	James Lofton RC	5	6	8	15	30	40	150	
311	Joe Pisarcik	4	4	5	5	8	10	20	
312	Bill Simpson AP	4	4	5	5	8	10	20	40
313	Haven Moses	4	4	5	5	8	10	20	40
314	Jim Merlo	4	4	5	5	8	10	20	40
315	Preston Pearson	4	4	5	5	8	10	20	
316	Larry Tearry	4	4	5	5	8	10	20	40
317	Tom Dempsey	4	4	5	5	8	10	20	
318	Greg Latta	4	4	5	5	8	10	20	
319	Redskins TL/J.Riggins	4	4	5	5	8	10	20	
320	Jack Ham	4	4	5	5	8	10	20	100
321	Harold Jackson	4	4	5	5	8	10	20	
322	George Roberts	4	4	5	5	8	10	20	
323	Ron Jaworski	4	4	5	5	8	10	20	150
324	Jim Otis	4	4	5	5	8	10	20	
325	Roger Carr	4	4	5	5	8	10	20	40
326	Jack Tatum	4	4	5	5	8	10	20	
327	Derrick Gaffney	4	4	5	5	8	10	20	
328	Reggie Williams	4	4	5	5	8	10	20	
329	Doug Dieken	4	4	5	5	8	10	20	
330	Efren Herrera	4	4	5	5	8	10	20	
331	Earl Campbell RB	4	4	5	6	10	12	30	150
332	Tony Galbreath RB	4	4	5	5	8	10	20	40
333	Bruce Harper RB	4	4	5	5	8	10	20	40
334	John James RB	4	4	5	5	8	10	15	40
335	Walter Payton RB	4	4	5	5	8	10	25	
336	Rickey Young RB	4	4	5	5	8	10	20	
337	Jeff Van Note	4	4	5	5	8	10	20	40
338	Chargers TL/J.Jefferson	4	4	5	5	8	10	20	
339	Stan Walters RC	4	4	5	5	8	10	20	
340	Louis Wright	4	4	5	5	8	10	20	50
341	Horace Ivory	4	4	5	5	8	10	20	50
342	Andre Tillman	4	4	5	5	8	10	20	40
343	Greg Coleman RC	4	4	5	5	8	10	20	40
344	Doug English RC	4	4	5	5	8	10	20	
345	Ted Hendricks	4	4	5	5	8	10	20	
346	Rich Saul	4	4	5	5	8	10	20	40
347	Mel Gray	4	4	5	5	8	10	20	60
348	Toni Fritsch	4	4	5	5	8	10	20	40
349	Cornell Webster	4	4	5	5	8	10	20	
350	Ken Houston	4	4	5	5	8	10	20	
351	Ron Johnson DB RC	4	4	5	5	8	10	20	40
352	Doug Kotar	4	4	5	5	8	10	20	50
353	Brian Sipe	4	4	5	5	8	10	20	50
354	Billy Brooks	4	4	5	5	8	10	20	
355	John Dutton	4	4	5	5	8	10	20	
356	Don Goode	4	4	5	5	8	10	20	
357	Detroit Lions TL	4	4	5	5	8	10	20	
358	Reuben Gant	4	4	5	5	8	10	20	40
359	Bob Parsons	4	4	5	5	8	10	20	40
360	Cliff Harris	4	4	5	5	8	10	40	
361	Raymond Clayborn	4	4	5	5	8	10	20	40
362	Scott Dierking	4	4	5	5	8	10	20	40
363	Bill Bryan	4	4	5	5	8	10	20	
364	Mike Livingston	4	4	5	5	8	10	20	40
365	Otis Sistrunk	4	4	5	5	8	10	20	
366	Charle Young	4	4	5	5	8	10	20	
367	Keith Wortman	4	4	5	5	8	10	20	40
368	Checklist 265-396	4	4	5	5	8	10	20	
369	Mike Michel	4	4	5	5	8	10	20	
370	Delvin Williams AP	4	4	5	5	8	10	20	40
371	Steve Furness	4	4	5	5	8	10	20	
372	Emery Moorehead	4	4	5	5	8	10	20	
373	Clarence Scott	4	4	5	5	8	10	20	40
374	Rufus Mayes	4	4	5	5	8	10	20	
375	Chris Hanburger	4	4	5	5	8	10	20	
376	Baltimore Colts TL	4	4	5	5	8	10	20	
377	Bob Avellini	4	4	5	5	8	10	20	
378	Jeff Siemon	4	4	5	5	8	10	20	50
379	Roland Hooks	4	4	5	5	8	10	20	
380	Russ Francis	4	4	5	5	8	10	20	60
381	Roger Wehrli	4	4	5	5	8	10	20	40
382	Joe Fields	4	4	5	5	8	10	20	

#	Player	VgEx 4	EX 5	ExMt 6	NM 7	NmMt 8	NmMt+ 8.5	MT 9	Gem 9.5/10
383	Archie Manning	4	4	5	5	8	10	20	
384	Rob Lytle	4	4	5	5	8	10	20	40
385	Thomas Henderson	4	4	5	5	8	10	80	
386	Morris Owens	4	4	5	5	8	10	20	
387	Dan Fouts	4	4	5	5	8	10	25	80
388	Chuck Crist	4	4	5	5	8	10	20	
389	Ed O'Neil	4	4	5	5	8	10	20	
390	Earl Campbell RC	10	12	20	30	60	80	350	2,000
391	Randy Grossman	4	4	5	5	8	10	20	
392	Monte Jackson	4	4	5	5	8	10	20	
393	John Mendenhall	4	4	5	5	8	10	20	
394	Miami Dolphins TL	4	4	5	5	8	10	20	
395	Isaac Curtis	4	4	5	5	8	10	20	40
396	Mike Bragg	4	4	5	5	8	10	20	
397	Doug Plank	4	4	5	5	8	10	20	
398	Mike Barnes	4	4	5	5	8	10	20	
399	Calvin Hill	4	4	5	5	8	10	20	40
400	Roger Staubach	4	5	6	10	20	30	50	
401	Doug Beaudoin	4	4	5	5	8	10	20	
402	Chuck Ramsey	4	4	5	5	8	10	20	40
403	Mike Hogan	4	4	5	5	8	10	20	
404	Mario Clark	4	4	5	5	8	10	20	40
405	Riley Odoms	4	4	5	5	8	10	20	40
406	Carl Eller	4	4	5	5	8	10	20	50
407	Packers TL/J.Lofton	4	4	5	5	8	10	20	
408	Mark Arneson	4	4	5	5	8	10	20	
409	Vince Ferragamo RC	4	4	5	5	8	10	20	
410	Cleveland Elam	4	4	5	5	8	10	20	
411	Donnie Shell RC	4	4	5	8	15	20	120	
412	Ray Rhodes	4	4	5	5	8	10	20	40
413	Don Cockroft	4	4	5	5	8	10	20	40
414	Don Bass	4	4	5	5	8	10	20	
415	Cliff Branch	4	4	5	5	8	10	20	
416	Diron Talbert	4	4	5	5	8	10	20	60
417	Tom Hicks	4	4	5	5	8	10	20	40
418	Roosevelt Leaks	4	4	5	5	8	10	20	
419	Charlie Joiner	4	4	5	5	8	10	20	80
420	Lyle Alzado	4	4	5	5	8	10	20	60
421	Sam Cunningham	4	4	5	5	8	10	20	
422	Larry Keller	4	4	5	5	8	10	20	50
423	Jim Mitchell TE	4	4	5	5	8	10	20	
424	Randy Logan	4	4	5	5	8	10	20	40
425	Jim Langer	4	4	5	5	8	10	20	
426	Gary Green	4	4	5	5	8	10	20	
427	Luther Blue	4	4	5	5	8	10	20	
428	Dennis Johnson	4	4	5	5	8	10	20	
429	Danny White	4	4	5	5	8	10	20	
430	Roy Gerela	4	4	5	5	8	10	20	
431	Jimmy Robinson	4	4	5	5	8	10	20	
432	Minnesota Vikings TL	4	4	5	5	8	10	60	
433	Oliver Davis	4	4	5	5	8	10	20	40
434	Lenvil Elliott	4	4	5	5	8	10	20	
435	Willie Miller RC	4	4	5	5	8	10	20	40
436	Brad Dusek	4	4	5	5	8	10	20	
437	Bob Thomas	4	4	5	5	8	10	20	
438	Ken Mendenhall	4	4	5	5	8	10	20	
439	Clarence Davis	4	4	5	5	8	10	20	40
440	Bob Griese	4	4	5	5	8	10	25	50
441	Tony McGee DT	4	4	5	5	8	10	20	40
442	Ed Taylor	4	4	5	5	8	10	20	40
443	Ron Howard	4	4	5	5	8	10	20	
444	Wayne Morris	4	4	5	5	8	10	20	
445	Charlie Waters	4	4	5	5	8	10	20	
446	Rick Danmeier	4	4	5	5	8	10	20	
447	Paul Naumoff	4	4	5	5	8	10	20	40
448	Keith Krepfle	4	4	5	5	8	10	20	
449	Rusty Jackson	4	4	5	5	8	10	20	40
450	John Stallworth	4	4	5	5	8	10	25	
451	New Orleans Saints TL	4	4	5	5	8	10	20	
452	Ron Mikolajczyk	4	4	5	5	8	10	20	40
453	Fred Dryer	4	4	5	5	8	10	20	40
454	Jim LeClair	4	4	5	5	8	10	20	
455	Greg Pruitt	4	4	5	5	8	10	20	40
456	Jake Scott	4	4	5	5	8	10	20	
457	Steve Schubert	4	4	5	5	8	10	20	
458	George Kunz	4	4	5	5	8	10	20	
459	Mike Williams	4	4	5	5	8	10	20	40
460	Dave Casper AP	4	4	5	5	8	10	40	
461	Sam Adams OL	4	4	5	5	8	10	20	40
462	Abdul Salaam	4	4	5	5	8	10	20	40

#	Player	VgEx 4	EX 5	ExMt 6	NM 7	NmMt 8	NmMt+ 8.5	MT 9	Gem 9.5/10
463	Terdell Middleton	4	4	5	5	8	10	20	40
464	Mike Wood	4	4	5	5	8	10	20	40
465	Bill Thompson AP	4	4	5	5	8	10	20	40
466	Larry Gordon	4	4	5	5	8	10	20	
467	Benny Ricardo	4	4	5	5	8	10	20	40
468	Reggie McKenzie	4	4	5	5	8	10	20	
469	Cowboys TL/T.Dorsett	4	4	5	5	8	10	25	
470	Rickey Young	4	4	5	5	8	10	20	
471	Charlie Smith WR	4	4	5	5	8	10	20	
472	Al Dixon	4	4	5	5	8	10	20	
473	Tom DeLeone	4	4	5	5	8	10	20	
474	Louis Breeden	4	4	5	5	8	10	20	
475	Jack Lambert	4	4	5	5	8	10	30	175
476	Terry Hermeling	4	4	5	5	8	10	20	
477	J.K. McKay	4	4	5	5	8	10	20	
478	Stan White	4	4	5	5	8	10	20	40
479	Terry Nelson	4	4	5	5	8	10	20	40
480	Walter Payton	5	6	12	20	35	40	125	
481	Dave Dalby	4	4	5	5	8	10	20	50
482	Burgess Owens	4	4	5	5	8	10	20	
483	Rolf Benirschke	4	4	5	5	8	10	20	40
484	Jack Dolbin	4	4	5	5	8	10	20	
485	John Hannah	4	4	5	5	8	10	20	
486	Checklist 397-528	4	4	5	5	8	10	50	
487	Greg Landry	4	4	5	5	8	10	20	50
488	St. Louis Cardinals TL	4	4	5	5	8	10	20	
489	Paul Krause	4	4	5	5	8	10	20	50
490	John James	4	4	5	5	8	10	20	40
491	Merv Krakau	4	4	5	5	8	10	20	
492	Dan Doornink	4	4	5	5	8	10	20	
493	Curtis Johnson	4	4	5	5	8	10	20	
494	Rafael Septien	4	4	5	5	8	10	40	
495	Jean Fugett	4	4	5	5	8	10	20	40
496	Frank LeMaster	4	4	5	5	8	10	20	
497	Allan Ellis	4	4	5	5	8	10	20	40
498	Billy Waddy RC	4	4	5	5	8	10	20	
499	Hank Bauer	4	4	5	5	8	10	20	
500	Terry Bradshaw	4	5	6	10	15	20	40	400
501	Larry McCarren	4	4	5	5	8	10	20	40
502	Fred Cook	4	4	5	5	8	10	20	
503	Chuck Muncie	4	4	5	5	8	10	20	80
504	Herman Weaver	4	4	5	5	8	10	20	40
505	Eddie Edwards	4	4	5	5	8	10	20	40
506	Tony Peters	4	4	5	5	8	10	20	40
507	Denver Broncos TL	4	4	5	5	8	10	20	40
508	Jimbo Elrod	4	4	5	5	8	10	20	
509	David Hill	4	4	5	5	8	10	20	
510	Harvey Martin	4	4	5	5	8	10	20	
511	Terry Miller	4	4	5	5	8	10	20	40
512	June Jones RC	4	4	5	5	8	10	20	50
513	Randy Cross	4	4	5	5	8	10	20	40
514	Duriel Harris	4	4	5	5	8	10	20	40
515	Harry Carson	4	4	5	5	8	10	20	
516	Tim Fox	4	4	5	5	8	10	20	
517	John Zook	4	4	5	5	8	10	20	
518	Bob Tucker	4	4	5	5	8	10	20	40
519	Kevin Long RC	4	4	5	5	8	10	20	
520	Ken Stabler	4	4	5	6	10	12	50	
521	John Bunting	4	4	5	5	8	10	20	
522	Rocky Bleier	4	4	5	5	8	10	20	
523	Noah Jackson	4	4	5	5	8	10	20	100
524	Cliff Parsley	4	4	5	5	8	10	20	
525	Louie Kelcher AP	4	4	5	5	8	10	20	50
526	Bucs TL/R.Bell	4	4	5	5	8	10	20	
527	Bob Brudzinski RC	4	4	5	5	8	10	20	
528	Danny Buggs	4	4	5	5	8	10	15	

— James Lofton #310 PSA 10 (Gem Mt) sold for $1,660 (eBay; 10/11)
— James Lofton #310 PSA 10 (Gem Mt) sold for $2,338 (eBay; 1/13)
— Wilbert Montgomery RC #85 PSA 10 (Gem Mint) sold for $519 (eBay: 6/12)
— Walter Payton #480 PSA 10 (Gem Mt) sold for $1,022 (eBay: 4/08)
— Walter Payton #480 PSA 10 (Gem Mt) sold for $905 (eBay: 7/09)
— Walter Payton #480 PSA 10 (Gem Mint) sold for $1869 (eBay: 6/12)
— Walter Payton #480 PSA 10 (Gem Mint) sold for $1350 (Bussineau; 6/12)
— Walter Payton RB #335 PSA 10 (Gem Mint) sold for $769 (eBay: 6/12)
— Roger Staubach #400 PSA 10 (Gem Mint) sold for $530 (eBay: 6/12)
— Roger Staubach #400 PSA 10 (Gem Mint) sold for $497.32 (eBay: 3/14)

FOOTBALL
1980 - Present

FOOTBALL

1980 Topps

		NmMt 8	NmMt+ 8.5	MT 9	Gem 9.5/10
160	Walter Payton	35	40	100	500
170	Ottis Anderson RC	10	12	20	250
195	Lester Hayes RC	25	30	80	350
200	Terry Bradshaw	15	20	30	400
225	Phil Simms RC	30	40	100	400
330	Tony Dorsett	10	12	30	150
418	Clay Matthews RC	15	20	30	100

— Terry Bradshaw #200 PSA 10 (Gem) sold for $1,003 (eBay; 4/08)

1981 Topps

		NmMt 8	NmMt+ 8.5	MT 9	Gem 9.5/10
100	Billy Sims RC	10	12	30	150
150	Kellen Winslow RC	12	15	40	200
194	Art Monk RC	40	50	60	400
202	Walter Payton SA	10	12	25	
216	Joe Montana RC	600	800	2,500	14,000
316	Dan Hampton RC	15	20	80	225
375	Terry Bradshaw	12	15	25	120
400	Walter Payton	25	30	80	400
422	Dwight Clark RC	25	30	40	
500	Tony Dorsett	10	12	20	60

— Joe Montana #216 BGS 9.5 (GemMt) typically sells for $2,500-$3,500

1982 Topps

		NmMt 8	NmMt+ 8.5	MT 9	Gem 9.5/10
44	Cris Collinsworth RC	10	12	25	60
51	Anthony Munoz RC	15	20	40	200
196	Matt Millen RC	6	8	12	25
204	Terry Bradshaw	10	12	25	80
257	J.Montana/Anderson LL	10	12	20	50
302	Walter Payton	20	25	50	200
303	Walter Payton IA	10	12	20	80
434	Lawrence Taylor RC	60	80	200	1,200
435	Lawrence Taylor IA	10	12	25	125
486	Ronnie Lott RC	60	80	100	400
487	Ronnie Lott IA	10	12	20	80
488	Joe Montana	20	35	50	150
489	Joe Montana IA	10	12	20	100

1983 Topps

		NmMt 8	NmMt+ 8.5	MT 9	Gem 9.5/10
4	Joe Montana RB	8	10	20	80
33	Jim McMahon RC	25	30	40	100
36	Walter Payton	10	12	30	150
38	Mike Singletary RC	50	60	100	350
133	Lawrence Taylor	8	10	15	40
169	Joe Montana DP	12	15	35	400
190	Joe Jacoby RC	12	15	40	200
294	Marcus Allen RC DP	25	30	50	400
356	Gary Anderson K RC DP	6	8	15	60
358	Terry Bradshaw DP	10	12	20	60

1984 Topps

		NmMt 8	NmMt+ 8.5	MT 9	Gem 9.5/10
63	John Elway RC	200	250	800	3,000
98	Marcus Allen	8	10	15	60
111	Howie Long RC	40	50	80	350
120	Mark Duper PB RC	8	10	15	60
123	Dan Marino RC	60	80	200	1,400
124	Dan Marino IR	12	15	30	100
129	Dwight Stephenson RC	8	12	30	120
143	Andre Tippett RC	8	12	25	

1984 Topps (continued)

		NmMt 8	NmMt+ 8.5	MT 9	Gem 9.5/10
162	Terry Bradshaw	8	10	20	60
202	D.Marino/Bartkow. LL	8	10	15	80
228	Walter Payton	25	35	150	
280	Eric Dickerson RC	30	40	80	800
286	Jackie Slater RC	8	10	20	150
300	Morten Andersen RC	8	10	20	150
353	Roger Craig RC	10	12	50	400
358	Joe Montana	15	20	35	250
359	Joe Montana IR	8	10	20	120
380	Darrell Green RC	25	30	40	250
381	Russ Grimm PB RC	8	10	25	80

— John Elway #63 BGS 10 (Pristine) sold for $3,615 (eBay; 3/08)
— John Elway #63 BGS 10 (Pristine) sold for $2,924 (eBay; 4/08)
— John Elway #63 in BGS 9.5 (Gem) typically sells for $250-$500
— Dan Marino #123 BGS 10 (Pristine) sold for $2,555 (eBay; 4/08)
— Dan Marino #123 BGS 10 (Pristine) sold for $1,637 (eBay; 8/08)
— Dan Marino #123 BGS 10 (Pristine) sold for $1,040 (eBay; 11/08)
— Dan Marino #123 in BGS 9.5 (Gem) typically sells for $250-$500
— Walter Payton #228 PSA 10 (Gem) sold for $1398 (eBay; 08/14)
— Walter Payton #228 PSA 10 (Gem) sold for $570 (eBay; 11/06)
— Dwight Stephenson #129 PSA 10 (Gem) sold for $2,610 (eBay; 4/07)

1984 Topps USFL

		NmMt 8	NmMt+ 8.5	MT 9	Gem 9.5/10
36	Jim Kelly XRC	250	300	400	1,200
52	Steve Young XRC	400	500	1,000	3,000
58	Reggie White XRC	150	▲400	▲600	
59	Anthony Carter XRC	12	15	40	
74	Herschel Walker XRC	100	125	▲400	
76	Marcus Dupree XRC	25	30		

— Herschel Walker #74 PSA 10 (Gem Mt) sold for $565 (eBay; 1/08)

1985 Topps

		NmMt 8	NmMt+ 8.5	MT 9	Gem 9.5/10
4	Dan Marino RB	10	12	25	200
24	Richard Dent RC	12	20	125	
33	Walter Payton	30	40	200	
80	Henry Ellard RC	8	10	20	150
157	Joe Montana	15	20	50	500
192	D.Marino/Montana LL	15	20	30	300
238	John Elway	15	25	80	
251	Warren Moon RC	▲40	▲50	80	500
253	Mike Munchak RC	15	20	50	
308	Mark Clayton AP RC	8	10	30	
314	Dan Marino	15	20	40	500
325	Irving Fryar RC	10	12	40	150
328	Craig James RC	8	10	30	

— Walter Payton #33 PSA 10 (Gem) sold for $2420 (eBay; 07/14)

1985 Topps USFL

		NmMt 8	NmMt+ 8.5	MT 9	Gem 9.5/10
45	Jim Kelly	20	25	50	150
49	Gary Clark XRC	10	12	25	80
65	Steve Young	30	35	60	300
75	Reggie White	20	25	40	150
80	Doug Flutie XRC	▲50	▲60	▲80	200
86	Herschel Walker	10	12	25	80
105	Marcus Dupree	12	15		

1986 Topps

		NmMt 8	NmMt+ 8.5	MT 9	Gem 9.5/10
11	Walter Payton	15	20	40	300
45	Dan Marino	10	12	30	400
112	John Elway	10	12	30	500
156	Joe Montana	15	20	60	1,000

1986 Topps (continued)

		NmMt 8	NmMt+ 8.5	MT 9	Gem 9.5/10
161	Jerry Rice RC	▲400	500	1,000	5,000
187	Bernie Kosar RC	10	12	40	200
255	Boomer Esiason RC	10	12	50	400
275	Reggie White RC	▲50	▲60	▲200	400
374	Steve Young RC	▲150	▲200	500	
388	Andre Reed RC	10	20	40	300
389	Bruce Smith RC	15	20	100	600

— Jerry Rice #161 BGS 9.5 (Gem Mt) typically sell for $1,800-$3,000
— Steve Young #374 BGS 9.5 (Gem Mt) sold for $1,350 (Mile High; 3/09)

1987 Topps

		NmMt 8	NmMt+ 8.5	MT 9	Gem 9.5/10
31	John Elway	8	10	15	60
45	Doug Flutie RC	10	12	25	80
46	Walter Payton	10	12	30	150
112	Joe Montana	10	12	25	60
115	Jerry Rice	15	20	25	80
125	Charles Haley RC	8	10	20	120
207	Gary Zimmerman RC	10	12	25	100
233	Dan Marino	8	10	15	60
264	Herschel Walker RC	8	10	15	40
296	Randall Cunningham RC	10	12	30	200
301	Reggie White	8	10	20	50
362	Jim Kelly RC	25	30	40	150
384	Steve Young	8	10	20	60

1988 Topps

		NmMt 8	NmMt+ 8.5	MT 9	Gem 9.5/10
23	John Elway	8	10	15	50
38	Joe Montana	8	10	15	50
43	Jerry Rice	6	8	12	30
144	Brian Bosworth RC	8	10	20	50
157	Chris Doleman RC	10	12	20	50
190	Dan Marino	8	10	15	30
327	Bo Jackson RC	50	60	80	400
352	Vinny Testaverde RC	8	10	20	50

1989 Pro Set

		NmMt 8	NmMt+ 8.5	MT 9	Gem 9.5/10
32	Thurman Thomas RC	8	10	12	30
89	Michael Irvin RC	8	10	12	35
183	Tim Brown RC	8	10	12	30
314	Cris Carter RC	8	10	12	30
486	Deion Sanders RC	8	10	12	30
490	Troy Aikman RC	15	20	30	80
494	Barry Sanders RC	15	20	25	80
498	Derrick Thomas RC	8	10	12	40

1989 Score Supplemental

		NmMt 8	NmMt+ 8.5	MT 9	Gem 9.5/10
333S	Sterling Sharpe RC	8	10	20	40
384S	Bo Jackson FB/BB	8	10	20	50
408S	Dermontti Dawson RC	8	10	15	50

1989 Topps

		NmMt 8	NmMt+ 8.5	MT 9	Gem 9.5/10
45	Thurman Thomas RC	8	10	12	30
121	Cris Carter RC	8	10	12	40
265	Tim Brown RC	8	10	12	40
383	Michael Irvin RC	8	10	12	40

1989 Topps Traded

		NmMt 8	NmMt+ 8.5	MT 9	Gem 9.5/10
30T	Deion Sanders RC	6	8	12	25
54T	Randall McDaniel RC	6	8	10	20

	NmMt 8	NmMt+ 8.5	MT 9	Gem 9.5/10
70T Troy Aikman RC	8	10	15	50
83T Barry Sanders RC	8	10	20	80
90T Derrick Thomas RC	6	8	10	20

1990 Action Packed Rookie Update

	NmMt 8	NmMt+ 8.5	MT 9	Gem 9.5/10
34 Emmitt Smith RC UER	50	60	80	1,000
38 Junior Seau RC	8	10	15	50

1990 Fleer Update

	NmMt 8	NmMt+ 8.5	MT 9	Gem 9.5/10
U40 Emmitt Smith RC	40	50	100	▼300
U102 Junior Seau RC	8	10	12	30

1990 Pro Set

	NmMt 8	NmMt+ 8.5	MT 9	Gem 9.5/10
673 Junior Seau RC	6	8	12	40
685 Emmitt Smith RC	12	15	20	60
800O Emmitt Smith/(Offensive ROY)	5	6	10	30

1990 Score Supplemental

	NmMt 8	NmMt+ 8.5	MT 9	Gem 9.5/10
65T Junior Seau	10	12	15	30
101T Emmitt Smith RC	▼100	▼125	250	▼2,500

1990 Topps

	NmMt 8	NmMt+ 8.5	MT 9	Gem 9.5/10
381 Junior Seau RC	6	8	15	40

1990 Topps Traded

	NmMt 8	NmMt+ 8.5	MT 9	Gem 9.5/10
27T Emmitt Smith RC	40	50	100	▼150
28T Junior Seau	5	6	8	25

1991 Action Packed Rookie Update

	NmMt 8	NmMt+ 8.5	MT 9	Gem 9.5/10
21 Brett Favre RC	8	10	40	▲125

1991 Pacific

	NmMt 8	NmMt+ 8.5	MT 9	Gem 9.5/10
551 Brett Favre RC	8	10	20	30

1991 Pro Set

	NmMt 8	NmMt+ 8.5	MT 9	Gem 9.5/10
762 Brett Favre RC	12	15	25	50
835 John Randle RC	10	12	20	30

1991 Pro Set Platinum

	NmMt 8	NmMt+ 8.5	MT 9	Gem 9.5/10
290 Brett Favre RC	10	12	20	40

1991 Stadium Club

	NmMt 8	NmMt+ 8.5	MT 9	Gem 9.5/10
94 Brett Favre RC UER	50	60	100	▼800

— Brett Favre #94 BGS 10 (Pristine) sold for $1,030 (eBay; 8/08)
— Brett Favre #94 BGS 10 (Pristine) sold for $1,000 (eBay; 2/09)

1991 Star Pics

	NmMt 8	NmMt+ 8.5	MT 9	Gem 9.5/10
55 Brett Favre	6	8	15	25

1991 Star Pics Autographs

	NmMt 8	NmMt+ 8.5	MT 9	Gem 9.5/10
55 Brett Favre	175	200	250	400

1991 Ultra

	NmMt 8	NmMt+ 8.5	MT 9	Gem 9.5/10
283 Brett Favre RC	20	25	40	100

1991 Ultra Update

	NmMt 8	NmMt+ 8.5	MT 9	Gem 9.5/10
U1 Brett Favre	12	15	25	100

1991 Upper Deck

	NmMt 8	NmMt+ 8.5	MT 9	Gem 9.5/10
13 Brett Favre RC	10	12	20	60
647 Brett Favre	8	10	15	30

1991 Wild Card Draft

	NmMt 8	NmMt+ 8.5	MT 9	Gem 9.5/10
119 Brett Favre	8	10	20	50

1992 Stadium Club

	NmMt 8	NmMt+ 8.5	MT 9	Gem 9.5/10
683 Brett Favre	100	125	150	500

— Brett Favre #683 BGS 10 (Pristine) sold for $1,946 (eBay; 8/08)

1992 Topps

	NmMt 8	NmMt+ 8.5	MT 9	Gem 9.5/10
696 Brett Favre	8	10	20	40

1992 Topps Gold

	NmMt 8	NmMt+ 8.5	MT 9	Gem 9.5/10
696 Brett Favre	25	30	250	300

1993 Action Packed

	NmMt 8	NmMt+ 8.5	MT 9	Gem 9.5/10
163 Drew Bledsoe RC	10	12	25	50
172 Jerome Bettis RC	10	12	25	50

1993 Bowman

	NmMt 8	NmMt+ 8.5	MT 9	Gem 9.5/10
264 Jerome Bettis RC	12	15	25	40
280 Drew Bledsoe RC FOIL	12	15	25	50

1993 Playoff

	NmMt 8	NmMt+ 8.5	MT 9	Gem 9.5/10
294 Jerome Bettis RC	10	12	20	▲50

1993 Playoff Contenders

	NmMt 8	NmMt+ 8.5	MT 9	Gem 9.5/10
124 Jerome Bettis RC	10	12	20	30

1993 Power Update Prospects

	NmMt 8	NmMt+ 8.5	MT 9	Gem 9.5/10
3 Trent Green RC	8	10	12	40
9 Jerome Bettis RC	8	10	12	40

1993 Select

	NmMt 8	NmMt+ 8.5	MT 9	Gem 9.5/10
166 Drew Bledsoe RC	6	8	10	20
172 Jerome Bettis RC	10	12	20	40

1993 SkyBox Premium

	NmMt 8	NmMt+ 8.5	MT 9	Gem 9.5/10
62 Jerome Bettis RC	10	12	20	35

1993 SP

	NmMt 8	NmMt+ 8.5	MT 9	Gem 9.5/10
6 Jerome Bettis RC	▲60	▲80	▲200	▲2,000
9 Drew Bledsoe RC	▲40	▲50	▲80	200
91 Mark Brunell RC	10	12	20	40
259 John Lynch RC	10	12	20	40

1993 Stadium Club

	NmMt 8	NmMt+ 8.5	MT 9	Gem 9.5/10
108 Jerome Bettis RC	10	12	20	40
280A Drew Bledsoe RC ERR	8	10	15	30
280B Drew Bledsoe RC COR	8	10	15	30

1993 Topps

	NmMt 8	NmMt+ 8.5	MT 9	Gem 9.5/10
130 Drew Bledsoe RC	8	10	15	30
166 Jerome Bettis RC	10	12	20	40

1993 Upper Deck

	NmMt 8	NmMt+ 8.5	MT 9	Gem 9.5/10
20 Jerome Bettis RC	10	12	15	25

1993 Upper Deck Rookie Exchange

	NmMt 8	NmMt+ 8.5	MT 9	Gem 9.5/10
RE2 Drew Bledsoe UER	8	10	15	25
RE7 Jerome Bettis	10	12	20	30

1994 Bowman

	NmMt 8	NmMt+ 8.5	MT 9	Gem 9.5/10
2 Marshall Faulk RC	15	20	40	120
68 Isaac Bruce RC	12	15	50	▼150

1994 Collector's Choice

	NmMt 8	NmMt+ 8.5	MT 9	Gem 9.5/10
14 Marshall Faulk RC	6	8	12	30

1994 Fleer Rookie Exchange

	NmMt 8	NmMt+ 8.5	MT 9	Gem 9.5/10
3 Marshall Faulk	15	20	30	100

1994 Pinnacle

	NmMt 8	NmMt+ 8.5	MT 9	Gem 9.5/10
198 Marshall Faulk RC	8	10	15	40

1994 Playoff

	NmMt 8	NmMt+ 8.5	MT 9	Gem 9.5/10
300 Larry Allen RC	25	40	200	500

1994 Playoff Contenders

	NmMt 8	NmMt+ 8.5	MT 9	Gem 9.5/10
104 Marshall Faulk RC	8	10	15	40

1994 Select

	NmMt 8	NmMt+ 8.5	MT 9	Gem 9.5/10
200 Marshall Faulk RC	8	10	20	40
SR1 Marshall Faulk SR	35	40	50	80

1994 SkyBox Impact

	NmMt 8	NmMt+ 8.5	MT 9	Gem 9.5/10
274 Marshall Faulk RC	8	10	15	25

1994 SkyBox Premium

	NmMt 8	NmMt+ 8.5	MT 9	Gem 9.5/10
158 Marshall Faulk RC	10	12	20	40

1994 SP

	NmMt 8	NmMt+ 8.5	MT 9	Gem 9.5/10
3 Marshall Faulk RC	20	30	80	▲300
5 Trent Dilfer RC	10	12	15	40

1994 SP Die Cuts

	NmMt 8	NmMt+ 8.5	MT 9	Gem 9.5/10
3 Marshall Faulk	20	25	40	400

1994 Stadium Club

	NmMt 8	NmMt+ 8.5	MT 9	Gem 9.5/10
288 Larry Allen RC	8	10	15	30
327 Marshall Faulk RC	8	10	12	40

1994 Topps

	NmMt 8	NmMt+ 8.5	MT 9	Gem 9.5/10
445 Marshall Faulk RC	6	8	12	40

1994 Ultra

	NmMt 8	NmMt+ 8.5	MT 9	Gem 9.5/10
133 Marshall Faulk RC	8	10	15	40

1994 Upper Deck

	NmMt 8	NmMt+ 8.5	MT 9	Gem 9.5/10
7 Marshall Faulk RC	8	10	15	60

1995 Absolute

	NmMt 8	NmMt+ 8.5	MT 9	Gem 9.5/10
182 Steve McNair RC	6	8	12	30

1995 Action Packed

	NmMt 8	NmMt+ 8.5	MT 9	Gem 9.5/10
36 Steve McNair RC	6	8	12	30

1995 Action Packed Rookies/Stars

	NmMt 8	NmMt+ 8.5	MT 9	Gem 9.5/10
90 Curtis Martin RC	6	8	12	30
92 Terrell Davis RC	6	8	12	30
101 Steve McNair RC	6	8	12	30

1995 Bowman

		NmMt 8	NmMt+ 8.5	MT 9	Gem 9.5/10
3	Steve McNair RC	10	12	20	60
301	Curtis Martin RC	8	10	20	40

1995 Bowman's Best

		NmMt 8	NmMt+ 8.5	MT 9	Gem 9.5/10
R3	Steve McNair RC	10	12	20	40
R5	Kerry Collins RC	8	10	12	30
R8	Joey Galloway RC	8	10	12	30
R74	Curtis Martin RC	12	15	30	▼80
R90	Antonio Freeman RC	8	10	12	25

1995 Bowman's Best Refractors

		NmMt 8	NmMt+ 8.5	MT 9	Gem 9.5/10
R3	Steve McNair	30	40	60	80
R74	Curtis Martin	40	50	80	100

1995 Crown Royale

		NmMt 8	NmMt+ 8.5	MT 9	Gem 9.5/10
78	Curtis Martin RC	8	10	15	60
126	Steve McNair RC	8	10	15	60
136	Terrell Davis RC	8	10	15	60

1995 Finest

		NmMt 8	NmMt+ 8.5	MT 9	Gem 9.5/10
264	Curtis Martin RC	10	12	40	100

1995 Flair

		NmMt 8	NmMt+ 8.5	MT 9	Gem 9.5/10
83	Steve McNair RC	6	8	12	60
124	Curtis Martin RC	6	8	12	60

1995 Playoff Contenders

		NmMt 8	NmMt+ 8.5	MT 9	Gem 9.5/10
126	Terrell Davis RC	6	8	10	40

1995 Select Certified

		NmMt 8	NmMt+ 8.5	MT 9	Gem 9.5/10
117	Curtis Martin RC	12	15	25	60
126	Terrell Davis RC	10	12	30	50

1995 Select Certified Mirror Gold

		NmMt 8	NmMt+ 8.5	MT 9	Gem 9.5/10
117	Curtis Martin	40	50	60	100
126	Terrell Davis	30	40	125	400

1995 SP

		NmMt 8	NmMt+ 8.5	MT 9	Gem 9.5/10
3	Steve McNair RC	12	15	50	60
5	Kerry Collins RC	10	12	25	50
6	Joey Galloway RC	10	12	25	50
18	Curtis Martin RC	12	15	50	▲400
99	Warren Sapp RC	10	12	25	60
103	Derrick Brooks RC	10	12	25	60
130	Terrell Davis RC	10	12	30	80
174	Ty Law RC	8	10	15	25

1995 SP Championship

		NmMt 8	NmMt+ 8.5	MT 9	Gem 9.5/10
14	Terrell Davis RC	10	12	20	80
19	Steve McNair RC	10	12	25	100
29	Curtis Martin RC	10	12	25	100

1996 Bowman's Best

		NmMt 8	NmMt+ 8.5	MT 9	Gem 9.5/10
147	Terrell Owens RC	25	30	50	400
148	Jonathan Ogden RC	12	15	25	40
162	Tedy Bruschi RC	15	20	30	60
164	Ray Lewis RC	60	80	200	800
165	Marvin Harrison RC	8	10	15	125
170	Eddie George RC	10	12	20	40
175	Zach Thomas RC	8	10	12	25
180	Keyshawn Johnson RC	8	10	15	40

1996 Bowman's Best Atomic Refractors

		NmMt 8	NmMt+ 8.5	MT 9	Gem 9.5/10
147	Terrell Owens	50	60	120	300
165	Marvin Harrison	50	60	120	
180	Keyshawn Johnson	25	30	60	150

1996 Bowman's Best Refractors

		NmMt 8	NmMt+ 8.5	MT 9	Gem 9.5/10
147	Terrell Owens	30	40	200	250
162	Tedy Bruschi	60	80	100	250
164	Ray Lewis	175	200	300	500
165	Marvin Harrison	30	40	80	
170	Eddie George	15	20	40	80
180	Keyshawn Johnson	12	15	30	60

1996 Collector's Choice

		NmMt 8	NmMt+ 8.5	MT 9	Gem 9.5/10
20	Ray Lewis RC	12	15	25	40

1996 Collector's Choice Update

		NmMt 8	NmMt+ 8.5	MT 9	Gem 9.5/10
U32	Ray Lewis	10	12	20	40

1996 Crown Royale

		NmMt 8	NmMt+ 8.5	MT 9	Gem 9.5/10
27	Marvin Harrison RC	10	12	20	50
39	Terrell Owens RC	10	12	20	80

1996 Finest

		NmMt 8	NmMt+ 8.5	MT 9	Gem 9.5/10
225	Keyshawn Johnson B RC	6	8	12	25
243	Marvin Harrison B RC	10	12	25	50
338	Terrell Owens B RC	10	12	40	300
344	Brian Dawkins B RC	▲20	▲40	80	▲400

1996 Finest Refractors

		NmMt 8	NmMt+ 8.5	MT 9	Gem 9.5/10
225	Keyshawn Johnson B	20	25	40	150
243	Marvin Harrison B	40	50	80	
338	Terrell Owens B	40	50	60	300

1996 Fleer

		NmMt 8	NmMt+ 8.5	MT 9	Gem 9.5/10
165	Ray Lewis RC	12	15	30	50

1996 Score Board Lasers

		NmMt 8	NmMt+ 8.5	MT 9	Gem 9.5/10
99	Ray Lewis RC	10	12	25	50

1996 Select Certified

		NmMt 8	NmMt+ 8.5	MT 9	Gem 9.5/10
91	Marvin Harrison RC	12	15	25	50
105	Keyshawn Johnson RC	8	10	15	30

1996 SP

		NmMt 8	NmMt+ 8.5	MT 9	Gem 9.5/10
1	Keyshawn Johnson RC	8	10	15	40
4	Jonathan Ogden RC	20	25	60	350
5	Eddie George RC	8	10	20	100
7	Terrell Owens RC	20	25	125	400
18	Marvin Harrison RC	15	20	60	150
126	Mike Alstott RC	8	10	20	40

1996 Stadium Club

		NmMt 8	NmMt+ 8.5	MT 9	Gem 9.5/10
351	Ray Lewis SP RC	20	25	▼60	125

1996 Topps Chrome

		NmMt 8	NmMt+ 8.5	MT 9	Gem 9.5/10
156	Marvin Harrison RC	15	20	50	▲150
159	Keyshawn Johnson RC	8	10	20	50
162	Eddie George RC	10	12	20	150
163	Jonathan Ogden RC	10	12	25	80

1996 Topps Chrome Refractors

		NmMt 8	NmMt+ 8.5	MT 9	Gem 9.5/10
156	Marvin Harrison	60	80	100	150
162	Eddie George	40	50	100	

1997 Bowman's Best

		NmMt 8	NmMt+ 8.5	MT 9	Gem 9.5/10
96	Jake Plummer RC	5	6	8	15
101	Tony Gonzalez RC	8	10	15	50
125	Warrick Dunn RC	5	6	8	15

1997 Pacific Philadelphia

		NmMt 8	NmMt+ 8.5	MT 9	Gem 9.5/10
199	Adam Vinatieri RC	80	100	150	400

1997 Pinnacle Certified

		NmMt 8	NmMt+ 8.5	MT 9	Gem 9.5/10
129	Tiki Barber RC	10	12	20	25
149	Tony Gonzalez RC	8	10	20	30

1997 Pinnacle Totally Certified Platinum Red

		NmMt 8	NmMt+ 8.5	MT 9	Gem 9.5/10
129	Tiki Barber RC	15	20	25	50
149	Tony Gonzalez RC	12	15	25	60

1997 SP Authentic

		NmMt 8	NmMt+ 8.5	MT 9	Gem 9.5/10
1	Orlando Pace RC	15	20	60	
10	Warrick Dunn RC	12	15	25	80
11	Tony Gonzalez RC	30	40	100	300
23	Jake Plummer RC	12	15	25	80
25	Corey Dillon RC	12	15	25	80
116	Jason Taylor RC	▲100	▲125	150	400
137	Tiki Barber RC	15	20	25	40
186	Ronde Barber RC	25	30	50	

1997 Topps Chrome

		NmMt 8	NmMt+ 8.5	MT 9	Gem 9.5/10
24	Tony Gonzalez RC	30	40	100	125

1998 Absolute Hobby

		NmMt 8	NmMt+ 8.5	MT 9	Gem 9.5/10
40	Randy Moss RC	15	20	30	120
165	Peyton Manning RC	25	30	50	250

1998 Absolute Retail

		NmMt 8	NmMt+ 8.5	MT 9	Gem 9.5/10
40	Randy Moss RC	8	10	15	40
165	Peyton Manning RC	15	50	60	200

1998 Aurora

		NmMt 8	NmMt+ 8.5	MT 9	Gem 9.5/10
71	Peyton Manning RC	20	25	50	150

1998 Black Diamond Rookies

		NmMt 8	NmMt+ 8.5	MT 9	Gem 9.5/10
91	Peyton Manning RC	25	60	80	200
97	Randy Moss RC	15	20	30	60

1998 Black Diamond Rookies Double

		NmMt 8	NmMt+ 8.5	MT 9	Gem 9.5/10
91	Peyton Manning	50	80	125	250

1998 Black Diamond Rookies Triple

		NmMt 8	NmMt+ 8.5	MT 9	Gem 9.5/10
91	Peyton Manning	80	100	150	500

1998 Bowman

		NmMt 8	NmMt+ 8.5	MT 9	Gem 9.5/10
1	Peyton Manning RC	60	100	200	800
27	Hines Ward RC	8	10	20	40
29	Ahman Green RC	8	10	15	25
181	Charles Woodson RC	8	10	15	25
182	Randy Moss RC	10	12	80	200

1998 Bowman Interstate

		NmMt 8	NmMt+ 8.5	MT 9	Gem 9.5/10
1	Peyton Manning	100	125	200	500
182	Randy Moss	20	40	60	150

1998 Bowman Rookie Autographs

		NmMt 8	NmMt+ 8.5	MT 9	Gem 9.5/10
A1	Peyton Manning	450	500	▲1,000	▲1,200

1998 Bowman Chrome Preview

		NmMt 8	NmMt+ 8.5	MT 9	Gem 9.5/10
BCP1	Peyton Manning	50	80	200	300

FOOTBALL

1998 Bowman Chrome Preview Refractors

		NmMt 8	NmMt+ 8.5	MT 9	Gem 9.5/10
BCP1	Peyton Manning	300	400	500	600

1998 Bowman Chrome

		NmMt 8	NmMt+ 8.5	MT 9	Gem 9.5/10
1	Peyton Manning RC	150	200	▼300	▼600
27	Hines Ward RC	12	15	60	125
181	Charles Woodson RC	10	12	20	40
182	Randy Moss RC	50	60	125	600

1998 Bowman Chrome Interstate

		NmMt 8	NmMt+ 8.5	MT 9	Gem 9.5/10
1	Peyton Manning	100	125	400	600
27	Hines Ward	15	20	30	60
182	Randy Moss	50	60	80	250

1998 Bowman Chrome Interstate Refractors

		NmMt 8	NmMt+ 8.5	MT 9	Gem 9.5/10
1	Peyton Manning	175	200	800	2,000
27	Hines Ward	60	80	100	200
182	Randy Moss	60	80	120	300

1998 Bowman Chrome Refractors

		NmMt 8	NmMt+ 8.5	MT 9	Gem 9.5/10
1	Peyton Manning	300	400	2,000	2,500
27	Hines Ward	40	50	80	125
182	Randy Moss	300	600	800	3,000

1998 Bowman's Best

		NmMt 8	NmMt+ 8.5	MT 9	Gem 9.5/10
101	Charles Woodson RC	8	10	15	30
109	Randy Moss RC	10	12	20	200
112	Peyton Manning RC	▲25	▲40	▲60	▼300
124	Hines Ward RC	10	12	20	50

1998 Bowman's Best Atomic Refractors

		NmMt 8	NmMt+ 8.5	MT 9	Gem 9.5/10
109	Randy Moss	100	120	150	300
112	Peyton Manning	250	300	400	600

1998 Bowman's Best Refractors

		NmMt 8	NmMt+ 8.5	MT 9	Gem 9.5/10
109	Randy Moss	40	50	60	120
112	Peyton Manning	60	80	100	200

1998 Bowman's Best Autographs

		NmMt 8	NmMt+ 8.5	MT 9	Gem 9.5/10
A	Peyton Manning	350	400	500	650
3	Peyton Manning	350	400	500	650

1998 Bowman's Best Performers

		NmMt 8	NmMt+ 8.5	MT 9	Gem 9.5/10
P1	Peyton Manning	25	30	150	250

1998 Collector's Edge First Place

		NmMt 8	NmMt+ 8.5	MT 9	Gem 9.5/10
81	Matt Hasselbeck RC	20	25	40	60
85	Peyton Manning RC	12	15	25	50

1998 Collector's Edge First Place Rookie Ink

		NmMt 8	NmMt+ 8.5	MT 9	Gem 9.5/10
A	Peyton Manning Blue	135	150	175	
B	Peyton Manning Black	135	150	175	

1998 Collector's Edge Masters

		NmMt 8	NmMt+ 8.5	MT 9	Gem 9.5/10
	Peyton Manning RC	20	25	30	50

1998 Crown Royale

		NmMt 8	NmMt+ 8.5	MT 9	Gem 9.5/10
	Peyton Manning RC	▲60	▲80	▲100	250
	Randy Moss RC	12	15	25	80

1998 E-X2001

		NmMt 8	NmMt+ 8.5	MT 9	Gem 9.5/10
	Peyton Manning RC	20	25	40	100
	Randy Moss RC	12	15	25	50

1998 E-X2001 Star Date 2001

		NmMt 8	NmMt+ 8.5	MT 9	Gem 9.5/10
15	Peyton Manning	15	20	30	60

1998 Finest

		NmMt 8	NmMt+ 8.5	MT 9	Gem 9.5/10
121	Peyton Manning RC	80	125	▼150	▼200
135	Randy Moss RC	40	50	80	400
148	Hines Ward RC	12	15	25	40

1998 Finest No-Protectors

		NmMt 8	NmMt+ 8.5	MT 9	Gem 9.5/10
121	Peyton Manning	35	40	60	120
135	Randy Moss	12	15	30	60

1998 Finest No-Protectors Refractors

		NmMt 8	NmMt+ 8.5	MT 9	Gem 9.5/10
121	Peyton Manning	100	120	175	400
135	Randy Moss	40	50	80	150

1998 Finest Refractors

		NmMt 8	NmMt+ 8.5	MT 9	Gem 9.5/10
121	Peyton Manning	60	80	200	1,000
135	Randy Moss	25	30	400	500

1998 Finest Undergrads

		NmMt 8	NmMt+ 8.5	MT 9	Gem 9.5/10
U20	Peyton Manning	25	30	60	200

1998 Flair Showcase Row 3

		NmMt 8	NmMt+ 8.5	MT 9	Gem 9.5/10
3	Peyton Manning RC	60	80	100	150
5	Randy Moss RC	10	12	40	100

1998 Flair Showcase Row 2

		NmMt 8	NmMt+ 8.5	MT 9	Gem 9.5/10
3	Peyton Manning	15	20	80	150
5	Randy Moss	10	12	40	100

1998 Flair Showcase Row 1

		NmMt 8	NmMt+ 8.5	MT 9	Gem 9.5/10
3	Peyton Manning	60	80	400	800
5	Randy Moss	25	30	150	250

1998 Flair Showcase Row 0

		NmMt 8	NmMt+ 8.5	MT 9	Gem 9.5/10
3	Peyton Manning	100	120	1,000	4,000
5	Randy Moss	50	60	800	2,000

1998 Fleer Brilliants

		NmMt 8	NmMt+ 8.5	MT 9	Gem 9.5/10
120	Peyton Manning RC	30	40	▼100	▼500
140	Randy Moss RC	15	20	▲40	100

1998 Fleer Brilliants Blue

		NmMt 8	NmMt+ 8.5	MT 9	Gem 9.5/10
120	Peyton Manning	40	50	80	150

1998 Leaf Rookies and Stars

		NmMt 8	NmMt+ 8.5	MT 9	Gem 9.5/10
199	Randy Moss RC	20	25	50	80
202	Hines Ward RC	20	25	40	80
233	Peyton Manning RC	40	50	60	120
270	Peyton Manning PT	25	30	40	80

1998 Leaf Rookies and Stars True Blue

		NmMt 8	NmMt+ 8.5	MT 9	Gem 9.5/10
233	Peyton Manning	40	50	80	200

1998 Metal Universe

		NmMt 8	NmMt+ 8.5	MT 9	Gem 9.5/10
189	Peyton Manning RC	▲20	▲30	▲80	▲400
190	Randy Moss RC	8	10	15	40

1998 Pacific

		NmMt 8	NmMt+ 8.5	MT 9	Gem 9.5/10
181	Peyton Manning RC	▲30	▲40	80	250

1998 Playoff Contenders Leather

		NmMt 8	NmMt+ 8.5	MT 9	Gem 9.5/10
37	Peyton Manning	40	50	80	▼200
52	Randy Moss	12	15	▲50	▲125

1998 Playoff Contenders Ticket

		NmMt 8	NmMt+ 8.5	MT 9	Gem 9.5/10
5	Priest Holmes RC	25	30	60	
87	Peyton Manning AU/200*	4,000	6,000	7,000	15,000
89	Fred Taylor AU/500*	60	80	250	300
92	Randy Moss AU/300*	4,000	6,000	7,000	10,000
94	Hines Ward AU/500*	400	500	600	1,500
97	Ahman Green AU/500*	40	50	100	

1998 Playoff Contenders Ticket Red

		NmMt 8	NmMt+ 8.5	MT 9	Gem 9.5/10
87	Peyton Manning	200	225	350	

1998 Playoff Momentum Hobby

		NmMt 8	NmMt+ 8.5	MT 9	Gem 9.5/10
98	Peyton Manning RC	40	50	80	▼300
131	Randy Moss RC	20	25	40	60

1998 Playoff Momentum Retail

		NmMt 8	NmMt+ 8.5	MT 9	Gem 9.5/10
146	Peyton Manning RC	20	50	80	150

1998 Playoff Prestige Hobby

		NmMt 8	NmMt+ 8.5	MT 9	Gem 9.5/10
165	Peyton Manning RC	▲40	▲50	▲60	300
173	Randy Moss RC	▲25	▲30	▲40	

1998 Playoff Prestige Retail

		NmMt 8	NmMt+ 8.5	MT 9	Gem 9.5/10
165	Peyton Manning RC	10	12	20	50
173	Randy Moss RC	6	8	10	30

1998 Revolution

		NmMt 8	NmMt+ 8.5	MT 9	Gem 9.5/10
58	Peyton Manning RC	▲50	60	80	800

1998 Score

		NmMt 8	NmMt+ 8.5	MT 9	Gem 9.5/10
233	Peyton Manning RC	50	60	80	▼150
235	Randy Moss RC	15	20	40	150
252	Hines Ward RC	8	10	12	25

1998 Score Showcase Artist's Proofs

		NmMt 8	NmMt+ 8.5	MT 9	Gem 9.5/10
PP123	Peyton Manning	60	125	150	400

1998 SkyBox Premium

		NmMt 8	NmMt+ 8.5	MT 9	Gem 9.5/10
231	Peyton Manning RC	50	60	80	150
240	Randy Moss RC	12	15	50	200

1998 SkyBox Thunder

		NmMt 8	NmMt+ 8.5	MT 9	Gem 9.5/10
239	Peyton Manning RC	15	▲50	100	300
242	Randy Moss RC	10	12	20	50

1998 SP Authentic

		NmMt 8	NmMt+ 8.5	MT 9	Gem 9.5/10
14	Peyton Manning RC	600	700	2,000	3,000
16	Fred Taylor RC	25	30	40	150
18	Randy Moss RC	500	600	1,200	2,000
23	Charles Woodson RC	250	300	500	2,000
27	Ahman Green RC	30	40	50	100
—	Peyton Manning #14 BGS 10 (PRISTINE) sold for $2460 (eBay; 6/07)				

1998 SP Authentic Die Cuts

		NmMt 8	NmMt+ 8.5	MT 9	Gem 9.5/10
11	Brian Griese	15	20	25	30
14	Peyton Manning	800	1,000	3,000	4,000
16	Fred Taylor	40	50	80	120
18	Randy Moss	250	300	500	800
23	Charles Woodson	200	250	300	400
27	Ahman Green	25	30	40	100

1998 SP Authentic Maximum Impact

		NmMt 8	NmMt+ 8.5	MT 9	Gem 9.5/10
SE11	Peyton Manning	50	60	80	200

1998 SPx Finite

		NmMt 8	NmMt+ 8.5	MT 9	Gem 9.5/10
181	Peyton Manning/1998 RC	▼300	600	800	1,500
239	Randy Moss/1998 RC	50	60	100	
287	Peyton Manning ET	30	40	60	150

1998 Stadium Club

		NmMt 8	NmMt+ 8.5	MT 9	Gem 9.5/10
182	Hines Ward RC	8	10	20	60
189	Randy Moss RC	10	12	▲50	▲150
195	Peyton Manning RC	40	50	80	▲300

1998 Stadium Club First Day

		NmMt 8	NmMt+ 8.5	MT 9	Gem 9.5/10
195	Peyton Manning	80	100	150	300

1998 Stadium Club Prime Rookies

		NmMt 8	NmMt+ 8.5	MT 9	Gem 9.5/10
PR10	Peyton Manning	12	15	60	150

1998 Topps

		NmMt 8	NmMt+ 8.5	MT 9	Gem 9.5/10
341	Hines Ward RC	10	12	20	▲125
352	Randy Moss RC	▼30	▼40	▼50	▼125
360	Peyton Manning RC	▼125	▼150	▼250	▼300

1998 Topps Autographs

		NmMt 8	NmMt+ 8.5	MT 9	Gem 9.5/10
A1	Randy Moss	250	300	400	1,000
A10B	Peyton Manning Bronze	450	500	600	900
A10G	Peyton Manning Gold	450	500	600	900

1998 Topps Chrome

		NmMt 8	NmMt+ 8.5	MT 9	Gem 9.5/10
35	Randy Moss RC	▼50	▼100	▼125	▼250
44	Charles Woodson RC	▼60	▼80	▼100	600
165	Peyton Manning RC	▼150	▼200	▼250	▼1,500

1998 Topps Chrome Refractors

		NmMt 8	NmMt+ 8.5	MT 9	Gem 9.5/10
35	Randy Moss	150	250	500	3,000
44	Charles Woodson	125	200	400	600
133	Brian Griese	12	15	30	60
152	Fred Taylor	25	30	40	60
165	Peyton Manning	3,000	4,000	6,000	30,000

1998 Topps Gold Label Class 1

		NmMt 8	NmMt+ 8.5	MT 9	Gem 9.5/10
20	Peyton Manning RC	40	50	80	200

1998 Topps Gold Label Class 1 Black

		NmMt 8	NmMt+ 8.5	MT 9	Gem 9.5/10
20	Peyton Manning	80	100	150	250

1998 Topps Gold Label Class 2

		NmMt 8	NmMt+ 8.5	MT 9	Gem 9.5/10
20	Peyton Manning	100	125	200	350

1998 Topps Gold Label Class 2 Black

		NmMt 8	NmMt+ 8.5	MT 9	Gem 9.5/10
20	Peyton Manning	80	100	125	150

1998 Topps Gold Label Class 3

		NmMt 8	NmMt+ 8.5	MT 9	Gem 9.5/10
20	Peyton Manning	80	125	200	350

1998 Topps Season Opener

		NmMt 8	NmMt+ 8.5	MT 9	Gem 9.5/10
1	Peyton Manning RC	80	100	200	400
11	Hines Ward RC	10	12	30	50
22	Randy Moss RC	12	15	40	200

1998 Topps Stars

		NmMt 8	NmMt+ 8.5	MT 9	Gem 9.5/10
67	Peyton Manning RC	▲40	▲50	100	300

1998 Topps Stars Bronze

		NmMt 8	NmMt+ 8.5	MT 9	Gem 9.5/10
67	Peyton Manning	25	40	100	400

1998 UD3

		NmMt 8	NmMt+ 8.5	MT 9	Gem 9.5/10
1	Peyton Manning FE	30	35	50	200
91	Peyton Manning FF	40	50	80	200
181	Peyton Manning FR RC	15	20	30	100
197	Randy Moss FR RC	10	12	20	60

1998 UD Choice

		NmMt 8	NmMt+ 8.5	MT 9	Gem 9.5/10
193	Peyton Manning RC	12	15	25	50
200	Randy Moss RC	6	8	12	25
256	Peyton Manning DN	15	20	30	60

1998 Ultra

		NmMt 8	NmMt+ 8.5	MT 9	Gem 9.5/10
201	Peyton Manning RC	30	40	▲60	120
207	Randy Moss RC	12	15	30	60
416	Peyton Manning	25	30	40	100

1998 Ultra Gold Medallion

		NmMt 8	NmMt+ 8.5	MT 9	Gem 9.5/10
201G	Peyton Manning	40	50	80	300
207G	Randy Moss	25	30	50	125

1998 Upper Deck

		NmMt 8	NmMt+ 8.5	MT 9	Gem 9.5/10
1	Peyton Manning RC	60	80	150	500
17	Randy Moss RC	30	40	50	125

1998 Upper Deck Game Jerseys

		NmMt 8	NmMt+ 8.5	MT 9	Gem 9.5/10
GJ16	Peyton Manning	150	250	300	1,600

1998 Upper Deck Encore

		NmMt 8	NmMt+ 8.5	MT 9	Gem 9.5/10
1	Peyton Manning RC	60	150	200	300
12	Randy Moss RC	15	20	30	60

1999 Black Diamond

		NmMt 8	NmMt+ 8.5	MT 9	Gem 9.5/10
114	Donovan McNabb RC	15	20	30	100
126	Torry Holt RC	10	12	15	60

1999 Bowman

		NmMt 8	NmMt+ 8.5	MT 9	Gem 9.5/10
168	Donovan McNabb RC	12	15	20	60

1999 Bowman Chrome

		NmMt 8	NmMt+ 8.5	MT 9	Gem 9.5/10
168	Donovan McNabb RC	10	12	25	50
174	Torry Holt RC	10	12	20	40

1999 Bowman Chrome Interstate

		NmMt 8	NmMt+ 8.5	MT 9	Gem 9.5/10
161	Edgerrin James	10	12	20	60
166	Daunte Culpepper	10	12	20	60
168	Donovan McNabb	12	15	30	100
174	Torry Holt	10	12	20	60

1999 Bowman Chrome Refractors

		NmMt 8	NmMt+ 8.5	MT 9	Gem 9.5/10
161	Edgerrin James	12	15	25	125
166	Daunte Culpepper	12	15	25	125
168	Donovan McNabb	25	30	60	300
174	Torry Holt	12	15	25	125

1999 Bowman's Best

		NmMt 8	NmMt+ 8.5	MT 9	Gem 9.5/10
110	Kurt Warner RC	20	25	100	400
118	Donovan McNabb RC	10	12	20	40
120	Torry Holt RC	8	10	15	30

1999 Bowman's Best Atomic Refractors

		NmMt 8	NmMt+ 8.5	MT 9	Gem 9.5/10
118	Donovan McNabb	60	80	120	400

1999 Bowman's Best Refractors

		NmMt 8	NmMt+ 8.5	MT 9	Gem 9.5/10
107	Daunte Culpepper	15	20	30	80
115	Edgerrin James	15	20	30	80
118	Donovan McNabb	40	50	60	150
120	Torry Holt	15	20	30	80

1999 Collector's Edge First Place

		NmMt 8	NmMt+ 8.5	MT 9	Gem 9.5/10
201PG	Kurt Warner Promo Gold	10	12	20	35
201PS	Kurt Warner Promo Silver	10	12	25	40

1999 Donruss

		NmMt 8	NmMt+ 8.5	MT 9	Gem 9.5/10
188	Kurt Warner RC	8	10	20	40

1999 Donruss Elite

		NmMt 8	NmMt+ 8.5	MT 9	Gem 9.5/10
178	Torry Holt RC	10	12	25	80
190	Donovan McNabb RC	15	20	40	120

1999 E-X Century

		NmMt 8	NmMt+ 8.5	MT 9	Gem 9.5/10
64	Donovan McNabb RC	12	15	25	80

1999 Finest

		NmMt 8	NmMt+ 8.5	MT 9	Gem 9.5/10
166	Donovan McNabb RC	10	12	15	40
175	Torry Holt RC	6	8	12	30

1999 Finest Refractors

		NmMt 8	NmMt+ 8.5	MT 9	Gem 9.5/10
151	Daunte Culpepper	8	10	20	40
152	Edgerrin James	10	12	25	40
166	Donovan McNabb	15	20	60	100

1999 Flair Showcase

		NmMt 8	NmMt+ 8.5	MT 9	Gem 9.5/10
182	Donovan McNabb RC	25	30	40	

1999 Fleer Focus

		NmMt 8	NmMt+ 8.5	MT 9	Gem 9.5/10
40	Kurt Warner RC	10	12	20	40
118	Donald Driver RC	▲100	▲125	▲150	▲200
172	Donovan McNabb RC	15	20	40	80

1999 Fleer Mystique

		NmMt 8	NmMt+ 8.5	MT 9	Gem 9.5/10
102	Donovan McNabb RC	15	20	25	30
105	Daunte Culpepper RC	10	12	25	80
109	Torry Holt RC	10	12	25	80

1999 Fleer Tradition

		NmMt 8	NmMt+ 8.5	MT 9	Gem 9.5/10
288	Donovan McNabb RC	10	12	20	60

1999 Leaf Certified

		NmMt 8	NmMt+ 8.5	MT 9	Gem 9.5/10
204	Daunte Culpepper RC	10	12	25	50
212	Donovan McNabb RC	15	20	40	100
222	Torry Holt RC	10	12	25	50

1999 Leaf Rookies and Stars

		NmMt 8	NmMt+ 8.5	MT 9	Gem 9.5/10
260	Daunte Culpepper RC	10	12	25	50
274	Donovan McNabb RC	15	20	40	100
288	Kurt Warner RC	15	20	50	
289	Torry Holt RC	10	12	25	50

1999 Metal Universe

		NmMt 8	NmMt+ 8.5	MT 9	Gem 9.5/10
213	Donovan McNabb RC	8	10	15	50

1999 Pacific

		NmMt 8	NmMt+ 8.5	MT 9	Gem 9.5/10
343	Kurt Warner RC/Tony Horne	12	15	50	150
434	Torry Holt RC	6	8	12	40
441	Donovan McNabb RC	8	10	15	60

1999 Paramount

		NmMt 8	NmMt+ 8.5	MT 9	Gem 9.5/10
100	Edgerrin James RC	6	8	12	30
182	Donovan McNabb RC	8	10	15	50

1999 Playoff Contenders SSD

		NmMt 8	NmMt+ 8.5	MT 9	Gem 9.5/10
118	Jeff Garcia AU/325* RC	60	80	125	200
146	Kurt Warner AU/1825* RC	▲400	▲500	▲600	1,600
152	R.Williams AU/725* RC	35	40	60	120
153	D.McNabb AU/525* RC	35	40	50	120
154	E.James AU/525* RC	30	35	60	200
155	Torry Holt AU/1025* RC	30	35	60	200
156	D.Culpepper AU/1025* RC	30	35	50	100
158	Champ Bailey AU/1725* RC	35	40	200	400

1999 Playoff Momentum SSD

		NmMt 8	NmMt+ 8.5	MT 9	Gem 9.5/10
144	Kurt Warner RC	20	25	40	80
152	Donovan McNabb RC	20	25	40	80

1999 SkyBox Molten Metal

		NmMt 8	NmMt+ 8.5	MT 9	Gem 9.5/10
93	Kurt Warner RC	▲40	▲50	▲60	▲150
133	Donovan McNabb RC	8	10	15	30
145	Donald Driver RC	25	30	50	100

1999 SP Authentic

		NmMt 8	NmMt+ 8.5	MT 9	Gem 9.5/10
91	Ricky Williams RC	20	25	40	80
95	Donovan McNabb RC	40	50	100	250
96	Torry Holt RC	▲50	▲60	100	▲150
111	Champ Bailey RC	25	80	100	400

1999 SP Authentic Excitement

		NmMt 8	NmMt+ 8.5	MT 9	Gem 9.5/10
91	Ricky Williams	25	30	60	100
94	Edgerrin James	20	25	50	100
95	Donovan McNabb	100	120	200	400
96	Torry Holt	25	30	60	125

1999 SP Signature

		NmMt 8	NmMt+ 8.5	MT 9	Gem 9.5/10
77	Donovan McNabb RC	20	25	40	80
80	Torry Holt RC	15	20	30	60

1999 SPx

		NmMt 8	NmMt+ 8.5	MT 9	Gem 9.5/10
17	Champ Bailey AU RC	30	40	60	
29	Torry Holt AU RC	35	40	50	▲250
32	Donovan McNabb AU RC	35	40	▲80	▲150
34	D.Culpepper AU/500 RC	30	40	50	100
35	Ricky Williams AU/500 RC	50	60	80	120

1999 Stadium Club

		NmMt 8	NmMt+ 8.5	MT 9	Gem 9.5/10
65	Donovan McNabb RC	10	12	25	50
66	Torry Holt RC	8	10	20	40

1999 Stadium Club Chrome

		NmMt 8	NmMt+ 8.5	MT 9	Gem 9.5/10
33	Donovan McNabb RC	12	15	30	60
34	Torry Holt RC	10	12	25	50

1999 Topps

		NmMt 8	NmMt+ 8.5	MT 9	Gem 9.5/10
41	Donovan McNabb RC	12	15	30	60
43	Torry Holt RC	10	12	25	50

1999 Topps Collection

		NmMt 8	NmMt+ 8.5	MT 9	Gem 9.5/10
330	Daunte Culpepper	8	10	20	60
339	Edgerrin James	8	10	20	60
341	Donovan McNabb	10	12	25	80
343	Torry Holt	8	10	20	60

1999 Topps Chrome

		NmMt 8	NmMt+ 8.5	MT 9	Gem 9.5/10
147	Donovan McNabb RC	15	20	25	80
149	Torry Holt RC	12	15	25	40

1999 Topps Chrome Refractors

		NmMt 8	NmMt+ 8.5	MT 9	Gem 9.5/10
135	Ricky Williams	12	15	25	40
145	Edgerrin James	40	50	100	300
147	Donovan McNabb	30	40	60	250

1999 Topps Gold Label Class 1

		NmMt 8	NmMt+ 8.5	MT 9	Gem 9.5/10
71	Torry Holt RC	8	10	15	40
75	Donovan McNabb RC	10	12	20	50

1999 UD Ionix

		NmMt 8	NmMt+ 8.5	MT 9	Gem 9.5/10
65	Donovan McNabb RC	10	12	15	40

1999 Ultra

		NmMt 8	NmMt+ 8.5	MT 9	Gem 9.5/10
265	Torry Holt RC	12	15	30	
266	Donovan McNabb RC	15	20	40	

1999 Upper Deck

		NmMt 8	NmMt+ 8.5	MT 9	Gem 9.5/10
235	Donovan McNabb RC	15	20	40	100
248	Torry Holt RC	12	15	30	60

1999 Upper Deck Encore

		NmMt 8	NmMt+ 8.5	MT 9	Gem 9.5/10
139	Kurt Warner RC	10	12	20	60
190	Donovan McNabb RC	15	20	30	150

1999 Upper Deck MVP

		NmMt 8	NmMt+ 8.5	MT 9	Gem 9.5/10
220	Donovan McNabb RC	8	10	15	50

1999 Upper Deck Retro

		NmMt 8	NmMt+ 8.5	MT 9	Gem 9.5/10
117	Donovan McNabb RC	8	10	15	30

2000 Absolute Coaches Honors

		NmMt 8	NmMt+ 8.5	MT 9	Gem 9.5/10
195	Tom Brady	175	600	700	

2000 Aurora

		NmMt 8	NmMt+ 8.5	MT 9	Gem 9.5/10
84	Tom Brady RC	200	250	500	▼600

2000 Black Diamond

		NmMt 8	NmMt+ 8.5	MT 9	Gem 9.5/10
126	Tom Brady RC	1,200	1,500	2,000	▼5,000
166	Brian Urlacher JSY RC	30	40	60	120

2000 Bowman

		NmMt 8	NmMt+ 8.5	MT 9	Gem 9.5/10
177	Shaun Alexander RC	6	8	10	15
178	Brian Urlacher RC	8	10	15	50
236	Tom Brady RC	▼2,500	▼3,000	▼4,000	▼8,000

2000 Bowman Chrome

		NmMt 8	NmMt+ 8.5	MT 9	Gem 9.5/10
178	Brian Urlacher RC	15	20	▲60	▲100
236	Tom Brady RC	4,000	6,000	12,000	25,000

2000 Bowman Chrome Refractors

		NmMt 8	NmMt+ 8.5	MT 9	Gem 9.5/10
236	Tom Brady	52,000	60,000	120,000	150,000

2000 Collector's Edge Supreme

		NmMt 8	NmMt+ 8.5	MT 9	Gem 9.5/10
176	Tom Brady RC	1,000	1,500	2,000	8,000
190	Brian Urlacher RC	20	25	30	60

2000 Crown Royale

		NmMt 8	NmMt+ 8.5	MT 9	Gem 9.5/10
110	Tom Brady RC	600	800	1,000	1,500

2000 Crown Royale Retail

		NmMt 8	NmMt+ 8.5	MT 9	Gem 9.5/10
110	Tom Brady RC	500	600	1,000	1,200

2000 Crown Royale Rookie Autographs

		NmMt 8	NmMt+ 8.5	MT 9	Gem 9.5/10
110	Tom Brady	2,500	3,000	3,500	4,000

2000 Crown Royale Rookie Royalty

		NmMt 8	NmMt+ 8.5	MT 9	Gem 9.5/10
2	Tom Brady	400	500	800	1,000

2000 Donruss

		NmMt 8	NmMt+ 8.5	MT 9	Gem 9.5/10
230	Tom Brady RC	1,500	2,000	2,500	3,000

2000 Donruss Elite

		NmMt 8	NmMt+ 8.5	MT 9	Gem 9.5/10
183	Tom Brady RC	1,500	2,000	3,000	8,000

2000 Donruss Elite Rookie Die Cuts

		NmMt 8	NmMt+ 8.5	MT 9	Gem 9.5/10
183	Tom Brady	2,000	2,200	2,500	3,000

2000 E-X

		NmMt 8	NmMt+ 8.5	MT 9	Gem 9.5/10
122	Tom Brady RC	4,000	5,000	15,000	20,000
140	Brian Urlacher RC	25	30	60	120

2000 Finest

		NmMt 8	NmMt+ 8.5	MT 9	Gem 9.5/10
151	Brian Urlacher RC	25	30	40	80

2000 Fleer Mystique

		NmMt 8	NmMt+ 8.5	MT 9	Gem 9.5/10
103	Tom Brady RC	400	500	600	2,000

2000 Fleer Tradition

		NmMt 8	NmMt+ 8.5	MT 9	Gem 9.5/10
309	Brian Urlacher RC	8	10	20	
352	T.Brady RC/Stachelski RC	▲200	▲250	300	▲1,200

2000 Fleer Tradition Glossy

		NmMt 8	NmMt+ 8.5	MT 9	Gem 9.5/10
352	Tom Brady/Stachelski	40	60	80	500

2000 Impact

		NmMt 8	NmMt+ 8.5	MT 9	Gem 9.5/10
27	Tom Brady RC	400	500	600	▲2,500

2000 Leaf Certified

		NmMt 8	NmMt+ 8.5	MT 9	Gem 9.5/10
157	Brian Urlacher RC	15	20	30	50
207	Tom Brady RC	2,000	2,500	3,000	5,000

2000 Leaf Certified Mirror Red

		NmMt 8	NmMt+ 8.5	MT 9	Gem 9.5/10
207	Tom Brady	3,000	4,000	5,000	6,000

2000 Leaf Certified Rookie Die Cuts

		NmMt 8	NmMt+ 8.5	MT 9	Gem 9.5/10
207	Tom Brady	5,000	6,000	8,000	

2000 Leaf Limited

		NmMt 8	NmMt+ 8.5	MT 9	Gem 9.5/10
378	Tom Brady RC	6,000	8,000	10,000	12,000

2000 Leaf Rookies and Stars

		NmMt 8	NmMt+ 8.5	MT 9	Gem 9.5/10
134	Tom Brady RC	2,000	2,500	3,000	
301	Michael Vick XRC	20	25	30	40
302	Drew Brees XRC	60	80	100	250
306	LaDainian Tomlinson XRC	15	20	50	

2000 Metal

		NmMt 8	NmMt+ 8.5	MT 9	Gem 9.5/10
267	Tom Brady RC	800	1,000	1,800	8,000

2000 Metal Emerald

		NmMt 8	NmMt+ 8.5	MT 9	Gem 9.5/10
267	Tom Brady UER/442 completions, not 441	3,000	4,000	10,000	

2000 Pacific

		NmMt 8	NmMt+ 8.5	MT 9	Gem 9.5/10
403	Tom Brady RC	300	400	500	800

2000 Pacific Autographs

		NmMt 8	NmMt+ 8.5	MT 9	Gem 9.5/10
403	Tom Brady/200*	1,000	2,000	3,000	3,500

2000 Pacific Omega

		NmMt 8	NmMt+ 8.5	MT 9	Gem 9.5/10
191	Tom Brady RC	1,200	1,500	2,000	8,000

2000 Pacific Prism Prospects

		NmMt 8	NmMt+ 8.5	MT 9	Gem 9.5/10
156	Tom Brady RC	2,000	2,500	3,000	

2000 Paramount

		NmMt 8	NmMt+ 8.5	MT 9	Gem 9.5/10
138	Tom Brady RC	250	300	600	▲2,000

2000 Paramount Draft Picks 325

		NmMt 8	NmMt+ 8.5	MT 9	Gem 9.5/10
138	Tom Brady	300	400	500	1,000

2000 Playoff Contenders

		NmMt 8	NmMt+ 8.5	MT 9	Gem 9.5/10
103	Brian Urlacher AU RC	100	125	250	
113	Shaun Alexander AU RC	20	25	40	
144	Tom Brady AU RC	50,000	60,000	100,000	600,000

2000 Playoff Contenders Round Numbers Autographs

		NmMt 8	NmMt+ 8.5	MT 9	Gem 9.5/10
11	M.Bulger/T.Brady	▲5,000	▲8,000	▲15,000	

2000 Playoff Momentum

		NmMt 8	NmMt+ 8.5	MT 9	Gem 9.5/10
180	Tom Brady RC	▲5,000	▲6,000	8,000	10,000

2000 Playoff Prestige

		NmMt 8	NmMt+ 8.5	MT 9	Gem 9.5/10
286	Tom Brady RC	800	1,000	1,500	2,000

2000 Press Pass Gold Zone

		NmMt 8	NmMt+ 8.5	MT 9	Gem 9.5/10
37	Tom Brady	60	80	125	300

2000 Press Pass Autographs

		NmMt 8	NmMt+ 8.5	MT 9	Gem 9.5/10
3	Tom Brady	5,000	6,000	8,000	15,000

2000 Private Stock

		NmMt 8	NmMt+ 8.5	MT 9	Gem 9.5/10
128	Tom Brady RC	400	600	2,500	3,000

2000 Private Stock Retail

		NmMt 8	NmMt+ 8.5	MT 9	Gem 9.5/10
128	Tom Brady RC	600	800	1,000	1,200

2000 Private Stock Premiere Date

		NmMt 8	NmMt+ 8.5	MT 9	Gem 9.5/10
128	Tom Brady	350	400	500	800

2000 Quantum Leaf

		NmMt 8	NmMt+ 8.5	MT 9	Gem 9.5/10
343	Tom Brady RC	400	500	▲800	2,000

2000 Revolution

		NmMt 8	NmMt+ 8.5	MT 9	Gem 9.5/10
128	Tom Brady RC	8,000	10,000	12,000	15,000

2000 Revolution First Look

		NmMt 8	NmMt+ 8.5	MT 9	Gem 9.5/10
22	Tom Brady	40	50	100	

2000 Score

		NmMt 8	NmMt+ 8.5	MT 9	Gem 9.5/10
288	Brian Urlacher RC	8	10	15	25
316	Tom Brady RC	▲250	▲300	▲500	1,000

2000 Score Scorecard

		NmMt 8	NmMt+ 8.5	MT 9	Gem 9.5/10
316	Tom Brady	300	400	500	

2000 SkyBox Dominion

		NmMt 8	NmMt+ 8.5	MT 9	Gem 9.5/10
234	T.Brady RC/Carmazzi RC	200	250	300	▲600

2000 SkyBox Dominion Extra

		NmMt 8	NmMt+ 8.5	MT 9	Gem 9.5/10
234	G.Carmazzi/T.Brady			100	350

2000 SP Authentic

		NmMt 8	NmMt+ 8.5	MT 9	Gem 9.5/10
118	Tom Brady RC	▼15,000	▼2,000	▼22,000	▼30,000
122	Brian Urlacher RC	50	60	▲250	▲400
140	Shaun Alexander RC	12	15	▲125	▲150

2000 SPx

		NmMt 8	NmMt+ 8.5	MT 9	Gem 9.5/10
130	Tom Brady RC	6,000	8,000	10,000	20,000
134	Brian Urlacher JSY AU RC	125	150	225	

2000 Stadium Club

		NmMt 8	NmMt+ 8.5	MT 9	Gem 9.5/10
170	Shaun Alexander RC	10	12	20	40

2000 Topps

		NmMt 8	NmMt+ 8.5	MT 9	Gem 9.5/10
383	Brian Urlacher RC	10	12	20	40

2000 Topps Chrome

		NmMt 8	NmMt+ 8.5	MT 9	Gem 9.5/10
241	Shaun Alexander RC	12	15	25	40
253	Brian Urlacher RC	▲50	▲150	▲300	▲500

2000 UD Graded

		NmMt 8	NmMt+ 8.5	MT 9	Gem 9.5/10
104	Tom Brady RC	2,000	2,500	3,000	8,000
111	Brian Urlacher RC	25	30	40	50
157	Shaun Alexander AU RC	35	40	60	100

2000 UD Ionix

		NmMt 8	NmMt+ 8.5	MT 9	Gem 9.5/10
77	Tom Brady RC	1,000	1,500	2,000	2,500

2000 Ultimate Victory

		NmMt 8	NmMt+ 8.5	MT 9	Gem 9.5/10
146	Tom Brady RC	1,500	2,000	2,500	▲8,000

2000 Ultimate Victory Parallel

		NmMt 8	NmMt+ 8.5	MT 9	Gem 9.5/10
146	Tom Brady	2,000	2,500	6,000	

2000 Ultra

		NmMt 8	NmMt+ 8.5	MT 9	Gem 9.5/10
234	Tom Brady RC	400	500	800	▲3,500
240	LaVar Arrington RC SP	50	60	100	175

2000 Ultra Gold Medallion

		NmMt 8	NmMt+ 8.5	MT 9	Gem 9.5/10
234	Tom Brady	500	800	1,200	2,000

2000 Upper Deck

		NmMt 8	NmMt+ 8.5	MT 9	Gem 9.5/10
254	Tom Brady RC	600	800	1,000	2,000

2000 Upper Deck Encore

		NmMt 8	NmMt+ 8.5	MT 9	Gem 9.5/10
254	Tom Brady RC	▲600	▲800	▲1,000	3,000

2000 Upper Deck Gold Reserve

		NmMt 8	NmMt+ 8.5	MT 9	Gem 9.5/10
215	Tom Brady RC	▲2,500	▲4,000	▲5,000	▲12,000

2000 Upper Deck MVP

		NmMt 8	NmMt+ 8.5	MT 9	Gem 9.5/10
192	Brian Urlacher RC	10	12	20	30

2000 Upper Deck Pros and Prospects

		NmMt 8	NmMt+ 8.5	MT 9	Gem 9.5/10
93	Brian Urlacher RC	30	40	60	100
124	Tom Brady RC	800	1,000	1,500	2,500

2000 Upper Deck Victory

		NmMt 8	NmMt+ 8.5	MT 9	Gem 9.5/10
326	Tom Brady RC	▲600	▲800	▲2,500	▲4,000

2000 Upper Deck Vintage Previews

		NmMt 8	NmMt+ 8.5	MT 9	Gem 9.5/10
14	T.Brady/J.R.Redmond	300	400	1,000	

2000 Vanguard

		NmMt 8	NmMt+ 8.5	MT 9	Gem 9.5/10
139	Tom Brady RC	600	1,000	1,600	3,500

2001 Bowman

		NmMt 8	NmMt+ 8.5	MT 9	Gem 9.5/10
164	Drew Brees RC	100	125	400	
200	Michael Vick RC	15	20	60	
210	LaDainian Tomlinson RC	15	20	▲80	

2001 Bowman Chrome

		NmMt 8	NmMt+ 8.5	MT 9	Gem 9.5/10
144	Drew Brees RC	▲800	1,000	1,600	2,000
180	Michael Vick RC	▲100	▲250	▲300	▲400
190	LaDainian Tomlinson RC	40	50	100	▲200

2001 Bowman Chrome Gold Refractors

		NmMt 8	NmMt+ 8.5	MT 9	Gem 9.5/10
144	Drew Brees	2,500	2,800	8,000	10,000
180	Michael Vick	200	225	800	1,000
190	LaDainian Tomlinson	200	225	400	500

2001 Bowman Chrome Xfractors

		NmMt 8	NmMt+ 8.5	MT 9	Gem 9.5/10
144	Drew Brees	1,200	1,500	2,500	4,000
180	Michael Vick	125	150	200	300
190	LaDainian Tomlinson	125	150	250	300

2001 Bowman Chrome Autographs

		NmMt 8	NmMt+ 8.5	MT 9	Gem 9.5/10
BCDB	Drew Brees	800	1,500	3,000	4,000
BCLT	LaDainian Tomlinson		400	500	600

2001 Bowman's Best

		NmMt 8	NmMt+ 8.5	MT 9	Gem 9.5/10
121	Drew Brees RC	100	200	400	1,500
124	LaDainian Tomlinson RC	25	30	50	150
125	Michael Vick RC	25	30	50	100

2001 Crown Royale

		NmMt 8	NmMt+ 8.5	MT 9	Gem 9.5/10
146	Michael Vick AU/250 RC	80	120	100	
150	Drew Brees AU/250 RC	500	600	800	1,500

2001 Crown Royale Crown Rookies

		NmMt 8	NmMt+ 8.5	MT 9	Gem 9.5/10
2	Drew Brees	10	12	40	50

2001 Donruss Elite

		NmMt 8	NmMt+ 8.5	MT 9	Gem 9.5/10
101	Michael Vick RC	15	25	50	
102	Drew Brees RC	150	250	400	500
114	LaDainian Tomlinson RC	25	30	100	

2001 eTopps

		NmMt 8	NmMt+ 8.5	MT 9	Gem 9.5/10
125	Drew Brees/1290	25	80	200	250
140	Michael Vick/5721	25	30	80	100
143	LaDainian Tomlinson/1536	20	25	30	40

2001 E-X

		NmMt 8	NmMt+ 8.5	MT 9	Gem 9.5/10
133	L.Tomlinson/1000 RC	30	40	60	100
136	Michael Vick/1000 RC	30	40	100	125

2001 Finest

		NmMt 8	NmMt+ 8.5	MT 9	Gem 9.5/10
127	Drew Brees RC	250	300	400	▲1,000
132	LaDainian Tomlinson RC	▲80	▲100	▲125	▲400
134	Michael Vick RC	30	40	50	150
136	Reggie Wayne RC	15	20	40	50

2001 Fleer Authority

		NmMt 8	NmMt+ 8.5	MT 9	Gem 9.5/10
101	Michael Vick RC	12	15	25	40
102	Drew Brees RC	30	50	80	400
113	LaDainian Tomlinson RC	12	15	25	40

2001 Fleer Legacy Rookie Postmarks Autographs

		NmMt 8	NmMt+ 8.5	MT 9	Gem 9.5/10
91	Michael Vick	200	250	300	450

Autographs

		NmMt 8	NmMt+ 8.5	MT 9	Gem 9.5/10
202	Drew Brees	175	200	350	

2001 Pacific

		NmMt 8	NmMt+ 8.5	MT 9	Gem 9.5/10
453	Drew Brees AU/1000 RC	▲500	▲600	▲800	1,500
459	L.Tomlinson AU/1500 RC	50	60	100	200

2001 Pacific Dynagon

		NmMt 8	NmMt+ 8.5	MT 9	Gem 9.5/10
102	Drew Brees AU RC	400	500	1,000	
108	LaDainian Tomlinson AU RC	80	100	150	

2001 Pacific Dynagon Retail

		NmMt 8	NmMt+ 8.5	MT 9	Gem 9.5/10
102	Drew Brees RC	10	12	20	30
108	LaDainian Tomlinson RC	10	12	20	30

2001 Playoff Contenders

		NmMt 8	NmMt+ 8.5	MT 9	Gem 9.5/10
124	Drew Brees AU/500* RC	4,000	6,000	10,000	15,000
150	L.Tomlinson AU/600* RC	200	250	450	800
157	Michael Vick AU/327* RC	175	200	400	700
166	Reggie Wayne AU/400* RC	125	150	200	400
190	Steve Smith AU/300* RC	120	150	300	450

2001 Quantum Leaf

		NmMt 8	NmMt+ 8.5	MT 9	Gem 9.5/10
201	Michael Vick RC	10	12	20	30
202	Drew Brees RC	40	50	100	300
210	LaDainian Tomlinson RC	8	10	15	25

2001 SAGE HIT

		NmMt 8	NmMt+ 8.5	MT 9	Gem 9.5/10
5	LaDainian Tomlinson	6	8	12	20
7	Michael Vick	6	8	12	20
15	Drew Brees	8	10	15	25

2001 SP Authentic

		NmMt 8	NmMt+ 8.5	MT 9	Gem 9.5/10
91	Michael Vick JSY AU RC	400	500	600	1,200
101	Drew Brees JSY RC	150	200	1,000	2,500
120	L.Tomlinson JSY/500 RC	200	250	400	700
146	Steve Smith AU RC	60	100	150	200

2001 SP Authentic Sign of the Times

		NmMt 8	NmMt+ 8.5	MT 9	Gem 9.5/10
DBR	Drew Brees	400	500	800	1,600

2001 SP Game Used Edition

		NmMt 8	NmMt+ 8.5	MT 9	Gem 9.5/10
91	Michael Vick JSY RC	40	50	60	80
93	Drew Brees JSY RC	50	80	125	200
96	LaDainian Tomlinson JSY RC	50	60	120	200

2001 SPx

		NmMt 8	NmMt+ 8.5	MT 9	Gem 9.5/10
95B	M.Vick JSY AU/250 RC	80	100	175	300
95G	M.Vick JSY AU/250 RC	80	100	175	300
101B	D.Brees JSY AU/250 RC	275	300	400	600
101G	D.Brees JSY AU/250 RC	275	300	400	600
122B	L.Tomlinson JSY/250 RC	50	60	100	
122G	L.Tomlinson JSY/250 RC	50	60	100	

2001 Topps

		NmMt 8	NmMt+ 8.5	MT 9	Gem 9.5/10
311	Michael Vick RC	12	15	50	60
328	Drew Brees RC	▼150	250	400	1,500
350	LaDainian Tomlinson RC	12	25	▲80	▲100

2001 Topps Rookie Premier Autographs

		NmMt 8	NmMt+ 8.5	MT 9	Gem 9.5/10
RPDB	Drew Brees	350	400	500	
RPMV	Michael Vick	350	400	600	

2001 Topps Chrome

		NmMt 8	NmMt+ 8.5	MT 9	Gem 9.5/10
221	LaDainian Tomlinson RC	▲400	▲500	▲800	▲1,000
229	Drew Brees RC	1,200	1,500	3,000	4,000
250	Reggie Wayne RC	100	120	300	
262	Michael Vick RC	▲200	▲250	400	

2001 Topps Chrome Refractors

		NmMt 8	NmMt+ 8.5	MT 9	Gem 9.5/10
221	LaDainian Tomlinson	125	300	500	1,200
229	Drew Brees	1,500	2,500	4,000	
262	Michael Vick	60	80	200	

2001 Topps Debut

		NmMt 8	NmMt+ 8.5	MT 9	Gem 9.5/10
101	Drew Brees AU RC	200	300	500	1,200
103	LaDainian Tomlinson AU RC	80	100	200	▲400
108	Michael Vick AU RC	40	80	150	200

2001 Topps Gallery

		NmMt 8	NmMt+ 8.5	MT 9	Gem 9.5/10
101	Michael Vick RC	10	12	15	30
103	LaDainian Tomlinson RC	10	12	15	30
115	Drew Brees RC	25	30	80	400

2001 Topps Heritage

		NmMt 8	NmMt+ 8.5	MT 9	Gem 9.5/10
116	Drew Brees RC	100	125	150	600
133	Michael Vick RC	25	30	40	60
136	LaDainian Tomlinson RC	25	30	40	80

2001 UD Game Gear

		NmMt 8	NmMt+ 8.5	MT 9	Gem 9.5/10
107	Drew Brees RC	20	25	50	80
108	LaDainian Tomlinson RC	25	30	50	100

2001 UD Graded

		NmMt 8	NmMt+ 8.5	MT 9	Gem 9.5/10
47	Drew Brees Action RC	35	40	100	300
47P	Drew Brees Portrait RC	35	40	100	300
53	L.Tomlinson Action RC	20	25	50	80
53P	L.Tomlinson Portrait RC	20	25	50	80
54	Michael Vick Action RC	15	20	40	80
54P	Michael Vick Portrait RC	15	20	40	80
56	Reggie Wayne Action RC	12	15	25	50
56P	Reggie Wayne Portrait RC	12	15	25	50

2001 Upper Deck

		NmMt 8	NmMt+ 8.5	MT 9	Gem 9.5/10
206	Drew Brees RC	25	30	100	200
230	LaDainian Tomlinson RC	20	25	40	60
239	Michael Vick RC	20	25	40	60

2001 UD Graded Rookie Autographs

		NmMt 8	NmMt+ 8.5	MT 9	Gem 9.5/10
47	Drew Brees	300	500	800	1,500
53	LaDainian Tomlinson	60	100	150	250
54	Michael Vick	40	50	60	80

2001 Upper Deck MVP

		NmMt 8	NmMt+ 8.5	MT 9	Gem 9.5/10
283	Michael Vick RC	10	12	20	30
287	Drew Brees RC	30	40	▲60	250
294	LaDainian Tomlinson RC	8	10	12	25

2001 Upper Deck Pros and Prospects

		NmMt 8	NmMt+ 8.5	MT 9	Gem 9.5/10
95	Drew Brees RC	40	80	100	250
104	LaDainian Tomlinson RC	40	50	60	80
135	Michael Vick JSY RC	40	50	60	120

2001 Upper Deck Top Tier

		NmMt 8	NmMt+ 8.5	MT 9	Gem 9.5/10
184	Michael Vick/1500 RC	20	25	40	60
227	L.Tomlinson/1500 RC	20	25	40	60

2001 Upper Deck Victory

		NmMt 8	NmMt+ 8.5	MT 9	Gem 9.5/10
374	Michael Vick RC	10	12	15	25
415	Drew Brees RC	25	30	80	100
416	LaDainian Tomlinson RC	10	12	15	25

2001 Upper Deck Vintage

		NmMt 8	NmMt+ 8.5	MT 9	Gem 9.5/10
204	Michael Vick RC	8	10	20	35
251	Drew Brees RC	40	50	100	400
252	LaDainian Tomlinson RC	10	25	30	50

2002 Bowman Chrome

		NmMt 8	NmMt+ 8.5	MT 9	Gem 9.5/10
99	Tom Brady	50	150	300	400
223	Brian Westbrook AU C RC	15	25	40	60
227	Dwight Freeney AU D RC	35	40	50	80
230	Ed Reed AU A RC	50	60	80	

2002 Finest

		NmMt 8	NmMt+ 8.5	MT 9	Gem 9.5/10
77	Julius Peppers RC	8	10	15	30
92	Dwight Freeney RC	8	10	12	20
102	Brian Westbrook RC	10	12	20	40
109	Ed Reed RC	12	15	40	200

2002 Finest Refractors

		NmMt 8	NmMt+ 8.5	MT 9	Gem 9.5/10
87	Jeremy Shockey	12	15	25	50
122	Clinton Portis AU	40	50	100	200

2002 Playoff Contenders

		NmMt 8	NmMt+ 8.5	MT 9	Gem 9.5/10
128	Dwight Freeney AU/410 RC	50	60	80	
129	Ed Reed AU/550 RC	80	100	200	

2002 SP Authentic

		NmMt 8	NmMt+ 8.5	MT 9	Gem 9.5/10
1	Tom Brady	100	200	250	500
157	Brian Westbrook RC	25	30	40	60
195	Ed Reed AU RC	50	▲100	▲250	▲500

2002 SPx

		NmMt 8	NmMt+ 8.5	MT 9	Gem 9.5/10
99	Ed Reed RC	15	20	30	50

2002 Topps Chrome

		NmMt 8	NmMt+ 8.5	MT 9	Gem 9.5/10
208	Ed Reed RC	25	30	200	1,000
214	Julius Peppers RC	15	20	200	▲800

2002 Topps Pristine

		NmMt 8	NmMt+ 8.5	MT 9	Gem 9.5/10
15	Tom Brady		100	150	500

2002 UD Graded

		NmMt 8	NmMt+ 8.5	MT 9	Gem 9.5/10

2002 Upper Deck

		NmMt 8	NmMt+ 8.5	MT 9	Gem 9.5/10
245	Clinton Portis RC	15	20	25	50

2003 Bowman

		NmMt 8	NmMt+ 8.5	MT 9	Gem 9.5/10
111	Carson Palmer RC	8	10	20	
171	Tony Romo RC	30	50	60	125
257	Troy Polamalu RC	40	50	60	80

2003 Bowman Chrome

		NmMt 8	NmMt+ 8.5	MT 9	Gem 9.5/10
144	Tony Romo RC	50	100	150	500
180	Rex Grossman RC	8	10	15	30
195	Andre Johnson RC	10	12	20	50
206	Willis McGahee RC	8	10	15	30
230	Jason Witten AU D RC	60	80	300	400
235	Larry Johnson AU B RC	35	40	80	
237	Carson Palmer AU A RC	40	50	60	

2003 Bowman Chrome Refractors

		NmMt 8	NmMt+ 8.5	MT 9	Gem 9.5/10
144	Tony Romo	80	100	500	800
195	Andre Johnson	20	25	40	80

2003 Finest

		NmMt 8	NmMt+ 8.5	MT 9	Gem 9.5/10
61	Troy Polamalu RC	30	40	80	▲250
119	Carson Palmer AU/399 RC	▼40	▼50	▼60	
127	Willis McGahee AU/399 RC	▼25	▼30	▼50	
139	Jason Witten AU RC	▲60	▲80	▲125	

2003 Fleer Tradition

		NmMt 8	NmMt+ 8.5	MT 9	Gem 9.5/10
299	Kings RC/Romo RC/St.P RC	12	15	20	30

2003 Leaf Limited

		NmMt 8	NmMt+ 8.5	MT 9	Gem 9.5/10
123	Tony Romo RC	40	50	▲200	▲250
145	Andre Johnson AU RC	60	80	120	

2003 Leaf Rookies and Stars

		NmMt 8	NmMt+ 8.5	MT 9	Gem 9.5/10
205	Tony Romo RC	40	50	80	125

2003 Playoff Contenders

		NmMt 8	NmMt+ 8.5	MT 9	Gem 9.5/10
117	Jason Witten AU/599 RC	175	250	400	800
126B	C.Palmer Blue AU/158 RC	200	250	400	600
127	Byron Leftwich AU/169 RC	50	60	100	175
134	Larry Johnson AU/344 RC	25	30	40	60
135	Will McGahee AU/369 RC	40	50	80	175
146	Anquan Boldin AU/524 RC	35	40	80	120
150	Dallas Clark AU/539 RC	35	40	50	60
156	Tony Romo AU/999 RC	250	300	350	600
190	Troy Polamalu AU/989 RC	300	▲400	▲1,000	

2003 Score

		NmMt 8	NmMt+ 8.5	MT 9	Gem 9.5/10
276	Carson Palmer RC	10	12	20	40

2003 SP Authentic

		NmMt 8	NmMt+ 8.5	MT 9	Gem 9.5/10
120	Troy Polamalu RC	▲250	▲300	▲400	▲600
199	Jason Witten RC	▲80	▲125	▲150	▲500
217	Tony Romo AU RC	225	250	300	400
244	Willis McGahee JSY RC	15	20	35	60
270	Carson Palmer JSY AU RC	▼30	▼100	▼150	

2003 SP Game Used Edition

		NmMt 8	NmMt+ 8.5	MT 9	Gem 9.5/10
91	Carson Palmer RC	20	25	40	60
111	Willis McGahee RC	12	15	25	40

2003 SP Signature

		NmMt 8	NmMt+ 8.5	MT 9	Gem 9.5/10
106	Tony Romo RC	50	50	60	80

2003 SPx

		NmMt 8	NmMt+ 8.5	MT 9	Gem 9.5/10
114	Tony Romo RC	35	40	▲100	▲125
184	Troy Polamalu RC	40	50	80	100
202	A.Johnson JSY AU/250 RC	150	175	250	350
207	B.Leftwich JSY AU/250 RC	25	30	50	60
208	McGahee JSY AU/450 RC	▼25	▼30	▼40	▼50
210	C.Palmer JSY AU/250 RC	40	50	80	120

2003 Topps

		NmMt 8	NmMt+ 8.5	MT 9	Gem 9.5/10
311	Carson Palmer RC	8	10	20	35

2003 Topps Chrome

		NmMt 8	NmMt+ 8.5	MT 9	Gem 9.5/10
166	Carson Palmer RC	12	15	25	50
215	Willis McGahee RC	8	10	20	30
227	Jason Witten RC	▲30	▲40	60	▲250
235	Andre Johnson RC	15	40	50	300
274	Troy Polamalu RC	▲250	▲300	▲400	▲500

2003 Topps Pristine

		NmMt 8	NmMt+ 8.5	MT 9	Gem 9.5/10
75	Carson Palmer C RC	10	12	20	35
76	Carson Palmer U	12	15	25	40
77	Carson Palmer R	15	20	30	50

2003 Topps Pristine Refractors

		NmMt 8	NmMt+ 8.5	MT 9	Gem 9.5/10
75	Carson Palmer C	12	15	25	40
76	Carson Palmer U	15	20	30	50
77	Carson Palmer R	35	40	60	100
111	Larry Johnson C	20	25	40	60
112	Larry Johnson U	25	30	50	80
113	Larry Johnson R	12	15	25	40

2003 Ultimate Collection

		NmMt 8	NmMt+ 8.5	MT 9	Gem 9.5/10
58	Tony Romo/750 RC	35	40	60	100
85	Carson Palmer AU/250 RC	100	120	150	250
95	Willis McGahee/250 RC	35	40	60	100
105	Andre Johnson/750 RC	15	20	30	▲100

2003 Ultra

		NmMt 8	NmMt+ 8.5	MT 9	Gem 9.5/10
161	Carson Palmer RC	8	10	20	30
164	Andre Johnson RC	10	12	15	25
182	Tony Romo RC	▲30	▲60	▲80	▲100

2003 Upper Deck

		NmMt 8	NmMt+ 8.5	MT 9	Gem 9.5/10
241	Carson Palmer RC	15	20	30	50
251	Willis McGahee RC	10	12	20	30
253	Andre Johnson RC	15	20	30	50
256	Tony Romo RC	25	30	50	80

2004 Absolute Memorabilia

		NmMt 8	NmMt+ 8.5	MT 9	Gem 9.5/10
225	Eli Manning RPM RC	40	50	80	120
227	Ben Roethlisberger RPM RC	50	60	100	150

2004 Bazooka

		NmMt 8	NmMt+ 8.5	MT 9	Gem 9.5/10
200	Eli Manning RC	10	12	15	30
210	Ben Roethlisberger RC	15	15	20	40

2004 Bowman

		NmMt 8	NmMt+ 8.5	MT 9	Gem 9.5/10
111	Eli Manning RC	30	40	50	200
114	Ben Roethlisberger RC	15	60	80	▲200

2004 Bowman Chrome

		NmMt 8	NmMt+ 8.5	MT 9	Gem 9.5/10
106	Tom Brady	50	80	100	250
111	Roethlisberger AU/199 RC	250	300	400	600
114	Matt Schaub RC	8	10	20	35
118	Larry Fitzgerald RC	▲80	150	200	500
179	Wes Welker RC	15	20	30	40
223	Philip Rivers AU/199 RC	100	125	150	500
225	Eli Manning AU/199 RC	200	225	300	500

2004 Bowman Chrome Refractors

		NmMt 8	NmMt+ 8.5	MT 9	Gem 9.5/10
118	Larry Fitzgerald	150	200	250	1,000
179	Wes Welker	35	40	50	60

2004 Bowman Chrome Super Bowl XXXIX Unsigned Draft Picks

		NmMt 8	NmMt+ 8.5	MT 9	Gem 9.5/10
111	Ben Roethlisberger	60	80	100	150
225	Eli Manning	40	50	60	100

2004 Bowman's Best

		NmMt 8	NmMt+ 8.5	MT 9	Gem 9.5/10
126	Eli Manning AU/199 RC	125	150	200	
130	Roethlisberger AU/199 RC	175	200	350	500

2004 eTopps

		NmMt 8	NmMt+ 8.5	MT 9	Gem 9.5/10
35	Ben Roethlisberger/2500	40	60	80	100
44	Eli Manning/3750	50	80	100	125

2004 E-X Rookie Die Cuts

		NmMt 8	NmMt+ 8.5	MT 9	Gem 9.5/10
41	Eli Manning No Ser.#	25	30	40	50
46	Ben Roethlisberger No Ser.#	35	40	50	60

2004 Finest

		NmMt 8	NmMt+ 8.5	MT 9	Gem 9.5/10
100	Larry Fitzgerald RC	60	100	150	250
108	Roethlisberger AU/399 RC	200	225	250	350
109	Philip Rivers AU/399 RC	60	80	200	300
110	Eli Manning AU/399 RC	125	150	200	▲500

2004 Finest Refractors

		NmMt 8	NmMt+ 8.5	MT 9	Gem 9.5/10
108	Ben Roethlisberger AU	250	300	400	500
109	Philip Rivers AU	80	100	200	400
110	Eli Manning AU	150	200	250	450

2004 Finest Gold Refractors

		NmMt 8	NmMt+ 8.5	MT 9	Gem 9.5/10
108	Ben Roethlisberger AU	350	400	600	1,500
110	Eli Manning AU	350	400	500	800

2004 Fleer Showcase

		NmMt 8	NmMt+ 8.5	MT 9	Gem 9.5/10
110	Eli Manning RC	25	30	40	60
113	Ben Roethlisberger RC	30	40	50	80

2004 Fleer Tradition

		NmMt 8	NmMt+ 8.5	MT 9	Gem 9.5/10
331	Eli Manning RC	10	12	20	35
332	Larry Fitzgerald RC	8	10	12	25
333	Ben Roethlisberger RC	10	12	20	40
337	Philip Rivers RC	8	10	12	25
351	Eli/Rivers/Roethlisberger	20	20	25	80
352	Fitz/Will/Ro.Will.WR	8	10	15	30

2004 Leaf Rookies and Stars

		NmMt 8	NmMt+ 8.5	MT 9	Gem 9.5/10
181	Willie Parker RC	6	8	12	20

2004 Playoff Contenders

		NmMt 8	NmMt+ 8.5	MT 9	Gem 9.5/10
106	Roethlisberger AU/541* RC	300	600	1,200	2,000
131	Eli Manning AU/372* RC	400	450	600	1,000
162	Philip Rivers AU/556* RC	▼300	▼400	▼500	▼800
169	Roy Williams AU/564* RC	25	30	60	
174	Steven Jackson AU/333* RC	50	60	▼80	150
188A	Willie Parker Blk AU RC	20	25	50	
193	Wes Welker AU RC	▼60	125	150	

2004 Playoff Prestige

		NmMt 8	NmMt+ 8.5	MT 9	Gem 9.5/10
151	Eli Manning RC	12	15	20	40
159	Ben Roethlisberger RC	15	20	▲40	60
220	Mike Williams SP RC	15	20	50	100

2004 SAGE

		NmMt 8	NmMt+ 8.5	MT 9	Gem 9.5/10
35	Ben Roethlisberger	10	12	15	25

2004 Score

		NmMt 8	NmMt+ 8.5	MT 9	Gem 9.5/10
371	Eli Manning RC	10	12	15	25
374	Philip Rivers RC	6	8	12	20
381	Ben Roethlisberger RC	10	12	20	▲100

2004 Score Glossy

		NmMt 8	NmMt+ 8.5	MT 9	Gem 9.5/10
371	Eli Manning	12	15	20	60
381	Ben Roethlisberger	20	20	25	200

2004 SP Authentic

		NmMt 8	NmMt+ 8.5	MT 9	Gem 9.5/10
135	Wes Welker RC	25	30	60	120
187	Matt Schaub JSY AU RC	175	200	250	350
213	Ben Roethlisberger JSY AU RC	1,000	1,200	1,500	
214	Philip Rivers JSY AU RC	400	500	▲1,000	
215	Larry Fitzgerald JSY AU RC	250	300	▲1,500	
216	Eli Manning JSY AU RC	600	1,000	1,200	

2004 SP Game Used Edition

		NmMt 8	NmMt+ 8.5	MT 9	Gem 9.5/10
171	Ben Roethlisberger RC	50	60	80	120
184	Eli Manning RC	50	60	80	150

2004 SPx

		NmMt 8	NmMt+ 8.5	MT 9	Gem 9.5/10
220	Roethlisberger JSY AU/375 RC	175	200	300	500
221	Eli Manning JSY AU/375 RC	150	175	250	500

2004 Topps

		NmMt 8	NmMt+ 8.5	MT 9	Gem 9.5/10
311	Ben Roethlisberger RC	40	100	150	500
350	Eli Manning RC	▲40	▲50	▲60	200
356	Matt Schaub RC	8	10	15	25
360	Larry Fitzgerald RC	8	10	15	25
375	Philip Rivers RC	8	10	15	25

2004 Topps Rookie Premiere Autographs

		NmMt 8	NmMt+ 8.5	MT 9	Gem 9.5/10
RPBR	Ben Roethlisberger	250	300	500	

2004 Topps Chrome

		NmMt 8	NmMt+ 8.5	MT 9	Gem 9.5/10
166	Ben Roethlisberger RC	200	250	500	1,200
205	Eli Manning RC	125	150	200	600
211	Matt Schaub RC				
215	Larry Fitzgerald RC	50	60	200	▲1,000
230	Philip Rivers RC	▼60	▼80	▼100	▼300

2004 Topps Chrome Gold Xfractors

		NmMt 8	NmMt+ 8.5	MT 9	Gem 9.5/10
166	Ben Roethlisberger	400	500	600	800
205	Eli Manning	200	250	300	500
230	Philip Rivers	250	300	400	1,600

2004 Topps Chrome Refractors

		NmMt 8	NmMt+ 8.5	MT 9	Gem 9.5/10
166	Ben Roethlisberger	150	200	800	1,000
205	Eli Manning	60	80	100	
230	Philip Rivers	60	80	300	350

2004 Topps Draft Picks and Prospects

		NmMt 8	NmMt+ 8.5	MT 9	Gem 9.5/10
150	Eli Manning RC	12	15	20	30
165	Ben Roethlisberger RC	15	20	25	30

2004 Topps Draft Picks and Prospects Chrome

		NmMt 8	NmMt+ 8.5	MT 9	Gem 9.5/10
150	Eli Manning	20	25	30	50
165	Ben Roethlisberger	25	30	40	75

2004 Topps Draft Picks and Prospects Gold Chrome

		NmMt 8	NmMt+ 8.5	MT 9	Gem 9.5/10
150	Eli Manning	60	60	80	120
165	Ben Roethlisberger	80	80	100	150

2004 Topps Pristine

		NmMt 8	NmMt+ 8.5	MT 9	Gem 9.5/10
51	Ben Roethlisberger C RC	20	25	35	▲200
52	Ben Roethlisberger U	25	30	50	▲300
53	Ben Roethlisberger R	30	35	50	▲300
87	Eli Manning C RC	15	20	25	40
88	Eli Manning U	20	25	35	60
89	Eli Manning R	25	30	40	60
108	Larry Fitzgerald C RC	10	12	15	30
109	Larry Fitzgerald U	▲80	▲100	▲125	▲200
110	Larry Fitzgerald R	▲80	▲100	▲125	▲250
129	Philip Rivers C RC	10	12	15	30
130	Philip Rivers U	12	15	20	40
131	Philip Rivers R	15	20	25	50

2004 Topps Pristine Refractors

		NmMt 8	NmMt+ 8.5	MT 9	Gem 9.5/10
51	Ben Roethlisberger C	35	40	50	60
52	Ben Roethlisberger U	40	50	80	125
53	Ben Roethlisberger R	100	120	150	250
87	Eli Manning C	30	40	50	80
88	Eli Manning U	30	40	50	60
89	Eli Manning R	30	40	50	60

2004 Topps Signature

		NmMt 8	NmMt+ 8.5	MT 9	Gem 9.5/10
80	Philip Rivers AU/299 RC	80	150	200	500
90	Eli Manning AU/299 RC	150	175	250	450
93	Roethlisberger AU/299 RC	200	250	300	500

2004 Topps Total

		NmMt 8	NmMt+ 8.5	MT 9	Gem 9.5/10
331	Philip Rivers RC	8	10	15	30
350	Eli Manning RC	10	12	20	40
375	Ben Roethlisberger RC	12	15	25	50

2004 Ultimate Collection

		NmMt 8	NmMt+ 8.5	MT 9	Gem 9.5/10
124	Steven Jackson AU RC	80	100	120	200
127	Ben Roethlisberger AU RC	500	600	800	1,600
128	Philip Rivers AU RC	400	500	600	800
129	Larry Fitzgerald AU RC	400	500	600	1,000
130	Eli Manning AU RC	400	500	600	800

2004 Ultimate Collection Ultimate Signatures

		NmMt 8	NmMt+ 8.5	MT 9	Gem 9.5/10
USBR	Roethlisberger/100	225	250	300	800
USEM	E.Manning/100	175	200	250	350
USPR	Philip Rivers/275	80	100	250	500

2004 Ultra Gold Medallion

		NmMt 8	NmMt+ 8.5	MT 9	Gem 9.5/10
201	Eli Manning L13	35	40	50	80
213	Ben Roethlisberger L13	25	30	40	60

2004 Upper Deck

		NmMt 8	NmMt+ 8.5	MT 9	Gem 9.5/10
201	Eli Manning RC	20	25	30	40
202	Larry Fitzgerald RC	12	15	25	40
204	Ben Roethlisberger RC	25	30	40	100
205	Philip Rivers RC	15	20	30	60

2004 Upper Deck Rookie Premiere

		NmMt 8	NmMt+ 8.5	MT 9	Gem 9.5/10
1	Eli Manning	8	10	15	30
2	Ben Roethlisberger	10	12	20	40
25	Matt Schaub	6	8	10	20

2005 Absolute Memorabilia

		NmMt 8	NmMt+ 8.5	MT 9	Gem 9.5/10
180	Aaron Rodgers RC	60	80	100	150

2005 Bazooka

		NmMt 8	NmMt+ 8.5	MT 9	Gem 9.5/10
190	Aaron Rodgers RC	▲100	▲125	200	500

2005 Bowman

		NmMt 8	NmMt+ 8.5	MT 9	Gem 9.5/10
112	Aaron Rodgers RC	150	200	300	250
114	Alex Smith QB RC	8	10	15	25

2005 Bowman Chrome

		NmMt 8	NmMt+ 8.5	MT 9	Gem 9.5/10
221	Aaron Rodgers AU/199 RC	4,000	4,500	5,000	5,500
252	Ryan Fitzpatrick AU F RC	25	30	50	200
259	Frank Gore AU B RC	40	50	80	120

2005 Donruss Classics

		NmMt 8	NmMt+ 8.5	MT 9	Gem 9.5/10
210	Aaron Rodgers RC	40	50	80	250

2005 Donruss Elite

		NmMt 8	NmMt+ 8.5	MT 9	Gem 9.5/10
101	Aaron Rodgers RC	100	120	150	

2005 Exquisite Collection

		NmMt 8	NmMt+ 8.5	MT 9	Gem 9.5/10
93	Frank Gore JSY AU RC	175	200	300	600
106	A.Rodgers JSY AU RC	2,000	2,200	2,800	6,000
114	R.Brown JSY AU/99 RC	250	300	500	800
117	C.Williams JSY AU/99 RC	100	125	200	300
118	A.Smith QB JSY AU/99 RC	300	350	450	

2005 Finest

		NmMt 8	NmMt+ 8.5	MT 9	Gem 9.5/10
121	Frank Gore RC	6	8	12	20
150	Marion Barber RC	10	12	15	25
151	Aaron Rodgers AU/299 RC	1,500	2,000	3,000	5,000
152	Alex Smith QB AU/299 RC	80	100	125	175
163	Brandon Jacobs AU RC	20	25	40	60

2005 Leaf Certified Materials

		NmMt 8	NmMt+ 8.5	MT 9	Gem 9.5/10
162	Aaron Rodgers RC	▲40	▲50	▲200	▲250

2005 Playoff Contenders

		NmMt 8	NmMt+ 8.5	MT 9	Gem 9.5/10
101	A.Rodgers AU/530* RC	2,500	2,800	3,200	6,000
106	Alex Smith QB AU/401* RC	80	100	125	250
129	Darren Sproles AU/454* RC	25	30	50	100
133	DeMarcus Ware AU RC	35	40	200	300
139	Frank Gore AU RC	▲200	▲300	▲400	▲500

2005 SAGE

		NmMt 8	NmMt+ 8.5	MT 9	Gem 9.5/10
37	Aaron Rodgers	10	12	15	50
50	Cadillac Williams	6	8	12	20

2005 SAGE HIT

		NmMt 8	NmMt+ 8.5	MT 9	Gem 9.5/10
8	Aaron Rodgers	6	8	12	20
24	Cadillac Williams	6	8	10	15

2005 Score

	NmMt 8	NmMt+ 8.5	MT 9	Gem 9.5/10
352 Aaron Rodgers RC	▲15	▲50	▲150	▲200

2005 Score Glossy

	NmMt 8	NmMt+ 8.5	MT 9	Gem 9.5/10
352 Aaron Rodgers	20	25	40	60

2005 SP Authentic

	NmMt 8	NmMt+ 8.5	MT 9	Gem 9.5/10
188 Marion Barber AU RC	12	15	25	50
190 Derek Anderson AU RC	12	15	25	40
219 DeMarcus Ware AU RC	▲60	▲80	▲100	250
224 Frank Gore JSY/899 AU RC	▲150	▲200	▲250	1,000
248 A.Smith QB JSY/299 AU RC	225	250	350	500
252 A.Rodgers JSY/99/AU RC	2,250	2,500	5,000	

2005 SPx

	NmMt 8	NmMt+ 8.5	MT 9	Gem 9.5/10
198B Kyle Orton JSY AU RC	25	30	50	
200B Frank Gore JSY AU RC	▲80	▲100	▲300	▲400
222 A.Smith QB JSY AU/250 RC	100	120	150	200
223 A.Rodgers JSY AU/250 RC	600	1,000	1,600	2,600

2005 Topps

	NmMt 8	NmMt+ 8.5	MT 9	Gem 9.5/10
431 Aaron Rodgers RC	200	250	▼400	▼800

2005 Topps Rookie Premiere Autographs

	NmMt 8	NmMt+ 8.5	MT 9	Gem 9.5/10
RPAS Alex Smith QB	80	100	125	175

2005 Topps Chrome

	NmMt 8	NmMt+ 8.5	MT 9	Gem 9.5/10
171 Jason Campbell RC	8	10	15	25
177 Frank Gore RC	60	100	200	▼600
190 Aaron Rodgers RC	500	600	▼1,500	2,500
194 Alex Smith QB RC	12	20	60	80
223 Marion Barber RC				

2005 Topps Chrome Black Refractors

	NmMt 8	NmMt+ 8.5	MT 9	Gem 9.5/10
194 Alex Smith QB	60	80	100	150

2005 Topps Chrome Gold Xfractors

	NmMt 8	NmMt+ 8.5	MT 9	Gem 9.5/10
190 Aaron Rodgers AU	4,000	5,000	6,000	10,000
194 Alex Smith QB	40	50	60	100

2005 Topps Chrome Refractors

	NmMt 8	NmMt+ 8.5	MT 9	Gem 9.5/10
170 Ronnie Brown				
190 Aaron Rodgers	2,000	2,500	4,000	5,000
194 Alex Smith QB	25	30	40	50

2005 Topps Draft Picks and Prospects

	NmMt 8	NmMt+ 8.5	MT 9	Gem 9.5/10
152 Aaron Rodgers RC	▲15	▲20	20	▲125

2005 Topps Draft Picks and Prospects Chrome

	NmMt 8	NmMt+ 8.5	MT 9	Gem 9.5/10
152 Aaron Rodgers	30	40	60	125

2005 Topps Heritage

	NmMt 8	NmMt+ 8.5	MT 9	Gem 9.5/10
344A Aaron Rodgers SP RC	25	30	50	80

2005 Topps Turkey Red

	NmMt 8	NmMt+ 8.5	MT 9	Gem 9.5/10
221 Aaron Rodgers RC	30	80	300	800

2005 Ultimate Collection

	NmMt 8	NmMt+ 8.5	MT 9	Gem 9.5/10
216 Frank Gore AU RC	30	40	50	100
232 Jason Campbell AU/150 RC	50	60	100	150
241 Alex Smith QB AU/99 RC	125	135	150	250
242 Aaron Rodgers AU/99 RC	800	900	1,500	3,500

2005 Ultra

	NmMt 8	NmMt+ 8.5	MT 9	Gem 9.5/10
201 Alex Smith QB L13 RC	25	30	40	60
202 Aaron Rodgers L13 RC	100	120	400	500
248 Frank Gore RC	8	10	15	25

2005 Upper Deck

	NmMt 8	NmMt+ 8.5	MT 9	Gem 9.5/10
202 Aaron Rodgers RC	35	40	60	125

2005 Upper Deck Kickoff

	NmMt 8	NmMt+ 8.5	MT 9	Gem 9.5/10
91 Aaron Rodgers RC	12	15	25	60

2005 Upper Deck Legends

	NmMt 8	NmMt+ 8.5	MT 9	Gem 9.5/10
101 Aaron Rodgers RC	50	60	300	400

2005 Upper Deck Rookie Debut

	NmMt 8	NmMt+ 8.5	MT 9	Gem 9.5/10
126 Aaron Rodgers RC	25	50	80	100

2005 Upper Deck Rookie Materials

	NmMt 8	NmMt+ 8.5	MT 9	Gem 9.5/10
91 Aaron Rodgers RC		30	40	50

2005 Upper Deck Rookie Premiere

	NmMt 8	NmMt+ 8.5	MT 9	Gem 9.5/10
4 Cadillac Williams				
16 Aaron Rodgers	80	100	150	▲400

2005 Upper Deck Rookie Premiere Gold

	NmMt 8	NmMt+ 8.5	MT 9	Gem 9.5/10
16 Aaron Rodgers	25	30	40	100

2006 Bowman

	NmMt 8	NmMt+ 8.5	MT 9	Gem 9.5/10
112 Matt Leinart RC	8	8	12	25
114 Jay Cutler RC	8	10	15	30

2006 Bowman Chrome

	NmMt 8	NmMt+ 8.5	MT 9	Gem 9.5/10
222 Jay Cutler RC	10	12	25	40
224 Matt Leinart RC	8	10	20	30

2006 Bowman Chrome Blue Refractors

	NmMt 8	NmMt+ 8.5	MT 9	Gem 9.5/10
222 Jay Cutler	25	30	40	80
223 Reggie Bush	25	30	40	60

2006 Bowman Chrome Refractors

	NmMt 8	NmMt+ 8.5	MT 9	Gem 9.5/10
222 Jay Cutler	15	20	30	50
223 Reggie Bush	15	20	30	50

2006 Bowman Chrome Rookie Autographs

	NmMt 8	NmMt+ 8.5	MT 9	Gem 9.5/10
223 Reggie Bush/199	40	50	60	

2006 Bowman Sterling

	NmMt 8	NmMt+ 8.5	MT 9	Gem 9.5/10
DHE Devin Hester AU RC	50	60	80	300
ML Matt Leinart JSY RC	20	25	30	50

2006 Finest

	NmMt 8	NmMt+ 8.5	MT 9	Gem 9.5/10
152 Matt Leinart AU/199 RC	25	30	50	80
153 Vince Young AU/199 RC	25	30	50	80
154 Jay Cutler AU/199 RC	40	60	100	125

2006 Fleer

	NmMt 8	NmMt+ 8.5	MT 9	Gem 9.5/10
146 Jay Cutler RC	6	8	12	20
173 Matt Leinart RC	6	8	12	20
197 Vince Young RC	6	10	12	20

2006 Playoff Contenders

	NmMt 8	NmMt+ 8.5	MT 9	Gem 9.5/10
115 Santonio Holmes AU RC	20	25	35	60
165 Devin Hester AU RC	30	40	50	60

2006 Playoff Prestige

	NmMt 8	NmMt+ 8.5	MT 9	Gem 9.5/10
198 Jay Cutler RC	8	10	15	
223 Matt Leinart RC	8	10	12	25
246 Vince Young RC	10	12	15	30

2006 SAGE

	NmMt 8	NmMt+ 8.5	MT 9	Gem 9.5/10
59 Vince Young	8	10	15	25

2006 SAGE HIT

	NmMt 8	NmMt+ 8.5	MT 9	Gem 9.5/10
10 Vince Young	8	10	15	25
11 Matt Leinart	8	10	12	20

2006 Score

	NmMt 8	NmMt+ 8.5	MT 9	Gem 9.5/10
331 Matt Leinart RC	6	8	10	15
340 Vince Young RC	8	10	12	20
350A Jay Cutler RC	6	8	10	15
350B Jay Cutler fact set	6	8	10	15

2006 SP Authentic

	NmMt 8	NmMt+ 8.5	MT 9	Gem 9.5/10
226 Jay Cutler AU/99 RC	▼50	▼60	▼80	
247 M.Drew JSY/999 AU RC				
252 R.Bush JSY/299 AU RC	▼40	▼50	▼100	

2006 SPx

	NmMt 8	NmMt+ 8.5	MT 9	Gem 9.5/10
183 Vince Young JSY AU RC	25	30	40	60
184 S.Holmes JSY AU RC	25	30	50	60
186 Matt Leinart JSY AU RC	25	30	50	80
203 Maurice Drew JSY AU RC	25	30	40	50
208 Brandon Marshall JSY AU RC	20	25	40	60

2006 SPx Rookie Autographs Gold

	NmMt 8	NmMt+ 8.5	MT 9	Gem 9.5/10
159 Jay Cutler	80	100	125	200

2006 Topps

	NmMt 8	NmMt+ 8.5	MT 9	Gem 9.5/10
353 Vince Young RC	8	10	15	25
354 Matt Leinart RC	8	10	15	25
365 Jay Cutler RC	10	12	20	35

2006 Topps Chrome

	NmMt 8	NmMt+ 8.5	MT 9	Gem 9.5/10
223 Vince Young RC	8	10	20	30
224 Matt Leinart RC	8	10	20	30
229 Jay Cutler RC	10	12	25	40
244 Santonio Holmes RC	8	10	20	30
247 Maurice Drew RC	10	12	20	30
252 Devin Hester RC	10	12	25	35

2006 Topps Chrome Black Refractors

	NmMt 8	NmMt+ 8.5	MT 9	Gem 9.5/10
221 Reggie Bush	25	30	40	60
229 Jay Cutler	25	30	40	60

2006 Topps Chrome Refractors

	NmMt 8	NmMt+ 8.5	MT 9	Gem 9.5/10
221 Reggie Bush	15	20	30	50
224 Matt Leinart	10	12	20	35
229 Jay Cutler	20	25	40	50
234 Vernon Davis	12	15	25	40
244 Santonio Holmes	10	12	20	35
247 Maurice Drew	15	20	30	40
263 Brandon Marshall	12	15	25	40
268 Joseph Addai	12	15	25	40

2006 Topps Chrome Special Edition Rookies

		NmMt 8	NmMt+ 8.5	MT 9	Gem 9.5/10
221	Reggie Bush	10	12	20	35
223	Vince Young	8	10	20	30
224	Matt Leinart	8	10	20	30
227	Laurence Maroney	15	20	30	50
228	DeAngelo Williams	8	10	20	30
229	Jay Cutler	12	15	25	40
247	Maurice Drew	10	12	20	35
268	Joseph Addai	15	20	30	50

2006 Topps Chrome Rookie Autographs

		NmMt 8	NmMt+ 8.5	MT 9	Gem 9.5/10
221	Reggie Bush A				
263	Brandon Marshall D	15	20	25	40

2006 Topps Heritage

		NmMt 8	NmMt+ 8.5	MT 9	Gem 9.5/10
320	Vince Young SP RC	10	12	20	30

2006 Topps Turkey Red

		NmMt 8	NmMt+ 8.5	MT 9	Gem 9.5/10
183A	Vince Young PS RC	8	10	18	30
229A	Matt Leinart TIB RC	8	10	15	25

2006 Ultra

		NmMt 8	NmMt+ 8.5	MT 9	Gem 9.5/10
201	Matt Leinart L13 RC	25	30	50	100
202	Vince Young L13 RC	25	30	50	100
206	Jay Cutler L13 RC	50	60	100	175

2006 Ultra Target Exclusive Rookies

		NmMt 8	NmMt+ 8.5	MT 9	Gem 9.5/10
201	Matt Leinart L13	25	30	40	50
202	Vince Young L13	25	30	40	50
203	Reggie Bush L13	30	40	50	60
206	Jay Cutler L13	30	40	50	60

2006 Upper Deck

		NmMt 8	NmMt+ 8.5	MT 9	Gem 9.5/10
210	Jay Cutler RC	15	20	30	50
216	Matt Leinart RC	10	12	20	35
225	Vince Young RC	10	12	20	35

2006 Upper Deck Exclusive Edition Rookies

		NmMt 8	NmMt+ 8.5	MT 9	Gem 9.5/10
210	Jay Cutler	8	10	12	20
216	Matt Leinart	6	8	12	20
219	Reggie Bush	8	10	15	25
225	Vince Young	8	10	15	25

2006 Upper Deck Rookie Premiere

		NmMt 8	NmMt+ 8.5	MT 9	Gem 9.5/10
2	Reggie Bush	8	10	15	25
15	Matt Leinart	8	10	12	20
26	DeAngelo Williams	6	8	10	15
30	Vince Young	8	10	15	25

2007 Artifacts

		NmMt 8	NmMt+ 8.5	MT 9	Gem 9.5/10
152	Adrian Peterson RC	20	25	40	60

2007 Bowman

		NmMt 8	NmMt+ 8.5	MT 9	Gem 9.5/10
26	Adrian Peterson RC	15	20	25	30

2007 Bowman Chrome

		NmMt 8	NmMt+ 8.5	MT 9	Gem 9.5/10
BC65	Adrian Peterson RC	25	40	80	200
BC66	Marshawn Lynch RC	8	12	20	25
BC75	Calvin Johnson RC	20	30	80	300

2007 Bowman Chrome Refractors

		NmMt 8	NmMt+ 8.5	MT 9	Gem 9.5/10
BC65	Adrian Peterson	50	80	150	300
BC66	Marshawn Lynch	10	12	15	25
BC75	Calvin Johnson	30	100	200	250

2007 Bowman Chrome Uncirculated Rookies

		NmMt 8	NmMt+ 8.5	MT 9	Gem 9.5/10
BC65	Adrian Peterson	25	30	60	100
BC75	Calvin Johnson	20	25	30	40

2007 Bowman Sterling

		NmMt 8	NmMt+ 8.5	MT 9	Gem 9.5/10
APE1	Adrian Peterson JSY RC	40	50	60	100
CJ01	Calvin Johnson JSY RC	20	25	35	▲80

2007 Donruss Elite

		NmMt 8	NmMt+ 8.5	MT 9	Gem 9.5/10
105	Adrian Peterson RC	40	50	80	
118	Calvin Johnson RC	25	30	50	

2007 Finest

		NmMt 8	NmMt+ 8.5	MT 9	Gem 9.5/10
112	Adrian Peterson RC	▲40	▲50	▲60	▲80
135	Calvin Johnson RC	25	40	100	300

2007 Finest Blue Refractors

		NmMt 8	NmMt+ 8.5	MT 9	Gem 9.5/10
102	Brady Quinn	12	15	25	40
112	Adrian Peterson	30	35	50	80

2007 Finest Refractors

		NmMt 8	NmMt+ 8.5	MT 9	Gem 9.5/10
112	Adrian Peterson	40	50	60	80
135	Calvin Johnson	15	20	35	60

2007 Finest Rookie Autographs

		NmMt 8	NmMt+ 8.5	MT 9	Gem 9.5/10
112	Adrian Peterson A	250	300	500	

2007 Playoff Contenders

		NmMt 8	NmMt+ 8.5	MT 9	Gem 9.5/10
104	A.Peterson AU/355* RC	300	350	400	700
123	C.Johnson AU/525* RC	150	200	250	500

2007 Playoff Prestige

		NmMt 8	NmMt+ 8.5	MT 9	Gem 9.5/10
155	Adrian Peterson RC	20	25	30	50

2007 SAGE HIT

		NmMt 8	NmMt+ 8.5	MT 9	Gem 9.5/10
28	Adrian Peterson	8	10	15	25

2007 Score

		NmMt 8	NmMt+ 8.5	MT 9	Gem 9.5/10
341	Adrian Peterson RC	8	10	15	25
351	Calvin Johnson RC	8	10	12	30

2007 SP Authentic

		NmMt 8	NmMt+ 8.5	MT 9	Gem 9.5/10
289	Adrian Peterson JSY AU RC	500	600		

2007 SP Chirography

		NmMt 8	NmMt+ 8.5	MT 9	Gem 9.5/10
101	Adrian Peterson AU/199 RC	125	150	200	300

2007 SPx

		NmMt 8	NmMt+ 8.5	MT 9	Gem 9.5/10
218	A.Peterson JSY AU/299 RC	250	300	400	
220	Ca.Johnson JSY AU/299 RC	100	120	250	

2007 Topps

		NmMt 8	NmMt+ 8.5	MT 9	Gem 9.5/10
301	Adrian Peterson RC	10	12	20	60
320	Calvin Johnson RC	8	10	15	25

2007 Topps Rookie Premiere Autographs

		NmMt 8	NmMt+ 8.5	MT 9	Gem 9.5/10
AP	Adrian Peterson	175	200	350	500

2007 Topps Chrome

		NmMt 8	NmMt+ 8.5	MT 9	Gem 9.5/10
TC181	Adrian Peterson RC	25	30	40	100
TC200	Calvin Johnson RC	80	125	200	500

2007 Topps Chrome Blue Refractors

		NmMt 8	NmMt+ 8.5	MT 9	Gem 9.5/10
TC181	Adrian Peterson	50	60	100	150

2007 Topps Chrome Red Refractors Uncirculated

		NmMt 8	NmMt+ 8.5	MT 9	Gem 9.5/10
TC181	Adrian Peterson	125	150	175	250

2007 Topps Chrome Refractors

		NmMt 8	NmMt+ 8.5	MT 9	Gem 9.5/10
TC181	Adrian Peterson	100	125	250	400
TC200	Calvin Johnson	150	250	400	500

2007 Topps Chrome White Refractors

		NmMt 8	NmMt+ 8.5	MT 9	Gem 9.5/10
TC181	Adrian Peterson	60	80	100	150
TC200	Calvin Johnson	60	80	100	500

2007 Topps Chrome Xfractors

		NmMt 8	NmMt+ 8.5	MT 9	Gem 9.5/10
TC181	Adrian Peterson	50	60	80	135
TC200	Calvin Johnson	50	60	80	100

2007 Topps Draft Picks and Prospects

		NmMt 8	NmMt+ 8.5	MT 9	Gem 9.5/10
135	Adrian Peterson RC	10	12	15	25

2007 Topps Draft Picks and Prospects Chrome Black

		NmMt 8	NmMt+ 8.5	MT 9	Gem 9.5/10
132	Calvin Johnson	8	10	15	25
135	Adrian Peterson	12	15	20	30

2007 Topps Draft Picks and Prospects Chrome Bronze

		NmMt 8	NmMt+ 8.5	MT 9	Gem 9.5/10
135	Adrian Peterson	15	20	25	40

2007 Ultimate Collection

		NmMt 8	NmMt+ 8.5	MT 9	Gem 9.5/10
101	Adrian Peterson AU/99 RC	250	300	400	500
103	Calvin Johnson AU/99 RC	150	175	200	250

2007 Ultra

		NmMt 8	NmMt+ 8.5	MT 9	Gem 9.5/10
205	Adrian Peterson L13 RC	25	30	40	60

2007 Ultra Retail

		NmMt 8	NmMt+ 8.5	MT 9	Gem 9.5/10
205	Adrian Peterson L13 RC	25	30	40	50

2007 Upper Deck

		NmMt 8	NmMt+ 8.5	MT 9	Gem 9.5/10
277	Calvin Johnson RC	12	15	25	40
279	Adrian Peterson RC	15	20	30	50

2007 Upper Deck Exclusive Edition Rookies

		NmMt 8	NmMt+ 8.5	MT 9	Gem 9.5/10
279	Adrian Peterson	8	10	15	25

2007 Upper Deck First Edition

		NmMt 8	NmMt+ 8.5	MT 9	Gem 9.5/10
104	Adrian Peterson RC	10	12	20	30

2007 Upper Deck Rookie Premiere

		NmMt 8	NmMt+ 8.5	MT 9	Gem 9.5/10
15	Calvin Johnson	8	10	12	25
21	Adrian Peterson	10	12	15	30

2008 Bowman Chrome

		NmMt 8	NmMt+ 8.5	MT 9	Gem 9.5/10
BC59	Matt Ryan RC	12	15	30	50
BC61	Joe Flacco RC	8	10	15	20

2008 Bowman Chrome Refractors

		NmMt 8	NmMt+ 8.5	MT 9	Gem 9.5/10
BC59	Matt Ryan	15	20	50	100
BC61	Joe Flacco	15	20	35	50
BC76	Chris Johnson	12	15	25	40

2008 Bowman Sterling Blue Refractor Rookie Autographs

		NmMt 8	NmMt+ 8.5	MT 9	Gem 9.5/10
BA1	Matt Ryan	80	100	125	150

2008 Bowman Sterling Gold Rookie Autographs

		NmMt 8	NmMt+ 8.5	MT 9	Gem 9.5/10
156	Chris Johnson/400	12	15	25	50

2008 Bowman Sterling Rookie Blue Refractors

		NmMt 8	NmMt+ 8.5	MT 9	Gem 9.5/10
BS1	Matt Ryan	12	15	25	50
BS2	Joe Flacco	12	15	25	40
BS7	Chris Johnson	8	10	15	30

2008 Donruss Classics

		NmMt 8	NmMt+ 8.5	MT 9	Gem 9.5/10
219	Joe Flacco AU/399 RC	30	40	50	60

2008 Donruss Elite

		NmMt 8	NmMt+ 8.5	MT 9	Gem 9.5/10
101	Matt Ryan AU/199 RC	80	100	125	175
105	Joe Flacco AU/299 RC	▼25	▼40	▼50	▼60

2008 Exquisite Collection

		NmMt 8	NmMt+ 8.5	MT 9	Gem 9.5/10
148	Jamaal Charles JSY AU RC	60	80	200	
168	Matt Ryan JSY AU RC	750	800	1,200	
170	Joe Flacco JSY AU RC	300	400	500	

2008 Finest

		NmMt 8	NmMt+ 8.5	MT 9	Gem 9.5/10
109	Matt Ryan RC	15	20	30	50
116	Chris Johnson RC	10	12	20	30

2008 Playoff Contenders

		NmMt 8	NmMt+ 8.5	MT 9	Gem 9.5/10
112	Chad Henne AU RC	20	25	40	60
115	Chris Johnson AU RC	25	30	60	120
123	Darren McFadden AU RC	30	35	60	100
151	Joe Flacco AU/220* RC	80	100	200	250
178	Matt Forte AU RC	35	40	50	80
179	Matt Ryan AU/246* RC	400	500	600	1,200

2008 Playoff National Treasures

		NmMt 8	NmMt+ 8.5	MT 9	Gem 9.5/10
111	Matt Ryan JSY AU RC	300	350	400	500

2008 Playoff Prestige

		NmMt 8	NmMt+ 8.5	MT 9	Gem 9.5/10
151	Joe Flacco RC	8	10	15	25
179	Matt Ryan RC	8	10	15	25

2008 Score

		NmMt 8	NmMt+ 8.5	MT 9	Gem 9.5/10
333	Matt Ryan RC	10	12	15	25
344	Joe Flacco RC	8	10	12	20
348	Chris Johnson RC	8	10	12	20

2008 SP Authentic

		NmMt 8	NmMt+ 8.5	MT 9	Gem 9.5/10
228	Matt Flynn AU RC				80
279	Jordy Nelson JSY AU RC	40	50	60	
295	Joe Flacco JSY AU RC	50	60	80	100
300	Matt Ryan JSY AU/499 RC	▲200	▲250	▲400	

2008 SP Rookie Edition

		NmMt 8	NmMt+ 8.5	MT 9	Gem 9.5/10
127	Joe Flacco RC	8	10	15	25
143	Matt Ryan RC	10	12	20	30
196	Matt Ryan 93	10	12	20	30

2008 SPx

		NmMt 8	NmMt+ 8.5	MT 9	Gem 9.5/10
153	Chris Johnson JSY AU RC	20	25	50	
162	Joe Flacco JSY AU RC	50	60	100	150

2008 Topps Rookie Premiere Autographs

		NmMt 8	NmMt+ 8.5	MT 9	Gem 9.5/10
RPADM	Darren McFadden	80	100	125	200
RPAJF	Joe Flacco	80	100	125	200
RPAJS	Jonathan Stewart	40	50	60	80
RPAMF	Matt Forte	40	50	60	80
RPAMR	Matt Ryan	80	100	120	150

2008 Topps Chrome

		NmMt 8	NmMt+ 8.5	MT 9	Gem 9.5/10
TC166	Matt Ryan RC	12	15	80	▼150
TC170	Joe Flacco RC	10	12	20	30

2008 Topps Chrome Copper Refractors

		NmMt 8	NmMt+ 8.5	MT 9	Gem 9.5/10
TC166	Matt Ryan	20	25	40	100

2008 Topps Chrome Refractors

		NmMt 8	NmMt+ 8.5	MT 9	Gem 9.5/10
TC166	Matt Ryan	15	20	125	300
TC170	Joe Flacco	12	15	25	50
TC186	Chris Johnson	8	10	20	40

2008 Topps Chrome Rookie Autographs

		NmMt 8	NmMt+ 8.5	MT 9	Gem 9.5/10
TC186	Chris Johnson E	20	25	40	50
TC187	Ray Rice B	25	30	40	50
TC191	Matt Forte E	25	30	40	50

2008 Upper Deck

		NmMt 8	NmMt+ 8.5	MT 9	Gem 9.5/10
219	Chris Johnson RC	8	10	15	20
251	Joe Flacco RC	10	12	15	25
305	Matt Ryan SP RC	20	25	35	50

2008 Upper Deck Draft Edition

		NmMt 8	NmMt+ 8.5	MT 9	Gem 9.5/10
50	Joe Flacco RC	10	12	15	25
74	Matt Ryan RC	10	12	15	25

2008 Upper Deck Rookie Premiere

		NmMt 8	NmMt+ 8.5	MT 9	Gem 9.5/10
4	Matt Ryan	8	10	15	25

2009 Bowman Chrome

		NmMt 8	NmMt+ 8.5	MT 9	Gem 9.5/10
111	Matthew Stafford RC	125	150	200	400

2009 Bowman Chrome Rookie Autographs

		NmMt 8	NmMt+ 8.5	MT 9	Gem 9.5/10
111	Matthew Stafford A	125	150	200	250

2009 Bowman Draft

		NmMt 8	NmMt+ 8.5	MT 9	Gem 9.5/10
111	Matthew Stafford RC	10	12	20	30

2009 Finest

		NmMt 8	NmMt+ 8.5	MT 9	Gem 9.5/10
61	Josh Freeman RC	8	10	12	20
73	Percy Harvin RC	8	10	12	20
80	Mark Sanchez RC	10	12	15	25
100	Matthew Stafford RC	60	100	▼150	400

2009 Playoff Contenders

		NmMt 8	NmMt+ 8.5	MT 9	Gem 9.5/10
101	M.Stafford AU/540* RC	100	125	150	300
156	Clay Matthews AU RC	80	100	125	150
176	Julian Edelman AU RC	200	250	300	500

2009 Playoff National Treasures

		NmMt 8	NmMt+ 8.5	MT 9	Gem 9.5/10
119	LeSean McCoy JSY AU RC	80	125	150	200
121	Matthew Stafford JSY AU RC	▲2,000	▲3,200	▲4,000	▲4,500
150	Clay Matthews AU RC	80	100	125	150

2009 Playoff Prestige

		NmMt 8	NmMt+ 8.5	MT 9	Gem 9.5/10
172A	Matthew Stafford RC	12	15	25	40

2009 Score

		NmMt 8	NmMt+ 8.5	MT 9	Gem 9.5/10
323	Chris Wells RC	10	12	15	25
371	Matthew Stafford RC	12	15	20	30

2009 SP Authentic

		NmMt 8	NmMt+ 8.5	MT 9	Gem 9.5/10
305	Julian Edelman AU RC	100	125	250	600
357	Clay Matthews AU/299 RC	50	60	80	125
403	M.Stafford JSY AU/499 RC	▲600	▲1,500	▲2,500	

2009 Topps

		NmMt 8	NmMt+ 8.5	MT 9	Gem 9.5/10
430A	Matthew Stafford RC	12	15	20	35

2009 Topps Chrome

		NmMt 8	NmMt+ 8.5	MT 9	Gem 9.5/10
TC155	Percy Harvin RC	8	10	15	25
TC210	Matthew Stafford RC	150	250	300	800

2009 Topps Chrome Blue Refractors

		NmMt 8	NmMt+ 8.5	MT 9	Gem 9.5/10
TC210	Matthew Stafford	100	150	200	800

2009 Topps Chrome Refractors

		NmMt 8	NmMt+ 8.5	MT 9	Gem 9.5/10
TC210	Matthew Stafford	150	250	400	1,200
TC220	Mark Sanchez	12	15	30	60

2009 Topps Chrome Xfractors

		NmMt 8	NmMt+ 8.5	MT 9	Gem 9.5/10
TC210	Matthew Stafford	25	30	50	80
TC220	Mark Sanchez	15	20	30	50

2009 Topps Chrome Rookie Autographs

		NmMt 8	NmMt+ 8.5	MT 9	Gem 9.5/10
TC210	Matthew Stafford B	▲400	▲500	▲1,000	▲1,500

2009 Topps Platinum

		NmMt 8	NmMt+ 8.5	MT 9	Gem 9.5/10
125	Matthew Stafford RC	10	12	20	30

2009 Upper Deck

		NmMt 8	NmMt+ 8.5	MT 9	Gem 9.5/10
305	Matthew Stafford RC	12	15	20	30

2010 Bowman Chrome Rookie Preview Inserts

		NmMt 8	NmMt+ 8.5	MT 9	Gem 9.5/10
BCR1	Tim Tebow	8	10	15	25
BCR3	Dez Bryant	8	10	15	25

2010 Donruss Rated Rookies

		NmMt 8	NmMt+ 8.5	MT 9	Gem 9.5/10
95	Tim Tebow	8	10	15	25
100	Victor Cruz	8	10	12	20

2010 Exquisite Collection Draft Picks

		NmMt 8	NmMt+ 8.5	MT 9	Gem 9.5/10
ERAD	Andy Dalton	50	60	80	100
ERCN	Cam Newton	125	150	200	300

2010 Finest

		NmMt 8	NmMt+ 8.5	MT 9	Gem 9.5/10
100	Tim Tebow RC	10	12	20	30
110	Dez Bryant RC	8	10	15	25

2010 Finest Atomic Refractor Rookies

		NmMt 8	NmMt+ 8.5	MT 9	Gem 9.5/10
FAR25	Tim Tebow	15	20	30	50

2010 Playoff Contenders

		NmMt 8	NmMt+ 8.5	MT 9	Gem 9.5/10
56	Danny Woodhead RC	8	10	15	30
101	Aaron Hernandez AU RC	▲100	▲150	▲200	▲500
105	Antonio Brown AU RC	200	250	300	▲800
151	Jimmy Graham AU/358* RC	60	80	100	125
186	Sean Lee AU RC	25	30	40	60

#		NmMt 8	NmMt+ 8.5	MT 9	Gem 9.5/10
199	Victor Cruz AU RC	25	30	40	50
204A	Ben Tate Cut AU RC	15	20	30	50
204B	Ben Tate Stnd AU RC	15	20	30	50
206A	C.J. Spiller BJ AU/372* RC	50	60	80	100
206B	C.J. Spiller WJ AU/372* RC	50	60	80	100
207A	Colt McCoy BJ AU/394* RC	25	30	50	80
207B	Colt McCoy WJ AU/394* RC	25	30	50	80
209A	D.Thomas Cut AU RC	40	50	80	120
209B	D.Thomas Fwd AU RC	40	50	80	120
211A	Dez Bryant BJ AU/360* RC	80	100	125	200
211B	Dez Bryant WJ AU/360* RC	80	100	125	200
214A	Eric Decker BJ AU/492* RC	30	40	50	60
214B	Eric Decker OJ AU/492* RC	30	40	50	60
228A	N.Suh BJ AU/326* RC	40	50	60	80
228B	N.Suh WJ AU/326* RC	40	50	60	80
229A	Gronkowski BJ AU/499* RC	60	80	100	300
229B	Gronkowski WJ AU/499* RC	60	80	100	300
232A	Bradford Fwd AU/377* RC	60	80	100	125
232B	Bradford Lft AU/377* RC	60	80	100	125
234A	Tim Tebow BJ AU/400* RC	60	80	150	250
234B	T.Tebow WJ AU/400* RC	60	80	150	250

2010 Playoff National Treasures

#		NmMt 8	NmMt+ 8.5	MT 9	Gem 9.5/10
311	Dez Bryant JSY AU RC	250	300	400	
329	Rob Gronkowski JSY AU RC	225	250	500	
332	Sam Bradford JSY AU RC	500	600	700	
334	Tim Tebow JSY AU RC	250	300	400	

2010 Score

#		NmMt 8	NmMt+ 8.5	MT 9	Gem 9.5/10
323	Colt McCoy RC	8	10	12	20
334	Dez Bryant RC	8	10	15	25
387	Sam Bradford RC	10	12	20	30
396	Tim Tebow RC	10	12	20	35

2010 SP Authentic

#		NmMt 8	NmMt+ 8.5	MT 9	Gem 9.5/10
102	Colt McCoy JSY AU/299 RC	25	30	35	
103	Dez Bryant JSY AU/299 RC	60	80	100	150
107	Bradford JSY AU/299 RC	40	50	60	80
108	Tim Tebow JSY AU/299 RC	100	125	150	200
128	Gronkowski JSY AU/499 RC	60	100	125	200

2010 SPx

#		NmMt 8	NmMt+ 8.5	MT 9	Gem 9.5/10
101	Sam Bradford JSY AU RC	350	400	500	600
102	Tim Tebow JSY AU RC	175	200	250	400
121	Rob Gronkowski JSY AU RC	100	150	200	250

2010 Topps

#		NmMt 8	NmMt+ 8.5	MT 9	Gem 9.5/10
148A	Rob Gronkowski RC Cutting to his right	8	10	12	20
194A	Colt McCoy RC helmet	8	10	15	25
300A	Sam Bradford RC passing	10	12	20	30
300B	Sam Bradford SP snap	60	80	100	125
425A	Dez Bryant RC leaping	8	10	15	25
440A	Tim Tebow RC leaping	10	12	20	40

2010 Topps Chrome

#		NmMt 8	NmMt+ 8.5	MT 9	Gem 9.5/10
C60A	Dez Bryant RC	10	12	15	25
C67	Jimmy Graham RC	8	10	15	25
C70A	Colt McCoy helm RC	10	12	15	25
C100A	Tim Tebow leap RC	8	10	15	25
C150A	Sam Bradford run RC	12	15	20	30
C150B	Sam Bradford snap SP	60	80	100	150

2010 Topps Chrome Purple Refractors

#		NmMt 8	NmMt+ 8.5	MT 9	Gem 9.5/10
C150	Sam Bradford	25	30	40	50

2010 Topps Chrome Refractors

#		NmMt 8	NmMt+ 8.5	MT 9	Gem 9.5/10
C3	Jahvid Best	12	15	20	30
C60	Dez Bryant	10	12	25	40
C70	Colt McCoy	10	12	20	30
C100	Tim Tebow	15	20	30	50
C150	Sam Bradford	15	20	30	40
C160	Ndamukong Suh	10	12	20	30

2010 Topps Chrome Rookie Autographs

#		NmMt 8	NmMt+ 8.5	MT 9	Gem 9.5/10
C60	Dez Bryant A	50	60	80	100
C87	Aaron Hernandez B	60	80	200	300
C100	Tim Tebow A	100	150	200	400
C112	Rob Gronkowski B	▼250	▼300	▼400	▼600
C160	Ndamukong Suh A	40	50	60	200

2010 Topps Platinum Rookie Autographs

#		NmMt 8	NmMt+ 8.5	MT 9	Gem 9.5/10
103	Jimmy Graham/999	25	30	40	60

2011 Bowman Chrome Rookie Preview Inserts

#		NmMt 8	NmMt+ 8.5	MT 9	Gem 9.5/10
BCR3	Cam Newton	10	12	20	40
BCR18	Cam Newton	10	12	20	40

2011 Donruss Elite

#		NmMt 8	NmMt+ 8.5	MT 9	Gem 9.5/10
115	Cam Newton RC	20	25	30	50

2011 Exquisite Collection

#		NmMt 8	NmMt+ 8.5	MT 9	Gem 9.5/10
152	Cam Newton JSY AU	500	600	800	1,000
154	Julio Jones JSY AU		250	400	600

2011 Exquisite Collection Draft Picks Bronze

#		NmMt 8	NmMt+ 8.5	MT 9	Gem 9.5/10
ERRW	Russell Wilson	100	125	150	175

2011 Finest

#		NmMt 8	NmMt+ 8.5	MT 9	Gem 9.5/10
125	Cam Newton RC	10	12	15	40

2011 Finest Refractors

#		NmMt 8	NmMt+ 8.5	MT 9	Gem 9.5/10
52	Colin Kaepernick	25	30	50	80
125	Cam Newton	20	25	40	60

2011 Finest Xfractors

#		NmMt 8	NmMt+ 8.5	MT 9	Gem 9.5/10
52	Colin Kaepernick	30	40	50	80
125	Cam Newton	25	30	50	80

2011 Finest Atomic Refractor Rookies

#		NmMt 8	NmMt+ 8.5	MT 9	Gem 9.5/10
FARAG	A.J. Green	8	10	12	20
FARCN	Cam Newton	15	20	25	50

2011 Finest Rookie Patch Autographs

#		NmMt 8	NmMt+ 8.5	MT 9	Gem 9.5/10
RAPCN	Cam Newton/100	60	80	100	125

2011 Finest Rookie Patch Autographs Refractors

#		NmMt 8	NmMt+ 8.5	MT 9	Gem 9.5/10
RAPAD	Andy Dalton	80	100	125	150

2011 Leaf Metal Draft

#		NmMt 8	NmMt+ 8.5	MT 9	Gem 9.5/10
RCCN1	Cam Newton	20	40	50	80

2011 Panini Plates and Patches

#		NmMt 8	NmMt+ 8.5	MT 9	Gem 9.5/10
201	C.Newton JSY AU/299 RC	80	100	125	150

2011 Panini Threads

#		NmMt 8	NmMt+ 8.5	MT 9	Gem 9.5/10
255	Cam Newton AU/300 RC	▼60	▼80	▼100	▼150

2011 Playoff Contenders

#		NmMt 8	NmMt+ 8.5	MT 9	Gem 9.5/10
137	J.J. Watt AU RC	250	300	▲600	▲800
203A	Ryan Mallett AU RC				
205A	Christian Ponder AU RC				
220A	Von Miller AU RC	40	50	60	80
221A	Julio Jones AU RC	100	125	150	300
222A	A.J. Green AU RC	50	60	80	150

#		NmMt 8	NmMt+ 8.5	MT 9	Gem 9.5/10
225A	Andy Dalton AU RC	▼30	▼40	▼60	▼100
227A	Colin Kaepernick AU RC	50	60	250	300
228A	Cam Newton AU RC	100	150	400	500

2011 Playoff National Treasures

#		NmMt 8	NmMt+ 8.5	MT 9	Gem 9.5/10
243	J.J. Watt AU RC	300	400	500	600
307	Von Miller JSY AU RC	60	80	100	400
323	Julio Jones JSY AU RC	1,200	1,500	1,800	▲3,000
326	Andy Dalton JSY AU RC	50	60	80	100
327	Kaepernick JSY AU RC	125	150	200	250
328	Cam Newton JSY AU RC	800	1,000	1,200	1,500
329	A.J. Green JSY AU RC	150	200	250	300

2011 Rookies and Stars

#		NmMt 8	NmMt+ 8.5	MT 9	Gem 9.5/10
251	Cam Newton AU RC	60	80	100	200

2011 Score

#		NmMt 8	NmMt+ 8.5	MT 9	Gem 9.5/10
315A	Cam Newton RC	8	10	15	25
320A	Colin Kaepernick RC	10	12	20	30

2011 SP Authentic

#		NmMt 8	NmMt+ 8.5	MT 9	Gem 9.5/10
89	A.J. Green	8	10	15	25
94	Cam Newton	10	12	20	30
100	Julio Jones	8	10	15	25
151	Cam Newton FW	8	10	15	25
203	A.J. Green JSY AU/299	60	80	100	
204	Cam Newton JSY AU/299	80	100	▲150	▲200
207	Julio Jones JSY AU/299	80	100	▲150	200
233	Kaepernick JSY AU/699	60	80	100	125

2011 SPx

#		NmMt 8	NmMt+ 8.5	MT 9	Gem 9.5/10
48	D.Murray JSY AU/225	20	25	30	50
64	Julio Jones JSY AU/150	60	80	100	120
67	A.J. Green JSY AU/150	30	40	50	100
68	Cam Newton JSY AU/150	80	100	125	200

2011 Topps

#		NmMt 8	NmMt+ 8.5	MT 9	Gem 9.5/10
200A	Cam Newton RC	10	12	20	30

2011 Topps Rookie Refractors

#		NmMt 8	NmMt+ 8.5	MT 9	Gem 9.5/10
TMB1	Cam Newton	10	12	20	30

2011 Topps Chrome

#		NmMt 8	NmMt+ 8.5	MT 9	Gem 9.5/10
1A	Cam Newton RC	10	12	20	40
104	J.J. Watt RC	10	12	20	40
131A	Julio Jones RC	8	10	12	25
150A	A.J. Green RC	8	10	12	25
173A	DeMarco Murray RC	8	10	12	25

2011 Topps Chrome Blue Refractors

#		NmMt 8	NmMt+ 8.5	MT 9	Gem 9.5/10
1	Cam Newton	50	100	300	400

2011 Topps Chrome Orange Refractors

#		NmMt 8	NmMt+ 8.5	MT 9	Gem 9.5/10
1	Cam Newton	25	30	200	300
25	Colin Kaepernick	20	25	40	80
51	Andy Dalton	12	15	25	40
150	A.J. Green	10	12	20	25
173	DeMarco Murray	10	12	20	40

2011 Topps Chrome Refractors

#		NmMt 8	NmMt+ 8.5	MT 9	Gem 9.5/10
1	Cam Newton	25	60	80	250
25	Colin Kaepernick	300	400	450	500
131	Julio Jones	10	12	20	30
150	A.J. Green	10	12	20	30
173	DeMarco Murray	10	12	20	30

2011 Topps Chrome Sepia Refractors

		NmMt 8	NmMt+ 8.5	MT 9	Gem 9.5/10
1	Cam Newton	100	125	150	250

2011 Topps Chrome Xfractors

		NmMt 8	NmMt+ 8.5	MT 9	Gem 9.5/10
1	Cam Newton	30	50	80	200
25	Colin Kaepernick	125	150	200	250
104	J.J. Watt	20	30	40	300

2011 Topps Chrome Finest Freshman

		NmMt 8	NmMt+ 8.5	MT 9	Gem 9.5/10
FFCM	Cam Newton	10	12	15	30

2011 Topps Chrome Rookie Autographs

		NmMt 8	NmMt+ 8.5	MT 9	Gem 9.5/10
1	Cam Newton A	125	150	200	250
25	Colin Kaepernick A	250	300	400	500

2011 Topps Chrome Rookie Autographs Refractors

		NmMt 8	NmMt+ 8.5	MT 9	Gem 9.5/10
1	Cam Newton	200	250	300	600

2011 Topps Legends

		NmMt 8	NmMt+ 8.5	MT 9	Gem 9.5/10
75	Cam Newton RC	10	12	20	30

2011 Topps Platinum

		NmMt 8	NmMt+ 8.5	MT 9	Gem 9.5/10
1	Cam Newton RC	10	12	25	40
86	J.J. Watt RC	6	10	20	40

2011 Topps Platinum Xfractors

		NmMt 8	NmMt+ 8.5	MT 9	Gem 9.5/10
1	Cam Newton	15	20	25	30
59	Colin Kaepernick	25	30	40	60
132	Andy Dalton	10	12	20	30

2011 Upper Deck

		NmMt 8	NmMt+ 8.5	MT 9	Gem 9.5/10
198	Cam Newton	10	12	20	35

2012 Bowman

		NmMt 8	NmMt+ 8.5	MT 9	Gem 9.5/10
150A	Andrew Luck RC	10	12	20	35

2012 Bowman Gold

		NmMt 8	NmMt+ 8.5	MT 9	Gem 9.5/10
150	Andrew Luck	15	20	30	60

2012 Bowman Sterling

		NmMt 8	NmMt+ 8.5	MT 9	Gem 9.5/10
5	Russell Wilson RC	▲50	▲60	▲125	▲200
100	Andrew Luck RC	15	20	30	50

2012 Certified

		NmMt 8	NmMt+ 8.5	MT 9	Gem 9.5/10
316	Andrew Luck JSY AU/299 RC	40	50	60	80
346	Russell Wilson JSY AU/499 RC	300	350	400	500

2012 Elite

		NmMt 8	NmMt+ 8.5	MT 9	Gem 9.5/10
101	Andrew Luck/699 RC	10	12	15	20
190	Russell Wilson/799 RC	▲100	▲125	▲150	▲200

2012 Elite Turn of the Century Autographs

		NmMt 8	NmMt+ 8.5	MT 9	Gem 9.5/10
101	Andrew Luck/99	80	125	200	300

2012 Finest

		NmMt 8	NmMt+ 8.5	MT 9	Gem 9.5/10
110	Andrew Luck RC	12	15	25	50
140	Russell Wilson RC	30	40	50	60

2012 Finest Prism Refractors

		NmMt 8	NmMt+ 8.5	MT 9	Gem 9.5/10
140	Russell Wilson	30	35	40	60

2012 Finest Refractors

		NmMt 8	NmMt+ 8.5	MT 9	Gem 9.5/10
140	Russell Wilson	20	25	35	50

2012 Finest Atomic Refractor Rookies

		NmMt 8	NmMt+ 8.5	MT 9	Gem 9.5/10
FARAL	Andrew Luck	20	25	30	50

2012 Leaf Draft Army All-American Bowl

		NmMt 8	NmMt+ 8.5	MT 9	Gem 9.5/10
AABAL1	Andrew Luck	10	12	15	25

2012 Leaf Metal Draft

		NmMt 8	NmMt+ 8.5	MT 9	Gem 9.5/10
TR1	Trent Richardson	15	20	25	40

2012 Leaf Metal Draft Prismatic Silver

		NmMt 8	NmMt+ 8.5	MT 9	Gem 9.5/10
TR1	Trent Richardson	20	25	30	50

2012 Leaf Valiant Draft

		NmMt 8	NmMt+ 8.5	MT 9	Gem 9.5/10
RW1	Russell Wilson	40	50	80	150

2012 Leaf Valiant Draft Blue

		NmMt 8	NmMt+ 8.5	MT 9	Gem 9.5/10
RW1	Russell Wilson	40	50	80	120

2012 Leaf Valiant Draft Army All-American Bowl Green

		NmMt 8	NmMt+ 8.5	MT 9	Gem 9.5/10
AL1	Andrew Luck	20	25	30	40

2012 Leaf Valiant Draft Army All-American Bowl Purple

		NmMt 8	NmMt+ 8.5	MT 9	Gem 9.5/10
AL1	Andrew Luck/125		40	60	80

2012 Leaf Young Stars Draft Autographs

		NmMt 8	NmMt+ 8.5	MT 9	Gem 9.5/10
RW1	Russell Wilson SP	40	50	80	120

2012 Momentum

		NmMt 8	NmMt+ 8.5	MT 9	Gem 9.5/10
101	A.Luck JSY AU/399 RC	40	50	100	150

2012 Panini Contenders

		NmMt 8	NmMt+ 8.5	MT 9	Gem 9.5/10
86A	Richard Sherman RC	15	▲50	▲80	▼125
155A	Kirk Cousins AU RC	80	100	125	300
201A	Andrew Luck AU/550* RC	▼100	▼125	▼150	▼200
201B	Andrew Luck AU SP/75*	▼300	▼500	▼800	▼1,000
204A	R.Tannehill AU/550* RC	80	100	▲200	500
204B	R.Tannehill AU SP/200*	100	125	150	600
211A	Doug Martin AU/550* RC	20	25	35	60
218A	Nick Foles AU/550* RC	80	100	125	150
225A	R.Wilson AU/550* RC	1,600	2,000	3,000	4,000
—	Andrew Luck AU/550* RC				
—	(ball in right hand only) #201A BGS 10 (Pristine) sold for $3,110 (eBay; 3/15)				

2012 Panini Contenders Playoff Ticket

		NmMt 8	NmMt+ 8.5	MT 9	Gem 9.5/10
201	Andrew Luck AU	1,000	1,200	1,500	2,500
218	Nick Foles AU	150	200	250	300
225	Russell Wilson AU	600	650	700	1,000

2012 Panini Contenders Rookie Stallions

		NmMt 8	NmMt+ 8.5	MT 9	Gem 9.5/10
1	Andrew Luck	10	12	20	35

2012 Panini National Treasures

		NmMt 8	NmMt+ 8.5	MT 9	Gem 9.5/10
257	Kirk Cousins AU RC	125	150	200	400
325	Russell Wilson JSY AU RC	8,000	10,000	15,000	20,000

2012 Panini Prizm

		NmMt 8	NmMt+ 8.5	MT 9	Gem 9.5/10
60	Peyton Manning	30	80	100	125
69	Aaron Rodgers	20	30	50	80
116	Tom Brady	150	200	300	1,000

		NmMt 8	NmMt+ 8.5	MT 9	Gem 9.5/10
118	Drew Brees	15	20	50	80
203A	Andrew Luck RC	12	15	25	40
230A	Russell Wilson RC	300	400	500	1,500

2012 Panini Prizm Autographs

203	Andrew Luck/250			
232	Ryan Tannehill/250			
277	Kirk Cousins/499			

2012 Panini Prizm Autographs Prizms

		NmMt 8	NmMt+ 8.5	MT 9	Gem 9.5/10	Pristine
230	Russell Wilson/99	200	250	300	350	400

2012 Prestige

		NmMt 8	NmMt+ 8.5	MT 9	Gem 9.5/10
229A	Andrew Luck RC	12	15	25	50

2012 Rookies and Stars

		NmMt 8	NmMt+ 8.5	MT 9	Gem 9.5/10
216	Andrew Luck JSY AU RC	50	60	80	100

2012 Score

		NmMt 8	NmMt+ 8.5	MT 9	Gem 9.5/10
304A	Andrew Luck RC	8	10	15	25

2012 SP Authentic

		NmMt 8	NmMt+ 8.5	MT 9	Gem 9.5/10
87	Russell Wilson	10	12	20	30
251	Nick Foles JSY AU/885	40	50	60	100
258	Kirk Cousins JSY AU/885	60	80	100	125
272	Russell Wilson JSY AU/885	125	150	200	300

2012 Topps

		NmMt 8	NmMt+ 8.5	MT 9	Gem 9.5/10
140A	Andrew Luck RC	10	12	20	40
140B	A.Luck SP rabbit foot	200	225	300	400
140D	A.Luck FS twst pass	10	12	20	40
165A	Russell Wilson RC	10	12	15	30

2012 Topps Rookie Refractors

		NmMt 8	NmMt+ 8.5	MT 9	Gem 9.5/10
TFHMAL	Andrew Luck	12	15	20	30

2012 Topps Chrome

		NmMt 8	NmMt+ 8.5	MT 9	Gem 9.5/10
1A	A.Luck RC passing	25	30	40	100
1B	Andrew Luck SP drop	80	100	135	250
23A	T.Richardson RC cut	8	10	15	30
40A	R.Wilson RC stands	100	125	150	200

2012 Topps Chrome Black Refractors

		NmMt 8	NmMt+ 8.5	MT 9	Gem 9.5/10
1	Andrew Luck	40	50	60	80
40	Russell Wilson	500	600	800	2,000

2012 Topps Chrome Blue Refractors

		NmMt 8	NmMt+ 8.5	MT 9	Gem 9.5/10
1	Andrew Luck	50	60	80	100
40	Russell Wilson	500	600	2,500	3,000

2012 Topps Chrome Camo Refractors

		NmMt 8	NmMt+ 8.5	MT 9	Gem 9.5/10
1	Andrew Luck	12	15	25	30
40	Russell Wilson	400	500	800	1,500

2012 Topps Chrome Orange Refractors

		NmMt 8	NmMt+ 8.5	MT 9	Gem 9.5/10
1	Andrew Luck	12	15	20	25
40	Russell Wilson	200	250	400	600

2012 Topps Chrome Pink Refractors

		NmMt 8	NmMt+ 8.5	MT 9	Gem 9.5/10
1	Andrew Luck	30	40	50	80
40	Russell Wilson	300	400	600	1,800

2012 Topps Chrome Prism Refractors

		NmMt 8	NmMt+ 8.5	MT 9	Gem 9.5/10
1	Andrew Luck	20	30	40	100
40	Russell Wilson	500	600	800	1,500

2012 Topps Chrome Purple Refractors

		NmMt 8	NmMt+ 8.5	MT 9	Gem 9.5/10
1	Andrew Luck	12	15	20	25
40	Russell Wilson	400	500	600	1,200

2012 Topps Chrome Refractors

		NmMt 8	NmMt+ 8.5	MT 9	Gem 9.5/10
1A	Andrew Luck/passing pose	12	20	25	30
40	Russell Wilson	300	400	700	2,000
147	Doug Martin	8	10	15	25
220	Tom Brady	80	200	400	

2012 Topps Chrome Sepia Refractors

		NmMt 8	NmMt+ 8.5	MT 9	Gem 9.5/10
1	Andrew Luck	30	40	50	60
40	Russell Wilson	800	1,000	1,500	2,000

2012 Topps Chrome Xfractors

		NmMt 8	NmMt+ 8.5	MT 9	Gem 9.5/10
1	Andrew Luck	12	15	20	25
40	Russell Wilson	250	300	400	800

2012 Topps Chrome 1957

		NmMt 8	NmMt+ 8.5	MT 9	Gem 9.5/10
1	Andrew Luck	12	15	40	50
2	Andrew Luck	12	15	40	50

2012 Topps Chrome 1965

		NmMt 8	NmMt+ 8.5	MT 9	Gem 9.5/10
1	Andrew Luck	12	15	40	50
42	Russell Wilson	▼100	▼125	▼200	▼300

2012 Topps Chrome 1984

		NmMt 8	NmMt+ 8.5	MT 9	Gem 9.5/10
	Andrew Luck	12	15	40	50
4	Russell Wilson	▼100	▼125	▼200	▼300

2012 Topps Chrome Red Zone Rookies Refractors

		NmMt 8	NmMt+ 8.5	MT 9	Gem 9.5/10
ZDC1	Andrew Luck	15	20	25	50
ZDC14	Russell Wilson	▲60	▲80	▲125	▲250

2012 Topps Chrome Rookie Autographs

		NmMt 8	NmMt+ 8.5	MT 9	Gem 9.5/10
0	Russell Wilson	400	500	1,000	▼2,000

2012 Topps Chrome Rookie Autographs Pink Refractors

	NmMt 8	NmMt+ 8.5	MT 9	Gem 9.5/10
Andrew Luck		600	800	1,200

2012 Topps Chrome Rookie Autographs Prism Refractors

	NmMt 8	NmMt+ 8.5	MT 9	Gem 9.5/10
Andrew Luck		150	200	300

2012 Topps Chrome Rookie Autographs Refractors

		NmMt 8	NmMt+ 8.5	MT 9	Gem 9.5/10
0	Russell Wilson	800	1,000	1,200	3,200
53	Nick Foles	60	80	100	150

2012 Topps Chrome Rookie Autographs Refractors Variations

		NmMt 8	NmMt+ 8.5	MT 9	Gem 9.5/10
	Andrew Luck	400	450	1,200	1,500
0	Russell Wilson	225	250	300	500

2012 Topps Magic

		NmMt 8	NmMt+ 8.5	MT 9	Gem 9.5/10
	Andrew Luck RC	10	12	20	40
1	Russell Wilson RC	▲30	▲50	▲60	▲150

2012 Topps Magic Autographs

		NmMt 8	NmMt+ 8.5	MT 9	Gem 9.5/10
2	Colin Kaepernick	30	40	80	250

2012 Topps Platinum

		NmMt 8	NmMt+ 8.5	MT 9	Gem 9.5/10
8	Russell Wilson RC	40	50	▼150	300
0	Andrew Luck RC	12	15	25	40

2012 Topps Platinum Orange Refractors

		NmMt 8	NmMt+ 8.5	MT 9	Gem 9.5/10
138	Russell Wilson	80	100	300	400
150	Andrew Luck	15	20	50	35

2012 Topps Platinum Xfractors

		NmMt 8	NmMt+ 8.5	MT 9	Gem 9.5/10
138	Russell Wilson	100	125	400	500
150	Andrew Luck	8	10	12	15

2012 Topps Platinum Rookie Die Cut

		NmMt 8	NmMt+ 8.5	MT 9	Gem 9.5/10
PDCAL	Andrew Luck	25	30	40	60

2013 Panini Prizm

		NmMt 8	NmMt+ 8.5	MT 9	Gem 9.5/10
64	Tom Brady	50	60	100	200
189	Russell Wilson	40	50	60	80
225	DeAndre Hopkins RC	60	80	100	400
292	Travis Kelce RC	80	125	▼150	▼500

2013 Topps Chrome

		NmMt 8	NmMt+ 8.5	MT 9	Gem 9.5/10
118	Travis Kelce RC	40	▼60	▼100	▼300

2013 Topps Chrome Refractors

		NmMt 8	NmMt+ 8.5	MT 9	Gem 9.5/10
118	Travis Kelce	60	100	200	800

2013 Topps Chrome Rookie Autographs

		NmMt 8	NmMt+ 8.5	MT 9	Gem 9.5/10
198	Le'Veon Bell/600	50	60	100	125

2014 Bowman

R8	Odell Beckham Jr. RC

2014 Bowman Chrome Rookie Autographs College Refractors

		NmMt 8	NmMt+ 8.5	MT 9	Gem 9.5/10
79	Odell Beckham Jr.	100	125	150	200

2014 Bowman Chrome Rookie Autographs College Blue Refractors

		NmMt 8	NmMt+ 8.5	MT 9	Gem 9.5/10
12	Johnny Manziel	80	100	125	150
14	Teddy Bridgewater	80	100	125	150
79	Odell Beckham Jr.	125	150	200	400

2014 Bowman Chrome

		NmMt 8	NmMt+ 8.5	MT 9	Gem 9.5/10
190A	Odell Beckham Jr. RC	8	10	12	20

2014 Bowman Chrome Rookie Autographs Refractors

		NmMt 8	NmMt+ 8.5	MT 9	Gem 9.5/10
RCRAAD	Aaron Donald	▲200	▲250	▲300	▲400
RCRADC	Derek Carr	50	60	80	200
RCRAJG	Jimmy Garoppolo	100	125	150	250
RCRAJM	Johnny Manziel	60	80	100	125
RCRAOB	Odell Beckham Jr.	60	80	100	150

2014 Bowman Chrome Rookie Autographs Blue Refractors

		NmMt 8	NmMt+ 8.5	MT 9	Gem 9.5/10
RCRAOB	Odell Beckham Jr.	80	100	125	150

2014 Finest

		NmMt 8	NmMt+ 8.5	MT 9	Gem 9.5/10
116	Jimmy Garoppolo RC	8	12	25	40

2014 Panini Contenders

		NmMt 8	NmMt+ 8.5	MT 9	Gem 9.5/10
208A	Carlos Hyde AU RC (ball in right arm)		50	60	80
214A	Derek Carr AU RC (ball at right shoulder)		200	300	▼600
221A	Jimmy Garoppolo AU RC (looking left)		500	600	1,000
227A	Odell Beckham Jr. AU RC (ball in left arm)	125	150	200	250

		NmMt 8	NmMt+ 8.5	MT 9	Gem 9.5/10
227B	Odell Beckham Jr. AU/206* (looking straight)	125	150	200	250
236A	Mike Evans AU RC (looking right)	40	50	▲100	▲200
237A	Sammy Watkins AU RC (ball in left arm)	30	40	50	60
239A	Teddy Bridgewater AU RC (looking left)	80	100	125	250

2014 Panini National Treasures

		NmMt 8	NmMt+ 8.5	MT 9	Gem 9.5/10
221	Martavis Bryant AU RC	40	50	60	80
274	Jimmy Garoppolo JSY AU RC	2,000	2,500	2,800	3,000
296	Derek Carr JSY AU RC	500	600	700	800

2014 Panini Prizm

		NmMt 8	NmMt+ 8.5	MT 9	Gem 9.5/10
36	Tom Brady	25	50	100	150
228	Aaron Donald RC	30	60	100	250

2014 SP Authentic

		NmMt 8	NmMt+ 8.5	MT 9	Gem 9.5/10
231	Jimmy Garoppolo JSY AU/350	▼100	▼125	▼150	▼200

2014 Topps

		NmMt 8	NmMt+ 8.5	MT 9	Gem 9.5/10
355A	Odell Beckham Jr. RC	3	4	5	10

2014 Topps Chrome

		NmMt 8	NmMt+ 8.5	MT 9	Gem 9.5/10
117A	Odell Beckham Jr. RC	12	15	20	30
175	Aaron Donald RC	20	50	100	200

2014 Topps Chrome Refractors

		NmMt 8	NmMt+ 8.5	MT 9	Gem 9.5/10
115	Derek Carr	30	40	50	200
117	Odell Beckham Jr.	25	30	40	50
150	Jimmy Garoppolo	25	30	40	100
173	Teddy Bridgewater	8	10	15	25

2014 Topps Chrome Rookie Autographs

		NmMt 8	NmMt+ 8.5	MT 9	Gem 9.5/10
115	Derek Carr SP	200	250	300	600
117	Odell Beckham Jr.	60	80	100	150
150	Jimmy Garoppolo	150	200	250	300
169	Johnny Manziel SP	40	50	60	80
175	Aaron Donald	30	40	300	500

2014 Topps Chrome Rookie Autographs Refractors

		NmMt 8	NmMt+ 8.5	MT 9	Gem 9.5/10
115	Derek Carr	100	120	300	400
173	Teddy Bridgewater	60	80	100	125

2015 Bowman

		NmMt 8	NmMt+ 8.5	MT 9	Gem 9.5/10
R22	Marcus Mariota RC	6	10	15	30
R23	Jameis Winston RC	5	8	12	25

2015 Bowman Chrome Rookie Autographs Refractors

		NmMt 8	NmMt+ 8.5	MT 9	Gem 9.5/10
RCRAAC	Amari Cooper	60	80	100	150
RCRAJW	Jameis Winston	50	60	80	100
RCRAMM	Marcus Mariota	60	80	100	150
RCRATG	Todd Gurley	60	80	100	150

2015 Panini Contenders

		NmMt 8	NmMt+ 8.5	MT 9	Gem 9.5/10
228A	Amari Cooper AU RC	60	80	100	125
238A	Todd Gurley AU RC	50	60	80	100

2015 Panini Contenders Draft Picks

		NmMt 8	NmMt+ 8.5	MT 9	Gem 9.5/10
122A	Jameis Winston AU RC SP1/(red jsy)			120	200
131A	Marcus Mariota AU RC SP1/(white jsy)	150	200	300	400

2015 Panini National Treasures

		NmMt 8	NmMt+ 8.5	MT 9	Gem 9.5/10
107	Jameis Winston JSY AU RC	400	500	600	▲2,500
140	Marcus Mariota JSY AU RC	400	500	600	1,500

2015 Topps Chrome Rookie Autographs

		NmMt 8	NmMt+ 8.5	MT 9	Gem 9.5/10
177	David Johnson	25	30	40	50

2015 Topps Chrome Rookie Autographs Camo Refractors

		NmMt 8	NmMt+ 8.5	MT 9	Gem 9.5/10
110	Todd Gurley	100	125	150	200

2015 Topps Chrome Rookie Autographs Pink Refractors

		NmMt 8	NmMt+ 8.5	MT 9	Gem 9.5/10
110	Todd Gurley	60	80	100	125

2015 Topps Chrome Rookie Autographs Refractors

		NmMt 8	NmMt+ 8.5	MT 9	Gem 9.5/10
110	Todd Gurley	50	60	80	100
150	Marcus Mariota	100	125	150	200

2016 Donruss Optic

		NmMt 8	NmMt+ 8.5	MT 9	Gem 9.5/10
62	Tom Brady	30	40	60	▲200
117	Tyreek Hill RC	25	50	100	250
156	Carson Wentz RR RC	15	20	25	60
162	Dak Prescott RR RC	60	80	125	▼250
168	Ezekiel Elliott RR RC	10	▲20	▲60	▲125

2016 Donruss Optic Holo

		NM 7	NmMt+ 8.5	MT 9	Gem 9.5/10
62	Tom Brady			200	300
156	Carson Wentz RR		25	50	400
168	Ezekiel Elliott RR		40	50	200

2016 Donruss Optic Rated Rookies Autographs

		NmMt 8	NmMt+ 8.5	MT 9	Gem 9.5/10
156	Carson Wentz	150	200	▲300	400
162	Dak Prescott			150	250
165	Derrick Henry			80	250
168	Ezekiel Elliott			125	200

2016 Elite Pen Pals

		NM 7	NmMt+ 8.5	MT 9	Gem 9.5/10
PPCW	Carson Wentz			150	250
PPDP	Dak Prescott			150	300
PPEE	Ezekiel Elliott			150	300

2016 Panini Contenders

		NmMt 8	NmMt+ 8.5	MT 9	Gem 9.5/10
232	Tyreek Hill AU RC	60	80	150	200
245	Adam Thielen AU RC	150	200	250	400

2016 Panini Contenders Draft Picks

		NmMt 8	NmMt+ 8.5	MT 9	Gem 9.5/10
105A	Ezekiel Elliott AU RC//(white jsy)			150	400
125A	Dak Prescott AU RC//(throwing)			150	300
127A	Carson Wentz AU RC//(white jsy)			150	400

2016 Panini National Treasures

		NmMt 8	NmMt+ 8.5	MT 9	Gem 9.5/10
102	Carson Wentz JSY AU RC	2,500	3,000	3,500	5,000
104	Ezekiel Elliott JSY AU RC		500	600	800

2016 Panini Prizm

		NmMt 8	NmMt+ 8.5	MT 9	Gem 9.5/10
218	Carson Wentz RC	▼60	▼80	▼100	▼400
238	Ezekiel Elliott RC	100	150	200	300
296	Tyreek Hill RC	60	80	100	▲300
298	Derrick Henry RC	100	150	200	800

2017 Classics

		NmMt 8	NmMt+ 8.5	MT 9	Gem 9.5/10
274	Patrick Mahomes II RC	100	150	200	▼600

2017 Classics Glossy

		NmMt 8	NmMt+ 8.5	MT 9	Gem 9.5/10
274	Patrick Mahomes II	250	400	500	1,000

2017 Donruss

		NmMt 8	NmMt+ 8.5	MT 9	Gem 9.5/10
318	Christian McCaffrey RR RC	40	50	60	200
327	Patrick Mahomes II RR RC	500	600	800	2,000
345	Deshaun Watson RR RC	40	50	80	200

2017 Donruss Rookie Gridiron Kings

2	Patrick Mahomes II				

2017 Donruss The Elite Series Rookies

		NmMt 8	NmMt+ 8.5	MT 9	Gem 9.5/10
7	Patrick Mahomes II	125	300	800	1,500

2017 Donruss The Rookies

		NmMt 8	NmMt+ 8.5	MT 9	Gem 9.5/10
7	Patrick Mahomes II	250	300	600	800

2017 Donruss Optic

		NmMt 8	NmMt+ 8.5	MT 9	Gem 9.5/10
177	Patrick Mahomes II RR RC	400	500	1,200	2,500
195	Deshaun Watson RR RC	40	50	200	600

2017 Donruss Optic Holo

		NmMt 8	NmMt+ 8.5	MT 9	Gem 9.5/10
168	Christian McCaffrey RR	100	125	150	300
177	Patrick Mahomes II RR	1,500	2,000	2,500	6,000
195	Deshaun Watson RR	50	60	125	400

2017 Donruss Optic Pink

		NmMt 8	NmMt+ 8.5	MT 9	Gem 9.5/10
195	Deshaun Watson RR	60	100	250	400

2017 Donruss Optic AKA

		NmMt 8	NmMt+ 8.5	MT 9	Gem 9.5/10
30	Patrick Mahomes II	250	300	500	1,000

2017 Donruss Optic The Rookies

		NmMt 8	NmMt+ 8.5	MT 9	Gem 9.5/10
7	Patrick Mahomes II	500	600	800	1,500

2017 Panini Contenders Optic

		NmMt 8	NmMt+ 8.5	MT 9	Gem 9.5/10
102	Deshaun Watson AU RC	600	1,000	1,500	2,000
103	Patrick Mahomes II AU RC	12,000	13,000	15,000	18,000
111	Christian McCaffrey AU RC	150	200	300	▼400
127	JuJu Smith-Schuster AU RC	60	80	100	125
186	George Kittle AU RC		250	300	800

2017 Panini Prizm

		NmMt 8	NmMt+ 8.5	MT 9	Gem 9.5/10
269	Patrick Mahomes II RC	2,000	2,500	3,000	4,000
279	Deshaun Watson RC	80	100	400	1,200

2017 Panini Prizm Rookie Autographs Prizms

		NmMt 8	NmMt+ 8.5	MT 9	Gem 9.5/10
RAPM	Patrick Mahomes II	300	400	500	1,200

2017 Panini Prizm Rookie Introductions Prizms

		NmMt 8	NmMt+ 8.5	MT 9	Gem 9.5/10
2	Patrick Mahomes II	▲200	▲250	▲400	▲1,000

2017 Select

		NmMt 8	NmMt+ 8.5	MT 9	Gem 9.5/10
303B	Josh Allen XRC	1,000	1,200	1,500	3,000

2018 Donruss

		NmMt 8	NmMt+ 8.5	MT 9	Gem 9.5/10
301	Sam Darnold RR RC	6	10	15	20
303	Baker Mayfield RR RC	25	30	80	150
304	Josh Allen RR RC	80	100	250	500
306	Saquon Barkley RR RC	8	12	25	50
317	Lamar Jackson RR RC	30	80	100	250

2018 Donruss Optic

		NmMt 8	NmMt+ 8.5	MT 9	Gem 9.5/10
49	Patrick Mahomes II	20	40	80	250
151	Sam Darnold RR RC	20	25	50	80
153	Baker Mayfield RR RC	50	80	100	250
156	Saquon Barkley RR RC	12	20	80	200
167	Lamar Jackson RR RC	▲50	▲80	▲150	400

2018 Donruss Optic Holo

		NmMt 8	NmMt+ 8.5	MT 9	Gem 9.5/10
49	Patrick Mahomes II	150	200	300	600
151	Sam Darnold RR	60	80	150	250
153	Baker Mayfield RR	100	125	200	500
156	Saquon Barkley RR	30	50	125	400
167	Lamar Jackson RR	300	400	500	1,000

2018 Panini Contenders Optic

		NmMt 8	NmMt+ 8.5	MT 9	Gem 9.5/10
101	Baker Mayfield AU RC	400	600	800	1,200
112	Lamar Jackson AU RC	1,000	1,200	1,500	2,000

2018 Panini Prizm

		NmMt 8	NmMt+ 8.5	MT 9	Gem 9.5/10
102	Patrick Mahomes II	▼80	▼100	200	▼400
201	Baker Mayfield RC	60	80	150	500
202	Saquon Barkley RC	40	50	125	400
203	Sam Darnold RC	40	50	80	200
205	Josh Allen RC	200	250	400	1,200
212	Lamar Jackson RC	100	300	400	800
213	Nick Chubb RC	20	30	50	80

2018 Panini Prizm Rookie Autographs Prizms

		NmMt 8	NmMt+ 8.5	MT 9	Gem 9.5/10
1	Baker Mayfield	300	400	▲800	▲1,500
2	Saquon Barkley	250	300	400	500
3	Sam Darnold	100	125	150	400
5	Josh Allen	1,000	1,200	1,500	4,000
12	Lamar Jackson	1,200	1,500	1,800	2,000

2019 Donruss

		NmMt 8	NmMt+ 8.5	MT 9	Gem 9.5/10
302	Kyler Murray RR RC	▲30	▲50	80	▲250

2019 Donruss Optic

		NmMt 8	NmMt+ 8.5	MT 9	Gem 9.5/10
1	Patrick Mahomes II	10	20	40	80
63	Tom Brady	12	30	50	80
152	Kyler Murray RR RC	50	80	▲200	400
163	D.K. Metcalf RR RC	30	50	100	150

2019 Donruss Optic Holo

		NmMt 8	NmMt+ 8.5	MT 9	Gem 9.5/10
152	Kyler Murray RR		250	300	1,200

2019 Panini Prizm

		NmMt 8	NmMt+ 8.5	MT 9	Gem 9.5/10
3	Josh Allen	10	15	80	125
18	Tom Brady	6	15	40	100
210	Patrick Mahomes II	▲30	▲40	▼80	▼125
301	Kyler Murray RC	▼125	▼200	▼300	▼500
302	Daniel Jones RC	30	40	80	▼100
322	Gardner Minshew II RC	10	15	40	100
323	Josh Jacobs RC	40	50	80	100

2020 Donruss

		NmMt 8	NmMt+ 8.5	MT 9	Gem 9.5/10
303	Justin Herbert RR RC	30	50	125	500

2020 Donruss Optic

151	Joe Burrow RR RC				
153	Justin Herbert RR RC				

2020 Panini Prizm Draft Picks

		NmMt 8	NmMt+ 8.5	MT 9	Gem 9.5/10
101	Tua Tagovailoa RC	10	20	60	150
102	Justin Herbert RC	10	30	80	300
105	Joe Burrow RC	10	20	60	150

GOLF
1927 - Present

1927 Churchman's Famous Golfers Large

		VgEx 4	EX 5	ExMt 6	NM 7
4	Walter Hagen	100	200	350	500
7	Bobby Jones	200	350	700	1,200

1927 Churchman's Famous Golfers Small

		EX 5	ExMt 6	NM 7	NmMt 8
13	Walter Hagen 13	50	100	250	750
14	Walter Hagen 14	50	100	250	750
27	Bobby Jones 27	125	250	600	1,000
28	Bobby Jones 28	125	250	600	1,000
33	Tom Morris	75	125	300	600
34	Edward Ray 34	15	25	50	150
35	Edward Ray 35	15	25	50	150
40	Freddie Tait	15	25	50	150
41	John Henry Taylor 41	20	30	60	150
42	John Henry Taylor 42	20	30	60	150
43	Cyril Tolley	15	25	50	150
44	Harry Vardon 44	30	50	150	300
45	Harry Vardon 45	30	50	150	300
46	Harry Vardon 46	30	50	150	300
47	Harry Vardon 47	30	50	150	300

1928 J.Millhoff and Co. Famous Golfers

		EX 5	ExMt 6	NM 7	NmMt 8
2	Walter Hagen	60	100	175	400
5	Harry Vardon	30	50	100	300
20	Bobby Jones	175	275	500	900

1930 Wills Cigarettes Famous Golfers

		EX 5	ExMt 6	NM 7	NmMt 8
7	Walter Hagen	75	125	150	300

1931 Churchman's Prominent Golfers Large

		EX 5	ExMt 6	NM 7	NmMt 8
3	Henry Cotton	25	60	100	
4	Walter Hagen	100	175	250	
5	Bobby Jones	150	250	500	800
6	Abe Mitchell	25	60	100	
8	Cyril Tolley	20	40	80	
11	Roger Wethered	25	60	100	

— Walter Hagen #4 PSA 8.5 (NmMt+) sold for $1,540 (eBay; 2/10)
— Walter Hagen #4 PSA 8 (NmMt) sold for $461 (eBay; 10/08)
— Harry Vardon #9 PSA 9 (MT) sold for $1,490 (eBay; 11/11)
— Harry Vardon #9 PSA 8 (NmMt) sold for $300 (eBay; 05/09)

1931 Churchman's Prominent Golfers Small

		VgEx 4	EX 5	ExMt 6	NM 7
16	Walter Hagen	25	40	75	200
25	Bobby Jones	60	100	175	325
35	Gene Sarazen	40	60	75	125

1981 Donruss

		NM 7	NmMt 8	MT 9	Gem 9.5/10
	COMMONS & MINOR STARS	5	10	15	60
1	Tom Watson RC	10	15	25	250
2	Lee Trevino RC	8	12	20	125
3	Curtis Strange RC	5	10	15	75
5	Ben Crenshaw RC	5	12	20	125
10	Raymond Floyd RC	5	10	15	200
13	Jack Nicklaus RC	15	40	40	225
20	Tom Kite RC	5	10	15	75
21	Jim Colbert RC	5	10	20	200
27	David Graham RC	5	10	30	175
29	Lon Hinkle RC	5	10	15	150
30	Johnny Miller RC	5	10	15	100
31	Dave Eichelberger RC	5	10	15	125
32	Wayne Levi SP RC	5	10	15	200
35	Jay Haas RC	5	10	15	150
36	Dan Halldorson SP RC	5	10	20	200
39	Mark Lye RC	5	10	20	125
47	Tom Weiskopf RC	5	10	15	150
48	Jim Simons RC	5	10	30	200
NNO	Jack Nicklaus SL	8	15	30	150
NNO	Tom Watson SL	5	10	40	250

1982 Donruss

		NM 7	NmMt 8	MT 9	Gem 9.5/10
	COMMONS & MINOR STARS	5	10	25	
1	Tom Kite	10	15	30	
3	Tom Watson	10	15	40	
16	Jack Nicklaus	15	30	50	
23	Lee Trevino	8	15	40	
53	Fred Couples RC	10	20	100	
55	Mark O'Meara RC	8	20	60	

— Jack Nicklaus #16 BGS 9.5 (Gem) sold for $145 (Mastro; 02/08)

1990 Pro Set

		NmMt 8	NmMt+ 8.5	MT 9	Gem 9.5/10
20	Payne Stewart RC	4	6	10	20
80	Arnold Palmer RC	4	6	10	
93	Jack Nicklaus	3	5	8	15

1992 Pro Set

		NmMt 8	NmMt+ 8.5	MT 9	Gem 9.5/10
E6	Vijay Singh RC	10	15	30	

1996 Niketown Promo

		NmMt 8	NmMt+ 8.5	MT 9	Gem 9.5/10
NNO	Tiger Woods	70	125	200	350

— Tiger Woods BGS 9.5 (Gem) sold for $4,155 (eBay; 5/09)

1996 Sports Illustrated for Kids II

		NmMt 8	NmMt+ 8.5	MT 9	Gem 9.5/10
536	Tiger Woods/Golf	400	500	750	2,500

1997-98 Grand Slam Ventures Masters Collection

		NmMt 8	NmMt+ 8.5	MT 9	Gem 9.5/10
1997	Tiger Woods XRC	60	75	350	500

1997-98 Grand Slam Ventures Masters Collection Gold Foil

		NmMt 8	NmMt+ 8.5	MT 9	Gem 9.5/10
1997	Tiger Woods	150	250	750	

— Tiger Woods #1997 BGS 9.5 (Gem) sold for $2,560 (eBay; 07/07)
— Tiger Woods #1997 BGS 9.5 (Gem) sold for $3,000 (eBay; 11/07)

2001 SP Authentic Preview

		NmMt 8	NmMt+ 8.5	MT 9	Gem 9.5/10
21	Tiger Woods STAR	15	20	25	50

2001 SP Authentic Preview Red

— Tiger Woods STAR #21 BGS 9 (Mint) sold for $1,505 (eBay; 06/08)

2001 SP Authentic

		NmMt 8	NmMt+ 8.5	MT 9	Gem 9.5/10
45	Tiger Woods AS AU/900 RC	15,000	20,000	25,000	100,000
46	D.Duval AS AU/900 RC	25	40	60	100
47	J.Parnevik AS AU/900 RC	15	30	40	75
62	S.Garcia AS AU/900 RC	80	100	125	150
78	R.Goosen AS AU/900 RC	20	40	60	100
136	David Toms AS AU/900	15	30	50	100

— #45 Tiger Woods BGS 10 (Pristine) sold for $16,610 (eBay; 3/08)
— #45 Tiger Woods BGS 10 (Pristine) sold for $10,417 (eBay; 5/09)

2001 SP Authentic Gold

— Tiger Woods #45 BGS 10 (Pristine) sold for $5,890 (eBay; 1/10)
— Tiger Woods #45 PSA 10 (Gem) sold for $4,540 (eBay; 11/07)
— Tiger Woods #45 PSA 10 (Gem) sold for $15,000 (eBay; 05/08)
— Tiger Woods #45 PSA 10 (Gem) sold for $10,000 (eBay; 10/09)
— Tiger Woods #45 PSA 10 (Gem) sold for $12,000 (eBay; 07/12)
— Tiger Woods #45 BGS 9.5 (Gem) sold for $10,000 (eBay; 02/08)
— Tiger Woods #45 BGS 9.5 (Gem) sold for $8,500 (eBay; 02/08)
— Tiger Woods #45 BGS 9.5 (Gem) sold for $4,533 (eBay; 10/09)
— Tiger Woods #45 BGS 9.5 (Gem) sold for $3,892 (eBay; 10/11)
— Tiger Woods #45 BGS 9.5 (Gem) sold for $4,999 (eBay; 4/13)
— Tiger Woods #45 BGS 9.5 (Gem) sold for $4,161 (eBay; 9/13)
— Tiger Woods #45 BGS 9.5 (Gem) sold for $3,870 (eBay; 9/13)
— Tiger Woods #45 BGS 9 (MT) sold for $8,900 (eBay; 02/08)
— Tiger Woods #45 BGS 9 (MT) sold for $8,500 (eBay; 06/08)
— Tiger Woods #45 BGS 9 (MT) sold for $6,000 (eBay; 08/08)
— Tiger Woods #45 BGS 9 (MT) sold for $4,500 (eBay; 04/08)
— Retief Goosen #78 BGS 9.5 (Gem) sold for $130 (eBay; 02/08)
— Retief Goosen #78 BGS 9.5 (Gem) sold for $125 (eBay; 03/08)
— Retief Goosen #78 BGS 9.5 (Gem) sold for $120 (eBay; 04/08)

2001 SP Authentic Sign of the Times

— Tiger Woods #TW BGS 9.5 (Gem) sold for $2,930 (eBay; 04/08)
— Tiger Woods #TW BGS 9.5 (Gem) sold for $750 (eBay; 05/11)
— Tiger Woods #TW PSA 10 (Gem) sold for $1,850 (eBay; 10/11)
— Tiger Woods #TW BGS 9 (Mint) sold for $1,900 (eBay; 06/08)
— Tiger Woods #TW BGS 9 (Mint) sold for $1,400 (eBay; 05/08)
— Tiger Woods #TW BGS 9 (Mint) sold for $999 (eBay; 5/09)
— Tiger Woods #TW BGS 9 (Mint) sold for $795 (eBay; 3/13)

2001 SP Authentic Sign of the Times Red

		NM 7	NmMt 8	NmMt+ 8.5	MT 9
TW1	T.Woods Bay Hill/273	250	400	600	800
TW2	T.Woods Player's/274	250	400	600	800

— Tiger Woods #TW1 PSA 10 (Gem) sold for $2,515 (eBay; 06/08)
— Tiger Woods #TW1 BGS 9.5 (Gem) sold for $2,025 (eBay; 06/08)
— Tiger Woods #TW1 SGC 10 (Gem) sold for $1,627 (eBay; 12/08)
— Tiger Woods #TW1 BGS 9.5 (Gem) sold for $1,230 (eBay; 11/08)
— Tiger Woods #TW1 BGS 9.5 (Gem) sold for $1,188 (eBay; 10/09)
— Tiger Woods #TW1 BGS 9 (Mint) sold for $1,190 (eBay; 06/08)
— Tiger Woods #TW1 BGS 9 (Mint) sold for $1,032 (eBay; 01/09)
— Tiger Woods #TW1 BGS 9 (Mint) sold for $807 (eBay; 5/09)
— Tiger Woods #TW2 BGS 10 (Pristine) sold for $3,300 (eBay; 12/08)
— Tiger Woods #TW2 BGS 10 (Pristine) sold for $3,030 (eBay; 2/10)
— Tiger Woods #TW2 BGS 9.5 (Gem) sold for $1,125 (eBay; 10/08)
— Tiger Woods #TW2 BGS 9.5 (Gem) sold for $762 (eBay; 09/26)
— Tiger Woods #TW2 BGS 9 (Mint) sold for $1,000 (eBay; 05/08)
— Tiger Woods #TW4 BGS 9.5 (Gem) sold for $2,220 (eBay; 08/12)
— Tiger Woods #TW5 BGS 9.5 (Gem) sold for $12,200 (eBay; 09/09)
— Tiger Woods #TW5 BGS 9.5 (Gem) sold for $9,560 (eBay; 05/08)
— Tiger Woods #TW7 BGS 9 (Mint) sold for $1,800 (eBay; 9/09)

2001 Upper Deck Promos

		NmMt 8	NmMt+ 8.5	MT 9	Gem 9.5/10
NNO	Tiger Woods	25	50	100	200

2001 Upper Deck

		NmMt 8	NmMt+ 8.5	MT 9	Gem 9.5/10
1	Tiger Woods RC	100	125	150	500

— Tiger Woods #1 BGS 10 (Pristine) sold for $1,010 (eBay; 04/08)
— Tiger Woods #1 BGS 10 (Pristine) sold for $550 (eBay; 02/09)
— Tiger Woods #1 BGS 10 (Pristine) sold for $500 (eBay; 03/08)
— Tiger Woods #1 BGS 10 (Pristine) sold for $500 (eBay; 05/09)
— Tiger Woods #1 BGS 10 (Pristine) sold for $493 (eBay; 03/09)
— Tiger Woods #1 BGS 10 (Pristine) sold for $485 (eBay; 03/08)
— Tiger Woods #1 BGS 10 (Pristine) sold for $430 (eBay; 06/08)
— Tiger Woods #1 BGS 10 (Pristine) sold for $415 (eBay; 06/08)
— Tiger Woods #1 BGS 10 (Pristine) sold for $409 (eBay; 04/09)
— Tiger Woods #1 BGS 10 (Pristine) sold for $375 (eBay; 06/08)
— Tiger Woods #1 BGS 10 (Pristine) sold for $305 (eBay; 05/08)
— Tiger Woods #1 BGS 10 (Pristine) sold for $235 (eBay; 11/07)
— Tiger Woods #1 BGS 10 (Pristine) sold for $230 (eBay; 06/08)
— Tiger Woods #1 BGS 10 (Pristine) sold for $215 (eBay; 11/07)
— Tiger Woods #1 BGS 10 (Pristine) sold for $215 (eBay; 11/07)
— Tiger Woods #1 BGS 10 (Pristine) sold for $215 (eBay; 01/08)
— Tiger Woods #1 BGS 10 (Pristine) sold for $205 (eBay; 01/08)
— Tiger Woods #1 BGS 10 (Pristine) sold for $155 (eBay; 01/08)
— Tiger Woods VM #151 BGS 10 (Pristine) sold for $181 (eBay; 02/09)
— Tiger Woods VM #151 BGS 10 (Pristine) sold for $124 (eBay; 03/09)

2001 Upper Deck Gallery

		NmMt 8	NmMt+ 8.5	MT 9	Gem 9.5/10
GG4	Tiger Woods	5	8	10	20

— Tiger Woods #GG4 BGS 10 (Pristine) sold for $105 (eBay; 06/08)
— Tiger Woods #GG4 BGS 10 (Pristine) sold for $32 (eBay; 5/11)

2001 Upper Deck Player's Ink

		NmMt 8	NmMt+ 8.5	MT 9	Gem 9.5/10
TW	Tiger Woods	600	800	1,000	1,200

— Tiger Woods #TW BGS 10 (Pristine) sold for $5,500 (eBay; 10/09)
— Tiger Woods #TW BGS 10 (Pristine) sold for $3,303 (eBay; 10/09)
— Tiger Woods #TW BGS 10 (Pristine) sold for $3,187 (eBay; 9/09)

2001 Upper Deck Stat Leaders

		NmMt 8	NmMt+ 8.5	MT 9	Gem 9.5/10
SL2	Tiger Woods	5	8	10	40
SL7	Tiger Woods	5	8	10	40
SL11	Tiger Woods	5	8	10	40
SL17	Tiger Woods	5	8	10	40

2001 Upper Deck Tiger's Tales

	NmMt 8	NmMt+ 8.5	MT 9	Gem 9.5/10
COMMON CARD (TT1-TT30)	5	5	5	15

2001 Upper Deck Heroes of Golf National Convention Promos

		NmMt 8	NmMt+ 8.5	MT 9	Gem 9.5/10
1TW	Tiger Woods	8	12	20	50

2001 Upper Deck Tiger Jam IV

		NmMt 8	NmMt+ 8.5	MT 9	Gem 9.5/10
TJ1	Tiger Woods	20	30	50	75
TJ2	Tiger Woods Silver	30	50	75	150

2002 SP Authentic

		NmMt 8	NmMt+ 8.5	MT 9	Gem 9.5/10
110	Phil Mickelson AU RC	400	600	2,000	8,000

2002 SP Authentic Limited

— Phil Mickelson #110 BGS 9 (MT) sold for $330 (eBay; 03/08)

2002 SP Game Used

		NmMt 8	NmMt+ 8.5	MT 9	Gem 9.5/10
80	Phil Mickelson AU Jsy T3 RC	500	800	1,500	3,000

2002 SP Game Used 01 Buybacks

— Tiger Woods #1 UD/18 PSA 9 (Mint) sold for $11,005 (eBay; 03/08)

2002 Upper Deck

		NmMt 8	NmMt+ 8.5	MT 9	Gem 9.5/10
41	Phil Mickelson RC	80	100	200	800

2003 SP Authentic

		NmMt 8	NmMt+ 8.5	MT 9	Gem 9.5/10
110	Annika Sorenstam AU/799 RC	150	200	250	600
125	Natalie Gulbis AU/1999 RC	15	20	25	40
127	Lorena Ochoa AU/1999 RC	15	20	25	50

2003 Upper Deck

		NmMt 8	NmMt+ 8.5	MT 9	Gem 9.5/10
48	Annika Sorenstam FL RC	6	8	10	25
57	Lorena Ochoa FL RC	6	8	10	25

— Tiger Woods #1 BGS 10 (Pristine) sold for $132 (eBay; 05/09)

2005 SP Authentic

		NmMt 8	NmMt+ 8.5	MT 9	Gem 9.5/10
104	Paula Creamer AU L1 RC	60	80	100	150

2005 SP Authentic Sign of the Times Single

		NmMt 8	NmMt+ 8.5	MT 9	Gem 9.5/10
TW	Tiger Woods	200	250	300	500

2014 SP Authentic

		NmMt 8	NmMt+ 8.5	MT 9	Gem 9.5/10
100	Rory McIlroy AU/299 RC	400	500	800	1,200

2015 Sports Illustrated for Kids

		NmMt 8	NmMt+ 8.5	MT 9	Gem 9.5/10
430	Jordan Spieth Golf	40	50	60	

HOCKEY

1910 - 1980

1910-11 C56

		PrFr 1	GD 2	VG 3	VgEx 4	EX 5	ExMt 6	NM 7	NmMt 8
1	Frank Patrick RC	250	▲500	▲600	1,000	2,000			
2	Percy Lesueur RC	300	400	500	800	3,000			
3	Gordon Roberts RC	100	150	250	400	600			
4	Barney Holden RC	80	120	200	300	500			
5	Frank(Pud) Glass RC	80	200	250	300	500			
6	Edgar Dey RC	80	120	200	300	500			
7	Marty Walsh RC	100	150	250	300	600	800		
8	Art Ross RC	500	800	1,000	1,500	5,000			
9	Angus Campbell RC	80	120	200	300	600			
10	Harry Hyland RC	125	175	300	400	800			
11	Herb Clark RC	60	150	200	300				
12	Art Ross RC	500	800	1,000	1,500	2,500	5,000		
13	Ed Decary RC	80	150	200	300	500	800		
14	Tom Dunderdale RC	150	200	300	500	800			
15	Fred Taylor RC	550	800	▲1,500	▲12,000				
16	Jos. Cattarinich RC	80	120	200	400	600			
17	Bruce Stuart RC	125	175	300	400	600	1,000		
18	Nick Bawlf RC	100	150	200	300	500	900		
19	Jim Jones RC	80	120	200	300	500	1,000		
20	Ernest Russell RC	125	175	300	400	800	1,500		
21	Jack Laviolette RC	80	120	200	300	600			
22	Riley Hern RC	100	150	250	400	600			
23	Didier(Pit) Pitre RC	▲150	▲250	▲400	▲500	▲800	3,000		
24	Skinner Poulin RC	60	100	200	300	400	800		
25	Art Bernier RC	60	150	250	300	500			
26	Lester Patrick RC	200	▲1,500		▲2,000	▲2,500			
27	Fred Lake RC	60	100	150	200	400			
28	Paddy Moran RC	200	400	500	700	1,250			
29	C.Toms RC	60	120	150	250	400			
30	Ernest(Moose) Johnson RC	150	250	400	600	800			
31	Horace Gaul RC	▲80	▲200	▲250	▲300	▲500			
32	Harold McNamara RC	100	▲200	▲300	▲400	▲600			
33	Jack Marshall RC	100	150	200	600	1,000			
34	Bruce Ridpath RC	60	150	200	250	500	1,000		
35	Jack Marshall RC	100	175	300	400	600			
36	Newsy Lalonde RC	500	600	1,000	2,500	3,000			

— Nick Bawlf #18 PSA 7 (NM) sold for $1,792.77 (eBay; 3/16)
— Art Bernier #25 PSA 6 (ExMt) sold for $1,366 (eBay; 3/16)
— Joesph Cattarinich #16 PSA 6 (ExMt) sold for $1,144 (eBay; 3/16)
— Frank Glass #5 PSA 6 (ExMt) sold foe $896 (eBay; 3/16)
— Harry Hyland RC #10 PSA 6 (ExMt) sold for $1,910 (eBay; 1/14)
— Skinner Poulin #24 PSA 7 (NrMt) sold for $2,911 (Mastro; 4/07)

1911-12 C55

		PrFr 1	GD 2	VG 3	VgEx 4	EX 5	ExMt 6	NM 7	NmMt 8
1	Paddy Moran	100	200	250	400	800			
2	Joe Hall RC	100	150	200	300	500			
3	Barney Holden	40	80	100	150	200	600		
4	Joe Malone RC	200	300	400	700	1,500	2,250		
5	Ed Oatman RC	50	80	100	150	▲250	▼600		
6	Tom Dunderdale	50	80	125	250	400	600		
7	Ken Mallen RC	50	80	100	150	200	500		
8	Jack MacDonald RC	100	120	150	200	300	800		
9	Fred Lake	30	40	60	100	200	400		
10	Albert Kerr RC	50	60	80	100	200	400		
11	Marty Walsh	50	100	150	250	300	400		
12	Hamby Shore RC	60	80	100	150	250	400		
13	Alex Currie RC	60	100	150	200	300	600		
14	Bruce Ridpath	40	60	80	100	200	300		
15	Bruce Stuart	50	80	150	200	300	500		
16	Percy Lesueur	80	150	200	250	400	600		
17	Jack Darragh RC	60	100	150	300	400	800		
18	Steve Vair RC	50	80	100	150	200	400		
19	Don Smith RC	50	80	125	150	300	600		
20	Fred Taylor	300	400	500	800	1,500	2,400		
21	Bert Lindsay RC	40	100	150	250	350	600		
22	H.L.(Larry) Gilmour RC	50	80	125	200	400	600		
23	Bobby Rowe RC	40	60	100	200	250	400		
24	Sprague Cleghorn RC	75	150	300	400	800	1,200		
25	Odie Cleghorn RC	50	80	125	250	300	600		

		PrFr 1	GD 2	VG 3	VgEx 4	EX 5	ExMt 6	NM 7	NmMt 8
26	Skene Ronan RC	50	100	150	200	250	400		
27A	W.Smaill RC Hand on stk	120	200	300	600	1,200			
27B	W.Smaill RC Hand on hip	150	300	800	1,200				
28	Ernest(Moose) Johnson	60	100	125	200	400	800		
29	Jack Marshall	50	100	150	200	300	600		
30	Harry Hyland	50	80	125	250	350	600		
31	Art Ross	300	500	700	1,000	1,500	2,000		
32	Riley Hern	60	100	150	250	350	600		
33	Gordon Roberts	60	80	100	150	200	400		
34	Frank Glass	50	80	125	200	300	400		
35	Ernest Russell	60	100	150	200	300	400		
36	James Gardner UER RC	50	80	125	250	400			
37	Art Bernier	40	60	100	150	250	500		
38	Georges Vezina RC	1,200	4,000	6,000	8,000	9,000	10,000		
39	G.(Henri) Dallaire RC	60	80	125	200	300	400		
40	R.(Rocket) Power RC	▲60	▲100	▲150	▲250	▲300	▲800		
41	Didier(Pit) Pitre	80	120	250	300	500			
42	Newsy Lalonde	250	400	500	800	1,000	2,000		
43	Eugene Payan RC	50	80	125	200	300	500		
44	George Poulin RC	50	80	125	200	300	600		
45	Jack Laviolette	80	150	200	300	500	▼1,500		

— Jack Darragh RC #17 PSA 7 (NM MT) sold for $1,085 (eBay, 1/14)
— Bert Lindsay #21 PSA 8 (NM MT) sold for $4,176 (eBay, 8/13)
— Ed Oatman RC #5 PSA 8 (NM MT) sold for $2,010 (eBay, 8/13)
— Walter Smaill #27A PSA 8 (NM MT) sold for $7,620 (eBay, 8/13)
— Fred Taylor #20 SCG 8 (NM MT) sold for $3,438 (Mile High; 1/16)%%Fred Taylor #20 PSA 6 (NM) sold for $1,812.50 (eBay, 2/14)
— George Vezina #38 SGC 8 (ExMt) sold for $1,910 (eBay, 07/09)
— George Vezina #38 SGC 96 (MT) sold for $100,000 (BMW, private sale)
— George Vezina #38 PSA 7 (NM) sold for $11,000 (Mastro, 12/08)
— George Vezina #38 SGC 20 (Fair) sold for $1,535 (eBay, 05/08)
— George Vezina #38 PSA 7 (NM) sold for $20,698.50 (eBay, 03/14)

1933-34 O-Pee-Chee V304A

		PrFr 1	GD 2	VG 3	VgEx 4	EX 5	ExMt 6	NM 7	NmMt 8
1	Danny Cox RC	35	60	100	150	250			
2	Joe Lamb RC	30	40	80	100	200			
3	Eddie Shore RC	200	350	450	1,000	1,800	3,000		
4	Ken Doraty RC	30	40	60	100	200			
5	Fred Hitchman RC	30	40	60	125	200	600		
6	Nels Stewart RC	120	200	300	500	800			
7	Walter Galbraith RC	50	80	100	150	200	400		
8	Dit Clapper RC	100	150	250	500	800			
9	Harry Oliver RC	60	100	150	250	400	600		
10	Red Horner RC	50	80	120	200	300			
11	Alex Levinsky RC	30	40	60	100	200	400		
12	Joe Primeau RC	100	200	250	300	600	1,000		
13	Ace Bailey RC	150	250	350	450	550	650		
14	George Patterson RC	30	40	60	100	150			
15	George Hainsworth RC	60	100	150	300	500			
16	Ott Heller RC	30	40	60	100	150			
17	Art Somers RC	30	40	60	100	150			
18	Lorne Chabot RC	60	100	125	250	400			
19	Johnny Gagnon RC	30	40	60	100	200	400		
20	Pit Lepine RC	30	40	60	100	150			
21	Wildor Larochelle RC	30	40	60	120	150	400		
22	Georges Mantha RC	30	40	60	120	175			
23	Howie Morenz RC	250	400	1,000	1,500	2,500			
24	Syd Howe RC	▲80	▲200	▲250	▲400	▲500	▲800		
25	Frank Finnigan RC	30	40	60	100	150			
26	Bill Touhey RC	30	40	60	100	150			
27	Cooney Weiland RC	80	100	150	250	350	500		
28	Leo Bourgeault RC	35	50	100	150	250			
29	Normie Himes RC	35	50	75	135	200	400		
30	Johnny Sheppard RC	30	40	60	100	150			
31	King Clancy RC	▲250	▲300	▲400	▲500	▲800	▲1,200		
32	Hap Day RC	50	80	150	200	300			
33	Busher Jackson RC	100	150	250	300	500	1,000		
34	Charlie Conacher RC	100	150	250	350	800			
35	Harold Cotton RC	50	60	100	150	200	350		
36	Butch Keeling RC	30	40	60	100	150			
37	Murray Murdoch RC	35	40	60	100	200			
38	Bill Cook	35	50	100	150	350	500		
39	Ching Johnson RC	60	100	150	250	▼400	▼600		
40	Hap Emms RC	30	40	60	100	150			

		PrFr 1	GD 2	VG 3	VgEx 4	EX 5	ExMt 6	NM 7	NmMt 8
41	Bert McInenly RC	30	40	60	100	150			
42	John Sorrell RC	50	100	150	200	250			
43	Bill Phillips RC	30	40	60	100	150	300		
44	Charley McVeigh RC	30	40	60	100	150			
45	Roy Worters RC	80	100	150	250	400			
46	Albert Leduc RC	35	50	80	120	200			
47	Nick Wasnie RC	30	40	60	100	150	500		
48	Armand Mondou RC	50	80	100	150	200			

— Ace Bailey #13 PSA 7 (NM) sold for $1,154 (eBay; 6/13)
— Dit Clapper #8 PSA 8 (NmMt) sold for $5,008 (eBay; 5/12)
— Dit Clapper #8 PSA 7.5 (NmMt) sold for $854 (eBay; 9/12)
— Butch Keeling #36 PSA 7 (NM) sold for $1,475 (eBay; 2/13)
— Cooney Weiland #27 PSA 7 (NM) sold for $1,283 (eBay; 2/16)

1933-34 O-Pee-Chee V304B

		PrFr 1	GD 2	VG 3	VgEx 4	EX 5	ExMt 6	NM 7	NmMt 8
49	Babe Siebert RC	50	80	120	▲300	▲800			
50	Aurel Joliat	125	200	300	400	600			
51	Larry Aurie RC	50	80	100	150	250	400		
52	Ebbie Goodfellow RC	35	60	100	150	250			
53	John Roach	30	50	80	125	200			
54	Bill Beveridge RC	30	50	80	125	200			
55	Earl Robinson RC	25	50	100	150	200	500		
56	Jimmy Ward RC	30	50	80	100	150			
57	Archie Wilcox RC	25	40	60	100	150	350		
58	Lorne Duguid RC	25	40	60	100	150	350		
59	Dave Kerr RC	30	80	100	150	200			
60	Baldy Northcott RC	30	50	80	125	200	400		
61	Marvin Wentworth RC	30	50	80	125	200	400		
62	Dave Trottier RC	30	50	80	125	150	250		
63	Wally Kilrea RC	25	40	60	100	150	350		
64	Glen Brydson RC	30	50	80	125	200			
65	Vernon Ayres RC	25	40	60	100	150			
66	Bob Gracie RC	25	40	60	100	150	400		
67	Vic Ripley RC	30	50	80	125	250			
68	Tiny Thompson RC	60	100	150	250	800			
69	Alex Smith RC	25	40	60	100	150			
70	Andy Blair RC	25	40	60	100	150			
71	Cecil Dillon RC	25	40	60	125	200	600		
72	Bun Cook RC	50	80	120	200	800			

— Tiny Thompson #68 PSA 7 (NM) sold for $1,865 (eBay; 4/16)

1933-34 V357 Ice Kings

	PrFr 1	GD 2	VG 3	VgEx 4	EX 5	ExMt 6	NM 7	NmMt 8
Dit Clapper RC	40	75	125	250	400	1,500		
Bill Brydge RC	25	30	50	80	150			
Aurel Joliat UER	50	100	200	300	400	700		
Andy Blair	25	30	50	80	100	150		
Earl Robinson RC	25	30	50	80	100	150		
Paul Haynes RC	25	30	50	80	100	150		
Ronnie Martin RC	25	30	50	80	100	150		
Babe Siebert RC	25	50	100	150	200	500		
Archie Wilcox RC	25	30	50	80	100	150		
Hap Day	35	50	80	125	250			
Roy Worters RC	50	80	150	200	350			
Nels Stewart RC	40	60	100	200	300	500		
King Clancy	40	80	120	200	300	600		
Marty Burke RC	30	40	60	100	200			
Cecil Dillon RC	25	30	50	80	100			
Red Horner RC	50	60	100	150	300			
Armand Mondou RC	25	30	50	80	100	150		
Paul Raymond RC	25	30	50	80	100			
Dave Kerr RC	25	30	50	80	100	150	250	
Butch Keeling RC	25	30	50	80	100	150	300	
Johnny Gagnon RC	25	30	50	80	100	150	250	
Ace Bailey RC	40	80	120	200	300			
Harry Oliver RC	30	40	60	100	150	250	400	
Gerald Carson RC	25	30	50	80	100	150	200	
Red Dutton RC	25	35	50	80	125	200		
Georges Mantha RC	25	30	50	80	100	200		
Marty Barry RC	40	50	80	125	175	250		
Wildor Larochelle RC	25	30	50	80	100	150		
Red Beattie RC	25	30	50	80	100	150		
Bill Cook	40	50	80	125	175	250		
Hooley Smith	50	60	100	150	200	350		
Art Chapman RC	25	30	50	80	100	150		
Harold Cotton RC	30	50	80	100	150	250		
Lionel Hitchman	30	40	60	100	150	250		
George Patterson RC	25	30	50	80	100	150		
Howie Morenz	150	250	400	800				
Jimmy Ward RC	25	30	50	80	100	150		
Charley McVeigh RC	25	35	50	80	125	175		
Glen Brydson RC	25	35	50	80	125	175		
Joe Primeau RC	100	125	200	300	500	800		
Joe Lamb RC	30	40	60	100	150	200	350	
Sylvio Mantha RC	50	60	100	150	225	350		
Cy Wentworth RC	30	40	60	100	200	400		
Normie Himes RC	25	35	50	80	125	175		
Doug Brennan RC	25	30	50	80	100	150		

		PrFr 1	GD 2	VG 3	VgEx 4	EX 5	ExMt 6	NM 7	NmMt 8
46	Pit Lepine RC	25	30	50	80	100			
47	Alex Levinsky RC	25	35	50	80	125	175		
48	Baldy Northcott RC	25	35	50	80	125	175		
49	Ken Doraty RC	25	35	50	80	125			
50	Bill Thoms RC	25	35	50	80	125			
51	Vernon Ayres RC	25	35	60	100	150			
52	Lorne Duguid RC	25	35	50	80	125			
53	Wally Kilrea RC	25	35	50	80	125			
54	Vic Ripley RC	25	35	50	80	125			
55	Hap Emms RC	25	35	50	80	125			
56	Duke Dutkowski RC	25	35	50	80	125			
57	Tiny Thompson	200	250	300	400	500	1,500		
58	Charlie Sands RC	25	35	50	80	125			
59	Larry Aurie RC	25	35	50	80	125			
60	Bill Beveridge RC	25	35	50	80	125			
61	Bill McKenzie RC	25	35	50	80	125			
62	Earl Roche RC	25	35	50	80	125			
63	Bob Gracie RC	25	35	50	80	125			
64	Hec Kilrea RC	25	35	50	80	125			
65	Cooney Weiland RC	125	150	200	250	400			
66	Bun Cook RC	40	60	100	150	300			
67	John Roach	25	35	50	80	125	175		
68	Murray Murdoch RC	25	35	50	80	125			
69	Danny Cox RC	25	35	50	80	125			
70	Desse Roche RC	25	35	50	80	150			
71	Lorne Chabot RC	125	150	200	300	400			
72	Syd Howe RC	40	60	100	150				

— Ace Bailey #22 PSA 7 (NrMt) sold for $756 (eBay; 9/12)
— Armand Mondou #17 PSA 8 (NmMt) sold for $1,127 (eBay; 9/12)
— Aurel Joliat #3 PSA 7 (NrMt) sold for $1,153 (eBay; 9/12)
— Bill Brydge #2 PSA 8 (NmMt) sold for $1,143 (eBay; 9/12)
— Hap Day #10 PSA 8 (NmMt) sold for $592 (eBay; 9/12)
— King Clancy #13 PSA 8 (NmMt) sold for $2,385 (Mile High; 1/12)
— Nels Stewart #12 PSA 8 (NmMt) sold for $1,432 (eBay; 9/14)

1935-36 O-Pee-Chee V304C

		PrFr 1	GD 2	VG 3	VgEx 4	EX 5	ExMt 6	NM 7	NmMt 8
73	Wilfred Cude RC	50	80	125	200	600			
74	Jack McGill RC	30	50	100	150				
75	Russ Blinco RC	30	50	80	150				
76	Hooley Smith	50	80	125	200				
77	Herb Cain RC	30	50	80	125	250			
78	Gus Marker RC	30	50	80	200				
79	Lynn Patrick RC	50	80	125	200				
80	Johnny Gottselig	30	50	80	125				
81	Marty Barry	35	60	100	150	300			
82	Sylvio Mantha	50	80	125	250				
83	Flash Hollett RC	30	50	80	200	500			
84	Nick Metz RC	30	50	80	125				
85	Bill Thoms	30	50	80	125				
86	Hec Kilrea	30	50	80	125				
87	Pep Kelly RC	30	50	80	125				
88	Art Jackson RC	30	50	80	125				
89	Allan Shields RC	30	50	80	150				
90	Buzz Boll	30	50	80	125				
91	Jean Pusie RC	30	50	80	125				
92	Roger Jenkins RC	30	50	80	125	400			
93	Arthur Coulter RC	▲50	▲100	▲200	▲300	▲1,000			
94	Art Chapman	30	50	80	125				
95	Paul Haynes	35	60	100	150				
96	Leroy Goldsworthy RC	50	80	125	200	250	300		

1936-37 O-Pee-Chee V304D

		PrFr 1	GD 2	VG 3	VgEx 4	EX 5	ExMt 6	NM 7	NmMt 8
97	Turk Broda RC	150	300	600	1,000	2,500			
98	Sweeney Schriner RC	▲50	▲150	▲200	▲300	▲800	▲1,200		
99	Jack Shill RC	25	40	60	100	150	200		
100	Bob Davidson RC	35	60	80	100	250	400		
101	Syl Apps RC	▲100	▲250	▲400	▲600	▲800	▲3,000		
102	Lionel Conacher	60	150	250	400	500			
103	Jimmy Fowler RC	35	60	100	150	250	400		
104	Al Murray RC	25	40	60	100	150			
105	Neil Colville RC	▲60	▲150	▲250	▲400	▲500			
106	Paul Runge RC	25	40	60	100	150	200		
107	Mike Karakas RC	30	50	80	125	175	250		
108	John Gallagher RC	25	40	60	100	150	250		
109	Alex Shibicky RC	35	60	100	150	200	300		
110	Herb Cain	35	60	100	150	200	300		
111	Bill McKenzie	25	40	60	100	150	200		
112	Harold Jackson	40	60	80	125	200	300		
113	Art Wiebe RC	25	40	60	100	150			
114	Joffre Desilets RC	25	40	60	100	150			
115	Earl Robinson	25	40	60	100	200	300		
116	Cy Wentworth	35	60	80	125	200	250		
117	Ebbie Goodfellow	25	40	60	100	175	300		
118	Eddie Shore	200	400	600	800	1,500			
119	Buzz Boll	25	40	60	100	150			
120	Wilfred Cude	30	50	80	120	200			
121	Howie Morenz	250	400	600	800	1,500	2,000		

		PrFr 1	GD 2	VG 3	VgEx 4	EX 5	ExMt 6	NM 7	NmMt 8
122	Red Horner	40	100	150	250	300	500		
123	Charlie Conacher	100	250	350	500	600			
124	Busher Jackson	50	120	200	250	300	400		
125	King Clancy	100	250	400	500	750	1,000		
126	Dave Trottier	30	50	80	125	200	300		
127	Russ Blinco	25	40	60	100	150			
128	Lynn Patrick	50	120	200	300	400			
129	Aurel Joliat	80	200	300	500	600	800		
130	Baldy Northcott	25	50	100	150	200	250		
131	Larry Aurie	25	40	100	150	225	300		
132	Hooley Smith	40	80	120	200	300	400		

— Turk Broda #97 PSA 8 (NmMt) sold for $3,6192.00 (eBay; 11/11)
— Charlie Conacher #123 SGC 9 (Mint) sold for $4,633.86.00 (Goodwin; 7/12)
— Aurel Joliat #129 SGC 8 (NRMint) sold for $1,036 (eBay; 3/14)
— Aurel Joliat #129 SGC 7 (NRMint) sold for $837 (eBay; 9/14)

1937-38 O-Pee-Chee V304E

		PrFr 1	GD 2	VG 3	VgEx 4	EX 5	ExMt 6	NM 7	NmMt 8
133	Turk Broda	100	150	250	400				
134	Red Horner	30	50	80	120				
135	Jimmy Fowler	25	35	50	60				
136	Bob Davidson	25	35	50	60				
137	Reg. Hamilton RC	25	35	50	60	200			
138	Charlie Conacher	80	120	200	300				
139	Busher Jackson	60	100	150	250				
140	Buzz Boll	25	35	50	60	200			
141	Syl Apps	60	100	150	250				
142	Gordie Drillon RC	60	100	200	300	400			
143	Bill Thoms	25	35	50	60				
144	Nick Metz	25	35	50	60				
145	Pep Kelly	25	35	50	60				
146	Murray Armstrong RC	25	35	50	60				
147	Murph Chamberlain RC	25	35	50	60				
148	Des Smith RC	25	35	50	60	200			
149	Wilfred Cude	30	50	80	100				
150	Babe Siebert	30	50	80	120				
151	Bill MacKenzie	25	40	60	80				
152	Aurel Joliat	80	120	200	300				
153	Georges Mantha	25	35	50	60				
154	Johnny Gagnon	25	35	50	60	200			
155	Paul Haynes	25	35	50	60				
156	Joffre Desilets	25	35	50	60				
157	George Allen Brown RC	25	35	50	60				
158	Paul Drouin RC	25	35	50	60				
159	Pit Lepine	▲30	50	60	80				
160	Toe Blake RC	150	250	300	500				
161	Bill Beveridge	30	50	80	100				
162	Allan Shields	25	35	50	60				
163	Cy Wentworth	30	50	80	120				
164	Stew Evans RC	25	35	50	60				
165	Earl Robinson	25	35	50	60				
166	Baldy Northcott	30	50	80	100				
167	Paul Runge	25	35	50	60				
168	Dave Trottier	25	35	50	60				
169	Russ Blinco	25	35	50	60	200			
170	Jimmy Ward	30	50	80	150				
171	Bob Gracie	25	35	50	60				
172	Herb Cain	30	50	80	120	250			
173	Gus Marker	25	35	50	60				
174	Walter Buswell RC	25	35	50	60				
175	Carl Voss	30	50	80	120				
176	Rod Lorraine RC	25	35	50	60				
177	Armand Mondou	25	35	50	60				
178	Cliff(Red) Goupille RC	25	35	50	60	200			
179	Jerry Shannon RC	25	35	50	60				
180	Tom Cook RC	30	50	80	120				

— Carl Voss #175 PSA 7 (NM) sold for $902 (eBay; 3/16)

1939-40 O-Pee-Chee V301-1

		PrFr 1	GD 2	VG 3	VgEx 4	EX 5	ExMt 6	NM 7	NmMt 8
1	Reg Hamilton	15	25	35	60				
2	Turk Broda	100	150	200	250	300			
3	Bingo Kampman RC	15	25	35	50				
4	Gordie Drillon	20	25	40	80				
5	Bob Davidson	15	25	35	50				
6	Syl Apps	30	50	80	120				
7	Pete Langelle RC	15	30	50	100				
8	Don Metz RC	15	25	35	50				
9	Pep Kelly	15	25	35	50				
10	Red Horner	20	30	50	80				
11	Wally Stanowsky RC	15	25	35	50				
12	Murph Chamberlain	15	25	35	50				
13	Bucko MacDonald	15	25	35	50				
14	Sweeney Schriner	20	30	50	80				
15	Billy Taylor RC	15	25	35	50				
16	Gus Marker	15	25	35	50				
17	Hooley Smith	20	30	50	80				
18	Art Chapman	15	25	35	50				
19	Murray Armstrong	15	25	35	50				

		PrFr 1	GD 2	VG 3	VgEx 4	EX 5	ExMt 6	NM 7	NmMt 8
20	Busher Jackson	20	30	50	80	150			
21	Buzz Boll	15	25	35	50				
22	Cliff(Red) Goupille	15	25	35	50				
23	Rod Lorraine	15	25	35	50				
24	Paul Drouin	15	25	35	50				
25	Johnny Gagnon	15	25	35	50				
26	Georges Mantha	15	25	40	60				
27	Armand Mondou	15	25	40	60				
28	Claude Bourque RC	15	25	40	60				
29	Ray Getliffe RC	15	25	40	60				
30	Cy Wentworth	15	25	40	60				
31	Paul Haynes	15	25	35	50				
32	Walter Buswell	15	25	35	50				
33	Ott Heller	15	25	35	50				
34	Arthur Coulter	15	25	35	60				
35	Clint Smith RC	20	30	50	80				
36	Lynn Patrick	20	30	50	80				
37	Dave Kerr	15	25	40	60				
38	Murray Patrick RC	15	25	35	50				
39	Neil Colville	20	30	50	80				
40	Jack Portland RC	15	25	35	50				
41	Flash Hollett	15	25	35	50				
42	Herb Cain	20	30	50	80				
43	Mud Bruneteau	15	25	35	50				
44	Joffre DeSilets	15	25	35	50				
45	Mush March	15	25	35	50				
46	Cully Dahlstrom RC	15	25	35	50				
47	Mike Karakas	15	25	35	60				
48	Bill Thoms	15	25	35	50				
49	Art Wiebe	15	25	35	50				
50	Johnny Gottselig	15	25	35	50				
51	Nick Metz	15	25	35	50				
52	Jack Church RC	15	25	35	50				
53	Bob Heron RC	15	25	35	50				
54	Hank Goldup RC	15	25	35	50	80			
55	Jimmy Fowler	15	25	35	50				
56	Charlie Sands	15	25	35	50				
57	Marty Barry	15	25	35	60				
58	Doug Young	15	25	35	50				
59	Charlie Conacher	30	60	100	150	250			
60	John Sorrell	15	25	35	50				
61	Tommy Anderson RC	15	25	35	50	135			
62	Lorne Carr	15	25	35	50				
63	Earl Robertson RC	15	25	60	80				
64	Wily Field RC	15	25	35	50				
65	Jimmy Orlando RC	15	25	35	50				
66	Ebbie Goodfellow	15	30	50	80	100			
67	Jack Keating RC	15	25	35	50	80			
68	Sid Abel RC	60	100	120	200	300			
69	Gus Giesebrecht RC	15	25	35	50				
70	Don Deacon RC	15	25	35	50	80			
71	Hec Kilrea	15	25	35	50				
72	Syd Howe	20	30	50	80				
73	Eddie Wares RC	15	25	35	50	80			
74	Carl Liscombe RC	15	25	35	50				
75	Tiny Thompson	20	30	50	80	150			
76	Earl Seibert RC	15	25	35	50				
77	Des Smith RC	15	25	35	50	80			
78	Les Cunningham RC	15	25	35	50				
79	George Allen RC	15	25	35	50				
80	Bill Carse RC	15	25	35	50				
81	Bill McKenzie	15	25	35	50				
82	Ab DeMarco RC	15	30	50	80	150			
83	Phil Watson	15	25	35	50				
84	Alf Pike RC	15	25	35	50				
85	Babe Pratt RC	15	25	40	60				
86	Bryan Hextall Sr. RC	15	25	40	60				
87	Kilby MacDonald RC	15	25	35	50				
88	Alex Shibicky	15	25	35	50	100			
89	Dutch Hiller RC	15	25	35	50				
90	Mac Colville	15	25	35	50				
91	Roy Conacher RC	20	30	50	80	125			
92	Cooney Weiland	20	30	50	80	125			
93	Art Jackson	15	25	35	50				
94	Woody Dumart RC	20	30	50	80	250			
95	Dit Clapper	30	50	80	120	200			
96	Mel Hill RC	15	25	35	50				
97	Frank Brimsek RC	50	80	120	200	300			
98	Bill Cowley RC	50	80	100	200	250			
99	Bobby Bauer RC	40	60	100	200				
100	Eddie Shore	100	150	250	400				

— Bryan Hextall #86 SGC 9 (Mint) sold for $1,705 (Mile High; 10/12)
— Bryan Hextall #86 PSA 8 (NM Mt) sold for $837 (eBay; 2/16)
— Rod Lorraine #23 SGC 9 (Mint) sold for $1,025 (Mile High; 5/12)
— Wally Stanowsky #11 SGC 8.5 (NmMt+) sold for $567 (Mile High; 5/12)

1951-52 Parkhurst

#	Name	GD 2	VG 3	VgEx 4	EX 5	ExMt 6	NM 7	NmMt 8	NmMt+ 8.5
1	Elmer Lach	80	150	300	400	650	1,250	4,000	
2	Paul Meger RC	25	60	100	200	300	400	3,500	
3	Butch Bouchard RC	▲150	▲250	▲500	▲600	▲800	▲1,000	▲2,000	
4	Maurice Richard RC	▲3,000	▲4,000	▲6,000	▲8,000	▲10,000			▲80,000
5	Bert Olmstead RC	40	100	150	200	▲400	600	▲1,500	
6	Bud MacPherson RC	15	25	40	80	125	250	700	
7	Tom Johnson RC	30	50	80	100	200	350	600	
8	Paul Masnick RC	15	25	40	80	100	200	300	
9	Calum Mackay RC	25	40	80	100	150	200	500	
10	Doug Harvey RC	▲400	▲600	▲800	▲1,000	▲1,500	▲2,000	▲3,000	
11	Ken Mosdell RC	15	25	40	80	125	250	800	
12	Floyd Curry RC	12	20	30	60	100	150	400	
13	Billy Reay RC	15	25	40	60	100	150	500	
14	Bernie Geoffrion RC	250	300	400	600	750	1,000	1,500	
15	Gerry McNeil RC	30	60	100	200	300	600	2,000	
16	Dick Gamble RC	15	30	50	80	120	200	350	
17	Gerry Couture RC	▲20	▲40	▲60	▲100	▲250	▲400	▲800	
18	Ross Robert Lowe RC	20	25	40	60	100	200	500	1,000
19	Jim Henry RC	20	40	50	60	100	175	400	
20	Victor Ivan Lynn RC	▲20	▲30	▲60	▲100	▲150	▲200	▲500	
21	Walter(Gus) Kyle RC	12	20	30	50	80	120	300	
22	Ed Sandford RC	12	20	30	50	100	150	250	
23	John Henderson RC	12	20	30	50	80	120	250	
24	Dunc Fisher RC	▲60	▲80	▲150	▲200	▲300	▲500	▲800	
25	Hal Laycoe RC	15	25	40	50	80	120	250	
26	Bill Quackenbush RC	20	40	50	80	120	200	400	
27	George Sullivan RC	▲20	▲30	▲40	▲60	▲100	▲150	▲400	
28	Woody Dumart RC	20	30	50	60	100	150	250	
29	Milt Schmidt	25	40	100	200	300	400	500	
30	Adam Brown RC	▲25	▲50	▲200	▲300	▲400	▲500	▲600	▲800
31	Pentti Lund RC	15	25	40	60	100	150	400	850
32	Ray Barry RC	12	20	30	50	80	100	250	
33	Ed Kryznowski UER RC	12	20	30	50	80	100	300	
34	Johnny Peirson RC	▲15	▲25	▲50	▲100	▲150	▲250	▲400	
35	Lorne Ferguson RC	12	20	30	50	80	120	250	
36	Clare(Rags) Raglan RC	▲15	▲25	▲40	▲80	▲150	▲300	▲500	
37	Bill Gadsby RC	▲60	▲100	▲200	▲250	▲300	▲500	▲1,000	
38	Al Dewsbury RC	12	20	40	50	80	120	400	
39	George Clare Martin RC	12	20	40	50	80	120	250	
40	Gus Bodnar RC	▲30	▲50	▲100	▲200	▲300	▲400	▲600	
41	Jim Peters RC	12	20	30	50	80	150	250	
42	Bep Guidolin RC	12	20	30	50	80	150	350	
43	George Gee RC	12	20	30	50	80	120	250	
44	Jim McFadden RC	15	30	50	80	150	200	300	
45	Fred Hucul RC	▲15	▲25	▲40	▲60	▲100	▲250	▲400	
46	Lee Fogolin	12	20	30	50	80	100	250	
47	Harry Lumley RC	50	60	100	▲200	▲300	▲400	▲800	▲1,500
48	Doug Bentley	25	50	80	100	200	400	800	
49	Bill Mosienko RC	▲60	▲100	▲150	▲200	▲500	▲600	▲800	
50	Roy Conacher	20	40	60	80	120	200	300	
51	Pete Babando	15	25	40	80	100	200	500	
52	B.Barilko/G.McNeil IA	▲150	▲300	▲800	▲1,000	▲1,500	▲2,000	▲3,000	
53	Jack Stewart	25	30	60	80	150	200	400	
54	Marty Pavelich RC	12	20	30	50	80	150	400	
55	Red Kelly RC	100	250	300	400	500	800	1,500	2,000
56	Ted Lindsay RC	▲200	▲400	▲500	▲600	▲800	▲1,000	▲1,500	
57	Glen Skov RC	12	20	30	50	80	250	1,200	
58	Benny Woit	12	20	30	50	80	175	400	
59	Tony Leswick RC	15	25	40	80	120	200	400	
60	Fred Glover RC	▲30	▲50	▲100	▲200	▲300	▲400	▲600	
61	Terry Sawchuk RC	▲1,200	▲3,000	▲4,000	▲5,000	▲6,000	▲8,000	▲25,000	
62	Vic Stasiuk RC	▲25	▲40	▲60	▲150	▲300	▲400	▲500	
63	Alex Delvecchio RC	80	150	▲300	▲400	▲600	800	1,500	2,000
64	Sid Abel	25	40	60	100	200	400	600	
65	Metro Prystai RC	12	20	30	50	80	150	400	
66	Gordie Howe RC	▲8,000	▲10,000	▲12,000				40,000	
67	Bob Goldham RC	15	25	40	60	125	200	400	
68	Marcel Pronovost RC	▲30	▲50	▲80	▲125	▲200	▲500	▲800	
69	Leo Reise	12	20	30	50	80	100	200	
70	Harry Watson RC	60	▲100	▲200	▲250	▲300	▲500	1,400	
71	Danny Lewicki RC	▲15	▲25	▲40	▲60	▲100	▲250	▲600	
72	Howie Meeker RC	▲60	▲125	▲200	▲300	▲400	▲600	▲2,000	
73	Gus Mortson RC	12	25	40	60	100	200	300	
74	Joe Klukay RC	15	30	50	80	120	250	1,000	
75	Turk Broda	60	100	200	▲300	▲600	▲2,000	▲4,000	
76	Al Rollins RC	25	40	60	80	100	350	1,500	
77	Bill Juzda RC	12	20	30	50	80	150	350	
78	Ray Timgren RC	12	20	30	50	80	150	300	
79	Hugh Bolton RC	▲25	▲40	▲80	▲250	▲400	▲500	▲800	
80	Fern Flaman RC	25	50	80	100	200	300	550	
81	Max Bentley	20	30	50	80	120	200	800	
82	Jim Thomson	12	20	30	50	80	150	300	
83	Fleming Mackell RC	15	30	50	80	100	200	400	
84	Sid Smith RC	20	30	50	80	125	250	400	
85	Cal Gardner RC	▲25	▲50	▲100	▲150	▲200	▲300	▲500	
86	Teeder Kennedy RC	40	60	100	150	250	400	750	2,400

#	Name	GD 2	VG 3	VgEx 4	EX 5	ExMt 6	NM 7	NmMt 8	NmMt+ 8.5
87	Tod Sloan RC	15	25	40	80	125	200	300	
88	Bob Solinger	15	30	50	80	100	200	300	
89	Frank Eddolls RC	12	20	30	50	80	150	300	
90	Jack Evans RC	12	20	30	60	80	120	250	
91	Hy Buller RC	12	20	30	50	80	150	700	
92	Steve Kraftcheck	12	20	30	50	80	100	300	
93	Don Raleigh	12	25	50	80	100	200	300	
94	Allan Stanley RC	▲50	▲80	▲150	▲200	▲300	▲400	▲1,000	
95	Paul Ronty RC	15	25	40	60	80	120	300	
96	Edgar Laprade RC	▲25	▲50	▲80	▲125	▲250	▲400	▲600	
97	Nick Mickoski RC	12	20	30	50	80	120	300	
98	Jack McLeod RC	12	20	30	50	80	150	350	
99	Gaye Stewart	12	20	30	50	80	150	300	
100	Wally Hergesheimer RC	15	30	50	▲100	▲125	▲200	▲400	
101	Ed Kullman RC	25	40	60	80	100	150	400	
102	Ed Slowinski RC	25	40	60	80	100	200	1,000	
103	Reg Sinclair RC	15	25	40	100	150	300	550	
104	Chuck Rayner RC	25	50	100	150	200	300	600	
105	Jim Conacher RC	▲30	▲80	▲100	▲150	▲250	▲400	▲1,000	

— Pete Babando #51 PSA 7.5 (NrMt) sold for $2,030 (eBay; 7/08)
— Bill Barilko/Gerry McNeil #53 PSA 9 (MT) sold for $5,612 (Memory Lane; 4/12)
— Bill Barilko/Gerry McNeil #53 PSA 8.5 (NmMt+) sold for $2,427 (Mile High; 5/12)
— Ray Barry #32 PSA 9 (MT) sold for $3,312 (Memory Lane; 7/12)
— Ray Barry #32 PSA 9 (MT) sold for $1,721 (eBay; 3/16)
(%%Doug Bentley #48 PSA 8.5 (NmMt+) sold for $1,332 (Mile High; 5/12)
— Doug Bentley #48 PSA 8.5 (NmMt+) sold for $7,200 (eBay; 8/08)
— Butch Bouchard #3 PSA 8.5 (NmMt+) sold for $7,200 (Mastro; 8/08)
— Turk Broda #75 PSA 8 (NmMt) sold for $3,065 (eBay; 3/14)
— Adam Brown #30 PSA 10 (Gem) sold for $6,000 (Mastro; 8/08)
— Adam Brown #30 PSA 9 (MT) sold for $1,256.50 (eBay; 5/16)
— Hy Buller #91 PSA 9 (MT) sold for $2,608.50 (eBay; 5/16)
— Roy Conacher #50 PSA 9 (MT) sold for $4,524 (eBay; 7/15)
— Gerry Couture RC #17 PSA 9 (Mt) sold for $2,216 (Memory Lane; 12/13)
— Alex Delvecchio #63 PSA 8 (NmMt) sold for $4,859 (eBay; 8/12)
— Alex Delvecchio #63 PSA 9 (MT) sold for $3,708 (eBay; 3/13)
— Jack Evans #90 PSA 9 (NmMt) sold for $2,379 (eBay; 6/12)
— Bill Gadsby #37 PSA 9 (MT) sold for $2,549 (Memory Lane; 5/13)
— George Gee #43 PSA 9 (MT) sold for $2,489 (Memory Lane; 7/12)
— Bob Goldman #67 PSA 10 (GEM) sold for $6,000 (Mastro; 8/08)
— Bep Guidolin #42 PSA 8.5 (NmMt+) sold for $6,000 (Mastro; 8/08)
— Doug Harvey #10 PSA 9 (MT) sold for $5,620 (eBay; 3/13)
— Doug Harvey #10 PSA 9 (MT) sold for $3,000 (eBay; 9/08)
— Jim Henry #19 PSA 9 (MT) sold for $2,005 (Mile High; 5/12)
— Jim Henry #19 PSA 9 (MT) sold for $3,204 (eBay; 10/08)
— Gordie Howe #66 SGC 9 (MT) sold for $29,372 (Goodwin; 9/15)
— Gordie Howe #66 SGC 8.5 (NmMt+) sold for $21,493 (Mile High; 7/15)
— Gordie Howe #66 PSA 8.5 (NmMt+) sold for $26,300 (eBay; 3/13)
— Fred Hucul #45 PSA 9 (MT) sold for $1,307 (eBay; 1/07)
— Fred Hucul #45 PSA 9 (MT) sold for $1,840 (eBay; 3/16)
— Tom Johnson #7 PSA 9 (MT) sold for $4,191 (eBay; 10/15)
— Ed Kryznowski #33 PSA 9 (Mint) sold for $1,034 (Memory Lane; 7/12)
— Hal Laycoe #25 PSA 9 (MT) sold for $1,367 (Mile High; 5/12)
— Hal Laycoe #25 PSA 9 (MT) sold for $2,480 (Mile High; 1/07)
— Danny Lewicki #71 PSA 9 (MT) sold for $2,263 (Memory Lane; 4/12)
— Ted Lindsay #56 PSA 9 (MT) sold for $7,714 (Memory Lane; 12/06)
— Ted Lindsay #56 SGC 9 (MT) sold for $2,323 (Goodwin; 3/13)
— Robert Lowe #18 PSA 9 (MT) sold for $2,738 (Mile High; 5/12)
— Harry Lumley #47 PSA 9 (MT) sold for $1,923 (eBay; 3/13)
— Jim McFadden #44 PSA 9 (MT) sold for $1,830 (eBay; 7/08)
— George Martin #39 PSA 9 (MT) sold for $1,627 (Memory Lane; 7/12)
— George Martin #39 PSA 9 (MT) sold for $2,534 (Memory Lane; 4/07)
— George Martin #39 PSA 9 (MT) sold for $1,704 (eBay; 10/08)
— Paul Meger #2 PSA 8 (NmMt) sold for $3,844 (Goodwin; 9/11)
— Ken Mosdell #11 PSA 9 (MT) sold for $3,300 (eBay; 9/08)
— Bill Mosienko #49 PSA 9 (MT) sold for $2,670 (Mile High; 5/12)
— Marcel Pronovost #68 PSA 8.5 (NmMt+) sold for $2,167 (Mile High; 5/12)
— Bill Quackenbush #26 PSA 9 (MT) sold for $3,600 (eBay; 9/08)
— Don Raleigh #93 PSA 9 (MT) sold for $1,700 (Memory Lane; 4/12)
— Maurice Richard #4 PSA 9 (MT) sold for $30,100 (eBay; 3/13)
— Maurice Richard #4 PSA 9 (MT) sold for $9,008 (eBay; 11/14)
— Maurice Richard #4 PSA 9 (MT) sold for $8,295 (Robert Edward; Fall 2013)
— Maurice Richard #4 PSA 5 (Ex) sold for $1,369 (eBay; 1/14)
— Maurice Richard #4 PSA 9 (MT) sold for $30,100 (eBay; 3/13)
— Maurice Richard #4 PSA 9 (MT) sold for $9,008 (eBay; 11/14)
— Maurice Richard #4 PSA 9 (MT) sold for $8,295 (Robert Edward; Fall 2013)
— Maurice Richard #4 PSA 5 (Ex) sold for $1,369 (eBay; 1/14)
— Paul Ronty #95 PSA 9 (MT) sold for $2,489 (Memory Lane; 4/12)
— Paul Ronty #95 PSA 9 (MI) sold for $1,262 (eBay; 3/20)
— Terry Sawchuk #61 PSA 9 (MT) sold for $6,600 (Mastro; 8/08)
— Terry Sawchuk #61 PSA 8.5 (NmMt+) sold for $4,041 (eBay; 11/15)
— Milt Schmidt #29 PSA 9 (MT) sold for $1,902 (Memory Lane; 7/12)
— Milt Schmidt #29 SGC 9 (MT) sold for $2,750 (eBay; 1/16)
— Allan Stanley #94 PSA 9 (MT) sold for $3,232 (Mile High; 5/12)
— Jack Stewart #53 PSA 9 (MT) sold for $2,520 (Mastro; 8/08)
— Jack Stewart #53 PSA 8.5 (NrMt+) sold for $772 (eBay; 2/14)

HOCKEY

1952-53 Parkhurst

#	Player	PrFr 1	GD 2	VG 3	VgEx 4	EX 5	ExMt 6	NM 7	NmMt 8
1	Maurice Richard	▲250	▲400	▲600	▲800	▲1,000	▲1,500	▲2,000	
2	Billy Reay	5	10	15	25	40	80	150	
3	Bernie Geoffrion UER	30	60	100	120	150	200	300	
4	Paul Meger	5	8	12	15	20	30	80	300
5	Dick Gamble	▲10	▲20	▲30	▲40	▲50	▲80	▲250	
6	Elmer Lach	8	15	25	30	40	60	120	300
7	Floyd(Busher) Curry	▲8	▲15	▲25	▲40	▲50	▲100	▲250	▲500
8	Ken Mosdell	5	10	15	20	25	40	80	250
9	Tom Johnson	5	10	15	20	25	40	80	300
10	Dickie Moore RC	▲50	▲100	▲150	▲200	▲250	▲400	▲600	▲2,000
11	Bud MacPherson	5	8	12	15	20	30	80	200
12	Gerry McNeil	12	25	40	50	60	80	175	
13	Butch Bouchard	5	10	20	30	40	50	200	300
14	Doug Harvey	25	40	50	80	100	200	300	600
15	John McCormack	5	8	12	15	20	30	80	
16	Pete Babando	5	8	12	15	20	30	100	300
17	Al Dewsbury	5	8	12	15	20	30	80	
18	Ed Kullman	▲6	▲10	▲15	▲30	▲40	▲50	▲100	200
19	Ed Slowinski	5	8	12	15	20	25	80	250
20	Wally Hergesheimer	5	10	15	20	25	40	80	250
21	Allan Stanley	10	20	30	40	50	60	120	250
22	Chuck Rayner	▲10	▲20	▲30	▲60	▲80	▲100	▲200	▲300
23	Steve Kraftcheck	5	8	12	15	25	50	80	200
24	Paul Ronty	5	8	12	15	20	30	80	175
25	Gaye Stewart	5	8	12	15	20	30	80	250
26	Fred Hucul	5	8	12	15	20	40	80	
27	Bill Mosienko	6	12	20	30	50	60	120	300
28	Jim Morrison RC	▲6	▲10	▲15	▲20	▲25	▲40	▲100	
29	Ed Kryznowski	▲6	▲10	▲15	▲20	▲30	▲50	▲100	300
30	Cal Gardner	5	10	15	20	25	40	60	200
31	Al Rollins	8	15	25	40	60	100	200	
32	Enio Sclisizzi RC	5	8	12	15	20	30	100	
33	Pete Conacher RC	5	10	15	20	40	50	100	250
34	Leo Boivin RC	▲10	▲20	▲30	▲60	▲150	▲300	▲500	▲1,000
35	Jim Peters	5	8	12	15	20	30	80	200
36	George Gee	5	8	12	20	40	60	100	200
37	Gus Bodnar	▲6	▲12	▲25	▲30	▲40	▲50	▲80	▲200
38	Jim McFadden	5	8	12	15	20	25	80	200
39	Gus Mortson	5	10	15	20	25	40	80	200
40	Fred Glover	5	8	12	15	20	25	60	225
41	Gerry Couture	5	8	12	25	50	80	150	250
42	Howie Meeker	12	20	30	40	60	80	120	500
43	Jim Thomson	5	8	12	15	20	30	80	200
44	Teeder Kennedy	12	25	40	50	60	100	200	
45	Sid Smith	5	10	15	20	30	▲50	▲125	400
46	Harry Watson	6	12	20	25	▲50	▲60	▲125	400
47	Fern Flaman	5	10	15	30	50	80	150	250
48	Tod Sloan	5	10	15	20	25	40	60	250
49	Leo Reise	5	8	12	15	25	40	80	200
50	Bob Solinger	5	8	12	15	25	50	150	250
51	George Armstrong RC	30	60	▲125	▲200	▲300	▲500	▲1,500	▲2,500
52	Dollard St.Laurent RC	▲6	▲12	▲20	▲25	▲30	▲60	▲125	▲400
53	Alex Delvecchio	20	25	40	80	100	150	250	
54	Gord Hannigan RC	▲6	▲10	▲15	▲20	▲30	▲60	▲100	▲300
55	Lee Fogolin	5	8	12	15	20	30	80	250
56	Bill Gadsby	6	12	20	25	30	50	100	225
57	Herb Dickenson RC	5	8	12	15	25	40	100	
58	Tim Horton RC	▲1,000	▲1,200	▲1,500	▲2,500				
59	Harry Lumley	12	25	40	▲60	▲100	▲200	▲300	▲500
60	Metro Prystai	12	10	20	25	50	80	100	200
61	Marcel Pronovost	5	10	15	30	50	100	▲200	
62	Benny Woit	5	8	12	▲20	▲40	▲100	▲200	▲400
63	Glen Skov	5	8	12	20	40	50	100	300
64	Bob Goldham	5	8	12	15	20	25	60	
65	Tony Leswick	5	8	12	15	20	30	80	250
66	Marty Pavelich	5	8	12	15	25	40	80	200
67	Red Kelly	20	30	40	60	100	120	175	300
68	Bill Quackenbush	6	12	20	▲30	▲50	▲100	▲150	
69	Ed Sandford	5	8	12	15	20	30	80	300
70	Milt Schmidt	8	15	25	30	40	60	150	
71	Hal Laycoe	5	10	▲20	▲30	▲40	▲50	▲100	▲250
72	Woody Dumart	▲6	▲12	▲20	▲30	▲40	▲60	▲150	▲300
73	Zellio Toppazzini	▲6	▲10	▲15	▲20	▲25	▲40	▲100	▲200
74	Jim Henry	5	10	15	20	25	50	80	200
75	Joe Klukay	5	8	12	15	20	30	80	200
76	Dave Creighton RC	5	10	15	▲30	▲40	▲50	▲80	200
77	Jack McIntyre	5	8	12	15	25	50	80	125
78	Johnny Peirson	▲6	▲10	▲15	▲20	▲40	▲60	▲125	
79	George Sullivan	5	10	15	20	▲30	▲60	▲100	▲300
80	Real Chevrefils RC	5	10	15	▲25	▲30	▲50	▲100	▲250
81	Leo Labine RC	▲8	▲15	▲25	▲30	▲40	▲60	▲100	400
82	Fleming Mackell	▲6	▲12	▲20	▲25	▲30	▲60	▲100	250
83	Pentti Lund	5	8	12	15	20	25	125	300
84	Bob Armstrong RC	▲8	▲15	▲25	▲50	▲60	▲80	▲125	
85	Warren Godfrey RC	5	8	12	15	20	40	60	
86	Terry Sawchuk	50	80	150	▲250	▲400	▲500	▲600	2,000
87	Ted Lindsay	20	40	60	80	100	120	200	500
88	Gordie Howe	200	300	▲400	▲500	▲800	▲2,000	▲3,000	▲4,000
89	Johnny Wilson RC	▲6	▲12	▲20	▲25	▲30	▲50	▲200	
90	Vic Stasiuk	5	10	15	20	25	40	80	200
91	Larry Zeidel	5	8	12	15	20	30	80	300
92	Larry Wilson RC	5	8	12	15	20	50	100	
93	Bert Olmstead	5	10	15	25	40	40	80	
94	Ron Stewart RC	▲10	▲15	▲25	▲40	▲60	▲100	▲250	▲400
95	Max Bentley	6	12	20	25	30	50	150	350
96	Rudy Migay RC	▲6	▲10	▲15	▲20	▲30	▲60	▲100	
97	Jack Stoddard	5	8	12	15	20	25	80	250
98	Hy Buller	5	8	12	15	20	50	100	
99	Don Raleigh UER	5	8	12	15	20	30	80	250
100	Edgar Laprade	5	10	15	20	25	50	80	
101	Nick Mickoski	5	8	12	15	20	30	80	
102	Jack McLeod UER	5	8	12	15	25	80	200	
103	Jim Conacher	6	10	15	20	25	50	100	225
104	Reg Sinclair	5	8	12	▲20	▲30	▲50	100	300
105	Bob Hassard RC	15	30	40	60	80	100		350

— Bob Armstrong #84 PSA 8 (NmMt) sold for $430.05 (Mile High; 11/11)
— George Armstrong #51 PSA 8 (NmMt) sold for $1,932.38 (eBay; 5/12)
— George Armstrong #51 PSA 8 (NmMt) sold for $1,221 (Mile High; 10/12)
— Dick Gamble #5 PSA 8 (NmMt) sold for $667 (eBay; 7/11)
— Bernie Geoffrion #5 PSA 8.5 (NmMt+) sold for $1,152 (eBay; 2/13)
— Tim Horton #58 PSA 8.5 (NmMt+) sold for $3,406.33 (eBay; 9/12)
— Tim Horton #58 PSA 8 (NmMt) sold for $3,270 (eBay; 2/14)
— Gordie Howe #88 SGC 9 (MT) sold for $3,828 (eBay; 7/12)
— Howie Meeker #42 PSA 9 (MT) sold for $1,096 (eBay; 3/16)
— Dickie Moore #10 PSA 8 (NmMt) sold for $1,377 (eBay; 7/11)

1953-54 Parkhurst

#	Player	PrFr 1	GD 2	VG 3	VgEx 4	EX 5	ExMt 6	NM 7	NmMt 8
1	Harry Lumley	▲40	▲60	▲125	▲200	▲300	▲500	▲1,000	
2	Sid Smith	▲6	▲8	▲15	▲25	▲40	▲125	▲200	
3	Gord Hannigan	5	6	12	20	25	40	60	
4	Bob Hassard	5	6	12	20	25	40	60	
5	Tod Sloan	5	6	12	20	25	40	60	175
6	Leo Boivin	5	6	12	20	25	40	100	300
7	Teeder Kennedy	10	15	25	▲60	▲80	▲125	▲200	▲300
8	Jim Thomson	5	6	12	20	25	40	60	225
9	Ron Stewart	5	6	12	20	▲30	▲60	▲80	200
10	Eric Nesterenko RC	6	10	20	30	40	60	100	400
11	George Armstrong	10	15	30	50	60	100	150	350
12	Harry Watson	6	10	20	30	40	60	80	300
13	Tim Horton	30	50	100	150	200	300	400	750
14	Fern Flaman	5	8	15	30	50	80		▼400
15	Jim Morrison	5	6	12	20	25	40	80	200
16	Bob Solinger	5	6	12	20	▲60	▲80	▲100	▲200
17	Rudy Migay	5	6	12	20	25	40	60	150
18	Dick Gamble	5	6	12	20		40	75	250
19	Bert Olmstead	5	8	15	25	30	50	80	300
20	Eddie Mazur RC	5	6	12	20	25	40	60	200
21	Paul Meger	5	6	12	20	25	40	60	150
22	Bud MacPherson	5	6	12	20	25	50	60	200
23	Dollard St.Laurent	5	6	12	20	25	40	60	300
24	Maurice Richard	▲80	▲125	▲250	▲600	▲800	▲1,000	▲1,500	3,500
25	Gerry McNeil	8	12	25	40	60	100	150	250
26	Doug Harvey	20	30	60	100	120	150	250	400
27	Jean Beliveau RC	350	500	800	▲1,000	▲2,000	▲4,000	▲5,000	▲7,000
28	Dickie Moore UER	12	20	40	60	80	125	200	400
29	Bernie Geoffrion	20	30	60	80	120	200	250	500
30	E.Lach/M.Richard	20	30	60	80	100	200	300	500
31	Elmer Lach	6	10	20	30	40	80	100	250
32	Butch Bouchard	5	8	15	25	30	50	80	300
33	Ken Mosdell	5	6	12	20	25	40	80	150
34	John McCormack	5	6	12	20	25	40	80	150
35	Floyd (Busher) Curry	5	6	12	20	25	40	60	150
36	Earl Reibel RC	5	6	12	20	25	40	80	200
37	Bill Dineen UER RC	8	12	25	40	50	80	120	400
38	Al Arbour UER RC	10	15	30	50	60	100	150	300
39	Vic Stasiuk	5	6	12	20	25	40	60	150
40	Red Kelly	10	15	30	50	60	100	150	250
41	Marcel Pronovost	5	8	15	25	30	50	80	200
42	Metro Prystai	5	6	12	20	25	40	60	150
43	Tony Leswick	5	6	12	20	25	40	80	▼150
44	Marty Pavelich	5	6	12	20	25	40	60	150
45	Benny Woit	5	6	12	20	25	40	60	150
46	Terry Sawchuk	▲150	▲200	▲250	▲300	▲400	▲500	▲600	▲1,200
47	Alex Delvecchio	▲15	▲30	▲40	▲60	▲125	▲200	▲250	▲500
48	Glen Skov	5	6	12	20	25	40	60	150
49	Bob Goldham	5	6	12	20	25	40	60	200
50	Gordie Howe	▲300	▲400	▲500	▲600	▲800	▲1,000	▲2,000	5,000
51	Johnny Wilson	5	6	12	20	25	40	▲80	
52	Ted Lindsay	10	15	30	50	60	100	150	300
53	Gump Worsley RC	60	▲125	▲200	▲300	▲500	▲800	▲1,000	▲2,000
54	Jack Evans	5	6	12	20	25	40	60	200
55	Max Bentley	6	10	20	30	▲60	▲80	▲125	▼250
56	Andy Bathgate RC	▲25	▲50	▲80	▲150	▲200	▲300	▲500	▲800
57	Harry Howell RC	15	25	50	80	100	120	200	400

#	Name	PrFr 1	GD 2	VG 3	VgEx 4	EX 5	ExMt 6	NM 7	NmMt 8
58	Hy Buller	5	6	12	20	25	40	80	150
59	Chuck Rayner	▲6	▲10	▲20	40	▲50	▲80	▲125	▲250
60	Jack Stoddard	5	6	12	20	30	50	100	200
61	Ed Kullman	5	6	12	20	25	50	120	300
62	Nick Mickoski	5	6	12	20	25	40	60	150
63	Paul Ronty	5	6	12	20	25	40	60	200
64	Allan Stanley	6	10	20	30	40	60	100	250
65	Leo Reise	5	6	12	20	▲30	▲50	▲80	150
66	Aldo Guidolin RC	5	6	12	20	25	40	60	200
67	Wally Hergesheimer	5	6	12	20	25	40	60	200
68	Don Raleigh	5	6	12	20	25	40	▲80	250
69	Jim Peters	5	6	12	20	25	40	60	300
70	Pete Conacher	5	6	12	20	30	40	60	200
71	Fred Hucul	5	6	12	20	25	40	60	250
72	Lee Fogolin	5	6	12	20	25	40	60	200
73	Larry Zeidel	5	6	12	20	25	40	60	200
74	Larry Wilson	5	6	12	20	30	50	100	150
75	Gus Bodnar	5	6	12	20	25	40	80	200
76	Bill Gadsby	6	10	20	30	40	60	100	250
77	Jim McFadden	5	6	12	20	25	40	60	200
78	Al Dewsbury	5	6	12	20	25	40	50	200
79	Clare Raglan	5	6	12	20	25	40	60	200
80	Bill Mosienko	6	10	20	30	▲60	▲80	▲125	200
81	Gus Mortson	5	6	12	20	25	40	60	200
82	Al Rollins	5	20	40	30	50	100	200	350
83	George Gee	5	6	12	20	25	40	60	200
84	Gerry Couture	5	6	12	20	25	40	▲80	150
85	Dave Creighton	5	6	12	20	25	40	60	175
86	Jim Henry	5	8	15	25	30	50	80	200
87	Hal Laycoe	5	6	12	20	25	40	60	200
88	Johnny Peirson UER	5	8	15	25	30	50	80	200
89	Real Chevrefils	5	6	12	20	25	40	60	150
90	Ed Sandford	5	6	12	20	25	40	60	150
91A	Fleming Mackell NoBio	5	8	15	25	30	50	80	150
91B	Fleming Mackell COR	200	250	350	450	600			
92	Milt Schmidt	6	10	20	30	40	100	150	300
93	Leo Labine	5	6	12	20	25	40	60	200
94	Joe Klukay	5	6	12	20	25	40	60	150
95	Warren Godfrey	5	6	12	20	25	50	100	200
96	Woody Dumart	5	8	15	25	30	50	80	350
97	Frank Martin RC	5	6	12	20	25	40	60	200
98	Jerry Toppazzini RC	5	6	12	20	25	50	150	300
99	Cal Gardner	5	6	12	20	25	40	60	500
100	Bill Quackenbush	15	25	50	80	100	150	300	900

— Andy Bathgate #56 PSA 9 (Mint) sold for $2,709 (Mile High; 1/12)
— Jean Beliveau RC #27 PSA 5.5 (Ex+) sold for $910 (eBay; 4/14)
— Alex Delvecchio #47 PSA 9 (MT) sold for $1,033 (eBay; 12/15)
— Al Dewsbury #78 PSA 10 (Gem) sold for $3,732 (Memory Lane; 4/12)
— Fern Flaman #14 PSA 9 (Mint) sold for $1,515 (Mile High; 1/12)
— Aldo Guidolin RC #66 PSA 9 (Mint) sold for $962 (eBay; 2/14)
— Red Kelly #40 PSA 9 (Mint) sold for $1,790 (Mile High; 1/12)
— Leo Labine #93 PSA 9 (Mint) sold for $562 (Mile High; 1/12)
— Hal Laycoe #87 PSA 10 (Gem Mt) sold for $3,023 (Mile High; 5/12)
— Harry Lumley #1 PSA 8 (NmMt) sold for $4,3034 (Mile High; 1/12)
— Harry Lumley #1 PSA 8 (NmMt) sold for $2,390 (eBay; 3/14)
— Bill Mosienko #1 PSA 9 (Mint) sold for $1,516 (eBay; 2/15)
— Eric Nesterenko #10 PSA 9 (Mint) sold for $825 (Mile High; 1/12)
— Bert Olmsted #19 PSA 9 (Mint) sold for $619 (Mile High; 1/12)
— Marty Pavelich #44 PSA 9 (Mint) sold for $494 (eBay; 1/08)
— Marcel Pronovost #41 PSA 9 (MT) sold for $896.99 (eBay; 3/16)
— Al Rollins #82 PSA 9 (Mint) sold for $619 (Mile High; 1/12)
— Sid Smith #2 PSA 8 (NmMt) sold for $704 (Mile High; 1/12)
— Vic Stasiuk #39 PSA 9 (MT) sold for $626.79 (eBay; 4/16)
— Johnny Wilson #51 PSA 9 (Mint) sold for $1,099 (Mile High; 1/12)
— Gump Worsley #82 PSA 8.5 (NmMt+) sold for $2,015 (eBay; 11/14)

1954-55 Parkhurst

#	Name	PrFr 1	GD 2	VG 3	VgEx 4	EX 5	ExMt 6	NM 7	NmMt 8
	Gerry McNeil	30	50	60	100	150	300	800	3,500
	Dickie Moore	10	15	25	40	50	100	150	350
	Jean Beliveau	▲50	▲80	▲150	▲250	▲400	▲500	▲1,000	▲2,500
	Eddie Mazur	5	8	12	20	25	40	80	
	Bert Olmstead	5	8	12	20	25	40	150	
	Butch Bouchard	8	12	20	25	40	60	120	
	Maurice Richard	50	75	120	200	250	300	400	1,200
	Bernie Geoffrion	15	25	40	60	80	100	200	
	John McCormack	5	8	12	20	25	40	80	
0	Tom Johnson	5	8	12	20	25	40	80	
1	Calum Mackay	8	10	15	25	40	80	150	
2	Ken Mosdell	5	8	12	20	25	40	100	
3	Paul Masnick	8	10	15	25	40	60	100	400
4	Doug Harvey	15	25	40	60	80	100	150	
5	Floyd(Busher) Curry	5	8	12	20	25	40	80	
6	Harry Lumley	8	12	15	25	35	60	80	
7	Harry Watson	10	15	20	25	40	50	80	
8	Jim Morrison	5	8	12	15	20	40	100	
9	Eric Nesterenko	5	8	12	15	20	40	80	
0	Fern Flaman	5	8	12	20	25	40	80	
1	Rudy Migay	5	8	12	20	25	30	60	

#	Name	PrFr 1	GD 2	VG 3	VgEx 4	EX 5	ExMt 6	NM 7	NmMt 8
22	Sid Smith	5	8	12	20	25	30	60	
23	Ron Stewart	5	8	12	20	25	40	80	150
24	George Armstrong	10	15	25	40	50	60	80	200
25	Earl Balfour RC	5	8	12	20	25	40	60	200
26	Leo Boivin	▲6	▲10	▲20	▲30	▲40	▲80	▲150	
27	Gord Hannigan	5	8	12	20	25	40	100	300
28	Bob Bailey RC	5	8	12	20	25	40	100	200
29	Teeder Kennedy	8	12	15	25	30	50	80	
30	Tod Sloan	5	8	12	20	25	40	80	250
31	Tim Horton	35	50	60	80	125	150	300	800
32	Jim Thomson	5	8	12	20	25	40	100	
33	Terry Sawchuk	40	60	80	100	150	250	350	800
34	Marcel Pronovost	5	8	12	20	25	40	80	
35	Metro Prystai	5	8	12	20	25	30	60	
36	Alex Delvecchio	10	15	25	40	50	60	100	300
37	Earl Reibel	5	8	12	20	25	40	80	
38	Benny Woit	5	8	12	20	25	40	80	
39	Bob Goldham	5	8	12	20	25	40	80	
40	Glen Skov	5	8	12	20	25	60	80	300
41	Gordie Howe	60	100	150	200	300	400	600	1,200
42	Red Kelly	10	15	25	40	50	60	80	250
43	Marty Pavelich	5	8	12	20	25	40	80	250
44	Johnny Wilson	▲6	▲10	▲15	▲30	▲60	▲100	▲150	▲400
45	Tony Leswick	▲6	▲10	▲15	▲30	▲60	▲80	▲125	▲250
46	Ted Lindsay	10	15	25	40	50	60	150	300
47	Keith Allen RC	5	8	12	20	25	40	60	
48	Bill Dineen	▲8	▲15	▲30	▲50	▲60	▲80	▲150	
49	Jim Henry	8	12	15	25	30	40	60	
50	Fleming Mackell	5	8	12	20	25	40	60	250
51	Bill Quackenbush	8	12	15	25	30	40	80	
52	Hal Laycoe	5	8	12	20	25	40	80	
53	Cal Gardner	5	8	12	20	25	40	80	250
54	Joe Klukay	5	8	12	20	25	40	100	
55	Bob Armstrong	5	8	12	20	25	40	80	
56	Warren Godfrey	▲10	▲20	▲30	▲50	▲60	▲80	▲150	
57	Doug Mohns RC	8	12	15	25	30	40	80	
58	Dave Creighton	15	25	40	60	80	100	200	
59	Milt Schmidt	8	12	15	25	35	50	100	
60	Johnny Peirson	5	8	12	20	25	30	80	
61	Leo Labine	8	10	15	25	40	60	120	
62	Gus Bodnar	5	8	12	20	25	40	80	
63	Real Chevrefils	5	8	12	20	25	40	80	
64	Ed Sandford	8	10	15	25	40	50	80	120
65	Johnny Bower UER RC	▲200	▲300	▲400	▲500	▲600	▲700	▲800	▲3,000
66	Paul Ronty	5	8	▲20	▲30	▲40	▲60	▲100	
67	Leo Reise	5	8	12	20	25	30	50	150
68	Don Raleigh	▲6	▲10	▲20	▲50	▲60	▲80	▲150	
69	Bob Chrystal	5	8	12	20	25	40	80	
70	Harry Howell	8	12	20	▲40	▲50	▲60	▲150	
71	Wally Hergesheimer	5	8	12	20	25	30	60	
72	Jack Evans	5	8	12	20	25	30	60	200
73	Camille Henry RC	5	8	12	20	25	40	80	
74	Dean Prentice RC	8	12	15	25	30	40	80	
75	Nick Mickoski	5	8	12	15	20	30	40	120
76	Ron Murphy RC	5	8	12	15	20	30	60	120
77	Al Rollins	8	12	15	25	30	50	100	
78	Al Dewsbury	5	8	12	20	25	30	60	
79	Lou Jankowski	5	8	12	20	25	30	60	200
80	George Gee	5	8	12	15	20	30	40	
81	Gus Mortson	5	8	12	15	▲25	▲40	▲80	200
82	Fred Saskamoose UER RC	15	25	40	60	80	125	200	400
83	Ike Hildebrand RC	5	8	12	20	25	40	60	
84	Lee Fogolin	5	8	12	20	25	40	60	150
85	Larry Wilson	5	8	12	20	25	40	80	
86	Pete Conacher	5	8	12	20	25	40	60	
87	Bill Gadsby	5	8	12	25	25	40	80	150
88	Jack McIntyre	5	8	12	20	25	40	80	
89	Busher Curry goes/up and over	5	8	12	20	25	40	60	
90	Delvecchio/Defense	8	12	15	25	35	50	120	
91	R.Kelly/H.Lumley	8	12	15	25	25	40	▼60	200
92	Lumley/Howe/Stewart	12	20	30	50	60	▲125	▲200	400
93	H.Lumley/R.Murphy	▲6	▲10	▲15	▲20	▲30	▲60	▲100	200
94	P.Meger/J.Morrison	▲6	▲10	▲15	▲20	▲30	▲40	60	250
95	D.Harvey/E.Nesterenko	▲10	▲15	▲25	▲40	▲80	▲100	▲150	▲250
96	T.Sawchuk/T.Kennedy	12	20	30	50	60	80	125	400
97	Plante/B.Bouchard/Reibel	12	20	30	50	60	80	100	400
98	J.Plante/Harvey/Sloan	12	20	30	50	60	80	150	400
99	J.Plante/T.Kennedy	12	20	30	50	60	80	125	400
100	T.Sawchuk/B.Geoffrion	25	40	60	80	120	150	400	1,000

— Alex Delvecchio #90 PSA 8 (NM) sold for $365 (eBay; 4/16)
— Camille Henry #73 PSA 9 (Mint) sold for $393 (eBay; 8/12)
— Ted Lindsay #46 PSA 9 (Mint) sold for $1,303 (eBay; 4/12)
— Gerry McNeil #1 PSA 8 (NrMt) sold for $3,633 (eBay; 8/12)

1954-55 Topps

#	Name	PrFr 1	GD 2	VG 3	VgEx 4	EX 5	ExMt 6	NM 7	NmMt 8
1	Dick Gamble	▲25	▲40	▲60	100	150	▲250	1,000	4,000
2	Bob Chrystal	▲8	▲15	▲25	▲40	▲80	▲150	600	2,000
3	Harry Howell	12	20	30	40	60	80	150	600
4	Johnny Wilson	6	10	15	20	30	80	100	400

#	Name	PrFr 1	GD 2	VG 3	VgEx 4	EX 5	ExMt 6	NM 7	NmMt 8
5	Red Kelly	20	30	60	100	150	200	300	550
6	Real Chevrefils	6	10	20	25	30	50	150	450
7	Bob Armstrong	▲8	▲15	▲25	▲40	▲80	▲125	▲200	▲400
8	Gordie Howe	▲300	▲500	▲1,000	▲1,500	▲2,000	▲3,000	▲5,000	▲8,000
9	Benny Woit	6	10	15	20	30	40	150	250
10	Gump Worsley	25	40	▲100	▲125	▲200	▲300	▲400	▲600
11	Andy Bathgate	▲15	▲25	▲50	80	▲125	▲200	▲300	▲500
12	Bucky Hollingworth RC	6	10	15	20	30	40	120	400
13	Ray Timgren	6	10	15	20	30	80	150	250
14	Jack Evans	6	10	15	20	30	40	100	300
15	Paul Ronty	6	15	20	30	▲50	60	▼100	▲250
16	Glen Skov	6	10	15	20	40	80	100	250
17	Gus Mortson	6	10	15	20	30	40	100	250
18	Doug Mohns RC	▼12	▼20	40	50	80	125	200	350
19	Leo Labine	10	12	20	30	40	80	200	500
20	Bill Gadsby	10	12	25	50	80	100	200	650
21	Jerry Toppazzini	8	12	20	30	60	80	100	350
22	Wally Hergesheimer	6	10	15	20	30	▲60	▲125	300
23	Danny Lewicki	6	10	15	20	30	60	150	200
24	Metro Prystai	6	10	15	25	50	80	150	250
25	Fern Flaman	8	12	20	40	50	100	150	350
26	Al Rollins	▲15	▲25	▲40	▲80	▲125	▲200	▲300	500
27	Marcel Pronovost	10	15	25	50	80	150	200	▲400
28	Lou Jankowski	6	10	15	20	30	60	150	300
29	Nick Mickoski	▲10	▲30	▲40	▲50	▲60	▲100	▲200	300
30	Frank Martin	6	15	30	40	50	100	150	300
31	Lorne Ferguson	6	10	15	20	30	40	100	300
32	Camille Henry RC	10	15	25	40	60	80	200	500
33	Pete Conacher	8	12	20	30	50	50	100	250
34	Marty Pavelich	6	10	15	20	40	100	150	300
35	Don McKenney RC	10	15	25	40	50	80	120	400
36	Fleming Mackell	8	12	20	30	40	50	100	300
37	Jim Henry	6	15	25	40	60	▲100	▲200	▲500
38	Hal Laycoe	6	10	15	20	50	100	150	300
39	Alex Delvecchio	20	30	40	60	80	100	200	550
40	Larry Wilson	6	10	15	20	30	40	100	250
41	Allan Stanley	12	20	30	50	80	100	175	650
42	George Sullivan	6	10	15	20	▲40	▲80	▲200	▲400
43	Jack McIntyre	6	10	15	20	30	40	100	250
44	Ivan Irwin RC	6	10	15	20	30	50	120	300
45	Tony Leswick	8	10	25	40	60	100	300	500
46	Bob Goldham	6	10	15	20	50	80	125	350
47	Cal Gardner	▲10	▲15	▲25	▲40	▲80	▲125	▲200	▲400
48	Ed Sandford	6	10	15	20	▲40	▲50	100	300
49	Bill Quackenbush	10	15	25	40	60	100	175	400
50	Warren Godfrey	6	10	15	25	50	80	150	300
51	Ted Lindsay	20	▲30	▲50	▲100	▲150	▲200	▲400	▲600
52	Earl Reibel	5	10	15	25	30	60	100	300
53	Don Raleigh	6	10	15	25	▲50	▲80	▲200	800
54	Bill Mosienko	10	15	25	40	60	100	200	500
55	Larry Popein	8	12	25	50	80	150	375	
56	Edgar Laprade	8	15	20	30	▲50	▲80	▲200	800
57	Bill Dineen	8	12	20	30	50	100	150	800
58	Terry Sawchuk	▲80	▲200	▲300	▲400	▲500	▲800	▲1,500	2,500
59	Marcel Bonin RC	10	15	20	50	150	250	500	2,000
60	Milt Schmidt	▼20	▼30	▼60	▼100	250	350	1,200	3,000

— Marcel Bonin #59 PSA 8 (NmMt) sold for $4,800 (Memory Lane; 5/08)
— Dick Gamble #1 PSA 8 (NmMt) sold for $5,141 (Goodwin & Co.; 12/08)
— Wally Hergesheimer #22 PSA 9 (MT) sold for $4,195 (Memory Lane; 9/07)
— Gordie Howe #8 SGC 96 (MT) sold for $13,200 (Mastro; 8/08)
— Gordie Howe #8 SGC 8.5 (NrMt+) sold for $2,398 (eBay; 4/14)
— Gordie Howe #8 SGC 7.5 (ExMt+) sold for $1,750 (eBay; 4/14)
— Red Kelly #5 SGC 96 (MT) sold for $6,955 (Memory Lane; 5/08)
— Edgar Laprade #56 PSA 8 (NmMt) sold for $4,365 (Memory Lane; 12/06)
— Edgar Laprade #56 PSA8 (NmMt) sold for $1,530 (Memory Lane; 9/07)
— Edgar Laprade #56 PSA 8 (NmMt) sold for $865 (Memory Lane; 5/08)
— Tony Leswick #42 PSA 8 (NmMt) sold for $2,035 (Memory Lane; 9/07)
— Ted Lindsay #51 PSA 9 (MT) sold for $2,726 (eBay; 6/12)
— Frank Martin #30 SGC 9 (MT) sold for $670 (eBay; 8/12)
— Nick Mickoski #29 PSA 9 (MT) sold for $810 (eBay; 7/08)
— Gus Mortson #17 PSA 9 (MT) sold for $3,466 (Memory Lane; 9/07)
— Gus Mortson #17 SGC 9 (MT) sold for $346.02 (eBay; 2/16)
— Larry Popein #55 PSA 7 (NM) sold for $560 (eBay; 11/07)
— Don Raleigh #53 PSA 9 (MT) sold for $9,650 (Mile High; 1/07)
— Don Raleigh #53 PSA 9 (MT) sold for $2,980 (Memory Lane; 5/07)
— Milt Schmidt #60 PSA 8 (NmMt) sold for $5,447 (Mile High; 1/07)
— Milt Schmidt #60 PSA 7.5 (NrMt+) sold for $1,752 (Goodwin & Co.; 12/08)
— Allan Stanley #41 SGC 96 (MT) sold for $3,600 (Memory Lane; 7/08)
— Jerry Toppazzini #21 PSA 9 (MT) sold for $2,252 (eBay; 3/13)

1955-56 Parkhurst

#	Name	PrFr 1	GD 2	VG 3	VgEx 4	EX 5	ExMt 6	NM 7	NmMt 8
1	Harry Lumley	40	60	100	200	400	900	3,000	
2	Sid Smith	6	8	10	15	30	100	300	
3A	Tim Horton	30	50	80	100	200	200	350	
4	George Armstrong	10	15	25	40	60	120	300	
5	Ron Stewart	6	8	10	15	30	100	300	
6	Joe Klukay	5	8	12	15	25	60	100	200
7	Marc Reaume	5	6	8	12	25	100	250	
8	Jim Morrison	5	6	8	12	25	60	100	300
9	Parker MacDonald RC	5	6	8	12	20	50	100	
10	Tod Sloan	5	6	8	12	30	80	150	
11	Jim Thomson	5	6	8	12	20	50	100	
12	Rudy Migay	5	6	8	12	20	50	100	300
13	Brian Cullen RC	6	8	10	15	25	50	120	
14	Hugh Bolton	5	6	8	12	20	50	100	
15	Eric Nesterenko	6	8	10	20	40	150	400	
16	Larry Cahan RC	5	6	8	12	20	50	100	300
17	Willie Marshall	5	6	8	12	20	50	200	
18	Dick Duff RC	12	20	30	50	80	175	1,000	
19	Jack Caffery RC	5	6	8	▲20	▲30	50	100	
20	Billy Harris RC	6	8	10	15	25	50	150	
21	Lorne Chabot OTG	6	8	10	15	25	50	100	
22	Harvey Jackson OTG	6	10	15	25	40	80	150	
23	Turk Broda OTG	12	20	30	40	60	100	300	
24	Joe Primeau OTG	6	8	12	20	30	50	150	300
25	Gordie Drillon OTG	6	8	10	15	25	50	150	500
26	Chuck Conacher OTG	6	8	12	20	30	100	150	300
27	Sweeney Schriner OTG	6	8	10	15	30	80	200	
28	Syl Apps OTG	6	8	12	20	30	80	150	
29	Teeder Kennedy OTG	8	12	20	30	40	80	150	
30	Ace Bailey OTG	8	12	20	30	50	80	175	350
31	Babe Pratt OTG	6	8	10	15	30	100	200	
32	Harold Cotton OTG	6	8	10	15	30	80	125	
33	King Clancy CO	12	20	30	50	80	150	250	
34	Hap Day	6	10	15	25	40	80	175	
35	Don Marshall RC	6	10	15	25	40	80	150	250
36	Jackie LeClair RC	6	8	10	15	30	100	200	
37	Maurice Richard	60	80	120	200	300	400	600	1,000
38	Dickie Moore	10	15	25	40	60	100	200	
39	Ken Mosdell	6	8	10	15	30	100	200	
40	Floyd(Busher) Curry	5	6	8	12	20	50	150	
41	Calum Mackay	5	6	8	12	20	50	100	400
42	Bert Olmstead	6	8	10	15	25	50	100	150
43	Bernie Geoffrion	15	25	50	100	150	200	300	600
44	Jean Beliveau	50	80	120	200	250	300	500	1,000
45	Doug Harvey	15	25	40	60	100	125	200	600
46	Butch Bouchard	6	8	10	15	25	50	120	200
47	Bud MacPherson	5	6	8	12	20	50	100	200
48	Dollard St.Laurent	5	6	8	12	20	50	100	300
49	Tom Johnson	6	8	10	15	25	50	100	200
50	Jacques Plante RC	200	▲500	▲1,000	▲3,000	▲4,000	▲8,000	▲10,000	
51	Paul Meger	5	6	8	12	20	50	100	400
52	Gerry McNeil	6	8	10	15	30	60	100	200
53	Jean-Guy Talbot RC	6	8	10	15	30	100	250	
54	Bob Turner	5	6	8	12	25	80	150	400
55	Newsy Lalonde OTG	8	12	20	30	50	120	250	500
56	Georges Vezina OTG	15	25	40	60	100	125	250	
57	Howie Morenz OTG	12	20	30	50	80	150	250	600
58	Aurel Joliat OTG	8	12	20	30	40	80	200	
59	George Hainsworth OTG	12	20	30	50	80	100	200	
60	Sylvio Mantha OTG	6	8	10	15	30	100	250	
61	Battleship Leduc OTG	6	8	10	15	30	100	200	
62	Babe Siebert OTG UER	6	8	12	20	30	50	100	200
63	Bill Durnan OTG RC	8	12	20	30	50	150	300	600
64	Ken Reardon OTG RC	8	12	20	30	50	150	300	
65	Johnny Gagnon OTG	6	8	10	15	30	60	150	400
66	Billy Reay OTG	6	8	10	15	30	100	400	
67	Toe Blake CO	6	10	15	25	40	150	250	
68	Frank Selke MG	6	8	12	20	30	80	200	
69	H.Bolton/C.Hodge	6	8	10	15	25	50	150	
70	H.Lumley/B.Geoffrion	8	12	20	30	50	150	300	
71	B.Bouchard/T.Johnson	10	15	25	40	60	100	200	
72	Rocket (Richard) Roars	10	15	30	50	80	200	500	
73	M.Richard/H.Lumley	12	20	30	40	60	150	300	
74	J.Beliveau/H.Lumley	8	12	20	30	50	80	200	500
75	Nesterenko/Smith/Plante	10	15	25	40	60	100	250	
76	Curry/Lumley/Morrison	6	8	10	15	30	100	300	500
77	Sloan/MacD/Harvey/Beliv	10	15	25	40	60	150	400	
78	Montreal Forum	40	60	100	120	200	450	1,200	
79	Maple Leaf Gardens	40	60	100	150	250	600	1,000	

— Tim Horton #3 SGC 9 (MT) sold for $12,103 (eBay; 4/11)
— Dick Duff #18 PSA 8 (NmMt) sold for $1,633 (eBay; 5/12)
— Harold Cotton OTG #32 PSA 9 (MT) sold for $4,118 (eBay; 8/12)
— Newsy Lalonde OTG #55 PSA 9 (MT) sold for $4,874 (Mile High; 10/12)
— Sloan/Macdonald/Harvey/Beliveau #77 PSA 8 (NmMt) sold for $2,782 (eBay; 8/12)

1957-58 Parkhurst

#	Name	PrFr 1	GD 2	VG 3	VgEx 4	EX 5	ExMt 6	NM 7	NmMt 8
M1	Doug Harvey	30	50	80	120	200	250	600	200
M2	Bernie Geoffrion	12	25	40	60	100	200	700	2,000
M3	Jean Beliveau	30	50	80	▲200	▲300	▲400	▲600	1,500
M4	Henri Richard RC	▲500	▲600	▲800	▲1,000	▲1,500	▲2,500	▼400	▲6,000
M5	Maurice Richard	40	60	100	150	250	400	550	1,250
M6	Tom Johnson	5	5	6	10	15	25	80	150
M7	Andre Pronovost RC	5	6	10	15	25	40	▲125	▲300
M8	Don Marshall	5	5	5	8	12	▲30	▲60	▲125
M9	Jean-Guy Talbot	5	5	5	8	12	20	50	100

		PrFr 1	GD 2	VG 3	VgEx 4	EX 5	ExMt 6	NM 7	NmMt 8
M10	Dollard St.Laurent	5	5	5	8	12	20	50	100
M11	Phil Goyette RC	5	6	10	15	25	40	100	350
M12	Claude Provost RC	5	6	10	15	25	50	150	250
M13	Bob Turner	5	5	5	8	12	20	50	120
M14	Dickie Moore	6	10	15	25	40	60	100	250
M15	Jacques Plante	40	60	▲125	▲200	▲400	▲500	▲600	▲1,500
M16	Toe Blake CO	5	6	▲15	▲20	▲30	▲50	100	200
M17	Charlie Hodge RC	8	12	20	30	50	80	150	300
M18	Marcel Bonin	5	6	8	▲15	▲30	▲40	▲80	▲150
M19	Bert Olmstead	5	5	6	10	15	25	80	120
M20	Floyd (Busher) Curry	5	5	5	8	12	20	50	100
M21	Len Broderick IA RC	5	6	10	15	25	40	80	200
M22	Brian Cullen scores	5	5	5	8	12	20	50	200
M23	Broderick/Harvey IA	5	6	10	15	25	40	60	150
M24	Geoffrion/Chadwick IA	5	8	12	20	30	50	100	200
M25	Olmstead/Chadwick IA	5	6	10	15	25	40	60	200
T1	George Armstrong	10	15	25	50	100	200	500	
T2	Ed Chadwick RC	30	40	60	100	135	225	600	
T3	Dick Duff	5	10	15	25	50	120	700	1,800
T4	Bob Pulford RC	30	40	60	▲150	▲250	▲500	▲1,500	▲3,000
T5	Tod Sloan	5	8	15	25	60	80	175	800
T6	Rudy Migay	5	5	6	10	▲20	▲40	▲80	▲200
T7	Ron Stewart	5	5	6	8	12	25	60	100
T8	Gerry James RC	5	6	6	10	15	25	80	120
T9	Brian Cullen	5	5	6	8	12	20	50	120
T10	Sid Smith	5	5	6	8	15	20	80	150
T11	Jim Morrison	5	5	6	8	12	20	50	100
T12	Marc Reaume	5	5	6	8	12	20	50	120
T13	Hugh Bolton	5	5	6	8	12	20	60	100
T14	Pete Conacher	5	5	5	8	12	20	50	100
T15	Billy Harris	5	5	5	8	12	20	50	150
T16	Mike Nykoluk RC	5	5	6	8	12	20	50	100
T17	Frank Mahovlich RC	▲200	▲400	▲600	▲800	▲1,000	▲1,500	▲2,000	▲3,000
T18	Ken Girard RC	5	5	6	8	12	20	50	100
T19	Al MacNeil RC	5	5	5	8	12	20	60	150
T20	Bob Baun RC	10	15	25	40	60	100	300	500
T21	Barry Cullen RC	5	5	8	12	20	50	80	150
T22	Tim Horton	25	30	50	80	120	200	350	500
T23	Gary Collins RC	5	5	5	8	12	20	60	100
T24	Gary Aldcorn RC	5	5	5	8	12	20	50	150
T25	Billy Reay CO	5	6	10	15	25	40	80	250

— George Armstrong #T1 PSA 8 (NmMtT) sold for $3,570 (eBay; 9/15)
— Pete Conacher #T14 PSA 9 (MT) sold for $410 (eBay; 8/12)
— Tom Johnson #M6 PSA 9 (MT) sold for $799 (eBay; 1/08)
— Don Marshall #M8 PSA 9 (MT) sold for $799 (eBay; 1/08)
— Rudy Migay #T6 PSA 10 (Gem Mt) sold for $1,500 (eBay; 3/13)
— Bert Olmstead #M19 PSA 10 (Gem Mt) sold for $1,317 (eBay; 4/15)
— Claude Provost #M12 PSA 10 (Gem MT) sold for $1,331 (eBay; 4/15)
— Billy Reay CO #T25 PSA 8.5 (NMMT+) sold for $356 (eBay; 7/12)

1957-58 Topps

	PrFr 1	GD 2	VG 3	VgEx 4	EX 5	ExMt 6	NM 7	NmMt 8
Real Chevrefils	6	8	12	20	25	60	400	1,000
Jack Bionda RC	5	6	8	12	20	30	60	500
Bob Armstrong	5	5	6	10	12	20	50	200
Fern Flaman	6	8	20	25	30	40	80	300
Jerry Toppazzini	6	8	10	40	50	60	80	250
Larry Regan RC	6	8	10	20	25	30	60	▼125
Bronco Horvath RC	6	8	10	15	25	40	100	450
Jack Caffery	5	6	8	12	15	20	80	150
Leo Labine	5	6	8	12	15	25	30	100
Johnny Bucyk RC	25	40	60	100	150	400	500	2,000
Vic Stasiuk	5	6	8	12	20	25	50	100
Doug Mohns	6	8	12	20	30	40	60	500
Don McKenney	5	6	8	12	20	40	50	250
Don Simmons RC	6	8	10	15	25	▲60	▲150	600
Allan Stanley	5	6	8	12	20	30	50	250
Fleming Mackell	5	6	8	12	15	25	30	▼125
Larry Hillman RC	5	6	8	12	15	50	▼80	200
Leo Boivin	5	6	8	12	15	25	30	100
Bob Bailey	5	5	6	10	12	20	40	100
Glenn Hall RC	100	125	200	250	300	▲500	▲800	▲2,000
Ted Lindsay	8	12	20	30	40	60	80	200
Pierre Pilote RC	10	15	25	50	80	150	250	550
Jim Thomson	5	6	8	12	20	25	60	200
Eric Nesterenko	5	6	8	12	20	25	60	200
Gus Mortson	▲10	▲12	▲20	▲30	▲50	▲100	▲200	▲600
Ed Litzenberger RC	5	6	8	12	20	30	60	▼125
Elmer Vasko RC	5	6	8	12	20	30	40	100
Jack McIntyre	5	5	6	10	12	20	30	100
Ron Murphy	5	6	8	12	15	25	40	300
Glen Skov	5	5	6	10	12	20	50	135
Hec Lalande RC	5	5	6	10	12	20	40	175
Nick Mickoski	5	5	6	10	12	20	60	150
Wally Hergesheimer	5	6	8	12	15	25	50	120
Alex Delvecchio	6	8	12	20	25	50	120	300
Terry Sawchuk UER	25	40	60	80	100	200	250	1,000
Guyle Fielder RC	5	6	8	12	15	25	30	150
Tom McCarthy	5	5	6	10	12	20	30	100

		PrFr 1	GD 2	VG 3	VgEx 4	EX 5	ExMt 6	NM 7	NmMt 8
38	Al Arbour	6	8	10	15	25	35	60	120
39	Billy Dea	5	5	6	10	12	25	60	150
40	Lorne Ferguson	5	5	6	10	12	25	50	200
41	Warren Godfrey	5	6	8	12	15	25	40	120
42	Gordie Howe	80	100	▲200	▲300	▲400	▲600	▲800	▲2,500
43	Marcel Pronovost	6	8	15	20	25	30	40	120
44	Bill McNeil RC	5	6	8	12	20	25	40	120
45	Earl Reibel	5	6	8	12	20	25	40	▼100
46	Norm Ullman RC	40	60	80	120	150	200	250	800
47	Johnny Wilson	5	5	6	10	12	30	50	120
48	Red Kelly	6	8	12	20	25	50	80	300
49	Bill Dineen	5	6	8	12	20	25	50	120
50	Forbes Kennedy RC	6	8	12	20	▲30	▲40	▲80	▲200
51	Harry Howell	8	12	20	25	30	40	60	200
52	Jean-Guy Gendron RC	5	6	8	12	15	25	▲60	100
53	Gump Worsley	10	15	25	40	50	80	100	250
54	Larry Popein	5	6	8	12	20	25	40	120
55	Jack Evans	5	▲8	▲12	▲15	▲25	▲40	▲60	▲125
56	George Sullivan	5	6	8	12	15	25	60	250
57	Gerry Foley RC	5	6	8	12	15	25	60	250
58	Andy Hebenton RC	5	6	8	12	15	25	50	120
59	Larry Cahan	5	5	6	10	12	20	40	▼100
60	Andy Bathgate	6	8	12	20	30	50	100	400
61	Danny Lewicki	6	8	12		25	30	50	150
62	Dean Prentice	6	8	10	15	25	40	60	250
63	Camille Henry	6	8	10	15	20	25	60	150
64	Lou Fontinato RC	6	8	12	20	25	40	60	250
65	Bill Gadsby	6	8	10	15	20	30	60	200
66	Dave Creighton	▲8	▲15	▲25	▲40	▲80	▲125	▲300	600

— Glenn Hall #20 SGC 9 (MT) sold for $1,860 (Greg Bussineau; Fall 2014)
— Ted Lindsay #21 PSA 9 (MT) sold for $1,346 (eBay; 3/13)
— Pierre Pilote #22 SGC 9 (MT) sold for $4,613 (Goodwin; 7/12)
— Pierre Pilote #22 PSA 8.5 (NmMt+) sold for $2,208 (eBay; 3/13)
— Terry Sawchuk UER #35 PSA 9 (MT) sold for $1,380 (Greg Bussineau; Fall 2013)
— Allan Stanley #15 PSA 9 (MT) sold for $1,803 (eBay; 3/14)
— Elmer Vasko #27 PSA 9 (MT) sold for $802 (eBay; 8/12)
— Elmer Vasko #27 PSA 9 (MT) sold for $672.78 (eBay; 2/14)

1958-59 Parkhurst

		PrFr 1	GD 2	VG 3	VgEx 4	EX 5	ExMt 6	NM 7	NmMt 8
1	Bob Pulford IA	5	8	12	20	▲50	▲80	150	600
2	Henri Richard	20	30	50	80	120	200	250	1,000
3	Andre Pronovost	5	5	6	10	15	20	80	120
4	Billy Harris	5	5	6	10	15	25	60	175
5	Albert Langlois RC	5	▲8	▲10	▲15	▲25	▲40	▲80	▲150
6	Noel Price RC	5	5	6	10	15	20	50	100
7	G.Armstrong/Johnson IA	5	6	8	12	20	30	50	120
8	Dickie Moore	5	6	10	15	25	40	60	175
9	Toe Blake CO	5	6	8	12	20	30	60	▲150
10	Tom Johnson	5	5	6	10	15	25	50	120
11	J.Plante/G.Armstrong	10	12	15	20	30	50	80	150
12	Ed Chadwick	5	6	10	15	25	40	60	150
13	Bob Nevin RC	5	6	8	12	20	30	60	175
14	Ron Stewart	5	5	6	10	15	25	60	120
15	Bob Baun	5	6	10	15	25	40	60	120
16	Ralph Backstrom RC	5	8	12	20	30	50	80	250
17	Charlie Hodge	5	6	10	15	25	40	60	120
18	Gary Aldcorn	5	5	6	10	15	20	50	100
19	Willie Marshall	5	5	6	10	15	20	50	120
20	Marc Reaume	5	5	6	10	15	20	50	100
21	Jacques Plante IA	10	15	20	25	40	60	80	200
22	Jacques Plante	40	50	80	120	150	250	300	600
23	Allan Stanley UER	5	6	8	12	20	30	60	120
24	Ian Cushenan RC	5	5	6	10	15	25	50	120
25	Billy Reay CO	5	5	6	10	15	25	50	120
26	Jacques Plante IA	10	15	20	30	40	60	80	200
27	Bert Olmstead	5	5	6	10	15	25	50	120
28	Bernie Geoffrion	8	12	20	35	50	80	120	250
29	Dick Duff	5	5	6	10	15	25	50	100
30	Ab McDonald RC	5	5	6	10	15	20	60	100
31	Barry Cullen	5	5	6	10	15	20	60	120
32	Marc Bonin	5	5	6	10	15	20	50	120
33	Frank Mahovlich	20	30	▲60	▲100	▲200	▲300	▲400	▲500
34	Jean Beliveau	20	30	50	80	100	150	200	500
35	J.Plante/Canadiens IA	6	10	15	25	40	60	80	150
36	Brian Cullen Shoots	5	5	6	10	15	25	50	120
37	Steve Kraftcheck	5	5	6	10	15	20	50	150
38	Maurice Richard	40	50	100	150	250	300	500	650
39	Jacques Plante IA	6	10	15	25	40	60	80	200
40	Bob Turner	5	5	6	10	▲20	▲30	▲60	▲150
41	Jean-Guy Talbot	5	5	6	10	15	20	50	100
42	Tim Horton	12	20	30	50	80	100	200	350
43	Claude Provost	5	5	6	10	15	25	▼40	▼80
44	Don Marshall	5	5	6	10	15	25	60	200
45	Bob Pulford	5	6	8	12	20	30	50	120
46	Johnny Bower UER	15	25	40	60	100	120	150	350
47	Phil Goyette	5	5	6	10	15	25	50	120
48	George Armstrong	5	6	10	15	25	40	60	150
49	Doug Harvey	8	12	20	30	50	80	100	250

50	Brian Cullen	5	6	10	15	25	40	100	200

— Bernie Geoffrion #28 PSA 9 (MT) sold for $528 (eBay; 5/12)
— Albert Langlois #5 PSA 9 (MT) sold for $468 (eBay; 5/12)
— Frank Mahovlich #5 PSA 9 (MT) sold for $910 (eBay; 4/15)
— J.Plante/Others IA #21 PSA 9 (MT) sold for $439 (eBay; 5/12)
— Jacques Plante #22 PSA 9 (MT) sold for $2,175 (eBay; 5/12)
— Andre Pronovost #3 PSA 9 (MT) sold for $718 (eBay; 2/14)
— Frank Mahovlich #33 PSA 9 (MT) sold for $2,662.00 (eBay; 5/12)
— Jean Beliveau #34 PSA 9 (MT) sold for $1,529 (eBay; 3/14)
— J.Plante/Canadiens IA #35 PSA 9 (MT) sold for $760.72 (eBay; 5/12)
— Steve Kraftcheck #37 PSA 9 (MT) sold for $720.00 (eBay; 8/12)

1958-59 Topps

		PrFr 1	GD 2	VG 3	VgEx 4	EX 5	ExMt 6	NM 7	NmMt 8
1	Bob Armstrong	5	6	10	15	25	100	300	
2	Terry Sawchuk	25	30	50	80	120	175	300	500
3	Glen Skov	5	5	5	8	12	20	80	300
4	Leo Labine	5	5	6	10	15	25	60	150
5	Dollard St.Laurent	5	5	5	8	12	20	100	250
6	Danny Lewicki	5	5	5	8	12	20	25	150
7	John Hanna RC	5	5	5	8	12	20	100	400
8	Gordie Howe UER	60	80	120	▲200	▲300	▲500	▲1,000	▲4,000
9	Vic Stasiuk	5	5	5	8	12	20	40	400
10	Larry Regan	5	5	5	8	12	20	30	100
11	Forbes Kennedy	5	5	5	8	12	20	60	200
12	Elmer Vasko	5	5	6	10	15	25	100	400
13	Glenn Hall	15	25	40	60	80	100	200	500
14	Ken Wharram RC	▲6	▲8	▲10	▲15	▲25	▲50	100	300
15	Len Lunde RC	5	5	5	8	12	20	60	200
16	Ed Litzenberger	5	5	6	10	15	25	40	100
17	Norm Johnson RC	▲6	▲8	▲10	▲20	▲30	▲40	▲80	▲200
18	Earl Ingarfield RC	5	5	5	8	12	20	60	300
19	Les Colwill RC	5	5	5	8	12	20	60	120
20	Leo Boivin	5	5	6	10	15	25	40	150
21	Andy Bathgate	5	6	10	15	25	40	60	250
22	Johnny Wilson	5	5	5	8	12	20	60	250
23	Larry Cahan	5	5	5	8	12	20	30	100
24	Marcel Pronovost	5	5	6	10	15	25	40	120
25	Larry Hillman	5	5	6	10	15	25	60	150
26	Jim Bartlett RC	5	5	5	8	12	20	30	120
27	Nick Mickoski	5	5	5	8	12	20	80	650
28	Larry Popein	5	5	5	8	12	20	100	1,000
29	Fleming Mackell	5	5	6	10	15	25	50	150
30	Eddie Shack RC	25	40	▼60	▼80	▼100	▼150	300	400
31	Jack Evans	5	5	5	8	12	20	50	120
32	Dean Prentice	5	5	6	10	15	25	60	500
33	Claude Laforge RC	5	5	5	8	12	20	60	300
34	Bill Gadsby	5	5	8	12	20	50	80	150
35	Bronco Horvath	5	5	6	10	15	25	50	120
36	Pierre Pilote	5	8	15	40	60	80	100	200
37	Earl Balfour	5	5	5	8	12	20	60	350
38	Gus Mortson	5	5	8	12	20	30	60	200
39	Gump Worsley	8	12	20	30	40	60	100	250
40	Johnny Bucyk	12	20	▲30	▲50	▲80	▲150	▲250	▲400
41	Lou Fontinato	5	5	6	10	15	25	80	200
42	Tod Sloan	5	5	5	8	12	20	60	300
43	Charlie Burns RC	5	5	5	8	12	20	▼80	400
44	Don Simmons	5	5	6	10	15	25	80	250
45	Jerry Toppazzini	5	5	5	8	12	20	60	150
46	Andy Hebenton	5	5	5	8	12	20	25	60
47	Pete Goegan UER	5	5	5	8	12	20	25	100
48	George Sullivan	5	5	5	8	12	20	60	200
49	Hank Ciesla RC	5	5	5	8	12	20	100	1,000
50	Doug Mohns	5	5	5	8	12	20	40	100
51	Jean-Guy Gendron	5	5	5	8	12	20	40	125
52	Alex Delvecchio	5	6	10	15	25	40	80	200
53	Eric Nesterenko	5	5	6	10	15	40	100	900
54	Camille Henry	5	5	6	10	15	25	60	400
55	Lorne Ferguson	5	5	5	8	12	30	60	150
56	Fern Flaman	5	5	6	10	15	25	60	150
57	Earl Reibel	5	5	5	8	15	40	100	
58	Warren Godfrey	5	5	5	8	12	30	60	300
59	Ron Murphy	5	5	5	8	12	30	80	300
60	Harry Howell	5	5	8	12	20	30	100	250
61	Red Kelly	5	6	10	15	25	40	80	250
62	Don McKenney	5	5	5	8	12	20	50	200
63	Ted Lindsay	5	6	10	15	25	40	100	550
64	Al Arbour	5	5	6	10	15	25	60	150
65	Norm Ullman	10	15	25	40	50	80	120	400
66	Bobby Hull RC	▲600	▲1,500	▲2,000	2,500	3,500	4,000	6,000	

— Bobby Hull #66 PSA 8 (NmMt) sold for $102,000 (REA, 4/17)
— Bobby Hull #66 PSA 8 (NmMt) sold for $13,010 (Mastro; 8/07)
— Earl Ingarfield #18 PSA 9 (Mint) sold for $762 (eBay; 8/13)
— Norm Johnson #17 PSA 7 (NrMt) sold for $1,284 (eBay; 11/14)
— Gus Mortson #18 PSA 9 (Mint) sold for $2,035 (eBay; 8/13)
— Earl Reibel #57 PSA 8 (NrMt) sold for $806 (eBay; 2/14)
— Ken Wharram RC #14 PSA 9 (Mint) sold for $2,229 (eBay; 3/14)
— Johnny Wilson #22 PSA 9 (Mint) sold for $791 (eBay; 6/13)

1959-60 Parkhurst

		VG 3	VgEx 4	EX 5	ExMt 6	NM 7	NmMt 8	NmMt+ 8.5	MT 9
1	Canadiens On Guard	40	60	70	80	200	350	450	800
2	Maurice Richard	100	120	150	250	400	800	1,000	2,000
3	Carl Brewer RC	20	▲40	▲50	▲80	▲125	▲200		
4	Phil Goyette	8	12	15	25	30	80	150	300
5	Ed Chadwick	10	15	20	30	40	100		
6	Jean Beliveau	50	80	100	150	200	350	450	1,500
7	George Armstrong	10	15	20	30	▲60	▲200	▲300	▲500
8	Doug Harvey	25	50	60	80	100	200	250	400
9	Billy Harris	8	15	25	40	50	100	150	250
10	Tom Johnson	8	12	15	25	40	100		
11	Marc Reaume	8	12	15	25	30	100	150	250
12	Marcel Bonin	8	12	15	25	30	80		
13	Johnny Wilson	8	12	15	25	30	120	150	200
14	Dickie Moore	12	20	30	50	80	150	250	400
15	Punch Imlach CO RC	12	20	25	40	50	150		
16	Charlie Hodge	10	15	25	50	80	150	200	300
17	Larry Regan	8	12	20	30	50	100	150	250
18	Claude Provost	8	12	15	25	30	120	150	250
19	Gerry Ehman RC	8	12	15	25	30	100	150	300
20	Ab McDonald	8	12	15	25	40	100	125	250
21	Bob Baun	8	12	15	25	30	100	125	300
22	Ken Reardon VP	8	12	15	25	30	80		
23	Tim Horton	30	50	60	80	100	250	350	600
24	Frank Mahovlich	40	60	80	100	150	250	300	500
25	Johnny Bower IA	12	20	25	40	50	150		
26	Ron Stewart	8	12	15	25	30	250		
27	Toe Blake CO	8	12	15	25	30	100		
28	Bob Pulford	8	12	15	25	30	80		
29	Ralph Backstrom	8	12	15	25	30	150		
30	Action Around the Net	10	15	20	30	40	150		
31	Bill Hicke RC	10	15	20	25	30	80		
32	Johnny Bower	30	50	60	80	120	250		
33	Bernie Geoffrion	20	30	40	60	80	200		
34	Ted Hampson RC	8	12	15	25	30	120		
35	Andre Pronovost	8	12	15	25	40	200		
36	Stafford Smythe CHC	8	12	15	25	50	150	200	250
37	Don Marshall	8	12	15	25	30	100		
38	Dick Duff	8	12	15	25	30	100		
39	Henri Richard	40	60	80	120	150	250	300	500
40	Bert Olmstead	8	12	15	25	30	100		
41	Jacques Plante	60	▲150	▲200	▲250	▲300	400	600	1,500
42	Noel Price	8	12	15	25	30	80		
43	Bob Turner	8	12	15	25	30	100		
44	Allan Stanley	12	20	25	40	50	100	125	300
45	Albert Langlois	8	12	15	25	50	150		
46	Officials Intervene	8	12	15	25	30	80		
47	Frank Selke MD	8	12	15	25	30	100		
48	Gary Edmundson RC	8	12	15	25	30	80	125	350
49	Jean-Guy Talbot	8	12	15	25	40	150		
50	King Clancy AGM	25	40	50	60	120	300		

— George Armstrong #7 PSA 9 (MT) sold for $514 (eBay; 8/09)
— Jean Beliveau #6 PSA 9 (Mt) sold for $783 (eBay; 5/12)
— Johnny Bower #32 PSA 9 (MT) sold for $840 (eBay; 3/07)
— Canadiens On Guard #1 PSA 8 (NmMt) sold for $470 (eBay; 10/08)
— Canadiens On Guard #1 PSA 9 (MT) sold for $1580.55 (eBay; 4/12)
— Charlie Hodge #16 PSA 10 (Gem) sold for $618 (eBay; 2/16)
— Tim Horton #23 PSA 9 (MT) sold for $1,034 (eBay; 5/07)
— Tim Horton #23 PSA 9 (MT) sold for $602 (eBay; 4/12)
— Jacques Plante #41 PSA 9 (MT) sold for $1,850 (eBay; 1/10)
— Jacques Plante #41 PSA 9 (MT) sold for $1,351 (eBay; 11/14)
— Maurice Richard #2 PSA 9 (MT) sold for $1331 (eBay; 11/14)
— Maurice Richard #2 PSA 9 (Mt) sold for $859.18 (Mile Hile; 1/12)

1959-60 Topps

		PrFr 1	GD 2	VG 3	VgEx 4	EX 5	ExMt 6	NM 7	NmMt 8
1	Eric Nesterenko	5	8	12	20	30	50	150	850
2	Pierre Pilote	5	6	10	15	25	40	60	150
3	Elmer Vasko	5	5	6	10	15	25	50	300
4	Peter Goegan	5	5	5	8	12	20	50	200
5	Lou Fontinato	5	5	6	10	15	25	50	150
6	Ted Lindsay	▲6	▲8	▲12	▲20	▲30	▲50	▲80	▲300
7	Leo Labine	5	5	6	10	15	25	50	
8	Alex Delvecchio	5	6	10	▲20	▲30	▲50	▲80	▲250
9	Don McKenney UER	5	5	5	8	12	20	50	120
10	Earl Ingarfield	5	5	5	8	12	20	50	100
11	Don Simmons	5	5	6	10	15	25	60	250
12	Glen Skov	5	5	5	8	12	20	50	120
13	Tod Sloan	5	5	5	8	12	25	80	350
14	Vic Stasiuk	5	5	5	8	12	20	50	120
15	Gump Worsley	6	10	15	25	40	60	80	200
16	Andy Hebenton	5	5	6	10	15	25	50	120
17	Dean Prentice	5	5	6	10	15	25	50	150
18	Action/Pronovost/Bartlett	5	5	5	8	12	20	50	100
19	Fleming Mackell	5	5	5	8	12	20	50	200
20	Harry Howell	5	5	6	10	15	25	60	120
21	Larry Popein	5	5	5	8	12	20	50	100

		PrFr 1	GD 2	VG 3	VgEx 4	EX 5	ExMt 6	NM 7	NmMt 8
22	Len Lunde	5	5	5	8	12	20	50	150
23	Johnny Bucyk	6	10	15	25	40	60	80	250
24	Jean-Guy Gendron	5	5	5	8	12	20	50	150
25	Barry Cullen	5	5	5	8	12	20	50	100
26	Leo Boivin	5	▲6	▲8	▲12	▲20	▲30	▲60	▲125
27	Warren Godfrey	5	5	5	8	12	20	50	80
28	G.Hall/C.Henry IA	5	6	10	15	25	40	50	200
29	Fern Flaman	5	5	6	10	15	25	50	120
30	Jack Evans	5	5	5	8	12	20	50	100
31	John Hanna	5	5	5	8	12	20	50	120
32	Glenn Hall	10	15	25	30	40	60	100	200
33	Murray Balfour RC	5	5	6	10	15	25	50	120
34	Andy Bathgate	5	6	10	15	25	40	60	250
35	Al Arbour	5	5	6	10	15	25	50	150
36	Jim Morrison	5	5	5	8	12	20	50	100
37	Nick Mickoski	5	5	5	8	12	20	40	150
38	Jerry Toppazzini	5	5	5	8	12	20	50	120
39	Bob Armstrong	5	5	5	8	12	20	50	100
40	Charlie Burns UER	5	5	5	8	20	50	60	150
41	Bill McNeil	5	5	5	8	12	20	50	100
42	Terry Sawchuk	20	25	40	60	80	10	150	200
43	Dollard St.Laurent	5	5	5	8	12	20	60	150
44	Marcel Pronovost	5	5	6	10	15	25	50	300
45	Norm Ullman	6	10	15	25	40	60	80	200
46	Camille Henry	5	5	6	10	15	30	100	300
47	Bobby Hull	50	80	100	150	250	450	600	850
48	G.Howe/Jack Evans IA	8	12	20	30	50	80	120	400
49	Lou Marcon RC	5	5	5	8	12	20	50	100
50	Earl Balfour	5	5	5	8	12	20	50	200
51	Jim Bartlett	5	5	5	8	12	20	50	200
52	Forbes Kennedy	5	5	5	8	12	20	50	200
53	Action Picture	5	5	5	8	12	20	50	120
54	G.Worsley/H.Howell IA	5	6	10	15	25	40	50	120
55	Brian Cullen	5	5	5	8	12	20	50	100
56	Bronco Horvath	5	5	6	10	15	25	50	100
57	Eddie Shack	10	15	25	▼40	60	80	100	200
58	Doug Mohns	5	5	6	10	15	25	50	350
59	George Sullivan	5	5	5	8	12	20	50	100
60	Pierre Pilote/Flem Mackell IA	5	5	5	8	12	20	50	100
61	Ed Litzenberger	5	5	5	8	12	20	80	150
62	Bill Gadsby	5	5	8	12	20	30	50	120
63	Gordie Howe	40	80	100	100	150	▲300	▲500	▲1,200
64	Claude Laforge	5	5	5	8	12	20	50	150
65	Red Kelly	5	6	10	15	25	40	100	250
66	Ron Murphy	5	8	12	20	35	50	150	

— John Buyck #23 SGC 9 (MT) sold for $467 (Goodwin; 1/12)
— Bill Gadsby #62 PSA 9 (Mint) sold for $249.50 (eBay; 4/16)
— Glenn Hall #32 SGC 9 (MT) sold for $467 (Goodwin; 1/12)
— Ed Litzenberger #61 PSA 9 (MT) sold for $732 (eBay; 5/12)
— Terry Sawchuk #42 PSA 9 (MT) sold for $1,365 (eBay; 2/14)
— Eddie Shack #57 PSA 9 (MT) sold for $897 (eBay; 6/12)
— Tod Sloan #13 PSA 9 (MT) sold for $797.50 (eBay; 2/14)
— Norm Ullman #45 PSA 9 (MT) sold for $1,221 (eBay; 2/13)
— Norm Ullman #45 SGC 9 (MT) sold for $464 (Goodwin; 1/12)

1960-61 Parkhurst

		VG 3	VgEx 4	EX 5	ExMt 6	NM 7	NmMt 8	NmMt+ 8.5	MT 9
1	Tim Horton	30	50	80	100	250	500		
2	Frank Mahovlich	25	30	50	80	125	350	400	800
3	Johnny Bower	15	20	30	50	100	200	600	
4	Bert Olmstead	8	10	12	20	30	100	125	200
5	Gary Edmundson	8	10	12	20	30	60	80	175
6	Ron Stewart	8	10	12	20	30	80	100	175
7	Gerry James	8	10	12	20	30	80	100	175
8	Gerry Ehman	8	10	12	20	30	60	80	175
9	Red Kelly	12	15	20	30	50	80	125	225
10	Dave Creighton	8	10	12	20	30	80	100	150
11	Bob Baun	8	10	12	20	30	80	100	175
12	Dick Duff	8	10	12	20	30	80	100	175
13	Larry Regan	8	10	12	20	25	60	80	175
14	Johnny Wilson	8	10	12	20	30	80	100	150
15	Billy Harris	8	10	12	20	30	80	100	150
16	Allan Stanley	8	10	12	20	30	60	80	120
17	George Armstrong	8	10	12	20	30	80	100	150
18	Carl Brewer	8	10	12	20	40	80	100	200
19	Bob Pulford	8	10	12	20	50	100	120	175
20	Gordie Howe	60	100	150	250	300	500	800	1,500
21	Val Fonteyne	8	10	12	20	25	60	80	175
22	Murray Oliver RC	8	10	12	20	30	80	100	150
23	Sid Abel CO	8	10	12	20	30	60	80	200
24	Jack McIntyre	8	10	12	20	25	60	80	175
25	Marc Reaume	8	10	12	20	30	80	100	175
26	Norm Ullman	15	20	30	50	80	150	200	250
27	Brian Smith	8	10	12	20	30	80	100	150
28	Gerry Melnyk UER RC	8	10	12	20	30	60	80	175
29	Marcel Pronovost	8	10	12	20	30	80	120	250
30	Warren Godfrey	8	10	12	20	30	80	125	200
31	Terry Sawchuk	30	40	60	80	150	200	250	400
32	Barry Cullen	8	10	12	20	30	60	80	150

		VG 3	VgEx 4	EX 5	ExMt 6	NM 7	NmMt 8	NmMt+ 8.5	MT 9
33	Gary Aldcorn	8	10	12	20	30	60	80	200
34	Pete Goegan	8	10	12	20	30	80	100	225
35	Len Lunde	8	10	12	20	30	80	100	175
36	Alex Delvecchio	12	15	20	30	60	100	150	250
37	John McKenzie RC	10	12	15	25	40	80	100	250
38	Dickie Moore	10	12	15	25	40	80	100	350
39	Albert Langlois	8	10	12	20	30	80	100	175
40	Bill Hicke	8	10	12	20	30	80	100	175
41	Ralph Backstrom	8	10	12	20	30	80	100	300
42	Don Marshall	8	10	12	20	30	80	100	200
43	Bob Turner	8	10	12	25	50	100	200	300
44	Tom Johnson	8	10	12	20	30	80	100	300
45	Maurice Richard	60	80	100	150	250	400	600	2,000
46	Bernie Geoffrion	15	20	30	50	80	120	150	400
47	Henri Richard	25	30	50	80	100	250	300	500
48	Doug Harvey	20	25	40	60	100	150	200	300
49	Jean Beliveau	25	40	50	80	125	250	300	550
50	Phil Goyette	8	10	12	20	30	80	125	250
51	Marcel Bonin	8	10	12	20	30	60	80	150
52	Jean-Guy Talbot	8	10	12	20	30	80	100	175
53	Jacques Plante	30	50	60	100	200	350	400	600
54	Claude Provost	8	10	12	20	30	80	100	250
55	Andre Pronovost	8	10	12	20	40	100		
56	Hicke/McDonald/Backstrom	8	10	12	20	30	80	125	200
57	Marsh/H.Richard/Moore	15	20	30	40	60	100	150	400
58	Provost/Pronovost/Goyette	8	10	12	20	30	100	150	200
59	Boom/Marshall/Beliveau	15	20	30	50	100	150	200	500
60	Ab McDonald	8	10	12	20	40	100	125	300
61	Jim Morrison	25	35	60	100	150	500		

— Gary Aldcorn #33 PSA 9 (MT) sold for $350 (eBay; 1/08)
— Johnny Bower #3 PSA 10 (GemMt) sold for $875 (eBay; 2/16)
— Phil Goyette #50 PSA 9 (MT) sold for $350 (eBay; 1/08)
— Bill Hicke #40 PSA 9 (MT) sold for $205 (eBay; 1/08)
— Albert Langlois #39 PSA 10 (GmMt) sold for $1005.00 (eBay; 8/12)
— John McKenzie #37 PSA 9 (MT) sold for $290 (eBay; 8/12)
— Allan Stanley #16 PSA 10 (GemMt) sold for $308.50 (eBay; 1/16)
— Norm Ullman #26 PSA 9 (MT) sold for $262 (eBay; 1/08)

1960-61 Topps

		VG 3	VgEx 4	EX 5	ExMt 6	NM 7	NmMt 8	NmMt+ 8.5	MT 9
1	Lester Patrick ATG	20	25	50	80	200	800		
2	Paddy Moran ATG	8	10	15	20	30	80		
3	Joe Malone ATG	10	12	20	30	40	80		
4	Ernest (Moose) Johnson ATG	6	8	12	20	30	80		
5	Nels Stewart ATG	10	12	20	30	50			
6	Bill Hay RC	6	8	12	20	40	150		
7	Eddie Shack	20	25	30	50	100	300		
8	Cy Denneny ATG	6	8	12	20	30	80	125	300
9	Jim Morrison	5	6	10	15	30	80		
10	Bill Cook ATG	6	8	12	25	50	100	150	225
11	Johnny Bucyk	15	20	25	40	80	250		
12	Murray Balfour	5	6	10	15	30	120		
13	Leo Labine	5	6	10	15	30	80		
14	Stan Mikita RC	250	350	400	500	600	1,000		
15	George Hay ATG	6	8	12	20	30	80		
16	Mervyn(Red) Dutton ATG	6	8	12	20	30	80		
17	Dickie Boon ATG UER	5	6	10	15	30	80		
18	George Sullivan	5	6	10	15	30	80		
19	Georges Vezina ATG	15	20	25	35	60	100	125	225
20	Eddie Shore ATG	15	20	25	30	50	100		
21	Ed Litzenberger	5	6	10	15	30	80		
22	Bill Gadsby	8	10	15	20	30	80		
23	Elmer Vasko	5	6	15	30	225			
24	Charlie Burns	5	6	10	30	60	250		
25	Glenn Hall	20	25	30	50	80	300		
26	Dit Clapper ATG	10	12	20	30	40	80	100	300
27	Art Ross ATG	15	20	25	40	60	100		
28	Jerry Toppazzini	5	6	10	15	30	80		
29	Frank Boucher ATG	6	8	12	20	30	80	100	225
30	Jack Evans	5	6	10	15	30	80		
31	Jean-Guy Gendron	5	6	10	15	40	120		
32	Chuck Gardiner ATG	8	10	15	25	40	80	100	250
33	Ab McDonald	5	6	10	20	30	80		
34	Frank Fredrickson ATG	6	8	12	25	50	100	150	300
35	Frank Nighbor ATG	8	10	15	25	40	100		
36	Gump Worsley	20	25	40	50	80	250		
37	Dean Prentice	6	8	12	20	30	80		
38	Hugh Lehman ATG	6	8	12	20	30	80		
39	Jack McCartan RC	10	12	20	30	100	300		
40	Don McKenney UER	5	6	10	20	30	80		
41	Ron Murphy	5	6	10	15	30	80		
42	Andy Hebenton	8	10	15	25	40	120		
43	Don Simmons	8	12	20	30	100			
44	Herb Gardiner ATG	6	8	12	20	30	80		
45	Andy Bathgate	8	10	15	25	40	150		
46	Cyclone Taylor ATG	10	12	30	40	60	150		
47	King Clancy ATG	15	20	25	40	80	200		
48	Newsy Lalonde ATG	10	12	20	30	50	100	125	250
49	Harry Howell	6	8	15	20	60	150		

HOCKEY

HOCKEY

		VG 3	VgEx 4	EX 5	ExMt 6	NM 7	NmMt 8	NmMt+ 8.5	MT 9
50	Ken Schinkel RC	5	6	10	15	50	200		
51	Tod Sloan	5	8	12	20	40	100		
52	Doug Mohns	8	10	15	25	60			
53	Camille Henry	6	8	12	20	30	125		
54	Bronco Horvath	5	6	10	15	30	150		
55	Tiny Thompson ATG	12	15	25	30	50	80		
56	Bob Armstrong	5	6	10	15	30	80		
57	Fern Flaman	6	8	12	20	50	150		
58	Bobby Hull	100	120	250	300	400	800	1,200	
59	Howie Morenz ATG	20	25	30	40	60	150		
60	Dick Irvin ATG	10	12	20	30	40	80		
61	Lou Fontinato	5	6	10	15	60			
62	Leo Boivin	6	8	12	20	40	100		
63	Moose Goheen ATG	6	8	12	20	30	80		
64	Al Arbour	6	8	12	20	60	120		
65	Pierre Pilote	10	12	20	40	50	120		
66	Vic Stasiuk	12	15	20	30	80	150		

— Johnny Bucyk #11 PSA 9 (MT) sold for $989 (eBay; 2/07)
— George Sullivan #18 PSA 9 (MT) sold for $502 (eBay; 4/12)
— Glenn Hall #25 PSA 9 (MT) sold for $636 (Goodwin; 2/07)
— Hugh Lehman #38 PSA 9 (MT) sold for $882 (eBay; 4/09)
— Lou Fontinato #61 PSA 8 (NMMT) sold for $908 (eBay; 8/12)
— Pierre Pilote #65 PSA 9 (MT) sold for $1,968.00 (Memory Lane; 6/12)

1961-62 Parkhurst

		VG 3	VgEx 4	EX 5	ExMt 6	NM 7	NmMt 8	NmMt+ 8.5	MT 9
1	Tim Horton	30	50	120	150	250	800		
2	Frank Mahovlich	25	30	40	80	100	300		
3	Johnny Bower	20	25	35	60	100	200		
4	Bert Olmstead	8	10	12	20	30	60		
5	Dave Keon RC	125	200	300	400	650	800	1,000	1,600
6	Ron Stewart	8	10	12	20	30	80	120	300
7	Eddie Shack	20	25	40	60	80	200	200	350
8	Bob Pulford	8	10	12	25	40	80		
9	Red Kelly	10	12	15	25	40	80		
10	Bob Nevin	8	10	12	20	25	60	100	175
11	Bob Baun	8	10	12	20	30	80	125	200
12	Dick Duff	8	10	12	25	40	80	100	175
13	Larry Keenan	8	10	12	20	30	60	125	200
14	Larry Hillman	8	10	12	20	25	60	100	200
15	Billy Harris	8	10	12	20	25	60	100	200
16	Allan Stanley	8	10	12	20	25	60	100	175
17	George Armstrong	8	10	12	20	30	80	125	175
18	Carl Brewer	8	10	12	20	25	60	100	200
19	Howie Glover	8	10	12	20	25	60	100	175
20	Gordie Howe	60	80	100	150	300	450	600	1,500
21	Val Fonteyne	8	10	12	20	30	50		
22	Al Johnson	8	10	12	20	30	80		
23	Pete Goegan	8	10	12	20	30	60	100	600
24	Len Lunde	8	10	12	20	30	80		
25	Alex Delvecchio	10	12	15	25	40	100	125	200
26	Norm Ullman	15	20	25	40	60	100	125	200
27	Bill Gadsby	8	10	12	20	30	50	100	175
28	Ed Litzenberger	8	10	12	20	30	80	100	200
29	Marcel Pronovost	8	10	12	20	30	80		
30	Warren Godfrey	8	10	12	20	25	60	100	175
31	Terry Sawchuk	25	30	50	80	150	250	300	400
32	Vic Stasiuk	8	10	12	20	30	80	100	175
33	Leo Labine	8	10	12	20	30	80	100	175
34	John McKenzie	8	10	12	20	30	80	100	175
35	Bernie Geoffrion	20	25	30	40	60	120	150	250
36	Dickie Moore	8	10	12	20	30	80	100	175
37	Albert Langlois	8	10	12	20	25	50	100	175
38	Bill Hicke	8	10	12	20	25	60	100	150
39	Ralph Backstrom	8	10	12	20	25	60	100	200
40	Don Marshall	8	10	12	20	30	60	80	125
41	Bob Turner	8	10	12	20	30	60	100	200
42	Tom Johnson	8	10	12	20	30	80	100	200
43	Henri Richard	20	25	35	60	80	150	200	350
44	Wayne Connelly UER RC	8	10	12	20	30	80	100	175
45	Jean Beliveau	25	30	50	100	150	250	300	400
46	Phil Goyette	8	10	12	20	30	80	100	175
47	Marcel Bonin	8	10	12	20	30	80	100	175
48	Jean-Guy Talbot	8	10	12	20	30	60	120	250
49	Jacques Plante	30	50	80	150	200	300	400	650
50	Claude Provost	8	10	12	20	30	80	100	150
51	Andre Pronovost UER	15	20	25	40	60	150		

— Bill Gadsby #27 PSA 10 (GmMt) sold for $1,025 (eBay; 8/12)
— Dave Keon #5 PSA 9 (Mint) sold for $1,365 (eBay; 2/13)
— Bert Olmstead #4 PSA 9 (Mint) sold for $186.50 (eBay; 3/16)
— Andre Pronovost #61 PSA 10 (GmMt) sold for $3,643.78 (Memory Lane; 4/12)

1961-62 Topps

		VG 3	VgEx 4	EX 5	ExMt 6	NM 7	NmMt 8	NmMt+ 8.5	MT 9
1	Phil Watson CO	20	25	40	60	100	550		
2	Ted Green RC	15	20	30	40	80	200		
3	Earl Balfour	6	8	10	12	30	80		
4	Dallas Smith RC	12	15	20	25	40	100		
5	Andre Pronovost UER	8	10	12	20	30	80		

		VG 3	VgEx 4	EX 5	ExMt 6	NM 7	NmMt 8	NmMt+ 8.5	MT 9
6	Dick Meissner	6	8	10	12	30	80		
7	Leo Boivin	8	10	12	15	30	60		
8	Johnny Bucyk	15	20	30	40	50	150		
9	Jerry Toppazzini	6	8	10	12	25	60	80	175
10	Doug Mohns	8	10	12	15	30	80		
11	Charlie Burns	6	8	10	15	25	60		
12	Don McKenney	6	8	10	20	100	250		
13	Bob Armstrong	6	8	10	15	40	150		
14	Murray Oliver	6	8	10	12	25	60		
15	Orland Kurtenbach RC	10	12	15	20	30	60	100	300
16	Terry Gray	6	8	10	12	25	60	80	175
17	Don Head	8	10	12	15	30	80		
18	Pat Stapleton RC	12	15	25	50	100	200	300	400
19	Cliff Pennington	6	8	10	12	25	40	100	300
20	Bruins Team Picture	15	20	30	40	50	100	135	400
21	E.Balfour/F.Flaman IA	8	12	20	25	50	120		
22	A.Bathgate/G.Hall IA	12	15	20	25	60	175		
23	Rudy Pilous CO RC	8	12	20	25	50	200		
24	Pierre Pilote	12	15	20	25	40	80	125	400
25	Elmer Vasko	6	8	10	12	25	60	125	350
26	Reg Fleming RC	8	10	12	15	30	80		
27	Ab McDonald	6	8	10	12	25	60	100	175
28	Eric Nesterenko	8	10	12	15	30	80	100	200
29	Bobby Hull	75	100	150	200	300	500	600	1,000
30	Ken Wharram	8	10	12	15	30	80	100	175
31	Dollard St.Laurent	6	8	10	12	25	60	100	250
32	Glenn Hall	20	25	40	60	100	200	300	400
33	Murray Balfour	6	8	10	12	25	60	100	200
34	Ron Murphy	6	8	10	12	25	40	80	175
35	Bill(Red) Hay	6	8	10	12	25	60		
36	Stan Mikita	30	40	60	100	150	300	400	750
37	Denis DeJordy RC	15	20	30	40	60	120		
38	Wayne Hillman	8	10	12	15	30	120		
39	Rino Robazzo	8	10	12	15	25	60		
40	Bronco Horvath	6	8	10	12	25	60		
41	Bob Turner	6	8	10	12	25	60		
42	Blackhawks Team Picture	15	20	30	40	60	120		
43	Ken Wharram IA	10	15	20	25	40	150		
44	St.Laurent/G.Hall IA	12	15	20	25	60	200	250	400
45	Doug Harvey CO	15	20	30	40	60	100	150	300
46	Junior Langlois	6	8	10	12	25	60	100	175
47	Irv Spencer	6	8	10	12	25	60	100	200
48	George Sullivan	8	10	12	15	25	60		
49	Earl Ingarfield	6	8	10	12	25	60	100	175
50	Gump Worsley	15	20	30	40	60	100	150	250
51	Harry Howell	8	10	12	15	30	80	100	175
52	Larry Cahan	6	8	10	12	25	60	100	175
53	Andy Bathgate	10	12	15	20	30	80	125	400
54	Dean Prentice	8	10	12	15	30	80	100	175
55	Andy Hebenton	6	8	10	12	25	60	100	175
56	Camille Henry	8	10	12	15	30	60	100	200
57	Jean-Guy Gendron	6	8	10	12	25	60		
58	Pat Hannigan	6	8	10	12	30	80	100	200
59	Ted Hampson	6	8	10	12	25	60		
60	Jean Ratelle RC	40	60	80	135	200	600	750	1,600
61	Al Lebrun	6	8	10	15	25	60	125	350
62	Rod Gilbert RC	50	60	100	125	200	400	600	2,000
63	Rangers Team Picture	15	20	30	40	80	800		
64	Meissner/Worsley IA	10	12	20	40	200			
65	Gump Worsley IA	15	20	30	80	150			
66	Checklist Card	50	60	80	120	200	600		

— Bob Armstrong #13 PSA 8.5 (NM MT+) sold for $173.99 (eBay; 3/16)
— Earl Balfour #3 PSA 9 (MT) sold for $305 (eBay; 8/08)
— Bruins Team Picture #20 PSA 9 (MT) sold for $648 (eBay; 3/07)
— Charlie Burns #11 PSA 9 (MT) sold for $279 (eBay; 2/16)
— Camile Henry #56 PSA 9 (MT) sold for $305 (eBay; 8/08)
— Camile Henry #56 PSA 10 (GemMT) sold for $639 (eBay; 3/17)
— Don McKenney #12 PSA 9 (MT) sold for $929 (eBay; 2/16)
— Stan Mikita #36 PSA 9 (MT) sold for $685 (eBay; 3/14)
— Stan Mikita #36 PSA 9 (MT) sold for $662 (ebay; 2/14)
— Stan Mikita #36 SGC 9 (MT) sold for $467.67 (Goodwin; 3/12)
— Dallas Smith #4 PSA 9 (MT) sold for $269.10 (eBay; 3/16)
— Jean Ratelle #60 SGC 10 (Gem) sold for $2,427 (Goodwin; 3/12)
— D.St.Laurent/G.Hall #44 PSA 9 (MT) sold for $940 (eBay; 8/09)
— Pat Stapleton #18 PSA 9 (MT) sold for $435 (eBay; 8/12)
— Bob Turner #41 PSA 9 (MT) sold for $299 (eBay; 2/16)
— Phil Watson #1 PSA 9 (MT) sold for $1,030 (eBay; 8/12)

1962-63 Parkhurst

		VG 3	VgEx 4	EX 5	ExMt 6	NM 7	NmMt 8	NmMt+ 8.5	MT 9
1	Billy Harris	10	12	20	30	50	120	150	350
2	Dick Duff	6	10	12	20	30	60	80	120
3	Bob Baun	6	10	12	20	30	60	80	120
4	Frank Mahovlich	12	15	30	50	80	125	200	300
5	Red Kelly	8	10	15	25	40	100	120	150
6	Ron Stewart	6	8	10	15	25	50	80	120
7	Tim Horton	12	15	25	40	80	150	225	350
8	Carl Brewer	6	8	10	15	25	40	80	120
9	Allan Stanley	6	8	10	20	30	60	80	120

		VG 3	VgEx 4	EX 5	ExMt 6	NM 7	NmMt 8	NmMt+ 8.5	MT 9
10	Bob Nevin	6	8	10	15	25	60	80	120
11	Bob Pulford	6	8	10	15	25	50	80	120
12	Ed Litzenberger	6	8	10	15	25	50	100	
13	George Armstrong	6	8	10	15	25	50	80	120
14	Eddie Shack	10	12	20	30	50	100	150	225
15	Dave Keon	12	15	25	40	75	125	150	250
16	Johnny Bower	10	12	20	30	50	100	150	200
17	Larry Hillman	6	8	10	15	25	40	60	100
18	Frank Mahovlich	12	15	25	40	60	100	125	250
19	Hank Bassen	6	8	10	15	25	40	80	120
20	Gerry Odrowski	6	8	10	15	25	50	60	100
21	Norm Ullman	6	8	10	20	30	60	100	150
22	Vic Stasiuk	6	8	10	15	25	40	80	120
23	Bruce MacGregor	6	8	10	15	25	40	80	120
24	Claude Laforge	6	8	10	15	25	50	80	120
25	Bill Gadsby	6	8	10	15	25	50	80	120
26	Leo Labine	6	8	10	15	25	50	80	120
27	Val Fonteyne	6	8	10	15	25	50	80	120
28	Howie Glover	6	8	10	15	25	50	80	120
29	Marc Boileau	6	8	10	15	25	50	80	120
30	Gordie Howe	60	80	100	150	300	400	500	900
31	Gordie Howe	60	80	100	150	200	300	400	800
32	Alex Delvecchio	8	10	15	25	40	60	100	150
33	Marcel Pronovost	6	8	10	15	25	50	80	120
34	Sid Abel CO	6	8	10	15	25	50	80	120
35	Len Lunde	6	8	10	15	25	50	80	100
36	Warren Godfrey	6	8	10	15	25	50	80	100
37	Phil Goyette	6	8	10	15	25	50	80	120
38	Henri Richard	12	15	25	40	100	175	200	250
39	Jean Beliveau	12	15	25	40	75	150	250	300
40	Bill Hicke	6	8	10	15	25	50	80	120
41	Claude Provost	6	8	10	15	25	100	120	150
42	Dickie Moore	6	8	10	15	25	50	80	120
43	Don Marshall	6	8	10	15	25	50	80	120
44	Ralph Backstrom	6	8	10	15	25	50	80	120
45	Marcel Bonin	6	8	10	20	25	50	80	120
46	Gilles Tremblay RC	10	12	20	30	50	80	125	175
47	Bobby Rousseau RC	8	10	15	25	40	100	150	200
48	Bernie Geoffrion	10	12	20	30	50	100	150	200
49	Jacques Plante	25	30	50	100	150	200	300	350
50	Tom Johnson	6	8	10	15	25	50	80	120
51	Jean-Guy Talbot	6	8	10	15	25	50	80	120
52	Lou Fontinato	6	8	10	15	25	100	120	150
53	Bernie Geoffrion	10	12	20	30	50	80	125	175
54	J.C.Tremblay RC	12	15	25	35	60	150	200	500
NNO	Zip Entry Game Card	60	80	100	150	250	400	500	600
NNO	Checklist Card	50	75	125	250	400	500		

— Sid Able #34 PSA 10 (Gem) sold for $192.50 (eBay; 12/15)
— Bob Baun #3 PSA 10 (Gem) sold for $219.50 (eBay; 12/15)
— Warren Godfrey #36 PSA 10 (Gem) sold for $1,031 (eBay; 9/12)
— Frank Mahovlich #4 PSA 10 (Gem) sold for $1,100 (eBay; 9/12)
— Frank Mahovlich #4 PSA 10 (Gem) sold for $637 (eBay; 3/14)
— Don Marshall #43 PSA 10 (Gem) sold for $797 (eBay; 8/07)
— Bob Nevin #10 PSA 10 (Gem) sold for $585 (eBay; 2/13)
— Jaques Plante #10 PSA 10 (Gem) sold for $1,099 (eBay; 3/13)
— Bobby Rousseau #47 PSA 9 (MT) sold for $515 (eBay; 12/06)
— Ron Stewart #6 PSA 10 (Gem) sold for $376 (eBay; 2/16)

1962-63 Topps

		VG 3	VgEx 4	EX 5	ExMt 6	NM 7	NmMt 8	NmMt+ 8.5	MT 9
1	Phil Watson CO	10	15	25	35	80	200		
2	Bob Perreault	10	15	25	35	60	200		
3	Bruce Gamble RC	10	15	30	40	60	300		
4	Warren Godfrey	6	8	10	15	30	80	100	150
5	Leo Boivin	8	10	12	15	30	80		
6	Doug Mohns	8	10	12	15	30	80	100	150
7	Ted Green	8	10	12	15	30	80		
8	Pat Stapleton	8	10	12	15	30	80		
9	Dallas Smith	8	10	12	15	30	60		
10	Don McKenney	6	8	10	15	30	80		
11	Johnny Bucyk	15	20	25	30	50	100	125	400
12	Murray Oliver	6	8	10	15	30	60		
13	Jerry Toppazzini	6	8	10	15	30	80		
14	Cliff Pennington	6	8	10	15	30	60		
15	Charlie Burns	6	8	10	15	30	100		
16	Jean-Guy Gendron	6	8	10	15	30	80		
17	Irv Spencer	6	8	10	15	30	60	100	300
18	Wayne Connelly	6	8	10	15	30	60	80	150
19	Andre Pronovost	6	8	10	15	30	80		
20	Terry Gray	6	8	10	15	30	80		
21	Tom Williams RC	8	10	12	15	30	80	100	150
22	Bruins Team	20	25	30	40	50	80		
23	Rudy Pilous CO	6	8	10	15	30	80		
24	Glenn Hall	25	30	35	50	100	150	200	400
25	Denis DeJordy	8	10	12	15	30	80	100	200
26	Jack Evans	6	8	10	15	30	80		
27	Elmer Vasko	6	8	10	15	30	80		
28	Pierre Pilote	10	12	15	20	30	80	100	200
29	Bob Turner	6	8	10	15	30	60	80	150

		VG 3	VgEx 4	EX 5	ExMt 6	NM 7	NmMt 8	NmMt+ 8.5	MT 9
30	Dollard St.Laurent	6	8	10	15	30	80		
31	Wayne Hillman	8	10	12	20	30	60		
32	Al McNeil	6	8	10	15	30	80		
33	Bobby Hull	50	60	80		200	350	450	1,000
34	Stan Mikita	30	40	50	80	150	200	250	400
35	Bill(Red) Hay	6	8	10	15	30	80		
36	Murray Balfour	6	8	10	15	30	80		
37	Chico Maki RC	10	12	15	20	40	80		
38	Ab McDonald	6	8	10	15	30	80		
39	Ken Wharram	8	10	12	15	30	80		
40	Ron Murphy	6	8	10	15	30	250		
41	Eric Nesterenko	6	8	10	15	30	80		
42	Reg Fleming	8	10	12	15	30	80		
43	Murray Hall	6	8	10	15	30	80	100	250
44	Blackhawks Team	20	25	30	40	50	100		
45	Gump Worsley	20	25	30	40	60	120		
46	Harry Howell	6	8	10	15	30	60	100	200
47	Albert Langlois	6	8	10	15	30	60	100	250
48	Larry Cahan	6	8	10	15	30	80		
49	Jim Neilson UER RC	10	12	15	20	40	80		
50	Al Lebrun	6	8	10	15	30	80		
51	Earl Ingarfield	6	8	10	15	30	60		
52	Andy Bathgate	10	12	15	20	30	80	100	200
53	Dean Prentice	8	10	12	15	30	80	100	175
54	Andy Hebenton	6	8	10	15	30	60		
55	Ted Hampson	6	8	10	15	30	60		
56	Dave Balon	6	8	10	15	30	60		400
57	Bert Olmstead	8	10	12	15	30	60	80	150
58	Jean Ratelle	25	30	35	50	60	120		
59	Rod Gilbert	25	30	35	50	80	150		
60	Vic Hadfield RC	25	30	35	50	80	150	200	300
61	Frank Paice RC TR	6	8	10	15	30	80		
62	Camille Henry	8	10	12	15	30	80		
63	Bronco Horvath	6	8	10	15	30	80		
64	Pat Hannigan	6	8	10	25	50	80		
65	Rangers Team	15	20	25	30	40	60	100	
66	Checklist Card	30	50	80	100	150	225	500	

— Denis DeJordy #25 PSA 10 (Gem) sold for $2,064.65 (Goodwin; 3/12)
— Vic Hadfield #60 PSA 10 (Gem) sold for $840 (eBay; 2/14)
— Bobby Hull #33 PSA 10 (Gem) sold for $5,118 (Mastro; 2/07)

1963-64 Parkhurst

		VG 3	VgEx 4	EX 5	ExMt 6	NM 7	NmMt 8	NmMt+ 8.5	MT 9
1	Allan Stanley	12	15	30	40	60		135	450
2	Don Simmons	6	8	10	20	30	60	80	150
3	Red Kelly	10	12	20	25	40	80	100	200
4	Dick Duff	6	8	10	20	30	50	80	120
5	Johnny Bower	15	20	25	50	80	100	150	250
6	Ed Litzenberger	6	8	10	20	30	60	80	120
7	Kent Douglas	6	8	10	20	30	60	80	200
8	Carl Brewer	6	8	10	20	30	60	80	120
9	Eddie Shack	15	20	25	40	80	120	150	250
10	Bob Nevin	6	8	10	20	30	60	80	120
11	Billy Harris	6	8	15	20	30	60	80	120
12	Bob Pulford	6	8	10	20	30	60	80	120
13	George Armstrong	6	8	10	20	40	100		
14	Ron Stewart	6	8	10	20	30	60	80	250
15	John McMillan	6	8	15	20	30	50	60	120
16	Tim Horton	20	40	50	60	100	150	200	350
17	Frank Mahovlich	20	25	30	50	80	150	200	350
18	Bob Baun	6	8	10	20	30	60	80	120
19	Punch Imlach ACO/GM	10	12	15	25	40	80	100	250
20	King Clancy ACO	10	12	15	25	50	100		
21	Gilles Tremblay	6	8	10	20	30	60	80	135
22	Jean-Guy Talbot	6	8	10	20	30	60	80	120
23	Henri Richard	20	25	30	50	100	150	175	300
24	Ralph Backstrom	6	8	10	20	30	60	80	250
25	Bill Hicke	6	8	10	20	30	50	80	200
26	Red Berenson RC	12	15	20	30	50	80	100	200
27	Jacques Laperriere RC	15	20	25	50	100	200	250	600
28	Jean Gauthier	6	8	10	20	30	60	80	120
29	Bernie Geoffrion	12	15	20	30	50	80	125	200
30	Jean Beliveau	20	25	30	60	100	150	200	350
31	J.C.Tremblay	6	8	10	20	30	60	80	120
32	Terry Harper RC	10	12	15	25	40	100	120	200
33	John Ferguson RC	20	25	30	60	100	175	225	400
34	Toe Blake CO	10	12	15	25	40	80	100	175
35	Bobby Rousseau	6	8	10	20	30	60	80	120
36	Claude Provost	6	8	10	20	30	60	80	120
37	Marc Reaume	6	8	10	20	30	80	100	150
38	Dave Balon	6	8	10	20	30	60		
39	Gump Worsley	12	15	20	30	50	100	175	300
40	Cesare Maniago RC	15	20	25	50	60	100	150	250
41	Bruce MacGregor	6	8	10	20	30	60	80	150
42	Alex Faulkner RC	50	60	100	150	200	400	500	900
43	Pete Goegan	6	8	10	20	30	60	80	120
44	Parker MacDonald	6	8	10	20	30	60	80	120
45	Andre Pronovost	6	8	10	20	30	50	80	120
46	Marcel Pronovost	6	8	10	20	30	60	80	120

HOCKEY

		VG 3	VgEx 4	EX 5	ExMt 6	NM 7	NmMt 8	NmMt+ 8.5	MT 9
47	Bob Dillabough	6	8	10	20	30	80		
48	Larry Jeffrey	6	8	10	20	30	50		
49	Ian Cushenan	6	8	10	20	30	60	80	120
50	Alex Delvecchio	10	12	15	25	40	100	125	250
51	Hank Ciesla	6	8	10	20	30	60	80	120
52	Norm Ullman	10	12	15	25	40	80	100	150
53	Terry Sawchuk	25	30	40	75	125	250		
54	Ron Ingram	6	8	10	20	30	60	80	150
55	Gordie Howe	80	100	150	250	400	600	800	1,800
56	Billy McNeil	6	8	10	20	30	60	80	150
57	Floyd Smith	6	8	10	20	30	60	80	120
58	Vic Stasiuk	6	8	10	20	30	60	80	120
59	Bill Gadsby	6	8	10	20	30	60	80	150
60	Doug Barkley	6	8	10	20	30	45	60	120
61	Allan Stanley	6	8	10	20	30	60	80	120
62	Don Simmons	6	8	10	20	30	50	60	100
63	Red Kelly	10	12	15	25	40	80	100	200
64	Dick Duff	6	8	10	20	30	80	100	350
65	Johnny Bower	15	20	25	50	80	100	200	400
66	Ed Litzenberger	6	8	10	20	30	50	60	100
67	Kent Douglas	6	8	10	20	30	60	80	120
68	Carl Brewer	6	8	10	20	30	50	60	100
69	Eddie Shack	15	20	25	40	80	100	150	200
70	Bob Nevin	6	8	10	20	30	60	80	120
71	Billy Harris	6	8	10	20	30	50	60	100
72	Bob Pulford	6	8	10	20	30	60	80	120
73	George Armstrong	6	8	10	20	30	60	80	120
74	Ron Stewart	6	8	10	20	30	50	60	100
75	Dave Keon	15	25	40	60	80	120	200	250
76	Tim Horton	15	20	25	40	80	120	200	400
77	Frank Mahovlich	15	20	25	40	60	100	120	300
78	Bob Baun	6	8	10	20	30	60	80	120
79	Punch Imlach ACO/GM	10	12	15	25	40	60	100	225
80	Gilles Tremblay	6	8	10	20	30	60	80	200
81	Jean-Guy Talbot	6	8	10	20	30	60	80	150
82	Henri Richard	20	25	30	60	80	100	150	300
83	Ralph Backstrom	6	8	10	20	30	50	60	100
84	Bill Hicke	6	8	10	20	30	50	60	120
85	Red Berenson RC	12	15	20	30	50	100	150	200
86	Jacques Laperriere RC	12	20	30	50	80	200		
87	Jean Gauthier	6	8	10	20	30	80	100	400
88	Bernie Geoffrion	12	15	20	30	50	125	150	200
89	Jean Beliveau	20	25	30	50	80	150	200	300
90	J.C.Tremblay	6	8	10	20	30	45	60	100
91	Terry Harper RC	10	12	15	25	40	60	80	150
92	John Ferguson RC	15	20	25	50	80	150		
93	Toe Blake CO	10	12	15	25	40	80	125	400
94	Bobby Rousseau	6	8	10	20	30	60	80	120
95	Claude Provost	6	8	10	20	30	50		100
96	Marc Reaume	6	8	10	20	30	60	80	100
97	Dave Balon	6	8	10	20	30	80	100	150
98	Gump Worsley	12	15	20	30	50	100	150	200
99	Cesare Maniago RC	30	40	60	100	175	300		800

— George Armstrong #73 PSA 10 (Gem) sold for $428.79 (eBay; 2/16)
— Ralph Backstrom #83 PSA 10 (Gem) sold for $560 (eBay; 7/08)
— Bob Baun #18 PSA 10 (Gem) sold for $852 (eBay; 9/12)
— Jean Beliveau #89 PSA 10 (Gem) sold for $2,260 (eBay; 7/08)
— Red Berenson #85 PSA 10 (Gem) sold for $1,683.33 (eBay; 9/12)
— Johnny Bower #5 PSA 10 (Gem) sold for $1,533.60 (eBay; 5/12)
— Johnny Bower #5 PSA 10 (Gem) sold for $673 (eBay; 3/14)
— Johnny Bower #65 PSA 10 (Gem) sold for $1,930.33 (eBay; 6/12)
— Bob Dillabough #47 PSA 9 (MT) sold for $803 (eBay; 3/14)
— Kent Douglas #7 PSA 10 (Gem) sold for $1,197 (eBay; 6/12)
— Alex Faulkner #42 PSA 10 (Gem) sold for $2,409 (eBay; 2/13)
— Alex Faulkner #42 PSA 10 (Gem) sold for $1,533 (eBay; 3/13)
— Alex Faulkner #42 PSA 10 (Gem) sold for $1,319 (eBay; 3/14)
— John Ferguson #33 PSA 10 (Gem) sold for $1,609.44 (eBay; 9/12)
— Glenn Hall #23 PSA 10 (Gem) sold for $3159 (eBay 4/27)
— Billy Harris #71 PSA 10 (Gem) sold for $259.90 (eBay; 2/16)
— Tim Horton #76 PSA 9 (MT) sold for $466.78 (eBay; 9/12)
— Gordie Howe #55 SGC 8.5 (NmMt+) sold for $372 (eBay; 3/14)
— Gordie Howe #55 PSA 9 (MT) sold for $1,856 (eBay; 9/12)
— Ed Litzenberger #6 PSA 10 (Gem) sold for $873 (eBay; 2/14)
— Frank Mahovlich #77 PSA 10 (Gem) sold for $2,180 (Memory Lane; 4/12)
— Cesare Maniago #40 PSA 10 (Gem) sold for $1,533.33 (eBay; 9/12)
— Cesare Maniago #99 PSA 9 (MT) sold for $668 (eBay; 3/14)
— Marcel Pronovost #46 PSA 10 (Gem) sold for $259 (eBay; 2/16)
— Henri Richard #82 PSA 10 (Gem) sold for $1,109 (eBay; 9/12)
— Henri Richard #82 PSA 10 (Gem) sold for $973 (eBay; 12/12)
— Henri Richard #82 PSA 10 (Gem) sold for $508 (eBay; 2/16)
— Terry Sawchuk #53 PSA 10 (Gem) sold for $436 (eBay; 9/12)
— Don Simmons #62 PSA 10 (Gem) sold for $1,297 (eBay; 6/12)
— Jean-Guy Talbot #81 PSA 9 (MT) sold for $514 (eBay; 12/06)
— Norm Ullman #52 PSA 10 (Gem) sold for $1,395 (eBay; 6/12)
— Norm Ullman #52 PSA 10 (Gem) sold for $342.76 (eBay; 2/16)
— Gump Worsley #98 PSA 10 (Gem) sold for $2,032 (eBay; 9/12)

1963-64 Topps

		VG 3	VgEx 4	EX 5	ExMt 6	NM 7	NmMt 8	NmMt+ 8.5	MT 9
1	Milt Schmidt CO	12	15	20	30	40	200		
2	Ed Johnston RC	15	20	25	35	50	80	100	300
3	Doug Mohns	8	10	12	15	30	80		
4	Tom Johnson	8	10	12	15	30	100		
5	Leo Boivin	8	10	12	15	30	80		
6	Bob McCord	6	8	10	12	30	80		
7	Ted Green	8	10	12	15	40	80		
8	Ed Westfall RC	15	20	25	30	40	80		
9	Charlie Burns	6	8	10	15	40	80		
10	Murray Oliver	8	10	12	15	30	60		
11	Johnny Bucyk	12	15	20	25	50	200		
12	Tom Williams	8	10	12	15	30	80		
13	Dean Prentice	8	10	12	15	30	80		
14	Bob Leiter	6	8	10	12	25	50	80	150
15	Andy Hebenton	6	8	10	12	25	50		
16	Jean-Guy Gendron	6	8	10	12	25	50		
17	Wayne Rivers	6	8	10	12	25	50		
18	Jerry Toppazzini	6	8	10	12	25	50		
19	Forbes Kennedy	6	8	10	12	25	50		
20	Orland Kurtenbach	8	10	12	15	30	80		
21	Bruins Team	20	25	30	40	60	200		
22	Billy Reay CO	8	10	12	15	30	60		
23	Glenn Hall	20	25	30	40	50	150	200	350
24	Denis DeJordy	8	10	12	15	30	80		
25	Pierre Pilote	8	10	12	15	30	80	120	300
26	Elmer Vasko	6	8	10	12	30	60		
27	Wayne Hillman	8	10	12	15	30	60	80	175
28	Al McNeil	6	8	10	12	25	50		
29	Howie Young	6	8	10	12	25	50		
30	Ed Van Impe RC	8	10	12	20	30	175		
31	Reg Fleming	8	10	12	15	25	50		
32	Bob Turner	6	8	10	12	25	50	60	200
33	Bobby Hull	50	60	100	150	250	350	450	500
34	Bill(Red) Hay	6	8	10	12	25	50		
35	Murray Balfour	6	8	10	12	25	50		
36	Stan Mikita	25	30	35	50	80	150	300	500
37	Ab McDonald	6	8	10	12	25	40	100	250
38	Ken Wharram	8	10	12	15	30	80		
39	Eric Nesterenko	8	10	12	15	30	60	100	350
40	Ron Murphy	6	8	10	12	25	50		
41	Chico Maki	6	8	10	12	25	50	60	200
42	John McKenzie	8	10	12	15	30	80		
43	Blackhawks Team	15	20	25	30	40	120		
44	George Sullivan	10	12	15	20	50	300		
45	Jacques Plante	25	30	40	60	100	200		
46	Gilles Villemure RC	15	20	25	30	40	100		
47	Doug Harvey	15	20	25	30	40	100		350
48	Harry Howell	8	10	12	15	30	80		
49	Albert Langlois	6	8	10	12	25	50	60	150
50	Jim Neilson	8	10	12	15	30	80		
51	Larry Cahan	6	8	10	12	25	50	60	150
52	Andy Bathgate	8	10	12	15	30	80	100	225
53	Don McKenney	6	8	10	12	25	50		
54	Vic Hadfield	8	10	12	15	30	80	100	175
55	Earl Ingarfield	6	8	10	12	25	50		
56	Camille Henry	6	8	10	12	25	50		
57	Rod Gilbert	15	20	25	30	40	100		
58	Phil Goyette	8	10	12	15	30	80	100	250
59	Don Marshall	8	10	12	15	30	60	80	150
60	Dick Meissner	6	8	10	12	25	50		
61	Val Fonteyne	6	8	10	12	25	50		
62	Ken Schinkel	6	8	10	12	25	50		
63	Jean Ratelle	15	20	25	30	40	80	100	300
64	Don Johns	6	8	10	12	25	50		
65	Rangers Team	20	25	30	40	50	125		
66	Checklist Card	40	50	80	100	200	400		

— Ab McDonald #37 PSA 9 (Mt) sold for $255 (eBay; 05/08)
— Glenn Hall #23 PSA 10 (GEM) sold for $3,195 (eBay; 4/16)
— Chico Maki #41 PSA 9 (Mt) sold for $365.28 (eBay; 5/12)
— Billy Reay #22 PSA 10 (GEM) sold for $1092 (eBay; 2/14)

1964-65 Topps

		VG 3	VgEx 4	EX 5	ExMt 6	NM 7	NmMt 8	NmMt+ 8.5	MT 9
1	Pit Martin RC	50	60	100	125	250	600	800	
2	Gilles Tremblay	12	15	20	25	50	225		
3	Terry Harper	12	15	20	30	80	150		
4	John Ferguson	20	25	30	40	60	120	250	
5	Elmer Vasko	10	12	15	20	60	150		
6	Terry Sawchuk UER	30	40	60	80	150	300		
7	Bill(Red) Hay	10	12	15	25	60	200		
8	Gary Bergman RC	15	25	40	70	100	300		
9	Doug Barkley	10	12	15	20	50	100	175	400
10	Bob McCord	10	12	15	20	50	100	150	400
11	Parker MacDonald	10	12	15	25	50	120		
12	Glenn Hall	25	30	50	100	200	350		
13	Albert Langlois	10	12	15	20	50	150		

		VG 3	VgEx 4	EX 5	ExMt 6	NM 7	NmMt 8	NmMt+ 8.5	MT 9
14	Camille Henry	20	30	50	80	150	350		
15	Norm Ullman	15	20	25	40	60	150		
16	Ab McDonald	10	15	15	40	60	120		
17	Charlie Hodge	10	12	15	20	80	175		
18	Orland Kurtenbach	10	12	15	25	60	150		
19	Dean Prentice	10	12	15	20	50	100		
20	Bobby Hull	100	150	200	350	500	800		
21	Ed Johnston	12	15	20	25	50	150		
22	Denis DeJordy	10	12	15	25	50	175		
23	Claude Provost	10	12	15	20	60	120		
24	Rod Gilbert	20	25	30	50	80	200		
25	Doug Mohns	10	12	25	40	60	100	150	300
26	Al McNeil	10	12	20	30	80	150		
27	Billy Harris	12	15	30	60	175	400		
28	Ken Wharram	12	15	25	50	120	400		
29	George Sullivan	10	12	15	20	50	80		
30	John McKenzie	10	12	15	40	50	100	150	450
31	Stan Mikita	40	50	60	100	150	300		
32	Ted Green	12	15	25	80	150	450		
33	Jean Beliveau	50	60	100	200	300	1,000		
34	Arnie Brown	10	12	15	20	50	100	150	400
35	Reg Fleming	10	12	15	20	40	120	175	400
36	Jim Mikol	10	12	15	20	50	80	125	400
37	Dave Balon	10	12	15	20	50	100		
38	Billy Reay CO	10	12	15	20	50	100	150	400
39	Marcel Pronovost	20	30	40	60	150	800		
40	Johnny Bower	25	30	40	50	80	175		
41	Wayne Hillman	10	5	20	30	50	80	125	700
42	Floyd Smith	10	12	15	25	50	80		
43	Toe Blake CO	15	20	25	50	80	200		
44	Red Kelly	15	20	25	30	50	120	175	400
45	Punch Imlach CO	15	20	25	30	50	120		
46	Dick Duff	15	20	25	30	50	120	150	250
47	Roger Crozier RC	25	30	40	60	100	225		
48	Henri Richard	40	60	100	150	250	1,200		
49	Larry Jeffrey	10	12	15	20	50	100		
50	Leo Boivin	10	12	15	20	50	100		
51	Ed Westfall	12	20	40	80	175	400		
52	Jean-Guy Talbot	10	12	20	30	40	135	175	400
53	Jacques Laperriere	12	15	20	30	50	135	175	500
54	1st Checklist	100	120	150	225	300	1,000		
55	2nd Checklist	120	200	350	600	1,200	1,500		
56	Ron Murphy	25	30	40	80	175	300		
57	Bob Baun	25	30	40	50	100	250		
58	Tom Williams SP	60	80	100	200	500	1,000		
59	Pierre Pilote SP	100	120	150	250	400	800		
60	Bob Pulford	25	30	35	50	100	250		
61	Red Berenson	25	30	35	50	100	200		
62	Vic Hadfield	25	30	35	50	100	300		
63	Bob Leiter	25	30	40	50	80	225		
64	Jim Pappin RC	25	30	40	60	150	250		
65	Earl Ingarfield	25	30	40	60	120	400		
66	Lou Angotti RC	25	30	40	60	175	600		
67	Rod Seiling RC	25	30	35	50	120	400		
68	Jacques Plante	60	80	100	175	250	500		
69	George Armstrong UER	40	50	60	80	120	250		
70	Milt Schmidt CO	25	30	35	50	100	250		
71	Eddie Shack	40	50	60	100	250	500		
72	Gary Dornhoefer SP RC	80	100	150	250	500	800		
73	Chico Maki SP	80	125	150	250	325	700		
74	Gilles Villemure SP	80	100	125	200	400	600		
75	Carl Brewer	25	30	35	50	100	300		
76	Bruce MacGregor	25	30	40	60	120	400		
77	Bob Nevin	25	30	40	60	120	300		
78	Ralph Backstrom	30	35	50	80	150	300		
79	Murray Oliver	20	25	40	60	100	250		
80	Bobby Rousseau SP	60	80	125	200	400			
81	Don McKenney	25	30	40	60	125	400		
82	Ted Lindsay	30	40	50	80	150	400		
83	Harry Howell	25	30	40	60	120	500		
84	Doug Robinson	20	25	30	60	120	300		
85	Frank Mahovlich	40	50	60	120	200	400		
86	Andy Bathgate	25	30	50	80	150	300		
87	Phil Goyette	25	30	40	60	100	250		
88	J.C. Tremblay	25	30	40	60	100	300		
89	Gordie Howe	200	250	300	400	600	1,750		
90	Murray Balfour	25	30	40	60	120	300		
91	Eric Nesterenko SP	60	100	120	175	400	1,000		
92	Marcel Paille SP RC	100	150	225	300	600	1,200		
93	Sid Abel CO	25	30	50	80	120	300		
94	Dave Keon	40	50	60	100	200	400		
95	Alex Delvecchio	30	40	50	80	150	400		
96	Bill Gadsby	25	30	40	60	175	350		
97	Don Marshall	25	30	35	50	100	500		
98	Bill Hicke SP	100	120	150	175	400	600		
99	Ron Stewart	25	30	40	50	120	300		
100	Johnny Bucyk	30	40	50	80	200	450		
101	Tom Johnson	25	30	35	50	100	250		
102	Tim Horton	70	80	100	150	350	700		
103	Jim Neilson	25	30	35	50	100	250		

		VG 3	VgEx 4	EX 5	ExMt 6	NM 7	NmMt 8	NmMt+ 8.5	MT 9
104	Allan Stanley	25	30	35	60	135	400		
105	Tim Horton AS SP	120	150	225	350	600	1,200		
106	Stan Mikita AS SP	100	120	150	250	400	750		
107	Bobby Hull AS	60	80	125	200	300	650		
108	Ken Wharram AS	25	30	40	60	150	500		
109	Pierre Pilote AS	25	30	40	80	120	250		
110	Glenn Hall AS	50	60	75	150	300	1,000		

— George Armstrong UER #69 PSA 9 sold for $698 (eBay; 12/15)
— Ralph Backstrom #78 PSA 9 (MT) sold for $483 (eBay; 2/07)
— Bob Baun #57 PSA 10 (Gem) sold for $4,207 (Memory Lane; 9/07)
— Toe Blake CO #43 PSA 9 sold for $359.10 (eBay; 3/16)
— Leo Boivin #50 PSA 9 (MT) sold for $491 (eBay; 3/07)
— Johnny Bucyk #100 PSA 9 (MT) sold for $1,617 (Memory Lane; 4/07)
— Checklist Card #54 PSA 9 (MT) sold for $3,271 (Memory Lane; 12/06)
— 2nd Checklist Card #55 PSA 8.5 (NmMt+) sold for $2,032 (eBay; 9/12)
— John Ferguson #4 PSA 9 (MT) sold for $1,042 (eBay; 3/07)
— Ted Green #32 PSA 8 (NmMt) sold for $890 (eBay; 2/07)
— Terry Harper #3 PSA 10 (Gem) sold for $1,789 (Memory Lane; 12/13)
— Terry Harper #3 PSA 9 (MT) sold for $519 (eBay; 12/06)
— Camille Henry #14 PSA 9 (MT) sold for $1,949 (eBay; 11/15)
— Wayne Hillman #41 PSA 9 (MT) sold for $545 (eBay; 12/06)
— Charlie Hodge #17 PSA 9 (MT) sold for $498 (eBay; 3/07)
— Harry Howell #83 PSA 9 (MT) sold for $1,013 (Goodwin; 2/07)
— Punch Imlach CO #45 PSA 9 (MT) sold for $607 (eBay; 12/06)
— Tom Johnson #101 PSA 9 (MT) sold for $1,241 (eBay; 9/12)
— Ed Johnston #21 PSA 9 (MT) sold for $775 (eBay; 6/12)
— Ed Johnston #21 PSA 9 (MT) sold for $675 (eBay; 3/16)
— Dave Keon #94 PSA 9 (MT) sold for $678.88 (eBay; 2/16)
— Bob Leiter #63 PSA 9 (MT) sold for $1,184 (Memory Lane; 6/12)
— Parker MacDonald #11 PSA 9 (MT) sold for $1,187 (Memory Lane; 4/07)
— Frank Mahovlich #85 PSA 9 (MT) sold for $2,563 (eBay; 9/12)
— Pit Martin #1 SGC 9 (MT) sold for $1,549 (Goodwin; 3/12)
— Jim Pappin #64 PSA 9 (MT) sold for $1,305 (Memory Lane; 4/07)
— Claude Provost #23 PSA 9 (MT) sold for $593 (eBay; 12/15)
— Bob Pulford #60 PSA 9 (MT) sold for $470 (eBay; 12/15)
— Terry Sawchuk #6 PSA 9 (MT) sold for $1,504 (eBay; 6/12)
— Milt Schmidt CO #70 PSA 9 (MT) sold for $888 (eBay; 2/16)
— Gilles Tremblay #2 PSA 9 (MT) sold for $1,435 (Memory Lane; 4/07)
— Norm Ullman #15 PSA 9 (MT) sold for $1,609 (eBay; 12/15)
— Ken Wharram AS #108 PSA 8.5 (NM MT+) sold for $569.99 (eBay; 12/15)
— Ken Wharram #28 PSA 9 (MT) sold for $1,024 (eBay; 3/16)

1965-66 Topps

		VG 3	VgEx 4	EX 5	ExMt 6	NM 7	NmMt 8	NmMt+ 8.5	MT 9
1	Toe Blake CO	25	35	40	60	150	700		
2	Gump Worsley	15	20	25	40	125	400		
3	Jacques Laperriere	6	8	10	12	25	60	80	135
4	Jean-Guy Talbot	6	8	10	20	50	200		
5	Ted Harris	6	8	20	50	80	200		
6	Jean Beliveau	25	30	35	50	80	150	200	400
7	Dick Duff	6	8	10	15	30	100		
8	Claude Provost DP	6	8	10	12	25	60		
9	Red Berenson	6	8	10	12	25	80		
10	John Ferguson	6	8	10	12	30	60		
11	Punch Imlach CO	6	8	10	12	40	120		
12	Terry Sawchuk	25	30	35	50	80	150	225	350
13	Bob Baun	6	8	10	12	25	50	80	150
14	Kent Douglas	6	8	10	12	25	60	80	150
15	Red Kelly	10	12	15	20	30	80	100	175
16	Jim Pappin	6	8	10	12	25	60	80	120
17	Dave Keon	15	20	25	30	60	150		
18	Bob Pulford	6	8	10	12	25	100		
19	George Armstrong	8	10	12	15	30	80	100	175
20	Orland Kurtenbach	6	8	10	12	25	60	80	150
21	Ed Giacomin RC	40	50	80	120	200	500		1,200
22	Harry Howell	6	8	10	12	25	80		500
23	Rod Seiling	6	8	10	12	25	80		
24	Mike McMahon	6	8	10	12	25	60		
25	Jean Ratelle	12	15	20	25	40	80	100	200
26	Doug Robinson	6	8	10	12	30	60		
27	Vic Hadfield	6	8	10	12	25	60	80	120
28	Garry Peters UER RC	6	8	10	12	25	60	80	120
29	Don Marshall	6	8	10	12	25	60	80	120
30	Bill Hicke	6	8	10	12	25	60	80	120
31	Gerry Cheevers RC	80	100	125	200	300	500		
32	Leo Boivin	6	8	10	12	25	60		
33	Albert Langlois	6	8	10	12	25	60		
34	Murray Oliver DP	6	8	10	12	25	60	80	150
35	Tom Williams	6	8	10	12	25	60	80	120
36	Ron Schock	6	8	10	12	25	100		
37	Ed Westfall	6	8	10	12	25	60		
38	Gary Dornhoefer	6	8	10	12	25	60		
39	Bob Dillabough	6	8	10	12	25	80		
40	Paul Popiel	6	8	10	12	25	60	80	150
41	Sid Abel CO	6	8	10	12	25	60		
42	Roger Crozier	6	8	10	15	30	100		
43	Doug Barkley	6	8	10	12	25	125		
44	Bill Gadsby	6	8	10	12	25	60	100	175
45	Bryan Watson RC	8	10	12	15	30	80	100	200

#	Player	VG 3	VgEx 4	EX 5	ExMt 6	NM 7	NmMt 8	NmMt+ 8.5	MT 9
46	Bob McCord	6	8	10	12	25	60		
47	Alex Delvecchio	8	10	12	15	30	80		
48	Andy Bathgate	8	10	12	15	30	80	100	300
49	Norm Ullman	8	10	12	15	30	100		
50	Ab McDonald	6	8	10	12	25	60		200
51	Paul Henderson RC	20	25	40	60	350	600		1,200
52	Pit Martin	6	8	10	12	25	60		
53	Billy Harris DP	6	8	10	12	25	80		
54	Billy Reay CO	6	8	15	20	25	60	100	200
55	Glenn Hall	15	20	30	50	120	400		
56	Pierre Pilote	8	10	12	15	30	100	120	200
57	Al McNeil	6	8	10	12	25	80		
58	Camille Henry	6	8	10	12	25	60	80	120
59	Bobby Hull	60	80	100	125	150	300	400	500
60	Stan Mikita	25	30	35	50	60	120	150	250
61	Ken Wharram	6	8	10	25	50	120		
62	Bill(Red) Hay	6	8	10	12	25	60		
63	Fred Stanfield RC	6	8	10	12	25	60	80	120
64	Dennis Hull RC DP	15	20	25	40	80	120	175	300
65	Ken Hodge RC	25	30	35	50	200	500		
66	Checklist Card	40	80	120	175	250	400		
67	Charlie Hodge	6	8	10	15	30	100		
68	Terry Harper	6	8	10	12	25	60		
69	J.C. Tremblay	6	8	10	12	25	100		
70	Bobby Rousseau DP	6	8	10	12	25	60		
71	Henri Richard	25	30	35	50	80	150	175	300
72	Dave Balon	6	8	10	12	25	60		
73	Ralph Backstrom	6	8	10	12	25	60	100	150
74	Jim Roberts RC	6	8	10	12	25	60		200
75	Claude Larose	6	8	10	12	25	60	80	150
76	Y.Cournoyer UER RC DP	50	80	100	200	350	500		
77	Johnny Bower DP	12	15	20	25	40	100	150	300
78	Carl Brewer	6	8	10	12	25	80	120	225
79	Tim Horton	25	30	35	50	100	250		
80	Marcel Pronovost	6	8	10	12	25	60		
81	Frank Mahovlich	25	30	35	50	80	120	175	300
82	Ron Ellis RC	15	20	25	40	60	150		
83	Larry Jeffrey	6	8	10	12	25	60	80	120
84	Peter Stemkowski RC	6	8	10	12	25	60	100	400
85	Eddie Joyal	6	8	10	12	25	60		120
86	Mike Walton RC	6	8	10	12	25	60	80	150
87	George Sullivan	6	8	10	12	25	60		
88	Don Simmons	6	8	10	12	25	60	100	175
89	Jim Neilson	6	8	10	12	25	60		
90	Arnie Brown	6	8	10	12	25	60		
91	Rod Gilbert	12	15	20	25	40	100	150	300
92	Phil Goyette	6	8	10	12	25	100		
93	Bob Nevin	6	8	10	12	25	60	100	175
94	John McKenzie	6	8	10	12	25	60	80	150
95	Ted Taylor RC	6	8	10	12	25	60		
96	Milt Schmidt CO DP	6	8	10	25	50	100	200	400
97	Ed Johnston	6	8	10	12	40	120		
98	Ted Green	6	8	10	15	40	80		
99	Don Awrey RC	6	8	10	20	50	200		
100	Bob Woytowich DP	6	8	10	12	25	60	100	250
101	Johnny Bucyk	10	12	15	20	60	100		
102	Dean Prentice	6	8	10	12	25	60		
103	Ron Stewart	6	8	10	12	25	60		
104	Reg Fleming	6	8	10	15	50	200		
105	Parker MacDonald	6	8	10	15	40	120		
106	Hank Bassen	6	8	10	12	25	60	80	150
107	Gary Bergman	6	8	10	12	25	60	80	250
108	Gordie Howe DP	40	50	60	100	175	600		
109	Floyd Smith	6	8	10	12	25	60		
110	Bruce MacGregor	6	8	10	12	25	60	80	150
111	Ron Murphy	6	8	10	12	25	80		
112	Don McKenney	6	8	10	12	25	60		
113	Denis DeJordy DP	6	8	10	12	25	60	100	250
114	Elmer Vasko	6	8	10	12	50	120		
115	Matt Ravlich	6	8	10	12	25	60	100	200
116	Phil Esposito RC	150	200	300	400	700	1,000	1,800	4,500
117	Chico Maki	6	8	10	12	25	60		
118	Doug Mohns	6	8	10	12	25	80		
119	Eric Nesterenko	6	8	10	12	25	60	100	250
120	Pat Stapleton	6	8	10	12	25	75	100	250
121	Checklist Card	50	75	150	200	250	400		
122	Gordie Howe 600 SP	125	200	225	250	400	800		
123	Toronto Maple Leafs SP	20	25	30	60	100	175		
124	Chicago Blackhawks SP	20	25	30	60	100	150		
125	Detroit Red Wings SP	30	40	50	80	150	350		
126	Montreal Canadiens SP	30	40	50	60	80	100	200	500
127	New York Rangers SP	30	40	50	80	200			
128	Boston Bruins SP	60	100	150	250	300	450		

— Toe Blake CO #1 PSA 9 (Mint) sold for $390 (eBay; 1/16)
— Gerry Cheevers #31 SGC 9 (Mint) sold for $3,149 (Goodwin; 3/12)
— Gerry Cheevers #31 PSA 9 (Mint) sold for $3,715 (eBay; 2/16)
— Yvan Cournoyer #76 PSA 10 (Gem) sold for $3,269 (eBay; 12/11)
— Yvan Cournoyer #76 PSA 9 (Mint) sold for $2,756 (eBay; 3/14)
— Yvan Cournoyer #76 PSA 9 (Mint) sold for $2,632.89 (eBay; 4/16)
— Kent Douglas #14 PSA 10 (Gem) sold for $426.99 (eBay; 3/16)

— Ron Ellis #82 PSA 10 (Gem) sold for $818 (eBay; 3/13)
— Ed Giacomin #21 SGC 8.5 (NrMt+) sold for $1,627 (Goodwin; 3/12)
— Phil Doyette #92 PSA 9 (Mint) sold for $415 (eBay; 3/16)
— Paul Henderson #51 PSA 9 (MT) sold for $1,419 (eBay; 10/15)
— Punch Imlach CO #11 PSA 8.5 (NrMt+) sold for $293.98 (eBay; 12/15)
— Pit Martin #53 PSA 10 (Gem) sold for $556.99 (eBay; 3/16)
— Mike McMahon #24 PSA 10 (Gem) sold for $528 (eBay; 2/07)
— Terry Sawchuk #12 SGC 9 (Mint) sold for $382 (Goodwin; 3/12)
— Pat Stapleton #120 PSA 9 (Mint) sold for $323 (eBay; 3/08)
— Peter Stemkowski #84 PSA 10 (Gem) sold for $719 (eBay; 3/16)
— George Sullivan #87 PSA 9 (Mint) sold for $388 (eBay; 3/08)
— Ted Taylor #95 PSA 9 (MT) sold for $278 (eBay; 12/06)

1966-67 Topps

#	Player	VG 3	VgEx 4	EX 5	ExMt 6	NM 7	NmMt 8	NmMt+ 8.5	MT 9
1	Toe Blake CO	25	30	40	80	500	1,250		
2	Gump Worsley	12	20	30	40	135	750		
3	Jean-Guy Talbot	6	8	10	40	150	800		
4	Gilles Tremblay	6	8	10	15	40	120		
5	J.C. Tremblay	8	10	12	20	50	200		
6	Jim Roberts	8	10	15	30	80			
7	Bobby Rousseau	6	8	10	15	100	250		
8	Henri Richard	20	25	30	50	80	350		
9	Claude Provost	6	8	10	12	40	200		
10	Claude Larose	8	10	12	15	60	300		
11	Punch Imlach CO	8	10	12	15	40	300		
12	Johnny Bower	15	20	25	30	80	400		
13	Terry Sawchuk	30	40	50	60	80	250		
14	Mike Walton	8	10	12	15	40	120		
15	Pete Stemkowski	6	8	10	15	30	120		
16	Allan Stanley	8	10	12	15	40	100		
17	Eddie Shack	20	25	30	40	60	150		
18	Brit Selby RC	8	10	12	15	40	100		
19	Bob Pulford	8	10	12	15	40	100		
20	Marcel Pronovost	8	10	12	15	40	350		
21	Emile Francis RC CO	12	15	20	25	60	350		
22	Rod Seiling	6	8	10	15	40	100		
23	Ed Giacomin	30	40	50	60	100	250		
24	Don Marshall	8	10	12	15	30	100		
25	Orland Kurtenbach	6	8	10	15	100	600		
26	Rod Gilbert	12	15	20	25	60	200		
27	Bob Nevin	6	8	10	15	30	100		
28	Phil Goyette	6	8	10	15	30	100		
29	Jean Ratelle	12	15	20	25	60	135		
30	Earl Ingarfield	6	8	10	15	30	300		
31	Harry Sinden RC CO	25	30	40	50	150	400		
32	Ed Westfall	8	10	12	15	40	150		
33	Joe Watson RC	8	10	12	15	40	150		
34	Bob Woytowich	6	8	10	15	30	100		
35	Bobby Orr RC	3,500	4,500	6,000	7,000	8,000	22,000		
36	Gilles Marotte RC	6	8	10	20	60	175		
37	Ted Green	8	10	12	15	40	100		
38	Tom Williams	6	8	10	15	30	200		
39	Johnny Bucyk	20	25	30	40	60	150		
40	Wayne Connelly	6	8	10	15	60	600		
41	Pit Martin	8	10	12	15	40	100		
42	Sid Abel CO	6	8	10	30	50	120		
43	Roger Crozier	8	10	12	15	40	200		
44	Andy Bathgate	8	10	12	15	40	120		
45	Dean Prentice	6	8	10	15	30	175		
46	Paul Henderson	10	12	15	20	80	150		
47	Gary Bergman	6	8	10	15	30	100		
48	Bryan Watson	8	10	12	15	40	120		
49	Bob Wall	6	8	10	15	30	150		
50	Leo Boivin	8	10	12	15	40	80		
51	Bert Marshall	6	10	15	30	100	350		
52	Norm Ullman	10	12	15	20	50	100		
53	Billy Reay CO	8	10	12	15	40	120		
54	Glenn Hall	15	20	25	30	60	300		
55	Wally Boyer	6	8	10	15	30	200		
56	Fred Stanfield	8	10	12	15	40	150		
57	Pat Stapleton	8	10	12	15	40	150		
58	Matt Ravlich	6	8	10	15	30	100		
59	Pierre Pilote	8	10	12	15	40	120		
60	Eric Nesterenko	8	10	12	15	40	200		
61	Doug Mohns	8	10	12	15	40	120		
62	Stan Mikita	25	30	40	50	100	400		
63	Phil Esposito	40	50	60	100	150	300		
64	Bobby Hull LL	40	50	60	100	200	450		
65	C.Hodge/Worsley	15	20	25	30	80	300		
66	Checklist Card	100	125	200	400	500	2,000		
67	Jacques Laperriere	8	10	12	15	100	400		
68	Terry Harper	6	8	10	15	30	135		
69	Ted Harris	6	8	10	15	30	120		
70	John Ferguson	8	10	12	25	80	300		
71	Dick Duff	8	10	12	20	60	200		
72	Yvan Cournoyer	25	30	40	50	100	200		
73	Jean Beliveau	30	40	50	60	150	300		
74	Dave Balon	6	8	10	15	30	100		

		VG 3	VgEx 4	EX 5	ExMt 6	NM 7	NmMt 8	NmMt+ 8.5	MT 9
75	Ralph Backstrom	8	10	12	15	40	120		
76	Jim Pappin	6	8	10	15	40	100		
77	Frank Mahovlich	20	25	30	40	80	600		
78	Dave Keon	20	25	30	40	80	200		
79	Red Kelly	12	15	20	25	50	100		
80	Tim Horton	25	30	40	50	80	200		
81	Ron Ellis	8	10	12	15	50	100		
82	Kent Douglas	6	8	10	15	40	150		
83	Bob Baun	8	10	12	15	50	100		
84	George Armstrong	10	12	15	20	50	120		
85	Bernie Geoffrion	15	20	25	30	50	250		
86	Vic Hadfield	8	10	12	15	40	200		
87	Wayne Hillman	6	8	10	15	30	120		
88	Jim Neilson	6	8	10	15	30	120		
89	Al McNeil	6	8	10	15	30	120		
90	Arnie Brown	6	8	10	15	30	200		
91	Harry Howell	8	10	12	15	40	120		
92	Red Berenson	8	10	12	15	40	100		
93	Reg Fleming	6	8	10	15	30	100		
94	Ron Stewart	6	8	10	15	30	120		
95	Murray Oliver	6	8	10	15	30	200		
96	Ron Murphy	6	8	10	15	30	100		
97	John McKenzie	8	10	12	15	50	125		
98	Bob Dillabough	6	8	10	15	30	100		
99	Ed Johnston	8	10	12	15	40	100		
100	Ron Schock	6	8	10	15	40	450		
101	Dallas Smith	6	8	10	15	30	100		
102	Alex Delvecchio	15	20	30	40	60	200		
103	Peter Mahovlich RC	20	25	30	40	80	200		
104	Bruce MacGregor	6	8	10	15	40	300		
105	Murray Hall	6	8	10	15	30	100		
106	Floyd Smith	6	8	10	15	30	120		
107	Hank Bassen	8	10	12	15	40	175		
108	Val Fonteyne	6	8	10	15	30	100		
109	Gordie Howe	80	100	150	250	350	1,500		
110	Chico Maki	6	8	10	15	30	175		
111	Doug Jarrett	6	8	12	20	60	150		
112	Bobby Hull	50	60	80	125	200	400		
113	Dennis Hull	8	10	12	15	60	200		
114	Ken Hodge	10	12	15	20	50	200		
115	Denis DeJordy	8	10	12	15	40	100		
116	Lou Angotti	6	8	10	15	30	150		
117	Ken Wharram	6	8	10	15	40	150		
118	Montreal Canadiens/Team Card	15	20	25	40	100	250		
119	Detroit Red Wings/Team Card	15	20	25	30	80	400		
120	Checklist Card	100	125	200	300	500			
121	Gordie Howe AS	40	50	60	80	225	700		
122	Jacques Laperriere AS	8	10	12	30	80	300		
123	Pierre Pilote AS	8	10	12	15	40	500		
124	Stan Mikita AS	15	20	50	100	250	350		
125	Bobby Hull AS	40	50	60	80	100	250		
126	Glenn Hall AS	20	25	30	40	80	250		
127	Jean Beliveau AS	20	25	40	80	150	500		
128	Allan Stanley AS	8	10	15	25	80	500		
129	Pat Stapleton AS	8	10	12	20	175	400		
130	Gump Worsley AS	20	25	30	60	150	350		
131	Frank Mahovlich AS	25	30	50	100	400			
132	Bobby Rousseau AS	25	30	40	120	400	2,500		

Andy Bathgate #44 PSA 9 (MT) sold for $891 (ebay; 3/14)
Jean Beliveau #73 PSA 8.5 (NmMt+) sold for $1,500 (ebay; 3/14)
Jean Beliveau AS #127 PSA 8 (NmMt) sold for $1,149 (Memory Lane; 9/07)
Wally Boyer #55 PSA 9 (Mint) sold for $829 (eBay; 3/16)
Gerry Cheevers #31 PSA 10 (Gem) sold for $3,558 (eBay; 5/09)
Wayne Connelly #40 PSA 8 (NmMt) sold for $774 (eBay; 5/12)
Denis DeJordy #115 PSA 9 (MT) sold for $1,812 (Mile High; 10/15)
Bernie Geoffrion #85 PSA 9 (MT) sold for $3,630 (Mile High; 10/15)
Bobby Hull AS #125 PSA 9 (MT) sold for $1,834 (eBay; 10/15)
Doug Jarrett #111 PSA 9 (MT) sold for $1,994 (Mile High; 10/15)
Frank Mahovlich AS #131 PSA 8 (NmMT) sold for $1,278 (eBay; 4/12)
Al McNeil #89 PSA 9 (Mint) sold for $844.95 (eBay; 3/14)
Stan Mikita AS #124 PSA 9 (MT) sold for $2,948 (Mile High; 10/15)
Bobby Orr #35 PSA 9 (MT) sold for $47,923 (Mastro; 4/07)
Bobby Orr #35 BGS 9.5 (GEM) sold for $5,789.44 (eBay; 5/12)
Pierre Pilote AS #123 PSA 9 (Mt) sold for $3,537 (Mile High; 10/15)
Pierre Pilote AS #123 PSA 9 (MT) sold for $1,118.88 (eBay; 1/16)
Jim Roberts #6 PSA 9 (MT) sold for $2,228 (Mile High; 10/15)
Bobby Rousseau #132 PSA 8 (NmMt) sold for $2,720 (eBay; 1/13)
Terry Sawchuk #13 PSA 9 (MT) sold for $1,312 (ebay; 1/14)
Terry Sawchuk #13 PSA 9 (MT) sold for $1,187 (Memory Lane; 9/07)
Eddie Shack #17 PSA 9 (MT) sold for $490 (eBay; 7/08)

1967-68 Topps

		VG 3	VgEx 4	EX 5	ExMt 6	NM 7	NmMt 8	NmMt+ 8.5	MT 9
1	Gump Worsley	20	25	35	60	100	300	500	
2	Dick Duff	6	8	10	30	150	500		
3	Jacques Lemaire RC	25	30	60	100	200	350		
4	Claude Larose	8	10	12	15	40	80		
5	Gilles Tremblay	6	8	10	12	25	40	50	120
6	Terry Harper	6	8	10	12	25	40	50	120

		VG 3	VgEx 4	EX 5	ExMt 6	NM 7	NmMt 8	NmMt+ 8.5	MT 9
7	Jacques Laperriere	6	8	10	12	25	50	60	200
8	Garry Monahan	6	8	10	12	25	40	50	100
9	Carol Vadnais RC	6	8	10	12	25	40	50	100
10	Ted Harris	6	8	10	12	25	40	50	100
11	Dave Keon	10	12	15	12	30	60	80	150
12	Pete Stemkowski	6	8	10	12	25	40		150
13	Allan Stanley	6	8	10	12	25	40	50	120
14	Ron Ellis	6	8	10	12	25	50	60	150
15	Mike Walton	6	8	10	12	25	40	50	100
16	Tim Horton	15	20	25	30	50	100		
17	Brian Conacher	6	8	10	12	25	40	50	100
18	Bruce Gamble	6	8	10	12	25	40	50	100
19	Bob Pulford	6	8	10	12	25	50		
20	Duane Rupp	6	8	10	12	25	40		
21	Larry Jeffrey	6	8	10	12	25	40		
22	Wayne Hillman	6	8	10	12	25	40		
23	Don Marshall	6	8	10	12	25	50		
24	Red Berenson	6	8	10	12	25	40	50	120
25	Phil Goyette	6	8	10	12	25	40	50	100
26	Camille Henry	6	8	10	12	25	40	50	80
27	Rod Seiling	6	8	10	12	25	40		
28	Bob Nevin	6	8	10	12	25	40	50	120
29	Bernie Geoffrion	15	20	25	30	40	50	60	120
30	Reg Fleming	6	8	10	12	25	40	60	120
31	Jean Ratelle	8	10	12	15	30	50	60	120
32	Phil Esposito	25	30	40	60	80	150	175	300
33	Derek Sanderson RC	30	40	50	80	150	300		
34	Eddie Shack	12	15	20	25	40	60	80	120
35	Ross Lonsberry RC	6	8	10	12	25	50	60	150
36	Fred Stanfield	6	8	10	12	25	40	50	100
37	Don Awrey UER	6	8	10	12	25	40	50	80
38	Glen Sather RC	15	20	25	30	50	100	125	250
39	John McKenzie	6	8	10	12	25	40	50	100
40	Tom Williams	6	8	10	12	25	40	50	100
41	Dallas Smith	6	8	10	12	25	40	60	120
42	Johnny Bucyk	10	12	15	20	30	60	100	175
43	Gordie Howe	30	40	50	80	125	350	450	800
44	Gary Jarrett	6	8	10	12	25	40		
45	Dean Prentice	6	8	10	12	25	40		
46	Bert Marshall	6	8	10	12	25	40		
47	Gary Bergman	6	8	10	12	25	40	60	120
48	Roger Crozier	6	8	10	12	25	50		
49	Howie Young	6	8	10	12	25	40	50	100
50	Doug Roberts	6	8	10	12	25	40	60	120
51	Alex Delvecchio	10	12	15	20	30	60		
52	Floyd Smith	6	8	10	12	25	40	60	120
53	Doug Shelton	6	8	10	12	25	40		
54	Gerry Goyer	6	8	10	12	25	40	50	150
55	Wayne Maki	6	8	10	12	25	60	80	120
56	Dennis Hull	6	8	10	12	25	50		
57	Dave Dryden RC	8	10	12	15	40	60	80	200
58	Paul Terbenche	6	8	10	12	25	40	50	200
59	Gilles Marotte	6	8	10	12	25	40	60	120
60	Eric Nesterenko	6	8	10	12	25	40	60	120
61	Pat Stapleton	6	8	10	12	25	40	50	100
62	Pierre Pilote	6	8	10	12	30	60	80	120
63	Doug Mohns	6	8	10	12	25	40		
64	Stan Mikita Triple	15	20	25	30	50	100		
65	G.Hall/D.DeJordy	10	12	15	20	30	80		
66	Checklist Card	50	60	100	150	250	450		
67	Ralph Backstrom	6	8	10	12	25	50		
68	Bobby Rousseau	6	8	10	12	25	40	60	120
69	John Ferguson	6	8	10	15	30	80	100	200
70	Yvan Cournoyer	15	20	25	30	50	80	100	200
71	Claude Provost	6	8	10	12	25	40	60	120
72	Henri Richard	12	15	20	25	40	80	100	200
73	J.C. Tremblay	6	8	10	12	25	50	60	150
74	Jean Beliveau	20	25	30	40	60	135	150	350
75	Rogatien Vachon RC	25	30	40	60	125	300	300	800
76	Johnny Bower	10	12	15	20	30	80	100	200
77	Wayne Carleton	6	8	10	12	25	40	60	120
78	Jim Pappin	6	8	10	12	25	40	50	100
79	Frank Mahovlich	12	15	20	25	40	100	120	200
80	Larry Hillman	6	8	10	12	25	40	50	100
81	Marcel Pronovost	6	8	10	12	25	60	80	120
82	Murray Oliver	6	8	10	12	25	40	60	120
83	George Armstrong	8	10	12	15	30	60	80	120
84	Harry Howell	6	8	10	12	25	40	60	100
85	Ed Giacomin	15	20	25	30	40	80	100	175
86	Gilles Villemure	6	8	10	12	40	80	100	150
87	Orland Kurtenbach	6	8	10	12	25	40	50	80
88	Vic Hadfield	6	8	10	12	25	40	50	100
89	Arnie Brown	6	8	10	12	25	40	60	120
90	Rod Gilbert	8	10	12	15	30	80	100	175
91	Jim Neilson	6	8	10	12	25	40	50	100
92	Bobby Orr	250	400	500	600	800	2,250	3,000	5,500
93	Skip Krake UER RC	6	8	10	12	25	40	50	100
94	Ted Green	6	8	10	12	25	40	50	100
95	Ed Westfall	6	8	10	12	25	40	50	100
96	Ed Johnston	6	8	10	12	25	40	50	100

#	Player	VG 3	VgEx 4	EX 5	ExMt 6	NM 7	NmMt 8	NmMt+ 8.5	MT 9
97	Gary Doak RC	6	8	10	12	30	40	50	100
98	Ken Hodge	6	8	10	12	30	50		
99	Gerry Cheevers	20	25	30	40	60	100	120	250
100	Ron Murphy	6	8	10	12	25	40	50	100
101	Norm Ullman	8	10	12	15	30	50	60	150
102	Bruce MacGregor	6	8	10	12	25	40	50	100
103	Paul Henderson	6	8	10	12	25	50		
104	Jean-Guy Talbot	6	8	10	12	25	40	60	120
105	Bart Crashley	6	8	10	12	25	40	50	100
106	Roy Edwards	6	8	10	12	25	50	60	135
107	Jim Watson	6	8	10	12	25	40	50	100
108	Ted Hampson	6	8	10	12	30	100		
109	Bill Orban	6	8	10	12	25	40	50	100
110	Geoffrey Powis	6	8	10	12	25	40	50	150
111	Chico Maki	6	8	10	12	25	40	50	100
112	Doug Jarrett	6	8	10	12	25	40	50	135
113	Bobby Hull	30	40	50	80	150	200	250	800
114	Stan Mikita	20	25	30	40	60	120	150	300
115	Denis DeJordy	6	8	10	12	25	40	50	100
116	Pit Martin	6	8	10	12	25	50		
117	Ken Wharram	6	8	10	12	25	40	50	100
118	Bobby Orr Calder	80	100	125	200	300	500	600	800
119	Harry Howell Norris	6	8	10	12	25	40	60	135
120	Checklist Card	60	80	100	150	250	400	500	800
121	Harry Howell AS	6	8	10	12	25	40	50	175
122	Pierre Pilote AS	6	8	10	12	30	60	75	120
123	Ed Giacomin AS	8	10	12	15	30	50	60	120
124	Bobby Hull AS	30	40	50	60	100	150	175	300
125	Ken Wharram AS	6	8	10	12	25	40	60	120
126	Stan Mikita AS	12	15	20	25	40	80	120	250
127	Tim Horton AS	10	12	15	20	30	80	100	150
128	Bobby Orr AS	125	150	200	250	350	500	800	1,500
129	Glenn Hall AS	10	12	15	20	30	50	60	120
130	Don Marshall AS	6	8	10	12	25	40	50	200
131	Gordie Howe AS	30	40	50	80	125	200	250	400
132	Norm Ullman AS	10	12	15	20	40	175		

— Checklist Card #66 PSA 9 (Mint) sold for $1,013 (eBay; 3/16)
— Ron Ellis #14 PSA 9 (Mint) sold for $365 (eBay; 3/08)
— Reg Flemming #30 PSA 10 (Gem) sold for $434 (eBay; 2/14)
— Harry Howell #84 PSA 10 (Gem) sold for $505 (eBay; 10/08)
— Harry Howell Norris #119 PSA 10 (Gem) sold for $640 (eBay; 8/12)
— Bruce MacGregor ##102 PSA 10 (Gem) sold for $364.44 (eBay; 2/16)
— Stan Mikita AS #126 PSA 10 (Gem) sold for $571.20 (Mile High 5/12)
— Bobby Orr AS #128 PSA 10 (Gem) sold for $6,655 (eBay; 2/12)
— Pierre Pilote AS #122 PSA 10 (Gem) sold for $711 (eBay; 8/07)
— Jean Ratelle #31 PSA 10 (Gem) sold for $298.98 (eBay; 8/12)
— Fred Stanfield #36 PSA 9 (Mint) sold for $359 (eBay; 3/08)
— J.C. Tremblay #73 PSA 10 (Gem) sold for $1,034 (eBay; 3/16)

1968-69 O-Pee-Chee

#	Player	VG 3	VgEx 4	EX 5	ExMt 6	NM 7	NmMt 8	NmMt+ 8.5	MT 9
1	Doug Harvey	25	30	40	80	350	400		
2	Bobby Orr	150	200	300	450	1,600			
3	Don Awrey UER	6	8	10	15	30	60		
4	Ted Green	6	8	10	15	30	60		
5	Johnny Bucyk	10	15	50	80	150			
6	Derek Sanderson	20	25	30	40	60	120		
7	Phil Esposito	20	25	30	40	60	120		
8	Ken Hodge	6	8	10	15	40	175		
9	John McKenzie	6	8	10	15	30	60	80	150
10	Fred Stanfield	6	8	10	20	30	80		
11	Tom Williams	6	8	10	15	30	50	60	175
12	Denis DeJordy	6	8	10	15	60	200		
13	Lou Angotti	6	8	10	15	30	60		
14	Gilles Marotte	6	8	10	15	30	60		
15	Pat Stapleton	6	8	10	15	40	125		
16	Bobby Hull	30	40	50	60	150	250		
17	Chico Maki	6	8	10	15	100	175		
18	Pit Martin	6	8	10	15	60	135		
19	Doug Mohns	6	8	10	15	40	150		
20	John Ferguson	6	8	12	30	80	600		
21	Jim Pappin	6	8	10	15	80	100		
22	Ken Wharram	6	8	10	15	30	60		
23	Roger Crozier	6	8	10	25	100			
24	Bob Baun	6	8	10	20	50	120		
25	Gary Bergman	6	8	12	30	80			
26	Kent Douglas	6	8	12	30	150	250		
27	Ron Harris	6	8	10	15	30	60		
28	Alex Delvecchio	8	10	12	20	60	200		
29	Gordie Howe	50	60	80	100	150	600	800	1,600
30	Bruce MacGregor	6	8	10	15	30	50	80	150
31	Frank Mahovlich	10	12	15	20	80	200		
32	Dean Prentice	6	8	10	15	30	60		
33	Pete Stemkowski	6	8	10	15	30	60		
34	Terry Sawchuk	20	25	40	50	100	200		
35	Larry Cahan	6	8	10	15	30	60		
36	Real Lemieux	6	8	10	15	30	60		
37	Bill White RC	6	8	10	15	30	60		
38	Gord Labossiere RC	6	8	10	15	30	60		
39	Ted Irvine RC	6	8	10	15	30	60		
40	Eddie Joyal	6	8	10	15	30	50	60	100
41	Dale Rolfe	6	8	10	15	30	60		
42	Lowell MacDonald RC	6	8	10	15	30	60		
43	Skip Krake UER	6	8	10	15	30	60		
44	Terry Gray	6	8	10	25	60	200		
45	Cesare Maniago	6	8	10	15	40	80	100	150
46	Mike McMahon	6	8	10	15	30	60		
47	Wayne Hillman	6	8	10	15	25	60		
48	Larry Hillman	6	8	10	15	30	60		
49	Bob Woytowich	6	8	15	30	125	250		
50	Wayne Connelly	6	8	10	15	30	60		
51	Claude Larose	6	8	10	15	30	175		
52	Danny Grant RC	10	12	15	20	80	175		
53	Andre Boudrias	6	8	10	15	30	60		
54	Ray Cullen RC	6	8	10	15	30	60	80	150
55	Parker MacDonald	6	8	10	15	30	300		
56	Gump Worsley	8	10	15	40	200	400		
57	Terry Harper	6	8	10	15	30	60		
58	Jacques Laperriere	6	8	10	15	30	60		
59	J.C. Tremblay	6	8	10	15	30	80		
60	Ralph Backstrom	6	8	10	20	60	120		
61	Checklist 2	60	80	150	250	350	600		
62	Yvan Cournoyer	10	12	15	20	50	175		
63	Jacques Lemaire	12	15	20	25	60	200		
64	Mickey Redmond RC	30	40	50	80	150	350		
65	Bobby Rousseau	6	8	10	15	30	80		
66	Gilles Tremblay	6	8	10	15	30	60		
67	Ed Giacomin	10	12	15	20	40	80		
68	Arnie Brown	6	8	10	15	30	60		
69	Harry Howell	6	8	12	25	60	200		
70	Al Hamilton	6	8	10	15	30	60		
71	Rod Seiling	6	8	12	25	100	300		
72	Rod Gilbert	6	8	10	15	40	80		
73	Phil Goyette	6	8	10	15	30	100		
74	Larry Jeffrey	6	8	10	15	30	80		
75	Don Marshall	6	8	10	15	30	60		
76	Bob Nevin	6	8	10	15	30	60		
77	Jean Ratelle	6	8	10	15	30	60		
78	Charlie Hodge	6	8	10	15	30	200		
79	Bert Marshall	6	8	10	15	30	60		
80	Billy Harris	6	8	10	15	30	100		
81	Carol Vadnais	6	8	10	15	30	60		
82	Howie Young	6	8	10	15	30	60		
83	John Brenneman	6	8	10	15	30	80		
84	Gerry Ehman	6	8	10	15	30			
85	Ted Hampson	6	8	10	15	30	60		
86	Bill Hicke	6	8	10	15	30	80		
87	Gary Jarrett	6	8	10	15	30	60		
88	Doug Roberts	6	8	10	15	30	50		
89	Bernie Parent RC	125	200	250	350	1,300	2,000		
90	Joe Watson	6	8	10	15	30	60		
91	Ed Van Impe	6	8	10	15	30	80		
92	Larry Zeidel	6	8	10	15	30	120		
93	John Miszuk	6	8	10	15	30	50		
94	Gary Dornhoefer	6	8	10	15	30	60		
95	Leon Rochefort	6	8	10	15	30	60		
96	Brit Selby	6	8	10	15	30	60		
97	Forbes Kennedy	6	8	10	15	30	60		
98	Ed Hoekstra RC	6	8	10	15	60	150		
99	Garry Peters	6	8	10	20	30	60		
100	Les Binkley RC	10	12	15	25	100	150		
101	Leo Boivin	6	8	10	20	30	80		
102	Earl Ingarfield	6	8	10	15	30	60		
103	Lou Angotti	6	8	10	15	30	60		
104	Andy Bathgate	6	8	10	15	30	100		
105	Wally Boyer	6	8	10	15	30	80		
106	Ken Schinkel	6	8	10	15	30	60		
107	Ab McDonald	6	8	10	15	30	150		
108	Charlie Burns	6	8	10	15	40	80		
109	Val Fonteyne	6	8	10	15	30	60	80	200
110	Noel Price	6	8	10	15	30	50	60	200
111	Glenn Hall	10	12	15	20	40	100		
112	Bob Plager RC	12	15	20	25	50	100		
113	Jim Roberts	6	8	10	15	30	60		
114	Red Berenson	6	8	10	15	30	60		
115	Larry Keenan	6	8	10	15	30	60		
116	Camille Henry	6	8	10	15	30	150		
117	Gary Sabourin	6	8	10	15	40	80		
118	Ron Schock	6	8	15	50	150	300		
119	Gary Veneruzzo	6	8	10	15	30	60		
120	Gary Melnyk	6	8	10	15	30	100		
121	Checklist 2	80	125	250	400	550			
122	Johnny Bower	8	15	15	25	80	300		
123	Tim Horton	12	15	20	25	50	100		
124	Pierre Pilote	6	8	10	15	30	60		
125	Marcel Pronovost	6	8	10	15	30	60		
126	Ron Ellis	6	8	10	15	30	80		
127	Paul Henderson	6	8	10	15	30	80		
128	Al Arbour	6	8	10	15	30	150		

#	Player	VG 3	VgEx 4	EX 5	ExMt 6	NM 7	NmMt 8	NmMt+ 8.5	MT 9
129	Bob Pulford	6	8	10	15	30	80		
130	Floyd Smith	6	8	10	15	30	80		
131	Norm Ullman	6	8	20	25	80			
132	Mike Walton	6	8	12	25	80			
133	Ed Johnston	6	8	12	25	150			
134	Glen Sather	8	10	12	20	60	120		
135	Ed Westfall	6	8	10	15	30	80		
136	Dallas Smith	6	8	10	15	30	60		
137	Eddie Shack	6	8	10	15	30	60		
138	Gary Doak	6	8	10	15	25	60	80	100
139	Ron Murphy	6	8	10	15	80	200		
140	Gerry Cheevers	10	12	15	20	50	100		
141	Bob Falkenberg	6	8	10	15	30	60		
142	Garry Unger DP RC	15	20	25	30	80	150		
143	Peter Mahovlich	6	8	10	15	30	60		
144	Roy Edwards	6	8	10	15	30	80		
145	Gary Bauman	6	8	10	15	100	200		
146	Bob McCord	6	8	10	15	30	60		
147	Elmer Vasko	6	8	10	15	30	60		
148	Bill Goldsworthy RC	6	8	10	15	30	100		
149	Jean-Paul Parise RC	6	8	10	15	40	120		
150	Dave Dryden	6	8	10	15	30	100		
151	Howie Young	6	8	10	15	25	50		
152	Matt Ravlich	6	8	10	15	30	120		
153	Dennis Hull	6	8	10	15	40	100		
154	Eric Nesterenko	6	8	10	15	30	60		125
155	Stan Mikita	15	20	25	30	50	100		
156	Bob Wall	6	8	10	15	30	80		
157	Dave Amadio	6	8	10	15	30	60		
158	Howie Hughes	6	8	10	15	60	120		
159	Bill Flett RC	6	8	10	15	30	80		
160	Doug Robinson	6	8	10	15	30	60		125
161	Dick Duff	6	8	10	15	25	40		
162	Ted Harris	6	8	10	15	30	60		
163	Claude Provost	6	8	10	15	25	50		
164	Rogatien Vachon	20	25	30	40	100	200		
165	Henri Richard	10	12	15	20	80	150		
166	Jean Beliveau	20	25	30	40	60	200		
167	Reg Fleming	6	8	10	15	30	80		
168	Ron Stewart	6	8	10	15	30	80		
169	Dave Balon	6	8	10	15	30	80		
170	Orland Kurtenbach	6	8	10	15	30	80		
171	Vic Hadfield	6	8	10	15	30	60		
172	Jim Neilson	6	8	10	15	25	40	50	120
173	Bryan Watson	6	8	10	15	30	60		
174	George Swarbrick	6	8	10	15	30	80		
175	Joe Szura	6	8	10	15	30	80		
176	Gary Smith RC	12	15	20	25	60	200		
177	Barclay Plager UER RC	8	10	12	15	40	80		
178	Tim Ecclestone	6	8	10	15	30	60		
179	Jean-Guy Talbot	6	8	10	15	25	50		
180	Ab McDonald	6	8	10	15	30	80		
181	Jacques Plante	20	25	30	40	50	120		
182	Bill McCreary	6	8	10	15	30	150		
183	Allan Stanley	6	8	10	15	25	50		
184	Andre Lacroix RC	6	8	10	15	60	175		
185	Jean-Guy Gendron	6	8	10	15	25	40	60	100
186	Jim Johnson RC	6	8	10	15	30	60		
187	Simon Nolet RC	6	8	10	15	60	80		
188	Joe Daley RC	6	8	12	20	80	150		
189	John Arbour	6	8	10	15	50	100		
190	Billy Dea	6	8	10	15	30	80		
191	Bob Dillabough	6	8	10	15	30	60		
192	Bob Woytowich	6	8	10	15	30	50	60	100
193	Keith McCreary RC	6	8	10	15	30	60		
194	Murray Oliver	6	8	10	15	30	60		
195	Larry Mickey	6	8	10	15	40	80		
196	Bill Sutherland	6	8	10	15	50	100		
197	Bruce Gamble	6	8	10	25	50	100		
198	Dave Keon	8	10	12	25	50	150		
199	Gump Worsley AS1	6	8	12	25	80			
200	Bobby Orr AS1	60	80	100	150	250	400	500	800
201	Tim Horton AS1	8	10	15	30	80	175		
202	Stan Mikita AS1	8	10	12	30	60	400		
203	Gordie Howe AS1	30	40	50	60	100	175	200	450
204	Bobby Hull AS1	25	30	40	50	80	175		
205	Ed Giacomin AS2	8	10	12	20	80	350		
206	J.C. Tremblay AS2	6	8	12	25	250	400		
207	Jim Neilson AS2	6	8	10	15	30	135		
208	Phil Esposito AS2	12	15	20	40	120	300		
209	Rod Gilbert AS2	6	8	12	30	100	500		
210	Johnny Bucyk AS2	6	8	10	15	80	250		
211	Stan Mikita Triple	8	10	12	30	60	200		
212	Worsley/Vachon Vezina	20	25	30	60	120	200		
213	Derek Sanderson Calder	25	30	40	50	100	250		
214	Bobby Orr Norris	60	80	100	150	250	800		
215	Glenn Hall Smythe	6	8	10	15	100	250		
216	Claude Provost Mast	8	10	12	15	80	200		

Ralph Backstrom #5 PSA 9 (MT) sold for $1,132 (eBay; 8/15)
Johnny Bucyk #5 PSA 9 (MT) sold for $626 (eBay; 8/12)

— Checklist #61 PSA 9 (MT) sold for $833 (eBay; 10/12)
— Roger Crozier #23 PSA 9 (MT) sold for $694 (eBay; 8/12)
— Alex Delvecchio #28 PSA 10 (Gem) sold for $1,490 (eBay; 4/15)
— Dave Dryden #150 PSA 9 (MT) sold for $1,040 (eBay; 2/13)
— Doug Harvey #1 PSA 8 (NmMt) sold for $1,649 (eBay; 8/12)
— Gordie Howe #29 PSA 9 (MT) sold for $1,584 (eBay; 3/15)
— Larry Hillman #48 PSA 9 (MT) sold for $611 (eBay; 3/14)
— Gordie Howe AS1#203 PSA 9 (MT) sold for $460 (eBay; 8/12)
— Gordie Howe #29 PSA 9 (MT) sold for $1,130 (eBay; 8/12)
— John McKenzie #9 PSA 10 (Gem) sold for $453 (eBay; 2/07)
— Bobby Orr #2 PSA 9 (MT) sold for $13,547 (Mile High; 12/13)
— Bobby Orr Norris #214 PSA 9 (Mt) sold for $1,775 (Mile High; 12/13)
— Bobby Orr Norris #214 PSA 9 (Mt) sold for $1,258 (eBay;2/16)
— Jim Pappin #21 PSA 9 (Mt) sold for $1040 (eBay; 2/13)
— Mickey Redmond RC #64 PSA 8 (NmMt) sold for $703.44 (eBay; 8/12)
— Mike Walton #132 PSA 9 (MT) sold for $465 (eBay; 8/12)

1968-69 Topps

#	Player	VG 3	VgEx 4	EX 5	ExMt 6	NM 7	NmMt 8	NmMt+ 8.5	MT 9
1	Gerry Cheevers	10	12	15	20	30	125		
2	Bobby Orr	80	100	200	300	400	1,200		
3	Don Awrey UER	6	8	10	12	15	30		
4	Ted Green	6	8	10	12	15	30		
5	Johnny Bucyk	6	8	10	15	30	100		
6	Derek Sanderson	12	15	20	25	30	80	100	175
7	Phil Esposito	15	20	25	30	40	80	120	300
8	Ken Hodge	6	8	10	12	15	150		
9	John McKenzie	6	8	10	12	15	30		
10	Fred Stanfield	6	8	10	12	15	30		
11	Tom Williams	6	8	10	12	15	30	40	100
12	Denis DeJordy	6	8	10	12	15	30	40	80
13	Doug Jarrett	6	8	10	12	15	30	40	80
14	Gilles Marotte	6	8	10	12	15	30		
15	Pat Stapleton	6	8	10	12	15	30		
16	Bobby Hull	25	25	30	50	80	150	200	300
17	Chico Maki	6	8	10	15	30	60		
18	Pit Martin	6	8	10	12	15	30	40	175
19	Doug Mohns	6	8	10	12	15	30	40	175
20	Stan Mikita	10	12	15	20	30	150		
21	Jim Pappin	6	8	10	12	15	30		
22	Ken Wharram	6	8	10	12	15	30		
23	Roger Crozier	6	8	10	12	25	40		
24	Bob Baun	6	8	10	12	15	30		
25	Gary Bergman	6	8	10	12	25	50		
26	Kent Douglas	6	8	10	15	25	60		
27	Ron Harris	6	8	10	12	15	30	40	80
28	Alex Delvecchio	6	8	10	12	15	40		
29	Gordie Howe	30	40	80	100	150	200		
30	Bruce MacGregor	6	8	10	12	15	30	40	80
31	Frank Mahovlich	8	10	12	15	20	50	75	135
32	Dean Prentice	6	8	10	12	15	30		
33	Pete Stemkowski	6	8	10	12	15	30	35	60
34	Terry Sawchuk	20	25	30	40	50	100	150	300
35	Larry Cahan	6	8	10	12	15	30	40	80
36	Real Lemieux	6	8	10	12	15	30		
37	Bill White RC	6	8	10	12	15	30		
38	Gord Labossiere	6	8	10	12	15	30	40	80
39	Ted Irvine	6	8	10	12	15	30	35	60
40	Eddie Joyal	6	8	10	12	15	30	35	60
41	Dale Rolfe	6	8	10	12	15	30	35	80
42	Lowell MacDonald RC	6	8	10	12	15	30	35	60
43	Skip Krake UER	6	8	10	12	15	30	40	80
44	Terry Gray	6	8	10	12	20	60		
45	Cesare Maniago	6	8	10	12	15	30	40	80
46	Mike McMahon	6	8	10	12	15	30		
47	Wayne Hillman	6	8	10	12	15	30		
48	Larry Hillman	6	8	10	12	15	30		
49	Bob Woytowich	6	8	10	12	15	30	40	80
50	Claude Connelly	6	8	10	12	15	30		
51	Claude Larose	6	8	10	12	15	30		
52	Danny Grant RC	6	8	10	12	15	80	120	150
53	Andre Boudrias	6	8	10	12	15	30	50	125
54	Ray Cullen RC	6	8	10	12	15	30	40	100
55	Parker MacDonald	6	8	10	12	15	30		
56	Gump Worsley	8	10	12	15	30	50		
57	Terry Harper	6	8	10	12	15	30	40	80
58	Jacques Laperriere	6	8	10	12	15	30	50	100
59	J.C. Tremblay	6	8	10	12	15	30	40	80
60	Ralph Backstrom	6	8	10	12	15	30		
61	Jean Beliveau	10	12	15	20	30	80	100	250
62	Yvan Cournoyer	8	10	12	15	20	50		
63	Jacques Lemaire	10	12	15	20	25	60		
64	Henri Richard	8	10	12	15	20	60		
65	Bobby Rousseau	6	8	10	12	15	30	40	80
66	Gilles Tremblay	6	8	10	12	15	30		
67	Ed Giacomin	8	10	12	15	20	50	60	120
68	Arnie Brown	6	8	10	12	15	30		
69	Harry Howell	6	8	10	12	20	50		
70	Jim Neilson	6	8	10	12	20	50		

#	Player	VG 3	VgEx 4	EX 5	ExMt 6	NM 7	NmMt 8	NmMt+ 8.5	MT 9
71	Rod Seiling	6	8	10	12	20	50		
72	Rod Gilbert	6	8	10	12	15	60	80	100
73	Phil Goyette	6	8	10	12	15	30	40	80
74	Vic Hadfield	6	8	10	12	15	35	50	100
75	Don Marshall	6	8	10	12	15	40		
76	Bob Nevin	6	8	10	12	15	40	50	80
77	Jean Ratelle	6	8	10	12	15	40	50	80
78	Charlie Hodge	6	8	10	12	15	30		
79	Bert Marshall	6	8	10	12	15	30	40	80
80	Billy Harris	6	8	10	12	15	30		
81	Carol Vadnais	6	8	10	12	15	30		
82	Howie Young	6	8	10	12	15	30		
83	John Brenneman	6	8	10	12	15	30	40	80
84	Gerry Ehman	6	8	10	12	15	30		
85	Ted Hampson	6	8	10	12	15	40		
86	Bill Hicke	6	8	10	12	15	40	50	80
87	Gary Jarrett	6	8	10	12	15	30		
88	Doug Roberts	6	8	10	12	15	40		
89	Bernie Parent RC	30	40	50	60	100	175	225	500
90	Joe Watson	6	8	10	12	15	30		
91	Ed Van Impe	6	8	10	12	15	40		
92	Larry Zeidel	6	8	10	12	15	30		
93	John Miszuk	6	8	10	12	15	30		
94	Gary Dornhoefer	6	8	10	12	15	40	50	150
95	Leon Rochefort	6	8	10	12	15	40	50	80
96	Brit Selby	6	8	10	12	15	40		
97	Forbes Kennedy	6	8	10	12	15	30	40	150
98	Ed Hoekstra	6	8	10	12	15	30		
99	Garry Peters	6	8	10	12	15	30	40	120
100	Les Binkley RC	8	10	12	15	20	50		
101	Leo Boivin	6	8	10	12	15	30		
102	Earl Ingarfield	6	8	10	12	15	30	40	135
103	Lou Angotti	6	8	10	12	15	30		
104	Andy Bathgate	6	8	10	12	15	30	40	80
105	Wally Boyer	6	8	10	12	15	40	50	100
106	Ken Schinkel	6	8	10	12	15	30	50	100
107	Ab McDonald	6	8	10	12	15	30		
108	Charlie Burns	6	8	10	12	15	30	50	100
109	Val Fonteyne	6	8	10	12	15	30	40	80
110	Noel Price	6	8	10	12	15	30	40	80
111	Glenn Hall	8	10	12	15	20	40	50	100
112	Bob Plager RC	8	10	12	15	30	60	80	100
113	Jim Roberts	6	8	10	12	15	30		
114	Red Berenson	6	8	10	12	15	30	40	80
115	Larry Keenan	6	8	10	12	15	30	40	80
116	Camille Henry	6	8	10	15	30	50		
117	Gary Sabourin	6	8	10	12	15	30		
118	Ron Schock	6	8	10	12	15	40		
119	Gary Veneruzzo	6	8	10	12	15	30	40	80
120	Gerry Melnyk	6	8	10	12	15	30	35	60
121	Checklist Card	40	50	60	80	150	200	250	350
122	Johnny Bower	8	10	12	15	20	80	60	150
123	Tim Horton	10	12	15	20	25	40	60	200
124	Pierre Pilote	6	8	10	12	15	30		
125	Marcel Pronovost	6	8	10	12	15	30	40	80
126	Ron Ellis	6	8	10	12	15	30		
127	Paul Henderson	6	8	10	12	30	40		
128	Dave Keon	6	8	10	12	15	40	50	100
129	Bob Pulford	6	8	10	12	20	50		
130	Floyd Smith	6	8	10	12	15	30	40	80
131	Norm Ullman	6	8	10	12	15	40		
132	Mike Walton	6	8	10	12	15	50		

— Bobby Hull #16 PSA 9 (MT) sold for $430 (eBay; 8/09)

1969-70 O-Pee-Chee

#	Player	VG 3	VgEx 4	EX 5	ExMt 6	NM 7	NmMt 8	NmMt+ 8.5	MT 9
1	Gump Worsley	20	25	40	50	150	400	500	800
2	Ted Harris	5	6	10	15	60	200		
3	Jacques Laperriere	5	6	10	15	50	200	250	350
4	Serge Savard RC	30	50	120	200	325	1,000		
5	J.C. Tremblay	5	6	8	10	25	100		
6	Yvan Cournoyer	5	6	8	10	25	50		
7	John Ferguson	5	6	8	10	30	120	135	250
8	Jacques Lemaire	5	6	8	10	50	200		
9	Bobby Rousseau	5	6	8	15	40	150		
10	Jean Beliveau	10	12	15	25	40	100	250	
11	Dick Duff	5	6	8	15	50	350		
12	Glenn Hall	6	8	10	12	25	60	80	120
13	Bob Plager	5	6	8	10	25	50	60	120
14	Ron Anderson	5	6	8	10	25	50	60	120
15	Jean-Guy Talbot	5	6	8	10	25	50		
16	Andre Boudrias	5	6	8	10	25	50	60	120
17	Camille Henry	5	6	8	10	25	50		
18	Ab McDonald	5	6	8	10	25	50	60	120
19	Gary Sabourin	5	6	8	10	25	50		
20	Red Berenson	5	6	8	15	50	120		
21	Phil Goyette	5	6	8	10	25	50	60	120
22	Gerry Cheevers	8	10	12	15	30	80		
23	Ted Green	5	6	8	10	25	50		
24	Bobby Orr	80	100	150	250	400	800		
25	Dallas Smith	5	6	8	10	25	50	60	120
26	Johnny Bucyk	6	8	10	12	25	50	80	135
27	Ken Hodge	5	6	8	10	25	50		
28	John McKenzie	5	6	8	10	25	50	60	135
29	Ed Westfall	5	6	8	10	40	80		
30	Phil Esposito	15	20	25	30	50	80	100	175
31	Checklist 2	50	60	100	150	275	400	450	700
32	Fred Stanfield	5	6	8	10	25	50		
33	Ed Giacomin	8	10	12	15	60	100		
34	Arnie Brown	5	6	8	10	25	50		
35	Jim Neilson	5	6	8	10	25	50	60	120
36	Rod Seiling	5	6	8	10	25	50		
37	Rod Gilbert	5	6	8	12	40	150		
38	Vic Hadfield	5	6	8	10	30	80		
39	Don Marshall	5	6	8	10	25	50		
40	Bob Nevin	5	6	8	10	25	50		
41	Ron Stewart	5	6	8	10	25	50	60	120
42	Jean Ratelle	5	6	8	10	25	80		
43	Walt Tkaczuk RC	5	6	8	10	25	50		
44	Bruce Gamble	5	6	8	10	25	50	60	120
45	Jim Dorey	5	6	8	10	25	50		
46	Ron Ellis	5	6	8	10	40	60		
47	Paul Henderson	5	6	8	10	25	150		
48	Brit Selby	5	6	8	10	25	50	60	135
49	Floyd Smith	5	6	8	10	25	50		
50	Mike Walton	5	6	8	10	25	50		
51	Dave Keon	5	6	8	15	50	120		
52	Murray Oliver	5	6	8	10	25	50		
53	Bob Pulford	5	6	8	10	25	50		
54	Norm Ullman	5	6	8	10	25	50	60	120
55	Roger Crozier	5	6	8	10	25	50		
56	Roy Edwards	5	6	8	10	25	50	60	120
57	Bob Baun	5	6	8	10	25	50		
58	Gary Bergman	5	6	8	10	25	60	80	150
59	Carl Brewer	5	6	8	10	25	50	60	120
60	Wayne Connelly	5	6	8	10	25	50	60	120
61	Gordie Howe	30	50	80	100	300	500	600	800
62	Frank Mahovlich	6	8	10	12	80	100	150	200
63	Bruce MacGregor	5	6	8	15	40	150		
64	Ron Harris	5	6	8	10	25	50	60	120
65	Pete Stemkowski	5	6	8	10	25	50		
66	Denis DeJordy	5	6	8	10	25	50	60	120
67	Doug Jarrett	5	6	8	10	25	50		
68	Gilles Marotte	5	6	8	10	25	50	60	120
69	Pat Stapleton	5	6	8	10	25	50	60	135
70	Bobby Hull	30	40	50	80	150	200	250	350
71	Dennis Hull	5	6	8	10	25	50		
72	Doug Mohns	5	6	8	15	50	200		
73	Howie Menard	5	6	8	10	25	50	60	120
74	Ken Wharram	5	6	8	10	25	50	60	120
75	Pit Martin	5	6	8	10	25	50		
76	Stan Mikita	10	12	15	25	60	250		
77	Charlie Hodge	5	6	8	10	25	50	60	120
78	Gary Smith	5	6	8	10	25	50		
79	Harry Howell	5	6	8	10	25	50	60	135
80	Bert Marshall	5	6	8	10	25	50	60	120
81	Doug Roberts	5	6	8	10	25	50		
82	Carol Vadnais	5	6	8	10	30	80		
83	Gerry Ehman	5	6	8	10	25	50		
84	Brian Perry	5	6	8	10	25	50	60	120
85	Gary Jarrett	5	6	8	10	25	50	60	120
86	Ted Hampson	5	6	8	10	25	50	60	120
87	Earl Ingarfield	5	6	8	10	25	50		
88	Doug Favell RC	8	10	12	15	50	175		
89	Bernie Parent	20	25	30	40	50	100	150	300
90	Larry Hillman	5	6	8	10	25	50		
91	Wayne Hillman	5	6	8	10	25	50		
92	Ed Van Impe	5	6	8	10	25	50	60	135
93	Joe Watson	5	6	8	10	25	50	60	120
94	Gary Dornhoefer	5	6	8	10	30	80		
95	Reg Fleming	5	6	8	10	25	50	60	120
96	Ralph McSweyn	5	6	8	10	25	50		
97	Jim Johnson	5	6	8	10	25	50		
98	Andre Lacroix	5	6	8	10	25	50		
99	Gerry Desjardins RC	6	8	10	12	25	60		
100	Dale Rolfe	5	6	8	10	25	50		
101	Bill White	5	6	8	10	25	50	60	150
102	Bill Flett	5	6	8	10	25	50		
103	Ted Irvine	5	6	8	10	25	80		
104	Ross Lonsberry	5	6	8	10	25	50		
105	Leon Rochefort	5	6	8	10	25	50		
106	Bryan Campbell	5	6	8	12	30	60		
107	Dennis Hextall RC	5	6	8	10	25	60		
108	Eddie Joyal	5	6	8	10	25	50		
109	Gord Labossiere	5	6	8	10	25	50		
110	Les Binkley	5	6	8	10	30	150	175	250
111	Tracy Pratt	5	6	8	10	25	60	80	150
112	Bryan Watson	5	6	8	10	25	50		
113	Bob Blackburn	5	6	8	10	25	50		

HOCKEY

#	Player	VG 3	VgEx 4	EX 5	ExMt 6	NM 7	NmMt 8	NmMt+ 8.5	MT 9
114	Keith McCreary	5	6	8	10	25	50		
115	Dean Prentice	5	6	8	10	25	50		
116	Glen Sather	5	6	8	10	25	50		
117	Ken Schinkel	5	6	8	10	25	50	60	135
118	Wally Boyer	5	6	8	10	25	50		
119	Val Fonteyne	5	6	8	10	25	50		
120	Ron Schock	5	6	8	10	25	50	60	120
121	Cesare Maniago	5	6	8	10	25	50	60	120
122	Leo Boivin	5	6	8	10	25	50		
123	Bob McCord	5	6	8	10	30	100		
124	John Miszuk	5	6	8	10	25	50		
125	Danny Grant	5	6	8	10	25	60		
126	Bill Collins	5	6	8	10	25	50		
127	Jean-Paul Parise	5	6	8	10	25	50	60	135
128	Tom Williams	5	6	8	10	25	50		
129	Charlie Burns	5	6	8	10	25	50	75	175
130	Ray Cullen	5	6	8	10	25	50		
131	Danny O'Shea	5	6	8	10	50	135		
132	Checklist 1	125	175	250	400	500			
133	Jim Pappin	5	6	8	10	12	25	30	50
134	Lou Angotti	5	6	8	10	12	15	20	30
135	Terry Cafery RC	5	6	8	10	12	15	20	30
136	Eric Nesterenko	5	6	8	10	12	30	40	80
137	Chico Maki	5	6	8	10	12	15	20	30
138	Tony Esposito RC	40	80	100	150	250	350	400	600
139	Eddie Shack	5	6	8	10	12	15	20	30
140	Bob Wall	5	6	8	10	12	30	40	60
141	Skip Krake RC	5	6	8	10	12	15	20	30
142	Howie Hughes	5	6	8	10	12	15	20	30
143	Jimmy Peters RC	5	6	8	10	12	20	30	50
144	Brent Hughes RC	5	6	8	10	12	25	30	50
145	Bill Hicke	5	6	8	10	12	15	20	30
146	Norm Ferguson RC	5	6	8	10	12	15	20	40
147	Dick Mattiussi RC	5	6	8	10	12	25	30	60
148	Mike Laughton RC	5	6	8	10	12	25	30	50
149	Gene Ubriaco RC	5	6	8	10	12	15	20	30
150	Bob Dillabough	5	6	8	10	12	20	30	50
151	Bob Woytowich	5	6	8	10	12	25	30	60
152	Joe Daley	5	6	8	10	12	25	30	60
153	Duane Rupp	5	6	8	10	12	30	30	60
154	Bryan Hextall RC	5	6	8	10	12	15	20	30
155	Jean Pronovost RC	5	6	8	10	12	20	25	40
156	Jim Morrison	5	6	8	10	12	20	25	40
157	Alex Delvecchio	6	8	10	12	12	25	30	50
158	Paul Popiel	5	6	8	10	12	20	25	40
159	Garry Unger	5	6	8	10	12	15	20	30
160	Garry Monahan	5	6	8	10	12	15	20	30
161	Matt Ravlich	5	6	8	10	12	15	20	30
162	Nick Libett RC	5	6	8	10	12	20	25	40
163	Henri Richard	6	8	10	12	12	30	40	175
164	Terry Harper	5	6	8	10	12	30	40	120
165	Rogatien Vachon	8	10	12	15	20	30	40	100
166	Ralph Backstrom	5	6	8	10	12	15	20	40
167	Claude Provost	5	6	8	10	12	15	20	30
168	Gilles Tremblay	5	6	8	10	12	15	40	50
169	Jean-Guy Gendron	5	6	8	10	12	20	25	40
170	Earl Heiskala RC	5	6	8	10	12	15	20	30
171	Garry Peters	5	6	8	10	15	40		
172	Bill Sutherland	5	6	8	10	12	15	20	30
173	Dick Cherry RC	5	6	8	10	12	15	20	30
174	Jim Roberts	5	6	8	10	12	20	25	40
175	Noel Picard RC	5	6	8	10	15	40		
176	Barclay Plager RC	5	6	8	10	12	15	20	30
177	Frank St. Marseille RC	5	6	8	10	12	15	20	30
178	Al Arbour	5	6	8	10	12	15	20	30
179	Tim Ecclestone	5	6	8	10	12	20	25	40
180	Jacques Plante	15	20	25	35	50	60	80	120
181	Bill McCreary	5	6	8	10	12	15	20	30
182	Tim Horton	8	10	12	15	20	30	40	60
183	Rick Ley RC	5	6	8	10	12	15	20	50
184	Wayne Carleton	5	6	8	10	12	15	20	30
185	Marv Edwards RC	5	6	8	10	12	20	25	40
186	Pat Quinn RC	8	10	12	15	20	60	80	135
187	Johnny Bower	6	8	10	12	15	50	80	100
188	Orland Kurtenbach	5	6	8	10	12	20	25	40
189	Terry Sawchuk UER	10	12	15	20	30	60	80	100
190	Real Lemieux	5	6	8	10	12	15	20	30
191	Dave Balon	5	6	8	10	12	15	20	30
192	Al Hamilton	5	6	8	10	12	30	40	80
193A	G.Howe Mr. HK ERR	30	40	50	60	80	100	150	250
193B	G.Howe Mr. HK COR	50	60	80	100	150	200		
194	Claude Larose	5	6	8	10	12	20	25	40
195	Bill Goldsworthy	5	6	8	10	12	30	40	80
196	Bob Barlow	5	6	8	10	12	30	40	80
197	Ken Broderick RC	5	6	8	10	12	30	40	60
198	Lou Nanne RC	5	6	8	10	12	20	25	40
199	Tom Polonic RC	5	6	8	10	12	25	30	60
200	Ed Johnston	5	6	8	10	12	15	20	30
201	Derek Sanderson	10	12	15	20	25	40	50	80
202	Gary Doak	5	6	8	10	12	15	20	50

#	Player	VG 3	VgEx 4	EX 5	ExMt 6	NM 7	NmMt 8	NmMt+ 8.5	MT 9
203	Don Awrey	5	6	8	10	12	20	20	30
204	Ron Murphy	5	6	8	10	12	25	30	60
205A	P.Esposito Double ERR	12	15	20	25	60			
205B	P.Esposito Double COR	12	15	20	50				
206	Alex Delvecchio Byng	5	6	8	10	12	25	30	50
207	J.Plante/G.Hall Vezina	15	20	25	30	50	60		
208	Danny Grant Calder	5	6	8	10	12	20	25	40
209	Bobby Orr Norris	30	40	50	80	150	200	250	350
210	Serge Savard Smythe	5	6	8	10	12	20	25	40
211	Glenn Hall AS	8	10	12	15	30	150		
212	Bobby Orr AS	30	40	50	60	80	120	150	250
213	Tim Horton AS	10	12	15	20	25	40	50	120
214	Phil Esposito AS	10	12	15	20	40	80		
215	Gordie Howe AS	25	30	40	50	80	120		
216	Bobby Hull AS	15	20	25	30	50	80		
217	Ed Giacomin AS	6	8	10	12	40			
218	Ted Green AS	5	6	8	10	12	20	25	40
219	Ted Harris AS	5	6	8	10	12	20	25	50
220	Jean Beliveau AS	10	12	15	30	80	400		
221	Yvan Cournoyer AS	5	6	8	10	12	25	50	
222	Frank Mahovlich AS	5	6	8	10	15	40	135	
223	Art Ross Trophy	5	6	12	20	60	250		
224	Hart Trophy	5	6	8	10	12	20	30	60
225	Lady Byng Trophy	5	6	8	12	25	100		
226	Vezina Trophy	5	6	8	10	12	30	35	40
227	Calder Trophy	5	6	8	12	30	200		
228	James Norris Trophy	5	6	8	12	25	80		
229	Conn Smythe Trophy	5	6	8	12	25	50		
230	Prince of Wales Trophy	5	6	8	10	12	20	25	50
231	The Stanley Cup	15	20	25	40	60	75	140	175

— Jean Beliveau #10 PSA 9 (MT) sold for $410 (eBay; 4/07)
— Checklist #31 PSA 10 (Gem) sold for $2,375 (Memory Lane; 4/07)
— Checklist #132 PSA 8 (NmMt) sold for $1,454 (eBay; 11/14)
— Gordie Howe #193A PSA 10 (Gem) sold for $3,216 (Memory Lane; 12/13)
— Bobby Hull #70 PSA 10 (Gem) sold for $2,092 (Memory Lane; 12/13)
— Eddie Joyal #108 PSA 10 (Gem) sold for $446 (eBay; 4/07)
— Cesare Maniago PSA 10 (Gem) sold for $265 (eBay; 05/08)
— Pit Martin #75 PSA 9 (MT) sold for $321 (eBay; 3/08)
— Keith Mcreary #114 PSA 10 (Gem) sold for $446 (eBay; 4/07)
— Bobby Orr #24 PSA 9 (MT) sold for $2,624 (Mile High; 12/13)
— Serge Savard RC #4 PSA 8 (NmMt) sold for $1,044 (eBay; 5/12)
— Gump Worsley #1 PSA 9 (MT) sold for $919 (eBay; 3/07)

1969-70 Topps

#	Player	VG 3	VgEx 4	EX 5	ExMt 6	NM 7	NmMt 8	NmMt+ 8.5	MT 9
1	Gump Worsley	8	10	12	15	25			
2	Ted Harris	5	6	8	10	15	30		
3	Jacques Laperriere	5	6	8	10	15	25	30	80
4	Serge Savard RC	10	12	15	20	40	120		
5	J.C. Tremblay	5	6	8	10	15	25	30	80
6	Yvan Cournoyer	5	6	8	10	15	40		
7	John Ferguson	5	6	8	10	15	25	30	80
8	Jacques Lemaire	5	6	8	10	15	40	50	100
9	Bobby Rousseau	5	6	8	10	15	80		
10	Jean Beliveau	8	10	12	15	60	100	135	300
11	Henri Richard	5	6	8	10	30	50	60	135
12	Glenn Hall	5	6	8	10	20	60		
13	Bob Plager	5	6	8	10	15	30		
14	Jim Roberts	5	6	8	10	15	30		
15	Jean-Guy Talbot	5	6	8	10	15	30		
16	Andre Boudrias	5	6	8	10	15	25	30	80
17	Camille Henry	5	6	8	10	15	25	30	80
18	Ab McDonald	5	6	8	10	15	30		
19	Gary Sabourin	5	6	8	10	15	50		
20	Red Berenson	5	6	8	10	15	50		
21	Phil Goyette	5	6	8	10	15	30		
22	Gerry Cheevers	6	8	10	12	20	50		
23	Ted Green	5	6	8	10	15	50		
24	Bobby Orr	50	60	100	150	200	300	350	1,400
25	Dallas Smith	5	6	8	10	15	25	30	80
26	Johnny Bucyk	5	6	8	10	15	35	50	125
27	Ken Hodge	5	6	8	10	15	50		
28	John McKenzie	5	6	8	10	15	50		
29	Ed Westfall	5	6	8	10	15	50		
30	Phil Esposito	10	12	15	20	35	60	80	200
31	Derek Sanderson	8	10	12	15	25	50		
32	Fred Stanfield	5	6	8	10	15	30		
33	Ed Giacomin	6	8	10	12	20	40	50	135
34	Arnie Brown	5	6	8	10	15	30		
35	Jim Neilson	5	6	8	10	15	25	30	60
36	Rod Seiling	5	6	8	10	15	25	30	60
37	Rod Gilbert	5	6	8	10	15	25	30	60
38	Vic Hadfield	5	6	8	10	15	40		
39	Don Marshall	5	6	8	10	15	60		
40	Bob Nevin	5	6	8	10	15	50		
41	Ron Stewart	5	6	8	10	15	50		
42	Jean Ratelle	5	6	8	10	15	30	35	80
43	Walt Tkaczuk RC	5	6	8	10	15	40		
44	Bruce Gamble	5	6	8	10	15	30		

HOCKEY

#		VG 3	VgEx 4	EX 5	ExMt 6	NM 7	NmMt 8	NmMt+ 8.5	MT 9
45	Tim Horton	8	10	12	15	25	60	80	175
46	Ron Ellis	5	6	8	10	15	30		
47	Paul Henderson	5	6	8	10	15	30	35	80
48	Brit Selby	5	6	8	10	15	30		
49	Floyd Smith	5	6	8	10	15	25	30	60
50	Mike Walton	5	6	8	10	15	30		
51	Dave Keon	5	6	8	10	15	40		
52	Murray Oliver	5	6	8	10	15	40		
53	Bob Pulford	5	6	8	10	15	25	30	60
54	Norm Ullman	5	6	8	10	15	30	40	80
55	Roger Crozier	5	6	8	10	15	50		
56	Roy Edwards	5	6	8	10	15	30		
57	Bob Baun	5	6	8	10	15	30	35	80
58	Gary Bergman	5	6	8	10	15	25	30	60
59	Carl Brewer	5	6	8	10	15	30	35	80
60	Wayne Connelly	5	6	8	10	15	30		
61	Gordie Howe	12	15	25	35	50	80	125	500
62	Frank Mahovlich	5	6	8	10	20	50	60	100
63	Bruce MacGregor	5	6	8	10	15	25	30	60
64	Alex Delvecchio	5	6	8	10	20	30	40	80
65	Pete Stemkowski	5	6	8	10	15	25	30	60
66	Denis DeJordy	5	6	8	10	15	30	35	80
67	Doug Jarrett	5	6	8	10	15	30	35	80
68	Gilles Marotte	5	6	8	10	15	30	35	80
69	Pat Stapleton	5	6	8	10	15	25	30	60
70	Bobby Hull	12	15	20	40	50	80	120	300
71	Dennis Hull	5	6	8	10	15	30	35	80
72	Doug Mohns	5	6	8	10	15	30		
73	Jim Pappin	5	6	8	10	15	40		
74	Ken Wharram	5	6	8	10	15	30	35	80
75	Pit Martin	5	6	8	10	15	30		
76	Stan Mikita	8	10	12	15	25	80	100	175
77	Charlie Hodge	5	6	8	10	15	30	35	80
78	Gary Smith	5	6	8	10	15	25	30	60
79	Harry Howell	5	6	8	10	15	30	35	80
80	Bert Marshall	5	6	8	10	15	30	35	80
81	Doug Roberts	5	6	8	10	15	25	30	60
82	Carol Vadnais	5	6	8	10	15	30		
83	Gerry Ehman	5	6	8	10	15	30		
84	Bill Hicke	5	6	8	10	15	25	30	60
85	Gary Jarrett	5	6	8	10	15	25	30	60
86	Ted Hampson	5	6	8	10	15	25	30	60
87	Earl Ingarfield	5	6	8	10	15	25	30	60
88	Doug Favell RC	6	8	10	12	25	60		
89	Bernie Parent	10	12	15	18	25	40	50	80
90	Larry Hillman	5	6	8	10	20	80		
91	Wayne Hillman	5	6	8	10	15	60		
92	Ed Van Impe	5	6	8	10	15	25	30	60
93	Joe Watson	5	6	8	10	15	30		
94	Gary Dornhoefer	5	6	8	10	15	30		
95	Reg Fleming	5	6	8	10	15	25	30	60
96	Jean-Guy Gendron	5	6	8	10	15	25	30	60
97	Jim Johnson	5	6	8	10	15	25	30	60
98	Andre Lacroix	5	6	8	10	15	30	35	80
99	Gerry Desjardins RC	5	6	8	10	15	30	35	80
100	Dale Rolfe	5	6	8	10	15	25	30	60
101	Bill White	5	6	8	10	15	25	30	60
102	Bill Flett	5	6	8	10	15	30		
103	Ted Irvine	5	6	8	10	15	25	30	60
104	Ross Lonsberry	5	6	8	10	15	40		
105	Leon Rochefort	5	6	8	10	15	25	30	60
106	Eddie Shack	5	6	8	10	15	40		
107	Dennis Hextall RC	5	6	8	10	15	30	35	60
108	Eddie Joyal	5	6	8	10	15	25	30	60
109	Gord Labossiere	5	6	8	10	15	25	30	60
110	Les Binkley	5	6	8	10	15	30	35	80
111	Tracy Pratt	5	6	8	10	15	30		
112	Bryan Watson	5	6	8	10	15	40		
113	Bob Woytowich	5	6	8	10	15	25	30	60
114	Keith McCreary	5	6	8	10	15	60		
115	Dean Prentice	5	6	8	10	15	30		
116	Glen Sather	5	6	8	10	15	30		
117	Ken Schinkel	5	6	8	10	15	50		
118	Wally Boyer	5	6	8	10	15	30	35	80
119	Val Fonteyne	5	6	8	10	15	30		
120	Ron Schock	5	6	8	10	15	25	30	60
121	Cesare Maniago	5	6	8	10	15	50		
122	Leo Boivin	5	6	8	10	15	30		
123	Bob McCord	5	6	8	10	15	50		
124	John Miszuk	5	6	8	10	15	30		
125	Danny Grant	5	6	8	10	15	30		
126	Claude Larose	5	6	8	10	15	50		
127	Jean-Paul Parise	5	6	8	10	15	30		
128	Tom Williams	5	6	8	10	15	25	30	60
129	Charlie Burns	5	6	8	10	15	80		
130	Ray Cullen	5	6	8	10	20	100		
131	Danny O'Shea	5	6	8	10	20	100		
132	Checklist Card	15	25	40	50	80	250		

— Bobby Hull #70 PSA 10 (GEM) sold for $780 (Mastro; 8/08)
— Bobby Orr #24 PSA 9 (MT) sold for $1,211780 (Mile High; 12/13)

1970-71 O-Pee-Chee

#		VG 3	VgEx 4	EX 5	ExMt 6	NM 7	NmMt 8	NmMt+ 8.5	MT 9
1	Gerry Cheevers	20	25	35	50	80	300	350	800
2	Johnny Bucyk	4	5	6	10	30	80		
3	Bobby Orr	60	80	125	200	400	800	1,600	2,200
4	Don Awrey	4	4	8	20	40	100		
5	Fred Stanfield	4	5	6	12	30	250		
6	John McKenzie	4	5	6	10	30	80		
7	Wayne Cashman RC	12	15	20	30	40	150	175	250
8	Ken Hodge	4	5	6	10	30	80		
9	Wayne Carleton	4	4	5	10	20	80		
10	Garnet Bailey RC	4	5	6	12	30	400		
11	Phil Esposito	20	25	30	40	50	100		
12	Lou Angotti	4	4	5	10	20	60	80	150
13	Jim Pappin	4	4	5	10	25	100		
14	Dennis Hull	4	5	8	15	25	100		
15	Bobby Hull	40	45	50	60	100	200	250	350
16	Doug Mohns	4	4	5	8	15	30	50	120
17	Pat Stapleton	4	5	6	10	30	300		
18	Pit Martin	4	5	6	10	50	80		135
19	Eric Nesterenko	4	5	6	10	20	40	50	200
20	Stan Mikita	15	20	20	30	40	80	125	225
21	Roy Edwards	4	5	6	10	20	40	50	80
22	Frank Mahovlich	10	12	15	25	50	250		
23	Ron Harris	4	4	5	8	15	30		
24	Checklist 1	150	200	250	300	400	600	800	1,000
25	Pete Stemkowski	4	4	5	8	15	25	40	125
26	Garry Unger	4	4	5	8	15	80		
27	Bruce MacGregor	4	4	5	8	15	50		
28	Larry Jeffrey	4	4	5	8	15	30		
29	Gordie Howe	30	40	60	80	100	200	300	600
30	Billy Dea	4	4	5	8	15	30	40	100
31	Denis DeJordy	4	5	6	10	20	50		
32	Matt Ravlich	4	5	8	12	40	135		
33	Dave Amadio	4	4	5	8	15	30	40	80
34	Gilles Marotte	4	4	5	10	30	60		
35	Eddie Shack	10	12	15	25	40	60	80	150
36	Bob Pulford	4	5	6	10	20	30		
37	Ross Lonsberry	4	5	6	10	20	40	50	120
38	Gord Labossiere	4	4	5	8	15	30	40	120
39	Eddie Joyal	4	4	5	8	15	30	40	100
40	Gump Worsley	10	12	15	25	40	80	125	250
41	Bob McCord	4	4	5	8	15	30		
42	Leo Boivin	4	5	6	10	20	30	40	80
43	Tom Reid RC	4	4	5	8	15	30	40	80
44	Charlie Burns	4	4	5	8	15	50		
45	Bob Barlow	4	4	5	8	15	30	40	80
46	Bill Goldsworthy	4	5	6	10	20	40	40	80
47	Danny Grant	4	5	6	10	20	30	40	100
48	Norm Beaudin RC	4	4	5	8	20	40	50	120
49	Rogatien Vachon	10	12	15	25	35	50	60	200
50	Yvan Cournoyer	10	12	15	25	35	60	80	135
51	Serge Savard	10	12	15	25	40	150		
52	Jacques Laperriere	4	8	10	15	30	100	125	175
53	Terry Harper	4	4	5	8	15	30	40	120
54	Ralph Backstrom	4	5	6	10	20	60		
55	Jean Beliveau	10	12	15	25	40	100		
56	Claude Larose	4	4	5	8	80	300		
57	Jacques Lemaire	10	12	15	25	40	80		
58	Peter Mahovlich	4	5	6	10	20	30	40	120
59	Tim Horton	12	15	20	40	50	80	100	200
60	Bob Nevin	4	4	5	8	15	30		
61	Dave Balon	4	4	5	10	20	60		
62	Vic Hadfield	4	5	6	10	20	30		
63	Rod Gilbert	10	12	15	25	40	80		
64	Ron Stewart	4	4	5	8	15	25		
65	Ted Irvine	4	4	5	8	15	40		
66	Arnie Brown	4	4	5	8	15	120		
67	Brad Park RC	20	25	30	60	75	250	300	1,400
68	Ed Giacomin	10	12	15	20	30	80		
69	Gary Smith	4	5	6	10	20	30		
70	Carol Vadnais	4	5	6	10	20	30	40	120
71	Doug Roberts	4	4	5	8	15	30		
72	Harry Howell	4	5	6	10	20	30		
73	Joe Szura	4	4	5	8	15	30	40	100
74	Mike Laughton	4	4	5	8	15	150		
75	Gary Jarrett	4	4	5	8	15	30	40	100
76	Bill Hicke	4	4	5	8	15	50		
77	Paul Andrea RC	4	4	5	8	20	80		
78	Bernie Parent	20	25	30	40	60	200		
79	Joe Watson	4	4	5	8	15	30	40	100
80	Ed Van Impe	4	4	5	8	15	60		
81	Larry Hillman	4	4	5	8	15	60		
82	George Swarbrick	4	4	5	8	15	60		
83	Bill Sutherland	4	4	5	8	15	40		
84	Andre Lacroix	4	5	6	10	20	80		
85	Gary Dornhoefer	4	4	5	10	20	30	50	100
86	Jean-Guy Gendron	4	4	5	8	15	30		

#	Player	VG 3	VgEx 4	EX 5	ExMt 6	NM 7	NmMt 8	NmMt+ 8.5	MT 9
87	Al Smith RC	4	5	6	10	25	50		
88	Bob Woytowich	4	4	5	8	15	30		
89	Duane Rupp	4	4	5	8	15	30		
90	Jim Morrison	4	4	5	8	15	50		
91	Ron Schock	4	4	5	8	15	60		
92	Ken Schinkel	4	4	5	8	15	30	40	120
93	Keith McCreary	4	4	5	8	15	40		
94	Bryan Hextall	4	5	6	10	25	60		
95	Wayne Hicks RC	4	4	5	8	15	40		
96	Gary Sabourin	4	4	5	8	15	30		
97	Ernie Wakely RC	4	5	6	10	20	80		
98	Bob Wall	4	4	5	8	15	40	50	100
99	Barclay Plager	4	5	6	10	20	40	50	100
100	Jean-Guy Talbot	4	4	5	8	15	30		
101	Gary Veneruzzo	4	4	5	8	15	30		
102	Tim Ecclestone	4	4	5	8	15	30	40	100
103	Red Berenson	4	5	6	10	20	60		
104	Larry Keenan	4	4	5	8	15	30	40	100
105	Bruce Gamble	4	4	5	8	15	100		
106	Jim Dorey	4	4	5	8	15	30		
107	Mike Pelyk RC	4	4	5	8	30	150		
108	Rick Ley	4	4	5	10	20	60		
109	Mike Walton	4	4	5	8	15	30		
110	Norm Ullman	10	12	15	25	30	100	125	175
111A	Brit Selby no trade	4	4	5	8	15	30	40	80
111B	Brit Selby trade	15	20	20	30	40	100		
112	Garry Monahan	4	4	5	8	15	100		
113	George Armstrong	10	12	15	25	40	80	125	200
114	Gary Doak	4	5	10	15	30	150		
115	Darryl Sly RC	4	4	5	8	15	30		
116	Wayne Maki	4	4	5	8	15	125		
117	Orland Kurtenbach	4	4	5	8	20	60		
118	Murray Hall	4	4	5	8	15	30		
119	Marc Reaume	4	4	5	8	15	30	40	350
120	Pat Quinn	10	12	15	25	40	60	80	200
121	Andre Boudrias	4	4	5	15	60	100		
122	Paul Popiel	4	4	5	8	15	150		
123	Paul Terbenche	4	4	5	8	15	40	50	80
124	Howie Menard	4	4	5	8	15	30		
125	Gerry Meehan RC	4	5	6	10	20	60		
126	Skip Krake	4	4	5	8	15	30		
127	Phil Goyette	4	4	5	8	15	50	60	150
128	Reg Fleming	4	4	5	8	15	30	40	100
129	Don Marshall	4	5	6	10	20	40		
130	Bill Inglis RC	4	4	5	8	15	40	50	100
131	Gilbert Perreault RC	60	80	125	250	300	1,750		
132	Checklist 2	50	100	150	300	350	1,200	1,350	1,500
133	Ed Johnston	4	5	6	10	40	50		
134	Ted Green	4	5	6	10	20	40		
135	Rick Smith RC	4	4	5	8	15	40		
136	Derek Sanderson	15	20	20	30	40	100	150	
137	Dallas Smith	4	5	8	20	30	100		
138	Don Marcotte RC	4	5	6	10	20	40	50	150
139	Ed Westfall	4	5	6	10	20	60		
140	Floyd Smith	4	4	5	8	15	30	35	60
141	Randy Wyrozub RC	4	4	5	8	15	30		
142	Cliff Schmautz RC	4	4	5	8	15	30		
143	Mike McMahon	4	4	5	8	15	30	40	150
144	Jim Watson	4	4	5	8	15	30		
145	Roger Crozier	4	5	6	10	20	40		
146	Tracy Pratt	4	4	5	8	15	30		
147	Cliff Koroll RC	4	5	6	10	20	50		
148	Gerry Pinder RC	4	5	6	10	20	30	40	60
149	Chico Maki	4	4	5	8	15	30	40	135
150	Doug Jarrett	4	4	5	8	15	30		
151	Keith Magnuson RC	10	12	15	20	25	50	60	150
152	Gerry Desjardins	4	5	6	10	20	30		
153	Tony Esposito	20	25	30	40	60	150	200	300
154	Gary Bergman	4	4	5	8	15	30	40	80
155	Tom Webster RC	4	5	6	10	20	30	40	60
156	Dale Rolfe	4	4	5	8	15	30		
157	Alex Delvecchio	10	12	15	20	25	50	60	100
158	Nick Libett	4	4	5	8	15	30		
159	Wayne Connelly	4	4	5	8	15	30	40	60
160	Mike Byers RC	4	4	5	8	15	30		
161	Bill Flett	4	4	5	8	15	30	40	60
162	Larry Mickey	4	4	5	8	15	30	40	80
163	Noel Price	4	4	5	8	15	30		
164	Larry Cahan	4	4	5	8	15	50		
165	Jack Norris RC	4	5	6	10	20	30	40	80
166	Ted Harris	4	4	5	8	15	30	40	60
167	Murray Oliver	4	4	5	8	15	30	40	80
168	Jean-Paul Parise	4	5	6	10	20	40	50	80
169	Tom Williams	4	4	5	8	15	30		
170	Bobby Rousseau	4	5	6	10	15	30		
171	Jude Drouin RC	4	5	6	10	20	50		
172	Walt McKechnie RC	4	5	6	10	20	30		
173	Cesare Maniago	4	5	6	10	20	100		
174	Rejean Houle RC	10	12	15	20	25	50	60	100
175A	M.Redmond trade	4	5	6	10	25	40	50	80

#	Player	VG 3	VgEx 4	EX 5	ExMt 6	NM 7	NmMt 8	NmMt+ 8.5	MT 9
175B	M.Redmond no trade	12	15	20	30	40	150		
176	Henri Richard	10	12	15	20	30	60	80	200
177	Guy Lapointe RC	15	20	30	40	50	125	150	250
178	J.C. Tremblay	4	5	6	10	20	30	40	60
179	Marc Tardif RC	10	12	15	25	50	60	80	100
180	Walt Tkaczuk	4	5	6	10	20	30	40	50
181	Jean Ratelle	6	8	12	15	25	60	80	100
182	Pete Stemkowski	4	4	5	8	15	30		
183	Gilles Villemure	4	5	6	10	20	30	35	60
184	Rod Seiling	4	4	5	8	15	30	35	60
185	Jim Neilson	4	4	5	8	15	30	35	60
186	Dennis Hextall	4	5	6	10	20	30	35	60
187	Gerry Ehman	4	4	5	8	15	30		
188	Bert Marshall	4	4	5	8	15	50		
189	Gary Croteau RC	4	4	5	8	15	30		
190	Ted Hampson	4	4	5	8	15	30		
191	Earl Ingarfield	4	4	5	8	15	30	40	60
192	Dick Mattiussi	4	4	5	8	15	30		
193	Earl Heiskala	4	4	5	8	15	30	40	80
194	Simon Nolet	4	4	5	8	15	30	40	60
195	Bobby Clarke RC	50	80	100	150	200	400	500	1,000
196	Garry Peters	4	4	5	8	15	30		
197	Lew Morrison RC	4	4	5	8	15	30	40	80
198	Wayne Hillman	4	4	5	8	15	40		
199	Doug Favell	10	12	15	25	40	100		
200	Les Binkley	4	5	6	10	20	30	50	150
201	Dean Prentice	4	5	6	8	15	30		
202	Jean Pronovost	4	5	6	10	25	80		
203	Wally Boyer	4	4	5	8	15	30		
204	Bryan Watson	4	4	5	8	15	30		
205	Glen Sather	4	5	6	10	25	40	50	80
206	Lowell MacDonald	4	4	5	8	15	30	40	80
207	Andy Bathgate	4	5	6	10	20	30	40	80
208	Val Fonteyne	4	4	5	8	15	30		
209	Jim Lorentz RC	4	4	5	8	15	30		
210	Glenn Hall	10	12	15	20	30	50	60	100
211	Bob Plager	4	5	6	10	20	40	50	60
212	Noel Picard	4	4	5	8	15	30		
213	Jim Roberts	4	5	6	10	25	40		
214	Frank St.Marseille	4	4	5	8	15	30	40	60
215	Ab McDonald	4	4	5	8	15	30		
216	Brian Glennie RC	4	4	5	8	15	30	40	80
217	Paul Henderson	4	5	6	10	20	35	50	80
218	Darryl Sittler RC	60	80	100	150	300	550	600	1,600
219	Dave Keon	8	10	12	20	35	50	60	125
220	Jim Harrison RC	4	4	5	8	15	30	40	125
221	Ron Ellis	4	5	6	10	20	30		
222	Jacques Plante	20	25	30	50	60	100		
223	Bob Baun	4	5	10	20	30	120		
224	George Gardner RC	4	4	5	8	15	30	40	60
225	Dale Tallon RC	4	5	6	10	20	40	50	80
226	Rosaire Paiement RC	4	4	5	8	15	30		
227	Mike Corrigan RC	4	4	5	8	15	30	40	80
228	Ray Cullen	4	4	5	8	15	30		
229	Charlie Hodge	4	5	6	10	20	40		
230	Len Lunde	4	4	5	8	15	30	40	80
231	Terry Sawchuk Mem	30	40	50	60	80	100	125	200
232	Bruins Team Champs	10	12	15	25	40	60	100	150
233	Espo/Cashmn/Hodge	15	20	20	25	35	60	80	150
234	Tony Esposito AS1	20	25	30	40	60	120		
235	Bobby Hull AS1	20	25	30	40	50	80		
236	Bobby Orr AS1	40	50	60	80	120	300	400	750
237	Phil Esposito AS1	12	15	20	30	40	80	100	200
238	Gordie Howe AS1	20	30	40	50	80	100		
239	Brad Park AS1	12	15	20	30	40	80		
240	Stan Mikita AS2	10	12	15	25	40	100		
241	John McKenzie AS2	4	5	8	10	25	125	150	200
242	Frank Mahovlich AS2	4	4	5	8	15	30	50	150
243	Carl Brewer AS2	4	4	5	8	15	30		
244	Ed Giacomin AS2	4	5	6	10	40	200		
245	J.Laperriere AS2	4	4	5	10	20	80		
246	Bobby Orr Hart	40	50	60	80	150	250	300	700
247	Tony Esposito Calder	20	25	30	40	60	100		
248A	B.Orr Norris Howe	50	60	80	120	200	350	500	
248B	B.Orr Norris no Howe	50	60	80	120	200	350	500	
249	Bobby Orr Ross	35	50	60	80	100	350	500	
250	Tony Esposito Vezina	20	25	30	40	60	120		
251	Phil Goyette Byng Trophy	4	4	5	8	15	30		
252	Bobby Orr Smythe	50	60	80	120	150	225	350	600
253	P.Martin Mastrtn Trophy	4	4	5	8	15	30		
254	Stanley Cup	12	15	20	30	40	50	60	100
255	Prince of Wales Trophy	4	5	6	10	20	30		
256	Conn Smythe Trophy	4	5	6	10	20	40	60	80
257	James Norris Trophy	4	5	6	10	20	30	40	80
258	Calder Trophy	4	5	6	10	20	30	40	80
259	Vezina Trophy	4	5	6	10	20	40		
260	Lady Byng Trophy	4	5	6	10	20	30	40	80
261	Hart Trophy	4	5	6	10	20	30	35	60
262	Art Ross Trophy	4	5	6	10	20	40		
263	Clarence Campbell Bowl	4	5	6	10	25	40		
264	John Ferguson	10	12	15	25	50	250		

— Art Ross Trophy #262 PSA 9 (MT) sold for $408 (eBay; 4/07)
— Bobby Orr Hart #246 PSA 9 (MT) sold for $681 (Mile High; 12/13)
— Bruins Team Champs #232 PSA 10 (Gem) sold for $929 (eBay; 1/14)
— Checklist 2 #132 PSA 10 (Gem) sold for $2,385 (Mile High; 12/13)
— Guy LaPointe #177 PSA 10 (Gem) sold for $1,209 (eBay; 9/15)
— Peter Mahovlich #58 PSA 10 (Gem) sold for $204 (eBay; 2/07)
— Bobby Orr #3 PSA 10 (Gem) sold for $7,036 (eBay; 5/12)
— Bobby Orr Norris #214 PSA 9 (Mt) sold for $1,775 (Mile High; 12/13)
— Bobby Orr Norris no Howe #248B PSA 10 (Gem) sold for $1,710 (eBay; 2/13)
— Bobby Orr Smythe #252 PSA 10 (Gem) sold for $1,955 (Memory Lane; 5/08)
— Jacques Plante #222 PSA 9 (MT) sold for $460 (eBay; 2/14)
— Terry Sawchuk Mem #231 PSA 10 (gem) sold for $1,135 (eBay; 2/16)
— Brad Park RC #67 PSA 9 (MT) sold for $1,730 (eBay; 4/09)

1970-71 Topps

#	Player	VG 3	VgEx 4	EX 5	ExMt 6	NM 7	NmMt 8	NmMt+ 8.5	MT 9
1	Gerry Cheevers	10	12	15	20	25	50		
2	Johnny Bucyk	5	6	8	10	12	30		
3	Bobby Orr	25	40	80	100	150	300	400	1,400
4	Don Awrey	5	6	8	10	12	15	25	40
5	Fred Stanfield	5	6	8	10	12	15	25	40
6	John McKenzie	5	6	8	10	12	15	25	40
7	Wayne Cashman RC	6	8	10	12	15	25	40	60
8	Ken Hodge	5	6	8	10	12	15	25	40
9	Wayne Carleton	5	6	8	10	12	15	25	40
10	Garnet Bailey RC	5	6	8	10	12	15	25	40
11	Phil Esposito	10	12	15	20	25	60	80	100
12	Lou Angotti	5	6	8	10	12	15	25	40
13	Jim Pappin	5	6	8	10	12	15	25	40
14	Dennis Hull	5	6	8	10	12	15	25	40
15	Bobby Hull	12	15	20	25	30	80	100	175
16	Doug Mohns	5	6	8	10	12	15	25	40
17	Pat Stapleton	5	6	8	10	12	15	20	30
18	Pit Martin	5	6	8	10	12	15	25	40
19	Eric Nesterenko	5	6	8	10	12	15	25	40
20	Stan Mikita	8	10	12	15	20	30	50	150
21	Roy Edwards	5	6	8	10	12	15	25	40
22	Frank Mahovlich	5	6	8	10	15	30	40	150
23	Ron Harris	5	6	8	10	12	15	25	40
24	Bob Baun	5	6	8	10	12	15	25	40
25	Pete Stemkowski	5	6	8	10	12	15	25	40
26	Garry Unger	5	6	8	10	12	15	25	40
27	Bruce MacGregor	5	6	8	10	12	15	25	40
28	Larry Jeffrey	5	6	8	10	12	15	25	40
29	Gordie Howe	20	25	40	50	60	80	100	150
30	Billy Dea	5	6	8	10	12	15	25	40
31	Denis DeJordy	5	6	8	10	12	15	25	40
32	Matt Ravlich	5	6	8	10	12	20	30	50
33	Dave Amadio	5	6	8	10	12	15	25	40
34	Gilles Marotte	5	6	8	10	12	15	20	30
35	Eddie Shack	5	6	8	10	12	15	25	50
36	Bob Pulford	5	6	8	10	12	15	20	30
37	Ross Lonsberry	5	6	8	10	12	15	20	30
38	Gord Labossiere	5	6	8	10	12	15	25	40
39	Eddie Joyal	5	6	8	10	12	15	25	40
40	Gump Worsley	5	6	8	10	12	20		
41	Bob McCord	5	6	8	10	12	15	20	40
42	Leo Boivin	5	6	8	10	12	15	25	40
43	Tom Reid	5	6	8	10	12	15	25	40
44	Charlie Burns	5	6	8	10	12	15	25	40
45	Bob Barlow	5	6	8	10	12	15	20	30
46	Bill Goldsworthy	5	6	8	10	12	15	20	30
47	Danny Grant	5	6	8	10	12	15	25	40
48	Norm Beaudin	5	6	8	10	12	15	20	30
49	Rogatien Vachon	6	8	10	12	12	20		50
50	Yvan Cournoyer	5	6	8	10	12	15	25	40
51	Serge Savard	5	6	8	10	12	15	30	50
52	Jacques Laperriere	5	6	8	10	12	15	20	30
53	Terry Harper	5	6	8	10	12	15	20	30
54	Ralph Backstrom	5	6	8	10	12	15	25	40
55	Jean Beliveau	8	10	12	20	30	50	60	80
56	Claude Larose UER	5	6	8	10	12	15	25	40
57	Jacques Lemaire	5	6	8	10	12	20	25	50
58	Peter Mahovlich	5	6	8	10	12	15	25	40
59	Tim Horton	8	10	12	15	25	40	50	80
60	Bob Nevin	5	6	8	10	12	15	25	40
61	Dave Balon	5	6	8	10	12	15	25	40
62	Vic Hadfield	5	6	8	10	12	15	25	40
63	Rod Gilbert	5	6	8	10	12	20	25	50
64	Ron Stewart	5	6	8	10	12	15	25	40
65	Ted Irvine	5	6	8	10	12	15	25	40
66	Arnie Brown	5	6	8	10	12	15	20	30
67	Brad Park RC	12	15	20	25	25	40	50	200
68	Ed Giacomin	5	6	8	10	12	20	25	50
69	Gary Smith	5	6	8	10	12	15	20	30
70	Carol Vadnais	5	6	8	10	12	15	25	40
71	Doug Roberts	5	6	8	10	12	15	20	30
72	Harry Howell	5	6	8	10	12	15	25	40
73	Joe Szura	5	6	8	10	12	15	20	30
74	Mike Laughton	5	6	8	10	12	15	20	30
75	Gary Jarrett	5	6	8	10	12	15	25	40
76	Bill Hicke	5	6	8	10	12	20		
77	Paul Andrea	5	6	8	10	12	15	25	40
78	Bernie Parent	8	10	12	15	20	40	50	100
79	Joe Watson	5	6	8	10	12	15	25	40
80	Ed Van Impe	5	6	8	10	12	15	25	40
81	Larry Hillman	5	6	8	10	12	15	25	40
82	George Swarbrick	5	6	8	10	12	15	25	40
83	Bill Sutherland	5	6	8	10	12	15	25	40
84	Andre Lacroix	5	6	8	10	12	15	25	40
85	Gary Dornhoefer	5	6	8	10	12	15	25	40
86	Jean-Guy Gendron	5	6	8	10	12	15	25	40
87	Al Smith	5	6	8	10	12	15	25	40
88	Bob Woytowich	5	6	8	10	12	15	25	40
89	Duane Rupp	5	6	8	10	12	15	25	40
90	Jim Morrison	5	6	8	10	12	15	25	40
91	Ron Schock	5	6	8	10	12	15	25	40
92	Ken Schinkel	5	6	8	10	12	15	25	40
93	Keith McCreary	5	6	8	10	12	15	25	40
94	Bryan Hextall	5	6	8	10	12	15	25	40
95	Wayne Hicks	5	6	8	10	12	15	25	40
96	Gary Sabourin	5	6	8	10	12	15	25	40
97	Ernie Wakely	5	6	8	10	12	15	25	40
98	Bob Wall	5	6	8	10	12	15	25	40
99	Barclay Plager	5	6	8	10	12	15	25	40
100	Jean-Guy Talbot	5	6	8	10	12	20		
101	Gary Veneruzzo	5	6	8	10	12	20		
102	Tim Ecclestone	5	6	8	10	12	15	25	40
103	Red Berenson	5	6	8	10	12	15	25	40
104	Larry Keenan	5	6	8	10	12	15	20	30
105	Bruce Gamble	5	6	8	10	12	20		
106	Jim Dorey	5	6	8	10	12	15	25	40
107	Mike Pelyk	5	6	8	10	12	15	25	40
108	Rick Ley	5	6	8	10	12	15	25	40
109	Mike Walton	5	6	8	10	12	15	25	40
110	Norm Ullman	5	6	8	10	12	20	25	50
111	Brit Selby	5	6	8	10	12	15	25	40
112	Garry Monahan	5	6	8	10	12	15	20	30
113	George Armstrong	5	6	8	10	12	20	25	50
114	Gary Doak	5	6	8	10	12	15	25	40
115	Darryl Sly	5	6	8	10	12	15	20	30
116	Wayne Maki	5	6	8	10	12	20		
117	Orland Kurtenbach	5	6	8	10	12	15	25	40
118	Murray Hall	5	6	8	10	12	15	20	30
119	Marc Reaume	5	6	8	10	12	15	25	40
120	Pat Quinn	5	6	8	10	12	30	40	60
121	Andre Boudrias	5	6	8	10	12	15	20	30
122	Paul Popiel	5	6	8	10	12	15	25	40
123	Paul Terbenche	5	6	8	10	12	15	25	40
124	Howie Menard	5	6	8	10	12	15	25	40
125	Gerry Meehan RC	5	6	8	10	12	25	30	50
126	Skip Krake	5	6	8	10	12	15	25	40
127	Phil Goyette	5	6	8	10	12	15	25	40
128	Reg Fleming	5	6	8	10	12	20		
129	Don Marshall	5	6	8	10	12	15	25	40
130	Bill Inglis	5	6	8	10	12	15	25	40
131	Gilbert Perreault RC	20	25	30	60	100	150	250	400
132	Checklist Card	20	25	30	40	80	150		

— Jean Beliveau #55 PSA 10 (GmMT) sold for $665 (eBay; 1/07)
— Gary Doak #114 PSA 10 (GmMT) sold for $535 (Memory Lane; 5/08)
— Gordie Howe #29 PSA 10 (GmMT) sold for $1,630 (eBay; 1/07)
— Orland Kurtenbach #117 PSA 10 (GmMT) sold for $535 (Memory Lane; 5/08)
— Gilbert Perreault RC #131 PSA 8 (NrMt) sold for $3,442.99 (eBay; 2/14)
— Doug Mohns #16 PSA 9 (MT) sold for $258 (eBay; 7/12)
— Brad Park #67 PSA 10 (GmMT) sold for $921.50 (eBay; 8/12)

1971-72 O-Pee-Chee

#	Player	VG 3	VgEx 4	EX 5	ExMt 6	NM 7	NmMt 8	NmMt+ 8.5	MT 9
1	Paul Popiel	6	8	10	15	30	200		
2	Pierre Bouchard RC	5	8	15	40	100	250		
3	Don Awrey	4	4	5	8	15	40	60	150
4	Paul Curtis RC	4	4	5	8	15	80		
5	Guy Trottier RC	4	4	5	10	20	50	60	135
6	Paul Shmyr RC	4	4	5	10	20	50	60	135
7	Fred Stanfield	4	4	5	8	15	50	60	120
8	Mike Robitaille RC	4	4	5	8	15	50	60	100
9	Vic Hadfield	4	4	5	10	20	30	60	100
10	Jim Harrison	4	4	5	8	15	40	60	100
11	Bill White	4	4	5	8	15	40	50	80
12	Andre Boudrias	4	4	5	8	25	60		
13	Gary Sabourin	4	4	5	8	15	40	80	150
14	Arnie Brown	5	6	10	15	30	80		
15	Yvan Cournoyer	6	8	10	15	30	60	80	175
16	Bryan Hextall	4	5	6	10	20	40	50	80
17	Gary Croteau	4	4	5	8	15	80		
18	Gilles Villemure	4	5	6	10	20	60		
19	Serge Bernier RC	4	5	6	10	20	50		
20	Phil Esposito	15	20	25	40	80	100	125	200
21	Tom Reid	4	4	5	8	15	40	60	120

#	Player	VG 3	VgEx 4	EX 5	ExMt 6	NM 7	NmMt 8	NmMt+ 8.5	MT 9
22	Doug Barrie RC	4	4	5	8	15	50	60	80
23	Eddie Joyal	4	4	5	8	15	50		
24	Dunc Wilson RC	6	8	10	15	30	100	125	250
25	Pat Stapleton	4	5	6	10	20	60		
26	Garry Unger	4	5	10	20	50	300		
27	Al Smith	4	5	6	10	20	40	50	80
28	Bob Woytowich	4	4	5	8	40	80		
29	Marc Tardif	4	5	6	10	20	60	80	150
30	Norm Ullman	6	8	10	15	30	80		
31	Tom Williams	4	4	5	8	40	250		
32	Ted Harris	4	4	5	8	15	40	50	80
33	Andre Lacroix	4	5	6	10	20	50		
34	Mike Byers	4	4	5	8	15	40	50	
35	Johnny Bucyk	6	8	10	15	30	150	200	400
36	Roger Crozier	4	5	6	10	20	50	60	120
37	Alex Delvecchio	8	10	12	20	30	80		
38	Frank St.Marseille	4	4	5	8	15	50	60	100
39	Pit Martin	4	5	6	10	20	40	50	80
40	Brad Park	12	15	15	25	35	50	60	120
41	Greg Polis RC	4	4	5	8	15	50		
42	Orland Kurtenbach	4	4	5	8	15	50	60	100
43	Jim McKenny RC	4	4	5	8	15	50	60	100
44	Bob Nevin	4	4	5	8	15	60	80	135
45	Ken Dryden RC	100	120	250	400	500	1,000	1,500	3,500
46	Carol Vadnais	4	5	6	10	20	50	60	100
47	Bill Flett	4	4	5	8	15	40	50	80
48	Jim Johnson	4	4	5	8	15	50	60	100
49	Al Hamilton	4	4	5	8	15	50		
50	Bobby Hull	30	40	50	60	80	100	125	300
51	Chris Bordeleau RC	4	4	5	8	15	60	80	175
52	Tim Ecclestone	4	4	5	8	15	40	50	80
53	Rod Seiling	4	4	5	8	15	40		
54	Gerry Cheevers	8	10	12	20	40	80		
55	Bill Goldsworthy	4	5	6	10	20	50	60	100
56	Ron Schock	4	4	5	8	15	50	60	100
57	Jim Dorey	4	4	5	8	15	40	50	80
58	Wayne Maki	4	4	5	8	15	40		
59	Terry Harper	4	4	5	8	15	50		
60	Gilbert Perreault	20	25	30	50	80	100	125	225
61	Ernie Hicke RC	4	4	5	8	15	40	50	80
62	Wayne Hillman	4	4	5	8	20	80	100	175
63	Denis DeJordy	4	5	6	10	20	80		
64	Ken Schinkel	4	4	5	8	15	50	60	100
65	Derek Sanderson	10	12	15	25	40	80	125	225
66	Barclay Plager	4	5	6	10	20	50	60	100
67	Paul Henderson	4	5	6	10	20	60	80	200
68	Jude Drouin	4	4	5	8	15	80	100	175
69	Keith Magnuson	4	5	6	10	20	40	50	80
70	Ron Harris	4	4	5	8	15	40	50	80
71	Jacques Lemaire	6	8	10	15	30	60	80	150
72	Doug Favell	4	5	6	10	20	60	80	150
73	Bert Marshall	4	4	5	8	15	30	40	80
74	Ted Irvine	4	4	5	8	15	40	50	80
75	Walt Tkaczuk	4	5	6	10	25	40	50	100
76	Bob Berry RC	6	8	10	15	30	60		
77	Syl Apps RC	6	8	10	15	30	60	80	150
78	Tom Webster	4	5	6	10	20	40	50	100
79	Danny Grant	4	5	6	10	20	60	80	150
80	Dave Keon	6	8	10	15	30			350
81	Ernie Wakely	4	5	6	10	20			150
82	John McKenzie	4	4	5	8	15	50	60	100
83	Ron Stackhouse RC	4	4	5	8	15			100
84	Peter Mahovlich	4	5	6	10	20			300
85	Dennis Hull	4	5	6	10	20	50	80	175
86	Juha Widing RC	4	4	5	8	15	50	60	100
87	Gary Doak	4	4	5	8	15	50	60	100
88	Phil Goyette	4	4	5	8	15	40	50	80
89	Lew Morrison	4	4	5	8	15	40	50	80
90	Ab DeMarco RC	4	4	5	8	15	40	50	80
91	Red Berenson	4	5	6	10	20	40	50	80
92	Mike Pelyk	4	4	5	8	15	50		
93	Gary Jarrett	4	4	5	8	15	30	40	60
94	Bob Pulford	4	5	6	10	20	40	50	100
95	Dan Johnson RC	4	4	5	8	15	30	40	60
96	Eddie Shack	6	8	10	15	30	50	60	120
97	Jean Ratelle	6	8	10	15	30	60	80	150
98	Jim Pappin	4	4	5	8	15	50	60	100
99	Roy Edwards	4	5	6	10	25	40	50	80
100	Bobby Orr	40	50	60	100	200	800		
101	Ted Hampson	4	4	5	8	15	40	50	80
102	Mickey Redmond	6	8	10	15	30	80		
103	Bob Plager	6	8	10	15	30	50	60	100
104	Barry Ashbee RC	4	5	6	10	20	50	60	150
105	Frank Mahovlich	8	10	12	20	40	100		
106	Dick Redmond RC	4	4	5	8	15	30	40	80
107	Tracy Pratt	4	4	5	8	15	30	40	80
108	Ralph Backstrom	4	5	6	10	15	30	40	80
109	Murray Hall	4	4	5	8	15	30	40	80
110	Tony Esposito	25	30	40	50	60	100	125	250
111	Checklist Card	250	300	400	700	900	2,000		
112	Jim Neilson	4	4	5	8	15	50	60	100
113	Ron Ellis	4	5	6	10	20	80		
114	Bobby Clarke	25	30	35	40	80	100	125	300
115	Ken Hodge	4	5	6	10	30	60		
116	Jim Roberts	4	5	6	10	30	80	100	175
117	Cesare Maniago	4	5	6	10	20	50	60	100
118	Jean Pronovost	4	5	6	10	20	50		
119	Gary Bergman	4	4	5	8	15	40	50	80
120	Henri Richard	8	10	12	20	30	80	100	175
121	Ross Lonsberry	4	4	5	8	15	50	60	100
122	Pat Quinn	4	5	6	10	20	60	80	150
123	Rod Gilbert	6	8	10	15	30	50	60	100
124	Walt McKechnie	4	5	6	10	20	50		
125	Stan Mikita	12	15	15	25	40	60	80	250
126	Ed Van Impe	4	4	5	8	15	30	40	60
127	Terry Crisp RC	8	10	12	20	30	40	50	80
128	Fred Barrett RC	4	4	5	8	15	40	50	80
129	Wayne Cashman	6	8	10	15	30	80		
130	J.C. Tremblay	4	5	6	10	40	80		
131	Bernie Parent	15	20	25	40	80	120	135	250
132	Bryan Watson	4	5	6	10	20	60		
133	Marcel Dionne RC	50	80	100	150	250	350	450	1,250
134	Ab McDonald	4	5	6	10	20	60	80	150
135	Leon Rochefort	4	5	6	10	20	30	40	60
136	Serge Lajeunesse RC	4	5	6	10	20	30	40	60
137	Joe Daley	5	6	8	12	25	40	50	80
138	Brian Conacher	4	5	6	10	20	60		
139	Bill Collins	4	5	6	10	20	60		
140	Nick Libett	4	5	6	10	20	80	100	150
141	Bill Sutherland	4	5	6	10	20	30	40	60
142	Bill Hicke	4	5	6	10	20	50	60	100
143	Serge Savard	8	10	12	20	30	80	80	150
144	Jacques Laperriere	5	6	8	12	40	100	120	175
145	Guy Lapointe	5	6	8	12	25	60		
146	Claude Larose UER	4	5	6	10	20	60		
147	Rejean Houle	5	6	8	12	25	60	80	120
148	Guy Lafleur UER RC	60	125	150	250	350	650	800	1,250
149	Dale Hoganson RC	4	5	6	10	20	40		80
150	Al McDonough RC	4	5	6	10	20	30	40	100
151	Gilles Marotte	4	5	6	10	20	30	40	100
152	Butch Goring RC	8	10	12	20	50	120		
153	Harry Howell	5	6	8	12	25	60	80	150
154	Real Lemieux	4	5	6	10	20	30	35	60
155	Gary Edwards RC	5	6	8	12	25	30	40	100
156	Rogatien Vachon	8	10	12	20	30	40	60	120
157	Mike Corrigan	4	5	6	10	20	60	80	150
158	Floyd Smith	4	5	6	10	20	40	50	100
159	Dave Dryden	5	6	8	12	25	60	80	150
160	Gerry Meehan	5	6	8	12	25	50		
161	Richard Martin RC	15	20	25	50	50			175
162	Steve Atkinson RC	4	5	6	10	20	60		
163	Ron Anderson	4	5	6	10	20	30	35	60
164	Dick Duff	5	6	8	12	25	50	60	100
165	Jim Watson	4	5	6	10	20	30	35	60
166	Don Luce RC	4	5	6	10	20	60		
167	Larry Mickey	4	5	6	10	20	60		
168	Larry Hillman	4	5	6	10	20	30	35	60
169	Ed Westfall	5	6	8	12	25	30	40	100
170	Dallas Smith	4	5	6	10	20	40	50	100
171	Mike Walton	4	5	6	10	20	40	50	100
172	Ed Johnston	5	6	8	12	25	40	50	80
173	Ted Green	5	6	8	12	25	50	60	100
174	Rick Smith	4	5	6	10	20	40	50	80
175	Reggie Leach RC	15	20	25	40	80	120		
176	Don Marcotte	4	5	6	10	20	50		
177	Bobby Sheehan RC	4	5	6	10	20	60		
178	Wayne Carleton	4	5	6	10	20	40	50	120
179	Norm Ferguson	4	5	6	10	20	30	35	60
180	Don O'Donoghue RC	4	5	6	10	20	30	40	80
181	Gary Kurt RC	5	6	8	12	25	40	50	80
182	Joey Johnston RC	4	5	6	10	20	40		
183	Stan Gilbertson RC	4	5	6	10	20	60	80	150
184	Craig Patrick RC	8	10	12	20	40	60	80	120
185	Gerry Pinder	4	5	6	10	20	30	35	60
186	Tim Horton	10	12	15	25	35	60	80	100
187	Darryl Edestrand RC	4	5	6	10	20	50		
188	Keith McCreary	4	5	6	10	20	50	60	100
189	Val Fonteyne	4	5	6	10	20	50	60	100
190	S.Kannegiesser RC	4	5	6	10	20	40		
191	Nick Harbaruk RC	4	5	6	10	20	60		
192	Les Binkley	5	6	8	10	20	30	35	60
193	Darryl Sittler	18	20	25	30	50	100	120	200
194	Rick Ley	4	5	6	10	20	60	80	150
195	Jacques Plante	25	30	35	40	50	100	120	200
196	Bob Baun	5	6	10	15	50	250		
197	Brian Glennie	4	5	6	10	20	40	50	80
198	Brian Spencer RC	8	10	12	20	35	50	60	175
199	Don Marshall	5	6	8	12	25	40	50	100
200	Denis Dupere RC	4	5	6	10	20	50	60	100
201	Bruce Gamble	5	6	8	12	25	30	35	60

		VG 3	VgEx 4	EX 5	ExMt 6	NM 7	NmMt 8	NmMt+ 8.5	MT 9
202	Gary Dornhoefer	4	5	6	10	20	30	40	80
203	Bob Kelly RC	5	6	8	12	25	60		
204	Jean-Guy Gendron	4	5	6	10	20	30	35	60
205	Brent Hughes	4	5	6	10	20	35	40	100
206	Simon Nolet	4	5	6	10	20	40	50	80
207	Rick MacLeish RC	15	20	25	30	40	60	80	150
208	Doug Jarrett	4	5	6	10	20	30	35	60
209	Cliff Koroll	4	5	6	10	20	40	50	80
210	Chico Maki	4	5	6	10	20	30	35	60
211	Danny O'Shea	4	5	6	10	20	30	40	80
212	Lou Angotti	4	5	6	10	20	30	40	880
213	Eric Nesterenko	5	6	8	12	25	30	35	60
214	Bryan Campbell	4	5	6	10	20	30	40	80
215	Bill Fairbairn RC	4	5	6	10	20	40	50	80
216	Bruce MacGregor	4	5	6	10	20	30	35	60
217	Pete Stemkowski	4	5	6	10	20	40	50	80
218	Bobby Rousseau	4	5	6	10	20	30	40	80
219	Dale Rolfe	4	5	6	10	20	30	35	60
220	Ed Giacomin	8	10	12	20	40	40	50	120
221	Glen Sather	5	6	8	12	25	30	50	80
222	Carl Brewer	5	6	8	12	25	30	40	80
223	George Morrison RC	4	5	8	15	50	200		
224	Noel Picard	4	5	6	10	20	30	35	60
225	Peter McDuffe RC	5	6	8	12	30	80		
226	Brit Selby	4	5	6	10	20	40	50	80
227	Jim Lorentz	4	5	6	10	20	30	40	80
228	Phil Roberto RC	4	5	6	10	20	40	50	80
229	Dave Balon	4	5	6	10	20	30	40	100
230	Barry Wilkins RC	4	5	6	10	20	35	40	80
231	Dennis Kearns RC	4	5	6	10	20	40	50	80
232	Jocelyn Guevremont RC	5	6	8	12	25	30	40	80
233	Rosaire Paiement	4	5	6	10	20	80	100	175
234	Dale Tallon	4	5	6	10	20	80		
235	George Gardner	4	5	6	10	20	50	60	100
236	Ron Stewart	4	5	6	10	20	30	35	60
237	Wayne Connelly	4	5	6	10	20	40	50	80
238	Charlie Burns	4	5	6	10	30	200		
239	Murray Oliver	4	5	6	10	20	30	40	80
240	Lou Nanne	5	6	8	12	25	30	40	100
241	Gump Worsley	8	10	12	20	35	50	60	100
242	Doug Mohns	4	5	6	10	20	50	60	100
243	Jean-Paul Parise	4	5	6	10	20	35	40	80
244	Dennis Hextall	5	6	8	15	60	250		
245	Bobby Orr Double	25	30	40	50	80	150	175	350
246	Gilbert Perreault Calder	12	15	15	25	40	80		
247	Phil Esposito Ross	8	10	12	20	30	60		
248	Giacmn/Ville Vezina	5	8	15	30	150	500		
249	Johnny Bucyk Byng	5	6	8	12	25	40	50	100
250	Ed Giacomin AS1	5	6	8	12	25	50	60	100
251	Bobby Orr AS1	25	30	35	40	80	150	250	500
252	J.C. Tremblay AS1	5	8	15	30	125	200		
253	Phil Esposito AS1 UER	10	12	15	25	40	60	80	200
254	Ken Hodge AS1	5	6	8	12	25	60		
255	Johnny Bucyk AS1	5	6	8	15	30	80		
256	Jacques Plante AS2 UER	12	15	15	30	50	80	100	200
257	Brad Park AS2	5	6	8	12	25	40	60	100
258	Pat Stapleton AS2	5	6	8	12	25	35		
259	Dave Keon AS2	5	6	8	15	30	200		
260	Yvan Cournoyer AS2	5	6	8	12	25	50	60	100
261	Bobby Hull AS2	15	20	25	30	40	80	100	200
262	Gordie Howe Retires	25	30	40	60	80	100	175	300
263	Jean Beliveau Retires	25	30	40	50	80	120	150	300
264	Checklist Card	60	80	120	150	200	300	400	1,000

— Jean Beliveau Retires #263 PSA 10 (Gem) sold for $1,499 (eBay; 2/14)
— Checklist Card #111 PSA 9 (MT) sold for $2,800 (eBay; 2/07)
— Checklist Card #264 PSA 9 (Mt) sold for $1,034 (eBay; 2/14)
— Marcel Dionne RC #133 BGS 9.5 (GemMT) sold for $1,629.30 (eBay; 12/15)
— Ted Hampson #101 PSA 10 (Gem) sold for $311 (eBay; 8/12)
— Bobby Hull #50 PSA 10 (Gem) sold for $1,063 (eBay; 11/15)
— Ed Johnston #172 PSA 10 (Gem) sold for $425 (eBay; 4/07)
— Andre Lacroix #33 PSA 10 (Gem) sold for $425 (eBay; 8/12)
— Peter Mahovlich #84 PSA 10 (Gem) sold for $684 (eBay; 8/12)
— Chico Maki #210 PSA 10 (Gem) sold for $375 (eBay; 8/07)
— Murray Oliver #239 PSA 10 (Gem) sold for $505 (eBay; 4/07)
— Bobby Orr #100 PSA 9 (MT) sold for $3,354 (eBay; 10/12)
— Bobby Orr #100 PSA 9 (MT) sold for $2,887 (Mile High; 12/13)
— Mike Pelyk #92 PSA 10 (Gem) sold for $526 (eBay; 8/12)
— Frank St.Marseille #38 PSA 10 (Gem) sold for $266 (eBay; 8/12)
— Gary Sabourin #13 PSA 10 (Gem) sold for $444 (eBay; 8/12)
— Serge Savard #143 PSA 10 (Gem) sold for $570 (eBay; 7/12)
— Ken Schinkel #64 PSA 10 (Gem) sold for $540 (eBay; 8/12)
— Jim Watson #165 PSA 10 (Gem) sold for $408 (eBay; 4/07)

1971-72 Topps

		VG 3	VgEx 4	EX 5	ExMt 6	NM 7	NmMt 8	NmMt+ 8.5	MT 9
1	Espo/Bucyk/B.Hull LL	12	15	30	50	60	80		
2	Orr/Espo/Bucyk LL	15	20	25	30	40	60	80	200
3	Espo/Orr/Bucyk LL	8	10	12	15	20	30	40	80
4	Espo/EJ/Cheev/Giaco LL	5	6	8	10	12	20	25	60
5	Giaco/Espo/Maniago LL	4	5	6	8	12	20	25	100

		VG 3	VgEx 4	EX 5	ExMt 6	NM 7	NmMt 8	NmMt+ 8.5	MT 9
6	Plante/Giaco/T.Espo LL	6	8	10	12	15	25	30	40
7	Fred Stanfield	4	5	6	8	12	15	20	40
8	Mike Robitaille RC	4	5	6	8	10	12	15	30
9	Vic Hadfield	4	5	6	8	12	15	20	40
10	Jacques Plante	8	10	12	15	20	25	30	60
11	Bill White	4	5	6	8	12	15	30	100
12	Andre Boudrias	4	5	6	8	10	12	15	30
13	Jim Lorentz	4	5	6	8	10	12	15	30
14	Arnie Brown	4	5	6	8	12	15	20	40
15	Yvan Cournoyer	4	5	6	8	12	15	20	40
16	Bryan Hextall	4	5	6	8	12	15	20	40
17	Gary Croteau	4	5	6	8	10	12	15	30
18	Gilles Villemure	4	5	6	8	12	15	20	40
19	Serge Bernier RC	4	5	6	8	12	15	20	40
20	Phil Esposito	6	8	10	12	15	25	30	80
21	Charlie Burns	4	5	6	8	12	15	20	40
22	Doug Barrie RC	4	5	6	8	12	15	20	40
23	Eddie Joyal	4	5	6	8	12	15	20	40
24	Rosaire Paiement	4	5	6	8	12	15	20	40
25	Pat Stapleton	4	5	6	8	12	15	20	40
26	Garry Unger	4	5	6	8	12	15	20	40
27	Al Smith	4	5	6	8	12	15	20	40
28	Bob Woytowich	4	5	6	8	12	15	20	40
29	Marc Tardif	4	5	6	8	12	15	20	40
30	Norm Ullman	4	5	6	8	12	15	20	40
31	Tom Williams	4	5	6	8	12	15	20	40
32	Ted Harris	4	5	6	8	12	15	20	40
33	Andre Lacroix	4	5	6	8	10	12	15	30
34	Mike Byers	4	5	6	8	12	15	20	40
35	Johnny Bucyk	4	5	6	8	12	15	30	100
36	Roger Crozier	4	5	6	8	12	15	20	40
37	Alex Delvecchio	4	5	6	8	12	15	20	40
38	Frank St.Marseille	4	5	6	8	12	15	20	40
39	Pit Martin	4	5	6	8	12	15	20	50
40	Brad Park	5	6	8	10	12	15	25	60
41	Greg Polis RC	4	5	6	8	12	15	20	40
42	Orland Kurtenbach	4	5	6	8	10	12	15	30
43	Jim McKenny RC	4	5	6	8	10	12	15	30
44	Bob Nevin	4	5	6	8	12	15	20	40
45	Ken Dryden RC	40	80	100	150	200	300	350	500
46	Carol Vadnais	4	5	6	8	12	15	20	40
47	Bill Flett	4	5	6	8	12	15	20	40
48	Jim Johnson	4	5	6	8	12	15	20	40
49	Al Hamilton	4	5	6	8	12	15	30	80
50	Bobby Hull	12	15	20	30	50	80	100	150
51	Chris Bordeleau RC	4	5	6	8	12	15	20	40
52	Tim Ecclestone	4	5	6	8	10	12	15	30
53	Rod Seiling	4	5	6	8	12	15	20	40
54	Gerry Cheevers	4	5	6	8	12	15	30	200
55	Bill Goldsworthy	4	5	6	8	12	15	20	40
56	Ron Schock	4	5	6	8	10	12	15	30
57	Jim Dorey	4	5	6	8	10	12	15	30
58	Wayne Maki	4	5	6	8	12	15	20	40
59	Terry Harper	4	5	6	8	12	15	20	40
60	Gilbert Perreault	8	10	12	15	20	30	40	80
61	Ernie Hicke RC	4	5	6	8	10	12	15	30
62	Wayne Hillman	4	5	6	8	10	12	15	30
63	Denis DeJordy	4	5	6	8	12	15	20	40
64	Ken Schinkel	4	5	6	8	12	15	25	60
65	Derek Sanderson	4	5	6	8	12	15	25	60
66	Barclay Plager	4	5	6	8	10	12	15	30
67	Paul Henderson	4	5	6	8	12	15	20	40
68	Jude Drouin	4	5	6	8	10	12	15	30
69	Keith Magnuson	4	5	6	8	10	12	15	30
70	Gordie Howe	12	15	20	40	80	100	125	150
71	Jacques Lemaire	4	5	6	8	12	15	30	60
72	Doug Favell	4	5	6	8	12	15	30	80
73	Bert Marshall	4	5	6	8	12	15	20	40
74	Gerry Meehan	4	5	6	8	12	15	20	40
75	Walt Tkaczuk	4	5	6	8	12	15	20	40
76	Bob Berry RC	4	5	6	8	12	15	20	40
77	Syl Apps Jr. RC	4	5	6	8	12	15	20	40
78	Tom Webster	4	5	6	8	10	12	15	30
79	Danny Grant	4	5	6	8	12	15	20	30
80	Dave Keon	4	5	6	8	10	12	15	30
81	Ernie Wakely	4	5	6	8	12	15	20	40
82	John McKenzie	4	5	6	8	12	15	25	80
83	Doug Roberts	4	5	6	8	12	15	20	40
84	Peter Mahovlich	4	5	6	8	12	15	20	30
85	Dennis Hull	4	5	6	8	12	15	30	60
86	Juha Widing RC	4	5	6	8	10	12	15	30
87	Gary Doak	4	5	6	8	12	15	20	40
88	Phil Goyette	4	5	6	8	12	15	20	40
89	Gary Dornhoefer	4	5	6	8	12	15	20	40
90	Ed Giacomin	4	5	6	8	12	15	30	40
91	Red Berenson	4	5	6	8	10	12	15	30
92	Mike Pelyk	4	5	6	8	10	12	15	30
93	Gary Jarrett	4	5	6	8	12	15	20	40
94	Bob Pulford	4	5	6	8	12	15	25	60
95	Dale Tallon	4	5	6	8	12	15	20	40

#		VG 3	VgEx 4	EX 5	ExMt 6	NM 7	NmMt 8	NmMt+ 8.5	MT 9
96	Eddie Shack	4	5	6	8	10	12	15	30
97	Jean Ratelle	4	5	6	8	12	15	30	60
98	Jim Pappin	4	5	6	8	12	15	20	40
99	Roy Edwards	4	5	6	8	12	15	20	40
100	Bobby Orr	15	20	30	50	100	150	200	350
101	Ted Hampson	4	5	6	8	12	15	20	40
102	Mickey Redmond	4	5	6	8	12	15	20	40
103	Bob Plager	4	5	6	8	12	15	40	60
104	Bruce Gamble	4	5	6	8	12	15	20	40
105	Frank Mahovlich	4	5	6	8	12	15	20	40
106	Tony Featherstone RC	4	5	6	8	12	15	20	40
107	Tracy Pratt	4	5	6	8	12	15	20	40
108	Ralph Backstrom	4	5	6	8	12	15	20	40
109	Murray Hall	4	5	6	8	12	15	20	40
110	Tony Esposito	12	15	20	25	30	40	50	100
111	Checklist Card	12	15	20	30	50	100	150	250
112	Jim Neilson	4	5	6	8	12	15	20	40
113	Ron Ellis	4	5	6	8	12	15	20	40
114	Bobby Clarke	12	15	20	25	50	80	100	150
115	Ken Hodge	4	5	6	8	12	15	30	100
116	Jim Roberts	4	5	6	8	12	15	20	40
117	Cesare Maniago	4	5	6	8	12	15	20	40
118	Jean Pronovost	4	5	6	8	10	12	15	30
119	Gary Bergman	4	5	6	8	10	12	15	30
120	Henri Richard	4	5	6	8	12	15	20	40
121	Ross Lonsberry	4	5	6	8	12	15	20	40
122	Pat Quinn	4	5	6	8	12	15	25	60
123	Rod Gilbert	4	5	6	8	12	15	20	40
124	Gary Smith	4	5	6	8	10	12	15	30
125	Stan Mikita	5	6	8	10	12	20	25	80
126	Ed Van Impe	4	5	6	8	12	15	30	60
127	Wayne Connelly	4	5	6	8	12	15	20	40
128	Dennis Hextall	4	5	6	8	12	15	20	40
129	Wayne Cashman	4	5	6	8	12	20	30	60
130	J.C. Tremblay	4	5	6	8	12	15	20	40
131	Bernie Parent	4	5	6	8	12	40	50	100
132	Dunc McCallum RC	5	6	8	10	20	40	50	150

— Espo/Bucyk/B. Hull LL #1 PSA 10 (Gem) sold for $2,000 (eBay; 7/08)
— Espo/Bucyk/B. Hull LL #1 PSA 9 (MT) sold for $367 (eBay; 3/08)
— Ken Dryden #45 PSA 10 (MT) sold for $2,375 (eBay; 9/12)

1972-73 O-Pee-Chee

#		VG 3	VgEx 4	EX 5	ExMt 6	NM 7	NmMt 8	NmMt+ 8.5	MT 9
1	Johnny Bucyk DP	6	8	12	20	25	100	120	250
2	Rene Robert RC	4	5	10	12	20	50		
3	Gary Croteau	4	5	6	10	15	30		
4	Pat Stapleton	4	5	6	10	15	25	30	60
5	Ron Harris	4	5	6	10	15	25	30	60
6	Checklist 1	30	40	50	60	80	100		
7	Playoff Game 1	4	5	10	15	30	150		
8	Marcel Dionne	12	15	20	25	35	50	60	200
9	Bob Berry	4	5	6	10	15	30		
10	Lou Nanne	4	5	6	10	15	30		
11	Marc Tardif	4	5	6	10	15	30		
12	Jean Ratelle	4	5	6	10	15	30		
13	Craig Cameron RC	4	5	6	10	15	30		
14	Bobby Clarke	25	30	40	40	50	60	80	150
15	Jim Rutherford RC	8	10	20	25	30			
16	Andre Dupont RC	4	5	6	10	15	30	40	60
17	Mike Pelyk	4	5	6	10	15	25	30	60
18	Dunc Wilson	4	5	6	10	15	30		
19	Checklist 2	30	40	50	60	80	100		
20	Playoff Game 2	4	5	6	10	15	30		
21	Dallas Smith	4	5	6	10	15	30		
22	Gerry Meehan	4	5	6	10	15	30		
23	Rick Smith UER	4	5	6	10	15	25	30	60
24	Pit Martin	4	5	6	10	15	30		
25	Keith McCreary	4	5	6	10	15	30		
26	Alex Delvecchio	4	5	6	10	15	30		
27	Gilles Marotte	4	5	6	10	15	25	30	60
28	Gump Worsley	4	5	6	10	15	40		
29	Yvan Cournoyer	4	5	6	10	15	40		
30	Playoff Game 3	4	5	6	10	15	30		
31	Vic Hadfield	4	5	6	10	15	25	30	60
32	Tom Miller RC	4	5	6	10	15	25	30	60
33	Ed Van Impe	4	5	6	10	15	30		
34	Greg Polis	4	5	6	10	15	30		
35	Barclay Plager	4	5	6	10	15	25	30	60
36	Ron Ellis	4	5	6	10	15	30		
37	Jocelyn Guevremont	4	5	6	10	15	30		
38	Playoff Game 4	4	5	6	10	15	25	30	80
39	Carol Vadnais	4	5	6	10	15	30		
40	Steve Atkinson	4	5	6	10	15	30		
41	Ivan Boldirev RC	4	5	6	10	15	30		
42	Jim Pappin	4	5	6	10	15	25	30	60
43	Phil Myre RC	6	8	12	20	25	40	50	80
44	Yvan Cournoyer IA	4	5	6	10	15	30	40	60
45	Nick Libett	4	5	6	10	15	30		
46	Juha Widing	4	5	6	10	15	30		

#		VG 3	VgEx 4	EX 5	ExMt 6	NM 7	NmMt 8	NmMt+ 8.5	MT 9
47	Jude Drouin	4	5	6	10	15	25	30	60
48A	Jean Ratelle IA Defense	4	5	6	10	15	30	40	60
48B	Jean Ratelle IA Centre	4	5	6	10	15	30	40	60
49	Ken Hodge	4	5	6	10	40			
50	Roger Crozier	4	5	6	10	25	30		
51	Reggie Leach	4	5	6	10	15	30	40	60
52	Dennis Hull	4	5	6	10	15	30		
53	Larry Hale RC	4	5	6	10	15	30		
54	Playoff Game 5	4	5	6	10	15	30		
55	Tim Ecclestone	4	5	6	10	15	25	30	60
56	Butch Goring	4	5	6	10	15	30	40	60
57	Danny Grant	4	5	6	10	15	30		
58	Bobby Orr IA	25	30	40	50	50	80	100	300
59	Guy Lafleur	30	40	50	60	80	150	200	500
60	Jim Neilson	4	5	6	10	15	30		
61	Brian Spencer	4	5	6	10	15	25	30	60
62	Joe Watson	4	5	6	10	15	25	30	60
63	Playoff Game 6	4	5	6	10	15	25	30	80
64	Jean Pronovost	4	5	6	10	15	30		
65	Frank St.Marseille	4	5	6	10	15	30		
66	Bob Baun	4	5	6	10	15	30		
67	Paul Popiel	4	5	6	10	15	25	30	60
68	Wayne Cashman	4	5	6	10	15	30		
69	Tracy Pratt	4	5	6	10	15	30		
70	Stan Gilbertson	4	5	6	10	15	20	25	50
71	Keith Magnuson	4	5	6	10	15	30		
72	Ernie Hicke	4	5	6	10	15	30		
73	Gary Doak	4	5	6	10	15	30		
74	Mike Corrigan	4	5	6	10	15	30		
75	Doug Mohns	4	5	6	10	15	25	30	60
76	Phil Esposito IA	6	8	12	20	25	40	50	100
77	Jacques Lemaire	4	5	6	10	15	30	40	80
78	Pete Stemkowski	4	5	6	10	15	30		
79	Bill Mikkelson RC	4	5	6	10	15	25	30	60
80	Rick Foley RC	4	5	6	10	15	25	30	60
81	Ron Schock	4	5	6	10	15	25	30	60
82	Phil Roberto	4	5	6	10	15	25	30	60
83	Jim McKenny	4	5	6	10	15	30		
84	Wayne Maki	4	5	6	10	15	25	30	60
85A	Brad Park IA Centre	6	8	12	20	25	40		
85B	Brad Park IA Defense	4	5	8	12	20	40		
86	Guy Lapointe	4	5	6	10	15	30	40	60
87	Bill Fairbairn	4	5	6	10	15	25	30	60
88	Terry Crisp	4	5	6	10	15	25	30	60
89	Doug Favell	4	5	6	10	15	25	30	60
90	Bryan Watson	4	5	6	10	15	20	25	50
91	Gary Sabourin	4	5	6	10	15	25	30	60
92	Jacques Plante	10	12	15	20	25	40	50	100
93	Andre Boudrias	4	5	6	10	15	20	25	50
94	Mike Walton	4	5	6	10	15	20	25	50
95	Don Luce	4	5	6	10	15	30		
96	Joey Johnston	4	5	6	10	15	20	25	50
97	Doug Jarrett	4	5	6	10	15	25	30	60
98	Bill MacMillan RC	4	5	6	10	15	30		
99	Mickey Redmond	4	5	6	10	15	30		
100	Rogatien Vachon UER	4	5	6	10	15	30	40	60
101	Barry Gibbs RC	4	5	6	10	15	30		
102	Frank Mahovlich DP	4	5	6	10	15	30	40	60
103	Bruce MacGregor	4	5	6	10	15	25	30	60
104	Ed Westfall	4	5	6	10	15	25	30	60
105	Rick MacLeish	4	5	8	12	20	35	40	80
106	Nick Harbaruk	4	5	6	10	15	25	30	60
107	Jack Egers RC	4	5	6	10	15	20	25	50
108	Dave Keon	4	5	6	10	15	30	40	80
109	Barry Wilkins	4	5	6	10	20	50		
110	Walt Tkaczuk	4	5	6	10	15	25	30	60
111	Phil Esposito	8	10	12	15	25	50	60	100
112	Gilles Meloche RC	6	8	12	20	25	40		
113	Gary Edwards	4	5	6	10	15	30	40	
114	Brad Park	8	10	20	25	30	40	60	80
115	Syl Apps DP	4	5	6	10	15	30		
116	Jim Lorentz	4	5	6	10	15	20	25	50
117	Gary Smith	4	5	6	10	15	20	25	50
118	Ted Harris	4	5	6	10	15	30		
119	Gerry Desjardins DP	4	5	6	10	15	25	30	60
120	Garry Unger	4	5	6	10	15	20	25	50
121	Dale Tallon	4	5	6	10	15	30		
122	Bill Plager RC	4	5	6	10	15	20	25	50
123	Red Berenson DP	4	5	6	10	15	20	25	50
124	Peter Mahovlich DP	4	5	6	10	15	20	25	50
125	Simon Nolet	4	5	6	10	15	30	35	60
126	Paul Henderson	4	5	6	10	15	30		
127	Hart Trophy Winners	4	5	6	10	15	20		50
128	Frank Mahovlich IA	4	5	6	10	15	30	35	60
129	Bobby Orr	35	40	50	80	100	250	350	800
130	Bert Marshall	4	5	6	10	15	30		
131	Ralph Backstrom	4	5	6	10	15	20	25	50
132	Gilles Villemure	4	5	6	10	15	20	25	50
133	Dave Burrows RC	4	5	6	10	15	20	25	50
134	Calder Trophy Winners	4	5	6	10	15	30	35	60

#	Player	VG 3	VgEx 4	EX 5	ExMt 6	NM 7	NmMt 8	NmMt+ 8.5	MT 9
135	Dallas Smith IA	4	5	6	10	15	20	25	50
136	Gilbert Perreault DP	8	10	12	15	20	30	35	60
137	Tony Esposito DP	8	10	12	15	25	40	50	100
138	Cesare Maniago DP	4	5	6	10	15	30		
139	Gerry Hart RC	4	5	6	10	15	20	25	50
140	Jacques Caron RC	4	5	6	10	15	30	40	60
141	Orland Kurtenbach	4	5	6	10	15	30		
142	Norris Trophy Winners	4	5	6	10	15	80		
143	Lew Morrison	4	5	6	10	15	30		
144	Arnie Brown	4	5	6	10	15	20	25	50
145	Ken Dryden DP	12	15	20	25	35	50	60	120
146	Gary Dornhoefer	4	5	6	10	15	20	25	50
147	Norm Ullman	4	5	8	12	20	30	35	80
148	Art Ross Trophy/Winners	4	5	6	10	15	20	25	50
149	Orland Kurtenbach IA	4	5	6	10	15	30	35	60
150	Fred Stanfield	4	5	6	10	15	30		
151	Dick Redmond DP	4	5	6	10	15	20	25	50
152	Serge Bernier	4	5	6	10	15	20	25	50
153	Rod Gilbert	4	5	8	12	20	30	35	60
154	Duane Rupp	4	5	6	10	15	20	25	50
155	Vezina Trophy Winners	4	5	6	10	15	30		
156	Stan Mikita IA	4	5	6	12	20	40	50	80
157	Richard Martin DP	4	5	8	12	20	30	40	80
158	Bill White DP	4	5	6	10	15	20	25	50
159	Bill Goldsworthy DP	4	5	6	10	15	25	30	60
160	Jack Lynch RC	4	5	6	10	15	30		
161	Bob Plager DP	4	5	6	10	15	25	30	60
162	Dave Balon UER	4	5	6	10	15	30		
163	Noel Price	4	5	6	10	15	30		
164	Gary Bergman DP	4	5	6	10	15	20	25	50
165	Pierre Bouchard	4	5	6	10	15	30		
166	Ross Lonsberry	4	5	6	10	15	20	25	50
167	Denis Dupere	4	5	6	10	15	30		
168	Byng Trophy Winners DP	4	5	6	10	15	20	25	50
169	Ken Hodge	4	5	6	10	15	30		
170	Don Awrey DP	4	5	6	10	15	25		
171	Marshall Johnston DP RC	4	5	6	10	15	40		
172	Terry Harper	4	5	6	10	15	30		
173	Ed Giacomin	4	5	8	10	15	25	35	60
174	Bryan Hextall DP	4	5	6	10	15	20	25	50
175	Conn Smythe/Trophy Winners	4	5	6	10	20	30	35	60
176	Larry Hillman	4	5	6	10	15	30		
177	Stan Mikita DP	6	8	12	20	25	40	50	80
178	Charlie Burns	4	5	6	10	15	30		
179	Brian Marchinko	4	5	6	10	15	30		
180	Noel Picard DP	4	5	6	10	15	20	25	50
181	Bobby Schmautz RC	4	5	6	10	15	30		
182	Richard Martin IA UER	4	5	6	10	15	30	40	80
183	Pat Quinn	4	5	6	10	15	30		
184	Denis DeJordy UER	4	5	6	10	15	20	25	50
185	Serge Savard	4	5	8	12	20	40		
186	Eddie Shack IA	4	5	6	10	15	30		
187	Bill Flett	4	5	6	10	15	30		
188	Darryl Sittler	15	20	25	30	40			
189	Gump Worsley IA	4	5	6	10	15	30	40	60
190	Checklist	25	30	40	50	60	80	100	200
191	Garnet Bailey DP	4	5	6	10	15	20	25	50
192	Walt McKechnie	4	5	6	10	15	20	25	50
193	Harry Howell	4	5	6	10	15	30		
194	Rod Seiling	4	5	6	10	15	30	35	60
195	Darryl Edestrand	4	5	6	10	15	30		
196	Tony Esposito IA	6	8	12	20	25	40		
197	Tim Horton	6	8	12	20	25	40		
198	Chico Maki DP	4	5	6	10	15	20	25	50
199	Jean-Paul Parise	4	5	6	10	15	30		
200	Germaine Gagnon UER RC	4	5	6	10	15	30		
201	Danny O'Shea	4	5	6	10	15	20	25	50
202	Richard Lemieux RC	4	5	6	10	15	30		
203	Dan Bouchard RC	8	10	20	25	30	40	50	100
204	Leon Rochefort	4	5	6	10	15	30		
205	Jacques Laperriere	4	5	6	10	15	25	30	60
206	Barry Ashbee	4	5	6	10	15	30		
207	Garry Monahan	4	5	6	10	15	30		
209	Dave Keon IA	4	5	8	12	20	40	50	80
210	Rejean Houle	4	5	6	10	15	30		
211	Dave Hudson RC	4	5	6	10	20	60		
212	Ted Irvine	4	5	6	10	15	25	30	60
213	Don Saleski RC	4	5	8	12	20	50		
214	Lowell MacDonald	4	5	6	10	15	20	25	50
215	Mike Murphy RC	4	5	6	10	15	30		
216	Brian Glennie	4	5	6	10	15	30		
217	Bobby Lalonde RC	4	5	6	10	15	30		
218	Bob Leiter	4	5	6	10	15	30		
219	Don Marcotte	4	5	6	10	25	60		
220	Jim Schoenfeld RC	10	12	20	25	30	60	80	125
221	Craig Patrick	4	5	6	10	15	30		
222	Cliff Koroll	4	5	6	10	15	30		
223	Guy Charron RC	4	5	6	10	15	20	25	50
224	Jim Peters	4	5	6	10	15	40		
225	Dennis Hextall	4	5	6	10	15	30		
226	Tony Esposito AS1	12	15	20	25	30			
227	Orr/Park AS1	25	30	40	60	80	150	250	500
228	Bobby Hull AS1	25	30	40	50	80	100	200	250
229	Rod Gilbert AS1	4	5	6	10	20	50		
230	Phil Esposito AS1	8	10	20	25	30	100		
231	Claude Larose UER	4	5	6	10	15	20	25	50
232	Jim Mair RC	4	5	6	10	15	20	25	50
233	Bobby Rousseau	4	5	6	10	15	20	25	50
234	Brent Hughes	4	5	6	10	15	30		
235	Al McDonough	4	5	6	10	15	20	25	50
236	Chris Evans RC	4	5	6	10	15	30		
237	Pierre Jarry RC	4	5	6	10	15	30		
238	Don Tannahill RC	4	5	6	10	15	60		
239	Rey Comeau RC	4	5	6	10	15	30		
240	Gregg Sheppard UER RC	4	5	6	10	15	30		
241	Dave Dryden	4	5	6	10	15	40	50	100
242	Ted McAneeley RC	4	5	6	10	15	30	40	100
243	Lou Angotti	4	5	6	10	15	30		
244	Len Fontaine RC	4	5	6	10	15	30		
245	Bill Lesuk RC	4	5	6	10	15	30		
246	Fred Harvey	4	5	6	10	15	30	35	60
247	Ken Dryden AS2	15	20	25	30	60	125		
248	Bill White AS2	4	5	6	10	15	30		
249	Pat Stapleton AS2	4	5	6	10	15	20	25	50
250	Ratelle/Cour/Hadfld LL	5	6	10	12	20	80		
251	Henri Richard	4	5	6	10	25	80		
252	Bryan Lefley RC	4	5	6	10	15	30	40	80
253	Stanley Cup Trophy	12	15	20	25	40	150		
254	Steve Vickers RC	6	8	12	20	25	40		
255	Wayne Hillman	4	5	6	10	15	30		
256	Ken Schinkel UER	4	5	6	10	15	30		
257	Kevin O'Shea RC	4	5	6	10	15	30		
258	Ron Low RC	12	15	20	25	40	60	80	100
259	Don Lever RC	8	12	20	25	80	150		
260	Randy Manery RC	4	5	6	10	15	30		
261	Ed Johnston	4	5	6	10	20	40		
262	Craig Ramsay RC	5	6	10	12	25	80		
263	Pete Laframboise RC	4	5	6	10	15	25	30	60
264	Dan Maloney RC	4	5	8	12	20	40		
265	Bill Collins	4	5	6	10	15	30		
266	Paul Curtis	4	5	6	10	15	30		
267	Bob Nevin	4	5	6	10	15	60		
268	Watson/Magnuson LL	4	5	6	10	20	50		
269	Jim Roberts	4	5	6	10	15	30		
270	Brian Lavender RC	4	5	6	10	20	30	50	40
271	Dale Rolfe	4	5	6	10	15	30		
272	Espo/Hadf/B.Hull LL	15	20	25	30	40			
273	Michel Belhumeur RC	6	8	12	20	25	40		
274	Eddie Shack	4	5	6	10	15	30		
275	W.Stephenson UER RC	8	10	20	25	30	50	60	100
276	Bruins Team	6	8	12	20	25	60		
277	Rick Kehoe RC	6	8	12	20	25	60		
278	Gerry O'Flaherty RC	4	5	6	10	15	40		
279	Jacques Richard RC	4	5	6	10	15	30		
280	Espo/Orr/Ratelle LL	20	25	30	40	60			
281	Nick Beverley RC	5	6	10	12	20	40	50	100
282	Larry Carriere RC	4	5	6	10	15	30		
283	Orr/Espo/Ratelle LL	20	25	30	40	60	250		
284	Rick Smith IA	4	5	6	10	15	30		
285	Jerry Korab RC	4	5	8	12	25	80		
286	Espo/Villem/Worsley LL	10	12	20	25	30			
287	Ron Stackhouse	4	5	6	10	15	30		
288	Barry Long RC	4	5	6	10	15	30		
289	Dean Prentice	4	4	6	10	15	100		
290	Norm Beaudin	6	8	12	20	25	40		
291	Mike Amodeo RC	6	8	12	20	25	40		
292	Jim Harrison	6	8	12	20	25	40	50	100
293	J.C. Tremblay	6	8	12	20	25	50	80	
294	Murray Hall	6	8	12	20	25	40		
295	Bart Crashley	6	8	12	20	25	40		
296	Wayne Connelly	6	8	12	20	25	40		
297	Bobby Sheehan	6	8	12	20	25	40		
298	Ron Anderson	6	8	12	20	25	40		
299	Chris Bordeleau	6	8	15	20	25	40		
300	Les Binkley	6	8	15	20	25	40	50	100
301	Ron Walters	6	8	15	20	25	40		
302	Jean-Guy Gendron	6	8	15	20	25	40		
303	Gord Labossiere	6	8	15	20	25	30	40	60
304	Gerry Odrowski	6	8	15	20	25	40	50	80
305	Mike McMahon	6	8	15	20	25	40		
306	Gary Kurt	6	8	15	20	25	40		
307	Larry Cahan	6	8	15	20	25	40	50	80
308	Wally Boyer	6	8	15	20	25	80		
309	Bob Charlebois RC	6	8	15	20	25	40		
310	Bob Falkenberg	6	8	15	20	25	40		
311	Jean Payette RC	6	8	15	20	25	40		
312	Ted Taylor	6	8	15	20	25	40		
313	Joe Szura	6	8	15	20	25	40		
314	George Morrison	6	8	15	20	25	40		
315	Wayne Rivers	6	8	15	20	25	50		

		VG 3	VgEx 4	EX 5	ExMt 6	NM 7	NmMt 8	NmMt+ 8.5	MT 9
316	Reg Fleming	6	8	15	20	25	60		
317	Larry Hornung RC	6	8	15	20	25	40		
318	Ron Climie RC	6	8	15	20	25	30	40	80
319	Val Fonteyne	6	8	15	20	25	40		
320	Michel Archambault RC	6	8	15	20	25	40	50	100
321	Ab McDonald	6	8	15	20	25	40		
322	Bob Leduc RC	6	8	15	20	25	40		
323	Bob Wall	6	8	15	20	25	40	50	80
324	Alain Caron RC	6	8	15	20	25	40		
325	Bob Woytowich	6	8	15	20	25	40	50	100
326	Guy Trottier	6	8	15	20	25	40		
327	Bill Hicke	6	8	15	20	25	40	50	100
328	Guy Dufour RC	6	8	15	20	25	30	40	60
329	Wayne Rutledge RC	6	8	15	20	25	40	50	80
330	Gary Veneruzzo	6	8	15	20	25	40	50	100
331	Fred Speck RC	6	8	15	20	25	40	50	100
332	Ron Ward RC	6	8	15	20	25	40		
333	Rosaire Paiement	6	8	15	20	25	40	50	100
334A	Checklist 3 ERR	60	80	100	120	150			
334B	Checklist 3 COR	50	60	80	100	125			
335	Michel Parizeau RC	6	8	15	20	25	40		
336	Bobby Hull	40	50	60	80	100	150	350	
337	Wayne Carleton	6	8	15	20	25	40		
338	John McKenzie	6	8	15	20	25	40		
339	Jim Dorey	6	8	15	20	25	50		
340	Gerry Cheevers	15	20	25	30	50	60	80	150
341	Gerry Pinder	15	20	25	30	50	120	150	150

— Guy Lafleur #59 PSA 10 (Gem) sold for $408 (eBay; 12/06)
— Brad Park #114 PSA 10 (Gem) sold for $127.50 (eBay; 8/12)
— Bobby Orr #129 PSA 10 (Gem) sold for $3,327.24 (Mile High; 12/13)
— Craig Ramsay #262 PSA 9 (MT) sold for $237.50 (eBay; 8/12)
— Rick Kehoe #277 PSA 10 (Gem) sold for $203.48 (eBay; 7/11)

1972-73 Topps

		VgEx 4	EX 5	ExMt 6	NM 7	NmMt 8	NmMt+ 8.5	MT 9	Gem 9.5/10
1	Bruins Team DP	5	6	8	12	20	25	30	250
2	Playoff Game 1	5	6	8	10	12	15	30	
3	Playoff Game 2	5	6	8	10	12	20	50	
4	Playoff Game 3	5	6	8	10	12	20	60	
5	Playoff Game 4 DP	5	6	8	10	12	15	20	60
6	Playoff Game 5 DP	5	6	8	10	12	15	20	60
7	Playoff Game 6 DP	5	6	8	10	12	15	20	60
8	Stanley Cup Trophy	5	6	8	10	12	15	30	150
9	Ed Van Impe DP	5	6	8	10	10	12	15	50
10	Yvan Cournoyer DP	5	6	8	10	12	15	20	120
11	Syl Apps DP	5	6	8	10	10	12	15	50
12	Bill Plager RC	5	6	8	10	10	12	15	50
13	Ed Johnston DP	5	6	8	10	10	12	15	40
14	Walt Tkaczuk	5	6	8	10	10	12	15	50
15	Dale Tallon DP	5	6	8	10	10	12	15	50
16	Gerry Meehan	5	6	8	10	12	15	20	60
17	Reggie Leach	5	6	8	10	10	12	15	50
18	Marcel Dionne DP	5	6	10	15	20	25	50	100
19	Andre Dupont RC	5	6	8	10	12	15	20	
20	Tony Esposito	6	8	10	15	25	30	40	100
21	Bob Berry DP	5	6	8	10	10	12	15	50
22	Craig Cameron	5	6	8	10	10	12	15	40
23	Ted Harris	5	6	8	10	10	12	15	50
24	Jacques Plante	6	8	10	15	20	25	40	120
25	Jacques Lemaire DP	5	6	8	10	10	12	15	50
26	Simon Nolet DP	5	6	8	10	10	12	15	50
27	Keith McCreary DP	5	6	8	10	10	12	15	40
28	Duane Rupp	5	6	8	10	10	12	15	50
29	Wayne Cashman	5	6	8	10	10	12	15	50
30	Brad Park	5	6	8	10	12	15	20	50
31	Roger Crozier	5	6	8	10	12	15	20	50
32	Wayne Maki	5	6	8	10	10	12	15	50
33	Tim Ecclestone	5	6	8	10	10	12	15	50
34	Rick Smith	5	6	8	10	10	12	15	50
35	Garry Unger DP	5	6	8	10	10	12	15	50
36	Serge Bernier DP	5	6	8	10	10	12	15	50
37	Brian Glennie	5	6	8	10	12	15	20	
38	Gerry Desjardins DP	5	6	8	10	10	12	15	50
39	Danny Grant	5	6	8	10	10	12	15	50
40	Bill White DP	5	6	8	10	10	12	15	50
41	Gary Dornhoefer DP	5	6	8	10	12	15	20	
42	Peter Mahovlich	5	6	8	10	12	15	20	60
43	Greg Polis DP	5	6	8	10	10	12	15	50
44	Larry Hale DP RC	5	6	8	10	10	12	15	50
45	Dallas Smith	5	6	8	10	10	12	15	50
46	Orland Kurtenbach DP	5	6	8	10	10	12	15	50
47	Steve Atkinson	5	6	8	10	12	15	20	
48	Joey Johnston DP	5	6	8	10	10	12	15	50
49	Gary Bergman	5	6	8	10	10	12	15	
50	Jean Ratelle	5	6	8	10	12	15	20	
51	Rogatien Vachon DP	5	6	8	10	10	12	15	50
52	Phil Roberto DP	5	6	8	10	12	15	20	
53	Brian Spencer DP	5	6	8	10	10	12	15	50
54	Jim McKenny DP	5	6	8	10	10	12	15	50
55	Gump Worsley	5	6	8	10	12	15	30	80
56	Stan Mikita DP	5	6	8	10	12	15	50	100
57	Guy Lapointe	5	6	8	10	12	15	20	
58	Lew Morrison DP	5	6	8	10	10	12	15	50
59	Ron Schock DP	5	6	8	10	10	12	15	50
60	Johnny Bucyk	5	6	8	10	12	15	25	60
61	Espo/Hadf/B.Hull LL	6	8	10	15	20	40		
62	Orr/Espo/Ratelle LL DP	6	8	10	15	20	25	40	
63	Espo/Orr/Ratelle LL DP	6	8	10	15	20	25	40	
64	Espo/Villem/Worsley LL	5	6	8	10	12	15	20	
65	Wtsn/Magn/Dorn LL	5	6	8	10	12	15	20	
66	Jim Neilson	5	6	8	10	12	15	20	
67	Nick Libett DP	5	6	8	10	10	12	15	50
68	Jim Lorentz	5	6	8	10	10	12	15	50
69	Gilles Meloche RC	5	6	8	10	12	15	25	60
70	Pat Stapleton	5	6	8	10	10	12	15	50
71	Frank St.Marseille DP	5	6	8	10	10	12	15	50
72	Butch Goring FTC	5	6	8	10	12	15	20	
73	Paul Henderson DP	5	6	8	10	10	12	15	50
74	Doug Favell	5	6	8	10	10	12	15	50
75	Jocelyn Guevremont DP	5	6	8	10	10	12	15	50
76	Tom Miller RC	5	6	8	10	10	12	15	50
77	Bill MacMillan	5	6	8	10	12	15	20	
78	Doug Mohns	5	6	8	10	10	12	15	50
79	Guy Lafleur DP	6	10	12	15	20	25	60	150
80	Rod Gilbert DP	5	6	8	10	10	12	15	50
81	Gary Doak	5	6	8	10	12	15	20	
82	Dave Burrows DP RC	5	6	8	10	10	12	15	50
83	Gary Croteau	5	6	8	10	12	15	20	
84	Tracy Pratt DP	5	6	8	10	12	15	20	
85	Carol Vadnais DP	5	6	8	10	10	12	15	50
86	Jacques Caron DP RC	5	6	8	10	10	12	15	50
87	Keith Magnuson	5	6	8	10	12	25	40	100
88	Dave Keon	5	6	8	10	12	15	30	80
89	Mike Corrigan	5	6	8	10	10	12	15	40
90	Bobby Clarke	10	12	15	20	25	30	60	
91	Dunc Wilson DP	5	6	8	10	10	12	15	50
92	Gerry Hart RC	5	6	8	10	12	15	20	50
93	Lou Nanne	5	6	8	10	12	15	20	
94	Checklist 1-176 DP	8	10	12	15	20	25	40	175
95	Red Berenson DP	5	6	8	10	12	15	20	
96	Bob Plager	5	6	8	10	10	12	15	50
97	Jim Rutherford RC	5	6	8	10	12	15	20	
98	Rick Foley DP RC	5	6	8	10	10	12	15	50
99	Pit Martin DP	5	6	8	10	10	12	15	50
100	Bobby Orr DP	15	25	40	80	100	150	200	450
101	Stan Gilbertson	5	6	8	10	10	12	15	50
102	Barry Wilkins	5	6	8	10	10	12	15	50
103	Terry Crisp DP	5	6	8	10	10	12	15	50
104	Cesare Maniago DP	5	6	8	10	10	12	15	50
105	Marc Tardif	5	6	8	10	10	12	15	50
106	Don Luce DP	5	6	8	10	10	12	15	50
107	Mike Pelyk	5	6	8	10	12	15	20	
108	Juha Widing DP	5	6	8	10	12	15	20	
109	Phil Myre DP RC	5	6	8	10	10	12	15	50
110	Vic Hadfield	5	6	8	10	12	15	20	
111	Arnie Brown DP	5	6	8	10	10	12	15	50
112	Ross Lonsberry DP	5	6	8	10	10	12	15	50
113	Dick Redmond	5	6	8	10	10	12	15	50
114	Gary Smith	5	6	8	10	12	15	20	
115	Bill Goldsworthy	5	6	8	10	12	15	20	
116	Bryan Watson	5	6	8	10	12	15	20	
117	Dave Balon DP	5	6	8	10	10	12	15	50
118	Bill Mikkelson DP RC	5	6	8	10	10	12	15	50
119	Terry Harper DP	5	6	8	10	12	15	20	
120	Gilbert Perreault DP	5	6	8	10	12	20	40	80
121	Tony Esposito AS1	5	6	8	10	12	20	30	60
122	Bobby Orr AS1	12	15	20	30	50	60	100	80
123	Brad Park AS1	5	6	8	10	10	12	15	50
124	Phil Esposito AS1	5	6	8	10	12	15	30	60
125	Rod Gilbert AS1	5	6	8	10	10	12	15	50
126	Bobby Hull AS1	10	12	15	25	40	50	50	
127	Ken Dryden AS2 DP	8	10	12	15	20	25	40	100
128	Bill White AS2 DP	5	6	8	10	10	12	15	50
129	Pat Stapleton AS2 DP	5	6	8	10	12	15	20	
130	Jean Ratelle AS2 DP	5	6	8	10	10	12	15	50
131	Yvan Cournoyer AS2 DP	5	6	8	10	10	12	15	50
132	Vic Hadfield AS2 DP	5	6	8	10	12	15	20	
133	Ralph Backstrom DP	5	6	8	10	10	12	15	50
134	Bob Baun DP	5	6	8	10	10	12	15	50
135	Fred Stanfield DP	5	6	8	10	10	12	15	50
136	Barclay Plager DP	5	6	8	10	10	12	15	50
137	Gilles Villemure	5	6	8	10	12	15	20	50
138	Ron Harris DP	5	6	8	10	10	12	15	50
139	Bill Flett DP	5	6	8	10	10	12	15	50
140	Frank Mahovlich	5	6	8	10	12	15	20	
141	Alex Delvecchio DP	5	6	8	10	10	12	15	50
142	Paul Popiel	5	6	8	10	10	12	15	50
143	Jean Pronovost DP	5	6	8	10	10	12	15	50
144	Denis DeJordy DP	5	6	8	10	10	12	15	50

HOCKEY

#	Player	VgEx 4	EX 5	ExMt 6	NM 7	NmMt 8	NmMt+ 8.5	MT 9	Gem 9.5/10
145	Richard Martin DP	5	6	8	10	10	12	15	40
146	Ivan Boldirev RC	5	6	8	10	12	15	20	
147	Jack Egers RC	5	6	8	10	10	12	15	50
148	Jim Pappin	5	6	8	10	10	12	15	50
149	Rod Seiling	5	6	8	10	10	12	15	50
150	Phil Esposito	6	8	10	15	25	30	50	150
151	Gary Edwards	5	6	8	10	10	12	15	50
152	Ron Ellis DP	5	6	8	10	10	12	15	50
153	Jude Drouin	5	6	8	10	10	12	15	40
154	Ernie Hicke DP	5	6	8	10	10	12	15	40
155	Mickey Redmond	5	6	8	10	10	12	15	50
156	Joe Watson DP	5	6	8	10	10	12	15	50
157	Bryan Hextall	5	6	8	10	10	12	15	50
158	Andre Boudrias	5	6	8	10	10	12	15	50
159	Ed Westfall	5	6	8	10	10	12	15	50
160	Ken Dryden	12	15	20	30	30	40	50	80
161	Rene Robert DP RC	5	6	8	10	10	12	15	50
162	Bert Marshall DP	5	6	8	10	10	12	15	50
163	Gary Sabourin	5	6	8	10	12	15	20	50
164	Dennis Hull	5	6	8	10	12	15	20	100
165	Ed Giacomin DP	5	6	8	10	12	15	20	60
166	Ken Hodge	5	6	8	10	10	12	15	50
167	Gilles Marotte DP	5	6	8	10	10	12	15	50
168	Norm Ullman DP	5	6	8	10	10	12	15	50
169	Barry Gibbs RC	5	6	8	10	10	12	15	50
170	Art Ross Trophy	5	6	8	10	12	15	20	
171	Hart Memorial Trophy	5	6	8	10	12	12	15	50
172	James Norris Trophy	5	6	8	12	12	15	30	
173	Vezina Trophy DP	5	6	8	12	15	20	25	60
174	Calder Trophy DP	5	6	8	12	15	20	25	
175	Lady Byng Trophy DP	5	6	8	12	20	25	30	
176	Conn Smythe Trophy DP	5	6	8	12	20	25	40	

— Bruins Team #1 PSA 10 (Gem) sold for $901 (eBay; 7/07)
— Bruins Team #1 PSA 10 (Gem) sold for $704 (eBay; 10/14)
— Espo/Orr/Ratelle LL #62 PSA 10 (Gem) sold for $323 (eBay; 9/12)
— Espo/Orr/Ratelle LL #63 PSA 10 (Gem) sold for $2,040 (eBay; 4/12)
— Playoff Game 3 PSA 10 (Gem) sold for $704 (Mile High; 10/12)

1973-74 O-Pee-Chee

#	Player	VG 3	VgEx 4	EX 5	ExMt 6	NM 7	NmMt 8	NmMt+ 8.5	MT 9
1	Alex Delvecchio	5	6	8	12	15	20	25	40
2	Gilles Meloche	4	5	6	10	15	60		
3	Phil Roberto	4	5	6	10	15	20		
4	Orland Kurtenbach	4	5	6	10	15	20		
5	Gilles Marotte	4	5	6	10	15	20		
6	Stan Mikita	5	6	8	12	15	30		
7	Paul Henderson	4	5	6	10	15	20	30	50
8	Gregg Sheppard	4	5	6	10	12	15	20	35
9	Rod Seiling	4	5	6	10	15	20		
10	Red Berenson	4	5	6	10	15	20		
11	Jean Pronovost	4	5	6	10	12	15	20	35
12	Dick Redmond	4	5	6	10	15	20	25	40
13	Keith McCreary	4	5	6	10	15	20		
14	Bryan Watson	4	5	6	10	15	20		
15	Garry Unger	4	5	6	10	15	20		
16	Neil Komadoski RC	4	5	6	10	15	20	25	40
17	Marcel Dionne	6	8	10	15	20	30	35	60
18	Ernie Hicke	4	5	6	10	12	15	20	30
19	Andre Boudrias	4	5	6	10	15	20	25	40
20	Bill Flett	4	5	6	10	15	20		
21	Marshall Johnston	4	5	6	10	12	15	20	30
22	Gerry Meehan	4	5	6	10	15	20		
23	Ed Johnston	4	5	6	10	15	20	30	40
24	Serge Savard	5	6	8	12	15	30	35	60
25	Walt Tkaczuk	4	5	6	10	12	15	20	35
26	Ken Hodge	4	5	6	10	15	20	25	40
27	Norm Ullman	5	6	8	12	15	30		
28	Cliff Koroll	4	5	6	10	15	20		
29	Rey Comeau	4	5	6	10	15	20	30	50
30	Bobby Orr	15	20	30	40	60	100	150	
31	Wayne Stephenson	4	5	6	10	15	20		
32	Dan Maloney	4	5	6	10	15	20		
33	Henry Boucha RC	4	5	6	10	15	20	25	40
34	Gerry Hart	4	5	6	10	12	15	20	35
35	Bobby Schmautz	4	5	6	10	15	20	25	40
36	Ross Lonsberry	4	5	6	10	15	20		
37	Ted McAneeley	4	5	6	10	15	20	25	40
38	Don Luce	4	5	6	10	12	15	20	35
39	Jim McKenny	4	5	6	10	15	20	25	40
40	Jacques Laperriere	4	5	6	10	12	15	20	30
41	Bill Fairbairn	4	5	6	10	15	20		
42	Craig Cameron	4	5	6	10	12	15	20	35
43	Bryan Hextall	4	5	6	10	12	15	20	35
44	Chuck Lefley RC	4	5	6	10	15	20		
45	Dan Bouchard	4	5	6	10	15	20		
46	Jean-Paul Parise	4	5	6	10	12	15	20	35
47	Barclay Plager	4	5	6	10	12	15	20	35
48	Mike Corrigan	4	5	6	10	12	15	20	30
49	Nick Libett	4	5	6	10	15	20		
50	Bobby Clarke	6	8	10	15	25	35	40	60
51	Bert Marshall	4	5	6	10	15	20		
52	Craig Patrick	4	5	6	10	12	15	20	30
53	Richard Lemieux	4	5	6	10	15	20		
54	Tracy Pratt	4	5	6	10	12	15	20	35
55	Ron Ellis	4	5	6	10	15	20		
56	Jacques Lemaire	5	6	8	12	15	30	35	50
57	Steve Vickers	4	5	6	10	15	20		30
58	Carol Vadnais	4	5	6	10	15	20	25	40
59	Jim Rutherford	4	5	6	10	15	20		
60	Rick Kehoe	4	5	6	10	15	20	25	40
61	Pat Quinn	4	5	6	10	15	20		
62	Bill Goldsworthy	4	5	6	10	15	20	25	40
63	Dave Dryden	4	5	6	10	15	20	30	60
64	Rogatien Vachon	5	6	8	12	15	30	35	60
65	Gary Bergman	4	5	6	10	15	20		
66	Bernie Parent	6	8	10	15	20	30	40	80
67	Ed Westfall	4	5	6	10	15	20		
68	Ivan Boldirev	4	5	6	10	12	15	20	35
69	Don Tannahill	4	5	6	10	15	20	25	40
70	Gilbert Perreault	6	8	10	15	20	40	50	100
71	Mike Pelyk	4	5	6	10	15	20	25	40
72	Guy Lafleur	8	10	12	20	30	40	60	100
73	Pit Martin	4	5	6	10	15	20		
74	Gilles Gilbert RC	5	6	8	12	15	30	40	80
75	Jim Lorentz	4	5	6	10	12	15	20	35
76	Syl Apps	4	5	6	10	12	15	20	30
77	Phil Myre	4	5	6	10	15	20		
78	Bill White	4	5	6	10	15	20		35
79	Jack Egers	4	5	6	10	12	15	20	35
80	Terry Harper	4	5	6	10	15	20		
81	Bill Barber RC	6	8	10	15	25	40	50	120
82	Roy Edwards	4	5	6	10	15	20	25	40
83	Brian Spencer	4	5	6	10	12	15	20	35
84	Reggie Leach	4	5	6	10	15	20		
85	Wayne Cashman	4	5	6	10	12	15	20	35
86	Jim Schoenfeld	5	6	8	12	15	20		35
87	Henri Richard	5	6	8	12	15	30	40	80
88	Dennis O'Brien RC	4	5	6	10	15	20		35
89	Al McDonough	4	5	6	10	12	15	20	35
90	Tony Esposito	6	8	10	15	20	30	40	80
91	Joe Watson	4	5	6	10	12	15	20	35
92	Flames Team	4	5	6	10	12	15	20	35
93	Bruins Team	4	5	6	10	15	20		
94	Sabres Team	4	5	6	10	12	15	20	30
95	Golden Seals Team	4	5	6	10	12	15	20	35
96	Blackhawks Team	4	5	6	10	15	20		
97	Red Wings Team	4	5	6	10	12	15	20	35
98	Kings Team	4	5	6	10	15	20		
99	North Stars Team	4	5	6	10	15	20		35
100	Canadiens Team	4	5	6	10	15	30	35	80
101	Islanders Team	4	5	6	10	12	15	20	35
102	Rangers Team	4	5	6	10	12	15	20	35
103	Flyers Team	4	5	6	10	15	20	25	40
104	Penguins Team	4	5	6	10	15	20	25	40
105	Blues Team	4	5	6	10	15	20		
106	Maple Leafs Team	4	5	6	10	15	20	30	60
107	Canucks Team	4	5	6	10	12	15	20	35
108	Vic Hadfield	4	5	6	10	15	20	25	40
109	Tom Reid	4	5	6	10	15	20	25	40
110	Hilliard Graves RC	4	5	6	10	15	20		
111	Don Lever	4	5	6	10	15	20		
112	Jim Pappin	4	5	6	10	15	20	25	40
113	Andre Dupont	4	5	6	10	15	20		
114	Guy Lapointe	4	5	6	10	15	20		
115	Dennis Hextall	4	5	6	10	15	20	25	40
116	Checklist 1	8	12	20	35	40	80		
117	Bob Leiter	4	5	6	10	15	20		
118	Ab DeMarco	4	5	6	10	15	20		
119	Gilles Villemure	4	5	6	10	15	20		
120	Phil Esposito	6	8	10	15	20	30	40	80
121	Mike Robitaille	4	5	6	10	15	20		
122	Real Lemieux	4	5	6	10	12	15	20	35
123	Jim Neilson	4	5	6	10	15	20		
124	Steve Durbano RC	4	5	6	10	12	15	20	30
125	Jude Drouin	4	5	6	10	12	15	20	30
126	Gary Smith	4	5	6	10	12	15	20	35
127	Cesare Maniago	4	5	6	10	12	15	20	35
128	Lowell MacDonald	4	5	6	10	15	20		
129	Checklist 2	8	12	20	25	30	40	50	100
130	Billy Harris RC	4	5	6	10	12	15	20	35
131	Randy Manery	4	5	6	10	15	20		
132	Darryl Sittler	6	8	10	15	20	40		
133	P.Espo/MacLeish LL	4	5	6	10	15	20	30	50
134	P.Espo/B.Clarke LL	4	5	6	10	15	20	25	40
135	P.Espo/B.Clarke LL	4	5	6	10	15	20		
136	K.Dryden/T.Espo LL	6	8	10	12	15	30	30	50
137	Schultz/Schnfeld LL	4	5	6	10	15	20		
138	P.Espo/MacLeish LL	4	5	6	10	15	20	30	60
139	Rene Robert	4	5	6	10	15	20		

		VG 3	VgEx 4	EX 5	ExMt 6	NM 7	NmMt 8	NmMt+ 8.5	MT 9
140	Dave Burrows	4	5	6	10	12	15	20	35
141	Jean Ratelle	5	6	8	12	15	30		
142	Billy Smith RC	15	20	25	35	50	125	225	700
143	Jocelyn Guevremont	4	5	6	10	15	20		
144	Tim Ecclestone	4	5	6	10	12	15	20	35
145	Frank Mahovlich	5	6	8	12	15	30	25	40
146	Rick MacLeish	5	6	8	12	15	20	25	40
147	Johnny Bucyk	5	6	8	12	15	30		
148	Bob Plager	4	5	6	10	15	20	25	40
149	Curt Bennett RC	4	5	6	10	12	15	20	35
150	Dave Keon	5	6	8	12	15	30		
151	Keith Magnuson	4	5	6	10	15	20	25	40
152	Walt McKechnie	4	5	6	10	15	20		
153	Roger Crozier	4	5	6	10	15	20		
154	Ted Harris	4	5	6	10	15	20		
155	Butch Goring	4	5	6	10	15	20	25	40
156	Rod Gilbert	5	6	8	12	15	40	50	60
157	Yvan Cournoyer	5	6	8	12	15	30	40	50
158	Doug Favell	4	5	6	10	15	20		
159	Juha Widing	4	5	6	10	12	15	20	35
160	Ed Giacomin	5	6	8	12	15	30		
161	Germaine Gagnon UER	4	5	6	10	12	15	20	35
162	Dennis Kearns	4	5	6	10	15	20		
163	Bill Collins	4	5	6	10	15	20		
164	Peter Mahovlich	4	5	6	10	15	20	30	60
165	Brad Park	5	6	8	12	15	30	35	60
166	Dave Schultz RC	6	8	10	15	20	30	40	60
167	Dallas Smith	4	5	6	10	15	20		
168	Gary Sabourin	4	5	6	10	15	20		
169	Jacques Richard	4	5	6	10	15	20	25	40
170	Brian Glennie	4	5	6	10	15	20	25	50
171	Dennis Hull	4	5	6	10	15	20	25	40
172	Joey Johnston	4	5	6	10	15	20		
173	Richard Martin	5	6	8	12	15	30		
174	Barry Gibbs	4	5	6	10	12	15	20	30
175	Bob Berry	4	5	6	10	15	20		
176	Greg Polis	4	5	6	10	15	20		
177	Dale Rolfe	4	5	6	10	15	20		
178	Gerry Desjardins	4	5	6	10	15	20	25	40
179	Bobby Lalonde	4	5	6	10	15	20		
180	Mickey Redmond	4	5	6	10	15	30		
181	Jim Roberts	4	5	6	10	15	20		
182	Gary Dornhoefer	4	5	6	10	15	20		
183	Derek Sanderson	5	6	8	12	15	30	35	60
184	Brent Hughes	4	5	6	10	12	15	20	30
185	Larry Romanchych RC	4	5	6	10	15	20		
186	Pierre Jarry	4	5	6	10	15	20		
187	Doug Jarrett	4	5	6	10	12	15	20	35
188	Bob Stewart RC	4	5	6	10	15	20		
189	Tim Horton	5	6	8	12	15	40	50	60
190	Fred Harvey	4	5	6	10	15	20		
191	Series A/Cand/Sabr	4	5	6	10	15	20	25	50
192	Series B/Flyrs/Stars	4	5	6	10	12	15	20	35
193	Series C/Hwks/Blues	4	5	6	10	15	20	25	40
194	Series D/Rngr/Bruins	4	5	6	10	15	40		
195	Series E/Cndn/Flyr	4	5	6	10	15	20		
196	Series F/Blckh/Rngr	4	5	6	10	15	20	25	40
197	Series G/Cndn/Hawk	4	5	6	10	15	25	30	60
198	Canadiens Champs	5	6	8	12	15	30		
199	Gary Edwards	4	5	6	10	15	20		
200	Ron Schock	4	5	6	10	15	20		
201	Bruce MacGregor	4	5	6	10	12	15	20	35
202	Bob Nystrom RC	5	6	8	12	15	20	30	50
203	Jerry Korab	4	5	6	10	12	15	20	35
204	Thommie Bergman RC	4	5	6	10	12	15	20	30
205	Bill Lesuk	4	5	6	10	15	20		
206	Ed Van Impe	4	5	6	10	12	15	20	35
207	Doug Roberts	4	5	6	10	12	15	20	35
208	Chris Evans	4	5	6	10	12	15	20	35
209	Lynn Powis RC	4	5	6	10	12	15	20	35
210	Denis Dupere	4	5	6	10	15	20	25	40
211	Dale Tallon	4	5	6	10	15	20		
212	Stan Gilbertson	4	5	6	10	15	20		
213	Craig Ramsay	4	5	6	10	15	20	25	40
214	Danny Grant	4	5	6	10	15	20		
215	Doug Volmar RC	4	5	6	10	12	15	20	35
216	Darryl Edestrand	4	5	6	10	15	20		
217	Pete Stemkowski	4	5	6	10	12	15	20	30
218	Lorne Henning RC	4	5	6	10	15	20		
219	Bryan McSheffrey RC	4	5	6	10	12	15	20	30
220	Guy Charron	4	5	6	10	15	20	25	40
221	Wayne Thomas RC	5	6	8	12	15	40	50	60
222	Simon Nolet	4	5	6	10	12	15	20	30
223	Fred O'Donnell RC	4	5	6	10	15	20	25	40
224	Lou Angotti	4	5	6	10	15	20		
225	Arnie Brown	4	5	6	10	15	20		
226	Garry Monahan	4	5	6	10	15	20	25	40
227	Chico Maki	4	5	6	10	12	15	20	35
228	Gary Croteau	4	5	6	10	12	15	20	30
229	Paul Terbenche	4	5	6	10	15	20		
230	Gump Worsley	5	6	8	12	15	20	30	50
231	Jim Peters	4	5	6	10	15	20	25	40
232	Jack Lynch	4	5	6	10	12	15	20	35
233	Bobby Rousseau	4	5	6	10	15	20		
234	Dave Hudson	4	5	6	10	15	20	25	40
235	Gregg Boddy RC	4	5	6	10	15	20	25	40
236	Ron Stackhouse	4	5	6	10	12	15	20	35
237	Larry Robinson RC	20	25	40	60	100	250	300	500
238	Bobby Taylor RC	5	6	8	12	15	30	40	60
239	Nick Beverley	4	5	6	10	15	20		
240	Don Awrey	4	5	6	10	12	15	20	35
241	Doug Mohns	4	5	6	10	15	20	25	40
242	Eddie Shack	5	6	8	12	15	20	25	40
243	Phil Russell RC	4	5	6	10	12	15	25	35
244	Pete Laframboise	4	5	6	10	15	20		
245	Steve Atkinson	4	5	6	10	15	20		
246	Lou Nanne	4	5	6	10	15	20	25	40
247	Yvon Labre RC	4	5	6	10	15	20		
248	Ted Irvine	4	5	6	10	15	20		
249	Tom Miller	4	5	6	10	15	20	25	50
250	Gerry O'Flaherty	4	5	6	10	15	20	25	40
251	Larry Johnston RC	4	5	6	10	15	20		
252	Michel Plasse RC	5	6	8	12	15	30	40	80
253	Bob Kelly	4	5	6	10	12	15	20	30
254	Terry O'Reilly RC	15	20	25	40	80	200		
255	Pierre Plante RC	4	5	6	10	15	20	25	40
256	Noel Price	4	5	6	10	15	20		
257	Dunc Wilson	4	5	6	10	15	20		
258	J.P. Bordeleau RC	4	5	6	10	15	20		
259	Terry Murray RC	4	5	6	10	15	20	30	60
260	Larry Carriere	4	5	6	10	15	20		
261	Pierre Bouchard	4	5	6	10	15	30		
262	Frank St.Marseille	4	5	6	10	15	20		
263	Checklist 3	8	12	20	35	50	120		
264	Fred Barrett	4	5	6	10	15	30	35	60

— Bob Nystrom RC #202 PSA 10 (MT) sold for $1,017 (eBay; 2/14)
— Larry Robinson #237 PSA 10 (MT) sold for $1,387.54 (Mile High; 5/12)
— Terry O'Reilly #254 PSA 9 (MT) sold for $145 (eBay; 2/07)

1973-74 Topps

		VG 3	VgEx 4	EX 5	ExMt 6	NM 7	NmMt 8	NmMt+ 8.5	MT 9
1	P.Espo/MacLeish LL	4	5	6	8	15	25	35	80
2	P.Espo/B.Clarke LL	4	5	6	8	12	20		60
3	P.Espo/B.Clarke LL	4	5	6	8	12	20	25	40
4	K.Dryden/T.Espo LL	4	5	6	8	12	20	25	40
5	Schultz/Schoenfeld LL	4	5	6	8	12	20	25	35
6	P.Espo/MacLeish LL	4	5	6	8	12	20	25	40
7	Paul Henderson DP	4	5	6	8	12	20	25	60
8	Gregg Sheppard DP UER	4	5	6	8	12	18		
9	Rod Seiling DP	4	5	6	8	12	18	20	30
10	Ken Dryden	10	15	20	25	30	40	60	120
11	Jean Pronovost DP	4	5	6	8	12	18	20	30
12	Dick Redmond	4	5	6	8	12	18		
13	Keith McCreary DP	4	5	6	8	12	18		
14	Ted Harris DP	4	5	6	8	12	18	20	30
15	Garry Unger	4	5	6	8	12	18		
16	Neil Komadoski RC	4	5	6	8	12	18	20	30
17	Marcel Dionne	5	6	8	10	15	25	30	50
18	Ernie Hicke DP	4	5	6	8	12	18	20	30
19	Andre Boudrias	4	5	6	8	12	18	25	50
20	Bill Flett	4	5	6	8	12	18	20	50
21	Marshall Johnston	4	5	6	8	12	18	20	30
22	Gerry Meehan	4	5	6	8	12	18		
23	Ed Johnston DP	4	5	6	8	12	18		
24	Serge Savard	4	5	6	8	12	18	20	30
25	Walt Tkaczuk	4	5	6	8	12	18		
26	Johnny Bucyk	4	5	6	8	12	18	20	30
27	Dave Burrows	4	5	6	8	12	18	20	30
28	Cliff Koroll	4	5	6	8	12	18		
29	Rey Comeau DP	4	5	6	8	12	18		
30	Barry Gibbs	4	5	6	8	12	18		
31	Wayne Stephenson	4	5	6	8	12	18	20	30
32	Dan Maloney DP	4	5	6	8	12	18	20	30
33	Henry Boucha DP	4	5	6	8	12	18	20	30
34	Gerry Hart	4	5	6	8	12	18		
35	Bobby Schmautz	4	5	6	8	12	18	20	30
36	Ross Lonsberry DP	4	5	6	8	12	18		
37	Ted McAneeley	4	5	6	8	12	18	20	30
38	Don Luce DP	4	5	6	8	12	18		
39	Jim McKenny DP	4	5	6	8	12	18	20	30
40	Frank Mahovlich	4	5	6	8	12	20	30	80
41	Bill Fairbairn	4	5	6	8	12	18	20	30
42	Dallas Smith	4	5	6	8	12	18		
43	Bryan Hextall	4	5	6	8	12	18		
44	Keith Magnuson	4	5	6	8	12	18	20	30
45	Dan Bouchard	4	5	6	8	12	18	20	30
46	Jean-Paul Parise DP	4	5	6	8	12	18	20	30
47	Barclay Plager	4	5	6	8	12	18	20	30
48	Mike Corrigan	4	5	6	8	12	18	20	30

#	Player	VG 3	VgEx 4	EX 5	ExMt 6	NM 7	NmMt 8	NmMt+ 8.5	MT 9
49	Nick Libett DP	4	5	6	8	12	18	20	30
50	Bobby Clarke	5	6	8	10	15	25		
51	Bert Marshall DP	4	5	6	8	12	18	20	30
52	Craig Patrick	4	5	6	8	12	18	20	30
53	Richard Lemieux	4	5	6	8	12	18		
54	Tracy Pratt DP	4	5	6	8	12	18		
55	Ron Ellis DP	4	5	6	8	12	18	20	30
56	Jacques Lemaire	4	5	6	8	12	18		
57	Steve Vickers DP	4	5	6	8	12	18	20	30
58	Carol Vadnais	4	5	6	8	12	18	20	30
59	Jim Rutherford DP	4	5	6	8	12	18	20	30
60	Dennis Hull	4	5	6	8	12	18		
61	Pat Quinn DP	4	5	6	8	12	18		
62	Bill Goldsworthy DP	4	5	6	8	12	18		
63	Fran Huck RC	4	5	6	8	12	18		
64	Rogatien Vachon DP	4	5	6	8	12	18	20	30
65	Gary Bergman DP	4	5	6	8	12	18		
66	Bernie Parent	4	5	6	8	12	20		
67	Ed Westfall	4	5	6	8	12	18		
68	Ivan Boldirev	4	5	6	8	12	18	20	30
69	Don Tannahill DP	4	5	6	8	12	18		
70	Gilbert Perreault	4	5	6	8	12	20	25	60
71	Mike Pelyk DP	4	5	6	8	12	18		
72	Guy Lafleur DP	5	6	8	10	15	30	40	80
73	Jean Ratelle	4	5	6	8	12	18		
74	Gilles Gilbert DP RC	4	5	6	8	12	20	25	50
75	Greg Polis	4	5	6	8	12	18		
76	Doug Jarrett DP	4	5	6	8	12	18		
77	Phil Myre DP	4	5	6	8	12	18	20	30
78	Fred Harvey DP	4	5	6	8	12	18	20	30
79	Jack Egers	4	5	6	8	12	18		
80	Terry Harper	4	5	6	8	12	18		
81	Bill Barber RC	5	6	8	10	15	25	30	50
82	Roy Edwards DP	4	5	6	8	12	18		
83	Brian Spencer	4	5	6	8	12	18	20	30
84	Reggie Leach DP	4	5	6	8	12	18	20	30
85	Dave Keon	4	5	6	8	12	18		
86	Jim Schoenfeld	4	5	6	8	12	18		
87	Henri Richard DP	4	5	6	8	12	18	20	30
88	Rod Gilbert DP	4	5	6	8	12	18	20	30
89	Don Marcotte DP	4	5	6	8	12	18	20	30
90	Tony Esposito	4	5	6	8	12	18		
91	Joe Watson	4	5	6	8	12	18	20	30
92	Flames Team	4	5	6	8	12	20	25	40
93	Bruins Team	4	5	6	8	12	20	25	40
94	Sabres Team DP	4	5	6	8	12	20	25	40
95	Golden Seals Team DP	4	5	6	8	12	18		
96	Blackhawks Team	4	5	6	8	12	20	25	40
97	Red Wings Team DP	4	5	6	8	12	20	30	100
98	Kings Team DP	4	5	6	8	12	18		
99	North Stars Team	4	5	6	8	12	20	25	40
100	Canadiens Team	4	5	6	8	12	20	25	40
101	Islanders Teams	4	5	6	8	12	20	25	40
102	Rangers Team DP	4	5	6	8	12	20	25	40
103	Flyers Team DP	4	5	6	8	12	18		
104	Penguins Team	4	5	6	8	12	20	25	40
105	Blues Team	4	5	6	8	12	18		
106	Maple Leafs Team	4	5	6	8	12	20	25	40
107	Canucks Team	4	5	6	8	12	20	25	40
108	Roger Crozier DP	4	5	6	8	12	18	20	30
109	Tom Reid	4	5	6	8	12	18	20	30
110	Hilliard Graves RC	4	5	6	8	12	18		
111	Don Lever	4	5	6	8	12	18		
112	Jim Pappin	4	5	6	8	12	18	20	30
113	Ron Schock DP	4	5	6	8	12	18	20	30
114	Gerry Desjardins	4	5	6	8	12	18	20	30
115	Yvan Cournoyer DP	4	5	6	8	12	18	20	30
116	Checklist Card	6	8	10	12	20	40		
117	Bob Leiter	4	5	6	8	12	18		
118	Ab DeMarco	4	5	6	8	12	18		
119	Doug Favell	4	5	6	8	12	18	20	30
120	Phil Esposito	4	5	6	8	12	18		
121	Mike Robitaille	4	5	6	8	12	18	20	30
122	Real Lemieux	4	5	6	8	12	18	20	30
123	Jim Neilson	4	5	6	8	12	18	20	30
124	Tim Ecclestone DP	4	5	6	8	12	18	20	30
125	Jude Drouin	4	5	6	8	12	18		
126	Gary Smith DP	4	5	6	8	12	18	20	30
127	Walt McKechnie	4	5	6	8	12	18	20	30
128	Lowell MacDonald	4	5	6	8	12	18		
129	Dale Tallon DP	4	5	6	8	12	18		
130	Billy Harris RC	4	5	6	8	12	18	20	30
131	Randy Manery DP	4	5	6	8	12	18	20	30
132	Darryl Sittler DP	4	5	6	8	12	20	25	40
133	Ken Hodge	4	5	6	8	12	18		
134	Bob Plager	4	5	6	8	12	18	20	30
135	Rick MacLeish	4	5	6	8	12	18	20	30
136	Dennis Hextall	4	5	6	8	12	18	20	30
137	Jacques Laperriere DP	4	5	6	8	12	18	20	30
138	Butch Goring	4	5	6	8	12	18	20	30

#	Player	VG 3	VgEx 4	EX 5	ExMt 6	NM 7	NmMt 8	NmMt+ 8.5	MT 9
139	Rene Robert	4	5	6	8	12	18		
140	Ed Giacomin	4	5	6	8	12	18		
141	Alex Delvecchio DP	4	5	6	8	12	18	20	30
142	Jocelyn Guevremont	4	5	6	8	12	18		
143	Joey Johnston	4	5	6	8	12	18	20	30
144	Bryan Watson DP	4	5	6	8	12	18	20	30
145	Stan Mikita	4	5	6	8	12	20	25	35
146	Cesare Maniago	4	5	6	8	12	18		
147	Craig Cameron	4	5	6	8	12	18	20	30
148	Norm Ullman DP	4	5	6	8	12	18	20	30
149	Dave Schultz RC	5	6	8	10	15	25		
150	Bobby Orr	10	15	20	25	35	50	60	350
151	Phil Roberto	4	5	6	8	12	18		
152	Curt Bennett	4	5	6	8	12	18	20	30
153	Gilles Villemure DP	4	5	6	8	12	18	20	30
154	Chuck Lefley	4	5	6	8	12	18	20	30
155	Richard Martin	4	5	6	8	12	18		
156	Juha Widing	4	5	6	8	12	18		
157	Orland Kurtenbach	4	5	6	8	12	18		
158	Bill Collins DP	4	5	6	8	12	18	20	30
159	Bob Stewart	4	5	6	8	12	18	20	30
160	Syl Apps	4	5	6	8	12	18		
161	Danny Grant	4	5	6	8	12	18		
162	Billy Smith RC	8	10	12	20	40	80		
163	Brian Glennie	4	5	6	8	12	18		
164	Pit Martin DP	4	5	6	8	12	18		
165	Brad Park	4	5	6	8	12	18		
166	Wayne Cashman DP	4	5	6	8	12	18		
167	Gary Dornhoefer	4	5	6	8	12	18		
168	Steve Durbano DP	4	5	6	8	12	18		
169	Jacques Richard	4	5	6	8	12	18	20	30
170	Guy Lapointe	4	5	6	8	12	18		
171	Jim Lorentz	4	5	6	8	12	18		
172	Bob Berry DP	4	5	6	8	12	18	20	30
173	Dennis Kearns	4	5	6	8	12	18		
174	Red Berenson	4	5	6	8	12	18		
175	Gilles Meloche DP	4	5	6	8	12	18	20	30
176	Al McDonough	4	5	6	8	12	18	20	30
177	Dennis O'Brien RC	4	5	6	8	12	18	20	30
178	Germaine Gagnon UER DP	4	5	6	8	12	18		
179	Rick Kehoe DP	4	5	6	8	12	18	20	30
180	Bill White	4	5	6	8	12	18		
181	Vic Hadfield DP	4	5	6	8	12	18		
182	Derek Sanderson	4	5	6	8	12	20	25	35
183	Andre Dupont DP	4	5	6	8	12	18		
184	Gary Sabourin	4	5	6	8	12	18		
185	Larry Romanchych RC	4	5	6	8	12	18	20	30
186	Peter Mahovlich	4	5	6	8	12	18		
187	Dave Dryden	4	5	6	8	12	18	20	30
188	Gilles Marotte	4	5	6	8	12	18		
189	Bobby Lalonde	4	5	6	8	12	18	20	30
190	Mickey Redmond	4	5	6	8	12	18		
191	Series A/Can 4/Sabres 2	4	5	6	8	12	18		
192	Series B/Flyers 4/Stars 2	4	5	6	8	12	18	20	30
193	Series C/'Hawks 4/Blues 1	4	5	6	8	12	18		
194	Series D/Rangrs 4/Bruins	4	5	6	8	12	18	20	30
195	Series E/Canad 4/Flyers 1	4	5	6	8	12	18		
196	Series F/'Hawks 4/Rangrs 1	4	5	6	8	12	18		
197	Series G/Canad 4/'Hawks 2	4	5	6	8	12	20		
198	Canadiens Champs	4	5	6	8	15	20		

— Paul Henderson #7 PSA 9 (MT) sold for $110.50 (eBay; 7/12)
— Gary Bergman #65 PSA 9 (MT) sold for $211.75 (eBay; 8/12)
— Bobby Orr #150 PSA 9 (MT) sold for $640.34 (eBay; 2/14)

1974-75 O-Pee-Chee

#	Player	VG 3	VgEx 4	EX 5	ExMt 6	NM 7	NmMt 8	NmMt+ 8.5	MT 9
1	P.Espo/Gldswrthy LL	5	6	8	12	30	80		
2	B.Orr/D.Hextall LL	6	8	10	15	30	135	150	250
3	P.Espo/B.Clarke LL	5	6	8	12	15	40		
4	Favell/B.Parent LL	4	5	6	10	12	20		
5	Watson/D.Schulz LL	4	5	6	10	12	20		
6	Redmond/MacLsh LL	4	5	6	10	12	20	25	40
7	Gary Bromley	4	5	6	10	12			
8	Bill Barber	5	6	8	12	20			
9	Emile Francis CO	4	5	6	10	12	30		
10	Gilles Gilbert	4	5	6	10	12	20		
11	John Davidson RC	6	8	10	15	20	40	50	100
12	Ron Ellis	4	5	6	10	12			
13	Syl Apps	4	5	6	10	12	20		
14	Richard/Lysiak TL	4	5	6	10	12	20	25	40
15	Dan Bouchard	4	5	6	10	12	25		
16	Ivan Boldirev	4	5	6	10	12			
17	Gary Coalter RC	4	5	6	10	12	20		
18	Bob Berry	4	5	6	10	12	20		
19	Red Berenson	4	5	6	10	12	20		
20	Stan Mikita	5	6	8	12	15	40	50	120
21	Fred Shero CO RC	5	6	10	15	25	80		
22	Gary Smith	4	5	6	10	12	20		
23	Bill Mikkelson	4	5	6	10	12	20		

#	Player	VG 3	VgEx 4	EX 5	ExMt 6	NM 7	NmMt 8	NmMt+ 8.5	MT 9
24	Jacques Lemaire UER	4	5	6	10	12			
25	Gilbert Perreault	5	6	8	12	15	30	35	60
26	Cesare Maniago	4	5	6	10	12			
27	Bobby Schmautz	4	5	6	10	12	20		
28	Espo/Orr/Bucyk TL	6	8	10	15	20	50	60	150
29	Steve Vickers	4	5	6	10	12	20		
30	Lowell MacDonald UER	4	5	6	10	25	80		
31	Fred Stanfield	4	5	6	10	12	20		
32	Ed Westfall	4	5	6	10	12			
33	Curt Bennett	4	5	6	10	12	20		
34	Bep Guidolin CO	4	5	6	10	12	20		
35	Cliff Koroll	4	5	6	10	12			
36	Gary Croteau	4	5	6	10	12			
37	Mike Corrigan	4	5	6	10	12			
38	Henry Boucha	4	5	6	10	12			
39	Ron Low	4	5	6	10	12	20		
40	Darryl Sittler	6	8	10	12	15	30		
41	Tracy Pratt	4	5	6	10	12			
42	Martin/Robert TL	4	5	6	10	12	20	25	40
43	Larry Carriere	4	5	6	10	12	20		
44	Gary Dornhoefer	4	5	6	10	12			
45	Denis Herron RC	5	6	8	12	15	25	30	60
46	Doug Favell	4	5	6	10	12	20		
47	Dave Gardner RC	4	5	6	10	12	20		
48	Morris Mott RC	4	5	6	10	12	20		
49	Marc Boileau CO	4	5	6	10	12	20		
50	Brad Park	5	6	8	12	15	30		
51	Bob Leiter	4	5	6	10	12	20		
52	Tom Reid	4	5	6	10	12	20		
53	Serge Savard	4	5	6	10	15	40		
54	Checklist 1-132 UER	12	20	25	40	100			
55	Terry Harper	4	5	6	10	12	20		
56	Joey Johnston LL	4	5	6	10	12	20	25	40
57	Guy Charron	4	5	6	10	12	20		
58	Pit Martin	4	5	6	10	12			
59	Chris Evans	4	5	6	10	12	20		
60	Bernie Parent	5	6	8	12	15			
61	Jim Lorentz	4	5	6	10	12	20		
62	Dave Kryskow RC	4	5	6	10	12	20		
63	Lou Angotti CO	4	5	6	10	12	20		
64	Bill Flett	4	5	6	10	12	20		
65	Vic Hadfield	4	5	6	10	12	20		
66	Wayne Merrick RC	4	5	6	10	12			
67	Andre Dupont	4	5	6	10	12			
68	Tom Lysiak RC	4	5	6	10	12	20		
69	Pappin/Mikita/Bord TL	4	5	6	10	12	20		
70	Guy Lapointe	4	5	6	10	12	20		
71	Gerry O'Flaherty	4	5	6	10	12	20		
72	Marcel Dionne	6	8	10	15	30			
73	Butch Deadmarsh RC	4	5	6	25	60			
74	Butch Goring	4	5	6	10	12	20		
75	Keith Magnuson	4	5	6	10	12	20		
76	Red Kelly CO	4	5	6	10	15	80		
77	Pete Stemkowski	4	5	6	10	12	20		
78	Jim Roberts	4	5	6	10	12	20		
79	Don Luce	4	5	6	10	12	20		
80	Don Awrey	4	5	6	10	12	20		
81	Rick Kehoe	4	5	6	10	12	20		
82	Billy Smith	6	8	10	12	15			
83	Jean-Paul Parise	4	5	6	10	12	20		
84	Rdmnd/Dnne/Hoga TL	4	5	6	10	12	20		
85	Ed Van Impe	4	5	6	10	12	20		
86	Randy Manery	4	5	6	10	12	20		
87	Barclay Plager	4	5	6	10	12	20		
88	Inge Hammarstrom RC	4	5	6	10	12	20		
89	Ab DeMarco	4	5	6	10	12	25	30	50
90	Bill White	4	5	6	10	12	20		
91	Al Arbour CO	4	5	6	10	12	20	30	60
92	Bob Stewart	4	5	6	10	12	20		
93	Jack Egers	4	5	6	10	12	20		
94	Don Lever	4	5	6	10	12	20		
95	Reggie Leach	4	5	6	10	12	20		
96	Dennis O'Brien	4	5	6	10	12	20		
97	Peter Mahovlich	4	5	6	10	12	20		
98	Grng/St.Mrsle/Kzk TL	4	5	6	10	12	20		
99	Gerry Meehan	4	5	6	10	12			
100	Bobby Orr	25	30	50	100	125	450	500	800
101	Jean Potvin RC	4	5	6	10	12	20		
102	Rod Seiling	4	5	6	10	12	20	25	50
103	Keith McCreary	4	5	6	10	12	20	25	60
104	Phil Maloney CO RC	4	5	6	10	12	20		
105	Denis Dupere	4	5	6	10	12	20		
106	Steve Durbano	4	5	6	10	12	20		
107	Bob Plager UER	4	5	6	10	12	20	25	50
108	Chris Oddleifson RC	4	5	6	10	12	20	25	60
109	Jim Neilson	4	5	6	10	12			
110	Jean Pronovost	4	5	6	10	12	20		
111	Don Kozak RC	4	5	6	10	12	20		
112	Gldswrthy/Hxtall TL	4	5	6	10	12	20	25	50
113	Jim Pappin	4	5	6	10	12	20		

#	Player	VG 3	VgEx 4	EX 5	ExMt 6	NM 7	NmMt 8	NmMt+ 8.5	MT 9
114	Richard Lemieux	4	5	6	10	12	20		
115	Dennis Hextall	4	5	6	10	12			
116	Bill Hogaboam RC	4	5	6	10	12	20		
117	Vrgrt/Schmt/Boud TL	4	5	6	10	12	20	25	50
118	Jimmy Anderson CO	4	5	6	10	12			
119	Walt Tkaczuk	4	5	6	10	12			
120	Mickey Redmond	4	5	6	10	12	20		
121	Jim Schoenfeld	4	5	6	10	12	20		
122	Jocelyn Guevremont	4	5	6	10	12	20		
123	Bob Nystrom	4	5	6	10	12	20		
124	Cour/F.Mahov/Lrse TL	4	5	6	10	12	20	25	60
125	Lew Morrison	4	5	6	10	12	20		
126	Terry Murray	4	5	6	10	12	20		
127	Richard Martin AS	4	5	6	10	12	20		
128	Ken Hodge AS	4	5	6	10	12	20		
129	Phil Esposito AS	4	5	6	10	12	20	30	80
130	Bobby Orr AS	8	10	12	40	80	200	225	350
131	Brad Park AS	4	5	6	10	12			
132	Gilles Gilbert AS	4	5	6	10	12			
133	Lowell MacDonald AS	4	5	6	10	12	20	25	40
134	Bill Goldsworthy AS	4	5	6	10	12			
135	Bobby Clarke AS	5	6	8	15	25	100		
136	Bill White AS	4	5	6	10	12	20		
137	Dave Burrows AS	4	5	6	10	12	20		
138	Bernie Parent AS	4	5	6	10	12	35		
139	Jacques Richard	4	5	6	10	12	20		
140	Yvan Cournoyer	4	5	6	10	12	20		
141	R.Gilbert/B.Park TL	4	5	6	10	12	20		
142	Rene Robert	4	5	6	10	12	20		
143	J. Bob Kelly RC	4	5	6	10	12	25		
144	Ross Lonsberry	4	5	6	10	12	20		
145	Jean Ratelle	4	5	6	10	12	20		
146	Dallas Smith	4	5	6	10	12	20		
147	Bernie Geoffrion CO	4	5	6	10	12	20	25	40
148	Ted McAneeley	4	5	6	10	12	20		
149	Pierre Plante	4	5	6	10	12	20		
150	Dennis Hull	4	5	6	10	12	20		
151	Dave Keon	4	5	6	10	12			
152	Dave Dunn RC	4	5	6	10	12	20		
153	Michel Belhumeur	4	5	6	10	12	20	25	40
154	Clarke/D.Schultz TL	4	5	6	10	12	20		
155	Ken Dryden	10	12	15	25	40	150		
156	John Wright RC	4	5	6	10	12			
157	Larry Romanchych	4	5	6	10	12	20		
158	Ralph Stewart RC	4	5	6	10	12			
159	Mike Robitaille	4	5	6	10	12	20		
160	Ed Giacomin	4	5	6	10	12	20		
161	Don Cherry CO RC	15	20	30	60	75	125	150	300
162	Checklist 133-264	10	12	20	30	50	100		
163	Rick MacLeish	4	5	6	10	12	20		
164	Greg Polis	4	5	6	10	12	20		
165	Carol Vadnais	4	5	6	10	12	20		
166	Pete Laframboise	4	5	6	10	12	20		
167	Ron Schock	4	5	6	10	12	20		
168	Lanny McDonald RC	10	12	20	40	60	300	500	800
169	Scouts Emblem	4	5	6	10	12			
170	Tony Esposito	5	6	8	12	15	40		
171	Pierre Jarry	4	5	6	10	12	20	25	40
172	Dan Maloney	4	5	6	10	12	20		
173	Peter McDuffe	4	5	6	10	12	20		
174	Danny Grant	4	5	6	10	12			
175	John Stewart RC	4	5	6	10	12	20		
176	Floyd Smith CO	4	5	6	10	12	20		
177	Bert Marshall	4	5	6	10	12			
178	Chuck Lefley UER	4	5	6	10	15	60		
179	Gilles Villemure	4	5	6	10	12	20		
180	Borje Salming RC	10	12	25	30	80	200		
181	Doug Mohns	4	5	6	10	12	20		
182	Barry Wilkins	4	5	6	10	12	20		
183	MacDonald/Apps TL	4	5	6	10	12	20	25	40
184	Gregg Sheppard	4	5	6	10	12	20	25	40
185	Joey Johnston	4	5	6	10	12			
186	Dick Redmond	4	5	6	10	12	20		
187	Simon Nolet	4	5	6	10	12	20		
188	Ron Stackhouse	4	5	6	10	12	20		
189	Marshall Johnston	4	5	6	10	12	20		
190	Richard Martin	4	5	6	10	12	20		
191	Andre Boudrias	4	5	6	10	12	20		
192	Steve Atkinson	4	5	6	10	12			
193	Nick Libett	4	5	6	10	12	20	25	40
194	Bob Murdoch Kings RC	4	5	6	10	12	20		
195	Denis Potvin RC	15	20	25	50	100	300	400	1,200
196	Dave Schultz	4	5	6	10	12	20		
197	Unger/Plante TL	4	5	6	10	12	20		
198	Jim McKenny	4	5	6	10	12	20		
199	Gerry Hart	4	5	6	10	12			
200	Phil Esposito	5	6	8	12	15	30	40	100
201	Rod Gilbert	4	5	6	10	12	20	25	60
202	Jacques Laperriere	4	5	6	10	12	25		
203	Barry Gibbs	4	5	6	10	12	20	30	100

#	Player	VG 3	VgEx 4	EX 5	ExMt 6	NM 7	NmMt 8	NmMt+ 8.5	MT 9
204	Billy Reay CO	4	5	6	10	12	20		
205	Gilles Meloche	4	5	6	10	12	20		
206	Wayne Cashman	4	5	6	10	12	20		
207	Dennis Ververgaert	4	5	6	10	12	20		
208	Phil Roberto	4	5	6	10	12	20		
209	Quarter Finals	4	5	6	10	12			
210	Quarter Finals	4	5	6	10	12	20		
211	Quarter Finals	4	5	6	10	12	20		
212	Quarter Finals	4	5	6	10	12	20		
213	Semi-Finals	4	5	6	10	12	20		
214	Semi-Finals	4	5	6	10	12	25		
215	Stanley Cup Finals	4	5	6	10	12	20		
216	Flyers Champions	4	5	6	10	12	25		
217	Joe Watson	4	5	6	10	12	20	25	50
218	Wayne Stephenson	4	5	6	10	12	20		
219	Sittlr/Ullmn/Hend TL	4	5	6	10	12	20		
220	Bill Goldsworthy	4	5	6	10	12	20		
221	Don Marcotte	4	5	6	10	12	20		
222	Alex Delvecchio CO	4	5	6	10	12			
223	Stan Gilbertson	4	5	6	10	12	20		
224	Mike Murphy	4	5	6	10	12	20		
225	Jim Rutherford	4	5	6	10	12	20		
226	Phil Russell	4	5	6	10	12	20		
227	Lynn Powis	4	5	6	10	12	20		
228	Billy Harris	4	5	6	10	12	20	25	50
229	Bob Pulford CO	4	5	6	10	12	25		
230	Ken Hodge	4	5	6	10	12	20		
231	Bill Fairbairn	4	5	6	10	12	20		
232	Guy Lafleur	6	8	10	15	20	40		
233	Harr/Stw/Ptvn TL UER	4	5	6	10	12	20		
234	Fred Barrett	4	5	6	10	12	20	25	40
235	Rogatien Vachon	4	5	6	10	12	20		
236	Norm Ullman	4	5	6	10	12	20		
237	Garry Unger	4	5	6	10	12	20		
238	Jack Gordon CO RC	4	5	6	10	12	20		
239	Johnny Bucyk	4	5	6	10	12	20	25	50
240	Bob Dailey RC	4	5	6	10	12	20		
241	Dave Burrows	4	5	6	10	12	20		
242	Len Frig RC	4	5	6	10	12	20	25	40
243	Henri Richard Mstrsn	4	5	6	10	25	100		
244	Phil Esposito Hart	4	5	6	10	12	20		
245	Johnny Bucyk Byng	4	5	6	10	12	20		
246	Phil Esposito Ross	4	5	6	12	20			
247	Wales Trophy	4	5	6	10	12	20		
248	Bobby Orr Norris	8	10	12	25	40	80	125	
249	Bernie Parent Vezina	4	5	6	10	15	40		
250	Philadelphia Flyers SC	4	5	6	10	12	20	30	60
251	Bernie Parent Smythe	4	5	6	10	12	40		
252	Denis Potvin Calder	6	8	10	12	15	30		
253	Campbell Trophy	4	5	6	10	12	20		
254	Pierre Bouchard	4	5	6	10	12	20		
255	Jude Drouin	4	5	6	10	12	20		
256	Capitals Emblem	4	5	6	10	12	20		
257	Michel Plasse	4	5	6	10	12	20		
258	Juha Widing	4	5	6	10	12			
259	Bryan Watson	4	5	6	10	12			
260	Bobby Clarke UER	6	8	10	15	20	60	80	150
261	Scotty Bowman CO RC	15	20	30	60	75	150		
262	Craig Patrick	4	5	6	10	12			
263	Craig Cameron	4	5	6	10	12	20		
264	Ted Irvine	4	5	6	10	12	20		
265	Ed Johnston	4	5	6	10	12	20		
266	Dave Forbes RC	4	5	6	10	12	20		
267	Red Wings Team CL	4	5	6	10	12	20	25	50
268	Rick Dudley RC	4	5	6	10	12	30		
269	Darcy Rota RC	4	5	6	10	12	20	25	50
270	Phil Myre	4	5	6	10	12			
271	Larry Brown RC	4	5	6	10	12	20		
272	Bob Neely RC	4	5	6	10	12	20		
273	Jerry Byers RC	4	5	6	10	12			
274	Penguins Team CL	4	5	6	10	12	20		
275	Glenn Goldup RC	4	5	6	10	12	20		
276	Ron Harris	4	5	6	10	12	20		
277	Joe Lundrigan RC	4	5	6	10	12	30		
278	Mike Christie RC	4	5	6	10	12	20		
279	Doug Rombough RC	4	5	6	10	12	20		
280	Larry Robinson	8	10	12	15	25	50		
281	Blues Team CL	4	5	6	10	12	20	25	40
282	John Marks RC	4	5	6	10	12	20		
283	Don Saleski	4	5	6	10	12	20	25	40
284	Rick Wilson RC	4	5	6	10	12	20		
285	Andre Savard RC	4	5	6	10	12			
286	Pat Quinn	4	5	6	10	12	20		
287	Kings Team CL	4	5	6	10	12	20		
288	Norm Gratton	4	5	6	10	12	20		
289	Ian Turnbull RC	4	5	6	10	12	60		
290	Derek Sanderson	4	5	6	10	12	20		
291	Murray Oliver	4	5	6	10	12	20		
292	Wilf Paiement RC	4	5	6	10	12	20		
293	Nelson Debenedet RC	4	5	6	10	12	20		
294	Greg Joly RC	4	5	6	10	12	25	30	50
295	Terry O'Reilly	4	5	6	10	12			
296	Rey Comeau	4	5	6	10	12	20	25	40
297	Michel Larocque RC	5	6	8	12	15	80		
298	Floyd Thomson RC	4	5	6	10	12	20		
299	Jean-Guy Lagace RC	4	5	6	10	12			
300	Flyers Team CL	4	5	6	10	12	30		
301	Al MacAdam RC	4	5	6	10	12	20		
302	George Ferguson RC	4	5	6	10	12	20		
303	Jimmy Watson RC	4	5	6	10	20	50		
304	Rick Middleton RC	8	10	12	25	40	100	120	300
305	Craig Ramsay UER	4	5	6	10	12	20		
306	Hilliard Graves	4	5	6	10	12			
307	Islanders Team CL	4	5	6	10	12	20		
308	Blake Dunlop RC	4	5	6	10	12	20		
309	J.P. Bordeleau	4	5	6	10	12	20		
310	Brian Glennie	4	5	6	10	12			
311	Checklist 265-396 UER	10	12	20	35	60	120		
312	Doug Roberts	4	5	6	10	12	20		
313	Darryl Edestrand	4	5	6	10	12			
314	Ron Anderson	4	5	6	10	12	20		
315	Blackhawks Team CL	4	5	6	10	12	20		
316	Steve Shutt RC	10	12	15	25	50	400	500	800
317	Doug Horbul RC	4	5	6	10	12	20	25	50
318	Billy Lochead RC	4	5	6	10	12	20		
319	Fred Harvey	4	5	6	10	12			
320	Gene Carr RC	4	5	6	10	12			
321	Henri Richard	4	5	6	10	12	50		
322	Canucks Team CL	4	5	6	10	12	20	25	40
323	Tim Ecclestone	4	5	6	10	12	20		
324	Dave Lewis RC	4	5	6	10	12	25		
325	Lou Nanne	4	5	6	10	12	20		
326	Bobby Rousseau	4	5	6	10	12	20		
327	Dunc Wilson	4	5	6	10	12	20		
328	Brian Spencer	4	5	6	10	12	20		
329	Rick Hampton RC	4	5	6	10	12	20		
330	Canadiens Team CL UER	4	5	6	10	12	30	35	50
331	Jack Lynch	4	5	6	10	12	20		
332	Garnet Bailey	4	5	6	10	12	20		
333	Al Sims RC	4	5	6	10	12	25		
334	Orest Kindrachuk RC	4	5	6	10	12	40		
335	Dave Hudson	4	5	6	10	12	20		
336	Bob Murray RC	4	5	6	10	12	20		
337	Sabres Team CL	4	5	6	10	12	20		
338	Sheldon Kannegiesser	4	5	6	10	12			
339	Bill MacMillan	4	5	6	10	12			
340	Paulin Bordeleau RC	4	5	6	10	12	20		
341	Dale Rolfe	4	5	6	10	12	20		
342	Yvon Lambert RC	4	5	6	10	12	50		
343	Bob Paradise RC	4	5	6	10	12	20		
344	Germaine Gagnon UER	4	5	6	10	12	20		
345	Yvon Labre	4	5	6	10	12	20		
346	Chris Ahrens RC	4	5	6	10	12	20		
347	Doug Grant RC	4	5	6	10	12	20		
348	Blaine Stoughton RC	4	5	6	10	12	20		
349	Gregg Boddy	4	5	6	10	12	25	30	60
350	Bruins Team CL	4	5	6	10	12	20		
351	Doug Jarrett	4	5	6	10	12	20	25	50
352	Terry Crisp	4	5	6	10	12	20	25	50
353	Glenn Resch UER RC	8	10	12	15	25	50	60	100
354	Jerry Korab	4	5	6	10	12	20		
355	Stan Weir RC	4	5	6	10	12	20		
356	Noel Price	4	5	6	10	12	20		
357	Bill Clement RC	6	8	10	20	30	60	80	135
358	Neil Komadoski	4	5	6	10	12			
359	Murray Wilson RC	4	5	6	10	12	20		
360	Dale Tallon UER	4	5	6	10	12	20		
361	Gary Doak	4	5	6	10	12			
362	Randy Rota RC	4	5	6	10	12			
363	North Stars Team CL	4	5	6	10	12	20		
364	Bill Collins	4	5	6	10	12	20		
365	Thommie Bergman UER	4	5	6	10	12	20		
366	Dennis Kearns	4	5	6	10	12	20		
367	Lorne Henning	4	5	6	10	12	20		
368	Gary Sabourin	4	5	6	10	12	20		
369	Mike Bloom RC	4	5	6	10	12			
370	Rangers Team CL	4	5	6	10	12	20		
371	Gary Simmons RC	5	6	8	12	15			
372	Dwight Bialowas RC	4	5	6	10	12	20		
373	Gilles Marotte	4	5	6	10	12	20		
374	Frank St.Marseille	4	5	6	10	12			
375	Garry Howatt	4	5	6	10	12	30		
376	Ross Brooks RC	4	5	6	10	12	20	25	60
377	Flames Team CL	4	5	6	10	12	20		
378	Bob Nevin	4	5	6	10	12	20		
379	Lyle Moffat RC	4	5	6	10	12	20		
380	Bob Kelly	4	5	6	10	12	20		
381	John Gould RC	4	5	6	10	12	20		
382	Dave Fortier RC	4	5	6	10	12	20		
383	Jean Hamel RC	4	5	6	10	12	20		

		VG 3	VgEx 4	EX 5	ExMt 6	NM 7	NmMt 8	NmMt+ 8.5	MT 9
384	Bert Wilson RC	4	5	6	10	12	20		
385	Chuck Arnason RC	4	5	6	10	12	20		
386	Bruce Cowick RC	4	5	6	10	12	20		
387	Ernie Hicke	4	5	6	10	12	20		
388	Bob Gainey RC	10	12	20	30	60	125	200	550
389	Vic Venasky RC	4	5	6	10	12	20		
390	Maple Leafs Team CL	4	5	6	10	12	25	30	60
391	Eric Vail RC	4	5	6	10	12	20		
392	Bobby Lalonde	4	5	6	10	12	20		
393	Jerry Butler RC	4	5	6	10	12	20		
394	Tom Williams	4	5	6	10	12	20		
395	Chico Maki	4	5	6	10	12	30		
396	Tom Bladon RC	4	5	6	12	20	40		

— Scotty Bowman CO RC #61 PSA 9 (MT) sold for $351.95 (eBay; 8/12)
— Bill Clement RC #357 PSA 9 (MT) sold for $305 (eBay; 8/12)
— Espo/Orr/Bucyk TL #28 PSA 10 (Gem) sold for $1,491 (eBay; 3/07)
— Espo/Orr/Bucyk TL #28 PSA 10 (Gem) sold for $562 (Mile High; 12/13)
— Espo/Orr/Bucyk TL #28 PSA 10 (Gem) sold for $510 (eBay; 12/06)
— Bob Gainey RC #388 PSA 10 (Gem) sold for $1,079 (eBay; 9/15)
— Rick Middleton RC #304 PSA 10 (Gem) sold for $764 (eBay; 7/12)
— Bobby Orr AS #130 PSA 10 (Gem) sold for $2,025 (eBay; 8/12)
— Bobby Orr AS #130 PSA 10 (Gem) sold for $1,952 (Mile High; 10/12)
— Bobby Orr AS #130 PSA 10 (Gem) sold for $1,626.73 (Mile High; 12/13)
— Bobby Orr Norris #248 BVG 10 (Gem) sold for $507.99 (eBay; 2/16)
— Denis Potvin RC #195 BVG 9.5 (GemMT) sold for $652.50 (eBay; 4/16)
— Steve Schutt RC #316 PSA 9 (MT) sold for $569 (eBay; 7/12)
— Billy Smith #82 PSA 10 (Gem) sold for $488 (eBay; 7/15)

1974-75 O-Pee-Chee WHA

		VG 3	VgEx 4	EX 5	ExMt 6	NM 7	NmMt 8	NmMt+ 8.5	MT 9
	COMMON CARD (1-66)	5	5	5	8	10	15	20	30
1	Gord/Mark/Marty Howe	15	20	25	40	60	125	150	200
2	Bruce MacGregor	5	5	5	8	10	15		
4	Ulf Nilsson RC	5	6	8	12	15	25	30	50
7	Rosaire Paiement	5	5	5	8	10	15		
8	Tom Webster	5	5	5	8	10	15		
11	Norm Beaudin	5	5	5	8	10	15	25	40
17	Anders Hedberg RC	5	6	8	12	15	30	40	60
19	Mike Pelyk	5	5	5	8	10	15	20	40
25	Danny Lawson RC	5	5	5	8	10	15	20	40
27	Gene Peacosh RC	5	5	5	8	10	15		
28	Fran Huck	5	5	5	8	10	15		
29	Al Hamilton	5	5	5	8	10	15	20	40
30	Gerry Cheevers	5	8	10	15	20	30	40	60
35	Pat Stapleton	5	6	8	12	15	25	30	50
38	Joe Daley	5	5	5	8	10	15	20	40
40	Frank Mahovlich	5	6	8	12	15	30	40	60
41	Rejean Houle	5	5	5	8	10	15	20	40
42	Ron Chipperfield RC	5	5	6	10	12	20		
48	Don McLeod RC	5	5	5	8	10	15	20	40
49	Vaclav Nedomansky RC	5	5	6	10	12	20	25	40
50	Bobby Hull	8	10	15	20	25	40	50	120
53	Checklist	6	10	15	20	25	40	50	80
54	Wayne Connelly	5	5	5	8	10	15		
56	Dennis Sobchuk RC	5	5	5	8	10	15	20	40
57	Paul Henderson	5	5	5	8	10	15	20	40
58	Andy Brown RC	5	5	6	10	12	20	25	50
60	Andre Lacroix	5	5	5	8	10	15	20	40
61	Gary Jarrett	5	5	5	8	10	15	20	40
62	Claude St.Sauveur RC	5	5	5	8	10	15		
63	Real Cloutier RC	5	5	6	10	12	20	25	50
64	Jacques Plante	8	10	15	20	25	40	50	100
65	Gilles Gratton RC	5	6	8	12	15	25		
66	Lars-Erik Sjoberg RC	5	6	8	12	25	40		

— Gordie/Mark/Marty Howe #1 PSA 10 (Gem) sold for $1,633 (eBay; 12/15)

1974-75 Topps

		VG 3	VgEx 4	EX 5	ExMt 6	NM 7	NmMt 8	NmMt+ 8.5	MT 9
1	P.Espo/Goldsworthy LL	4	5	6	8	15	40		
2	B.Orr/D.Hextall LL	4	5	6	20	25	30		50
3	P.Espo/B.Clarke LL	4	5	6	8	12	20	25	50
4	D.Favell/B.Parent LL	4	5	6	8	12	20		
5	B.Watson/D.Schultz LL	4	5	6	8	12	18		
6	M.Redmond/R.Mac LL	4	5	6	8	10	12	15	30
7	Gary Bromley RC	4	5	6	8	10	12	15	30
8	Bill Barber	4	5	6	8	12	20		
9	Emile Francis CO	4	5	6	8	12	18		
10	Gilles Gilbert	4	5	6	8	12	20		
11	John Davidson RC	5	6	8	10	15	25		
12	Ron Ellis	4	5	6	8	12	18		
13	Syl Apps	4	5	6	8	10	12	15	30
14	Richard/Lysiak/McCrry TL	4	5	6	8	12	18		
15	Dan Bouchard	4	5	6	10	15	50		
16	Ivan Boldirev	4	5	6	8	12	18		
17	Gary Coalter RC	4	5	6	8	12	18		
18	Bob Berry	4	5	6	8	12	18		
19	Red Berenson	4	5	6	10	15			
20	Stan Mikita	4	5	6	8	12	20		
21	Fred Shero CO RC	4	5	6	8	12	15	20	35

		VG 3	VgEx 4	EX 5	ExMt 6	NM 7	NmMt 8	NmMt+ 8.5	MT 9
22	Gary Smith	4	5	6	8	10	12	15	30
23	Bill Mikkelson	4	5	6	8	12	18		
24	Jacques Lemaire UER	4	5	6	8	12	20		
25	Gilbert Perreault	4	5	6	8	12	20	25	50
26	Cesare Maniago	4	5	6	8	10	12	15	30
27	Bobby Schmautz	4	5	6	8	12	18		
28	Espo/Orr/Bucyk TL	5	6	8	10	15	25	30	60
29	Steve Vickers	4	5	6	8	12	18		
30	Lowell MacDonald	4	5	6	8	12	18		
31	Fred Stanfield	4	5	6	8	10	12	15	30
32	Ed Westfall	4	5	6	10	15			
33	Curt Bennett	4	5	6	8	10	12	15	30
34	Bep Guidolin CO	4	5	6	8	12	18		
35	Cliff Koroll	4	5	6	8	10	12	15	30
36	Gary Croteau	4	5	6	8	10	12	15	30
37	Mike Corrigan	4	5	6	8	10	12	15	30
38	Henry Boucha	4	5	6	10	15			
39	Ron Low	4	5	6	8	10	12	15	30
40	Darryl Sittler	4	5	6	8	12	15	20	40
41	Tracy Pratt	4	5	6	8	12	18		
42	R.Martin/R.Robert TL	4	5	6	8	12	18		
43	Larry Carriere	4	5	6	8	10	12	15	30
44	Gary Dornhoefer	4	5	6	8	12	18		
45	Denis Herron RC	4	5	6	8	12	15	20	35
46	Doug Favell	4	5	6	8	12	18		
47	Dave Gardner RC	4	5	6	8	10	12	15	30
48	Morris Mott RC	4	5	6	8	10	12	15	30
49	Marc Boileau CO	4	5	6	8	10	12	15	30
50	Brad Park	4	5	6	8	12	20		
51	Bob Leiter	4	5	6	8	10	12	15	30
52	Tom Reid	4	5	6	8	12	18		
53	Serge Savard	4	5	6	8	12	15	20	35
54	Checklist 1-132	5	6	8	10	15	25		
55	Terry Harper	4	5	6	8	10	12	15	30
56	Johnston/McKechnie TL	4	5	6	8	10	12	15	30
57	Guy Charron	4	5	6	8	10	12	15	30
58	Pit Martin	4	5	6	8	12	18		
59	Chris Evans	4	5	6	8	12	18		
60	Bernie Parent	4	5	6	8	12	20		
61	Jim Lorentz	4	5	6	8	12	18		
62	Dave Kryskow RC	4	5	6	8	12	18		
63	Lou Angotti CO	4	5	6	10	15	30		
64	Bill Flett	4	5	6	8	12	18		
65	Vic Hadfield	4	5	6	10	15	30		
66	Wayne Merrick RC	4	5	6	10	15	35		
67	Andre Dupont	4	5	6	10	15	35		
68	Tom Lysiak RC	4	5	6	8	12	20		
69	Pappin/Mikita/Bord TL	4	5	6	8	12	18		
70	Guy Lapointe	4	5	6	10	12	15		30
71	Gerry O'Flaherty	4	5	6	8	12	18		
72	Marcel Dionne	4	5	6	8	12	20		
73	Butch Deadmarsh RC	4	5	6	10	15	35		
74	Butch Goring	4	5	6	8	10	12	15	30
75	Keith Magnuson	4	5	6	8	12	18		
76	Red Kelly CO	4	5	6	8	12	18		
77	Pete Stemkowski	4	5	6	8	12	18		
78	Jim Roberts	4	5	6	10	12	15		30
79	Don Luce	4	5	6	8	10	12	15	30
80	Don Awrey	4	5	6	8	12	18		
81	Rick Kehoe	4	5	6	8	10	12	15	30
82	Billy Smith	4	5	6	8	12	15	20	40
83	Jean-Paul Parise	4	5	6	8	12	18		
84	Redmnd/Dionne/Hog TL	4	5	6	8	12	18		
85	Ed Van Impe	4	5	6	8	12	18		
86	Randy Manery	4	5	6	10	12	15		30
87	Barclay Plager	4	5	6	10	15	30		
88	Inge Hammarstrom RC	4	5	6	8	12	18		
89	Ab DeMarco	4	5	6	8	12	18		
90	Bill White	4	5	6	8	10	12	15	30
91	Al Arbour CO	4	5	6	8	12	20		
92	Bob Stewart	4	5	6	8	12	18		
93	Jack Egers	4	5	6	8	12	18		
94	Don Lever	4	5	6	8	10	12	15	30
95	Reggie Leach	4	5	6	8	12	18		
96	Dennis O'Brien	4	5	6	8	10	12	15	30
97	Peter Mahovlich	4	5	6	8	12	18		
98	Goring/St.Mars/Kozak TL	4	5	6	8	10	12	15	30
99	Gerry Meehan	4	5	6	8	10	12	15	30
100	Bobby Orr	12	15	20	25	40	60	80	120
101	Jean Potvin RC	4	5	6	8	12	18		
102	Rod Seiling	4	5	6	8	12	18		
103	Keith McCreary	4	5	6	8	10	12	15	30
104	Phil Maloney CO RC	4	5	6	8	10	12	15	30
105	Denis Dupere	4	5	6	8	12	18		
106	Steve Durbano	4	5	6	8	12	18		
107	Bob Plager UER	4	5	6	8	10	12	15	30
108	Chris Oddleifson RC	4	5	6	8	12	18		
109	Jim Neilson	4	5	6	8	12	18		
110	Jean Pronovost	4	5	6	8	10	12	15	30
111	Don Kozak RC	4	5	6	8	10	12	15	30

#	Player	VG 3	VgEx 4	EX 5	ExMt 6	NM 7	NmMt 8	NmMt+ 8.5	MT 9
112	Goldswrthy/Grant/Hex	4	5	6	8	12	18		
113	Jim Pappin	4	5	6	8	12	18		
114	Richard Lemieux	4	5	6	8	10	12	15	30
115	Dennis Hextall	4	5	6	8	12	18		
116	Bill Hogaboam	4	5	6	8	12	18		
117	Canucks Leaders	4	5	6	8	12	18		
118	Jimmy Anderson CO	4	5	6	8	12	18		
119	Walt Tkaczuk	4	5	6	8	12	18		
120	Mickey Redmond	4	5	6	10	15			
121	Jim Schoenfeld	4	5	6	8	12	20		
122	Jocelyn Guevremont	4	5	6	8	10	12	15	30
123	Bob Nystrom	4	5	6	8	12	20		
124	Cour/F.Mahv/Larose TL	4	5	6	8	12	15	20	35
125	Lew Morrison	4	5	6	10	15	25		
126	Terry Murray	4	5	6	8	12	18		
127	Richard Martin	4	5	6	8	12	18		
128	Ken Hodge AS	4	5	6	8	12	18		
129	Phil Esposito AS	4	5	6	8	12	20		
130	Bobby Orr AS	5	6	8	10	15	30	40	100
131	Brad Park AS	4	5	6	10	15			
132	Gilles Gilbert AS	4	5	6	10	15	80		
133	Lowell MacDonald AS	4	5	6	8	10	12	15	30
134	Bill Goldsworthy AS	4	5	6	8	12	18		
135	Bobby Clarke AS	4	5	6	8	12	20		
136	Bill White AS	4	5	6	10	15	25		
137	Dave Burrows AS	4	5	6	8	12	18		
138	Bernie Parent AS	4	5	6	8	12	20		
139	Jacques Richard	4	5	6	8	10	12	15	30
140	Yvan Cournoyer	4	5	6	8	10	12	15	30
141	R.Gilbert/B.Park TL	4	5	6	8	12	15	20	35
142	Rene Robert	4	5	6	8	10	12	15	30
143	J. Bob Kelly RC	4	5	6	10	15	25		
144	Ross Lonsberry	4	5	6	8	12	18		
145	Jean Ratelle	4	5	6	8	12	18		
146	Dallas Smith	4	5	6	8	10	12	15	30
147	Bernie Geoffrion CO	4	5	6	8	12	15	20	35
148	Ted McAneeley	4	5	6	8	10	12	15	30
149	Pierre Plante	4	5	6	8	12	18		
150	Dennis Hull	4	5	6	8	12	18		
151	Dave Keon	4	5	6	8	12	15	20	35
152	Dave Dunn RC	4	5	6	8	10	12	15	30
153	Michel Belhumeur	4	5	6	8	12	18		
154	B.Clarke/D.Schultz TL	4	5	6	8	12	20		
155	Ken Dryden	6	8	10	12	20	30	35	50
156	John Wright RC	4	5	6	8	12	18		
157	Larry Romanchych	4	5	6	8	10	12	15	30
158	Ralph Stewart	4	5	6	10	15	25		
159	Mike Robitaille	4	5	6	8	10	12	15	30
160	Ed Giacomin	4	5	6	8	12	15	20	35
161	Don Cherry CO RC	8	10	12	15	30	40	50	60
162	Checklist 133-264	5	6	8	10	15	25		
163	Rick MacLeish	4	5	6	8	10	12	15	30
164	Greg Polis	4	5	6	10	15	25		
165	Carol Vadnais	4	5	6	8	12	18		
166	Pete Laframboise	4	5	6	8	10	12	15	30
167	Ron Schock	4	5	6	8	10	12	15	30
168	Lanny McDonald RC	5	6	8	10	15	40	50	80
169	Scouts Emblem	4	5	6	8	12	18		
170	Tony Esposito	4	5	6	8	12	25	30	60
171	Pierre Jarry	4	5	6	8	12	18		
172	Dan Maloney	4	5	6	8	10	12	15	30
173	Peter McDuffe	4	5	6	8	10	12	15	30
174	Danny Grant	4	5	6	8	10	12	15	30
175	John Stewart	4	5	6	8	10	12	15	30
176	Floyd Smith CO	4	5	6	8	10	12	15	30
177	Bert Marshall	4	5	6	8	12	18		
178	Chuck Lefley UER	4	5	6	8	12	18		
179	Gilles Villemure	4	5	6	8	10	12	15	30
180	Borje Salming RC	5	6	8	12	20	25	30	80
181	Doug Mohns	4	5	6	8	12	18		
182	Barry Wilkins	4	5	6	8	10	12	15	30
183	MacDonald/S.Apps TL	4	5	6	8	12	18		
184	Gregg Sheppard	4	5	6	8	10	12	15	30
185	Joey Johnston	4	5	6	8	12	18		
186	Dick Redmond	4	5	6	8	10	12	15	30
187	Simon Nolet	4	5	6	8	10	12	15	30
188	Ron Stackhouse	4	5	6	8	12	18		
189	Marshall Johnston	4	5	6	8	10	12	15	30
190	Richard Martin	4	5	6	8	12	15	20	35
191	Andre Boudrias	4	5	6	8	12	18		
192	Steve Atkinson	4	5	6	10	12	20		
193	Nick Libett	4	5	6	8	12	18		
194	Bob Murdoch RC	4	5	6	8	10	12	15	30
195	Denis Potvin RC	10	12	15	20	30	50		
196	Dave Schultz	4	5	6	8	12	20		
197	G.Unger/P.Plante TL	4	5	6	8	12	18		
198	Jim McKenny	4	5	6	8	12	18		
199	Gary Hart	4	5	6	8	12	18		
200	Phil Esposito	4	5	6	8	12	20	30	60
201	Rod Gilbert	4	5	6	8	12	20		

#	Player	VG 3	VgEx 4	EX 5	ExMt 6	NM 7	NmMt 8	NmMt+ 8.5	MT 9
202	Jacques Laperriere	4	5	6	8	10	12	15	30
203	Barry Gibbs	4	5	6	8	10	12	15	30
204	Billy Reay CO	4	5	6	8	10	12	15	30
205	Gilles Meloche	4	5	6	8	12	18		
206	Wayne Cashman	4	5	6	8	10	12	15	30
207	Dennis Ververgaert RC	4	5	6	8	12	18		
208	Phil Roberto	4	5	6	8	10	12	15	30
209	Quarter Finals	4	5	6	8	12	18		
210	Quarter Finals	4	5	6	8	12	18		
211	Quarter Finals	4	5	6	8	10	12	15	30
212	Quarter Finals	4	5	6	8	10	12	15	30
213	Stanley Cup Semifinals	4	5	6	8	10	12	15	30
214	Stanley Cup Semifinals	4	5	6	8	12	18		
215	Stanley Cup Finals	4	5	6	8	12	18		
216	Flyers Champions	4	5	6	8	12	15	20	35
217	Joe Watson	4	5	6	8	12	18		
218	Wayne Stephenson	4	5	6	10	15	25		
219	Sittler/Ullman/Hend TL	4	5	6	8	12	18		
220	Bill Goldsworthy	4	5	6	8	12	18		
221	Don Marcotte	4	5	6	8	12	18		
222	Alex Delvecchio CO	4	5	6	8	12	18		
223	Stan Gilbertson	4	5	6	8	10	12	15	30
224	Mike Murphy	4	5	6	8	10	12	15	30
225	Jim Rutherford	4	5	6	8	12	18		
226	Phil Russell	4	5	6	8	10	12	15	30
227	Lynn Powis	4	5	6	8	10	12	15	30
228	Billy Harris	4	5	6	8	10	12	15	30
229	Bob Pulford CO	4	5	6	8	10	12	15	30
230	Ken Hodge	4	5	6	8	12	18		
231	Bill Fairbairn	4	5	6	8	10	12	15	30
232	Guy Lafleur	5	6	8	10	15	30	40	100
233	Harris/Stew/Potvin TL	4	5	6	8	12	20		
234	Fred Barrett	4	5	6	8	10	12	15	30
235	Rogatien Vachon RC	4	5	6	8	12	15	20	35
236	Norm Ullman	4	5	6	8	12	20		
237	Garry Unger	4	5	6	10	15			
238	Jack Gordon CO RC	4	5	6	8	10	12	15	30
239	Johnny Bucyk	4	5	6	8	12	15	20	35
240	Bob Dailey RC	4	5	6	8	10	12	15	30
241	Dave Burrows	4	5	6	8	12	18		
242	Len Frig RC	4	5	6	8	12	12	15	30
243	Henri Richard Mast.	4	5	6	10	15	30		
244	Phil Esposito Hart	4	5	6	8	12	15	20	40
245	Johnny Bucyk Byng	4	5	6	8	12	18		
246	Phil Esposito Ross	4	5	6	8	12	20		
247	Prince of Wales Trophy	4	5	6	8	12	18		
248	Bobby Orr Norris	5	6	8	10	15	25	25	40
249	Bernie Parent Vezina	4	5	6	8	12	15	20	40
250	Flyers Stanley Cup	4	5	6	8	12	15	20	40
251	Bernie Parent Smythe	4	5	6	8	12	15	20	40
252	Denis Potvin Calder	4	5	6	8	12	20		
253	Flyers Campbell Trophy	4	5	6	8	12	18		
254	Pierre Bouchard	4	5	6	8	12	18		
255	Jude Drouin	4	5	6	8	12	18		
256	Capitals Emblem	4	5	6	8	12	20		
257	Michel Plasse	4	5	6	8	12	18		
258	Juha Widing	4	5	6	10	12	20		
259	Bryan Watson	4	5	6	10	12	20		
260	Bobby Clarke	5	6	8	10	15	25		
261	Scotty Bowman CO RC	8	10	12	15	25	40	50	80
262	Craig Patrick	4	5	6	10	15	25		
263	Craig Cameron	4	5	6	10	15			
264	Ted Irvine	4	5	6	12	20			

1975-76 O-Pee-Chee

#	Player	VG 3	VgEx 4	EX 5	ExMt 6	NM 7	NmMt 8	NmMt+ 8.5	MT 9
1	Stanley Cup Finals	4	5	6	12	20	50		
2	Semi-Finals/Phil/Isln	4	5	6	10	12	25		
3	Semi-Finals/Buf/Mont	4	5	6	10	12	25	30	50
4	Quarter Finals/Isln/Pitt	4	5	6	10	12	20		
5	Quarter Finals/Mont/Van	4	5	6	10	12	20		
6	Quarter Finals/Buf/Chi	4	5	6	10	12	20	30	80
7	Quarter Finals/Phil/Tor	4	5	6	10	12	30		
8	Curt Bennett	4	5	6	10	12	20		
9	Johnny Bucyk	4	5	6	10	12	20		
10	Gilbert Perreault	5	6	8	12	15	25		
11	Darryl Edestrand	4	5	6	10	12	20		
12	Ivan Boldirev	4	5	6	10	12	20	25	40
13	Nick Libett	4	5	6	10	12	20	25	40
14	Jim McElmury RC	4	5	6	10	12	20		
15	Frank St.Marseille	4	5	6	10	12	20		
16	Blake Dunlop	4	5	6	10	12	20		
17	Yvon Lambert	4	5	6	10	12	20		
18	Gerry Hart	4	5	6	10	12	20		
19	Steve Vickers	4	5	6	10	12	20		
20	Rick MacLeish	4	5	6	10	12	20		
21A	Bob Paradise NoTR	4	5	6	10	12	20	25	40
21B	Bob Paradise TR	4	5	6	10	12	20		
22	Red Berenson	4	5	6	10	12	20		

HOCKEY

#	Player	VG 3	VgEx 4	EX 5	ExMt 6	NM 7	NmMt 8	NmMt+ 8.5	MT 9
23	Lanny McDonald	5	6	8	12	15	25	35	60
24	Mike Robitaille	4	5	6	10	12	20		
25	Ron Low	4	5	6	10	12	20	25	40
26A	Bryan Hextall NoTR	4	5	6	10	12	20		
26B	Bryan Hextall TR	4	5	6	10	12	20		
27A	Carol Vadnais NoTR	4	5	6	10	12	20		
27B	Carol Vadnais TR	4	5	6	10	12	20		
28	Jim Lorentz	4	5	6	10	12	20	25	40
29	Gary Simmons	4	5	6	10	12	20		
30	Stan Mikita	4	5	6	10	12	20		
31	Bryan Watson	4	5	6	10	12	20		
32	Guy Charron	4	5	6	10	12	20		
33	Bob Murdoch	4	5	6	10	12	20		
34	Norm Gratton	4	5	6	10	12	20		
35	Ken Dryden	10	12	15	25	35	60	75	135
36	Jean Potvin	4	5	6	10	12	20	25	40
37	Rick Middleton	4	5	6	10	12	20		
38	Ed Van Impe	4	5	6	10	12	20		
39	Rick Kehoe	4	5	6	10	12	20	25	40
40	Garry Unger	4	5	6	10	12	20		
41	Ian Turnbull	4	5	6	10	12	20		
42	Dennis Ververgaert	4	5	6	10	12	20		
43	Mike Marson RC	4	5	6	10	12	20	25	50
44	Randy Manery	4	5	6	10	12	20		
45	Gilles Gilbert	4	5	6	10	12	20		
46	Rene Robert	4	5	6	10	12	20	25	40
47	Bob Stewart	4	5	6	10	12	20		
48	Pit Martin	4	5	6	10	12	20	25	40
49	Danny Grant	4	5	6	10	12	20	25	40
50	Peter Mahovlich	4	5	6	10	12	20		
51	Dennis Patterson RC	4	5	6	10	12	20	25	40
52	Mike Murphy	4	5	6	10	12	20	25	40
53	Dennis O'Brien	4	5	6	10	12	20	25	40
54	Garry Howatt	4	5	6	10	12	20		
55	Ed Giacomin	4	5	6	10	12	20		
56	Andre Dupont	4	5	6	10	12	20		
57	Chuck Arnason	4	5	6	10	12	20		
58	Bob Gassoff RC	4	5	6	10	12	20		
59	Ron Ellis	4	5	6	10	12	20		
60	Andre Boudrias	4	5	6	10	12	20		
61	Yvon Labre	4	5	6	10	12	20		
62	Hilliard Graves	4	5	6	10	12	20	25	40
63	Wayne Cashman	4	5	6	10	12	20		
64	Danny Gare RC	4	5	6	10	12	20		
65	Rick Hampton	4	5	6	10	12	20	25	40
66	Darcy Rota	4	5	6	10	12	20		
67	Bill Hogaboam	4	5	6	10	12	20		
68	Denis Herron	4	5	6	10	12	20		
69	Sheldon Kannegiesser	4	5	6	10	12	20		
70	Yvan Cournoyer UER	4	5	6	10	12	20	30	50
71	Ernie Hicke	4	5	6	10	12	20		
72	Bert Marshall	4	5	6	10	12	20	25	40
73	Derek Sanderson	4	5	6	10	12	20		
74	Tom Bladon	4	5	6	10	12	20		
75	Ron Schock	4	5	6	10	12	20		
76	Larry Sacharuk RC	4	5	6	10	12	20		
77	George Ferguson	4	5	6	10	12	20		
78	Ab DeMarco	4	5	6	10	12	20		
79	Tom Williams	4	5	6	10	12	20	25	40
80	Phil Roberto	4	5	6	10	12	20		
81	Bruins Team CL	4	5	6	10	12	20		
82	Seals Team CL	4	5	6	10	12	20	25	50
83	Sabres Team CL	4	5	6	10	12	20		
84	Blackhawks Team CL	4	5	6	10	12	20		
85	Flames Team CL	4	5	6	10	12	20		
86	Kings Team CL	4	5	6	10	12	20		
87	Red Wings Team CL	4	5	6	10	12	20		
88	Scouts Team CL	4	5	6	10	12	20		
89	North Stars Team CL	4	5	6	10	12	20		
90	Canadiens Team CL	4	5	6	10	15	60		
91	Maple Leafs Team CL	4	5	6	10	12	40		
92	Islanders Team CL	4	5	6	10	12	20		
93	Penguins Team CL	4	5	6	10	12	20		
94	Rangers Team CL	4	5	6	10	12	20		
95	Flyers Team CL	4	5	6	10	12	20		
96	Blues Team CL	4	5	6	10	12	20		
97	Canucks Team CL	4	5	6	10	12	20		
98	Capitals Team CL	4	5	6	10	12			
99	Checklist 1-110	6	8	10	15	40	80		
100	Bobby Orr	15	20	25	30	50	100	150	300
101	Germain Gagnon UER	4	5	6	10	12	20		
102	Phil Russell	4	5	6	10	12	20		
103	Billy Lochead	4	5	6	10	12	20		
104	Robin Burns RC	4	5	6	10	12	20	25	40
105	Gary Edwards	4	5	6	10	12	20	25	40
106	Dwight Bialowas	4	5	6	10	12	20		
107	Doug Risebrough UER RC	4	5	6	10	15	35	50	80
108	Dave Lewis	4	5	6	10	12	20		
109	Bill Fairbairn	4	5	6	10	12	20		
110	Ross Lonsberry	4	5	6	10	12	20		

#	Player	VG 3	VgEx 4	EX 5	ExMt 6	NM 7	NmMt 8	NmMt+ 8.5	TMT 9
111	Ron Stackhouse	4	5	6	10	12	20		
112	Claude Larose	4	5	6	10	12	20	25	40
113	Don Luce	4	5	6	10	12	20	25	40
114	Errol Thompson RC	4	5	6	10	12	20	25	40
115	Gary Smith	4	5	6	10	12	20		
116	Jack Lynch	4	5	6	10	12	.		
117	Jacques Richard	4	5	6	10	12	20		
118	Dallas Smith	4	5	6	10	12	20		
119	Dave Gardner	4	5	6	10	12	20		
120	Mickey Redmond	4	5	6	10	12	20		
121	John Marks	4	5	6	10	12	20		
122	Dave Hudson	4	5	6	10	12	20		
123	Bob Nevin	4	5	6	10	12	20		
124	Fred Barrett	4	5	6	10	12	20		
125	Gerry Desjardins	4	5	6	10	12	20		
126	Guy Lafleur UER	6	8	10	15	25	50	60	100
127	Jean-Paul Parise	4	5	6	10	12	20		
128	Walt Tkaczuk	4	5	6	10	12	20		
129	Gary Dornhoefer	4	5	6	10	12	20	25	40
130	Syl Apps	4	5	6	10	12	20		
131	Bob Plager	4	5	6	10	12	20		
132	Stan Weir	4	5	6	10	12	20		
133	Tracy Pratt	4	5	6	10	12	20		
134	Jack Egers	4	5	6	10	12	20	25	40
135	Eric Vail	4	5	6	10	12	20		
136	Al Sims	4	5	6	10	12	20		
137	Larry Patey RC	4	5	6	10	12	20	25	40
138	Jim Schoenfeld	4	5	6	10	12	20		
139	Cliff Koroll	4	5	6	10	12	20	25	40
140	Marcel Dionne	5	6	8	12	15	25		
141	Jean-Guy Lagace	4	5	6	10	12	20		
142	Juha Widing	4	5	6	10	12	20	25	40
143	Lou Nanne	4	5	6	10	12	20		
144	Serge Savard	4	5	6	10	12	20		
145	Glenn Resch	4	5	6	10	12	20		
146	Ron Greschner RC	4	5	6	10	12	20		
147	Dave Schultz	4	5	6	10	12	20		
148	Barry Wilkins	4	5	6	10	12	20		
149	Floyd Thomson	4	5	6	10	12	20		
150	Darryl Sittler	5	6	8	12	15	30	35	60
151	Paulin Bordeleau	4	5	6	10	12	20	25	40
152	Ron Lalonde RC	4	5	6	10	12	20	25	40
153	Larry Romanchych	4	5	6	10	12	20		
154	Larry Carriere	4	5	6	10	12	20	25	40
155	Andre Savard	4	5	6	10	12	20		
156	Dave Hrechkosy RC	4	5	6	10	12	20		
157	Bill White	4	5	6	10	12	20		
158	Dave Kryskow	4	5	6	10	12	20		
159	Denis Dupere	4	5	6	10	12	20		
160	Rogatien Vachon	4	5	6	10	12	20	25	50
161	Doug Rombough	4	5	6	10	12	20		
162	Murray Wilson	4	5	6	10	12	20		
163	Bob Bourne RC	4	5	6	10	12	25	30	50
164	Gilles Marotte	4	5	6	10	12	20		
165	Vic Hadfield	4	5	6	10	12	20	25	50
166	Reggie Leach	4	5	6	10	12	20		
167	Jerry Butler	4	5	6	10	12	20		
168	Inge Hammarstrom	4	5	6	10	12	20		
169	Chris Oddleifson	4	5	6	10	12	20		
170	Greg Joly	4	5	6	10	12	20		
171	Checklist 111-220	6	8	10	12	25	80		
172	Pat Quinn	4	5	6	10	12	20		
173	Dave Forbes	4	5	6	10	12	20	25	40
174	Len Frig	4	5	6	10	12	20		
175	Richard Martin	4	5	6	10	12	20		
176	Keith Magnuson	4	5	6	10	12	20	25	40
177	Dan Maloney	4	5	6	10	12	20		
178	Craig Patrick	4	5	6	10	12	20		
179	Tom Williams	4	5	6	10	12	20		
180	Bill Goldsworthy	4	5	6	10	12	20		
181	Steve Shutt	4	5	6	10	12	20	30	60
182	Ralph Stewart	4	5	6	10	12	20	25	40
183	John Davidson	4	5	6	10	12	20		
184	Bob Kelly	4	5	6	10	12	20		
185	Ed Johnston	4	5	6	10	12	20		
186	Dave Burrows	4	5	6	10	12	20		
187	Dave Dunn	4	5	6	10	12	20		
188	Dennis Kearns	4	5	6	10	12	20		
189	Bill Clement	4	5	6	10	12	20		
190	Gilles Meloche	4	5	6	10	12	20	25	40
191	Bob Leiter	4	5	6	10	12	20	25	40
192	Jerry Korab	4	5	6	10	12	20		
193	Joey Johnston	4	5	6	10	12	20		
194	Walt McKechnie	4	5	6	10	12	20		
195	Wilf Paiement	4	5	6	10	12	20		
196	Bob Berry	4	5	6	10	12	20	25	40
197	Dean Talafous RC	4	5	6	10	12	20		
198	Guy Lapointe	4	5	6	10	12	20		
199	Clark Gillies RC	5	6	12	40	60	150	200	300
200A	Phil Esposito NoTR	5	6	8	12	15			

#	Name	VG 3	VgEx 4	EX 5	ExMt 6	NM 7	NmMt 8	NmMt+ 8.5	TMT 9
200B	Phil Esposito TR	4	5	6	10	12	30		
201	Greg Polis	4	5	6	10	12	20		
202	Jimmy Watson	4	5	6	10	12	20		
203	Gord McRae RC	4	5	6	10	12	20	25	40
204	Lowell MacDonald	4	5	6	10	12	20		
205	Barclay Plager	4	5	6	10	12	20		
206	Don Lever	4	5	6	10	12	20		
207	Bill Mikkelson	4	5	6	10	12	20		
208	Espo/Lafleur/Martin LL	4	5	6	10	12	20		
209	Clarke/Orr/P.Mahv LL	5	6	8	12	60	150	250	500
210	Orr/Espo/Dionne LL	5	8	12	30	50	350		
211	Schltz/Dupnt/Rssll LL	4	5	6	10	12	25		
212	Espo/Martin/Grant LL	4	5	6	10	12	20		
213	Parnt/Vach/Drydn LL	5	6	8	12	15	30		
214	Barry Gibbs	4	5	6	10	12	20		
215	Ken Hodge	4	5	6	10	12	20		
216	Jocelyn Guevremont	4	5	6	10	12	20		
217	Warren Williams RC	4	5	6	10	12	20		
218	Dick Redmond	4	5	6	10	12	20		
219	Jim Rutherford	4	5	6	10	12	20		
220	Simon Nolet	4	5	6	10	12	20		
221	Butch Goring	4	5	6	10	12	20		
222	Glen Sather	4	5	6	10	12	20		
223	Mario Tremblay UER RC	4	5	6	10	20	60		
224	Jude Drouin	4	5	6	10	12	20		
225	Rod Gilbert	4	5	6	10	12	20		
226	Bill Barber	4	5	6	10	12	20		
227	Gary Inness RC	4	5	6	10	12	20	25	40
228	Wayne Merrick	4	5	6	10	12	20		
229	Rod Seiling	4	5	6	10	12	20		
230	Tom Lysiak	4	5	6	10	12	20		
231	Bob Dailey	4	5	6	10	12	20		
232	Michel Belhumeur	4	5	6	10	12	20		
233	Bill Hajt RC	4	5	6	10	12	20		
234	Jim Pappin	4	5	6	10	12	20		
235	Gregg Sheppard	4	5	6	10	12	20		
236A	Gary Bergman NoTR	4	5	6	10	12			
236B	Gary Bergman TR	4	5	6	10	12			
237	Randy Rota	4	5	6	10	12	20	25	40
238	Neil Komadoski	4	5	6	10	12			
239	Craig Cameron	4	5	6	10	12	20		
240	Tony Esposito	5	6	8	12	15	25	30	60
241	Larry Robinson	5	6	8	12	20	40	50	80
242	Billy Harris	4	5	6	10	12	20		
243A	Jean Ratelle NoTR	4	5	6	10	12			
243B	Jean Ratelle TR	4	5	6	10	12	20		
244	Ted Irvine UER	4	5	6	10	12	20	25	40
245	Bob Neely	4	5	6	10	12	20		
246	Bobby Lalonde	4	5	6	10	12	20	25	40
247	Ron Jones RC	4	5	6	10	12	20		
248	Rey Comeau	4	5	6	10	12	20		
249	Michel Plasse	4	5	6	10	12	20		
250	Bobby Clarke	5	6	8	12	20	40		
251	Bobby Schmautz	4	5	6	10	12	20		
252	Peter McNab RC	4	5	6	10	12	20	25	50
253	Al MacAdam	4	5	6	10	12	20		
254	Dennis Hull	4	5	6	10	12	20		
255	Terry Harper	4	5	6	10	12	20		
256	Peter McDuffe	4	5	6	10	12	20	25	40
257	Jean Hamel	4	5	6	10	12	20		
258	Jacques Lemaire	4	5	6	10	12	20		
259	Bob Nystrom	4	5	6	10	12	20		
260A	Brad Park NoTR	4	5	6	10	12	20		
260B	Brad Park TR	4	5	6	10	12	20		
261	Cesare Maniago	4	5	6	10	12	20	25	40
262	Don Saleski	4	5	6	10	12	20	25	40
263	J. Bob Kelly	4	5	6	10	12	20		
264	Bob Hess RC	4	5	6	10	12	20		
265	Blaine Stoughton	4	5	6	10	12	20	25	40
266	John Gould	4	5	6	10	12	20		
267A	Checklist 221-330	6	8	10	15	30	80		
267B	Checklist 331-396	6	8	10	15	30	80		
268	Dan Bouchard	4	5	6	10	12	20		
269	Don Marcotte	4	5	6	10	12	20		
270	Jim Neilson	4	5	6	10	12	20		
271	Craig Ramsay	4	5	6	10	12	20		
272	Grant Mulvey RC	4	5	6	10	12	30		
273	Larry Giroux RC	4	5	6	10	12	20		
274	Real Lemieux	4	5	6	10	12	20		
275	Denis Potvin	5	6	8	12	20	30	35	50
276	Don Kozak	4	5	6	10	12	20		
277	Tom Reid	4	5	6	10	12	20		
278	Bob Gainey	5	6	8	12	15	25		
279	Nick Beverley	4	5	6	10	12	20		
280	Jean Pronovost	4	5	6	10	12	20		
281	Joe Watson	4	5	6	10	12	20		
282	Chuck Lefley	4	5	6	10	12			
283	Borje Salming	5	6	8	12	15	30	35	60
284	Garnet Bailey	4	5	6	10	12	20	25	40
285	Gregg Boddy	4	5	6	10	12	20		
286	Bobby Clarke AS1	4	5	6	10	12	25		
287	Denis Potvin AS1	4	5	6	10	12	20		
288	Bobby Orr AS1	10	12	15	25	40	80	100	200
289	Richard Martin AS1	4	5	6	10	12	20	30	50
290	Guy Lafleur AS1	5	6	8	12	15	30		
291	Bernie Parent AS1	4	5	6	10	12	20		
292	Phil Esposito AS2	4	5	6	10	12	20		
293	Guy Lapointe AS2	4	5	6	10	12	20		
294	Borje Salming AS2	4	5	6	10	12	20		
295	Steve Vickers AS2	4	5	6	10	12	20		
296	Rene Robert AS2	4	5	6	10	12	20		
297	Rogatien Vachon AS2	4	5	6	10	12	25		
298	Buster Harvey RC	4	5	6	10	12	20		
299	Gary Sabourin	4	5	6	10	12	20		
300	Bernie Parent	4	5	6	10	12	20		
301	Terry O'Reilly	4	5	6	10	12	20		
302	Ed Westfall	4	5	6	10	12	20		
303	Pete Stemkowski	4	5	6	10	12	20		
304	Pierre Bouchard	4	5	6	10	12	20		
305	Pierre Larouche RC	5	6	8	12	15	30		
306	Lee Fogolin RC	4	5	6	10	12	20	25	40
307	Gerry O'Flaherty	4	5	6	10	12	20		
308	Phil Myre	4	5	6	10	12	20		
309	Pierre Plante	4	5	6	10	12	20		
310	Dennis Hextall	4	5	6	10	12	20		
311	Jim McKenny	4	5	6	10	12	20		
312	Vic Venasky	4	5	6	10	12	20		
313	Vail/Lysiak TL	4	5	6	10	12	20		
314	P.Espo/Orr/Bucyk TL	10	12	15	20	30	60	80	135
315	R.Martin/R.Robert TL	4	5	6	10	12	20		
316	Hrchsy/Ptey/Weir TL	4	5	6	10	12	20		
317	S.Mikita/J.Pappin TL	4	5	6	10	12	20		
318	D.Grant/M.Dionne TL	4	5	6	10	12	20		
319	Nolet/Prmnt/Charn TL	4	5	6	10	12			
320	Nevin/Wdng/Brry TL	4	5	6	10	12	20	25	40
321	Gldswrthy/Hextall TL	4	5	6	10	12	20		
322	Lafleur/P.Mahov TL	4	5	6	10	12	20		
323	Nystrom/Potvin/Gill TL	4	5	6	10	12	20		
324	Vick/Gilbert/Ratelle TL	4	5	6	10	12	20		
325	R.Leach/B.Clarke TL	4	5	6	10	12	30		50
326	Pronovost/Schock TL	4	5	6	10	12	20		
327	G.Unger/L.Sacharuk TL	4	5	6	10	12	20		
328	Darryl Sittler TL	4	5	6	10	12	25	30	50
329	Lever/Boudrias TL	4	5	6	10	12	20		
330	Williams/Bailey TL	4	5	6	10	12	20		
331	Noel Price	4	5	6	10	12	20		
332	Fred Stanfield	4	5	6	10	12	20		
333	Doug Jarrett	4	5	6	10	12	20	25	40
334	Gary Coalter	4	5	6	10	12	20		
335	Murray Oliver	4	5	6	10	12	20		
336	Dave Fortier	4	5	6	10	12	20		
337	Terry Crisp UER	4	5	6	10	12	20		
338	Bert Wilson	4	5	6	10	12	20	25	40
339	John Grisdale RC	4	5	6	10	12	20	25	40
340	Ken Broderick	4	5	6	10	12	20		
341	Frank Spring RC	4	5	6	10	12	20		
342	Mike Korney RC	4	5	6	10	12	20		
343	Gene Carr	4	5	6	10	12	20		
344	Don Awrey	4	5	6	10	12	20		
345	Pat Hickey	4	5	6	10	12	20		
346	Colin Campbell RC	4	5	6	10	12	20		
347	Wayne Thomas	4	5	6	10	12	20		
348	Bob Gryp RC	4	5	6	10	12	20		
349	Bill Flett	4	5	6	10	12	20		
350	Roger Crozier	4	5	6	10	12	20	25	40
351	Dale Tallon	4	5	6	10	12	20		
352	Larry Johnston	4	5	6	10	12	20		
353	John Flesch RC	4	5	6	10	12	20		
354	Lorne Henning	4	5	6	10	12	20		
355	Wayne Stephenson	4	5	6	10	12	20	25	40
356	Rick Wilson	4	5	6	10	12	20		
357	Garry Monahan	4	5	6	10	12	20		
358	Gary Doak	4	5	6	10	12	20	25	40
359A	Pierre Jarry NoTR	4	5	6	10	12			
359B	Pierre Jarry TR	4	5	6	10	12	20		
360	George Pesut RC	4	5	6	10	12	20		
361	Mike Corrigan	4	5	6	10	12	20		
362	Michel Larocque	4	5	6	10	12	20		
363	Wayne Dillon	4	5	6	10	12	20		
364	Pete Laframboise	4	5	6	10	12	20	25	40
365	Brian Glennie	4	5	6	10	12	20		
366	Mike Christie	4	5	6	10	12	20		
367	Jean Lemieux RC	4	5	6	10	12	20		
368	Gary Bromley	4	5	6	10	12	20	25	50
369	J.P. Bordeleau	4	5	6	10	12	20		
370	Ed Gilbert RC	4	5	6	10	12	20		
371	Chris Ahrens	4	5	6	10	12	20		
372	Billy Smith	5	6	8	12	15	25		
373	Larry Goodenough RC	4	5	6	10	12	20		
374	Leon Rochefort	4	5	6	10	12	20		

		VG 3	VgEx 4	EX 5	ExMt 6	NM 7	NmMt 8	NmMt+ 8.5	TMT 9
375	Doug Gibson RC	4	5	6	10	12	20		
376	Mike Bloom	4	5	6	10	12	20		
377	Larry Brown	4	5	6	10	12	20		
378	Jim Roberts	4	5	6	10	12	20		
379	Gilles Villemure	4	5	6	10	12	20	25	40
380	Dennis Owchar RC	4	5	6	10	12	20		
381	Doug Favell	4	5	6	10	12	20		
382	Stan Gilbertson UER	4	5	6	10	12	20		
383	Ed Kea RC	4	5	6	10	12	20		
384	Brian Spencer	4	5	6	10	12	20		
385	Mike Veisor RC	4	5	6	10	12	20		
386	Bob Murray	4	5	6	10	12	20		
387	Andre St.Laurent RC	4	5	6	10	12	20	25	40
388	Rick Chartraw RC	4	5	6	10	12	20		
389	Orest Kindrachuk RC	4	5	6	10	12	20	25	40
390	Dave Hutchinson RC	4	5	6	10	12	20		
391	Glenn Goldup	4	5	6	10	12	20		
392	Jerry Holland RC	4	5	6	10	12	20		
393	Peter Sturgeon RC	4	5	6	10	12	20		
394	Alain Daigle RC	4	5	6	10	12	20		
396	Harold Snepsts RC	10	12	15	25	40	80		

— Espo/Orr/Bucyk TL #314 PSA 10 (Gem) sold for $1,531 (eBay; 3/07)
— Espo/Orr/Bucyk TL #314 PSA 10 (Gem) sold for $510 (eBay; 12/06)
— Orr/Espo/Dionne LL #210 PSA 10 (Gem) sold for $618.80 (Mile High; 12/13)

1975-76 O-Pee-Chee WHA

		VG 3	VgEx 4	EX 5	ExMt 6	NM 7	NmMt 8	NmMt+ 8.5	MT 9
	COMMON CARD (1-132)	5	5	6	8	10	15		
1	Bobby Hull	8	12	20	30	40	60		
2	Dale Hoganson	5	5	6	8	10	20		
4	Ron Chipperfield	5	5	6	8	10	20		
5	Paul Shmyr	5	5	6	8	10	15	20	30
7	Mark Howe RC	20	25	30	40	50	150		
9	Bryon Baltimore	5	5	6	8	10	15	20	30
11	Nick Harbaruk	5	5	6	8	10	20		
12	John Garrett RC	6	8	10	12	15	25	30	60
13	Lou Nistico	5	5	6	8	10	15	20	30
15	Veli-Pekka Ketola RC	5	6	8	10	12	20	25	40
16	Real Cloutier	5	5	6	8	10	15	20	30
18	Duane Rupp	5	5	6	8	10	15	20	30
19	Robbie Ftorek RC	6	8	12	15	20	30	35	60
20	Gerry Cheevers	6	8	12	15	20	30	35	80
22	Bruce MacGregor	5	5	6	8	10	15	20	30
24	Gene Peacosh	5	5	6	8	10	15	20	30
28	C.Abrahamsson RC	5	6	8	10	12	20	25	40
31	Bryan Campbell	5	5	6	8	10	15	20	30
33	Al McDonough	5	5	6	8	10	15	20	30
34	Jacques Plante	6	10	15	25	40	60		
37	Ken Baird	5	5	6	8	10	15	20	30
40	Anders Hedberg	5	5	6	8	10	15	20	40
41	Rick Smith	5	5	6	8	10	15	20	30
44	Richard Brodeur RC	6	8	10	12	15	25	30	60
47	Jim Harrison	5	5	6	8	10	20	25	40
53	Murray Heatley	5	5	6	8	10	15	20	30
55	Jim Shaw	5	5	6	8	10	15	20	30
56	Larry Pleau RC	5	5	6	8	10	15	20	40
59	Butch Deadmarsh	5	5	6	8	10	15	20	30
62	J.C. Tremblay AS	5	5	6	8	10	15	20	30
63	Kevin Morrison AS	5	5	6	8	10	15	20	30
64	Andre Lacroix AS	5	5	6	8	10	15	20	30
65	Bobby Hull AS	6	10	15	20	25	40	50	80
66	Gordie Howe AS	6	10	15	20	25	60		
67	Gerry Cheevers AS	5	6	8	10	12	20		
69	Barry Long AS	5	5	6	8	10	15	20	30
70	Serge Bernier AS	5	5	6	8	10	15	20	30
80	Kevin Morrison	5	5	6	8	10	15	20	30
83	Ulf Nilsson	5	5	6	8	10	15	20	40
85	N.Lapointe RC UER	5	5	6	8	10			
88	Al McLeod	5	5	6	8	10	15	20	30
90	Barry Long	5	5	6	8	10	15	20	40
97	Dave Keon	5	5	6	8	10	15	20	40
99	Rick Jodzio	5	5	6	8	10	15	20	30
100	Gordie Howe	12	15	20	30	50	80	100	150
101	Joe Daley	5	5	6	8	10	15	20	40
102	Wayne Muloin	5	5	6	8	10	15	20	30
106	Rosaire Paiement	5	5	6	8	10	15	20	30
107	John Sheridan RC	5	6	8	10	12	20		
108	Nick Fotiu RC	6	8	10	12	15	25		
110	Frank Mahovlich	5	5	6	8	12	25	30	60
114	Jack Norris	5	5	6	8	10	15	20	40
119	Cam Newton	5	5	6	8	10	15	20	30
121	Fran Huck	5	5	6	8	10	15	20	30
122	Tony Featherstone	5	5	6	8	10	15	20	30
125	Heikki Riihiranta	5	5	6	8	10	15	25	50
129	Jacques Locas	5	5	6	8	10	15		
131	Checklist Card	10	12	20	30	50	80	100	150
132	Ernie Wakely	6	8	10	12	20			

— Gordie Howe AS #66 PSA 10 (Gem) sold for $668 (eBay; 8/12)
— Dave Keon #97 PSA 10 (Gem) sold for $99 (Sirius Sports; 6/12)
— Jacques Plante #34 PSA 9 (MT) sold for $110 (Sirius Sports; 6/12)

1975-76 Topps

		VG 3	VgEx 4	EX 5	ExMt 6	NM 7	NmMt 8	NmMt+ 8.5	MT 9
1	Stanley Cup Finals	4	5	6	8	15	25		
2	Semi-Finals	4	5	6	8	12	18		
3	Semi-Finals	4	5	6	8	12	18		
4	Quarter Finals	4	5	6	8	12	15	20	30
5	Quarter Finals	4	5	6	10	15			
6	Quarter Finals	4	5	6	8	12	15	20	30
7	Quarter Finals	4	5	6	8	12	15	20	30
8	Curt Bennett	4	5	6	8	10	12	15	25
9	Johnny Bucyk	4	5	6	8	10	12	15	25
10	Gilbert Perreault	4	5	6	8	12	18		
11	Darryl Edestrand	4	5	6	8	10	12	15	25
12	Ivan Boldirev	4	5	6	8	10	12	15	25
13	Nick Libett	4	5	6	8	10	12	15	25
14	Jim McElmury RC	4	5	6	8	10	12	15	25
15	Frank St.Marseille	4	5	6	8	10	12	15	25
16	Blake Dunlop	4	5	6	10	15			
17	Yvon Lambert	4	5	6	8	10	12	15	25
18	Gerry Hart	4	5	6	8	10	12	15	25
19	Steve Vickers	4	5	6	8	12	18		
20	Rick MacLeish	4	5	6	10	15			
21	Bob Paradise	4	5	6	8	10	12	15	25
22	Red Berenson	4	5	6	8	10	12	15	25
23	Lanny McDonald	4	5	6	8	10	20	30	50
24	Mike Robitaille	4	5	6	8	10	12	15	25
25	Ron Low	4	5	6	8	12	18		
26	Bryan Hextall	4	5	6	8	10	12	15	25
27	Carol Vadnais	4	5	6	8	10	12	15	25
28	Jim Lorentz	4	5	6	8	10	12	15	25
29	Gary Simmons	4	5	6	10	15			
30	Stan Mikita	4	5	6	8	12	20	25	40
31	Bryan Watson	4	5	6	8	10	12	15	25
32	Guy Charron	4	5	6	8	10	12	15	25
33	Bob Murdoch	4	5	6	8	10	12	15	25
34	Norm Gratton	4	5	6	8	10	12	15	25
35	Ken Dryden	6	8	10	12	20	30	40	60
36	Jean Potvin	4	5	6	8	12	18		
37	Rick Middleton	4	5	6	10	15			
38	Ed Van Impe	4	5	6	8	10	12	15	25
39	Rick Kehoe	4	5	6	8	10	12	15	25
40	Garry Unger	4	5	6	8	10	12	15	25
41	Ian Turnbull	4	5	6	8	10	12	15	25
42	Dennis Ververgaert	4	5	6	8	12	18		
43	Mike Marson	4	5	6	8	10	12	15	25
44	Randy Manery	4	5	6	10	15			
45	Gilles Gilbert	4	5	6	8	10	12	15	25
46	Rene Robert	4	5	6	8	10	12	15	25
47	Bob Stewart	4	5	6	8	10	12	15	25
48	Pit Martin	4	5	6	8	12	18		
49	Danny Grant	4	5	6	8	10	12	15	25
50	Peter Mahovlich	4	5	6	10	15			
51	Dennis Patterson RC	4	5	6	8	10	12	15	25
52	Mike Murphy	4	5	6	8	10	12	15	25
53	Dennis O'Brien	4	5	6	8	10	12	15	25
54	Garry Howatt	4	5	6	8	10	12	15	25
55	Ed Giacomin	4	5	6	8	12	20	25	35
56	Andre Dupont	4	5	6	10	15			
57	Chuck Arnason	4	5	6	8	10	12		25
58	Bob Gassoff RC	4	5	6	10	15			
59	Ron Ellis	4	5	6	8	10	12	15	25
60	Andre Boudrias	4	5	6	8	10	12	15	25
61	Yvon Labre	4	5	6	8	10	12	15	25
62	Hilliard Graves	4	5	6	8	10	12	15	25
63	Wayne Cashman	4	5	6	8	12	18		
64	Danny Gare RC	4	5	6	8	12	20	25	35
65	Rick Hampton	4	5	6	8	10	12		25
66	Darcy Rota	4	5	6	8	10	12	15	25
67	Bill Hogaboam	4	5	6	8	10	12	15	25
68	Denis Herron	4	5	6	8	10	12	15	25
69	Sheldon Kannegiesser	4	5	6	8	10	12	15	25
70	Yvan Cournoyer UER	4	5	6	8	10	12	15	25
71	Ernie Hicke	4	5	6	8	12	18		
72	Bert Marshall	4	5	6	8	10	12	15	25
73	Derek Sanderson	4	5	6	8	12	20	25	35
74	Tom Bladon	4	5	6	8	10	12	15	25
75	Ron Schock	4	5	6	8	10	12	15	25
76	Larry Sacharuk RC	4	5	6	8	10	12	15	25
77	George Ferguson	4	5	6	8	10	12	15	25
78	Ab DeMarco	4	5	6	8	10	12	15	25
79	Tom Williams	4	5	6	8	12	18		
80	Phil Roberto	4	5	6	8	10	12	15	25
81	Bruins Team CL	4	5	6	8	12	20	25	35
82	Seals Team CL	4	5	6	8	12	20	25	35
83	Sabres Team CL UER	4	5	6	8	12	20	25	35
84	Blackhawks CL UER	4	5	6	8	12	20	25	35
85	Flames Team CL	4	5	6	8	12	20	25	35
86	Kings Team CL	4	5	6	8	12	20	25	35

HOCKEY

#	Name	VG 3	VgEx 4	EX 5	ExMt 6	NM 7	NmMt 8	NmMt+ 8.5	MT 9
87	Red Wings Team CL	4	5	6	8	12	20	25	35
88	Scouts Team CL UER	4	5	6	8	12	20	25	35
89	North Stars Team CL	4	5	6	8	12	20	25	35
90	Canadiens Team CL	4	5	6	8	12	20	25	35
91	Maple Leafs Team CL	4	5	6	8	12	20	25	35
92	Islanders Team CL	4	5	6	8	12	20	25	35
93	Penguins Team CL	4	5	6	8	12	20	25	35
94	Rangers Team CL	4	5	6	8	12	20	25	35
95	Flyers Team CL UER	4	5	6	8	12	20	25	35
96	Blues Team CL	4	5	6	8	12	20	25	35
97	Canucks Team CL	4	5	6	8	12	20	25	35
98	Capitals Team CL	4	5	6	8	12	20	25	35
99	Checklist 1-110	5	6	8	10	15	25		
100	Bobby Orr	8	10	12	15	25	40	60	100
101	Germaine Gagnon UER	4	5	6	8	10	12	15	25
102	Phil Russell	4	5	6	8	10	12	15	25
103	Billy Lochead	4	5	6	8	10	12	15	25
104	Robin Burns	4	5	6		10	15		
105	Gary Edwards	4	5	6	8	10	12	15	25
106	Dwight Bialowas	4	5	6	8	10	12	15	25
107	D.Risebrough UER RC	4	5	6	8	12	20	25	35
108	Dave Lewis	4	5	6		10	15		
109	Bill Fairbairn	4	5	6		10	15		
110	Ross Lonsberry	4	5	6	8	10	12	15	25
111	Ron Stackhouse	4	5	6	8	12	18		
112	Claude Larose	4	5	6	8	10	12	15	25
113	Don Luce	4	5	6	8	10	12	15	25
114	Errol Thompson RC	4	5	6	8	10	12	15	25
115	Gary Smith	4	5	6	8	10	12	15	25
116	Jack Lynch	4	5	6	8	10	12	15	25
117	Jacques Richard	4	5	6		10	15		
118	Dallas Smith	4	5	6		10	15		
119	Dave Gardner	4	5	6	8	10	12	15	25
120	Mickey Redmond	4	5	6	8	10	12	15	25
121	John Marks	4	5	6	8	10	12	15	25
122	Dave Hudson	4	5	6	8	10	12	15	25
123	Bob Nevin	4	5	6	8	12	18		
124	Fred Barrett	4	5	6	8	10	12	15	25
125	Gerry Desjardins	4	5	6		10	15		
126	Guy Lafleur UER	5	6	8	10	15	25	30	40
127	Jean-Paul Parise	4	5	6	8	10	12	15	25
128	Walt Tkaczuk	4	5	6	8	10	12	15	25
129	Gary Dornhoefer	4	5	6	8	10	12	15	25
130	Syl Apps	4	5	6	8	10	12	15	25
131	Bob Plager	4	5	6	8	10	12	15	25
132	Stan Weir	4	5	6	8	10	12	15	25
133	Tracy Pratt	4	5	6	8	10	12	15	25
134	Jack Egers	4	5	6	8	10	12	15	25
135	Eric Vail	4	5	6	8	10	12	15	25
136	Al Sims	4	5	6	8	10	12	15	25
137	Larry Patey	4	5	6	8	10	12	15	25
138	Jim Schoenfeld	4	5	6	8	10	12	15	25
139	Cliff Koroll	4	5	6	8	10	12	15	25
140	Marcel Dionne	4	5	6	8	12	20	30	50
141	Jean-Guy Lagace	4	5	6	8	10	12	15	25
142	Juha Widing	4	5	6	8	10	12	15	25
143	Lou Nanne	4	5	6	8	10	12	15	25
144	Serge Savard	4	5	6	8	10	12	15	25
145	Glenn Resch	4	5	6	8	12	20	25	40
146	Ron Greschner RC	4	5	6	8	12	20	25	35
147	Dave Schultz	4	5	6	8	10	12	15	25
148	Barry Wilkins	4	5	6	8	10	12	15	25
149	Floyd Thomson	4	5	6	8	10	12	15	25
150	Darryl Sittler	4	5	6	8	10	12	15	25
151	Paulin Bordeleau	4	5	6	8	10	12	15	25
152	Ron Lalonde RC	4	5	6	8	10	12	15	25
153	Larry Romanchych	4	5	6	8	10	12	15	25
154	Larry Carriere	4	5	6	8	12	18		
155	Andre Savard	4	5	6	8	10	12	15	25
156	Dave Hrechkosy RC	4	5	6	8	10	12	15	25
157	Bill White	4	5	6	8	10	12	15	25
158	Dave Kryskow	4	5	6	8	10	12	15	25
159	Denis Dupere	4	5	6	8	12	18		
160	Rogatien Vachon	4	5	6	8	12	20	25	35
161	Doug Rombough	4	5	6	8	10	12	15	25
162	Murray Wilson	4	5	6	8	10	12	15	25
163	Bob Bourne RC	4	5	6	8	12	20	25	35
164	Gilles Marotte	4	5	6		10	15		
165	Vic Hadfield	4	5	6		10	15		
166	Reggie Leach	4	5	6	8	10	12	15	25
167	Jerry Butler	4	5	6		10	15		
168	Inge Hammarstrom	4	5	6	8	12	18		
169	Chris Oddleifson	4	5	6	8	12	18		
170	Greg Joly	4	5	6	8	10	12	15	25
171	Checklist 111-220	5	6	10	12	20			
172	Pat Quinn	4	5	6		10	15		
173	Dave Forbes	4	5	6	8	10	12	15	25
174	Len Frig	4	5	6	8	10	12	15	25
175	Richard Martin	4	5	6	8	10	12	15	25
176	Keith Magnuson	4	5	6	8	10	12	15	25
177	Dan Maloney	4	5	6	8	10	12	15	25
178	Craig Patrick	4	5	6	8	10	12	15	25
179	Tom Williams	4	5	6	10	15			
180	Bill Goldsworthy	4	5	6	8	10	12	15	25
181	Steve Shutt	4	5	6	8	10	12	15	25
182	Ralph Stewart	4	5	6	8	12	18		
183	John Davidson	4	5	6	8	12	20	25	40
184	Bob Kelly	4	5	6	8	10	12	15	25
185	Ed Johnston	4	5	6	8	10	12	15	25
186	Dave Burrows	4	5	6	8	10	12	15	25
187	Dave Dunn	4	5	6	8	10	12	15	25
188	Dennis Kearns	4	5	6	8	10	12	15	25
189	Bill Clement	4	5	6	8	12	20	25	40
190	Gilles Meloche	4	5	6	8	10	12	15	25
191	Bob Leiter	4	5	6	8	10	12	15	25
192	Jerry Korab	4	5	6	8	10	12	15	25
193	Joey Johnston	4	5	6	8	10	12	15	25
194	Walt McKechnie	4	5	6	8	10	12	15	25
195	Wilf Paiement	4	5	6	8	10	12	15	25
196	Bob Berry	4	5	6	8	10	12	15	25
197	Dean Talafous RC	4	5	6	8	10	12	15	25
198	Guy Lapointe	4	5	6	8	10	12	15	25
199	Clark Gillies RC	4	5	6	8	12	20	30	50
200	Phil Esposito	4	5	6	8	12	20	25	40
201	Greg Polis	4	5	6	8	10	12	15	25
202	Jimmy Watson	4	5	6	10	15			
203	Gord McRae RC	4	5	6	8	12	18		
204	Lowell MacDonald	4	5	6	8	10	12	15	25
205	Barclay Plager	4	5	6	8	10	12	15	25
206	Don Lever	4	5	6	8	12	18		
207	Bill Mikkelson	4	5	6	8	10	12	15	25
208	Espo/Lafleur/Martin LL	4	5	6	8	12	20	25	40
209	Clarke/Orr/P.Mahov LL	4	5	6	8	12	25	30	125
210	Orr/Espo/Dionne LL	4	5	6	8	12	30		
211	Schultz/Dupont/Rusl LL	4	5	6	8	10	12	15	25
212	Espo/Martin/Grant LL	4	5	6	10	15			
213	Parent/Vach/Dryden LL	4	5	6	8	12	25	30	50
214	Barry Gibbs	4	5	6	10	15			
215	Ken Hodge	4	5	6	8	10	12	15	25
216	Jocelyn Guevremont	4	5	6	8	10	12	15	25
217	Warren Williams RC	4	5	6	8	10	12	15	25
218	Dick Redmond	4	5	6	8	10	12	15	25
219	Jim Rutherford	4	5	6	8	10	12	15	25
220	Simon Nolet	4	5	6	8	10	12	15	25
221	Butch Goring	4	5	6	8	10	12	15	25
222	Glen Sather	4	5	6	8	10	12	15	25
223	Mario Tremblay RC	4	5	6	8	12	20		
224	Jude Drouin	4	5	6	10	15			
225	Rod Gilbert	4	5	6	8	10	12	15	25
226	Bill Barber	4	5	6	8	10	12	15	25
227	Gary Inness RC	4	5	6	8	10	12	15	25
228	Wayne Merrick	4	5	6	8	10	12	15	25
229	Rod Seiling	4	5	6	8	10	12	15	25
230	Tom Lysiak	4	5	6	8	10	12	15	25
231	Bob Dailey	4	5	6	8	10	12	15	25
232	Michel Belhumeur	4	5	6	10	15			
233	Bill Hajt RC	4	5	6	8	10	12	15	25
234	Jim Pappin	4	5	6	8	10	12	15	25
235	Gregg Sheppard	4	5	6	8	10	12	15	25
236	Gary Bergman	4	5	6	8	10	12	15	25
237	Randy Rota	4	5	6	8	10	12	15	25
238	Neil Komadoski	4	5	6	10	15			
239	Craig Cameron	4	5	6	8	10	12	15	25
240	Tony Esposito	4	5	6	8	12	20		
241	Larry Robinson	4	5	6	10	15			
242	Billy Harris	4	5	6	8	10	12	15	25
243	Jean Ratelle	4	5	6	8	10	12	15	25
244	Ted Irvine UER	4	5	6	8	10	12	15	25
245	Bob Neely	4	5	6	8	10	12	15	25
246	Bobby Lalonde	4	5	6	8	10	12	15	25
247	Ron Jones RC	4	5	6	8	10	12	15	25
248	Rey Comeau	4	5	6	8	10	12	15	25
249	Michel Plasse	4	5	6	8	10	12	15	25
250	Bobby Clarke	4	5	6	8	12	25	30	50
251	Bobby Schmautz	4	5	6	8	10	12	15	25
252	Peter McNab RC	4	5	6	8	12	20	25	35
253	Al MacAdam	4	5	6	8	10	12	15	25
254	Dennis Hull	4	5	6	8	10	12	15	25
255	Terry Harper	4	5	6	8	10	12	15	25
256	Peter McDuffe	4	5	6	8	10	12	15	25
257	Jean Hamel	4	5	6	10	15			
258	Jacques Lemaire	4	5	6	10	15			
259	Bob Nystrom	4	5	6	8	10	12	15	25
260	Brad Park	4	5	6	8	12	20		
261	Cesare Maniago	4	5	6	8	10	12	15	25
262	Don Saleski	4	5	6	8	10	12	15	25
263	J. Bob Kelly	4	5	6	8	12	18		
264	Bob Hess RC	4	5	6	8	10	12	15	25
265	Blaine Stoughton	4	5	6	8	12	18		
266	John Gould	4	5	6	8	10	12	15	25

		VG 3	VgEx 4	EX 5	ExMt 6	NM 7	NmMt 8	NmMt+ 8.5	MT 9
267	Checklist 221-330	5	6	8	10	15	25	40	60
268	Dan Bouchard	4	5	6	8	10	12	15	25
269	Don Marcotte	4	5	6	8	12	18		
270	Jim Neilson	4	5	6	8	10	12	15	25
271	Craig Ramsay	4	5	6	8	10	12	15	25
272	Grant Mulvey RC	4	5	6	8	10	12	15	25
273	Larry Giroux RC	4	5	6	8	10	12	15	25
274	Real Lemieux	4	5	6	10	15			
275	Denis Potvin	4	5	6	8	12	25	30	50
276	Don Kozak	4	5	6	10	15			
277	Tom Reid	4	5	6	8	12	18		
278	Bob Gainey	4	5	6	8	12	20	30	50
279	Nick Beverley	4	5	6	10	15			
280	Jean Pronovost	4	5	6	8	10	12	15	25
281	Joe Watson	4	5	6	10	15			
282	Chuck Lefley	4	5	6	8	10	12	15	25
283	Borje Salming	4	5	6	8	12	25	30	50
284	Garnet Bailey	4	5	6	8	10	12	15	25
285	Gregg Boddy	4	5	6	8	10	12	15	25
286	Bobby Clarke AS1	4	5	6	8	12	20		
287	Denis Potvin AS1	4	5	6	8	12	20	25	40
288	Bobby Orr AS1	5	6	8	12	20	40	80	300
289	Richard Martin AS1	4	5	6	8	10	12	15	25
290	Guy Lafleur AS1	4	5	6	8	12	20	30	50
291	Bernie Parent AS1	4	5	6	8	10	12	15	25
292	Phil Esposito AS2	4	5	6	8	12	20	25	35
293	Guy Lapointe AS2	4	5	6	8	10	12	15	25
294	Borje Salming AS2	4	5	6	8	12	20	25	35
295	Steve Vickers AS2	4	5	6	8	10	12	15	25
296	Rene Robert AS2	4	5	6	8	10	12	15	25
297	Rogatien Vachon AS2	4	5	6	8	12	20	25	35
298	Buster Harvey RC	4	5	6	8	10	12	15	25
299	Gary Sabourin	4	5	6	8	10	12	15	25
300	Bernie Parent	4	5	6	8	10	12	15	25
301	Terry O'Reilly	4	5	6	8	10	12	15	25
302	Ed Westfall	4	5	6	8	10	12	15	25
303	Pete Stemkowski	4	5	6	10	15			
304	Pierre Bouchard	4	5	6	8	12	18		
305	Pierre Larouche RC	4	5	6	8	12	20	30	50
306	Lee Fogolin RC	4	5	6	8	10	12	15	25
307	Gerry O'Flaherty	4	5	6	8	10	12	15	25
308	Phil Myre	4	5	6	8	10	12	15	25
309	Pierre Plante	4	5	6	8	10	12	15	25
310	Dennis Hextall	4	5	6	10	15			
311	Jim McKenny	4	5	6	8	10	12	15	25
312	Vic Venasky	4	5	6	8	10	12	15	25
313	Flames Leaders	4	5	6	8	12	15	20	30
314	Espo/Orr/Bucyk TL	4	5	6	8	12	25	30	50
315	Sabres Leaders	4	5	6	8	12	15	20	30
316	Seals Leaders	4	5	6	8	12	15	20	30
317	S.Mikita/J.Pappin TL	4	5	6	8	12	15	20	30
318	D.Grant/M.Dionne TL	4	5	6	8	12	15	20	30
319	Scouts Leaders	4	5	6	8	12	15	20	30
320	Kings Leaders	4	5	6	8	12	15	20	30
321	North Stars Leaders	4	5	6	8	12	15	20	30
322	Lafleur/P.Mahov TL	4	5	6	8	12	20	25	35
323	Nystrom/Potvin/Gill TL	4	5	6	8	12	20		
324	Vick/Gilbert/Ratelle TL	4	5	6	10	15			
325	R.Leach/B.Clarke TL	4	5	6	8	12	15	20	30
326	Penguins Leaders	4	5	6	10	15			
327	Blues Leaders	4	5	6	10	15			
328	Darryl Sittler TL	4	5	6	10	15			
329	Canucks Leaders	4	5	6	8	12	15	20	30
330	Capitals Leaders	4	5	6	8	12	18	20	30

— Stan Mikita #30 PSA 10 (Gem) sold for $99.98 (eBay; 4/12)
— Bobby Orr #100 PSA 10 (Gem) sold for $1,047 (eBay; 5/12)
— Bobby Orr #100 PSA 10 (Gem) sold for $564 (eBay; 11/15)
— Bobby Orr AS #288 PSA 10 (Gem) sold for $924.63 (Memory Lane; 4/12)

1976-77 O-Pee-Chee

		VG 3	VgEx 4	EX 5	ExMt 6	NM 7	NmMt 8	NmMt+ 8.5	MT 9
1	Leach/Lafleur/Larou LL	5	6	8	12	15	60		
2	Clarke/Lafleur/Perr LL	5	6	8	12	15	25	30	50
3	Lafleur/Clarke/Perr LL	5	6	8	10	12	25		
4	Durbno/Watsn/Schltz LL	4	5	6	10	12	20		
5	Espo/Lafleur/Potvin LL	5	6	8	10	12	30		
6	Dryden/Resch/Laroc LL	5	6	8	10	12	20	30	60
7	Gary Doak	4	5	6	8	10	12	20	
8	Jacques Richard	4	5	6	8	10	12	20	
9	Wayne Dillon	4	5	6	10	12	20	25	50
10	Bernie Parent	4	5	6	10	12	20		
11	Ed Westfall	4	5	6	10	12	15	20	30
12	Dick Redmond	4	5	6	10	12	20		
13	Bryan Hextall	4	5	6	10	12	20		
14	Jean Pronovost	4	5	6	10	12	15	20	30
15	Peter Mahovlich	4	5	6	10	12	20		
16	Danny Grant	4	5	6	10	12	15	20	30
17	Phil Myre	4	5	6	10	12	15	20	30
18	Wayne Merrick	4	5	6	10	12	20		

		VG 3	VgEx 4	EX 5	ExMt 6	NM 7	NmMt 8	NmMt+ 8.5	MT 9
19	Steve Durbano	4	5	6	10	12	15	20	30
20	Derek Sanderson	4	5	6	10	12	20		
21	Mike Murphy	4	5	6	10	12	15	20	30
22	Borje Salming	5	6	8	10	12	20	30	60
23	Mike Walton	4	5	6	10	12	15	20	30
24	Randy Manery	4	5	6	10	12	15	20	30
25	Ken Hodge	4	5	6	10	12	15	20	30
26	Mel Bridgman RC	4	5	6	10	12	20	25	50
27	Jerry Korab	4	5	6	10	12	15	20	30
28	Gilles Gratton	4	5	6	10	12	20		
29	Andre St.Laurent	4	5	6	10	12	20		
30	Yvan Cournoyer	4	5	6	10	12	20	25	50
31	Phil Russell	4	5	6	10	12	20		
32	Dennis Hextall	4	5	6	10	12	20		
33	Lowell MacDonald	4	5	6	10	12	20		
34	Dennis O'Brien	4	5	6	10	12	20		
35	Gerry Meehan	4	5	6	10	12	15	20	30
36	Gilles Meloche	4	5	6	10	12	15	20	30
37	Wilf Paiement	4	5	6	10	12	15	20	30
38	Bob MacMillan RC	4	5	6	10	12	20		
39	Ian Turnbull	4	5	6	10	12	20		
40	Rogatien Vachon	4	5	6	10	12	20	25	50
41	Nick Beverley	4	5	6	10	12	20		
42	Rene Robert	4	5	6	10	12	15	20	30
43	Andre Savard	4	5	6	10	12	15	20	30
44	Bob Gainey	5	6	8	10	12	20	25	50
45	Joe Watson	4	5	6	10	12	20		
46	Billy Smith	5	6	8	10	12	20	25	40
47	Darcy Rota	4	5	6	10	12	20		
48	Rick Lapointe RC	4	5	6	10	12	15	20	30
49	Pierre Jarry	4	5	6	10	12	20		
50	Syl Apps	4	5	6	10	12	15	20	30
51	Eric Vail	4	5	6	10	12	15	20	30
52	Greg Joly	4	5	6	10	12	15	20	30
53	Don Lever	4	5	6	10	12	15	20	30
54	Bob Murdoch Seals	4	5	6	10	12	20		
55	Denis Herron	4	5	6	10	12	15	20	30
56	Mike Bloom	4	5	6	10	12	15	20	30
57	Bill Fairbairn	4	5	6	10	12	20		
58	Fred Stanfield	4	5	6	10	12	20		
59	Steve Shutt	4	5	6	10	12	20		
60	Brad Park	4	5	6	10	12	20		
61	Gilles Villemure	4	5	6	10	12	20		
62	Bert Marshall	4	5	6	10	12	20		
63	Chuck Lefley	4	5	6	10	12	20		
64	Simon Nolet	4	5	6	10	12	15	20	30
65	Reggie Leach RB	4	5	6	10	12	20		
66	Darryl Sittler RB	4	5	6	10	12	20		
67	Bryan Trottier RB	5	6	8	10	15	30	40	60
68	Garry Unger RB	4	5	6	10	12	15	20	30
69	Ron Low	4	5	6	10	12	20		
70	Bobby Clarke	5	6	8	10	12	25	30	50
71	Michel Bergeron RC	4	5	6	10	12	15	20	30
72	Ron Stackhouse	4	5	6	10	12	15	20	30
73	Bill Hogaboam	4	5	6	10	12	20		
74	Bob Murdoch Kings	4	5	6	10	12	15	20	30
75	Steve Vickers	4	5	6	10	12	20		
76	Pit Martin	4	5	6	10	12	15	20	30
77	Gerry Hart	4	5	6	10	12	20		
78	Craig Ramsay	4	5	6	10	12	20		
79	Michel Larocque	4	5	6	10	12	20		
80	Jean Ratelle	4	5	6	10	12	20		
81	Don Saleski	4	5	6	10	12	15	20	30
82	Bill Clement	4	5	6	10	12	20		
83	Dave Burrows	4	5	6	10	12	15	20	30
84	Wayne Thomas	4	5	6	10	12	15	20	30
85	John Gould	4	5	6	10	12	20		
86	Dennis Maruk RC	5	6	8	10	12	20	25	50
87	Ernie Hicke	4	5	6	10	12	20		
88	Jim Rutherford	4	5	6	10	12	15	20	30
89	Dale Tallon	4	5	6	10	12	20		
90	Rod Gilbert	4	5	6	10	12	20		
91	Marcel Dionne	5	6	8	10	12	25	30	40
92	Chuck Arnason	4	5	6	10	12	15	20	30
93	Jean Potvin	4	5	6	10	12	20		
94	Don Luce	4	5	6	10	12	20		
95	Johnny Bucyk	4	5	6	10	12	20	25	40
96	Larry Goodenough	4	5	6	10	12	20		
97	Mario Tremblay	4	5	6	10	12	20		
98	Nelson Pyatt	4	5	6	10	12	20		
99	Brian Glennie	4	5	6	10	12	20		
100	Tony Esposito	5	6	8	10	12	25	30	50
101	Dan Maloney	4	5	6	10	12	15	20	30
102	Dunc Wilson	4	5	6	10	12	20		
103	Dean Talafous	4	5	6	10	12	20		
104	Ed Staniowski	4	5	6	10	12	15	20	30
105	Dallas Smith	4	5	6	10	12	15	20	30
106	Jude Drouin	4	5	6	10	12	15	20	30
107	Pat Hickey	4	5	6	10	12	20		
108	Jocelyn Guevremont	4	5	6	10	12	15	20	30

#	Player	VG 3	VgEx 4	EX 5	ExMt 6	NM 7	NmMt 8	NmMt+ 8.5	MT 9
109	Doug Risebrough	4	5	6	10	12	20		
110	Reggie Leach	4	5	6	10	12	20		
111	Dan Bouchard	4	5	6	10	12	15	20	30
112	Chris Oddleifson	4	5	6	10	12	20		
113	Rick Hampton	4	5	6	10	12	20		
114	John Marks	4	5	6	10	12	15	20	30
115	Bryan Trottier RC	15	25	40	60	80	150	200	600
116	Checklist 1-132	6	8	10	12	20	35	50	80
117	Greg Polis	4	5	6	10	12	20		
118	Peter McNab	4	5	6	10	12	20	25	40
119	Jim Roberts Mont	4	5	6	10	12	15	20	30
120	Gerry Cheevers	5	6	8	10	12	20	25	40
121	Rick MacLeish	4	5	6	10	12	20		
122	Billy Lochead	4	5	6	10	12	15	20	30
123	Tom Reid	4	5	6	10	12	15	20	30
124	Rick Kehoe	4	5	6	10	12	15	20	30
125	Keith Magnuson	4	5	6	10	12	20		
126	Clark Gillies	4	5	6	10	12	20	25	40
127	Rick Middleton	4	5	6	10	12	20		
128	Bill Hajt	4	5	6	10	12	20		
129	Jacques Lemaire	4	5	6	10	12	20		
130	Terry O'Reilly	4	5	6	10	12	20		
131	Andre Dupont	4	5	6	10	12	20		
132	Flames Team	5	6	8	10	12	20		
133	Bruins Team	5	6	8	10	12	20		
134	Sabres Team	5	6	8	10	12	20		
135	Seals Team	5	6	8	10	12	20		
136	Blackhawks Team	5	6	8	10	12	20	25	40
137	Red Wings Team	5	6	8	10	12	20	25	40
138	Scouts Team	5	6	8	10	12	20		
139	Kings Team	5	6	8	10	12	20		
140	North Stars Team	5	6	8	10	12	20		
141	Canadiens Team	5	6	8	10	12	20	25	40
142	Islanders Team	5	6	8	10	12	20		
143	Rangers Team	5	6	8	10	12	20	25	40
144	Flyers Team	5	6	8	10	12	20	25	40
145	Penguins Team	5	6	8	10	12	20		
146	Blues Team	5	6	8	10	12	20	25	40
147	Maple Leafs Team	5	6	8	10	12	20		
148	Canucks Team	5	6	8	10	12	20		
149	Capitals Team	5	6	8	10	12	20	25	40
150	Dave Schultz	4	5	6	10	12	20	25	50
151	Larry Robinson	5	6	8	10	12	25	30	40
152	Al Smith	4	5	6	10	12	15	20	30
153	Bob Nystrom	4	5	6	10	12	15	20	30
154	Ron Greschner	4	5	6	10	12	20		
155	Gregg Sheppard	4	5	6	10	12	20		
156	Alain Daigle	4	5	6	10	12	15	20	30
157	Ed Van Impe	4	5	6	10	12	20		
158	Tim Young RC	4	5	6	10	12	15	20	30
159	Bryan Lefley	4	5	6	10	12	20		
160	Ed Giacomin	4	5	6	10	12	20	25	50
161	Yvon Labre	4	5	6	10	12	20		
162	Jim Lorentz	4	5	6	10	12	15	20	30
163	Guy Lafleur	6	8	10	12	20	40	50	80
164	Tom Bladon	4	5	6	10	12	20		
165	Wayne Cashman	4	5	6	10	12	20		
166	Pete Stemkowski	4	5	6	10	12	20		
167	Grant Mulvey	4	5	6	10	12	15	20	30
168	Yves Belanger	4	5	6	10	12	15	20	30
169	Bill Goldsworthy	4	5	6	10	12	15	20	30
170	Denis Potvin	5	6	8	10	12	25	30	40
171	Nick Libett	4	5	6	10	12	15	20	30
172	Michel Plasse	4	5	6	10	12	20		
173	Lou Nanne	4	5	6	10	12	15	20	30
174	Tom Lysiak	4	5	6	10	12	15	20	30
175	Dennis Ververgaert	4	5	6	10	12	15	20	30
176	Gary Simmons	4	5	6	10	12	20		
177	Pierre Bouchard	4	5	6	10	12	15	20	30
178	Bill Barber	4	5	6	10	12	20	25	40
179	Darryl Edestrand	4	5	6	10	12	20		
180	Gilbert Perreault	5	6	8	10	12	20		
181	Dave Maloney RC	4	5	6	10	12	20	25	40
182	Jean-Paul Parise	4	5	6	10	12	20		
183	Jim Harrison	4	5	6	10	12	20		
184	Pete Lopresti	4	5	6	10	12	15	20	30
185	Don Kozak	4	5	6	10	12	15	20	30
186	Guy Charron	4	5	6	10	12	15	20	30
187	Stan Gilbertson	4	5	6	10	12	20		
188	Bill Nyrop	4	5	6	10	12	20		
189	Bobby Schmautz	4	5	6	10	12	15	20	30
190	Wayne Stephenson	4	5	6	10	12	20		
191	Brian Spencer	4	5	6	10	12	15	20	30
192	Gilles Marotte	4	5	6	10	12	15	20	30
193	Lorne Henning	4	5	6	10	12	15	20	30
194	Bob Neely	4	5	6	10	12	15	20	30
195	Dennis Hull	4	5	6	10	12	15	20	30
196	Walt McKechnie	4	5	6	10	12	15	20	30
197	Curt Ridley	4	5	6	10	12	20		
198	Dwight Bialowas	4	5	6	10	12	15	20	30

#	Player	VG 3	VgEx 4	EX 5	ExMt 6	NM 7	NmMt 8	NmMt+ 8.5	MT 9
199	Pierre Larouche	4	5	6	10	12	20		
200	Ken Dryden	6	8	10	15	30	60	80	150
201	Ross Lonsberry	4	5	6	10	12	20		
202	Curt Bennett	4	5	6	10	12	20		
203	Hartland Monahan	4	5	6	10	12	20		
204	John Davidson	5	6	8	10	12	20	25	50
205	Serge Savard	4	5	6	10	12	20		
206	Garry Howatt	4	5	6	10	12	15	20	30
207	Darryl Sittler	5	6	8	10	12	20	25	40
208	J.P. Bordeleau	4	5	6	10	12	15	20	30
209	Henry Boucha	4	5	6	10	12	20		
210	Richard Martin	4	5	6	10	12	20		
211	Vic Venasky	4	5	6	10	12	15	20	30
212	Buster Harvey	4	5	6	10	12	20		
213	Bobby Orr	15	20	25	30	50	120	135	300
214	Martin/Perreault/Robert	5	6	8	10	12	20	25	50
215	Barber/Clarke/Leach	5	6	8	10	12	20	30	
216	Gillies/Trottier/Harris	5	6	8	10	12	20	25	40
217	Gainey/Jarvis/Roberts	4	5	6	10	12	20		
218	Bicentennial Line	4	5	6	10	12	20		
219	Bob Kelly	4	5	6	10	12	20		
220	Walt Tkaczuk	4	5	6	10	12	15	20	30
221	Dave Lewis	4	5	6	10	12	15	20	30
222	Danny Gare	4	5	6	10	12	20		
223	Guy Lapointe	4	5	6	10	12	20		
224	Hank Nowak	4	5	6	10	12	15	20	30
225	Stan Mikita	5	6	8	10	12	20	25	50
226	Vic Hadfield	4	5	6	10	12	20		
227	Bernie Wolfe	4	5	6	10	12	15	20	30
228	Bryan Watson	4	5	6	10	12	15	20	30
229	Ralph Stewart	4	5	6	10	12	20		
230	Gerry Desjardins	4	5	6	10	12	20		
231	John Bednarski	4	5	6	10	12	20		
232	Yvon Lambert	4	5	6	10	12	20		
233	Orest Kindrachuk	4	5	6	10	12	20		
234	Don Marcotte	4	5	6	10	12	15	20	30
235	Bill White	4	5	6	10	12	20		
236	Red Berenson	4	5	6	10	12	20		
237	Al MacAdam	4	5	6	10	12	20		
238	Rick Blight	4	5	6	10	12	15	20	30
239	Butch Goring	4	5	6	10	12	20		
240	Cesare Maniago	4	5	6	10	12	20		
241	Jim Schoenfeld	4	5	6	10	12	20		
242	Cliff Koroll	4	5	6	10	12	20		
243	Scott Garland	4	5	6	10	12	20		
244	Rick Chartraw	4	5	6	10	12	20		
245	Phil Esposito	5	6	8	10	12	20	25	40
246	Dave Forbes	4	5	6	10	12	15	20	30
247	Jimmy Watson	4	5	6	10	12	20		
248	Ron Schock	4	5	6	10	12	20		
249	Fred Barrett	4	5	6	10	12	15	20	30
250	Glenn Resch	5	6	8	10	12	20	25	50
251	Ivan Boldirev	4	5	6	10	12	20		
252	Billy Harris	4	5	6	10	12	15	20	30
253	Lee Fogolin	4	5	6	10	12	15	20	30
254	Murray Wilson	4	5	6	10	12	15	20	30
255	Gilles Gilbert	4	5	6	10	12	20		
256	Gary Dornhoefer	4	5	6	10	12	20		
257	Carol Vadnais	4	5	6	10	12	15	20	30
258	Checklist 133-264	10	15	20	30	40	200		
259	Errol Thompson	4	5	6	10	12	20		
260	Garry Unger	4	5	6	10	12	20		
261	J. Bob Kelly	4	5	6	10	12	20		
262	Terry Harper	4	5	6	10	12	15	20	30
263	Blake Dunlop	4	5	6	10	12	20		
264	Canadiens Champs	4	5	6	10	12	20		
265	Richard Mulhern	4	5	6	10	12	15	20	30
266	Gary Sabourin	4	5	6	10	12	20		
267	Bill McKenzie UER RC	4	5	6	10	12	20		
268	Mike Corrigan	4	5	6	10	12	15	20	30
269	Rick Smith	4	5	6	10	12	20		
270	Stan Weir	4	5	6	10	12	15	20	30
271	Ron Sedlbauer	4	5	6	10	12	15	20	30
272	Jean Lemieux	4	5	6	10	12	20		
273	Hilliard Graves	4	5	6	10	12	20		
274	Dave Gardner	4	5	6	10	12	20		
275	Tracy Pratt	4	5	6	10	12	15	20	30
276	Frank St.Marseille	4	5	6	10	12	15	20	30
277	Bob Hess	4	5	6	10	12	15	20	30
278	Bobby Lalonde	4	5	6	10	12	15	20	30
279	Tony White	4	5	6	10	12	20		
280	Rod Seiling	4	5	6	10	12	20		
281	Larry Romanchych	4	5	6	10	12	15	20	30
282	Ralph Klassen	4	5	6	10	12	20		
283	Gary Croteau	4	5	6	10	12	15	20	30
284	Neil Komadoski	4	5	6	10	12	20		
285	Ed Johnston	4	5	6	10	12	15	20	30
286	George Ferguson	4	5	6	10	12	20		
287	Gerry O'Flaherty	4	5	6	10	12	20		
288	Jack Lynch	4	5	6	10	12	15	20	30

#	Name	VG 3	VgEx 4	EX 5	ExMt 6	NM 7	NmMt 8	NmMt+ 8.5	MT 9
289	Pat Quinn	4	5	6	10	12	15	20	30
290	Gene Carr	4	5	6	10	12	15	20	30
291	Bob Stewart	4	5	6	10	12	15	20	30
292	Doug Favell	4	5	6	10	12	15	20	30
293	Rick Wilson	4	5	6	10	12	20		
294	Jack Valiquette	4	5	6	10	12	15	20	30
295	Garry Monahan	4	5	6	10	12	20		
296	Michel Belhumeur	4	5	6	10	12	20		
297	Larry Carriere	4	5	6	10	12	15	20	30
298	Fred Ahern	4	5	6	10	12	20		
299	Dave Hudson	4	5	6	10	12	20		
300	Bob Berry	4	5	6	10	12	15	20	30
301	Bob Gassoff	4	5	6	10	12	15	20	30
302	Jim McKenny	4	5	6	10	12	20		
303	Gord Smith	4	5	6	10	12	15	20	30
304	Garnet Bailey	4	5	6	10	12	15	20	30
305	Bruce Affleck	4	5	6	10	12	20		
306	Doug Halward	4	5	6	10	12	20		
307	Lew Morrison	4	5	6	10	12	20		
308	Bob Sauve RC	5	6	8	10	12	20	25	50
309	Bob Murray RC	4	5	6	10	12	20		
310	Claude Larose	4	5	6	10	12	15	20	30
311	Don Awrey	4	5	6	10	12	15	20	30
312	Bill MacMillan	4	5	6	10	12	20		
313	Doug Jarvis RC	4	5	6	10	12	30	35	80
314	Dennis Owchar	4	5	6	10	12	15	20	30
315	Jerry Holland	4	5	6	10	12	15	20	30
316	Guy Chouinard RC	4	5	6	10	12	20	25	40
317	Gary Smith	4	5	6	10	12	15	20	30
318	Pat Price	4	5	6	10	12	15	20	30
319	Tom Williams	4	5	6	10	12	15	20	30
320	Larry Patey	4	5	6	10	12	15	20	30
321	Claire Alexander	4	5	6	10	12	15	20	30
322	Larry Bolonchuk	4	5	6	10	12	15	20	30
323	Bob Sirois	4	5	6	10	12	20		
324	Joe Zanussi	4	5	6	10	12	20		
325	Joey Johnston	4	5	6	10	12	15	20	30
326	J.P. LeBlanc	4	5	6	10	12	15	20	30
327	Craig Cameron	4	5	6	10	12	15	20	30
328	Dave Fortier	4	5	6	10	12	15	20	30
329	Ed Gilbert	4	5	6	10	12	15	20	30
330	John Van Boxmeer	4	5	6	10	12	15	20	30
331	Gary Inness	4	5	6	10	12	15	20	30
332	Bill Flett	4	5	6	10	12	20		
333	Mike Christie	4	5	6	10	12	15	20	30
334	Denis Dupere	4	5	6	10	12	20		
335	Sheldon Kannegiesser	4	5	6	10	12	15	20	30
336	Jerry Butler	4	5	6	10	12	15	20	30
337	Gord McRae	4	5	6	10	12	15	20	30
338	Dennis Kearns	4	5	6	10	12	15	20	30
339	Ron Lalonde	4	5	6	10	12	20		
340	Jean Hamel	4	5	6	10	12	15	20	30
341	Barry Gibbs	4	5	6	10	12	20		
342	Mike Pelyk	4	5	6	10	12	20		
343	Rey Comeau	4	5	6	10	12	15	20	30
344	Jim Neilson	4	5	6	10	12	20		
345	Phil Roberto	4	5	6	10	12	20		
346	Dave Hutchinson	4	5	6	10	12	20		
347	Ted Irvine	4	5	6	10	12	15	20	30
348	Lanny McDonald UER	5	6	8	10	12	20	30	60
349	Jim Moxey	4	5	6	10	12	15	20	30
350	Bob Dailey	4	5	6	10	12	15	20	30
351	Tim Ecclestone	4	5	6	10	12	20		
352	Len Frig	4	5	6	10	12	20		
353	Randy Rota	4	5	6	10	12	20		
354	Juha Widing	4	5	6	10	12	15	20	30
355	Larry Brown	4	5	6	10	12	20		
356	Floyd Thomson	4	5	6	10	12	20		
357	Richard Nantais	4	5	6	10	12	20		
358	Inge Hammarstrom	4	5	6	10	12	15	20	30
359	Mike Robitaille	4	5	6	10	12	20		
360	Rejean Houle	4	5	6	10	12	15	20	30
361	Ed Kea	4	5	6	10	12	15	20	30
362	Bob Girard	4	5	6	10	12	15	20	30
363	Bob Murray Vancv	4	5	6	10	12	15	20	30
364	Dave Hrechkosy	4	5	6	10	12	15	20	30
365	Gary Edwards	4	5	6	10	12	15	20	30
366	Harold Snepsts	5	6	8	10	12	20	25	40
367	Pat Boutette RC	4	5	6	10	12	20	25	40
368	Bob Paradise	4	5	6	10	12	15	20	30
369	Bob Plager	4	5	6	10	12	15	20	30
370	Tim Jacobs	4	5	6	10	12	15	20	30
371	Pierre Plante	4	5	6	10	12	15	20	30
372	Colin Campbell	4	5	6	10	12	15	20	30
373	Dave Williams RC	8	10	15	20	30	60	100	200
374	Ab DeMarco	4	5	6	10	12	20		
		VG 3	VgEx 4	EX 5	ExMt 6	NM 7	NmMt 8	NmMt+ 8.5	MT 9
375	Mike Lampman	4	5	6	10	12	15	20	30
376	Mark Heaslip	4	5	6	10	12	15	20	30
377	Checklist Card	6	8	10	12	20	50	60	100
378	Bert Wilson	4	5	6	10	12	20		

#	Name	VG 3	VgEx 4	EX 5	ExMt 6	NM 7	NmMt 8	NmMt+ 8.5	MT 9
379	Bntt/Lysk/Qnn/St.S TL	4	5	6	10	12	20		
380	Gre/Perrlt/Mrtin TL	4	5	6	10	12	15	20	30
381	Bucyk/Ratle/O'Rei TL	4	5	6	10	12	20		
382	Mrtn/Tln/Rsll/Kroll TL	4	5	6	10	12	20		
383	Seals/McAd/Mrdch TL	4	5	6	10	12	20		
384	Charron/Durbano TL	4	5	6	10	12	20		
385	Brgrn/McKch/Wtsn TL	4	5	6	10	12	20		
386	Dione/Htch/Corrig TL	4	5	6	10	12	15	20	30
387	Hoga/Yng/O'Brien TL	4	5	6	10	12	15	20	30
388	Laflr/P.Mahv/Rise TL	5	6	8	10	12	20	25	50
389	Gillies/Potvin/How TL	4	5	6	10	12	20	25	50
390	Gilbert/Vick/Espo TL	4	5	6	10	12	20		
391	Leach/Clarke/Barber TL	4	5	6	10	12	20		
392	Lrch/Apps/Schck TL	4	5	6	10	12	20		
393	Lefly/Ungr/Gssf TL	4	5	6	10	12	20		
394	Thmpsn/Sittlr/Will TL	4	5	6	10	12	20		
395	Vgrt/Odl/Krns/Snpst TL	4	5	6	10	12	20		
396	Pyatt/Mhn/Lbr/Whte TL	4	5	6	10	12	20		

— Guy Lafleur #163 PSA 10 (Gem) sold for $262 (Memory Lane; 4/12)
— Bobby Orr #213 PSA 10 (Gem) sold for $949 (Memory Lane; 4/07)
— Bobby Orr #213 PSA 10 (Gem) sold for $756.84 (Mile High; 12/13)
— Brian Trottier RC #155 PSA 10 (Gem) sold for $2,033 (eBay; 3/13)

1976-77 O-Pee-Chee WHA

#	Name	GD 2	VG 3	VgEx 4	EX 5	ExMt 6	NM 7	NmMt 8	MT 9
	COMMON CARD (1-132)	4	4	5	6	8	10	12	
2	Tardit/Trembl/Nils LL	4	4	5	6		10	12	
3	Tardif/B.Hull/Nils LL	4	5	6	8	12	15	20	40
9	Ulf Nilsson	4			6	10	12	15	
14	Tom Webster	4	4	5	6	8	10	12	25
15	Marty Howe	4	4	5	6	10	12	15	30
20	Joe Daley	4	4	5	6	8	12	15	
21	Gary Veneruzzo	4	4	5	6	8	10	12	25
23	Mike Antonovich	4	4	5	6	8	10	12	30
27	Poul Popiel	4	4	5	6	8	10	12	25
28	Renald Leclerc	4	4	5	6	8	10	12	25
30	Lars-Erik Sjoberg	4	4	5	6	8	10	12	25
33	Tim Sheehy	4	4	5	6	8	10	12	25
34	Brent Hughes	4	4	5	6	8	10	12	25
37	Rosaire Paiement	4	4	5	6	8	10	12	25
39	Hugh Harris	4	4	5	6	8	10	12	25
41	Rich Leduc	4	4	5	6	8	10	12	25
46	Joe Noris RC	4	4	5	6	8	10	12	25
50	Gordie Howe	8	10	15	20	25	30	40	80
52	Dave Keon	4			6	10	12	15	
54	Bryan Maxwell	4	4	5	6	8	10		
60	Gene Peacosh	4	4	5	6	8	10	12	25
62	J.C. Tremblay AS	4	4	5	6	8	10	12	25
63	Lars-Erik Sjoberg AS	4	4	5	6	8	10	12	25
65	Bobby Hull AS	6	8	10	12	20	25	35	80
67	Chris Abrahamsson AS	4	4	5	6	8	10	12	25
72	Gordie Howe AS	6	8	10	12	20	25	40	150
73	Bob Nevin	4	4	5	6	8	10	12	25
81	Frank Hughes	4	4	5	6	8	10	12	25
82	Reg Thomas	4	4	5	6	8	10	12	25
84	Paul Henderson	4			6	10	12	15	
91	Garry Swain	4	4	5	6	8	10	12	25
95	Mark Howe	5	6	8	10	12	15	20	40
96	Peter Marrin RC	4	4	5	6	10	12	15	
98	Paulin Bordeleau	4	4	5	6	8	10	12	25
100	Bobby Hull	6	8	10	12	20	25	40	80
101	Rick Ley	4	4	5	6	8	10	12	25
105	John French	4	4	5	6	8	10	12	25
106	John Hughes	4	4	5	6	8	10		
111	Frank Mahovlich	5	6	8	10	15	20	30	60
115	Rich Preston	4	4	5	6	8	10	12	25
117	Checklist Card	4		6	8	12	20	40	100
125	Anders Hedberg	4	4	5	6	10	12	15	
126	Norm Ullman	4	4	5	6	10	12	15	35
127	Steve Sutherland	4	4	5	6	8	10	12	25
128	John Schella	4	4	5	6	8	10	12	25
129	Don McLeod	4	4	5	6	8	10	12	25
130	Canadian Finals	4	5	6	8	12	15	20	40
132	World Trophy Final	5	6	8	10	12	15	20	40

1976-77 Topps

#	Name	VG 3	VgEx 4	EX 5	ExMt 6	NM 7	NmMt 8	NmMt+ 8.5	MT 9
1	Leach/Lafleur/Larou LL	4	5	6	8	10	20	25	
2	Clarke/Lafleur/Perr/ LL	4	5	6	8	10	20	25	
3	Lafleur/Clarke/Perr LL	4	5	6	8	10	15	20	
4	Durbno/Watsn/Schultz LL	4	5	6	8	10	15	20	
5	Espo/Lafleur/Potvin LL	4	5	6	8	10	12	15	
6	Dryden/Resch/Laroc LL	4	5	6	8	10	12	15	
7	Gary Doak	4	5	6	8	10	12	15	
8	Jacques Richard	4	5	6	8	10	12	15	
9	Wayne Dillon	4	5	6	8	10	12	15	20
10	Bernie Parent	4	5	6	8	10	12	15	25
11	Ed Westfall	4	5	6	8	10	12	15	20
12	Dick Redmond	4	5	6	8	10	12	15	

#	Player	VG 3	VgEx 4	EX 5	ExMt 6	NM 7	NmMt 8	NmMt+ 8.5	MT 9
13	Bryan Hextall	4	5	6	8	10	12	15	20
14	Jean Pronovost	4	5	6	8	10	12	15	20
15	Peter Mahovlich	4	5	6	8	10	12	15	20
16	Danny Grant	4	5	6	8	10	12	15	
17	Phil Myre	4	5	6	8	10	12	15	20
18	Wayne Merrick	4	5	6	8	10	12	15	
19	Steve Durbano	4	5	6	8	10	12	15	20
20	Derek Sanderson	4	5	6	8	10	12	15	
21	Mike Murphy	4	5	6	8	10	12	15	
22	Borje Salming	4	5	6	8	10	12	15	25
23	Mike Walton	4	5	6	8	10	12	15	20
24	Randy Manery	4	5	6	8	10	12	15	20
25	Ken Hodge	4	5	6	8	10	12	15	
26	Mel Bridgman RC	4	5	6	8	10	12	15	20
27	Jerry Korab	4	5	6	8	10	12	15	20
28	Gilles Gratton	4	5	6	8	10	12	15	20
29	Andre St.Laurent	4	5	6	8	10	12	15	
30	Yvan Cournoyer	4	5	6	8	10	12	15	
31	Phil Russell	4	5	6	8	10	12	15	
32	Dennis Hextall	4	5	6	8	10	12	15	
33	Lowell MacDonald	4	5	6	8	10	12	15	20
34	Dennis O'Brien	4	5	6	8	10	12	15	
35	Gerry Meehan	4	5	6	8	10	12	15	
36	Gilles Meloche	4	5	6	8	10	12	15	
37	Wilf Paiement	4	5	6	8	10	12	15	
38	Bob MacMillan RC	4	5	6	8	10	12	15	
39	Ian Turnbull	4	5	6	8	10	12	15	
40	Rogatien Vachon	4	5	6	8	10	12	15	
41	Nick Beverley	4	5	6	8	10	12	15	
42	Rene Robert	4	5	6	8	10	12	15	20
43	Andre Savard	4	5	6	8	10	12	15	20
44	Bob Gainey	4	5	6	8	10	12	15	
45	Joe Watson	4	5	6	8	10	12	15	20
46	Billy Smith	4	5	6	8	10	12	15	25
47	Darcy Rota	4	5	6	8	10	12	15	
48	Rick Lapointe RC	4	5	6	8	10	12	15	
49	Pierre Jarry	4	5	6	8	10	12	15	
50	Syl Apps	4	5	6	8	10	12	15	20
51	Eric Vail	4	5	6	8	10	12	15	20
52	Greg Joly	4	5	6	8	10	12	15	
53	Don Lever	4	5	6	8	10	12	15	
54	Bob Murdoch Seals	4	5	6	8	10	12	15	
55	Denis Herron	4	5	6	8	10	12	15	
56	Mike Bloom	4	5	6	8	10	12	15	20
57	Bill Fairbairn	4	5	6	8	10	12	15	
58	Fred Stanfield	4	5	6	8	10	12	15	
59	Steve Shutt	4	5	6	8	10	12	15	25
60	Brad Park	4	5	6	8	10	12	15	25
61	Gilles Villemure	4	5	6	8	10	12	15	
62	Bert Marshall	4	5	6	8	10	12	15	20
63	Chuck Lefley	4	5	6	8	10	12	15	
64	Simon Nolet	4	5	6	8	10	12	15	
65	Reggie Leach RB	4	5	6	8	10	12	15	
66	Darryl Sittler RB	4	5	6	8	10	12	15	
67	Bryan Trottier RB	5	6	8	10	12	15	20	30
68	Garry Unger RB	4	5	6	8	10	12	15	20
69	Ron Low	4	5	6	8	10	12	15	
70	Bobby Clarke	5	6	8	10	12	15	20	25
71	Michel Bergeron RC	4	5	6	8	10	12	15	
72	Ron Stackhouse	4	5	6	8	10	12	15	
73	Bill Hogaboam	4	5	6	8	10	12	15	20
74	Bob Murdoch Kings	4	5	6	8	10	12	15	
75	Steve Vickers	4	5	6	8	10	12	15	
76	Pit Martin	4	5	6	8	10	12	15	20
77	Gerry Hart	4	5	6	8	10	12	15	
78	Craig Ramsay	4	5	6	8	10	12	15	20
79	Michel Larocque	4	5	6	8	10	12	15	20
80	Jean Ratelle	4	5	6	8	10	12	15	20
81	Don Saleski	4	5	6	8	10	12	15	20
82	Bill Clement	4	5	6	8	10	12	15	20
83	Dave Burrows	4	5	6	8	10	12	15	
84	Wayne Thomas	4	5	6	8	10	12	15	20
85	John Gould	4	5	6	8	10	12	15	20
86	Dennis Maruk RC	4	5	6	8	10	12	15	25
87	Ernie Hicke	4	5	6	8	10	12	15	20
88	Jim Rutherford	4	5	6	8	10	12	15	
89	Dale Tallon	4	5	6	8	10	12	15	
90	Rod Gilbert	4	5	6	8	10	12	15	
91	Marcel Dionne	4	5	6	8	10	15	20	25
92	Chuck Arnason	4	5	6	8	10	12	15	
93	Jean Potvin	4	5	6	8	10	12	15	20
94	Don Luce	4	5	6	8	10	12	15	20
95	Johnny Bucyk	4	5	6	8	10	12	15	20
96	Larry Goodenough	4	5	6	8	10	12	15	20
97	Mario Tremblay	4	5	6	8	10	12	15	
98	Nelson Pyatt RC	4	5	6	8	10	12	15	
99	Brian Glennie	4	5	6	8	10	12	15	
100	Tony Esposito	4	5	6	8	10	12	15	30
101	Dan Maloney	4	5	6	8	10	12	15	20
102	Barry Wilkins	4	5	6	8	10	12	15	

#	Player	VG 3	VgEx 4	EX 5	ExMt 6	NM 7	NmMt 8	NmMt+ 8.5	MT 9
103	Dean Talafous	4	5	6	8	10	12	15	20
104	Ed Staniowski RC	4	5	6	8	10	12	15	20
105	Dallas Smith	4	5	6	8	10	12	15	
106	Jude Drouin	4	5	6	8	10	12	15	
107	Pat Hickey	4	5	6	8	10	12	15	
108	Jocelyn Guevremont	4	5	6	8	10	12	15	20
109	Doug Risebrough	4	5	6	8	10	12	15	20
110	Reggie Leach	4	5	6	8	10	12	15	
111	Dan Bouchard	4	5	6	8	10	12	15	20
112	Chris Oddleifson	4	5	6	8	10	12	15	
113	Rick Hampton	4	5	6	8	10	12	15	
114	John Marks	4	5	6	8	10	12	15	
115	Bryan Trottier RC	10	12	15	25	30	80	100	150
116	Checklist 1-132	5	6	8	10	15	20	30	
117	Greg Polis	4	5	6	8	10	12	15	
118	Peter McNab	4	5	6	8	10	12	15	20
119	Jim Roberts	4	5	6	8	10	12	15	
120	Gerry Cheevers	4	5	6	8	10	12	15	
121	Rick MacLeish	4	5	6	8	10	12	15	20
122	Billy Lochead	4	5	6	8	10	12	15	
123	Tom Reid	4	5	6	8	10	12	15	20
124	Rick Kehoe	4	5	6	8	10	12	15	20
125	Keith Magnuson	4	5	6	8	10	12	15	20
126	Clark Gillies	4	5	6	8	10	12	15	20
127	Rick Middleton	4	5	6	8	10	12	15	
128	Bill Hajt	4	5	6	8	10	12	15	
129	Jacques Lemaire	4	5	6	8	10	12	15	
130	Terry O'Reilly	4	5	6	8	10	12	15	20
131	Andre Dupont	4	5	6	8	10	12	15	
132	Flames Team CL	4	5	6	8	10	12	15	
133	Bruins Team CL	4	5	6	8	10	12	15	
134	Sabres Team CL	4	5	6	8	10	12	15	40
135	Seals Team CL	4	5	6	8	10	12	15	
136	Blackhawks Team CL	4	5	6	8	10	12	15	40
137	Red Wings Team CL	4	5	6	8	10	12	15	
138	Scouts Team CL	4	5	6	8	10	12	15	
139	Kings Team CL	4	5	6	8	10	12	15	
140	North Stars Team CL	4	5	6	8	10	12	15	
141	Canadiens Team CL	4	5	6	8	10	12	15	
142	Islanders Team CL	4	5	6	8	10	12	15	
143	Rangers Team CL	4	5	6	8	10	12	15	
144	Flyers Team CL	4	5	6	8	10	12	15	
145	Penguins Team CL	4	5	6	8	10	12	15	
146	Blues Team CL	4	5	6	8	10	12	15	
147	Maple Leafs Team CL	4	5	6	8	10	12	15	
148	Canucks Team CL	4	5	6	8	10	12	15	
149	Capitals Team CL	4	5	6	8	10	12	15	
150	Dave Schultz	4	5	6	8	10	12	15	20
151	Larry Robinson	5	6	8	10	12	15	20	25
152	Al Smith	4	5	6	8	10	12	15	
153	Bob Nystrom	4	5	6	8	10	12	15	20
154	Ron Greschner UER	4	5	6	8	10	12	15	
155	Gregg Sheppard	4	5	6	8	10	12	15	
156	Alain Daigle	4	5	6	8	10	12	15	20
157	Ed Van Impe	4	5	6	8	10	12	15	20
158	Tim Young RC	4	5	6	8	10	12	15	20
159	Gary Bergman	4	5	6	8	10	12	15	
160	Ed Giacomin	4	5	6	8	10	12	15	20
161	Yvon Labre	4	5	6	8	10	12	15	20
162	Jim Lorentz	4	5	6	8	10	12	15	20
163	Guy Lafleur	5	6	8	10	12	15	20	50
164	Tom Bladon	4	5	6	8	10	12	15	
165	Wayne Cashman	4	5	6	8	10	12	15	
166	Pete Sternkowski	4	5	6	8	10	12	15	
167	Grant Mulvey	4	5	6	8	10	12	15	20
168	Yves Belanger RC	4	5	6	8	10	12	15	
169	Bill Goldsworthy	4	5	6	8	10	12	15	
170	Denis Potvin	5	6	8	10	15	20	25	40
171	Nick Libett	4	5	6	8	10	12	15	
172	Michel Plasse	4	5	6	8	10	12	15	
173	Lou Nanne	4	5	6	8	10	12	15	20
174	Tom Lysiak	4	5	6	8	10	12	15	20
175	Dennis Ververgaert	4	5	6	8	10	12	15	
176	Gary Simmons	4	5	6	8	10	12	15	20
177	Pierre Bouchard	4	5	6	8	10	12	15	
178	Bill Barber	4	5	6	8	10	12	15	25
179	Darryl Edestrand	4	5	6	8	10	12	15	
180	Gilbert Perreault	4	5	6	8	10	12	15	30
181	Dave Maloney RC	4	5	6	8	10	12	15	20
182	Jean-Paul Parise	4	5	6	8	10	12	15	
183	Bobby Sheehan	4	5	6	8	10	12	15	20
184	Pete Lopresti RC	4	5	6	8	10	12	15	20
185	Don Kozak	4	5	6	8	10	12	15	
186	Guy Charron	4	5	6	8	10	12	15	
187	Stan Gilbertson	4	5	6	8	10	12	15	
188	Bill Nyrop RC	4	5	6	8	10	12	15	
189	Bobby Schmautz	4	5	6	8	10	12	15	20
190	Wayne Stephenson	4	5	6	8	10	12	15	
191	Brian Spencer	4	5	6	8	10	12	15	
192	Gilles Marotte	4	5	6	8	10	12	15	

#		VG 3	VgEx 4	EX 5	ExMt 6	NM 7	NmMt 8	NmMt+ 8.5	MT 9
193	Lorne Henning	4	5	6	8	10	12	15	20
194	Bob Neely	4	5	6	8	10	12	15	
195	Dennis Hull	4	5	6	8	10	12	15	
196	Walt McKechnie	4	5	6	8	10	12	15	20
197	Curt Ridley RC	4	5	6	8	10	12	15	
198	Dwight Bialowas	4	5	6	8	10	12	15	20
199	Pierre Larouche	4	5	6	8	10	12	15	
200	Ken Dryden	6	8	10	12	15	30	40	80
201	Ross Lonsberry	4	5	6	8	10	12	15	
202	Curt Bennett	4	5	6	8	10	12	15	
203	Hartland Monahan RC	4	5	6	8	10	12	15	20
204	John Davidson	4	5	6	8	10	12	15	
205	Serge Savard	4	5	6	8	10	12	15	
206	Garry Howatt	4	5	6	8	10	12	15	20
207	Darryl Sittler	4	5	6	8	10	15	20	25
208	J.P. Bordeleau	4	5	6	8	10	12	15	20
209	Henry Boucha	4	5	6	8	10	12	15	
210	Richard Martin	4	5	6	8	10	12	15	20
211	Vic Venasky	4	5	6	8	10	12	15	20
212	Buster Harvey	4	5	6	8	10	12	15	
213	Bobby Orr	8	10	12	15	20	30	40	80
214	Martin/Perrlt/Robert	4	5	6	8	10	12	15	30
215	Barber/Clarke/Leach	4	5	6	8	10	12	15	
216	Gillies/Trottier/Harris	4	5	6	8	10	15	20	
217	Gainey/Jarvis/Roberts	4	5	6	8	10	12	15	
218	MacDon/Apps/Pronvst	4	5	6	8	10	12	15	
219	Bob Kelly	4	5	6	8	10	12	15	20
220	Walt Tkaczuk	4	5	6	8	10	12	15	
221	Dave Lewis	4	5	6	8	10	12	15	20
222	Danny Gare	4	5	6	8	10	12	15	
223	Guy Lapointe	4	5	6	8	10	12	15	
224	Hank Nowak RC	4	5	6	8	10	12	15	
225	Stan Mikita	4	5	6	8	10	15	20	30
226	Vic Hadfield	4	5	6	8	10	12	15	
227	Bernie Wolfe RC	4	5	6	8	10	12	15	
228	Bryan Watson	4	5	6	8	10	12	15	
229	Ralph Stewart	4	5	6	8	10	12	15	
230	Gerry Desjardins	4	5	6	8	10	12	15	20
231	John Bednarski RC	4	5	6	8	10	12	15	
232	Yvon Lambert	4	5	6	8	10	12	15	
233	Orest Kindrachuk	4	5	6	8	10	12	15	
234	Don Marcotte	4	5	6	8	10	12	15	
235	Bill White	4	5	6	8	10	12	15	
236	Red Berenson	4	5	6	8	10	12	15	20
237	Al MacAdam	4	5	6	8	10	12	15	
238	Rick Blight RC	4	5	6	8	10	12	15	20
239	Butch Goring	4	5	6	8	10	12	15	
240	Cesare Maniago	4	5	6	8	10	12	15	
241	Jim Schoenfeld	4	5	6	8	10	12	15	20
242	Cliff Koroll	4	5	6	8	10	12	15	
243	Mickey Redmond	4	5	6	8	10	12	15	
244	Rick Chartraw	4	5	6	8	10	12	15	
245	Phil Esposito	4	5	6	8	10	15	20	30
246	Dave Forbes	4	5	6	8	10	12	15	20
247	Jimmy Watson	4	5	6	8	10	12	15	
248	Ron Schock	4	5	6	8	10	12	15	20
249	Fred Barrett	4	5	6	8	10	12	15	
250	Glenn Resch	4	5	6	8	10	12	15	
251	Ivan Boldirev	4	5	6	8	10	12	15	20
252	Billy Harris	4	5	6	8	10	12	15	
253	Lee Fogolin	4	5	6	8	10	12	15	
254	Murray Wilson	4	5	6	8	10	12	15	
255	Gilles Gilbert	4	5	6	8	10	12	15	
256	Gary Dornhoefer	4	5	6	8	10	12	15	
257	Carol Vadnais	4	5	6	8	10	12	15	
258	Checklist 133-264	5	6	8	10	15	20	30	
259	Errol Thompson	4	5	6	8	10	12	15	
260	Garry Unger	4	5	6	8	10	12	15	
261	J. Bob Kelly	4	5	6	8	10	12	15	
262	Terry Harper	4	5	6	8	10	12	15	
263	Blake Dunlop	4	5	6	8	10	12	15	
264	Canadiens Champs	4	5	6	8	12	15	20	

1977-78 O-Pee-Chee

#		VG 3	VgEx 4	EX 5	ExMt 6	NM 7	NmMt 8	NmMt+ 8.5	MT 9
	COMMON CARD (1-396)	4	5	6	8	10	15		
1	Shutt/Lafleur/Dionne LL	4	5	6	8	10	15	20	40
2	Lafleur/Dionne/Sal/ LL	4	5	6	8	10	15	20	35
3	Lafleur/Dionne/Shutt LL	4	5	6	8	10	15	20	35
4	Williams/Polonich/Gassoff LL	4	5	6	8	10	12	15	25
5	McDonald/Espo/Will LL	4	5	6	8	10	12	15	25
6	Laroc/Dryden/Resch LL	4	5	6	8	10	15	20	40
7	Perr/Shutt/Lafleur/ LL	4	5	6	8	10	15	20	35
8	Dryden/Vach/Parent/ LL	4	5	6	8	10	15	20	40
9	Brian Spencer	4	5	6	8	10	15	20	
10	Denis Potvin	4	5	6	8	10	15	20	40
11	Nick Fotiu	4	5	6	8	10	12	15	25
12	Bob Murray	4	5	6	8	10	12	15	25
13	Pete Lopresti	4	5	6	8	10	15	20	

#		VG 3	VgEx 4	EX 5	ExMt 6	NM 7	NmMt 8	NmMt+ 8.5	MT 9
14	J. Bob Kelly	4	5	6	8	10	12	15	25
15	Rick MacLeish	4	5	6	8	10	12	15	25
16	Terry Harper	4	5	6	8	10	15	20	
17	Willi Plett RC	4	5	6	8	10	15	20	40
18	Peter McNab	4	5	6	8	10	15	20	25
19	Wayne Thomas	4	5	6	8	10	12	15	25
20	Pierre Bouchard	4	5	6	8	10	15	20	25
21	Dennis Maruk	4	5	6	8	10	15	20	
22	Mike Murphy	4	5	6	8	10	12	15	25
23	Cesare Maniago	4	5	6	8	10	15	20	
24	Paul Gardner RC	4	5	6	8	10	15	20	25
25	Rod Gilbert	4	5	6	8	10	15	20	25
26	Orest Kindrachuk	4	5	6	8	10	12	15	25
27	Bill Hajt	4	5	6	8	10	12	15	25
28	John Davidson	4	5	6	8	10	15	20	35
29	Jean-Paul Parise	4	5	6	8	10	12	15	25
30	Larry Robinson	4	5	6	8	10	15	20	40
31	Yvon Labre	4	5	6	8	10	12	15	25
32	Walt McKechnie	4	5	6	8	10	12	15	25
33	Rick Kehoe	4	5	6	8	10	15	20	25
34	Randy Holt	4	5	6	8	10	12	15	25
35	Garry Unger	4	5	6	8	10	15	20	
36	Lou Nanne	4	5	6	8	10	12	15	25
37	Dan Bouchard	4	5	6	8	10	12	15	25
38	Darryl Sittler	4	5	6	8	10	15	20	40
39	Bob Murdoch	4	5	6	8	10	12	15	25
40	Jean Ratelle	4	5	6	8	10	15	20	25
41	Dave Maloney	4	5	6	8	10	12	15	25
42	Danny Gare	4	5	6	8	10	15	20	
43	Jimmy Watson	4	5	6	8	10	12	15	25
44	Tom Williams	4	5	6	8	10	15	20	
45	Serge Savard	4	5	6	8	10	15	20	25
46	Derek Sanderson	4	5	6	8	10	15	20	
47	John Marks	4	5	6	8	10	12	15	25
48	Al Cameron	4	5	6	8	10	15	20	
49	Dean Talafous	4	5	6	8	10	12	15	25
50	Glenn Resch	4	5	6	8	10	15	20	35
51	Ron Schock	4	5	6	8	10	12	15	25
52	Gary Croteau	4	5	6	8	10	12	15	25
53	Gerry Meehan	4	5	6	8	10	12	15	25
54	Ed Staniowski	4	5	6	8	10	12	15	25
55	Phil Esposito UER	4	5	6	8	10	15	20	40
56	Dennis Ververgaert	4	5	6	8	10	12	15	25
57	Rick Wilson	4	5	6	8	10	12	15	25
58	Jim Lorentz	4	5	6	8	10	12	15	25
59	Bobby Schmautz	4	5	6	8	10	12	15	25
60	Guy Lapointe AS2	4	5	6	8	10	12	15	25
61	Ivan Boldirev	4	5	6	8	10	15	20	25
62	Bob Nystrom	4	5	6	8	10	15	20	
63	Rick Hampton	4	5	6	8	10	12	15	25
64	Jack Valiquette	4	5	6	8	10	12	15	25
65	Bernie Parent	4	5	6	8	10	15	20	
66	Dave Burrows	4	5	6	8	10	15	20	
67	Butch Goring	4	5	6	8	10	12	15	25
68A	Checklist 1-132 ERR	4	5	6	8	10	20	30	
68B	Checklist 1-132 COR								
69	Murray Wilson	4	5	6	8	10	12	15	25
70	Ed Giacomin	4	5	6	8	10	15	20	35
71	Flames Team/(checklist back)	4	5	6	8	10	15	20	35
72	Bruins Team/(checklist back)	4	5	6	8	10	15	20	
73	Sabres Team/(checklist back)	4	5	6	8	10	15	20	
74	Blackhawks Team/(checklist back)	4	5	6	8	10	15	20	
75	Barons Team/(checklist back)	4	5	6	8	10	15	20	
76	Rockies Team/(checklist back)	4	5	6	8	10	15	20	35
77	Red Wings Team/(checklist back)	4	5	6	8	10	15	20	35
78	Kings Team/(checklist back)	4	5	6	8	10	15	20	
79	North Stars Team/(checklist back)	4	5	6	8	10	15	20	35
80	Canadiens Team/(checklist back)	4	5	6	8	10	15	20	35
81	Islanders Team/(checklist back)	4	5	6	8	10	15	20	35
82	Rangers Team/(checklist back)	4	5	6	8	10	15	20	35
83	Flyers Team/(checklist back)	4	5	6	8	10	15	20	35
84	Penguins Team/(checklist back)	4	5	6	8	10	15	20	
85	Blues Team/(checklist back)	4	5	6	8	10	15	20	
86	Maple Leafs Team/(checklist back)	4	5	6	8	10	15	20	35
87	Canucks Team/(checklist back)	4	5	6	8	10	15	20	35
88	Capitals Team/(checklist back)	4	5	6	8	10	15	20	35
89	Keith Magnuson	4	5	6	8	10	12	15	25
90	Walt Tkaczuk	4	5	6	8	10	15	20	25
91	Bill Nyrop	4	5	6	8	10	12	15	25
92	Michel Plasse	4	5	6	8	10	15	20	25
93	Bob Bourne	4	5	6	8	10	15	20	
94	Lee Fogolin	4	5	6	8	10	12	15	25
95	Gregg Sheppard	4	5	6	8	10	15	20	
96	Hartland Monahan	4	5	6	8	10	12	15	25
97	Curt Bennett	4	5	6	8	10	15	20	
98	Bob Dailey	4	5	6	8	10	15	20	
99	Bill Goldsworthy	4	5	6	8	10	12	15	25
100	Ken Dryden	4	5	6	10	15	40	50	150
101	Grant Mulvey	4	5	6	8	10	12	15	25
102	Pierre Larouche	4	5	6	8	10	12	15	25

HOCKEY

#	Player	VG 3	VgEx 4	EX 5	ExMt 6	NM 7	NmMt 8	NmMt+ 8.5	MT 9
103	Nick Libett	4	5	6	8	10	15	20	
104	Rick Smith	4	5	6	8	10	12	15	25
105	Bryan Trottier	5	6	8	10	15	20	25	50
106	Pierre Jarry	4	5	6	8	10	12	15	25
107	Red Berenson	4	5	6	8	10	12	15	25
108	Jim Schoenfeld	4	5	6	8	10	12	15	25
109	Gilles Meloche	4	5	6	8	10	12	15	25
110	Lanny McDonald	4	5	6	8	10	15	20	35
111	Don Lever	4	5	6	8	10	12	15	25
112	Greg Polis	4	5	6	8	10	12	15	25
113	Gary Sargent RC	4	5	6	8	10	15	20	
114	Earl Anderson	4	5	6	8	10	12	15	25
115	Bobby Clarke	4	5	6	8	10	15	25	40
116	Dave Lewis	4	5	6	8	10	12	15	25
117	Darcy Rota	4	5	6	8	10	12	15	25
118	Andre Savard	4	5	6	8	10	12	15	25
119	Denis Herron	4	5	6	8	10	15	20	
120	Steve Shutt	4	5	6	8	10	15	20	35
121	Mel Bridgman	4	5	6	8	10	15	20	
122	Buster Harvey	4	5	6	8	10	15	20	
123	Roland Eriksson	4	5	6	8	10	12	15	25
124	Dale Tallon	4	5	6	8	10	12	15	25
125	Gilles Gilbert	4	5	6	8	10	12	15	25
126	Billy Harris	4	5	6	8	10	12	15	25
127	Tom Lysiak	4	5	6	8	10	12	15	25
128	Jerry Korab	4	5	6	8	10	12	15	25
129	Bob Gainey	4	5	6	8	10	15	20	35
130	Wilf Paiement	4	5	6	8	10	15	20	
131	Tom Bladon	4	5	6	8	10	12	15	25
132	Ernie Hicke	4	5	6	8	10	15	20	
133	J.P. LeBlanc	4	5	6	8	10	15	20	
134	Mike Milbury RC	4	5	8	10	15	25	30	80
135	Pit Martin	4	5	6	8	10	12	15	25
136	Steve Vickers	4	5	6	8	10	15	20	
137	Don Awrey	4	5	6	8	10	12	15	25
138	Bernie Wolfe	4	5	6	8	10	12	15	25
139	Doug Jarvis	4	5	6	8	10	12	15	25
140	Borje Salming	4	5	6	8	10	15	20	
141	Bob MacMillan	4	5	6	8	10	12	15	25
142	Wayne Stephenson	4	5	6	8	10	15	20	
143	Dave Forbes	4	5	6	8	10	12	15	25
144	Jean Potvin	4	5	6	8	10	12	15	25
145	Guy Charron	4	5	6	8	10	12	15	25
146	Cliff Koroll	4	5	6	8	10	12	15	25
147	Danny Grant	4	5	6	8	10	12	15	25
148	Bill Hogaboam	4	5	6	8	10	12	15	25
149	Al MacAdam	4	5	6	8	10	12	15	25
150	Gerry Desjardins	4	5	6	8	10	12	15	25
151	Yvon Lambert	4	5	6	8	10	12	15	25
152	Rick Lapointe	4	5	6	8	10	15	20	
153	Ed Westfall	4	5	6	8	10	15	20	
154	Carol Vadnais	4	5	6	8	10	15	20	
155	Johnny Bucyk	4	5	6	8	10	15	20	
156	J.P. Bordeleau	4	5	6	8	10	12	15	25
157	Ron Stackhouse	4	5	6	8	10	12	15	
158	Glen Sharpley	4	5	6	8	10	15	20	
159	Michel Bergeron	4	5	6	8	10	15	20	
160	Rogatien Vachon	4	5	6	8	10	15	20	35
161	Fred Stanfield	4	5	6	8	10	12	15	25
162	Gerry Hart	4	5	6	8	10	15	20	
163	Mario Tremblay	4	5	6	8	10	12	15	25
164	Andre Dupont	4	5	6	8	10	12	15	25
165	Don Marcotte	4	5	6	8	10	12	15	25
166	Wayne Dillon	4	5	6	8	10	12	15	25
167	Claude Larose	4	5	6	8	10	15	20	
168	Eric Vail	4	5	6	8	15	25	30	
169	Tom Edur	4	5	6	8	10	12	15	25
170	Tony Esposito	4	5	6	8	10	15	20	40
171	Andre St.Laurent	4	5	6	8	10	15	20	
172	Dan Maloney	4	5	6	8	10	12	15	25
173	Dennis O'Brien	4	5	6	8	10	12	15	25
174	Blair Chapman	4	5	6	8	10	12	15	25
175	Dennis Kearns	4	5	6	8	10	12	15	25
176	Wayne Merrick	4	5	6	8	10	15	20	
177	Michel Larocque	4	5	6	8	10	12	15	25
178	Bob Kelly	4	5	6	8	10	12	15	25
179	Dave Farrish	4	5	6	8	10	15	20	
180	Richard Martin AS2	4	5	6	8	10	12	15	25
181	Gary Doak	4	5	6	8	10	15	20	
182	Jude Drouin	4	5	6	8	10	12	15	25
183	Barry Dean	4	5	6	8	10	12	15	25
184	Gary Smith	4	5	6	8	10	15	20	
185	Reggie Leach	4	5	6	8	10	12	15	25
186	Ian Turnbull	4	5	6	8	10	12	15	25
187	Vic Venasky	4	5	6	8	10	15	20	
188	Wayne Bianchin	4	5	6	8	10	12	15	25
189	Doug Risebrough	4	5	6	8	10	15	20	
190	Brad Park	4	5	6	8	10	15	20	35
191	Craig Ramsay	4	5	6	8	10	12	15	25
192	Ken Hodge	4	5	6	8	10	12	15	25
193	Phil Myre	4	5	6	8	10	15	20	
194	Garry Howatt	4	5	6	8	10	12	15	25
195	Stan Mikita	4	5	6	8	10	15	20	40
196	Garnet Bailey	4	5	6	8	10	12	15	25
197	Dennis Hextall	4	5	6	8	10	15	20	
198	Nick Beverley	4	5	6	8	10	15	20	
199	Larry Patey	4	5	6	8	10	15	20	
200	Guy Lafleur	4	5	6	10	15	25	30	100
201	Don Edwards RC	4	5	6	8	10	15	20	80
202	Gary Dornhoefer	4	5	6	8	10	12	15	25
203	Bob Paradise	4	5	6	8	10	12	15	25
204	Alex Pirus	4	5	6	8	10	12	15	25
205	Peter Mahovlich	4	5	6	8	10	12	15	25
206	Bert Marshall	4	5	6	8	10	12	15	25
207	Gilles Gratton	4	5	6	8	10	12	15	25
208	Alain Daigle	4	5	6	8	10	15	20	
209	Chris Oddleifson	4	5	6	8	10	12	15	25
210	Gilbert Perreault	4	5	6	8	10	15	20	60
211	Mike Palmateer RC	4	5	6	10	15	30	40	80
212	Billy Lochead	4	5	6	8	10	12	15	25
213	Dick Redmond	4	5	6	8	10	15	20	
214	Guy Lafleur RB	4	5	6	8	10	15	20	35
215	Ian Turnbull RB	4	5	6	8	10	12	15	25
216	Guy Lafleur RB	4	5	6	8	10	15	20	35
217	Steve Shutt RB	4	5	6	8	10	12	15	25
218	Guy Lafleur RB	4	5	6	8	10	15	20	35
219	Lorne Henning	4	5	6	8	10	12	15	25
220	Terry O'Reilly	4	5	6	8	10	12	15	25
221	Pat Hickey	4	5	6	8	10	12	15	25
222	Rene Robert	4	5	6	8	10	12	15	25
223	Tim Young	4	5	6	8	10	12	15	25
224	Dunc Wilson	4	5	6	8	10	15	20	
225	Dennis Hull	4	5	6	8	10	12	15	25
226	Rod Seiling	4	5	6	8	10	15	20	
227	Bill Barber	4	5	6	8	10	12	15	25
228	Dennis Polonich	4	5	6	8	10	12	15	25
229	Billy Smith	4	5	6	8	10	15	20	35
230	Yvan Cournoyer	4	5	6	8	10	12	15	
231	Don Luce	4	5	6	8	10	12	15	25
232	Mike McEwen RC	4	5	6	8	10	15	20	
233	Don Saleski	4	5	6	8	10	12	15	25
234	Wayne Cashman	4	5	6	8	10	12	15	25
235	Phil Russell	4	5	6	8	10	12	15	25
236	Mike Corrigan	4	5	6	8	10	12	15	25
237	Guy Chouinard	4	5	6	8	10	12	15	25
238	Steve Jensen	4	5	6	8	10	12	15	25
239	Jim Rutherford	4	5	6	8	10	12	15	25
240	Marcel Dionne	4	5	6	8	10	15	20	40
241	Rejean Houle	4	5	6	8	10	12	15	25
242	Jocelyn Guevremont	4	5	6	8	10	12	15	25
243	Jim Harrison	4	5	6	8	10	12	15	25
244	Don Murdoch	4	5	6	8	10	15	20	
245	Rick Green RC	4	5	6	8	10	12	15	25
246	Rick Middleton	4	5	6	8	10	15	20	
247	Joe Watson	4	5	6	8	10	12	15	25
248	Syl Apps	4	5	6	8	10	15	20	
249	Checklist 133-264	4	5	6	10	20	40		
250	Clark Gillies	4	5	6	8	10	15	20	
251	Bobby Orr	6	10	12	15	25	60	80	150
252	Nelson Pyatt	4	5	6	8	10	12	15	25
253	Gary McAdam	4	5	6	8	10	12	15	25
254	Jacques Lemaire	4	5	6	8	10	12	15	25
255	Bob Girard	4	5	6	8	10	12	15	25
256	Ron Greschner	4	5	6	8	10	12	15	25
257	Ross Lonsberry	4	5	6	8	10	12	15	25
258	Dave Gardner	4	5	6	8	10	12	15	25
259	Rick Blight	4	5	6	8	10	12	15	25
260	Gerry Cheevers	4	5	6	8	10	15	20	35
261	Jean Pronovost	4	5	6	8	10	15	20	
262	Cup Semi-Finals	4	5	6	8	10	12	15	25
263	Cup Semi-Finals	4	5	6	8	10	12	15	25
264	Canadiens Champs	4	5	6	8	10	12	15	25
265	Rick Bowness RC	4	5	6	8	12	20	25	40
266	George Ferguson	4	5	6	8	10	12	15	25
267	Mike Kitchen RC	4	5	6	8	10	12	15	25
268	Bob Berry	4	5	6	8	10	12	15	25
269	Greg Smith RC	4	5	6	8	10	12	15	25
270	Stan Jonathan RC	4	5	6	8	10	15	20	40
271	Dwight Bialowas	4	5	6	8	10	12	15	25
272	Pete Stemkowski	4	5	6	8	10	12	15	
273	Greg Joly	4	5	6	8	10	12	15	25
274	Ken Houston RC	4	5	6	8	10	12	15	25
275	Brian Glennie	4	5	6	8	10	12	15	25
276	Ed Johnston	4	5	6	8	10	12	15	25
277	John Grisdale	4	5	6	8	10	12	15	25
278	Craig Patrick	4	5	6	8	10	12	15	25
279	Ken Breitenbach RC	4	5	6	8	10	12	15	25
280	Fred Ahern	4	5	6	8	10	12	15	25
281	Jim Roberts	4	5	6	8	10	12	15	25
282	Harvey Bennett RC	4	5	6	8	10	15	20	

#		VG 3	VgEx 4	EX 5	ExMt 6	NM 7	NmMt 8	NmMt+ 8.5	MT 9
283	Ab DeMarco	4	5	6	8	10	12	15	25
284	Pat Boutette	4	5	6	8	10	12	15	25
285	Bob Plager	4	5	6	8	10	12	15	25
286	Hilliard Graves	4	5	6	8	10	12	15	25
287	Gordie Lane RC	4	5	6	8	10	12	15	25
288	Ron Andruff	4	5	6	8	10	12	15	25
289	Larry Brown	4	5	6	8	10	12	15	25
290	Mike Fidler	4	5	6	8	10	12	15	25
291	Fred Barrett	4	5	6	8	10	12	15	25
292	Bill Clement	4	5	6	8	10	12	15	25
293	Errol Thompson	4	5	6	8	10	12	15	25
294	Doug Grant	4	5	6	8	10	12	15	25
295	Harold Snepsts	4	5	6	8	10	15	20	35
296	Rick Bragnalo	4	5	6	8	10	15	20	
297	Bryan Lefley	4	5	6	8	10	12	15	25
298	Gene Carr	4	5	6	8	10	12	15	25
299	Bob Stewart	4	5	6	8	10	15	20	
300	Lew Morrison	4	5	6	8	10	12	15	25
301	Ed Kea	4	5	6	8	10	12	15	25
302	Scott Garland	4	5	6	8	10	15	20	
303	Bill Fairbairn	4	5	6	8	10	12	15	25
304	Larry Carriere	4	5	6	8	10	12	15	25
305	Ron Low	4	5	6	8	10	12	15	25
306	Tom Reid	4	5	6	8	10	12	15	25
307	Paul Holmgren RC	4	5	6	8	10	15	20	40
308	Pat Price	4	5	6	8	10	12	15	25
309	Kirk Bowman	4	5	6	8	10	15	20	
310	Bobby Simpson	4	5	6	8	10	12	15	25
311	Ron Ellis	4	5	6	8	10	12	15	25
312	R.Bourbonnais (Federko)	4	5	6	8	10	15	20	35
313	Bobby Lalonde	4	5	6	8	10	12	15	25
314	Tony White	4	5	6	8	10	12	15	25
315	John Van Boxmeer	4	5	6	8	10	12	15	25
316	Don Kozak	4	5	6	8	10	12	15	25
317	Jim Neilson	4	5	6	8	10	12	15	25
318	Terry Martin	4	5	6	8	10	12	15	25
319	Barry Gibbs	4	5	6	8	10	15	20	
320	Inge Hammarstrom	4	5	6	8	10	12	15	25
321	Darryl Edestrand	4	5	6	8	10	12	15	25
322	Flames Logo	4	5	6	8	10	15	20	35
323	Bruins Logo	4	5	6	8	10	15	20	35
324	Sabres Logo	4	5	6	8	10	15	20	35
325	Blackhawks Logo	4	5	6	8	10	15	20	35
326	Barons Logo	4	5	6	8	10	15	20	35
327	Rockies Logo	4	5	6	8	10	15	20	35
328	Red Wings Logo	4	5	6	8	10	15	20	35
329	Kings Logo	4	5	6	8	10	15	20	35
330	North Stars Logo	4	5	6	8	10	15	20	35
331	Canadiens Logo	4	5	6	8	10	15	20	35
332	Islanders Logo	4	5	6	8	10	15	20	35
333	Rangers Logo	4	5	6	8	10	15	20	35
334	Flyers Logo	4	5	6	8	10	15	20	35
335	Penguins Logo	4	5	6	8	10	15	20	35
336	Blues Logo	4	5	6	8	10	15	20	35
337	Maple Leafs Logo	4	5	6	8	10	15	20	35
338	Canucks Logo	4	5	6	8	10	15	20	35
339	Capitals Logo	4	5	6	8	10	15	20	35
340	Chuck Lefley	4	5	6	8	10	12	15	25
341	Garry Monahan	4	5	6	8	10	12	15	25
342	Bryan Watson	4	5	6	8	10	12	15	25
343	Dave Hudson	4	5	6	8	10	12	15	25
344	Neil Komadoski	4	5	6	8	10	12	15	25
345	Gary Edwards	4	5	6	8	10	12	15	25
346	Rey Comeau	4	5	6	8	10	15	20	
347	Bob Neely	4	5	6	8	10	12	15	25
348	Jean Hamel	4	5	6	8	10	12	15	25
349	Jerry Butler	4	5	6	8	10	15	20	
350	Mike Walton	4	5	6	8	10	12	15	25
351	Bob Sirois	4	5	6	8	10	12	15	25
352	Jim McElmury	4	5	6	8	10	12	15	25
353	Dave Schultz	4	5	6	8	10	12	15	25
354	Doug Palazzari	4	5	6	8	10	12	15	25
355	David Shand	4	5	6	8	10	12	15	25
356	Stan Weir	4	5	6	8	10	12	15	25
357	Mike Christie	4	5	6	8	10	12	15	25
358	Floyd Thomson	4	5	6	8	10	12	15	25
359	Larry Goodenough	4	5	6	8	10	15	20	
360	Bill Riley	4	5	6	8	10	15	20	
361	Doug Hicks	4	5	6	8	10	15	20	
362	Dan Newman	4	5	6	8	10	15	20	
363	Rick Chartraw	4	5	6	8	10	15	20	
364	Tim Ecclestone	4	5	6	8	10	15	20	
365	Don Ashby	4	5	6	8	10	12	15	25
366	Jacques Richard	4	5	6	8	10	12	15	25
367	Yves Belanger	4	5	6	8	10	12	15	25
368	Ron Sedlbauer	4	5	6	8	10	12	15	25
369	Jack Lynch UER (Collins)	4	5	6	8	10	15	20	
370	Doug Favell	4	5	6	8	10	12	15	25
371	Bob Murdoch	4	5	6	8	10	12	15	25
372	Ralph Klassen	4	5	6	8	10	15	20	

#		VG 3	VgEx 4	EX 5	ExMt 6	NM 7	NmMt 8	NmMt+ 8.5	MT 9
373	Richard Mulhern	4	5	6	8	10	12	15	25
374	Jim McKenny	4	5	6	8	10	15	20	
375	Mike Bloom	4	5	6	8	10	12	15	25
376	Bruce Affleck	4	5	6	8	10	15	20	
377	Gerry O'Flaherty	4	5	6	8	10	12	15	25
378	Ron Lalonde	4	5	6	8	10	12	15	25
379	Chuck Arnason	4	5	6	8	10	12	15	25
380	Dave Hutchinson	4	5	6	8	10	12	15	25
381A	Checklist ERR Topps	4	5	6	10	20	35	40	
381B	Checklist COR No Topps	4	5	6	10	20	25	30	60
382	John Gould	4	5	6	8	10	12	15	25
383	Dave Williams	4	5	6	8	10	15	20	40
384	Len Frig	4	5	6	8	10	12	15	25
385	Pierre Plante	4	5	6	8	10	12	15	25
386	Ralph Stewart	4	5	6	8	10	12	15	25
387	Gord Smith	4	5	6	8	10	12	15	25
388	Denis Dupere	4	5	6	8	10	12	15	25
389	Randy Manery	4	5	6	8	10	12	15	25
390	Lowell MacDonald	4	5	6	8	10	12	15	25
391	Dennis Owchar	4	5	6	8	10	12	15	25
392	Jim Roberts RC	4	5	6	8	10	12	15	25
393	Mike Veisor	4	5	6	8	10	15	20	
394	Bob Hess	4	5	6	8	10	12	15	25
395	Curt Ridley	4	5	6	8	10	15	15	25
396	Mike Lampman	4	5	6	8	10	15	20	

— Mike Milbury RC #134 PSA 10 (Gem) sold for $169.66 (eBay; 4/12)

1977-78 O-Pee-Chee WHA

#		VG 3	VgEx 4	EX 5	ExMt 6	NM 7	NmMt 8	NmMt+ 8.5	MT 9
	COMMON CARD (1-66)	4	5	6	8	10	12	15	25
1	Gordie Howe	15	20	25	30	40	100		
2	Jean Bernier RC	5	6	8	10	12	20		
3	Anders Hedberg	5	8	10	12	15	50		
4	Ken Broderick	4	5	6	8	10	12		
5	Joe Noris	5	6	8	10	12	20		
6	Blaine Stoughton	5	6	8	10	12	20		
7	Claude St.Sauveur	5	6	8	10	12	20		
8.	Real Cloutier	4	5	6	8	10	15	20	30
9	Joe Daley	4	5	6	8	10	15	20	30
11	Wayne Rutledge	4	5	6	8	10	15	20	30
12	Mark Napier	4	5	6	8	10	15	20	30
14	Don McLeod	4	5	6	8	10	12	15	30
15	Ulf Nilsson	4	5	6	8	10	15		
16	Blair MacDonald	4	5	6	8	10	12		
17	Mike Rogers	4	5	6	8	10	12	15	30
18	Gary Inness	4	5	6	8	10	12		
19	Larry Lund	4	5	6	8	10	12		
20	Marc Tardif	4	5	6	8	10	12	15	30
21	Lars-Erik Sjoberg	4	5	6	8	10	12		
22	Bryan Campbell	4	5	6	8	10	12		
23	John Garrett	4	5	6	8	10	12	15	30
25	Mark Howe	5	6	8	10	12	20	25	40
28	Dave Dryden	4	5	6	8	10	12		
29	Reg Thomas	4	5	6	8	10	12		
30	Andre Lacroix	4	5	6	8	10	12	15	30
31	Paul Henderson	4	5	6	8	10	12		
33	Juha Widing	4	5	6	8	10	12	15	30
35	Robbie Ftorek	4	5	6	10	12			
37	Terry Ruskowski	4	5	6	8	10	12		
38	Richard Brodeur	4	5	6	8	10	15	20	40
39	Willy Lindstrom RC	4	5	6	8	10	15	20	50
40	Al Hamilton	4	5	6	10	12			
41	John McKenzie	4	5	6	8	10	12	15	30
42	Wayne Wood	4	5	6	8	10	12		
44	J.C. Tremblay	4	5	6	8	10	12		
45	Gary Bromley	4	5	6	10	12			
47	Bobby Sheehan	4	5	6	10	12			
48	Don Larway RC	4	5	6	8	10	12		
49	Al Smith	4	5	6	8	10	12	15	30
50	Bobby Hull	6	8	10	12	20	40		
56	Jim Park RC	4	5	6	8	10	12	15	30
57	Dan Labraaten RC	4	5	6	8	10	12		
58	Checklist Card	5	6	8	10	12	25		
59	Paul Shmyr	4	5	6	8	10	12		
60	Serge Bernier	4	5	6	8	10	12	15	30
61	Frank Mahovlich	5	6	8	10	12	20	25	80
62	Michel Dion	4	5	6	8	10	12		
63	Poul Popiel	4	5	6	8	10	12		
64	Lyle Moffat	4	5	6	10	12			
65	Marty Howe	4	5	6	8	10	12	20	
66	Don Burgess	5	8	10	12	15	40		

1977-78 Topps

#		VG 3	VgEx 4	EX 5	ExMt 6	NM 7	NmMt 8	NmMt+ 8.5	MT 9
1	Shutt/Lafleur/Dionne LL	4	5	6	8	10	15	25	40
2	Lafleur/Dionne/Sal LL	4	5	6	8	10	12	15	20
3	Lafleur/Dionne/Shutt LL	4	5	6	8	10	12	15	20
4	Williams/Polnch/Gasff LL	4	5	6	8	10	12	15	20
5	McDonald/Espo/Will LL	4	5	6	8	10	12	15	20

#		VG 3	VgEx 4	EX 5	ExMt 6	NM 7	NmMt 8	NmMt+ 8.5	MT 9
6	Laroc/Dryden/Resch LL	4	5	6	8	10	12	15	20
7	Perr/Shutt/Lafleur LL	4	5	6	8	10	12	15	20
8	Dryden/Vach/Parent LL	4	5	6	8	10	12	15	20
9	Brian Spencer	4	5	6	8	10	12	15	20
10	Denis Potvin AS2	4	5	6	8	10	12	15	20
11	Nick Fotiu	4	5	6	8	10	12	15	20
12	Bob Murray	4	5	6	8	10	12	15	20
13	Pete Lopresti	4	5	6	8	10	12	15	20
14	J. Bob Kelly	4	5	6	8	10	12	15	20
15	Rick MacLeish	4	5	6	8	10	12		
16	Terry Harper	4	5	6	8	10	12	15	20
17	Willi Plett RC	4	5	6	8	10	12	15	20
18	Peter McNab	4	5	6	8	10	12	15	20
19	Wayne Thomas	4	5	6	8	10	12	15	20
20	Pierre Bouchard	4	5	6	8	10	12	15	20
21	Dennis Maruk	4	5	6	8	10	12	15	20
22	Mike Murphy	4	5	6	8	10	12	15	20
23	Cesare Maniago	4	5	6	8	10	12	15	20
24	Paul Gardner RC	4	5	6	8	10	12	15	20
25	Rod Gilbert	4	5	6	8	10	12	15	20
26	Orest Kindrachuk	4	5	6	8	10	12	15	20
27	Bill Hajt	4	5	6	8	10	12	15	20
28	John Davidson	4	5	6	8	10	12	15	20
29	Jean-Paul Parise	4	5	6	8	10	12	15	20
30	Larry Robinson AS1	4	5	6	8	10	12	15	20
31	Yvon Labre	4	5	6	8	10	12	15	20
32	Walt McKechnie	4	5	6	8	10	12	15	20
33	Rick Kehoe	4	5	6	8	10	12	15	20
34	Randy Holt RC	4	5	6	8	10	12	15	20
35	Garry Unger	4	5	6	8	10	12	15	20
36	Lou Nanne	4	5	6	8	10	12		
37	Dan Bouchard	4	5	6	8	10	12	15	20
38	Darryl Sittler	4	5	6	8	10	12	15	25
39	Bob Murdoch	4	5	6	8	10	12	15	20
40	Jean Ratelle	4	5	6	8	10	12	15	20
41	Dave Maloney	4	5	6	8	10	12	15	20
42	Danny Gare	4	5	6	8	10	12		
43	Jimmy Watson	4	5	6	8	10	12	15	20
44	Tom Williams	4	5	6	8	10	12	15	20
45	Serge Savard	4	5	6	8	10	12	15	20
46	Derek Sanderson	4	5	6	8	10	12		
47	John Marks	4	5	6	8	10	12		
48	Al Cameron RC	4	5	6	8	10	12	15	20
49	Dean Talafous	4	5	6	8	10	12	15	20
50	Glenn Resch	4	5	6	8	10	12	15	20
51	Ron Schock	4	5	6	8	10	12	15	20
52	Gary Croteau	4	5	6	8	10	12		
53	Gerry Meehan	4	5	6	8	10	12	15	20
54	Ed Staniowski	4	5	6	8	10	12	15	20
55	Phil Esposito	4	5	6	8	10	12	15	25
56	Dennis Ververgaert	4	5	6	8	10	12	15	20
57	Rick Wilson	4	5	6	8	10	12	15	20
58	Jim Lorentz	4	5	6	8	10	12	15	20
59	Bobby Schmautz	4	5	6	8	10	12		
60	Guy Lapointe AS2	4	5	6	8	10	12	15	20
61	Ivan Boldirev	4	5	6	8	10	12	15	20
62	Bob Nystrom	4	5	6	8	10	12	15	20
63	Rick Hampton	4	5	6	8	10	12	15	20
64	Jack Valiquette	4	5	6	8	10	12	15	20
65	Bernie Parent	4	5	6	8	10	12		
66	Dave Burrows	4	5	6	8	10	12		
67	Butch Goring	4	5	6	8	10	12	15	20
68	Checklist 1-132	4	5	6	10	12	15		
69	Murray Wilson	4	5	6	8	10	12	15	20
70	Ed Giacomin	4	5	6	8	10	12	15	20
71	Flames Team CL	4	5	6	8	10	12	15	20
72	Bruins Team CL	4	5	6	8	10	12	15	20
73	Sabres Team CL	4	5	6	8	10	12	15	20
74	Blackhawks Team CL	4	5	6	8	10	12	15	20
75	Barons Team CL	4	5	6	8	10	12	15	20
76	Rockies Team CL	4	5	6	8	10	12	15	20
77	Red Wings Team CL	4	5	6	8	10	12	15	20
78	Kings Team CL	4	5	6	8	10	12		
79	North Stars Team CL	4	5	6	8	10	12	15	20
80	Canadiens Team CL	4	5	6	8	10	12	15	20
81	Islanders Team CL	4	5	6	8	10	12	15	20
82	Rangers Team CL	4	5	6	8	10	12	15	20
83	Flyers Team CL	4	5	6	8	10	12	15	20
84	Penguins Team CL	4	5	6	8	10	12	15	20
85	Blues Team CL	4	5	6	8	10	12	15	20
86	Maple Leafs Team CL	4	5	6	8	10	12	15	20
87	Canucks Team CL	4	5	6	8	10	12	15	20
88	Capitals Team CL	4	5	6	8	10	12	15	20
89	Keith Magnuson	4	5	6	8	10	12	15	20
90	Walt Tkaczuk	4	5	6	8	10	12	15	20
91	Bill Nyrop	4	5	6	8	10	12	15	20
92	Michel Plasse	4	5	6	8	10	12	15	20
93	Bob Bourne	4	5	6	8	10	12		
94	Lee Fogolin	4	5	6	8	10	12	15	20
95	Gregg Sheppard	4	5	6	8	10	12	15	20

#		VG 3	VgEx 4	EX 5	ExMt 6	NM 7	NmMt 8	NmMt+ 8.5	MT 9
96	Hartland Monahan	4	5	6	8	10	12	15	20
97	Curt Bennett	4	5	6	8	10	12	15	20
98	Bob Dailey	4	5	6	8	10	12	15	20
99	Bill Goldsworthy	4	5	6	8	10	12	15	20
100	Ken Dryden AS1	4	5	6	8	10	12	15	25
101	Grant Mulvey	4	5	6	8	10	12	15	20
102	Pierre Larouche	4	5	6	8	10	12	15	20
103	Nick Libett	4	5	6	8	10	12		
104	Rick Smith	4	5	6	8	10	12	15	20
105	Bryan Trottier	5	6	8	10	12	15	20	25
106	Pierre Jarry	4	5	6	8	10	12	15	20
107	Red Berenson	4	5	6	8	10	12	15	20
108	Jim Schoenfeld	4	5	6	8	10	12	15	20
109	Gilles Meloche	4	5	6	8	10	12	15	20
110	Lanny McDonald AS2	4	5	6	8	10	12	15	20
111	Don Lever	4	5	6	8	10	12	15	20
112	Greg Polis	4	5	6	8	10	12	15	20
113	Gary Sargent RC	4	5	6	8	10	12	15	20
114	Earl Anderson RC	4	5	6	8	10	12	15	20
115	Bobby Clarke	4	5	6	8	10	12	15	20
116	Dave Lewis	4	5	6	8	10	12	15	20
117	Darcy Rota	4	5	6	8	10	12		
118	Andre Savard	4	5	6	8	10	12	15	20
119	Denis Herron	4	5	6	8	10	12	15	20
120	Steve Shutt AS1	4	5	6	8	10	12	15	20
121	Mel Bridgman	4	5	6	8	10	12		
122	Buster Harvey	4	5	6	8	10	12	15	20
123	Roland Eriksson RC	4	5	6	8	10	12	15	20
124	Dale Tallon	4	5	6	8	10	12		
125	Gilles Gilbert	4	5	6	8	10	12	15	20
126	Billy Harris	4	5	6	8	10	12	15	20
127	Tom Lysiak	4	5	6	8	10	12	15	20
128	Jerry Korab	4	5	6	8	10	12	15	20
129	Bob Gainey	4	5	6	8	10	12	15	20
130	Wilf Paiement	4	5	6	8	10	12	15	20
131A	Tom Bladon Standing	4	5	6	8	10	12	15	25
131B	Tom Bladon Skating	4	5	6	8	10	12	15	20
132	Ernie Hicke	4	5	6	8	10	12	15	20
133	J.P. LeBlanc	4	5	6	8	10	12	15	20
134	Mike Milbury RC	4	5	6	8	10	12	15	25
135	Pit Martin	4	5	6	8	10	12	15	20
136	Steve Vickers	4	5	6	8	10	12	15	20
137	Don Awrey	4	5	6	8	10	12	15	20
138A	Bernie Wolfe MacAdam	4	5	6	8	10	12		
138B	Bernie Wolfe COR	4	5	6	8	10	12	15	20
139	Doug Jarvis	4	5	6	8	10	12	15	20
140	Borje Salming AS1	4	5	6	8	10	12		
141	Bob MacMillan	4	5	6	8	10	12	15	20
142	Wayne Stephenson	4	5	6	8	10	12	15	20
143	Dave Forbes	4	5	6	8	10	12	15	20
144	Jean Potvin	4	5	6	8	10	12	15	20
145	Guy Charron	4	5	6	8	10	12	15	20
146	Cliff Koroll	4	5	6	8	10	12	15	20
147	Danny Grant	4	5	6	8	10	12	15	20
148	Bill Hogaboam UER	4	5	6	8	10	12	15	20
149A	Al MacAdam ERR Wolfe	4	5	6	8	10	12	15	20
149B	Al MacAdam COR	4	5	6	8	10	12	15	20
150	Gerry Desjardins	4	5	6	8	10	12	15	20
151	Yvon Lambert	4	5	6	8	10	12	15	20
152A	Rick Lapointe ERR	4	5	6	8	10	12	15	20
152B	Rick Lapointe COR	4	5	6	8	10	12	15	20
153	Ed Westfall	4	5	6	8	10	12	15	20
154	Carol Vadnais	4	5	6	8	10	12	15	20
155	Johnny Bucyk	4	5	6	8	10	12		
156	J.P. Bordeleau	4	5	6	8	10	12	15	20
157	Ron Stackhouse	4	5	6	8	10	12	15	20
158	Glen Sharpley RC	4	5	6	8	10	12		
159	Michel Bergeron	4	5	6	8	10	12	15	20
160	Rogatien Vachon AS2	4	5	6	8	10	12	15	20
161	Fred Stanfield	4	5	6	8	10	12	15	20
162	Gerry Hart	4	5	6	8	10	12	15	20
163	Mario Tremblay	4	5	6	8	10	12	15	20
164	Andre Dupont	4	5	6	8	10	12	15	20
165	Don Marcotte	4	5	6	8	10	12	15	20
166	Wayne Dillon	4	5	6	8	10	12	15	20
167	Claude Larose	4	5	6	8	10	12	15	20
168	Eric Vail	4	5	6	8	10	12		
169	Tom Edur	4	5	6	8	10	12	15	20
170	Tony Esposito	4	5	6	8	10	12	15	20
171	Andre St.Laurent	4	5	6	8	10	12	15	20
172	Dan Maloney	4	5	6	8	10	12	15	20
173	Dennis O'Brien	4	5	6	8	10	12	15	20
174	Blair Chapman RC	4	5	6	8	10	12	15	20
175	Dennis Kearns	4	5	6	8	10	12	15	20
176	Wayne Merrick	4	5	6	8	10	12	15	20
177	Michel Larocque	4	5	6	8	10	12	15	20
178	Bob Kelly	4	5	6	8	10	12	15	20
179	Dave Farrish RC	4	5	6	8	10	12		
180	Richard Martin AS2	4	5	6	8	10	12	15	20
181	Gary Doak	4	5	6	8	10	12	15	20

#	Player	VG 3	VgEx 4	EX 5	ExMt 6	NM 7	NmMt 8	NmMt+ 8.5	MT 9
182	Jude Drouin	4	5	6	8	10	12	15	20
183	Barry Dean RC	4	5	6	8	10	12	15	20
184	Gary Smith	4	5	6	8	10	12		
185	Reggie Leach	4	5	6	8	10	12	15	20
186	Ian Turnbull	4	5	6	8	10	12		
187	Vic Venasky	4	5	6	8	10	12	15	20
188	Wayne Bianchin RC	4	5	6	8	10	12	15	20
189	Doug Risebrough	4	5	6	8	10	12	15	20
190	Brad Park	4	5	6	8	10	12	15	20
191	Craig Ramsay	4	5	6	8	10	12	15	20
192	Ken Hodge	4	5	6	8	10	12	15	20
193	Phil Myre	4	5	6	8	10	12		
194	Garry Howatt	4	5	6	8	10	12	15	20
195	Stan Mikita	4	5	6	8	10	12	15	30
196	Garnet Bailey	4	5	6	8	10	12		
197	Dennis Hextall	4	5	6	8	10	12	15	20
198	Nick Beverley	4	5	6	8	10	12	15	20
199	Larry Patey	4	5	6	8	10	12	15	20
200	Guy Lafleur AS1	4	5	6	8	10	12	15	25
201	Don Edwards RC	4	5	6	8	10	12	15	30
202	Gary Dornhoefer	4	5	6	8	10	12		
203	Stan Gilbertson	4	5	6	8	10	12	15	20
204	Alex Pirus RC	4	5	6	8	10	12	15	20
205	Peter Mahovlich	4	5	6	8	10	12	15	20
206	Bert Marshall	4	5	6	8	10	12	15	20
207	Gilles Gratton	4	5	6	8	10	12	15	20
208	Alain Daigle	4	5	6	8	10	12	15	20
209	Chris Oddleifson	4	5	6	8	10	12	15	20
210	Gilbert Perreault AS2	4	5	6	8	10	12	15	40
211	Mike Palmateer RC	4	5	6	8	12	20		
212	Billy Lochead	4	5	6	8	10	12	15	20
213	Dick Redmond	4	5	6	8	10	12	15	20
214	Guy Lafleur RB	4	5	6	8	10	12	15	25
215	Ian Turnbull RB	4	5	6	8	10	12	15	20
216	Guy Lafleur RB	4	5	6	8	10	12	15	25
217	Steve Shutt RB	4	5	6	8	10	12	15	20
218	Guy Lafleur RB	4	5	6	8	10	12	15	25
219	Lorne Henning	4	5	6	8	10	12	15	20
220	Terry O'Reilly	4	5	6	8	10	12	15	20
221	Pat Hickey	4	5	6	8	10	12	15	20
222	Rene Robert	4	5	6	8	10	12		
223	Tim Young	4	5	6	8	10	12	15	20
224	Dunc Wilson	4	5	6	8	10	12		
225	Dennis Hull	4	5	6	8	10	12		
226	Rod Seiling	4	5	6	8	10	12		
227	Bill Barber	4	5	6	8	10	12	15	20
228	Dennis Polonich RC	4	5	6	8	10	12	15	20
229	Billy Smith	4	5	6	8	10	12	15	25
230	Yvan Cournoyer	4	5	6	8	10	12	15	20
231	Don Luce	4	5	6	8	10	12	15	20
232	Mike McEwen RC	4	5	6	8	10	12	15	20
233	Don Saleski	4	5	6	8	10	12	15	20
234	Wayne Cashman	4	5	6	8	10	12	15	20
235	Phil Russell	4	5	6	8	10	12		
236	Mike Corrigan	4	5	6	8	10	12	15	20
237	Guy Chouinard	4	5	6	8	10	12	15	20
238	Steve Jensen RC	4	5	6	8	10	12		
239	Jim Rutherford	4	5	6	8	10	12	15	20
240	Marcel Dionne AS1	4	5	6	8	10	12	15	25
241	Rejean Houle	4	5	6	8	10	12		
242	Jocelyn Guevremont	4	5	6	8	10	12		
243	Jim Harrison	4	5	6	8	10	12	15	20
244	Don Murdoch RC	4	5	6	8	10	12		
245	Rick Green RC	4	5	6	8	10	12	15	20
246	Rick Middleton	4	5	6	8	10	12	15	20
247	Joe Watson	4	5	6	8	10	12	15	20
248	Syl Apps	4	5	6	8	10	12		
249	Checklist 133-264	4	5	6	10	12	15	20	25
250	Clark Gillies	4	5	6	8	10	12		
251	Bobby Orr	6	8	10	12	15	25	30	60
252	Nelson Pyatt	4	5	6	8	10	12	15	20
253	Gary McAdam RC	4	5	6	8	10	12	15	20
254	Jacques Lemaire	4	5	6	8	10	12	15	20
255	Bill Fairbairn	4	5	6	8	10	12	15	20
256	Ron Greschner	4	5	6	8	10	12	15	20
257	Ross Lonsberry	4	5	6	8	10	12	15	20
258	Dave Gardner	4	5	6	8	10	12	15	20
259	Rick Blight	4	5	6	8	10	12	15	20
260	Gerry Cheevers	4	5	6	8	10	12	15	20
261	Jean Pronovost	4	5	6	8	10	12	15	20
262	Mon/NYI Semi-Finals	4	5	6	8	10	12	15	20
263	Bruins Semi-Finals	4	5	6	8	10	12	15	20
264	Canadiens Champs	4	5	6	8	10	12	15	20

1978-79 O-Pee-Chee

#	Player	VG 3	VgEx 4	EX 5	ExMt 6	NM 7	NmMt 8	NmMt+ 8.5	MT 9
	COMMON CARD (1-396)	4	4	5	8	10	15	20	
	Mike Bossy HL	6	8	12	15	40	120	135	200
	Phil Esposito HL	4	5	6	8	10	15	20	
	Guy Lafleur HL	4	5	6	8	10	15	20	
4	Darryl Sittler HL	4	5	6	8	10	15	20	
5	Garry Unger HL	4	5	6	8	10	15	20	
6	Gary Edwards	4	5	6	8	10	15	20	
7	Rick Blight	4	5	6	8	10	15	20	
8	Larry Patey	4	5	6	8	10	15	20	
9	Craig Ramsay	4	5	6	8	10	15	20	30
10	Bryan Trottier	5	6	8	10	12	15	20	40
11	Don Murdoch	4	5	6	8	10	15	20	
12	Phil Russell	4	5	6	8	10	15	20	
13	Doug Jarvis	4	5	6	8	10	15	20	
14	Gene Carr	4	5	6	8	10	15	20	
15	Bernie Parent	4	5	6	8	10	15	20	35
16	Perry Miller	4	5	6	8	10	15	20	
17	Kent-Erik Andersson RC	4	5	6	8	10	15	20	
18	Gregg Sheppard	4	5	6	8	10	15	20	
19	Dennis Owchar	4	5	6	8	10	15	20	
20	Rogatien Vachon	4	5	6	8	10	15	20	
21	Dan Maloney	4	5	6	8	10	15	20	
22	Guy Charron	4	5	6	8	10	15	20	
23	Dick Redmond	4	5	6	8	10	15	20	
24	Checklist 1-132	5	6	8	10	12	20	30	60
25	Anders Hedberg	4	5	6	8	10	15	20	
26	Mel Bridgman	4	5	6	8	10	15	20	
27	Lee Fogolin	4	5	6	8	10	15	20	
28	Gilles Meloche	4	5	6	8	10	15	20	
29	Garry Howatt	4	5	6	8	10	15	20	
30	Darryl Sittler	4	5	6	8	10	15	20	
31	Curt Bennett	4	5	6	8	10	15	20	
32	Andre St.Laurent	4	5	6	8	10	15	20	
33	Blair Chapman	4	5	6	8	10	15	20	
34	Keith Magnuson	4	5	6	8	10	15	20	35
35	Pierre Larouche	4	5	6	8	10	15	20	
36	Michel Plasse	4	5	6	8	10	15	20	
37	Gary Sargent	4	5	6	8	10	15	20	
38	Mike Walton	4	5	6	8	10	15	20	
39	Robert Picard RC	4	5	6	8	10	15	20	
40	Terry O'Reilly	4	5	6	8	10	15	20	
41	Dave Farrish	4	5	6	8	10	15	20	
42	Gary McAdam	4	5	6	8	10	15	20	
43	Joe Watson	4	5	6	8	10	15	20	
44	Yves Belanger	4	5	6	8	10	15	20	35
45	Steve Jensen	4	5	6	8	10	15	20	
46	Bob Stewart	4	5	6	8	10	15	20	
47	Darcy Rota	4	5	6	8	10	15	20	
48	Dennis Hextall	4	5	6	8	10	15	20	
49	Bert Marshall	4	5	6	8	10	15	20	
50	Ken Dryden	5	6	10	12	20	50	60	80
51	Peter Mahovlich	4	5	6	8	10	15	20	
52	Dennis Ververgaert	4	5	6	8	10	15	20	30
53	Inge Hammarstrom	4	5	6	8	10	15	20	30
54	Doug Favell	4	5	6	8	10	15	20	30
55	Steve Vickers	4	5	6	8	10	15	20	
56	Syl Apps	4	5	6	8	10	15	20	
57	Errol Thompson	4	5	6	8	10	15	20	
58	Don Luce	4	5	6	8	10	15	20	30
59	Mike Milbury	4	5	6	8	10	15	20	
60	Yvan Cournoyer	4	5	6	8	10	15	20	35
61	Kirk Bowman	4	5	6	8	10	15	20	
62	Billy Smith	4	5	6	8	10	15	20	
63	Lafleur/Bossy/Shutt LL	5	6	8	10	12	20	30	
64	Trott/Lafleur/Sitt LL	4	5	6	8	10	15	20	
65	Lafleur/Trott/Sitt LL	4	5	6	8	10	15	20	40
66	Schltz/Will/Polnich LL	4	5	6	8	10	15	20	35
67	Bossy/Espo/Shutt LL	5	6	8	10	12	20	25	40
68	Dryden/Parent/Gilb LL	5	6	8	10	12	20	25	40
69	Lafleur/Barber/Sitt LL	5	6	8	10	12	20	25	40
70	Parent/Dryden/Espo LL	5	6	8	10	12	20	25	40
71	Bob Kelly	4	5	6	8	10	15	20	
72	Ron Stackhouse	4	5	6	8	10	15	20	
73	Wayne Dillon	4	5	6	8	10	15	20	
74	Jim Rutherford	4	5	6	8	10	15	20	
75	Stan Mikita	4	5	6	8	10	15	20	35
76	Bob Gainey	4	5	6	8	10	15	20	35
77	Gerry Hart	4	5	6	8	10	15	20	
78	Lanny McDonald	4	5	6	8	10	15	20	
79	Brad Park	4	5	6	8	10	15	20	
80	Richard Martin	4	5	6	8	10	15	20	30
81	Bernie Wolfe	4	5	6	8	10	15	20	
82	Bob MacMillan	4	5	6	8	10	15	20	
83	Brad Maxwell RC	4	5	6	8	10	15	20	
84	Mike Fidler	4	5	6	8	10	15	20	
85	Carol Vadnais	4	5	6	8	10	15	20	
86	Don Lever	4	5	6	8	10	15	20	
87	Phil Myre	4	5	6	8	10	15	20	
88	Paul Gardner	4	5	6	8	10	15	20	30
89	Bob Murray	4	5	6	8	10	15	20	30
90	Guy Lafleur	5	6	8	10	12	20	25	50
91	Bob Murdoch	4	5	6	8	10	15	20	30
92	Ron Ellis	4	5	6	8	10	15	20	
93	Jude Drouin	4	5	6	8	10	15	20	

#	Player	VG 3	VgEx 4	EX 5	ExMt 6	NM 7	NmMt 8	NmMt+ 8.5	MT 9
94	Jocelyn Guevremont	4	5	6	8	10	15	20	
95	Gilles Gilbert	4	5	6	8	10	15	20	30
96	Bob Sirois	4	5	6	8	10	15	20	30
97	Tom Lysiak	4	5	6	8	10	15	20	
98	Andre Dupont	4	5	6	8	10	15	20	
99	Per-Olov Brasar RC	4	5	6	8	10	15	20	30
100	Phil Esposito	4	5	6	8	10	15	20	
101	J.P. Bordeleau	4	5	6	8	10	15	20	
102	Pierre Mondou RC	4	5	6	8	10	15	20	
103	Wayne Bianchin	4	5	6	8	10	15	20	
104	Dennis O'Brien	4	5	6	8	10	15	20	30
105	Glenn Resch	4	5	6	8	10	15	20	35
106	Dennis Polonich	4	5	6	8	10	15	20	
107	Kris Manery RC	4	5	6	8	10	15	20	
108	Bill Hajt	4	5	6	8	10	15	20	
109	Jere Gillis RC	4	5	6	8	10	15	20	30
110	Garry Unger	4	5	6	8	10	15	20	
111	Nick Beverley	4	5	6	8	10	15	20	
112	Pat Hickey	4	5	6	8	10	15	20	
113	Rick Middleton	4	5	6	8	10	15	20	
114	Orest Kindrachuk	4	5	6	8	10	15	20	
115	Mike Bossy RC	12	20	25	40	80	200	250	650
116	Pierre Bouchard	4	5	6	8	10	15	20	30
117	Alain Daigle	4	5	6	8	10	15	20	
118	Terry Martin	4	5	6	8	10	15	20	30
119	Tom Edur	4	5	6	8	10	15	20	
120	Marcel Dionne	4	5	6	8	10	20	25	40
121	Barry Beck RC	4	5	6	8	10	15	20	
122	Billy Lochead	4	5	6	8	10	15	20	
123	Paul Harrison RC	4	5	6	8	10	15	20	30
124	Wayne Cashman	4	5	6	8	10	15	20	
125	Rick MacLeish	4	5	6	8	10	15	20	
126	Bob Bourne	4	5	6	8	10	15	20	30
127	Ian Turnbull	4	5	6	8	10	15	20	
128	Gerry Meehan	4	5	6	8	10	15	20	
129	Eric Vail	4	5	6	8	10	15	20	30
130	Gilbert Perreault	4	5	6	8	10	15	20	30
131	Bob Dailey	4	5	6	8	10	15	20	
132	Dale McCourt RC	4	5	6	8	10	15	20	
133	John Wensink RC	4	5	6	8	10	15	20	
134	Bill Nyrop	4	5	6	8	10	15	20	
135	Ivan Boldirev	4	5	6	8	10	15	20	30
136	Lucien DeBlois RC	4	5	6	8	10	15	20	
137	Brian Spencer	4	5	6	8	10	15	20	
138	Tim Young	4	5	6	8	10	15	20	
139	Ron Sedlbauer	4	5	6	8	10	15	20	30
140	Gerry Cheevers	4	5	6	8	10	15	20	
141	Dennis Maruk	4	5	6	8	10	15	20	
142	Barry Dean	4	5	6	8	10	15	20	
143	Bernie Federko RC	5	6	10	15	30	80	100	300
144	Stefan Persson RC	4	5	6	8	10	15	20	30
145	Wilf Paiement	4	5	6	8	10	15	20	
146	Dale Tallon	4	5	6	8	10	15	20	30
147	Yvon Lambert	4	5	6	8	10	15	20	
148	Greg Joly	4	5	6	8	10	15	20	
149	Dean Talafous	4	5	6	8	10	15	20	
150	Don Edwards	4	5	6	8	10	15	20	
151	Butch Goring	4	5	6	8	10	15	20	
152	Tom Bladon	4	5	6	8	10	15	20	
153	Bob Nystrom	4	5	6	8	10	15	20	
154	Ron Greschner	4	5	6	8	10	15	20	
155	Jean Ratelle	4	5	6	8	10	15	20	
156	Russ Anderson RC	4	5	6	8	10	15	20	
157	John Marks	4	5	6	8	10	15	20	
158	Michel Larocque	4	5	6	8	10	15	20	
159	Paul Woods RC	4	5	6	8	10	15	20	
160	Mike Palmateer	4	5	6	8	10	15	20	30
161	Jim Lorentz	4	5	6	8	10	15	20	
162	Dave Lewis	4	5	6	8	10	15	20	
163	Harvey Bennett	4	5	6	8	10	15	20	
164	Rick Smith	4	5	6	8	10	15	20	
165	Reggie Leach	4	5	6	8	10	15	20	
166	Wayne Thomas	4	5	6	8	10	15	20	30
167	Dave Forbes	4	5	6	8	10	15	20	
168	Doug Wilson RC	5	6	8	10	12	30	40	100
169	Dan Bouchard	4	5	6	8	10	15	20	
170	Steve Shutt	4	5	6	8	10	15	20	
171	Mike Kaszycki RC	4	5	6	8	10	15	20	
172	Denis Herron	4	5	6	8	10	15	20	
173	Rick Bowness	4	5	6	8	10	15	20	
174	Rick Hampton	4	5	6	8	10	15	20	
175	Glen Sharpley	4	5	6	8	10	15	20	
176	Bill Barber	4	5	6	8	10	15	20	
177	Ron Duguay RC	5	6	8	10	12	25	30	80
178	Jim Schoenfeld	4	5	6	8	10	15	20	
179	Pierre Plante	4	5	6	8	10	15	20	
180	Jacques Lemaire	4	5	6	8	10	15	20	
181	Stan Jonathan	4	5	6	8	10	15	20	
182	Billy Harris	4	5	6	8	10	15	20	
183	Chris Oddleifson	4	5	6	8	10	15	20	
184	Jean Pronovost	4	5	6	8	10	15	20	
185	Fred Barrett	4	5	6	8	10	15	20	
186	Ross Lonsberry	4	5	6	8	10	15	20	30
187	Mike McEwen	4	5	6	8	10	15	20	
188	Rene Robert	4	5	6	8	10	15	20	
189	J. Bob Kelly	4	5	6	8	10	15	20	
190	Serge Savard	4	5	6	8	10	15	20	
191	Dennis Kearns	4	5	6	8	10	15	20	
192	Flames Team	4	5	6	8	10	15	20	30
193	Bruins Team	4	5	6	8	10	15	20	
194	Sabres Team	4	5	6	8	10	15	20	
195	Blackhawks Team	4	5	6	8	10	15	20	30
196	Rockies Team	4	5	6	8	10	15	20	30
197	Red Wings Team	4	5	6	8	10	15	20	
198	Kings Team	4	5	6	8	10	15	20	30
199	North Stars Team	4	5	6	8	10	15	20	
200	Canadiens Team	4	5	6	8	10	15	20	30
201	Islanders Team	4	5	6	8	10	15	20	
202	Rangers Team	4	5	6	8	10	15	20	
203	Flyers Team	4	5	6	8	10	15	20	
204	Penguins Team	4	5	6	8	10	15	20	
205	Blues Team	4	5	6	8	10	15	20	30
206	Maple Leafs Team	4	5	6	8	10	15	20	30
207	Canucks Team	4	5	6	8	10	15	20	
208	Capitals Team	4	5	6	8	10	15	20	30
209	Danny Gare	4	5	6	8	10	15	20	
210	Larry Robinson	4	5	6	8	10	15	20	
211	John Davidson	4	5	6	8	10	15	20	
212	Peter McNab	4	5	6	8	10	15	20	
213	Rick Kehoe	4	5	6	8	10	15	20	30
214	Terry Harper	4	5	6	8	10	15	20	
215	Bobby Clarke	4	5	6	8	10	15	20	30
216	Bryan Maxwell UER	4	5	6	8	10	15	20	
217	Ted Bulley RC	4	5	6	8	10	15	20	
218	Red Berenson	4	5	6	8	10	15	20	
219	Ron Grahame	4	5	6	8	10	15	20	30
220	Clark Gillies	4	5	6	8	10	15	20	
221	Dave Maloney	4	5	6	8	10	15	20	
222	Derek Smith RC	4	5	6	8	10	15	20	30
223	Wayne Stephenson	4	5	6	8	10	15	20	
224	John Van Boxmeer	4	5	6	8	10	15	20	
225	Dave Schultz	4	5	6	8	10	15	20	
226	Reed Larson RC	4	5	6	8	10	15	20	
227	Rejean Houle	4	5	6	8	10	15	20	
228	Doug Hicks	4	5	6	8	10	15	20	30
229	Mike Murphy	4	5	6	8	10	15	20	
230	Pete Lopresti	4	5	6	8	10	15	20	
231	Jerry Korab	4	5	6	8	10	15	20	
232	Ed Westfall	4	5	6	8	10	15	20	30
233	Greg Malone RC	4	5	6	8	10	15	20	
234	Paul Holmgren	4	5	6	8	10	15	20	
235	Walt Tkaczuk	4	5	6	8	10	15	20	30
236	Don Marcotte	4	5	6	8	10	15	20	
237	Ron Low	4	5	6	8	10	15	20	30
238	Rick Chartraw	4	5	6	8	10	15	20	30
239	Cliff Koroll	4	5	6	8	10	15	20	
240	Borje Salming	4	5	6	8	10	15	20	
241	Roland Eriksson	4	5	6	8	10	15	20	
242	Ric Seiling RC	4	5	6	8	10	15	20	
243	Jim Bedard RC	4	5	6	8	10	15	20	
244	Peter Lee RC	4	5	6	8	10	15	20	
245	Denis Potvin	4	5	6	8	10	15	20	30
246	Greg Polis	4	5	6	8	10	15	20	
247	Jimmy Watson	4	5	6	8	10	15	20	
248	Bobby Schmautz	4	5	6	8	10	15	20	
249	Doug Risebrough	4	5	6	8	10	15	20	
250	Tony Esposito	4	5	6	8	10	15	20	40
251	Nick Libett	4	5	6	8	10	15	20	
252	Ron Zanussi RC	4	5	6	8	10	15	20	
253	Andre Savard	4	5	6	8	10	15	20	
254	Dave Burrows	4	5	6	8	10	15	20	
255	Ulf Nilsson	4	5	6	8	10	15	20	
256	Richard Mulhern	4	5	6	8	10	15	20	
257	Don Saleski	4	5	6	8	10	15	20	
258	Wayne Merrick	4	5	6	8	10	15	20	30
259	Checklist 133-264	5	6	8	10	12	20	30	
260	Guy Lapointe	4	5	6	8	10	15	20	
261	Grant Mulvey	4	5	6	8	10	15	20	
262	Stanley Cup Semifinals	4	5	6	8	10	15	20	40
263	Stanley Cup Semifinals	4	5	6	8	10	15	20	30
264	Stanley Cup Finals	4	5	6	8	10	15	20	30
265	Bob Sauve	4	5	6	8	10	15	20	
266	Randy Manery	4	5	6	8	10	15	20	
267	Bill Fairbairn	4	5	6	8	10	15	20	
268	Garry Monahan	4	5	6	8	10	15	20	
269	Colin Campbell	4	5	6	8	10	15	20	
270	Dan Newman	4	5	6	8	10	15	20	30
271	Dwight Foster RC	4	5	6	8	10	15	20	30
272	Larry Carriere	4	5	6	8	10	15	20	
273	Michel Bergeron	4	5	6	8	10	15	20	30

		VG 3	VgEx 4	EX 5	ExMt 6	NM 7	NmMt 8	NmMt+ 8.5	MT 9
274	Scott Garland	4	5	6	8	10	15	20	
275	Bill McKenzie	4	5	6	8	10	15	20	
276	Garnet Bailey	4	5	6	8	10	15	20	
277	Ed Kea	4	5	6	8	10	15	20	
278	Dave Gardner	4	5	6	8	10	15	20	
279	Bruce Affleck	4	5	6	8	10	15	20	
280	Bruce Boudreau RC	4	5	6	8	10	15	20	
281	Jean Hamel	4	5	6	8	10	15	20	
282	Kurt Walker RC	4	5	6	8	10	15	20	
283	Denis Dupere	4	5	6	8	10	15	20	
284	Gordie Lane	4	5	6	8	10	15	20	
285	Bobby Lalonde	4	5	6	8	10	15	20	
286	Pit Martin	4	5	6	8	10	15	20	
287	Jean Potvin	4	5	6	8	10	15	20	
288	Jimmy Jones RC	4	5	6	8	10	15	20	
289	Dave Hutchinson	4	5	6	8	10	15	20	
290	Pete Stemkowski	4	5	6	8	10	15	20	
291	Mike Christie	4	5	6	8	10	15	20	30
292	Bill Riley	4	5	6	8	10	15	20	
293	Rey Comeau	4	5	6	8	10	15	20	
294	Jack McIlhargey RC	4	5	6	8	10	15	20	
295	Tom Younghans RC	4	5	6	8	10	15	20	
296	Mario Faubert RC	4	5	6	8	10	15	20	
297	Checklist Card	5	6	8	10	12	20	30	
298	Rob Palmer RC	4	5	6	8	10	15	20	
299	Dave Hudson	4	5	6	8	10	15	20	
300	Bobby Orr	6	8	12	20	35	80	100	175
301	Lorne Stamler RC	4	5	6	8	10	15	20	
302	Curt Ridley	4	5	6	8	10	15	20	
303	Greg Smith	4	5	6	8	10	15	20	
304	Jerry Butler	4	5	6	8	10	15	20	
305	Gary Doak	4	5	6	8	10	15	20	30
306	Danny Grant	4	5	6	8	10	15	20	30
307	Mark Suzor RC	4	5	6	8	10	15	20	
308	Rick Bragnalo	4	5	6	8	10	15	20	
309	John Gould	4	5	6	8	10	15	20	
310	Sheldon Kannegiesser	4	5	6	8	10	15	20	
311	Bobby Sheehan	4	5	6	8	10	15	20	
312	Randy Carlyle RC	5	6	8	10	15	40		
313	Lorne Henning	4	5	6	8	10	15	20	
314	Tom Williams	4	5	6	8	10	15	20	30
315	Ron Andruff	4	5	6	8	10	15	20	
316	Bryan Watson	4	5	6	8	10	15	20	
317	Willi Plett	4	5	6	8	10	15	20	
318	John Grisdale	4	5	6	8	10	15	20	
319	Brian Sutter RC	5	6	10	12	25	30	60	
320	Trevor Johansen RC	4	5	6	8	10	15	20	30
321	Vic Venasky	4	5	6	8	10	15	20	
322	Rick Lapointe	4	5	6	8	10	15	20	
323	Ron Delorme RC	4	5	6	8	10	15	20	
324	Yvon Labre	4	5	6	8	10	15	20	
325	Bryan Trottier AS UER	5	6	8	10	12	20	25	40
326	Guy Lafleur AS	4	5	6	8	10	15	20	35
327	Clark Gillies AS	4	5	6	8	10	15	20	30
328	Borje Salming AS	4	5	6	8	10	15	20	30
329	Larry Robinson AS	4	5	6	8	10	15	20	30
330	Ken Dryden AS	5	6	8	10	12	25	30	40
331	Darryl Sittler AS	4	5	6	8	10	15	20	53
332	Terry O'Reilly AS	4	5	6	8	10	15	20	30
333	Steve Shutt AS	4	5	6	8	10	15	20	30
334	Denis Potvin AS	4	5	6	8	10	15	20	30
335	Serge Savard AS	4	5	6	8	10	15	20	30
336	Don Edwards AS	4	5	6	8	10	15	20	30
337	Glenn Goldup	4	5	6	8	10	15	20	
338	Mike Kitchen	4	5	6	8	10	15	20	
339	Bob Girard	4	5	6	8	10	15	20	
340	Guy Chouinard	4	5	6	8	10	15	20	
341	Randy Holt	4	5	6	8	10	15	20	
342	Jim Roberts	4	5	6	8	10	15	20	
343	Dave Logan RC	4	5	6	8	10	15	20	
344	Walt McKechnie	4	5	6	8	10	15	20	
345	Brian Glennie	4	5	6	8	10	15	20	
346	Ralph Klassen	4	5	6	8	10	15	20	
347	Gord Smith	4	5	6	8	10	15	20	
348	Ken Houston	4	5	6	8	10	15	20	
349	Bob Manno RC	4	5	6	8	10	15	20	
350	Jean-Paul Parise	4	5	6	8	10	15	20	
351	Don Ashby	4	5	6	8	10	15	20	
352	Fred Stanfield	4	5	6	8	10	15	20	
353	Dave Taylor RC	6	10	15	20	25	50	60	100
354	Nelson Pyatt	4	5	6	8	10	15	20	
355	Blair Stewart RC	4	5	6	8	10	15	20	
356	David Shand	4	5	6	8	10	15	20	
357	Hilliard Graves	4	5	6	8	10	15	20	
358	Bob Hess	4	5	6	8	10	15	20	
359	Dave Williams	4	5	6	8	10	15	20	
360	Larry Wright RC	4	5	6	8	10	15	20	
361	Larry Brown	4	5	6	8	10	15	20	
362	Gary Croteau	4	5	6	8	10	15	20	
363	Rick Green	4	5	6	8	10	15	20	

		VG 3	VgEx 4	EX 5	ExMt 6	NM 7	NmMt 8	NmMt+ 8.5	MT 9
364	Bill Clement	4	5	6	8	10	15	20	
365	Gerry O'Flaherty	4	5	6	8	10	15	20	
366	John Baby RC	4	5	6	8	10	15	20	
367	Nick Fotiu	4	5	6	8	10	15	20	
368	Pat Price	4	5	6	8	10	15	20	
369	Bert Wilson	4	5	6	8	10	15	20	
370	Bryan Lefley	4	5	6	8	10	15	20	
371	Ron Lalonde	4	5	6	8	10	15	20	
372	Bobby Simpson	4	5	6	8	10	15	20	
373	Doug Grant	4	5	6	8	10	15	20	
374	Pat Boutette	4	5	6	8	10	15	20	
375	Bob Paradise	4	5	6	8	10	15	20	
376	Mario Tremblay	4	5	6	8	10	15	20	
377	Darryl Edestrand	4	5	6	8	10	15	20	
378	Andy Spruce RC	4	5	6	8	10	15	20	
379	Jack Brownschidle RC	4	5	6	8	10	15	20	
380	Harold Snepsts	4	5	6	8	10	15	20	30
381	Al MacAdam	4	5	6	8	10	15	20	
382	Neil Komadoski	4	5	6	8	10	15	20	
383	Don Awrey	4	5	6	8	10	15	20	
384	Ron Schock	4	5	6	8	10	15	20	
385	Gary Simmons	4	5	6	8	10	15	20	30
386	Fred Ahern	4	5	6	8	10	15	20	
387	Larry Bolonchuk	4	5	6	8	10	15	20	
388	Brad Gassoff RC	4	5	6	8	10	15	20	
389	Chuck Arnason	4	5	6	8	10	15	20	
390	Barry Gibbs	4	5	6	8	10	15	20	
391	Jack Valiquette	4	5	6	8	10	15	20	
392	Doug Halward	4	5	6	8	10	15	20	
393	Hartland Monahan	4	5	6	8	10	15	20	
394	Rod Seiling	4	5	6	8	10	15	20	
395	George Ferguson	4	5	6	8	10	15	20	
396	Al Cameron	4	5	6	8	10	15	20	

— Randy Carlyle RC #312 PSA 9 (Mt) sold for $643.99 (eBay; 2/14)
— Randy Carlyle RC #312 PSA 10 (Gem) sold for $512 (eBay; 4/12)
— Bernie Federko RC #143 PSA 10 (Gem) sold for $1,830 (eBay; 3/12)
— Doug Wilson RC #168 PSA 10 (Gem) sold for $714 (eBay; 9/15)

1978-79 Topps

		VG 3	VgEx 4	EX 5	ExMt 6	NM 7	NmMt 8	NmMt+ 8.5	MT 9
1	Mike Bossy HL	6	8	10	12	15	30		
2	Phil Esposito HL	4	5	6	8	10	12	15	20
3	Guy Lafleur HL	4	5	6	8	10	12	15	20
4	Darryl Sittler HL	4	5	6	8	10	12	15	20
5	Garry Unger HL	4	5	6	8	10	12	15	20
6	Gary Edwards	4	5	6	8	10	12	15	20
7	Rick Blight	4	5	6	8	10	12	15	20
8	Larry Patey	4	5	6	8	10	12	15	20
9	Craig Ramsay	4	5	6	8	10	12		
10	Bryan Trottier	5	6	8	10	12	15	20	25
11	Don Murdoch	4	5	6	8	10	12	15	20
12	Phil Russell	4	5	6	8	10	12	15	20
13	Doug Jarvis	4	5	6	8	10	12	15	20
14	Gene Carr	4	5	6	8	10	12	15	20
15	Bernie Parent	4	5	6	8	10	12	15	20
16	Perry Miller	4	5	6	8	10	12	15	20
17	Kent-Erik Andersson RC	4	5	6	8	10	12	15	20
18	Gregg Sheppard	4	5	6	8	10	12	15	20
19	Dennis Owchar	4	5	6	8	10	12	15	
20	Rogatien Vachon	4	5	6	8	10	12	15	20
21	Dan Maloney	4	5	6	8	10	12	15	20
22	Guy Charron	4	5	6	8	10	12	15	20
23	Dick Redmond	4	5	6	8	10	12	15	20
24	Checklist 1-132	4	5	6	8	10	12	15	25
25	Anders Hedberg	4	5	6	8	10	12	15	20
26	Mel Bridgman	4	5	6	8	10	12	15	
27	Lee Fogolin	4	5	6	8	10	12	15	
28	Gilles Meloche	4	5	6	8	10	12	15	20
29	Garry Howatt	4	5	6	8	10	12	15	20
30	Darryl Sittler	4	5	6	8	10	12	15	20
31	Curt Bennett	4	5	6	8	10	12	15	20
32	Andre St.Laurent	4	5	6	8	10	12	15	20
33	Blair Chapman	4	5	6	8	10	12	15	
34	Keith Magnuson	4	5	6	8	10	12	15	20
35	Pierre Larouche	4	5	6	8	10	12	15	20
36	Michel Plasse	4	5	6	8	10	12	15	
37	Gary Sargent	4	5	6	8	10	12	15	20
38	Mike Walton	4	5	6	8	10	12	15	20
39	Robert Picard RC	4	5	6	8	10	12	15	20
40	Terry O'Reilly	4	5	6	8	10	12	15	20
41	Dave Farrish	4	5	6	8	10	12	15	
42	Gary McAdam	4	5	6	8	10	12	15	
43	Joe Watson	4	5	6	8	10	12	15	20
44	Yves Belanger	4	5	6	8	10	12	15	20
45	Steve Jensen	4	5	6	8	10	12	15	
46	Bob Stewart	4	5	6	8	10	12	15	20
47	Darcy Rota	4	5	6	8	10	12	15	
48	Dennis Hextall	4	5	6	8	10	12	15	20
49	Bert Marshall	4	5	6	8	10	12	15	20

#	Player	VG 3	VgEx 4	EX 5	ExMt 6	NM 7	NmMt 8	NmMt+ 8.5	MT 9
50	Ken Dryden	5	6	8	10	12	15	20	25
51	Peter Mahovlich	4	5	6	8	10	12	15	20
52	Dennis Ververgaert	4	5	6	8	10	12	15	20
53	Inge Hammarstrom	4	5	6	8	10	12	15	
54	Doug Favell	4	5	6	8	10	12	15	20
55	Steve Vickers	4	5	6	8	10	12	15	
56	Syl Apps	4	5	6	8	10	12	15	20
57	Errol Thompson	4	5	6	8	10	12	15	20
58	Don Luce	4	5	6	8	10	12	15	20
59	Mike Milbury	4	5	6	8	10	12	15	20
60	Yvan Cournoyer	4	5	6	8	10	12	15	20
61	Kirk Bowman	4	5	6	8	10	12	15	20
62	Billy Smith	4	5	6	8	10	12	15	20
63	Lafleur/Bossy/Shutt LL	4	5	6	8	10	12	20	25
64	Trott/Lafleur/Sitt LL	4	5	6	8	10	12	15	
65	Lafleur/Trott/Sitt LL	4	5	6	8	10	12	15	20
66	Schltz/Wil/Polnich LL	4	5	6	8	10	12	15	20
67	Bossy/Espo/Shutt LL	4	5	6	8	10	12	15	20
68	Dryden/Parent/Gilb LL	4	5	6	8	10	12	15	20
69	Lafleur/Barber/Sitt LL	4	5	6	8	10	12	15	20
70	Parent/Dryden/Espo LL	4	5	6	8	10	12	15	20
71	Bob Kelly	4	5	6	8	10	12	15	20
72	Ron Stackhouse	4	5	6	8	10	12	15	20
73	Wayne Dillon	4	5	6	8	10	12	15	20
74	Jim Rutherford	4	5	6	8	10	12	15	20
75	Stan Mikita	4	5	6	8	10	12	15	25
76	Bob Gainey	4	5	6	8	10	12	15	20
77	Gerry Hart	4	5	6	8	10	12	15	20
78	Lanny McDonald	4	5	6	8	10	12	15	20
79	Brad Park	4	5	6	8	10	12	15	20
80	Richard Martin	4	5	6	8	10	12	15	
81	Bernie Wolfe	4	5	6	8	10	12	15	
82	Bob MacMillan	4	5	6	8	10	12	15	20
83	Brad Maxwell RC	4	5	6	8	10	12	15	20
84	Mike Fidler	4	5	6	8	10	12	15	20
85	Carol Vadnais	4	5	6	8	10	12	15	
86	Don Lever	4	5	6	8	10	12	15	20
87	Phil Myre	4	5	6	8	10	12	15	20
88	Paul Gardner	4	5	6	8	10	12	15	20
89	Bob Murray	4	5	6	8	10	12	15	20
90	Guy Lafleur	4	5	6	8	10	12	20	25
91	Bob Murdoch	4	5	6	8	10	12	15	20
92	Ron Ellis	4	5	6	8	10	12	15	
93	Jude Drouin	4	5	6	8	10	12	15	20
94	Jocelyn Guevremont	4	5	6	8	10	12	15	20
95	Gilles Gilbert	4	5	6	8	10	12	15	20
96	Bob Sirois	4	5	6	8	10	12	15	20
97	Tom Lysiak	4	5	6	8	10	12	15	20
98	Andre Dupont	4	5	6	8	10	12	15	20
99	Per-Olov Brasar RC	4	5	6	8	10	12	15	20
100	Phil Esposito	4	5	6	8	10	12	15	25
101	J.P. Bordeleau	4	5	6	8	10	12	15	20
102	Pierre Mondou RC	4	5	6	8	10	12	15	20
103	Wayne Bianchin	4	5	6	8	10	12	15	20
104	Dennis O'Brien	4	5	6	8	10	12	15	20
105	Glenn Resch	4	5	6	8	10	12	15	20
106	Dennis Polonich	4	5	6	8	10	12	15	20
107	Kris Manery RC	4	5	6	8	10	12	15	
108	Bill Hajt	4	5	6	8	10	12	15	20
109	Jere Gillis RC	4	5	6	8	10	12	15	20
110	Garry Unger	4	5	6	8	10	12	15	20
111	Nick Beverley	4	5	6	8	10	12	15	20
112	Pat Hickey	4	5	6	8	10	12	15	20
113	Rick Middleton	4	5	6	8	10	12	15	20
114	Orest Kindrachuk	4	5	6	8	10	12	15	20
115	Mike Bossy RC	10	12	15	30	50	60	80	120
116	Pierre Bouchard	4	5	6	8	10	12	15	20
117	Alain Daigle	4	5	6	8	10	12	15	20
118	Terry Martin	4	5	6	8	10	12	15	20
119	Tom Edur	4	5	6	8	10	12	15	20
120	Marcel Dionne	4	5	6	8	10	12	15	25
121	Barry Beck RC	4	5	6	8	10	12	15	20
122	Billy Lochead	4	5	6	8	10	12	15	20
123	Paul Harrison	4	5	6	8	10	12	15	20
124	Wayne Cashman	4	5	6	8	10	12	15	
125	Rick MacLeish	4	5	6	8	10	12	15	
126	Bob Bourne	4	5	6	8	10	12	15	20
127	Ian Turnbull	4	5	6	8	10	12	15	20
128	Gerry Meehan	4	5	6	8	10	12	15	20
129	Eric Vail	4	5	6	8	10	12	15	20
130	Gilbert Perreault	4	5	6	8	10	12	15	20
131	Bob Dailey	4	5	6	8	10	12	15	20
132	Dale McCourt RC	4	5	6	8	10	12	15	
133	John Wensink RC	4	5	6	8	10	12	15	
134	Bill Nyrop	4	5	6	8	10	12	15	20
135	Ivan Boldirev	4	5	6	8	10	12	15	20
136	Lucien DeBlois RC	4	5	6	8	10	12	15	20
137	Brian Spencer	4	5	6	8	10	12	15	20
138	Tim Young	4	5	6	8	10	12	15	20
139	Ron Sedlbauer	4	5	6	8	10	12	15	20
140	Gerry Cheevers	4	5	6	8	10	12	15	20
141	Dennis Maruk	4	5	6	8	10	12	15	20
142	Barry Dean	4	5	6	8	10	12	15	
143	Bernie Federko RC	5	6	8	10	12	15	20	30
144	Stefan Persson RC	4	5	6	8	10	12	15	20
145	Wilf Paiement	4	5	6	8	10	12	15	20
146	Dale Tallon	4	5	6	8	10	12	15	20
147	Yvon Lambert	4	5	6	8	10	12	15	20
148	Greg Joly	4	5	6	8	10	12	15	20
149	Dean Talafous	4	5	6	8	10	12	15	20
150	Don Edwards AS2	4	5	6	8	10	12	15	20
151	Butch Goring	4	5	6	8	10	12	15	20
152	Tom Bladon	4	5	6	8	10	12	15	20
153	Bob Nystrom	4	5	6	8	10	12	15	20
154	Ron Greschner	4	5	6	8	10	12	15	20
155	Jean Ratelle	4	5	6	8	10	12	15	20
156	Russ Anderson RC	4	5	6	8	10	12	15	20
157	John Marks	4	5	6	8	10	12	15	20
158	Michel Larocque	4	5	6	8	10	12	15	20
159	Paul Woods RC	4	5	6	8	10	12	15	20
160	Mike Palmateer	4	5	6	8	10	12	15	20
161	Jim Lorentz	4	5	6	8	10	12	15	20
162	Dave Lewis	4	5	6	8	10	12	15	20
163	Harvey Bennett	4	5	6	8	10	12	15	
164	Rick Smith	4	5	6	8	10	12	15	20
165	Reggie Leach	4	5	6	8	10	12	15	20
166	Wayne Thomas	4	5	6	8	10	12	15	20
167	Dave Forbes	4	5	6	8	10	12	15	20
168	Doug Wilson RC	5	6	8	10	12	15	20	25
169	Dan Bouchard	4	5	6	8	10	12	15	20
170	Steve Shutt	4	5	6	8	10	12	15	20
171	Mike Kaszycki RC	4	5	6	8	10	12	15	20
172	Denis Herron	4	5	6	8	10	12	15	
173	Rick Bowness	4	5	6	8	10	12	15	
174	Rick Hampton	4	5	6	8	10	12	15	20
175	Glen Sharpley	4	5	6	8	10	12	15	20
176	Bill Barber	4	5	6	8	10	12	15	20
177	Ron Duguay RC	4	5	6	8	10	12	15	25
178	Jim Schoenfeld	4	5	6	8	10	12	15	20
179	Pierre Plante	4	5	6	8	10	12	15	20
180	Jacques Lemaire	4	5	6	8	10	12	15	20
181	Stan Jonathan	4	5	6	8	10	12	15	20
182	Billy Harris	4	5	6	8	10	12	15	20
183	Chris Oddleifson	4	5	6	8	10	12	15	20
184	Jean Pronovost	4	5	6	8	10	12	15	20
185	Fred Barrett	4	5	6	8	10	12	15	20
186	Ross Lonsberry	4	5	6	8	10	12	15	20
187	Mike McEwen	4	5	6	8	10	12	15	20
188	Rene Robert	4	5	6	8	10	12	15	20
189	J. Bob Kelly	4	5	6	8	10	12	15	20
190	Serge Savard AS2	4	5	6	8	10	12	15	20
191	Dennis Kearns	4	5	6	8	10	12	15	20
192	Flames Team CL	4	5	6	8	10	12	15	20
193	Bruins Team CL	4	5	6	8	10	12	15	20
194	Sabres Team CL	4	5	6	8	10	12	15	20
195	Blackhawks Team CL	4	5	6	8	10	12	15	20
196	Rockies Team CL	4	5	6	8	10	12	15	20
197	Red Wings Team CL	4	5	6	8	10	12	15	20
198	Kings Team CL	4	5	6	8	10	12	15	20
199	North Stars Team CL	4	5	6	8	10	12	15	20
200	Canadiens Team CL	4	5	6	8	10	12	15	20
201	Islanders Team CL	4	5	6	8	10	12	15	20
202	Rangers Team CL	4	5	6	8	10	12	15	20
203	Flyers Team CL	4	5	6	8	10	12	15	20
204	Penguins Team CL	4	5	6	8	10	12	15	20
205	Blues Team CL	4	5	6	8	10	12	15	20
206	Maple Leafs Team CL	4	5	6	8	10	12	15	20
207	Canucks Team CL	4	5	6	8	10	12	15	20
208	Capitals Team CL	4	5	6	8	10	12	15	20
209	Danny Gare	4	5	6	8	10	12	15	20
210	Larry Robinson	4	5	6	8	10	12	15	25
211	John Davidson	4	5	6	8	10	12	15	20
212	Peter McNab	4	5	6	8	10	12	15	20
213	Rick Kehoe	4	5	6	8	10	12	15	20
214	Terry Harper	4	5	6	8	10	12	15	20
215	Bobby Clarke	4	5	6	8	10	12	15	25
216	Bryan Maxwell UER	4	5	6	8	10	12	15	20
217	Ted Bulley	4	5	6	8	10	12	15	20
218	Red Berenson	4	5	6	8	10	12	15	
219	Ron Grahame	4	5	6	8	10	12	15	20
220	Clark Gillies AS1	4	5	6	8	10	12	15	20
221	Dave Maloney	4	5	6	8	10	12	15	20
222	Derek Smith RC	4	5	6	8	10	12	15	20
223	Wayne Stephenson	4	5	6	8	10	12	15	20
224	John Van Boxmeer	4	5	6	8	10	12	15	20
225	Dave Schultz	4	5	6	8	10	12	15	20
226	Reed Larson RC	4	5	6	8	10	12	15	20
227	Rejean Houle	4	5	6	8	10	12	15	20
228	Doug Hicks	4	5	6	8	10	12	15	20
229	Mike Murphy	4	5	6	8	10	12	15	20

#	Card	VG 3	VgEx 4	EX 5	ExMt 6	NM 7	NmMt 8	NmMt+ 8.5	MT 9
230	Pete Lopresti	4	5	6	8	10	12	15	20
231	Jerry Korab	4	5	6	8	10	12	15	
232	Ed Westfall	4	5	6	8	10	12	15	20
233	Greg Malone RC	4	5	6	8	10	12	15	20
234	Paul Holmgren	4	5	6	8	10	12	15	20
235	Walt Tkaczuk	4	5	6	8	10	12	15	20
236	Don Marcotte	4	5	6	8	10	12	15	20
237	Ron Low	4	5	6	8	10	12	15	20
238	Rick Chartraw	4	5	6	8	10	12	15	20
239	Cliff Koroll	4	5	6	8	10	12	15	20
240	Borje Salming	4	5	6	8	10	12	15	20
241	Roland Eriksson	4	5	6	8	10	12	15	20
242	Ric Seiling RC	4	5	6	8	10	12	15	20
243	Jim Bedard RC	4	5	6	8	10	12	15	20
244	Peter Lee RC	4	5	6	8	10	12	15	20
245	Denis Potvin	4	5	6	8	10	12	15	25
246	Greg Polis	4	5	6	8	10	12	15	
247	Jimmy Watson	4	5	6	8	10	12	15	20
248	Bobby Schmautz	4	5	6	8	10	12	15	
249	Doug Risebrough	4	5	6	8	10	12	15	20
250	Tony Esposito	4	5	6	8	10	12	15	20
251	Nick Libett	4	5	6	8	10	12	15	
252	Ron Zanussi RC	4	5	6	8	10	12	15	20
253	Andre Savard	4	5	6	8	10	12	15	20
254	Dave Burrows	4	5	6	8	10	12	15	20
255	Ulf Nilsson	4	5	6	8	10	12	15	20
256	Richard Mulhern	4	5	6	8	10	12	15	20
257	Don Saleski	4	5	6	8	10	12	15	20
258	Wayne Merrick	4	5	6	8	10	12	15	20
259	Checklist 133-264	4	5	6	8	10	12	15	25
260	Guy Lapointe	4	5	6	8	10	12	15	20
261	Grant Mulvey	4	5	6	8	10	12	15	20
262	Stanley Cup: Semis	4	5	6	8	10	12	15	20
263	Stanley Cup: Semis	4	5	6	8	10	12	15	20
264	Stanley Cup Finals	4	5	6	8	10	12	15	20

– Mike Bossy RC #115 BGS 9.5 (Gem) sold for $302 (eBay; 6/12)

– Mike Bossy RC #115 PSA 10 (Gem) sold for $1,302 (Memory Lane; 6/12)

1979-80 O-Pee-Chee

#	Card	VG 3	VgEx 4	EX 5	ExMt 6	NM 7	NmMt 8	NmMt+ 8.5	MT 9
	Bossy/Dionne/Lafleur LL	6	10	12	15	40	135		
	Trott/Lafleur/Dionne LL	4	5	6	8	15	25	30	
	Trott/Dionne/Lafleur LL	4	6	8	10	15	60	80	
	Williams/Holt/Schultz LL	4	4	5	6	10	25		
	Bossy/Dionne/Gardner LL	4	6	8	12	20	30	50	150
	Dryden/Resch/Parent LL	4	5	6	8	15	25	30	100
	Lafleur/Bossy/Trott/ LL	4	5	6	8	15	25	30	
	Dryden/Espo/Parent LL	4	5	6	8	15	60	80	120
	Greg Malone	4	4	5	6	10	15	20	
	Rick Middleton	4	4	5	6	10	15	20	50
	Greg Smith	4	4	5	6	10	15	20	35
	Rene Robert	4	4	5	6	10	15	20	
	Doug Risebrough	4	4	5	6	10	15	20	
	Bob Kelly	4	4	5	6	10	15	20	
	Walt Tkaczuk	4	4	5	6	10	15	20	35
	John Marks	4	4	5	6	10	15	20	
	Willie Huber RC	4	4	5	6	10	15	20	35
	Wayne Gretzky UER RC 80 GP not 60	2,500	3,000	▼4,000	8,000	▼10,000	▼30,000		100,000
	Ron Sedlbauer	4	4	5	6	10	15	20	35
	Glenn Resch AS2	4	4	5	6	10	15	20	35
	Blair Chapman	4	4	5	6	10	15	20	
	Ron Zanussi	4	4	5	6	10	15	20	35
	Brad Park	4	5	6	8	12	30		
	Yvon Lambert	4	4	5	6	10	15	20	35
	Andre Savard	4	4	5	6	10	15	20	
	Jimmy Watson	4	4	5	6	10	15	20	
	Hal Philipoff RC	4	4	5	6	10	15	20	
	Dan Bouchard	4	4	5	6	10	15	20	
	Bob Sirois	4	4	5	6	10	15	20	35
	Ulf Nilsson	4	4	5	6	10	15	20	
	Mike Murphy	4	4	5	6	10	15	20	
	Stefan Persson	4	4	5	6	10	15	20	
	Garry Unger	4	4	5	6	10	15	20	35
	Rejean Houle	4	4	5	6	10	15	20	35
	Barry Beck	4	4	5	6	10	15	20	
	Tim Young	4	4	5	6	10	15	20	
	Rick Dudley	4	4	5	6	10	15	20	35
	Wayne Stephenson	4	4	5	6	10	15	20	
	Peter McNab	4	4	5	6	10	15	20	35
	Borje Salming AS2	4	4	5	6	10	15	20	
	Tom Lysiak	4	4	5	6	10	15	20	
	Don Maloney RC	4	4	5	6	10	15	20	40
	Mike Rogers	4	4	5	6	10	15	20	
	Dave Lewis	4	4	5	6	10	15	20	
	Peter Lee	4	4	5	6	10	15	20	35
	Marty Howe	4	4	5	6	10	15	20	40
	Serge Bernier	4	4	5	6	10	15	20	
	Paul Woods	4	4	5	6	10	15	20	

#	Card	VG 3	VgEx 4	EX 5	ExMt 6	NM 7	NmMt 8	NmMt+ 8.5	MT 9
49	Bob Sauve	4	4	5	6	10	15	20	
50	Larry Robinson AS1	4	5	6	8	12	40		
51	Tom Gorence RC	4	4	5	6	10	15	20	35
52	Gary Sargent	4	4	5	6	10	15	20	
53	Thomas Gradin RC	4	4	5	6	10	15	20	
54	Dean Talafous	4	4	5	6	10	15	20	
55	Bob Murray	4	4	5	6	10	15	20	35
56	Bob Bourne	4	4	5	6	10	15	20	
57	Larry Patey	4	4	5	6	10	15	20	
58	Ross Lonsberry	4	4	5	6	10	15	20	35
59	Rick Smith UER	4	4	5	6	10	15	20	35
60	Guy Chouinard	4	4	5	6	10	15	20	35
61	Danny Gare	4	4	5	6	10	15	20	
62	Jim Bedard	4	4	5	6	10	15	20	
63	Dale McCourt UER	4	4	5	6	10	15	20	
64	Steve Payne RC	4	4	5	6	10	30		
65	Pat Hughes RC	4	4	5	6	10	15	20	35
66	Mike McEwen	4	4	5	6	10	15	20	35
67	Reg Kerr RC	4	4	5	6	10	15	20	35
68	Walt McKechnie	4	4	5	6	10	15	20	
69	Michel Plasse	4	4	5	6	10	15	20	
70	Denis Potvin AS1	4	4	5	6	10	15	20	
71	Dave Dryden	4	4	5	6	10	15	20	40
72	Gary McAdam	4	4	5	6	10	15	20	35
73	Andre St.Laurent	4	4	5	6	10	15	20	
74	Jerry Korab	4	4	5	6	10	15	20	
75	Rick MacLeish	4	4	5	6	10	15	20	40
76	Dennis Kearns	4	4	5	6	10	15	20	
77	Jean Pronovost	4	4	5	6	10	15	20	35
78	Ron Greschner	4	4	5	6	10	15	20	
79	Wayne Cashman	4	4	5	6	10	15	20	35
80	Tony Esposito	4	5	6	8	12	15	20	35
81	Jets Logo CL	5	8	10	12	20	30	40	80
82	Oilers Logo CL	6	10	12	20	25	40	50	150
83	Stanley Cup Finals	4	5	8	30	40	50		
84	Brian Sutter	4	4	5	6	10	15	20	40
85	Gerry Cheevers	4	4	5	6	10	15	20	
86	Pat Hickey	4	4	5	6	10	15	20	
87	Mike Kaszycki	4	4	5	6	10	15	20	35
88	Grant Mulvey	4	4	5	6	10	15	20	
89	Derek Smith	4	4	5	6	10	15	20	35
90	Steve Shutt	4	4	5	6	10	15	20	
91	Robert Picard	4	4	5	6	10	15	20	
92	Dan Labraaten	4	4	5	6	10	15	20	
93	Glen Sharpley	4	4	5	6	10	15	20	
94	Denis Herron	4	4	5	6	10	15	20	
95	Reggie Leach	4	4	5	6	10	15	20	
96	John Van Boxmeer	4	4	5	6	10	15	20	
97	Tiger Williams	4	4	5	6	10	20	25	50
98	Butch Goring	4	4	5	6	10	15	20	35
99	Don Marcotte	4	4	5	6	10	15	20	
100	Bryan Trottier AS1	4	5	6	8	12	30	40	
101	Serge Savard AS2	4	4	5	6	10	15	20	
102	Cliff Koroll	4	4	5	6	10	15	20	
103	Gary Smith	4	4	5	6	10	15	20	
104	Al MacAdam	4	4	5	6	10	15	20	
105	Don Edwards	4	4	5	6	10	15	20	35
106	Errol Thompson	4	4	5	6	10	15	20	
107	Andre Lacroix	4	4	5	6	10	15	20	
108	Marc Tardif	4	4	5	6	10	15	20	35
109	Rick Kehoe	4	4	5	6	10	15	20	35
110	John Davidson	4	4	5	6	10	15	20	
111	Behn Wilson RC	4	4	5	6	10	15	20	35
112	Doug Jarvis	4	4	5	6	10	15	20	35
113	Tom Rowe RC	4	4	5	6	10	15	20	35
114	Mike Milbury	4	4	5	6	10	15	20	
115	Billy Harris	4	4	5	6	10	15	20	
116	Greg Fox RC	4	4	5	6	10	15	20	
117	Curt Fraser RC	4	4	5	6	10	15	20	35
118	Jean-Paul Parise	4	4	5	6	10	15	20	
119	Ric Seiling	4	4	5	6	10	15	20	35
120	Darryl Sittler	4	4	5	6	10	15	20	
121	Rick Lapointe	4	4	5	6	10	15	20	
122	Jim Rutherford	4	4	5	6	15	30	20	
123	Mario Tremblay	4	4	5	6	10	15	20	40
124	Randy Carlyle	4	4	5	6	10	15	20	40
125	Bobby Clarke	4	5	6	8	12	20	25	
126	Wayne Thomas	4	4	5	6	10	20	20	
127	Ivan Boldirev	4	4	5	6	10	15	20	35
128	Ted Bulley	4	4	5	6	10	15	20	
129	Dick Redmond	4	4	5	6	10	15	20	35
130	Clark Gillies AS1	4	4	5	6	10	30		
131	Checklist 1-132	6	10	15	25	40	60		
132	Vaclav Nedomansky	4	4	5	6	10	15	20	
133	Richard Mulhern	4	4	5	6	10	15	20	
134	Dave Schultz	4	4	5	6	10	15	20	
135	Guy Lapointe	4	4	5	6	10	15	20	
136	Gilles Meloche	4	4	5	6	10	15	20	
137	Randy Pierce RC	4	4	5	6	10	15	20	35

#	Player	VG 3	VgEx 4	EX 5	ExMt 6	NM 7	NmMt 8	NmMt+ 8.5	MT 9
138	Cam Connor	4	4	5	6	10	15	20	
139	George Ferguson	4	4	5	6	10	15	20	35
140	Bill Barber	4	4	5	6	10	15	20	
141	Terry Ruskowski UER	4	4	5	6	10	15	20	
142	Wayne Babych RC	4	4	5	6	10	15	20	35
143	Phil Russell	4	4	5	6	10	15	20	
144	Bobby Schmautz	4	4	5	6	10	15		80
145	Carol Vadnais	4	4	5	6	10	30		
146	John Tonelli RC	4	6	8	10	20	50	80	100
147	Peter Marsh RC	4	4	5	6	10	15	20	35
148	Thommie Bergman	4	4	5	6	10	15	20	35
149	Richard Martin	4	4	5	6	10	15	20	
150	Ken Dryden AS1	5	8	10	12	15	50	60	200
151	Kris Manery	4	4	5	6	10	15	20	35
152	Guy Charron	4	4	5	6	10	15	20	
153	Lanny McDonald	4	4	5	6	10	15	20	40
154	Ron Stackhouse	4	4	5	6	10	15	20	
155	Stan Mikita	4	5	6	8	12	20	25	40
156	Paul Holmgren	4	4	5	6	10	15	20	35
157	Perry Miller	4	4	5	6	10	15	20	
158	Gary Croteau	4	4	5	6	10	15	20	
159	Dave Maloney	4	4	5	6	10	15	20	
160	Marcel Dionne AS2	4	5	6	8	12	20	25	
161	Mike Bossy RB	4	5	6	8	20	25		
162	Don Maloney RB	4	4	5	6	10	15	20	
163	Whalers Logo CL	5	8	10	12	15	25	40	80
164	Brad Park RB	4	4	5	6	10	15	20	
165	Bryan Trottier RB	4	4	5	6	10	15	20	
166	Al Hill RC	4	4	5	6	10	15	20	35
167	Gary Bromley UER	4	4	5	6	10	15	20	35
168	Don Murdoch	4	4	5	6	10	15	20	35
169	Wayne Merrick	4	4	5	6	10	15	20	
170	Bob Gainey	4	4	5	6	10	20	25	40
171	Jim Schoenfeld	4	4	5	6	10	15	20	
172	Gregg Sheppard	4	4	5	6	10	15	20	35
173	Dan Bolduc RC	4	4	5	6	10	15	20	
174	Blake Dunlop	4	4	5	6	10	25		
175	Gordie Howe	6	10	12	25	30	50	75	350
176	Richard Brodeur	4	4	5	6	10	15	20	40
177	Tom Younghans	4	4	5	6	10	15	20	35
178	Andre Dupont	4	4	5	6	10	15	20	35
179	Ed Johnstone RC	4	4	5	6	10	15	20	
180	Gilbert Perreault	4	4	5	6	10	20		
181	Bob Lorimer RC	4	4	5	6	10	15	20	
182	John Wensink	4	4	5	6	10	15	20	
183	Lee Fogolin	4	4	5	6	10	15	20	
184	Greg Carroll RC	4	4	5	6	10	15	20	
185	Bobby Hull	6	10	12	15	25	60		
186	Harold Snepsts	4	4	5	6	10	15	20	
187	Peter Mahovlich	4	4	5	6	10	15	20	
188	Eric Vail	4	4	5	6	10	15	20	35
189	Phil Myre	4	4	5	6	10	15	20	
190	Wilf Paiement	4	4	5	6	10	15	20	
191	Charlie Simmer RC	5	8	10	12	20	30	40	60
192	Per-Olov Brasar	4	4	5	6	10	15	20	35
193	Lorne Henning	4	4	5	6	10	15	20	
194	Don Luce	4	4	5	6	10	15	20	
195	Steve Vickers	4	4	5	6	10	15	20	35
196	Bob Miller RC	4	4	5	6	10	15	20	
197	Mike Palmateer	4	4	5	6	10	15	20	
198	Nick Libett	4	4	5	6	10	15	20	
199	Pat Ribble RC	4	4	5	6	10	15	20	
200	Guy Lafleur AS1	5	8	10	12	20	60	80	
201	Mel Bridgman	4	4	5	6	10	30		
202	Morris Lukowich RC	4	4	5	6	10	15	20	35
203	Don Lever	4	4	5	6	10	15	20	
204	Tom Bladon	4	4	5	6	10	15	20	35
205	Garry Howatt	4	4	5	6	10	15	20	
206	Bobby Smith RC	5	8	10	12	20	40	50	150
207	Craig Ramsay	4	4	5	6	10	15	20	
208	Ron Duguay	4	4	5	6	10	15	20	35
209	Gilles Gilbert	4	4	5	6	10	15	20	
210	Bob MacMillan	4	4	5	6	10	15	20	
211	Pierre Mondou	4	4	5	6	10	15	20	
212	J.P. Bordeleau	4	4	5	6	10	15	20	35
213	Reed Larson	4	4	5	6	10	15	20	35
214	Dennis Ververgaert	4	4	5	6	10	15	20	
215	Bernie Federko	4	5	6	8	15	25	30	
216	Mark Howe	4	6	8	10	15	25		
217	Bob Nystrom	4	4	5	6	10	15	20	
218	Orest Kindrachuk	4	4	5	6	10	15	20	
219	Mike Fidler	4	4	5	6	10	15	20	35
220	Phil Esposito	4	4	5	6	10	15	20	
221	Bill Hajt	4	4	5	6	10	15	20	35
222	Mark Napier	4	4	5	6	10	30		
223	Dennis Maruk	4	4	5	6	10	15	20	
224	Dennis Polonich	4	4	5	6	10	15	20	35
225	Jean Ratelle	4	4	5	6	10	15	20	
226	Bob Dailey	4	4	5	6	10	15	20	
227	Alain Daigle	4	4	5	6	10	15	20	
228	Ian Turnbull	4	4	5	6	10	15	20	35
229	Jack Valiquette	4	4	5	6	10	15	20	
230	Mike Bossy AS2	5	8	10	12	20	40	60	
231	Brad Maxwell	4	4	5	6	10	15	20	
232	Dave Taylor	4	5	6	8	15	25	30	
233	Pierre Larouche	4	4	5	6	10	15	20	40
234	Rod Schutt RC	4	4	5	6	10	15	20	
235	Rogatien Vachon	4	4	5	6	10	15	20	
236	Ryan Walter RC	4	4	5	6	10	15	20	60
237	Checklist 133-264 UER	8	12	25	50	80	250		
238	Terry O'Reilly	4	4	5	6	10	15	20	
239	Real Cloutier	4	4	5	6	10	15	20	
240	Anders Hedberg	4	4	5	6	10	15	20	
241	Ken Linseman RC	4	5	6	8	15	25	30	
242	Billy Smith	4	4	5	6	10	15	20	
243	Rick Chartraw	4	4	5	6	10	15	20	
244	Flames Team	4	5	6	8	12	20	25	
245	Bruins Team	4	5	6	8	12	20	25	
246	Sabres Team	4	5	6	8	12	20	25	
247	Blackhawks Team	4	5	6	8	12	20	25	
248	Rockies Team	4	5	6	8	12	20	25	
249	Red Wings Team	4	5	6	8	12	20	25	50
250	Kings Team	4	5	6	8	12	20	25	
251	North Stars Team	4	5	6	8	12	20	25	50
252	Canadiens Team	5	8	10	12	20	50		
253	Islanders Team	4	5	6	8	15	100		
254	Rangers Team	4	5	6	8	12	20	25	
255	Flyers Team	4	5	6	8	12	20	25	50
256	Penguins Team	4	5	6	8	12	20	25	
257	Blues Team	4	5	6	8	12	20	25	
258	Maple Leafs Team	4	5	6	8	15	25	30	
259	Canucks Team	4	5	6	8	15	25	30	
260	Capitals Team	4	5	6	8	12	30	40	
261	Nordiques Team	5	8	10	12	30	40	50	80
262	Jean Hamel	4	4	5	6	10	15	20	
263	Stan Jonathan	4	4	5	6	10	15	20	
264	Russ Anderson	4	4	5	6	10	15	20	35
265	Gordie Roberts RC	4	4	5	6	10	15	20	
266	Bill Flett	4	4	5	6	10	15	20	35
267	Robbie Ftorek	4	4	5	6	10	15	20	
268	Mike Amodeo	4	4	5	6	10	15	20	35
269	Vic Venasky	4	4	5	6	10	15	20	
270	Bob Manno	4	4	5	6	10	15	20	
271	Dan Maloney	4	4	5	6	10	15	20	
272	Al Sims	4	4	5	6	10	15	20	
273	Greg Polis	4	4	5	6	10	15	20	
274	Doug Favell	4	4	5	6	15	20	25	
275	Pierre Plante	4	4	5	6	10	15	20	
276	Bob Murdoch	4	4	5	6	10	15	20	35
277	Lyle Moffat	4	4	5	6	10	30		
278	Jack Brownschidle	4	4	5	6	10	15	20	
279	Dave Keon	4	4	5	6	15	20	25	35
280	Darryl Edestrand	4	4	5	6	10	15	20	35
281	Greg Millen RC	4	6	8	10	20	30		
282	John Gould	4	4	5	6	10	15	20	
283	Rich Leduc	4	4	5	6	10	15	20	
284	Ron Delorme	4	4	5	6	10	15	20	40
285	Gord Smith	4	4	5	6	10	15	20	
286	Nick Fotiu	4	4	5	6	10	15	20	
287	Kevin McCarthy RC	4	4	5	6	10	15	20	90
288	Jimmy Jones	4	4	5	6	10	15	20	
289	Pierre Bouchard	4	4	5	6	10	15	20	
290	Wayne Bianchin	4	4	5	6	10	15	20	50
291	Garry Lariviere	4	4	5	6	10	15	20	
292	Steve Jensen	4	4	5	6	10	15	20	
293	John Garrett	4	4	5	6	10	15	20	
294	Hilliard Graves	4	4	5	6	10	15	20	35
295	Bill Clement	4	4	5	6	10	15	20	
296	Michel Larocque	4	4	5	6	10	30		40
297	Bob Stewart	4	4	5	6	10	15	20	
298	Doug Patey RC	4	4	5	6	10	15	20	35
299	Dave Farrish	4	4	5	6	10	15	20	
300	Al Smith	4	4	5	6	10	15	20	
301	Billy Lochead	4	4	5	6	15	20	25	
302	Dave Hutchinson	4	4	5	6	10	15	20	
303	Bill Riley	4	4	5	6	10	15	20	
304	Barry Gibbs	4	4	5	6	10	15	20	
305	Chris Oddleifson	4	4	5	6	10	15	20	
306	J. Bob Kelly UER	4	4	5	6	10	30		
307	Al Hangsleben RC	4	4	5	6	10	15	20	40
308	Curt Brackenbury RC	4	4	5	6	10	15	20	35
309	Rick Green	4	4	5	6	10	15	20	
310	Ken Houston	4	4	5	6	10	15	20	
311	Greg Joly	4	4	5	6	10	15	20	35
312	Bill Lesuk	4	4	5	6	10	15	20	
313	Bill Stewart RC	4	4	5	6	10	15	20	40
314	Rick Ley	4	4	5	6	10	15	20	
315	Brett Callighen RC	4	4	5	6	10	15	20	35

		VG 3	VgEx 4	EX 5	ExMt 6	NM 7	NmMt 8	NmMt+ 8.5	MT 9
316	Michel Dion	4	4	5	6	10	15	20	
317	Randy Manery	4	4	5	6	10	15	20	35
318	Barry Dean	4	4	5	6	10	20	25	
319	Pat Boutette	4	4	5	6	10	15	20	
320	Mark Heaslip	4	4	5	6	10	15	20	
321	Dave Inkpen	4	4	5	6	10	15	20	
322	Jere Gillis	4	4	5	6	10	15	20	
323	Larry Brown	4	4	5	6	10	15	20	
324	Alain Cote RC	4	4	5	6	10	15	20	35
325	Gordie Lane	4	4	5	6	10	15	20	
326	Bobby Lalonde	4	4	5	6	10	15	20	
327	Ed Staniowski	4	4	5	6	10	20	25	
328	Ron Plumb	4	4	5	6	10	15	20	
329	Jude Drouin	4	4	5	6	10	15	20	
330	Rick Hampton	4	4	5	6	10	15	20	35
331	Stan Weir	4	4	5	6	10	15	20	
332	Blair Stewart	4	4	5	6	10	15	20	
333	Mike Polich RC	4	4	5	6	10	15	20	35
334	Jean Potvin	4	4	5	6	10	15	20	35
335	Jordy Douglas RC	4	4	5	6	10	15	20	35
336	Joel Quenneville RC	4	4	5	6	10	15	20	
337	Glen Hanlon RC	4	5	6	8	10	20	25	
338	Dave Hoyda RC	4	4	5	6	10	15	20	
339	Colin Campbell	4	4	5	6	10	15	20	
340	John Smrke	4	4	5	6	10	15	20	
341	Brian Glennie	4	4	5	6	10	15	20	
342	Don Kozak	4	4	5	6	10	15	20	
343	Yvon Labre	4	4	5	6	10	15	20	
344	Curt Bennett	4	4	5	6	10	15	20	
345	Mike Christie	4	4	5	6	10	20	25	
346	Checklist 265-396	5	8	12	40	60			
347	Pat Price	4	4	5	6	10	15	20	35
348	Ron Low	4	4	5	6	10	15	20	
349	Mike Antonovich	4	4	5	6	10	15	20	35
350	Roland Eriksson	4	4	5	6	10	15	20	
351	Bob Murdoch	4	4	5	6	10	15	20	
352	Rob Palmer	4	4	5	6	10	15	20	
353	Brad Gassoff	4	4	5	6	10	15	20	35
354	Bruce Boudreau	4	4	5	6	10	15	20	35
355	Al Hamilton	4	4	5	6	10	15	20	
356	Blaine Stoughton	4	4	5	6	10	15	20	35
357	John Baby	4	4	5	6	10	15	20	
358	Gary Inness	4	4	5	6	10	30		35
359	Wayne Dillon	4	4	5	6	10	15	20	
360	Darcy Rota	4	4	5	6	10	15	20	
361	Brian Engblom RC	4	4	5	6	10	30		
362	Bill Hogaboam	4	4	5	6	10	15	20	
363	Dave Debol RC	4	4	5	6	10	15	20	
364	Pete Lopresti	4	4	5	6	10	15	20	
365	Gerry Hart	4	4	5	6	10	15	20	
366	Syl Apps	4	4	5	6	10	15	20	
367	Jack McIlhargey	4	4	5	6	10	15	20	
368	Willy Lindstrom	4	4	5	6	10	15	20	35
369	Don Laurence RC	4	4	5	6	10	15	20	35
370	Chuck Luksa RC	4	4	5	6	10	15	20	
371	Dave Semenko RC	5	8	10	12	15	40	60	100
372	Paul Baxter RC	4	4	5	6	10	15	20	
373	Ron Ellis	4	4	5	6	10	15	20	
374	Leif Svensson RC	4	4	5	6	10	15	20	60
375	Dennis O'Brien	4	4	5	6	10	15	20	
376	Glenn Goldup	4	4	5	6	10	15	20	
377	Terry Richardson	4	4	5	6	10	15	20	
378	Peter Sullivan	4	4	5	6	10	15	20	35
379	Doug Hicks	4	4	5	6	10	15	20	
380	Jamie Hislop RC	4	4	5	6	10	15	20	30
381	Jocelyn Guevremont	4	4	5	6	10	15	20	
382	Willi Plett	4	4	5	6	10	15	20	
383	Larry Goodenough	4	4	5	6	10	15	20	35
384	Jim Warner RC	4	4	5	6	10	15	20	40
385	Rey Comeau	4	4	5	6	10	15	20	
386	Barry Melrose RC	4	6	8	10	12	30	40	100
387	Dave Hunter RC	4	4	5	6	10	15	20	40
388	Wally Weir RC	4	4	5	6	10	15	20	35
389	Mario Lessard RC	4	4	5	6	10	15	20	40
390	Ed Kea	4	4	5	6	10	15	20	35
391	Bob Stephenson RC	4	4	5	6	10	15	20	30
392	Dennis Hextall	4	4	5	6	10	15	20	35
393	Jerry Butler	4	4	5	6	10	15	20	
394	David Shand	4	4	5	6	10	15	20	
395	Rick Blight	4	4	5	6	10	15	20	
396	Lars-Erik Sjoberg	4	4	6	8	12	25	30	

— Wayne Gretzky RC #18 BGS 9.5 (Gem) sold for $50,000 (eBay; 7/08)
— Wayne Gretzky RC #18 BGS 9.5 (Gem) sold for $11,789 (Memory Lane; 6/12)
— Billy Harris #115 PSA 10 (Gem Mt) sold for $11,789 (Memory Lane; 6/12)
— Billy Harris #115 PSA 10 (Gem Mt) sold for $3,174 (eBay; 1/13)

1979-80 Topps

		VG 3	VgEx 4	EX 5	ExMt 6	NM 7	NmMt 8	NmMt+ 8.5	MT 9
1	Bossy/Dionne/Lafleur LL	4	4	5	6	8	25		
2	Trott/Lafleur/Dionne LL	4	4	5	6	8	12	15	
3	Trott/Dionne/Lafleur LL	4	4	5	6	10	15	25	
4	Williams/Holt/Schultz LL	4	4	5	6	8	12	15	
5	Bossy/Dionne/Gardner LL	4	4	5	6	8	12	15	
6	Dryden/Resch/Parent LL	4	4	5	6	8	12	15	
7	Lafleur/Bossy/Trott/ LL	4	4	5	6	8	12	15	
8A	Dryden/Espo/Par LL ERR	4	4	5	8	15	40		
8B	Dryden/Espo/Par LL COR	4	4	5	6	10	25	35	
9	Greg Malone	4	4	5	6	10	15	20	
10	Rick Middleton	4	4	5	6	8	12	15	
11	Greg Smith	4	4	5	6	8	12	15	30
12	Rene Robert	4	4	5	6	8	12	15	
13	Doug Risebrough	4	4	5	6	8	12	15	30
14	Bob Kelly	4	4	5	6	8	12	15	
15	Walt Tkaczuk	4	4	5	6	8	12	15	30
16	John Marks	4	4	5	6	8	12	15	
17	Willie Huber RC	4	4	5	6	8	12	15	30
18	Wayne Gretzky RC	1,500	2,000	2,500	3,000	5,000	▼8,000	20,000	80,000
19	Ron Sedlbauer	4	4	5	6	8	12	15	30
20	Glenn Resch AS2	4	4	5	6	8	12	15	
21	Blair Chapman	4	4	5	6	8	12	15	
22	Ron Zanussi	4	4	5	6	8	12	15	30
23	Brad Park	4	4	5	6	10	15	20	
24	Yvon Lambert	4	4	5	6	8	12	15	
25	Andre Savard	4	4	5	6	8	12	15	
26	Jimmy Watson	4	4	5	6	10	15	20	
27	Hal Philipoff RC	4	4	5	6	8	12	15	
28	Dan Bouchard	4	4	5	6	8	12	15	
29	Bob Sirois	4	4	5	6	8	12	15	30
30	Ulf Nilsson	4	4	5	6	10	15	20	
31	Mike Murphy	4	4	5	6	10	15	20	
32	Stefan Persson	4	4	5	6	8	12	15	
33	Garry Unger	4	4	5	6	8	12	15	30
34	Rejean Houle	4	4	5	6	8	12	15	30
35	Barry Beck	4	4	5	6	8	12	15	
36	Tim Young	4	4	5	6	8	12	15	30
37	Rick Dudley	4	4	5	6	8	12	15	
38	Wayne Stephenson	4	4	5	6	8	12	15	30
39	Peter McNab	4	4	5	6	10	15	20	
40	Borje Salming AS2	4	4	5	6	8	12	15	
41	Tom Lysiak	4	4	5	6	8	12	15	30
42	Don Maloney RC	4	4	5	6	8	12	15	30
43	Mike Rogers	4	4	5	6	10	15	20	
44	Dave Lewis	4	4	5	6	8	12	15	
45	Peter Lee	4	4	5	6	8	12	15	30
46	Marty Howe	4	4	5	6	8	12	15	
47	Serge Bernier	4	4	5	6	8	12	15	30
48	Paul Woods	4	4	5	6	10	15	20	
49	Bob Sauve	4	4	5	6	8	12	15	30
50	Larry Robinson AS1	4	4	5	6	8	12	15	
51	Tom Gorence RC	4	4	5	6	8	12	15	30
52	Gary Sargent	4	4	5	6	8	12	15	30
53	Thomas Gradin RC	4	4	5	6	10	15	20	
54	Dean Talafous	4	4	5	6	8	12	15	
55	Bob Murray	4	4	5	6	8	12	15	30
56	Bob Bourne	4	4	5	6	8	12	15	
57	Larry Patey	4	4	5	6	8	12	15	30
58	Ross Lonsberry	4	4	5	6	10	15	20	
59	Rick Smith	4	4	5	6	8	12	15	30
60	Guy Chouinard	4	4	5	6	8	12	15	30
61	Danny Gare	4	4	5	6	8	12	15	
62	Jim Bedard	4	4	5	6	8	12	15	
63	Dale McCourt	4	4	5	6	10	15	20	
64	Steve Payne RC	4	4	5	6	8	12	15	
65	Pat Hughes RC	4	4	5	6	10	15	20	
66	Mike McEwen	4	4	5	6	8	12	15	30
67	Reg Kerr RC	4	4	5	6	8	12	15	
68	Walt McKechnie	4	4	5	6	8	12	15	30
69	Michel Plasse	4	4	5	6	8	12	15	
70	Denis Potvin AS1	4	4	5	6	8	12	15	
71	Dave Dryden	4	4	5	6	8	12	15	
72	Gary McAdam	4	4	5	6	8	12	15	30
73	Andre St.Laurent	4	4	5	6	8	12	15	
74	Jerry Korab	4	4	5	6	10	15	20	
75	Rick MacLeish	4	4	5	6	8	12	15	30
76	Dennis Kearns	4	4	5	6	8	12	15	
77	Jean Pronovost	4	4	5	6	8	12	15	30
78	Ron Greschner	4	4	5	6	10	15	20	
79	Wayne Cashman	4	4	5	6	8	12	15	30
80	Tony Esposito	4	4	5	6	8	15	25	30
81	Cup Semi-Finals	4	4	5	6	8	40		
82	Cup Semi-Finals	4	4	5	6	8	12	15	
83	Stanley Cup Finals	4	4	5	6	10	15	20	
84	Brian Sutter	4	4	5	6	8	12	15	
85	Gerry Cheevers	4	4	5	6	8	12	15	30
86	Pat Hickey	4	4	5	6	10	15	20	

#	Player	VG 3	VgEx 4	EX 5	ExMt 6	NM 7	NmMt 8	NmMt+ 8.5	MT 9
87	Mike Kaszycki	4	4	5	6	8	12	15	
88	Grant Mulvey	4	4	5	6	8	12	15	30
89	Derek Smith	4	4	5	6	8	12	15	30
90	Steve Shutt	4	4	5	6	8	12	15	
91	Robert Picard	4	4	5	6	10	15	20	
92	Dan Labraaten	4	4	5	6	8	12	15	
93	Glen Sharpley	4	4	5	6	8	12	15	30
94	Denis Herron	4	4	5	6	8	12	15	
95	Reggie Leach	4	4	5	6	8	12	15	
96	John Van Boxmeer	4	4	5	6	8	12	15	
97	Tiger Williams	4	4	5	6	8	12	15	
98	Butch Goring	4	4	5	6	8	12	15	30
99	Don Marcotte	4	4	5	6	8	12	15	30
100	Bryan Trottier AS1	4	4	5	6	8	12	15	
101	Serge Savard AS2	4	4	5	6	10	15	20	
102	Cliff Koroll	4	4	5	6	8	12	15	30
103	Gary Smith	4	4	5	6	8	12	15	30
104	Al MacAdam	4	4	5	6	10	15	20	
105	Don Edwards	4	4	5	6	8	12	15	30
106	Errol Thompson	4	4	5	6	8	12	15	
107	Andre Lacroix	4	4	5	6	8	12	15	
108	Marc Tardif	4	4	5	6	8	12	15	30
109	Rick Kehoe	4	4	5	6	8	12	15	30
110	John Davidson	4	4	5	6	8	12	15	
111	Behn Wilson RC	4	4	5	6	8	12	15	30
112	Doug Jarvis	4	4	5	6	8	12	15	30
113	Tom Rowe RC	4	4	5	6	10	15	20	
114	Mike Milbury	4	4	5	6	8	12	15	
115	Billy Harris	4	4	5	6	8	12	15	30
116	Greg Fox RC	4	4	5	6	8	12	15	30
117	Curt Fraser RC	4	4	5	6	8	12	15	
118	Jean-Paul Parise	4	4	5	6	8	12	15	
119	Ric Seiling	4	4	5	6	8	12	15	
120	Darryl Sittler	4	4	5	6	8	12	15	
121	Rick Lapointe	4	4	5	6	8	12	15	
122	Jim Rutherford	4	4	5	6	8	12	15	
123	Mario Tremblay	4	4	5	6	8	12	15	30
124	Randy Carlyle	4	4	5	6	8	12	15	
125	Bobby Clarke	4	4	5	6	10	15	20	
126	Wayne Thomas	4	4	5	6	8	12	15	30
127	Ivan Boldirev	4	4	5	6	8	12	15	
128	Ted Bulley	4	4	5	6	8	12	15	
129	Dick Redmond	4	4	5	6	8	12	15	30
130	Clark Gillies AS1	4	4	5	6	8	12	15	
131	Checklist 1-132	4	4	5	8	10	30		
132	Vaclav Nedomansky	4	4	5	6	8	12	15	30
133	Richard Mulhern	4	4	5	6	10	15	20	
134	Dave Schultz	4	4	5	6	10	15	20	
135	Guy Lapointe	4	4	5	6	8	12	15	
136	Gilles Meloche	4	4	5	6	8	12	15	
137	Randy Pierce RC	4	4	5	6	8	12	15	30
138	Cam Connor	4	4	5	6	8	12	15	30
139	George Ferguson	4	4	5	6	10	15	20	30
140	Bill Barber	4	4	5	6	8	12	15	
141	Mike Walton	4	4	5	6	8	12	15	
142	Wayne Babych RC	4	4	5	6	8	12	15	30
143	Phil Russell	4	4	5	6	8	12	15	
144	Bobby Schmautz	4	4	5	6	10	15	20	
145	Carol Vadnais	4	4	5	6	10	15	20	
146	John Tonelli RC	4	4	5	8	10	15	25	60
147	Peter Marsh RC	4	4	5	6	8	12	15	
148	Thommie Bergman	4	4	5	6	8	12	15	
149	Richard Martin	4	4	5	6	8	12	15	30
150	Ken Dryden AS1	4	4	5	8	10	15	30	100
151	Kris Manery	4	4	5	6	8	12	15	30
152	Guy Charron	4	4	5	6	10	15	20	
153	Lanny McDonald	4	4	5	6	8	12	15	30
154	Ron Stackhouse	4	4	5	6	8	12	15	
155	Stan Mikita	4	4	5	6	8	12	15	
156	Paul Holmgren	4	4	5	6	10	15	20	
157	Perry Miller	4	4	5	6	8	12	15	30
158	Gary Croteau	4	4	5	6	8	12	15	30
159	Dave Maloney	4	4	5	6	8	12	15	30
160	Marcel Dionne AS2	4	4	5	6	8	12	15	80
161	Mike Bossy RB	4	4	5	6	8	12	15	
162	Don Maloney RB	4	4	5	6	10	15	20	
163	Ulf Nilsson RB	4	4	5	6	8	12	15	
164	Brad Park RB	4	4	5	6	8	12	15	
165	Bryan Trottier RB	4	4	5	6	10	15	20	
166	Al Hill RC	4	4	5	6	8	12	15	30
167	Gary Bromley	4	4	5	6	8	12	15	30
168	Don Murdoch	4	4	5	6	10	15	20	
169	Wayne Merrick	4	4	5	6	10	15	20	
170	Bob Gainey	4	4	5	6	8	12	15	
171	Jim Schoenfeld	4	4	5	6	8	12	15	30
172	Gregg Sheppard	4	4	5	6	8	12	15	
173	Dan Bolduc RC	4	4	5	6	8	12	15	
174	Blake Dunlop	4	4	5	6	8	12	15	
175	Gordie Howe	5	6	8	15	25	50	60	80
176	Richard Brodeur	4	4	5	6	8	12	15	30

#	Player	VG 3	VgEx 4	EX 5	ExMt 6	NM 7	NmMt 8	NmMt+ 8.5	MT 9
177	Tom Younghans	4	4	5	6	8	12	15	
178	Andre Dupont	4	4	5	6	10	15	20	
179	Ed Johnstone RC	4	4	5	6	8	12	15	30
180	Gilbert Perreault	4	4	5	6	8	12	15	
181	Bob Lorimer RC	4	4	5	6	10	15	20	
182	John Wensink	4	4	5	6	8	12	15	
183	Lee Fogolin	4	4	5	6	10	15	20	
184	Greg Carroll RC	4	4	5	6	8	12	15	30
185	Bobby Hull	4	5	6	10	15	25	30	50
186	Harold Snepsts	4	4	5	6	8	12	15	30
187	Peter Mahovlich	4	4	5	6	8	12	15	30
188	Eric Vail	4	4	5	6	8	12	15	30
189	Phil Myre	4	4	5	6	10	15	20	
190	Wilf Paiement	4	4	5	6	10	15	20	
191	Charlie Simmer RC	4	4	5	6	10	15	25	
192	Per-Olov Brasar	4	4	5	6	10	15	20	30
193	Lorne Henning	4	4	5	6	8	12	15	
194	Don Luce	4	4	5	6	8	12	15	
195	Steve Vickers	4	4	5	6	8	12	15	30
196	Bob Miller RC	4	4	5	6	8	12	15	
197	Mike Palmateer	4	4	5	6	8	12	15	
198	Nick Libett	4	4	5	6	10	15	20	
199	Pat Ribble RC	4	4	5	6	8	12	15	
200	Guy Lafleur AS1	4	4	5	6	8	30	40	
201	Mel Bridgman	4	4	5	6	10	15	20	
202	Morris Lukowich RC	4	4	5	6	8	12	15	
203	Don Lever	4	4	5	6	10	15	20	
204	Tom Bladon	4	4	5	6	8	12	15	30
205	Garry Howatt	4	4	5	6	8	12	15	30
206	Bobby Smith RC	4	4	5	8	10	15	20	
207	Craig Ramsay	4	4	5	6	8	12	15	30
208	Ron Duguay	4	4	5	6	8	12	15	
209	Gilles Gilbert	4	4	5	6	10	15	20	30
210	Bob MacMillan	4	4	5	6	8	12	15	
211	Pierre Mondou	4	4	5	6	8	12	15	
212	J.P. Bordeleau	4	4	5	6	10	15	20	30
213	Reed Larson	4	4	5	6	10	15	20	30
214	Dennis Ververgaert	4	4	5	6	8	12	15	
215	Bernie Federko	4	4	5	6	8	12	15	
216	Mark Howe	4	4	5	6	8	12	15	
217	Bob Nystrom	4	4	5	6	8	12	15	30
218	Orest Kindrachuk	4	4	5	6	10	15	20	
219	Mike Fidler	4	4	5	6	8	12	15	30
220	Phil Esposito	4	4	5	6	8	12	15	
221	Bill Hajt	4	4	5	6	8	12	15	30
222	Mark Napier	4	4	5	6	8	12	15	30
223	Dennis Maruk	4	4	5	6	10	15	20	
224	Dennis Polonich	4	4	5	6	8	12	15	
225	Jean Ratelle	4	4	5	6	8	12	15	30
226	Bob Dailey	4	4	5	6	8	12	15	
227	Alain Daigle	4	4	5	6	8	12	15	
228	Ian Turnbull	4	4	5	6	8	12	15	
229	Jack Valiquette	4	4	5	6	10	15	20	
230	Mike Bossy AS2	4	4	5	6	10	12	20	80
231	Brad Maxwell	4	4	5	6	8	12	15	30
232	Dave Taylor	4	4	5	8	10	15	20	
233	Pierre Larouche	4	4	5	6	10	15	20	30
234	Rod Schutt RC	4	4	5	6	10	15	20	
235	Rogatien Vachon	4	4	5	6	10	15	20	
236	Ryan Walter RC	4	4	5	6	8	12	15	30
237	Checklist 133-264	4	4	5	8	10	60		
238	Terry O'Reilly	4	4	5	6	8	12	15	30
239	Real Cloutier	4	4	5	6	8	12	15	30
240	Anders Hedberg	4	4	5	6	10	15	20	
241	Ken Linseman RC	4	4	5	6	8	12	15	
242	Billy Smith	4	4	5	6	10	15		
243	Rick Chartraw	4	4	5	6	8	12	15	
244	Flames Team	4	4	5	6	8	12	15	
245	Bruins Team	4	4	5	6	8	12	15	35
246	Sabres Team	4	4	5	6	8	12	15	
247	Blackhawks Team	4	4	5	6	8	12	15	
248	Rockies Team	4	4	5	6	8	12	15	
249	Red Wings Team	4	4	5	6	8	12	15	35
250	Kings Team	4	4	5	6	8	12	15	
251	North Stars Team	4	4	5	6	8	12	15	
252	Canadiens Team	4	4	5	6	8	20	25	
253	Islanders Team	4	4	5	6	8	12	15	
254	Rangers Team	4	4	5	6	8	12	15	
255	Flyers Team	4	4	5	6	8	12	15	
256	Penguins Team	4	4	5	6	8	12	15	35
257	Blues Team	4	4	5	6	10	15		
258	Maple Leafs Team	4	4	5	6	8	12	15	
259	Canucks Team	4	4	5	6	8	12	15	
260	Capitals Team	4	4	5	6	8	12	15	
261	New NHL Entries CL	4	5	6	10	20	40	50	
262	Jean Hamel	4	4	5	6	8	12	15	
263	Stan Jonathan	4	4	5	6	8	12	15	
264	Russ Anderson	4	4	5	6	8	12	15	35

— Wayne Gretzky #18 PSA 10 (Gem) sold for $30,209 (Mastro; 4/07)
— Wayne Gretzky #18 BGS 9.5 (Gem) sold for $22,000 (eBay; 1/14)

HOCKEY

1980 - Present

1980-81 O-Pee-Chee

		NmMt 8	NmMt+ 8.5	MT 9	Gem 9.5/10
2	Ray Bourque RB	20	25	60	120
3	Wayne Gretzky RB	50	60	150	250
9	Ken Morrow OLY RC	12	15	25	60
31	Mike Liut RC	30	40	80	100
39	Brian Propp RC	20	30	100	
67	Michel Goulet RC	50	80	150	700
87	Wayne Gretzky AS2	40	50	100	300
140	Ray Bourque RC	600	1,000	2,500	10,000
162	Gretzky/Dionne/Lafleur LL	20	25	60	125
163	Dionne/Gretzky/Lafleur LL	20	25	80	125
182	Wayne Gretzky TL	20	25	60	250
187	Mike Foligno RC	20	30	50	
195	Mike Gartner RC	50	100	150	300
242	Rick Vaive RC	30	40	80	
250	Wayne Gretzky	250	350	600	750
279	Pete Peeters RC	20	30	60	
289	Mark Messier UER RC	▼600	▼1,000	▼2,500	8,000
344	Rod Langway RC	30	40	125	
385	Richard Sevigny RC	20	30	60	

1980-81 Topps

		NmMt 8	NmMt+ 8.5	MT 9	Gem 9.5/10
2	Ray Bourque RB/65 Points.; Record for Rookie Defenseman	12	25	40	
3	Wayne Gretzky RB/Youngest 50-goal Scorer	30	50	80	
57	Michel Goulet RC	10	15	30	
87	Wayne Gretzky AS2	30	50	80	
140	Ray Bourque RC	40	60	250	
162	Gretz/Dion/Lafl LL	10	15	30	
163	Gretz/Dion/Lafl LL	15	30	50	
182	Wayne Gretzky TL/Oilers Scoring Leaders (checklist back)	15	25	50	
195	Mike Gartner RC	20	30	40	
250	Wayne Gretzky UER/(1978-79 GP should be 80 not 60)	80	100	150	

1981-82 O-Pee-Chee

		NmMt 8	NmMt+ 8.5	MT 9	Gem 9.5/10
2	Ray Bourque	30	40	175	300
3	Denis Savard RC	50	60	120	300
106	Wayne Gretzky	60	80	200	400
107	Jari Kurri RC	100	150	250	350
108	Glenn Anderson RC	20	30	150	250
111	Paul Coffey RC	200	250	350	550
117	Kevin Lowe RC	25	30	100	
118	Mark Messier	30	40	80	135
120	Andy Moog RC	60	80	100	250
125	Wayne Gretzky SA	50	80	100	300

1981-82 Topps

		NmMt 8	NmMt+ 8.5	MT 9	Gem 9.5/10
5	Ray Bourque	6	12	25	40
16	Wayne Gretzky	25	50	80	100
18	Jari Kurri RC	6	15	40	60
W75	Denis Savard RC	10	15	20	40
W100	Larry Murphy RC	6	10	20	30
W105	Dino Ciccarelli RC	12	15	25	

1982-83 O-Pee-Chee

		NmMt 8	NmMt+ 8.5	MT 9	Gem 9.5/10
1	Wayne Gretzky HL	10	12	25	60
99	Wayne Gretzky TL	8	10	20	50
105	Grant Fuhr RC	60	80	150	300
106	Wayne Gretzky	50	80	150	
107	Wayne Gretzky IA	25	50	80	
111	Jari Kurri	8	10	20	40
117	Mark Messier	10	12	20	40
123	Ron Francis RC	50	60	120	300
164	Neal Broten RC	10	15	25	100
235	Wayne Gretzky LL	8	10	20	60
237	W.Gretzky/M.Goulet LL	8	10	20	50
240	Wayne Gretzky LL	8	10	20	50
242	Wayne Gretzky LL	8	10	20	60
243	Wayne Gretzky LL	8	10	20	60
307	Joe Mullen RC	10	15	40	150
380	Dale Hawerchuk RC	20	25	30	150

1983-84 O-Pee-Chee

		NmMt 8	NmMt+ 8.5	MT 9	Gem 9.5/10
22	Wayne Gretzky TL			15	40
23	M.Messier/W.Gretzky HL	40	50	80	150
29	Wayne Gretzky	50	80	150	200
65	Phil Housley RC	8	12	30	100
160	Bernie Nicholls RC	8	10	50	80
185	Guy Carbonneau RC	12	15	60	100
203	Wayne Gretzky Hart	8	10	15	40
204	Wayne Gretzky Ross	8	10	15	40
212	Wayne Gretzky RB	8	10	15	40
215	Wayne Gretzky LL	8	10	20	80
216	Wayne Gretzky LL	8	10	20	100

		NmMt 8	NmMt+ 8.5	MT 9	Gem 9.5/10
126	Wayne Gretzky TL	15	20	40	80
148	Larry Murphy RC	25	30	150	
161	Dino Ciccarelli RC	50	80	100	300
269	Peter Stastny RC	40	60	120	200
277	Dale Hunter RC	25	30	50	80
383	Wayne Gretzky LL	15	25	100	
384	Wayne Gretzky LL	15	25	100	
392	Wayne Gretzky RB	20	30	60	

1984-85 O-Pee-Chee

		NmMt 8	NmMt+ 8.5	MT 9	Gem 9.5/10
17	Dave Andreychuk RC	10	15	40	200
18	Tom Barrasso RC	10	15	40	150
67	Steve Yzerman RC	400	500	▲1,200	▼3,000
121	Pat Verbeek RC	12	15	30	60
129	Pat LaFontaine RC	15	20	40	150
185	Doug Gilmour RC	50	80	150	400
208	Wayne Gretzky AS	12	15	25	150
243	Wayne Gretzky	20	30	60	150
259	Chris Chelios RC	50	80	100	250
327	Cam Neely RC	80	100	150	250
357	Wayne Gretzky TL	8	12	20	50
373	Wayne Gretzky Ross	6	12	20	50
374	Wayne Gretzky Hart	6	12	20	50
380	Wayne Gretzky LL	10	12	20	50
381	Wayne Gretzky LL	10	12	20	40
382	Wayne Gretzky LL	10	12	20	40
383	Wayne Gretzky LL	10	12	20	50
385	Steve Yzerman LL	20	25	60	150
388	Wayne Gretzky RB	8	15	25	60

— Steve Yzerman #67 BGS 10 (Pristine) sold for $2,465 (eBay; 7/08)
— Steve Yzerman #67 BGS 10 (Pristine) sold for $2,300 (eBay; 7/07)
— Chris Chelios #259 BGS 10 (Pristine) sold for $410 (eBay, 05/08)

1984-85 Topps

		NmMt 8	NmMt+ 8.5	MT 9	Gem 9.5/10
13	Dave Andreychuk SP RC	8	10	15	40
14	Tom Barrasso RC	8	10	15	40
49	Steve Yzerman RC	▼150		▼300	2,500
51	Wayne Gretzky	8	12	25	

1985-86 O-Pee-Chee

		NmMt 8	NmMt+ 8.5	MT 9	Gem 9.5/10
9	Mario Lemieux RC	▼2,000	▼3,000	▼6,000	
29	Steve Yzerman	25	40	60	120
110	Pelle Lindbergh Mem.	20	25	40	80
120	Wayne Gretzky	40	60	80	225
122	Kelly Hrudey RC	12	15	25	50
210	Al Iafrate RC	15	20	30	60
237	Al MacInnis RC	30	40	80	
257	Wayne Gretzky LL	15	25	50	100
258	Wayne Gretzky LL	15	25	50	100
259	Wayne Gretzky LL	15	25	50	100
262	Mario Lemieux LL	40	60	80	500

HOCKEY

1985-86 Topps

		NmMt 8	NmMt+ 8.5	MT 9	Gem 9.5/10
9	Mario Lemieux RC	800	1,000	2,000	20,000
29	Steve Yzerman	15	20	30	
110	Pelle Lindbergh SP	12	15	30	
120	Wayne Gretzky	20	30	60	

1986-87 O-Pee-Chee

		NmMt 8	NmMt+ 8.5	MT 9	Gem 9.5/10
3	Wayne Gretzky	30	40	100	200
9	John Vanbiesbrouck RC	20	30	50	120
11	Steve Yzerman	25	30	60	150
53	Patrick Roy RC	1,000	1,500	▼3,000	
122	Mario Lemieux	50	60	100	200
149	Wendel Clark RC	50	80	150	200
259	Wayne Gretzky LL	10	15	25	50
260	Wayne Gretzky LL	10	15	25	50

1986-87 Topps

		NmMt 8	NmMt+ 8.5	MT 9	Gem 9.5/10
3	Wayne Gretzky	30	40	60	
9	John Vanbiesbrouck DP RC	12	20	40	
53	Patrick Roy RC	▼400	600	▲1,000	10,000
122	Mario Lemieux	25	40	75	
149	Wendel Clark DP RC	12	20	40	

1987-88 O-Pee-Chee

		NmMt 8	NmMt+ 8.5	MT 9	Gem 9.5/10
15	Mario Lemieux	25	30	50	100
42	Luc Robitaille RC	30	40	60	200
53	Wayne Gretzky	25	50	100	250
56	Steve Yzerman	12	15	25	60
123	Adam Oates RC	15	20	40	100
163	Patrick Roy	20	25	40	100
169	Ron Hextall RC	15	20	30	120
215	Mike Vernon RC	15	20	35	80
227	Claude Lemieux RC	12	20	30	80
243	Vincent Damphousse RC	12	20	30	80

1987-88 Topps

		NmMt 8	NmMt+ 8.5	MT 9	Gem 9.5/10
15	Mario Lemieux	15	25	30	50
42	Luc Robitaille RC	15	20	25	40
53	Wayne Gretzky	10	20	40	
123	Adam Oates RC	10	15	25	
163	Patrick Roy	20	25	30	60
169	Ron Hextall RC	10	15	25	40

1988-89 O-Pee-Chee

		NmMt 8	NmMt+ 8.5	MT 9	Gem 9.5/10
1	Mario Lemieux	12	15	25	100
16	Joe Nieuwendyk RC	10	15	40	100
66	Brett Hull RC	▼150	300	▼400	▲8,000
116	Patrick Roy	12	15	25	35
120	Wayne Gretzky UER	15	20	40	200
122	Brendan Shanahan RC	40	50	100	250
181	Bob Probert RC	12	20	30	100
194	Pierre Turgeon RC	10	12	25	120
196	Steve Yzerman	8	12	25	50

1988-89 Topps

		NmMt 8	NmMt+ 8.5	MT 9	Gem 9.5/10
1	Mario Lemieux DP	6	10	20	
16	Joe Nieuwendyk RC	10	15	30	
66	Brett Hull DP RC	▼60	100	▼150	3,000
116	Patrick Roy DP	8	12	25	
120	Wayne Gretzky Sweater	15	25	40	250
122	Brendan Shanahan RC	15	20	50	
181	Bob Probert DP RC	10	15	30	
194	Pierre Turgeon RC	10	12	25	

1989-90 O-Pee-Chee

		NmMt 8	NmMt+ 8.5	MT 9	Gem 9.5/10
89	Trevor Linden RC	10	12	20	40
113	Joe Sakic RC	▼50		200	1,000
136	Brian Leetch RC	10	12	20	75
156	Wayne Gretzky	8	10	20	
232	Theo Fleury RC	10	12	30	50

1989-90 Topps

		NmMt 8	NmMt+ 8.5	MT 9	Gem 9.5/10
113	Joe Sakic RC	15	20	50	
136	Brian Leetch RC	8	12	20	60

1990-91 O-Pee-Chee

		NmMt 8	NmMt+ 8.5	MT 9	Gem 9.5/10
7	Jeremy Roenick RC	5	5	12	25
120	Wayne Gretzky	2	4	6	15

1990-91 OPC Premier

		NmMt 8	NmMt+ 8.5	MT 9	Gem 9.5/10
30	Sergei Fedorov RC	▲20		▼30	▼150
38	Wayne Gretzky			▲40	▲200
50	Jaromir Jagr RC	▼80		▼125	600
51	Curtis Joseph RC	▲8	▲10	▲20	▲60
74	Mike Modano RC	25		40	▼150
100	Jeremy Roenick RC	6	▲15	▲25	40
114	Mats Sundin RC	▲25		▲40	▲100

1990-91 Score

		NmMt 8	NmMt+ 8.5	MT 9	Gem 9.5/10
120	Mike Modano RC	6	8	12	20
179	Jeremy Roenick RC	6	8	12	20
428	Jaromir Jagr RC	25	30	50	▼150
439	Martin Brodeur RC	30	40	60	300
440	Eric Lindros RC	▲25		▲40	200

1990-91 Score Rookie Traded

		NmMt 8	NmMt+ 8.5	MT 9	Gem 9.5/10
20T	Sergei Fedorov RC	5	6	8	15
70T	Jaromir Jagr		▲40	▲60	▲125
88T	Eric Lindros	8	10	▲20	▲30

1990-91 Topps

		NmMt 8	NmMt+ 8.5	MT 9	Gem 9.5/10
171	Curtis Joseph RC	8	10	15	25
348	Mike Modano RC	8	10	15	25

1990-91 Upper Deck

		NmMt 8	NmMt+ 8.5	MT 9	Gem 9.5/10
24	Alexander Mogilny RC	5	6	10	15
46	Mike Modano RC	6	8	12	20
55	Ed Belfour RC	6	8	12	20
63	Jeremy Roenick RC	5	6	10	15
178	Mark Recchi RC	5	6	10	15
356	Jaromir Jagr RC	30	40	▼50	▲300
365	Mats Sundin RC	5	6	10	20
458	Felix Potvin RC	6	8	12	25
525	Sergei Fedorov YG RC UER	40	8	50	▼150
526	Pavel Bure YG RC	▼25	▼30	50	▼250

1990-91 Upper Deck French

		NmMt 8	NmMt+ 8.5	MT 9	Gem 9.5/10
356	Jaromir Jagr RC	10	12	20	40
525	Sergei Fedorov YG RC UER	8	10	15	40
526	Pavel Bure YG RC	12	15	25	50

1991-92 OPC Premier

		NmMt 8	NmMt+ 8.5	MT 9	Gem 9.5/10
117	Nicklas Lidstrom RC	5	10	15	40
118A	V.Konstantinov ERR RC	10	15	25	40

1991-92 Upper Deck

		NmMt 8	NmMt+ 8.5	MT 9	Gem 9.5/10
21	Teemu Selanne CC RC	25	30	50	200
26	Nicklas Lidstrom CC RC	8	10	15	30
64	Peter Forsberg RC	▼20	30	40	200
335	Dominik Hasek RC	▼30	50	60	▲400
345	John LeClair RC	6	8	12	20
652	Nikolai Khabibulin RC	6	8	12	20
655	Alexei Kovalev RC	6	8	12	20
698	Keith Tkachuk RC	6	8	12	20

1991-92 Upper Deck French

		NmMt 8	NmMt+ 8.5	MT 9	Gem 9.5/10
21	Teemu Selanne RC CC	8	10	15	30
26	Nicklas Lidstrom RC CC	8	10	15	30
64	Peter Forsberg RC	8	10	15	30
335	Dominik Hasek RC	8	10	15	30

1991-92 Upper Deck Czech World Juniors

		NmMt 8	NmMt+ 8.5	MT 9	Gem 9.5/10
50	Paul Kariya	▼15		25	60

1992-93 Upper Deck

		NmMt 8	NmMt+ 8.5	MT 9	Gem 9.5/10
234	Markus Naslund RC	6	8	10	15
586	Paul Kariya RC	15	20	▼40	200
591	Chris Pronger RC	15		30	150
617	Saku Koivu RC	6	8	12	20

1994-95 Finest

		NmMt 8	NmMt+ 8.5	MT 9	Gem 9.5/10
41	Wayne Gretzky	10	12	20	30
125	Miikka Kiprusoff RC	20	20	25	50

1994-95 SP

		NmMt 8	NmMt+ 8.5	MT 9	Gem 9.5/10
181	Jarome Iginla RC	12	15	50	175
SP1	Wayne Gretzky 2500	10	15	25	50

1996-97 Black Diamond

		NmMt 8	NmMt+ 8.5	MT 9	Gem 9.5/10
160	Joe Thornton RC	250	▲400	▲500	

1996-97 Upper Deck

		NmMt 8	NmMt+ 8.5	MT 9	Gem 9.5/10
370	Joe Thornton RC	50		▼100	▼500

1997-98 Black Diamond

		NmMt 8	NmMt+ 8.5	MT 9	Gem 9.5/10
114	Daniel Sedin RC	12	20	30	60
131	Roberto Luongo RC	12	15	25	50
136	Henrik Sedin RC	12	20	30	60
150	Vincent Lecavalier RC	12	15	25	40

1997-98 SP Authentic

		NmMt 8	NmMt+ 8.5	MT 9	Gem 9.5/10
186	Zdeno Chara RC	▲400		▲2,000	

1997-98 Zenith

		NmMt 8	NmMt+ 8.5	MT 9	Gem 9.5/10
81	Patrik Elias RC	5	5	20	
95	Vincent Lecavalier RC	25	50	100	175
97	Roberto Luongo RC	25	40	80	100
99	Alex Tanguay RC	6	12	25	40

1998-99 SP Authentic

		NmMt 8	NmMt+ 8.5	MT 9	Gem 9.5/10
95	Milan Hejduk RC	20	25	30	60

1998-99 Upper Deck

		NmMt 8	NmMt+ 8.5	MT 9	Gem 9.5/10
234	Martin St. Louis RC	10	12	20	30

2000-01 SP Game Used

		NmMt 8	NmMt+ 8.5	MT 9	Gem 9.5/10
70	Marian Gaborik RC	35	40	50	80

2000-01 Upper Deck

		NmMt 8	NmMt+ 8.5	MT 9	Gem 9.5/10
198	Dany Heatley YG RC	15	20	30	50
229	Marian Gaborik YG RC	30	50	80	▼200

2001-02 SP Authentic

		NmMt 8	NmMt+ 8.5	MT 9	Gem 9.5/10
145	Pavel Datsyuk RC	60	80	100	200
175	Ilya Kovalchuk AU RC	135	150	175	300

2001-02 Upper Deck

		NmMt 8	NmMt+ 8.5	MT 9	Gem 9.5/10
211	Ilya Kovalchuk YG RC	50	60	80	200
422A	Pavel Datsyuk YG RC	60	80	200	300
422B	Pavel Datsyuk YG RC	60	80	100	200

2002-03 Pacific Exclusive

		NmMt 8	NmMt+ 8.5	MT 9	Gem 9.5/10
196	Rick Nash AU RC	25	30	40	80
197	Henrik Zetterberg AU RC	30	40	50	100

2002-03 SP Authentic

		NmMt 8	NmMt+ 8.5	MT 9	Gem 9.5/10
184	Rick Nash AU RC	30	50	80	100
186	Henrik Zetterberg AU RC	60	80	100	
191	Jason Spezza AU RC	▲60	▲80	▲125	▲200

2002-03 SP Game Used

		NmMt 8	NmMt+ 8.5	MT 9	Gem 9.5/10
73	Rick Nash RC	10	20	25	40
75	Henrik Zetterberg RC	8	15	25	35
82	Jason Spezza RC	10	20	25	40
97	Ryan Miller RC	10	20	25	40

2002-03 Upper Deck

		NmMt 8	NmMt+ 8.5	MT 9	Gem 9.5/10
232	Rick Nash YG RC	175	200	250	400
234	Henrik Zetterberg YG RC	150	175	▲800	▲2,000
429	Tim Thomas YG RC	60	80	200	400

— Henrik Zetterberg #234 BGS 10 (Pristine) sold for $675 (eBay; 4/15)

— Rick Nash #232 BGS 10 (Pristine) sold for $456.44 (eBay; 4/12)

2003-04 Black Diamond

		NmMt 8	NmMt+ 8.5	MT 9	Gem 9.5/10
198	Marc-Andre Fleury RC	35	40	60	80

2003-04 SP Authentic

		NmMt 8	NmMt+ 8.5	MT 9	Gem 9.5/10
137	Eric Staal AU RC	40	50	100	▲200
146	Patrice Bergeron AU RC	40	50	100	400
153	Marc-Andre Fleury AU RC	▲150	▲200	▲500	▲1,000
158	Alexander Semin AU RC	20	25	30	▲100

2003-04 Upper Deck

		NmMt 8	NmMt+ 8.5	MT 9	Gem 9.5/10
204	Patrice Bergeron YG RC	▲400	80	▲600	▲3,000
206	Eric Staal YG RC	40	50	60	▲400
221	Brent Burns YG RC	▲100	▲150	▲250	▲800
234	Marc-Andre Fleury YG RC	100	150	500	▲3,000
454	Ryan Kesler YG RC	25	30	▲60	▲300

2003-04 Upper Deck Trilogy

		NmMt 8	NmMt+ 8.5	MT 9	Gem 9.5/10
143	Patrice Bergeron RC	15	20	25	40
180	Marc-Andre Fleury RC	25	30	35	50

2004-05 SP Authentic Rookie Redemptions

		NmMt 8	NmMt+ 8.5	MT 9	Gem 9.5/10
RR5	Dion Phaneuf	20	30	60	100
RR24	Sidney Crosby	150	200	250	▲800
RR30	Alexander Ovechkin	100	125	250	600
RR40	Mike Richards	15	20	25	40
RR45	Ryan Getzlaf	20	25	30	50

2005-06 Artifacts

		NmMt 8	NmMt+ 8.5	MT 9	Gem 9.5/10
224	Sidney Crosby RC	200	350	400	1,500
230	Alexander Ovechkin RC	60	80	100	150

2005-06 Beehive

		NmMt 8	NmMt+ 8.5	MT 9	Gem 9.5/10
101	Sidney Crosby RC UER				
	Typo 'talent it tow'	40	50	▲300	▲500
102	Alexander Ovechkin RC	60	80	▲200	▲400

2005-06 Black Diamond

		NmMt 8	NmMt+ 8.5	MT 9	Gem 9.5/10
155	Duncan Keith RC	15	20	30	60
156	Henrik Lundqvist RC	20	25	30	50
191	Alexander Ovechkin RC	▲600	▲800	▲1,000	▲1,500
192	Zach Parise RC	20	25	35	50
193	Sidney Crosby RC	150	200	▲1,200	▲2,000
194	Dion Phaneuf RC	15	20	30	50
195	Jeff Carter RC	15	20	25	50
196	Corey Perry RC	25	30	35	50
199	Mike Richards RC	20	25	30	50

2005-06 McDonald's Upper Deck

		NmMt 8	NmMt+ 8.5	MT 9	Gem 9.5/10
51	Sidney Crosby		80	▼125	▲400

2005-06 Parkhurst

		NmMt 8	NmMt+ 8.5	MT 9	Gem 9.5/10
657	Sidney Crosby RC	35	40	50	120
669	Alexander Ovechkin RC	20	25	30	40

2005-06 SP Authentic

		NmMt 8	NmMt+ 8.5	MT 9	Gem 9.5/10
131	Ryan Getzlaf AU RC	▲50	▲80	▲200	▲400
132	Corey Perry AU RC	▲40	▲50	▲80	▲200
139	Thomas Vanek AU RC	30	35	40	60
140	Dion Phaneuf AU RC	30	35	40	80
142	Cam Ward AU RC	15	20	25	40
145	Brent Seabrook AU RC	25	30	40	80
147	Duncan Keith AU RC	60	▲100	▲300	▲400
155	Jim Howard AU RC	30	35	40	60
167	Zach Parise AU RC	50	60	80	150
171	Henrik Lundqvist AU RC	60	80	100	200
177	Jeff Carter AU RC	30	35	40	80
178	Mike Richards AU RC	20	25	30	50
181	Sidney Crosby AU RC	▲1,500	▲3,000	▲8,000	▲15,000
188	Alexander Steen AU RC	25	30	35	60
190	Alex Ovechkin AU RC	1,000	2,000	▲6,000	▲15,000

— Sidney Crosby #190 BGS 10 (Pristine) sold for $2,010 (eBay, 06/13)

— Alexander Ovechkin #190 BGS 10 (Pristine) sold for $1,280 (eBay, 05/08)

2005-06 SP Game Used

		NmMt 8	NmMt+ 8.5	MT 9	Gem 9.5/10
101	Sidney Crosby RC	125	▲200	▲500	▲1,000
111	Alexander Ovechkin RC	80	▲150	▲400	▲800

2005-06 SPx

		NmMt 8	NmMt+ 8.5	MT 9	Gem 9.5/10
164	Dion Phaneuf JSY AU RC	35	40	60	
173	Henrik Lundqvist JSY AU RC	▲60	▲80	▲200	▲300
190	Alex Ovechkin JSY AU/499 RC	800	1,000	1,500	2,500
191	Sidney Crosby JSY AU/499 RC	500	1,000	2,000	2,500

2005-06 UD Rookie Class

		NmMt 8	NmMt+ 8.5	MT 9	Gem 9.5/10
1	Sidney Crosby			▲200	▲500
2	Alexander Ovechkin	100	150	▼300	500

2005-06 Ultimate Collection

		NmMt 8	NmMt+ 8.5	MT 9	Gem 9.5/10
91	Sidney Crosby AU RC	650	1,000	2,000	3,500
92	Alexander Ovechkin AU RC	500	1,000	2,000	3,000
97	Henrik Lundqvist AU RC	60	80	125	250
101	Ryan Getzlaf AU RC	35	40	50	100
105	Dion Phaneuf AU RC	30	40	50	100

2005-06 Ultra

		NmMt 8	NmMt+ 8.5	MT 9	Gem 9.5/10
251	Sidney Crosby RC		300	400	▲800
252	Alexander Ovechkin RC		300	▲500	▲1,200
269	Henrik Lundqvist RC	12	15	20	40

2005-06 Upper Deck

		NmMt 8	NmMt+ 8.5	MT 9	Gem 9.5/10
201	Sidney Crosby YG RC	1,000	1,500	2,500	5,000
216	Henrik Lundqvist YG RC	40	50	80	200
443	Alexander Ovechkin YG RC	▲2,000	▲2,500	▲3,000	▲8,000
452	Ryan Getzlaf YG RC	12	15	25	60

2005-06 Upper Deck Ice

		NmMt 8	NmMt+ 8.5	MT 9	Gem 9.5/10
103	Alexander Ovechkin RC	800	900	1,000	
105	Corey Perry RC	250	300	400	
106	Sidney Crosby RC	3,000	3,200	3,500	
107	Ryan Getzlaf RC	25	30	40	80
109	Dion Phaneuf RC	15	20	30	50
110	Cam Ward RC	12	15	25	40
115	Zach Parise RC	25	30	40	60
117	Mike Richards RC	20	25	30	50
123	Brent Seabrook RC	10	12	25	50
137	Henrik Lundqvist RC	25	30	40	60
148	Duncan Keith RC	12	15	20	30
251	Pekka Rinne RC	12	15	30	50
260	Corey Crawford RC	12	15	20	30

2005-06 Upper Deck MVP

		NmMt 8	NmMt+ 8.5	MT 9	Gem 9.5/10
393	Sidney Crosby RC	40	50	100	300
394	Alexander Ovechkin RC	40	50	100	300

2005-06 Upper Deck Trilogy

		NmMt 8	NmMt+ 8.5	MT 9	Gem 9.5/10
211	Sidney Crosby RC	100	200	500	1,000
220	Alexander Ovechkin RC	40	50	80	125

2005-06 Upper Deck Victory

		NmMt 8	NmMt+ 8.5	MT 9	Gem 9.5/10
264	Alexander Ovechkin RC	40	50	100	150
285	Sidney Crosby RC	20	30	50	150

2006-07 Black Diamond

		NmMt 8	NmMt+ 8.5	MT 9	Gem 9.5/10
200	Anze Kopitar RC	20	25	30	50

		NmMt 8	NmMt+ 8.5	MT 9	Gem 9.5/10
202	Phil Kessel RC	20	25	30	50
205	Jordan Staal RC	20	25	30	50
206	Paul Stastny RC	25	30	40	50
210	Evgeni Malkin RC	50	60	80	150

2006-07 Flair Showcase

		NmMt 8	NmMt+ 8.5	MT 9	Gem 9.5/10
322	Evgeni Malkin RC	25	30	40	60

2006-07 SP Authentic

		NmMt 8	NmMt+ 8.5	MT 9	Gem 9.5/10
163	Phil Kessel AU RC	40	50	60	100
184	Anze Kopitar AU RC	50	60	80	125
196	Evgeni Malkin AU RC	150	175	200	600
198	Jordan Staal AU RC	30	35	50	100
200	Kristopher Letang AU RC	35	40	50	80

2006-07 The Cup

		NmMt 8	NmMt+ 8.5	MT 9	Gem 9.5/10
169	Jordan Staal JSY AU/99 RC	250	400	600	750
170	Phil Kessel JSY AU/99 RC	250	350	500	700
171	Evgeni Malkin JSY AU/99 RC	1,400	1,800	2,400	3,200
172	Paul Stastny JSY AU/99 RC	300	500	700	900
173	Anze Kopitar JSY AU/99 RC	400	600	750	1,000

2006-07 Ultra

		NmMt 8	NmMt+ 8.5	MT 9	Gem 9.5/10
251	Evgeni Malkin RC	10	15	20	60

2006-07 Upper Deck

		NmMt 8	NmMt+ 8.5	MT 9	Gem 9.5/10
204	Phil Kessel YG RC	25	30	40	80
216	Anze Kopitar YG RC	25	30	40	80
222	Shea Weber YG RC	15	20	40	80
239	Jordan Staal YG RC	15	20	25	40
240	Kristopher Letang YG RC	20	25	40	80
486	Evgeni Malkin YG RC	300	400	500	1,000
487	Joe Pavelski YG RC	12	20	100	300
495	Evgeni Malkin YG CL	30	60	150	300

2006-07 Upper Deck Trilogy

		NmMt 8	NmMt+ 8.5	MT 9	Gem 9.5/10
149	Evgeni Malkin RC	50	60	80	120

2007-08 Black Diamond

		NmMt 8	NmMt+ 8.5	MT 9	Gem 9.5/10
191	Jonathan Toews RC	40	50	80	100
194	Carey Price RC	40	50	60	100
200	Patrick Kane RC	30	40	50	100

2007-08 O-Pee-Chee

		NmMt 8	NmMt+ 8.5	MT 9	Gem 9.5/10
517	Jonathan Toews RC	12	20	40	60
518	Patrick Kane RC	10	15	25	40

2007-08 SP Authentic

		NmMt 8	NmMt+ 8.5	MT 9	Gem 9.5/10
177	Jonathan Quick RC	125	150	300	400
203	Jonathan Toews AU RC	175	200	250	400
204	Patrick Kane AU RC	135	150	175	250
225	Carey Price AU RC	100	125	150	500

2007-08 SP Authentic Sign of the Times

		NmMt 8	NmMt+ 8.5	MT 9	Gem 9.5/10
STCP	Carey Price	40	50	75	125
STJT	Jonathan Toews	80	100	125	300

2007-08 Ultra

		NmMt 8	NmMt+ 8.5	MT 9	Gem 9.5/10
251	Carey Price RC	30	35	50	80
252	Jonathan Toews RC	35	40	50	100
260	Patrick Kane RC	30	35	50	80

2007-08 Upper Deck

		NmMt 8	NmMt+ 8.5	MT 9	Gem 9.5/10
202	Bobby Ryan YG RC	12	15	20	40
207	Milan Lucic YG RC	10	12	15	40
208	David Krejci YG RC	12	15	20	50
210	Patrick Kane YG RC	400	600	800	▲3,000
223	Jonathan Bernier YG RC	15	20	25	50
227	Carey Price YG RC	400	500	▲600	1,500
228	Jaroslav Halak YG RC	8	10	12	40
249	Nicklas Backstrom YG RC	15	20	40	150
453	Ondrej Pavelec YG RC	12	15	20	30
456	Tuukka Rask YG RC	20	30	60	200
462	Jonathan Toews YG RC	200	250	400	▲2,000

2007-08 Upper Deck Ice

		NmMt 8	NmMt+ 8.5	MT 9	Gem 9.5/10
212	Jonathan Toews/99 RC	500	600	700	1,250
214	Carey Price/99 RC	700	800	900	1,250
217	Nicklas Backstrom/99 RC	100	125	150	250
221	Patrick Kane/99 RC	300	350	400	600

2008-09 Black Diamond

		NmMt 8	NmMt+ 8.5	MT 9	Gem 9.5/10
154	Claude Giroux RC	12	15	20	40
209	Steven Stamkos RC	40	50	80	150

2008-09 SP Authentic

		NmMt 8	NmMt+ 8.5	MT 9	Gem 9.5/10
178	Max Pacioretty RC	50	60	80	150
237	Claude Giroux AU RC	50	60	80	250
243	T.J. Oshie AU RC	20	25	30	80
244	Drew Doughty AU RC	50	60	80	150
247	Steven Stamkos AU RC	175	200	250	350

2008-09 Ultra

		NmMt 8	NmMt+ 8.5	MT 9	Gem 9.5/10
251	Steven Stamkos RC	20	25	35	50

2008-09 Upper Deck

		NmMt 8	NmMt+ 8.5	MT 9	Gem 9.5/10
202	Blake Wheeler YG RC	15	20	40	100
205	Jakub Voracek YG RC	12	20	40	80
218	T.J. Oshie YG RC	12	15	25	30
220	Drew Doughty YG RC	20	25	40	100
235	Claude Giroux YG RC	25		80	125
245	Steven Stamkos YG RC	100	150	▼250	▲800

2008-09 Upper Deck Ice

		NmMt 8	NmMt+ 8.5	MT 9	Gem 9.5/10
161	Claude Giroux RC	40	50	60	100

2008-09 Upper Deck Trilogy

		NmMt 8	NmMt+ 8.5	MT 9	Gem 9.5/10
163	Steven Stamkos RC	40	50	60	100

2009-10 Black Diamond

		NmMt 8	NmMt+ 8.5	MT 9	Gem 9.5/10
222	John Tavares RC	30	40	50	100

2009-10 SP Authentic

		NmMt 8	NmMt+ 8.5	MT 9	Gem 9.5/10
201	John Tavares AU RC	125	150	200	300
203	Matt Duchene AU RC	40	50	60	100
209	Erik Karlsson AU RC	60	80	100	150
223	Jamie Benn AU RC	40	50	60	100
259	Logan Couture AU RC	35	40	50	100

2009-10 The Cup

		NmMt 8	NmMt+ 8.5	MT 9	Gem 9.5/10
178	Matt Duchene JSY AU RC/99	100	200	300	500
180	John Tavares JSY AU RC/99	1,800	2,000	2,500	4,000

2009-10 Upper Deck

		NmMt 8	NmMt+ 8.5	MT 9	Gem 9.5/10
201	John Tavares YG RC	150		300	600
202	Victor Hedman YG RC	80		200	600
203	Matt Duchene YG RC	20	25	30	80
210	Erik Karlsson YG RC	25	30	40	200
212	Jamie Benn YG RC	30	40	50	120
214	Tyler Myers YG RC	8	10	20	40
452	Brad Marchand YG RC	100		125	200
487	Logan Couture YG RC	10	12	20	40
493	James Reimer YG RC	15	20	30	50
494	Michael Grabner YG RC	10	12	20	40
499	Braden Holtby YG RC	12	15	25	40

2009-10 Upper Deck Ice

		NmMt 8	NmMt+ 8.5	MT 9	Gem 9.5/10
170	Jamie Benn RC	175	200	250	400
183	Matt Duchene RC	175	200	250	350
184	John Tavares RC	500	600	700	800

2009-10 Upper Deck MVP

		NmMt 8	NmMt+ 8.5	MT 9	Gem 9.5/10
377	John Tavares RC	30	35	40	60

2009-10 Upper Deck Victory

		NmMt 8	NmMt+ 8.5	MT 9	Gem 9.5/10
318	John Tavares RC	10	12	15	25

2010-11 Black Diamond

		NmMt 8	NmMt+ 8.5	MT 9	Gem 9.5/10
218	P.K. Subban RC	25	30	40	60
220	Jordan Eberle RC	30	35	50	80
221	Tyler Seguin RC	25	30	40	60
222	Taylor Hall RC	20	25	50	100

2010-11 SP Authentic

		NmMt 8	NmMt+ 8.5	MT 9	Gem 9.5/10
71	P.K. Subban AU RC	50	80	100	150
77	Brayden Schenn AU RC	20	25	30	60

		NmMt 8	NmMt+ 8.5	MT 9	Gem 9.5/10
280	Taylor Hall AU RC	80	100	150	200
281	Jordan Eberle AU RC	60	80	100	200
301	Tyler Seguin AU RC	80	100	125	225

2010-11 Upper Deck

		NmMt 8	NmMt+ 8.5	MT 9	Gem 9.5/10
211	Jeff Skinner YG RC	20	25	30	60
219	Taylor Hall YG RC	60	80	▲200	▲500
220	Jordan Eberle YG RC	10	20	30	60
231	P.K. Subban YG RC	40	60	80	150
240	Sergei Bobrovsky YG RC	8	12	15	60
247	Nazem Kadri YG RC	20	25	30	80
456	Tyler Seguin YG RC	60	80	100	200
466	Magnus Paajarvi YG RC	12	15	20	30
486	Robin Lehner YG RC	25	30	40	50

— Taylor Hall #219 BGS 10 (Pristine) sold for $269 (eBay; 9/12)

— Jordan Eberle #220 BGS 10 (Pristine) sold for $217 (eBay; 10/12)

— Tyler Seguin #456 BGS 10 (Pristine) sold for $239 (eBay; 7/12)

2010-11 Upper Deck 20th Anniversary Parallel

		NmMt 8	NmMt+ 8.5	MT 9	Gem 9.5/10
219	Taylor Hall YG	60	80	100	150
456	Tyler Seguin YG	60	80	100	150
549	Jordan Eberle CWJ	60	80	100	150

2010-11 Upper Deck Exclusives

		NmMt 8	NmMt+ 8.5	MT 9	Gem 9.5/10
219	Taylor Hall YG	175	200	250	
456	Tyler Seguin YG	275	300	325	450

2010-11 Upper Deck Ice

		NmMt 8	NmMt+ 8.5	MT 9	Gem 9.5/10
102	Derek Stepan/99 B RC	80	100	125	200
103	P.K. Subban/99 B RC	300	350	400	500
104A	Tyler Seguin/99 B RC	350	400	450	600
105	Taylor Hall/99 B RC	600	650	700	900
110	Jordan Eberle/99 S RC	350	400	450	550

2011-12 Black Diamond

		NmMt 8	NmMt+ 8.5	MT 9	Gem 9.5/10
250	Ryan Nugent-Hopkins RC	25	30	40	80

2011-12 Panini Contenders

		NmMt 8	NmMt+ 8.5	MT 9	Gem 9.5/10
218	Ryan Nugent-Hopkins AU RC	40	50	80	100

2011-12 SP Authentic

		NmMt 8	NmMt+ 8.5	MT 9	Gem 9.5/10
221	Gustav Nyquist AU RC	30	40	50	80
228	Mark Scheifele AU RC	20	25	30	40
238	Brandon Saad AU RC	25	30	35	50
245	Ryan Johansen AU RC	25	30	40	60
247	Gabriel Landeskog AU RC	50	60	80	120
248	Nugent-Hopkins AU RC	80	100	150	200

2011-12 The Cup

		NmMt 8	NmMt+ 8.5	MT 9	Gem 9.5/10
180	Nugent-Hopkins JSY AU/99 RC	1,000	1,300	2,000	2,500

2011-12 Ultimate Collection

		NmMt 8	NmMt+ 8.5	MT 9	Gem 9.5/10
121	Ryan Nugent-Hopkins AU/99 RC	150	200	250	300

2011-12 Upper Deck

		NmMt 8	NmMt+ 8.5	MT 9	Gem 9.5/10
207	Brandon Saad YG RC	12	15	20	60
208	Gabriel Landeskog YG RC	20	25	30	▲300
214	Ryan Nugent-Hopkins YG RC	▲60		100	▲300
226	Adam Henrique YG RC	15	20	25	40
229	Mika Zibanejad YG RC			100	400
234	Sean Couturier YG RC	15	20	25	40
245	Cody Hodgson YG RC	15	20	25	30
248	Mark Scheifele YG RC	12	15	40	80
465	Ryan Johansen YG RC	15	20	25	35
468	Gustav Nyquist YG RC	15	20	30	40
476	Louis Leblanc YG RC	12	15	25	35

— Ryan Nugent-Hopkins #214 BGS 10 (Pristine) sold for $385 (eBay; 9/12)

— Ryan Nugent-Hopkins #214 BGS 10 (Pristine) sold for $412 (eBay; 2/12)

2011-12 Upper Deck Canvas

		NmMt 8	NmMt+ 8.5	MT 9	Gem 9.5/10
C98	Ryan Nugent-Hopkins YG	50	60	80	120

2011-12 Upper Deck Ice

		NmMt 8	NmMt+ 8.5	MT 9	Gem 9.5/10
98	Gabriel Landeskog RC	200	225	250	350
100	Ryan Nugent-Hopkins RC	500	550	600	800

2012-13 Upper Deck Ice

		NmMt 8	NmMt+ 8.5	MT 9	Gem 9.5/10
46	Chris Kreider/99 RC	80	100	125	150

2013-14 Black Diamond

		NmMt 8	NmMt+ 8.5	MT 9	Gem 9.5/10
229	Nathan MacKinnon RC	25	30	50	100

2013-14 SP Authentic

		NmMt 8	NmMt+ 8.5	MT 9	Gem 9.5/10
249	Tyler Johnson RC	15	20	25	50
265	Nail Yakupov AU RC	30	40	50	80
268	Morgan Rielly AU RC	20	25	30	60
269	Filip Forsberg AU RC	50	60	80	100
274	Tyler Toffoli AU RC	20	25	30	60
276	Vladimir Tarasenko AU RC	50	80	150	300
312	Nathan MacKinnon AU RC	500	600	1,000	2,000
313	Jacob Trouba AU RC	20	25	30	60
319	Mikael Granlund AU RC	20	25	30	60

2013-14 Upper Deck

		NmMt 8	NmMt+ 8.5	MT 9	Gem 9.5/10
220	Olli Maatta YG RC	12	15	20	40
222	Jonathan Huberdeau YG RC	12	20	40	80
228	Seth Jones YG RC	12	15	30	80
230	Vladimir Tarasenko YG RC	30	40	60	▲250
238	Nathan MacKinnon YG RC	500	600	1,000	2,000
242	Sean Monahan YG RC	15	20	25	60
246	Tyler Toffoli YG RC			100	150
451	Filip Forsberg YG RC	25	30	35	60
466	Petr Mrazek YG RC	12	15	20	30
470	Aleksander Barkov YG RC			▲150	▲500

		NmMt 8	NmMt+ 8.5	MT 9	Gem 9.5/10
477	Brendan Gallagher YG RC	15	20	25	40
483	Nikita Kucherov YG RC	80	100	150	500
485	Martin Jones YG RC	12	15	20	30
486	John Gibson YG RC	15	20	30	60
492	Tyler Johnson YG RC	15	20	25	40

2013-14 Upper Deck Canvas

		NmMt 8	NmMt+ 8.5	MT 9	Gem 9.5/10
C114	Nathan MacKinnon YG	60	80	125	300
C119	Tomas Hertl YG	20	25	30	50
C257	Nathan MacKinnon POE	100	125	150	200

2013-14 Upper Deck Ice

		NmMt 8	NmMt+ 8.5	MT 9	Gem 9.5/10
119	Filip Forsberg/99 RC	150	200	250	300
123	Nathan MacKinnon/99 RC	600	700	800	1,000
124	Vladimir Tarasenko/99 RC	300	350	400	500
128	Nail Yakupov/99 RC	200	250	300	350
129	Alex Galchenyuk/99 RC	400	450	500	600
130	Aleksander Barkov/99 RC	150	175	200	300
131	Tomas Hertl/99 RC	150	175	200	300
133	Seth Jones/99 RC	100	125	150	200

2014-15 Black Diamond

		NmMt 8	NmMt+ 8.5	MT 9	Gem 9.5/10
231	Johnny Gaudreau RC	25	30	50	100

2014-15 SP Authentic

		NmMt 8	NmMt+ 8.5	MT 9	Gem 9.5/10
294	Kevin Hayes AU RC	25	30	50	100
309	Aaron Ekblad AU RC	40	50	60	100
313	Jonathan Drouin AU RC	50	60	100	150

2014-15 Upper Deck

		NmMt 8	NmMt+ 8.5	MT 9	Gem 9.5/10
211	Johnny Gaudreau YG RC	60	80	100	▲250
214	Teuvo Teravainen YG RC	15	20	25	40
223	Leon Draisaitl YG RC	600		800	▲3,000
225	Aaron Ekblad YG RC	25	30	40	80
236	Anthony Duclair YG RC	10	12	20	40
248	Evgeny Kuznetsov YG RC	12	15	30	60
457	Darnell Nurse YG RC	10	12	20	40
477	Jonathan Drouin YG RC	40	50	60	150
478	Andrei Vasilevskiy YG RC			300	600
494	Bo Horvat YG RC			300	600
495	David Pastrnak YG RC	400	500	600	1,500

2014-15 Upper Deck Canvas

		NmMt 8	NmMt+ 8.5	MT 9	Gem 9.5/10
C94	Sam Reinhart YG	20	25	30	50
C96	Johnny Gaudreau YG	40	50	60	100
C98	Teuvo Teravainen YG	35	40	50	80
C104	Leon Draisaitl YG	60	100	200	350
C105	Aaron Ekblad YG	35	40	50	80
C110	Anthony Duclair YG	15	20	25	40
C117	Evgeny Kuznetsov YG	25	30	35	60
C214	Jonathan Drouin YG	35	40	50	80
C225	David Pastrnak YG	100	200	300	400

2014-15 Upper Deck Ice

		NmMt 8	NmMt+ 8.5	MT 9	Gem 9.5/10
157	Anthony Duclair/249 RC	20	25	40	80

		NmMt 8	NmMt+ 8.5	MT 9	Gem 9.5/10
158	Evgeny Kuznetsov/249 RC	35	40	60	125
159	David Pastrnak/99 RC	200	250	300	400
160	Sam Reinhart/99 RC	200	250	300	350
161	Leon Draisaitl/99 RC	125	150	175	200
162	Aaron Ekblad/99 RC	200	250	300	400
163	Curtis Lazar/99 RC	125	150	175	200
164	Bo Horvat/99 RC	150	200	225	250
165	Teuvo Teravainen/99 RC	150	200	225	250
166	Jonathan Drouin/99 RC	200	250	300	400
167	Johnny Gaudreau/99 RC	400	450	500	600
168	Andre Burakovsky/99 RC	125	150	175	200

2015-16 Upper Deck

		NmMt 8	NmMt+ 8.5	MT 9	Gem 9.5/10
201	Connor McDavid YG RC	▲1,500	▲2,000	▲2,500	▲5,000
204	Max Domi YG RC			▲40	▲100
206	Mikko Rantanen YG RC	20	30	50	100
221	Artemi Panarin YG RC	100	125	150	400
228	Dylan Larkin YG RC	50	60	80	200
451	Jack Eichel YG RC	125	150	200	▲500

2015-16 Upper Deck Canvas

		NmMt 8	NmMt+ 8.5	MT 9	Gem 9.5/10
C91	Jack Eichel YG			200	300
C98	Mikko Rantanen YG	20	30	40	80
C211	Connor McDavid YG			1,000	2,000
C270	Connor McDavid POE		80	100	250

2016-17 Upper Deck

		NmMt 8	NmMt+ 8.5	MT 9	Gem 9.5/10
201	Auston Matthews YG RC	500	600	1,000	2,500
205	Brayden Point YG RC	20	25	50	80
210	Sebastian Aho YG RC	60		125	400
451	Patrik Laine YG RC	20	30	100	▲200
458	Mathew Barzal YG RC			▲200	▲400
468	Mitch Marner YG RC	300		400	800

2016-17 Upper Deck Canvas

		NmMt 8	NmMt+ 8.5	MT 9	Gem 9.5/10
C35	Connor McDavid	10	15	25	50
C91	Mitch Marner YG	30	50	100	200
C106	Patrik Laine YG	30	50	100	200
C211	Auston Matthews YG	80	100	200	400
C214	William Nylander YG	20	30	50	100
C235	Jake Guentzel YG	25	50	80	150

2017-18 Upper Deck

		NmMt 8	NmMt+ 8.5	MT 9	Gem 9.5/10
201	Nico Hischier YG RC	20	25	60	200
247	Brock Boeser YG RC	▼40	60	80	200

2018-19 Upper Deck

		NmMt 8	NmMt+ 8.5	MT 9	Gem 9.5/10
201	Rasmus Dahlin YG RC			60	200
202	Roope Hintz YG RC	20	25	30	50
207	Dillon Dube YG RC	15	20	25	50
210	Mackenzie Blackwood YG RC	15	20	30	60
214	Filip Hronek YG RC	15	20	30	50
216	Max Comtois YG RC	15	25	30	50
217	Eeli Tolvanen YG RC	15	20	30	50
218	Oskar Lindblom YG RC	15	25	30	50
219	Anthony Cirelli YG RC	15	25	40	80

		NmMt 8	NmMt+ 8.5	MT 9	Gem 9.5/10
221	Evan Bouchard YG RC	15	25	40	80
225	Ryan Donato YG RC	10	15	20	40
226	Michael Rasmussen YG RC	10	15	20	40
228	Travis Dermott YG RC	10	20	25	40
230	Henri Jokiharju YG RC	15	20	25	40
231	Dennis Cholowski YG RC	10	15	25	40
244	Kristian Vesalainen YG RC	12	15	25	40
246	Miro Heiskanen YG RC	50	60	80	150
248	Elias Pettersson YG RC	125		200	▲400
249	Jesperi Kotkaniemi YG RC	▼30	▼50	▼60	200
491	Carter Hart YG RC	60	80	100	250

2018-19 Upper Deck Canvas

		NmMt 8	NmMt+ 8.5	MT 9	Gem 9.5/10
C101	Miro Heiskanen YG	15	25	40	100
C218	Carter Hart YG	60	80	125	200
C223	Jesperi Kotkaniemi YG	50	60	80	125

2019-20 Upper Deck

		NmMt 8	NmMt+ 8.5	MT 9	Gem 9.5/10
201	Jack Hughes YG RC	▼80	▼125	200	▲400
207	Victor Olofsson YG RC	20	30	▲50	▲125
210	Ilya Mikheyev YG RC	15	30	40	100
222	Rasmus Sandin YG RC	20	30	▲50	▲200
225	Alexandre Texier YG RC	15	20	▲30	▲80
226	Ryan Poehling YG RC	15	20	30	60
228	Adam Fox YG RC	100		250	600
237	Cody Glass YG RC	15	20	▲60	▲125
246	Dominik Kubalik YG RC	▼20	▼30	▼50	▼150
249	Quinn Hughes YG RC	80	100	150	400
451	Kirby Dach YG RC			▼100	300
454	Cayden Primeau YG RC			80	▼250
458	John Marino YG RC	15	20	25	60
463	Barrett Hayton YG RC	15	20	30	▲200
466	Elvis Merzlikins YG RC	▲40		▲50	▲200
471	Nick Suzuki YG RC	▲150		200	▲500
478	Filip Zadina YG RC	20	40	60	200
493	Cale Makar YG RC	150	200	250	600
499	Kaapo Kakko YG RC	▼50	80	100	▲300
528	Igor Shesterkin YG RC	▼60	▼100	▼150	500

2020-21 Upper Deck

		NmMt 8	NmMt+ 8.5	MT 9	Gem 9.5/10
201	Alexis Lafreniere YG RC	200		300	800
205	Bowen Byram YG RC	60		125	▲400
209	Josh Norris YG RC	20		80	400
211	Vitek Vanecek YG RC			60	200
234	Connor McMichael YG RC	25		60	▼250
235	Jason Robertson YG RC			80	▼400
237	Nick Robertson YG RC			60	250
239	Peyton Krebs YG RC	20		60	250
243	Vitali Kravtsov YG RC			60	300
451	Kirill Kaprizov YG RC	250		400	▼1,000
455	Alexander Romanov YG RC			60	300
461	Ilya Sorokin YG RC			200	400
462	Nils Hoglander YG RC				250
469	K'Andre Miller YG RC				300
482	Tim Stutzle YG RC			150	▲600
484	Pius Suter YG RC				250

GAMING

1993 Magic The Gathering Alpha

		NmMt 8	NmMt+ 8.5	MT 9	Gem 9.5/10
1	Animate Wall R :W:	150	300	350	500
2	Armageddon R :W:	900	950	1,700	
3	Balance R :W:	800	900	2,300	10,000
5	Black Ward U :W:	40	60	250	400
6	Blaze of Glory R :W:	300	400	600	2,300
7	Blessing R :W:	200	300	500	1,400
8	Blue Ward U :W:	30	60	100	300
9	Castle U :W:	30	100	125	500
14	Consecrate Land U :W:	30	40	125	
15	Conversion U :W:	40	50	75	175
16	Crusade R :W:	400	500	600	
19	Farmstead R :W:	300	350	400	450
20	Green Ward U :W:	30	40	60	
25	Island Sanctuary R :W:	300	400	500	1,000
26	Karma U :W:	50	80	175	200
27	Lance U :W:	60	100	150	
29	Northern Paladin R :W:	145	200	500	
31	Personal Incarnation R :W:	200	300	500	
32	Purelace R :W:	75	125	200	500
33	Red Ward U :W:	20	60	100	
34	Resurrection U :W:	30	75	100	250
35	Reverse Damage R :W:	100	150	500	
36	Righteousness R :W:	150	200	300	400
38	Savannah Lions R :W:	450	600	800	1,000
39	Serra Angel U :W:	500	750	2,000	4,000
40	Swords to Plowshares U :W:	200	250	500	
41	Veteran Bodyguard R :W:	150	200	250	
42	Wall of Swords U :W:	20	30	40	
43	White Knight U :W:	50	300	400	500
44	White Ward U :W:	20	30	40	300
45	Wrath of God R :W:	400	600	800	1,200
46	Air Elemental U :B:	40	120	175	600
47	Ancestral Recall R :B:	3,500	4,500	18,000	35,000
48	Animate Artifact U :B:	60	75	100	250
50	Braingeyser R :B:	900	1,000	2,600	4,300
51	Clone U :B:	125	150	250	400
52	Control Magic U :B:	200	250	500	600
53	Copy Artifact R :B:	400	500	600	
54	Counterspell U :B:	400	600	900	
56	Drain Power R :B:	200	300	400	
57	Feedback U :B:	30	50	200	350
61	Lifetap U :B:	40	80	100	125
62	Lord of Atlantis R :B:	300	500	1,000	2,500
63	Magical Hack R :B:	150	200	600	
64	Mahamoti Djinn R :B:	500	600	1,000	
65	Mana Short R :B:	300	600	1,300	
67	Phantasmal Forces U :B:	30	50	125	
69	Phantom Monster U :B:	20	30	100	150
70	Pirate Ship R :B:	150	200	500	
74	Psionic Blast U :B:	80	100	200	
77	Siren's Call U :B:	20	40	100	180
78	Sleight of Mind R :B:	400	600	800	1,500
80	Stasis R :B:	200	300	400	
81	Steal Artifact U :B:	20	35	50	
82	Thoughtlace R :B:	150	180	300	1,600
83	Time Walk R :B:	3,000	8,000	12,000	20,000
84	Timetwister R :B:	2,000	5,900	12,000	25,000
87	Vesuvan Doppleganger R :B:	800	1,000	2,000	3,500
88	Volcanic Eruption R :B:	100	150	300	
89	Wall of Air U :B:	20	30	90	120
90	Wall of Water U :B:	20	30	40	
91	Water Elemental U :B:	30	40	60	
92	Animate Dead U :K:	200	350	400	600
93	Bad Moon R :K:	200	300	1,000	1,300
94	Black Knight U :K:	200	300	500	1,200
95	Bog Wraith U :K:	75	100	200	1,500
96	Contract from Below R :K:	250	300	500	
97	Cursed Land U :K:	35	50	150	
99	Darkpact R :K:	200	400	500	
100	Deathgrip U :K:	50	80	150	200
101	Deathlace R :K:	150	200	300	900
102	Demonic Attorney R :K:	200	300	500	
103	Demonic Hordes R :K:	150	200	300	650
104	Demonic Tutor U :K:	500	1,000	1,500	
107	Evil Presence U :K:	50	75	150	750
110	Gloom U :K:	60	100	125	
112	Hypnotic Specter U :K:	400	500	600	
113	Lich R :K:	400	500	600	
114	Lord of the Pit R :K:	300	500	700	3,000
115	Mind Twist R :K:	400	450	750	
116	Nether Shadow R :K:	150	200	300	500
117	Nettling Imp U :K:	20	30	75	
118	Nightmare R :K:	400	500	600	
123	Royal Assassin R :K:	300	400	1,100	1,800
124	Sacrifice U :K:	20	30	80	
126	Scavenging Ghoul U :K:	20	30	60	
127	Sengir Vampire U :K:	75	90	200	
128	Simulacrum U :K:	20	35	80	
132	Wall of Bone U :K:	20	30	40	
133	Warp Artifact R :K:	100	120	150	
135	Will-O'-The-Wisp R :K:	150	200	500	700
136	Word of Command R :K:	200	250	400	
137	Zombie Master R :K:	250	300	400	500
138	Burrowing U :R:	50	75	150	350
139	Chaoslace R :R:	200	250	500	1,000
141	Dragon Whelp U :R:	80	150	250	1,300
142	Dwarven Demolition Team U :R:	50	100	200	750
144	Earth Elemental U :R:	40	60	100	400
146	Earthquake R :R:	250	300	400	500
148	Fire Elemental U :R:	30	50	80	
151	Flashfires U :R:	70	125		
152	Fork R :R:	550	825	1,000	2,000
153	Goblin Balloon Brigade U :R:	40	60	80	200
154	Goblin King R :R:	350	500	650	
155	Granite Gargoyle R :R:	250	300	450	600
160	Keldon Warlord U :R:	150	200	300	
162	Mana Flare R :R:	125	180	750	2,300
163	Manabarbs R :R:	100	150	300	1,300
165	Orcish Artillery U :R:	25	30	70	
166	Orcish Oriflamme U :R:	20	35	50	
167	Power Surge R :R:	100	125	170	
168	Raging River R :R:	200	250	500	1,000
170	Roc of Kher Ridges R :R:	300	400	500	
171	Rock Hydra R :R:	150	200	250	
172	Sedge Troll R :R:	400	500	800	
174	Shivan Dragon R :R:	2,900	3,700	6,800	10,000
175	Smoke R :R:	150	400	500	
176	Stone Giant U :R:	20	35	50	
178	Tunnel U :R:	20	40	60	
179	Two-Headed Giant of Foriys R :R:	125	180	300	
180	Uthden Troll U :R:	30	60	100	250
181	Wall of Fire U :R:	20	30	40	
182	Wall of Stone U :R:	20	30	40	
183	Wheel of Fortune R :R:	800	1,000	3,500	
184	Aspect of Wolf R :G:	150	200	500	1,800
185	Berserk U :G:	200	450	700	900
186	Birds of Paradise R :G:	2,600	4,700	6,000	30,000
187	Camouflage U :G:	60	100	250	300
188	Channel U :G:	120	150	400	
189	Cockatrice R :G:	150	200	350	
191	Elvish Archers R :G:	200	250	350	
192	Fastbond R :G:	400	500	700	
194	Force of Nature R :G:	500	700	1,000	
195	Fungusaur R :G:	200	250		
196	Gaea's Liege R :G:	200	250		
200	Hurricane U :G:	80	100		
201	Ice Storm U :G:	100	140	150	300
202	Instill Energy U :G:	150	200	250	
204	Kudzu R :G:	150	200		
205	Ley Druid U :G:	30	50	100	180
206	Lifeforce U :G:	30	50	100	175
207	Lifelace R :G:	100	200	300	
208	Living Artifact R :G:	100	150	300	800
209	Living Lands R :G:	100	150	200	
211	Lure U :G:	60	80	100	
212	Natural Selection R :G:	150	200	300	
214	Regrowth U :G:	50	70	160	
218	Thicket Basilisk U :G:	20	30	50	
219	Timber Wolves R :G:	150	200	400	600
221	Tsunami U :G:	20	35	50	
222	Verduran Enchantress R :G:	150	200	500	1,000
223	Wall of Brambles U :G:	20	30	40	
224	Wall of Ice U :G:	20	30	40	
226	Wanderlust U :G:	20	30	50	
228	Web R :G:	100	150	200	
230	Ankh of Mishra R	300	400	950	2,400
231	Basalt Monolith U	150	300	450	900
232	Black Lotus R	50,000	80,000	100,000	250,000
233	Black Vise U	200	500	1,200	2,800
234	Celestial Prism U	30	60	120	200
235	Chaos Orb R	4,200	4,800	7,200	
236	Clockwork Beast R	150	175	800	
237	Conservator U	40	60	80	300
238	Copper Tablet U	100	150	200	250
239	Crystal Rod U	50	75	100	
240	Cyclopean Tomb R	300	400	600	
241	Dingus Egg R	80	120	250	
242	Disrupting Scepter R	400	600	700	800
243	Forcefield R	600	800	1,200	10,000
244	Gauntlet of Might R	1,000	1,200		
245	Glasses of Urza U	40	50		
246	Helm of Chatzuk R	100	150	400	
247	Howling Mine R	400	500	700	900
248	Icy Manipulator U	300	400	500	800
249	Illusionary Mask R	350	400	750	
250	Iron Star U	40	60	80	100
251	Ivory Cup U	20	30	40	200
252	Jade Monolith R	100	150	325	
253	Jade Statue U	100	130		
254	Jayemdae Tome R	500	700	1,100	
255	Juggernaut U	150	200	300	
256	Kormus Bell R	200	300	500	1,000
257	Library of Leng U	60	80	100	
258	Living Wall U	30	50	150	450
259	Mana Vault R	1,400	1,500	2,000	3,700
260	Meekstone R	200	250	400	600
261	Mox Emerald R	2,000	5,000	9,000	23,000
262	Mox Jet R	2,500	6,000	9,000	25,000
263	Mox Pearl R	5,800	8,000	10,000	15,000
264	Mox Ruby R	2,000	5,700	11,000	23,000
265	Mox Sapphire R	3,200	7,000	15,000	
266	Nevinyrral's Disk R	400	1,000	1,700	4,000
267	Obsianus Golem U	15	25	50	
268	Rod of Ruin U	20	30	80	
269	Sol Ring U	150	400	1,000	2,000
270	Soul Net U	40	80	200	
271	Sunglasses of Urza R	100	150	170	
272	The Hive R	300	400	500	
273	Throne of Bone U	20	30	50	
274	Time Vault R	900	2,000	3,000	4,000
275	Winter Orb R	300	400	500	
276	Wooden Sphere U	30	40	80	
277	Badlands R	1,500	3,800	4,000	5,800
278	Bayou R	2,000	3,000	4,000	7,000
279	Plateau R	1,000	2,000	2,500	3,100
280	Savannah R	800	1,100	2,000	5,000
281	Scrubland R	1,000	2,500	2,700	6,300
282	Taiga R	1,500	2,500	4,000	8,000
283	Tropical Island R	3,000	3,500	4,000	6,000
284	Tundra R	3,000	3,800	5,600	7,550
285	Underground Sea R	5,000	6,000	11,000	21,000

1993 Magic The Gathering Beta

		NmMt 8	NmMt+ 8.5	MT 9	Gem 9.5/10
1	Animate Wall R :W:	15	25	30	75
2	Armageddon R :W:	150	225	300	500
3	Balance R :W:	150	180	200	500
4	Benalish Hero C :W:	5	10	15	25
5	Black Ward U :W:	8	15	20	
6	Blaze of Glory R :W:	40	100	125	350
7	Blessing R :W:	20	40	60	125
8	Blue Ward U :W:	8	15	20	30
9	Castle U :W:	12	20	25	50
10	Circle of Protection Black C :W:	8	15	20	30
11	Circle of Protection Blue C :W:	8	15	20	40
12	Circle of Protection Green C :W:	8	15	20	30
13	Circle of Protection Red C :W:	8	15	20	30
14	Circle of Protection White C :W:	8	15	20	30
15	Consecrate Land U :W:	15	25	30	75
16	Conversion U :W:	8	15	20	
17	Crusade R :W:	50	100	125	500
18	Death Ward C :W:	8	15	20	30
19	Disenchant C :W:	15	20	25	40
20	Farmstead R :W:	20	40	50	125
21	Green Ward U :W:	8	15	20	
22	Guardian Angel C :W:	8	15	20	30
23	Healing Salve C :W:	8	15	20	30
24	Holy Armor C :W:	8	15	20	30
25	Holy Strength C :W:	8	15	20	30
26	Island Sanctuary R :W:	20	50	60	150
27	Karma U :W:	8	15	20	
28	Lance U :W:	8	15	20	
29	Mesa Pegasus C :W:	8	15	20	30
30	Northern Paladin R :W:	40	80	100	250
31	Pearled Unicorn C :W:	8	15	20	30
32	Personal Incarnation R :W:	20	30	40	
33	Purelace R :W:	12	20	25	50
34	Red Ward U :W:	8	15	20	30
35	Resurrection U :W:	8	15	20	30
36	Reverse Damage R :W:	20	40	50	125
37	Righteousness R :W:	20	40	50	125
38	Samite Healer C :W:	8	15	20	30
39	Savannah Lions R :W:	80	100	150	500
40	Serra Angel U :W:	80	150	175	400
41	Swords to Plowshares U :W:	30	75	100	300
42	Veteran Bodyguard R :W:	20	30	40	
43	Wall of Swords U :W:	8	15	20	30
44	White Knight U :W:	20	30	40	
45	White Ward U :W:	8	15	20	30
46	Wrath of God R :W:	300	400	500	600
47	Air Elemental U :B:	8	10	15	20
48	Ancestral Recall R :B:	3,500	5,000	6,600	12,500
49	Animate Artifact U :B:	8	15	20	
50	Blue Elemental Blast C :B:	8	15	20	30
51	Braingeyser R :B:	130	150	200	350
52	Clone U :B:	20	40	50	
53	Control Magic U :B:	15	25	30	
54	Copy Artifact R :B:	50	120	150	400
55	Counterspell U :B:	40	80	100	
56	Creature Bond C :B:	8	15	20	30
57	Drain Power R :B:	20	50	60	150
58	Feedback U :B:	8	15	20	30
59	Flight C :B:	8	15	20	30
60	Invisibility C :B:	8	15	20	30
61	Jump C :B:	8	15	20	30
62	Lifetap U :B:	8	15	20	30
63	Lord of Atlantis R :B:	50	120	150	350
64	Magical Hack R :B:	20	40	50	
65	Mahamoti Djinn R :B:	50	100	125	400
66	Mana Short R :B:	50	100	125	350
67	Merfolk of the Pearl Trident C :B:	8	15	20	
68	Phantasmal Forces U :B:	8	15	20	
69	Phantasmal Terrain C :B:	8	15	20	30
70	Phantom Monster U :B:	8	15	20	30
71	Pirate Ship R :B:	20	40	50	125
72	Power Leak C :B:	8	15	20	30
73	Power Sink C :B:	8	15	20	30
74	Prodigal Sorcerer C :B:	8	15	20	30
75	Psionic Blast U :B:	40	80	100	250
76	Psychic Venom C :B:	8	15	20	
77	Sea Serpent C :B:	8	15	20	30
78	Siren's Call U :B:	8	15	20	30
79	Sleight of Mind R :B:	20	30	40	100
80	Spell Blast C :B:	8	15	20	30
81	Stasis R :B:	50	100	125	350

#	Card	NmMt 8	NmMt+ 8.5	MT 9	Gem 9.5/10
82	Steal Artifact U :B:	8	15	20	
83	Thoughtlace R :B:	20	30	40	100
84	Time Walk R :B:	1,500	6,100	4,900	12,250
85	Timetwister R :B:	1,000	1,750	2,500	3,000
86	Twiddle C :B:	8	15	20	30
87	Unsummon C :B:	8	15	20	30
88	Vesuvan Doppelganger R :B:	100	200	250	7,000
89	Volcanic Eruption R :B:	15	25	30	75
90	Wall of Air U :B:	8	15	20	30
91	Wall of Water U :B:	8	15	20	
92	Water Elemental U :B:	8	15	20	
93	Animate Dead U :K:	20	40	70	90
94	Bad Moon R :K:	100	150	200	400
95	Black Knight U :K:	20	30	50	
96	Bog Wraith U :K:	8	15	20	
97	Contract from Below :K:	40	80	100	250
98	Cursed Land U :K:	8	15	20	30
99	Dark Ritual C :K:	20	50	60	150
100	Darkpact R :K:	20	40	50	
101	Deathgrip U :K:	8	15	20	
102	Deathlace R :K:	20	30	40	100
103	Demonic Attorney R :K:	20	30	40	100
104	Demonic Hordes R :K:	50	100	125	400
105	Demonic Tutor U :K:	100	125	200	300
106	Drain Life C :K:	8	15	20	30
107	Drudge Skeletons C :K:	8	15	20	30
108	Evil Presence U :K:	8	15	20	30
109	Fear C :K:	8	15	20	30
110	Frozen Shade C :K:	8	15	20	30
111	Gloom U :K:	8	15	20	30
112	Howl from Beyond C :K:	8	15	20	30
113	Hypnotic Specter U :K:	50	80	100	225
114	Lich R :K:	75	125	150	400
115	Lord of the Pit R :K:	75	125	150	400
116	Mind Twist R :K:	125	225	300	750
117	Nether Shadow R :K:	40	80	100	250
118	Nettling Imp U :K:	8	15	20	30
119	Nightmare R :K:	50	100	150	400
120	Paralyze C :K:	8	15	20	30
121	Pestilence C :K:	8	15	20	30
122	Plague Rats C :K:	8	15	20	30
123	Raise Dead C :K:	8	15	20	30
124	Royal Assassin R :K:	100	200	250	650
125	Sacrifice U :K:	8	15	20	
126	Scathe Zombies C :K:	8	15	20	30
127	Scavenging Ghoul U :K:	8	15	20	
128	Sengir Vampire U :K:	30	60	70	150
129	Simulacrum U :K:	8	15	20	
130	Sinkhole C :K:	40	100	125	300
131	Terror C :K:	8	15	20	30
132	Unholy Strength C :K:	8	15	20	30
133	Wall of Bone U :K:	8	15	20	30
134	Warp Artifact R :K:	15	25	30	60
135	Weakness C :K:	8	15	20	30
136	Will-O'-The-Wisp R :K:	50	100	125	350
137	Word of Command R :K:	75	125	150	400
138	Zombie Master R :K:	50	80	100	250
139	Burrowing U :R:	8	15	20	
140	Chaoslace R :R:	15	25	30	60
141	Disintegrate C :R:	8	15	20	30
142	Dragon Whelp U :R:	20	40	60	125
143	Dwarven Demolition Team U :R:	10	20	30	
144	Dwarven Warriors C :R:	8	15	20	30
145	Earth Elemental U :R:	8	15	20	
146	Earthbind C :R:	8	15	20	30
147	Earthquake R :R:	40	80	100	250
148	False Orders C :R:	8	15	20	30
149	Fire Elemental U :R:	8	15	20	30
150	Fireball C :R:	10	20	25	40
151	Firebreathing C :R:	8	15	20	30
152	Flashfires U :R:	10	20	30	60
153	Fork R :R:	80	150	200	350
154	Goblin Balloon Brigade U :R:	8	15	20	40
155	Goblin King R :R:	50	100	125	350
156	Granite Gargoyle R :R:	30	50	60	175
157	Gray Ogre C :R:	8	15	20	30
158	Hill Giant C :R:	8	15	20	30
159	Hurloon Minotaur C :R:	8	15	20	30
160	Ironclaw Orcs C :R:	8	15	20	30
161	Keldon Warlord U :R:	8	15	20	
162	Lightning Bolt C :R:	20	50	120	150
163	Mana Flare R :R:	75	125	150	400
164	Manabarbs R :R:	20	30	40	
165	Mons's Goblin Raiders C :R:	8	15	20	30
166	Orcish Artillery U :R:	10	20	25	40
167	Orcish Oriflamme U :R:	10	20	25	40
168	Power Surge R :R:	20	40	60	150
169	Raging River R :R:	40	80	100	250
170	Red Elemental Blast C :R:	10	20	25	40
171	Roc of Kher Ridges R :R:	20	40	50	125
172	Rock Hydra R :R:	30	50	60	175
173	Sedge Troll R :R:	40	80	100	1,400
174	Shatter C :R:	8	15	20	30
175	Shivan Dragon R :R:	175	250	300	750
176	Smoke R :R:	20	40	50	125
177	Stone Giant U :R:	8	15	20	
178	Stone Rain C :R:	8	15	20	30
179	Tunnel U :R:	8	15	20	
180	Two-Headed Giant of Foriys R :R:	50	100	125	350
181	Uthden Troll U :R:	8	15	20	
182	Wall of Fire U :R:	8	15	20	30
183	Wall of Stone U :R:	8	15	20	
184	Wheel of Fortune R :R:	150	300	400	800
185	Aspect of Wolf R :G:	20	30	40	100
186	Berserk U :G:	130	150	180	250
187	Birds of Paradise R :G:	400	500	600	800
188	Camouflage U :G:	12	20	25	
189	Channel U :G:	15	25	30	
190	Cockatrice R :G:	25	40	50	
191	Craw Wurm C :G:	8	15	20	40
192	Elvish Archers R :G:	40	100	125	350

#	Card	NmMt 8	NmMt+ 8.5	MT 9	Gem 9.5/10
193	Fastbond R :G:	80	150	175	450
194	Fog C :G:	8	15	20	
195	Force of Nature R :G:	80	150	175	400
196	Fungusaur R :G:	20	30	40	
197	Gaea's Liege R :G:	20	40	50	125
198	Giant Growth C :G:	8	15	20	30
199	Giant Spider C :G:	8	15	20	30
200	Grizzly Bears C :G:	10	15	25	50
201	Hurricane U :G:	10	20	25	
202	Ice Storm U :G:	30	60	80	150
203	Instill Energy U :G:	8	15	20	40
204	Ironroot Treefolk :G:	8	15	20	30
205	Kudzu R :G:	20	30	40	100
206	Ley Druid U :G:	8	15	20	30
207	Lifeforce U :G:	8	15	20	30
208	Lifelace R :G:	15	25	30	
209	Living Artifact R :G:	20	30	40	100
210	Living Lands R :G:	20	30	40	100
211	Llanowar Elves C :G:	20	50	60	150
212	Lure U :G:	8	15	20	30
213	Natural Selection R :G:	50	100	125	350
214	Regeneration C :G:	8	15	20	30
215	Regrowth U :G:	40	80	100	250
216	Scryb Sprites C :G:	8	15	20	30
217	Shanodin Dryads C :G:	8	15	20	30
218	Stream of Life C :G:	8	15	20	30
219	Thicket Basilisk U :G:	8	15	20	30
220	Timber Wolves R :G:	15	25	30	75
221	Tranquility C :G:	8	15	20	30
222	Tsunami U :G:	8	15	20	30
223	Verduran Enchantress R :G:	40	80	100	250
224	Wall of Brambles U :G:	8	15	20	
225	Wall of Ice U :G:	8	15	20	30
226	Wall of Wood C :G:	8	15	20	
227	Wanderlust U :G:	8	15	20	
228	War Mammoth C :G:	8	15	20	30
229	Web R :G:	15	25	30	60
230	Wild Growth C :G:	8	15	20	30
231	Ankh of Mishra R	50	120	150	350
232	Basalt Monolith U	10	20	30	60
233	Black Lotus R	18,000	22,000	33,000	75,000
234	Black Vise U	20	35	50	
235	Celestial Prism U	8	15	20	
236	Chaos Orb R	400	450	500	700
237	Clockwork Beast R	20	30	40	100
238	Conservator U	8	15	20	
239	Copper Tablet U	10	20	30	60
240	Crystal Rod U	8	15	20	
241	Cyclopean Tomb R	75	125	150	400
242	Dingus Egg R	20	40	50	
243	Disrupting Scepter R	40	80	100	250
244	Forcefield R	350	400	500	2,550
245	Gauntlet of Might R	100	175	225	650
246	Glasses of Urza U	8	15	20	30
247	Helm of Chatzuk R	15	25	30	60
248	Howling Mine R	100	175	200	500
249	Icy Manipulator U	50	80	100	350
250	Illusionary Mask R	150	300	400	850
251	Iron Star U	8	15	20	30
252	Ivory Cup U	8	15	20	30
253	Jade Monolith R	20	30	40	100
254	Jade Statue U	15	25	30	75
255	Jayemdae Tome R	25	40	50	125
256	Juggernaut U	25	40	50	125
257	Kormus Bell R	20	30	40	100
258	Library of Leng U	8	15	20	30
259	Living Wall U	8	15	20	
260	Mana Vault R	100	200	250	600
261	Meekstone R	30	50	60	175
262	Mox Emerald R	1,500	2,500	4,000	5,000
263	Mox Jet R	1,500	2,500	4,000	12,000
264	Mox Pearl R	1,500	1,800	2,000	4,500
265	Mox Ruby R	1,500	2,000	2,500	4,500
266	Mox Sapphire R	2,000	5,500	7,200	16,000
267	Nevinyrral's Disk R	150	275	350	750
268	Obsianus Golem U	8	15	20	
269	Rod of Ruin U	8	15	20	
270	Sol Ring U	90	150	200	500
271	Soul Net U	8	15	20	30
272	Sunglasses of Urza R	20	30	40	100
273	The Hive R	20	30	40	100
274	Throne of Bone U	8	15	20	30
275	Time Vault R	600	800	1,000	1,250
276	Winter Orb R	75	125	175	500
277	Wooden Sphere U	8	15	20	30
278	Badlands R	800	1,000	1,200	1,500
279	Bayou R	1,000	1,300	1,500	2,000
280	Plateau R	650	800	1,000	2,000
281	Savannah R	800	850	950	1,100
282	Scrubland R	800	1,000	1,200	1,500
283	Taiga R	600	750	900	1,100
284	Tropical Island R	1,000	1,500	2,000	3,000
285	Tundra R	1,800	2,000	2,500	3,500
286	Underground Sea R	3,000	4,000	4,500	5,000
287	Volcanic Island R	3,000	4,000	5,000	10,000
288	Plains v1 L	8	15	20	30
289	Plains v2 L	8	15	20	30
290	Plains v3 L	8	15	20	30
291	Island v1 L	8	15	20	30
292	Island v2 L	8	15	20	30
293	Island v3 L	8	15	20	30
294	Swamp v1 L	8	15	20	30
295	Swamp v2 L	8	15	20	30
296	Swamp v3 L	8	15	20	30
297	Mountain v1 L	8	15	20	30
298	Mountain v2 L	8	15	20	30
299	Mountain v3 L	8	15	20	30
300	Forest v1 L	8	15	20	30
301	Forest v2 L	8	15	20	30
302	Forest v3 L	8	15	20	30

1999 Pokemon Base 1st Edition

#	Card	NmMt 8	NmMt+ 8.5	MT 9	Gem 9.5/10
1	Alakazam HOLO R/Thin Stamp	600	1,000	1,300	5,500
2	Blastoise HOLO R/Thin Stamp	1,700	2,200	3,000	7,000
3	Chansey HOLO R/Thin Stamp	600	900	1,200	5,000
4	Charizard HOLO R/Thin Stamp	7,800	10,000	12,000	30,000
5	Clefairy HOLO R/Thin Stamp	500	800	1,200	2,000
6	Gyarados HOLO R/Thin Stamp	400	800	1,200	2,000
7	Hitmonchan HOLO R/Thin Stamp	250	350	600	1,800
8	Machamp HOLO R/Thin Stamp	200	300	400	1,000
9	Magneton HOLO R/Thin Stamp	300	350	750	5,300
10	Mewtwo HOLO R/Thin Stamp	700	1,200	2,000	6,000
11	Nidoking HOLO R/Thin Stamp	200	300	800	4,000
12	Ninetales HOLO R/Thin Stamp	200	300	700	3,000
13	Poliwrath HOLO R/Thin Stamp	200	300	450	3,100
14	Raichu HOLO R/Thin Stamp	200	1,600	5,000	
15	Venusaur HOLO R/Thin Stamp	400	500	3,000	8,000
16	Zapdos HOLO R/Thin Stamp	200	300	1,000	2,500
17	Beedrill R/Thick Stamp	80	100	250	1,000
18	Dragonair R/Thick Stamp	40	60	80	800
19	Dugtrio R/Thick Stamp	30	40	50	450
20	Electabuzz R/Thick Stamp	30	40	50	400
21	Electrode R/Thick Stamp	30	40	75	600
22	Pidgeotto R/Thick Stamp	20	30	40	350
23	Arcanine U/Thick Stamp	30	40	40	100
24	Charmeleon U/Thick Stamp	25	40	60	450
25	Dewgong U/Thick Stamp	15	20	30	65
26	Dratini U/Thick Stamp	15	20	25	450
27	Farfetch'd U/Thick Stamp	15	20	30	75
28	Growlithe U/Thick Stamp	20	30	35	300
29	Haunter U/Thick Stamp	25	30	30	250
30	Ivysaur U/Thick Stamp	20	30	40	150
31	Jynx U/Thick Stamp	15	20	25	300
32	Kadabra U/Thick Stamp	20	30	40	200
33	Kakuna (UER) U/Thick Stamp	10	15	20	70
34	Machoke U/Thick Stamp	15	20	30	70
35	Magikarp U/Thick Stamp	15	20	30	70
36	Magmar U/Thick Stamp	15	20	25	70
37	Nidorino U/Thick Stamp	10	15	20	70
38	Poliwhirl U/Thick Stamp	15	20	25	75
39	Porygon U/Thick Stamp	20	25	30	70
40	Raticate U/Thick Stamp	20	30	50	50
41	Seel U/Thick Stamp	15	20	25	40
42	Wartortle U/Thick Stamp	30	40	75	800
43	Abra C/Thick Stamp	5	10	15	45
44	Bulbasaur (UER) C/Thick Stamp	30	45	55	200
45	Caterpie (UER) C/Thick Stamp	10	15	20	80
46	Charmander C/Thick Stamp	20	25	35	100
47	Diglett C/Thick Stamp	10	15	20	30
48	Doduo C/Thick Stamp	10	15	20	40
49	Drowzee C/Thick Stamp	10	15	20	45
50	Gastly C/Thick Stamp	10	15	20	45
51	Koffing C/Thick Stamp	10	15	20	40
52	Machop C/Thick Stamp	10	15	20	40
53	Magnemite C/Thick Stamp	10	15	20	40
54	Metapod (UER) C/Thick Stamp	10	15	20	45
55	Nidoran-M C/Thick Stamp	10	15	20	35
56	Onix C/Thick Stamp	10	15	20	40
57	Pidgey C/Thick Stamp	10	15	20	40
58	Pikachu (Red cheeks Error) C Thick Stamp	40	50	75	350
58	Pikachu (Yellow cheeks Corr.) C Thick Stamp	20	30	50	150
59	Poliwag C/Thick Stamp	10	15	20	40
60	Ponyta C/Thick Stamp	10	15	20	40
61	Rattata C/Thick Stamp	10	15	20	40
62	Sandshrew C/Thick Stamp	10	15	20	40
63	Squirtle C/Thick Stamp	15	20	30	80
64	Starmie C/Thick Stamp	10	15	20	40
65	Staryu C/Thick Stamp	10	15	20	40
66	Tangela C/Thick Stamp	10	15	20	40
67	Voltorb (UER) C/Thick Stamp	10	15	20	45
68	Vulpix (UER) C/Thick Stamp	15	20	25	45
69	Weedle C/Thick Stamp	10	15	20	45
70	Clefairy Doll R/Thick Stamp	20	30	45	500
71	Computer Search R/Thick Stamp	60	80	100	450
72	Devolution Spray R/Thick Stamp	20	30	40	750
73	Impostor Professor Oak R Thick Stamp	20	40	60	350
74	Item Finder R/Thick Stamp	15	20	25	500
75	Lass R/Thick Stamp	60	80	100	1,000
76	Pokemon Breeder R/Thick Stamp	20	25	35	300
77	Pokemon Trader R/Thick Stamp	20	30	40	350
78	Scoop Up R/Thick Stamp	20	25	35	200
79	Super Energy Removal R/Thick Stamp	20	30	40	300
80	Defender U/Thick Stamp	5	10	15	20
81	Energy Retrieval U/Thick Stamp	10	15	20	20
82	Full Heal U/Thick Stamp	10	15	20	50
83	Maintenance U/Thick Stamp	10	15	20	50
84	Plus Power U/Thick Stamp	10	15	20	120
85	Pokemon Center U/Thick Stamp	10	15	20	50
86	Pokemon Flute U/Thick Stamp	10	15	20	300
87	Pokedex U/Thick Stamp	10	15	20	120
88	Professor Oak U/Thick Stamp	15	20	30	450
89	Revive U/Thick Stamp	10	15	25	80
90	Super Potion U/Thick Stamp	10	15	25	80
91	Bill C/Thick Stamp	10	15	20	45
92	Energy Removal C/Thick Stamp	10	15	20	50
93	Gust of Wind C/Thick Stamp	10	15	25	55
94	Potion C/Thick Stamp	10	15	25	50
95	Switch C/Thick Stamp	10	15	25	50
96	Double Colorless Energy U Thick Stamp	10	15	25	120
97	Fighting Energy/Thick Stamp	5	10	15	30
98	Fire Energy/Thick Stamp	5	10	15	30
99	Grass Energy/Thick Stamp	5	10	15	30
100	Lightning Energy/Thick Stamp	5	10	15	30
101	Psychic Energy/Thick Stamp	5	10	15	30
102	Water Energy/Thick Stamp	5	10	15	30